A THE
American
Century
Dictionary

D0034115

LAURENCE URDANG is a distinguished lexicographer and publisher, and the founder and editor of *Verbatim, the Language Quarterly.* His many publication credits include *The Oxford Thesaurus: American Edition, The Random House Dictionary of the English Language,* Unabridged Edition, *The Random House College Dictionary,* and scores of other dictionaries and language-reference books.

A THE American Century Dictionary

Edited by Laurence Urdang

WARNER BOOKS

NEW YORK   BOSTON

The American Century Dictionary. Warner Books Paperback Edition

Copyright © 1995 by Oxford University Press, Inc.
All rights reserved.

This work was previously published in hardcover under the title, *The Oxford Dictionary: American Edition*, by Oxford University Press, Inc., 198 Madison Avenue, New York, NY 10016.

Oxford is a registered trademark of Oxford University Press

Cover design by Jerry Pfeiffer
Interior illustrations by John Flagg

Warner Books, Inc.
1271 Avenue of the Americas
New York, NY 10020

Visit our Web site at
www.warnerbooks.com

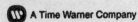 A Time Warner Company

Printed in the United States of America

First Warner Books Printing: August, 1996
Reissued: August, 1997

15

GUIDE TO THE USE OF
THE DICTIONARY

Main Entries

All main entries are listed in letter-by-letter alphabetic order and are set in **boldface**, or, for foreign terms, in ***boldface italic***.

Cross-references are shown in small capitals.

an·aes·the·si·a /an′əsTHē′ZHə/ *n.* var., esp. *Brit.*, of ANESTHESIA

They refer to forms that are themselves main entries. They are given for frequent alternate or variant spellings, former names of places, unusual plural forms, and so on.

Main entries that are spelled alike but have different origins (homographs) are shown as separate entries with a superscript number.

box[1] ... container
box[2] ... take part in boxing
box[3] ... small evergreen tree

If a capitalized main entry has a sense that is spelled lower case, these are marked with a boldface lower-case letter followed by a hyphen and enclosed in parentheses.

Java /jä′və, jav′ə/ *n.* **1** main island ... **2** (often **j-**) **a** a coffee grown ... **b** *Slang.* any coffee

If a main entry is lower case but has a sense that is capitalized, this is shown as follows:

jack /jak/ *n.* **1** device ... **6** (*cap.*) familiar form of *John*

See additional details under **Biographical Entries; Geographical Entries**

Alternative Forms

Alternative forms or spellings that would be alphabetically very close

(within five entries) to a main entry may be included as part of the main entry.

good·bye or **good-bye**
pret·er·it or **pret·er·ite**

They may also follow the part of speech, in parentheses.

ma·ha·ra·jah /mä′hərä′jə/ *n.* (also **ma′ha·ra′ja**)

If the alternative is frequent and alphabetically distant, it is entered as a main entry, with pronunciation and a cross reference back to the main spelling or form.

aer·o·plane /ar′əplān′, er′-/ *n. Brit.* var. of AIRPLANE

Pronunciations

Pronunciations are enclosed in slashes following the entry. Most general vocabulary items are pronounced, as are variants and biographical and geographical entries. Primary stress is indicated by a dark stroke (′) immediately following the stressed syllable; secondary stress is indicated by a light stroke (′) following the syllable. A hyphen is inserted between vowel symbols in some cases, if necessary for clarity.

When an entry has more than one pronunciation in common use, a variant pronunciation is shown, separated from the first pronunciation by a comma. If no qualifying note is given, then each pronunciation, regardless of the order in which it is given, is considered equally acceptable.

If the pronunciation of only one part of the entry varies, only the variant portion is shown.

cu·li·nar·y /kəl′əner′ē, kyo͞o′lə-/

A hyphen after the variant portion indicates a pronunciation of an initial syllable or syllables; one before the variant indicates final syllable(s); and hyphens before and after the variant indicate internal syllables.

If a particular part of speech of an entry has its own pronunciation, that pronunciation is given immediately preceding the first definition for that part of speech.

record *n.* /rek′ərd/ **1a** evidence ... —*v.* /rikôrd′/ **7** set down in writing

A partial pronunciation of a compound main entry is given if one of the parts is not a main entry.

Cats′kill′ Moun′tains /kat′skil/
pitched′ bat′tle /piCHt/

Each word of a compound entry is given with stress marks.

Pronunciations (usually partial ones) are given for derivatives that are significantly different in vowel quality or stress pattern from the main entry.

If an entry is a compound of another main entry (with a common prefix, suffix, or other word(s) added), only stressed syllables and syllabication are shown. The pronunciation is based on the root element in the compound form.

hand′bag′
ma·chine′ read′a·ble

See the Key to Pronunciation at the end of this guide.

Syllable Breaks

All multi-syllable main entries, alternative forms, inflected forms, and derivatives are shown with syllable breaks marked by centered dots.

Parts of Speech

Part-of-speech labels are given for main vocabulary entries, including open, closed, and hyphenated compounds, and geographical entries. Biographical entries do not carry part-of-speech labels, but any derivative forms they may have do.

Jef′fer·son ... —**Jef′fer·so′ni·an**
/-sō′nēən/ *adj.*

If a main entry has more than one part of speech, an em-dash precedes each new part-of-speech label.

care /ker/ *n.* **1** worry ...
—*v.* (**cared, car·ing**) **5** feel concern

Plurals and Inflected Forms

Inflected forms are given in boldface for non-regular formations of verbs (as for irregulars like *go* and verbs ending in -*e*), non-regular plurals of nouns, and non-regular comparative and superlative degrees of adjectives. For verbs, the inflected forms given are the simple past and present participle (-*ing*) forms, with any variants they may have.

trot /trät/ *v.* (**trot·ted, trot·ting**)

Where three forms are given they are the simple past, past participle, and present participle.

give /giv/ *v.* (**gave, giv·en, giv·ing**)

The inflected form for multi-syllable words is usually shortened to include only the changed part.

pre·fer /prifər′/ *v.* (·**ferred, ·fer·ring**)

Plurals for one-syllable words are given as follows:

elk /elk/ *n.* (*pl.* same or -**s**)
fez /fez/ *n.* (*pl.* ·**zes**)

Labels

All labels, such as *Math.*, *Colloq.*, *Brit.*, *Slang.*, and so on, appear in italic followed by a period. If the label applies to an entire multi-sense entry, the label precedes the first definition number. If it applies to only a single sense, it follows that definition number. If the label applies to all parts of speech, it precedes the first part of speech.

Aussie /ŏ′sē, ŏz′ē/ *Colloq. n.* **1** Australian **2** Australia —*adj.* **3** Australian

See the list at the end of this guide for abbreviated labels used in this dictionary.

Definitions

If a main entry has multiple senses, they are numbered sequentially with boldface numerals through the whole entry (including all parts of speech and idioms). The most frequent senses of the word are given first. Special field labels, such as *Hist., Math.,* or *Chem.,* are given as needed.

If a numbered sense of a word can be subdivided into closely related meanings, each of these is preceded by a boldface letter.

case¹ /kās/ *n.* **1** instance ... **2** hypothetical or actual situation **3a** person's illness ... **b** such a person

Idioms and Phrasal Verbs

Idiomatic phrases and phrasal verbs are printed in boldface type and listed alphabetically after all other senses, but before any derivatives. They are preceded by a sense number and followed by a definition. When an idiom or phrasal verb has multiple senses, the idiom is followed by a colon. Separate senses follow, each marked with a letter.

make ... **27 make up: a** act to overcome ... **b** be reconciled

Derivatives

Derivatives are shown in boldface following all senses and any idioms, preceded by a dash. They are shown with syllable breaks and stress marks. Pronunciations are given where

needed. They are followed by a part-of-speech label. If the derivative is a verb, its inflected forms are given in parentheses, if applicable. If the derivative is an adjective, the comparative and superlative forms are given in parentheses, if applicable.

Etymologies

Etymologies, where given, are enclosed in square brackets at the end of an entry. Languages referred to in them are generally abbreviated. References to other main entries appear in small capitals.

See the list at the end of this guide for the abbreviations used in this dictionary.

Biographical Entries

Only the family name or surname has been pronounced. When more than one person is included under the same family name, the individuals are arranged in chronological order by birth.

Da·vis /dā′vəs/ **1 Jefferson** 1808–89 ... **2 Bette** ... 1908–89

For U.S. presidents, kings, emperors, noted British prime ministers, and so on, the term of office or dates of reign are given in parentheses after the name of the office. A date followed by a dash and space indicates that the person is still alive or still in office at the time of printing.

Nicknames and other forms of given names usually used are shown after the surname, with the real name in parentheses.

Ber·ra /ber′ə/, **"Yogi" (Lawrence Peter)**
Bi·ko /bē′kō/, **Steve (Stephen)**

Pseudonyms, stage names, and so on, are given as follows:

Augustus /ôgəs′təs/ (born **Gaius Octavianus;** also known as **Octavian**)

Hope /hōp/, **Bob** (born **Leslie Townes Hope**)

Saints are listed under their name, followed by **St.**

Bernard, St.

All B.C. dates are so marked. Other dates are A.D., either marked as such (as needed for clarity) or unmarked.

Geographical Entries

Entries are listed alphabetically by the name, not by feature.

Ni·ag′a·ra Falls

Cod, Cape
Fun·dy, Bay of

The common, not the official, name is used for the main entry of countries (e.g., **China**, not **People's Republic of China**). In some cases the alternate name is a cross-reference entry.

Population figures for U.S. cities and states are based on the 1990 U.S. Census.

Pronunciations for foreign names are as they are used in the United States. If a name is not in common use, the foreign pronunciation is given.

Va·duz /fädo͞ots′/

KEY TO PRONUNCIATION

a	<u>a</u>nd, c<u>a</u>t, m<u>a</u>n	N	nasal in <u>un</u>, v<u>in</u> (French)
ā	b<u>ai</u>l, w<u>a</u>de, sl<u>ay</u>	OE	f<u>eu</u> (French); sch<u>ö</u>n (German)
ä	<u>a</u>rt, <u>a</u>lms, f<u>a</u>ther, hurr<u>ah</u>	Y	<u>ü</u>ber (German); p<u>u</u>r (French)
e	<u>e</u>tch, l<u>e</u>t; <u>ai</u>r c<u>a</u>re	b	<u>b</u>oot, ru<u>bb</u>er, ta<u>b</u>
ē	<u>ea</u>sy, f<u>ee</u>t, m<u>e</u>, lobb<u>y</u>	d	<u>d</u>ate, ru<u>dd</u>er, ru<u>d</u>e
i	<u>i</u>t, w<u>i</u>tch	f	<u>f</u>ate, re<u>f</u>er, pu<u>ff</u>
ī	<u>eye</u>, t<u>i</u>de, m<u>y</u>	g	<u>g</u>o, bi<u>gg</u>er, ba<u>g</u>
ō	<u>o</u>ver, c<u>o</u>ve, g<u>o</u>	h	<u>h</u>ot, ca<u>h</u>oots
ô	<u>aw</u>l, f<u>a</u>ll, r<u>aw</u>	j	<u>j</u>ack, ma<u>g</u>ic, hu<u>g</u>e
oi	<u>oi</u>l, f<u>oi</u>l, b<u>oy</u>	k	<u>c</u>ut, ba<u>k</u>er, ba<u>ck</u>
ŏŏ	h<u>oo</u>k, p<u>u</u>ll	l	<u>l</u>ap, ce<u>ll</u>ar, ca<u>ll</u>; also syllabic <u>l</u>
ōō	<u>oo</u>ze, l<u>oo</u>se, shampo<u>o</u>		in crad<u>le</u> (no schwa), sett<u>le</u>
ou	<u>ou</u>ch, c<u>ou</u>ch, n<u>ow</u>	m	<u>m</u>ain, ru<u>mm</u>age, co<u>m</u>e
ə	<u>u</u>p, b<u>u</u>t, <u>a</u>bove, ban<u>a</u>na	n	<u>n</u>ew, ho<u>n</u>or, ca<u>n</u>; also syllabic
ər	<u>ear</u>n, f<u>ur</u>; p<u>er</u>haps, moth<u>er</u>		<u>n</u> in maide<u>n</u> (no schwa)
CH	<u>ch</u>urch, cat<u>ch</u>er	p	<u>p</u>ut, sto<u>pp</u>er, loo<u>p</u>
NG	si<u>ng</u>er, lo<u>ng</u>	r	<u>r</u>oot, ca<u>rr</u>y, ca<u>r</u>
SH	<u>sh</u>ape, wa<u>sh</u>er, ca<u>sh</u>	s	<u>s</u>it, me<u>ss</u>y, ma<u>ss</u>
TH	<u>th</u>ing, pa<u>th</u>	t	<u>t</u>ake, ma<u>tt</u>er, la<u>t</u>e
TH	<u>th</u>is, mo<u>th</u>er, la<u>th</u>e	v	<u>v</u>ase, ne<u>v</u>er, ca<u>v</u>e
ZH	lei<u>s</u>ure, sei<u>z</u>ure, bei<u>g</u>e	w	<u>w</u>ait, q<u>u</u>ick
A	<u>a</u>mi (French)	y	<u>y</u>es, be<u>y</u>ond
KH	lo<u>ch</u> (Scottish); i<u>ch</u> (German)	z	<u>z</u>ebra, la<u>z</u>y, fu<u>s</u>e

GENERAL ABBREVIATIONS

abbreviation	*abbr.*	interjection	*interj.*
ablative	*abl.*	irregularly	irreg.
accusative	*acc.*	lower case	*l.c.*
adjective	*adj.*	masculine	*masc.*
adverb	*adv.*	modern	mod.
alteration	alter.	neuter	*neut.*
anno domini	A.D.	nominative	*nom.*
apparently	appar.	north	N
assimilation	assim.	noun	*n.*
attributive	*attrib.*	obsolete	obs.
before Christ	B.C.	origin,	
capital	*cap.*	originally	orig.
century	cent.	participle	*part.*
circa	c.	passive	*pass.*
combining form	*comb. form*	perhaps	perh.
comparative	*comp.*	plural	*pl.*
conjunction	*conj.*	possibly	poss.
contraction	*contr.*	preposition	*prep.*
dative	*dat.*	present	*pres.*
derivative	deriv.	probably	prob.
dialect, dialectal	dial.	pronoun	*pron.*
diminutive	dim.	reflexive	*refl.*
east	E	related to	rel. to
equivalent	equiv.	respelling,	
et cetera	etc.	respelled	resp.
euphemism	euphem.	singular	*sing.*
feminine	*fem.*	south	S
figurative	*fig.*	superlative	*superl.*
flourished	fl.	ultimately	ult.
following	foll.	uncertain	uncert.
frequentative	freq.	usually	usu.
from	fr.	variant	var.
genitive	*gen.*	verb	*v.*
imitative	imit.	west	W

SUBJECT OR REGISTER LABEL ABBREVIATIONS

Aeronautics	*Aeron.*	Literary	*Lit.*
Anatomy	*Anat.*	Mathematics	*Math.*
Anglo-Indian	*Anglo-Ind.*	Mechanics	*Mech.*
Antiquities	*Antiq.*	Medicine	*Med.*
Archaeological	*Archaeol.*	Meteorology	*Meteorol.*
Architecture	*Archit.*	Military	*Milit.*
Astrology	*Astrol.*	Mineralogy	*Mineral.*
Astronautics	*Astronaut.*	Music	*Mus.*
Astronomy	*Astron.*	Mythology	*Myth.*
Australian English	*Austral.*	Nautical	*Naut.*
Biblical	*Bibl.*	Northern English	*No. Engl.*
Biochemistry	*Biochem.*	Obsolete	*Obs.*
Biology	*Biol.*	Offensive	*Offens.*
Botany	*Bot.*	Old-fashioned	*Old-fash.*
British	*Brit.*	Parliament, Parliamentary	*Parl.*
Canadian English	*Canad.*	Pharmacy, Pharmacology	*Pharm.*
Chemistry	*Chem.*	Philosophy	*Philos.*
Chinese	*Chin.*	Phonetics	*Phonet.*
Cinematography	*Cinematog.*	Photography	*Photog.*
Colloquial	*Colloq.*	Physiology	*Physiol.*
Computer technology	*Comp.*	Poetic	*Poet.*
Derogatory	*Derog.*	Political, Politics	*Polit.*
Dialect	*Dial.*	Prosody	*Pros.*
Ecclesiastical	*Eccles.*	Psychiatry	*Psychiat.*
Economics	*Econ.*	Psychology	*Psychol.*
Egyptian	*Egypt.*	Religion	*Relig.*
Electrical	*Electr.*	Rhetorical	*Rhet.*
English	*Eng.*	Roman	*Rom.*
Euphemism	*Euphem.*	Roman Catholic Church	*RC Ch.*
Fiction	*Fict.*	Science	*Sci.*
Geology	*Geol.*	South African English	*S. Afr.*
Geometry	*Geom.*	Statistics	*Stat.*
Grammar	*Gram.*	Stock Exchange	*Stock Exch.*
Greek	*Gk.*	Surgery	*Surg.*
Historic(al)	*Hist.*	Symbol	*Symb.*
Improperly	*Improp.*	Theater	*Theat.*
Ironic	*Iron.*	Theology	*Theol.*
Jocular	*Joc.*	Trademark	*Tdmk.*
Knitting	*Knit.*	Zoology	*Zool.*
Linguistics	*Ling.*		

LANGUAGE ABBREVIATIONS
IN ETYMOLOGIES

Note: Some elements are used in combination, e.g.: AmerInd = American Indian; or prefixed by H = High, M = Middle, Mod = Modern, O = Old, e.g.: OE = Old English, HGer = High German.

Aboriginal	Aborig	Korean	Kor
African	Afr	Late Greek	LGk
Afrikaans	Afrik	Late Latin	LL
American	Amer	Latin	L
Anglo-	Ang	Lithuanian	Lith
Arabic	Ar	Louisiana French	LaFr
Aramaic	Aram	Low German	LGer
Bulgarian	Bulg	Medieval Greek	MGk
Canadian	Can	Medieval Latin	MedL
Celtic	Celt	Mexican	Mex
Chinese	Chin	Neo-Latin	NeoL
Danish	Dan	Norwegian	Norw
Dutch	Du	Pennsylvania German	PaGer
Egyptian	Egypt	Persian	Pers
English	E	Polish	Pol
Eskimo	Esk	Portuguese	Port
Finnish	Finn	Provençal	Prov
French	Fr	Prussian	Pruss
Frisian	Fris	Romance	Rom
Gallo-	Gallo	Rumanian	Rum
German	Ger	Russian	Russ
Germanic	Gmc	Sanskrit	Skt
Gothic	Goth	Scandinavian	Scand
Greek	Gk	Scots Gaelic	ScotGael
Hawaiian	Haw	Scottish	Scot
Hebrew	Heb	Semitic	Sem
Icelandic	Icel	Slavic	Slav
Indian	Ind	Spanish	Sp
Irish	Ir	Swedish	Sw
Italian	It	Turkish	Turk
Japanese	Japn	Vulgar Latin	VL

A

a, A /ā/ *n.* (*pl.* **a's; A's, As**) first letter of the English alphabet; a vowel

a /ā, ə/ *adj.* (also **an** /an/ before a vowel sound) **1** one; some; any **2** one like (*a Hercules*) **3** one single (*not a chance*) **4** per (*twice a year; seven a side*) [OE *ān* one]

a or **a.** *abbr.* **1** about **2** acre **3** *Mus.* alto **4** ampere(s) **5** answer

A or **A.** *abbr.* **1** a blood type **2** top grade, indicating excellence **3** America(n) **4** April **5** *Baseball.* assist(s) **6** August

A *abbr.* angstrom

a-¹ *prefix* **1** to; toward (*ashore; aside*) **2** (with verb in pres. part. or infin.) doing or being (*ahunting, abuzz*) **3** on (*afire*) **4** in (*nowadays*) [OE *an, on,* ON]

a-² *prefix* (also **an-** before a vowel sound) not; without (*amoral; anarchy*) [Gk]

AA *abbr.* **1** Alcoholics Anonymous **2** anti-aircraft

Aa·chen /äKH'ən/ *n.* city in Germany. Pop. 241,900

aard·vark /ärd'värk'/ *n.* anteating mammal [Afrik]

Aar·on /ar'ən, er'ən/ brother of Moses; traditional founder of the Jewish priesthood

ab- *prefix* off; away; from (*abduct*) [L]

A.B. *abbr.* Bachelor of Arts [L *artium baccalaureus*]

a·back /əbak'/ *adv.* as in **take aback** surprise; confuse [OE]

ABACUS

aba·cus /ab'əkəs, əbak'əs/ *n.* (*pl.* **·cus·es** or **·ci** /-sī'/) frame with wires along which beads are slid for calculating [L fr. Gk]

a·baft /əbaft'/ *adv. Naut.* in the stern half of a vessel [OE]

a·ban·don /əban'dən/ *v.* **1** give up **2** forsake; desert **—n. 3** freedom from inhibitions **—a·ban'don·ment** *n.* [Fr, rel. to AD + BAN]

a·ban·doned /əban'dənd/ *adj.* **1** deserted; forsaken **2** unrestrained; profligate

a·base /əbās'/ *v.* (**·based, ·bas·ing**) humiliate; degrade **—a·base'ment** *n.* [Fr, rel. to AD + BASE²]

a·bashed /əbasht'/ *adj.* embarrassed; disconcerted **—a·bash'ed·ly** /-bASH'ədlē/*adv.* [OFr *abaissier*]

a·bate /əbāt'/ *v.* (**·bat·ed, ·bat·ing**) **1** make or become less strong, etc.; diminish **2** *Law.* stop **—a·bate'ment** *n.* [MFr *abatre* fr. L *battuere* beat]

ab·at·toir /ab'ətwär', ab'ətwär'/ *n.* slaughterhouse [Fr *abatre* slaughter + *-oir* -ORY]

abbé /abā'/ *n.* (in France) abbot or priest [Fr fr. L, rel. to ABBOT]

ab·bess /ab'əs/ *n.* head of a community of nuns

ab·bey /ab'ē/ *n.* **1** building(s) occupied by a community of monks or nuns **2** the community itself

ab·bot /ab'ət/ *n.* head of a community of monks [OE fr. L *abbas*]

abbr. (also **abbrev.**) *abbr.* abbreviation

ab·bre·vi·ate /əbrē'vē·āt'/ *v.* (**·at·ed, ·at·ing**) shorten, esp. represent (a word, etc.) by a part of it **—ab·bre·vi·a'tion** *n.* [L, rel. to BRIEF]

ab·bre·vi·at·ed /əbrē'vēā'tid/ *adj.* brief; small

ABC /ā'bē'sē'/ *n.* (*pl.* **ABCs** or **ABC's**) **1** the alphabet **2** rudiments of a subject

ab·di·cate /ab'dikāt'/ *v.* (**·cat·ed, ·cat·ing**) **1** give up or renounce (a throne) **2** renounce (a duty, right, etc.) **—ab'di·ca'tion** *n.* [L *dicare* declare]

ab·do·men /ab'dəmən, abdō'-/ *n.* **1** the belly, including the stomach, bowels, etc. **2** the hinder part of an insect, etc. **—ab·dom'i·nal** /abdäm'ənəl/ *adj.* [L]

ab·duct /əbdəkt', ab-/ *v.* carry off illegally; kidnap **—ab·duc'tion, ab·duc'tor** *n.* [L *ducere* lead]

a·beam /əbēm'/ *adv.* at right angles to a vessel's or an aircraft's length

A·bel /ā'bəl/ (in the Bible) son of Adam and Eve; killed by his brother, Cain

Ab·e·lard /ab'əlärd'/, **Peter** 1079–1142; French scholar, theologian, and philosopher

Ab·er·deen /ab'ərdēn'/ *n.* city in Scotland, United Kingdom. Pop. 190,500

ab·er·ra·tion /ab'ərā'SHən/ *n.* **1** abnormal behavior; moral or mental lapse **2** distortion of an image because of an optical defect **—ab·er'rant** /əber'ənt/ *adj.*

a·bet /əbet'/ *v.* (**·bet·ted, ·bet·ting**) encourage or assist (an offender or offense) **—a·bet'tor** or **a·bet'ter** *n.* [Fr, rel. to AD + BAIT]

a·bey·ance /əbā'əns/ *n.* temporary disuse [MFr, rel. to AD + *baer* gape; yawn]

ab·hor /əbhôr', ab-/ *v.* (**·horred, ·hor·ring**) detest; regard with disgust **—ab·hor'rence** *n.* [L, rel. to HORROR]

ab·hor·rent /əbhôr'ənt, ab-/ *adj.* disgusting or hateful

a·bide /əbīd'/ *v.* (**·bode** or **·bid·ed, ·bid·ing**) **1** tolerate; endure **2** remain; continue **3** *(foll. by* by*)* **a** act in accordance with **b** keep (a promise) [OE *a-* intensive prefix + BIDE]

a·bid·ing /əbī'diNG/ *adj.* enduring; permanent

Ab·i·djan /ab'ijän'/ *n.* administrative center of Ivory Coast (Côte d'Ivoire). Pop. 1,850,000

Ab·i·lene /ab'əlēn'/ *n.* city in Texas. Pop. 106,654

a·bil·i·ty /əbil'ətē/ *n.* (*pl.* **·ties**) **1** capacity or power **2** skill; talent [Fr, rel. to ABLE]

-ability *suffix* forming nouns of quality from or corresponding to adjectives in -ABLE

ab·ject /ab'jekt'/ *adj.* miserable; wretched; degraded; despicable **—ab·jec'tion** *n.*; **ab·ject'ly** *adv.*; **ab·ject'ness** *n.* [L *-ject-* fr. *jacere* throw]

ab·jure /abjŏŏr'/ *v.* (**·jured, ·jur·ing**) renounce on oath **—ab'ju·ra'tion** n.; **ab·jur'a·to'ry** adj.; **ab·jur'er** n. [L *jurare* swear]

ab·la·tive /ab'lətiv/ *Gram.* n. 1 case (in Latin) of nouns and pronouns indicating an agent, instrument, or location —adj. 2 of or in the ablative [L *ablatus* taken away]

a·blaze /əblāz'/ adj. & adv. 1 on fire 2 glittering; glowing 3 greatly excited

a·ble /ā'bəl/ adj. (**a·bler, a·blest**) 1 having the capacity or power (*able to come*) 2 talented; clever **—a'bly** adv. [L *habilis*]

-able suffix (also **·ble, ·ible**) forming adjectives meaning: 1 that may or must be (*eatable; payable*) 2 that can be made the subject of (*dutiable; objectionable*) 3 relevant to or in accordance with (*fashionable; seasonable*) [L *-abilis*]

a'ble-bod'ied adj. fit; healthy

a'ble sea'man n. (also **a'ble-bod'ied sea'man**) ordinary trained seaman

ab·lu·tion /əbloo'sHən/ n. (usu. *pl.*) 1 ceremonial washing of the hands, sacred vessels, etc. 2 *Colloq.* ordinary bodily washing [L *abluere ablut-* wash away]

-ably suffix forming adverbs corresponding to adjectives in -ABLE

ABM abbr. anti-ballistic missile

ab·ne·gate /ab'nigāt/ v. (**·gat·ed, ·gat·ing**) give up or renounce (a pleasure, right, etc.) **—ab'ne·ga'tion** n. [L *negare* deny]

ab·nor·mal /abnôr'məl/ adj. deviating from the norm; exceptional **—ab'nor·mal'i·ty** /-mal'itē/ n. (*pl.* **·ties**); **ab·nor'mal·ly** adv. [Fr, rel. to ANOMALOUS]

a·board /əbôrd', əbörd'/ adv. & prep. on or into (a vessel, aircraft, etc.)

a·bode /əbōd'/ n. 1 dwelling place —v. 2 *past* and *past perf.* of ABIDE

a·bol·ish /əbäl'isH/ v. put an end to (esp. a custom or institution) [L *abolere* destroy]

ab·o·li·tion /ab'əlisH'ən/ n. 1 abolishing or being abolished 2 *US Hist.* (often *cap.*) the abolition of slavery **—ab'o·li'tion·ist** n.

A-bomb /ā'bäm'/ n. ATOM BOMB

a·bom·i·na·ble /əbäm'ənəbəl/ adj. 1 detestable; loathsome 2 *Colloq.* very unpleasant **—a·bom'i·na·bly** adv. [L *abominari* deprecate]

a·bom·i·nate /əbäm'ənāt/ v. (**·nat·ed, ·nat·ing**) detest; loathe **—a·bom'i·na'tion** n. [L, rel. to ABOMINABLE]

ab·o·rig·i·nal /ab'ərij'ənəl/ adj. 1 inhabiting a land from the earliest times, esp. before the arrival of colonists 2 of aborigines —n. 3 aboriginal inhabitant [L, rel. to ORIGINAL]

ab·o·rig·i·ne /ab'ərij'ənē/ n. aboriginal inhabitant

a·bort /əbôrt'/ v. 1 miscarry 2 effect abortion 3 end or cause (a project, mission, space flight, etc.) to end before completion [L *aboriri* miscarry]

a·bor'tion n. natural or (esp.) induced expulsion of a fetus from the womb before it is able to survive independently **—a·bor'tion·ist** n.

a·bor'tive adj. fruitless; unsuccessful

a·bound /əbound'/ v. be plentiful; be rich; teem [L *undare* move in waves]

about /əbout'/ prep. 1 on the subject of 2 near to 3 around 4 associated with —adv. 5 approximately 6 nearby 7 in every directio[n] 8 almost; nearly [OE]

a·bout'·face' n. 1 turn made to face in the op[posite] posite direction 2 change of opinion or policy (usu. abrupt or diametrically opposite) **—in** [in]teri. 3 *Milit.* command to make an about-face —v. (**a·bout'-face'**) (**faced, fac·ing**) 4 *Milit[ary]* make an about-face

a·bove /əbəv'/ prep. 1 over; on the top of higher than 2 higher in rank, importance etc., than 3 beyond (*above suspicion*) —adv. 4 at or to a higher point; overhead 5 earlie[r] on a page or in a book —adj. 6 preceding —n. 7 (prec. by *the*) preceding text 8 above all most of all; more than anything else [OE]

a·bove'board' adj. & adv. without conceal[ment]; open or openly

ab·ra·ca·dab·ra /ab'rəkədab'rə/ interj. wor[d] used in conjuring [L fr. Gk]

a·brade /əbrād'/ v. (**·brad·ed, ·brad·ing**) scrape or wear away by rubbing [L *rader[e]* scrape]

A·bra·ham /ā'brəham'/ Hebrew patriarch

ab·ra·sion /əbrā'zHən/ n. 1 result of abrad[ing] 2 resulting damaged area; scrape

ab·ra·sive /əbrā'siv, -ziv/ adj. 1 tending t[o] rub or abrade 2 irritating or hurtful in manne[r] —n. 3 abrasive substance **—a·bra'sive·l[y]** adv.; **a·bra'sive·ness** n.

a·breast /əbrest'/ adv. 1 side by side and fac[ing] ing the same way 2 (foll. by *of*) up to date

a·bridge /əbrij'/ v. (**·bridged, ·bridg·ing**) shorten (a book, film, etc.) **—a·bridg'men[t]** or **a·bridge'ment** n. [L, rel. to ABBREVIATE]

a·broad /əbrôd'/ adv. 1 in or to a foreig[n] country or countries 2 widely 3 in circulatio[n]

ab·ro·gate /ab'rəgāt'/ v. (**·gat·ed, ·gat·ing**) repeal; abolish (a law, etc.) **—ab'ro·ga'tion** ab'ro·ga'tor n. [L *rogare* propose a law]

ab·rupt /əbrəpt'/ adj. 1 sudden; hasty 2 cur[t] 3 steep **—ab·rupt'ly** adv.; **ab·rupt'ness** n[.] [L, rel. to RUPTURE]

ABS abbr. anti-lock braking system

ab·scess /ab'ses'/ n. swelling containing pu[s] [L, rel. to AB- + CEDE]

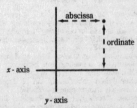

ABSCISSA and ORDINATE

ab·scis·sa /absis'ə/ n. (*pl.* **·sas** or **·sa[s]** /-sē/) *Math.* (in a system of coordinates) shortest distance from a point to the vertica[l] or *y*-axis [L *abscindere* cut off]

ab·scond /abskänd', əb-/ v. depart hurriedl[y] and furtively, esp. to avoid arrest **—ab·scond[']er** n. [L *abscondere* hide from]

ab·seil /ab'sāl'/ v. 1 descend by slippin[g] down a rope —n. 2 descent made by absei[l]ing [Ger *ab* down + *Seil* rope]

ab·sence /ab'səns/ n. 1 being away 2 tim[e] of this 3 lack [L *absentia*]

ab·sent adj. /ˈabˈsənt/ 1 not present 2 not existing; lacking 3 inattentive —v. /ˈabˈsentˈ, abˈsent/ 4 go or stay away —**abˈsentˈly** adv.

ab·sen·tee /ˈabˈsənˈtē/ n. person not present

ab·sen·tee·ism n. habitual absence from work, school, etc.

ab·sen·tee land·lord n. one who lets a property while living elsewhere

ab·sent-mind·ed adj. forgetful or inattentive —**abˈsent-mindˈed·ly** adv.; **abˈsent-mindˈed·ness** n.

ab·sinthe /ˈabˈsinTH/ n. aniseed-flavored liqueur based on wormwood [Fr fr. L fr. Gk]

ab·so·lute /ˈabˈsəlōōt/ adj. 1 complete; utter 2 unconditional 3 not relative or comparative 4 (of a legal decree, etc.) final [L, rel. to ABSOLVE]

ab·so·lute·ly /ˈabˈsəlōōtˈlē, ˈabˈsəlōōtˈlē/ adv. 1 completely; utterly 2 in an absolute sense 3 Colloq. definitely; yes

abˈso·lute ma·jorˈi·ty n. majority over all rivals combined

abˈso·lute pitch (also **perˈfect pitch**) n. ability to identify or sound any given note

abˈso·lute zeˈro n. theoretical lowest possible temperature, calculated as −273.15° C (or −459.67° F or 0° K)

ab·so·lu·tion /ˈabˈsəlōōˈSHən/ n. formal forgiveness of sins

abˈso·lutˈism n. principle or practice of absolute government —**abˈso·lutˈist** n.

ab·solve /əbzälvˈ, -zölvˈ/ v. (-**solved, -solving**) free from blame, obligation, etc. [L, rel. to SOLVE]

ab·sorb /əbsôrbˈ, -zôrbˈ/ v. 1 incorporate as part of itself or oneself 2 take in; suck up 3 reduce the effect or intensity of; cushion 4 consume 5 engross the attention of —**ab·sorbˈing** adj. [L sorbere swallow; suck in]

ab·sor·bent /əbsôrbˈənt, -zôrbˈ-/ adj. 1 tending to absorb —n. 2 absorbent substance or organ —**ab·sorˈben·cy** n.

ab·sorp·tion /əbsôrpˈSHən, -zôrpˈ-/ n. 1 absorbing or being absorbed 2 mental engrossment —**ab·sorpˈtive** adj.

ab·stain /əbstānˈ/ v. refrain (from) —**ab·stainˈer** n.; **ab·stenˈtion** /-stenˈSHən/ n. [L tenere hold]

ab·ste·mi·ous /əbstēˈmēəs/ adj. moderate or temperate, esp. in eating and drinking —**ab·steˈmi·ous·ly** adv.; **ab·steˈmi·ous·ness** n. [L, rel. to AB-, temetum strong drink]

ab·sti·nence /ˈabˈstənəns/ n. abstaining, esp. from food or alcohol —**abˈsti·nent** adj., rel. to ABSTAIN]

ab·stract adj. /abstraktˈ, abˈstrakt/ 1 of or existing in thought or theory rather than matter or practice; not concrete 2 (of a word, esp. a noun) denoting a quality, condition, etc., not a concrete object 3 (of art) achieving its effect by form and color rather than by realism —v. /abstraktˈ, abˈstraktˈ/ 4 extract; remove 5 summarize —n. /abˈstrakt/ 6 summary 7 abstract work of art —**abˈstractˈly** adv.; **abˈstractˈness** n. [L, rel. to TRACT[1]]

ab·stract·ed /abstrakˈtid/ adj. inattentive; distracted —**ab·stractˈed·ly** adv.; **ab·stractˈed·ness** n.

ab·strac·tion /abstrakˈSHən/ n. 1 removal or taking away 2 abstract or visionary idea 3 absent-mindedness

ab·struse /abstrōōsˈ/ adj. hard to understand; profound —**ab·struseˈly** adv.; **ab·struseˈness** n. [L abstrudere abstrus- conceal; thrust away]

ab·surd /əbsərdˈ, -zərdˈ/ adj. wildly illogical or inappropriate; ridiculous —**ab·surdˈi·ty** n. (pl. -**ties**); **ab·surdˈly** adv.; **ab·surdˈness** n. [L surdus deaf; insensible]

A·bu Dha·bi /äˈbōō däbˈē/ n. capital of United Arab Emirates. Pop. 363,400

A·bu·ja /äbōōˈjä/ n. capital of Nigeria. Pop. 298,300

a·bun·dance /əbənˈdəns/ n. plenty; more than enough; a lot —**a·bunˈdant** adj.; **a·bunˈdant·ly** adv. [L, rel. to ABOUND]

a·buse v. /əbyōōzˈ/ (-**bused, -bus·ing**) 1 use improperly; misuse 2 insult verbally 3 maltreat —n. /əbyōōsˈ/ 4 misuse 5 insulting language 6 unjust or corrupt practice 7 maltreatment —**a·busˈer** n.; **a·buˈsive** adj.; **a·buˈsive·ly** adv.; **a·buˈsive·ness** n. [L, rel. to USE]

a·but /əbətˈ/ v. (-**but·ted, -but·ting**) (of land) border on [ME fr. OF abuter touch at the end]

a·but·ment /əbətˈmənt/ n. lateral supporting structure of a bridge, arch, etc.

a·bys·mal /əbizˈməl/ adj. 1 Colloq. extremely bad 2 profound; utter —**a·bysˈmal·ly** adv. [L, rel. to ABYSS]

a·byss /əbisˈ/ n. 1 deep chasm 2 immeasurable depth [L fr. Gk: bottomless]

Ac symb. actinium

AC abbr. 1 (also **ac, A.C., a.c.**) alternating current 2 air conditioning

ac- prefix var. of AD- before c and qu

-ac suffix forming adjectives often (or only) used as nouns (cardiac; maniac) [L -acus fr. Gk -akos]

a·ca·cia /əkāˈSHə/ n. 1 tree with yellow or white flowers, esp. one yielding gum arabic 2 locust tree [L fr. Gk]

ac·a·de·mi·a /akˈədēˈmēə/ n. the academic world; scholastic life

ac·a·dem·ic /akˈədemˈik/ adj. 1 scholarly; of learning 2 of no practical relevance; theoretical —n. 3 teacher or scholar in a university, etc. —**acˈa·demˈi·cal·ly** adv.

ac·a·de·mi·cian /akˈədəmiSHˈən, əkadˈə-/ n. 1 person in academia, esp. one on a college-level faculty 2 member of an Academy [Fr académicien]

a·cad·e·my /əkadˈəmē/ n. (pl. -**mies**) 1 place of specialized training 2 (usu. cap.) society or institution of distinguished scholars, artists, scientists, etc. (National Academy of Arts & Sciences) [Gk Akadēmeia the place in Athens where Plato taught]

a·can·thus /əkanˈTHəs/ n. (pl. -**thus·es** or -**thi** /-THī/) herbaceous plant with spiny leaves [L fr. Gk]

a cap·pel·la /äˈkəpelˈə/ adj. & adv. (of choral singing) unaccompanied [It: in church style]

A·ca·pul·co /akˈəpōōlˈkō, äk-, -pōōlˈ-/ n. Pacific coast city in Mexico; resort. Pop. 301,900

ac·cede /aksēdˈ/ v. (-**ced·ed, -ced·ing**) 1 take office 2 assent or agree [L, rel. to CEDE]

ac·cel·er·ate /akselˈərātˈ/ v. (-**at·ed, -at·ing**) move or cause to move or happen more quickly —ac'cel·er·a'tion n. [L, rel. to CE-LERITY]

ac·cel'er·a'tor n. 1 device for increasing speed, esp. the pedal controlling the speed of a vehicle's engine 2 Physics. apparatus for imparting high speeds to charged particles

ac·cent n. /ak'sent'/ 1 particular (esp. local or national) mode of pronunciation 2 distinctive feature or emphasis 3 prominence given to a syllable by stress or pitch 4 mark on a letter or word to indicate pitch, stress, or vowel quality; diacritic —v. /ak'sent', aksent'/ 5 emphasize (a word, syllable, etc.) 6 write or print accents on (words, etc.) 7 accentuate [L -cent- fr. cantus song]

ac·cen·tu·ate /aksen'CHŌŌ-āt'/ v. (·at·ed, ·at·ing) emphasize; make prominent —ac·cen'tu·a'tion n. [MedL, rel. to ACCENT]

ac·cept /aksept'/ v. 1 willingly receive 2 answer affirmatively 3 regard favorably; treat as welcome 4 believe in [L -cept- fr. capere take]
• Usage: Accept, which means 'to take what is offered,' is often confused with except, which (as a verb) means 'to exclude.'

ac·cept·a·ble /aksep'təbəl/ adj. 1 worth accepting; welcome 2 tolerable —ac·cept'a·bil'i·ty, ac·cept'a·ble·ness n.; ac·cept'a·bly adv. [Fr, rel. to ACCEPT]

ac·cept·ance /aksep'təns/ n. 1 willingness to accept 2 affirmative answer to an invitation, etc.

ac·cess /ak'ses'/ n. 1 way of approach or entry 2 right or opportunity to reach or use or visit; accessibility —v. 3 Comp. gain access to (data, etc.) 4 accession [Fr, rel. to ACCEDE]

ac·ces·si·ble /akses'əbəl/ adj. 1 reachable or obtainable; readily available 2 easy to understand —ac·ces'si·bil'i·ty n.; ac·ces'si·bly adv.

ac·ces·sion /aksesH'ən/ n. 1 taking office, esp. as monarch 2 thing added, esp. to a collection —v. 3 record the addition of (a new item) to a library, etc.

ac·ces·so·ry /akses'ərē/ n. (pl. ·ries) 1 additional or extra thing 2 (usu. pl.) small attachment, fitting, or subsidiary item of dress (e.g., shoes, gloves) 3 person who aids or is privy to an (esp. illegal) act [MedL, rel. to ACCEDE]

ac'cess time' n. Comp. time taken to retrieve data from storage

ac·ci·dent /ak'sədənt/ n. 1 unfortunate and unintended event 2 harmful or damaging event [L accident- fr. accidere befall]

ac·ci·den·tal /ak'sədent'l/ adj. 1 happening by chance or accident —n. 2 Mus. sign indicating a note's momentary departure from the key signature —ac'ci·den'tal·ly adv.

ac'ci·dent-prone' adj. apparently predisposed to accidents

ac·claim /əklām'/ v. 1 welcome or applaud enthusiastically; hail —n. 2 applause; welcome; public praise [L acclamare, rel. to CLAIM]

ac·cla·ma·tion /ak'ləmā'sHən/ n. 1 loud and eager assent 2 supporting voice vote

ac·cli·mate /əklī'mit, ak'ləmāt'/ v. (also ac·cli·ma·tize /əklī'mətīz/) (·mat·ed or ·ma·tized, ·mat·ing or ·ma·tiz·ing) adapt to a

new climate or conditions —ac'cli·ma'tion or ac·cli'ma·ti·za'tion n. [Fr acclimater]

ac·co·lade /ak'əlād/ n. praise given [L collum neck]

ac·com·mo·date /əkäm'ədāt'/ v. (·dat·ed, ·dat·ing) 1 provide lodging or room for 2 adapt; harmonize; reconcile 3 do a favor for [L, rel. to COMMODE]

ac·com'mo·dat'ing adj. obliging; compliant

ac·com'mo·da'tion n. 1 lodgings; space 2 adaptation; settlement; compromise

ac·com·pa·ni·ment /əkəm'pənēmənt/ n. 1 instrumental or orchestral support for a sole instrument, voice, or group 2 accompanying thing —ac·com'pa·nist n.

ac·com·pa·ny /əkəm'pənē/ v. (·nied, ·ny·ing) 1 go with; escort 2 supplement 3 Mus play an accompaniment for (a person) [Fr, rel to COMPANION]

ac·com·plice /əkäm'plis, -kəm'-/ n. partne in a crime [L, rel. to COMPLEX]

ac·com·plish /əkäm'plisH, -kəm'-/ v. succeed in doing; achieve; complete [L, rel. t COMPLETE]

ac·com'plished adj. clever; skilled

ac·com'plish·ment n. 1 completion (of a task etc.) 2 acquired, esp. social, skill 3 thing achieved

ac·cord /əkôrd'/ v. 1 be consistent or in har mony 2 grant (permission, a request, etc. —n. 3 agreement; harmony 4 of one's own accord voluntarily [L cor cord- heart]

ac·cord·ance /əkôr'dəns/ n. conformity —ac·cord'ant adj.

ac·cord·ing /əkôrd'iNG/ adv. 1 (foll. by to as stated by 2 in proportion to

ac·cord·ing·ly /əkôrd'iNGlē/ adv. 1 as cir cumstances suggest or require 2 conse quently

ACCORDION

ac·cor·di·on /əkôrd'ēən/ n. musical reed in strument with bellows, keys, and button —ac·cor'di·on·ist n. [prob. It accordare ha monize]

ac·cost /əkôst', əkäst'/ v. 1 approach and ad dress (a person), esp. boldly 2 (of a prost tute) solicit [L costa side]

ac·count /əkount'/ n. 1 narration; descrip tion (an account of his trip) 2 arrangement a a bank, etc., for depositing and withdrawin money, credit, etc. 3 record or statement c financial transactions 4 CHARGE ACCOUN —v. 5 consider as 6 account for: a serv as or provide an explanation for b make u a specified portion of 7 on account: a (c goods) to be paid for later b (of money) i part payment 8 on account of because of 9 on no account under no circumstances 10 take into account consider [Fr, rel. to COUNT[1]]

ac·count·a·ble /əkount'əbəl/ adj. 1 respon

sible; required to account for one's conduct **2** understandable —**ac·count'a·bil'i·ty** *n.*

ac·count·ant /əkoʊnt'nt/ *n.* professional keeper or verifier of accounts —**ac·count'an·cy, ac·count'ing** *n.*

ac·cou·ter·ments /əkoʊ'tərmənts/ *n.* (also **ac·cou'tre·ments** /-trə-/) **1** clothing **2** soldier's equipment [Fr]

Ac·cra /əkrä'/ *n.* capital of Ghana. Pop. 949,100

ac·cred·it /əkred'it/ *v.* **1** attribute **2** send (a delegate) with credentials **3** believe —**ac·cred'i·ta'tion** *n.* [Fr, rel. to CREDIT]

ac·cre·tion /əkrē'SHən/ *n.* **1** growth or increase by addition or natural growth **2** the resulting whole **3** matter so added [L *-cret-* fr. *crescere* grow]

ac·crue /əkroʊ'/ *v.* (**·crued, ·cru·ing**) come as a natural increase or advantage [L, rel. to ACCRETION]

acct. *abbr.* **1** account **2** accountant

ac·cu·mu·late /əkyoʊm'yəlāt'/ *v.* (**·lat·ed, ·lat·ing**) amass; collect —**ac·cu'mu·la'tion** *n.*; **ac·cu'mu·la'tive** *adj.*; **ac·cu'mu·la'tor** *n.* [L, rel. to CUMULUS]

ac·cu·ra·cy /ak'yərəsē/ *n.* exactness or careful precision [L *cura* care]

ac·cu·rate /ak'yərət/ *adj.* careful; precise; conforming exactly with the truth or a standard —**ac'cu·rate·ly** *adv.*

ac·curs·ed /əkərst', əkərs'əd/ *adj.* **1** under a curse; *Colloq.* detestable; annoying [OE *a-* intensive prefix, CURSE]

ac·cu·sa·tion /ak'yəzā'SHən/ *n.* accusing or being accused —**ac·cu·sa·to·ry** /əkyoʊ' zətôr'ē/ *adj.* [Fr, rel. to ACCUSE]

ac·cu·sa·tive /əkyoʊ'zətiv/ *Gram.* *n.* **1** case expressing the object of an action —*adj.* **2** of or in this case

ac·cuse /əkyoʊz'/ *v.* (**·cused, ·cus·ing**) charge with a fault or crime; blame —**ac·cus'er** *n.* [L *accusare* rel. to CAUSE]

ac·cus·tom /əkəs'təm/ *v.* make used to [Fr, rel. to CUSTOM]

ac·cus·tomed /əkəs'təmd/ *adj.* **1** used to a thing **2** customary; usual

ace /ās/ *n.* **1** playing card with a single spot, often of greatest value **2a** person who excels in some activity **b** pilot who has shot down many enemy aircraft **3** *Tennis.* unreturnable stroke (esp. a service) **4** *Golf.* hole in one —*adj.* **5** *Slang.* excellent —*v.* (**aced, ac·ing**) **6** defeat **7** *Colloq.* earn a grade of A in (a course, examination) **8 within an ace of** on the verge of [ME *as* fr. L: a unit]

a·cer·bic /əsər'bik/ *adj.* harsh and sharp, esp. in speech or manner —**a·cer'bi·ty** *n.* (*pl.* **·ties**) [L *acerbus* sour; bitter]

a·ce·ta·min·o·phen /əsē'tamin'əfən/ *n.* common drug used to reduce pain and fever

ac·e·tate /as'ətāt'/ *n.* **1** salt or ester of acetic acid **2** fabric made from this

a·ce·tic /əsēt'ik/ *adj.* of or like vinegar [L *acetum* vinegar]

a·ce'tic ac'id *n.* clear liquid acid giving vinegar its characteristic taste

ac·e·tone /as'ətōn'/ *n.* colorless volatile liquid that dissolves organic compounds, esp. paints, varnishes, etc.

a·cet·y·lene /əset'l-ēn', -ən/ *n.* gas burning with a bright flame, used esp. with oxygen in welding

ache /āk/ *n.* **1** continuous dull pain **2** mental distress —*v.* (**ached, ach·ing**) **3** suffer an ache [OE]

A·che·be /äCHā'bā/, **Chinua** (born **Albert Chinualumgu**) 1930– ; Nigerian author; Nobel prize 1989

Ach·e·son /aCH'əsən/, **Dean** 1893–1971; US statesman

a·chieve /əCHēv'/ *v.* (**·chieved, ·chiev·ing**) **1** get, esp. by effort **2** accomplish —**a·chiev'a·ble** *adj.*; **a·chiev'er** *n.* [OFr *achever*, rel. to CHIEF]

a·chieve·ment /əCHēv'mənt/ *n.* **1** something achieved **2** act of achieving

A·chil'les heel' /əkil'ēz/ *n.* person's weak or vulnerable point [for *Achilles*, Gk hero in the *Iliad*]

Achil'les ten'don *n.* tendon connecting the heel with the calf muscles

ach·ro·mat·ic /ak'rəmat'ik/ *adj.* *Optics.* transmitting light without separation into constituent colors —**ach'ro·mat'i·cal·ly** *adv.*; **a·chro·ma·tism** /əkrō'mətiz'əm/ *n.* [rel. to A-, CHROME]

ac·id /as'id/ *n.* **1** any of a class of substances that are usu. sour and corrosive, turn litmus red, and react with a base to make a salt **2** any sour substance **3** *Slang.* the drug LSD —*adj.* **4** sour **5** biting; sharp **6** *Chem.* having the properties of an acid —**a·cid·ic** /əsid'ik/ *adj.*; **a·cid·i·fy** /əsid'əfī'/ *v.* (**·fied, ·fy·ing**); **a·cid'i·ty** *n.*; **ac'id·ly** *adv.* [L *acidus* sour fr. *acer* sharp]

ac'id rain' *n.* acidic rainwater, esp. from industrial waste gases

ac'id rock' *n.* rock music associated with psychedelic drugs

ac'id test' *n.* severe or conclusive test

a·cid·u·lous /əsij'ələs/ *adj.* somewhat acid

ack·ack /ak'ak'/ *Colloq.* *adj.* **1** anti-aircraft —*n.* **2** anti-aircraft gun

ac·knowl·edge /aknäl'ij/ *v.* (**·edged, ·edg·ing**) **1** recognize; accept as truth **2** confirm the receipt of (a letter, etc.) **3** respond to **4** express appreciation for **5** recognize the validity of —**ac·knowl'edg·ment** or **ac·knowl'edge·ment** *n.* [*ac-* fr. AD- + KNOWLEDGE]

ac·me /ak'mē/ *n.* highest point [Gk]

ac·ne /ak'nē/ *n.* skin condition causing pimples [Gk]

ac·o·lyte /ak'əlīt'/ *n.* **1** person assisting a priest **2** assistant; beginner [Gk *akolouthos* follower]

A·con·ca·gua /äk'ənkäg'wə/ *n.* highest mountain in W hemisphere, in the Andes in Argentina; 22,831 ft.

ac·o·nite /ak'ənīt'/ *n.* any of various poisonous plants [Gk *akoniton*]

a·corn /ā'kôrn', -kərn/ *n.* fruit of the oak, with a smooth nut in a cuplike base [OE]

a·cous·tic /əkoʊ'stik/ *adj.* **1** of sound or the sense of hearing **2** (of a musical instrument, etc.) without electrical amplification —**a·cous'ti·cal·ly** *adv.* [Gk *akouein* hear]

a·cous·tics /əkoʊ'stiks/ *n. pl.* **1** properties or qualities (of a room, etc.) in transmitting sound **2** (usu. as *sing.*) science of sound —**ac·ous·ti·cian** /ak'oʊstish'ən/ *n.*

ac·quaint /əkwänt'/ *v.* make aware of or familiar with [L, rel. to AD- + COGNIZANCE]

ac·quaint·ance /əkwänt′ns/ *n.* **1** being acquainted **2** person one knows slightly —**ac·quain′tance·ship′** *n.*

ac·qui·esce /ak′wē-es′/ *v.* (**·esced, ·esc·ing**) **1** agree, esp. by default **2** accept (an arrangement, etc.) —**ac′qui·es′cence** *n.*; **ac′qui·es′cent** *adj.* [L, rel. to AD- + QUIET]

ac·quire /əkwīr′/ *v.* (**·quired, ·quir·ing**) gain for oneself; come into possession of —**ac·quir′a·ble** *adj.*; **ac·quire′ment** *n.* [L, rel. to AD- + -*quirere* fr. *quaerere* seek]

ac·quired′ im·mune′ de·fi′cien·cy syn′drome *n.* AIDS

ac·qui·si·tion /ak′wəzish′ən/ *n.* **1** thing acquired **2** acquiring or being acquired [L, rel. to ACQUIRE]

ac·quis·i·tive /əkwiz′ətiv/ *adj.* keen to acquire things

ac·quit /əkwit′/ *v.* (**·quit·ted, ·quit·ting**) **1** declare not guilty **2** behave or perform in a specified way (*acquitted herself well*) **3** discharge (a duty or responsibility) —**ac·quit′tal** *n.* [L, rel. to AD- + QUIT]

a·cre /ā′kər/ *n.* measure of land (43,560 sq. ft.) [OE]

a·cre·age /ā′k(ə)rij/ *n.* a number of acres

ac·rid /ak′rid/ *adj.* bitterly pungent —**a·crid·i·ty** /əkrid′itē/ *n.* [L *acr-* fr. *acer* sharp; pungent]

ac·ri·mo·ni·ous /ak′rəmō′nēəs/ *adj.* bitter in manner or temper —**ac′ri·mo′ny** *n.*

ac·ro·bat /ak′rəbat′/ *n.* one performing gymnastic feats —**ac·ro·bat′ic** *adj.*; **ac′ro·bat′i·cal·ly** *adv.* [Gk *akrobatos* fr. *akro-* highest + *-batos* fr. *bainein* walk]

ac·ro·bat·ics /ak′rəbat′iks/ *n. pl.* **1** acrobatic feats **2** maneuvers requiring skill

ac·ro·nym /ak′rənim′/ *n.* pronounceable word formed from the first or first few letters of other words (e.g., *laser, NATO*) [Gk *akros* end; top + *onyma* var. of *onoma* name]

A·crop·o·lis /əkräp′əlis/ *n.* citadel of Athens, site of the Parthenon [Gk *akro-* on high + *polis* city]

a·cross /əkrôs′/ *prep.* **1** to or on the other side of **2** from one side to another side of **3** into contact with —*adv.* **4** to or on the other side **5** from one side to another **6** so as to be understood [rel. to CROSS]

• Usage: Avoid the pronunciation of *across* with a *t*-sound at the end of the word, which many regard as unacceptable.

a·cross′-the-board′ *adj.* **1** (of a bet) covering all possibilities **2** affecting all

a·cros·tic /əkrôs′tik/ *n.* poem, etc., in which certain letters (usu. the first and last in each line) form a word or words [Gk *akros* end; top + *stikhos* row]

a·cryl·ic /əkril′ik/ *adj.* **1** of synthetic material made from acrylic acid —*n.* **2** acrylic fiber

act /akt/ *n.* **1** something done; a deed **2** process of doing **3** unit of entertainment **4** pretense **5** main division of a play, etc. **6** law —*v.* **7** behave **8** perform an action or function; take action **9** affect **10** perform a part in a play, film, etc. **11 act up** *Colloq.* misbehave; give trouble **12 get one's act together** *Slang* become properly organized [L *actus* fr. *agere* do]

ACTH *abbr.* hormone that stimulates the adrenal glands [adrenocorticotropic hormone]

act·ing /ak′tiNG/ *n.* **1** art or occupation of an actor —*adj.* **2** serving temporarily

ac·tin·i·um /aktin′ēəm/ *n.* *Chem.* radioactive metallic element; *symb.* **Ac** [Gk *aktis* ray]

ac·tion /ak′shən/ *n.* **1** process of doing or acting **2** forcefulness or energy **3** exertion of energy or influence **4** deed; act **5** series of events in a story, play, etc **6** *Slang.* exciting activity **7** battle; fighting (*killed in action*) **8** mechanism of an instrument **9** lawsuit

ac·tion·a·ble /ak′shənəbəl/ *adj.* giving cause for legal action

ac·ti·vate /ak′təvāt′/ *v.* (**·vat·ed, ·vat·ing**) **1** make active **2** *Chem.* cause reaction in **3** make radioactive —**ac′ti·va′tor** *n.*

ac·tive /ak′tiv/ *adj.* **1** marked by action; energetic **2** *Gram.* designating the form of a verb whose subject performs the action (e.g., *saw* in *he saw a film*) —*n.* **3** *Gram.* active form or voice of a verb —**ac′tive·ly** *adv.* [L, rel. to ACT]

ac′tiv·ism′ *n.* policy of energetic action, esp. for a political cause —**ac′tiv·ist** *n.*

ac·tiv·i·ty /aktiv′ətē/ *n.* (*pl.* **·ties**) **1** busy or energetic action **2** (often *pl.*) occupation or pursuit

ac·tor /ak′tər/ *n.* (*fem.* **ac·tress** /ak′tris/) person who acts in a play, film, etc. [L, rel. to ACT]

ac·tu·al /ak′CH(ōō)əll/ *adj.* **1** existing in fact; real **2** current [L, rel. to ACT]

ac·tu·al·i·ty /ak′CHŌŌ-al′ətē/ *n.* (*pl.* **·ties**) **1** reality **2** (*pl.*) existing conditions

ac·tu·al·ly /ak′CH(ōō)əlē/ *adv.* **1** in fact; really **2** strange as it may seem

ac·tu·ar·y /ak′CHŌŌ-er′ē/ *n.* (*pl.* **·ar·ies**) statistician, esp. one who calculates insurance risks and premiums —**ac·tu·ar′i·al** *adj.* [L *actuarius* bookkeeper]

ac·tu·ate /ak′CHŌŌ-āt′/ *v.* (**·at·ed, ·at·ing**) **1** cause to function **2** cause to act [L, rel. to ACT]

a·cu·i·ty /əkyōō′ətē/ *n.* sharpness; acuteness [MedL, rel. to ACUTE]

a·cu·men /əkyōō′mən, ak′yəmən/ *n.* keen insight or discernment [L: sharpness]

ac·u·punc·ture /ak′yəpəNGK′CHər/ *n.* medical treatment using needles in parts of the body —**ac′u·punc′tur·ist** *n.* [L *acu* needle + PUNCTURE]

a·cute /əkyōōt′/ *adj.* (**·cut·er, ·cut·est**) **1** serious; severe **2** (of senses) keen; penetrating **3** (of a disease) coming quickly to a crisis; not chronic **4** (of an angle) less than 90° —*n.* **5** ACUTE ACCENT —**a·cute′ly** *adv.*; **a·cute′ness** *n.* [L *acutus* pointed; sharpened]

a·cute′ ac′cent *n.* diacritical mark (′) placed over certain letters to show pronunciation, stress, etc.

-acy *suffix* forming nouns of state or quality (*accuracy; piracy*), or an instance of it (*conspiracy; fallacy*) [L *-acia; -atia*]

ad- *prefix* implying motion or direction to; reduction or change into; addition, adherence, increase, or intensification [L]

A.D. *abbr.* (also **AD**) of the Christian era [ANNO DOMINI]

ad /ad/ *n.* *Colloq.* advertisement [abbr.]

ad·age /ad′ij/ *n.* proverb [Fr fr. L]

a·da·gio /ədäzн′(ē)ō/ *adv. & adj. Mus.* **1** in

slow time —*n.* (*pl.* ·**gios**) **2** such a movement or passage [It: at ease]

Ad·am /ad'əm/ the first man [Heb: man]

ad·a·mant /ad'əmənt/ *adj.* stubbornly resolute; unyielding —**ad'a·mant·ly** *adv.* [L *adamas adamant·* untameable fr. Gk]

Ad·ams /ad'əmz/ **1 Samuel** 1722–1803; US patriot **2 John** 1735–1826; 2nd US president (1797–1801) **3 John Quincy** 1767–1848; 6th US president (1825–29) **4 Ansel** 1902–84; US photographer

Ad'am's ap'ple *n.* projection of cartilage at the front of the neck, esp. of a man

A·da·na /äd'ənä/ *n.* city in Turkey. Pop. 916,200

a·dapt /ədapt'/ *v.* **1** fit; adjust (one thing to another) **2** adjust (oneself) to new conditions —**a·dapt'a·ble** *adj.*; **ad'ap·ta'tion, a·dap'tor** *n.* [L, rel. to AD- + APT]

● **Usage:** Avoid confusing this with *adopt.*

add /ad/ *v.* **1** join (one thing to another) to increase or supplement **2** (also **add up**) put together (numbers) to find their total **3** say further **4 add up** *Colloq.* make sense [L *addere*]

Ad·dams /ad'əmz/, **Jane** 1860–1935; US social reformer and feminist

ad·dend /ad'end/ *n.* number added to another

ad·den·dum /əden'dəm/ *n.* (*pl.* ·**da**) thing to be added, as at the end of a book

ad·der /ad'ər/ *n.* small venomous snake, esp. the common viper [OE, orig. *nadder*]

ad·dict /ad'ikt/ *n.* **1** person addicted, esp. to a drug **2** *Colloq.* devotee —*v.* **3** become an addict —**ad·dic'tion** *n.*; **ad·dic'tive** *adj.* [L, rel. to AD- + *dicere* determine; fix]

Ad·dis A·ba·ba /ad'is ab'əbə/ *n.* capital of Ethiopia. Pop. 1,732,000

Ad·di·son /ad'əsən/, **Joseph** 1672–1719; English poet, dramatist, and essayist

ad·di·tion /ədisH'ən/ *n.* **1** adding **2** person or thing added **3 in addition** also; as well (as) [L, rel. to ADD]

ad·di·tion·al /ədisH'(ə)nəl/ *adj.* added; extra; supplementary —**ad·di'tion·al·ly** *adv.*

ad·di·tive /ad'ətiv/ *n.* **1** substance added to improve another, esp. to color, flavor, or preserve food —*adj.* **2** involving addition [L, rel. to ADD]

ad·dle /ad'l/ *v.* (·**dled, ·dling**) **1** confuse **2** (of an egg) become rotten [OE: filth]

addn. *abbr.* addition

ad·dress /ə'dres', ad'res/ **1** place where a person lives, an organization is situated, or their mail is sent **2** *Comp.* location of an item of stored information **3** speech to an audience —*v.* /ədres'/ **4** write postal directions on (an envelope, etc.) **5** speak or write to, esp. formally **6** direct one's attention to **7** *Golf.* take aim at (the ball) [Fr, rel. to AD- + EQUATE]

ad·dress·ee /ad'res'ē', ədres'ē'/ *n.* person to whom a letter, etc., is addressed

ad·duce /əd(y)ōōs'/ *v.* (·**duced, ·duc·ing**) name as an instance or as proof or evidence —**ad·duc'i·ble** or **ad·duce'a·ble** *adj.* [L AD- + *ducere* lead]

Ad·e·laide /ad'l·ād'/ *n.* city in Australia. Pop. 1,023,600

A·den /äd'n, ād'n/ *n.* economic capital of Yemen. Pop. 318,000

A·den, Gulf of /äd'n, ād'n/ *n.* arm of the Arabian Sea S of the Arabian Peninsula

A·de·nau·er /äd'n·ou'ər, ad'-/, **Konrad** 1876–1967; first chancellor of the Federal Republic of Germany (1949–63)

ad·e·noids /ad'n·oidz/ *n.* area of lymphatic tissue between the nose and the throat —**ad·e·noi'dal** /ad'n·oid'l/ *adj.* [Gk *adēn* gland]

a·dept *adj.* /ədept'/ **1** skillful —*n.* (ad·ept) /ad'ept'/ **2** adept person —**a·dept'ly** *adv.*; **a·dept'ness** *n.* [L *adept·* fr. *adipisci* attain]

ad·e·quate /ad'ikwət/ *adj.* sufficient, satisfactory —**ad·e·qua·cy** /ad'əkwəsē/ *n.*; **ad'e·quate·ly** *adv.* [L, rel. to AD- + EQUATE]

ad·here /adhēr'/ *v.* (·**hered, ·her·ing**) **1** stick fast to a substance, etc. **2** behave according to (a rule, etc.) **3** give allegiance [L *haerere* to stick; cling]

ad·her·ent /adhēr'ənt, ədher-/ *n.* **1** supporter —*adj.* **2** sticking; adhering —**ad·her'ence** *n.*

ad·he·sion /adhē'zHən, əd-/ *n.* **1** adhering **2** unnatural union of body tissues

ad·he·sive /adhē'siv/ *adj.* **1** sticky; causing adhesion —*n.* **2** adhesive substance —**ad·he'sive·ness** *n.*

ad hoc /ad' häk', hōk'/ *adv. & adj.* for one particular occasion or use [L]

a·dieu /əd(y)ōō'/ *interj.* (*pl.* **a·dieus** or **a·dieux**) goodbye [MFr: to God]

ad in·fi·ni·tum /ad' in'fənīt'əm/ *adv.* without limit; for ever [L]

ad·i·os /ad'ēōs', ä'dēōs'/ *interj.* goodbye [Sp: to God]

ad·i·pose /ad'əpōs'/ *adj.* of fat; fatty —**ad'i·pos'i·ty** /-päs'ətē/ *n.* [L *adip·* fr. *adeps* fat]

Ad'i·ron'dack Moun'tains /ad'ərän'dak/ *n.* part of the Appalachian range, in NE N.Y.

adj. *abbr.* adjective

ad·ja·cent /əjā'sənt/ *adj.* lying near; adjoining —**ad·ja'cen·cy** *n.* [L *jacere* to lie]

ad·jec·tive /aj'iktiv/ *n.* word used to describe or modify a noun or pronoun —**ad·jec·ti·val** /aj'ikti'vəl/ *adj.*; **ad'jec·ti'val·ly** *adv.* [L *jacere* to lie]

ad·join /əjoin'/ *v.* be next to and joined with —**ad·join'ing** *adj.* [L *jungere* join]

ad·journ /əjərn'/ *v.* **1** postpone; suspend (a meeting, etc.) temporarily **2** (of a meeting) break and disperse or (foll. by **to**) transfer to another place —**ad·journ'ment** *n.* [L AD- + *diurnus* daily]

ad·judge /əjəj'/ *v.* (·**judged, ·judg·ing**) **1** pronounce judgment on (a matter) **2** pronounce or award judicially —**ad·judg'ment** or **ad·judge'ment** *n.* [L *judicare* to judge]

ad·ju·di·cate /əjōōd'ikāt'/ *v.* (·**cat·ed, ·cat·ing**) **1** act as judge in a competition, court, etc. **2** adjudge —**ad·ju·di·ca'tion** *n.*; **ad·ju'di·ca'tive** *adj.*; **ad·ju'di·ca'tor** *n.*

ad·junct /aj'əNGkt'/ *n.* subordinate or incidental thing [L, rel. to ADJOIN]

ad·jure /əjōōr'/ *v.* (·**jured, ·jur·ing**) beg or command —**ad'ju·ra'tion** *n.* [L *adjurare* put to oath, rel. to JURY]

ad·just /əjəst'/ *v.* **1** order or position; regulate; arrange **2** adapt **3** settle **4** assess (insured loss or damages) —**ad·just'a·ble** *adj.*;

ad·just'er or **ad·jus'tor, ad·just'ment** n. [L *adjuxtare* fr. *juxta* near]

ad·ju·tant /aj'ətənt/ n. **1** army officer assisting a superior **2** assistant [L *adjutant-* fr. *adjutare* to help]

Ad·ler /ad'lər/, **Alfred** 1870–1937; Austrian psychiatrist

ad lib /ad' lib'/ v. **(libbed, lib·bing) 1** improvise —*adj.* **2** improvised —*adv.* **3** as one pleases; to any desired extent [abbr. of L *ad libitum* according to pleasure]

ad loc *abbr.* to or at that place [L *ad locum*]

ad·man /ad'man'/ n. (*pl.* **·men**) man working in advertising

ad·min·is·ter /ədmin'əstər/ v. **1** manage **2** deliver or dispense, esp. formally (a punishment, sacrament, etc.) **3** dispense medicine or treatment (to) **4** direct the taking of (an oath) [L AD- + MINISTER]

ad·min·is·trate /ədmin'əstrāt/ v. **(·trat·ed, ·trat·ing)** manage; act as an administrator —**ad·min'is·tra'tive** *adj.*; **ad·min'is·tra'tive·ly** *adv.*

ad·min·is·tra'tion n. **1** administering; management **2** government in power

ad·min'is·tra'tor n. **1** manager **2** *Law.* person appointed to manage the estate of one who has died

ad·mi·ra·ble /ad'm(ə)rəbəl/ *adj.* deserving admiration; excellent —**ad'mi·ra·bly** *adv.*

ad·mi·ral /ad'm(ə)rəl/ n. **1a** commander-in-chief of a fleet **1b** high-ranking naval officer **2** any of various butterflies [Ar, rel. to AMIR]

ad·mi·ral·ty /ad'm(ə)rəltē/ n. (*pl.* **·ties**) *Brit. Hist.* committee superintending the Royal Navy

ad·mi·ra'tion /ad'mərāSHən/ n. respect; warm approval or pleasure

ad·mire /ədmīr'/ v. **(·mired, ·mir·ing) 1** regard with approval, respect, or satisfaction **2** express admiration of —**ad·mir'er** n.; **ad·mir'ing** *adj.*; **ad·mir'ing·ly** *adv.* [L AD- + *mirari* wonder at]

ad·mis·si·ble /ədmis'əbəl/ *adj.* **1** (of an idea, etc.) worth accepting or considering **2** *Law.* allowable as evidence [L, rel. to ADMIT]

ad·mis·sion /ədmisH'ən/ n. **1** acknowledgment **2a** process or right of entering **b** charge for this

● Usage: *Admission* more often refers to the price paid or the right to enter: *Admission was $3. Admittance* more often refers to physical entry: *No Admittance.* In modern usage they are often used interchangeably.

ad·mit /ədmit'/ v. **(·mit·ted, ·mit·ting) 1** acknowledge; recognize as true **2** confess **3** allow (a person) entrance, access, etc. **4** accommodate —**ad·mit'tance** n. [L *mittere* send]

ad·mit·ted·ly /ədmit'ədlē/ *adv.* as must be admitted

ad·mix·ture /admiks'CHər/ n. **1** thing added, esp. a minor ingredient **2** mixture

ad·mon·ish /ədmän'isH/ v. **1** warn **2** urge; advise **3** scold mildly —**ad·mon'ish·ment, ad·mo·ni·tion** /ad'mənisH'ən/ n.; **ad·mon'i·to'ry** /-tôrē/ *adj.* [L *monere* warn]

ad nau·se·am /ad nô'zēəm/ *adv.* excessively; disgustingly [L: to sickness]

a·do /ədo͞o'/ n. fuss; trouble [fr. AT + DO[1]; orig. in *much ado* much to do]

a·do·be /ədō'bē/ n. **1** sun-dried brick **2** clay for making these **3** building of adobe [Sp]

ad·o·les·cent /ad'l·es'ənt/ *adj.* **1** between childhood and adulthood —n. **2** adolescent person —**ad'o·les'cence** n. [L *adolescent-* fr. *adolescere* grow up]

A·do·nis /ədän'əs, -dō'nəs/ n. **1** *Gk. Myth.* handsome youth loved by Aphrodite **2** any very handsome young man

a·dopt /ədäpt'/ v. **1** legally take another's child as one's own **2** choose **3** take over (another's idea, etc.) —**a·dop'tion** n. [L AD- + OPT]

● Usage: Avoid confusing this with *adapt.*

a·dop·tive /ədäp'tiv/ *adj.* by adoption

a·dor·a·ble /ədôr'əbəl/ *adj. Colloq.* delightful; charming

a·dore /ədôr'/ v. **(·dored, ·dor·ing) 1** love intensely **2** worship as divine **3** *Colloq.* like very much —**ad·o·ra'tion, a·dor'er** n. [L *adorare* worship]

a·dorn /ədôrn'/ v. add beauty to; decorate —**a·dorn'ment** n. [L AD- + *ornare* decorate]

ADP *abbr.* **1** automatic data processing **2** adenosine diphosphate, a nucleic acid essential to living cells

a·dre·nal /ədrēn'l/ *adj.* **1** at or near the kidneys **2** of the adrenal glands —n. **3** (in full **ad·re'nal gland'**) either of two ductless glands above the kidneys, secreting epinephrine [fr. AD- + RENAL]

A·dren·a·lin /ədren'l-ən/ n. *Tdmk.* epinephrine

A·dri·at·ic Sea /ā'drē·at'ik/ n. arm of the Mediterranean Sea between the Balkan Peninsula and Italy

a·drift /ədrift'/ *adv. & adj.* **1** drifting **2** powerless; aimless

a·droit /ədroit'/ *adj.* dexterous; skillful —**a·droit'ly** *adv.*; **a·droit'ness** n. [Fr *à droit* according to right]

ad·sorb /adsôrb', -zôrb'/ v. (usu. of a solid) hold (molecules of a gas or liquid, etc.) to its surface, as a thin film —**ad·sor'bent** *adj.* & n.; **ad·sorp·tion** /-sôrp'SHən, -zôrp'-/ n. [fr. AD- + ABSORB]

ad·u·late /aj'ŏŏlāt/ v. **(·lat·ed, ·lat·ing)** flatter obsequiously —**ad·u·la'tion** n. [L *adulation-* fr. *adulare* fawn on]

a·dult /ədəlt', ad'əlt'/ *adj.* **1** mature; grown-up **2** of or for adults —n. **3** adult person —**a·dult'hood** n. [L *adultus* grown]

a·dul·ter·ate /ədəl'tərāt'/ v. **(·at·ed, ·at·ing)** debase by adding other substances —**a·dul'ter·ant** *adj.* & n.; **a·dul'ter·a'tion** n. [L *adulterare* corrupt]

a·dul·ter·er /ədəl'tərər/ n. (*fem.* **a·dul'ter·ess**) person who commits adultery

a·dul·ter·y /ədəl'tərē/ n. voluntary sexual intercourse between a married person and a person other than his or her spouse —**a·dul'ter·ous** *adj.*

ad·um·brate /ad'əmbrāt, ədəm'-/ v. **(·brat·ed, ·brat·ing) 1** indicate faintly or in outline **2** foreshadow **3** overshadow —**ad'um·bra'tion** n. [L AD- + *umbra* shade]

ad·vance /ədvans'/ v. **(·vanced, ·vanc·ing) 1** move or put forward; progress **2** pay or lend (money) beforehand **3** promote **4** present (a suggestion, etc.) —n. **5** progress **6** prepayment; loan **7** (*pl.*) amorous approaches **8** rise in price —*adj.* **9** beforehand **10 in advance** abroad in place or time —**ad·vance′ ment** *n.* [L AB- + *ante* before]

ad·vanced *adj.* **1** greater **2** further ahead **3** beyond elementary stages

ad·van·tage /əd·van′tij/ *n.* **1** beneficial feature **2** benefit, profit **3** superiority **4** *Tennis.* the next point after deuce —*v.* (·taged, ·taging) **5** benefit; favor **6 take advantage of:** **a** make good use of **b** exploit, esp. unfairly **c** *Euphem.* seduce —**ad·van·ta·geous** /ad′vəntā′jəs, -van′-/ *adj.* [Fr, rel. to ADVANCE]

Ad·vent /ad′vent′/ *n.* **1** season before Christmas **2** coming of Christ **3** (a-) important arrival [L *adventus* fr. *venire* come]

ad·ven·ti·tious /ad′ventiSH′əs/ *adj.* accidental; casual [L, rel. to ADVENT]

ad·ven·ture /ədven′CHər/ *n.* **1** unusual and exciting experience **2** daring enterprise —*v.* (·tured, ·tur·ing) **3** dare; venture —**ad·ven′ tur·ous** *adj.*; **ad·ven′tur·ous·ly** *adv.*; **ad·ven′tur·ous·ness** *n.* [L, rel. to ADVENTURE]

ad·ven·tur·er /ədven′CH(ə)rər/ *n.* (*fem.* **ad·ven′tur·ess**) **1** person who seeks adventure **2** financial speculator

ad·verb /ad′vərb′/ *n.* word indicating manner, degree, circumstance, etc., used to modify a verb, an adjective, or another adverb (e.g., *gently, quite, then*) —**ad·ver′bi·al** *adj.* [L *verbum* word, rel. to VERB]

ad·ver·sar·y /ad′və(r)ser′ē/ *n.* (*pl.* ·sar·ies) enemy; opponent —**ad·ver·sar′i·al** *adj.*

ad·verse /advərs′/ *adj.* unfavorable; harmful —**ad·verse′ly** *adv.* [L *adversus* against]

• Usage: *Adverse* is most often used before a noun to mean 'contrary; unfavorable': *She had an adverse reaction to my suggestion. Averse* is most often used after a verb to mean 'opposed; reluctant': *He was not averse to changing the schedule.*

ad·ver·si·ty /advər′sətē/ *n.* misfortune; distress

ad·vert /ad′vərt/ *v.* call attention to

ad·ver·tise /ad′vərtīz/ *v.* (·tised, ·tis·ing) **1** promote (goods or services) publicly to increase sales **2** make generally known **3** place an advertisement [MFr *avertir*, rel. to ADVERSE]

ad·ver·tise·ment /ad′vərtīz′mənt, ədvərt′ əzmənt/ *n.* public announcement

ad·vice /ədvīs′/ *n.* recommendation about how to act

ad·vis·a·ble /ədvī′zəbəl/ *adj.* to be recommended; expedient —**ad·vis·a·bil′i·ty** *n.*

ad·vise /ədvīz′/ *v.* (·vised, ·vis·ing) **1** give advice to **2** recommend **3** inform —**ad·vis′ er** or **ad·vi′sor** *n.* [L AD- + *visus* fr. *videre* see]

ad·vis·ed·ly /ədvī′zədlē/ *adv.* deliberately

ad·vi·so·ry /ədvī′z(ə)rē/ *adj.* **1** giving advice —*n.* (*pl.* ·ries) **2** information, esp. warning about a storm

ad·vo·cate *n.* /ad′vəkət/ **1** person who supports or speaks in favor **2** person who pleads for another, esp. in a court of law —*v.* /-kāt′/ (·cat·ed, ·cat·ing) **3** recommend by argument [L AD- + *vocare* call]

adz /adz/ *n.* (also **adze**) tool like an ax for coarsely shaping timber [OE]

Ae·ge·an Sea /ijē′ən, ē-/ *n.* arm of the Mediterranean Sea between Greece and Turkey

ae·gis /ē′jis/ *n.* protection; support [Gk *aigis* shield of Zeus or Athena]

Ael·fric /al′frik/ c. 955 – c. 1020; English monk, writer, and grammarian

ae·on /ē′ən, ē′än/ *n.* var. of EON

aer·ate /ar′āt′, er′āt′/ *v.* (·at·ed, ·at·ing) **1** charge (a liquid) with carbon dioxide **2** expose to air —**aer·a′tion, aer′a′tor** *n.* [L fr. Gk *aēr* air]

aer·i·al /ar′ēəl, er′-/ *n.* **1** radio or TV antenna —*adj.* **2** by, in, or from the air **3** in the air **4** of or like air —**aer′i·al·ly** *adv.* [Gk, rel. to AIR]

aer′i·al·ist *n.* tightrope walker or trapeze acrobat

aer·ie /ar′ē, er′ē/ *n.* (also **ey′rie**) **1** lofty nest of a bird of prey **2** house, etc., perched high up [AngFr, OFr *airie* fr. L *ager* field]

aero- comb. form air; aircraft [Gk *aero-* fr. *aēr* air]

aer·o·bat·ics /ar′əbat′ik, er′-/ *n. pl.* spectacular flying of aircraft, esp. to entertain [fr. AERO-, after ACROBATICS]

aer·o·bic /arō′bik, er-, ər-/ *adj.* requiring air or oxygen to function [Gk AERO- + *bios* life]

aer·o·bics *n. pl.* vigorous exercises designed to increase oxygen intake

aer·o·dy·nam·ics /ar′ōdīnam′iks, er′-/ *n. pl.* (usu. treated as *sing.*) dynamics of solid bodies moving through air —**aer′o·dy·nam′ic** *adj.*

aer·o·nau·tics /ar′ənôt′iks, er′-/ *n.* (usu. treated as *sing.*) science or practice of motion in the air —**aer′o·nau′tic, aer′o·nau′ti·cal** *adj.* [fr. AERO- + NAUTICAL]

aer·o·plane /ar′əplān′, er′-/ *n. Brit.* var. of AIRPLANE

aer·o·sol /ar′əsäl′, er′-, -sôl′/ *n.* **1** pressurized container for releasing a substance as a fine spray **2** minute particles suspended in gas [fr. AERO- + SOL]

aer·o·space /ar′əspās′, er′-/ *n.* **1** earth's atmosphere and outer space —*adj.* **2** designed for use in aerospace

Aes·chy·lus /es′kələs/ c. 525 – c. 456 B.C.; Greek tragedian

Ae·sop /ē′säp′, -səp/ 6th cent. B.C.; Greek fable writer

aes·thete /es′THēt′/ *n.* (also **es′thete**) person who has or professes a special appreciation of beauty [Gk *aisthētēs* one who perceives]

aes·thet·ic /esTHet′ik/ *adj.* **1** of or sensitive to beauty **2** artistic; tasteful —*n.* **3** (*pl.*) philosophy of beauty, esp. in art —**aes·thet′i· cal·ly** *adv.*; **aes·thet′i·cism** *n.*

a·far /əfär′/ *adv.* at or to a distance

AFB *abbr.* Air Force Base

af·fa·ble /af′əbəl/ *adj.* **1** friendly **2** courteous —**af′fa·bil′i·ty** *n.*; **af′fa·bly** *adv.* [L *affabilis* courteous]

af·fair /əfer′, əfar′/ *n.* **1** matter, concern, or thing to attend to **2** celebrated or notorious happening **3** *Colloq.* thing or event **4** amorous relationship **5** (*pl.*) public or private business [OFr *à faire* to do fr. L]

af·fect /əfekt′/ *v.* **1** produce an effect on **2** move emotionally **3** pretend **4** pose as or use for effect —*n.* /af′ekt/ **5** *Psychol.* emotion;

feeling —af·fect'ing adj.; af·fect'ing·ly adv. [L affectare to pursue; aim at]

● Usage: The verb affect means 'influence': His insults affected her deeply. It should not be confused with the verb effect, meaning 'bring about, accomplish': We effected a compromise. Effect as a noun means 'result': The compromise had a bad effect. The movie has good special effects. The noun affect, which means 'emotion', is a term used in psychology and psychiatry.

af·fec·ta·tion /af'ek'tā'sнən/ n. 1 artificial manner or behavior 2 pretense

af·fect·ed /əfek'tid/ adj. 1 pretended; artificial 2 full of affectation

af·fec·tion /əfek'sнən/ n. 1 good will; fond feeling 2 disease; diseased condition

af·fec·tion·ate /əfek'sнənət/ adj. loving; fond —af·fec'tion·ate·ly adv.

af·fi·da·vit /af'ədā'vit/ n. written statement confirmed by oath [L: has stated on oath]

af·fil·i·ate v. /əfil'ē·āt'/ (·at·ed, ·at·ing) 1 attach, adopt, or connect as a member or branch —n. /əfil'ē·ət'/ 2 affiliated person, etc. —af·fil'i·a'tion n. [L, rel. to FILIAL]

af·fin·i·ty /əfin'ətē/ n. (pl. ·ties) 1 liking or attraction; feeling of kinship 2 relationship, esp. by marriage 3 similarity of structure or character suggesting a relationship [L affinitas relationship by marriage]

af·firm /əfarm'/ v. 1 assert; state as a fact 2 Law. make a solemn declaration in place of an oath —af·fir·ma'tion n. [L, rel. to FIRM[1]]

af·fir·ma·tive /əfər'mətiv/ adj. 1 affirming; expressing approval —n. 2 affirmative statement or word

af·firm'a·tive ac'tion n. policies intended to promote the hiring of members of minority groups, etc.

af·fix v. /əfiks'/ 1 attach; fasten 2 add in writing —n. /af'iks'/ 3 addition 4 Gram. prefix or suffix [L, rel. to FIX]

af·flict /əflikt'/ v. distress physically or mentally —af·flic'tion n. [L afflictus fr. affligere to crush; strike down or against]

af·flu·ent /af'lōō'ənt/ adj. wealthy, rich —af'flu·ence n. [L, rel. to FLUENT]

af·ford /əfôrd'/ v. 1 have enough money, time, etc., to spare 2 be in a position 3 provide [OE geforthian to accomplish fr. ge- + FORTH]

af·for·est /əfôr'əst, afär'-, ə-/ v. plant with trees —af·for'es·ta'tion n.

af·fray /əfrā'/ (also fray) n. loud brawl [AngFr: break the peace]

af·front /əfrənt'/ n. 1 open insult —v. 2 insult openly [L, rel. to FRONT]

af·ghan /af'gan/ n. 1 crocheted or knitted shawl or throw 2 (also Af'ghan hound') breed of large dog with long silky coat

Af·ghan /af'gan/ n. 1a native or national of Afghanistan b person of Afghan descent 2 official language of Afghanistan —adj. 3 of Afghanistan [Pashto]

Af·ghan·i·stan /afgan'istan'/ n. republic in central Asia. Capital: Kabul. Pop. 18,052,000

a·fi·cio·na·do /əfisн'(ē)ənäd'ō/ n. (pl. ·dos) devotee of a sport or pastime [Sp]

a·field /əfēld'/ adv. to or at a distance from home

a·flame /əflām'/ adv. & adj. 1 in flames 2 very excited

a·float /əflōt'/ adv. & adj. 1 floating 2 at sea

a·flut·ter /əflət'ər/ adj. excited; in a flutter

a·foot /əfŏŏt'/ adv. & adj. in operation; progressing

afore- comb. form before; previously (aforementioned; aforesaid)

a·fore·thought /əfôr'тнôt'/ adj. premeditated

a·foul /əfoul'/ adj. & adv. 1 entangled with 2 run or fall afoul of conflict with

a·fraid /əfrād'/ adj. 1 alarmed; frightened 2 Colloq. politely regret (I'm afraid we're late) [orig. past part. of AFFRAY]

a·fresh /əfresн'/ adv. anew

Af·ri·ca /af'rikə/ n. second largest continent, S of Europe —Af'ri·can n. & adj.

Af'ri·can A·mer'i·can n. 1 US citizen of black African ethnic heritage —adj. 2 of such a person

Af'ri·can vi'o·let n. houseplant with velvety leaves and blue, purple, or pink flowers

Af·ri·kaans /af'rikäns'/ n. language derived from Dutch, spoken in S Africa [Du]

Af·ri·ka·ner /af'rikän'ər/ n. Afrikaans-speaking white person in S Africa

Af·ro /af'rō/ adj. 1 (of hair) tightly curled and bushy —n. (pl. ·ros) 2 Afro hairstyle

Afro- comb. form African

Af'ro·A·mer'i·can n. & adj. var. of AFRICAN AMERICAN

Af'ro·Car'ib·be·an n. 1 Caribbean person of African descent —adj. 2 of Afro-Caribbeans

Af·ro·cen·trism /af'rosen'trizm/ n. theory that African history and culture are principal sources of Western civilization

aft /aft/ adv. Naut. & Aeron. at or toward the stern or tail [OE]

af·ter /af'tər/ prep. 1 following in time; later than (after a week) 2 in view of; in spite of (after all my efforts I still lost) 3 behind 4 in pursuit or quest of 5 about; concerning 6 in allusion to 7 in imitation of 8 next in importance to —conj. 9 later than —adv. 10 later 11 behind —adj. 12 later; following 13 Naut. nearer the stern [OE]

af'ter·birth' n. placenta, etc., discharged from the womb after childbirth

af'ter·burn'er n. device for rocket or jet engine that burns exhaust gases and unused fuel

af'ter·care' n. care for a convalescent after leaving a hospital

af'ter·ef·fect' n. delayed effect following an accident, trauma, etc.

af'ter·life' n. life after death

af'ter·math' /af'tərmaтн'/ n. consequences, esp. unpleasant [fr. AFTER + math mowing fr. OE]

af'ter·noon' n. time from noon to evening

af'ter·thought' n. thing thought of or added later

af·ter·ward /af'tərwərd/ adv. (also af'ter·wards') later; subsequently

Ag symb. silver [L argentum]

a·gain /əgen', əgän'/ adv. 1 another time; once more 2 as previously 3 in addition 4 further; besides 5 on the other hand 6 again and again repeatedly [OE]

a·gainst /əgenst', əgänst'/ prep. 1 in opposition to 2 into collision or in contact with 3 in contrast to **4** in anticipation of **5** as a compensating factor to [fr. AGAIN]

A·ga Khan /äg′ə KHän′, kän′/ title of the leader of a division of Islam

a·gape /əgāp′/ adj. gaping; open-mouthed [fr. A·¹ + GAPE]

a·gar /ä′gär/ n. (also **a′gar-a′gar**) a gelatinous substance from seaweed, used as a thickening agent in culturing bacteria, etc. [Malay]

Ag·as·siz /ag′əsē/, **(Jean) Louis** 1807–73; Swiss-born US naturalist

Ag·as·siz, Lake /ag′əsē/ n. Hist. prehistoric lake in central N America

ag·ate /ag′ət/ n. **1** hard, usu. streaked, chalcedony **2** (also **ag′gie**) a playing marble [Gk achatēs]

a·gave /əgäv′ē/ n. (also **cen′tu·ry plant′**) a desert plant thought to bloom once every 100 years [Agave woman in Gk myth]

-age suffix forming nouns denoting: **1** action (breakage) **2** condition (bondage) **3** aggregate or number (acreage) **4** cost (postage) **5** place or abode (anchorage) [L -aticus]

age /āj/ n. **1** length of time that a person or thing has existed **2** Colloq. (often pl.) a long time (waited for ages) **3** distinct historical or geological period **4** old age —v. (**aged, aging** or **age·ing**) **5** show or cause to show signs of advancing age **6** grow old **7** mature **8** of age adult [L aetas]

a·ged adj. **1** /ājd/ of the age of (aged 3) **2** /ā′jid/ old

ag·ism /ā′jiz′əm/ n. prejudice on grounds of age —**age′ist** adj. & n.

age′less /āj′ləs/ adj. **1** never growing or appearing old **2** eternal —**age′less·ness** n.

a·gen·cy /ā′jənsē/ n. (pl. -cies) **1** business or premises of an agent **2** action; intervention **3** governmental department [L, rel. to ACT]

a·gen·da /əjen′də/ n. (pl. -das) **1** list of items to deal with at a meeting **2** things to be done

a·gent /ā′jənt/ n. **1** person who acts for another in business, etc. **2** person or thing that exerts power or produces an effect **3** person from an agency

a·gent pro·vo·ca·teur /ä′jänt prəväk′ətər′/ n. (pl. **a·gents pro·vo·ca·teurs** /pronunc. same) person who tempts suspected offenders to self-incriminating action [Fr: provoking agent]

age′ of con·sent′ n. age at which consent to sexual intercourse is valid in law

age′-old′ adj. very long-standing

ag·gie /ag′ē/ n. var. of AGATE, 2

ag·glom·er·ate v. /əgläm′ərāt′/ (·at·ed, ·at·ing) **1** collect into a mass —n. /-ərit/ **2** mass of fused fragments —adj. /-ərət/ **3** collected into a mass —**ag·glom′er·a′tion** n. [L glomer- fr. glomus ball of yarn]

ag·glu·ti·nate /əglo̅o̅t′n·āt′/ v. (·nat·ed, ·nat·ing) stick as with glue —**ag·glu′ti·na′tion** n.; **ag·glu·ti·na·tive** /əglo̅o̅t′n-āt′iv, -ətiv/ adj. [L, rel. to GLUTEN]

ag·gran·dize /əgran′dīz′, ag′rən-/ v. (·dized, ·diz·ing) increase the power, rank, or wealth of —**ag·gran·dize·ment** /əgran′dəzmənt, -dīz′-/ n. [Fr, rel. to GRAND]

ag·gra·vate /ag′rəvāt′/ v. (·vat·ed, ·vat·ing) **1** make worse **2** Colloq. annoy —**ag·gra·va′tion** n. [L gravis heavy]

• Usage: Aggravate means 'to make worse or

Aga Khan / agriculture

less endurable,' as, Our misery was aggravated by the terrible heat. The sense of 'to irritate or annoy' is colloquial.

ag·gre·gate n. /ag′rigət/ **1** total amount assembled **2** crushed stone used in making concrete —adj. /-gət/ **3** combined; collective: total —v. /-gāt′/ (·gat·ed, ·gat·ing) **4** combine into a mass **5** amount to —**ag·gre·ga′tion** n.; **ag·gre·ga·tive** adj. [L greg- fr. grex flock]

ag·gres·sion /əgresH′ən/ n. **1** unprovoked attack **2** hostile or destructive behavior —**ag·gres·sor** /əgres′ər/ n. [L aggression- fr. aggredi to attack]

ag·gres·sive /əgres′iv/ adj. **1** given to aggression; hostile **2** forceful; self-assertive —**ag·gres′sive·ly** adv.; **ag·gres′sive·ness** n.

ag·grieve /əgrēv′/ v. (·grieved, ·griev·ing) injure, esp. unjustly [rel. to AGGRAVATE]

a·ghast /əgast′/ adj. filled with dismay or horror [ME agast fr. OE gǣstan to frighten]

ag·ile /aj′əl, aj′īl′/ adj. quick-moving; nimble —**a·gil·i·ty** /əjil′ətē/ n. [L agilis, rel. to ACT]

ag·i·tate /aj′ətāt′/ v. (·tat·ed, ·tat·ing) **1** disturb or excite **2** campaign, esp. politically —**ag′i·ta′tion, ag′i·ta′tor** n. [L agitatus fr agitare, rel. to ACT]

a·glow /əglō′/ adj. glowing

ag·nos·tic /agnäs′tik, əg-/ n. **1** person who believes that the existence of God is not provable —adj. /-gät/ **2** of agnosticism —**ag·nos′ti·cism** n. [fr. A- + Gk gnotos known]

a·go /əgō′/ adv. earlier; in the past [orig. agone gone by]

a·gog /əgäg′/ adj. eager; expectant [Fr en in + gogue fun]

ag·o·nize /ag′ənīz′/ v. (·nized, ·niz·ing) suffer or cause to suffer agony

ag·o·ny /ag′ənē/ n. (pl. ·nies) **1** extreme mental or physical suffering **2** severe struggle [Gk agōn struggle]

A·gra /äg′rə/ n. city in India; site of the Taj Mahal. Pop. 899,200

a·grar·i·an /əgrer′ēən, əgrar′-/ adj. **1** of the land or its cultivation **2** of landed property [L agrari- fr. ager field]

a·gree /əgrē′/ v. (·greed, ·gree·ing) **1** hold the same opinion (as) **2** consent **3** become or be in harmony **4** be healthful (for) **5** Gram. have the same number, gender, case, or person as **6** reach agreement (about) [L AD- + gratus pleasing]

• Usage: Note the distinction between agree to, which a person does in regard to a plan, scheme, or project; and agree with, which a person does with another person or a thing: Jessica agrees with Sally that it is a good idea; Spicy foods do not agree with me. Agree with is also used for two things: The verb agrees with the noun in person and number.

a·gree·a·ble /əgrē′əbəl/ adj. **1** pleasing; pleasant **2** willing to agree —**a·gree′a·bly** adv.

a·gree′ment n. **1** act or state of agreeing **2** arrangement or contract

ag·ri·busi·ness /ag′rəbiz′nis, -niz/ n. large-scale farming and related commerce, as food-processing, distribution, etc.

ag·ri·cul·ture /ag′rikəl′CHər/ n. cultivation of the soil and rearing of animals —**ag′ri·cul′**

tur·al adj.; **ag'ri·cul'tur·al·ist** n. [L agricul-
tura fr. ager field + cultura CULTURE]

a·gron·o·my /əgrän'əmē/ n. science of soil
management and crop production —**a·gron'-
o·mist** n. [Gk agros land]

a·ground /əground'/ adj. & adv. on or on to
the bottom in shallow water

A·guas·ca·lien·tes /äg'wäskälyen'tās/ n.
state in central Mexico. Capital: Aguascalien-
tes. Pop. 719,700

a·gue /ā'gyōō/ n. **1** Hist. malarial fever **2**
shivering fit [L, rel. to ACUTE]

ah /ä/ interj. expression of surprise, pleasure,
realization, etc.

a·ha /ähä'/ interj. expression of surprise, triumph, mockery, etc.

a·head /əhed'/ adv. **1** further forward in
space or time **2** in the lead

a·hem /əhem'/ interj. used to attract attention, gain time, etc.

Ah·mad·a·bad /äm'ədəbäd/ n. city in W India. Pop. 2,872,900

a·hoy /əhoi'/ interj. Naut. call used in hailing

A·hu·ra Maz·da /ähōōr'ä mäz'dä/ supreme
deity of Zoroastrianism

AI abbr. **1** artificial insemination **2** artificial intelligence

aid /ād/ n. **1** help **2** person or thing that
helps —v. **3** help **4** promote [L AD- + juvare
help]

aide /ād/ n. **1** aide-de-camp **2** assistant [Fr]

aide-de-camp /ād' də kamp', kän'/ n. (pl.
aides-de-camp, pronunc. same) officer assisting a senior officer [Fr]

AIDS /ādz/ n. acquired immune deficiency
syndrome, a viral syndrome marked by increased susceptibility to infection, certain can-
cers, etc. [abbr.]

Ai·ken /ā'kən/, Conrad 1889–1973; US poet

ail /āl/ v. **1** trouble or afflict **2** be ill [OE]

ai·le·ron /ā'lərän'/ n. hinged control flap on
an airplane wing [Fr aile wing + -eron dim. suf-
fix]

ail·ment /āl'mənt/ n. minor illness or disorder

aim /ām/ v. **1** intend or try; attempt **2** direct
or point (a weapon, remark, etc.) —n. **3** purpose or object **4** the directing of a weapon,
etc., at an object **5 take aim** direct a weapon,
etc., at a target [ME aimen fr. L aestimare es-
timate]

aim·less /ām'ləs/ adj. without aim or purpose —**aim'less·ly** adv.; **aim'less·ness** n.

ain't /ānt/ contr. Colloq. **1** am, is, or are not
2 have or has not
• Usage: This form is regarded as highly informal, if not outright incorrect, and should be
avoided in formal contexts.

air /ar, er/ n. **1** mixture mainly of oxygen and
nitrogen surrounding the earth **2** distinctive
impression **3** (pl.) pretentiousness **4** tune **5**
light wind —v. **6** expose to fresh air **7** express and discuss publicly **8** broadcast **9** by
air by or in an aircraft **10 in the air** prevalent
11 up in the air uncertain —**air'less** adj.;
air'less·ness n. [Gk aēr]

air'bag' n. car safety device in which a bag
automatically inflates upon collision to cushion the driver or passengers

air'base' n. base for military aircraft

air'borne' adj. **1** transported by air **2** (of aircraft) in the air after taking off

air' con·di'tion·ing n. system for regulating
the humidity, ventilation, and temperature in a
building, car, etc. —**air'-con·di'tion** v.; **air'-
con·di'tioned** adj.; **air' con·di'tion·er** n.

air'craft' n. (pl. same) machine capable of
flight, esp. an airplane or helicopter

air'craft' car'ri·er n. warship carrying and
used as a base for aircraft

Aire·dale /ar'dāl, er'-/ n. large breed of a
rough-coated terrier [Airedale in Yorkshire]

air'field' n. area with runway(s) for aircraft

air' force' n. branch of armed forces carrying
out airborne military operations

air'head' n. Slang. stupid or foolish person

air'lift' n. **1** emergency transport of supplies
by air —v. **2** transport thus

air'line' n. public air transport system or company

air'lin'er n. large passenger aircraft

air'lock' n. **1** stoppage of the flow by an air
bubble in a pump or pipe **2** compartment between areas at different pressures

air'mail' n. (also **air mail**) **1** system of transporting mail by air **2** mail carried by air

air'man' n. (pl. -**men**) pilot or member of an
aircraft crew

air' mass' n. a relatively uniform body of air
over a large area

air'plane' n. powered heavier-than-air flying
vehicle with fixed wings [Fr AERO- + PLANE¹]

air' pock'et n. apparent vacuum causing an
aircraft to drop suddenly

air'port' n. airfield, usu. with facilities to service aircraft, process passengers, handle
cargo, etc.

air' raid' n. attack by aircraft on ground targets

air' ri'fle n. rifle using compressed air to fire
pellets

air'ship' n. power-driven aircraft lighter than
air

air'sick' adj. nauseous from air travel

air'space' n. air above a country and subject
to its jurisdiction

air' speed' n. aircraft's speed relative to the
air

air'strip' n. strip of ground for the take-off and
landing of aircraft

air' tight' adj. **1** impermeable to air **2** unassailable

air' traf'fic con·trol'ler n. official who controls air traffic by radio

air'waves' n. pl. Colloq. radio waves used in
broadcasting

air'way' n. **1** recognized route of aircraft **2**
breathing passage

air'wom'an n. (pl. -**wom'en**) woman pilot or
member of an aircraft crew

air'wor'thy adj. (of an aircraft) fit to fly —**air'-
wor'thi·ness** n.

air'y adj. (-i·er, -i·est) **1** well-ventilated;
breezy **2** flippant; superficial **3** light as air **4**
ethereal —**air'i·ly** adv.; **air'i·ness** n.

aisle /īl/ n. passage between rows of pews,
seats, etc. [Fr fr. L ala wing]

aitch /āCH/ n. the letter H [ME fr. OFr ache]

Aix-en-Pro·vence /äks äN prōväNs'/ n. city
in France. Pop. 126,900

a·jar /əjär'/ *adv. & adj.* slightly open [A-¹ + obs. *char* fr. OE *cerr* a turn]

AK postal abbr. for Alaska

a.k.a. *abbr.* also known as

Ak·bar /ak'bər, -bär'/, **Jalaludin Muhammad** 1542–1605; Mogul emperor of India (1556–1605)

Akh·na·ton /äknä'tən/ see AMENHOTEP, IV

A·ki·hi·to /ä'kihē'tō/ 1933– ; emperor of Japan

ARMS AKIMBO

a·kim·bo /əkim'bō/ *adv.* (of the arms) with hands on the hips and elbows turned outwards [ME *in kenebowe*, prob. fr. ON]

a·kin /əkin'/ *adj.* 1 related by blood 2 similar

Ak·ron /ak'rən/ *n.* city in Ohio. Pop. 223,019

ak·va·vit /äk'vəvēt/ *n.* var. of AQUAVIT

Al *symb.* aluminum

AL postal abbr. for Alabama

-al *suffix* 1 (also **-i·al**) forming adjectives meaning 'relating to, of the kind of' (*central; dictatorial*) 2 forming nouns, esp. of verbal action (*removal*) [L *-alis*]

à la /ä'lä, äl'ə, al'ə/ *prep.* in the manner of [Fr fr. À LA MODE]

Ala. abbr. for Alabama

Al·a·bam·a /al'əbam'ə/ *n.* S state of the US. Capital: Montgomery. Pop. 4,040,587. Abbr. **AL; Ala.** —**Al'a·bam'i·an, Al'a·bam'an** *n. & adj.*

al·a·bas·ter /al'əbas'tər/ *n.* 1 translucent usu. white form of gypsum, used for carving, etc. —*adj.* 2 of alabaster 3 white or smooth [Gk *alabastros*]

à la carte /äl'ə kärt', al'ə/ *adv. & adj.* with individually priced dishes [Fr]

a·lac·ri·ty /əlak'rətē/ *n.* briskness; cheerful readiness [L *alacritas* brisk]

à la king /a lä kiNG'/ *adv. & adj.* in a cream sauce

à la mode /äl'ə mōd, al'ə/ *adv. & adj.* 1 in fashion; fashionable 2 served in a particular way, as with a scoop of ice cream [Fr: in the style of]

Al·a·ric /al'ərik/ c. 370–410; king of the Visigoths (395–410); captured Rome (410)

a·larm /əlärm'/ *n.* 1 warning of danger, etc. 2 warning sound or device 3 apprehension —*v.* 4 frighten or disturb 5 warn —**a·larm'ing** *adj.*; **a·larm'ing·ly** *adv.* [OIt *all'arme!* to arms!]

a·larm' clock *n.* clock that rings at a set time

a·larm'ist *n.* person stirring up alarm

a·las /əlas'/ *interj.* expressing grief, pity, etc.

A·las·ka /əlas'kə/ *n.* northwesternmost state of the US. Capital: Juneau. Pop. 550,043. Abbr. **AK** —**A·las'kan** *n. & adj.*

A·las·ka, Gulf of *n.* inlet of the N Pacific on the S coast of Alaska

alb /alb/ *n.* long white vestment worn by Christian priests [L *alba (vestis)* white (garment)]

al·ba·core /al'bəkôr'/ *n.* long-finned edible tuna [Ar *al bakūrah* the tuna]

Al·ba·ni·a /albā'nēə, ôl-/ *n.* republic on the W coast of the Balkan Peninsula. Capital: Tiranë. Pop. 3,357,000 —**Al·ba'ni·an** *n. & adj.*

Al·ba·ny /ôl'bənē/ *n.* capital of N.Y. state, in the E part. Pop. 101,082

al·ba·tross /al'bətrôs'/ *n.* 1 long-winged, web-footed sea bird 2 encumbrance [alter. of *algatross* fr. Port *alcatraz* fr. Ar *al-ghattas* sea eagle]

Al·bee /ôl'bē, al'-/, **Edward** 1928– ; US dramatist

al·be·it /ôlbē'it, al-/ *conj.* though [*although it be*]

Al·ber·ta /albərt'ə/ *n.* province in W Canada. Capital: Edmonton. Pop. 2,662,000

Al·ber·tus Mag·nus, St. /albərt'əs mag'nəs/ c. 1200–80; Dominican theologian, philosopher, and scientist

al·bi·no /albī'nō/ *n.* (*pl.* **-nos**) 1 person or animal lacking pigment in the skin and hair (which are white) and the eyes (usu. pink) 2 plant lacking normal coloring —**al·bi·nism** /al'bəniz'əm, albī'-/ *n.* [Port, rel. to *albo* white]

al·bum /al'bəm/ *n.* 1 blank book for photographs, stamps, etc. 2 long-playing phonograph record [L: blank tablet, fr. *albus* white]

al·bu·men /albyōō'mən, al'byōō'-/ *n.* 1 egg white 2 substance found between the skin and germ of many seeds 3 ALBUMIN [L, rel. to ALBUM]

al·bu·min /albyōō'mən, al'byōō'-/ *n.* (also **al·bu'men**) water-soluble protein found in egg white, milk, blood, etc. —**al·bu'min·ous** *adj.*

Al·bu·quer·que /al'bəkər'kē/ *n.* city in N. Mex. Pop. 384,736

Al·ca·traz /al'kətraz'/ *n.* island in San Francisco Bay; site of a former federal prison

al·che·my /al'kəmē/ *n.* medieval chemistry, esp. seeking to turn base metals into gold —**al'che·mist** *n.* [OFr fr. Ar fr. Gk *kemeia* transmutation]

Al·ci·bi·a·des /al'səbī'ədēz'/ c. 450–404 B.C.; Athenian general and statesman

al·co·hol /al'kəhôl'/ *n.* 1 colorless volatile inflammable liquid, esp. as the intoxicant in wine, beer, spirits, etc., and as a solvent, fuel, etc. 2 liquor containing this [Ar *al-kuhl*]

al·co·hol·ic /al'kəhôl'ik, -häl'-/ *adj.* 1 of, like, containing, or caused by alcohol —*n.* 2 person suffering from alcoholism

al·co·hol·ism /al'kəhôl'iz'əm, -hä'-/ *n.* condition resulting from addiction to alcohol

Al·cott /ôl'kət, al'-, -kät'/, **Louisa May** 1832–88; US novelist

al·cove /al'kōv'/ *n.* recess, esp. in the wall of a room [Ar: the vault]

Al·cuin /al'kwin/ c. 735–804; English scholar and theologian

al den·te /äl den'tä, al/ *adj.* (of pasta, etc.) cooked so as to be still firm when bitten [It: literally, to the tooth]

al·der /ôl'dər/ *n.* tree related to the birch [OE]

al·der·man /ôl'dərmən/ *n.* (in some cities) councilman [OE *ealdor* chief + MAN]

ale /āl/ *n.* beverage like beer, but usu. stronger [OE]

a·le·a·to·ry /ā'lēətôr'ē/ *adj.* depending on chance [L *alea* DIE²]

a·lem·bic /əlem'bik/ *n.* 1 *Hist.* apparatus used in distilling 2 means of refining [Gk *ambix* cup]

A·lep·po /əlep'ō/ *n.* city in Syria. Pop. 1,445,900

a·lert /ələrt'/ *adj.* 1 watchful; vigilant 2 nimble; attentive —*n.* 3 alarm 4 state or period of special vigilance —*v.* 5 warn 6 on the alert vigilant —**a·lert'ly** *adv.*; —**a·lert'ness** *n.* [Fr fr. Il *all'erta* on the lookout]

Al·eut /əloōt'/ *n.* 1 native people of the Aleutian Islands and parts of the western Alaskan peninsula 2 their language

A·leu·tian Is·lands /əloō'SHən/ *n.* (also **Aleutians**) chain of Alaskan islands separating the Bering Sea from the Pacific Ocean

Al·ex·an·der /al'igzan'dər/ name of three Russian czars: 1 **Alexander I** 1777–1825; reigned 1801–25 2 **Alexander II** (called **"the Liberator"**) 1818–81; reigned 1855–81 3 **Alexander III** 1845–94; reigned 1881–94

Al'ex·an'der Nev·ski /n(y)ef'skē/ c. 1220–63; Russian national hero and saint

Al'ex·an'der the Great 356–323 B.C.; king of Macedon (336–323); conqueror of the Persian Empire

Al·ex·an·dri·a /al'igzan'drēə/ *n.* 1 seaport in N Egypt on the Nile. Pop. 3,170,000 2 city in Va. Pop. 111,183

al·fal·fa /alfal'fə/ *n.* cloverlike plant used for fodder [Ar: green fodder]

Al·fred /al'frəd/ (**"the Great"**) 849–899; Anglo-Saxon king (871–89)

al·fres·co /alfres'kō/ *adv. & adj.* in the open air [It]

al·gae /al'jē/ *n. pl.* (*sing.* **alga** /al'gə/) nonflowering stemless water plant, esp. seaweed and plankton [L]

al·ge·bra /al'jəbrə/ *n.* branch of mathematics that uses letters, etc., to represent numbers and quantities —**al'ge·bra'ic** /al'jəbrā'ik/ *adj.* [ult. fr. Ar *al-jabr* reunion of broken parts]

Al·ge·ri·a /aljēr'ēə/ *n.* republic in NW Africa. Capital: Algiers. Pop. 26,401,000 —**Al·ge'ri·an** *n. & adj.*

Al·giers /aljērz'/ *n.* seaport and cap. of Algeria, in NW Africa. Pop. 1,507,200

Al·gon·qui·an /algoNG'kēən,-kwēən/ *n.* (*pl.* same or **-ans**) 1 family of languages spoken by Native Americans of the NE Mid-Atlantic and N Central regions 2 speaker of one of these languages —*adj.* 3 of or pertaining to this language family or these people

al·go·rithm /al'gəriTH'əm/ *n.* process or set of rules used for calculation, etc., esp. with a computer —**al'go·rith'mic** *adj.* [Pers, name of a 9th-cent. mathematician *al-Khuwārizmī*]

A·li /älē', alē'/, **Muhammad** (born **Cassius Marcellus Clay, Jr.**) 1942– ; US heavyweight boxer; three-time world champion

a·li·as /ā'lēəs/ *adv.* 1 also named or known as —*n.* 2 assumed name [L: at another time]

al·i·bi /al'əbī'/ *n.* (*pl.* **-bis**) 1 claim or proof that one was elsewhere when a crime, etc.,

was committed 2 *Colloq.* excuse [L: in another place]

Al·i·can·te /al'ikant'ē/ *n.* seaport in Spain on the Mediterranean. Pop. 261,300

al·ien /ā'lēən/ *adj.* 1 unfamiliar; unacceptable or repugnant 2 foreign 3 of beings from other worlds —*n.* 4 foreign-born resident who is not a citizen 5 being from another world [L *alius* other]

al·ien·a·ble /ā'lēənəbəl/ *adj.* *Law.* transferable to new ownership

al·ien·ate /ā'lēənāt'/ *v.* (**·at·ed, ·at·ing**) 1 estrange; make hostile 2 transfer ownership of 3 divert (affection) —**al'ien·a'tion** *n.*

A·li·ghie·ri /al'əgyer'ē/, **Dante** see DANTE

a·light¹ /əlīt'/ *adj.* 1 on fire 2 lit up; excited [OE]

a·light² *v.* (**·light·ed** *or* **·lit, ·light·ing**) 1 descend from a vehicle 2 come to earth; settle [OE]

a·lign /əlīn'/ *v.* (also **a·line'**) 1 put or bring into line 2 ally (oneself, etc.) with (a cause, party, etc.) 3 adjust —**a·lign'ment** *n.* [Fr fr. L *linea* line]

a·like /əlīk'/ *adj.* 1 similar; like —*adv.* 2 in a similar way

al·i·men·ta·ry /al'əment'ərē, -men'trē/ *adj.* of or providing food or nourishment [L *alere* nourish]

al'i·men'ta·ry ca·nal' *n.* passage along which food passes during digestion

al·i·mo·ny /al'əmō'nē/ *n.* money payable to a spouse or former spouse after separation or divorce

a·line /əlīn'/ *v.* (**·lined, ·lin·ing**) var. of ALIGN

a·lit /əlit'/ *v. past* of ALIGHT

a·live /əlīv'/ *adj.* 1 living 2 lively; active 3 (foll. by *to*) aware of; alert 4 (foll. by *with*) swarming or teeming with [OE]

al·ka·li /al'kəlī'/ *n.* (*pl.* **-lis**) 1 any of a class of substances that liberate hydroxide ions in water and turn litmus blue; base 2 *Chem.* any substance that reacts with or neutralizes acids —**al'ka·line'** /-lən, -līn'/ *adj.*; —**al·ka·lin'i·ty** *n.* [Ar: calcined ashes]

al·ka·lize /al'kəlīz'/ *v.* (**·lized, ·liz·ing**) make into an alkali; neutralize the acidity of

al·ka·loid /al'kəloid'/ *n.* nitrogenous compound of plant origin, e.g., morphine, quinine

al·kyd /al'kid/ *n.* (also **al'kyd res'in**) sticky resin used in glues and paints

all /ôl/ *adj.* 1 whole amount, quantity, or extent of (*all day; all his life*) 2 any whatever (*beyond all doubt*) 3 greatest possible (*with all respect*) —*n.* 4 every one of (*all my sons*) 5 all concerned; everything (*all were present; all is lost*) 6 (foll. by *of*): a the whole of (*take all of it*) b every one of (*all of us*) 7 (in games) each (*two goals all*) —*pron.* 8 whole quantity (*drink all of the milk*) —*adv.* 9 entirely; quite (*dressed all in black*) 10 (foll. by *the* + compar.) to that or the utmost extent (*if they go, all the better*) 11 **after all** still; nevertheless 12 **all in** *Colloq.* exhausted 13 **all in all** everything considered 14 **all the same** nevertheless 15 **all there** *Colloq.* mentally alert or normal 16 **at all** in any way; to any extent [OE]

Al·lah /al'ə, äl'ə, älä'/ *n.* the Muslim and Arab name of God [Ar]

all'-A·mer'i·can (also **all'-A·mer'i·ca**) *adj.* 1 representing the United States as a whole 2 typically or entirely American —*n.* 3 US student-athlete recognized for excellence in a sport

all'-a·round' *adj.* (of a person) versatile

al·lay /əlā'/ *v.* 1 diminish (fear, suspicion, etc.) 2 alleviate (pain, etc.) [OE]

all'-clear' *n.* signal that danger, etc., is over

al·le·ga·tion /al'igā'SHən/ *n.* 1 assertion, esp. unproved 2 alleging [L *allegare* adduce]

al·lege /əlej'/ *v.* (**·leged, ·leg·ing**) 1 declare, esp. without proof 2 advance as an argument or excuse [OFr *esligier* clear at law, confused in sense with L *allegare* adduce]

al·leged /əlejd', lej'id/ *adj.* 1 said to be but unproved 2 so-called —**al·leg·ed·ly** /-lej'idlē/ *adv.*

Al·le·ghe·ny Moun·tains /al'əgā'nē/ *n.* part of the Appalachian Mountains, in E US

al·le·giance /əlē'jəns/ *n.* 1 loyalty (to a person, cause, etc.) 2 the duty of a subject [OFr, rel. to LIEGE]

al·le·go·ry /al'igôr'ē/ *n.* (*pl.* **·ries**) story whose characters are represented symbolically —**al·le·gor'i·cal** *adj.;* **al'le·go·rize'** *v.* (**·rized, ·riz·ing**) [Gk *allēgoria* other speaking]

al·le·gret·to /al'igret'ō, äl'-/ *Mus. adv. & adj.* 1 in a fairly brisk tempo —*n.* (*pl.* **·tos**) 2 such a passage or movement [It, dim. of ALLEGRO]

al·le·gro /əleg'rō, əlā'grō/ *Mus. adv. & adj.* 1 in a brisk tempo —*n.* (*pl.* **·gros**) 2 such a passage or movement [It: lively]

al·le·lu·ia /al'əlōō'yə/ *interj. & n.* var. of HALLELUJAH

Al·len /al'ən/ 1 **Ethan** 1738–89; American Revolutionary War leader 2 **Woody** (born **Allen Stewart Konigsberg**) 1935– ; US film director, writer, and actor

Al·len·de Gos·sens /äyen'dā gô'sens/, **Salvador** 1908–73; Chilean president (1970–73)

Al·len·town /al'əntoun'/ *n.* city in Penn. Pop. 105,090

Al'len wrench' *n.* hexagonal right-angled bar for turning a screw (**Al'len screw'**) with a hexagonal socket in its head [for *Allen*, manufacturer]

al·ler·gen /al'ərjin/ *n.* anything causing an allergic reaction —**al·ler·gen'ic** *adj.* [Ger fr. Gk]

al·ler·gic /ələr'jik/ *adj.* 1a having an allergy to b *Colloq.* having a strong dislike for 2 caused by an allergy —**al·ler'gi·cal·ly** *adv.*

al·ler·gy /al'ərjē/ *n.* (*pl.* **·gies**) 1 adverse reaction to certain substances, esp. particular foods, pollen, fur, or dust 2 *Colloq.* aversion [Ger fr. Gk *allos* other + *-ergia* activity]

al·le·vi·ate /əlē'vē-āt'/ *v.* (**·at·ed, ·at·ing**) make (pain, etc.) less severe —**al·le'vi·a'tion** *n.* [L *levare* raise]

al·ley /al'ē/ *n.* (*pl.* **·leys**) 1 narrow streetlike passageway 2 place for bowling, etc. —**al'ley·way** *n.* [Fr *aller* go]

al·li·ance /əlī'əns/ *n.* union or agreement to cooperate, esp. of States by treaty, families by marriage, etc. [OFr, rel. to ALLY]

al·lied /əlīd', al'īd/ *adj.* 1 associated in an alliance 2 connected; related

al·li·ga·tor /al'əgāt'ər/ *n.* large reptile of the crocodile family with a head broader than a crocodile's [Sp *el lagarto* lizard]

ALLIGATOR

al'li·ga·tor pear' *n.* AVOCADO

al·lit·er·a·tion /əlit'ərā'SHən/ *n.* repetition of the same letter or sound at the beginning of adjacent or closely connected words (e.g., *cool, calm, and collected*) —**al·lit'er·ate'** *v.* (**·at·ed, ·at·ing**); **al·lit·er·a·tive** /əlit'ərātiv, -ərā'tiv/ *adj.;* **al·lit'er·a'tive·ly** *adv.;* **al·lit'er·a'tive·ness** *n.* [MedL, rel. to LETTER]

al·lo·cate /al'əkāt'/ *v.* (**·cat·ed, ·cat·ing**) assign or devote to (a purpose, person, or place) —**al'lo·ca'tion** *n.* [MedL, rel. to *locus* place]

al·lot /əlät'/ *v.* (**·lot·ted, ·lot·ting**) apportion or distribute to (a person), esp. as a share —**al·lot'ment** *n.* [ME fr. MFr]

all'-out' *adj.* enthusiastic; energetic (*all-out effort*)

al·low /əlou'/ *v.* 1 permit 2 assign a limited amount 3 provide or set aside for a purpose —**al·low'a·ble** *adj.;* **al·low'a·bly** *adv.* [OFr *a(l)louer* place, and perh. *allouer* praise, ult. fr. L *locus* place, *laudare* praise]

al·low·ance /əlou'əns/ *n.* 1 amount or sum allowed 2 amount given, esp. to a child, as spending money 3 **make allowances** make excuses

al·loy /al'oi, əloi'/ *n.* 1 mixture of two or more metals 2 inferior metal mixed esp. with gold or silver —*v.* 3 mix (metals) 4 debase by admixture [OFr, rel. to ALLY]

all'-pur'pose *adj.* having many uses

all' right' *adj.* 1 acceptable 2 unharmed —*interj.* 3 yes; very well —*adv.* 4 satisfactorily 5 definitely

• Usage: See note at ALRIGHT.

all'spice' *n.* 1 aromatic spice obtained from the berry of the pimento tree 2 the berry

all'-time' *adj.* unsurpassed

al·lude /əlōōd'/ *v.* (**·lud·ed, ·lud·ing**) refer to, esp. indirectly or briefly [L, rel. to AD- + *ludere* play]

al·lure /əlōōr'/ *v.* (**·lured, ·lur·ing**) 1 attract, charm, or entice —*n.* 2 personal charm; fascination —**al·lure'ment** *n.* [Fr, rel. to AD- + LURE]

al·lu·sion /əlōō'ZHən/ *n.* passing or indirect reference —**al·lu'sive** /-siv/ *adj.* [L, rel. to ALLUDE]

al·lu·vi·um /əlōō'vēəm/ *n.* (*pl.* **·vi·ums** or **·vi·a** /-vēə/) deposit of usu. fine fertile soil left behind by a flood —**al·lu'vi·al** *adj.* [L *alluere* wash against]

al·ly *n.* /al'ī, əlī'/ (*pl.* **·lies**) 1 state, person, etc., formally cooperating or united with another, esp. in war —v. /əlī'/ (·lied, ·ly·ing) 2 combine for a purpose [OFr fr. L alligare bind]

al·ma ma·ter /al'mə mät'ər/ n. 1 university, school, or college that one attended 2 school song [L: bounteous mother]

al·ma·nac /ôl'mənak, al'-/ n. calendar, usu. with astronomical data [MedL fr. Gk or Ar]

Al-Ma·nam·ah /al'mənam'ə/ n. see MANAMA

al-Man·su·ra /al'mansoor'ə/ n. (also El Mansura) city in Egypt. Pop. 316,900

Al·ma·ty /äl'mätē'/ n. (formerly Alma-Ata) capital of Kazakhstan. Pop. 1,156,200

al·might·y /ôlmīt'ē/ adj. 1 having complete power 2 (the Almighty) God 3 Slang. very great (almighty crash)

al·mond /ä(l)m'ənd, a(l)m'-/ n. 1 nutlike kernel of a fruit allied to the peach and plum 2 tree bearing this [Gk amygdalē]

al·most /ôl'mōst, ôlmōst'/ adv. all but; very nearly [OE, rel. to ALL + MOST]
• Usage: See note at MOST.

alms /ä(l)mz/ n. pl. donation of money or food to the poor [Gk eleēmosynē]

alms·house /ä(l)mz'hous'/ n. Hist. institution for the poor

al·oe /al'ō/ n. plant of the lily family with toothed fleshy leaves [OE fr. Gk]

a·loft /əlôft'/ adj. & adv. 1 high up; overhead 2 upwards [ON]

a·lo·ha /əlō'hə, -hä/ interj. word of welcome or farewell [Haw: love]

a·lone /əlōn'/ adj. 1 without others 2 lonely —adv. 3 only; exclusively [earlier al one, rel. to ALL + ONE]

a·long /əlôNG'/ prep. 1 beside or through (part of) the length of —adv. 2 onward; into a more advanced state 3 with oneself or others 4 beside or through part or the whole length of a thing 5 all along from the start 6 get along: a move ahead b succeed c get by d be on good terms [OE, orig. adj.: facing against]

a·long·side /əlôNG'sīd'/ adv. 1 at or to the side —prep. 2 close to the side of

a·loof /əlōōf'/ adj. 1 distant; unsympathetic —adv. 2 away; apart [fr. A⁻¹ + LUFF]

a·loud /əloud'/ adv. audibly

alp /alp/ n. high mountain [fr. ALPS]

ALPACA 1

al·pac·a /alpak'ə/ n. 1 shaggy S American mammal related to the llama 2 its wool; fabric made from this [Sp fr. Quechua]

al·pha /al'fə/ n. 1 first letter of the Greek alphabet (A, α) 2 alpha and omega beginning and end [L fr. Gk]

al·pha·bet /al'fəbet'/ n. set of letters used in writing a language —al'pha·bet'i·cal adj.; al'pha·bet'i·cal·ly adv. [Gk ALPHA + BETA]

al·pha·nu·mer·ic /al'fən(y)ōōmer'ik/ adj. containing both letters and numbers

al'pha par'ti·cle n. helium nucleus emitted by a radioactive substance

al·pine /al'pīn/ adj. of mountainous regions or (cap.) the Alps

Alps /alps/ n. mountain range of central Europe extending from France to Austria and the Balkan Peninsula

al·read·y /ôlred'ē/ adv. 1 before the time in question 2 as early as or as soon as this [fr. ALL + READY]

al·right /ôlrīt', ôl'rīt'/ adv. ALL RIGHT
• Usage: All right is the spelling accepted by most authorities, who consider the popular alright, formed on the model of already and altogether, to be wrong.

ALS abbr. AMYOTROPHIC LATERAL SCLEROSIS

al·so /ôl'sō/ adv. in addition; besides [OE, rel. to ALL + SO¹]

al'so·ran' n. 1 loser in a race or election 2 undistinguished person

alt. abbr. 1 alternate 2 altimeter 3 altitude

al·tar /ôl'tər/ n. 1 table or flat block for sacrifice or offering to a deity 2 table for religious purposes in a church, etc. [L altus high]

al'tar·piece n. painting, screen, etc., above or behind an altar

al·ter /ôl'tər/ v. make or become different; change —al'ter·a'tion n. [L alter other]

alter. abbr. 1 alternate 2 alternative

al·ter·cate /ôl'tərkāt'/ v. (·cat·ed, ·cat·ing) dispute; wrangle —al'ter·ca'tion n. [L altercari quarrel]

al·ter·e·go /ôl'tər ē'gō/ n. (pl. ·gos) 1 one's hidden or second self 2 intimate friend [L: other self]

al·ter·nate v. /ôl'tərnāt'/ (·nat·ed, ·nat·ing) 1 occur or cause to occur by turns 2 go back and forth —adj. /ôl'tərnət/ 3 every other 4 alternating —al'ter·nate·ly adv.; al'ter·na'tion n. [L alternare do by turns, rel. to ALTER]
• Usage: The adjective and noun alternate (and the adverb, alternately) are used to refer to 'every other one; first one, then the other': Alternate recruits were chosen for special training. Because Jones was on leave, an alternate served for him. The recruits were selected alternately. The adjective and noun alternative (and the adverb, alternatively) refer to 'choice': The alternative route leads north of the lake. As the main route is blocked, we have no alternative. Alternatively, we could take the southern route.

al'ter·nat'ing cur'rent n. electric current reversing its direction at regular intervals

al·ter·na·tive /ôltər'nətiv/ adj. 1 available as another choice 2 unconventional (alternative medicine) —n. 3 any of two or more possibilities 4 choice —al·ter'na·tive·ly adv.
• Usage: See note at ALTERNATE.

al·ter·na·tor /ôl'tərnāt'ər/ n. dynamo that generates an alternating current

al·though /ôlT͟Hō'/ conj. THOUGH [fr. ALL + THOUGH]

al·tim·e·ter /altim'ətər, al'təmēt'ər/ *n.* instrument indicating altitude reached

al·ti·tude /al'tət(y)ōōd'/ *n.* height, esp. of an object above sea level or above the horizon [L *altus* high]

al·to /al'tō/ *n.* (*pl.* ·tos) 1 CONTRALTO 2a highest adult male singing voice, above tenor b singer with this voice 3 instrument pitched second or third highest in its family [It fr. L *altus* high]

al·to·geth·er /ōl'təgeTH'ər/ *adv.* 1 totally; completely 2 on the whole 3 in total 4 in the altogether *Colloq.* naked [fr. ALL + TOGETHER]

Al·too·na /altōō'nə/ *n.* city in Penn. Pop. 51,881

al·tru·ism /al'trōō-iz'əm/ *n.* unselfishness as a principle of action —**al'tru·ist** *n.*; **al'tru·is'tic** *adj.*; **al'tru·is'ti·cal·ly** *adv.* [Fr *altruisme* fr. L *alter*]

al·um /al'əm/ *n.* sulfate of aluminum, potassium, etc. [L *alumen*]

a·lu·mi·na /əlōō'mənə/ *n.* aluminum oxide occurring naturally as corundum and emery

a·lu·mi·num /əlōō'mənəm/ *n.* silvery light and malleable metallic element; *symb.* Al

a·lum·nus /əlum'nəs/ *n.* (*pl.* ·ni /-nī, -nē/; *fem.* ·na, *pl.* ·nae /-nī, -nē/) graduate of a school, college, etc. [L: nursling; pupil]

al·ways /ōl'wāz, -wēz/ *adv.* 1 at all times; on all occasions 2 whatever the circumstances 3 repeatedly; often [fr. ALL + WAY]

al·Zar·qa *n.* see ZARQA

Alz'hei'mer's dis·ease' /älts'hī'mərz, alts'-/ *n.* brain disorder causing senility [for A. *Alzheimer*, German neurologist]

am /am/ *v.* 1st person sing. present of BE

Am *symb.* americium

AM *abbr.* 1 (also A.M., a.m.) *Latin. ante meridiem* time between midnight and noon 2 airmail 3 amplitude modulation 4 *Latin. anno mundi* in the year of the world 5 (also M.A.) *Latin. artium magister* master of arts

Am. *abbr.* 1 America 2 American

a·mal·gam /əmal'gəm/ *n.* 1 mixture or blend 2 alloy of mercury and another metal, used in dentistry [Gk *malagma* emollient]

a·mal·ga·mate /əmal'gəmāt'/ *v.* (·mat·ed, ·mat·ing) mix; unite —**a·mal'ga·ma'tion** *n.*

a·man·u·en·sis /əman'yōō-en'sis/ *n.* (*pl.* ·en'ses /-sēz/) usu. *Joc.* secretary [L *a manu* at hand]

am·a·ranth /am'əranTH/ *n.* 1 plant with small green, red, or purple tinted flowers 2 imaginary unfading flower —**am'a·ran'thine** /am'əran'THən, -THīn/ *adj.* [Gk *amarantos* unfading]

Am·a·ril·lo /am'əril'ō/ *n.* city in Texas. Pop. 157,615

am·a·ryl·lis /am'əril'is/ *n.* bulbous plant with lilylike flowers [Gk, name of a shepherdess]

a·mass /əmas'/ *v.* heap together; accumulate [Fr, rel. to AD- + MASS]

am·a·teur /am'ətər, -CHŌŌr, -CHər/ *n.* person who engages in a pursuit as a pastime rather than a profession, or performs with limited skill —**am'a·teur'ish** *adj.*; **am'a·teur'ish·ly** *adv.*; **am'a·teur'ish·ness, am'a·teur'ism** *n.* [L *amator* lover]

A·ma·ti /əmät'ē, ä-/ family of Italian violinmakers, including: 1 **Andrea** c. 1520 – c. 1580 and his grandson 2 **Nicolò** 1596–1684

am·a·to·ry /am'ətôr'ē/ *adj.* of sexual love [L *amare* love]

a·maze /əmāz'/ *v.* (·mazed, ·maz·ing) surprise greatly; fill with wonder —**a·maze'ment** *n.*; **a·maz'ing** *adj.*; **a·maz'ing·ly** *adv.* [OE *āmasian*]

Am·a·zon /am'əzän', -zən/ *n.* 1 female warrior of a mythical race 2 (a-) large, strong, or athletic woman —**Am'a·zo'ni·an** /am'əzō'nēən/ *adj.* [L fr. Gk]

Am'a·zon' Riv'er /am'əzän', -zən/ *n.* river in N South America flowing 3,900 mi. E from the Andes to the Atlantic

am·bas·sa·dor /ambas'ədər, -dôr'/ *n.* 1 diplomat sent abroad to represent a country's interests 2 promoter (*ambassador of peace*) —**am·bas'sa·do'ri·al** *adj.*; **am·bas'sa·dor·ship'** *n.* [MFr, ult. fr. L *ambactus* servant]

am·ber /am'bər/ *n.* 1a yellow translucent fossilized resin used in jewelry b color of this —*adj.* 2 of or like amber [OFr fr. Ar]

am·ber·gris /am'bərgris', -grē(s)'/ *n.* waxlike secretion of the sperm whale, used in perfumes [MFr: gray amber]

am·bi·ance /am'bēəns/ *n.* (also **am'bi·ence**) surroundings or atmosphere [L *ambire* go around]

am·bi·dex·trous /am'bədek'strəs/ *adj.* able to use either hand equally well —**am'bi·dex·ter'i·ty** /-ter'itē/ *n.*; **am'bi·dex'trous·ly** *adv.* [L *ambi-* on both sides + *dexter* on the right]

am·bi·ent /am'bēənt/ *adj.* surrounding

am·big·u·ous /ambig'yōōəs/ *adj.* 1 having an obscure or double meaning 2 difficult to classify —**am·big·u'i·ty** *n.* (*pl.* ·ties); **am·big'u·ous·ly** *adv.* [L *ambi-* both ways + *agere* drive; act]

am·bi·tion /ambiSH'ən/ *n.* 1 determination to succeed 2 object of this [L *ambitio* canvassing for votes]

am·bi·tious /ambiSH'əs/ *adj.* 1 full of ambition or high aims 2 strongly determined —**am·bi'tious·ly** *adv.*

am·biv·a·lence /ambiv'ələns/ *n.* simultaneous conflicting feelings —**am·biv'a·lent** *adj.*; **am·biv'a·lent·ly** *adv.* [L *ambi-* both + *valentia* vigor]

am·ble /am'bəl/ *v.* (·bled, ·bling) 1 move at an easy pace —*n.* 2 such a pace [L *ambulare* walk]

am·bro·si·a /ambrō'ZHə/ *n.* 1 *Gk. & Rom. Myth.* the food of the gods 2 sublimely delicious food, etc. [Gk: not mortal]

am·bu·lance /am'byələns, -lans/ *n.* vehicle equipped for conveying patients to a hospital [L *ambulare* walk]

am·bu·la·to·ry /am'byələtôr'ē/ *adj.* 1 of or for walking 2 able to walk [L *ambulare* walk]

am·bus·cade /am'bəskäd', am'bəskäd'/ *n. & v.* (·cad·ed, ·cad·ing) AMBUSH

am·bush /am'bōōsH/ *n.* 1 surprise attack by persons hiding 2 hiding place for this —*v.* 3 attack from an ambush; waylay [Fr, rel. to IN-¹ + *boscos* woods]

a·me·ba /əmē'bə/ *n.* (*pl.* ·bas or ·bae /-bē/) var. of AMOEBA

a·me·lio·rate /əmē'lēərāt'/ *v.* (·rat·ed, ·rat·ing) make or become better —**a·mel'io·ra'tion** *n.*; **a·mel'io·ra'tive** *adj.* [fr. AD- + L *melior* better]

a·men /ämen', ā-/ *interj.* (esp. at the end of a prayer, etc.) so be it [ChL fr. Heb: certainly]

a·me·na·ble /əmē'nəbəl, əmen'-/ *adj.* 1 responsive; docile 2 accountable to law, etc. —**a·me'na·bil'i·ty, a·me'na·ble·ness** *n.*; **a·me'na·bly** *adv.* [MFr, rel. to AD- + L *minari* drive animals]

a·mend /əmend'/ *v.* 1 make minor alterations in to improve 2 correct an error in (a document, etc.) 3 reform (oneself) —**a·mend'a·ble** *adj.* [L *emendare*]

a·mend'ment *n.* alteration in or addition to a document, resolution, etc.

a·mends /əmen(d)z'/ *n.* compensation; reparation

A·men·ho·tep /äm'ənhō'tep'/ name of four Egyptian pharaohs: 1 **Amenhotep I** (also **Amenophis**) reigned 1546–26 B.C. 2 **Amenhotep II** reigned 1450–25 B.C. 3 **Amenhotep III** reigned 1417–1379 B.C. 4 **Amenhotep IV** (also **Akhnaton; Ikhnaton**) reigned 1379–62 B.C.

a·men·i·ty /əmen'itē/ *n.* (*pl.* **-ties**) 1 pleasant or useful feature or facility 2 pleasantness (of a place, etc.) 3 polite actions [L *amoenus* pleasant]

Am·er·a·sian /am'ərā'ZHən/ *n.* person of American and (esp. East) Asian descent

a·merce /əmərs'/ *v.* (**-merced, -merc·ing**) punish by a fine —**a·merce'ment** *n.* [Fr *a merci* be at the mercy]

A·mer·i·ca /əmer'ikə, -mar'-/ *n.* 1 popular term for the United States of America 2 (also **the Americas**) the continents of N and S America and nearby islands, considered together [fr. *Amerigo* Vespucci, Italian navigator]

A·mer·i·can /əmer'ikən/ *adj.* 1 of America, esp. the US —*n.* 2 native, citizen, or inhabitant of America, esp. the US —**A·mer'i·can·ize'** *v.*; **A·mer'i·can·i·za'tion** *n.*

A·mer·i·ca·na /əmer'əkä'nə/ *n.* objects, media, etc., that have to do with the US

A·mer·i·can In'di·an *n.* (also **Am'er·ind', Am'er·in'di·an**) member of any of the aboriginal peoples inhabiting N or S America or the W Indies

A·mer·i·can·ism /əmer'ikəniz'əm/ *n.* 1 custom or other cultural characteristic typical of people of the US 2 word or phrase originating or occurring principally in the US 3 devotion to the customs, etc., of the US

A·mer·i·can Rev·o·lu'tion *n.* war (1775–83) fought by the American colonies against Great Britain to gain their independence

A·mer·i·can Sa·mo·a /səmō'ə/ *n.* the part of Samoa belonging to the US. Capital: Pago Pago. Pop. 49,600. See also WESTERN SAMOA —**Sa·mo'an** *n.* & *adj.*

am·er·i·ci·um /am'əriSH'ēəm, -ris'-/ *n.* artificial radioactive metallic element; *symb.* Am

am·e·thyst /am'əTHist'/ *n.* semiprecious stone of a violet or purple variety of quartz [Gk: preventing drunkenness]

a·mi·a·ble /ā'mēəbəl/ *adj.* friendly and pleasant; likeable —**a'mi·a·bil'i·ty** *n.*; **a'mi·a·bly** *adv.* [L, rel. to AMICABLE]

am·i·ca·ble /am'ikəbəl/ *adj.* (esp. of an arrangement, relations, etc.) friendly —**am'i·**

ca·bil'i·ty *n.*; **am'i·ca·bly** *adv.* [L *amicus* friend]

a·mid /əmid'/ *prep.* (also **a·midst** /əmidst'/) in the middle of; among [OE]

am·ide /am'īd/ *n.* compound formed from ammonia

a·mid·ships /əmid'SHips/ *adv.* in or into the middle of a ship [fr. AMID + SHIP]

Am·i·ens /āmyan'/ *n.* city in France. Pop. 136,400

a·mi·go /əmē'gō/ *n.* (*pl.* **-gos**) friend [Sp]

A·min /ämēn'/, **Idi** 1925– ; president of Uganda (1971–79)

a·mine /əmēn', am'ēn'/ *n.* compound formed from ammonia

a·mi'no ac'id /əmē'nō/ *n. Biochem.* any of a group of nitrogenous organic acids forming the basic constituents of proteins [fr. AMINE + ACID]

a·mir /əmēr'/ *n.* var. of EMIR

a·miss /əmis'/ *adj.* 1 wrong; out of order —*adv.* 2 wrong(ly); inappropriately [perh. fr. ON *à mis* so as to miss]

am·i·ty /am'ətē/ *n.* friendship [L *amicus* friend]

Am·man /ämän'/ *n.* capital of Jordan. Pop. 1,213,300

am·me·ter /am'ēt'ər/ *n.* instrument for measuring electric current in amperes [fr. AMPERE + -METER]

am·mo /am'ō/ *n. Slang.* ammunition [abbr.]

am·mo·nia /əmōn'yə/ *n.* 1 pungent strongly alkaline gas 2 solution of ammonia in water [as *sal ammoniac*]

am·mu·ni·tion /am'yəniSH'ən/ *n.* 1 supply of bullets, shells, grenades, etc. 2 information usable in an argument [MFr ult. fr. L]

am·ne·sia /amnē'ZHə/ *n.* loss of memory —**am·ne'si·ac'** /-ZHē-ak', -zē-ak'/ *n.* [Gk]

am·nes·ty /am'nəstē/ *n.* (*pl.* **-ties**) 1 general pardon, esp. for political offenses —*v.* (**-tied, -ty·ing**) 2 grant an amnesty to [Gk *amnēstia* oblivion]

am·ni·o·cen·te·sis /am'nē-ōsentē'sis/ *n.* (*pl.* **-te·ses** /-tē'sēz/) sampling of amniotic fluid to determine health of a fetus [fr. AMNION + Gk *kentēsis* pricking]

am·ni·on /am'nē-än/ *n.* (*pl.* **-ni·ons** or **-ni·a** /-nē-ə/) innermost membrane enclosing an embryo —**am'ni·ot'ic** /-ät'ik/ *adj.* [Gk *amnos* lamb]

a·moe·ba /əmē'bə/ *n.* (*pl.* **-bas** or **-bae** /-bē/; also **a·me'ba**) microscopic aquatic amorphous one-celled organism —**a·moe'bic** *adj.* [Gk: change]

a·mok /əmək', əmäk'/ *adv.* (also **a·muck'**) as in **run amok** run wild [Malay]

a·mong /əməNG'/ *prep.* (also **a·mongst** /əməNGst'/) 1 surrounded by; with 2 included in 3 to each of (usu. three or more) 4 from the joint resources of 5 with one another [OE: in a crowd]

● Usage: See note at BETWEEN.

a·mor·al /āmôr'əl, -mär'-/ *adj.* 1 not involving morality 2 without moral principles —**a'mo·ral'i·ty** *n.*; **a·mor'al·ly** *adv.*

● Usage: See note at IMMORAL.

am·o·rous /am'ərəs/ *adj.* of, showing, or feeling sexual love —**am'o·rous·ly** *adv*; **am'o·rous·ness** *n.* [L *amor* love]

a·mor·phous /əmôr'fəs/ *adj.* 1 of no definite

shape 2 vague 3 *Chem.* noncrystalline —a·mor'phous·ly *adv.*; a·mor'phous·ness *n.* [Gk *a-* not + *morphē* form]

am·or·tize /am'ərtīz/ *v.* (·tized, ·tiz·ing) gradually extinguish (a debt) by regular installments [L *ad mortem* to death]

a·mount /əmount'/ *n.* 1 quantity, esp. a total in number, size, value, extent, etc. —*v.* 2 be equivalent to in number, significance, etc. [OFr *amonter* ascend]

a·mour /əmoor'/ *n.* (esp. illicit) love affair [Fr: love fr. L *amare*]

a·mour pro·pre /amoor' prō'p(r)/ *n.* self-respect [Fr]

amp /amp/ *n.* 1 amperage 2 ampere 3 amplifier [abbr.]

am·per·age /am'p(ə)rij/ *n.* strength of an electric current in amperes

am·pere /am'pēr/ *n.* unit of electric current [for A.M. *Ampère*, French physicist]

am·per·sand /am'pərsand/ *n.* the sign '&' (*and*) [corruption of *and* PER SE *and*]

am·phet·a·mine /amfet'əmēn', -mən/ *n.* synthetic drug used esp. as a stimulant

am·phib·i·an /amfib'ēən/ *adj.* 1 of a class of vertebrates living both on land and in water —*n.* 2 vertebrate of this class 3 vehicle or aircraft able to operate both on land and in water —am·phib'i·ous *adj.*; am·phib'i·ous·ly *adv.* [Gk *amphi-* both + *bios* life]

am·phi·the·a·ter /am(p)'fəthē'ətər/ *n.* circular building with tiers of seats surrounding a central space [Gk *amphi-* around + *theatron*]

am·pho·ra /am'fərə/ *n.* (*pl.* -rae /-rē', -rī'/) narrow-necked Greek or Roman vessel with two handles [Gk *amphoreus*]

AMPHORA

am·ple /am'pəl/ *adj.* (·pler, ·plest) 1 plentiful; abundant; extensive 2 *Euphem.* large; stout 3 more than enough —am'ply *adv.* [L *amplus*]

am·pli·fi·er /am'pləfī'ər/ *n.* electronic device for increasing the strength of electrical signals, esp. for conversion into sound

am·pli·fy /am'pləfī'/ *v.* (·fied, ·fy·ing) 1 increase the strength of (sound, electrical signals, etc.) 2 expand, develop (a story, etc.) —am'pli·fi·ca'tion *n.* [L *amplificare*]

am·pli·tude /am'plət(y)ōōd'/ *n.* 1 maximum departure from average of an oscillation, alternating current, etc. 2 extent; scope 3 abundance [L, rel. to AMPLE]

am'pli·tude mod·u·la'tion *n.* modulation of a wave by variation of its amplitude; *abbr.* AM

am·pule /am'pyōōl/ *n.* (also am'poule, am·pul /am'pōōl/) sealed capsule holding a solution for injection [Fr fr. L *ampulla* bottle]

am·pu·tate /am'pyətāt'/ *v.* (·tat·ed, ·tat·ing) cut off surgically (a limb, etc.) —am'pu·ta'tion *n.* [L *ambi-* about + *putare* prune]

am·pu·tee /am'pyōōtē'/ *n.* person who has had a limb amputated

Am·rit·sar /am'rit'sər/ *n.* city in NW India. Pop. 709,500

Am·ster·dam /am'stərdam/ *n.* capital of the Netherlands. Pop. 702,400

amt. *abbr.* amount

Am·trak /am'trak'/ *n.* US passenger railroad system

a·muck /əmək'/ *adv.* var. of AMOK

am·u·let /am'yələt/ *n.* charm worn against evil [L]

a·muse /əmyōōz'/ *v.* (·mused, ·mus·ing) 1 cause to laugh or smile 2 interest or occupy —a·mus'ing *adj.*; a·mus'ing·ly *adv.* [MFr *á* at + *muser* stare]

a·muse'ment *n.* 1 thing that amuses 2 being amused

a·muse'ment ar·cade' *n.* indoor area with game machines, etc.

a·muse'ment park' *n.* park equipped with carnival rides and other entertainments

a·my·o·troph'ic lat'er·al scle·ro'sis /ā'mīətrāf'ik, -trō'fik, āmī'ə-/ (also Lou Gehrig's disease) *n.* incurable degenerative disease leading to paralysis; *abbr.* ALS

an /ən, an/ *adj.* see A

an- *prefix* 1 see A-[2] 2 var. of AD- before *n*

-an *suffix* (also -ian) forming adjectives and nouns, esp. from names of places, systems, classes, etc. (*Mexican; Anglican; Devonian*) [L -*anus*]

an'a·bol'ic ste'roid /an'əbäl'ik/ *n.* synthetic steroid hormone used to increase muscle size

a·nab·o·lism /ənab'əliz'əm/ *n.* synthesis of complex molecules in living organisms from simpler ones [Gk *anabolē* ascent]

a·nach·ro·nism /ənak'rəniz'əm/ *n.* 1a attribution of a custom, event, etc., to the wrong period b thing thus attributed 2 out-of-date person or thing —a·nach'ro·nis'tic *adj.* [Gk *ana-* against + *khronos* time]

an·a·con·da /an'əkän'də/ *n.* large nonpoisonous snake killing its prey by constriction [Sinhalese]

a·nae·mi·a /ənē'mēə/ *n.* var. of ANEMIA

a·nae·mic /ənē'mik/ *adj.* var. of ANEMIC

an·aer·o·bic /an'erō'bik/ *adj.* able to live without air or oxygen —an·aer·obe /an'erōb'/ *n.*; an'aer·o'bi·cal·ly *adv.*

an·aes·the·si·a /an'isTHē'ZHə/ *n.* var., esp. *Brit.*, of ANESTHESIA —an·aes·thet·ic /an'isTHet'ik/ *n.* & *adj.*

an·a·gram /an'əgram'/ *n.* word or phrase formed by transposing the letters of another —an'a·gram·mat'ic, an'a·gram·mat'i·cal *adj.*; an'a·gram·mat'i·cal·ly *adv.*; an'a·gram'ma·tize *v.* (·tized, ·tiz·ing) [Gk *ana* again + *gramma* letter]

An·a·heim /an'əhīm'/ *n.* city in Calif., near Los Angeles. Pop. 266,406

a·nal /ān'l/ *adj.* of or near the anus

an·al·ge·si·a /an'l-jē'ZHə, -zēə/ *n.* absence or relief of pain [Gk]

an·al·ge·sic /an'l-jē'zik/ *adj.* 1 relieving pain —*n.* 2 analgesic drug

an·a·log /an'əlȯg', -äg/ (also an'a·logue) *n.* analogous thing

an'a·log com·pu'ter *n.* computer using physical variables, e.g., voltage, to represent numbers (cf. DIGITAL)

a·nal·o·gize /ənal'əjīz'/ *v.* (·gized, ·giz·ing) use, represent, or explain by analogy

a·nal·o·gous /ənal'əgəs/ *adj.* partially similar [Gk *analogos* proportionate]

a·nal·o·gy /ənal'əjē/ *n.* (*pl.* -gies) 1 correspondence; partial similarity 2 arguing or reasoning from parallel cases —an'a·log'i·cal *adj.*; **an'a·log'i·cal·ly** *adv.* [Gk *analogia* proportion]

a·nal·y·sis /ənal'əsis/ *n.* (*pl.* **·ses** /-sēz'/) **1a** detailed examination of elements or structure **b** statement of the result of this **2** *Chem.* determination of the constituent parts of a mixture or compound **3** psychoanalysis —**an'a·lyt'ic, an·a·lyt'i·cal** *adj.*; **an·a·lyt'i·cal·ly** *adv.* [Gk *ana* up + *lyein* loosen]

an·a·lyst /an'əlist/ *n.* **1** person skilled in (esp. chemical or computer) analysis **2** psychoanalyst

an·a·lyze /an'əlīz'/ *v.* (**·lyzed, ·lyz·ing**) **1** examine in detail; determine the parts or ingredients of (a substance, sentence, etc.) **2** psychoanalyze —**an'a·lyz'a·ble** *adj.*; **an'a·lyz'er** *n.*

an·a·pest /an'əpest'/ *n.* metrical foot consisting of two short or unstressed syllables followed by one long or stressed syllable —**an'a·pes'tic** *adj.* [Gk *anapaistos* reversed (dactyl)]

an·ar·chism /an'ərkiz'əm, an'är'-/ *n.* political theory that all government and laws should be abolished —**an'ar·chist'** *n.*; **an'ar·chis'tic** *adj.* [Fr. rel. to ANARCHY]

an·ar·chy /an'ərkē, an'är'-/ *n.* disorder, esp. political —**an·ar·chic** /anär'kik/ *adj.*; **an·ar'chi·cal·ly** *adv.* [Gk *an-* without + *arkhē* rule]

anat. *abbr.* **1** anatomical **2** anatomy

a·nath·e·ma /ənaTH'əmə/ *n.* (*pl.* **·mas**) **1** detested thing or person **2** ecclesiastical curse [Gk: thing devoted (i.e., to evil)]

a·nath·e·ma·tize /ənaTH'əmə·tīz'/ *v.* (**·tized, ·tiz·ing**) curse

a·nat·o·mize /ənat'əmīz'/ *v.* (**·mized, ·miz·ing**) dissect to study the structure or parts of

a·nat·o·my /ənat'əmē/ *n.* (*pl.* **·mies**) **1** science of animal or plant structure **2** such a structure **3** analysis —**an'a·tom'ic, an·a·tom·i·cal** /an'ətäm'ikəl/ *adj.*; **a·nat'o·mist'** *n.* [Gk *ana-* up + *temnein* cut]

An·ax·ag·o·ras /an'aksag'ərəs/ c. 500 – c. 428 B.C.; Greek philosopher

ANC *abbr.* African National Congress

-ance *suffix* forming nouns expressing: **1** quality or state or an instance of one (*arrogance*; *resemblance*) **2** action (*assistance*) [OFr fr. L *-antia*]

an·ces·tor /an'ses'tər/ *n.* **1** person, animal, or plant from which another has descended or evolved **2** prototype or forerunner —**an·ces'tral** *adj.*; **an·ces'tral·ly** *adv.*; **an·ces'tress** *n. fem.* [L *ante-* before + *cedere* go]

an·ces·try /an'ses'trē/ *n.* (*pl.* **·tries**) **1** family descent; lineage **2** ancestors collectively

an·chor /aNG'kər/ *n.* **1** metal device for mooring a ship or a balloon **2** stabilizing thing **3** *Sports.* last contestant in a relay race **4** person who hosts a news or other broadcast that includes several reporters **5** major store in a shopping center or mall —*v.* **6** secure with an anchor **7** fix firmly **8** serve as an anchor [Gk *ankyra*]

an·chor·age /aNG'kərij/ *n.* **1** place for anchoring **2** anchoring or lying at anchor

An'chor·age *n.* seaport in Alaska. Pop. 226,338

an·cho·rite /aNG'kərīt'/ *n.* hermit; religious recluse [Gk *ana* + *chōrein* retire]

an·chor·man /aNG'kərman'/ *n.* (*pl.* **·men** also **an'·chor;** *fem.* **an'chor·wom'an,** *pl.* **·w·men; an'chor·per'son**) coordinator, esp. o reports in a news broadcast

an·cho·vy /an'CHŌ'vē/ *n.* (*pl.* **·vies**) sma strong-flavored fish of the herring family [S and Port *anchova*]

an·cient /ān'sHənt, -CHənt/ *adj.* **1** of long ag esp. before the fall of the Roman Empire —*n* the West **2** having lived or existed long —*n* **3** very old person [OFr fr. L *ante* before]

an·cil·lary /an'səler'ē/ *adj.* subordinate; au: iliary; accessory [L *ancilla* handmaid]

-ancy *suffix* forming nouns denoting a qualit (*constancy*) or state (*infancy*) [L *-antia*]

and /and, ən(d)/ *conj.* **1** connecting word clauses, or sentences to be taken jointly (*y and I*) **2** implying: **a** progression (*better an better*) **b** causation (*hit him and he cries*) great duration (*cried and cried*) **d** a grea number (*miles and miles*) **e** addition (*two an two*) **3** *Colloq.* to (*try and come*) **4** and/o either or both of two stated alternatives [OF]

An·da·man Is·lands /an'dəmən, -man'/ group of Indian islands in the Bay of Benga W of the Malay Peninsula

an·dan·te /ändän'tā, -dänt'ē/ *Mus. adv. adj.* **1** in a moderately slow tempo —*n.* such a passage or movement [It: walking]

Andersen /an'dərsən, än'dərsən/, **Han Christian** 1805–75; Danish writer

An·der·son /an'dərsən/ **1 Sherwood** 1876 1941; US writer **2 Maxwell** 1888–1959; U dramatist **3 Marian** 1902–93; US contralto **Jack** 1922– ; US newspaper columnist

An·des /an'dēz/ *n.* mountain range in V South America from Colombia to Cape Hor —**An'de·an** *n. & adj.*

and·i·ron /an'dī'ərn/ *n.* one of a pair of su ports for logs in a fireplace [OFr *andier*]

An·dor·ra /andôr'ə/ *n.* tiny republic in E rope between France and Spain. Pop. 57,10C

An·drew, St. /an'drōō'/ one of the twelv Apostles; patron saint of Scotland

an·dro·gen /an'drəjən/ *n.* substance that r inforces masculine characteristics —**an'dr gen'ic** *adj.*

an·drog·y·nous /andräj'ənəs/ *adj.* **1** he maphrodite **2** *Bot.* with stamens and pistils i the same flower [Gk *andros* man + *gy woman*]

an·droid /an'droid/ *n.* robot with a huma appearance [Gk *andros* man + -OID]

An·dro·pov /andrō'pôf'/, **Yuri** 1914–8 president of USSR (1983–84)

an·ec·dote /an'ikdōt'/ *n.* short, esp. true, a count or story —**an'ec·dot'al** *adj.* [Gk *ane dotos* unpublished]

a·ne·mi·a /ənē'mēə/ *n.* deficiency of re blood cells or their hemoglobin [Gk: withou blood]

a·ne·mic /ənē'mik/ *adj.* **1** of or sufferin from anemia **2** pale; listless **3** weak —**a·n mi·cal·ly** *adv.*

an·e·mom·e·ter /an'əmäm'ətər/ *n.* instr ment for measuring wind force [Gk *anem* wind + METER]

a·nem·o·ne /ənem'ənē/ *n.* plant of the bu tercup family with flowers [Gk: wind-flower

an·er·oid /an'əroid'/ *adj.* **1** (of a baromete

measuring air pressure by its action on the lid of a box containing a vacuum —*n.* 2 aneroid barometer [Gk *a-* not + *něros* water]

an·es·the·sia /an'əsTHē"ZHə/ *n.* absence of sensation, esp. artificially induced before surgery [Gk: without feeling]

an·es·thet·ic /an'əsTHet'ik/ *n.* 1 substance producing anesthesia —*adj.* 2 producing anesthesia

an·es·the·tist /ənes'THətist/ *n.* doctor specialized in administering anesthetics

an·eu·rysm /an'yərizəm/ *n.* (also **an'eu·rism'**) abnormal localized enlargement of an artery [Gk *ana-* up + *eurys* wide]

a·new /ən(y)ōō'/ *adv.* 1 again 2 in a different way

an·gel /ān'jəl/ *n.* 1a attendant or messenger of God b representation of this in human form with wings 2 virtuous or obliging person 3 *Slang.* financial backer of a play, etc. —**an·gel'ic, an·gel·i·cal** *adj.*; **an·gel'i·cal·ly** *adv.* [Gk *angelos* messenger]

An'gel Falls' *n.* waterfall in SE Venezuela; world's highest: 3,212 ft.

An·ge·lou /än'jəlōō', -lō'/, Maya 1928– ; US novelist and poet

an·ger /aNG'gər/ *n.* 1 extreme or passionate displeasure —*v.* 2 make angry [ON *angr* grief]

an·gi·na /anji'nə/ *n.* (in full **an·gi'na pec'to·ris** /pek'tərəs/) chest pain brought on by exertion, caused by an inadequate blood supply to the heart [Gk *anchonē* strangulation]

an·gi·o·plas·ty /an'jēōplas'tē/ *n.* surgical repair or replacement of damaged blood vessels [Gk *aggeion* vessel + *-plastia* formation]

an·gi·o·sperm /an'jēōspərm'/ *n.* plant propagation by seeds in pods [Gk *aggeion* vessel + *sperm*]

acute   right   obtuse

ANGLE¹ 1

an·gle¹ /aNG'gəl/ *n.* 1 space between two meeting lines or surfaces, esp. as measured in degrees 2 corner 3 point of view —*v.* (**·gled, ·gling**) 4 move or place obliquely 5 present (information) in a biased way [L *angulus*]

an·gle² *v.* (**·gled, ·gling**) 1 fish with hook and line 2 seek an objective indirectly (*angled for a loan*) —**ang'ler** *n.* [OE]

An·gles /aNG'gəlz/ *n.* N German tribe that settled in E Britain in the 5th cent. A.D.

An·gli·can /aNG'glikən/ *adj.* 1 of the Church of England —*n.* 2 member of the Anglican Church. —**An'gli·can·ism'** *n.* [MedL *Anglicanus*, rel. to ANGLES]

An·gli·cism /aNG'gləsizəm/ *n.* peculiarly English word or custom [L *Anglicus*, rel. to ANGLES]

An·gli·cize /aNG'gləsīz'/ *v.* (**·cized, ·ciz·ing**) make English in language, pronunciation, character, etc.

An·glo /aNG'glō/ *n.* (*pl.* **·glos**) 1 English-speaking person 2 *SW US.* a non-Hispanic white person

Anglo- *comb. form* 1 English 2 Anglican

An'glo-French' *adj.* 1 English (or British) and French —*n.* 2 French language as developed in England after the Norman Conquest

An·glo·phile /aNG'gləfīl'/ *n.* person who greatly admires England or the English

An·glo-Sax·on /aNG'glōsak'sən/ *adj.* 1 of the English Saxons before the Norman Conquest 2 of English descent —*n.* 3 Anglo-Saxon person 4 Old English 5 *Colloq.* plain (esp. crude) English

An·go·la /aNG'gō'lə, an-/ *n.* republic in SW Africa. Capital: Luanda. Pop. 10,609,000 —**An·go'lan** *n. & adj.*

An·go·ra /aNGgôr'ə, an-/ *n.* 1 fabric or wool from the hair of the Angora goat or rabbit 2 long-haired variety of cat, goat, or rabbit [*Angora* (Ankara) in Turkey]

an·gry /aNG'grē/ *adj.* (**·gri·er, ·gri·est**) 1 feeling, showing, or suggesting anger 2 (of a wound, etc.) inflamed; painful 3 stormy —**an'gri·ly** *adv.*

ang·strom /aNG'strəm/ *n.* unit of length equal to 10⁻¹⁰ meter [for A. *Ångström*, Swedish physicist]

an·guish /aNG'gwisH/ *n.* 1 severe mental suffering 2 pain; agony —**an'guished** *adj.* [L *angustia* tightness]

an·gu·lar /aNG'gyələr/ *adj.* 1 having sharp corners or (of a person) features 2 measured by angle —**an'gu·lar'i·ty** *n.* [L, rel. to ANGLE¹]

an·i·line /an'əlin/ *n.* colorless oily liquid used in making dyes, drugs, and plastics [Ger *Anil* fr. L *an-nil* indigo, former source]

an·i·mad·vert /an'əmadvərt'/ *v. Lit.* criticize; censure —**an'i·mad·ver'sion** /-vər'zHən/ *n.* [L *animus* mind + *advertere* turn]

an·i·mal /an'əməl/ *n.* 1 living organism, esp. other than man, that feeds and usu. has sense organs and a nervous system and can move quickly 2 brutish person —*adj.* 3 of or like an animal [L *animalis* having breath]

an'i·mal·ism' *n.* 1 nature and activity of animals 2 belief that humans are mere animals

an·i·mate /an'əmit/ 1 having life 2 lively —*v.* /an'əmāt'/ (**·mat·ed, ·mat·ing**) 3 enliven 4 give life to —**an'i·mat'ed** *adj.*; **an'i·mat'ed·ly** *adv.*; **an'i·ma'tor** *n.* [L *anima* breath]

an'i·ma'tion *n.* 1 vivacity; ardor 2 being alive 3 technique of producing a moving picture from a sequence of drawings or puppet poses, etc.

an·i·mism /an'əmiz'əm/ *n.* belief that inanimate and natural phenomena have souls —**an'i·mist'** *n.*; **an'i·mis'tic** *adj.*

an·i·mos·i·ty /an'əmäs'ətē/ *n.* (*pl.* **·ties**) spirit or feeling of hostility [L, rel. to ANIMUS]

an·i·mus /an'əməs/ *n.* animosity; ill feeling [L: spirit; mind; passion]

an·i·on /an'ī'ən/ *n.* negatively charged ion —**an·i·on·ic** /an'ī-än'ik/ *adj.* [Gk *ana* up + ION]

an·ise /an'əs/ *n.* plant with aromatic seeds [Gk *anison*]

An·ka·ra /äNG'kərə, aNG'-/ *n.* capital of Turkey. Pop. 2,559,500

ankh /aNGk/ *n.* cross with a loop at the top [Egypt: soul]

an·kle /aNG'kəl/ *n.* 1 joint connecting the foot with the leg 2 this part of the leg [OE]

an·klet /aNG'klit/ *n.* 1 ornament worn around the ankle 2 short sock

an·ky·lo·sis /aNG'kələ'sis/ *n.* stiffening of a joint by fusion of the bones —**an'ky·lot'ic** /-lot'ik/ *adj.* [Gk *ankylos* crooked]

ANKH

an·nals /an'əlz/ *n. pl.* 1 narrative of events year by year 2 historical records —**an'nal·ist** *n.* [L *annus* year]

An·nap·o·lis /ənap'(ə)ləs/ *n.* seaport and capital of Md. on Chesapeake Bay. Site of the US Naval Academy. Pop. 33,187

Ann Ar·bor /an är'bər/ *n.* city in Mich. Pop. 109,592

Anne /an/ 1665–1714; queen of England (1702–14)

Anne, St. traditional name for the mother of the Virgin Mary

an·neal /ənēl'/ *v.* heat (metal or glass) and cool slowly, esp. to toughen it [OE *anēlan* kindle]

Anne Bol·eyn see BOLEYN, ANNE

an·ne·lid /an'əlid/ *n.* segmented worm, e.g., the earthworm [L *anulus* ring]

An·nen·berg /an'ənbərg'/, **Walter** 1908– ; US publisher and philanthropist

Anne of Cleves /klēvz/ 1515–57; 4th wife of Henry VIII

an·nex *v.* /əneks', an'eks'/ 1 add as a subordinate part 2 incorporate (territory) into one's own —*n.* /an'eks/ 3 something added, as to a building —**an'nex·a'tion** *n.* [L *nectere* bind]

an·ni·hi·late /ənī'əlāt'/ *v.* (·lat·ed, ·lat·ing) completely destroy or defeat —**an·ni'hi·la'tion**, **an·ni'hi·la'tor** *n.* [L *nihil* nothing]

an·ni·ver·sa·ry /an'əvər'sərē/ *n.* (*pl.* ·ries) 1 date of an event in a previous year 2 celebration of this [L *annus* year + *vertere* versturn]

An·no Do·mi·ni /an'ō däm'ənē, -nī'/ *adv.* era after Christ's birth; Christian era; *abbr.* A.D. [L: in the year of the Lord]

an·no·tate /an'ətāt'/ *v.* (·tat·ed, ·tat·ing) add explanatory notes to —**an'no·ta'tion** *n.* [L *nota* mark]

an·nounce /ənouns'/ *v.* (·nounced, ·nounc·ing) 1 make publicly known 2 make known the arrival or imminence of 3 be a sign of —**an·nounce'ment** *n.* [L *nuntius* messenger]

an·nounc'er *n.* person who announces, esp. in broadcasting

an·noy /ənoi'/ *v.* irritate or distress slightly —**an·noy'ance** *n.*; **an·noy'ing** *adj.*; **an·noy'ing·ly** *adv.* [L *in odio* hateful]

an·nu·al /an'yŌŌəl, -yəl/ *adj.* 1 calculated by the year 2 occurring yearly 3 living or lasting (only) a year —*n.* 4 book, etc., published yearly 5 plant that lives only a year —**an'nu·al·ly** *adv.* [L *annus* year]

an·nu·i·ty /ən(y)ŌŌ'ətē/ *n.* (*pl.* ·ties) 1 investment yielding a fixed annual sum 2 the sum paid

an·nul /ənəl'/ *v.* (·nulled, ·nul·ling) 1 declare invalid 2 cancel; abolish —**an·nul'ment** *n.* [L *nullus* none]

an·nu·lar /an'yələr/ *adj.* ring-shaped [L *anulus* ring]

an'nu·lar e·clipse' *n.* solar eclipse in which a ring of sunlight remains visible

an·nun·ci·a·tion /ənən'sē·ā'sHən/ *n.* 1 announcement, esp. (*cap.*) that made by the angel Gabriel to Mary that she would be the mother of Jesus 2 festival of this [L, rel. to ANNOUNCE]

an·ode /an'ōd'/ *n.* positive electrode in an electrolytic cell, etc. [Gk *anodos* way up]

an·o·dize /an'ədīz'/ *v.* (·dized, ·diz·ing) coat (metal) with a protective layer by electrolysis

an·o·dyne /an'ədīn'/ *adj.* 1 pain-relieving 2 mentally soothing —*n.* 3 anodyne drug, etc. [Gk *an-* without + *odynē* pain]

a·noint /ənoint'/ *v.* 1 apply oil or ointment to, esp. ritually 2 smear [L *in-* on + *unguere* anoint]

a·nom·a·lous /ənäm'ələs/ *adj.* irregular; deviant; abnormal [Gk *an-* not + *homalos* even]

a·nom·a·ly /ənäm'əlē/ *n.* (*pl.* ·lies) anomalous thing; irregularity

a·non /ənän'/ *adv. Archaic.* soon; shortly [OE *on ān* into one]

anon. *abbr.* anonymous

a·non·y·mous /ənän'əməs/ *adj.* 1 of unknown name or authorship 2 without character; featureless —**an·o·nym'i·ty** *n.* [Gk *an-* without + *onyma* name]

a·noph·e·les /ənof'əlēz'/ *n.* a mosquito that transmits malaria to man [Gk: harmful]

an·o·rak /an'ərak'/ *n.* waterproof usu. hooded jacket [Esk]

an·o·rex·i·a /an'ərek'sēə/ *n.* lack of appetite, esp. (an·o·rex'i·a ner·vo'sa /nərvō'sə, -zə/) an obsessive desire to lose weight by refusing to eat —**an'o·rex'ic** *adj. & n.* [Gk *an-* without + *orexis* appetite]

an·oth·er /ənəTH'ər/ *adj.* 1 an additional; one more 2 person like 3 a different —*pron.* 4 additional, other, or different person or thing [earlier *an other*]

A·nou·ilh /änŌŌ'ē/, **Jean** 1910–87; French dramatist

An·selm, St. /an'selm'/ c. 1033–1109; archbishop of Canterbury (1093–1109)

an·swer /an'sər/ *n.* 1 something said or done in reaction to a question, statement, or circumstance 2 solution to a problem —*v.* 3 make an answer or response (to) 4 suit a purpose or need 5 be responsible 6 correspond, esp. to a description 7 answer back *Colloq.* answer insolently —**an'swer·a·ble** *adj.* [OE: swear against (a charge)]

ant /ant/ *n.* small usu. wingless insect living in social colonies and proverbial for industry [OE]

-ant *suffix* 1 forming adjectives denoting attribution of an action (*repentant*) or state (*arrogant*) 2 forming agent nouns (*assistant*) [L *-ant-*, pres. part. stem of verbs]

ant·ac·id /antas'id/ *adj.* 1 preventing or correcting acidity —*n.* 2 antacid agent

an·tag·o·nism /antag'əniz'əm/ *n.* active hostility [Fr, ult. fr. Gk] an·tag′o·nist *n.* opponent or adversary —an·tag′o·nis′tic *adj.*

an·tag′o·nize′ *v.* (·nized, ·niz·ing) make hostile; provoke

An·tal′ya /äntäl′yə/ *n.* seaport in Turkey. Pop. 378,200

An·ta·na·na·ri·vo /än′tənan′ərē′vō/ *n.* capital of Madagascar. Pop. 802,400

Ant·arc·ti·ca /äntärk′tikə, ·ärt′ikə/ *n.* 1 ice-covered continent surrounding the South Pole 2 (the Antarctic) region of Antarctica and surrounding oceans —ant·arc′tic *adj.* [L fr. Gk, rel. to ARCTIC]

Ant·arc′tic Cir′cle *n.* parallel of latitude 66° 32′ S, delimiting the Antarctic region

an·te /an′tē/ *n.* 1 stake put up by a player in poker, etc., before receiving cards 2 amount payable in advance —*v.* (·ted or ·teed, ·teing) 3 put up as an ante

ante- *prefix* before; preceding [L: before]

ant′eat′er *n.* any of various mammals feeding on ants and termites

an·te·bel′lum /an′tēbel′əm/ *adj.* before the American Civil War (1861–65) [L]

an·te·ced·ent /an′təsēd′nt/ *n.* 1 preceding thing or circumstance 2 *Gram.* word or phrase, etc., to which another word (esp. a relative pronoun) refers 3 (*pl.*) person's past history or ancestors —*adj.* 4 previous [L ANTE- + *cedere* go]

an′te·cham′ber /an′tē-/ *n.* ante-room

an′te·date′ /an′tē-/ *v.* (·dat·ed, ·dat·ing) 1 precede in time 2 assign an earlier date to

an·te·di·lu·vi·an /an′tidəlōō′vēən/ *adj.* 1 of the time before the Flood 2 *Colloq.* very old or out of date [L ANTE- + *diluvium* deluge]

an·te·lope /ant′l·ōp′/ *n.* swift-moving deer-like ruminant, e.g., the gazelle and wildebeest [MGk *antholops*]

an·ten·na /anten′ə/ *n.* 1 (*pl.* ·nae /-nē/) each of a pair of feelers on the heads of insects, crustaceans, etc. 2 (*pl.* ·nas) structure of wires, rods, etc., for sending and receiving radio waves [L: sail yard]

an·te·ri·or /antēr′ēər/ *adj.* 1 nearer the front 2 prior [L fr. *ante* before]

an·te·room /an′tirōōm′/ *n.* small room leading to a main one

an′tʰem /an′THəm/ *n.* 1 elaborate choral composition usu. based on a passage of scripture 2 solemn hymn of praise, etc., esp. national anthem [L fr. Gk, rel. to ANTIPHON]

an·ther /an′THər/ *n.* part of a stamen containing pollen [Gk *anthēros* flowering]

ant′hill′ *n.* moundlike nest built by ants or termites

an·thol·o·gy /anTHäl′əjē/ *n.* (*pl.* ·gies) collection of poems, essays, stories, etc. —thol′o·gist *n.*; an·thol′o·gize (·gized, ·giz·ing) *v.* [Gk *anthos* flower + *logia* collection]

An·tho·ny /an′THənē/, Susan B(rownell) 1820–1906; US suffragist

an·thra·cite /an′THrəsīt′/ *n.* type of hard coal burning with little flame and smoke [Gk, rel. to ANTHRAX]

an·thrax /an′THraks/ *n.* disease of sheep and cattle transmissible to humans [Gk: coal; carbuncle]

an·thro·po·cen·tric /an′THrəpəsen′trik/ *adj.* regarding mankind as the focal point of existence [Gk *anthrōpos* man]

an·thro·poid /an′THrəpoid′/ *adj.* 1 human in form 2 apelike —*n.* 3 anthropoid ape

an·thro·pol·o·gy /an′THrəpäl′əjē/ *n.* the study of mankind, esp. its societies and customs —an·thro·po·log′i·cal /-pəläj′ikəl/ *adj.*; an′thro·po·log′i·cal·ly *adv.*; an′thro·pol′o·gist *n.*

an·thro·po·mor·phism /an′THrəpəmôr′fiz′əm/ *n.* attribution of human characteristics to a god, animal, or thing —an′thro·po·mor′phic *adj.*; an′thro·po·mor′phi·cal·ly *adv.* [Gk *anthrōpos* man + *morphē* form]

an·thro·po·mor·phous /an′THrəpəmôr′fəs/ *adj.* human in form

an·ti /an′tē, an′tī/ *prep.* 1 opposed to —*n.* (*pl.* ·tis) 2 person opposed to a policy, etc.

anti- *prefix* 1 opposed to (*anticlerical*) 2 preventing (*antifreeze*) 3 opposite of (*antithesis*) [Gk: against]

an′ti·a·bor′tion *adj.* opposing abortion —an′ti·a·bor′tion·ist *n.*

an′ti·air′craft *adj.* (of a gun or missile) for use to attack enemy aircraft

an·ti·bi·ot·ic /an′tēbī·ät′ik, an′tī-, -bē-/ *n.* 1 substance that can inhibit or destroy susceptible microorganisms —*adj.* 2 functioning as an antibiotic [Gk *bios* life]

an′ti·bod′y *n.* (*pl.* ·ies) a blood protein produced in response to and then counteracting antigens

an·tic /an′tik/ *n.* (usu. *pl.*) foolish behavior or action [It *antico* ANTIQUE]

An·ti·christ /an′tikrīst′/ *n.* enemy of Christ —an·ti·chris·tian /an′tikris′CHən, an′tī′-/ *adj.*

an·tic·i·pate /antis′əpāt′/ *v.* (·pat·ed, ·pat·ing) 1 deal with or use before the proper time 2 expect; foresee 3 forestall (a person or thing) 4 look forward to —an·tic′i·pa′tion *n.*; an·tic′i·pa·to′ry *adj.* [L *anti-* before + *capere* take]

an·ti·cli·max /an′tiklī′maks, an′tī-/ *n.* disappointingly trivial conclusion to something significant —an′ti·cli·mac′tic /-klīmak′tik/ *adj.*; an′ti·cli·mac′ti·cal·ly *adv.*

an·ti·dote /an′tidōt′/ *n.* 1 medicine, etc., used to counteract poison 2 anything counteracting something unpleasant [Gk *antidotos* given against]

an·ti·freeze /an′tifrēz′, an′tī-/ *n.* substance added to water to lower its freezing point, esp. in a vehicle's radiator

an·ti·gen /an′tijən/ *n.* foreign substance that causes the body to produce antibodies [Gk *-genēs* produced]

An·ti·gua and Bar·bu·da /antē′gwə; bärbōōd′ə/ *n.* island state in the West Indies. Capital: St. John's. Pop. 64,000

an·ti·he·ro /an′tē hēr′ō/ *n.* (*pl.* ·roes) (in a story) central character lacking conventional heroic qualities

an·ti·his·ta·mine /an′tihis′təmēn′, an′tī-, -mən/ *n.* drug used in treating allergies

an·ti·knock /an′tinäk′, an′tī-/ *n.* substance added to motor fuel to eliminate knocking noise produced by premature combustion

An·til·les /antil´ēz/ *n.* chain of islands in the Caribbean Sea

an·ti·lock /an´tē läk´/ *adj.* (of brakes) designed to prevent locking (and skidding) when applied suddenly

an·ti·log·a·rithm /an´tiläg´əriᴛʜˈəm, an´tī-, -lôg´-/ *n.* (also **an·ti·log** /an´tilôg´, -läg´/) number to which a logarithm belongs

an·ti·mat·ter /an´timat´ər, an´tī-/ *n.* matter composed solely of antiparticles

an·ti·mo·ny /an´təmō´nē/ *n.* brittle silvery metallic element used esp. in alloys; *symb.* Sb [MedL]

an·ti·par·ti·cle /an´tipärt´ikəl, an´tī-/ *n.* elementary particle with the same mass but opposite charge, etc., to another particle

an·ti·pas·to /an´tipäs´tō/ *n.* assorted appetizers, esp. of marinated vegetables [It: before food]

an·tip·a·thy /antip´əᴛʜē/ *n.* (*pl.* **-thies**) strong aversion or dislike **—an·ti·pa·thet·ic** /an´tipəᴛʜet´ik/ *adj.* [Gk, rel. to PATHETIC]

an·ti·per·spi·rant /an´tipər´sp(ə)rənt, an´tī-/ *n.* substance preventing or reducing perspiration

an·ti·phon /an´tifən, -fän´/ *n.* **1** hymn sung alternately by two groups **2** phrase from this **—an·tiph´o·nal** *adj.* [Gk *phōnē* sound]

an·tip·o·des /antip´ədēz´/ *n. pl.* places diametrically opposite to one another on the earth, esp. (also *cap.*) Australasia in relation to N America or Europe **—an·tip´o·de´an** *adj.* & *n.* [Gk: having the feet opposite]

An·tip·o·des *n.* **1** term for Australia and New Zealand, considered together **2** group of islands SE of New Zealand

an·ti·quar·i·an /an´tikwer´ēən/ *adj.* **1** of or dealing in antiques or rare books **—n.** **2** antiquary **—an´ti·quar´i·an·ism** *n.*

an·ti·quar·y /an´tikwer´ē/ *n.* (*pl.* **-ies**) student or collector of antiques, etc. [L, rel. to ANTIQUE]

an·ti·quat·ed /an´tikwāt´id/ *adj.* old-fashioned; out-dated

an·tique /antēk´/ *n.* **1** old object, piece of furniture, usu. more than 100 years old **—adj.** **2** of or from an early date **3** out of date **—v.** (**·tiqued, ·tiqu·ing**) **4** condition to resemble an antique [L *antiquus* ancient]

an·tiq·ui·ty /antik´wətē/ *n.* (*pl.* **-ties**) **1** ancient times, esp. before the Middle Ages **2** great age **3** (usu. *pl.*) relics from ancient times [L, rel. to ANTIQUE]

an·ti·Sem·ite /an´tisem´īt´, an´tī-/ *n.* person prejudiced against Jews **—an´ti·Se·mit´ic** /-səmit´ik/ *adj.*; **an´ti·Se·mit´i·cal·ly** *adv.*; **an´ti·Sem´i·tism** /-sem´ətiz´əm/ *n.*

an·ti·sep·tic /an´tisep´tik/ *adj.* **1** counteracting sepsis, esp. by destroying germs **2** sterile; uncontaminated **3** lacking character **—n.** **4** antiseptic agent

an·ti·se·rum /an´tisēr´əm, an´tī-/ *n.* serum with a high antibody content

an·ti·so·cial /an´tisō´SHəl, an´tī-/ *adj.* **1** harmful to society **2** not sociable

an·tith·e·sis /antiᴛʜ´əsis/ *n.* (*pl.* **-ses** /-sēz/) **1** direct opposite **2** contrast **—an´ti·thet´i·cal** /an´tiᴛʜet´ikəl/ *adj.*; **an´ti·thet´i·cal·ly** *adv.* [Gk *anti* + *tithēnai* set against]

an·ti·tox·in /an´titäk´sin/ *n.* antibody counteracting a toxin **—an´ti·tox´ic** *adj.*

an·ti·trust /an´tītrəst´/ *adj.* against the formation of large trusts or cartels

an·ti·vi·ral /an´tivī´rəl, an´tī-/ *adj.* effective against viruses

ANTLERS

ant·ler /ant´lər/ *n.* branched horn of a stag or other deer **—ant´lered** *adj.* [MFr]

An·to·ni·nus Pi·us /an´tənī´nəs pī´əs/ 86–161; Roman emperor (137–161)

An·to·ny /an´tənē/, **Mark (Marcus Antonius)** c. 83–30 B.C.; Roman general and political leader

an·to·nym /an´tənim´/ *n.* word opposite in meaning to another **—an·ton´y·mous** *adj.* [Gk *anti* opposite, *onyma* name]

Ant·werp /ant´twərp´/ *n.* seaport in Belgium. Pop. 467,500

A·nu·bis /ənōō´bis, ənyōō´-/ *n.* *Egypt. Myth.* god of the dead

a·nus /ā´nəs/ *n.* (*pl.* **·nus·es** or **·ni** /-nī´/) excretory opening at the end of the alimentary canal [L]

ANVIL

an·vil /an´vəl/ *n.* iron block on which metals are shaped [OE]

anx·i·e·ty /aNGzī´ətē/ *n.* (*pl.* **-ties**) **1** being anxious **2** worry or concern **3** eagerness; troubled desire [L *anxietas* fr. *angere* choke]

anx·ious /aNGK´SHəs/ *adj.* **1** mentally troubled **2** causing or marked by anxiety **3** eager; uneasily wanting **—anx´ious·ly** *adv.* [L *anxius*]

an·y /en´ē/ *adj.* **1** one, no matter which, of three or more **2** some, no matter how much or many or of what sort **3** whichever; every **4** appreciable; significant **—pron.** **5** any one **6** any number or amount **—adv.** **7** at all [OE *ænig*]

an·y·bod·y /en´ēbäd´ē, -bäd´ē/ *n.* & *pron.* **1** any person **2** person of importance

an·y·how´ *adv.* **1** anyway **2** in a disorderly manner or state

an·y´one´ *pron.* anybody

an·y´thing´ *pron.* **1** any thing; thing of any sort **2** anything but not at all

an·y´way´ *adv.* **1** in any way or manner **2** at any rate **3** nevertheless; anyhow

an·y·where' *adv.* **1** in or to any place —*pron.* **2** any place

A-OK /ā'ōkā'/ *adj.* (also **A'·O·kay'**) *Colloq.* all right; fine; proper

A1 /ā' wən'/ *n.* (also **A-1, A one, A-one,** or **A number 1**) **1** *Colloq.* first-rate; excellent **2 from A to Z** from beginning to end

a·or·ta /āôr'tə/ *n.* (*pl.* **-tas**) main artery carrying oxygenated blood to the body from the heart —**a·or'tic** *adj.* [Gk *aortē,* rel. to *aeirein* raise]

a·pace /əpās'/ *adv. Lit.* swiftly [MFr *à pas*]

A·pach·e /əpACH'ē/ *n.* member of a N American Indian tribe [MexSp]

a·part /əpärt'/ *adv.* **1** separately; not together **2** into pieces **3** to or on one side; aside **4** to or at a distance —*adj.* **5 apart from: a** excluded; separate **b** beside; not considering **c** in addition to [OFr *à part* to one side]

a·part·heid /əpär'tāt', -tīt'/ *n.* (in S Africa) racial segregation or discrimination [Afrik]

a·part·ment /əpärt'mənt/ *n.* room or suite of rooms for use as a dwelling [Fr fr. It *appartare* separate]

ap·a·thy /ap'əTHē/ *n.* lack of interest; indifference —**ap·a·thet·ic** /ap'əTHet'ik/ *adj.* [Gk *a-* without + PATHOS]

ape /āp/ *n.* **1** monkeylike primate, e.g., the gorilla, chimpanzee, orangutan, or gibbon **2** imitator —*v.* (**aped, ap·ing**) **3** imitate; mimic —**ape'like** *adj.* [OE]

Ap·en·nines /ap'ənīnz'/ *n.* mountain range extending the length of the Italian peninsula

a·pe·ri·tif /ä'per'ətēf', əper'ətēf'/ *n.* alcoholic drink taken before a meal [Fr fr. L *aperire* open]

ap·er·ture /ap'ərCHŏŏr', -CHər/ *n.* opening or gap [L *aperire* open]

a·pex /ā'peks'/ *n.* (*pl.* **-pex·es** or **ap·i·ces** /ap'əsēz'/) **1** highest point **2** tip or pointed end —**ap·i·cal** /ap'əkəl, ā'pəkəl/ *adj.* [L]

a·pha·si·a /əfā'ZHə/ *n.* loss of verbal understanding or expression —**a·pha·sic** /-fā'zik/ *adj.* & *n.* [Gk *aphatos* speechless]

aph·e·li·on /afēl'yən/ *n.* (*pl.* **-ons** or **-li·a** /-lēə/) point in an orbit furthest from the sun [Gk *aph-* from + *hēlios* sun]

a·phid /ā'fid/ *n.* small insect infesting and damaging plants

aph·o·rism /af'əriz'əm/ *n.* short effective saying —**aph'o·ris'tic** *adj.* [Gk *aphorismos* definition]

aph·ro·dis·i·ac /af'rədē'zē-ak, -diz'ē-/ *adj.* **1** arousing sexual desire —*n.* **2** aphrodisiac substance [Gk *Aphroditē* goddess of love]

Aph·ro·di·te /af'rədī'tē/ *n. Gk. Myth.* goddess of beauty and love, identified with Roman Venus

A·pi·a /äpē'ə/ *n.* capital of Western Samoa. Pop. 32,900

a·pi·ar·y /ā'pē·er'ē/ *n.* (*pl.* **·ar·ies**) place where bees are kept —**a'pi·a·rist** /-ərist/ *n.* [L *apis* bee]

ap·i·cal /ā'pikəl/ *adj.* of, at, or forming an apex

a·piece /əpēs'/ *adv.* for each one [ME, fr. A + PIECE]

a·plomb /əpläm', əpləm'/ *n.* skillful self-assurance; poise [Fr: straight as a plummet]

APO *abbr.* (U.S.) Army post office

a·poc·a·lypse /əpäk'əlips'/ *n.* **1** violent or destructive event **2** (**the Apocalypse**) Revela-

tion, the last book of the New Testament **3** revelation, esp. about the end of the world —**a'poc·a·lyp'tic** *adj.* [Gk *apokalyptein* reveal]

A·poc·ry·pha /əpäk'rəfə/ *n. pl.* **1** books included in the Septuagint and Vulgate versions of the Old Testament but not in the Hebrew Bible **2** (**a-**) writings, etc., not considered genuine [Gk *apokryptein* hide away]

a·poc·ry·phal /əpäk'rəfəl/ *adj.* of doubtful authenticity

ap·o·gee /ap'əjē/ *n.* point in an orbit furthest from the earth [Gk *apo-* from + *gē* earth]

a·po·lit·i·cal /ā'pəlit'ikəl/ *adj.* not interested in or concerned with politics

A·pol·lo /əpäl'ō/ *n. Gk. & Rom. Myth.* god associated with prophecy, poetry, healing, etc.

Ap·ol·lo·ni·us /ap'əlō'nēəs/ *n.* (**of Rhodes**) 3rd cent. B.C.; Greek poet

a·pol·o·get·ic /əpäl'əjet'ik/ *adj.* showing or expressing regret —**a·pol'o·get'i·cal·ly** *adv.*

a·pol·o·gist /əpäl'əjist/ *n.* person who defends something by argument

a·pol·o·gize' *v.* (**·gized, ·giz·ing**) make an apology; express regret

a·pol·o·gy /əpäl'əjē/ *n.* (*pl.* **·gies**) **1** statement of regret for an offense or failure **2** (also **ap·o·lo·gi·a** /ap'əlō'jē/) explanation or defense **3** (foll. by *for*) poor specimen of [Gk *apo-* from + *logos* speech]

ap·o·phthegm /ap'əTHem'/ *n.* APHORISM [L fr. Gk]

ap·o·plex·y /ap'əplek'sē/ *n.* sudden paralysis caused by blockage or rupture of a brain artery; stroke —**ap'o·plec'tic** *adj.* [Gk, fr. *plēssein* strike]

a·pos·ta·sy /əpäs'təsē/ *n.* (*pl.* **·sies**) renouncing of a belief or faith, abandoning of principles, etc. [Gk: defection]

a·pos·tate /əpäs'tāt'/ *n.* person who renounces a former belief, faith, etc. —**a·pos'ta·tize** *v.* (**·tized, ·tiz·ing**)

a pos·te·ri·o·ri /ä' pōstēr'ē-ôr'ē, ä', -ī'/ *adj.* **1** (of reasoning) proceeding from effects to causes; inductive —*adv.* **2** inductively [L: from what comes after]

a·pos·tle /əpäs'əl/ *n.* **1** (*cap.*) any of the twelve men sent out by Christ to preach the gospel **2** leader, esp. of a new movement [Gk *apostolos* messenger]

ap·os·tol·ic /ap'əstäl'ik/ *adj.* **1** of the Apostles or their teaching **2** of the pope

a·pos·tro·phe /əpäs'trəfē/ *n.* **1** punctuation mark (') indicating: **a** omission of letters or numbers (e.g., *can't; May '92*) **b** possessive case (e.g., *Harry's book; boys' coats*) **c** certain plurals (*1900's; cross the t's*) **2** exclamatory passage addressed to (an often absent) person or thing —**a·pos'tro·phize'** *v.* (**·phized, ·phiz·ing**) [Gk: turning away]

a·poth·e·car·y /əpäTH'əker'ē/ *n.* (*pl.* **·car·ies**) pharmacist [Gk *apothēkē* storehouse]

a·po·the·o·sis /əpäTH'ē-ō'sis/ *n.* (*pl.* **·o·ses** /-sēz/) **1** elevation to divine status; deification **2** glorification of a thing; sublime example [Gk *theos* god]

Ap·pa·la·chi·an Moun·tains /ap'ələ'CH(ē)ən, -laCH'-/ *n.* mountain range in E US, running 1,500 mi. SW to NE

Ap·pa·la·chi·an Trail' *n.* scenic trail in E US extending 2,000 mi. from Maine to Ga.

ap·pall /əpôl'/ *v.* (·palled, ·pal·ling) greatly dismay or horrify [MFr *apallir* grow pale, rel. to PALE[1]]

ap·pa·rat·us /ap'ərat'əs, -rāt'əs/ *n.* 1 equipment for a particular function, esp. scientific or technical 2 political or other complex organization [L *apparare* prepare]

ap·par·el /əpar'əl, -per'-/ *n.* 1 clothing; dress —*v.* (·eled or ·elled, ·el·ing or ·el·ling) 2 dress; attire [ME fr. MFr *apareillier*, perh. rel. to L *apparare* prepare]

ap·par·ent /əpar'ənt, -per'-/ *adj.* 1 readily visible; obvious 2 seeming —**ap·par'ent·ly** *adv.* [L, rel. to APPEAR]

ap·pa·ri·tion /ap'ərish'ən/ *n.* remarkable or unexpected thing that appears; phantom

ap·peal /əpēl'/ *v.* 1 request earnestly or formally; plead 2 be attractive or interesting 3 beseech earnestly 4 *Law.* apply (to a higher court) for reconsideration of a legal decision —*n.* 5 act of appealing 6 request for public support, esp. financial 7 *Law.* referral of a case to a higher court 8 attractiveness [L *appellare* speak to]

ap·pear /əpēr'/ *v.* 1 become or be visible 2 seem 3 present oneself publicly or formally 4 be presented to the public [L *apparere*]

ap·pear·ance /əpēr'əns/ *n.* 1 act of appearing 2 outward form as perceived 3 semblance 4 **keep up appearances** maintain an impression or pretense 5 **make** (or **put in**) **an appearance** be present, esp. briefly

ap·pease /əpēz'/ *v.* (·peased, ·peas·ing) 1 make calm or quiet, esp. pacify (a potential aggressor) by making concessions 2 satisfy (an appetite, scruples) —**ap·pease'ment, ap·peas'er** *n.* [OFr *à* to + *pais* PEACE]

ap·pel·lant /əpel'ənt/ *n.* person who appeals to a higher court

ap·pel·late /əpel'āt/ *adj.* (esp. of a court) concerned with appeals

ap·pel·la·tion /ap'əlā'shən/ *n. Formal.* 1 name or title 2 nomenclature

ap·pend /əpend'/ *v.* attach; affix; add; esp. to a written document [L *appendere* hang]

ap·pend·age /əpen'dij/ *n.* thing attached; addition

ap·pen·dec·to·my /ap'əndek'təmē/ *n.* (*pl.* ·mies) surgical removal of the appendix [fr. APPENDIX + -ECTOMY]

ap·pen·di·ci·tis /əpen'dəsīt'əs/ *n.* inflammation of the appendix

ap·pen·dix /əpen'diks/ *n.* 1 (*pl.* ·dix·es) tissue forming a tube-shaped sac attached to the large intestine 2 (*pl.* ·di·ces /-dəsēz'/ or ·dix·es) addition to a book, etc. [L, rel. to APPEND]

ap·per·tain /ap'ərtān'/ *v.* relate, belong, or be appropriate [MFr fr. L *pertinere* belong]

ap·pe·tite /ap'ətīt'/ *n.* 1 natural craving, esp. for food or sexual activity 2 inclination or desire [L *appetere* seek; desire]

ap·pe·tiz·er /ap'ətī'zər/ *n.* small amount of food to stimulate the appetite, esp. before a main course

ap·pe·tiz·ing /ap'ətī'ziNG/ *adj.* stimulating the appetite, esp. for food; tasty

ap·plaud /əplôd'/ *v.* 1 express strong approval, esp. by clapping 2 commend; approve (a person or action) [L *applaudere* clap hands]

ap·plause /əplôz'/ *n.* approval, esp. as shown by clapping the hands

ap·ple /ap'əl/ *n.* 1 roundish firm edible fruit with crisp flesh 2 tree bearing this 3 **apple of one's eye** cherished person or thing [OE]

ap'ple·jack *n.* brandy distilled from fermented cider

ap'ple·pie' or'der *n.* extreme neatness

ap'ple·sauce' *n.* 1 sauce from crushed, cooked apples 2 *Colloq.* nonsense

Ap·ple·ton /ap'əltən/ *n.* city in Wis. Pop. 65,695

ap·pli·ance /əplī'əns/ *n.* device for a specific task [rel. to APPLY]

ap·pli·ca·ble /ap'likəbəl, əplik'-/ *adj.* that may be applied; relevant; appropriate —**ap'pli·ca·bil'i·ty** *n.* [MedL, rel. to APPLY]

ap·pli·cant /ap'likənt/ *n.* person who applies for something, esp. a job

ap·pli·ca·tion /ap'likā'shən/ *n.* 1 formal request 2 act of applying 3 substance applied 4a relevance b use 5 diligence

ap·pli·ca·tor /ap'likāt'ər/ *n.* device for applying ointment, etc.

ap·plied /əplīd'/ *adj.* practical, not merely theoretical (*applied science*)

ap·pli·qué /ap'ləkā'/ *n.* 1 cutting out of fabric patterns and attaching them to another fabric —*v.* (·quéd, ·qué·ing) 2 decorate with appliqué [Fr: applied]

ap·ply /əplī'/ *v.* (·plied, ·ply·ing) 1 formally request 2 be relevant 3 make use of; employ 4 put or spread on 5 devote [L *applicare* attach; join]

ap·point /əpoint'/ *v.* 1 assign a job or office to 2 fix (a time, place, etc.) 3 equip; furnish —**ap·point'ee** *n.* [MFr *apointer* point]

ap·point'ment *n.* 1 appointing or being appointed 2 arrangement for meeting or consultation 3 post or office open to applicants 4 person appointed 5 (usu. *pl.*) furniture; fittings; equipment

Ap'po·mat'tox Court'house /ap'əmat'əks/ *n.* former town in Va.; site of Lee's surrender to Grant (1865) ending American Civil War

ap·por·tion /əpôr'shən/ *v.* share out; assign as a share —**ap·por'tion·ment** *n.* [MFr fr. L]

ap·pose /əpōz'/ *v.* (·posed, ·pos·ing) put side by side [L *apponere* place near]

ap·po·site /ap'əzit/ *adj.* apt; appropriate; well expressed —**ap'po·site·ly** *adv.;* **ap'po·site·ness** *n.* [L *apponere* apply; place near]

ap·po·si·tion /ap'əzish'ən/ *n.* juxtaposition, esp. of words or phrases sharing a syntactic function (e.g., *William the Conqueror; my friend Sue*)

ap·prais·al /əprā'zəl/ *n.* appraising or being appraised

ap·praise /əprāz'/ *v.* (·praised, ·prais·ing) 1 estimate the value or quality of 2 set a price on (esp. officially) [ME fr. MFr *aprisier*]

● Usage: *Appraise*, which means 'evaluate,' should not be confused with *apprise*, which means 'inform': *The house was appraised at $2 million. We were apprised of the value.*

ap·pre·cia·ble /əprē'shəbəl/ *adj.* significant; considerable [Fr, rel. to APPRECIATE]

ap·pre·ci·ate /əprē'shēāt', -prish'ē-/ *v.* (·at-

ed, ·at·ing) 1 esteem highly; value **2** be grateful for **3** understand; recognize **4** rise in value —**ap·pre'cia·tive** /-pre'sнətiv, -prisн'ət-/ *adj.*; **ap·pre'ci·a'tor** *n.*; **ap·pre'cia·to'ry** *adj.* [L *pretium* price]

ap·pre·ci·a'tion *n.* **1** favorable or grateful recognition **2** sensitive estimation or judgment **3** rise in value [Fr, rel. to APPRECIATE]

ap·pre·hend /ap'rihend'/ *v.* **1** seize; arrest **2** understand; perceive [L *prehendere* grasp]

ap·pre·hen·sion /ap'rihen'sнən/ *n.* **1** uneasiness; dread **2** understanding **3** arrest; capture

ap·pre·hen·sive /ap'rihen'siv/ *adj.* uneasily fearful —**ap'pre·hen'sive·ly** *adv.*; **ap'pre·hen'sive·ness** *n.*

ap·pren·tice /əprent'əs/ *n.* **1** person learning a trade by working in it for an agreed period at low wages **2** novice —*v.* (·ticed, ·tic·ing) **3** engage as an apprentice —**ap·pren'tice·ship'** *n.* [OFr *apprendre* learn, prob. fr. L *apprehendere* seize]

ap·prise /əpriz'/ *v.* (also **ap·prize'**) (·prised or ·prized, ·pris·ing or ·priz·ing) *Formal.* inform [Fr *appris* learned; taught]
● Usage: See note at APPRAISE.

ap·proach /əprōcн'/ *v.* **1** come near or nearer (to) in space or time **2** tentatively propose to **3** be similar or approximate to **4** set about (a task, etc.) —*n.* **5** act or means of approaching **6** approximation [L *prope* near]

ap·proach·a·ble /əprō'cнəbəl/ *adj.* **1** friendly; easy to talk to **2** able to be approached

ap·pro·ba·tion /ap'rəbā'sнən/ *n.* approval; consent [L *approbare* approve]

ap·pro·pri·ate *adj.* /əprō'prēət/ **1** suitable; proper —*v.* /əprō'prēāt'/ (·at·ed, ·at·ing) **2** take, esp. without authority **3** devote (money, etc.) to special purposes —**ap·pro'pri·ate·ly** *adv.*; **ap·pro'pri·a'tion** *n.* [L *proprius* own]

ap·prov·al /əprōō'vəl/ *n.* **1** approving consent; favorable opinion **3 on approval** (of goods supplied) returnable if not satisfactory

ap·prove /əprōōv'/ *v.* (·proved, ·prov·ing) **1** confirm; sanction **2** regard with favor [L *approbare*]

approx. *abbr.* approximate(ly)

ap·prox·i·mate *adj.* /əprак'səmət/ **1** fairly correct; close to the actual —*v.* /-səmāt'/ (·mat·ed, ·mat·ing) **2** bring or come near (esp. in quality, number, etc.) —**ap·prox'i·mate'ly** *adv.*; **ap·prox'i·ma'tion** *n.* [L *proximus* nearest]

ap·pur·te·nance /əpərt'n-əns/ *n.* (usu. *pl.*) belonging; accessory [L *pertinere* belong to]

APR *abbr.* annual or annualized percentage rate (esp. of interest on loans or credit)

Apr. *abbr.* April

a·près-ski /äp'rā' skē'/ *French. n.* **1** social activities following a day's skiing —*adj.* **2** (of clothes, drinks, etc.) suitable for these

a·pri·cot /ap'rikät', ā'pri-/ *n.* **1a** small, juicy, soft, orange-yellow peachlike fruit **b** tree bearing it **2** its color —*adj.* **3** orange-yellow [Port and Sp fr. Ar, ult. fr. L *praecox* early-ripening]

A·pril /ā'prəl/ *n.* fourth month of the year [L]

A'pril Fool's' Day' *n.* 1st of April, when unsuspecting people are tricked —**A'pril Fool'** *n.*

a pri·o·ri /ä' prē·ôr'ē, ā'-/ *adj.* **1** (of reasoning) from causes to effects; deductive **2** (of concepts, etc.) logically independent of experience **3** assumed without investigation —*adv.* **4** deductively **5** as far as one knows [L: from what is before]

a·pron /ā'prən/ *n.* **1** garment for covering and protecting the front of the clothes **2** *Theat.* part of a stage in front of the curtain **3** area on an airfield for maneuvering or loading [orig. *napron,* fr. MFr *nape* tablecloth]

ap·ro·pos /ap'rəpō'/ *adj.* **1** appropriate **2** *Colloq.* in respect of —*adv.* **3** appropriately [Fr *à propos* to the purpose]

apse /aps'/ *n.* large arched or domed recess at the end of a church [L fr. Gk *hapsis* arch; vault]

apt /apt/ *adj.* **1** appropriate; suitable **2** tending; likely **3** clever; quick to learn [L *aptus* fitted]

apt. *abbr.* apartment

ap·ti·tude /ap'tət(y)ōōd'/ *n.* **1** natural talent **2** ability or fitness [MFr, rel. to APT]

A·pu·lei·us /ap'yəlē'əs/ *fl.* 150; Roman writer

aq·ua /ак'wə, äk'-/ *n.* **1** water **2** the color aquamarine

Aq'ua-Lung' *n. Tdmk.* portable breathing apparatus for divers [L *aqua* water]

aq'ua·ma·rine' *n.* **1** bluish-green beryl **2** its color —*adj.* **3** bluish-green [L *aqua marina* sea water]

aq·ua·naut /ак'wənôt'/ *n.* person trained to work under water [L *aqua* water + *-naut*]

aq'ua·plane' *n.* **1** board for riding on water, pulled by a speedboat —*v.* (·planed, ·plan·ing) **2** ride on this **3** (of a vehicle) glide uncontrollably on a wet surface [L *aqua* water + PLANE¹]

a·quar·i·um /əkwer'ēəm, -kwar'-/ *n.* (*pl.* ·ums or ·i·a /-ēə/) **1** tank of water for keeping and showing fish, etc. **2** building for exhibiting live fish, etc. [L *aquarius* of water]

A·quar·i·us /əkwer'ēəs, -kwar'-/ *n.* **1** constellation and eleventh sign of the zodiac (the Water-carrier) **2** person born under this sign

a·quat·ic /əkwat'ik, əkwät'-/ *adj.* **1** growing or living in water **2** (of a sport) played in or on water [L *aqua* water]

aq·ua·vit /ак'wəvēt'/ *n.* (also **ak'va·vit'**) vodkalike Scandinavian liquor flavored with caraway

aq·ua vi·tae /ä'kwə vī'tē, vē'tē/ *n.* strong alcoholic spirit [L: water of life]

aq·ue·duct /ак'wədəkt'/ *n.* water pipe, esp. on a bridge on columns across a valley [L *aquae ductus* conduit]

a·que·ous /ā'kwēəs, ак'wē-/ *adj.* of or like water

a'que·ous hu'mor *n.* clear fluid in the eye between the lens and the cornea

aq·ui·cul·ture /ак'wəkəl'cнər/ *n.* HYDRO-PONICS [L *aqua* water + (*agri*)*culture*]

aq·ui·fer /ак'wəfər'/ *n.* water-bearing underground formation [L *aqua* water + *ferre* carry]

aq·ui·line /ак'wəlīn'/ *adj.* **1** of or like an eagle **2** (of a nose) curved [L *aquila* eagle]

A·qui·nas /əkwī'nəs/, **St. Thomas** 1225–74; Christian theologian

Ar *symb.* argon

AR *abbr.* **1** accounts receivable **2** postal abbr. for Arkansas

Ar·ab /ar'əb/ *n.* **1** member of a Semitic people originating in Arabia, now widespread throughout the Middle East **2** horse of a breed orig. native to Arabia

ar·a·besque /ar'əbesk'/ *n.* **1** *Ballet.* posture with one leg extended horizontally backwards and arms outstretched **2** design of intertwined leaves, scrolls, etc. [Fr fr. It *arabesco* Arabian]

A·ra'bi·an   Pen·in'su·la /ərā'bēən/ *n.* (also called **A·ra'bi·a**) large, mainly arid peninsula in SW Asia between the Red Sea and the Persian Gulf

ARABESQUE 2

A·ra'bi·an Sea' *n.* portion of the Indian Ocean between the Arabian Peninsula and India

Ar·a·bic /ar'əbik/ *n.* **1** Semitic language of the Arabs —*adj.* **2** of the Arabs (esp. their language or literature)

ar'a·bic nu'mer·al *n.* any of the numerals 0–9

ar·a·ble /ar'əbəl/ *adj.* (of land) suitable for crop production [L *arāre* plow]

a·rach·nid /ərak'nid/ *n.* arthropod of a class comprising spiders, scorpions, etc. [Gk *arachnē* spider]

Ar·a·fat /ar'əfat'/, **Yasser** 1929– ; Palestinian political leader; Nobel prize 1994

A·rak /ərāk'/ *n.* city in Iran. Pop. 265,349

Ar·al Sea /ar'əl/ *n.* inland sea in SW Asia

Ar·a·ma·ic /ar'əmā'ik/ *n.* **1** branch of the Semitic family of languages, esp. the language of Syria, used as a lingua franca in the Near East —*adj.* **2** of or in Aramaic [Gk *Aramaios* of Aram (Heb name of Syria)]

Ar·a·rat, Mt. /ar'ərat'/ *n.* mountain in E Turkey; traditionally considered the landing site of Noah's Ark

Ar·be·la /ärbē'lə/ (also **Ar·bil** /ər'bil/) *n.* see ERBIL

ar·bi·ter /är'bətər/ *n.* arbitrator; judge [L: witness]

ar·bi·trar·y /är'bitrer'ē/ *adj.* **1** random **2** capricious **3** despotic —**ar'bi·trar'i·ly** *adv.*; **ar'bi·trar'i·ness** *n.*

ar·bi·trate /är'bətrāt'/ *v.* (**·trat·ed, ·trat·ing**) decide by arbitration

ar'bi·tra'tion *n.* settlement of a dispute by an impartial third party

ar'bi·tra'tor *n.* person appointed to arbitrate

ar·bor /är'bər/ *n.* shady garden alcove enclosed by trees, etc. [OFr fr. L *herba*]

ar·bo·re·al /ärbôr'ēəl/ *adj.* of or living in trees [L *arbor* tree]

ar·bo·re·tum /är'bərēt'əm/ *n.* (*pl.* **·tums** or **·ta** /-tə/) place cultivating and displaying rare trees

ar'bor vi'tae /vīt'ē/ *n.* any of various evergreen conifers [L: tree of life]

ar·bu·tus /ärbyoot'əs/ *n.* **1** tree or shrub with clusters of flowers and strawberrylike berries **2** plant with fragrant white or pink flowers (**trail'ing ar·bu'tus**) [L]

arc /ärk/ *n.* **1** part of the circumference of a circle or other curve **2** luminous discharge between two electrodes —*v.* (**arced** or

arcked, arc·ing or **arck·ing**) **3** form an arc; move in a curve [L *arcus* bow]

ar·cade /ärkād'/ *n.* **1** covered walk, esp. lined with shops **2** series of arches supporting or set along a wall [Fr fr. It, rel. to ARC]

ar·cane /ärkān'/ *adj.* mysterious; secret [L *arcanus* hidden]

arch¹ /ärCH/ *n.* **1** curved structure as an opening, as a support for a bridge, floor, etc. **2** any arch-shaped curve —*v.* **3** span like an arch **4** form an arch [L *arcus* arc]

arch² *adj.* **1** principal **2** mischievous —**arch'ly** *adv.*; **arch'ness** *n.* [Gk *arkhos* chief]

arch- *comb. form* chief; principal (**archbishop, archenemy**) [fr. ARCH²]

-arch *comb. form* used as a suffix (*patriarch*) [fr. ARCH²]

ar·chae·ol·o·gy /är'kē·äl'əjē/ *n.* (also **ar'che·ol'o·gy**) study of ancient cultures, esp. by the excavation and analysis of physical remains —**ar'chae·o·log'i·cal** *adj.*; **ar'chae·o·log'i·cal·ly** *adv.*; **ar'chae·ol·o·gist** *n.* [Gk *archaiologia* ancient history]

ar·cha·ic /ärkā'ik/ *adj.* **1** old **2** (of a word, etc.) no longer in ordinary use **3** of an early period of culture —**ar·cha'i·cal·ly** *adv.* [Gk *archaios* ancient]

ar·cha·ism /är'kē·iz'əm, -kā-/ *n.* **1** use of the archaic, esp. in language or art **2** archaic word or expression —**ar'cha·ist** *n.*; **ar'cha·is'tic** *adj.*

arch·an·gel /är'kān'jəl/ *n.* angel of the highest rank

Arch·an'gel *n.* see ARKHANGELSK

arch·bish·op /ärch'bish'əp/ *n.* bishop of the highest rank —**arch'bish'op·ric** /-rik'/ *n.*

arch·dea·con /ärchdē'kən/ *n.* church dignitary next below a bishop —**arch'dea'con·ry** *n.* (*pl.* **·ries**)

arch·di·o·cese /ärchdī'əsis, -sēz'/ *n.* diocese of an archbishop —**arch'di·oc'e·san** /-äs'əsən/ *adj.*

arch·duke /ärch'd(y)ook'/ *n. Hist.* chief duke (esp. formerly as the title of a son of the Emperor of Austria) —**arch'duch'ess** *n. fem.*; **arch'duch'y** /-dəCH'ē/ *n.* (*pl.* **·ies**) [MFr *archeduc*]

arch·en·e·my /ärCH' en'əmē/ *n.* (*pl.* **·mies**) **1** chief enemy **2** the Devil

ar·che·ol·o·gy /är'kē·äl'əjē/ *n.* var. of ARCHAEOLOGY

arch·er /är'CHər/ *n.* **1** person who shoots with a bow and arrows **2** (**the Archer**) zodiacal sign or constellation Sagittarius [L *arcus* bow]

ar'cher·y *n.* shooting with a bow and arrows, esp. as a sport

ar·che·type /är'kitīp'/ *n.* original model; prototype —**ar'che·typ'al, ar'che·typ'i·cal** *adj.* [Gk *typos* stamp; mold]

ar·chi·pel·a·go /är'kəpel'əgō', är'CHə-/ *n.* (*pl.* **·gos**) **1** group of islands **2** sea with many islands [Gk *archi-* chief + *pelagos* sea]

ar·chi·tect /är'kitekt'/ *n.* **1** designer of buildings, etc., supervising their construction **2** person who plans a specified thing [Gk *archi-* chief + *tektōn* builder]

ar·chi·tec·ton·ics /är'kitekton'iks/ *n. pl.* (used as *sing.*) **1** science of architecture **2** systematized structure —**ar'chi·tec·ton'ic** *adj.*

ar·chi·tec·ture /är'kitek'CHər/ *n.* **1** design

and construction of buildings **2** style of a building **3** buildings collectively **—ar'chi·tec'tur·al** *adj.*; **ar'chi·tec'tur·al·ly** *adv.*

ar·chi·trave /är'kitrāv/ *n.* (in classical architecture) main beam resting across the tops of columns [It *archi-* ARCH- + L *trabs* beam]

ar·chive /är'kīv/ *n.* (usu. *pl.*) **1** collection of documents or records **2** place for these **—v.** (**·chived, ·chiv·ing**) **3** place or store in an archive **4** *Comp.* transfer (data) to a less frequently used file **—ar'chi·vist** /är'kəvist, är'kī-/ *n.* [Gk *arkheia* public records]

arch'way' *n.* arched entrance or passage

-archy *comb. form* ruling (*monarchy*)

Arc·tic /ärk'tik, ärt'ik/ *adj.* **1** of the north polar regions **2** (**a-**) *Colloq.* very cold **—n.** **3** Arctic regions [Gk *arktos* Great Bear]

Arc'tic Cir'cle *n.* parallel of latitude 66° 32' N, delimiting the Arctic region

Arc'tic O'cean *n.* ocean N of N America, Europe, and Asia. Area: 5,500,000 sq. mi.

Ar·da·bil /ärd'äbēl'/ *n.* (also **Ar'de·bil'**) city in Iran. Pop. 282,000

ar·dent /ärd'nt/ *adj.* **1** eager; fervent; passionate **2** burning **—ar'dent·ly** *adv.* [L *ardere* burn]

ar·dor /ärd'ər/ *n.* (also esp. *Brit.* **ar'dour**) zeal; enthusiasm; passion

ar·du·ous /är'jŌŌəs/ *adj.* hard to accomplish; laborious; strenuous **—ar'du·ous·ly** *adv.*; **ar'du·ous·ness** *n.* [L: steep]

are /är/ *v. pl. & 2nd sing. present of* BE

a·re·a /är'ēə, er'ēə/ *n.* **1** extent or measure in square units of a surface **2** region **3** space for a specific purpose **4** scope or range [L: vacant space]

a·re·na /ərē'nə/ *n.* **1** central part of an amphitheater, etc. **2** scene of conflict; sphere of action [L: sand]

aren't /ärnt/ *v. contr.* **1** are not **2** (in *interrog.*) *Colloq.* am not (*Aren't I coming too?*)

A·re·qui·pa /är'əkē'pə/ *n.* city in Peru. Pop. 621,700

Ar·es /är'ēz/ *n. Gk. Myth.* god of war, identified with Roman Mars

Ar·gen·ti·na /är'jəntē'nə/ *n.* republic in SE S America. Capital: Buenos Aires. Pop. 33,070,000 **—Ar·gen·tine** /är'jəntēn, -tīn'/ *n. & adj.*; **Ar·gen·tin·e·an** /är'jəntin'ēən/ *n. & adj.*

ar·gon /är'gän/ *n.* inert gaseous element; *symb.* Ar [Gk *argos* idle]

ar·go·sy /är'gəsē/ *n.* (*pl.* **·sies**) *Poet.* large merchant ship [It *Ragusea nave* ship of Ragusa]

ar·got /är'gət, -gō/ *n.* jargon of a group or class [Fr]

ar·gue /är'gyŌŌ/ *v.* (**·gued, ·gu·ing**) **1** exchange views forcefully; quarrel **2** maintain by reasoning; indicate **3** persuade **—ar'gu·a·ble** *adj.*; **ar'gu·a·bly** *adv.* [L *arguere* make clear; prove]

ar'gu·ment *n.* **1** (esp. quarrelsome) exchange of views; dispute **2** reason given; reasoning process

ar'gu·men·ta'tion *n.* methodical reasoning; debate

ar·gu·men·ta·tive /är'gyəment'ətiv/ *adj.* given to arguing

Ár·hus /ôr'hŌŌz'/ *n.* city in E Jutland, in Denmark. Pop. 200,200

a·ri·a /är'ēə/ *n.* solo song in an opera, etc. [It]

ar·id /ar'id/ *adj.* **1** dry; parched **2** uninteresting **—a·rid·i·ty** /əridətē/ *n.* [L *arere* be dry]

A·ries /ar'ēz/ *n.* **1** constellation and first sign of the zodiac (the Ram) **2** person born under this sign [L: ram]

a·right /ərīt'/ *adv.* rightly

A·ri·os·to /är'ē-äs'tō, -ô'stō/, **Ludovico** 1474–1533; Italian poet

a·rise /ərīz'/ *v.* (**a·rose, a·ris·en** /əriz'ən/, **a·ris·ing**) **1** originate **2** result **3** emerge **4** rise, esp. from the dead or from kneeling [OE]

Ar·is·ti·des /ar'əstīd'ēz/ (called **"the Just"**) fl. 5th cent. B.C.; Athenian statesman and general

ar·is·toc·ra·cy /ar'əstäk'rəsē/ *n.* (*pl.* **·cies**) **1** ruling class; nobility **2a** government by an elite **b** state so governed [Gk *aristokratia* rule by the best]

ar·is·to·crat /əris'təkrat', ar'əs-/ *n.* member of the aristocracy **—ar·is'to·crat'ic** *adj.*; **a·ris'to·crat'i·cal·ly** *adv.*

Ar·is·toph·a·nes /ar'əstäf'ənēz/ *c.* 450 – *c.* 385 B.C.; Greek comic dramatist

Ar·is·tot·le /ar'əstät'l, ar'əstät'l/ 384–322 B.C.; Greek philosopher, pupil of Plato

a·rith·me·tic *n.* /əriТН'mə·tik/ **1** science of numbers **2** use of numbers; computation **—***adj.* /ar'iТНmet'ik/ **3** (also **ar'ith·met'i·cal**) of arithmetic [Gk *arithmos* number]

ar'ith·met'ic mean' *n.* AVERAGE, 2

ar'ith·met'ic pro·gres'sion *n.* sequence of numbers with constant intervals (e.g., 9, 7, 5, 3, etc.)

Ariz. *abbr. for* Arizona

Ar·i·zo·na /ar'əzō'nə/ *n.* SW state of the US. Capital: Phoenix. Pop. 3,665,118. Abbr. **Ariz.**; **AZ** **—Ar·i·zo'nan, Ar·i·zo'ni·an** *n. & adj.*

ark /ärk/ *n.* ship in which Noah escaped the Flood with his family and animals [OE fr. L *arca* chest]

Ark. *abbr. for* Arkansas

Ar·kan·sas /är'kənsô'/ *n.* S state of the US. Capital: Little Rock. Pop. 2,350,725. Abbr. **AR**; **Ark.** **—Ar·kan·san** /ärkan'sən/ *n. & adj.*

Ar·khan·gelsk /är'kaNGelsk'/ *n.* (also **Arch'-an'gel**) city in Russia. Pop. 428,200

Ark' of the Cov'e·nant *n.* chest or cupboard containing the tables of Jewish Law

Ar·ling·ton /är'liNGtən/ *n.* **1** city in Texas. Pop. 261,721 **2** Va. suburb of Washington, D.C. Pop. 170,936

arm¹ /ärm/ *n.* **1** upper limb of the human body from shoulder to hand **2** forelimb or tentacle of an animal **3a** sleeve of a garment **b** arm support of a chair, etc. **4** extension **5** at arm's length at a distance **6** with open arms cordially **—arm'ful** *n.* [OE]

arm² /ärm/ *n.* **1** (usu. *pl.*) weapon **2** branch of the military **—v.** **3** supply or equip with weapons **4** make (a bomb, etc.) ready **5** take up arms go to war **6** under arms equipped for war **7** up in arms **a** ready to fight **b** angry; indignant [L *arma* weapons]

ar·ma·da /ärmä'də/ *n.* fleet of warships, esp. (**Spanish Armada**) sent by Spain against England in 1588 [Sp fr. L]

ar·ma·dil·lo /är'mədil'ō/ *n.* (*pl.* **·los**) tropical American mammal with a covering of bony plates [Sp dim. *armado* armed]

Ar·ma·ged·don /är′məgĕd′n/ *n.* **1** in the Bible, site of final battle between the forces of good and evil (Rev. 16:16) **2** any huge battle or struggle

ar·ma·ment /är′məmənt/ *n.* **1** (often *pl.*) military equipment **2** equipping for war **3** force equipped [L, rel. to ARM²]

ar·ma·ture /är′məCHər, -CHŏŏr/ *n.* **1** rotating part of a dynamo or electric motor **2** iron bar placed across the poles of a horseshoe magnet to preserve its power **3** metal framework on which a clay, etc., sculpture is molded [L *armatura* armor]

arm′band′ *n.* band worn around the upper arm to hold up a shirtsleeve, as identification, etc.

arm′chair′ *n.* **1** chair with arm supports **2** theoretical rather than active

Ar·me·ni·a /ärmē′nēə/ *n.* country in W Asia; formerly part of the USSR. Capital: Yerevan. Pop. 3,426,000 —**Ar·me′ni·an** *n. & adj.*

arm′hole′ *n.* each of two holes for arms in a garment

ar·mi·stice /är′məstəs/ *n.* truce, esp. permanent [L *arma* arms + *sistere* stop]

Ar′mi·stice Day *n.* former name for VETERANS DAY

arm′let *n.* ornamental band worn around the arm

ar·mor /är′mər/ *n.* **1** protective usu. metal covering formerly worn in fighting **2** (in full **ar′mor-plate′**) protective metal covering for an armed vehicle, ship, etc. **3** armed vehicles collectively —*v.* **4** protect with armor —**ar′mored** *adj.* [L *armatura*]

ar·mo·ri·al /ärmôr′ēəl/ *adj.* of heraldry or coats of arms [rel. to ARMOR]

ar·mor·y /är′mərē/ *n.* (*pl.* **·mor·ies**) arsenal

arm′pit′ *n.* hollow under the arm at the shoulder

arm′rest′ *n.* support for the arm

Arm·strong /ärm′strông/ *n.* **1 (Daniel) Louis ("Satchmo")** 1900–71; US jazz musician **2 Neil** 1930– ; US astronaut; first man to walk on the moon

ar·my /är′mē/ *n.* (*pl.* **·mies**) **1** organized armed land force **2** very large number [MFr fr. L *arma* weapons]

Arn·hem /ärn′hem′, är′nəm/ *n.* city in the Netherlands on the Rhine River. Pop. 131,703

Ar·nold /är′nəld/ *n.* **1 Benedict** 1741–1801; American Revolutionary War general who became a traitor **2 Matthew** 1822–88; English poet and essayist

a·ro·ma /ərō′mə/ *n.* smell (esp. a pleasing one), often of food [Gk: spice]

ar·o·mat·ic /ar′əmat′ik/ *adj.* **1** fragrant; spicy —*n.* **2** aromatic substance [L fr. Gk, rel. to AROMA]

a·rose /ərōz′/ *v.* past of ARISE

a·round /əround′/ *adv.* **1** on every side; about **2** *Colloq.* **a** in existence; available **b** near at hand **3** here and there **4** in circumference —*prep.* **5** on or along the circuit of **6** on every side of **7** here and there; in or near **8** on the other side of **9** at a time near to

a·rouse /ərouz′/ *v.* (·**roused**, ·**rous·ing**) **1** induce (esp. an emotion) **2** awake from sleep **3** stir into activity **4** stimulate sexually —**a·rous′al** *n.* [*a-* intensive prefix + ROUSE]

ar·peg·gio /ärpej′(ē)ō/ *n.* (*pl.* ·**gios**) *Mus.* notes of a chord played in succession [It *arpa* harp]

ar·raign /ərān′/ *v.* indict; accuse —**ar·raign′ment** *n.* [OFr fr. VL *rationare* reason]

ar·range /ərānj′/ *v.* (·**ranged**, ·**rang·ing**) **1** put into order; classify **2** plan or provide for **3** agree about **4** *Mus.* adapt (a composition) for a particular manner of performance [MFr, rel. to RANGE]

ar·range′ment *n.* **1** arranging or being arranged **2** manner of this **3** something arranged; agreement **4** (usu. *pl.*) plans; measures **5** *Mus.* composition adapted for performance in a particular way

ar·rant /ar′ənt/ *adj. Lit.* downright; utter [var. of ERRANT]

ar·ras /ar′əs/ *n. Hist.* rich tapestry or wall hanging [*Arras*, France]

ar·ray /ərā′/ *n.* **1** imposing or well-ordered series or display **2** ordered arrangement, esp. of troops —*v.* **3** deck; adorn **4** set in order; marshal (forces) [OFr]

ar·rears /ərērz′/ *n. pl.* **1** amount (esp. of work, rent, etc.) still outstanding or uncompleted **2 in arrears** behind, esp. in payment [MFr, prob. ult. fr. L *ad retro* backward]

ar·rest /ərest′/ *v.* **1** lawfully seize (a suspect, etc.) **2** stop or check the progress of **3** attract (a person's attention) —*n.* **4** arresting or being arrested **5** stoppage **6 under arrest** arrested; in custody —**ar·rest′ing** *adj.* [MFr, prob. fr. L *restare* remain]

ar·riv·al /ərī′vəl/ *n.* **1** arriving; appearance on the scene **2** person or thing that has arrived

ar·rive /ərīv′/ *v.* (·**rived**, ·**riv·ing**) **1** reach a destination **2** (foll. by *at*) reach (a conclusion, etc.) **3** *Colloq.* become successful **4** *Colloq.* (of a child) be born **5** (of a time) come [VL *arripare* come to land, fr. L *ripa* shore]

ar·ri·ve·der·ci /ärē′vəder′CHē/ *interj.* goodbye [It]

ar·ri·viste /ar′ivēst′/ *n.* ambitious or ruthless person [Fr, rel. to ARRIVE]

ar·ro·gant /ar′əgənt/ *adj.* aggressively assertive or presumptuous —**ar′ro·gance** *n.*; **ar′ro·gant·ly** *adv.* [rel. to ARROGATE]

ar·ro·gate /ar′əgāt′/ *v.* (·**gat·ed**, ·**gat·ing**) claim (power, etc.) without right —**ar′ro·ga′tion** *n.* [L *rogare* ask]

ar·row /ar′ō/ *n.* **1** pointed slender missile shot from a bow **2** representation of this, esp. indicating direction [OE]

ar′row·head′ *n.* pointed tip of an arrow

ar′row·root′ *n.* **1** nutritious starch **2** plant yielding this

ar·se·nal /är′sən-l, är′snəl/ *n.* **1** store, esp. of weapons **2** place for the storage and manufacture of weapons and ammunition [Ar: workshop]

ar·se·nic *n.* /är′s(ə)nik/ **1** *Chem.* brittle semimetallic element; *symb.* As **2** nonscientific name for arsenic trioxide, a poisonous white powder used in weed-killers, insecticides, etc. —*adj.* /ärsen′ik/ **3** of or containing arsenic —**ar·sen′i·cal** *adj. & n.* [Gk, perh. ult. fr. Pers *zar* gold]

ar·son /är′sən/ *n.* crime of deliberately setting fire to property —**ar′son·ist** *n.* [L *ardere ars-* burn]

art[1] /ärt/ *n.* **1a** human creative skill or its application **b** work showing this 2 (*pl.*; prec. by *the*) branches of creative activity concerned with the production of imaginative designs, sounds, or ideas, e.g., painting, music, writing, etc. 3 creative activity resulting in visual representation 4 human skill as opposed to nature 5 skill; knack 6 (*pl.*; usu. prec. by *the*) LIBERAL ARTS [L *ars* art-]

art[2] *v. Archaic. 2nd pres. indic.* of BE (*thou art*)

Ar·ta·xerx·es /ärt′əzərk′sēz/ name of three Persian kings: **1 Artaxerxes I** reigned 464-424 B.C.; son of Xerxes I **2 Artaxerxes II** reigned 404-358 B.C. **3 Artaxerxes III** reigned 358-338 B.C.

art′ de′co /ärt dek′ō, är(t)′ dākō′/ *n.* decorative art style of 1920-40, with geometric motifs, strong colors, and modern materials like plastic, etc.

Ar·te·mis /är′təmis/ *n. Gk. Myth.* goddess of the moon and the hunt, identified with the Roman Diana

ar·te·ri·al /ärtēr′ēəl/ *adj.* **1** of or like an artery 2 (esp. of a road) main; important [MFr, rel. to ARTERY]

ar·te·rio·scle·ro·sis /ärtēr′ē-ōsklərō′sis/ *n.* loss of elasticity and thickening of artery walls, esp. in old age [fr. ARTERY + SCLEROSIS]

ar·te·ry /är′tərē/ *n.* (*pl.* ·**ries**) 1 any of the blood vessels carrying blood from the heart 2 main road or railway line [L fr. Gk. prob. fr. *airein* lift; raise]

ar·te′sian well′ /ärtē′ZHən/ *n.* well in which water rises to the surface by natural pressure [*Artois*, former Fr province]

art·ful /ärt′fəl/ *adj.* crafty; deceitful —**art′ful·ly** *adv.*; **art′ful·ness** *n.*

ar·thri·tis /ärTHrīt′is/ *n.* inflammation of a joint or joints —**ar·thrit′ic** /-THrit′ik/ *adj.* & *n.* [Gk *arthron* joint]

ar·thro·pod /är′THrəpäd/ *n.* invertebrate with a segmented body and jointed limbs [Gk *arthron* joint + *pous* pod- foot]

Ar·thur /är′THər/ legendary king of Britain, 5th or 6th cent. —**Ar·thu′ri·an** *adj.*

Ar·thur /är′THər/, **Chester Alan** 1830-86; 21st US president (1881-85)

ar·ti·choke /ärt′əCHŌk/ *n.* 1 plant allied to the thistle 2 (**globe′ ar′ti·choke**) its partly edible flower head [It fr. Ar]

ar·ti·cle /ärt′ikəl/ *n.* 1 item or thing 2 nonfictional journalistic essay 3 clause or item in an agreement or contract 4 *Gram.* definite or indefinite article [MedL *articulus* fr. L *artus* joint]

ar·tic·u·lar /ärtik′yələr/ *adj.* of a joint or joints [L, rel. to ARTICLE]

ar·tic·u·late *adj.* /ärtik′yələt/ **1** fluent and clear in speech 2 (of sound or speech) having clearly distinguishable parts 3 having joints —*v.* /-yəlāt′/ (·lat·ed, ·lat·ing) 4 pronounce distinctly 5 speak or express clearly 6 be connected by joints —**ar·tic′u·late·ly** *adv.*; **ar·tic′u·late·ness**, **ar·tic′u·la′tion** *n.*

ar·ti·fact /ärt′əfakt′/ *n.* man-made object, esp. tool [L *arte factum* made with skill]

ar·ti·fice /ärt′əfis/ *n.* 1 trick or clever device

2 cunning 3 skill; ingenuity [L *ars art- art + facere* make]

ar·ti·fi·cer /ärtif′əsər, ärt′əfisər/ *n.* 1 craftsman 2 skilled worker

ar·ti·fi·cial /ärt′əfiSH′əl/ *adj.* 1 not natural; man-made; synthetic 2 imitating nature 3 affected; insincere —**ar′ti·fi·ci·al·i·ty** /-fiSH′ē-al′ətē/ *n.*; **ar′ti·fi′cial·ly** *adv.* [L, rel. to ARTIFICE]

ar′ti·fi′cial in·sem′i·na′tion *n.* injection of semen into the uterus by artificial means

ar′ti·fi′cial in·tel′li·gence *n.* use of computers for tasks normally regarded as needing human intelligence

ar′ti·fi′cial res′pi·ra′tion *n.* manual or mechanical stimulation of breathing

ar·til·ler·y /ärtil′(ə)rē/ *n.* 1 heavy guns used in land warfare 2 branch of the army using these —**ar·til′ler·y·man** (*pl.* ·**men**) *n.* [OFr *artillier* equip]

ar·ti·san /ärt′əzən, -sən/ *n.* skilled manual worker or craftsman [It *artigiano* fr. L *ars art-*]

art·ist /ärt′ist/ *n.* 1 practitioner of any of the arts, esp. painting 2 professional performer, esp. a singer or dancer 3 person using skill or taste —**art′ist·ry** *n.* [MFr *artiste* fr. L *ars art-*]

ar·tis·tic /ärtis′tik/ *adj.* 1 having natural skill in art 2 skillfully or tastefully done 3 of art or artists 4 sensitive; discriminating —**ar·tis′ti·cal·ly** *adv.*

art·less /ärt′ləs/ *adj.* 1 guileless; ingenuous 2 natural 3 clumsy —**art′less·ly** *adv.*; **art′less·ness** *n.*

art nou·veau /är(t) nōōvō′/ *n.* art style of the late 19th cent., with flowing lines

art′work′ *n.* 1 illustrative material in or for printed matter 2 works of art collectively

art′y *adj.* (·i·er, ·i·est) *Colloq.* pretentiously or affectedly artistic

A·ru·ba /ärōō′bä/ *n.* island in the Netherlands Antilles off the NW coast of Venezuela

a·rum /ar′əm, er′əm/ *n.* plant with arrow-shaped leaves [Gk *aron*]

Ar·y·an /ar′ēən, er′ēən/ *n.* 1 hypothetical source of the languages of the Indo-European family; Proto-Indo-European 2 *Improp.* (in Nazi ideology) non-Jewish Caucasian [Skt]

as /az, əz/ *adv.* & *conj.* 1 (*adv.* as antecedent in main sentence; *conj.* in relative clause expressed or implied) to the extent to which . . . is or does, etc. (*as tall as he; as tall as he is; as recently as last week*) —*conj.* 2 (with relative clause expressed or implied) (with antecedent *so*) expressing result or purpose (*came early so as to meet us*) 3 although (*good as it is* although it is good) 4a in the manner in which; as if (*do as you like; rose as one man*) **b** in the capacity or form of (*I speak as your friend; Olivier as Hamlet*) **c** while (*arrived as I was eating*) **d** since; seeing that (*as you are here, we can talk*) **e** for instance (*capital cities, as Albany*) 5 and so (*he is a writer, as is his wife*) —*rel. pron.* (with verb of relative clause expressed or implied) that; who; which (*I had the same trouble as you*) 7 (with a sentence as referent) a fact that (*he lost, as you know*) 8 as for with regard to 9 as if (or *though*) as would be the case if (*acts as if he were in charge*) 10 as is in the same form 11

as it were in a way; to some extent **12 as well** in addition; moreover [OE: ALSO]
● *Usage:* See note at LIKE[1].

As *symb.* arsenic

a.s.a.p. (also **ASAP**) *abbr.* as soon as possible

as·bes·tos /asbes'təs, az-/ *n.* **1** fibrous silicate mineral **2** this as a heat-resistant or insulating material [Gk: unquenchable]

as·cend /əsend'/ *v.* **1** move or slope upwards; rise **2** climb; go up **3** ascend the throne become king or queen [L *scandere* climb]

as·cen·dan·cy *n.* (also **as·cen·den·cy**) dominant power or control

as·cen·dant /əsen'dənt/ *adj.* (also **as·cen·dent**) **1** rising **2** *Astron.* rising toward the zenith **3** predominant **4 in the ascendant** gaining or having power or authority

as·cen·sion /əsen'SHən/ *n.* **1** ascent **2** (*cap.*) ascent of Christ into heaven

as·cent /əsent'/ *n.* **1** ascending, rising, or progressing **2** upward slope or path, etc.

as·cer·tain /as'ərtān'/ *v.* find out for certain —**as'cer·tain'ment** *n.* [MFr, rel. to CERTAIN]

as·cet·ic /əset'ik/ *adj.* **1** severely abstinent; self-denying —*n.* **2** person who forgoes all comforts and luxuries, esp. for religious reasons —**as·cet'i·cism** /-əsiz'əm/ *n.* [Gk *askein* exercise; work]

ASCII /as'kē/ *abbr. Comp.* American Standard Code for Information Interchange

a·scor'bic ac'id /əskôr'bik/ *n.* vitamin C [fr. A-[2] + SCORBUTIC]

ASCOT

as·cot /as'kət, -kät'/ *n.* a necktie with very broad ends hanging from the knot

a·scribe /əskrīb'/ *v.* (·**scribed**, ·**scrib·ing**) **1** attribute **2** regard as belonging, esp. a trait —**a·scrip·tion** /əskrip'SHən/ *n.* [L *scribere* write]

a·sep·sis /āsep'sis/ *n.* **1** absence of harmful microorganisms **2** method of achieving asepsis in surgery —**a·sep'tic** *adj.*

a·sex·u·al /āsek'sHŌŌəl/ *adj.* **1** without sex, sexual organs, or sexuality **2** (of reproduction) not involving the fusion of gametes —**a·sex'u·al·ly** *adv.*

ash[1] /asH/ *n.* **1** powdery residue left after burning **2** (*pl.*) human remains after cremation **3** grayish color [OE]

ash[2] *n.* **1** tree with silver-gray bark **2** its hard, pale wood [OE]

a·shamed /əsHāmd'/ *adj.* **1** embarrassed by shame **2** hesitant; reluctant out of shame [OE]

ash'can' *n.* receptacle for ashes, esp. from a coal fire

Ashe /asH/, **Arthur** 1943–93; US tennis player

ash'en *adj.* like ashes, esp. gray or pale

Ash·ga·bat /asH'kəbat/ *n.* (also **Ashkhabad**) capital of Turkmenistan. Pop. 412,200

ash·lar /asH'lər/ *n.* **1** cut stone used in building; masonry made of these **2** thin slabs of masonry used for facing walls [L *axis* board]

a·shore /əsHôr'/ *adv.* toward or on the shore or land

ash·ram /asH'ram', äsH'räm', asH'rəm/ *n.* place of religious retreat for Hindus [Skt]

ash'tray' *n.* small receptacle for cigarette ash, butts, etc.

Ash' Wednes'day *n.* first day of Lent

ash'y *adj.* (·**i·er**, ·**i·est**) **1** ASHEN **2** covered with ashes

A·sia /ā'zHə/ *n.* largest continent, bounded by Europe and the Arctic, Pacific, and Indian oceans —**A'sian** *n.* & *adj.*

A'sia Mi'nor *n. Hist.* peninsula in W Asia bounded by the Black and Mediterranean seas, roughly equivalent to modern-day Turkey

A·si·at·ic /ā'zHē-at'ik/ *n.* **1** *Offens.* Asian person —*adj.* **2** Asian

a·side /əsīd'/ *adv.* **1** to or on one side; away; apart —*n.* **2** words spoken aside, esp. confidentially to the audience by an actor

As·i·mov /az'əmôf', -môv'/, **Isaac** 1920–92; Russian-born US scientist and writer

as·i·nine /as'ənīn'/ *adj.* like an ass, esp. stupid or stubborn —**as'i·nin'i·ty** /-nin'ətē/ *n.* [L *asinus* ass]

ask /ask/ *v.* **1** call for an answer to or about **2** seek to obtain **3** invite **4** (foll. by *for*) seek to obtain, meet, or be directed to (*ask for help; asking for you; ask for the men's room*) **5 ask after** inquire about (esp. a person) [OE]

a·skance /əskans'/ *adv.* **1** sideways or squinting **2** with suspicion

a·skew /əskyōō'/ *adv.* **1** awry; crookedly —*adj.* **2** oblique; awry

a·slant /əslant'/ *adv.* **1** obliquely or at a slant —*prep.* **2** obliquely across —*adj.* **3** oblique; slanting

a·sleep /əslēp'/ *adj.* & *adv.* **1** in or into a state of sleep **2** inactive; inattentive **3** (of a limb, etc.) numb **4** *Euphem.* dead

As·ma·ra /äsmär'ə/ *n.* (also **Asmera**) capital of Eritrea. Pop. 342,700

asp /asp/ *n.* small venomous snake of N Africa or southern Europe [Gk *aspis*]

as·par·a·gus /əspar'əgəs/ *n.* **1** plant of the lily family **2** edible shoots of this [L fr. Gk]

as·pect /as'pekt'/ *n.* **1** view, feature, etc. **2** appearance **3** view in a particular direction [L *aspicere* look at]

asp·en /as'pən/ *n.* poplar with leaves that tremble in the slightest wind [OE]

as·per·i·ty /əspər'itē/ *n.* (*pl.* ·**ties**) **1** sharpness of temper or tone **2** roughness of surface [L *asper* rough]

as·per·sion /əspər'zHən/ *n.* attack on a person's reputation [L *aspergere* besprinkle]

as·phalt /as'fôlt'/ *n.* **1** mixture of pitch with sand or gravel for surfacing roads, etc. —*v.* **2** surface with asphalt [L fr. Gk]

as·pho·del /as'fədel'/ *n.* plant of the lily family [L fr. Gk]

as·phyx·i·ate /asfik'sē-āt'/ *v.* (·**at·ed**, ·**at·ing**) suffocate —**as·phyx'i·a'tion** *n.* [Gk *a-* not + *sphyzein* pulse; throb]

as·pic /as'pik/ *n.* savory jelly used esp. to contain game, eggs, etc. [Fr: ASP]

as·pi·dis·tra /as'pədis'trə/ *n.* house plant with broad tapering leaves [Gk *aspis* shield]

as·pi·rant /as′pərənt, əspī′rʹrənt/ *adj.* 1 aspiring —*n.* 2 person who aspires

as·pi·rate /as′pərət/ *adj.* 1 pronounced with an exhalation of breath with the sound of *h* —*n.* 2 sound of *h*; consonant pronounced in this way —*v.* /-rāt′/ (·rat·ed, ·rat·ing) 3 pronounce with breath or with initial *h* 4 draw (fluid) by suction

as·pi·ra·tion /as′pərā′sHən/ *n.* 1 ambition or desire 2 drawing breath or *Phonet.* aspirating

as′pi·ra′tor *n.* apparatus for aspirating fluid [L, rel. to ASPIRE]

as·pire /əspīr′/ *v.* (·pired, ·pir·ing) have ambition or a strong desire [L *aspirare* breathe upon]

as·pi·rin /as′p(ə)rin/ *n.* 1 white powder, acetylsalicylic acid, used to reduce pain and fever 2 tablet of this [Ger]

ass /as/ *n.* 1a four-legged long-eared mammal related to the horse b donkey 2 stupid person [OE, prob. fr. L]

As·sad /äsäd′/, **Hafiz al-** 1928– ; president of Syria (1971–)

as·sail /əsāl′/ *v.* attack physically or verbally —**as·sail′ant** *n.* [L *salire* leap]

as·sas·sin /əsas′in/ *n.* killer, esp. of a political or religious leader [Ar: hashish-eater]

as·sas·si·nate /əsas′ənāt′/ *v.* (·nat·ed, ·nating) kill for political or religious motives —**as·sas′si·na′tion** *n.*

as·sault /əsôlt′/ *n.* 1 violent physical or verbal attack 2 *Law.* threat or display of violence against a person —*v.* 3 make an assault on [MedL, rel. to ASSAIL]

as·say /as′ā, asā′/ *n.* 1 testing of a metal or ore to determine its ingredients and quality —*v.* /asā′/ 2 make an assay of (a metal or ore) [MFr, var. of *essai* ESSAY]

as·sem·blage /əsem′blij/ *n.* 1 assembling 2 assembled group 3 /as′imbläzH′/ work of art consisting of a collection of diverse objects

as·sem·ble /əsem′bəl/ *v.* (·bled, ·bling) 1 gather together; collect 2 fit together (components, a whole) —**as·sem′bler** *n.* [L *ad* to + *simul* together]

as·sem·bly /əsem′blē/ *n.* (*pl.* ·blies) 1 assembling 2 assembled group, esp. as a deliberative body 3 whole made from components

as·sem′bly line′ *n.* manufacturing process in which a complex product is assembled by workers who perform separate tasks

as·sent /əsent′, a-/ *v.* 1 express agreement —*n.* 2 consent or approval —**as·sent′er** *n.* [L *sentire* think; feel]

as·sert /əsərt′/ *v.* 1 declare; state clearly 2 enforce a claim to 3 **assert oneself** insist on one's rights [L *asserere -sert-*]

as·ser·tion /əsər′sHən/ *n.* declaration; forthright statement

as·ser′tive *adj.* tending to be forthright; positive —**as·ser′tive·ly** *adv.*; **as·ser′tive·ness** *n.*

as·sess /əses′/ *v.* 1 estimate the size or quality of 2 estimate the value of (property, etc.) for taxation —**as·ses′sor** *n.* [L *assidere -sess-* sit by]

as·sess′ment *n.* 1 assessing 2 amount due as a result of a tax assessment

as·set /as′et/ *n.* 1 useful or valuable person or thing 2 (usu. *pl.*) property and possessions [OFr *asez* fr. L *satis* enough]

as·sev·er·ate /əsev′ərāt′/ *v.* (·at·ed, ·at-

ing) declare solemnly —**as·sev′er·a′tion** *n.* [L *asseverare* affirm; assert]

as·sid·u·ous /əsij′ŏŏəs/ *adj.* 1 persevering; hard-working 2 attending closely —**as·si·du·i·ty** /as′ədyŏŏ′ətē/ *n.*; **as·sid′u·ous·ly** *adv.* [L, rel. to ASSESS]

as·sign /əsīn′/ *v.* 1 allot as a share or responsibility 2 appoint to a position, task, etc. 3 ascribe or attribute to 4 *Law.* transfer formally (a right, property) —*n.* 5 *Law.* assignee —**as·sign′er** or *Law.* **as·sign′or** *n.* [L *assignare* mark out; assign]

as·sig·na·tion /as′ignā′sHən/ *n.* appointment to meet, esp. in secret

as·sign·ee /as′īnē′, asī-/ *n.* *Law.* person to whom a right or property is assigned

as·sign′ment *n.* 1 task or mission 2 assigning or being assigned

as·sim·i·late /əsim′əlāt′/ *v.* (·lat·ed, ·lating) 1 absorb or be absorbed, either physically or mentally 2 make similar; cause to resemble —**as·sim′i·la·ble** *adj.*; **as·sim′i·la′tion** *n.*; **as·sim′i·la′tive** /-lativ/ *adj.*; **as·sim′i·la′tor** *n.*; **as·sim′i·la·to′ry** *adj.* [L *similis* like]

as·sist /əsist′/ *v.* 1 help —*n.* 2 *Colloq.* act of help —**as·sis′tance** *n.* [L *assistere* stand by]

as·sis′tant /əsis′tənt/ *n.* person who helps, esp. as a subordinate

assn. *abbr.* association

assoc. *abbr.* 1 associate 2 association

as·so·ci·ate /v. /əsō′sHē-āt′, -sō′sē-/ (·at·ed, ·at·ing) 1 connect mentally 2 join or combine, esp. for a common purpose 3 meet frequently or deal with —/əsō′sHēət, -sō′sē-/ 4 partner; colleague 5 friend; companion 6 subordinate member of a society, etc. 7 degree awarded by a junior college —*adj.* /əsō′sHēət, -sō′sē-/ 8 joined or allied 9 of lower status —**as·so′ci·a′tive** /-sHē-āt′iv, -sō′sē-, -sō′sHativ/ *adj.* [L *socius* allied]

as·so·ci·a·tion /əsō′sē-ā′sHən, -sHē-/ *n.* 1 group organized for a joint purpose; society 2 associating or being associated 3 companionship 4 mental connection of ideas [MedL, rel. to ASSOCIATE]

as·so·nance /as′ənəns/ *n.* resemblance of sound (often of vowels) between two words or syllables; e.g., *book* and *tour; saw* and *caught* —**as′so·nant** *adj.* [Fr fr. L *assonare* resound]

as·sort /əsôrt′/ *v.* 1 classify or arrange in sorts 2 suit or harmonize with [MFr, rel. to SORT]

as·sort′ed *adj.* 1 of various sorts; mixed 2 classified

as·sort′ment *n.* diverse group or mixture

asst. *abbr.* assistant

as·suage /əswāj′/ *v.* (·suaged, ·suag·ing) 1 calm or soothe 2 appease (an appetite) —**as·suage′ment** *n.* [OFr, ult. fr. L *suavis* sweet]

as·sume /əsŏŏm′/ *v.* (·sumed, ·sum·ing) 1 take to be true 2 simulate (ignorance, etc.) 3 undertake (an office, responsibility, etc.) 4 take or put on (an aspect, attribute, etc.) [L *assumere* take to; receive]

as·sumed′ *adj.* 1 taken on to deceive 2 taken for granted

as·sum′ing *adj.* arrogant; presumptuous

as·sump·tion /əsəm(p)'sHən/ *n.* **1** assuming **2** thing assumed **3** (*cap.*) reception of the Virgin Mary bodily into heaven

as·sur·ance /əsHŏŏr'əns/ *n.* **1** emphatic declaration; guarantee **2** *esp. Brit.* insurance, esp. life insurance **3** certainty **4** self-confidence; assertiveness

as·sure /əsHŏŏr'/ *v.* (·sured, ·sur·ing) **1** convince **2** confirm confidently **3** guarantee **4** *esp. Brit.* insure (esp. a life) [OFr fr. L, rel. to SECURE]

● Usage: See note at INSURE.

as·sured' *adj.* **1** guaranteed **2** confident **3a** beneficiary of insurance **b** insured person —**as·sur·ed·ly** /əsH'ŏŏr'idlē/ *adv.*

A·staire /əstar', əster'/, **Fred** (born **Frederick Austerlitz**) 1899–1987; US dancer, singer, and actor

as·ta·tine /as'tətēn/ *n.* radioactive element; *symb.* **At** [Gk *astatos* unstable]

as·ter /as'tər/ *n.* plant with bright daisylike flowers [Gk: star]

as·ter·isk /as'tərisk/ *n.* **1** symbol (*) used to mark words to indicate omission, symbolize a footnote, etc. —*v.* **2** mark with an asterisk [Gk: little star]

● Usage: Avoid the pronunciation "as-tuhr-riks," which many regard as unacceptable.

a·stern /əstərn'/ *adv.* **1** in or to the rear of a ship or aircraft **2** backwards

as·ter·oid /as'təroid/ *n.* any of the minor planets orbiting the sun, mainly between the orbits of Mars and Jupiter [Gk, rel. to ASTER]

asth·ma /az'mə/ *n.* respiratory condition marked by wheezing —**asth·mat'ic** /-matik/ *n. & adj.* [Gk]

a·stig·ma·tism /əstig'mətiz'əm/ *n.* eye or lens defect resulting in distorted images —**as·tig·mat·ic** /as'tigmat'ik/ *adj.* [fr. A-² + STIGMA]

a·stir /əstər'/ *adj. & adv.* **1** in motion **2** out of bed

as·ton·ish /əstän'isH/ *v.* surprise greatly; amaze —**as·ton'ish·ing** *adj.*; **as·ton'ish·ing·ly** *adv.*; **as·ton'ish·ment** *n.* [ME, prob. fr. L *ex*- forth + *tonare* thunder]

As·tor /as'tər/, **John Jacob** 1763–1848; German-born US fur trader and capitalist

as·tound /əstound'/ *v.* astonish greatly —**as·tound'ing** *adj.*; **as·tound'ing·ly** *adv.*

a·strad·dle /əstrad'l/ *adv.* astride

as·tra·khan /as'trəkən', -kən/ *n.* dark curly fleece of young Astrakhan lambs [ASTRAKHAN in Russia]

As·tra·khan /as'trəkən/ *n.* city in Russia at the mouth of the Volga River. Pop. 511,900

as·tral /as'trəl/ *adj.* of the stars; starry [L *astrum* star]

a·stray /əstrā'/ *adv. & adj.* **1** off the right path or road **2** in or into error [OFr *estraie*]

a·stride /əstrīd'/ *adv. & adj.* **1** in a position with a leg on each side —*prep.* **2** astride of **3** extending across

as·trin·gent /əstrin'jənt/ *adj.* **1** contracting body tissues **2** severe; austere —*n.* **3** astringent substance —**as·trin'gen·cy** *n.* [L *astringere* draw tight]

astro- *comb. form* star [Gk *astron*]

as·tro·labe /as'trəlāb'/ *n.* instrument for-

merly used to measure the altitude of stars, etc. [Gk: star-taking]

as·trol·o·gy /əsträl'ŏjē/ *n.* study of supposed planetary, astral, and solar influence on human affairs —**as·trol'o·ger** *n.*; **as·tro·log·i·cal** /as'trəläj'ikəl/ *adj.*; **as·trol'o·gist** *n.* [Gk ASTRO- star + -LOGY]

as·tro·naut /as'trənôt', -nät'/ *n.* crew member of a spacecraft —**as·tro·nau'ti·cal** *adj.*; **as·tro·nau'tics** *n.* [Gk ASTRO- star + *nautēs* sailor]

as·tro·nom·i·cal /as'trənäm'ikəl/ *adj.* (also **as·tro·nom'ic**) **1** of astronomy **2** vast; gigantic —**as·tro·nom'i·cal·ly** *adv.*

as·tro·nom·i·cal u·nit *n.* unit of distance equal to the mean distance between the earth and the sun: approx. 93,000,000 miles

as·tron·o·my /əsträn'əmē/ *n.* the scientific study of celestial bodies —**as·tron'o·mer** *n.* [Gk ASTRO- star + *nomia* law]

as·tro·phys·ics /as'trōfiz'iks/ *n. pl.* (treated as *sing.*) the study of the physics and physical properties of celestial bodies —**as·tro·phys'i·cal** *adj.*; **as·tro·phys'i·cist** /-fiz'əsist/ *n.* [Gk *astro-* star]

As·tu·ri·as /äst(y)ŏŏr'ēəs/, **Miguel Angel** 1899–1974; Guatemalan novelist and poet

as·tute /əst(y)ŏŏt'/ *adj.* shrewd —**as·tute'ly** *adv.*; **as·tute'ness** *n.* [L *astus* craft; cunning]

A·sun·ción /äsŏŏn'sē-ōn'/ *n.* capital of Paraguay. Pop. 607,700

a·sun·der /əsən'dər/ *adv.* apart

As·wan /aswän'/ *n.* city in Egypt; site of the Aswan Dam on the Nile River. Pop. 191,500

a·sy·lum /əsī'ləm/ *n.* **1** sanctuary; protection, esp. for fugitives **2** *Hist.* institution for the mentally ill or destitute [Gk *a-* without + *sylon* right of seizure]

a·sym·me·try /āsim'ətrē/ *n.* lack of symmetry —**a·sym·met·ric** /ā'səme'trik/ *adj.*; **a'sym·met'ri·cal** *adj.*; **a'sym·met'ri·cal·ly** *adv.* [Gk]

A·syut /äsyŏŏt'/ *n.* city in Egypt. Pop. 273,200

at /at, ət/ *prep.* **1** expressing position (*at the corner*) **2** expressing a time (*at dawn*) **3** expressing a point in a scale (*at his best*) **4** expressing engagement in an activity, etc. (*at war*) **5** expressing a value or rate (*sell at $10 each*) **6a** with or with reference to (*annoyed at losing; came at a run*) **b** by means of (*starts at a touch*) **7** expressing direction (*aim at the target*) [OE]

At *symb.* astatine

A·ta·ca·ma Des·ert /ät'əkäm'ə, at'-/ *n.* arid region in N Chile

A·ta·türk /at'ətərk'/, **Kemal** (born **Mustafa Kemal**) 1881–1938; founder of Turkish republic; president (1923–38)

at·a·vism /at'əviz'əm/ *n.* **1** reappearance of a remote ancestral characteristic; throwback **2** reversion to an earlier type —**at·a·vis·tic** /at'əvis'tik/ *adj.* [L *atavus* ancestor]

a·tax·i·a /ətak'sēə, ā-/ *n. Med.* imperfect control of bodily movements —**a·tax'ic** *adj.* [Gk *a-* without + *taxis* order]

ate /āt/ *v.* past of EAT

-ate¹ *suffix* forming nouns denoting status, function, or office (*doctorate; consulate*) [L]

-ate² *suffix* forming adjectives with the sense 'having' (*foliate*) or 'full of' (*passionate*) [L participial ending -*atus*]

a·te·lier /at'l-yā'/ *n.* workshop or artist's studio [Fr]

Ath·a·bas·ka, Lake /ATH'əbas'kə/ *n.* lake in W Canada

a·the·ism /ā'THē-iz'əm/ *n.* belief that there is no God —**a'the·ist** *n.*; **a'the·is'tic** *adj.* [Gk *a-* not + *theos* god]

A·the·na /əthē'nə/ *n.* Gk. Myth. goddess of wisdom, identified with Roman Minerva

Ath·ens /aTH'ənz/ *n.* capital of Greece. Pop. 748,100 —**A·the·ni·an** /əTHē'nēən/ *n.* & *adj.*

ath·er·o·scle·ro·sis /aTH'ərōsklərō'sis/ *n.* degeneration of the arteries caused by a buildup of fatty deposits [Gk *athērōma* grainy tumor + SCLEROSIS]

a·thirst /əTHərst'/ *adj.* Poet. **1** eager **2** thirsty

ath·lete /aTH'lēt'/ *n.* person who engages in athletics, exercise, etc. [Gk *āthlein* contend for a prize]

ath'lete's foot' *n.* fungal foot condition

ath·let·ic /aTHlet'ik/ *adj.* **1** of athletes or athletics **2** physically strong or agile —**ath·let'i·cal·ly** *adv.*; **ath·let'i·cism** /-let'əsiz'əm/ *n.* [L fr. Gk, rel. to ATHLETE]

ath·let'ics *n. pl.* (treated as *sing.* or *pl.*) physical exercises, games, sports, etc.

-athon *suffix* forming nouns with the sense 'prolonged activity' (*sellathon; dance-athon*) [fr. (MAR)ATHON]

-ation *suffix* **1** forming nouns denoting an action or an instance of it (*flirtation*) **2** forming nouns denoting a result or product of action (*plantation; starvation*) [L -atio]

At·lan·ta /ətlant'ə, at-/ *n.* capital of Ga., in the N central part. Pop. 394,017

At·lan·tic In'tra·coast'al Wa'ter·way /ətlant'ik, at-/ *n.* navigational system of sheltered waterways along the E US coast

At·lan'tic O'cean *n.* ocean separating the Americas from Europe and Africa. Area 31,530,000 sq. mi.; greatest width 4,150 mi.

at·las /at'ləs/ *n.* book of maps or charts [Gk ATLAS]

At'las *n.* Gk. Myth. giant condemned to support the heavens on his shoulders

At'las Moun'tains *n.* mountain range in NW Africa

ATM *abbr.* computerized terminal allowing a customer to transact business with a bank [automated teller machine]

at·mos·phere /at'məsfēr'/ *n.* **1** gases enveloping the earth, any other planet, etc. **2** air in a room, etc. **3** pervading tone or mood of a place, situation, or work of art **4** unit of pressure equal to mean atmospheric pressure at sea level, or 101,325 pascals —**at·mo·spher·ic** /at'məsfer'ik/ *adj.*; **at'mos·pher'i·cal·ly** *adv.* [Gk *atmos* vapor + SPHERE]

at·mos·pher·ics /at'məsfer'iks/ *n. pl.* **1** electrical atmospheric disturbance, esp. caused by lightning **2** interference with telecommunications caused by this

at·oll /a'tôl',ā'-,tāl'/ *n.* ring-shaped coral reef enclosing a lagoon [Fr, fr. native language of MALDIVES]

at·om /at'əm/ *n.* **1a** smallest particle of a chemical element that can take part in a chemical reaction **b** this as a source of nuclear energy **2** minute portion or thing [Gk *atomos* indivisible]

at'om bomb' *n.* (also **a·tom'ic bomb'**) bomb in which energy is released by nuclear fission

a·tom·ic /ətäm'ik/ *adj.* **1** of or using atomic energy or atomic bombs **2** of atoms

a·tom'ic en'er·gy *n.* nuclear energy

a·tom'ic num'ber *n.* number of protons in the nucleus of an atom

a·tom'ic weight' *n.* weight or mass of one atom of an element based on an average of the mass of all of its isotopes

at·om·ize /at'əmīz'/ *v.* (**·ized, ·iz·ing**) reduce to atoms or fine particles

at·om·iz·er /at'əmī'zər/ *n.* device for dispensing liquid, insecticide, cologne, etc., as a fine spray

a·ton·al /ātōn'l/ *adj.* Mus. not written in any key or mode —**a'to·nal'i·ty** *n.*

a·tone /ətōn'/ *v.* (**·toned, ·ton·ing**) make amends [back formation fr. ATONEMENT]

a·tone'ment *n.* atoning [*at one* + -MENT]

ATP *abbr.* biochemical functioning as an energy source in all living cells [adenosine triphosphate]

a·tri·um /ā'trēəm/ *n.* (*pl.* **·tri·a** /-trēə/.) **1a** central court of an ancient Roman house **b** (usu. skylit) central court rising through several stories **2** either of the two upper cavities of the heart [L]

a·tro·cious /ətrō'SHəs/ *adj.* **1** very bad or unpleasant; awful **2** wicked —**a·tro'cious·ly** *adv.*; **a·tro'cious·ness** *n.* [L, rel. to ATROCITY]

a·troc·i·ty /əträs'ətē/ *n.* (*pl.* **·ties**) **1** wicked or cruel act **2** extreme wickedness [L *atrox* cruel; fierce]

at·ro·phy /a'trəfē/ *n.* **1** wasting away, esp. through disuse; emaciation —*v.* (**·phied, ·phy·ing**) **2** suffer atrophy or cause atrophy in [Gk *a-* without + *trophē* food]

at·ro·pine /a'trəpēn'/ *n.* poisonous alkaloid in deadly nightshade [Gk *Atropos*, the Fate who cut the thread of life]

at·tach /ətacH'/ *v.* **1** fasten; affix; join **2** attribute or be attributable; assign **3** accompany; form part of **4** join **5** seize by legal authority [OFr fr. Gmc]

at·ta·ché /at'əSHā', a'tə-; ətasH'ā/ *n.* specialist member of an ambassador's staff

at·ta·ché' case' *n.* rectangular case for papers, folders, etc.

at·tach'ment *n.* **1** thing attached, esp. for a purpose **2** affection; devotion **3** attaching or being attached **4** legal seizure

at·tack /ətak'/ *v.* **1** try to hurt or defeat using force **2** criticize adversely **3** act harmfully upon **4** vigorously apply oneself to —*n.* **5** act of attacking **6** offensive operation **7** sudden onset of an illness —**at·tack'er** *n.* [MFr fr. It]

at·tain /ətān'/ *v.* **1** reach; gain; accomplish **2** arrive at —**at·tain'ment** *n.* [L *attingere* reach]

at·tar /a'tär', at'ər/ *n.* perfume made from flower petals, often rose petals [Pers]

at·tempt /ətempt'/ *v.* **1** try to do or achieve —*n.* **2** attempting; endeavor **3** attack or assault [L *attemptare* try]

At·ten·bor·ough /at'n-b(ə)rə/ *n.* **1** (Sir) Richard 1923– ; English film actor, producer, and director; brother of: **2** (Sir) David 1926– ; English naturalist, writer, and television producer

at·tend /ətend′/ v. **1** be present (at) **2** escort **3** turn or apply one's mind **4** deal with **5** pay attention [L attendere stretch toward]

at·tend·ance /əten′dəns/ n. **1** attending or being present **2** number present

at·tend·ant /əten′dənt/ n. **1** person escorting or providing a service —adj. **2** accompanying **3** waiting; serving

at·tend·ee /ətendē′, ə-/ n. person who attends

at·ten·tion /əten′sHən/ n. **1** act or faculty of applying one's mind; notice **2** consideration; care **3** (pl.) **a** courtesies **b** sexual advances **4** erect stance, esp. military attitude of readiness

at·ten·tive /əten′iv/ adj. **1** concentrating; paying attention **2** assiduously polite —**at·ten′tive·ly** adv.; **at·ten′tive·ness** n.

at·ten·u·ate /əten′yōō-āt′/ v. (·at·ed, ·at·ing) **1** make thin **2** reduce in force, value, etc. —**at·ten′u·a′tion** n. [L tenuis thin]

at·test /ətest′/ v. **1** certify the validity of **2** bear witness to —**at·tes·ta·tion** /a′tes′tā′sHən, at′əstā′-/ n. [L testis witness]

at·tic /at′ik/ n. space or room at the top of a house, under the roof [fr. ATTIC, with ref. to an architectural feature]

At′tic adj. **1** of ancient Athens or Attica, or the form of Greek used there —n. **2** Greek as used by the ancient Athenians [Gk Attikos]

At·ti·la /at′l-ə, ətil′ə/ 406–453; king of the Huns (434–453); called the "Scourge of God"

at·tire /ətīr′/ n. **1** clothes —v. (·tired, ·tir·ing) **2** dress [OFr à tire in order]

at·ti·tude /at′ət(y)ōōd/ n. **1** opinion or way of thinking **2** behavior reflecting this **3** bodily posture; pose **4** position of an aircraft, etc., relative to given points [Fr fr. It fr. L, rel. to APT]

at·ti·tu·di·nize /at′ət(y)ōōd′n-īz′/ v. (·nized, ·niz·ing) adopt (esp. affected) attitudes; pose

Att·lee /at′lē/, **Clement Richard** 1883–1967; British prime minister (1945–51)

at·tor·ney /ətər′nē/ (also **at·tor′ney-at-law′**) n. (pl. ·neys) **1** lawyer **2** person empowered to act on another's behalf [AngFr attourner assign]

at·tor′ney-gen·er·al n. (pl. **at·tor′neys-gen′er·al**) chief legal officer in the US and some other governments

at·tract /ətrakt′/ v. **1** (of a magnet, etc.) draw to itself or oneself **2** arouse interest or admiration in [L trahere draw]

at·trac·tion /ətrak′sHən/ n. **1** attracting or being attracted **2** attractive quality **3** person or thing that attracts **4** Physics. tendency of bodies to attract each other

at·trac′tive adj. **1** attracting (esp. interest or admiration) **2** aesthetically pleasing; good-looking —**at·trac′tive·ly** adv.; **at·trac′tive·ness** n.

at·tri·bute v. /ətrib′yōōt, -yət/ (·but·ed, ·but·ing) **1** regard as belonging to, written or said by, etc. **2** ascribe to (a cause) —n. /a′trəbyōōt′/ **3** characteristic quality ascribed to a person or thing **4** object symbolizing or appropriate to a person, office, or status —**at·trib′ut·a·ble** /-yətəbəl/ adj.; **at·tri·bu·tion** /a′trəbyōō′sHən/ n. [L tribuere allot]

at·trib·u·tive /ətrib′yətiv/ adj. Gram. (of an adjective or noun) preceding the word described, as old in the old dog —**at·trib′u·tive·ly** adv.

at·tri·tion /ətrisH′ən/ n. **1** gradual wearing down (war of attrition) **2** abrasion; friction [L terere trit- rub; wear away]

At·tucks /at′əks/, **Crispus** c. 1723–70; American patriot; killed in the Boston Massacre

at·tune /ət(y)ōōn′/ v. (·tuned, ·tun·ing) **1** adjust to a situation, etc. **2** Mus. bring into tune [rel. to TUNE]

atty. abbr. attorney

ATV abbr. vehicle designed to travel over any surface [all terrain vehicle]

At·wood /at′wŏŏd′/, **Margaret** 1939– ; Canadian writer and critic

a·typ·i·cal /ā′tip′ikəl/ adj. not typical —**a·typ′i·cal·ly** adv.

Au symb. gold [L aurum]

au·burn /ô′bərn/ adj. reddish-brown [orig. yellowish white: fr. L albus white]

Auck·land /ô′klənd/ n. seaport in New Zealand. Pop. 315,900

auc·tion /ôk′sHən/ n. **1** sale in which articles are sold to the highest bidder —v. **2** (also **auc′tion off′**) sell by auction [L augere auctincrease]

auc·tion·eer /ôk′sHənēr′/ n. person who conducts auctions, esp. for a living

au·da·cious /ôdā′sHəs/ adj. **1** daring; bold **2** impudent —**au·dac·i·ty** /ôdas′ətē/ n. [L audax bold]

Au·den /ôd′n/, **W(ystan) H(ugh)** 1907–73; British-born US poet

au·di·ble /ôd′əbəl/ adj. able to be heard —**au′di·bil′i·ty** n.; **au′di·bly** adv. [L audire hear]

au·di·ence /ôd′ēəns/ n. **1** assembled listeners or spectators, esp. at a play, concert, etc. **2** people addressed by a film, book, etc. **3** formal interview with a superior [L, rel. to AUDIBLE]

au·di·o /ô′dēō′/ n. **1** sound or its reproduction **2** sound portion of a television program, motion picture, etc. [L audire hear]

au′di·o fre′quen·cy n. sound at a frequency perceivable by the human ear

au·di·o·phile /ô′dēōfīl′/ n. person who enjoys high-quality sound recordings and equipment

au′di·o·vi′su·al adj. (of teaching methods, etc.) using both sight and sound

au·dit /ôd′it/ n. **1** official scrutiny of accounts —v. **2** conduct an audit of **3** take a university course for no credit

au·di·tion /ôdisH′ən/ n. **1** test of a performer's suitability or ability —v. **2** assess or be assessed at an audition [L audire hear]

au·di·tor /ôd′ətər/ n. **1** person who audits accounts **2** student who audits a course [AngFr fr. L]

au·di·to·ri·um /ôd′ətôr′ēəm/ n. (pl. ·ums) **1** part of a theater, etc., for the audience **2** assembly hall in an institution [L]

au·di·to·ry /ôd′ətôr′ē/ adj. of hearing

Au·du·bon /ôd′əbon, -bän′/, **John James** 1785–1851; US naturalist and artist

au fait /ō fā′/ adj. conversant [Fr: to the fact]

Aug. abbr. August

au·ger /ô′gər/ n. tool for boring in wood [OE]

aught[1] /ôt/ *n.* anything [OE]

aught[2] *n.* zero [ME fr. *a naught*]

aug·ment /ôgment'/ *v.* make or become greater; increase **—aug'men·ta'tion** *n.*; **aug·men'ta·tive** *adj.*; **aug·ment'er** *n.* [L *augere*]

au gra·tin /ō grat'n, ō grät'n, ô/ *adj.* cooked with a crust of breadcrumbs and usu. melted cheese [Fr]

Augs·burg /ouks'bŏŏrk, ôgz'bərg/ *n.* city in Germany. Pop. 256,900

au·gur /ô'gər/ *v.* 1 portend; serve as an omen **—n.** 2 *Hist.* Roman religious soothsayer [L]

au·gu·ry /ô'gyərē/ *n.* (*pl.* **·ries**) 1 omen 2 interpretation of omens

au·gust /ôgəst', ô'gəst/ *adj.* venerable; imposing [L]

Au·gust /ô'gəst/ *n.* eighth month of the year [L *Augustus*, first Roman emperor]

Au·gus·ta /ôgəs'tə/ *n.* capital of Maine, in the S part. Pop. 21,325

Au·gus·tan /ôgəs'tən/ *adj.* 1 of the reign of Augustus, esp. as a flourishing literary period 2 (of literature) refined and classical in style [L: see AUGUSTUS]

Au·gus·tine /ô'gəstēn, ôgəs'tən/ 1 Saint 354–430; early Christian writer; bishop of Hippo in North Africa 2 Saint died c. 604; first archbishop of Canterbury **—Au·gus·tin'i·an** *adj.*

Au·gus·tus /ôgəs'təs/ (born **Gaius Octavianus;** also known as **Octavian**) 63 B.C.–A.D. 14; first Roman emperor (27 B.C.–A.D. 14)

au jus /ō zhŏŏ', ō zhys'/ *adv. & adj.* (of meat) served with its own gravy

auk /ôk/ *n.* black and white diving bird, e.g., the guillemot, puffin, etc. [Scan fr. ON]

auld lang syne /ôl(d)' lang' zīn'/ *n.* old times remembered fondly [Scot: old long since]

Aung San Suu Kyi /oung' sän' sŏŏ' chē'/ 1945– ; Burmese political leader; Nobel prize 1991

aunt /ant, änt/ *n.* 1 sister of one's father or mother 2 uncle's wife [L *amita*]

au·ra /ôr'ə/ *n.* (*pl.* **·ras**) 1 distinctive atmosphere 2 subtle emanation [Gk: breeze]

au·ral /ôr'əl/ *adj.* of the ear or hearing **—au'ral·ly** *adv.* [L *auris* ear]

Au·rang·a·bad /ourANG'(g)əbäd'/ *n.* (also **Aurungabad**) city in India. Pop. 572,634

Au·re'li·us, Marcus see MARCUS AURELIUS

au·re·ole /ôr'ē-ōl'/ *n.* (also **au·re·o·la** /ôrē'ələ/) 1 halo, esp. in a religious painting 2 corona around the sun [L: golden (crown)]

au re·voir /ō'rəvwär', ôr'əv-/ *interj. & n. French.* goodbye

au·ri·cle /ôr'ikəl/ *n.* 1 either atrium of the heart 2 external part of the ear **—au·ric·u·lar** /ôrik'yələr/ *adj.* [L *auricula* ear]

au·ro·ra /ôrôr'ə, ə-/ *n.* (*pl.* **·ras** or **·rae** /-rē/) luminous phenomenon, usu. of streamers of light in the night sky above the northern (**au·ro'ra bo·re·al'is** /bôr'ē-al'əs/) or southern (**au·ro'ra aus·tra'lis** /ôstrā'ləs/) magnetic pole [L: dawn; goddess of dawn]

Au·ro·ra /ərôr'ə, -rôr'ə/ *n.* 1 city in Colo. Pop. 222,103 2 city in Ill. Pop. 99,581

aus·cul·ta·tion /ô'skəltā'shən/ *n.* listening, esp. to sounds from the heart, lungs, etc., for purposes of diagnosis [L *auscultare* listen]

aus·pice /ô'spis/ *n.* (*pl.* **·pi·ces** /-pəsiz, -pəsēz'/) 1 (*pl.*) patronage 2 omen; premo-

37   **aught / autoclave**

nition [L *auspicium* divination from the flight of birds]

aus·pi·cious /ôspish'əs/ *adj.* promising well; favorable **—aus·pi'cious·ly** *adv.*; **aus·pi'cious·ness** *n.*

Aus·sie /ô'sē, ôz'ē/ *Colloq. n.* 1 Australian 2 Australia **—adj.** 3 Australian

Aus·ten /ô'stən/, **Jane** 1775–1817; English novelist

aus·tere /ôstēr'/ *adj.* 1 severely simple 2 morally strict 3 stern; grim **—aus·tere'ly** *adv.* [Gk *austēros*]

aus·ter·i·ty /ôster'ətē/ *n.* (*pl.* **·ties**) 1 sternness; severity 2 hardship; strict economy

Aus·tin /ô'stən/, **Stephen** 1793–1836; American pioneer in Texas

Aus'tin *n.* capital of Tex., in the E central part. Pop. 465,622

Aus·tral·a·sia /ôs'trəlā'zhə, äs'-, -shə/ *n.* region of Australia, New Zealand, and nearby islands in the S Pacific Ocean

Aus·tral·ia /ôstrāl'yə, äs-/ *n.* 1 continent SE of Asia, bounded by the Coral and Tasman seas, and the Indian and Pacific oceans 2 commonwealth of the states and territories of Australia and Tasmania. Capital: Canberra. Pop. 17,562,000 **—Aus·tral'i·an** *n. & adj.*

Aus·tri·a /ô'strēə, äs'-/ *n.* landlocked republic of central Europe. Capital: Vienna. Pop. 7,857,000 **—Aus'tri·an** *n. & adj.*

auth. *abbr.* author

au·then·tic /ôthen'tik/ *adj.* 1 of undisputed origin; genuine 2 reliable; trustworthy **—au·then'ti·cal·ly** *adv.*; **au·then·tic·i·ty** /ô'thentis'ətē/ *n.* [Gk *authentikos*]

au·then·ti·cate /ôthen'tikāt'/ *v.* (**·cat·ed, ·cat·ing**) establish as true, genuine, or valid **—au·then'ti·ca'tion** *n.*

au·thor /ô'thər/ *n.* 1 writer, esp. of books 2 originator of an idea, event, etc. **—au'thor·ship'** *n.* [L *auctor*]

au·thor·i·tar·i·an /ôthôr'əter'ēən, ə-, -thär'-/ *adj.* 1 favoring or enforcing strict obedience to authority **—n.** 2 authoritarian person **—au·thor'i·tar'i·an·ism'** *n.*

au·thor·i·ta·tive /ôthôr'ətāt'iv, ə-, -thär'-/ *adj.* 1 reliable, esp. having authority 2 official

au·thor·i·ty /ôthôr'ətē, ə-, -thär'-/ *n.* (*pl.* **·ties**) 1 power or right to enforce obedience 2 (esp. *pl.*) body having authority 3 influence based on recognized knowledge or expertise 4 expert [L *auctoritas*]

au'thor·ize *v.* (**·ized, ·iz·ing**) 1 officially approve; sanction 2 give authority to 3 justify **—au'thor·i·za'tion** *n.*

Au'thor·ized Ver'sion *n.* English translation of the Bible made in 1611

au·tism /ô'tizəm/ *n.* condition characterized by self-absorption and social withdrawal **—au·tis'tic** *adj.* [rel. to AUTO-]

au·to /ô't/ō *n.* (*pl.* **·tos**) automobile

auto- *comb. form* 1 self 2 one's own 3 of or by oneself or itself [Gk *autos* self]

au·to·bi·og·ra·phy /ô't'əbīäg'rəfē/ *n.* (*pl.* **·phies**) 1 written account of one's own life 2 this as a literary genre **—au'to·bi·og'ra·pher** *n.*; **au'to·bi'o·graph'i·cal** *adj.*

au·to·clave /ô'təklāv'/ *n.* sterilizer using steam [L *clavus* nail or *clavis* key]

au·toc·ra·cy /ôtäk′rəsē/ *n.* (*pl.* ·**cies**) dictatorship [Gk *kratos* power]

au·to·crat /ôt′əkrat′/ *n.* **1** absolute ruler **2** dictatorial person —**au′to·crat′ic** *adj.*; **au′to·crat′i·cal·ly** *adv.*

au·to·da·fé /out′ō də fā′, ôt′-/ *n.* (*pl.* **au·tos-da-fé** /out′ōz, ôt′ōz/) **1** *Hist.* ceremonial judgment of heretics by the Spanish Inquisition **2** public burning of heretics [Port: act of the faith]

au·to·di·dact /ô′tōdī′dakt/ *n.* self-taught person [Gk *didaktos* that may be taught]

au·to·graph /ôt′əgraf′/ *n.* **1** signature, esp. that of a celebrity —*v.* **2** sign or write on in one's own hand —**au′to·graph′ic** or **au′to·graph′i·cal** *adj.*; **au′to·graph′i·cal·ly** *adv.* [Gk *graphein* write]

au·to·im·mune /ôt′ōimyoon′/ *adj.* (of a disease) caused by antibodies produced against substances naturally present in the body

au·to·mate /ôt′əmāt/ *v.* (·**mat·ed**, ·**mat·ing**) convert to or operate by automation

au·to·mat·ic /ôt′əmat′ik/ *adj.* **1** working by itself, without direct human intervention **2** done spontaneously **3** inevitable; unavoidable **4** (of a firearm) able to be loaded and fired continuously **5** (of a vehicle or its transmission) using gears that change automatically —*n.* **6** automatic machine, firearm, or tool **7** vehicle with automatic transmission —**au′to·mat′i·cal·ly** *adv.* [Gk, rel. to AUTOMATON]

au′to·mat′ic pi′lot *n.* device for keeping an aircraft or ship on a set course

au·to·ma·tion /ôt′əmā′shən/ *n.* use of automatic manufacturing equipment

au·tom·a·tism /ôtäm′ətiz′əm/ *n.* involuntary, unthinking action [Gk, rel. to AUTOMATON]

au·tom·a·ton /ôtäm′ətän′, -tən/ *n.* (*pl.* ·**tons** or ·**ta** /-tə/) **1** machine controlled automatically; robot **2** person acting like a robot [Gk: acting of itself]

au·to·mo·bile /ôt′əməbēl′, ôt′əmōbēl′/ *n.* passenger vehicle with an engine and four wheels; car [Fr]

au′to·mo′tive *adj.* **1** of motor vehicles **2** powered by an internal engine

au′to·nom′ic ner′vous sys′tem /ô′tənəm′ik/ *n.* nervous system controlling involuntary bodily functions, as respiration, heartbeat, etc. [Gk, rel. to AUTONOMOUS]

au·ton·o·mous /ôtän′əməs/ *adj.* **1** having self-government **2** acting or free to act independently —**au·ton′o·mous·ly** *adv.* [Gk *nomos* law]

au·ton·o·my /ôtän′əmē/ *n.* **1** self-government **2** personal freedom —**au′to·nom′ic** *adj.*

au′to·pi′lot *n.* AUTOMATIC PILOT

au·top·sy /ô′täp′sē/ *n.* (*pl.* ·**sies**) postmortem [Gk *autopsia* seeing with one's own eyes]

au·tumn /ôt′əm/ *n.* **1** season between summer and winter **2** time of imminent decline —**au·tum·nal** /ôtəm′nəl/ *adj.* [L *autumnus*]

aux·il·ia·ry /ôgzil′(y)ərē/ *adj.* **1** subsidiary; additional **2** giving help **3** supplementing —*n.* (*pl.* ·**ries**) **4** auxiliary person or thing **5** (also **aux·il′ia·ry verb′**) verb used to form tenses or moods of other verbs (e.g., *have* in *I have seen*) [L *auxilium* help]

aux·in /ôk′sən/ *n.* plant hormone that regulates growth

AV *abbr.* audiovisual

a·vail /əvāl′/ *v.* **1** help; be of use **2** make use of; profit by —*n.* **3** use; profit [L *valere* be strong]

a·vail·a·ble /əvā′ləbəl/ *adj.* at one's disposal; obtainable —**a·vail′a·bil′i·ty** *n.*

av·a·lanche /av′əlanch/ *n.* **1** rapidly sliding mass of snow and ice on a mountain **2** sudden overwhelming amount [Fr]

a·vant-garde /äv′än(t)′gärd′, av′-/ *n.* **1** pioneers or (esp. artistic) innovators —*adj.* **2** new; pioneering [Fr: vanguard]

av·a·rice /av′(ə)rəs/ *n.* extreme greed for wealth —**av′a·ri′cious** /-rish′əs/ *adj.* [L *avarus* greedy]

a·vast /əvast′/ *interj.* stop! [Du *houd vast* hold fast]

av·a·tar /av′ətär′/ *n.* (in Hindu mythology) descent of a deity, etc., to earth in bodily form [Skt: descent]

avdp. *abbr.* avoirdupois

Ave. *abbr.* Avenue

A·ve Ma·ri·a /ä′vä märē′ə/ *n. RC Ch.* name of a prayer [L: Hail, Mary]

a·venge /əvenj′/ *v.* (·**venged**, ·**veng·ing**) **1** inflict retribution on behalf of **2** take vengeance for (an injury) —**a·veng′er** *n.* [OFr fr. L *vindicare*]

av·e·nue /av′ən(y)oo′/ *n.* **1** broad, esp. treelined, road or street **2** approach [Fr fr. L *advenire* come to]

a·ver /əvər′/ *v.* (·**verred**, ·**ver·ring**) assert; affirm —**a·ver′ment**, **a·ver′ral** *n.* [L *verus* true]

av·er·age /av′(ə)rij/ *n.* **1** usual amount, extent, or rate **2** amount obtained by adding two or more numbers and dividing by how many there are —*adj.* **3** usual; ordinary **4** mediocre **5** constituting an average —*v.* (·**aged**, ·**ag·ing**) **6** amount on average to **7** do on average **8** estimate the average of **9 average out (at)** result in an average (of) **10** on average as an average rate or estimate [Ar: damaged goods]

● Usage: See note at MEAN³.

A·ver·ro·ës /əver′ō-ēz, av′ərō′-/ c. 1126-98; Spanish-born Islamic philosopher, judge, and physician (Arabic name **ibn-Rushd**)

a·verse /əvərs′/ *adj.* opposed; disinclined [L *vertere vers-* turn]

● Usage: See note at ADVERSE.

a·ver·sion /əvər′zhən, -shən/ *n.* **1** dislike or unwillingness **2** object of this

a·vert /əvərt′/ *v.* **1** turn away (one's eyes or thoughts) **2** prevent or ward off (esp. danger)

avg. *abbr.* average

a·vi·an /ā′vēən/ *adj.* relating to or characteristic of birds [L *avis* bird]

a·vi·ar·y /ā′vē·er′ē/ *n.* (*pl.* ·**ries**) large cage or building for keeping birds [L *avis* bird]

a·vi·a·tion /ā′vēā′shən/ *n.* science or practice of flying aircraft [L, rel. to AVIARY]

a·vi·a·tor /ā′vēāt′ər/ *n.* person who flies aircraft —**a′vi·a′trix** /-triks/ *n. fem.*

A·vi·cen·na /av′əsen′ə/ 980-1037; Persian-born Islamic philosopher and physician (Arabic name **ibn-Sina**)

av·id /av′id/ *adj.* eager; greedy —**a·vid′i·ty** *n.*; **av′id·ly** *adv.* [L *avere* crave]

a·vi·on·ics /ā′vē-än′iks/ *n. pl.* (usu. treated as *sing.*) electronics as applied to aviation [fr. AVI(ATION) + (ELECTR)ONICS]

av·o·ca·do /av′əkäd′ō, äv′-/ *n.* (*pl.* **-dos**) (also **al′li·ga·tor pear′**) 1 dark green edible pear-shaped fruit with yellowish-green creamy flesh 2 tree bearing it [Sp fr. Aztec]

av·o·ca·tion /av′əkā′sHən/ *n.* hobby —**av′o·ca′tion·al** *adj.* [L *a-* away + *vocation-* calling]

a·void /əvoid′/ *v.* 1 keep away or refrain from 2 escape; evade 3 *Law.* quash; annul —**a·void′a·ble** *adj.*; **a·void′a·bly** *adv.*; **a·void′ance** *n.* [AngFr]

av·oir·du·pois /av′ərdəpoiz′/ *n.* system of weights based on a pound of 16 ounces or 7,000 grains [OFr: goods of weight]

a·vow /əvou′/ *v.* declare; confess —**a·vow′al** *n.*; **a·vow′ed·ly** /-ədlē/ *adv.* [L *advocare* call]

a·vun·cu·lar /əvəNG′kyələr/ *adj.* like or of an uncle, esp. in manner [L *avunculus* uncle]

aw /ô/ *interj.* 1 sound of disappointment 2 sound of objection

a·wait /əwāt′/ *v.* 1 wait for 2 be in store for [ONFr, rel. to WAIT]

a·wake /əwāk′/ *v.* (**a·woke** or **a·waked,** **a·waked** or **a·wok·en, a·wak·ing**) 1 cease to sleep or arouse from sleep 2 become or make alert, aware, or active —*adj.* 3 not asleep 4 alert; aware [OE]

a·wak·en /əwā′kən/ *v.* AWAKE —**a·wak′en·ing** *n.*

a·ward /əwôrd′/ *v.* 1 give or order to be given as a payment or prize —*n.* 2 thing or amount awarded 3 judicial decision [AngFr]

a·ware /əwer′, əwar′/ *adj.* conscious; having knowledge; knowledgeable —**a·ware′ness** *n.* [OE]

a·wash /əwäsH′, əwôsH′/ *adj. & adv.* 1 so as to be level with the surface of and just covered by water 2 overflowing; abounding

a·way /əwā′/ *adv.* 1 to or at a distance from 2 into nonexistence 3 constantly; persistently 4 without delay 5 out of one's possession 6 aside —*adj.* 7 absent 8 distant 9 **away with** go or take away 10 **do away with: a** get rid of **b** kill [OE]

awe /ô/ *n.* 1 reverential fear or wonder —*v.* (**awed, aw·ing**) 2 inspire with awe [ON]

a·weigh /əwā′/ *adj.* (of an anchor) clear of the bottom

awe′-in·spir′ing *adj.* awesome; magnificent

awe·some /ô′səm/ *adj.* 1 inspiring awe; dreaded 2 *Colloq.* impressive —**awe′some·ly** *adv.*; **awe′some·ness** *n.*

aw·ful /ô′fəl/ *adj.* 1 very bad or unpleasant 2 as an intensifier 3 *Poet.* inspiring awe —*adv.* 4 *Colloq.* very —**aw′ful·ness** *n.*

aw·ful·ly /ô′f(ə)lē/ *adv.* 1 badly; unpleasantly 2 *Colloq.* very

a·while /ə(h)wīl′/ *adv.* for a short time

awk·ward /ôk′wərd/ *adj.* 1 difficult to use or deal with 2 clumsy; ungainly 3 embarrassed or embarrassing —**awk′ward·ly** *adv.*; **awk′ward·ness** *n.* [ME *fr.* ON]

awl /ôl/ *n.* small tool for piercing holes [OE]

awn /ôn/ *n.* bristly head of a sheath of barley and other grasses [ON]

awn·ing /ô′niNG/ *n.* sheet of canvas, etc., stretched on a frame as a shelter against the sun or rain

a·woke /əwōk′/ *v. past* of AWAKE

a·wok·en /əwō′kən/ *v. past part.* of AWAKE

AWOL /ā′wôl/ *abbr.* absent without official leave

a·wry /ərī′/ *adv.* 1 crookedly; askew 2 amiss; wrong —*adj.* 3 crooked; unsound

ax /aks/ (also **axe**) *n.* 1 chopping tool with a handle and heavy blade 2 (**the ax**) dismissal; abandonment of a project, etc. —*v.* (**axed, ax·ing**) 3 cut (esp. costs or staff) drastically; abandon (a project) 4 **an ax to grind** private ends to serve [OE]

ax·i·al /ak′sēəl/ *adj.* of, forming, or placed around an axis

ax·il /ak′səl/ *n.* upper angle between a leaf and stem [L *axilla* armpit]

ax·i·om /ak′sēəm/ *n.* 1 established or accepted principle 2 self-evident truth —**ax′i·o·mat′ic** *adj.*; **ax′i·o·mat′i·cal·ly** *adv.* [Gk *axios* worthy]

ax·is /ak′sis/ *n.* (*pl.* **ax·es** /-sēz/) 1 imaginary line about which a body rotates 2 line that divides a regular figure symmetrically 3 fixed reference line for the measurement of coordinates, etc. 4 (**the Axis**) alliance of Germany, Italy, and later Japan, in World War II [L: axle]

ax·le /ak′səl/ *n.* 1 spindle on which a wheel is fixed or turns 2 shaft connecting such spindles [OE, perh. fr. ON]

AXOLOTL

ax·o·lotl /ak′səlät′l/ *n.* newtlike salamander of SW N America [Nahuatl]

ax·on /ak′sän/ *n.* part of a nerve cell that transmits impulses away from the cell body [Gk: axis]

a·ya·tol·lah /ī′ətō′lə, -təl′ə/ *n.* Shiite religious leader [Pers fr. Ar: token of God]

aye /ī/ *adv.* 1 *Archaic.* or *Dial.* yes —*n.* 2 affirmative answer or vote [prob. fr. *I,* expressing assent]

Ayer /ā′ər/, **A(lfred) J(ules)** 1910–89 British philosopher

AZ postal abbr. for Arizona

a·za·lea /əzāl′yə/ *n.* a kind of rhododendron [Gk *azaleos* dry]

Az·er·bai·jan /az′ərbīzHän′, -jän′/ *n.* republic on the W coast of the Caspian Sea, formerly part of the USSR. Capital: Baku. Pop. 7,237,000 —**Az′er·bai·ja′ni** *n.*

az·i·muth /az′əməTH/ *n.* angular distance from a north or south point of the horizon to the intersection with the horizon of a vertical circle passing through a given celestial body —**az′i·muth′al** *adj.* [MFr fr. Ar]

A·zores, the /ā′zôrz/ *n.* island group in the N Atlantic Ocean, W of Portugal; autonomous region of Portugal

A·zov, Sea of /az'ôf, a'zôf'/ *n.* N arm of the Black Sea bordered by Ukraine and SW Russia

AZT *abbr. Tdmk.* drug for use against AIDS [azidothymidine]

Az·tec /az'tek'/ *n.* **1** member of the native Mexican people overthrown by the Spanish in 1519 **2** language of this people —*adj.* **3** of the Aztecs or their language [Nahuatl]

az·ure /azₕ'ər/ *n.* **1** deep sky-blue color **2** *Poet.* clear sky —*adj.* **3** deep sky-blue [OFr fr. Ar fr. Pers *lazhuward*]

B

---

b, B /bē/ *n.* (*pl.* **b's; B's, Bs**) second letter of the English alphabet; a consonant

B *symb.* boron

b or b. *abbr.* **1** *Physics.* **a** bar(s) **b** barn(s) **2** black **3** bachelor **4** *Baseball.* base; baseman **5** *Mus.* bass; basso **6** bay **7** billion **8** book **9** born **10** breadth **11** brother; brotherhood

B or B. *abbr.* **1** Bible **2** British

Ba *symb.* barium

B.A. *abbr.* Bachelor of Arts

baa /bä, ba/ *v.* (**baaed** or **baa'd**) **1** bleat —*n.* **2** sheep's cry [imit.]

Ba·al /bā'əl, bāl/ *n.* Semitic nature deity

bab·ble /bab'ər/ *v.* (**·bled, ·bling**) **1** talk, chatter, or say incoherently or excessively **2** (of a stream, etc.) murmur **3** repeat or divulge foolishly; blab —*n.* **4** babbling **5** murmur of voices, water, etc. [ME, prob. orig. imit.]

babe /bāb/ *n.* **1** *Lit.* baby **2** innocent or helpless person **3** *Slang.* young woman

ba·bel /bā'bəl, bab'əl/ *n.* **1** confused noise, esp. of voices **2** scene of confusion [Heb: Babylon (Gen. 11)]

Ba·ber /bä'bər/ (also spelled **Babar; Babur**) 1483–1530; founder of Mogul empire; conquered India 1526

ba·boon /baboōn'/ *n.* dog-faced African and Arabian monkey with a short tail [MFr or MedL]

ba·by /bā'bē/ *n.* (*pl.* **·bies**) **1** very young child **2** childish person **3** youngest member of a family, etc. **4** very young animal **5** *Slang.* sweetheart **6** one's special concern —*v.* (**·bied, ·by·ing**) **7** treat like a baby; pamper —**ba'by·hood'** *n.*; **ba'by·ish** *adj.* [ME, prob. imit. of child's *ba ba*]

ba'by boom' *n. Colloq.* temporary increase in the birthrate

ba'by boom'er *n.* person born in a baby boom, esp. that in the US from c. 1946–1960

ba'by car'riage *n.* (also **ba'by bug'gy**) wheeled vehicle for pushing around an infant

ba'by grand' *n.* small grand piano

ba'by·sit' *v.* (**·sat, ·sit·ting**) look after a child while its parents are out —**ba'by·sit'ter** *n.*

ba'by talk' *n.* childish speech, esp. as simulated by adults

Ba·call /bəkôl'/, **Lauren** (born Betty Joan Perske) 1924– ; US actress

bac·ca·lau·re·ate /bak'əlôr'ēət, -lär'-/ *n.* college or university degree awarded to a person who has completed an undergraduate course of studies [MedL *baccalaureus* bachelor]

bac·cha·nal *n.* /bä'kənäl', bak'ənəl'/ **1a** (also **bac'cha·na'li·a** /-nə'lēə/) drunken revelry **b** reveler **2** priest or follower of Bacchus —*adj.* /bak'ənəl/ **3** of or like Bacchus **4** drunkenly riotous —**bac'cha·na'li·an** *adj.* [fr. BACCHUS]

Bac·chus /bak'əs/ *Gk. Myth.* god of wine and revelry —**Bac·chic** *adj.*

Bach /bäKH, bäk/ family of German composers, including: **1 Johann Sebastian** 1685–1750; and his sons: **2 Wilhelm Friedemann** 1710–84; **3** C(arl) P(hilipp) E(manuel) 1714–88; **4 Johann Christoph Friedrich** 1732–95; **5 Johann Christian** 1735–82

bach·e·lor /bacH'(ə)lər/ *n.* unmarried man —**bach'e·lor·hood'** *n.* [MedL *baccalaris* tenant farmer; squire]

bach'e·lor's de·gree' *n.* baccalaureate, esp. Bachelor of Arts, Bachelor of Science, Bachelor of Law, etc.

ba·cil·lus /bəsil'əs/ *n.* (*pl.* **·li** /-lī'/) rod-shaped bacterium, esp. one causing disease —**ba·cil·la·ry** /bas'əler'ē, bəsil'ərē/ *adj.* [L, dim. of *baculus* stick]

back /bak/ *n.* **1a** rear surface of the human body from shoulder to hip **b** upper surface of an animal's body **2** spine **3** backlike surface; reverse **4** more distant part **5** defensive player in football, etc. —*adv.* **6** to the rear **7** in or into a previous state, place, or time **8** at a distance **9** in return —*v.* **10** give moral or financial support to **11** bet on **12** move backward **13** put or serve as a back, background, or support to **14** *Mus.* accompany —*adj.* **15** situated at or toward the rear; remote; subsidiary **16** past; not current **17** backward **18** **back and forth** to and fro **19** **back down** withdraw from confrontation **20** **back off** retreat **21** **back out** withdraw from a commitment **22** **back up:** **a** support **b** *Comp.* duplicate **23** **get** (or **put**) **a person's back up** annoy a person **24** **turn one's back on** abandon; ignore —**back'er** *n.*; **back'less** *adj.* [OE]

back'ache' *n.* ache in the back

back'bit'ing *n.* malicious talk —**back'bite'** *v.* (**·bit, ·bit·ten, ·bit·ing**)

back'bone' *n.* **1** spine **2** chief support **3** firmness of character

back'-break'ing *adj.* extremely hard

back' burn'er *n.* as in **on the back burner** receiving or meriting little attention

back'date' *v.* (**·dat·ed, dat·ing**) **1** make retroactively valid **2** put an earlier date to

back' door' *n.* secret or surreptitious means

back'drop' *n.* **1** scenic cloth at back of a stage, often painted **2** any background scene or situation

back'field' *n. Football.* players behind the line

back'fire' *v.* (**·fired, ·fir·ing**) **1** (of an engine or vehicle) make an explosive noise as the result of premature fuel ignition **2** (of a plan, etc.) fail adversely

back' for·ma'tion *n.* **1** formation of a word from its seeming derivative (e.g., *laze* from *lazy*) **2** word so formed

back·gam·mon /bak'gam'ən/ *n.* board game with pieces moved according to throws of the dice [fr. BACK + obs. form of GAME¹]

back'ground' *n.* **1** part of a scene or picture furthest from the observer **2** inconspicuous or subordinate position **3** person's education, experience, origin, etc. **4** explanatory or contributory information or events

back'hand' *adj.* **1** (of a stroke, catch, etc.) made with the hand across one's body —*n.* **2** such a stroke, catch, etc.

back'hand'ed *adj.* **1** made with the back of the hand **2** indirect

back'ing *n.* **1** support, esp. financial or moral **2** material used for a thing's back or support **3** musical accompaniment, esp. to a pop singer

back'lash' *n.* **1** violent, usu. hostile, reaction **2** sudden recoil in a mechanism

back'log' *n.* arrears of work

back' num'ber *n.* **1** out-of-date issue of a periodical **2** *Slang.* out-of-date person or thing

back'pack' *n.* **1** knapsack —*v.* **2** travel or hike with this —back'pack'er *n.*

back'ped'al *v.* (·aled, ·al·ing) **1** pedal backward **2** retreat from one's position, etc.

back'rest' *n.* support for the back

back'seat' *n.* less prominent or important position

back'-seat' driv'er *n.* person eager to advise without taking or having responsibility

back'side' *n.* **1** back **2** *Colloq.* buttocks

back'slap'per *n.* overly friendly person —back'slap'ping *n.*

back'slide' *v.* (·slid, ·slid·ing) return to bad habits, etc. —back'slid'er *n.*

back'space' *v.* (·spaced, ·spac·ing) move a typewriter carriage, cursor, etc., back one or more spaces

back'spin' *n.* backward spin as on a golf ball, billiard ball, etc.

back'stage' *adv.* & *adj.* behind the scenes

back'stairs' *adj.* (also back·stair) underhand; secret

back'stop' *n. Baseball, etc.* screen or shield for keeping a ball within the playing area

back'stroke' *n.* **1** swimming stroke done on the back —*v.* (·stroked, ·strok·ing) **2** swim using the backstroke

back'talk' *n.* insolent response

back'-to-back' *adj.* **1** one right after another —*adv.* **2** continuously

back'track' *v.* **1** retrace one's steps **2** reverse one's policy or opinion

back'up' *n.* **1** support; reserve **2** *Comp.* a making of spare copies of data for safety b copy so made

back·ward /bak'wərd/ *adv.* (also back'wards) **1** away from one's front **2a** with the back foremost **b** in reverse of the usual way **3** into a worse state **4** into the past **5** back toward an earlier position —*adj.* **6** toward the rear or starting-point **7** reversed **8** slow to develop or progress **9** hesitant; shy **10** backward and forward or backwards and forwards to and fro; back and forth **11** bend (or fall or lean) over backwards *Colloq.*

make every effort, esp. to be fair or helpful —back'ward·ly *adv.*; back'ward·ness *n.*

back'wash' *n.* **1** receding waves made by a vessel or its propeller **2** repercussions

back'wa'ter *n.* **1** peaceful, secluded, or dull place **2** stagnant water

back'woods' *n. pl.* **1** remote uncleared forest land **2** remote region —back'woods'man *n.* (*pl.* ·men)

ba·con /bā'kən/ *n.* cured meat from the back or sides of a pig [OFr fr. Gmc]

Ba·con /bā'kən/ **1** Roger c. 1214–94; English philosopher and scientist **2** Francis 1561–1626; English statesman and philosopher

bac·te·ri·cide /baktē'rəsīd'/ *n.* substance for killing bacteria —bac·te'ri·ci'dal *adj.*

bac·te·ri·ol·o·gy /baktēr'ē·äl'əjē/ *n.* the study of bacteria —bac·te'ri·o·log'i·cal /-əläj'ikəl/ *adj.*; bac·te'ri·o·log'i·cal·ly *adv.*; bac·te'ri·ol'o·gist *n.*

bac·te·ri·um /baktēr'ēəm/ *n.* (*pl.* ·ri·a /-rēə/) one-celled microorganism lacking an organized nucleus, esp. one causing disease —bac·te'ri·al *adj.* [Gk: little stick]

bad /bad/ *adj.* (worse, worst) **1** inadequate; defective **2** unpleasant **3** harmful **4** (of food) spoiled; decayed **5** ill; injured **6** regretful; guilty **7** serious; severe **8a** morally unacceptable **b** naughty **9** not valid —*n.* **10** ill fortune; ruin —*adv.* **11** *Colloq.* badly **12** not (or not so or not too) bad *Colloq.* fairly good **13** too bad *Colloq.* regrettable [ME, perh. rel. to OE *bæddel*]

● Usage: The problem with *bad* and *good* vs. *badly* and *well* usually arises with special verbs (called copulas) like *feel*, *seem*, etc.: *I feel bad* and *I feel well* are the standard forms accepted by all. Technically, *I feel badly* means 'There is something wrong with my sense of touch.' See note at GOOD.

bad' blood' *n.* ill feeling

bad' debt' *n.* debt that is not recoverable

bade /bad/ *alter. past* of BID

bad' egg' *n.* person of bad character

Ba·den-Pow·ell /bād'n-pō'əl, -pou'əl/, (Lord) Robert Stephenson Smyth 1857–1941; English general; founder of the Boy Scout movement (1908)

bad' faith' *n.* intent to deceive

badge /baj/ *n.* **1** small flat emblem worn to signify office, membership, etc., or as decoration **2** thing that reveals a condition or quality

bad·ger /baj'ər/ *n.* **1** nocturnal burrowing mammal with a black and white striped head —*v.* **2** pester; harass

bad' hat' *n.* person of bad character

bad·i·nage /bad'n-äzH'/ *n.* playful ridicule [Fr]

Bad·lands /bad'lan(d)z'/ *n.* barren, eroded region in southwestern S. Dak. and NW Nebr.

bad' lot' *n.* person of bad character

bad·ly /bad'lē/ *adv.* (worse, worst) **1** in a bad manner **2** *Colloq.* very much **3** severely

bad'man' *n.* (*pl.* ·men) robber or bandit, esp. of the western US in the 19th century

bad·min·ton /bad'mint'n/ *n.* racket game played by hitting a shuttlecock back and forth across a net [*Badminton* in S England]

bad'-mouth' *v. Slang.* abuse verbally; put down

bad' news' *n. Colloq.* unpleasant or troublesome person or thing

bad'-tem'pered *adj.* irritable

Baf·fin Bay /baf'in/ *n.* part of the Arctic Ocean between Greenland and Baffin Island

Baf'fin Is'land *n.* Canadian island in the Arctic Ocean off the W coast of Greenland

baf·fle /baf'əl/ *v.* (**·fled, ·fling**) 1 perplex 2 frustrate; hinder —*n.* 3 device that checks flow of fluid, sound waves, etc. —**baf'fle·ment** *n.*

bag /bag/ *n.* 1 soft open-topped receptacle 2 piece of luggage 3 woman's handbag 4 (*pl.*) *Colloq.* large amount 5 amount of game shot by one person or in one hunt 6 (usu. *pl.*) baggy skin under the eyes 7 *Slang.* particular interest —*v.* (**bagged, bag·ging**) 8 *Colloq.* secure 9 put in a bag 10 (cause to) hang loosely; bulge 11 **in the bag** *Colloq.* achieved; secured —**bag'ful** *n.* (*pl.* **·fuls**)

bag·a·telle /bag'ətel'/ *n.* mere trifle [Fr fr. It]

ba·gel /bā'gəl/ *n.* ring-shaped bread roll of dough that is boiled, then baked [Yiddish]

bag·gage /bag'ij/ *n.* 1 luggage 2 *Joc.* or *Derog.* girl or woman [OFr]

bag·gy /bag'ē/ *adj.* (**·gi·er, ·gi·est**) hanging loosely —**bag'gi·ly** *adv.*; **bag'gi·ness** *n.*

Bagh·dad /bag'dad', bagdad'/ *n.* capital of Iraq. Pop. 3,841,300

bag' la'dy *n.* derelict woman who carries her belongings in shopping bags

BAGPIPE

bag'pipe' *n.* (usu. *pl.*) musical instrument consisting of a windbag connected to reeded pipes

ba·guette /baget'/ *n.* long thin French loaf [Fr fr. It]

bah /bä/ *interj.* expression of contempt or disbelief

Ba·ha·mas /bəhäm'əz/ *n.* country comprising a group of Atlantic islands SE of Florida. Capital: Nassau. Pop. 264,000 —**Ba·ha·mi·an** /bəhä'mēən/ *n. & adj.*

Bah·rain /bärän', bäkHrän'/ *n.* sheikdom comprising a group of islands in the Persian Gulf. Capital: Manama. Pop. 531,000

Bai·kal, Lake /bīkäl', -kôl/ *n.* lake in S Russia, in Asia; deepest in the world: 5,700 ft.

bail[1] /bāl/ *n.* 1 money pledged against the temporary release of an untried prisoner 2 this release 3 person(s) providing bail —*v.*

4 release or secure the release of (a prisoner) on payment of bail 5 release from a difficulty; rescue 6 **on bail** released after payment of bail —**bail'a·ble** *adj.* [OFr fr. L *baiulare* carry]

bail[2] *n.* 1 bar holding the paper against a typewriter platen 2 hooplike wire handle of a pail [ME fr. ON]

bail[3] *v.* 1 scoop water out of (a boat, etc.) 2 **bail out: a** parachute from a flying aircraft **b** leave or desert an undesirable situation [MFr fr. L *baiulare* carry]

bai·liff /bā'lif/ *n.* 1 sheriff's officer who executes writs, etc. 2 officer serving in a court [OFr, rel. to BAIL[1]]

bai·li·wick /bā'lēwik/ *n.* 1 district of a bailiff 2 person's particular interest [BAILIFF + obs. *wick* district]

bait /bāt/ *n.* 1 food used to entice prey 2 allurement —*v.* 3 harass, torment, or annoy (a person or chained animal) 4 put bait on (a hook, trap, etc.) [ON]

bait'-and-switch' *n.* sales technique in which customer is lured by an attractive offer, then sold another item of lesser value or higher cost

baize /bāz/ *n.* usu. green woolen felted material, used for coverings [Fr *baies* pl. of *bai* bay-colored]

Ba'ja Ca'li·for'nia /bä'hä/ *n.* peninsula in W Mexico extending into the Pacific, enclosing the Gulf of California

Ba'ja Ca'li·for'nia Sur' /sŏŏr'/ *n.* NW state of Mexico; S part of Baja California. Capital: La Paz. Pop. 317,800

bake /bāk/ *v.* (**baked, bak·ing**) cook or become cooked by dry heat, esp. in an oven —**bak'er** *n.* [OE]

baked' beans' *n. pl.* beans baked with molasses, seasoning, and, often, salt pork

bak'er's doz'en *n.* thirteen

Ba·kers·field /bā'kərzfēld'/ *n.* city in Calif. Pop. 174,820

bak·er·y /bā'k(ə)rē/ *n.* (*pl.* **·ies**) place where bread and cakes are made or sold

Bakh·ta·ran /bak'tərän'/ *n.* city in Iran. Pop. 560,500

bak'ing pow'der *n.* mixture of sodium bicarbonate, cream of tartar, etc., used as a raising agent

bak'ing so'da *n.* sodium bicarbonate, used as a raising agent in baking and as an antacid

bak·la·va /bäk'ləvä'/ *n.* rich pastry of flaky dough, honey, and nuts [Turk]

bak·sheesh /bak'sHēsH, bak'sHēsH'/ *n.* gratuity; tip [Pers]

Ba·ku /bäkōō'/ *n.* (also **Ba'ky**) capital of Azerbaijan. Pop. 1,080,500

bal·a·cla·va /bal'əkläv'ə/ *n.* usu. woolen covering for the whole head and neck, except for the face [*Balaklava*, in the Crimea, battle site 1854]

ba·la·lai·ka /bal'əlī'kə/ *n.* guitarlike stringed instrument with a triangular body [Russ]

bal·ance /bal'əns/ *n.* 1a even distribution of weight or amount **b** stability of body or mind 2 apparatus for weighing, esp. one with a central pivot, beam, and two scales 3 counteracting weight or force 4 decisive weight or amount (*balance of opinion*) 5 amount outstanding 6 amount left over 7a *Art.* harmony and proportion **b** *Mus.* relative volume of sources of sound **8 (the Balance)** zodiacal sign or constellation Libra —*v.* (**·anced, ·anc·ing**) **9** bring into, keep, or be in equilibrium **10** offset or compare (one thing) with another **11** counteract, equal, or neutralize the weight or importance of **12** make well-proportioned and harmonious **13a** compare and esp. equalize the debits and credits of (an account) **b** (of an account) have credits and debits equal **14 in the balance** uncertain; at a critical stage **15 on balance** all things considered [OFr fr. L *bilanx* scales]

bal′ance of pay′ments *n.* difference in value between payments into and out of a country

bal′ance of pow′er *n.* situation of nearly equal distribution of power among the chief states of the world

bal′ance of trade′ *n.* difference in value between imports and exports

bal′ance sheet′ *n.* statement giving the balance of an account

Bal·an·chine /balˈənCHēn, -SHēn′/, **George** 1904–83; Russian-born US ballet dancer and choreographer

Bal·bo·a /balbōˈə/, **Vasco Núñez de** 1475–1517; Spanish explorer of America

bal·co·ny /balˈkənē/ *n.* (*pl.* **·nies**) **1** enclosed platform on the outside of a building with access from an upper floor **2** upper tier of seats in a theater, etc. —**bal′co·nied** *adj.* [It]

bald /bôld/ *adj.* **1** lacking some or all hair on the scalp **2** lacking the usual hair, feathers, leaves, etc. **3** having white feathers on the head (*bald eagle*) **4** plain; direct —**bald′ing** *adj.*; **bald′ly** *adv.*; **bald′ness** *n.* [ME]

bal·der·dash /bôlˈdərdasH/ *n.* nonsense

Bald·win /bôlˈdwin/ **1 Stanley** 1867–1947; British prime minister (1923–29; 1935–37) **2 James** 1924–87; US novelist

bale /bāl/ *n.* **1** tightly bound bundle of merchandise or hay —*v.* (**baled, bal·ing**) **2** make up into bales [ME fr. MFr, perh. rel. to Gmc *balla* ball]

Bâle /bäl/ *n.* BASEL

Bal′e·ar′ic Is′lands /balˈē-arˈik/ *n.* group of islands in the W Mediterranean Sea, a province of Spain

ba·leen /bəlēn′/ *n.* whalebone [L *balaena* whale]

bale·ful /bālˈfəl/ *adj.* **1** menacing in look, manner, etc. **2** malignant; destructive —**bale′ful·ly** *adv.*; **bale′ful·ness** *n.* [OE, rel. to archaic *bale* evil]

Bal·four /balˈfər, -fôr′/, **Arthur James** 1848–1930; British statesman; prime minister (1902–05)

Ba·li /bälˈē, balˈē/ *n.* Indonesian island E of Java

Ba·lik·pa·pan /bälˈikpäpˈän′/ *n.* seaport in Indonesia on Borneo. Pop. 280,700

balk /bôk/ *n.* **1** obstacle **2** heavy timber **3** *Baseball.* feigned pitch, an illegal motion —*v.* **4** stop; refuse to proceed **5** *Baseball.* commit a balk **6** deter from proceeding [ME fr. OE]

Bal′kan Pen·in′su·la /bôlˈkən/ *n.* peninsula in S Europe between the Adriatic and Black seas

Bal′kan States′ *n.* (also called **Bal′kans**) countries of the Balkan Peninsula: Albania, Bulgaria, Greece, Rumania, former Yugoslavia, and European Turkey

ball[1] /bôl/ *n.* **1** sphere, esp. for use in a game **2a** spherical object; material in the shape of a ball **b** rounded part of the body **3** ammunition for a cannon, musket, etc. **4** *Baseball.* single delivery of a ball that is not struck by the batter and is not called a strike by the umpire —*v.* **5** form into a ball **6 on the ball** *Colloq.* alert; efficient [ON]

ball[2] *n.* **1** formal social gathering for dancing **2** *Slang.* enjoyable time [Fr fr. L fr. Gk *ballizein* dance]

bal·lad /balˈəd/ *n.* **1** poem or song narrating a popular story **2** slow sentimental song —**bal′lad·eer′, bal′lad·ry** *n.* [Prov. rel. to BALL[2]]

ball′-and-sock′et joint′ *n.* joint in which a rounded end pivots in a concave socket

bal·last /balˈəst/ *n.* **1** heavy material stabilizing a ship, the car of a balloon, etc. **2** coarsely crushed stone as the bed of a railway track or road —*v.* **3** provide with ballast [LGer or Scand]

ball′ bear′ing *n.* **1** bearing in which friction is relieved by a ring of steel balls **2** one of these balls

ball′boy′ *n.* (*fem.* **ball′girl′**) *Tennis.* boy or girl who retrieves balls

ball′cock′ *n.* floating ball on a hinged arm controlling the water intake in a cistern

bal·le·ri·na /balˈərēˈnə/ *n.* female ballet dancer [It, rel. to BALL[2]]

bal·let /balā′, balˈā′/ *n.* **1** dramatic or representational style of dancing to music **2** particular piece or performance of ballet —**bal·let·ic** /baletˈik/ *adj.* [Fr fr. It, rel. to BALL[2]]

ball′game′ *n.* **1** game played with a ball **2** *Colloq.* affair; matter; set of circumstances

bal·lis′tic mis′sile *n.* guided missile that is powered and controlled by gravity, atmospheric conditions, etc.

bal·lis·tics /balisˈtiks/ *n. pl.* (usu. treated as *sing.*) **1** science of projectiles and firearms **2 go ballistic** *Colloq.* to become suddenly very angry —**bal·lis′tic** *adj.*

ball′ joint′ BALL-AND-SOCKET JOINT

bal·loon /bəlōōn′/ *n.* **1** small inflatable rubber toy or decoration **2** large bag filled with light gas to allow it to rise, often carrying a basket for passengers **3** *Colloq.* balloon shape enclosing dialogue in a comic strip or cartoon —*v.* **4** (cause to) swell out like a balloon **5** travel by balloon —**bal·loon′ist** *n.* [Fr or It: large ball]

bal·lot /balˈət/ *n.* **1** occasion or system of voting, in writing and usu. secret **2** total of such votes **3** paper, etc., on which a vote is recorded —*v.* **4** give a vote **5** take a ballot of [It *ballotta*, rel. to BALLOON]

bal′lot-box′ *n.* sealed box for completed ballot-papers

ball′park′ *n.* **1** stadium where baseball is played **2** *Colloq.* sphere of activity, etc. —*adj.* **3** *Colloq.* approximate **4 in the ballpark** *Colloq.* within acceptable range of being correct

ball′point′ *n.* (in full **ball′point′ pen′**) pen with a tiny ball as its writing point

ball′room′ *n.* large room for dancing

bal·ly·hoo /balˈēhōō′/ *n.* **1** loud noise or fuss **2** noisy publicity —*v.* (**·hooed, ·hoo·ing**) **3** publicize blatantly

balm /bä(l)m/ *n.* aromatic, soothing ointment or oil [L, rel. to BALSAM]

balm·y /bä(l)′mē/ *adj.* (·i·er, ·i·est) 1 mild and fragrant; soothing 2 *Slang.* esp. *Brit.* slightly crazy; eccentric —**balm′i·ly** *adv.*; **balm′i·ness** *n.*

ba·lo·ney /bəlō′nē/ *n.* 1 var. of BOLOGNA 2 nonsense

bal·sa /bôl′sə/ *n.* 1 (in full **bal′sa wood′**) tough lightweight wood used for making rafts, models, etc. 2 tropical American tree yielding it [Sp: raft]

bal·sam /bôl′səm/ *n.* 1 resin exuded from various trees and shrubs 2 ointment, esp. containing oil or turpentine 3 tree or shrub yielding balsam —**bal·sam·ic** /bôlsam′ik/ *adj.* [Gk *balsamon*]

Bal·tic Sea /bôl′tik/ *n.* sea in N Europe W of Lithuania, Latvia, and Estonia

Bal·ti·more /bôl′təmôr′/ *n.* city in Md. Pop. 736,014

Bal·ti·more, Lord see CALVERT

bal·us·ter /bal′əstər/ *n.* short post or pillar supporting a rail [Gk *balaustion* wild-pomegranate flower]

bal·us·trade /bal′əstrād′/ *n.* railing supported by balusters —**bal′us·trad′ed** *adj.*

Bal·zac /bôl′zak, bal′-/, Honoré de 1799–1850; French novelist

Ba·ma·ko /bam′əkō/ *n.* capital of Mali. Pop. 745,800

bam·boo /bambōō′/ *n.* 1 tropical woody grass with jointed, hollow stems 2 its stem, used for canes, furniture, etc. [Du fr. Malay]

bam′boo cur′tain *n. Hist.* term for the political barrier enclosing Communist-controlled SE Asia

bam·boo·zle /bambōō′zəl/ *v.* (·zled, ·zling) *Colloq.* cheat; mystify —**bam·boo′zle·ment** *n.*

ban /ban/ *v.* (**banned, ban·ning**) 1 forbid, prohibit, esp. formally 2 formal prohibition [OE: summon]

ba·nal /bənal′, banal′, bān′l/ *adj.* trite; commonplace —**ba·nal·i·ty** /bənal′ətē/ *n.* (*pl.* ·ties); **ba′nal·ly** *adv.* [Fr, rel. to BAN]

ba·nan·a /bənan′ə/ *n.* 1 long curved soft fruit with a yellow skin 2 treelike plant bearing it 3 **go bananas** *Slang.* go mad 4 **top banana** (esp. in vaudeville) featured comedian [Port or Sp, fr. a W Afr language]

ba·nan′a re·pub′lic *n. Derog.* small state, esp. in Central America, dependent on foreign capital

band¹ /band/ *n.* 1 flat, thin strip or loop of paper, metal, cloth, etc., put around something, esp. to hold or decorate it 2a strip of material on a garment b stripe 3 range of frequencies, wavelengths, or values —*v.* 4 put a band on [MFr fr. Gmc or perh. ON]

band² *n.* 1 organized group, esp. of nonclassical musicians —*v.* 2 unite [MFr fr. It *banda*]

band·age /ban′dij/ *n.* 1 strip of material used to bind a wound —*v.* (·aged, ·ag·ing) 2 bind with a bandage [Fr, rel. to BAND¹]

Band′-Aid′ *n.* 1 *Tdmk.* adhesive strip with gauze panel for covering minor cuts, etc. 2 (also **band-aid**) any temporary or makeshift remedy

ban·dan·na /bandan′ə/ *n.* (also **ban·dan′a**) large patterned handkerchief [Port fr. Hindi]

Ban·dar Se·ri Be·ga·wan /bən′dər ser′ē bəgä′wən/ *n.* capital of Brunei. Pop. 21,500

b. & b. *abbr.* (also **B. & B., B. and B., b. and b.**) bed and breakfast

band′box′ *n.* box to hold collars, etc.

ban·deau /bandō′/ *n.* (*pl.* ·deaux /-dōz′/) narrow ribbon [Fr]

ban·dit /ban′dit/ *n.* robber or outlaw, esp. one attacking travelers, etc. —**ban′dit·ry** *n.* [It]

ban·do·leer /ban′dəlēr′/ *n.* (also **ban′do·lier′**) shoulder belt with loops or pockets for cartridges [MFr]

band′saw′ *n.* mechanical saw with a blade formed by an endless band

bands′man *n.* (*pl.* ·men) player in a band

band′stand′ *n.* outdoor platform for musicians

Ban·dung /ban′dŏŏng/ *n.* city in Indonesia on Java. Pop. 1,462,600

band′wag′on *n.* 1 vehicle carrying a band in a parade 2 **climb** (or **jump**) **on the bandwagon** join a popular or successful cause, etc.

ban·dy /ban′dē/ *v.* (·died, ·dy·ing) 1 pass (a story, rumor, etc.) to and fro 2 discuss disparagingly 3 exchange (blows, insults, etc.) [perh. fr. MFr]

ban′dy-leg′ged *adj.* having legs bowed so as to be wide apart at the knees [perh. fr. obs. *bandy* curved stick]

bane /bān/ *n.* 1 cause of ruin or trouble 2 *Archaic.* (except in *comb.*) poison (*ratsbane*) —**bane′ful** *adj.* [OE]

bang /baNG/ *n.* 1 loud short sound 2 sharp blow 3 (usu. *pl.*) fringe of hair cut straight across the forehead —*v.* 4 strike or shut noisily 5 (cause to) make a bang 6 *Slang.* thrill —*adv.* 7 with a bang 8 *Colloq.* exactly 9 abruptly [ON, prob. orig. imit.]

Ban·ga·lore /baNG′gəlôr′/ *n.* city in SW India. Pop. 2,650,700

Bang·kok /baNG′käk′, -kök′/ *n.* capital of Thailand. Pop. 5,876,000

Ban·gla·desh /baNG′glədesH′, bäNG′-/ *n.* republic in S Asia, on the N coast of the Bay of Bengal. Capital: Dhaka. Pop. 110,602,000 —**Ban·gla·desh′i** *n.*

ban·gle /baNG′gəl/ *n.* rigid bracelet or anklet [Hindi *bangri*]

Ban·gui /bäNG-gē′/ *n.* capital of Central African Republic. Pop. 451,700

ban·ish /ban′isH/ *v.* 1 condemn to exile 2 dismiss (esp. from one's mind) —**ban′ish·ment** *n.* [Gmc, rel. to BAN]

BANISTER

ban·is·ter /ban′əstər/ *n.* (also **ban′nis·ter**) (usu. *pl.*) handrail on uprights beside a staircase [corruption of BALUSTER]

Ban·jer·ma·sin /bän'jərmäs'in/ *n.* seaport in Indonesia on Borneo. Pop. 381,300

45

Banjermasin / barbel

ban·jo /ban'jō/ *n.* (*pl.* ·jos or ·joes) guitar-like stringed instrument with a circular body —**ban'jo·ist** *n.* [US southern corruption of *bandore* fr. Gk *pandoura* lute]

Ban·jul /bän'jŏŏl'/ *n.* capital of the Gambia. Pop. 44,200

bank¹ /bäNGk/ *n.* 1 sloping ground, esp. beside a river 2 mass of cloud, fog, snow, etc. —*v.* 3 heap or rise into banks 4 pack (a fire) tightly for slow burning 5a (of a vehicle, aircraft, etc.) round a curve with one side higher than the other b cause to do this [ON, rel. to BENCH]

bank² *n.* 1 establishment for depositing, withdrawing, and borrowing money 2 kitty in some gambling games 3 storage place —*v.* 4 deposit or keep (money, etc.) in a bank 5 **bank on** *Colloq.* rely on —**bank'a·ble** *adj.* [Fr *banque* or It *banca*, rel. to BANK¹]

bank³ *n.* 1 row of similar objects, e.g., lights, switches, oars —*v.* 2 arrange in a row or rows [Fr *banc* fr. Gmc, rel. to BANK¹]

bank'book' *n.* book in which bank deposits and withdrawals are recorded

bank'er *n.* 1 owner or manager of a bank 2 keeper of the bank in some gambling games

bank'ing *n.* business of running a bank

bank'note' *n.* piece of paper money

bank·rupt /baNG'krəpt/ *adj.* 1 legally declared insolvent 2 drained of or lacking in (emotion, morals, etc.) —*n.* 3 insolvent person —*v.* 4 make bankrupt —**bank'rupt·cy** *n.* (*pl.* ·cies) [It *banca rotta* broken bank]

ban·ner /ban'ər/ *n.* 1 large sign bearing a slogan or design, esp. in a demonstration or procession; flag 2 newspaper headline occupying most or all the page width [L *bandum* standard]

ban·nis·ter /ban'əstər/ *n.* var. of BANISTER

Ban·nis·ter /ban'əstər/, (Sir) **Roger Gilbert** 1929– ; British athlete; first to run mile in under four minutes (1954)

banns /banz/ *n. pl.* notice announcing an intended marriage, read out in a parish church [pl. of BAN]

ban·quet /baNG'kwit/ *n.* 1 sumptuous, esp. formal, feast or dinner —*v.* 2 attend, or entertain with, a banquet; feast [Fr dim. of *banc* bench]

ban·quette /baNGket'/ *n.* upholstered bench, esp. in a restaurant or bar [Fr fr. It]

ban·shee /ban'SHē, banSHē'/ *n.* *Ir.* & *Scot.* wailing female spirit warning of death in a house [Ir: fairy woman]

ban·tam /bant'əm/ *n.* 1 a kind of small domestic fowl 2 small but aggressive person [appar. fr. *Bäntän* in Java]

ban'tam·weight' *n.* *Sports.* weight class for competitors; in professional boxing, includes fighters up to 118 lbs.

ban·ter /bant'ər/ *n.* 1 good-humored teasing —*v.* 2 tease 3 exchange banter

Ban·tu /ban'tōō/ *n.* (*pl.* same or ·tus) 1 member of an extensive black ethnic group of central and southern Africa 2 any of a family of languages spoken by them —*adj.* 3 of these peoples or their languages

ban·yan /ban'yən/ *n.* Indian fig tree with self-rooting branches [Port fr. Skt: trader]

ba·o·bab /bā'əbab', bou'bab'/ *n.* African tree with a massive trunk and large pulpy fruit [prob. Afr dial.]

bap·tism /bap'tiz'əm/ *n.* 1 symbolic admission to the Christian Church, with water and usu. name-giving 2 any initiation —**bap·tis'mal** /-tiz'məl/ *adj.* [Gk *baptizein* baptize]

Bap'tist *n.* Christian advocating baptism by total immersion

bap·tis·ter·y /bap'tistrē/ *n.* (*pl.* ·ies) 1 part of a church or separate church building used for baptism 2 (in a Baptist chapel) receptacle used for immersion

bap·tize /bap'tīz'/ *v.* (·tized, ·tiz·ing) 1 administer baptism to 2 give a name or nickname to

bar¹ /bär/ *n.* 1 long piece of rigid material, used esp. to confine or obstruct 2 something of similar form 3a counter for serving alcohol, etc. b room or building containing it c small shop or stall serving refreshments 4a barrier b restriction 5a railed enclosure in a court of law b lawyers collectively 6 any of the sections into which a piece of music is divided by vertical lines —*v.* (**barred, bar·ring**) 7 fasten with a bar or bars 8 shut or keep in or out 9 obstruct; prevent —*prep.* 10 except [Fr]

bar² *n.* esp. *Meteorol.* unit of pressure, 10⁵ newtons per square meter, approx. one atmosphere [Gk *baros* weight]

Bar·ab·bas /barab'əs/ (in the Bible) prisoner released instead of Jesus

barb /bärb/ *n.* 1 sharp backward-facing projection from an arrow, fishhook, etc. 2 hurtful remark —*v.* 3 furnish with a barb —**barbed** *adj.* [L *barba* beard]

Bar·ba·dos /bärbād'ōs, -ōz/ *n.* island country in the E West Indies. Capital: Bridgetown. Pop. 259,000 —**Bar·ba'di·an** /-dēən/ *n.* & *adj.*

bar·bar·i·an /bärber'ēən/ *n.* 1 uncultured or brutish person 2 member of a primitive tribe, etc. —*adj.* 3 rough and uncultured 4 uncivilized —**bar'bar'i·an·ism'** *n.* [Gk *barbaros* foreign]

bar·bar·ic /bärber'ik/ *adj.* 1 uncultured; brutal 2 primitive

bar·ba·rism /bär'bəriz'əm/ *n.* 1 barbaric state or act 2 nonstandard word or expression

bar·bar·i·ty /bärber'ətē/ *n.* (*pl.* ·ties) 1 savage cruelty 2 brutal act

Bar·ba·ros·sa /bär'bərōs'ə/ see FREDERICK I

bar·ba·rous /bär'bərəs/ *adj.* BARBARIC

Bar·ba·ry Coast /bär'barē/ *n.* Mediterranean coast of the former Barbary States, in N Africa

Bar'ba·ry States' *n. Hist.* Morocco, Algiers, Tunis, and Tripoli; pirate refuges between 1520–1830

bar·be·cue /bär'bikyōō'/ *n.* 1a food cooked over charcoal or an open fire out of doors b meat prepared in a spicy sauce to be cooked this way 2 party at which such fare is featured 3 grill, etc., used for this —*v.* (·cued, ·cu·ing) 4 cook this way [Sp fr. Haitian]

barbed' wire' *n.* (also **barb'wire'**) wire with interwoven sharp spikes, used in fences and barriers

bar·bel /bär'bəl/ *n.* fleshy filament at the mouth of some fishes [L, rel. to BARB]

bar·bell /bär'bel'/ *n.* iron bar with removable weights at each end, used for weightlifting

bar·ber /bär'bər/ *n.* 1 person who cuts men's hair, etc., by profession —*v.* 2 cut the hair (of), shave, etc. —**bar'ber·shop**' *n.* [MedL *barba* beard]

bar·ber·ry /bär'ber'ē/ *n.* (*pl.* ·ries) 1 shrub with yellow flowers and red berries 2 its berry [Fr *berberis*]

bar·bi·tu·rate /bärbicH'ərət/ *n.* soporific or sedative drug from barbituric acid [Ger, fr. the name *Barbara*]

bar·ca·role /bär'kərōl'/ *n.* 1 gondoliers' song 2 music imitating this [It *barca* boat]

Bar·ce·lo·na /bär'səlō'nə/ *n.* seaport in NE Spain on the Mediterranean. Pop. 1,623,500

bar' code' *n.* machine-readable striped code on packaging, etc.; universal product code

bard /bärd/ *n.* 1 *Poet.* poet 2 *Hist.* Celtic minstrel —**bard'ic** *adj.* [Celt]

bare /bar, ber/ *adj.* 1 unclothed; 2 leafless; unfurnished; empty 3 plain; unadorned 4 scanty; just sufficient —*v.* (**bared, bar·ing**) 5 uncover, reveal —**bare'ness** *n.* [OE]

bare'back' *adj.* & *adv.* without a saddle

bare'faced' *adj.* shameless, impudent

bare'foot' *adj.* & *adv.* (also **bare'foot'ed**) wearing nothing on the feet

bare'head'ed *adj.* & *adv.* wearing nothing on the head

Ba·reil·ly /bərāl'ē/ *n.* city in N India. Pop. 583,500

bare·ly /bar'lē, ber'-/ *adv.* 1 scarcely 2 scantily 3 obviously

bar·gain /bär'gən/ *n.* 1 agreement on the terms of a sale, etc. 2 this from the buyer's viewpoint 3 something costing less than expected —*v.* 4 discuss the terms of a sale, etc. 5 **bargain for** (or **on**) be prepared for; expect 6 **in** (or **into**) **the bargain** moreover; besides [Fr fr. Gmc]

barge /bärj/ *n.* 1 long flat-bottomed cargo boat on a canal or river 2 long ornamental pleasure boat —*v.* (**barged, barg·ing**) 3 intrude rudely or awkwardly [MedL *barga*]

Ba·ri /bär'ē/ *n.* (also **Ba'ri del'le Pu'glie** /del'ə pōōl'yä/) seaport in SE Italy on the Adriatic. Pop. 353,000

bar·i·tone /bar'ətōn'/ *n.* 1a second lowest adult male singing voice b singer with this voice 2 instrument pitched second lowest in its family [Gk *barus* heavy + *tonos* tone]

bar·i·um /bar'ēəm, ber'-/ *n.* white soft metallic element; *symb.* **Ba** [Gk *barus* heavy]

bark¹ /bärk/ *n.* 1 sharp explosive cry of a dog, fox, etc. 2 sound like this —*v.* 3 (of a dog, etc.) give a bark 4 speak or utter sharply or brusquely 5 **bark up the wrong tree** misguide one's efforts [OE]

bark² *n.* 1 tough outer skin of tree trunks, branches, etc. —*v.* 2 graze (one's shin, etc.) 3 strip bark from [Scand]

bar'keep'er *n.* 1 owner of a BAR¹, 2 bartender

bark'er *n.* person at a sideshow, etc., employed to proclaim its attractions to draw an audience

bar·ley /bär'lē/ *n.* 1 cereal used as food and in spirits 2 its grain [OE]

bar'maid' *n.* female bartender

bar'man' *n.* male bartender

bar mitz·vah /bär mits'və/ *n.* (see also BAT MITZVAH) 1 religious initiation ceremony of a Jewish boy at 13 2 boy undergoing this —*v.* 3 administer bar mitzvah to [Heb: son of the commandment]

barn /bärn/ *n.* farm building for storing grain, etc. [OE: barley house]

bar·na·cle /bär'nikəl/ *n.* 1 marine crustacean clinging to rocks, ships' bottoms, etc. 2 tenacious attendant or follower [Fr or MedL]

Bar·nard /bär'nərd/, **Christiaan Neethling** 1922– ; South African surgeon; performed first human heart transplant (1967)

Bar·na·ul /bär'nəōl'/ *n.* city in Russia on the Ob River. Pop. 606,800

barn'storm' *v.* tour rural areas as an actor or political campaigner —**barn'storm'er** *n.*

Bar·num /bär'nəm/, **P(hineas) T(aylor)** 1810–91; US showman and circus owner

barn'yard' *n.* area around a barn

Ba·ro·da /bərōd'ə/ *n.* city in W India. Pop. 1,021,100

ba·rom·e·ter /bəräm'ətər/ *n.* 1 instrument measuring atmospheric pressure, used in meteorology 2 anything that reflects change —**bar'o·met'ric** /-əme'trik/ *adj.* [Gk *baros* weight + -METER]

bar·on /bar'ən/ *n.* 1 member of the lowest order of nobility 2 powerful businessman, entrepreneur, etc. —**ba·ro·ni·al** /bərō'nēəl/ *adj.* [MedL: man]

bar·on·ess *n.* 1 woman holding the rank of baron 2 baron's wife or widow

bar·on·et /bar'ənət/ *n.* member of the lowest hereditary titled British order —**bar'on·et'cy** *n.* (*pl.* ·cies)

bar·o·ny /bar'ənē/ *n.* (*pl.* ·nies) domain or rank of a baron

ba·roque /bərōk'/ *adj.* 1 highly ornate and extravagant in style, typical of European art, decoration, and music of the 17th and 18th cent. 2 of this period —*n.* 3 baroque style or art [Port, orig. misshapen pearl]

Bar·qui·si·me·to /bär'kēsēmä'tō/ *n.* city in N Venezuela. Pop. 602,600

bar·rack /bar'ək, ber'-/ *n.* (often *pl.*) 1 housing for soldiers 2 large bleak building —*v.* 3 lodge (soldiers, etc.) in barracks [It or Sp]

bar·ra·cu·da /bar'əkōōd'ə/ *n.* (*pl.* same or ·das) voracious tropical marine fish [Sp]

bar·rage /bəräZH'/ *n.* 1 concentrated artillery bombardment 2 rapid succession of questions or criticisms *v.* (·**raged, ·rag·ing**) 3 subject to a barrage [Fr *barrer* BAR¹]

Bar·ran·qui·lla /bä'ränkē'(l)yə/ *n.* seaport in Colombia on the Magdalena River. Pop. 896,600

barre /bär/ *n.* horizontal bar at waist level, used in dance exercises [Fr]

bar·rel /bar'əl/ *n.* 1 cylindrical usu. convex container 2 its contents 3 measure of capacity (31.5 gallons) 4 cylindrical tube forming part of an object, e.g., a gun or a pen —*v.* (·**reled** or **·relled, ·rel·ing** or **·rel·ling**) 5 put into a barrel or barrels 6 move along at high speed 7 **over a barrel** *Colloq.* helpless, at a person's mercy [Fr]

bar'rel or'gan *n.* mechanical musical instrument in which air is blown into pipes from bellows controlled by a crank

bar·ren /bar'ən/ *adj.* **1a** unable to bear young (of land, a tree, etc.) **b** unproductive **2** unprofitable, dull —**bar'ren·ness** *n.* [Fr]

Bar·rett /bar'it/, **Elizabeth** see BROWNING

bar·rette /bərĕt'/ *n.* clasp for the hair

bar·ri·cade /bar'əkād'/ *n.* **1** barrier, esp. improvised —*v.* (**·cad·ed, ·cad·ing**) **2** block or defend with this [Fr *barrique* cask]

Bar·rie /bar'ē/, (Sir) J(ames) M(atthew) 1860–1937; Scottish dramatist and novelist

bar·ri·er /bar'ēər/ *n.* **1** fence, etc., that bars advance or access **2** obstacle [Rom. rel. to BAR¹]

bar·ring /bär'ING/ *prep.* except; not including

bar·ris·ter /bar'əstər/ *n.* (in England) advocate entitled to practice in the higher courts [fr. BAR¹; cf. MINISTER]

bar'room' *n.* establishment serving alcoholic drinks at a bar

bar·row¹ /bar'ō/ *n.* **1** two-wheeled handcart **2** WHEELBARROW [OE, rel. to BEAR¹]

bar·row² *n.* ancient grave-mound [OE]

Bar·ry·more /bar'ēmôr'/ family of US actors: **1 Lionel** 1878–1954 **2 Ethel** 1879–1959 **3 John** 1882–1942

bar'tend'er *n.* person serving alcoholic drinks at a bar

bar·ter /bär'tər/ *v.* **1** trade in goods without using money **2** exchange (goods) —*n.* **3** trade by bartering [perh. fr. Fr]

Barth /bärt/, (for **2**) bärTH/ **1 Karl** 1886–1968; Swiss Protestant theologian **2 John** 1930– ; US writer

Barthes /bärt/, **Roland** 1915–80; French writer and critic

Bar·tók /bär'tôk', -täk'/, **Béla** 1881–1945; Hungarian composer

Bar·ton /bärt'n/, **Clara** 1821–1912; US founder of the American Red Cross

bar·y·on /bar'ēän'/ *n.* heavy elementary particle (i.e., a nucleon or a hyperon) [Gk *barus* heavy]

Ba·rysh·ni·kov /bərisH'nikôf'/, **Mikhail** 1948– ; Russian-born US ballet dancer

ba·sal /bā'səl, -zəl/ *adj.* of, at, or forming a base

ba'sal me·tab'o·lism *n.* amount of energy consumed by an organism while at rest

ba·salt /bəsôlt', bā'sôlt'/ *n.* a dark volcanic rock —**ba·sal'tic** *adj.* [L *basaltes* fr. Gk]

base¹ /bās/ *n.* **1a** part supporting from beneath or serving as a foundation **b** notional support or foundation (*power base*) **2** principle or starting point **3** headquarters **4** main or important ingredient **5** *Math.* number in terms of which other numbers or logarithms are expressed **6** *Chem.* substance capable of combining with an acid to form a salt **7** *Baseball.* any of the four bags, etc., placed at the corners of the diamond to mark the runner's circuit —*v.* (**based, bas·ing**) **8** found or establish **9** station —*adj.* **10** serving as a base [Gk *basis* stepping]

base² *adj.* **1** cowardly; despicable **2** menial; low **3** low in quality **4** (of a metal) low in value —**base'ly** *adv.*; **base'ness** *n.* [L *bassus*]

base'ball' *n.* **1** game played by two opposing teams on a diamond-shaped field marked at each corner with a base, the object being to outscore the opponent in the number of players completing a circuit of the bases **2** ball used in this

base'board' *n.* vertical wooden trim at the bottom of a wall in a room

base' hit' *n. Baseball.* fair ball enabling its batter to reach base without an error or the forcing out of a teammate

Ba·sel /bäz'əl/ *n.* (also **Bâle; Basle**) city in Switzerland on the Rhine River. Pop. 171,000

base'less *adj.* unfounded, groundless

base'line' *n.* **1** line used as a base or starting point **2** line marking each end of a tennis or basketball court **3** *Baseball.* running path between bases

base'ment *n.* floor of a building below ground level

base' on balls' *n. Baseball.* advance to first base by a batter to whom a pitcher has thrown four balls; walk

base' pay' *n.* amount paid for a slated period, excluding overtime, etc.

bash /basH/ *v.* **1** strike bluntly or heavily —*n.* **2** *Slang.* party [imit.]

bash'ful *adj.* shy; diffident —**bash'ful·ly** *adv.*; **bash'ful·ness** *n.* [as ABASHED]

bas·ic /bā'sik/ *adj.* **1** serving as a base; fundamental —*n.* **2** (usu. *pl.*) fundamental facts or principles —**ba'si·cal·ly** *adv.*

BASIC *n.* computer programming language using familiar English words [Beginner's All-purpose Symbolic Instruction Code]

Ba·sie /bā'sē/, **"Count"** (**William**) 1904–84; US jazz pianist, composer, and bandleader

ba·sil /baz'əl, bāz'-/ *n.* aromatic herb used as flavoring [Gk *basilikos* royal]

Bas·il, St. /baz'əl, bē'zəl/ *c.* 330–379; early Christian bishop

ba·sil·i·ca /bəsil'ikə/ *n.* **1** ancient Roman hall with an apse and colonnades, used as a court of law, etc. **2** similar building as a Christian church [Gk *basilikē* (*stoa*) royal (portico)]

ba·sin /bā'sən/ *n.* **1** shallow open vessel for holding liquids or preparing food **2** sink **3** hollow depression **4** sheltered mooring area **5** area drained by a river —**ba'sin·ful** *n.* (*pl.* **-fuls**) [MedL *ba(s)cinus*]

ba·sis /bā'səs/ *n.* (*pl.* **·ses** /-sēz'/) **1** foundation or support **2** main principle or ingredient **3** starting-point [Gk, rel. to BASE¹]

bask /bask/ *v.* **1** relax in warmth and light **2** revel in this [ON, rel. to BATHE]

bas·ket /bas'kət/ *n.* **1** container made of interwoven cane, reed, wire, etc. **2** amount held by this **3** the goal in basketball, or a goal scored [Fr]

bas'ket·ball' *n.* **1** game in which goals are scored by putting the ball through a net suspended from a circular rim **2** ball used in this

bas'ket case' *n. Colloq.* completely helpless person

bas·ket·ry /bas'kətrē/ *n.* **1** art of weaving cane, etc. **2** work so produced

bas'ket weave' *n.* flat, open woven pattern

bas'ket·work' *n.* BASKETRY

bas' mitz'vah /bäs/ BAT MITZVAH

Basque /bask/ *n.* **1** member of a people of the Western Pyrenees **2** their language —*adj.* **3** of the Basques or their language [L *Vasco*]

Bas·ra /bäs'rə, bäz'-/ *n.* city in SE Iraq. Pop. 616,700

bas-re·lief /bä' rilēf'/ *n.* sculpture or carving with figures projecting slightly from the background [Fr and It]

bass¹ /bās/ *n.* **1a** lowest adult male singing voice **b** singer with this voice **2** instrument pitched lowest in its family **3** low-frequency output of a radio, record player, etc. —*adj.* **4** lowest in musical pitch **5** deep-sounding —**bass'ist** *n.* [fr. BASE² altered after It *basso*]

bass² /bas/ *n.* (*pl.* same or **bass·es**) **1** common perch **2** other spiny-finned fish of the perch family [OE]

bas·set /bas'it/ *n.* sturdy hunting dog with a long body and short legs [Fr dim. of *bas* low]

Basse-terre /bäs ter'/ *n.* capital of St. Kitts and Nevis. Pop. 18,500

Basse-Terre /bäs ter'/ *n.* capital of Guadeloupe. Pop. 14,100

bas·si·net /bas'ənet'/ *n.* infant's basketlike cradle, usu. hooded [Fr dim. of *bassin* BASIN]

bas·so /bas'ō, bäs'ō/ *n.* (*pl.* -sos) singer with a bass voice [It: BASS¹]

BASSOON

bas·soon /bəsōōn'/ *n.* bass instrument of the oboe family —**bas·soon'ist** *n.* [It, rel. to BASS¹]

bast /bast/ *n.* fiber from the inner bark of a tree, used for ropes, etc. [OE]

bas·tard /bas'tərd/ *often Offens. n.* **1** person born of an unmarried mother **2** *Slang.* unpleasant or despicable person **3** something inferior, irregular, etc. —*adj.* **4** illegitimate by birth **5** unauthorized; counterfeit; hybrid —**bas'tard·y** *n.* [Fr fr. MedL]

bas'tard·ize *v.* (·**ized, ·iz·ing**) **1** corrupt; debase **2** declare (a person) illegitimate —**bas'-tard·i·za'tion** *n.*

baste¹ /bāst/ *v.* (**bast·ed, bast·ing**) moisten (meat) with cooking juices, etc., during cooking

baste² *v.* (**bast·ed, bast·ing**) sew with large loose stitches; tack [Fr fr. Gmc]

bas·tion /bas'CHən/ *n.* **1** projecting part of a fortification **2** thing regarded as protecting [It *bastire* build]

Ba·su'to·land /bəsōō'tōōland', -tōland'/ *n.* see LESOTHO

bat¹ /bat/ *n.* **1** implement with a handle, used for hitting balls in games **2** player's turn with this **3** blow —*v.* (**bat·ted, bat·ting**) **4** hit with or as with a bat **5** take a turn at batting [OE fr. Fr]

bat² *n.* mouselike nocturnal flying mammal [Scand]

bat³ *v.* (**bat·ted, bat·ting**) blink [var. of obs. *bate* flutter]

batch /bacH/ *n.* **1** group of things or persons considered or dealt with together **2** quantity of loaves of bread, cakes, etc., produced at one baking **3** *Comp.* group of records processed as one unit —*v.* **4** arrange or deal with in batches [rel. to BAKE]

bat·ed /bāt'id/ *adj.* as in **with bated breath** very anxiously [as ABATE]

bath /baTH/ *n.* (*pl.* **baths** /baTHz, baTHs/) **1** TUB, 3 **2** act of washing the body in a bathtub **3** BATHHOUSE **4** liquid for immersing or treating something [OE]

bathe /bāTH/ *v.* (**bathed, bath·ing**) **1** immerse in water, esp. to swim or wash **2** soak **3** (of sunlight, etc.) envelop [OE]

bath'house /baTH-/ *n.* public building with baths

bath'ing suit /bāTH'iNG/ *n.* garment worn for swimming

bath-mat /baTH'mat'/ *n.* cloth for standing on after a bath or shower

ba·thos /bā'THäs/ *n.* lapse in mood from the sublime to the absurd or trivial; anticlimax —**ba·thet'ic** /bəTHet'ik/ *adj.* [Gk: depth]

bath'robe /baTH-/ *n.* loose-fitting absorbent robe worn after bathing

bath'room /baTH'rōōm', -rŏŏm'/ *n.* room with a toilet and sink, and often with a bathtub or shower

bath' salts *n. pl.* soluble powder or crystals for scenting or softening bath water

bath·y·scaphe /baTH'əskaf', -skäf'/ *n.* (also **bath'y·scaph'**) manned vessel for deep-sea diving [Gk *bathus* deep + *skaphos* ship]

bath·y·sphere /baTH'əsfēr'/ *n.* vessel for deep-sea observation [Gk *bathus* deep + SPHERE]

ba·tik /bətēk'/ *n.* **1** method of dyeing textiles by applying wax to parts to be left uncolored **2** cloth so treated [Javanese: painted]

Ba·tis·ta /bətē'stə/, Fulgencio 1901–73; president of Cuba (1940–44; 1954–59)

ba·tiste /batēst'/ *n.* fine linen or cotton cloth [Fr fr. *Baptiste*, name of the first maker]

bat mitz·vah /bät mits'və, bäs-/ *n.* (also **bath mitz'vah, bas mitz'vah**) (see also BAR MITZ-VAH) **1** religious initiation ceremony of a Jewish girl at 13 **2** girl undergoing this —*v.* **3** administer bat mitzvah to [Heb: daughter of the commandment]

ba·ton /bətän', ba-/ *n.* **1** thin stick for conducting an orchestra **2** short stick passed on in a relay race **3** stick carried by a drum major **4** staff of office [Fr fr. L]

Bat·on Rouge /bat'n rōōzh'/ *n.* capital of La., in the SE part. Pop. 219,531

bat·tal·ion /bətal'yən/ *n.* army unit, part of a division [It *battaglia* BATTLE]

bat·ten¹ /bat'n/ *n.* **1** narrow flat strip of wood used as a stiffener, etc. **2** horizontal strip of wood to which laths, etc., are fastened **3** wooden strip covering joints between boards **4** strip for securing tarpaulin over a ship's hatchway —*v.* **5** strengthen or fasten with battens [Fr, rel. to BATTER]

bat·ten² *v.* thrive at the expense of (another) [ON]

bat·ter¹ /bat'ər/ *v.* **1** strike hard and repeatedly **2** subject to long-term violence —**bat'-ter·er** *n.* [Fr *battre* beat, rel. to BATTLE]

bat·ter² *n.* mixture of flour, egg, and milk or water, used for pancakes, etc. [Fr, rel. to BATTER¹]

bat·ter³ *n.* player who bats, as in baseball

bat′ter·ing ram′ *n.* beam used in breaking down doors, gates, etc.

bat·ter·y /bat′ərē/ *n.* (*pl.* **·ies**) **1** electrically charged cell or cells as a source of current **2** set of similar units of equipment; series; sequence **3** emplacement for heavy guns **4** *Law.* unlawful physical violence against a person [L, rel. to BATTLE]

bat·tle /bat′l/ *n.* **1** prolonged fight between armed forces **2** difficult struggle; contest —*v.* (**·tled, ·tling**) **3** engage in battle; fight [L *battuere* beat]

bat′tle·ax′ *n.* (also **·axe′**) **1** large ax used in ancient warfare **2** *Colloq. & Offens.* formidable older woman

Bat′tle Creek′ *n.* city in Mich. Pop. 53,540

bat′tle cruis′er *n.* warship of higher speed and lighter armor than a battleship

bat′tle cry′ *n.* cry or slogan used in a campaign

bat′tle·dore′ /bat′l-dòr′/ *n. Hist.* (In full bat′tle·dore′ and shut′tle·cock′) game like badminton, played with a shuttlecock and rackets [perh. fr. Prov *batedor* beater]

bat′tle·field′ *n.* (also **bat′tle·ground′**) scene of a battle

BATTLEMENT

bat·tle·ment /bat′l-mənt/ *n.* (usu. *pl.*) recessed parapet along the top of a fortification [Fr *batailler* fortify]

bat′tle·roy′al *n.* (*pl.* **bat′tles·roy′al**) **1** battle of many combatants; free fight **2** heated argument

bat′tle·ship′ *n.* heavily armored warship

bat·ty /bat′ē/ *adj.* (**·ti·er, ·ti·est**) *Slang.* crazy [fr. BAT²]

bau·ble /bò′bəl/ *n.* showy, worthless trinket or toy [Fr *ba(u)bel* toy]

Bau·de·laire /bōd-ler′/, **Charles** 1821–67; French poet and critic

baux·ite /bòk′sīt/ *n.* claylike ore, source of aluminum [Fr fr. *Les Baux* in S. France]

bawd /bòd/ *n.* woman who runs a brothel [see BAWDY]

bawd·y *adj.* (**·i·er, ·i·est**) **1** humorously indecent —*n.* **2** such talk or writing —**bawd′i·ly** *adv.*; **bawd′i·ness** *n.* [*bawd* brothel keeper, fr. Fr *baudetrot*]

bawd′y·house′ *n.* brothel

bawl /bòl/ *v.* **1** speak or shout noisily **2** weep loudly **3 bawl out** *Colloq.* reprimand angrily [ME fr. Gmc]

bay¹ /bā/ *n.* broad curving inlet of a large body of water [Sp *bahia*]

bay² *n.* **1** laurel with deep green leaves **2** (*pl.*) bay wreath, for a victor or poet [L *baca* berry]

bay³ *n.* **1** recess; alcove in a wall **2** compartment or specially allocated area [Fr *baer* gape]

bay⁴ *adj.* **1** (esp. of a horse) dark reddish-brown —*n.* **2** bay horse [L *badius*]

bay⁵ *v.* **1** bark or howl loudly and plaintively —*n.* **2** sound of this, esp. of hounds in close pursuit **3** at bay cornered; unable to escape **4** keep at bay hold off (a pursuer) [Fr *bayer* to bark]

Ba·ya·món /bī′əmòn′/ *n.* city in N Puerto Rico. Pop. 220,300

bay′ber·ry *n.* (*pl.* **·ries**) fragrant N American tree

bay′ leaf′ *n.* leaf of the bay tree, used for flavoring

bay·o·net /bā′ənet′/ *n.* **1** stabbing blade attachable to the muzzle of a rifle **2** fitting pushed into a socket and twisted —*v.* (**·net·ed** or **·net·ted, ·net·ing** or **·net·ting**) **3** stab with a bayonet [Fr, perh. fr. *Bayonne* in SW France]

bay·ou /bī′ōō, bī′ō/ *n.* sluggish, marshy inlet, lake, etc. [AmInd *bayuk* small stream]

bay′ rum′ *n.* perfume distilled orig. from bayberry leaves in rum

bay′ win′dow *n.* **1** window projecting outward from a wall **2** *Colloq.* paunch

ba·zaar /bəzär′/ *n.* **1** oriental market **2** fundraising sale, esp. for charity [Pers]

ba·zoo·ka /bəzōō′kə/ *n.* **1** antitank rocket launcher **2** musical instrument invented by comedian Bob Burns

BB *n.* (also **BB gun**) pelletlike shot, .18 in. in diameter, used in an air rifle

bbl. *abbr.* barrel

BC *abbr.* (also **b.c.**) **1** before (the birth of) Christ **2** British Columbia

bdrm. *abbr.* bedroom

be /bē/ *v.* (*sing. pres.* **am, is**; *pl. pres.* **are**; *sing. past* **was**; *pl. past* **were**; *pres. part.* **being**; *past part.* **been**) **1** exist; live **2** occur; take place **3** occupy a position **4** remain; continue **5** linking subject and predicate, expressing: **a** identity (*she is the person*) **b** condition (*he is ill*) **c** state or quality (*he is kind*) **d** opinion (*I am against hanging*) **e** total (*two and two are four*) **f** cost or significance (*it is $5 to enter; it is nothing to me*) **6** *v. aux.* **a** with a past part. to form the passive (*it was done; it is said*) **b** with a pres. part. to form progressive tenses (*we are coming*) **c** with an infinitive to express duty or commitment, intention, possibility, destiny, or hypothesis (*I am to tell you; we are to wait here; he is to come at four; it was not to be found; they were never to meet again; if I were to die*) [OE]

be- *prefix* forming verbs: **1a** all over; all around (*besieged*) **b** thoroughly; excessively (*belabor*) **2** expressing transitive action (*bemoan*) **3a** affect with (*befog*) **b** treat as (*befriend*) **c** having (*bejeweled*) [OE: BY]

beach /bēch/ *n.* **1** pebbly or sandy shore —*v.* **2** run or haul (a boat, etc.) on to a beach

beach′·comb·er /bēch′kō′mər/ *n.* person who searches beaches for articles of value

beach′head′ *n.* fortified position set up on a beach by landing forces

bea·con /bē′kən/ *n.* **1** visible warning or guiding device (lighthouse, navigation buoy, etc.) **2** radio transmitter whose signal is used for guidance [OE]

bead /bēd/ *n.* **1a** small usu. rounded piece

of glass, stone, etc., for threading to make necklaces, etc., or sewing on to fabric, etc. **b** (*pl.*) bead necklace; rosary **2** drop of liquid **3** front sight of a gun **4** inner edge of a pneumatic tire gripping the rim of the wheel —*v.* **5** adorn with or as with beads **6 draw a bead on** take aim at —**bead′y** *adj.* (**·i·er, ·i·est**) [OE: prayer]

bead′ing *n.* **1** *Archit.* molding like a string of beads **2** decoration of beads on clothing, handbags, etc. **3** bead of a tire

bea·gle /bē′gəl/ *n.* small short-haired hound [Fr]

beak /bēk/ *n.* **1a** bird's horny projecting jaws **b** similar jaw of a turtle, etc. **2** proboscis of an insect [Fr fr. Celt]

beak·er /bē′kər/ *n.* **1** tall cup or tumbler **2** lipped glass vessel for scientific experiments [ON]

beam /bēm/ *n.* **1** long sturdy piece of timber or metal used in building, etc. **2** ray or shaft of light **3** series of radio or radar signals as a guide to a ship or aircraft **4** crossbar of a balance **5** ship's breadth —*v.* **6** emit or direct (light, approval, etc.) **7a** shine **b** look or smile radiantly **8 off the beam** *Colloq.* mistaken **9 on the beam** *Colloq.* on the right track [OE: tree]

bean /bēn/ *n.* **1a** plant with edible seeds in long pods **b** seed or pod of this **2** similar seed of coffee, etc. **3 full of beans** *Colloq.* lively; exuberant [OE]

bean′bag′ *n.* **1** small bag filled with dried beans and used as a ball **2** large bag filled usu. with polystyrene pieces and used as a chair

bean′ count′er *n. Colloq.* accountant or bookkeeper

bean′pole′ *n.* **1** support for bean plants **2** *Colloq.* tall, thin person

bear¹ /ber/ *v.* (**bore**, **borne** or **born, bearing**) **1** carry, bring, or take **2** show; have, esp. characteristically **3a** produce; yield (fruit, etc.) **b** give birth to **4a** sustain (a weight, responsibility, cost, etc.) **b** endure (an ordeal, difficulty, etc.) **5a** tolerate **b** admit of **6** in a given direction (*bear left*) **7 bear down (on): a** bring pressure down (on) **b** press downward **8 bear on** (or **upon**) be relevant to **9 bear out** support as evidence **10 bear up** endure **11 bear with** tolerate **12 bear witness** testify —**bear′a·ble** *adj.*; **bear′a·bly** *adv.*; **bear·er** *n.* [OE]

bear² *n.* **1** any of several large heavy mammals with thick fur **2** rough or uncouth person **3** person who sells shares hoping to repurchase them more cheaply **4 Great Bear; Little Bear** constellations near the North Pole [OE]

beard /bērd/ *n.* **1** facial hair on the chin, etc. **2** similar tuft on an animal —*v.* **3** oppose; defy —**beard′ed, beard′less** *adj.* [OE]

Beards·ley /bērdz′lē/, **Aubrey Vincent** 1872–98; English artist and illustrator

bear·ing /ber′iNG/ *n.* **1** posture; attitude; mien **2** relevance **3** part of a machine supporting a rotating or sliding part **4a** (often *pl.*) direction or position relative to a fixed point **b** (*pl.*) knowledge of one's relative position

Bé·ar·naise′ sauce′ /bā′ərnāz′/ *n.* rich egg-yolk sauce for meat or fish [Fr]

bear·skin /ber′skin/ *n.* fur or hide of a bear, esp. as a rug, coat, etc.

beast /bēst/ *n.* **1** animal, esp. a wild mammal **2** brutal, coarse, or objectionable person [L *bestia*]

beast′ly *adj.* (**·li·er, ·li·est**) **1** *Colloq.* objectionable; unpleasant **2** like a beast; brutal —**beast′li·ness** *n.*

beast′ of bur′den *n.* any animal, as a horse, elephant, etc., used for carrying

beast′ of prey′ *n.* animal that hunts animals for food

beat /bēt/ *v.* (**beat, beat·en, beat·ing**) **1** strike persistently and violently **2a** overcome; surpass **b** be too hard for; perplex **3** whisk (eggs, etc.) vigorously **4** shape (metal, etc.) by blows **5** (of the heart, etc.) pulsate rhythmically **6a** indicate (a tempo) by tapping, etc. **b** sound (a signal, etc.) by striking a drum (*beat a tattoo*) **7** move or cause (wings) to move up and down **8** make (a path, etc.) by trampling —*n.* **9a** main stress accent in music or verse **b** rhythm indicated by a conductor **10** stroke or blow or measured sequence of strokes **11** police officer's route or area —*adj.* **12** *Slang.* exhausted; tired out **13 beat down** cause (a seller) to lower the price by bargaining **14 beat it** *Slang.* go away **15 beat off** drive back (an attack, etc.) **16 beat up** thrash, esp. with punches and kicks —**beat′a·ble** *adj.* [OE]

beat′en *adj.* **1** shaped or decorated by beating **2** defeated utterly **3** much traversed

beat′er *n.* implement for beating, as batter, eggs, etc.

be·a·tif·ic /bē′ətif′ik/ *adj.* **1** *Colloq.* blissful **2** making blessed [L *beatus* blessed]

be·at·i·fy /bē·at′əfī′/ *v.* (**·fied, ·fy·ing**) **1** *RC Ch.* declare (a person) to be "blessed," often as a step towards canonization **2** make happy —**be·at′i·fi·ca′tion** /-fikā′SHən/ *n.*

be·at·i·tude /bē·at′ət(y)ōōd′/ *n.* **1** perfect bliss or happiness **2** (*pl.*) blessings in Matt. 5:3–11

beat·nik /bēt′nik/ *n.* member of socially unconventional group, esp. in the 1950s

Be·a·trix /bā′ətriks/ 1938– ; queen of the Netherlands (1980–)

beat′-up′ *adj. Colloq.* dilapidated

beau /bō/ *n.* **1** (*pl.* **beaux** /bōz/) *Old-fash.* boyfriend [L *bellus* pretty]

Beau′fort scale′ /bō′fərt/ *n.* scale of wind speed ranging from 0 (calm) to 12 (hurricane) [for the Brit. admiral who originated it]

Beau′fort Sea′ /bō′fərt/ *n.* part of the Arctic Ocean NE of Alaska

Beau·jo·lais /bō′zHəlā′/ *n.* red or white wine from the Beaujolais district of France

Beau·mar·chais /bō′märSHā′/, **Pierre Augustin Caron de** 1732–99; French dramatist

Beau·mont /bō′mänt′/, **Francis** 1584–1616; English dramatist

Beau·mont /bō′mänt′/ *n.* city in Texas. Pop. 114,323

beau·te·ous /byōōt′ēəs/ *adj.* beautiful —**beau′te·ous·ly** *adv.*; **beau′te·ous·ness** *n.*

beau·ti·cian /byōōtiSH′ən/ *n.* specialist in beauty treatment

beau·ti·ful /byōōt′əfəl/ *adj.* having beauty; pleasing to the eye, ear, or mind, etc. —**beau′ti·ful·ly** *adv.*

beau·ti·fy /byŏŏt'əf ī'/ v. (**·fied, ·fy·ing**) make beautiful; adorn —**beau'ti·fi·ca'tion** n.

beau·ty /byŏŏt'ē/ n. (pl. **·ties**) 1 combination of shape, color, sound, etc., that pleases the senses 2a Colloq. excellent specimen b attractive feature; advantage [L bellus pretty]

beau'ty par'lor n. (also **beau'ty sa·lon'** or **shop'**) establishment for coiffure, manicure, etc.

Beau·voir, Simone de see DE BEAUVOIR

bea·ver /bē'vər/ n. 1a amphibious broad-tailed rodent b its fur c hat of this 2 top hat —v. 3 Colloq. work hard [OE]

Bea·ver·ton /bē'vərtən/ n. city in Ore. Pop. 53,310

be·bop /bē'bäp/ n. type of 1940s jazz with complex harmony and rhythms [imit.]

be·calm /bikä(l)m'/ v. deprive (a ship) of wind

be·came /bikām'/ v. past of BECOME

be·cause /bikôz', -kaz'/ conj. 1 for the reason that; since 2 **because of** on account of; by reason of [fr. BY + CAUSE]

bé·cha·mel /bāsH'əmel'/ n. a kind of thick white sauce [for its creator]

beck /bek/ n. as in **at a person's beck and call** subject to a person's constant orders [fr. BECKON]

Beck·et /bek'it/, **St. Thomas à** c. 1118–70; archbishop of Canterbury; murdered for opposing Henry II

Beck·ett /bek'it/, **Samuel Barclay** 1906–89; Irish dramatist, novelist, and poet

beck·on /bek'ən/ v. 1 summon by gesture 2 entice [OE]

be·come /bikəm'/ v. (**·came, ·come, ·com·ing**) 1 begin to be 2a look well on; suit b be appropriate to 3 **become of** happen to [OE, rel. to BE + COME]

bed /bed/ n. 1 piece of furniture for sleeping on 2 garden plot, esp. for flowers 3 bottom of the sea, a river, etc. 4 foundations of a road or railway 5 stratum; layer —v. (**bed·ded, bed·ding**) 6 put or go to bed 7 plant in a garden bed 8 arrange as a layer 9 **bed of roses** life of ease [OE]

bed' and board' n. lodging and food

bed' and break'fast n. 1 room and breakfast in a hotel, etc. 2 establishment providing this

be·daz·zle /bidaz'əl/ v. (**·zled, ·zling**) 1 dazzle 2 bewilder

bed'bug' n. biting parasite infesting beds, etc.

bed'clothes' n. pl. (also **bed'lin'en**) sheets, blankets, etc., for a bed

bed·ding /bed'iNG/ n. 1 mattress and bed-clothes 2 geological strata

Bede, St. /bēd/ c. 673–735; English monk, theologian, and historian (called "the Venerable Bede")

be·deck /bidek'/ v. adorn

be·dev·il /bidev'əl/ v. (**·iled, ·il·ing**) 1 trouble; vex 2 confound; confuse 3 torment; abuse —**be·dev'il·ment** n.

bed'fel'low n. 1 person who shares a bed 2 associate

be·dim /bedim', bi-/ v. (**·dimmed, ·dim·ming**) make dim

bed·lam /bed'ləm/ n. uproar and confusion [St Mary of Bethlehem, name of a hospital in London]

Bed·ou·in /bed'ōōən/ n. (also **Bed·u·in**)

(pl. same) 1 nomadic desert Arab 2 wandering person [Ar: desert dwellers]

bed'pan' n. portable toilet for use in bed

be·drag·gled /bidrag'əld/ adj. disheveled; untidy

bed'rid'den adj. confined to bed by infirmity

bed'rock' n. 1 solid underlying rock 2 basic principles

bed'room' n. room for sleeping

bed'side' n. 1 space beside a bed, esp. of a patient 2 **bedside manner** (esp. doctor's) way with patients

bed'sore' n. sore developed by lying in bed

bed'spread' n. decorative cover for a bed

bed·stead /bed'sted'/ n. framework of a bed

bed'time' n. usual time for going to bed

bed'wet'ting n. involuntary urination when asleep in bed

bee /bē/ n. 1 four-winged stinging insect, collecting nectar and pollen and producing wax and honey 2 meeting for work or amusement 3 **a bee in one's bonnet** obsession [OE]

beech /bēcH/ n. 1 large, smooth, gray tree with glossy leaves 2 its hard wood [OE]

Bee·cher /bē'cHər/, **Henry Ward** 1813–87; US clergyman and abolitionist

beech'nut' n. fruit of the beech

beef /bēf/ n. (pl. **beeves** or **beefs**) 1 flesh of the ox, bull, or cow for eating 2 Colloq. male muscle 3 ox, etc., bred for beef 4 (pl. **beefs**) Slang. complaint —v. 5 Slang. complain 6 **beef up** Slang. strengthen; reinforce [L bos bovis ox]

beef·bur·ger /bēf'bər'gər/ n. HAMBURGER

beef'cake' n. Colloq. muscular male form as provocative display [fr. CHEESECAKE]

beef'steak' n. thick slice of beef for broiling

beef'y adj. (**·i·er, ·i·est**) 1 like beef 2 solid; muscular —**beef'i·ness** n.

bee'hive' n. 1 shelter for a colony of bees 2 busy place

bee'keep'er n. keeper of bees —**bee'keep'ing** n.

bee'line' n. most direct route

Be·el·ze·bub /bē·el'zəbəb'/ n. the Devil [Heb: lord of the flies]

been /bin, ben/ v. past part. of BE

beep /bēp/ n. 1 high-pitched sound of a horn or electronic device —v. 2 emit a beep [imit.]

beep'er n. portable radio device that beeps when receiving a message

beer /bēr/ n. 1 alcoholic drink made by brewing fermented malt, etc., flavored with hops 2 brewed nonalcoholic drink (**root beer, ginger beer**) [OE]

Beer·bohm /bēr'bōm'/, **"Max"** (**Sir**) **Henry Maximilian** 1872–1956; English caricaturist, essayist, and critic

Beer·she·ba /bərsHē'bə/ n. city in Israel. Pop. 113,800

bees·wax /bēz'waks'/ n. wax secreted by bees to make honeycombs

beet /bēt/ n. plant with an edible root [OE]

Bee·tho·ven /bā'tō'vən/, **Ludwig van** 1770–1827; German composer

bee·tle¹ /bēt'l/ n. insect with hard protective outer wings [OE, rel. to BITE]

bee·tle² adj. 1 projecting; shaggy; scowling (**beetle brows**) —v. 2 (**·tled, ·tling**) (of brows, cliffs, etc.) project; overhang

bee·tle³ *n.* heavy tool for ramming, crushing, etc. [OE, rel. to BEAT]

bee′tle-browed′ *adj.* with shaggy, projecting, or scowling eyebrows

Bee·ton / bēt′n/, **Isabella Mary** 1836–65; English cookbook writer

beeves / bēvz/ *n. pl.* of BEEF

be·fall / bifôl′/ *v.* (**-fell**, **-fall·en**, **-fall·ing**) happen; happen to [OE, rel. to BE- + FALL]

be·fit / bifit′/ *v.* (**-fit·ted**, **-fit·ting**) be appropriate or suitable for

be·fog / bifôg′, -fäg′/ *v.* (**-fogged**, **-fog·ging**) 1 confuse; obscure 2 envelop in fog

be·fore / bifôr′/ *conj.* 1 earlier than the time when 2 rather than that —*prep.* 3 earlier than 4 in front of; ahead of 5 in the face of 6 rather than 7 in the presence of 8 for the attention of —*adv.* 9 previously; already 10 ahead [OE, rel. to BY + FORE]

be·fore′hand′ *adv.* in advance; in readiness

be·friend / bifrend′/ *v.* act as a friend to; help

be·fud·dle / bifud′l/ *v.* (**-dled**, **-dling**) 1 make drunk 2 confuse

beg / beg/ *v.* (**begged**, **beg·ging**) 1a ask for b live by begging 2 (of a dog) sit up with the front paws raised expectantly 3 take leave (*I beg to differ*) 4 beg off ask to be excused from something [rel. to BID]

be·get / biget′/ *v. Archaic.* (**-got** or **-gat**, **-got·ten** or **-got**, **-get·ting**) 1 father; procreate 2 cause [OE, rel. to BE- + GET]

beg·gar / beg′ər/ *n.* 1 person who lives by begging —*v.* 2 make poor 3 be too extraordinary for (*beggar description*) —**beg′gar·ly** *adj.*; **beg′gar·y** *n.*

be·gin / bigin′/ *v.* (**-gan**, **-gun**, **-gin·ning**) 1 perform the first part of; start 2 come into being 3 start at a certain time 4 be begun [OE]

Be·gin / bāgēn′, bā′gin/, **Menachem** 1913–92; prime minister of Israel (1977–84); Nobel prize 1978

be·gin′ner *n.* trainee; learner

be·gin′ning *n.* 1 time or place at which anything begins 2 source; origin 3 first part

be·gone / bigôn′/ *interj.* go away at once!

be·go·nia / bigôn′yə/ *n.* garden plant with bright flowers and leaves [*Bégon*, name of a patron of science]

be·got′ / bigät′/ *v. past* and alter. *past part.* of BEGET

be·got·ten / bigät′n/ *v. past part.* of BEGET

be·grudge / bigrəj′/ *v.* (**-grudged**, **-grudg·ing**) 1 resent; be dissatisfied at 2 envy (a person) the possession of —**be·grudg′ing·ly** *adv.*

be·guile / bigil′/ *v.* (**-guiled**, **-guil·ing**) 1 charm; amuse 2 willfully divert; seduce 3 delude; cheat —**be·guil′er**, **be·guile′ment** *n.*; **be·guil′ing** *adj.*

be·guine / bigēn′/ *n.* popular dance of W Indian origin [MFr *béguin* infatuation]

be·gun / bigən′/ *v. past part.* of BEGIN

be·half / bihaf′/ *n.* as in **in** (or **on**) **behalf of** in the interests of; for [earlier *bihalve* on the part of]

Be·han / bē′ən/, **Brendan** 1923–64; Irish dramatist and poet

be·have / bihāv′/ *v.* (**-haved**, **-hav·ing**) 1 act or react (in a specified way) 2 conduct oneself properly 3 work well (in a specified way) [fr. BE- + HAVE]

be·hav·ior / bihā′vyər/ *n.* way of behaving or acting —**be·hav′ior·al** *adj.*

be·hav′ior·al sci′ence *n.* the study of human behavior

be·head / bihed′/ *v.* cut the head off

be·held / biheld′/ *v. past* and *past part.* of BEHOLD

be·he·moth / bihē′məTH, bē′əməTH/ *n.* huge creature or thing [Heb (Job 40:15)]

be·hest / bihest′/ *n.* command; request [OE]

be·hind / bihīnd′/ *prep.* 1 in or to the rear of 2 on the far side of 3 hidden or implied by 4 in the past in relation to 5 late regarding 6 inferior to; weaker than 7 in support of 8 responsible for —*adv.* 9 in or to the rear; farther back 10 on the farther side 11 remaining 12 in arrears 13 late in finishing a task, etc. 14 in an inferior position —*n.* 15 *Colloq.* buttocks [OE]

be·hold / bihōld′/ *v.* (**-held**, **-hold·ing**) see; look at [OE, rel. to BE- + HOLD]

be·hold′en *adj.* under obligation

be·hoove / bihŏŏv′/ *v.* (**-hooved**, **-hoov·ing**) 1 be incumbent on 2 befit [OE, rel. to BE- + HEAVE]

beige / bāZH/ *n.* 1 pale sandy color —*adj.* 2 of this color [Fr]

Bei·jing / bājinG′, -ZHinG′/ *n.* (formerly Peking) capital of China. Pop. 5,769,600

be·ing / bē′inG/ *n.* 1 existence 2 nature or essence 3 person or creature

Bei·ra / bā′rə/ *n.* city in Mozambique. Pop. 298,800

Bei·rut / bārŏŏt′/ *n.* capital of Lebanon. Pop. 1,910,000

be·jew·el / bijŏŏ′əl/ *v.* (**-eled**, **-el·ing**) adorn with jewels

be·la·bor / bēlā′bər, bi-/ *v.* 1 beat repeatedly 2 labor (a subject)

Bel·a·rus / bel′ərŏŏs′/ *n.* (formerly Byelorussia, part of the USSR) republic in E Europe. Capital: Minsk. Pop. 10,321,000

be·lat·ed / bilāt′əd/ *adj.* late or too late —**be·lat′ed·ly** *adv.*

be·lay / bilā′/ *v.* (**-layed**, **-lay·ing**) 1 secure (a rope) by winding it around a cleat 2 *Naut.* stop; cease 3 secure by means of a rope [Du *beleggen*]

bel can·to / bel kan′tō/ *n.* lyrical rich-toned style of operatic singing [It: fine song]

belch / belCH/ *v.* 1 emit gas from the stomach noisily through the mouth 2 (of a chimney, gun, etc.) send (smoke, etc.) out or up —*n.* 3 act of belching

be·lea·guer / bilē′gər/ *v.* 1 besiege 2 vex; harass [Du *leger* camp]

Bel·fast / bel′fast, belfast′/ *n.* capital of Northern Ireland, United Kingdom. Pop. 354,400

bel·fry / bel′frē/ *n.* (*pl.* **-fries**) 1 bell tower 2 space for bells in a church tower [Gmc, prob. peace-protector]

Bel·gium / bel′jəm/ *n.* monarchy in W Europe, on the North Sea. Capital: Brussels. Pop. 10,021,000 —**Bel′gian** *n.* & *adj.*

Bel·go·rod / b(y)el′gəräd/ *n.* city in W Russia. Pop. 311,400

Bel·grade / bel′grād′, -gräd/ *n.* capital of Serbia. Pop. 1,136,700 be·lie /bilī'/ v. (·lied, ·ly·ing) 1 give a false impression of 2 fail to fulfill or justify [OE, rel. to BE- + LIE²]

be·lief /bilēf'/ n. 1 firm opinion; acceptance 2 religious conviction 3 trust or confidence [rel. to BELIEVE]

be·lieve /bilēv'/ v. (·lieved, ·liev·ing) 1 accept as true or as conveying the truth 2 think; suppose 3a (foll. by *in*) have faith in the existence of b trust in as a policy —be·liev'a·ble *adj.*; be·liev'a·bly *adv.*; be·liev'er *n.* [OE]

be·lit·tle /bilit'l/ v. (·tled, ·tling) disparage; make appear insignificant —be·lit'tle·ment *n.*

Be·lize /bəlēz'/ *n.* country in N Central America. Capital: Belmopan. Pop. 196,000

bell /bel/ *n.* 1 hollow, esp. cup-shaped, usu. metal object sounding a note when struck 2 such a sound, esp. as a signal 3 thing resembling a bell, esp. in sound or shape —v. 4 provide with a bell [OE]

Bell /bel/, **Alexander Graham** 1847–1922; Scottish-born US inventor of the telephone

bel·la·don·na /bel'ədän'ə/ *n.* 1 deadly nightshade 2 drug from this [It: fair lady]

bell'bot'tom *n.* 1 marked flare below the knee (of a trouser leg) 2 (*pl.*) trousers with these —bell'bot'tomed *adj.*

bell'boy' *n.* BELLMAN

belle /bel/ *n.* beautiful woman [Fr, fem. of BEAU]

bel·les-let·tres /bel let(rə)'/ *n. pl.* literary writings or studies [Fr: fine letters]

Belle·vue /bel'vyoo'/ *n.* city in Wash. Pop. 86,874

bell'hop' *n.* BELLMAN

bel·li·cose /bel'ikōs'/ *adj.* eager to fight; warlike [L *bellum* war]

bel·lig·er·ence /bilij'ərəns/ *n.* 1 aggressive behavior 2 status of a belligerent

bel·lig·er·ent /bilij'ərənt/ *adj.* 1 engaged in war or conflict 2 quarrelsome; pugnacious —n. 3 belligerent nation or person [L *belligerare* wage war]

Bel·li·ni /belē'nē/ family of Italian painters, including: 1 **Jacopo** c. 1400–70 2 **Gentile** c. 1429–1507 3 **Giovanni** c. 1430–1516

bell' jar' *n.* bell-shaped glass cover or container

bell'man *n.* (*pl.* ·men) (also esp. *Formerly.* **bell·boy, bell·hop**) hotel worker who carries guests' luggage, runs errands, etc.

bel·low /bel'ō/ v. 1 emit a deep, loud roar 2 utter loudly —n. 3 loud roar

Bel·low /bel'ō/, **Saul** 1915– ; Canadian-born US novelist

BELLOWS 1

bel·lows /bel'ōz/ *n. pl.* (also treated as *sing.*) 1 device for driving air into or through something 2 expandable part, e.g., of a camera [rel. to BELLY]

bell·weth·er /bel'weth'ər/ *n.* 1 leading sheep of a flock 2 leader; model

bel·ly /bel'ē/ *n.* (*pl.* ·lies) 1 trunk below the chest, containing the stomach and bowels 2 stomach 3 front of the body from waist to groin 4 underside of an animal 5 cavity or bulging part —v. (·lied, ·ly·ing) 6 swell; bulge [OE: bag]

bel'ly·ache' *n.* 1 *Colloq.* stomach pain —v. (·ached, ·ach·ing) 2 *Slang.* complain noisily or persistently

bel'ly·but'ton *n. Colloq.* navel

bel'ly dance' *n.* oriental dance performed by a woman, with voluptuous belly movements —bel'ly danc'er, bel'ly danc'ing *n.*

bel'ly·flop' *n. Colloq.* dive with the belly landing flat on the water

bel'ly·ful' *n.* (*pl.* ·fuls) 1 enough to eat 2 *Colloq.* more than one can tolerate

bel'ly laugh' *n.* loud, unrestrained laugh

Bel·mo·pan /bel'mōpan'/ *n.* capital of Belize. Pop. 5,300

Be·lo Ho·ri·zon·te /bā'lō hôr'izänt'ē/ *n.* city in SE Brazil. Pop. 1,442,500

be·long /bilông'/ v. 1a (foll. by *to*) be the property of b be correctly assigned to 2 be a member of 3 fit socially [fr. BE- + obs. *long* belong]

be·long'ings *n. pl.* possessions; luggage

be·lov·ed /biləv'id, -ləvd'/ *adj.* 1 much loved —n. 2 much loved person

be·low /bilō'/ *prep.* 1 lower in position, amount, status, etc., than 2 beneath the surface of 3 unworthy of —adv. 4 at or to a lower point or level 5 further on a page or in a book [*be-* BY + LOW¹]

Bel·shaz·zar /belshaz'ər/ 6th cent. B.C.; son of Nebuchadnezzar; last king of Babylon

belt /belt/ *n.* 1 strip of leather, etc., worn esp. around the waist 2 continuous band in machinery; conveyor belt 3 region or extent 4 *Slang.* heavy blow —v. 5 put a belt around; fasten with a belt 6 *Slang.* hit hard 7 **below the belt** unfair(ly) 8 **belt out** *Slang.* sing (a song) loudly 9 **tighten one's belt** economize 10 **under one's belt** securely acquired [OE]

be·moan /bimōn'/ v. lament; complain about

be·muse /bimyooz'/ v. (·mused, ·mus·ing) puzzle; bewilder [fr. BE- + MUSE]

Be·na·res /bənär'is, -ēz/ *n.* see VARANASI

bench /bench/ *n.* 1 long seat usu. of wood or stone 2 strong worktable 3a judge's seat b court of law c judges collectively 4 seat where players of football, etc., sit when not in the game —v. 5 not use or remove (a player) from a game 6 **on the bench: a** active as a judge in a court b not playing in a game [OE]

bench'mark' *n.* 1 surveyor's mark as a reference point 2 standard or point of reference

bench'war'rant *n.* order for arrest issued by a judge or court

bend¹ /bend/ v. (bent, bend·ing) 1a force or adapt (something straight) into a curve or angle b (of an object) be so altered 2 curve; incline; stoop 3 interpret or modify (a rule) to suit oneself 4 turn (one's steps, eyes, or energies) in a new direction 5 be flexible; submit; force to submit —n. 6 curve; departure from a straight course 7 bent part 8 (*pl.*)

Colloq. decompression sickness —**bend′a·ble** *adj.*; **bend′y** *adj.* (·i·er, ·i·est) [OE]

bend² *n.* any of various rope knots [OE, rel. to BIND]

bend′er *n. Slang.* wild drinking spree

be·neath /binēTH/ *prep.* **1** unworthy of **2** below; under —*adv.* **3** below; underneath [OE, rel. to BE- + NETHER]

Ben·e·dict, St. /ben′ədikt/ *c.* 480–*c.* 550; Italian monk; founder of Western monasticism

ben·e·dic·tion /ben′ədik′sHən/ *n.* blessing, esp. at the end of a religious service or as a special Roman Catholic service —**ben′e·dic′to·ry** /-tôrē/ *adj.* [L *benedicere* bless]

ben·e·fac·tion /ben′əfak′sHən/ *n.* **1** donation; gift **2** giving or doing good [L, rel. to BENEFIT]

ben·e·fac·tor /ben′əfak′tər/ *n.* (*fem.* **ben′e·fac′tress**) person giving (esp. financial) support

ben·e·fice /ben′əfəs/ *n.* a living from a church office

ben·e·fi·cent /bənef′əsənt/ *adj.* doing good; generous; kind —**be·nef′i·cence** *n.*; **be·nef′i·cent·ly** *adv.*

ben·e·fi·cial /ben′əfisH′əl/ *adj.* advantageous; having benefits —**ben′e·fi′cial·ly** *adv.*

ben·e·fi·ci·ar·y /ben′əfisH′ē·er′ē, ·fisH′ärē/ *n.* (*pl.* ·ies) **1** person who benefits, esp. from a will **2** holder of a benefice

ben·e·fit /ben′əfit/ *n.* **1** favorable or helpful factor, etc. **2** (often *pl.*) insurance or social security payment **3** public performance, game, etc., in aid of a charitable cause —*v.* (·fit·ed, ·fit·ing) **4** help; bring advantage to **5** receive benefit [L *benefactum* fr. *bene* well + *facere* do]

Ben·e·lux /ben′ləks/ *n.* Belgium, the Netherlands, and Luxembourg

Be·nét /bənā′/, **Stephen Vincent** 1898–1943; US poet

be·nev·o·lent /bənev′ələnt/ *adj.* **1** well-wishing; actively friendly and helpful **2** charitable —**be·nev′o·lence** *n.*; **be·nev′o·lent·ly** *adv.* [Fr fr. L *bene volens* well-wishing]

Ben·gal, Bay of /ben·gôl′, bENG-/ *n.* part of the Indian Ocean between India and Burma

Ben·gha·zi /ben·gäz′ē/ *n.* city in Libya, on Gulf of Sidra. Pop. 446,300

Ben-Gu·ri·on /ben gŏŏr′ēən, David 1886–1973; Polish-born first prime minister of Israel (1948–53; 1955–63)

be·night·ed /bənīt′id/ *adj.* intellectually or morally ignorant —**be·night′ed·ly** *adv.*; **be·night′ed·ness** *n.*

be·nign /binīn′/ *adj.* **1** gentle; mild; kindly **2** fortunate; salutary **3** (of a tumor, etc.) not malignant —**be·nign′ly** *adv.* [L *benignus*]

be·nig·nant /binig′nənt/ *adj.* **1** kindly, esp. to inferiors **2** salutary; beneficial —**be·nig′nan·cy** *n.*

be·nig·ni·ty /binig′nətē/ *n.* (*pl.* ·ties) kindliness

Be·nin /bənēn′, -nin′/ *n.* republic in W Africa. Capital: Porto-Novo. Pop. 4,928,000

Ben·ny /ben′ē/, **Jack** 1894–1974; US comedian

bent¹ /bent/ *v.* **1** *past* and *past part.* of BEND¹ —*adj.* **2** curved; angular **3** *Slang.* dishonest;

illicit **4** set on doing or having —*n.* **5** inclination; bias **6** talent

bent² *n.* **1** reedy grass with stiff stems **2** stiff flower stalk of a grass [OE]

Ben·tham /ben′THəm/, **Jeremy** 1748–1832; English philosopher and jurist

Ben·ton /bent′n/, **Thomas Hart** 1782–1858; US politician

bent′wood′ *n.* wood artificially shaped for making furniture

be·numb /binəm′/ *v.* **1** make numb; deaden **2** paralyze (the mind or feelings)

Benz /benz, bents/, **Karl Friedrich** 1844–1929; German engineer and car manufacturer

ben·zene /ben′zēn, benzēn′/ *n.* colorless volatile liquid used as a solvent, etc. [ult. fr. Ar *lubān jāwī* incense of Java]

be·queath /bikwēTH′, -kwēTH′/ *v.* **1** leave to a person in a will **2** hand down to posterity [fr. BE- + QUOTH]

be·quest /bikwest′/ *n.* **1** bequeathing; bestowal by will **2** thing bequeathed [fr. BE- + obs. *quiste* saying]

be·rate /birāt′/ *v.* (·rat·ed, ·rat·ing) scold; rebuke

Ber·ber /bər′bər/ *n.* **1** member of a Caucasian people of N Africa **2** language of these people —*adj.* **3** of the Berbers or their language [Ar]

be·reave /birēv′/ *v.* (·reaved or ·reft, ·reav·ing) deprive of a relation, friend, etc., esp. by death —**be·reave′ment** *n.* [OE, fr. *reave* deprive of]

be·ret /bərā′/ *n.* round, flattish, brimless cap of felt [Fr, rel. to BIRETTA]

berg /bərg/ *n.* ICEBERG

Ber·gen /ber′gən, bər′-/ *n.* seaport in Norway, on the North Sea. Pop. 216,000

Berg·man /bərg′mən, berg′män/ **1 Ingrid** 1915–82; Swedish-born US actress **2 Ingmar** 1918– ; Swedish film and theater director

Berg·son /berg′sən/, **Henri** 1859–1941; French philosopher

beri·beri /ber′ē·ber′ē/ *n.* nerve disease caused by a deficiency of vitamin B₁ [Sinhalese]

Ber·ing /bēr′iNG, ber′-/, **Vitus Jonassen** 1681–1741; Danish navigator and explorer

Ber′ing Sea′ *n.* extension of the N Pacific Ocean between Siberia and Alaska

Ber′ing Strait′ *n.* body of water separating Asia (Russia) from North America (Alaska)

Berke·ley /bär′klē, bar′-/, **George** 1685–1753; Irish philosopher and bishop

Berke·ley /bär′klē/ *n.* city in Calif. Pop. 102,724 —**Berke′ley·ite** *n.*

berke·li·um /bərkē′lēəm/ *n.* artificial radioactive metallic element; *symb.* **Bk** [*Berkeley,* Calif., where first identified]

Ber·lin /bərlin′/, **Irving** (born **Israel Baline**) 1888–1989; Russian-born US songwriter

Ber·lin /bərlin′/ *n.* capital of Germany. Pop. 3,433,700 —**Ber·lin′er** *n.*

Ber·li·oz /ber′lē·ōz′/, **Hector Louis** 1803–69; French composer

Ber·mu·da /bərmyŏŏd′ə/ *n.* (also **Bermu′das**) group of islands in the Atlantic, 570 mi. E of the US —**Ber·mu′dan, Ber·mu′di·an** /-dēən/ *n. & adj.*

Ber·mu′da shorts′ *n. pl.* (also **Ber·mu′das**) close-fitting knee-length shorts

Ber·mu′da Tri·an′gle *n.* area in the Atlantic

Ocean bounded by Puerto Rico, Bermuda, and Melbourne, Fla., where many ships and planes are said to have disappeared mysteriously

55

Bern / betoken

Bern /bərn, bern/ *n.* (also **Berne**) capital of Switzerland. Pop. 134,600 —**Ber·nese** /bərnēz', -nēs'/ *n.* & *adj.*

Ber·na·dette, St. /bər'nədet'/ 1844–79; French peasant girl who had visions of the Virgin Mary at Lourdes

Ber·nard, St. /bərnärd', bər'närd, bər'nərd/ c. 996 – c. 1081; French monk; founded Alpine hospices for travelers

Ber·nard of Clair·vaux /bərnärd' əv klärvō'/ 1090–1153; French theologian and abbot

Bern·hardt /bərn'härt', **Sarah** (born Henriette Rosine Bernard) 1844–1923; French actress

Ber·ni·ni /bərnē'nē/, **Gianlorenzo** 1598–1680; Italian sculptor, painter, and architect

Bern·stein /bərn'stīn, -stēn/, **Leonard** 1918–90; US composer, conductor, and pianist

Ber·ra /ber'ə/, **"Yogi" (Lawrence Peter)** 1925– ; US baseball player and manager

ber·ry /ber'ē/ *n.* (*pl.* **·ries**) **1** any small, roundish, juicy, stoneless fruit **2** *Bot.* fruit with its seeds enclosed in pulp (e.g. banana, tomato) [OE]

Ber·ry /ber'ē/, **Chuck (Charles Edward)** 1931– ; US rock and roll musician

ber·serk /bə(r)zərk'/ *adj.* wild; frenzied; in a rage [orig. Norse warrior]

berth /bərth/ *n.* **1** bunk on a ship, train, etc. **2** place for a ship to moor or be at anchor **3** *Colloq.* job —*v.* **4** moor (a ship); be moored **5** provide a sleeping place for **6** give a wide **berth to** stay away from [prob. fr. a special use of BEAR¹]

ber·yl /ber'əl/ *n.* transparent precious stone, esp. emerald, aquamarine [Gk *bērullos*]

be·ryl·li·um /bəril'ēəm/ *n.* hard white metallic element; *symb.* **Be**

be·seech /bisēch'/ *v.* (**be·sought** or **be·seeched, be·seech·ing**) ask earnestly for [fr. BE- + SEEK]

be·set /biset'/ *v.* (**·set, ·set·ting**) **1** attack or harass persistently **2** surround [OE *be-* + *settan* set]

be·side /bisīd'/ *prep.* **1** at the side of; near **2** compared with **3** irrelevant to **4 beside oneself** frantic [OE, rel. to BY + SIDE]

be·sides /bisīdz'/ *prep.* **1** in addition to; apart from —*adv.* **2** also; moreover

be·siege /bisēj'/ *v.* (**·sieged, ·sieg·ing**) **1** lay siege to **2** crowd around eagerly **3** harass

be·smirch /bismərch'/ *v.* **1** soil **2** dishonor

be·sot·ted /bisät'id/ *adj.* **1** infatuated **2** intoxicated; stupefied

be·sought /bisôt'/ *v. past* and *past part.* of BESEECH

be·span·gle /bispaNG'gəl/ *v.* (**·gled, ·gling**) adorn with spangles

be·spat·ter /bispat'ər/ *v.* **1** spatter all over **2** slander; defame

be·speak /bispēk'/ *v.* (**·spoke, ·spo·ken** or **·spoke, speak·ing**) **1** engage in advance **2** suggest; be evidence of

best /best/ *adj.* **1** *superl.* of GOOD **2** of the most excellent or desirable kind —*adv.* **3** *superl.* of WELL¹ **4** in the best manner **5** to the greatest degree **6** most usefully, advisedly, etc. —*n.* **7** utmost; that which is best **8** chief merit or advantage **9** winning majority of (games played, etc.) **10** one's best clothes —*v.* **11** *Colloq.* defeat, outwit, outbid, etc. **12** at best on the most optimistic view **13 get the best of** defeat; outwit **14 had best** or **better** would find it wisest to **15 make the best of** derive what limited advantage one can from [OE]

bes·tial /bes'chəl, bēs'chəl, -tyəl/ *adj.* **1** brutish; cruel **2** of or like a beast —**bes'ti·al·i·ty** /-chēal'ətē, -tēal'ətē/ *n.* (*pl.* **·ties**) [L, rel. to BEAST]

bes·ti·ar·y /bes'chēer'ē, bēs'-, -tē-/ *n.* (*pl.* **·ies**) medieval treatise on beasts [MedL, rel. to BEAST]

be·stir /bistər'/ *v.* (**·stirred, ·stir·ring**) exert or rouse oneself

best' man' *n.* bridegroom's chief attendant

be·stow /bistō'/ *v.* confer (a gift, right, etc.) —**be·stow'al** *n.* [OE *stow* a place]

be·strew /bistrōō'/ *v.* (**·strewed** or **·strewn** /strōōn/, **·strew·ing**) **1** strew (a surface) **2** lie scattered over

be·stride /bistrīd'/ *v.* (**·strode, ·strid·den, ·strid·ing**) **1** sit astride on **2** stand astride over

best'sell'er *n.* **1** book, etc., sold in large numbers **2** author of such a book —**best'-sell' ing** *adj.*

bet /bet/ *v.* (**bet** or **bet·ted, bet·ting**) **1** risk a sum of money on the result of an event, esp. a horse race, game, contest, etc. **2** risk (a sum) thus **3** *Colloq.* feel sure —*n.* **4** act of betting **5** money, etc., staked **6** *Colloq.* choice or possibility —**bet'tor** or **bet'ter** *n.*

bet. *abbr.* between

be·ta /bāt'ə/ *n.* second letter of the Greek alphabet (B, β) [L fr. Gk]

be'ta block'er *n.* drug preventing unwanted stimulation of the heart, used to treat angina and high blood pressure

be·take /bitāk'/ *v.* (**·took, ·tak·en, ·tak·ing**) move (oneself)

be'ta par'ti·cle *n.* fast-moving electron emitted by radioactive decay

be'ta·tron /bāt'əträn'/ *n.* apparatus for accelerating electrons in a circular path [fr. BETA + ELECTRON]

be·tel /bēt'l/ *n.* leaf chewed in E Asia with the betel nut [Port fr. Malayalam]

be'tel nut' *n.* seed of a tropical palm

bête noire /bāt n(ə)wär', bet/ *n.* (*pl.* **bêtes noires,** pronunc. same) person or thing one hates or fears [Fr: black beast]

Be·thes·da /bəthez'də/ *n.* Md. suburb of Washington, D.C. Pop. 62,936

be·think /bĭthĬNGk'/ *v.* (**·thought, ·think·ing**) **1** reflect; stop to think **2** be reminded by reflection [OE, rel. to BE- + THINK]

Be·thune /bəthōōn'/, **Mary McLeod** 1875–1955; US educator

be·tide /bitīd'/ *v.* (**·tid·ed, ·tid·ing**) happen to; befall [fr. BE- + *tide* befall]

be·times /bitīmz'/ *adv. Lit.* early; in good time

Bet·je·man /bech'əmən/, **(Sir) John** 1906–84; English poet; poet laureate (1972–84)

be·to·ken /bitō'kən/ *v.* be a sign of; indicate [OE, rel. to BE- + TOKEN]

be·took /bitŏok′/ *v. past of* BETAKE

be·tray /bitrā′/ *v.* **1** be disloyal or treacherous to **2** reveal involuntarily or treacherously; be evidence of **3** lead astray **—be·tray′al, be·tray′er** *n.* [fr. BE- + obs. *tray* fr. L *tradere* hand over]

be·troth /bitrōTH′, -trŏTH′/ *v.* engage to marry **—be·troth′al** *n.*; **be·troth′ed** *n.* & *adj.* [fr. BE- + TRUTH]

bet·ter /bet′ər/ *adj.* **1** *compar.* of GOOD **2** of a more excellent or desirable kind **3** partly or fully recovered from illness **4** greater **—***adv.* **5** *compar.* of WELL[1] **6** in a more excellent or desirable manner **7** to a greater degree **8** more advisedly **—***n.* **9** more excellent or preferred thing **10** (*pl.*) one's superiors **—***v.* **11** surpass **12** improve **13 better off** in preferred or more desirable circumstances **14 get the better of** defeat; outwit **15 had better** or **best** would find it wisest to [OE]

bet′ter·ment *n.* improvement

bet·tor /bet′ər/ *n.* (also **bet′ter**) person who bets

be·tween /bitwēn′/ *prep.* **1a** at a position in the region bounded by two points in space, time, etc. **b** along the extent of such an area **2** separating **3a** shared by **b** by joint action **4** connecting **5** to and from **6** taking one of **—***adv.* (also **in-between**) **7** at a point or in the area bounded by two or more other points (*not far or thin but in-between*) **8** between you and me in confidence [OE, rel. to BY + TWO] ● Usage: **1** *Between* is reserved for two things, people, etc.: *I must choose between the two candidates. Among* is used only when more than two are involved: *Agreement was reached among all the countries.* But if the relationship of them in pairs is to be emphasized, then *between* is proper: *There is great respect between the signers of the treaty.* **2** *Between you and I* is incorrect; the preposition *between* should be followed only by the objective case of the pronoun: *me, her, him, them.*

be·twixt /bitwikst′/ *adv.* as in **betwixt and between** neither one thing nor the other [OE]

bev·el /bev′əl/ *n.* **1** slope from the horizontal or vertical; sloping surface or edge **2** tool for marking angles **—***v.* (**·eled** or **·elled, ·el·ing** or **·el·ling**) **3** reduce (a square edge) to a sloping edge **4** slope at an angle [Fr]

bev′el gear *n.* gear meshing with another at an angle

bev·er·age /bev′(ə)rij/ *n.* drink [L *bibere* drink]

bev·y /bev′ē/ *n.* (*pl.* **·ies**) group (of quails, larks, women, etc.)

be·wail /biwāl′/ *v.* lament; wail over

be·ware /biwar′, -wer′/ *v.* (only in *imper.* or *infin.*) be cautious (of) [fr. BE + *ware* cautious]

BEVEL GEARS

be·wil·der /biwil′dər/ *v.* perplex; confuse **—be·wil′der·ing** *adj.*; **be·wil′der·ing·ly** *adv.*; **be·wil′der·ment** *n.* [fr. BE- + obs. *wilder* lose one's way]

be·witch /biwicH′/ *v.* **1** enchant **2** cast a spell on

bey /bā/ *n.* title of respect for a Turkish dignitary [Turk: lord]

be·yond /bē·änd′/ *prep.* **1** at or to the farther side of **2** outside the scope or understanding of **3** more than **—***adv.* **4** at or to the farther side **5** further on **—***n.* **6 the great beyond** the unknown after death [OE, rel. to BY + YON]

bez·el /bez′əl/ *n.* **1** sloped edge of a chisel **2** oblique faces of a cut gem **3** groove holding a watch crystal or gem [Fr]

Bho·pal /bōpäl′/ *n.* city in central India. Pop. 1,063,700

Bhu·tan /bōōtän′, -tan′/ *n.* monarchy in the Himalayas, NE of India. Capital: Thimphu. Pop. 1,511,000

Bhut·to /bōō′tō/ **1 Zulfikar Ali** 1928–79; president of Pakistan (1971–73) and prime minister (1973–77); father of: **2 Benazir** 1953– ; prime minister of Pakistan (1988–90; 1993–)

Bi *symb.* bismuth

bi- *comb. form* forming nouns, adjectives, and verbs, meaning: **1** division into two (*bisect*) **2** having two (*biplane*) **3a** occurring twice during every one **b** occurring once during every two (*bicentennial*) **c** lasting for two (*biennial*) [L]

Bia·ly·stok /bē·äl′ēstôk′/ *n.* city in E Poland. Pop. 272,100

bi·an·nu·al /bī·an′yōōəl/ *adj.* occurring twice a year

bi·as /bī′əs/ *n.* **1** predisposition; prejudice **2** edge cut obliquely across the weave of a fabric **—***v.* (**·ased, ·as·ing**) **3** prejudice **4 on the bias** obliquely; diagonally [Fr]

bi·ath·lon /bī·aTH′lən, -län′/ *n.* athletic contest in skiing and shooting or cycling and running [fr. BI-, after PENTATHLON]

bib /bib/ *n.* **1** covering fastened around a child's neck while eating **2** top front part of an apron, dungarees, etc.

Bib. *abbr.* **1** Bible **2** biblical

Bi·ble /bī′bəl/ *n.* **1a** (*prec. by the*) Christian scriptures of Old and New Testaments **b** Jewish scripture, equivalent to the Old Testament **2** (**b-**) authoritative book **—bib′li·cal** (also *cap.*) /bib′likəl/ *adj.* [Gk *biblia* books]

bibl. or **Bibl.** *abbr.* biblical

bibliog. *abbr.* bibliography

bib·li·og·ra·phy /bib′lē·äg′rəfē/ *n.* (*pl.* **·phies**) **1** list of books on a specific subject, by a particular author, etc. **2** the study of books, their authorship, editions, etc. **—bib′li·og·ra·pher** *n.*; **bib′li·o·graph′ic** *adj.*; **bib′li·o·graph′i·cal** /·ägraf′ikəl/ *adj.* [Gk, rel. to BIBLE]

bib·li·o·phile /bib′lē·əfīl′/ *n.* lover or collector of books

bib·u·lous /bib′yələs/ *adj.* tending to drink alcoholic beverages [L *bibere* drink]

bi·cam·er·al /bīkam′ərəl/ *adj.* (of a legislative body) having two chambers [fr. BI- + L *camera* chamber]

bi·carb /bī′kärb/ *n. Colloq.* BICARBONATE [abbr.]

bi·car·bon·ate /bīkär′bənət/ *n.* (in full **bi·car′bon·ate of so′da**) sodium bicarbonate used as an antacid or in baking powder

bi·cen·ten·ni·al /bī′senten′ēəl/ *adj.* **1** taking place once every 200 years **—***n.* **2** bicentennial celebration

bi·ceps /bī′seps/ *n.* (*pl.* same or **·ceps**)

muscle with two heads or attachments, esp. that bending the elbow [L *bi-* two + *caput* head]

bick·er /bik'ər/ *v.* argue pettily

bi·con·cave /bīkän'kāv/ *adj.* (of a lens) concave on both sides

bi·con·vex /bīkän'veks/ *adj.* (of a lens) convex on both sides

bi·cus·pid /bīkas'pid/ *adj.* 1 having two cusps —*n.* 2 the premolar tooth in humans [fr. BI- + CUSP]

bi·cy·cle /bī'sik'əl, -sikəl, -sīk'-/ *n.* 1 pedal-driven two-wheeled vehicle —*v.* (·cled, ·cling) 2 ride a bicycle [Gk *kuklos* wheel]

bid /bid/ *v.* (**bid** or **bade**, **bid·den**, **bid·ding**) 1a make an offer (of) b offer a service for a stated price 2 command; invite 3 utter (a greeting or farewell) to 4 *Cards.* state before play how many tricks one intends to make —*n.* 5 act of bidding 6 amount bid 7 *Colloq.* attempt; effort —**bid'da·ble** *adj.*; **bid'der** *n.* [OE]

bid'ding *n.* 1 command; request; invitation 2 bids at an auction or in a card game

bid·dy /bid'ē/ *n.* (*pl.* **·dies**) *Colloq.* & *Offens.* (old) woman [fr. name *Bridget*]

bide /bīd/ *v.* (**bid·ed** or **bode**, **bid·ed**, **bid·ing**) 1 wait; abide 2 **bide one's time** delay action [OE]

bi·det /bidā'/ *n.* low basin for sitting on to wash the genital area [Fr: pony]

Bie·le·feld /bē'ləfelt'/ *n.* city in Germany. Pop. 319,000

bi·en·ni·al /bī-en'ēəl/ *adj.* 1 lasting for or recurring every two years —*n.* 2 event that takes place every two years 3 plant that lives for two years [L *annus* year]

bier /bēr/ *n.* movable frame for a coffin [OE]

Bierce /bērs/, **Ambrose** 1842 – c. 1914; US writer

bi·fo·cals /bīfō'kəls/ *n. pl.* eyeglass lenses with one part for close vision and the other for distant vision

bi·fur·cate /bī'fərkāt'/ *v.* (·cat·ed, ·cat·ing) 1 fork —*adj.* 2 forked; branched —**bi'fur·ca'tion** *n.* [L *furca* fork]

big /big/ *adj.* (**big·ger**, **big·gest**) 1a of considerable size, amount, intensity, etc. b of a large or the largest size 2 important 3 adult; elder 4a *Colloq.* boastful (*big words*) b generous c ambitious; grandiose 5 advanced in pregnancy —*adv.* 6 *Colloq.* impressively or grandly —**big'gish** *adj.*; **big'ness** *n.*

big·a·my /big'əmē/ *n.* crime of marrying while still married to another person —**big'a·mist** *n.*; **big'a·mous** *adj.* [Gk *gamos* marriage]

Big Ap'ple *n. Slang.* New York City

big' bang' the'o·ry *n.* theory that the universe began with the explosion of dense matter

big'·heart'ed *adj.* generous

big'horn' *n.* wild sheep with large, curving horns

bight /bīt/ *n.* 1 bay, inlet, etc. 2 loop or other part of a rope that is not an end [OE]

big'mouth' *n.* loud, talkative, opinionated person

big·ot /big'ət/ *n.* obstinate believer who is intolerant of others —**big'ot·ed** *adj.*; **big'ot·ry** *n.* [Fr]

big' shot' *n.* (also **big' wheel, big'wig'**) *Slang.* important person

---

Big' Sur' /sər'/ *n.* Pacific coastal region of great natural beauty, from Carmel to San Simeon, Calif.

big' top' *n.* main tent in a circus

bike /bīk/ *Colloq. n.* 1 bicycle or motorcycle —*v.* (**biked, bik·ing**) 2 ride a bike —**bik'er** *n.*

bi·ki·ni /bikē'nē/ *n.* brief two-piece swimsuit for women [*Bikini*, Pacific atoll]

Bi·ko /bē'kō/, **Steve (Stephen)** 1946–77; South African black activist

bi·lat·er·al /bīlat'ərəl/ *adj.* 1 of, on, or with two sides 2 affecting or between two parties, countries, etc. —**bi·lat'er·al·ly** *adv.*

Bil·ba·o /bilbou', -bä'ō/ *n.* seaport in N Spain. Pop. 368,700

bile /bīl/ *n.* 1 bitter digestive fluid secreted by the liver 2 bad temper; peevish anger —**bil·i·ar·y** /bil'ē-er'ē/ *adj.* [L *bilis*]

bilge /bilj/ *n.* 1a the part of a ship's bottom closest to the keel b (in full **bilge' wa'ter**) filthy water that collects there 2 *Slang.* nonsense [prob. var. of BULGE]

bi·lin·gual /bīliNG'gwəl/ *adj.* 1 able to speak two languages 2 spoken or written in two languages —*n.* 3 bilingual person —**bi·lin'gual·ism'** *n.* [L BI- + *lingua* tongue]

bil·ious /bil'ēəs/ *adj.* 1 affected by a disorder of the bile 2 bad-tempered [L, rel. to BILE]

bilk /bilk/ *v.* 1 cheat 2 elude 3 avoid paying

bill[1] /bil/ *n.* 1 statement of charges for goods or services 2 draft of a proposed law 3 poster; placard 4 program of entertainment 5 piece of paper money —*v.* 6 send a statement of charges to 7 put in the program; announce [MedL *bulla* seal]

bill[2] *n.* 1 bird's beak —*v.* 2 (of doves, etc.) stroke bills 3 **bill and coo** exchange caresses [OE]

bill[3] *n. Hist.* weapon with a hooked blade [OE]

bill'board' *n.* large outdoor advertising sign

bil·let /bil'it/ *n.* 1 place where troops, etc., are lodged 2 job —*v.* 3 quarter (soldiers, etc.) [AngFr dim. of BILL[1]]

bil·let-doux /bēyā dōō', -/ *n.* (*pl.* **bil·lets-doux** /-dōōz'/) love letter [Fr: sweet note]

bil·liards /bil'yərdz/ *n.* 1 game played on a cloth-covered table in which a stick is used to propel a ball at other object balls 2 (*loosely*) any game played on such a table using hard balls, e.g., pool [Fr *billard*, orig. a cue]

Bil·lings /bil'iNGz/ *n.* city in Mont. Pop. 81,151

bil·lion /bil'yən/ *adj.* & *n.* 1 a thousand million (10^9) 2 (*pl.*) *Colloq.* a very large number —**bil'lionth** *adj.* & *n.* [Fr]

bil·lion·aire /bil'yəner'/ *n.* person who has over a billion dollars, pounds, etc. [after MILLIONAIRE]

bill' of ex·change' *n.* written order to pay a sum of money on a given date to the drawer or to a named payee

bill' of fare' *n.* menu

bill' of lad'ing *n.* detailed list of a ship's cargo

Bill' of Rights' *n.* first ten amendments to the U.S. Constitution, guaranteeing civil rights

bill' of sale' *n.* receipt showing transfer of ownership

bil·low /bil′ō/ *n.* **1** wave **2** any large mass —*v.* **3** rise or surge in billows —**bil′low·y** *adj.* [ON]

bil·ly /bil′ē/ *n.* (*pl.* **·lies**) (also **bil′ly club′**) policeman's truncheon [OE *bill* sword + -Y]

bil′ly goat′ *n.* male goat

bi·me·tal·lic /bī′mətal′ik/ *adj.* using or made of two metals [Fr]

bi·month·ly /bīmənth′lē/ *adv. & adj.* **1** occurring once in two months **2** (*loosely*) twice a month **3** periodical published every two months, or two times a month

bin /bin/ *n.* large receptacle for rubbish or storage [OE]

bi·na·ry /bī′nərē, -nerē/ *adj.* **1** of two parts; dual **2** of a number system with the base 2, in which quantities are represented by combinations of 0 and 1 —*n.* (*pl.* **·ries**) **3** something having two parts **4** binary number [L *bini* two together]

bind /bīnd/ *v.* (**bound, bind·ing**) **1** tie or fasten tightly **2** restrain forcibly **3** (cause to) cohere **4** compel; impose a duty on **5** fasten (the pages of a book) in a cover **6** ratify (a bargain, agreement, etc.) **7** bandage —*n.* **8** *Colloq.* nuisance; restriction [OE]

bind′er *n.* **1** cover for loose papers, etc. **2** substance that binds things together **3** reaping machine that binds grain into sheaves **4** bookbinder

bind′er·y *n.* (*pl.* **·ies**) bookbinder's workshop

bind′ing *n.* **1** thing that binds, esp. the covers, glue, etc., of a book —*adj.* **2** obligatory

binge /binj/ *n. Slang.* **1** bout of excessive eating, drinking, etc.; spree —*v.* (**binged, bing·ing**) **2** indulge in a binge

bin·go /biNG′gō/ *n.* gambling game in which each player has a card with numbers to be marked off as they are called

bin·na·cle /bin′ikəl/ *n.* case for a ship's compass [L *habitaculum* dwelling]

bin·oc·u·lar /bīnäk′yələr/ *adj.* for both eyes [L *bini* two together + *oculus* eye]

bin·oc·u·lars /bənäk′yələrz, bī-/ *n. pl.* instrument with a lens for each eye for viewing distant objects

bi·no·mi·al /bīnō′mēəl/ *n.* **1** algebraic expression of the sum or the difference of two terms —*adj.* **2** name of an animal or plant consisting of two terms, one generic, the other specific **3** of two terms [Gk *nomos* part]

bio. *abbr.* **1** biography **2** biological **3** biology

bio- *comb. form* **1** life (*biography*) **2** biological; of living things [Gk *bios* life]

bi·o·chem·is·try /bī′ōkem′əstrē/ *n.* study of the chemistry of living organisms —**bi′o·chem′i·cal** *adj.*; **bi′o·chem′i·cal·ly** *adv.*; **bi′o·chem′ist** *n.*

bi·o·de·grad·a·ble /bī′ōdigrād′əbəl/ *adj.* capable of being decomposed by bacteria or other living organisms

bi·o·en·gin·eer·ing /bī′ō·en′jənēr′iNG/ *n.* **1** application of engineering techniques to biological processes **2** use of artificial tissues, organs, etc., to replace parts of the body

bi·o·feed·back /bī′ōfēd′bak/ *n.* techniques to monitor and attempt to control involuntary body processes such as heartbeat, blood pressure, etc.

biog. *abbr.* **1** biographical **2** biography

bi·o·gen·e·sis /bī′ōjen′əsəs/ *n.* **1** hypothesis that a living organism arises only from a similar living organism **2** synthesis of substances by living organisms —**bi′o·ge·net′ic** /-net′ik/ *adj.*; **bi′o·ge·net′i·cal·ly** *adv.*

bi·og·ra·phy /bī·äg′rəfē/ *n.* (*pl.* **·phies**) account of a person's life, written usu. by another —**bi·og′ra·pher** *n.*; **bi·o·graph·i·cal** /bī′əgraf′ikəl/ *adj.* [Fr, rel. to BIO-]

bi·o·log′i·cal clock′ *n.* innate mechanism controlling rhythmic physiological activities

bi·o·log′i·cal war′fare *n.* use of toxins or microorganisms against an enemy

bi·ol·o·gy /bīäl′əjē/ *n.* the study of living organisms —**bi·o·log·i·cal** /bī′əläj′ikəl/ *adj.*; **bi′o·log·i·cal·ly** *adv.*; **bi·ol′o·gist** *n.* [Ger, rel. to BIO-]

bi·o·mass /bī′ōmas′/ *n.* living organisms and organic materials, considered collectively

bi·on·ic /bī·än′ik/ *adj.* having electronically or mechanically operated body parts —**bi·on′ic·al·ly** *adv.* [fr. *bio-* + electronic]

bi·on·ics *n. pl.* (treated as *sing.*) the study of mechanical systems that function like living organisms

bi·o·phys·ics /bī′ōfiz′iks/ *n. pl.* (treated as *sing.*) science of the laws of physics applied to biological phenomena —**bi′o·phys′i·cal** *adj.*; **bi′o·phys′i·cist** *n.*

bi·op·sy /bī′äp′sē/ *n.* (*pl.* **·sies**) examination of tissue severed for diagnosis [Gk *bios* life + *opsis* sight]

bi·o·rhythm /bī′ōriTH′əm/ *n.* any recurring biological cycle thought to affect the physical or mental state

bi·o·sphere /bī′əsfēr′/ *n.* regions of the earth's crust and atmosphere occupied by living things [Ger, rel. to BIO-]

bi·o·syn·the·sis /bī′ōsin′THəsis/ *n.* production of organic molecules by living organisms —**bi′o·syn·thet′ic** /-sinTHet′ik/ *adj.*

bi·o·tech·nol·o·gy /bī′ōteknäl′əjē/ *n.* branch of technology exploiting biological processes in industry, medicine, etc.

bi·o·tin /bī′ətin/ *n.* vitamin of the B complex [Gk *bios* life]

bi·par·ti·san /bīpärt′əzən/ *adj.* of or involving two parties

bi·par·tite /bīpär′tīt′/ *adj.* **1** of two parts **2** shared by or involving two parties [L *bipartire* divide in two]

bi·ped /bī′ped′/ *n.* **1** two-footed animal —*adj.* **2** two-footed —**bi·ped′al** *adj.* [L *bipes -edis*]

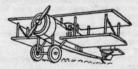

BIPLANE

bi·plane /bī′plān′/ *n.* airplane with two sets of wings, one above the other

birch /bərCH/ *n.* **1** tree with pale, hard wood and thin, peeling bark **2** its wood **3** bundle of birch twigs used for flogging —*v.* **4** beat with a birch [OE]

bird /bərd/ *n.* **1** two-legged, feathered,

winged vertebrate, egg-laying and usu. able to fly **2 a bird in the hand** something secured or certain **3 birds of a feather** similar people **4 for the birds** Colloq. trivial; uninteresting [OE]

bird'bath' n. basin with water for birds to bathe in

bird'brain' n. Colloq. stupid or flighty person —**bird'brained'** adj.

bird·ie /bərd'ē/ n. Golf. hole played in one under par

bird's'-eye view' n. detached view from above

bird'watch'er n. person who observes wild birds as a hobby —**bird'watch'ing** n.

bi·ret·ta /bəret'ə/ n. square, usu. black, cap worn by Roman Catholic priests [L birrus cape]

Bir·ming·ham n. **1** /bər'miNGəm/ city in central England. Pop. 1,024,100 **2** /bər'miNGham'/ city in Ala. Pop. 265,968

birth /bərTH/ n. **1** emergence of a baby or young from its mother's body **2** beginning **3** origin (of noble birth) **4 give birth to: a** produce (young) **b** be the originator of [ON]

BIRETTA

birth' cer·tif'i·cate n. official document detailing a person's birth

birth' con·trol' n. contraception

birth'day' n. **1** day on which one was born **2** anniversary of this **3 birth'day' suit** in the clothes one was born in; naked

birth'mark' n. colored mark on one's body at or from birth

birth'place' n. place where one was born

birth' rate' n. number of live births per thousand of population per year

birth'right' n. inherited rights, esp. to property

birth'stone' n. gem popularly associated with the month of one's birth

Bis·cay, Bay of /biskā'/ n. inlet of the Atlantic between Spain and France

bis·cuit /bis'kit/ n. **1** quick-baking bread made in small buns **2** chiefly Brit. cracker or cookie [L bis twice + coquere cook]

bi·sect /bīsekt'/ v. divide into two (strictly; equal) parts —**bi·sec'tor** n. [fr. BI- + L sectum fr. secare cut]

bi·sex·u·al /bīsek'SHŌŌəl/ adj. **1** feeling or involving sexual attraction to people of both sexes **2** hermaphrodite —n. **3** bisexual person —**bi·sex'u·al·ism**/, bi·sex'u·al'i·ty /-al'itē/ n.; **bi·sex'u·al·ly** adv.

Bish·kek /bisHkek'/ n. capital of Kyrgyzstan. Pop. 641,400

bish·op /bisH'əp/ n. **1** senior clergyman in charge of a diocese **2** Chess. piece that is moved diagonally [Gk episkopos overseer]

bish·op·ric /bisH'əprik/ n. office or diocese of a bishop

Bis·marck /biz'märk/, **Otto Eduard Leopold von** 1815–98; Prussian statesman; 1st chancellor of a unified Germany (1871–90); also called the "Iron Chancellor"

Bis·marck /biz'märk/ n. capital of N. Dak., in the S central part. Pop. 49,256

bis·muth /biz'məTH/ n. metallic element used in alloys, medicine, etc.; symb. Bi [Ger]

bi·son /bī'sən/ n. (pl. same) wild hump-

backed ox of Europe or N America [L fr. Gmc]

bisque¹ /bisk/ n. rich soup, esp. of lobster [Fr]

bisque² n. BISCUIT, 2

Bis·sau /bisou'/ n. capital of Guinea-Bissau. Pop. 125,000

bis·tro /bē'strō, bis'trō/ n. (pl. -tros) small restaurant [Fr]

bit¹ /bit/ n. **1** small piece or quantity **2** (prec. by a) fair amount **3** short or small time, distance, or amount **4 bit by bit** gradually **5 do one's bit** make a useful contribution **6 two bits** one quarter; 25 cents [OE]

bit² n. **1** metal mouthpiece of a bridle **2** tool or piece for boring or drilling (see illustration at BRACE AND BIT) **3** cutting or gripping part of a plane, pincers, etc. [OE]

bit³ n. Comp. unit of information in a binary system [binary digit]

bitch /biCH/ n. **1** female dog or other canine animal **2** Slang. Offens. spiteful woman **3** Slang. unpleasant or difficult thing —v. **4** speak scathingly or spitefully **5** complain [OE]

bitch'y adj. (·i·er, ·i·est) Slang. spiteful —**bitch'i·ly** adv.; **bitch'i·ness** n.

bite /bīt/ v. (bit, bit·ten, bit·ing) **1** cut or puncture with the teeth **2** detach thus **3** (of an insect, etc.) sting **4** Colloq. accept bait or an inducement **5** be harsh **6** cause smarting pain **7** be sharp or effective **8** act of biting **9** wound, etc., made by biting **10a** mouthful of food **b** snack **11** taking of bait by a fish **12** pungency (esp. of flavor) **13 bite the bullet** face something painful or unpleasant without flinching **14 bite the dust** Slang. die **15 bite a person's head off** Colloq. respond angrily **16 bite one's lip** repress emotion **17 bite one's tongue** remain silent [OE]

bit' part' n. minor role

bit·ter /bit'ər/ adj. **1** having a sharp pungent taste; not sweet **2** causing, showing, or feeling mental pain or resentment **3a** harsh; resentful **b** piercingly cold —**bit'ter·ly** adv.; **bit'ter·ness** n. [OE]

bit·tern /bit'ərn/ n. wading bird of the heron family [OFr butor fr. L buteo]

bit·ters /bit'ərz/ n. bitter-tasting alcoholic liquor used as a flavoring

bit'ter·sweet' adj. **1** sweet with a bitter aftertaste —n. **2** such sweetness **3** plant of the nightshade family, with red berries

bi·tu·men /bət(y)ŌŌ'mən, bī'-/ n. tarlike mixture of hydrocarbons derived from petroleum —**bi·tu'mi·nous** adj. [L]

bi·tu'mi·nous coal' n. soft coal burning with a smoky flame

bi·valve /bī'valv'/ n. aquatic mollusk with a hinged double shell, e.g., the oyster

biv·ou·ac /biv'(ə)wak'/ n. **1** temporary open encampment without tents —v. (·acked, ·ack·ing) **2** make or camp in a bivouac [Fr, prob. fr. Ger]

biz /biz/ n. Colloq. business

bi·zarre /bizär'/ adj. strange; eccentric; grotesque [Fr]

Bi·zet /bēzā'/, **Georges** 1838–75; French composer

Bk *symb.* berkelium

bk. *abbr.* 1 bank 2 book

blab /blab/ *v.* (**blabbed, blab-bing**) 1 talk foolishly or indiscreetly 2 reveal (a secret) —**blab'ber-mouth** *n.* [imit.]

black /blak/ *adj.* 1 colorless from lack of reflected light (like soot); completely dark 2 (also *cap.*) of the human population with dark-colored skin, esp. of African origin 3 (of the sky, etc.) heavily overcast 4 angry; gloomy 5 wicked; sinister; deadly 6 ominous 7 comic but sinister (*black comedy*) 8 (of coffee or tea) without milk —*n.* 9 black color or pigment 10 black clothes 11 (also *cap.*) member of a dark-skinned race, esp. an African —*v.* 12 make black 13 **black out** become unconscious 14 **in the black** profitable —**black'ish** *adj.*; **black'ly** *adv.*; **black'ness** *n.* [OE]

black'-and-blue' *adj.* bruised

black'ball' *v.* reject (a candidate) in a ballot

black'belt' *n.* 1 highest grade of proficiency in judo, karate, etc. 2 holder of this grade, entitled to wear a black belt

black'ber'ry *n.* (*pl.* -ries) 1 black, fleshy, edible fruit of the bramble 2 the plant yielding it

black'bird' *n.* common thrush of which the male is black with an orange beak

black'board' *n.* board with a smooth, dark surface for writing on with chalk

Black-burn /blak'bərn/ *n.* city in NW England. Pop. 110,300

Black' Death' *n.* (prec. by *the*) 14th-century plague in Europe

black' e-con'o-my *n.* unofficial and untaxed trade

black'en *v.* 1 make or become black or dark 2 defame; slander

Black' Eng'lish *n.* variety of English spoken by some black Americans

black' eye' *n.* 1 bruised skin around the eye 2 stigma of dishonor

black'-eyed' Su'san *n.* daisy with yellow petals and dark brown center

black-guard /blag'ard, -ärd'/ *n.* villain; scoundrel —**black'guard-ly** *adj.*

Black' Hawk' 1767–1838; American Indian leader

black'head' *n.* black-topped pimple on the skin

Black' Hills' *n.* mountains in NE Wyo. and western S. Dak.

black' hole' *n.* theoretical region of space from which matter and radiation cannot escape owing to strong gravitational pull

black' ice' *n.* thin layer of invisible ice on a road, etc.

black'jack' *n.* 1 short club, often covered in black leather, used as a weapon 2 card game in which players bet on reaching a score of 21 3 ace and a ten or face card in this game

black'light' *n.* invisible light used to make fluorescent materials glow in the dark

black'list' *n.* 1 list of people in disfavor, etc. —*v.* 2 put on a blacklist

black' mag'ic *n.* magic supposed to invoke evil spirits

black'mail' *n.* 1a extortion of payment in return for silence **b** payment so extorted —*v.*

2 (try to) extort money from by blackmail —**black'mail'er** *n.* [obs. *mail* rent]

black' mark' *n.* mark of discredit

black' mar'ket *n.* illicit trade in rationed, prohibited, or scarce commodities —**black' mar'ke-teer'** *n.*

Black' Mass' *n.* worship of Satan

black'out' *n.* 1 temporary loss of consciousness or memory 2 loss of electric power, radio reception, etc. 3 compulsory darkness as a precaution against air raids 4 suppression of news 5 sudden darkening of a theater stage for dramatic effect

Black-pool /blak'pōōl/ *n.* resort town in NW England. Pop. 149,000

Black' Pow'er *n.* movement, esp. of the 1960s, for black rights and political power

Black' Sea' *n.* sea enclosed by Turkey, the Balkan Peninsula, Ukraine, and SW Russia

black' sheep' *n.* *Colloq.* member of a family, group, etc., regarded as a disgrace or failure

black-smith /blak'smiTH/ *n.* worker who forges and shapes iron implements

Black-stone /blak'stōn/, (**Sir**) **William** 1723–80; English jurist

black'thorn' *n.* thorny shrub bearing white blossom and sloes

black' tie' *n.* 1 black bow tie worn with a dinner jacket 2 *Colloq.* man's formal evening dress

black'top' *n.* 1 asphalt paving mixture —*v.* (·**topped, ·top·ping**) 2 pave with blacktop

Black-well /blak'wel', -wəl/, **Elizabeth** 1821–1910; US physician

black' wid'ow *n.* venomous spider of which the female devours the male

blad-der /blad'ər/ *n.* 1a sac in some animals, esp. that holding urine **b** this adapted for various uses 2 inflated blister in seaweed, etc. [OE]

blade /blād/ *n.* 1 cutting part of a knife, etc. 2 flattened part of an oar, propeller, etc. 3a flat narrow leaf of grass, etc. **b** broad, thin part of a leaf 4 sword [OE]

Blake /blāk/, **William** 1757–1827; English artist and poet

blame /blām/ *v.* (**blamed, blam-ing**) 1 assign fault or responsibility to 2 fix responsibility for (an error, etc.) on —*n.* 3 responsibility for an error, etc. 4 blaming or attributing of responsibility 5 **be to blame** be responsible for an error —**blame'a-ble, blame'less** *adj.*; **blame'wor'thy** /-wər'THē/ *adj.* [Fr. rel. to BLASPHEME]

Blanc, Mont /môn blän/ *n.* highest mountain in the Alps, on the France-Italy-Switzerland border: 15,771 ft.

blanch /blanCH/ *v.* 1 make or become white or pale 2 prepare (almonds, vegetables, etc.) by scalding briefly in boiling water [Fr, rel. to BLANK]

bland /bland/ *adj.* 1a mild; not irritating **b** tasteless; insipid 2 gentle in manner; suave —**bland'ly** *adv.*; **bland'ness** *n.* [L *blandus* smooth]

blan-dish /blan'diSH/ *v.* flatter; coax —**blan'dish-ment** *n.* [L, rel. to BLAND]

blank /blaNGk/ *adj.* 1a (of paper) not written or printed on **b** (of a document) with spaces left for a signature or details 2 empty 3 having (temporarily) no knowledge, etc. 4 complete —n. 5a unfilled space, esp. in a document b document having blank spaces 6 (in full blank′ car′tridge) cartridge containing gunpowder but no bullet 7 blank out obliterate; erase 8 draw a blank get no response; fail —blank′ly adv.; blank′ness n. [Fr blanc white, fr. Gmc]

blank′ check′ n. 1 signed check left for the payee to fill in the amount 2 check without writing 3 Colloq. freedom of action

blan·ket /blaNG′kit/ n. 1 sheet, esp. woven, used for warmth, as a bed covering, etc. 2 thick covering mass or layer —adj. 3 covering everything; inclusive —v. 4 cover 5 obstruct; suppress [Fr, rel. to BLANK]

blank′ verse′ n. unrhymed verse, esp. iambic pentameters

Blan·tyre /blan′tīr′/ n. city in Malawi. Pop. 333,100

blare /bler/ v. (blared, blar·ing) 1 sound or utter loudly 2 make the sound of a trumpet —n. 3 blaring sound [LGer or Du, imit.]

blar·ney /blär′nē/ n. 1 cajoling talk; flattery —v. (·neyed, ·ney·ing) 2 flatter; cajole [Blarney, castle in Ireland]

bla·sé /bläzā′/ adj. bored or indifferent [Fr]

blas·pheme /blas·fēm′, blas′fēm/ v. (·phemed, ·phem·ing) 1 use religious names irreverently; treat a religious or sacred subject irreverently 2 talk irreverently about [Gk blasphēmein]

blas·phe·my /blas′fəmē/ n. (pl. ·mies) 1 irreverent talk or treatment of a religious or sacred thing 2 instance of this —blas′phe·mous adj.

blast /blast/ n. 1 strong gust of air 2a explosion b destructive wave of air from this 3 loud note from a wind instrument, car horn, etc. 4 Colloq. severe reprimand —v. 5 blow up with explosives 6 wither; shrivel —interj. 7 expressing annoyance 8 at full blast at maximum volume, speed, etc. 9 blast off (of a rocket) take off from a launching site [OE]

blast′ fur′nace n. smelting furnace into which hot air is driven

blast′off′ n. (also blast′-off′) launching of a rocket, etc.

bla·tant /blāt′nt/ adj. 1 flagrant; unashamed 2 loudly obtrusive —bla′tant·ly adv. [coined by Spenser]

blaze¹ /blāz/ n. 1 bright flame or fire 2 violent outburst (of passion, etc.) 3 brilliant display —v. (blazed, blaz·ing) 4 burn or shine brightly or fiercely 5 be consumed with anger, excitement, etc. 6 blaze away shoot continuously [OE: torch]

blaze² n. 1 white mark on an animal's face 2 mark cut on a tree, esp. to show a route —v. (blazed, blaz·ing) 3 mark (a tree or a path) with blazes

blaz′er n. solid-color jacket, usu. with shiny metal buttons

bla·zon /blā′zən/ v. 1 proclaim —n. 2 coat of arms —bla′zon·ment, bla′zon·ry n. [Fr, orig. shield]

bldg. abbr. building

bleach /blēCH/ v. 1 whiten in sunlight or by a chemical process —n. 2 bleaching substance or process [OE]

bleach′ers n. pl. inexpensive seats in a stadium, not sheltered from the sun, rain, etc.

bleak /blēk/ adj. 1 exposed; windswept 2 dreary; grim [ON]

blear·y /blēr′ē/ adj. (·i·er, ·i·est) 1 dim; blurred 2 indistinct [LGer]

blear′y-eyed′ adj. having dim sight

bleat /blēt/ v. 1 (of a sheep, goat, or calf) make a wavering cry —n. 2 bleating cry [OE]

bleed /blēd/ v. (bled, bleed·ing) 1 emit blood 2 draw blood from surgically 3 Colloq. extort money from 4 empty (a system) of excess air or fluid —bleed′er n. [OE]

bleep /blēp/ n. 1 high-pitched sound made by an electronic device —v. 2 make a bleep 3 obliterate obscenities with a bleep, as on a TV performance

blem·ish /blem′iSH/ n. 1 flaw, defect, or stain —v. 2 spoil, mark, or stain [Fr]

blench /blenCH/ v. flinch; quail [OE]

blend /blend/ v. 1 mix together as required 2 become one 3 (esp. of colors) merge imperceptibly; harmonize —n. 4 mixture [ON]

blend′er n. kitchen appliance for liquidizing, chopping, or puréeing food

bless /bles/ v. (blessed or blest, bless·ing) 1 ask God to look favorably on, esp. by making the sign of the cross over 2 consecrate (food, etc.) 3 glorify (God) 4 thank 5 make happy or successful 6 (God) bless you! exclamation of endearment, gratitude, etc., or to a person who has just sneezed [OE]

bless·ed /bles′id/ adj. (also blessed /blest/ or Poet. blest) 1 holy 2 Euphem. cursed (blessed nuisance!) 3 RC Ch. beatified —bless′ed·ness n.

bless′ing n. 1 invocation of (esp. divine) favor 2 grace said at a meal 3 benefit

blew /bloō/ v. past of BLOW¹

blight /blīt/ n. 1 plant disease caused by insects, etc. 2 such an insect 3 harmful or destructive force 4 ugly, deteriorated area (urban blight) —v. 5 affect with blight 6 harm; destroy 7 spoil

blimp /blimp/ n. small, nonrigid airship

blind /blīnd/ adj. 1 lacking the power of sight 2a without adequate discernment b unwilling or unable to accept 3 not governed by purpose or reason 4a concealed b closed at one end 5 (of flying) using instruments only —v. 6 deprive of sight 7 rob of judgment 8 overawe —n. 9 shade for a window 10 obstruction to sight or light 11 hiding place of a hunter, observer, etc., of wildlife —blind′ly adv.; blind′ness n. [OE]

blind′ date′ n. Colloq. date between two people who have not previously met 2 either of such people

blind·fold /blin(d)′fōld′/ v. 1 cover the eyes with a cloth, etc. —n. 2 cloth so used —adj. & adv. 3 blindfolded 4 without due care [orig. blindfelled struck blind]

blind′side′ v. strike or attack unexpectedly

blind′ spot′ n. 1 point on the retina insensitive to light 2 area where vision or understanding is lacking

blink /bliNGk/ v. 1 shut and open the eyes quickly 2 prevent (tears) by blinking 3 (of a light) go on and off —n. 4 act of blinking 5 momentary gleam or glimpse 6 blink at ignore **7 on the blink** *Slang.* not working properly [Du, var. of BLENCH]

blink'er *n.* 1 (usu. *pl.*) each of two screens on a bridle preventing lateral vision 2 device that blinks —*v.* 3 obscure with blinkers

blintz /blints/ *n.* thin pancake with various fillings [Yiddish *blintze* fr. Russ *blinets* small pancake]

blip /blip/ *n.* 1 temporary minor deviation or error 2 spot of light on a radar screen [imit.]

bliss /blis/ *n.* 1 perfect joy 2 being in heaven —**bliss'ful** *adj.*; **bliss'ful·ly** *adv.*; **bliss'ful·ness** *n.* [OE]

blis·ter /blis'tər/ *n.* 1 small bubble on the skin filled with watery fluid and caused by heat or friction. 2 similar swelling on plastic, wood, etc. —*v.* 3 come up in blisters 4 raise a blister on 5 attack sharply —**blis'ter·ing·ly** *adv.*; **blis'ter·y** *adj.*

blithe /blīTH, blīTH/ *adj.* (also **blithe'some** /-səm/) 1 cheerful; happy 2 careless; casual —**blithe'ful** *adj.*; **blithe'ful·ly** *adv.*; **blithe'ful·ness** *n.*; **blithe'ly** *adv.*; **blithe'ness** *n.* [OE]

blitz /blits/ *n.* 1 intensive or sudden (esp. aerial) attack —*v.* 2 inflict a blitz on [abbr. of Ger *Blitzkrieg* lightning war]

bliz·zard /bliz'ərd/ *n.* severe snowstorm

bloat /blōt/ *v.* inflate; swell [ON]

blob /bläb/ *n.* 1 small drop or spot *v.* (**blobbed, blob·bing**) 2 spatter with blobs

bloc /bläk/ *n.* group of governments, factions, etc., sharing a common purpose [Fr, rel. to BLOCK]

block /bläk/ *n.* 1 solid piece of hard material, esp. stone or wood 2 this as a base for chopping, etc. 3 obstruction 4 two or more pulleys mounted in a case 5 piece of wood or metal engraved for printing —*v.* 6 obstruct; impede **7 block out:** a shut out (light, noise, a memory, view, etc.) b sketch roughly; plan —**block'er** *n.* [LGer or Du]

block·ade /bläkād'/ *n.* 1 blocking of a place by an enemy to prevent entry and exit —*v.* (**·ad·ed, ·ad·ing**) 2 subject to a blockade

block' and tack'le *n.* system of pulleys and ropes, esp. for lifting

block·bust·er /bläk'bəs'tər/ *n. Slang.* 1 thing of great power, esp. a very successful film, book, etc. 2 highly destructive bomb

block'bust'ing *n.* unethical real estate sales practice of spreading rumors that a minority-group member is buying a nearby home

block'head' *n.* stupid person

block'house' *n.* 1 reinforced concrete shelter 2 *Hist.* small fort of timber

Bloem·fon·tein /bloom'fän'ten'/ *n.* judicial capital of South Africa. Pop. 104,400

blond /bländ/ *adj.* (also *fem.* **blonde**) 1 (of a person, hair, or complexion) light-colored; fair —*n.* 2 person, esp. a man, with fair hair [L *blondus* yellow]

blood /bləd/ *n.* 1 usu. red fluid circulating in the arteries and veins of animals 2 bloodshed 3 passion; temperament 4 race; descent; parentage 5 relationship; relations 6 source of new ideas, energy, etc., from new or younger people **7 in cold blood** cruelly; deliberately; unremorsefully [OE]

blood' bank' *n.* store of blood for transfusion

blood' bath' *n.* massacre

blood' count' *n.* number of corpuscles in a specific amount of blood

blood'cur'dling /kər'dliNG/ *adj.* horrifying

blood' group' *n.* any of the types of human blood

blood'hound' *n.* 1 large keen-scented dog used in tracking 2 *Colloq.* detective

blood'less *adj.* 1 without blood or bloodshed 2 unemotional 3 pale 4 feeble —**blood'less·ly** *adv.*; **blood'less·ness** *n.*

blood'mo·bile' *n.* truck equipped to collect blood from donors to a blood bank

blood' mon'ey *n.* 1 money paid as compensation for a death 2 money paid to a killer 3 money paid to an informer

blood' poi'son·ing *n.* diseased condition caused by microorganisms in the blood

blood' pres'sure *n.* pressure of the blood in the arteries, etc., measured for diagnosis

blood' re·la'tion *n.* (also **blood' rel'a·tive**) relative by birth

blood'shed' *n.* killing

blood'shot' *adj.* (of an eyeball) inflamed

blood'stain' *n.* stain caused by blood —**blood'stained'** *adj.*

blood'stream' *n.* blood in circulation

blood'suck'er *n.* 1 leech 2 extortionist —**blood'suck'ing** *adj.*

blood'thirst'y *adj.* (**·i·er, ·i·est**) eager for bloodshed

blood' ves'sel *n.* vein, artery, or capillary carrying blood

blood'y *adj.* (**·i·er, ·i·est**) 1 of, like, running with, or smeared with blood 2a involving bloodshed b bloodthirsty; cruel 3 *Brit. Slang.* damned; in the extreme 4 red —*adv. Brit. Slang.* as an intensifier 5 terribly; very; awfully (*bloody awful*) —*v.* (**·ied, ·y·ing**) 6 stain with blood —**blood'i·ly** *adv.*; **blood'i·ness** *n.*

bloom /bloom/ *n.* 1a flower, esp. cultivated b state of flowering 2 one's prime 3 healthy glow of the complexion 4 fine powder on fresh fruit and leaves —*v.* 5 bear flowers; be in flower 6 be in one's prime; flourish [ON]

Bloom·er /bloo'mər/, **Amelia Jenks** 1818–94; US reformer

bloom·ers /bloo'mərz/ *n. pl.* women's long, loose underpants or knee-length trousers [name of the originator]

Bloom·field /bloom'feld/, **Leonard** 1887–1949; US linguist

bloom'ing *adj.* 1 flourishing; healthy 2 *Slang.* euphem. for BLOODY, 3 —*adv.* 3 *Slang.* euphem. for BLOODY, 5

Bloo·ming·ton /bloo'miNGtən/ *n.* 1 city in Minn. Pop. 86,335 2 city in Ind. Pop. 60,633

blos·som /bläs'əm/ *n.* 1 flower or mass of flowers, esp. of a fruit tree 2 promising stage —*v.* 3 start flourishing 4 mature; thrive [OE]

blot /blät/ *n.* 1 spot or stain of ink, etc. 2 disgraceful act or quality 3 blemish —*v.* (**blot·ted, blot·ting**) 4 make a blot on; stain 5 soak up moisture, as with blotting paper 6 **blot out:** a obliterate b obscure (a view, sound, etc.) [prob. Scand]

blotch /bläCH/ *n.* 1 discolored or inflamed patch on the skin 2 irregular patch of color —*v.* 3 cover with blotches —**blotch'y** *adj.* (**·i·er, ·i·est**) [obs. *plotch* + BLOT]

blot·ter / blăt′ər/ *n.* sheet of blotting paper

blot′ting pa′per *n.* absorbent paper for drying wet ink

blouse / blous, blouz/ *n.* **1** woman's shirtlike garment **2** upper part of a military uniform —*v.* (**bloused, blous·ing**) **3** make (a bodice, etc.) full like a blouse [Fr]

blow¹ /blō/ *v.* (**blew, blown, blow·ing**) **1** send forth air esp. from the mouth **2** drive or be driven by blowing **3** (esp. of the wind) move rapidly **4** expel by breathing **5** sound or be sounded by blowing **6** clear (the nose) by expelling air **7** puff; pant **8** *Slang.* depart suddenly (from) **9** shatter, etc., by an explosion **10** make or shape (glass or a bubble) by blowing **11a** fail from overloading (*the fuse has blown*) **b** break or burst suddenly **12** break into with explosives **13a** *Slang.* squander (*blew $20*) **b** bungle (an opportunity, etc.) **c** reveal (a secret, etc.) —*n.* **14** act of blowing **15** a gust of wind or air **b** exposure to fresh air **16 blow a gasket** *Slang.* lose one's temper **17 blow hot and cold** *Colloq.* vacillate **18 blow in** *Colloq.* arrive unexpectedly **19 blow a person's mind** *Slang.* cause to have hallucinations, etc.; astound **20 blow over** (of trouble, etc.) fade away **21 blow one's top** *Colloq.* explode in rage **22 blow up: a** explode **b** *Colloq.* rebuke strongly **c** inflate (a tire, etc.) **d** *Colloq.* enlarge (a photograph) **e** *Colloq.* exaggerate **f** *Colloq.* lose one's temper —**blow′er** *n.* [OE]

blow² *n.* **1** hard stroke with a hand or weapon **2** sudden shock or misfortune

blow′-by-blow′ *adj.* (of a narrative, etc.) detailed [orig. of a boxing match]

blow′-dry′ *v.* (**-dried, -dry·ing**) **1** arrange (the hair) while drying it with a hand-held hair dryer —*n.* **2** act of doing this

blow′fly *n.* (*pl.* **-flies**) fly that lays its eggs on meat or flesh

blow′gun′ *n.* (also **blow′pipe′**) narrow tube for blowing darts by a puff of breath

blow′-hole′ *n.* **1** nostril of a whale **2** hole or vent for air, smoke, etc.

blown /blōn/ *v. past part.* of BLOW¹

blow′out′ *n.* *Colloq.* **1** sudden bursting of a tire **2** *Colloq.* big party

blow′pipe′ *n.* **1** tube for blowing air through **2** var. of BLOWGUN

blow′torch′ *n.* device with a very hot flame for burning off paint, plumbing, etc.

blow′up′ *n.* **1** *Colloq.* enlargement (of a photograph, etc.) **2** explosion

blow·zy /blou′zē/ *adj.* (**-zi·er, -zi·est**) slovenly [obs. *blowze* beggar's wench]

BLT *abbr.* bacon, lettuce, and tomato sandwich

blub·ber /blŭb′ər/ *n.* **1** whale fat —*v.* **2** sob loudly **3** sob out (words) [prob. imit.]

blud·geon /blŭj′ən/ *n.* **1** heavy club —*v.* **2** beat with a bludgeon **3** coerce

blue /blōō/ *adj.* **1** having the color of a clear sky **2** sad; depressed **3** pornographic (*a blue film*) **4** puritanical (*blue laws*) —*n.* **5** blue color or pigment **6** blue clothes or material (*dressed in blue*) **7** once in a blue moon very rarely **8** out of the blue unexpectedly [Fr fr. Gmc]

blue′ ba′by *n.* newborn with a blue complexion owing to a congenital heart defect

---

blue′bell′ *n.* woodland plant with bell-shaped blue flowers

blue′ber′ry *n.* (*pl.* **-ries**) small blue-black edible fruit of various plants

blue′bird′ *n.* blue songbird of N America

blue′ blood′ *n.* aristocrat

blue′ cheese′ *n.* cheese with veins of blue mold

blue′-col′lar *adj.* (of a worker or work) manual; industrial

blue′grass′ *n.* **1** grass with a bluish cast, esp. Kentucky bluegrass **2** a kind of instrumental country-and-western music

Blue′grass Re′gion *n.* area in central Ky. noted for thoroughbred horse breeding

blue′jack′et *n.* enlisted person in the (esp. U.S.) navy

blue′ jay′ *n.* common blue-backed crested bird

blue′ jeans′ *n.* blue denim trousers

blue′ law′ *n.* puritanical law, esp. one restricting business on Sunday

blue′ moon′ *n.* very long time

blue′nose′ *n.* *Colloq.* puritanical person

blue′-pen′cil *v.* edit (a manuscript, film, etc.)

blue′point′ *n.* common oyster of US NE coastal waters

blue′print′ *n.* **1** photographic print of plans in white on a blue background **2** detailed plan

blues /blōōz/ *n. pl.* (prec. by *the*) **1** bout of depression **2** melancholic musical style originated by black Americans —**blues′y** *adj.*

bluff¹ /blŭf/ *v.* **1** feign strength, confidence, etc. —*n.* **2** act of bluffing **3 call a person's bluff** challenge a person to prove a claim [Du *bluffen* brag]

bluff² *adj.* **1** blunt; frank **2** steep and broad in front —*n.* **3** steep cliff or headland

blun·der /blŭn′dər/ *n.* **1** serious or foolish mistake —*v.* **2** make a blunder **3** move clumsily; stumble [prob. Scand]

blun·der·buss /blŭn′dərbŭs′/ *n. Hist.* short, large-bored gun [Du *donderbus* thunder gun]

blunt /blŭnt/ *adj.* **1** not sharp or pointed **2** direct; outspoken —*v.* **3** make less sharp —**blunt′ly** *adv.*; **blunt′ness** *n.* [prob. Scand]

blur /blŭr/ *v.* (**blurred, blur·ring**) **1** make or become unclear or less distinct; smear —*n.* **2** blurred object, sound, memory, etc. [perh. rel. to BLEARY]

blurb /blŭrb/ *n.* promotional description, esp. of a book [coined by G. Burgess 1907]

blurt /blŭrt/ *v.* utter abruptly, thoughtlessly, or tactlessly

blush /blŭsh/ *v.* **1a** become pink in the face from embarrassment or shame **b** (of the face) redden thus **2** feel embarrassed or ashamed **3** redden —*n.* **4** act of blushing **5** pink tinge **6** at first blush on initial appearance [OE]

blush·er /blŭsh′ər/ (also **blush, blush′-on′**) *n.* rouge

blus·ter /blŭs′tər/ *v.* **1** behave pompously or boisterously **2** (of the wind, etc.) blow fiercely —*n.* **3** bombastic talk —**blus′ter·y** *adj.*

blvd. *abbr.* boulevard

BM *abbr.* bowel movement

BO *abbr.* body odor

bo·a /bō′ə/ *n.* **1** large snake that kills by crushing and suffocating **2** long stole of feathers or fur [L]

Bo·ad·i·ce·a /bō′ədəsē′ə/ (also **Boudic′ca**)

d. 62; queen of the ancient Britons; led revolt against Romans (61)

boar /bôr/ *n.* **1** male wild pig **2** uncastrated male pig [OE]

board /bôrd/ *n.* **1** long, flat, thin piece of sawn timber **2** provision of regular meals for payment **3** official administrative body of a company, etc. **4** (*pl.*) stage of a theater **5** side of a ship **6** pasteboard —*v.* **7** go on or onto a ship, train, etc. **8** receive or provide with meals **9** close up with boards **10 go by the board** be neglected or discarded **11 on board** on or on to a ship, aircraft, etc. —**board′er** *n.* [OE]

board′ing·house *n.* establishment providing board and lodging for pay

board′walk *n.* usu. raised, wooden promenade along a public beach

boast /bōst/ *v.* **1** talk about oneself with excessive pride **2** own or have with pride —*n.* **3** act of boasting **4** thing one is proud of —**boast′er** *n.*; **boast′ful** *adj.*; **boast′ful·ly** *adv.*; **boast′ful·ness** *n.* [AngFr]

boat /bōt/ *n.* **1** small vessel propelled on water by an engine, oars, or sails **2** (*loosely*) any ship **3** long, low pitcher for sauce, etc. —*v.* **4** go in a boat, esp. for pleasure **5 in the same boat** having the same problems —**boat rock the boat** upset smooth normality —**boat′man** *n.* (*pl.* **-men**) [OE]

boat′er *n.* flat-topped straw hat with a full brim

boat′house *n.* waterside shed for housing a boat or boats

boat′ing *n.* rowing or sailing as recreation

boat′ peo′ple *n. pl.* refugees traveling by sea

boat·swain /bō′sən/ *n.* (also **bo′sun, bo′sun**) ship's officer in charge of equipment and crew

bob /bäb/ *v.* (**bobbed, bob·bing**) **1** move quickly up and down **2** cut (the hair) in a bob —*n.* **3** jerking or bouncing movement, esp. upward **4** short hairstyle with the hair hanging evenly above the shoulders **5** weight on a pendulum, chain, cord, etc.

bob·bin /bäb′in/ *n.* reel for thread [Fr]

bob·ble /bäb′əl/ *n. Sports.* fumble of the ball [dim. of BOB]

bob·by /bäb′ē/ *n.* (*pl.* **-bies**) *Brit. Colloq.* police officer [Sir *Robert* Peel, 19th-cent. statesman]

bob′by pin′ *n.* hairpin with one side straight and the other wavy

bob′by socks′ *n. pl.* (also **bob′by sox′**) *Colloq.* short socks as worn by schoolgirls in the 1940s and '50s —**bob′by-sox′er** or **bob′by sox′er** *n.*

bob′cat′ *n.* (*pl.* **-cats** or **same**) wildcat of N America with a short tail

bob′sled′ *n.* **1** racing sled —*v.* (**·sled·ded, ·sled·ding**) **2** race in a bobsled

Boc·cac·ci·o /bəkäCH′(ē)ō/, **Giovanni** 1313–75; Italian poet and humanist

Bo·chum /bō′kəm, -KHŏŏm/ *n.* city in Germany. Pop. 396,500

bode¹ /bōd/ *v.* (**bod·ed, bod·ing**) **1** be a sign of; portend **2 bode well** (or **ill**) be a good (or bad) sign [OE]

bode² *v. past of* BIDE

bo·de·ga /bōdā′gə/ *n.* small store selling groceries, etc. [Sp]

bod·ice /bäd′əs/ *n.* part of a woman's dress above the waist [orig. *pair of bodies*]

BODICE

bod·i·ly /bäd′l-ē/ *adj.* **1** of the body —*adv.* **2** as a whole body **3** in the flesh; in person

bod·kin /bäd′kin/ *n.* **1** blunt, thick needle for drawing tape, etc., through a hem **2** dagger

bod·y /bäd′ē/ *n.* (*pl.* **·ies**) **1** whole physical structure of a person or animal, including the bones, flesh, and organs **2** TRUNK, 2 **3** main or central part; bulk or majority **4a** group regarded as a unit **b** collection **5** quantity **6** piece of matter **7** full or substantial quality of flavor, tone, etc. [OE]

bod′y bag′ *n.* plastic bag used to enclose a dead body for transport

bod′y-build′ing *n.* exercises to enlarge and strengthen the muscles

bod′y·guard′ *n.* person or group escorting and protecting another

bod′y lan′guage *n.* communication through gestures and poses

bod′y pol′i·tic *n.* nation or state as an entity

bod′y shop′ *n.* workshop where bodies of cars are repaired

bod′y stock′ing *n.* tightfitting garment covering the torso

bod′y·suit′ *n.* close-fitting all-in-one garment for women, worn esp. for sport

Boer /bôr, bŏŏr/ *n.* **1** S African of Dutch descent —*adj.* **2** of the Boers [Du: farmer]

Bo·e·thi·us /bō·ē′THēəs/, **Anicius Manlius Severinus** c. 480–524; Roman statesman and philosopher

bog /bäg, bôg/ *n.* **1** wet, spongy ground; marsh —*v.* (**bogged, bog·ging**) **2** impede —**bog′gy** *adj.* (**·gi·er, ·gi·est**) [Ir or Gaelic *bogach*]

Bo·gart /bō′gärt/, **Humphrey** 1899–1957; US actor

bo·gey¹ /bō′gē/ *n.* (also **bo′gy**) (*pl.* **·geys** or **·gies**) *Golf.* score of one stroke more than par at any hole [perh. fr. *Bogey*, as an imaginary player]

bo·gey² /bō′gē, bŏŏg′ē, bŏŏ′gē/ *n.* (also **bo′gy**) (*pl.* **·geys** or **·gies**) evil or mischievous spirit; devil [orig. (*Old*) *Bogey* the Devil]

bo·gey·man /bŏŏg′ēman′, bō′gē-, bŏŏ′gē-/ *n.* (also **bo′gy·man′**) frightening person, etc.

bog·gle /bäg′əl/ *v.* (**·gled, ·gling**) *Colloq.* **1** be startled or baffled (*the mind boggles*) **2** pause (at) **3** baffle [prob. dial. *boggle* BOGEY²]

bo·gie /bō′gē/ *n.* wheeled undercarriage of a locomotive, etc.

Bo·go·tá /bō′gətä′/ *n.* capital of Colombia. Pop. 3,974,800

bo·gus /bō′gəs/ *adj.* sham; spurious

bo·gy /bō′gē/ *var. of* BOGEY²

bo·gy·man /bŏŏg′ēman′/ *n.* var. of BOGEY-MAN

Bo·he·mi·an /bōhē′mēən/ *n.* **1** native of Bohemia; a Czech **2** (also **b-**) socially unconventional person, esp. an artist or writer —*adj.* **3** of Bohemia or its people **4** (also **b-**) socially unconventional —**bo·he′mi·an·ism′** *n.* [*Bohemia*, part of Czech Republic]

Bohr /bôr/, Niels 1885–1962; Danish nuclear physicist

boil¹ /boil/ *v.* **1** (of a liquid) start to bubble up and turn into vapor on reaching a certain temperature **2** (of a vessel) contain boiling liquid **3** cause to boil **4** cook in boiling liquid **5** be very angry —*n.* **6** act or process of boiling; boiling-point **7 boil down: a** reduce in volume by boiling **b** reduce to essentials [L *bulla* bubble]

boil² *n.* inflamed pus-filled swelling under the skin [OE]

boil′er *n.* **1** apparatus for heating and storing water **2** tank for turning water to steam **3** tub for boiling laundry, etc.

boil′ing point′ *n.* **1** temperature at which a liquid begins to boil; for water, 212° F. or 100° C. **2** time when one loses one's temper

Boi·se /boi′sē, -zē/ *n.* capital of Idaho, in the SW part. Pop. 125,738

bois·ter·ous /boi′st(ə)rəs/ *adj.* **1** noisily exuberant; rough **2** (of the sea, etc.) stormy —**bois′ter·ous·ly** *adv.*; **bois′ter·ous·ness** *n.*

bo·la /bō′lä/ *n.* (*pl.* **-las**) strong cord with heavy balls at the ends, used in S America to entangle the legs of cattle, etc. [Sp: ball]

bold /bōld/ *adj.* **1** confidently assertive; adventurous; brave **2** impudent **3** vivid —**bold′ly** *adv.*; **bold′ness** *n.* [OE]

bole /bōl/ *n.* trunk of a tree [ON]

bo·le·ro /bəler′ō/ *n.* (*pl.* **-ros**) **1** Spanish dance, or the music for it, in triple time **2** woman's short, open jacket [Sp]

Bol·eyn /bŏolĭn′, bŏŏl′ən/, **Anne** 1507–36; 2nd wife of Henry VIII; mother of Elizabeth I

Bol·í·var /bəlē′vär′, bäl′əvər/, **Simón** 1783–1830; Venezuelan patriot and statesman; S American liberator

Bo·liv·i·a /bəliv′ēə/ *n.* republic in W South America. Capitals: La Paz; Sucre. Pop. 7,739,000 —**Bo·liv′i·an** *n. & adj.*

boll /bōl/ *n.* round seedpod of cotton, flax, etc. [Du]

bo·lo·gna /bəlō′nē, -lōn′yə/ *n.* (also **bo·lo·ney** /bəlō′nē/) sausage of finely ground meats and flavorings

Bo·lo·gna /bəlōn′yə/ *n.* city in N Italy. Pop. 411,800 —**Bo·lo·gnese** /bō′lənēz′/ *n. & adj.*

bo·lo·ney /bəlō′nē/ *n.* (also **ba·lo′ney**) *Slang.* nonsense

Bol·she·vik /bōl′sнəvik, bäl′-/ *n.* **1** *Hist.* member of the radical faction of the Russian Social Democratic Party that became the Communist Party in 1918 **2** Russian Communist **3** any revolutionary socialist —*adj.* **4** of the Bolsheviks **5** Communist —**Bol′she·vism, Bol′she·vist** *n.* [Russ: member of the majority]

bol·ster /bōl′stər/ *n.* **1** long, cylindrical pillow —*v.* **2** encourage; support; prop up [OE]

bolt¹ /bōlt/ *n.* **1** sliding bar and socket used to fasten a door, etc. **2** metal threaded pin used with a nut to hold things together **3** discharge of lightning **4** sudden run, as to escape **5** short, metal arrow for shooting from a crossbow **6** roll of fabric, paper, etc. —*v.* **7** fasten with a bolt **8** fasten together with bolts **9a**

dash off suddenly **b** (of a horse) suddenly gallop out of control **10** gulp down (food) unchewed —*adv.* **11** (usu. **bolt′ up′right**) rigidly; stiffly **12 bolt from the blue** complete surprise [OE]

BOLTS¹ 2

bolt² *v.* sift (flour, etc.) [Fr]

Bol·ton /bōlt′n/ *n.* city in NW England. Pop. 143,900

bomb /bäm/ *n.* **1** container filled with explosive, incendiary material, etc., designed to explode and cause damage **2** *Colloq.* utter failure —*v.* **3** attack with bombs **4** *Colloq.* fail completely [Gk *bombos* hum]

bom·bard /bämbärd′/ *v.* **1** attack with heavy guns, bombs, etc. **2** question persistently **3** *Physics.* direct a stream of high-speed particles at —**bom·bard′ment** *n.* [L, rel. to BOMB]

bom·bar·dier /bäm′bə(r)dēr′/ *n.* crew member in an aircraft who aims and releases bombs

bom·bast /bäm′bast′/ *n.* pompous language; exaggeration —**bom·bas′tic** *adj.* [earlier *bombace* cotton wool]

Bom·bay /bämbā′/ *n.* seaport in W India on the Arabian Sea. Pop. 9,909,500

bomb·er /bäm′ər/ *n.* **1** aircraft equipped to drop bombs **2** person using bombs

bomb′shell′ *n.* **1** overwhelming surprise **2** artillery bomb **3** *Slang.* very attractive woman

bo·na fi·de /bō′nə fīd′, fīd′ē/ *adj.* **1** genuine; sincere —*adv.* **2** genuinely; sincerely [L]

bo·nan·za /bənan′zə/ *n.* **1** source of wealth **2** rich lode [Sp: fair weather]

Bo·na·parte /bō′nəpärt′/ *see* NAPOLEON

bon·bon /bän′bän′/ *n.* piece of candy [Fr *bon* good]

bond /bänd/ *n.* **1** thing or force that unites or (usu. *pl.*) restrains **2** binding agreement **3** certificate issued by a government or a company promising to repay borrowed money at a fixed rate of interest **4** (also **bail′ bond′**) financial deposit made by or for a suspect guaranteeing appearance in court **5** state of taxable goods in a warehouse until payment of duty —*v.* **6** hold or bind together **7** supply a bond for **8** place (goods) in bond [var. of BAND]

bond·age /bän′dij/ *n.* slavery [AngL, rel. to BONDSMAN]

bond′ pa′per *n.* high-quality writing paper

bonds·man /bän(d)z′mən/ *n.* (*pl.* **-men**; *fem.* **wom′an,** *pl.* **·wom′en**) **1** slave **2** person who provides bond (sense 4) [OE *bonda* husbandman]

bone /bōn/ *n.* **1** any piece of hard tissue making up the skeleton in vertebrates **2** (often **bare′bones′**) essentials; basic structure —*v.* (**boned, bon·ing**) **3** remove the bones from **4** *bone up Colloq.* study intensively **5 have a bone to pick** have cause for dispute **6 make no bones about: a** be frank about **b** not hesitate or scruple —**bone′less** *adj.* [OE]

bone′ chi′na *n.* fine china made of clay mixed with bone ash

bone′-dry′ *adj.* completely dry

bone′ meal′ *n.* crushed bones, esp. as a fertilizer

bone′ of con·ten′tion *n.* source of dispute

bon·fire /bän′fīr′/ *n.* large open-air fire [fr. BONE + FIRE]

bong /bäNG, bôNG/ *n.* 1 deep reverberating sound, as from a gong —*v.* 2 make such a sound

BONGOS

bon·go /bäNG′gō, bôNG′-/ *n.* (*pl.* ·gos) either of a pair of drums usu. held between the knees and played with the fingers [AmerSp]

bo·ni·to /bənē′tō/ *n.* (*pl.* ·tos) food fish related to the tuna [Sp]

bon mot /bôn′ mō′/ *n.* (*pl.* bons mots /bôn′ mōz′/) *French.* witty saying

Bonn /bän, bôn/ *n.* city, seat of government of Germany. Pop. 292,200

bon·net /bän′ət/ *n.* hat tied under the chin, worn by babies and women [Fr]

Bon·ne·ville Salt Flats /bän′ivil′/ *n.* barren salt flatland in NW Utah

bon·ny /bän′ē/ *adj.* (·ni·er, ·ni·est) esp. *Scot. & No. Engl.* 1a physically attractive b healthy-looking c good; pleasant [perh. fr. Fr *bon* good]

bon·sai /bän′sī′, bōnsī′/ *n.* (*pl.* same) 1 dwarfed tree or shrub 2 art of growing these [Japn]

bo·nus /bō′nəs/ *n.* (*pl.* ·nus·es) extra benefit or payment [L: good]

bon voyage /bôn′ voiäzH′/ *interj. French.* expression of good wishes to a departing traveler

bon·y /bōn′ē/ *adj.* (·i·er, ·i·est) 1 thin with prominent bones 2 having many bones 3 of or like bone —**bon′i·ness** *n.*

boo /bōō/ *interj.* 1 expression of disapproval, etc. 2 sound intended to startle —*n.* 3 utterance of *boo*, esp. to a performer —*v.* (**booed, boo·ing**) 4 utter boos 5 jeer at by booing

boob /bōōb/ *n.* (also **boo′by**) fool

boo′-boo′ *n.* 1 silly mistake 2 slight bruise [baby talk]

boo′by prize′ /bōō′bē/ *n.* prize given for finishing last

boo′by trap′ *n.* 1 trap set to trick an unsuspecting victim, esp. an explosive device —*v.* 2 rig a booby trap on

boo·dle /bōōd′l/ *n. Slang.* money, goods, etc., esp. gained or used dishonestly [Du *boedel* possessions]

boo·gie /bōōg′ē, bōō′gē/ *v.* (·gied, ·gie·ing) *Slang.* 1 dance to pop music 2 leave; go

boog·ie-woog·ie /bōōg′ē-wōōg′ē/ *n.* style of playing blues or jazz, esp. on the piano

book /bōōk/ *n.* 1 written or printed work with pages bound along one side 2 bound set of tickets, stamps, matches, etc. 3 (*pl.*) set of records or accounts 4 main division of a large literary work 5 libretto, script, etc. 6 record of bets —*v.* 7 reserve (a seat, etc.) in advance 8 engage (an entertainer, etc.) 9 record officially the charge against (an offender) 10 **bring to book** call to account 11 **go by the book** proceed by the rules [OE]

book′bind′er *n.* person who binds books —**book′bind′ing** *n.*

book′case′ *n.* set of open or closed shelves for books

book′end′ *n.* prop used to keep books upright

book·ie /bōōk′ē/ *n. Colloq.* BOOKMAKER

book′ing *n.* reservation or engagement

book·ish /bōōk′ish/ *adj.* 1 studious; fond of reading 2 having knowledge mainly from books

book′keep′er *n.* person who keeps accounts —**book′keep′ing** *n.*

book·let /bōōk′lit/ *n.* small book, usu. with a paper cover

book′mak′er *n.* professional taker of bets —**book′mak′ing** *n.*

book′mark′ *n.* thing used to mark a reader's place

book′ match′es *n. pl.* usu. paper matches in a stiff paper folder

book·mo·bile /bōōk′mōbēl′/ *n.* van of truck, containing a lending library, that visits local neighborhoods

book′plate′ *n.* decorative personalized label stuck inside the front cover of a book

book′sell′er *n.* dealer in books

book′shelf′ *n.* shelf for books

book′store′ *n.* (also **book′shop′**) retail store selling books

book′worm′ *n.* 1 *Colloq.* devoted reader 2 larva feeding on the paper and glue in books

boom¹ /bōōm/ *n.* 1 deep resonant sound —*v.* 2 make or speak with a boom

boom² *n.* 1 period of economic prosperity or activity —*v.* 2 be suddenly prosperous 3 increase; flourish

boom³ *n.* 1 pivoted spar to which a sail is attached 2 long pole carrying a microphone, camera, etc. 3 barrier across a harbor, etc. [Du: beam]

boom′ box′ *n. Colloq.* portable stereo with powerful speakers

boo·mer·ang /bōō′məraNG′/ *n.* 1 flat, V-shaped, hardwood missile able to return to its thrower 2 plan that recoils on its originator —*v.* 3 (of a plan, etc.) backfire [Aborig]

boon¹ /bōōn/ *n.* advantage; blessing [ON]

boon² *adj.* intimate; favorite (usu. *boon companion*) [Fr *bon* fr. L *bonus* good]

boon·docks /bōōn′doks′/ *n. pl.* (also **boon′ies**) *Colloq.* 1 wilderness or remote rural area 2 poor neighborhood [Tagalog: mountain]

boon·dog·gle /bōōn′dog′əl/ *n.* 1 trivial work done to appear busy —*v.* (·gled, ·gling) 2 engage in boondoggle

Boone /bōōn/, **Daniel** c. 1735–1820; American pioneer

boor /bōōr/ *n.* ill-mannered person —**boor′ish** *adj.*; **boor′ish·ly** *adv.*; **boor′ish·ness** *n.* [LGer or Du]

boost /bōōst/ *v.* 1 promote or encourage 2 increase; assist 3 push from below —*n.* 4 act or result of boosting

boost′er *n.* 1 device for increasing power or

voltage 2 auxiliary engine or rocket for initial speed 3 dose, injection, etc., to reinforce an earlier one

boot[1] / bōot/ *n.* 1 outer foot covering reaching above the ankle —*v.* 2 kick 3 dismiss from employment 4 start or reset (a computer) [ON]

boot[2] *n.* as in **to boot** as well; in addition [OE]

boot′black *n.* person who polishes boots and shoes

booth / bōoTH/ *n.* 1 small, temporary structure used as a stall at a fair, market, etc. 2 enclosure for telephoning, voting, etc. 3 cubicle in a restaurant, etc. [ON]

boot·ie / bōot′tē/ *n.* (also **boot′ee**) baby's soft shoe

boot′leg *adj.* 1 (esp. of alcohol) smuggled; illicit —*v.* (**·legged, ·leg·ging**) 2 illicitly make or deal in esp. untaxed goods, as alcohol —**boot′leg′ger** *n.*

boot′less *adj.* to no advantage

boot′strap[′] *n.* 1 loop used to pull a boot on 2 **pull oneself up by one's bootstraps** better oneself by sheer energy and without help

boo·ty / bōot′ē/ *n.* 1 loot; spoil 2 *Colloq.* prize or gain [Ger]

booze / bōoz/ *Colloq. n.* 1 alcoholic drink —*v.* (**boozed, booz·ing**) 2 drink alcohol, esp. to excess —**booz′er** *n.*; **booz′y** *adj.* (**·i·er, ·i·est**) [Du]

bop[1] / bäp/ *n.* 1 BEBOP —*v.* (**bopped, bop·ping**) 2 dance, esp. to pop music —**bop′per** *n.* [abbr.]

bop[2] *Colloq. v.* (**bopped, bop·ping**) 1 hit or punch —*n.* 2 blow or hit

bor. *abbr.* borough

bo·rax / bôr′aks/ *n.* salt used in making glass and china and as an antiseptic [Fr ult. fr. Pers]

Bor·deaux / bôrdō′/ *n.* 1 seaport in SW France. Pop. 213,300 2 (*pl.* same *·dōz*[′]) wine (esp. red) from the Bordeaux district in SW France

bor·der / bôrd′ər/ *n.* 1 edge or boundary, or the part near it 2 line or region separating two countries 3 strip around an edge —*v.* 4 be a border to 5 provide with a border 6 adjoin; come close to being [Fr fr. Gmc, rel. to BOARD]

bor′der·land[′] *n.* 1 district near a border 2 area subject to debate

bor′der·line[′] *n.* 1 line dividing two conditions 2 line marking a boundary —*adj.* 3 on the borderline 4 barely acceptable

bore[1] / bôr/ *v.* (**bored, bor·ing**) 1 make (a hole), esp. with a revolving tool 2 make a hole in, hollow out —*n.* 3 hollow of a firearm barrel or of a cylinder in an internal-combustion engine 4 diameter of this [OE]

bore[2] *n.* 1 tiresome or dull person or thing —*v.* (**bored, bor·ing**) 2 weary by tedious talk or dullness

bore[3] *n.* high tidal wave in an estuary [Scand]

bore[4] *v.* past of BEAR[1]

bore·dom / bôr′dəm/ *n.* state of being bored

Bor·ges / bôr′hās/, Jorge Luis 1899–1986; Argentine writer

Bor·gia / bôr′jə, -zhə/ 1 Cesare 1476–1507; Italian Renaissance cardinal, soldier, and politician; his sister: 2 Lucrezia 1480–1519; patron of the arts

bo′ric ac′id / bôr′ik/ *n.* acid derived from borax, used as an antiseptic

born / bôrn/ *adj.* 1 existing as a result of birth

2 of natural ability or quality 3 destined 4 (in *comb.*) of a certain status by birth (*French-born*) [past part. of BEAR[1]]

Born / bôrn/, Max 1882–1970; German physicist; Nobel prize 1954

born′·a·gain[′] *adj.* converted to or with revived enthusiasm, esp. for fundamentalist Christianity

borne / bôrn/ *v.* 1 past part. of BEAR[1] —*adj.* 2 (in *comb.*) carried by

Bor·ne·o / bôr′nē·ō′/ *n.* island in the Malay Archipelago

bo·ron / bôr′än/ *n.* nonmetallic usu. crystalline element; *symb.* B [fr. BORAX, after *carbon*]

bor·ough / bər′ō/ *n.* 1 incorporated municipality 2 one of the five administrative districts of New York City [OE]

bor·row / bär′ō, bôr′ō/ *v.* 1a acquire temporarily, promising or intending to return b obtain money thus 2 take (another's idea, invention, etc.) —**bor′row·er** *n.* [OE]

borscht / bôr′sH(t)/ *n.* Russian soup mainly of beets [Russ]

BORZOI

bor·zoi / bôr′zoi′/ *n.* large, silky-coated dog [Russ: swift]

Bosch / bäsH, bôsH/, Hieronymus c. 1450–1516; Dutch painter

bosh / bäsH, bôsH/ *n. & interj. Colloq.* nonsense [Turk: empty]

Bos·ni·a and Her·ce·go·vi·na / bäz′nēə; hərt′səgōvē′nə, -gō′vinə/ *n.* (also **Bosnia-Herzegovina**) republic on the Balkan Peninsula, formerly part of Yugoslavia. Capital: Sarajevo. Pop. 4,397,000

bo·som / bōoz′əm/ *n.* 1a person's breast b *Colloq.* each of a woman's breasts c enclosure formed by the breast and arms 2 emotional center —*adj.* 3 close (*bosom friend*) [OE]

Bos·po·rus / bäs′pərəs/ *n.* strait connecting the Sea of Marmara and the Black Sea

boss[1] / bôs/ *n.* 1 employer, manager, or supervisor 2 one in control of a political organization —*v.* 3 give orders to; order about [Du *baas*]

boss[2] *n.* decorative round knob, stud, etc. [Fr]

bos·sa no·va / bäs′ə nō′və/ *n.* 1 Brazilian dance like the samba 2 music for this [Port: new flair]

boss′y *adj.* (**·i·er, ·i·est**) *Colloq.* domineering —**boss′i·ness** *n.*

Bos·ton / bô′stən/ *n.* capital and chief city of Mass., on the E coast. Pop. 574,283 —**Bos·ton·i·an** / bôstō′nēən/ *n. & adj.*

bo·sun / bō′sən/ *n.* (also **bo′sun**) var. of BOATSWAIN

Bos·well / bäz′wel′, -wəl/, James 1740–95; Scottish writer; biographer of Samuel Johnson

bot. *abbr.* 1 botanical 2 botany

bot·a·ny / bät′n·ē/ *n.* the study of plant:

—**bo·tan·ic** /bətan'ik/ adj.; **bo·tan'i·cal** adj.; **bot'a·nist** n. [Gk botanē plant]

botch /bäch/ v. 1 bungle; do badly 2 patch clumsily —n. 3 bungled or spoilt work

both /bōth/ adj. & pron. 1 the two, not only one —adv. 2 with equal truth in two cases [ON]

● Usage: Avoid using *both* when *each* is intended: Q: Which pie would you prefer? A: May I have a little of each? (not "of both"); *Each brother* (not "Both brothers") blamed the other.

both·er /bäTH'ər/ v. 1 trouble; worry; disturb 2 take the time or trouble —n. 3 person or thing that bothers; nuisance 4 trouble; worry —**both'er·some** adj. [Ir bodhraim deafen]

Both·ni·a, Gulf of /bäTH'nēə/ n. arm of the Baltic Sea between Sweden and Finland

Bot·swa·na /bätswän'ə/ n. republic in southern Africa. Capital: Gaborone. Pop. 1,359,000

Bot·ti·cel·li /bät'əCHel'ē/, Sandro 1445–1510; Italian painter

bot·tle /bät'l/ n. 1 container, esp. glass or plastic, for storing liquid 2 amount filling it —v. (**·tled, ·tling**) 3 put into, or preserve in, bottles or jars 4 (foll. by *up*) conceal or restrain (esp. a feeling) **5 hit the bottle** *Slang.* drink heavily [MedL, rel. to BUTT⁴]

bot'tle·neck n. 1 narrow congested area, esp. on a road 2 any impedance to progress

bot·tom /bät'əm/ n. 1a lowest point or part b base c underneath part 2 *Colloq.* buttocks 3 seat of a chair, etc. 4 lower part of a scale or measure 5 ground below water 6 basis or origin —adj. 7 lowest; last **8 at bottom** basically —**bot'tom·less** adj [OE]

bot'tom line' n. *Colloq.* underlying truth; ultimate, esp. financial, criterion

bot·u·lism /bäCH'əliz'əm/ n. poisoning caused by a bacillus in badly preserved food [L *botulus* sausage]

Bou·di·ca /bōōdik'ə/ see BOADICEA

bou·doir /bōō'dwär/ n. woman's private sitting room or bedroom [Fr *bouder* sulk]

bouf·fant /bōōfänt'/ adj. (of a dress, hair, etc.) puffed out [Fr]

bou·gain·vil·le·a /bōō'gənvil'ēə/ n. tropical plant with large colored bracts [*Bougainville*, name of a navigator]

bough /bou/ n. main branch of a tree [OE]

bought /bôt/ v. past and past part. of BUY

bouil·lon /bōōl'yän', bōōl'yən/ n. clear broth [Fr *bouillir* to boil]

boul·der /bōl'dər/ n. large rock [Scand]

Boul·der /bōl'dər/ n. city in Colo. Pop. 83,312

bou·le·vard /bōōl'əvärd'/ n. broad tree-lined avenue [Fr fr. Ger]

Bou·lez /bōōlez'/, Pierre 1925– ; French composer and conductor

bounce /bouns/ v. (**bounced, bounc·ing**) 1 (cause to) rebound 2 *Slang.* (of a check) be returned by a bank when there are no funds to meet it 3 jump, move, or rush boisterously —n. 4a rebound b power of rebounding 5 *Colloq.* energy; liveliness **6 the bounce** *Slang.* dismissal from a job —**bounc'y** adj. (**·i·er, ·i·est**)

bounc·er n. *Slang.* doorman ejecting troublemakers from a bar, nightclub, etc.

bounc'ing adj. (esp. of a baby) big and healthy

bound¹ /bound/ v. 1 spring, leap **2** (of a ball, etc.) bounce —n. 3 springy leap 4 bounce [Fr *bondir* fr. L *bombus* hum]

bound² n. (usu. pl.) 1 limitation; restriction 2 border; boundary —v. 3 limit **4** be the boundary of **5 out of bounds** outside a permitted area —**bound'less** adj. [Fr fr. MedL]

bound³ adj. 1 on one's way 2 (in *comb.*) going in a specified direction [ON: ready]

bound⁴ adj. 1 tied 2 likely (*bound to come soon*) 3 having a binding **4** certain (*bound to lose*) [past and past part. of BIND]

bound·a·ry /boun'd(ə)rē/ n. (pl. **·ries**) line marking the limits of an area, etc.

bound'en du'ty n. *Archaic.* solemn responsibility [archaic past part. of BIND]

bound'er n. *Brit.* cad

boun·te·ous /bount'ēəs/ adj. BOUNTIFUL [Fr, rel. to BOUNTY]

boun·ti·ful /bount'əfəl/ adj. 1 generous 2 ample

boun·ty /bount'ē/ n. (pl. **·ties**) 1 generosity 2 reward or premium 3 gift [Fr fr. L *bonus* good]

bou·quet /bōkā', bōō-/ n. 1 bunch of flowers 2 scent of wine, etc. 3 compliment [Fr *bois* wood]

bour·bon /bər'bən/ n. whiskey made with corn mash [*Bourbon* County, Kentucky]

bour·geois /bōōr'zHwä'/ adj. 1 conventional 2 materialistic 3 capitalist —n. (pl. same) 4 bourgeois person [Fr]

bour·geoi·sie /bōōr'zHwäzē'/ n. 1 capitalist class 2 middle class [Fr]

Bourke-White /bōōr'k wīt', bər'-/, Margaret 1906–71; US photojournalist

Bourne·mouth /bôrn'məTH/ n. seaside resort city in S England. Pop. 148,400

bout /bout/ n. 1 period; interval 2 attack 3 wrestling or boxing match [obs. *bought* bending]

bou·tique /bōōtēk'/ n. small shop selling fashionable clothes, perfumes, etc. [Fr]

bou·ton·niere /bōō'tənēr', -yar'/ n. flower for a buttonhole [Fr: buttonhole]

Bou·tros-Gha·li /bōō'trōs gälē'/, Boutros 1922– ; Egyptian statesman; Secretary-General of the United Nations (1992–)

bo·vine /bō'vīn'/ adj. 1 of cattle 2 stupid; dull [L *bos bovis* ox]

bow¹ /bō/ n. 1 slipknot with a double loop 2 ribbon tied in a decorative knot 3 curved piece of wood, etc., with a string stretched across its ends, for shooting arrows 4 rod with horsehairs stretched along its length, for playing a stringed musical instrument 5 shallow curve or bend —v. 6 use a bow on (a stringed instrument) [OE]

bow² /bou/ v. 1 incline the head or body, esp. in greeting or acknowledgment 2 submit 3 cause (the head, etc.) to incline —n. 4 act of bowing **5 take a bow** acknowledge applause [OE]

bow³ /bou/ n. 1 (also pl.) front end of a vessel or boat 2 rower nearest the front [LGer or Du, rel. to BOUGH]

bowd·ler·ize /bōd'lərīz', boud'-/ v. (**·ized, ·iz·ing**) delete suggestive parts from (a book, etc.) —**bowd'ler·i·za'tion** n. [for T. *Bowdler*, expurgator of Shakespeare]

bow·el /bou′əl/ *n.* **1** (often *pl.*) INTESTINE **2** (*pl.*) innermost parts **3 move one's bowels** defecate [L *botulus* sausage]

bow·er /bou′ər/ *n.* arbor; copselike enclosure [OE: dwelling]

bow·ie knife /bō′ē, bōō′ē/ *n.* a kind of hunting knife with a broad, heavy blade [for James *Bowie*, its designer]

bowl[1] /bōl/ *n.* **1a** usu. round deep basin for food or liquid **b** contents of a bowl **2** hollow part of a tobacco pipe, spoon, etc. **3** amphitheater —**bowl′ful** *n.* (*pl.* **-fuls**) [OE]

bowl[2] *n.* **1** spell or turn of bowling —*v.* **2a** roll (a ball, etc.) **b** play at bowling **3** go along rapidly **4 bowl over** : a knock down **b** *Colloq.* impress greatly; overwhelm [L *bulla* bubble]

bow·leg /bō′legs/ *n. pl.* bandy legs —**bow·leg·ged** /bō·leg′id/ *adj.*

bowl·er[1] /bō′lər/ *n.* player at bowling

bowl·er[2] *n.* man's hard, round, felt hat [for *Bowler*, a hatter]

bowl·ing /bō′liNG/ *n.* **1** game in which a player rolls a ball, usu. along a wooden lane, to knock over as many pins as possible; ten-pins **2** duckpins **3** lawn bowling

bowl′ing al′ley *n.* wooden lane used in ten-pins, duckpins, etc.

bowl′ing green *n.* lawn for lawn bowling

bow·man /bō′mən/ *n.* (*pl.* **-men**) archer

bow·sprit /bou′sprit, bō′-/ *n.* spar running forward from a ship's bow

bow·string /bō′striNG/ *n.* string of an archer's bow

bow tie /bō′ tī′/ *n.* necktie in the form of a bow

box[1] /bäks/ *n.* **1a** container, usu. rectangular, flat-sided, and firm **b** amount contained in a box **2** special seating area in a theater, etc. **3** facility at a post office, periodical, etc., for receiving mail, replies to advertising, etc. **4** enclosure for a jury in a courtroom **5** *Baseball.* designated area for a given player **6** rectangular area on a printed page —*v.* **7** put in or provide with a box **8** confine —**box′like** *adj.* [LL *buxis*, rel. to BOX[3]]

box[2] *v.* **1a** take part in boxing **b** fight (an opponent) at boxing **c** slap (esp. a person's ears) —*n.* **3** hard blow, esp. on the ears

box[3] *n.* (also **box′wood**′) **1** small evergreen tree with dark green leaves **2** its fine hard wood [L *buxus* fr. Gk *pyxos*]

box′ car′ *n.* enclosed railroad freight car

box′er *n.* **1** person who boxes, esp. as a sport **2** medium-sized short-haired dog with a snub nose

box′ing *n.* fighting with the fists, esp. as a sport

box′ing glove′ *n.* each of a pair of heavily padded mittens worn in boxing

box′ of′fice *n.* **1** ticket office at a theater, etc. **2** receipts taken at a box office **3** attracting power of a performer, play, etc.

boy /boi/ *n.* **1** male child; son **2** young man **3** (*formerly*) male servant, etc. —*interj.* **4** expressing pleasure, surprise, etc. —**boy′hood**′, **boy′ish·ness** *n.*; **boy′ish** *adj.*; **boy′ish·ly** *adv.*

boy·cott /boi′kät′/ *v.* **1** refuse to have social or commercial relations with (a person, country, etc.) —*n.* **2** such a refusal [Capt. *Boycott*, so treated in 1880]

boy′friend′ *n.* person's regular male companion or lover

Boy′ Scouts′ *n.* international organization aimed at building character through outdoor and other activities for boys and young men

bps *abbr. Comp.* bits or bytes per second

Br *symb.* bromine

bra /brä/ *n.* undergarment worn by women to support the breasts [abbr. of BRASSIERE]

brace /brās/ *n.* **1** device that clamps or fastens tightly **2** metal or wooden strut serving to strengthen a framework **3** (*pl.*) *Brit.* straps passing over the shoulders to support trousers **4** (often *pl.*) wire device for straightening the teeth **5** pair (esp. of game) **6** connecting mark { or } in printing **7** handle for a drilling bit (auger) **8** support for a weakened part of the body —*v.* (**braced, brac·ing**) **9** make steady by supporting **10** fasten tightly to make firm **11** invigorate; refresh **12** prepare for a difficulty, shock, etc. [L *bracchia* arms]

bit   brace

BRACE AND BIT

brace′ and bit′ *n.* revolving tool for boring, with a D-shaped central handle

brace·let /brā′slət/ *n.* **1** ornamental band or chain worn on the wrist or arm **2** (*pl.*) *Slang.* handcuffs

brack·en /brak′ən/ *n.* **1** large coarse fern **2** mass of these [ON]

brack·et /brak′it/ *n.* **1** support projecting from a vertical surface **2** either of the marks [or] enclosing words or figures **3** group or classification —*v.* **4** enclose in brackets **5** group or classify together [L *bracae* breeches]

brack·ish /brak′ish/ *adj.* (of water) slightly salty [LGer or Du]

bract /brakt/ *n.* leaflike and often brightly colored part of a plant, growing below the flower [L *bractea* thin sheet]

brad /brad/ *n.* thin wire nail with a small head [ON]

Brad·bur·y /brad′ber′ē, -b(ə)rē/, **Ray** 1920– ; US science-fiction writer

Brad·ford /brad′fərd/, **William** 1590–1657; English Puritan; governor of Plymouth colony (Mass.)

Brad·ford /brad′fərd/ *n.* city in N England. Pop. 295,000

Brad·ley /brad′lē/, **Omar Nelson** 1893–1981; US general during World War II

Bra·dy /brā′dē/, **Matthew B.** 1823–96; US Civil War photographer

brae /brā/ *n. Scot.* hillside [ON]

brag /brag/ *v.* (**bragged, brag·ging**) **1** talk boastfully —*n.* **2** boastful statement or talk

brag·gart /brag′ərt/ *n.* **1** boastful person —*adj.* **2** boastful

Bra·he /brä′(hē)/, **Tycho** 1546–1601; Danish astronomer

Brah·ma /bräm′ə/ *n.* supreme Hindu divinity [Skt: creator]

Brah·man /bräm′ən/ *n.* (*pl.* ·**mans**) 1 (also **Brah′min**) member of the highest or priestly Hindu caste 2 member of one of the established New England families regarded as elite and aristocratic —**Brah·man′ic** /-man′ik/ *adj.*; **Brah′man·ism′** *n.*

Brahms /brämz/, **Johannes** 1833–97; German composer

braid /brād/ *n.* 1 woven band as edging or trimming 2 interwoven strands of hair; plait —*v.* 3 interweave —**braid′ing** *n.* [OE]

Braille /brāl/ *n.* system of writing and printing for the blind, with patterns of raised dots [for its inventor]

brain /brān/ *n.* 1 organ of soft nervous tissue in the skull of vertebrates, the center of sensation and of intellectual and nerve activity 2a *Colloq.* intelligent person **b** (often *pl.*) intelligence —*v.* 3 strike hard on the head so as to dash out the brains [OE]

brain′child′ *n. Colloq.* clever idea or invention

brain′ death′ *n.* irreversible brain damage causing the end of independent respiration and regarded as indicative of death —**brain′ dead′** *adj.*

brain′ drain′ *n. Colloq.* loss of skilled personnel by emigration

brain′less *adj.* foolish

brain′storm *n.* 1 spontaneous ingenious idea or inspiration —*v.* 2 meet with others to try to create a brainstorm —**brain′storm′ing** *n.*

brain′wash′ *v.* implant ideas or esp. ideology into (a person) by repetition, etc. —**brain′wash′ing** *n.*

brain′ wave′ *n.* 1 (usu. *pl.*) electrical impulse in the brain 2 *Colloq.* sudden bright idea

brain′y *adj.* (·i·er, ·i·est) intellectually clever

braise /brāz/ *v.* (**braised, brais·ing**) stew slowly with a little liquid in a closed container [Fr *braise* live coals]

brake /brāk/ *n.* 1 device for stopping or slowing a wheel, vehicle, etc. —*v.* (**braked, brak·ing**) 2 apply a brake [prob. obs. *brake* curb]

brake′man *n.* (*pl.* ·**men**) railroad employee assisting a train conductor

bram·ble /bram′bəl/ *n.* wild thorny shrub, esp. the blackberry —**bram′bly** *adj.* [OE]

Bramp·ton /bram(p)′tən/ *n.* city in Ontario, Canada. Pop. 234,400

bran /bran/ *n.* grain husks separated from flour [Fr]

branch /branCH/ *n.* 1 limb of a tree 2 lateral extension or subdivision, esp. of a river, road, or railway 3 subdivision of a family, knowledge, etc. 4 local office, etc., of a large business —*v.* 5 diverge 6 divide into branches 7 branch out extend one's field of interest —**branch′less, branch′like′** *adj.* [LL *branca* paw]

brand /brand/ *n.* 1a particular make of goods **b** (also **brand′ name′**) identifying trade mark, label, etc. 2 characteristic kind 3 identifying mark burned esp. on livestock 4 iron used for this 5 piece of burning or charred wood 6 stigma; mark of disgrace —*v.* 7 mark with a hot iron 8 stigmatize —**brand′er** *n.*; **brand′less** *adj.* [OE]

Bran·deis /bran′dīs′/, **Louis Dembitz** 1856–1941; US jurist

bran·dish /bran′disH/ *v.* wave or flourish as a threat or display [Fr fr. Gmc]

brand′-new′ *adj.* completely new

Bran·do /bran′dō/, **Marlon** 1924– ; US actor

Brandt /bränt, brant/, **Willy** 1913–92; chancellor of West Germany (1969–74)

bran·dy /bran′dē/ *n.* (*pl.* ·**dies**) strong alcoholic spirit distilled from wine or fermented fruit juice [Du *brandewijn*]

brash /brasH/ *adj.* vulgarly self-assertive; impudent —**brash′ly** *adv.*; **brash′ness** *n.* [Brit dial.]

Bra·sil·ia /brəzil′yə/ *n.* capital of Brazil. Pop. 411,300

brass /bras/ *n.* 1 yellow alloy of copper and zinc 2 brass objects collectively 3 brass wind instruments 4 *Colloq.* effrontery 5 *Slang* esp. military officers of high rank —*adj.* 6 made of brass —**brass′y** *adj.* (·i·er, ·i·est); **brass′i·ly** *adv.*; **brass′i·ness** *n.* [OE]

bras·siere /brəzēr′/ *n.* (also **bras·sière** BRA [Fr]

brass′ tacks′ *n. pl. Slang* essential details

brat /brat/ *n.* child, esp. an ill-behaved one

Bra·ti·sla·va /brät′isläv′ə/ *n.* capital of Slovakia. Pop. 441,500

bra·va·do /brəvä′dō/ *n.* show of boldness [Sp]

brave /brāv/ *adj.* 1 able or ready to face and endure danger, disgrace, or pain 2 splendid; spectacular —*n.* 3 N American Indian warrior —*v.* (**braved, brav·ing**) 4 face bravely or defiantly —**brave′ly** *adv.*; **brave′ness, brav′er·y** *n.* [ult. L *barbarus* barbarian]

bra·vo /brä′vō/ *interj.* 1 expressing approval —*n.* (*pl.* ·**vos**) 2 cry of 'bravo' [Fr fr. It]

bra·vu·ra /brəv(y)ŏŏr′ə/ *n.* 1 brilliance of execution 2 passage of (esp. vocal) music requiring brilliant technique [It]

brawl /brôl/ *n.* 1 noisy quarrel or fight —*v.* 2 engage in a brawl [Prov]

brawn /brôn/ *n.* 1 muscular strength 2 muscle; lean flesh —**brawn′y** *adj.* (·i·er, ·i·est) [Fr fr. Gmc]

bray /brā/ *n.* 1 cry of a donkey —*v.* 2 make such a sound [Fr *braire*]

braze /brāz/ *v.* (**brazed, braz·ing**) solder with an alloy of brass and zinc [Fr *braser*]

bra·zen /brā′zən/ *adj.* 1 shameless; insolent 2 of or like brass 3 harsh in sound —*v.* 4 **brazen out** face or undergo defiantly —**bra′zen·ly** *adv.*; **bra′zen·ness** *n.* [OE]

bra·zier[1] /brā′zHər/ *n.* metal pan or stand holding burning coals [Fr, rel. to BRAISE]

bra·zier[2] *n.* worker in brass {fr. BRASS}

Bra·zil /brəzil′/ *n.* republic in S America, on the Atlantic Ocean. Capital: Brasilia. Pop. 151,381,000 —**Bra·zil′ian** /-yən/ *n.* & *adj.*

Bra·zil′ nut′ *n.* large, three-sided edible nut from a S American tree

Braz·za·ville /braz′əvil′/ *n.* capital of Congo. Pop. 937,600

breach /brēCH/ *n.* 1 breaking or nonobservation of a law, contract, etc. 2 breaking of relations; quarrel 3 opening; gap —*v.* 4 break through; make a gap in 5 break (a law, contract, etc.) [Gmc, rel. to BREAK]

breach′ of prom′ise *n.* breaking of a promise, esp. to marry

breach′ of the peace′ *n.* crime of causing a public disturbance

bread /bred/ *n.* **1** baked dough of flour and water, usu. leavened with yeast **2** necessary food **3** *Slang.* money —*v.* **4** coat with breadcrumbs for cooking **5 break bread** [OE]

breadth /bredTH/ *n.* **1** distance or measurement from side to side of a thing **2** size; extent [OE, rel. to BROAD]

bread'win'ner *n.* person who works to support a family

break /brāk/ *v.* (**broke, bro·ken, break·ing**) **1** separate into pieces under a blow or strain; shatter **2** make or become inoperative **3** interrupt **4** stop for an interval **5** fail to keep (a law, promise, etc.) **6** make or become subdued or weak; (cause to) yield **7** weaken the effect of (a fall, blow, etc.) **8** surpass (a record) **9** (foll. by *with*) end a friendship with (a person, etc.) **10a** be no longer subject to (a habit) **b** free (a person) from a habit **11** reveal or be revealed **12** (of fine weather) change suddenly **13** (of waves) curl over and foam **14** (of the day) dawn **15** (of clouds) disperse **16** (of a storm) begin violently **17** *Electr.* disconnect (a circuit) **18a** (of the voice) change with emotion; falter **b** (of a boy's voice) change at puberty **19a** divide (a set, etc.) **b** change money for smaller bills or coins **20** ruin financially **21** decipher (a code) **22** burst forth **23** escape or emerge from (prison, bounds, cover, etc.), esp. by a sudden effort —*n.* **24** act or instance of breaking **25** point of breaking; gap **26** interval; interruption; pause **27** sudden dash (esp. to escape) **28** *Colloq.* piece of luck; fair chance **29 break down: a** fail; collapse **b** suppress (resistance) **c** analyze into components **30 break even** make neither profit nor loss **31 break in: a** enter by force **b** interrupt **c** accustom to a habit, etc. **d** wear until comfortable e tame (an animal); accustom (a horse) to a saddle, etc. **32 break into: a** enter forcibly **b** burst forth with **33 break off** bring to an end **34 break out:** a escape by force, esp. from prison **b** become covered in a rash, etc. **35 break up:** a disperse; disband **b** (cause to) terminate a relationship **c** *Colloq.* collapse from laughter, tears, etc. —**break'a·ble** *adj.* [OE]

break·age /brā'kij/ *n.* **1** broken thing **2a** damage caused by breaking **b** insurance paid for this **3** act or instance of breaking

break'down' *n.* **1** mechanical failure **2** loss of (esp. mental) health **3** collapse **4** analysis

break'er *n.* heavy breaking wave

break·fast /brek'fəst/ *n.* **1** first meal of the day —*v.* **2** have breakfast

break'-in' *n.* forced entry, esp. with criminal intent

break'neck' *adj.* (of speed) dangerously fast

break'through' *n.* **1** major advance or discovery **2** act of breaking through an obstacle, etc.

break'up' *n.* **1** disintegration or collapse **2** dispersal

break'wa'ter *n.* barrier breaking the force of waves

breast /brest/ *n.* **1a** either of two milk-secreting organs on a woman's chest **b** corresponding part of a man's body **2a** chest **b** corresponding part of an animal **3** part of a garment that covers the breast **4** breast as a source of emotion —*v.* **5** contend with [OE]

breast'bone' *n.* thin, flat, vertical bone in the chest between the ribs; sternum

breast'-feed' *v.* (**-fed, -feed·ing**) feed (a baby) from the breast

breast'plate' *n.* armor covering the breast

breast' stroke' *n.* swimming stroke made by extending both arms forward and sweeping them back

breath /breTH/ *n.* **1a** air drawn into or expelled from the lungs **b** respiration **2a** slight movement of air **b** whiff (of perfume, etc.) **3** whisper; murmur (esp. of scandal) **4** spirit; vitality **5 catch one's breath:** a cease breathing momentarily in surprise, etc. **b** rest to restore normal breathing **6 hold one's breath** cease breathing temporarily **7 take one's breath away** surprise; delight, etc. **8 under one's breath** in a whisper [OE]

breathe /brēTH/ *v.* (**breathed, breath·ing**) **1** draw air into and expel it from the lungs **2** be or seem alive **3** utter or sound; express —**breath'a·ble** *adj.*

breath·er /brē'THər/ *n.* *Colloq.* brief rest

breath'ing space' *n.* time to recover; pause

breath·less /breTH'ləs/ *adj.* **1** panting; out of breath **2** holding the breath, as from excitement **3** still; windless —**breath'less·ly** *adv.*; **breath'less·ness** *n.*

breath'tak'ing *adj.* astounding; awe-inspiring —**breath'tak·ing·ly** *adv.*

Brecht /breKHt, brekt/, **Bertolt** 1898–1956; German dramatist, producer, and poet

bred /bred/ *v.* *past* and *past part.* of BREED

Bre·da /brādä'/ *n.* city in the Netherlands. Pop. 124,800

breech /brēCH/ *n.* back part of a rifle or gun barrel [OE]

breech' birth' *n.* (also **breech' de·liv'er·y**) delivery of a baby with the buttocks or feet foremost

breech·es /briCH'iz, brē'CHiz/ *n. pl.* short trousers

breech'es bu'oy *n.* lifebuoy with canvas breeches for the user's legs

breed /brēd/ *v.* (**bred, breed·ing**) **1** (of animals) produce young **2** propagate; raise (animals) **3** result in; give rise to **4** bring up; train —*n.* **5** stock of similar animals or plants **6** race; lineage **7** sort; kind —**breed'er** *n.* [OE]

breed'er re·ac'tor *n.* nuclear reactor creating surplus fissile material

breed'ing *n.* **1** raising of offspring **2** good manners, esp. as reflective of ancestry

breeze /brēz/ *n.* **1** gentle wind **2** *Colloq.* easy task —*v.* (**breezed, breez·ing**) **3** *Colloq.* saunter casually [prob. Sp and Port *briza*]

breeze'way' *n.* open covered passage between parts of a residence

breez'y *adj.* (**·i·er, ·i·est**) **1** slightly windy **2** *Colloq.* cheerful; light-hearted; casual

Brem·en /brem'ən/ *n.* port in NW Germany. Pop. 551,200

Brem·er·ha·ven /brem'ərhäv'ən/ *n.* seaport in NW Germany. Pop. 130,400

Bren·dan, St. /bren'dən/ *c.* 486 – *c.* 575; Irish abbot

Bre·scia /brä'sнə/ *n.* city in N Italy. Pop. 196,800

Brest /brest/ *n.* **1** seaport in W France. Pop. 153,100 **2** city in SW Belarus. Pop. 277,000

breth·ren /breтн'rin/ *n. Formal.* *pl.* of BROTHER

Breu·ghel see BRUEGEL

breve /brēv, brev/ *n.* **1** *Mus.* note twice the length of a whole note **2** mark (˘) indicating a short or unstressed vowel [var. of BRIEF]

bre·vi·ary /brē'vē·er'ē/ *n.* (*pl.* **-ies**) book containing the Roman Catholic daily office [L, rel. to BRIEF]

brev·i·ty /brev'ətē/ *n.* **1** conciseness **2** shortness (of time, etc.) [AngFr, rel. to BRIEF]

brew /brōō/ *v.* **1a** make (beer, etc.) by infusion, boiling, and fermentation **b** make (tea, etc.) by infusion **2** undergo these processes **3** gather force **4** concoct (a plan, etc.) —*n.* **5** liquid or amount brewed; concoction —**brew'er** *n.* [OE]

brew·er·y /brōō'ərē, brōōr'ē/ *n.* (*pl.* **-ies**) factory for brewing beer, etc.

brew'pub' *n.* informal bar or restaurant that serves beer made on the premises

Brezh·nev /brezн'nef, -nyəf/, **Leonid** 1906–83; president of the USSR (1977–82)

bri·ar /brī'ər/ *n.* var. of BRIER[1] or BRIER[2]

bribe /brīb/ *v.* (**bribed, brib·ing**) **1** persuade to act improperly by a gift of money, etc. —*n.* **2** money or services offered in bribing —**brib'er·y** *n.* [Fr *briber* beg]

bric-a-brac /brik' ə brak'/ *n.* (also **bric-à-brac**) cheap ornaments, etc. [Fr]

brick /brik/ *n.* **1** small, usu. rectangular, block of fired or sun-dried clay used in building **2** brick-shaped thing —*v.* **3** build or pave with brick —*adj.* **4** built of brick [LGer or Du]

brick'bat' *n.* **1** piece of brick, esp. as a thrown weapon **2** insult

brick'lay·er *n.* person who builds with bricks, esp. for a living —**brick'lay·ing** *n.*

brid·al /brīd'l/ *adj.* of a bride or wedding [OE]

Brid·al·veil /brīd'l·vāl'/ *n.* waterfall in Yosemite National Park, Calif.: 620 ft. high

bride /brīd/ *n.* woman on her wedding day and during the period just before and after it [OE]

bride'groom' *n.* man on his wedding day and during the period just before and after it [OE]

brides·maid /brīdz'mād'/ *n.* girl or unmarried woman attending a bride at her wedding

bridge[1] /brij/ *n.* **1** structure providing a way across a river, road, railway, etc. **2** thing joining or connecting **3** operational superstructure on a ship **4** upper bony part of the nose **5** piece on a stringed instrument over which the strings are stretched **6** BRIDGEWORK —*v.* (**bridged, bridg·ing**) **7** be or make a bridge over **8** burn one's bridges (**behind one**) proceed to act without possibility of retreat [OE]

bridge[2] *n.* card game derived from whist

bridge'head' *n.* fortified position held on the enemy's side of a river or other obstacle

bridge' loan' *n.* loan to cover the interval between buying one house and selling another

Bridge·port /brij'pôrt', -pōrt'/ *n.* city in Conn. Pop. 141,686

Bridg·es /brij'iz/, **Robert** 1844–1930; English poet and literary critic

Bridg·et, St. /brij'it/ **1** (also **Bride; Brigid**) c. 450 – c. 525; Irish abbess **2** (also **Brigid; Birgitta**) c. 1303–73; Swedish nun and visionary

Bridge·town /brij'toun/ *n.* capital of Barbados. Pop. 6,100

bridge'work' *n.* dental structure covering a gap

BRIDLE 1

bri·dle /brīd'l/ *n.* **1** headgear for controlling a horse, including reins and bit **2** restraining thing —*v.* (**·dled, ·dling**) **3** put a bridle on **4** curb; restrain **5** express anger, offense, etc., by throwing back the head [OE]

bri'dle path' *n.* path for horseback riding

Brie /brē/ *n.* a kind of soft cheese [*Brie* in N France]

brief /brēf/ *adj.* **1** of short duration **2** concise; abrupt; brusque **3** scanty —*n.* **4** (*pl.*) short or legless underwear **5** summary of a law case —*v.* **6** inform or instruct in advance —**brief'ly** *adv.*; **brief'ness** *n.* [L *brevis* short]

brief'case' *n.* flat flexible document case

bri·er[1] /brī'ər/ *n.* (also **bri'ar**) wild rose or other prickly bush [OE]

bri·er[2] *n.* (also **bri'ar**) **1** white heath of S Europe **2** tobacco pipe made from its root [Fr *bruyère*]

brig[1] /brig/ *n.* two-masted square-rigged ship [abbr. of BRIGANTINE]

brig[2] *n.* naval prison

bri·gade /brigād'/ *n.* **1** part of a military division, usu. three battalions **2** group organized for a special purpose [It *briga* strife]

brig·a·dier' gen·er·al /brigədēr'/ *n.* (*pl.* **brig·a·dier' gen·er·als**) *Milit.* officer ranking just below major general

brig·and /brig'and/ *n.* member of a robber band; bandit —**brig'and·age** /-ij/ *n.* [It *brigante*, rel. to BRIGADE]

brig·an·tine /brig'antēn'/ *n.* type of two-masted ship [Fr or It, rel. to BRIGAND]

bright /brīt/ *adj.* **1** emitting or reflecting much light; shining **2** intense; vivid **3** clever **4** cheerful —*adv.* **5** esp. *Poet.* brightly —**bright'ly** *adv.*; **bright'ness** *n.* [OE]

bright'en *v.* make or become brighter

Brigh·ton /brīt'n/ *n.* seaside resort city in SE England. Pop. 138,000

bril·liant /bril'yənt/ *adj.* **1** very bright; sparkling **2** outstandingly talented **3** showy **4** *Colloq.* excellent —*n.* **5** diamond of the finest cut with many facets —**bril'liance** *n.*; **bril'liant·ly** *adv.* [Fr *briller* shine, fr. It]

bril·lian·tine /bril'yəntēn'/ *n.* dressing for making the hair glossy [Fr, rel. to BRILLIANT]

brim /brim/ *n.* **1** edge or lip of a vessel **2** projecting edge of a hat —*v.* (**brimmed, brim·ming**) **3** fill or be full to the brim —**brim′less** *adj.*

brim·ful *adj.* (also **brim′full**) filled to the brim

brim·stone /brim′stōn′/ *n.* sulfur [fr. BURN[1] + STONE]

brin·dled /brind′ld/ *adj.* brown or tawny with streaks of another color [Scand]

brine /brīn/ *n.* **1** water saturated or strongly impregnated with salt **2** sea water —**brin′y** *adj.* (**·i·er, ·i·est**) [OE]

bring /briNG/ *v.* (**brought, bring·ing**) **1** come carrying; lead; accompany; convey **2** cause or result in **3** be sold for; produce as income **4 bring about** cause to happen **5 bring forth** give birth to **6 bring off** achieve successfully **7 bring out: a** emphasize; make evident **b** publish **8 bring up: a** rear (a child) **b** vomit **c** call attention to [OE]

brink /briNGk/ *n.* extreme edge; verge [ON]

brink′man·ship′ *n.* (also **brinks′man·ship′**) pursuit (esp. habitual) of action to the brink of catastrophe

bri·quette /briket′/ *n.* block of compressed charcoal as fuel [Fr dim., rel. to BRICK]

Bris·bane /briz′bən, -bān′/ *n.* seaport in W Australia. Pop. 1,334,746

brisk /brisk/ *adj.* **1** quick; lively; keen **2** bracing —*v.* **3** make or grow brisk —**brisk′ly** *adv.*; **brisk′ness** *n.* [prob. Fr BRUSQUE]

bris·ket /bris′kət/ *n.* animal's breast, esp. as a cut of meat [Fr]

bris·tle /bris′əl/ *n.* **1** short stiff hair, esp. one on an animal's back, used in brushes —*v.* (**·tled, ·tling**) **2** (of hair) stand upright **3** show irritation **4** be covered or abundant (in) —**bris′tly** *adj.* (**·tli·er, ·tli·est**) [OE]

Bris·tol /bris′tol/ *n.* seaport on the Avon River in SW England. Pop. 420,200

Brit /brit/ *n.* Colloq. British person [abbr.]

Brit. *abbr.* British.

Brit·ain /brit′n/ *n.* GREAT BRITAIN —**Bri·tan·nic** /britan′ik/ *adj.*

Bri·tan·nia /britan′yə/ *n.* personification of Britain, esp. as a helmeted woman with shield and trident [L]

britch·es /briCH′iz/ *n. pl.* var. of BREECHES

Brit·i·cism /brit′əsiz′əm/ *n.* word or idiom used or originating in Britain [after Gallicism]

Brit·ish /brit′iSH/ *adj.* **1** of Great Britain, the British Commonwealth, or its people —*n.* **2** (prec. by the; treated as pl.) the British people [OE]

Brit·ish Co·lum·bi·a /kələm′bēə/ *n.* province in W Canada, on the Pacific Ocean. Capital: Victoria. Pop. 3,535,000

Brit′ish Em′pire *n.* Hist. countries under the control or leadership of the British crown

Brit′ish ther′mal u′nit *n.* unit of heat equal to approx. 252 calories; abbr. BTU

Brit′ish Vir′gin Is′lands *n.* islands in the Caribbean Sea, NE of Puerto Rico; British possession

Brit·on /brit′n/ *n.* **1** native or inhabitant of Great Britain **2** Celtic inhabitant of S Britain before the Roman conquest [LL Brittones]

Brit·ten /brit′n/ *n.* (**Edward**) **Benjamin** 1913–76; English composer

brit·tle /brit′l/ *adj.* **1** hard and fragile; apt to

break —*n.* **2** hard candy of molasses and nuts —**brit′tle·ness** *n.* [OE]

Br·no /bər′nō/ *n.* city in E Czech Republic. Pop. 388,000

broach /brōCH/ *v.* **1** raise for discussion **2** pierce (a cask) to draw liquor —*n.* **3** bit for boring [L broccus projecting]

broad /brôd/ *adj.* **1** large in extent from one side to the other; wide **2** extensive; wide-ranging **3** full and clear **4** explicit **5** general —*n.* **6** broad part **7** Slang. woman —**broad′ly** *adv.*; **broad′ness** *n.* [OE]

broad·cast /brôd′kast′/ *v.* (**·cast** or **·cast·ed, ·cast·ing**) **1** transmit by radio or television **2** take part in such a transmission **3** sow (seed, etc.) widely **4** disseminate (information) widely —*n.* **5** radio or television program or transmission —**broad′cast′er, broad′cast′ing** *n.*

broad′cloth′ *n.* fine cloth of wool, cotton, or silk

broad·en /brôd′n/ *v.* make or become broader

broad′ jump′ *n.* former name for LONG JUMP

broad′loom′ *adj.* (esp. of carpet) woven in broad widths

broad′-mind′ed *adj.* tolerant; liberal

broad′sheet′ *n.* large-sized newspaper

broad·side /brôd′sīd′/ *n.* **1** vigorous verbal attack **2** simultaneous firing of all guns from one side of a ship **3** side of a ship above the water

broad′-spec′trum *adj.* (of a drug) effective against many organisms

broad′sword′ *n.* broad-bladed sword, for cutting rather than thrusting

Broad·way /brôd′wā′/ *n.* **1** avenue in New York City, a section of which has many theaters near it **2** US dramatic theater, etc., epitomized

bro·cade /brōkād′/ *n.* **1** rich fabric woven with a raised pattern —*v.* (**·cad·ed, ·cad·ing**) **2** weave in this way [It brocco twisted thread]

broc·co·li /bräk′(ə)lē/ *n.* green plant with edible flower-heads [It]

bro·chure /brōsHŏŏr′/ *n.* booklet [Fr brocher stitch]

Brock·ton /bräk′tən/ *n.* city in Mass. Pop. 92,788

Brod·sky /bräd′skē, brät′-/, **Joseph** 1940– ; Russian-born US poet

brogue[1] /brōg/ *n.* **1** strong outdoor shoe with ornamental perforations **2** rough shoe of untanned leather [Gaelic and Ir brōg fr. ON]

brogue[2] *n.* marked accent, esp. Irish [perh. rel. to BROGUE[1]]

broil /broil/ *v.* **1** grill (meat) **2** make or become very hot [Fr bruler burn]

broil′er *n.* **1** young chicken for broiling **2** cooking appliance with heat source above the food

broke /brōk/ *v.* **1** past of BREAK —*adj.* **2** Colloq. having no money

bro·ken /brō′kən/ *v.* **1** past part. of BREAK —*adj.* **2** having been broken **3** reduced to despair; beaten **4** (of language) badly spoken, esp. by a foreigner **5** interrupted **6** tamed —**bro′ken·ly** *adv.*; **bro′ken·ness** *n.*

bro′ken-down′ *adj.* **1** worn out by age, use, etc. **2** not functioning

bro′ken-heart′ed *adj.* overwhelmed with grief

bro′ken home′ *n.* family disrupted by divorce or separation

bro′ker *n.* 1 agent; middleman 2 member of a stock exchange dealing in stocks, bonds, equities, etc. —**bro′ker·age, brok′ing** *n.* [AngFr]

bro·mide /brō′mīd′/ *n.* 1 any binary compound of bromine 2 such a compound used as a sedative 3 trite, boring remark

bro·mine /brō′mēn′/ *n.* poisonous liquid element with a choking smell; *symb.* Br [Gk *brōmos* stink]

bron·chi·al /bräng′kēəl/ *adj.* of the bronchi (see BRONCHUS) or of the smaller tubes into which they divide

bron·chi·tis /bräNGkīt′is/ *n.* inflammation of the mucous membrane in the bronchial tubes

bron·chus /bräNG′kəs/ *n.* (*pl.* ·chi /-kī′/) either of the two main divisions of the windpipe [L fr. Gk]

bron·co /bräNG′kō/ *n.* (*pl.* ·cos) wild or half-tamed horse of the western US [Sp: rough]

Bron·të /bränt′ē, brän′tā/ family of English novelists: 1 **Charlotte** 1816–55 2 **Emily** 1818–48 3 **Anne** 1820–49

bron·to·sau·rus /bränt′əsôr′əs/ *n.* (*pl.* ·rus·es) immense plant-eating dinosaur with a long tail [Gk *brontē* thunder + *sauros* lizard]

Bronx, the /bräNGks/ *n.* one of the five boroughs of New York City. Pop. 1,223,400

bronze /bränz/ *n.* 1 alloy of copper and tin 2 its brownish color 3 thing of bronze, esp. a sculpture —*adj.* 4 made of or resembling bronze —*v.* (bronzed, bronz·ing) 5 tan in the sun 6 coat with bronze to preserve, as baby shoes [Fr fr. It]

brooch /brōCH/ *n.* ornamental pin [Fr *broche*, rel. to BROACH]

brood /brood/ *n.* 1 young, esp. birds born or hatched at one time 2 *Colloq.* children in a family —*v.* 1 worry; ponder (esp. resentfully) 4 (of a bird) sit on eggs to hatch them —**brood′er** *n.*; **brood′y** *adj.* (·i·er, ·i·est) [OE]

brook[1] /brook/ *n.* small stream [OE]

brook[2] *v.* tolerate; allow [OE]

Brook·lyn /brook′lən/ *n.* one of the five boroughs of New York City. Pop. 2,314,300

broom /broom, broom/ *n.* 1 long-handled brush for sweeping 2 shrub with bright yellow flowers [OE]

broom′stick′ *n.* handle of a broom

bros. *abbr.* brothers

broth /brôTH/ *n.* thin soup of meat or fish stock [OE]

broth·el /brôTH′əl/ *n.* premises for prostitution [orig.: worthless fellow, fr. OE]

broth·er /brəTH′ər/ *n.* 1 male sibling 2 close male friend or associate 3 (*pl.* also **breth·ren**) member of a male religious order, esp. a monk —**broth′er·li·ness** *n.*; **broth′er·ly** *adj.* [OE]

broth·er·hood /brəTH′ərhood/ *n.* 1 relationship between brothers 2 association of people with a common interest

broth′er-in-law′ *n.* (*pl.* broth′ers-in-law′) 1 one's wife's or husband's brother 2 one's sister's or sister-in-law's husband

brought /brôt/ *v. past* and *past part.* of BRING

brou·ha·ha /broo′hä′hä′/ *n.* commotion; sensation [Fr]

brow /brou/ *n.* 1 forehead 2 eyebrow 3 summit of a hill, edge of a cliff, etc. [OE]

brow′beat′ *v.* (·beat, ·beat·en, ·beat·ing) intimidate; bully

Brown /broun/, **John** 1800–59; US abolitionist

brown /broun/ *adj.* 1 having the color of dark wood, chocolate, or rich soil 2 darkskinned or suntanned —*n.* 3 brown color or pigment 4 brown clothes or material —*v.* 5 make or become brown 6 browned off *Colloq.* fed up; disheartened —**brown′ish** *adj.* [OE]

brown′ bag′ *n.* 1 plain brown paper sack —*v.* (·bagged, ·bag·ging) 2 carry one's lunch to work, school, etc.

brown·ie /broun′ē/ *n.* 1 small square of chocolate cake with nuts 2 benevolent elf 3 (*cap.*) member of a junior group in Girl Scouts

Brown′ie point′ *n. Colloq.* notional mark awarded for good conduct, etc.

Brown·ing /brou′niNG/ English poets 1 **Elizabeth Barrett** 1806–61; her husband: 2 **Robert** 1812–89

brown′out′ *n.* reduction of voltage owing to a power shortage

brown′ rice′ *n.* unpolished rice

brown′stone′ *n.* reddish-brown sandstone, used in building

brown′ sug′ar *n.* unrefined or partially refined sugar

Browns·ville /brounz′vil/ *n.* city in Texas. Pop. 98,962

browse /brouz/ *v.* (browsed, brows·ing) 1 read desultorily or look over goods for sale 2 feed on leaves, twigs, etc. —*n.* 3 twigs, shoots, etc., as fodder [OFr *brost* bud; shoot]

Bruce, Robert the /broos/ ROBERT I

Brue·gel /broi′gəl/ (also **Breughel; Brue·ghel**), **Pieter** c. 1525–69; Flemish artist

Bruges /brooZH, bryZH/ *n.* (also **Brugge**) city in NW Belgium. Pop. 117,100

bruise /brooz/ *n.* 1 injury and discoloration of the skin 2 similar damage on a fruit, etc. —*v.* (bruised, bruis·ing) 3a inflict a bruise on b hurt 4 be susceptible to bruising [orig.: crush, fr. OE]

bruis·er *n. Colloq.* 1 large, tough-looking person 2 professional boxer

bruit /broot/ *v.* spread (a report or rumor) [Fr: noise]

brunch /brənCH/ *n.* esp. late morning meal [breakfast and lunch]

Bru·nei /broonī′/ *n.* sultanate on the NW coast of Borneo in the Malay Archipelago. Capital: Bandar Seri Begawan. Pop. 268,000

Bru·nel·les·chi /broon′l-es′kē/, **Filippo** 1377–1446; Italian architect

bru·nette /broonet′/ *n.* (*masc.* **bru·net′**) 1 woman with dark brown hair —*adj.* 2 having dark brown hair [Fr dim.]

Bruns·wick /brənz′wik/ *n.* city in Germany. Pop. 258,800

brunt /brənt/ *n.* chief impact of an attack, task, etc.

brush /brəSH/ *n.* 1 implement with bristles, hair, wire, etc., set into a handle, for cleaning, painting, arranging the hair, etc. 2 act of brushing 3 short esp. unpleasant encounter 4 fox's bushy tail 5 piece of carbon or metal as an electrical contact, esp. with a moving part 6 BRUSHWOOD, 2 —v. 7 sweep, scrub, treat, or tidy with a brush 8 remove or apply with a brush 9 graze in passing 10 **brush aside** dismiss curtly or lightly 11 **brush up** renew one's memory or skill in (a subject) [Fr]

brush'-off' n. abrupt dismissal

brush'wood' n. 1 undergrowth, thicket 2 cut or broken twigs, etc.

brush'work' n. 1 use of the brush in painting 2 painter's style in this

brusque /brəsk/ adj. abrupt or offhand —**brusque'ly** adv.; **brusque'ness** n. [It *brusco* sour]

Brus·sels /brəs'əlz/ n. capital of Belgium, site of European parliament. Pop. 954,000

Brus'sels sprout' /brəs'əlz/ n. 1 plant with small, edible, cabbagelike buds 2 such a bud [*Brussels* in Belgium]

bru·tal /brōōt'l/ adj. 1 savagely cruel 2 harsh; merciless —**bru·tal'i·ty** /-tal'itē/ n. (pl. **·ties**); **bru'tal·ly** adv. [Fr, rel. to BRUTE]

bru'tal·ize' v. (**·ized**, **·iz·ing**) 1 make brutal 2 treat brutally

brute /brōōt/ n. 1 brutal or violent person 2 animal —adj. 3 unthinking 4 cruel; stupid —**brut'ish** adj.; **brut'ish·ly** adv.; **brut'ish·ness** n. [L *brutus* stupid]

Bru·tus /brōōt'əs/, **Marcus Junius** 85–42 B.C.; Roman senator; an assassin of Julius Caesar

Bry·an /brī'ən/, **William Jennings** 1860–1925; US political leader and orator

Bry·ansk /brē·änsk'/ n. city in W Russia. Pop. 458,900

Bry·ant /brī'ənt/, **William Cullen** 1794–1878; US poet

Bryn·ner /brin'ər/, **Yul** 1915–85; Russian-born US actor

B.S. abbr. (also **BS**, **B.Sc.**) Bachelor of Science

BTU abbr. (also **Btu**, **B.T.U.**, **B.t.u.**, **btu**) BRITISH THERMAL UNIT(S)

bub·ble /bəb'əl/ n. 1 thin liquid enclosure of air or gas 2 air-filled cavity in a fluid or solidified liquid 3 transparent canopy 4 visionary or unrealistic project —v. (**·bled**, **·bling**) 5 rise in or send up bubbles 6 make the sound of boiling —**bub'bly** adj. (**·bli·er**, **·bli·est**)

bub'ble gum' n. chewing gum that can be blown into bubbles

Bu·ber /bōō'bər/, **Martin** 1878–1965; Austrian-born Israeli religious philosopher

bu·bo /b(y)ōō'bō/ n. (pl. **·boes**) inflamed swelling in the armpit or groin [Gk *boubon* groin]

bu·bon'ic plague' /b(y)ōōbän'ik/ n. contagious disease with fever, weakness, and buboes

Bu·ca·ra·man·ga /bōō'kərəmäNG'gə/ n. city in N Colombia. Pop. 341,500

buc·ca·neer' /bək'ənēr'/ n. pirate —**buc'ca·neer'ing** n. & adj. [Fr]

Bu·chan·an /byōōkan'ən/, **James** 1791–1868; 15th US president (1857–61)

Bu·cha·rest /bōō'kərest'/ n. capital of Romania. Pop. 2,064,500

Buck /bək/, **Pearl S**(ydenstricker) 1892–1973; US writer

buck¹ /bək/ n. 1 male deer, hare, rabbit, etc. 2 *Colloq.* dandy —v. 3 (of a horse) jump upwards with its back arched 4 throw (a rider) in this way 5 (foll. by *up*) *Colloq.* cheer up [OE]

buck² n. *Colloq.* dollar

buck³ n. *Slang.* 1 (in poker) article placed before the next dealer 2 **pass the buck** *Colloq.* shift responsibility (to another)

buck'board' n. small four-wheeled carriage without springs

buck·et /bək'it/ n. 1 a round, open container with a handle, for carrying or drawing water, etc. b amount contained in this 2 (pl.) *Colloq.* large quantities, esp. of rain or tears 3 bucketlike scoop of a water wheel, dredger, etc. —v. *Colloq.* 4 (esp. of rain) pour heavily 5 move or drive fast or bumpily [AngFr]

buck'et seat' n. seat for one person, esp. in a car

buck·le /bək'əl/ n. 1 clasp with a hinged pin for securing a belt, strap, etc. —v. (**·led**, **·ling**) 2 fasten with a buckle 3 (cause to) crumple under pressure 4 **buckle down** make a determined effort [L *buccula* cheekstrap]

buck·ler /bək'lər/ n. *Hist.* small, round shield

buck·min·ster·ful·ler·ene /bək'minstər'fōōl'ərēn'/ n. (also **buck'y·ball'**) carbon molecule whose rounded structure resembles a geodesic dome [for R. *Buckminster Fuller*, designer of geodesic dome]

buck·ram /bək'rəm/ n. coarse linen, etc., stiffened with paste [Fr *boquerant*]

BUCKSAW

buck'saw' n. wood-cutting saw blade set in an adjustable frame

buck'shot' n. coarse lead shot

buck'skin' n. 1 leather from a buck's skin 2 thick, smooth cotton or woolen cloth

buck'tooth' n. (pl. **·teeth**) upper projecting tooth —**buck'tooth'ed** /-tōōTHt'/ adj.

buck'wheat' n. seed of a plant used to make flour or as an alternative to rice [Du: beechwheat]

buck·y·ball /bək'ēbôl'/ n. see BUCKMINSTERFULLERENE

bu·col·ic /byōōkäl'ik/ adj. 1 of shepherds; rustic; pastoral —n. 2 (usu. pl.) pastoral poem or poetry [Gk *boukolos* herdsman]

bud /bəd/ n. 1 shoot from which a stem, leaf, or flower develops 2 flower or leaf not fully open —v. (**bud·ded, bud·ding**) 3 form buds 4 begin to grow or develop —**bud′like′** adj.

Bu·da·pest /bōōd′əpest′/ n. capital of Hungary. Pop. 2,018,000

Bud·dha /bōōd′ə, bŏŏd′ə/ (born **Siddhartha Gautama**) c. 563 – c. 483 B.C.; Indian philosopher; founder of Buddhism

Bud·dhism /bōōd′iz′əm, bŏŏd′-/ n. Asian religion or philosophy founded by Gautama Buddha —**Bud′dhist** n. & adj.

bud·dy /bəd′ē/ n. (pl. **-dies**) Colloq. friend or mate [perh. fr. BROTHER]

budge /bəj/ v. (**budged, budg·ing**) 1 move slightly 2 (cause to) change an opinion [Fr bouger]

bud·ger·i·gar /bəj′(ə)rēgär′/ n. (also **budg′ie**) small parrot, often kept as a pet [Aborig]

bud·get /bəj′it/ n. 1 amount of money needed or available 2 estimate or plan of revenue and expenditure —v. 3 allow or arrange for —**budg′et·ar′y** adj. [L bulga bag]

Bue·nos Ai·res /bwä′nəs er′ēz/ n. capital of Argentina. Pop. 2,961,000

buff /bəf/ adj. 1 of a yellowish beige color —n. 2 this color 3 Colloq. enthusiast 4 velvety dull-yellow leather —v. 5 polish (metal, etc.) 6 make (leather) velvety 7 **in the buff** Colloq. naked [orig.: buffalo, fr. Fr buffle]

buf·fa·lo /bəf′əlō′/ n. (pl. same or **-loes**) 1 wild ox of Africa or Asia 2 N American bison [Gk boubalos ox]

Buf·fa·lo /bəf′əlō′/ n. city in N.Y. Pop. 328,123

buff·er[1] /bəf′ər/ n. 1 thing that deadens impact, esp. a device on a train or at the end of a track 2 substance that maintains the constant acidity of a solution, as in a medication 3 Comp. temporary memory area for data —v. 4 Comp. store temporarily —**buff′ered** adj.

buff·er[2] n. 1 person who buffs (metal, etc.) 2 cloth, etc., for buffing 3 shock absorber

buff′er state′ n. (also **buff′er zone′**) small state or area between two larger ones, regarded as reducing friction

buf·fet[1] /bəfā′, bŏŏfā′/ n. 1 counter where people serve themselves food 2 self-service meal of several dishes set out at once 3 sideboard [Fr: stool]

buf·fet[2] /bəf′it/ v. 1 strike repeatedly —n. 2 blow, esp. of the hand 3 shock [Fr dim. of bufe blow]

buf′fet car′ /bəfā′/ n. railroad car serving refreshments

buf·foon /bəfōōn′/ n. clownish or stupid person —**buf·foon′er·y** n. [L buffo clown]

bug /bəg/ n. 1a any of various insects with mouthparts modified for piercing and sucking b Colloq. any insect Slang. 2 virus; infection 3 concealed microphone 4 error in a computer program or system, etc. 5 obsession, enthusiasm, etc. —v. (**bugged, bug·ging**) 6 conceal a microphone in 7 annoy

bug′bear′ n. 1 cause of annoyance 2 object of baseless fear [bug bogey]

bug·gy /bəg′ē/ n. (pl. **-gies**) 1 small, esp. open, horsedrawn carriage 2 (also **ba′by bug′gy**) BABY CARRIAGE

bu·gle /byōō′gəl/ n. 1 brass military instrument like a small trumpet —v. (**-gled, -gling**) 2 sound a bugle —**bu′gler** n. [L buculus young bull]

BUGLE 1

build /bild/ v. (**built, build·ing**) 1 construct or cause to be constructed 2 establish or develop 3 base (hopes, theories, etc.) —n. 4 physical proportions 5 **build in** incorporate 6 **build up**: a increase in size or strength b praise; boost —**build′er** n. [OE]

build′ing n. 1 permanent fixed structure 2 construction of these

build′up′ n. (also **build′-up′**) 1 favorable advance publicity 2 gradual approach to a climax 3 accumulation

built /bilt/ v. past and past part. of BUILD

built′-in′ adj. integral

built′-up′ adj. 1 (of a locality) densely developed 2 increased in height by addition

Bu·jum·bu·ra /bōō′jambŏŏr′ə/ n. capital of Burundi. Pop. 240,500

Bu·la·wa·yo /bōōl′əwī′ō/ n. city in SW Zimbabwe. Pop. 495,300

bulb /bəlb/ n. 1a globular base of the stem of some plants, sending roots downward and leaves upward b plant grown from this, e.g., a daffodil 2 object or part shaped like a bulb [L bulbus fr. Gk: onion]

bul·bous /bəl′bəs/ adj. bulb-shaped; fat or bulging

Bul·finch /bŏŏl′finCH/, **Charles** 1763–1844; US architect

Bul·gar·i·a /bəlgar′ēə, bŏŏl-/ n. republic in SE Europe, on the Black Sea. Capital: Sofia. Pop. 8,985,000 —**Bul·gar′i·an** n. & adj.

bulge /bəlj/ n. 1 irregular swelling —v. (**bulged, bulg·ing**) 2 swell —**bulg′y** adj. [L bulga bag]

bu·li·ma·rex·i·a /byōōlē′mərek′sēə/ n. disorder in which gorging alternates with self-induced vomiting —**bu·li′ma·rex′ic** adj. [BULIM(IA) + A(NO)REXIA]

bu·lim·i·a /b(y)ōōlim′ēə, -lē′mēə/ n. 1 disorder marked by overeating 2 BULIMAREXIA [Gk bous ox + limos hunger]

bulk /bəlk/ n. 1a magnitude (esp. large) b large mass, body, etc. c large quantity 2 greater part; majority 3 roughage —v. 4 seem (in size or importance) (bulks large) 5 make (a book, etc.) seem thicker 6 **in bulk** in large quantities [ON]

bulk′head′ n. upright fixed partition in a ship, aircraft, etc. —**bulk′head′ed** adj.

bulk′y adj. (**-i·er, -i·est**) awkwardly large —**bulk′i·ness** n.

bull[1] /bŏŏl/ n. 1a male bovine animal b male of the whale, elephant, etc. 2 (**the Bull**) zodiacal sign or constellation Taurus 3 person who buys shares hoping to sell them at a profit 4 Slang. nonsense 5 **take the bull by the horns** face danger or a challenge boldly —**bull′ish** adj.; **bull′ish·ly** adv.; **bull′ish·ness** n. [ON]

bull[2] n. papal edict [L bulla seal]

bull·dog —n. 1 short-haired heavy-jowled sturdy dog —v. (**·dogged, ·dog·ging**) 2 catch and wrestle a steer to the ground —adj. 3 tenacious

BULLDOG 1

bull·doze /bŏŏl'dōz'/ v. (**·dozed, ·doz·ing**) 1 clear with a bulldozer 2 *Colloq.* make (one's way) forcibly

bull'doz·er n. powerful tractor with a broad vertical blade at the front for clearing ground

bul·let /bŏŏl'ət/ n. small pointed missile fired from a rifle, revolver, etc. [Fr dim. of *boule* ball]

bul·le·tin /bŏŏl'ət·n/ n. 1 short, official news report 2 society's regular notice of information, etc. [It dim., rel. to BULL²]

bull'let·proof' adj. 1 designed to protect from bullets —v. 2 make impervious to bullets

bull'fight' n. public baiting, and usu. killing, of bulls —bull'fight'er, bull'fight'ing n.

bull'frog' n. large N American frog with a booming croak

bull'head'ed adj. obstinate, blundering

bull'horn' n. portable voice amplifier

bul·lion /bŏŏl'yən/ n. 1 gold or silver in bulk, before coining or being valued by weight 2 gold or silver in ingots [Fr, rel. to BOIL¹]

bul·lock /bŏŏl'ək/ n. castrated male of domestic cattle; steer [OE dim. of BULL¹]

bull'pen' n. 1 large cell where prisoners are kept temporarily 2 *Baseball.* area where pitchers warm up 3 area of newspaper office where copy editors, etc., work

bull'ring' n. arena for bullfights

bull's'-eye' n. 1 center of a target 2 direct hit

bul·ly¹ /bŏŏl'ē/ n. (pl. **·lies**) 1 person intimidating others —v. (**·lied, ·ly·ing**) 2 persecute; intimidate [Du]

bul·ly² n. corned beef [Fr, rel. to BOIL¹]

bul·rush /bŏŏl'rəsh'/ n. 1 a kind of tall rush 2 *Bibl.* papyrus [perh. fr. BULL¹ + RUSH²]

Bult·mann /bŏŏlt'män, -mən/, **Rudolf Karl** 1884–1976; German Lutheran theologian

bul·wark /bŏŏl'wərk/ n. 1 defensive wall, esp. of earth 2 protecting person or thing 3 (usu. pl.) ship's side above deck [LGer or Du]

bum /bəm/ *Colloq.* n. 1 loafer or tramp 2 enthusiast, as ski bum, etc. —v. (**bummed, bum·ming**) 3 loaf or wander around 4 cadge —adj. (**bum·mer, bum·mest**) 5 of poor quality 6 misleading 7 **on the bum:** a living as a tramp b not working [Ger *Bummler* loafer]

bum·ble /bəm'bəl/ v. (**·bled, ·bling**) 1 speak in a rambling way 2 bungle; blunder —bum'bler n. [fr. BOOM¹]

bum·ble·bee /bəm'bəlbē'/ n. large bee with a loud hum

bump /bəmp/ n. 1 dull-sounding blow or collision 2 swelling so caused 3 uneven patch

on a road, etc. —v. 4 hit or come against with a bump 5 move along joltingly 6 **bump into** *Colloq.* meet by chance 7 **bump off** *Slang.* murder —bump'y adj. (**·i·er, ·i·est**)

bump'er¹ n. horizontal bar at the front or back of a motor vehicle for protecting its body

bump·er² adj. unusually abundant (*bumper crop*)

bump'er stick'er n. sign bearing a motto, slogan, joke, advertisement, etc., for sticking on a car's (rear) bumper

bump·kin /bəm(p)'kin/ n. rustic or socially inept person [Du]

bump·tious /bəm(p)'shəs/ adj. offensively self-assertive or conceited —bump'tious·ly adv.; bump'tious·ness n. [fr. BUMP, after *fractious*]

bun /bən/ n. 1 small bread, roll, or cake 2 hair coiled and pinned to the head

bunch /bənch/ n. 1 things gathered together 2 *Colloq.* group of people; gang —v. 3 gather into close folds 4 (often **bunch' to·geth'er**) form into a group or crowd

Bunche /bənch/, **Ralph** 1904–71; US diplomat at the United Nations; Nobel prize 1950

bun·combe /bung'kəm/ n. nonsense; bunkum [*Buncombe* County, N.C.]

bun·dle /bən'dəl/ n. 1 things tied or fastened together 2 set of nerve fibers, etc. 3 *Slang.* large amount of money —v. (**·dled, ·dling**) 4 tie or make into a bundle 5 move carelessly 6 send away hurriedly [LGer or Du]

bung /bəng/ n. stopper, esp. for a cask [Du]

bun·ga·low /bəng'gəlō'/ n. one-storied house [Gujarati: of Bengal]

bun·gee /bən'jē/ n. elastic cord or rope; shock cord

bun'gee jump'ing n. sport of leaping from a height while secured by bungee cords and harness

bun·gle /bəng'gəl/ v. (**·gled, ·gling**) 1 mismanage or fail at (a task) 2 work badly or clumsily —n. 3 bungled attempt or work —bun'gler n.

Bu·nin /bōōn'yēn/, **Ivan** 1870–1953; Russian poet and prose-writer; Nobel prize 1933

bun·ion /bən'yən/ n. swelling on the foot, esp. at the base of the big toe [Fr]

bunk¹ /bəngk/ n. 1 shelflike bed against a wall, esp. in a ship 2 any place to sleep —v. 3 sleep, esp. in a makeshift bed

bunk² n. *Slang.* nonsense; humbug [shortening of BUNCOMBE]

bun·ker /bəng'kər/ n. 1 container for fuel aboard a ship 2 reinforced underground shelter 3 sandy hollow in a golf course

bun·kum /bəng'kəm/ n. nonsense; humbug [fr. BUNCOMBE]

bun·ny /bən'ē/ n. (pl. **·nies**) child's name for a rabbit [dial. *bun* rabbit]

Bun'sen burn'er /bun'sən/ n. single-jet adjustable gas burner used in a laboratory [for R.W. *Bunsen*, German chemist]

bunt /bənt/ n. 1 *Baseball.* batter's tapping of a pitched ball to make it roll to an open part of the infield —v. 2 to bat in such a way [nasalized BUTT¹]

bun·ting¹ /bən'ting/ n. small bird related to the finches

bun·ting² *n.* 1 flags and other decorations 2 loosely woven fabric for these

Bu·ñuel /bōōnwel'/, **Luis** 1900–83; Spanish film director

Bun·yan /bən'yən/ 1 **John** 1628–88; English writer 2 **Paul** US lumberjack of folk legend

buoy /bōō'ē, boi/ *n.* 1 anchored float as a navigation mark, etc. 2 lifebuoy —*v.* 3a keep afloat b encourage; uplift 4 mark with a buoy [Du, perh. fr. L *boia* collar]

buoy·ant /boi'ənt, bōō'yənt/ *adj.* 1 able or apt to keep afloat 2 resilient; exuberant —**buoy'an·cy** *n.*; **buoy'ant·ly** *adv.* [Fr or Sp, rel. to BUOY]

bur /bər/ *n.* 1a prickly, clinging seed case or flowerhead b any plant having these 2 clinging person 3 var. of BURR 2 [Scand]

bur. *abbr.* bureau

Bur·bank /bər'baNGk/ *n.* city in Calif., near Los Angeles. Pop. 93,643

Bur·bank /bər'baNGk/, **Luther** 1849–1926; US horticulturist

bur·den¹ /bər'dən/ *n.* 1 load, esp. a heavy one 2 oppressive duty, expense, emotion, etc. 3 capacity, as of a cargo ship —*v.* 4 load with a burden; oppress —**bur'den·some** *adj.* [OE, rel. to BIRTH]

bur·den² *n.* 1 refrain of a song 2 main theme of a speech, book, etc. [MF *bourdon* droning sound]

bur·dock /bər'dək/ *n.* plant with prickly flowers and leaves [fr. BUR + DOCK³]

bu·reau /byōōr'ō/ *n.* (*pl.* **·reaus** or **·reaux** /-rōz/) 1 chest of drawers 2a office or department for specific business b government department [Fr, orig.: baize]

bu·reau·cra·cy /byōōräk'rəsē/ *n.* (*pl.* **·cies**) 1a government by administrative officials b state, etc., so governed 2 government officials, esp. regarded as oppressive and inflexible 3 conduct typical of these —**bu'reau·crat'** /-rōkrat'/ *n.*; **bu'reau·crat'ic** *adj.*; **bu'reau·crat'i·cal·ly** *adv.*

bur·geon /bər'jən/ *v.* grow rapidly; flourish [L *burra* wool]

burg·er /bər'gər/ *n. Colloq.* hamburger

Bur·gess /bər'jəs/, **Anthony** 1917–93; English writer and critic

bur·gher /bər'gər/ *n.* citizen of a town [Ger or Du]

bur·glar /bər'glər/ *n.* person who commits burglary [AngFr]

bur'glar·ize' *v.* (**·ized, ·iz·ing**) commit burglary on or in

bur·gla·ry /bər'glərē/ *n.* (*pl.* **·ries**) 1 illegal entry with intent to commit a felony, as theft 2 instance of this

bur·gle /bər'gəl/ *v.* (**·gled, ·gling**) commit burglary (on or in)

bur·go·mas·ter /bər'gəmas'tər/ *n.* mayor of a Dutch or Flemish town [Du]

Bur·gos /bōōr'gōs/ *n.* city in N Spain. Pop. 160,400

Bur·gun·dy /bər'gəndē/ *n.* (*pl.* **·dies**) (also **b-**) 1 red or white wine from Burgundy in E France 2 dark red color of this

bur·i·al /ber'ēəl/ *n.* burying of a corpse

Burke /bərk/, **Edmund** 1729–97; British man of letters and politician

Bur·ki·na Fa·so /bōōrkē'nə fäs'ō/ *n.* republic in W Africa. Capital: Ouagadougou. Pop. 9,515,000

bur·lesque /bərlesk'/ *n.* 1 comic imitation; parody 2 variety show with striptease —*adj.* 3 of or using burlesque —*v.* (**·lesqued, ·lesqu·ing**) 4 parody [It *burla* mockery]

Bur·ling·ton /bər'liNGtən/ *n.* city in SE Ontario, Canada. Pop. 129,600

bur·ly /bər'lē/ *adj.* (**·li·er, ·li·est**) large and sturdy [OE]

Bur·ma /bər'mə/ *n.* (also called **Myanmar** /mēän'mär/) republic in SE Asia, bordering the Bay of Bengal. Capital: Rangoon (Yangon). Pop. 43,446,000 —**Bur·mese** /bər'mēz'/ *n. & adj.*

burn¹ /bərn/ *v.* (**burned** or **burnt, burning**) 1 (cause) to be consumed or destroyed by fire 2 blaze or glow with fire 3 (cause) to be injured or damaged by fire, heat, radiation, acid, etc. 4 use or be used as fuel, etc. 5 char in cooking 6 produce (a hole, mark, etc.) by fire or heat 7 make, be, or feel hot, esp. painfully 8 (cause to) feel great emotion or passion —*n.* 9 mark or injury caused by burning 10 **burn down** destroy or be destroyed by burning 11 **burn out: a** (cause to) fail by burning b suffer exhaustion 12 **burn up: a** consume or be consumed by fire b *Slang.* rage [OE]

burn² *n. Scot.* brook [OE]

Bur·na·by /bər'nəbē/ *n.* city in W Canada. Pop. 158,900

burn'er *n.* part of a stove, lamp, etc., emitting heat or light

Bur·nett /bərnet', bər'nət/, **Frances Hodgson** 1849–1924; English-born US novelist

burn'ing *adj.* 1 ardent; intense 2 hotly discussed; vital; urgent

bur·nish /bər'nish/ *v.* polish by rubbing [Fr *brunir* fr. *brun* brown]

bur·noose /bərnōōs'/ *n.* Arab or Moorish hooded cloak [Ar fr. Gk]

burn'out' *n.* 1 extinguishing of a rocket motor when fuel is exhausted 2 physical or mental exhaustion

Burns /bərnz/, **Robert** 1759–96; Scottish poet

Burn·side /bərn'sīd'/, **Ambrose Everett** 1824–81; American Civil War general for Union forces

burnt /bərnt/ *v.* var. *past* and *past part.* of BURN¹

burp /bərp/ *Colloq. v.* 1 belch 2 make (a baby) belch —*n.* 3 belch [imit.]

burr /bər/ *n.* 1a whirring sound b rough sounding of the letter *r* 2 (also **bur**) a rough edge on metal or paper b surgeon's or dentist's small drill 3 var. of BUR —*v.* 4 make a burr

BURNOOSE

Burr /bər/, **Aaron** 1756–1836; US vice-president (1801–05)

bur·ri·to /bərē'tō/ *n.* tortilla with a savory filling of beans, meat, cheese, etc. [MexSp: little burro]

bur·ro /bər'ō/ *n.* (*pl.* **·ros**) small donkey [Sp]

Bur·roughs /bər'ōz/, **Edgar Rice** 1875–1950; US writer

bur·row /bərʹō/ *n.* **1** hole or tunnel dug by an animal as a dwelling or shelter —*v.* **2** make a burrow **3** make (a hole, one's way, etc.) (as) by digging **4** investigate; search [appar. var. of BOROUGH]

bur·sa /barʹsə/ *n.* (*pl.* **·sae** /-sē/ or **·sas**) *Anat.* sac or cavity containing fluid to lubricate movement between tendon and bone [L: pouch fr. Gk *byrsa* skin]

Bur·sa /bŏŏrsäʹ/ *n.* city in NW Turkey. Pop. 834,600

bur·sar /barʹsər/ *n.* treasurer, esp. of a college [MedL *bursarius* fr. *bursa* purse]

bur·si·tis /bərsīʹtəs/ *n.* inflammation of a bursa

burst /barst/ *v.* (**burst, burst·ing**) **1** (cause to) break violently apart; open forcibly from within **2** break in, out, through, etc., suddenly or by force **3** be full to overflowing **4** appear or come suddenly **5** suddenly begin to shed (tears) or utter **6** seem about to explode from effort, excitement, etc. —*n.* **7** act of bursting **8** sudden issue or outbreak **9** sudden effort, spurt **10** volley of gunfire [OE]

Bur·ton /bartʹn/ **1** (Sir) **Richard Francis** 1821–90; English explorer and anthropologist **2 Richard** (born **Richard Jenkins**) 1925–84; Welsh actor

Bu·run·di /bərŏŏnʹdē/ *n.* republic in central Africa, at N end of Lake Tanganyika. Capital: Bujumbura. Pop. 5,657,000

bur·y /berʹē/ *v.* (**·ied, ·y·ing**) **1** place (a corpse) in the earth, a tomb, or the sea **2** put or hide under ground **3** cover up; conceal **4** involve deeply [OE]

bus¹ /bəs/ *n.* (*pl.* **bus·es** or **bus·ses**) **1** large passenger vehicle, usu. traveling a fixed route —*v.* (**bused** or **bussed, bus·ing** or **bus·sing**) **2** go by bus [abbr. of OMNIBUS]

bus² *v.* (**bussed, buss·ing**) work as a busboy or busgirl

bus. *abbr.* business

bus'boy *n.* (*fem.* **bus'girl**) person who brings water, etc., to customers in a restaurant, removes used dishes, etc.

bus·by /bazʹbē/ *n.* (*pl.* **·bies**) tall fur hat worn with dress military uniform

bush /bŏŏsh/ *n.* **1** shrub or clump of shrubs **2** thing like a bush, esp. a clump of hair **3** (esp. in Australia and Africa) uncultivated area; woodland or forest —**bush'y** *adj.* (**·i·er, ·i·est**); **bush'i·ly** *adv.*; **bush'i·ness** *n.* [OE and ON]

Bush /bŏŏsh/, **George Herbert Walker** 1924– ; 41st US president (1989–93)

bushed /bŏŏsht/ *adj. Colloq.* tired out

bush·el /bŏŏshʹəl/ *n.* measure of capacity equivalent to 4 pecks [Fr]

bush·ing /bŏŏshʹing/ *n.* metal lining for a hole enclosing a revolving shaft [fr. Du *busse* box]

bush' league' *adj. Slang.* unimportant; second rate

bush'man *n.* (*pl.* **·men**) **1** traveler or dweller in the Australian bush **2** (*cap.*) member or language of a S African aboriginal people

bush'mas'ter *n.* large pit viper of S America

busi·ness /bizʹnəs, -nəz/ *n.* **1** one's regular occupation or profession **2** one's own concern **3** task or duty **4** matter or affair **5** commercial firm [OE, rel. to BUSY]

busi'ness·like *adj.* efficient; systematic

busi·ness·man /bizʹnəsman', -nəz-, -mən/ *n.* (*pl.* **·men**); *fem.* **busi·ness·wom·an** (*pl.* **·wom'en**) person engaged in trade or commerce

bus'ing *n.* (also **bus'sing**) transportation by bus, esp. of children to schools outside their neighborhood to achieve racial balance

bus'man *n.* (*pl.* **·men**) **1** bus driver **2 busman's holiday** leisure time spent in an activity closely resembling one's work

buss /bəs/ *n.* & *v.* kiss

bust¹ /bəst/ *n.* **1** human chest, esp. of a woman; bosom **2** sculpture of a person's head, shoulders, and chest —**bust'y** *adj.* (**·i·er, ·i·est**) [Fr fr. It]

bust² *v.* (**bust·ed, bust·ing**) *Colloq.* **1** break; burst **2** raid; search **3** arrest **4** strike; hit —*adj.* **5** broken; burst **6** bankrupt **7 bust up** (esp. of a married couple) separate [var. of BURST]

bust'er *n. Slang.* **1** person who breaks up something —*interj.* **2** term of address to an adversary or source of irritation [fr. BUST²]

bus·tle¹ /basʹəl/ *v.* (**·tled, ·tling**) **1** (cause to) move busily and energetically —*n.* **2** excited or energetic activity [perh. fr. obs. *busk* prepare]

bus·tle² *n.* padding worn under a skirt to puff it out behind

bus·y /bizʹē/ *adj.* (**·i·er, ·i·est**) **1** occupied or engaged **2** full of activity **3** (of a person) in use **4** overly intricate —*v.* (**·ied, ·y·ing**) **5** keep busy; occupy —**bus'i·ly** *adv.*; **bus'y·ness** *n.* [OE]

bus·y·bod·y /bizʹēbäd'ē/ *n.* (*pl.* **·ies**) meddlesome person

but /bət/ *conj.* **1** nevertheless; however **2** on the other hand; on the contrary **3** except; otherwise than **4** unless —*prep.* **5** except; apart from; other than —*adv.* **6** only; no more than **7 but for** except for; if not for [OE]

bu·tane /byōōʹtān'/ *n.* flammable gas used as fuel

butch /bŏŏch/ *adj. Slang.* **1** masculine; tough-looking **2** (of a lesbian) masculine

butch·er /bŏŏchʹər/ *n.* **1** person who deals in meat **2** slaughterer **3** brutal murderer —*v.* **4** slaughter or cut up (an animal) for food **5** kill wantonly or cruelly **6** *Colloq.* ruin through incompetence —**butch'er·y** *n.* (*pl.* **·ies**) [Fr *boc* BUCK¹]

but·ler /bətʹlər/ *n.* principal manservant of a household [Fr *bouteille* bottle]

But·ler /bətʹlər/ **1 Samuel** 1612–80; English poet **2 Samuel** 1835–1902; English novelist

butt¹ /bət/ *v.* **1** push or strike with the head or horns **2** (cause to) meet end to end —*n.* **3** push with the head **4** joint where two ends meet **5 butt in** interrupt; meddle [Fr fr. Gmc]

butt² *n.* **1** object of ridicule, etc. **2a** mound behind a target **b** (*pl.*) shooting-range [Fr *but* goal]

butt³ *n.* **1** thicker end, esp. of a tool or weapon **2** stub of a cigarette, etc. **3** buttocks [Du]

butt⁴ *n.* cask [L *buttis*]

but·ter /bətʹər/ *n.* **1** solidified churned cream, used as a spread and in cooking **2** substance of similar texture —*v.* **3** spread, cook, or serve with butter **4 butter up** *Colloq.* seek to influence by flattery [Gk *bouturon*]

but´ter bean´ *n.* flat, dried, white wax or lima bean

but´ter cream´ *n.* mixture of butter, confectioners' sugar, etc., used in decorating or as a filling for a cake

but´ter-cup´ *n.* wild plant with yellow cup-shaped flowers

but´ter-fat´ *n.* fat from whole milk

but·ter-fin´gers *n. Colloq.* person prone to drop things

but·ter·fly /bət´ərflī´/ *n.* (*pl.* **·flies**) **1** insect with four usu. brightly colored wings **2** (*pl.*) *Colloq.* nervous sensation in the stomach —*v.* (**·flied**, **·fly·ing**) **3** prepare meat for cooking by splitting open and spreading apart

but´ter-fly stroke´ *n.* stroke in which a prone swimmer raises both arms at once and brings them forward and downward together

but´ter-milk´ *n.* liquid left after churning butter

but´ter-scotch´ *n.* brittle toffee made from butter, brown sugar, etc.

but·ter·y¹ /bət´ərē/ *n.* (*pl.* **·ies**) room where food is stored; larder [rel. to BUTT⁴]

but·ter·y² *adj.* like or containing butter

but·tock /bət´ək/ *n.* **1** each of the two fleshy protuberances at the rear of the human trunk **2** (*pl.*) rump [*butt* ridge]

but·ton /bət´n/ *n.* **1** small disk, etc., sewn to a garment as a fastener or worn as an ornament **2** small, round knob, etc., pressed to operate electronic equipment —*v.* **3** fasten with buttons **4 button up:** *Colloq.* **a** complete satisfactorily **b** be silent [Fr fr. Gmc]

but´ton-down´ *adj.* **1** (of a collar) buttoned to the shirt front **2** conservative

but´ton-hole´ *n.* **1** slit in cloth for a button **2** flower worn in a lapel buttonhole —*v.* (**·holed**, **·hol·ing**) **3** *Colloq.* accost and detain (a reluctant listener)

but·tress /bə´trəs/ *n.* **1** projecting support for a wall **2** prop —*v.* **3** support [rel. to BUTT¹]

bux·om /bək´səm/ *adj.* (of a woman) large-bosomed [ME *buhsum* pliant, rel. to BOW²]

buy /bī/ *v.* (**bought, buying**) **1** obtain, esp. in exchange for money **2** bribe **3** gain **4** *Slang.* believe in; accept **5** be a buyer for a store, etc. —*n.* **6** *Colloq.* purchase **7** *Colloq.* bargain **8 buy off** pay to get rid of **9 buy out** pay for ownership, all interest, etc. **10 buy up** buy as much as possible of [OE]

buy´er *n.* **1** person employed to purchase stock for a store, etc. **2** customer

buy´er's mar´ket *n.* (also **buy´ers' mar´ket**) trading conditions favorable to buyers

buy´out´ *n.* purchase of a controlling share in a company, etc.

buzz /bəz/ *n.* **1** hum of a bee, etc. **2** similar sound of a buzzer **3** low murmur, as of conversation **4** *Slang.* hurried activity **5** *Slang.* telephone call **6** *Slang.* thrill —*v.* **7** hum **8a** summon with a buzzer **b** *Slang.* telephone **9** move busily **10** (of a place) appear busy or full of excitement **11 buzz off** *Slang.* go or hurry away

buz·zard /bəz´ərd/ *n.* large bird of the hawk family [L *buteo* falcon]

buzz´er *n.* electrical device that emits a buzz as a signal

buzz´saw *n.* saw with disk-shaped blade driven by a motor

buzz´word´ *n. Colloq.* fashionable technical or specialist word; catchword

BVM *abbr. RC Ch.* Blessed Virgin Mary

by /bī/ *prep.* **1** near; beside **2** through the agency or means of **3** not later than **4** through; via **5** during **6** to the extent of **7** according to **8** with the succession of **9** in respect of **10** expressing dimensions of an area, etc. (*three feet by two*) **11** inclining to (*north by north-west*) **12** expressing a multiplier or divisor (*multiply 2 by 3; divide 6 by 3*) —*adv.* **13** near **14** aside; in reserve (*put $5 by*) **15** past (*marched by*) **16 by and by** before long; eventually **17 by and large** on the whole **18 by the by** (or **bye**) incidentally [OE]

by- *prefix* subordinate; incidental (*byroad*)

Byd·goszcz /bid´gôsн´/ *n.* city in N Poland. Pop. 382,000

bye¹ /bī/ *n.* status of an unpaired competitor in a sport, who proceeds to the next round by default [fr. BY as a noun]

bye² *interj.* (also **bye´-bye´**) *Colloq.* GOODBYE [abbr.]

Bye·lo·rus·sia /byel´ōrusн´ə/ *n.* see BELARUS

by·gone /bī´gôn´, -gän´/ *adj.* **1** past; antiquated —*n.* **2 let bygones be bygones** forgive and forget past quarrels

by´-law´ *n.* regulation made by a society or corporation [obs. *by* town]

by´line´ *n.* line naming the writer of a newspaper article, etc.

by´pass´ *n.* **1** main road passing around a town or its center **2** secondary channel or pipe, etc., used in emergencies **3** alternative passage for the circulation of blood through the heart —*v.* **4** avoid; go around (a town, difficulty, etc.)

by´play´ *n.* secondary action, esp. in a play

by´-prod´uct *n.* **1** incidental product made in the manufacture of something else **2** secondary result

Byrd /bərd/, **Richard Evelyn** 1888–1957; US admiral and polar explorer

by´road´ *n.* minor road

By·ron /bī´rən/, (**Lord**) **George Gordon** 1788–1824; English poet

by´stand´er *n.* person present but not taking part; onlooker

byte /bīt/ *n. Comp.* group of eight binary digits, often representing one character

by´way´ *n.* secondary or secluded path

by´word´ *n.* **1** person or thing as a notable example **2** familiar saying

Byz·an·tine /biz´əntēn´, -tīn, bəzan´tin´/ *adj.* **1** of Byzantium or the E Roman Empire **2** of its highly decorated style of architecture **3** (of a situation, etc.) complex; inflexible; underhand —*n.* **4** citizen of Byzantium or the E Roman Empire

Byz·an·tine Em´pire *n. Hist.* the E Roman Empire from the fall of the Western Empire (A.D. 476) to the fall of Constantinople (1453)

By·zan·ti·um /bizan´sнē-əm, -tē-əm/ *n.* see ISTANBUL

C

c, C /sē/ *n.* (*pl.* **c's; C's, Cs**) third letter of the English alphabet; a consonant

C /sē/ *n.* (*pl.* **Cs** or **C's**) **1** *Mus.* first note of diatonic scale of C major **2** third hypothetical person or example **3** third-highest category, etc. **4** *symb.* carbon **5** *Rom. num.* one hundred

c or **c.** *abbr.* **1** calorie **2** carat **3** cent **4** century **5** (also **ca.**) circa **6** *Algebra.* (as **c**) third known quantity

C or **C.** *abbr.* **1** Catholic **2** Celsius **3** Centigrade **4** College **5** Congress **6** (also ©) copyright

Ca *symb.* calcium

CA postal abbr. for California

cab /kab/ *n.* **1** taxi **2** driver's compartment in a truck, train, crane, etc. [abbr. of *cabriolet* carriage]

ca·bal /kəbal′, -bäl′/ *n.* conspiring political clique [Fr fr. L]

cab·a·ret /kab′ərā′/ *n.* entertainment in a nightclub or restaurant [Fr: tavern]

cab·bage /kab′ij/ *n.* vegetable with a round head and green or purple leaves [Fr *caboche* head]

cab·by /kab′ē/ *n.* (also **cab′bie**) (*pl.* **·bies**) *Colloq.* taxidriver

cab·in /kab′in/ *n.* **1** small shelter or house, esp. of wood **2** room or compartment in an aircraft or ship [Fr fr. L]

cab·i·net /kab′ənit/ *n.* **1a** cupboard or case for storage or display **b** casing of a radio, television, etc. **2** committee of senior ministers in a government [dim. of CABIN]

cab′i·net·mak′er *n.* skilled carpenter

ca·ble /kā′bəl/ *n.* **1a** encased group of insulated wires or fibers for transmitting electricity, etc. **b** insulated wire for transmission of television signals, etc. **2** thick rope of wire or hemp **3** cablegram —*v.* (**·bled, ·bling**) **4** transmit (a message) or inform (a person) by cablegram [L *capulum* halter; lasso]

ca′ble car′ *n.* small cabin conveyed by overhead cable for transport on an incline

ca·ble·gram /kā′bəlgram′/ *n.* telegraph message sent by undersea cable

ca′ble read′y *adj.* (of a TV, VCR, etc.) designed for direct connection to a coaxial cable TV system

ca′ble tel′e·vi·sion *n.* television transmission by cable to subscribers

ca·boo·dle /kəbōōd′l/ *n. Slang.* as in **the whole caboodle** the whole lot

ca·boose /kəbōōs′/ *n.* crew car at rear of a freight train [Du]

Cab·ot /kab′ət/, **John** (born **Giovanni Caboto**) 1425–c. 1498; Italian explorer

Ca·bri·ni /kəbrē′nē/, **St. Frances Xavier ("Mother Cabrini")** 1850–1917; Italian-born US nun

ca·ca·o /kəkā′ō, -kä′-/ *n.* (*pl.* **·os**) **1** seed from which cocoa and chocolate are made **2** tree bearing these [Sp fr. Nahuatl]

cache /kaSH/ *n.* **1** hiding place **2** things hidden there [Fr *cacher* hide]

ca·chet /kaSHā′/ *n.* **1** prestige **2** distinguishing mark or seal [Fr *cacher* hide]

cack·le /kak′əl/ *n.* **1** clucking of a hen, etc. **2** raucous laugh —*v.* (**·led, ·ling**) **3** make such a sound [imit.]

ca·coph·o·ny /kəkäf′ənē/ *n.* (*pl.* **·nies**) harsh discordant sound —**ca·coph′o·nous** *adj.* [Gk *kakos* bad + *phōnē* sound]

cac·tus /kak′təs/ *n.* (*pl.* **·ti** /-tī′/ or **·tus·es**) plant with a thick fleshy stem and usu. spines but no leaves [L fr. Gk]

cad /kad/ *n.* man who behaves dishonorably —**cad′dish** *adj.* [abbr. of CADDIE]

ca·dav·er /kədav′ər/ *n.* corpse [L *cadere* fall]

ca·dav′er·ous *adj.* corpselike; very pale and thin

CAD/CAM /kad′ kam′/ *abbr.* computer-aided design/computer-aided manufacturing; designating computer systems aiding in design, drafting, engineering, etc.

cad·die /kad′ē/ (also **cad′dy**) *n.* (*pl.* **·dies**) **1** person paid to carry a golfer's clubs —*v.* (**·died, ·dy·ing**) **2** act as a caddie [Fr CADET]

cad·dy[1] /kad′ē/ *n.* (*pl.* **·dies**) small container for tea [Malay]

cad·dy[2] *n.* var. of CADDIE

ca·dence /kād′ns/ *n.* **1** rhythm; measure or beat of a sound or movement **2** tonal inflection **3** closing musical phrase [L *cadere* fall]

ca·den·za /kəden′zə/ *n.* virtuoso passage for a soloist [It, rel. to CADENCE]

ca·det /kədet′/ *n.* young military or police trainee [Fr, ult. fr. L *caput* head]

cadge /kaj/ *v.* (**cadged, cadg·ing**) *Colloq.* **1** get or seek by begging **2** borrow without intent to repay

Cad·il·lac /kad′l-ak′, käd′ē-yäk′/, **Antoine de la Mothe** c. 1656–1730; French explorer; founder of Detroit, Mich.

Cá·diz /kədiz′/ *n.* seaport in SW Spain. Pop. 153,600

cad·mi·um /kad′mēəm/ *n.* soft bluish-white metallic element; *symb.* **Cd** [Gk *kadmeia* Cadmean (earth)]

cad·re /kad′rē, käd′-, -rā′/ *n.* core unit, esp. of military personnel [Fr fr. L *quadrum* square]

CADUCEUS

ca·du·ce·us /kədōō′sēəs/ *n.* (*pl.* **·ce·i** /-sēī′/) winged staff of Mercury; symbol of the medical profession [L]

Caen /kän/ *n.* city in NW France. Pop. 115,600

Cae·sar /sē′zər/ *n.* **1** (**Gaius Julius**) 100–44 B.C.; Roman general and statesman; assassinated on the Ides of March **2** title of Roman emperors **3** autocrat

Cae·sar·e·an /sizer′ēən/ (also **Ce·sar′i·an**) *adj.* **1** (of birth) effected by Caesarean section —*n.* **2** (in full **Cae·sar′e·an sec′tion**) delivery of a child by cutting through the mother's abdomen [for Julius CAESAR, who was supposedly born this way]

cae·su·ra /sizHōōr′ə, -zōōr′ə/ *n.* (*pl.* **·ras**)

pause in a line of verse —**cae·su′ral** adj. [L caedere cut]

ca·fé /kafā′/ n. small coffeehouse or restaurant [Fr]

caf·e·te·ri·a /kaf′ətēr′ēə/ n. self-service restaurant [AmerSp: coffee shop]

caf·feine /kafēn′, kaf′ēn/ n. alkaloid stimulant in tea leaves and coffee beans [Fr café coffee]

caf·tan /kaf′tan′/ n. (also **kaf′tan**) 1 long tunic worn by men in the Near East 2 any robelike dress or shirt [Turk]

cage /kāj/ n. 1 structure of bars or wires, esp. for confining animals or birds 2 similar open framework, as in a mine, etc. —v. (**caged, cag·ing**) 3 place or keep in a cage [L cavea]

ca·gey /kā′jē/ adj. (also **cag′y**) (**·i·er, ·i·est**) Colloq. cautious and noncommittal —**ca′gi·ly** adv.; **ca′gi·ness** n.

Cag·ney /kag′nē/, **James** 1904–86; US actor

Ca·guas /kä′(g)wäs/ n. city in Puerto Rico. Pop. 133,400

ca·hoots /kəhōōts′/ n. pl. Slang. as in **in cahoots** in collusion

CAI abbr. computer-aided instruction

Cain /kān/ n. 1 Biblical son of Adam and Eve; killed his brother, Abel 2 **raise Cain** Colloq. make trouble

Caine /kān/, **Michael** (born **Maurice Micklewhite**) 1933– ; English actor

cairn /kern/ n. mound of stones as a monument or landmark [Gaelic]

Cai·ro /kī′rō/ n. capital of Egypt. Pop. 6,452,000

cais·son /kā′sän′, -sən/ n. watertight chamber for underwater construction work [It cassone]

ca·jole /kəjōl′/ v. (**·joled, ·jol·ing**) persuade by flattery, deceit, etc. —**ca·jol′er·y** n. [Fr]

cake /kāk/ n. 1 baked mixture of flour, butter, eggs, sugar, etc., and often iced 2 food or other item in a flat round shape —v. (**caked, cak·ing**) 3 form into a compact mass 4 cover (with a hard or sticky mass) 5 **a piece of cake** Colloq. something easily achieved [ON]

cal. abbr. 1 calorie(s) 2 calender

cal·a·bash /kal′əbasH/ n. 1 gourd-bearing tree of tropical America 2 such a gourd, esp. as a vessel for water, etc. [MFr fr. Sp]

cal·a·mine /kal′əmīn′/ n. a zinc oxide skin lotion [Fr fr. L]

ca·lam′i·ty /kəlam′ətē/ n. (pl. **·ties**) disaster; great misfortune —**ca·lam′i·tous** adj. [MFr fr. L]

Ca·lam′i·ty Jane′ /jān/ (born **Martha Jane Cannary**) c. 1852–1903; US frontierswoman

cal·cif·er·ous /kalsif′ərəs/ adj. yielding calcium salts, esp. calcium carbonate

cal·ci·fy /kal′səfī′/ v. (**·fied, ·fy·ing**) 1 harden by the depositing of calcium salts 2 convert or be converted to calcium carbonate —**cal′ci·fi·ca′tion** n.

cal·cine /kal′sīn, kalsīn′/ v. (**·cined, ·cin·ing**) decompose or be decomposed by strong heat [Medl calcinare heat, fr. L calx lime]

cal·cite /kal′sīt′/ n. natural crystalline calcium carbonate [L, rel. to calx lime]

cal·ci·um /kal′sēəm/ n. soft gray metallic element occurring in limestone, marble, chalk, etc.; symb. **Ca** [L calx lime]

cal′ci·um car′bon·ate n. white insoluble solid occurring as chalk, marble, etc.

cal·cu·late /kal′kyəlāt′/ v. (**·lat·ed, ·lat·ing**) 1 ascertain or forecast, esp. by arithmetic 2 plan deliberately —**cal′cu·la·ble** adj.; **cal′cu·la′tion** n. [L, rel. to CALCULUS]

cal′cu·lat′ed adj. done by plan or intentionally

cal′cu·lat′ing adj. scheming

cal·cu·la·tor /kal′kyəlāt′ər/ n. device (esp. a handheld one) for making mathematical calculations

cal·cu·lus /kal′kyələs/ n. (pl. **·lus·es** or **·li** /-lī′, -lē′/) 1 particular method of higher mathematics 2 stone or mineral mass in kidneys, etc. [L: small stone (used on an abacus)]

Cal·cut·ta /kalkət′ə/ n. seaport on the Hooghly River in E India. Pop. 10,916,000

Cal·der /kôl′dər/, **Alexander** 1898–1976; US sculptor

cal·en·dar /kal′əndər/ n. 1 system for organizing the year into set intervals 2 annual chart, etc., showing days, weeks, and months 3 timetable of dates, events, etc. [L Kalendae first day of the month]

cal·en·der /kal′əndər/ n. 1 machine in which cloth, paper, etc., is rolled to glaze or smooth it —v. 2 press in a calender [MFr fr. L cylindrus cylinder]

calf[1] /kaf/ n. (pl. **calves**) 1 young cow or bull 2 young of other animals, e.g., the elephant, deer, and whale [OE]

calf[2] n. (pl. **calves**) fleshy hind part of the human leg below the knee [ON]

calf′skin′ n. calf leather

Cal·ga·ry /kal′gərē/ n. city in S Alberta, Canada. Pop. 710,700

Cal·houn /kalhōōn′/, **John C.** 1782–1850; US politician; championed states' rights

Ca·li /kä′lē/ n. city in SW Colombia. Pop. 1,323,900

cal·i·ber /kal′əbər/ n. 1 diameter of a gun bore, tube, bullet, etc. 2 strength or quality of ability, dependability, etc. [MFr, ult. fr. Gk kalapous shoe last]

cal·i·brate /kal′əbrāt′/ v. (**·brat·ed, ·brat·ing**) 1 mark (a gauge) with a scale of readings 2 correlate readings of (an instrument or system of measurement) with a standard —**cal′i·bra′tion** n.

cal·i·co /kal′ikō′/ n. (pl. **·cos**) 1 printed cotton fabric —adj. 2 of calico 3 multicolored [Calicut in India]

Calif. abbr. California

Cal·i·for·nia /kal′ifôr′nyə/ n. W state of the US. Capital: Sacramento. Pop. 29,760,021. Abbr. **CA; Cal.; Calif.** —**Cal′i·for′ni·an** n. & adj.

Cal′i·for′nia, Gulf of n. inlet of the Pacific enclosed by Baja California

cal·i·for·ni·um /kal′əfôr′nēəm/ n. artificial radioactive metallic element; symb. **Cf** [CALIFORNIA, where discovered]

Ca·lig·u·la /kəlig′yələ/ (born **Gaius Caesar**) 12–41; Roman emperor (37–41)

cal·i·per /kal′əpər/ n. (often pl.) device for

CALIPER

ca·liph /kā′ləf, kal′əf/ *n.* esp. *Hist.* chief Muslim civil and religious ruler —**ca′liph·ate** *n.* [Ar: successor (of Muhammad)]

cal·is·then·ics /kal′əsTHen′iks/ *n. pl.* fitness exercises —**cal′is·then′ic** *adj.* [Gk *kallos* beauty + *sthenos* strength]

ca·lix /kā′liks, kal′iks/ *n.* var. of CALYX

calk /kôk/ *v.* var. of CAULK

call /kôl/ *v.* **1a** cry; shout; speak loudly **b** (of a bird, etc.) emit its characteristic sound **2** communicate with by telephone or radio **3** summon **4** pay a brief visit **5** order to take place (*called a meeting*) **6** name; describe as **7** (foll. by *for*) demand **8** stop (a game) **9** guess the outcome of tossing a coin, etc. —*n.* **10** shout; cry **11** characteristic cry of a bird, etc. **12** brief visit **13** act of telephoning **14** invitation, summons **15** signal on a bugle, etc. **16** option of buying stock at a fixed price at a given date **17 call off: a** cancel (an arrangement) **b** order (an attacker or pursuer) to desist **18 call up: a** telephone **b** summon to military service **19 on call** ready or available [OE fr. ON]

Cal·la·ghan /kal′əhan′/, (Lord) (Leonard) James 1912– ; British prime minister (1976–79)

Ca·llao /kəyou′/ *n.* seaport in W Peru. Pop. 588,600

Cal·las /kal′əs, käl′-/, **Maria** 1923–77; US operatic soprano

call′er *n.* visitor or telephoner

call′ girl *n.* prostitute by appointment

cal·lig·ra·phy /kəlig′rəfē/ *n.* art of fine handwriting —**cal·lig′ra·pher** *n.*; **cal′li·graph′ic** *adj.*; **cal·lig′ra·phist** *n.* [Gk *kallos* beauty + *graphein* write]

call′ing *n.* profession or vocation

cal·los·i·ty /kəläs′ətē/ *n.* (*pl.* **-ties**) area of hard thick skin [L, rel. to CALLUS]

cal·lous /kal′əs/ *adj.* **1** unfeeling; insensitive **2** (also **cal′loused**) (of skin) hardened —**cal′lous·ly** *adv.*; **cal′lous·ness** *n.* [L, rel. to CALLUS]

cal·low /kal′ō/ *adj.* inexperienced; immature [OE: bald]

cal·lus /kal′əs/ *n.* (*pl.* **-lus·es**) area of hard thick skin [L]

calm /kä(l)m/ *adj.* **1** tranquil; quiet; windless **2** serene; not agitated —*n.* **3** calm condition or period —*v.* **4** make or become calm —**calm′ly** *adv.*; **calm′ness** *n.* [Gk *kauma* heat]

Ca·lo·o·can /kal′ōō′kän/ *n.* city on Luzon in the Philippines. Pop. 746,000

ca·lo·ric /kəlôr′ik, -lär′-/ *adj.* pertaining to heat or calories

cal·o·rie /kal′(ə)rē/ *n.* (*pl.* **-ries**) unit of quantity of heat or food energy [Fr fr. L *calor* heat]

cal·o·rif·ic /kal′ərif′ik/ *adj.* producing heat

ca·lum·ni·ate /kəlum′nē·āt′/ *v.* (**·at·ed, ·at·ing**) malign; slander [L]

cal·um·ny /kal′əmnē/ *n.* (*pl.* **-nies**) slander —**ca·lum′ni·ous** *adj.* [L]

cal·va·dos /kal′vədōs, kal′vədōs′/ *n.* apple brandy [*Calvados* in France]

calve /kav/ *v.* (**calved, calv·ing**) give birth to a calf [OE, rel. to CALF¹]

Cal·vert /kal′vərt/ family of English colonial administrators of Maryland: **1** (Lord) George (1st Baron Baltimore) c. 1580–1632 **2** Leonard 1606–47 **3** Charles (3rd Baron Baltimore) 1637–1715

calves /kavz/ *n. pl.* of CALF¹, CALF²

Cal·vin /kal′vən/, **John** 1509–64; French Protestant theologian and reformer

Cal·vin·ism /kal′vəniz′əm/ *n.* theology of Calvin or his followers, stressing predestination and divine grace —**Cal′vin·ist** *n.* & *adj.*; **Cal′vin·is′tic** *adj.* [for John CALVIN]

ca·lyp·so /kəlip′sō/ *n.* (*pl.* **-sos**) W Indian syncopated folk music

ca·lyx /kā′liks/ *n.* (*pl.* **ca·ly·ces** /-ləsēz′/ or **ca·lyx·es**) (also **ca′lix**) **1** sepals forming the protective case of a flower in bud **2** cuplike cavity or structure [Gk: husk]

cam /kam/ *n.* projection on a wheel to effect a particular motion [Du *kam* comb]

CAM see CAD/CAM

Ca·ma·güey /käm′əgwā′/ *n.* city in central Cuba. Pop. 279,000

ca·ma·ra·de·rie /käm′əräd′ərē, kām′-/ *n.* warm comradeship [Fr]

cam·ber /kam′bər/ *n.* **1** convex surface of a road, etc. —*v.* **2** build with a camber [L *camur* curved]

Cam·bo·di·a /cambōd′ēə/ *n.* (also called **Kam′pu·che′a**) republic in SE Asia on E coast of the Gulf of Thailand. Capital: Phnom Penh. Pop. 8,974,000 —**Cam·bo′di·an** *n.* & *adj.*

Cam·bri·an /kam′brēən, käm′-/ *adj.* **1** Welsh **2** *Geol.* of the first period in the Paleozoic era —*n.* **3** this period [ult. fr. Welsh *Cymry* Welsh people]

cam·bric /kām′brik/ *n.* fine linen or cotton fabric [*Cambrai* in France]

Cam·bridge /kām′brij/ *n.* **1** city in Mass., near Boston. Pop. 95,802 **2** city in SE England; site of Cambridge University. Pop. 104,000

cam·cor·der /kam′kôrd′ər/ *n.* video camera with sound [fr. CAMERA + RECORDER]

Cam·den /kam′dən/ *n.* city in N.J. Pop. 87,492

came /kām/ *v. past* of COME

cam·el /kam′əl/ *n.* long-legged ruminant with one hump (**Arabian camel** or **dromedary**) or two humps (**Bactrian camel**) [Gk]

ca·mel·li·a /kəmēl′yə/ *n.* evergreen shrub with shiny leaves and showy flowers [*Camellus*, name of a botanist]

Cam·em·bert /kam′əmber′/ *n.* a creamy pungent cheese [*Camembert* in France]

cam·e·o /kam′ē·ō′/ *n.* (*pl.* **·os**) **1** relief carving with a background of a different color **2** brief character part in a play or film played by a distinguished actor [It fr. Fr fr. MedL]

cam·er·a /kam′(ə)rə/ *n.* **1** apparatus for taking still or motion photographs **2** equipment for converting images into electrical signals **3 in camera** *Law.* in private —**cam′er·a·man′** *n.* (*pl.* **·men′**) [L, rel. to CHAMBER]

Cam·e·roon /kam′ərōōn′/ *n.* republic in W Africa bordering the Gulf of Guinea. Capital: Yaoundé. Pop. 12,622,000

cam·i·sole /kam′isōl′/ *n.* woman's lightweight undervest [Fr fr. LL, rel. to CHEMISE]

cam·o·mile /kam′əmīl′, -mēl′/ *n.* var. of CHAMOMILE

cam·ou·flage /kam'əflãzн', -fläj'/ *n.* 1 disguising of soldiers, tanks, etc., so that they blend into the background 2 such a disguise 3 misleading or evasive behavior —*v.* (·**flaged**, ·**flag·ing**) 4 hide by camouflage [Fr *camoufler* disguise]

camp[1] /kamp/ *n.* 1 base for troops 2 temporary accommodation of huts, tents, etc. 3 supporters —*v.* 4 set up or spend time in a camp [L *campus* level ground; field]

camp[2] *adj. Colloq.* amusingly tasteless or exaggerated —**camp'y** *adj.* (·**i·er**, ·**i·est**)

cam·paign /kam'pān'/ *n.* 1 organized course of action 2 military operations —*v.* 3 take part in a campaign —**cam·paign'er** *n.* [L, rel. to CAMP[1]]

cam·pa·ni·le /kam'pənē'lē/ *n.* bell tower (usu. freestanding), esp. in Italy [It *campana* bell, fr. L]

Camp' Da·vid /dā'vid/ *n.* official US presidential retreat in Catoctin Mts. of Md., about 70 mi. NW of Washington, D.C.

Cam·pe·che /kampä'CHā, -pē'CHē/ *n.* state of Mexico, in the SE part. Capital: Campeche. Pop. 535,200

camp·er /kam'pər/ *n.* 1 person who camps 2 large motor vehicle with beds, etc.

cam·phor /kam'fər/ *n.* pungent white crystalline substance used in making celluloid, medicine, and mothballs [Fr, ult. fr. Skt]

Cam·pi·nas /kampē'nəs/ *n.* city in SE Brazil. Pop. 566,500

camp'site' *n.* place for camping

cam·pus /kam'pəs/ *n.* (*pl.* ·**pus·es**) grounds of a university, college, or other institution [L: field]

cam·shaft /kam'sнaft'/ *n.* shaft with one or more cams

Ca·mus /kämy'/, **Albert** 1913–60; French writer

can[1] /kan, kən/ *v. aux.* (*past* **could**) 1a be able to; know how to b be potentially capable of 2 be permitted to [OE: know]
   • Usage: In formal style, *can* is used in the sense 'be able': *I can do anything you can do. May* means 'be permitted': *Mother said I may go to the movies.* For one sense of *may* vs. *might*, see note at MAY.

can[2] /kan/ *n.* 1 metal vessel for liquid 2 sealed tin container of food or drink 3 (prec. by *the*) *Slang.* **a** prison **b** toilet —*v.* (**canned, can·ning**) 4 put or preserve in a can 5 **in the can** *Colloq.* completed [OE]

Can·a·da /kan'ədə/ *n.* country of N America, bounded on the E by the Atlantic Ocean, on the S by the US, on the W by the Pacific Ocean. Capital: Ottawa. Pop. 27,296,900 —**Ca·na·di·an** /kanā'dēən/ *n. & adj.*

Can'a·da goose' *n.* wild N American goose with a brownish-gray body and white neck and breast

Ca·na'di·an ba'con *n.* smoked pork loin, usu. sliced

Ca·na'di·an·ism' *n.* word, phrase, or usage uniquely Canadian

ca·nal /kənal'/ *n.* 1 artificial inland waterway 2 tubular duct in a plant or animal [L *canalis*]

Ca·na·let·to /kan'l-et'ō/ (born **Giovanni Antonio Canale**) 1697–1768; Italian painter

ca·na·pé /kan'əpā, -pē'/ *n.* small piece of bread or pastry with savory topping [Fr]

ca·nard /kənärd'/ *n.* unfounded rumor or story [Fr: duck]

ca·nar·y /kəner'ē/ *n.* (*pl.* ·**ies**) small songbird with yellow feathers [*Canary* Islands]

Ca·nar'y Is'lands *n.* mountainous islands in the Atlantic Ocean off the NW coast of Africa

ca·nas·ta /kanas'tə/ *n.* card game using two decks and resembling rummy [Sp: basket]

Ca·nav·er·al, Cape /kənav'(ə)rəl/ *n.* cape on the east-central coast of Fla.; site of NASA Kennedy Space Center

Can·ber·ra /kan'b(ə)rə/ *n.* capital of Australia. Pop. 278,900

can·can /kan'kan'/ *n.* lively stage dance with high kicking [Fr]

can·cel /kan'səl/ *v.* (·**celed** or ·**celled**, ·**cel·ing** or ·**cel·ling**) 1 revoke or discontinue (an arrangement) 2 delete; mend; invalidate 3 neutralize; counterbalance 4 *Math.* strike out (an equal factor) on each side of an equation, etc. —**can'cel·la'tion** *n.* [L *cancellus* lattice]

can·cer /kan'sər/ *n.* 1 malignant tumor of body cells 2 evil influence; corruption 3 (*cap.*) **a** constellation and fourth sign of the zodiac (the Crab) **b** person born under this sign —**can'cer·ous** *adj.* [L: crab]

can·de·la·brum /kan'dələ'brəm, -lä'-/ *n.* (*pl.* ·**bra** or ·**brums**) (also **can'de·la'bra**, *pl.* ·**bras**) branched candlestick or lamp-holder [L]

CANDELABRUM

Can·di·a /kan'dēə/ *n.* 1 former name of CRETE 2 former name of IRÁKLION

can·did /kan'did/ *adj.* 1 frank; open 2 (of a photograph) taken informally —**can'did·ly** *adv.*; **can'did·ness** *n.* [L *candidus* white]

can·di·date /kan'(d)ədāt', -dət/ *n.* nominee, office-seeker, or entrant —**can'di·da·cy** *n.* [L: white-robed]

can·dle /kan'dl/ *n.* 1 cylinder or block of wax or tallow with a central wick which gives light when burning 2 **cannot hold a candle to** is much inferior to [L *candela*]

can'dle·pow'er *n.* unit of luminous intensity

can'dle·stick' *n.* holder for one or more candles

can·dor /kan'dər/ *n.* frankness; openness [L]

can·dy /kan'dē/ *n.* (*pl.* ·**dies**) 1 a sweet solid confection variously of sugar, chocolate, fruit, etc.; sweet —*v.* (·**died, ·dy·ing**) 2 preserve (fruit, etc.) in candy [MFr, ult. fr. Skt]

can'dy·strip'er *n. Colloq.* volunteer hospital orderly, often a teenager [fr. the typical uniform]

cane /kān/ *n.* 1a hollow jointed stem of giant reeds or grasses b solid stem of slender palms 2 SUGAR CANE 3 cane used for wickerwork, etc. 4 walking stick or rod —*v.* (**caned, can·ing**) 5 beat with a cane 6 weave cane into (a chair, etc.) [Gk *kanna* reed]

ca·nine /kā'nīn/ *adj.* 1 of a dog or dogs —*n.* 2 dog 3 (in full **ca'nine tooth'**) pointed tooth between incisors and premolars [L *canis* dog]

can·is·ter /kan'əstər/ *n.* 1 small container

for tea, etc. **2** cylinder of shot, tear gas, etc. [Gk *kanastron* wicker basket]

can·ker /kaNG´kər/ *n.* **1** destructive disease of trees and plants **2** ulcerous ear disease of animals **3** corrupting influence —*v.* **4** infect with canker **5** corrupt —**can´ker·ous** *adj.* [L, rel. to CANCER]

can·na·bis /kan´əbəs/ *n.* **1** hemp plant **2** parts of it used as a narcotic [L fr. Gk]

canned /kand/ *adj.* **1** sold in a can **2** prerecorded

can·nel·lo·ni /kan´l-lō´nē/ *n. pl.* tubes of pasta stuffed with meat, cheese, etc., and baked [It]

can·ner·y /kan´ərē/ *n.* (*pl.* **·ies**) canning factory

can·ni·bal /kan´əbəl/ *n.* person or animal that eats its own species —**can´ni·bal·ism´** *n.*; **can´ni·bal·is´tic** *adj.* [Sp fr. Carib]

can´ni·bal·ize *v.* (**·ized** or **·iz·ing**) use (a machine, etc.) for spare parts —**can´ni·bal·i·za´tion** /-əzā´sHən/ *n.*

can·non /kan´ən/ *n.* (*pl.* usu. same) large, heavy, esp. mounted gun [It, rel. to CANE]

can·non·ade /kan´ənäd´/ *n.* **1** period of continuous heavy gunfire —*v.* (**·ad·ed, ad·ing**) **2** bombard with a cannonade [It, rel. to CANNON]

can´non·ball´ *n. Hist.* iron ball fired by a cannon

can´non·fod´der /-fäd´ər/ *n.* soldiers regarded as expendable

can·not /kanät´, kə-; kan´ät´/ *v. aux.* can not

can·ny /kan´ē/ *adj.* (**·ni·er, ·ni·est**) shrewd, worldly-wise —**can´ni·ly** *adv.*; **can´ni·ness** *n.* [fr. CAN¹]

ca·noe /kənōō´/ *n.* **1** long narrow boat with pointed ends, usu. paddled —*v.* (**·noed, ·noe·ing**) **2** travel in a canoe —**ca·noe´ist** *n.* [Sp fr. Carib]

ca·no´la oil´ /kanō´lə/ *n.* cooking oil derived from the seed of a variety of the rape plant [abbr. Canada oil low acid]

can·on /kan´ən/ *n.* **1a** general principle or criterion **b** church decree or law **2** member of a cathedral chapter **3** writings accepted as authoritative **4** *Mus.* melody shared successively by different parts [OE fr. Gk *kanōn* rule]

ca·ñon /kan´yən/ *n.* var. of CANYON [Sp]

ca·non·i·cal /kənän´ikəl/ *adj.* (also **ca·non´ic**) **1a** according to canon law **b** included in the canon of Scripture **2** authoritative; accepted [MedL, rel. to CANON]

can·on·ize /kan´əniz´/ *v.* (**·ized, ·iz·ing**) declare officially to be or regard as a saint —**can´on·i·za´tion** *n.* [MedL, rel. to CANON]

can·o·py /kan´əpē/ *n.* (*pl.* **·pies**) **1** covering suspended over a throne, bed, etc. **2** overhanging rooflike projection or shelter [Gk: mosquito net]

Ca·no·va /kanō´və/, **Antonio** 1757–1822; Italian sculptor

canst /kanst/ *v. Archaic. 2nd person sing.* of CAN¹

cant¹ /kant/ *n.* **1** insincere pious or moral talk **2** language peculiar to a class, profession, etc.; jargon [prob. fr. L, rel. to CHANT]

cant² /kant/ *n.* **1** slanting surface; bevel **2** oblique push or jerk **3** tilted position —*v.* **4** push or pitch out of level; tilt [LGer or MDu: edge]

can't /kant/ *v. contr.* can not

can·ta·loupe /kant´əlōp´/ *n.* (also **can´ta·loup**) small round ribbed melon [*Cantaluppi* near Rome, where it was first grown in Europe]

can·tan·ker·ous /kantaNG´kərəs/ *adj.* bad-tempered; quarrelsome —**can·tan´ker·ous·ly** *adv.*; **can·tan´ker·ous·ness** *n.*

can·ta·ta /kəntät´ə/ *n.* composition with vocal solos and usu. choral and orchestral accompaniment [It, rel. to CHANT]

can·teen /kantēn´/ *n.* **1** employee restaurant **2** military club or store **3** water flask [It: cellar]

cant·er /kant´ər/ *n.* **1** horse's pace between a trot and a gallop —*v.* **2** go at a canter [*Canterbury gallop* of medieval pilgrims]

Can·ter·bur·y /kan´tərber´ē, -brē/ *n.* city in SE England; seat of the archbishop who heads the Anglican Church. Pop. 115,600

can·ti·cle /kant´ikəl/ *n.* song or chant with a biblical text [L *canticum* CHANT]

can·ti·le·ver /kant´l-ē´vər/ *n.* **1** support bracket, beam, etc., projecting from a wall **2** beam or girder fixed at one end only —**can´ti·le´vered** *adj.*

can·to /kant´ō/ *n.* (*pl.* **·tos**) division of a long poem [L *cantus*, rel. to CHANT]

can·ton /kan´tn, -tän´/ *n.* subdivision of a country, esp. of Switzerland [Fr: corner, rel. to CANT²]

Can·ton /kant´n/ *n.* city in Ohio. Pop. 84,161

can·tor /kant´ər/ *n.* soloist in a synagogue [L: singer]

Ca·nute /kən(y)ōōt´/ (**Cnut; Knut**) d. 1035; Danish king of England (1017–35), Denmark (1018–35), and Norway (1028–35)

can·vas /kan´vəs/ *n.* **1** strong coarse cloth used for tents, painting, etc. **2** a painting on canvas, esp. in oils —*v.* **3** cover with canvas [L, rel. to CANNABIS]

can·vass /kan´vəs/ *v.* **1** ascertain the opinions of —*n.* **2** canvassing, esp. of voters —**can´vass·er** *n.* [orig. sp. var. of CANVAS]

can·yon /kan´yən/ *n.* (also **ca´ñon**) deep gorge [Sp *cañón* tube]

cap /kap/ *n.* **1** soft brimless hat **2a** cover like a cap **b** top for a bottle, jar, pen, camera lens, etc. **3** dental crown —*v.* (**capped, capping**) **4a** put a cap on **b** cover the top or end of **c** set a limit to **5** form the top of **6** surpass, excel **7** cap in hand humbly [LL *cappa* hooded cloak]

cap. *abbr.* **1** capacity **2** capital (city) **3** capital (letter)

ca·pa·bil·i·ty /kā´pəbil´ətē/ *n.* (*pl.* **·ties**) **1** ability; power **2** undeveloped or unused faculty

ca·pa·ble /kā´pəbəl/ *adj.* **1** competent; able **2a** having the ability, fitness, etc., for **b** admitting of (explanation, improvement, etc.) —**ca´pa·bly** *adv.* [L *capere* take]

ca·pa·cious /kəpā´sHəs/ *adj.* roomy —**ca·pa´cious·ly** *adv.*; **ca·pa´cious·ness** *n.* [L *capax*, rel. to CAPABLE]

ca·pac·i·tance /kəpas´itəns/ *n.* **1** ability to store electric charge **2** ratio of change in the electric charge in a system to the corresponding change in its potential

ca·pac·i·tor /kəpas′itər/ *n.* device for storing electric charge; condenser

ca·pac·i·ty /kəpas′ətē/ *n.* (*pl.* **·ties**) **1a** power to contain, receive, experience, or produce **b** maximum containable, producible, etc. **2** mental power **3** position or function **4** legal competence **5 to capacity** fully [L, rel. to CAPACIOUS]

ca·par·i·son /kəpar′əsən/ *Lit. n.* **1** (usu. *pl.*) horse's trappings —*v.* **2** adorn [Sp: saddlecloth]

cape[1] /kāp/ *n.* sleeveless cloak [L *cappa* CAP]

cape[2] *n.* headland; promontory [L *caput* head]

Cape′ Horn′ *n.* S tip of S America

Cape′ of Good′ Hope′ *n.* cape at the S tip of Africa

ca·per[1] /kā′pər/ *v.* **1** jump or run playfully —*n.* **2** playful leap **3a** prank **b** *Slang.* planned theft [L *caper* he-goat]

ca·per[2] *n.* **1** bramblelike shrub **2** (*pl.*) its pickled buds used esp. in a sauce [Gk *kapparis*]

Ca·pet /kāpe′, kəpā′, kā′pət/, **Hugh (Hugo)** 938–996; king of France (987–996)

Cape′ Town′ *n.* legislative capital of South Africa. Pop. 776,600

Cape′ Verde′ /vərd/ *n.* republic comprising a group of islands in the Atlantic Ocean, W of Africa. Capital: Praia. Pop. 346,000

cap·il·lar·y /kap′əler′ē/ *adj.* **1** of or like a hair **2** (of a tube) of very small diameter **3** of the branching blood vessels connecting arteries and veins —*n.* (*pl.* **·ies**) **4** capillary tube **5** capillary blood vessel [L *capillus* hair]

cap′il·la′ry ac′tion *n.* rise or depression of a liquid in contact with a solid owing to surface tension, etc.

Doric   Ionic   Corinthian

CAPITAL 5

cap·i·tal /kap′ət-l/ *n.* **1** chief town or city of a country or region **2** money for starting or funding business **3** accumulated wealth **4** capital letter **5** head of a column or pillar —*adj.* **6** principal; most important **7** involving punishment by death **8** (of letters of the alphabet) large in size or in a different style, used to begin sentences and names, etc. [L *caput capitis* head]

cap′i·tal gain′ *n.* profit from the sale of investments or property

cap′i·tal·ism′ *n.* economic and political system dependent on private capital and profit-making

cap′i·tal·ist *n.* **1** person investing or possessing capital **2** advocate of capitalism —*adj.* **3** of or favoring capitalism —**cap′i·tal·is′tic** *adj.*

cap′i·tal·ize′ *v.* (**·ized, ·iz·ing**) **1** (foll. by *on*) use to one's advantage **2** convert into or provide with capital **3a** write (a letter of the al-

phabet) as a capital **b** begin (a word) with a capital letter —**cap′i·tal·i·za′tion** *n.* [Fr, rel. to CAPITAL]

ca·pit·u·late /kəpich′əlāt′/ *v.* (**·lat·ed, ·lat·ing**) surrender —**ca·pit′u·la′tion** *n.* [MedL: put under headings]

ca·po /kä′pō/ *n.* (*pl.* **·pos**) device fitted across the strings of a guitar, etc., to raise their pitch equally [It *capo tasto* head stop]

ca·pon /kā′pän′, ·pən/ *n.* castrated rooster fattened for eating [L *capo*]

Ca·pone /kəpōn′/, **Al (Alphonse)** 1899–1947; Italian-born US gangster

Ca·po·te /kəpōt′ē/, **Truman** 1924–84; US writer

cap·puc·ci·no /kap′əCHē′nō/ *n.* (*pl.* **·nos**) espresso coffee with steamed milk [It, ref. to color of Capuchin monk's robe]

Cap·ra /kap′rə/, **Frank** 1897–1991; Italian-born US film director

ca·price /kəprēs′/ *n.* **1** whim **2** lively or fanciful work of art, music, etc. [It *capriccio* sudden start]

ca·pri·cious /kəprish′əs, -prē′sHəs/ *adj.* subject to whims; unpredictable —**ca·pri′cious·ly** *adv.*; **ca·pri′cious·ness** *n.*

Cap·ri·corn /kap′rikôrn′/ *n.* **1** constellation and tenth sign of the zodiac (the Goat) **2** person born under this sign [L *caper, capri* goat + *cornu* horn]

cap·size /kap′sīz′, kapsīz′/ *v.* (**·sized, ·siz·ing**) (of a boat) be overturned; overturn

cap·stan /kap′stən, -stan′/ *n.* vertical cylinder for winding a cable, etc. [Prov]

cap·sule /kap′səl, -s(y)ōōl′/ *n.* **1** small digestible case enclosing medicine **2** detachable compartment of a spacecraft **3** dry fruit that releases its seeds when ripe —*adj.* **4** concise; condensed —**cap′su·lar** *adj.* [L *capsa* case]

cap′sul·ize′ *v.* (**·ized, ·iz·ing**) put (information, etc.) in compact form

Capt. *abbr.* Captain

cap·tain /kap′tən/ *n.* **1** chief, leader, or commander **2** *Milit.* officer ranking just above lieutenant (US Army) or commander (US Navy) —*v.* **3** be captain of; lead —**cap′tain·cy** *n.* (*pl.* **·cies**) [L *caput* head]

cap·tion /kap′sHən/ *n.* **1** wording appended to an illustration, cartoon, film, etc. **2** heading of a chapter, article, etc. —*v.* **3** provide with a caption [L *capere* take]

cap·tious /kap′sHəs/ *adj.* faultfinding —**cap′tious·ly** *adv.*; **cap′tious·ness** *n.* [L, rel. to CAPTION]

cap·ti·vate /kap′təvāt′/ *v.* (**·vat·ed, ·vat·ing**) fascinate; charm —**cap′ti·va′tion** *n.* [L, rel. to CAPTIVE]

cap·tive /kap′tiv/ *n.* **1** confined or imprisoned person or animal —*adj.* **2** taken prisoner; held —**cap·tiv′i·ty** *n.* [L *captum* fr. *capere* take]

cap·tor /kap′tər/ *n.* person who captures [L, rel. to CAPTIVE]

cap·ture /kap′cHər/ *v.* (**·tured, ·tur·ing**) **1** take prisoner; seize **2** portray, as on film, etc. **3** record (data) for use in a computer —*n.* **4** act of capturing [L, rel. to CAPTIVE]

cap·y·ba·ra /kap′ibär′ə, -bar′ə/ *n.* semiaquatic S American rodent [Tupi]

car /kär/ *n.* **1** motor vehicle **2** (in *comb.*) vehicle of specific kind (*streetcar*) **3** railroad carriage **4** passenger compartment of an elevator, balloon, etc. [Fr fr. L]

Ca·ra·cas /kərakʹəs, -räkʹ-/ n. capital of Venezuela. Pop. 1,824,900

car·a·cul /karʹəkəl/ n. var. of KARAKUL

ca·rafe /kərafʹ, -räfʹ/ n. glass, etc., container for water or wine [Fr fr. Ar]

car·a·mel /kärʹməl; karʹəməl, -melʹ/ n. **1a** burnt sugar or syrup, used as a flavoring or coloring **b** a kind of soft, chewy candy **2** light-brown color [Fr fr. Sp]

car·a·pace /karʹəpās/ n. upper shell of a tortoise or crustacean [Fr fr. Sp]

car·at /karʹət/ n. **1** unit of weight for precious stones (200 mg) **2** KARAT [Fr ult. fr. Gk keras horn]

Ca·ra·vag·gio /kär'əväjʹ(ē)ō/, **Michelangelo Merisi da** 1573–1610; Italian painter

car·a·van /karʹəvan/ n. people traveling together, esp. across a desert [Fr fr. Pers]

car·a·van·se·ry /kar'əvanʹsərē/ n. Near Eastern inn, usu. with a central court [Pers: caravan place]

car·a·vel /karʹəvel/ n. Hist. **1** small, light, fast ship **2** CARVEL-BUILT [Gk karabos literally, horned beetle]

car·a·way /karʹəwā/ n. plant with edible seeds and tiny white flowers [Sp fr. Ar]

car·bide /kärʹbīd/ n. binary compound of carbon

car·bine /kärʹbēn, -bīn/ n. light rifle, orig. for cavalry use [Fr]

car·bo·hy·drate /kär'bəhīʹdrāt/ n. energy-producing organic compound of carbon, hydrogen, and oxygen (e.g., starch, sugar)

car·bol·ic /kärbälʹik/ n. phenol [fr. CARBON]

car·bon /kärʹbən/ n. **1** nonmetallic element occurring naturally as diamond, graphite, and charcoal, and in all organic compounds; symb. **C 2a** CARBON COPY **b** CARBON PAPER [L carbo charcoal]

car·bon·ate /kärʹbənāt/ n. **1** Chem. salt of carbonic acid —v. (·at·ed, ·at·ing) **2** charge with carbon dioxide [Fr, rel. to CARBON]

car'bon cop'y n. **1** copy made with carbon paper **2** exact copy

car'bon dat'ing n. determining the age of an organic object by measuring radioactive carbon isotopes

car'bon di·ox'ide n. gas occurring naturally in the atmosphere and formed by respiration

car·bon·ic /kärbänʹik/ adj. containing carbon

car·bon'ic ac'id n. weak acid formed from carbon dioxide in water

car·bon·if·er·ous /kär'bənifʹərəs/ adj. producing carbon or coal

car'bon mon·ox'ide /mənäksʹid/ n. toxic gas formed by the incomplete burning of carbon

car'bon pa'per n. carbon-coated paper used for making copies

car·bo·run·dum /kär'bərənʹdəm/ n. Tdmk. compound of carbon and silicon used esp. as an abrasive [fr. CARBON + CORUNDUM]

car'boy' n. large globular glass bottle usu. in a wicker frame [Pers]

car·bun·cle /kärʹbuŋʹkəl/ n. severe skin abscess —**car·bun'cu·lar** adj. [L, rel. to CARBON]

car·bu·ret·or /kärʹb(y)ərāt'ər/ n. device for

mixing gasoline and air to make an explosive mixture in an internal-combustion engine

car·cass /kärʹkəs/ n. **1** dead body of an animal **2** framework [Fr]

car·cin·o·gen /kärsinʹəjən, kärʹsənəjen/ n. substance producing cancer —**car'ci·no·gen'ic** adj. [rel. to CARCINOMA]

car·ci·no·ma /kär'sənōʹmə/ n. (pl. ·mas or ·ma·ta) cancerous tumor [Gk karkinos crab]

card /kärd/ n. **1** thick, stiff paper, plastic, etc. **2** piece of this for writing or printing on **3** rectangular piece of paper or plastic for identity, etc. **4a** PLAYING CARD **b** (pl.) card-playing **5** program of events **6** odd or amusing person **7** card up one's sleeve plan or secret weapon in reserve **8 in the cards** possible or likely **9 put (or lay) one's cards on the table** reveal one's resources, intentions, etc. [Gk chartēs papyrus leaf]

card'board' n. pasteboard or stiff paper, esp. for making boxes

car·di·ac /kärʹdē·ak/ adj. pertaining to the heart [Gk kardia heart]

Car·diff /kärʹdif/ n. capital of Wales, United Kingdom, in the SE part. Pop. 266,300

car·di·gan /kärʹdigən/ n. sweater that buttons up the front [for the 7th Earl of Cardigan]

car·di·nal /kärdʹn·əl, -nəl/ adj. **1** chief; fundamental **2** deep scarlet —n. **3** (as a title cap.) RC Ch. high-ranking ecclesiastic appointed by the pope to his council (the College of Cardinals) **4** small scarlet songbird [L cardo cardinis hinge]

car'di·nal num'ber n. number denoting quantity (1, 2, 3, etc.), as opposed to an ORDINAL NUMBER (first, second, etc.)

car·di·o·gram /kärʹdēəgram'/ n. record of heart movements [Gk kardia heart]

car·di·o·graph /kärʹdēəgraf'/ n. instrument recording heart movements —**car'di·og'ra·phy** n.

car·di·ol·o·gy /kär'dē·älʹəjē/ n. branch of medicine concerned with the heart —**car'di·ol'o·gist** n.

car·di·o·pul'mo·nar'y re·sus'ci·ta'tion /kär'dē·ōpōōl'mənerē/ n. emergency medical procedure to restore normal heartbeat and breathing to victims of heart failure, drowning, etc.; abbr. **CPR**

car·di·o·vas·cu·lar /kär'dē·ōvas'kyələr/ adj. of the heart and blood vessels

card'sharp' n. (also **card'sharp'er**) swindler at card-games

care /ker/ n. **1** worry; anxiety **2** cause of this **3** serious attention; caution **4** looking after; charge —v. (**cared, car·ing**) **5** feel concern or interest **6** wish or be willing (to) **7 care for:** a provide for; look after **b** like **8 take care** be careful **9 take care of** look after [OE: sorrow]

ca·reen /kərēnʹ/ v. **1** turn (a ship) on one side for repair, etc. **2** tilt; lean over **3** swerve about [L carina keel]

ca·reer /kərērʹ/ n. **1** one's occupational progress through life **2** profession or occupation —v. **3** move or swerve about wildly [L, rel. to CAR]

care'free' adj. lighthearted; joyous

care'ful adj. **1** painstaking; thorough **2** cautious **3** taking care; not neglecting —**care′-ful·ly** *adv.*; **care′ful·ness** *n.*

care′giv·er *n.* one who attends to the personal needs of children, the sick, the elderly, etc.

care′less *adj.* **1** lacking care or attention **2** unthinking, insensitive **3** light-hearted —**care′less·ly** *adv.*; **care′less·ness** *n.*

ca·ress /kəres′/ *v.* **1** touch or stroke gently or lovingly —*n.* **2** loving or gentle touch [L *carus* dear]

car·et /kar′ət/ *n.* mark (∧) indicating an insertion in printing or writing [L: is lacking]

care′tak·er *n.* person employed to look after a house, building, etc.

care′worn′ *adj.* showing the effects of prolonged worry

car·go /kär′gō/ *n.* (*pl.* **·goes** or **·gos**) goods carried on a ship or aircraft [Sp, rel. to CHARGE]

Car·ib /kar′ib/ *n.* family of languages of the Carib Indians of Central and S America

Car·ib·be·an Sea /kar′əbē′ən, kərib′ēən/ *n.* arm of the Atlantic Ocean enclosed by the W Indies, northern S America, and Central America

car·i·bou /kar′əbōō′/ *n.* (*pl.* same) N American reindeer [Fr fr. AmerInd]

car·i·ca·ture /kar′ikəchŏŏr′, -chər/ *n.* **1** comically exaggerated representation, esp. of a person **2** ridiculously poor imitation or version —*v.* (**·tured, ·tur·ing**) **3** make a caricature of —**car′i·ca·tur′ist** *n.* [It *caricare* exaggerate]

car·ies /kar′ēz′/ *n.* (*pl.* same) decay of a tooth or bone [L]

car·il·lon /kar′əlän′, -lən/ *n.* set of bells [Fr]

car′ing *adj.* kind; humane

car′jack′ing *n.* theft of an automobile by threatening and forcing the driver out

Car·lyle /kärlīl′, kär′līl′/, **Thomas** 1795–1881; Scottish historian and political philosopher

Car·mi·chael /kär′mī′kəl/, **"Hoagy"** (Howard Hoagland) 1899–81; US jazz pianist, composer, and singer

car·mine /kär′mən, -mīn′/ *adj.* **1** of vivid crimson color —*n.* **2** this color [prob. fr. L *carmesinum* CRIMSON]

car·nage /kär′nij/ *n.* great slaughter, esp. in battle [L, rel. to CARNAL]

car·nal /kärn′l/ *adj.* **1** pertaining to the body or flesh; worldly **2** sensual; sexual —**car′nal′i·ty** *n.* [L *caro carnis* flesh]

car·na·tion /kärnā′shən/ *n.* **1** fragrant flower of various colors **2** rosy pink —*adj.* **3** rosy pink [It, rel. to CARNAL, because of the flesh color]

Car·né /kärnā′/, **Marcel** 1909– ; French film director

Car·ne·gie /kär′nəgē, kärneg′ē/, **Andrew** 1835–1919; Scottish-born US industrialist and philanthropist

car·ne·lian /kärnēl′yən/ *n.* dull red variety of quartz [Fr]

car·ni·val /kär′nəvəl/ *n.* **1** festive event **2** festival preceding Lent **3** fair with contests, rides, etc. [It *carnevale* fr. L *carnem levare* put away meat]

car·ni·vore /kär′nəvôr′/ *n.* carnivorous animal or plant

car·niv·o·rous /kärniv′ərəs/ *adj.* feeding on flesh —**car·niv′or·ous·ly** *adv.*; **car·niv′or·ous·ness** *n.* [L, rel. to CARNAL + *vorare* devour]

car·ob /kar′əb/ *n.* chocolatelike seed pod or a Mediterranean tree [Ar *karrūba*]

car·ol /kar′əl/ *n.* **1** joyous song, esp. a Christmas hymn —*v.* (**·oled** or **·olled, ·ol·ing** or **·ol·ling**) **2** sing carols [Fr]

Car·o·li·na /kar′əlī′nə/ *n.* **1** N. or S. Carolina **2** /kär′əlē′nə/ city in NE Puerto Rico. Pop. 177,900

Car·o·line Is·lands /kar′əlīn′, ker′-, -lin/ *n.* group of islands in the Pacific, E of the Philippines; US trusteeship

Car·o·lus Mag·nus /kar′ələs mag′nəs/ CHARLEMAGNE

car·o·tene /kar′ətēn′/ *n.* orange-colored pigment found in carrots, tomatoes, etc., source of vitamin A [L, rel. to CARROT]

ca·rot·id /kərät′id/ *n.* **1** either of two main arteries carrying blood to the head and neck —*adj.* **2** of these arteries [L fr. Gk]

ca·rouse /kərouz′/ *v.* (**·roused, ·rous·ing**) **1** have a lively drinking party —*n.* (also **ca·rous′al**) **2** such a party; carousal [Ger *gar aus* (drink) right out]

car·ou·sel /kar′əsel′/ *n.* **1** merry-go-round **2** rotating luggage delivery system used at airports, etc. [Fr. fr. It]

carp[1] /kärp/ *n.* (*pl.* same) freshwater food fish [Prov or L]

carp[2] *v.* find fault; complain pettily —**carp′er** *n.* [ON: brag]

car·pal /kär′pəl/ *adj.* **1** pertaining to bones in the wrist —*n.* **2** wristbone [fr. CARPUS]

Car·pa·thi·an Moun·tains /kärpā′thēən/ *n.* mountain range in central Europe

car·pel /kär′pəl/ *n.* female reproductive organ of a flower [Gk *karpos* fruit]

car·pen·ter /kär′pəntər/ *n.* person skilled in woodworking —**car′pen·try** *n.* [L *carpentum* wagon]

car·pet /kär′pət/ *n.* **1a** thick fabric for covering floor or stairs **b** piece of this **2** thing resembling this (*carpet of snow*) —*v.* (**·pet·ed, ·pet·ing**) **3** cover with or as with carpet **4** on the carpet being reprimanded **5** sweep under the carpet conceal (a problem or difficulty) [L *carpere* pluck]

car′pet·bag·ger *n. Colloq.* **1** *US Hist.* Northerner who went South after the Civil War for personal gain **2** political candidate, etc., without local connections **3** unscrupulous opportunist

car′pet·ing *n.* **1** material for carpets **2** carpets collectively

car′port′ *n.* roofed open-sided shelter for a car

car·pus /kär′pəs/ *n.* (*pl.* **·pi** /-pī/) small bones forming the wrist in humans and similar parts in other mammals [L fr. Gk]

Car·rac·ci /kärächē′/ family of Italian painters: **1** Ludovico 1555–1619 **2** Agostino 1557–1602 **3** Annibale 1560–1609

car·rel /kar′əl/ *n.* small library cubicle [Fr fr. MedL]

Car·re·ras /kərer′äs′/, José 1946– ; Spanish operatic tenor

car·riage /kar′ij/ *n.* **1** railway passenger vehicle **2** wheeled horse-drawn passenger vehicle **3** carrying part of a machine (e.g., a typewriter) **4** gun carriage **5** bearing; deportment [Fr. rel. to CARRY]

car·ri·er /ˈkarˈēər/ *n.* **1** person or thing that carries **2** transport or freight company **3** person or animal that may transmit disease, etc. **4** AIRCRAFT-CARRIER

car′ri·er pi′geon *n.* pigeon trained to carry messages

car·ri·on /ˈkarˈēən/ *n.* dead, putrefying flesh [L *caro* flesh]

Car·roll /ˈkarˈəl/, **Lewis** (pseudonym of **Charles Lutwidge Dodgson**) 1832–98; English writer

car·rot /ˈkarˈət/ *n.* **1a** plant with a tapering orange-colored root **b** this as a vegetable **2** incentive [Gk *karōton*]

car·ry /ˈkarˈē/ *v.* (**·ried**, **·ry·ing**) **1** support or hold up, esp. while moving **2** convey with one or have on one's person **3** conduct or transmit **4** take (a process, etc.) to a specified point; prolong (*carry a joke too far*) **5** entail (*carries 6% interest*) **6** *Math.* transfer (a figure) to a column of higher value **7** hold in a specified way (*carry oneself erect*) **8** publish or broadcast **9** keep a regular stock of **10** (of sound) be audible at a distance **11** win victory or acceptance for (a proposal, etc.) **12** endure the weight of; support **13** be pregnant with —*n.* (*pl.* **·ries**) **14** act of carrying **15** *Golf.* distance a ball travels in the air **16** carry away: **a** remove **b** inspire **c** deprive of self-control (*got carried away*) **17 carry the day** be victorious or successful **18 carry on: a** continue **b** engage in (conversation or business) **c** *Colloq.* behave strangely or excitedly **19 carry weight** be influential or important [AngFr. rel. to CAR]

car′sick /ˈkärˈsik/ *adj.* nauseous from car travel —**car′sick′ness** *n.*

Car·son /ˈkärˈsən/ **1 "Kit" (Christopher)** 1809–68; US frontiersman **2 Rachel** 1907–64; US zoologist and ecologist

Car′son Cit′y /ˈkärˈsən/ *n.* capital of Nev., in the W part, near the Calif. border. Pop. 40,443

cart /ˈkärt/ *n.* **1** open vehicle for carrying loads, usu. pushed or pulled —*v.* **2** convey in a cart **3 put the cart before the horse** reverse the proper order or procedure [ON]

Car·ta·ge·na /ˈkärtˈəjēˈnə, -häˈ-/ *n.* **1** seaport in N Colombia. Pop. 491,400 **2** seaport in SE Spain. Pop. 166,700

carte blanche /ˈkärt blänSH′/ *n.* full discretionary power; freehand [Fr: blank paper]

car·tel /ˈkärtˈel′/ *n.* association of suppliers, etc., to control prices [It dim., rel. to CARD]

Car·ter /ˈkärtˈər/, **Jimmy** (born **James Earl**) 1924– ; 39th US president (1977–81)

Car·thage /ˈkärˈTHij/ *n.* ancient city-state in N Africa, near present-day Tunis —**Car·tha·gin′i·an** *n. & adj.*

Car·tier /ˈkärtẏə′, kärtˈēˈä′/, **Jacques** 1491–1557; French explorer

car·ti·lage /ˈkärtˈl-ij/ *n.* firm, flexible skeletal tissue —**car·ti·lag·i·nous** /ˈkärtˈl-ajˈənəs/ *adj.* [Fr fr. L]

car·tog·ra·phy /ˈkärtägˈrəfē/ *n.* making of maps —**car·tog′ra·pher** *n.*; **car·to·graph′ic** *adj.* [Fr *carte* map]

car·ton /ˈkärtˈn/ *n.* light esp. cardboard box or container [Fr, rel. to CARTOON]

car·toon /ˈkärtō̄on′/ *n.* **1** humorous, often

topical drawing in a newspaper, etc. **2** sequence of drawings telling a story **3** animated sequence of these on film —**car·toon′ist** *n.* [It, rel. to CARD]

car·touche /ˈkärtō̄osh′/ *n.* scroll-like ornament [Fr, rel. to CARTOON]

car·tridge /ˈkärˈtrij/ *n.* **1** case containing bullet or explosive charge **2** sealed container of film, etc. **3** ink-container for insertion in a pen, etc. [Fr, rel. to CARTOON]

cart′wheel′ *n.* **1** wheel of a cart **2** circular sideways handspring

Ca·ru·so /ˈkarōō′sō, -zō/, **Enrico** 1873–1921; Italian operatic tenor

carve /ˈkärv/ *v.* (**carved, carv·ing**) **1** produce or shape by cutting **2** cut patterns, etc. **3** cut (meat, etc.) into slices —**carv′er** *n.* [OE]

car·vel-built /ˈkärvəl′-/ *adj.* (of a vessel) made with planks flush, not overlapping [fr. CARAVEL]

Car·ver /ˈkärˈvər/, **George Washington** 1864–1943; US botanist and educator

carv′ing *n.* carved object, esp. an artifact

Cas·a·blan·ca /ˈkasˈəblaNGˈkə, kazˈ-/ *n.* seaport in NW Morocco. Pop. 2,139,200

Ca·sals /ˈkəsälz′/, **Pablo** 1876–1973; Spanish cellist, conductor, and composer

Cas·a·no·va /ˈkasˈənō′və, kazˈ-/ **1 Giovanni Jacopo** 1725–98; Italian adventurer **2** any notorious womanizer

cas·cade /ˈkaskād′/ *n.* **1** small waterfall, esp. one of series **2** thing falling or arranged like a cascade —*v.* (**·cad·ed, ·cad·ing**) **3** fall in or like a cascade [fr. L *cadere* fall]

Cas·cade′ Range′ *n.* mountain range extending from N California to W Canada

case¹ /ˈkās/ *n.* **1** instance of something occurring **2** hypothetical or actual situation **3a** person's illness, circumstances, etc., as regarded by a doctor, social worker, etc. **b** such a person **4** matter under investigation **5** litigation **6a** sum of the arguments on one side, esp. in a trial **b** set of arguments (*have a good case*) **c** valid set of arguments (*have no case*) **7** *Gram.* a relation of a word to other words in a sentence **b** form of a noun, adjective, or pronoun expressing this **8 in any case** whatever the truth is; whatever may happen **9 in case** in the event that; if [L *casus* from *cadere* fall]

case² *n.* **1** container or enclosing covering **2** this with its contents —*v.* (**cased, cas·ing**) **3** enclose in a case **4** *Slang.* reconnoiter (a house, etc.) before burgling it [L *capsa* box]

case′hard·en *v.* **1** harden the surface of (esp. iron by carbonizing) **2** make callous

case′ment *n.* window or part thereof hinged at its outer frame [AngL, rel. to CASE²]

case′work′ *n.* social work concerned with family and background —**case′work′er** *n.*

cash /ˈkaSH/ *n.* **1** money in coins or bills **2** (also **cash down**) full payment at time of purchase —*v.* **3** give or obtain cash for (a bill, check, etc.) **4 cash in: a** obtain cash for **b** *Colloq.* profit (from); take advantage (of) [L, rel. to CASE²]

Cash /ˈkaSH/, **Johnny** 1932– ; US country music singer and songwriter

cash′ cow′ *n. Colloq.* product, business, etc., generating steady profits, used to fund other enterprises

ca·shew /kaSH′ōō, kəSHōō′/ *n.* **1** evergreen tree bearing kidney-shaped nuts **2** this edible nut [Port from Tupi]

cash′ flow′ *n.* movement of money into and out of a business

cash·ier /kaSHēr′/ *n.* person dealing with cash transactions in a store, bank, etc.

cash·mere /kaSH′mēr′, kazH′-/ *n.* **1** fine soft wool, esp. that of a Kashmir goat **2** material made from this [*Kashmir* in Asia]

cash′ reg·is·ter *n.* device for recording sales, usu. with money drawer

cas·ing /kā′siNG/ *n.* protective or enclosing cover or material

ca·si·no /kəsē′nō/ *n.* (*pl.* **·nos**) place for gambling [It dim. of *casa* house]

cask /kask/ *n.* **1** barrel, esp. for alcohol **2** its contents [Fr *casque* or Sp *casco* helmet]

cas·ket /kas′kit/ *n.* **1** coffin **2** lidded box for jewels, etc. [L, rel. to CASE²]

Cas·pi·an Sea /kas′pēən/ *n.* inland salt lake between Asia and extreme SE Europe

Cas·satt /kəsat′/, **Mary** 1845–1926; US painter

cas·sa·va /kəsä′və/ *n.* **1** plant with starchy roots **2** starch or flour from these, used, e.g., in tapioca [Taino]

cas·se·role /kas′ərōl′/ *n.* **1** covered dish for baking **2** food so cooked —*v.* (·**roled**, ·**rol·ing**) **3** cook in a casserole [Fr, poss. fr. Gk *kuathion* little cup]

cas·sette /kəset′/ *n.* encased magnetic tape, film, etc., ready for insertion in a VCR, camera, etc. [Fr dim., rel. to CASE²]

cas·si·a /kasH′ə, kas′ēə/ *n.* **1** tree from the leaves of which senna is extracted **2** cinnamonlike bark of this used as a spice [Gk *kasia* fr. Heb]

Cas·sius /kasH′əs/, **Gaius** d. 42 B.C.; Roman general; an assassin of Julius Caesar

cas·sock /kas′ək/ *n.* long clerical robe [Fr fr. It]

cas·so·war·y /kas′əwer′ē/ *n.* (*pl.* ·**ies**) large flightless Australasian bird [Malay]

cast /kast/ *v.* (**cast, cast·ing**) **1** throw, esp. deliberately or forcefully **2a** direct or cause (one's eyes, a glance, light, a shadow, a spell, etc.) to fall **b** express (doubts, aspersions, etc.) **3** throw outward (a fishing line, etc.) **4** let down (an anchor, etc.) **5** register (a vote) **6a** shape (molten metal, etc.) in a mold **b** make thus **7a** assign (an actor) to a role **b** allocate roles in (a play, etc.) —*n.* **8** throwing of a missile, dice, line, net, etc. **9a** object made in a mold **b** molded case to support a broken limb **10** actors in a play, etc. **11** **cast about** (or **around**) search (for) **12** **cast adrift** leave to drift **13** **cast aside** abandon **14** **cast off: a** abandon **b** untie (a vessel) from its mooring **15** **cast up** deposit on the shore [ON]

cas·ta·net /kas′tənet′/ *n.* (usu. *pl.*) each of a pair of hand-held pieces of wood clicked together, as by Spanish dancers [L, rel. to CHESTNUT]

cast′a·way *n.* **1** shipwrecked person —*adj.* **2** shipwrecked

caste /kast/ *n.* **1** Hindu hereditary class **2** exclusive social class or system of classes [Sp and Port, rel. to CHASTE]

cas·tel·lat·ed /kas′təlāt′id/ *adj.* **1** having battlements **2** castlelike —**cas′tel·la′tion** *n.* [MedL, rel. to CASTLE]

cast′er *n.* var. of CASTOR

cas·ti·gate /kas′tigāt′/ *v.* (·**gat·ed**, ·**gat·ing**) rebuke or punish severely —**cas′ti·ga′tion**, **cas′ti·ga′tor** *n.* [L *castus* pure]

cast′ing *n.* cast, esp. of molten metal

cast′ i′ron *n.* hard alloy of iron cast in a mold

CASTLE 1

cas·tle /kas′əl/ *n.* **1** large fortified building with towers and battlements **2** *Chess.* ROOK² **3 castles in the air** daydreaming; impractical scheme [L *castellum*]

cast′off′ *adj.* **1** abandoned; discarded —*n.* **2** castoff thing, esp. a garment

cas·tor /kas′tər/ *n.* (also **cast′er**) **1** small swiveled wheel, as on furniture [fr. CAST]

Cas·tor /kas′tər/ *n. Gk. Myth.* brother of Pollux, one of the twins called Dioscuri or Gemini

cast′or oil *n.* oil from the seeds of a tropical plant, used as a purgative and lubricant

cas·trate /kas′trāt′/ *v.* (·**trat·ed**, ·**trat·ing**) remove the testicles of; geld —**cas·tra′tion** *n.* [L *castrare*]

Cas·tries /kastrē′, käs′trēs′/ *n.* capital of St. Lucia. Pop. 11,100

Cas·tro /kas′trō/, **Fidel** 1927– ; Cuban president (1976–)

cas·u·al /kazH′ōōəl/ *adj.* **1** accidental; chance **2** not regular or permanent (*casual work*) **3a** unconcerned **b** careless **4** (of clothes) informal —**cas′u·al·ly** *adv.*; **cas′u·al·ness** *n.* [Fr and L, rel. to CASE¹]

ca·su·al·ty /kazH′əltē, kazH′(ə)wəl-/ *n.* (*pl.* ·**ties**) **1** person killed or injured in a war or accident **2** thing lost or destroyed [MedL, rel. to CASUAL]

ca·su·ist /kazH′ōō·ist/ *n.* person who uses clever but false reasoning in matters of conscience, etc. —**cas′u·is′tic** *adj.*; **cas′u·ist·ry** *n.* [L, rel. to CASE¹]

cat /kat/ *n.* **1** small soft-furred four-legged domesticated animal **2** wild animal of the same family **3 let the cat out of the bag** reveal a secret **4 rain cats and dogs** rain hard [L *cattus*]

CAT *abbr.* computerized axial tomography

cata- *prefix* **1** down **2** wrongly [Gk]

cat·a·clysm /kat′əkliz′əm/ *n.* violent upheaval or disaster —**cat′a·clys′mic** *adj.* [Gk *klyzein* wash]

cat·a·comb /kat′əkōm′/ *n.* (often *pl.*) underground cemetery, esp. Roman [Fr fr. L]

cat·a·falque /kat′əfō(l)k, -falk/ *n.* platform on which a body in a coffin rests, as in state funerals [Fr fr. It]

Cat·a·lan /kat′l-an/ *n.* **1** native or language

of Catalonia in Spain —*adj.* **2** of Catalonia [Fr fr. Sp]

cat·a·lep·sy /kat′l-ep′sē/ *n.* trance or seizure with unconsciousness and rigidity of the body —**cat′a·lep′tic** *adj. & n.* [Gk *lēpsis* seizure]

Cat·a·li·na Is·land /kat′l-ē′nə/ *n.* see SANTA CATALINA ISLAND

cat·a·log /kat′l-ôg′, -äg′/ (also **cat·a·logue**) *n.* **1** complete alphabetical or otherwise ordered list of items, often with a description of each —*v.* (·**logued**, ·**log·uing**) **2** make a catalog of **3** enter in a catalog [Gk *katalegein* count up]

ca·tal·pa /kətal′pə, -tôl′-/ *n.* tree with long pods and showy flowers [AmerInd]

ca·tal·y·sis /kətal′əsis/ *n.* (*pl.* ·**ses** /-sēz/) acceleration of a chemical reaction by a catalyst [Gk *lyein* set free]

cat·a·lyst /kat′l-ist/ *n.* **1** substance that speeds up a chemical reaction **2** person or thing that precipitates change

cat·a·lyt·ic /kat′l-it′ik/ *adj.* of or involving catalysis

cat·a·lyt′ic con·vert′er *n.* device in a vehicle's exhaust system for neutralizing pollutant gases

cat·a·ma·ran /kat′əməran′/ *n.* **1** boat with parallel twin hulls **2** raft of yoked logs or boats [Tamil]

Ca·ta·nia /kətän′yə, -tän′-/ *n.* seaport in Sicily, Italy. Pop. 364,200

cat·a·pult /kat′əpəlt′, -poolt′/ *n.* **1** *Milit. Hist.* machine for hurling large stones, etc. **2** device for launching a glider, etc. —*v.* **3a** hurl from or launch with a catapult **b** fling forcibly **4** leap or be hurled forcibly [L fr. Gk]

cat·a·ract /kat′ərakt′/ *n.* **1** large waterfall **2** eye condition in which the lens becomes opaque [Gk *katarraktēs* waterfall; down-rushing]

ca·tas·tro·phe /kətas′trəfē/ *n.* great and usu. sudden disaster —**cat·a·stroph·ic** /kat′əsträf′ik/ *adj.*; **cat′a·stroph′i·cal·ly** *adv.* [Gk *strephein* turn]

cat·a·to·nia /kat′ətō′nēə/ *n.* **1** schizophrenia with intervals of catalepsy and sometimes violence **2** catalepsy —**cat′a·ton′ic** /-tän′ik/ *adj. & n.* [Gk, rel. to CATA- + TONE]

cat′ bur′glar *n.* burglar who enters by climbing to an upper story

cat′call′ *n.* shrill whistle of disapproval

catch /kacH/ *v.* (**caught, catch·ing**) **1** capture in a trap, one's hands, etc. **2** detect or surprise (esp. a guilty person) **3** intercept and hold (a moving thing) **4a** contract (a disease) from an infected person **b** acquire (a quality, etc.) **5a** reach in time and board (a train, bus, etc.) **b** be in time to see, etc. (a person or thing about to leave or finish) **6** apprehend or notice (esp. a thing occurring quickly or briefly) **7** (cause to) become fixed, entangled, or checked **8** draw the attention of; captivate (*caught his eye*) **9** begin to burn —*n.* **10** act of catching **11a** amount of a thing caught, esp. of fish **b** thing or person won or worth winning **12a** question, trick, etc., intended to deceive, incriminate, etc. **b** unexpected or hidden difficulty or disadvantage **13** device for fastening a door or window, etc. **14 catch fire** see FIRE **15 catch hold of** grasp; seize **16 catch on:** *Colloq.* **a** become popular **b** un-

91 | **catalepsy / cathode**

derstand **17 catch up: a** reach a person, etc., ahead **b** make up arrears **c** pick up hurriedly **d** (often in *passive*) involve; entangle (*caught up in crime*) [L *captare* try to catch]

catch-22 *n.* (often *attrib.*) *Colloq.* frustratingly contradictory or paradoxical situation [fr. title of J. Heller novel]

catch′all′ *n.* (often *attrib.*) thing designed to be all-inclusive

catch′ing *adj.* infectious

catch′ phrase′ *n.* CATCHWORD

catch′word′ *n.* phrase, word, or slogan in frequent current use

catch′y *adj.* (·**i·er**, ·**i·est**) (of a tune) engaging; easy to remember

cat·e·chism /kat′əkiz′əm/ *n.* **1** principles of a religion in the form of questions and answers **2** book containing this [ChL, rel. to CATECHIZE]

cat·e·chize /kat′əkīz′/ *v.* (·**chized**, ·**chiz·ing**) instruct by using a catechism [Gk *katēchein* cause to hear]

cat·e·gor·i·cal /kat′əgôr′ikəl, -gär′-/ *adj.* unconditional; absolute; explicit —**cat′e·gor′i·cal·ly** *adv.* [rel. to CATEGORY]

cat·e·go·rize /kat′əgərīz′/ *v.* (·**rized**, ·**riz·ing**) place in a category

cat·e·go·ry /kat′əgôr′ē/ *n.* (*pl.* ·**ries**) class or division (of things, ideas, etc.) [Gk: statement]

ca·ter /kā′tər/ *v.* **1** supply food **2** provide what is needed or desired **3** pander to [AngFr *acatour* buyer, fr. L *captare*, rel. to CATCH]

cat′er·cor′nered /kat′ər-/ *adj. & adv.* in a diagonal (position)

ca·ter·er /kā′tərər/ *n.* professional supplier of food for social events, etc.

cat·er·pil·lar /kat′ə(r)pil′ər/ *n.* larva of a butterfly or moth [AngFr: hairy cat]

cat·er·waul /kat′ərwôl′/ *v.* **1** howl like a cat —*n.* **2** this noise [fr. CAT + *waul* imit.]

cat′fish′ *n.* (*pl.* same) freshwater fish with whiskerlike barbels around the mouth

cat′gut′ *n.* material used for surgical sutures, etc., made of animal intestines (but not cat)

ca·thar·sis /kəTHär′sis/ *n.* (*pl.* ·**ses** /-sēz/) **1** emotional release in drama or art **2** *Psychol.* freeing and elimination of repressed emotion [Gk *katharos* clean]

ca·thar·tic /kəTHär′tik/ *adj.* effecting catharsis

ca·the·dral /kəTHē′drəl/ *n.* principal church of a diocese [Gk *kathedra* seat]

Cath·er /kaTH′ər/, **Willa** 1876–1947; US novelist

Cath·er·ine, St. /kaTH′(ə)rən/, **of Alexandria** died c. 307; early Christian martyr

Cath·er·ine II, "the Great" 1729–96; German-born empress of Russia (1762–96)

Cath·er·ine de Med′i·ci /də med′əCHē, mədē′CHē/ (also **Ca·the·rine′ de′ Mé·di·cis′**) 1519–89; queen of Henry II of France, born in Florence

Cath·er·ine of Ar′a·gon 1485–1536; 1st wife of Henry VIII; mother of Mary I

cath·e·ter /kaTH′ətər/ *n.* tube inserted into a body cavity for introducing or removing fluid [Gk *kathienai* send down]

cath·ode /kaTH′ōd′/ *n.* *Electr.* **1** negative

electrode in an electrolytic cell **2** positive terminal of a battery [Gk *kathodos* way down]

cath′ode ray′ *n.* beam of electrons from the cathode of a vacuum tube

cath·o·lic /kaTH′(ə)lik/ *adj.* **1** all-embracing; of wide sympathies or interests **2** of interest or use to all; universal —*n.* **3** (*cap.*) Roman Catholic —**Ca·thol·i·cism** /kəTHäl′əsiz′əm/ *n.*; **cath·o·lic·i·ty** /kaTH′(ə)lis′ətē/ *n.* [Gk *holos* whole]

Cat·i·line /kat′l-īn′/ (**Lucius Sergius Catalina**) died c. 62 B.C.; Roman political conspirator

cat·i·on /kat′ī′ən/ *n.* positively charged ion —cat′i·on′ic /-ī′än′ik/ *adj.* [fr. CATA- + ION]

cat·kin /kat′kin/ *n.* small spike of usu. hanging flowers on a willow, hazel, etc. [Du: kitten]

cat′nap′ *n.* **1** short sleep —*v.* (·**napped**, ·**nap·ping**) **2** have a catnap

cat′nip′ *n.* mintlike herb that attracts cats [fr. CAT + dial. *nip* catmint]

Ca·to /kāt′ō/, **Marcus Porcius** (called **"the Elder"** or **"the Censor"**) 234–149 B.C.; Roman statesman, orator, and writer

cat-o′-nine-tails *n. Hist.* whip with nine knotted lashes

CAT′ scan′ *abbr.* diagnostic x-ray made from a computerized combination of several single x-ray images [computerized axial tomography]

cat′s′ cra′dle *n.* child's game of forming patterns from a loop of string

Cats′kill′ Moun′tains /kat′skil′/ *n.* part of the Appalachian Mountains in SE N.Y., along the W bank of the Hudson River

cat′s′-paw′ *n.* person used as a tool by another

cat·sup /kat′səp, keCH′əp/ *n.* var. of KETCHUP

Catt /kat/, **Carrie Chapman Lane** 1859–1947; US suffragist

cat·tle /kat′l/ *n. pl.* ruminant animals with horns and cloven hoofs, usu. bred for milk or meat [AngFr *catel*, rel. to CAPITAL]

cat·ty /kat′ē/ *adj.* (·**ti·er**, ·**ti·est**) spiteful —cat′ti·ly *adv.*; cat′ti·ness *n.*

Ca·tul·lus /kətəl′əs/, **Gaius Valerius** c. 84–c. 54 B.C.; Roman poet

CATV *abbr.* community access television

cat′walk′ *n.* narrow pathway or platform

Cau·ca·sian /kôkā′ZHən/ *adj.* **1** of the white or light-skinned race **2** of the Caucasus —*n.* **3** Caucasian person [CAUCASUS]

Cau·ca·soid /kô′kəsoid′/ *adj.* of Caucasians

Cau·ca·sus, the /kô′kəsəs/ *n.* mountain range in SW Russia and Georgia; part of the traditional division between Europe and Asia

cau·cus /kô′kəs/ *n.* (*pl.* **·es**) meeting of party members, esp. in the Senate, etc., to decide policy [perh. fr. Algonquian]

cau·dal /kôd′l/ *adj.* pertaining to a tail [L *cauda* tail]

caught /kôt/ *v. past* and *past part.* of CATCH

caul·dron /kôl′drən/ *n.* (also **cal·dron**) large deep vessel for boiling [L *calidus* warm]

cau·li·flow·er /käl′əflour′, kôl′-, -flou′ər/ *n.* cabbage with a large white flower-head [It *cavolfiore* flowered cabbage]

caulk /kôk/ *v.* (also **calk**) stop up the seams of a boat, etc.) with a pliable sealant —caulk′ing *n.* [L *calcare* tread on]

caus·al /kô′zəl/ *adj.* **1** of or forming a cause

2 pertaining to cause and effect —caus′al·ly *adv.*

cau·sal·i·ty /kôzal′ətē/ *n.* relation of cause and effect

cau·sa·tion /kôzā′SHən/ *n.* **1** act of causing **2** CAUSALITY

caus·a·tive /kô′zətiv/ *adj.* acting as or expressing a cause

cause /kôz/ *n.* **1** thing or person that produces an effect **2** reason or motive for an effect or action **3** principle, belief, or purpose **4** *Law.* a case for trial —*v.* (**caused, caus·ing**) **5** be the cause of; bring about; produce [L *causa*]

cause cé·lè·bre /kôz′ səleb′(rə)/ *n.* (*pl.* **causes cé·lè·bres** /kôz′ səleb′rəz/) *French.* court case, etc., that attracts much interest

cau·se·rie /kō′zərē′/ *n.* informal article or talk [Fr]

cause·way /kôz′wā′/ *n.* raised road across low ground or water [AngFr *caucie* fr. L *calx* lime + WAY]

caus·tic /kô′stik/ *adj.* **1** corrosive; burning **2** sarcastic; biting —*n.* **3** caustic substance —caus′ti·cal·ly *adv.* [Gk *kaustikos* fr. *kaiein* burn]

cau·ter·ize /kôt′ərīz′/ *v.* (·**ized, ·iz·ing**) burn (tissue), esp. to stop bleeding [Fr, rel. to CAUSTIC]

cau·tion /kô′SHən/ *n.* **1** attention to safety; prudence; carefulness **2** a warning —*v.* **3** warn or admonish [L *cautio*]

cau·tion·ar·y /kô′SHəner′ē/ *adj.* giving or serving as a warning

cau·tious /kô′SHəs/ *adj.* having or showing caution —cau′tious·ly *adv.*; cau′tious·ness *n.*

cav·al·cade /kav′əlkād′/ *n.* procession or assembly of riders, vehicles, etc. [It *cavalcata* horseback raid]

cav·a·lier /kav′əlēr′/ *n.* **1** courtly gentleman **2** *Hist.* knight; horseman —*adj.* **3** offhand; supercilious [rel. to CAVALCADE]

cav·al·ry /kav′əlrē/ *n.* (*pl.* **·ries**) (usu. treated as *pl.*) soldiers on horseback or in armored vehicles [rel. to CAVALCADE]

cave /kāv/ *n.* **1** large hollow in the side of a cliff, hill, etc., or underground —*v.* (**caved, cav·ing**) **2** explore caves **3 cave in: a** (cause to) collapse **b** yield; give up [L *cavus* hollow]

ca·ve·at /kav′ē·ät′, käv′-/ *n.* warning; proviso [L: let him beware]

ca′ve·at′ emp′tor /em(p)′tôr′/ *Latin.* let the buyer beware; i.e., at time of purchase

cave′man′ *n.* prehistoric person who lived in caves

cav·ern /kav′ərn/ *n.* cave, esp. a large or dark one —cav′ern·ous *adj.* [L *caverna*, rel. to CAVE]

cav·i·ar /kav′ē·är′/ *n.* roe of sturgeon or other large fish, eaten as a delicacy [It fr. Turk]

cav·il /kav′əl/ *v.* (·**iled, ·il·ing**) **1** make petty objections; carp —*n.* **2** petty objection [L *cavillari* quibble]

cav·i·ty /kav′ətē/ *n.* (*pl.* **·ties**) **1** hollow within a solid body **2** decayed part of a tooth [L, rel. to CAVE]

ca·vort /kəvôrt′/ *v.* caper excitedly

Ca·vour /kəvoõr′/, **Camillo Benso** 1810–61; Italian statesman

caw /kô/ *n.* 1 harsh cry of a rook, crow, etc. —*v.* 2 utter this cry [imit.]

cay·enne /kī-en', kā-/ *n.* powdered red pepper [Tupi]

Cay·enne /kī-en', kā-/ *n.* capital of French Guiana. Pop. 37,100

cay·man /kā'mən/ *n.* (also **cai'man;** *pl.* **·mans**) S American alligatorlike reptile [Sp and Port fr. Carib]

CB *abbr.* citizens' band, used of radio frequencies for civilian use

cc *abbr.* (also **c.c.**) 1 cubic centimeter(s) 2 copy; copies (to)

CCTV *abbr.* closed circuit television

CCU *abbr.* coronary care unit

Cd *symb.* cadmium

CD *abbr.* 1 certificate of deposit 2 compact disc

CDC *abbr.* Centers for Disease Control (and Prevention)

CD-ROM /sē'dē'räm'/ *abbr. Comp.* metal-coated disk read by laser, used for storage and retrieval of text, images, etc. [compact disk read-only memory]

CDT *abbr.* central daylight time

Ce *symb.* cerium

cease /sēs/ *v.* (**ceased, ceas·ing**) stop; bring or come to an end [L *cessare*]

cease'-fire' *n.* 1 period of truce 2 order to stop firing

cease'less *adj.* without end —**cease'less·ly** *adv.*

Ceau·ses·cu /CHOUSHESH'kōō/, **Nicolae** 1918–89; president of Romania (1974–89)

Ce·bú /sābōō'/ *n.* seaport on Cebú Island in the Philippines. Pop. 610,000

ce·cum /sē'kəm/ *n.* (*pl.* **·ca**) pouch at the junction of the small and large intestines [L *caecus* blind]

ce·dar /sē'dər/ *n.* 1 spreading evergreen conifer 2 its hard fragrant wood [Gk *kedros*]

Ce'dar Rap'ids *n.* city in Iowa. Pop. 108,751

cede /sēd/ *v.* (**ced·ed, ced·ing**) *Formal.* give up one's rights to or possession of [L *cedere* yield]

ce·dil·la /sədil'ə/ *n.* mark written under *c,* esp. in French, to show it has an *s* sound (as in *façade*) [Sp dim. of *zeda* Z]

ceil·ing /sē'liNG/ *n.* 1 upper interior surface of a room or compartment 2 upper limit 3 maximum altitude reachable

Cel·e·bes /sel'əbēz'/ *n.* see SULAWESI

cel·e·brant /sel'əbrənt/ *n.* person who performs a rite, esp. the priest at the Eucharist

cel·e·brate /sel'əbrāt'/ *v.* (**·brat·ed, ·brat·ing**) 1 mark with or engage in festivities 2 perform (a rite or ceremony) 3 praise publicly —**cel'e·bra'tion,** **cel·e·bra'tor** *n.*; **cel·e·bra·to·ry** /sələb'rətôr'ē/ *adj.* [L *celeber* renowned]

ce·leb·ri·ty /sələb'rətē/ *n.* (*pl.* **·ties**) 1 well-known person 2 fame [L, rel. to CELEBRATE]

ce·ler·i·ty /sələr'ətē/ *n.* swiftness [L *celer* swift]

cel·er·y /sel'(ə)rē/ *n.* plant with crisp, long leaf-stalks used as a vegetable [Gk *selinon* parsley]

ce·les·ta /səles'tə/ *n.* small keyboard instrument with bell-like sound [Fr, rel. to CELESTIAL]

ce·les·tial /səles'CHəl/ *adj.* 1 of the sky or

heavenly bodies 2 divinely good; sublime [L *caelum* sky]

cel·i·bate /sel'əbət/ *adj.* 1a unmarried b committed to sexual abstention 2 having no sexual relations —*n.* 3 celibate person —**cel'i·ba·cy** /-əbəsē/ *n.* [L *caelebs* unmarried]

cell /sel/ *n.* 1 small room, esp. in a prison or monastery 2 tiny compartment 3 smallest structural and functional unit of living matter, consisting of cytoplasm and a nucleus 4 vessel containing electrodes for current-generation or electrolysis [L *cella* room]

cel·lar /sel'ər/ *n.* storage room below ground level [L *cellarius,* rel. to CELL]

Cel·li·ni /CHəlē'nē/, **Benvenuto** 1500–71; Italian goldsmith and sculptor

cel·lo /CHel'ō/ *n.* (*pl.* **·los**) bass instrument of the violin family, held between the legs of the seated player —**cel'list** *n.* [abbr. of VIOLONCELLO]

cel·lo·phane /sel'əfān'/ *n.* thin transparent wrapping material made from cellulose

cel·lu·lar /sel'yələr/ *adj.* consisting of cells; of open texture; porous —**cel'lu·lar'i·ty** /-lar'ətē/ *n.* [Fr, rel. to CELL]

CELLO

cel·lu·lar phone' *n.* (also **cell phone**) mobile radio-telephone that can operate over a wide region via a network of local transmitters, each serving a local area (cell)

cel·lu·lite /sel'yəlīt'/ *n.* lumpy fat, esp. on the hips and thighs [Fr, rel. to CELL]

cel·lu·loid /sel'yəloid'/ *n.* 1 plastic made from camphor and cellulose nitrate 2 movie film

cel·lu·lose /sel'yəlōs'/ *n.* 1 carbohydrate forming plant-cell walls, used in textile fibers 2 paint or lacquer consisting of esp. cellulose acetate or nitrate in solution [L, rel. to CELL]

Cel·si·us /sel'sē-əs/ *adj.* of a scale of temperature on which water freezes at 0° and boils at 100° [name of an astronomer]

Celt /kelt, selt/ *n.* member of an ethnic group, including inhabitants of Ireland, Wales, Scotland, etc. [L fr. Gk]

Celt·ic /kel'tik, sel'-/ *adj.* 1 of the Celts —*n.* 2 group of Celtic languages, including Gaelic, Welsh, Cornish, etc.

ce·ment /siment'/ *n.* 1 powder of calcined lime and clay, mixed with water to form mortar or used in concrete 2 similar substance for bonding things 3 uniting factor or principle 4 substance used in filling teeth, etc. —*v.* 5a unite with or as with cement b establish or strengthen (a friendship, etc.) 6 apply cement to [L *caedere* cut]

cem·e·ter·y /sem'əter'ē/ *n.* (*pl.* **·ies**) burial ground [Gk *koimētērion* place of rest]

cen·o·taph /sen'ətaf'/ *n.* tomblike monument to a person whose body is elsewhere [Gk *kenos* empty + *taphos* tomb]

Ce·no·zo·ic /sē'nəzō'ik, sen'ə-/ *adj.* 1 of the most recent geological era, marked by the evolution and development of mammals, etc. —*n.* 2 this era [Gk *kainos* new + *zóion* animal]

cen·ser /sen'sər/ *n.* vessel for burning incense [AngFr, rel. to INCENSE[1]]

cen·sor /sen'sər/ *n.* 1 person authorized to suppress or expurgate books, films, etc., on grounds of obscenity, security, etc. —*v.* 2 act as a censor of 3 make deletions or changes in —**cen·so·ri·al** /sensôr'ēəl/ *adj.*; **cen'sor·ship** *n.* [L *censere* assess]

cen·so·ri·ous /sensôr'ēəs/ *adj.* severely critical —**cen·so'ri·ous·ly** *adv.*

cen·sure /sen'shər/ *v.* (·**sured, sur·ing**) 1 criticize harshly; reprove —*n.* 2 hostile criticism; disapproval [L, rel. to CENSOR]

cen·sus /sen'səs/ *n.* (*pl.* ·**sus·es**) official count of population, etc. [L, rel. to CENSOR]

cent /sent/ *n.* 1 one-hundredth of a dollar 2 coin of this value; penny [L *centum* 100]

CENTAUR

cen·taur /sen'tôr'/ *n.* creature in Greek mythology with the upper half of a man and the lower half of a horse [L fr. Gk]

cen·te·nar·i·an /sen'tən·er'ēən/ *n.* 1 person a hundred or more years old —*adj.* 2 a hundred or more years old

cen·te·nar·y /senten'ərē, sen'tn·er'ē/ *n.* (*pl.* ·**ries**) 1 hundredth anniversary —*adj.* 2 of a centenary 3 occurring every hundred years [L *centeni* 100 each]

cen·ten·ni·al /senten'ēəl/ *adj.* 1 lasting for a hundred years 2 occurring every hundred years —*n.* 3 CENTENARY [L *centum* 100: cf. BIENNIAL]

cen·ter /sent'ər/ *n.* 1 middle point or part 2 pivot or axis of rotation 3 place or buildings forming a central point or a main area for an activity 4 point of concentration or dispersion; nucleus; source 5 political party or group holding moderate opinions —*v.* (·**tered, ter·ing**) 6 have as its main center 7 place in the center 8 concentrate [Gk *kentron* sharp point]

cen'ter·board' *n.* keellike board that can be lowered through a boat's hull

cen'ter·fold' *n.* magazine center spread, esp. with nude photographs

cen'ter of grav'i·ty *n.* (also **cen'ter of mass'**) point at which the weight of a body is in balance

cen'ter·piece' *n.* 1 ornament for the middle of a table 2 principal item

centi- *comb. form* 1 one-hundredth 2 hundred [L *centum* 100]

cen·ti·grade /sen'təgrād/ *adj.* CELSIUS [L *centum* 100 + GRADE]

cen·time /sän'tēm, -tēm'/ *n.* 1 one-hundredth of a franc 2 coin of this value [L *centum* 100]

cen·ti·me·ter /sen'təmēt'ər/ *n.* one hundredth of a meter

cen·ti·pede /sen'təpēd/ *n.* arthropod with segmented wormlike body and many legs [L *pes pedis* foot]

cen·tral /sen'trəl/ *adj.* 1 pertaining to the center 2 essential; most important —**cen·tral·i·ty** /sentral'ətē/ *n.*; **cen'tral·ly** *adv.*

Cen'tral Af'ri·can Re·pub'lic *n.* republic in Central Africa. Capital: Bangui. Pop. 2,930,000

Cen'tral A·mer'i·ca *n.* continental North America from S of Mexico to South America

cen'tral·ize *v.* (·**ized, ·iz·ing**) 1 concentrate (esp. administration) at a single center 2 subject to this system —**cen'tral·i·za'tion** *n.*

cen'tral ner'vous sys'tem *n.* brain and spinal cord

Cen'tral Val'ley *n.* valley in W central Calif. between the Sacramento and San Joaquin rivers

cen·trif·u·gal /sentrif'(y)əgəl/ *adj.* moving or tending to move from a center —**cen·trif'u·gal·ly** *adv.* [fr. CENTER + L *fugere* flee]

cen·trif'u·gal force' *n.* apparent force that acts outwards on a body moving about a center

cen·tri·fuge /sen'trifyōōj/ *n.* rapidly rotating machine designed to separate substances, as particles in a liquid

cen·trip·e·tal /sentrip'ət·l/ *adj.* moving or tending to move toward a center —**cen·trip'e·tal·ly** *adv.* [fr. CENTER + L *petere* seek]

cen·trip'e·tal force' *n.* force acting on a body causing it to move toward a center

cen·trist /sen'trist/ *n. Polit.* person holding moderate views —**cen'trism** *n.*

cen·tu·ri·on /sent(y)ŏŏr'ēən/ *n.* commander of 100 men in the ancient Roman army [L, rel. to CENTURY]

cen·tu·ry /sen'ch(ə)rē/ *n.* (*pl.* ·**ries**) 1a 100 years b any 100 year span reckoned from the birth of Christ (*twentieth century* 1901–2000; *fifth century* B.C. 500–401 B.C.) 2 company in the ancient Roman army, orig. of 100 men [L *centuria*, rel. to CENT]

CEO *abbr.* chief executive officer

ce·phal·ic /səfal'ik/ *adj.* of or in the head [Gk *kephalē* head]

ceph·a·lo·pod /sef'ələpod'/ *n.* mollusk with a distinct tentacled head, e.g., the octopus [fr. CEPHALIC + Gk *pous podos* foot]

ce·ram·ic /səram'ik/ *adj.* 1 made of (esp.) baked clay 2 pertaining to ceramics —*n.* 3 ceramic article or product [Gk *keramos* pottery]

ce·ram'ics *n. pl.* 1 ceramic products collectively 2 (usu. treated as *sing.*) art of making ceramic articles

ce·re·al /sēr'ēəl/ *n.* 1a grain used for food b wheat, corn, rye, etc., producing this 2 breakfast food made from a cereal —*adj.* 3 of edible grain [L *Ceres* goddess of agriculture]

cer·e·bel·lum /ser'əbel'əm/ *n.* (*pl.* ·**lums** or ·**la**) part of the brain at the back of the skull [L dim. of CEREBRUM]

ce·re·bral /sərē'brəl, ser'ə-/ *adj.* 1 pertaining to the brain 2 intellectual; unemotional [rel. to CEREBRUM]

ce·re'bral pal'sy *n.* paralysis from brain damage before or at birth, with muscular spasm and involuntary movements

ce·re·brum /sərē′brəm, ser′ə-/ *n.* (*pl.* **-bra**) principal part of the brain in vertebrates, at the front of the skull [L]

cer·e·mo·ni·al /ser′əmō′nēəl/ *adj.* 1 of or with ceremony; formal —*n.* 2 order of rites or ceremonies —**cer′e·mo′ni·al·ly** *adv.*

cer·e·mo·ni·ous /ser′əmō′nēəs/ *adj.* fond of or characterized by ceremony; formal —**cer′e·mo′ni·ous·ly** *adv.*

cer·e·mo·ny /ser′əmō′nē/ *n.* (*pl.* **-nies**) 1 formal procedure, esp. at a public event or anniversary 2 formalities, esp. ritualistic 3 excessively polite behavior 4 **stand on ceremony** insist on formality [L *caerimonia* worship]

Ce·res /sēr′ēz/ *n. Rom. Myth.* goddess of agriculture, identified with Greek Demeter

ce·rise /sərēs′, -rēz′/ *n.* light clear red [Fr, rel. to CHERRY]

ce·ri·um /sēr′ēəm/ *n.* silvery metallic element; symb. **Ce** [*Ceres,* name of an asteroid]

cer·tain /sərt′n/ *adj.* **1a** confident; convinced **b** indisputable 2 sure; destined (*certain to win*) 3 unerring; reliable 4 unspecified (*of a certain age*) 5 a degree of (*a certain reluctance*) —*pron.* 6 (as *pl.*) some but not all (*certain of them knew*) 7 **for certain** without doubt [L *certus*]

cer·tain·ly /sərt′n-lē/ *adv.* 1 without any doubt 2 (in answer) yes; by all means

cer·tain·ty /sərt′n-tē/ *n.* (*pl.* **-ties**) 1 undoubted fact or prospect 2 absolute conviction 3 reliable thing or person

cer·ti·fi·a·ble /sərt′əfī′əbəl/ *adj.* 1 able or needing to be certified 2 *Colloq.* insane

cer·tif·i·cate /sərtif′ikət/ *n.* formal document attesting a fact, qualification, or legality —**cer·ti·fi·ca·tion** /sər′tifəkā′sHən/ *n.* [L, rel. to CERTIFY]

cer′ti·fied check′ *n.* check guaranteed by a bank

cer·ti·fy /sərt′əfī/ *v.* (**-fied, -fy·ing**) 1 attest (to), esp. formally 2 declare by certificate 3 officially declare insane [L *certus* definite]

cer·ti·tude /sərt′ət(y)ōōd′/ *n.* feeling of certainty [L, rel. to CERTAIN]

ce·ru·le·an /sərōō′lēən/ *adj. & n. Lit.* deep sky-blue [L *caeruleus*]

Cer·van·tes /sərvan′tēz, servän′tās′/, **Miguel de** (full surname **Cervantes Saavedra**) 1547-1616; Spanish writer

cer·vi·cal /sər′vikəl/ *adj.* pertaining to the neck or the cervix (*cervical vertebrae*) [rel. to CERVIX]

cer·vix /sər′viks/ *n.* (*pl.* **-vices** /-vəsēz/) necklike structure, esp. the neck of the womb [L]

ce·si·um /sē′zēəm/ *n.* soft silver-white element; symb. **Cs** [L *caesius* blue-gray]

ces·sa·tion /sesā′sHən/ *n.* ceasing or pause [L, rel. to CEASE]

ces·sion /sesH′ən/ *n.* 1 ceding 2 territory, etc., ceded [L, rel. to CEDE]

cess·pool /ses′pōōl′/ *n.* pit for waste or sewage

ce·ta·cean /sitā′sHən/ *n.* 1 marine mammal, e.g., the whale —*adj.* 2 pertaining to cetaceans [Gk *kētos* whale]

Cey·lon /silon′, sā-/ *n.* SRI LANKA

Cé·zanne /sāzän′/, **Paul** 1839-1906; French painter

Cf *symb.* californium

CF *abbr.* cystic fibrosis

cf. *abbr.* compare [L *confer*]

CFA *abbr.* chartered financial analyst

CFC *abbr.* CHLOROFLUOROCARBON

cfm *abbr.* cubic feet per minute

cfs *abbr.* cubic feet per second

cg. *abbr.* centigram(s)

Cha·blis /sHablē′, sHä-/ *n.* dry white wine, originally from Chablis in France

cha-cha /CHä′CHä/ *n.* (also **cha′-cha-cha′**) 1 Latin-American dance 2 music for this [AmerSp]

Chad /CHad/ *n.* republic in N central Africa. Capital: N'Djamena. Pop. 5,961,000 —**Chad′i·an** *n. & adj.*

chafe /CHāf/ *v.* (**chafed, chaf·ing**) 1 make or become sore or damaged by rubbing 2 make or become annoyed; fret [L *calefacere* make warm]

chaff /CHaf/ *n.* 1 corn husks 2 chopped hay, straw, etc. 3 lighthearted teasing 4 worthless things —*v.* 5 tease; banter [OE]

chaf′ing dish′ *n.* vessel in which food is cooked or kept warm at table

Cha·gall /sHəgäl′/, **Marc** 1887-1985; Russian-born French painter and graphic artist

cha·grin /sHəgrin′/ *n.* 1 acute annoyance or disappointment —*v.* 2 affect with chagrin [Fr]

chain /CHān/ *n.* **1a** connected flexible series of esp. metal links **b** thing resembling this 2 (*pl.*) fetters; restraining force 3 sequence; series 4 group of associated hotels, restaurants, stores, etc. —*v.* 5 secure or confine with a chain [L *catena*]

cha·in′ gang′ *n. Hist.* team of convicts chained together for work

chain′ re·ac′tion *n.* 1 self-sustaining chemical or nuclear reaction 2 series of events, each caused by the previous one

chain′ saw′ *n.* motor-driven saw with cutting teeth on a looped chain

chair /CHer/ *n.* 1 seat for one person usu. with a back 2 professorship **3a** chairperson **b** seat or office of a chairperson —*v.* 4 preside over (a meeting) [Gk *kathedra*]

chair′lift′ *n.* chairs on a cable, for carrying passengers up and down a mountain, etc.

chair′man *n.* (*pl.* **-men**; *fem.* **-wom′an**, *pl.* **-wom′en**) person chosen to preside over a meeting, committee, board, etc.

chair′per·son *n.* chairman or chairwoman

chaise longue /sHāz lônG′/ *n.* (*pl.* **chaise longues** or **chaises longues**, pronunc. same) lounging chair with a long seat [Fr: long chair]

cha·let /sHalā′/ *n.* 1 Swiss house or cottage with overhanging eaves 2 house in a similar style [SwissFr]

chal·ice /CHal′is/ *n.* 1 goblet 2 Eucharistic cup [L CALIX]

chalk /CHôk/ *n.* 1 white soft limestone 2 similar substance, sometimes colored, for writing or drawing —*v.* 3 rub, mark, draw, or write with chalk 4 (foll. by *up*) register or gain (success, etc.) —**chalk′y** *adj.* (**-i·er, -i·est**); **chalk′i·ness** *n.* [L *calx* lime]

chal·lenge /CHal'ənj/ *n.* **1** summons to take part in a contest to prove or justify something, etc. **2** demanding or difficult task **3** objection made to a jury member —*v.* (**·lenged, ·leng·ing**) **4** issue a challenge to **5** dispute; deny **6** be stimulatingly difficult **7** object to (a jury member, evidence, etc.) —**chal'leng·er** *n.*; **chal'leng·ing** *adj.* [L *calumnia* calumny]

cham·ber /CHām'bər/ *n.* **1a** hall used by a legislative or judicial body **b** body that meets in it **2** (*pl.*) judge's room **3** *Archaic.* room, esp. a bedroom **4** cavity or compartment in the body, machinery, etc. [Gk *kamara* vault]

Cham·ber·lain /CHām'bərlən/, **(Arthur) Neville** 1869–1940; · British prime minister (1937–40)

cham·ber·lain /CHām'bərlin/ *n.* officer managing a royal or noble household [Gmc, rel. to CHAMBER]

cham'ber·maid' *n.* woman whose work is to clean bedrooms

cham'ber mu·sic *n.* music for or performed by a small ensemble

cham'ber of com'merce *n.* ·association to promote local commercial interests

cha·me·le·on /kəmēl'ēən, -yən/ *n.* small lizard able to change color for camouflage [Gk: ground-lion]

cham·ois /SHam'ē, SHamwä'/ *n.* (*pl.* same) **1** agile European and Asian mountain antelope **2** soft leather from sheep, goats, deer, etc. [Fr]

cham·o·mile /kam'əmīl', -mēl'/ *n.* (also **cam'o·mile**) aromatic plant with daisylike flowers used esp. to make tea [Gk: earth-apple]

champ[1] /CHamp, CHämp/ *v.* **1** munch or chew noisily **2 champ at the bit** be restlessly impatient [imit.]

champ[2] /CHamp/ *n. Colloq.* champion [abbr.]

cham·pagne /SHampān'/ *n.* **1** white sparkling wine, originally made in Champagne **2** pale cream color [*Champagne*, former province in E France]

Cham·paign /SHampān'/ *n.* city in Ill. Pop. 63,502

cham·pi·on /CHam'pēən/ *n.* **1** person or thing that has defeated or surpassed all rivals **2** defender of a cause or another person —*v.* **3** support the cause of; defend [ult. fr. L *campus* field]

cham'pi·on·ship' *n.* **1** (often *pl.*) contest to decide the champion **2** position of champion

Cham·plain /SHamplān'/, **Samuel de** 1567–1635; French explorer and colonial statesman in Canada

Cham·plain, Lake *n.* lake in NE US between Vermont and New York

chance /CHans/ *n.* **1** possibility **2** (often *pl.*) probability **3** opportunity **4** fortune; fate —*adj.* **5** fortuitous; accidental —*v.* (**chanced, chanc·ing**) **6** risk **7** happen (*I chanced to find it*) **8 by any chance** perhaps **9 by chance** fortuitously **10 chance on** (or **upon**) happen to find, meet, etc. **11 stand a chance** have a prospect of success, etc. [ult. fr. L *cadere* fall]

chan·cel /CHan'səl/ *n.* part of a church near the altar [L *cancelli* grating]

chan·cel·ler·y /CHan's(ə)lərē, -səlrē/ *n.* (*pl.* **·ies**) **1** chancellor's department, staff, or residence **2** office attached to an embassy or consulate

chan·cel·lor /CHan's(ə)lər/ *n.* high governmental or university official [L *cancellarius* secretary]

chan·cer·y /CHan's(ə)rē/ *n.* (*pl.* **·ies**) **1** *Law.* court of equity **2** *RC Ch.* administrative offices of a bishop **3** chancellery [contr. of CHANCELLERY]

chan·cy /CHan'sē/ *adj.* (**·i·er, ·i·est**) uncertain; risky

chan·de·lier /SHan'dəlēr'/ *n.* ornamental branched lighting fixture [Fr, rel. to CANDLE]

Chan·di·garh /CHən'digär'/ *n.* city in N India. Pop. 503,000

Chan·dler /CHand'lər/, **Raymond** 1888–1959; US novelist

Cha·nel /SHənel'/, **"Coco" (Gabrielle Bonheur)** 1883–1971; French couturière

Chang /CHaNG/ *n.* (also **Chang Jiang**; formerly **Yang·tze** /yaNG'(t)sē'/) largest river of China, flowing 3,400 mi. from Tibet to the East China Sea near Shanghai; important commercial route

Chang·chun /CHäNG'CHŏŏn'/ *n.* city in NE China. Pop. 1,679,300

change /CHānj/ *n.* **1a** making or becoming different **b** alteration or modification **2a** money exchanged for money in larger units or a different currency **b** money returned as the balance of that given in payment **c** coins **3** new experience; variety (*need a change*) **4** substitution of one thing for another (*change of scene*) —*v.* (**changed, chang·ing**) **5** undergo, show, or subject to change; make or become different **6a** take or use another instead of (*change one's socks*) **b** give up or get rid of in exchange (*changed the car for a van*) **7** give money in exchange for **8** put fresh clothes or coverings on **9** exchange **10 change hands** pass to a different owner **11 change one's mind** adopt a different opinion or plan **12 change one's tune** voice a revised opinion —**change'less** *adj.* [L *cambire* barter]

change'a·ble *adj.* **1** inconstant **2** that can change or be changed

change·ling /CHānj'liNG/ *n.* (esp. in folklore) child secretly substituted for another

change'o·ver *n.* change from one system to another

Chang·sha /CHäNG'SHä'/ *n.* city in SE China. Pop. 1,113,200

chan·nel /CHan'l/ *n.* **1** body of water joining two seas, etc. **2** medium of communication; agency **3** band of frequencies in radio and television transmission **4** course in which anything moves **5a** hollow bed of water **b** navigable part of a waterway —*v.* (**·neled, ·nel·ing**) **6** guide; direct [L, rel. to CANAL]

Chan'nel Is'lands *n.* group of British islands in the English Channel near the NE coast of France

chant /CHant/ *n.* **1** intoned phrase or song **2a** simple tune for unmetrical words, e.g., psalms **b** song, esp. monotonous or repetitive —*v.* **3** sing or intone (a psalm, etc.) [L *cantare* fr. *canere* sing]

chan·ti·cleer /CHant'iklēr'/ *n.* name given to

Cha·nu·kah /KHä′nəkə, hä-/ *n.* var. of HA- NUKKAH

cha·os /kā′äs′/ *n.* utter confusion —**cha·ot′ ic** *adj.*; **cha·ot′i·cal·ly** *adv.* [L fr. Gk]

chap[1] /CHap/ *n. Colloq.* man or boy; fellow [abbr. of *chapman* peddler]

chap[2] *v.* (**chapped, chap·ping**) 1 (esp. of the skin) develop cracks or soreness —*n.* 2 (usu. *pl.*) crack in the skin, etc.

chap. *abbr.* chapter

chap·ar·ral /SHap′əral′/ *n.* dense tangled brushwood [Sp]

chap·el /CHap′əl/ *n.* 1 smaller chamber for worship in a large church, with its own altar 2 this attached to a private house, etc. [MedL *cappella* cloak: for a sanctuary in which St. Martin's cloak was preserved]

chap·er·on /SHap′ərōn′/ *n.* 1 companion, esp. for younger people, ensuring propriety on social occasions —*v.* 2 act as chaperon to [Fr fr. *chape* cope, rel. to CAPE[1]]

chap·lain /CHap′lin/ *n.* cleric attached to a chapel, institution, ship, etc. —**chap′lain·cy** *n.* (*pl.* ·**cies**) [L, rel. to CHAPEL]

chap·let /CHap′lit/ *n.* 1 garland or circlet for the head 2 short string of beads; rosary [L, rel. to CAP]

Chap·lin /CHap′lən/, **Charlie** 1889–1977; English film actor and director

chap·ter /CHap′tər/ *n.* 1 main division of a book 2 division of an organization, as a local branch [L dim. of *caput* head]

char /CHär/ *v.* (**charred, char·ring**) 1 make or become black by burning; scorch 2 burn to charcoal [fr. CHARCOAL]

char·ac·ter /kar′iktər/ *n.* 1 collective distin- guishing qualities or characteristics 2a moral strength b reputation, esp. good reputation 3a person in a novel, play, etc. b dramatic role 4 *Colloq.* person, esp. an eccentric one 5 printed or written letter, symbol, etc. [Gk *char- aktēr*]

char·ac·ter·is·tic /kar′iktəris′tik/ *adj.* 1 typ- ical; distinctive —*n.* 2 notable feature or qual- ity —**char′ac·ter·is′ti·cal·ly** *adv.*

char′ac·ter·ize *v.* (·**ized, ·iz·ing**) 1a de- scribe the character of b describe as 2 be characteristic of —**char′ac·ter·i·za′tion** *n.*

cha·rade /SHərād′/ *n.* 1 (usu. *pl.*, treated as *sing.*) game of guessing a word from acted clues 2 absurd pretense [Prov *charra* chat- ter]

char·coal /CHär′kōl′/ *n.* 1a dark gray or black form of carbon from partially burnt wood, etc. b piece of this for drawing c a drawing in charcoal 2 (in full **char·coal gray**) dark gray

charge /CHärj/ *v.* (**charged, charg·ing**) 1a ask (an amount) as a price b ask (a person) for an amount as a price 2 assign the cost of to (a person or account) 3a accuse (of an of- fense) b make an accusation 4 instruct or urge 5 entrust (with) 6 make a rushing at- tack (on) 7a give an electric charge to b store energy in (a battery) 8 load or fill, as with fuel, energy, strong feelings, etc. —*n.* 9 price asked for services or goods 10 accusation 11a task; duty b care; custody c person or thing entrusted 12a impetuous rush or at- tack, esp. in battle b signal for this 13 appro-

priate explosive for a gun 14a property of matter causing electrical phenomena b quan- tity of this carried by the body c energy stored chemically for conversion into electricity 15 **in charge** having command 16 **take charge** assume control —**charge′a·ble** *adj.* [L *carrus* CAR]

charge′ ac·count′ *n.* agreement, usu. with a retailer, whereby a customer may purchase goods and be billed for them

charge′ card′ *n.* CREDIT CARD

char·ger /CHär′jər/ *n.* 1 battle horse 2 ap- paratus for charging a battery

CHARIOT

char·i·ot /CHar′ēət/ *n. Hist.* two-wheeled vehicle drawn by horses, used in ancient war- fare and racing [Fr, rel. to CAR] —**char′i·o· teer′** *n.*

cha·ris·ma /kəriz′mə/ *n.* personal or oracu- lar power to inspire or attract others; excep- tional charm —**char′is·mat′ic** *adj.* [Gk *charis* grace]

char·i·ta·ble /CHar′ətəbəl/ *adj.* 1 generous in giving to those in need 2 of or relating to a charity or charities 3 generous in judging oth- ers —**char′i·ta·bly** *adv.*

char·i·ty /CHar′ətē/ *n.* (*pl.* ·**ties**) 1 giving voluntarily to those in need 2 organization for good or the needy 3a kindness; benevolence b tolerance [L *caritas* fr. *carus* dear]

char·la·tan /SHär′lət̯n/ *n.* person falsely claiming knowledge or skill —**char′la·tan· ism′** *n.* [It: babbler]

Char·le·magne /SHär′ləmän/ (**Carolus Magnus** or **Charles the Great**) 742–814; king of the Franks (768–814) and Holy Roman Emperor (800–814)

Char·le·roi /SHär′lərwä′, SHär′ləroi/ *n.* city in S Belgium. Pop. 206,200

Charles[1] /CHärlz/ name of two kings of Eng- land, Scotland, and Ireland: 1 **Charles I** 1600–49; reigned 1625–49 2 **Charles II** 1630–85; reigned 1660–85

Charles[2] name of four kings of Spain, includ- ing: 1 **Charles I** 1500–58; reigned 1516–56 and (as Charles V) Holy Roman Emperor (1519–56) 2 **Charles II** 1661–1700; reigned 1665–1700

Charles, Prince of Wales 1948– ; first son of Elizabeth II; heir apparent to the throne of the United Kingdom

Charles VII 1403–61; king of France (1422– 61) crowned with the help of Joan of Arc

Charles Mar·tel /märtel′/ *c.* 688–741; ruler of the Franks (714–741)

Charles·ton /CHärl′stən/ *n.* 1 capital of W. Va., in the W part. Pop. 57,287 2 port city in S. Car. Pop. 80,414

Char·lotte /SHär′lət/ *n.* city in N. Car. Pop. 395,934

Char·lotte·town /SHÄr′lət-toun′/ *n.* capital of the Canadian province of Prince Edward Island. Pop. 15,400

charm /CHÄrm/ *n.* **1** power or quality of delighting, arousing admiration, or influencing; fascination; attractiveness **2** trinket or a bracelet, etc. **3** object, act, or word(s) supposedly having magic power —*v.* **4** delight; captivate **5** obtain or gain by charm (*charmed his way into power*) —**charm′er** *n.* [L *carmen* song]

charm′ing *adj.* delightful —**charm′ing·ly** *adv.*

chart /CHärt/ *n.* **1** geographical map or plan, esp. for navigation **2** information table, graph, or diagram **3** (usu. *pl.*) *Colloq.* listing of best-selling pop recordings —*v.* **4** make a chart of; map [L *charta*, rel. to CARD]

char·ter /CHär′tər/ *n.* **1** document granting rights, issued esp. by a government **2** written constitution, rules, etc. —*v.* **3** grant a charter to **4** hire (an aircraft, ship, etc.) for private use [L *chartula*, rel. to CHART]

char′ter mem′ber *n.* founding or original member

char·treuse /SHärtrōōz′, -trōōs′/ *n.* pale green or yellow brandy-based liqueur [*Chartreuse*, monastery in S France]

char·y /CHAr′ē/ *adj.* (**·i·er, ·i·est**) **1** cautious; wary **2** sparing; ungenerous [OE, rel. to CARE]

chase[1] /CHās/ *v.* (**chased, chas·ing**) **1** run after; pursue **2** force to run away or flee **3** *Colloq.* a try to attain **b** court persistently —*n.* **4** pursuit **5** (prec. by *the*) hunting, esp. as a sport [L *captare*, rel. to CATCH]

chase[2] *v.* (**chased, chas·ing**) emboss or engrave (metal) [Fr, rel. to CASE[2]]

Chase, Salmon P. 1808–73; chief justice of the US Supreme Court (1864–73)

chas′er *n. Colloq.* drink taken after another of a different kind

chasm /kaz′əm/ *n.* deep cleft or opening in the earth, rock, etc.; gulf [L fr. Gk]

chas·sis /CHas′ē, SHas′ē/ *n.* (*pl.* same /-sēz/) **1** frame of a motor vehicle, carriage, etc. **2** frame for radio, etc., components [L, rel. to CASE[2]]

chaste /CHāst/ *adj.* **1** abstaining from extramarital or all sexual intercourse **2** pure; virtuous **3** simple; unadorned —**chaste′ly** *adv.*; **chaste′ness** *n.* [L *castus*]

chast·en /CHā′sən/ *v.* **1** subdue; restrain **2** discipline; punish

chas·tise /CHastīz′, CHas′tīz/ *v.* (**·tised, ·tis·ing**) **1** rebuke severely **2** punish, esp. by beating —**chas·tise′ment** *n.*

chas·ti·ty /CHas′tətē/ *n.* being chaste

cha·su·ble /CHaz′(y)əbəl/ *n.* sleeveless usu. ornate outer clerical vestment [L *casubla*]

chat /CHat/ *v.* (**chatted, chat·ting**) **1** talk in a light familiar way —*n.* **2** pleasant informal talk [shortening of CHATTER]

châ·teau /SHatō′/ *n.* (*pl.* **·teaux** /-tōz′/) large French country house or castle [Fr fr. L *castellum*]

Cha·teau·bri·and /SHätō′brē·än′/, **François-René (Vicomte de)** 1768–1848; French writer and diplomat

chat·e·laine /SHat′l-ān′/ *n.* mistress of a large house [MedL *castellanus*]

Chat·ta·hoo′chee Riv′er /CHat′əhōō′CHē/ *n.* river in SE US, flowing 430 mi. S from NE Ga.

Chat·ta·noo·ga /CHat′ənōō′gə/ *n.* city in Tenn. Pop. 152,466

chat·tel /CHat′l/ *n.* (usu. *pl.*) movable property [OFr, rel. to CATTLE]

chat·ter /CHat′ər/ *v.* **1** talk quickly, incessantly, or trivially **2** (of a bird, monkey, etc.) emit short sounds **3** (of teeth) click repeatedly together —*n.* **4** chattering talk or sounds [imit.]

chat′ter·box *n.* talkative person

chat′ty *adj.* (**·ti·er, ·ti·est**) **1** fond of chatting **2** resembling chat —**chat′ti·ly** *adv.*; **chat′ti·ness** *n.*

Chau·cer /CHô′sər/, **Geoffrey** c. 1342–1400; English poet

chauf·feur /SHō′fər, SHōfər′/ *n.* **1** person employed to drive a car —*v.* **2** drive (a car or person) as a chauffeur [Fr: stoker]

chau·vin·ism /SHō′vəniz′əm/ *n.* **1** exaggerated or aggressive patriotism **2** excessively partisan support or loyalty [*Chauvin*, name of extremist Fr patriot]

chau·vin·ist /SHō′vənist/ *n.* **1** person exhibiting chauvinism **2** (in full **male′ chauv′in·ist′**) man who shows prejudice against women —**chau·vin·is′tic** *adj.*; **chau·vin·is′ti·cal·ly** *adv.*

Ch.E. *abbr.* chemical engineer

cheap /CHēp/ *adj.* **1** low in price **2** charging low prices; offering good value **3** of poor quality; inferior **4** costing little effort —*adv.* **5** cheaply **6 on the cheap** cheaply —**cheap′ly** *adv.*; **cheap′ness** *n.* [OE: price; bargain]

cheap′en *v.* make or become cheap; depreciate; degrade

cheap′ shot′ *n.* unfair or cruel action or remark

cheap′skate′ *n. Colloq.* stingy person

cheat /CHēt/ *v.* **1a** deceive or trick **b** deprive of **2** gain unfair advantage by deception or breaking rules —*n.* **3** person who cheats **4** deception; disappointment **5 cheat on** *Colloq.* be sexually unfaithful to [fr. ME *chet*]

Che·bok·sa·ry /CHeb′əksär′ē/ *n.* port in Russia on the Volga River. Pop. 436,000

check /CHek/ *v.* **1a** examine the accuracy or quality of **b** make sure; verify **2** stop or slow the motion of; curb **3** *Chess.* directly threaten (the opposing king) **4** mark for verification; agree on comparison **5** deposit (luggage, etc.) for safekeeping or shipment —*n.* **6** means or act of testing or ensuring accuracy, quality, etc. **7a** stopping or slowing of motion **b** rebuff or rebuke **8a** pattern of small squares **b** fabric so patterned **9** signed document ordering payment of a sum from a deposit account **10** *Chess.* exposure of a king to direct attack **11** restaurant bill **12** token of identification for left luggage, etc. **13 check in: a** arrive or register at a hotel, airport, etc. **b** record the arrival of **14 check into:** a register one's arrival at (a hotel, etc.) **b** investigate **15 check off** mark on a list **16 check on** examine; verify; keep watch on **17 check out** leave a hotel, etc., after paying [OFr *eschec* check (in chess), fr. Pers: king]

checked /CHekt/ *adj.* having a pattern of squares

check'er[1] *n.* 1 person, etc. that examines, esp. in a factory, etc. 2 cashier in supermarket, etc.

check·er[2] *n.* 1 (often *pl.*) pattern of squares often alternately colored —*v.* 2 mark with checkers 3 (check'ered) with varied fortunes (*checkered career*)

check'er·board' *n.* square board or surface with pattern of 64 squares, used to play checkers and chess

check'ers *n.* 1 game in which two players maneuver small disks on a checkerboard 2 pieces used in this game

check'ing ac·count' *n.* bank account used for payments via written orders (checks)

check·mate /cʜɛkˈmāt'/ *n.* 1 Chess. position from which a king cannot move or escape —*v.* (·mat·ed, ·mat·ing) 2 Chess. put into checkmate 3 frustrate [MFr, rel. to CHECK + Pers *māt* is dead]

check'out' *n.* 1 departing a hotel, etc. 2 pay counter in a supermarket, etc.

check'point' *n.* barrier or gate for inspection

check'up' *n.* thorough (esp. medical) examination

ched·dar /cʜɛdˈər/ *n.* a kind of firm smooth cheese [*Cheddar* in England]

cheek /cʜēk/ *n.* 1a side of the face below the eye b side-wall of the mouth 2 impertinence; cool confidence 3 Slang. buttock 4 cheek by jowl close together; intimate [OE]

cheek'bone' *n.* bone below the eye

cheek'y *adj.* (·i·er, ·i·est) impertinent —cheek'i·ly *adv.*; cheek'i·ness *n.*

cheep /cʜēp/ *n.* 1 weak shrill cry of a young bird —*v.* 2 make such a cry [imit.]

cheer /cʜēr/ *n.* 1 shout of encouragement or applause 2 spirits; disposition (*full of good cheer*) 3 Colloq. expression of good wishes on parting or before drinking —*v.* 4a applaud with shouts b urge on with shouts 5 shout for joy 6 gladden; comfort [LL *cara* face, fr. Gk]

cheer'ful *adj.* 1 in good spirits; noticeably happy 2 bright; pleasant —cheer'ful·ly *adv.*; cheer'ful·ness *n.*

cheer'lead'er *n.* person who leads cheers or applause, as at a game

cheer'less *adj.* gloomy; dreary

cheer'y *adj.* (·i·er, ·i·est) cheerful —cheer'i·ly *adv.*; cheer'i·ness *n.*

cheese /cʜēz/ *n.* 1 food made from curds of milk 2 cake of this with rind —chees'y *adj.* [L *caseus*]

cheese'burg'er *n.* hamburger with cheese on it

cheese'cake' *n.* 1 dessert cake made with sweetened cream cheese, etc. 2 Slang. display, esp. a photo of a woman's legs, to arouse interest or notice

cheese'cloth' *n.* thin loosely woven cloth

chees'y *adj.* (·i·er, ·i·est) 1 of or like cheese 2 Slang. inferior in quality

chee·tah /cʜēˈta/ *n.* swift spotted leopardlike feline [Hindi]

chef /sʜɛf/ *n.* cook, esp. the chief cook [Fr]

Che·khov /cʜɛkˈôf', -ôv'/, Anton 1860–1904; Russian writer

Chel·ya·binsk /cʜɛlyäˈbinsk/ *n.* city in S Russia. Pop. 1,148,300

chem. *abbr.* 1 chemical 2 chemist 3 chemistry

chem·i·cal /kɛmˈikəl/ *adj.* 1 pertaining to chemistry or chemicals —*n.* 2 substance obtained or used in chemistry —chem'i·cal·ly *adv.* [Fr or MedL, rel. to ALCHEMY]

chem·i·cal en·gi·neer'ing *n.* studies or activities involving the creation and operation of industrial chemical plants

chem·i·cal war'fare *n.* warfare using poison gas and other chemicals

che·mise /sʜəmēz'/ *n.* woman's loose-fitting undergarment or dress [LL *camisa* shirt]

chem·ist /kɛmˈist/ *n.* expert in chemistry [Fr, rel. to ALCHEMY]

chem·is·try /kɛmˈistrē/ *n.* (*pl.* ·tries) 1 branch of science dealing with substances, as the elements, their compounds, and reactions 2 chemical composition and properties of a substance 3 Colloq. personal accord or attraction

Chem·nitz /kɛmˈnits/ *n.* (formerly Karl-Marx-Stadt) city in Germany. Pop. 294,200

che·mo·ther·a·py /kēˈmōthər'əpē/ *n.* treatment of disease, esp. cancer, by chemical substances

Cheng·chou *n.* see ZHENGZHOU

Cheng·du /cʜʌNGˈdōō/ *n.* city in central China. Pop. 1,713,300

che·nille /sʜənēl'/ *n.* 1 tufty velvety cord or yarn 2 fabric of this [Fr: caterpillar, fr. L *canicula* little dog]

Che·ops /kēˈäps/ (also Khu'fu) fl. early 26th cent. B.C.; Egyptian king who built the great pyramid at Giza

Che·re·po·vets /cʜɛrˈəpəv(y)ets'/ *n.* city in NW Russia. Pop. 315,900

cher·ish /cʜɛrˈisʜ/ *v.* 1 protect or tend lovingly 2 hold dear; cling to (hopes, feelings, etc.) [Fr *cher* dear, fr. L *carus*]

Cher·nen·ko /cʜɛrnyɛNGˈkō/, Konstantin 1911–85; president of the USSR (1984–85)

che·root /sʜərōōt'/ *n.* cigar with both ends open [Fr fr. Tamil]

cher·ry /cʜɛrˈē/ *n.* (*pl.* ·ries) 1a small, round fruit with a hard, smooth pit b tree bearing this or grown for its ornamental flowers c its wood 2 bright red color [Gk *kerasos*]

cher·ub /cʜɛrˈəb/ *n.* 1 (*pl.* ·u·bim) angelic being, often depicted as a winged child or its head 2 beautiful or innocent child —che·ru·bic /cʜərōōˈbik/ *adj.* [ult. fr. Heb]

cher·vil /cʜʌrˈvəl/ *n.* herb used for flavoring [Gk *chairephyllon*]

Ches·a·peake /cʜɛsˈəpēk'/ *n.* city in Va. Pop. 151,976

Ches·a·peake Bay' *n.* inlet of the Atlantic Ocean on coast of E US

chess /cʜɛs/ *n.* game for two played on a chessboard with varied pieces [OFr, rel. to CHECK]

chess'board' *n.* checkered board of 64 squares on which chess is played

chess·man /cʜɛsˈman', -mən/ *n.* (*pl.* ·men) any of the pieces with which chess is played

chest /cʜɛst/ *n.* 1 large strong box 2a part of the body enclosed by the ribs b front surface of the body from the neck to the bottom of the ribs 3 small cabinet 4 get a thing off one's chest Colloq. unburden oneself of secrets, one's thoughts, etc., by communicating them [L *cista* fr. Gk]

Ches·ter·ton /CHĕs′tərtən/, **G(ilbert) K(eith)** 1874–1936; English writer and critic

chest·nut /CHĕs′nət′, -nət/ *n.* **1a** glossy hard brown edible nut **b** tree bearing it **2** HORSE CHESTNUT **3** wood of any chestnut **4** horse of a reddish-brown color **5** *Colloq.* stale joke, etc. —*adj.* **6** reddish-brown [Gk *kastanea* nut]

Che·tu·mal /CHā′tŏŏmäl′/ *n.* capital of the Mexican state of Quintana Roo. Pop. 111,400

Che·va·lier /SHəval′yā, SH(ə)välyā′/, **Maurice** 1888–1972; French singer and actor

CHEVRON

chev·ron /SHĕv′rən/ *n.* V-shaped line or stripe [ult. fr. L *caper* goat]

chew /CHŏŏ/ *v.* **1** work (food, etc.) between the teeth —*n.* **2** something chewed or to chew [OE]

chew′ing gum′ *n.* flavored gum for chewing

chew′y *adj.* (·i·er, ·i·est) needing or inviting much chewing —**chew′i·ness** *n.*

Chey·enne /SHīan′, -en′/ *n.* capital of Wyo., in the SE part. Pop. 50,008

chi /kī/ *n.* twenty-second letter of the Greek alphabet (X, χ) [Gk]

Chia·i /jē-ī′/ *n.* city in W Taiwan. Pop. 257,600

Chiang Kai-shek /CHĂNG′ kī′SHĕk′/ 1887–1975; president of China (1928–31; 1943–49) and Taiwan (1950–75)

Chi·an·ti /kē·än′tē, -än′tē/ *n.* dry red wine, originally from the Chianti area in Italy

Chi·a·pas /CHē·äp′əs, CHäp′əs/ *n.* state in SE Mexico, on the Pacific Ocean. Capital: Tuxtla. Pop. 3,210,500

chi·a·ro·scu·ro /kē·är′əsk(y)ŏŏr′ō, -är′-/ *n.* treatment of light and shade in drawing and painting [It: clear dark]

Chi·ba /CHē′ba/ *n.* city in Japan, on SE Honshu. Pop. 834,500

chic /SHēk/ *adj.* **1** stylish; elegant —*n.* **2** stylishness; elegance [Fr]

Chi·ca·go /SHiˈkäg′ō, -kô′gō/ *n.* city in Ill.; commercial center. Pop. 2,783,726 —**Chi·ca′go·an** *n.*

chi·ca·ner·y /SHikā′nərē/ *n.* (*pl.* ·ies) trickery; deception [Fr]

Chi·ca·no /CHikä′nō/ *n.* & *adj.* (*pl.* ·nos; *fem.* **Chi·ca′na**, *pl.* ·nas) Mexican American

chick /CHik/ *n.* **1** young bird **2** *Slang.* young woman [OE, rel. to CHICKEN]

chick·en /CHik′ən/ *n.* **1a** common domestic fowl **b** its flesh as food **2** young bird of a domestic fowl —*adj.* **3** *Colloq.* cowardly —*v.* **4** (foll. by *out*) *Colloq.* withdraw through cowardice [OE]

chick′en feed′ *n.* **1** food for poultry **2** *Colloq.* trivial amount, esp. of money

chick·en·pox /CHik′ənpäks′/ *n.* infectious disease, esp. of children, with a rash of small blisters

chick′en·wire′ *n.* light wire netting with a hexagonal mesh

chick′ pea′ *n.* yellow pealike seed used as a vegetable [L *cicer* + PEA]

chick′weed′ *n.* small weed with tiny white flowers

Chi·cla·yo /CHiklī′ō/ *n.* city in NW Peru. Pop. 419,600

chi·cle /CHik′əl/ *n.* milky juice of a tropical tree, used in chewing gum [Sp fr. Nahuatl]

chic·o·ry /CHik′ərē/ *n.* (*pl.* ·ries) **1** plant with leaves used in salads **2** its root, roasted and ground and used with or instead of coffee [Gk *kikhorion*]

chide /CHīd/ *v.* (**chid·ed** or **chid, chid·ed** or **chid** or **chid·den, chid·ing**) scold; rebuke [OE]

chief /CHēf/ *n.* **1a** leader or ruler **b** head of a tribe, clan, etc. **2** head of a department; highest official —*adj.* **3** first in position, importance, etc. **4** prominent; leading [L *caput* head]

chief′ly *adv.* above all; mainly

chief·tain /CHēf′tən/ *n.* leader of a tribe, clan, etc. [L, rel. to CHIEF]

chif·fon /SHifän′/ *n.* light sheer fabric of silk, nylon, etc. [Fr *chiffe* rag]

Chif·ley /CHif′lē/, **Joseph Benedict** 1885–1951; prime minister of Australia (1945–49)

chig·ger /CHig′gər/ *n.* tiny larva of a mite whose bite causes severe itching

chi·gnon /SHēn′yän, SHēnyän′/ *n.* coil of hair at the back of a woman's head [Fr]

chi·hua·hua /CHəwä′wə, -wä/ *n.* dog of a very small smooth-haired breed [CHIHUAHUA]

Chi·hua·hua /CHəwä′wä, -wə/ *n.* state in N central Mexico, bordering Texas and N. Mexico. Capital: Chihuahua. Pop. 2,441,900

chil·blain /CHil′blān′/ *n.* painful itching swelling on a hand, foot, etc., from exposure to cold [fr. CHILL + *blain* inflamed sore; blister]

child /CHīld/ *n.* (*pl.* **chil·dren** /CHil′drən/) **1a** young human being below the age of puberty **b** unborn or newborn human being **2** one's son or daughter **3** descendant, follower, or product of **4** childish person —**child′less** *adj.* [OE]

child′birth′ *n.* giving birth to a child

child′care′ *n.* the care of children, esp. by a paid service or individual

child·hood /CHīld′hŏŏd′/ *n.* state or period of being a child

child·ish /CHīl′dish/ *adj.* **1** pertaining to a child **2** immature; silly —**child′ish·ly** *adv.*; **child′ish·ness** *n.*

child·like′ *adj.* having the good qualities of a child, such as innocence, frankness, etc.

child′s play′ *n.* easy task

Chil·e /CHil′ē, CHē′lā/ *n.* republic on W coast of S America. Capital: Santiago. Pop. 13,599,000 —**Chil′e·an** *n.* & *adj.*

chil·i /CHil′ē/ *n.* (*pl.* ·ies) **1** hot-tasting dried pod of a certain red pepper, used as a spice **2** spicy dish made usu. with ground beef, powdered chili pepper, and often beans (also **chile; chile con carne**) [Sp fr. Aztec]

Chi·lin *n.* JILIN

chill /CHil/ *n.* **1a** unpleasant cold sensation; lowered body temperature **b** feverish cold **2** unpleasant coldness (of air, water, etc.) **3** depressing influence **4** coldness of manner —*v.*

5 make or become cold **6** depress; horrify **7** preserve (food or drink) by cooling **8** chill (out) *Colloq.* calm down; behave more quietly —*adj.* **9** *Lit.* chilly [OE]

chill'y *adj.* (·i-er, ·i-est) **1** somewhat cold **2** unfriendly; unemotional

Chil·pan·cin·go /CHil'pənsiNG'gō/ *n.* capital of the Mexican state of Guerrero. Pop. 136,200

Chi·lung /jē'lŏŏNG/ *n.* (formerly Keelung) seaport in N Taiwan. Pop. 352,900

Chim·bo·te /CHimbō'tā/ *n.* city in NW Peru on the Santa River. Pop. 296,600

chime /CHīm/ *n.* **1** bell, as in a clock, or set of tuned bells **2** sounds made by this —*v.* (chimed, chim·ing) **3** (of bells) ring **4** show (the time) by chiming **5** chime in interject a remark [OE, rel. to CYMBAL]

chi·me·ra /kīmēr'ə/ *n.* **1** *Gk. Myth.* monster with **2** a lion's head, goat's body, and serpent's tail **2** wild or fantastic conception —**chi·me'ri·cal** /-mer'ikəl/ *adj.* [L fr. Gk]

chim·ney /CHim'nē/ *n.* (*pl.* ·neys) **1** channel conducting smoke up and away from a fire **2** part of this above a roof **3** glass tube protecting the flame of a lamp **4** vertical split or crack in a rockface [L *caminus* oven, fr. Gk]

chim·pan·zee /CHim'pan'zē', -pən-; -pan'zē/ *n.* (also *Colloq.* chimp) small African humanlike ape [Fr fr. Bantu]

chin /CHin/ *n.* **1** front of the lower jaw —*v.* **2** pull (oneself) up while grasping a bar so as to touch the chin to the bar **3** keep one's chin up *Colloq.* remain cheerful [OE]

Chi·na /CHī'nə/ *n.* (official name People's Republic of China; *abbr.* PRC) country in E Asia. Capital: Beijing. Pop. 1,165,888,000

chi·na /CHī'nə/ *n.* **1** fine white or translucent ceramic ware, porcelain, etc. **2** things made of this —*adj.* **3** made of china [orig. fr. CHINA]

Chi·nan *n.* JINAN

chin·chil·la /CHinCHil'ə/ *n.* **1** small S American rodent **2** its soft gray fur [Sp *chinche* bug]

chine /CHīn/ *n.* **1** backbone **2** cut of meat containing all or part of this [L *spina* SPINE]

Chi·nese /CHīnēz'/ *adj.* **1** of China —*n.* **2** Chinese language **3** (*pl.* same) **a** native or national of China **b** person of Chinese descent

Chi'nese lan'tern *n.* collapsible paper lantern

chink[1] /CHiNGk/ *n.* narrow opening; slit [rel. to *chine* narrow ravine]

chink[2] *v.* **1** (cause to) make a sound like glasses or coins striking together —*n.* **2** this sound [imit.]

chi·no /CHē'nō/ *n.* **1** strong cotton fabric **2** (usu. *pl.*) casual pants made from this

chintz /CHints/ *n.* printed multicolored usu. glazed cotton fabric [Hindi fr. Skt]

chintz'y *adj.* (·ier, ·iest) **1** like chintz **2** *Colloq.* showy but inferior **3** *Slang.* stingy

chip /CHip/ *n.* **1** small piece hewn by chopping, etc. **2** place or mark where a piece has been broken off **3** thin slice of potato, etc., fried crisp **4** counter used in some games to represent money **5** MICROCHIP —*v.* (chipped, chip·ping) **6** cut or break (a piece from a hard material) **7** cut pieces off **8** be apt to break at the edge **9** chip in *Colloq.* contribute (money, etc.) **10** chip off the old block child resembling its parent, esp. in char-

101 chilly / chlorofluorocarbon

acter **11** a chip on one's shoulder *Colloq.* resentful or combative inclination **12** when the chips are down *Colloq.* when it comes to the point of danger, urgency, hard times, etc. [OE]

chip·munk /CHip'məNGk/ *n.* striped N American ground squirrel [Algonquian]

chip·per /CHip'ēr/ *adj. Colloq.* healthy and spry

Chi·rac /SHiräk', -rak'/, **Jacques** 1932– ; prime minister of France (1974–76; 1986–88)

Chi·ri·co /kē'rikō', kir'-/, **Giorgio de** 1888–1978; Greek-born Italian painter

chiro- *comb. form* hand [Gk *cheir* hand]

chi·ro·man·cy /kī'rōman'sē/ *n.* palmistry [Gk *mantis* seer]

chi·rop·o·dy /kərăp'ədē/ *n.* PODIATRY —**chi·rop'o·dist** *n.* [Gk *pous podos* foot]

chi·ro·prac·tic /kī'rəprak'tik/ *n.* treatment of bodily disorders by manipulation of esp. the spinal column —**chi'ro·prac'tor** *n.* [Gk *prāktikos* fr. *prāssein* do]

chirp /CHərp/ *v.* **1** (of small birds, grasshoppers, etc.) utter a short sharp note **2** speak or utter merrily —*n.* **3** chirping sound [imit.]

chir·rup /CHər'əp, CHēr'-/ *v.* (·rupped, ·rup·ping) **1** chirp, esp. repeatedly —*n.* **2** chirruping sound [imit.]

chis·el /CHiz'əl/ *n.* **1** hand tool with a squared beveled blade for shaping —*v.* (·eled, ·el·ing) **2** cut or shape with a chisel **3** *Slang.* cheat —**chis'el·er** *n.* [L *caedere* cut]

chis'eled *adj.* **1** cut or shaped with a chisel **2** (of facial features) clear-cut; fine

Chis·holm Trail /CHiz'əm/ *n.* post-Civil War cattle trail from San Antonio, Texas, to Abilene, Kan.

Chi·si·nau *n.* KISHINEV

chit /CHit/ *n.* note indicating a (small) sum owed, etc. [Hindi fr. Skt]

Chi·ta /CHitä'/ *n.* city in SE Russia. Pop. 377,000

chit-chat /CHit'CHat'/ *n. Colloq.* light conversation; gossip [reduplication of CHAT]

chi·tin /kī'tən/ *n.* tough outer covering of insects, etc.

Chit·ta·gong /CHit'əgäNG', -gôNG'/ *n.* port in SE Bangladesh. Pop. 13,634,000

chit·ter·lings or **chit·lin(g)s** /CHit'linz/ *n. pl.* small intestine of pigs, used as food

chiv·al·rous /SHiv'əlrəs/ *adj.* **1** gallant; honorable **2** of or showing chivalry —**chiv'al·rous·ly** *adv.* [OFr *chevaler* knight]

chiv·al·ry /SHiv'əlrē/ *n.* **1** medieval knightly system with its religious, moral, and social code **2** selfless gallantry —**chi'val·ric** *adj.*

chive /CHīv/ *n.* plant with long onion-flavored leaves [L *caepa* onion]

chla·myd·i·a /kləmid'ēə/ *n.* venereal disease caused by a parasitic microorganism

chlo·ride /klôr'īd'/ *n.* **1** compound with chlorine **2** bleaching agent containing this

chlo·ri·nate /klôr'ənāt'/ *v.* (·nat·ed, ·nat·ing) impregnate or treat with chlorine —**chlo·ri·na'tion** *n.*

chlo·rine /klôr'ēn'/ *n.* poisonous gaseous element used for purifying water; *symb.* Cl [Gk *chlōros* green]

chlo·ro·fluor·o·car·bon /klôr'ōflôr'ōkär' bən, -flôr'-/ *n.* gaseous compound of chlorine, fluorine, carbon, and hydrogen used in refrigerants, etc.; *abbr.* CFC

chlo·ro·form /klôr'əfôrm/ *n.* 1 colorless volatile liquid formerly used as general anesthetic —*v.* 2 render unconscious with this [fr. CHLORINE + *formic acid*]

chlo·ro·phyll /klôr'əfil'/ *n.* green pigment found in most plants [Gk *chlōros* green + *phyllon* leaf]

chock /CHäk/ *n.* 1 block or wedge to check the motion of a wheel, etc. —*v.* 2 make fast with chocks [OFr]

chock'-full' *adj.* crammed full

choc·o·late /CHÔK'(ə)lət, CHäK'-/ *n.* 1a food preparation made from ground cacao seeds and usu. sweetened b candy or drink made of or coated with this 2 deep brown color —*adj.* 3 made from chocolate [Aztec *chocolatl*]

choice /CHOis/ *n.* 1a act of choosing b thing or person chosen 2 range from which to choose 3 power or opportunity to choose —*adj.* 4 of superior quality [Gmc, rel. to CHOOSE]

choir /kwīr/ *n.* 1 regular group of singers, esp. in a church 2 part of the church for these singers [L, rel. to CHORUS]

choke /CHōk/ *v.* (**choked, chok·ing**) 1 stop the breathing of, esp. by constricting the windpipe or (of gas, smoke, etc.) by being unbreathable 2 suffer a stoppage of breath 3 make or become speechless from emotion 4 retard the growth of or kill (esp. plants) 5 (foll. by *back*) suppress (feelings) with difficulty 6 block or clog 7 *Colloq.* fail out of fear —*n.* 8 air-intake control in a carburetor 9 **choke up** overwhelm emotionally [OE]

chok'er *n.* close-fitting necklace

cho·ler /käl'ər/ *n. Rare.* anger; irascibility [Gk *cholera* cholera]

chol·er·a /käl'ərə/ *n.* infectious often fatal bacterial disease of the small intestine [Gk]

chol·er·ic /käl'ärik, kəler'ik/ *adj.* irascible

cho·les·ter·ol /kəles'tərôl', -rōl'/ *n.* sterol found in blood and most body tissues; high concentrations promote arterial blockage [Gk CHOLERA + *stereos* stiff]

chomp /CHômp, CHämp/ *v.* CHAMP[1] [imit.]

Chom·sky /CHäm'skē/, (**Avram**) **Noam** 1928– ; US linguist, philosopher, and political activist

Chong·jin /CHəNG'jin'/ *n.* seaport in North Korea. Pop. 520,000

Chong·qing /CHəNG'CHiNG', -kiNG'/ *n.* (formerly **Chungking**) city in S central China. Pop. 2,266,800

Chon·ju /jän'jōō'/ *n.* city in SW South Korea. Pop. 517,100

choose /CHōōz/ *v.* (**chose, chos·en, choos·ing**) 1 select out of a greater number 2 select one or another 3 decide 4 select as (*was chosen leader*) [OE]

choos'y *adj.* (**·i·er, ·i·est**) *Colloq.* fastidious; fussy —**choos'i·ness** *n.*

chop[1] /CHäp/ *v.* (**chopped, chop·ping**) 1 cut by the blow of a sharp tool 2 cut into small pieces —*n.* 3 cutting blow 4 thick slice of meat (esp. pork or lamb) usu. including a rib [rel. to CHAP[2]]

chop[2] *n.* (usu. *pl.*) jaw

Cho·pin /SHŌ'pan', SHŌpaN'/, **Frédéric** 1810–49; Polish-born French composer

chop·per /CHäp'ər/ *n.* 1 ax, knife, cutter, etc. 2 *Colloq.* helicopter

chop'py *adj.* (**·pi·er, ·pi·est**) (of the sea, etc.) fairly rough —**chop'pi·ly** *adv.*; **chop'pi·ness** *n.* [fr. CHOP[1]]

chop'stick' *n.* each of a pair of sticks used as eating utensils, esp. in the Far East [pidgin E fr. Chin *chop* quick]

chop su·ey /CHäp sōō'ē/ *n.* (*pl.* **·eys**) Chinese-style dish of meat, bean sprouts, etc. [Chin: mixed bits]

cho·ral /kôr'əl/ *adj.* pertaining to a choir or chorus [MedL, rel. to CHORUS]

cho·rale /kəral', -räl'/ *n.* 1 simple stately hymn tune; harmonized form of this 2 choir [Ger fr. L, rel. to CHORAL]

c.h. or **C.H.** *abbr.* 1 clearing house 2 courthouse

chord[1] /kôrd/ *n.* group of notes sounded together [orig. *cord* fr. ACCORD]

chord[2] *n.* straight line joining the ends of an arc or curve [var. of CORD]

chor·date /kôr'dāt'/ *n.* 1 animal having a cartilaginous skeletal rod at some stage of its development —*adj.* 2 of chordates [L *chorda* CHORD[2] + -ATE[2]]

chore /CHôr/ *n.* tedious or routine task [fr. CHAR[2]]

cho·re·o·graph /kôr'ēəgraf'/ *v.* plan or write dance movements, as for a ballet, etc. —**cho·re'og'ra·pher** *n.*

cho·re·og·ra·phy /kôr'ēäg'rəfē/ *n.* design or arrangement of a ballet, etc. —**cho're·o·graph'ic** *adj.* [Gk *choreia* dance]

cho·ris·ter /kôr'əstər/ *n.* member of a choir [Fr, rel. to CHOIR]

chor·tle /CHôrt'l/ *n.* 1 gleeful chuckle —*v.* (**·tled, ·tling**) 2 utter or express with a chortle [prob. fr. CHUCKLE + SNORT]

cho·rus /kôr'əs/ *n.* 1 group of singers or dancers who perform together 2 music composed for such a group 3 refrain of a song 4 *Theat.* a group of performers who comment on the action b utterance made by this group —*v.* 5 speak or utter simultaneously [L fr. Gk]

chose /CHōz/ *v.* past of CHOOSE

cho·sen /CHō'zən/ *v.* past part. of CHOOSE

Chou En-lai /jō' en'lī'/ (also **Zhou Enlai**) 1898–1976; prime minister of China (1949–76)

chow[1] /CHou/ *n.* 1 *Slang.* food 2 dog of a Chinese breed with long woolly hair [Chin *chowchow*]

chow·der /CHou'dər/ *n.* thick or hearty soup, usu. with potatoes and often clams or fish, etc.

chow mein /CHou mān'/ *n.* Chinese-style dish of fried noodles with shredded meat, shrimps, etc., and vegetables [Chin *chao mian* fried flour]

Chré·tien de Troyes /krātyan' də trwä'/ 12th cent.; French poet

Christ /krīst/ *n.* 1 title given to Jesus 2 Messiah as prophesied in the Old Testament [Gk: anointed]

Christ·church /krīs(t)'CHərCH/ *n.* city on South Island, New Zealand. Pop. 292,500

chris·ten /kris'ən/ *v.* 1 baptize 2 give a name to 3 *Colloq.* use for the first time —**chris'ten·ing** *n.* [L, rel. to CHRISTIAN]

Chris·ten·dom /krɪsʹəndəm/ *n.* Christians worldwide

Chris·tian /krɪsʹCHən/ *n.* 1 adherent of Christianity —*adj.* 2 of Christ's teaching 3 believing in or following the religion of Christ 4 showing compassionate qualities [L *Christianus* of CHRIST]

Chris·ti·an·i·ty /krɪsʹCHē-anʹətē/ *n.* 1 Christians collectively; the Christian religion 2 being a Christian

Chris'tian name' *n.* forename, esp. as given at baptism

Chris'tian Sci'ence *n.* Christian group that practices a system of spiritual healing —**Chris'tian Sci'en·tist** *n.*

Chris·tie /krɪsʹtē/, (**Dame**) Agatha 1890–1976; English writer

Christ·mas /krɪsʹməs/ *n.* 1 annual festival of Christ's birth (Dec. 25) 2 period around this [OE, rel. to CHRIST + MASS²]

chro·mat·ic /krōmatʹik/ *adj.* 1 of color; in colors 2 *Mus.* (of a scale) ascending or descending by semitones —**chro·mat'i·cal·ly** *adv.* [Gk *chrōmatikos* fr. *chrōma* color]

chro·ma·tin /krōʹmətin/ *n.* chromosome material in a cell nucleus that can be stained for microscopic examination [Gk, rel. to CHROME]

chrome /krōm/ *n.* 1 chromium, esp. as plating 2 pigment made from chromium compounds [Gk *chrōma* color]

chro·mi·um /krōʹmēəm/ *n.* metallic element used as a reflective and anti-corrosive coating; *symb.* Cr

chro·mo·some /krōʹməsōm/ *n.* threadlike structure, usu. found in the cell nucleus of animals and plants, carrying genes [Gk, rel. to CHROME + *sōma* body]

chron·ic /kränʹik/ *adj.* 1 (esp. of an illness) long-lasting 2 continual 3 *Colloq.* habitual; inveterate (*a chronic liar*) —**chron'i·cal·ly** *adv.* [Gk *chronos* time]

chron·i·cle /kränʹikəl/ *n.* 1 register of events in order of occurrence —*v.* (·cled, ·cling) 2 record (events) thus [Gk *chronika*, rel. to CHRONIC]

chro·nol·o·gy /krənälʹəjē/ *n.* (*pl.* ·gies) 1 science of determining dates 2a arrangement of events, etc., in order of occurrence b table or document displaying this —**chron'o·log'i·cal** *adj.*; **chro'no·log'i·cal·ly** *adv.* [Gk *chronos* time + -LOGY]

chro·nom·e·ter /krənämʹətər/ *n.* very accurate clock or watch [CHRONO(LOGY) + -METER]

chrys·a·lis /krɪsʹəlis/ *n.* (*pl.* ·lis·es) 1 pupa of a butterfly or moth 2 case enclosing it [Gk *chrysallis*]

chrys·an·the·mum /krɪsanʹTHəməm/ *n.* garden plant of the daisy family blooming in autumn [Gk fr. *chrysos* gold + *anthemon* flower]

chub·by /CHəbʹē/ *adj.* (·bi·er, ·bi·est) plump and rounded

chuck¹ /CHək/ *v.* 1 *Colloq.* fling or throw carelessly or casually 2 touch playfully, esp. under the chin —*n.* 3 playful touch under the chin 4 toss [perh. fr. Fr *choquer* knock]

chuck² *n.* 1 cut of beef from neck to ribs 2 device for holding a drill bit, etc. [var. of CHOCK]

chuck·le /CHəkʹəl/ *v.* (·led, ·ling) 1 laugh quietly or inwardly —*n.* 2 quiet or suppressed laugh [ME *chuck* cluck]

chug /CHəg/ *v.* (**chugged, chug·ging**) 1 emit a regular muffled explosive sound, as of an engine running slowly 2 move with this sound —*n.* 3 chugging sound [imit.]

Chuk·chi Sea /CHəkʹCHē, CHŏŏkʹ-/ *n.* part of the Arctic Ocean N of the Bering Strait

chuk'ka boot' *n.* ankle-high leather boot

Chu·la Vis·ta /CHŏŏʹlə visʹtə/ *n.* city in Calif. Pop. 135,163

chum /CHəm/ *n.* *Colloq.* close friend —**chum'my** *adj.* (·mi·er, ·mi·est); **chum'mi·ly** *adv.*; **chum'mi·ness** *n.* [abbr. of *chamber-fellow*]

chump /CHəmp/ *n.* *Colloq.* foolish person [blend of CHUNK + LUMP¹]

Chung·king /CHŏŏNGʹkiNGʹ/ CHONGQING

chunk /CHəNGk/ *n.* 1 thick piece cut or broken off 2 substantial amount [var. of CHUCK²]

chunk·y *adj.* (·i·er, ·i·est) 1 consisting of or resembling chunks; thick; substantial 2 small and sturdy —**chunk'i·ness** *n.*

church /CHərCH/ *n.* 1 building for public worship, esp. Christian 2 public worship (*met after church*) 3 (*cap.*) a body of Christians b clergy or clerical profession 4 religious matters, as opposed to secular [Gk *kyriakon* (*dōma*) Lord's (house)]

church'go·er /CHərCHʹgōʹər/ *n.* person attending church regularly

Church·ill /CHərʹCHilʹ/ 1 John (1st Duke of Marlborough) 1650–1722; British military commander, called "Corporal John" 2 (Sir) Winston 1874–1965; British statesman; prime minister of Great Britain (1940–45; 1951–55)

Church' of Eng'land *n.* Anglican Church, headed by the English sovereign

church'yard' *n.* enclosed ground adjoining a church, often used for burials

churl /CHərl/ *n.* ill-bred or surly person —**churl'ish** *adj.*; **churl'ish·ly** *adv.*; **churl'ish·ness** *n.* [OE: man]

churn /CHərn/ *n.* 1 container or machine for making butter —*v.* 2 agitate (milk or cream) in a churn 3 produce (butter) in a churn 4 upset; agitate 5 **churn out** produce in large quantities [OE]

chute¹ /sHŏŏt/ *n.* sloping channel or slide for sending things to a lower level [L *cadere* fall]

chute² *n.* parachute [abbr.]

chut·ney /CHətʹnē/ *n.* (*pl.* ·neys) pungent condiment of fruits, vinegar, spices, etc. [Hindi]

chutz·pah /KHŏŏtʹspə, hŏŏtʹ-/ *n.* *Slang.* brashness; audacity [Yiddish]

chyme /kīm/ *n.* acid pulp formed from partly digested food [Gk *chymos* juice]

CIA *abbr.* Central Intelligence Agency

ci·ca·da /sikäʹdə, -käʹ-/ *n.* large transparent-winged insect that makes a chirping sound [L]

cic·a·trice or **cic·a·trix** /sikʹətris, -triks/ *n.* (*pl.* ·tri'ces /-trīʹsēs/ or ·trix'es) scar [L]

Cic·e·ro /sisʹərōʹ/, **Marcus Tullius** 106–43 B.C.; Roman statesman and writer

Cid, El /el sidʹ/ (**Rodrigo Díaz de Vivar**) c. 1043–99; Spanish hero in the war against the Moors

-cide *suffix* 1 person or substance that kills

(*regicide*; *insecticide*) **2** killing of (*infanticide*) [L *caedere* kill]

ci·der /sī'dər/ *n.* juice of pressed apples [Heb: strong drink]

ci·gar /sigär'/ *n.* tight roll of tobacco leaves for smoking [Sp]

cig·a·rette /sig'əret'/ *n.* roll of finely cut tobacco in paper for smoking [Fr dim.]

cil·i·um /sil'ēəm/ *n.* (*pl.* ·**i'a**) **1** minute hair-like cellular structure **2** eyelash [L: eyelash]

cinch /sinCH/ *n.* **1** saddle strap **2** *Colloq.* sure thing; easy task **3** fasten (a saddle) **4** make (something) certain [Sp *cincha* saddle girth]

cin·cho·na /sinGkō'nə, sinCHō'-/ *n.* **1** S American evergreen tree or shrub **2** its bark, containing quinine [Peruvian Countess of *Chinchón*]

Cin·cin·nat·i /sin'sinat'ē/ *n.* city in Ohio. Pop. 364,040

cinc·ture /sinGk'CHər/ *n.* girdle; belt [L *cingere* gird]

cin·der /sin'dər/ *n.* **1** residue of coal, wood, etc., after burning **2** (*pl.*) ashes [OE *sinder* slag]

Cin·der·el·la /sin'dərel'ə/ *n.* person or thing of unrecognized or disregarded merit or beauty [name of a girl in a fairy tale]

cin·e·ma /sin'əmə/ *n.* **1** movies collectively **2** art or industry of producing movies —**cin'e·mat'ic** *adj.* [Fr, rel. to Gk *kīnēma* motion]

cin·e·ma·tog·ra·phy /sin'əmətäg'rəfē/ *n.* photographic art in the making of movies —**cin'e·ma·tog'ra·pher** *n.*; **cin'e·mat'o·graph'ic** *adj.*

cin·na·bar /sin'əbär'/ *n.* bright red mercuric sulfide [L fr. Gk]

cin·na·mon /sin'əmən/ *n.* **1** aromatic spice from the bark of a SE Asian tree **2** this tree **3** yellowish-brown [LGk *kinnamon* fr. Sem]

ci·pher /sī'fər/ *n.* **1a** secret or disguised writing **b** thing so written **c** key to it **2** the symbol *0*; zero **3** person or thing of no importance [Ar *sifr*]

cir·ca /sər'kə/ *prep.* (preceding an approximate date) about [L]

cir·ca·di·an /sərkād'ēən/ *adj. Physiol.* occurring once per day [L *circa* about + *dies* day]

cir·cle /sər'kəl/ *n.* **1** round plane figure whose circumference is everywhere equidistant from its center **2** line, route, enclosure, or structure in the rounded shape of this figure **3** group with shared interests, as social, literary, etc. —*v.* (·**cled**, ·**cling**) **4** move in a circle **5a** revolve around **b** form a circle around [L dim., rel. to CIRCUS]

cir·clet /sər'klit/ *n.* **1** small circle **2** circular band, esp. as an ornament

cir·cuit /sər'kit/ *n.* **1** boundary line or course around an area or thing **2a** path of an electric current **b** apparatus through which current passes **3** regular course of travel for work, as of a preacher **4** auto racing track **5** itinerary or sphere of operation (*election circuit; cabaret circuit*) [L *circum* around + *ire* go]

cir'cuit break'er *n.* automatic device for interrupting an electric circuit

cir·cu·i·tous /sərkyoō'itəs/ *adj.* **1** indirect **2** going a long way around

cir·cuit·ry /sər'kətrē/ *n.* (*pl.* ·**ries**) **1** system of electric circuits **2** equipment forming this

cir·cu·lar /sər'kyələr/ *adj.* **1a** having the form of a circle **b** moving (roughly) in a circle back to the starting-point **2** (of reasoning) using the point it is trying to prove as evidence for its conclusion, hence invalid —*n.* **3** distributed letter, leaflet, etc. —**cir·cu·lar'i·ty** *n.* [L, rel. to CIRCLE]

cir'cu·lar·ize' *v.* (·**ized**, ·**iz·ing**) distribute circulars to

cir·cu·late /sər'kyəlāt/ *v.* (·**la·ted**, ·**la·ting**) **1** be in or put into circulation; spread **2** move about among guests, etc. [L, rel. to CIRCLE]

cir'cu·la'tion *n.* **1** movement within or around, esp. of blood from and to the heart **2a** distribution, as of newspapers, etc. **b** number of copies sold **3** *Colloq.* **in** (or **out of**) **circulation** active (or not active) socially

cir·cu·la·to·ry /sər'kyəlätôr'ē/ *adj.* pertaining to circulation, esp. of blood

circum- *comb. form* around; about [L]

circum. *abbr.* circumference

cir·cum·cise /sər'kəmsīz'/ *v.* (·**cised**, ·**cis·ing**) cut off the foreskin or clitoris of —**cir'cum·ci'sion** /-sizH'ən/ *n.* [L *circum* around + *caedere* cut]

cir·cum·fer·ence /sərkəm'f(ə)rəns/ *n.* **1** enclosing boundary, esp. of a circle **2** distance around —**cir'cum·fer·en'tial** /-fəren'CHəl/ *adj.* [L *ferre* carry]

cir·cum·flex /sər'kəmfleks'/ *n.* mark (ˆ) placed over a vowel [L, rel. to FLEX]

cir·cum·lo·cu·tion /sər'kəmlōkyoō'sHən/ *n.* roundabout expression; evasive talk

cir·cum·nav·i·gate /sər'kəmnav'igāt'/ *v.* (·**gat·ed**, ·**gat·ing**) sail around (esp. the world) —**cir'cum·nav'i·ga'tion** *n.*

cir·cum·scribe /sər'kəmskrīb', sər'kəmskrīb'/ *v.* (·**scribed**, ·**scrib·ing**) **1** encircle or outline **2** lay down limits of; confine —**cir·cum·scrip'tion** /-skrip'sHən/ *n.* [L *scribere* write]

cir·cum·spect /sər'kəmspekt'/ *adj.* cautious —**cir'cum·spec'tion** *n.*; **cir'cum·spect'ly** *adv.* [L *specere* look]

cir·cum·stance /sər'kəmstans'/ *n.* **1** fact, occurrence, or condition, esp. (*pl.*) accompanying an event; (bad) luck (*victim of circumstance(s)*) **2** (*pl.*) one's financial condition **3** ceremony; fuss **4 under the circumstances** the state of affairs being what it is **5 under no circumstances** not at all; never [L *stare* stand]

cir·cum·stan·tial /sər'kəmstan'sHəl/ *adj.* **1** having to do with or based upon circumstances **2** giving particulars —**cir'cum·stan·ti·al'i·ty** *n.*

cir·cum·vent /sər'kəmvent'/ *v.* evade; find a way around —**cir·cum·ven'tion** *n.* [L *venire* come]

cir·cus /sər'kəs/ *n.* (*pl.* ·**es**) **1** traveling show of acrobats, clowns, animals, etc. **2** *Colloq.* **a** scene of lively action **b** disorderly or ridiculous situation [L: ring]

cir. or **circ.** *abbr.* **1** circle **2** circular (as **circ.**) circulation

cir·rho·sis /sirō'sis/ *n.* chronic liver disease [Gk *kirrhos* tawny]

cir·rus /sēr'əs/ *n.* (*pl.* **cir·ri** /-ī/) white wispy cloud at high altitude [L: curl]

cis·tern /sis'tərn/ *n.* tank for storing water [L *cista* box, fr. Gk]

cit. *abbr.* 1 citation 2 cited 3 citizen

cit·a·del /sit'əd-l, -ədel'/ *n.* fortress, usu. on high ground [MFr *citadelle*]

ci·ta·tion /sītā'SHən/ *n.* 1 passage quoted 2 description of the reasons for an award

cite /sīt/ *v.* (**cit·ed, cit·ing**) 1 mention as an example, etc. 2 quote (a book, etc.) in support 3 summon to appear in court [LL *citare* summon, fr. L *ciere* set in motion]

cit·i·zen /sit'əzən/ *n.* member of a country, state, city, etc. —**cit'i·zen·ry** /-rē/ *n.*; **cit'i·zen·ship** *n.* [OFr, rel. to CITY]

cit·ric /si'trik/ *adj.* derived from citrus fruit

cit'ric ac'id *n.* sharp-tasting acid in citrus

cit·ron /si'trən/ *n.* 1 tree with large lemon-like fruits 2 this fruit [Fr fr. L CITRUS]

cit·ro·nel·la /si'trənel'ə/ *n.* a fragrant oil used in insect repellents, soap, etc.

cit·rus /si'trəs/ *n.* (*pl.* **·es**) 1 tree of a group including the lemon, orange, and grapefruit 2 fruit of such a tree [L]

Cit'rus Heights' *n.* suburb of Sacramento, Calif. Pop. 107,439

cit·y /sit'ē/ *n.* (*pl.* **·ies**) 1 important population or commercial center; large town 2 (in the US) incorporated municipality governed according to state charter 3 its inhabitants, collectively [L *civitas*]

cit'y hall' *n.* building that houses municipal government offices

Ciu·dad Gua·ya·na /sē'ōōdäd gwäyä'nä/ *n.* see SANTO TOMÉ DE GUAYANA

Ciu·dad' Juá'rez /(h)wär'es/ *n.* city in Mexico. Pop. 544,500

Ciu·dad' Vic·to'ria /vēktōr'ēə/ *n.* capital of the Mexican state of Tamaulipas. Pop. 207,800

civ·et /siv'ət/ *n.* 1 (in full **civ'et cat'**) catlike animal of Central Africa 2 strong musky perfume obtained from it [MFr ult. fr. Ar]

civ·ic /siv'ik/ *adj.* pertaining to a city or citizens —**civ'i·cal·ly** *adv.* [L *civis* citizen]

civ·ics /siv'iks/ *n. pl.* (usu. treated as *sing*) study of rights and duties of citizenship

civ·il /siv'əl/ *adj.* 1 of or belonging to citizens 2 nonmilitary 3 courteous; not rude 4 *Law.* concerning private rights and not criminal offenses —**civ'il·ly** *adv.* [L *civilis*]

civ'il en·gi·neer' *n.* one who designs or maintains roads, bridges, dams, etc.

ci·vil·ian /səvil'yən/ *n.* 1 person not in the armed services or police force —*adj.* 2 of or for civilians

ci·vil·i·ty /səvil'ətē/ *n.* (*pl.* **·ties**) 1 courtesy 2 act of politeness [L, rel. to CIVIL]

civ·i·li·za·tion /siv'ələzā'SHən, -lī-/ *n.* 1 advanced stage or system of social development 2 peoples of the world that are regarded as having this 3 a people or nation (esp. of the past) regarded as an element of social evolution (*Inca civilization*)

civ·i·lize /siv'əlīz'/ *v.* (**·lized, ·liz·ing**) 1 bring out of a barbarous or primitive stage of society 2 enlighten; refine and educate [Fr, rel. to CIVIL]

civ'il lib'er·ty *n.* (often *pl.*) freedom of action subject to the law

civ'il rights' *n. pl.* rights of citizens to freedom, due process of law, etc.

civ'il ser'vant *n.* member of the civil service

civ'il ser'vice *n.* government employees, excluding military and elective or appointed office

civ'il war' *n.* war between citizens of the same country

civ·vies /siv'ēz/ *n. pl. Slang.* civilian clothes [abbr.]

cl *abbr.* centiliter(s)

Cl *symb.* chlorine

clack /klak/ *v.* 1 make a sharp sound, as of boards —*n.* 2 clacking noise or talk [imit.]

clad /klad/ *adj.* 1 clothed 2 provided with cladding [*past part.* of CLOTHE]

clad·ding /klad'iNG/ *n.* covering or coating

claim /klām/ *v.* 1 declare; assert 2 demand as one's due or property 3 represent oneself as having or achieving (*claim victory*) 4 entail or cost (*fire claimed two victims*) 5 (of a thing) deserve (attention, etc.) —*n.* 6 personal demand or request; demand —*v.* 3 make a claim) 7 right or title 8 assertion 9 thing claimed —**claim'ant** *n.* [L *clamare* call out]

clair·voy·ance /klervoi'əns/ *n.* supposed faculty of perceiving the future or things beyond normal sensory perception —**clair·voy'ant** *n. & adj.* [Fr, rel. to CLEAR + *voir* see]

clam /klam/ *n.* 1 edible bivalve mollusk —*v.* (**clammed, clam·ming**) 2 *Colloq.* refuse to talk [rel. to CLAMP]

clam'bake' *n.* social gathering at which steamed clams, etc., are served

clam·ber /klam'(b)ər/ *v.* climb laboriously using hands and feet [ME, rel. to CLIMB]

clam·my /klam'ē/ *adj.* (**·mi·er, ·mi·est**) unpleasantly damp and sticky —**clam'mi·ly** *adv.*; **clam'mi·ness** *n.* [ME *clam* to daub]

clam·or /klam'ər/ *n.* 1 loud or vehement shouting or noise 2 protest; demand —*v.* 3 make a clamor —**clam'or·ous** *adj.* [L, rel. to CLAIM]

clamp *n.* 1 device, esp. a brace or band of iron, etc., for gripping or locking —*v.* 2 strengthen or fasten with a clamp; fix firmly 3 **clamp down on** become stricter (about); suppress [LGer or Du]

clan /klan/ *n.* 1 group of people with a common ancestor 2 group with a strong common interest [Gaelic]

clan·des·tine /klandes'tən/ *adj.* surreptitious; secret [L]

CLAMP 1

clang /klaNG/ *n.* 1 loud resonant metallic sound —*v.* 2 (cause to) make a clang [imit.: cf. L *clangere* resound]

clangor /klaNG'ər/ *n.* prolonged clanging —**clan'gor·ous** *adj.*

clank /klaNGk/ *n.* 1 sound as of metal on metal —*v.* 2 (cause to) make this sound [imit.]

clan·nish /klan'isH/ *adj. often Derog.* (of a family or group) associating closely or too closely

clap /klap/ *v.* (**clapped, clap·ping**) 1 strike the palms of one's hands together, esp. repeatedly as applause 2 strike (the hands) together in this way —n. 3 act of clapping, esp. as applause 4 explosive sound, esp. of thunder 5 slap; pat [OE]

clap′per n. tongue or striker of a bell

Clap·ton /klap′tən/, **Eric** 1945– ; British guitarist and composer

clap′trap′ n. insincere or foolish talk

claque /klak/ n. hired applauders [Fr]

Clare of As·si·si, St. /klar, kler/ 1194–1253; Italian nun

clar·et /klar′ət/ n. 1 red wine, esp. from Bordeaux 2 purplish-red [Fr, rel. to CLARIFY]

clar·i·fy /klar′əfī′/ v. (**·fied, ·fy·ing**) make or become clear —**clar′i·fi·ca′tion** n. [L, rel. to CLEAR]

clar·i·net /klar′ənet′/ n. woodwind instrument with a single reed —**clar′i·net′ist** or **clar′i·net′tist** n. [Fr, prob. fr. clarion]

clar·i·on /klar′ēən/ n. clear, rousing sound [L, rel. to CLEAR]

clar·i·ty /klar′ətē/ n. clearness

Clark /klärk/ **1 George Rogers** 1752–1818; US frontiersman and soldier **2 William** 1770–1838; US explorer (with Meriwether Lewis) of the American continent (1804–06)

Clarke /klärk/, **Arthur C(harles)** 1917– ; English writer of science fiction and scientific researcher

clash /klasH/ n. 1 loud jarring sound as of metal objects struck together 2a conflict b discord of colors, etc. —v. 3 (cause to) make this sound 4 collide; coincide awkwardly 5 come into conflict with or be discordant [imit.]

clasp /klasp/ n. 1 device with interlocking parts for fastening 2a embrace b grasp; handshake —v. 3 fasten with or as with a clasp 4a grasp; hold closely b embrace [OE]

class /klas/ n. 1 any set of persons or things grouped, graded, or differentiated from others (first class; economy class) 2 division or order of society (middle class) 3 Colloq. distinction; high quality 4a group of students taught together b occasion when they meet c their course of instruction 5 Biol. next grouping of organisms below a division or phylum —v. 6 assign to a class or category —**class′less** adj. [L classis assembly]

class′-con′scious adj. aware of social divisions or one's place in them —**class′ con′scious·ness** n.

clas·sic /klas′ik/ adj. 1 first-class; lasting 2 very typical (a classic case) 3a of ancient Greek and Latin literature, art, etc. b (of style) simple; harmoniously ordered 4 famous as typical or established —n. 5 classic writer, artist, work, or example 6 (pl.) ancient Greek and Latin literature 7 famous or typical exemplar [L classicus, rel. to CLASS]

● Usage: It is useful to maintain the distinction between classic 'typical; excellent as an example' and classical 'of antiquity, esp. Greek and Roman; (of music) traditionally formal and sophisticated (contrasted with popular)'. A classic case of favoritism. The building is in classical style. We speak of great art as being classic, not classical (unless its reliance on old forms is to be stressed). A classical education exposes a student to classical literature and languages (especially Latin and Greek); a classic education would refer to one that is an established, traditional system.

class·i·cal /klas′ikəl/ adj. **1a** of ancient Greek or Roman literature or art **b** (of a language) having the form used by ancient standard authors **2** (of music) conforming to certain standards of form, genre, etc. **3** restrained in style —**class′i·cal·ly** adv.

clas·si·cism /klas′əsiz′əm/ n. **1** adherence to a classic style **2** classical scholarship —**clas′si·cist** n.

clas·si·fy /klas′əfī′/ v. (**·fied, ·fy·ing**) **1a** arrange in classes or categories **b** assign to a class or category **2** designate as officially secret —**clas′si·fi′able** adj.; **clas′si·fi·ca′tion** n. [Fr, rel. to CLASS]

class′mate′ n. person in the same class at school

class′room′ n. room where a class of students is taught

class′y adj. (**·i·er, ·i·est**) Colloq. superior; stylish —**class′i·ly** adv.; **class′i·ness** n.

clat·ter /klat′ər/ n. sound as of hard objects struck together [OE]

Claude Lor·raine /klōd′ lōren′/ (born **Claude Gellée**) 1600–82; French landscape painter

Clau·di·us /klôd′ēəs/ 10 B.C.–A.D. 54; Roman emperor (41–54)

clause /klôz/ n. **1** Gram. part of a sentence with subject and predicate **2** single statement in a treaty, law, contract, etc. —**claus′al** adj. [L clausula, rel. to CLOSE]

Clau·se·witz /klou′zəvits′/, **Karl von** 1780–1831; Prussian general and military theorist

claus·tro·pho·bi·a /klôs′trəfō′bēə/ n. abnormal fear of confined places —**claus′tro·pho′bic** adj. [rel. to CLOISTER + PHOBIA]

clav·i·chord /klav′ikôrd′/ n. small keyboard instrument with soft tone [MedL, rel. to CLAVICLE]

clav·i·cle /klav′ikəl/ n. COLLARBONE [L dim. of clavis key]

claw /klô/ n. **1a** pointed nail on an animal's foot **b** foot with claws **2** pincer of a shellfish —v. **3** scratch, maul, or pull with claws or fingernails [OE]

clay /klā/ n. **1** stiff sticky earth, used for making bricks, pottery, etc. **2** Poet. substance of the human body —**clay′ey** adj. [OE]

Clay /klā/ **1 Henry** (called the "Great Compromiser") 1777–1852; US politician **2 Cassius** see ALI, MUHAMMAD

clean /klēn/ adj. **1** free from dirt or impurities; unsoiled **2** clear; unused; pristine (clean air) **3** not obscene or indecent **4** attentive to personal hygiene and cleanliness **5** complete; clear-cut **6** Colloq. showing no record of crime, disease, etc. **7** fair (a clean fight) **8** streamlined; well-formed —adv. **9** completely; outright; simply **10** in a clean manner —v. **11** make or become clean **12** clean up: **a** make tidy **b** Slang. acquire as or make a profit **13** come clean Colloq. confess fully —**clean·li·ness** /klen′lēnis/ n.; **clean′ness** n. [OE]

clean′-cut′ adj. **1** sharply outlined or defined **2** (of a person) neat; groomed

clean′er n. **1** person or thing that cleans **2**

establishment for cleaning clothes, etc. **3 take to the cleaners** *Slang.* defraud or rob

clean·ly /klen'lē/ *adj.* (**·li·er, ·li·est**) habitually clean; with clean habits —**clean'li·ness** *n.*

cleanse /klenz/ *v.* (**cleansed, cleans·ing**) make clean or pure —**cleans'er** *n.*

clear /klēr/ *adj.* **1** free from dirt or contamination **2** (of weather, the sky, etc.) cloudless; fair **3** transparent **4** easily seen or heard; distinct; evident (*a clear voice; it is clear that*) **5** logical and alert (*clear mind*) **6** confident; convinced **7** free from guilt **8** (of a road, etc.) unobstructed **9** net, without deduction **10** free; unhampered —*adv.* **11** in a clear manner **12** completely (*got clear away*) **13** away; out of contact (*keep clear*) —*v.* **14** make or become clear **15** make free from obstruction, etc. **16** show (a person) to be innocent **17** approve for a special duty, access, etc. **18** pass over or by safely **19** make (an amount of money) as a net gain **20** pass through **21 clear the air** remove suspicion, tension, etc. **22 clear with** get approval or authorization from **23 in the clear** free from suspicion or difficulty —**clear'ly** *adj.*; **clear'ness** *n.* [L *clarus*]

clear·ance /klēr'əns/ *n.* **1** space allowed or residual for the passing of two objects **2** special authorization **3** clearing by customs

clear'-cut' *adj.* sharply defined

clear'ing *n.* open area in a forest

clear'ing·house' *n.* **1** *Banking.* establishment where checks and accounts are exchanged and resolved **2** central place for collecting and distributing information

Clear·wa·ter /klēr'wôt'ər, -wät'ər/ *n.* city in Fla. Pop. 98,784

cleat /klēt/ *n.* **1** piece of metal, wood, etc., for fastening ropes to, or for strength **2** projecting piece for traction [OE]

cleav·age /klē'vij/ *n.* **1** hollow between a woman's breasts **2** division; splitting

cleave¹ /klēv/ *v.* (**clove, cleft, or cleaved; cloven, cleft, or cleaved; cleav·ing**) *Lit.* chop apart; split, esp. along the grain [OE]

cleave² *v.* (**cleaved, cleav·ing**) (foll. by *to*) *Lit.* stick fast; adhere [OE]

CLEAVER

cleav·er /klē'vər/ *n.* heavy cutting or chopping tool

clef /klef/ *n. Mus.* symbol indicating the pitch of notes on a staff [L *clavis* key]

cleft¹ /kleft/ *adj.* split; divided [past part. of CLEAVE¹]

cleft² *n.* split; fissure [OE, rel. to CLEAVE¹]

cleft' pal'ate *n.* congenital split in the roof of the mouth

cle·ma·tis /klem'ətəs, kləmat'əs/ *n.* climbing plant with white, pink, or purple flowers [Gk]

Cle·men·ceau /klem'ənsō'/, **Georges Eugène Benjamin** 1841–1929; prime minister of France (1906–09; 1917–20)

Clem·ens /klem'ənz/, **Samuel Langhorne** see TWAIN, MARK

clem·ent /klem'ənt/ *adj.* **1** (of weather) mild **2** merciful —**clem'en·cy** *n.* [L *clemens*]

clench /klenCH/ *v.* **1** close (teeth, fingers, etc.) tightly **2** grasp firmly —*n.* **3** clenching [OE]

Cle·o·pat·ra /klē'əpa'trə/ (Cleopatra VII) 69–30 B.C.; queen of Egypt (47–30)

CLERESTORY

clere·sto·ry /klēr'stôr'ē/ *n.* (*pl.* **·ries**) upper tier of openings or windows in a cathedral or large church [rel. to CLEAR + STORY (of a building)]

cler·gy /klər'jē/ *n.* (*pl.* **·gies**) ordained religious ministers, etc., collectively [Fr, rel. to CLERIC]

cler·ic /kler'ik/ *n.* member of the clergy [Gk *klērikos* fr. *klēros* lot; heritage]

cler·i·cal /kler'ikal/ *adj.* **1** pertaining to clergy **2** pertaining to clerks or office work

clerk /klərk/ *n.* **1** person employed to record or keep proceedings, accounts, etc. **2** secretary or agent of a court, etc. —*v.* **3** work as clerk [OE, rel. to CLERIC]

Cleve·land /klēv'lənd/, (**Stephen**) **Grover** 1837–1908; 22nd and 24th US president (1885–89; 1893–97)

Cleve·land /klēv'lənd/ *n.* city in Ohio. Pop. 505,616

clev·er /klev'ər/ *adj.* (**·er·er, ·er·est**) skillful; talented; quick; adroit; ingenious —**clev'er·ly** *adv.*; **clev'er·ness** *n.* [ME, prob. fr. Scand]

cli·ché /klēshā'/ *n.* hackneyed phrase or idea —**cli·chéd'** *adj.* [Fr]

click /klik/ *n.* **1** slight sharp sound —*v.* **2** (cause to) make a click [imit.]

cli·ent /klī'ənt/ *n.* **1** person using services of a lawyer, architect, or other professional person **2** customer [L *cliens clientis*]

cli·en·tele /klī'əntel', klē'än-/ *n.* **1** clients collectively **2** customers [Fr and L, rel. to CLIENT]

cliff /klif/ *n.* steep rockface, esp. on a coast [OE]

cliff'hang'er *n.* very suspenseful story, ending, etc.

cli·mac·ter·ic /klīmak'tərik, klī'mak'terik/ *n.* crucial period of life, as menopause [Gk, rel. to CLIMAX]

cli·mate /klī'mət/ *n.* **1** prevailing weather conditions of an area **2** region with particular weather conditions **3** prevailing trend of opinion or feeling —**cli·mat·ic** /klīmat'ik/ *adj.*; **cli·mat'i·cal·ly** *adv.* [Gk *klīma* slope]

cli·max /klī'maks/ *n.* 1 point of greatest intensity or interest; culmination 2 orgasm —**cli·mac'tic** /-mak'tik/ *adj.* [Gk: ladder]

climb /klīm/ *v.* 1 ascend; mount; go or come up 2 grow up a wall, etc., by clinging or twining 3 progress —*n.* 4 ascent by climbing 5 hill, etc., climbed or to be climbed —**climb'er** *n.* [OE]

clime /klīm/ *n. Lit.* 1 region 2 climate [L, rel. to CLIMATE]

clinch /klinCH/ *v.* 1 confirm or settle (an argument, bargain, etc.) 2 *Boxing.* become closely engaged 3 secure (a nail or rivet) by driving the point sideways when through —*n.* 4 clinching action or state 5 *Colloq.* embrace [var. of CLENCH]

clinch'er *n. Colloq.* point or remark that settles an argument, etc.

cling /kliNG/ *v.* (**clung, cling·ing**) 1 adhere 2 be unwilling to give up; be dependent on (a habit, idea, friend, etc.) 3 maintain grasp; keep hold —**cling'y** *adj.* (**·i·er, ·i·est**) [OE]

clin·ic /klin'ik/ *n.* 1 private or specialized hospital 2 treatment center 3 instructional session [Gk *klīnē* bed]

clin'i·cal *adj.* 1 of or for the treatment of patients 2 dispassionate; detached —**clin'i·cal·ly** *adv.* [Gk, rel. to CLINIC]

clink /kliNGk/ *n.* 1 sharp ringing sound 2 *Slang.* jail —*v.* 3 (cause to) make a clink [Du: imit.]

clink'er *n.* 1 mass of slag or lava 2 hard residue from burnt coal 3 *Slang.* mistake [Du, rel. to CLINK, 1]

Clin·ton /klint'n/ 1 **DeWitt** 1769–1828; governor of NY state (1817–21; 1825–28); promoter of the Erie Canal 2 **William Jefferson** (**"Bill"**) 1946– ; 42nd US president (1993–); his wife: 3 **Hillary Rodham** 1947–

clip¹ /klip/ *n.* 1 device for holding together or attaching 2 piece of jewelry fastened by a clip 3 set of attached cartridges for a firearm —*v.* (**clipped, clip·ping**) 4 fix with a clip [OE]

clip² *v.* (**clipped, clip·ping**) 1 cut (hair, wool, etc.) short with shears or scissors 2 trim or remove the hair or wool of 3 *Colloq.* hit smartly 4 cut short or omit 5 cut from a newspaper, etc. 6 *Slang.* swindle; rob —*n.* 7 act of clipping 8 *Colloq.* smart blow 9 brief portion from a movie, tape, etc. 10 *Colloq.* speed, esp. rapid [ON]

clip'board' *n.* small board with a spring clip for holding papers

clip'joint' *n. Slang.* club, etc., charging exorbitant prices

clip'per *n.* 1 (usu. *pl.*) tool for clipping hair, etc. 2 *Hist.* fast sailing ship

clip'ping *n.* piece clipped, esp. from a newspaper

clique /klēk, klik/ *n.* small exclusive group of people —**cliqu'ey, cliqu'ish** *adj.* [Fr]

cli·to·ris /klit'ərəs, klitōr'əs/ *n.* erectile part of the female genitals —**cli'to·ral** *adj.* [L fr. Gk]

Clive /klīv/, **Robert** 1725–74; British general and colonial administrator in India

cloak /klōk/ *n.* 1 outdoor usu. long and sleeveless over-garment 2 covering (*cloak of*

snow) —*v.* 3 cover with a cloak 4 conceal; disguise [ult. fr. MedL *clocca* bell (shaped)]

clob·ber /kläb'bər/ *v. Slang.* 1 hit; beat up 2 defeat

cloche /klōSH/ *n.* woman's closefitting bell-shaped hat [Fr: bell]

clock /kläk/ *n.* 1 instrument for measuring and showing time 2 measuring device resembling this —*v.* 3 *Colloq.* **a** attain or register (a stated time, distance, or speed) **b** time (a race, etc.) [MedL *clocca* bell]

clock'wise' *adj. & adv.* in the direction that the hands of a clock turn

clock'work' *n.* 1 mechanism of or like a clock 2 like clockwork regularly; automatically

clod /kläd/ *n.* 1 lump of earth, clay, etc. 2 *Slang.* stupid person [OE]

clod'hop'per *n. Colloq.* large heavy shoe

clog /kläg, klôg/ *n.* 1 shoe with a thick wooden sole —*v.* (**clogged, clog·ging**) 2 obstruct or become obstructed; choke

clois·ter /kloi'stər/ *n.* 1 covered walk around a courtyard, with the side open to the courtyard 2 monastery or convent 3 monastic life or seclusion —*v.* 4 seclude —**clois'tered, clois'tral** /-strəl/ *adj.* [L *claustrum* barrier]

clomp /klämp/ *v.* var. of CLUMP, 3

clone /klōn/ *n.* 1a organisms produced asexually from one stock or ancestor, with matching genetic material **b** one such organism 2 *Colloq.* person or thing regarded as identical to another —*v.* (**cloned, clon·ing**) 3 propagate as a clone —**clon'al** *adj.* [Gk *klōn* twig]

clonk /kläNGk, klôNGk/ *n.* 1 abrupt heavy sound of impact —*v.* 2 make this sound 3 *Colloq.* hit [imit.]

close¹ /klōs/ *adj.* 1 at a short distance or interval 2a having a strong or immediate relation or connection **b** in intimate association **c** corresponding almost exactly (*close resemblance*) 3 in or almost in contact (*close combat*) 4 dense; compact 5 (of a contest) nearly even or equal; narrowly decided 6 rigorous (*close reasoning*) 7 concentrated; searching 8 (of air, etc.) stuffy; humid —*adv.* 9 at only a short distance or interval —**close'ly** *adv.*; **close'ness** *n.* [L *clausus* fr. *claudere* shut]

close² /klōz/ *v.* (**closed, clos·ing**) 1a shut **b** block up 2 bring or come to an end 3 end the day's business 4 bring or come closer or into contact —*n.* 5 conclusion; end 6 **close down** discontinue business 7 **close in: a** enclose **b** come nearer 8 **close up: a** move closer **b** shut **c** block up **d** (of an aperture) grow smaller [L, rel. to CLOSE¹]

closed'-cir'cuit *adj.* (of television) transmitted by cable to a restricted set of receivers

close'-knit' /klōs-/ *adj.* tightly interlocked; closely united

close'shave' *n. Colloq.* narrow escape

clos·et /kläz'it/ *n.* 1 small room 2 cupboard 3 (*attrib.*) secret (*closet drinker*) —*v.* (**·et·ed, ·et·ing**) 4 shut away [MFr dim., rel. to CLOSE²]

close-up /klōs'əp/ *n.* photograph, etc., taken close

clo·sure /klō'ZHər/ *n.* 1 closing 2 closed state 3 procedure for ending a debate and taking a vote [L, rel. to CLOSE²]

clot /klät/ *n.* 1 thick mass of coagulated liquid, etc., esp. of blood —v. **(clot·ted, clot·ting)** 2 form into clots [OE]

cloth /klôth/ n. 1 woven or felted material 2 piece of this, esp. for a particular purpose 3 fabric for clothes 4 (prec. by *the*) the clergy [OE]

clothe /klōᴛʜ/ v. **(clothed or clad, clothing)** 1 provide with clothes 2 cover as with clothes [OE]

clothes /klō(ᴛʜ)z/ n. pl. garments worn to cover the body and limbs [OE]

cloth·ier /klō´ᴛʜēər/ n. seller of clothes

cloth·ing /klō´ᴛʜiNG/ n. clothes collectively

clo·ture /klō´CHər/ n. Parl. ending of debate by calling for an immediate vote

cloud /kloud/ n. 1 visible mass of condensed watery vapor floating high above the ground 2 mass of smoke or dust 3 (foll. by *of*) mass of insects, etc. 4 state of gloom, trouble, or suspicion —v. 5 cover, darken, or trouble 6 become overcast, gloomy, or unclear 7 **on cloud nine** *Colloq.* extremely happy 8 **under a cloud** out of favor, under suspicion 9 **(with one's head) in the clouds** daydreaming —**cloud´less** adj. [OE]

cloud´burst´ n. sudden violent rainstorm

cloud´y adj. **(·i·er, ·i·est)** 1 (of the sky, weather) covered with clouds; overcast 2 not transparent; unclear —**cloud´i·ly** adv.; **cloud´i·ness** n.

Clou·et /klōō-ā´/, Jean c. 1485–1541; French portrait painter

clout /klout/ n. 1 heavy blow 2 *Colloq.* influence or power —v. 3 hit hard [OE]

clove¹ /klōv/ n. dried bud of a tropical plant used as a spice [L *clavus* nail (fr. its shape)]

clove² n. small segment of a compound bulb, esp. of garlic [OE, rel. to CLEAVE¹]

clove³ v. past of CLEAVE¹

clo·ven /klō´vən/ adj. split; divided [past part. of CLEAVE¹]

clo·ver /klō´vər/ n. three-leaved fodder plant [OE]

Clo·vis /klō´vəs/ 465–511; king of the Franks (481–511)

clown /kloun/ n. 1 comic entertainer, esp. in a circus 2 foolish or playful person —v. 3 behave like a clown

cloy /kloi/ v. satiate or sicken with sweetness, richness, etc. [OFr *encloyen* nail up, fr. L *clavus* nail]

CLU abbr. chartered life underwriter

club /kləb/ n. 1 heavy stick with a thick end, esp. as a weapon 2 headed stick used in golf 3 association of persons meeting periodically 4 members' organization or premises 5a playing card of the suit denoted by a black trefoil b (pl.) this suit 6 commercial organization for subscribers —v. **(clubbed, clubbing)** 7 beat with or as with a club [ON]

club´foot´ n. congenitally deformed foot

club´house´ n. 1 building used by a club 2 locker room used by a sports team

club´ sand´wich n. sandwich with two layers between three slices of toast or bread

club´ so´da n. carbonated water

cluck /klək/ n. 1 guttural cry like that of a hen —v. 2 emit cluck(s) [imit.]

clue /klōō/ n. 1 fact or idea that guides or suggests in a problem or investigation 2 piece of evidence 3 verbal hint in a crossword —v.

(clued, clu·ing) 4 provide a clue to [var. of OE *clew*]

clump /kləmp/ n. 1 cluster or mass —v. 2 form a clump 3 (also **clomp**) walk with a heavy tread [LGer or Du]

clum·sy /kləm´zē/ adj. **(·si·er, ·si·est)** 1 awkward in movement or shape 2 difficult to handle or use 3 tactless —**clum´si·ly** adv.; **clum´si·ness** n. [ME *clumsen* numb with cold]

clung /kləNG/ v. past and past part. of CLING

clunk /kləNGk/ n. 1 dull metallic sound —v. 2 make such a sound [imit.]

clus·ter /kləs´tər/ n. 1 aggregated or close group or bunch —v. 2 bring into, come into, or be in cluster(s) [OE]

clutch¹ /kləCH/ v. 1 grasp tightly 2 try desperately to seize —n. 3 tight grasp 4 (pl.) cruel or relentless grasp or control 5a (in a vehicle) device for engaging and disengaging the engine b control operating this [OE]

clutch² n. 1 set of eggs for hatching 2 brood of chickens [ON: hatch]

clut·ter /klət´ər/ n. 1 untidy things; debris 2 untidy state —v. 3 crowd untidily [rel. to CLOT]

cm abbr. centimeter(s)

Cm symb. curium

Cmdr. abbr. commander

CNS abbr. central nervous system

Cnut /kənōōt´, -nyōōt´/ CANUTE

Co symb. cobalt

CO abbr. 1 postal abbr. for Colorado 2 Commanding Officer

co- prefix added to: 1 nouns, with the sense 'joint, mutual' (*co-author*) 2 adjectives and adverbs, with the sense 'jointly, mutually' (*co-equal*) 3 verbs, with the sense 'together with another or others' (*cooperate*) [L, var. of COM-]

Co. abbr. 1 company 2 county

c/o abbr. care of

coach /kōCH/ n. 1 bus, usu. comfortably equipped for long journeys 2 railroad carriage 3 closed horse-drawn carriage 4a instructor or trainer in a sport, etc. b private tutor —v. 5 train or teach as a coach [Fr fr. Magyar]

co·ag·u·late /kō-ag´yəlāt´/ v. **(·lat·ed, ·lat·ing)** 1 change from fluid to semisolid 2 clot; curdle —**co·ag´u·lant** /-lənt/, **co·ag·u·la´tion** n. [L *coagulum* rennet, fr. CO- + *agere* set in motion]

Co·a·hui·la /kō´əwē´lə, kwäwē´lə/ n. N state of Mexico, bordering Texas. Capital: Saltillo. Pop. 1,972,300

coal /kōl/ n. 1 hard black mineral used as fuel 2 piece of this 3 **haul** (or **rake, drag,** or **call**) **over the coals** reprimand [OE]

co·a·lesce /kō´əles´/ v. **(·lesced, ·lesc·ing)** come together and form a whole —**co·a·les´cence** n.; **co·a·les´cent** adj. [L *alere* nourish]

co·a·li·tion /kō´əlish´ən/ n. temporary alliance, esp. of political parties [MedL, rel. to COALESCE]

coal´ tar´ n. thick black oily liquid distilled from coal and used in dyes, etc.

coarse /kôrs/ adj. 1 rough or loose in texture; made of large particles 2 lacking refinement; crude —**coarse´ly** adv.; **coarse´ness** n.

coars·en /kôr′sən/ v. make or become coarse

coast /kōst/ n. 1 land near the sea; seashore —v. 2 ride or move, usu. downhill, without the use of power 3 make progress without much effort 4 the coast is clear there is no danger —**coast′al** adj. [L costa side]

coast·er /kō′stər/ n. small pad or mat for a bottle or glass

coast′line n. line of the seashore

coat /kōt/ n. 1 outer garment with sleeves, usu. extending below the hips 2 animal's fur or hair 3 single covering of paint, etc. —v. 4 cover with a coat or layer 5 form a covering to [OFr fr. Gmc]

coat′ hang·er HANGER, 2

coat′ing n. applied layer

coat′ of arms′ n. heraldic bearings or shield of a person, family, etc.

coat′tail′ n. each flap at the back of a coat

coax /kōks/ v. 1 persuade gradually or by flattery 2 obtain thus 3 manipulate carefully or slowly [obs. cokes a fool]

co·ax·i·al /kō·ak′sēəl/ adj. 1 having a common axis 2 Electr. (of a cable or line) having two concentric conductors separated by an insulator

cob /käb/ n. 1 CORNCOB 2 sturdy horse with short legs [ME cobbe male swan]

co·balt /kō′bôlt′/ n. 1 silvery-white metallic element; symb. Co 2a pigment made from this b its deep-blue color [Ger, prob. kobold demon in mines]

cob·ble¹ /käb′əl/ n. 1 (in full **cob′ble· stone′**) small rounded stone used for paving —v. (**·bled, ·bling**) 2 pave with cobbles [fr. COB]

cob·ble² v. (**·bled, ·bling**) 1 mend or patch up (esp. shoes) 2 join or assemble roughly [fr. COBBLER]

cob·bler¹ /kob′lər/ n. person who mends shoes professionally

cob·bler² n. deep-dish fruit pie

Co·blenz /kō′blens′/ n. (also **Koblenz**) city in Germany. Pop. 108,700

COBRA

co·bra /kō′brə/ n. venomous snake of Africa and Asia [L colubra snake]

cob′web′ n. 1 fine network spun by a spider from liquid it secretes 2 thread of this —**cob′ web′by** adj. [OE coppe spider]

co·ca /kō′kə/ n. 1 S American shrub 2 its dried leaves, chewed as a stimulant [Sp fr. Quechua]

co·caine /kōkān′/ n. drug from coca, an anesthetic and stimulant

coc·cyx /käk′siks/ n. (pl. **coc·cy·ges** /-səjēz′/) small triangular bone at the base of the spinal column [Gk: cuckoo (fr. its shape's resemblance to the bird's bill)]

Co·cha·bam·ba /kō′CHəbäm′bə/ n. city in Bolivia. Pop. 403,600

Co·chin /kōCHin′/ n. seaport in SW India. Pop. 564,000

Co·chise /kōchēs′/ c. 1812–74; Apache Indian chief

cock /käk/ n. 1 male bird, esp. a rooster 2a firing lever in a gun b cocked position of this 3 tap or valve controlling flow —v. 4 turn or move (the eye or ear) attentively or knowingly 5 set aslant; turn up the brim of (a hat) 6 raise the cock of (a gun) [OE]

cock·ade /käkäd′/ n. rosette, etc., worn in the hat as a badge [Fr, rel. to COCK]

cock′-and-bull′ sto′ry n. absurd or incredible account

cock·a·too /käk′ətōō′/ n. crested parrot [Du fr. Malay]

cock·er (span′iel) n. small breed of dog with a silky coat [rel. to COCK]

cock·er·el /käk′ərəl/ n. young rooster [ME, dim. of COCK]

cock·eyed /käk′īd′/ adj. Colloq. 1 crooked, askew 2 absurd; not practical [fr. COCK]

cock′fight′ n. fight between cocks as sport

cock·le /käk′əl/ n. 1a edible bivalve shellfish b its shell 2 **warm the cockles of one's heart** make one contented [MFr fr. L fr. Gk, rel. to CONCH]

cock·ney /käk′nē/ n. (pl. **·neys**) 1 native of London, esp. of the East End 2 dialect or accent used there [ME cokeney cock's egg]

cock′pit′ n. 1 compartment for the pilot (and crew) of an airplane or other craft 2 place for cockfights

cock·roach /käk′rōCH/ n. dark-brown beetlelike verminous insect [Sp cucaracha]

cock′sure′ adj. arrogantly confident [fr. COCK]

cock′tail′ n. 1 mixed alcoholic drink 2 appetizer of shrimp, fruit, etc. 3 any hybrid mixture

cock′y adj. (**·i·er, ·i·est**) Colloq. conceited; arrogant —**cock′i·ly** adv.; **cock′i·ness** n. [fr. COCK]

co·co /kō′kō/ n. (pl. **·cos**) coconut palm [Port and Sp: grimace]

co·coa /kō′kō/ n. 1 powder made from crushed cacao seeds 2 drink made from this [altered fr. CACAO]

co′coa but′ter n. fatty substance obtained from the cocoa bean

co·co·nut /kō′kənət′/ n. fruit of the coconut palm, with hard shell and edible white lining enclosing milky juice

co·coon /kəkōōn′/ n. 1 silky case spun by insect larvae for protection as pupae 2 protective covering [Prov coco shell]

Coc·teau /käktō′/, **Jean** 1889–1963; French dramatist and film director

cod /käd/ n. (pl. same or -s) sea fish used as food

COD abbr. cash or collect on delivery

Cod, Cape /käd/ n. peninsula on SE coast of Mass.; popular resort area

co·da /kō′də/ n. 1 added final musical passage 2 any concluding section [L cauda tail]

cod·dle /käd′l/ v. (**·dled, ·dling**) 1 protect attentively; pamper 2 cook (an egg) in water below boiling point

code /kōd/ n. 1 system of words, letters, symbols, signals, etc., used for secrecy or brevity **2** system of laws, etc. **3** standard of moral behavior —*v.* (**cod·ed, cod·ing**) **4** put into code [L CODEX]

co·deine /kōˈdēn/ *n.* analgesic alkaloid from morphine [Gk *kōdeia* poppy-head]

co·dex /kōˈdeks/ *n.* (*pl.* **·di·ces** /-dəsēz′/) ancient manuscript text in book form [L: tablet; book]

cod′fish′ *n.* COD

cod·ger /käjˈər/ *n. Colloq.* older, often eccentric person

cod·i·cil /kädˈəsəl/ *n.* addition to a will [L dim. of CODEX]

cod·i·fy /kädəfī′, kō′-/ *v.* (**·fied, ·fy·ing**) arrange (laws, etc.) systematically into a code —**cod′i·fi·ca′tion, cod′i·fi′er** *n.*

cod′-liv′er oil′ *n.* oil from cod livers, rich in vitamins D and A

cod′piece *n. Hist.* bag or flap at front of a man's breeches [ME *cod* scrotum + PIECE]

Co·dy /kōdˈē/, **"Buffalo Bill" (William Frederick)** 1846–1917; US army scout and showman

co·ed /kōˈed′/ *Colloq. n.* **1** often *Offens.* female student —*adj.* **2** coeducational [abbr.]

co·ed·u·ca·tion /kōˈej′əkāˈsHən/ *n.* education of both sexes together —**co′ed·u·ca′tion·al** *adj.*

co·ef·fi·cient /kōˈəfiSHˈənt/ *n.* **1** *Math.* quantity placed before and multiplying an algebraic expression **2** *Physics.* multiplier or factor by which a property is measured (*coefficient of expansion*) [rel. to CO- + EFFICIENT]

coe·len·ter·ate /silentˈərāt′/ *n.* marine animal with tube- or cup-shaped body, e.g., jellyfish [Gk *koilos* hollow + *enteron* intestine]

co·e·qual /kō-ēˈkwəl/ *adj. & n. Formal* or *Lit.* equal

co·erce /kō-ərs′/ *v.* (**·erced, ·erc·ing**) persuade or restrain by force —**co·er′ci·ble** *adj.*; **co·er′cion** /-ərˈzHən, -ərˈsHən/ *n.*; **co·er′cive** *adj.* [L *coercere* restrain]

co·e·val /kō-ēˈvəl/ *Formal. adj.* **1** of the same age; contemporary —*n.* **2** coeval person or thing —**co·e′val·ly** *adv.* [L *aevum* age]

co·ex·ist /kōˈigzist′/ *v.* **1** exist together **2** show mutual tolerance —**co′ex·ist′ence** *n.*; **co′ex·is′tent** *adj.*

co·ex·ten·sive /kōˈiksten′siv/ *adj.* extending over the same space or time

cof·fee /kôfˈē, käfˈē/ *n.* **1a** drink made from roasted and ground beanlike seeds of a tropical shrub **b** cup of this **2a** the shrub **b** its seeds **3** pale brown [Turk fr. Ar]

cof′fee break′ *n.* brief respite from work

cof′fee·cake′ *n.* sweet cake served with coffee or as dessert

cof′fee·house′ *n.* cafe or small club, often with entertainment

cof′fee shop′ *n.* small informal restaurant

cof′fee ta′ble *n.* small low table

cof·fer /kôfˈər, käfˈər/ *n.* **1** large strong box for valuables **2** (*pl.*) treasury; funds [L *cophinus* basket]

cof′fer·dam′ *n.* watertight enclosure for underwater work

cof·fin /kôfˈin, käfˈin/ *n.* box in which a corpse is buried or cremated [L fr. Gk]

cog /käg, kôg/ *n.* **1** each of a series of projections on a wheel or bar transferring motion

111   **codeine / coitus**

by engaging with another series **2** unimportant worker [prob. Scand]

co·gent /kōˈjənt/ *adj.* (of an argument, etc.) convincing; compelling —**co′gen·cy** *n.*; **co′gent·ly** *adv.* [L *cogere* drive; collect]

cog·i·tate /käjˈətāt′/ *v.* (**·tat·ed, ·tat·ing**) ponder; meditate —**cog′i·ta′tion** *n.*; **cog′i·ta′tive** *adj.* [L *cogitare*]

cog·nac /kōnˈyak′/ *n.* high-quality brandy, esp. from Cognac in France

cog·nate /kägˈnāt′/ *adj.* **1** related to or descended from a common ancestor **2** (of a word) having the same derivation —*n.* **3** cognate word [L *cognatus*]

cog·ni·tion /kägniSHˈən/ *n.* **1** knowing, perceiving, or conceiving as an act or faculty **2** result of this —**cog·ni′tion·al, cog′ni·tive** *adj.* [L *cognitio*, rel. to COGNIZANCE]

cog·ni·zance /kägˈnəzəns/ *n.* **1** knowledge or awareness; perception **2** sphere of observation or concern [L *cognoscere* get to know]

cog′ni·zant *adj.* (foll. by *of*) having knowledge or being aware

cog·no·men /kägˈnəmən, kägnōˈ-/ *n.* a name, esp. nickname [L]

cog′wheel′ *n.* wheel with cogs

co·hab·it /kōhabˈit/ *v.* (**·it·ed, ·it·ing**) (esp. of an unmarried couple) live together —**co′hab·i·ta′tion** *n.* [L *habitare* dwell]

Co·han /kōˈhan/, **George M(ichael)** 1878–1942; US singer, songwriter, and dramatist

co·here /kōhēr′/ *v.* (**·hered, ·her·ing**) **1** stick together; remain united **2** be logical or consistent [L *haerere* stick]

co·her·ent /kōhērˈənt, -herˈ-/ *adj.* **1** intelligible and articulate **2** (of an argument, etc.) consistent **3** *Optics.* of waves with a fixed phase relationship —**co·her′ence** *n.*; **co·her′ent·ly** *adv.*

co·he·sion /kōhēˈzHən/ *n.* tendency to cohere —**co·he′sive** *adj.*

co·hort /kōˈhôrt′/ *n.* **1** band of warriors **2** associates banded together [L]

coif /kwäf/ *v.* dress or arrange (the hair) [OFr *coiffe*]

coif·fure /kwäfyŏŏr′/ *n.* hairstyle [Fr]

coil /koil/ *v.* **1** arrange or be arranged in spirals or concentric rings **2** move sinuously —*n.* **3** something so arranged, as rope **4** *Electr.* wire in a spiral [Fr, perh. rel. to CULL]

Co·im·ba·tore /koimˈbətôr′, -tōr-/ *n.* city in SW India. Pop. 853,400

coin /koin/ *n.* **1** stamped disk of metal used as money **2** metal money, collectively —*v.* **3** make (coins) by stamping **4** invent (esp. a new word or phrase) —**coin·age** /koiˈnij/ *n.* [L *cuneus* wedge]

co·in·cide /kōˈinsīd′/ *v.* (**·cid·ed, ·cid·ing**) **1** occur at the same time **2** occupy the same space **3** agree or be identical [L, rel. to INCIDENT]

co·in·ci·dence /kō-inˈsədəns, -dens′/ *n.* **1** coinciding **2** remarkable concurrence of events, etc., apparently by chance —**co·in′ci·dent** *adj.*

co·in·ci·den·tal /kō-inˈsədentˈl/ *adj.* in the nature of or resulting from a coincidence —**co·in′ci·den′tal·ly** *adv.*

co·i·tus /kōˈitəs, kō-ēˈtəs/ *n.* sexual intercourse —co'i·tal *adj.* [L: coming together; uniting]

coke[1] /kōk/ *n.* solid fuel made by extracting gases from coal [OE, rel. to COAL]

coke[2] *n. Slang.* cocaine [abbr.]

col- *prefix* var. of COM- before *l*

col. *abbr.* column

Col. *abbr.* Colonel

co·la /kō'lə/ *n.* (also ko'la) 1 W African tree whose seeds yield an extract containing caffeine 2 carbonated drink flavored with this [W Afr]

COLA *abbr.* cost-of-living allowance (or adjustment)

col·an·der /kəl'əndər, käl'-/ *n.* perforated cooking vessel to drain liquid [L *colum* strainer]

Col·bert /kôlber'/, Jean Baptiste 1619–83; chief minister to Louis XIV of France (1661–83)

cold /kōld/ *adj.* 1 of or at a low temperature 2 not heated 3 feeling cool or chilly 4 lacking friendliness or affection 5 depressing, uninteresting 6 *Colloq.* unconscious (*out cold*) 7 (in games) far from finding what is sought —*n.* 8a prevalence of low temperature b cold weather or environment 9 viral infection of the nose or throat with sneezing, etc. —*adv.* 10 completely (*stopped cold*) 11 in cold blood without emotion; deliberately 12 out in the cold ignored; neglected —cold'ly *adv.*; cold'ness *n.* [OE]

cold'-blood'ed *adj.* 1 having a body temperature varying with that of the environment 2 deliberately cruel —cold'-blood'ed·ly *adv.*; cold'-blood'ed·ness *n.*

cold' cream' *n.* cleansing preparation for the skin

cold' cuts' *n.* sliced meats and cheeses, as for sandwiches

cold' feet' *n. pl. Colloq.* loss of nerve

cold' shoul'der *n.* (prec. by *the*) intentional unfriendliness

cold' sore' *n.* inflammation and blisters from a viral infection

cold' tur'key *n. Slang.* abrupt withdrawal from addictive drugs

cold' war' *n.* conflict between nations without actual fighting

Cole /kōl/, Nat "King" 1919–65; US popular singer and pianist

Cole·ridge /kō'lərij/, Samuel Taylor 1772–1834; English poet, critic, and philosopher

cole·slaw /kōl'slô'/ *n.* dressed salad of sliced raw cabbage [Du *koolsla* cabbage salad]

Co·lette /kəlet'/ (born Sidonie Gabrielle Claudine Colette) 1873–1954; French novelist

co·le·us /kō'lēəs/ *n.* decorative plant with variegated leaves [Gk *koleos* sheath]

col·ic /käl'ik/ *n.* severe spasmodic abdominal pain —col'ick·y *adj.* [L fr. Gk, rel. to COLON[2]]

Co·li·ma /kəlē'mə/ *n.* state in SW Mexico, on the Pacific Ocean. Capital: Colima. Pop. 428,500

co·li·tis /kōlīt'is, kə-/ *n.* colon inflammation

col·lab·o·rate /kəlab'ərāt'/ *v.* (·rat·ed, ·rat-ing) 1 work together 2 cooperate with an enemy —col·lab'o·ra'tion *n.*; col·lab'o·ra-tive /-ərətiv/ *adj.*; col·lab'o·ra·tor *n.* [LL, rel. to LABOR]

col·lage /kəläzh'/ *n.* art work with various materials fixed to a backing [Fr: gluing]

col·lapse /kəlaps'/ *n.* 1 falling down or in of a structure 2 sudden failure of physical or mental breakdown; exhaustion —*v.* (·lapsed, ·laps·ing) 3 (cause to) undergo collapse 5 *Colloq.* lie or sit after strenuous effort 6 fold up —col·lap'si·ble *adj.* [L *collapsus* fr. *collabi* fall]

col·lar /käl'ər/ *n.* 1 garment part encircling the neck 2 band of leather, etc., for an animal's neck 3 encircling part, device, etc. —*v.* 4 capture; seize, as by the collar [L *collum* neck]

col'lar·bone' *n.* bone joining the breastbone and shoulderblade

col·late /kəlāt', kō'lāt', käl'āt'/ *v.* (·lat·ed, ·lat·ing) 1 assemble in order 2 compare (texts, statements, etc.) —col'la·tor *n.* [L, rel. to CONFER]

col·lat·er·al /kəlat'ərəl/ *n.* 1 security pledged as a guarantee of repayment 2 person having the same ancestor as another but by a different line —*adj.* 3 descended from the same ancestor but by a different line 4 side by side; parallel 5a additional but subordinate b contributory —col·lat'er·al·ly *adv.* [MedL, rel. to LATERAL]

col·la·tion /kəlā'shən, kō-/ *n.* 1 collating 2 light meal [L, rel. to COLLATE]

col·league /käl'ēg/ *n.* fellow worker; associate [L *collega* fr. *legere* gather]

col·lect /kəlekt'/ *v.* 1 bring or come together; assemble; accumulate 2 systematically acquire, esp. as a hobby 3 obtain (contributions, etc.) 4a *refl.* regain control of oneself b concentrate (one's thoughts) c (as collected *adj.*) not perturbed or distracted —*adj.* & *adv.* 5 (of a telephone call) to be paid for by the receiver [L *collectus* fr. *legere* gather]

col·lect·i·ble /kəlek'təbəl/ *adj.* (also col-lect'a·ble) 1 worth collecting —*n.* 2 item sought by collectors

col·lec'tion *n.* 1 collecting or being collected 2 things collected 3 money collected, esp. at a meeting or service

col·lec'tive *adj.* 1 pertaining to a group or society as a whole; joint; shared —*n.* 2 cooperative enterprise 3 COLLECTIVE NOUN —col-lec'tive·ly *adv.*

col·lec'tive bar'gain·ing *n.* negotiation of wages, etc. by an organized body of employees

col·lec'tive noun' *n.* singular noun denoting a collection or number of individuals (e.g., *assembly, family, troop*)

col·lec'tiv·ism' *n.* collective ownership of land and the means of production —col·lec'tiv·ist *n.* & *adj.*

col·lec'tor *n.* 1 person who collects things of interest 2 person who collects payment due

col·leen /käl'ēn/ *n.* girl [Ir *cailín*]

col·lege /käl'ij/ *n.* 1 establishment for further, higher, or professional education 2 major branch of a university 3 organized body of

col·le·giate /kəlēj'(ē)ət/ *adj.* pertaining to a college

col·lide /kəlīd'/ *v.* (**·lid·ed**, **·lid·ing**) come into collision or conflict [L *collidere* clash]

col·lie /käl'ē/ *n.* long-haired dog, orig. bred in Scotland [perh. fr. *coll* COAL]

COLLIE

col·lier·y /käl'yərē/ *n.* (*pl.* **·ies**) esp. *Brit.* coal mine and its buildings

col·li·sion /kəlizH'ən/ *n.* 1 violent impact of a moving body with another or with a fixed object 2 clashing of interests, etc. [L, rel. to COLLIDE]

col·loid /käl'oid/ *n.* substance consisting of microscopic particles suspended in a liquid or other medium **—col·loi·dal** /kəloid'l/ *adj.* [Gk *kolla* glue]

col·lo·qui·al /kəlō'kwēəl/ *adj.* of informal or familiar conversation **—col·lo'qui·al·ism** *n.*; **col·lo'qui·al·ly** *adv.* [L, rel. to COLLOQUY]

col·lo·qui·um /kəlō'kwēəm/ *n.* (*pl.* **·ums** or **·qui·a**) academic conference or seminar [L, rel. to COLLOQUY]

col·lo·quy /käl'əkwē/ *n.* (*pl.* **·quies**) *Lit.* conversation; talk [L *loqui* speak]

col·lude /kəlōōd'/ *v.* (**·lud·ed**, **·lud·ing**) conspire together **—col·lu'sion** /-lōō'zHən/ *n.*; **col·lu'sive** *adj.* [L *ludere lusi* play]

Colo. *abbr.* Colorado

co·logne /kəlōn'/ *n.* perfumed water for the face, etc. [Fr. *eau de cologne* water of COLOGNE]

Co·logne *n.* (German name **Köln**) city in W Germany. Pop. 953,551

Co·lom·bi·a /kəlem'bēə/ *n.* republic on the NW coast of S America. Capital: Bogotá. Pop. 34,252,000 **—Co·lom'bi·an** *n.* & *adj.*

Co·lom·bo /kəlem'bō/ *n.* capital of Sri Lanka. Pop. 615,000

co·lon[1] /kō'lən/ *n.* punctuation mark (:), used esp. to set off something to follow [Gk: clause]

co·lon[2] *n.* lower and greater part of the large intestine [L fr. Gk]

colo·nel /karn'l/ *n.* *Milit.* officer ranking just below brigadier general **—colo'nel·cy** *n.* (*pl.* **·cies**) [It *colonnello*, rel. to COLUMN]

co·lo·ni·al /kəlō'nēəl/ *adj.* 1 pertaining to a colony or colonies 2 pertaining to colonialism **—**n.** 3 inhabitant of a colony

co·lo·ni·al·ism *n.* policy of acquiring or maintaining colonies esp. for economic advantage **—co·lo'ni·al·ist** *n.* & *adj.*

colo·nist /käl'ənist/ *n.* settler in or inhabitant of a colony

col·o·nize *v.* (**·nized**, **·niz·ing**) establish a colony in **—col'o·ni·za'tion** *n.*

col·on·nade /käl'ənäd'/ *n.* row of columns, esp. supporting a wall or roof **—col'on·nad'ed** *adj.* [Fr, rel. to COLUMN]

COLONNADE

col·o·ny /käl'ənē/ *n.* (*pl.* **·nies**) 1a settlement or settlers in a new country, fully or partly subject to the mother country b their territory 2 people of one nationality, vocation, interest, etc., forming a community 3 group of animals, plants, etc., living close together [L *colonia* farm]

co·lo·phon /käl'əfən, -fän'/ *n.* publisher's imprint [Gk: summit]

color /kəl'ər/ *n.* 1 sensation produced by visible wavelengths of light 2 one, or any mixture, of the constituents into which light can be separated as in a spectrum or rainbow 3 coloring substance, esp. paint 4 use of colors in photography, etc. 5 skin pigmentation, esp. when dark 6 ruddiness 7 (*pl.*) appearance or aspect (*saw them in their true colors*) 8 (*pl.*) insignia, symbol, flag, etc. 9 richness or variety in music, literature, etc. **—**v.** 10 apply color to 11 influence 12 misrepresent; exaggerate 13 take on color; blush 14 **show one's true colors** reveal one's true character or intentions [L *color*]

Col·o·ra·do /käl'ərad'ō, -räd'ō/ *n.* mountainous state of the W US. Capital: Denver. Pop. 3,294,394. Abbr. **CO** **—Col·o·ra'dan, Col'o·ra'do·an** *n.* & *adj.*

Col'o·rad'o Riv'er *n.* river flowing 1,450 mi. SW from Colo. into the Gulf of California

Col'o·rad'o Springs' *n.* city in Colo. Pop. 281,140

col·or·a'tion *n.* coloring [L, rel. to COLOR]

col·or·a·tu·ra /kal'ərət(y)ŏŏr'ə/ *n.* 1 elaborate ornamentation of a vocal melody 2 soprano skilled in this [It, rel. to COLOR]

col'or-blind' *adj.* unable to distinguish certain colors **—col'or-blind'ness** *n.*

col·ored /kəl'ərd/ *adj.* 1 having color 2 often *Offens.* wholly or partly of nonwhite descent

col'or·fast' *adj.* having color or dye not prone to fading

col'or·ful *adj.* 1 full of color; bright 2 fascinating; vivid **—col'or·ful·ly** *adv.*

col'or·ing *n.* 1 appearance as regards color, esp. complexion 2 use of color 3 substance giving color

col'or·ize *v.* (**·ized**, **·iz·ing**) convert finished black-and-white films to color using computer technology

col'or·less *adj.* 1 without color 2 lacking character or interest

col'or line' *n.* social or other barrier imposed on racial grounds

co·los·sal /kəläs'əl/ *adj.* huge **—co·los'sal·ly** *adv.* [rel. to COLOSSUS]

co·los·sus /kəläs′əs/ n. (pl. ·si /-ī′/ or ·sus·es) 1 statue much bigger than life size 2 prodigious empire, personage, etc. [L fr. Gk: statue]

co·los·to·my /kələs′təmē/ n. (pl. ·mies) Med. surgical opening from the colon through the abdominal wall to provide an artificial anus [fr. COLON?]

colt /kōlt/ n. young male horse —**colt′ish** adj. [OE]

Colt /kōlt/, **Samuel** 1814–62; US developer of the Colt revolver

Col·trane /kōltrān′, kōl′trān/, **John William** 1926–67; US jazz musician

Co·lum·ba, St. /kələm′bə/ c. 521–597; Irish abbot and missionary

Co·lum·bi·a /kələm′bēə/ n. 1 capital of S. Car., in the central part. Pop. 98,052 2 city in Mo. Pop. 69,101

Co·lum·bi·a Riv·er n. river flowing 1,200 mi. from W Canada through Wash., and along the Wash.-Ore. border into the Pacific

col·um·bine /käl′əmbīn′/ n. garden plant with purple-blue flowers like a cluster of doves [L columba dove]

Co·lum·bus /kələm′bəs/, **Christopher** 1451–1506; Italian-born explorer for Spain; initiated European colonization of America (1492)

Co·lum·bus /kələm′bəs/ n. capital of Ohio, in the central part. Pop. 632,910

col·umn /käl′əm/ n. 1 supporting upright or pillar, usu. circular 2 column-shaped object, stream, etc. 3 vertical division of a printed page 4 part of a newspaper, etc., regularly devoted to a particular subject 5 vertical row of figures in accounts, etc. 6 line of troops, vehicles, etc. —**co·lum·nar** /kələm′nər/ adj.; **col′umned** adj. [L columna]

col·um·nist /käl′əmnist/ n. journalist contributing regularly to a newspaper, etc.

com- prefix (also **co-, col-, con-,** or **cor-**) with; together; jointly; or used as an intensive [L com- fr. cum with]

co·ma /kō′mə/ n. (pl. ·mas) prolonged deep unconsciousness [L fr. Gk]

co·ma·tose /kō′mətōs′/ adj. 1 in a coma 2 drowsy; sleepy

comb /kōm/ n. 1a toothed strip of rigid material for grooming the hair b similar curved decorative strip worn in the hair 2 tool used or shaped like a comb 3 red fleshy crest of a fowl, esp. a cock —v. 4 draw a comb through 5 dress (wool, etc.) 6 Colloq. search (a place) thoroughly [OE]

com·bat /kom′bat′/ n. 1 fight; struggle; contest —v. (·bat·ed, ·bat·ing) 2 oppose; strive against [L battuere strike]

com·bat·ant /kəmbat′nt/ n. 1 person engaged in fighting —adj. 2 fighting 3 for fighting

com·bat′ive adj. pugnacious

com·bi·na·tion /käm′bənā′sHən/ n. 1 combining or being combined 2 combined set 3 sequence used to open a combination lock [L, rel. to COMBINE]

com·bi·na′tion lock′ n. lock operated by a preset sequence of numbers, etc.

com·bine v. /kəmbīn′/ (·bined, ·bin·ing) 1 join together; unite 2 possess (qualities usually distinct) together 3 form or cause to form a chemical compound —n. /käm′bīn′/ 4 (in full **com′bine har′vest·er**) machine that reaps and threshes in one operation 5 combination of esp. commercial interests [L bini a pair]

comb·ings /kō′miNGz/ n. pl. hairs combed off

com·bin′ing form′ n. linguistic element used in combination with another to form a word (e.g., Anglo-'English')

com·bo /käm′bō/ n. (pl. ·bos) Slang. small jazz or dance band [abbr. of COMBINATION]

com·bus·ti·ble /kəmbəs′təbəl/ adj. 1 capable of or used for burning —n. 2 combustible substance —**com·bus′ti·bil′i·ty** n. [LL combustibilis fr. comburere burn up]

com·bus·tion /kəmbəs′cHən/ n. 1 burning 2 chemical generation of light and heat

Comdr. abbr. commander

come /kəm/ v. (came, com·ing) 1 move, be brought towards, or reach a place 2 reach a specified situation or result (came to no harm) 3 reach or extend to a specified point 4 traverse or accomplish (have come a long way) 5 happen (how did you come to break your leg?) 6 live or occur (May comes after Claudius) 7 be recallable (it will come to me) 8 be available (comes in three sizes) 9 become (come loose) 10 (foll. by from, of) a be descended from b be the result of (that comes of complaining) 11 Colloq. when a specified time is reached (come next month) 12 come about happen 13 come across (or upon) meet or find by chance 14 come along: a make progress b arrive 15 come around (or round): a pay an informal visit b regain consciousness c be won over 16 come away become detached 17 come by: a call on a visit b obtain 18 come down lose position or wealth 19 come into: a achieve prominence, etc. b receive, esp. as an heir 20 come off: a (of an action) succeed; occur b fare (badly, well, etc.) c be detached or detachable (from) 21 come out: a emerge; become known b be produced or issued c be removed d declare oneself openly e declare that one is a homosexual 22 come through: a complete successfully b do what is required 23 come to: a recover consciousness b amount to 24 come up: a arise; present itself b be mentioned or discussed c (foll. by with) produce (an idea, etc.) 25 come upon: a meet or find by chance b attack by surprise [OE]

come′back′ n. 1 return to a previous (esp successful) state 2 Slang. rejoinder

co·me·di·an /kəmēd′ēən/ n. humorous entertainer or actor [MFr]

co·me·di·enne /kəmēd′ē·en′/ n. female comedian [Fr fem.]

come′down′ n. 1 loss of status 2 disappointment

com·e·dy /käm′ədē/ n. (pl. ·dies) 1a play, film, etc., of amusing character, usu. with a happy ending b such works as a dramatic genre 2 humor; amusing doings, behavior, etc. —**co·me·dic** /kəmēd′ik/ adj. [Gk, rel. to COMIC]

come·ly /kəm′lē/ adj. (·li·er, ·li·est) good looking —**come′li·ness** n. [OE]

come′-on′ n. Slang. enticement

co·mes·ti·bles /kəmes'təbəlz/ *n. pl. Formal or Joc.* food [Fr fr. L]

com·et /käm'it/ *n. Astron.* object moving in a path around the sun, usu. with a luminous tail [Gk *komētēs*]

come·up·pance /kəm'əp'əns/ *n. Colloq.* deserved punishment [*come up* + -ANCE]

com·fort /kəm'fərt/ *n.* **1a** state of physical well-being **b** (usu. *pl.*) things that make life easy or pleasant **2** relief of suffering; consolation **3** that giving consolation —*v.* **4** soothe; console [L *fortis* strong]

com·fort·a·ble /kəm'fərtəbəl, kəmf'tərbəl/ *adj.* **1** giving ease **2** free from discomfort; at ease in body, mind, condition, etc. —**com'fort·a·bly** *adv.*

com·fort·er /kəm'fərtər/ *n.* **1** person who comforts **2** quilted bedspread

com·fy /kəm'fē/ *adj.* (·fi·er, ·fi·est) *Colloq.* comfortable [abbr.]

com·ic /käm'ik/ *adj.* **1** pertaining to comedy **2** funny —*n.* **3** comedian **4a** COMIC STRIP **b** (*pl.*) newspaper section with comic strips —**com'i·cal** *adj.*; **com'i·cal·ly** *adv.* [Gk *kōmos* revel]

com'ic strip' *n.* sequence of cartoon drawings that tell a story, as in a newspaper

com·ing /kəm'iNG/ *adj.* **1** approaching; next (*the coming week*) —*n.* **2** arrival

com·i·ty /käm'itē/ *n.* (*pl.* ·ties) *Formal.* courtesy; friendship [L *comis* courteous]

comm. *abbr.* **1** commerce **2** commission **3** committee **4** community

com·ma /käm'ə/ *n.* punctuation mark (,) indicating a pause or break [Gk: clause]

com·mand /kəmand'/ *v.* **1** give a formal order or instruction to **2** have authority or control over **3** have at one's disposal or within reach (a skill, resources, etc.) **4** deserve and get (sympathy, respect, etc.) **5** look down over or on —*n.* **6** order; instruction **7** mastery; control **8** exercise or tenure of authority, esp. military **9a** body of troops, etc. **b** district under a commander [L COM- + *mandare* trust]

com·man·dant /käm'əndant', -dänt'/ *n.* commanding officer, as of a fort or special unit [Fr or It or Sp, rel. to COMMAND]

com·man·deer /käm'əndēr'/ *v.* seize (esp. goods) for military or other use [Afrik *kommanderen*]

com·mand·er /kəman'dər/ *n.* **1** person who commands **2** *US Navy.* officer ranking just below captain

com·mand'er in chief' *n.* (*pl.* **com·mand'ers in chief'**) supreme commander, esp. of a nation's forces

com·mand'ing *adj.* **1** impressive **2** (of a position) giving a wide view **3** (of an advantage, etc.) substantial (*commanding lead*)

com·mand'ment *n.* divine command, esp. one of the TEN COMMANDMENTS

com·man·do /kəman'dō/ *n.* (*pl.* ·**dos**) *Milit.* member of a special unit trained for raids [Port, rel. to COMMAND]

com·mem·o·rate /kəmem'ərāt'/ *v.* (·rat·ed, ·rat·ing) **1** preserve in memory by a celebration or ceremony **2** be a memorial of —**com·mem'o·ra'tion** *n.*; **com·mem'o·ra'tive** /-ərətiv, -ərā'tiv/ *adj.* [L, rel. to MEMORY]

com·mence /kəmens'/ *v.* (·menced, ·menc·ing) begin [L, rel. to COM- + INITIATE]

com·mence'ment *n.* **1** beginning **2** graduation ceremony

com·mend /kəmend'/ *v.* **1** praise **2** entrust; commit **3** recommend —**com'men·da'tion** *n.* [L, rel. to MANDATE]

com·mend·a·ble /kəmen'dəbəl/ *adj.* praiseworthy —**com·mend'a·bly** *adv.*

com·men·su·ra·ble /kəmen's(ə)rəbəl, -sH(ə)rə-/ *adj.* measurable by the same standard —**com·men'su·ra·bil'i·ty** *n.* [L, rel. to MEASURE]

com·men·su·rate /kəmen's(ə)rət, -sH(ə)rət/ *adj.* **1** coextensive **2** proportionate

com·ment /käm'ent/ *n.* **1** brief critical or explanatory remark or note; opinion **2** commenting; criticism (*aroused much comment*) —*v.* **3** make (esp. critical) remarks [L]

com·men·tar·y /käm'ənter'ē/ *n.* (*pl.* ·**ies**) **1** descriptive account of an event or performance as it happens **2** explanatory notes [L]

com·men·ta·tor /käm'əntāt'ər/ *n.* person who provides a commentary, esp. on news [L]

com·merce /käm'ərs/ *n.* financial transactions; trading [L *mercari* deal; trade]

com·mer·cial /kəmər'sHəl/ *adj.* **1** pertaining to commerce **2** seeking profit —*n.* **3** television or radio advertisement —**com·mer'cial·ly** *adv.*

com·mer'cial·ism *n.* **1** commercial practices **2** emphasis on financial profit

com·mer'cial·ize *v.* (·ized, ·iz·ing) **1** exploit or spoil for profit **2** make commercial —**com·mer'cial·i·za'tion** *n.*

com·min·gle /kəmiNG'gəl/ *v.* (·gled, ·gling) mingle together

com·mis·er·ate /kəmiz'ərāt'/ *v.* (·at·ed, ·at·ing) express or feel sympathy (with) —**com·mis·er·a'tion** *n.* [L, rel. to MISER]

com·mis·sar·y /käm'əser'ē/ *n.* (*pl.* ·**ies**) **1** *Milit.* store for food and supplies **2** cafeteria, as in a film studio [L, rel. to COMMIT]

com·mis·sion /kəmisH'ən/ *n.* **1a** authority to perform a task, etc. **b** person(s) entrusted with such authority **c** task, etc., given to such person(s) **2** order for something to be produced specially **3** *Milit.* a warrant conferring rank of officer **b** rank so conferred **4** pay or percentage paid to an agent **5** act of committing (a crime, etc.) —*v.* **6** empower by commission **7a** give (an artist, etc.) a commission for a piece of work **b** order (a work) to be made **8** bring (a ship, etc.) into operation **9** in (or out of) commission ready (or not ready) for service [L, rel. to COMMIT]

com·mis·sion·er /kəmisH'(ə)nər/ *n.* **1** leader appointed by a commission **2** member of a government commission **3** government representative [MedL, rel. to COMMISSION]

com·mit /kəmit'/ *v.* (·mit·ted, ·mit·ting) **1** do or make (a crime, blunder, etc.) **2** entrust or consign for safe keeping, treatment, etc. **3** send (a person) to prison **4** pledge or bind (esp. oneself) [L *committere*]

com·mit'ment *n.* **1** obligation **2** committing or being committed **3** dedication

com·mit·tee /kəmit'ē/ *n.* body of persons appointed for a special function [fr. COMMIT + -EE]

com·mode /kəmōd'/ *n.* **1** toilet **2** chest of drawers [L *commodum* convenience]

com·mo·di·ous /kəmō′dēəs/ *adj.* roomy

com·mod·i·ty /kəmäd′ətē/ *n.* (*pl.* **·ties**) article of trade, esp. a raw material or product [L, rel. to COMMODE]

com·mo·dore /käm′ədôr′/ *n.* **1** *US Navy Hist.* naval officer above captain **2** commander of a division of a fleet **3** president of a yacht club [Fr, rel. to COMMANDER]

com·mon /käm′ən/ *adj.* (·er, ·est) **1a** occurring often **b** ordinary; not special **2** general; public **3** low-class; inferior **4** familiar (*common cold*) **5** *Math.* belonging to two or more quantities (*common denominator*) —*n.* **6** piece of open public land **7 in common: a** in joint use; shared **b** of joint interest —**com′mon·ly** *adv.* [L *communis*]

com·mon·al·i·ty /käm′ənal′ətē/ *n.* (*pl.* **·ties**) **1** sharing of an attribute **2** common occurrence **3** (also com′mon·al·ty) **a** the common people **b** body of people or members

com·mon·er /käm′ənər/ *n.* one of the common people; not a noble [MedL, rel. to COMMON]

com′mon law′ *n.* unwritten law based on custom and precedent

Com′mon Mar′ket *n.* EUROPEAN UNION

com′mon noun′ *n. Gram.* name denoting a class of objects or a concept

com′mon·place′ *adj.* **1** trite; ordinary —*n.* **2** event, topic, etc., that is ordinary or usual **3** trite remark [translation of L *locus communis*]

com·mons /käm′ənz/ *n. pl.* **1** dining hall, as at a college **2** common people

com′mon sense′ *n.* sound practical sense

com′mon·wealth′ *n.* **1a** independent state or community, esp. a democratic republic **b** official designation for four US states (Ky., Mass., Penn., Va.) **2** (the Com′monwealth′) association of the UK with states previously part of the British Empire **3** federation of states

com·mo·tion /kəmō′SHən/ *n.* confused and noisy disturbance; uproar [L, rel. to COM- + *movere* move]

com·mu·nal /kəmyōōn′l, käm′yən-l/ *adj.* shared between members of a group or community —**com·mu′nal·ly** *adv.* [L, rel. to COMMUNE[1]]

com·mune[1] /käm′yōōn/ *n.* **1** group of people sharing accommodation, goods, etc. **2** district in France, etc. [MedL, rel. to COMMON]

com·mune[2] /kəmyōōn′/ *v.* (·muned, ·mun·ing) **1** speak intimately **2** feel in close touch (with nature, etc.) [MFr, rel. to COMMON]

com·mu·ni·ca·ble /kəmyōō′nikəbəl/ *adj.* (esp. of a disease) able to be passed on [L, rel. to COMMUNICATE]

com·mu·ni·cant /kəmyōō′nikənt/ *n.* person who receives Holy Communion [rel. to COMMUNICATE]

com·mu·ni·cate /kəmyōō′nikāt/ *v.* (·cat·ed, ·cat·ing) **1** impart; transmit **2** succeed in conveying information **3** relate socially; have dealings **4** be connected (*communicating rooms*) —**com·mu′ni·ca′tor** *n.*; **com·mu′ni·ca·to′ry** /-kətôr′ē/ *adj.* [L, rel. to COMMON]

com·mu′ni·ca′tion *n.* **1a** communicating or being communicated **b** information communicated **c** letter, message, etc. **2** connection

or means of access **3** social dealings **4** (*pl.*) science and practice of transmitting information

com·mu·ni·ca·tive /kəmyōō′nikətiv/ *adj.* ready to talk and impart information

com·mu·nion /kəmyōōn′yən/ *n.* **1** sharing of thoughts, feelings, etc.; fellowship **2** sharing in common (*communion of interests*) **3** (*cap.*) HOLY COMMUNION **4** Christian denomination (*Methodist communion*) [L, rel. to COMMON]

com·mu·ni·qué /kəmyōō′nikā′/ *n.* official communication [Fr: communicated]

com·mu·nism /käm′yəniz′əm/ *n.* **1a** social system in which property is commonly owned **b** political theory advocating this **2** (usu. *cap.*) the form of socialist society advocated by Marx and Lenin, as formerly in the USSR [Fr, rel. to COMMON]

com·mu·nist /käm′yənist/ *n.* **1** person advocating communism **2** (usu. *cap.*) supporter or member of a Communist Party —*adj.* **3** pertaining to communism **4** (usu. *cap.*) pertaining to Communists or a Communist party —**com′mu·nis′tic** *adj.*

com·mu·ni·ty /kəmyōō′nətē/ *n.* (*pl.* **·ties**) **1** body of people living in one locale **2** body of people having religion, ethnic origin, profession, etc., in common **3** fellowship (*community of interest*) [L, rel. to COMMON]

com·mu′ni·ty col′lege *n.* junior college serving a limited region

com·mute /kəmyōōt′/ *v.* (·mut·ed, ·mut·ing) **1** travel some distance to and from work **2** change (a punishment) to one less severe —**com·mut′able** *adj.*; **com′mu·ta′tion** *n.* [L *mutare* change]

com·mut′er *n.* person who regularly travels to and from work

Com·o·ros /käm′ərōz′, kəmôr′ōz/ *n.* republic comprising three of the Comoro Islands, in the Indian Ocean between Africa and Madagascar. Capital: Moroni. Pop. 497,000 —**Com′o·ran, Co·mo′ri·an** *n.* & *adj.*

comp. *abbr.* **1** companion **2** comparative **3** compensation **4** compilation **5** compiled **6** compiler **7** complete **8** composite **9** composition **10** compositor **11** comprehensive

com·pact[1] *adj.* /kəmpakt′, käm′pakt′/ **1** closely or neatly packed together **2** small and economically designed **3** concise **4** (of a person) small but well-proportioned —*v.* /kəmpakt′, käm′pakt′/ **5** make compact —*n.* /käm′pakt′/ **6** small flat case for face powder **7** car that is smaller than standard size, and usu. more economical —**com·pact′ly** *adv.*; **com·pact′ness** *n.* [L *pangere* fasten]

com·pact[2] /käm′pakt′/ *n.* agreement; contract [L, rel. to PACT]

com′pact disk′ *n.* disk on which information or sound is recorded digitally and reproduced by reflection of laser light; *abbr.* CD

com·pan·ion /kəmpan′yən/ *n.* **1** person who accompanies or associates with another **2** partner; sharer **3** person employed to live with and assist another **4** thing that goes with another [L *panis* bread]

com·pan′ion·a·ble *adj.* sociable; friendly —**com·pan′ion·a·bly** *adv.*

com·pan′ion·ship *n.* friendship; being together

com·pan′ion·way′ *n.* ship stairway

com·pa·ny /kəmp'(ə)nē/ *n.* (*pl.* **·nies**) **1a** number of people assembled **b** guest(s) **2a** commercial business **b** partners in this **3** actors, etc., working together **4** subdivision of a battalion **5** personnel or complement (*the ship's company*) **6** being with another or others **7 keep a person company** remain with a person to be sociable **8 part company** cease to associate with [Fr. rel. to COMPANION]

com·pa·ra·ble /käm'p(ə)rəbəl, kəmpar'əbəl/ *adj.* able or fit to be compared —**com'pa·ra·bil'i·ty** *n.*; **com'pa·ra·bly** *adv.* [L, rel. to COMPARE]

com·par·a·tive /kəmpar'ətiv/ *adj.* **1** as perceived or estimated by comparison; relative (*in comparative comfort*) **2** of or involving comparison (*a comparative study*) **3** *Gram.* (of an adjective or adverb) expressing a higher degree (e.g., *braver, more quickly*) —*n.* **4** *Gram.* comparative expression or word —**com·par'a·tive·ly** *adv.* [L, rel. to COMPARE]

com·pare /kəmper'/ *v.* (**·pared, ·par·ing**) **1** express similarities in; liken to **2** estimate the similarity in **3** bear comparison **4** *Gram.* form comparative and superlative degrees of (an adjective or adverb) —*n.* **5** comparison (*beyond compare*) **6 compare notes** exchange ideas or opinions [L *compar* equal]
  • **Usage:** Traditionally, *compare to* is used when similarities are being stressed in otherwise dissimilar things: *Shall I compare thee to a summer's day? Compare with* applies when either differences or similarities are being stressed in similar things: *Compare this text with that one to see where they differ and where they agree.* For *compare* vs. *contrast*, see note at CONTRAST.

com·par·i·son /kəmpar'əsən/ *n.* **1** comparing **2** illustration or example of similarity **3** capacity for being likened (*there's no comparison*) **4** *Gram.* positive, comparative, and superlative forms or degrees of adjectives and adverbs

com·part·ment /kəmpärt'mənt/ *n.* **1** partitioned space within a larger space **2** watertight division of a ship [L, rel. to PART]

com·part·men·tal /kəmpärt'ment'l, käm'pärt-/ *adj.* of or divided into compartments or categories

com·part·men·tal·ize /kəmpärt'ment'l-īz', käm'-/ *v.* (**·ized, ·iz·ing**) divide into compartments or categories

com·pass /kəm'pəs/ *n.* **1** instrument showing the direction of magnetic north and bearings from it **2** instrument within two hinged legs for taking measurements and describing circles **3** circumference or boundary [L *passus* pace]

com·pas·sion /kəmpasH'ən/ *n.* pity inclining one to help or be merciful [ChL, rel. to PASSION]

com·pas'sion·ate *adj.* showing compassion; sympathetic —**com·pas'sion·ate·ly** *adv.*

com·pat·i·ble /kəmpat'əbəl/ *adj.* **1a** able to coexist; well-suited **b** consistent **2** (of equipment, etc.) able to be used in combination —**com·pat'i·bil'i·ty** *n.* [MedL, rel. to PASSION]

com·pa·tri·ot /kəmpā'trēət/ *n.* fellow-countryman [L, rel. to PATRIOT]

com·pel /kəmpel'/ *v.* (**·pelled, ·pel·ling**) **1** force; constrain **2** arouse irresistibly —**com·pel'ling·ly** *adv.* [L *pellere* drive]

com·pen·di·ous /kəmpen'dēəs/ *adj.* comprehensive but brief [L, rel. to COMPENDIUM]

com·pen·di·um /kəmpen'dēəm/ *n.* (*pl.* **·ums** or **·di·a**) concise summary or abridgment [L]

com·pen·sate /käm'pənsāt/ *v.* (**·sat·ed, ·sat·ing**) **1** pay **2** make amends **3** counterbalance **4** offset disability, hardship, etc., by adjusting —**com·pen·sa·to·ry** /kəmpen'sətôr'ē/ *adj.* [L *pendere* weigh]

com·pen·sa'tion *n.* **1** compensating or being compensated **2** money, etc., given as recompense

com·pete /kəmpēt'/ *v.* (**·pet·ed, ·pet·ing**) **1** take part in a contest **2** contend; vie [L *petere* seek]

com·pe·tence /käm'pətəns/ *n.* (also **com'pe·ten·cy**) **1** ability; being competent **2** legal capacity

com·pe·tent /käm'pətənt/ *adj.* adequately qualified or capable —**com'pe·tent·ly** *adv.* [L, rel. to COMPETE]

com·pe·ti·tion /käm'pətisH'ən/ *n.* **1** competing **2** event in which people compete **3** the others competing; opposition [L, rel. to COMPETE]

com·pet·i·tive /kəmpet'ətiv/ *adj.* **1** of or involving competition **2** (of prices, etc.) comparing favorably **3** driven to win —**com·pet'i·tive·ness** *n.*

com·pet'i·tor *n.* person who competes; rival, esp. in business

com·pile /kəmpīl'/ *v.* (**·piled, ·pil·ing**) **1** collect and arrange into a list, book, etc. **2** produce (a book, etc.) thus —**com·pi·la'tion** *n.* [L *compilare* plunder]

com·pil'er *n.* person who compiles

com·pla·cent /kəmplā'sənt/ *adj.* smugly self-satisfied or contented —**com·pla'cence, com·pla'cen·cy** *n.*; **com·pla'cent·ly** *adv.* [L *placere* please]

com·plain /kəmplān'/ *v.* **1** express dissatisfaction **2a** say that one is suffering from (an ailment) **b** state a grievance [L *plangere* lament]

com·plain·ant /kəmplā'nənt/ *n.* plaintiff

com·plaint /kəmplānt'/ *n.* **1** complaining **2** grievance; accusation **3** ailment

com·plai·sant /kəmplā'sənt, -zənt/ *adj.* willing to please; acquiescent —**com·plai'sance** *n.* [Fr, rel. to COMPLACENT]

com·ple·ment *n.* /käm'pləmənt/ **1** thing that completes; counterpart **2** full number needed —*v.* /-ment'/ **3** complete **4** form a complement to [L *complere* fill up]

com·ple·men·ta·ry /käm'pləment'ərē, -men'trē/ *adj.* **1** completing; forming a complement **2** (of two or more things) complementing each other

com·plete /kəmplēt'/ *adj.* **1** having all its parts; entire **2** finished —*v.* (**·plet·ed, ·plet·ing**) **3** finish **4** make whole **5** fill in (a form, etc.) —**com·plete'ly** *adv.*; **com·plete'ness, com·ple'tion** *n.* [L, rel. to COMPLEMENT]

com·plex *n.* /käm'pleks/ **1** building, series of rooms, etc., of related parts **2** *Psychol.* group of usu. repressed feelings or thoughts that influence behavior **3** preoccupation; feeling of inadequacy —*adj.* /ˈkämpleks, kəm-, kämˈpleks/ **4** complicated —**com·plex·i·ty** /kəmˈpleksˈətē/ *n.* (*pl.* **·ties**) [LL *complexus*]

com·plex·ion /kəmˈplekˈshən/ *n.* **1** natural appearance of skin, esp. of the face **2** aspect; interpretation [L, rel. to COMPLEX]

com·pli·ance /kəmˈplīˈəns/ *n.* **1** obedience to a request, command, etc. **2** capacity to yield

com·pli·ant *adj.* obedient; yielding —**com·pliˈant·ly** *adv.*

com·pli·cate /ˈkämˈpləkāt/ *v.* (**·cat·ed, ·cat·ing**) make difficult or complex [L *plicare* to fold]

com·pli·cat·ed *adj.* **1** complex **2** difficult to explain, understand, etc.

com·pli·ca·tion /ˌ/ *n.* **1** involved or confused condition; difficulty **2** (often *pl.*) aggravating consequence [L, rel. to COMPLICATE]

com·plic·i·ty /kəmˈplisˈətē/ *n.* partnership in wrongdoing [Fr, rel. to COMPLEX]

com·pli·ment *n.* /ˈkämˈpləmənt/ **1a** polite expression of praise **b** act implying praise **2** (in *pl.*) formal greetings —*v.* /ˈ-ment/ **3** congratulate; praise [L, rel. to COMPLEMENT]

com·pli·men·ta·ry /ˌkämˈpləmentˈarē, -menˈtrē/ *adj.* **1** expressing a compliment **2** given free

com·ply /kəmˈplī/ *v.* (**·plied, ·ply·ing**) act in accordance [L *complere* fill up]

com·po·nent /kəmˈpōnənt/ *n.* part of a larger whole [L, rel. to COMPOUND[1]]

com·port /kəmˈpôrt/ *v. refl.* **1** conduct oneself; behave **2** comport with suit; befit —**com·portˈment** *n.* [L *portare* carry]

com·pose /kəmˈpōz/ *v.* (**·posed, ·pos·ing**) **1** create in music or writing **2** constitute; make up **3** arrange artistically, neatly, etc. **4a** (often *refl.*) calm **b** (as **composed** *adj.*) calm; self-possessed **5** *Printing.* **a** set (type) **b** put (an article, etc.) in type **6 composed of** made up of —**com·posˈed·ly** /-pōˈzədlē/ *adv.* [Fr, rel. to POSE]

com·pos·er *n.* person who composes (esp. music)

com·pos·ite /ˈkämˈpäzˈit, kəm-/ *adj.* **1** made up of parts or different materials **2** (of a plant) having a head of many flowers forming one bloom —*n.* **3** composite thing or plant [L, rel. to COMPOSE]

com·po·si·tion /ˌkämˈpəzishˈən/ *n.* **1a** putting together; composing **b** thing composed, esp. music **2** constitution of a substance **3** school essay **4** artistic arrangement **5** compound artificial substance —**com·po·siˈtion·al** *adj.*

com·pos·i·tor /kəmˈpäzˈətər/ *n.* person who sets type for printing [L, rel. to COMPOSE]

com·post /ˈkämˈpōst/ *n.* **1** mixture of decayed organic matter for fertilizing soil —*v.* **2** treat with compost **3** make into compost [L, rel. to COMPOSE]

com·po·sure /kəmˈpōˈzhər/ *n.* tranquil manner [fr. COMPOSE]

com·pote /ˈkämˈpōt/ *n.* fruit preserved or cooked in syrup [Fr, rel. to COMPOSE]

com·pound[1] *n.* /ˈkämˈpound/ **1** mixture of two or more things **2** word made up of two or more existing words **3** substance chemically formed from two or more elements —*adj.*

/ˈkämˈpound, kämˈpound, kəm-/ **4** made up of two or more ingredients **5** combined; collective —*v.* /kämˈpound, kämˈpound/ **6** mix or combine (ingredients or elements) **7** increase or complicate (difficulties, etc.) **8** make up (a composite whole) [L *componere* put together]

com·pound[2] /ˈkämˈpound/ *n.* enclosure or fenced-in space [Malay *kampong*]

com·pound fracˈture *n.* bone fracture that pierces the skin

com·pound inˈter·est *n.* interest paid on principle and its accumulated interest

com·pre·hend /ˌkämˈprihend/ *v.* **1** grasp mentally; understand **2** include —**com·pre·henˈsi·ble** *adj.*; **com·pre·henˈsion** *n.* [L *prehendo* seize]

com·pre·henˈsive *adj.* **1** including all or nearly all; inclusive **2** (of insurance) providing protection against most risks —**com·pre·henˈsive·ly** *adv.*; **com·pre·henˈsive·ness** *n.*

com·press *v.* /kəmˈpres/ **1** squeeze together **2** bring into a smaller space or shorter time —*n.* /ˈkämˈpres/ **3** pad applied to a wound —**com·pressˈi·ble** /kəmˈpresˈəbəl/ *adj.* [L, rel. to PRESS[1]]

com·presˈsion *n.* compressing

com·presˈsor *n.* machine for compressing air or other gases

com·prise /kəmˈprīz/ *v.* (**·prised, ·pris·ing**) **1** include **2** consist of **3** make up; compose [Fr, rel. to COMPREHEND]

com·pro·mise /ˈkämˈprəmīz/ *n.* **1** mutual settlement of a dispute **2** intermediate state between conflicting opinions, actions, etc. —*v.* (**·mised, ·mis·ing**) **3a** settle a dispute by mutual concession **b** modify one's opinions, demands, etc. **4** bring into disrepute or danger by indiscretion [L, rel. to PROMISE]

comp·trol·ler /kənˈtrōˈlər, kämˈp)ˈtrōˈlər/ *n.* financial officer [var. of CONTROLLER]

com·pul·sion /kəmˈpəlˈshən/ *n.* **1** compelling or being compelled; obligation **2** irresistible urge [L, rel. to COMPEL]

com·pul·sive /kəmˈpəlˈsiv/ *adj.* **1** resulting or acting (as if) from compulsion **2** irresistible —**com·pulˈsive·ly** *adv.*; **com·pulˈsive·ness** *n.* [MedL, rel. to COMPEL]

com·pul·so·ry /kəmˈpəlˈs(ə)rē/ *adj.* **1** required by law or a rule **2** essential —**com·pulˈso·ri·ly** *adv.*

com·punc·tion /kəmˈpəNGk)ˈshən/ *n.* **1** pricking of conscience **2** slight regret; scruple [ChL, rel. to POINT]

com·pute /kəmˈpyo͞ot/ *v.* (**·put·ed, ·put·ing**) **1** reckon or calculate **2** use a computer —**com·pu·taˈtion** *n.* [L *putare* reckon]

com·putˈer *n.* electronic device for storing and processing data, making calculations, or controlling machinery

com·putˈer·ize *v.* (**·ized, ·iz·ing**) **1** equip with a computer **2** store, perform, or produce by computer —**com·putˈer·i·zaˈtion** *n.*

com·putˈer-litˈer·ate *adj.* able to use computers

com·putˈer sciˈence *n.* the study of the principles and uses of computers

com·putˈer viˈrus *n.* self-replicating software sequence maliciously introduced into a program to corrupt or destroy data

com·rade /ˈkämˈrad, -rad/ *n.* **1** associate or companion **2** fellow socialist or Communist

—**com'rade·ly** *adj.*; **com'rade·ship** *n.* [Sp fr. *camara* room]

Comte /kōnt/, **Auguste** 1798–1857; French philosopher

con¹ /kän/ *Slang. n.* **1** confidence trick —*v.* (**conned, con·ning**) **2** swindle; deceive [abbr.]

con² *n.* **1** (usu. *pl.*) reason against —*prep.* & *adv.* **2** against (cf. PRO²) [L *contra* against]

con³ *n. Slang.* convict [abbr.]

con- *prefix* var. of COM- before *n*

Co·na·kry /kän'əkrē/ *n.* capital of Guinea. Pop. 705,300

con·cat·e·na·tion /känkat'n-ā'sHən, kən-/ *n.* series of linked things or events [L *catena* chain]

con·cave /känkāv', kän'kāv/ *adj.* curved like the interior of a circle or sphere (see illustration at CONVEX) —**con·cav'i·ty** /-kav'ətē/ *n.* [L, rel. to CAVE]

con·ceal /kənsēl'/ *v.* **1** keep secret **2** hide —**con·ceal'ment** *n.* [L *celare* hide]

con·cede /kənsēd'/ *v.* (·**ced·ed, ·ced·ing**) **1** admit to be true **2** admit defeat in **3** grant (a right, privilege, etc.) [L, rel. to CEDE]

con·ceit /kənsēt'/ *n.* **1** personal vanity; pride **2** *Lit.* a metaphoric comparison **b** fanciful notion [fr. CONCEIVE]

con·ceit'ed *adj.* vain —**con·ceit'ed·ly** *adv.*

con·ceiv·a·ble /kənsē'vəbəl/ *adj.* capable of being grasped or imagined —**con·ceiv'a·bly** *adv.*

con·ceive /kənsēv'/ *v.* (·**ceived, ·ceiv·ing**) **1** become pregnant (with) **2** imagine; think; devise [L *concipere* contain; hold]

con·cen·trate /kän'səntrāt'/ *v.* (·**trat·ed, ·trat·ing**) **1** focus one's attention or thought **2** bring together to one point **3** increase the strength of —*n.* **4** concentrated substance [L, rel. to CENTER]

con·cen·tra'tion *n.* **1** concentrating or being concentrated **2** mental attention **3** something concentrated

con·cen·tra'tion camp' *n.* camp holding political prisoners

con·cen·tric /kənsen'trik, kän-/ *adj.* having a common center —**con·cen'tri·cal·ly** *adv.* [Fr or MedL, rel. to CENTER]

Con·cep·ción /kən'sep'sē·ōn'/ *n.* city in Chile. Pop. 311,500

con·cept /kän'sept'/ *n.* general notion; abstract idea [L, rel. to CONCEIVE]

con·cep·tion /kənsep'sHən/ *n.* **1** conceiving or being conceived **2** idea; plan **3** understanding; inkling (*has no conception*) —**con·cep'tion·al** *adj.* [Fr fr. L, rel. to CONCEPT]

con·cep·tu·al /kənsep'CHŌŌəl/ *adj.* pertaining to conceptions or concepts —**con·cep'tu·al·ly** *adv.*

con·cep·tu·al·ize' *v.* (·**ized, ·iz·ing**) form a concept or idea of —**con·cep'tu·al·i·za'tion** *n.*

con·cern /kənsərn'/ *v.* **1a** be relevant or important to **b** relate to; be about **2** interest or involve oneself **3** worry; affect —*n.* **4** anxiety; worry **5** matter of interest or importance **6** business; firm [L *cernere* sift]

con·cerned' *adj.* **1** involved; interested **2** troubled; anxious —**con·cern'ed·ly** /-sərn'ədlē/ *adv.*

con·cern'ing *prep.* about; regarding

con·cert /kän'sərt/ *n.* **1** musical or dance performance **2** stage performance of a comedian, storyteller, etc. **3** agreement **4** combination of voices or sounds [It, rel. to CONCERTO]

con·cert·ed /kənsərt'əd/ *adj.* jointly arranged or planned

CONCERTINA

con·cer·ti·na /kän'sərtē'nə/ *n.* musical instrument like an accordion but smaller

con·cer·to /kənCHer'tō/ *n.* (*pl.* ·**tos** or ·**ti** /-tē/) composition for solo instrument(s) and orchestra [It]

con·ces·sion /kənsesH'ən/ *n.* **1a** conceding **b** thing conceded **2** right to sell goods in a particular territory —**con·ces'sion·ar·y** *adj.* [L, rel. to CONCEDE]

conch /kängk, känCH, kÓNGk/ *n.* **1** spiral shell of various marine gastropod mollusks **2** any such gastropod [L *concha* fr. Gk]

con·ci·erge /kÓNSyerzH'/ *n.* **1** hotel staff person who arranges special services for guests **2** porter, as in an apartment building [Fr]

con·cil·i·ate /kənsil'ē·āt'/ *v.* (·**at·ed, ·at·ing**) **1** make calm and amenable; pacify; gain the goodwill of **2** reconcile —**con·cil·i·a'tion**, **con·cil'i·a·tor** *n.*; **con·cil'i·a·to·ry** /-ətôr'ē/ *adj.* [L, rel. to COUNCIL]

con·cise /kənsīs'/ *adj.* brief but comprehensive —**con·cise'ly** *adv.*; **con·cise'ness** *n.*; **con·ci'sion** /-sizH'ən/ *n.* [L *caedere* cut]

con·clave /kän'klāv', käNG'-/ *n.* **1** private meeting **2** *RC Ch.* assembly of cardinals for the election of a pope [L *clavis* key]

con·clude /kənklŌŌd'/ *v.* (·**clud·ed, ·clud·ing**) **1** bring or come to an end **2** infer **3** settle (a treaty, etc.) [L *concludere*, rel. to CLOSE¹]

con·clu·sion /kənklŌŌ'zHən/ *n.* **1** ending; end **2** judgment reached by reasoning **3** summing-up **4** settling (of peace, etc.) [L, rel. to CONCLUDE]

con·clu·sive /kənklŌŌ'siv/ *adj.* decisive; convincing —**con·clu'sive·ly** *adv.* [L, rel. to CONCLUDE]

con·coct /kənkäkt'/ *v.* **1** make by mixing ingredients **2** invent —**con·coc'tion** *n.* [L *coquere* cook]

con·com·i·tant /kənkäm'ətənt/ *adj.* **1** accompanying; occurring together —*n.* **2** accompanying thing —**con·com'i·tance** *n.* [L *comes comititis* companion]

con·cord /kän'kôrd', käNG'-/ *n.* agreement; harmony —**con·cor'dant** /kənkôrd'nt/ *adj.* [L *cordis* fr. *cor* heart]

Con·cord /käNG'kərd, -kôrd/ *n.* **1** capital of N. Hamp., in the S central part. Pop. 36,006 **2** city in Calif. Pop. 111,348 con·cor·dance /kənkôrd'ns/ n. 1 agreement 2 index of words used in a book or by an author [MedL, rel. to CONCORD]

con·course /kän'kôrs, käNG'-/ n. 1 crowd; gathering 2 large open area for public use [L, rel. to CONCUR]

con·crete adj. /känkrēt', kən-, kän'krēt'/ 1a existing in a material form; real b specific; definite 2 Gram. (of a noun) denoting a material object as opposed to a quality, state, etc. —n. /kän'krēt', känkrēt'/ 3 mixture of gravel, sand, cement, and water, used for building [L concretus fr. crescere grow]

con·cre·tion /kənkrē'SHən, kän-/ n. 1 hard solid mass 2 forming of this [L, rel. to CONCRETE]

con·cu·bine /käNG'kyoŏbīn'/ n. 1 Lit. mistress 2 (in some societies) secondary or subordinate wife —con·cu·bi·nage /kənkyoŏ'bənij/ n. [L cubare lie down]

con·cu·pis·cence /kənkyoŏ'pəsəns/ n. lust —con·cu'pis·cent adj. [L cupiscere desire]

con·cur /kənkər'/ v. (-curred, -cur·ring) 1 agree (with) 2 coincide [L currere run]

con·cur·rent /kənkər'ənt, -kə'rənt/ adj. (often followed by with) existing or active at the same time or together —con·cur'rence n.; con·cur'rent·ly adv.

con·cus·sion /kənkəSH'ən/ n. 1 injury to the brain or spinal cord from a blow, fall, etc. 2 violent shock or shaking

con·demn /kəndem'/ v. 1 express utter disapproval of 2a find guilty; convict b sentence (to) 3 pronounce (a building, etc.) unfit for use 4 doom or assign (to something unpleasant) —con'dem·na'tion n.; con·dem'na·to'ry adj. [L, rel. to DAMN]

con·den·sa·tion /kän'densä'SHən/ n. 1 condensing or being condensed 2 condensed liquid (esp. water) 3 abridgment [L, rel. to CONDENSE]

con·dense /kəndens'/ v. (-densed, -dens·ing) 1 make denser or more concentrated 2 express in fewer words 3 reduce or be reduced from a gas or vapor to a liquid [L, rel. to DENSE]

con·dens·er n. 1 apparatus or vessel for condensing vapor 2 Electr. CAPACITOR

con·de·scend /kän'dəsend'/ v. 1 be gracious enough (to do a thing unworthy of one) 2 pretend to be on equal terms with (an inferior) 3 patronize —con·de·scen'sion n. [L, rel. to DESCEND]

con'de·scend'ing adj. having a patronizing attitude —con·de·scend'ing·ly adv.

con·dign /kəndīn'/ adj. (of punishment) severe and well-deserved [L dignus worthy]

con·di·ment /kän'dəmənt/ n. seasoning or relish for food [L condire pickle]

con·di·tion /kəndiSH'ən/ n. 1 stipulation; term or terms 2a state of fitness b ailment; abnormality (heart condition) 3 (in pl.) circumstances; atmosphere —v. 4a bring into a good or desired state b make fit (esp. dogs or horses) 5 teach or accustom 6 on condition that with the stipulation that [L dicere say]

con·di'tion·al adj. 1 dependent or tentative; not absolute 2 Gram. (of a clause, noun, etc.) expressing a condition —con·di'tion·al·ly adv. [L, rel. to CONDITION]

con·di'tion·er n. agent that conditions, esp. the hair

con·do·lence /kəndō'ləns/ n. (often pl.) expression of sympathy

con·dom /kän'dəm/ n. prophylactic or contraceptive sheath worn on the penis

con·do·min·i·um /kän'dəmin'ēəm/ n. 1 joint sovereignty 2 building or complex containing individually owned apartments [L dominium lordship]

con·done /kəndōn'/ v. (-doned, -don·ing) forgive or overlook [L donare give]

con·dor /kon'dər, -dôr'/ n. large S American vulture [Sp fr. Quechua]

con·du·cive /kənd(y)oŏ'siv/ adj. contributing or helping (toward something)

con·duct n. /kän'dəkt'/ 1 behavior 2 activity or manner of directing or managing —v. /kəndəkt'/ 3 guide, direct, or manage (a business, etc.) 4 be the conductor of (an orchestra, etc.) 5 transmit (heat, electricity, etc.) 6 refl. behave [L ductus fr. ducere lead]

con·duc·tance /kəndək'təns/ n. ability to conduct electricity

con·duc·tion /kəndək'SHən/ n. transmission of heat, electricity, etc., through a substance —con·duc'tive adj.; con·duc·tiv·i·ty /kän'dəktiv'itē/ n. [L, rel. to CONDUCT]

con·duc·tor /kəndək'tar/ n. 1 person who directs an orchestra, etc. 2 person in charge of passengers, as on a train 3 thing that conducts heat or electricity [L, rel. to CONDUCT]

con·duit /kän'd(y)oŏot/ n. 1 channel or pipe conveying liquids 2 tube protecting electric wires [MedL, rel. to CONDUCT]

cone /kōn/ n. 1 solid figure with a circular (or other curved) plane base, tapering to a point 2 thing or holder of similar shape 3 dry, scaly fruit of a conifer [L fr. Gk]

con·fec·tion /kənfek'SHən/ n. sweet dish or candy [L conficere prepare]

con·fed·er·a·cy /kənfed'(ə)rəsē/ n. (pl. -cies) 1 league or alliance 2 (the Confederacy) the group of 11 southern states that seceded from the US in 1860–61 [Fr, rel. to CONFEDERATE]

con·fed·er·ate adj. /kənfed'(ə)rət/ 1 allied —n. /kənfed'(ə)rət/ 2 ally or accomplice 3 (cap.) supporter of the Confederacy —v. /-fed'ərāt'/ (-at·ed, -at·ing) 4 bring or come into alliance [L, rel. to FEDERAL]

Con·fed'er·ate States' of A·mer'i·ca n. pl. CONFEDERACY, 2

con·fed·er·a·tion /kənfed'ərā'SHən/ n. 1 union or alliance 2 confederating or being confederated

con·fer /kənfər'/ v. (-ferred, -fer·ring) 1 grant or bestow 2 converse; consult —con·fer'ra·ble adj. [L conferre bring together]

con·fer·ence /kän'f(ə)rəns/ n. 1 consultation 2 meeting [Fr or MedL, rel. to CONFER]

con·fer'ment n. conferring of a degree, honor, etc.

con·fess /kənfes'/ v. 1a acknowledge or admit b admit (to) 2 admit reluctantly 3a declare (one's sins) to a priest b (of a priest) hear the confession of [AngFr, OFr confesser fr. L confiteri]

con·fes'sion n. 1a act of confessing b thing confessed 2 declaration of one's beliefs

con·fes'sion·al n. 1 enclosed stall in a church

in which the priest hears confessions —*adj.*
2 of confession

con·fes·sor /kənfes'ər/ *n.* priest who hears
confessions

con·fet·ti /kənfet'ē/ *n.* bits of colored paper
thrown during celebrations [It]

con·fi·dant /kän'fədant', -dänt'/ *n.* (*fem.*
·dante) person trusted with knowledge of
one's private affairs [rel. to CONFIDE]

con·fide /kənfīd'/ *v.* (**·fid·ed, ·fid·ing**) 1
(foll. by *in*) talk confidentially to 2 tell in confidence 3 entrust (an object of care, a task,
etc.) to [L *confidere* trust]

con·fi·dence /kän'fədəns/ *n.* 1 firm trust 2a
feeling of reliance or certainty **b** sense of self-
reliance; boldness 3 something told as a secret [L, rel. to CONFIDE]

con'fi·dence game' *n.* swindle in which the
victim is persuaded to trust the swindler
—**con'fi·dence man'** *n.*

con·fi·dent /kän'fədənt/ *adj.* feeling or
showing confidence; bold —**con'fi·dent·ly**
adv. [It, rel. to CONFIDE]

con·fi·den·tial /kän'fədən'SHəl/ *adj.* sensitive, secret, or shared in trust —**con'fi·den·**
ti·al'i·ty /-den'SHē·al'ətē/ *n.*; **con·fi·den'tial·**
ly *adv.*

con·fig·u·ra·tion /kənfig'yərā'SHən/ *n.* arrangement in a particular form [L, rel. to FIG-
URE]

con·fine *v.* /kənfīn'/ (**·fined, ·fin·ing**) 1
keep in or restrict 2 imprison —*n.* /kän'-
fīn/ 3 (usu. *pl.*) limit; boundary [L *finis*
limit]

con·fine'ment *n.* 1 confining or being confined 2 time of childbirth

con·firm /kənfərm'/ *v.* 1 settle the truth or
correctness of 2 encourage (a person) in (an
opinion, etc.) 3 establish or make formally
valid 4 administer the religious rite of confirmation to [L, rel. to FIRM[1]]

con·fir·ma·tion /kän'fərmā'SHən/ *n.* 1 confirming or being confirmed 2 rite confirming
a baptized person as a church member

con·firmed' *adj.* firmly settled in some habit
or condition (*confirmed bachelor*)

con·fis·cate /kän'fəskāt'/ *v.* (**·cat·ed, ·cat·**
ing) take or seize by authority —**con'fis·ca'**
tion *n.* [L, rel. to FISCAL]

con·fla·gra·tion /kän'fləgrā'SHən/ *n.* great
and destructive fire [L, rel. to FLAGRANT]

con·flate /kənflāt'/ *v.* (**·flat·ed, ·flat·ing**)
blend or fuse together (esp. two variant texts
into one) —**con·fla'tion** *n.* [L *conflatus* fr.
flare blow]

con·flict /kän'flikt/ *n.* 1a state of opposition
b fight; struggle —*v.* /kənflikt'/ 2 clash; be
incompatible [L *flictus* fr. *fligere* strike]

con·flu·ence /kän'flōō'əns, kənflōō'-/ *n.* 1
place where two rivers meet 2 coming together [L *fluere* flow]

con·form /kənfôrm'/ *v.* 1 comply with rules
or general custom 2 comply with; be in accordance with 3 make similar [L, rel. to
FORM]

con·form'a·ble *adj.* 1 similar 2 consistent 3
adaptable

con·for·ma·tion /kän'fərmā'SHən/ *n.* way a
thing is formed; shape

con·form'ist *n.* 1 person who conforms to established practice —*adj.* 2 conforming; conventional —**con·form'ism** *n.*

con·form·i·ty /kənfôr'mətē/ *n.* 1 accordance with established practice 2 agreement;
suitability

con·found /kənfound'/ *v.* 1 perplex; baffle 2
confuse (in one's mind) [L *confusus* fr. *confun-
dere* mix up]

con·front /kənfrənt'/ *v.* 1a face in hostility
or defiance **b** face up to and deal with 2 present itself to 3 (foll. by *with*) bring (a person)
face to face with 4 meet or stand facing
—**con·fron·ta'tion** *n.*; **con·fron·ta'tion·al**
adj. [Fr fr. MedL]

Con·fu·cius /kənfyōō'SHəs/ (also **K'ung Fu-**
tzu) 551–479 B.C.; Chinese philosopher
—**Con·fu'cian** *adj.*

con·fuse /kənfyōōz'/ *v.* (**·fused, ·fus·ing**) 1
perplex; bewilder 2 mix up in the mind; mistake (one for another) 3 make indistinct (*confuse the issue*) —**con·fus'ed·ly** /-fyōō'zədlē/
adv.; **con·fus'ing** *adj.* [rel. to CONFOUND]

con·fu'sion *n.* confusing or being confused

con·fute /kənfyōōt'/ *v.* (**·fut·ed, ·fut·ing**)
prove to be in error —**con·fu·ta'tion** *n.* [L]

Cong. *abbr.* 1 Congress 2 Congressional 3
Congregational

con·ga /käNG'gə/ *n.* 1 Latin American dance
with a line of dancers 2 tall narrow drum
beaten with the hands [Sp *conga: fem.* of the
Congo]

con·geal /kənjēl'/ *v.* 1 make or become
semi-solid by cooling 2 coagulate —**con·ge·**
la·tion /kän'jəlā'SHən/ *n.* [Fr fr. L *gelare*
freeze]

con·ge·nial /kənjēn'yəl/ *adj.* 1 pleasantly sociable 2 suited or agreeable —**con·ge'ni·al'**
i·ty /-jē'nē·al'ətē/ *n.*; **con·gen'ial·ly** *adv.* [fr.
COM- + GENIAL]

con·gen·i·tal /kənjen'it·l/ *adj.* (esp. of disease) existing from birth —**con·gen'i·tal·ly**
adv. [L, rel. to COM-]

con·ger /käNG'gər/ *n.* large marine eel [Gk
gongros]

con·ge·ries /kän'jərēz', kənjər'ēz/ *n.* (*pl.*
same) disorderly collection; heap [L *congerere* heap together]

con·gest /kənjest'/ *v.* affect with congestion
[L *congerere* heap together]

con·ges'tion *n.* abnormal accumulation or obstruction

con·glom·er·ate *adj.* /kəngläm'ərət/ 1 gathered into a rounded mass —*n.* /kəngläm'
ərət/ 2 heterogeneous mass 3 group or corporation —*v.* /-rāt/ (**·at·ed, ·at·ing**) 4 collect into a coherent mass —**con·glom'er·a'**
tion /-ā'SHən/ *n.* [L *glomus glomeris* ball]

Con·go /käNG'gō/ *n.* 1 republic in central Africa. Capital: Brazzaville. Pop. 2,692,000 2 former name of Zaire —**Con·go·lese** /käNG'
gəlēz', -lēs'/ *n.* & *adj.*

Con'go Riv'er *n.* river in central Africa flowing
3,000 mi. from SE Zaire to the Atlantic

con·grat·u·late /kəNGGraCH'əlāt', -graj'-/ *v.*
(**·lat·ed, ·lat·ing**) express pleasure at the
good fortune or excellence of (a person)
—**con·grat'u·la·to'ry** /-ələtôr'ē/ *adj.* [L *gratus* pleasing]

con·grat·u·la'tion *n.* 1 congratulating 2 (usu.
pl.) expression of this

con·gre·gate /käNG'grigāt'/ *v.* (**·gat·ed,**

·gat·ing) collect or gather into a crowd [L *grex gregis* flock]

con·gre·ga·tion *n.* 1 gathering of people, esp. for religious worship 2 body of persons regularly attending a particular church, etc. [L, rel. to CONGREGATE]

con·gre·ga·tion·al *adj.* 1 of a congregation 2 (*cap.*) of or adhering to Congregationalism, a Christian denomination of individual churches that are largely self-governing —Con·gre·ga′tion·al·ist *n.*

con·gress /käNG′grəs/ *n.* 1 formal meeting of delegates for discussion 2 (*cap.*) national legislative body of the US —con·gres′sion·al /kən-gresH′ən-l/ *adj.* [L *congressus* assembly fr. *congredi* meet]

con·gress·man /käNG′grəsmən/ *n.* (*pl.* ·men; *fem.* ·wom·an, *pl.* ·wom′en) member of the US Congress

Con·greve /kän′grēv′, käNG′-/, William 1670–1729; English dramatist

con·gru·ent /kän·grōō′ənt, käNG′grōōənt/ *adj.* 1 suitable; agreeing 2 *Geom.* coinciding when superimposed —con·gru·ence *n.* [L *congruere* agree]

con·gru·ous /käNG′grōōəs/ *adj.* suitable; fitting —con·gru′i·ty *n.* [L, rel. to CONGRUENT]

con·ic /kän′ik/ *adj.* of a cone

con′i·cal *adj.* cone-shaped

co·ni·fer /kän′əfər/ *n.* tree usu. bearing cones —co·nif′er·ous *adj.* [L, rel. to CONE]

conj. *abbr.* conjunction

con·jec·ture /kənjek′CHər/ *n.* 1 formation of an opinion on incomplete information; guessing 2 guess —*v.* (·tured, ·tur·ing) 3 guess —con·jec′tur·al *adj.* [L *conjectura* fr. *jacere* throw]

con·join /kənjoin′/ *v. Formal.* join; combine

con·joint /kənjoint′/ *adj. Formal.* associated; conjoined

con·ju·gal /kän′jəgəl/ *adj.* pertaining to marriage [L *conjunx* spouse]

con·ju·gate *v.* /kän′jəgāt′/ (·gat·ed, ·gat·ing) 1 *Gram.* list the different forms of (a verb) 2a unite b become fused —*adj.* /kän′jəgət/ 3 joined together; fused [L *jugum* yoke]

con·ju·ga·tion *n. Gram.* system of verbal inflection

con·junct /kənjəNGkt′/ *adj.* joined together; combined; associated [L fr. *juntus* joined]

con·junc·tion /kənjəNGk′sHən/ *n.* 1 joining; connection 2 *Gram.* connective word (e.g. *and, but, if*) 3 combination (of events or circumstances)

con·junc·ti·va /kän′jəNGktī′və/ *n.* (*pl.* ·vas) mucous membrane of the eye

con·junc′tive *adj.* 1 serving to join 2 *Gram.* of the nature of a conjunction

con·junc·ti·vi·tis /kənjəNGk′tivī′tis/ *n.* inflammation of the conjunctiva

con·jure /kän′jər/ *v.* (·jured, ·jur·ing) 1 perform seemingly magical tricks 2 summon (a spirit or demon) to appear 3 conjure up produce as if by magic 4 evoke —con′jur·or or con′jur·er *n.* [L *jurare* swear]

conk /käNGk, kôNGk/ *v. Colloq.* 1 hit on the head 2 conk out: a (of a machine, etc.) break down b (of a person) be exhausted and fall asleep [perh. fr. CONCH]

con′ man′ *n.* confidence man

Conn. *abbr.* Connecticut

con·nect /kənekt′/ *v.* 1 join (two things, or one thing with another) 2 be joined, joinable 3 associate mentally or practically 4 (of a flight, etc.) be timed to arrive before (another scheduled departure) 5 put into communication 6 *Colloq.* hit or strike effectively —con·nec′tor *n.* [L *nectere* bind]

Con·nect·i·cut /kənet′ikət/ *n.* NE state of the US. Capital: Hartford. Pop. 3,287,116. Abbr. Conn.; CT; Ct.

Con·nect′i·cut Riv′er *n.* river flowing 400 mi. from N. Hamp. into Long Island Sound

con·nec·tion /kənek′sHən/ *n.* 1 connecting or being connected 2 meeting point 3 link, esp. by telephone 4 connecting flight, etc. 5 (often *pl.*) relevant or helpful acquaintance 6 relation of ideas

con·nec·tive /kənek′tiv/ *adj.* connecting, esp. of body tissue connecting, separating, etc., organs, etc.

Con·ner·y /kän′ərē/, Sean (born Thomas Connery) 1930– ; Scottish-born actor

conn′ing tow′er /kän′iNG/ 1 superstructure of a submarine containing the periscope 2 armored wheelhouse of a warship

con·nive /kəniv′/ *v.* (·nived, ·niv·ing) 1 (foll. by *at*) disregard or tacitly consent to (a wrongdoing) 2 conspire —con·niv′ance *n.* [L *conivere* shut the eyes]

con·nois·seur /kän′əsər′, -sōōr′/ *n.* expert judge in matters of taste [Fr *connaître* know]

Con·nors /kän′ərz/, James Scott (Jimmy) 1952– ; US tennis player

con·note /kənōt′/ *v.* (·not·ed, ·not·ing) imply in addition to the literal or primary meaning —con·no·ta·tion /känōtā′sHən/ *n.*; con·no·ta·tive /kän′ətā′tiv/ *adj.* [MedL, rel. to NOTE]

● *Usage: Connote* means 'suggest': *Home connotes warmth and security. Denote* refers to the literal meaning: *Home denotes a place where someone lives.*

con·nu·bi·al /kənōō′bēəl/ *adj.* pertaining to marriage [L *nubere* marry]

con·quer /käNG′kər/ *v.* 1a overcome militarily b be victorious 2 strive and prevail —con′quer·or *n.* [L *conquirere* win]

con·quest /kän′kwest′, käNG′-/ *n.* 1 conquering or being conquered 2 something won 3 person whose affection has been won

Con·rad /kän′rad′/, Joseph 1857–1924; Polish-born British novelist

Con·rail /kän′rāl′/ *n.* Consolidated Rail Corporation, US freight railroad system

con·san·guin·e·ous /kän′saNG·gwin′ēəs, -san-/ *adj.* descended from the same ancestor; akin —con′san·guin′i·ty *n.* [L *sanguis* blood]

con·science /kän′CHəns/ *n.* 1 moral sense of right and wrong 2 in all conscience by any reasonable standard [L, rel. to SCIENCE]

con·sci·en·tious /kän′sHē·en′sHəs/ *adj.* diligent and scrupulous —con′sci·en′tious·ly *adv.*; con′sci·en′tious·ness *n.* [MedL, rel. to CONSCIENCE]

con·sci·en′tious ob·jec′tor *n.* person refraining from military service on moral grounds

con·scious /kän′sHəs/ *adj.* 1 awake and aware of one's surroundings and identity 2 aware; knowing; intentional 3 (in *comb.*)

aware of; concerned with (*fashion-conscious*)
—con'scious·ly *adv.*; con'scious·ness *n.* [L
scire know]

con·script *v.* /kənskript'/ **1** summon for
compulsory (esp. military) service —*n.* /kän'
skript'/ **2** conscripted person —con·scrip·
tion /kənskrip'shən/ *n.* [L *scribere* write]

con·se·crate /kän'sikrāt'/ *v.* (·crat·ed,
·crat·ing) **1** make or declare sacred **2** (foll.
by *to*) devote to (a purpose) —con'se·cra'
tion *n.* [L, rel. to SACRED]

con·sec·u·tive /kənsek'(y)ətiv/ *adj.* follow·
ing continuously; in sequence —con·sec'u·
tive·ly *adv.* [L *secutus* fr. *sequi* follow]

con·sen·sus /kənsen'səs/ *n.* general agree·
ment or opinion [L, rel. to CONSENT]

con·sent /kənsent'/ *v.* **1** express willing·
ness; agree —*n.* **2** voluntary agreement; per·
mission [L *sentire* feel]

con·se·quence /kän'səkwəns, -kwens'/ *n.* **1**
result or effect of what has gone before **2** im·
portance **3** take the consequences accept
the results of one's choice or action [L, rel. to
CONSECUTIVE]

con·se·quent /kän'sikwənt, -kwent'/ *adj.* fol·
lowing as a result or consequence

con·se·quen·tial /kän'sikwen'shəl/ *adj.* **1**
consequent; resulting indirectly **2** important

con'se·quent'ly *adv.* & *conj.* as a result;
therefore

con·ser·van·cy /kənsər'vənsē/ *n.* (*pl.*
·cies) body controlling a port, river, etc., or
preserving the environment [L, rel. to CON·
SERVE]

con·ser·va·tion /kän'sərvā'shən/ *n.* preser·
vation, esp. of the natural environment —con'
ser·va'tion·ist *n.* [L, rel. to CONSERVE]

con·ser·va·tive /kənsər'vətiv/ *adj.* **1a**
averse to rapid change **b** *Polit.* tending to fa·
vor strict adherence to a traditional, limited
role for government **c** moderate; avoiding ex·
tremes **2** (of an estimate, etc.) purposely low
3 tending to conserve —*n.* **4** conservative
person —con·ser'va·tism *n.* [L, rel. to CON·
SERVE]

con·ser·va·to·ry /kənsər'vətor'ē/ *n.* (*pl.*
·ries) **1** greenhouse **2** music school [L and
It, rel. to CONSERVE]

con·serve *v.* /kənsərv'/ (·served, ·serv·
ing) **1** safeguard against harm, damage, or
waste, esp. for later use —*n.* /kän'sərv/ **2**
fresh fruit jam [L *servare* keep]

con·sid·er /kənsid'ər/ *v.* **1** contemplate;
weigh; evaluate **2** look attentively at **3** take
into account; regard **4** regard as; deem **5** (as
considered *adj.*) deliberated (*a considered
opinion*) **6** all things considered taking ev·
erything into account [Fr fr. L]

con·sid·er·a·ble *adj.* **1** much (*considerable
pain*) **2** notable; important —con·sid'er·a·
bly *adv.*

con·sid·er·ate *adj.* thoughtful or solicitous to·
ward others —con·sid'er·ate·ly *adv.* [L, rel.
to CONSIDER]

con·sid·er·a·tion /kənsid'ərā'shən/ *n.* **1**
careful thought **2** thoughtfulness **3** fact or
thing taken into account **4** compensation; pay·
ment or reward

con·sid·er·ing *prep.* & *conj.* **1** in view of; be·
cause of —*adv.* **2** *Colloq.* all in all (*not so bad,
considering*)

con·sign /kənsīn'/ *v.* **1** hand over; deliver **2**

assign; commit **3** transmit or send (goods)
[L, rel. to SIGN]

con·sign·ment /kənsīn'mənt/ *n.* **1** consign·
ing or being consigned **2** goods consigned **3**
on consignment with payment due after sale
(of goods)

con·sist /kənsist'/ *v.* be composed; have as
ingredients or essentials [L *sistere* stop]

con·sis·ten·cy /kənsis'tənsē/ *n.* (*pl.* ·cies)
1 degree of density, thickness, etc., esp. of liq·
uids **2** being consistent [L, rel. to CONSIST]

con·sis·tent *adj.* **1** compatible or in harmony
with **2** (of a person) constant —con·sist'ent·
ly *adv.* [L, rel. to CONSIST]

con·so·la·tion /kän'sələ'shən/ *n.* **1** consol·
ing or being consoled **2** consoling thing or
person —con·sol·a·to·ry /kənsō'lətōr'ē,
-säl'ə-/ *adj.*

con·sole[1] /kənsōl'/ *v.* (·soled, ·sol·ing)
comfort, esp. in grief or disappointment [L,
rel. to SOLACE]

con·sole[2] /kän'sōl'/ *n.* **1** panel for switches,
controls, etc. **2** appliance cabinet **3** cabinet
with the keyboards and stops of an organ [Fr]

con·sol·i·date /kənsäl'ədāt'/ *v.* (·dat·ed,
·dat·ing) **1** make or become strong or secure
2 combine together —con·sol'i·da'tion,
con·sol'i·da'tor *n.* [L, rel. to SOLID]

con·som·mé /kän'səmā'/ *n.* clear soup from
meat stock [Fr]

con·so·nant /kän'sənənt/ *n.* **1** speech sound
in which the breath is at least partly ob·
structed **2** letter(s) representing this —*adj.*
3 consistent (with)

con·sort[1] *n.* /kän'sôrt'/ **1** wife or husband,
esp. of royalty —*v.* /kənsôrt'/ **2** keep com·
pany (with) [L, rel. to SORT]

con·sort[2] /kän'sôrt'/ *n.* small group of play·
ers, singers, or instruments [var. of CONCERT]

con·sor·ti·um /kənsôr'sh(ē)əm, -sôrt'ēəm/
n. (*pl.* ·ti·a or ·ti·ums) association, esp. of
several firms [L, rel. to CONSORT[1]]

con·spic·u·ous /kənspik'yōōəs/ *adj.* **1**
clearly visible; attracting notice **2** consider·
able —con·spic'u·ous·ly *adv.* [L *specere*
look]

con·spir·a·cy /kənspêr'əsē/ *n.* (*pl.* ·cies) **1**
secret plan to commit a crime; plot **2** conspir·
ing [L, rel. to CONSPIRE]

con·spir·a·tor /kənspêr'ətər/ *n.* person who
takes part in a conspiracy —con·spir·a·to·ri·
al /-tôr'ēəl/ *adj.*

con·spire /kənspīr'/ *v.* (·spired, ·spir·ing)
1 collude for an unlawful or harmful act **2** (of
events) seem to be working together [L *spi·
rare* breathe]

con·sta·ble /kän'stəbəl, kən'-/ *n.* **1** peace of·
ficer in a small town **2** *Brit.* police officer [LL
comes stabuli count of the stable]

Con·sta·ble /kän'stəbəl/, **John** 1776–1837;
English painter

con·stab·u·lar·y /kənstab'yələr'ē/ *n.* (*pl.*
·ies) constables, collectively [MedL, rel. to
CONSTABLE]

con·stan·cy /kän'stənsē/ *n.* dependability;
faithfulness [L, rel. to CONSTANT]

con·stant /kän'stənt/ *adj.* **1** continuous **2**
occurring frequently **3** faithful; dependable
—*n.* **4** anything that does not vary —con'
stant·ly *adv.* [L *stare* stand]

Con·stan·ta /kônstänt′sä/ *n.* seaport in Romania on the Black Sea. Pop. 350,500

Con·stan·tine /kän′stäntēn, -tīn′/, (called "the Great") c. 274–337; Roman emperor (306–337); sanctioned Christian worship

Con·stan·tine /kän′stäntēn, kôn′stäntēn/ *n.* city in Algeria. Pop. 440,900

Con·stan·ti·no·ple /kän′stantən-ō′pəl/ *n.* IsTANBUL

con·stel·la·tion /kän′stəlā′SHən/ *n.* 1 group of associated stars 2 configuration or assemblage, etc. [L *stella* star]

con·ster·na·tion /kän′stərmä′SHən/ *n.* anxiety; dismay [L *sternare* throw down]

con·sti·pate /kän′stəpāt′/ *v.* (·pat·ed, ·pat·ing) affect with constipation [L *stipare* cram]

con·sti·pa′tion *n.* difficulty in emptying the bowels

con·stit·u·en·cy /kənstiCH′ŏŏənsē/ *n.* (*pl.* ·cies) 1 body of voters who elect a representative 2 area so represented

con·stit·u·ent /kənstiCH′ŏŏənt/ *adj.* 1 composing; constituting 2 able to make or change a constitution (*constituent assembly*) 3 electing —*n.* 4 member of a constituency 5 component [L, rel. to CONSTITUTE]

con·sti·tute /kän′stit(y)ŏŏt′/ *v.* (·tut·ed, ·tut·ing) 1 be the components or essence of; compose 2 amount to (*constitutes a warning*) 3 give legal or constitutional form to [L *constituere* establish]

con·sti·tu·tion /kän′stit(y)ŏŏ′SHən/ *n.* 1 act or method of constituting; composition 2 body of fundamental governing principles 3 person's inherent health, strength, etc. [L, rel. to CONSTITUTE]

con′sti·tu′tion·al *adj.* 1 pertaining to a constitution 2 inherent (*constitutional weakness*) —*n.* 3 walk taken regularly for health —**con′sti·tu·tion·al′i·ty** *n.*; **con′sti·tu′tion·al·ly** *adv.*

con·strain /kənstrān′/ *v.* 1 compel 2a confine forcibly b restrict severely 3 force; embarrass [L *stringere* tie]

con·straint /kənstrānt′/ *n.* 1 constraining or being constrained 2 restriction 3 self-control

con·strict /kənstrikt′/ *v.* make narrow or tight; compress —**con·stric′tion** *n.*; **con·stric′tive** *adj.* [L, rel. to CONSTRAIN]

con·stric·tor /kənstrik′tər/ *n.* snake that kills by compressing

con·struct *v.* /kənstrəkt′/ 1 make by fitting together; build —*n.* /kän′strəkt′/ 2 thing constructed, esp. by the mind —**con·struc′tor** /kənstrək′tər/ *n.* [L *constructus* fr. *struere* build]

con·struc·tion /kənstrək′SHən/ *n.* 1 constructing or being constructed 2 thing constructed 3 interpretation or explanation 4 particular arrangement of words —**con·struc′tion·al** *adj.*

con·struc′tive *adj.* 1 tending to form a basis for ideas 2 helpful; positive —**con·struc′tive·ly** *adv.*

con·strue /kənstrŏŏ′/ *v.* (·strued, ·stru·ing) 1 interpret 2 analyze the syntax of (a sentence) 3 translate literally [L, rel. to CONSTRUCT]

con·sul /kän′səl/ *n.* official appointed by a government to protect its citizens and inter-ests in a foreign city 2 *Hist.* either of two chief magistrates in ancient Rome —**con′sul·ar** /-s(ə)lər/ *adj.*; **con′sul·ship** *n.* [L]

con·sul·ate /kän′sələt/ *n.* 1 official building of a consul 2 position of consul

con·sult /kənsəlt′/ *v.* 1 seek information or advice from 2 solicit the counsel of 3 take into account (feelings, interests, etc.) 4 provide professional advice —**con·sul′ta·tive** /-tätiv/ *adj.* [L *consulere* take counsel]

con·sult·ant /kənsəl′tnt/ *n.* person providing professional advice, strategy, etc. —**con·sul′tan·cy** *n.*

con·sul·ta·tion /kän′səltä′SHən/ *n.* 1 meeting for professional advice 2 act or process of consulting

con·sume /kəns(y)ŏŏm′/ *v.* (·sumed, ·sum·ing) 1 eat or drink 2 destroy 3 preoccupy; possess (*consumed with rage*) 4 use up —**con·sum′a·ble** *adj.* & *n.* [L *consumere*]

con·sum′er *n.* person who consumes, esp. one who uses a product or service

con·sum′er·ism *n.* movement to protect consumers' interests —**con·sum′er·ist** *adj.*

con·sum·mate *v.* /kän′səmāt′/ (·mat·ed, ·mat·ing) 1 complete; make perfect 2 complete (a marriage) by sexual intercourse —*adj.* /kän′səmit, kənsəm′it/ 3 complete; perfect —**con′sum·ma′tion** *n.* [L *summus* utmost]

con·sump·tion /kənsəmp′SHən/ *n.* 1 consuming or being consumed 2 amount consumed 3 use by a particular group 4 *Archaic.* tuberculosis 5 purchase and use of goods, etc. [Fr, rel. to CONSUME]

cont. *abbr.* 1 contents 2 continued

con·tact *n.* /kän′takt′/ 1 state or condition of touching, meeting, or communicating 2 person useful to deal with 3 connection for the passage of an electric current —*v.* /kän′takt′, kəntakt′/ 4 get in touch with [L *contactus* fr. *tangere* touch]

con′tact lens′ *n.* small lens placed directly on the eyeball to correct vision

con·ta·gion /kəntā′jən/ *n.* 1a spreading of disease by bodily contact b contagious disease 2 moral corruption [rel. to CONTACT]

con·ta·gious /kəntā′jəs/ *adj.* 1a (of a person) likely to transmit a disease by contact b (of a disease) transmitted in this way 2 (of emotions, etc.) likely to spread

con·tain /kəntān′/ *v.* 1 hold or be capable of holding within itself; include 2 (of measures) be equal to (*a gallon contains eight pints*) 3 prevent from moving or extending 4 control or restrain (feelings, etc.) [L *tenere* hold]

con·tain′er *n.* box, jar, etc., for holding things

con·tain′er·ize *v.* (·ized, ·iz·ing) pack in or transport by container —**con·tain′er·i·za′tion** *n.*

con·tain′ment *n.* prevention of hostile incursion

con·tam·i·nate /kəntam′ənāt′/ *v.* (·nat·ed, ·nat·ing) 1 pollute; taint 2 infect —**con·tam′i·nant** /-nənt/, **con·tam′i·na′tion**, **con·tam′i·na·tor** *n.* [L *-taminare*, rel. to *tangere* touch]

con·tem·plate /kän′təmplāt′/ *v.* (·plat·ed, ·plat·ing) 1 survey mentally or visually 2 regard (an event) as possible 3 intend 4 meditate —**con·tem·pla′tion** *n.*; **con·tem′pla·tive** /-təm′plətiv/ *adj.* [L]

con·tem·po·ra·ne·ous /kəntem′pərā′nēəs/ *adj.* existing or occurring at the same time —**con·tem′po·ra·ne′i·ty** /-rənē′ətē,-rənā′ətē/ *n.*; **con·tem′po·ra′ne·ous·ly** *adv.* [L, rel. to COM- + *tempus* time]

con·tem·po·rar·y /kəntem′pərer′ē/ *adj.* **1** living or occurring at the same time **2** of about the same age **3** modern in style —*n.* (*pl.* ·ies) **4** contemporary person or thing [MedL, rel. to CONTEMPORANEOUS]

con·tempt /kəntempt′/ *n.* **1** feeling of scorn or extreme reproach **2** being so regarded **3** disrespect shown to a court, etc. [L *contemp-tus* fr. *temnere* despise]

con·tempt·i·ble /kəntemp′təbəl/ *adj.* de-serving contempt —**con·tempt′i·bly** *adv.*

con·temp·tu·ous /kəntemp′CHŌōəs/ *adj.* feeling or showing contempt —**con·temp′tu·ous·ly** *adv.*; **con·temp′tu·ous·ness** *n.*

con·tend /kəntend′/ *v.* **1** fight; argue **2** compete **3** assert; maintain —**con·tend′er** *n.* [L, rel. to TEND¹]

con·tent¹ /kəntent′/ *adj* **1** satisfied; ade-quately happy **2** willing —*v.* **3** satisfy —*n.* **4** satisfied state [L, rel. to CONTAIN]

con·tent² /kän′tent′/ *n.* **1** (usu. *pl.*) what is contained, as in a vessel, book, house, etc. **2** amount contained (*high fat content*) **3** sub-stance (of a speech, etc.) as distinct from form **4** capacity or volume [MedL, rel. to CONTAIN]

con·tent·ed /kəntent′id/ *adj.* happy; satis-fied —**con·tent′ed·ly** *adv.*; **con·tent′ed·ness** *n.*

con·ten·tion /kəntenSHən/ *n.* **1** dispute or argument; rivalry **2** assertion [L, rel. to CON-TEND]

con·ten′tious *adj.* **1** quarrelsome **2** likely to cause an argument

con·tent·ment /kəntent′mənt/ *n.* satisfied state; tranquil happiness

con·test *n.* /kän′test′/ **1** contending; strife **2** a competition —*v.* /kəntest′/ **3** dispute **4** contend or compete for [L *testis* witness]

con·test·ant /kəntes′tənt/ *n.* person taking part in a contest

con·text /kän′tekst′/ *n.* **1** parts that sur-round or clarify a word or passage **2** relevant circumstances —**con·tex·tu·al** /kənteks′CHŌōəl/ *adj.*; **con·tex′tu·al·ize′** *v.* (·ized, ·iz-ing) [L, rel. to TEXT]

con·tig·u·ous /kəntig′yŌōəs/ *adj.* touching; in contact —**con·ti·gu·i·ty** /kän′tigyŌō′ətē/ *n.* [L, rel. to CONTACT]

con·ti·nent¹ /kän′tn-ənt/ *n.* any of the main continuous land masses on earth (Europe, Asia, Africa, N and S America, Australia, Ant-arctica) —**con′ti·nen′tal** /-tənent′l/ *adj.* [L, rel. to CONTAIN]

con·ti·nent² *adj.* **1** able to control one's bow-els and bladder **2** exercising self-restraint, esp. sexually —**con′ti·nence** *n.* [L, rel. to CONTAIN]

con′ti·nen′tal break′fast *n.* light breakfast of coffee, rolls, etc.

Con·ti·nen′tal Di·vide′ *n.* (also called **Great′ Di·vide′**) line in the Rocky Mountains mark-ing separation of westward-flowing and east-ward-flowing rivers

con′ti·nen′tal shelf′ *n.* area of shallow seabed bordering a continent

con·tin·gen·cy /kəntin′jənsē/ *n.* (*pl.* ·cies)

1 event that may or may not occur **2** uncer-tainty or chance [L, rel. to CONTINGENT]

con·tin′gent *adj.* **1** conditional; dependent (on an uncertain event or circumstance) **2** that may or may not occur —*n.* **3** body (of troops, ships, etc.) forming a part **4** group or faction [L, rel. to CONTACT]

con·tin·u·al /kəntin′yŌōəl/ *adj.* constantly or frequently recurring; inescapable —**con·tin′u·al·ly** *adv.* [Fr, rel. to CONTINUE]

● Usage: Careful users distinguish *continual* 'repeating at intervals' and *continuous* 'going on uninterruptedly': *The coast is continually pounded by storms. The eternal flame burns con-tinuously.*

con·tin·u·ance /kəntin′yŌōəns/ *n.* **1** contin-uing in existence or operation **2** duration **3** *Law.* delay; postponement

con·tin·u·a·tion /kəntin′yŌō-ā′SHən/ *n.* **1** continuing or being continued **2** part that con-tinues something else

con·tin·ue /kəntin′yŌō/ *v.* (·ued, ·u·ing) **1** maintain; not stop **2** resume or prolong (a nar-rative, journey, etc.) **3** be a sequel to **4** re-main [L, rel. to CONTAIN]

con·ti·nu·i·ty /kän′tn-(y)Ōō′itē/ *n.* (*pl.* ·ties) **1** state of being continuous **2** a logical sequence

con·tin′u·ous *adj.* uninterrupted; unbroken —**con·tin′u·ous·ly** *adv.* [L, rel. to CONTAIN]

● Usage: See note at CONTINUAL.

con·tin·u·um /kəntin′(y)Ōōəm/ *n.* (*pl.* ·ua or ·u·ums) thing having a continuous struc-ture [L, rel. to CONTINUOUS]

con·tort /kəntôrt′/ *v.* twist or force out of normal shape —**con·tor′tion** *n.* [L *torquere* twist]

con·tor′tion·ist *n.* entertainer who adopts contorted postures

con·tour /kän′tŌor′/ *n.* **1** outline —*v.* **2** shape to the outward form of a thing [It *con-tornare* draw in outline]

contra- *comb. form* against; opposite [L]

con·tra·band /kän′trəband′/ *n.* **1** smuggled goods —*adj.* **2** forbidden from import or ex-port [Sp fr. It]

con·tra·cep·tion /kän′trəsep′SHən/ *n.* pre-vention of pregnancy, esp. by artificial means —**con′tra·cep′tive** *adj.* [fr. CONTRA- + CON-CEPTION]

con·tract *n.* /kän′trakt′/ **1** written or spoken agreement, esp. one enforceable by law **2** document recording this —*v.* /kəntrakt′/ **3** make or become smaller or shorter **4a** make a contract **b** arrange (work) to be done by contract **5** become affected by (a disease) —**con·tract′i·ble** *adj.* [L *contractus*, rel. to TRACT¹]

con·trac·tile /kəntrak′tīl′, -təl/ *adj.* capable of or producing contraction —**con·trac·til·i·ty** /kän′trak′til′-ətē/ *n.*

con·trac·tion /kəntrak′SHən/ *n.* **1** contract-ing or being contracted **2** *Med.* shortening of the uterine muscles during childbirth **3** short-ened form of a word or words (e.g., *he's*)

con·trac·tor /kän′trak′tər, kəntrak′tər/ *n.* person who makes a contract, as to provide services

con·trac·tu·al /kəntrak'CHŌŌəl/ *adj.* pertaining to a contract —**con·trac'tu·al·ly** *adv.*

con·tra·dict /kän'trədikt'/ *v.* 1 deny (a statement) 2 deny a statement made by (a person) 3 be in opposition to or in conflict with —**con·tra·dic'tion** *n.*; **con·tra·dic'to·ry** *adj.* [L *dictus* fr. *dicere* say]

con·tra·dis·tinc·tion /kän'trədistiNG'SHən/ *n.* distinction made by contrast

con·trail /kän'trāl/ *n.* white vapor trail left by jet engines [con(densation) trail]

con·tral·to /kəntral'tō/ *n.* (*pl.* -tos) 1 lowest female singing voice 2 singer with this voice [It, rel. to CONTRA- + ALTO]

con·trap·tion /kəntrap'SHən/ *n.* machine or device, esp. an odd one

con·tra·pun·tal /kän'trəpənt'l/ *adj. Mus.* of or in counterpoint —**con'tra·pun'tal·ly** *adv.* [fr. It]

con·trar·i·wise /kän'trer'ēwīz', kän'trer'ē-/ *adv.* 1 on the other hand 2 in the opposite way

con·trar·y /kän'trer'ē, kəntrer'ē/ *adj.* 1 opposed in nature or tendency 2 willful 3 (of a wind) unfavorable 4 opposite in position or direction —*n.* 5 (prec. by *the*) the opposite —*adv.* 6 (foll. by *to*) quite the opposite of (*contrary to expectations*) 7 **on the contrary** expressing denial of what has just been implied or stated —**con'trar·i·ness** /-trer'ēnəs, -trer'-/ *n.* [L, rel. to CONTRA-]

con·trast *n.* /kän'trast'/ 1a juxtaposition or comparison showing differences b difference so revealed 2 thing or person having different qualities 3 range of color or tone in a picture —*v.* /kəntrast', kän'trast'/ 4 set together so as to reveal a contrast [It fr. L *stare* stand]

• Usage: *Compare* means 'note the similarities' while *contrast* connotes 'note the differences.'

con·tra·vene /kän'trəvēn'/ *v.* (·vened, ·ven·ing) 1 infringe (a law, etc.) 2 (of things) conflict with —**con·tra·ven'tion** /-ven'SHən/ *n.* [L *venire* come]

con·tre·temps /kän'trətäN'/ *n.* (*pl.* same /-täNz/) unfortunate and embarrassing encounter, occurrence, etc. [Fr]

con·trib·ute /kəntrib'yŏŏt/ *v.* (·ut·ed, ·ut·ing) 1 give (time, money, etc.) toward a common purpose; help play a part in 2 supply (an article, etc.) for publication —**con·trib'u·tor** *n.*; **con·trib'u·to'ry** *adj.* [L, rel. to TRIBUTE]

con'tri·bu'tion *n.* 1 act of contributing 2 thing contributed

con·trite /kəntrīt'/ *adj.* penitent; feeling great guilt —**con·trite'ly** *adv.*; **con·tri'tion** /-trisH'ən/ *n.* [L, rel. to TRITE]

con·triv·ance /kəntrī'vəns/ *n.* 1 something contrived, esp. a plan or mechanical device 2 act of contriving

con·trive /kəntrīv'/ *v.* (·trived, ·triv·ing) 1 devise; plan or make resourcefully or with skill 2 manage [Fr fr. L]

con·trived' *adj.* artificial; forced

con·trol /kəntrōl'/ *n.* 1 power of directing 2 power of restraining, esp. self-restraint 3 means of restraint 4 (usu. *pl.*) means of regulating 5 (usu. *pl.*) switches and other devices by which a machine is controlled 6 place where something is overseen 7 standard of comparison in an experiment —*v.* (·trolled, ·trol·ling) 8 have control of; regulate 9 hold in check —**con·trol'la·ble** *adj.* [MedL: keep copy of accounts, rel. to CONTRA- + ROLL]

con·trol·ler /kəntrō'lər/ *n.* 1 person or thing that controls 2 person in charge 3 financial officer of a business, etc.

con·tro·ver·sial /kän'trəvər'SHəl/ *adj.* causing or subject to controversy [L, rel. to CONTROVERT]

con·tro·ver·sy /kän'trəvər'sē/ *n.* (*pl.* ·sies) prolonged argument or dispute [L, rel. to CONTROVERT]

con·tro·vert /kän'trəvərt'/ *v.* dispute; deny [L *vertere* turn]

con·tu·ma·cious /kän't(y)əmā'SHəs/ *adj.* stubbornly or willfully disobedient —**con·tu·ma·cy** /kənt(y)ŏŏ'məsē, känt't(y)ə-/ *n.* (*pl.* ·cies) [L *tumere* swell]

con·tu·me·ly /kän'tyŏŏməl'ē, kənt(y)ŏŏm'əlē/ *n.* 1 insolent language or treatment 2 insult [L, rel. to CONTUMACIOUS]

con·tuse /kənt(y)ŏŏz'/ *v.* (·tused, ·tus·ing) bruise —**con·tu'sion** /t(y)ŏŏ'zHən/ *n.* [L *contusus* fr. *tundere* hit]

co·nun·drum /kənən'drəm/ *n.* 1 riddle, esp. one with a pun in its answer 2 puzzling question

con·ur·ba·tion /kän'ərbā'SHən/ *n.* extended urban area [L *urbs* city]

con·va·lesce /kän'vəles'/ *v.* (·lesced, ·lesc·ing) recover health after illness —**con·va·les'cence** *n.*; **con·va·les'cent** *adj. & n.* [L *valere* be well]

con·vec·tion /kənvek'SHən/ *n.* heat transfer by upward movement of a heated and less dense medium [L *vehere* carry]

con·vene /kənvēn'/ *v.* (·vened, ·ven·ing) 1 summon or arrange (a meeting, etc.) 2 assemble [L *venire* come]

con·ven·ience /kənvēn'yəns/ *n.* 1 state of being convenient; suitability 2 useful or helpful thing 3 **at one's convenience** as suitable [L, rel. to CONVENE]

con·ven·ient /kənvēn'yənt/ *adj.* serving one's comfort or interests; suitable —**con·ven'ient·ly** *adv.*

con·vent /kän'vənt, -vent'/ *n.* 1 religious community, esp. of nuns 2 premises for this [L, rel. to CONVENE]

con·ven·tion /kənven'SHən/ *n.* 1 general custom or customary practice 2 assembling of many people with a common interest 3 a formal agreement, esp. between nations [L, rel. to CONVENE]

con·ven·tion·al /kənven'SHənl/ *adj.* 1 depending on or according with convention 2 (of a person) bound by social conventions 3 usual or commonplace 4 (of weapons, etc.) nonnuclear —**con·ven·tion·al'i·ty** *n.* (*pl.* ·ties); **con·ven'tion·al·ly** *adv.*

con·verge /kənvərj'/ *v.* (·verged, ·verg·ing) 1 come together or toward the same point 2 approach from different directions —**con·ver'gence** *n.*; **con·ver'gent** *adj.* [L *vergere* incline]

con·ver·sant /kənvər'sənt/ *adj.* well acquainted (with) [Fr, rel. to CONVERSE[1]]

con·ver·sa·tion /kän'vərsā'SHən/ *n.* 1 informal spoken communication 2 instance of this —**con'ver·sa'tion·al** *adj.*; **con'ver·sa'tion·**

al·ist *n.*; **con'ver·sa'tion·al·ly** *adv.* [L, rel. to CONVERSE¹]

con·verse¹ /kənvʉrs'/ *v.* (**·versed, ·vers·ing**) talk [L, rel. to CONVERT]

con·verse² /kän'vʉrs/ *adj.* 1 opposite; contrary; reversed —*n.* 2 something opposite or contrary —**con·verse'ly** /kən-, kän-/ *adv.* [L, rel. to CONVERT]

con·ver·sion /kənvʉr'zhən/ *n.* converting or being converted [L, rel. to CONVERT]

con·vert *v.* /kənvʉrt'/ 1 change in form or function 2 cause (a person) to change belief, etc. 3 change (moneys, etc.) 4 modify structurally 5 (in various sports) score a point or points —*n.* /kän'vʉrt'/ 6 person changed to a different belief, etc. [L *vertere* turn]

con·vert·i·ble /kənvʉr'təbəl/ *adj.* 1 able to be converted —*n.* 2 car with a folding roof —**con·vert·i·bil'i·ty** *n.* [L, rel. to CONVERT]

CONVEX and CONCAVE

con·vex /känveks', kän'veks'/ *adj.* curved like the exterior of a circle or sphere —**con·vex'i·ty** *n.* [L]

con·vey /kənvā'/ *v.* 1 transport or carry 2 communicate or transmit (an idea, meaning, etc.) —**con·vey'a·ble** *adj.* [L *via* way]

con·vey·ance /kənvā'əns/ *n.* 1 conveying or being conveyed 2 means of transport; vehicle

con·vict *v.* /kənvikt'/ 1 prove to be guilty 2 declare guilty by a legal process —*n.* /kän'vikt'/ 3 prison inmate [L *convictus* fr. *vincere* conquer]

con·vic·tion /kənvik'shən/ *n.* 1 convicting or being convicted 2a being convinced b firm belief [L, rel. to CONVICT]

con·vince /kənvins'/ *v.* (**·vinced, ·vinc·ing**) firmly persuade —**con·vinc'ing** *adj.*; **con·vinc'ing·ly** *adv.* [L, rel. to CONVICT]

con·viv·i·al /kənviv'ēəl/ *adj.* fond of good company; sociable and lively —**con·viv·i·al'i·ty** *n.* [L *vivere* live]

con·vo·ca·tion /kän'vōkā'shən/ *n.* 1 convoking or being convoked 2 large formal gathering [L, rel. to CONVOKE]

con·voke /kənvōk'/ *v.* (**·voked, ·vok·ing**) *Formal.* call together [L *vocare* call]

con·vo·lut·ed /kän'vəlo͞o'tid/ *adj.* 1 coiled; twisted 2 complex [L *convolutus* fr. *volvere* roll]

con·vo·lu·tion /kän'vəlo͞o'shən/ *n.* 1 coiling; twisting 2 complexity

con·voy /kän'voi'/ *n.* group of ships, vehicles, etc., traveling together or under escort [Fr, rel. to CONVEY]

con·vulse /kənvəls'/ *v.* (**·vulsed, ·vuls·ing**) 1 (usu. *passive*) affect with convulsions 2 cause to laugh uncontrollably —**con·vul'sive** *adj.*; **con·vul'sive·ly** *adv.* [L *convulsus* fr. *vellere* pull]

con·vul·sion /kənvəl'shən/ *n.* 1 (usu. *pl.*) violent body spasm 2 violent disturbance 3 (in *pl.*) uncontrollable laughter

coo /ko͞o/ *n.* 1 soft murmuring sound as of a dove —*v.* (**cooed, coo·ing**) 2 emit a coo 3 talk or say in a soft voice [imit.]

cook /ko͝ok/ *v.* 1 prepare (food) by heating it 2 (of food) undergo cooking 3 *Colloq.* falsify (accounts, etc.) —*n.* 4 person who cooks 5 **be cooking** *Colloq.* be happening, proceeding, or thriving 6 **cook up** *Colloq.* concoct [L *coquere*]

Cook /ko͝ok/, (Captain) James 1728–79; English explorer of the Pacific

cook'book' *n.* book of recipes, etc.

cook·er·y /ko͝ok'ərē/ *n.* art or practice of cooking

cook·ie /ko͝ok'ē/ *n.* small, baked, sweet cake [prob. Du *koekje*]

cook'ie-cut'ter *adj.* made or done to an unchanging pattern; unvarying

Cook Is·lands *n.* group of islands in the S Pacific belonging to New Zealand

cool /ko͞ol/ *adj.* 1 of or at a fairly low temperature; fairly cold 2 calm; unexcited 3 lacking enthusiasm 4 calmly audacious 5a *Slang.* meeting approval b wonderful; great —*n.* 6 coolness 7 *Slang.* calmness; composure —*v.* 8 make or become cool 9 **cool it** *Slang.* calm down —**cool'ly** *adv.*; **cool'ness** *n.* [OE]

cool·ant /ko͞o'lənt/ *n.* cooling agent, esp. fluid

cool·er /ko͞o'lər/ *n.* 1 container in which a thing is cooled or kept cold 2 cold drink 3 *Slang.* prison cell

Cool·idge /ko͞o'lij/, (John) Calvin 1872–1933; 30th US president (1923–29)

coo·lie /ko͞o'lē/ *n.* unskilled native laborer in the Far East [perh. fr. *Kulī*, tribe in India]

coon /ko͞on/ *n.* raccoon [abbr.]

coop /ko͞op/ *n.* 1 cage for keeping poultry —*v.* 2 confine (a person) [L *cupa* cask]

co·op /kō'äp'/ *n. Colloq.* COOPERATIVE, 3, 4, 5 [abbr.]

Coop·er /ko͞o'pər, ko͝op'ər/, James Fenimore 1789–1851; US novelist

co·op·er·ate /kō·äp'ərāt'/ *v.* (**·at·ed, ·at·ing**) 1 work or act together with 2 do as one is asked —**co'op·er·a'tion** *n.* [rel. to CO-]

co·op·er·a·tive /kō·äp'(ə)rətiv/ *adj.* 1 willing to cooperate 2 of or characterized by cooperation 3 (of a business) owned and run jointly by its members, with profits shared —*n.* 4 (often **co-op**) a apartment building owned by tenant shareholders b apartment in such a building 5 cooperative farm, society, or business

co·opt /kō·äpt'/ *v.* 1 appoint to membership of a body by invitation 2 take over or appropriate —**co·op'tion** /-äp'shən/ *n.*; **co·op'tive** *adj.* [L *cooptare* fr. *optare* choose]

co·or·di·nate *v.* /kō·ôrd'n·āt'/ (**·nat·ed, ·nat·ing**) 1 cause to function together efficiently 2 work or act together effectively —*adj.* /kō·ôrd'nət/ 3 equal in rank or importance —*n.* /kō·ôrd'nət/ 4 *Math.* each of a system of values used to fix the position of a point, line, or plane —**co·or'di·na'tion, co·or'di·na'tor** *n.* [L *ordo*, rel. to ORDER]

coot /ko͞ot/ *n.* 1 aquatic bird with short wings and tail 2 *Colloq.* crotchety person [prob. LGer]

cop /käp/ *Slang. n.* 1 police officer —*v.* (**copped, cop·ping**) 2 catch or arrest (an offender) 3 take; seize 4 **cop out** withdraw;

give up; renege **5 cop a plea** *Colloq.* plea-bargain [Fr *caper* seize]

cope[1] /kōp/ *v.* (**coped, cop·ing**) deal effectively or contend with; manage [Fr, rel. to COUP]

cope[2] *n.* priest's cloaklike vestment [L *cappa* CAP]

Co·pen·ha·gen /kō′pənhä′gən, -häg′ən/ *n.* capital of Denmark. Pop. 1,337,100

Co·per·ni·cus /kəpər′nikəs/, **Nicolaus** 1473–1543; Polish astronomer; promulgated theory of the solar system

cop·i·er /käp′ēər/ *n.* machine that makes copies

co·pi·lot /kō′pī′lət/ *n.* assistant pilot in an aircraft

cop·ing /kō′piNG/ *n.* top (usu. sloping) course of masonry in a wall [fr. COPE[2]]

co·pi·ous /kō′pēəs/ *adj.* 1 abundant 2 productive —**co′pi·ous·ly** *adv.* [L *copia* plenty]

Cop·land /kō′plənd/, **Aaron** 1900–90; US composer

Cop·ley /käp′lē/, **John Singleton** 1738–1815; US painter

cop′-out′ *n.* cowardly evasion

cop·per /käp′ər/ *n.* 1 malleable red-brown metallic element; *symb.* Cu 2 bronze coin —*adj.* 3 made of or colored like copper [L *cuprum*]

cop′per·head′ *n.* venomous N American or Australian snake

Cop·po·la /käp′ələ/, **Francis Ford** 1939– ; US film director and producer

co·pra /kō′prə/ *n.* dried coconut meat [Port fr. Malayalam]

copse /käps/ *n.* (**also cop·pice** /käp′əs/) area dense with trees or shrubs

cop·ter /käp′tər/ *n.* helicopter [abbr.]

cop·u·la /käp′yələ/ *n.* (*pl.* **-las**) connecting word, esp. a form of the verb *be* linking subject and predicate [L]

cop·u·late /käp′yəlāt′/ *v.* (**-lat·ed, -lat·ing**) have sexual intercourse —**cop·u·la′tion** *n.*

cop·y /käp′ē/ *n.* (*pl.* **-ies**) 1 thing made to imitate another 2 issue of a publication 3 material to be printed; reading matter (*the crisis will make exciting copy*) —*v.* (**cop·ied, cop·y·ing**) 4 make a copy of 5 imitate [L *copia* plenty]

cop′y·cat′ *n. Colloq.* imitator

cop′y·right′ *n.* 1 exclusive legal right to print, publish, perform, or record material —*adj.* 2 protected by copyright —*v.* 3 secure copyright for (material)

cop′y·writ′er *n.* writer of promotional or advertising copy

co·quette /kōket′/ *n.* female who flirts —**co·quet′tish** *adj.* [Fr dim., rel. to COCK[1]]

cor- *prefix* var. of COM- before *r*

cor·al /kôr′əl, kär′-/ *n.* 1 hard red, pink, or white calcareous substance secreted by marine polyps —*adj.* 2 red or pink, like coral 3 made of coral [Gk *korallion*]

Cor′al Sea′ *n.* part of the S Pacific, NE of Australia

cor·bel /kôr′bəl/ *n.* jutting support of stone, timber, etc. [L *corvus* crow]

cord /kôrd/ *n.* 1a thick stringlike material **b** piece of this 2 similar structure 3a ribbed fabric, esp. corduroy **b** (in *pl.*) corduroy trousers 4 unit of measure for stacked firewood; 128 cu. ft. [Gk *khordē* string]

Cor·day d′Ar·mont /kôrdā′därmôN′/, **Charlotte** 1768–93; French political assassin

cor·dial /kôr′jəl/ *adj.* 1 warm; friendly —*n.* 2 liqueur —**cor·di·al·i·ty** /kôr′jē·al′ətē/ *n.*; **cor′dial·ly** *adv.* [L *cor cordis* heart]

cord·ite /kôr′dīt′/ *n.* smokeless explosive [fr. CORD, because of its appearance]

cord·less /kôrd′ləs/ *adj.* battery-powered

Cór·do·ba /kôr′dəbə, -əvə/ *n.* 1 (also **Cor′do·va**) city in S Spain. Pop. 300,200 2 city in central Argentina. Pop. 1,179,000

cor·don /kôrd′n/ *n.* 1 protective line or circle of police, soldiers, guards, etc. 2 ornamental cord or braid —*v.* 3 enclose or separate with a cordon of police, etc. [It and Fr, rel. to CORD]

cor·du·roy /kôr′dəroi′/ *n.* 1 thick cotton fabric with velvety ribs 2 (*pl.*) corduroy trousers [*cord* ribbed fabric]

core /kôr/ *n.* 1 central part of certain fruits, containing the seeds 2 central or most important part of anything 3 inner central region of the earth —*v.* (**cored, cor·ing**) 4 remove the core from —**cor′er** *n.*

co·re·spon·dent /kôrispän′dənt/ *n.* person cited in a divorce case as having committed adultery with the respondent

Cor·fu /kôrfōō′/ *n.* island off the NW coast of Greece

cor·gi /kôr′gē/ *n.* (*pl.* **-gis**) dog of a short-legged breed with a foxlike head [Welsh]

co·ri·an·der /kôr′ēan′dər/ *n.* 1 aromatic plant 2 its seeds used for flavoring [Gk *koriandron*]

Co·rin·thi·an /kərin′THēən/ *adj.* of the most ornate order of Greek architecture, characterized by a large capital decorated with acanthus leaves (see illustration at CAPITAL) [*Corinth,* ancient Greek city]

Cor·i·o·la·nus /kôr′ēəlä′nəs/, **Gaius** (or **Gnaeus**) **Marcius** 5th cent. B.C.; legendary Roman general

cork /kôrk/ *n.* 1 buoyant light-brown bark of a S European oak 2 stopper for a bottle, made of this —*adj.* 3 made of cork —*v.* 4 stop, as with a cork [Ar *qurq* fr. L *quercus* oak]

Cork /kôrk/ *n.* seaport in Ireland. Pop. 127,000

cork′screw′ *n.* 1 spiral device for extracting corks from bottles 2 thing with a spiral shape —*v.* 3 move spirally; twist

cor·mo·rant /kôr′mərənt/ *n.* diving black sea bird [L *corvus marinus* sea-raven]

corn[1] /kôrn/ *n.* 1a cereal plant, originally of America, with kernels growing in rows on a core (cob) enclosed by a leaflike husk **b** kernels of this plant 2 grain or seed of a cereal plant 3 *Brit.* grain, esp. wheat or a chief crop 4 *Colloq.* something corny or trite [OE]

corn[2] *n.* painful area of hardened skin, esp. on the toe [L *cornu* horn]

corn′ball′ *adj. Slang.* CORNY

corn′cob′ *n.* cylindrical center of a corn ear

cor·ne·a /kôr′nēə/ *n.* transparent covering at the front of the eyeball —**cor′ne·al** *adj.* [MedL, rel. to CORN[2]]

corned /kôrnd/ *adj.* (esp. of beef) preserved in salt or brine [fr. CORN[1]]

Cor·neille /kôrnā′/, **Pierre** 1606–84; French dramatist

cor·ner /kôr′nər/ *n.* 1 place where sides or

edges meet **2** projecting angle, esp. where two streets meet **3** internal space or recess formed by the meeting of two sides, esp. of a room **4** difficult position **5** secluded place, region, or quarter **6** monopoly on a stock or commodity —*v.* **7** force into a difficult or inescapable position **8** establish a monopoly in **9** (esp. of or in a vehicle) go around a corner [L, rel. to CORN²]

cor'ner·stone' *n.* **1** stone at the corner of a building, often laid with ceremony **2** indispensable part or basis

cor·net /kôr'net'/ *n.* brass instrument resembling a trumpet but shorter and wider —**cor·net'ist** *n.* [L *cornu*, rel. to CORN²]

corn'flow'er *n.* plant with deep-blue flowers

cor·nice /kôr'nis/ *n.* ornamental molding just below a ceiling [Fr fr. It]

Corn·ish /kôrn'ish/ *adj.* **1** pertaining to Cornwall, England, or its people —*n.* **2** Celtic language of Cornwall

corn' meal' *n.* coarse ground corn

corn' starch' *n.* starchy flour from corn, used in cooking

corn' syr'up *n.* sweet syrup processed from corn

cor·nu·co·pi·a /kôr'n(y)əkō'pēə/ *n.* **1** horn overflowing with flowers, fruit, etc., as a symbol of plenty **2** abundant supply [L, rel. to CORN² + COPIOUS]

Corn·wall /kôrn'wôl/ *n.* county in SW England

Corn·wal·lis /kôrnwäl'əs/, **Charles (1st Marquis)** 1738–1805; British general who surrendered to George Washington at Yorktown

corn'y *adj.* (**·i·er, ·i·est**) *Colloq.* tritely humorous —**corn'i·ly** *adv.*; **corn'i·ness** *n.* [fr. CORN¹]

co·rol·la /kərä1'ə, -rō'lə/ *n.* petals forming a flower [L dim. of CORONA]

cor·ol·lar·y /kôr'əler'ē/ *n.* (*pl.* **·ies**) **1** proposition that follows from one already proved **2** natural consequence [L: gratuity, rel. to COROLLA]

co·ro·na /kərō'nə/ *n.* (*pl.* **nas** or **·nae** /-nē/) **1** halo around the sun or moon **2** ionized gas around the sun, visible during total solar eclipse —**cor·o'nal** *adj.* [L: crown]

Co·ro·na·do /kôr'ənäd'ō/, **Francisco Vásquez de** 1510–54; Spanish explorer

cor·o·nar·y /kôr'əner'ē, kär'-/ *adj.* **1** *Anat.* resembling or encircling like a crown, esp. of the heart's arteries —*n.* (*pl.* **·ies**) **2** CORONARY THROMBOSIS [L, rel. to CORONA]

cor'o·nar'y throm·bo'sis *n.* obstruction caused by a blood clot in a coronary artery

cor·o·na·tion /kôr'ənā'shən, kär'-/ *n.* ceremony of crowning [MedL, rel. to CORONA]

cor·o·ner /kôr'ənər, kär'-/ *n.* official holding inquests on deaths thought to be violent or accidental [AngFr, rel. to CROWN]

cor·o·net /kôr'ənet', kär'-/ *n.* small crown or band worn on the head [Fr dim., rel. to CROWN]

Co·rot /kərō'/, **(Jean-Baptiste) Camille** 1796–1875; French landscape painter

corp. *abbr.* corporation

cor·po·ra /kôr'pərə/ *n.* *pl.* of CORPUS

cor·po·ral¹ /kôr'p(ə)rəl/ *n.* *Milit.* noncommissioned officer ranking just below sergeant [Fr fr. It]

---

129   **cornerstone / corroborate**

cor·po·ral² *adj.* of the human body —**cor·po·ral·i·ty** /kôr'pəral'ətē/ *n.* [L *corpus* body]

cor'po·ral pun'ish·ment *n.* physical punishment

cor·po·rate /kôr'p(ə)rət/ *adj.* **1** forming a corporation **2** enjoined or united [L, rel. to CORPORAL²]

cor·po·ra'tion *n.* group of people legally chartered to act as an individual, esp. in business

cor·po·re·al /kôrpôr'ēəl/ *adj.* bodily; physical; material —**cor'po·re·al'i·ty** *n.*; **cor·po're·al·ly** *adv.* [L, rel. to CORPORAL²]

corps /kôr/ *n.* (*pl.* same /kôrz/) **1** special military body or subdivision **2** special personnel (*diplomatic corps*) [Fr, rel. to CORPSE]

corpse /kôrps/ *n.* dead body [L, rel. to CORPUS]

cor·pu·lent /kôr'pyələnt/ *adj.* physically bulky; fat —**cor'pu·lence** *n.* [L, rel. to CORPUS]

cor·pus /kôr'pəs/ *n.* (*pl.* **·po·ra** /-pərə/) body or collection of writings, texts, etc. [L: body]

Cor·pus Chris·ti /kôr'pəs kris'tē/ *n.* city in Texas. Pop. 257,453

cor·pus·cle /kôr'pəs'əl/ *n.* vertebrate cell, esp. in blood —**cor·pus'cu·lar** *adj.* [L dim. of CORPUS]

corr. *abbr.* **1** correction **2** correspondence

cor·ral /kəral'/ *n.* **1** pen for cattle, horses, etc. —*v.* (**·ralled, ·ral·ling**) **2** put or keep in a corral [Sp and Port, rel. to KRAAL]

cor·rect /kərekt'/ *adj.* **1** true; accurate **2** proper and expected —*v.* **3** set right; amend **4** mark errors in **5a** admonish (a person) **b** punish (a person or fault) **6** counteract (a harmful quality) —**cor·rect'ly** *adv.*; **cor·rect'ness** *n.* [L *correctus* fr. *regere* guide]

cor·rec·tion /kərek'shən/ *n.* **1** correcting or being corrected **2** thing substituted for what is wrong **3** *Formal.* punishment —**cor·rec'tion·al** *adj.* [L, rel. to CORRECT]

cor·rec·tive /kərek'tiv/ *adj.* **1** serving to correct or counteract something harmful —*n.* **2** corrective measure or thing [L, rel. to CORRECT]

Cor·reg·gio /kərej'(ē)ō/, **Antonio Allegri da** c. 1489–1534; Italian painter

cor·re·late /kôr'əlāt, kär'-/ *v.* (**·lat·ed, ·lat·ing**) **1** have or bring into a mutual relation or dependence —*n.* **2** each of two complements —**cor're·la'tion** *n.* [rel. to RELATION]

cor·rel·a·tive /kərel'ətiv/ *adj.* **1** having a mutual relation **2** *Gram.* used together (as *neither* and *nor*) —*n.* **3** correlative word or thing

cor·re·spond /kôr'əspänd', kär'-/ *v.* **1a** be similar or equivalent (to) **b** be in agreement (with); not contradict **2** exchange letters (with) —**cor·re·spond'ing·ly** *adv.* [Fr fr. MedL]

cor·re·spon·dence /kôr'əspän'dəns, kär'-/ *n.* **1** agreement or similarity **2a** exchange of letters **b** letters

cor·re·spond·ent /kôr'əspän'dənt, kär'-/ *n.* **1** person who writes letters **2** reporter or news source, esp. abroad

cor·ri·dor /kôr'ədər, kär'-, -dôr'/ *n.* passage giving access into rooms, compartments, etc. [Fr fr. It]

cor·rob·o·rate /kəräb'ərāt'/ *v.* (**·rat·ed,**

·rat·ing) confirm or give support to (a statement or belief, etc.) —**cor·rob·o·ra·tion** n.; **cor·rob·o·ra·tive** adj.; **cor·rob·o·ra·tor** n. [L robur strength]

cor·rode /kərōd'/ v. (**·rod·ed, ·rod·ing**) 1 wear away, esp. by chemical action 2 destroy gradually [L rodere gnaw]

cor·ro·sion /kərō'zHən/ n. 1 corroding or being corroded 2 corroded area —**cor·ro'sive** adj. & n.

cor·ru·gate /kôr'əgāt, kär'-/ v. (**·gat·ed, ·gat·ing**) form into ridges and grooves —**cor·ru·ga'tion** n. [L rugare wrinkle]

cor·rupt /kərəpt'/ adj. 1 dishonest, esp. being bribed 2 immoral; wicked 3 (of a text, etc.) made unreliable by errors or alterations —v. 4 make or become corrupt —**cor·rupt'i·ble** adj.; **cor·rupt·i·bil'i·ty** n.; **cor·rup'tion** /-rəp'sHən/ n.; **cor·rup'tive** adj.; **cor·rupt'ly** adv. [L corruptus fr. rumpere break]

cor·sage /kôrsäzH', -säj'/ n. small bouquet worn by women [Fr, rel. to CORPSE]

cor·sair /kôr'ser'/ n. 1 pirate ship 2 pirate [Fr, rel. to COURSE]

cor·set /kôr'sit/ n. close-fitting undergarment for support —**cor'set·ry** n. [Fr dim., rel. to CORPSE]

Cor·si·ca /kôr'sikə/ n. island in the Mediterranean Sea, W of Italy, a department of France. Capital: Ajaccio —**Cor'si·can** n. & adj.

Cor·tés (or **Cortez**) /kôrtez', kôr'tez/, Hernando 1485–1547; Spanish conquistador

cor·tex /kôr'teks/ n. (pl. **·ti·ces** /-təsēz'/) outer part of an organ, esp. of the brain or kidneys —**cor'ti·cal** /-tikəl/ adj. [L: bark]

cor·ti·sone /kôr'tizōn'/ n. hormone used esp. in treating inflammation and allergy [abbr. of chemical name]

co·run·dum /kərən'dəm/ n. extremely hard crystallized alumina, used esp. as an abrasive [Tamil fr. Skt]

cor·us·cate /kôr'əskāt, kär'-/ v. (**·cat·ed, ·cat·ing**) sparkle —**cor·us·ca'tion** n. [L]

cos abbr. cosine

co·se·cant /kōsē'kənt, -kant'/ n. Math. ratio of the hypotenuse (in a right triangle) to the side opposite an acute angle

co·sig·na·to·ry /kōsig'nətôr'ē/ n. (pl. **·ries**) party signing something jointly

co·sine /kō'sīn'/ n. Math. ratio of the side adjacent to an acute angle (in a right triangle) to the hypotenuse

cos·met·ic /käzmet'ik/ adj. 1 beautifying; enhancing 2 only superficially improving 3 (of surgery or a prosthesis) imitating, restoring, or enhancing normal appearance —n. 4 cosmetic preparation, esp. for the face —**cos·met'i·cal·ly** adv. [Gk: ornament]

cos·mic /käz'mik/ adj. pertaining to the cosmos or its scale; universal

cos·mog·o·ny /käzmäg'ənē/ n. (pl. **·nies**) 1 origin of the universe 2 theory about this [Gk kosmos universe + -gonos begetting]

cos·mol·o·gy /käzmäl'əjē/ n. science or theory of the universe —**cos'mo·log'i·cal** /-məlöj'ik-l/ adj.; **cos·mol'o·gist** n. [fr. COSMOS + -LOGY]

cos·mo·naut /käz'mənôt'/ n. Soviet or Russian astronaut [fr. COSMOS + Gk nautēs sailor]

cos·mo·pol·i·tan /käz'məpäl'ət-n/ adj. 1 of,

from, or knowing many parts of the world; sophisticated —n. 2 cosmopolitan person —**cos'mo·pol'i·tan·ism** n. [Gk politēs citizen]

cos·mos /käz'məs, -mōs/ n. the universe, esp. as a well-ordered whole [Gk]

Cos·sack /käs'ak', -ək/ n. member of a people of southern Russia [Turk quzzāq]

cost /kôst/ v. (**cost, cost·ing**) 1 be obtainable for (a sum); have as a price 2 involve as a loss or sacrifice (it cost him his life) —n. 3 what a thing costs; price 4 loss or sacrifice 5 **at all costs** (or **at any cost**) no matter what [L constare stand at a price]

Cos·ta Bra·va /kō'stə bräv'ə/ n. Mediterranean coastal resort region of NE Spain

Cos·ta del Sol /del sōl'/ n. Mediterranean coastal resort region on the S coast of Spain

Cos·ta Me·sa /kō'stə mā'sə, käs'tə/ n. city in Calif. Pop. 96,357

Cos·ta Ri·ca /kō'stə rē'kə, kôs'-/ n. republic in Central America. Capital: San José. Pop. 3,161,000 —**Cos'ta Ri'can** n. & adj.

cost'-ef·fec'tive adj. producing good results for the expenditure

cost'ly adj. (**·li·er, ·li·est**) costing much; expensive —**cost'li·ness** n.

cost' of liv'ing n. level of prices, esp. of basic necessities

cos·tume n. /käs't(y)ōōm'/ 1 style of dress, esp. of a particular place or time 2 set of clothes 3 clothes for a role —v. /käst(y)ōōm, käst'(y)ōōm'/ (**·tumed, ·tuming**) 4 provide with a costume [L, rel. to CUSTOM]

cot[1] /kät/ n. light or portable bed [Hindi]

cot[2] abbr. cotangent

co·tan·gent /kōtan'jənt/ n. Math. ratio of the side adjacent to an acute angle (in a right triangle) to the opposite side

Côte d'A·zur /kōt' dəzoor'/ n. RIVIERA

Côte d'I·voire /kōt' dēvwär'/ n. IVORY COAST

co·te·rie /kōt'ərē, kōt'ərē'/ n. exclusive circle or clique [Fr]

Co·to·nou /kōt'n-ōō'/ n. official capital of Benin. Pop. 487,000

cot·tage /kät'ij/ n. small simple house, esp. in the country [AngFr]

cot'tage cheese' n. soft white cheese made from milk curds

cot·ter /kät'ər/ n. 1 securing bolt or wedge 2 (in full **cot'ter pin'**) split pin that can be opened after passing through a hole

cot·ton /kät'n/ n. 1 soft white fibrous substance covering the seeds of certain plants 2 such a plant, esp. of the mallow family 3 thread or cloth from this [Fr fr. Ar]

cot'ton gin' n. machine for separating cotton seeds from raw fibers

cot'ton·tail' n. N American rabbit with a fluffy tail

cot'ton·wood' n. N American poplar tree with fibrous seeds

cot·y·le·don /kät'l-ēd'n/ n. embryonic leaf in seed-bearing plants [Gk kotylē cup]

couch /kouCH/ n. 1 upholstered piece of furniture for several people; sofa —v. 2 express (in certain terms) [ME couchen fr. L collocare put in place]

couch' po·ta·to n. Slang. lazy person

cou·gar /kōō'gər/ n. large wild cat of N and

S America (also **moun'tain li'on** or pu'ma)
[Fr fr. Guarani]

131

cough / countryside

cough /kôf/ v. 1 expel air, etc., from the lungs with a sudden sharp sound 2 (of an engine, etc.) make a similar sound —n. 3 act of coughing 4 condition of respiratory organs causing coughing 5 **cough up** *Slang.* give forth (money or information) reluctantly [imit., rel. to Du *kuchen*]

could /kŏŏd, kəd/ v. 1 past of CAN[1] 2 *Colloq.* feel inclined to (*I could murder him*)

could·n't /kŏŏd'nt/ v. contr. could not

cou·lomb /kŏŏ'läm', -lōm/ n. unit of electric charge [for C. *Coulomb*, French physicist]

coun·cil /koun'səl/ n. advisory, deliberative, or administrative body —**coun'cil·man** (*pl.* **·men;** *fem.* **·wom·an,** *pl.* **·wom'en**) n. [L con*cilium*]

coun·cil·or /koun's(ə)lər/ n. member of a (esp. local) council

coun·sel /koun'səl/ n. 1 advice, esp. formally given 2 (*pl.* same) legal adviser —v. (**·seled** or **·selled,** **·sel·ing** or **·sel·ling**) 3 advise 4 give, esp. professional, advice on personal problems 5 recommend (a course of action) —**coun'sel·ing** n. [L *consilium*]

coun·sel·or /koun's(ə)lər/ n. 1 adviser or professional guide 2 lawyer

count[1] /kount/ v. 1 determine, esp. one-by-one, the total number of 2 repeat numbers in order 3 include or be included 4 consider or regard to be (lucky, etc.) 5 be worth (*counts for little*) —n. 6a counting or being counted b total of reckoning 7 *Law.* each charge in an indictment 8 **count against** be reckoned to the disadvantage of 9 **count one's blessings** be grateful for what one has 10 **count on** (or upon) rely on; expect 11 **count out: a** count aloud b complete a count of ten seconds over (a fallen boxer, etc.) c *Colloq.* exclude; disregard [L, rel. to COMPUTE]

count[2] n. noble corresponding to an English earl [L *comes* companion]

count·a·ble /koun'təbəl/ adj. that can be counted

count'down' n. 1 act of counting backward to zero 2 preparatory or waiting period before an event

coun·te·nance /kount'n-əns/ n. 1 the face or facial expression —v. (**·nanced,** **·nanc·ing**) 2 approve; abide [Fr, rel. to CONTAIN]

count·er[1] /koun'tər/ n. 1 flat, horizontal surface in a store, etc., across which business is conducted 2a small disk for boardgames b token representing a coin; chip 3 apparatus for counting 4 **under the counter** surreptitiously, esp. sold illegally [rel. to COUNT[1]]

count·er[2] v. 1a oppose; contradict b meet by countermove 2 *Boxing.* give a return blow —adv. 3 in the opposite direction or manner —adj. 4 opposite —n. 5 countermove [rel. to COUNTER-]

counter- comb. form denoting: 1 retaliation, opposition, or rivalry (*counter-threat*) 2 opposite direction (*counterclockwise*) 3 correspondence (*counterpart*) [L *contra* against]

coun'ter·act' v. hinder or neutralize by contrary action —**coun'ter·ac'tion** n.; **coun'ter·ac'tive** adj.

coun'ter·at·tack' n. & v. attack in reply

coun'ter·bal'ance n. 1 weight or influence balancing another —v. (**·anced,** **·anc·ing**) 2 act as a counterbalance to

coun'ter·clock'wise adv. & adj. circling in a direction opposite to that of the hands of a clock

coun'ter·cul'ture n. unconventional aspects of society, emphasizing nontraditional forms and values

coun'ter·es'pi·o·nage' n. action taken against enemy spying

coun·ter·feit /koun'tərfit/ adj. 1 made in imitation; not genuine; forged —n. 2 forgery; imitation —v. 3 imitate fraudulently; forge [Fr]

coun'ter·in·tel'li·gence n. COUNTERESPIONAGE

coun·ter·mand /koun'tərmand/ v. revoke (a command) [L, rel. to MANDATE]

coun·ter·pane /koun'tərpān/ n. bedspread [MedL *culcita puncta* quilted mattress]

coun'ter·part' n. 1 complement or equivalent to another 2 duplicate

coun'ter·point' n. 1 art or practice of combining melodies according to fixed rules 2 melody combined with another 3 contrasting element [MedL *contrapunctum* marked opposite]

coun'ter·poise' n. 1 counterbalance 2 state of equilibrium —v. (**·poised,** **·pois·ing**) 3 counterbalance [L *pensum* weight]

coun'ter·pro·duc'tive adj. having the opposite of the desired effect

coun'ter·rev'o·lu'tion n. revolution opposing a former one —**coun'ter·rev·o·lu'tion·ar'y** (*pl.* **·ies**) n. & adj.

coun'ter·sign' v. 1 add a signature to (a document) for confirmation —n. 2 password, esp. in reply [It, rel. to SIGN]

coun'ter·sink' v. (**·sunk,** **·sink·ing**) 1 enlarge (a hole) so that a screw or bolt can be inserted flush with the surface 2 put (a screw, etc.) in such a hole

coun'ter·ten'or n. 1 male alto singing voice 2 singer with this voice [It, rel. to CONTRA-]

coun·ter·vail /koun'tərvāl/ v. *Lit.* 1 counterbalance 2 oppose, usu. successfully [L *valere* have worth]

coun'ter·weight' n. counterbalancing weight

count·ess /koun'təs/ n. 1 wife or widow of a count or earl 2 woman holding the rank of count or earl [L *comitissa*, rel. to COUNT[2]]

count·less /kount'ləs/ adj. too many to be counted

coun·tri·fied /kən'trifīd'/ adj. rustic

coun·try /kən'trē/ n. (*pl.* **·tries**) 1 nation or its territory 2 (often *attrib.*) rural area 3 land of a person's birth or citizenship 4 region with regard to its aspect, associations, etc. (*mountainous country*) 5 national population, esp. as voters [MedL *contrata* (*terra*) (land) lying opposite]

coun'try-and-west'ern n. style of popular music orig. of the southern US

coun'try club' n. social and sporting club, usu. with a golf course

coun'try·man n. (*pl.* **·men;** *fem.* **·wom·an,** *pl.* **·wom'en**) (also **fel'low-coun'try·man**) person of one's own country

coun'try mu'sic n. COUNTRY-AND-WESTERN

coun'try·side' n. rural areas

coun·ty /koun'tē/ *n.* (*pl.* **·ties**) **1** administrative division in some countries **2** political and administrative division of a state in the US —*adj.* **3** of or like the gentry [L *comitatus*, rel. to COUNT²]

coup /kōō/ *n.* (*pl.* **coups** /kōōz/) **1** successful stroke or move **2** COUP D'ÉTAT [LL *colpus* blow]

coup de grâce /kōō' də gräs'/ *n.* **1** merciful death blow **2** decisive or finishing stroke [Fr]

coup d'é·tat /kōō' dätä'/ *n.* (*pl.* **coups d'é·tat** /kōō' dätä(z)'/') violent or illegal seizure of power [Fr]

coupe /kōōp/ *n.* car with a hard roof and two doors [Fr *couper* cut]

Cou·pe·rin /kōōp'(ə)raN'/, François 1668–1733; French composer

cou·ple /kəp'əl/ *n.* **1a** two **b** about two (*a couple of hours*) **2a** two people married or considered a pair **b** pair of partners in a dance, etc. —*v.* (**·pled, ·pling**) **3** link together **4** associate in thought or speech **5** copulate [L *copula* tie, bond]

cou·plet /kəp'lit/ *n.* two successive lines of verse, usu. paired and sometimes rhyming [Fr dim., rel. to COUPLE]

cou·pling /kəp'liNg/ *n.* link or device connecting two things, as railroad cars, etc.

cou·pon /k(y)ōō'pän'/ *n.* **1** small, detachable printed form, as on bonds, etc. **2** discount voucher presented at purchase [Fr *couper* cut]

cour·age /kər'ij, kə'rij/ *n.* ability to disregard fear; bravery [L *cor* heart]

cou·ra·geous /kərā'jəs/ *adj.* brave —**cou·ra'geous·ly** *adv.*

cou·ri·er /kŏŏr'ēər, kər'-/ *n.* special messenger [L *currere* run]

course /kôrs/ *n.* **1** onward movement or progression **2** direction taken **3** stretch of land or water **4** series of lessons on a subject **5** each successive part of a meal **6** sequence of medical treatment, etc. **7** line of conduct **8** horizontal layer of masonry, brick, etc. **9** water channel —*v.* (**coursed, cours·ing**) **10** (esp. of liquid) run, esp. fast **11** in the course of during **12** of course naturally; as is or was to be expected; admittedly [L *cursus*, rel. to COURIER]

cours·er /kôr'sər/ *n. Poet.* swift horse

court /kôrt/ *n.* **1** (in full **court' of law'**) a judicial body hearing legal cases **b** COURTROOM **2** quadrangular area for games **3a** residential yard off the street **b** COURTYARD **4** the milieu or attendants of a sovereign **5** attention paid to a person for favor (*paid court to her*) —*v.* **6** try to win affection or favor of **7** seek to win (applause, fame, etc.) **8** invite (misfortune) by one's actions [L, rel. to COHORT]

cour·te·ous /kart'ēəs/ *adj.* polite; considerate —**cour'te·ous·ly** *adv.*; **cour'te·ous·ness** *n.* [Fr, rel. to COURT]

cour·te·san /kôrt'əzən, -zan'/ *n.* prostitute, esp. for wealthy clients [It, rel. to COURT]

cour·te·sy /kart'əsē/ *n.* (*pl.* **·sies**) courteous behavior or act [Fr, rel. to COURTEOUS]

court'house' *n.* **1** judicial building **2** county administrative building

cour·ti·er /kôrt'ēər/ *n.* person who attends a sovereign's court [AngFr, rel. to COURT]

court·ly /kôrt'lē/ *adj.* (**·li·er, ·li·est**) dignified; refined —**court'li·ness** *n.*

court'-mar'tial *n.* (*pl.* **courts'-mar'tial**) **1** military judicial court —*v.* (**·tialed, ·tial·ing**) **2** try by this

court' or'der *n.* direction issued by a court or judge

court'room' *n.* room for judicial proceedings

court'ship' *n.* **1** process or period of wooing **2** courting behavior of animals, birds, etc.

court'yard' *n.* area enclosed by walls or buildings

cous·cous /kōōs'kōōs'/ *n.* N African spicy grain dish often with meat or fruit added [Fr fr. Ar]

cous·in /kəz'ən/ *n.* **1** (also **first' cous'in**) child of one's uncle or aunt **2** person of a kindred race or nation [L *consobrinus*]

cou·ture /kōōtŏŏr'/ *n.* design and manufacture of fashionable clothes [Fr]

cou·tu·ri·er /kōōtŏŏr'ēər, -tŏŏr'ē-ā'/ *n.* fashion designer

cove /kōv/ *n.* **1** small inlet or bay **2** sheltered recess [OE]

co·ven /kəv'ən/ *n.* assembly of witches [rel. to CONVENT]

cov·e·nant /kəv'ənənt/ *n.* **1** agreement; contract **2** *Law.* sealed contract, esp. a deed of covenant —*v.* **3a** make a covenant **b** promised by a covenant **4** agree, esp. by legal covenant [Fr, rel. to CONVENE]

Cov·en·try /käv'əntrē, kuv'-/ *n.* city in central England. Pop. 322,600

cov·er /kəv'ər/ *v.* **1** protect or conceal with a cloth, lid, etc. **2a** extend over the surface of **b** strew thickly or thoroughly **c** lie over **3** protect; clothe **4** include; comprise; deal with **5** travel (a specified distance) **6** describe as a reporter **7** be enough to defray (*$20 should cover it*) **8a** protect oneself **b** (foll. by *for*) stand in for **9a** aim a gun, etc., at **b** protect —*n.* **10** thing that covers, esp.: **a** lid **b** book's outer binding **c** envelope or wrapping (*under separate cover*) **11** shelter **12a** pretense; screen **b** pretended identity **13** cover up conceal (facts) **14** take cover find shelter [L *cooperire*]

cov·er·age /kəv'(ə)rij/ *n.* **1** area or amount covered **2** amount of publicity received by an event, etc.

cov·er·all' *n.* (usu. *pl.*) full-length protective garment

cov'er charge' *n.* entry or service charge in a restaurant, nightclub, etc.

cov·er·let /kəv'ərlit/ *n.* bedspread [AngFr, rel. to COVER + *lit* bed]

cov'er sto'ry *n.* story featured on the front cover of a magazine, etc.

co·vert /kō'vərt', kōvərt', kəv'ərt/ *adj.* **1** secret or disguised (*covert glance*) —*n.* **2** shelter, esp. a thicket hiding game —**co·vert'ly** *adv.* [Fr, rel. to COVER]

cov'er-up' *n.* concealment of facts

cov·et /kəv'it/ *v.* desire greatly (another's possession) [Fr, rel. to CUPID]

cov·et·ous /kəv'ətəs/ *adj.* coveting; grasping —**cov'et·ous·ly** *adv.*

co·vey /kəv'ē/ *n.* (*pl.* **·eys**) **1** brood of partridges **2** small group of people [OFr *cover* hatch fr. L *cubare* lie down]

cow¹ /kou/ *n.* **1** fully grown female of domestic cattle, raised esp. for milk **2** female of other large animals, esp. the elephant, whale, and seal [OE]

cow² *v.* intimidate or dispirit [ON]

cow·ard /kou′ərd/ *n.* person lacking courage [L *cauda* tail]

Cow·ard /kou′ərd/, **(Sir) Noel** 1899–1973; English dramatist, actor, and composer

cow·ard·ice /kou′ərdis/ *n.* lack of courage

cow′ard·ly *adj.* 1 lacking courage 2 (of an action) done against one who cannot retaliate

cow′boy′ *n.* (*fem.* **cow′girl′**) person who tends cattle, esp. in the western US

cow·er /kou′ər/ *v.* crouch or shrink in fear [LGer]

cow′hide′ *n.* 1 cow's hide 2 leather or whip made from this

COWL

cowl /koul/ *n.* monk's cloak [L *cucullus*]

cow′lick′ *n.* projecting lock of hair

cowl·ing /kou′liNG/ *n.* removable cover of a vehicle or aircraft engine

Cow·per /kōō′pər, kōōp′ər, kou′pər/, **William** 1731–1800; English poet

cow′pox′ *n.* disease of cows, whose virus was formerly used in smallpox vaccination

cox·comb /käks′kōm′/ *n.* ostentatiously conceited man —**cox′comb·ry** *n.* (*pl.* -**ries**) [*cock's comb*]

cox·swain /käk′sən, -swän′/ *n.* person who steers a racing shell [*cock* ship's boat + SWAIN]

coy /koi/ *adj.* 1 affectedly shy 2 irritatingly reticent —**coy′ly** *adv.*; **coy′ness** *n.* [Fr, rel. to QUIET]

coy·o·te /kī-ōt′ē, kī′ōt′/ *n.* (*pl.* same or -**tes**) N American wolflike wild dog [MexSp]

coz·en /kaz′ən/ *v. Lit.* 1 cheat; defraud 2 beguile 3 act deceitfully —**coz′en·age** *n.*

co·zy /kō′zē/ *adj.* (-**zi·er**, -**zi·est**) *Brit.* **co·sy** 1 comfortable and warm; snug —*n.* (*pl.* -**zies**) 2 cover to keep a teapot hot —**co′zi·ly** *adv.*; **co′zi·ness** *n.*

cp. *abbr.* compare

CPA or **C.P.A.** *abbr.* Certified Public Accountant

cpd. *abbr.* compound

CPI *abbr.* consumer price index

Cpl. *abbr.* Corporal

CPR *abbr.* cardiopulmonary resuscitation

Cr *symb.* chromium

crab /krab/ *n.* 1 crustacean with four pairs of legs and two pincers 2 (**the Crab**) sign or constellation Cancer 3 (in full **crab louse**) parasitic louse transmitted sexually to esp. pubic hair 4 *Slang.* peevish person —*v.* (**crabbed, crab·bing**) 5 *Slang.* complain —**crab′like** *adj.* [OE]

crab′ ap′ple *n.* 1 small sour apple 2 tree bearing this

crab·bed /krab′id/ *adj.* 1 peevish 2 (of handwriting) hard to read [fr. CRAB]

crab′by *adj.* (-**bi·er**, -**bi·est**) irritable; complaining —**crab′bi·ly** *adv.*; **crab′bi·ness** *n.*

crack /krak/ *n.* 1a sharp explosive noise b sudden break in vocal pitch 2 sharp blow 3 narrow opening; break; split 4 *Colloq.* joke or malicious remark 5 *Colloq.* attempt 6 *Slang.* potent crystalline form of cocaine —*v.* 7 break without separating the parts 8 make or cause to make a sharp explosive sound 9 break with a sharp sound 10 give way or cause to give way (under torture, etc.) 11 (of the voice) change pitch sharply 12 *Colloq.* find the solution to 13 tell (a joke, etc.) 14 *Colloq.* hit sharply —*adj.* 15 *Colloq.* excellent; first-rate (*crack shot*) 16 **crack down (on)** *Colloq.* take severe measures against 17 **crack of dawn** daybreak 18 **cracked** crazy 19 **crack up** *Colloq.* a collapse under strain b laugh heartily [OE]

crack′down′ *n. Colloq.* severe countermeasures

crack′er *n.* 1 loud firework 2 thin crisp biscuit

crack′ers *adj. Slang.* crazy

crack·le /krak′əl/ *v.* (-**led**, -**ling**) 1 make repeated slight cracking sound —*n.* 2 such a sound —**crack′ly** *adj.* [fr. CRACK]

crack′pot′ *Slang. n.* 1 eccentric person —*adj.* 2 mad; unworkable

crack′up′ *n. Colloq.* mental breakdown

Crac·ow /krak′ou, kräk′ōōf/, *n.* (also **Krak′ów**) city in Poland on the Vistula River. Pop. 750,600

-cracy *comb. form* denoting a particular form of government, etc. (*bureaucracy*) [L -*cratia*]

cra·dle /krād′l/ *n.* 1a baby's bed, esp. on rockers b place where something begins or is fostered 2 supporting framework or structure —*v.* (-**dled**, -**dling**) 3 contain or shelter as in a cradle [OE]

crafts·man /kraf(t)s′mən/ *n.* (*pl.* -**men**; *fem.* **wom′an**, *pl.* **wom′en**) skilled worker; artisan —**crafts′man·ship** *n.*

craft′y *adj.* (-**i·er**, -**i·est**) cunning; artful; wily —**craft′i·ly** *adv.*; **craft′i·ness** *n.*

crag /krag/ *n.* steep or rugged rock [Celt]

crag′gy *adj.* (-**gi·er**, -**gi·est**) (of facial features, landscape, etc.) rugged —**crag′gi·ness** *n.*

Cra·io·va /krī-ō′və/ *n.* city in SW Romania. Pop. 303,500

cram /kram/ *v.* (**crammed, cram·ming**) 1a fill to bursting; stuff b force (a thing) in or into 2 prepare intensively for an examination [OE]

cramp /kramp/ *n.* 1 painful involuntary muscular contraction —*v.* 2 affect with cramp 3 confine narrowly 4 restrict 5 **cramp one's style** hinder a person from acting freely or naturally [LGer or Du]

cramped /krampt/ *adj.* 1 (of a space) too small 2 (of handwriting) small and with the letters close together

Cra·nach /krän′äKH′/, **Lucas ("the Elder")** 1472–1553; German painter

cran·ber·ry /kran′ber′ē/ *n.* (*pl.* -**ries**) 1 small, edible sour red berry 2 shrub on which it grows [Ger *Kranbeere* crane-berry]

crane /krān/ *n.* **1** machine with a long hoisting arm **2** tall wading bird with long legs, neck, and bill —*v.* (**craned, cran·ing**) **3** stretch out (one's neck) to see [OE]

Crane /krān/, **Stephen** 1871–1900; US writer

cra·ni·um /krā′nēəm/ *n.* (*pl.* **-ums** or **-ni·a** /-nēə/) skull, esp. the part enclosing the brain —**cra′ni·al** *adj.*; **cra·ni·ol′o·gy** *n.* [MedL fr. Gk]

crank /kraNGk/ *n.* **1** part of an axle or shaft bent at right angles for converting reciprocal into circular motion or vice versa **2** eccentric person —*v.* **3** cause to move by means of a crank **4 crank up** start [OE]

crank′case′ *n.* case enclosing a crankshaft

crank′shaft′ *n.* shaft driven by a crank

crank′y *adj.* (**-i·er, -i·est**) crotchety —**crank′i·ly** *adv.*; **crank′i·ness** *n.*

Cran·mer /kran′mər/, **Thomas** 1489–1556; archbishop of Canterbury; leader of Church of England reforms

cran·ny /kran′ē/ *n.* (*pl.* **-nies**) chink; crevice —**cran′nied** *adj.* [Fr]

crap /krap/ *n. Slang.* **1** nonsense; rubbish **2** feces —*v.* (**crapped, crap·ping**) **3** defecate —**crap′py** *adj.* (**-pi·er, -pi·est**) [Du]

crape /krāp/ *n.* crêpe, usu. of black silk, formerly used for mourning [fr. CRÊPE]

craps /kraps/ *n. pl.* (also **crap game**) gambling dice game

crap·u·lent /krap′yələnt/ *adj.* suffering the effects of drunkenness —**crap′u·lence** *n.*; **crap′u·lous** *adj.* [L *crapula* inebriation]

crash[1] /krasH/ *v.* **1** (cause to) make a loud smashing noise **2** throw, drive, move, or fall with a loud smash **3** collide or fall, or cause (a vehicle, etc.) to collide or fall, violently **4** collapse financially **5** *Comp.* (of a system) fail suddenly **6** *Slang.* sleep, esp. on a floor, etc. —*n.* **7** loud and sudden smashing noise **8** violent collision or fall, esp. of a vehicle **9** ruin, esp. financial **10** *Comp.* sudden failure (of a system) —*adj.* **11** done rapidly or urgently [imit.]

crash[2] *n.* coarse plain fabric of linen, cotton, etc. [Russ]

crash′-land′ *v.* land or cause (an aircraft, etc.) to land without landing gear or not on a runway —**crash′-land′ing** *n.*

crass /kras/ *adj.* gross; grossly stupid —**crass′ly** *adv.*; **crass′ness** *n.* [L *crassus* thick]

Cras·sus /kras′əs/, **Marcus Licinius** c. 115–53 B.C.; Roman politician and military commander

-crat *comb. form* member or supporter of a type of government, etc.

crate /krāt/ *n.* **1** slatted wooden case for transporting goods **2** *Slang.* old aircraft or other vehicle —*v.* (**crat·ed, crat·ing**) **3** pack in a crate [perh. fr. Du]

cra·ter /krā′tər/ *n.* **1** volcano mouth **2** bowl-shaped cavity, esp. from a shell or bomb **3** hollow on the surface of a planet or moon —*v.* **4** form a crater in [Gk: mixing bowl]

-cratic *comb. form* (also **-cratical**) denoting a type of government, etc. (*autocratic*)

cra·vat /krəvat′/ *n.* necktie [Serbo-Croatian: Croat]

crave /krāv/ *v.* (**craved, crav·ing**) long or beg for [OE]

cra·ven /krā′vən/ *adj.* cowardly [prob. Fr *cravanté* defeated]

crav′ing *n.* strong desire or longing

craw /krô/ *n.* **1** crop of a bird or insect **2** **stick in one's craw** be unacceptable [LGer or Du]

craw·fish /krô′fisH/ *n.* CRAYFISH

Craw·ford /krô′fərd/, **Joan** (born **Lucille le Seuer**) 1908–77; US actress

crawl /krôl/ *v.* **1** move slowly, esp. on hands and knees near the ground **2** walk or move slowly **3** *Colloq.* behave obsequiously **4** be or appear to be covered or filled with crawling or moving things or people —*n.* **5** crawling **6** slow rate of movement **7** high-speed overarm swimming stroke

cray·fish /krā′fisH/ *n.* (*pl.* **same**) small lobsterlike freshwater crustacean [Fr *crevice*]

cray·on /krā′än′, -ən/ *n.* **1** stick or pencil of colored chalk, wax, etc. —*v.* **2** draw with crayons [Fr *craie* chalk]

craze /krāz/ *v.* (**crazed, craz·ing**) **1** produce fine surface cracks on (pottery glaze, etc.); develop such cracks **n.** **2** fashion; rage **3 crazed** insane [perh. fr. ON]

cra·zy /krā′zē/ *adj.* (**-zi·er, -zi·est**) *Colloq.* **1** insane; mad; foolish **2** extremely enthusiastic —**cra′zi·ly** *adv.*; **cra′zi·ness** *n.*

Cra′zy Horse c. 1849–77; Sioux Indian leader

creak /krēk/ *n.* **1** harsh scraping or squeaking sound —*v.* **2** make a creak **3a** move stiffly or with a creaking noise **b** be poorly constructed (*plot creaks*) [imit.]

creak′y *adj.* (**-i·er, -i·est**) **1** liable to creak **2** stiff; frail; decrepit —**creak′i·ness** *n.*

cream /krēm/ *n.* **1** fatty part of milk **2** its yellowish-white color **3** creamlike cosmetic, etc. **4** (usu. prec. by *the*) best part of something —*v.* **5** make creamy **6** form a cream or scum —*adj.* **7** pale yellowish white [ME *creme* fr. ChL *chrisma* oil for anointing]

cream′ cheese′ *n.* soft white cheese made from cream and unskimmed milk

cream·er·y /krē′m(ə)rē/ *n.* (*pl.* **-ies**) factory or store for dairy products

cream′ of tar′tar *n.* white, crystalline mineral used in medicine, baking powder, etc.

cream′y *adj.* (**-i·er, -i·est**) **1** like cream **2** rich in cream —**cream′i·ly** *adv.*; **cream′i·ness** *n.*

crease /krēs/ *n.* **1** line caused by folding or crushing —*v.* (**creased, creas·ing**) **2** make creases in **3** develop creases [fr. CREST]

cre·ate /krē·āt′/ *v.* (**-at·ed, -at·ing**) **1** bring into existence; cause **2** originate [L *creare*]

cre·a·tion *n.* **1** creating or being created **2a** (usu. **the Creation**) God's creating of the universe **b** (usu. *cap.*) all created things; the universe **3** product of the imagination, art, fashion, etc.

cre·a′tion·ism′ *n.* theory of the origin of life on earth in accord with the Biblical account

cre·a′tive *adj.* **1** inventive; imaginative **2** able to create —**cre·a′tive·ly** *adv.*; **cre·a′tive·ness**, **cre′a·tiv′i·ty** *n.*

cre·a·tor /krē·āt′ər/ *n.* **1** person who creates **2** (**the Creator**) God

crea·ture /krē′CHər/ *n.* **1** any living being, esp. an animal **2** person of a specified kind

cre·dence /krēd´ns/ n. 1 belief 2 give credence to believe 3 lend credence to make believable [MedL, rel. to CREDO]

cre·den·tial /kriden´SHəl/ n. (usu. pl.) certificates, references, etc., attesting to a person's qualifications, position, etc. [MedL, rel. to CREDENCE]

cred·i·bil·i·ty /kred´əbil´ətē/ n. 1 being credible 2 reputation; status

cred·i·ble /kred´əbəl/ adj. believable; worthy of belief [L, rel. to CREDO]

• Usage: See note at INCREDIBLE.

cred·it /kred´it/ n. 1 source of honor, pride, etc. 2 acknowledgment or token of merit or achievement 3 good reputation 4a person's financial reliability b power to obtain goods, etc., before payment 5 (usu. pl.) indicated acknowledgment of a contribution 6 reputation for solvency and honesty in business 7a entry in an account of a sum paid into it b sum entered —v. (·it·ed, ·it·ing) 8 believe 9 enter on the credit side of an account 10 credit a person with ascribe (a good quality) to a person 11 do credit to (or do a person credit) enhance the reputation of 12 on credit with an arrangement to pay later 13 to one's credit in one's favor [It or L, rel. to CREDO]

cred·it·a·ble /kred´itəbəl/ adj. bringing credit or honor —cred´it·a·bly adv.

cred´it card´ n. plastic card from a bank, etc., authorizing the purchase of goods on credit

cred·i·tor /kred´ətər/ n. person to whom a debt is owing [L, rel. to CREDIT]

cre·do /krēd´ō, krād´-/ n. (pl. ·dos) creed [L: I believe]

cred·u·lous /krej´ələs/ adj. too ready to believe; gullible —cre·du·li·ty /krid(y)ōō´litē/ n.; cred´u·lous·ly adv. [L, rel. to CREDO]

• Usage: See note at INCREDIBLE.

creed /krēd/ n. 1 set of principles or beliefs 2 system of religious belief 3 formal summary of Christian doctrine [L, rel. to CREDO]

creek /krēk, krik/ n. 1 stream 2 up the creek Slang. in difficulties [ON and Du]

creel /krēl/ n. fisherman's large wicker basket

creep /krēp/ v. (crept, creep·ing) 1 move with the body prone and close to the ground 2 move stealthily or timidly 3 slowly overcome 4 Colloq. act obsequiously 5 (of a plant) grow along the ground or up a wall, etc. 6 (of flesh) shiver; shudder —n. 7 act or spell of creeping 8 Slang. unpleasant person 9 the creeps feeling of revulsion or fear [OE]

creep´ing adj. developing slowly and steadily

creep´y adj. (·i·er, ·i·est) Colloq. feeling or causing horror, revulsion, or fear —creep´i·ly adv.; creep´i·ness n.

cre·mate /krē´māt, krimāt´/ v. (·mat·ed, ·mat·ing) burn (a corpse, etc.) to ashes —cre·ma´tion n. [L cremare burn]

cre·ma·to·ri·um /krē´mətôr´ēəm, krem´ə-/ n. (pl. ·ri·a or ·ri·ums) place where corpses are cremated

crème de la crème /krem´ də lä krem´/ n. French. best part; elite

crème de menthe /krem´ də menTH´, krēm´, mint´/ n. French. peppermint liqueur

cren·el·ate or cren·el·late v. (·at·ed or ·lat-

ed, ·at·ing or ·lat·ing) fashion with or as with battlements —cren·el·la´tion n. [Fr crenel embrasure]

Cre·ole /krē´ōl´/ n. 1 descendant of European settlers in the W Indies or Central or S America 2 white descendant of French settlers, esp. in Louisiana 3 person of mixed European and black descent 4 language arising from two coexisting languages —adj. 5 of Creoles 6 (usu. creole) of Creole origin, etc. (creole cooking) [Fr fr. Sp]

cre·o·sote /krē´əsōt/ n. dark brown distillation of wood or coal tar used as wood preservative, antiseptic, etc. [Gk kreas flesh + sōtēr preserver]

crepe or crêpe /krāp/ n. 1 fine gauzy wrinkled fabric 2 thin pancake often with a sweet filling 3 hard-wearing wrinkled rubber used for the soles of shoes [L, rel. to CRISP]

crepe´ pa´per n. thin crinkled paper

crept /krept/ v. past and past part. of CREEP

cre·scen·do /kriSHen´dō/ n. (pl. ·dos) 1 Mus. gradual increase in loudness 2 progress toward a climax —adv. & adj. 3 increasing in loudness [It, rel. to CRESCENT]

cres·cent /kres´nt/ n. 1 curved sickle shape as of the waxing or waning moon (see illustration at MOON PHASES) 2 thing of this shape [L crescere grow]

cress /kres/ n. any of various plants with pungent edible leaves [OE]

crest /krest/ n. 1a comb, tuft, etc., on a bird's or animal's head b plume, etc., on a helmet, etc. 2 top of a mountain, wave, roof, etc. 3 heraldic device, as on seals, etc. —v. 4 reach the crest of 5 (of a wave) form a crest —crest´ed adj. [L crista]

crest·fall·en /krest(t)´fôl´ən/ adj. dejected; dispirited

cre·ta·ceous /krita´SHəs/ adj. 1 of or like chalk 2 (cap.) Geol. of the last period of the Mesozoic era, during which chalk deposits formed —n. 3 (cap.) Geol. this era or system [L creta chalk]

Crete /krēt/ n. (also Can´di·a) Greek island in the Mediterranean Sea, SE of the mainland

cre·tin /krēt´n/ n. 1 deformed and mentally deficient person 2 Colloq. stupid person —cre´tin·ism´ n.; cre´tin·ous adj. [Fr crétin, rel. to CHRISTIAN]

cre·tonne /krē´tän´, kritän´/ n. heavy cotton upholstery fabric, usu. with a floral pattern [Creton in Normandy]

cre·vasse /krəvas´/ n. deep open crack, esp. in a glacier [Fr]

crev·ice /krev´is/ n. narrow opening or fissure, esp. in rock [Fr, rel. to CREVASSE]

crew /krōō/ n. 1 (often treated as pl.) a people manning a ship, aircraft, train, etc. b these as distinct from the captain or officers c people working together; team 2 Colloq. work gang —v. 3 supply or act as a crew on a crew member for [L crescere increase]

crew´ cut´ n. close-cropped hair style

crew·el /krōō´əl/ n. thin worsted yarn for tapestry and embroidery

crew´el·work´ n. design in crewel

crew´neck´ n. round close-fitting neckline

crib /krib/ n. 1 baby's small bed with high sides 2 rack for animal fodder 3 Colloq. study aid or notes used furtively by students —*v.* (cribbed, crib·bing) (also *absol.*) 4 *Colloq.* copy unfairly 5 confine in a small space [OE]

crib·bage /krib'ij/ *n.* card game for up to four players

crib' death' see SUDDEN INFANT DEATH SYNDROME

crick /krik/ *n.* sudden painful stiffness, esp. in the neck

Crick /krik/, **Francis Harry Compton** 1916– ; English biophysicist; Nobel prize 1962

crick·et[1] /krik'it/ *n.* grasshopperlike chirping insect [Fr. imit.]

crick·et[2] *n.* team game played with balls, bats, and wickets

cried /krīd/ *v. past* and *past part.* of CRY

cri·er /krī'ər/ *n.* (also cry'er) 1 person who cries 2 official making public announcements in a court of law or street [rel. to CRY]

crime /krīm/ *n.* 1a offense punishable by law b illegal acts 2 evil or shameful act (*crime against humanity*) [L *crimen*]

Cri·me·a /krīmē'ə/ *n.* peninsula of Ukraine extending into the Black Sea —**Cri·me'an** *adj.*

crim·i·nal /krim'ən-l/ *n.* 1 person guilty of a crime —*adj.* 2 pertaining to crime 3 guilty of crime 4 *Law.* of or concerning criminal offenses 5 *Colloq.* scandalous; deplorable —crim·i·nal'i·ty /-al'ətē/ *n.*; crim'i·nal·ly *adv.* [L, rel. to CRIME]

crim·i·nol·o·gy /krim'ənäl'əjē/ *n.* the study of crime —**crim·i·nol'o·gist** *n.*

crimp /krimp/ *v.* 1 press into small folds; corrugate 2 make waves in (hair) —*n.* 3 crimped thing or form 4 **put a crimp in** deter [LGer or Du]

crim·son /krim'zən/ *adj.* 1 of a rich deep red —*n.* 2 this color [ult. fr. Ar, rel. to *qirmiz*]

cringe /krinj/ *v.* (cringed, cring·ing) shrink in fear; cower [rel. to CRANK]

crin·kle /kriNG'kəl/ *n.* 1 wrinkle; crease —*v.* (·kled, ·kling) 2 form crinkles (in) —crin'kly *adj.* [rel. to CRINGE]

crin·o·line /krin'l-in/ *n.* stiff fabric of horsehair, etc., used for linings, hats, etc. [Fr fr. L *crinis* hair + *linum* thread]

crip·ple /krip'əl/ *n.* 1 *Offens.* permanently lame person —*v.* (·pled, ·pling) 2 make a cripple of 3 disable, weaken, or damage seriously [OE]

cri·sis /krī'sis/ *n.* (*pl.* ·ses /-sēz/) 1 time of danger or great difficulty 2 decisive moment; turning point [Gk: decision]

crisp /krisp/ *adj.* 1 brittle and easily crumbled 2a (of air) bracing b (of style or manner) lively; brisk and decisive c (of paper) stiff and crackling —*v.* 3 make or become crisp —crisp'ly *adv.*; crisp'ness *n.* [L *crispus* curled]

crisp'y *adj.* (·i·er, ·i·est) crisp —crisp'i·ness *n.*

criss'cross' *n.* 1 pattern of crossing lines —*adj.* 2 crossing; in crossed lines —*adv.* 3 crosswise; at cross purposes —*v.* 4a intersect repeatedly b move crosswise [*Christ's cross*]

cri·te·ri·on /krītēr'ēən/ *n.* (*pl.* ·ri·a /-rēə/)

comparative standard of judgment [Gk: means of judging]

● *Usage:* Careful use maintains the singular as *criterion* and the plural *criteria.*

crit·ic /krit'ik/ *n.* 1 person who criticizes 2 person who reviews literary, artistic, etc., works [L *criticus* fr. Gk *kritēs* judge]

crit·i·cal /krit'ikəl/ *adj.* 1a faultfinding; censorious b expressing or involving criticism 2 providing textual criticism (*critical edition of Milton*) 3a of or at a crisis; dangerous b decisive; crucial 4 (of a nuclear reactor) maintaining a self-sustaining chain reaction —crit'i·cal·ly *adv.*; crit'i·cal·ness *n.*

crit·i·cism /krit'əsiz'əm/ *n.* 1a faultfinding; censure b critical remark, etc. 2a work of a critic b judgmental analysis

crit·i·cize /krit'əsīz/ *v.* (·cized, ·ciz·ing) 1 find fault with; censure 2 discuss critically

cri·tique /kritēk'/ *n.* expression of critical analysis [Fr, rel. to CRITIC]

croak /krōk/ *n.* 1 deep hoarse sound, esp. of a frog —*v.* 2 utter or speak with a croak 3 *Slang.* die —croak'i·ly *adv.*; croak'i·ness *n.*; croak'y *adj.* [imit.]

Cro·at /krō'at', -ät'-ət; krōt/ (also Cro·a·tian /krōā'sʜən/) *n.* 1a native of Croatia b person of Croatian descent 2 Slavonic dialect of the Croats —*adj.* 3 of the Croats or their dialect [Serbo-Croatian *Hrvat*]

Cro·a·tia /krōā'sʜə/ *n.* republic on the Balkan Peninsula, formerly part of Yugoslavia. Capital: Zagreb. Pop. 4,808,000

cro·chet /krōsʜā'/ *n.* 1 needlework in which yarn is hooked to make a lacy patterned fabric —*v.* (·cheted /-sʜād'/, ·chet·ing /-sʜā'iNG/) 2 make using crochet [Fr dim. of *croche* hook]

crock /kräk/ *n.* 1 earthenware pot or jar 2 broken piece of this [OE]

crock·er·y /kräk'ərē/ *n.* earthenware or china dishes, plates, etc. [rel. to CROCK]

Crock·ett /kräk'it/, **Davy (David)** 1786–1836; US frontiersman and soldier

croc·o·dile /kräk'ədīl'/ *n.* 1 large tropical amphibious reptile with thick scaly skin, a long tail, and long jaws 2 its skin [Gk *krokodilos*]

croc'o·dile tears' *n. pl.* insincere grief

cro·cus /krō'kəs/ *n.* (*pl.* ·cus·es) early spring plant with white, yellow, or purple flowers [L fr. Gk]

Croe·sus /krē'səs/ 6th cent. B.C.; legendarily wealthy king of Lydia

crois·sant /krē'sänt', kr(w)äsäN'/ *n.* crescent-shaped breakfast roll [Fr, rel. to CRESCENT]

Crom·well /kräm'wel', -wəl/ 1 **Thomas** c. 1485–1540; chief minister to Henry VIII 2 **Oliver** 1599–1658; Lord Protector of England (1653–58)

crone /krōn/ *n.* withered old woman [ME fr. MDu *kroonie* old sheep]

Cro·nin /krō'nən/, **A(rchibald) J(oseph)** 1896–1981; Scottish novelist

cro·ny /krō'nē/ *n.* (*pl.* ·nies) friend; companion [Gk *khronios* long-lasting]

crook /krŏŏk/ *n.* 1 hooked staff of a shepherd or bishop 2a bend; curve; hook b hooked or curved thing 3 *Colloq.* swindler; criminal —*v.* 4 bend; curve [ON]

crook′ed *adj.* 1 not straight or level; bent 2 *Colloq.* not straightforward; dishonest; criminal —**crook′ed·ly** *adv.*; **crook′ed·ness** *n.*

croon /krōōn/ *v.* sing, hum, or say in a low sentimental voice —**croon′er** *n.* [LGer or Du]

crop /kräp/ *n.* 1a produce of cultivated plants, esp. cereals b season's yield 2 group, yield, etc., of one time or place (*a new crop of students*) 3 handle of a whip 4 predigestive pouch in a bird's gullet —*v.* (**cropped, cropping**) 5a cut off b bite off 6 cut (hair, etc.) short 7 **crop up** occur unexpectedly [OE]

crop′per *n.* 1 crop-producing plant of a specified quality 2 **come a cropper** *Slang.* fail badly

cro·quet /krōkā′/ *n.* lawn game in which wooden balls are driven through hoops with mallets [perh. a dial. form of Fr *crochet* hook]

cro·quette /krōket′/ *n.* ball of breaded and fried mashed potato, etc. [Fr *croquer* crunch]

Cros·by /krôz′bē/, **Bing** (born Harry Lillis Crosby) 1904–77; US singer and actor

cro·sier /krō′zHər/ *n.* (also **cro′zier**) bishop's ceremonial hooked staff [Fr *croisier* cross-bearer and *crossier* crook-bearer]

cross /krôs/ *n.* 1 upright post with a transverse bar, as used in antiquity for crucifixion 2a (**the Cross**) cross on which Christ was crucified b representation, ornament, etc. 3 mark like a cross 4 cross-shaped military, etc., decoration 5a hybrid b crossing of breeds, etc. 6 mixture of two things 7 trial; affliction —*v.* 8 go across 9 intersect; (cause to) be across 10 cancel or delete by drawing lines across 11 make the sign of the cross on or over 12a pass in opposite or different directions b (of letters, etc.) be sent at the same time 13a cause to interbreed b cross-fertilize (plants) —*adj.* 14 peevish; angry 15 transverse; reaching from side to side 16 intersecting 17 **at cross purposes** misunderstanding; conflicting 18 **cross one's fingers** (or **keep one's fingers crossed**): a put one finger across another to ward off bad luck b trust in good luck 19 **cross one's heart** make a solemn pledge, esp. by crossing one's front 20 **cross one's mind** occur to one 21 **cross wires** (or **get one's wires crossed**): a become wrongly connected by telephone b have a misunderstanding —**cross′ly** *adv.*; **cross′ness** *n.* [L *crux*]

cross′bar′ *n.* horizontal bar, esp. that on a man's bicycle

cross-bow /krôs′bō′/ *n.* bow fixed on a wooden stock with a groove for an arrow

cross′breed′ *n.* 1 hybrid breed of animals or plants 2 individual hybrid —*v.* 3 produce by crossing

cross′-check′ *v.* 1 check by alternative method(s) —*n.* 2 such a check

cross′-coun′try *adj.* & *adv* 1 across open country 2 not keeping to main roads

cross′cut′ *adj.* 1 cut across the main grain —*n.* 2 diagonal cut, path, etc.

cross′-dress′ing *n.* dressing in the clothes of the opposite sex —**cross′-dress′** *v.*; **cross′-dress′er** *n.*

cross′-ex·am′ine *v.* esp. *Law.* question confrontationally —**cross′-ex·am′in·a′tion** *n.*

cross′-eyed′ *adj.* having one or both eyes turned inward

cross′-fer′til·ize *v.* (**-ized, -iz·ing**) 1 fertilize (an animal or plant) from one of a different species 2 interchange ideas, etc. —**cross′-fer′ti·li·za′tion** *n.*

cross′ fire′ *n.* 1 firing in two crossing directions 2a attack or criticism from all sides b combative exchange of views

cross′hatch′ *v.* shade with crossing parallel lines

cross′ing *n.* 1 place where things (esp. roads) cross 2 place for crossing a street, etc. 3 journey over water, mountains, etc.

cross′o′ver *n.* 1 point or place of crossing 2 overlapping, esp. from one style or genre to another —*adj.* 3 that overlaps, esp. from one style or genre to another

cross′piece′ *n.* transverse beam.

cross′-re·fer′ *v.* (**-ferred, -fer·ring**) refer from one part of a book, etc., to another

cross′ ref′er·ence *n.* reference from one part of a book, etc., to another

cross′road′ *n.* (usu. *pl.*) 1 intersection of two or more roads 2 **at the crossroads** at the critical point

cross′ sec′tion *n.* 1a a cutting across a solid b plane surface so produced c drawing, etc., of this 2 representative sample —**cross′-sec′tion·al** *adj.*

cross′wise′ (also **cross′ways′**) *adj.* & *adv.* 1 in the form of a cross; intersecting 2 diagonal or diagonally

cross′word′ *n.* (also **cross′word puz′zle**) printed grid of squares and blanks for vertical and horizontal words to be filled in from clues

crotch /kräCH/ *n.* fork, esp. between legs (of a person, trousers, etc.) [rel. to CROOK]

crotch·et·y /kräCH′itē/ *adj.* (**-i·er, -i·est**) peevish; irritable

crouch /krouCH/ *v.* 1 lower the body with limbs close to the chest; be in this position —*n.* 2 crouching; crouching position [ON, rel. to CROOK]

croup /krōōp/ *n.* childhood inflammation of the larynx, etc., with a hard cough [imit.]

crou·pi·er /krōō′pēər, -pē-ā′/ *n.* person running a gaming table [Fr]

crou·ton /krōō′tän′/ *n.* cube of toasted bread served with soup, etc. [Fr, rel. to CRUST]

crow¹ /krō/ *n.* 1 large black bird with a powerful black beak 2 **as the crow flies** in a straight line [OE]

crow² *v.* (**crowed, crow·ing**) 1 (of a cock) utter a loud cry 2 gloat; show glee —*n.* 3 cry of a cock [OE]

crow′bar′ *n.* iron bar with a flattened end, used as a lever

crowd /kroud/ *n.* 1 large gathering of people 2 spectators; audience 3 *Colloq.* particular set of people —*v.* 4a (cause to) come together in a crowd b force one's way 5a force or compress into a confined space b fill or make full of 6 *Colloq.* come aggressively close to —**crowd′ed** *adj.*; **crowd′ed·ness** *n.* [OE]

crown /kroun/ *n.* 1 monarch's jeweled headdress 2 (*cap.*) a monarch as head of state b power or authority of the monarchy 3a wreath for the head as an emblem of victory b award or distinction, esp. in sport 4 crown-shaped ornament, etc. 5 top part of the head, a hat, etc. 6 highest or central part 7a part of a tooth visible outside the gum **b** artificial replacement for this —**v. 8** put a crown on (a person or head) **9** invest with royal authority **10** be a crown to; rest on top of **11** *Slang.* hit on the head **12** promote (a piece in checkers) to king **13** crowning (cause) to be the reward, summit, or finishing touch to (*crowning glory*) [L *corona*]

crown' prince' *n.* male heir to a throne

crown' prin'cess *n.* **1** wife of a crown prince **2** female heir to a throne

crow's'-foot' *n.* (*pl.* -feet) wrinkle at the outer corner of the eye

crow's'-nest' *n.* lookout perch on a sailing ship's masthead

cro·zier /krō′zhər/ *n.* var. of CROSIER

cru·ces /krōō′sēz/ *n. pl.* of CRUX

cru·cial /krōō′shəl/ *adj.* **1** decisive; critical **2** very important —**cru′cial·ly** *adv.* [L *crux crucis* cross]

cru·ci·ble /krōō′səbəl/ *n.* **1** melting pot for metals, etc. **2** severe or fateful test [MedL, rel. to CRUCIAL]

cru·ci·fix /krōō′səfiks/ *n.* model of a cross with the crucified Jesus on it [L *cruci fixus* fixed to a cross]

cru·ci·fix·ion /krōō′səfik′shən/ *n.* **1** crucifying or being crucified **2** (*cap.*) crucifixion of Christ [ChL, rel. to CRUCIFIX]

cru·ci·form /krōō′səfôrm′/ *adj.* cross-shaped [L *crux crucis* cross]

cru·ci·fy /krōō′səfī′/ *v.* (**-fied**, **-fy·ing**) **1** put to death by fastening to a cross **2** persecute; torment **3** *Slang.* defeat thoroughly; humiliate [Fr, rel. to CRUCIFIX]

crud /krəd/ *n. Slang.* **1** deposit of dirt, grease, etc. **2** unpleasant person —**crud′dy** *adj.* (**-di·er**, **-di·est**) [var. of CURD]

crude /krōōd/ *adj.* **1a** in the natural state; not refined **b** unpolished; lacking finish **2a** rude; blunt **b** offensive; indecent **3** inexact —*n.* **4** natural mineral oil —**crude′ly** *adv.*; **crude′ness, cru′di·ty** *n.* [L *crudus* raw]

cru·di·tés /krōō′dită′/ *n. pl.* hors d'œuvre of mixed raw vegetables [Fr]

cru·el /krōō′əl/ *adj.* **1** causing pain or suffering, esp. deliberately **2** harsh; severe —**cru′el·ly** *adv.*; **cru′el·ness** *n.*; **cru′el·ty** *n.* (*pl.* -ties) [Fr, rel. to CRUDE]

cru·et /krōō′it/ *n.* small containers for use at table, esp. of glass [AngFr dim., rel. to CROCK]

cruise /krōōz/ *v.* (**cruised, cruis·ing**) **1** voyage for pleasure, calling at ports **2** travel at a leisurely or steady speed **3** achieve an objective, esp. win a race, etc., with ease **4** *Slang.* search for a sexual partner in bars, streets, etc. —*n.* **5** voyage [Du, rel. to CROSS]

cruise' con·trol' *n.* mechanism for setting and maintaining the speed of an automobile, etc.

crumb /krəm/ *n.* **1a** small fragment, esp. of bread **b** small particle (*crumb of comfort*) **2** bread without crusts **3** *Slang.* objectionable person —*v.* **4** cover with or break into breadcrumbs [OE]

crum·ble /krəm′bəl/ *v.* (**-bled, -bling**) break or fall into small fragments —**crum′bly** (**-bli·er, -bli·est**) *adj.*; **crum′bli·ness** *n.*

crumb′y *adj.* (**-i·er, -i·est**) **1** like or covered in crumbs **2** CRUMMY

crum·my /krəm′ē/ *adj.* (**-mi·er, -mi·est**) *Slang.* dirty; squalid; inferior; worthless —**crum′mi·ness** *n.* [var. of CRUMBY]

crum·ple /krəm′pəl/ *v.* (**-pled, -pling**) **1** crush or become crushed into creases or wrinkles **2** collapse; give way —*n.* **3** crease or wrinkle [obs. *crump* curl up]

crunch /krənCH/ *v.* **1a** crush noisily with the teeth **b** grind under foot, wheels, etc. —*n.* **2** crunching; crunching sound **3** *Colloq.* decisive event or moment [imit.]

crunch′y /krən′CHē/ *adj.* (**-i·er, -i·est**) hard and crisp —**crunch′i·ness** *n.*

crup·per /krəp′ər/ *n.* strap looped under a horse's tail to hold the harness back [ME, fr. OFr *crope* rump]

cru·sade /krōōsād′/ *n.* **1** *Hist.* any of several medieval Christian military expeditions that attempted to recapture the Holy Land from the Muslims **2** vigorous campaign for a cause —*v.* (**-sad·ed, -sad·ing**) **3** engage in a crusade —**cru·sad′er** *n.* [Fr, rel. to CROSS]

crush /krəsH/ *v.* **1** compress with force or violence, so as to break, bruise, etc. **2** reduce to powder by pressure **3** defeat or subdue completely —*n.* **4** act of crushing **5** crowded mass of people **6** *Colloq.* infatuation [Fr]

crust /krəst/ *n.* **1a** hard outer part of bread **b** dry scrap of bread **2** pastry covering of a pie **3** hard surface over a soft thing **4** outer portion of the earth **5** hard residue or deposit [L *crusta* rind; shell]

crus·ta·cean /krə′stā′shən/ *n.* **1** esp. aquatic arthropod with a hard shell, e.g., the crab, lobster, and shrimp —*adj.* **2** of crustaceans

crust′y *adj.* (**-i·er, -i·est**) **1** having a crisp crust **2** irritable; curt —**crust′i·ly** *adv.*; **crust′i·ness** *n.*

crutch /krəCH/ *n.* **1** usu. T-shaped support for a lame person **2** support depended upon [OE]

crux /krəks, krōōks/ *n.* (*pl.* **crux·es**) decisive point at issue [L: cross]

cru·za·do /krōōzä′dō/ *n.* (*pl.* **-dos**) chief monetary unit of Brazil [Port]

cry /krī/ *v.* (**cried, cry·ing**) **1** make a loud or shrill sound, esp. to express pain, appeal for help, etc. **2** shed tears; weep **3** say or exclaim loudly or excitedly **4** (of an animal, esp. a bird) make a loud call —*n.* (*pl.* **cries**) **5** loud shout or scream of grief, pain, etc. **6** spell of weeping **7** loud excited utterance **8** urgent appeal **9a** public demand or opinion **b** rallying call **10** call of an animal **11** cry out for need as an obvious requirement or solution [L *quiritare*]

cry′ba′by *n.* **1** childish complainer **2** person who weeps frequently

cry·er /krī′ər/ *n.* var. of CRIER

cry′ing *adj.* (of injustice, etc.) flagrant

cry·o·gen·ics /krī′ə′jen′iks/ *n.* branch of physics dealing with very low temperatures —**cry·o·gen′ic** *adj.* [Gk *kryos* frost + *-genēs* born]

crypt /kript/ *n.* vault, esp. beneath a church, used usu. as a burial place [L *crypta* fr. Gk *kryptos* hidden]

cryp·tic /krip′tik/ *adj.* obscure in meaning; secret; mysterious —**cryp′ti·cal·ly** *adv.*

cryp·to·gram /krip′təgram′/ *n.* text written in cipher [rel. to CRYPT]

cryp·tog·ra·phy /kriptäg'rəfē/ *n.* art of writing or solving ciphers —**cryp·to'gra·pher** *n.*; **cryp·to·graph'ic** *adj.*

crys·tal /kris'təl/ *n.* **1a** transparent colorless mineral, esp. quartz **b** piece of this **2a** highly transparent glass **b** articles of this **3** substance with a definite internal structure and a solid form enclosed by symmetrical plane faces —*adj.* **4** made of, like, or clear as crystal [Gk *krystallos*]

crys·tal·line /kris'tələn/ *adj.* **1** of, like, or clear as crystal **2** having the structure and form of a crystal

crys'tal·lize *v.* (**·lized, ·liz·ing**) **1** form into crystals **2** (of ideas or plans) make or become definite —**crys'tal·li·za'tion** *n.*

Cs *symb.* cesium

CST *abbr.* central standard time

CT, Ct. *abbr.* Connecticut (postal abbr. **CT**)

ct. *abbr.* count

ctn. *abbr.* carton

Cu *symb.* copper [L *cuprum*]

cu. *abbr.* cubic

cub /kəb/ *n.* **1** young of a fox, bear, lion, etc. **2** *Colloq.* (also **cub' re·port'er**) young newspaper reporter

Cu·ba /kyoo'bə/ *n.* island country in the Caribbean Sea, S of Florida. Capital: Havana. Pop. 10,848,000 —**Cu'ban** *n.* & *adj.*

cub·by·hole /kəb'ēhōl'/ *n.* very small, enclosed space [LGer]

cube /kyoob/ *n.* **1** solid of six equal square sides **2** cube-shaped block **3** product of a number multiplied by its square —*v.* (**cubed, cub·ing**) **4** find the cube of (a number) **5** cut (food, etc.) into small cubes [L fr. Gk]

cube' root' *n.* number for which a given number is the cube (sense 3)

cu·bic /kyoo'bik/ *adj.* **1** cube-shaped **2** of three dimensions **3** involving the cube (and no higher power) of a number

cu·bi·cal /kyoo'bikəl/ *adj.* cube-shaped

cu·bi·cle /kyoo'bikəl/ *n.* small enclosed space; compartment [L *cubare* lie down]

cub·ism /kyoo'biz'əm/ *n.* geometric style in art, esp. painting —**cu'bist** *n.* & *adj.*

cu·bit /kyoo'bit/ *n.* ancient measure about the length of a forearm [L *cubitum* elbow]

cuck·old /kək'əld, -ōld'/ *n.* **1** husband of an adulterous wife —*v.* **2** make a cuckold of —**cuck'old·ry** *n.* [Fr]

cuck·oo /koo'koo, koo'-/ *n.* **1** bird with characteristic cry, and known to lay its eggs in the nests of other birds —*adj.* **2** *Slang.* crazy [Fr, imit.]

cu·cum·ber /kyoo'kəm'bər/ *n.* long green fleshy fruit, used in salads and for pickles [Fr fr. L]

Cú·cu·ta /koo'kətə/ *n.* city in E Colombia. Pop. 357,000

cud /kəd/ *n.* half-digested food returned to the mouth of ruminants for further chewing [OE]

cud·dle /kəd'l/ *v.* (**·dled, ·dling**) **1** hug; fondle **2** nestle together; lie close and snug

cud'dly *adj.* (**·dli·er, ·dli·est**) **1** (of a person, toy, etc.) soft and yielding **2** given to cuddling **3** warmly winsome or lovable

cud·gel /kəj'əl/ *n.* short thick stick used as a weapon [OE]

cue¹ /kyoo/ *n.* **1a** last words of an actor's line as a signal to another to enter or speak **b** sim-

---

139   **cryptography / cum**

ilar signal to a musician, etc. **2a** stimulus to perception, etc. **b** signal for action **c** hint on appropriate behavior —*v.* (**cued, cu·ing** or **cue·ing**) **3** give a cue to **4** put (audio equipment) in readiness **5** give information to **6** on cue at the correct moment

cue² *n. Billiards.* long rod for striking a ball [var. of QUEUE]

Cuer·na·va·ca /kwer'nəvä'kə/ *n.* capital of the Mexican state of Morelos. Pop. 348,900

cuff¹ /kəf/ *n.* **1** end part of a sleeve **2** turned-up trouser hem **3** (*pl.*) *Colloq.* handcuffs **4 off the cuff** *Colloq.* impromptu

cuff² *v.* **1** strike with an open hand —*n.* **2** such a blow [perh. imit.]

cuff' link' *n.* two joined studs, etc., for fastening a cuff

cui·sine /kwizēn'/ *n.* style or method of cooking [Fr]

cul'-de-sac' /kəl'dəsak'/ *n.* (*pl.* **culs-de-sac** or **cul-de-sacs**) **1** alley with a dead end **2** futile course [Fr: sack-bottom]

-cule *suffix* forming (orig. diminutive) nouns (*molecule*) [L *-culus*]

Cu·lia·cán /kool'yəkän'/ *n.* capital of the Mexican state of Sinaloa. Pop. 602,100

cu·li·nar·y /kəl'əner'ē, kyoo'lə-/ *adj.* pertaining to cooking [L *culina* kitchen]

cull /kəl/ *v.* **1** gather or derive (*knowledge culled from books*) **2** extract or pick out selectively [Fr, rel. to COLLECT]

cul·mi·nate /kəl'mənāt'/ *v.* (**·nat·ed, ·nat·ing**) reach its highest or final point —**cul'mi·na'tion** *n.* [L *culmen* top]

cu·lottes /k(y)ŏŏ'läts'/ *n. pl.* women's trousers cut like a skirt [Fr: knee-breeches]

cul·pa·ble /kəl'pəbəl/ *adj.* deserving blame —**cul'pa·bil'i·ty** *n.* [L *culpa* blame]

cul·prit /kəl'prit/ *n.* guilty person [perh. fr. AngFr *culpable*: see CULPABLE]

cult /kəlt/ *n.* **1** religious system, sect, etc., esp. ritualistic **2a** devotion to a person or thing (*cult of aestheticism*) **b** fashion **c** exotically fashionable (*cult film*) [L, rel. to CULTIVATE]

cul·ti·vate /kəl'tivāt'/ *v.* (**·vat·ed, ·vat·ing**) **1** prepare and use (soil, etc.) for crops or gardening **2a** raise (crops) **b** culture (bacteria, etc.) —**cul·ti·va'tion** *n.* [MedL *cultivatus* fr. L *colere* till]

cul'ti·vat'ed *adj.* **1** improved (the mind, manners, etc.) **2** nurtured (a person, friendship, etc.)

cul·tur·al /kəl'CHərəl/ *adj.* of or relating to intellectual or artistic matters, or to a specific culture —**cul'tur·al·ly** *adv.*

cul·ture /kəl'CHər/ *n.* **1a** intellectual and artistic achievement or expression **b** refined appreciation of the arts, etc. **2** customs, achievements, etc., of a particular civilization or group **3** quantity of microorganisms and nutrient material supporting their growth —*v.* (**·tured, ·tur·ing**) **4** maintain (bacteria, etc.) in suitable growth conditions [L, rel. to CULTIVATE]

cul'tured *adj.* having refined taste, etc.

cul·vert /kəl'vərt/ *n.* channel carrying water under a road, etc.

cum /kŏŏm, kəm/ *prep.* (usu. *comb.*) with; combined with; also used as (*bedroom-cum-study*) [L]

cum. *abbr.* cumulative

Cum·ber·land Gap /kəm′bərlənd/ *n.* narrow natural pass through the Appalachian Mountains

Cum·ber·land Road′ *n.* see NATIONAL ROAD

cum·ber·some /kəm′bərsəm/ *adj.* (also **cum·brous** /kəm′brəs/) inconveniently bulky, etc. **2** formed by accumulation —*v.* **4** restraint [*cumber* hinder]

cum·in /kəm′ən, k(y)o͞o′mən/ *n.* (also **cum′ min**) **1** plant with aromatic seeds **2** these as flavoring [Gk *kyminon*]

cum·mer·bund /kəm′ərbənd/ *n.* waist sash [Hindi and Pers]

Cum·mings /kəm′iNGz/, **Edward Estlin** ("e e cummings") 1894–1962; US poet

cum·quat /kəm′kwät/ *n.* var. of KUMQUAT

cu·mu·la·tive /kyo͞o′ myəlātiv/ *adj.* **1** increasing progressively in amount, force, etc. **2** formed by successive additions (*learning is a cumulative process*) —**cu′ mu·la·tive·ly** *adv.*

CUMMERBUND

cu·mu·lus /kyo͞o′myələs/ *n.* (*pl.* **-li** /-lī′/) cloud formation of rounded masses heaped up on a flat base [L: heap]

cu·ne·i·form /kyo͞oně′əfôrm′, kyo͞o′n(ē)ə-/ *adj.* **1** wedge-shaped **2** of or using wedge-shaped writing —*n.* **3** cuneiform writing [L *cuneus* wedge]

cun·ning /kən′iNG/ *adj.* **1** deceitful; clever; crafty **2** ingenious —*n.* **3** craftiness; deception **4** skill; ingenuity —**cun′ning·ly** *adv.* [ON, rel. to CAN¹]

cup /kəp/ *n.* **1** small bowl-shaped container for drinking from **2a** its contents **b** CUPFUL **3** cup-shaped thing **4** cup-shaped trophy as a prize —*v.* (**cupped, cup·ping**) **5** form (esp. the hands) into the shape of a cup **6** take or hold as in a cup **7** one's cup of tea *Colloq.* what interests or suits one [MedL *cuppa*]

cup·board /kəb′ərd/ *n.* recess or piece of furniture with a door and (usu.) shelves

cup·ful /kəp′fo͞ol′/ *n.* (*pl.* **-s**) amount held by a cup, esp. a half-pint or 8-ounce measure

Cu·pid /kyo͞o′pid/ *n.* **1** Roman god of love, represented as a winged naked boy archer **2** (also **c-**) representation of Cupid [L *cupere* desire]

cu·pid·i·ty /kyo͞opid′ətē/ *n.* greed; avarice [L, rel. to CUPID]

CUPOLA

cu·po·la /kyo͞o′pələ/ *n.* dome forming or adorning a roof [It fr. L *cupa* cask]

cu·pric /k(y)o͞o′prik/ *adj.* of copper

cur /kər/ *n.* **1** mangy ill-tempered dog **2** contemptible person [perh. fr. ON *kurr* grumbling]

cur. *abbr.* **1** currency **2** current

cur·a·ble /kyo͞or′əbəl/ *adj.* able to be cured —**cur·a·bil′i·ty** *n.*

Cu·ra·çao /k(y)o͞orʹəsō′, -sou′/ *n.* **1** main island of the Netherlands Antilles, off the coast of Venezuela. Capital: Willemstad **2** (**c-**) orange-flavored liqueur, originally made there

cu·ra·re /k(y)o͞orär′ē/ *n.* extract of various plants, used by American Indians to poison arrows [Carib]

cu·rate /kyo͞or′ət/ *n.* assistant to a parish priest [MedL *curatus*, rel. to CURE]

cu·ra·tive /kyo͞or′ətiv/ *adj.* **1** tending or able to cure —*n.* **2** curative agent [MedL, rel. to CURATE]

cu·ra·tor /kyo͞orät′ər, kyo͞orāt′ər/ *n.* keeper or custodian of a museum, etc. [AngL, rel. to CURE]

curb /kərb/ *n.* **1** check; restraint **2** strap, etc., to restrain a horse **3** enclosing border **4** street edge or sidewalk border —*v.* **5** restrain [Fr, rel. to CURVE]

curd /kərd/ *n.* (often *pl.*) coagulated acidic milk product made into cheese or eaten as food

cur·dle /kərd′l/ *v.* (**-dled, -dling**) **1** form into curds; congeal **2** make one's blood curdle horrify one [frequent. of CURD]

cure /kyo͞or/ *v.* (**cured, cur·ing**) **1** restore to health; relieve (*cured of pleurisy*) **2** eliminate (disease, evil, etc.) **3** preserve (meat, fruit, etc.) by salting, drying, etc. —*n.* **4** restoration to health **5** thing effecting a cure **6** course of treatment [L *cura* care]

cure′-all′ *n.* panacea

cur·few /kər′fyo͞o/ *n.* signal or time after which people must remain indoors [Fr, rel. to COVER + L FOCUS]

cu·rie /kyo͞or′ē, ko͞orē′/ *n.* unit of radioactivity [for M. and P. CURIE]

Cu·rie /kyo͞orē′, ko͞orē′/ **1 Pierre** 1859–1906; French physicist, codiscoverer of radium with his wife: **2 Marie** 1867–1934

cu·ri·o /kyo͞or′ē-ō′/ *n.* (*pl.* **-os**) rare or unusual object [abbr. of CURIOSITY]

cu·ri·os·i·ty /kyo͞or′ē-äs′ətē/ *n.* (*pl.* **-ties**) **1** eager desire to know; inquisitiveness **2** strange, rare, etc., object [L, rel. to CURIOUS]

cu·ri·ous /kyo͞or′ēəs/ *adj.* **1** eager to learn; inquisitive **2** strange; surprising; odd —**cu′ ri·ous·ly** *adv.* [L, rel. to CURE]

Cu·ri·ti·ba /ko͞or′itē′bə, -və/ *n.* city in SE Brazil. Pop. 843,700

cu·ri·um /kyo͞or′ēəm/ *n.* artificial radioactive metallic element; *symb.* Cm [for M. and P. CURIE]

curl /kərl/ *v.* **1** bend or coil into a spiral **2** move in a spiral form —*n.* **3** lock of curled hair **4** anything spiral or curved inward **5a** curling movement **b** being curled **6** curl one's lip express scorn **7** curl up lie or sit with the knees drawn up [Du]

cur·lew /kər′l(y)o͞o/ *n.* wading bird, usu. with a long slender bill [Fr]

cur·li·cue /kər′likyo͞o/ *n.* decorative curl or twist [fr. CURLY + CUE² or Q¹]

curl′ing *n.* game played on ice with round flat stones

curl·y *adj.* (**·i·er, ·iest**) 1 having or arranged in curls 2 moving in curves —**curl'i·ness** *n.*

cur·mud·geon /kərmuj'ən/ *n.* bad-tempered person —**cur·mud'geon·ly** *adj.*

cur·rant /kər'ənt, kə'rənt/ *n.* 1 small seedless dried grape 2a any of various shrubs producing red, white, or black berries **b** such a berry [AngFr fr. *Corinth* in Greece]

cur·ren·cy /kər'ənsē, kə'rən-/ *n.* (*pl.* **·cies**) 1a money in use in a country **b** other commodity used as money 2 being current; prevalence

cur·rent /kər'ənt, kə'rənt/ *adj.* 1 belonging to the present; happening now —*n.* 2 narrow force of moving water, air, etc. 3a ordered movement of electrically charged particles **b** quantity representing the intensity of this —**cur'rent·ness** *n.* [L *currere* run]

cur'rent·ly *adv.* at the present time; now

cur·ric·u·lum /kərik'yələm/ *n.* (*pl.* **·la** or **·lums**) subjects in a course of study [L: course]

cur·ry[1] /kər'ē, kə'rē/ *n.* (*pl.* **·ries**) 1 powder of various spices or the savory dishes prepared with it —*v.* (**·ried, ·ry·ing**) 2 prepare or flavor with this powder [Tamil]

cur·ry[2] *v.* (**·ried, ·ry·ing**) 1 groom (a horse) with a currycomb 2 treat (tanned leather) to improve it 3 **curry favor** ingratiate oneself [Gmc, rel. to READY]

cur'ry·comb' *n.* metal serrated device for grooming horses

curse /kərs/ *n.* 1 solemn invocation of divine wrath 2 supposed resulting evil 3 violent or profane exclamation or oath 4 thing causing evil or harm —*v.* (**cursed, curs·ing**) 5a utter a curse against **b** (in *imper.*) may God curse 6 afflict with 7 swear profanely [OE]

cur·sive /kər'siv/ *adj.* 1 (of writing) with joined characters —*n.* 2 cursive writing [MedL: running, rel. to CURRENT]

cur·sor /kər'sər/ *n. Comp.* positional indicator on a screen [L: runner, rel. to CURSIVE]

cur·so·ry /kər'sərē/ *adj.* hasty; hurried —**cur'so·ri·ly** *adv.*; **cur'so·ri·ness** *n.* [L, rel. to CURSOR]

curt /kərt/ *adj.* noticeably or rudely brief —**curt'ly** *adv.*; **curt'ness** *n.* [L *curtus* short]

cur·tail /kərtāl'/ *v.* cut short; reduce —**cur·tail'ment** *n.* [corruption of obs. adj. *curtal*, rel. to CURT]

cur·tain /kərt'n/ *n.* 1 piece of cloth, etc., hung as a screen, esp. at a window 2a rise or fall of a stage curtain **b** CURTAIN CALL 3 partition or cover 4 (*pl.*) *Slang.* the end —*v.* 5 shut off with curtain(s) [L *cortina*]

cur'tain call' *n.* audience's applause summoning actors to take a bow

Cur·tin /kərt'n/, **John** 1885–1945; prime minister of Australia (1941–45)

Cur·tiss /kərt'əs/, **Glenn** 1878–1930; US air pioneer and aircraft designer

curt·sy /kərt'sē/ (also **curt·sey**) —*n.* (*pl.* **·sies**) 1 deferential bending and lowering of the body by a girl or woman —*v.* (**·sied, ·sy·ing**) 2 make a curtsy [var. of COURTESY]

cur·va·ceous /kərvā'sHəs/ *adj. Colloq.* (esp. of a woman) having a shapely figure

cur·va·ture /kər'vəCHər/ *n.* curving or degree of curve [Fr fr. L, rel. to CURVE]

curve /kərv/ *n.* 1 line or surface of which no

---

part is straight or flat 2 curved line trail, etc. —*v.* (**curved, curv·ing**) 3 bend or shape to form a curve —**curved** *adj.*; **curv'y** *adj.* (**·i·er, ·i·est**); **curv'i·ness** *n.* [L *curvus* curved]

cush·ion /koosh'ən/ *n.* 1 bag stuffed with soft material, for sitting or leaning on, etc. 2 protection against shock; measure to soften a blow 3 margin of security, advantage, etc. —*v.* 4 provide or protect with cushion(s) 5 mitigate the adverse effects of [L *culcita* mattress]

cush·y /koosh'ē/ *adj.* (**·i·er, ·i·est**) *Colloq.* easy and pleasant [Hindi *khush* pleasant]

cusp /kəsp/ *n.* point at which two curves meet, e.g., the horn of a moon [L *cuspis* point; apex]

cus·tard /kəs'tərd/ *n.* pudding or sweet sauce of eggs or flavored cornstarch and milk [obs. *crustade*, rel. to CRUST]

Cus·ter /kəs'tər/, **George Armstrong** 1839–76; US cavalry general

cus·to·di·an /kəstō'dēən/ *n.* 1 caretaker 2 maintenance worker —**cus·to'di·an·ship'** *n.*

cus·to·dy /kəs'tədē/ *n.* 1 guardianship; protective care 2 imprisonment 3 **take into custody** arrest —**cus·to'di·al** /kəstō'dēəl/ *adj.* [L *custodia* fr. *custos* guard]

cus·tom /kəs'təm/ *n.* 1a usual behavior **b** particular established way of behaving 2 *Law.* established usage having the force of law 3 (*pl.*; also treated as *sing.*) **a** duty on imports and exports **b** officials or area administering this [OFr *costume* fr. L *consuescere*]

cus·tom·ar·y /kəs'tomer'ē/ *adj.* in accordance with custom; usual —**cus'tom·ar'i·ly** *adv.* [MedL, rel. to CUSTOM]

cus'tom·er *n.* 1 person who buys goods or services 2 *Colloq.* person of a specified kind (*tough customer*) [AngFr, rel. to CUSTOM]

cus'tom·ize' *v.* (**·ized, ·iz·ing**) make or modify to order; personalize

cut /kət/ *v.* (**cut, cut·ting**) 1 penetrate or wound with a sharp-edged instrument 2 divide or be divided with a knife, etc. 3 trim or detach by cutting 4 reduce (wages, time, etc.) or cease (services, etc.) 5a make (a coat, gem, key, record, etc.) by cutting **b** make (a path, tunnel, etc.) by removing material 6 perform; make 7 cross; intersect 8 traverse, esp. as a shorter way 9 deliberately ignore (a person one knows) 10 deliberately miss (a class, etc.) 11 *Cards.* divide (a deck) into two parts 12 switch off; cease; stop —*n.* 13 cutting 14 division or wound made by cutting 15 stroke with a knife, etc. 16 reduction; cessation 17 hurtful remark or act 18 style of hair, garment, etc., achieved by cutting 19 particular piece of butchered meat 20 *Colloq.* commission; share of profits 21 **a cut above** *Colloq.* noticeably superior to 22 **be cut out** be suited 23 **cut corners** do perfunctorily or incompletely, esp. to save time 24 **cut (a person) down to size** *Colloq.* deflate pretensions 25 **cut in** interrupt 26 **cut one's losses** abandon an unprofitable scheme 27 **cut no ice** *Slang.* have no influence 28 **cut one's teeth on** acquire experience from [OE]

cut' and dried' *adj.* fixed and unalterable

cu·ta·ne·ous /kyootā'nēəs/ *adj.* of the skin [L, rel. to CUTICLE]

cut'a·way' *adj.* **1** (of a diagram, etc.) with parts of the interior exposed **2** man's formal coat that curves back to the tails

cut'back' *n.* cutting back, esp. a reduction in expenditure

cute /kyōot/ *adj. Colloq.* endearingly attractive —**cute'ly** *adv.*; **cute'ness** *n.* [shortening of ACUTE]

cu·ti·cle /kyōo'tikəl/ *n.* dead skin at the base of a fingernail or toenail [L dim. of *cutis* skin]

CUTAWAY 2

cut'lass /kət'ləs/ *n. Hist.* short sword with a slightly curved blade [ult. fr. L *cultellus* knife]

cut·ler·y /kət'lərē/ *n.* knives, forks, and spoons for use at table [AngFr, rel. to CUT]

cut'let /kət'lit/ *n.* **1** small piece of veal, etc., for frying **2** flat cake of minced meat, fish, etc. [Fr dim. fr. L *costa* rib]

cut'off' *n.* **1** point at which something is cut off **2** diverging path or shortcut —*adj.* **3** designating something cut off, shortened, etc. **4** designating an (arbitrary) end or limit (*cutoff date*)

cut'throat' *n.* **1** murderer —*adj.* **2** (of competition) ruthless and intense

cut'ting *n.* **1** piece cut from a plant for propagation —*adj.* **2** hostile; wounding —**cut'ting·ly** *adv.*

cut·tle·fish /kət'l-fish'/ *n.* (*pl.* same or -es) mollusk with ten arms and ejecting a black fluid when threatened [OE]

Cuz·co /kōos'kō/ *n.* city in S Peru. Pop. 275,000

c.w.o. *abbr.* cash with order

-cy *suffix* denoting state, condition, or status (*idiocy; captaincy*) [L -*cia*, Gk -*kia*]

cy·a·nide /sī'ənīd'/ *n.* highly poisonous substance used in mineral extraction

cy·a·no·sis /sī'ənō'sis/ *n.* bluish skin due to oxygen-deficient blood

cy·ber·net·ics /sī'bərnet'iks/ *n. pl.* (usu. treated as *sing.*) science of communications and control systems in machines and living things —**cy·ber·net'ic** *adj.* [Gk *kybernētēs* steersman]

cy·ber·punk /sī'bərpəNGk'/ *n.* science fiction writing combining high-tech plots with unconventional or nihilistic social values [fr. CYBER(NETICS) + PUNK]

cy·borg /sī'bôrg/ *n. Sci. Fict.* human being integrating electro-mechanical devices to enhance biological functions [cybernetic organism]

cy·cla·men /sik'ləmən, sī'klə-/ *n.* plant with pink, red, or white flowers [L fr. Gk]

cy·cle /sī'kəl/ *n.* **1a** recurrent round or period (of events, phenomena, etc.) **b** time needed for this **2** *Electr.* HERTZ **3** series of related songs, poems, etc. **4** bicycle, tricycle, etc. —*v.* (**·cled, ·cling**) **5** ride a bicycle, etc. [Gk *kyklos* circle]

cy·clic /sī'klik, sik'lik/ (also **cy·cli·cal** /sī'kli·kəl, sik'li-/) *adj.* **1a** recurring in cycles **b** belonging to a chronological cycle **2** with constituent atoms forming a ring —**cy'cli·cal·ly** *adv.*

cy·clist /sī'klist/ *n.* rider of a bicycle

cyclo- *comb. form* circle, cycle, or cyclic

cy·clone /sī'klōn/ *n.* large-scale low-pressure system similar to a hurricane —**cy·clon'ic** /-klän'ik/ *adj.* [Gk *kyklōma* wheel]

cy·clo·tron /sī'kləträn/ *n.* apparatus for acceleration of charged atomic and subatomic particles revolving in a magnetic field

cyg·net /sig'nit/ *n.* young swan [L *cygnus* swan fr. Gk]

cyl·in·der /sil'əndər/ *n.* **1** uniform solid or hollow body with straight sides and a circular cross-section **2** thing of this shape —**cy·lin·dri·cal** /səlin'drikəl/ *adj.* [L *cylindrus* fr. Gk]

cym·bal /sim'bəl/ *n.* brass or bronze disk struck to make a ringing sound [L fr. Gk]

Cym·be·line /sim'bəlēn/ *n.* died c. 42; British chieftain

cyn·ic /sin'ik/ *n.* **1** person with a pessimistic view of human nature **2** person who believes the worst about people's motives —**cyn'i·cal** *adj.*; **cyn'i·cal·ly** *adv.*; **cyn'i·cism** /-əsiz'əm/ *n.* [Gk *kynikos* dog-like]

cy·no·sure /sī'nəshŏor', sin'ə-/ *n.* center of attraction or admiration [Gk: dog's tail (name for Ursa Minor)]

cy·press /sī'prəs/ *n.* conifer with hard wood and dark foliage [Gk *kyparissos*]

Cy·prus /sī'prəs/ *n.* island republic in the Mediterranean Sea, S of Turkey. Capital: Nicosia. Pop. 756,000

Cyr·a·no de Ber·ge·rac /ser'ənō də ber'zHərak'/, **Savinien** 1619–55; French soldier and writer

Cyr·il, St. /ser'əl/ 826–869; Greek missionary to the Slavs; invented the Cyrillic alphabet

Cy·ril·lic /səril'ik/ *adj.* **1** of the alphabet used by Slavonic peoples of the Orthodox Church, now used esp. for Russian and Bulgarian —*n.* **2** this alphabet [for St. CYRIL]

Cy·rus the Great /sī'rəs/ d. 529 B.C.; king of Persia (559–529 B.C.)

cyst /sist/ *n.* sac formed in the body, containing liquid matter [Gk *kystis* bladder]

cys'tic *adj.* **1** of the bladder **2** like a cyst

cys'tic fi·bro'sis *n.* hereditary disease usu. with respiratory infections

-cyte *comb. form* mature cell (*leukocyte*) [Gk *kytos* vessel]

cy·tol·o·gy /sītäl'əjē/ *n.* the study of cells [Gk *kytos* vessel]

cy·to·plasm /sīt'əplaz'əm/ *n.* protoplasmic content of a cell apart from its nucleus

czar /zär, (t)sär/ *n.* (also **tsar**) **1** emperor; king **2** autocratic ruler **3** (often *cap.*) former title for emperors of Russia [L *Caesar*]

Czech /cHek/ *n.* **1** native or national of the Czech Republic **2** language of the Czech Republic —*adj.* **3** of the Czech Republic, its people, or language [Bohemian *Čech*]

Czech·o·slo·va·ki·a /cHek'əslävä'kēə/ *n.* former republic in central Europe (1918–93); divided into Czech Republic and Slovakia

Czech' Re·pub'lic /cHek/ *n.* republic in central Europe, the W part of the former Czechoslovakia. Capital: Prague. Pop. 10,400,000

Cze·sto·cho·wa /cHen'stəkō'və/ *n.* city in S Poland. Pop. 258,300

D

d, D /dē/ (*pl.* **d's; D's, Ds**) fourth letter of the English alphabet; a consonant

d or d. *abbr.* **1** daughter **2** day **3** deceased; died **4** degree **5** departs **5** diameter **6** *Brit. Hist.* pence; penny

D or D. *abbr.* **1** December **2** Democrat **3** *symb.* (as D) deuterium **4** *Rom. num.* (as D) five hundred

'd *v. contr.* contraction for *had* or *would*, usu. after pronouns (*I'd; he'd*)

D.A. *abbr.* district attorney

dab /dab/ *v.* (**dabbed, dab'bing**) **1** repeatedly press briefly and lightly with a cloth, etc. **2** apply by dabbing —*n.* **3** dabbing **4** small amount thus applied [imit.]

dab·ble /dab'əl/ *v.* (**·bled, ·bling**) **1** engage (in an activity, etc.) superficially **2** move the feet, hands, etc., in esp. shallow liquid —**dab'bler** *n.* [fr. DAB]

da·cha /däCH'ə/ *n.* Russian country cottage [Russ]

dachs·hund /däks'hŏont', -hŏond/ *n.* dog of a short-legged long-bodied breed [Ger: badger-dog]

dac·tyl /dak'təl/ *n.* metrical foot consisting of one long syllable followed by two short syllables —**dac·tyl'ic** *adj.* [Gk: finger]

dad /dad/ *n. Colloq.* father [imit. of a child's *da da*]

dad·dy /da'dē/ *n.* (*pl.* **·dies**) *Colloq.* father [fr. DAD]

da·do /dā'dō/ *n.* (*pl.* **·dos**) **1** lower, differently decorated, part of an interior wall **2** plinth of a column [It, rel. to DIE²]

dae·mon /dē'mən/ *n.* var. of DEMON, 4

daf·fo·dil /daf'ədil'/ *n.* spring bloom with a yellow trumpet-shaped flower [rel. to ASPHODEL]

daft /daft/ *adj. Colloq.* silly; foolish; crazy [OE: meek]

dag·ger /dag'ər/ *n.* **1** short pointed knife for stabbing **2** printing reference symbol (†) **3 look daggers** at glare angrily at

da·guerre·o·type /dəger'(ē)ətīp'/ *n.* early photograph using a silvered plate and mercury vapor [for *Daguerre*, its inventor]

Dahl /däl/, Roald 1916–90; British writer

dahl·ia /dal'yə, däl'-, dāl-/ *n.* large-flowered showy garden plant [for *Dahl*, botanist]

dai·ly /dā'lē/ *adj.* **1** done or occurring every day or weekday —*adv.* **2** every day —*n.* (*pl.* **·lies**) *Colloq.* **3** daily newspaper

dain·ty /dānt'ē/ *adj.* **1** delicately pretty **2** delicate; small **3** (of food) choice **4** fastidious; discriminating —*n.* (*pl.* **·ties**) **5** choice delicacy —**dain'ti·ly** *adv.*; **dain'ti·ness** *n.* [L *dignitas* DIGNITY]

dai·qui·ri /dī'kərē, dak'ə-/ *n.* (*pl.* **·ris**) cocktail of rum, lime juice, etc. [*Daiquiri* in Cuba]

dair·y /der'ē/ *n.* (*pl.* **·ies**) **1** place for processing, distributing, or selling milk and its products —*adj.* **2** pertaining to dairy products (and sometimes eggs) [OE]

da·is /dā'is, dī'-/ *n.* raised platform, usu. at the front of a hall [L DISCUS disk; (later) table]

dai·sy /dā'zē/ *n.* (*pl.* **·sies**) **1** small wild plant with white-petaled flowers **2** plant with similar flowers [OE: *day's eye*]

Da·kar /dəkär', dak'är'/ *n.* capital of Senegal. Pop. 1,729,800

Da·ko·ta /dəkō'tə/ *n.* language of the Sioux Indians of N America

Da·lai La·ma /dä'lī lä'mə, -lē/ title of the leader of Tibetan Buddhism

dale /dāl/ *n.* valley [OE]

Da·li /dä'lē, dälē'/, Salvador 1904–89; Spanish surrealist painter

Da·lian /däl'yen'/ *n.* (formerly **Tairen; Lüda**) city in NE China. Pop. 1,723,300

Dal·las /dal'əs/ *n.* city in Texas. Pop. 1,006,877 —**Dal'las·ite'** *n.*

dal·ly /dal'ē/ *v.* (**·lied, ·ly·ing**) **1** delay; waste time **2** flirt; trifle —**dal'li·ance** *n.* [Fr]

DALMATIAN

Dal·ma·tian /dalmā'SHən/ *n.* large white spotted short-haired dog [*Dalmatia* in Croatia]

dam¹ /dam/ *n.* **1** barrier across river, etc., forming a reservoir or preventing flooding —*v.* (**dammed, dam·ming**) **2** provide or confine with a dam **3** block up; obstruct [LGer or Du]

dam² *n.* mother, esp. of a four-footed animal [var. of DAME]

dam·age /dam'ij/ *n.* **1** harm or injury **2** (*pl.*) *Law.* financial compensation for loss or injury **3** (prec. by *the*) *Slang.* cost —*v.* (**·aged, ·aging**) **4** inflict damage on [L *damnum*]

dam'age con·trol' *n.* intervention to repair or limit physical damage or adverse effects

Da·mas·cus /dəmas'kəs/ *n.* capital of Syria. Pop. 1,451,000

dam·ask /dam'əsk/ *n.* **1** reversible figured woven fabric, esp. white table linen —*adj.* **2** made of damask **3** velvety pink —*v.* **4** weave with figured designs [for DAMASCUS]

dame /dām/ *n.* **1** *Brit. cap.* woman's honorific title **2** *Slang.* woman [L *domina* lady]

dam·mit /dam'it/ *interj. Colloq.* damn it

damn /dam/ *v.* **1** curse (a person or thing) **2** doom to hell; cause the damnation of **3** criticize harshly —*n.* **4** uttered curse **5** *Slang.* negligible amount —*adj. & adv.* **6** *Colloq.* DAMNED **7 damning** (of circumstance, evidence, etc.) showing or proving to be guilty **8 damn with faint praise** commend feebly, and so imply disapproval [L *damnum* loss]

dam·na·ble /dam'nəbəl/ *adj.* hateful; annoying —**dam'na·bly** *adv.*

dam·na'tion *n.* eternal punishment in hell

damned *adj. Colloq.* **1** damnable —*adv.* **2** extremely (*damned hot*) **3 do one's damnedest** do one's utmost

damp /damp/ *adj.* **1** slightly wet —*n.* **2** moisture, esp. unwanted —*v.* **3** make damp; moisten **4a** temper; mute (*damp enthusiasm*) **b** make (a fire) burn less strongly by reducing the flow of air —**damp′ness** *n.* [LGer]

damp·en /dam′pən/ *v.* **1** make or become damp **2** temper; lessen

damp′er *n.* **1** discouraging person or thing **2** device that reduces or lessens **3 put a damper on** take the vigor or enjoyment out of

dam·sel /dam′zəl/ *n. Archaic* or *Lit.* young unmarried woman [Fr dim., rel. to DAME]

dam·sel·fly /dam′zəlflī′/ *n.* insect like a dragonfly but with wings folded when resting

Da·na /dā′nə/, **Richard Henry** 1815–82; US adventurer, lawyer, and writer

Da·nang /dänäNG′, dənaNG′/ *n.* seaport in central Vietnam. Pop. 370,700

dance /dans/ *v.* (**danced, danc·ing**) **1** move rhythmically, usu. to music **2** skip or jump about **3** perform (a specified dance, role, etc.) **4** bob up and down —*n.* **5a** dancing as an art form **b** style or form of this **6** social gathering for dancing **7** lively motion —**dance′a·ble** *adj.*; **danc′er** *n.* [Fr]

dan·de·li·on /dan′dl-ī′ən/ *n.* wild plant with jagged leaves and a yellow flower [Fr *dent-de-lion*: lion's tooth]

dan·der /dan′dər/ *n. Colloq.* **1** temper; indignation **2 get one's dander up** become angry

dan·dle /dan′dl/ *v.* (**·dled, ·dling**) bounce (a child) on one's knees, etc.

dan·druff /dan′drəf/ *n.* flakes of dead skin on or from the scalp

dan·dy /dan′dē/ *n.* (*pl.* **·dies**) **1** man greatly devoted to style and fashion **2** *Colloq.* excellent thing —*adj.* (**·di·er, ·di·est**) **3** *Colloq.* splendid [perh. fr. the name *Andrew*]

Dane /dān/ *n.* **1** native or national of Denmark **2** *Hist.* Viking invader of England in the 9th–11th cent. [ON]

dan·ger /dān′jər/ *n.* **1** liability or exposure to harm **2** thing that causes or may cause harm [earlier 'power', fr. L *dominus* lord]

dan·ger·ous /dān′jərəs/ *adj.* involving or causing danger —**dan′ger·ous·ly** *adv.*

dan·gle /daNG′gəl/ *v.* (**·gled, ·gling**) **1** be loosely suspended and able to sway **2** hold or carry thus **3** hold out (hope, temptation, etc.) enticingly [imit.]

Dan·ish /dā′niSH/ *adj.* **1** of Denmark or the Danes —*n.* **2** Danish language **3** (prec. by *the*; treated as *pl.*) the Danish people [L, rel. to DANE]

Dan′ish past′ry *n.* pastry topped with icing, fruit, nuts, etc.

dank /daNGk/ *adj.* disagreeably damp and cold —**dank′ness** *n.* [prob. Scand]

d'An·nun·zio /dänōōnt′sē-ō/, **Gabriele** 1863–1938; Italian novelist, dramatist, and poet

Dan·te /dän′tā′, dant′ē/ (surname **Alighieri**) 1265–1321; Italian poet

Dan·ton /däNtôN′/, **Georges Jacques** 1759–94; French revolutionary

Dan·ube /dan′yōōb/ *n.* river in central and S Europe flowing from SW Germany 1,720 mi. into the Black Sea

dap·per /dap′ər/ *adj.* **1** neat and precise, esp. in dress **2** sprightly [LGer or Du *dapper* strong]

dap·ple /dap′əl/ *v.* (**·pled, ·pling**) **1** mark or become marked with spots of color or shade —*n.* **2** dappled effect

Dar·da·nelles /därd′n-elz′/ *n.* strait connecting the Aegean Sea with the Sea of Marmara

Dare /dar, der/, **Virginia** b. 1587; first child born in America of European parents

dare /der/ *v.* (**dared, dar·ing**) **1** have the courage or impudence (to) **2** face bravely —*n.* **3** challenge **4** challenge, esp. to prove courage **5 I dare say** it is probable [OE]

dare′dev′il *n.* **1** recklessly daring person —*adj.* **2** recklessly daring —**dare′dev′il·ry** *n.*

Dar es Sa·laam /där′ es səläm′/ *n.* capital of Tanzania. Pop. 1,360,900

dar·ing /der′iNG/ *n.* **1** adventurous courage —*adj.* **2** adventurous —**dar′ing·ly** *adv.*

Da·ri·us I /dərī′əs/ (called **"the Great"**) c. 550–486 B.C.; king of Persia (521–486)

dark /därk/ *adj.* **1** with little or no light **2** of deep or somber color **3** (of a person) with dark coloring **4** gloomy; dismal **5** evil; sinister **6** secret; mysterious —*n.* **7** absence of light —**dark′ly** *adv.*; **dark′ness** *n.* [OE]

dark·en /där′kən/ *v.* make or become dark or darker

dark′ horse′ *n.* little-known contestant

dark′room′ *n.* darkened room for photographic work

dar·ling /där′liNG/ *n.* **1** beloved, lovable, or endearing person or thing **2** favorite —*adj.* **3** beloved; lovable **4** charming or pretty [OE, rel. to DEAR]

darn¹ /därn/ *v.* **1** mend (cloth, etc.) by filling a hole with stitching —*n.* **2** darned area

darn² *v., interj., adj., & adv. Colloq.* euphemism for DAMN —**darned** *adj.*

Dar·row /dar′ō/, **Clarence** 1857–1938; US lawyer

dart /därt/ *n.* **1** small pointed missile **2** (*pl.*; usu. treated as *sing.*) indoor game of throwing these at a dartboard to score points **3** sudden rapid movement **4** tapering tuck in a garment —*v.* **5** move, send, or go suddenly or rapidly [Fr fr. Gmc]

dart′board′ *n.* circular target in darts

Dar·win /där′wən/, **Charles** 1809–82; English naturalist; proponent of evolution

dash /daSH/ *v.* **1** rush **2** strike or fling forcefully, esp. so as to shatter **3** ruin (*dashed their hopes*) —*n.* **4** rush or onset; sudden advance **5** horizontal stroke (—) in writing or printing to mark a pause, etc. **6** impetuous vigor; zest **7** sprinting race **8** longer signal of two in Morse code (see also DOT, 1b) **9** slight admixture **10 dash off: a** depart hastily **b** write or draw hurriedly [imit.]

dash′board′ *n.* instrument panel of a vehicle

dash′ing *adj.* **1** spirited; lively **2** showy —**dash′ing·ly** *adv.*

das′tard·ly /das′tärdlē/ *adj.* cowardly; despicable —**das′tard·li·ness** *n.*

DAT *abbr.* digital audio tape

da·ta /dat′ə, dāt′ə/ *n. pl.* (usu. treated as *sing.*, although orig. the *pl.* of *datum*) **1** known facts as a basis for conclusions; information **2** quantities or characters operated on by a computer, etc. [L *data* fr. *dare* give]

● Usage: In origin, *data* is the plural of the

Latin word **datum**. **Data** is used as a singular in contexts where it means 'information': *The data is being prepared for the meeting*. It is used as a plural chiefly in technical senses and when individual items of information are to be stressed: *The data we gathered on earthquakes are being fed into the computer*.

data′base′ *n.* structured set of data held in a computer

da′ta cap′ture *n.* entering or inputting of data for use by a computer

da′ta pro′cess·ing *n.* series of operations on data, esp. by a computer —**da′ta pro′ces·sor** *n.*

date[1] /dāt/ *n.* 1 day of the month, esp. as a number 2 particular day or year 3 day noted at the head of a document, etc. 4 period to which a work of art, etc., belongs 5 *Colloq.* a appointment, esp. social b person to be met at this —*v.* (**dat·ed, dat·ing**) 6 mark with a date 7 assign a date to (an object, event, period, etc.) 8 have its origins at a particular time 9 appear or expose as old-fashioned 10 *Colloq.* a make a date with b go out together as sexual partners 11 **out of date** old-fashioned; obsolete 12 **to date** until now 13 **up to date** fashionable; current [Fr, rel. to DATA]

date[2] *n.* 1 dark oval single-stoned fruit 2 (in full **date′-palm′**) tree bearing it [Gk, rel. to DACTYL, fr. the shape of the leaf]

date′line′ *n.* date and place of writing at the head of a newspaper article, etc.

date′ rape′ *n.* sexual assault involving two people who have met socially

da·tive /dā′tiv/ *n. Gram.* 1 case expressing the indirect object or recipient —*adj.* 2 of or in this case [L, rel. to DATA]

da·tum /dāt′əm, dat′əm/ see DATA

daub /dôb, däb/ *v.* 1 spread (paint, etc.) crudely or roughly 2 paint crudely or unskillfully —*n.* 3 paint, etc., daubed on a surface [L, rel. to DE- + ALB]

Dau·det /dōdā′/, **Alphonse** 1840–97; French writer

daugh·ter /dô′tər/ *n.* 1 girl or woman in relation to her parent(s) 2 female descendant —**daugh′ter·ly** *adj.* [OE]

daugh′ter-in-law′ *n.* (*pl.* **daugh′ters-in-law′**) son's wife

Dau·mier /dōmyā′/, **Honoré** 1808–78; French painter

daunt /dônt, dänt/ *v.* discourage; intimidate —**daunt′ing** *adj.* [L *domitare* fr. *domare* tame]

daunt·less /dônt′ləs, dänt′-/ *adj.* intrepid

dau·phin /dô′fin/ *n. Hist.* eldest son of the King of France [Fr fr. L *delphinus* DOLPHIN, as a family name]

Da·vao /dä′vou′, dävou′/ *n.* seaport on Mindanao in the Philippines. Pop. 850,000

dav·en·port /dav′ənpôrt′/ *n.* large sofa [name of the maker]

Dav·en·port /dav′ənpôrt′/ *n.* city in Iowa. Pop. 95,333

Da·vid /dā′vəd/ died c. 970 B.C.; second king of Israel (c. 1010 – c. 970 B.C.); father of Solomon

Da·vid /dävēd′/, **Jacques-Louis** 1748–1825; French painter

da Vin′ci, Leonardo LEONARDO DA VINCI

Da·vis /dā′vəs/ 1 **Jefferson** 1808–89; president of the Confederate States of America

(1861–65) 2 **Bette** (born **Ruth Elizabeth**) 1908–89; US actress 3 **Sammy, Jr.** 1925–90; US entertainer 4 **Miles (Dewey)** 1926–91; US jazz musician

daw·dle /dôd′l/ *v.* (**·dled, ·dling**) 1 walk slowly and idly 2 waste time; procrastinate

dawn /dôn/ *n.* 1 daybreak 2 beginning or birth of something —*v.* 3 (of a day) begin; grow light 4 begin to become obvious (to) [OE]

day /dā/ *n.* 1 time between sunrise and sunset 2a 24 hours as a unit of time b corresponding period on other planets (*Martian day*) 3 daylight (*clear as day*) 4 time during which work is normally done (*eight-hour day*) 5a (also *pl.*) historical period (*in those days*) b (prec. by *the*) present time (*issues of the day*) 6 prime of a person's life (*in my day*) 7 a future time (*will do it one day*) 8 date of a specific event, etc. (*graduation day*) 9 battle or contest (*win the day*) 10 **all in a day's work** part of normal routine 11 **call it a day** end a period of activity 12 **day by day** gradually 13 **day in, day out** routinely; constantly 14 **not one's day** time when things go badly (for a person) 15 **one of these days** soon 16 **(it's)** one of those days day when things go badly 17 **that will be the day** *Colloq.* that will never happen [OE]

Da·yan /dī-än′, dä-yän′/, **Moshe** 1915–81; Israeli politician and general

day′bed′ *n.* bed for daytime rest

day′break′ *n.* first light in the morning

day′ care′ *n.* 1 supervision and care for young children or others who need assistance in daily living 2 facility providing such care —**day′-care′** *adj.*

day′dream′ *n.* 1 pleasant fantasy or reverie —*v.* 2 indulge in this —**day′dream·er** *n.*

day′light′ *n.* 1 light of day 2 dawn 3 visible gap or space

day′light sav′ing(s) time′ *n.* standard time advanced by one hour

day′ school′ *n.* school for pupils living at home

day′ time′ *n.* part of the day when there is natural light

day′-to-day′ *adj.* mundane; routine

Day·ton /dāt′n/ *n.* city in Ohio. Pop. 182,044

day′-trip′ *n.* trip completed in one day —**day′-trip′per** *n.*

daze /dāz/ *v.* (**dazed, daz·ing**) 1 stupefy; bewilder —*n.* 2 state of bewilderment [ON]

daz·zle /daz′əl/ *v.* (**·zled, ·zling**) 1 blind or confuse temporarily with a sudden bright light 2 impress or overpower with knowledge, ability, etc. —*n.* 3 bright confusing light —**daz′zling** *adj.*; **daz′zling·ly** *adv.* [fr. DAZE]

dB *abbr.* decibel(s)

DBMS *abbr. Comp.* data base management system

DC *abbr.* (also **dc**) direct current

D.C., DC *abbr.* District of Columbia (postal abbr. DC). See also WASHINGTON, D.C.

DD *abbr.* Doctor of Divinity

D.D.S. *abbr.* doctor of dental surgery (or science)

DDT *abbr.* an insecticide; use outlawed in the US [fr. the chemical name]

DE postal abbr. for Delaware

de- *prefix* 1 forming verbs and their derivatives: **a** down; away (*descend*) **b** completely (*denude*) **2** added to form verbs and nouns implying removal or reversal (*de-ice; decentralization*) [L]

dea·con /dē′kən/ *n.* (*fem.* **dea′con·ess**) assistant to a priest, minister, etc. [Gk *diakonos* servant]

de·ac·ti·vate /dē-ak′təvāt′/ *v.* (·**vat·ed, ·vat·ing**) make inactive or less reactive

dead /ded/ *adj.* **1** no longer alive **2** *Colloq.* extremely tired or unwell **3** numb (*fingers feel dead*) **4** insensitive to **5** no longer effective or in use; extinct **6** lacking force or vigor **7** quiet; lacking activity (*dead season*) **8** (of a microphone, etc.) not transmitting sounds **9** (of a ball in a game) not in play **10** abrupt; complete (*come to a dead stop; dead certainty*) —*adv.* **11** absolutely; completely (*dead on target; dead tired*) —*n.* **12** time of silence or inactivity (*dead of night*) **13 dead to the world** *Colloq.* fast asleep; unconscious [OE]

dead′beat′ *adj. Slang.* evader or shirker of debts

dead·en /ded′n/ *v.* **1** deprive of or lose vitality, force, brightness, sound, feeling, etc. **2** make insensitive

dead′ end′ *n.* **1** closed end of road, passage, etc. **2 dead-end** hopeless situation, job, etc.

dead′ heat′ *n.* race in which competitors tie

dead′ let′ter *n.* law or practice no longer observed or recognized

dead′line′ *n.* time limit

dead′lock′ *n.* **1** state of unresolved conflict —*v.* **2** bring or come to a standstill

dead′ly *adj.* (·**li·er, ·li·est**) **1** causing or able to cause fatal injury or serious damage **2** intense; extreme **3** (of aim, etc.) true; effective **4** *Colloq.* dreary; dull —*adv.* **5** as if dead **6** extremely

dead′ly night′shade *n.* poisonous plant with purple-black berries

dead′pan′ *adj. & adv.* lacking expression or emotion

dead′ reck′on·ing *n.* calculation of a ship's position from direction, compass, etc.

Dead′ Sea′ *n.* inland salt lake between Israel and Jordan

dead′wood′ *n. Colloq.* ineffectual person(s) or thing(s)

deaf /def/ *adj.* **1** wholly or partly unable to hear **2** refusing to listen or comply **3 turn a deaf ear** be unresponsive —**deaf′ness** *n.* [OE]

deaf′en·ing *adj.* (of noise) oppressing or making deaf, esp. temporarily —**deaf′en·ing·ly** *adv.*

deal /dēl/ *v.* (**dealt, deal·ing**) **1a** take measures to resolve, placate, etc. **b** do business with; associate with **c** discuss or treat (a subject) **2** behave in specified way **3** sell **4a** distribute to several people **b** distribute cards to players **5** administer (*was dealt a blow*) —*n.* **6** *Colloq.* business arrangement; transaction **7** treatment (*a rough deal*) [OE]

deal′er *n.* **1** trader in (esp. retail) goods **2** player dealing at cards

deal′ings *n. pl.* contacts; transactions

dealt /delt/ *v. past* and *past part.* of DEAL

dean /dēn/ *n.* **1a** college or university official

with disciplinary and advisory functions **b** head of a university faculty or department or of a medical school **2** head of a cathedral or collegiate church [L *decanus*]

Dean /dēn/, **James** 1931–55; US actor

dear /dēr/ *adj.* **1a** beloved; much esteemed **b** as a merely polite or ironic form (*dear boy*) **2** as a formula of address, esp. beginning a letter (*Dear Sir*) **3** precious; cherished **4** (usu. *superl.*) earnest (*my dearest wish*) —*n.* **5** (esp. as a form of address) dear person —*adv.* **6** at great cost (*will cost me dear*) —*interj.* **7** expressing surprise, dismay, pity, etc. (*oh dear!*) **8 for dear life** desperately —**dear′ly** *adv.* [OE]

Dear·born /dēr′bôrn′, -bərn/ *n.* city in Mich., near Detroit. Pop. 89,286

dearth /dərᴛʜ/ *n.* scarcity; lack

death /deᴛʜ/ *n.* **1** irreversible ending of life; dying or being killed **2** instance of this **3** destruction; ending (*death of our hopes*) **4** being dead (*eyes closed in death*) **5** (usu. *cap.*) personification of death, esp. as a skeleton **6** lack of spiritual life **7 at death's door** close to death **8 be the death of** be annoying or harmful to **9 fate worse than death** *Colloq.* very unpleasant experience [OE]

death′bed′ *n.* bed where a person dies

death′blow′ *n.* **1** blow causing death **2** event, etc., that destroys or ends something

death′ly *adj.* (·**li·er, ·li·est**) **1** suggestive of death —*adv.* **2** in a deathly way

death′ row′ *n.* part of a prison for those sentenced to death

death′trap′ *n. Colloq.* dangerous building, vehicle, etc.

Death′ Val′ley *n.* desert basin in E Calif.; lowest elevation: 282 ft. below sea level

deb /deb/ *n. Colloq.* debutante [abbr.]

de·ba·cle /dibäk′əl, -bak′-, dābäk′(l)/ *n.* utter defeat, collapse, or chaos [Fr]

de·bar /dēbär′/ *v.* (·**barred, ·bar·ring**) exclude; prohibit —**de·bar′ment** *n.* [Fr, rel. to BAR[1]]

de·bark /dēbärk′/ *v.* land from a ship —**de·bar·ka′tion** *n.* [Fr *débarquer*]

de·base /dēbās′/ *v.* (·**based, ·bas·ing**) lower in quality, value, or character —**de·base′ment** *n.* [fr. DE- + (A)BASE]

de·bat·a·ble /dibā′təbəl/ *adj.* questionable; disputable [rel. to DEBATE]

de·bate /dibāt′/ *v.* (·**bat·ed, ·bat·ing**) **1** discuss or dispute, esp. formally **2** consider aspects of (a question) —*n.* **3** formal discussion on a particular matter **4** discussion [Fr, rel. to BATTLE]

de·bauch /dibôᴄʜ′/ *v.* **1** corrupt; pervert —*n.* **2** bout of sensual indulgence [Fr]

de·bauch·ee /dibô′ᴄʜē′/ *n.* debauched person

de·bauch·er·y /dibô′ᴄʜərē/ *n.* sensual overindulgence

de Beau·voir /də bōvwär′/, **Simone** 1908–86; French existentialist philosopher, novelist, and feminist

de·ben·ture /diben′ᴄʜər/ *n.* acknowledgment of indebtedness, esp. a bond for repayment at fixed intervals [L *debere* owe]

de·bil·i·tate /dibil′ətāt′/ *v.* (·**tat·ed, ·tat·ing**) enfeeble; enervate —**de·bil·i·ta′tion** *n.* [L *debilis* weak]

de·bil·i·ty /dĭbĭl´ĭtē/ *n.* feebleness, esp. of health

deb·it /deb´ĭt/ *n.* 1 entry in an account recording a sum owed 2 sum recorded 3 total of such sums 4 debit side of an account —*v.* 5 enter on the debit side of an account [L *debitum* DEBT]

deb·o·nair /deb´əner´/ *adj.* stylishly self-assured or carefree [Fr]

de·brief /dēbrēf´/ *v. Colloq.* question (a diplomat, pilot, etc.) about a completed mission or undertaking —**de·brief´ing** *n.*

de·bris /dəbrē´, dā-/ *n.* scattered fragments, esp. of wreckage [Fr *briser* break]

Debs /debz/, **Eugene** 1855–1926; US labor leader

debt /det/ *n.* 1 money, etc., owed (*debt of gratitude*) 2 state of owing (*in debt; get into debt*) [L *debita* fr. *debere* owe]

debt·or /det´ər/ *n.* person owing money, etc.

de·bug /dēbug´/ *v.* (**·bugged, ·bug·ging**) *Colloq.* 1 remove concealed microphones from (a room, etc.) 2 remove defects from (a computer program, etc.)

de·bunk /dēbungk´/ *v. Colloq.* expose (a person, claim, etc.) as spurious or false —**de·bunk´er** *n.*

De·bus·sy /deb´yōōsē´, dā´byōō-/, (**Achille**) **Claude** 1862–1918; French composer

de·but /dābyōō´, dā´byōō/ *n.* first public appearance (as a performer, etc.) [Fr]

deb·u·tante /deb´yōōtänt´/ *n.* (usu. wealthy) young woman making her social debut

Dec. *abbr.* December

deca- *comb. form* ten [Gk *deka* ten]

dec·ade /dek´ād´, dikād´/ *n.* 1 period of ten years 2 series or group of ten [Gk, rel. to DECA-]

dec·a·dence /dek´ədəns/ *n.* 1 moral or cultural decline 2 immoral behavior —**dec´a·dent** *adj. & n.*; **dec´a·dent·ly** *adv.* [L, rel. to DECAY]

de·caf·fein·at·ed /dēkaf´ənāt´id/ *adj.* with caffeine removed or reduced

Dec·a·logue /dek´əlôg´, -läg´/ *n.* Ten Commandments [Gk, rel. to DECA- + *logos* word; reason]

de·camp /dikamp´/ *v.* 1 depart suddenly; abscond 2 break up or leave camp [Fr, rel. to CAMP[1]]

de·cant /dikant´/ *v.* gradually pour off or transfer by pouring [Gk *kanthos* lip of jug]

de·cant·er /dikan´tər/ *n.* stoppered glass container for wine, etc.

de·cap·i·tate /dikap´ətāt´/ *v.* (**·tat·ed, ·tat·ing**) behead —**de·cap·i·ta´tion** *n.* [L, rel. to CAPITAL]

de·cath·lon /dikaTH´lən, -län´/ *n.* track-and-field contest of ten events for all competitors —**de·cath´lete´** /-lēt´/ *n.* [fr. DECA- + Gk *athlon* contest]

De·ca·tur /dikāt´ər/, **Stephen** 1779–1820; US naval officer

De·ca·tur /dikāt´ər/ *n.* city in Ill. Pop. 83,885

DECANTER

de·cay /dikā´/ *v.* 1 (cause to) rot or decompose 2 decline or cause to decline in quality, power, etc. 3 (of a substance) undergo

change by radioactivity —*n.* 4 rotten state 5 deterioration 6 radioactive change [L *cadere* fall]

de·ceased /disēst´/ *adj.* 1 dead —*n.* 2 (usu. prec. by *the*) person who has died, esp. recently

de·ceit /disēt´/ *n.* 1 deception, esp. by concealing the truth 2 dishonest trick [L *capere* take]

de·ceit·ful /disēt´fəl/ *adj.* using deceit —**de·ceit´ful·ly** *adv.*; **de·ceit´ful·ness** *n.*

de·ceive /disēv´/ *v.* (**·ceived, ·ceiv·ing**) 1 make (a person) believe what is false; purposely mislead 2 be unfaithful to, esp. sexually —**de·ceiv´er** *n.*

de·cel·er·ate /dēsel´ərāt´/ *v.* (**·at·ed, ·at·ing**) (cause to) reduce speed —**de·cel´er·a´tion** *n.* [fr. DE- + ACCELERATE]

De·cem·ber /disem´bər/ *n.* twelfth month of the year [L *decem* ten, orig. 10th month of Roman year]

de·cen·cy /dē´sənsē/ *n.* (*pl.* **·cies**) 1 correct, honorable, or caring behavior 2 (in *pl.*) proprieties; manners [L, rel. to DECENT]

de·cent /dē´sənt/ *adj.* 1a conforming with standards of decency b free of obscenity 2 respectable 3 acceptable; good enough 4 kind; obliging —**de´cent·ly** *adv.* [L *decere* fitting]

de·cen·tral·ize /dēsen´trəlīz´/ *v.* (**·ized, ·iz·ing**) 1 transfer (power, etc.) from central to local authority 2 reorganize to give greater local autonomy —**de·cen´tral·i·za´tion** *n.*

de·cep·tion /disep´SHən/ *n.* 1 deceiving or being deceived 2 thing that deceives [L, rel. to DECEIVE]

de·cep·tive /disep´tiv/ *adj.* likely to deceive; misleading —**de·cep´tive·ly** *adv.*; **de·cep´tive·ness** *n.*

deci- *comb. form* one-tenth [L *decimus* tenth]

dec·i·bel /des´əbel´, -bəl/ *n.* unit used to measure relative sound levels

de·cide /disīd´/ *v.* (**·cid·ed, ·cid·ing**) 1 resolve after consideration 2 resolve or settle (an issue, etc.) 3 give a judgment —**de·cid´a·ble** *adj.* [L *caedere* cut]

de·cid·ed /disīd´id/ *adj.* 1 definite; unquestionable 2 positive; resolute

de·cid·ed·ly *adv.* undoubtedly; undeniably

de·cid·u·ous /disij´ŏŏəs/ *adj.* 1 (of a tree) shedding leaves annually 2 (of leaves, horns, teeth, etc.) shed periodically [L *cadere* fall]

dec·i·mal /des´(ə)məl/ *adj.* 1 based on the number ten —*n.* 2 decimal fraction [L *decem* ten]

dec´i·mal point´ *n.* dot placed before the fraction in a decimal fraction

dec·i·mate /des´əmāt´/ *v.* (**·mat·ed, ·mat·ing**) destroy a large proportion of —**dec´i·ma´tion** *n.*

de·ci·pher /disī´fər/ *v.* 1 convert (coded information) into intelligible language 2 determine the meaning of (unclear handwriting, etc.) —**de·ci´pher·a·ble** *adj.*

de·ci·sion /disizH´ən/ *n.* 1 act or process of deciding 2 resolution made after consideration 3a settlement of a question b formal judgment [L, rel. to DECIDE]

de·ci·sive /disī´siv/ *adj.* 1 conclusive; settling an issue 2 quick to decide —**de·ci´sive-**

ly *adv.*; **de·ci′sive·ness** *n.* [MedL, rel. to DE-
CIDE]

deck /dek/ *n.* **1** flooring on a ship **2** floor or
compartment of a bus, etc. **3** section for playing disks, tapes, etc., in a sound system **4**
pack of cards **5** *Slang.* ground —*v.* **6** decorate [Du: cover]

-decker *comb. form* having a specified number
of decks or layers (*double-decker*)

de·claim /diklām′/ *v.* speak or say as if addressing an audience —**dec′la·ma′tion** *n.*;
de·clam′a·to′ry *adj.* [L *declamare*]

dec·la·ra·tion /dek′lərā′SHən/ *n.* **1** declaring
2 formal or emphatic statement [L, rel. to DE-
CLARE]

Dec′la·ra′tion of In′de·pen′dence *n.* document signed July 4, 1776, that proclaimed the
independence of the American colonies as the
United States of America

de·clare /dikler′/ *v.* (·clared, ·clar·ing) **1**
announce openly or formally **2** pronounce **3**
assert emphatically **4** acknowledge possession of (dutiable goods, income, etc.) **5** admit
to being —**de·clar′a·tive, de·clar′a·to′ry**
/-tô′rē/ *adj.*; **de·clar′er** *n.* [L *clarare* make
clear]

de·clas·si·fy /dēklas′əfī′/ *v.* (·fied, ·fy·ing)
declare (information, etc.) to be no longer secret —**de·clas′si·fi·ca′tion** /-fikā′SHən/ *n.*

de·clen·sion /diklen′SHən/ *n.* **1** *Gram.* a
form of a noun, pronoun, or adjective to show
its grammatical case **b** class of nouns with the
same inflections **2** declining [L, rel. to DE-
CLINE]

dec·li·na·tion /dek′lənā′SHən/ *n.* **1** downward bend or turn **2** angular distance of a star,
etc., north or south of the celestial equator **3**
deviation of a compass needle from true north
—**dec′li·na′tion·al** *adj.* [L, rel. to DECLINE]

de·cline /diklīn′/ *v.* (·clined, ·clin·ing) **1**
deteriorate; lose strength or vigor **2** politely
refuse (an invitation, challenge, etc.) **3** slope
or bend downward; droop **4** *Gram.* state the
forms of (a noun, pronoun, or adjective) —*n.*
5 gradual loss of vigor or excellence **6** deterioration [L *declinare* bend]

de·cliv·i·ty /dikliv′itē/ *n.* (*pl.* ·ties) downward slope [L *clivus* slope]

de·coc·tion /dikäk′SHən/ *n.* **1** boiling down
to extract an essence **2** the resulting liquid [L
coquere boil]

de·code /dēkōd′/ *v.* (·cod·ed, ·cod·ing) decipher —**de·cod′er** *n.*

dé·col·le·tage /dā′kälətäzH′, dek′(ə)lə-/ *n.*
low neckline of a woman's dress, etc. [Fr *collet*
collar]

dé·col·le·té /dākäl′ətā′, dek′(ə)lə-/ *adj.* (also
dé′col·le·tée′) (of a dress, woman, etc.) having or wearing a low neckline

de·com·pose /dē′kəmpōz′/ *v.* (·posed,
·pos·ing) **1** rot **2** separate (a substance,
light, etc.) into its elements —**de′com·po·si′**
tion *n.*

de·com·press /dē′kəmpres′/ *v.* subject to
decompression

de·com·pres·sion /dē′kəmpresH′ən/ *n.* **1**
release from compression **2** gradual reduction of high pressure on a deep-sea diver, etc.

de·con·ges·tant /dē′kənjes′tənt/ *n.* medicine, etc., that relieves nasal congestion

de·con·tam·i·nate /dē′kəntam′ənāt/ *v.*
(·nat·ed, ·nat·ing) remove contamination
from —**de′con·tam′i·na′tion** *n.*

dé·cor /dākôr′, dā′kôr′/ (also **de·cor′**)
furnishings and decoration of a room, stage
set, etc. [Fr, rel. to DECORATE]

dec·o·rate /dek′ərāt′/ *v.* (·rat·ed, ·rat·ing)
1 beautify; adorn **2** paint, wallpaper, etc. **3**
give a medal or award to —**dec′o·ra·tive**
/-ərətiv/ *adj.*; **dec′o·ra·tive·ly** *adv.*; **dec′o·ra′**
tor *n.* [L *decorare*]

dec·o·ra·tion *n.* **1** decorating **2** thing that dec-
orates **3** honorary medal, etc. **4** (*pl.*) festive
flags, tinsel, etc.

Dec′o·ra′tion Day′ *n.* MEMORIAL DAY

de·co·rous /dek′(ə)rəs/ *adj.* having or showing decorum —**dec′o·rous·ly** *adv.*; **dec′o·**
rous·ness *n.* [L *decorus* seemly]

de·co·rum /dikôr′əm/ *n.* appropriate or dignified behavior [rel. to DECOROUS]

dé·cou·page /dā′kōōpäzH′/ *n.* art of decorating by use of paper cutouts, etc., glued to a
surface

de·coy *n.* /dē′koi, dikoi′/ **1** person or thing
used as a lure; bait; enticement —*v.* /dikoi′,
dē′koi′/ **2** lure or distract, esp. using a decoy
[Du *de kooi* the cage]

de·crease *v.* /dikrēs′, dē′krēs′/ (·creased,
·creas·ing) **1** make or become smaller or
fewer —*n.* /dē′krēs′, dikrēs′/ **2** decreasing
3 amount of this —**de·creas′ing·ly** *adv.* [L,
rel. to DE- + *crescere* grow]

de·cree /dikrē′/ *n.* **1** official order **2** legal
judgment or decision, esp. in divorce cases
—*v.* (·creed, ·cree·ing) **3** legally ordain [L
decernere decide; judge]

de·crep·it /dikrep′it/ *adj.* **1** weakened by age
or infirmity **2** dilapidated —**de·crep′i·tude**
n. [L *crepare* creak]

de·crim·i·nal·ize /dēkrim′ənəlīz′/ *v.* (·ized,
·iz·ing) cease to treat as criminal —**de·crim′**
i·nal·i·za′tion *n.*

de·cry /dikrī′/ *v.* (·cried, ·cry·ing) denounce

ded·i·cate /ded′əkāt′/ *v.* (·cat·ed, ·cat·ing)
1 devote (esp. oneself) to a task or purpose
2 address (a book, etc.) to a friend, patron,
etc. **3** devote (a building, etc.) to a deity, saint,
etc. **4** devote (oneself) single-mindedly to a
cause, etc. —**ded′i·ca′tor** *n.*; **ded′i·ca·to′ry**
/-kətô′rē/ *adj.* [L *dedicare* declare]

ded′i·ca′tion *n.* **1** dedicating or being dedicated **2** words of tribute in a book, etc. [L,
rel. to DEDICATE]

de·duce /did(y)ōōs′/ *v.* (·duced, ·duc·ing)
infer logically —**de·duc′i·ble** *adj.* [L *dedu-
cere* lead away; bring out]

de·duct /didəkt′/ *v.* subtract, take away, or
withhold (an amount, portion, etc.) [L *dedu-
cere deduct*]

de·duct′i·ble *adj.* that may be deducted, esp.
from taxable income

de·duc·tion /didək′SHən/ *n.* **1a** deducting **b**
amount deducted **2a** inferring of particular instances from a general law or principle **b** conclusion so reached [L, rel. to DEDUCT]

de·duc′tive *adj.* of or reasoning by deduction
—**de·duc′tive·ly** *adv.* [L, rel. to DEDUCT]

deed /dēd/ *n.* **1** thing done intentionally or
consciously **2** brave or conspicuous act or feat

3 action (*kind in word and deed*) **4** legal document used esp. for transferring ownership of property [OE, rel. to DO[1]]

deem /dēm/ *v.* consider; judge [OE]

deep /dēp/ *adj.* **1** extending far down or in **2a** to or at a specified depth (*6 feet deep*) **b** in a specified number of ranks (*soldiers drawn up six deep*) **3** situated or coming from far down, back, or in (*deep sigh*) **4** low-pitched or full-toned **5** intense; extreme **6** fully absorbed; overwhelmed **7** profound; difficult to understand —*n.* **8** (prec. by *the*) *Poet.* sea **9** abyss or chasm —*adv.* **10** deeply; far down or in —**deep′ly** *adv.* [OE]

deep·en /dē′pən/ *v.* make or become deep or deeper

deep′ freeze′ *n.* **1** cabinet for freezing and keeping food for long periods —*v.* (as **deep-freeze**) (**froze, fro·zen, freez·ing**) **2** freeze or store in a deep freeze

deep′-fry′ *v.* (**-fried, -fry·ing**) immerse in boiling fat to cook

deer /dēr/ *n.* (*pl.* same) four-footed grazing animal, the male of which usu. has antlers [OE]

deer′skin′ *n.* leather from a deer's skin

de·es·ca·late /dē′es′kəlāt/ *v.* (**-lat·ed, -lat·ing**) make or become less intense —**de·es′ca·la′tion** *n.*

de·face /difās′/ *v.* (**faced, fac·ing**) disfigure —**de·face′ment** *n.* [OFr, rel. to FACE]

de fac·to /di fak′tō/ *adv.* **1** in fact (whether by right or not) —*adj.* **2** existing or so in fact (*a de facto ruler*) [L: from the fact]

de·fal·ca·tion /dē′falkā′shən, -fôl-/ *n.* **1** misappropriation of money **2** amount misappropriated —**de·fal′cate** *v.* (**·cat·ed, ·cat·ing**)

de Fal·la, Manuel see FALLA

de·fame /difām′/ *v.* (**·famed, ·fam·ing**) libel; slander —**def·a·ma·tion** /def′əmā′shən/ *n.*; **de·fam·a·to·ry** /difam′ətôr′ē/ *adj.* [L *fama* report]

de·fault /difôlt′/ *n.* **1** failure to appear, pay, or act as one should —*v.* **2** fail to fulfill (esp. a legal) obligation **3 by default** because of a lack of an alternative or opposition —**de·fault′er** *n.* [OFr, rel. to FAIL]

de·feat /difēt′/ *v.* **1** overcome in battle, a contest, etc. **2** frustrate; baffle **3** reject (a motion, etc.) by voting —*n.* **4** vanquishing or being vanquished [L, rel. to DIS- + *facere* do]

de·feat′ism *n.* undue readiness to accept defeat —**de·feat′ist** *n.* & *adj.*

def·e·cate /def′əkāt/ *v.* (**·cat·ed, cat·ing**) evacuate the bowels —**def′e·ca′tion** *n.* [L *faex faecis* dregs]

de·fect *n.* /dē′fekt′/ **1** fault; imperfection; shortcoming —*v.* /difekt′/ **2** leave one's country or cause for another —**de·fec′tion** /fek′shən/, **de·fec′tor** *n.* [L *deficere -fect-* fail]

de·fec′tive *adj.* having defect(s); imperfect —**de·fec′tive·ness** *n.* [LL, rel. to DEFECT]

de·fend /difend′/ *v.* **1** resist an attack made on; protect **2** uphold by argument **3** conduct a defense in a lawsuit **4** compete to retain (a title, etc.) —**de·fend′er** *n.* [L *defendere*]

de·fen·dant /difen′dənt/ *n.* person, etc., sued or accused in a court of law [OFr, rel. to DEFEND]

---

de·fense /difens′, dē′fens′/ *n.* **1** defending; protection **2** means of this **3** justification; vindication **4** defendant's case or counsel in a lawsuit **5** defending play or players —**de·fense′less** *adj.*; **de·fense′less·ly** *adv.*; **de·fense′less·ness** *n.* [L, rel. to DEFEND]

de·fense′ mech′a·nism *n.* **1** body's resistance to disease **2** usu. unconscious mental process to avoid anxiety

de·fen·si·ble /difen′səbəl/ *adj.* **1** justifiable; supportable by argument **2** able to be defended militarily —**de·fen′si·bil′i·ty** *n.*; **de·fen′si·bly** *adv.* [L, rel. to DEFEND]

de·fen′sive *adj.* **1** done or intended for defense **2** overreacting to criticism —**de·fen′sive·ly** *adv.*; **de·fen′sive·ness** *n.* [MedL, rel. to DEFEND]

de·fer[1] /difər′/ *v.* (**·ferred, ·fer·ring**) postpone —**de·fer′ment, de·fer′ral** *n.* [ME, orig. the same as DIFFER]

de·fer[2] *v.* (**·ferred, ·fer·ring**) yield or make concessions to [L *deferre* carry away]

def·er·ence /def′ərəns/ *n.* courteous regard; respect; compliance

def·er·en·tial /def′ərən′shəl/ *adj.* respectful —**def′er·en′tial·ly** *adv.*

de·fi·ance /difī′əns/ *n.* open disobedience; bold resistance [OFr, rel. to DEFY]

de·fi·ant /difī′ənt/ *adj.* showing defiance; disobedient —**de·fi′ant·ly** *adv.*

de·fi·cien·cy /difish′ənsē/ *n.* (*pl.* **·cies**) **1** being deficient **2** lack or shortage **3** thing lacking

de·fi·cient /difish′ənt/ *adj.* incomplete or insufficient [L *deficere* fail; lack]

def·i·cit /def′əsit/ *n.* **1** amount by which a thing (esp. money) is too small **2** excess of liabilities over assets [Fr fr. L *deficere* lack]

de·file[1] /difīl′/ *v.* (**·filed, ·fil·ing**) **1** make dirty; pollute **2** desecrate; profane —**de·file′ment** *n.* [earlier *defoul*, fr. OFr *defouler* trample down]

de·file[2] *n.* **1** narrow gorge or pass —*v.* (**·filed, ·fil·ing**) **2** march in file [Fr]

de·fine /difīn′/ *v.* **1** give the meaning of (a word, etc.) **2** describe or explain the scope of **3** outline —**de·fin′a·ble** *adj.* [L *definire* limit]

def·i·nite /def′(ə)nət/ *adj.* **1** certain; sure **2** clearly defined; not vague; precise —**def′i·nite·ly** *adv.* [L, rel. to DEFINE]

def′i·nite ar′ti·cle *n. Gram.* the specifying word preceding a noun (*the* in English)

def·i·ni·tion /def′ənish′ən/ *n.* **1** defining **2** stated meaning of a word, etc. **3** distinctness in outline of an image [L, rel. to DEFINE]

de·fin′i·tive *adj.* **1** (of an answer, verdict, etc.) decisive; unconditional; final **2** (of a book, etc.) most authoritative

de·flate /diflāt′/ *v.* (**·flat·ed, ·flat·ing**) **1** empty (a flexible container, as a tire, balloon, etc.) of air, gas, etc.; be so emptied **2** (cause to) lose confidence or conceit **3** subject (a currency or economy) to deflation [fr. DE- + (IN)FLATE]

de·fla′tion *n.* **1** deflating or being deflated **2** reduction of money in circulation, raising its unit value —**de·fla′tion·ar′y** *adj.*

de·flect /diflekt′/ *v.* **1** divert or turn aside

from a course or purpose 2 (cause to) deviate —de·flec′tion /-flek′SHən, de·flec′tor n. [L *deflectere* bend aside]

de·flow·er /dēflou̇′, flou̇′ər/ v. *Lit.* 1 deprive of virginity 2 ravage; spoil [L, rel. to FLOWER]

De·foe /difō′/, Daniel 1660–1731; English novelist and journalist

de·fo·li·ate /dēfō′lē·āt′/ v. (·at·ed, ·at·ing) destroy the leaves of (trees or plants) —de·fo′li·ant /-lēant′/, de·fo′li·a′tion n. [MedL *defoliare*]

de·form /difôrm′/ v. make ugly or misshapen; disfigure —de·for·ma′tion n.; de·formed′ adj.; de·for′mi·ty n. (pl. ·ties) [L, rel. to FORM]

de·fraud /difrôd′/ v. cheat by fraud [L, rel. to FRAUD]

de·fray /difrā′/ v. pay for (a cost or expense) —de·fray′al n. [OFr *defroier*]

de·frost /difrôst′, dē-/ v. 1 remove frost or ice from (a refrigerator, windshield, etc.) 2 unfreeze (frozen food) 3 become unfrozen

deft /deft/ adj. neat; dexterous; adroit —deft′ly adv.; deft′ness n. [ME, var. of DAFT 'meek']

de·funct /difəNGkt′/ adj. 1 no longer active or used 2 dead or extinct [L *functus* performed]

de·fuse /dēfyōōz′/ v. (·fused, ·fus·ing) 1 remove the fuse from (a bomb, etc.) 2 reduce tensions in (a crisis, difficulty, etc.)

de·fy /difī′/ v. (·fied, ·fy·ing) 1 resist openly; refuse to obey 2 (of a thing) utterly thwart (*defies solution*) 3 challenge (a person) to do or prove something [OFr, rel. to L *fides* faith]

deg. abbr. degree

De·gas /dägä′/, (Hilaire) Edgar 1834–1917; French painter

de Gaulle /də gōl′, gôl′/, Charles André Joseph Marie 1890–1970; president of France (1959–69)

de·gen·er·ate adj. /dijen′(ə)rət/ 1 fallen from normality or goodness; immoral; degraded —n. /dijen′(ə)rət/ 2 degraded person —v. /dijen′ərāt′/ (·at·ed, ·at·ing) 3 become degenerate —de·gen′er·a·cy /-əsē/ n. [L *degenerare* decline, rel. to *genus* race]

de·gen·er·a·tion /dijen′ərā′SHən, dē-/ n. 1 becoming degenerate 2 *Med.* morbid deterioration of body tissue, etc. [LL, rel. to DEGENERATE]

de·grade /digrād′/ v. (·grad·ed, ·grad·ing) 1 humiliate; dishonor 2 reduce to a lower rank —deg·ra·da·tion /deg′rədāSHən/ n.; de·grad′ing adj. [L, rel. to GRADE]

de·gree /digrē′/ n. 1 stage in a scale, series, or process 2 stage in intensity or amount (*in some degree*) 3 unit of measurement of an angle or arc, with 360 degrees completing a circle 4 unit of temperature, hardness, etc. 5 extent of burns 6 academic rank 7 grade of crime 8 by degrees gradually [OFr fr. L *gradus* step]

de·hu·man·ize /dē(h)yōō′mənīz′/ v. (·ized, ·iz·ing) 1 take human qualities away from 2 make impersonal —de·hu′man·i·za′tion n.

de·hy·drate /dēhī′drāt′/ v. (·drat·ed, ·drat·ing) 1 remove water from (esp. foods) 2

make or become dry, esp. too dry —de′hy·dra′tion n. [Gk *hydōr* water]

de·ice /dē′īs′/ v. (·iced, ·ic·ing) 1 remove ice from 2 prevent the formation of ice on —de·ic′er n.

de·i·fy /dē′əfī, dā′-/ v. (·fied, ·fy·ing) make a god or idol of —de′i·fi·ca′tion /-fikā′SHən/ n. [L *deus* god]

deign /dān/ v. think fit; condescend [L *dignus* worthy]

de·ism /dē′iz′əm, dā′-/ n. reasoned belief in the existence of a god —de′ist /-ist/ n.; de·is′tic adj. [L *deus* god]

de·i·ty /dē′ətē, dā′-/ n. (pl. ·ties) 1 god or goddess 2 divine status or nature 3 (the Deity) God [OFr fr. L *deus* god]

dé·jà vu /dā′ zHä′ vōō′/ n. feeling of having already experienced a situation [Fr: already seen]

de·ject /dijekt′/ v. make sad; depress —de·ject′ed·ly adv.; de·jec′tion /-jek′SHən/ n. [L *jacere* throw]

de jure /dā′ jŏŏr′ə/ adj. 1 rightful —adv. 2 rightfully; by right [L]

de Klerk /də klerk′, klərk′/, F(rederik) W(illem) 1936– ; president of South Africa (1989–94); Nobel prize 1993

de Koo·ning /də kōō′niNG/, Willem 1904– ; Dutch-born US painter

Del. abbr. Delaware

De·la·croix /del′əkrwä′/, (Ferdinand Victor) Eugène 1798–1863; French painter

de la Mare /də lə mar′, mer′/, Walter 1873–1956; English poet and novelist

Del·a·ware /del′əwar′, -wer′/ n. middle Atlantic state of the US. Capital: Dover. Pop. 666,168. Abbr. DE; Del. —Del′a·war′e·an n. & adj.

Del′a·ware Bay n. arm of the Atlantic Ocean between E coast of Del. and SW coast of N.J.

Del′a·ware Riv′er n. river flowing SE from S N.Y. into Delaware Bay

de·lay /dilā′/ v. 1 postpone; defer 2 make or be late; tarry —n. 3 deferring or being deferred 4 time lost by this 5 hindrance [OFr]

de·lec·ta·ble /dilek′təbəl/ adj. delightful; delicious —de·lec′ta·bly adv. [L *delectare*]

de·lec·ta·tion /dē′lek′tā′SHən, del′ik-/ n. pleasure; enjoyment

del·e·gate n. /del′igət, -gāt′/ 1 elected representative sent to a conference 2 member of a committee or delegation —v. /del′igāt′/ (·gat·ed, ·gat·ing) 3a commit (power, etc.) to an agent or deputy b entrust (a task) to another 4 send or authorize (a person) as a representative [L *delegare* assign]

del·e·ga·tion /del′igā′SHən/ n. 1 group representing others 2 delegating or being delegated

de·lete /dilēt′/ v. (·let·ed, ·let·ing) remove (a letter, word, etc.), esp. by crossing out —de·le′tion n. [L *delere*]

del·e·te·ri·ous /del′itēr′ēəs/ adj. harmful [Gk]

delft /delft/ n. (also delft′ware′) glazed, usu. blue and white, earthenware [*Delft* in Holland]

Del·hi /del′ē/ n. city in N India. Pop. 7,174,800

del·i /del′ē/ n. (pl. ·is) *Colloq.* delicatessen

de·lib·er·ate adj. /dilib′(ə)rət/ 1a intentional

b considered; careful **2** (of movement, thought, etc.) unhurried; cautious —*v.* /dilib'ərāt'/ (·at·ed, ·at·ing) **3** think carefully; consider —**de·lib'er·ate·ly** *adv.*; **de·lib'er·a'tive** *adj.* [L *deliberare* consider]

de·lib·er·a·tion /dilib'ərā'sHən/ *n.* **1** careful consideration; discussion **2** careful slowness

De·libes /dəlēb'/, (Clément) Léo 1836–91; French composer

del·i·ca·cy /del'ikəsē/ *n.* (*pl.* ·cies) **1** being delicate or fine **2** sensitivity **3** a choice food [ME, fr. DELICATE]

del·i·cate /del'ikət/ *adj.* **1** fine in texture, quality, etc.; slender; slight **2** subtle or faint **3** susceptible; weak; tender **4** requiring care or tact; tricky **5** (of an instrument) highly sensitive —**del'i·cate·ly** *adv.* [L]

del·i·ca·tes·sen /del'ikətes'ən/ *n.* **1** store selling cold cuts, prepared foods, cheeses, etc. **2** such foods [Ger fr. Fr]

de·li·cious /dilisH'əs/ *adj.* highly enjoyable, esp. to taste or smell —**de·li'cious·ly** *adv.* [L *deliciae* delights]

de·light /dilīt'/ *v.* **1** please greatly **2** take great pleasure in —*n.* **3** great pleasure **4** thing that delights —**de·light'ed, de·light'ful** *adj.*; **de·light'ful·ly** *adv.* [L *delectare*]

de·lim·it /dilim'it/ *v.* fix the limits or boundary of —**de·lim'i·ta'tion** /-itā'sHən/ *n.* [L, rel. to LIMIT]

de·lin·e·ate /dilin'ē·āt'/ *v.* (·at·ed, ·at·ing) portray by drawing, etc., or in words —**de·lin'e·a'tion** *n.* [L *linea* line]

de·lin·quent /diliNG'kwənt/ *n.* **1** offender —*adj.* **2** guilty of a minor crime or misdeed **3** failing in one's duty **4** overdue —**de·lin'quen·cy** *n.* [L *delinquere* offend]

del·i·quesce /del'ikwes'/ *v.* (·quesced, ·quesc·ing) become liquid, esp. by absorbing moisture from the air —**del·i·ques'cence** *n.*; **del·i·ques'cent** *adj.* [L, rel. to LIQUID]

de·lir·i·ous /dilēr'ēəs/ *adj.* **1** affected with delirium **2** wildly excited; ecstatic —**de·lir'i·ous·ly** *adv.*

de·lir·i·um /dilēr'ēəm/ *n.* **1** disorder involving incoherence, hallucinations, etc., caused by fever, intoxication, etc. **2** great excitement; ecstasy [L *delirare* be crazy; literally, go out of the furrow]

de·lir'i·um tre·mens /trem'ənz, trē'mənz/ *n.* (also **D.T.'s**) psychosis of chronic alcoholism involving tremors and hallucinations

De·li·us /dē'lēəs/, Frederick 1862–1934; English composer

de·liv·er /diliv'ər/ *v.* **1a** distribute (letters, goods, etc.) to their destination(s) **b** hand over **2** save, rescue, or set free **3a** give birth to **b** assist in giving birth **4** utter (an opinion, speech, etc.) **5** yield; resign (*delivered his soul up*) **6** launch or aim (a blow, etc.) [L *liber* free]

de·liv·er·ance /diliv'(ə)rəns/ *n.* rescuing or being rescued

de·liv·er·y /diliv'ərē/ *n.* (*pl.* ·ies) **1** delivering or being delivered **2** regular distribution of letters, etc. **3** thing delivered **4** childbirth **5** style of throwing a ball, delivering a speech, etc. [AngFr, rel. to DELIVER]

dell /del/ *n.* small usu. wooded valley [OE]

del·la Rob·bi·a /del'ə rō'bēə, räb'ēə/ family

---

151   **deliberation / demijohn**

of Italian sculptors and ceramicists, including: **1** Luca 1400–82; his nephew: **2** Andrea 1434–1525

Del·mar·va Pen·in·su·la /delmär'və/ *n.* peninsula between the Atlantic Ocean and Chesapeake Bay; includes parts of Delaware, Maryland, Virginia.

del·phin·i·um /delfin'ēəm/ *n.* (*pl.* ·ums) garden plant with tall spikes of usu. blue flowers [Gk, rel. to DOLPHIN]

del·ta /del'tə/ *n.* **1** triangular area of earth, alluvium, etc., at the mouth of a river **2** fourth letter of the Greek alphabet (Δ, δ) [Gk]

de·lude /dilōōd'/ *v.* (·lud·ed, ·lud·ing) deceive; mislead [L *deludere* play false; mock]

del·uge /del'(y)ōōj', ·(y)ōōzH'/ *n.* **1** great flood **2** (**the Deluge**) the biblical Flood (Genesis 6:8) **3** overwhelming rush **4** heavy fall of rain —*v.* (·uged, ·ug·ing) **5** flood or inundate [L *diluvium*]

de·lu·sion /dilōō'zHən/ *n.* **1** false belief, hope, etc. **2** hallucination —**de·lu'sive** /-siv/, **de·lu'so·ry** /-sərē/ *adj.* [L *deludere*]

de·luxe /diləks', -lōōks'/ *adj.* luxurious; superior; sumptuous [Fr: of luxury]

delve /delv/ *v.* (**delved, delv·ing**) search or research energetically or deeply [OE]

Dem. *abbr.* Democrat; Democratic (Party)

de·mag·ne·tize /dēmag'nətīz'/ *v.* (·tized, ·tiz·ing) remove the magnetic properties of —**de·mag'ne·ti·za'tion** *n.*

dem·a·gogue /dem'əgäg'/ *n.* (also **dem'a·gog'**) political agitator appealing to mob instincts —**dem'a·gog'ic** /-gäj'ik/ *adj.*; **dem'a·gogu'er·y** *n.*; **dem·a·go·gy** /-gäg'ē, ·gäj'ē, ·gō'jē/ *n.* [Gk: leader of the people]

de·mand /dimand'/ *v.* **1** insistent and urgent request **2** market for a commodity **3** urgent claim —*v.* **4** ask insistently **5** require **6** insist on **7** require skill, effort, attention, etc. **8** in **demand** sought after **9** on **demand** as soon as requested [AngFr fr. L, rel. to MANDATE]

de·mar·ca·tion /dē'märkā'sHən/ *n.* **1** marking of a boundary or limits **2** boundary or limit —**de·mar·cate** /dimär'kāt', dē'mär-/ *v.* (·cat·ed, ·cat·ing) [Sp *demarcar*]

de·mean¹ /dimēn'/ *v.* lower the dignity of; debase [rel. to DEMEAN²]

de·mean² *v.* behave or conduct (oneself) [OFr *demener* conduct, fr. L *minari* threaten]

de·mean·or /dimēn'ər/ *n.* apparent behavior or bearing [rel. to DEMEAN²]

de' Me·di·ci see MEDICI; MARIE DE MÉDICIS

de·ment·ed /dimen'tid/ *adj.* insane —**de·ment'ed·ly** *adv.* [L *mens* mind]

de·men·tia /dimen'sHə/ *n.* chronic insanity [L: madness]

de·mer·it /dimer'it/ *n.* fault or transgression, esp. when penalized

de·mesne /dimān', -mēn'/ *n.* territory; domain [OFr, rel. to DOMAIN]

De·me·ter /dimē'tər/ *n.* Gk. Myth. goddess of agriculture, identified with Roman Ceres

demi· *prefix* half; partly [Fr fr. L *dimidius* half]

dem·i·god /dem'ēgäd'/ *n.* **1** partly divine being **2** godlike person

dem·i·john /dem'ējän'/ *n.* large bottle usu. in a wicker casing [Fr]

de·mil·i·ta·rize /dēmil'ətərīz'/ v. (·rized, ·riz·ing) remove an army from (a frontier, zone, etc.) —**de·mil'i·ta·ri·za'tion** n.

De Mille /də mil'/ 1 Cecil B(lount) 1881–1959; US film producer and director 2 Agnes 1909–93; US choreographer

dem·i·monde /dem'ēmänd'/ n. 1 class of women of doubtful morality 2 any semi-respectable group [Fr: half-world]

de·mise /dimīz'/ n. 1 death; termination 2 Law. transfer of an estate, title, etc., by demising —v. (·mised, ·mis·ing) 3 Law. transfer (an estate, title, etc.) by will, lease, or death [AngFr, rel. to DISMISS]

dem·i·tasse /dem'itäs'/ n. small cup, esp. for strong coffee

dem·o /dem'ō/ n. (pl. ·os) Colloq. 1 DEMONSTRATION, 3 2 noncommercial recording made to display one's talent

de·mo·bi·lize /dēmō'bəlīz'/ v. (·lized, ·liz·ing) disband (troops, ships, etc.) —**de·mo'bi·li·za'tion** n.

de·moc·ra·cy /dimäk'rəsē/ n. (pl. ·cies) 1 government by the people, directly or through elected representatives 2 country, etc., so governed [Gk dēmokratia rule of the people]

dem·o·crat /dem'əkrat'/ n. 1 advocate of democracy 2 (cap.) member of the Democratic Party

dem·o·crat·ic /dem'əkrat'ik/ adj. 1 of, like, practicing, or being a democracy 2 favoring social equality —**dem'o·crat'i·cal·ly** adv.

Dem'o·crat'ic Par'ty n. one of the two main political parties in the US

de·moc·ra·tize /dimäk'rətīz'/ v. (·tized, ·tiz·ing) make democratic —**de·moc'ra·ti·za'tion** n.

De·moc·ri·tus /dimäk'rətəs/ c. 460–c. 370 B.C.; Greek philosopher

de·mod·u·late /dēmäd'yŏŏlāt'/ v. extract a (modulating signal) —**de·mod'u·la'tion** n.

de·mog·ra·phy /dimäg'rəfē/ n. the study of the statistics of births, deaths, disease, etc. —**dem·o·graph·ic** /dem'əgraf'ik/ adj.; **dem'o·graph'i·cal·ly** adv. [Gk dēmos the people +-GRAPHY]

de·mol·ish /dimäl'ish/ v. 1 destroy 2 refute (an argument, theory, etc.) —**dem·o·li·tion** /dem'əlish'ən, dē'mə-/ n. [L demolari]

de·mon /dē'mən/ n. 1 evil spirit or devil 2 evil or remorseless person —**de·mon·ic** /dimän'ik/ adj. [Gk daimōn deity]

de·mon·e·tize /dē'män'ətīz, -mən'-/ v. (·tized, ·tiz·ing) 1 divest (a currency, standard, etc.) of value 2 withdraw (a coin, etc.) from use —**de·mon'e·ti·za'tion** n. [Fr, rel. to DE- + MONEY]

de·mo·ni·ac /dimō'nē·ak'/ adj. 1 fiercely energetic or frenzied 2 of or like demons —**de·mo·ni·a·cal** /dē'mənī'əkəl/ adj.; **de'mo·ni'a·cal·ly** adv. [ChL, rel. to DEMON]

de·mon·stra·ble /dimän'strəbəl/ adj. able to be shown or proved —**de·mon'stra·bly** adv.

dem·on·strate /dem'ənstrāt'/ v. (·strat·ed, ·strat·ing) 1 show (feelings, etc.) 2 present and explain by experiment, use, etc. 3 logically prove or be proof of 4 take part in a public rally for a cause —**dem'on·stra'tor** n. [L monstrare show]

dem·on·stra·tion n. 1 show of feeling, etc. 2 (esp. political) public meeting, march, etc. 3 presentation or exhibition of an experiment, product, etc. 4 proof by logic, argument, etc.

de·mon·stra·tive /dimän'strətiv/ adj. 1 showing feelings readily; affectionate 2 indicative, exemplifying, or proving 3 Gram. (of an adjective or pronoun) indicating the person or thing referred to (e.g., this, that, those) —**de·mon'stra·tive·ly** adv.; **de·mon'stra·tive·ness** n.

de·mor·al·ize /dimôr'əlīz', -mär'-/ v. (·ized, ·iz·ing) destroy the morale of; dishearten —**de·mor'al·i·za'tion** n. [Fr]

De·mos·the·nes /dimäs'thənēz'/ 384–322 B.C.; Athenian orator and statesman

de·mote /dimōt'/ v. (·mot·ed, ·mot·ing) reduce to a lower rank or class —**de·mo'tion** n. [fr. DE- + (PRO)MOTE]

Demp·sey /demp'sē/, **Jack (William)** 1895–1983; US boxer

de·mur /dimər'/ v. (·murred, ·mur·ring) raise objections [L morari delay]

de·mure /dimyŏŏr'/ adj. (·mur·er, ·mur·est) 1 quiet; reserved; modest 2 coy —**de·mure'ly** adv.; **de·mure'ness** n. [Fr, rel. to DE-MUR]

de·mur·rer /dimər'ər/ n. Law. objection raised or exception taken

de·mys·ti·fy /dēmis'təfī'/ v. (·fied, ·fy·ing) remove the mystery from; clarify —**de·mys'ti·fi·ca'tion** /-fikā'shən/ n.

den /den/ n. 1 wild animal's lair 2 place of crime or vice 3 homey, informal room [OE]

de·na·ture /dēnā'CHər/ v. (·tured, ·tur·ing) 1 change the properties of (a protein, etc.) by heat, acidity, etc. 2 make (alcohol) undrinkable [DE- + NATURE]

den·drite /den'drīt/ n. Anat. part of a nerve cell that carries impulses toward the cell

den·gue /deNG'gā, -gē'/ n. infectious tropical viral fever [WInd Sp fr. Swahili]

Deng Xiao·ping /deNG' sHou'piNG'/ (also **Teng Hsiao-p'ing**) 1904– ; vice-premier of China (1973–76; 1977–80)

de·ni·al /dinī'əl/ n. 1 denying the truth or existence of a thing 2 refusal of a request or wish 3 disavowal of a leader, etc.

de·nier /dənyā'/ n. unit of weight measuring the fineness of silk, nylon, etc. [OFr, orig. name of a small coin, fr. L denarius]

den·i·grate /den'igrāt'/ v. (·grat·ed, ·grat·ing) blacken the reputation of —**den'i·gra'tion** n. [L nigrare make black]

den·im /den'əm/ n. hard-wearing usu. blue cotton twill used for jeans, overalls, etc. [Fr de Nîmes (fabric) of NÎMES, France]

De Ni·ro /də nēr'ō/, **Robert** 1943– ; US actor

den·i·zen /den'əzən/ n. inhabitant, occupant, or frequenter [OFr fr. L de intus from within]

Den·mark /den'märk'/ n. republic in N Europe on the North Sea. Capital: Copenhagen. Pop. 5,167,000

de·nom·i·nate /dēnäm'ənāt'/ v. (·nat·ed, ·nat·ing) give a name to; call; describe as [L nominare name]

de·nom·i·na·tion n. 1 church or religious sect 2 class of measurement or money 3 name, esp. a characteristic or class name

—de·nom'i·na'tion·al adj. [L, rel. to DENOMINATE]

de·nom·i·na·tor /dinäm'ənā'tər/ n. number below the line in a fraction; divisor [L, rel. to DENOMINATE]

de·note /dinōt'/ v. (·not·ed, ·not·ing) 1 be a sign of; indicate; mean 2 stand as a name for; signify —de'no·ta'tion /-tā'SHən/ n. [L notare mark]

● Usage: See note at CONNOTE.

de·noue·ment /dā'nōō'mäN'/ n. (also dé'noue·ment') culmination of a plot or complicated situation [Fr, fr. L nodus knot]

de·nounce /dinouns'/ v. (·nounced, ·nounc·ing) 1 expressly accuse or condemn; censure 2 inform against —de·nounce'ment n. [OFr fr. L nuntius messenger]

Den·pa·sar /dənpäs'är'/ n. city in Indonesia on Bali. Pop. 261,300

dense /dens/ adj. 1 closely compacted; crowded together; thick 2 Colloq. stupid —dense'ly adv.; dense'ness n. [L densus]

den·si·ty /den'sətē/ n. (pl. ·ties) 1 denseness of a thing, substance, crowd, etc. 2 Physics. degree of consistency measured by the quantity of mass per unit volume

dent /dent/ n. 1 slight hollow as made by a blow or pressure 2 noticeable adverse effect —v. 3 mark with a dent [ME, var. of DINT]

dent. abbr. 1 dental 2 dentist 3 dentistry

den·tal /dent'l/ adj. 1 of the teeth or dentistry 2 (of a consonant) produced with the tongue's tip against the upper front teeth (as th) or the ridge of the teeth (as n, s, t) [L dens dent- tooth]

den'tal floss' n. thread used to clean between the teeth

den·ti·frice /dent'əfris/ n. toothpaste or tooth powder [L, rel. to DENTAL + fricare rub]

den·tin /den'tin/ n. (also den'tine /-tēn, -tin/) dense tissue forming the bulk of a tooth

den·tist /den'tist/ n. person qualified to treat, extract, etc., teeth —den'tist·ry n.

den·ti·tion /dentisH'ən/ n. 1 type, number, and arrangement of teeth 2 teething

den·ture /den'CHər/ n. removable artificial tooth or teeth

de·nude /din(y)ōōd'/ v. (·nud·ed, ·nud·ing) make naked; bare; strip —den·u·da·tion /den'yōōdā'SHən/ n. [L nudus naked]

de·nun·ci·a·tion /dinən'sē-ā'SHən/ n. denouncing; public condemnation [L, rel. to DENOUNCE]

Den·ver /den'vər/ n. capital of Colo., in the central part. Pop. 467,610

de·ny /dinī'/ v. (·nied, ·ny·ing) 1 declare untrue or nonexistent 2 repudiate or disclaim 3 withhold (a thing) from [OFr fr. L denegare]

de·o·dor·ant /dē·ō'dərənt/ n. substance for concealing unwanted smells

de·o'dor·ize v. (·ized, ·iz·ing) remove or destroy the smell of —de·o'dor·i·za'tion n.

de·ox·y·ri·bo·nu·cle'ic   ac'id   /dēok'sirībōnōōklē'ik,-nyō-, -ok'si rī'-/ n. DNA [fr. DE- + OXYGEN + RIBONUCLEIC ACID]

de·part /dipärt'/ v. 1a go away; leave b set out (for) 2 deviate (from) 3 die [OFr fr. L partire divide]

de·part·ed /dipärt'id/ adj. 1 bygone —n. 2 Euphem. dead person or people

153   denominator / deposit

de·part·ment /dipärt'mənt/ n. 1 separate part of a complex whole, esp.: a branch of administration b division of a school, college, etc., by subject c section of a large store 2 Colloq. area of special expertise —de'part·men'tal /-ment'əl/ adj.; de'part·men'tal·ly adv. [Fr, rel. to DEPART]

de·part'ment store' n. retail store offering a variety of merchandise by department

de·par·ture /dipär'CHər/ n. 1 departing 2 deviation (from the truth, a standard, etc.) 3 new course of action or thought

de·pend /dipend'/ v. 1 be controlled or determined by 2 rely on [OFr fr. L pendere hang]

de·pend·a·ble /dipen'dəbəl/ adj. reliable —de·pend'a·bil'i·ty,   de·pend'a·ble·ness n.; de·pend'a·bly adv.

de·pen·dence /dipen'dəns/ n. 1 depending or being dependent, esp. financially 2 reliance; trust

de·pen·den·cy /dipen'dənsē/ n. (pl. ·cies) 1 country or province controlled by another 2 addiction

de·pen·dent /dipen'dənt/ adj. 1 depending; conditional 2 unable to do without (esp. a drug) 3 (of a clause, etc.) subordinate; not independent —n. (also de·pen'dant) 4 person supported by another, esp. financially

de·pict /dipikt'/ v. 1 represent in drawing, painting, etc. 2 portray in words; describe —de·pic'ter or de·pic'tor n.; de·pic'tion /-pik'sHən/ n. [L pingere paint]

de·pil·a·to·ry /dipil'ətôr'ē/ adj. 1 removing unwanted hair —n. (pl. ·ries) 2 depilatory substance [L DE- + pilus hair]

de·plete /diplēt'/ v. (·plet·ed, ·plet·ing) reduce in numbers, force, or quantity; exhaust —de·ple'tion n. [L plere fill]

de·plor·a·ble /diplôr'əbəl/ adj. woefully bad —de·plor'a·bly adv.

de·plore /diplôr'/ v. (·plored, ·plor·ing) 1 regret deeply 2 find exceedingly bad [L plorare wail]

de·ploy /diploi'/ v. 1 station or spread out (troops) 2 use (arguments, forces, etc.) effectively —de·ploy'ment n. [Fr fr. L DIS- + plicare fold]

de·po·lit·i·cize /dē'pəlit'isīz/ v. (·cized, ·ciz·ing) make nonpolitical —de·po·lit'i·ci·za'tion n.

de·pop·u·late /dēpäp'yəlāt'/ v. (·lat·ed, ·lat·ing) reduce the population of —de·pop'u·la'tion n.

de·port /dipôrt'/ v. 1 remove forcibly or exile to another country 2 behave (in a specified manner) —de'por·ta'tion /-pôrtā'SHən/ n. [L portare carry]

de·por·tee /di'pôrtē'/ n. deported person

de·port·ment /dipôrt'mənt/ n. bearing; behavior [Fr, rel. to DEPORT]

de·pose /dipōz'/ v. (·posed, ·pos·ing) 1 remove from office, esp. dethrone 2 Law. testify, esp. under oath [OFr fr. L deponere put aside; deposit]

de·pos·it /dipäz'it/ n. 1a money in a bank account b anything stored for safekeeping 2 payment made as an initial pledge 3 natural layer of accumulated matter —v. (·it·ed, ·it·ing) 4 put or lay down 5 pay (a sum) into a bank account 6 pay (a sum) as part of a larger sum or as a pledge —de·pos'i·tor n. [L *deponere, -posit-* put aside]

de·po·si·tion /dep'əzisH'ən/ n. 1 deposing 2 sworn evidence; giving of this [L, rel. to DEPOSIT]

de·pos·i·to·ry /dipäz'ətôr'ē/ n. (pl. ·ries) safe place where things are kept [L, rel. to DEPOSIT]

de·pot /dep'ō, dē'pō/ n. 1 storehouse, esp. for military supplies 2 railway or bus station [Fr fr. L, rel. to DEPOSIT]

de·prave /diprāv'/ v. (·praved, ·prav·ing) corrupt, esp. morally —de·prav'i·ty /-prav' itē/ n. (pl. ·ties) [L *pravus* crooked]

dep·re·cate /dep'rikāt'/ v. (·cat·ed, ·cat·ing) express disapproval of; deplore —dep' re·ca'tion n.; dep're·ca·to·ry /-kətôr'ē/ adj. [L, rel. to PRAY]

de·pre·ci·ate /diprē'sHē-āt'/ v. (·at·ed, ·at·ing) 1 diminish in value 2 belittle —de·pre' ci·a'tion n. [L, rel. to PRICE]

dep·re·da·tion /dep'rədā'sHən/ n. despoiling; ravaging [L, rel. to PREY]

de·press /dipres'/ v. 1 make dispirited or sad 2 push down; lower 3 reduce the value of —de·press'ing adj.; de·press'ing·ly adv. [L *premere* press]

de·pres·sant /dipres'ənt/ adj. 1 reducing activity, esp. of a body function —n. 2 depressant substance

de·pres·sion /dipresH'ən/ n. 1 extreme melancholy, often with physical symptoms 2 *Econ.* long period of high unemployment, low economic activity, etc. 3 area of low atmospheric pressure 4 hollow on a surface 5 pressing down

de·pres·sive /dipres'iv/ adj. 1 tending to depress (*depressive influence*) 2 of or tending toward depression —n. 3 person suffering from depression

de·prive /diprīv'/ v. (·prived, ·priv·ing) 1 prevent from having or enjoying 2 take from —dep·ri·va·tion /dep'rəvä'sHən/ n. [OFr fr. L *privare*]

de·pro·gram /dēprō'gram/ v. (·grammed or ·gramed, ·gram·ming or ·gram·ing) rid of or counteract beliefs, indoctrination by a cult, etc.

dept. abbr. department

depth /depTH/ n. 1a deepness b measurement from the top down, the surface inward, or front to back 2 difficulty; abstruseness 3 intensity of emotion, etc. 4 abyss 5 (pl.) lowest, inmost, or central part 6 in depth thoroughly [OE, rel. to DEEP]

depth' charge' n. antisubmarine bomb that explodes at a set depth

dep·u·ta·tion /dep'yətā'sHən/ n. delegation [L, rel. to DEPUTE]

de·pute /dipyōōt'/ v. (·put·ed, ·put·ing) 1 assign to a deputy 2 authorize as representative [OFr fr. L *putare* think]

dep·u·tize /dep'yətīz'/ v. (·tized, ·tiz·ing) create as a deputy

dep·u·ty /dep'yətē/ n. (pl. ·ties) person appointed to act for another [var. of DEPUTE]

De Quin·cey /də kwin'sē/, Thomas 1785–1859; English essayist and critic

de·rail /dirāl'/ v. cause (a train, etc.) to leave the rails —de·rail'ment n. [Fr, rel. to RAIL[1]]

DERAILLEUR

de·rail·leur /dərāl'ər/ n. type of gear-shifting mechanism on a bicycle [Fr]

De·rain /dəraN'/, André 1880–1954; French painter

de·range /dirānj'/ v. (·ranged, ·rang·ing) 1 make insane 2 disorder; disturb —de·range' ment n. [Fr, rel. to RANGE]

der·by /dər'bē, (Brit.) där'bē/ n. (pl. ·bies) 1 any of several important horse races, esp. annual 2 competition between various entrants 3 bowler hat [for Earl of *Derby*, who founded such a race]

Der·by /där'bē/ n. city in central England. Pop. 220,700

de·reg·u·late /dēreg'yəlāt'/ v. (·lat·ed, ·lat·ing) remove regulations from —de·reg·u·la'tion n.

der·e·lict /der'əlikt'/ adj. 1 dilapidated 2 abandoned 3 negligent —n. 4 vagrant 5 ship abandoned at sea [L, rel. to RELINQUISH]

der·e·lic·tion /der'əlik'sHən/ n. 1 neglect; failure to carry out obligations 2 abandoning or being abandoned

de·ride /dirīd'/ v. (·rid·ed, ·rid·ing) mock —de·ri'sion /-rizH'ən/ n. [L *ridere* laugh]

de rigueur /də' rigər'/ adj. required by fashion or etiquette [Fr]

de·ri·sive /dirī'siv, -ziv/ adj. derisory —de·ri'sive·ly adv.; de·ri'sive·ness n. [fr. DERIDE]

de·ri·so·ry /dirī'sərē, -zə-/ adj. (also de·ri' sive) scoffing; ironical

der·i·va·tion /der'əvā'sHən/ n. 1 deriving or being derived 2 formation or tracing of a word

de·riv·a·tive /diriv'ətiv/ adj. 1 not original —n. 2 derived word or thing

de·rive /dirīv'/ v. (·rived, ·riv·ing) 1 get or trace from a source 2 arise from; originate in [L *derivare* lead off, fr. *rivus* stream]

der·ma·bra·sion /dər'məbrā'zHən/ n. *Med.* surgical scraping of upper layers of skin, for blemish removal, etc.

der·ma·ti·tis /dər'məti'tis/ n. inflammation of the skin [Gk *derma* skin + -ITIS]

der·ma·tol·o·gy /dər'mətäl'əjē/ n. the study of skin diseases —der'ma·to·log'i·cal /-toläj'ikəl/ adj.; der'ma·tol'o·gist n. [fr. DERMATITIS + -LOGY]

der·mis /dər'mis/ n. layer of living tissue below the epidermis [fr. EPIDERMIS]

der·o·gate /der'əgāt'/ v. (·gat·ed, ·gat·ing) (foll. by *from*) *Formal.* detract from (merit, right, etc.) —der'o·ga'tion n. [L *rogare* ask]

de·rog·a·to·ry /dirāg'ətôr'ē/ adj. disparaging —de·rog'a·to'ri·ly adv.

der·rick /der′ik/ *n.* **1** pivoting crane for heavy weights **2** framework over an oil well, etc. [for *Derrick*, a London hangman]

DERRICK 2

der·ring·er /der′injər/ *n.* short-barreled pocket pistol [for *Deringer*, gunsmith who invented it]

der·vish /dər′vish/ *n.* member of an ascetic Muslim fraternity [Turk fr. Pers: poor]

de Sade /də säd′/, **Marquis** see SADE

de·sa·li·nate /dēsal′ənāt′/ *v.* (·nat·ed, ·nat·ing) remove the salt from (esp. sea water) —de′sal·i·na′tion *n.* [fr. SALINE]

des·cant *n.* /des′kant/ **1** melody above the basic melody —*v.* /des′kant′, deskant′/ **2** sing **3** discourse on [L *cantus* song, rel. to CHANT]

Des·cartes /dākärt′/, **René** 1596–1650; French philosopher and mathematician

de·scend /disend′/ *v.* **1** go or come down **2** slope downward **3** descend on: a attack b visit **4** descend to stoop to (an unworthy act) —de·scend′ent *adj.* [L *scandere* climb]

de·scen·dant /disen′dənt/ *n.* person or thing descended from another [Fr, rel. to DESCEND]

de·scent /disent′/ *n.* **1** act or way of descending **2** downward slope **3** lineage, family origin **4** decline; fall

de·scribe /diskrīb′/ *v.* (·scribed, ·scrib·ing) **1** state the characteristics, appearance, etc., of **2** outline; delineate —de·scrib′er *n.* [L *scribere* write]

de·scrip·tion /diskrip′shən/ *n.* **1a** describing or being described **b** representation, esp. in words **2** sort; kind —de·scrip′tive *adj.*; de·scrip′tive·ly *adv.* [L, rel. to DESCRIBE]

de·scry /diskrī′/ *v.* (·scried, ·scry·ing) *Lit.* catch sight of; discern [OFr, rel. to CRY]

des·e·crate /des′ikrāt′/ *v.* (·crat·ed, ·crat·ing) violate (a sacred place, etc.) with violence, profanity, etc. —des′e·cra′tion, des′e·cra′tor *n.* [fr. DE- + (CON)SECRATE]

de·seg·re·gate /dēseg′rigāt′/ *v.* (·gat·ed, ·gat·ing) abolish racial segregation in —de·seg′re·ga′tion *n.*

de·sen·si·tize /dēsen′sitīz′/ *v.* (·tized, ·tiz·ing) reduce or destroy the sensitivity of —de·sen′si·ti·za′tion *n.*

des·ert[1] /dizərt′/ *v.* **1** leave without intending to return **2** forsake; abandon **3** run away (esp. from military service) —de·sert′er, de·ser′tion /-zər′shən/ *n.* [L *deserere* *sert*- leave]

des·ert[2] /dez′ərt/ *n.* **1** dry, barren, esp. sandy region **2** inhospitable place; wilderness [L *desertum*, rel. to DESERT[1]]

des·ert[3] /dizərt′/ *n.* (*pl.*) deserved reward or punishment (*just deserts*) [OFr, rel. to DESERVE]

de·serve /dizərv′/ *v.* (·served, ·serv·ing) be worthy of —de·serv′ed·ly /-zər′vidlē/ *adv.* [OFr fr. L *servire* serve]

De Si·ca /də sē′kə/, **Vittorio** 1901–74; Italian film director and actor

des·ic·cate /des′ikāt/ *v.* (·cat·ed, ·cat·ing) dry out —des′ic·ca′tion *n.* [L *siccus* dry]

de·sid·er·a·tum /dizid′ərā′təm/ *n.* (*pl.* ·ta /-tə/) something lacking but desirable [L, rel. to DESIRE]

de·sign /dizīn′/ *n.* **1** plan or sketch for making something **2** lines or shapes forming a pattern or decoration **3** arrangement or layout —*v.* **4** produce a design for **5** intend, tailor, or gear **6** by design on purpose —de·sign′er *n.* [L *signum* mark]

des·ig·nate *v.* /dez′ignāt′/ (·nat·ed, ·nat·ing) **1** appoint **2** specify **3** describe as; style —*adj.* /dez′ignət/ **4** appointed but not yet installed —des′ig·na′tion *n.* [L, rel. to DESIGN]

des′ig·nat·ed driv′er *n.* one member of a group who abstains from alcohol in order to drive the others safely

des′ig·nat·ed hit′ter *n.* *Baseball.* batter in the lineup who hits for the pitcher; *abbr.* DH

de·sign·ing /dizī′ning/ *adj.* crafty; scheming

de·sir·a·ble /dizī′rəbəl/ *adj.* **1** worth having or doing **2** sexually attractive —de·sir′a·bil′i·ty, de·sir′a·ble·ness *n.*; de·sir′a·bly *adv.*

de·sire /dizīr′/ *n.* **1a** longing or wish expression of this; request **2** sexual appetite **3** something desired —*v.* (·sired, ·sir·ing) **4** long for; wish **5** request [OFr fr. L *desiderare* long for]

de·sir·ous /dizī′rəs/ *adj.* desiring

de·sist /dizist, -sist′/ *v.* abstain; cease [L *desistere*]

desk /desk/ *n.* piece of furniture with a writing surface and often drawers [L, rel. to DISCUS]

desk′top′ *n.* **1** working surface of a desk **2** *Comp.* working area on a screen for selecting different programs, etc. —*adj.* **3** for use or done on top of a desk

Des Moines /dimoin′/ *n.* capital of Iowa, in the central part. Pop. 193,187

des·o·late *adj.* /des′ələt, dez′-/ **1** left alone; solitary **2** uninhabited; ruined; dreary **3** forlorn; wretched —*v.* /des′əlāt/ (·lat·ed, ·lat·ing) **4** devastate; lay waste **5** make wretched —des′o·late·ly *adv.*; des′o·late·ness *n.* [L *solus* alone]

des·o·la·tion /des′əlā′shən/ *n.* **1** desolating or being desolated **2** loneliness, grief, etc. **3** neglected, ruined, or empty state

de So·to /də sōt′ō/, **Hernando** 1496–1542; Spanish explorer

de·spair /disper′/ *n.* **1** complete loss or absence of hope —*v.* **2** lose or be without hope [L *sperare* hope]

des·patch /dispach′/ *n.* & *v.* var. of DISPATCH

des·per·a·do /des′pərä′dō/ *n.* (*pl.* ·dos or ·does) bold and reckless criminal; outlaw [as DESPERATE]

des·per·ate /des′p(ə)rət/ *adj.* **1** reckless or dangerous from despair **2** extremely serious or bad **3** drastic **4** urgently desirous —**des′per·ate·ly** adv.; **des′per·ate·ness, des′per·a′tion** n. [L, rel. to DESPAIR]

de·spi·ca·ble /dispik′əbəl, des′-/ adj. vile; contemptible —**des·pi′ca·bly** adv. [L despicere look down, fr. specere spect- look at]

de·spise /dispīz′/ v. (·spised, ·spis·ing) **1** regard as inferior or contemptible **2** hate [L, rel. to DESPICABLE]

de·spite /dispīt′/ prep. in spite of [L, rel. to DESPICABLE]

de·spoil /dispoil′/ v. Lit. plunder; rob; deprive —**de·spo·li·a·tion** /dispō′lē·ā′sHən/ n. [L, rel. to SPOIL]

de·spon·dent /dispän′dənt/ adj. in low spirits; dejected —**de·spon′dence, de·spon′den·cy** n.; **de·spon′dent·ly** adv. [L spondere promise]

des·pot /des′pət, -pät′/ n. **1** absolute ruler **2** tyrant —**des·pot·ic** /dispät′ik/ adj.; **des·pot′i·cal·ly** adv.; **des·pot·ism** /des′pətiz′əm/ n. [Gk despotēs master]

des·sert /dizərt′/ n. course usu. at the end of a meal, esp. cake, ice cream, etc. [Fr, rel. to DIS- + SERVE]

des·ti·na·tion /des′tənā′sHən/ n. place a person or thing is bound for [L, rel. to DESTINE]

des·tine /des′tin/ v. (·tined, ·tin·ing) preordain; intend [Fr fr. L]

des·ti·ny /des′tənē/ n. (pl. ·nies) **1** fate or the power of inevitability **2** particular person's fate or lot [Fr fr. L]

des·ti·tute /des′tat(y)ōōt′/ adj. **1** in utter poverty **2** lacking —**des′ti·tu′tion** n. [L]

de·stroy /distroi′/ v. **1** pull or break down; demolish **2** kill (esp. an animal) **3** ruin or spoil **4** defeat [OFr fr. L struere struct- build]

de·stroy′er n. **1** person or thing that destroys **2** fast warship

de·struct /distrəkt′/ v. Aeron. destroy or be destroyed deliberately, esp. for safety

de·struc·tion /distrək′sHən/ n. **1** destroying or being destroyed —**de·struc′tive** adj.; **de·struc′tive·ly** adv.; **de·struc′tive·ness** n. [L, rel. to DESTROY]

de·sue·tude /des′wit(y)ōōd′/ n. state of disuse [L suescere be accustomed]

des·ul·to·ry /des′əltôr′ē/ adj. **1** turning from one subject to another **2** disconnected —**des′ul·to′ri·ly** adv. [L desultor circus rider who jumps from horse to horse]

de·tach /ditacH′/ v. unfasten or disengage and remove —**de·tach′a·ble** adj. [OFr, rel. to ATTACH]

de·tached′ adj. **1** impartial; unemotional **2** separate

de·tach′ment n. **1a** aloofness; indifference **b** impartiality **2** detaching or being detached **3** troops deployed for a specific purpose [Fr, rel. to DETACH]

de·tail /ditāl′, dē′tāl′/ **1** small particular; item; minor element **2** these collectively **3** attention to such particulars **4** small military detachment —v. /ditāl′/ **5** give particulars or circumstances of **6** assign for special duty **7** itemize [OFr taillier cut]

de·tain /ditān′/ v. **1** keep waiting; delay **2** hold (a person) in custody —**de·tain′ee** /-tān′ē/, **de·tain′ment** n. [L tenere hold]

de·tect /ditekt′/ v. discover or perceive

—**de·tect′a·ble** adj.; **de·tec′tion, de·tec′tor** n. [L tegere tect- cover]

de·tec′tive n. person who investigates, esp. crimes

dé·tente /dātänt′/ n. easing of tension, esp. between nations [Fr: relaxation]

de·ten·tion /diten′CHən/ n. detaining or being detained [L, rel. to DETAIN]

de·ten′tion home′ n. short-term prison for youthful offenders

de·ter /ditər′/ v. (·terred, ·ter·ring) discourage or prevent, esp. through fear —**de·ter′ment** n. [L terrere frighten]

de·ter·gent /ditər′jənt/ n. **1** cleansing agent —adj. **2** cleansing [L tergere wipe]

de·te·ri·o·rate /ditēr′ēərāt′/ v. (·rat·ed, ·rat·ing) become worse —**de·te′ri·o·ra′tion** n. [L deterior worse]

de·ter·mi·nant /ditər′mənənt/ adj. **1** determining **2** determining factor, etc. [L, rel. to DETERMINE]

de·ter·mi·nate /ditər′mənət/ adj. limited; fixed in scope or nature

de·ter·mi·na·tion /ditər′mənā′sHən/ n. **1** firmness of purpose **2** process of determining

de·ter·mine /ditər′mən/ v. (·mined, ·min·ing) **1** find out or establish precisely **2** decide or resolve **3** be the decisive factor [L terminus boundary]

de·ter′mined adj. resolute; unflinching —**de·ter′mined·ly** /-mənədlē/ adv.

de·ter·rent /ditər′ənt/ adj. **1** deterring —n. **2** dissuading thing or factor —**de·ter′rence** n.

de·test /ditest′/ v. loathe —**de·test′a·ble** adj.; **de·tes·ta·tion** /dē′testā′sHən/ n. [L detestari curse; denounce]

de·throne /dēTHrōn′/ v. (·throned, ·thron·ing) remove from a throne; depose —**de·throne′ment** n.

det·o·nate /det′n-āt′/ v. (·nat·ed, ·nat·ing) set off (an explosive); be set off —**det′o·na′tion, det′o·na′tor** n. [L tonare thunder]

de·tour /dē′tōōr′/ n. **1** divergence from a usual route —v. **2** take or cause to take a detour [OFr, rel. to TURN]

de·tox·i·fy /dētäk′sifī′/ v. (·fied, ·fy·ing) remove poison or harmful substances from —**de·tox′i·fi·ca′tion** /-fikā′sHən/ n. [L toxicum poison]

de·tract /ditrakt′/ v. take away (something valuable, appealing, etc.) from —**de·trac′tion** /-trak′sHən/ n.; **de·trac′tor** n. [L tractus drawn]

det·ri·ment /de′trəmənt/ n. **1** harm; damage **2** cause of this —**det′ri·men′tal** adj. [L terere rub away]

de·tri·tus /ditrī′təs/ n. gravel, sand, etc., from erosion; debris [L, rel. to DETRIMENT]

De·troit /ditroit′, dē′troit′/ n. city in Mich. Pop. 1,027,974

deuce /d(y)ōōs/ n. **1** two on dice or playing-cards **2** Tennis. score of 40 all [L duo duos two]

deu·te·ri·um /d(y)ōōtēr′ēəm/ n. stable isotope of hydrogen [Gk deuteros second]

Deutsche mark /doicH′əmärk′/ n. (also **Deutsch′mark′**) chief monetary unit of Germany [Ger: German mark]

De Va·le·ra /dev′ələr′ə,-lir′ə/, Eamon 1882–1975; US-born president of Ireland (1959–73)

de·val·ue /dēval′yōō/ v. (·ued, ·u·ing) reduce the value of —**de·val′u·a′tion** n.

dev·as·tate /dev′əstāt′/ v. (·tat·ed, ·tat·ing) 1 cause great destruction to 2 overwhelm with shock or grief —**dev′a·stat′ing** adj.; **dev′as·ta′tion** n. [L vastare lay waste]

de·vel·op /divel′əp/ v. (·oped, ·op·ing) 1a make or become bigger, fuller, etc. b bring or come to an active, visible, or mature state 2 begin to exhibit or suffer from 3a build on (land) b convert (land) to new use 4 treat (film, etc.) to make the image visible —**de·vel′op·er** n. [OFr]

de·vel·op·ment n. 1 developing or being developed 2 thing that has developed; new event or circumstance 3 full-grown state 4 group of buildings —**de·vel′op·men′tal** adj.

De·vi /dā′vē/ (also **Dur·ga, Ka·li, U·ma**) Hinduism. goddess and wife of Shiva

de·vi·ant /dē′vēənt/ adj. 1 deviating from what is normal, esp. sexually —n. 2 deviant person or thing —**de′vi·ance, de′vi·an·cy** n.

de·vi·ate /dē′vēāt′/ v. (·at·ed, ·at·ing) diverge (from a course of action, rule, etc.) —**de·vi·a′tion** n. [L via way]

de·vice /divīs′/ n. 1 thing for a special purpose 2 plan, scheme, or trick 3 design, esp. heraldic 4 leave one to one's own devices allow to do as one wishes [OFr fr. L, rel. to DEVISE]

dev·il /dev′əl/ n. 1 (often cap.) supreme spirit of evil; Satan 2a evil spirit; demon b personified evil 3a wicked person b mischievous person 4 Colloq. person of a specified kind (lucky devil) 5 mischievousness —v. (·viled or ·villed, ·vil·ing or vil·ling) 6 prepare (food) with spicy seasoning 7 harass; pester —**dev′il·ish** adj.; **dev′il·ish·ly** adv. [Gk diabolos accuser; slanderer]

dev′il·may-care′ adj. reckless

dev′il·ment n. mischief; wild spirits

dev′il's ad′vo·cate n. person who argues against a proposition to test it

dev′il's-food′ cake′ n. very rich, dark chocolate cake

dev·il·try or **dev·il·ry** /dev′əltrē; dev′əlrē/ n. (pl. ·tries or ·ries) reckless mischief

de·vi·ous /dē′vēəs/ adj. 1 not straightforward; shifty 2 winding; crooked —**de′vi·ous·ly** adv.; **de′vi·ous·ness** n. [L via way]

de·vise /divīz′/ v. (·vised, ·vis·ing) 1 carefully plan or invent 2 Law. leave (real estate) by will [OFr fr. L dividere divide]

de·void /divoid′/ adj. (foll. by of) lacking or free from [Fr, rel. to VOID]

de·volve /divälv′, vôlv′/ v. (·volve, ·volv·ing) pass (work or duties) or be passed to (a deputy, etc.) [L volvere roll]

De·vo·ni·an /divō′nēən/ adj. 1 of the fourth period of the Palaeozoic era —n. 2 this period [Devon in England]

de·vote /divōt′/ v. (·vot·ed, ·vot·ing) (foll. by to) apply or give over to (a particular activity, etc.) [L devovere vow]

de·vot·ed adj. loving; loyal —**de·vot′ed·ly** adv.

dev·o·tee /dev′ətē′, -tā′/ n. zealous enthusiast or supporter

de·vo·tion /divō′sHən/ n. 1 great love or loyalty 2a religious worship b (pl.) prayers —**de·vo′tion·al** adj. [L, rel. to DEVOTE]

de·vour /divour′/ v. 1 eat voraciously 2 engulf; destroy [L vorare swallow]

de·vout /divout′/ adj. earnestly religious or sincere —**de·vout′ly** adv.; **de·vout′ness** n. [L, rel. to DEVOTE]

dew /d(y)ōō/ n. 1 condensed water vapor forming on cool surfaces at night 2 similar glistening moisture —**dew′y** adj. (·i·er, ·i·est) [OE]

dew′ber·ry n. (pl. ·ries) bluish fruit like the blackberry

dew′drop′ n. drop of dew

Dew·ey /d(y)ōō′ē/ 1 **Melvil** 1851–1931; US librarian; devised decimal system for classifying books 2 **John** 1859–1952; US philosopher and educational theorist

dew′lap′ n. loose fold of skin hanging from the throat of cattle, dogs, etc. [ME, fr. DEW + LAP¹]

dew′ point′ n. temperature at which dew forms

dex·ter·i·ty /dekster′itē/ n. skill in using one's hands, mind, etc. [L dexter handy; skillful]

dex·ter·ous /dek′strəs/ adj. (also **dex′trous**) having or showing dexterity —**dex′ter·ous·ly** or **dex′trous·ly** adv.; **dex′ter·ous·ness** or **dex′trous·ness** n.

dex·trose /dek′strōs′/ n. form of glucose [L dexter right-hand]

DH abbr. DESIGNATED HITTER

Dha·ka /däk′ə/ n. capital of Bangladesh. Pop. 3,397,200

dho·ti /dō′tē/ n. (pl. ·tis) loincloth worn by male Hindus [Hindi]

di-¹ comb. form two; double [Gk dis twice]

di-² prefix var. of DIS- before g

di-³ prefix form of DIA- before a vowel

dia- prefix (also **di-** before a vowel) 1 through (diaphanous) 2 apart (diacritical) 3 across (diameter) [Gk dia by; of; through]

dia. abbr. diameter

di·a·be·tes /dī′əbē′tēz, -bē′təs/ n. any of several metabolic disorders marked by increased urine production and high blood sugar —**di′a·bet′ic** /-bet′ik/ adj. & n. [L fr. Gk]

di·a·bol·i·cal /dī′əbäl′ikəl/ adj. (also **di·a·bol′ic**) 1 of the Devil 2 devilish; inhumanly cruel or wicked 3 extremely bad, clever, or annoying —**di′a·bol′i·cal·ly** adv. [Gk, rel. to DEVIL]

di·a·crit·ic /dī′əkrit′ik/ n. (also **di·a·crit′i·cal mark′**) sign (e.g., an acute accent) indicating the sound of a letter —**di′a·crit′i·cal** adj. [Gk, rel. to CRITIC]

di·a·dem /dī′ədem′/ n. crown or ornamental headband [Gk diadein bind]

diag. abbr. diagonal

Di·a·ghi·lev /dē·äg′əlef′/, **Sergei Pavlovich** 1872–1929; Russian ballet impresario

di·ag·nose /dī′əgnōs′, -nōz′/ v. (·nosed, ·nos·ing) make a diagnosis of (a disease, fault, etc.)

di·ag·no·sis /dī′əgnō′sis/ n. (pl. ·ses /-sēz′/) 1 identification of a disease 2 formal statement of this —**di′ag·nos′tic** /-näs′tik/ adj.; **di′ag·nos′ti·cal·ly** adv.; **di′ag·nos·ti′cian** /-nästi′sHən/ n. [Gk: distinguishing, fr. gignōskein know]

di·ag·nos·tics /dī′əgnäs′tiks/ n. Comp. programs used to identify faults in hardware or software

di·ag·o·nal /dī-ag′ənəl/ *adj.* 1 crossing a straight-sided figure from corner to corner 2 slanting; oblique —*n.* 3 straight line joining two opposite corners —**di·ag·o·nal·ly** *adv.* [Gk *gōnia* angle]

di·a·gram /dī′əgram′/ *n.* 1 outline drawing, plan, etc. —*v.* (·gramed or ·grammed, ·gram·ing or ·gram·ming) 2 represent in or as a diagram —**di·a·gram·mat′ic** /-gramat′ik/ *adj.*; **di·a·gram·mat′i·cal·ly** *adv.* [Gk *diagraphein* mark out by lines]

di·al /dī′(ə)l/ *n.* 1 plate with a scale for indicating weight, volume, etc. 2 rotary numbered disk on a telephone for calling a number 3 display of a clock or watch, marking the hours, etc. 4 adjustment control on an appliance —*v.* (·aled or ·alled, ·al·ing or ·al·ling) 5 select by means of a dial [ME fr. L *dies* day]

di·a·lect /dī′əlekt′/ *n.* 1 regional form of speech 2 variety of language with nonstandard vocabulary, pronunciation, or grammar —**di·a·lec′tal** *adj.* [Gk *legein* speak]

di·a·lec·tic /dī′əlek′tik/ *n.* 1 logical test or argumentation often considering opposites —**di·a·lec′ti·cal** *adj.*; **di·a·lec′ti·cal·ly** *adv.* [Gk, rel. to DIALECT]

di·a·logue /dī′əlôg′, -läg′/ *n.* (also **di′a·log**) 1a conversation b this in written form 2 interchange of opinions [Gk *logos* word; speech]

di′al tone /dī′əl/ *n.* sound indicating that a telephone line is ready for dialing a number

di·al·y·sis /dī-al′əsis/ *n.* (*pl.* ·ses /-sēz′/) separation of particles in a liquid by use of a membrane, esp. for purification of the blood [Gk: separation]

diam. *abbr.* diameter

di·am·e·ter /dī-am′ətər/ *n.* 1 straight line through the center of a circle or sphere to its edges 2 length of this [Gk *metron* measure]

di·a·met·ri·cal /dī′əme′trikəl/ *adj.* (also **di′a·met′ric**) 1 of or along a diameter 2 (of opposites, etc.) absolute —**di·a·met′ri·cal·ly** *adv.* [Gk, rel. to DIAMETER]

di·a·mond /dī′(ə)mənd/ *n.* 1 very hard transparent crystallized carbon 2 gem cut from this 3 four-sided figure, esp. in the shape of a rhombus 4a playing card of the suit denoted by a red rhombus, ♦ b (*pl.*) this suit 5 *Baseball.* the playing field, esp. the infield [L fr. Gk, rel. to ADAMANT]

di′a·mond·back′ *adj.* bearing diamond-shaped marks on the back, as certain rattlesnakes

Di·an·a /dīan′ə/ *n.* ARTEMIS

di·a·per /dī′(ə)pər/ *n.* absorbent wrapping for a baby not yet toilet trained [Gk *aspros* white]

di·aph·a·nous /dī-af′ənəs/ *adj.* very sheer; delicate [Gk *diaphanēs* transparent]

di·a·phragm /dī′əfram/ *n.* 1 muscular partition between the thorax and abdomen in mammals 2 cervical contraceptive device 3 vibrating disk that produces sound as in a speaker 4 aperture device in a camera —**di′a·phrag·mat′ic** /-fragmat′ik/ *adj.* [Gk *phragma* fence]

di·a·rist /dī′ərist/ *n.* person who keeps a diary

di·ar·rhe·a /dī′ərē′ə/ *n.* condition of excessively frequent and loose bowel movements [Gk *diarrhein* flow through]

di·a·ry /dī′(ə)rē/ *n.* (*pl.* ·ries) daily record of or book for events or thoughts [L *dies* day]

Di·as or **Di·az** /dē′əs, dē′äsh/, **Bartolomeu** c. 1450–1500; Portuguese navigator and explorer

di·a·stase /dī′əstāz′, -stäs′/ *n.* enzyme converting starch to sugar [Gk *diastasis* separation]

di·as·to·le /dīas′təlē′/ *n.* normal rhythmic expansion of the heart's chambers as they fill with blood —**di·as·tol′ic** /-əstäl′ik/ *adj.* [Gk *stellein* send]

di·a·tom /dī′ətäm′/ *n.* single-celled alga found as plankton and forming fossil deposits —**di′a·to·ma′ceous** /-təmā′SHəs/ *adj.* [Gk: cut in half]

di·a·tom·ic /dī′ətäm′ik/ *adj.* consisting of two atoms

di·a·ton·ic /dī′ətän′ik/ *adj. Mus.* relating to a standard major or minor scale of eight notes [Gk, rel. to TONIC]

di·a·tribe /dī′ətrīb′/ *n.* forceful verbal attack or criticism [Gk *tribein* rub]

dib·ble /dib′əl/ *n.* gardening tool for making holes

dice /dīs/ *n. pl.* 1a small cubes with faces bearing 1–6 spots, used in games or gambling b (treated as *sing.*) one of these cubes (also *die*) 2 game played with dice —*v.* (diced, dic·ing) 3 cut into small cubes [OFr, pl. of DIE²]

di·chot·o·my /dīkät′əmē/ *n.* (*pl.* ·mies) division into two, esp. a sharply defined one [Gk *dicho-* apart + *-tomy* cutting]

dick /dik/ *n. Slang.* detective [perh. an abbr.; perh. fr. *Richard*]

Dick·ens /dik′ənz/, **Charles** 1812–70; English novelist

dick·er /dik′ər/ *v.* bargain; haggle

dick·ey /dik′ē/ *n.* (also **dick′y**) (*pl.* ·eys or ·ies) *Colloq.* false shirt-front [*Dicky*, nickname for *Richard*]

Dick·in·son /dik′ənsən/, **Emily** 1830–86; US poet

dict. *abbr.* 1 dictionary 2 dictation

dic·ta /dik′tə/ *n. pl.* of DICTUM

dic·tate *v.* /dik′tāt′, diktāt′/ (·tat·ed, ·tat·ing) 1 say or read aloud (material to be written down or recorded) 2 state or order authoritatively or peremptorily —*n.* /dik′tāt′/ 3 requirement or imperative —**dic·ta′tion** *n.* [L *dictare* fr. *dicere* say]

dic·ta·tor /dik′tā′tər, diktā′-/ *n.* omnipotent ruler —**dic′ta·to′ri·al** /-tātôr′ēəl/ *adj.*; **dic′ta′tor·ship′** *n.* [L, rel. to DICTATE]

dic·tion /dik′SHən/ *n.* 1 manner of enunciation 2 choice of words [L *dicere dict-* say]

dic·tion·ar·y /dik′SHənər′ē/ *n.* (*pl.* ·ies) 1 reference publication listing (usu. alphabetically) and explaining the words of a language or equivalents in another language 2 reference publication on a special topic, esp. alphabetically arranged 3 *Comp.* list of words, codes, etc., used by a program [MedL, rel. to DICTION]

dic·tum /dik′təm/ *n.* (*pl.* ·ta /-tə/ or ·tums)

did /did/ *v.* past of DO[1]

di·dac·tic /dīdak'tik/ *adj.* 1 meant to instruct 2 (of a person) tediously pedantic —**di·dac'ti·cal·ly** *adv.*; **di·dac'ti·cism** /-ti'sizəm/ *n.* [Gk *didaskein* teach]

did·dle /did'l/ *v.* (**-dled, -dling**) *Colloq.* 1 swindle 2 waste time [perh. fr. *Diddler*, name of a character in a 19th-cent. play]

Di·de·rot /dēd'ərō'/, **Denis** 1713–84; French philosopher, writer, and critic

didn't /did'nt/ *v. contr.* did not

die[1] /dī/ *v.* (**died, dy·ing**) 1 cease to live; expire 2**a** come to an end; fade away **b** cease to function **c** (of a flame) go out 3 suffer; languish (died of boredom) 4 long (for) intensely (*dying for a drink*) 5 **die down** (or out or away) become fainter or weaker 6 **die off** die one after another [ON]

die[2] *n.* 1 DICE, 1b 2 (*pl.* **dies**) engraved stamping device 3 **the die is cast** an irrevocable step has been taken [OFr fr. L *datum*]

die'-hard (also **die·hard**) *n.* conservative or stubborn person

di·er·e·sis /dī·er'əsis/ *n.* (*pl.* **-ses** /-sēz'/) mark (as in *naïve*) over a vowel to indicate that it is sounded separately [Gk: division]

die·sel /dē'zəl/ *n.* 1 (in full **die'sel en'gine**) internal-combustion engine that burns fuel ignited by the compression of air 2 vehicle driven by a diesel engine 3 (of a gasoline engine) continue to run after the ignition is off [*Diesel*, name of an engineer]

di·et[1] /dī'ət/ *n.* 1 range of foods habitually eaten by a person or animal 2 food to which a person is restricted —*v.* (**-et·ed, -et·ing**) 3 restrict oneself to a special diet, esp. for weight loss —**di'e·tar'y** /-əter'ē/ *adj.*; **di'e·ter** *n.* [Gk *diaita* way of life]

di·et[2] *n.* legislative assembly in certain countries [L, perh. rel. to *dies* day]

di·e·tet·ic /dī'ətet'ik/ *adj.* of diet and nutrition [Gk, rel. to DIET[1]]

di·e·tet·ics /dī'ətet'iks/ *n. pl.* (usu. treated as *sing.*) the study of diet and nutrition

di·e·ti·tian /dī'ətish'ən/ *n.* (also **di'e·ti'cian**) expert in dietetics

Die·trich /dē'trik, -triкн/, **Marlene** (born **Maria Magdelene von Losch**) 1901–92; German-born US actress and singer

dif- *prefix* var. of DIS-[1] before *f*

dif·fer /dif'ər/ *v.* 1 be unlike or distinguishable 2 disagree [L *differe* separate; delay; differ]

dif·fer·ence /dif'(ə)rəns/ *n.* 1 being different or unlike 2 degree or nature of this 3 quantity by which amounts differ 4 disagreement; dispute

dif·fer·ent /dif'(ə)rənt/ *adj.* unlike; distinct; separate; unusual —**dif'fer·ent·ly** *adv.*

• Usage: Many critics, possibly on the grounds of logic, hold that *different than* is an improper usage for *different from*: *Her opinion is quite different from his.* Still, *different than* is widely used and appears in good writing.

dif·fer·en·tial /dif'ərən'sнəl/ *adj.* 1 of, exhibiting, or depending on a difference —*n.* 2 difference between things of the same kind 3 DIFFERENTIAL GEAR

dif'fer·en'tial gear' *n.* gear enabling a vehicle's rear wheels to revolve at different speeds on corners

dif·fer·en·ti·ate /dif'ərən'sнēat/ *v.* (**-at·ed, -at·ing**) 1 constitute a difference between or in 2 recognize as different; distinguish —**dif'fer·en·ti·a'tion** *n.*

dif·fi·cult /dif'əkəlt, -kəlt/ *adj.* 1 needing much effort or skill 2 troublesome; perplexing 3 (of a person) demanding or vexing

dif·fi·cul·ty /dif'əkəltē, -kəl'tē/ *n.* (*pl.* **-ties**) 1 being difficult 2**a** difficult thing; problem; hindrance **b** distress, esp. financial [L *difficultas*]

dif·fi·dent /dif'ədənt/ *adj.* shy; lacking self-confidence —**dif'fi·dence** *n.*; **dif'fi·dent·ly** *adv.* [L *diffidere* distrust]

dif·frac·tion /difrak'sнən/ *v.* the breaking up as a beam of light, into a series of dark and light bands, high and low intensities, or colored spectra —**dif·frac'tive** *adj.* [L *diffringere*, rel. to FRACTION]

dif·fuse *adj.* /difyōōs'/ 1 spread out; not concentrated 2 not concise; wordy —*v.* /difyōōz'/ (**-fused, -fus·ing**) 3 disperse or spread widely —**dif·fuse'ly** *adv.*; **dif·fuse'ness** *n.*; **dif·fus'i·ble** *adj.*; **dif·fu'sion** /-fyōō'zнən/ *n.*; **dif·fu'sive** *adj.* [L *diffusus* spread abroad]

dig /dig/ *v.* (**dug, dig·ging**) 1 break up and remove or turn over (ground, etc.) 2 (foll. by *up*) break up the soil of 3 make (a hole, tunnel, etc.) by digging 4 study; investigate; research 5 obtain or discover by digging 6 *Slang.* like; understand 7 thrust (a sharp object); prod or nudge 8 make one's way by digging —*n.* 9 piece of digging 10 thrust or poke 11 *Colloq.* pointed remark 12 **dig in** *Colloq.* begin eating [OE]

di·gest *v.* /dījest', dī-/ 1 assimilate (food) in the stomach and bowels 2 understand and absorb mentally 3 condense; summarize —*n.* /dī'-/ 4 periodical synopsis of current literature or news 5 condensation; summary —**di·gest'i·ble** *adj.*; **di·ges'tive** *adj.* [L *digerere -gest-* separate]

di·ges'tion /dījes'cнən, dī-/ *n.* 1 process of digesting 2 capacity to digest food

dig·it /dij'ət/ *n.* 1 any numeral from 0 to 9 2 finger or toe [L: finger; toe]

dig·i·tal /dij'ət-l/ *adj.* 1 of digits 2 (of a clock, watch, etc.) giving a reading by displayed digits 3 *Comp.* operating on data represented by digits 4 (of a recording) with sound electronically represented by digits —**dig'i·tal·ly** *adv.* [L, rel. to DIGIT]

dig·i·tal·is /dij'ətal'is/ *n.* drug prepared from the foxglove, used to stimulate the heart [NeoL, rel. to DIGIT, fr. the shape of the flowers]

dig'i·tize' /dij'ətīz'/ *v.* (**-tized, -tiz·ing**) convert (data, etc.) into digital form, esp. for a computer —**dig'i·ti·za'tion** *n.*

dig·ni·fied /dig'nəfīd'/ *adj.* having or showing dignity

dig·ni·fy /dig'nəfī'/ *v.* (**-fied, -fy·ing**) confer dignity on; ennoble [L *dignus* worthy]

dig·ni·tar·y /dig'nəter'ē/ *n.* (*pl.* **-ies**) person of high rank or office [fr. DIGNITY]

dig·ni·ty /dig'nətē/ *n.* (*pl.* **-ties**) 1 composed and serious manner 2 worthiness; nobleness **3** high rank or position [L *dignus* worthy]

di·graph /dī'graf'/ *n.* two letters representing one sound, e.g., *ph* as in *phone* [fr. DI-[1] + -GRAPH]

di·gress /dīgres'/ *v.* depart from the main subject in speech or writing —**di·gres'sion** /-gresH'ən/ *n.* [L *digredi -gress-* go off]

Di·jon /dē·zHôN', -zHäN'/ *n.* city in France. Pop. 151,600

Di·jon' mus'tard *n.* mild, brownish mustard paste, orig. made in Dijon, France

dike /dīk/ *n.* (also **dyke**) embankment built to prevent flooding [OE fr. ON, rel. to DITCH]

di·lap·i·dat·ed /dəlap'ədāt'id/ *adj.* in disrepair or ruin —**di·lap·i·da'tion** *n.* [L DIS- + *lapidare* throw stones at]

di·la·ta·tion /dī'lətā'sHən, dil'ə-/ *n.* **1** dilating of the cervix, e.g., for surgical curettage **2** dilation [fr. DILATE]

di·late /dī'lāt', dīlāt'/ *v.* (**·lat·ed, ·lat·ing**) **1** make or become wider or larger **2** speak or write at length —**di'la'tion** *n.* [L *latus* wide]

dil·a·to·ry /dil'ətôr'ē/ *adj.* given to or causing delay [L *dilatorius*, rel. to DIFFER]

di·lem·ma /dəlem'ə/ *n.* situation in which a difficult choice has to be made; predicament [Gk *lēmma* premise]

dil·et·tante /dil'ətänt', dil'ətänt'(ē)/ *n.* (*pl.* **·tantes** or **·tan·ti** /-tän'tē/) dabbler in a subject —**dil'et·tan'tism** *n.* [It *dilettare* fr. L *delectare* DELIGHT]

dil·i·gent /dil'əjənt/ *adj.* **1** hardworking **2** showing care and effort —**dil'i·gence** *n.*; **dil'i·gent·ly** *adv.* [Fr fr. L *diligere* love; esteem]

dill /dil/ *n.* herb with aromatic leaves and seeds [OE]

dil·ly·dal·ly /dil'ē·dal'ē/ *v.* (**·lied, ·ly·ing**) *Colloq.* **1** dawdle **2** vacillate [reduplication of DALLY]

di·lute /dīlōōt', də-/ *v.* (**·lut·ed, ·lut·ing**) **1** reduce the strength of (a fluid) by adding water, etc. **2** weaken or reduce in effect —*adj.* **3** diluted —**di·lu'tion** *n.* [L *diluere -lut-* wash away]

dim /dim/ *adj.* (**dim·mer, dim·mest**) **1a** faintly luminous or visible; not bright **b** indistinct **2** not clearly perceived nor remembered **3** *Colloq.* stupid —*v.* (**dimmed, dim·ming**) **4** make or become dim **5** take a dim view of *Colloq.* disapprove of —**dim'ly** *adv.*; **dim'ness** *n.* [OE]

Di·Mag·gi·o /dimaj'(ē)ō, -mazH'ō/, Joe (Joseph Paul) 1914– ; US baseball player

dime /dīm/ *n.* coin worth ten cents (US & Canada) [L *decima* tenth (part)]

di·men·sion /dimen'sHən, dī-/ *n.* **1** measurable extent, as length, breadth, etc. **2** (*pl.*) size; extent **3** aspect; facet —**di·men'sion·al** *adj.* [L *dimetiri -mens-* measure out]

di·min·ish /dəmin'ish/ *v.* **1** make or become smaller or less **2** lessen the reputation of (a person) [L *deminuere* make smaller]

di·min·u·en·do /dəmin'yōō·en'dō/ *Mus. n.* (*pl* **·dos**) **1** gradual decrease in loudness —*adv. & adj.* **2** decreasing in loudness [It, rel. to DIMINISH]

dim·i·nu·tion /dim'ən(y)ōō'sHən/ *n.* **1** diminishing or being diminished **2** decrease [L, rel. to DIMINISH]

di·min·u·tive /dəmin'yətiv/ *adj.* **1** tiny **2** (of a word or suffix) implying smallness or affection —*n.* **3** diminutive word or suffix

dim·mer /dim'ər/ *n.* (in full **dim'mer switch**) device for varying the brightness of an electric light

dim·ple /dim'pəl/ *n.* **1** small hollow, esp. in the cheek or chin —*v.* (**·pled, ·pling**) **2** form dimples (in) [prob. OE]

dim sum /dim' səm', sŏŏm/ *n.* Chinese steamed or fried filled dumplings

dim'wit' *n. Colloq.* stupid person —**dim'·wit'ted** *adj.*

din /din/ *n.* prolonged loud confused noise [OE]

dine /dīn/ *v.* (**dined, din·ing**) **1a** eat dinner **b** (foll. by *on, upon*) eat for dinner **2** provide a dinner for [OFr *diner*, prob. fr. L DIS- away + *jejunus* fasting]

din·er /dī'nər/ *n.* **1** person who dines **2** railroad dining car **3** informal restaurant

di·nette /dīnet'/ *n.* small room or alcove for eating meals

ding /diNG/ *v.* **1** make a ringing sound —*n.* **2** ringing sound [imit.]

din·ghy /diNG'(g)ē/ *n.* (*pl.* **·ghies**) small boat for rowing or sailing [Hindi]

din·go /diNG'gō/ *n.* (*pl.* **·goes**) wild Australian dog [Austral native name]

din·gy /din'jē/ *adj.* (**·gi·er, ·gi·est**) dirty-looking; drab —**din'gi·ly** *adv.*; **din'gi·ness** *n.*

din·ky /diNG'kē/ *adj.* (**·ki·er, ·ki·est**) *Colloq.* small [Scot *dink*]

din·ner /din'ər/ *n.* **1** main meal of the day, either at midday or in the evening **2** formal evening meal or banquet [OFr, rel. to DINE]

din'ner jack'et *n.* man's short formal jacket for evening wear

di·no·saur /dī'nəsôr'/ *n.* **1** extinct, often enormous, reptile of the Mesozoic era **2** outmoded person or thing [Gk *deinos* terrible + *sauros* lizard]

dint /dint/ *n.* as in **by dint of** by force or means of [OE and ON]

di·o·cese /dī'əsis, -sēz', -sēs'/ *n.* district administered by a bishop —**di·oc·e·san** /dī·äs'əsən/ *adj.* [Gk *dioikēsis* administration]

Di·o·cle·tian /dī'əklē'sHən/ 245–313; Roman emperor (284–305)

di·ode /dī'ōd'/ *n.* semiconductor or radio tube allowing the flow of current in one direction only and having two terminals [fr. DI-[1] + (ELECTR)ODE]

Di·og·e·nes /dī·äj'ənēz'/ c. 400–c. 325 B.C.; Greek philosopher

Di·o·ny·sian /dī'ənisH'ən, -nī's'sēən/ *adj.* wildly pagan; sensual [Gk DIONYSUS]

Di·o·ny·si·us I /dī'ənisH'(ē)əs, -nī'sēəs/ c. 430–367 B.C.; tyrant of Syracuse

Di·o·ny·sus /dī'əni'səs/ (also called **Bacchus**) *Gk. & Rom. Myth.* god of wine

di·o·ra·ma /dī'əram'ə, -räm'ə/ *n.* three-dimensional scenic display with a painted backdrop [Gk DIA- through + *horāma* view]

dip /dip/ *v.* (**dipped, dip·ping**) **1** put or lower briefly into liquid, etc. **2** go below a surface or level **3** (of income, activity, etc.) decline slightly **4** slope or extend downward **5** (foll. by *into*) look cursorily into (a book, subject, etc.) **6** (foll. by *into*) reach into and remove **7** lower or be lowered, esp. in salute —*n*. **8** dipping or being dipped **9** liquid or sauce for dipping **10** brief swim **11** downward slope or hollow in a road, skyline, etc. [OE]

diph·the·ri·a /dif'нEr'ēə, dip-/ *n*. acute infectious bacterial disease with inflammation, esp. of the throat [Gk *diphthera* skin; hide]

diph·thong /dif'тнŏng, dip'-/ *n*. two vowels pronounced as one syllable (as in *coin, loud, toy*) [Gk DI·¹ + *phthongos* voice; sound]

di·plo·ma /diplō'mə/ *n*. certificate of graduation or degree awarded by a college, school, etc. [Gk: folded paper, fr. *diplous* double]

di·plo·ma·cy /diplō'məsē/ *n*. **1** management of or skill in international relations **2** tact [Fr, rel. to DIPLOMAT]

dip·lo·mat /dip'ləmat'/ *n*. **1** member of a diplomatic service **2** tactful person —**dip'lo·mat'ic** *adj*.; **dip'lo·mat'i·cal·ly** *adv*. [Fr, rel. to DIPLOMA]

di·pole /dī'pōl'/ *n*. **1** two equal and oppositely charged or magnetized poles separated by a distance **2** type of radio antenna

dip·per /dip'ər/ *n*. **1** diving bird, esp. the water ouzel **2** ladle **3** (*cap*.) **a** (also called **Big' Dip'per**) part of the constellation Ursa Major **b** (also called **Lit'tle Dip'per**) part of the constellation Ursa Minor

dip·so·ma·ni·a /dip'səmā'nēə/ *n*. alcoholism —**dip'so·ma'ni·ac** /-nēak/ *n*. [Gk *dipsa* thirst]

dip·stick /dip'stik/ *n*. rod for measuring depth, esp. of oil in a vehicle's crankcase

Dir. *abbr*. **1** direction **2** director

dire /dīr/ *adj*. **1a** calamitous; dreadful **b** ominous **c** *Colloq*. very bad **2** urgent [L]

di·rect /dərekt', dī-/ *adj*. **1** extending or moving in a straight line or by the shortest route **2** straightforward; frank **3** with nothing or no one in between; personal **4** (of descent) lineal; not collateral **5** complete; exact —*adv*. **6** in a direct way or manner —*v*. **7** control; govern or guide **8** order **9** tell or show (someone) the way to **10** point, aim, or turn (a blow, attention, or remark) **11** supervise the performing, staging, etc., of (a film, play, etc.) —**di·rect'ness** *n*. [L *derigere* arrange]

di·rect' cur'rent *n*. electric current flowing in one direction only

di·rec'tion /dərek'sнən, dī-/ *n*. **1** directing; supervision **2** order or instruction **3** line of movement, sight, etc. **4** tendency of a theme, argument, etc. —**di·rec'tion·al** *adj*.

di·rec'tive /dərek'tiv, dī-/ *n*. **1** order from an authority —*adj*. **2** serving to direct

di·rect'ly *adv*. **1a** at once; without delay **b** soon; shortly **2** exactly (*directly opposite*) **3** in a direct manner

di·rect' ob'ject *n*. primary object of the action of a transitive verb

di·rec·tor /dərek'tər, dī-/ *n*. **1** person who directs or controls, esp. a member of the board of a corporation **2** person who directs a film, play, etc. —**di·rec·to'ri·al** /-tôr'ēəl/ *adj*.; **di·rec'tor·ship** *n*.

di·rec·tor·ate /dərek'tərət, dī-/ *n*. **1** board of directors **2** office of director

di·rec·to·ry /dərek'tərē, dī-/ *n*. (*pl*. ·ries) listing of names, etc., of members, subscribers, tenants, etc. [L, rel. to DIRECT]

dirge /dərj/ *n*. lament for the dead [L *dirige* direct, used in the Office for the Dead]

di·ri·gi·ble /dir'əjəbəl, dərij'əbəl/ *n*. see AIRSHIP [L, rel. to DIRECT]

dirk /dərk/ *n*. dagger

dirn·dl /dərn'dəl/ *n*. **1** dress with a close-fitting bodice and full skirt **2** full skirt of this kind [Ger]

dirt /dərt/ *n*. **1** unclean matter that soils **2** earth; soil **3** foul or malicious words or talk [ME, perh. fr. ON *drit* excrement]

dirt'·cheap' *adj*. & *adv*. *Colloq*. very inexpensive(ly)

dirt'y *adj*. (·i·er, ·i·est) **1** soiled, unclean **2** causing dirtiness **3** sordid; lewd; obscene **4** nasty; unfair **5** (of weather) rough **6** (of color) muddied; dingy —*adv*. **7** in a dirty manner —*v*. (·ied, ·y·ing) **8** make or become dirty —**dirt'i·ly** *adv*.; **dirt'i·ness** *n*.

dis or **diss** *v*. (**dissed, dis·sing**) *Colloq*. insult; disregard or reject [fr. DISRESPECT]

dis- *prefix* forming nouns, adjectives, and verbs implying: **1** negation or direct opposite (*dishonest*) **2** reversal (*disorient*) **3** removal of a thing or quality (*dismember*) **4** separation (*distinguish*) **5** completeness or intensification (*disgruntled*) **6** expulsion from (*disbar*) [OFr *des-* or L *dis-*]

dis·a·bil·i·ty /dis'əbil'itē/ *n*. (*pl*. ·ties) **1** physical or mental incapacity **2** lack of some capacity, etc., preventing action

dis·a·ble /disā'bəl/ *v*. (·bled, ·bling) deprive of an ability or function —**dis·a'ble·ment** *n*.

dis·a·buse /dis'əbyooz'/ *v*. (·bused, ·bus·ing) rid of a mistaken idea

dis·ad·van·tage /dis'ədvant'ij/ *n*. **1** unfavorable circumstance or condition; detriment —*v*. **2** cause disadvantage to —**dis'ad·van·ta'geous** /-ad'ventā'jəs/ *adj*.

dis'ad·van'taged *adj*. lacking normal opportunities through poverty, disability, etc.

dis·af·fect·ed /dis'əfek'tid/ *adj*. discontented; no longer loyal —**dis'af·fect'** *v*.; **dis'af·fec'tion** *n*.

dis·a·gree /dis'əgrē'/ *v*. (·greed, ·gree·ing) **1** hold a different opinion **2** (of factors) not correspond **3** make ill —**dis'a·gree'ment** *n*.

dis·a·gree·a·ble /dis'əgrē'əbəl/ *adj*. **1** unpleasant **2** bad-tempered —**dis'a·gree'a·bly** *adv*.

dis·al·low /dis'əlou'/ *v*. refuse to allow or accept

dis·ap·pear /dis'əpēr'/ *v*. **1** cease to be visible **2** cease to exist or be in circulation or use —**dis'ap·pear'ance** *n*.

dis·ap·point /dis'əpoint'/ *v*. **1** fail to fulfill the desire or expectation of **2** frustrate (a hope, etc.) —**dis'ap·point'ed, dis'ap·point'ing** *adj*.; **dis'ap·point'ment** *n*.

dis·ap·pro·ba·tion /dis'ap'rəbā'sнən/ *n*. *Formal*. disapproval

dis·ap·prove /dis'əproov'/ *v*. (·proved, ·prov·ing) have or express an unfavorable opinion —**dis'ap·prov'al** *n*.

dis·arm /disärm'/ *v*. **1** take weapons, etc., away from **2** reduce or give up one's own weapons **3** render harmless **4** charm; win over —**dis·arm'ing** *adj*.; **dis·arm'ing·ly** *adv*.

dis·ar·ma·ment /disär'məmənt/ *n.* reduction of armaments

dis·ar·range /dis'ərānj'/ *v.* (·ranged, ·ranging) bring into disorder —**dis'ar·range'ment** *n.*

dis·ar·ray /dis'ərā'/ *n. & v.* disorder

dis·as·so·ci·ate /dis'əsō'shē·āt, -sō'sē-/ *v.* (·at·ed, ·at·ing) DISSOCIATE —**dis'as·so'ci·a'tion** *n.*

di·sas·ter /dizas'tər/ *n.* 1 great or sudden misfortune; catastrophe 2 *Colloq.* complete failure —**di·sas'trous** /-trəs/ *adj.*; **di·sas'trous·ly** *adv.* [L fr. Gk *astron* star]

dis·a·vow /dis'əvou'/ *v.* disclaim knowledge of or responsibility for —**dis'a·vow'al** *n.*

dis·band /disband'/ *v.* break up; disperse —**dis·band'ment** *n.*

dis·bar /disbär'/ *v.* (·barred, ·bar·ring) deprive (a lawyer) of the right to practice —**dis·bar'ment** *n.*

dis·be·lieve /dis'bəlēv'/ *v.* (·lieved, ·liev·ing) be unable or unwilling to believe; be skeptical —**dis'be·lief'** /-bəlēf'/ *n.*; **dis'be·liev'ing** *adj.*; **dis'be·liev'ing·ly** *adv.*

dis·burse /disbûrs'/ *v.* (·bursed, ·burs·ing) pay out (money) —**dis·burs'al, dis·burse'ment** *n.* [OFr *desbourser*]

disc /disk/ *n.* var. spelling of DISK

dis·card /diskärd'/ *v.* 1 reject as unwanted 2 remove or put aside —*n.* /dis'kärd/ 3 something discarded, esp. an unwanted playing card [fr. DIS- + CARD]

dis·cern /disûrn', diz-/ *v.* perceive clearly with the mind or senses —**dis·cern'i·ble** *adj.* [L *cernere* separate]

dis·cern'ing *adj.* having good judgment —**dis·cern'ing·ly** *adv.*; **dis·cern'ment** *n.*

dis·charge /discHärj'/ *v.* (·charged, ·charg·ing) 1 release (a prisoner) 2 dismiss from office or employment 3 fire (a gun, etc.) 4 throw; eject 5 emit; pour out 6 (foll. by *into*) flow 7 carry out (a duty or obligation) 8 relieve oneself of (a debt) 9 release an electrical charge from —*n.* /dis'cHärj, -cHärj'/ 10 discharging or being discharged 11 certificate of release or dismissal 12 matter discharged; pus, etc. 13 release of an electric charge, esp. with a spark

dis·ci·ple /disī'pəl/ *n.* 1 follower of a leader, teacher, etc. 2 *Christianity.* early follower of Christ [L *capere* hold]

dis·ci·pli·nar·i·an /dis'əplənər'ēən/ *n.* enforcer of or believer in firm discipline

dis·ci·pline /dis'əplən/ *n.* 1 control or order exercised over people or animals, e.g., over members of an organization 2 training or way of life aimed at self-control and conformity 3 branch of learning 4 punishment —*v.* (·plined, ·plin·ing) 5 punish 6 train in obedience —**dis'ci·plin·ar'y** /-plīner'ē/ *adj.* [L, rel. to DISCIPLE]

disc' jock'ey *n.* var. of DISK JOCKEY

dis·claim /disklām'/ *v.* 1 deny or disown 2 renounce legal claim to

dis·claim'er *n.* renunciation; statement disclaiming something

dis·close /disklōz'/ *v.* (·closed, ·clos·ing) make known; expose —**dis·clo'sure** *n.*

dis·co /dis'kō/ *n. & adj. Colloq.* (*pl.* ·cos) DISCOTHEQUE

dis·col·or /diskəl'ər/ *v.* cause to change from its normal color; stain —**dis'col·or·a'tion** *n.*

dis·com·fit /diskəm'fit/ *v.* (·fit·ed, ·fit·ing) disconcert; frustrate —**dis·com'fi·ture** /ficHər/ *n.* [OFr fr. L DIS- + *conficere* prepare]

dis·com·fort /diskəm'fərt/ *n.* 1 lack of comfort; slight unease or pain 2 cause of this —*v.* 3 make uncomfortable

dis·com·mode /dis'kəmōd'/ *v.* inconvenience [L DIS- + *commodare* make suitable]

dis·com·pose /dis'kəmpōz'/ *v.* (·posed, ·pos·ing) disturb the composure of —**dis'com·po'sure** /-pō'zHər/ *n.*

dis·con·cert /dis'kənsərt'/ *v.* discompose

dis·con·nect /dis'kənekt'/ *v.* break the connection or functioning of —**dis'con·nec'tion** /-nek'sHən/ *n.*

dis·con·nect·ed /dis'kənek'tid/ *adj.* 1 separated and not functioning 2 incoherent and illogical

dis·con·so·late /diskän'səlat/ *adj.* forlorn; inconsolably disappointed —**dis·con'so·late·ly** *adv.* [L, rel. to DIS- + CONSOLE]

dis·con·tent /dis'kəntent'/ *n.* 1 dissatisfaction; grievance —*v.* 2 dissatisfy —**dis'con·tent'ment** *n.*

dis·con·tin·ue /dis'kəntin'yōō/ *v.* (·ued, ·u·ing) 1 come or bring to an end 2 give up; cease from (doing something) —**dis'con·tin'u·ance** *n.*

dis·con·tin·u·ous /dis'kəntin'yōōəs/ *adj.* disconnected —**dis'con·ti·nu'i·ty** /-känt'n-(y)ōō'ətē/ *n.*

dis·cord /dis'kôrd/ *n.* 1 disagreement; strife 2 harsh noise 3 lack of harmony —**dis·cor'dant** *adj.* [L DIS- + *cor cord-* heart]

dis·co·theque /dis'kətak'/ *n.* (also dis'co) club for dancing to recorded music [Fr: record library]

dis·count /dis'kount/ *n.* 1 amount deducted from a customary price —*v.* /diskount'/ 2 disregard as unreliable or unimportant 3 deduct an amount from (a price, etc.)

dis·coun·te·nance /diskount'n·əns/ *v.* (·nanced, ·nanc·ing) 1 embarrass 2 refuse to approve of

dis·cour·age /diskər'ij/ *v.* (·aged, ·ag·ing) 1 deprive of courage or confidence 2 dissuade; deter 3 show disapproval of —**dis·cour'age·ment** *n.*; **dis·cour'ag·ing** *adj.*

dis·course /dis'kôrs/ *n.* 1 conversation 2 presented treatment of a subject —*v.* /diskôrs'/ (·coursed, ·cours·ing) 3 converse 4 speak or write at length on a subject [L *currere curs-* run]

dis·cour·te·ous /diskərt'ēəs/ *adj.* lacking courtesy —**dis·cour'te·ous·ly** *adv.*; **dis·cour'te·sy** *n.* (*pl.* ·sies)

dis·cov·er /diskəv'ər/ *v.* 1 find out or become aware of 2 be first to find or find out —**dis·cov'er·er** *n.* [L, rel. to DIS- + COVER]

dis·cov·er·y /diskəv'(ə)rē/ *n.* (*pl.* ·ies) 1 discovering or being discovered 2 person or thing discovered

dis·cred·it /diskred'it/ *v.* 1 harm to reputation 2 cause of this —*v.* (·it·ed, ·it·ing) 3 harm the good reputation of 4 cause to be disbelieved 5 refuse to believe

dis·cred·it·a·ble /diskred'itəbəl/ *adj.* bringing discredit; shameful —**dis·cred'it·a·bly** adv.

dis·creet /diskrēt'/ adj. 1 tactful; prudent 2 unobtrusive —**dis·creet'ly** adv.; **dis·creet'ness** n. [L, rel. to DISCERN]

● Usage: *Discreet* 'prudent; cautious' and *discrete* 'separate' are different words with different meanings, and their distinction is maintained in careful speech and writing.

dis·crep·an·cy /diskrep'ənsē/ n. (pl. ·cies) difference; inconsistency —**dis·crep'ant** adj. [L *discrepare* be discordant]

dis·crete /diskrēt'/ adj. distinct; separate —**dis·crete'ness** n. [L, rel. to DISCERN]

dis·cre·tion /diskresH'ən/ n. 1 being discreet 2 freedom or authority to act according to one's judgment —**dis·cre'tion·ar'y** /-er'ē/ adj. [L, rel. to DISCERN]

dis·crim·i·nate /diskrim'ənāt'/ v. (·nat·ed, ·nat·ing) 1 make or see a distinction 2 treat unfavorably or favorably, esp. on the basis of race, gender, etc. —**dis·crim'i·na'tion** n.; **dis·crim'i·na·to'ry** /-ənətôr'ē/ adj. [L *discriminare*, rel. to DISCERN]

dis·crim'i·nat'ing adj. showing good judgment or taste

dis·cur·sive /diskər'siv/ adj. tending to digress; rambling [L *currere curs-* run]

DISCUS THROWER

dis·cus /dis'kəs/ n. (pl. ·cus·es) *Sports*. heavy disk thrown in competition [L fr. Gk]

dis·cuss /diskəs'/ v. talk or write about —**dis·cuss'ant, dis·cus'sion** /-kəsH'ən/ n. [L *discutere -cuss-* disperse; shatter]

dis·dain /disdān'/ n. 1 scorn; contempt —v. 2 regard with disdain 3 refrain or refuse out of disdain —**dis·dain'ful** adj.; **dis·dain'ful·ly** adv. [L, rel. to DIS- + DEIGN]

dis·ease /dizēz'/ n. 1 unhealthy condition of the body or mind, plants, etc. 2 particular kind of illness —**dis·eased'** adj. [Fr, rel. to DIS- + EASE]

dis·em·bark /dis'əmbärk'/ v. get off or unload from a ship, aircraft, bus, etc. —**dis'em·bar·ka'tion** /-em'bär'kā'sHən/ n.

dis·em·bod·ied /dis'əmbäd'ēd/ adj. free of a body or concrete form —**dis·em·bod'i·ment** n.

dis·em·bow·el /dis'əmboul', -bou'əl/ v. (·eled or ·elled, ·el·ing or ·el·ling) remove the bowels or entrails of —**dis'em·bow·el'ment** n.

dis·en·chant /dis'incHant'/ v. disillusion —**dis'en·chant'ment** n.

dis·en·cum·ber /dis'inkəm'bər/ v. free from encumbrance

dis·en·fran·chise /dis'infran'cHīz'/ v. (also

163   **discreet / disinfect**

dis·fran·chise) (·chised, ·chis·ing) deprive of the right to vote, be represented, etc. —**dis·en·fran'chise·ment** n.

dis·en·gage /dis'inGāj'/ v. (·gaged, ·gag·ing) 1 detach; loosen; release 2 remove (troops) from battle, etc. 3 become detached —**dis'en·gage'ment** n.

dis·en·tan·gle /dis'intanG'gəl/ v. (·gled, ·gling) free or become free of tangles or complications —**dis'en·tan'gle·ment** n.

dis·fa·vor /disfā'vər/ n. 1 disapproval or dislike 2 being disliked

dis·fig·ure /disfig'yər/ v. (·ured, ·ur·ing) spoil the appearance of —**dis·fig'ure·ment** n.

dis·fran·chise /disfran'cHīz/ v. var. of DIS·ENFRANCHISE

dis·gorge /disgôrj'/ v. (·gorged, ·gorg·ing) 1 vomit 2 pour forth —**dis·gorge'ment** n.

dis·grace /disgrās'/ n. 1 shame; ignominy 2 shameful or very bad person or thing —v. (·graced, ·grac·ing) 3 bring shame or discredit on —**dis·grace'ful** adj.; **dis·grace'ful·ly** adv. [L, rel. to DIS- + GRACE]

dis·grun·tled /disgrənt'ld/ adj. discontented; resentful —**dis·grun'tle·ment** n. [fr. DIS- + GRUNT]

dis·guise /disgīz'/ v. (·guised, ·guis·ing) 1 conceal the identity of; make unrecognizable —n. 2 costume, manner, etc., used to disguise 3 disguised state [Fr, rel. to DIS- + GUISE]

dis·gust /disgəst'/ n. 1 strong aversion; repugnance —v. 2 cause disgust in —**dis·gust'ing** adj.; **dis·gust'ing·ly** adv. [Fr or It, rel. to DIS- + GUSTO]

dish /disH/ n. 1a a shallow flat-bottomed container for food b its contents c particular kind of food or preparation 2 (pl.) plates, pans, etc., used for a meal 3 dish-shaped object or cavity —v. 4 **dish out** (or **up**): a distribute or serve, in or as in dishes b *Colloq*. present as a fact or argument [OE fr. L *discus*]

dis·har·mo·ny /dis·här'mənē/ n. lack of harmony; discord —**dis·har·mo'ni·ous** /dis'här'mō'nēəs/ adj.

dis·heart·en /dis·härt'n/ v. cause to lose courage, hope, or confidence

di·shev·eled /disHev'əld/ adj. untidy —**di·shev'el·ment** n. [fr. DIS- + *chevel* 'hair', fr. L *capillus*]

dis·hon·est /disän'ist/ adj. fraudulent or insincere —**dis·hon'est·ly** adv.; **dis·hon'es·ty** n.

dis·hon·or /disän'ər/ n. 1 loss of honor or respect; disgrace 2 thing causing this —v. 3 disgrace —**dis·hon'or·a·ble** adj.; **dis·hon'or·a·bly** adv.

dish' rag n. cloth for washing dishes

dish'wash'er n. machine or person that washes dishes

dis·il·lu·sion /dis'əloo'zHən/ v. 1 free from an illusion or belief 2 shatter an ideal —**dis'il·lu'sion·ment** n.

dis·in·cline /dis'inklīn'/ v. (·clined, ·clin·ing) make reluctant —**dis'in·cli·na'tion** /-klənā'sHən/ n.

dis·in·fect /dis'infekt'/ v. cleanse; sterilize —**dis'in·fec'tant, dis'in·fec'tion** /-fek'sHən/ n.

dis·in·for·ma·tion /dis'in'fərmə'sʜən/ *n.* false information deliberately issued to deceive

dis·in·gen·u·ous /dis'injen'yōŏəs/ *adj.* insincere; not candid —**dis'in·gen'u·ous·ly** *adv.*

dis·in·her·it /dis'inher'ət/ *v.* deprive of the right of inheritance

dis·in·te·grate /disint'əgrāt'/ *v.* (**·grat·ed, ·grat·ing**) separate into component parts or fragments; break up —**dis·in'te·gra'tion** *n.*

dis·in·ter /dis'intər'/ *v.* (**·terred, ·ter·ring**) dig up (esp. a corpse) —**dis'in·ter'ment** *n.*

dis·in·ter·est·ed /disin'trəstid/ *adj.* 1 impartial 2 uninterested —**dis·in'ter·est** *n.*; **dis·in'ter·est·ed·ly** *adv.*

  • Usage: *Disinterested* means 'not having a personal interest; impartial': *As the referee, I was disinterested in the outcome of the game.* *Uninterested* means 'not interested; indifferent; unconcerned': *Bored beyond belief, I was uninterested in the outcome of the game.*

dis·joint /disjoint'/ *v.* 1 destroy the integrity of 2 take apart at the joints —**dis·joint'ed** *adj.*

disk /disk/ (also **disc**) *n.* 1a flat thin circular object b round flat or apparently flat surface, mark, etc. 2 layer of cartilage between vertebrae 3 phonograph record 4 flat circular computer storage device (often **disc** for optical devices) [L DISCUS]

disk' brake' *n.* brake employing the friction of pads against a disk

disk' drive' *n. Comp.* mechanism for inserting a floppy disk to read or write data

dis·kette /disket'/ *n. Comp.* FLOPPY, 2

disk' jock'ey (also **disc' jock'ey**) *n.* radio host of recorded pop music

disk' op·er·at·ing sys'tem *n. Comp.* software that controls personal computers; *abbr.* DOS

dis·like /dislīk'/ *v.* (**·liked, ·lik·ing**) 1 have an aversion to —*n.* 2 not liking 3 object of this

dis·lo·cate /dis'lōkāt, dislō'-/ *v.* (**·cat·ed, ·cat·ing**) 1 disturb the normal connection of (esp. a joint in the body) 2 disrupt —**dis'lo·ca'tion** *n.*

dis·lodge /disläj'/ *v.* (**·lodged, ·lodg·ing**) disturb or move —**dis·lodg'ment** *n.*

dis·loy·al /disloi'əl/ *adj.* not loyal; unfaithful —**dis·loy'al·ly** *adv.*; **dis·loy'al·ty** *n.*

dis·mal /diz'məl/ *adj.* gloomy; miserable; dreary —**dis'mal·ly** *adv.* [MedL *dies mali* unlucky days]

dis·man·tle /dismant'l/ *v.* (**·tled, ·tling**) take to pieces; pull down

dis·may /dismā'/ *n.* 1 intense disappointment or despair —*v.* 2 fill with dismay [Fr fr Gmc, rel. to DIS- + MAY]

dis·mem·ber /dismem'bər/ *v.* 1 remove the limbs from 2 partition or divide up —**dis·mem'ber·ment** *n.*

dis·miss /dismis'/ *v.* 1 send away, esp. from one's presence 2 terminate the employment of 3 put from one's mind or emotions 4 consider unimportant, minor, etc. 5 *Law.* refuse further hearing to (a case) —**dis·miss'al** *n.*; **dis·mis'sive** /-mis'iv/ *adj.*; **dis·mis'sive·ly** *adv.*; **dis·mis'sive·ness** *n.* [L DIS- + *mittere miss*- send]

dis·mount /dismount'/ *v.* get down from a horse, bicycle, etc.

Dis·ney /diz'nē/, **Walt (Walter Elias)** 1901–66; US animator and film producer

dis·o·be·di·ent /dis'ōbēd'ēənt/ *adj.* disobeying; rebellious —**dis'o·be'di·ence** *n.*; **dis'o·be'di·ent·ly** *adv.*

dis·o·bey /dis'ōbā'/ *v.* refuse or fail to obey

dis·o·blige /dis'əblīj'/ *v.* (**·bliged, ·blig·ing**) refuse to help or cooperate with

dis·or·der /disôr'dər/ *n.* 1 lack of order; disarray 2 public disturbance; riot 3 ailment or disease —*v.* 4 destroy the order of —**dis·or'dered** *n.*

dis·or·der·ly /disôr'dərlē/ *adj.* 1 untidy; confused 2 unruly —**dis·or'der·li·ness** *n.*

dis·or·ga·nize /disôr'gənīz'/ *v.* (**·nized, ·niz·ing**) 1 throw into disorder 2 organize badly —**dis·or'ga·ni·za'tion** *n.*; **dis·or'gan·ized** *adj.*

dis·o·ri·ent /disôr'ē·ent', -ôr'-/ *v.* confuse (a person), esp. as to his or her bearings —**dis·o'ri·en·ta'tion** /-entā'sʜən/ *n.*

dis·own /disōn'/ *v.* deny or give up any connection with; repudiate

dis·par·age /dispar'ij/ *v.* (**·aged, ag·ing**) 1 criticize; belittle 2 bring discredit on —**dis·par'age·ment** *n.* [Fr, rel. to DIS- + *parage* rank]

dis·pa·rate /dis'pərət/ *adj.* essentially different; not comparable —**dis'pa·rate·ness** *n.* [L *disparare* separate]

dis·par·i·ty /dispar'ətē/ *n.* (*pl.* **·ties**) inequality; difference; incongruity

dis·pas·sion·ate /dispasʜ'ənət/ *adj.* free from emotion; impartial —**dis·pas'sion·ate·ly** *adv.*

dis·patch /dispacʜ'/ (also **des·patch**) *v.* 1 send off to a destination or for a purpose 2 perform (a task, etc.) promptly 3 kill; execute —*n.* 4 dispatching or being dispatched 5a official message, esp. military b news report 6 promptness [It *dispacciare* or Sp *despachar*]

dis·pel /dispel'/ *v.* (**·pelled, ·pel·ling**) drive away (fears, etc.) [L *pellere* drive]

dis·pens·a·ble /dispen'səbəl/ *adj.* 1 that can be given out 2 not important

dis·pen·sa·ry /dispen'sərē/ *n.* (*pl.* **·ries**) place where first aid and medicines are dispensed

dis·pen·sa·tion /dis'pensā'sʜən, -pən-/ *n.* 1 dispensing or distributing 2 exemption from penalty, rule, etc. 3 divine ordering or management of the world

dis·pense /dispens'/ *v.* (**·pensed, ·pens·ing**) 1 distribute; deal out 2 administer 3 make up and give out (medicine, etc.) 4 (foll. by *with*) do without —**dis·pens'er** *n.* [Fr fr. L *pendere pens*- weigh]

dis·perse /dispərs'/ *v.* (**·persed, ·pers·ing**) 1 go, send, drive, or scatter widely or in different directions 2 break up or dispel —**dis·pers'al, dis·per'sion** /-pər'zʜən/ *n.*; **dis·per'sive** *adj.* [L, rel. to DIS- + *spargere* scatter]

dis·pir·it /dispir'it/ *v.* make despondent; deject —**dis·pir'it·ing, dis·pir'it·ed** *adj.*

dis·place /displās'/ *v.* (**·placed, ·plac·ing**) 1 move from its place 2 remove from office 3 take the place of; oust

dis·placed' per'son *n.* refugee in war, etc., or from persecution

dis·place·ment *n.* **1** displacing or being displaced **2** amount of fluid displaced by an object floating or immersed in it

dis·play /displā′/ *v.* **1** exhibit; show **2** reveal; betray —*n.* **3** displaying **4a** exhibition or show **b** thing(s) displayed **5** ostentation **6** mating rituals of some birds, etc. [OFr fr. L *plicare* fold]

dis·please /displēz′/ *v.* (·**pleased**, ·**pleas·ing**) dissatisfy; annoy —**dis·plea′sure** /-pleZH′ər/ *n.*

dis·port /dispôrt′/ *v.* play; frolic; enjoy oneself [AngFr *porter* fr. L *portare* carry]

dis·pos·a·ble /dispō′zəbəl/ *adj.* **1** intended for one-time or limited use, then disposed of **2** able to be disposed of

dis·pos·al /dispō′zəl/ *n.* **1** disposing of, e.g., waste **2 at one's disposal** available

dis·pose /dispōz′/ *v.* (·**posed**, ·**pos·ing**) **1** make willing; incline **2** arrange suitably **3** have a specified inclination **4 dispose of: a** get rid of **b** finish **c** kill [MFr, rel. to POSE]

dis·po·si·tion /dis′pəZISH′ən/ *n.* **1** natural tendency; temperament **2** ordering; arrangement

dis·pos·sess /dis′pəzes′/ *v.* **1** deprive (a person) of **2** dislodge; oust —**dis′pos·ses′sion** /-zeSH′ən/ *n.*

dis·pro·por·tion /dis′prəpôr′SHən/ *n.* lack of proportion —**dis′pro·por′tion·al** *adj.*; **dis′pro·por′tion·al·ly** *adv.*

dis·pro·por·tion·ate /dis′prəpôr′SHənət/ *adj.* **1** out of proportion **2** relatively too large or small, etc. —**dis′pro·por′tion·ate·ly** *adv.*

dis·prove /disproov′/ *v.* (·**proved**, ·**prov·ing**) prove (something) to be false

dis·put·a·ble /dispyoo′təbəl/ *adj.* open to question; uncertain —**dis·pu′ta·bly** *adv.*

dis·pu·ta·tion /dis′pyoota′SHən/ *n.* debate, esp. formal argument

dis·pu·ta·tious *adj.* argumentative

dis·pute /dispyoot′/ *v.* (·**put·ed**, ·**put·ing**) **1** debate; argue **2** question the truth or validity of; oppose **3** contend for —*n.* **4** controversy; debate **5** quarrel **6 in dispute** being argued about —**dis·pu′tant** *n.* [L *disputare*]

dis·qual·i·fy /diskwäl′əfī′/ *v.* (·**fied**, ·**fy·ing**) debar or pronounce ineligible, unsuitable, or unqualified —**dis·qual′i·fi·ca′tion** /-fikā′ SHən/ *n.*

dis·qui·et /diskwī′ət/ *v.* **1** make anxious —*n.* **2** anxiety; uneasiness

dis·qui·si·tion /dis′kwəzISH′ən/ *n.* formal treatise or discourse [L *quaerere quaesit*-seek]

Dis·rae·li /dizrā′lē/, **Benjamin (Earl of Beaconsfield)** 1804–81; prime minister of Great Britain (1868; 1874–80)

dis·re·gard /dis′rigärd′/ *v.* **1** ignore **2** treat as unimportant —*n.* **3** indifference; neglect

dis·re·pair /dis′rəper′/ *n.* poor condition due to lack of repairs

dis·rep·u·ta·ble /disrep′yətəbəl/ *adj.* **1** of bad reputation **2** shabby in appearance —**dis·rep′u·ta·bly** *adv.*

dis·re·pute /dis′rəpyoot′/ *n.* lack of good reputation; disgrace

dis·re·spect /dis′rispekt′/ *n.* lack of respect; discourtesy —**dis·re·spect′ful** *adj.*; **dis·re·spect′ful·ly** *adv.*

dis·robe /disrōb′/ *v.* (·**robed**, ·**rob·ing**) undress

dis·rupt /disrəpt′/ *v.* **1** interrupt the continuity or order of **2** break apart —**dis·rup′tion** /-rəp′SHən/ *n.*; **dis·rup′tive** *adj.*; **dis·rup′tive·ly** *adv.* [L, rel. to RUPTURE]

dis·sat·is·fy /disat′əsfī′/ *v.* (·**fied**, ·**fy·ing**) make discontented; fail to satisfy —**dis·sat′is·fac′tion** /-fak′SHən/ *n.*

dis·sect /disekt′, dī-/ *v.* **1** cut open, esp. for examination or a post mortem **2** analyze or criticize in detail —**dis·sec′tion** /-sek′SHən/ *n.* [L *dissecare*]

dis·sem·ble /disem′bəl/ *v.* (·**bled**, ·**bling**) be hypocritical or insincere [L *simulare* SIMULATE]

dis·sem·i·nate /disem′ənāt′/ *v.* (·**nat·ed**, ·**nat·ing**) spread (esp. ideas) widely —**dis·sem′i·na′tion** *n.* [L, rel. to DIS- + SEMEN]

dis·sen·sion /disen′SHən/ *n.* disagreement or quarreling [L, rel. to DISSENT]

dis·sent /disent′/ *v.* **1** disagree, esp. openly **2** differ, esp. from the established or official opinion —*n.* **3** such disagreement or an instance of it —**dis·sent′er** *n.* [L, rel. to DIS- + *sentire* feel]

dis·ser·ta·tion /dis′ərtā′SHən/ *n.* detailed treatise, esp. one submitted toward an academic degree [L *dissertare* discuss]

dis·ser·vice /dis·sər′vis/ *n.* harm or injustice

dis·si·dent /dis′ədənt/ *n.* **1** person disagreeing, esp. with the established government, system, etc. —*adj.* **2** dissenting —**dis′si·dence** *n.* [L *dissidere* sit apart]

dis·sim·i·lar /dis(-s)im′ələr/ *adj.* unlike —**dis·sim′i·lar′i·ty** /-lar′ärē/ *n.* (*pl.* ·**ties**)

dis·sim·u·late /disim′yəlāt/ *v.* (·**lat·ed**, ·**lat·ing**) dissemble —**dis·sim′u·la′tion** *n.* [L *dissimulare* disguise]

dis·si·pate /dis′əpāt′/ *v.* **1** disperse; disappear **2** squander —**dis′si·pat′ed** *adj.*; **dis′si·pa′tion** *n.* [L *dissipare -pat*-]

dis·so·ci·ate /disō′SHē-āt′, -sē-āt′/ *v.* (·**at·ed**, ·**at·ing**) **1** disconnect or separate **2** become disconnected —**dis·so′ci·a′tion** *n.*; **dis·so′ci·a·tive** /-SHē-āt′iv, -sē-, -SHətiv/ *adj.* [L *dissociare*]

dis·so·lute /dis′əloot′/ *adj.* lax in morals; dissipated [L, rel. to DISSOLVE]

dis·so·lu′tion *n.* dissolving or being dissolved

dis·solve /dizälv′, -zôlv′/ *v.* (·**solved**, ·**solv·ing**) **1** make or become liquid, esp. by dispersion in a liquid **2** (cause to) disappear gradually **3** dismiss (an assembly) **4** put an end to (a partnership, marriage, etc.) **5** be overcome (by tears, laughter, etc.) [L, rel. to DIS- + *solvere solut*- loosen]

dis·so·nant /dis′ənənt/ *adj.* **1** harsh-toned; unharmonious **2** incongruous —**dis′so·nance** *n.* [L *dis-* + *sonus* sound]

dis·suade /diswād′/ *v.* (·**suad·ed**, ·**suad·ing**) discourage; persuade against —**dis·sua′sion** /-swā′ZHən/ *n.*; **dis·sua′sive** /-siv, -ziv/ *adj.* [L, rel. to DIS- + *suadere* advise]

dis·taff /dis′taf′/ *n.* stick holding wool or flax for spinning [OE]

dis·tance /dis′təns/ *n.* **1** being far off; remoteness **2** space between two points **3** distant point or place **4** aloofness; estrangement —*v.* (·**tanced**, ·**tanc·ing**) **5** place or cause to seem far off; be aloof [L, rel. to DIS- + *stare* stand]

dis·tant /dis'tənt/ *adj.* 1 far away; at a specified distance 2 remote in time, relationship, etc. 3 aloof —**dis'tant·ly** *adv.*

dis·taste /distāst'/ *n.* dislike; aversion —**dis·taste'ful** *adj.*; **dis·taste'ful·ly** *adv.*; **dis·taste'ful·ness** *n.*

dist. atty. *abbr.* district attorney

dis·tem·per /distem'pər/ *n.* viral disease that affects pets [L, rel. to DIS- + *temperare* be moderate]

dis·tend /distend'/ *v.* swell out by pressure from within —**dis·ten'sion** /-ten'shən/ *n.* [L, rel. to DIS- + *tendere* stretch]

dis·till /distil'/ *v.* (**·tilled**, **·til·ling**) 1 purify or extract the essence from (a substance) by vaporizing and condensing 2 extract the essential meaning of (an idea, etc.) 3 make (esp. liquor) by distilling raw materials 4 fall or cause to fall in drops —**dis·til·la'tion** /-təlā'shən/, **dis·till'er** *n.* [L, rel. to DE- + *stillare* drip]

dis·till·er·y /distil'ərē/ *n.* (*pl.* **·ies**) place where alcoholic liquor is distilled

dis·tinct /distiNGkt'/ *adj.* 1 not identical; separate; different 2 clearly perceptible 3 unmistakable —**dis·tinct'ly** *adv.* [L, rel. to DIS- TINGUISH]

dis·tinc·tion /distiNGk'shən/ *n.* 1 discriminating or distinguishing 2 difference between two things 3 thing that differentiates 4 honor, award, title, etc. 5 excellence [L, rel. to DISTINGUISH]

dis·tinc·tive /distiNGk'tiv/ *adj.* distinguishing; notable —**dis·tinc'tive·ly** *adv.*; **dis·tinc'tive·ness** *n.*

dis·tin·guish /distiNG'(g)wish/ *v.* 1 differentiate; see or draw distinctions 2 be a mark or property of; characterize 3 discern 4 make prominent —**dis·tin'guish·a·ble** *adj.* [L *distinguere*]

dis·tin'guished *adj.* 1 famous 2 dignified

dis·tort /distôrt'/ *v.* 1 pull or twist out of shape 2 misrepresent (facts, etc.) 3 transmit (sound, etc.) inaccurately —**dis·tor'tion** /-tôr'shən/ *n.* [L *torquere* *tort-* twist]

dis·tract /distrakt'/ *v.* 1 draw away the attention of 2 confuse; derange 3 amuse, esp. to divert from pain, etc. —**dis·tract'ed**, **dis·tract'ing** *adj.*; **dis·tract'ed·ly** *adv.* [L DIS- + *trahere* *tract-* draw]

dis·trac·tion /distrak'shən/ *n.* 1a distracting or being distracted b thing that distracts 2 relaxation; amusement 3 mental confusion; madness

dis·trait /distrā'/ *adj.* (*fem.* **dis·traite** /distrāt'/) inattentive; distraught [Fr fr. L, rel. to DISTRACT]

dis·traught /distrôt'/ *adj.* extremely agitated [ME, var. of DISTRAIT]

dis·tress /distres'/ *n.* 1 anguish; suffering 2 poverty —*v.* 3 cause distress to; make unhappy —**dis·tress'ful** *adj.* [OFr fr. L *distringere* draw asunder]

dis·tressed /distrest'/ *adj.* 1 suffering from distress 2 (of furniture, clothing, etc.) aged, damaged, etc., artificially

dis·trib·ute /distrib'yŏŏt, -yət/ *v.* (**·ut·ed**, **·ut·ing**) 1 give or deal out 2 scatter; put at different points 3 arrange; classify —**dis'tri·bu'tion** *n.* [L *distribuere*]

dis·trib·u·tor /distrib'yətər/ *n.* 1 person, company, etc., that distributes, esp. from a manufacturer to retailers 2 device in an internal-combustion engine for passing current to spark plugs

dis·trict /dis'trikt/ *n.* 1 geographical or administrative unit 2 region or neighborhood [L *distringere* draw asunder]

dis'trict at·tor'ney *n.* prosecuting attorney for a government

Dis'trict of Co·lum'bi·a /kələm'bēə/ *n.* federal district in the E United States; coextensive with the national capital, Washington. Abbr. DC; D.C.

dis·trust /distrəst'/ *n.* 1 lack of trust; suspicion —*v.* 2 have no trust in —**dis·trust'ful** *adj.*; **dis·trust'ful·ly** *adv.*

dis·turb /distərb'/ *v.* 1 break the rest, calm, or quiet of 2 agitate; worry 3 move from a settled position [L DIS- + *turbare* tumult]

dis·tur·bance /distərb'əns/ *n.* 1 disturbing or being disturbed 2 tumult; uproar

dis·u·nite /dis'yŏŏnīt', dishŏŏ-/ *v.* (**·nit·ed**, **·nit·ing**) 1 undo the unity of 2 separate —**dis·u'ni·ty** /-yŏŏ'nitē/ *n.* (*pl.* **·ties**)

dis·use *n.* /disyŏŏs'/ 1 disused state —*v.* /-yŏŏz'/ (**·used**, **·us·ing**) 2 cease to use

ditch /dich/ *n.* 1 long narrow excavation esp. for drainage —*v.* 1 make a ditch 3 *Slang.* abandon; discard [OE]

dith·er /diTH'ər/ *v.* 1 hesitate; be indecisive —*n.* 2 *Colloq.* state of agitation or hesitation —**dith'er·er** *n.* [var. of *didder* DODDER]

dit·sy /dit'sē/ (also **dit'zy**) (**·si·er** or **·zi·er**, **·si·est** or **·zi·est**) *adj. Colloq.* silly; inane

dit·to /dit'ō/ *n.* (*pl.* **·tos**) *Colloq.* (said to avoid repetition) the same [L *dictus* said]

dit'to mark' *n.* mark (″) used to indicate that something written above is to be repeated

dit·ty /dit'ē/ *n.* (*pl.* **·ties**) short simple song [L, rel. to DICTATE]

ditz /dits/ *n. Slang.* ditsy person

di·u·ret·ic /dī'(y)əret'ik/ *adj.* 1 causing increased output of urine —*n.* 2 diuretic drug [Gk DIA- + *ourein* urinate]

di·ur·nal /dī'ərn'l/ *adj.* 1 of the day or daytime 2 daily —**di·ur'nal·ly** *adv.* [L *diurnalis* fr. *dies* day]

div. *abbr.* 1 divided 2 division

di·va /dē'və/ *n.* (*pl.* **·vas**) woman opera singer; prima donna [It fr. L: goddess]

di·van /divan', dī'van'/ *n.* low couch [ult. fr. Pers *dīwān* account book]

dive /dīv/ *v.* (**dived** or **dove**, **div·ing**) 1 plunge head first into water 2a (of an aircraft, person, etc.) plunge steeply downward b (of a submarine) submerge; go deeper 3 (foll. by *into*) *Colloq.* become enthusiastic about (a subject, meal, etc.) —*n.* 4 act of diving; plunge 5 steep descent or fall 6 *Colloq.* disreputable nightclub, bar, etc. —**div'er** *n.* [OE]

di·verge /dīvərj'/ *v.* (**·verged**, **·verg·ing**) 1a spread out from a central point; become dispersed b take different paths 2a depart from a set course b (of opinions, etc.) differ

—di·ver′gence *n.*; **di·ver′gent** *adj.* [L DI-² + *vergere* incline]

di·vers /dī′vərz/ *adj. Lit.* various; several [L, rel. to DIVERSE]

di·verse /divors′, də-/ *adj.* varied **—di·verse′ly** *adv.*; **di·verse′ness** *n.* [L DI-² + *vertere* vers- turn]

di·ver·si·fy /dīvər′səfī′, də-/ *v.* (**·fied, ·fy·ing**) 1 make diverse; vary 2 spread or expand one's enterprises, etc. **—di·ver′si·fi·ca′tion** /-fikā′shən/ *n.*

di·ver·sion /dəvər′zhən, dī-, -shən/ *n.* 1 diverting or being diverted 2 diverting of attention 3 recreation **—di·ver′sion·ar·y** /-erē/ *adj.*

di·ver·si·ty /dīvər′sitē, də-/ *n.* variety

di·vert /dīvərt′, də-/ *v.* 1a turn aside; deflect **b** distract (attention) 2 amuse [L, rel. to DIVERSE]

di·ver·tic·u·li·tis /dī′vərtik′yəlī′tis/ *n. Med.* painful inflammation of diverticula

di·ver·tic·u·lum /dī′vərtik′yələm/ *n.* (*pl.* **·la** /-lə/) *Anat.* blind sac or branch of a canal or cavity, as in the wall of the colon

di·vest /dīvest′/ *v.* 1 unclothe; strip 2 deprive; rid 3 *Commerce.* sell off [L *vestire* dress]

di·vide /dəvīd′/ *v.* (**·vid·ed, ·vid·ing**) 1 separate into parts; break up; split 2 distribute; deal; share 3 make separate; classify 4 cause to disagree 5 *Math.* find how many times (a number) contains or is contained in another **—n.** 6 dividing line 7 watershed [L *dividere*]

div·i·dend /div′ədend′/ *n.* 1 share of profits paid to stockholders 2 number to be divided 3 benefit [L, rel. to DIVIDE]

div·i·na·tion /div′ənā′shən/ *n.* supposed supernatural insight into the future, etc. [L *divinare* soothsay]

di·vine /divīn′/ *adj.* 1a of, from, or like God or a god **b** sacred 2 *Colloq.* excellent; delightful **—v.** (**·vined, ·vin·ing**) 3 discover by intuition or guessing 4 foresee **—n.** 5 theologian or clergyman **—di·vine′ly** *adv.* [L *divinus*]

di·vin′ing rod′ *n.* rod for finding underground water, etc.

di·vin·i·ty /dəvin′itē/ *n.* (*pl.* **·ties**) 1 being divine 2 god; godhead 3 theology 4 (**the Divinity**) God

di·vis·i·ble /dəviz′əbəl/ *adj.* capable of being divided **—di·vis′i·bil′i·ty** *n.*

di·vi·sion /dəvizh′ən/ *n.* 1 dividing or being divided 2 operation of dividing one number by another 3 one of the parts into which a thing is divided 4 unit of administration, organization, etc. **—di·vi′sion·al** *adj.*

di·vi′sion sign′ *n.* sign (÷) indicating that one quantity is to be divided by another

di·vi·sive /dəvī′siv/ *adj.* causing disagreement **—di·vi′sive·ly** *adv.*; **di·vi′sive·ness** *n.* [L *divisus*]

di·vi·sor /dəvī′zər/ *n.* number by which another is divided

di·vorce /dəvôrs′/ *n.* 1 legal dissolution of a marriage 2 break; distance **—v.** (**·vorced, ·vorc·ing**) 3a legally dissolve the marriage of **b** separate by divorce **c** end one's marriage with 4 out of touch with (*divorced from reality*) [L *divortium* fr. *divertere* turn away]

di·vor·cé /dəvôr′sā′, -sē′/ *n.* divorced man

di·vor·cée /dəvôr′sā′, -sē′/ *n.* (also **di′vor·cee′** /-sē′/) divorced woman

div·ot /div′ət/ *n.* piece of turf cut out, esp. by a golf stroke

di·vulge /dīvəlj′, də-/ *v.* (**·vulged, ·vulg·ing**) disclose (a secret, etc.) **—di·vul′gence** *n.* [L *divulgare* publish]

div·vy /div′ē/ *v.* (**·vied, ·vy·ing**) *Colloq.* divide (up)

Dix·ie /dik′sē/ *n.* (also **Dix·ie·land**) southern states of the US, esp. those of the Confederacy

Dix′ie·land′ *n.* 1 traditional form of jazz 2 DIXIE

Di·yar·ba·kir /dē·är′bäkēr′/ *n.* city on the Tigris River in Turkey. Pop. 381,100

diz·zy /diz′ē/ *adj.* (**·zi·er, ·zi·est**) 1a giddy **b** feeling confused 2 causing giddiness **—v.** (**·zied, ·zy·ing**) 3 make dizzy 4 bewilder **—diz′zi·ly** *adv.*; **diz′zi·ness** *n.* [OE]

DJ *abbr.* disk jockey

djel·la·ba /jəläb′ə/ *n.* (also **jel·la′ba**) loose hooded cloak (as) worn by Arab men [Ar]

Dji·bou·ti /jibōōt′ē/ *n.* 1 republic in E Africa. Capital: Djibouti. Pop. 557,000 2 capital of Djibouti. Pop. 290,000

DM *abbr.* DEUTSCHE MARK

D.M.D. *abbr.* doctor of dental medicine [L *Doctor Medicinae Dentalis*]

DNA *abbr.* deoxyribonucleic acid, the material that carries genetic information in chromosomes

DNA fin′ger·print′ing *n.* identification, esp. in a legal case, by analysis and comparison of DNA from body tissue

Dni·pro·pe·trovsk /(də)n(y)ep′rō′pətröfsk′/ *n.* city in Ukraine on the Dnieper River. Pop. 1,189,000

do¹ /dōō/ *v.* (**did, done, do·ing**) 1 perform; carry out; complete (work, etc.) 2 produce; make; provide 3 grant 4 act; behave; proceed 5 work at 6 be suitable or acceptable; suffice 7 deal with; attend to 8a traverse (a certain distance) **b** travel at a specified speed 9 *Colloq.* serve (a prison term) 10 cook completely 11 *Slang.* take (an illegal drug) **—v. aux.** 12 in questions and negative statements or commands (*do you understand? I don't smoke; don't be silly*) 13 used in place of a verb (*you know her better than I do*) 14 used for emphasis (*they did go*) 15 have to do with be concerned or connected with 16 do away with: **a** get rid of; abolish **b** kill 17 do in: *Slang.* **a** kill **b** exhaust; tire out 18 do over *Colloq.* redecorate; refurbish 19 dos and don'ts rules of behavior 20 do up: **a** fasten **b** *Colloq.* adorn; dress up 21 do without manage without; forgo **—do′a·ble** *adj.* [OE]

do² /dō/ *n. Mus.* first note of a major scale

DOA *abbr.* dead on arrival

DOB *abbr.* date of birth

Do·ber·man pin·scher /dō′bərmən pin′shər/ *n.* large dog of a smooth-coated breed [Ger, for *Dobermann* name of a breeder + *pinscher* terrier]

doc /däk/ *n. Colloq.* doctor

do·cent /dō′sənt/ *n.* informative tour guide, as at a museum

doc·ile /däs′əl, -īl′/ *adj.* submissive; easily

managed —doc'ile·ly *adv.*; do·cil'i·ty /-sil'itē/ *n.* [L *docere* teach]

dock[1] /däk/ *n.* 1 waterway for vessels alongside a pier or wharf 2 loading platform —*v.* 3 bring or come into dock 4a join (spacecraft) together in space b become joined thus [MDu *docke*]

dock[2] *n.* enclosure in a criminal court for the accused [Flemish *dok* cage]

dock[3] *v.* 1 cut short (an animal's tail) 2 take away part of (wages, supplies, etc.) [OE]

dock·et /däk'it/ *n.* 1 schedule of cases in a law court 2 agenda; schedule

dock'yard' *n.* shipyard

doc·tor /däk'tar/ *n.* 1 qualified practitioner of medicine; physician 2 person who holds a doctorate —*v. Colloq.* 3 treat medically 4 fix; mend (machinery, etc.) 5 adulterate 6 tamper with; falsify [L *docere* teach]

doc·tor·al /däk'taral/ *adj.* of or for the degree of doctor

doc·tor·ate /däk'tarat/ *n.* highest university degree

Doc'tor of Phi·los'o·phy *n.* highest advanced degree awarded in various disciplines; *abbr.* Ph.D.

doc·tri·naire /däk'traner'/ *adj.* applying theory or doctrine dogmatically [Fr, rel. to DOCTRINE]

doc·trine /däk'trin/ *n.* 1 what is taught; body of instruction 2a religious, political, etc., tenet b creed or philosophy —**doc'tri·nal** /-trīnǝl/ *adj.* [L, rel. to DOCTOR]

doc·u·dra·ma /däk'yōōdrä'mǝ/ *n.* television drama based on real events [blend of DOCU(MENTARY) + DRAMA]

doc·u·ment *n.* /däk'yǝmǝnt/ 1 written record or evidence of events, agreement, ownership, etc. —*v.* /däk'yǝment'/ 2 prove by or support with documents 3 record in a document —**doc'u·men·ta'tion** /-mǝntä'SHǝn/ *n.* [L *docere* teach]

doc·u·men·ta·ry /däk'yǝment'ǝrē/ *adj.* 1 consisting of documents 2 providing a factual record or report —*n.* (*pl.* ·ries) 3 documentary film, etc.

DOD *abbr.* Department of Defense

dod·der /däd'ǝr/ *v.* tremble or totter, esp. from age —**dod'der·ing** *adj.* [obs. dial. *dadder*]

do·dec·a·he·dron /dōdek'ǝhē'drǝn/ *n.* (*pl.* ·drons or ·dra /-drǝ/) *Geom.* solid figure with twelve faces [Gk *dōdeka* twelve, *hedra* base]

dodge /däj/ *v.* (**dodged, dodg·ing**) 1 move quickly to elude a pursuer, blow, etc. 2 evade by cunning or trickery —*n.* 3 quick movement to avoid something 4 clever trick or expedient —**dodg'er** *n.*

DODECAHEDRON

Dodg·son /däj'sǝn/, **Charles Lutwidge** see Lewis CARROLL

do·do /dō'dō/ *n.* (*pl.* ·**dos**) extinct flightless bird [Port *doudo* stupid]

doe /dō/ *n.* (*pl.* same or -s) female deer, reindeer, rabbit, etc. [OE]

DOE *abbr.* 1 Department of Energy 2 (also **d.o.e.**) depending on experience

do·er /dōō'ǝr/ *n.* 1 person who does something 2 person who takes decisive action

does /dǝz/ *v.* 3rd pers. sing. of DO[1]

does·n't /dǝz'nt/ *v. contr.* does not

doff /däf, dôf/ *v.* remove (a hat or clothes) [ME, fr. *do off*]

dog /dôg, däg/ *n.* 1 four-legged domesticated animal related to the fox and wolf 2 *Colloq.* a despicable person b person of a specified kind (*lucky dog*) 3 mechanical device for gripping —*v.* (**dogged, dog·ging**) 4 follow closely; pursue 5 go to the dogs *Slang.* be ruined [OE]

dog' days' *n. pl.* hottest period of the year

dog'-eared' *adj.* (of pages, etc.) with turned-down or worn corners

dog'-eat'-dog' *adj. Colloq.* ruthlessly competitive

dog'fight' *n.* 1 close combat between fighter aircraft 2 rough fight

dog·fish /dôg'fisн, däg'-/ *n.* (*pl.* same or -es) a kind of small shark

dog·ged /dôg'id, däg'-/ *adj.* tenacious; grimly persistent —**dog'ged·ly** *adv.*; **dog'ged·ness** *n.*

dog·ger·el /dôg'(ǝ)rǝl, däg'-/ *n.* poor or trivial verse [ME, appar. fr. DOG]

dog'gy bag' /dôg'gē, dä'-/ *n.* bag for leftovers in a restaurant, etc.

dog'house' *n.* 1 dog's shelter 2 **in the doghouse** *Slang.* in disgrace or trouble

do·gie /dō'gē/ *n.* orphan or stray calf

dog·ma /dôg'mǝ, däg'-/ *n.* 1 principle, tenet, or creed, esp. of a church or political party 2 rigid or authoritarian belief [Gk *dokein* seem; think]

dog·mat·ic /dôgmat'ik, däg·/ *adj.* asserting or imposing opinions; rigidly certain —**dog·mat'i·cal·ly** *adv.*

dog·ma·tism /dôg'mǝtiz'ǝm, däg-/ *n.* tendency to be dogmatic —**dog'ma·tist** *n.*

do'-good'er *n.* well-meaning but unrealistic or patronizing altruist or reformer

dog'pad'dle *n.* 1 casual swimming stroke with arms kept under water —*v.* (**·dled, ·dling**) 2 do the dog-paddle

dog·wood /dôg'wŏŏd, däg'-/ *n.* flowering tree or shrub

Do·ha /dō'hǝ/ *n.* capital of Qatar. Pop. 217,300

doi·ly /doi'lē/ *n.* (*pl.* ·**lies**) small lacy, sometimes paper decorative mat [*Doiley*, name of a London textile merchant]

do·ing /dōō'iNG/ *v.* 1 *pres. part.* of DO[1] —*n.* 2 action 3 effort

do'-it-your·self' *adj.* of or for a task, craft, etc., accomplishable by a nonspecialist

Dol·by /dōl'bē, dôl'-/ *n. Tdmk.* electronic noise-reduction system used esp. in audio recording [for its inventor]

dol·drums /dōl'drǝmz, dôl'-/ *n. pl.* 1 low spirits 2 period of inactivity 3 equatorial ocean region with little or no wind [perh. fr. obs. *dold* stupid, or fr. DULL]

dole /dōl/ *n.* 1 *Colloq.* unemployment benefits 2 distribution from a charity —*v.* (**doled, dol·ing**) 3 distribute sparingly [OE]

dole·ful /dōl'fǝl/ *adj.* 1 mournful; sad 2

dreary; dismal —**dole′ful·ly** adv.; **dole′ful·ness** n. [L dolor grief]

doll /däl/ n. **1** small model of a human or other figure, as a child's toy **2** Colloq. pretty or cherished woman —v. **3** (foll. by up) Colloq. dress smartly [pet form of Dorothy]

dol·lar /däl′ər/ n. chief monetary unit in the US, Canada, etc. [LGer daler fr. Ger Taler, a coin]

Doll·fuss /dôl′fŏŏs′/, **Engelbert** 1892–1934; chancellor of Austria (1932–34)

dol·lop /däl′əp/ n. shapeless lump of food, etc. [perh. fr. Scand]

dol·ly /däl′ē/ n. (pl. **·lies**) **1** child's name for a doll **2** movable platform for a motion picture camera **3** small cart for freight

dol·men /dōl′mən, dôl′-/ n. prehistoric tomb with a large flat stone laid on upright ones [Fr]

do·lo·mite /dō′ləmīt′, däl′ə-/ n. mineral or rock of calcium magnesium carbonate [for de Dolomieu, a Fr geologist]

do·lor /dō′lər/ n. Lit. sorrow; distress —**do′lor·ous** adj. [L dolor pain]

DOLPHINS

dol·phin /däl′fin, dôl′-/ n. porpoiselike sea mammal with a slender snout [Gk delphin]

dolt /dōlt/ n. stupid person —**dolt′ish** adj. [appar. fr. obs. dold stupid, rel. to DULL]

-dom suffix forming nouns denoting: **1** condition (freedom) **2** rank; domain (earldom) **3** class, fraternity, etc., of people (officialdom) [OE]

do·main /dəmān′, dō-/ n. **1** area under one rule; realm **2** sphere of control or influence [Fr domaine, rel. to L dominus lord]

dome /dōm/ n. **1** rounded (usu. hemispherical) vault forming a roof **2** any top-rounded thing —**domed** adj. [L domus house]

do·mes·tic /dəmes′tik/ adj. **1** of the home, household, or family affairs **2** of one's own country **3** (of an animal) tamed —n. **4** household servant —**dom·es′ti·cal·ly** adv. [L domus home]

do·mes·ti·cate /dəmes′tikāt′/ v. (**·cat·ed, ·cat·ing**) **1** tame (an animal) to live with humans **2** adapt or accustom to a household —**do·mes′ti·ca′tion** n. [MedL, rel. to DOMESTIC]

do·mes·tic·i·ty /dō′mestis′itē/ n. **1** being domestic **2** domestic or home life

do·mi·cile /däm′əsīl′, dō′mə-/ n. dwelling-place; residence —**do′mi·ciled′** adj. [L domus home]

dom·i·nant /däm′ənənt/ adj. **1** dominating; prevailing —n. **2** Mus. fifth note of the diatonic scale of any key —**dom′i·nance** n.; **dom′i·nant·ly** adv.

dom·i·nate /däm′ənāt′/ v. (**·nat·ed, ·nat·ing**) **1** command; control **2** be the most influential or obvious **3** (of a high place) over-

look —**dom′i·na′tion** n. [L dominari be in power]

dom·i·neer·ing /däm′ənēr′iNG/ adj. behaving arrogantly or tyrannically —**dom′i·neer′ing·ly** adv. [Fr, rel. to DOMINATE]

Do·min·go /dəmiNG′gō/, **Placido** 1941– ; Spanish operatic tenor

Dom·i·nic, St. /däm′ənik/ c. 1170–1221; Spanish priest; founder of Dominican religious order

Dom·i·ni·ca /däm′inē′kə, dəmin′ikə/ n. island republic in the E West Indies. Capital: Roseau. Pop. 71,500

Do·min·i·can Re·pub′lic /dəmin′ikən/ n. republic in the West Indies, the E part of the island of Hispaniola. Capital: Santo Domingo. Pop. 7,471,000

do·min·ion /dəmin′yən/ n. **1** sovereignty; control **2** realm; domain [L dominus lord]

dom·i·no /däm′ənō′/ n. (pl. **·noes**) **1** small oblong piece marked with 0 – 6 dots in each half **2** (pl.) game played with these **3** mask for the eyes [Fr, prob. rel. to L dominus]

Dom·i·no /däm′ənō′/, **"Fats" (Antoine)** 1928– ; US pianist, singer, and songwriter

dom′i·no the′o·ry n. (also **dom′i·no ef·fect′**) theory that one event precipitates others in causal sequence

Do·mi·tian /dəmiSH′ən/ 51–96; Roman emperor (81–96)

don¹ /dän/ n. **1** Brit. university teacher, esp. a senior member of a college at Oxford or Cambridge **2** (cap.) Spanish title of respect [Sp fr. L dominus lord]

don² v. (**donned, don·ning**) put on (clothing) [do on]

do·nate /dō′nāt′/ v. (**·nat·ed, ·nat·ing**) give (money, etc.), esp. to charity [fr. DONATION]

Don·a·tel·lo /dän′ətel′ō/ 1386–1466; Italian sculptor

do·na·tion /dōnā′SHən/ n. **1** donating or being donated **2** thing or amount donated [L donum gift]

done /dən/ adj. **1** completed **2** cooked **3** (often foll. by in) Colloq. tired out **4** be done with have or be finished with **5** done for: Colloq. a doomed; dead **b** in serious trouble [past part. of DO¹]

Do·netsk /dən(y)etsk′/ n. city in E Ukraine. Pop. 1,121,000

Don·i·zet·ti /dō′nə(d)zet′ē, dän′ə(d)-/, **Gaetano** 1797–1848; Italian composer

Don Juan /dän (h)wän′/ n. seducer of women

don·key /däNG′kē, dəNG′-, dôNG′-/ n. (pl. **·keys**) **1** domestic ass **2** Colloq. stupid person [perh. fr. Duncan]

Donne /dən/′, **John** 1572–1631; English poet and priest

don·ny·brook /dän′ēbrŏŏk′/ n. wild fight; free-for-all

do·nor /dō′nər/ n. person who donates

Don′ Riv′er /dän/ n. river in SW Russia flowing 1,200 mi. S into the Sea of Azov

don't /dōnt/ v. contr. **1** do not —n. **2** prohibition (dos and don'ts)

do·nut /dō′nət, -nət′/ n. DOUGHNUT

doo·dle /dōōd′l/ v. (**·dled, ·dling**) **1** scribble or draw, esp. absent-mindedly —n. **2**

such a scribble or drawing [orig. foolish person]

doom /dŏŏm/ n. **1a** grim fate or destiny **b** death; ruin **2** judgment; condemnation —v. **3** condemn or destine, esp. to misfortune or destruction [OE *dōm* STATUTE]

dooms·day /dŏŏmz'dā'/ n. Judgment Day

door /dôr/ n. **1a** movable barrier for closing and opening the entrance to a building, room, cupboard, etc. **b** this as representing a house, etc. **2a** entrance or exit; doorway **b** means of access [OE]

door'bell' n. bell, chime, etc., at an entrance door, rung by visitors to announce their presence

door'knob' n. knob turned to open a door

door'man' n. (pl. **·men**) person on duty at the door to an apartment house, etc.

door'mat' n. **1** mat at an entrance for wiping shoes **2** Colloq. submissive person

door'step' n. step or area in front of the outer door of a house, etc.

door'stop' n. device for keeping a door open or to prevent it from striking a wall

door'way' n. opening or access shut by a door

dope /dōp/ n. **1a** Slang. narcotic **b** drug, etc., given to a horse, athlete, etc., to improve performance **2** thick liquid used as a lubricant, etc. **3** varnish **4** Slang. stupid person **5** Slang. information —v. (**doped, dop·ing**) **6** give or add a drug to [Du: sauce]

dop·ey /dō'pē/ adj. (also **dop'y**) (**·i·er, ·i·est**) Colloq. **1** half asleep or stupefied as if by a drug **2** stupid —**dop'i·ly** adv.; **dop'i·ness** n.

Dor·ic /dôr'ik, där'-/ adj. of the simplest order of Greek architecture (see illustration at CAPITAL) [fr. *Dōris* in Greece]

dork /dôrk/ n. Slang. stupid, foolish, or awkward person —**dork'y** adj. (**·i·er, ·i·est**)

dor·mant /dôr'mənt/ adj. **1** inactive or temporarily so; sleeping **2** (of plants) alive but not growing —**dor'man·cy** n. [L *dormire* sleep]

DORMER

dor·mer /dôr'mər/ n. projecting upright window in a sloping roof [MFr, rel. to DORMITORY]

dor·mi·to·ry /dôr'mətôr'ē/ n. (pl. **·ries**) group sleeping area or building, esp. in a school or institution [L *dormire* sleep]

dor·mouse /dôr'mous/ n. (pl. **·mice**) small mouselike rodent

dor·sal /dôr'səl/ adj. of or on the back [L *dorsum* back]

Dort·mund /dôrt'mŏŏnt, -mənd/ n. city in W Germany. Pop. 599,100

do·ry /dôr'ē/ n. small flat-bottomed boat with flared sides

DOS abbr. DISK OPERATING SYSTEM

dos·age /dō'sij/ n. **1** size of a dose **2** giving of a dose

dose /dōs/ n. **1** single portion of medicine **2** brief experience of something **3** amount of radiation received —v. (**dosed, dos·ing**) **4** treat with or give doses of medicine to [Gk *dosis* gift]

Dos Pas·sos /dəs pas'əs/, John 1896–1970; US novelist

dos·sier /dôs'ē-ā', däs'-/ n. file of specific information, as on a person [Fr fr. L *dorsum* back, fr. label on file's spine]

Do·sto·ev·sky /däs'təyef'skē, -yev'-/ (also **Dostoyevsky**), Fyodor Mikhailovich 1821–81; Russian novelist

dot /dät/ n. **1a** small spot or mark **b** this as part of a letter, code, as a decimal point, etc. **2** shorter signal of the two in Morse code —v. (**dot·ted, dot·ting**) **3** mark with dot(s) **4** partly cover as with dots **5 on the dot** exactly on time [OE]

DOT abbr. Department of Transportation

dot·age /dō'tij/ n. feeble-minded senility

dot·ard /dō'tard/ n. senile person

dote /dōt/ v. (**dot·ed, dot·ing**) (foll. by *on*) be excessively fond of —**dot'ing** adj.; **dot'ing·ly** adv.

dot'-ma'trix adj. Comp. denoting a technique in which characters are formed by varying the pattern of metal pins arrayed in a matrix, then struck against an inked ribbon for transfer to paper

Dou·a·la /dŏŏ-äl'ə/ n. seaport in Cameroon. Pop. 810,000

dou·ble /dəb'əl/ adj. **1** consisting of two parts, things, levels, etc. **2** twice as much or many **3** twice the usual size, quantity, strength, etc. —adv. **4** at or to twice the amount, size, etc. **5** two together —n. **6** double quantity **7** counterpart; person who strongly resembles another **8** (pl.) game between two pairs of players —v. (**·bled, ·bling**) **9** make or become double; multiply by two **10** amount to twice as much as **11** fold or bend over on itself **12** play a twofold role **13** Colloq. **on the double** running; hurrying **14 double back** turn back in the opposite direction **15 double up: a** (cause to) bend or curl up with pain or laughter **b** share quarters, a task, etc. —**dou'bly** adv. [L *duplus*]

dou'ble a'gent n. spy working for rival interests

dou'ble-bar'reled adj. **1** (of a gun) having two barrels **2** having two aspects, elements, etc.

dou'ble-bass' /-bā'/ n. largest instrument of the violin family

dou'ble boil'er n. two-part cooking utensil, with the lower pot for boiling water

dou'ble-breast'ed /-brest'əd/ adj. (of a coat, etc.) overlapping at the front closure

dou'ble-cross' v. **1** deceive or betray (a supposed ally) —n. **2** act of doing this —**dou'ble-cross'er** n.

dou'ble-deal'ing n. **1** deceit, esp. in business —adj. **2** practicing deceit

dou'ble-deck'er /-dek'ər/ n. **1** bus having an upper and lower deck **2** Colloq. sandwich made with three pieces of bread

dou'ble-edged' adj. **1** presenting both a danger and an advantage **2** having two cutting edges

dou·ble en·ten·dre /dəb'əl äntän'drə, dōōb'(ə)läntänd'(rə)/ *n.* French. ambiguous phrase open to usu. risqué interpretation

dou'ble-joint'ed *adj.* (esp. of a person) supple enough to allow unusual bending

dou'ble stan'dard *n.* rule, treatment, etc., not impartially applied

dou·blet /dəb'lit/ *n.* 1 *Hist.* man's short close-fitting jacket 2 one of a pair of similar things [MFr, rel. to DOUBLE]

DOUBLET 1

dou'ble take' *n.* delayed reaction

dou'ble-talk' *n.* (usu. deliberately) ambiguous or misleading speech

dou·bloon /dəblōōn'/ *n.* former Spanish gold coin [Sp, rel. to DOUBLE]

doubt /dout/ *n.* 1 uncertainty; undecided state of mind 2 skepticism —*v.* 3 feel uncertain or undecided about 4 call in question 5 **no doubt** certainly; probably 6 **without doubt (or a doubt)** certainly [L *dubitare* hesitate]

doubt·ful /dout'fəl/ *adj.* 1 feeling doubt 2 causing doubt 3 unreliable —**doubt'ful·ly** *adv.*; **doubt'ful·ness** *n.*

doubt·less *adv.* certainly; probably —**doubt' less·ly** *adv.*; **doubt'less·ness** *n.*

douche /dōōsh/ *n.* 1 jet of liquid applied to part of the body for cleansing or medicinal purposes 2 implement for producing this —*v.* (**douched, douch·ing**) 3 use a douche [L, rel. to DUCT]

dough /dō/ *n.* 1 thick mixture of flour, etc., and liquid for baking 2 *Slang.* money —**dough'y** *adj.* (·i·er, ·i·est) [OE]

dough·nut /dō'nət, -nət'/ *n.* (also **do'nut**) small fried cake of sweetened dough typically ring-shaped

dough·ty /dou'tē/ *adj. Lit.* valiant [OE]

Doug·las /dəg'ləs/, **Stephen A(rnold)** 1813–61; US political leader and orator

Doug'las fir' *n.* large N American evergreen tree valued for its lumber [for botanist D. *Douglas*]

Doug·lass /dəg'ləs/, **Frederick** c. 1817–95; US abolitionist and former slave

dour /dour, dōōr/ *adj.* 1 gloomy; sullen 2 severe [ME fr. L *durus* hard]

douse /dous/ *v.* (**doused, dous·ing**) **1a** throw liquid over **b** immerse 2 extinguish (a light)

dove¹ /dəv/ *n.* 1 bird with short legs, a small head, and a large breast 2 advocate of peace [OE]

dove² /dōv/ *v. past* of DIVE

Do·ver /dō'vər/ *n.* capital of Del., in the central part. Pop. 27,630

dove·tail /dəv'tāl/ *n.* 1 mortise and tenon joint shaped like a dove's spread tail —*v.* 2 join with dovetails 3 fit together; combine neatly

DOVETAIL 1

dow·a·ger /dou'əjər/ *n.* 1 widow with a title or property from her late husband 2 dignified elderly woman [MFr, rel. to DOWER]

dow·dy /dou'dē/ *adj.* (·di·er, ·di·est) 1 (of clothes) unattractively dull 2 dressed dowdily —**dow'di·ly** *adv.*; **dow'di·ness** *n.*

dow·el /dou'əl, doul/ *n.* 1 cylindrical peg for fastening components together, for hanging clothes on, etc. —*v.* (·eled or ·elled, ·el·ing or ·el·ling) 2 fit with a dowel [MLGer]

dow·er /dou'ər, dour/ *n.* 1 widow's share for life of a husband's estate 2 dowry [L *dos* dowry]

down¹ /doun/ *adv.* 1 into or toward a lower place, esp. to the ground 2 in a lower place or position 3 to or in a place regarded as lower, esp. southward 4 in or into a low or weaker position or condition 5 (of a computer system) not operating 6 from an earlier to a later time 7 to a finer or thinner consistency or smaller amount or size 8 lower in value or price 9 into a more settled state 10 in writing or recorded form 11 paid or done as a deposit or part (*$10 down*) —*prep.* 12 downward along, through, or into 13 from the top to the bottom of 14 farther along —*adj.* 15 directed downward —*v.* 16 knock or bring down 17 swallow —*n.* 18 act of putting down 19 setback; misfortune 20 *Football.* one of a series of plays 21 **down and out** destitute 22 **down with** expressing rejection of a specified person or thing [OE *dun* hill]

down² *n.* 1 fine soft feathers or hairs 2 fluffy substance [ON]

down³ *n.* (often *pl.*) open rolling land [OE]

down'beat' *n.* 1 *Mus.* accented beat, usu. the first of the bar —*adj.* 2 pessimistic; gloomy

down'cast' *adj.* 1 dejected 2 (of eyes) looking downwards

Down' East' *n.* nickname for: 1 New England 2 specifically, Maine, esp. its coast 3 Canadian maritime provinces

down·er /dou'nər/ *n. Slang.* 1 depressant or tranquilizing drug 2 depressing experience; failure

down'fall' *n.* 1 fall from prosperity or power 2 cause of this

down'grade' *v.* (·grad·ed, ·grad·ing) reduce in rank or status

down·heart·ed /dounhär'tid/ *adj.* dejected —**down'heart'ed·ly** *adv.*; **down'heart'ed·ness** *n.*

down'hill' *adv.* 1 toward the bottom of a hill —*adj.* 2 sloping down; declining 3 **go downhill** *Colloq.* deteriorate

down′ pay′ment *n.* initial partial payment

down′pour′ *n.* heavy fall of rain

down′right′ *adj.* 1 utter 2 plain; straightforward —*adv.* 3 thoroughly

down′size′ *v.* (**·sized, ·siz·ing**) reduce in size (esp. of personnel)

down′stage′ *adj. & adv.* nearer the front of a theater stage

down′stairs′ *adv.* 1 down the stairs 2 to or on a lower floor —*adj.* 3 situated downstairs 4 lower floor

down′state′ *adv. & adj.* in, to, or from a more southern part of a US state

down′stream′ *adv. & adj.* in the direction in which a stream, etc., flows

Down′ syn′drome /doun/ *n.* (also **Down's′ syn′drome**) congenital disorder with mental retardation and physical abnormalities [for John *Down*, British physician]

down′-to-earth′ *adj.* practical; realistic

down′town′ *adj.* 1 of the central part of a town or city —*n.* 2 downtown area —*adv.* 3 in or into this area

down-trod-den /doun′träd′n/ *adj.* oppressed

down′turn′ *n.* decline, esp. economically

down·ward /doun′word/ *adv.* (also **down′wards**) 1 toward what is lower, inferior, etc. —*adj.* 2 moving or extending downward

down′y *adj.* (**·i·er, ·i·est**) 1 of, like, or covered with down 2 soft and fluffy

dow·ry /dou′rē/ *n.* (*pl.* **·ries**) property or money brought by a bride to her husband [AngFr fr. Fr *douaire* DOWER]

dowse /douz/ *v.* (**dowsed, dows·ing**) search for underground water, etc., using a rod that dips when over the right spot —**dows′er** *n.*

dox·ol·o·gy /däksäl′əjē/ *n.* (*pl.* **·gies**) liturgical hymn of praise to God —**dox·o·log′i·cal** /-äläj′ikal/ *adj.* [Gk *doxa* glory]

Doyle /doil/, **(Sir) Arthur Conan** 1859–1930; Scottish novelist

doz. *abbr.* dozen

doze /dōz/ *v.* (**dozed, doz·ing**) 1 sleep lightly; be half asleep —*n.* 2 short light sleep 3 **doze off** fall lightly asleep

doz·en /dəz′ən/ *n.* 1 twelve 2 set of twelve 3 *Colloq.* (*pl.*) very many [L *duodecim* twelve]

DP *abbr.* 1 data processing 2 displaced person

DPT *abbr.* (vaccination against) diphtheria, pertussis, and tetanus

Dr. *abbr.* Doctor

drab /drab/ *adj.* (**drab·ber, drab·best**) 1 dull; uninteresting 2 of a dull brownish color —**drab′ly** *adv.*; **drab′ness** *n.* [MFr *drap* cloth]

drach·ma /drak′mə/ *n.* (*pl.* **·mas**) 1 chief monetary unit of Greece 2 silver coin of ancient Greece [Gk *drachmē*]

Dra·co /drā′kō/ 7th cent. B.C.; Athenian lawgiver

Dra·co·ni·an /drəkō′nēən/ *adj.* very harsh; cruel [DRACO]

draft /draft/ *n.* 1 preliminary written version of a speech, document, etc. 2a written order for payment by a bank **b** drawing of money by this 3 conscription 4 current of air 5 pulling; traction 6 depth of water needed to float a vessel 7a single act of drinking or inhaling **b** amount drunk thus —*v.* 8 prepare a draft of (a document, etc.) 9 select for a special duty or purpose 10 conscript [phonetic spelling of *draught*, rel. to DRAW]

draft′ beer′ *n.* beer drawn from a barrel or cask

draft·ee /draftē′/ *n.* person drafted for military service

drafts·man /draf(t)′smən/ *n.* (*pl.* **·men** /-mən/) person who makes drawings, plans, or sketches —**drafts′man·ship** *n.*

draft′y *adj.* (**·i·er, ·i·est**) (of a room, etc.) letting in sharp currents of air —**draft′i·ness** *n.*

drag /drag/ *v.* (**dragged, drag·ging**) 1 pull along with effort 2 trail or allow to trail along the ground 3 (of time, a meeting, etc.) pass slowly or tediously 4 search the bottom of (a river, etc.) with grapnels, nets, etc. 5 *Colloq.* take along (an esp. unwilling person) 6 draw on (a cigarette, etc.) —*n.* 7 obstruction; retarding force 8 *Colloq.* tiresome person, duty, etc. 9 *Slang.* inhalation 10 *Slang.* women's clothes worn by men 11 (foll. by *out* or *on*) protract [ME, perh. fr. ON]

drag′net′ *n.* 1 net drawn through a river or across the ground to trap fish or game 2 systematic hunt for criminals, etc.

drag·on /drag′ən/ *n.* mythical monster, usu. depicted as a fire-breathing winged reptile [Gk: serpent]

drag·on·fly′ *n.* (*pl.* **·flies**) insect with a long body and two pairs of transparent, veined wings

dra·goon /drəgōōn′/ *n.* 1 cavalryman —*v.* 2 (foll. by *into*) coerce or bully [Fr *dragon*, rel. to DRAGON]

drag′ race′ *n.* car race on a straight course from a standing start —**drag′ rac′er, drag′ rac′ing** *n.*

drain /drān/ *v.* 1 draw off liquid from 2 draw off (liquid) 3 flow or trickle away 4 dry or become dry as liquid flows away 5 exhaust 6 drink all of; empty —*n.* 7a channel or pipe carrying off liquid, sewage, etc. **b** tube for drawing off discharge, etc. 8 constant outflow or expenditure 9 **down the drain** *Colloq.* lost; wasted [OE, rel. to DRY]

drain·age /drā′nij/ *n.* 1 draining 2 system of drains 3 what is drained off

drain′pipe′ *n.* pipe for carrying off water, etc.

drake /drāk/ *n.* male duck

Drake /drāk/, **(Sir) Francis** c. 1540–96; English navigator and explorer

dram /dram/ *n.* 1 small drink of liquor 2 measure of weight (apothecaries' 1/8 ounce; avoirdupois 1/16 ounce) [L fr. Gk *drachmē* handful]

dra·ma /dräm′ə, dram′ə/ *n.* 1 play for stage or broadcasting 2 art of writing, acting, or presenting plays 3 dramatic event or quality [L fr. Gk: action]

Dram·a·mine /dram′əmēn/ *n. Tdmk.* drug for motion sickness

dra·mat·ic /drəmat′ik/ *adj.* 1 pertaining to drama 2 sudden and exciting or unexpected 3 vividly striking 4 (of a gesture, etc.) theatrical —**dra·mat′i·cal·ly** *adv.* [Gk, rel. to DRAMA]

dra·mat·ics /drəmat′iks/ *n. pl.* (often treated as *sing.*) 1 performance of plays 2 exaggerated behavior

dra·ma·tist /dram'ətist, dräm'-/ *n.* writer of dramas

dram·a·tize /dram'ətīz, dräm'-/ *v.* (·tized, ·tiz·ing) 1 turn (a novel, etc.) into a play 2 make a dramatic scene of 3 act, react, etc., with exaggeration or for notice **—dra'ma·ti·za'tion** *n.*

drank /draNGk/ *v. past of* DRINK

drape /drāp/ *v.* (**draped, drap·ing**) 1 hang or cover loosely; adorn with cloth, etc. 2 arrange in folds **—n.** 3 (*pl.*) curtains [MFr fr. L *drappus* cloth]

drap·er·y /drā'p(ə)rē/ *n.* (*pl.* **·ies**) clothing or hangings arranged in folds

dras·tic /dras'tik/ *adj.* extreme or harsh in effect; severe **—dras'ti·cal·ly** *adv.* [Gk *drastikos* active]

draught /draft/ *n. & v.* esp. *Brit.* var. of DRAFT

draw /drô/ *v.* (**drew, drawn, draw·ing**) 1 pull or cause to move toward or after one 2 pull (a thing) up, over, or across 3 pull open or shut 4 attract; bring; take in 5 inhale from, as a pipe, etc. 6 take out; remove 7 obtain or take from a source 8a make (a line, picture, etc.) b represent (something) in a picture, etc. 9 finish (a contest or game) with equal scores 10 infer (a conclusion) 11 elicit; evoke 12 bring out or extract (liquid) 13 (of a chimney, etc.) promote or allow a draft 14 (foll. by *on*) call on (a person or a person's skill, etc.) 15 write out or compose (a check, contract, etc.) 16 formulate or perceive (a comparison or distinction) **—n.** 17 act of drawing 18 attraction 19 raffle, lottery, etc. 20 game ending in a tie 21 **draw out:** a prolong b elicit 22 **draw up:** a draft (a document, etc.) b come to a halt [OE]

draw'back' *n.* disadvantage

draw'bridge' *n.* bridge that can be drawn up or moved aside

draw·er /drô'ər/ *n.* 1 person or thing that draws 2 /drôr/ lidless boxlike storage compartment, sliding in and out of a desk, dresser, etc. 3 (*pl.* **·ers** /drôrz/) underpants

draw·ing /drô'iNG/ *n.* 1 art of representing by line with a pencil, etc. 2 picture made thus

draw'ing card' *n.* someone or something that draws patrons; attraction

draw'ing room' *n. Old-fash.* room in a private house for receiving guests [earlier *withdrawing room*]

drawl /drôl/ *v.* 1 speak with drawn-out vowel sounds **—n.** 2 drawling utterance [LGer or Du *dralen* linger]

drawn /drôn/ *v.* 1 *past part.* of DRAW **—adj.** 2 looking strained and tense

draw'string' *n.* string or cord threaded through a waistband, bag opening, etc., for pulling it tighter or shut

dray /drā/ *n.* low cart without sides for heavy loads [rel. to DRAW]

dread /dred/ *v.* 1 fear greatly, esp. in advance **—n.** 2 great fear or apprehension **—adj.** 3 dreaded [OE]

dread'ful /dred'fəl/ *adj.* 1 much feared 2 *Colloq.* very bad **—dread'ful·ly** *adv.*

dread·locks /dred'läks/ *n. pl.* hair style with long, thin braids or twisted locks

dream /drēm/ *n.* 1 scenes or feelings in the mind of a sleeping person 2 daydream or fantasy 3 ideal; aspiration 4 beautiful or ideal person or thing **—v.** (**dreamed or dreamt**

/dremt/, **dream·ing**) 5 experience a dream 6 imagine as in a dream 7 (with *neg.*) consider possible (*would not dream of it*) 8 unrealistic 9 **dream up** imagine; invent 10 like a dream *Colloq.* easily; effortlessly **—dream'er** *n.* [OE: joy]

dream'land' *n.* ideal or imaginary land

dream'y *adj.* (**·i·er, ·i·est**) 1 given to daydreaming or fantasy 2 dreamlike; vague 3 *Colloq.* delightful **—dream'i·ly** *adv.*; **dream'i·ness** *n.*

drear·y /drēr'ē/ *adj.* (**·i·er, ·i·est**) dismal; dull; gloomy **—drear'i·ly** *adv.*; **drear'i·ness** *n.* [OE]

dredge¹ /drej/ *n.* 1 apparatus used to scoop from a river or sea bed **—v.** (**dredged, dredg·ing**) 2 bring (up) or search (for) with a dredge 3 clean with or use a dredge

dredge² *v.* (**dredged, dredg·ing**) sprinkle with flour, sugar, etc. [ME, perh. fr. Fr: sweetmeat]

dregs /dregz/ *n. pl.* 1 sediment; grounds 2 worthless part [ON]

Drei·ser /drī'zər/, **Theodore** 1871–1945; US novelist

drench /drenCH/ *v.* wet thoroughly; soak [OE]

Dres·den /drez'dən/ *n.* city in SE Germany. Pop. 490,600

dress /dres/ *v.* 1a put clothes on b have and wear clothes 2 arrange or adorn (hair, a store window, etc.) 3 treat (a wound) esp. with a dressing 4 prepare (food) for cooking or eating 5 finish the surface of (fabric, leather, stone, etc.) 6 align (troops) **—n.** 7 woman's garment of a bodice and skirt 8 clothing, esp. a whole outfit **—adj.** 9 pertaining to dresses 10 pertaining to formal clothes 11 **dress down:** a reprimand or scold b dress informally 12 **dress up:** a put on special clothes b make more attractive or interesting [AngFr *dresser,* ult. rel. to DIRECT]

dres·sage /dresäZH', drə-/ *n.* training of a horse in obedience and deportment [Fr]

dress' cir'cle *n.* lowest tier above the orchestra in a theater

dress'er *n.* 1 chest of drawers for clothes 2 person who dresses in a specified way 3 person employed to dress actors, etc. [AngFr *dresser* prepare]

dress'ing *n.* 1 putting clothes on 2a sauce for salads b stuffing for cooked poultry, etc. 3 bandage, ointment, etc., for a wound

dress'ing-down' *n. Colloq.* scolding

dress'ing gown' *n.* loose robe worn when one is not fully dressed

dress' re·hears'al *n.* final rehearsal in full costume

dress'y *adj.* (**·i·er, ·i·est**) (of clothes or a person) smart; elegant **—dress'i·ness** *n.*

drew /drōō/ *v. past of* DRAW

Drey·fus /drī'fəs/, **Alfred** 1859–1935; French army officer falsely accused of treason

drib·ble /drib'əl/ *v.* (**·bled, ·bling**) 1 allow saliva to flow from the mouth 2 flow in drops 3 *Sports.* move (a ball) with slight touches or taps **—n.** 4 act of dribbling 5 dribbling flow [obs. *drib* DRIP]

dribs' and drabs' /dribz, drabz/ *n. pl. Colloq.* small scattered amounts

dried /drīd/ v. past and past part. of DRY

dri·er[1] /drī′ər/ adj. comp. of DRY

dri·er[2] n. see DRYER

dri·est /drī′əst/ adj. superl. of DRY

drift /drift/ n. 1a slow movement or variation b this caused by a current 2 perceived intent or meaning of what is said, etc. 3 mass of wind-blown snow, etc. 4 deviation of a ship, aircraft, etc., from its course —v. 5 be carried by or as if by a current 6 progress without plan 7 pile or be piled into drifts [OE *drifen* drive]

drift′er n. aimless person

drift′wood′ n. wood afloat or washed ashore

drill[1] /dril/ n. 1 tool or machine for boring holes 2 military marching 3 routine procedure in an emergency 4 thorough training, esp. by repetition —v. 5a make a hole in or through with a drill b make (a hole) with a drill 6 train or be trained by drill [Du]

drill[2] n. 1 machine for making furrows, sowing, and covering seed 2 small furrow 3 row of seeds sown by a drill —v. 4 plant in drills

drill[3] n. coarse twilled cotton or linen fabric [L *trilix* having three threads]

drill′press′ n. machine tool for drilling or boring

dri·ly /drī′lē/ adv. (also **dry′ly**) in a dry manner

drink /driNGk/ v. (**drank, drunk, drink·ing**) 1a swallow (liquid) b swallow the contents of (a vessel) 2 take alcohol, esp. to excess —n. 3 liquid for drinking 4a alcoholic liquor b sip, glass, etc., of this c excessive use of alcohol 5 drink in listen eagerly to 6 drink to toast (a person) —**drink′a·ble** adj.; **drink′er** n. [OE]

drip /drip/ v. (**dripped, drip·ping**) 1 fall or let fall in drops, drip continually 2 be so wet as to shed drops —n. 3a liquid falling in drops b sound of dripping 4 Colloq. dull or ineffectual person [OE]

drip′-dry′ v. (**-dried, -dry·ing**) 1 dry or leave to dry with no need for ironing —adj. 2 able to be drip-dried

drive /drīv/ v. (**drove, driv·en, driv·ing**) 1 urge forward, esp. forcibly 2a compel b force into a specified state c urge to overwork 3a operate and direct (a vehicle) b convey or be conveyed in a vehicle c be competent to drive 4 (of wind, etc.) carry along, propel, esp. rapidly 5 force (a screw, nail, etc.) into place 6 (of power) operate (machinery) 7 hit a ball to make it go fast or a great distance —n. 8 journey or excursion in a vehicle 9a route b driveway 10a motivation and energy b inner urge (*sex drive*) 11 organized effort 12 transmission of power to machinery, wheels, etc. 13 drive at intend; mean 14 drive home effect or conclude forcibly [OE]

drive′-in′ adj. 1 (of a bank, movie theater, etc.) used while sitting in one's car —n. 2 such a site

driv·el /driv′əl/ n. 1 silly talk; nonsense —v. (**-eled** or **-elled, -el·ing** or **-el·ling**) 2 talk drivel [OE]

driv·en /driv′ən/ v. 1 past part. of DRIVE —adj. 2 compelled; inspired

driv·er /drī′vər/ n. 1 person who drives a vehicle 2 golf club for driving long shots from a tee

drive′way′ n. path for vehicles from a street to a building or house

driz·zle /driz′əl/ n. 1 very fine rain —v. (**-zled, -zling**) 2 (cause to) fall in very fine drops —**driz′zly** adj. [perh. fr. OE *drēosan* fall]

droll /drōl/ adj. quaintly amusing; odd —**droll′er·y** /-erē/ n. (pl. **-ies**); **droll′ness** n.; **droll′y** adv. [MFr fr. MDu]

drom·e·dar·y /dräm′ əder′ē/ n. (pl. **-ies**) one-humped (esp. Arabian) camel bred for riding [Gk *dromas -ados* runner]

drone /drōn/ n. 1 nonworking male of the honeybee 2 idler 3 deep humming sound 4 monotonous speaking tone —v. (**droned, dron·ing**) 5 make a deep humming sound 6 speak or utter monotonously [OE]

drool /drool/ v. 1 slobber; dribble 2 admire extravagantly [fr. DRIVEL]

droop /droop/ v. 1 sag; hang down; flag 2 weary visibly —n. 3 drooping —**droop′y** adj. [ON, rel. to DROP]

drop /dräp/ n. 1a globule of liquid b very small amount of liquid 2a abrupt slope b degree of this c act of dropping d fall in prices, temperature, etc. e deterioration 3 globular gemstone, piece of candy, etc. 4 curtain or scenery let down on to a stage 5 (pl.) medicine used in drops —v. (**dropped, drop·ping**) 6 fall or let fall in drops; shed 7 let go 8a sink from exhaustion or injury b die 9a (cause to) cease or lapse; abandon b Colloq. cease to associate with or discuss 10 set down; deposit 11 utter casually 12 send casually 13a lower (*voice dropped*) b (of a person) jump down lightly 14 omit (a letter) in speech (*drop one's h's*) 15 lose (a game, point, etc.) 16 dismiss or omit 17 mail or ship 18 at the drop of a hat promptly; with little provocation 19 drop in (or by) Colloq. visit casually 20 drop off: a fall asleep b drop (a passenger) 21 drop out Colloq. cease to participate —**drop′let** n. [OE]

drop′-out′ n. person who has withdrawn from conventional society, school, etc.

drop·per /dräp′ər/ n. device for dispensing liquid in drops

drop·pings /dräp′iNGz/ n. pl. dung of animals

drop·sy /dräp′sē/ n. Old-fash. edema —**drop′si·cal** /-səkəl/ adj. [L fr. Gk *hydrōps* fr. *hydrōr* water]

dross /dräs, drôs/ n. 1 rubbish 2 scum from melted metals [OE]

drought /drout/ n. prolonged absence of rain [OE]

drove[1] /drōv/ v. past of DRIVE

drove[2] n. 1 (pl.) a moving crowd b great number 2 herd or flock driven or moving together —**drov′er** n. [OE, rel. to DRIVE]

drown /droun/ v. 1 suffocate by submersion in liquid 2 submerge; flood; drench 3 overpower (sound) with louder sound [prob. OE]

drowse /drouz/ v. (**drowsed, drows·ing**) 1 be lightly asleep —n. 2 nap [OE]

drows·y /drou′zē/ adj. (**-i·er, -i·est**) sleepy; almost asleep —**drows′i·ly** adv.; **drows′i·ness** n. [OE]

drub /drəb/ v. (**drubbed, drub·bing**) [1]

beat; thrash 2 defeat thoroughly —**drub′ bing** *n.* [Ar *darb* blow]

drudge /drəj′/ *n.* **1** person who does dull, laborious, or menial work —*v.* (**drudged, drudg·ing**) **2** work laboriously; toil —**drudg′er·y** *n.*

drug /drəg′/ *n.* **1** medicinal substance **2** (esp. addictive) narcotic, hallucinogen, or stimulant —*v.* (**drugged, drug·ging**) **3** add a drug to (food or drink) **4a** give a drug to b stupefy [MFr]

drug′gist *n.* pharmacist [rel. to DRUG]

drug′store′ *n.* retail store for pharmaceuticals and other items

Dru·id /drōō′id/ *n.* adherent of an ancient Celtic religion —**Dru·id′ic** *adj.*; **Dru′id·ism** *n.* [L fr. Celt]

drum /drəm/ *n.* **1** hollow cylindrical percussion instrument covered at one end or both **2** percussion section **3** repetitive sound made by a drum **4** thing resembling a drum, esp. a metal container —*v.* (**drummed, drum·ming**) **5** play a drum **6** beat or tap continuously with the fingers, etc. **7 drum into** drive (a lesson or facts) into (a person) by persistence **8 drum out** expel for wrongdoing **9 drum up** summon or get by vigorous effort —**drum′mer** *n.* [LGer]

drum′ ma′jor *n.* leader of a marching band

drum′ ma′jor·ette′ *n.* female baton-twirling member of a parading group

drum′stick′ *n.* **1** stick for beating drums **2** lower leg of a dressed fowl

drunk /drəNGk′/ *adj.* **1** lacking control from drinking alcohol **2** overcome with joy, success, power, etc. —*n.* **3** drunkard [*past part.* of DRINK]

drunk·ard /drəNG′kərd/ *n.* person who is habitually drunk

drunk·en /drəNG′kən/ *adj.* **1** DRUNK, 1 **2** caused by or involving drunkenness —**drunk′en·ly** *adv.*; **drunk′en·ness** *n.*

drupe /drōōp/ *n.* fleshy stone fruit, e.g., the olive and plum [L fr. Gk]

dry /drī/ *adj.* (**dri·er, dri·est**) **1** free from moisture, esp.: a with moisture having evaporated, drained away, etc. b (of eyes) free from tears c (of a climate, etc.) with relatively little rain **2** (of wine) not sweet **3a** plain; unelaborated (*dry facts*) b uninteresting **4** (of humor) subtle; understated **5** prohibiting the sale of alcohol —*v.* (**dried, dry·ing**) **6** make or become dry **7 dry out: a** make or become fully dry **b** treat or be treated for alcoholism **8 dry up: a** make or become utterly dry **b** *Colloq.* cease talking **c** become unproductive **d** (of supplies) run out —**dry′ly, dri′ly** *adv.*; **dry′ness** *n.* [OE]

dry·ad /drī′ad′/ *n.* wood nymph [Gk *drys* tree]

dry′ cell′ *n.* electric battery with dry electrolyte

dry′-clean′ *v.* clean (clothes, etc.) using solvents and no water —**dry′-clean′er, dry′-clean′ing** *n.*

Dry·den /drīd′n/, **John** 1631–1700; English poet

dry′ dock′ *n.* dock that can be pumped dry for building or repairing ships

dry′er *n.* device or substance for drying or accelerating drying

dry′ goods′ *n. pl.* textiles

dry′ ice′ *n.* carbon dioxide frozen solid for use as a refrigerant

dry′ rot′ *n.* decay in wood; fungi causing this

dry′ run′ *n. Colloq.* rehearsal

DST *abbr.* daylight saving(s) time

dt′s or **D.T.′s** *abbr. Slang.* delirium tremens

du·al /d(y)ōō′əl/ *adj.* **1** in two parts; twofold **2** double —**du·al′i·ty** /-al′itē/ *n.* [L *duo* two]

dub¹ /dəb′/ *v.* (**dubbed, dub·bing**) **1** make (a person) a knight by touching his shoulders with a sword **2** give a (person) a name, nickname, etc. —**dub′ber** *n.* [OE]

dub² *v.* **1** provide (a film, etc.) with an, esp. translated, soundtrack **2** add (sound effects or music) to a film or broadcast —**dub′ber** *n.* [abbr. of DOUBLE]

Du·bai /dōōbī′/ *n.* city in United Arab Emirates. Pop. 585,200

Dub·ček /dōōb′CHek′/, **Alexander** 1921–92; political leader of the former Czechoslovakia

du·bi·e·ty /d(y)ōōbī′ətē/ *n.* doubt [L, rel. to DUBIOUS]

du·bi·ous /d(y)ōō′bēəs/ *adj.* **1** hesitating; doubtful **2** questionable; suspicious **3** unreliable —**du′bi·ous·ly** *adv.*; **du′bi·ous·ness** *n.* [L *dubium* doubt]

Dub·lin /dəb′lin/ *n.* capital of the Republic of Ireland. Pop. 477,700 —**Dub′lin·er** *n. & adj.*

Du Bois /d(y)ōō bois′/, **W(illiam) E(dward) B(urghardt)** 1868–1963; US sociologist, writer, and educator

Du·buque /dəbyōōk′/ *n.* city in Iowa. Pop. 57,546

du·cal /d(y)ōō′kəl/ *adj.* of or like a duke [MFr fr. LL, rel. to DUKE]

duc·at /dək′ət/ *n.* **1** former gold coin of Europe **2** *Slang.* ticket to a performance [MedL *ducatus* DUCHY]

Du·champ /dy SHäN′/, **Marcel** 1887–1968; French-born US painter and sculptor

duch·ess /dəCH′is/ *n.* **1** duke's wife or widow **2** woman holding the title of a duchy [OFr, rel. to DUKE]

duch·y /dəCH′ē/ *n.* (*pl.* **-ies**) territory of a duke or duchess [MedL *ducatus*, rel. to DUKE]

duck¹ /dək′/ *n.* (*pl.* same or **-s**) **1a** swimming bird, esp. the domesticated mallard or wild duck **b** its flesh as food —*v.* **2** bend down, esp. to avoid being seen or hit **3** dip one's own or another person's head briefly under water **4** *Colloq.* dodge (a task, etc.) [OE]

duck² *n.* **1** strong linen or cotton fabric **2** (*pl.*) trousers made of this [Du]

duck′ling *n.* young duck

duck′pins′ *n. pl.* (*treated as sing.*) game similar to bowling played with small broad pins and a smaller ball [fr. the shape of the pins]

duck·y /dək′ē/ *adj.* (**-i·er, -i·est**) *Slang.* marvelous; acceptable

duct /dəkt/ *n.* channel or tube for conveying a fluid, a cable, etc. [L *ductus* fr. *ducere* lead]

duc·tile /dək′təl, -tīl′/ *adj.* **1** (of metal) capable of being drawn into wire; pliable **2** easily molded —**duc·til′i·ty** /-til′itē/ *n.* [L, rel. to DUCT]

dud /dəd′/ *n. Colloq.* **1** bomb, etc., that fails to explode **2** failure; flop

dude /dōōd/ *n.* **1** *Slang.* male person **2** dandy **3** city-dweller staying on a ranch

duds /dədz/ *n. pl. Colloq.* clothes

due /d(y)ōō/ *adj.* **1** owing or payable **2** merited; appropriate **3** deserved **4** expected or scheduled at a certain time **5** proper —*n.* **6** what one owes or is owed **7** (*pl.*) fee or amount payable —*adv.* **8** (of a direction) exactly; directly **9 due to** because of [MFr fr. L *debere* owe]

du·el /d(y)ōō′əl/ *n.* **1** armed contest between two people, usu. to the death **2** any contest between two —*v.* **·eled** or **·elled, ·el·ing** or **·el·ling** **3** fight a duel —**du′el·ist** or **du′el·list** *n.* [L *duellum,* early form of *bellum* war]

due′ pro′cess (of law′) *n. Law.* procedures to ensure individual rights and justice

du·et /d(y)ōō·et′/ *n.* musical composition for two performers [L *duo* two]

duf·fer /dəf′ər/ *n. Colloq.* incompetent or unskilled person, esp. at golf

duf′fle bag′ /dəf′əl/ *n.* usu. cylindrical bag for personal items, clothing, etc.

Du·fy /dyfē′/, **Raoul** 1877–1953; French painter

dug /dəg/ *v.* past and past part. of DIG

dug·out *n.* **1** ground shelter, esp. for troops, or at a baseball field **2** canoe made from a tree trunk

DUI *abbr.* driving under the influence (of alcohol or drugs)

Duis·burg /d(y)ōōs′bŏŏrk/, -bərg/ *n.* river port at the junction of the Rhine and Ruhr rivers in Germany. Pop. 535,400

duke /d(y)ōōk/ *n.* **1** person holding a hereditary title of the nobility **2** prince ruling a duchy —**duke′dom** *n.* [L *dux* leader]

dul·cet /dəl′sit/ *adj.* sweet-sounding [L *dulcis* sweet]

dul·ci·mer /dəl′səmər/ *n.* metal stringed instrument played by plucking or striking with hammers [L *dulce melos* sweet song]

dull /dəl′/ *adj.* **1** tedious; not interesting **2** (of color, light, sound, etc.) not bright, vivid, or clear **3** (of a pain) not acute **4** slow-witted; stupid **5** not sharp; blunt —*v.* **6** make or become dull —**dull′ness** *n.*; **dull′y** *adv.* [OE]

dull·ard /dəl′ərd/ *n.* stupid person

Dul·les /dəl′əs/, **John Foster** 1888–1959; US secretary of state (1953–59)

Du·luth /dəlōōTH′/ *n.* city in Minn. Pop. 85,493

du·ly /d(y)ōō′lē/ *adv.* **1** in due time or manner **2** rightly; properly

Du·mas /d(y)ōōmä′/ French novelists: **1** Alexandre (called "**Dumas père**") 1802–70; his son: **2** Alexandre (called "**Dumas fils**") 1824–95

Du Mau·ri·er /d(y)ə môr′ē-ā′, -mär′-/ **1** George Louis Palmella Busson 1834–96; French-born English illustrator and novelist; his granddaughter: **2** (**Dame**) **Daphne** 1907–89; English novelist

dumb /dəm′/ *adj.* **1** unable to speak; mute **2** silenced by surprise, shyness, etc. **3** *Colloq.* stupid; ignorant [OE]

dumb′bell′ *n.* **1** short bar with a weight at each end, for muscle-building, etc. **2** *Slang.* stupid person

dumb·found /dəm′found′/ *v.* (also **dum′found′**) make speechless with surprise [fr. DUMB + (CON)FOUND]

dumb′wait′er *n.* hand-operated elevator between floors of a house, etc.

dum-dum /dəm′dəm′/ *n.* soft-nosed bullet that expands on impact [*Dum-Dum* in India]

dum·my /dəm′ē/ *n.* (*pl.* **·mies**) **1** a model of a human figure, esp. as used to display clothes **b** such a model used by a ventriloquist **2** imitation or stand-in object **3** *Colloq.* stupid person **4** *Bridge.* partner of the declarer, whose cards are exposed and played by the declarer —*adj.* **5** sham; imitation [fr. DUMB]

dump /dəmp/ *n.* **1** place for depositing rubbish **2** *Colloq.* shabby or dreary place **3** temporary store of ammunition, etc. —*v.* **4** put down firmly or clumsily **5** deposit as rubbish **6** *Colloq.* abandon or get rid of **7** sell (excess goods) to a foreign market at a low price **8 dump on** abuse or exploit

dump·ling /dəm′pliNG/ *n.* **1** ball of boiled or steamed dough, usu. served with stew, soup, etc. **2** dessert of usu. baked dough filled with fruit

dumps *n. pl. Colloq.* low spirits [LGer or Du, prob. rel. to DAMP]

Dump·ster /dəmp′stər/ *n. Tdmk.* trash receptacle for community or commercial use, usu. emptied by truck

dump′y *adj.* (**·i·er, ·i·est**) short and stout

dun[1] /dən/ *adj.* **1** grayish-brown —*n.* **2** dun color [OE]

dun[2] *v.* (**dunned, dun·ning**) **1** make persistent demands on a debtor for payment —*n.* **2** such a demand

Dun·can /dəNG′kən/, **Isadora** 1878–1927; US dancer

dunce /dəns/ *n.* stupid or ignorant person [DUNS SCOTUS]

Dun·dee /dən′dē′/ *n.* seaport on the Firth of Tay in Scotland, United Kingdom. Pop. 174,300

dune /d(y)ōōn/ *n.* bank of sand formed by the wind [MDu, rel. to DOWN[3]]

dung /dəNG/ *n.* excrement of animals; manure [OE]

dun·ga·ree /dəNG′gərē′/ *n.* **1** coarse cotton cloth **2** (*pl.*) overalls or trousers of this [Hindi]

dun·geon /dən′jən/ *n.* underground prison cell [MFr *donjon* keep of a castle; ult. fr. L *dominus* lord]

dunk /dəNGk/ *v.* **1** dip (food) into liquid before eating **2** immerse [Ger *tunken* dip]

Duns Sco·tus /dən′skōt′əs/, **John** c. 1265–1308; Scottish theologian

du·o /d(y)ōō′ō/ *n.* (*pl.* **·os**) **1** pair of performers **2** duet [It fr. L: two]

du·o·de·num /d(y)ōō′ədē′nəm, d(y)ōō-äd′n-əm/ *n.* (*pl.* **·nums**) first part of the small intestine below the stomach —**du′o·de′nal** *adj.* [L *duodeni* twelve, ref. to its length as twelve fingers' breadth]

dupe /d(y)ōōp/ *n.* **1** victim of deception —*v.* (**duped, dup·ing**) **2** deceive; trick [Fr, ult. fr. L *upupa* hoopoe, a bird considered stupid]

du·ple /d(y)ōō′pəl/ *adj.* of two parts [L *duplus* double]

du·plex /d(y)ōō′pleks/ *n.* **1** two-floor apartment **2** house divided for two families [L: double]

du·pli·cate *adj.* /d(y)ōō′plikət/ **1** identical **2a** having two identical parts **b** doubled —*n.* /-kət/ **3** identical thing, esp. a copy —*v.*

/-kāt/ (·cat·ed, ·cat·ing) **4** make or be an exact copy of **5** repeat, esp. unnecessarily —**du'pli·ca'tion** /-kā'sHən/, **du'pli·ca'tor** *n.* [L, rel. to DUPLEX]

du·plic·i·ty /d(y)ŏ͝oplis'itē/ *n.* deceitfulness —**du·plic'i·tous** *adj.* [L, rel. to DUPLEX]

du Pont /dŏo͞pänt'/, **Eleuthère I.** 1771–1834; French-born US industrialist

du·ra·ble /d(y)ŏor'əbəl/ *adj.* lasting; hard-wearing; tough —**du'ra·bil'i·ty** *n.* [L *durus* hard]

du·ra ma·ter /d(y)ŏor'ə mā'tər/ *n.* outermost membrane of the brain and spinal cord [MedL: hard mother, translation of Ar]

Du·ran·go /d(y)ŏoranG'gō/ *n.* state in N central Mexico. Capital: Durango. Pop. 1,349,400

Du·rant /dərant'/ US historians: **1 Will** 1885–1981; his wife: **2 Ariel** 1898–1981

du·ra·tion /d(y)ŏorā'sHən/ *n.* time taken by an event, process, etc. [MedL fr. L *durare* last]

Dur·ban /dər'bən/ *n.* seaport in South Africa. Pop. 634,300

Dü·rer /d(y)ŏor'ər/, **Albrecht** 1471–1528; German painter and engraver

du·ress /d(y)ŏores'/ *n.* **1** coercive circumstances **2** imprisonment [L *durus* hard]

Durey /dyre'/, **Louis** 1888–1979; French composer

Dur·ga /dŏor'gä/ see DEVI

Dur·ham /dər'əm, dŏor'-/ *n.* city in N. Car. Pop. 136,600

dur·ing /d(y)ŏor'iNG/ *prep.* throughout or at some point in [L *durus* hard]

Durk·heim /dyrkem'/, **Émile** 1858–1917; French sociologist

Du·shan·be /d(y)ŏosHäm'bä/ *n.* capital of Tadzhikistan. Pop. 582,400

dusk /dəsk/ *n.* darker stage of twilight —**dusk'y** *adj.* (·i·er, ·i·est)

Düs·sel·dorf /d(y)ŏo͞o'soldôrf/, dY'-/ *n.* port on the Rhine River in Germany. Pop. 575,800

dust /dəst/ *n.* **1** finely powdered earth or other material **2** dead person's remains —*v.* **3** wipe the dust from (furniture, etc.) **4** sprinkle with powder, sugar, etc. **5 bite the dust** die [OE]

dust' bowl' *n.* arid region losing topsoil from drought and erosion

dust' jack'et *n.* paper cover on a hardback book

dust'pan' *n.* receptacle for (brushed) dust

dust'y *adj.* (·i·er, ·i·est) **1** full of or covered with dust **2** (of a color) dull or muted —**dust'i·ness** *n.*

Dutch /dəCH/ *adj.* **1** of the Netherlands or its people or language —*n.* **2** the Dutch language **3** (prec. by *the*; treated as *pl.*) the people of the Netherlands **4 go Dutch** share expenses **5 in Dutch** *Colloq.* in trouble —**Dutch'man** *n.* (*pl.* ·men; *fem.* ·wom'an, *pl.* ·wom'en) [Du]

Dutch' door' *n.* door horizontally divided so that either half can be opened or closed

Dutch' elm' dis·ease' *n.* fungus disease of elm trees

Dutch' treat' *n.* outing, etc., at which people pay for themselves

Dutch' un'cle *n.* kind but firm adviser

du·te·ous /d(y)ŏo͞o'tēəs/ *adj. Lit.* dutiful —**du'te·ous·ly** *adv.*

du·ti·a·ble /d(y)ŏo͞o'tēəbəl/ *adj.* requiring the payment of duty

du·ti·ful /d(y)ŏo͞o'təfəl/ *adj.* doing one's duty; obedient —**du'ti·ful·ly** *adv.*

du·ty /d(y)ŏo͞o'tē/ *n.* (*pl.* ·ties) **1** moral or legal obligation; responsibility **2** tax on certain imports, etc. **3** assigned or expected job or function **4 on** (or **off**) **duty** at (or temporarily done with) work [AngFr, rel. to DUE]

Du·va·lier /dŏo͞o'välyā'/, **François ("Papa Doc")** 1907–71; president of Haiti (1957–71)

du·vet /dŏovā'/ *n.* thick soft quilt filled with down, etc. [Fr]

D.V.M. *abbr.* doctor of veterinary medicine

Dvo·řák /(də)vôr'zHäk/, **Antonin** 1841–1904; Czech composer

dwarf /dwôrf/ *n.* (*pl.* **dwarfs** or **dwarves** /dwôrvz/) **1** person, animal, or plant much below normal size **2** small mythological being with magical powers **3** small usu. dense star —*v.* **4** stunt in growth **5** make seem small —**dwarf'ish** *adj.*; **dwarf'ism** *n.* [OE]

dweeb /dwēb/ *n. Slang.* unattractive or socially inept person

dwell /dwel/ *v.* (**dwelt** or **dwelled**, **dwell·ing**) **1** live; reside **2 dwell on** (or **upon**) think, write, or speak about at length —**dwell'er** *n.* [OE: lead astray]

dwell'ing *n.* house; residence

DWI *abbr.* driving while intoxicated

dwin·dle /dwind'l/ *v.* (·dled, ·dling) become gradually less or smaller [OE]

Dy *symb.* dysprosium

dye /dī/ *n.* **1** substance used to change the color of hair, fabric, etc. **2** color so produced —*v.* (**dyed, dye·ing**) **3** color with dye —**dy'er** *n.* [OE]

dyed'-in-the-wool' *adj.* out and out; unchangeable

dy'ing /dī'iNG/ *adj.* of, or at the time of, death (*dying words*)

Dyl·an /dil'ən/, **Bob** (born **Robert Allen Zimmerman**) 1941– ; US singer and songwriter

dy·nam·ic /dīnam'ik/ *adj.* **1** energetic; active **2** *Physics.* **a** of a motive force **b** of force in actual operation **3** of dynamics —**dy·nam'i·cal·ly** *adv.* [Gk *dynamis* power]

dy·nam·ics *n. pl.* **1** (usu. treated as *sing.*) mathematical study of motion and its causes **2** motive forces in any sphere

dy·na·mism /dī'nəmiz'əm/ *n.* energy; dynamic power

dy·na·mite /dī'nəmīt'/ *n.* **1** high explosive mixture containing nitroglycerin —*v.* (·mit·ed, ·mit·ing) **2** charge or blow up with dynamite

dy·na·mo /dī'nəmō'/ *n.* (*pl.* ·mos) **1** electric generator **2** *Colloq.* energetic person [abbr. of *dynamo-electric machine*]

dy·nas·ty /dī'nəstē/ *n.* (*pl.* ·ties) **1** line of hereditary rulers **2** succession of related leaders, repeated championships, etc. —**dy·nas'tic** /-nas'tik/ *adj.* [L fr. Gk]

dys- *prefix* bad; difficult [Gk]

dys·en·ter·y /dis'əntər'ē/ *n.* inflammation of the intestines, causing severe diarrhea [Gk *dysentera* bad bowels]

dys·func·tion /disfəNGk'sHən/ *n.* abnormality or impairment of functioning

dys·lex·i·a /dislek′sēə/ *n.* abnormal difficulty in reading and spelling —**dys·lex′ic** /-sik/, **dys·lec′tic** *adj.* & *n.* [Gk *lexis* word; speech]

dys·pep·si·a /dispep′sēə/ *n.* indigestion —**dys·pep′tic** *adj.* & *n.* [Gk *pepsis* digestion]

dys·pro·si·um /disprō′zēəm/ *n.* metallic element of the lanthanide series; *symb.* Dy [Gk *dysprositos* hard to get at]

dz. *abbr.* dozen(s)

Dzer·zhinsk /dərzHinsk′, jər-/ *n.* city in Russia. Pop. 286,700

Dzer·zhin·sky /jərzHin′skē/, **Feliks** 1877–1926; Russian Bolshevik who led the Soviet security police

E

e, E /ē/ *n.* (*pl.* **e's; E's, Es**) fifth letter of the English alphabet; a vowel

e or **e.** *abbr.* **1** eldest **2** electron **3** entrance **4** *Baseball.* error(s)

E or **E.** *abbr.* **1** Earl **2** Earth **3** east; eastern **4** Easter **5** *Physics.* energy **6** English

e- *prefix* var. of EX-[1] before certain consonants

each /ēcH/ *adj.* **1** every one of two or more persons or things, regarded separately —*pron.* **2** each person or thing [OE]
   ● Usage: See note at BOTH.

each′ oth′er *pron.* one another

Ead·wig /ed′wēg, -wig/ (also spelled **Edwy**) d. 959; king of England (955–957)

ea·ger /ē′gər/ *adj.* keen; enthusiastic —**ea′ger·ly** *adv.*; **ea′ger·ness** *n.* [L *acer* keen]

ea′ger bea′ver *n. Colloq.* very avid person

ea·gle /ē′gəl/ *n.* **1a** large bird of prey with keen vision **b** this as a symbol, esp. of the US **2** *Golf.* score of two strokes under par on a hole [L *aquila*]

ea′gle eye′ *n.* keen sight; watchfulness —**ea′gle-eyed′** *adj.*

ea·glet /ē′glit/ *n.* young eagle

ear[1] /ēr/ *n.* **1** organ of hearing, esp. its external part **2** faculty for discriminating sounds **3** attention, esp. sympathetic **4** all ears listening attentively **5 have (or keep) an ear to the ground** be alert to news, rumors, or trends **6 up to one's ears** *Colloq.* deeply involved or occupied [OE]

ear[2] *n.* seed-bearing head of a cereal plant [OE]

ear′ache′ *n.* pain in the inner ear

ear′drum′ *n.* membrane of the middle ear

ear·ful /ēr′fŏŏl′/ *n.* (*pl.* **-fuls**) *Colloq.* **1** prolonged amount of talking **2** strong reprimand

Ear·hart /er′härt′, ēr′-/, **Amelia** 1898–1937; US aviator

earl /ərl′/ *n.* British nobleman ranking between marquis and viscount —**earl′dom** *n.* [OE]

ear·ly /ər′lē/ *adj.* & *adv* (**·li·er, ·li·est**) **1** before the usual or expected time **2a** not far along in the day or night, or in time **b** prompt **3** not far along in a period or process —**ear′li·ness** *n.* [OE, rel. to ERE]

ear′ly bird′ *n. Colloq.* person who arrives, gets up, etc., early

ear′ly on′ *adv.* at an early stage

ear·mark /ēr′märk′/ *v.* **1** set aside for a special purpose —*n.* **2** identifying mark

ear′muffs′ *n. pl.* paired ear coverings for protection against cold

earn /ərn′/ *v.* **1** bring in as income or interest **2** be entitled to or obtain as reward —**earn′er** *n.* [OE]

ear·nest /ər′nist/ *adj.* **1** intensely serious **2 in earnest** serious or seriously; with determination —**ear′nest·ly** *adv.*; **ear′nest·ness** *n.* [OE]

earn′ings *n. pl.* money earned

ear·phone /ēr′fōn′/ *n.* device applied to the ear to receive a radio, etc., communication

ear′ring *n.* jewelry worn on the ear

ear·shot /ēr′sHät′/ *n.* hearing range

ear′split′ting *adj.* excessively loud

earth /ərTH′/ *n.* **1a** (also *cap.*) the planet on which we live **b** land and sea, as distinct from sky **2a** the ground **b** soil **3** *Relig.* this world, as distinct from heaven or hell **4 come back** (or **down**) **to earth** return to realities **5 on earth** *Colloq.* existing anywhere; absolutely —**earth′ward** or **earthwards** *adv.*; **earth′ward** *adj.* [OE]

earth′en *adj.* made of earth or baked clay

earth·en·ware /ər′THənwer′/ *n.* pottery made of fired clay

earth′ling /ərTH′lING/ *n.* inhabitant of the earth, esp. in science fiction

earth′ly /ərTH′lē/ *adj.* **1** of the earth or human life on it; terrestrial **2** (usu. with *neg.*) *Colloq.* remotely possible (*no earthly use*)

earth′quake′ *n.* convulsion of the earth's surface as a result of underground faults or volcanic action

earth′work′ *n.* artificial bank of earth in fortification, road building, etc.

earth′worm′ *n.* common worm living in the ground

earth·y /ərTH′ē/ *adj.* (**·i·er, ·i·est**) **1** of or like earth or soil **2** down-to-earth **3** coarse; crude (*earthy humor*) —**earth′i·ness** *n.*

ease /ēz/ *n.* **1** facility; effortlessness **2** relaxed manner **3** freedom from hardship or worries —*v.* (**eased, eas·ing**) **4** relieve from pain or anxiety **5a** make or become less burdensome or severe **b** facilitate; smooth **c** slow down **d** move or be moved carefully into place [L, rel. to ADJACENT]

ea·sel /ē′zəl/ *n.* frame or tripod to hold an artist's work, etc. [Du *ezel* ass]

EASEL

ease·ment /ēz′mənt/ *n.* **1** legal right of way or similar right over another's land **2** easing or relieving [OFr, rel. to EASE]

eas·i·ly /ē′zəlē/ *adv.* **1** without difficulty **2** by far **3** very probably

east /ēst′/ *n.* **1a** point of the horizon where

the sun rises at the equinoxes **b** compass point corresponding to this **c** direction in which this lies **2** (usu. **the East**) **a** Asia, or specifically the Orient **b** eastern part of the US **3** eastern part of a country, state, etc. —*adj.* **4** toward, at, near, or facing the east **5** from the east —*adv.* **6** toward, at, or near the east **7** (foll. by *of*) farther east than [OE]

East′ Chi′na Sea′ *n.* part of the N Pacific E of mainland China and N of Taiwan

Eas·ter /ē′stər/ *n.* festival (held on a Sunday in March or April) of Christ's resurrection [OE]

east′er·ly *adj. & adv.* **1** in an eastern position or direction **2** (of a wind) from the east —*n.* (*pl.* -**lies**) **3** such a wind

east′ern *adj.* of or in the east —**east′ern·most** *adj.*

east′ern·er *n.* native or inhabitant of the east

East′ Ger′ma·ny *n.* German state created in 1949, under Communist government; unified with West Germany in 1990

East′ Los′ An′ge·les *n.* suburb of Los Angeles, Calif. Pop. 126,379

East·man /ēst′mən/, **George** 1854–1932; US inventor

east·ward /ēst′wərd/ *adj. & adv* (also **east′wards**) toward the east

East·wood /ēs′twŏŏd′/, **Clint** 1930– ; US actor and director

East′ York′ *n.* city in Canada, near Toronto. Pop. 102,700

eas·y /ē′zē/ *adj.* (**·i·er, ·i·est**) **1** not difficult; not requiring great effort **2** free from pain, trouble, or anxiety **3** natural; unaffected **4** relaxed and pleasant **5** compliant —*adv.* **6** with ease; in an effortless or relaxed manner — in*terj.* **7** go or move carefully **8 take it easy: a** proceed gently **b** relax; work less —**eas′i·ness** *n.* [OFr, rel. to EASE]

eas′y chair′ *n.* comfortable armchair

eas′y·go′ing *adj.* placid and tolerant

eat /ēt/ *v.* (**ate, eat·en, eat·ing**) **1 a** take into the mouth, chew, and swallow **b** consume food; have a meal **2 a** destroy gradually **b** begin to consume or diminish (resources, etc.) **3** *Slang.* vex (*what's eating you?*) —*n.* **4** (*pl.*) *Slang.* food **5 eat one's heart out** suffer from excessive longing or envy —**eat′a·ble** *adj.*; **eat′er** *n.* [OE]

eaves /ēvz/ *n. pl.* underside of a projecting roof [OE]

eaves·drop /ēvz′dräp′/ *v.* (**·dropped, ·dropping**) listen to a private conversation —**eaves′drop′per** *n.*

ebb /eb/ *n.* **1** movement of the tide out to sea —*v.* **2** flow out to sea; recede **3** decline [OE]

eb·o·ny /eb′ənē/ *n.* **1** heavy hard dark wood of a tropical tree —*adj.* **2** made of ebony **3** black like ebony [Gk *ebenos* ebony tree]

e·bul·li·ent /iboŏl′yənt, ibal′-/ *adj.* exuberant —**e·bul′lience, e·bul′lien·cy** *n.*; **e·bul′lient·ly** *adv.* [L *ebullire* boil over]

EC *abbr.* European Community (cf. EUROPEAN UNION)

ec·cen·tric /iksen′trik, ek-/ *adj.* **1** odd or capricious in behavior or appearance **2** not quite circular or concentric —*n.* **3** eccentric person **4** disk at the end of a shaft for changing rotatory into backward-and-forward motion —**ec·cen′tri·cal·ly** *adv.*; **ec·cen·tric·i·ty** /ek′sen′tris′itē/ *n.* [*-ekkentros* out of center]

eccl. *abbr.* ecclesiastical

ec·cle·si·as·tic /iklē′zē-as′tik/ *n.* **1** clergyman —*adj.* **2** ECCLESIASTICAL [Gk *ekklēsia* church]

ec·cle′si·as′ti·cal *adj.* pertaining to the church or clergy

ech·e·lon /esh′əlän/ *n.* **1** level in an organization, in society, etc. **2** those occupying it **3** formation in staggered parallels of troops, aircraft, etc. [OFr: ladder, fr. L *scala*]

e·chi·no·derm /ikī′nədərm′/ *n.* (usu. spiny) sea animal of the group including the starfish and sea urchin [Gk *echinos* sea urchin + *derma* skin]

ech·o /ek′ō/ *n.* (*pl.* -**oes**) **1 a** repetition of a sound by reflection of sound waves **b** sound so produced **2** reflected radio or radar beam —*v.* (**·oed, ·o·ing**). **3 a** (of a place) resound with an echo **b** (of a sound) be repeated; resound **4 a** repeat **b** confirm or second [L fr. Gk]

e·cho·ic /ekō′ik/ *adj.* (of a word) onomatopoeic

é·clair /ākler/ *n.* small elongated pastry filled with custard [Fr: lightning]

é·clat /āklä′/ *n.* **1** striking presentation or effect **2** conspicuous success [Fr]

ec·lec·tic /iklek′tik/ *adj.* **1** selecting ideas, style, etc., from various sources —*n.* **2** eclectic person or philosopher —**ec·lec′ti·cal·ly** *adv.*; **ec·lec′ti·cism** /-təsiz′əm/ *n.* [Gk, rel. *legein* pick out]

e·clipse /iklips′/ *n.* **1** obscuring of light from one heavenly body by another **2** loss of light, importance, or prominence —*v.* (**·clipsed, ·clips·ing**) **3** (of a heavenly body) cause the eclipse of (another) **4** outshine; surpass [Gk *ekleipsis*]

e·clip·tic /iklip′tik/ *n.* sun's apparent path among the stars during the year

ec·logue /ek′lôg, -läg/ *n.* short pastoral poem [Gk *eklogē* selection]

Eco /ek′ō/, **Umberto** 1932– ; Italian novelist and expert in semiotics

eco- *comb. form* ecology; ecological (*ecoclimate*)

ecol. *abbr.* **1** ecological **2** ecologist **3** ecology

e·col·o·gy /ikäl′əjē/ *n.* **1** the study of the relations of organisms to one another and to their surroundings **2** the study of the interaction of people with their environment —**ec·o·log·i·cal** /ē′kəläji′ikəl, ek′-/ *adj.*; **ec′o·log′i·cal·ly** *adv.*; **e·col′o·gist** *n.* [Gk *oikos* house]

econ. *abbr.* **1** economics **2** economist **3** economy

e·co·nom·ic /ē′kənäm′ik, ek′ə-/ *adj.* **1** of economics **2** profitable or cost effective **3** connected with trade and industry (*economic geography*) —**ec′o·nom′i·cal·ly** *adv.* [Gk, rel. to ECONOMY]

• **Usage:** *Economic* is usually reserved for the sense 'concerning economics': *Economic experts met in Geneva*. *Economical* serves as a more formal word for 'thrifty': *It is more economical to buy the larger box of detergent.*

ec′o·nom′i·cal *adj.* sparing; avoiding waste —**ec′o·nom′i·cal·ly** *adv.*

ec·o·nom·ics *n. pl.* (as *sing.*) **1** science of the production and distribution of wealth **2** application of this to a particular **subject**

e·con·o·mist /ikän′əmist, ē-/ n. expert on or student of economics

e·con·o·mize /ikän′əmīz, ē-/ v. (·mized, ·miz·ing) 1 be economical; reduce expenditure 2 (foll. by on) use sparingly

e·con·o·my /ikän′əmē, ē-/ n. (pl. ·mies) 1a community's system of wealth creation b particular kind of this (a capitalist economy) 2a careful management of (esp. financial) resources; frugality b instance of this 3 sparing or careful use (economy of language) [Gk oikonomia household management]

e·con′o·my class′ n. cheapest class of air travel, accommodations, etc.

ec·o·sys·tem /ē′kōsis′təm, ek′ō-/ n. community of interacting organisms and their environment

ec·sta·sy /ek′stəsē/ n. (pl. ·sies) overwhelming joy or rapture —**ec·stat′ic** /-stat′ik/ adj.; **ec·stat′i·cal·ly** adv. [Gk ekstasis standing outside oneself]

ecto- comb. form outside [Gk ektos]

ec·to·morph /ek′təmôrf′/ n. person with a lean body [Gk morphē form]

-ectomy comb. form denoting the surgical removal of part of the body (appendectomy) [Gk ektomē excision]

Ec·ua·dor /ek′wədôr′/ n. republic in NW South America. Capital: Quito. Pop. 10,607,000 —**Ec′ua·dor′an**, **Ec′ua·do′ri·an** /-rēən/ n. & adj.

ec·u·men·i·cal /ek′yəmen′ikəl/ adj. 1 of or representing the whole Christian world 2 seeking worldwide Christian unity —**ec′u·men′i·cal·ly** adv.; **ec′u·me·nism′** /-yŏŏ′mənizəm/ n. [Gk oikoumenikos of the inhabited earth]

ec·ze·ma /eg′zəmə, ek′sə-, igzē′-/ n. inflammation of the skin, with itching and discharge [L fr. Gk]

ed. abbr. 1 edited by 2 edition 3 editor 4 education

-ed¹ suffix forming adjectives: 1 from nouns, meaning 'having, wearing, etc.' (talented; trousered) 2 from phrases of adjective and noun (good-humored) [OE]

-ed² suffix forming: 1 past tense and past participle of most verbs (needed) 2 participial adjectives (escaped prisoner) [OE]

E·dam /ē′dəm/ n. round cheese with a red rind [Edam in Holland]

ed·dy /ed′ē/ n. (pl. ·dies) 1 circular movement of water causing a small whirlpool 2 movement of wind, smoke, etc., resembling this —v. (·died, ·dy·ing) 3 whirl around in eddies [OE ed- again; back + ēa water]

Ed·dy /ed′ē/, **Mary Baker** 1821–1910; US founder of the Christian Science movement

e·del·weiss /ād′l-vīs′/ n. Alpine plant with white flowers [Ger: noble white]

e·de·ma /idē′mə/ n. accumulation of excess fluid in body tissues [Gk oideō swell]

E·den /ēd′n/, **(Robert) Anthony** 1897–1977; prime minister of Great Britain (1955–57)

E·den /ēd′n/ n. 1 Bibl. abode of Adam and Eve at the Creation 2 any place of bliss [Heb: delight]

Ed·gar /ed′gər/ 944–975; king of England (959–975)

edge /ej/ n. 1 boundary line or margin of an area or surface 2 narrow surface of a thin object 3 meeting line of surfaces 4a sharpened side of a blade b sharpness 5 brink of a precipice 6 edgelike thing 7 effectiveness; boldness 8 Colloq. advantage —v. (edged, edg·ing) 9 advance, esp. gradually or furtively 10a provide with an edge or border b form a border to 11 on edge tense and irritable [OE]

edge·wise /ej′wīz′/ adv. (also edge′ways′) 1 with edge uppermost or foremost 2 get a word in edgewise interject in a dominated conversation

edg′ing n. thing forming an edge or border

edg′y adj. (·i·er, ·i·est) irritable; anxious —**edg′i·ly** adv.; **edg′i·ness** n.

ed·i·ble /ed′əbəl/ adj. fit to be eaten —**ed′i·bil′i·ty** n. [L edere eat]

e·dict /ē′dikt/ n. order proclaimed by author-ity [L edicere proclaim]

ed·i·fice /ed′əfis/ n. building, esp. an imposing one [L aedis dwelling; temple]

ed·i·fy /ed′əfī′/ v. (·fied, ·fy·ing) improve morally or intellectually —**ed′i·fi·ca′tion** /-fikā′sнən/ n. [L aedificare build]

Ed·in·burgh /ed′n-bər′ə, -brə/ n. capital of Scotland, United Kingdom. Pop. 420,200

Ed·i·son /ed′əsən/, **Thomas Alva** 1847–1931; US inventor

ed·it /ed′it/ v. 1 assemble, prepare, or modify (written material for publication) 2 be editor of (a newspaper, etc.) 3 take extracts from and collate (a film, etc.) to form a unified sequence 4 reword; correct [L editus published, fr. edere give out]

e·di·tion /idisн′ən/ n. 1 edited or published form of a book, etc. 2 copies of a book, newspaper, etc., issued at one time

ed·i·tor /ed′itər/ n. 1 person who edits 2 person who directs preparation of a newspaper or a periodical (or section thereof) or a news program 3 person who selects or commissions material for publication —**ed′i·tor·ship′** n.

ed·i·to·ri·al /ed′itôr′ēəl/ adj. 1 of editing or editors —n. 1 article or column giving a newspaper's views on a current topic —**ed′i·to′ri·al·ly** adv.

Ed·mon·ton /ed′məntən/ n. capital of the Canadian province of Alberta. Pop. 839,900

Ed·mund /ed′mənd/ name of two kings of England: 1 **Edmund I** 921–946; reigned 939–946 2 **Edmund II** (called "Ironside") c. 980–1016; reigned 1016

EDT abbr. eastern daylight time

ed·u·cate /ej′əkāt′/ v. (·cat·ed, ·cat·ing) 1 give intellectual, factual, or edifying instruction to 2 provide education for —**ed′u·ca·ble** /-kəbəl/ adj.; **ed′u·ca·bil′i·ty** n.; **ed′u·ca′tive** /-kā′tiv/ adj.; **ed′u·ca′tor** n. [L educare rear]

ed·u·cat′ed adj. 1 having had an (esp. good) education 2 well-taught; informed 3 based on experience or study (educated guess)

ed·u·ca′tion n. 1 systematic instruction, schooling, etc. 2 particular kind of or stage in education 3 development of character or mental powers; formative experience —**ed′u·ca′tion·al** adj.; **ed′u·ca′tion·al·ly** adv.

e·duce /id(y)ŏŏs′/ v. (·duced, ·duc·ing) bring out or develop —**e·duc′tion** /-dək′sнən/ n. [L educere draw out]

Ed·ward /ed′wərd/ name of eight kings of

England or Great Britain, including: **1 Edward I** 1239–1307; reigned 1272–1307 **2 Edward VII** 1841–1910; son of Queen Victoria; reigned 1901–10 **3 Edward VIII** 1894–1972; king of Great Britain (1936); abdicated, became Duke of Windsor

Ed·wards /ĕd′wərdz/, **Jonathan** 1703–58; Colonial American theologian

Ed·wy see EADWIG

-ee *suffix* forming nouns denoting: **1** person affected by the verbal action (*employee; payee*) **2** person concerned with or described as (*absentee; refugee*) [Fr -é in past part.]

EEC *abbr.* European Economic Community

EEG *abbr.* electroencephalogram

eel /ēl/ *n.* snakelike fish [OE]

EEOC *abbr.* Equal Employment Opportunity Commission

-eer *suffix* forming: **1** nouns meaning 'person concerned with' (*auctioneer*) **2** verbs meaning 'be concerned with' (*electioneer*) [Fr -*ier* fr. L -*arius*]

ee·rie /ēr′ē/ *adj.* (·**ri·er**, ·**ri·est**) unsettling and strange; weird —**ee′ri·ly** *adv.*; **ee′ri·ness** *n.* [OE]

ef- var. of EX-¹ before *f*

ef·face /ifas′/ *v.* (·**faced**, ·**fac·ing**) **1** rub or wipe out **2** treat as unimportant —**ef·face′ment** *n.* [MFr., rel. to FACE]

ef·fect /ifekt′/ *n.* **1** result; consequence **2** efficacy; influence **3** impression produced on a spectator, hearer, etc. **4** (*pl.*) property **5** physical phenomenon —*v.* **6** bring about **7 in effect:** **a** operative **b** for practical purposes **8 take effect** become operative [L *efficere* make; cause]

● Usage: See note at *affect.*

ef·fec·tive /ifek′tiv/ *adj.* **1** producing the intended result **2** impressive; striking **3** actual; existing **4** operative —**ef·fec′tive·ly** *adv.*; **ef·fec′tive·ness** *n.*

ef·fec·tu·al /ifek′CHŌōəl/ *adj.* **1** producing the required effect **2** valid —**ef·fec′tu·al·ly** *adv.*

ef·fec·tu·ate /ifek′CHŌōāt′/ *v.* (·**at·ed**, ·**at·ing**) effect —**ef·fec′tu·a′tion** *n.*

ef·fem·i·nate /ifem′ənət/ *adj.* (of a man) womanish in appearance or manner —**ef·fem′i·na·cy** /-nəsē/ *n.*; **ef·fem′i·nate·ly** *adv.* [L *femina* woman]

ef·fer·vesce /ef′ərves′/ *v.* (·**vesced**, ·**vesc·ing**) **1** give off bubbles of gas **2** be lively —**ef′fer·ves′cence** *n.*; **ef′fer·ves′cent** *adj.* [L, rel. to FERVENT]

ef·fete /ifēt′/ *adj.* feeble; languid; effeminate —**ef·fete′ly** *adv.*; **ef·fete′ness** *n.* [L]

ef·fi·ca·cious /ef′ikā′sHəs/ *adj.* producing the desired effect —**ef·fi·ca·cy** /ef′ikəsē/ *n.* [L *efficax*, rel. to EFFICIENT]

ef·fi·cient /ifisH′ənt/ *adj.* **1** productive with minimum waste or effort **2** capable; acting effectively —**ef·fi′cien·cy** *n.*; **ef·fi′cient·ly** *adv.* [L *facere* make; do]

ef·fi·gy /ef′əjē/ *n.* (*pl.* ·**gies**) sculpture or model of a person [L *effigies* fr. *fingere* fashion; shape]

ef·flu·ent /ef′lōō′ənt/ *adj.* **1** flowing out —*n.* **2** waste discharged into a river, etc.

ef·flu·vi·um /eflōō′vēəm/ *n.* (*pl.* ·**vi·a**) unpleasant or noxious vapor or odor [L *fluere* flow]

ef·fort /ef′ərt/ *n.* **1** use of physical or mental energy **2** determined attempt **3** force exerted —**ef′fort·less** *adj.*; **ef′fort·less·ly** *adv.*; **ef′fort·less·ness** *n.* [OFr *forcier* force, rel. to L *fortis* strong]

ef·fron·ter·y /ifrənt′ərē/ *n.* (*pl.* ·**ies**) impudent audacity [OFr *esfront* shameless, fr. L *frons front-* forehead]

ef·ful·gent /efəl′jənt, ifōōl′-/ *adj. Lit.* radiant —**ef·ful′gence** *n.* [L *fulgere* shine]

ef·fuse /ifyōōz′/ *v.* (·**fused**, ·**fus·ing**) pour forth (liquid, light, etc.) —**ef·fu′sive** /-fyōō′siv/ *adj.*; **ef·fu′sive·ly** *adv.*; **ef·fu′sive·ness** *n.* [L *effundere effus-* pour out]

ef·fu·sion /ifyōō′ZHən/ *n.* **1** outpouring **2** unrestrained verbiage [L, rel. to EFFUSE]

e.g. *abbr.* for example [L *exempli gratia*]

e·gal·i·tar·i·an /igal′əter′ēən/ *adj.* **1** of or advocating equal social and political rights for all types of people —*n.* **2** egalitarian person —**e·gal′i·tar′i·an·ism** *n.* [Fr *égal* EQUAL]

egg¹ /eg/ *n.* **1a** often encased body produced by females of birds, insects, etc., capable of developing into a new individual **b** egg of the domestic hen, used for food **2** *Biol.* ovum **3** *Colloq.* person or thing of a specified kind (*good egg*) **4 with egg on one's face** *Colloq.* looking foolish [ON]

egg² *v.* urge; incite [ON, rel. to EDGE]

egg·head /eg′hed′/ *n. Colloq.* intellectual

egg·plant /eg′plant′/ *n.* plant with purple or white egg-shaped fruit used as a vegetable

egg white′ *n.* white part around the yolk of an egg

eg·lan·tine /eg′ləntīn′, -tēn′/ *n.* sweetbrier [L *acus* needle]

e·go /ē′gō/ *n.* (*pl.* ·**gos**) **1** the self; the part of the mind that has self-awareness **2** self-esteem; self-conceit [L: I]

e·go·cen·tric /ē′gōsen′trik/ *adj.* self-centered

e·go·ism /ē′gōiz′əm/ *n.* **1** self-interest as the basis of behavior **2** EGOTISM —**e′go·ist** /-ist/ *n.*; **e′go·is′tic**, **e′go·is′ti·cal** *adj.*; **e′go·is′ti·cal·ly** *adv.*

● Usage: An *egoist* is one who is self-centered or selfish; an *egotist* is one who brags about himself or herself.

e·go·tism /ē′gotiz′əm/ *n.* **1** self-conceit **2** self-ishness —**e′go·tist** /-tist/ *n.*; **e′go·tis′tic**, **e′go·tis′ti·cal** *adj.*; **e′go·tis′ti·cal·ly** *adv.*

e′go trip′ *n. Colloq.* activity to boost one's own self-esteem and self-conceit

e·gre·gious /igrē′jəs/ *adj.* extremely bad [L: preeminent, fr. *grex greg-* flock]

e·gress /ē′gres′/ *n. Formal.* exit [L *egressus* escape; departure]

e·gret /ē′grit, ē′gret′, igret′/ *n.* a kind of heron with long white feathers [Fr *aigrette*]

E·gypt /ē′jipt/ *n.* republic in NE Africa, on the Mediterranean and Red seas. Capital: Cairo. Pop. 55,979,000

E·gyp·tian /ējip′sHən/ *adj.* **1** of Egypt —*n.* **2** native of Egypt **3** language of the ancient Egyptians

eh /ā, e/ *interj. Colloq.* **1** expressing surprise **2** asking for repetition or explanation

Eich·mann /īk′mən, īкн-/, **(Karl) Adolf** 1906–62; German Nazi official

ei·der /ī′dər/ *n.* any of various large northern ducks [Icel fr. ON]

ei'der·down' *n.* **1** down from the eider duck **2** quilt stuffed with this

Eif·fel /ī'fəl/, **Alexandre Gustave** 1832–1923; French engineer; designed Eiffel Tower

eight /āt/ *adj.* & *n.* **1** one more than seven **2** symbol for this (8, viii, VIII) —**eighth** /ā(t)TH/ *adj.* & *n.* [OE]

eight·een /ā(t)tēn'/ *adj.* & *n.* **1** one more than seventeen **2** symbol for this (18, xviii, XVIII) —**eight'eenth** *adj.* & *n.* [OE]

eight·y /ā'tē/ *adj.* & *n.* (*pl.* **·ies**) **1** eight times ten **2** symbol for this (80, lxxx, LXXX) **3** (*pl.*) numbers from 80 to 89, esp. as years —**eight'i·eth** *adj.* & *n.* [OE]

Eind·ho·ven /īnt'hō'vən/ *n.* city in the Netherlands. Pop. 192,900

Ein·stein /īn'stīn'/, **Albert** 1879–1955; German-born US physicist; developed theory of relativity

ein·stein·i·um /īnstī'nēəm/ *n.* artificial radioactive metallic element; *symb.* **Es** [for A. EINSTEIN]

Eir·e /er'ə, ī'rə/ *n.* see IRELAND

Ei·sen·how·er /ī'zənhou'ər/, **Dwight David** ("Ike") 1890–1969; US general and 34th US president (1953–61)

Ei·sen·stein /ī'zənstīn'/, **Sergei** 1898–1948; Soviet film director

ei·ther /ē'THər, ī'THər/ *adj.* & *pron.* **1** one or the other of two **2** each of two —*adv.* & *conj.* **3** as one possibility or alternative **4** any more than the other [OE]

e·jac·u·late /ijak'yəlāt'/ *v.* (**·lated, ·lat·ing**) **1** exclaim **2** emit (semen) in orgasm —**e·jac'u·la'tion** *n.*; **e·jac'u·la·to'ry** /-lətôr'ē/ *adj.* [L *ejaculari* dart out, fr. *jacere* throw]

e·ject /ijekt'/ *v.* **1** expel; compel to leave **2** (of a pilot, etc.) cause oneself to be propelled from an aircraft in an emergency **3** cause to be removed —**e·jec'tion** /-jek'SHən/ *n.* [L *ejicere eject-* throw out]

eke /ēk/ *v.* (**eked, ek·ing**) (foll. by *out*) make (a living) or support (an existence) with difficulty [OE]

EKG *abbr.* electrocardiogram [L, ult. fr. Gk *elektron + kardio + gram*]

e·lab·o·rate /ilab'(ə)rət/ **1** minutely worked out **2** complicated —*v.* /-rāt'/ (**·rat·ed, ·rat·ing**) **3** work out or explain in detail —**e·lab'o·rate·ly** *adv.*; **e·lab'o·rate·ness,** *n.* **e·lab·o·ra'tion** *n.* [L, rel. to LABOR]

élan /ālän', älan'/ *n.* French. brisk style; dash

e·land /ē'lənd/ *n.* (*pl.* same or **·lands**) large African antelope [Afrik fr. Du]

e·lapse /ilaps'/ *v.* (**·lapsed, ·laps·ing**) (of time) pass by [L *elabi elaps-* slip away]

e·las·tic /ilas'tik/ *adj.* **1** able to return to its normal bulk or shape after contraction, dilation, etc.; flexible —*n.* **2** elastic cord or fabric —**e·las'ti·cal·ly** *adv.*; **e'las·tic'i·ty** /-tis'ətē, ē'-/ *n.* [Gk *elaunein* set in motion; drive]

e·late /ilāt'/ *v.* (**·lat·ed, ·lat·ing**) make delighted —**e·lat'ed·ly** /-ədlē/ *adv.*; **e·la'tion** *n.* [L *efferre elat-*]

El·ba /el'bə/ *n.* island in the Mediterranean Sea between Italy and Corsica; site of Napoleon's first exile

el·bow /el'bō'/ *n.* **1** joint between the forearm and the upper arm **2** elbow-shaped bend —*v.* **3** jostle or thrust (a person or oneself) [OE, rel. to ELL + BOW¹]

el'bow grease' *n. Colloq.* vigorous physical effort; hard work

el'bow·room' *n.* sufficient room to move or work in

El·brus, Mount /elbrōōz'/ *n.* mountain in the Caucasus range; highest mountain in Europe: 18,481 ft.

El Cid see CID, EL

eld·er¹ /el'dər/ *adj.* **1** (of persons, esp. when related) senior; of greater age —*n.* **2** older of two persons **3** (*pl.*) persons older and usu. venerable **4** church official [OE, rel. to OLD]

eld·er² *n.* tree with white flowers and dark berries [OE]

el'der·ber'ry *n.* (*pl.* **·ries**) berry of the elder tree

eld'er·ly *adj.* rather old; past middle age

eld'est /el'dist/ *adj.* first-born; oldest

El Do·ra·do /el' dərä'dō/ (also **El'do·ra'do**) *n.* (*pl.* **·dos**) **1** imaginary land of great wealth **2** place of abundance or opportunity [Sp *el dorado* the gilded]

El·ea·nor of Aq·ui·taine /el'ənər, -nôr', ak' witän'/ *c.* 1122–1204; queen of France (1137–52) and England (1154–89)

elec. *abbr.* **1** electrical **2** electricity

e·lect /ilekt'/ *v.* **1** choose **2** choose by voting —*adj.* **3** chosen **4** select; choice **5** (after the noun) chosen but not yet in office (*president elect*) [L *eligere elect-* choose]

e·lec·tion /ilek'SHən/ *n.* **1** electing or being elected **2** occasion of this

e·lec·tion·eer /ilek'SHənēr'/ *v.* work for a candidate for election

e·lec·tive /ilek'tiv/ *adj.* **1** chosen or derived from election **2** (of a body) empowered to elect **3** optional

e·lec·tor /ilek'tər, -tôr'/ *n.* **1** qualified voter in an election **2** member of the electoral college —**e·lec'tor·al** *adj.*

e·lec'tor·al col'lege *n.* ad hoc assembly that formally elects the US president

e·lec·tor·ate /ilek't(ə)rət/ *n.* body of qualified voters

e·lec·tric /ilek'trik/ *adj.* **1** of, worked by, or charged with electricity; producing electricity **2** causing or charged with excitement [Gk *ēlektron* amber]

e·lec'tri·cal *adj.* of electricity —**e·lec'tri·cal·ly** *adv.*

e·lec'tric chair' *n.* electrified chair used for capital punishment

e·lec·tri·cian /ilek'triSH'ən, ē'lek-/ *n.* person who installs or maintains electrical equipment

e·lec·tric·i·ty /ilek'tris'ətē/ *n.* **1** form of energy occurring in elementary particles (electrons, protons, etc.) **2** science of electricity **3** supply of electricity **4** excitement

e·lec·tri·fy /ilek'trəfī'/ *v.* (**·fied, ·fy·ing**) **1** charge with electricity **2** convert to the use of electric power **3** cause sudden excitement —**e·lec'tri·fi·ca'tion** /-fikā'SHən/ *n.*

electro- *comb. form* of, by, or caused by electricity [rel. to ELECTRIC]

e·lec·tro·car·di·o·gram /ilek'trōkär'dēəgram'/ *n.* record traced by an electrocardiograph; *abbr.* **EKG**

e·lec·tro·car·di·o·graph /ilek'trōkär'dēəgraf'/ *n.* instrument recording electric currents generated by a heartbeat

e·lec·tro·cute /ilek'trəkyōōt'/ v. (·cut·ed, ·cut·ing) kill by electric shock —e·lec'tro·cu'tion n. [ELECTRO- + (EXE)CUTE]

e·lec·trode /ilek'trōd'/ n. conductor through which electricity enters or leaves an electrolyte, gas, vacuum, etc. [ELECTRO- + Gk hodos way]

e·lec·tro·en·ceph·a·lo·gram /ilek'trō-insef'(ə)logram'/ n. record traced by an electroencephalograph; abbr. EEG

e·lec·tro·en·ceph·a·lo·graph /ilek'trō-insef'(ə)lograf'/ n. instrument that records electrical activity of the brain

e·lec·trol·y·sis /ilekträl'əsis/ n. 1 chemical decomposition by electric action 2 destruction of tumors, hair roots, etc., by this process —e·lec·tro·lyt·ic /ilek'trəlit'ik/ adj.

elec·tro·lyte /ilek'trəlīt'/ n. substance in solution able to conduct electricity, as in a battery

e·lec·tro·lyze /ilek'trəlīz/ v. (·lyzed, ·lyz·ing) subject to or treat by electrolysis

e·lec·tro·mag·net /ilek'trōmag'nit/ n. soft metal core made into a magnet by a surrounding coil carrying an electric current —e·lec'tro·mag·net'ic /-net'ik/ adj.; e·lec'tro·mag·net'i·cal·ly adv.; e·lec·tro·mag·net·ism n.

e·lec·tro·mo·tive /ilek'trəmō'tiv/ adj. producing or tending to produce an electric current

e·lec·tro·mo·tive force' n. force set up in an electric circuit by a difference in potential

e·lec·tron /ilek'trän'/ n. stable atomic particle with a negative electrical charge

e·lec·tron·ic /ilekträn'ik/ adj. 1a produced by or involving the flow of electrons b of electrons or electronics 2 (of music, etc.) produced by electronic means 3 (of mail) sent by a computer system —e·lec·tron'i·cal·ly adv.

e·lec·tron·ics /ilekträn'iks/ n. pl. (treated as sing.) science dealing with the movement, action, and use of electrons

e·lec'tron mi'cro·scope n. microscope with high magnification and resolution, using electron beams instead of light

e·lec·tro·plate /ilek'trəplāt'/ v. (·plat·ed, ·plat·ing) coat with a thin layer of metal by electrolysis

e·lec·tro·shock /ilek'trəshaäk'/ adj. (of therapy) by means of electric shocks

el·ee·mos·y·nar·y /el'imäs'əner'ē, el'/ adj. pertaining to charity [ult. fr. Gk eleēmosynē alms]

el·e·gant /el'igənt/ adj. 1 tasteful; refined; graceful 2 ingeniously simple —el'e·gance n.; el'e·gant·ly adv. [L, rel. to ELECT]

el·e·gi·ac /el'əjī'ək, ilē'jēak'/ adj. (also el·e·gi'a·cal) 1 used for elegies 2 mournful —n. 3 (pl.) elegiac verses

el·e·gy /el'əjē/ n. (pl. ·gies) sorrowful poem or song, esp. for the dead [L fr. Gk]

elem. abbr. elementary

el·e·ment /el'əmənt/ n. 1 component part; factor, often basic or essential 2 Chem. any of the substances that cannot be resolved by chemical means into simpler substances 3 a being's natural environment 4 Electr. wire that heats up in an electric appliance 5 (pl.) weather forces, esp. wind and storm 6 (pl.) rudiments of learning (an art, etc.) [L]

el·e·men·tal adj. 1 of or like the elements or the forces of nature; powerful 2 essential; basic

el·e·men·ta·ry /el'əment'(ə)rē/ adj. basic; simple; rudimentary

el·e·men·ta·ry par'ti·cle n. Physics. subatomic particle, esp. one not known to consist of simpler ones

el·e·men·ta·ry school' n. school teaching basic subjects, usually for six or eight years

el·e·phant /el'əfənt/ n. largest land animal, with a flexible snout or trunk and usu. ivory tusks [Gk elephās]

el·e·phan·ti·a·sis /el'əfəntī'əsis/ n. skin disease causing gross enlargement of parts affected

el·e·phan·tine /el'əfan'tēn', -tīn/ adj. 1 of elephants 2a huge b clumsy

elev. abbr. elevation

el·e·vate /el'əvāt'/ v. (·vat·ed, ·vat·ing) 1 raise; lift up 2 raise in rank, etc. 3 raise morally or intellectually [L elevare lift up]

el'e·va'tion n. 1 elevating or being elevated 2 angle with the horizontal 3 height above sea level, etc. 4 high position 5 drawing or diagram showing one side of a building

el'e·va'tor n. 1 usu. boxlike apparatus for raising and lowering people, freight, etc., between floors 2 person or thing that elevates 3 Aeron. device on an airplane's tail to control vertical motion

e·lev·en /ilev'ən/ adj. & n. 1 one more than ten 2 symbol for this (11, xi, XI) —e·lev'enth adj. & n. [OE]

elf /elf/ n. (pl. elves) mythological being, esp. one that is small and mischievous —elf'in, elf'ish adj. [OE]

El·gar /el'gär', -gər/, (Sir) Edward 1857–1934; British composer

El Gi·za n. see GIZA

El Gre·co /el grek'ō/ (born Domenikos Theotokopoulos) 1541–1614; Cretan-born Spanish painter

e·lic·it /ilis'it/ v. draw out (facts, a response, etc.); prompt [L elicere]

e·lide /ilīd'/ v. (·lid·ed, ·lid·ing) omit (a vowel or syllable) in pronunciation [L elidere elis- crush out; strike out]

el·i·gi·ble /el'əjəbəl/ adj. 1 fit or entitled to be chosen 2 desirable or suitable for marriage —el'i·gi·bil'i·ty n. [L, rel. to ELECT]

E·li·jah /ilī'jə/ 9th cent. B.C.; Hebrew prophet

e·lim·i·nate /ilim'ənāt'/ v. (·nat·ed, ·nat·ing) 1 remove; get rid of 2 exclude from consideration 3 excrete —e·lim'i·na'tion, e·lim'i·na'tor n. [L limen threshold]

El·i·ot /el'ēət/ 1 George (pseudonym of Mary Ann Evans) 1819–80; English novelist 2 T(homas) S(tearns) 1888–1965; US-born British poet and dramatist

E·li·sha /ilī'shə/ 9th cent. B.C.; Hebrew prophet

e·li·sion /ilizh'ən/ n. omission of a vowel or syllable in pronunciation [L, rel. to ELIDE]

e·lite /ilēt', ālēt'/ n. best or select group or class [MFr, rel. to ELECT]

e·lit·ism /ilēt'iz'əm, ā-/ n. recourse to or advocacy of leadership or dominance by a select group —e·lit'ist n. & adj.

e·lix·ir /ilik'sər/ n. 1a alchemist's hypothetical substance to change metals into gold or prolong life b remedy for all ills 2 aromatic medicinal drug [MedL fr. Ar]

E·liz·a·beth /iliz'əbəth/ n. city in N.J. Pop. 110,002

E·liz·a·beth I /iliz'əbəth/ 1533–1603; queen of England and Ireland (1558–1603)

Elizabeth II 1926– ; queen of the United Kingdom (1952–)

Elizabeth, St. (in the Bible) mother of John the Baptist

E·liz·a·be·than /iliz'əbē'тнən/ adj. 1 of the time of Queen Elizabeth I or II —n. 2 person of the time of Elizabeth I in England

elk /elk/ n. (pl. same or -s) large deer of northern parts of Europe, N America, and Asia [OE]

ell /el/ n. 1 right-angled extension to a building 2 something L-shaped, e.g., a pipe elbow 3 Hist. measure equal to 45 in. [OE: forearm]

El·ling·ton /el'iNGtən/, "Duke" (Edward Kennedy) 1899–1974; US jazz pianist, composer, and band-leader

el·lipse /ilips'/ n. closed symmetrical oval figure

el·lip·sis /ilip'sis/ n. (pl. ·ses /-sēz'/) 1 omission of words within a construction or sense 2 set of three dots indicating omission of words [Gk elleipsis deficit]

el·lip·ti·cal /ilip'tikal/ adj. (also el·lip'tic) 1 of or in the form of an ellipse 2 marked by ellipsis 3 ambiguous —el·lip'ti·cal·ly adv.

El·lis /el'əs/, (Henry) Havelock 1859–1939; English psychologist

El·lis Is·land /el'əs/ n. island in N.Y. Harbor; former processing center for European immigrants

elm /elm/ n. 1 tall tree with rough serrated leaves 2 its wood [OE]

El Man·su·ra see AL-MANSURA

El Mon·te /el mänt'ē/ n. city in Calif. Pop. 106,209

El Ni·ño /el nēn'yō/ n. occasional warm Pacific current that affects weather patterns

el·o·cu·tion /el'əkyōō'shən/ n. art of clear and expressive speech [L eloquori speak out; utter]

e·lon·gate /ilôNG'gāt/ v. (·gat·ed, ·gat·ing) lengthen; extend —e·lon·ga'tion n. [L longus long]

e·lope /ilōp'/ v. (·loped, ·lop·ing) run away to get married secretly —e·lope'ment n. [AngFr]

el·o·quence /el'əkwəns/ n. fluent and effective use of language —el'o·quent adj.; el'o·quent·ly adv. [L eloquori speak out]

El Pas·o /el pas'ō/ n. city in Texas. Pop. 515,342

El Sal·va·dor /el sal'vədôr'/ n. republic in NW Central America. Capital: San Salvador. Pop. 5,460,000 —Sal'va·do'ran, Sal'va·do'ri·an /-rēan/ n. & adj.

else /els/ adv. 1 besides (someone else) 2 instead (what else) 3 otherwise; if not (or else you'll be late) [OE]

else'where' adv. in or to some other place

e·lu·ci·date /ilōō'sədāt'/ v. (·dat·ed, ·dat·ing) throw light on; explain —e·lu'ci·da'tion n. [L, rel. to LUCID]

e·lude /ilōōd'/ v. (·lud·ed, ·lud·ing) 1 escape adroitly; avoid 2 slip from (a person, memory, etc.) [L ludere play; deceive]

e·lu·sive /ilōō'siv/ adj. 1 difficult to capture 2 difficult to remember or pin down —e·lu'sive·ness n.

elves /elvz/ n. pl. of ELF

E·ly·si·um /iliz'ēəm, -lizh'-, -lē'zē-/ n. 1 (also E·ly'si·an Fields') Gk. Myth. abode of the blessed after death 2 place of ideal happiness —E·ly'si·an /-lizh'ən/ adj. [L fr. Gk]

em /em/ n. Printing. unit of measurement equal to the width of an M

'em pron. Colloq. them

em- prefix see EN-

e·ma·ci·ate /imā'shē·āt'/ v. (·at·ed, ·at·ing) make abnormally thin or feeble —e·ma'ci·a'tion n. [L macies leanness]

e-mail /ē'māl'/ n. (also E·mail) ELECTRONIC, 3

em·a·nate /em'ənāt'/ v. (·nat·ed, ·nat·ing) issue; originate —em'a·na'tion n. [L emanare flow out]

e·man·ci·pate /imän'səpāt'/ v. (·pat·ed, ·pat·ing) 1 free from social or political restraint 2 free from inhibitions 3 free from slavery —e·man'ci·pa'tion n. [L: free from possession, fr. manus hand + capere seize]

e·mas·cu·late /imäs'kyəlāt'/ v. (·lat·ed, ·lat·ing) 1 deprive of force or vigor 2 castrate —e·mas'cu·la'tion /-lā'shən/ n. [L, rel. to MALE]

em·balm /embä(l)m'/ v. preserve (a corpse) from decay [OFr, rel. to BALM]

em·bank·ment /embaNGk'mənt/ n. bank constructed to keep back water or carry a road, railway, etc.

em·bar·go /embär'gō/ n. (pl. ·goes) 1 order barring ships from a port or ports 2 official suspension of trade —v. (·goes, ·go·ing) 3 place under embargo [Sp, rel. to BAR¹]

em·bark /embärk'/ v. 1 put or go on board a ship or aircraft (to a destination) 2 (foll. by on) begin an enterprise —em'bar·ka'tion n. [MFr fr. OFr barque a sailboat]

em·bar·rass /embar'əs/ v. 1 make (a person) feel awkward or ashamed 2 cause to be unable to pay 3 encumber —em·bar'rass·ing adj.; em·bar'rass·ment n. [perh. fr. It imbarrare bar in, or fr. Port baraça cord]

em·bas·sy /em'bəsē/ n. (pl. ·sies) 1a residence or offices of an ambassador b ambassador and staff 2 deputation to a foreign government [OFr, rel. to AMBASSADOR]

em·bat·tled /embat'ld/ adj. 1 prepared or arrayed for battle 2 under attack or in trying circumstances

em·bed /embed'/ v. (also im·bed) (·bed·ded, ·bed·ding) fix firmly in; implant

em·bel·lish /embel'ish/ v. 1 beautify; adorn 2 enhance (a story, etc.) with fictitious additions —em·bel'lish·ment n. [MFr, rel. to bel fr. L bellus pretty]

em·ber /em'bər/ n. small piece of glowing coal, etc., in a fire [OE]

em·bez·zle /embez'əl/ v. (·zled, ·zling) divert (money, etc.) fraudulently to one's own use —em·bez'zle·ment, em·bez'zler n. [AngFr]

em·bit·ter /embit'ər/ v. arouse bitter feelings in —em·bit'ter·ment n.

em·bla·zon /emblā'zən/ v. 1 portray or

adorn conspicuously 2 adorn (a heraldic shield) —em·bla'zon·ment n.

em·blem /em'bləm/ n. 1 symbol 2 heraldic or representative device —em'blem·at'ic /at'ik/ adj. [Gk emballein insert]

em·bod·y /embäd'ē/ v. (·ied, ·y·ing) 1 make (an idea, etc.) actual or discernible 2 (of a thing) be a tangible expression of 3 include; comprise —em·bod'i·ment n.

em·bold·en /embōl'dən/ v. make bold; encourage

em·bo·lism /em'bəliz'əm/ n. obstruction of an artery by a clot, air bubble, etc. [L fr. Gk]

em·boss /embôs', -bäs'/ v. carve or decorate with a design in relief [rel. to BOSS²]

em·bou·chure /äm'booshoor'/ n. Mus. technique for applying the mouth to a wind instrument [Fr, rel. to bouche mouth]

em·brace /embrās'/ v. (·braced, ·brac·ing) 1a hold closely in the arms b (of two people) embrace each other 2 clasp; enclose 3 accept eagerly 4 adopt or include; comprise —n. 5 act of embracing; clasp —em·brace'a·ble adj. [OFr, rel. to BRACE¹]

em·broi·der /embroi'dər/ v. 1 decorate (cloth, etc.) with needlework 2 embellish (a narrative) —em·broi'der·er n. [MFr fr. Gmc]

em·broi'der·y n. (pl. ·ies) 1 art of embroidering 2 embroidered work 3 embellishment

em·broil /embroil'/ v. involve (a person, etc.) in a conflict or difficulties —em·broil'ment n. [MFr brouiller mix]

em·bry·o /em'brē·ō'/ n. (pl. ·os) 1a unborn or unhatched offspring b human organism in the first eight weeks from conception 2 rudimentary plant in a seed 3 thing in a rudimentary stage —em'bry·on'ic /em'brē·än'ik/ adj. [Gk bryein swell]

em·bry·ol·o·gy /em'brē·äl'əjē/ n. the study of embryos —em'bry·ol'o·gist n.

e·mend /imend'/ v. edit (a text, etc.) to make corrections —e·men·da·tion /ēməndā'shən/ n. [L emendare fr. mendum fault]

em·er·ald /em'(ə)rəld/ n. 1 deep-green gem 2 color of this —adj. 3 deep green [Gk smaragdos]

e·merge /ēmərj'/ v. (·merged, ·merg·ing) 1 come up or out into view or notice 2 become known; be revealed 3 become recognized or prominent —e·mer'gence n.; e·mer'gent adj. [L emergere bring forth; rise]

e·mer·gen·cy /ēmər'jənsē/ n. (pl. ·cies) sudden state of danger, etc., requiring immediate action [MedL, rel. to EMERGE]

e·mer·i·tus /imer'ətəs/ adj. (fem. e·mer'i·ta) retired but retaining one's title as an honor (emeritus professor) [L merere earn; deserve]

Em·er·son /em'ərsən/, Ralph Waldo 1803–82; US philosopher, essayist, and poet

em·er·y /em'(ə)rē/ n. coarse corundum for polishing metal, etc. [Gk smēris polishing powder]

e·met·ic /ēmet'ik/ adj. 1 that causes vomiting —n. 2 emetic medicine [Gk emetos vomiting]

em·i·grant /em'igrənt/ n. 1 person who emigrates —adj. 2 emigrating

em·i·grate /em'igrāt'/ v. (·grat·ed, ·grat·ing) leave one's own country to settle in another —em'i·gra'tion n. [L emigrare]

● Usage: A person emigrates from ('leaves') one country, and immigrates to ('enters') another. The difference between the two is based on point of view.

é·mi·gré /em'igrā'/ n. emigrant, esp. a political exile [Fr fr. L]

em·i·nence /em'ənəns/ n. 1 distinction; high station 2 (cap.) RC Ch. title of address to a cardinal [L eminere stand out]

em·i·nent /em'ənənt/ adj. distinguished; notable; outstanding [L eminere stand out]

● Usage: Eminent means 'important'; outstanding; famous': Roosevelt was an eminent statesman. Imminent means 'about to occur': A blizzard is imminent, so prepare yourselves. Immanent means 'inherent; inborn': Her immanent goodness prevented her from doing evil.

em'i·nent do·main' n. Law. right of a government to purchase private property, as land, for public use

e·mir /imēr', ā-/ n. (also a·mir') title of various Muslim rulers [Fr fr. Ar]

em·is·sar·y /em'əser'ē/ n. (pl. ·ies) person sent on a diplomatic mission [L, rel. to EMIT]

e·mit /ēmit'/ v. (·mit·ted, ·mit·ting) give or send out (heat, light, sound, etc.); discharge —e·mis·sion /ēmish'ən/ n. [L emittere fr. miss-]

e·mol·li·ent /imäl'yənt/ adj. 1 that softens or soothes the skin, etc. —n. 2 softening substance, as an ointment [L mollis soft]

e·mol·u·ment /imäl'yəmənt/ n. fee from employment; salary [L]

e·mote /imōt'/ v. (·mot·ed, ·mot·ing) show excessive emotion

e·mo·tion /imō'shən/ n. 1 strong feeling such as love, anger, or fear 2 emotional intensity or sensibility [MFr, rel. to MOTION]

e·mo·tion·al adj. 1 of or expressing emotions 2 especially liable to emotion 3 arousing emotion —e·mo'tion·al·ism' n.; e·mo'tion·al·ly adv.

em·pa·thize /em'pəthīz'/ v. (·thized, ·thiz·ing) exercise empathy

em·pa·thy /em'pəthē/ n. capacity to identify with a person or object —em·pa·thet·ic /em'pəthet'ik/ adj. [Gk empatheia affection]

Em·ped·o·cles /emped'əklēz'/ c. 493 – c. 433 B.C.; Greek philosopher

em·per·or /em'pərər/ n. sovereign of an empire [L imperare command]

em·pha·sis /em'fəsis/ n. (pl. ·ses /-sēz'/) 1 importance or prominence given to a thing 2 stress laid on a word, syllable, etc., to make the meaning clear or show importance [L fr. Gk]

em·pha·size /em'fəsīz'/ v. (·sized, ·siz·ing) put emphasis on; stress

em·phat·ic /imfat'ik, em-/ adj. 1 forcibly expressive 2 of words: a bearing the stress b used to give emphasis —em·phat'i·cal·ly adv.

em·phy·se·ma /em'fəsē'mə, -zē'mə/ n. disease of the lungs causing breathing difficulty [Gk emphysan inflate]

em·pire /em'pīr'/ n. 1 large group of territories or countries under a single authority 2 supreme dominion 3 large organization considered powerful [L imperium dominion]

em·pir·i·cal /impēr'ikəl/ adj. (also em·pir'

ic) based on observation, experience, or experiment, not on theory —em·pir'i·cal·ly *adv.*; em·pir'i·cism' /-siz'əm/ *n.*; em·pir'i·cist *n. & adj.* [Gk *empeiria* experience]

em·place·ment /implās'mənt/ *n.* 1 putting in position 2 platform for guns [Fr, rel. to PLACE]

em·ploy /imploi', em-/ *v.* 1 use the services of (a person) in return for payment 2 use to good effect 3 keep (a person) occupied —em·ploy'a·ble *adj.*; em·ploy'er *n.* [L *implicare* involve; entangle]

em·ploy·ee /emploi'ē', im-, -ploi'ē'/ *n.* (also em·ploy'e) person employed for wages

em·ploy'ment *n.* 1 employing or being employed 2 occupation

em·po·ri·um /empôr'ēəm/ *n.* (*pl.* -ums or ·ri·a /-rēə/) market or store offering a wide variety of goods [Gk *emporos* merchant]

em·pow·er /impou'ər, -pour'/ *v.* give authority to

em·press /em'pris/ *n.* 1 wife or widow of an emperor 2 woman emperor [OFr fr. L, rel. to EMPEROR]

emp·ty /em(p)'tē/ *adj.* (·ti·er, ·ti·est) 1 containing nothing 2 unoccupied or unfurnished 3 hollow; insincere 4 without purpose 5 vacuous (*an empty head*) —*v.* (·tied, ·ty·ing) 6 remove the contents of 7 become empty 8 (of a river) discharge itself —*n.* (*pl.* ·ties) *Colloq.* 9 empty bottle, etc. —emp'ti·ly *adv.*; emp'ti·ness *n.* [OE]

emp'ty-hand'ed *adj.* bringing or taking nothing

em·py·re·an /empər'ēən/ *n.* the highest heaven, as the sphere of fire or abode of God [Gk *pyr* fire]

EMT *abbr.* emergency medical technician

EMU

e·mu /ē'myōō/ *n.* (*pl.* ·mus) flightless Australian bird [Port]

em·u·late /em'yəlāt'/ *v.* (·lat·ed, ·lat·ing) 1 try to equal or excel 2 imitate —em'u·la'tion *n.*; em·u·la'tive /-lə'tiv/ *adj.*; em'u·la'tor *n.* [L *aemulari* rival]

e·mul·si·fy /iməl'səfī'/ *v.* (·fied, ·fy·ing) convert into an emulsion —e·mul'si·fi·ca'tion /-fika'sHən/ *n.*; e·mul'si·fi'er *n.*

e·mul·sion /iməl'sHən/ *n.* fine dispersion of one liquid in another, esp. as paint, medicine, etc. [L *mulgere* milk]

en /en/ *n. Printing.* unit of measurement equal to half an em [for the letter N]

en-[1] *prefix* (also em- before *b*, *p*) forming verbs: IN-[2]: 1 from nouns, meaning 'put into or on' (*engulf; entrust; embed*) 2 from nouns or adjectives, meaning 'bring into the condition of' (*enslave*) 3 from verbs: a in the sense

'in; into; on' (*enfold*) b as an intensifier (*entangle*) [OFr en- fr. L *in*-]

en-[2] *prefix* (also em- before *b*, *p*) in; inside (*energy; empathy*) [Gk]

-en *suffix* forming verbs: 1 from adjectives, usu. meaning 'make or become so or more so' (*deepen; moisten*) 2 from nouns (*happen; strengthen*) [OE]

en·a·ble /enā'bəl/ *v.* (·bled, ·bling) 1 give (a person, etc.) the means or authority 2 make possible

en·act /enakt'/ *v.* 1a ordain; decree b make (a bill, etc.) law 2 play (a part) —en·act'ment *n.*

e·nam·el /enam'əl/ *n.* 1 glasslike opaque coating for metal, etc. 2a smooth hard coating b a kind of hard gloss paint 3 hard coating of a tooth —*v.* (·eled or ·elled, ·el·ing or ·el·ling) 4 inlay, coat, etc., with enamel [AngFr fr. Gmc]

en·am·or /enam'ər/ *v.* as in **enamored of** inspire with love or delight for [Fr *amour* love]

en·camp /enkamp', en-/ *v.* settle in a (esp. military) camp —en·camp'ment *n.*

en·cap·su·late /enkap's(y)əlāt'/ *v.* (·lat·ed, ·lat·ing) 1 enclose in or as in a capsule 2 express briefly; summarize —en·cap'su·la'tion *n.* [rel. to CAPSULE]

en·case /enkās'/ *v.* (·cased, ·cas·ing) enclose in or as in a case —en·case'ment *n.*

-ence *suffix* forming nouns expressing: 1 a quality or state or an instance of this (*patience*) 2 an action (*reference*) [OFr fr. L -*entia*]

en·ceph·a·li·tis /ensef'əlī'tis/ *n.* inflammation of the brain [Gk *enkephalos* brain]

en·ceph·a·lo·gram /ensef'(ə)ləgram'/ *n.* ELECTROENCEPHALOGRAM

en·ceph·a·lo·graph /ensef'(ə)ləgraf'/ *n.* ELECTROENCEPHALOGRAPH

en·chant /enCHant'/ *v.* 1 charm; delight 2 bewitch —en·chant'ed·ly, en·chant'ing·ly *adv.*; en·chant'er, en·chant'ress /-CHan'tris/, en·chant'ment *n.*; en·chant'ing *adj.*

en·cir·cle /ensər'kəl/ *v.* (·cled, ·cling) 1 surround 2 form a circle around —en·cir'cle·ment *n.*

en·clave /en'klāv', än'-/ *n.* territory surrounded by foreign territory [L *clavis* key]

en·close /enklōz'/ *v.* (·closed, ·clos·ing) 1a surround with a wall, fence, etc. b shut in 2 put in a receptacle [L, rel. to INCLUDE]

en·clo·sure /enklō'zHər/ *n.* 1 act of enclosing 2 enclosed space or area 3 thing enclosed with a letter [Fr, rel. to ENCLOSE]

en·code /enkōd'/ *v.* (·cod·ed, ·cod·ing) put into code

en·co·mi·um /inkō'mēəm, en-/ *n.* (*pl.* ·ums) formal or high-flown praise —en·co'mi·as'tic /-as'tik/ *adj.* [Gk *kōmos* revelry]

en·com·pass /enkəm'pəs/ *v.* 1 contain; include 2 surround

en·core /än'kôr'/ *n.* 1 audience's demand for continuation of performing, usu. by applause 2 such a reprise [Fr: once again]

en·coun·ter /enkoun'tər/ *v.* 1 meet unexpectedly 2 meet as an adversary —*n.* 3 meeting by chance or in conflict [L *contra* against]

en·cour·age /enkər'ij/ *v.* (·aged, ·ag·ing) 1 give courage or confidence to 2 urge 3 promote —en·cour'age·ment *n.* [MFr]

en·croach /enkrōCH/ *v.* intrude **—en·croach′ment** *n.* [OFr *croc* CROOK]

en·crust /enkrəst′/ *v.* cover with or form a crust [Fr]

en·cum·ber /enkəm′bər/ *v.* be a burden to or hindrance [MFr fr. Rom]

en·cum·brance /enkəm′brəns/ *n.* burden

ency. (also **encyc.**) *abbr.* encyclopedia

-ency *suffix* forming nouns denoting quality or state (*efficiency; fluency; presidency*) [L *-entia*]

en·cyc·li·cal /ensik′likəl/ *n.* papal essay to bishops [Gk, rel. to CYCLE]

en·cy·clo·pe·di·a /ensī′kləpē′dēə/ *n.* (also **·pae′di·a**) reference publication giving information on many subjects or on many aspects of one subject [Gk *enkyklios* all-around + *paideia* education]

en·cy·clo·pe′dic *adj.* (also **·pae′dic**) (of knowledge or information) comprehensive

end /end/ *n.* **1a** extreme limit **b** extremity **2** extreme part or surface of a thing **3** finish **4** latter part **5** death; destruction **6** result **7** goal **8** (prec. by *the*) *Colloq.* the limit of durability **—v. 9** bring or come to an end; finish **10** result **11 make ends meet** live within one's income **12 on end: a** upright **b** continuously [OE]

en·dan·ger /endān′jər/ *v.* place in danger

en·dan′gered spe′cies *n.* species threatened by extinction

en·dear /endēr′/ *v.* make dear **—en·dear′ing** *adj.*; **en·dear′ing·ly** *adv.*

en·dear′ment *n.* **1** an expression of affection **2** liking; affection

en·deav·or /endev′ər/ *v.* **1** try earnestly **—n.** **2** earnest attempt [fr. EN-[1] + Fr *devoir* duty]

en·dem·ic /endem′ik/ *adj.* prevalent among a particular people or in a particular region **—en·dem′i·cal·ly** *adv.* [Gk *en-* in + *dēmos* the people]

● **Usage:** See note at EPIDEMIC.

end′ing *n.* **1** end or final part, esp. of a story **2** inflected final part of a word

en·dive /en′dīv′, än′dēv′/ *n.* plant with overlapping white leaves, used in salads [Gk *entybon*]

end·less /end′ləs/ *adj.* **1** infinite; without end **2** continual **3** innumerable **4** (of a belt, chain, etc.) having the ends joined for continuous action over wheels, etc. **—end′less·ly** *adv.* [OE, rel. to END]

end′most′ *adj.* nearest the end

endo- *comb. form* internal [Gk *endon* within]

en·do·crine /en′dəkrən, -krī′n/ *adj.* (of a gland) secreting directly into the blood [Gk *krinein* separate]

en·do·morph /en′dōmôrf′/ *n.* person with a heavy, rounded body [Gk *morphē* form]

en·dorse /endôrs′/ *v.* (**·dorsed, ·dors·ing**) **1** approve **2** sign or write on (a document), esp. sign the back of (a check) **3** recommend commercially **—en·dorse′ment** *n.* [L *dorsum* back]

en·dow /endou′/ *v.* **1** bequeath or give a permanent income to (an institution, etc.) **2** provide with talent, ability, etc. [OFr fr. L *dotare* dower]

en·dow′ment *n.* **1** endowing **2** endowed income

end′ prod′uct *n.* final result

end′ ta′ble *n.* table at the end of a sofa

en·due /end(y)ōō′/ *v.* (**·dued, ·du·ing**) provide (a person) with (qualities, etc.) [L *inducere* introduce; cover; put on clothes]

en·dur·ance /end(y)ŏŏr′əns/ *n.* ability to withstand prolonged strain, pain, etc. [Fr, rel. to ENDURE]

en·dure /end(y)ŏŏr′/ *v.* (**·dured, ·dur·ing**) **1** undergo (a difficulty, etc.) **2** tolerate **3** last **—en·dur′able** *adj.* [OFr fr. L *durus* hard]

end·ways /end′wāz′/ *adv.* (also **end′wise′**) **1** with end uppermost or foremost **2** end to end

en·e·ma /en′əmə/ *n.* introduction of fluid into the rectum, esp. to medicate, evacuate the lower bowel, etc. [Gk: injection]

en·e·my /en′əmē/ *n.* (*pl.* **·mies**) **1** person manifestly hostile to another **2a** hostile nation or army **b** member of this [L *inimicus* unfriendly; hostile]

en·er·get·ic /en′ərjet′ik/ *adj.* full of energy; vigorous **—en′er·get′i·cal·ly** *adv.* [Gk, rel. to ENERGY]

en·er·gize /en′ərjīz′/ *v.* (**·gized, ·giz·ing**) **1** give energy to **2** provide (a device) with energy for operation

en·er·gy /en′ərjē/ *n.* (*pl.* **·gies**) **1** capacity for activity; force; vigor **2** capacity of matter or radiation to do work [Gk *energein* be active]

en·er·vate /en′ərvāt′/ *v.* (**·vat·ed, ·vat·ing**) deprive of vigor or vitality **—en′er·va′tion** *n.* [L *enervare* weaken]

en·fee·ble /enfē′bəl/ *v.* (**·bled, ·bling**) make feeble **—en·fee′ble·ment** *n.*

en·fi·lade /en′fəlād′/ *n.* gunfire directed along a line of battle [Fr L *filum* thread]

en·fold /enfōld′/ *v.* **1** wrap; envelop **2** clasp; embrace

en·force /enfôrs′/ *v.* (**·forced, ·forc·ing**) **1** compel observance of (a law, etc.) **2** impose (an action or one's will) on **—en·force′a·ble** *adj.*; **en·force′ment** *n.* [L, rel. to FORCE]

en·fran·chise /enfran′CHīz/ *v.* (**·chised, ·chis·ing**) **1** give (a person) the right to vote **2** free (a slave, etc.) **—en·fran′chise·ment** *n.* [OFr, rel. to FRANK]

en·gage /enɡāj′/ *v.* (**·gaged, ·gag·ing**) **1a** (usu. *passive*) occupy **b** hold fast; seize **2** (usu. *passive*) bind by a promise, esp. of marriage **3** hire **4a** interlock (parts of a gear, etc.) **b** (of a gear, etc.) become interlocked **5a** come into battle with **b** bring (troops) into battle with **6** take part (*engage in politics*) **—en·gaged′** *adj.* [OFr, rel. to GAGE[1]]

en·gage′ment *n.* **1** engaging or being engaged **2** appointment **3** betrothal **4** battle

en·gag′ing *adj.* attractive; charming **—en·gag′ing·ly** *adv.*

En·gels /eNG′(g)əlz/, **Friedrich** 1820–95; German political philosopher

en·gen·der /enjen′dər/ *v.* give rise to; produce [OFr fr. L *generare* beget]

en·gine /en′jin/ *n.* **1** mechanical contrivance, esp. as a source of power **2** locomotive [L *ingenium* nature; quality]

● **Usage:** *Engine* refers to a power-generating machine fueled by combustion, as an automobile engine or steam engine. *Motor* is also used of a car's engine, and is also used specifically of *electric motors.*

en·gi·neer /en′jənēr′/ *n.* **1** person skilled in a branch of engineering **2** person in charge of engines, etc. (*ship's engineer*) **3** contriver —*v.* **4** contrive; bring about [MedL, rel. to ENGINE]

en·gi·neer′ing *n.* application of science to the design, building, and use of machines, etc.

Eng·land /iNG′(g)lənd/ *n.* largest division of the United Kingdom. Capital: London. Pop. 44,876,000

● Usage: See note at GREAT BRITAIN.

Eng·lish /iNG′glisH/ *adj.* **1** of England or its people or language —*n.* **2** language of England, now used in the UK, US, Canada, etc. **3** (prec. by *the*; treated as *pl.*) the people of England **4** (often **e-**) spin imparted to a ball [OE]

Eng′lish Chan′nel *n.* strait between England and France, connecting the Atlantic Ocean and the North Sea

ENGLISH HORN

Eng′lish horn′ *n. Mus.* double-reed woodwind instrument similar to an oboe but larger and a fifth lower in pitch

Eng·lish·man /iNG′glisHmən/ *n.* (*pl.* **·men**; *fem.* **wom′an**, *pl.* **wom′en**) native or citizen of England

en·gorged /enGôrjd′/ *adj.* **1** crammed full **2** congested with fluid, esp. blood [MFr, rel. to EN-[1] + GORGE]

engr. *abbr.* **1** engineer **2** engraved

en·grave /enGrāv′/ *v.* (**·graved**, **·grav·ing**) **1** carve (a text or design) on a hard surface **2** inscribe (a surface) thus **3** impress deeply (on a person's memory) —**en·grav′er** *n.* [fr. GRAVE[2]]

en·grav′ing *n.* print made from an engraved plate

en·gross /enGrōs′/ *v.* absorb the attention of; occupy fully —**en·gross′ing** *adj.*; **en·gross′ment** *n.* [AngFr]

en·gulf /enGəlf′/ *v.* flow over and swamp; overwhelm —**en·gulf′ment** *n.*

en·hance /enhans′/ *v.* (**·hanced**, **·hanc·ing**) intensify; improve —**en·hance′ment** *n.* [AngFr fr. L *altus* high]

e·nig·ma /inig′mə/ *n.* **1** puzzling thing or person **2** riddle; paradox —**en·ig·mat·ic** /en′igmat′ik/ *adj.*; **en′ig·mat′i·cal·ly** *adv.* [L fr. Gk]

en·join /enjoin′/ *v.* **1** command; order **2** *Law.* prohibit by injunction (from doing a thing) [L *injungere* attach]

en·joy /enjoi′/ *v.* **1** take pleasure in **2** have the use or benefit of **3** experience **4** enjoy oneself experience pleasure —**en·joy′ment** *n.* [OFr]

en·joy′a·ble *adj.* pleasant —**en·joy′a·bly** *adv.*

en·large /enlärj′/ *v.* (**·larged**, **·larg·ing**) **1** make or become larger or wider **2** describe in greater detail **3** reproduce on a larger scale —**en·large′ment** *n.* [OFr, rel. to LARGE]

en·larg′er *n.* apparatus for enlarging photographs

en·light·en /enlīt′n/ *v.* **1** inform (about a subject) **2** (as **enlightened** *adj.*) progressive

en·light′en·ment *n.* **1** enlightening or being enlightened **2** (**the Enlightenment**) 18th-cent. philosophy of reason and individualism

en·list /enlist′/ *v.* **1** enroll in the armed services **2** secure as a means of help or support —**en·list′ment** *n.*

en·liv·en /enlī′vən/ *v.* make lively or cheerful; brighten (a picture, etc.); invigorate —**en·liv′en·ment** *n.*

en masse /än mas′/ *adv. French.* all together

en·mesh /enmesH′/ *v.* entangle in or as in a net

en·mi·ty /en′mətē/ *n.* (*pl.* **·ties**) **1** state of being an enemy **2** hostility [Rom, rel. to ENEMY]

En·ni·us /en′ēəs/, **Quintus** 239–169 B.C.; Roman poet and dramatist

en·no·ble /enō′bəl/ *v.* (**·bled**, **·bling**) make noble —**en·no′ble·ment** *n.* [OFr, rel. to NOBLE]

en·nui /änwē′/ *n.* mental weariness; boredom [Fr, rel. to ANNOY]

e·nor·mi·ty /inôr′mətē/ *n.* (*pl.* **·ties**) **1** monstrous wickedness; appallingness **2** great size [L *enormitas*]

e·nor·mous /inôr′məs/ *adj.* extremely large —**e·nor′mous·ly** *adv.* [L *enormis*, rel. to NORM]

e·nough /inəf′, ē-/ *adj.* **1** as much or as many as required —*n.* **2** sufficient amount or quantity —*adv.* **3** adequately **4** quite (*well enough*) **5** sure enough as expected [OE]

en·quire /enkwī′ər/ *v.* var. of INQUIRE

en·quir′y *n.* (*pl.* **·ies**) var. of INQUIRY

en·rage /enrāj′/ *v.* (**·raged**, **·rag·ing**) make furious [MFr, rel. to RAGE]

en·rap·ture /enrap′cHər/ *v.* (**·tured**, **·tur·ing**) delight intensely

en·rich /enricH′/ *v.* **1** make rich or richer **2** increase the strength, value, or contents of —**en·rich′ment** *n.* [OFr, rel. to RICH]

en·roll /enrōl′/ *v.* **1** enlist **2a** write the name of (a person) on a list **b** incorporate as a member **c** sign up —**en·roll′ment** *n.* [OFr, rel. to ROLL]

en route /än rōōt′, en-, in-/ *adv. French.* on the way

Ens. *abbr.* Ensign

En·sche·de /en′skədə/ *n.* city in the Netherlands. Pop. 146,500

en·sconce /enskäns′/ *v.* (**·sconced**, **·sconc·ing**) establish or settle comfortably [Du *schans* small fortification]

en·sem·ble /änsäm′bəl/ *n.* **1a** thing viewed as the sum of its parts **b** general effect of this **2** set of clothes worn together **3** group of performers working together [L *simul* at the same time]

en·shrine /enshrīn′/ *v.* (**·shrined**, **·shrin·ing**) **1** enclose in a shrine **2** cherish; idolize —**en·shrine′ment** *n.*

en·shroud /epsHroud′/ *v.* **1** cover with or as with a shroud **2** obscure

en·sign /en′sən, -sīn′/ *n.* **1** banner or flag, esp. the military or naval flag of a nation **2** *US*

en·slave /enslāv'/ *v.* (·**slaved**, ·**slav·ing**) make (a person) a slave —**en·slave'ment** *n.*

en·snare /ensner'/ *v.* (·**snared**, ·**snar·ing**) catch in or as in a snare —**en·snare'ment** *n.*

en·sue /ensoo'/ *v.* (·**sued**, ·**su·ing**) happen later or as a result [OFr *fr.* L *sequori* follow]

en·sure /enshoor'/ *v.* (·**sured**, ·**sur·ing**) 1 make certain 2 protect —**en·sur'er** *n.* [AngFr, rel. to ASSURE]
● Usage: See note at INSURE.

-ent *suffix* 1 forming adjectives denoting attribution of an action (*consequent*) or state (*existent*) 2 forming agent nouns (*president*) [L *-ent-* pres. part. stem of verbs]

en·tail /entāl'/ *v.* 1 necessitate or involve unavoidably 2 *Law.* bequeath (an estate) to a specified line of beneficiaries [ME, rel. to TAIL]

en·tan·gle /entang'gəl/ *v.* (·**gled**, ·**gling**) 1 catch or hold fast in a snare, bushes, etc. 2 involve in difficulties 3 complicate —**en·tan'gle·ment** *n.*

en·tente /äntänt'/ *n.* friendly understanding between countries [OFr: intention]

en·ter /en'tər/ *v.* 1 go or come in or into 2 come on stage 3 penetrate 4 write (name, details, etc.) in a list, book, etc. 5 register for; compete in 6a become a member of (a society or profession) b enroll in a school, etc. 7 present before a court 8 engage; subscribe; take part in 9 begin; begin to deal with [L *intra* within]

en·ter·prise /en'tərprīz'/ *n.* 1 undertaking, esp. a challenging one 2 initiative 3 business firm or venture [L *prehendere* grasp]

en'ter·pris'ing *adj.* showing enterprise; resourceful; energetic —**en'ter·pris'ing·ly** *adv.*

en·ter·tain /en'tərtān'/ *v.* 1 divert; amuse 2a receive as a guest b receive guests 3 consider; be drawn to [L *tenere* hold]

en'ter·tain'er *n.* person who entertains, esp. professionally

en'ter·tain'ing *adj.* amusing; diverting —**en'ter·tain'ing·ly** *adv.*

en'ter·tain'ment *n.* 1 entertaining or being entertained 2 thing that entertains; performance

en·thrall /enthrôl'/ *v.* captivate; please greatly —**en·thrall'ment** *n.* [fr. EN-¹ + THRALL]

en·throne /enthrōn'/ *v.* (·**throned**, ·**thron·ing**) place on a throne —**en·throne'ment** *n.*

en·thuse /enth(y)ooz'/ *v.* (·**thused**, ·**thus·ing**) *Colloq.* be or make enthusiastic

en·thu·si·asm /enth(y)oo'zē·az'əm/ *n.* strong interest; great eagerness —**en·thu'si·ast'** /-ast'/ *n.*; **en·thu'si·as'tic** *adj.*; **en·thu'si·as'ti·cal·ly** *adv.* [Gk *entheos* inspired by a god]

en·tice /entīs'/ *v.* (·**ticed**, ·**tic·ing**) attract by the offer of pleasure or reward —**en·tice'ment** *n.*; **en·tic'ing** *adj.*; **en·tic'ing·ly** *adv.* [OFr *enticier* fr. L *titio* burning brand]

en·tire /entīr'/ *adj.* whole; complete; unbroken [L, rel. to INTEGER]

en·tire'ly *adv.* 1 wholly 2 solely

en·tire'ty *n.* (*pl.* ·**ties**) completeness; wholeness

en·ti·tle /entīt'l/ *v.* (·**tled**, ·**tling**) 1 give (a person) a just claim or right 2 give a title to —**en·ti'tle·ment** *n.* [LL, rel. to TITLE]

en·ti·ty /en'tītē/ *n.* (*pl.* ·**ties**) 1 thing with distinct existence 2 thing's existence in itself [L *ens ent-* being]

en·tomb /entoom', in-/ *v.* place in a tomb —**en·tomb'ment** *n.* [MFr, rel. to TOMB]

en·to·mol·o·gy /en'təmäl'əjē/ *n.* the study of insects —**en·to·mo·log'i·cal** /-məläj'ikəl/ *adj.*; **en·to·mol'o·gist** *n.* [Gk *entomon* insect]

en·tou·rage /än'tooräzh'/ *n.* people attending an important person [Fr, rel. to TOUR]

en·trails /en'trālz, -trəlz/ *n. pl.* bowels; intestines [L *inter* among]

en·trance¹ /en'trans/ *n.* 1 place for entering 2 going or coming in 3 admittance 4 coming of an actor on stage [MFr, rel. to ENTER]

en·trance² /entrans', in-/ *v.* (·**tranced**, ·**tranc·ing**) 1 enchant; delight 2 put into a trance —**en·trance'ment** *n.*; **en·tranc'ing** *adj.*; **en·tranc'ing·ly** *adv.*

en·trant /en'trənt/ *n.* person who enters, esp. a competition [Fr, rel. to ENTER]

en·trap /entrap'/ *v.* (·**trapped**, ·**trap·ping**) 1 catch in or as in a trap 2 beguile —**en·trap'ment** *n.* [MFr, rel. to EN-¹ + TRAP]

en·treat /entrēt'/ *v.* ask earnestly; beg —**en·treat'y** *n.* (*pl.* ·**ies**) [MFr, rel. to EN-¹ + TREAT]

en·trée /än'trā'/ *n.* 1 main dish 2 right of admission [Fr]

en·trench /entrench'/ *v.* establish firmly (in a position, office, etc.) —**en·trench'ment** *n.*

en·trenched' *adj.* (of an attitude, etc.) not easily changed

en·tre·pre·neur /än'trəp(r)ənər', -n(y)oor'/ *n.* person who undertakes a commercial risk for profit —**en·tre·pre·neur'i·al** *adj.* [Fr, rel. to ENTERPRISE]

en·tro·py /en'trəpē/ *n.* 1 *Physics.* measure of disorganization or degradation in the universe that reduces available energy 2 tendency of available energy to dwindle [Gk, rel. to EN-² + *tropē* transformation]

en·trust /entrəst'/ *v.* give into the care of another

en·try /en'trē/ *n.* (*pl.* ·**tries**) 1a going or coming in b liberty to do this 2 place of entrance 3 item entered in a diary, list, etc. 4 registered competitor [L *intrare* ENTER]

en'try-lev'el *adj.* at the beginning or lowest level of a ranked series

en·twine /entwīn'/ *v.* (·**twined**, ·**twin·ing**) twine around; interweave

en·nu·mer·ate /ēn(y)oo'mərāt', i-/ *v.* (·**at·ed**, ·**at·ing**) 1 specify (items) 2 count —**e·nu'mer·a'tion** *n.*; **e·nu'mer·a'tive** /-rətiv/ *adj.* [L, rel. to NUMBER]

e·nun·ci·ate /ēnən'sē·āt', i-/ *v.* (·**at·ed**, ·**at·ing**) 1 pronounce clearly 2 express in definite terms —**e·nun'ci·a'tion** *n.* [L *nuntiare* announce]

en·vel·op /envel'əp, in-/ *v.* 1 wrap up or cover completely 2 completely surround —**en·vel'op·ment** *n.* [OFr]

en·ve·lope /en'vəlōp', än'-/ *n.* 1 paper or other, usu. sealable container for a letter, etc. 2 wrapper; covering

En·ver Pa·sha /en'ver' päsh'ə, pəshä'/ 1881–1922; Turkish political and military leader

en·vi·a·ble /en'vēəbəl/ *adj.* likely to excite

envy; desirable —**en′vi·a·bil′i·ty** *n.*; **en′vi·a·bly** *adv.*

en·vi·ous /en′vēəs/ *adj.* feeling or showing envy —**en′vi·ous·ly** *adv.* [AngFr, rel. to ENVY]

en·vi·ron·ment /envī′rə(n)mənt, -vī′ər(n)-/ *n.* 1 surroundings, esp. as affecting lives or activity 2 circumstances of living —**en·vi′ron·men′tal** *adj.*; **en·vi′ron·men·tal·ly** *adv.* [OFr *environ* surroundings]

en·vi′ron·men′tal·ist *n.* person concerned with safeguarding the natural environment —**en·vi′ron·men·tal·ism** *n.*

en·vi·rons /envī′rənz, in-, -vī′ərnz/ *n. pl.* district around a town, etc.

en·vis·age /enviz′ij/ *v.* (·aged, ·ag·ing) have a mental picture of [Fr, rel. to VISAGE]

en·voy /en′voi/, än′-/ *n.* 1 messenger or representative 2 diplomat ranking below ambassador [Fr *envoyer* send, fr. L *via* way]

en·vy /en′vē/ *n.* (*pl.* ·vies) 1 discontent aroused by another's gains, success, etc. 2 object of this feeling —*v.* (·vied, ·vy·ing) 3 feel envy of (a person, etc.) [L *invidia* envy, fr. *videre* see]

en·zyme /en′zīm/ *n.* protein catalyst of a specific biochemical reaction [MGk *enzymos* leavened]

EOE *abbr.* equal opportunity employer

e.o.m. or **E.O.M.** *abbr.* end of the month

e·on /ē′än′, -ən/ *n.* 1 long or indefinite period 2 an age [L fr. Gk]

EPA *abbr.* Environmental Protection Agency

EPAULET

ep·au·let /ep′əlet/ *n.* (also ep′au·lette′) ornamental shoulder piece, esp. on a uniform [Fr *épaule* shoulder]

é·pée /āpā′, ep′ā/ *n.* Fencing. sword with a protected tip [Fr fr. L *spatha* sword]

e·phem·er·al /ifem′(ə)rəl/ *adj.* of brief life; transitory [Gk, rel. to EPI- + *hēmera* day]

epi- *prefix* 1 upon 2 above 3 in addition [Gk]

ep·ic /ep′ik/ *n.* 1 long narrative poem about heroic deeds 2 grand or extended story, film, etc. —*adj.* 3 of or like an epic 4 grand; heroic [Gk *epos* song]

ep·i·cene /ep′isēn/ *adj.* having characteristics of both sexes or of neither sex [Gk *koinos* common]

ep·i·cen·ter /ep′isen′tər/ *n.* 1 point on the earth's surface directly above an earthquake 2 central or focal point [Gk, rel. to CENTER]

ep·i·cure /ep′ikyŏŏr′/ *n.* person with refined tastes, esp. in food and drink [MedL, rel. to EPICUREAN]

ep·i·cu·re·an /ep′ikyŏŏr′ēən/ *n.* 1 devotee of (esp. sensual) enjoyment —*adj.* 2 pertaining to or fond of good food [Gk *Epicurus*, name of a philosopher]

E·pi·cu·rus /ep′ikyŏŏr′əs/ 341–270 B.C.; Greek philosopher

ep·i·dem·ic /ep′idem′ik/ *n.* 1 widespread occurrence of a disease at a particular time —*adj.* 2 in the nature of an epidemic [Gk *epi* against + *dēmos* the people]

● Usage: A disease that breaks out, affects a large number of people, and then subsides is *epidemic*: *The 1918 flu epidemic killed millions.* A disease that persists in a particular area is *endemic*: *Malaria is endemic in the tropics.*

ep·i·de·mi·ol·o·gy /ep′idē′mēäl′əjē/ *n.* the study of epidemic diseases and their control —**ep′i·de′mi·ol′o·gist** *n.*

ep·i·der·mis /ep′idər′mis/ *n.* outer layer of the skin —**ep′i·der′mal** *adj.* [Gk *derma* skin]

ep·i·glot·tis /ep′iglät′əs/ *n.* flap of cartilage above the root of the tongue, depressed during swallowing to cover the windpipe —**ep′i·glot′tal** *adj.* [Gk *glōtta* tongue]

ep·i·gram /ep′igram/ *n.* pointed or witty saying —**ep′i·gram·mat′ic** /-grəmat′ik/ *adj.* [Gk, rel. to -GRAM]

ep·i·graph /ep′igraf′/ *n.* inscription [Gk, rel. to -GRAPH]

ep·i·lep·sy /ep′əlep′sē/ *n.* nervous disorder often with convulsions or loss of consciousness [Gk *lambanein* take; seize]

ep·i·lep·tic /ep′əlep′tik/ *adj.* 1 pertaining to epilepsy —*n.* 2 person with epilepsy

ep·i·logue /ep′əlôg, -läg/ *n.* (also ep′i·log) *n.* concluding narrative part, commentary, speech, etc. [Gk *logos* speech]

ep·i·neph·rine /ep′ənef′rin, -rēn/ *n.* 1 hormone secreted by the adrenal medulla that increases heart rate, blood pressure, etc. 2 natural or synthetic form of this used medicinally to stimulate the heart, relax bronchial muscles, etc.

e·piph·a·ny /ēpif′ənē/ *n.* (*pl.* ·nies) 1 (*cap.*) a manifestation of Christ to the Magi b (also **Twelfth Day**) festival of this on January 6 2 moment of striking personal realization or insight [Gk *phainein* appear]

e·pis·co·pa·cy /ipis′kəpəsē/ *n.* (*pl.* ·cies) 1 government by bishops 2 (prec. by *the*) bishops collectively

e·pis·co·pal /ipis′kəpəl/ *adj.* of or headed by a bishop or bishops [ChL, rel. to BISHOP]

E·pis·co·pa·lian /ipis′kəpāl′yən/ *adj.* 1 of or pertaining to the Episcopal Church —*n.* 2 member of this church

e·pis·co·pate /ipis′kəpət/ *n.* 1 the office of a bishop 2 (prec. by *the*) bishops collectively [ChL, rel. to BISHOP]

ep·i·sode /ep′əsōd′/ *n.* 1 event or period as part of a sequence 2 dramatic installment 3 incident or period in a narrative —**ep′i·sod′ic** /-əsäd′ik/ *adj.*; **ep′i·sod′i·cal·ly** *adv.* [Gk *eisodos* entry]

e·pis·tle /ipis′əl/ *n.* 1 letter 2 (*cap.*) any of the apostles' letters in the New Testament [Gk *epistolē* fr. *stellein* send]

e·pis·to·lar·y /ipis′təler′ē/ *adj.* of or in the form of a letter or letters [L, rel. to EPISTLE]

ep·i·taph /ep′itaf′/ *n.* memorial words as a tomb inscription [Gk *taphos* tomb]

ep·i·the·li·um /ep′ithē′lēəm/ *n.* (*pl.* ·ums or ·a /-ə/) tissue forming the outer layer of the body and lining many hollow structures —**ep′i·the′li·al** /-əl/ *adj.* [Gk *thēlē* teat]

ep·i·thet /ep′iтнet/ *n.* 1 characterizing adjective, etc. 2 term of abuse [Gk *tithēmi* place]

e·pit·o·me /ipit′əmē/ *n.* 1 person or thing

embodying a quality, etc. 2 thing representing another in miniature [Gk *temnein* cut]

e·pit·o·mize /ipit′əmīz′/ v. (·mized, ·mizing) perfectly exemplify

ep·och /ep′ək, -äk′/ n. 1 notable period of history 2 beginning of an era —ep′och·al adj. [Gk: pause]

ep·ox·y /ipäk′sē/ adj. 1 designating a resin used in adhesives, insulation, coatings, etc. —n. (pl. ·ies) 2 epoxy resin [fr. EPI- + OXYGEN]

ep·si·lon /ep′sələn′/ n. fifth letter of the Greek alphabet (E, ε) [Gk]

Ep′som salts′ /ep′səm/ n. magnesium sulfate used as a purgative, etc. [*Epsom* in S. England]

Ep′stein-Barr′ vi′rus /ep′stēn bär′/ n. *Med.* herpes virus that causes infectious mononucleosis [for Brit. pathologists who isolated it]

e·qua·ble /ek′wəbəl/ adj. not varying; even; uniform —e′qua·bil′i·ty n.; eq′ua·bly adv. [rel. to EQUAL]

e·qual /ē′kwəl/ adj. 1 the same in quantity, quality, size, degree, level, etc. 2 evenly balanced 3 having the same rights or status —n. 4 person or thing equal to another —v. (·qualed or ·qualled, ·qual·ing or ·qual·ling) 5 be equal to 6 achieve something that is equal to —e·qual′i·ty /-kwôl′ətē, -kwäl-/ n. (pl. ·ties); e′qual·ly adv. [L *aequalis*]

e·qual·ize /ē′kwəlīz′/ v. (·ized, ·iz·ing) make or become equal —e′qual·i·za′tion n.

e·qua·nim·i·ty /ek′wənim′ətē, ē′kwə-/ n. composure; evenness in temperament [L *aequus* even + *animus* mind]

e·quate /ikwāt′/ v. (·quat·ed, ·quat·ing) 1 regard as equal or equivalent 2 be equal or equivalent (with) —e·quat′a·ble adj. [L *aequare aequat-* make equal]

e·qua·tion /ikwā′ZHən/ n. 1 equating or making equal; being equal 2 statement that two mathematical expressions are equal

e·qua·tor /ikwā′tər/ n. imaginary line around the earth or other body, equidistant from the poles —e·qua·to·ri·al /ī′kwätôr′ēəl/ adj. [L: equalizer]

E·qua·to′ri·al Guin′ea n. republic in W Africa. Capital: Malabo. Pop. 367,000

e·ques·tri·an /ikwes′trēən/ adj. 1 of horseback riding 2 on horseback —n. (fem. e·ques′tri·enne′ /-trēen′/) 3 rider or performer on horseback —e·ques′tri·an·ism′ n. [L *equestris* fr. *equus* horse]

equi- comb. form equal [L, rel. to EQUAL]

e·qui·dis·tant /ē′kwidis′tənt, ek′wi-/ adj. at equal distances

e·qui·lat·er·al /ē′kwilat′ərəl, ek′wi-/ adj. having all sides equal in length (see illustration at TRIANGLE)

e·qui·lib·ri·um /ē′kwilib′rēəm, ek′wi-/ n. (pl. ·a /-ə/ or ·ums) 1 state of physical balance 2 state of composure [L *libra* balance]

e·quine /ē′kwīn′, ek′wīn′/ adj. of or like a horse [L *equus* horse]

e·qui·nox /ē′kwinäks′, ek′wi-/ n. time or date (twice each year) at which the sun crosses the celestial equator, when day and night are of equal length —e′qui·noc′tial /-näk′SHəl/ adj. [L *nox noctis* night]

e·quip /ikwip′/ v. (·quipped, ·quip·ping) supply with what is needed [OFr, prob. fr. ON *skipa* to man a ship]

e·qui·page /ek′wəpij/ n. *Hist.* carriage and horses with attendants [MFr, rel. to EQUIP]

e·quip′ment n. 1 necessary tools, clothing, etc. 2 equipping or being equipped [Fr, rel. to EQUIP]

e·qui·poise /ek′wəpoiz′/ n. 1 equilibrium 2 counterbalance or what achieves this

eq·ui·ta·ble /ek′witəbəl/ adj. fair; just —eq′ui·ta·bly adv. [Fr, rel. to EQUITY]

eq·ui·ta·tion /ek′witā′SHən/ n. horsemanship [L *equitare* ride (a horse)]

eq·ui·ty /ek′witē/ n. (pl. ·ties) 1 fairness; justice 2 value of property less debt 3a value of the shares issued by a company b (pl.) stocks and shares not bearing fixed interest [L *aequitas*, rel. to EQUAL]

e·quiv·a·lent /ikwiv′(ə)lənt/ adj. 1 equal; tantamount —n. 2 equivalent thing, amount, etc. —e·quiv′a·lence n. [L, rel. to VALUE]

e·quiv·o·cal /ikwiv′əkəl/ adj. 1 of double or doubtful meaning 2 uncertain; questionable —e·quiv′o·cal·ly adv. [L *vocare* call]

e·quiv·o·cate /ikwiv′əkāt′/ v. (·cat·ed, ·cat·ing) use ambiguity to conceal the truth —e·quiv′o·ca′tion, e·quiv′o·ca′tor n. [L, rel. to EQUIVOCAL]

Er symb. erbium

ER abbr. 1 emergency room 2 Elizabeth Regina

-er[1] suffix forming nouns from nouns, adjectives, and verbs, denoting: 1 person, animal, or thing that does (*talker*) 2 person or thing that is (*foreigner*) 3 person concerned with (*plumber*) 4 person from (*villager*) [OE]

-er[2] suffix forming the comparative of adjectives (*wider*) and adverbs (*faster*) [OE]

e·ra /ēr′ə, er′ə/ n. 1 period reckoned from a noteworthy event 2 significant historical period [L: number (pl. of *aes* money)]

ERA abbr. 1 *Baseball.* earned run average 2 Equal Rights Amendment

e·rad·i·cate /irad′ikāt′/ v. (·cat·ed, ·cat·ing) root out; destroy completely —e·rad′i·ca·ble /-ikəbəl/ adj.; e·rad′i·ca′tion, e·rad′i·ca′tor n. [L *eradicare* fr. *radix* root]

e·rase /irās′/ v. (·rased, ·ras·ing) 1 rub out; obliterate 2 remove recorded material from (magnetic medium) [L *radere ras-* scrape]

e·ras′er n. thing that erases, esp. a piece of rubber for removing pencil marks

E·ras·mus /iraz′məs/, **Desiderius** c. 1469–1536; Dutch humanist and theologian

e·ra·sure /irā′SHər/ n. 1 erasing 2 part erased

Er·bil /er′bil′/ n. (also **Arbil; Arbela; Irbil**) city in Iraq. Pop. 333,900

er·bi·um /ər′bēəm/ n. metallic element of the lanthanide series; symb **Er** [*Ytterby* in Sweden]

ere /er/ prep. & conj. *Poet.* before (of time) (*ere noon; ere they come*) [OE]

e·rect /irekt′/ adj. 1 upright; vertical —v. 2 set up; build —e·rec′tion /irek′SHən/ n.; e·rect′ly adv.; e·rect′ness n. [L *erigere erect-* raise up]

e·rec·tile /irek′təl, -tīl′/ adj. that can become erect (esp. of body tissue when engorged) [Fr, rel. to ERECT]

Er·furt /er'fŏŏrt'/ *n.* city in Germany. Pop. 289,000

erg /ərg'/ *n. Physics.* unit of work or energy [Gk *ergon* work]

er·go /ər'gō, er'-/ *adv. Latin.* therefore

er·go·nom·ics /ər'gənäm'iks/ *n.* the study of the relationship between people and their working environment —**er'go·nom'ic** *adj.* [Gk *ergon* work]

Er·ic /er'ik/ ("the Red") c. 940-c. 1010; Norse explorer

Er·ic·son /er'iksən/ (also **Er'ics·son; Er'iks·son**), Leif early 11th cent.; Norse explorer

E·rie /ēr'ē/ *n.* city in Penn. Pop. 108,718

E'rie, Lake' *n.* southernmost of the Great Lakes, between Lake Ontario and Lake Huron

E'rie Ca·nal' *n.* canal in N.Y. from Buffalo to Albany, connecting Lake Erie with the Hudson River

Er·i·tre·a /er'itrē'ə, -trā'ə/ *n.* republic in E Africa, formerly a province of Ethiopia. Capital: Asmara. Pop. 3,421,000

er·mine /ər'mən/ *n.* (*pl.* same or **·mines**) 1 an Old World weasel 2 its white winter fur [OFr *h.*]

erne /ərn/ *n.* SEA EAGLE

Ernst /ernst/, Max 1891-1976; German artist

e·rode /irōd'/ *v.* (**·rod·ed, ·rod·ing**) wear away; destroy gradually —**e·ro·sion** /irō'ZHən/ *n.*; **e·ro'sive** /-siv/ *adj.* [L *rodere ros-gnaw*]

e·rog·e·nous /iräj'ənəs/ *adj.* (of a part of the body) particularly sensitive to sexual stimulation [Gk EROS + -GENOUS]

Eros /ēr'əs, er'əs/ *n. Gk. Myth.* god of love, identified with Roman Cupid

e·rot·ic /irät'ik/ *adj.* of or causing sexual desire or excitement —**e·rot'i·cal·ly** *adv.* [Gk EROS sexual love]

e·rot·i·ca /irät'ikə/ *n. pl.* erotic literature or art

e·rot·i·cism /irät'əsiz'əm/ *n.* 1 erotic character 2 use of or response to erotic images or stimulation

err /ər'/ *v.* 1 be mistaken or incorrect 2 do wrong; sin [L *errare* stray]
  ● Usage: Traditionally, the correct pronunciation rhymes with *her*, though the pronunciation that rhymes with *hair* is quite common.

er·rand /er'ənd/ *n.* short outing for a specific purpose [OE]

er·rant /er'ənt/ *adj.* 1 erring 2 *Lit.* traveling in search of adventure (*knight errant*) —**er'rant·ry** *n.* [MFr fr. L *iter* journey, perh. also rel. to ERR]

er·rat·ic /irat'ik/ *adj.* 1 inconsistent or odd in conduct, opinions, etc 2 uncertain in movement —**er·rat'i·cal·ly** *adv.* [L, rel. to ERR]

er·ra·tum /irä'təm, -rä't-/ *n.* (*pl.* **·ta** /-tə/) error in printing or writing [L, rel. to ERR]

er·ro·ne·ous /irō'nēəs/ *adj.* incorrect —**er·ro'ne·ous·ly** *adv.* [L, rel. to ERR]

er·ror /er'ər/ *n.* 1 mistake; untruth 2 moral transgression 3 degree of inaccuracy [L, rel. to ERR]

er·satz /er'säts', -zäts'/ *adj. & n.* substitute; imitation [Ger]

Erse /ərs'/ *adj.* 1 Gaelic —*n.* 2 the Gaelic language [early Scots form of IRISH]

erst·while /ərst'(h)wīl'/ *adj.* former; previous [rel. to ERE]

e·ruc·ta·tion /irək'tä'sHən/ *n.* belching [L *eructare* belch forth; vomit]

er·u·dite /er'(y)ədīt'/ *adj.* learned —**er'u·dite'ly** *adv.*; **er'u·di'tion** /-di'sHən/ *n.* [L *eruditus* instructed, rel. to RUDE]

e·rupt /irəpt'/ *v.* 1 break out suddenly or dramatically 2 forcefully eject lava, water, etc. 3 (of a rash, etc.) appear on the skin —**e·rup·tion** /irəp'sHən/ *n.*; **e·rup'tive** /-tiv/ *adj.* [L *erumpere erupt-* break out]

-ery *suffix* (also **-ry**) forming nouns denoting: 1 class or kind (*machinery; citizenry*) 2 calling (*dentistry*) 3 state or condition (*slavery*) 4 place of work or cultivation or breeding (*brewery; nursery*) 5 behavior (*mimicry*) 6 often *Derog.* all that has to do with (*popery*) [OFr *-erie*]

e·ryth·ro·cyte /irĭTH'rəsīt'/ *n.* red blood cell [Gk *erythros* red + -CYTE]

Es *symb.* einsteinium

es·ca·late /es'kəlāt'/ *v.* (**·lat·ed, ·lat·ing**) 1 increase or develop (usu. rapidly) by stages 2 make or become more intense —**es'ca·la'tion** *n.* [fr. ESCALATOR]

es'ca·la'tor *n.* mechanical staircase that moves up or down continuously [prob. fr. L *scala* ladder]

es·ca·pade /es'kəpād'/ *n.* reckless adventure or caper [Fr fr. Prov or Sp, rel. to ESCAPE]

es·cape /iskāp'/ *v.* (**·caped, ·cap·ing**) 1 get free of restriction, control, or a person 2 leak 3 succeed in avoiding punishment, etc. 4 avoid 5 elude the notice or memory of 6 (of words, etc.) issue unawares from (a person, etc.) —*n.* 7 act or instance of escaping 8 means of escaping 9 temporary relief or diversion [LL *cappa* cloak]

es·cap·ee /iskā'pē', es'kā-/ *n.* person who has escaped

es·cape'ment *n.* part of a clock, etc., that connects and regulates the motive power [Fr, rel. to ESCAPE]

es·cape' ve·loc'i·ty *n.* minimum velocity needed to escape a gravitational field

es·cap·ism *n.* pursuit of distraction and relief from reality —**es·cap'ist** *n. & adj.*

es·carp·ment /iskärp'mənt/ *n.* long steep slope [MFr fr. It, rel. to SCARP]

es·chew /isCHŏŏ'/ *v.* avoid; abstain from —**es·chew'al** *n.* [Gmc, rel. to SHY[1]]

Es·con·di·do /es'kəndēd'ō/ *n.* city in Calif. Pop. 108,635

es·cort *n.* /es'kôrt'/ 1 persons, vehicle, etc., accompanying a person for protection or as a mark of status 2 person accompanying a person of the opposite sex socially —*v.* /iskôrt', es'kôrt'/ 3 act as an escort to [Fr fr. It]

es·crow /es'krō/ *n.* legal arrangement in which a third party provides security, as by holding deposited funds, etc., until certain conditions are met

es·cutch·eon /iskəCH'ən/ *n.* shield or emblem bearing a coat of arms [L *scutum* shield]

Es·fa·han /es'fəhän'/ *n.* see ISFAHAN

Es·ki·mo /es'kəmō'/ *n.* (*pl.* same or **·mos**) see INUIT

Es·ki·se·hir /es'kisĭhĕr'/ *n.* city in Turkey. Pop. 413,100

ESL *abbr.* English as a second language

e·soph·a·gus /isäf'əgəs, ēsäf'-/ *n.* (*pl.* **-gi**

/jĭ, gī/) passage for food from the pharynx to the stomach

es·o·ter·ic /es'əter'ik/ adj. intelligible only to those with special knowledge —es'o·ter'i·cal·ly adv. [Gk esōteros inner]

ESP abbr. extrasensory perception

es·pa·drille /es'pədril'/ n. light canvas shoe with a sole usu. of twisted rope [Prov, rel. to esparto, a grass]

es·pal·ier /ispal'yər,-yā'/ n. 1 latticework for training the branches of a tree or shrub 2 tree or shrub so trained [Fr fr. It]

es·pe·cial /ispesh'(ə)l/ adj. special [L, rel. to SPECIAL]

es·pe·cial·ly adv. 1 in particular 2 much more than in other cases

Es·pe·ran·to /es'pəränt'ō, -rant'ō/ n. an artificial language intended for universal use [L sperare hope]

es·pi·o·nage /es'pēənäzH',-näj'/ n. spying or use of spies [MFr, rel. to SPY]

es·pla·nade /es'plənäd',-nād'/ n. long open level area for strolling [L planus level]

es·pous·al /ispou'zəl/ n. 1 espousing of (a cause, etc.) 2 Archaic. marriage; betrothal

es·pouse /ispouz'/ v. (·poused, ·pous·ing) 1 adopt or support (a cause, doctrine, etc.) 2 Archaic. (usu. of a man) marry [L spondere spons- betroth]

es·pres·so /espres'ō/ n. (pl. ·sos) strong black coffee made under steam pressure [It: pressed out]

es·prit /esprē'/ n. French. 1 sprightliness; wit 2 esprit de corps /də kôr'/ devotion to and pride in one's group [Fr fr. L, rel. to SPIRIT]

es·py /ispī'/ v. (·pied, ·py·ing) catch sight of [OFr, rel. to SPY]

Esq. abbr. Esquire

-esque suffix forming adjectives meaning 'in the style of' or 'resembling' (Kafkaesque) [Fr fr. It fr. Gmc]

es·quire /es'kwīr'/ n. title added to a surname, esp. a lawyer's, when no other title is used, as on letters [MFr fr. L scutum shield]

-ess suffix forming nouns denoting females (actress; lioness) [Gk -issa]

es·say n. /es'ā/ 1 short piece of writing on a given subject 2 Formal. attempt —v. /esā', es'ā'/ 3 attempt —es'say·ist n. [L exigere try; consider; weigh]

Es·sen /es'ən/ n. city in Germany. Pop. 627,000

es·sence /es'əns/ n. 1 fundamental nature; inherent characteristics 2a extract obtained by distillation, etc. b perfume [L esse be]

es·sen·tial /isen'SHəl/ adj. 1 necessary; indispensable 2 of or constituting the essence of a person or thing —n. 3 (esp. pl.) basic or indispensable element or thing —es·sen'tial·ly adv. [L, rel. to ESSENCE]

EST abbr. eastern standard time

est. abbr. 1 established 2 estimate 3 estimated

-est suffix forming the superlative of adjectives (happiest) and adverbs (soonest) [OE]

es·tab·lish /istab'lish/ v. 1 set up on a permanent basis; institute; install 2 achieve permanent acceptance for (a custom, belief, etc.) 3 place (a fact, etc.) beyond dispute [L stabilire make firm]

es·tab'lish·ment n. 1 establishing or being established 2 organization or its facilities, site, etc. 3 (the Establishment) authority or social group with influence and resisting change

es·tate /istāt'/ n. 1 property consisting of much land and usu. a large house 2 person's assets and liabilities, esp. at death [Fr estat, fr. L stare stat- stand]

es·teem /istēm'/ v. 1 have a high regard for 2 Formal. consider —n. 3 high regard; favor [L, rel. to ESTIMATE]

es·ter /es'tər/ n. Chem. a compound produced by replacing the hydrogen of an acid by an organic radical [Ger]

es·ti·ma·ble /es'təməbəl/ adj. worthy of esteem; admirable [L, rel. to ESTEEM]

es·ti·mate n. /es'təmət/ 1 approximate judgment, esp. of cost, value, size, etc. 2 statement of approximate charge for work to be undertaken —v. /es'təmāt/ (·mat·ed, ·mat·ing) 3 form an estimate or opinion of 4 make a rough calculation —es'ti·ma'tor n. [L aestimare value; appraise]

es'ti·ma'tion n. 1 estimating 2 judgment of worth [L, rel. to ESTIMATE]

Es·to·ni·a /estō'nēə/ n. republic in N Europe on the Baltic Sea, formerly part of the USSR. Capital: Tallinn. Pop. 1,592,000

Es·to·ni·an /estō'nēən/ n. 1a native or national of Estonia b person of Estonian descent 2 language of Estonia —adj. 3 of Estonia, its people, or language

es·trange /istrānj'/ v. (·tranged, ·trang·ing) 1 alienate; make hostile or indifferent 2 (as estranged adj.) no longer living with one's spouse —es·trange'ment n. [OFr fr. L, rel. to STRANGE]

es·tro·gen /es'trəjən/ n. female sex hormone controlling estrus, etc.

es·trus /es'trəs/ n. time during the female reproductive cycle in mammals of most receptivity to mating

es·tu·ar·y /es'CHOO·er'ē/ n. (pl. ·ies) wide tidal river mouth [L aestus tide]

e·ta /ā'tə, ē'tə/ n. seventh letter of the Greek alphabet (H, η) [Gk]

ETA abbr. estimated time of arrival

et al. /et al, äl, ôl/ abbr. and others [L et alii]

etc. abbr. ET CETERA

et cet·er·a /et set'ərə, se'trə/ adv. and the rest; and so on [L]

● Usage: Avoid the pronunciation "ek set-uhr-uh," which many regard as unacceptable.

etch /eCH/ v. 1a reproduce (a picture, etc.) by engraving it on a metal plate with acid b engrave (a plate) in this way 2 practice this craft 3 impress deeply (esp. on the mind) —etch'er n. [Du etsen fr. Ger]

etch'ing n. 1 print made from an etched plate 2 art of producing these plates

ETD abbr. estimated time of departure

e·ter·nal /itərn'l/ adj. 1 existing always; without an end or (usu.) beginning 2 unchanging —e·ter'nal·ly adv. [L aeternus]

e·ter·ni·ty /itər'nətē/ n. (pl. ·ties) 1 infinite (esp. future) time 2 endless life after death 3 being eternal [L, rel. to ETERNAL]

-eth var. of -TH

eth·ane /eth'ān/ n. Chem. a colorless, odorless, flammable gas

Eth·el·red II /ˈeTHʹəlred/ (called "**the Un-ready**") c. 969–1016; king of England (978–1016)

e·ther /ˈeʹTHər/ *n.* **1** *Chem.* colorless volatile organic liquid used as an anesthetic or solvent **2** clear sky; upper regions of the atmosphere **3** medium formerly assumed to permeate all space [Gk *aithein* burn]

e·the·re·al /iˈTHirʹeəl/ *adj.* **1** light and airy **2** highly delicate, esp. in appearance **3** heavenly —**e·theʹre·al·ly** *adv.* [Gk, rel. to ETHER]

eth·ic /ˈeTHʹik/ *n.* set of moral principles [Gk, rel. to ETHOS]

eth·i·cal *adj.* **1** relating to morals, esp. as concerning human conduct **2** morally correct —**ethʹi·cal·ly** *adv.*

eth·ics *n. pl.* (also treated as *sing.*) **1** moral philosophy **2a** moral principles **b** set of these

E·thi·o·pi·a /ˈeʹTHēoʹpēə/ *n.* republic in E Africa. Capital: Addis Ababa. Pop. 54,077,000 —**E·thi·oʹpi·an** *n. & adj.*

eth·nic /ˈeTHʹnik/ *n.* **1** having a common national or cultural tradition **2** denoting origin by birth or descent rather than nationality (*ethnic Turks*) **3** of a nonnative cultural tradition —**ethʹni·cal·ly** *adv.* [Gk *ethnos* nation]

eth·nic cleansʹing *n.* *Euphem.* military action aimed at annihilating or driving out certain ethnic or racial groups

eth·nol·o·gy /eTHnälʹəjē/ *n.* the comparative study of peoples —**eth·no·logʹi·cal** /-nəläjʹikəl/ *adj.*; **eth·nolʹo·gist** *n.*

e·thos /ˈēʹTHäs/ *n.* characteristic spirit or attitudes of a community, etc. [Gk *ēthos* character]

eth·yl /ˈeTHʹəl/ *n.* a radical derived from ethane, present in alcohol and ether [Ger, rel. to ETHER]

eth·yl·ene /ˈeTHʹəlēn/ *n.* *Chem.* a colorless, flammable gas, usu. obtained from petroleum or natural gas

e·ti·ol·o·gy /ˈēʹtēˈälʹəjē/ *n.* study of the causes of disease —**e·ti·o·logʹi·cal** /-əläjʹikəl/ *adj.* [Gk *aitia* cause]

et·i·quette /etʹiket/ *n.* conventional rules of social behavior or professional conduct [Fr, rel. to TICKET]

Et·na, Mount /etʹnə/ *n.* active volcano in E Sicily; 11,122 ft.

E·trus·can /itrəsʹkən/ *adj.* **1** of ancient Etruria in Italy —*n.* **2** native of Etruria **3** language of Etruria [L *Etruscus*]

et seq. *abbr.* (also **et seqq.**) and the following (pages, etc.) [L *et sequens*]

-ette *suffix* forming nouns meaning: **1** small (*kitchenette*) **2** imitation or substitute (*leatherette*) **3** female (*majorette*) [Fr]

é·tude /ˈāʹt(y)ōōd/ *n.* musical composition designed to enhance playing technique [Fr: study]

etym. *abbr.* etymology

et·y·mol·o·gy /etʹəmälʹəjē/ *n.* (*pl.* **-gies**) **1a** derivation and development of a word **b** account of this **2** the study of word origins —**etʹy·mo·logʹi·cal** /-məläjʹikəl/ *adj.*; **etʹy·mo·logʹi·cal·ly** *adv.*; **et·y·molʹo·gist** *n.* [Gk *etymos* true]

Eu *symb.* europium

EU *abbr.* EUROPEAN UNION

eu- *comb. form* well; easily [Gk]

eu·ca·lyp·tus /yōōʹkəlipʹtəs/ *n.* (*pl.* **-tus·es** or **-ti** /-tīʹ/) **1** tall evergreen Australasian tree **2** its oil, used as an antiseptic, etc. [Gk EU- + *kalyptos* covered]

Eu·cha·rist /yōōʹkərist/ *n.* **1** *Christianity.* sacrament in which consecrated bread and wine are consumed **2** consecrated elements, esp. the bread —**Euʹcha·risʹtic** *adj.* [Gk: thanksgiving]

Eu·clid /yōōʹklid/ 3rd cent. B.C.; Greek mathematician

Eu·gene /yōōjēnʹ/ *n.* city in Ore. Pop. 112,669

eu·gen·ics /yōōjenʹiks/ *n. pl.* (also treated as *sing.*) measures intended to improve the qualities of a human population by control of inherited characteristics —**eu·genʹic** *adj.*; **eu·genʹi·cal·ly** *adv.* [Gk *eugenes* wellborn]

Eu·gé·nie /yōōʹjenē, yōōjāʹnē/ 1826–1920; Spanish-born empress of France (1853–71); wife of Napoleon III

eu·lo·gize /yōōʹləjīz/ *v.* (**-gized, -giz·ing**) praise in speech or writing —**euʹlo·gisʹtic** /-jisʹtik/ *adj.*; **euʹlo·gist**, **euʹlo·giz·er** *n.*

eu·lo·gy /yōōʹləjē/ *n.* (*pl.* **-gies**) **1** speech or writing in praise of a person **2** extolling [L fr. Gk]

eu·nuch /yōōʹnək/ *n.* castrated man [Gk: bedchamber attendant]

eu·phe·mism /yōōʹfəmizʹəm/ *n.* **1** mild or vague expression substituted for a harsher or more direct one (e.g., *pass for die*) **2** use of such expressions —**euʹphe·misʹtic** *adj.*; **euʹphe·misʹti·cal·ly** *adv.* [Gk *phēmē* speaking]

eu·pho·ny /yōōʹfənē/ *n.* (*pl.* **-nies**) pleasantness of sound, esp. of a word or phrase —**eu·phoʹni·ous** /-fōʹnēəs/ *adj.* [Gk *phōnē* sound]

eu·pho·ri·a /yōōfôrʹēə/ *n.* intense feeling of well-being and excitement —**eu·phorʹic** *adj.* [Gk]

Eu·phra·tes /yōōfrātʹēz/ *n.* river flowing 1,700 mi. from central Turkey to the Persian Gulf

Eur·a·sian /yōōrāʹzHən/ *adj.* **1** of mixed European and Asian parentage **2** of Europe and Asia —*n.* **3** Eurasian person

eu·re·ka /yōōrēʹkə/ *interj.* I have found it! (announcing a discovery, etc.) [Gk *heurēka* fr. *heuriskein* find]

Eu·rip·i·des /yōōripʹədēz/ 480 – c. 406 B.C.; Greek dramatist

Euro- *comb. form* Europe; European [abbr.]

Eu·rope /yōōrʹəp/ *n.* continent between the Atlantic Ocean and Asia, bounded by the Ural and Caucasus mountains and the Black and Caspian seas

Eu·ro·pe·an /yōōrʹəpēʹən/ *adj.* **1** of or in Europe **2** originating in, native to, or characteristic of Europe —*n.* **3** native or inhabitant of Europe [Gk *Eurōpē* Europe]

Eu·ro·peʹan Unʹion *n.* (formerly **Eu·ro·peʹan Com·muʹni·ty**) official name of a confederation of independent European countries

eu·ro·pi·um /yōōrōʹpēəm/ *n.* metallic element of the lanthanide series; *symb.* Eu [fr. EUROPE]

Eu·sta·chian tubeʹ /yōōstāʹsH(ē)ən, -stāʹkēən/ *n.* tube from the pharynx to the middle ear [*Eustachio*, name of an anatomist]

eu·tha·na·sia /yōōʹTHənəʹzHə/ *n.* bringing about of a gentle death in the case of incurable and painful condition [Gk *thanatos* death]

e·vac·u·ate /ivak'yōō-āt/ v. (·at·ed, ·at·ing) 1a remove (people) from a place b empty (a place) 2 make empty 3 withdraw from (a place) 4 empty (the bowels, etc.) —e·vac·u·a'tion, e·vac·u·ee' /-ē/ n. [L vacuus empty]

e·vade /ivād'/ v. (·vad·ed, ·vad·ing) 1 escape from; avoid, esp. by guile or trickery 2 avoid doing, answering, etc. [L evadere go out; escape]

e·val·u·ate /ival'yōō-āt/ v. (·at·ed, ·at·ing) 1 assess; appraise 2 determine the number or amount of —e·val'u·a'tion n. [Fr, rel. to VALUE]

ev·a·nes·cent /ev'ənes'ənt/ adj. quickly fading —ev'a·nes'cence n. [L evanescere vanish]

e·van·gel·i·cal /ē'van'jel'ikəl, ev'ən-/ adj. 1 Christianity. of or according to the teaching of the gospel 2 maintaining the doctrine of salvation by faith —n. 3 believer in this —e·van·gel'i·cal·ism' n.; e'van·gel'i·cal·ly adv. [Gk, rel. to EU-, ANGEL]

e·van·ge·list /ivan'jəlist/ n. 1 writer of one of the Bible's four Gospels 2 preacher of the gospel —e·van·ge·lism' n.; e·van·ge·lis'tic adj.

e·van·ge·lize /ivan'jəliz'/ v. (·lized, ·liz·ing) 1 preach the gospel to 2 convert to Christianity —e·van·ge·li·za'tion n.

Ev·ans /ev'ənz/ 1 (Sir) **Arthur John** 1851–1941; British archaeologist 2 (**Dame**) **Edith** 1888–1976; English actress

Ev·ans·ton /ev'ənstən/ n. city in Ill. Pop. 73,233

Ev·ans·ville /ev'ənzvil'/ n. city in Ind. Pop. 126,272

e·vap·o·rate /ivap'ərāt'/ v. (·rat·ed, ·rat·ing) 1 turn from solid or liquid into vapor 2 (cause to) lose moisture as vapor 3 (cause to) disappear —e·vap'o·ra·ble adj.; e·vap'o·ra'tion, e·vap'o·ra'tor n. [L, rel. to VAPOR]

e·va·sion /ivā'zHən/ n. 1 evading 2 evasive answer [L, rel. to EVADE]

e·va·sive /ivā'siv/ adj. 1 seeking to evade 2 not direct in one's answers, etc. —e·va'sive·ly adv.; e·va'sive·ness n.

eve /ēv/ n. 1 evening or day before a holiday, etc. 2 time just before an event (eve of the election) 3 Archaic. evening [EVEN²]

Eve /ēv/ Biblical first woman; wife of Adam

e·ven¹ /ē'vən/ adj. 1 level; smooth 2a uniform in quality; constant b equal in amount or value c equally balanced 3 (of a person's temper, etc.) equable; calm 4 (of a number) divisible by two without a remainder —adv. 5 not so much as (never even opened) 6 as little, unimportant, etc., a one as (even you must realize it) —v. 7 make or become even 8 even so nevertheless 9 even though despite the fact that 10 get (or be) even with have one's revenge on —e'ven·ly adv.; e'ven·ness n. [OE]

e·ven² n. Poet. evening [OE]

e'ven·hand'ed adj. impartial

eve·ning /ēv'niNG/ n. close of the day, esp. from about 6 p.m. or sunset [OE, rel. to EVEN²]

eve'ning star' n. planet, esp. Venus, conspicuous in the west after sunset

e·ven mon·ey /ē'vən/ n. betting without odds given

e·vent /ivent'/ n. 1 thing that happens 2 fact

of a thing's occurring 3 item in a competitive program 4 at all events (or in any event) whatever happens 5 in the event of if (a specified thing) happens 6 in the event that if it happens that [L evenire -vent- come out]

event·ful /ivent'fəl/ adj. marked by noteworthy events —e·vent'ful·ly adv.; e·vent'ful·ness n.

e·ven·tide /ē'vəntīd/ n. Poet. EVENING [rel. to EVEN²]

e·ven·tu·al /iven'CHŌŌəl/ adj. occurring in due course; ultimate —e·ven'tu·al·ly adv. [fr. EVENT]

e·ven·tu·al·i·ty /iven'CHŌŌal'itē/ n. (pl. ·ties) possible event or outcome

e·ven·tu·ate /iven'CHŌŌ-āt'/ v. (·at·ed, ·at·ing) result

ev·er /ev'ər/ adv. 1 at all times; always 2 at any time 3 (used for emphasis) in any way; at all (how ever did you do it?) 4 (in comb.) constantly (ever-present) 5 (foll. by so) very; very much (ever so easy) 6 ever since throughout the period since [OE]

Ev·er·est, Mount /ev'(ə)rəst/ n. Himalayan peak on the Nepal-Tibet border; highest in the world: 29,028 ft.

Ev·er·glades /ev'ərglādz'/ n. vast region of swampland in S Fla.

ev'er·green' adj. 1 retaining green leaves all year around —n. 2 evergreen plant

ev'er·last'ing adj. lasting forever or for a long time

ev'er·more' adv. forever; always

eve·ry /ev'rē/ adj. 1 each single 2 each at a specified interval 3 every now and then (or again) from time to time 4 every other each second in a series 5 every so often occasionally [OE, rel. to EVER, EACH]

eve·ry·bod·y /ev'rēbäd'ē, -bəd'ē/ pron. every person

• **Usage:** As with everyone, with which it is interchangeable, traditionalists insist that everybody must use a singular pronoun of reference: Everybody must bring his (not their) own book. This construction is perceived as sexist by some, hence: Everybody must bring his or her own book, but the his or her is often considered awkward. Others find that the plural pronoun simply makes more sense: Everybody must bring their own book. This last violates strict logic, but it is standard in British English and may soon prevail elsewhere. In some sentences, only they makes grammatical sense: Everybody agreed to condemn the dictator, and it was about time they did.

eve'ry·day' adj. 1 occurring every day 2 used on ordinary days 3 commonplace

eve'ry one' n. each one

eve'ry·one' pron. everybody

eve'ry·thing' pron. 1 all things 2 most important thing

eve'ry·where' adv. 1 in every place 2 in many places

e·vict /ivikt'/ v. expel (a tenant, etc.) by legal process —e·vic'tion /-vik'sHən/ n. [L evincere evict- conquer]

ev·i·dence /ev'ədəns/ n. 1 available facts, circumstances, etc., determining truth or validity 2 statements, information, etc., admissible as testimony in a court of law —v.

(**·denced, ·denc·ing**) **3** be evidence of **4 in evidence** conspicuous [L *videre* see]

ev·i·dent /ev′ədənt/ *adj.* plain or obvious; manifest [L, rel. to EVIDENCE]

ev·i·dent·ly /ev′ədəntlē, -dent′-; ev′ədent′lē/ *adv.* **1** seemingly; as it appears **2** as shown by evidence

e·vil /ē′vəl/ *adj.* **1** morally bad; wicked **2** harmful **3** disagreeable —*n.* **4** evil thing **5** wickedness —**e′vil·ly** *adv.* [OE]

e·vil·do·er /ē′vəldōō′ər/ *n.* sinner —**e′vil·do′ing** *n.*

e·vince /ivins′/ *v.* (**·vinced, ·vinc·ing**) indicate; display (a quality, feeling, etc.) [L *evincere* conquer]

e·vis·cer·ate /ivis′ərāt/ *v.* (**·at·ed, ·at·ing**) disembowel —**e·vis′cer·a′tion** *n.* [L, rel. to VISCERA]

e·voc·a·tive /ivāk′ətiv/ *adj.* evoking (esp. feelings or memories) —**e·voc′a·tive·ly** *adv.*; **e·voc′a·tive·ness** *n.*

e·voke /ivōk′/ *v.* (**·voked, ·vok·ing**) inspire or draw forth (memories, a response, etc.) —**ev·o·ca·tion** /ev′əkā′SHən/ *n.* [L *vocare* call]

ev·o·lu·tion /ev′əlōō′SHən, ē′və-/ *n.* **1** gradual development **2** development of species from earlier forms, as an explanation of origins **3** unfolding of events, etc. —**ev′o·lu′tion·ar′y** /-er′ē/ *adj.* [L, rel. to EVOLVE]

ev·o·lu·tion·ist /ev′əlōō′SHənist, ē′və-/ *n.* person who regards evolution as explaining the origin of species

e·volve /ivälv′, ivôlv′/ *v.* (**·volved, ·volv·ing**) **1** develop gradually and naturally **2** devise (a theory, plan, etc.) **3** unfold [L *evolvere* roll out; unfold]

ewe /yōō/ *n.* female sheep [OE]

ew·er /yōō′ər/ *n.* water jug with a wide mouth [L *aquae* water]

ex /eks/ *n. Colloq.* former husband or wife [see EX-¹]

ex-¹ *prefix* (also e- before some consonants, ef- before *f*) **1** forming verbs meaning: **a** out, forth (*exclaim*) **b** upward (*extol*) **c** thoroughly (*excruciating*) **d** bring into a state (*exasperate*) **e** remove or free from (*expatriate*) **2** forming nouns meaning 'former' (*ex-president; ex-wife*) [L fr. *ex* out of]

ex-² *prefix* out (*exodus*) [Gk]

ex·ac·er·bate /igzas′ərbāt, eksas′-/ *v.* (**·bat·ed, ·bat·ing**) **1** make (pain, etc.) worse **2** annoy; irritate —**ex·ac′er·ba′tion** *n.* [L *exacerbare* fr. *acerbus* bitter]

ex·act /igzakt′/ *adj.* **1** accurate; correct in all details **2** precise —*v.* **3** enforce payment of (money, etc.) **4** demand; insist on; require —**ex·act′ly** *adv.*; **ex·act′ness** *n.* [L *exigere exact-* require]

ex·act·ing *adj.* **1** making great demands **2** requiring much effort

ex·ac·tion /igzak′SHən/ *n.* **1** exacting or being exacted **2a** illegal or exorbitant demand; extortion **b** sum or thing exacted

ex·act·i·tude /igzak′tit(y)ōōd/ *n.* exactness; precision

ex·ag·ger·ate /igzaj′ərāt′/ *v.* (**·at·ed, ·at·ing**) **1** to make seem larger or greater **2** emphasize; overdo —**ex·ag′ger·a′tion** *n.* [L *agger* heap]

ex·alt /egzôlt′/ *v.* **1** raise in rank or power **2** praise highly **3** make lofty or noble —**ex·al·ta·tion** /eg′zôltā′SHən/ *n.* [L *altus* high]

ex·am /igzam′/ *n. Colloq.* examination

ex·am·i·na·tion /igzam′ənā′SHən/ *n.* **1** examining or being examined **2** detailed inspection **3** test **4** formal questioning in court

ex·am·ine /igzam′ən/ *v.* (**·ined, ·in·ing**) **1** inquire into the nature or condition of **2** look closely at **3** test by questioning **4** check the health of (a patient) [L *examinare* weigh; test]

ex·am·ple /igzam′pəl/ *n.* **1** thing characteristic of its kind or illustrating a rule **2** model **3** circumstance or treatment seen as a warning to others **4** illustrative problem or exercise **5 for example** by way of illustration [L *exemplum*]

ex·as·per·ate /igzas′pərāt/ *v.* (**·at·ed, ·at·ing**) irritate intensely —**ex·as′per·a′tion** *n.* [L *asper* rough]

ex·ca·vate /eks′kəvāt/ *v.* (**·vat·ed, ·vat·ing**) **1a** make (a hole or channel) **b** dig out material from (the ground) **2** reveal or extract by digging —**ex·ca·va′tion, ex′ca·va′tor** *n.* [L *excavare* hollow out]

ex·ceed /iksēd′/ *v.* **1** be more or greater than **2** go beyond or do more than is warranted **3** surpass [L *excedere -cess-* go beyond]

ex·ceed·ing·ly *adv.* extremely —**ex·ceed′ing** *adj.*

ex·cel /iksel′/ *v.* (**·celled, ·cel·ling**) **1** surpass **2** be preeminent [L *excellere* be eminent]

ex·cel·lence /ek′sələns/ *n.* **1** outstanding merit or quality [L, rel. to EXCEL]

ex·cel·len·cy /ek′sələnsē/ *n.* (*pl.* **·cies**) **1** (*cap.*) title used in addressing or referring to certain high officials **2** EXCELLENCE

ex·cel·lent /ek′sələnt/ *adj.* extremely good

ex·cept /iksept′/ *v.* **1** exclude —*prep.* **2** not including; other than —*conj.* **3** unless [L *excipere -cept-* take out]

● **Usage:** See note at ACCEPT.

ex·cept′ing *prep.* EXCEPT, 2

ex·cep·tion /iksep′SHən/ *n.* **1** excepting or being excepted **2** thing to be excepted **3** instance that does not follow a rule **4 take exception** object

ex·cep·tion·a·ble /iksep′SHənəbəl/ *adj.* open to objection

ex·cep·tion·al /iksep′SHən-l/ *adj.* **1** forming an exception; unusual **2** outstanding —**ex·cep′tion·al·ly** *adv.*

ex·cerpt *n.* /ek′sərpt′, eg′zərpt′/ **1** extract from a book, film, etc. —*v.* /eksərpt′, egzərpt′/ **2** take excerpts from [L *carpere* pluck]

ex·cess *n.* /ikses′, ek′ses′/ **1** exceeding **2** amount by which one thing exceeds another **3a** overstepping of accepted limits; overindulgence **b** (*pl.*) immoderate behavior —*adj.* /ek′ses, ikses′/ **4** (usu. *pl.*) that exceeds a limited or prescribed amount **5 in** (or **to**) **excess** exceeding the proper amount or degree **6 in excess of** more than; exceeding [L, rel. to EXCEED]

ex·ces·sive /ikses′iv/ *adj.* too much or too great —**ex·ces′sive·ly** *adv.*

ex·change /iks′CHänj′/ *n.* **1** giving of one thing and receiving of another in its place **2** giving of money for its equivalent in a different currency **3** center where telephone connections are made **4** place where merchants, bankers, etc., transact business **5** short conversation —*v.* (·changed, ·chang·ing) **6** give or receive (one thing) in place of another **7** give and receive as equivalents **8** make an exchange **9** in exchange as a thing exchanged (for) —**ex·change′a·ble** *adj.* [AngFr. rel. to CHANGE]

ex·change′ rate′ *n.* value of one currency in terms of another

ex·cheq·uer /eks′CHek′ər, ikscHek′ər/ *n.* **1** royal or national treasury **2** financial reserves; funds [OFr *eschequier* chessboard]

ex·cise /iksīz′/ *v.* (·cised, ·cis·ing) remove; cut out —**ex·ci·sion** /eksi′ZHən/ *n.* [L *excidere* cut out]

ex·cise or **ex·cise tax** /ek′sīz/ *n.* tax on goods produced or sold within the country of origin [MedL *accisa* tax fr. L *accidere* cut into]

ex·cit·a·ble /iksī′təbəl/ *adj.* easily excited —**ex·cit·a·bil′i·ty** *n.*; **ex·cit′a·bly** *adv.*

ex·cite /iksīt′/ *v.* (·cit·ed, ·cit·ing) **1a** rouse the emotions of (a person) **b** arouse (feelings, etc.) **2** provoke; stimulate —**ex·cit′ed·ly** *adv.* [L *citare* put in motion]

ex·cite′ment *n.* **1** excited state of mind **2** exciting thing

ex·cit′ing *adj.* arousing great interest or enthusiasm —**ex·cit′ing·ly** *adv.*

ex·claim /iksklām′/ *v.* **1** cry out suddenly **2** utter by exclaiming [L *exclamare*]

ex·cla·ma·tion /ekskləmä′sHən/ *n.* **1** exclaiming **2** word(s) exclaimed [L, rel. to EXCLAIM]

ex′cla·ma′tion point′ or **mark′** *n.* punctuation mark (!) indicating exclamation

ex·clam·a·to·ry /iksklam′ətôr′ē/ *adj.* of or serving as an exclamation

ex·clude /iksklōōd′/ *v.* (·clud·ed, ·clud·ing) **1** keep out (a person or thing) from a place, group, privilege, etc. **2** remove from consideration —**ex·clu′sion** /-klōō′ZHən/ *n.* [L *excludere* shut out]

ex·clu·sive /iksklōō′siv, -ziv/ *adj.* **1** excluding other things **2** restricted; off-limits to some **3** high-class **4** not obtainable or published elsewhere —*n.* **5** article, etc., published by only one newspaper, etc. **6** exclusive of not including —**ex·clu′sive·ly** *adv.*; **ex·clu′sive·ness, ` ex·clu·siv′i·ty** /eks′klōōsiv′itē/ *n.* [MedL, rel. to EXCLUDE]

ex·com·mu·ni·cate /eks′kəmyōō′nikāt′/ *v.* (·cat·ed, ·cat·ing) officially exclude (a person) from membership and esp. sacraments of church —**ex′com·mu·ni·ca′tion** *n.* [L, rel. to COMMON]

ex·co·ri·ate /ekskôr′ē-āt′/ *v.* (·at·ed, ·at·ing) censure severely —**ex·co′ri·a′tion** *n.* [L *corium* hide]

ex·cre·ment /eks′krəmənt/ *n.* digestive waste; dung —**ex′cre·men′tal** /-əl/ *adj.* [L, rel. to EXCRETE]

ex·cres·cence /ikskres′əns/ *n.* **1** abnormal or morbid outgrowth **2** ugly addition —**ex·cres′cent** *adj.* [L *crescere* grow]

ex·cre·ta /ikskrē′tə/ *n. pl.* feces and urine [L, rel. to EXCRETE]

ex·crete /ikskrēt′/ *v.* (·cret·ed, ·cret·ing) (of an animal or plant) expel (waste matter) —**ex·cre′tion** *n.*; **ex′cre·to·ry** *adj.* [L *excernere* -cret- sift out]

ex·cru·ci·at·ing /ikskrōō′sHē-āt′iNG/ *adj.* causing acute mental or physical pain —**ex·cru′ci·at′ing·ly** *adv.* [L EX- + *cruciare* crucify]

ex·cul·pate /ek′skəlpāt′/ *v.* (·pat·ed, ·pat·ing) free from blame; clear of a charge —**ex′cul·pa′tion** *n.*; **ex·cul′pa·to·ry** /-pətôr′ē/ *adj.* [L *culpare* blame]

ex·cur·sion /ikskər′ZHən/ *n.* **1** short pleasure trip **2** deviation [L *excurrere* run out]

ex·cur·sive /ikskər′siv/ *adj. Lit.* digressive

ex·cuse *v.* /ikskyōōz′/ (·cused, ·cus·ing) **1** try to lessen the blame attaching to (a person, act, or fault) **2** (of an action, circumstance, etc.) serve as a reason to judge (a person or act) less severely **3** release (a person) from a duty, etc. **4** forgive **5** leave or allow to leave —*n.* /ikskyōōs′/ **6** reason put forward to account for a misdeed or offense **7** apology —**ex·cus′a·ble** /-skyōō′zəbəl/ *adj.* [L *causa* cause; reason; excuse]

ex·e·cra·ble /ek′sikrəbəl/ *adj.* abominable [L, rel. to EXECRATE]

ex·e·crate /ek′sikrāt′/ *v.* (·crat·ed, ·crat·ing) **1** express or feel abhorrence for **2** denounce; curse —**ex′e·cra′tion** *n.* [L *exsecrari* curse, rel. to SACRED]

ex·e·cute /ek′sikyōōt′/ *v.* (·cut·ed, ·cut·ing) **1** carry out; perform **2** carry out a design for (a product of art or skill) **3** carry out a death sentence on **4** make legally valid by signing, sealing, etc. —**ex′e·cu′tion** *n.* [L *exsequi* follow up]

ex′e·cu′tion·er *n.* official who carries out a death sentence

ex·ec·u·tive /igzek′yətiv/ *n.* **1** person or body with managerial or administrative responsibility **2** branch of government concerned with executing laws, agreements, etc. —*adj.* **3** concerned with executing laws, agreements, etc., or with other administration or management [MedL, rel. to EXECUTE]

ex·ec·u·tor /igzek′yətər/ *n.* (*fem.* **ex·ec′u·trix′** /-triks/) person appointed to fulfill provisions of a will —**ex·ec′u·to′ri·al** /-tôr′ēəl/ *adj.*

ex·e·ge·sis /ek′sijē′sis/ *n.* (*pl.* ·ses /-sēz/) critical explanation of a text, esp. of Scripture —**ex′e·get′ic** /-jet′ik/ , **ex′e·get′i·cal** *adj.* [Gk *hēgeisthai* lead]

ex·em·plar /igzem′plär′, -plər/ *n.* **1** model **2** typical or specimen instance [L: image; copy]

ex·em·pla·ry /igzem′plərē/ *adj.* fit to be imitated; outstandingly good

ex·em·pli·fy /igzem′pləfī′/ *v.* (·fied, ·fy·ing) **1** illustrate by example **2** be an example of —**ex·em′pli·fi·ca′tion** /-fikā′sHən/ *n.*

ex·empt /igzempt′/ *adj.* **1** free from an obligation imposed on others —*v.* **2** (foll. by *from*) make free from obligation —**ex·emp′tion** /-zemp′SHən/ *n.* [L *eximere* -empt- take out]

ex·er·cise /ek′sərsīz′/ *n.* **1** activity requiring physical effort, done to sustain or improve health **2** mental or spiritual activity, esp. to develop a faculty **3** task devised as exercise **4** use or application of a mental faculty, right, ability, etc. **5** military drill or maneuvers —*v.* (·cised, ·cis·ing) **6** use or apply (a faculty, right, etc.) **7** perform (a function) **8** train or tone one's body by physical exertion **9** tax the powers of **10** perplex; worry [L *exercere* keep busy; practice; work]

ex·ert /igzʌrt'/ *v.* **1** bring to bear; use **2** *refl.* strive —**ex·er'tion** /-zər'ʃHən/ *n.* [L *exserere exsert-* put forth]

ex·hale /eks·hāl'/ *v.* (**·haled**, **·hal·ing**) **1** breathe out **2** emit vapor —**ex'ha·la'tion** /-hälə'ʃHən/ *n.* [Fr fr. L *halare* breathe]

ex·haust /igzȯst'/ *v.* **1** consume or use up the whole of **2** tire out **3** study or expound (a subject) completely —*n.* **4** waste gases, etc., expelled from an engine after combustion **5** (also **ex·haust' pipe'**) pipe or system by which these are expelled —**ex·haust'i·ble** *adj.* [L *haurire haust-* drain]

ex·haus·tion /igzȯs'CHən/ *n.* **1** exhausting or being exhausted **2** total loss of strength

ex·haus·tive /igzȯs'tiv/ *adj.* thorough; comprehensive —**ex·haus'tive·ly** *adv.*; **ex·haus'tive·ness** *n.*

ex·hib·it /igzib'it/ *v.* (**·it·ed**, **·it·ing**) **1** show or reveal **2** display (a quality, etc.) —*n.* **3** item displayed —**ex·hib'i·tor** *n.* [L *exhibere -hibit-*]

ex·hi·bi·tion /ek'səbiSH'ən/ *n.* **1** display (esp. public) of works of art, etc. **2** exhibiting or being exhibited **3** display of behavior

ex'hi·bi'tion·ism' *n.* **1** tendency toward attention-seeking behavior **2** *Psychol.* compulsion to expose one's genitals in public —**ex'hi·bi'tion·ist'** *n.*

ex·hil·a·rate /igzil'ərāt'/ *v.* (**·rat·ed**, **·rat·ing**) enliven; gladden —**ex·hil'a·rat'ing** *adj.*; **ex·hil'a·ra'tion** *n.* [L *hilarare* cheer]

ex·hort /igzȯrt'/ *v.* urge strongly or earnestly —**ex'hor·ta'tion** /-zȯrtā'ʃHən/ *n.* [L *exhortari* encourage]

ex·hume /igz'(y)o͞om', iks(h)yo͞om'/ *v.* (**·humed**, **·hum·ing**) dig up (esp. a buried corpse) —**ex'hu·ma'tion** /-mā'ʃHən/ *n.* [L *humare* inter]

ex·i·gen·cy /eksij'ənsē/ *n.* (*pl.* **·cies**) (also **ex'i·gence**) **1** urgent need or demand **2** emergency —**ex'i·gent** *adj.* [L *exigere* require]

ex·ig·u·ous /igzig'yo͞oəs, eksig'-/ *adj.* scanty; small —**ex'i·gu'i·ty** /-gyo͞o'itē/ *n.* [L]

ex·ile /ek'sīl', egʹzīl'/ *n.* **1** expulsion from one's native land **2** long absence abroad **3** exiled person —*v.* (**·iled**, **·il·ing**) **4** send into exile [Fr fr. L]

ex·ist /igzist'/ *v.* **1** have a place in objective reality **2** occur; be found **3** continue in being; live [L *existere*]

ex·is'tence *n.* **1** fact or manner of being or existing **2** continuance in life or being **3** all that exists —**ex·is'tent** *adj.*

ex·is·ten·tial /eg'zisten'sHəl/ *adj.* **1** of or relating to existence **2** *Philos.* concerned with human existence as viewed by existentialism —**ex'is·ten'tial·ly** *adv.*

ex·is·ten'tial·ism' *n.* philosophical theory emphasizing the existence of the individual as a free and self-determining agent —**ex'is·ten'tial·ist** *n.* & *adj.*

ex·it /eg'zit, ek'sit/ *n.* **1** passage or door by which to leave a room, etc. **2** act or right of going out **3** place to leave a highway **4** actor's departure from the stage —*v.* **5** go out of a room, etc. **6** leave the stage [L *exire exit-* go out]

exo- *comb. form* external [Gk *exō* outside]

ex·o·dus /ek'sədəs, egʹzədəs/ *n.* **1** mass departure **2** (*cap.*) Biblical departure of the Israelites from Egypt [Gk *exodos* fr. *hodos* way]

ex·of·fi·cio /eks' əfiSH'ē-ō'/ *adv.* & *adj.* by virtue of one's office [L]

ex·on·er·ate /igzän'ərāt'/ *v.* (**·at·ed**, **·at·ing**) free or declare free from blame —**ex·on'er·a'tion** *n.* [L *exonerare* fr. *onus* burden]

ex·or·bi·tant /igzȯr'bətənt/ *adj.* (of a price, demand, etc.) grossly excessive —**ex·or'bi·tance** *n.*; **ex·or'bi·tant·ly** *adv.* [L, rel. to ORBIT]

ex·or·cise /ek'sȯrsīz'/ *v.* (also **·cize**) (**·cised** or **·cized**, **·cis·ing** or **·ciz·ing**) **1** expel (a supposed evil spirit) by prayers, etc. **2** free (a person or place) in this way —**ex'or·cism'** /-siz'əm/, **ex'or·cist** *n.* [Gk *horkos* oath]

ex·ot·ic /igzät'ik/ *adj.* **1** introduced from a foreign country; not native **2** strange or unusual **3** intriguingly different; colorful —*n.* **4** exotic person or thing —**ex·ot'i·cal·ly** *adv.* [Gk *exōtikos*]

ex·pand /ikspand'/ *v.* **1** increase in size or importance **2** spread out **3** give a fuller account [L *pandere pans-* spread]

ex·panse /ikspans'/ *n.* wide continuous area

ex·pan·si·ble /ikspan'səbəl/ *adj.* (also **ex·pand'a·ble**) that can be expanded

ex·pan·sion /ikspan'sHən/ *n.* **1** expanding or being expanded **2** enlargement of the scale or scope of a business

ex·pan'sion·ism' *n.* advocacy of expansion, esp. of a nation's territory —**ex·pan'sion·ist** *n.* & *adj.*

ex·pan·sive /ikspan'siv/ *adj.* **1** able or tending to expand **2** extensive **3** (of a person, etc.) effusive; open —**ex·pan'sive·ly** *adv.*; **ex·pan'sive·ness** *n.*

ex·pa·ti·ate /ikspā'sHē-āt'/ *v.* (**·at·ed**, **·at·ing**) speak or write at length —**ex·pa'ti·a'tion** *n.* [L *exspatiari* wander]

ex·pa·tri·ate /ekspā'trēat'/ *v.* **1** living abroad **2** exiled —*n.* /-ət'/ **3** expatriate person —*v.* /-āt'/ (**·at·ed**, **·at·ing**) **4** expel (a person) from his or her native country —**ex·pa'tri·a'tion** *n.* [L *patria* native land]

ex·pect /ikspekt'/ *v.* **1a** regard as likely **b** look for as appropriate or one's due **2** suppose **3** be expecting be pregnant (with) [L *spectare* look at]

ex·pec·tan·cy /ikspek'tənsē/ *n.* (*pl.* **·cies**) **1** state of expectation **2** prospect

ex·pec·tant /ikspek'tənt/ *adj.* hopeful; expecting —**ex·pec'tant·ly** *adv.*

ex·pec·ta·tion /ek'spektā'sHən/ *n.* **1** expecting or anticipation **2** thing expected **3** probability of an event

ex·pec·to·rant /ekspek'tərənt/ *n.* medicine for promoting the expulsion of phlegm

ex·pec·to·rate /ekspek'tərāt'/ *v.* (**·rat·ed**, **·rat·ing**) cough or spit out (phlegm, etc.) —**ex·pec'to·ra'tion** *n.* [L *pectus pector-* breast]

ex·pe·di·ent /ikspē'dēənt/ *adj.* **1** advantageous, advisable —*n.* **2** means of attaining an end; resource —**ex·pe'di·ence**, **ex·pe'di·en·cy** *n.* [rel. to EXPEDITE]

ex·pe·dite /ek'spədīt'/ *v.* (**·dit·ed**, **·dit·ing**)

1 assist the progress of 2 accomplish (business) quickly [L *expedire* fr. *pes ped-* foot]

ex-pe-di-tion /ek'spədiSH'ən/ *n.* 1 journey or voyage for a particular purpose, esp. exploration 2 people undertaking this —**ex'pe-di'tion-ar'y** /-er'ē/ *adj.* [L, rel. to EXPEDITE]

ex-pe-di-tious /ek'spədiSH'əs/ *adj.* acting or done with speed and efficiency

ex-pel /ikspel'/ *v.* (-pelled, -pel-ling) 1 deprive of membership, participation, etc. 2 force out; eject [L *pellere puls-* drive]

ex-pend /ikspend'/ *v.* spend or use up [L *pendere pens-* weigh]

ex-pend-a-ble /ikspen'dəbəl/ *adj.* that may be sacrificed or dispensed with; not worth saving

ex-pen-di-ture /ikspen'dəCHər/ *n.* 1 spending or using up 2 thing (esp. money) expended

ex-pense /ikspens'/ *n.* 1a cost incurred b amount paid to reimburse this 2 thing on which money is spent [L *expensa*, rel. to EXPEND]

ex-pen-sive /ikspen'siv/ *adj.* costing or charging much —**ex-pen'sive-ly** *adv.*; **ex-pen'sive-ness** *n.*

ex-pe-ri-ence /ikspēr'ēəns/ *n.* 1 living and how it shapes a person 2 observation of or practical acquaintance with facts or events 3 knowledge or skill resulting from this 4 event or activity participated in or observed (*a rare experience*) —*v.* (-enced, -enc-ing) 5 have experience of; undergo 6 feel [L *experiri -pert-* try]

ex-pe-ri-enced *adj.* 1 having had much experience 2 skilled from experience

ex-per-i-ment *n.* /iksper'əmənt/ 1 procedure for testing a hypothesis, etc. —*v.* /-ment'/ 2 make an experiment —**ex-per'i-men-ta'tion** /-məntā'sHən/, **ex-per'i-ment'er** *n.* [L, rel. to EXPERIENCE]

ex-per-i-men-tal *adj.* 1 based on or making use of experiment 2 used in experiments —**ex-per'i-men'tal-ly** *adv.*

ex-pert /ek'spərt'/ *adj.* 1 having special knowledge or skill —*n.* 2 person with special knowledge or skill —**ex'pert-ly** *adv.*; **ex'pert-ness** *n.* [L, rel. to EXPERIENCE]

ex-per-tise /ek'spərtēz', -tēs'/ *n.* expert skill, knowledge, or judgment [Fr]

ex-pi-ate /ek'spē-āt'/ *v.* (-at-ed, -at-ing) pay the penalty for or make amends for (wrongdoing) —**ex-pi-a-ble** /ek'spēəbəl/ *adj.*; **ex'pi-a'tion** *n.*; **ex'pi-a-to'ry** /-ətôr'ē/ *adj.* [L *expiare*, rel. to PIOUS]

ex-pire /ikspīr'/ *v.* (-pired, -pir-ing) 1 (of a period of time, validity, etc.) come to an end 2 cease to be valid 3 die 4 exhale —**ex-pi-ra'tion** /-spərā'sHən/, **ex-pi-ry** *n.* (*pl.* -ries) [L *spirare* breathe]

ex-plain /iksplān'/ *v.* 1a make clear or intelligible b make known in detail 2 account for (one's conduct, etc.) 3 explain away minimize the significance of by explanation [L *ex-planare* fr. *planus* flat]

ex-pla-na-tion /ek'splənāsHən/ *n.* 1 explaining 2 statement or circumstance that explains something

ex-plan-a-to-ry /iksplan'ətôr'ē/ *adj.* serving or designed to explain

ex-ple-tive /ek'splətiv/ *n.* swearword or exclamation [L *explere* fill out]

199   expedition / exposure

ex-pli-ca-ble /iksplik'əbəl, ek'splik-/ *adj.* that can be explained

ex-pli-cate /ek'splikāt'/ *v.* (-cat-ed, -cat-ing) 1 develop the meaning of (an idea, etc.) 2 explain (esp. a text) —**ex'pli-ca'tion** *n.* [L *explicare -plicat-* unfold]

ex-plic-it /iksplis'it/ *adj.* 1 expressly stated; not merely implied; stated in detail 2 definite 3 outspoken —**ex-plic'it-ly** *adv.*; **ex-plic'it-ness** *n.* [L, rel. to EXPLICATE]

ex-plode /iksplōd'/ *v.* (-plod-ed, -plod-ing) 1a burst suddenly with a loud noise owing to release of internal energy b cause (a bomb, etc.) to explode 2 give vent suddenly to emotion, esp. anger 3 increase suddenly or rapidly 4 show (a theory, etc.) to be false or baseless 5 show the components of (a drawing of a mechanism) somewhat separated [L *explodere -plos-* hiss off the stage]

ex-ploit *n.* /ek'sploit'/ 1 daring feat —*v.* /iksploit'/ 2 make use of (a resource, etc.) 3 take advantage of (esp. a person) for one's own ends —**ex'ploi-ta'tion** /-tā'sHən/ *n.*; **ex-ploit'a-tive** /-ətiv/ *adj.*; **ex-ploit'er** *n.* [L, rel. to EXPLICATE]

ex-plore /iksplôr'/ *v.* (-plored, -plor-ing) 1 travel through (a country, etc.) to learn about it 2 inquire into —**ex'plo-ra'tion** *n.*; **ex-plor'a-to'ry** /-ətôr'ē/ *adj.*; **ex-plor'er** *n.* [L *explorare* search out]

ex-plo-sion /iksplō'zHən/ *n.* 1 exploding 2 loud noise caused by this 3 sudden outbreak of feeling 4 rapid or sudden increase

ex-plo-sive /iksplō'siv, -ziv/ *adj.* 1 able, tending, or likely to explode 2 dangerously tense —*n.* 3 substance that can explode —**ex-plo'sive-ly** *adv.*; **ex-plo'sive-ness** *n.*

ex-po-nent /ikspō'nənt/ *n.* 1 person who promotes an idea, etc. 2 practitioner of an activity, profession, etc. 3 type or representative 4 raised symbol beside a numeral indicating how many of the number are to be multiplied together (e.g., $2^3 = 2 \times 2 \times 2$) [L *exponere* EXPOUND]

ex-po-nen-tial /ek'spənen'sHəl/ *adj.* 1 of or indicated by a mathematical exponent 2 (of an increase, etc.) more and more rapid —**ex'po-nen'tial-ly** *adv.*

ex-port *v.* /ekspôrt'/ 1 sell or send to another country —*n.* /ek'spôrt/ 2 exporting 3 exported article or service —**ex'por-ta'tion** /-pôrtā'sHən/, **ex-port'er** *n.* [L *portare* carry]

ex-pose /ikspōz'/ *v.* (-posed, -pos-ing) 1 uncover or leave unprotected 2 (foll. by *to*) a put at risk of b subject to (an influence, etc.) 3 *Photog.* subject (a film) to light 4 reveal 5 exhibit; display [L *ponere* put]

ex-po-sé /ek'spōzā'/ *n.* revelation of something discreditable [Fr]

ex-po-si-tion /ek'spəzisH'ən/ *n.* 1 explanatory account 2 explanation or commentary 3 large public exhibition [L, rel. to EXPOUND]

ex post facto /eks' pōst' fak'tō/ *adj.* & *adv.* with retroactive action or force [L: from the thing done afterward]

ex-pos-tu-late /ikspäs'CHəlāt'/ *v.* (-lat-ed, -lat-ing) make a protest; remonstrate —**ex-pos'tu-la'tion** *n.* [L, rel. to POSTULATE]

ex-po-sure /ikspō'zHər/ *n.* 1 exposing or being exposed 2 physical condition resulting from being exposed to the elements 3 *Photog.* a exposing film to light b duration of this c section of film so affected

ex·pound /ikspound'/ *v.* 1 set out in detail 2 explain or interpret [L *ponere posit-* place; put]

ex·press /ikspres'/ *v.* 1 represent or make known in words or by gestures, conduct, etc. 2 communicate 3 represent by symbols 4 send by express service —*adj.* 5 operating at high speed 6 definitely stated 7 delivered by a specially fast service —*adv.* 8 at high speed 9 by express shipment —*n.* 10 fast train, etc. 11 service for rapid package delivery —**ex·press'i·ble** *adj.*; **ex·press'ly** *adv.* [L *exprimere -press-* squeeze out]

ex·pres·sion /ikspresH'ən/ *n.* 1 expressing or being expressed 2 word or phrase expressed 3 person's facial appearance, indicating feeling 4 depiction or conveying of feeling, etc., in art 5 *Math.* collection of symbols expressing a quantity —**ex·pres'sion·less** *adj.* [rel. to EXPRESS]

ex·pres'sion·ism *n.* style of painting, music, drama, etc., seeking to express emotion rather than the external world —**ex·pres'sion·ist** *n.* & *adj.*

ex·pres·sive /ikspres'iv/ *adj.* 1 full of expression 2 serving to express —**ex·pres'sive·ly** *adv.*; **ex·pres'sive·ness** *n.*

ex·press'way *n.* high-speed highway

ex·pro·pri·ate /iksprō'prē-āt'/ *v.* (·at·ed, ·at·ing) take away (property) from its owner for official or public reasons —**ex·pro'pri·a'tion** *n.* [L *proprius* proper; one's own]

ex·pul·sion /ikspəl'sHən/ *n.* expelling or being expelled [L, rel. to EXPEL]

ex·punge /ikspənj'/ *v.* (·punged, ·pung·ing) erase; remove [L *expungere* prick out (for deletion)]

ex·pur·gate /ek'spərgāt'/ *v.* (·gat·ed, ·gat·ing) remove objectionable matter from (a book, etc.) —**ex'pur·ga'tion, ex'pur·ga'tor** *n.* [L, rel. to PURGE]

ex·qui·site /ekskwiz'it, ek'skwiz-/ *adj.* 1 extremely beautiful or delicate 2 keenly felt 3 highly refined —**ex'qui·site·ly** *adv.* [L *exquirere -quisit-* seek out]

ex·tant /ek'stant, ekstant'/ *adj.* still in existence [L *ex(s)tare* stand out]

ex·tem·po·ra·ne·ous /ikstem'pərā'nēəs/ *adj.* spoken or done without preparation —**ex·tem'po·ra'ne·ous·ly** *adv.* [fr. EXTEMPORE]

ex·tem·po·re /ikstem'pərē/ *adj.* & *adv.* without preparation [L: at the moment]

ex·tem·po·rize /ikstem'pəriz'/ *v.* (·rized, ·riz·ing) improvise —**ex·tem'po·ri·za'tion** *n.*

ex·tend /ikstend'/ *v.* 1 lengthen or make larger in space or time 2 stretch or lay out at full length 3 reach or encompass 4 (foll. by *to*) go so far as to include 5 offer (an invitation, hospitality, etc.) —**ex·tend'i·ble, ex·ten'si·ble** *adj.* [L *extendere -tens-* stretch out]

ex·tend'ed fam'i·ly *n.* family including nearby relatives

ex·ten·sion /iksten'sHən/ *n.* 1 extending or being extended 2 part enlarging or added on

3 subsidiary telephone 4 additional interval

ex·ten·sive /iksten'siv/ *adj.* 1 covering a large area 2 far-reaching —**ex·ten'sive·ly** *adv.*; **ex·ten'sive·ness** *n.*

ex·tent /ikstent'/ *n.* 1 space over which a thing extends 2 range; scope; degree [AngFr, rel. to EXTEND]

ex·ten·u·ate /iksten'yoō-āt'/ *v.* (·at·ed, ·at·ing) make (guilt or an offense) seem less serious —**ex·ten'u·a'tion** *n.* [L *tenuis* thin]

ex·te·ri·or /ikstēr'ēər/ *adj.* 1 of or on the outer side 2 coming from outside —*n.* 3 outward aspect or surface 4 outward demeanor [L]

ex·ter·mi·nate /ikstər'mənāt'/ *v.* (·nat·ed, ·nat·ing) destroy utterly (esp. a living thing) —**ex·ter·mi·na'tion, ex·ter'mi·na'tor** *n.* [L *terminus* boundary]

ex·ter·nal /ikstərn'l/ *adj.* 1a of or on the outside or visible part b in or coming from the outside or an outside source 2 foreign 3 not subjective or individual 4 for use on the outside of the body —*n.* 5a (*pl.*) outward features or aspect b external circumstances c inessentials —**ex·ter'nal·ly** *adv.* [L *externus* outer]

ex·ter·nal·ize /ikstərn'l-īz'/ *v.* (·ized, ·iz·ing) give or attribute external existence to —**ex·ter'nal·i·za'tion** *n.*

ex·tinct /ikstiNGkt'/ *adj.* 1 that has died out; defunct 2 (of a volcano) that no longer erupts [L *ex(s)tinguere -stinct-* quench]

ex·tinc·tion /ekstiNGk'sHən/ *n.* 1 making or becoming extinct 2 extinguishing or being extinguished 3 annihilation

ex·tin·guish /ikstiNG'gwisH/ *v.* 1 cause (a flame, light, etc.) to die out 2 destroy —**ex·tin'guish·a·ble** *adj.*; **ex·tin'guish·er** *n.*

ex·tir·pate /ek'stərpāt'/ *v.* (·pat·ed, ·pat·ing) root out; eradicate —**ex·tir·pa'tion** *n.* [L *ex(s)tirpare* fr. *stirps* stem of tree]

ex·tol /ikstōl'/ *v.* (also **ex·toll'**) (·tolled, ·tol·ling) praise enthusiastically [L *tollere* raise]

ex·tort /ikstôrt'/ *v.* obtain by coercion [L *torquere* tort- twist]

ex·tor·tion /ekstôr'sHən/ *n.* act of extorting, esp. money —**ex·tor'tion·ate /-sHənit/** *adj.*; **ex·tor'tion·ate·ly** *adv.*; **ex·tor'tion·er, ex·tor'tion·ist** *n.*

ex·tra /ek'strə/ *adj.* 1 additional; more than usual, necessary, or expected —*adv.* 2 more than usually 3 additionally (*was charged extra*) —*n.* 4 extra thing 5 thing for which an extra charge is made 6 performer in a minor role [prob. fr. EXTRAORDINARY]

extra- *comb. form* 1 outside; beyond 2 beyond the scope of [L *extra* outside]

ex·tract *v.* /ikstrakt'/ 1 remove or take out 2 obtain (money, an admission, etc.) using pressure 3 select (a part of a book, etc.) 4 obtain (juice, etc.) by pressure, distillation, etc. 5 derive (pleasure, etc.) —*n.* /ek'strakt'/ 6 short passage from a book, etc. 7 concentrated ingredient [L *trahere tract-* draw]

ex·trac'tion *n.* 1 extracting or being extracted 2 lineage; descent —**ex·trac'tor** *n.* [L, rel. to EXTRACT]

ex·tra·cur·ric·u·lar /ek'strəkərik'yələr/ *adj.* not part of the normal curriculum

ex·tra·dite /ek'strədīt'/ *v.* (**·dit·ed, ·dit·ing**) return (a person accused or convicted of a crime) to the country, state, etc., in which the crime was committed —**ex'tra·dit'a·ble** *adj.*; **ex'tra·di'tion** *n.* [Fr, rel. to TRADITION]

ex·tra·mar·i·tal /ek'strəmar'ət-l/ *adj.* (esp. of sexual relations) occurring outside marriage

ex·tra·ne·ous /ikstrā'nēəs/ *adj.* 1 of external origin 2 separate; irrelevant; unrelated [L *extraneus*]

ex·tra·or·di·nar·y /ikstrôrd'n·er'ē, ek'strəôrd'-/ *adj.* 1 unusual or remarkable 2 unusually great 3 (of a meeting, official, etc.) special or additional —**ex·tra·or'di·nar'i·ly** /-er'ilē/ *adv.* [L]

ex·trap·o·late /ikstrap'əlāt'/ *v.* (**·lat·ed, ·lat·ing**) calculate or derive approximately from known data, etc. —**ex·trap'o·la'tion** *n.* [fr. EXTRA- + (INTER)POLATE]

ex·tra·sen·so·ry /ek'strəsen'sərē/ *adj.* outside the known senses

ex·tra·ter·res·tri·al /ek'strətəres'trēəl/ *adj.* 1 outside the earth or its atmosphere or from there —*n.* 2 (in science fiction) being from outer space

ex·trav·a·gant /ikstrav'əgənt/ *adj.* 1 spending money excessively 2 excessive; absurd 3 costing much —**ex·trav'a·gance** *n.*; **ex·trav'a·gant·ly** *adv.* [L *vagari* wander]

ex·trav·a·gan·za /ikstrav'əgan'zə/ *n.* spectacular theatrical production [It: extravagance]

ex·treme /ikstrēm'/ *adj.* 1 of a high or the highest degree 2 severe 3 outermost 4 on the far left or right of a political party —*n.* 5 either of two opposite things; pole; end 6 highest degree 7 *Math.* first or last term of a ratio or series —**ex·treme'ly** *adv.* [L]

ex·trem·ist *n.* person with radical views —**ex·trem'ism** *n.*

ex·trem·i·ty /ikstrem'itē/ *n.* (*pl.* **·ties**) 1 extreme point; end 2 (*pl.*) the hands and feet 3 extreme adversity [L, rel. to EXTREME]

ex·tri·cate /ek'strikāt'/ *v.* (**·cat·ed, ·cat·ing**) free or disentangle from a difficulty, etc. —**ex'tri·ca·ble** *adj.*; **ex'tri·ca'tion** *n.* [L *tricae* perplexities]

ex·trin·sic /ekstrin'sik/ *adj.* 1 coming from outside; not inherent or intrinsic 2 extraneous —**ex·trin'si·cal·ly** *adv.* [L *extrinsecus* outwardly]

ex·tro·vert /ek'strəvərt'/ *n.* outgoing and externally oriented person —**ex'tro·ver'sion** *n.*; **ex'tro·vert'ed** *adj.* [L *vertere* turn]

ex·trude /ikstrōōd'/ *v.* (**·trud·ed, ·trud·ing**) thrust or force out, as through a small opening —**ex·tru'sion** *n.*; **ex·tru'sive** *adj.* [L *extrudere -trus-* thrust out]

ex·u·ber·ant /igz(y)ōō'bərənt/ *adj.* 1 lively; high-spirited 2 (of a plant, etc.) prolific —**ex·u'ber·ance** *n.*; **ex·u'ber·ant·ly** *adv.* [L *uber* fertile]

ex·ude /igz(y)ōōd'/ *v.* (**·ud·ed, ·ud·ing**) 1 ooze out 2 freely show (a spirit, emotion, etc.) —**ex·u·da'tion** *n.* [L *sudare* sweat]

ex·ult /igzəlt'/ *v.* be joyful —**ex·ul·ta'tion** /·zəltā'SHən/ *n.*; **ex·ul'tant** *adj.*; **ex·ul'tant·ly** *adv.* [L *ex(s)ultare* fr. *saltare* leap]

eye /ī/ *n.* 1 organ of sight 2 eye characterized by the color of the iris 3 tissues around the eye (*black eye*) 4 (*sing.* or *pl.*) sight 5a particular visual ability b discernment (*good eye for detail*) 6 calm region at the center of a hurricane 7 hole of a needle —*v.* (**eyed, eye·ing** or **ey·ing**) 8 watch or observe closely 9 **have an eye** or **eyes for** be interested in; wish to acquire 10 **see eye to eye** agree 11 **with an eye to** with a view to [OE]

eye'ball' *n.* 1 ball of the eye within the lids and socket —*v.* 2 *Slang.* look or stare (at)

eye'brow' *n.* 1 line of hair on the ridge above the eye socket 2 **raise one's eyebrows** show surprise, disbelief, or disapproval

eye'-catch'ing *adj. Colloq.* striking

eye'ful /ī'fool'/ *n.* (*pl.* **·fuls**) *Colloq.* 1 visually striking person or thing 2 **get an eyeful** (of) good and thorough look

eye'glass'es *n.* pair of framed lenses to assist defective sight

eye'lash' *n.* each of the hairs growing on the edges of the eyelids

eye'let /ī'lit/ *n.* 1 small hole for string, rope, etc., to pass through 2 metal ring strengthening this [OFr *oillet* fr. L *oculus*]

eye'lid' *n.* either of the skin folds closing to cover the eye

eye'lin'er *n.* cosmetic for the eyes, usu. applied in a thin line next to the lashes

eye'-o'pen·er *n. Colloq.* enlightening experience; startling revelation

eye'piece' *n.* lens or lenses to which the eye is applied at the end of an optical instrument

eye'sight' *n.* faculty or power of seeing

eye'sore' *n.* ugly thing

eye'tooth' *n.* canine tooth in the upper jaw

eye'wash' *n.* 1 solution to cleanse the eyes 2 *Slang.* nonsense; insincere talk

eye'wit'ness /ī'wit'nəs/ *n.* person who saw a thing happen

ey·rie /âr'ē, ēr'ē/ *n.* see AERIE

Ey·senck /ī'zeNGk/, **Hans Jürgen** 1916–92; German-born British psychologist

---

F

f, F /ef/ *n.* (*pl.* **f's; F's, Fs**) sixth letter of the English alphabet; a consonant

F /ef/ *symb.* fluorine

f or **f.** *abbr.* 1 farthing 2 father 3 fathom 4 feet 5 female; feminine 6 filly 7 fine 8 focal length 9 folio 10 (*pl.* **ff.**) following 11 franc(s)

F or **F.** *abbr.* 1 Fahrenheit 2 farad(s) 3 February 4 franc(s) 5 France; French 6 Friday

fa /fä/ *n. Mus.* fourth note of a major scale

FAA *abbr.* Federal Aviation Administration

Fa·ber·gé /fab'ərzhā'/, **Peter Carl** 1846–1920; Russian goldsmith and jeweler

fa·ble /fā'bəl/ *n.* 1a fictional, esp. supernatural, story **b** moral tale, esp. with animals as characters **2** lie [L *fabula* story]

fa'bled *adj.* celebrated; legendary

fab·ric /fab'rik/ *n.* **1** woven material; cloth **2** essential structure [L *fabrica* craft]

fab·ri·cate /fab'rikāt'/ *v.* (·cat·ed, ·cat·ing) **1** construct, esp. from components **2** invent (a story, etc.) —**fab'ri·ca'tion, fab'ri·ca·tor** *n.* [L, rel. to FABRIC]

fab·u·lous /fab'yələs/ *adj.* **1** astounding **2** *Colloq.* marvelous **3** legendary —**fab'u·lous·ly** *adv.* [L, rel. to FABLE]

fa·çade or **fa·cade** /fəsäd', fa–/ *n.* **1** face or front of a building **2** outward appearance, esp. a deceptive one [Fr, rel. to FACE]

face /fās/ *n.* **1** front of the head from fore-head to chin **2** facial expression **3a** surface; side **b** dial of a clock, etc. **4** aspect —*v.* (**faced, fac·ing**) **5** look or be positioned to-ward or in a certain direction **6** be opposite **7** meet resolutely; confront **8** install the surface of (a thing) **9** *face the music Colloq.* accept bravely unpleasant consequences **10** *face up to* accept bravely **11** *in the face of* despite **12** *lose face* be humiliated **13** *save face* avoid humiliation [L *facies*; face; face]

face'·less /fās'ləs/ *adj.* without identity; char-acterless

face'·lift' *n.* **1** (also *face' lift'ing*) cosmetic surgery to remove wrinkles, etc. **2** improve-ment in appearance, efficiency, etc., often su-perficial

fac·et /fas'it/ *n.* **1** aspect **2** side of a cut gem [Fr, rel. to FACE]

fa·ce·tious /fəsē'shəs/ *adj.* intending or intended to be amusing; not serious —**fa·ce'tious·ly** *adv.* [L *facetus* witty]

FACET 2

face' val'ue *n.* **1** nominal value of money **2** seeming value

fa·cial /fā'shəl/ *adj.* **1** of or for the face —*n.* beauty treatment for the face —**fa'cial·ly** *adv.*

fa'cial tis'sue *n.* soft paper handkerchief

fac·ile /fas'əl/ *adj.* **1** easily achieved but of little value **2** glib; fluent [L *facere* do]

fa·cil·i·tate /fəsil'ətāt'/ *v.* (·tat·ed, ·tat·ing) ease (a process, etc.) —**fa·cil'i·ta'tion** *n.* [L, rel. to FACILE]

fa·cil·i·ty /fəsil'ətē/ *n.* (*pl.* ·ties) **1** ease **2** fluency; dexterity **3** opportunity or equipment for doing something **4** building or technical station **5** (the facilities) bathroom; restroom [L, rel. to FACILE]

fac·ing /fā'sing/ *n.* **1** garment lining **2** outer covering on a wall, etc.

fac·sim·i·le /faksim'əlē/ *n.* exact copy, esp. of writing, printing, a picture, etc. [L: make like]

fact /fakt/ *n.* **1** thing known to exist or be true **2** truth; reality [L *factum* fr. *facere* do]

fac·tion /fak'shən/ *n.* small organized dis-senting group within a larger one —**fac'tion·al** *adj.*; **fac'tion·al·ism** *n.* [L, rel. to FACT]

fac·tious /fak'shəs/ *adj.* of, characterized by, or inclined to faction [L, rel. to FACTION]

fac·ti·tious /faktish'əs/ *adj.* **1** contrived **2** ar-tificial [L, rel. to FACT]

fac·tor /fak'tər/ *n.* **1** circumstance or ele-ment contributing to a result **2** whole num-ber, etc., that when multiplied with another produces a given number —*v.* **3** *Math.* de-termine the quantities that, when multiplied together, produce a given quantity [L *facere* do; make]

fac·to·ri·al /faktôr'ēəl/ *n.* **1** product of a number and all the whole numbers below it —*adj.* **2** of a factor or factorial

fac·to·ry /fak't(ə)rē/ *n.* (*pl.* ·ries) place where goods are manufactured [L *facere* make; do]

fac·to·tum /faktō'təm/ *n.* (*pl.* ·tums) per-son who does many varied tasks [MedL, fr. L *facere* make; do, *totus* all]

facts' of life' *n. pl.* information about sexual functions and practices

fac·tu·al /fak'chōōəl/ *adj.* based on or con-cerned with fact —**fac'tu·al·ly** *adv.*

fac·ul·ty /fak'əltē/ *n.* (*pl.* ·ties) **1** aptitude for a particular activity **2** inherent mental, sen-sory, or physical power **3** teaching staff [L, rel. to FACILE]

fad /fad/ *n.* short-lived fashion; craze —**fad'dish** *adj.* [prob. fr. *fiddle-faddle*]

fade /fād/ *v.* (**fad·ed, fad·ing**) **1** lose or cause to lose color, light, or sound; slowly di-minish **2** lose freshness or strength **3** cause (a photographic image, recorded sound, etc.) to appear or disappear gradually —*n.* **4** ac-tion of fading **5** *fade away* diminish; disap-pear [Fr *fade* dull]

Faer·oe Is·lands /far'ō, fer'ō/ *n.* group of Danish islands in the N Atlantic between Great Britain and Iceland

fag·ot or **fag·got** *n.* bundle of sticks, etc. [OFr]

Fahd /fäd/ 1922– ; king of Saudi Arabia (1982–)

Fahr·en·heit /far'ənhīt'/ *adj.* of a scale of temperature on which water freezes at 32° and boils at 212° [for G. *Fahrenheit*, German phys-icist]

fa·ience /fā·äns', fī–/ *n.* decorated and glazed earthenware and porcelain [Fr fr. *Faenza* in Italy]

fail /fāl/ *v.* **1** not succeed **2** be or judge to be unsuccessful in (an examination, etc.) **3** be unable; neglect (*fail to appear*) **4** disappoint **5** become weaker; cease functioning **6** be-come bankrupt **7** without fail for certain; whatever happens [L *fallere* deceive]

fail'ing *n.* **1** fault; weakness —*prep.* **2** in de-fault of; lacking

fail'-safe' *adj.* equipped to revert to a safe con-dition in case of malfunction

fail·ure /fāl'yər/ *n.* **1** lack of success; failing **2** unsuccessful person or thing **3** nonper-formance or inaction **4** breaking down or ceasing to function (*heart failure*) **5** bank-ruptcy; insolvency [AngFr, rel. to FAIL]

fain /fān/ *adj. Archaic.* **1** willing; obliged —*adv.* **2** gladly (esp. *would fain*) [OE]

faint /fānt/ *adj.* **1** indistinct; dim; pale **2** weak or giddy **3** slight **4** feeble; timid —*v.* **5** lose consciousness —*n.* **6** act or state of fainting —**faint'ly** *adv.*; **faint'ness** *n.* [OFr, rel. to FEIGN]

faint'heart'ed *adj.* cowardly; timid

fair¹ /fer/ *adj.* **1** just; equitable; in accor-dance with the rules **2** blond; light or pale **3a** moderate in quality or amount **b** satisfactory

4 (of weather) fine; (of the wind) favorable 5 *Baseball.* falling within the baselines 6 beautiful —*adv.* 7 in a just manner 8 exactly; completely —**fair′ness** *n.* [OE]

fair[2] *n.* 1 usu. outdoor festival for public entertainment 2 periodic market, often with entertainments 3 exposition, esp. commercial [OFr fr. LL *feriae* festivals]

Fair·banks /far′baNGks, fer′-/, **Douglas** (born **Julius Ullman**) 1883–1939; US actor

Fair·banks /far′baNGks, fer′-/ *n.* city in Alaska. Pop. 30,843

fair′ game′ *n.* legitimate target or object

fair·ing /fer′iNG/ *n.* streamlining structure added to a ship, aircraft, vehicle, etc.

fair′ly *adv.* 1 in a fair manner 2 moderately; rather

fair′ play′ *n.* just treatment or behavior

fair·way /fer′wā′/ *n. Golf.* well-mowed part of a hole between a tee and its green

fair·y /fer′ē/ *n.* (*pl.* -ies) small winged legendary being [OFr]

fair′y god′moth′er *n.* imaginary woman who provides magical assistance

fair′y tale′ *n.* 1 tale about fairies 2 incredible story; lie

Fai·sal /fī′səl/ name of two kings of Iraq: 1 **Faisal I** 1885–1933; reigned 1921–33 2 **Faisal II** 1935–58; reigned 1939–58

Fai·sa·la·bad /fī′sälˈəbäd/ *n.* (formerly Lyallpur) city in Pakistan. Pop. 1,104,200

fait ac·com·pli /fetäkôNplēˈ/ *n.* (*pl. faits accomplis* /fezäkôNplēˈ/) *French.* thing that has been done and is irreversible

faith /fāTH/ *n.* 1 complete trust or confidence 2 unquestioning, esp. religious, belief 3 religion or creed 4 loyalty; trustworthiness [L *fides* trust]

faith·ful /fāTH′fəl/ *adj.* 1 showing faith 2 loyal; trustworthy 3 accurate —**faith′ful·ly** *adv.*; **faith′ful·ness** *n.*

faith′less /fāTH′ləs/ *adj.* 1 false; unreliable; disloyal 2 without religious faith —**faith′less·ly** *adv.*; **faith′less·ness** *n.*

fake /fāk/ *n.* 1 false or counterfeit thing or person —*adj.* 2 counterfeit; not genuine —*v.* (**faked, fak′ing**) 3 make a fake or imitation of 4 feign —**fak′er** *n.*

fa·kir /fəkēr′, fākēr′/ *n.* Muslim or (rarely) Hindu religious beggar or ascetic [Ar: poor man]

fal·con /fal′kən, fôl′-/ *n.* small hawk sometimes trained to hunt —**fal′con·ry** *n.* [LL *falco*]

Falk′land Is′lands /fô(l)′klənd/ *n.* (Spanish name **Is·las Mal·vin·as**) island group in the Atlantic Ocean E of Argentina; British possession

fall /fôl/ *v.* (**fell, fall·en, fall·ing**) 1 go or come down freely; descend 2 topple (over) 3 hang or slope down 4a sink lower; decline b subside 5 occur 6 (of the face) show dismay or disappointment 7 yield to temptation 8 take or have a particular direction or place 9 be classed among 10 come by chance or duty 11 pass into a specified condition (*fall apart*) 12 be captured 13 die 14 attack 15 begin (*fell to wondering*) —*n.* 16 act of falling 17 that which falls or has fallen, e.g., snow 18 overthrow 19a succumbing to temptation b (**the Fall**) *Bibl.* Adam's sin and its results 20 (also *cap.*) autumn 21 (esp. *pl.*) waterfall 22

throw in wrestling 23 **fall back on** have recourse to 24 **fall behind:** a lag b be in arrears 25 **fall for** *Colloq.* be captivated or deceived by 26 **fall off** decrease 27 **fall out:** a (of the hair, teeth, etc.) become detached b *Milit.* come out of formation 28 **fall short** be deficient 29 **fall through** fail; not happen 30 **fall to** begin, e.g., eating or working [OE]

Fal·la /fä′yə/, **Manuel de** 1876–1946; Spanish composer

fal·la·cy /fal′əsē/ *n.* (*pl.* -cies) 1 mistaken belief 2 faulty reasoning; misleading argument —**fal·la·cious** /fälä′sHəs/ *adj.* [L *fallere* deceive]

fall′ guy′ *n. Slang.* easy victim; scapegoat

fal·li·ble /fal′əbəl/ *adj.* capable of making mistakes —**fal′li·bil′i·ty** *n.*; **fal′li·bly** *adv.* [MedL, rel. to FALLACY]

fall′ing·out′ *n.* estrangement; parting of the ways

fall′ing star′ *n.* meteor

Fal·lo·pi·an tube /fälō′pēən/ *n.* either of two tubes along which ova travel from the ovaries to the womb [for G. *Fallopius*, Italian anatomist]

fall′out′ *n.* radioactive nuclear debris

fal·low /fal′ō/ *adj.* 1 (of land) plowed but left unsown 2 uncultivated [OE]

false /fôls/ *adj.* 1 wrong; incorrect 2 spurious; artificial 3 improperly so called (*false acacia*) 4 deceptive 5 (foll. by *to*) deceitful, treacherous, or unfaithful —**false′ly** *adv.*; **false′ness** *n.* [L *falsus*]

false·hood /fôls′hŏŏd/ *n.* 1 untrue thing 2a act of lying b lie

fal·set·to /fôlset′ō/ *n.* male singing voice above the normal range [It dim., rel. to FALSE]

fal·si·fy /fôl′səfī/ *v.* (-**fied, -fy·ing**) 1 fraudulently alter 2 misrepresent —**fal′si·fi·ca′tion** /-fikā′sHən/ *n.* [MFr fr. MedL, rel. to FALSE]

fal·si·ty /fôl′sətē/ *n.* being false

fal·ter /fôl′tər/ *v.* 1 stumble; go unsteadily 2 lose courage 3 speak hesitatingly

fame /fām/ *n.* renown; being famous —**famed** *adj.* [L *fama* talk; report]

fa·mil·ial /fəmil′yəl/ *adj.* of a family or its members

fa·mil·iar /fəmil′yər/ *adj.* 1a well known b often met (with) 2 well acquainted 3 informal, esp. presumptuously so —*n.* 4 close friend —**fa·mil′i·ar′i·ty** /-ēer′itē/ *n.*; **fa·mil′iar·ly** *adv.* [L, rel. to FAMILY]

fa·mil·iar·ize /fəmil′yərīz/ *v.* (-**ized, -iz·ing**) make conversant or well acquainted —**fa·mil′iar·i·za′tion** *n.*

fam·i·ly /fam′(ə)lē/ *n.* (*pl.* -lies) 1 set of relations, esp. parents and children 2 descendants of a common ancestor 3 close-knit organization 4 group of similar objects, people, etc. 5 group of related genera of animals or plants [L *familia* household]

fam′i·ly leave′ *n.* time off from work to attend to the needs of family members

fam′i·ly plan′ning *n.* birth control

fam′i·ly room′ *n.* room in a home for relaxation and entertainment

fam′i·ly tree′ *n.* genealogical chart

fam·ine /fam′ən/ *n.* extreme scarcity, esp. of food [L *fames* hunger]

fam·ish /fam′isн/ v. make or become extremely hungry —**fam′ished** adj. [Rom, rel. to FAMINE]

fa·mous /fā′məs/ adj. 1 celebrated; well-known 2 Colloq. excellent —**fa′mous·ly** adv. [L, rel. to FAME]

fan¹ /fan/ n. 1 apparatus, usu. with rotating blades, for ventilation 2 wide, flat device waved to cool oneself —v. (**fanned, fan·ning**) 3 blow air on, with, or as with a fan 4 spread out [L vannus winnowing basket]

fan² n. devotee; follower [abbr. of FANATIC]

fa·nat·ic /fənat′ik/ n. 1 person obsessively devoted to a belief, activity, etc.; zealot —adj. 2 excessively enthusiastic —**fa·nat′i·cal** adj.; **fa·nat′i·cal·ly** adv.; **fa·nat′i·cism** n. [L fanum temple]

fan·ci·er /fan′sēər/ n. connoisseur

fan·ci·ful /fan′sifəl/ adj. 1 imaginary 2 indulging in fancies —**fan′ci·ful·ly** adv.

fan·cy /fan′sē/ n. (pl. ·**cies**) 1 inclination 2 whim 3 supposition 4a faculty of imagination b mental image —adj. (·**ci·er, ·ci·est**) 5 ornamental 6 extravagant —v. (·**cied, ·cy·ing**) 7 be inclined to suppose; imagine 8 desire; value highly 9 **take a fancy** to become fond of —**fan′ci·ly** adv.; **fan′ci·ness** n. [contr. of FANTASY]

fan′cy-free′ adj. without (esp. emotional) commitments

fan·dan·go /fandaNG′gō/ n. (pl. ·**goes** or ·**gos**) 1 lively Spanish dance for two 2 music for this [Sp]

fan·fare /fan′fer′/ n. short ceremonious sounding of trumpets, etc. [Fr]

fang /faNG/ n. 1 canine tooth, esp. of a dog or wolf 2 tooth of a venomous snake [OE]

fan·ny /fan′ē/ n. (pl. ·**nies**) Slang. the buttocks

fan′ny pack′ n. pouch worn around the waist

fan·ta·size /fan′təsīz′/ v. (·**sized, ·siz·ing**) 1 daydream 2 imagine

fan·tas·tic /fantas′tik/ adj. 1 Colloq. excellent; extraordinary 2 extravagantly fanciful 3 grotesque —**fan·tas′ti·cal·ly** adv.

fan·ta·sy /fan′tasē/ n. (pl. ·**sies**) 1 imagination, esp. when unrelated to reality 2 mental image; daydream 3 fanciful or supernatural literature [Gk phantasia appearance; idea]

far /fär/ (**far·ther, far·thest**) adv. 1 at, to, or by a great distance 2 a long way (off) in space or time 3 to a great extent or degree; by much —adj. 4 remote; distant 5 more distant 6 extreme 7 **as far as** right up to (a place) 8 **by far** by a great amount 9 **a far cry** a long way 10 **so far:** a to such an extent; to this point b until now 11 **so far so good** satisfactory up to now [OE]

far·ad /far′ad, ·əd/ n. SI unit of capacitance [for M. FARADAY]

Far·a·day /far′ədē/, **Michael** 1791–1867; British chemist and physicist

far·a·way /fär′əwā′/ adj. 1 remote 2 (of a look or voice) dreamy; distant

farce /färs/ n. 1a comedy with a ludicrously improbable situational plot b this branch of drama 2 absurdly futile proceedings; pretense —**far′ci·cal** /·sikəl/ adj. [L farcire to stuff, used metaphorically of interludes, etc.]

fare /fer/ n. 1a price of a journey on public transport b fare-paying passenger 2 food —v. (**fared, far·ing**) 3 progress; get on [OE]

Far′ East′ n. E Asia, including China, Japan, North and South Korea, Mongolia, and adjacent areas

fare·well /ferwel′/ interj. 1 goodbye —n. 2 leave-taking —adj. /fer′wel′/ 3 parting; final

far-fetched /fär′feснt′/ adj. straining credulity; preposterous

far′-flung′ adj. 1 widely scattered 2 remote

Far·go /fär′gō/ n. city in N. Dak. Pop. 74,111

Fa·ri·da·bad /fərēd′əbäd′/ n. city in India. Pop. 613,800

fa·ri·na /fərē′nə/ n. flour or meal of cereal, potatoes, etc. —**far·i·na·ceous** /far′ənā′shəs/ adj. [L]

farm /färm/ n. 1 land and its buildings under one management for growing crops, rearing animals, etc. 2 such land, etc., for a specified purpose (trout farm) —v. 3a use (land) for growing crops, rearing animals, etc. b be a farmer; work on a farm 4 (foll. by out) delegate or subcontract (work) to others —**farm′er, farm′ing** n. [MedL firma fixed payment, fr. L firmare make firm]

farm′hand′ n. worker on a farm

farm′house′ n. house attached to a farm

far·o /fer′ō/ n. gambling game played with cards [Fr pharaon name of game, perh. fr. picture of a pharaoh on one of the cards]

far′-off′ /fär′ôf′/ adj. remote

Fa·rouk /fərōōk′/ 1920–65; king of Egypt (1936–52)

far′-out′ adj. 1 distant 2 Slang. avant-garde; unconventional 3 Slang. excellent

far·ra·go /fərä′gō/ n. (pl. ·**gos** or ·**goes**) medley; hodgepodge [L: mixed grains]

Far·ra·gut /far′əgət/, **David Glasgow** 1801–70; US naval commander

far′-reach′ing /fär′ adj. widely influential or applicable

far·ri·er /far′ēər/ n. blacksmith [L ferrum iron]

far·row /far′ō/ n. 1 litter of pigs 2 birth of a litter —v. 3 (of a sow) produce (pigs) [OE]

far′-sight′ed /fär′ adj. 1 having foresight; prudent 2 seeing distant objects more clearly than closer ones

far·ther /fär′тнәr/ adj. 1 more distant in space or time 2 to a greater extent; more —adv. 3 comp. of FAR (superl. farthest) 4 more distant or advanced 5 more; additional ● Usage: Some traditionalists insist that farther, farthest should be used only in referring to actual physical distance: We went farther into the jungle. They say that further, furthest should be restricted to figurative or abstract senses: They are giving my proposal further consideration. Although farther, farthest are not used figuratively, further, furthest are in fact common in both senses: The corral furthest from the house is the biggest.

far·thing /fär′тнiNG/ n. former small British coin of little value [OE, rel. to FOURTH]

fas·ces /fas′ēz/ n. pl. (usu. used with sing. verb) Rom. Hist. bundle of rods containing an ax with its blade pro-

FASCES

truding, symbol of office for Roman magistrates [L, pl. of *fascis* bundle]

fas·ci·a /ˈfāˈSHēə, fāˈSHēə/ *n.* (also **fa·ci·a**) (*pl.* **·as** or **·ci·ae** /-SHē-ē/) **1** long flat surface in classical architecture **2** flat surface, usu. of wood, covering the ends of rafters [L: band; bandage]

fas·ci·nate /ˈfasˈənāt/ *v.* (**·nat·ed, ·nat·ing**) **1** capture the interest of; attract **2** charm; allure —**fas'ci·na'tion** *n.* [L *fascinum* spell]

fas·cism /ˈfasHˈizəm/ *n.* extreme totalitarian right-wing nationalist movement or philosophy, as instituted in Italy (1922–43) —**fas'cist** *n.* & *adj.*; **fas·cis·tic** /faSHisˈtik/ *adj.* [It *fascio* bundle; organized group]

fash·ion /ˈfaSHˈən/ *n.* **1** current popular custom or style, esp. in dress **2** manner of doing something —*v.* **3** make or form **4** after a **fashion** to some extent [L *factio*, rel. to FACT]

fash'ion·a·ble *adj.* **1** following or suited to current fashion; modish **2** of or favored by people who follow current fashion —**fash'ion·a·ble·ness** *n.*; **fash'ion·a·bly** *adv.*

Fass·bind·er /ˈfäsˈbin(d)ər/, **Rainer Werner** 1946–82; German film director

fast[1] /fast/ *adj.* **1** rapid; quick-moving **2** capable of or intended for high speed **3** (of a clock, etc.) ahead of the correct time **4** firm; firmly fixed or attached **5** (of a color) not fading **6** pleasure-seeking; dissolute **7** (of photographic film, etc.) needing only short exposure —*adv.* **8** quickly; in quick succession **9** firmly; tightly **10** soundly; completely (*fast asleep*) [OE]

fast[2] *v.* **1** abstain from food or certain food for a time —*n.* **2** act or period of fasting [OE]

fast·en /ˈfasˈən/ *v.* **1** make or become fixed or secure; tie **2** lock securely; shut in **3** direct (a look, thoughts, etc.) or fix attention (on) —**fas'ten·er** *n.* [OE, rel. to FAST[1]]

fast'en·ing *n.* device that fastens something; fastener

fast' food' *n.* food that is quickly prepared and served informally

fas·tid·i·ous /fasˈtidˈēəs/ *adj.* **1** excessively discriminatory; fussy **2** easily disgusted; squeamish —**fas·tid'i·ous·ly** *adv.*; **fas·tid'i·ous·ness** *n.* [L *fastidium* loathing]

fast'ness *n.* stronghold [OE]

fat /fat/ *n.* **1** natural oily or greasy substance found esp. in animal bodies **2** part of meat, etc., containing this **3** needless or dispensable matter —*adj.* (**fat·ter, fat·test**) **4** corpulent; plump **5** containing much fat **6a** thick **b** substantial (*fat check*) **7** *Colloq. Iron.* very little; not much (*fat chance*) **8** chew the fat *Slang.* talk; chat —**fat''less** *adj.*; **fat'ness** *n.*; **fat'tish** *adj.* [OE]

fa·tal /ˈfātˈl/ *adj.* **1** causing or ending in death **2** ruinous —**fa'tal·ly** *adv.* [L, rel. to FATE]

fa·tal·ism /ˈfātˈlˌizəm/ *n.* **1** belief in predetermination **2** submissive acceptance —**fa'tal·ist** *n.*; **fa'tal·is'tic** *adj.*; **fa'tal·is'ti·cal·ly** *adv.*

fa·tal·i·ty /fātalˈətē, fə-/ *n.* (*pl.* **·ties**) **1** death by accident, war, etc. **2** fatal influence

fat' cat' *n. Slang.* person of influence, esp. from wealth or position

fate /fāt/ *n.* **1** supposed power predetermining events **2a** the future so determined **b** individual's destiny or fortune **3** death; destruc-

tion —*v.* (**fat·ed, fat·ing**) **4** preordain [L *fatum*]

fate·ful /ˈfātˈfəl/ *adj.* **1** important; decisive **2** controlled by fate —**fate'ful·ly** *adv.*

Fates /fāts/ *n. Gk. & Rom. Myth.* trio of goddesses personifying destiny

fa·ther /ˈfäˈT͟Hər/ *n.* **1** male parent **2** (usu. *pl.*) forefather **3** originator; early leader **4** (also *cap.*) (often as a title or form of address) priest **5** (*cap.*) *Christianity.* first person of the Trinity **6** (usu. *pl.*) elders (*city fathers*) —*v.* **7** beget **8** originate (a scheme, etc.) —**fa'ther·hood** *n.*; **fa'ther·less** *adj.* [OE]

fa'ther·fig·ure *n.* older man respected and trusted like a father

fa'ther-in-law' *n.* (*pl.* **fa'thers-in-law'**) father of one's husband or wife

fa'ther·land' *n.* one's native country

fa'ther·ly *adj.* like or of a father

fath·om /ˈfaT͟Hˈəm/ *n.* **1** measure of length (six feet), used esp. in depth soundings —*v.* **2** comprehend **3** measure the depth of —**fath'om·a·ble, fath'om·less** *adj.* [OE]

fa·tigue /fətēgˈ/ *n.* **1** extreme tiredness **2** weakness in metals, etc. **3a** nonmilitary army work duty **b** (*pl.*) clothing worn for this —*v.* (**·tigued, ·tigu·ing**) **4** cause fatigue in [L *fatigare* exhaust]

Fa·ti·ma /fatˈəmə/ *c.* 606–632; youngest daughter of the prophet Muhammad

fat·ten /ˈfatˈn/ *v.* make or become fat

fat·ty /fatˈē/ *adj.* (**·ti·er, ·ti·est**) like or containing fat

fat'ty ac'id *n.* organic compound that bonds to glycerol to form a fat molecule

fat·u·ous /ˈfaCHˈōōəs/ *adj.* hopelessly foolish; purposeless; idiotic —**fa·tu·i·ty** /fat(y)ōˈətē/ *n.* (*pl.* **·ties**); **fat'u·ous·ly** *adv.*; **fat'u·ous·ness** *n.* [L *fatuus*]

fat·wa /ˈfatˈwä/ *n.* legal decision or ruling by an Islamic religious leader [Ar]

fau·cet /ˈfôˈsit/ *n.* valve for controlling flow of water from a pipe [MFr *fausset* vent-peg]

Faulk·ner /ˈfôkˈnər/, **William** 1897–1962; US novelist

fault /fôlt/ *n.* **1** defect or imperfection **2** responsibility for wrongdoing, error, etc. **3** transgression; offense **4** *Tennis.* invalid service **5** break in rock strata —*v.* **6** find fault with; blame **7 at fault** guilty; to blame **8 find fault** criticize; complain **9 to a fault** to excess [L *fallere* deceive]

fault'find'ing *n.* continual criticizing

fault'less *adj.* perfect —**fault'less·ly** *adv.*

fault'y *adj.* (**·i·er, ·i·est**) having faults; imperfect —**fault'i·ly** *adv.*; **fault'i·ness** *n.*

faun /fôn/ *n.* ancient Roman rural deity with goat's horns, legs, and tail [L *Faunus*]

fau·na /ˈfôˈnə/ *n.* (*pl.* **·nas** or **·nae** /-nē, -nīˈ/) animal life of a region or period [L *Fauna*, name of a rural goddess]

Fau·ré /ˈfôrāˈ/, **Gabriel** 1845–1924; French composer

Faust /foust/ (also **Faus·tus**) died *c.* 1540; German astronomer and necromancer —**Faus'ti·an** /-tēən/ *adj.*

faux pas /ˈfō päˈ/ *n.* (*pl.* same /päz/) *French.* tactless social mistake; blunder [Fr: false step]

fa·vor /ˈfāˈvər/ *n.* **1** kind act **2** approval;

friendly regard **3** partiality **4** small gift or novelty —*v.* **5** regard or treat with favor or partiality **6** support; promote; prefer **7** be to the advantage of; facilitate **8** resemble [L *favere* be favorable; befriend]

fa·vor·a·ble /fāˈvər(ə)bəl/ *adj.* **1** well-disposed; propitious; approving **2** promising; auspicious **3** helpful; suitable —**faˈvor·a·bly** *adv.*

fa·vor·ite /fāvˈ(ə)rit/ *adj.* **1** preferred to all others —*n.* **2** favorite person or thing **3** *Sports.* competitor thought most likely to win

faˈvor·it·ism *n.* unfair partiality

fawn[1] /fôn/ *n.* **1** deer in its first year **2** light yellowish brown —*adj.* **3** fawn-colored [L, rel. to FETUS]

fawn[2] *v.* **1** behave servilely; cringe **2** (of esp. a dog) show extreme affection [OE]

fax /faks/ *n.* **1** transmission of an image of a document, etc., electronically **2** copy produced by this —*v.* **3** transmit in this way [abbr. of FACSIMILE]

Fay·ette·ville /fāˈətvəl, -vilˈ/ *n.* city in N. Car. Pop. 75,695

faze /fāz/ *v.* (**fazed, faz·ing**) disconcert; disorientate

FBI *abbr.* Federal Bureau of Investigation

FCC *abbr.* Federal Communications Commission

FDA *abbr.* Food and Drug Administration

FDIC *abbr.* Federal Deposit Insurance Corporation

Fe *symb.* iron [L *ferrum*]

fe·al·ty /fēˈəltē/ *n.* (*pl.* **·ties**) **1** fidelity to a feudal lord **2** allegiance [L, rel. to FIDELITY]

fear /fēr/ *n.* **1a** panic or distress caused by a real or impending danger, pain, etc. **b** cause of this **2** danger —*v.* **3** feel fear **4** (foll. by *for*) feel anxiety about —**fearˈless** *adj.*; **fearˈless·ly** *adv.*; **fearˈless·ness** *n.* [OE]

fear·ful /fērˈfəl/ *adj.* **1** afraid **2** terrible; awful —**fearˈful·ly** *adv.*; **fearˈful·ness** *n.*

fear·some /fērˈsəm/ *adj.* frightening —**fearˈsome·ly** *adv.*; **fearˈsome·ness** *n.*

fea·si·ble /fēˈzəbəl/ *adj.* practicable; possible —**fea·si·bilˈi·ty** *n.*; **feaˈsi·bly** *adv.* [L *facere* do]

feast /fēst/ *n.* **1** large or sumptuous meal **2** sensual or mental pleasure **3** religious festival —*v.* **4** partake of a feast; dine sumptuously **5** **feast one's eyes** on look with pleasure at [L *festus* joyful; festive]

feat /fēt/ *n.* remarkable act or achievement [L, rel. to FACT]

feath·er /feTHˈər/ *n.* **1** one of the structures forming a bird's plumage, with a horny stem and fine strands —*v.* **2** cover or line with feathers **3** turn (an oar, propeller blades, etc.) to be parallel to the direction of forward motion **4** **feather in one's cap** a personal achievement **5** **feather one's nest** enrich oneself **6** **in fine** (or **high**) **feather** in good spirits —**featherˈy** *adj.* [OE]

featherˈbedˈding *n.* coercion, as by a union, for the hiring or retaining of unnecessary workers

featherˈing *n.* **1** bird's plumage **2** feathers of an arrow **3** featherlike thing

featherˈweight *n.* **1** *Sports.* weight class for competitors; in professional boxing, includes fighters of 126 lbs. or less **2** very light person or thing

fea·ture /fēˈCHər/ *n.* **1** distinctive or characteristic part of a thing **2** part of the face **3** specialized article in a newspaper, etc. **4** (in full **feaˈture film**') main movie showing on a theater program —*v.* (**·tured, ·tur·ing**) **5** make a feature of; emphasize **6** (of a performance) star —**feaˈture·less** *adj.* [L *factura* formation, rel. to FACT]

Feb. *abbr.* February

fe·brile /febˈril', -rəl, fēˈbrəl/ *adj.* of fever; feverish [L *febris* fever]

Feb·ru·ar·y /febˈrōō-erˈē, feb'yōō-/ *n.* (*pl.* **·ies**) second month of the year in the Gregorian calendar [L *februa* purification feast]

fe·ces /fēˈsēz'/ *n. pl.* waste matter discharged from the bowels —**fe·cal** /fēˈkəl/ *adj.* [L *faeces* grounds; dregs]

feck·less /fekˈləs/ *adj.* **1** feeble; ineffective **2** unthinking; irresponsible [Scot *feck* fr. *effeck* var. of EFFECT]

fe·cund /fekˈənd, fēˈkənd/ *adj.* prolific; fertile —**fe·cunˈdi·ty** /-ditē'/ *n.* [L]

fed /fed/ *v.* **1** *past* and *past part.* of FEED **2** **fed up** discontented; bored

fed. *abbr.* **1** federal **2** federation

fed·er·al /fedˈ(ə)rəl/ *adj.* **1** of a system of government with self-governing states but a central authority **2** of such a federation, as the national government of the US —**fedˈer·al·ism**', fedˈer·al·ist, fedˈer·al·i·zaˈtion *n.*; **fedˈer·al·ize** /-īz/ *v.* (**·ized, iz·ing**); **fedˈer·al·ly** *adv.* [L *foedus* league; treaty]

Fedˈer·al Disˈtrict of Mexˈi·co *n.* national government district in central Mexico

Fed·er·al Re·serveˈ Sysˈtem *n.* national banking system in the US controlling credit and interest rates to commercial banks

fed·er·ate /fedˈərāt'/ *v.* (**·at·ed, ·at·ing**) unite on a federal basis

fed·er·aˈtion *n.* **1** federal system or group **2** act of federating [L, rel. to FEDERAL]

fe·do·ra /fədôrˈə/ *n.* soft felt hat with a curled brim

fee /fē/ *n.* **1** payment made for professional advice or services **2** entrance or access charge [OFr var. of *fief*, ult. fr. Gmc]

fee·ble /fēˈbəl/ *adj.* (**·bler, ·blest**) **1** weak; infirm **2** lacking strength, effectiveness, etc. —**feeˈble·ness** *n.*; **feeˈbly** *adv.* [L *flebilis* lamentable]

feeˈble-mindˈed *adj.* mentally deficient

feed /fēd/ *v.* (**fed, feed·ing**) **1a** supply with food **b** put food into the mouth of **2** give as food, esp. to animals **3** (of animals) eat **4** nourish or be nourished by; benefit from **5a** stoke with fuel **b** supply (material) to a machine, etc. **c** flow into **6** gratify (vanity, etc.) **7** provide (advice, information, etc.) to —*n.* **8** food, esp. for animals or infants —**feedˈer** *n.* [OE]

feedˈback' *n.* **1** response or comment from others **2** *Electronics.* return of a fraction of an output signal to the input

feel /fēl/ *v.* (**felt, feel·ing**) **1a** examine or search by touch **b** have the sensation of touch **2** perceive or ascertain by touch **3** experience, exhibit, or be affected by (an emotion, conviction, etc.) **4** have an impression **5** consider; think **6** seem **7** be consciously; consider oneself (*feel happy*) **8** (foll. by *for*) have sympathy or pity —n. 9 feeling; testing by touch 10 attendant sensation 11 sense of touch 12 feel like have a wish or inclination for 13 feel up to be ready to face or deal with 14 feel one's way proceed cautiously 15 have a feel for have an instinct or aptitude for [OE]

feel'er /n. 1 organ in certain animals for sensing or searching for food 2 tentative proposal

feel'ing /n. 1a capacity to feel; sense of touch b physical sensation 2a emotional reaction b (pl.) emotional susceptibilities 3 particular sensitivity 4a intuition or notion b general sentiment 5 sympathy; compassion 6 emotional sensibility or intensity —adj. 7 sensitive; sympathetic; heartfelt —**feel'ing·ly** adv.

feet /fēt/ n. pl. of FOOT

feign /fān/ v. simulate; pretend [L fingere fictmold; contrive]

feint /fānt/ n. 1 sham attack or diversionary blow 2 pretense —v. 3 make a feint [OFr, rel. to FEIGN]

feld·spar /fel(d)'spär'/ n. common aluminum silicate of potassium, sodium, or calcium [Ger Feld field + Spat(h) spar]

fe·lic·i·tate /fəlis'ətāt'/ v. (·tat·ed, ·tat·ing) Formal. congratulate —**fe·lic'i·ta'tion** n. [L felix happy]

fe·lic·i·tous /fəlis'ətəs/ adj. Formal. appropriate to the occasion; apt; well-chosen

fe·lic·i·ty /fəlis'itē/ n. (pl. ·ties) 1 intense happiness 2a capacity for apt expression b well-chosen phrase [L felix happy]

fe·line /fē'līn'/ adj. 1 of the cat family 2 catlike —n. 3 animal of the cat family [L feles cat]

fell¹ /fel/ v. past of FALL

fell² v. 1 cut down (esp. a tree) 2 strike or knock down [OE]

fell³ adj. Poet. 1 ruthless; destructive 2 at (or in) one fell swoop in a single (orig. deadly) action [OFr, rel. to FELON]

Fel·li·ni /fəlē'nē/, Federico 1920–93; Italian film director

fel·low /fel'ō/ n. 1 man; boy 2 comrade 3 counterpart; one of a pair 4 holder of a fellowship 5 member of a certain learned society —adj. 6 of the same group, etc. [OE fr. ON]

fel·low·ship /fel'ōship/ n. 1 friendly association with others; companionship 2 body of associates 3 endowment for a student or scholar to study

fel·on /fel'ən/ n. person who has committed a felony [OFr felun wicked person]

fel·o·ny /fel'ənē/ n. (pl. ·nies) serious, often violent, crime —**fe·lo·ni·ous** /fəlō'nēəs/ adj.

felt¹ /felt/ n. 1 cloth of matted and pressed fibers of wool, etc. —v. 2 make into felt [OE]

felt² v. past and past part. of FEEL

FEMA /fē'mə/ abbr. Federal Emergency Management Agency

fe·male /fē'māl'/ adj. 1 of the sex that can give birth or produce eggs 2 (of plants) fruitbearing 3 of women or female animals or plants 4 (of a connector part, etc.) hollow to receive an inserted part —n. 5 female person, animal, or plant [L dim. of femina woman, assimilated to male]

fem·i·nine /fem'ənin/ adj. 1 of women 2 having womanly qualities 3 of or denoting the female gender —n. 4 feminine gender or word —**fem'i·nin'i·ty** n. [L, rel. to FEMALE]

fem'i·nism' n. advocacy of women's rights and sexual equality —**fem'i·nist** n. & adj.

fe·mur /fē'mər/ n. (pl. ·murs or fem·o·ra /fem'ərə/) thighbone —**fem·o·ral** /fem'ərəl/ adj. [L]

fen /fen/ n. low marshy land [OE]

fence /fens/ n. 1 barrier, railing, etc., enclosing a field, garden, etc. 2 Slang. dealer in stolen goods —v. (fenced, fenc·ing) 3 surround with or as with a fence 4 enclose, separate, or seal with or as with a fence 5 practice fencing with a sword 6 be evasive 7 Slang. deal in (stolen goods) —**fenc'er** n. [ME, fr. DEFENSE]

fenc'ing n. 1 set of, or material for, fences 2 swordfighting, esp. as a sport

fend /fend/ v. 1 (foll. by for) look after (esp. oneself) 2 ward (off) [ME, fr. DEFEND]

fend'er n. 1 low frame bordering a fireplace 2 shieldlike parts over the wheels of a vehicle

fen·nel /fen'l/ n. yellow-flowered fragrant herb used for flavoring [L faenum hay]

fe·ral /fēr'əl, fer'-/ adj. 1 wild; untamed 2 savage [L ferus wild]

Fer·ber /fər'bər/, Edna 1885–1968; US writer

Fer·di·nand II /fərd'n-and'/ ("the Catholic") 1452–1516; founder of the Spanish monarchy (1506); husband of Isabella I

fer·ment n. /fər'ment'/ 1 excitement; unrest 2a fermentation b fermenting agent —v. /fərment'/ 3 undergo or subject to fermentation 4 excite; stir up [L fermentum yeast]

fer·men·ta·tion /fər'məntā'shən/ n. 1 breakdown of a substance by yeasts and bacteria, esp. of sugar in making alcohol 2 agitation; excitement

Fer·mi /fer'mē/, Enrico 1901–54; Italianborn US nuclear physicist

fer·mi·um /fer'mēəm, far'-/ n. transuranic artificial radioactive metallic element; symb. Fm [for E. FERMI]

FERN

fern /fərn/ n. (pl. same or -s) flowerless plant usu. having feathery fronds [OE]

fe·ro·cious /fərō'shəs/ adj. fierce; savage —**fe·ro'cious·ly** adv.; **fe·roc·i·ty** /fərās'ətē/ n. [L ferox]

-ferous comb. form forming adjectives with the sense 'bearing,' 'having' (odoriferous) [L fero bear]

Fer·ra·ra /fərär'ə/ n. city in Italy. Pop. 140,600

fer·ret /fer'ət/ n. 1 small polecat used in catching rabbits, rats, etc. —v. 2 hunt with ferrets 3 rummage; search out (secrets, criminals, etc.) [L fur thief]

fer·ric /fer'ik/ adj. of iron [L ferrum iron]

Fer'ris wheel /fer'əs/ n. revolving vertical

amusement-ride wheel with passenger cars [for G.W. *Ferris*, American inventor]

ferro- *comb. form* **1** iron **2** (of alloys) containing iron [rel. to FERRIC]

fer·rous /fer′əs/ *adj.* containing iron

fer·rule /fer′ool′/ *n.* ring or cap on the end of a stick, umbrella, etc. [L *viria* bracelet]

fer·ry /fer′ē/ *n.* (also **fer′ry·boat′**) (*pl.* **-ries**) **1** boat or aircraft for esp. regular transport, esp. across water **2** craft for this —*v.* (**·ried, ·ry·ing**) **3** convey or go in a ferry **4** transport, esp. regularly, from place to place [OE *ferian*, perh. rel. to ON *ferja*]

fer·tile /fart′l/ *adj.* **1** (of soil) abundantly productive; fruitful **2a** (of a seed, egg, etc.) capable of growth **b** (of animals and plants) able to reproduce **3** inventive —**fer·til′i·ty** /-til′itē/ *n.* [Fr fr. L]

fer·til·ize /fart′l-īz/ *v.* (**·ized, ·iz·ing**) **1** make (soil, etc.) fertile **2** cause (an egg, female animal, etc.) to develop or gestate by mating, etc. —**fer′til·i·za′tion** *n.*

fer′til·iz·er *n.* substance added to soil to make it more fertile

fer·vent /fər′vant/ *adj.* ardent; intense —**fer′ven·cy** *n.*; **fer′vent·ly** *adv.* [L *fervere* boil]

fer·vid /fər′vid/ *adj.* ardent; intense —**fer′vid·ly** *adv.* [L, rel. to FERVENT]

fer·vor /fər′vər/ *n.* passion; zeal [L: heat]

fes·tal /fes′tal/ *adj.* **1** joyous; merry **2** of a feast or festival [L, rel. to FEAST]

fes·ter /fes′tər/ *v.* **1** make or become septic **2** rot; stagnate **3** cause continuing anger or bitterness [L FISTULA]

fes·ti·val /fes′tavəl/ *n.* **1** day or period of celebration **2** series of cultural events [Fr, rel. to FESTIVE]

fes·tive /fes′tiv/ *adj.* **1** of or characteristic of a festival **2** joyous —**fes′tive·ly** *adv.*; **fes′tive·ness** *n.* [L, rel. to FEAST]

fes·tiv·i·ty /festiv′itē/ *n.* (*pl.* **·ties**) **1** gaiety; rejoicing **2** (*pl.*) celebration; party

fes·toon /festoon′/ *n.* **1** curved hanging chain of flowers, leaves, ribbons, etc. —*v.* **2** adorn or drape with [It, rel. to FESTIVE]

fet·a /fet′ə/ *n.* soft white Greek-style cheese [Gk *pheta*]

fetch /fecH/ *v.* **1** go for and bring back **2** be sold for (a price) [OE]

fetch′ing *adj.* attractive —**fetch′ing·ly** *adv.*

fete /fāt, fet/ *n.* (also **fête**) **1** outdoor fundraising event with stalls and amusements, etc. **2** festival **3** saint's day —*v.* (**fet·ed, fet·ing**) **4** honor or entertain lavishly [Fr, rel. to FEAST]

fet·id /fet′id/ *adj.* stinking [L *fetere* stink]

fe·tish /fet′isH/ *n.* **1** *Psychol.* **a** abnormal object of sexual desire **b** preoccupation with this **2** object worshiped as magic —**fet′ish·ism′**, **fet′ish·ist** *n.*; **fet′ish·is·tic** *adj.* [Port *feitiço* charm]

fet·lock /fet′läk′/ *n.* back of a horse's leg above the hoof with a tuft of hair [ult. rel. to FOOT]

fet·ter /fet′ər/ *n.* **1** shackle for the ankles **2** (*pl.*) captivity **3** restraining device —*v.* **4** put into fetters **5** restrict [OE]

fet·tle /fet′l/ *n.* condition or trim (*in fine fettle*) [OE]

fe·tus /fēt′əs/ *n.* (*pl.* **·tus·es**) unborn mammalian offspring, esp. a human embryo of eight weeks or more —**fe·tal** /fēt′l/ *adj.* [L *fetus* offspring]

feud /fyood/ *n.* **1** prolonged hostility, esp. between families, tribes, etc. —*v.* **2** conduct a feud [Gmc, rel. to FOE]

feu·dal /fyood′l/ *adj.* of, like, or according to the feudal system —**feu′dal·ism′** *n.*

feu′dal sys′tem *n.* medieval system of land tenure with allegiance and service due to the landowner

fe·ver /fē′vər/ *n.* **1a** abnormally high temperature, often with delirium **b** disease characterized by this (*scarlet fever*) **2** nervous excitement; agitation —**fe′vered** *adj.* [L *febris*]

fe′ver·ish /fē′vərisH/ *adj.* **1** having symptoms of fever **2** excited; restless —**fe′ver·ish·ly** *adv.*; **fe′ver·ish·ness** *n.*

fe′ver pitch′ *n.* state of extreme excitement

few /fyoo/ *adj.* **1** not many —*n.* (as *pl.*) **2** (prec. by *a*) some but not many **3** not many **4** (prec. by *the*) **a** the minority **b** the elect **5 not a few** a considerable number [OE]

● **Usage:** The comparative of *few*, *fewer*, properly refers to a countable quantity: *Express checkout is for 10 items or fewer.* Formally, *less* is confined to uncountable, mass quantities: *less salt; fewer people; less water; fewer potatoes; less time and trouble; fewer problems.* People rarely use *fewer* for *less*, but often use *less* where *fewer* is preferred (*10 items or less*), a usage frowned on by purists.

fey /fā/ *adj.* strange; otherworldly; whimsical [OE: doomed to die]

fez /fez/ *n.* (*pl.* **·zes**) flat-topped conical red cap, once commonly worn in Turkey, etc. [Turk]

Fez /fez, fes/ *n.* (also **Fès**) city in Morocco. Pop. 448,800 [OE]

ff *abbr. Mus.* fortissimo

ff. *abbr.* **1** folios **2** following pages, etc.

FHA *abbr.* Federal Housing Administration

fi·an·cé /fē′än′sā′/ *n.* (*fem.* **fi·an·cée** pronunc. same) person one is engaged to [Fr fr. L *fidere* trust]

fi·as·co /fē·as′kō/ *n.* (*pl.* **·cos**) ludicrous or humiliating failure; disaster [It: bottle]

fi·at /fē′ät′, fī′at′, -ət/ *n.* **1** authorization **2** decree [L: let it be done]

fib /fib/ *n.* **1** trivial lie —*v.* (**fibbed, fibbing**) **2** tell a fib —**fib′ber** *n.* [perh. fr. *fible-fable*, a reduplication of FABLE]

fi·ber /fī′bər/ *n.* **1** thread or filament forming tissue or textile **2** piece of threadlike glass **3** substance formed of fibers, or able to be spun, woven, etc. **4** structure; character (*moral fiber*) **5** roughage [Fr fr. L *fibra*]

fi′ber·board′ *n.* board of compressed wood or other plant fibers

fi′ber·glass′ *n.* **1** fabric made from woven glass fibers **2** plastic reinforced by glass fibers

fi′ber op′tics *n. pl.* optics using thin glass fibers, usu. for the transmission of modulated light to carry signals

fi·bril /fī′brəl/ *n.* small fiber [L dim. of *fibra* FIBER]

fi·broid /fī′broid/ *adj.* of, like, or containing fibrous tissue, as some benign tumors

FEZ

fi·bro·sis /fībrō′sis/ *n.* thickening and scarring of connective tissue [fr. FIBER, -OSIS]

fib·u·la /fib′yələ/ *n.* (*pl.* **fib·u·lae** /-lē′ or ·las**) small outer bone between the knee and the ankle —**fib′u·lar** *adj.* [L: brooch; pin; clasp]

-fic *suffix* forming adjectives meaning 'producing,' 'making' (*prolific; pacific*) [L *facere* make]

FICA /fī′kə/ *abbr.* Federal Insurance Contributions Act

-fication *suffix* forming nouns of action from verbs in *-fy* (*purification; simplification*)

fiche /fēsh/ *n.* (*pl.* same or **-s**) microfiche

fick·le /fik′əl/ *adj.* inconstant; changeable; unreliable —**fick′le·ness** *n.* [OE]

fic·tion /fik′shən/ *n.* **1** nonfactual or imaginative literature, esp. novels **2** invented idea, thing, etc. —**fic′tion·al** *adj.*; **fic′tion·al·ize** /-shənəlīz′/ *v.* (**·ized, ·iz·ing**) [L *fictum* deception; falsehood]

fic·ti·tious /fiktish′əs/ *adj.* imaginary; unreal; not genuine

fid·dle /fid′l/ *n.* **1** *Colloq.* stringed instrument played with a bow, esp. a violin —*v.* (**·dled, ·dling**) **2** adjust; tinker; tamper **3** falsify **4 as fit as a fiddle** in very good health **5 play second** (or **first**) **fiddle** take a subordinate (or leading) role [OE]

fid·dler /fid′lər, -l-ər/ *n.* **1** fiddle player **2** small N American crab

fid·dle·sticks /fid′l-stiks/ *interj.* nonsense

fi·del·i·ty /fadel′ətē, fī-/ *n.* **1** faithfulness; loyalty **2** strict accuracy **3** precision in sound reproduction [L *fides* faith]

fid·get /fij′it/ *v.* move or act restlessly or nervously —**fid′get·y** *adj.* [obs. or dial. *fidge* twitch]

fi·du·ci·ar·y /fid(y)ōō′shēerē̆, -shərē̆/ *adj.* **1** of a trust, trustee, or trusteeship **2** held or given in trust —*n.* (*pl.* **·ies**) **3** trustee [L *fiducia* trust]

fie /fī/ *interj. Archaic.* expressing disgust, rejection, etc. [MFr fr. L]

Fied·ler /fēd′lər/, **Arthur** 1894–1979; US orchestra conductor

fief /fēf/ *n.* land held under the feudal system or in fee [OFr]

fief·dom /fēf′dəm/ *n.* **1** fief **2** province of control; domain

field /fēld/ *n.* **1** area of esp. cultivated enclosed land **2** area rich in some natural product **3** tract for a game, etc. **4** participants in a contest, race, or sport **5** expanse of ice, snow, sea, sky, etc. **6** area of activity or study **7** *Physics.* region in which a force is effective **8** range of perception **9** area or region regarded as natural **10** background of a picture, coin, flag, etc. —*v.* **11** *Baseball.* play (a ball) as part of the defense **12** deal with (questions, an argument, etc.) **13 play the field** *Colloq.* not restrict one's activities to one sphere or object [OE]

field′er *n. Baseball.* person in a defensive position

field′ glass·es *n. pl.* binoculars

Field·ing /fēl′diNG/, **Henry** 1707–54; English novelist

Fields /fēldz/, **W.C.** (born **William Claude Dukenfield**) 1880–1946; US comedian in vaudeville and films

field′work′ *n.* practical surveying, science, sociology, etc., conducted in the natural environment —**field′work′er** *n.*

fiend /fēnd/ *n.* **1** evil spirit; demon **2** wicked or cruel person **3** *Slang.* devotee —**fiend′ish** *adj.*; **fiend′ish·ly** *adv.* [OE]

fierce /fērs/ *adj.* (**fierc·er, fierc·est**) **1** violently aggressive or frightening **2** eager; intense **3** unpleasantly extreme —**fierce′ly** *adv.*; **fierce′ness** *n.* [L *ferus* savage]

fi·er·y /fī′(ə)rē̆/ *adj.* (**·i·er, ·i·est**) **1** consisting of or flaming with fire **2** bright red **3** hot; burning **4** spirited

fi·es·ta /fē-es′tə/ *n.* holiday, festivity, or religious festival [Sp]

fife /fīf/ *n.* small shrill flute used in military music [Ger *Pfeife* PIPE or Fr *fifre*]

fif·teen /fiftēn′/ *adj. & n.* **1** one more than fourteen **2** symbol for this (15, xv, XV) **3** size, etc., denoted by fifteen —**fif′teenth′** *adj. & n.* [OE, rel. to FIVE, -TEEN]

fifth /fi(f)TH/ *adj. & n.* **1** next after fourth **2** any of five equal parts of a thing **3** *Mus.* interval or chord spanning five consecutive notes in a diatonic scale (e.g., C to G) **4** (**the Fifth**) *Slang.* FIFTH AMENDMENT —**fifth′ly** *adv.* [OE, rel. to FIVE]

Fifth′ A·mend′ment *n.* fifth amendment to the US Constitution, esp. the part providing that a person need not give evidence against himself or herself in a criminal case

fif·ty /fif′tē/ *adj. & n.* (*pl.* **·ties**) **1** five times ten **2** symbol for this (50, l, L) **3** (*pl.*) numbers from 50 to 59, esp. as years —**fif′ti·eth** /-əTH/ *adj. & n.* [OE]

fif′ty-fif′ty *adj.* **1** equal —*adv.* **2** equally

fig /fig/ *n.* **1** soft pulpy fruit with many seeds **2** tree bearing figs [L *ficus*]

fig. *abbr.* figure

fight /fīt/ *v.* (**fought, fight·ing**) **1** contend or contend with in war, battle, single combat, etc. **2** engage in (a battle, duel, etc.) **3** contend or resist; not submit to **4** strive to achieve something or to overcome (disease, fire, etc.) —*n.* **5a** combat **b** boxing match **c** battle; conflict; struggle **6** power or inclination to fight **7 fight off** repel with effort [OE]

fight′er *n.* **1** person or animal that fights **2** fast military aircraft designed for attacking other aircraft

fig·ment /fig′mənt/ *n.* invented or imaginary thing [L *fingere* mold; feign]

fig·u·ra·tive /fig′(y)ərətiv/ *adj.* **1** metaphorical, not literal **2** characterized by figures of speech **3** of pictorial or sculptural representation —**fig′u·ra·tive·ly** *adv.* [L, rel. to FIGURE]

fig·ure /fig′yər/ *n.* **1** external form or bodily shape **2a** silhouette; human form **b** person of a specified kind or appearance **3** space enclosed by one or more lines or surfaces, e.g., a triangle or sphere **4** numerical symbol or number, esp. 0 – 9 **5** amount; estimated value **6** (in full **figure of speech**) any literary device drawing on the imagination of a reader, etc., e.g., hyperbole —*v.* (**·ured, ·ur·ing**) **7** appear or be mentioned, esp. prominently **8** calculate; do arithmetic **9** *Colloq.* conclude or guess; venture **10** make sense; be likely **11 figure on** count on; expect **12 figure out**

work out by arithmetic or logic [L *figura* shape]

fig·ure·head' *n.* 1 nominal leader 2 wooden bust or figure at a ship's prow

fig·ure skat'ing *n.* skating in prescribed patterns —**fig·ure skat'er** *n.*

fig·u·rine /fig'yərēn'/ *n.* statuette [It, rel. to FIGURE]

Fi·ji /fē'jē/ *n.* independent archipelago in the S Pacific, N of New Zealand. Capital: Suva. Pop. 748,000 —**Fi'ji·an** *n.* & *adj.*

fil·a·ment /fil'əmənt/ *n.* 1 threadlike body or fiber 2 conducting wire or thread in an electric bulb, etc. —**fil'a·men'tous** /-men'təs/ *adj.* [L *filum* thread]

fil·bert /fil'bərt/ *n.* HAZELNUT

filch /filCH/ *v.* pilfer; steal

file¹ /fīl/ *n.* 1 folder, box, etc., for holding loose papers 2 papers kept in this 3 *Comp.* collection of (usu. related) data stored under one name 4 line of people or things —*v.* (**filed, fil·ing**) 5 place (papers) in a file or among records 6 submit an application, etc. [L *filum* thread]

file² *n.* 1 tool with a roughened surface for smoothing or shaping —*v.* (**filed, fil·ing**) 2 smooth or shape with a file [OE]

fi·let /filā', fil'ət/ *n.* 1 FILLET 2 (in full **fi·let' mig·non'** / filā' minyōn' /) thick slice of beef tenderloin, usu. grilled

fil·i·al /fil'ēəl/ *adj.* of or due from a son or daughter —**fil'i·al·ly** *adv.* [L *filius* son, *filia* daughter]

fil·i·bus·ter /fil'əbəs'tər/ *n.* 1 obstruction of progress in a legislative assembly by prolonged speaking 2 person who engages in this —*v.* 3 act as a filibuster (against) [Du, rel. to FREEBOOTER]

fil·i·gree /fil'əgrē'/ *n.* 1 fine ornamental work in gold, etc., wire 2 similar tracery —*v.* (**·greed, ·gree·ing**) 3 decorate with filigree —**fil'i·greed'** *adj.* [L *filum* thread, *granum* seed]

fil·ing /fī'liNG/ *n.* particle rubbed off by a file

Fil·i·pi·no /fil'əpē'nō/ *n.* (*pl.* **·nos**) 1 native or national of the Philippines —*adj.* 2 of the Philippines or Filipinos [Sp: Philippine]

fill /fil/ *v.* 1 make or become full 2 occupy completely; spread over or through 3 drill and put a filling into (a decayed tooth) 4 appoint a person to hold or (of a person) hold (a post) 5 carry out or supply (an order, commission, etc.) 6 occupy or use up (vacant time) 7 (esp. of food) satiate —*n.* 8 as much as one wants or can bear 9 enough to fulfill something 10 *Colloq.* inform (a person) more fully 11 **fill in:** a complete (a form, document, etc.) b fill (a hole, etc.) completely c act as a substitute 12 **fill out:** a enlarge to the required size b become enlarged or plump c fill in (a document, etc.) [OE]

fill'er *n.* 1 material used to fill or to increase bulk 2 small news item

fil·let /fil'it/ *n.* 1 (also **fi·let** /filā'/) a boneless piece of meat or fish b tenderloin, as of beef 2 strip; band —*v.* (**·let·ed, ·let·ing**) 3 (also **fi·let'**) remove bones from (fish or meat) [L *filum* thread]

fill'ing *n.* material that fills a cavity, sandwich, pie, etc.

fil·lip /fil'əp/ *n.* 1 stimulus; incentive 2 flick with a finger or thumb —*v.* (**·liped, ·lip·ing**) 3 flick

Fill·more /fil'môr', -mōr'/, Millard 1800–74; 13th US president (1850–53)

fil·ly /fil'ē/ *n.* (*pl.* **·lies**) young female horse [ON]

film /film/ *n.* 1 thin coating or covering layer 2 strip or sheet of plastic, etc., coated with light-sensitive emulsion for exposure in a camera 3 story, episode, etc., on motion-picture film; MOVIE 4 slight veil or haze, etc. —*v.* 5 make a motion picture of 6 cover or become covered with or as with a film [OE]

film'strip' *n.* series of transparencies in a strip for projection

film'y *adj.* (**·i·er, ·i·est**) 1 thin and translucent 2 covered with or as with a film

fil·ter /fil'tər/ *n.* 1 porous device for removing impurities, etc., from a fluid passed through it 2 screen or attachment for absorbing or modifying light, x-rays, etc. 3 device for suppressing unwanted electrical or sound waves —*v.* 4 (cause to) pass through a filter 5 make way gradually [Gmc, rel. to FELT²]

filth /filTH/ *n.* 1 repugnant or extreme dirt 2 obscenity —**filth'i·ly** *adv.*; **filth'i·ness** *n.*; **filth'y** *adj.* (**·i·er, ·i·est**) [OE, rel. to FOUL]

fil·trate /fil'trāt'/ *v.* (**·trat·ed, ·trat·ing**) 1 filter —*n.* 2 filtered liquid —**fil·tra'tion** *n.* [rel. to FILTER]

fin /fin/ *n.* 1 flat external organ of esp. fish, for propelling, steering, etc. 2 similar projection on an aircraft, car, etc. 3 swimmer's flipper —**fin'ny** *adj.* [OE]

fi·na·gle /fənā'gəl/ *v.* (**·gled, ·gling**) *Colloq.* act or obtain with guile or craft —**fi·na'gler** *n.* [dial. *fainaigue* cheat]

fi·nal /fīn'l/ *adj.* 1 situated at the end; coming last 2 conclusive; decisive —*n.* 3 last or deciding heat or game 4 examination at the end of a class at school, etc. —**fi'nal·ly** *adv.*; **fi·nal'i·ty** /-nal'itē/ *n.* (*pl.* **·ties**) [L *finis* end]

fi·na·le /fənal'ē/ *n.* last movement or section of a piece of music or drama, etc. [It, rel. to FINAL]

fi·nal·ist /fīn'əlist/ *n.* competitor in a final

fi·nance /fī'nans, fənans'/ *n.* 1 management of money 2 monetary support for an enterprise 3 (*pl.*) money resources —*v.* (**·nanced, ·nanc·ing**) 4 provide capital for —**fi·nan'cial** /-nan'sHəl/ *adj.*; **fi·nan'cial·ly** *adv.* [MFr *finer* settle; pay, fr. L *finis* end]

fi·nan·cier /fin'ansēr', fənan'-/ *n.* capitalist [Fr, rel. to FINANCE]

finch /finCH/ *n.* one of a group of small, seed-eating birds, incl. sparrows, goldfinches, canaries, etc. [OE]

find /fīnd/ *v.* (**found, find·ing**) 1a discover or get by chance or effort b become aware of 2 succeed in obtaining 3 seek out and provide or supply 4 *Law.* (of a jury, judge, etc.) decide and declare 5 reach by a natural process —*n.* 6 discovery of treasure, etc. 7 valued thing or person newly discovered 8 **find out:** a discover or detect b get information; determine —**find'er** *n.* [OE]

● Usage: See note at LOCATE.

find'ing *n.* conclusion reached by an inquiry, etc.

fine¹ /fīn/ *adj.* 1 of high quality; excellent 2 good; satisfactory 3 pure; refined 4 in good health 5 (of weather, etc.) bright and clear 6 thin; sharp 7 in small particles —*adv.* 8 finely 9 *Colloq.* very well —**fine'ly** *adv.*; **fine'ness** *n.* [Fr *fin* fr. L *finis* end]

fine² *n.* 1 money to be paid as a penalty —*v.* (**fined, fin·ing**) 2 punish by a fine [Fr *fin* settlement of a dispute, fr. L *finis* end]

fine' arts' *n. pl.* poetry, music, and the visual arts

fin·er·y /fī'nərē/ *n.* showy dress or decoration [fr. FINE¹]

fi·nesse /fines'/ *n.* 1 stylish refinement 2 subtle manipulation 3 artfulness; poise; tact —*v.* (**·nessed, ·ness·ing**) 4 use or achieve by finesse [Fr, rel. to FINE¹]

fine'-tune' *v.* (**·tuned, ·tun·ing**) make small adjustments to

fin·ger /fiNG'gər/ *n.* 1 any of the terminal projections of the hand (usu. excluding the thumb) 2 part of a glove for a finger 3 fingerlike object or structure —*v.* 4 touch, feel, or turn about with the fingers 5 *Slang.* accuse; identify as a culprit 6 *Mus.* use the fingers in a particular way in playing an instrument 7 **put one's finger on** locate or identify exactly —**fin'ger·ing** *n.* [OE]

Fin'ger Lakes' /fiNG'gər/ *n.* chain of long, thin lakes in N central N.Y. W of Syracuse

fin'ger·nail' *n.* nail of each finger

fin'ger·print' *n.* 1 impression of a fingertip on a surface, used in detecting crime —*v.* 2 record the fingerprints of

fin'ger·tip' *n.* 1 tip of a finger 2 **have at one's fingertips** have immediately available or at one's command

fin·i·al /fin'ēəl/ *n.* ornamental top or end of a roof, gable, etc. [AngFr fr. L *finis* end]

fin·ick·y /fin'ikē/ *adj.* (also **fin'i·cal** /·ikəl/, **fin'ick·ing**) 1 very particular; fastidious 2 detailed —**fin'ick·i·ness** *n.* [perh. fr. FINE¹]

fi·nis /fin'is/ *n.* end of a book, movie, etc. [L]

fin·ish /fin'iSH/ *v.* 1a bring or come to an end or the end of; complete; cease **b** *Colloq.* kill; vanquish **c** consume or complete consuming (food or drink) 2 treat the surface of (cloth, woodwork, etc.) —*n.* 3a end; last stage; completion **b** ending point 4 method, material, etc., used for surface treatment of wood, cloth, etc. 5 **finish with** have no more to do with using, etc. [L *finis* end]

fi·nite /fī'nīt'/ *adj.* 1 limited; not infinite 2 (of a part of a verb) having a specific number and person [L, rel. to FINISH]

Fin·land /fin'lənd/ *n.* republic in N Europe. Capital: Helsinki. Pop. 5,033,000

Finn /fin/ *n.* native or national of Finland; person of Finnish descent [OE]

Finn·ish /fin'iSH/ *adj.* 1 of the Finns or their language —*n.* 2 language of the Finns

fiord /fē·ôrd', fyôrd/ *n.* (also **fjord**) long narrow sea inlet with steep cliffs [Norw]

fir /fər'/ *n.* 1 evergreen coniferous tree with needles growing singly on the stems 2 its wood [OE or ON]

fire /fīr/ *n.* 1a combustion of substances with oxygen, giving out light and heat **b** flame; incandescence 2 burning fuel in a grate, furnace, etc. 3 fervor; spirit; ardor 4 burning heat; fever —*v.* (**fired, fir·ing**) 5 shoot (a gun, missile, etc.) 6 produce (a warning, salute, etc.) by shooting guns, etc. 7 (of a gun, etc.) be discharged 8 deliver or utter rapidly

9 dismiss (an employee) 10 (of an engine) undergo ignition 11 stimulate 12 bake; dry; cure (pottery, bricks, etc.) 13 **catch (on) fire** begin to burn 14 **under fire** under attack [OE]

fire'arm' *n.* gun, pistol, or rifle

fire'ball' *n.* 1 large meteor 2 ball of flame or lightning 3 *Colloq.* energetic person

fire'bomb' *n.* 1 incendiary bomb —*v.* 2 use incendiary bombs on

fire·brand /fīr'brand'/ *n.* 1 piece of burning wood 2 person causing trouble or unrest

fire'break' *n.* obstacle to the spread of fire in a forest, etc., esp. an open space

fire'crack'er *n.* explosive firework

fire' drill' *n.* rehearsal of the procedures to be used in case of fire

fire' en'gine *n.* vehicle carrying hoses, firefighters, etc.

fire' es·cape' *n.* emergency staircase for use in a fire

fire' ex·tin'guish·er *n.* portable apparatus for putting out a fire

fire'fight'er *n.* FIREMAN, 1

fire'fly' *n.* (*pl.* **-flies**) beetle emitting phosphorescent light, e.g., the lightning bug

fire-man /fīr'mən/ *n.* (*pl.* **-men**) 1 member of a fire brigade 2 person who tends a furnace

Fi·ren·ze /fērent'sā, fəren'zə/ *n.* see FLORENCE

fire-place /fīr'plās'/ *n.* 1 place for a domestic fire, esp. a recess in a wall 2 structure surrounding this

fire'pow'er *n.* destructive capacity of guns, etc.

fire'proof' *adj.* 1 able to resist fire or great heat —*v.* 2 make fireproof

fire'side' *n.* 1 area around a fireplace 2 home or home life

fire'storm' *n.* high wind or storm following a fire caused by bombs

fire'trap' *n.* building with no precautions against fire

fire'wa'ter *n. Facetious.* strong alcoholic liquor

fire'wood' *n.* wood as fuel

fire'works' *n.* 1 devices that burn or explode spectacularly when lit 2 outburst of passion, esp. anger

fir'ing *n.* 1 discharge of guns 2 fuel

fir'ing line' *n.* 1 front line in a battle 2 position of dangerous action

firm¹ /fərm'/ *adj.* 1a solid; compact **b** fixed; stable 2a resolute; determined **b** steadfast; constant 3 (of an offer, etc.) definite; not conditional —*adv.* 4 firmly —*v.* 5 make or become firm, secure, compact, or solid —**firm'ly** *adv.*; **firm'ness** *n.* [L *firmus* strong; stable]

firm² *n.* business concern or its partners [L *firmare* strengthen; confirm]

fir·ma·ment /fər'məmənt/ *n. Lit.* the sky regarded as a vault or arch [L, rel. to FIRM¹]

first /fərst'/ *adj.* 1 earliest in time or order 2 foremost in rank or importance 3 most willing or likely 4 basic or evident —*n.* 5 person or thing first mentioned or occurring 6 first gear 7 first place in a competition —*adv.* 8 before any other person or thing 9 before someone or something else 10 for the first time 11 **at first** at the beginning [OE]

● Usage: *First, second, third,* etc., serve as both adjectives and adverbs. Thus, one can say *First, do your homework; second, help clean the house.* It is not necessary to use *firstly,* etc., where *first,* etc., will do, but it is not wrong. One should make sure not to mix them: *first, second, third;* not *first, secondly, thirdly.* Also see note at FORMER.

first' aid' *n.* emergency medical treatment

first'born' *adj.* 1 eldest —*n.* 2 person's eldest child

first' class' *n.* 1 best group or category 2 best accommodation offered 3 mail given priority —*adj.* & *adv.* 4 first-class: a of or by the first class b excellent

first' cous·in *n.* see COUSIN

first' fam'i·ly *n.* immediate family of a US president or state governor

first'hand' *adj.* & *adv.* from the original source; direct

first' la'dy *n.* wife of the US president

first·ly /fərst'lē/ *adv.* in the first place; first

first' name' *n.* personal or given name

first' per'son see PERSON

first'-rate' *adj.* 1 excellent 2 *Colloq.* very well

firth /fərTH'/ *n.* narrow inlet of sea [ON, rel. to FIORD]

fis·cal /fis'kəl/ *adj.* 1 of public revenue 2 financial —**fis'cal·ly** *adv.* [L *fiscus* treasury]

fish /fiSH/ *n.* (*pl.* same or *-es*) 1 vertebrate cold-blooded animal with gills and fins living wholly in water 2 fish as food 3 (**the Fish** or **Fishes**) sign or constellation Pisces —*v.* 4 try to catch fish 5 **fish for** seek 6 **fish out** retrieve from a narrow place [OE]

fish·er·man /fiSH'ərmən/ *n.* (*pl.* **·men**) man who catches fish as a livelihood or for sport

fish·er·y /fiSH'ərē/ *n.* (*pl.* **·ies**) 1 place where fish are caught or reared 2 industry of fishing or breeding fish

fish'hook' *n.* barbed hook for catching fish

fish'ing rod' *n.* tapering usu. jointed rod for fishing

fish' meal' *n.* ground dried fish as fertilizer or animal feed

fish'net' *n.* 1 net for fishing 2 knitted material resembling this

fish·tail /fiSH'tāl'/ *v.* (of a vehicle, etc.) move its end from side to side

fish'y *adj.* (**·i·er, ·i·est**) 1 of or like fish 2 *Slang.* dubious; suspicious; not quite right —**fish'i·ly** *adv.*; **fish'i·ness** *n.*

fis·sile /fis'əl, -īl'/ *adj.* 1 capable of undergoing nuclear fission 2 tending to split [L, rel. to FISSURE]

fis·sion /fiSH'ən/ *n.* 1 splitting of a heavy atomic nucleus, with a release of energy 2 cell division as a mode of reproduction —**fis'sion·a·ble** *adj.* [L, rel. to FISSURE]

fis·sure /fiSH'ər/ *n.* crack or split, usu. long and narrow [L *findere fiss-* cleave]

fist /fist/ *n.* tightly closed hand —**fist'ful** *n.* (*pl.* **-fuls**) [OE]

fist·i·cuffs /fis'tikəfs'/ *n. pl.* fighting with the fists [prob. fr. obs. *fisty* (fr. FIST), CUFF[2]]

fis·tu·la /fis'CHələ/ *n.* (*pl.* **·las** or **·lae** /-lē'/) abnormal or artificial passage, as between an organ and the body surface [L: pipe]

fit[1] /fit/ *adj.* (**fit·ter, fit·test**) 1a well suited b qualified; competent; worthy c in suitable condition; ready d good enough 2 in good health or condition 3 proper; becoming; right

—*v.* (**fit** or **fit·ted, fit·ting**) 4 be or make of the right shape and size for 5 equip with 6 befit; become —*n.* 7 way in which a garment, component, etc., fits 8 **fit in:** a be compatible; accommodate b find space or time for 9 **fit out** equip —**fit'ly** *adv.*; **fit'ness, fit'ter** *n.*

fit[2] *n.* 1 sudden esp. epileptic seizure with unconsciousness or convulsions 2 sudden brief bout or burst 3 **by** (or **in**) **fits and starts** spasmodically; fitfully 4 **have a fit** *Colloq.* be greatly surprised or outraged [ME]

fit·ful /fit'fəl/ *adj.* spasmodic; intermittent —**fit'ful·ly** *adv.*

fit'ting *n.* 1 trying-on of a garment for adjustment 2 fixture —*adj.* 3 proper; becoming; right —**fit'ting·ly** *adv.*

Fitz·ger·ald /fitsjer'əld/ 1 F(rancis) Scott 1896–1940; US writer 2 Ella 1918– ; US jazz singer

five /fīv/ *adj.* & *n.* 1 one more than four 2 symbol for this (5, v, V) [OE]

fix /fiks/ *v.* 1 make firm or stable; fasten; secure 2 decide; specify (a price, date, etc.) 3 repair 4 implant 5 (foll. by *on, upon*) direct (the eyes, etc.) 6 determine the exact nature, position, etc., of 7 make or become rigid 8 *Colloq.* prepare (food or drink) 9 *Colloq.* punish; deal with (a person) 10 *Colloq.* arrange the outcome of (a sporting event) —*n.* 11 *Colloq.* dilemma; predicament 12 position found by bearings, etc. 13 *Slang.* dose of an addictive drug 14 **fix up:** a repair; provide with b arrange; organize c accommodate —**fix'a·ble** *adj.*; **fix'er** *n.* [L *fixus* fixed, fr. *figere* fasten]

fix·ate /fik'sāt'/ *v.* (**·at·ed, ·at·ing**) 1 direct one's gaze on 2 *Psychol.* cause (a person) to become abnormally attached to a person or thing [L, rel. to FIX]

fix·a'tion *n.* 1 state of being fixated 2 obsession; monomania

fix·a·tive /fik'sətiv/ *adj.* 1 tending to fix or secure —*n.* 2 fixative substance

fix·ed·ly /fik'sidlē/ *adv.* intently

fix'ings *n. pl. Colloq.* 1 apparatus or equipment 2 trimmings for a dish, dress, etc.

fix·i·ty /fik'sitē/ *n.* fixed state; stability; permanence

fix·ture /fiks'CHər/ *n.* something fixed in position

fizz /fiz/ *v.* 1 make a hissing or spluttering sound 2 (of a drink) effervesce —*n.* 3 effervescence 4 *Colloq.* effervescent drink —**fizz'y** *adj.* (**·i·er, ·i·est**) [perh. imit., or fr. FIZZLE]

fiz·zle /fiz'əl/ *v.* (**·zled, ·zling**) 1 make a feeble hiss —*n.* 2 such a sound 3 **fizzle out** end feebly [perh. imit., or fr. ON *fisa* break wind]

fjord /fē·ôrd', fyôrd/ *n.* var. of FIORD

FL postal abbr. for Florida

fl. *abbr.* 1 floruit 2 fluid

Fla. *abbr.* Florida

flab /flab/ *n. Colloq.* fat; flabbiness —**flab'by** *adj.* (**·bi·er, ·bi·est**); **flab'bi·ness** /-bēnəs/ *n.*

flab·ber·gast /flab'ərgast'/ *v. Colloq.* astonish; dumbfound

flac·cid /flak'sid, flas'id/ *adj.* limp; flabby; drooping —**flac·cid'i·ty** *n.* [L *flaccus* limp]

flag[1] /flag/ *n.* 1 usu. oblong or square piece of cloth, etc., as an emblem or signal —*v.*

(flagged, flag·ging) 2a grow tired; lag b hang down; droop 3 inform or communicate by flag or similarly 4 **flag down** signal to stop

flag² n. (also **flag·stone**) 1 flat paving stone 2 (pl.) pavement of these [prob. Scand]

flag³ n. plant with a bladed leaf (esp. the iris)

flag·el·late /flaj′əlāt′/ v. (·lat·ed, ·lat·ing) scourge; flog —**flag′el·la′tion** n.

fla·gel·lum /fləjel′əm/ n. (pl. ·la /-lə/) long lashlike appendage on some microscopic organisms [L: whip]

flag·on /flag′ən/ n. large vessel for wine, etc., usu. with a handle, spout, and lid [L flasco FLASK]

flag′pole′ n. (also **flag′staff′**) pole on which a flag may be hoisted

fla·grant /flā′grənt/ adj. blatant; notorious; scandalous —**fla′gran·cy** n.; **fla′grant·ly** adv. [L flagrare blaze; burn]

flag′ship′ n. 1 ship with an admiral on board 2 leading or primary member, office, etc.

flag′stone′ n. FLAG²

flail /flāl/ n. 1 wooden staff with a short heavy stick swinging from it, used for threshing —v. 2 wave or swing wildly 3 beat [L flagellum whip]

flair /fler/ n. 1 natural talent in a specific area 2 style; finesse [OFr flairier smell, fr. L fragrare]

flak /flak/ n. 1 antiaircraft fire 2 adverse criticism; abuse 3 Slang. press agent [Ger Fliegerabwehrkanone, literally, 'aviator-defense-gun']

flake /flāk/ n. 1 small thin light piece of falling snow, etc. 2 thin piece peeled or split off 3 Colloq. disorganized or eccentric person —v. (**flaked, flak·ing**) 4 take off or come away in flakes

flak′y adj. (·i·er, ·i·est) 1 of, like, or in flakes 2 Slang. crazy; eccentric

flambé /flämbā′/ adj. French. (of food) covered with alcohol and set alight briefly [Fr, rel. to FLAME]

flam·boy·ant /flamboi′ənt/ adj. 1 ostentatious; showy 2 floridly decorated or colored —**flam·boy′ance** n.; **flam·boy′ant·ly** adv. [Fr, rel. to FLAMBÉ]

flame /flām/ n. 1a ignited tongue of fire b glow from burning 2 brilliant orange-red color 3a strong passion, esp. love b Colloq. sweetheart —v. (**flamed, flam·ing**) 4 burn; blaze [L flamma]

fla·men·co /fləmeNG′kō/ n. (pl. ·cos) 1 style of Spanish gypsy guitar music with singing 2 dance performed to this [Sp: Flemish]

flame′proof′ /flām′pr ̄oof/ adj. 1 treated to resist open flame —v. 2 make flameproof

flame′throw′er n. weapon for throwing a spray of flame

flam′ing adj. 1 emitting flames 2 bright-colored

fla·min·go /fləmiNG′gō/ n. (pl. ·gos or ·goes) tall long-necked wading bird with mainly pink plumage [perh. Prov., rel. to FLAME, or Sp: Flemish, for their supposed coloring]

flam·ma·ble /flam′əbəl/ adj. able to burn —**flam′ma·bil′i·ty** n. [L, rel. to FLAME]
• Usage: See note at INFLAMMABLE.

Flan·ders /flan′dərz/ region of western Europe in coastal Belgium and vicinity

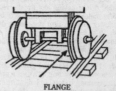

FLANGE

flange /flanj/ n. projecting flat rim, etc., for strengthening or attachment

flank /flaNGk/ n. 1 side of the body between ribs and hip 2 side of a mountain, building, etc. 3 side of an array of troops —v. 4 be at or move along the side of [OFr fr. Gmc]

flan·nel /flan′l/ n. 1 woven woolen usu. napless fabric 2 (pl.) flannel garments, esp. trousers [Welsh gwlanen fr. gulân wool]

flan′nel·ette′ /-et′/ n. napped cotton fabric like flannel

flap /flap/ v. (**flapped, flap·ping**) 1 move or be moved back and forth or up and down; beat 2 sway; flutter —n. 3 piece of cloth, wood, etc., attached by one side, e.g., the folded part of an envelope or a table leaf 4 motion of a wing, arm, etc. 5 Colloq. agitation; panic 6 Aeron. hinged section on the trailing edge of a wing [ME, perh. imit.]

flap′jack′ /flap′jak′/ n. pancake

flap′per n. Colloq. (in the 1920s) young unconventional woman

flare /fler/ v. (**flared, flar·ing**) 1 widen gradually 2 (cause to) blaze brightly and unsteadily 3 burst out, esp. angrily —n. 4a dazzling irregular flame or light b sudden outburst of flame 5 flame, firework, or bright light used as a signal, etc. 6 gradual widening, esp. of a skirt or trousers 7 **flare up** burst into a sudden blaze, anger, activity, etc.

flare′up′ n. sudden outburst

flash /flasH/ v. 1 (cause to) emit a brief or sudden light; (cause to) gleam 2 send or reflect like a sudden flame 3a burst suddenly into view or perception b move swiftly 4a send (news, etc.) by radio, telegraph, etc. b signal to (a person) with lights 5 Colloq. show ostentatiously —n. 6 sudden bright light or flame, e.g., of lightning 7 an instant 8 sudden brief feeling, display of wit, etc. 9 NEWSFLASH 10 Photog. FLASHLIGHT 1 11 bright patch of color [ME, prob. imit.]

flash′back′ n. scene set in a time earlier than the main action

flash′ing n. (usu. metal) strip used to prevent water penetration at a roof joint, etc.

flash′light′ n. portable electric light

flash′ point′ n. temperature at which vapor from oil, etc., will ignite in air

flash′y adj. (·i·er, ·i·est) showy; gaudy; cheaply attractive —**flash′i·ly** adv.; **flash′i·ness** n.

flask /flask/ n. 1 narrow-necked bulbous bot

FLAMINGO

tle **2** thin beverage container for concealment in a pocket [LL *fiasca* FLAGON]

flat¹ /flat/ *adj.* (**flat·ter, flat·test**) **1a** horizontally level **b** even; smooth; unbroken **c** level and shallow **2** unqualified; downright **3** dull; lifeless; monotonous vocally **4** (of a carbonated drink) having lost its effervescence **5a** *Mus.* below true or normal pitch **b** semitone lower **6** (of a tire) punctured; deflated —*adv.* **7** at full length; spread out **8** *Colloq.* **a** completely; absolutely **b** exactly (*five minutes flat*) **9** *Mus.* below the true or normal pitch —*n.* **10** flat part or thing (*flat of the hand*) **11** (usu. *pl.*) level ground, esp. exposed bottom at low tide **12** *Mus.* a note lowered a semitone **b** sign (♭) indicating this **13** *Theat.* flat scenery on a frame **14** *Colloq.* flat tire **15** flat out: **a** at top speed **b** directly; bluntly —**flat′ly** *adv.*; **flat′ness** *n.*; **flat′tish** *adj.* [ON]

flat² *n.* apartment on one floor [obs. *flet* floor; dwelling, fr. Gmc, rel. to FLAT¹]

flat′bed′ *n.* truck, railroad car, etc., with a flat surface for cargo

flat′fish′ *n.* sole, halibut, or other species of fish with a very slender body and both eyes on one side

flat′foot′ *n.* **1** foot with a flattened arch **2** *Slang.* police officer

flat′foot′ed /-fŏŏt′əd/ *n.* **1** having flat feet **2** *Colloq.* unprepared

flat′i·ron *n.* *Hist.* iron for pressing clothes, etc.

flat·ten /flat′n/ *v.* **1** make or become flat **2** *Colloq.* knock down

flat·ter /flat′ər/ *v.* **1** compliment unduly, esp. for gain or advantage **2** congratulate or delude **3** enhance the appearance of **4** cause to feel honored —**flat′ter·er** *n.*; **flat′ter·ing** *adj.*; **flat′ter·ing·ly** *adv.* [Fr]

flat′ter·y *n.* exaggerated or insincere praise

flat·u·lent /flăcH′ələnt/ *adj.* **1** having or producing intestinal gas **2** (of speech) inflated; pretentious —**flat′u·lence** *n.* [L *flatus* blowing]

flat′ware *n.* eating utensils; tableware

flat′worm′ *n.* worm with a flattened body

Flau·bert /flōbêr′/, **Gustave** 1821–80; French writer

flaunt /flônt, flänt/ *v.* display proudly; show off; parade

● Usage: *Flaunt* means 'put on a showy display': *Maddy kept on flaunting her engagement ring.* It should not be confused with *flout* 'scoff at, mock': *Students who flout the rules in Ms. Martin's class are given extra homework assignments.*

flau·tist /flôt′ist, flou′-/ *n.* flute player [It, rel. to FLUTE]

fla·vor /flā′vər/ *n.* **1** mingled sensation of smell and taste **2** characteristic quality —*v.* **3** give flavor to; season —**fla′vor·less** *adj.*; **fla′vor·some** /-səm/ *adj.* [Fr]

fla′vor·ing *n.* substance used to flavor food or drink

flaw /flô/ *n.* **1** imperfection; blemish; fault **2** crack, chip, etc. —*v.* **3** crack; damage; spoil —**flaw′less** *adj.*; **flaw′less·ly** *adv.* [ON]

flax /flaks/ *n.* **1** blue-flowered plant cultivated for its textile fiber and its seeds **2** flax fibers [OE]

flax·en /flak′sən/ *adj.* **1** of flax **2** (of hair) pale yellow

flay /flā/ *v.* **1** strip the skin or hide off **2** criticize severely [OE]

flea /flē/ *n.* small, wingless parasitic insect that moves very quickly by jumping

flea′ mar′ket *n.* usu. outdoor market selling second-hand goods, etc.

fleck /flek/ *n.* **1** spot; particle; speck —*v.* **2** mark with flecks [ON, or LGer or Du]

fled /fled/ *v.* *past* and *past part.* of FLEE

fledg·ling /flej′lING/ *n.* **1** young bird **2** inexperienced person

flee /flē/ *v.* (**fled, flee·ing**) **1** run away (from); leave abruptly **2** vanish [OE]

fleece /flēs/ *n.* **1** woolly coat of a sheep, etc. **2** soft fabric —*v.* (**fleeced, fleec·ing**) **3** strip of money, valuables, etc.; swindle **4** shear (sheep, etc.) —**fleec′i·ness** *n.*; **fleec′y** *adj.* (**·i·er, ·i·est**) [OE]

fleet /flēt/ *n.* **1** warships under one commander-in-chief **2** vehicles under one ownership —*adj.* **3** swift [OE]

fleet′ing *adj.* transitory; brief —**fleet′ing·ly** *adv.*

Flem·ing /flem′iNG/ **1** (**Sir**) **Alexander** 1881–1955; English bacteriologist; discovered penicillin **2** **Ian** 1908–64; English novelist

Flem·ish /flem′isH/ *adj.* **1** of Flanders —*n.* **2** language of Flanders, esp. the Dutch language of N Belgium [Du]

flesh /flesH/ *n.* **1a** soft substance between the skin and bones of an animal or a human **b** plumpness; fat **2** the body, esp. as sinful **3** pulpy substance of a fruit, etc. **4** yellowish pink color **5** animal or human life **6** flesh out make substantial **7** in the flesh in person **8** one's own flesh and blood near relatives [OE]

flesh′ and blood′ *n.* **1** the body or its substance **2** humankind or human nature —*adj.* **3** real, not imaginary

flesh′ly *adj.* (**·li·er, ·li·est**) **1** bodily; sensual **2** mortal **3** worldly

flesh′y *adj.* (**·i·er, ·i·est**) of flesh; plump; pulpy —**flesh′i·ness** *n.*

Fletch·er /flecH′ər/, **John** 1579–1625; English dramatist

FLEUR-DE-LIS

fleur-de-lis /flər′ də lē′/ *n.* (also **fleur-de-lys**) (*pl.* **fleurs-**, pronunc. same) lily-like emblem used on the former royal arms of France [Fr: flower of lily]

flew /flōō/ *v.* *past* of FLY¹

flex /fleks/ *v.* **1** bend (a joint, limb, etc.) or be bent **2** move (a muscle) or (of a muscle) be moved to bend a joint [L *flexus* fr. *flectere* bend]

flex·i·ble /flek′səbəl/ *adj.* **1** capable of bending without breaking; pliable **2** adaptable;

variable —**flex′i·bil′i·ty** n.; **flex′i·bly** adv. [L *flexibilis*, rel. to FLEX, 1]

flex′time′ n. (also **flex′i·time′** /-sētim′/) system of flexible working hours [fr. FLEXIBLE + TIME]

flick /flik/ n. **1a** light sharp blow **b** sudden release of a bent digit **2** sudden movement or jerk, esp. of the wrist **3** *Slang.* a movie **b** (*pl.; prec. by the*) the movies —v. **4** strike or move off with a flick [imit.]

flick′er v. **1** (of light or flame) shine or burn unsteadily **2** flutter **3** (of hope, etc.) waver —n. **4** unsteady movement or light **5** brief spell (of hope, etc.) [OE]

fli·er /flī′ər/ n. (also **fly′er**) **1** airman or airwoman **2** thing that flies in a specified way **3** printed advertisement for distribution by hand or by mail

flight¹ /flīt/ n. **1a** act or manner of flying **b** movement or passage through air **2a** journey through air or in space **b** airline journey **3** series, esp. of stairs [OE, rel. to FLY¹]

flight² n. fleeing; hasty retreat [OE]

flight′ at·ten′dant n. airline staff member who assists passengers during a flight

flight′less adj. (of a bird, etc.) unable to fly

flight′y adj. (**·i·er, ·i·est**) frivolous; fickle —**flight′i·ness** n.

flim·sy /flim′zē/ adj. (**·i·er, ·i·est**) **1** insubstantial; rickety **2** unconvincing **3** (of clothing) thin —**flim′si·ly** adv.; **flim′si·ness** n.

flinch /flinCH/ v. draw back in fear, etc.; wince [Fr fr. Gmc]

fling /flinG/ v. (**flung, fling·ing**) **1** throw or hurl forcefully or hurriedly **2** put or send suddenly or violently —n. **3** act of flinging; throw **4** bout of wild behavior **5** whirling Scottish dance [ON]

flint /flint/ n. **1a** hard gray siliceous stone **b** piece of this, esp. as a primitive tool or weapon **2** piece of hard alloy used to give a spark —**flint′y** adj. (**·i·er, ·i·est**) [OE]

Flint /flint/ n. city in Mich. Pop. 140,761

flip /flip/ v. (**flipped, flip·ping**) **1** flick or toss (a coin, pellet, etc.) so that it spins in the air **2** turn over; flick —n. **3** act of flipping —adj. **4** *Colloq.* glib; flippant **5** flip one's lid *Slang.* lose self-control; go mad **6** flip through riffle through [prob. fr. FILLIP]

flip′-flop′ n. **1** repeated reversal of belief, policy, etc. **2** (usu. rubber) sandal with a thong between the toes —v. (**-flopped, -flop·ping**) **3** repeatedly reverse one's opinion or policy [imit.]

flip·pant /flip′ənt/ adj. frivolous; disrespectful; offhand —**flip′pan·cy** n.; **flip′pant·ly** adv. [fr. FLIP]

flip′per n. **1** broad flat limb of a turtle, etc., adapted for swimming **2** similar flexible foot attachment to assist swimming

flirt /flərt/ v. **1** try to attract sexually but without serious intent **2** toy (with); trifle —n. **3** person who flirts —**flir·ta·tion** /flərtā′sHən/, **flir·ta′tious·ness** /-tā′sHəsnəs/ n.; **flir·ta′tious** adj.; **flir·ta′tious·ly** adv. [imit.]

flit /flit/ v. (**flit·ted, flit·ting**) move lightly, softly, or rapidly [ON, rel. to FLEET]

float /flōt/ v. **1** (cause to) rest or move on the surface of a liquid **2** *Colloq.* move in a leisurely way **3a** start or launch (a company, scheme, etc.) **b** offer (stock, etc.) on the stock market **4** circulate or cause (a rumor or idea) to circulate —n. **5** thing that floats, esp.: **a** raft **b** buoyant object used in fishing **c** buoyant device, control, etc. **6** decorated platform or tableau in a parade —**float′a·ble** adj. [OE]

floc·cu·lent /fläk′yələnt/ adj. like or in tufts of wool, etc.; downy —**floc′cu·lence** n. [L *floccus* + *-ulent*]

flock /fläk/ n. **1** animals of one kind as a group or unit **2** large crowd of people **3** religious congregation —v. **4** congregate; mass; troop [OE]

floe /flō/ n. sheet of floating ice [Norw]

flog /fläg/ v. (**flogged, flog·ging**) beat with a whip, stick, etc.

flood /fləd/ n. **1a** overflowing or influx of water, esp. over land; inundation **b** the water that overflows **2** outpouring; torrent **3** (also **flood′tide′**) inflow of the tide **4** *Bibl.* (*cap.*) deluge sent by God —v. **5** overflow, cover, or be covered with or as if with a flood **6** irrigate, deluge, or overfill **7** come in great quantities [OE]

flood′gate′ n. **1** gate for admitting or excluding water, esp. in a lock **2** (usu. *pl.*) last restraint against tears, rain, anger, etc.

flood′light′ n. **1** large powerful light to illuminate a building, lot, etc. —v. **2** illuminate with floodlights —**flood′lit** adj.

floor /flôr/ n. **1** lower surface of a room **2a** bottom of the sea, a cave, etc. **b** any level area **3** one level of a building; story **4a** place where an assembly meets **b** right to speak next in a debate (*have the floor*) **5** minimum of prices, wages, etc. —v. **6** provide with a floor **7** knock or bring (a person) down **8** *Colloq.* confound; baffle **9** *Colloq.* overcome [OE]

floor′ing n. material to make or cover a floor

floor′ show′ n. nightclub entertainment

flop /fläp/ v. (**flopped, flop·ping**) **1** sway about heavily or loosely **2** fall or sit awkwardly or suddenly **3** *Slang.* fail; collapse **4** make a dull soft thud or splash —n. **5** flopping movement or sound **6** *Slang.* failure [var. of FLAP]

flop′py adj. (**·pi·er, ·pi·est**) tending to flop; flaccid —n. (*pl.* **·pies**) **2** (in full **flop′py disk′**) *Comp.* flexible disk for storage of data —**flop′pi·ness** n.

flo·ra /flôr′ə/ n. (*pl.* **·ras** or **·rae** /-ē′, -ī′/) plant life of a region or period [L *Flora* goddess of flowers]

flo·ral /flôr′əl/ adj. of, decorated with, or depicting flowers —**flo′ral·ly** adv. [L]

Flor·ence /flôr′əns, flär′-/ n. city in Italy on the Arno River. Pop. 408,400 —**Flor·en·tine** /flôr′əntēn′, -tīn′/ n. & adj.

flor·id /flôr′id, flär′-/ adj. **1** reddish **2** elaborately ornate; showy —**flor′id·ly** adv.; **flor′id·ness** n. [L, rel. to FLOWER]

Flor·i·da /flôr′ədə, flär′-/ n. peninsular SE state of the US. Capital: Tallahassee. Pop. 12,937,926. Abbr. **FL; Fla.** —**Flo·rid·i·an** /flōrid′ēən/ n. & adj.

Flor′i·da, Straits of n. channel at the S tip of Fla., separating Fla. from Cuba

Flor′i·da Keys′ n. chain of coral islands extending SW from the S tip of Fla. into the Gulf of Mexico

flo·rist /flôr'ist/ *n.* person who sells or grows flowers [L. *flos* FLOWER]

floss /flôs, fläs/ *n.* **1** rough silk of a silkworm's cocoon **2** silk thread used in embroidery **3** DENTAL FLOSS —*v.* **4** clean (teeth) with dental floss —**floss'y** *adj.* [Fr *floche*]

flo·ta·tion /flōtā'SHən/ *n.* act or state of floating [fr. FLOAT]

flo·til·la /flôtil'ə/ *n.* small fleet of naval vessels or boats [Sp]

flot'sam and jet'sam *n.* wreckage found floating [AngFr, rel. to FLOAT]

flot'sam and jet'sam *n.* odds and ends

flounce¹ /flouns/ *v.* (**flounced, flounc·ing**) **1** go or move angrily or impatiently —*n.* **2** flouncing movement

flounce² *n.* frill on a dress, skirt, etc. [alter. of *frounce* pleat, fr. Fr]

floun·der¹ /floun'dər/ *v.* **1** struggle helplessly as if wading in mud **2** do a task clumsily

floun·der² *n.* (*pl.* same) edible flatfish [AngFr, prob. fr. Scand]

flour /flour/ *n.* **1** meal or powder from ground wheat, etc. **2** any fine powder —**flour'y** *adj.* (·i·er, ·i·est); **flour'i·ness** *n.* [alter. spelling of FLOWER 'best part of the meal']

flour·ish /flər'isH/ *v.* **1a** grow vigorously; thrive **b** prosper **c** be in one's prime **2** wave; brandish —*n.* **3** showy gesture **4** ornamental curve in handwriting **5** *Mus.* ornate passage or fanfare [L *florere* fr. *flos* FLOWER]

flout /flout/ *v.* **1** disobey (the law, etc.) contemptuously; scorn —*n.* **2** scornful remark or act [Du *fluiten* whistle, rel. to FLUTE]

• Usage: See note at FLAUNT.

flow /flō/ *v.* **1** glide along as a stream **2** gush out; run; be spilled **3** circulate **4** move smoothly or steadily **5** (of a garment, hair, etc.) hang gracefully **6** proceed (from) **7** be plentiful —*n.* **8a** flowing movement or mass **b** flowing liquid **c** outpouring; stream **9** rise of a tide or river (*ebb and flow*) [OE]

flow' chart' *n.* diagram of movement, stages, production, etc.

flow·er /flou'ər, flour/ *n.* **1** part of a plant from which the fruit or seed is developed **2** blossom, esp. used for decoration **3** plant cultivated for its blossoms —*v.* **4** bloom; blossom **5** reach a peak **6 the flower of** the best of —**flow'ered** *adj.* [L *flos floris* flower]

flow'er·pot' *n.* pot for growing a plant

flow'er·y *adj.* **1** florally decorated **2** (of style, speech, etc.) high-flown; ornate —**flow'er·i·ness** *n.*

flow·ing /flō'iNG/ *adj.* **1** (of style, etc.) fluent; easy **2** smoothly continuous **3** (of hair, etc.) unconfined —**flow'ing·ly** *adv.*

flown /flōwn/ *v.* past part. of FLY¹

fl. oz. *abbr.* fluid ounce(s)

flu /flōō/ *n. Colloq.* influenza

fluc·tu·ate /flək'CHŌō·āt'/ *v.* (·at·ed, ·at·ing) vary irregularly; rise and fall —**fluc'tu·a'tion** *n.* [L *fluctus* wave]

flue /flōō/ *n.* **1** smoke duct in a chimney **2** channel for conveying heat

flu·ent /flōō'ənt/ *adj.* **1** flowing; smooth **2** verbally facile, esp. in a foreign language —**flu'en·cy** *n.*; **flu'ent·ly** *adv.* [L *fluere* flow]

fluff /fləf/ *n.* **1** soft fur, feathers, or fabric par-

ticles, etc. **2** *Slang.* mistake in a performance, etc. —*v.* **3** shake into or become a soft mass **4** *Colloq.* bungle —**fluff'y** *adj.* (·i·er, ·i·est) **fluff'i·ness** *n.* [prob. dial. alter. of *flue* fluff]

flu·id /flōō'id/ *n.* **1** substance, esp. gas or liquid, whose shape is determined by its container —*adj.* **2** able to flow and alter shape freely **3** constantly changing —**flu·id'i·ty** *n.*; **flu'id·ly** *adv.*; **flu'id·ness** *n.* [L, rel. to FLUENT]

flu'id ounce' *n.* one-sixteenth of a pint

fluke¹ /flōōk/ *n.* lucky accident —**fluk'y** *adj.* (·i·er, ·i·est)

fluke² *n.* **1** parasitic flatworm **2** flatfish, esp. a flounder [OE]

fluke³ *n.* **1** triangular, pointed tip of an anchor **2** lobe of a whale's tail [perh. fr. FLUKE²]

flum·mox /fləm'əks/ *v. Colloq.* bewilder; disconcert

flung /fləNG/ *v.* past and past part. of FLING

flunk /fləNGk/ *v. Colloq.* fail a course or examination

flunk·y /fləNG'kē/ *n.* (also **flun'key**) (*pl.* ·kies) usu. *Derog.* **1** liveried servant **2** toady **3** underling

flu·o·resce /flŏŏres'/ *v.* (·resced, ·resc·ing) exhibit fluorescence [rel. to FLUORESCENCE]

flu·o·res·cence /flŏŏres'əns/ *n.* **1** light radiation from certain substances **2** property of absorbing invisible light and emitting visible light —**flu'o·res'cent** *adj.* [rel. to FLUORITE + -*escence* of *opalescence*]

flu'o·res'cent lamp' *n.* esp. tubular lamp giving light by fluorescence

flu·o·ri·date /flŏŏr'ədāt', flŏŏr'-/ *v.* (·dat·ed, ·dat·ing) add fluoride to (drinking water, etc.), esp. to prevent tooth decay —**fluor'i·da'tion** *n.*

flu·o·ride /flŏŏr'īd, flŏŏr'-/ *n.* compound of fluorine

flu·o·rine /flŏŏr'ēn, flŏŏr'-/ *n.* poisonous pale-yellow gaseous element; *symb.* F [rel. to FLUORITE]

flu·o·rite /flŏŏr'īt, flŏŏr'-/ *n.* mineral form of calcium fluoride [fr. *fluor* + -RITE; L: flow, for its use as flux]

flu·o·ro·car·bon /flŏŏr'əkär'bən, flŏŏr'-/ *n.* compound of a hydrocarbon with fluorine atoms

flur·ry /flər'ē, flə'rē/ *n.* (*pl.* ·ries) **1** gust or squall **2** sudden burst of activity, etc.; commotion —*v.* (·ried, ·ry·ing) **3** confuse; agitate [FLUTTER + HURRY]

flush¹ /fləsH/ *v.* **1** blush; redden **2** cause to glow or blush (*flushed with pride*) **3a** cleanse (a drain, wound, etc.) by a flow of water **b** dispose of in this way **4** rush out; spurt —*n.* **5** blush or glow **6a** rush of water **b** cleansing thus **7** rush of esp. elation or triumph **8** freshness; vigor **9** sudden feeling of heat —*adj.* **10** level; in the same plane **11** *Colloq.* having plenty of money [perh. fr. FLUSH³]

flush² *n.* hand of cards all of one suit, esp. in poker [L *fluxus* FLUX]

flush³ *v.* **1** cause (esp. a game bird) to fly up **2** flush out drive out

flus·ter /fləs'tər/ *v.* **1** make or become nervous or confused —*n.* **2** confused or agitated state

flute /floōt/ *n.* **1** high-pitched tubelike wind instrument with fingerholes and keys **2** channel or groove —*v.* **flut'ing, flut'ist** *n.;* **flut'y** *adj.* [Fr]

FLUTE 1

flut·ter /flət'ər/ *v.* **1** flap (the wings) rapidly in flying or trying to fly **2** fall quiveringly **3** wave or flap quickly **4** (of the pulse, etc.) beat feebly or irregularly —*n.* **5** act of fluttering **6** tremulous excitement [OE]

flux /fləks/ *n.* **1** process of flowing or flowing out **2** continuous change **3** substance to aid fusion, as in soldering [L *fluxus* fr. *fluere* flow]

fly[1] /flī/ *v.* (**flew, flown, fly·ing**) **1a** move through the air under control, esp. with wings **b** move through the air or space **2** operate a flying vehicle **3** travel in a flying vehicle **4** wave or flutter **5** flee (from) **6** spring violently —*n.* (*pl.* **flies**) **7a** concealing flap, esp. over a zipper on clothing **b** this fastening **8** flap at a tent entrance **9** (*pl.*) *Theat.* space above a stage **10 fly off the handle** *Colloq.* lose one's temper [OE]

fly[2] *n.* (*pl.* **flies**) **1** insect with two usu. transparent wings **2** (esp. artificial) fly as bait in fishing **3** *Baseball.* ball batted high in the air —*v.* (**flied, fly·ing**) **4** *Baseball.* hit a fly ball [OE]

fly'-by-night' *adj.* **1** unreliable; irresponsible —*n.* **2** person who evades a debt

fly'-fish' *v.* fishing with artificial flies as bait

fly'ing *adj.* **1** fluttering, waving, or hanging loose **2** designed for rapid movement **3** (of an animal) leaping with winglike membranes, etc. —*n.* **4** flight, esp. in an aircraft **5 with flying colors** with thorough success; easily

fly'ing but'tress *n.* (usu. arched) supporting piece from the outside of a wall extending out and down to the ground

fly'ing fish' *n.* fish with winglike fins for gliding through the water

fly'ing sau'cer *n.* supposed alien spaceship; UFO

fly'leaf' *n.* blank leaf at the beginning or end of a book

fly'pa'per *n.* sticky paper for catching flies

fly'weight' *n.* *Sports.* weight class for competitors; in professional boxing, includes fighters up to 112 lbs.

fly'wheel' *n.* weighted wheel on a revolving shaft to regulate machinery or accumulate power

Fm *symb.* fermium

FM *abbr.* frequency modulation

f-num·ber *n. Photog.* ratio of the focal length to the effective diameter of a lens [fr. focal number]

foal /fōl/ *n.* **1** young of a horse or related animal —*v.* **2** give birth to (a foal) [OE]

foam /fōm/ *n.* **1** mass of small bubbles formed on or in liquid **2** froth of saliva or sweat **3** substance light or spongelike in tex-

ture —*v.* **4** emit or run with foam; froth —**foam'y** *adj.* (**·i·er, ·i·est**) [OE]

fob[1] /fäb/ *n.* **1** chain of a pocket watch **2** small pocket **3** ornament on a watch chain, etc. [Ger]

fob[2] *v.* (**fobbed, fob·bing**) as in **fob off** deceive into accepting something inferior [cf. obs. *fop* dupe]

fo·cal /fō'kəl/ *adj.* of or at a focus [L, rel. to FOCUS]

fo'cal length' *n.* distance between the center of a lens and its point of focus

fo'cal point' *n.* **1** FOCUS, 1 **2** center of interest or activity

Foch /fôsн/, **Ferdinand** 1851–1929; French general

fo'c's'le /fōk'səl/ *n.* var. of FORECASTLE

fo·cus /fō'kəs/ *n.* (*pl.* **·cus·es** or **·ci** /fō'sī'/) **1** point at which rays or waves meet after reflection or refraction **2a** point at which an object must be situated for a lens or mirror to give a well-defined image **b** adjustment of the eye or a lens to give a clear image **c** state of clear definition **3** FOCAL POINT —*v.* (**·cused** or **·cussed, cus·ing** or **cus·sing**) **4** bring into focus **5** adjust the focus of (a lens or eye) **6** concentrate or be concentrated on [L: hearth]

fo'cus group' *n.* group meeting to discuss a particular issue, problem, etc.

fod·der /fäd'ər/ *n.* dried hay, straw, etc., as animal food [OE]

foe /fō/ *n.* enemy [OE]

fog /fôg, fäg/ *n.* **1** cloud of water droplets or smoke suspended at or near the earth's surface **2** uncertain or confused position or state —*v.* (**fogged, fog·ging**) **3** cover or become covered with or as with fog [perh. a back formation fr. FOGGY]

fo·gey /fō'gē/ *n.* var. of FOGY

fog·gy /fō'gē, fäg'ē/ *adj.* (**·gi·er, ·gi·est**) **1** full of fog **2** of or like fog **3** vague; indistinct —**fog'gi·ness** *n.* [perh. fr. Scand *fogg* long grass]

fog'horn' *n.* horn warning ships in fog

fo·gy /fō'gē/ *n.* (also **fo'gey**) (*pl.* **·gies** or **·geys**) dull old-fashioned person

foi·ble /foi'bəl/ *n.* minor weakness or idiosyncrasy [Fr, rel. to FEEBLE]

foil[1] /foil/ *v.* frustrate; baffle; defeat [perh. fr. Fr *fouler* trample]

foil[2] *n.* **1** very thin sheet of metal **2** person or thing setting off another by contrast [L *folium* leaf]

foil[3] *n.* light blunt fencing sword

foist /foist/ *v.* force (a thing or oneself) on an unwilling person [Du *vuisten* take in the hand]

Fo·kine /fōk'yin, fōkēn'/, **Michel** 1880–1942; Russian-born US dancer and choreographer

fold[1] /fōld/ *v.* **1** bend or close (a flexible thing) over upon itself **2** become or be able to be folded **3** make compact by folding **4** enfold **5** bring together or clasp (the arms) **6** fail; cease operation —*n.* **7** crease made by folding **8** folded part [OE]

fold[2] *n.* **1** enclosure for sheep **2** religious group or congregation [OE]

-fold *suffix* forming adjectives and adverbs from cardinal numbers, meaning: **1** in an amount multiplied by (*repaid tenfold*) **2** with so many parts (*threefold blessing*) [orig. 'folded in so many layers']

fold′er *n.* 1 folding cover or holder for papers 2 folding brochure, leaflet, etc.

fo·li·age /fō′l(ē)ij/ *n.* leaves; leafage [Fr *feuillage* fr. *feuille* leaf]

fo·li·o /fō′lēō/ *n.* (*pl.* -os) 1 leaf of paper, esp. numbered only on the front 2 sheet of paper folded once making two leaves of a book 3 page number 4 book size, about 12 by 15 inches [fr. L *folium* leaf]

folk /fōk/ *n.* (*pl.* same or -s) 1 (treated as *pl.*) people in general or of a specified class (*townsfolk*) 2 (*pl.*) one's parents or relatives 3 (treated as *sing.*) a people or nation 4 (*pl.*) common people 5 of popular origin (*folk art*) [OE]

folk′ dance′ *n.* dance of popular origin

folk′lore′ *n.* 1 traditional beliefs and stories of a people 2 the study of these

folk′ song′ *n.* song of popular or traditional origin or style —**folk′ sing′er** *n.*

folk·sy /fōk′sē/ *adj.* (-si·er, -si·est) 1 of or like folk art, culture, etc. 2 friendly; unpretentious —**folk′si·ness** *n.*

folk′ tale′ *n.* 1 traditional story 2 false or inventive story

fol·li·cle /fäl′ikəl/ *n.* small sac or vesicle in the body, esp. one containing a hair root [L dim. of *follis* bellows]

fol·low /fäl′ō/ *v.* 1 go or come after (a person or thing ahead) 2 go along (a road, etc.) 3 come after in order or time 4 take as a guide or leader 5 conform to 6 practice (a trade or profession) 7 understand 8 take an interest in 9 provide with a sequel or successor 10a be necessarily true as a consequence b result 11 **follow through: a** continue to a conclusion **b** continue the movement of a stroke after hitting a ball 12 **follow up: a** develop b investigate further [OE]

fol′low·er *n.* 1 supporter or devotee 2 person who follows

fol′low·ing *prep.* 1 after in time; as a sequel to —*n.* 2 supporters or devotees —*adj.* 3 that follows or comes after

fol′low-through′ *n.* action of following through

fol′low-up′ *n.* subsequent or continued action

fol·ly /fäl′ē/ *n.* (*pl.* -lies) 1 foolishness 2 foolish act, behavior, idea, etc. [Fr *folie* fr. *fol* mad; FOOL]

fo·ment /fō′ment′, fōment′/ *v.* instigate or stir up (trouble, discontent, etc.) —**fo′men·ta′tion** /-tā′sнən/ *n.* [LL *fomentare* fr. L *fovere* heat]

fond /fänd/ *adj.* 1 cherished 2 affectionate 3 fond of having a liking for —**fond′ly** *adv.*; **fond′ness** *n.* [obs. *fon* fool; be foolish]

Fon·da /fänd′ə/ family of US actors, including: 1 **Henry** 1905–82; his daughter: 2 **Jane** 1937–

fon·dle /fän′dəl/ *v.* (-dled, -dling) caress [rel. to FOND]

fon·due /fänd(y)o͞o′/ *n.* dish of melted cheese, etc., for dipping [Fr: melted, rel. to FUSE[1]]

font[1] /fänt/ *n.* receptacle for baptismal water [L *fons fontis* fountain]

font[2] *n.* set of printing type of same face and size

fon·ta·nel /fänt′ənel′/ *n.* (also **fon′ta·nelle′**) membranous space in an infant's skull at the angles of the parietal bones [L *fontanella* little FOUNTAIN]

Fon·teyn /fäntān′/, (**Dame**) **Margot** (born **Margaret Hookham**) 1919–91; English prima ballerina

food /fo͞od/ *n.* 1a substance ingested to maintain life and growth **b** solid food 2 mental stimulus (*food for thought*) [OE]

food′ chain′ *n.* series of organisms each dependent on the next for food

food′ pro′ces·sor *n.* machine for chopping and mixing food

food′ stamp′ *n.* government coupon redeemable for groceries by the needy

food′stuff′ *n.* substance used as food

fool /fo͞ol/ *n.* 1 rash, unwise, or stupid person 2 *Hist.* jester; clown 3 dupe —*v.* 4 deceive 5 trick; cheat 6 joke or tease 7 play or trifle [L *follis* bellows]

fool′har′dy *adj.* (-di·er, -di·est) rashly or foolishly bold; reckless —**fool′har′di·ly** *adv.*; **fool′har′di·ness** *n.*

fool·ish /fo͞o′lish/ *adj.* lacking good sense or judgment; unwise —**fool′ish·ly** *adv.*; **fool′ish·ness** *n.*

fool′proof′ *adj.* (of a procedure, mechanism, etc.) incapable of misuse or mistake

fools·cap /fo͞olz′kap′/ *n.* inexpensive writing paper, usu. 8-1/2 by 14 inches, bound as a pad [fr. a watermark of a *fool's cap*]

foot /fo͞ot/ *n.* (*pl.* **feet**) 1a part of the leg below the ankle **b** part of a sock, etc., covering this 2 lowest or endmost part 3 step or pace (*fleet of foot*) 4 (*pl.* **feet** or **foot**) measure of length (12 inches) 5 metrical unit of verse —*v.* 6 pay (a bill) 7 **have one's** (*or* **feet on the ground**) be practical 8 **on foot** walking 9 **put one's foot down** *Colloq.* insist firmly [OE]

foot·age /fo͞ot′ij/ *n.* 1 length in feet 2 a length of videotape, film, etc., ready for presentation

foot′-and-mouth′ dis·ease′ *n.* contagious viral disease of cattle, etc.

foot′ball′ *n.* 1 team game played with an inflated oval ball 2 ball used in this —**foot′ball·er** *n.*

foot′bridge′ *n.* bridge for pedestrians

foot′fall′ *n.* sound of a footstep

foot′hill′ *n.* any of the low hills at the base of a mountain or range

foot′hold′ *n.* 1 secure place for a foot when climbing, etc. 2 secure initial position

foot′ing *n.* 1 foothold; secure position 2 operational basis 3 relative position or status

foot′less *adj.* 1 having no foot or feet 2 having no base —**foot′less·ly** *adv.*; **foot′less·ness** *n.*

foot·lights /fo͞ot′līts′/ *n. pl.* floor-level lights at the front of a stage

foot′lock·er *n.* small trunk, often kept at the foot of a bed

foot′loose′ *adj.* free to act as one pleases

foot′note′ *n.* note printed at the foot of a page

foot′path′ *n.* path for pedestrians

foot′print′ *n.* 1 impression left by a foot or shoe 2 surface area, as of a desk occupied by a computer, printer, etc.

foot'step' *n.* **1** step taken in walking **2** footfall **3** follow in a person's footsteps do as another did before

foot'stool' *n.* stool for resting the feet on when sitting

foot'wear' *n.* shoes, socks, etc.

foot'work' *n.* use or agility of the feet in sports, dancing, etc.

fop /fäp/ *n.* dandy —**fop'per·y** *n.*; **fop'pish** *adj.* [perh. fr. obs. *fop* fool]

for /fôr, far/ *prep.* **1** in the interest or to the benefit of; intended to go to (*for your own good*) **2** in defense, support, or favor of (*vote for the issue*) **3** suitable or appropriate to (*a dance for beginners*) **4** with regard to (*ready for bed*) **5** representing or in place of (*acting for my client*) **6** in exchange with; at the price of; corresponding to (*sold for $5; word for word*) **7** as a consequence of (*fined for speeding*) **8a** with a view to; in the hope or quest of (*did it for the money*) **b** on account of (*could not speak for laughing*) **9** to reach; toward (*left for Rome*) **10** through or over (a distance or period) **11** as being (*for the last time*) **12** in spite of (*nothing to show for it*) **13** considering; in the case of (*good for a beginner*) —*conj.* **14** because; since [OE, reduced form of FORE]

for- *prefix* forming verbs, etc., meaning: **1** away; off (*forswear*) **2** prohibition (*forbid*) **3** abstention or neglect (*forgo*) [OE]

for·age /fôr'ij, fär'-/ *n.* **1** food for horses or cattle **2** searching for food —*v.* **3** search for food; rummage **4** collect food from [Gmc, rel. to FODDER]

for·ay /fôr'ā', fär'-/ *n.* **1** sudden attack; raid —*v.* **2** make a foray [Fr, rel. to FORAGE]

for·bade /fôrbad'/ *v.* (also **for·bad'**) *past of* FORBID

for·bear' /fôrber'/ *v.* (·**bore**, ·**borne**, ·**bearing**) *Formal.* abstain or desist (from) [OE, rel. to BEAR¹]

for·bear² *v.* var. of FOREBEAR

for·bear·ance /fôrber'əns/ *n.* patient self-control; tolerance

for·bid /farbid'/ *v.* (·**bade** or ·**bad**, ·**bid·den**, ·**bid·ding**) **1** order (someone) not (to do something) **2** refuse to allow [OE, rel. to BID]

for·bid'ding *adj.* stern; threatening —**for·bid'ding·ly** *adv.*

for·bore /fôrbôr'/ *v. past of* FORBEAR¹

for·borne /fôrbôrn'/ *v. past part. of* FORBEAR¹

force /fôrs/ *n.* **1** power; strength; impetus; intense effort **2** coercion; compulsion **3a** military strength **b** organized body of soldiers, police, etc. **4a** moral, intellectual, or legal power, influence, or validity **b** person, etc., with such power **5** influence tending to cause a change in the motion of a body —*v.* (**forced**, **forc·ing**) **6** compel or coerce **7** break open or into by force **8** drive or propel violently or against resistance **9** impose or press on (a person) **10** cause, produce, or attain by effort (*forced a smile*) **11** strain or increase to the utmost **12** in force: a valid **b** in great strength or numbers [L *fortis* strong]

force'-feed' *v.* (·**fed**, ·**feed·ing**) force to take food

force·ful /fôrs'fəl/ *adj.* vigorous; powerful; impressive —**force'ful·ly** *adv.*; **force'ful·ness** *n.*

for·ceps /fôr'seps', -səps/ *n.* (*pl.* same) surgical pincers [L]

FORCEPS

for·ci·ble /fôr'səbəl/ *adj.* done by or involving force; forceful —**for'ci·bly** *adv.* [Fr, rel. to FORCE, 1]

ford /fôrd/ *n.* **1** shallow water crossing, as in a river —*v.* **2** cross (water) at a ford —**ford'a·ble** *adj.* [OE]

Ford /fôrd/ **1 Henry** 1863–1947; US automobile manufacturer **2 Ford Madox** (born **Ford Hermann Hueffer**) 1873–1939; English novelist **3 John** (born **Sean O'Feeney**) 1895–1973; US film director **4 Gerald R(udolph)** 1913– ; 38th US president (1974–77)

fore /fôr/ *adj.* **1** situated in front —*n.* **2** front part; bow of a ship —*interj.* **3** *Golf.* warning to players ahead [OE]

fore- *prefix* forming: **1** verbs meaning: **a** in front (*foreshorten*) **b** beforehand (*forewarn*) **2** nouns meaning: **a** in front of (*forecourt*) **b** front part of (*forehead*)

fore' and aft' *adj.* (of a sail or rigging) lengthwise

fore'arm' *n.* the arm from the elbow to the wrist or fingertips

fore·bear /fôr'ber'/ *n.* (also **for'bear'**) (usu. *pl.*) ancestor [fr. FORE + obs. *beer*, rel. to BE]

fore·bode /fôrbōd'/ *v.* (·**bod·ed**, ·**bod·ing**) **1** be an advance sign of; portend **2** have a premonition of (usu. evil)

fore·bod'ing *n.* expectation of trouble

fore'cast' *v.* (·**cast** or ·**cast·ed**, **cast·ing**) **1** predict —*n.* **2** prediction, esp. of weather —**fore'cast'er** *n.*

fore·cas·tle /fōk'səl/ *n.* (also **fo'c's'le**) forward part of a ship

fore·close /fôrklōz'/ *v.* (·**closed**, ·**clos·ing**) **1** stop (a mortgage) from being redeemable; repossess when a loan is not duly repaid **2** exclude —**fore·clo'sure** /-klō'zhər/ *n.* [OFr *fors* outside + CLOSE²]

fore'fa'ther *n.* ancestor

fore'fin'ger *n.* finger next to the thumb

fore'foot' *n.* front foot of an animal

fore'front' *n.* **1** leading position **2** foremost part

fore·go' *v.* (·**went**, ·**gone**, ·**go·ing**) var. of FORGO

fore·go'ing *adj.* preceding

fore·gone' con·clu'sion *n.* easily predictable result

fore'ground' *n.* **1** area nearest the observer **2** most conspicuous position

fore'hand' *n.* **1** (in tennis, etc.) stroke played with the palm of the hand facing forward **2** of or made with a forehand

fore·head /fär'əd, fôr'əd; fôr'hed'/ *n.* the part of the face above the eyebrows

● Usage: Traditionally, the word is pronounced with the stress on the first syllable and with the *h* silent, as it is still by many, especially older speakers. But the pronunciation in which *head* is made more apparent, with *h* sounded and the secondary stress, is very common.

for·eign /fôr'ən, fär'-/ *adj.* 1 of, from, in, or characteristic of a country or language other than one's own. 2 dealing with other countries (*foreign service*) 3 unfamiliar; alien 4 coming from outside (*foreign body*) —**for'eign·ness** *n.* [L *foris* outside]

for·eign·er *n.* person born in or coming from another country

fore'leg' *n.* front leg of an animal

fore'lock' *n.* lock of hair just above the forehead

fore·man /fôr'mən/ *n.* (*pl.* ·men) 1 worker supervising others 2 presiding juror in a legal trial

fore'mast' *n.* mast nearest the bow of a ship

fore'most' *adj.* 1 most notable; best 2 first; front —*adv.* 3 most importantly (*first* and *foremost*) [OE]

fo·ren·sic /fəren'sik, -zik/ *adj.* 1 of or used in courts of law 2 of or involving the use of scientific examinaion in compiling legal evidence —**fo·ren'si·cal·ly** *adv.* [L *forensis*, rel. to FORUM]

fore'play' *n.* stimulation preceding sexual intercourse

fore'run'ner *n.* 1 predecessor 2 herald

fore·sail /fôr'sāl', -səl/ *n.* principal sail on a foremast

fore·see' *v.* (·saw, ·seen, ·see·ing) see or be aware of beforehand —**fore·see'a·ble** *adj.*

fore·shad'ow *v.* be a warning or indication of (a future event)

fore·short'en *v.* show or portray with shortened visual perspective

fore'sight' *n.* 1 regard or provision for the future 2 foreseeing

fore'skin' *n.* fold of skin covering the end of the penis

for·est /fôr'əst, fär'-/ *n.* 1 large area of trees and undergrowth —*v.* 2 plant with trees —**for'est·er** *n.* [L *forestis*, rel. to FOREIGN]

fore·stall /fôrstôl'/ *v.* prevent by advance action; anticipate [fr. FORE- + STALL¹]

for·est·ry /fôr'əstrē, fär'-/ *n.* science or management of forests

fore'taste' *n.* small preliminary experience of something

fore·tell' *v.* (·told, ·tell·ing) predict; prophesy

fore'thought' *n.* 1 care or provision for the future 2 deliberate intention

for·ev'er *adv.* always; continually; persistently

fore·warn' *v.* warn beforehand

fore'wom·an *n.* (*pl.* ·wom'en) 1 female worker supervising others 2 jury spokeswoman

fore·word /fôr'wərd/ *n.* introductory remarks in a book, often not by the author

for·feit /fôr'fit/ *n.* 1 penalty 2 thing surrendered as a penalty —*adj.* 3 lost or surrendered as a penalty —*v.* 4 lose the right to or surrender as a penalty —**for'fei·ture**

/-fəchər/ *n.* [Fr *forfaire* transgress, fr. L *foris* outside + *facere* DO]

for·gath·er /fôrgaTH'ər/ *v.* assemble; associate [Du]

for·gave /fôrgāv'/ *v. past of* FORGIVE

forge¹ /fôrj/ *v.* (forged, forg·ing) 1 make or write in fraudulent imitation 2 shape (metal) by heating and hammering —*n.* 3 furnace or workshop for melting or refining metal —**forg'er** *n.* [fr. OFr *forgier* fr. L *fabricare*, rel. to FABRIC]

forge² *v.* (forged, forg·ing) 1 move forward gradually or steadily 2 **forge ahead:** a take the lead b strive and progress [perh. alter. of FORCE, 1]

forg·er·y /fôr'jərē/ *n.* (*pl.* ·ies) 1 act of forging 2 forged document, etc.

for·get /fôrget'/ *v.* (·got, ·got·ten or ·got, ·get·ting) 1 lose remembrance of 2 neglect; overlook 3 cease to think of —**for·get'ta·ble** *adj.* [OE]

for·get·ful /fôrget'fəl/ *adj.* 1 apt to forget; absent-minded 2 neglectful —**for·get'ful·ly** *adj.*; **for·get'ful·ness** *n.*

for·get'-me-not' *n.* plant with small blue flowers

for·give /fôrgiv'/ *v.* (·gave, ·giv·en, ·giv·ing) cease to feel angry or resentful toward; pardon —**for·giv'a·ble** *adj.*; **for·give'ness** *n.* [OE]

for·giv'ing *adj.* inclined to forgive

for·go /fôrgō'/ *v.* (also **fore·go'**) (·went, ·gone, ·go·ing) go without; relinquish [OE]

for·got /fôrgät'/ *v. past of* FORGET

for·got'ten *v. past part. of* FORGET

fork /fôrk/ *n.* 1 pronged implement for use in eating 2 similar tool used for digging, lifting, etc. 3a divergence of a branch, road, etc., into two parts b place of this c either part —*v.* 4 diverge into two parts 5 serve, dig, lift, etc., with a fork 6 **fork out** *Slang.* pay, esp. reluctantly [L *furca* pitchfork]

fork'lift truck' *n.* vehicle with prongs for lifting and carrying loads

for·lorn /fərlôrn'/ *adj.* 1 sad and abandoned 2 in a pitiful state —**for·lorn'ly** *adv.* [FOR- + *lorn* past part. of obs. *leese* LOSE]

form /fôrm/ *n.* 1 shape; arrangement of parts; visible aspect 2 person or animal as visible or tangible 3 mode of existence or manifestation 4 kind or variety 5 document to be filled in 6 correct procedure 7a athletic or performing condition or technique b beauty or perfection of execution 8 state or disposition (*in great form*) 9 any of the spellings, inflections, etc., of a word 10 arrangement; style —*v.* 11 make or be made 12 make up; constitute 13 develop or establish 14 mold or organize to become (*form a circle*) —**form'less** *adj.*; **form'less·ly** *adv.*; **form'less·ness** *n.* [L *forma*]

-form *comb. form* forming adjectives meaning 'having the form of' (*cruciform*)

for·mal /fôr'məl/ *adj.* 1 in accordance with rules, convention, or ceremony 2 precise or symmetrical (*formal garden*) 3 prim; stiff 4 explicit or official (*formal agreement*) —**for'mal·ly** *adv.* [L, rel. to FORM]

form·al·de·hyde /fôrmal'dəhīd'/ *n.* colorless pungent gas used in solution as a disinfectant and preservative [fr. *formic acid* + *aldehyde*]

for·mal·ism *n.* strict adherence to external

form without regard to content, esp. in art —for'mal·ist /-ist/ n.

221

formality / fossil

for·mal·i·ty /fôrmal'ətē/ n. (pl. ·ties) 1a formal, esp. meaningless, procedure or custom b thing done simply to comply with a rule 2 rigid observance of rules or convention

for'mal·ize v. (·ized, ·iz·ing) 1 give definite form to 2 make formal —for'mal·i·za'tion n.

for·mat /fôr'mat'/ n. 1 shape and size (of a book, etc.) 2 style or arrangement —v. (·mat·ed or ·mat·ted, ·mat·ing or ·mat·ting) 3 arrange or put into a format [L formatus shaped, rel. to FORM]

for·ma·tion /fôrmā'SHən/ n. 1 forming 2 thing formed 3 particular arrangement (e.g., of troops) [L, rel. to FORM]

for·ma·tive /fôr'mətiv/ adj. serving to form or fashion

for·mer /fôr'mər/ attrib. adj. 1 of the past; earlier; previous 2 (the former) the first or first-mentioned of two [rel. to FOREMOST]

• Usage: When two previously listed items are referred to, the one that was said first is the former, the one that comes next is the latter: Having an atlas and a dictionary, I keep the former in the bookcase and the latter on my desk. If there are three or more, first, second, and last should be used, even if all are not mentioned: Of the atlas, thesaurus, and dictionary, I find the last most useful.

for'mer·ly adv. in former times

For·mi·ca /fôrmī'kə/ n. Tdmk. durable plastic laminate used for surfaces

for·mi·da·ble /fôrmid'əbəl, fôr'mid-/ adj. 1 inspiring dread, awe, or respect 2 hard to overcome or deal with —for'mi·da·bly adv. [L formidare fear]

for·mu·la /fôr'myələ/ n. (pl. ·las or ·lae /-lē', -lī'/) 1 chemical symbols showing constituents of a substance 2 mathematical rule expressed in symbols 3 fixed form of esp. ceremonial or polite words 4 list of ingredients 5 liquid, prepared baby food —for'mu·la'ic /-lā'ik/ adj. [L, dim. of forma FORM]

for·mu·late /fôr'myəlāt'/ v. (·lat·ed, ·lat·ing) 1 express in a formula 2 express precisely —for'mu·la'tion n.

for·ni·cate /fôr'nikāt'/ v. (·cat·ed, ·cat·ing) (of an unmarried couple) have sexual intercourse —for'ni·ca'tion, for'ni·ca'tor n. [L fornix brothel]

for·sake /fôrsāk', fər-/ v. (·sook, ·sak·en, ·sak·ing) 1 give up; renounce 2 desert; abandon [OE]

for·sooth /fərsooTH'/ adv. Archaic or Joc. indeed [OE, rel. to FOR + SOOTH]

For·ster /fôr'stər/, E(dward) M(organ) 1879–1970; English novelist

for·swear /fôrswer'/ v. (·swore, ·sworn, ·swear·ing) 1 renounce 2 commit perjury [OE]

For·syth /fôr'sīTH', fôrsīTH'/, Frederick 1938– ; English novelist

for·syth·i·a /fərsiTH'ēə/ n. shrub with bright yellow flowers in early spring [Forsyth, name of a botanist]

fort /fôrt/ n. fortified military building or position [L fortis strong]

For·ta·le·za /fôrt'əlā'zə/ n. seaport in Brazil. Pop. 648,800

Fort Col·lins /käl'inz/ n. city in Colo. Pop. 87,758

forte¹ /fôrt, fôr'tā'/ n. person's strong point or specialty [fem. of Fr FORT]

for·te² /fôr'tā', fôrtē'/ adj. & adv. Mus. loud(ly) [It, rel. to FORT]

forth /fôrTH/ adv. Archaic. 1 forward; into view (come forth) 2 onward in time (from this time forth) [OE]

forth·com'ing adj. 1 coming or available soon 2 produced when wanted 3 (of a person) candid

forth'right adj. outspoken; straightforward [OE]

forth·with' /fôrTHwiTH', -wiTH'/ adv. without delay [fr. FORTH]

for·ti·fy /fôrt'əfī'/ v. (·fied, ·fy·ing) 1 provide with military defense 2 strengthen physically, mentally, or morally 3 strengthen (wine) with alcohol 4 increase the nutritive value of (food, esp. with vitamins) —for'ti·fi·ca'tion /-fikā'SHən/, for'ti·fi'er n. [L fortis strong]

for·tis·si·mo /fôrtis'əmō'/ adj. & adv. Mus. very loud(ly) [It, superl. of FORTE²]

for·ti·tude /fôrt'ət(y)ood'/ n. courage in trouble or pain [L fortis strong]

Fort Lau·der·dale /lôd'ərdāl'/ n. city in Fla. Pop. 149,377

fort·night /fôrt'nīt'/ n. (esp. Brit.) two weeks —fort'night'ly adj. & adv. [OE: fourteen nights]

for·tress /fôr'tris/ n. fortified building or town [L fortis strong]

for·tu·i·tous /fôrt(y)oo'ətəs/ adj. happening by, esp. lucky, chance; accidental —for·tu'i·tous·ly adv.; for·tu'i·tous·ness n.; for·tu'i·ty /-ətē/ n. (pl. ·ties) [L forte by chance]

for·tu·nate /fôr'CHənət/ adj. 1 lucky 2 auspicious —for'tu·nate·ly adv. [L fortunatus, rel. to FORTUNE]

for·tune /fôr'CHən/ n. 1a chance or luck in human affairs b person's destiny 2 luck that befalls a person or enterprise 3 good luck 4 amassing of wealth; riches [L fortuna]

for'tune-tell'er n. person who claims to foretell one's destiny —for'tune-tell'ing n.

Fort Wayne /wān/ n. city in Ind. Pop. 173,072

Fort Worth /wərTH'/ n. city in Texas. Pop. 447,619

for·ty /fôr'tē/ adj. & n. (pl. ·ties) 1 four times ten 2 symbol for this (40, xl, XL) 3 (pl.) numbers from 40 to 49, esp. as years —for'ti·eth /-ith/ adj. & n. [OE, rel. to FOUR]

fo·rum /fôr'əm/ n. 1 place, agency, or meeting for public discussion 2 public square in an ancient Roman city [L]

for·ward /fôr'wərd/ adj. 1 onward; toward the front; ahead 2 bold; presumptuous 3 relating to the future (forward contract) —n. 4 Sports. player positioned near the opponent's goal —adv. 5 to the front; into prominence 6 in advance; ahead 7 onward 8a (also forwards) toward the front in the direction one is facing b in the normal direction of motion —v. 9 send (a letter, etc.) on to a further destination 10 help to advance; promote [OE, rel. to FORTH + -WARD]

for·went /fôrwent'/ v. past of FORGO

fos·sil /fäs'əl/ n. 1 remains or impression of

a (usu. prehistoric) plant or animal hardened in rock 2 *Colloq.* antiquated or unchanging person or thing —*adj.* 3 of or like a fossil; antiquated —**fos′sil·ize** /-īz/ *v.* (·ized, ·iz·ing); **fos′sil·i·za′tion** *n.* [L *fossilis* dug up]

fos′sil fu′el *n.* natural fuel extracted from the ground

fos·ter /fôs′tər, fäs′-/ *v.* 1a promote the growth or development of b encourage or harbor (a feeling) 2 bring up (another's child) 3 (of circumstances) be favorable to —*adj.* 4 having a family connection by fostering (*foster brother*) 5 concerned with fostering a child (*foster care*) [OE, rel. to FOOD]

Fos·ter /fô′stər, fäs′tər/, **Stephen** 1826–64; US composer

Fou·cault /fōōkō′/, **Michel** 1929–84; French philosopher

fought /fôt/ *v.* past and past part. of FIGHT

foul /foul/ *adj.* 1 offensive; loathsome; stinking 2 soiled; filthy 3 noxious 4 obscenely abusive 5 against the rules 6 (of the weather) rough; stormy —*n.* 7 *Sports.* ball, play, etc., that goes against the rules set —*adv.* 8 unfairly —*v.* 9 make or become foul 10 *Sports.* commit a foul against (a player) 11 (cause to) become entangled or blocked 12 bungle —**foul′ly** *adv.*; **foul′ness** *n.* [OE]

foul′mouthed′ *adj.* using obscene or offensive language

foul′ play′ *n.* 1 treacherous or violent act, esp. murder 2 unfair play in games

foul′-up′ *n.* muddle; bungle

found[1] /found/ *v.* past and past part. of FIND

found[2] *v.* 1 establish; initiate; originate 2 construct or base (a story, theory, rule, etc.) on —**found′er** *n.* [L *fundus* bottom]

found[3] *v.* 1a melt and mold (metal) b fuse (materials for glass) 2 make by founding —**found′er** *n.* [L *fundere* pour]

foun·da·tion /foundā′sʜən/ *n.* 1a solid ground or base beneath a building b lowest part of a building 2 material base 3 basis; underlying principle 4a establishment (esp. of an endowed institution) b college, hospital, etc., so founded [L, rel. to FOUND[2]]

found·er /foun′dər/ *v.* 1 (of a ship) fill with water and sink 2 (of a plan, etc.) fail 3 (of a horse or its rider) stumble; fall lame [rel. to FOUND[2]]

found·ling /found′liɴɢ/ *n.* abandoned infant of unknown parentage [rel. to FIND]

found·ry /foun′drē/ *n.* (*pl.* ·ries) workshop for or business of casting metal

fount /fount/ *n. Poet.* spring or fountain; source [back formation fr. FOUNTAIN]

foun·tain /fount′n/ *n.* 1a spouting jet or jets of water as an ornament or for drinking b structure for this 2 spring 3 source [L *fontana* fr. *fons fontis* spring]

foun′tain pen′ *n.* pen with a split nib and reservoir for ink

four /fôr/ *adj.* & *n.* 1 one more than three 2 symbol for this (4, iv, IV) 3 **on all fours** on hands and knees [OE]

four′fold′ *adj.* & *adv.* 1 four times as much or as many 2 of four parts

four′-let′ter word′ *n.* obscene word, esp. of four letters

four·some /fôr′səm/ *n.* group of four people

four′square′ *adj.* 1 solidly based 2 steady; resolute —*adv.* 3 steadily; resolutely

four·teen /fôr(t)tēn′/ *adj.* & *n.* 1 one more than thirteen 2 symbol for this (14, xiv, XIV) —**four′teenth′** *adj.* & *n.* [OE, rel. to FOUR + -TEEN]

fourth /fôrth/ *adj.* & *n.* 1 next after third 2 any of four equal parts of a thing —**fourth′ly** *adv.* [OE, rel. to FOUR]

fourth′ di·men′sion *n.* time, considered as a dimension along with length, width, and depth

fourth′ es·tate′ *n.* journalism; journalists collectively

Fourth′ of Ju·ly′ *n.* INDEPENDENCE DAY

four′-wheel′ drive′ *n.* system transferring power to all four wheels of a vehicle

fowl /foul/ *n.* (*pl.* same or -s) 1 domestic birds, esp. chicken, kept for eggs and meat 2 flesh of these birds as food 3 any bird [OE]

Fowles /foulz/, **John** 1926– ; English novelist

fox /fäks/ *n.* 1a wild canine animal with a bushy tail and red or gray fur b its fur 2 cunning person —*v.* 3 deceive; trick [OE]

Fox /fäks/, **George** 1624–91; English founder of the Society of Friends (Quakers)

foxed /fäkst/ *adj.* (of book pages) discolored with brown spots, esp. from age

fox′glove′ *n.* tall plant with purple or white flowers like glove fingers

fox′hole′ *n.* hole in the ground dug as a shelter, etc., in battle

fox′hound′ *n.* hound bred and trained to hunt foxes

fox′ ter′ri·er *n.* a kind of shorthaired terrier

fox′trot′ *n.* 1 ballroom dance with slow and quick steps 2 music for this —*v.* (·trot·ted, ·trot·ting) 3 perform this

fox′y *adj.* (·i·er, ·i·est) 1 foxlike; sly; cunning 2 *Slang.* attractive; sexy —**fox′i·ly** *adv.*; **fox′i·ness** *n.*

foy·er /foi′ər, foi′ā′/ *n.* entrance hall in a hotel, theater, etc. [Fr: hearth; home; fr. L FOCUS]

FPO *abbr.* (on mail to service personnel) fleet (or field) post office

fps (also **f.p.s.**) *abbr.* 1 feet per second 2 foot-pound-second 3 frames per second

Fr *symb.* francium

fr. *abbr.* 1 fragment 2 franc 3 from

Fr. *abbr.* 1 Father 2 French

fra·cas /frā′kəs, frak′əs/ *n.* noisy disturbance or quarrel [Fr fr. It]

frac·tion /frak′sʜən/ *n.* 1 part of a whole number (e.g., 1/2, 0.5) 2 small part, piece, or amount —**frac′tion·al** *adj.*; **frac′tion·al·ly** *adv.* [L *fraction-* fr. *frangere* break]

frac·tious /frak′sʜəs/ *adj.* irritable; peevish [fr. FRACTION in obs. sense 'brawling']

frac·ture /frak′ʜʜər/ *n.* 1 breakage, esp. of a bone —*v.* (·tured, ·tur·ing) 2 cause or suffer a fracture in [L, rel. to FRACTION]

frag·ile /fraj′əl, -īl/ *adj.* 1 easily broken 2 delicate —**fra·gil′i·ty** /-jil′ətē/ *n.* [L, rel. to FRACTURE]

frag·ment /frag′mənt/ *n.* 1 part broken off 2 incomplete portion (of a book, etc.) —*v.* 3 break or separate into fragments —**frag·men′tal** /-men′təl/, **frag·men·tar′y** /-mən′ter′ē/ *adj.*; **frag·men·ta′tion** /-tā′sʜən/ *n.* [L, rel. to FRACTION]

fra·grance /frā′grəns/ n. 1 sweetness of smell 2 sweet scent —**fra′grant** adj. [L *fragrare* smell sweet]

frail /frāl/ adj. 1 fragile; delicate 2 morally weak —**frail′ly** adv.; **frail′ness** n. [L, rel. to FRAGILE]

frail·ty /frāl′tē/ n. (pl. ·ties) 1 frail quality 2 weakness; foible

frame /frām/ n. 1 case or border enclosing a picture, window, door, etc. 2 basic rigid supporting structure of a building, vehicle, etc. 3 (pl.) structure of eyeglasses holding the lenses 4 human or animal body structure 5a structure; construction b order or supporting system 6 single image on film, tape, etc. 7 *Bowling.* unit of play —v. (**framed, framing**) 8a set in a frame b serve as a frame for 9 construct; devise 10 adapt; fit 11 *Slang.* concoct a false charge or evidence against; devise a plot against 12 formulate (words) [OE: be helpful]

frame′-up n. *Colloq.* conspiracy to implicate or convict an innocent person

frame′work n. 1 essential supporting structure 2 basic system; apparatus

franc /fraNGk/ n. unit of currency of France, Belgium, Switzerland, etc. [Fr, rel. to FRANK]

France /frans/ n. republic in W Europe. Capital: Paris. Pop. 57,289,000

France /frans/, **Anatole** (pseudonym of Jacques Anatole Thibault) 1844–1924; French writer

fran·chise /fran′CHīz′/ n. 1 right to vote in elections; citizenship 2 authorization to sell a company's services or goods, etc., in a particular area —v. (**·chised, ·chis·ing**) 3 grant a franchise to [Fr *franc* FRANK]

Fran·cis of As·si·si, St. /fran′sis; əsis′ē, əsē′ zē/ c. 1181–1226; Italian monk; founder of Franciscan religious order

fran·ci·um /fran′sēəm/ n. radioactive metallic element; *symb.* **Fr** [France, where first identified]

Franck /fräNGk/, **César** 1822–90; Belgian-born French composer

Fran·co- *comb. form* French [L, rel. to FRANK]

frank /fraNGk/ adj. 1 candid; outspoken 2 undisguised; open —v. 3 mark (a letter) to record the payment of postage —n. 4 franking signature or mark —**frank′ly** adv.; **frank′ness** n. [LL *francus* free, rel. to FRANK]

Frank /fraNGk/ n. member of the Germanic people that conquered Gaul in the 6th cent. —**Frank′ish** adj. [OE]

Frank /fraNGk/, **Anne** 1929–45; German-born Jewish girl, living in Amsterdam; wrote diary during Nazi occupation

Frank·en·stein /fraNG′kənstīn′/ n. thing that becomes terrifying to its maker; ill-conceived monster [name of title character in a novel by MARY SHELLEY]

Frank·fort /fraNGk′fərt/ n. capital of Ky., in the N central part. Pop. 25,968

Frank·furt (am Main) /fraNGk′fərt/ n. 1 (also Frankfurt am Main) city in Germany on the Main River. Pop. 644,900 2 city in Germany on the Oder River. Pop. 70,000

frank·furt·er /fraNGk′fərt′ər/ n. (also **frank**) seasoned smoked sausage [for FRANKFURT]

Frank·furt·er /fraNGk′fərt′ər/, **Felix** 1882–1965; Austrian-born US Supreme Court justice

frank·in·cense /fraNG′kinsens/ n. aromatic gum resin burnt as incense [Fr, rel. to FRANK in obs. sense 'high quality' + INCENSE¹]

Frank·lin /fraNG′klən/ 1 **Benjamin** 1706–90; US statesman, writer, inventor, and diplomat 2 **Aretha** 1943– ; US soul and gospel singer

fran·tic /frant′ik/ adj. hurried; anxious; desperate —**fran′ti·cal·ly** adv. [L, rel. to FRENETIC]

Franz Jo·sef I /fränz yō′zəf/ 1830–1916; emperor of Austria (1848–1916) and king of Hungary (1867–1916)

frappé /frapā′/ n. (also **frappe** /frap/) *French.* drink made with shaved ice

fra·ter·nal /frətərn′l/ adj. 1 of brothers; brotherly; comradely 2 (of twins) developed from separate ova and not identical —**fra·ter′ nal·ly** adv. [L *frater* brother]

fra·ter·ni·ty /frətər′nətē/ n. (pl. ·ties) 1 group with common interests or of the same professional class 2 male students' society 3 brotherliness [L, rel. to FRATERNAL]

frat·er·nize /frat′ərnīz′/ v. (·nized, ·niz·ing) 1 associate with 2 enter into friendly relations with enemies, etc. —**frat′er·ni·za′tion** n. [Fr and L, rel. to FRATERNAL]

frat·ri·cide /fra′trəsīd/ n. 1 killing of one's brother or sister 2 person who does this —**frat′ri·ci′dal** adj. [L, rel. to FRATERNAL]

Frau /frou/ n. (pl. **Frau·en** /frou′ən/) German form of address equivalent to *Mrs.* [Ger]

fraud /frôd/ n. 1 criminal deception 2 dishonest artifice or trick 3 impostor [L *fraus fraudis*]

fraud·u·lent /frô′jələnt/ adj. of, involving, or guilty of fraud —**fraud′u·lence** n.; **fraud′u·lent·ly** adv. [L, rel. to FRAUD]

fraught /frôt/ adj. 1 filled or charged with (danger, etc.) 2 *Colloq.* distressing; tense [Du *vracht* FREIGHT]

Fräu·lein /froi′līn/ n. German form of address for an unmarried woman [Ger]

fray¹ /frā/ v. 1 wear through or become worn; esp. (of woven material) unravel at the edge 2 become strained [L *fricare* rub]

fray² n. brawl [rel. to AFFRAY]

Fra·zer /frā′zər/, (Sir) **James George** 1854–1941; Scottish anthropologist

fraz·zle /fraz′əl/ *Colloq.* n. 1 worn, exhausted, or shriveled state —v. (·zled, ·zling) 2 wear out; exhaust

freak /frēk/ n. 1 abnormal person or thing 2a *Colloq.* unconventional person b fanatic (*health freak*) —v. *Colloq.* 3 **freak out:** a lose self-control b become irate c (cause to) undergo hallucinations, etc., esp. as a result of drug abuse —**freak′ish, freak′y** adj. (·i·er, ·i·est)

freck·le /frek′əl/ n. 1 small brown spot on the skin —v. (·led, ·ling) 2 spot or be spotted with freckles —**freck′ly** adj. [ON]

Fred·er·ick I /fred′(ə)rik/, (called "**Barbarossa**") c. 1123–90; Holy Roman emperor (1152–90)

Fred·er·ick II /fred′(ə)rik/ (called **"the Great"**) 1712–86; king of Prussia (1740–86)

Fred·er·ick Wil·liam /fred′(ə)rik wil′yəm/ (called **"the Great Elector"**) 1620–88; elector of Brandenburg (1640–88); helped consolidate Prussian power

Fred·er·ic·ton /fred′riktən/ *n.* capital of the Canadian province of New Brunswick. Pop. 46,502

free /frē/ *adj.* (**fre·er** /frē′ər/, **fre·est**) 1 not under another's control; at liberty 2 autonomous; democratic 3a unrestricted; not confined or fixed b not imprisoned c released from duties, etc. d independent; unattached 4a exempt from b not containing 5 permitted; at liberty (to) 6 costing nothing 7 not in use 8 lavish 9 frank; unreserved 10 (of literary style) informal; unmetrical 11 (of translation) not literal —*adv.* 12 in a free manner 13 without cost or payment —*v.* 14 make free; liberate 15 relieve 16 disentangle; clear —**free′ly** *adv.* [OE]

● Usage: As *free* means 'without charge,' and a *gift* is 'something given without charge,' the expression "free gift" is poor usage.

-free *comb. form* free of or from (*worry-free; duty-free*)

free·bie /frē′bē/ *n. Colloq.* thing given free of charge

free·boot·er /frē′bōō′tər/ *n.* pirate [Du *vrijbuiter*, rel. to FREE + BOOTY]

free′-born′ *adj.* not born a slave

freed·man /frēd′mən/ *n.* (*pl.* **-men**) emancipated slave

free·dom /frē′dəm/ *n.* 1 condition of being free or unrestricted 2 political or civic liberty 3 liberty of action 4 exemption from 5 unrestricted use of (a house, etc.) [OE]

free′ en′ter·prise *n.* freedom of private business from governmental control

free′ fall′ *n.* fall to earth without aid or hindrance

free′-for-all′ *n.* chaotic fight, discussion, etc.

free′hand′ *adj.* 1 (of a drawing, etc.) done without special instruments —*adv.* 2 in a freehand manner

free′hold′ *n.* 1 complete ownership of property for life 2 such land or property —**free′hold′er** *n.*

free·lance or **free-lance** /frē′lans′/ *n.* 1 (also **free′lanc′er**) person, usu. self-employed, working for several employers on particular assignments —*v.* (**·lanced, ·lanc·ing**) 2 act as a freelance —*adv.* 3 as a freelance [*free lance*, a medieval mercenary]

free·load·er /frē′lō′dər/ *n. Colloq.* person who imposes on others, as for meals —**free′load′** *v.*

free′ mar′ket *n.* market with unrestricted competition

free′ speech′ *n.* right of expression

free′-stand′ing *adj.* not supported by another structure

free′style′ *n.* 1a swimming race in which any stroke may be used b crawl stroke 2 wrestling allowing almost any hold

free′think′er *n.* person who rejects dogma or authority —**free′think′ing** *n. & adj.*

Free·town /frē′toun/ *n.* capital of Sierra Leone. Pop. 469,800

free′ trade′ *n.* trade without import restrictions, etc.

free′ verse′ *n.* verse without traditional meter or rhyme

free′way′ *n.* toll-free divided highway with controlled access

free′ will′ *n.* power of acting independently or voluntarily —**free′-will′** *adj.*

freeze /frēz/ *v.* (**froze, fro·zen, freez·ing**) 1a turn solid or into ice by cold b become rigid from the cold 2 be or feel very cold 3 cover or become covered with ice 4 chill (food) below its freezing point 5 make or become motionless through fear, surprise, etc. 6 make (assets, etc.) unavailable 7 fix (prices, wages, etc.) at a certain level 8 stop (the movement in a recorded image) —*n.* 9 period or state of frost 10 fixing or stabilization of prices, wages, etc. 11 (in full **freeze frame**) still image from film or tape [OE]

freeze′-dry′ *v.* (**·dried, ·dry·ing**) preserve (food) by freezing, then drying in a vacuum

freez′er *n.* refrigerated, insulated container for freezing and preserving food

freez′ing point′ *n.* temperature at which a liquid freezes; for water, 32° F. or 0° C.

freight /frāt/ *n.* 1 transport of goods 2 goods transported; cargo 3 charge for such transport —*v.* 4 transport as or load with freight [LGer or Du *vrecht*]

freight′er *n.* ship for carrying freight

Fre·mont /frē′mänt/ *n.* city in Calif. Pop. 173,339

Fré·mont /frē′mänt/, **John Charles** 1813–90; US explorer and politician

French /french/ *adj.* 1 of France, its people, or language 2 having French characteristics —*n.* 3 the French language 4 (the French) (*pl.*) the people of France —**French′man** /-mən/ *n.* (*pl.* **-men;** *fem.* **·wom′an,** *pl.* **·wom′en**) [OE, rel. to FRANK]

French′ bread′ *n.* long, slender bread loaf

French′ Ca·na′di·an *n.* Canadian whose principal language is French

French′ cuff′ *n.* buttonless shirtsleeve folded back and fastened with a cuff link

French′ doors′ *n.* pair of glass-paned doors for a single doorway, each hinged at one side to close in the middle

French′ dress′ing *n.* sweet, orange-colored, creamy salad dressing

French′ fries′ *n. pl.* (or **French′ fried′ po·ta′toes**) potatoes cut in strips and deep-fried

FRENCH HORN

French′ horn′ *n.* coiled brass wind instrument with a mellow tone

French′ kiss′ *n.* open-mouthed kiss

French′ leave′ *n.* departure without permission

fre·net·ic /frənet′ik/ *adj.* frantic; frenzied —**fre·net′i·cal·ly** *adv.* [Gk *phrenētikos* mad]

fren·zy /fren′zē/ *n.* (*pl.* **·zies**) wild or delirious excitement, agitation, or fury —**fren′zied** *adj.*; **fren′zied·ly** *adv.* [MedL, rel. to FRENETIC]

fre·quen·cy /frē′kwənsē/ *n.* (*pl.* **·cies**) 1 number of occurrences 2 frequent occurrence 3 rate of recurrence (of a vibration, etc.) [rel. to FREQUENT]

fre′quen·cy mod·u·la′tion *n. Radio.* modulation by varying carrier-wave frequency; *abbr.* FM

fre·quent *adj.* /frē′kwənt/ 1 occurring often or in close succession 2 habitual; constant —*v.* /frēkwent′, frē′kwent/ 3 attend or go to habitually —**fre′quent·ly** *adv.* [L *frequens frequentis* crowded]

fres·co /fres′kō/ *n.* (*pl.* **·cos**) watercolor painting done on wet plaster [It: fresh]

fresh /fresH/ *adj.* 1 newly made or obtained 2a other; different; new b additional (*fresh supplies*) 3 lately arrived 4 not stale, musty, spoiled, etc. 5 (of food) not preserved 6 not salty (*fresh water*) 7 pleasant and refreshing 8 (of wind) brisk 9 *Colloq.* impudent 10 inexperienced —*adv.* 11 newly; recently (esp. in *comb.*: *fresh-baked*) —**fresh′ly** *adv.*; **fresh′ness** *n.* [OE *fersc* and Fr *freis*]

fresh·en /fresHən/ *v.* 1 make or become fresh 2 (foll. by *up*) wash, change clothes, etc.

fresh·man /fresH′mən/ *n.* (*pl.* **·men**) first-year student, member, etc.

fresh′wa′ter *adj.* (of fish, etc.) not of the sea

Fres·no /frez′nō/ *n.* city in Calif. Pop. 354,202

fret[1] /fret/ *v.* (**fret·ted, fret·ting**) 1 be worried or distressed 2 worry; vex 3 wear or consume by gnawing or rubbing —*n.* 4 worry; vexation [OE, rel. to FOR + EAT]

fret[2] *n.* ornamental pattern of straight lines joined usu. at right angles [Fr *freter*]

FRETS[3]

fret[3] *n.* ridge on the fingerboard of a guitar, etc.

fret·ful /fret′fəl/ *adj.* anxious; irritable —**fret′ful·ly** *adv.*

fret′work *n.* ornamental design work of interlacing lines

Freud /froid/ 1 **Sigmund** 1856–1939; Austrian neurologist; founder of psychoanalysis —**Freud′i·an** *n.* & *adj.* 2 **Lucian** 1922– ; German-born British painter

Freud′i·an slip′ *n.* unintentional verbal error, thought to reveal subconscious feelings

F.R.G. *abbr.* Federal Republic of Germany

fri·a·ble /frī′əbəl/ *adj.* easily crumbled —**fri′a·bil′i·ty** *n.* [L *friare* crumble]

fri·ar /frī′ər/ *n.* male priest or monk, esp. mendicant [L *frater* brother]

fric·as·see /frik′əsē′/ *n.* 1 stewed or fried pieces of meat served in a thick sauce —*v.* (**·seed, ·see·ing**) 2 cook (meat) this way [Fr]

fric·a·tive /frik′ətiv/ *adj.* 1 (of a consonant) sounded by friction of the breath against the lips, throat, etc. (e.g., *f*, *th*) 2 such a consonant —*n.* (e.g., *f*, *th*) [L *fricare* rub]

fric·tion /frik′sHən/ *n.* 1 rubbing of one object against another 2 the resistance encountered in so moving 3 clash of personalities, opinions, etc. —**fric′tion·al** *adj.* [L, rel. to FRICATIVE]

Fri·day /frī′dā, -dē/ *n.* day of the week following Thursday; *abbr* Fri.; F [OE]

fridge /frij/ *n. Colloq.* REFRIGERATOR

Frie·dan /fridan′/, **Betty** 1921– ; US feminist and writer

Fried·man /frēd′mən/, **Milton** 1912– ; US economist

friend /frend/ *n.* 1 person one likes and socializes with 2 sympathizer; helper 3 (*cap.*) Quaker [OE]

friend′ly *adj.* (**·li·er, ·li·est**) 1 well-disposed; kindly; cordial 2 on amicable terms 3 (in *comb.*) serving or helping (*user-friendly*) —*adv.* 4 in a friendly manner —**friend′li·ness** *n.*

friend′ship′ *n.* friendly relationship or feeling

fri·er /frī′ər/ *n.* var. of FRYER

frieze /frēz/ *n. Archit.* horizontal decorative or sculpted band usu. at the top of a wall [ult. fr. L *Phrygium* (*opus*) Phrygian (work)]

frig·ate /frig′it/ *n.* naval escort vessel or light warship [Fr fr. It]

fright /frīt/ *n.* 1 sudden or extreme fear 2 instance of this (*gave me a fright*) 3 repellent-looking person or thing [OE]

fright·en /frīt′ən/ *v.* 1 fill with fright 2 repel by fright —**fright′en·ing** *adj.*; **fright′en·ing·ly** *adv.*

fright·ful /frīt′fəl/ *adj.* 1a dreadful; shocking b ugly 2 extreme —**fright′ful·ly** *adv.*

frig·id /frij′id/ *adj.* 1 freezing or very cold 2 unfriendly; cold 3 (of a woman) sexually unresponsive —**fri·gid′i·ty** *n.*; **frig′id·ly** *adv.* [L *frigus* coldness]

frill /fril/ *n.* 1 strip of gathered or pleated material as an ornamental edging 2 (*pl.*) unnecessary embellishments —**frill′y** *adj.* (**·i·er, ·i·est**)

fringe /frinj/ *n.* 1 border of tassels or loose threads 2 outer edge 3 periphery (*fringes of society*) 4 unimportant area or part —*v.* (**fringed, fring·ing**) 5 adorn with or serve as a fringe [L *fimbria*]

fringe′ ben·e·fit *n.* compensation for work additional to pay, as insurance

frip·per·y /frip′ərē/ *n.* (*pl.* **·ies**) showy finery, esp. in dress [Fr *friperie*]

Fris·bee /friz′bē/ *n. Tdmk.* plastic disk thrown with spin as an outdoor game [perh. fr. *Frisbie* bakery pie tins]

frisk /frisk/ *v.* search (a person) for a weapon, etc., by feeling [Fr *frisque* lively]

frisk·y /fris′kē/ *adj.* (**·i·er, ·i·est**) lively; playful —**frisk′i·ly** *adv.*; **frisk′i·ness** *n.*

frit·ter[1] /frit′ər/ *v.* waste (money, time, etc.) triflingly [obs. *fritter*(s) fragments]

frit·ter[2] *n.* vegetable or meat patty dipped in batter and fried [Fr *friture* fr. L *frigere* FRY, 1]

friv·o·lous /friv′ələs/ *adj.* 1 not serious; silly; shallow 2 trifling; trivial —**fri·vol′i·ty** /-*val′-*/

ātē/ n. (pl. ·ties); **friv′o·lous·ly** adv.; **friv′o·lous·ness** n. [L]

frizz /frĭz/ v. 1 form (hair) into tight curls —n. 2 frizzed hair or state —**friz′zy** (·zi·er, ·zi·est) adj. [Fr friser]

friz·zle[1] /frĭz′əl/ v. (·zled, ·zling) fry or cook with a sizzling noise [obs. frizz, rel. to FRY, 1, + imit. ending]

friz·zle[2] v. (·zled, ·zling) 1 form into tight curls —n. 2 frizzled hair —**friz′zly** (·zli·er, ·zli·est) adj. [perh. rel. to FRIZZ]

fro /frō/ adv. back (now only in to and fro) [ON, rel. to FROM]

frock /frăk/ n. 1 woman's or girl's dress 2 monk's or priest's gown 3 smock [Fr fr. Gmc]

frog[1] /frŏg, frăg/ n. 1 smooth-skinned tailless amphibian with long hind legs 2 **frog in one's throat** Colloq. hoarseness [OE]

frog[2] n. ornamental coat-fastening of a button and loop

frog′man n. (pl. ·men) person trained for underwater combat, demolition, etc.

Frois·sart /f(r)wäsär′/, Jean c. 1333– c. 1400; French historian

frol·ic /frăl′ik/ v. (·icked, ·ick·ing) 1 play cheerfully —n. 2 cheerful play 3 merriment [Du vrolijk fr. MDu vro glad]

frol·ic·some /frăl′iksəm/ adj. merry; playful

from /frəm, frăm/ prep. expressing separation or origin, as: 1 person, place, time, etc., that is the starting point (journey from home) 2 place, object, etc., at a specified distance, etc. (10 miles from Rome) 3a source (book from the library) b giver or sender (not heard from her) 4 thing or person avoided, deprived, etc. (took his gun from him) 5 reason; cause; motive (died from fatigue) 6 thing distinguished or unlike (know black from white) 7 lower limit (from 10 to 20 boats) 8 state changed for another (from poor to rich) 9 adverb or preposition of time or place (from long ago; from abroad) [OE]

frond /frănd/ n. leaflike part of a fern or palm [L frons frondis leaf]

front /frŭnt/ n. 1 side, part, or position most prominent or most forward 2 foremost line of action, battle, etc. 3 edge or border area 4 demeanor; bearing 5a covering behavior b pretext 6 person, etc., as a cover for subversive or illegal activities 7 forward edge of advancing cold or warm air —adj. 8 of the front 9 situated in front —v. 10 have the front facing or directed toward 11 Slang. act as a front or cover for 12 provide with or have a front (fronted with stone) 13 **in front of:** a ahead of; in advance of b in the presence of [L frons frontis face]

front·age /frŭn′tij/ n. 1 front of a building 2 land or boundary next to a street, water, etc.

fron·tal /frŭnt′l/ adj. 1 of or on the front 2 of the forehead

fron·tier /frŏntēr′/ n. 1a border between two countries b district on each side of this 2 forefront of knowledge in a subject 3 border between settled and unsettled country —**fron·tiers′man** /-mən/ (pl. ·men) n.

fron·tis·piece /frŏnt′əspēs′/ n. illustration facing the title page of a book [L, rel. to FRONT + specere look]

front′ of′fice n. administrative and management personnel of a business

front′ run′ner n. favorite in a race, etc.

frosh /frăsh, frŏsh/ n. Colloq. first-year student in a college or 4-year high-school

frost /frŏst, fräst/ n. 1a frozen dew or vapor b consistent temperature below freezing point —v. 2 cover or become covered with frost 3 make (glass) nontransparent by roughening its surface [OE, rel. to FREEZE]

Frost /frŏst/, Robert 1874–1963; US poet

frost′bite n. injury from skin exposure to cold —**frost′bit′ten** /-bit′ən/ adj.

frost′ing n. icing

frost′y adj. (·i·er, ·i·est) 1 cold with frost 2 covered with or as with frost 3 unfriendly in manner —**frost′i·ly** adv.; **frost′i·ness** n.

froth /frŏTH/ n. 1 foam 2 idle or amusing talk, etc. —v. 3 emit or gather froth —**froth′y** adj. (·i·er, ·i·est) [ON]

frown /froun/ v. 1 wrinkle one's brows, esp. in displeasure or concentration 2 disapprove —n. 3 look of displeasure or concentration [Fr]

frow·zy /frou′zē/ adj. (also **frow′sy**) (·zi·er, ·zi·est) slovenly; untidy

froze /frōz/ v. past of FREEZE

fro·zen /frō′zn/ v. past part. of FREEZE

fruc·ti·fy /frŭk′təfī′/ v. (·fied, ·fy·ing) 1 bear fruit 2 make fruitful [L, rel. to FRUIT]

fruc·tose /frŭk′tōs, frŏŏk′-, -tōz′/ n. sugar in honey, fruits, etc. [L, rel. to FRUIT]

fru·gal /frŏŏ′gəl/ adj. 1 sparing; thrifty 2 slight; meager; scanty —**fru·gal′i·ty** /-gal′ ātē/ n.; **fru′gal·ly** adv. [L]

fruit /frŏŏt/ n. 1a seed-bearing part of a plant or tree; this as food b these collectively 2 (usu. pl.) vegetables, grains, etc., as food (fruits of the earth) 3 (usu. pl.) profits; rewards —v. 4 (cause to) bear fruit —**fruit′i·ly** adv.; **fruit′i·ness** /-ēnəs/ n.; **fruit′y** adj. (·i·er, ·i·est) [L fructus fr. frui enjoy]

fruit′ cake′ n. cake containing dried fruit

fruit·ful /frŏŏt′fəl/ adj. 1 producing much fruit 2 successful; profitable —**fruit′ful·ly** adv.

fru·i·tion /frŏŏ·ish′ən/ n. 1 bearing of fruit 2 realization of aims or hopes [L, rel. to FRUIT]

fruit·less /frŏŏt′ləs/ adj. 1 useless; unsuccessful 2 not bearing fruit —**fruit′less·ly** adv.

frump /frŭmp/ n. dowdy, unattractive woman —**frump′ish, frump′y** adj. (·i·er, ·i·est) [perh. dial. frumple wrinkle]

frus·trate /frəs′trāt′/ v. (·trat·ed, ·trat·ing) 1 make (efforts) ineffective 2 prevent (a person) from achieving a purpose —**frus′trat·ing·ly** adv.; **frus·tra′tion** n. [L frustra in vain]

frus′tra′ted adj. 1 thwarted 2 discontented as a result of being thwarted 3 disappointed

fry /frī/ v. (fried, fry·ing) 1 cook or be cooked in hot fat —n. (pl. fries) 2 (pl.) short for French fried potatoes 3 usu. outdoor party with fried food [L frigere]

Frye /frī/, (Herman) Northrop 1912–91; Canadian literary critic

fry′er n. (also **fri′er**) 1 person who fries 2 vessel for frying 3 chicken for frying

FSLIC abbr. Federal Savings and Loan Insurance Corporation

ft. or ft abbr. foot; feet

Fu·ad /fŏŏ-äd'/ name of two kings of Egypt: 1 Fuad I 1868–1936; reigned 1922–36 2 Fuad II 1952– ; reigned 1952–53

fuch·sia /fyŏŏ'SHə/ *n.* 1 shrub with drooping red, purple, or white flowers 2 purplish red [for L. *Fuchs*, German botanist]

fud·dle /fəd'l/ *v.* (·dled, ·dling) 1 confuse or stupefy, esp. with alcohol. —*n.* 2 confusion 3 intoxication

fud·dy-dud·dy /fəd'ē dəd'ē/ *adj.* 1 old-fashioned or quaintly fussy —*n.* (*pl.* ·dies) 2 such a person

fudge /fəj/ *n.* 1 soft, chewy candy made of milk, sugar, butter, etc. —*v.* (fudged, fudging) 2 make or do clumsily or dishonestly; fake (*fudge the results*)

fueh·rer /fyŏŏ'ər/ *n.* var. of FÜHRER

fu·el /fyŏŏ'əl, fyŏŏl/ *n.* 1 material for burning or as a source of heat or power 2 food as a source of energy 3 thing that sustains or inflames passion, etc. —*v.* (·eled or ·elled, ·el·ing or ·el·ling) 4 supply with or get fuel [Fr fr. L]

Fuen·tes /fwen'tās/, **Carlos** 1928– ; Mexican novelist and writer

fu·gi·tive /fyŏŏ'jətiv/ *n.* 1 person who flees from justice or an enemy —*adj.* 2 fleeing 3 transient; fleeting [L *fugere* flee]

fugue /fyŏŏg/ *n.* piece of music in which a short melody or phrase is introduced by one part and taken up and developed by others —fu'gal /-gəl/ *adj.* [L *fuga* flight]

füh·rer /fyŏŏ'ər/ *n.* (also **fueh·rer**) tyrannical leader [Ger]

Fu·ji, Mount /fŏŏ'jē/ *n.* dormant, conical volcano in central Japan; 12,388 ft.

Fu·ku·o·ka /fŏŏ'kŏŏ-ō'ka/ *n.* city in Japan, on Kyushu. Pop. 1,249,300

-ful *comb. form* forming: 1 adjectives from a nouns, meaning full of or having qualities of (*masterful*) b adjectives (*direful*) c verbs, meaning 'apt to' (*forgetful*) 2 nouns (*pl.* ·fuls) meaning 'amount that fills' (*spoonful*)

Ful·bright /fŏŏl'brīt'/, (**James**) **William** 1905–95; US senator

ful·crum /fŏŏl'krəm, fol'-/ *n.* (*pl.* ·crums or ·cra) support point for a lever (see illustration at LEVER) [L *fulcire* to prop]

ful·fill /fŏŏlfil'/ *v.* (·filled, ·fill·ing) 1 carry out (a task, prophecy, promise, etc.) 2 satisfy (conditions, a desire, prayer, etc.) 3 complete —ful·fill'ment *n.* [OE, rel. to FULL¹ + FILL]

full¹ /fŏŏl/ *adj.* 1 holding all it can 2 having eaten all one can or wants 3 abundant; rich; satisfying 4 having an abundance 5 complete (*in full bloom*) 6 (of tone) deep and clear 7 plump; rounded (*full figure*) 8 (of clothes) ample; hanging in folds —*adv.* 9 very (*knows full well*) 10 fully (*a full six miles*) 11 **in full:** a without abridgment b to or for the full amount 12 **in full view** entirely visible —full'ness *n.* [OE]

full² *v.* clean and thicken (cloth) [ult. fr. L *fullo* one who fulls]

full'back' *n.* Football. offensive player positioned behind the quarterback

full'-blood'ed *adj.* 1 not hybrid 2 vigorous; lively

full'-blown' *adj.* fully developed

Ful·ler /fŏŏl'ər/ 1 (**Sarah**) **Margaret** 1810–50; US writer, critic, and reformer 2

R(ichard) **Buckminster** 1895–1983; US designer and architect

Ful·ler·ton /fŏŏl'ərtən/ *n.* city in Calif. Pop. 114,144

full' house' *n.* 1 maximum attendance at a theater, etc. 2 hand in poker with three of a kind and a pair

full' moon' *n.* moon with its whole disk illuminated

full'-scale' *adj.* not reduced in size

full'-time' *adj.* 1 for or during the whole of the working week —*adv.* 2 on such a basis

ful·mi·nate /fŏŏl'mənāt'/ *v.* (·nat·ed, ·nat·ing) 1 criticize loudly and forcefully 2 explode violently; flash —ful'mi·na'tion *n.* [L *fulmen* lightning]

ful·some /fŏŏl'səm/ *adj.* excessive; cloying —ful'some·ly *adv.* [fr. FULL¹]

● Usage: Contrary to its appearance, the traditional meaning of *fulsome* is 'disgusting; excessive.' Despite that, it is used so often to mean 'generous; abundant' that many now accept this newer sense.

Ful·ton /fŏŏl'tn/, **Robert** 1765–1815; US inventor; developed first successful steamboat

fum·ble /fam'bəl/ *v.* (·bled, ·bling) 1 use the hands awkwardly; grope about 2 handle clumsily —*n.* 3 act of fumbling [LGer *fummeln*]

fume /fyŏŏm/ *n.* 1 (usu. *pl.*) exuded gas, smoke, or vapor, esp. when harmful or unpleasant —*v.* (fumed, fum·ing) 2 emit fumes or as fumes 3 exhibit repressed rage [L *fumus* smoke]

fu·mi·gate /fyŏŏ'migāt'/ *v.* (·gat·ed, ·gat·ing) disinfect or purify with fumes —fu'mi·ga'tion, fu'mi·ga'tor *n.* [L, rel. to FUME]

fun /fən/ *n.* 1 lively or playful amusement 2 source of this 3 pleasure —*adj.* 4 *Colloq.* amusing; enjoyable 5 **make fun of** (or **poke fun at**) ridicule; tease [obs. *fon* dupe; rel. to FOND]

Fu·na·bash·i /fŏŏ'nəbäSH'ē/ *n.* city in Japan. Pop. 535,600

Fu·na·fu·ti /f(y)ŏŏ'nəf(y)ŏŏt'ē/ *n.* capital of Tuvalu. Pop. 2,800

func·tion /fəNGK'SHən/ *n.* 1a role, activity, or purpose b official or professional duty 2 public or social occasion 3 *Math.* quantity whose value depends on the varying values of others —*v.* 4 fulfill a function; operate 5 manage or cope [L *functio* fr. *fungi* perform]

func'tion·al *adj.* 1 of or serving a function 2 practical rather than attractive 3 affecting the function of a bodily organ but not its structure —func'tion·al·ly *adv.*

func'tion·al il·lit'er·ate *n.* person with very limited reading ability, hence unable to function well in many kinds of work

func·tion·ar·y /fəNGK'SHəner'ē/ *n.* (*pl.* ·ies) official performing certain duties

fund /fənd/ *n.* 1 permanently available supply 2 sum of money, esp. for a purpose 3 (*pl.*) money available —*v.* 4 provide with money 5 make (a debt) permanent at fixed interest [L *fundus* bottom]

fun·da·men·tal /fən'dəment'l/ *adj.* 1 of or being a base or foundation; essential; primary —*n.* 2 (usu. *pl.*) principles —fun'da·men'tal·ly *adv.* [L, rel. to FOUND²]

fun·da·men·tal·ism' *n.* strict adherence to traditional religious beliefs —**fun·da·men·tal·ist** /-ist/ *n. & adj.*

fund'-rais·er *n.* person or event raising money for a cause, enterprise, etc. —**fund'-rais'ing** *n.*

Fun·dy, Bay of /fən'dē/ *n.* inlet of the Atlantic between Nova Scotia and New Brunswick

fu·ner·al /fyŏŏ'n(ə)rəl/ *n.* ceremonial burial or cremation of a corpse [L *funus funeris*]

fu'ner·al di·rec'tor *n.* undertaker

fu'ner·al home' *n.* (also **fu'ner·al par'lor**) establishment where corpses are prepared for funerals

fu·ne·re·al /fyŏŏnēr'ēəl/ *adj.* 1 of or appropriate to a funeral 2 dismal; dark —**fu·ne're·al·ly** *adv.*

fun·gi·cide /fən'jəsīd', faNG'gə-/ *n.* substance that kills fungus —**fun'gi·ci'dal** /-dəl/ *adj.*

fun·gus /faNG'gəs/ *n.* (*pl.* **·gi** /-jī/ or **·gus·es**) type of plant, as mushroom, mold, mildew, etc., without chlorophyll and reproducing by spores —**fun'gal** /-gəl/, **fun'gous** *adj.* [L]

fu·nic·u·lar /fyŏŏnik'yələr/ *adj.* 1 (of a mountain railway) operating by cable with ascending and descending cars counterbalanced —*n.* 2 funicular railway [L *funiculus*, dim. of *funis* rope]

funk /faNGk/ *n. Slang.* 1 fear; panic 2 dejected state

funk·y /faNG'kē/ *adj.* (**·i·er, ·i·est**) *Colloq.* 1 (esp. of jazz or rock music) earthy, bluesy, with a heavy rhythm 2 foul-smelling; gamy 3 amusingly unconventional

fun·nel /fən'l/ *n.* 1 tube with a widening at the top, for pouring liquid, etc., into a small opening 2 metal chimney, as on a steam engine —*v.* (**·neled** or **·nelled, ·nel·ing** or **·nel·ling**) 3 guide or move through or as through a funnel [Prov *fonilh* fr. L (*in*)*fundibulum*]

fun·ny /fən'ē/ *adj.* (**·ni·er, ·ni·est**) 1 amusing; comical 2 strange; peculiar —**fun'ni·ly** *adv.*; **fun'ni·ness** *n.* [fr. FUN]

fun'ny bone' *n.* part of the elbow over which a sensitive nerve passes

fur /fər/ *n.* 1 a thick, soft animal hair b hide with fur on it [Fr fr. Gmc]

fur·be·low /fər'bəlō'/ *n.* 1 (*pl.*) showy ornaments 2 gathered strip or border of a skirt or petticoat [Fr *falbala*]

fur·bish /fər'bISH/ *v.* 1 renovate 2 polish [Fr fr. Gmc]

fu·ri·ous /fyŏŏr'ēəs/ *adj.* 1 very angry 2 raging; frantic —**fu'ri·ous·ly** *adv.* [L, rel. to FURY]

furl /fərl/ *v.* 1 roll or gather up and secure (a sail, etc.) 2 become furled [Fr *ferler*]

fur·long /fər'lôNG/ *n.* measure of distance (220 yards or 1/8 of a mile) [OE, rel. to FURROW + LONG¹]

fur·lough /fər'lō/ *n.* 1 leave of absence, esp. military —*v.* 2 grant furlough to [Du, rel. to FOR- + LEAVE¹]

furn. *abbr.* furnished

fur·nace /fər'nis/ *n.* enclosed structure for intense heating [L *fornax* fr. *fornus* oven]

fur·nish /fər'nISH/ *v.* 1 provide with furniture 2 supply [Fr fr. Gmc]

fur'nish·ings *n. pl.* 1 furniture, rugs, decor, etc., in a house, room, etc. 2 items of dress or accessories

fur·ni·ture /fər'niCHər/ *n.* movable equipment of a house, room, etc., e.g., tables, beds [Fr, rel. to FURNISH]

fu·ror /fyŏŏr'ər/ *n.* 1 uproar; fury 2 craze [L, rel. to FURY]

fur·ri·er /fər'ēər, fə'rē-/ *n.* dealer in or dresser of furs [Fr]

fur·row /fər'ō, fə'rō/ *n.* 1 narrow trench made by a plow 2 rut; groove; wrinkle —*v.* 3 plow 4 make furrows in [OE]

fur·ry /fər'ē, fə'rē/ *adj.* (**·ri·er, ·ri·est**) like or covered with fur

fur·ther /fər'THər/ (see also FARTHER) *adv.* (**·thest**) 1 more distant in space or time 2 to a greater extent; more 3 in addition —*adj.* 4 more distant or advanced 5 more; additional (*further details*) —*v.* 6 promote; favor (a scheme, etc.) [OE, rel. to FORTH]

● Usage: See note at FARTHER.

fur'ther·more' *adv.* in addition; besides

fur·tive /fər'tiv/ *adj.* sly; stealthy —**fur'tive·ly** *adv.*; **fur'tive·ness** *n.* [L *fur* thief]

fu·ry /fyŏŏr'ē/ *n.* (*pl.* **·ries**) 1 a wild and passionate anger b fit of rage 2 violence of a storm, disease, etc. 3 *Gk. Myth.* (*cap.*) (*usu. pl.*) avenging goddess [L *furia*]

furze /fərz/ *n.* GORSE [OE]

fuse¹ /fyŏŏz/ *v.* (**fused, fus·ing**) 1 melt with intense heat 2 blend into one whole by melting —*n.* 3 device in an electric circuit to interrupt any excessive current [L *fusus* melted fr. *fundere* melt]

fuse² (also **fuze**) *n.* device of combustible matter for igniting an explosive [L *fusus* spindle]

fu·se·lage /fyŏŏ'sələzh', -zə-/ *n.* body of an airplane [Fr fr. *fuseau* spindle]

Fu·shun /fŏŏ'sHŏŏn'/ *n.* city in China. Pop. 1,202,400

fus·i·ble /fyŏŏ'zəbəl/ *adj.* that can be melted —**fus'i·bil'i·ty** *n.* [L, rel. to FUSE¹]

fu·sil·ier /fyŏŏ'zəlēr'/ *n. Hist.* soldier armed with a light musket [ult. fr. L *focus* fire]

fu·sil·lade /fyŏŏ'səlād', -läd'/ *n.* period of continuous discharge of firearms

fu·sion /fyŏŏ'ZHən/ *n.* 1 fusing or melting 2 blending; coalition 3 NUCLEAR FUSION [L, rel. to FUSE¹]

fuss /fəs/ *n.* 1 excited commotion; bustle 2 excessive concern about a trivial thing 3 sustained protest or dispute —*v.* 4 behave with nervous concern 5 agitate; worry 6 **make a fuss of** (or **over**) treat (a person or animal) affectionately —**fuss'er** *n.*

fuss'budg·et *n.* compulsively fussy or unduly meticulous person

fuss·y /fəs'ē/ *adj.* (**·i·er, ·i·est**) 1 inclined to fuss 2 overly detailed or elaborate 3 fastidious —**fuss'i·ly** *adv.*; **fuss'i·ness** *n.*

fus·tian /fəs'CHən/ *n.* pompous language [Fr]

fus·ty /fəs'tē/ *adj.* (**·ti·er, ·ti·est**) 1 musty; stuffy 2 antiquated —**fust'i·ness** *n.* [Fr *fust* cask, fr. L *fustis* cudgel]

fu·tile /fyŏŏt'l, -tīl'/ *adj.* useless; ineffectual —**fu·til'i·ty** /-til'ətē/ *n.* [L *futilis* leaky; futile]

futon /fōō′tän′/ *n.* folding cushion or mattress placed on a floor for use as a bed [Japn]

fu·ture /fyōō′CHər/ *adj.* **1** due to happen, be, or become **2a** of time to come **b** *Gram.* (of a tense) describing an event yet to happen —*n.* **3** time to come **4** future events **5** prospect of success, etc. **6** *Gram.* future tense [L *futurus* future part. of *sum* be]

fu·ture per·fect *n. Gram.* tense giving the sense 'will have done'

fu·tur·is·tic /fyōō′CHəris′tik/ *adj.* suitable for the future; ultra-modern

fu·tu·ri·ty /fyōō·t(y)ōōr′ətē, -CHŌŌr′-/ *n.* (*pl.* **·ties**) **1** future time **2** future events

futz /fəts/ *v. Colloq.* (foll. by *around*) trifle; play

fuze /fyōōz/ *n.* var. of FUSE²

fuzz /fəz/ *n.* **1** fluff **2** fluffy or frizzed hair **3** *Slang.* police officer [prob. LGer or Du]

fuzz′y *adj.* (**·i·er**, **·i·est**) **1** like fuzz; fluffy **2** blurred; indistinct **3** unclear in thought; confused —**fuzz′i·ly** *adv.*; **fuzz′i·ness** *n.*

FY *abbr.* fiscal year

-fy *suffix* forming: **1** verbs from nouns, meaning: **a** make; produce (*beautify*) **b** make into (*liquefy*) **2** verbs from adjectives, meaning 'bring or come into a state' (*solidify*) **3** verbs in a causative sense (*horrify; stupefy*) [Fr *-fier* fr. L *facere* make]

FYI *abbr.* for your information

G

g, G /jē/ *n.* (*pl.* **g's; G's, Gs**) **1** seventh letter of the English alphabet; a consonant **2** *Mus.* (*cap.*) fifth note of the diatonic scale of C major

g or **g.** *abbr.* **1** gauge **2** gender **3** general **4** gold **5** good **6** grain(s) **7** gram(s)

G or **G.** *abbr.* **1** gauss **2** gay **3** German **4** giga- **5** gravity **6** gulf **7** (of a movie) classified as suitable for general audiences

Ga *symb.* gallium

Ga., GA abbr. for Georgia (postal abbr. **GA**)

gab *n. Colloq.* talk; chatter [var. of GOB¹]

gab·ar·dine /gab′ərdēn′/ *n.* (also **gab′er·dine′**) type of twilled cloth [Fr *gavardine*]

gab·ble /gab′əl/ *v.* (**·bled**, **·bling**) **1** talk or utter unintelligibly or too fast —*n.* **2** fast unintelligible talk —**gab′bler** *n.* [Du. imit.]

GABLE

ga·ble /gā′bəl/ *n.* triangular upper part of a wall at the end of a ridged roof —**ga′bled** *adj.* [ON and Fr]

Ga·ble /gā′bəl/, **(William) Clark** 1901–60; US actor

Ga·bon /gabôN′/ *n.* republic in W Africa. Capital: Libreville. Pop. 1,253,000 —**Gab·o·nese** /gab′ənēz′, -nēs′/ *n. & adj.*

Ga·bo·ro·ne /gäb′ərō′nē/ *n.* capital of Botswana. Pop. 133,800

gad /gad/ *v.* (**gad·ded, gad·ding**) wander about idly or in search of pleasure [obs. *gadling* companion]

gad′a·bout′ *n.* person who gads about

Gad·da·fi /gədä′fē/ see QADHAFI

gad′fly′ *n.* (*pl.* **·flies**) **1** fly that bites cattle and horses **2** provocative or irritating person [obs. *gad* spike]

gadg·et /gaj′it/ *n.* mechanical device or tool —**gadg′et·ry** /-itrē/ *n.*

gad·o·lin·i·um /gad′l-in′ēəm/ *n.* metallic element of the lanthanide series; *symb.* **Gd** [for J. *Gadolin*, Finnish chemist]

Gae·a /jē′ə, gī′ə/ *n.* (also **Gai·a**) *n. Gk. Myth.* earth goddess

Gael·ic /gā′lik, gal′ik/ *n.* **1** Celtic language of Ireland and Scotland —*adj.* **2** of the Celts or the Celtic languages —**Gael** *n.*

gaff /gaf/ *n.* **1** stick with an iron hook for landing large fish **2** spar for a fore-and-aft sail [Prov *gaf* hook]

gaffe /gaf/ *n.* blunder; indiscreet act or remark [Fr]

gag /gag/ *n.* **1** thing thrust into or tied across the mouth to prevent speaking **2** joke **3** thing restricting free speech —*v.* (**gagged, gagging**) **4** apply a gag to **5** silence; deprive of free speech **6** choke; retch

Ga·ga·rin /gəgär′ən/, **Yuri** 1934–68; Russian cosmonaut; first man in space

gage¹ /gāj/ *n.* **1** pledge; thing deposited as security **2** symbol of a challenge to fight, esp. a glove thrown down [Gmc, rel. to WAGE]

gage² *n.* GAUGE
● Usage: See note at GAUGE.

Gage /gāj/, **Thomas** 1721–87; British general

gag·gle /gag′əl/ *n.* **1** flock of geese **2** disorganized group [imit.]

gai·e·ty /gā′ətē/ *n.* **1** being cheerful **2** merrymaking **3** bright appearance [Fr, rel. to GAY]

gai·ly /gā′lē/ *adv.* in a merry or careless manner

gain /gān/ *v.* **1** obtain or win **2** acquire; earn **3** get more of; improve **4** benefit; profit **5** (of a clock, etc.) display a later time **6** come closer to **7** reach (a desired place) —*n.* **8** increase of wealth, etc.; profit **9** betterment; improvement **10** increase in amount **11** gain ground: **a** advance **b** come nearer (a person pursued) [Fr fr. Gmc]

Gaines·ville /gānz′vil′, -vəl/ *n.* city in Fla. Pop. 84,770

gain·ful /gān′fəl/ *adj.* **1** (of employment) paid **2** lucrative —**gain′ful·ly** *adv.*

gain·say /gān′sā′, gänsā′/ *v.* deny; contradict [ON, rel. to AGAINST + SAY]

Gains·bor·ough /gānz′b(ə)rə/, **Thomas** 1727–88; English painter

gait /gāt/ *n.* manner of running or walking [ON]

gai·ter /gā′tər/ *n.* covering of cloth, leather, etc., for the lower leg [Fr *guêtre*]

gal /gal/ *n. Colloq.* girl

gal. *abbr.* gallon(s)

ga·la /gā′lə, gal′ə, gä′lə/ *n.* festive occasion or gathering [ult. fr. Fr *gale* rejoicing, fr. Gmc]

ga·lac·tic /gəlak′tik/ *adj.* of a galaxy or galaxies

Ga·lá′pa·gos Is′lands /gəläp′əgəs/ *n.* Pacific archipelago, W of Ecuador

gal·ax·y /gal′əksē/ *n.* (*pl.* **·ies**) **1** independent system of stars, gas, dust, etc., in space **2** (the Galaxy) Milky Way [Gk *gala* milk]

Gal·braith /gal′brāth/, **John Kenneth** 1908– ; Canadian-born US economist

gale /gāl/ *n.* **1** very strong wind or storm **2** outburst, esp. of laughter

Ga·len /gā′lən/ c. 130–c. 201; Greek physician

Gal·i·lee, Sea of /gal′ilē′/ *n.* lake in NE Israel

Gal·i·le·o /gal′əlē′ō, -lā′ō/ 1564–1642; Italian astronomer

gall¹ /gôl/ *n.* **1** impudence **2** bitterness **3** bile [ON]

gall² *n.* **1** sore made by chafing —*v.* **2** rub sore **3** vex [LGer or Du *galle*]

gall³ *n.* growth produced by insects, etc., on plants and trees [L *galla*]

gal·lant *adj.* /gal′ənt/ **1** brave **2** fine; stately **3** /gəlant′, -länt′/ solicitous to women; chivalrous —*n.* /gəlant′, länt′/ **4** ladies' man —**gal·lant·ly** /gal′əntlē/ *adv.* [Fr *galer* make merry]

gal·lant·ry /gal′əntrē/ *n.* (*pl.* **·ries**) **1** bravery **2** courtesy to women **3** polite act or speech

gall blad·der /gôl′ blad′ər/ *n.* organ storing bile

gal·le·on /gal′yən/ *n. Hist.* sailing ship of war or for cargo [Fr or Sp, rel. to GALLEY]

gal·ler·i·a /gal′ərē′ə/ *n.* arcade, usu. with several stores under a single roof [It]

gal·ler·y /gal′(ə)rē/ *n.* (*pl.* **·ies**) **1** room or building showing works of art **2** balcony, esp. in a church, hall, etc. **3a** highest balcony in a theater with cheapest seats **b** people occupying these seats **4** long narrow room or passage **5** group of spectators [Fr *galerie*]

gal·ley /gal′ē/ *n.* **1** *Hist.* single-decked sailing vessel usu. rowed by slaves or criminals **2** kitchen of a ship or plane **3** *Printing.* (in full **gal′ley proof′**) typeset copy before division into pages [L *galea*]

Gal·lic /gal′ik/ *adj.* **1** French or typically French **2** of Gaul or the Gauls [L *Gallicus*]

gal·li·um /gal′ēəm/ *n.* soft bluish-white metallic element; *symb.* Ga [L *Gallia* France, country of its discoverer]

gal·li·vant /gal′əvant′/ *v.* wander around seeking amusement

gal·lon /gal′ən/ *n.* **1** liquid measure equivalent to four quarts **2** (*pl.*) *Colloq.* large amount [Fr]

gal·lop /gal′əp/ *n.* **1** fastest pace of a horse, etc., with all the feet off the ground together in each stride —*v.* **2** (of a horse, etc., or its rider) go at a gallop **3** move, talk, etc., very quickly [Fr, rel. to WALLOP]

gal·lows /gal′ōz/ *n. pl.* (usu. treated as *sing.*) structure for hanging criminals [ON]

gall·stone /gôl′stōn/ *n.* small hard mass forming in the gall bladder

ga·lore /gəlôr′/ *adv.* in plenty; abundantly [Ir]

ga·losh /gəläsh′/ *n.* (usu. *pl.*) waterproof overshoe [Fr]

Gais·wor·thy /gôlz′wər′thē/, **John** 1867–1933; English novelist and dramatist

ga·lumph /gəlumf′/ *v. Colloq.* move noisily or clumsily [coined by Lewis Carroll, perh. fr. GALLOP + TRIUMPH]

gal·van·ic /galvan′ik/ *adj.* **1a** producing an electric current by chemical action **b** (of electricity) produced by chemical action **2** dramatically stimulating —**gal·van′i·cal·ly** *adv.*

gal·va·nize /gal′vənīz′/ *v.* (**·nized, ·niz·ing**) **1** rouse forcefully, esp. by shock or excitement **2** coat (iron) with zinc to protect against rust —**gal·va·ni·za′tion** *n.* [*Galvani*, name of a physiologist]

gal·va·nom·e·ter /gal′vənäm′ətər/ *n.* instrument for measuring small electric currents —**gal′va·no·met′ric** /-nōmet′rik/ *adj.*

Gal·ves·ton Bay /gal′vəstən/ *n.* inlet of the Gulf of Mexico on the coast of Texas, SE of Houston

Ga·ma /gäm′ə/, **Vasco da** c. 1469–1524; Portuguese navigator

Gam·bi·a, the /gam′bēə, gäm′-/ *n.* republic in W Africa. Capital: Banjul. Pop. 921,000

gam·bit /gam′bit/ *n.* **1** *Chess.* opening strategy of sacrifice for positional advantage **2** trick or device; ploy [It *gambetto* tripping up]

gam·ble /gam′bəl/ *v.* (**·bled, ·bling**) **1** play games of chance for money **2** bet (a sum of money) **3** risk much in the hope of great gain **4** act in the hope of —*n.* **5** risky undertaking —**gam′bler** *n.*

gam·bol /gam′bəl/ *v.* **1** skip or jump about playfully —*n.* **2** frolic; caper [Fr *gambade* leap, fr. It *gamba* leg]

GAMBREL ROOF

gam′brel roof′ /gam′brəl/ *n.* gabled roof with each side having two different angles of slope, the lower steeper than the upper

game¹ /gām/ *n.* **1** form of play or sport, esp. a competitive one with rules **2** portion of such play forming a scoring unit **3** (*pl.*) series of athletic, etc., contests **4** jest **5** *Colloq.* **a** scheme **b** type of activity or business **6a** wild animals or birds hunted for sport or food **b** their flesh as food —*adj.* **7** eager and willing —*v.* (**gamed, gam·ing**) **8** gamble for money stakes **9** game is up scheme is exposed or foiled —**game′ly** *adv.* [OE]

game² *adj.* injured; lame

game′cock′ *n.* rooster bred and trained for fighting

game′keep′er *n.* person employed to care for game

games·man·ship /gāmz′mənship/ *n.* skill in

ga·mete /gămēt´, găm´ēt´/ *n.* reproductive cell able to unite with another for sexual reproduction —**ga·met·ic** /gəmet´ik/ *adj.* [Gk: wife]

gam·in /găm´ən/ (*fem.* **ga´mine,** pronunc. same) *n.* **1** street urchin **2** child, esp. a girl, with mischievous charm [Fr]

gam·ma /găm´ə/ *n.* third letter of the Greek alphabet (Γ, γ) [Gk]

gam´ma ra·di·a´tion *n.* (also **gam´ma rays´**) electromagnetic radiation of wavelength shorter than x-rays

gam·ut /găm´ət/ *n.* **1** entire range or scope **2 run the gamut** perform the complete range of experience or perform [MedL *gamma ut,* words used for a scale of musical notes]

gam·y /gā´mē/ *adj.* (·i·er, ·i·est) **1** smelling or tasting like game **2** slightly spoiled

gan·der /găn´dər/ *n.* **1** male goose **2** *Slang.* look; glance [OE]

Gan·dhi /găn´dē/ **1 Mahatma** (born Mohandes Karamchand) 1869–1948; Indian nationalist and spiritual leader **2 Indira** 1917–84; prime minister of India (1966–77; 1980–84); her son: **3 Rajiv** 1944–91; prime minister of India (1984–89)

gang /găng/ *n.* **1** band of persons associating for some (usu. antisocial or criminal) purpose **2** set of workers, slaves, or prisoners **3 gang up on** *Colloq.* attack in a group [ON]

Gan·ges Riv·er /găn´jēz´/ *n.* sacred river of the Hindus, flowing SE from N India to the Bay of Bengal at Calcutta

gan·gling /găng´gling/ *adj.* (also **gan·gly** /găng´glē/; ·gli·er, ·gli·est) tall and thin; lanky [freq. of OE *gang go*]

gan·gli·on /găng´glēən/ *n.* (*pl.* ·gli·a /glēə/ or ·ons) structure containing an assemblage of nerve cells —**gan´gli·on´ic** /-än´ik/ *adj.* [Gk]

gang´plank´ *n.* movable plank for boarding or disembarking from a ship

gan·grene /găng´grēn, găng·grēn´/ *n.* death of body tissue, usu. from loss of circulation —**gan´gre·nous** /-grənəs/ *adj.* [Gk *gang-graina*]

gang·ster /găng´stər/ *n.* member of a criminal gang

gang´way´ *n.* **1** narrow walkway **2a** opening in a ship's bulwarks **b** bridge from ship to shore

gan·net /găn´it/ *n.* diving sea bird [OE]

gant·let /gänt´lit/ *n.* var. of GAUNTLET²

gan·try /găn´trē/ *n.* (*pl.* ·tries) bridgelike structure supporting a traveling crane, rocket-launching equipment, etc. [prob. *gawn,* a dial. form of GALLON, + TREE]

GAO *abbr.* General Accounting Office

gap /găp/ *n.* **1a** empty space **b** deficiency **2** breach; opening **3** wide divergence in views, etc. —**gap´py** *adj.* [ON]

gape /gāp/ *v.* (**gaped, gap·ing**) **1a** open one's mouth wide **b** be or become wide open; split **2** stare at —*n.* **3** open mouth **4** rent; opening [ON]

ga·rage /gəräzh´, -räj´/ *n.* **1** shelter for a vehicle or vehicles **2** establishment that services vehicles —*v.* (·raged, ·rag·ing) **3** put or keep in a garage [Fr]

garb /gärb/ *n.* **1** clothing, esp. distinctive —*v.* **2** dress [Gmc, rel. to GEAR]

gar·bage /gär´bij/ *n.* **1** trash; waste **2** nonsense; anything worthless [AngFr]

gar·ble /gär´bəl/ *v.* (·bled, ·bling) distort or confuse (facts, messages, etc.) [It fr. Ar]

Gar·bo /gär´bō/, **Greta** (born Greta Gustafsson) 1905–90; Swedish-born US actress

Gar·cí·a Lor·ca /gärsē´ə lôr´kə/, **Federico** 1899–1936; Spanish poet and dramatist

Gar·cí·a Már·quez /gärsē´ə mär´käs/, **Gabriel** 1928– ; Colombian writer

gar·den /gärd´n/ *n.* **1** ground for growing flowers, fruit, or vegetables **2** (esp. *pl.*) grounds laid out for public enjoyment —*v.* **3** cultivate or tend a garden —**gar´den·er, gar´den·ing** *n.* [Gmc, rel. to YARD²]

Gar´den Grove´ *n.* city in Calif. Pop. 143,050

gar·de·nia /gärdēn´yə/ *n.* tree or shrub with large fragrant flowers [*Garden,* name of a naturalist]

gar´den var·i·e·ty *adj.* common; ordinary

Gard·ner /gärd´nər/, **Erle Stanley** 1899–1970; US writer

Gar·field /gär´fēld´/, **James Abram** 1831–81; 20th US president (1881); assassinated

gar·gan·tu·an /gärgan´choöən/ *adj.* gigantic [fr. *Gargantua,* a giant in a book by Rabelais]

gar·gle /gär´gol/ *v.* (·gled, ·gling) **1** wash (the throat) with a liquid kept in motion by exhaling through it —*n.* **2** liquid for gargling [Fr, rel. to GARGOYLE]

GARGOYLE

gar·goyle /gär´goil´/ *n.* grotesque carved face or figure, esp. as a spout from the gutter on a building [Fr: throat]

Gar·i·bal·di /gar´əböl´dē/, **Giuseppe** 1807–82; Italian hero of the movement to unify Italy

gar·ish /ger´ish, gar´-/ *adj.* showy; gaudy —**gar´ish·ly** *adv.*; **gar´ish·ness** *n.* [obs. *gaure* stare]

gar·land /gär´lənd/ *n.* **1** wreath of flowers, etc. —*v.* **2** adorn or crown with garlands [Fr]

Gar·land *n.* city in Texas. Pop. 180,650

Gar·land, Judy (born Frances Gumm) 1922–69; US singer and actress

gar·lic /gär´lik/ *n.* plant of the onion family with pungent bulb used to flavor food —**gar´lick·y** *adj.* [OE: spear-leek]

gar·ment /gär´mənt/ *n.* article of dress [Fr, rel. to GARNISH]

gar·ner /gär´nər/ *v.* **1** collect **2** store [L, rel. to GRANARY]

gar·net /gär´nit/ *n.* glassy silicate mineral, esp. a red kind used as a gem [MedL *granatum* pomegranate]

gar·nish /gär´nish/ *v.* **1** decorate (esp. food) —*n.* **2** decoration, esp. to food [Fr *garnir* fr. Gmc]

ga·rote or **gar·rotte** /gərät´/ *v.* (·rot·ed or

·rot·ted, ·rot·ing or ·rot·ting) 1 execute or kill by strangulation, esp. with wire —*n.* 2 device used for this [Fr or Sp]

gar·ret /gar'it/ *n.* attic or room in a roof [OFr *garite* watchtower]

gar·ri·son /ger'əsən/ *n.* 1 troops stationed in a town, etc., to defend it —*v.* 2 provide with or occupy as a garrison [Fr *garir* defend, fr. Gmc]

Gar·ri·son /ger'əsən/, **William Lloyd** 1805–79; US editor and abolitionist

gar·ru·lous /ger'ələs/ *adj.* talkative —**gar·ru·li·ty** /gərōō'lətē/, **gar'ru·lous·ness** *n.*; **gar'ru·lous·ly** *adv.* [L]

gar·ter /gär'tər/ *n.* band worn to keep a sock or stocking up [Fr]

Gar·vey /gär'vē/, **Marcus Mosiah** 1887–1940; Jamaican leader of the "Back to Africa" movement in the US

Gar·y /ger'ē/ *n.* city in Ind. Pop. 116,646

gas /gas/ *n.* (*pl.* **·es** or **·ses**) 1 any airlike substance (not solid or liquid) moving freely to fill available space 2 such a substance used as fuel 3 nitrous oxide or other anesthetic gas 4 poisonous gas 5 *Colloq.* a gasoline b accelerator (of a car) 6 *Slang.* enjoyable or amusing thing or person —*v.* (**gassed, gassing**) 7 expose to gas, esp. to immobilize or kill —**gas·e·ous** /gaSH'əs, gas'ēəs/ *adj.* [Du invented word based on Gk *khaos* CHAOS]

gas' cham'ber *n.* room for execution by gas

gash /gaSH/ *n.* 1 long deep cut or wound —*v.* 2 slash; cut [Fr]

gas·ket /gas'kit/ *n.* sheet or ring of rubber, etc., for sealing a joint [Fr *garcette*]

gas' mask' *n.* respirator as a protection against poison gas, noxious fumes, etc.

gas·o·line /gas'əlēn, gas'əlēn'/ *n.* refined petroleum used as a liquid fuel in motor vehicles, etc.

gasp /gasp/ *v.* 1 catch one's breath with an open mouth as in exhaustion or astonishment 2 utter with gasps —*n.* 3 convulsive catching of breath [ON]

gas'sy *adj.* (**·si·er, ·si·est**) 1 of or like gas 2 full of gas

gas·tric /gas'trik/ *adj.* of the stomach [Fr, rel. to GASTRO-]

gas·tri·tis /gastrīt'is/ *n.* inflammation of the stomach

gastro- *comb. form* stomach [Gk *gastēr* stomach]

gas·tron·o·my /gasträn'əmē/ *n.* science or art of good eating and drinking —**gas'tro·nom'ic** /-näm'ik/, **gas'tro·nom'i·cal** *adj.*; **gas'tro·nom'i·cal·ly** *adv.*

gas·tro·pod /gas'trəpäd'/ *n.* mollusk that moves by means of a ventral muscular organ, e.g., a snail [fr. GASTRO- + Gk *pod-* fr. *pous* foot]

gate /gāt/ *n.* 1 barrier, usu. hinged, to close an entrance through a wall, fence, etc. 2 gateway 3 means of entrance or exit 4 place of access to aircraft at an airport 5 device regulating the passage of water in a lock, etc. 6a number of paying spectators b amount of money taken thus —**gat·ed** /gāt'id/ *adj.* [OE]

gate'crash'er *n.* uninvited guest at a social affair —**gate'crash'** *v.*

gate'house' *n.* house standing at a gateway, esp. to a large house or park

Gates /gāts/ 1 **Horatio** c. 1728–1806; general in the American Revolution 2 **Bill (William Henry)** 1955– ; US computer entrepreneur

gate'way' *n.* 1 opening closed by a gate 2 means of access

gath·er /gaTH'ər/ *v.* 1 bring or come together; accumulate 2 harvest 3 infer or deduce 4 increase (*gather speed*) 5 summon up 6 draw together in folds or wrinkles —*n.* 7 fold; pleat [OE]

gath'er·ing *n.* assembly

Ga·tun Lake /gətōōn'/ *n.* artificial lake forming part of the Panama Canal

gauche /gōSH/ *adj.* socially awkward; tactless —**gauche'ness** *n.* [Fr]

gau·che·rie /gōSH'(ə)rē'/ *n.* gauche manners or act [Fr, fr. GAUCHE]

gau·cho /gou'CHō/ *n.* (*pl.* **·chos**) cowboy from the South American pampas [Sp fr. Quechua]

gaud·y /gô'dē/ *adj.* (**·i·er, ·i·est**) tastelessly showy —**gaud'i·ly** *adv.*; **gaud'i·ness** *n.* [obs. *gaud* ornament, fr. L *gaudere* rejoice]

gauge /gāj/ *n.* (also, in technical use, **gage**) 1 standard measure, esp. of capacity, fineness, diameter, etc. 2 instrument for measuring 3 distance between rails of a railroad 4 criterion; test —*v.* (**gauged** or **gaged, gaug·ing** or **gag·ing**) 5 measure 6 judge; estimate [Fr]

• Usage: The form *gage* is found in some technical writing, but in ordinary English, *gauge* prevails.

Gau·guin /gōgaN'/, **(Eugène) Paul** 1848–1903; French painter

Gau·ha·ti /gouhät'ē/ *n.* city in India on the Brahmaputra River. Pop. 577,600

Gaul /gôl/ *n.* 1 province of the Roman Empire, in W Europe 2 inhabitant of ancient Gaul [Fr fr. Gmc]

Gaul'ish *adj.* 1 of the Gauls —*n.* 2 their language

Gaulle see DE GAULLE

gaunt /gônt, gänt/ *adj.* 1 lean; haggard 2 grim; desolate —**gaunt'ness** *n.*

gaunt·let[1] /gônt'lit, gänt'-/ *n.* 1 stout glove with a long loose wrist 2 *Hist.* armored glove 3 throw down the **gauntlet** issue a challenge [Fr dim. of *gant* glove]

gaunt·let[2] *n.* (also **gant·let** /gant'lit/) as in run the **gauntlet** 1 undergo harsh criticism 2 pass between two rows of people and receive punishing blows [Sw *gatlopp* fr. *gata* lane + *lopp* course]

Gau·ta·ma /gout'əmə, gôt'-/ family name of the BUDDHA

gauze /gôz/ *n.* thin transparent fabric of silk, cotton, etc. —**gauz'y** *adj.* (**·i·er, ·i·est**)

gave /gāv/ *v.* past of GIVE

gav·el /gav'əl/ *n.* hammer used by a judge, etc., to summon attention

ga·votte /gəvät'/ *n.* 1 old French dance 2 music for this [Fr fr. Prov]

gawk /gôk/ *v.* stare stupidly; gape [obs. *gaw* GAZE]

gawk'y *adj.* (**·i·er, ·i·est**) awkward or ungainly —**gawk'i·ly** *adv.*; **gawk'i·ness** *n.*

gay /gā/ *adj.* 1 lighthearted; cheerful 2 brightly colored 3 homosexual —*n.* 4 (esp. male) homosexual —**gay'ness** *n.* [Fr]

gay·e·ty /gā'itē/ *n.* var. of GAIETY

gaze /gāz/ *v.* (gazed, gaz·ing) 1 look fixedly —*n.* 2 intent look

ga·ze·bo /gəzē'bō/ *n.* (*pl.* -bos) open-sided pavilion, etc., with a wide view [perh. fr. GAZE]

ga·zelle /gəzel'/ *n.* (*pl.* same or -zelles) type of swift, graceful antelope [Ar *gazāl*]

ga·zette /gəzet'/ *n.* 1 newspaper (used in the title) 2 *Brit.* official publication with announcements, etc. [Fr fr. It]

gaz·et·teer /gaz'ətēr'/ *n.* geographical index or dictionary [It, rel. to GAZETTE]

Ga·zi·an·tep /gäz'ēän'tep'/ *n.* city in Turkey. Pop. 603,400

gaz·pa·cho /gəspäCH'ō/ *n.* (*pl.* -chos) cold Spanish-style vegetable soup [Sp]

GB *abbr.* Great Britain

Gd *symb.* gadolinium

Gdansk /gədänsk', -dansk'/ *n.* seaport in Poland, on the Baltic. Pop. 465,400

GDP *abbr.* gross domestic product

Gdy·nia /gədin'ēə/ *n.* seaport in Poland, on the Baltic. Pop. 251,500

Ge *symb.* germanium

gear /gēr/ *n.* 1 (often *pl.*) a set of toothed wheels that work together, as in a vehicle **b** particular setting of these (*first gear*) 2 equipment; clothing, etc. —*v.* 3 adjust or adapt (to) 4 **gear up** make ready; prepare [ON]

gear' shift' *n.* lever used to engage or change gear

gear'wheel' *n.* toothed wheel in a set of gears

geck·o /gek'ō/ *n.* (*pl.* -os) tropical lizard [Malay]

gee /jē/ *interj.* (also geez /jēz/, gee whiz') *Colloq.* expression of surprise, etc. [abbr. of JESUS]

geese /gēs/ *n.* *pl.* of GOOSE

gee·zer /gē'zər/ *n.* *Slang.* person, esp. an old man [dial. *guiser* mummer]

ge·fil'te fish' /gəfil'tə/ *n.* cakes or balls of minced and seasoned usu. freshwater fish [Yiddish]

Geh·rig /ger'ig/, **Lou** (Henry Louis) 1903–41; US baseball player

Gei'ger count'er /gī'gər/ *n.* device for detecting and measuring radioactivity [for H. *Geiger*, German physicist]

gei·sha /gā'SHə, gē'-/ *n.* (*pl.* same or -shas) Japanese woman trained to entertain men [Japn]

gel /jel/ *n.* 1 semisolid jellylike colloid 2 jellylike substance —*v.* (gelled, gel·ling) 3 form a gel 4 see JELL [fr. GELATIN]

gel·a·tin /jel'ət·n/ *n.* (also gel'a·tine /-tēn'/) transparent jellylike substance derived from skin, tendons, etc., used in cooking, photography, etc. —**ge·lat'i·nous** /-lat'ənəs/ *adj.* [It, rel. to JELLY]

gel·cap /jel'kap'/ *n.* *Pharm.* capsule-shaped tablet with gel coating for ease of swallowing [gelatin + capsule]

geld /geld/ *v.* castrate [ON]

geld'ing *n.* gelded animal, esp. a horse

Gel·sen·kir·chen /gel'zənkēr'KHən, -kən/ *n.* city in Germany. Pop. 293,700

gem /jem/ *n.* 1 precious stone, esp. cut and polished 2 thing or person of great beauty or worth [L *gemma* bud; jewel]

Gem·i·ni /jem'ənī/ *n.* (*pl.* -nis) 1 constel-

---

lation and third sign of the zodiac (the Twins) 2 person born under this sign [L: twins]

gem'stone' *n.* precious stone used as a gem

ge·müt·lich /gəmOET'liKH/ *adj.* friendly; cozy [Ger]

Gen. *abbr.* General

-gen *comb. form* that which produces (*hydrogen; antigen*) [Gk *-genēs* born]

gen·darme /ZHän'därm'/ *n.* (in Frenchspeaking countries) police officer [Fr *gens d'armes* men of arms]

gen·der /jen'dər/ *n.* 1 *Gram.* a classification corresponding to the two sexes and sexlessness **b** grouping of words in some languages according to this, as masculine, feminine, neuter 2 a person's sex [L GENUS]

gen'der gap' *n.* disparities between men and women in salary, opportunities, etc.

gene /jēn/ *n.* unit in a chromosome determining heredity [Ger]

ge·ne·al·o·gy /jē'nēal'əjē/ *n.* (*pl.* -gies) 1 descent traced continuously from an ancestor 2 study of family descent —**ge'ne·a·log'i·cal** /-läj'ikəl/ *adj.*; **ge'ne·a·log'i·cal·ly** *adv.*; **ge' ne·al'o·gist** *n.* [Gk *genea* race]

gen·er·a /jen'ərə/ *n.* *pl.* of GENUS

gen·er·al /jen'(ə)rəl/ *adj.* 1 including or affecting all or most parts or cases 2 prevalent; usual 3 not partial, particular, or local 4 not restricted, specialized, or detailed —*n.* 5 *Milit.* **a** officer ranking above colonel **b** specifically, officer ranking above lieutenant general 6 commander of an army 7 leader or strategist 8 **in general: a** as a normal rule; usually **b** for the most part [L *generalis*]

gen·er·a·lis·si·mo /jen'(ə)rəlisəmō'/ *n.* (*pl.* -mos) commander of combined armed forces (in certain countries) [It superl.]

gen·er·al·i·ty /jen'əral'itē/ *n.* (*pl.* -ties) 1 general statement or rule 2 general applicability 3 lack of detail 4 main body or majority

gen·er·al·ize /jen'(ə)rəlīz'/ *v.* (-ized, -iz·ing) 1 speak in general or indefinite terms 2 reduce to a general statement 3 derive or assume (a rule, etc.) from particular cases —**gen·er·al·i·za'tion** *n.*

gen·er·al·ly *adv.* 1 usually; in most respects or cases 2 without regard to particulars or exceptions

gen'er·al prac·ti'tion·er *n.* community or nonspecialist doctor; *abbr.* GP

Gen·er·al Sar·mien·to /hä'näräl' särmyän' tō/ *n.* city in Argentina. Pop. 646,900

gen·er·ate /jen'ərāt'/ *v.* (-at·ed, -at·ing) bring into existence; produce [L, rel. to GENUS]

gen·er·a'tion *n.* 1 all the people born at about the same time 2 stage in a family history 3 stage in (esp. technological) development 4 average time for a new human generation (about 30 years) 5 production, as of electricity 6 procreation [L, rel. to GENERATE]

Gen'er·a'tion X' term for those born from approx. 1965 to 1975 [fr. novel by Douglas Coupland]

gen·er·a·tive /jen'ərətiv/ *adj.* 1 of procreation 2 productive

gen·er·a·tor /jen'ərātər/ *n.* 1 machine for converting mechanical into electrical energy 2 apparatus for producing gas, steam, etc.

ge·ner·ic /jəner′ik/ *adj.* 1 characteristic of or relating to an entire class 2 (of a product) not having a trade or brand name 3 *Biol.* characteristic of or belonging to a genus —*n.* 4 generic product —**ge·ner′i·cal·ly** *adv.* [L, rel. to GENUS]

gen·er·ous /jen′(ə)rəs/ *adj.* 1 giving or given freely 2 magnanimous 3 abundant —**gen′er·os′i·ty** /jē′nē′ətē/ *n.*; **gen′er·ous·ly** *adv.* [L, rel. to GENUS]

gen·e·sis /jen′əsis/ *n.* 1 origin; mode of formation 2 (*cap.*) first book of the Old Testament, with an account of the Creation [Gk *gen* be produced]

ge·net·ic /jənet′ik/ *adj.* 1 of genetics or genes 2 or in origin —**ge·net′i·cal·ly** *adv.* [fr. GENESIS]

ge·net′ic code′ *n.* arrangement of genetic information in chromosomes

ge·net′ic en′gi·neer′ing *n.* manipulation of DNA to modify hereditary features

ge·net′ic fin′ger·print′ing *n.* identifying individuals by DNA patterns

ge·net·ics /jənet′iks/ *n. pl.* (treated as *sing.*) the study of heredity and inherited characteristics —**ge·net′i·cist** /-əsist/ *n.*

Ge·ne·va /jənē′və/ *n.* city in Switzerland. Pop. 167,200

Ge·ne′va, Lake′ of *n.* lake between SW Switzerland and France

Gen·ghis Khan /jeNG′gəs kän′, geNG′gəs/ *n.* c. 1162–1227; Mongol leader; conquered most of Asia and part of E Europe

gen·i·al /jēn′yəl/ *adj.* 1 sociable; cordial 2 (of climate) mild and warm; conducive to growth —**ge·ni·al·i·ty** /jē′nē·al′ətē/ *n.*; **ge′nial·ly** *adv.* [L, rel. to GENIUS]

ge·nie /jē′nē/ *n.* (in Arabian tales) spirit or goblin with magical powers [Fr *génie* GENIUS: cf. JINN]

gen·i·tal /jen′ət·l/ *adj.* 1 of reproduction or the reproductive organs —*n.* 2 (*pl.*) external reproductive organs [L *genitalis* of birth fr. *gignere* beget]

gen·i·ta·li·a /jen′ətāl′yə/ *n. pl.* genitals [L, neut. *pl.* of *genitalis*: see GENITAL]

gen·i·tive /jen′ətiv/ *Gram.* *n.* 1 case expressing possession or close association —*adj.* 2 of or in this case [L, rel. to GENITAL]

ge·nius /jēn′yəs/ *n.* (*pl.* **·nius·es**) 1a exceptional intellectual or creative power or other ability b person with this 2 guardian spirit of a person, place, etc. [L]

genl. *abbr.* general

Gen·o·a /jen′əwə/ *n.* seaport in Italy. Pop. 701,000

gen·o·cide /jen′əsīd′/ *n.* deliberate extermination of a people or nation —**gen′o·ci′dal** *adj.* [Gk *genos* race + -CIDE]

-genous *comb. form* forming adjectives meaning 'produced' (*endogenous*)

gen·re /zHän′rə/ *n.* 1 kind or style of art, etc. 2 painting of scenes from ordinary life [Fr, rel. to GENDER]

gent /jent/ *n. Colloq.* gentleman

gen·teel /jentēl′/ *adj.* affectedly refined or stylish —**gen·teel′ly** *adv.* [Fr *gentil*, rel. to GENTLE]

gen·tian /jen′cHən/ *n.* mountain plant usu. with blue flowers [L *gentiana*]

Gen·tile /jen′tīl′/ (also g-) *adj.* 1 not Jewish —*n.* 2 person who is not Jewish [L *gentilis* fr. *gens* family]

gen·til·i·ty /jentil′ətē/ *n.* 1 social superiority 2 genteel manners or behavior [Fr, rel. to GENTLE]

gen·tle /jent′l/ *adj.* (**·tler**, **·tlest**) 1 not rough or severe; mild; kind 2 moderate (*gentle breeze*) 3 courteous; refined —**gen′tle·ness** *n.*; **gent′ly** *adv.* [L, rel. to GENTILE]

gen·tle·man /jent′l·mən/ *n.* (*pl.* **·men**) 1 man (in polite address) 2 well-mannered, honorable man 3 man of good social standing 4 (*pl.*) form of address to men in an audience —**gen′tle·man·ly** *adj.*

gen·tri·fi·ca·tion /jen′trəfikā′sHən/ *n.* renovation of a deteriorating urban area into housing, etc., for the well-to-do —**gen′tri·fy** /-fī/ *v.* (**·fied**, **·fy·ing**)

gen·try /jen′trē/ *n. pl.* 1 well-born or affluent people 2 particular group of people [Fr, rel. to GENTLE]

gen·u·flect /jen′yəflekt′/ *v.* bend the knee, esp. in worship —**gen′u·flec′tion** /-flək′sHən/ *n.* [L *genu* knee + *flectere* bend]

gen·u·ine /jen′yōō·in, -in′/ *adj.* 1 really coming from its reputed source, etc.; not sham 2 sincere —**gen′u·ine·ly** *adv.*; **gen′u·ine·ness** *n.* [L]

ge·nus /jē′nəs/ *n.* (*pl.* **gen·er·a** /jen′ərə/ or **·nus·es**) 1 *Zool.* taxonomic category, usu. of several species, with common structural characteristics 2 kind; class [L *genus*]

geo- *comb. form* earth [Gk *gē* earth]

ge·o·cen·tric /jē′ōsen′trik/ *adj.* 1 considered as viewed from the earth's center 2 having the earth as the center —**ge′o·cen′tri·cal·ly** *adv.*

ge·ode /jē′ōd/ *n.* 1 cavity lined with crystals 2 rock containing this [Gk *geōdēs* earthlike]

ge·o·de·sic /jē′ədes′ik, -dē′zik/ *adj.* 1 (also **ge′o·det′ic** /-det′ik/) of geodesy 2 (of a dome) constructed as a framework of interlocked polygons

ge·od·e·sy /jēäd′əsē/ *n.* the study of the shape and area of the earth [Gk *geōdaisia*]

ge·o·graph·i·cal /jē′əgraf′ikəl/ *adj.* (also **ge′o·graph′ic**) of geography —**ge′o·graph′i·cal·ly** *adv.*

ge′o·graph′ic in′for·ma′tion sys′tem(s) (also GIS) *n.* computerized system utilizing precise locational data for mapping, navigation, etc.

ge·og·ra·phy /jēäg′rəfē/ *n.* 1 science of the earth's physical features, resources, climate, population, etc. 2 features or terrain of a region —**ge·og′ra·pher** *n.* [L fr. Gk]

geol. *abbr.* 1 geologic 2 geological 3 geologist 4 geology

ge·ol·o·gy /jēäl′əjē/ *n.* science of the earth's crust, strata, origin of its rocks, etc. —**ge′o·log′i·cal** /-əloj′ikəl/ *adj.*; **ge·o·log′i·cal·ly** *adv.*; **ge·ol′o·gist** *n.*

geom. *abbr.* geometric; geometry

ge·o·met·ric /jē′əme′trik/ *adj.* (also **ge′o·met′ri·cal**) 1 of geometry 2 (of a design, etc.) with regular lines and shapes —**ge′o·met′ri·cal·ly** *adv.*

ge′o·met′ric pro·gres′sion *n.* numeric series with a constant ratio between quantities (as 1, 3, 9, 27)

ge·om·e·try /jēäm′ətrē/ *n.* study of the properties and relations of lines, surfaces, and solids —**ge·o·me·tri·cian** /jē-äm′ətrĭsh′ən, jē′əmə-/ *n.* [fr. GEO- + -METRY]

ge·o·phys·ics /jē′ōfĭz′ĭks/ *n. pl.* (treated as *sing.*) physics of the earth

George III /jôrj/ 1738–1820; king of England (1760–1820) during American Revolution

George, St. died c. 337; patron saint of England

George·town /jôrg′toun/ *n.* capital of Guyana. Pop. 150,400

Geor·gia /jôr′jə/ *n.* 1 S state of the US. Capital: Atlanta. Pop. 6,478,216. Abbr. **GA; Ga.** 2 republic in E Europe, formerly part of the USSR. Capital: Tbilisi. Pop. 5,482,000 —**Geor′gian** *n. & adj.*

ge·o·sta·tion·ar·y /jē′ōstā′shənĕr′ē/ (also **ge·o·syn·chro·nous** /jē′ōsĭng′krənəs/) *adj.* pertaining to a satellite orbiting so that it remains in a fixed position above a point on the earth's surface

ge·ra·ni·um /jərā′nēəm/ *n.* 1 widely cultivated garden plant with red, white, or pink flowers 2 herb or shrub bearing fruit shaped like a crane's bill [Gk *geranos* crane]

ger·bil /jûr′bəl/ *n.* (also **jer′bil**) mouselike rodent with long hind legs [Fr, rel. to *jerboa*]

ger·i·at·ric /jĕr′ē-ă′trĭks/ *adj.* of old people [Gk *gēras* old age + *iatros* doctor]

ger·i·at·rics /jĕr′ē-ă′trĭks/ *n. pl.* (usu. treated as *sing.*) branch of medicine or social science dealing with the health and care of old people

germ /jûrm/ *n.* 1 microorganism, esp. one causing disease 2 seed 3 kernel; originating element —**germ′y** *adj.* (·i·er, ·i·est) [L *germen* sprout]

Ger·man /jûr′mən/ *n.* 1a native or national of Germany b person of German descent 2 language of Germany —*adj.* 3 of Germany or its people or language [L *Germanus*]

ger·mane /jərmān′/ *adj.* relevant [L *germanus* related]

Ger·man·ic /jərmăn′ĭk/ *adj.* 1 having German characteristics 2 of the Germans 3 of the Scandinavians, Anglo-Saxons, or Germans —*n.* 4 branch of Indo-European languages that includes English, German, Dutch, and the Scandinavian languages 5 the primitive language of Germanic peoples

ger·ma·ni·um /jərmā′nēəm/ *n.* brittle grayish-white semi-metallic element; *symb.* Ge [for *Germany*]

Ger′man mea′sles *n. pl.* disease like mild measles; rubella

Ger′man shep′herd *n.* breed of large dog related to the wolfhound

Ger·ma·ny /jûr′mənē/ *n.* republic in W Europe. Capital: Berlin; seat of government: Bonn. Pop: 79,122,000

ger·mi·cide /jûr′məsīd′/ *n.* substance that destroys germs —**ger′mi·ci′dal** *adj.*

ger·mi·nal /jûr′mən-l/ *adj.* 1 of germs 2 in the earliest stage of development [rel. to GERM]

ger·mi·nate /jûr′mənāt′/ *v.* (·nat·ed, ·nat·ing) 1 sprout; bud; develop 2 cause to do this —**ger′mi·na′tion** *n.* [L, rel. to GERM]

Ge·ron·i·mo /jərän′əmō′/ c. 1829–1909; Apache Indian chief

ger·on·tol·o·gy /jĕr′əntŏl′əjē/ *n.* study of old age and aging [Gk *gerōn* old man + -LOGY]

ger·ry·man·der /jĕr′ēmăn′dər/ *v.* manipulate voting district boundaries for political advantage [for E. *Gerry*, 19th cent. governor of Mass.]

Gersh·win /gûrsh′wən/ 1 **Ira** 1896–1983; US lyricist; collaborator with his brother: 2 **George** 1898–1937; US composer and pianist

ger·und /jer′ənd/ *n. Gram.* verbal noun, in English ending in -*ing* (e.g., *Do you mind my asking?; Dancing is her favorite exercise*) [L]

Ge·sta·po /gəstäp′ō/ *n. Hist.* Nazi secret police [Ger, fr. *Geheime Staatspolizei*]

ges·ta·tion /jestā′shən/ *n.* 1 process or period in the uterus between conception and birth 2 development of a plan, idea, etc. —**ges′tate** *v.* (·tat·ed, ·tat·ing) [L *gestare* carry]

ges·tic·u·late /jestĭk′yəlāt′/ *v.* (·lat·ed, ·lat·ing) use gestures instead of or to reinforce speech —**ges·tic′u·la′tion** *n.* [L, rel. to GESTURE]

ges·ture /jes′chər/ *n.* 1 meaningful movement of a limb or the body 2 use of such movements, esp. for communication 3 action to evoke a response or convey intention, usu. friendly —*v.* (·tured, ·tur·ing) 4 gesticulate [L *gestura* fr. *gerere* wield]

get /get/ *v.* (**got**, **got** or **got·ten**, **get·ting**) 1 come into possession of; acquire; obtain; receive; earn 2 fetch or procure 3 go to ride on (a bus, train, etc.) 4 (cause to) reach some state or become (*got them ready*) 5 establish contact by telephone, etc. 6 experience or suffer; be subjected to (*get sick*) 7 succeed in bringing, placing, coming, or going (*get there somehow*) 8 (with *have*) a possess (*have not got a penny*) b be bound or obliged (*have got to see you*) 9 induce; prevail upon (*got them to help me*) 10 *Colloq.* understand (a person or an argument) (*have you got that?*) 11 *Colloq.* punish; retaliate against; kill (*I'll get you for that*) 12 *Colloq.* a annoy b affect emotionally c attract 13 develop an inclination (*getting to like it*) 14 begin (*get going*) 15 conceive (an idea, etc.) 16 get along (or on): a live harmoniously b fare; manage 17 **get around** (or **about**): a travel extensively or fast b begin walking, etc. (esp. after illness) 18 **get at**: a reach; get hold of b *Colloq.* imply 19 **get away with**: a escape blame or punishment for b steal 20 **get back** at retaliate against 21 **get by** *Colloq.* manage well enough 22 **get off**: a *Colloq.* (cause to) be acquitted; escape with little or no punishment b start c alight from (a bus, etc.) 23 **get on** enter (a bus, airplane, etc.) 24 **get out**: a leave or escape or help to do this b manage to go outdoors c alight from a vehicle d make or become known 25 **get out of** avoid or escape (a duty, etc.) 26 **get over** recover from (an illness, upset, etc.) 27 **get through**: a manage; survive b succeed in communicating with; make contact [ON]

get′a·way′ *n.* escape, esp. after a crime

get′-to·geth′er *n. Colloq.* social gathering

Get·ty /get′ē/, **J(ean) Paul** 1892–1976; US industrialist

Get·tys·burg /get′ēzbərg/ *n.* American Civil War battlesite in Penn.

get′-up′ *n. Colloq.* style of dress, garb, etc.

gew·gaw /gyŏŏ′gô/ *n.* trinket

gey·ser /ˈgīˈzər/ n. intermittent hot spring [Icel *Geysir* fr. *geysa* to gush]

Gha·na /ˈgänə/ n. republic in W Africa. Capital: Accra. Pop. 15,237,000 —**Gha·na·ian**, **Ghan·i·an** n. & adj.

ghast·ly /ˈgas(t)lē/ adj. (·li·er, ·li·est) 1 horrible; frightful 2 *Colloq.* terrible 3 deathlike; pallid —**ghast′li·ness** n. [obs. *gast* terrify]

Ghent /gent/ n. port in Belgium. Pop. 230,200

gher·kin /ˈgərˈkin/ n. small pickled cucumber [Du]

ghet·to /ˈgetˈō/ n. (pl. ·tos) 1 part of a city occupied principally by one minority group 2 *Hist.* Jewish quarter in a city [It]

ghost /gōst/ n. 1 supposed apparition of a dead person or animal; disembodied spirit 2 shadow or semblance 3 secondary optical image or blur —v. 4 act as ghost-writer —**ghost′li·ness** n.; **ghost′ly** adj. (·li·er, ·li·est) [OE]

ghost′ town′ n. town with few or no remaining inhabitants

ghost′·writ′er n. person who writes (a book, etc.) for the credited author —**ghost′·write** v. (·wrote, ·writ·ten, ·writ·ing); **ghost′writ′ing** n.; **ghost′writ′ten** adj.

ghoul /gōōl/ n. 1 person morbidly interested in death, etc. 2 evil spirit in Muslim folklore, preying on corpses —**ghoul′ish** adj.; **ghoul′ish·ly** adv. [Ar]

GI n. soldier in the US army [abbr. of government (or general) issue]

gi·ant /ˈjīˈənt/ n. 1 (*fem.* **gi′ant·ess**) imaginary being of superhuman size 2 person or thing of great size, ability, courage, etc. —adj. 3 very large [Gk *gigas*]

gib·ber /ˈjibˈər/ v. jabber inarticulately [imit.]

gib′ber·ish n. unintelligible or meaningless speech; nonsense

gib·bet /ˈjibˈit/ n. *Hist.* 1 gallows 2 post with an arm from which the body of an executed criminal was hung [Fr *gibet*]

gib·bon /ˈgibˈən/ n. long-armed SE Asian anthropoid ape [Fr]

Gib·bon /ˈgibˈən/, Edward 1737–94; English historian

gib·bous /ˈgibˈəs/ adj. 1 convex 2 (esp. of the moon) appearing greater than a semicircle and less than a circle (see illustration at MOON PHASES) [L *gibbus* hump]

gibe /jīb/ v. (also **jibe**) (gibed, gib·ing) 1 jeer; mock —n. 2 jeering remark; taunt [perh. fr. Fr *giber* handle roughly]

gib·lets /ˈjibˈlits/ n. pl. edible organs, etc., of a bird [Fr *gibelet* game stew]

Gi·bral·tar /jiˈbrôlˈtər/ n. 1 British crown colony near the S tip of Spain 2 (**Strait of**) strait between Europe and Africa at the W end of the Mediterranean Sea

gid·dy /ˈgidˈē/ adj. (·di·er, ·di·est) 1 tending to fall or stagger; dizzy 2a mentally intoxicated (*giddy with success*) b excitable; flighty 3 causing dizziness —**gid′di·ly** /-dəlē/ adv.; **gid′di·ness** n. [OE]

Gide /zhēd/, André 1869–1951; French writer and critic

Giel·gud /ˈgēlˈgŏŏd/, (Sir) (Arthur) John 1904– ; English actor and director

gift /gift/ n. 1 thing given; present 2 natural ability or talent 3 giving [ON, rel. to GIVE]

gift′-wrap′ v. (·wrapped, ·wrap·ping) wrap with decorative paper for presentation as a gift

gig¹ /gig/ n. 1 light two-wheeled one-horse carriage 2 light ship's boat

gig² n. *Colloq.* engagement to play music, etc.

giga- comb. form one billion (10⁹) [Gk, rel. to GIANT]

gi·gan·tic /jīˈganˈtik/ adj. enormous; huge [L, rel. to GIANT]

gig·gle /ˈgigˈəl/ v. (·gled, ·gling) 1 laugh in a usu. high-pitched or nervous burst —n. 2 such a laugh —**gig′gly** adj. (·gli·er, ·gli·est) [imit.]

GI·GO /ˈgīˈgō/ n. *Comp.* abbr. for garbage in, garbage out, implying that quality of data input determines quality of the results

gig·o·lo /ˈjigˈəlō/ n. (pl. ·los) woman's paid male escort or lover [Fr]

Gi·jón /hēˈhōn/ n. seaport in Spain on the Bay of Biscay. Pop. 259,100

Gil·bert /ˈgilˈbərt/, (Sir) W(illiam) S(chwenck) 1836–1911; English dramatist; collaborated with composer (Sir) Arthur Sullivan

gild /gild/ v. (gild·ed or gilt, gild·ing) 1 cover thinly with gold 2 give a false brilliance to [OE, rel. to GOLD]

gill¹ /gil/ n. (usu. pl.) respiratory organ in a fish, etc. [ON]

gill² /jil/ n. unit of liquid measure equal to 1/4 pint [Fr]

Gil·les·pie /gəˈlesˈpē/, "Dizzy" (John Birks) 1917–93; US jazz trumpet player

gilt /gilt/ adj. 1 thinly covered with gold —n. 2 gilding [fr. GILD]

gilt′-edged′ adj. (of securities, etc.) very reliable

gim·bals /ˈgimˈbəlz, ˈjim′-/ n. pl. contrivance of rings and pivots for keeping instruments horizontal in ships, aircraft, etc. [var. of *gimmal* fr. Fr *gemel* double finger-ring]

gim·crack /ˈjimˈkrak′/ adj. 1 showy but flimsy and worthless —n. 2 showy ornament; gewgaw

gim·let /ˈgimˈlit/ n. boring tool with a pointed screw tip [Fr]

gim·mick /ˈgimˈik/ n. trick or device, esp. to attract attention or publicity —**gim′mick·ry** n.; **gim′mick·y** adj.

gim·py /ˈgimˈpē/ adj. (·i·er, ·i·est) *Slang.* lame

gin¹ /jin/ n. distilled alcoholic beverage typically flavored with juniper berries [Du *geneva*, rel. to JUNIPER]

gin² n. 1 snare; trap 2 (in full **cot′ton gin′**) machine separating cotton from its seeds —v. (ginned, gin·ning) 3 process (cotton) in a gin [Fr, rel. to ENGINE]

gin·ger /ˈjinˈjər/ n. 1a pungent root used as a spice or flavoring b plant having this root 2 light reddish-yellow 3 vigor; mettle —**gin′ger** adj. [OE and Fr, ult. fr. Skt]

gin′ger ale′ n. ginger-flavored carbonated drink

gin′ger beer′ n. usu. nonalcoholic carbonated drink made with ginger and syrup

gin′ger·bread′ n. 1 ginger-flavored cake —adj. 2 architecturally over-decorated

gin·ger·ly /ˈjinˈjərlē/ adv. 1 in a careful or

cautious manner —*adj.* 2 showing great care or caution [perh. fr. Fr *gensor* delicate]

ging·ham /GING'əm/ *n.* smooth-finish, patterned cotton cloth [Du fr. Malay]

gin·gi·vi·tis /jin'jəvīt'is/ *n.* inflammation of the gums [L *gingiva* GUM² + -ITIS]

gink·go /GING'kō/ *n.* (*pl.* -goes) tree with fan-shaped leaves and yellow flowers [Chin: silver apricot]

gin rum·my /jin' rəm'ē/ *n.* form of the card game rummy

Gins·berg /ginz'bərg/, **Allen** 1926– ; US poet

gin·seng /jin'seNG', -saNG'/ *n.* plant of E Asia and N America whose root is used as a medicinal tonic [Chin]

Gior·gio·ne /jôrjō'nā/ c. 1478–1511; Italian painter

Giot·to /jät'ō, jē-ät'ō/ c. 1267–1337; Italian painter

Gip·sy /jip'sē/ *n.* var. of GYPSY

gi·raffe /jəraf'/ *n.* (*pl.* same or -raffes) four-legged African animal with long neck and forelegs [Fr, ult. fr. Ar]

gird /gərd/ *v.* (**gird·ed** or **girt, gird·ing**) 1 encircle or secure with a belt or band 2 enclose or encircle 3 **gird** (or **gird up**) one's **loins** prepare for action [OE]

gird'er *n.* iron or steel support beam

gir·dle /gərd'l/ *n.* 1 belt worn around the waist 2 corset 3 thing that surrounds —*v.* (**-dled, -dling**) 4 surround with a girdle [OE]

girl /gərl/ *n.* 1 female child; daughter 2 young woman 3 girlfriend 4 (*formerly*) female servant —**girl'hood** *n.*; **girl'ish, girl'y** *adj.* [ME *girle* young child]

girl'friend *n.* 1 person's regular female companion or lover 2 female friend

Girl' Scout' *n.* member of the Girl Scouts of America, youth organization that promotes skills, character, etc.

girt /gərt/ *v.* see GIRD

girth /gərTH/ *n.* 1 distance around a thing 2 band around the body of a horse to secure the saddle, etc. [ON, rel. to GIRD]

GIS *abbr.* geographic information system(s)

Gis·card d'Es·taing /ZHēskär' destaN'/, **Valéry** 1926– ; president of France (1974–81)

Gish /giSH/, **Lillian** 1896–1993; US actress

gis·mo /giz'mō/ *n.* (also **giz'mo**) (*pl.* -mos) *Slang.* gadget

gist /jist/ *n.* substance or essence of a matter [OFr *giste* fr. L *jacere* LIE¹]

give /giv/ *v.* (**gave, giv·en, giv·ing**) 1 transfer the possession of; hand over as a present 2a transfer temporarily; provide with (*give him the dog to hold*) b administer (medicine) c deliver (a message) 3a confer; grant; provide b pledge (*gave his word*) 4 perform; execute; conduct 5 yield to pressure; collapse 6 yield as a product or result (*gives an average of 7*) 7 devote; dedicate (*gave his life to the cause*) 8 offer; show (*give me an example*) 9 be a source of; cause (*gave me a cold*) 10 (as *given*) assumed; granted; specified (*given the circumstances*) —*n.* 11 capacity to yield or comply; elasticity 12 **give and take** exchange of words, ideas, blows, etc. 13 **give away**: a transfer as a gift b hand over (a bride) to a bridegroom c reveal 14 **give in** yield; acknowledge defeat 15 **give off** emit

237

gingham / glass

(fumes, etc.) 16 **give** or **take** *Colloq.* more or less 17 **give out**: a emit b make public c be exhausted d run short e distribute 18 **give rise to** cause 19 **give up**: a resign; surrender b part with c renounce or cease (an activity) 20 **give way**: a yield under pressure; collapse b give precedence —**giv'er** *n.*; **giv'ing** *adj.* [OE]

Gi·za /gē'zə/ *n.* city in Egypt. Pop. 2,156,000

giz·mo /giz'mō/ *n.* (*pl.* -mos) var. of GISMO

giz·zard /giz'ərd/ *n.* part of a bird's stomach that grinds food [Fr]

gla·cé /glasā'/ *adj.* 1 (of fruit, esp. cherries) candied 2 (of cloth, etc.) smooth; polished [Fr]

gla·cial /glā'SHəl/ *adj.* 1 of ice; icy 2 *Geol.* characterized or produced by ice [L *glacies* ice]

gla·cier /glā'SHər/ *n.* massive ice sheet covering a mountain slope or valley [Fr, rel. to GLACIAL]

glad /glad/ *adj.* (**glad·der, glad·dest**) 1 pleased 2 expressing or causing pleasure 3 ready and willing —**glad'ly** *adv.*; **glad'ness** *n.* [OE]

glad·den /glad'n/ *v.* make glad

glade /glād/ *n.* open space in a forest

glad·i·a·tor /glad'ē-āt'ər/ *n. Hist.* trained fighter in ancient Roman spectacles —**glad'i·a·to'ri·al** /-ətôr'ēəl/ *adj.* [L *gladius* sword]

gla·di·o·lus /glad'ē-ō'ləs/ *n.* (*pl.* -**li** /-lī/, -lē, -lī'/) plant of the lily family with sword-shaped leaves and spikes of flowers [L, dim. of *gladius* sword]

Glad·stone /glad'stən, -stōn'/, **William Ewart** 1809–98; prime minister of Great Britain (1868–74; 1880–85; 1886; 1892–94)

Glad'stone bag' *n.* boxlike traveling case opening into two compartments [for W. GLADSTONE]

glam·or·ize /glam'ərīz/ *v.* (**-ized, -iz·ing**) make glamorous or attractive

glam·our /glam'ər/ *n.* (also **glam'or**) 1 physical or cosmetic beauty 2 excitement; adventure (*glamour of travel*) —**glam'or·ous** *adj.*; **glam'or·ous·ly** *adv.* [var. of GRAMMAR in obs. sense 'magic']

glance /glans/ *v.* (**glanced, glanc·ing**) 1 look briefly; direct one's eye 2 strike at an angle and glide off an object (*glancing blow*) 3 (of light, etc.) flash or dart —*n.* 4 brief look 5 flash or gleam 6 **at a glance** immediately upon looking

gland /gland/ *n.* organ or specialized cells that secrete substances [L *glandulae* fr. *glans* acorn]

glan·du·lar /glan'jələr/ *adj.* of a gland or glands

glare /gler/ *v.* (**glared, glar·ing**) 1 look fiercely or fixedly 2 shine dazzlingly —*n.* 3a strong fierce light b oppressive public attention 4 fierce or fixed look [LGer or Du]

glar'ing *adj.* 1 blatant; conspicuous 2 shining oppressively —**glar'ing·ly** *adv.*

Glas·gow /glas'kō, glaz'gō/ *n.* seaport on the Clyde River in Scotland, United Kingdom. Pop. 765,000 —**Glas·we·gian** /glaswē'jən, -jēən/ *n. & adj.*

glass /glas/ *n.* 1 hard, brittle, usu. transparent substance made by fusing sand with soda and lime, etc. 2 objects made of this, collectively 3a drinking or other vessel b its contents 4 (*pl.*) a spectacles b binoculars —**glass′ful** *n.* (*pl.* ·**fuls**) [OE]

glass′ ceil′ing *n.* barrier hindering promotion, esp. of women and minorities, to high executive positions

glass·ware /glas′wer′/ *n.* articles made of glass

glass′y *adj.* (·**i·er**, ·**i·est**) 1 like glass 2 (of the eye, expression, etc.) abstracted; dull; fixed

glau·co·ma /glouko̅o̅′mə, glô-/ *n.* eye condition with increased pressure in the eyeball and gradual loss of sight [Gk *glaukos* grayish blue]

glaze /glāz/ *v.* (**glazed**, **glaz·ing**) 1 fit a window, etc.) with glass or (a building) with windows 2 cover with a clear, shiny finish 3 (of the eyes) become glassy —*n.* 4 vitreous substance for glazing pottery 5 shiny coating [fr. GLASS]

gla·zier /glā′zHər, -zēər/ *n.* person whose trade is repairing window glass, etc.

gleam /glēm/ *n.* 1 faint or brief light or show —*v.* 2 emit gleams; shine [OE]

glean /glēn/ *v.* 1 acquire (facts, etc.) in small amounts 2 gather (grain left by reapers) [Fr]

Glea·son /glē′sən/, Jackie 1916–87; US comedian and actor

glee /glē/ *n.* mirth; delight [OE]

glee′ club′ *n.* group that sings choral music

glee·ful /glē′fəl/ *adj.* joyful —**glee′ful·ly** *adv.*; **glee′ful·ness** *n.*

glen /glen/ *n.* narrow valley [Gaelic]

Glen·dale /glen′dāl′/ *n.* 1 city in Calif. Pop. 180,038 2 city in Ariz. Pop. 148,134

Glen·dow·er /glendou′ər/ (also **Glyndwr** /glinddōr′/, **Owen** c. 1355 – c. 1417; legendary hero of Welsh nationalism

Glenn /glen/, **John Herschel, Jr.** 1921– ; US astronaut and senator

glib /glib/ *adj.* (**glib·ber**, **glib·best**) speaking or spoken quickly or smoothly but with questionable sincerity —**glib′ly** *adv.*; **glib′ness** *n.* [obs. *glibbery* slippery, perh. imit.]

glide /glīd/ *v.* (**glid·ed**, **glid·ing**) 1 move smoothly and continuously 2 *Aeron.* fly without engine power 3 pass gradually or imperceptibly 4 cause to glide —*n.* 5 gliding movement [OE]

glid′er *n.* 1 light aircraft without an engine 2 suspended chair for swinging

glim·mer /glim′ər/ *v.* 1 shine faintly or intermittently —*n.* 2 feeble or wavering light 3 (also **glim′mer·ing**) small sign (of hope, etc.) [prob. Scand]

glimpse /glimps/ *n.* 1 brief view or look 2 faint transient appearance —*v.* (**glimpsed**, **glimps·ing**) 3 have a brief view of [rel. to GLIMMER]

glint /glint/ *v.* 1 flash; glitter —*n.* 2 flash; sparkle [prob. Scand]

glis·san·do /glisän′dō/ *n.* (*pl.* ·**di** /-dē/ or ·**dos**) *Mus.* continuous sliding effect of adjacent notes [It fr. Fr *glissant* sliding]

glis·ten /glis′ən/ *v.* 1 shine like a wet or polished surface —*n.* 2 glitter; sparkle [OE]

glitch /glicH/ *n.* *Slang.* sudden irregularity or malfunction (of equipment, etc.)

glit·ter /glit′ər/ *v.* 1 shine with a bright re-

flected light; sparkle 2 be showy or splendid —*n.* 3 sparkle 4 showiness 5 sparkling material as decoration —**glit′ter·y** *adj.* [ON]

glitz /glits/ *n.* *Slang.* showy glamour —**glitz′y** *adj.* (·**i·er**, ·**i·est**) [fr. GLITTER + RITZY]

gloam·ing /glō′miNG/ *n.* twilight [OE]

gloat /glōt/ *v.* look or think (over) with greed, malice, etc.

glob /gläb/ *n.* soft mass or lump [perh. fr. GOB² + BLOB]

glob·al /glō′bəl/ *adj.* 1 worldwide 2 all-embracing —**glob′al·ly** *adv.* [Fr, rel. to GLOBE]

glob′al warm′ing *n.* increase in the average temperature of the earth's atmosphere caused by the greenhouse effect

globe /glōb/ *n.* 1a (prec. by *the*) the earth b spherical representation of it with a map on the surface 2 spherical object [L *globus*]

globe′-trot′ter *n.* *Colloq.* person who travels widely —**globe′-trot′ting** *n.* & *adj.*

glob·u·lar /gläb′yələr/ *adj.* 1 globe-shaped 2 composed of globules

glob·ule /gläb′yōōl/ *n.* small round particle or drop [L *globulus*]

GLOCKENSPIEL

glock·en·spiel /gläk′ənspēl′, -sHpēl′/ *n.* musical instrument with metal bars or tubes, played with hammers [Ger: bell-play]

gloom /glōōm/ *n.* 1 darkness; obscurity 2 melancholy; despondency

gloom′y *adj.* (·**i·er**, ·**i·est**) 1 dark; unlit 2 depressed or depressing —**gloom′i·ly** *adv.*; **gloom′i·ness** *n.*

glo·ri·fy /glôr′əfī′/ *v.* (·**fied**, ·**fy·ing**) 1 make glorious 2 make seem better or more splendid than it is 3 invest with more attractiveness, importance, etc., than is merited 4 extol —**glo·ri·fi·ca′tion** /-fikā′sHən/ *n.* [L, rel. to GLORY]

glo·ri·ous /glôr′ēəs/ *adj.* 1 possessing or conferring glory; illustrious 2 splendid; excellent —**glo′ri·ous·ly** *adv.*

glo·ry /glôr′ē/ *n.* (*pl.* ·**ries**) 1 renown; honor 2 adoring praise 3 resplendent majesty, beauty, etc. 4 thing that brings renown, distinction, or pride 5 heavenly bliss and splendor —*v.* (·**ried**, ·**ry·ing**) 6 pride oneself (in) [L *gloria*]

gloss¹ /glôs, gläs/ *n.* 1 surface luster 2 deceptively attractive appearance —*v.* 3 make glossy 4 **gloss over** cover or pass over quickly, esp. to conceal

gloss² *n.* 1 explanatory comment added to a text, e.g., in the margin 2 interpretation or paraphrase —*v.* 3 add a gloss to (a text word, etc.) [L *glossa* tongue]

glos·sa·ry /glòs'ərē, gläs'-/ n. (pl. ·ries) list defining technical or special words [L, rel. to GLOSS²]

glos·so·la·li·a /glòs'ōlā'lēə/ n. incoherent utterance associated with religious rapture; speaking in tongues

gloss'y adj. (·i·er, ·i·est) 1 smooth and shiny 2 printed on such paper —n. (pl. ·ies) 3 glossy magazine or photograph —**gloss'i·ly** adv.; **gloss'i·ness** n.

glot·tal stop /glòt''l stäp'/ n. sound produced by the sudden opening or shutting of the glottis

glot·tis /glät'is/ n. opening between the vocal cords —**glot'tal** adj. [Gk]

Glouces·ter /glàs'tər, glòs'-/ n. city on the Severn River in England. Pop. 108,200

glove /gləv/ n. 1 hand covering for protection, warmth, etc., usu. with separate fingers 2 Baseball. hand protection worn by fielders 3 Boxing. padded mitten worn by fighters —v. (gloved, glov·ing) 4 cover or provide with gloves [OE]

glove' com·part'ment n. storage receptacle in the dashboard of a car, etc.

glow /glō/ v. 1a emit light and heat without flame b shine thus 2a (of the body) be heated b show or feel strong emotion 3 show a warm color —n. 4 glowing state 5 bright warm color 6 feeling of satisfaction or well-being [OE]

glow·er /glou'ər/ v. 1 look angrily (at) 2 look dark or threatening —n. 3 glowering look

glow-worm /glō'wərm'/ n. beetle whose wingless female emits light from the end of the abdomen

glu·cose /glōō'kōs', -kōz'/ n. sugar found in the blood, fruit juice, etc. [Gk gleukos sweet wine]

glue /glōō/ n. 1 adhesive substance —v. (glued, glu·ing or glue·ing) 2 fasten or join with glue 3 keep or put very close —**glue'y** adj. (glu·i·er, glu·i·est) [L glus, rel. to GLUTEN]

glum /gləm/ adj. (glum·mer, glum·mest) dejected; sullen —**glum'ly** adv.; **glum'ness** n. [var. of GLOOM]

glut /glət/ v. (glut·ted, glut·ting) 1 feed or indulge to the full; satiate 2 fill to excess —n. 3 supply exceeding demand 4 full indulgence; surfeit [Fr gloutir swallow, rel. to GLUTTON]

glu·ten /glōōt'n/ n. mixture of proteins present in cereal grains; sticky protein residue [L gluten glue]

glu·ti·nous /glōōt'n-əs/ adj. sticky; like glue [L, rel. to GLUTEN]

glut·ton /glət'n/ n. 1 greedy eater 2 insatiably eager person —**glut'ton·ous** adj.; **glut'ton·ous·ly** adv. [L gluttire SWALLOW¹]

glut'ton·y n. greed or excess in eating [Fr, rel. to GLUTTON]

glyc·er·in /glis'ərin/ n. (also **glyc'er·ol** /-əròl'/, **glyc'er·ine** /-in, -ēn'/) thick, sweet, colorless liquid used as medicine, ointment, etc., and in explosives [Gk glukeros sweet]

gly·co·gen /glī'kəjən/ n. substance in animal tissues that is converted to glucose for energy

gm abbr. (also **gm.**) gram(s)

G'-man' n. FBI agent [fr. Government]

GMT abbr. Greenwich Mean Time

gnarled /närld/ adj. knobbly; twisted; rugged [var. of knarled, rel. to KNURL]

gnash /nasH/ v. grind (the teeth) together [ON]

gnat /nat/ n. small two-winged biting fly [OE]

gnaw /nó/ v. 1a wear away by biting b bite persistently 2a corrode; wear away b (of pain, fear, etc.) torment —**gnaw'ing** adj. [OE]

gneiss /nīs/ n. coarse-grained metamorphic rock of feldspar, quartz, and mica [Ger]

gnome /nōm/ n. dwarfish legendary spirit or goblin living underground —**gnom'ish** adj. [Fr]

gno·mic /nō'mik/ adj. of aphorisms; sententious [Gk gnōmē opinion]

GNP abbr. gross national product

gnu /n(y)ōō/ n. (pl. same or -s) oxlike antelope; wildebeest [Bushman nqu]

go /gō/ v. (went, gone, go·ing) 1 start or be moving; travel; proceed 2 engage in (went skiing) 3 lead or extend to (the road goes to London) 4 leave; depart 5 move, act, work, etc. 6 make a specified movement or sound (go like this with your foot; gun went bang) 7 be or proceed in a specified state (go hungry) 8a pass into a specified condition (went to sleep) b Colloq. die 9 (of time or distance) pass; elapse; be traversed (ten days to go; the last mile went quickly) 10a be told, sung, or taken in a certain way (so the story goes; the tune goes like this) b be suitable; fit; match (the shoes don't go with the hat) c be regularly kept; belong (the forks go here) 11 turn out; proceed in a certain way (test went well) 12a be sold (for) b (of money) be spent 13a leave; be gotten rid of (you'll have to go) b fail; decline 14 be acceptable, accepted, or permitted (whatever she says goes) 15 be guided (by, with, or on) (nothing to go on) 16 attend regularly (goes to school) 17 act or proceed to a certain point (go no further) 18 (of a number) be capable of being contained in another (6 into 5 won't go) 19a be allotted or awarded (to) b be allotted (to or toward) (go toward expenses) 20 be known or called (I go by the name Tom) 21 apply to (that goes for me too) —n. (pl. goes) 22 spirit; vigor (a lot of go in her) 23 Colloq. success (made a go of it) 24 Colloq. turn; attempt (I'll have a go) —adj. 25 Colloq. functioning properly (all systems are go) 26 go about set to work at 27 go ahead proceed without hesitation 28 go along with agree to or with 29 go back on fail to keep (a promise, etc.) 30 go down: a subside b decrease in price c sink; set; fall d (of a computer) fail e be recorded in writing f be swallowed g find acceptance 31 go for: a proceed to fetch b avail or yield (went for nothing) c prefer; choose d Colloq. strive to attain (go for it!) e Colloq. attack (the dog went for him) 32 go in for take as one's style, pursuit, etc. 33 go into: a enter (a profession, hospital, etc.) b take up; discuss 34 go off: a depart b explode 35 go on: a continue; persevere b Colloq. talk at great length c proceed (went on to become a star) 36 go out: a leave a room, house, etc. b be extinguished c be broadcast d be courting 37 go over: a inspect b do again c be received 38 go

through: a discuss or scrutinize in detail **b** perform **c** undergo **d** *Colloq.* use up; spend **39 go under** sink; fail; succumb **40 on the go** *Colloq.* in constant motion or activity —**go′er** *n.* [OE]

goad /gōd/ *v.* **1** urge on with a goad **2** irritate; stimulate —*n.* **3** spiked stick for urging cattle forward **4** anything that incites [OE]

go′-a-head′ *n.* permission to proceed

goal /gōl/ *n.* **1** object of ambition or effort; destination **2a** *Sports.* receiving structure or area at which the ball, puck, etc., is directed for a score **b** point won

goal′keep′er *n.* (also **goal-ie** /gō′lē/; **goal′tend′er**) player defending a goal

goat /gōt/ *n.* **1** hardy domesticated mammal with horns and (in the male) a beard **2** lecherous man **3** scapegoat **4** (**the Goat**) zodiacal sign or constellation Capricorn **5 get a person's goat** *Colloq.* irritate a person [OE]

goa-tee /gōtē′/ *n.* small pointed beard

goat′herd /gōt′hərd′/ *n.* person who tends goats

goat′skin′ *n.* **1** skin of a goat **2** garment or bottle made of goatskin

gob¹ /gäb/ *n.* **1** clot of slimy matter **2** *Colloq.* (*pl.*) lots; many [Fr *go(u)be* mouthful]

gob² *n.* *US Navy Slang.* sailor

gob-ble¹ /gäb′əl/ *v.* (·**bled**, ·**bling**) eat hurriedly and noisily [fr. GOB¹]

gob-ble² *v.* (·**bled**, ·**bling**) (of a male turkey) make a characteristic guttural sound

gob-ble-dy-gook /gäb′əldēgōōk′/ *n.* (also **gob′ble-de-gook′**) pompous or unintelligible jargon [prob. imit. of a turkey]

go′-be-tween′ *n.* intermediary

Go-bi /gō′bē/ *n.* desert in E Asia, mostly in Mongolia

gob-let /gäb′lit/ *n.* drinking vessel with a stem and foot [Fr dim. of *gobel* cup]

gob-lin /gäb′lən/ *n.* mischievous ugly dwarflike creature of folklore [AngFr]

god /gäd/ *n.* **1** (**God**) (in Christian and other monotheistic religions) creator and ruler of the universe **2a** being or spirit worshiped as immortal and with supernatural power over nature, human fortunes, etc. **b** image, idol, etc., symbolizing a god **3** adored or greatly admired person —**god′less, god′like** *adj.*; **god′less-ness** *n.* [OE]

Go-dard /gōdär′/, **Jean-Luc** 1930– ; French film director

god′child′ *n.* (*pl.* ·**chil-dren**) person in relation to his or her godparent

God-dard /gäd′ərd/, **Robert Hutchings** 1882–1945; US rocket scientist

god′daugh′ter *n.* female godchild

god-dess /gäd′əs/ *n.* **1** female deity **2** adored woman

god′fa′ther *n.* **1** male godparent **2** patriarch of a criminal organization

god′-for-sak′en *adj.* **1** desolate; barren **2** wretched; dismal

god′head′ *n.* (also *cap.*) **1a** state of being God or a god **b** divine nature **2** deity **3** God

Go-di-va /gədī′və/, **Lady** d. 1080; legendary English noblewoman

god′ly *adj.* (·**li-er**, ·**li-est**) pious; devout —**god′li-ness** *n.*

god′moth′er *n.* female godparent

god′par′ent *n.* person who sponsors a child at baptism

god′send′ *n.* unexpected but welcome event or acquisition

god′son′ *n.* male godchild

Go-du-nov /gōd′n-ôf, gôd′-/, **Boris** 1550–1605; czar of Russia (1598–1605)

Goeb-bels /gœ′bəlz, gər′-/, **Paul Joseph** 1897–1945; German director of Nazi propaganda under Hitler

Goe-ring /gœ′ïNG, gər′-/, **Hermann Wilhelm** 1893–1946; German Nazi leader; directed air force

Goe-the /gœ′tə, gər′-/, **Johann Wolfgang von** 1749–1832; German poet and statesman

go′-get′ter *n.* *Colloq.* aggressively enterprising person

gog-gle /gäg′əl/ *v.* (·**gled**, ·**gling**) **1** look with wide-open eyes —*adj.* **2** (of the eyes) protuberant or rolling —*n.* **3** (*pl.*) spectacles for protecting the eyes [prob. imit.]

go′-go′ *adj.* *Colloq.* (of a dancer, music, etc.) lively, erotic, and rhythmic

Go-gol /gō′gəl, gô′gôl′/, **Nikolai Vasilievich** 1809–52; Russian novelist and dramatist

Goi-â-ni-a /goi-an′ēə, -än′-/ *n.* city in central Brazil. Pop. 703,300

go-ing /gō′ïNG/ *n.* **1** act or process of going **2a** condition of the ground for walking, riding, etc. **b** progress affected by this —*adj.* **3** in or into action (*set the clock going*) **4** current (*the going rate*) **5 get going** start steadily talking, working, etc. **6 going on** approaching (an age) **7 going to** intending to; about to

go′ing-o′ver *n.* **1** *Colloq.* inspection or overhaul **2** *Slang.* thrashing

go′ings-on′ *n. pl.* actions or behavior, esp. disapproved of

goi-ter /goi′tər/ *n.* (also **goi′tre**) enlargement of the thyroid gland [L *guttur* throat]

gold /gōld/ *n.* **1** precious yellow metallic element; *symb.* **Au 2** color of gold **3a** coins or articles of gold **b** wealth —*adj.* **4** made wholly or partly of gold **5** colored like gold [OE]

gold-en /gōl′dən/ *adj.* **1a** made or consisting of gold **b** yielding gold **2** colored or shining like gold **3** precious; excellent

gold′en age′ *n.* period of a nation's greatest prosperity, cultural achievement, etc.

gold′en mean′ *n.* principle of moderation

gold′en par′a-chute *n.* *Business.* contract assuring an executive generous compensation upon termination

gold′en re-triev′er *n.* breed of retriever with a golden-colored coat

gold′en-rod′ *n.* plant with a spike of yellow flowers

gold′en rule′ *n.* principle of conduct: 'Do unto others as you would have them do unto you'

gold-finch /gōld′finCH/ *n.* songbird with a yellow band across each wing

gold′fish′ *n.* (*pl.* same or ·**fish-es**) bright orange fish, often kept in fish bowls

Gol-ding /gōl′diNG/, **(Sir) William** 1911–93; English writer

gold′ leaf′ *n.* gold beaten into a very thin sheet

gold′ med′al *n.* medal of gold, usu. awarded as first prize

gold′ mine′ *n.* **1** place where gold is mined **2** source of great wealth

gold-smith /gōld′smiTH/ *n.* worker in gold

Gold·smith /gṓld'smĭTH'/, **Oliver** 1728–74; Irish writer

gold' stan·dard *n.* system valuing currency in terms of gold

Gold·wyn /gṓld'wən/, **Samuel** (born Schmuel Gelbfishz) 1882–1974; Polish-born US film producer

golf /gălf, gôlf/ *n.* **1** game in which a small hard ball is hit with clubs into a series of 18 or 9 holes using the fewest possible strokes —*v.* **2** play golf —**golf'er** *n.*

Go·li·ath /gəlī'əTH/, (in the Bible) Philistine giant killed by David

gol·ly /găl'ē/ *interj.* expression of surprise

Go·mel /gō'məl, gô'-/ *n.* city in SE Belarus. Pop. 503,300

Gom·pers /găm'pərz/, **Samuel** 1850–1924; English-born US labor leader

go·nad /gō'nad/ *n.* animal organ producing gametes, esp. the testis or ovary [Gk *gonē* seed]

GONDOLA 1

gon·do·la /găn'dələ/ *n.* **1** flat-bottomed boat rowed on Venetian canals **2** car suspended from an airship, balloon, or cable [It]

gon·do·lier /găn'dəlēr'/ *n.* oarsman on a gondola

gone /gŏn, gän/ *adj.* **1** departed; left **2a** lost; hopeless **b** dead **3** *Slang.* completely enthralled or entranced, esp. by music, drugs, etc. [past part. of GO[1]]

gon·er /gō'nər, gän'-/ *n.* *Colloq.* person or thing doomed or irrevocably lost

gong /gôNG, gŏNG/ *n.* **1** metal disk giving a resonant note when struck **2** saucer-shaped bell [Malay]

gon·or·rhea /găn'ərē'ə/ *n.* venereal disease with inflammatory discharge [Gk: semen-flux]

goo /gōō/ *n.* *Colloq.* **1** sticky or slimy substance **2** sickening sentimentality

good /gŏŏd/ *adj.* (bet·ter, best) **1** having the right or desired qualities; adequate **2** efficient; competent **3a** kind **b** morally excellent; virtuous **c** well-behaved **4** enjoyable; agreeable (*good party; good news*) **5** thorough; considerable **6** not less than (*waited a good hour*) **7** beneficial **8** valid; sound —*n.* **9** that which is good; what is beneficial or morally right (*only good can come of it*) **10** (*pl.*) **a** movable property or merchandise **b** (prec. by *the*) *Colloq.* what one has undertaken to supply (esp. *deliver the goods*) **c** *Slang.* evidence; proof of wrongdoing —*adv.* **11** *Colloq.* well (*doing pretty good*) **12 as good as** practically **13** for good (finally); permanently **14 good for: a** beneficial to **b** able to perform **c** able to be trusted to pay **d** worth **15** to the good having as profit or benefit [OE]

• Usage: The adverb for *good* is *well: He is a good worker who does his job well.* A problem arises because *well* is also an adjective meaning 'healthy, fine,' and most critics agree that *good* is informal in its place: *I feel well* (vs. informal "I feel good"). Q: *How are you? A: Very well, thank you* (vs. informal "good"). See note at BAD.

good-bye or **good-bye** /gŏŏdbī'/ *interj.* (also **good'by'** or **good·by'**) **1** expressing good wishes on parting, ending a telephone conversation, etc. —*n.* (*pl.* -byes or -bys) **2** parting; farewell [fr. *God be with you!*]

good' faith' *n.* sincerity of intention

Good' Fri'day *n.* Friday before Easter Sunday, commemorating the crucifixion of Jesus

good'-heart'ed *adj.* kindly; well-meaning

good'-hu'mored *adj.* cheerful; amiable —**good'-hu'mored·ly** *adv.*

good·ie *n.* var. of GOODY

good'ly *adj.* (-li·er, -li·est) **1** handsome **2** of imposing size, etc. —**good'li·ness** *n.* [OE]

Good·man /gŏŏd'mən/, **Benny (Benjamin David)** 1909–86; US jazz clarinetist and bandleader

good'-na'tured *adj.* friendly; easygoing —**good'-na'tured·ly** *adv.*

good·ness /gŏŏd'nəs/ *n.* **1** virtue; excellence **2** kindness **3** what is beneficial in a thing —*interj.* **4** expressing surprise, anger, etc. [OE]

good·will' *n.* **1** kindly feeling **2** established reputation of a business, etc., as an asset

good·y /gŏŏd'ē/ *n.* (*pl.* -ies) **1** *Colloq.* (usu. *pl.*) something good or attractive, esp. to eat —*interj.* **2** expressing childish delight

good'y-good'y *n.* (*pl.* -ies) **1** smugly virtuous person —*adj.* **2** smugly virtuous

goo·ey /gōō'ē/ *adj.* (-i·er, -i·est) *Colloq.* **1** viscous; sticky **2** sentimental [fr. GOO]

goof /gōōf/ *Slang.* *n.* **1** foolish or stupid person **2** mistake —*v.* **3** bungle; blunder **4** (foll. by *off, around*) waste time; avoid duty [L *gufus* coarse]

goof'y *adj.* (-i·er, -i·est) *Slang.* silly or odd; eccentric

goon /gōōn/ *n.* **1** *Slang.* stupid person **2** *Colloq.* ruffian hired by racketeers, etc.

goose /gōōs/ *n.* (*pl.* geese) **1a** large water bird with webbed feet and a broad bill **b** female of this **c** flesh of a goose as food **2** simpleton [OE]

goose·ber·ry /gōōs'ber'ē, gōōz'-/ *n.* (*pl.* -ries) **1** yellowish-green berry with juicy flesh **2** thorny shrub bearing this

goose' flesh' *n.* (also **goose' pim'ples; goose' bumps'**) bristling state of the skin produced by cold, fright, etc.

goose'-step' *n.* **1** military marching step with knees kept stiff —*v.* (-stepped, -step·ping) **2** march thus

GOP *abbr.* Grand Old Party (Republican Party)

go·pher /gō'fər/ *n.* American burrowing rodent; ground squirrel

Gor·ba·chev /gôr'bəchôf', -CHŏv'/, **Mikhail S.** 1931– ; president of the USSR (1988–91)

Gor·di·mer /gôrd'əmər/, **Nadine** 1923– ; South African novelist; Nobel prize 1991

Gor·don /gôrd'n/, **Charles George** 1833–85; British general and colonial administrator

gore[1] /gôr/ *n.* blood shed and clotted [OE: dirt]

gore[2] *v.* (gored, gor·ing) pierce with a horn, tusk, etc.

gore[3] *n.* wedge-shaped piece in a garment [OE: triangle of land]

gorge /gôrj/ *n.* 1 narrow opening between cliffs, etc. 2 act of gorging 3 contents of the stomach —*v.* (gorged, gorg·ing) 4 feed or devour greedily 5 satiate (oneself) [Fr: throat]

gor·geous /gôr′jəs/ *adj.* 1 richly colored; sumptuous 2 *Colloq.* very pleasant; splendid 3 *Colloq.* strikingly beautiful —**gor′geous·ly** *adv.* [Fr]

gor·gon /gôr′gən/ *n.* 1 *Gk. Myth.* each of three snake-haired sisters (esp. Medusa) with the power to turn to stone anyone who looked at them 2 frightening or repulsive woman [Gk *gorgos* terrible]

go·ril·la /gəril′ə/ *n.* largest anthropoid ape, native to Africa [Gk, perh. fr. Afr]

Gor·ky /gôr′kē/, **Maxim** (pseudonym of Aleksei Maksimovich Peshkov) 1868–1936; Russian writer and revolutionary

gorp /gôrp/ *n.* mixture of nuts, raisins, etc., eaten as a snack

gorse /gôrs/ *n.* (also called **furze**) *n.* a spiny evergreen shrub native to Europe

gor·y /gôr′ē/ *adj.* (·i·er, ·i·est) 1 involving bloodshed; sanguinary 2 covered in gore —**gor′i·ly** *adv.*; **gor′i·ness** *n.*

gosh /gäsh/ *interj.* expressing surprise [euphemism for GOD]

gos·ling /gäz′liNG, -lin/ *n.* young goose [ON, rel. to GOOSE]

gos·pel /gäs′pəl/ *n.* 1 teaching of Christ 2 (*cap.*) a record of Christ's life in the first four books of the New Testament b each of these books c portion from one of them read at a service 3 (also **gos′pel truth′**) thing regarded as absolutely true 4 (in full **gos′pel mu′sic**) style of religious singing originated by black Americans [OE, rel. to GOOD + SPELL[1] news]

gos·sa·mer /gäs′əmər/ *n.* 1 filmy substance of small spiders' webs 2 delicate filmy material —*adj.* 3 light and flimsy

gos·sip /gäs′əp/ *n.* 1a unconstrained talk or writing, esp. about persons, rumors, etc. b idle talk 2 person who indulges in gossip —*v.* 3 talk or write gossip —**gos′sip·y** *adj.* [OE, orig. 'godparent,' hence 'familiar acquaintance']

got /gät/ *v. past* and *past part.* of GET

Gö·te·borg /yoE′təbôr′(yə)/ *n.* (also **Gothenburg**) seaport in Sweden. Pop. 432,100

Goth /gäth/ *n.* member of a Germanic tribe that invaded the Roman Empire in the 3rd–5th cent. [OE *Gota* and Gk *Gothoi*]

Goth·ic /gäTH′ik/ *adj.* 1 of the Goths 2 *Archit.* of a style prevalent in W Europe in the 12th–16th cent., characterized by pointed arches 3 (of a novel, etc.) with supernatural or horrifying events —*n.* 4 language of the Goths 5 Gothic architecture [L, rel. to GOTH]

Got·land /gät′lənd/ *n.* island in the Baltic, a province of Sweden

got·ten /gät′ən/ *v. past part.* of GET

Gou·da /gōō′də, goud′ə/ *n.* a mild Dutch cheese [*Gouda* in Holland]

gouge /gouj/ *n.* 1 chisel with a concave blade —*v.* (gouged, goug·ing) 2 cut with or as with a gouge 3 brutally scoop out [LL *gubia*]

gou·lash /gōō′läsh/ *n.* highly seasoned Hungarian meat stew [Magyar *gulyás-hús* herdsman's meat]

Gou·nod /gōōnō′/, **Charles François** 1818–93; French composer

gourd /gôrd, goōrd/ *n.* 1a fleshy usu. large fruit with a hard skin b climbing or trailing plant bearing this 2 hollowed gourd shell used as a drinking vessel, etc. [L *cucurbita*]

gour·mand /goōr′mänd′, -mənd/ *n.* glutton [Fr]

gour·met /goōrmā′/ *n.* connoisseur of good food [Fr]

gout /gout/ *n.* inflammation of the smaller joints, esp. of the big toe —**gout′y** *adj.* [L *gutta* drop]

gov·ern /gəv′ərn/ *v.* 1 rule or control with authority; conduct the affairs of 2 influence or determine 3 be a standard or principle for 4 check or control (esp. passions) [Gk *kybernan* steer]

gov·er·nance /gəv′ərnəns/ *n.* act or manner of governing [Fr, rel. to GOVERN]

gov·ern·ess /gəv′ərnəs/ *n.* woman employed to teach children in a private household

gov·ern·ment /gəv′ə(r)n)mənt′/ *n.* 1 act, manner, or system of governing 2 governing personnel —**gov′ern·men′tal** /-men′təl/ *adj.*

gov·er·nor /gəv′ə(r)nər/ *n.* 1 ruler 2 official governing a province, town, colony, etc. 3 executive head of a US state —**gov′er·nor·ship** *n.*

govt. *abbr.* government

gown /goun/ *n.* 1 loose flowing garment, esp. a woman's long dress or nightgown 2 official or academic robe [L *gunna* fur]

Go·ya /goi′ə/, **Francisco** 1746–1828; Spanish artist

GP *abbr.* general practitioner

GPO *abbr.* 1 Government Printing Office 2 General Post Office

gr *abbr.* (also **gr.**) 1 gram(s) 2 grains 3 gross

grab /grab/ *v.* (grabbed, grab·bing) 1 seize suddenly 2 take greedily or unfairly 3 *Slang.* attract the attention of; impress 4 snatch (at) —*n.* 5 sudden clutch or attempt to seize [LGer or Du]

grace /grās/ *n.* 1 attractiveness in manner, movement, proportion, etc.; elegance 2 courteous goodwill 3 attractive feature; charm (*social graces*) 4 *Christianity.* the favor of God 5 goodwill; favor 6 delay granted as a favor 7 short thanksgiving before or after a meal 8 (*cap.*) (prec. by *His, Her, Your*) form of address for a duke, duchess, or archbishop —*v.* (graced, grac·ing) 9 add grace to; confer honor on [L *gratia*]

grace′ful *adj.* having or showing grace or elegance —**grace′ful·ly** *adv.*; **grace′ful·ness** *n.*

grace′less *adj.* lacking grace, elegance, or charm

gra·cious /grā′shəs/ *adj.* 1 kind; indulgent and beneficent to inferiors 2 (of God) merciful; benign 3 elegant; luxurious —**gra′**

cious·ly adv.; **gra'cious·ness** n. [L, rel. to GRACE]

243

gradate / grange

gra·date /grādāt′/ v. (**-dat·ed, -dat·ing**) 1 (cause to) pass gradually from one shade to another 2 arrange in steps or grades of size, etc.

gra·da'tion n. (usu. pl.) 1 stage, change, or degree in rank, intensity, etc. 2 arrangement in such degrees —**gra·da'tion·al** adj. [L, rel. to GRADE]

grade /grād/ n. **1a** certain degree in rank, merit, proficiency, etc. **b** class or rank 2 mark indicating the quality of a student's work 3 class in school 4 gradient; slope —v. (**grad·ed, grad·ing**) 5 arrange in grades 6 give a grade to (a student, examination paper, etc.) 7 reduce (a road, etc.) to easy gradients [L gradus step]

gra·di·ent /grā'dēənt/ n. 1 stretch of road, railway, etc., that slopes 2 degree of such a slope [prob. fr. GRADE after salient]

grad·u·al /graj'ōōəl/ adj. 1 progressing by degrees 2 not rapid, steep, or abrupt —**grad'u·al·ly** adv. [L, rel. to GRADE]

grad·u·al·ism n. policy of gradual reform

grad·u·ate n. /graj'ōōət/ 1 person holding an academic degree or certificate —v. /graj'ōōāt′/ (**-at·ed, -at·ing**) 2 obtain an academic degree 3 move up to (a higher status, etc.) 4 mark out in degrees or parts 5 arrange in gradations —**grad·u·a'tion** n. [MedL graduare, rel. to GRADE]

• Usage: Older, traditional use is 'to be graduated from': She will be graduated from college in June. More general use is 'to graduate from': He will graduate from high school in two years. Avoid using graduate as a transitive verb: He graduated high school last week.

graf·fi·ti /grəfē'tē/ n. pl. (sing. **graf·fi'to**) writing or drawing scribbled, scratched, or sprayed on a surface [It graffio a scratch]

graft¹ /graft/ n. 1 Bot. shoot or scion inserted into a slit of stock, from which it receives sap 2 Surg. piece of tissue, organ, etc., transplanted surgically —v. 3 insert (a scion) as a graft 4 transplant (living tissue) 5 insert or fix (a thing) permanently (in or on) [Gk graphion stylus]

graft² n. 1 practices, esp. bribery, used to secure illicit gains in politics or business —v. 2 seek or make such gains

Gra·ham /grā'əm/ 1 **Martha** 1893–1991; US dancer and choreographer 2 **Billy (William Franklin)** 1918– ; US Protestant evangelical preacher

gra·ham crack·er /grā'əm/ n. sweetened whole-wheat cracker [for S. Graham, US nutritionist]

Gra·hame /grā'əm/, **Kenneth** 1859–1932; Scottish writer

Grail /grāl/ n. (also **Ho'ly Grail'**) (in medieval legend) cup or platter used by Christ at the Last Supper [MedL gradalis dish]

grain /grān/ n. 1 fruit or seed of a cereal 2 kernels of wheat or any allied grass used as food 3 small hard particle of salt, sand, etc. 4 measure of weight (0.0648 gram) 5 smallest possible quantity 6 texture 7 pattern of lines of fiber in wood or paper —**grain'y** adj. (**-i·er, -i·est**) [L granum]

gram /gram/ n. metric measure of mass (one

thousandth of a kilogram) [Gk gramma small weight]

-gram comb. form forming nouns denoting a thing written or recorded (often in a certain way) (anagram; epigram; telegram) [Gk gramma thing written]

gram·mar /gram'ər/ n. 1 study or rules of a language's inflections, forms, etc. 2 observance or application of such rules 3 book on grammar —**gram·mar·i·an** /grəmer'ēən/ n.; **gram·mat'i·cal** /-mat'ikəl/ adj.; **gram·mat'i·cal·ly** adv. [Gk gramma letter]

gram'mar school' n. elementary school

Gra·na·da /grənäd'ə/ n. city in S Spain. Pop. 254,000

gran·a·ry /grā'nərē, gran'ə-/ n. (pl. **-ries**) storehouse for threshed grain [L, rel. to GRAIN]

grand /grand/ adj. 1 magnificent; imposing; dignified 2 main; of chief importance 3 of the highest rank (Grand Duke) 4 excellent; enjoyable 5 (in comb.) (in names of family relationships) denoting the second degree of ascent or descent (granddaughter) —n. 6 (pl. same) Slang. thousand dollars —**grand'ly** adv.; **grand'ness** n. [L grandis full-grown]

Grand' Banks' n. extensive shoal SE of Newfoundland; excellent fishing grounds

Grand' Can'yon n. massive gorge of the Colorado River in NW Ariz.

grand'child n. (pl. **-child·ren**) child of one's son or daughter

grand'daugh'ter n. female grandchild

gran·dee /grandē'/ n. 1 highest Spanish or Portuguese nobleman 2 person of high station [Sp and Port grande, rel. to GRAND]

gran·deur /gran'jər, gran'd(y)ōōr'/ n. 1 majesty; splendor 2 nobility of character; dignity [Fr, rel. to GRAND]

grand'fa'ther n. 1 male grandparent 2 founder; originator —v. 3 Law. exempt from new legislation —**grand'fa'ther·ly** adj.

grand'fa'ther n. (or **grand'fa'ther's) clock'** n. clock in a tall wooden case, driven by weights

gran·dil·o·quent /grandil'əkwənt/ adj. pompous or inflated in language —**gran·dil'o·quence** n.; **gran·dil'o·quent·ly** adv. [L, rel. to GRAND + loqui speak]

gran·di·ose /gran'dēōs′/ adj. 1 producing or meant to produce an imposing effect 2 ambitious in scale —**gran'di·ose'ly** adv.; **gran'di·os'i·ty** /-äs'ätē/ n. [It, rel. to GRAND]

grand' ju'ry n. jury to examine evidence and decide whether to indict a suspect

grand' mas'ter n. chessplayer of the highest rank

grand'moth'er n. female grandparent —**grand'moth·er·ly** adj.

grand'par'ent n. parent of one's father or mother

grand' pi·a'no n. large pianoforte with horizontal strings

Grand' Rap'ids n. city in Mich. Pop. 189,126

grand' slam' n. 1 Sports. winning of all of a group of matches, etc. 2 Baseball. home run with bases loaded 3 Bridge. winning of 13 tricks

grand'son' n. male grandchild

grand'stand' n. main stand for spectators

grange /grānj/ n. 1 farm and its buildings 2

gran·ite /gran'it/ *n.* granular crystalline rock of quartz, mica, etc., used for building [It *granito*, rel. to GRAIN]

gran·ny /gran'ē/ *n.* (also **gran'nie**) (*pl. ·nies*) *Colloq.* grandmother

gra·no·la /grənō'lə/ *n.* breakfast or snack food, a mixture of rolled oats, nuts, dried fruits, etc.

grant /grant/ *v.* **1a** consent to fulfill (a request, etc.) **b** allow (a person) to have (a thing) **2** give formally; transfer legally **3** admit as true; concede (that) —*n.* **4** process of granting **5** sum of money officially given **6 take for granted: a** cease to appreciate through familiarity **b** assume to be true or valid [Fr *gr(e)anter* var. of *creanter* fr. L *credere* trust]

Grant /grant/ **1** Ulysses S(impson) 1822–85; Union general in American Civil War and 18th US president (1869–77) **2** Cary (born **Alexander Archibald Leach**) 1904–86; English-born US actor

gran·u·lar /gran'yələr/ *adj.* of or like grains or granules —**gran'u·lar'i·ty** /-lar'ətē/ *n.* [L, rel. to GRANULE]

gran·u·late /gran'yəlāt'/ *v.* (**·lat·ed, ·lat·ing**) form into grains —**gran'u·la'tion** *n.*

gran·ule /gran'yōōl'/ *n.* small grain [L dim. of *granum*, rel. to GRAIN]

grape /grāp/ *n.* berry growing in clusters on a vine, eaten as fruit and used in making wine [Fr, prob. fr. *grappe* hook]

grape'fruit' *n.* (*pl.* same) large round usu. yellow citrus fruit

grape'vine' *n.* **1** vine **2** the means of transmission of a rumor

graph /graf/ *n.* **1** diagram showing the relation between variable quantities, usu. along two axes —*v.* **2** plot or trace on a graph [abbr. of *graphic formula*]

-graph *comb. form* forming nouns and verbs meaning: **1** thing written, composed, etc., in a specified way (*photograph*) **2** instrument that records (*seismograph*)

-grapher *comb. form* forming nouns denoting a person concerned with a subject (*lexicographer*) [Gk *graphein* write]

graph·ic /graf'ik/ *adj.* **1** of or relating to the visual or descriptive arts, esp. writing and drawing **2** vividly realistic —**graph'i·cal·ly** *adv.* [Gk *graphein* write]

-graphic *comb. form* (also **-graphical**) forming adjectives corresponding to nouns ending in *-graphy*

graph'ic arts' *n. pl.* technical arts involving design and visual representation

graph·ics /graf'iks/ *n. pl.* (usu. treated as *sing.*) **1** products of the graphic arts **2** use of diagrams in calculation, design, and illustration **3** *Comp.* visual and display hardware, techniques, etc.

graph·ite /graf'īt'/ *n.* crystalline allotropic form of carbon used as a lubricant, in pencils, etc. [Ger *Graphit* fr. Gk *graphein* write]

gra·phol·o·gy /grafäl'əjē/ *n.* the study of handwriting, esp. as a supposed guide to character —**graph·ol'o·gist** *n.* [Gk, rel. to GRAPHIC]

-graphy *comb. form* forming nouns denoting: **1** descriptive science (*lexicography*) **2** technique of producing images (*photography*) **3** style or method of writing, etc. (*calligraphy*)

grap·nel /grap'nəl/ *n.* **1** device with iron claws, for dragging or grasping **2** small anchor with several flukes [Fr *grapon*, rel. to GRAPE]

grap·ple /grap'əl/ *v.* (**·pled, ·pling**) **1** try to manage (a difficult problem, etc.) **2** grip with the hands in a struggle; wrestle —*n.* **3** contest at close quarters **4** clutching instrument; grapnel [Fr *grapil*, rel. to GRAPNEL]

grap'pling i'ron *n.* (also **grap'pling hook'**) GRAPNEL

grasp /grasp/ *v.* **1a** clutch at; seize greedily **b** hold firmly **2** (foll. by *at*) try to seize **3** understand or realize (a fact or meaning) —*n.* **4** firm hold; grip **5** mastery; insight [earlier *grapse*, rel. to GROPE]

grasp'ing *adj.* greedy

grass /gras/ *n.* **1a** any of a group of wild plants with green blades that are eaten by ruminants **b** plant of the family that includes cereals, reeds, and bamboos **2** pasture land **3** lawn **4** *Slang.* marijuana —**grass'y** *adj.* (**·i·er, ·i·est**) [OE]

Grass /gräs/, **Günter** 1927– ; German novelist and dramatist

grass·hop·per /gras'häp'ər/ *n.* jumping and chirping insect

grass·land /gras'land, -land'/ *n.* large open area covered with grass, esp. used for grazing

grass' roots' *n.* **1** fundamental level or source **2** ordinary people; rank and file of an organization

grate¹ /grāt/ *v.* (**grat·ed, grat·ing**) **1** reduce to small particles by rubbing on a serrated surface **2** rub with a harsh scraping sound **3a** sound harshly **b** have an irritating effect —**grat'er** *n.* [Fr fr. Gmc]

grate² *n.* metal frame confining fuel in a fireplace [L *cratis* hurdle]

grate·ful /grāt'fəl/ *adj.* **1** thankful; feeling or showing gratitude **2** pleasant; acceptable —**grate'ful·ly** *adv.* [obs. *grate* fr. L *gratus*]

grat·i·fy /grat'əfī'/ *v.* (**·fied, ·fy·ing**) **1a** please; delight **b** please by compliance **2** yield to (a feeling or desire) —**grat'i·fi·ca'tion** /-fikā'sHən/ *n.* [L, rel. to GRATEFUL]

grat·ing¹ /grāt'iNG/ *n.* **1** framework of parallel or crossed metal bars **2** *Optics.* set of parallel wires, lines ruled on glass, etc.

grat·ing² *adj.* **1** harsh-sounding; rasping **2** irritating —**grat'ing·ly** *adv.*

grat·is /grat'is, grä'tis, grä'-/ *adv. & adj.* free; without charge [L]

grat·i·tude /grat'ət(y)ōōd'/ *n.* being thankful; appreciation [L, rel. to GRATEFUL]

gra·tu·i·tous /grət(y)ōō'ətəs/ *adj.* **1** given or done free of charge **2** uncalled-for —**gra·tu'i·tous·ly** *adv.*; **gra·tu'i·tous·ness** *n.* [L: spontaneous]

gra·tu'i·ty *n.* (*pl.* **·ties**) money given for service; tip [L, rel. to GRATEFUL]

grave¹ /grāv/ *n.* **1** trench for the burial of a corpse **2** any burial place **3** (prec. by *the*) death [OE]

grave² *adj.* **1a** serious; weighty; important **b** solemn; somber **2** critical; threatening —*n.* **3** GRAVE ACCENT —**grave'ly** *adv.* [L *gravis* heavy]

grave' ac'cent /gräv/ *n.* a mark (`) placed over a vowel to denote pronunciation, length, etc.

grav·el /grav'əl/ *n.* **1** mixture of coarse sand and small stones, used for paths, etc. —*v.* (**·eled** or **·elled, ·el·ing** or **·el·ling**) **2** lay or strew with gravel [Fr dim., perh. of *grave* shore]

grav'el·ly *adj.* **1** of or like gravel **2** (of a voice) deep and rough-sounding

Graves /grävz/, **Robert** 1895–1985; English poet, novelist, and critic

grave'stone' *n.* stone marking a grave

grave'yard' *n.* burial ground

grave'yard' shift' *n.* worker's shift beginning late at night

grav·i·tate /grav'ətāt'/ *v.* (**·tat·ed, ·tat·ing**) **1** move or be attracted to **2** move or tend by force of gravity toward [rel. to GRAVE²]

grav·i·ta'tion *n. Physics.* **1** force of attraction between particles of matter in the universe **2** effect of this, esp. the falling of bodies to the earth **3** gravitating —**grav'i·ta'tion·al** *adj.*

grav·i·ty /grav'itē/ *n.* **1** gravitation, esp. on earth **2** property of having weight **3a** importance; seriousness **b** solemnity [L, rel. to GRAVE²]

gra·vy /grā'vē/ *n.* (*pl.* **·vies**) **1** juices exuding from meat during and after cooking **2** sauce made from these [perh. fr. a misreading of Fr *grané* fr. *grain* spice; GRAIN]

gra'vy train' *n. Slang.* source of easy financial benefit

gray /grā/ (also **grey**) *adj.* **1** of a color intermediate between black and white **2** dull; dreary **3** having gray hair **4** anonymous; unidentifiable —*n.* **5a** gray color or pigment **b** something gray in color —*v.* **6** make or become gray —**gray'ish** *adj.*; **gray'ness** *n.* [OE]

Gray /grā/, **Thomas** 1716–71; English poet

gray a're·a *n.* situation or topic not clearly defined

gray' mat'ter *n.* **1** the darker tissues of the brain and spinal cord **2** *Colloq.* intelligence

Graz /gräts/ *n.* city in Austria. Pop. 232,200

graze¹ /grāz/ *v.* (**grazed, graz·ing**) **1** (of cattle, sheep, etc.) eat growing grass **2** feed (cattle, etc.) on growing grass **3** *Slang.* pilfer and consume food while shopping [OE, rel. to GRASS]

graze² *v.* (**grazed, graz·ing**) **1** rub or scrape (part of the body, esp. the skin) **2** touch lightly in passing —*n.* **3** abrasion [perh. fr. GRAZE¹]

Gr. Br. or **Gr. Brit.** *abbr.* Great Britain

grease /grēs/ *n.* **1** oily or fatty matter **2** melted animal fat —*v.* (**greased, greas·ing**) **3** smear or lubricate with grease **4** **grease the palm of** *Colloq.* bribe [L *crassus* fat]

grease'paint' *n.* stage makeup

greas·y /grē'sē, -zē/ *adj.* (**·i·er, ·i·est**) **1a** of or like grease; oily **b** smeared, covered, or saturated with grease **2** unctuous —**greas'i·ly** *adv.*; **greas'i·ness** *n.*

great /grāt/ *adj.* **1** of a size, amount, extent, or intensity considerably above the normal or average **2** important; preeminent; grand; imposing **3** remarkable in ability, character, etc. **4** (foll. by *at*) adroit; skilled **5** enthusiastic (*great believer in tolerance*) **6** *Colloq.* very pleasurable; enjoyable (*had a great time*) **7**

(in *comb.*) (in names of family relationships) denoting one degree further removed upward or downward (*great-uncle; great-great-grandchild*) —*n.* **8** outstanding person or thing —**great'ly** *adv.*; **great'ness** *n.* [OE]

Great' Ba'sin *n.* vast desert region in the western US

Great' Brit'ain /brit'n/ *n.* **1** island, NW Europe, comprising England, Scotland, and Wales **2** popular term for the United Kingdom
• Usage: *Great Britain* is the overall name given to the island that comprises *England, Scotland, Wales*; the *United Kingdom* includes the foregoing and *Northern Ireland*; the *British Isles* include the *United Kingdom* together with the *Channel Islands* and all the other surrounding islands—the *Isles of Scilly, Isle of Man*, and the *Orkney* and *Shetland Islands*. The all-encompassing adjective is *British*, which is unlikely to offend anyone. *Welsh, Scottish*, and *English* should be used with care; it is safest to use *British* if unsure.

great' cir'cle *n.* circle on a sphere whose plane passes through the sphere's center

Great' Dane' *n.* dog of a large shorthaired breed

Great' Di·vide' *n.* see CONTINENTAL DIVIDE

Great'er An·til'les /antil'ēz/ *n.* collective term for the larger islands in the Caribbean Sea (Cuba, Hispaniola, Jamaica, and Puerto Rico). See also LESSER ANTILLES

Great'er Sun'da Is'lands /sən'də, sŏon'də/ *n.* a chain of islands in the Malay Archipelago, including Borneo, Java, Sumatra, and Sulawesi

Great' Lakes' *n.* five freshwater lakes in N central US and S Canada: Superior, Michigan, Huron, Erie, and Ontario

Great' Plains' *n.* dry, grassy highlands extending from N Canada to S Texas, E of the Rocky Mountains

Great' Salt' Lake' *n.* inland salt sea in NW Utah

Great' Salt' Lake' Des'ert *n.* arid region in NW Utah

Great' Smo'ky Moun'tains *n.* part of the Appalachian Mountains, forming the boundary between Tenn. and N. Car.

grebe /grēb/ *n.* a kind of diving bird [Fr]

Gre·cian /grē'sнən/ *adj.* Greek (usu. with reference to ancient Greece) [L *Graecia* Greece]

Gre·co, El see EL GRECO

Greece /grēs/ *n.* republic in S Europe at the S end of the Balkan Peninsula. Capital: Athens. Pop. 10,288,000

greed /grēd/ *n.* excessive desire, esp. for wealth [fr. GREEDY]

greed'y *adj.* (**·i·er, ·i·est**) **1** having or showing greed **2** very eager —**greed'i·ly** *adv.*; **greed'i·ness** *n.* [OE]

Greek /grēk/ *n.* **1a** native or national of Greece **b** person of Greek descent **2** language of Greece —*adj.* **3** of Greece or its people or language [OE ult. fr. Gk *Graikoi*]

Gree·ley /grē'lē/, **Horace** 1811–72; US journalist and politician

green /grēn/ *adj.* **1** of the color between blue and yellow in the spectrum **2** covered with leaves or grass **3** unripe or unseasoned **4** inexperienced **5** gullible **6** jealous; envious **7** pertaining to protection of the environment

—n. 8 green color or pigment **9a** piece of public grassy land **b** grassy area used for a special purpose (*putting green*) **10** (*pl.*) green vegetables **—v. 11** make or become green **—green'ish** *adj.*; **green'ly** *adv.*; **green'ness** *n.* [OE]

green'back' *n.* bill of US paper currency

Green' Bay' *n.* city in Wis. Pop. 96,466

Greene /grēn/ **1 Nathanael** 1742–86; general in the American Revolution **2 (Henry) Graham** 1904–91; English novelist

green·er·y /grē'nərē/ *n.* green foliage or growing plants

green'gro·cer *n. esp. Brit.* retailer of fruit and vegetables

green'horn' *n.* inexperienced person

green'house' *n.* structure with sides and roof mainly of glass, for growing plants

green'house' ef·fect' *n.* atmospheric trapping of the sun's warmth near the earth, caused by gaseous pollutants

Green·land /grēn'lənd, -land'/ *n.* island NE of N America, largest in the world; territory of Denmark **—Greenland'ic** *adj.*

Green'land Sea' *n.* part of the Arctic Ocean, NE of Greenland and N of Iceland

green' pep'per *n.* mild green-colored fruit of the sweet or bell pepper

green'room' *n.* room in a theater, studio, etc., for performers when not on stage

Greens·bo·ro /grēnz'bər'ə/ *n.* city in N. Car. Pop. 183,521

green·sward /grēn'swôrd'/ *n.* expanse of grassy turf

Green'wich Mean' Time' /gren'iCH, -ij/ *n.* local time on the meridian of Greenwich, England, used as an international basis of time reckoning

green'y *adj.* greenish

Greer /grēr/, **Germaine** 1939– ; Australian feminist and writer

greet /grēt/ *v.* **1** address politely or welcomingly on meeting or arrival **2** receive or acknowledge in a specified way **3** (of a sight, sound, etc.) become apparent to or noticed by [OE]

greet'ing *n.* **1** act or instance of welcoming; salutation **2** words, gestures, etc., used to greet a person **3** (often *pl.*) message of goodwill

gre·gar·i·ous /griger'ēəs, -gar'-/ *adj.* **1** fond of company **2** living in flocks or communities **—gre·gar'i·ous·ly** *adv.*; **gre·gar'i·ous·ness** *n.* [L *grex gregis* flock]

Gre·go'ri·an cal'en·dar /grigôr'ēən/ *n.* calendar now in use, introduced in 1582 by Pope Gregory XIII

Gre·go'ri·an chant' *n.* plainsong ritual music [for GREGORY I]

Greg·o·ry I, St. /greg'(ə)rē/ **("the Great")** c. 540–604; pope (590–604); inventor of Gregorian chant

Greg·o·ry XIII 1502–85; pope (1572–85); promulgated modern calendar

grem·lin /grem'lin/ *n.* imaginary mischievous sprite regarded as responsible for random mechanical faults, etc.

Gre·na·da /grənād'ə/ *n.* country in the E West Indies. Capital: St. George's. Pop. 90,900

gre·nade /grənād'/ *n.* small bomb thrown by hand (**hand' gre·nade'**) or shot from a rifle [Fr, rel. to POMEGRANATE]

Gre·no·ble /grənō'bəl/ *n.* city in SE France. Pop. 154,000

Gren·ville /gren'vəl, -vil'/, **George** 1712–70; British prime minister (1763–65)

grew /grōō/ *v. past of* GROW

grey /grā/ *adj., n., & v.* var. of GRAY

Grey /grā/ **1 (Lady) Jane** 1537–54; queen of England (July 1553); executed by Mary I **2 Zane** 1875–1939; US writer

GREYHOUND

grey'hound' *n.* dog of a swift, slender breed [OE: bitch-hound]

grid /grid/ *n.* **1** grating **2** system of squares printed on a map for reference **3** network of lines, electric-power connections, gas supply lines, etc. **4** perforated electrode controlling electron flow in a radio tube **5** rectangular arrangement of city streets [fr. GRIDIRON]

grid·dle /grid'l/ *n.* iron plate placed over a source of heat for baking, etc. [L *cratis* hurdle]

grid·i·ron /grid'ī'ərn/ *n.* **1** framework of metal bars for grilling **2** football field [rel. to GRIDDLE]

grid'lock' *n.* **1** traffic jam in which vehicular movement is blocked by stoppage of cross-traffic **2** complete standstill in action or progress **—grid'locked'** *adj.*

grief /grēf/ *n.* **1** intense sorrow **2** cause of this **3** **come to grief** meet with disaster [Fr, rel. to GRIEVE]

Grieg /grēg/, **Edvard** 1843–1907; Norwegian composer

griev·ance /grē'vəns/ *n.* cause for complaint [Fr, rel. to GRIEF]

grieve /grēv/ *v.* (**grieved, griev·ing**) **1** cause grief to **2** suffer grief [L, rel. to GRAVE²]

griev·ous /grē'vəs/ *adj.* **1** (of pain, etc.) severe **2** causing grief **3** flagrant; heinous **—griev'ous·ly** *adv.* [Fr, rel. to GRIEVE]

● Usage: Avoid pronouncing *grievous* with an extra syllable, as "gree-vee-uhs," which many regard as unacceptable.

grif·fin /grif'ən/ *n.* creature of fable with an eagle's head and wings and a lion's body [L *gryphus* fr. Gk]

Grif·fith /grif'əTH/, **D(avid) W(ark)** 1875–1948; US film director

grill /gril/ *n.* **1** griddle or grate for cooking food **2** food cooked on a grill **3** restaurant specializing in grilled food **—v. 4** cook or be cooked on or under a grill **5** subject to severe questioning [Fr, rel. to GRIDDLE]

grille /gril/ *n.* (also **grill**) grating or latticed screen

grim /grim/ *adj.* (**grim·mer, grim·mest**) **1** of stern or forbidding appearance **2** harsh;

merciless 3 joyless (*a grim truth*) —**grim′ly** *adv.*; **grim′ness** *n.* [OE]

grim·ace /grĭm′əs, grĭmās′/ *n.* 1 distortion of the face made in disgust, etc., or to amuse —*v.* (·**aced**, ·**ac·ing**) 2 make a grimace [Fr fr. Sp]

grime /grīm/ *n.* 1 soot or dirt ingrained in a surface —*v.* (grimed, grim·ing) 2 blacken with grime; befoul —**grim′i·ness** *n.*; **grim′y** *adj.* (·i·er, ·i·est) [LGer or Du]

Grimm /grĭm/ German philologists and folklorists, brothers: 1 Jacob Ludwig Karl 1785–1863 2 Wilhelm Karl 1786–1859

grin /grĭn/ *v.* (grinned, grin·ning) 1 smile broadly, showing the teeth 2 express by grinning —*n.* 3 act of grinning 4 **grin and bear it** accept pain, bad luck, etc., stoically [OE]

grind /grīnd/ *v.* (ground, grind·ing) 1 reduce to particles or powder by crushing 2a sharpen or smooth by friction b rub or rub together gratingly 3 oppress 4 work or study hard —*n.* 5 act or instance of grinding 6 *Colloq.* hard, dull work 7 size of ground particles 8 **grind out** produce with effort [OE]

grind′er *n.* 1 person or thing that grinds, esp. a machine 2 molar tooth

grind′stone′ *n.* 1 thick rotating stone disk used for sharpening, etc. 2 a kind of stone used for this 3 **keep one's nose to the grindstone** work hard and continuously

grip /grĭp/ *v.* (gripped, grip·ping) 1 grasp tightly 2 compel the attention of —*n.* 3 firm hold; tight grasp 4 power of holding attention 5 intellectual control 6a part of a machine that grips b handle 7 traveling bag 8 **come (or get) to grips with** begin to deal with [OE]

gripe /grīp/ *v.* (griped, grip·ing) 1 *Colloq.* complain 2 affect with gastric pain —*n.* 3 (usu. *pl.*) colic 4 *Colloq.* complaint [OE]

gris·ly /grĭz′lē/ *adj.* (·li·er, ·li·est) causing horror, disgust, or fear —**gris′li·ness** *n.* [OE]

grist /grĭst/ *n.* grain to be ground [OE, rel. to GRIND]

gris·tle /grĭs′əl/ *n.* tough flexible animal tissue; cartilage —**gris′tly** *adj.* [OE]

grit /grĭt/ *n.* 1 particles of stone or sand, esp. as irritating or hindering 2 coarse sandstone 3 pluck; endurance —*v.* (grit·ted, grit·ting) 4 clench (the teeth) 5 make a grating sound —**grit′ter** *n.*; **grit′ty** *adj.* (·ti·er, ·ti·est) [OE]

grits /grĭts/ *n. pl.* 1 HOMINY 2 coarsely ground grain [OE]

griz·zled /grĭz′əld/ *adj.* 1 (of hair) gray or streaked with gray 2 having grizzled hair [*grizzle* gray fr. Fr *grisel*]

griz·zly /grĭz′lē/ *adj.* (·zli·er, ·zli·est) grayish, as hair —*n.* (*pl.* ·zlies) 2 (in full **griz′zly bear′**) variety of large brown bear of N America and N Russia

groan /grōn/ *v.* 1 make a deep sound expressing pain, grief, or disapproval —*n.* 2 sound made in groaning [OE]

gro·cer /grō′sər/ *n.* dealer in food and household provisions [AngFr *grosser* fr. L *grossus* GROSS]

gro·cer·y /grō′s(ə)rē/ *n.* (*pl.* ·ies) 1 grocer's store 2 (*pl.*) goods, esp. food, sold by a grocer

Gro·dno /grōd′nō, gräd′-/ *n.* city in W Belarus. Pop. 284,800

grog /gräg/ *n.* mixture of rum and water [fr. *Old Grog*, nickname of Edward Vernon, Brit. admiral who first ordered it served]

grog·gy /gräg′ē/ *adj.* (·gi·er, ·gi·est) dazed; unsteady —**grog′gi·ly** *adv.*; **grog′gi·ness** *n.*

groin /groin/ *n.* 1 area from the belly to the upper legs 2 *Archit.* a edge formed by intersecting vaults b arch supporting a vault

grom·met /grăm′ət, grŏm′-/ *n.* metal, plastic, etc., eyelet for protecting a hole in cloth [Fr]

Gro·my·ko /grəmē′kō/, **Andrei** 1909–89; Russian diplomat

Gro·ning·en /grō′nĭnGən/ *n.* city in the N Netherlands. Pop. 168,700

groom /grōōm, grŏŏm/ *n.* 1 caretaker of horses 2 BRIDEGROOM —*v.* 3a curry or tend (a horse) b give a neat appearance to (a person, etc.) 4 (of an ape, etc.) clean and comb the fur of (its fellow) 5 prepare or train for a particular purpose

groove /grōōv/ *n.* 1 channel or elongated hollow 2 *Colloq.* comfortable routine or successful run —*v.* (grooved, groov·ing) 3 make a groove or grooves in [Du]

groov′y *adj.* (·i·er, ·i·est) *Slang.* excellent

grope /grōp/ *v.* (groped, grop·ing) 1 feel about or search blindly 2 search mentally —*n.* 3 act of groping [OE]

Gro·pi·us /grō′pēəs/, **Walter** 1883–1969; German-born US architect

gros·grain /grō′grā′/ *n.* corded fabric of silk, etc. [Fr: coarse grain, rel. to GROSS + GRAIN]

gross /grōs/ *adj.* 1 overfed; bloated 2 (of a person, manners, or morals) coarse; unrefined; indecent 3 flagrant 4 total; without any reductions (*gross tonnage*) 5 *Slang.* extremely unpleasant or offensive —*v.* 6 generate as gross income —*n.* 7 (*pl.* same) amount equal to twelve dozen 8 **gross out** be offensive or disgusting —**gross′ly** *adv.*; **gross′ness** *n.* [L *grossus*]

gross′ do·mes′tic prod′uct *n.* total value of goods produced and services provided in a country in one year; *abbr.* GDP

gross′ na′tion·al prod′uct *n.* gross domestic product plus the total of net income from abroad; *abbr.* GNP

gro·tesque /grōtesk′/ *adj.* 1 comically or repulsively distorted 2 incongruous; absurd —*n.* 3 decorative form interweaving human and animal features —**gro·tesque′ly** *adv.*; **gro·tesque′ness** *n.* [It, rel. to GROTTO]

grot·to /grăt′ō/ *n.* (*pl.* ·toes or ·tos) 1 cave 2 artificial ornamental cave [It *grotta* fr. Gk *kryptē* CRYPT]

grouch /grouch/ *Colloq.* *v.* 1 grumble —*n.* 2 discontented person —**grouch′y** *adj.* (·i·er, ·i·est) [rel. to GRUDGE]

ground[1] /ground/ *n.* 1a solid surface of the earth b part of this specified in some way (*low ground*) 2 latitude; scope (*the book covers a lot of ground*) 3 (often *pl.*) reason; justification 4 designated area (often *comb.*: *fishing grounds*) 5 (*pl.*) land attached to a house, etc. 6 area or basis for agreement, etc. (*common ground*) 7 (*pl.*) residual particles, esp. of coffee 8 *Electr.* connection of a circuit to the earth —*adj.* 9 (of animals) living on or in the ground; (of plants) dwarfish or trailing —*v.*

10a refuse authority for (a pilot or an aircraft) to fly b *Colloq.* forbid (a child) to visit friends, etc., as punishment 11a run (a ship) aground; strand b (of a ship) run aground 12 instruct thoroughly (in a subject) 13 *Electr.* connect (a circuit) to the ground 14 **break new** (or **fresh**) **ground** treat a subject previously not dealt with 15 **get off the ground** *Colloq.* make a successful start 16 **hold one's ground** not retreat 17 **on the grounds of** because of [OE]

ground[2] *v. past* and *past part.* of GRIND

ground' con·trol' *n.* personnel directing the landing, etc., of aircraft, etc.

ground' cov'er *n.* low-growing plants covering the surface of the soil

ground' floor' *n.* floor of a building at ground level

ground'ing *n.* basic training or instruction

ground'less *adj.* without motive or basis

ground' speed' *n.* aircraft's speed relative to the ground

ground' swell' *n.* 1 heavy or rolling sea 2 (**ground'swell'**) surge of feeling or support

ground'wa'ter *n.* water found in soil or in pores, crevices, etc., in rock

ground'work' *n.* preliminary or basic work

group /grо̄о̄p/ *n.* 1 persons or things close together or considered or classed together —*v.* 2 form or be formed into a group 3 place in a group or groups [It *gruppo*]

group'ie /grо̄о̄p′ē/ *n. Colloq.* ardent follower of a touring pop- or rock-music group, celebrity, or an activity

group' ther'a·py *n.* psychological therapy in which a group discusses personal problems

grouse[1] /grous/ *n.* (*pl.* same) game bird with a plump body and feathered legs

grouse[2] *Colloq. v.* (**groused, grous·ing**) 1 grumble; complain —*n.* 2 complaint [perh. rel. to GROUCH]

grout /grout/ *n.* creamlike mortar used between ceramic tiles

grove /grōv/ *n.* small wood or group of trees [OE]

grov·el /gräv′əl, grəv′-/ *v.* (**-eled** or **-elled, -el·ing** or **-el·ling**) 1 behave obsequiously 2 lie or crawl in subservience [obs. *grovelling* fr. ON *á grúfu* face down]

grow /grō/ *v.* (**grew, grown, grow·ing**) 1 increase in size, height, quantity, degree, etc. 2 develop in life or naturally 3a produce (plants, etc.) by cultivation b allow (a beard, etc.) to develop 4 **grow on** become gradually more favored by 5 **grow up** mature —**grow'er** *n.* [OE]

growl /groul/ *v.* 1a make a low guttural sound, usu. of anger b murmur angrily —*n.* 2 growling sound 3 angry murmur [prob. imit.]

grown /grōn/ *v. past part.* of GROW

grown'-up' *adj.* 1 adult —*n.* (also **grown' up'**) 2 adult person

growth /grōTH/ *n.* 1 act or process of growing 2 increase in size or value 3 something that has grown or is growing 4 abnormal mass of tissue, as a tumor, wart, etc.

Groz·ny /grôz′nē, gräz′-/ *n.* city in Russia. Pop. 401,400

grub /grəb/ *n.* 1 larva of an insect 2 *Colloq.* food —*v.* (**grubbed, grub·bing**) 3 dig superficially 4 extract, as by digging [OE]

grub'by *adj.* (**·bi·er, ·bi·est**) dirty —**grub'bi·ly** *adv.*; **grub'bi·ness** *n.*

grudge /grəj/ *n.* 1 persistent feeling of ill will or resentment —*v.* (**grudged, grudg·ing**) 2 be resentfully unwilling to give or allow [Fr]

gru·el /grо̄о̄′əl/ *n.* thin porridge [Fr fr. Gmc]

gru·el·ing /grо̄о̄′(ə)liNG/ *adj.* extremely demanding or tiring

grue·some /grо̄о̄′səm/ *adj.* horrible; grisly —**grue'some·ly** *adv.* [Scand]

gruff /grəf/ *adj.* 1a (of a voice) low and harsh b having a gruff voice 2 surly —**gruff'ly** *adv.*; **gruff'ness** *n.* [LGer or Du *grof* coarse]

grum·ble /grəm′bəl/ *v.* (**·bled, ·bling**) 1 complain peevishly 2 rumble —*n.* 3 complaint 4 rumble —**grum'bler** *n.* [obs. *grumme*]

grump·y /grəm′pē/ *adj.* (**·i·er, ·i·est**) morosely irritable —**grump'i·ly** *adv.*; **grump'i·ness** *n.* [imit.]

grunge /grənj/ *n.* 1 *Slang.* dirt; filth; trash —*adj.* 2 pertaining to a youthful style associated with the wearing of disheveled clothing, etc. —**grun'gy** *adj.* (**·gi·er, ·gi·est**)

grunt /grənt/ *n.* 1 low guttural sound made by a pig 2 similar sound —*v.* 3 make a grunt [OE, imit.]

Gru·yère /grо̄о̄yer′, grē-/ *n.* a firm pale cheese [*Gruyère* in Switzerland]

gr. wt. *abbr.* gross weight

GSA *abbr.* 1 General Services Administration 2 Girl Scouts of America

Gua·da·la·ja·ra /gwäd′l-əhär′ə/ *n.* capital of the Mexican state of Jalisco. Pop. 2,884,000

Gua·dal·ca·nal /gwäd′l-kanal′/ *n.* largest of the Solomon Islands; site of a World War II battle

Gua·da·lu·pe /gwäd′l-о̄о̄′pä/ *n.* city in Mexico. Pop. 370,500

Gua·de·loupe /gwäd′l-о̄о̄p′/ *n.* island dependency of France in the Caribbean Sea

Guam /gwäm/ *n.* largest island of the Marianas, in the N Pacific E of the Philippines; US possession. Pop. 133,200 —**Gua·ma'ni·an** /-mä′nēən/ *n.* & *adj.*

Gua·na·jua·to /gwän′ə(h)wät′ō/ *n.* state in central Mexico. Capital: Guanajuato. Pop. 3,982,600

gua·no /gwä′nō/ *n.* (*pl.* **-nos**) excrement of sea birds, bats, etc., used as fertilizer [Sp fr. Quechua]

Guan·tá·na·mo /gwäntän′əmō/ *n.* city in Cuba; site of a US naval base. Pop. 197,900

Gua·ra·ni /gwär′änē′/ (also **Gua'ra·ni'**) *n.* (*pl.* **-nis, -nies, -ni**) 1 member of the native Indian people of Paraguay 2 their language; principal vernacular of Paraguay

guar·an·tee /gar′əntē′/ (also **guar'an·ty'**, *pl.* **-ties**) *n.* 1a formal promise or assurance, esp. of quality or performance b document assuring this —*v.* (**·teed, ·tee·ing**) 2 give or serve as a guarantee for 3 give a promise or assurance [rel. to WARRANT]

● Usage: *Guarantee* and *guaranty* are interchangeable for both noun and verb. Many manufacturers use *warranty* in their place. *Warrantee* means 'the person to whom a warranty is made'; it is not a spelling variant of *warranty*.

guaranteeor / gum

guar·an·tor /ˈgarˈəntôrˈ/ *n.* person who gives a guarantee or guaranty

guard /gärd/ *v.* 1 watch over and protect or defend 2 supervise (prisoners, etc.) and prevent from escaping 3 keep (thoughts or speech) in check 4 take precautions —*n.* 5 state of vigilance 6 person who protects or keeps watch 7 soldiers, etc., protecting a place or person; escort 8 defensive posture [Gmc, rel. to WARD]

guard·ed *adj.* (of a remark, etc.) cautious —**guard'ed·ly** *adv.*

guard·i·an /ˈgärˈdēən/ *n.* 1 protector; keeper 2 person having legal custody of another, esp. a minor —**guard'i·an·ship'** *n.* [Fr, rel. to WARD, WARDEN]

Gua·te·ma·la /gwätˈəmälˈə/ *n.* republic in N Central America. Capital: Guatemala City. Pop. 9,442,000 —**Gua'te·ma'lan** *n.* & *adj.*

Gua·te·ma'la Cit'y *n.* capital of Guatemala. Pop. 1,076,700

gua·va /ˈgwävˈə/ *n.* 1 edible pale orange fruit with pink flesh 2 tree bearing this [Sp]

Guay·a·quil /ˈgwīˈəkēlˈ/ *n.* seaport in Ecuador. Pop. 1,508,400

gu·ber·na·to·ri·al /ˌg(y)ōōˈbərˈ(ə)nətôrˈēəl/ *adj.* of or relating to a governor [L *gubernator* governor]

Guern·sey /ˈgərnˈzē/ *n.* (*pl.* **-seys**) one of a breed of dairy cattle from Guernsey in the Channel Islands

Guer·re·ro /gerˈrerˈō/ *n.* S state of Mexico. Capital: Chilpancingo. Pop. 2,620,600

guer·ril·la /gərilˈə/ *n.* (also **gue·ril'la**) member of a (usu. political) group taking part in irregular fighting [Sp, dim. of *guerra* war]

guess /ges/ *v.* 1 estimate without calculation or measurement 2 conjecture; think likely 3 conjecture or estimate correctly 4 make a conjecture about —*n.* 5 estimate; conjecture

guess'work' *n.* process of or results attained by guessing

guest /gest/ *n.* 1 person invited to visit, have a meal, etc., at another's expense 2 visiting customer [ON]

Gue·va·ra /g(w)əvärˈə, gā-/, **Ernesto** ("Che") 1928–67; Argentine guerrilla leader active in Cuban revolution

guff /gəf/ *n. Colloq.* foolish or insolent talk [imit.]

guf·faw /gəfôˈ/ *n.* 1 boisterous laugh —*v.* 2 utter a guffaw [imit.]

guid·ance /ˈgīdˈəns/ *n.* 1 advice or helpful direction 2 guiding or being guided

guide /gīd/ *n.* 1 person who leads or shows the way 2 person who conducts tours 3 adviser 4 directing principle 5 book with essential information on a subject 6 thing marking a position —*v.* (**guid·ed, guid·ing**) 7 act as guide to 8 be the principle or motive of [Fr fr. Gmc]

guide'book' *n.* book of information about a place for tourists, etc.

guid'ed mis'sile *n.* missile under remote control or directed by equipment within itself

guide' dog' *n.* dog trained to guide a blind person

guide'line' *n.* principle directing action

guild /gild/ *n.* 1 association of people for mutual aid or the pursuit of a common goal 2 medieval association of craftsmen or merchants [LGer Gw or Du *gilde*]

guil·der /ˈgilˈdər/ *n.* chief monetary unit of the Netherlands [alter. of Du *gulden* golden]

guile /gīl/ *n.* cunning or sly behavior; deceit —**guile'ful, guile'less** *adj.* [Fr fr. Scand]

guil·lo·tine /ˈgilˈətēn, gēˈə-/ *n.* 1 machine with a heavy blade that drops vertically, used for beheading —*v.* (·**tined**, ·**tin·ing**) 2 use a guillotine on [for *Guillotin*, French inventor]

guilt /gilt/ *n.* 1 fact of having committed a specified or implied offense 2 feeling of having done wrong —**guilt'less** *adj.* [OE]

guilt·y *adj.* (·**i·er**, ·**i·est**) 1 responsible for a wrong 2 affected by guilt 3 causing a feeling of guilt (*a guilty secret*) 4 having committed a (specified) offense —**guilt'i·ly** *adv.*; **guilt'i·ness** *n.* [OE, rel. to GUILT]

guin·ea /ˈginˈē/ *n.* former British gold coin worth 21 shillings [*Guinea* in W Africa]

Guin·ea /ˈginˈē/ *n.* republic in W Africa. Capital: Conakry. Pop. 7,232,000

Guin'ea, Gulf' of *n.* part of the Atlantic on the central W coast of Africa

Guin·ea-Bis·sau /ˈginˈē bisouˈ/ *n.* republic in W Africa. Capital: Bissau. Pop. 1,015,000

guin'ea fowl' *n.* fowl with slate-colored white-spotted plumage

guin'ea pig' *n.* 1 domesticated S American rodent, bred as a pet and for experimental study 2 subject used in an experiment

Guin·ness /ˈginˈəs/, (Sir) **Alec** 1914– ; English actor

guise /gīz/ *n.* 1 assumed appearance; pretense 2 garb [Gmc, rel. to WISE²]

gui·tar /gitärˈ/ *n.* usu. six-stringed musical instrument played with the fingers or a plectrum —**gui·tar'ist** *n.* [Gk *kithara* harp]

Gui·yang /ˈgwäˈyäNGˈ/ *n.* (formerly **Kuei'yang; Kwei'yang**) city in China. Pop. 1,018,600

Gu·ja·ra·ti /ˌgōōjˈəräˈtē, gōōˈjə-/ *n.* language of western India

Guj·ran·wa·la /ˌgōōjˈrənwälˈə/ *n.* city in Pakistan. Pop. 658,800

guich /ɡəlCH/ *n.* deep, narrow ravine

gulf /gəlf/ *n.* 1 deep ocean inlet with a narrow mouth 2 deep hollow; chasm 3 wide difference of feelings, opinion, etc. [Gk *kolpos*]

Gulf' Stream' *n.* warm ocean current flowing N from Gulf of Mexico toward Europe

gull¹ /gəl/ *n.* web-footed sea bird, usu. with white plumage [prob. Welsh *gwylan*]

gull² *v.* dupe; fool [perh. fr. obs. *gull* yellow fr. ON]

gul·let /ˈgəlˈit/ *n.* 1 esophagus 2 throat [L *gula* throat]

gul·li·ble /ˈgəlˈəbəl/ *adj.* easily persuaded or deceived —**gull'i·bil'i·ty** *n.* [fr. GULL²]

gul·ly /ˈgəlˈē/ *n.* (*pl.* ·**lies**) water-worn ravine [Fr *goulet*, rel. to GULLET]

gulp /gəlp/ *v.* 1 swallow hastily or greedily 2 swallow with difficulty —*n.* 3 act of gulping 4 large mouthful of a drink [Du *gulpen*, imit.]

gum¹ /gəm/ *n.* 1 viscous secretion of some trees and shrubs 2 adhesive substance 3 chewing gum —*v.* (**gummed, gum·ming**) 4 fasten with gum 5 apply gum to 6 **gum up**

Colloq. interfere with the smooth running of
—**gum′my** *adj.* (·**mi·er**, ·**mi·est**) [LL
gumma]

gum² *n.* (usu. *pl.*) firm flesh around the roots
of the teeth [OE]

gum′ ar′a·bic /ar′əbik/ *n.* gum exuded by
some kinds of acacia

gum′drop′ *n.* flavored candy drop made with
gelatin, etc.

gump·tion /gəmp′SHən/ *n. Colloq.* 1 resourcefulness; initiative 2 courage

gun /gən/ *n.* 1 weapon consisting of a metal
tube from which projectiles are propelled with
explosive force 2 starting pistol 3 device for
discharging insecticide, grease, etc. —*v.*
(**gunned, gun·ning**) 4 shoot or shoot at
with a gun 5 *Colloq.* (of an engine, etc.) cause
to speed up 6 **gun for** (also **go gunning for**)
seek out determinedly to attack or rebuke 7
go great guns *Colloq.* proceed vigorously or
successfully 8 **stick to one's guns** *Colloq.*
maintain one's position under attack [ME,
perh. orig. fr. Norse woman's name *Gunn-
hildr*, applied to cannon, etc.]

gun′boat′ *n.* small vessel with heavy guns

gun′fight′ *n.* fight with firearms, esp. hand-
guns —**gun′fight′er** *n.*

gun′fire′ *n.* firing of a gun or guns

gung′-ho′ /guNG′hō/ *adj. Colloq.* zealous; arrogantly eager [Chin *gonghe* work together]

gunk /gəNGk/ *n. Colloq.* thick, greasy, or
messy substance or residue —**gunk′y** *adj.* (·**i·
er**, ·**i·est**)

gun·man /gən′mən/ *n.* (*pl.* ·**men**) man
armed with a gun, esp. when committing a
crime

gun′-met′al *n.* 1 a dull bluish-gray color 2
(usu. **gun′ met′al**) alloy formerly used for
guns

gun·nel /gən′l/ *n.* var. of GUNWALE

gun·ner /gən′ər/ *n.* 1 artillery soldier 2 *Naval.* warrant officer in charge of a battery, magazine, etc. 3 member of an aircraft crew who
operates a gun

gun′ner·y *n.* 1 construction and management
of large guns 2 firing of guns

gun·ny /gən′ē/ *n.* (*pl.* ·**nies**) coarse fabric
of hemp or jute [Hindi and Marathi]

gun′ny-sack′ /gən′ēsak′/ *n.* sack made of
gunny

gun′pow′der *n.* explosive powder used in cartridges, fireworks, etc.

gun′run′ner *n.* person engaged in smuggling
firearms —**gun′run′ning** *n.*

gun′shot′ *n.* shot fired from a gun

gun′smith′ *n.* maker and repairer of small firearms

gun·wale /gən′l/ *n.* (also **gun′nel**) upper
edge of the side of a boat or ship [WALE used
to support guns]

gup·py /gəp′ē/ *n.* (*pl.* ·**pies**) freshwater fish
of the W Indies and S America frequently kept
in aquariums [for R. *Guppy*, man who helped
classify them]

gur·gle /gər′gəl/ *v.* (·**gled**, ·**gling**) 1 make
a bubbling sound, as with water 2 utter with
such a sound —*n.* 3 gurgling sound [prob.
imit.]

gu·ru /gŏŏr′ŏŏ, gŏŏrŏŏ′/ *n.* (*pl.* ·**rus**) 1

Hindu spiritual teacher or leader 2 influential
or revered teacher [Hindi]

gush /gəsh/ *v.* 1 emit or flow in a sudden and
copious stream 2 speak or behave effusively
—*n.* 3 sudden or copious stream 4 effusive
manner —**gush′er** *n.* [prob. imit.]

gus·set /gəs′it/ *n.* piece inserted into a garment, etc., to strengthen or enlarge it [Fr]

gust /gəst/ *n.* 1 sudden strong rush of wind
2 burst of rain, laughter, etc. —*v.* 3 blow in
gusts —**gust′y** *adj.* (·**i·er**, ·**i·est**) [ON]

Gus·ta·vus A·dol·phus /gəstäv′əs ədōl′fəs,
1594–1632; king of Sweden (1611–32)

gus·to /gəs′tō/ *n.* zest; enjoyment [L *gustus*
taste]

gut /gət/ *n.* 1 the intestine 2 (*pl.*) the bowel
or entrails 3 (*pl.*) *Colloq.* personal courage 4
Slang. stomach; belly 5 (*pl.*) a contents b
essence 6 material for violin strings, fishing
line, etc. —*adj.* 7a instinctive (*a gut reaction*)
b fundamental (*a gut issue*) —*v.* (**gut·ted**,
gut·ting) 8 remove or destroy the interior of
(a house, etc.) 9 remove the intestines of (a
fish) [OE]

Gut·en·berg /gŏŏt′n-bərg/, **Johannes** c.
1400–68; German printer; pioneered use of
movable type

Guth·rie /gəTH′rē/, **Woody** 1912–67; US
folk-singer and songwriter

gut·less /gət′ləs/ *adj. Colloq.* lacking courage

gut·sy /gət′sē/ *adj.* (·**si·er**, ·**si·est**) *Colloq.* 1
courageous 2 greedy

gut·ter /gət′ər/ *n.* 1 shallow trough or channel to carry off rainwater, as on a house or
along a street 2 (prec. by *the*) poor or degraded background or environment —*v.* 3
flow in a stream 4 (of a candle) burn unsteadily and melt away rapidly [L *gutta* drop]

gut·tur·al /gət′ərəl/ *adj.* 1 throaty; harsh-
sounding 2 *Phonet.* (of a consonant, as *k*, *g*)
produced in the throat or by the back of the
tongue and palate 3 of the throat —**gut′tur-
al·ly** *adv.* [L *guttur* throat]

guy¹ /gī/ *n. Colloq.* man; fellow [*Guy* Fawkes,
English conspirator]

guy² *n.* 1 rope or chain to secure a tent or
steady a load, etc. —*v.* 2 secure with a guy
or guys [prob. LGer]

Guy·a·na /gī-än′ə, -an′ə/ *n.* republic on the
NE coast of S America. Capital: Georgetown.
Pop. 748,000

guz·zle /gəz′əl/ *v.* (·**zled**, ·**zling**) eat or drink
greedily [prob. Fr *gosiller* fr. *gosier* throat]

Gwa·li·or /gwäl′ē-ôr′/ *n.* city in India. Pop.
693,000

Gyan·dzha /gyän′jə/ *n.* city in Azerbaijan.
Pop. 282,000

gybe /jīb/ *v.* (**gybed, gyb·ing**) JIBE

gym /jim/ *n. Colloq.* 1 gymnasium 2 physical
education

gym·na·si·um /jimnā′zēəm/ *n.* (*pl.* ·**ums** or
·**si·a** /-zēə/) room or building equipped for
indoor sports and training [Gk *gymnos* naked]

gym·nas·tics /jimnas′tiks/ *n. pl.* (also treated
as *sing.*) 1 athletic exercises or competitive
sports displaying tumbling, agility, flexibility,
etc. 2 other forms of physical or mental agility
—**gym′nast** /-nast/ *n.*; **gym·nas′tic** *adj.*;
gym·nas′ti·cal·ly *adv.*

gym·no·sperm /jim′nəspərm/ *n.* any of a

group of plants having seeds unprotected by an ovary, including conifers, ginkgos, etc. [Gk *gymnos* naked]

gyn. *abbr.* **1** gynecological **2** gynecologist **3** gynecology

gy·ne·col·o·gy /ɡī´niˈkäl´əjē/ *n.* science and medical specialty dealing with physiological functions and diseases of women —**gy·ne·co·log´i·cal** /-kəläj´ikəl/ *adj.*; **gy·ne·col´o·gist** *n.* [Gk *gynē* woman + -LOGY]

gyp·sum /jip´səm/ *n.* mineral used esp. to make plaster of Paris [Gk *gypsos*]

Gyp·sy /jip´sē/ *n.* (also **Gip´sy**; *pl.* **-sies**) member of a nomadic people perhaps of Hindu origin with dark skin and hair [fr. EGYPTIAN, once believed to be their origin]

gyp´sy moth´ *n.* Old World moth found in the US that is destructive to trees

gy·rate /jī´rāt/ *v.* (**-rat·ed**, **-rat·ing**) move in a circle or spiral; revolve; whirl —**gy·ra´tion**, **gy·ra´tor** *n.*; **gy·ra·to·ry** /-rətôr´ē/ *adj.* [Gk, rel. to GYRO-]

gy·ro /jē´rō, zhē´-/ *n.* Greek-style roasted lamb served in pita bread

gyro- *comb. form* rotation [Gk *gyros* ring]

gy·ro·scope /jī´rəskōp´/ *n.* rotating wheel whose axis is free to turn and that can maintain absolute direction despite change of position, esp. used in stabilization, navigation, etc.

GYROSCOPE

H

h, H /āCH/ *n.* (*pl.* **h's**; **H's**, **Hs**) eighth letter of the English alphabet; a consonant

H *abbr. Slang.* heroin

h or **h.** *abbr.* **1** harbor **2** hard; hardness **3** heavy sea **4** height **5** high **6** (also *cap.*) *Baseball.* hit(s) **7** (also *cap.*) hour(s) **8** hundred(s) **9** husband

ha /hä´/ *interj.* (also **hah**) expressing surprise, derision, triumph, etc. [imit.]

Ha *symb.* hahnium

ha. *abbr.* hectare(s)

Haar·lem /här´ləm/ *n.* city in the Netherlands. Pop. 149,500

ha·be·as cor·pus /hä´bēəs kôr´pəs/ *n. Law.* writ requiring that a person detained be brought before a court, esp. to investigate the lawfulness of the detention [traditional opening words of the writ: L: you have the body (person)]

hab·er·dash·er /hab´ə(r)dasH´ər/ *n.* dealer in men's furnishings —**hab·er·dash·er·y** *n.* (*pl.* **-ies**) [prob. AngFr]

ha·bil·i·ment /həbil´əmənt/ *n.* (usu. *pl.*) clothes [Fr fr. *habiller* fit out]

hab·it /hab´it/ *n.* **1** settled or regular tendency or practice **2** addiction **3** mental constitution or attitude **4** dress, esp. of a religious order [L *habitus* fr. *habere* have]

hab·it·a·ble /hab´itəbəl/ *adj.* suitable for living in —**hab·it·a·bil´i·ty** *n.* [L *habitare* inhabit]

hab·i·tat /hab´itat/ *n.* natural home of an animal or plant [L: it dwells]

hab·i·ta·tion /hab´itā´sHən/ *n.* **1** inhabiting **2** house or home

hab´it-form´ing *adj.* addictive

ha·bit·u·al /həbicH´ōōəl/ *adj.* **1** done constantly or as a habit **2** regular; usual **3** given to a (specified) habit —**ha·bit´u·al·ly** *adv.*

ha·bit·u·ate /həbicH´ōō·āt´/ *v.* (**-at·ed**, **-at·ing**) accustom (to) —**ha·bit´u·a´tion** *n.* [L, rel. to HABIT]

ha·bit·u·é /həbicH´ōō·ā´/ *n.* habitual visitor or resident [Fr]

ha·ček /hä´CHek/ *n.* diacritic (ˇ) placed over a letter in some languages to indicate a modified sound [Czech, dim. of *hák* hook]

ha·ci·en·da /häs´ē·en´də/ *n.* (in Spanish-speaking regions) an estate, or specifically the main house of an estate [Sp, fr. L *facienda* things to be done]

hack¹ /hak/ *v.* **1** cut or chop roughly **2** deliver cutting blows **3** cut (one's way) through foliage, etc. **4** *Slang.* cope with; tolerate **5** emit dry, harsh coughs —*n.* **6** gash or wound [OE]

hack² *n.* **1a** HACKNEY **b** horse let out for hire **2** person hired to do dull routine work, esp. writing —*adj.* **3** used as a hack **4** typical of a hack; commonplace [abbr. of HACKNEY]

hack´er *n.* **1** person or thing that hacks or cuts roughly **2** *Colloq.* person with advanced skills in using and exploiting computer technology

hack·le /hak´əl/ *n.* **1a** (*pl.*) erectile hairs on an animal's neck, rising when it is angry or alarmed **b** feather(s) on the neck of a domestic rooster, etc. **2 make one's hackles rise** cause one to be angry or indignant [OE]

hack·ney /hak´nē/ *n.* (*pl.* **-neys**) horse for ordinary riding [*Hackney*, place in London]

hack·neyed /hak´nēd/ *adj.* (of a phrase, etc.) made trite by overuse

HACKSAW

hack´saw´ *n.* saw for cutting metal, having a narrow blade set in a frame

had /had/ *v. past* and *past part.* of HAVE

had·dock /had´ək/ *n.* (*pl.* same) N Atlantic marine fish used as food [prob. Fr]

Ha·des /hā´dēz/ *n. Gk. Myth.* the underworld [Gk, orig. a name of Pluto]

had·n't /had´ənt/ *v. contr.* had not

haf·ni·um /haf´nēəm/ *n.* silvery lustrous metallic element; *symb.* **Hf** [L *Hafnia* Copenhagen]

haft /haft/ *n.* handle of a dagger, knife, etc. [OE]

hag /hag/ *n.* **1** ugly old woman **2** witch [OE]

hag·gard /hag′ərd/ *adj.* looking exhausted and distraught [Fr *hagard* wild hawk]

hag·gle /hag′əl/ *v.* (**-gled, ·gling**) **1** bargain persistently **2** haggling —**hag′gler** *n.* [ON]

hagio- *comb. form* of saints [Gk *hagios* holy]

Hague, The /hāg/ *n.* city and seat of government of the Netherlands. Pop. 444,200

hah var. of HA

ha-ha /hä′hä′/ *interj.* words representing laughter [OE]

hah·ni·um /hän′ēəm/ *n.* artificially produced radioactive element; *symb.* **Ha** [for O. *Hahn,* German chemist]

Hai·fa /hī′fə/ *n.* seaport in Israel. Pop. 223,900

hai·ku /hī′kōō/ *n.* (*pl.* same) Japanese three-line poem of 17 syllables [Japn]

hail¹ /hāl/ *n.* **1** pellets of frozen rain **2** (foll. by *of*) barrage or onslaught —*v.* **3** come down forcefully, as hail [OE]

hail² *v.* **1** signal to (a taxi, etc.) to stop **2** greet enthusiastically; acclaim **3** hail from originate or come (*hails from Boston*) —*interj.* **4** *Archaic* or *joc.* expressing greeting —*n.* **5** act of hailing [ON *heill,* rel. to WASSAIL]

Hai·le Se·las·sie /hī′lē səläs′ē, -läs′-/ (born **Tafari Makonnen**) 1892–1975; emperor of Ethiopia (1930–74)

hail′stone′ *n.* pellet of hail

hail′storm′ *n.* period of heavy hail

Hai·phong /hī′fông′/ *n.* seaport in Vietnam. Pop. 456,000

hair /her/ *n.* **1a** any of the fine threadlike strands growing from the skin of mammals **b** these collectively (*has long hair*) **2** elongated cell growing from a plant **3** very small extent **4** get in a person's hair *Slang.* annoy a person **5** let one's hair down *Colloq.* abandon restraint **6** make a person's hair stand on end horrify a person —**hair′less** *adj.;* **hair′like** *adj.* [OE]

hair′brush′ *n.* brush for tidying the hair

hair′cut′ *n.* style or act of cutting the hair

hair·do /her′dōō′/ *n.* (*pl.* **-dos**) style or act of styling the hair

hair′dress′er *n.* person who cuts and styles hair, esp. for a living —**hair′dress′ing** *n.*

hair′line′ *n.* **1** edge of hair growth, esp. on the forehead **2** (**hair′line′ crack**) very narrow line or crack

hair′net′ *n.* piece of netting for confining the hair

hair′piece′ *n.* toupee

hair′pin′ *n.* U-shaped pin for fastening the hair

hair′-rais′ing *adj.* terrifying

hair's′ breadth′ *n.* a tiny amount or margin

hair′-split′ting *adj. & n.* quibbling

hair′style′ *n.* particular way of arranging the hair —**hair′styl′ist** *n.*

hair′y *adj.* (**·i·er, ·i·est**) **1** covered with hair **2** *Colloq.* frightening; dangerous; tricky —**hair′i·ness** *n.*

Hai·ti /hā′tē/ *n.* republic in the West Indies, the W part of the island of Hispaniola. Capital:

hajj /haj/ *n.* Islamic pilgrimage to Mecca —**haj·ji** or **had·ji** /hä′jē/ *n.* [Ar]

hake /hāk/ *n.* (*pl.* same) marine food fish resembling the cod

Hak·luyt /hak′lōōt, hak′l-wit′/, **Richard** c. 1552–1616; English geographer

hal·berd /hal′bərd/ *n. Hist.* weapon combining spear and battleaxe [Fr fr. Ger]

hal·cy·on /hal′sēən/ *adj.* calm; peaceful; happy (*halcyon days*) [Gk: kingfisher, reputed to calm the sea]

hale /hāl/ *adj.* strong and healthy, esp. as in **hale and hearty** [var. of WHOLE]

Hale /hāl/, **Nathan** 1755–76; American Revolutionary War officer hanged by British for spying

HALBERD

half /haf/ *n.* (*pl.* **halves** /havz/) **1** either of two equal parts into which a thing is divided **2** *Sports.* either of two equal periods of play —*adj.* **3** amounting to or forming half —*adv.* **4** to the extent of half; partly (*half cooked*) **5** not half: **a** not nearly (*not half long enough*) **b** not at all (*not half bad*) [OE]

half′-and-half′ *adj.* **1** being half one thing and half another —*n.* **2** mixture of milk and cream for coffee

half′-back′ *n. Football.* player on offense positioned behind the quarterback

half′-baked′ *adj.* not thoroughly thought out; foolish

half′-breed′ *n. Offens.* person with parents of different ethnic or racial origin

half′ broth·er *n.* brother with whom one has only one parent in common

half′heart·ed *adj.* lacking enthusiasm —**half′heart′ed·ly** *adv.;* **half′heart′ed·ness** *n.*

half′-life′ *n.* time required for half the atoms of a radioactive material to disintegrate

half′-mast′ *n.* (also **half′-staff′**) position of a flag halfway down its staff, esp. denoting mourning

half·pen·ny /hāp′nē/ *n.* (*pl.* **·pen·nies** or **·pence** /hā′pəns/) former British coin worth half a penny

half′ sis·ter *n.* sister with whom one has only one parent in common

half′-staff′ *n.* HALF-MAST

half′ time′ *n.* **1** midpoint of a game or contest **2** interlude at this time

half′tone′ *n.* **1** process whereby a photographic image is reproduced as varying gray tones composed of closely spaced black dots **2** plate or illustration using this process

half′-truth′ *n.* statement that (esp. deliberately) conveys only part of the truth

half′way′ *adv.* **1** at a point midway between two others **2** partially (*halfway acceptable*) —*adj.* **3** situated halfway

half′way house′ *n.* facility assisting ex-prisoners, etc., in readjusting to society

half′wit′ *n.* foolish or stupid person —**half′wit′ted** *adj.*

hal·i·but /hal′əbət/ *n.* (*pl.* same) large ma

rine flatfish used as food [fr. HOLY (perh. because eaten on holy days) + *butt* flat-fish]

Hal·i·fax /hal'ifaks/ *n.* capital of the Canadian province of Nova Scotia. Pop. 320,500

hal·i·to·sis /hal'itō'sis/ *n.* bad-smelling breath [L *halitus* breath]

hall /hôl/ *n.* **1** entrance area at the front of a house, etc. **2** large room or building for meetings, concerts, etc. **3** college building or residence for students **4** HALLWAY [OE]

Hal·le /häl'ə/ *n.* city in Germany. Pop. 310,200

hal·le·lu·jah /hal'əlōō'yə/ *interj.* expression of joy or praise

Hal·ley /hal'ē, hā'lē/, **Edmund** 1656–1742; English astronomer

hal·liard /hal'yərd/ *n.* var. of HALYARD

hall·mark /hôl'märk/ *n.* **1** mark of purity, as stamped into gold, silver, and platinum **2** distinctive feature —**hall'marked** *adj.* [for Goldsmiths' Hall, London]

hal·low /hal'ō/ *v.* **1** make holy; consecrate **2** honor as holy [OE, rel. to HOLY]

Hal·low·e'en /hal'ōēn'/ *n.* (also **Hal·low·een**) *n.* Oct. 31, eve of All Saints' Day

hal·lu·ci·nate /həlōō'sənāt'/ *v.* (·nat·ed, ·nat·ing) experience hallucinations [L *hallucinari* wander mentally]

hal·lu·ci·na'tion *n.* perception of sights, sounds, etc., not actually present —**hal·lu'ci·na·to'ry** /-nətôr'ē/ *adj.*

hal·lu·ci·no·gen /həlōō'sənəjən/ *n.* drug causing hallucinations —**hal·lu'ci·no·gen'ic** /-jen'ik/ *adj.*

hall·way /hôl'wā/ *n.* entrance hall or corridor

ha·lo /hā'lō/ *n.* (*pl.* ·**loes**) **1** disk or circle of light depicted around the head of a sacred person **2** circle of light around a luminous body, esp. the sun or moon —*v.* (·loed, ·loing) **3** surround with a halo [Gk *halos* circular threshing-floor]

ha·lo·gen /hal'əjən/ *n.* any of the nonmetallic elements (fluorine, chlorine, bromine, iodine, and astatine) that form a salt (e.g., sodium chloride) when combined with a metal [Gk *halo-* fr. *hals* salt + -GEN]

Hals /häls/, **Frans** c. 1580–1666; Dutch painter

Hal·sey /hôl'zē/, **William Frederick ("Bull")** 1882–1959; US admiral

Häl·sing·borg /hel'siNGbôrg'/ *n.* seaport in Sweden. Pop. 109,900

halt¹ /hôlt/ *n.* **1** stop (often temporary) —*v.* **2** bring to a stop [Ger, rel. to HOLD]

halt² *v.* **1** proceed hesitantly —*adj.* **2** lame —**halt'ing·ly** *adv.* [OE]

hal·ter /hôl'tər/ *n.* **1** bridle and rope for leading or tying up a horse, etc. **2a** (also **hal'ter top'**) woman's upper garment with a loop around the neck **b** loop on such a garment [OE]

halve /hav/ *v.* (**halved, halv·ing**) **1** divide into two halves **2** reduce by half

halves /havz/ *n. pl.* of HALF

hal·yard /hal'yərd/ *n.* (also **hal'liard**) rope or tackle for raising or lowering a sail, flag, etc. [archaic *hale* drag forcibly]

ham /ham/ *n.* **1** upper part of a pig's leg salted, etc., for food **2** back of the thigh **3** unsubtle actor **4** amateur radio operator —*v.*

(**hammed, ham·ming**) **5** (usu. **ham it up**) *Colloq.* overact [OE]

Ham·a·dan /ham'ədän', -dan'/ *n.* city in Iran. Pop. 272,500

Ha·ma·mat·su /häm'əmät'sōō/ *n.* city in Japan, on Honshu. Pop. 550,000

Ham·burg /ham'bərg/ *n.* port on the Elbe River in Germany. Pop. 1,652,400

ham·burg·er /ham'bərgər/ *n.* **1** ground beef **2** patty of this cooked and usu. served on a bread roll [*Hamburg* in Germany]

Ham·hung /häm'hōōNG'/ *n.* city in North Korea. Pop. 701,000

Ham·il·ton /ham'əltən/, **Alexander** 1755–1804; first US Secretary of the Treasury

ham·let /ham'lət/ *n.* small village [MFr *hamelet*, dim. of *ham* village]

Hamm /häm/ *n.* (also **Hamm in Westfalen**) city in Germany. Pop. 179,600

Ham·mar·skjold /häm'ərSHōld, ham'-/, **Dag** 1905–61; Swedish statesman; Secretary General of the United Nations (1953–61)

claw   ball-peen   tack

HAMMER 1a

ham·mer /ham'ər/ *n.* **1a** tool with a heavy metal head used for driving nails, etc. **b** similar device, as for firing the cartridge in a gun **2** *Track & Field.* metal ball attached to a wire, thrown for distance —*v.* **3** hit or beat with or as with a hammer **4a** drive in (nails) **b** fasten or secure by hammering (*hammered the lid down*) **5** inculcate (ideas, knowledge, etc.) forcefully or repeatedly **6** *Colloq.* defeat utterly **7** hammer away (at) persist (in) **8** hammer out: **a** make flat or smooth by hammering **b** work out details of (a plan, etc.) laboriously [OE]

Ham·mer /ham'ər/, **Armand** 1898–1990; US businessman; promoted US-USSR ties

ham'mer and sick'le *n.* symbols for the industrial worker and peasant, used as an emblem of Communism, esp. by the former USSR

ham'mer·head' *n.* **1** head of a hammer **2** shark with a flattened head and eyes on its lateral extensions

Ham·mer·stein /ham'ərstīn'/, **Oscar, II** 1895–1960; US lyricist and librettist

ham'mer·toe' *n.* deformed toe bent permanently downward

Ham·mett /ham'ət/, **(Samuel) Dashiell** 1894–1961; US writer

ham·mock /ham'ək/ *n.* hanging bed of canvas, etc., suspended by cords at the ends [Sp fr. Carib]

Ham·mu·ra·bi /ham'ərab'ē, häm'-/ fl. 18th cent. B.C.; king of Babylonia; promulgated code of laws

ham·per¹ /ham'pər/ *n.* receptacle of basketwork, etc., usu. with a lid [Fr *hanap* goblet]

ham·per² v. prevent the free movement of; hinder

Hamp·ton /ˈhamptən/ n. city in Va. Pop. 133,793

ham·ster /ˈham(p)stər/ n. mouselike rodent with a short tail and large cheek pouches [Ger]

ham·string /ˈhamˌstriNG/ n. 1 each of five tendons at the back of the knee 2 great tendon at the back of the hock in quadrupeds 3 (loosely) muscle at the back of the thigh —v. (·strung, ·string·ing) 4 cripple by or as by cutting the hamstrings of (a person or animal) 5 impair the activity or efficiency of

Ham·sun /ˈhämˌsən/, **Knut** (pseudonym of **Knut Pedersen**) 1859–1952; Norwegian novelist

Han·cock /ˈhanˌkäk/, **John** 1737–93; noted signer of the US Declaration of Independence

hand /hand/ n. 1a part of the human arm below the wrist b (in other primates) end part of a forelimb 2a (often pl.) control; management; custody (in good hands) b active support (give me a hand) 3 pointer of a clock, etc. 4 right or left side or direction 5a skill b person skillful in some respect 6 penmanship or its style 7 pledge of marriage 8 manual or ship's worker 9 source, as for news (at first hand) 10a playing cards dealt to a player b round of play 11 applause —adj. 12 held or done by hand —v. 13 deliver or give over with or as with the hand 14 at hand: a close by b about to happen 15 by hand: a by a person, not a machine b delivered personally 16 hand down: a pass ownership or use of to a later generation, etc. b Law. issue a ruling or verdict 17 hand it to Colloq. award deserved praise to 18 hands down with no difficulty 19 on hand available 20 on the one (or the other) hand from one (or another) point of view 21 out of hand: a out of control b peremptorily (refused out of hand) [OE]

hand·bag n. woman's purse or pocketbook

hand·ball n. game in which a ball is struck by hand against a wall

hand·bill n. printed notice distributed by hand

hand·book n. short manual or guidebook

hand·cart n. small cart pushed or drawn by hand

hand·cuff n. 1 (usu. pl.) device for securing a prisoner's wrist(s) —v. 2 put handcuffs on

Han·del /ˈhandl/, **George Frederick** 1685–1759; German-born composer; lived in England from 1712

hand·ful n. (pl. ·fuls) 1 quantity that fills the hand 2 small number or amount 3 Colloq. troublesome person or task

hand·gre·nade n. GRENADE

hand·gun n. small firearm fired with one hand

hand·i·cap /ˈhandēˌkap/ n. 1 physical or mental disability 2 thing that makes progress or success difficult 3a disadvantage imposed on a superior competitor to make chances more equal b race, etc., in which this is imposed —v. (·capped, ·cap·ping) 4 impose a handicap on 5 place at a disadvantage —**hand'i·capped** adj. [hand i' (in) cap describing a kind of lottery]

hand·i·craft /ˈhandēˌkraft/ n. work requiring manual and artistic skill

hand' in glove' adj. in collusion or association

hand' in hand' adv. 1 in close association 2 holding hands

hand·i·work /ˈhandēˌwərk/ n. work done or a thing made by hand or by a particular person [OE]

hand·ker·chief /ˈhaNGkərchif, -chēf/ n. cloth for wiping one's nose, etc.

han·dle /ˈhandl/ n. 1 part by which a thing is held, carried, or controlled 2 Slang. name or nickname —v. (·dled, ·dling) 3 touch, feel, operate, or move with the hands 4 manage; deal with 5 deal in; sell 6 treat (a subject) 7 (of a car) be readily controlled [OE, rel. to HAND]

han·dle·bar n. (usu. pl.) steering bar of a bicycle, etc.

han·dler n. 1 person who handles or deals in something 2 person who trains and looks after an animal

hand·made adj. made by hand, not machine

hand·me·down n. article of clothing, etc., passed on from another person

hand·out n. 1 thing given free to a needy person 2 statement given to the press, etc. 3 paper distributed to a school class, etc.

hand·rail n. narrow rail for holding as a support

hand·set n. telephone mouthpiece and earpiece as one unit

hand·shake n. clasping of a person's hand as a greeting, etc.

hand·some /ˈhan(d)səm/ adj. (·som·er, ·som·est) 1 good-looking 2 (of an object) imposing; attractive 3a generous (handsome present) b (of a price, fortune, etc.) considerable —**hand'some·ly** adv.

hand·spring n. somersault during which the hands touch the ground

hand·stand n. supporting oneself on one's hands with one's feet in the air

hand·to·hand' adj. (of fighting) at close quarters

hand·work n. work done with the hands —**hand'worked** adj.

hand·writ·ing n. 1 writing done with a pen, pencil, etc. 2 individual's style of this —**hand'writ·ten** /-ˈritn/ adj.

hand·y /ˈhandē/ adj. (·i·er, ·i·est) 1 convenient to handle or use; useful 2 easily available 3 clever with the hands —**hand'i·ly** adv.; **hand'i·ness** n.

Han·dy /ˈhandē/, **W(illiam) C(hristopher)** 1873–1958; US musician

hand·y·man n. (pl. ·men') person who does odd jobs

hang /haNG/ v. (**hung** or **hanged** (sense 6), **hang·ing**) 1 secure or cause to be supported from above, esp. with the lower part free 2 set up (a door, etc.) on hinges 3 place or attach on or to a wall 4 Colloq. blame (a thing on a person) (can't hang that on me) 5 (foll. by with) decorate by suspending pictures, etc. 6 kill by suspending by the neck with a rope, etc. 7 let droop (hang one's head) 8 remain static in the air 9 remain present or imminent —n. 10 way a thing hangs or falls 11 get the hang of Colloq. understand the technique or meaning of 12 hang around: a linger; loiter b associate (with) 13 hang back show reluc-

15 **hang on: a** continue to hold or grasp **b** *Colloq.* wait for a short time **c** *Colloq.* continue; persevere **d** depend 16 **hang out** *Slang.* spend time; frequent 17 **hang together** make sense 18 **hang up: a** hang from a hook, etc. **b** end a telephone conversation **c** *Colloq.* be a psychological problem or obsession for [OE]
• Usage: If a person is suspended by the neck until dead, that person is *hanged*. Pictures, draperies, and the like are *hung*.

hang·ar /haNG′ər, -gər/ *n.* building for housing aircraft, etc. [Fr]

hang′dog′ *adj.* shamefaced

hang·er *n.* 1 person or thing that hangs 2 device on which something is hung

hang′er-on′ *n.* (*pl.* **hang′ers-on′**) follower, esp. an unwelcome one

hang′-glid′er *n.* kitelike glider controlled in flight by a person suspended beneath it —**hang′-glide′** *v.* (-glid·ed, -glid·ing); **hang′-glid′ing** *n.*

hang′ing *n.* 1 execution by suspending by the neck 2 tapestry, etc., hung on a wall, etc.

hang·man /haNG′man/ *n.* (*pl.* -men) executioner who hangs condemned persons

hang′nail′ *n.* torn skin near a fingernail

hang′out′ *n.* *Slang.* place frequented by a person; haunt

hang′o·ver *n.* 1 stomach upset, headache, etc., from drinking too much alcohol 2 survival from the past

hang′-up′ *n.* *Colloq.* emotional problem or inhibition

Hang·zhou /häNG′jō′/ *n.* (formerly Hang′chou′) seaport in China. Pop. 1,099,700

hank /haNGk/ *n.* coil or skein of yarn or thread [ON]

hank·er /haNG′kər/ *v.* long for; crave —**hank′er·ing** *n.* [fr. obs. *hank*]

han·ky-pan·ky /haNG′kē paNG′kē/ *n.* *Colloq.* 1 sexual relations, esp. illicit ones 2 financial dishonesty

Han·ni·bal /han′əbəl/ 247–182 B.C.; Carthaginian general; opposed Rome

Ha·noi /hanoi′/ *n.* capital of Vietnam. Pop. 1,088,900

Han·o·ver /han′ō′vər/ *n.* city in Germany. Pop. 513,000

han·som /han′səm/ *n.* two-wheeled horse-drawn cab [for A. *Hansom*, its designer]

Ha·nuk·kah /KHän′əkə, hän′-/ *n.* (also Ha·nu·kah, Cha·nu·kah) 8-day Jewish festival of lights, commemorating the purification of the Temple [Heb: dedication]

hap·haz·ard /haphaz′ərd/ *adj.* done, etc., by chance; random —**hap·haz′ard·ly** *adv.* [archaic *hap* chance; luck; fr. ON *happ* + HAZARD]

hap·less /hap′ləs/ *adj.* unlucky —**hap′less·ly** *adv.;* **hap′less·ness** *n.*

hap·loid /hap′loid/ *adj.* (of an organism or cell) with a single set of chromosomes [Gk *haplous* single + *eidos* form]

hap·pen /hap′ən/ *v.* 1 occur 2 have (good or bad) fortune (*I happened to meet her*) 3 be the (esp. unwelcome) fate or experience of (*what happened to you?*) 4 happen on (or upon) meet or discover by chance 5 **as it happens** in fact; in reality [rel. to HAPHAZARD]

hap′pen·ing *n.* event

hap·py /hap′ē/ *adj.* (-pi·er, -pi·est) 1 feeling or showing pleasure or contentment 2a

fortunate; lucky **b** (of words, behavior, etc.) apt; pleasing —**hap′pi·ly** *adv.;* **hap′pi·ness** *n.*

hap′py camp′er *n.* *Colloq.* contented, satisfied person

hap′py-go-luck′y *adj.* cheerfully casual

hap′py hour′ *n.* time at which a bar, etc., sells drinks at reduced prices

ha·ra-ki·ri /har′ə kir′ē, kar′ē/ *n.* (also, loosely, **ha·ri-ka·ri** /har′ē kar′ē/) ritual suicide by disembowelment [Japn *hara* belly + *kiri* cutting]

ha·rangue /həraNG′/ *n.* 1 lengthy and vehement speech —*v.* (·rangued, ·rangu·ing) 2 make a harangue; lecture [Fr *arenge* fr. MedL]

Ha·ra·re /hərär′rä/ *n.* capital of Zimbabwe. Pop. 863,000

ha·rass /həras′, har′əs/ *v.* 1 trouble and annoy continually 2 make repeated attacks on —**ha·rass′ment** or **ha′rass·ment** *n.* [Fr]
• Usage: Traditionally, the preferred pronunciation has the stress on the first syllable, as "HAIR-uhs," but the pronunciation that puts the stress on the second syllable is very widely used.

Har·bin /härbin′/ *n.* city in NE China. Pop. 2,443,400

har·bin·ger /här′binjər/ *n.* 1 person or thing that announces or signals the approach of another 2 forerunner [Gmc, rel. to HARBOR]

har·bor /här′bər/ *n.* 1 place of shelter for ships 2 shelter; refuge —*v.* 3 give shelter to (esp. a criminal) 4 hold in one's mind [OE: army shelter]

hard /härd/ *adj.* 1 firm and solid 2a difficult to understand, explain, or accomplish **b** not easy 3 difficult to bear 4 unfeeling; uncompromising 5 severe; harsh (*hard winter*) 6 assiduous; intense (*hard worker*) 7a (of liquor) strongly alcoholic **b** (of drugs) potent and addictive 8 (of water) having a relatively high content of mineral salts 9 stark and unavoidable (*hard facts*) 10a (of currency, prices, etc.) not likely to fall in value **b** (of money) cash —*adv.* 11 strenuously; intensely; copiously (*try hard; raining hard*) 12 **be hard on: a** be difficult for **b** be severe in one's treatment or criticism of 13 **hard by** close by —**hard′ness** *n.* [OE]

hard′-and-fast′ *adj.* (of a rule or distinction) unalterable; strict

hard′back′ *adj.* 1 bound in boards covered with cloth, etc. —*n.* 2 hardback book

hard′ball′ *n.* 1 baseball, as opposed to (slow-pitch) softball 2 **play hardball** employ a strategy of aggressive or ruthless competition

hard′-bit′ten *adj.* tough and cynical

hard′-boiled′ *adj.* 1 (of an egg) boiled until the white and yolk are solid 2 *Colloq.* (of a person) tough; shrewd

hard′ cop′y *n.* material printed out on paper, as from a computer file

hard′ core′ *n.* 1 essential nucleus 2 the most loyal and committed members of a group, movement, etc. —*adj.* 3 forming a nucleus 4 uncompromising 5 (of pornography) explicit; obscene

hard′ disk′ *n.* *Comp.* (also **hard′ drive′**) rigid magnetic data-storage disk

hard·en /härd'n/ v. **1** make or become hard or harder **2** become or make (one's attitude, etc.) less sympathetic

hard'hat' n. **1** protective helmet worn esp. by construction workers **2** *Colloq.* a construction worker **b** any blue-collar worker, esp. one politically conservative —adj. **3** *Colloq.* pertaining to or typical of hardhats

hard'head'ed adj. practical; not sentimental —**hard'head'ed·ly** adv.; **hard'head'ed·ness** n.

hard'heart'ed adj. unfeeling —**hard'heart'ed·ly** adv.; **hard'heart'ed·ness** n.

har·di·hood /här'dēhŏŏd'/ n. boldness; daring

Har·ding /härd'iNG/, **Warren Gamaliel** 1865–1923; 29th US president (1921–23)

hard' la'bor n. heavy manual work as a punishment, esp. in a prison

hard' line' n. **1** unyielding adherence to a policy —adj. **2** (**hard'-line'**) unyielding; uncompromising —**hard'-lin'er** n.

hard'ly adv. **1** scarcely; only just **2** only with difficulty

hard'-nosed' adj. *Colloq.* realistic; uncompromising

hard'-pressed' adj. **1** closely pursued **2** burdened; under pressure

hard'scrab'ble adj. yielding meager returns for much effort

hard' sell' n. aggressive salesmanship

hard'ship' n. **1** severe suffering or privation **2** instance or cause of this

hard'top' n. **1** style of car with a rigid top and no roof supports between the side windows **2** car with a removable rigid top

hard' up' adj. short of money

hard·ware /härd'wer'/ n. **1** tools and household articles of metal, etc. **2** heavy machinery or armaments **3** mechanical and electronic components of a computer, etc.

hard'wood' n. close-grained, dense wood, as from a deciduous broad-leaved tree

hard'-work'ing adj. diligent

har·dy /här'dē/ adj. (**·di·er**, **·di·est**) **1** robust; enduring **2** (of a plant) able to grow in the open air all year —**har'di·ly** adv.; **har'di·ness** n. [Fr *hardi* made bold]

Har·dy /härd'ē/ **1 Thomas** 1840–1928; English novelist and poet **2 Oliver** 1892–1957; US comedian; partner of STAN LAUREL

hare /her/ n. rodentlike mammal with long hind legs, long ears, and a divided upper lip [OE]

hare'brained' adj. rash; ill-advised

hare'lip' n. congenital cleft in the upper lip

har·em /har'əm, her'-/ n. **1** women of a traditional Muslim household **2** their quarters [Ar: sanctuary]

hark /härk/ v. **1** (usu. *imper.*) *Archaic.* listen attentively **2 hark back** revert to an earlier topic [OE]

har·le·quin /här'lik(w)in/ n. **1** (*cap.*) mute character in pantomime, usu. masked and dressed in a diamond-patterned costume —adj. **2** in varied colors [Fr]

har·lot /här'lət/ n. prostitute —**har'lot·ry** n. [Fr: knave]

harm /härm/ n. **1** hurt; damage —v. **2** cause harm to **3 out of harm's way** to safety [OE]

harm'ful adj. causing or likely to cause harm —**harm'ful·ly** adv.; **harm'ful·ness** n.

harm·less /härm'ləs/ adj. **1** not able or likely to cause harm **2** inoffensive —**harm'less·ly** adv.; **harm'less·ness** n.

har·mon·ic /härmän'ik/ adj. **1** of or relating to harmony; harmonious —n. **2** *Mus.* overtone that forms a composite note with another note —**har·mon'i·cal·ly** adv.

har·mon·i·ca /härmän'ikə/ n. rectangular musical instrument with reeds, played by blowing or sucking air through; mouth organ

har·mo·ni·ous /härmō'nēəs/ adj. **1** sweetsounding; tuneful **2** forming a pleasing or consistent whole **3** free from disagreement or dissent —**har·mo'ni·ous·ly** adv.

har·mo·nize /här'mənīz/ v. (**·nized**, **·niz·ing**) **1** add notes to (a melody) to produce harmony **2** bring into or be in harmony **3** make or form a pleasing or consistent whole —**har'mo·ni·za'tion** n.

har·mo·ny /här'mənē/ n. (*pl.* **·nies**) **1** combination of simultaneously sounded musical notes to produce chords **2** apt or esthetic arrangement of parts **3** agreement; concord [Gk *harmonia* joining]

Harms·worth /härmz'wərTH/, **Alfred** (**Viscount Northcliffe**) 1865–1922; English journalist and publisher

har·ness /här'nəs/ n. **1** equipment of straps, etc., by which a horse is fastened to a cart, etc., and controlled **2** similar fastening to support a person climbing, etc. —v. **3a** put a harness on **b** attach by harness (to) **4** make use of (natural resources), esp. to produce energy [Fr *harneis* military equipment]

harp /härp/ n. **1** upright stringed instrument plucked with the fingers —v. **2 harp on** or **upon** talk repeatedly and tediously —**harp'ist** n. [OE]

har·poon /härpŏŏn'/ n. **1** barbed spear with a rope attached for catching whales, etc. —v. **2** spear with a harpoon [Gk *harpē* sickle; hook]

harp·si·chord /härp'sikôrd'/ n. pianolike instrument in which strings are plucked mechanically —**harp'si·chord'ist** n. [L *harpa* harp + *chorda* string]

har·py /här'pē/ n. (*pl.* **·pies**) **1** *Gk. Myth.* monster with a woman's head and body and a bird's wings and claws **2** shrewish woman [fr. Gk *harpazein* snatch away]

har·ri·dan /har'ədən/ n. bad-tempered old woman

har·ri·er /har'ēər/ n. **1** hound used for hunting hares **2** cross-country runner [fr. HARE, HARRY]

Har·ris /har'əs/, **Joel Chandler** 1848–1908; US writer

Har·ris·burg /har'əsbərg/ n. capital of Penn., in the SE part. Pop. 52,376

Har·ri·son /har'əsən/ **1 William Henry** 1773–1841; 9th US president (1841) **2 Benjamin** 1833–1901; 23rd US president (1889–93) **3** (**Sir**) **Rex** 1908–90; English actor **4 George** 1943– ; British rock guitarist and composer

har·row /har'ō/ n. **1** heavy frame with iron teeth dragged over plowed land —v. **2** draw

har·ry /här′ē/ v. (·ried, ·ry·ing) 1 ravage; despoil 2 harass [OE]

harsh /härsH/ adj. 1 unpleasantly rough or sharp, esp. to the senses 2 severe; cruel —**harsh′en** v.; **harsh′ly** adv.; **harsh′ness** n. [LGer]

Hart /härt/, **Lorenz** 1895–1943; US lyricist

Harte /härt/, **(Francis) Bret** 1836–1902; US writer

Hart·ford /härt′fərd/ n. capital of Conn., in the N central part. Pop. 139,739

har·um-scar·um /her′əm sker′əm/ Colloq. adj. 1 wild and reckless —adv. 2 in a reckless way [rhyming formation on HARE + SCARE]

har·vest /här′vist/ n. 1a process of gathering in crops, etc. b season of this 2 season's yield 3 product of any action —v. 4 gather as harvest; reap —**har′ves·ter** n. [OE]

Har·vey /här′vē/, **William** 1578–1657; British physician and anatomist

has /haz; has (before to)/ v. 3rd sing. present of HAVE

has′-been n. person or thing of declined importance

hash /hasH/ n. 1 dish of cooked meat and usu. vegetables cut into small pieces and reheated 2a mixture; jumble b mess 3 hash out settle by conferring or debating [Fr hacher cut up]

hash·ish /hasH′ēsH/, ·isH, häsHēsH/ n. (also Slang. hash) resinous product of hemp, smoked or chewed as a narcotic [Ar]

has·n't /haz′ənt/ v. contr. has not

HASP

hasp /hasp/ n. hinged metal clasp fitting over a staple and secured by a padlock [OE]

has·si·um /has′sēəm/ n. radioactive element; symb. Hs

has·sle /has′əl/ Colloq. n. 1 trouble; problem; argument —v. (·sled, ·sling) 2 harass; annoy [orig. a dial. word]

has·sock /has′ək/ n. thick firm cushion for sitting or for the feet [OE]

haste /hāst/ n. 1 urgency of movement or action; excessive hurry —v. (hast·ed, hast·ing) 2 Archaic. HASTEN. 3 make haste hurry; be quick [Fr fr. Gmc]

hast·en /hā′sən/ v. 1 make haste; hurry 2 bring about sooner

hast·y /hā′stē/ adj. (·i·er, ·i·est) 1 hurried; acting too quickly 2 said, made, or done too quickly or too soon; rash —**hast′i·ly** adv.; **hast′i·ness** n.

hat /hat/ n. 1 (esp. outdoor) covering for the head 2 keep under one's hat keep secret 3 pass the hat (around) collect contributions of money 4 take one's hat off to acknowledge admiration for [OE]

hatch¹ /hacH/ n. 1 opening or door in an aircraft, etc. 2a HATCHWAY b cover for this [OE]

hatch² v. 1a (of a young bird, fish, etc.) emerge from the egg b (of an egg) produce a young animal 2 incubate (an egg) 3 devise (a plot, etc.) —n. 4 act of hatching 5 brood hatched [earlier hacche, fr. Gmc]

hatch′back n. car with a sloping back hinged at the top to form a door

hatch·et /hacH′it/ n. light short-handled axe [Fr hachette]

hatch′et job′ n. malicious attack on someone's character; ruthless criticism

hatch′et man′ n. (pl. ·men) person employed to harm or dismiss another

hatch′way n. opening in a ship's deck for cargo

hate /hāt/ v. (hat·ed, hat·ing) 1 dislike intensely 2a dislike b be reluctant (to do something) (I hate to disturb you) —n. 3 hatred 4 hated person or thing [OE]

hate′ful adj. arousing hatred —**hate′ful·ly** adv.; **hate′ful·ness** n.

Hath·a·way /haTH′əwā′/, **Anne** c. 1557–1623; wife of William Shakespeare

ha·tred /hā′trid/ n. extreme dislike or ill will

hat·ter /hat′ər/ n. maker or seller of hats

hat′ trick′ n. three successes, etc., in a single game

haugh·ty /hô′tē/ adj. (·ti·er, ·ti·est) arrogant and disdainful —**haugh′ti·ly** adv.; **haugh′ti·ness** n. [haught, haut fr. Fr: high]

haul /hôl/ v. 1 pull or drag forcibly 2 transport by truck, cart, etc. —n. 3 hauling 4 amount gained or acquired 5 distance to be traversed [Fr haler fr. ON hala]

haunch /hônCH, hänCH/ n. 1 fleshy part of the buttock with the thigh 2 leg and loin of a deer, etc., as food [Fr fr. Gmc]

haunt /hônt, hänt/ v. 1 (of a ghost) visit a place) regularly 2 frequent (a place) 3 linger in the mind of —n. 4 place frequented by a person or animal [Fr fr. Gmc]

haunt′ing adj. (of a memory, melody, etc.) tending to linger in the mind

Haupt·mann /houpt′män′/, **Gerhart** 1862–1946; German dramatist

Hau·sa /hou′sä/ n. (pl. ·sas, ·sa) n. 1 members of an Islamic people native to N Nigeria and S Niger 2 their language

haute cuisine /ōt′ kwizēn′/ n. fancy, esp. French-style cooking [Fr]

hau·teur /ōtər′/ n. haughtiness [Fr]

Ha·van·a /həvan′ə/ n. capital of Cuba. Pop. 2,077,900

have /hav, haf (before to)/ v. (had, hav·ing) 1 as an auxiliary verb with past part. to form the perfect, pluperfect, and future perfect tenses, and the conditional mood (has, had, will have seen; had I known, I would have gone) 2 own or be able to use 3 hold in a certain relationship (has a sister) 4 contain as a part or quality 5a experience (have a nice day) b be subjected to a specified act or condition (book has a page missing) c cause (a person or thing) to be in a particular state or to take particular action (had us worried; had a copy made) 6a engage in (an activity) (have an argument) b hold (a meeting, party, etc.) 7 eat or drink (had a beer) 8 (with neg.) accept or tolerate (*I won't have it*) **9a** feel (*have no doubt*) **b** show (mercy, pity, etc.) **10a** give birth to (offspring) **b** conceive mentally (an idea, etc.) **11** receive; obtain (*not a ticket to be had*) **12** *Slang.* **a** get the better of (*I had him there*) **b** cheat; deceive (*you were had*) —*n.* **13** (usu. *pl.*) *Colloq.* person with wealth or resources **14** have it in for *Colloq.* be hostile or ill-disposed toward **15** have it out (with) *Colloq.* attempt to settle a dispute; argue **16** have on wear (clothes) **17** have to be obliged to; must [OE]

Ha·vel /hä′vəl/, **Václav** 1936– ; Czech dramatist; president of Czech Republic (1993–)

ha·ven /hā′vən/ *n.* **1** refuge **2** harbor; port [OE]

have′-not′ *n.* (usu. *pl.*) person lacking wealth or resources

have·n't /hav′ənt/ *v. contr.* have not

hav·er·sack /hav′ərsak′/ *n.* stout canvas bag carried on the back or over the shoulder [Ger *Habersack* oats-sack]

hav·oc /hav′ək/ *n.* widespread destruction; great disorder [MFr *havot*]

haw /hô/ *n.* hawthorn berry [OE]

Ha·wai·i /həwä′ē, -wī′ē, -wô′ē/ *n.* **1** Pacific state of the US comprising 8 islands. Capital: Honolulu. Pop. 1,108,229. Abbr. HI **2** largest island of the state of Hawaii —**Ha·wai′ian** /-wä′yən, -wī′ən/ *n. & adj.*

hawk[1] /hôk/ *n.* **1** bird of prey with a curved beak, rounded short wings, and a long tail **2** *Polit.* person who advocates warlike policies —**hawk′ish** *adj.*; **hawk′ish·ly** *adv.*; **hawk′ish·ness** *n.* [OE]

hawk[2] *v.* carry about or offer (goods) for sale [back formation fr. HAWKER]

hawk[3] *v.* **1** clear the throat noisily **2** bring (phlegm, etc.) up from the throat [imit.]

Hawke /hôk/, **Robert James Lee ("Bob")** 1929– ; Australian prime minister (1983–91)

hawk′er *n.* person who travels about selling goods [LGer or Du]

hawk-eyed /hôk′īd′/ *adj.* keen-sighted

Hawk·ing /hôk′iNG/, **Stephen** 1942– ; British physicist

Hawks /hôks/, **Howard** 1896–1977; US film director and producer

haw·ser /hô′zər/ *n.* thick rope or cable for mooring or towing a ship [Fr *haucier* hoist, fr. L *altus* high]

haw·thorn /hô′THôrn/ *n.* thorny shrub with small dark-red berries [rel. to HAW + THORN]

Haw·thorne /hô′THôrn/, **Nathaniel** 1804–64; US writer

hay /hā/ *n.* **1** grass mown and dried for fodder **2** hit the hay *Slang.* go to bed [OE]

Hay /hā/, **John** 1838–1905; US statesman

Hay·dn /hīd′n/, **Franz Joseph** 1732–1809; Austrian composer

Hayes /hāz/, **1 Rutherford B(irchard)** 1822–93; 19th US president (1877–81) **2 Helen** 1900–93; US actress

hay′ fe′ver *n.* allergy with respiratory symptoms caused by pollen or dust

hay′stack′ *n.* packed pile of hay

Hay·ward /hā′wərd/ *n.* city in Calif. Pop. 111,498

hay′wire′ *adj. Colloq.* **1** out of control; awry **2** crazy

haz·ard /haz′ərd/ *n.* **1** danger or risk **2** source of this **3** *Golf.* obstacle, as a bunker —*v.* **4** risk —**haz′ard·ous** *adj.*; **haz′ard·ous·ly** *adv.* [Ar *az-zahr* chance; luck]

haze /hāz/ *n.* **1** thin atmospheric vapor **2** mental obscurity or confusion [back formation fr. HAZY]

ha·zel /hā′zəl/ *n.* **1** shrub bearing round brown edible nuts **2** greenish brown [OE]

ha′zel·nut′ *n.* nut of the hazel

ha·zy /hā′zē/ *adj.* (·**zi·er**, ·**zi·est**) **1** misty **2** vague; indistinct **3** confused; uncertain —**haz′i·ly** *adv.*; **haz′i·ness** *n.*

H′-bomb′ /āCH′bäm′/ *n.* HYDROGEN BOMB

hdbk. *abbr.* handbook

HDPE *abbr.* high density polyethylene

HDTV *abbr.* HIGH-DEFINITION TELEVISION

he /hē/ *pron.* (*pl.* **they**) **1** the man, boy, or male animal previously named or in question **2** person or creature of unspecified sex —*n.* **3** male; man **4** (in *comb.*) male (*he-goat*) [OE]
● Usage: See note at EVERYBODY.

He *symb.* helium

head /hed/ *n.* **1** uppermost part of the human body, or foremost or upper part of an animal's body, containing the brain, mouth, and sense organs **2a** seat of intellect **b** mental aptitude or tolerance (*a good head for business*) **3** thing like a head in form or position; top **4** person in charge **5** front, upper, top, or foremost part **6** individual person or animal as a unit **7a** side of a coin bearing the image of a head **b** (usu. *pl.*) this as a choice in a coin toss **8** source of a river, etc. **9** height or length of a head as a measure **10** promontory (esp. in place-names) —*adj.* **11** chief; principal —*v.* **12** be at the head or front of **13** be in charge of **14** face, move, or direct in a specified direction (*head north*) **15** come to a head: **a** be ready to burst, as a pimple **b** reach a crisis **16** go to one's head: **a** (of an alcoholic drink) make one slightly drunk **b** make one conceited **17** head off: **a** get ahead of so as to intercept **b** forestall **18** keep (or lose) one's head remain (or fail to remain) calm **19** off the top of one's head *Colloq.* impromptu **20** over one's head: **a** beyond one's understanding **b** to a higher authority [OE]

head′ache′ *n.* **1** persistent pain in the head **2** *Colloq.* worrying problem —**head′ach′y** *adj.*

head′board′ *n.* upright panel at the head of a bed

head′hunt′ing *n.* **1** (as among certain peoples) collecting of the heads of dead enemies as trophies **2** *Colloq.* recruitment of staff from other organizations —**head′hunt′er** *n.*

head′ing *n.* **1a** title at the head of a page, chapter, etc. **b** section of a subject of discourse, etc. **2** direction of a moving ship or airplane

head·land /hed′lənd, -land′/ *n.* promontory

head′light′ *n.* **1** road-illuminating light at the front of a vehicle **2** beam from this

head′line′ *n.* **1** heading at the top of an article or page, esp. in a newspaper **2** (*pl.*) most important items in a news bulletin —*v.* (·**lined**, ·**lin·ing**) **3** star as a performer —**head′lin′er** *n.*

head′long′ *adv. & adj.* **1** with the head foremost **2** in a rush

head′mas′ter *n.* (*fem.* **head′mis′tress**) head of a private school

head'-on' *adj. & adv.* **1** with the front foremost (*head-on crash*) **2** in direct confrontation

head' o'ver heels' *n.* **1** turning over completely in forward motion, as in a somersault —*adv.* **2** utterly

head'phones' *n. pl.* set of earphones fitting over the head

head'quar'ters *n.* (as *sing.* or *pl.*) administrative center of an organization

head'rest' *n.* support for the head, esp. on a seat

head'room' *n.* space or clearance above a vehicle, person's head, etc.

head-set /hed'set'/ *n.* headphones, often with a microphone attached

head-shrink-er /hed'SHriNG'kər/ *n.* (also **shrink**) *Slang.* psychiatrist

head' start' *n.* advantage granted or gained at an early stage

head'stone' *n.* stone set up at the head of a grave

head'strong' *adj.* self-willed

head'wa'ters *n. pl.* upper streams of a river

head'way' *n.* **1** progress **2** ship's rate of progress

head' wind' *n.* wind blowing from directly in front

head'word' *n.* word forming a heading, as of a dictionary entry

head'y *adj.* (**·i·er, ·i·est**) **1** (of liquor) potent **2** intoxicating; exciting **3** impulsive; rash —**head'i·ly** *adv.*; **head'i·ness** *n.*

heal /hēl/ *v.* **1** become sound or healthy again **2** cause to heal **3** put right (differences, etc.) —**heal'er** *n.* [OE, rel. to WHOLE]

health /helTH/ *n.* **1** state of being well in body or mind **2** person's mental or physical condition **3** soundness, esp. financial or moral [OE, rel. to WHOLE]

health' food' *n.* food thought to promote good health, as being pure or unprocessed

health'ful *adj.* conducive to good health; beneficial —**health'ful·ly** *adv.*; **health'ful·ness** *n.*

health'y *adj.* (**·i·er, ·i·est**) **1** having, showing, or promoting good health **2** indicative of (esp. moral or financial) health **3** substantial (*a healthy margin*) —**health'i·ly** *adv.*; **health'i·ness** *n.*

heap /hēp/ *n.* **1** disorderly pile **2** (esp. *pl.*) *Colloq.* large number or amount **3** *Slang.* dilapidated vehicle —*v.* **4** collect or be collected in a pile **5** load copiously (with) **6** give or offer copiously [OE]

hear /hēr/ *v.* (**heard** /hərd/**, hear·ing**) **1** perceive with the ear **2** listen to **3** *Law.* judge (a case, etc.) **4** be told or informed; learn **5** grant (a prayer) **6 hear a person out** listen to attentively **7 hear from** be contacted by **8 will not hear of** will not allow —**hear'er** *n.* [OE]

hear'ing *n.* **1** faculty of perceiving sounds **2** range of audible sounds **3** opportunity to state one's case **4** preliminary appearance before a court

hear'ing aid' *n.* device worn by a partially deaf person to amplify sound

hear·ken /här'kən/ *v.* listen carefully (to) [OE, rel. to HARK]

hear·say /hēr'sā/ *n.* rumor; gossip

hearse /hərs/ *n.* vehicle for conveying the coffin at a funeral [Fr *herse* harrow, fr. L *hirpex* large rake]

Hearst /hərst/, **William Randolph** 1863–1951; US newspaper publisher

heart /härt/ *n.* **1** hollow muscular organ maintaining the circulation of blood by rhythmic contraction and dilation **2** region of the heart; the breast **3a** center of thought, feeling, and emotion (esp. love) **b** capacity for feeling emotion **4** courage or enthusiasm (*take heart*) **5** mood or feeling (*change of heart*) **6** central or essential part of something **7a** conventional representation of a heart (♥) **b** playing card of the suit denoted by this symbol in red **c** (*pl.*) this suit **8 at heart:** a in one's inmost feelings **b** basically **9 break a person's heart** overwhelm a person with sorrow **10 by heart** from memory **11 take to heart:** a heed earnestly **b** be much affected by [OE]

heart'ache' *n.* emotional anguish

heart' at·tack' *n.* sudden or acute disorder or failure of the heart

heart'beat' *n.* pulsation of the heart

heart'break' *n.* overwhelming distress —**heart'break'ing, heart'bro'ken** *adj.*

heart'burn' *n.* burning sensation in the chest from indigestion

heart·en /härt'n/ *v.* make or become more cheerful —**heart'en·ing** *adj.*

heart'felt' *adj.* sincere; deeply felt

hearth /härTH/ *n.* **1** floor of a fireplace **2** the home [OE]

heart'land', -land' /n.* central or vital part of an area

heart'less /härt'ləs/ *adj.* unfeeling; pitiless —**heart'less·ly** *adv.*

heart'-rend'ing *adj.* very distressing

heart'sick' *adj.* despondent

heart'strings' *n. pl.* one's deepest feelings

heart'throb' *n.* person for whom one has (esp. immature) romantic feelings

heart'-to-heart' *adj.* **1** (of a conversation, etc.) candid; intimate —*n.* **2** candid or personal conversation

heart'warm'ing *adj.* emotionally rewarding or uplifting

heart'y *adj.* (**·i·er, ·i·est**) **1** strong; vigorous **2** (of a meal or appetite) large **3** warm; friendly —**heart'i·ly** *adv.*; **heart'i·ness** *n.*

heat /hēt/ *n.* **1** condition of being hot **2** *Physics.* energy arising from the motion of molecules **3** hot weather **4** warmth of feeling; anger; excitement **5** most intense part or period of activity (*heat of battle*) **6** trial round in a race, etc. —*v.* **7** make or become hot or warm **8** inflame **9 in heat** (of mammals, esp. females) sexually receptive [OE]

heat'ed *adj.* angry; impassioned —**heat'ed·ly** *adv.*

heat'er *n.* any device furnishing heat

heath /hēTH/ *n.* **1** area of flattish uncultivated land with low shrubs **2** plant growing on a heath, esp. heather [OE]

Heath /hēTH/, **(Sir) Edward** 1916– ; prime minister of Great Britain (1970–74)

hea·then /hē'THən/ *n.* **1** person not believing in the biblical God, i.e., not a Christian, Jew, or Muslim **2** person regarded as lacking religious or moral principles —*adj.* **3** of heathens **4** having no religion [OE]

heath·er /heTH′ər/ *n.* any of various shrubs growing esp. on moors and heaths

heat′ light′ning *n.* flashes of lightning without thunder, as from a distant summer storm

heat′proof *adj.* **1** able to resist great heat —*v.* **2** make heatproof

heat′stroke *n.* fever, rapid pulse, dry skin, etc., caused by excessive heat

heat′ wave′ *n.* period of unusually hot weather

heave /hēv/ *v.* (**heaved** or esp. *Naut.* **hove, heav·ing**) **1** lift or haul with great effort **2** utter with effort (*heaved a sigh*) **3** *Colloq.* throw **4** rise and fall rhythmically or spasmodically **5** *Naut.* haul by rope **6** retch —*n.* **7** heaving **8** (*pl.*, with the) **a** respiratory disease of horses **b** *Colloq.* spasm of vomiting [OE]

heav·en /hev′ən/ *n.* **1** place regarded in some religions as the abode of God and of the blessed after death **2** place or state of supreme bliss **3** *Colloq.* delightful feeling, state, etc. **4** (*pl.*, with the) the sky as seen from the earth, esp. at night —**heav′en·ward** /-wərd/, **heav′en·wards** *adv.* [OE]

heav′en·ly *adj.* **1** of heaven; divine **2** of the heavens or sky **3** very pleasing; wonderful

heav·y /hev′ē/ *adj.* (**·i·er, ·i·est**) **1** of great or unusually high weight; difficult to lift **2** of great density; abundant; considerable (*heavy crop; heavy traffic*) **3** severe; intense (*heavy fighting*) **4** prodigious; overindulgent (*heavy drinker*) **5** (of machinery, artillery, etc.) very large of its kind; large in caliber, etc. **6** demanding much physical effort (*heavy work*) **7** serious or somber **8** tedious **9a** hard to digest **b** hard to read or understand **10** oppressive; taxing (*heavy demands*) —*n.* (*pl.* **·ies**) **11** *Colloq.* villain; thug —*adv.* **12** in a heavy manner —**heav′i·ly** *adv.*; **heav′i·ness** *n.*; **heav′y·ish** *adj.* [OE]

heav′y-du′ty *adj.* intended to withstand hard use

heav′y·go′ing *n.* slow or difficult progress

heav′y-hand′ed *adj.* **1** clumsy **2** overbearing; oppressive —**heav′y-hand′ed·ly** *adv.*; **heav′y-hand′ed·ness** *n.*

heav′y-heart′ed *adj.* sad; doleful

heav′y in′dus·try *n.* industry producing metal, machinery, etc.

heav′y met′al *n.* **1** metal of high density **2** rock music with a pounding rhythm, featuring loud guitars

heav′y·set′ *adj.* large or stocky in build

heav′y wa′ter *n.* water composed of deuterium and oxygen

heav′y·weight *n.* **1** *Sports.* weight class for competitors; in professional boxing, fighters usu. above 195 lbs. **2** person, etc., of above average weight **3** person of influence or importance

He·bra·ic /hibrā′ik/ *adj.* of Hebrew or the Hebrews

He·brew /hē′brōō/ *n.* **1** member of an ancient Semitic people **2a** language of this people **b** modern form of this, used esp. in Israel —*adj.* **3** of or in Hebrew **4** of the Hebrews or the Jews [Heb: one from the other side of the river]

Heb·ri·des /heb′rədēz′/ *n.* group of islands off the W coast of Scotland

heck /hek/ *interj.* mild exclamation of surprise or dismay [a form of HELL]

heck·le /hek′əl/ *v.* (**·led, ·ling**) **1** interrupt and harass (a public speaker) —*n.* **2** act of heckling —**heck′ler** *n.* [var. of HACKLE]

hec·tare /hek′ter/ *n.* metric unit of square measure, 100 ares (2.471 acres or 10,000 square meters) [Fr, rel. to HECTO- + *are*]

hec·tic /hek′tik/ *adj.* **1** busy and confused; excited **2** feverish —**hec′ti·cal·ly** *adv.* [Gk *hektikos* habitual]

hecto- *comb. form* hundred [Gk *hekaton*]

hec·tor /hek′tər/ *v.* **1** bully; intimidate —*n.* **2** bully [fr. *Hector* in Homer's *Iliad*]

he'd /hēd/ *v. contr.* **1** he had **2** he would

hedge /hej/ *n.* **1** fence or boundary of dense bushes or shrubs **2** protection against possible loss —*v.* (**hedged, hedg·ing**) **3** surround or bound with a hedge **4** enclose **5a** reduce one's risk of loss on (a bet or speculation) through compensating transactions **b** avoid committing oneself [OE]

hedge′hog′ *n.* PORCUPINE

he·do·nism /hēd′n·iz′əm/ *n.* **1** belief in pleasure as humankind's proper aim **2** behavior based on this —**hed′on·ist** /-ist/ *n.*; **he′do·nis′tic** *adj.* [Gk *hēdonē* pleasure]

heed /hēd/ *v.* **1** attend to; take notice of —*n.* **2** careful attention —**heed′ful, heed′less** *adj.*; **heed′less·ly** *adv.* [OE]

hee-haw /hē′hô′/ *n.* **1** bray of a donkey —*v.* **2** make a braying sound [imit.]

heel[1] /hēl/ *n.* **1** back of the foot below the ankle **2a** sock part covering this **b** shoe part supporting this **3** thing like a heel in form or position **4** crust end of a loaf of bread **5** *Colloq.* scoundrel —*v.* **6** fit or renew a heel on (a shoe, etc.) **7** (of a dog) follow or accompany closely **8 at** (or **on**) **the heels of** following closely after **9 kick up one's heels** have fun or go on a spree **10 down at the heel** (of a person) shabby **11 take to one's heels** run away [OE]

heel[2] *v.* **1** (of a sailing vessel, etc.) lean (over) **2** cause (a vessel) to do this [obs. *heeld*, fr. Gmc]

heft·y /hef′tē/ *adj.* (**·i·er, ·i·est**) **1** (of a person) big and strong **2** (of a thing) large; heavy; powerful —**heft′i·ly** *adv.*; **heft′i·ness** *n.* [*heft* weight, rel. to HEAVE]

He·gel /hā′gəl/, **Georg Wilhelm Friedrich** 1770–1831; German philosopher

he·ge·mo·ny /hijem′ənē, hej′əmō′nē/ *n.* dominating leadership, esp. by one government over another; predominance [Gk *hēgemōn* leader]

He·gi·ra /hejī′rə, hej′ərə/ *n.* (also **He·ji′ra**) **1** Muhammad's flight from Mecca in AD 622 **2** Muslim era reckoned from this date [Ar *hijra* departure]

Hei·deg·ger /hīd′igər/, **Martin** 1889–1976; German philosopher

Hei·del·berg /hīd′l-bərg′/ *n.* city in Germany. Pop. 136,800

heif·er /hef′ər/ *n.* young cow that has not had a calf [OE]

Hei·fetz /hī′fəts/, **Jascha** 1901–87; Russian-born US violinist

height /hīt/ *n.* **1** measurement from base to top or head to foot **2** elevation above the ground or a recognized level **3** considerable elevation **4** high place or area **5** acme **6a** most intense part or period (*battle at its height*) **b** extreme example (*the height of fashion*) [OE]

● Usage: Avoid the pronunciation of *height* with a *th*-sound at the end, which many regard as unacceptable.

height·en /hīt'n/ *v.* make or become higher or more intense

Heim·lich ma·neu·ver /hīm'lik/ *n.* emergency technique to aid a choking victim by applying pressure to the abdomen just below the ribcage [for E.M. *Heimlich*, US physician who devised it]

Hei·ne /hī'nə/, **(Christian) Heinrich** 1797–1856; German poet

hei·nous /hā'nəs/ *adj.* utterly odious or wicked [Fr *haïr* hate]

Heinz /hīnz/, **Henry John** 1844–1919; US food manufacturer

heir /er/ *n.* (*fem.* **heir·ess** /er'is/) person entitled to property or title as a legal successor [L *heres*]

heir' ap·par'ent *n.* heir whose claim cannot be set aside by the birth of another heir

heir·loom /er'lōōm/ *n.* **1** possession or property in a family for several generations **2** piece of property as part of an inheritance

He·ji·ra /hiji'rə/ *n.* var. of HEGIRA

held /held/ *v. past* and *past part.* of HOLD[1]

Hel·e·na /hel'ənə/ *n.* capital of Mont., in the W central part. Pop. 24,569

he·li·cal /hel'ikəl, hē'li-/ *adj.* spiral

hel·i·ces /hel'isēz/ *n. pl.* of HELIX

he·li·cop·ter /hel'ikäp'tər/ *n.* wingless aircraft obtaining lift and propulsion from horizontally rotating overhead blades [Gk, rel. to HELIX + *pteron* wing]

helio- *comb. form* sun [Gk *hēlios* sun]

he·li·o·cen·tric /hē'lēōsen'trik/ *adj.* **1** regarding the sun as center **2** considered as viewed from the sun's center

he·li·o·trope /hē'lēətrōp'/ *n.* plant with fragrant purple flowers [Gk, rel. to HELIO- + *trepein* turn]

hel·i·port /hel'əpôrt'/ *n.* place where helicopters take off and land

he·li·um /hē'lēəm/ *n.* light inert gaseous element used in airships and as a refrigerant; *symb.* He [rel. to HELIO-]

he·lix /hē'liks/ *n.* (*pl.* **he'li·ces**) spiral curve (like a corkscrew) or coiled curve (like a watch spring) [L fr. Gk]

he'll /hēl/ *v. contr.* he will; he shall

hell /hel/ *n.* **1** place regarded in some religions as the abode of the dead or of devils and condemned sinners **2** place or state of misery or wickedness **3** come hell or high water regardless of the difficulties **4a** (one) hell of a **b** *Colloq.* outstanding example of (*one hell of a party*) [OE]

hell'bent' *adj.* recklessly determined

hel·le·bore /hel'əbôr'/ *n.* evergreen plant with usu. white, purple, or green flowers, e.g., the Christmas rose [Gk (*h*)*elleborus*]

Hel·le·nism /hel'əniz'əm/ *n.* (esp. ancient) Greek character or culture —**Hel·len'ic** /-len'ik/ *adj.*; **Hel'len·ist** *n.*

Hel·len·is·tic /hel'ənis'tik/ *adj.* of Greek history, language, and culture of the late 4th to the late 1st cent. B.C.

Hel·ler /hel'ər/, **Joseph** 1923– ; US writer

hell'hole' *n.* oppressive or unbearable place

hell'ish *adj.* **1** of or like hell **2** extremely difficult or unpleasant —**hell'ish·ly** *adv.*; **hell' ish·ness** *n.*

Hell·man /hel'mən/, **Lillian** 1905–84; US dramatist

hel·lo /həlō', helō', hel'ō/ *interj.* **1** expression of informal greeting, or of surprise, or to call attention —*n.* (*pl.* **·los**) **2** cry of "hello" [var. of earlier *hollo* fr. MFr *hola* ahoy there]

helm /helm/ *n.* **1** tiller or wheel for controlling a ship's rudder **2** at the helm in control; at the head of an organization, etc. [OE]

hel·met /hel'mət/ *n.* protective head covering worn by a soldier, motorcyclist, etc. [Fr fr. Gmc]

helms·man /helmz'mən/ *n.* (*pl.* **·men**) person who steers a ship

help /help/ *v.* **1** provide with the means toward what is needed or sought **2** be of use or service to **3** contribute to remedying (a pain or difficulty) **4** prevent or remedy (*it can't be helped*) **5** (usu. with *neg.*) refrain from **6** serve with food —*n.* **7** helping or being helped **8** person or thing that helps **9** domestic assistant or assistance **10** remedy or escape **11** help oneself take without permission —**help'er** *n.* [OE]

help·ful /help'fəl/ *adj.* giving help; useful —**help'ful·ly** *adv.*; **help'ful·ness** *n.*

help'ing *n.* portion of food at a meal

help·less /help'ləs/ *adj.* **1** lacking help or protection; defenseless **2** unable to act without help —**help'less·ly** *adv.*; **help'less·ness** *n.*

help'mate' *n.* (also **help'meet'**) helpful companion or partner

Hel·sin·ki /hel'siNGkē/ *n.* capital of Finland. Pop. 496,300

hel·ter-skel·ter /hel'tər skel'tər/ *adv.* **1** in disorderly haste —*adj.* **2** disorderly [imit.]

hem[1] /hem/ *n.* **1** border of cloth where the edge is turned and sewn down —*v.* (**hemmed, hem·ming**) **2** turn and sew in the edge of (cloth, etc.) **3** hem in confine; restrict [OE]

hem[2] *interj.* **1** slight coughing sound to call attention or express hesitation —*n.* **2** utterance of this —*v.* (**hemmed, hem·ming**) **3** say *hem*; hesitate in speech **4** hem and haw hesitate; be evasive [imit.]

he'·man' *n.* (*pl.* **·men**) masterful or muscular man

he·ma·tol·o·gy /hē'mətäl'əjē/ *n.* the study of the blood —**he'ma·tol'o·gist** *n.*

hemi- *comb. form* half [Gk]

Hem·ing·way /hem'iNGwā'/, **Ernest** 1899–1961; US writer

hem·i·sphere /hem'əsfēr'/ *n.* **1** half a sphere **2** half of the earth, esp. as divided by the equator or by a line passing through the poles —**hem'i·spher'i·cal** /-fēr'ikəl, -sfer'-/, **hem'i·spher'ic** *adj.* [Gk, rel. to HEMI- + SPHERE]

hem'line' *n.* lower edge of a skirt, etc.

hem·lock /hem'läk'/ *n.* **1** poisonous plant with fernlike leaves and small white flowers **2** poison made from this [OE]

he·mo·glo·bin /hē'məglō'bin/ *n.* oxygen-carrying substance in red blood cells [fr. *glob-ulin*]

he·mo·phil·i·a /hē'məfil'ēə/ *n.* hereditary condition in which the blood does not clot normally, resulting in severe bleeding from even a slight injury [Gk *haima* blood + *philia* loving]

he·mo·phil·i·ac /hē'məfil'ē-ak'/ *n.* person with hemophilia

hem·or·rhage /hem'(ə)rij/ *n.* 1 profuse loss of blood from a ruptured blood vessel —*v.* (·rhaged, ·rhag·ing) 2 suffer a hemorrhage [Gk *haima* blood + *rhēgnynai* burst]

hem·or·rhoids /hem'əroidz'/ *n.* swollen, often painful or bleeding veins in the wall of the anus; piles [Gk *haima* blood + *rheein* flow]

hemp /hemp/ *n.* 1 (in full **In'di·an hemp'**) Asian herbaceous plant 2 its fiber used to make rope and stout fabrics 3 narcotic drug made from the hemp plant [OE]

hem·stitch /hem'stiCH/ *n.* 1 decorative stitch —*v.* 2 hem with this stitch

hen /hen/ *n.* female bird, esp. of a domestic fowl [OE]

hence /hens/ *adv.* 1 from this time 2 for this reason 3 *Archaic.* from here [OE]

hence'forth' *adv.* (also **hence'for'ward**) from this time onward

hench·man /henCH'mən/ *n.* (*pl.* ·men) trusted supporter, esp. a criminal [OE *hengst* horse + MAN]

Hen·drix /hen'driks/, **Jimi** 1942–70; US rock guitarist

hen·na /hen'ə/ *n.* 1 tropical shrub 2 reddish hair dye made from this —*v.* (·naed, ·na·ing) 3 dye with henna [Ar]

hen'peck' *v.* (of a wife) constantly nag (her husband)

Hen·ry /hen'rē/ 1 **"the Navigator"** 1394–1460; Portuguese prince; sponsor of geographic expeditions 2 **Henry VIII** 1491–1547; king of England (1509–47) 3 **Patrick** 1736–99; US patriot and orator

Hen·son /hen'sən/, **Jim** 1936–90; US puppeteer; creator of the Muppets

hep /hep/ *adj.* var. of HIP²

he·pat·ic /hipat'ik/ *adj.* of the liver [Gk *hē-par* liver]

hep·a·ti·tis /hep'ətīt'is/ *n.* inflammation of the liver [rel. to HEPATIC]

Hep·burn /hep'bərn/ 1 **Katharine** 1909– ; US actress 2 **Audrey** 1929–93; Belgian-born US actress

He·phaes·tus /hifes'təs/ *n. Gk. Myth.* god of fire and the forge

hepta- *comb. form* seven [Gk]

hep·ta·gon /hep'tagän'/ *n.* plane figure with seven sides and angles —**hep·tag'o·nal** /-tag'ənl/ *adj.* [Gk, rel. to HEPTA- + *gōnia* angle]

hep·tath·lon /heptaTH'län/ *n. Track & Field.* seven-event competition, esp. for women

her /hər/ *pron.* 1 objective case of SHE (*I like her*) 2 *Colloq.* she (*it's her all right; am older than her*) —*poss. pron.* 3 of or belonging to her or herself (*her house; her own business*) [OE dat. and gen. of SHE]

He·ra /hēr'ə, her'ə/ *n. Gk. Myth.* goddess, wife and sister of Zeus, equivalent to the Roman Juno

Her·a·cles /her'əklēz'/ *n.* HERCULES

Her·a·cli·tus /her'əklīt'əs/ c. 500 B.C.; Greek philosopher

He·rak·li·on /herak'lēən/ *n.* see IRÁKLION

her·ald /her'əld/ *n.* 1 official messenger bringing news 2 forerunner; harbinger —*v.* 3 proclaim the approach of; usher in —**he·ral·dic** /həral'dik/ *adj.* [Fr fr. Gmc]

her·ald·ry /her'əldrē/ *n.* (*pl.* ·ries) art or knowledge of coats of arms, genealogies, etc.

herb /(h)ərb/ *n.* 1 any nonwoody seed-bearing plant 2 plant with leaves, seeds, or flowers used for flavoring, food, medicine, scent, etc. —**her·ba·ceous** /hərbā'SHəs/, **herb'al** *adj.*; **herb'al·ist** *n.*; **herb'y** *adj.* (·i·er, ·i·est) [L *herba*]

her·bi·cide /(h)ər'bəsīd'/ *n.* poison used to destroy unwanted vegetation

her·bi·vore /(h)ər'bəvôr'/ *n.* animal that feeds on plants —**her·biv·o·rous** /(h)ər'biv'ərəs/ *adj.* [L *herba* plant + *vorare* devour]

Her·cu·le·an /hər'kyəlē'ən/ *adj.* having or requiring great strength or effort [for HERCULES]

Her·cu·les /hər'kyəlēz'/ (also **Her'a·cles'**) *n. Gk. & Rom. Myth.* legendary hero of extraordinary strength

herd /hərd/ *n.* 1 a number of animals, esp. cattle, feeding, traveling, or kept together 2 (prec. by the) *Derog.* common crowd; rabble —*v.* 3 (cause to) go in a herd 4 look after (sheep, cattle, etc.) [OE]

herds·man /hərdz'mən/ *n.* (*pl.* ·men) man who owns or tends a herd

here /hēr/ *adv.* 1 in or at or to this place or position 2 indicating a person's presence or a thing offered (*my son here; here is your coat*) 3 at this point —*n.* 4 this place 5 neither here nor there of no importance [OE]

here'a·bouts' *adv.* (also **here'a·bout'**) near this place

here·af'ter *adv.* 1 from now on; in the future —*n.* 2 the future 3 life after death

here' and now' *adv.* at this very moment; immediately

here' and there' *adv.* in various places

here'by' *adv.* by this means; as a result of this

he·red·i·tar·y /həred'əter'ē/ *adj.* 1 (of a disease, instinct, etc.) able to be passed down genetically 2a descending by inheritance b holding a position by inheritance [L, rel. to HEIR]

he·red·i·ty /həred'ətē/ *n.* 1a passing on of physical or mental characteristics genetically b these characteristics 2 genetic constitution

here·in /hērin'/ *adv.* in this matter, book, etc.

her·e·sy /her'əsē/ *n.* (*pl.* ·sies) 1 esp. *RC Ch.* religious belief or practice contrary to orthodox doctrine 2 nonconforming opinion [Gk *hairesis* choice]

her·e·tic /her'ətik'/ *n.* 1 person believing in or practicing religious heresy 2 holder of an unorthodox opinion —**he·ret·i·cal** /həret'ikəl/ *adj.*

here'to·fore' *adv.* before this time

here'u·pon' *adv.* after this; in consequence of this

here·with' *adv.* with this (esp. of an enclosure in a letter, etc.)

her·i·tage /her'itij/ *n.* 1 what is or may be inherited 2 inherited circumstances, benefits, etc. **3** historic buildings, traditions, etc., deemed valuable

her·maph·ro·dite /hərmaf'rədīt/ *n.* **1** person, animal, or plant having both male and female reproductive organs —*adj.* **2** combining aspects of both sexes —**her·maph·ro·dit'ic** /-maf'rədit'ik/ *adj.* [for *Hermaphroditus*, son of *Hermes* and *Aphrodite* who became joined in one body to a nymph]

Her·mes /hər'mēz/ *n. Gk. Myth.* divine messenger of the gods, equivalent to the Roman Mercury

her·met·ic /hərmet'ik/ *adj.* with an airtight closure —**her·met'i·cal·ly** *adv.* [for HERMES, regarded as the founder of alchemy]

her·mit /hər'mit/ *n.* person (esp. an early Christian) living in solitude and austerity —**her·mit'ic** *adj.* [Gk *erēmos* solitary]

her·mit·age /hər'mitij/ *n.* **1** hermit's dwelling **2** secluded dwelling

her'mit crab' *n.* crab that lives in a cast-off mollusk shell

Her·mo·si·llo /er'mōsē'yō/ *n.* capital of the Mexican state of Sonora. Pop. 449,400

her·ni·a /hər'nēə/ *n.* protrusion of part of an organ through the wall of the body cavity containing it [L]

he·ro /hēr'ō/ *n.* (*pl.* **-roes**) **1** person noted or admired for nobility, courage, outstanding achievements, etc. **2** chief male character in a play, story, etc. [Gk *hērōs*]

Her·od /her'əd/ dynasty ruling in Palestine at the time of Jesus Christ, including: **1** Herod ("the Great") c. 74–4 B.C.; king of Judea (37–4 B.C.) **2** Herod Antipas 22 B.C.–A.D. c. 40; ruler of Galilee (4 B.C.–A.D. 40); son of Herod the Great **3** Herod Agrippa I 10 B.C.–A.D. 44; king of Judea (41–44)

He·rod·o·tus /həräd'ətəs/ fl. 5th cent. B.C.; Greek historian; called "the Father of History"

he·ro·ic /hērō'ik/ *adj.* **1** of, fit for, or like a hero; very brave —*n.* **2** (*pl.*) a high-flown language or sentiments **b** unduly bold behavior —**he·ro'i·cal·ly** /-lē/ *adv.*

her·o·in /her'ō·in/ *n.* addictive drug derived from morphine, often used as a narcotic [Ger, rel. to HERO, fr. the effect on the user's self-esteem]

her·o·ine /her'ō·in/ *n.* **1** woman noted or admired for nobility, courage, outstanding achievements, etc. **2** chief female character in a play, story, etc. [Gk, rel. to HERO]

her'o·ism' *n.* heroic conduct or qualities [Fr *héroïsme*, rel. to HERO]

HERON

her·on /her'ən/ *n.* long-legged wading bird with a long S-shaped neck [Fr fr. Gmc]

her·pes /hər'pēz/ *n.* virus disease causing skin blisters [Gk *herpein* creep]

her'pes zos'ter /zos'tər/ *n.* (also **shin'gles**) painful viral inflammation of the nerve ganglia

Herr /her/ *n.* (*pl.* **Herr·en** /her'ən/) German form of address equivalent to *Mister* [Ger]

Her·rick /her'ik/, **Robert** 1591–1674; English poet

her·ring /her'iNG/ *n.* (*pl.* same or **·rings**) N Atlantic fish used as food [OE]

HERRINGBONE

her'ring·bone' *n.* stitch or weave having a zigzag pattern

hers /hərz/ *poss. pron.* **1** the one or ones belonging to or associated with her (*it is hers; hers are over there*) **2** of hers or belonging to her (*friend of hers*)

her·self /hərself'/ *pron.* **1a** *emphat. form of* SHE or HER (*she herself will do it*) **b** *refl. form of* HER (*she has hurt herself*) **2** in her normal state of body or mind (*does not feel herself today*) [OE, rel. to HER + SELF]

hertz /hərts/ *n.* (*pl.* same) international unit of frequency, equal to one cycle per second [for H.R. *Hertz*, German physicist]

Her·zl /hert'səl/, **Theodor** 1860–1904; Austrian founder of the Zionist movement

he's /hēz/ *v. contr.* **1** he is **2** he has

He·si·od /hē'sēəd, hes'ē-/ c. 700 B.C.; Greek poet

hes·i·tant /hez'ətənt/ *adj.* hesitating; irresolute —**hes'i·tance, hes'i·tan·cy** *n.*; **hes'i·tant·ly** *adv.*

hes·i·tate /hez'ətāt'/ *v.* (**·tat·ed, ·tat·ing**) **1** show or feel indecision or uncertainty; pause in doubt **2** be reluctant (*hesitate to say*) —**hes'i·ta'tion** *n.* [L *haesitare* fr. *haerere* stick]

Hess /hes/, **(Walter) Rudolf** 1894–1987; German Nazi official

Hes·se /hes'ə/, **Hermann** 1877–1962; German-born Swiss novelist and poet

hetero- *comb. form* other; different [Gk *heteros* other]

het·er·o·dox /het'ərədäks'/ *adj.* not orthodox —**het'er·o·dox'y** *n.* (*pl.* **·ies**) [fr. HETERO- + Gk *doxa* opinion fr. *dokein* think]

het·er·o·ge·ne·ous /het'ərəjē'nēəs/ *adj.* **1** diverse in character; differing **2** varied in content —**het'er·o·ge·ne'i·ty** /-rōjənē'ətē/ *n.* [L fr. Gk *genos* kind]

het·er·o·sex·u·al /het'ərōsek'sHŌŌəl/ *adj.* **1** feeling or involving sexual attraction to the opposite sex —*n.* **2** heterosexual person —**het'er·o·sex·u·al'i·ty** /-al'itē/ *n.*

heu·ris·tic /hyŏŏris'tik/ *adj.* **1** allowing or assisting to discover **2** proceeding to a solution by trial and error [Gk *heuriskein* find]

hew /hyŌŌ/ *v.* (**hewed, hewn** /hyŌŌn/ or **hewed, hew·ing**) **1** chop or cut with an ax, sword, etc. **2** cut into shape [OE]

hex /heks/ *v.* **1** cause (a person) bad luck —*n.* **2** evil magic spell [Ger]

hexa- *comb. form* six [Gk]

hex·a·dec·i·mal /ˈhekˈsədesˈəməl/ *adj.* (esp. *Comp.*) of a system of numerical notation that has 16 (the figures 0 to 9 and the letters A to F) rather than 10 as a base

hex·a·gon /ˈhekˈsəgän/ *n.* plane figure with six sides and six angles —**hex·ag·o·nal** /heksagˈən-l/ *adj.* [Gk, rel. to HEXA- + *gōnia* angle]

hex·a·gram /ˈhekˈsəgram/ *n.* figure formed by two intersecting equilateral triangles

hex·am·e·ter /heksamˈətər/ *n.* line of verse with six metrical feet

hey /hā/ *interj.* call for attention or expressing joy, surprise, inquiry, etc. [imit.]

hey·day /ˈhāˈdā/ *n.* time of greatest success or prosperity [LGer]

Hey·er·dahl /ˈhīˈərdäl/, **Thor** 1914– ; Norwegian explorer and ethnologist

Hf *symb.* hafnium

HF *abbr.* high frequency

Hg *symb.* mercury

hgt. *abbr.* height

hgwy. *abbr.* highway

HHS *abbr.* (Department of) Health and Human Services

hi /hī/ *interj.* call for attention or as a greeting

HI postal abbr. for Hawaii

Hi·a·le·ah /hīˈalēˈə/ *n.* city in Fla. Pop. 188,004

hi·a·tus /hīˈātəs/ *n.* (*pl.* **·tus·es**) break or gap in a series or sequence [L *hiare* gape]

hi·ba·chi /hēbäˈCHē, hibä′-/ *n.* portable charcoal-burning grill [Japn *hi* fire + *bachi* bowl]

hi·ber·nate /ˈhīˈbärnāt′/ *v.* (**·nat·ed, ·nat·ing**) (of an animal) spend the winter in a dormant state —**hi′ber·na′tion** *n.* [L *hibernus* wintry]

Hi·ber·ni·an /hībärˈnēən/ *adj.* 1 of Ireland —*n.* 2 native of Ireland [L *Hibernia* Ireland]

hi·bis·cus /hibisˈkəs, hī-/ *n.* (*pl.* **·cus·es**) cultivated shrub with large bright-colored flowers [Gk *hibiskos* marsh mallow]

hic·cup /hikˈəp, -əp/ *n.* (also **hic·cough** /hikˈəf, -əp/) *n.* 1 involuntary spasm of the diaphragm causing an abrupt sound —*v.* (**·cupped** or **·cupped, ·cup·ing** or **·cup·ping**) 2 make a hiccup [imit.]

hick /hik/ *n.* country bumpkin [familiar form of *Richard*]

Hick·ok /hikˈäk′/, **"Wild Bill"** (James Butler) 1837–76; US frontiersman

hick·o·ry /hikˈ(ə)rē/ *n.* (*pl.* **·ries**) 1 N American tree yielding wood and nutlike edible fruits 2 the tough heavy wood of this [earlier *pohickery*, fr. Algonquian]

hid /hid/ *v. past of* HIDE¹

Hi·dal·go /hidalˈgō/ *n.* central E state of Mexico. Capital: Pachuca. Pop. 1,888,400

hid·den /hidˈən/ *v.* 1 *past part.* of HIDE¹ —*adj.* 2 concealed; secret

hid′den a·gen′da *n.* secret motivation; ulterior motive

hide¹ /hīd/ *v.* (**hid, hid·den** or **hid, hid·ing**) 1 put or keep out of sight 2 conceal oneself 3 keep secret 4 conceal —**hid′er** *n.* [OE]

hide² *n.* animal's skin, esp. when tanned or dressed [OE]

hide′-and-seek′ *n.* game in which players hide and another searches for them

hide′a·way′ *n.* hiding place or place of retreat

hide′bound′ *adj.* 1 narrow-minded 2 constricted by tradition

hid·e·ous /hidˈēəs/ *adj.* very ugly; revolting —**hid′e·ous·ly** *adv.*; **hid′e·ous·ness** *n.* [AngFr *hidous*]

hide′out′ *n.* hiding place

hi·er·ar·chy /hīˈ(ə)rärˈkē/ *n.* (*pl.* **·chies**) system of grades of status or authority ranked one above the other —**hi′er·ar′chi·cal** /-kikəl/ *adj.* [Gk *hieros* sacred + *archos* ruler]

hi·er·o·glyph·ic /hīˈ(ə)rəglifˈik/ *adj.* 1 depicted with pictures representing words or sounds, as used in ancient Egyptian —*n.* 2 (*pl.*) hieroglyphic writing

hi-fi /hīˈfī′/ *adj.* 1 of high fidelity —*n.* (*pl.* **·fis**) 2 set of high-fidelity equipment [abbr.]

Hi·ga·shi·o·sa·ka /higäˈSHE-ōsäkˈə/ *n.* city in Japan, on Honshu. Pop. 517,200

high /hī/ *adj.* 1a of great vertical extent b of a specified height (*waist-high*) 2 far above ground or sea level (*high altitude*) 3 above the normal level 4a of exalted quality b lavish (*high living*) 5 of exalted rank 6 great; intense; extreme (*high praise; high temperature*) 7 *Colloq.* intoxicated 8 shrill in pitch 9 (of a period, age, time, etc.) at its peak (*high noon; high summer* —*n.* 10 high; or the highest, level or figure 11 area of high atmospheric pressure 12 *Slang.* euphoric or intoxicated state —*adv.* 13 far up; aloft 14 in or to a high degree 15 at a high price 16 (of a sound) at or to a high pitch 17 **high and low** everywhere 18 **high on** enthusiastic about [OE]

high′ball′ *n.* alcoholic drink mixed with water or a soft beverage, served with ice in a tall glass

high′ beam′ *n.* full illumination of a headlight on a vehicle

high′brow′ *Colloq. adj.* 1 intellectual; cultural —*n.* 2 intellectual or cultured person

high′ chair′ *n.* infant's chair with long legs and a tray for meals

high′-class′ *adj.* of high quality

high′-def·i·ni′tion tel′e·vi·sion (also **HDTV**) *n.* television transmission system delivering very sharp screen images

high′-end′ *adj. Colloq.* 1 most technically advanced; state of the art 2 pertaining to or attracting high-income consumers

high·fa·lu·tin /hīˈfəlootˈn/ *adj.* (also **high′fa·lu′ting**) *Colloq.* pompous; haughty; pretentious

high′ fi·del′i·ty *n.* high-quality sound reproduction with little distortion

high′ five′ *n.* gesture in which two people slap each other's raised palm, esp. out of elation

high′-flown′ *adj.* (of language, etc.) extravagant; bombastic

high′ fre′quen·cy *n.* frequency, esp. in radio, of 3 to 30 megahertz

high′-hand′ed *adj.* overbearing —**high′-hand′ed·ly** *adv.*; **high′-hand′ed·ness** *n.*

high′ jinks′ *n. pl.* boisterous fun

high·land /hīˈlənd/ *n.* 1 (usu. *pl.*) area of high land 2 (**the Highlands**) mountainous part of Scotland —*adj.* 3 of or in a highland or the Highlands —**high′land·er, High′land·er** *n.* [OE: promontory, rel. to HIGH]

high'-lev'el *adj.* (of negotiations, etc.) conducted by high-ranking people

high'light' *n.* 1 light-colored, bright, or reflective area 2 moment or detail of vivid interest; outstanding feature —*v.* 3 bring into prominence; draw attention to 4 mark with a highlighter pen

high'ly *adv.* 1 in or to a high degree 2 favorably

high'-mind'ed *adj.* having high moral principles —**high'-mind'ed·ly** *adv.*; **high'-mind'ed·ness** *n.*

high'-oc'cu·pan·cy ve'hi·cle (also **HOV**) *n.* commuter vehicle carrying several (or many) passengers

high'-pitched' *adj.* 1 (of a sound) high in frequency 2 (of a roof) steep

high'-pow'ered *adj.* 1 having great power or energy 2 important; influential

high' pres'sure *n.* 1 high degree of energy or exertion 2 atmospheric condition with the pressure above average —*adj.* 3 (**high'-pres'sure**) using forceful or insistent techniques

high' priest' *n.* (*fem.* **high' priest'ess**) 1 chief priest 2 *Colloq.* influential leader

high'-rise' *adj.* 1 (of a building) having many stories —*n.* 2 such a building

high' school' *n.* secondary school, including grades 9 or 10 through 12

high' seas' *n.* open seas not under any country's jurisdiction

high'-spir'it·ed *adj.* vivacious; cheerful

high'-strung' *adj.* very sensitive or nervous; edgy

high'-tech' *adj.* 1 pertaining to high technology 2 of a style incorporating elements of industrial architecture and interiors

high' tech·nol'o·gy *n.* advanced technological development, esp. in electronics

high'-ten'sion *adj.* carrying a high voltage

high' tide' *n.* time or level of the tide at its peak

high'way' *n.* 1a public road b main route 2 direct course of action (*the highway to success*)

high·way·man / hī'wāmən/ *n.* (*pl.* **-men**) *Hist.* robber of travelers

high' wire' *n.* high tightrope

hi·jack / hī'jak'/ *v.* 1 seize control of (a vehicle, etc.), esp. to force it to a different destination 2 seize (goods) in transit —*n.* 3 a hijacking —**hi'jack'er** *n.*

hike / hīk/ *n.* 1 long walk, esp. in the country 2 rise in prices, etc. —*v.* (**hiked, hik·ing**) 3 go for a hike 4 walk laboriously 5 pull up (clothing, etc.) 6 raise (prices, etc.) —**hik'er** *n.*

hi·lar·i·ous / hilar'ēəs, -ler'-/ *adj.* 1 exceedingly funny 2 boisterously merry —**hi·lar'i·ous·ly** *adv.*; **hi·lar'i·ty** /-ətē, -ler'-/ *n.* [Gk *hilaros* cheerful]

hill / hil/ *n.* 1 naturally raised area of land, lower than a mountain 2 (often in *comb.*) heap; mound (*anthill*) 3 sloping stretch of road 4 **over the hill** past the prime of life —**hill'y** *adj.* (**·i·er, ·i·est**); **hill'i·ness** *n.* [OE]

Hil·la·ry / hil'ərē/, (Sir) Edmund 1919– ; New Zealand mountaineer; scaled Mt. Everest (1953)

hill·bil·ly / hil'bil'ē/ *n.* often *Derog.* person from a remote mountain or rural area, esp. of the southern US

hill'side' *n.* sloping side of a hill

hill'top' *n.* top of a hill

hilt / hilt/ *n.* 1 handle of a sword, dagger, etc. 2 **up to the hilt** completely [OE]

Hil·ton / hilt'n/, **James** 1900–54; English novelist

Hil·wan / hilwän'/ *n.* city in Egypt. Pop. 352,300

him / him/ *pron.* 1 *objective case* of HE (*I saw him*) 2 *Colloq.* he (*it's him again; taller than him*) [OE, dat. of HE]

Him·a·la·yas / him'əlā'əz, himäl'(ə)yəz/ *n.* mountain range extending 1,500 mi. between India and Tibet

Himm·ler / him'lər/, **Heinrich** 1900–45; German leader of the Nazi secret police

him·self / himself'/ *pron.* 1a *emphat. form* of HE or HIM (*he himself will do it*) b *refl. form* of HIM (*he has hurt himself*) 2 in his normal state of body or mind (*does not feel himself today*) [OE, rel. to HIM + SELF]

hind / hīnd/ *adj.* at the back (*hind leg*) [OE *hindan* fr. behind]

Hin·de·mith / hin'dəmit/, **Paul** 1895–1963; German composer

Hin·den·burg / hin'dənbərg/, **Paul von** 1847–1934; German field marshall; president of the Weimar Republic (1925–34)

hin·der / hin'dər/ *v.* impede; delay [OE]

Hin·di / hin'dē/ *n.* 1 group of spoken dialects of N India 2 literary form of Hindustani, an official language of India

hind·most / hīn(d)'mōst'/ *adj.* furthest behind

hind·quar·ters / hīn(d)'kwô(r)t'ərz/ *n. pl.* hind legs and rump of a quadruped

hin·drance / hin'drəns/ *n.* 1 hindering; being hindered 2 thing that hinders

hind·sight / hīn(d)'sīt'/ *n.* wisdom after the event

Hin·du / hin'dōō/ *n.* (*pl.* **-dus**) 1 follower of Hinduism —*adj.* 2 of Hindus or Hinduism [Urdu *Hind* India]

Hin·du·ism / hin'dōōizm'/ *n.* main religious and social system of India

Hin·du Kush' / kōōsH'/ *n.* mountain range mostly in NE Afghanistan, extending W from the Himalayas

Hin·du·sta·ni / hin'dōō'stän'ē, -stan'ē/ *n.* language based on Hindi, a lingua franca in much of India [fr. HINDU + *stän* country]

HINGE 1

hinge / hinj/ *n.* 1 movable joint on which a door, lid, etc., turns or swings —*v.* (**hinged, hing·ing**) 2 depend (on) 3 attach or be attached by a hinge [rel. to HANG]

hint / hint/ *n.* 1 slight or indirect indication or suggestion 2 bit of helpful information 3 trace; suggestion —*v.* 4 suggest slightly or indirectly [obs. *hent* grasp]

hin·ter·land /hint'ərland/ *n.* 1 district beyond a coast or river's banks 2 remote region [Ger]

hip[1] /hip/ *n.* projection of the pelvis and the upper part of the thighbone [OE]

hip[2] *adj.* (also **hep**) (**hip·per, hip·pest**) *Slang.* trendy; stylish

hip'bone' *n.* bone forming the hip

hip'hop' *n.* US urban subculture noted for rap music, graffiti art, etc. [fr. HIP[2]]

hip·pie /hip'ē/ *n.* (also **hip'py**) (*pl.* **·pies**) (esp. in the 1960s) person rejecting social convention, esp. in wearing the hair long, advocating sexual freedom, drug-taking, etc. [fr. HIP[2]]

hip·po /hip'ō/ *n.* (*pl.* **·pos**) *Colloq.* hippopotamus

Hip·poc·ra·tes /hipäk'rətēz/ *c.* 460–*c.* 377 B.C.; Greek physician; called "Father of Medicine"

Hip'po·crat'ic oath' /hip'əkrat'ik/ *n.* statement of ethics of the medical profession [for HIPPOCRATES]

hip·po·pot·a·mus /hip'əpät'əməs/ *n.* (*pl.* **·mus·es** or **·mi** /-mī'/) African mammal with a heavy body, short legs, and thick skin, living by rivers, lakes, etc. [Gk *hippos* horse + *potamos* river]

hip·py /hip'ē/ *n.* var. of HIPPIE

hire /hīr/ *v.* (**hired, hir·ing**) 1 pay for the temporary use of (a thing) 2 take into employment —*n.* 3 hiring or being hired 4 payment for this —**hir'a·ble, hire'a·ble** *adj.* [OE]

hire·ling /hīr'liNG/ *n.* person who works (only) for money

Hi·ro·hi·to /hē'rōhē'tō/ (also called Sho'wa) 1901–89; emperor of Japan (1926–89)

Hi·ro·shi·ma /hē'rəSHē'mə, hērō'SHimə/ *n.* seaport in Japan on Honshu; target of first atomic bomb, 1945. Pop. 1,090,000

hir·sute /hər'sōōt', hēr'-; hər'sōōt'/ *adj.* hairy [L]

his /hiz/ *poss. pron.* 1 of or belonging to him or himself (*his house; his own business*) 2 the one or ones belonging to or associated with him (*it is his; his are over there*) 3 of his of or belonging to him (*friend of his*) [OE, gen. of HE]

His·pan·ic /hispan'ik/ *adj.* 1 pertaining to Spain or to Spain and Portugal 2 pertaining to Spanish-speaking countries and regions and their culture —*n.* 3 person of Spanish descent living in the US [L *Hispania* Spain]

His·pan·io·la /his'pənyō'lə/ *n.* island in the Caribbean Sea, comprising the republic of Haiti and the Dominican Republic

hiss /his/ *v.* 1 make a sharp prolonged *s*-sound 2 express disapproval of by hisses —*n.* 3 sharp *s*-sound [imit.]

hist. *abbr.* 1 historian 2 historical 3 history

his·ta·mine /his'təmēn'/ *n.* chemical compound released by body tissues, etc., as in allergic reactions [fr. HISTOLOGY + AMINE]

his·tol·o·gy /histäl'əjē/ *n.* the study of tissue structure [Gk *histos* web + -LOGY]

his·to·ri·an /histôr'ēən, -tär'-/ *n.* writer of or one learned in history

his·tor·ic /histôr'ik, -tär'-/ *adj.* famous or important in history, or potentially so

● Usage: In precise use, *historic* and *historical* have different meanings: the former means 'important; notable'; the latter, 'relating to history.' An event can be either, depending on whether it is viewed as part of history or as extremely important; but things like summit meetings, battles, etc., are typically described as *historic.*

his·tor·i·cal /histôr'ikəl, -tär'-/ *adj.* 1 of or concerning history 2 (of the study of a subject) showing its development 3 factual, not fictional or legendary 4 belonging to the past, not the present —**his·tor'i·cal·ly** *adv.*

his·to·ric·i·ty /his'təris'itē/ *n.* historical truth or authenticity

his·to·ri·og·ra·phy /histôr'ē·äg'rəfē/ *n.* the writing and researching of history —**his·to'ri·og'ra·pher** *n.*

his·to·ry /his't(ə)rē/ *n.* (*pl.* **·ries**) 1 continuous record of (esp. public) events 2a past events b study and interpretation of past events 3 eventful past (*this house has a history*) 4 past record 5 **make history** do something memorable [Gk *historia* inquiry]

his·tri·on·ic /his'trē·än'ik/ *adj.* 1 theatrical; dramatic —*n.* 2 (*pl.*) overwrought or self-dramatizing behavior [L *histrio* actor]

hit /hit/ *v.* (**hit, hit·ting**) 1a strike with a blow or projectile b (of a moving body) strike with force c strike (a target, etc.) 2 cause to suffer; affect adversely 3 knock (*hit his head*) 4 achieve (*can't hit the high notes*) 5a *Colloq.* encounter (*hit a snag*) b arrive at (*hit town*) c indulge heavily in, esp. liquor (*hit the bottle*) 6 occur forcefully to 7a propel (a ball, etc.) with a bat, etc. b *Baseball.* score or reach base in this way (*hit a home run*) —*n.* 8a blow; stroke b collision 9 shot, etc., that hits its target 10 *Baseball.* BASE HIT 11 *Colloq.* popular success 12 **hit it off** *Colloq.* get along well (with a person) 13 **hit the nail on the head** state the truth exactly 14 **hit the road** *Slang.* depart 15 **hit the spot** be satisfying [OE fr. ON]

hit'-and-run' *adj.* 1 (of a driver, raider, etc.) causing damage or injury and leaving the scene immediately 2 perpetrated by such a person or people

hitch /hiCH/ *v.* 1 fasten or be fastened with a loop, hook, etc. 2 move (a thing) slightly or with a jerk 3 *Colloq.* a HITCHHIKE b obtain (a ride) by hitchhiking —*n.* 4 temporary obstacle or snag 5 abrupt pull or push 6 noose or knot of various kinds 7 *Colloq.* free ride in a vehicle 8 *Colloq.* period of military service 9 **get hitched** *Colloq.* marry

Hitch·cock /hiCH'käk/, (**Sir**) **Alfred** 1899–1980; English film director

hitch'hike' *v.* (**·hiked, ·hik·ing**) travel by seeking free rides from passing vehicles —**hitch'hik'er** *n.*

hith·er /hiTH'ər/ *adv. Formal.* to or toward this place [OE]

hith·er·to /hiTH'ərtōō'/ *adv.* until this time

Hit·ler /hit'lər/, **Adolf** (born **Adolf Schicklgruber**) 1889–1945; Austrian-born Nazi leader of Germany (1933–45)

hit' man' *n. Slang.* hired killer

hit'-or-miss' *adj.* liable to error; random

Hit·tite /hit'īt/ *n.* 1 member or language of

an ancient people of Asia Minor and Syria —*adj.* **2** of the Hittites [Heb]

HIV *abbr.* human immunodeficiency virus, any of several viruses causing AIDS

hive /hīv/ *n.* beehive [OE]

hives /hīvz/ *n. pl.* allergic skin eruption of itchy, red patches

HMO *abbr.* health maintenance organization

Ho *symb.* holmium

hoard /hôrd/ *n.* **1** stock or store (esp. of money or food) —*v.* **2** amass and store —**hoard′er** *n.* [OE]

hoarse /hôrs/ *adj.* **1** (of the voice) rough and deep; husky; croaking **2** having such a voice —**hoarse′ly** *adv.*; **hoarse′ness** *n.* [ON]

hoar·y /hôr′ē/ *adj.* (**·i·er**, **·i·est**) **1a** (of hair) gray or white with age **b** having such hair; aged **2** old and trite (*hoary joke*) [OE]

hoax /hōks/ *n.* **1** humorous or malicious deception —*v.* **2** deceive (a person) with a hoax [perh. fr. HOCUS-POCUS]

Hobbes /häbz/, **Thomas** 1588–1679; English philosopher

hob·ble /häb′əl/ *v.* (**·bled**, **·bling**) **1** walk lamely; limp **2** restrain by tying the legs together —*n.* **3** uneven or infirm gait **4** rope, etc., for hobbling a horse, etc. [prob. LGer]

hob·by /häb′ē/ *n.* (*pl.* **·bies**) leisure-time activity pursued for pleasure [fr. *Robin*, used as a horse's name]

hob′by·horse′ *n.* **1** child's toy consisting of a stick with a horse's head or a rocking horse **2** favorite subject or idea

hob·gob·lin /häb′gäb′lin/ *n.* mischievous imp; bogy [fr. HOBBY + GOBLIN]

hob·nail /häb′nāl′/ *n.* heavy-headed nail for soles of workshoes, etc. [fr. *hob* peg + NAIL]

hob·nob /häb′näb′/ *v.* (**·nobbed**, **·nobbing**) mix socially or informally [*hab nab* have or not have]

ho·bo /hō′bō/ *n.* (*pl.* **·boes** or **·bos**) tramp; vagrant

Ho Chi Minh /hō′ CHē′ min′/ (born Nguyen That Thanh) 1890–1969; Vietnamese leader; president of N Vietnam (1954–69)

Ho′ Chi′ Minh′ Cit′y *n.* (formerly Saigon) city in Vietnam. Pop. 3,169,100

hock¹ /häk/ *n.* joint of a quadruped's hind leg between the knee and the fetlock [OE]

hock² *v. Colloq.* **1** pawn; pledge **2 in hock** in pawn; in debt [Du]

hock·ey /häk′ē/ *n.* team sport played on ice skates or on a field, with angled sticks and a puck or ball

ho·cus-po·cus /hō′kəs pō′kəs/ *n.* deception; trickery [L sham]

hod /häd/ *n.* **1** V-shaped trough on a pole used for carrying bricks, etc. **2** portable receptacle for coal [Fr *hotte* pannier]

hodge·podge /häj′päj′/ *n.* jumble; mixture [Fr *hochepot* shake pot]

Hodg·kin's dis·ease′ /häj′kinz/ *n.* malignant disease usu. characterized by enlargement of the lymph nodes [for T. *Hodgkin*, English physician]

hoe /hō/ *n.* **1** long-handled tool with a blade, used for weeding, etc. —*v.* (**hoed**, **hoe·ing**) **2** weed (crops); loosen (earth) with a hoe [Fr fr. Gmc]

hog /hôg, häg/ *n.* **1** adult swine, esp. domesticated and raised for market **2** greedy person —*v.* (**hogged**, **hog·ging**) **3** take greedily or

selfishly **4** go (the) whole hog do something completely or thoroughly —**hog′gish** *adj.* [OE]

Ho·garth /hō′gärTH/, **William** 1697–1764; English painter and engraver

hogs·head /hôgz′hed′, hägz′-/ *n.* **1** large cask holding from 63 to 140 gallons **2** measure of capacity (63 gallons) [fr. HOG + HEAD; reason unknown]

hog′wash′ *n.* nonsense; rubbish

hoi pol·loi /hoi′ pəloi′/ *n.* the masses; the common people [Gk: the many]

hoist /hoist/ *v.* **1** raise or haul up, esp. with ropes, pulleys, etc. —*n.* **2** act of hoisting; lift **3** apparatus for hoisting [earlier *hoise*, prob. fr. LGer]

hoi·ty-toi·ty /hoi′tē toi′tē/ *adj.* haughty [obs. *hoit* romp]

Hok·kai·do /häkī′dō/ *n.* (formerly Yezo) large island in N Japan

ho·kum /hō′kəm/ *n.* **1** sentiment, low comedy, or false information used for effect, as in a play, speech, etc. **2** nonsense; rubbish

Hol·bein /hōl′bīn′, hôl′-/ German artists: **1** **Hans ("the Elder")** c. 1465–1524; his son: **2** **Hans ("the Younger")** c. 1497–1543; worked in England

hold¹ /hōld/ *v.* (**held**, **hold·ing**) **1a** keep fast; grasp (esp. in the hands or arms) **b** keep or sustain in a particular position, state, or condition **c** grip so as to control **2** have the capacity for; contain (*holds two pints*) **3** possess; gain; have, esp.: **a** be the owner or tenant of (land, property, etc.) **b** gain or have gained (a qualification, record, etc.) **c** have the position of (a job, office, etc.) **d** occupy defensively **4** remain intact (*roof held under the storm*) **5** celebrate or conduct (a meeting, conversation, etc.) **6a** engross to dominate (*held the stage*) **7** keep (a person, etc.) to (a promise, etc.) **8** (of weather) continue as is **9** think; believe; assert **10** regard with a specified feeling (*held him in contempt*) **11** restrain (*hold your fire*) **12** be able to drink (alcohol) without effect **13** *Law.* rule; decide —*n.* **14** grasp; grip **15** influence or power over **16** thing to hold by **17 hold** (a thing) **against** (a person) regard as discreditable to **18 hold forth** speak at length or tediously **19 hold it** (or on) stop action or movement **20 hold the line** not hang up (the telephone) **21 hold off** delay **22 hold out: a** offer (an inducement, etc.) **b** maintain resistance **c** persist or last **23 hold out on** *Colloq.* withhold from (a person) **24 hold one's own** maintain one's position; not be beaten **25 hold up: a** support; sustain **b** exhibit; display **c** hinder; obstruct **d** (stop and) rob by force **26 hold water** (of reasoning) be sound or valid **27 no holds barred** no restrictions of method **28 take hold** (of a custom or habit) become established —**hold′er** *n.* [OE]

hold² *n.* cargo area in a ship or aircraft [OE, rel. to HOLLOW]

hold′ing *n.* **1** tenure of land **2** stocks, property, etc., held

hold′ing com′pa·ny *n.* company created to hold and control the shares of other companies

hold'up' *n.* **1** stoppage or delay **2** robbery by force

hole /hōl/ *n.* **1a** empty space in a solid body **b** opening in or through something **2** animal's burrow **3** small or dingy place **4** difficult situation **5** *Golf.* **a** receptacle in the ground into which the ball is to be hit **b** one complete playing area from tee to green **6 hole up** hide; retire —**hol'ey** *adj.* [OE]

-holic *comb. form* person with a powerful obsession or craving, as *chocoholic*, one who craves chocolate [clip fr. *alcoholic*]

hol·i·day /häl'ədā'/ *n.* **1** day of festivity or recreation when no work is done, esp. a national or religious festival **2** (often *pl.*) *Brit.* vacation —*adj.* **3** pertaining to a holiday [OE, rel. to HOLY + DAY]

ho·li·er-than-thou /hō'lēər ᴛʜən ᴛʜou'/ *adj.* self-righteous

ho·li·ness /hō'lēnis/ *n.* **1** being holy or sacred **2** (*cap.*) title of address for the pope [OE, rel. to HOLY]

Hol·ins·hed /häl'insʜed/, **Raphael** died c. 1580; English chronicler

ho·lism /hō'lizəm/ *n.* (also **who'lism'**) **1** *Philos.* theory that certain wholes are greater than the sum of their parts **2** *Med.* treating of the whole person rather than symptoms of a disease, usu. emphasizing nutrition —**ho·lis'tic** /-lis'tik/ *adj.* [Gk *holos* whole]

Hol·land /häl'ənd/ *n.* see NETHERLANDS, THE

hol'lan·daise sauce' /häl'əndāz'/ *n.* creamy sauce of butter, egg yolks, vinegar, etc. [Fr]

hol·ler /häl'ər/ *v. & n. Colloq.* shout [Fr *holà* hello!]

hol·low /häl'ō/ *adj.* **1a** having a cavity **b** sunken **2** (of a sound) echoing **3** empty; hungry **4** meaningless **5** insincere —*n.* **6** hollow place; hole **7** valley; basin —*v.* **8** make hollow; excavate —**hol'low·ly** *adv.*; **hol'low·ness** *n.* [OE]

hol·ly /häl'ē/ *n.* (*pl.* **-lies**) evergreen shrub with glossy leaves and red berries [OE]

hol·ly·hock /häl'ēhäk'/ *n.* tall plant with showy flowers [fr. HOLY + obs. *hock* mallow]

Hol·ly·wood /häl'ēwood/ *n.* **1** city in Fla. Pop. 121,697 **2** part of Los Angeles, Calif.; center of US motion-picture industry

Holmes /hō(l)mz/ **1** Oliver Wendell 1809–94; US writer and physician; his son: **2** Oliver Wendell 1841–1935; US jurist

hol·mi·um /hōl'mēəm/ *n.* metallic element of the lanthanide series; *symb.* Ho [L *Holmia* Stockholm]

ho·lo·caust /hō'ləkôst', häl'ə-/ *n.* **1** large-scale destruction, esp. by fire or nuclear war **2** (**the Holocaust**) systematic killing of European Jews by the Nazis, 1939–45 [Gk *holos* whole + *kaustos* burnt]

ho·lo·gram /hō'ləgram', häl'ə-/ *n.* three-dimensional photographic image using laser technology [Gk *holos* whole + -GRAM]

ho·lo·graph /hō'ləgraf', häl'ə-/ *adj.* **1** wholly written by hand by its author —*n.* **2** holograph document —**hol'o·graph'ic** *adj.* [Gk *holos* whole + -GRAPH]

ho·log·ra·phy /hōläg'rəfē/ *n.* the study or production of holograms

Holst /hōlst/, **Gustav** 1874–1934; English composer

hol·ster /hōl'stər/ *n.* leather case for a pistol or revolver, worn on a belt, etc. [Du]

ho·ly /hō'lē/ *adj.* (**·li·er, ·li·est**) **1** morally and spiritually excellent or perfect **2** belonging to or devoted to God **3** consecrated; sacred [OE, rel. to WHOLE]

Ho'ly Com·mu'nion *n.* Christian sacrament in which participants consume bread and wine consecrated as the body and blood of Christ or as symbols of them

Ho'ly Ghost' *n.* HOLY SPIRIT

Ho'ly Grail' *n.* GRAIL

Ho'ly Land' *n.* (formerly Palestine) region in which Judaism and Christianity developed; largely within modern-day Israel and its occupied territories

Ho'ly Ro'man Em'pire *n. Hist.* empire of W central Europe from 800 until 1806

Ho'ly Spir'it *n. Christianity.* third person of the Trinity

hom·age /(h)äm'ij/ *n.* tribute; honor [L *homo* man]

hom·burg /häm'bərg/ *n.* man's felt hat with a narrow curled brim and a lengthwise dent in the crown [*Homburg* in Germany]

home /hōm/ *n.* **1** place where one lives; fixed residence **2** family circumstances (*comes from a good home*) **3** native land **4** institution caring for people or animals **5** place where a thing originates, is kept, or is native or most common **6** *Baseball.* HOME PLATE —*adj.* **7** of or connected with one's home **8** in one's own country **9** *Sports.* played on one's own field, etc. —*adv.* **10** to, at, or in one's home or country **11** to the point aimed at (*drove the nail home*) —*v.* (**homed, hom·ing**) **12** (esp. of a trained pigeon) return home **13** (of a missile, etc.) be guided toward a destination or target **14 at home: a** in one's house or native land **b** at ease **c** familiar or well informed [OE]

home'com'ing *n.* **1** arrival at home **2** annual reunion of alumni held by some colleges, high schools, etc.

home' e·co·nom'ics *n. pl.* study of household management

home'grown' *adj.* grown or produced at home or locally

home'land' *n.* one's native land

home·less /hōm'ləs/ *adj.* **1** lacking a home —*n.* **2** (with **the**) homeless people as a group —**home'less·ness** *n.*

home'ly *adj.* (**·li·er, ·li·est**) **1** simple; plain **2** unattractive —**home'li·ness** *n.*

home'made' *adj.* made at home

ho·me·op·a·thy /hō'mēäp'əᴛʜē/ *n.* treatment of disease by minute doses of drugs that in a healthy person would produce symptoms of the disease —**ho'me·o·path'** /-əpaᴛʜ'/ *n.*; **ho'me·o·path'ic** *adj.* [Gk *homoios* like + *pathy*, rel. to PATHOS]

home' plate' *n.* (also **home**) *Baseball.* base pitched to and at which runs are scored

Ho·mer /hō'mər/ **1** 8th cent. B.C.; Greek epic poet **2** Winslow 1836–1910; US painter

Ho·mer·ic /hōmer'ik/ *adj.* **1** of or in the style of Homer **2** of Bronze Age Greece as described in Homer's poems

home'sick' *adj.* longing for home —**home'sick'ness** *n.*

home·spun /hōm′spun/ *adj.* **1** made of yarn spun at home **2** plain; simple —*n.* **3** homespun cloth

home·stead /hōm′sted/ *n.* **1** home and adjoining land **2** house

home·ward /hōm′wərd/ *adv.* (also home′wards) **1** toward home —*adj.* **2** going toward home

home·work *n.* **1** work to be done at home, esp. by a school pupil **2** preparatory work or study; research

hom·ey /hō′mē/ *adj.* (also hom′y) (·i·er, ·i·est) suggesting home; cozy —hom′ey·ness, hom′i·ness *n.*

ho·mi·cide /häm′əsīd, hō′mə-/ *n.* **1** killing of a human being by another **2** person who kills a human being —ho′mi·ci′dal *adj.* [L *homo* man + -CIDE]

hom·i·ly /häm′əlē/ *n.* (*pl.* ·lies) **1** sermon **2** moralizing discourse —hom′i·let′ic /-let′ik/ *adj.* [Gk *homilia*]

hom·i·nid /häm′ənid/ *adj.* **1** of the primate family including humans and their fossil ancestors —*n.* **2** member of this family [L *homo hominis* man]

hom·i·noid /häm′ənoid/ *adj.* **1** like a human —*n.* **2** animal resembling a human

hom·i·ny /häm′ənē/ *n.* (also hom′in·y grits′ or grits) dried, coarsely ground corn kernels, usu. boiled for food

homo- *comb. form* same [Gk *homos* same]

ho·mo·ge·ne·ous /hō′məjē′nēəs/ *adj.* **1** of the same kind **2** consisting of parts all of the same kind; uniform —ho′mo·ge·ne′i·ty /-jənē′ətē, -nā′-/ *n.*; ho′mo·ge·ne·ous·ly *adv.* [fr. HOMO- + Gk *genos* kind]

ho·mog·e·nize /həmäj′əniz′/ *v.* (·nized, ·niz·ing) **1** make homogeneous **2** treat (milk) so that the fat droplets are emulsified and the cream does not separate

hom·o·graph /häm′əgraf′, hō′mə-/ *n.* word spelled like another but of different meaning and (usu.) origin (e.g., POLE¹, POLE²) [HOMO- + -GRAPH]

ho·mol·o·gous /həmäl′əgəs/ *adj.* **1a** having the same relation, relative position, etc. **b** corresponding **2** *Biol.* (of organs, etc.) similar in position and structure but not necessarily in function [fr. HOMO- + Gk *logos* ratio]

hom·o·nym /häm′ənim′/ *n.* **1** word spelled or pronounced like another but of different meaning **2** namesake [fr. HOMO- + Gk *onyma* name]

ho·mo·pho·bi·a /hō′məfō′bēə/ *n.* hatred or fear of homosexuals —ho′mo·phobe′ *n.*; ho′mo·pho′bic *adj.*

ho·mo·phone /häm′əfōn′, hō′mə-/ *n.* word pronounced like another but of different meaning and usu. different spelling and origin (e.g., *pair*, *pear*) [fr. HOMO- + Gk *phōnē* sound]

Ho·mo sa·pi·ens /hō′mō sap′ēənz, sā′pē-/ *n.* modern humans regarded as a species [L: wise man]

ho·mo·sex·u·al /hō′məsek′sнōōəl/ *adj.* **1** feeling or involving sexual attraction to people of the same sex —*n.* **2** homosexual person —ho′mo·sex·u·al′i·ty /-al′ətē/ *n.* [HOMO- + SEXUAL]

Homs /hômz, hôms/ *n.* city in Syria. Pop. 518,000

hom·y /hō′mē/ *adj.* var. of HOMEY

hon·cho /hän′сно/ *n.* (*pl.* ·chos) *Slang.* leader or chief, esp. an influential one

269   **homespun / honorable**

Hon·du·ras /händ′yŏŏr′əs/ *n.* republic in NE Central America. Capital: Tegucigalpa. Pop. 4,996,000 —Hon·du′ran *n.* & *adj.*

hone /hōn/ *n.* **1** sharpening stone —*v.* (honed, hon·ing) **2** sharpen on or as on a hone [OE]

Ho·neck·er /hō′nəkər/, Erich 1912–94; head of state in E Germany (1976–89)

hon·est /än′ist/ *adj.* **1** fair and just **2** free of deceit and untruthfulness; sincere **3** fairly earned (*an honest living*) **4** blameless but undistinguished —hon′es·ty *n.* [L *honestus*]

hon·est·ly *adv.* **1** in an honest way **2** really

hon·ey /hən′ē/ *n.* (*pl.* ·eys) **1** sweet sticky yellowish fluid made by bees from nectar **2** color of this **3** sweetness **4** (form of address) darling [OE]

HONEYCOMB 1

hon·ey·comb *n.* **1** bees' wax structure of hexagonal cells for honey and eggs **2** pattern arranged hexagonally —*v.* **3** fill with cavities or tunnels **4** mark with a honeycomb pattern [OE]

hon·ey·dew *n.* a variety of melon

hon·eyed /hən′ēd/ *adj.* (of words, etc.) sweet; sweet-sounding

hon·ey·moon /hən′ē/ *n.* **1** vacation taken by a newly married couple **2** initial period of enthusiasm or goodwill —*v.* **3** spend a honeymoon —hon′ey·moon′er *n.*

hon·ey·suck·le /hən′ēsək′əl/ *n.* climbing shrub with fragrant cream or pink flowers

Hong Kong /häng′ käng′, hông′ kông′/ *n.* **1** British crown colony (to 1997) bordering SE China. Capital: Victoria. Pop. 5,799,000 **2** major island of this colony

Ho·ni·a·ra /hō′nē·är′ə/ *n.* capital of the Solomon Islands. Pop. 30,500

honk /hôngk, hängk/ *n.* **1** sound of a car horn **2** cry of a goose —*v.* **3** (cause to) make a honk [imit.]

honk·y-tonk /hôNG′kē tôNG′k′, häNG′kē täNG′k′/ *n.* **1** ragtime piano music **2** cheap or disreputable nightclub, etc.

Hon·o·lu·lu /hän′əlŌŌ′lŌŌ, hōn′-/ *n.* capital of Hawaii, on the S coast of the island of Oahu. Pop. 365,272

honor /än′ər/ *n.* **1** high respect; public regard **2** adherence to what is right or accepted behavior **3** nobleness of mind **4** official award **5a** exalted position **b** privilege; prerogative **c** (*cap.*) (prec. by *your*, *his*, etc.) title of a judge, etc. **6** source of respect or high regard **7a** chastity (of a woman) **b** reputation for this **8** (*pl.*) specialized degree course or special distinction in academics —*v.* **9** respect highly **10** confer honor on **11** accept; accede to; pay **12** do the honors perform the duties of a host to guests, etc. [L *honor* repute]

hon·or·a·ble /än′(ə)rəbəl/ *adj.* **1** deserving, bringing, or showing honor **2** (*cap.*) title given to certain officials, etc. —hon′or·a·bly adv.

hon·o·rar·i·um /ˌänˈərərˈēəm/ n. (pl. ·ums or ·i·a /-ēə/) fee, esp. a voluntary special payment for professional services rendered [L, rel. to HONOR]

hon·or·ar·y /ˈänˈərerˈē/ adj. 1 conferred as an honor 2 (of an office or its holder) unpaid

hon·or·if·ic /ˌänˈərifˈik/ adj. 1 conferring honor 2 implying respect

Hon·shu /ˈhänˈSHŌō/ n. chief island in Japan, in the central part

hooch /hōōCH/ n. Slang. inferior or illicit whiskey [Esk]

hood¹ /hŏŏd/ n. 1 covering for the head and neck, esp. as part of a garment 2 hinged front cover, usu. over a car's engine —v. 3 cover with or as with a hood [OE]

hood² n. Slang. gangster [abbr. of HOODLUM]

Hood, Mt. n. inactive volcanic peak in the Cascade Range in NW Ore.

’hood /hŏŏd/ n. Colloq. neighborhood, esp. in a low-income urban district

-hood suffix forming nouns: 1 of condition or state (childhood; falsehood) 2 designating a group (sisterhood; neighborhood) [OE]

hood·lum /ˈhŏŏdˈləm, hŏŏd′-/ n. gangster or other lawless person

hood·wink /ˈhŏŏdˈwiNGk/ v. deceive; delude [fr. HOOD¹ blindfold]

hoo·ey /hōōˈē/ n. Colloq. nonsense

hoof /hŏŏf, hōōf/ n. (pl. hoofs or hooves) horny part of the foot of a horse, etc. [OE]

hook /hŏŏk/ n. 1a bent or curved piece of metal, etc., for catching or hanging things on b fishhook 2 sharp bend 3 something moving in a curving path —v. 4 element or tactic to capture interest 5 grasp or secure with hook(s) 6 draw in; entice 7 Sports. send (the ball) in a curving path 8 by hook or by crook by one means or another 9 off the hook: a out of difficulty or trouble b (of a telephone receiver) not on its rest [OE]

hoo·kah /ˈhŏŏkˈə/ n. pipe with a long tube passing through water to cool the smoke [Urdu fr. Ar: casket]

hooked /hŏŏkt/ adj. 1 hook-shaped 2 Slang. captivated or addicted

hook′er n. Slang. prostitute

hook′up′ n. connection, esp. electronic

hook′worm′ n. worm with hooklike mouthparts, infesting humans and animals

hook·y /hŏŏkˈē/ n. (also hook′ey) as in play hooky Slang. play truant

hoo·li·gan /ˈhōōˈligən/ n. hoodlum; ruffian —hoo′li·gan·ism n.

hoop /hŏŏp/ n. 1 circular band of metal, wood, etc., esp. as part of a framework 2 hoop-shaped item, as a basketball rim —v. 3 bind or encircle with hoop(s) [OE]

hoo·ray /hŏŏrāˈ/ interj. HURRAH

hoot /hŏŏt/ n. 1 cry of an owl 2 sound made by a car's horn, etc. 3 shout expressing scorn or disapproval 4a Slang. laughter b cause of this —v. 5 utter or make a hoot 6 greet or drive away with scornful hoots [imit.]

Hoo·ver /hōōˈvər/ 1 Herbert Clark 1874–1964; 31st US president (1929–33) 2 J(ohn) Edgar 1895–1972; director of the Federal Bureau of Investigation (1924–72)

hooves /hŏŏvz/ n. pl. of HOOF

hop¹ /häp/ v. (hopped, hop·ping) 1 spring with two or (as of a frog) all feet at once 2 (of a person) jump on one foot 3 Colloq. get on; board —n. 4 hopping movement 5 Colloq. informal dance 6 short journey, esp. a flight [OE]

hop² n. 1 climbing plant bearing cones 2 (pl.) its ripe cones, used to flavor beer [LGer or Du]

hope /hōp/ n. 1 expectation and desire for a thing 2 person or thing giving cause for this 3 what is hoped for —v. 4 expect and desire 5 feel fairly confident [OE]

Hope /hōp/, Bob (born Leslie Townes Hope) 1903– ; English-born US comedian

hope′ful adj. 1 feeling, causing, or inspiring hope 2 likely to succeed —n. 3 person likely to succeed

hope′ful·ly adv. 1 in a hopeful manner 2 it is to be hoped

• Usage: This word, which originally meant 'in a hopeful manner,' has come to mean 'it is hoped that': Hopefully, we shall come out of this alive. Purists refuse to allow such a sense. But in fact, it functions as a "sentence adverb," and, like nevertheless, moreover, and others, causes no grammatical problems. Its usage is too frequent to be denied, though it is important to be aware that some strongly object to it.

hope′less adj. 1 feeling or admitting no hope 2 incompetent —hope′less·ly adv.; hope′less·ness n.

Hop·kins /ˈhäpˈkinz/, Gerard Manley 1844–89; English poet

hop·per /ˈhäpˈər/ n. 1 container tapering downward to an opening for discharging its contents 2 hopping insect

Hop·per /ˈhäpˈər/, Edward 1882–1967; US painter

hop·scotch /ˈhäpˈskäCH/ n. children's game of hopping over marked-out squares to retrieve a stone [fr. HOP¹ + SCOTCH]

Hor·ace /ˈhôrˈəs, härˈ-/ (Quintus Horatius Flaccus) 65–8 B.C.; Roman poet

horde /hôrd/ n. large group; pack [Turk ordū camp]

hore·hound /ˈhôrˈhound/ n. plant yielding a bitter juice used in cough drops, etc. [OE: hoary herb]

ho·ri·zon /hərīˈzən/ n. 1 line at which earth and sky appear to meet 2 (usu. pl.) limit of mental perception, possibility, etc. 3 on the horizon just imminent or becoming apparent [Gk horizein limit]

hor·i·zon·tal /ˈhôrˈəzäntˈl, härˈ-/ adj. 1 parallel to the plane of the horizon; at right angles to the vertical 2 level; flat —n. 3 horizontal line, plane, etc. —hor′i·zon·tal′i·ty /-tالˈətē/ n.; hor′i·zon′tal·ly adv.

hor·mone /ˈhôrˈmōn/ n. 1 substance produced in an organism and transported in tissue fluids to stimulate some action 2 similar synthetic substance —hor·mon′al adj. [Gk hormān impel]

horn /hôrn/ n. 1a hard outgrowth from the head of esp. hoofed animals, often curved and tapering to a point b hornlike projection, or thing shaped like a horn 2 substance of which horns are made 3 brass wind instrument 4

horn·blende /hôrn'blend'/ *n.* dark-brown, black, or green mineral found in rock [Ger]

hor·net /hôr'nit/ *n.* large stinging wasp [LGer or Du]

horn' of plen'ty *n.* a cornucopia

horn'pipe' *n.* lively dance, esp. associated with sailors

horn'-rimmed' *adj.* (esp. of eyeglasses) having rims made of horn or a similar substance

horn'y *adj.* (**·i·er, ·i·est**) 1 of or like horn 2 hard or callused 3 *Slang.* lustful **—horn'i·ness** *n.*

ho·rol·o·gy /hərāl'əjē/ *n.* art of measuring time or making clocks, watches, etc. **—hor'o·log'i·cal** /-älij'ikəl/ *adj.* [Gk *hōra* time]

hor·o·scope /hôr'əskōp', här'-/ *n.* 1 forecast of a person's future from a zodiacal diagram 2 chart used for this [Gk *hōra* time + *skopos* observer]

Hor·o·witz /hôr'əwits, här'-/, **Vladimir** 1904–89; Russian-born US pianist

hor·ren·dous /hären'dəs/ *adj.* horrifying **—hor·ren'dous·ly** *adv.* [L, rel. to HORRIBLE]

hor·ri·ble /hôr'əbal, här'-/ *adj.* 1 causing or likely to cause horror 2 *Colloq.* very bad; deplorable **—hor'ri·bly** *adv.* [L *horrere* bristle; shudder at]

hor·rid /hôr'id, här'-/ *adj.* 1 horrible; revolting 2 very unpleasant

hor·rif·ic /hôrif'ik, här'-/ *adj.* horrifying **—hor·rif'i·cal·ly** *adv.*

hor·ri·fy /hôr'əfī', här'-/ *v.* (**·fied, ·fy·ing**) arouse horror in; shock **—hor'ri·fy'ing** *adj.*

hor·ror /hôr'ər, här'-/ *n.* 1 painful feeling of loathing and fear 2 intense dislike 3 person or thing causing horror

hors d'œuvre /ôr darv', ôr dœ'vr/, *n.* food served as an appetizer [Fr: outside the work]

horse /hôrs/ *n.* 1 four-legged mammal with mane and tail, used for riding, to pull loads, etc. 2 VAULTING HORSE 3 supporting frame 4 **from the horse's mouth** *Colloq.* (of information, etc.) from the original or an authoritative source 5 **horse around** play foolishly or annoyingly [OE]

horse'back' *n.* 1 back of a horse 2 **on horseback** mounted on a horse

horse' chest'nut *n.* 1 tree with upright conical clusters of flowers 2 dark brown nutlike fruit of this

horse'fly' *n.* (*pl.* **·flies**) any of various biting insects troublesome esp. to horses

horse'hair' *n.* hair from the mane or tail of a horse, used for padding, etc.

horse·man /hôrs'mən/ *n.* (*pl.* **·men**) skilled rider of horses **—horse'man·ship** *n.*

horse'play' *n.* boisterous play

horse'pow'er *n.* (*pl.* same) unit of measure for the power of an engine, equal to 550 foot-pounds per second

horse' race' *n.* race between horses with riders **—horse' rac'ing** *n.*

horse'rad'ish *n.* plant with a pungent root, used in relish, etc.

horse' sense' *n.* common sense

horse'shoe' *n.* 1 U-shaped iron plate nailed to a horse's hoof for protection 2 thing of this shape 3 (*pl.*) game in which horseshoes are tossed to encircle a stake

horse'tail' *n.* 1 horse's tail 2 plant resembling this

horse'whip' *n.* 1 whip for driving horses **—v.** (**·whipped, ·whip·ping**) 2 beat with a horse-whip

horse'wom·an *n.* (*pl.* **·wom·en**) 2 skilled woman rider of horses

hors'y *adj.* (**·i·er, ·i·est**) 1 of or like a horse 2 concerned with or devoted to horses

hor·ti·cul·ture /hôrt'ikal'CHər/ *n.* art of garden cultivation **—hor'ti·cul'tur·al** *adj.*; **hor'ti·cul'tur·ist** *n.* [L *hortus* garden + CULTURE]

Ho·rus /hôr'əs/ *n. Egypt. Myth.* sun god

ho·san·na /hōzan'ə, -zän'-/ *n. & interj.* shout of adoration to God [Heb]

hose /hōz/ *n.* 1 flexible tube for conveying a fluid 2 (*pl.*) hosiery **—v.** (**hosed, hos·ing**) 3 water, spray, or drench with a hose [OE]

ho·sier·y /hō'ZH(ə)rē/ *n.* stockings and socks

hosp. *abbr.* 1 hospice 2 hospital

hos·pice /häs'pis/ *n.* 1 home where people who are ill (esp. terminally) or destitute are cared for 2 lodging for travelers, esp. one kept by a religious order [L, rel. to HOST²]

hos·pi·ta·ble /häs'pitəbəl, häspit'-/ *adj.* giving hospitality **—hos'pi·ta·bly** *adv.* [L, rel. to HOST²]

hos·pi·tal /häs'pit'l/ *n.* institution providing medical care for ill and injured people [L, rel. to HOST²]

Hos·pi·ta·let /(h)äs'pit'l-et'/ *n.* city in Spain. Pop. 269,200

hos·pi·tal·i·ty /häs'pətal'ətē/ *n.* welcoming treatment of guests or strangers

hos·pi·tal·ize /häs'pit'l-īz'/ *v.* (**·ized, ·iz·ing**) send or admit (a patient) to a hospital **—hos'pi·tal·i·za'tion** *n.*

host¹ /hōst/ *n.* large number of people or things [L *hostis* enemy; army]

host² *n.* 1 person who receives or entertains another as a guest 2 master of ceremonies 3 *Biol.* animal or plant having a parasite **—v.** 4 be host to (a person) or of (an event) [L *hospes hospitis* host; guest]

host³ *n.* (also *cap.*) bread consecrated in the Eucharist [L *hostia* victim]

hos·tage /häs'tij/ *n.* person seized or held as security for the fulfillment of a condition [OF fr. L *obses*]

hos·tel /häst'l/ (also **youth' host'el**) *n.* inexpensive lodging esp. for travelers, hikers, etc. [MedL, rel. to HOSPITAL]

hos·tel·ry /häst'ərē/ *n.* (*pl.* **·ries**) inn

host·ess /hō'stis/ *n.* 1 woman who receives or entertains a guest 2 woman employed to welcome customers at a restaurant, etc. [rel. to HOST²]

hos·tile /häst'l, häs'tīl'/ *adj.* 1 of an enemy 2 unfriendly; opposed **—hos'tile·ly** *adv.* [L, rel. to HOST²]

hos·til·i·ty /hästil'ətē/ *n.* (*pl.* **·ties**) 1 being hostile; enmity 2 (*pl.*) acts of warfare

hot /hät/ *adj.* (**hot·ter, hot·test**) 1 having a relatively high temperature 2 causing a sensation of heat 3 (of a person) feeling heat 4a ardent; passionate; excited b eager; keen (*in hot pursuit*) c angry or upset 5 (of news, etc.)

fresh 6 (of a competitor) thriving; winning 7 *Electr.* carrying current 8 *Slang.* stolen, esp. recently 9 **hot under the collar** angry —**hot′ly** *adv.*; **hot′ness** *n.* [OE]

hot′ air′ *n. Slang.* empty or boastful talk

hot′ bed′ *n.* 1 environment conducive to (esp. vice, intrigue, etc.) 2 bed of earth heated by fermenting manure

hot′-blood′ed *adj.* passionate

hot′ but′ton *n. Colloq.* contemporary theme, issue, etc., that attracts immediate popular notice

hot′ cake′ *n.* 1 pancake 2 **sell** (or **go**) **like hot cakes** *Colloq.* be sold (or go) quickly

hot′ dog′ *n.* mild sausage, esp. on a soft roll

ho-tel /hōtel′/ *n.* establishment providing lodging and meals for travelers [Fr. rel. to HOSTEL]

ho-tel-ier /ō′təlyā′, hōtL′ER/ *n.* hotel-keeper

hot′ head′ *n.* impetuous person —**hot′ head′ed** *adj.*; **hot′ head′ed-ness** *n.*

hot′ house′ *n.* 1 heated building for growing tender plants 2 environment conducive to rapid development

hot′ line′ *n.* dedicated telephone, etc., line, esp. for emergencies

hot′ plate′ *n.* heated metal plate for cooking or warming food

hot′ po-ta′to *n. Colloq.* contentious matter

hot′ rod′ *n.* car modified for extra power and speed

hot′ seat′ *n. Slang.* 1 difficult or pressured situation 2 electric chair

hot′-tem′pered *adj.* impulsively angry

hot′ tub′ *n.* tub of heated, circulating water for therapy or recreation, usu. able to accommodate several people

hot′-wa′ter bot′tle *n.* (usu. rubber) container filled with hot water, used to apply heat

Hou-di-ni /hōōdē′nē/, **Harry** (pseudonym of **Erik Weisz**) 1874–1926; Hungarian-born US magician and escape artist

hound /hound/ *n.* 1 dog used in hunting —*v.* 2 harass or pursue [OE]

hour /our/ *n.* 1 twenty-fourth part of a day and night; 60 minutes 2 time of day; point in time 3 period for a specific purpose (*lunch hour*) 4 time for action, etc. 5 specific time on the clock (*buses leave on the hour*) 6 **after hours** after closing time [Gk *hōra*]

hour′glass′ *n.* time-measuring device in which sand trickles down from one part of a glass container to another through a narrow tube

hour-ly /our′lē/ *adj.* 1 done or occurring every hour 2 reckoned hour by hour (*hourly wage*) —*adv.* 3 every hour 4 frequently

house *n.* /hous/ (*pl.* **hous′es** /hou′ziz/) 1 building for human habitation 2 building for a special purpose 3 royal family or dynasty 4 firm or institution 5 legislative or deliberative assembly 6 audience for a performance 7 *Astrol.* sign of the zodiac —*v.* /houz/ (**housed, hous′ing**) 8 provide with a house or other

HOURGLASS

accommodation 9 store 10 enclose or encase 11 **like a house on fire** vigorously; fast 12 **on the house** free [OE]

house-boat /hous′bōt′/ *n.* boat equipped for living in

house′break′ing *n.* criminal breaking into a building —**house′break′er** *n.*

house′bro′ken *adj.* (of pets) trained to excrete only outdoors or only in proper places

house′coat′ *n.* woman's informal indoor robe

house′fly′ *n.* (*pl.* **-flies**) common fly

house′hold′ *n.* 1 occupants of a house as a unit 2 house and its affairs —**house′hold′er** *n.*

house′hold′ word′ *n.* familiar name, person, or thing

house′-hus′band *n.* married man whose main job is managing household duties

house′keep′er *n.* person employed to manage a household

house′keep′ing *n.* maintenance or management of a house, hotel, etc.

house′maid′ *n.* female servant in a house

House′ of Lords′ *n.* chamber of the British Parliament that is mainly hereditary

house′plant′ *n.* plant grown indoors

house′warm′ing *n.* party celebrating a move to a new home

house′wife′ *n.* (*pl.* **-wives′**) married woman whose main job is managing household duties —**house′wife′ly** *adj.*

house′work′ *n.* regular housekeeping chores —**house′work′er** *n.*

hous-ing /hou′ziNG/ *n.* 1a dwellings collectively b provision of these 2 shelter; lodging 3 rigid casing for machinery, etc.

Hous-man /hous′mən/, **A(lfred) E(dward)** 1859–1936; English poet

Hous-ton /(h)yōō′stən/ *n.* city in Texas. Pop. 1,630,553

Hous-ton /(h)yōō′stən/, **Samuel** 1793–1863; US soldier and frontiersman; president of the Republic of Texas (1836–38)

HOV *abbr.* HIGH-OCCUPANCY VEHICLE

hove /hōv/ *v. past* of HEAVE

hov-el /həv′əl, häv′-/ *n.* small miserable dwelling

hov-er /həv′ər, häv′-/ *v.* 1 remain in place in the air 2 wait close at hand; linger [obs. *hove* hover]

hov′er-craft′ *n.* (*pl.* same) vehicle traveling on a cushion of air provided by a downward blast

how /hou/ *interrog. adv.* 1 by what means; in what way 2 in what condition, esp. of health 3 to what extent or degree (*how far? how did it go?*) —*adv.* 4 in whatever way —*conj.* 5 *Colloq.* that (*told us how he'd been in India*) 6 **how about** *Colloq.* would you like (*how about a quick swim?*) 7 **how do you do?** a formal greeting [OE]

how-dah /houd′ə/ *n.* (usu. canopied) seat for riding on an elephant or camel [Urdu *hawda*]

Howe /hou/ 1 **Elias** 1819–67; US inventor of sewing machine 2 **Julia Ward** 1819–1910; US reformer and writer

How-ells /hou′əlz/, **William Dean** 1837–1920; US writer and editor

how-ev′er *adv.* 1a in whatever way b to whatever extent 2 nevertheless

how·it·zer /hou′ətsər/ *n.* short-barreled cannon for the high-angle firing of shells [Czech *houfnice* catapult]

howl /houl/ *n.* **1** long doleful cry of a dog, etc. **2** loud cry of pain, rage, derision, or laughter **3** *Colloq.* amusing spectacle or joke —*v.* **4** make a howl **5** weep loudly [imit.]

howl′er *n.* glaring mistake

How-rah /hou′rə/ *n.* city in India, on the Hooghly River. Pop. 946,700

how·so·ev·er /hou′sōev′ər/ *adv.* **1** in whatever way **2** to whatever extent

Hox·ha /hôj′ə/, **Enver** 1908–85; Communist leader of Albania (1954–85)

hoy·den /hoid′n/ *n.* boisterous girl [Du *heiden*, rel. to HEATHEN]

h.p. *abbr.* (also **hp**) horsepower

HQ *abbr.* headquarters

hr. *abbr.* (*pl.* **hrs.**) hour

H.R. *abbr.* **1** home rule **2** home run **3** House of Representatives

Hs *symb.* hassium

HS *abbr.* high school

HST *abbr.* **1** Hawaii(an) Standard Time **2** hypersonic transport

Huang /hwäNG/ *n.* (also **Yel′low Riv′er**) river flowing 2,800 mi. from W China into the Yellow Sea

hub /həb/ *n.* **1** central part of a wheel, rotating on or with the axle **2** center of interest, activity, etc.

hub-bub /həb′əb′/ *n.* confused noise; disturbance [perh. of Ir orig.]

hub·by /həb′ē/ *n.* (*pl.* **-bies**) *Colloq.* husband [abbr.]

Hub·li /hōōb′lē/ *n.* city in SW India. Pop. 647,600

hu·bris /hyōō′bris/ *n.* arrogant pride or presumption —**hu·bris′tic** *adj.* [Gk]

huck·le·ber·ry /hək′əlber′ē/ *n.* **1** low-growing N American shrub **2** blue or black fruit of this [prob. an alter. of *hurtleberry*]

huck·ster /hək′stər/ *n.* **1** aggressive salesman; hawker —*v.* **2** hawk (goods) [LGer]

HUD *abbr.* (Department of) Housing and Urban Development

Hud·ders·field /həd′ərzfēld/ *n.* city in N central England. Pop. 148,500

hud·dle /həd′l/ *v.* (**·dled, ·dling**) **1** crowd together **2** curl up one's body —*n.* **3** confused or crowded mass **4a** close or secret conference **b** *Football.* conference of the offensive team before a down [perh. fr. LGer]

Hud·son /həd′sən/, **Henry** d. 1611; English explorer

Hud′son Bay′ inland sea in NE Canada, an arm of the Atlantic

Hud′son Riv′er *n.* river rising in eastern N.Y., flowing S into New York Bay

hue /hyōō/ *n.* **1** color; tint **2** variety or shade of color [OE]

hue′ and cry′ *n.* loud outcry [Fr *huer* shout]

huff /həf/ *n.* **1** fit of petty annoyance —*v.* **2** blow air, steam, etc. **3** (esp. **huff and puff**) bluster ineffectually —**huff′y** *adj.* (**·i·er, ·i·est**) [imit. of blowing]

hug /həg/ *v.* (**hugged, hug·ging**) **1** embrace tightly, esp. with affection **2** keep close to; fit tightly around —*n.* **3** firm embrace [prob. Scand]

huge /(h)yōōj/ *adj.* **1** extremely large **2** (of an abstract thing) very great —**huge′ly** *adv.*; **huge′ness** *n.* [Fr *ahuge*]

Hughes /(h)yōōz/ **1** (**James**) **Langston** 1902–67; US writer **2** **Howard** 1905–76; US businessman and aviator **3** **Ted** 1930– ; English poet; poet laureate (1984–)

Hu·go /(h)yōō′gō/, **Victor** 1802–85; French writer

Hu·gue·not /hyōō′gənät′/ *n.* French Protestant of the 16th or 17th cent. [Fr]

huh /hə, hən/ *interj.* expression of disgust, surprise, etc. [imit.]

hu·la /hōō′lə/ *n.* (also **hu′la-hu′la**) Polynesian dance with flowing arm and hip movements [Hawaiian]

hulk /həlk/ *n.* **1** body of a dismantled ship **2** large clumsy-looking person or thing [OE]

hulk′ing *adj.* bulky; clumsy

hull¹ /həl/ *n.* body of a ship, airship, etc. [perh. rel. to HOLD²]

hull² /həl/ *n.* **1** outer covering of a fruit, as the pod of peas, the husk of grain, etc. —*v.* **2** remove the hulls from (fruit, etc.) [OE]

Hull /həl/ *n.* port on the Humber River in England. Pop. 325,500

hul·la·ba·loo /həl′əbəlōō′/ *n.* uproar [reduplication of *hullo*]

hul·lo /həlō′/ *n.* var. of HELLO

hum /həm/ *v.* (**hummed, hum·ming**) **1** make a low steady buzzing sound **2** sing with closed lips **3** *Colloq.* be active (*really made things hum*) —*n.* **4** humming sound [imit.]

hu·man /(h)yōō′mən/ *adj.* **1** of or belonging to the species *Homo sapiens* **2** consisting of human beings **3** of or characteristic of mankind, esp. as being fallible, etc. **4** showing warmth, sympathy, etc. —*n.* **5** human being [L *humanus*]

• Usage: See note at MAN.

hu′man be′ing *n.* man, woman, or child

hu·mane /(h)yōōmān′/ *adj.* **1** benevolent; compassionate **2** inflicting the minimum of pain **3** (of learning) tending to civilize —**hu·mane′ly** *adv.*; **hu·mane′ness** *n.*

hu·man·ism /(h)yōō′məniz′əm/ *n.* **1** nonreligious philosophy based on liberal human values **2** (often *cap.*) literary culture, esp. that of the Renaissance —**hu′man·ist** /-ist/ *n.*; **hu′man·is′tic** *adj.*

hu·man·i·tar·i·an /(h)yōōman′əter′ēən/ *n.* **1** person who seeks to promote human welfare —*adj.* **2** pertaining to humanitarians —**hu·man′i·tar′i·an·ism** *n.*

hu·man·i·ty /(h)yōōman′ətē/ *n.* (*pl.* **·ties**) **1a** the human race **b** being human **2** humaneness; benevolence **3** (*pl.*) subjects concerned with human culture, e.g., literature and history

hu·man·ize /(h)yōōmənīz′/ *v.* (**·ized, ·iz·ing**) make human or humane —**hu′man·i·za′tion** *n.* [Fr, rel. to HUMAN]

hu′man·kind′ *n.* human beings collectively

hu′man·ly *adv.* **1** by human means **2** in a human manner

hu′man na′ture *n.* general characteristics and feelings of mankind

hu′man rights′ *n. pl.* rights held to be common to all human beings

hum·ble /həm′bəl/ *adj.* **1** having or showing low self-esteem **2** of low social or political rank **3** modest in size, pretensions, etc. —*v.* (**·bled, ·bling**) **4** make humble; abase **5** eat **humble pie** apologize humbly; accept humiliation —**hum′ble·ness** *n.*; **hum′bly** *adv.* [L *humilis*, rel. to HUMUS]

hum·bug /həm′bəg/ *n.* **1** lying or deception; hypocrisy **2** impostor —*v.* (**·bugged, ·bugging**) **3** like an impostor **4** deceive; hoax —*interj.* **5** nonsense!

hum·ding·er /həm′diNG′ər/ *n. Colloq.* excellent or remarkable person or thing

hum·drum /həm′drəm/ *adj.* commonplace; dull; monotonous [reduplication of HUM]

Hume /(h)yōōm/, **David** 1711–76; Scottish philosopher, economist, and historian

hu·mer·us /hyōō′mərəs/ *n.* (*pl.* **·mer·i** /-rī′, -rē′/) bone of the upper arm —**hu′mer·al** *adj.* [L: shoulder]

hu·mid /(h)yōō′mid/ *adj.* (of the air or climate) full of moisture [L *humidus*]

hu·mid·i·fy /(h)yōōmid′əfī′/ *v.* (**·fied, ·fy·ing**) make (air, etc.) humid

hu·mid·i·ty /(h)yōōmid′itē/ *n.* (*pl.* **·ties**) **1** dampness **2** degree of moisture, esp. in the atmosphere

hu·mil·i·ate /(h)yōōmil′ē·āt′/ *v.* (**·at·ed, ·at·ing**) injure the dignity or self-respect of —**hu·mil′i·at′ing** *adj.*; **hu·mil′i·a′tion** *n.* [L, rel. to HUMBLE]

hu·mil·i·ty /(h)yōōmil′itē/ *n.* humbleness; meekness [Fr, rel. to HUMILIATE]

hum·ming·bird /həm′iNGbərd/ *n.* tiny bird that makes a humming sound with its wings

hum·mock /həm′ək/ *n.* hillock; hump

hum·mus /həm′əs, hōōm′-/ *n.* dip or appetizer made from ground chickpeas and sesame seeds, lemon, and garlic [Turk]

hu·mon·gous /hyōōməNG′gəs/ (also **hu·mun′gous**) *adj. Slang.* tremendously large; huge

hu·mor /(h)yōō′mər/ *n.* **1a** quality of being amusing **b** the expression of the comic in literature, speech, etc. **2** (in full **sense of humor**) ability to perceive or express what is funny **3** state of mind; inclination (*bad humor*) **4** *Obs.* each of the four fluids (blood, phlegm, choler, melancholy), thought to determine a person's physical and mental qualities —*v.* **5** gratify or indulge (a person or taste, etc.) —**hu′mor·ist** *n.*; **hu′mor·less** *adj.*; **hu′mor·less·ly** *adv.*; **hu′mor·less·ness** *n.* [L *humor* moisture]

hu·mor·ous /(h)yōō′mərəs/ *adj.* showing humor or a sense of humor —**hu′mor·ous·ly** *adv.*

hump /həmp/ *n.* **1** rounded protuberance on a camel's back **2** abnormality on a person's back **3** rounded raised mass of earth, etc. —*v.* **4** make into an arch shape [prob. LGer or Du]

hump′back′ *n.* **1** (also **hunch′back′**) a deformed back with a hump **b** person with this **2** whale with a dorsal fin forming a hump —**hump′backed′** *adj.*

Hum·per·dinck /həm′pərdiNGK′/, **Engelbert** 1854–1921; German composer

bu·mus /(h)yōō′məs/ *n.* organic constituent of soil formed by decayed vegetation [L: soil]

Hun /hən/ *n.* member of a warlike Asiatic

nomadic people who ravaged Europe in the 4th–5th cent. [OE]

hunch /hənCH/ *v.* **1** bend or arch into a hump —*n.* **2** intuitive feeling or idea **3** hump

hunch′back′ *n.* HUMPBACK, 1 —**hunch′backed′** *adj.*

hun·dred /hən′drəd/ *adj.* & *n.* (*pl.* **hun′dreds** or (in sense 1) **hun′dred**) (*sing.*, *prec.* by *a* or *one*) **1** ten times ten **2** symbol for this (100, c, C) **3** (*pl.*) the years of a specified century (*the seventeen hundreds*) —**hun′dred·fold** *adj.* & *adv.*; **hun′dredth** /-dredTH/ *adj.* & *n.* [OE]

hun′dred·weight′ *n.* (*pl.* same or **·weights′**) **1** unit of weight equal to 100 lbs. **2** unit of weight equal to 50 kg

hung /həNG/ *v.* past and past part. of HANG
● Usage: See note at HANG.

Hun·gar·i·an /həNG′ger′ēən/ *n.* **1a** native or national of Hungary **b** person of Hungarian descent **2** language of Hungary —*adj.* **3** of Hungary or its people or language [MedL]

Hun·ga·ry /həNG′gərē/ *n.* republic in central Europe. Capital: Budapest. Pop. 10,318,000

hun·ger /həNG′gər/ *n.* **1a** discomfort or exhaustion caused by lack of food **b** need for food **2** strong desire —*v.* **3** crave or desire **4** feel hunger —**hun′gry** *adj.*; **hun′gri·ly** *adv.* [OE]

hung′ju′ry *n.* jury unable to reach a verdict

hunk /həNGk/ *n.* **1** large piece cut off **2** *Colloq.* physically attractive man —**hunk′y** *adj.* (**·i·er, ·i·est**) [prob. Du]

hunt /hənt/ *v.* **1a** pursue and kill (wild animals) for sport or food **b** (of an animal) chase (its prey) **2** seek; search —*n.* **3** practice or instance of hunting **4** search —**hunt′er** or (*fem.*) **hunt′ress, hunt′ing** *n.*; **hunts′man** /-mən/ *n.* (*pl.* **·men**) [OE]

Hun·ting·ton /hənt′iNGtən/ *n.* town in N.Y. Pop. 191,474

Hun′ting·ton Beach′ *n.* city in Calif. Pop. 181,519

Hunts·ville /hənts′vil′/ *n.* city in Ala. Pop. 159,789

hur·dle /hərd′l/ *n.* **1a** each of a series of light barriers to be leapt over by athletes in a race **b** (*pl.*) race with these **2** obstacle or difficulty —*v.* (**·dled, ·dling**) **3** run in a hurdle race —**hur′dler** *n.* [OE]

hur·dy-gur·dy /hər′dē·gər′dē/ *n.* (*pl.* **·dies**) BARREL ORGAN [imit.]

hurl /hərl/ *v.* **1** throw with great force **2** utter (abuse, etc.) vehemently [imit.]

hur·ly-bur·ly /hər′lē·bər′lē/ *n.* boisterous activity [reduplication of HURL]

Hu·ron, Lake /(h)yōōr′än′, -ən/ *n.* one of the Great Lakes, E of Mich.

hur·rah /hōōrä′, -rô′/ *interj.* & *n.* (also **hoo·ray; hur·ray** /hōōrā′/) exclamation of joy or approval

hur·ri·cane /hər′ikän′, hə′ri-, -kən/ *n.* storm with a violent wind; tropical cyclone [Sp and Port fr. Carib]

hur′ri·cane lamp′ *n.* oil lamp designed to stay lit in a high wind

hur·ry /hər′ē, hə′rē/ *n.* **1** great or eager haste **2** (with *neg.* or *interrog.*) need for haste (*there is no hurry*) —*v.* (**·ried, ·ry·ing**) **3** move or act hastily **4** cause to hurry **5** do rapidly —**hur′ried·ly** *adv.* [imit.]

hurt /hərt/ v. **(hurt, hurt·ing) 1** cause pain or injury to **2** cause mental pain or distress to **3** suffer pain —n. **4** injury **5** harm; wrong [Fr *hurter* knock]

hurt·ful /hərt'fəl/ adj. causing (esp. mental) hurt —**hurt'ful·ly** adv.

hur·tle /hərt'l/ v. (·tled, ·tling) move or hurl rapidly or noisily [fr. HURT in the obs. sense 'strike hard']

Husain /hŏŏsän'/ *see* HUSSEIN

hus·band /həz'bənd/ n. **1** married man, esp. in relation to his wife —v. **2** use (resources) economically [OE: house-dweller]

hus·band·ry /həz'bəndrē/ n. **1** farming **2** management of resources

hush /həSH/ v. **1** make or become silent or quiet —*interj.* **2** call for silence —n. **3** expectant stillness or silence [*husht*, an obs. exclamation, taken as a past part.]

hush'-hush' adj. highly secret

hush' pup'py n. (pl. ·pies) ball of cornmeal dough, deep-fried

husk /həsk/ n. **1** dry outer covering of some fruits or seeds **2** worthless outside part of a thing —v. **3** remove husk(s) from [prob. LGer]

husk·y¹ /həs'kē/ adj. (·i·er, ·i·est) **1** (of a person or voice) dry in the throat; hoarse **2** (of a person) burly and strong —**husk'i·ly** adv.; **husk'i·ness** n. [HUSK + -Y]

husk·y² n. (pl. ·ies) dog of a breed used in the Arctic for pulling sleds [perh. fr. corruption of ESKIMO]

Hus·sein /hŏŏsän'/ (also **Husain**) **1** ibn Talal 1935– ; king of Jordan (1953–) **2 Saddam** 1937– ; political leader of Iraq (1979–)

Hus·serl /həs'ərl/, **Edmund** 1859–1938; German philosopher

hus·sy /həs'ē/ n. (pl. ·sies) impudent or promiscuous girl or woman [contr. of HOUSEWIFE]

hus·tings /həs'tiNGz/ n. election campaign or proceedings [OE: house of assembly, fr. ON]

hus·tle /həs'əl/ v. (·tled, ·tling) **1** jostle; bustle **2** force or hurry along **3** *Slang.* a. solicit business **b** engage in prostitution **4** obtain by energetic activity —n. **5** act or instance of hustling —**hus'tler** n. [Du]

Hus·ton /(h)yŏŏ'stən/, **John** 1906–87; US film director

hut /hət/ n. simple or crude house or shelter [Fr *hutte* fr. Gmc]

hutch /həCH/ n. **1** box or cage for rabbits, etc. **2** cupboard [Fr *huche*]

Hutch·in·son /həCH'insən/, **Anne** 1591–1643; English-born American colonist and religious leader

Hux·ley /hək'slē/, **Aldous** 1894–1963; English novelist

hwy. *abbr.* highway

hy·a·cinth /hī'əsinTH/ n. **1** bulbous plant with clusters of fragrant (esp. purplish blue) flowers **2** purplish blue [Gk *hyakinthos*]

hy·brid /hī'brid/ n. **1** offspring of two plants or animals of different species or varieties **2** thing composed of diverse elements —adj. **3** bred as a hybrid **4** heterogeneous —**hy'brid·ism'** n. [L]

hy·brid·ize /hī'bridīz'/ v. (·ized, ·iz·ing) **1** subject (a species, etc.) to crossbreeding **2a**

produce hybrids **b** (of an animal or plant) interbreed —**hy'brid·i·za'tion** n.

Hy·der·a·bad /hīd'ərəbäd'/ n. **1** city in W India. Pop. 2,991,900 **2** city on the Indus River in Pakistan. Pop. 751,500

hy·dra /hī'drə/ n. **1** freshwater polyp with a tubular body and tentacles **2** something hard to destroy [Gk: water serpent]

hy·dran·gea /hīdrān'jə/ n. shrub with globular clusters of white, pink, or blue flowers [Gk HYDRO- + *angeion* vessel]

hy·drant /hī'drənt/ n. outlet (esp. along a street) with a nozzle for a hose, for drawing water from a main [see HYDRO-]

hy·drate /hī'drāt'/ n. **1** compound combining water with another compound or an element —v. (·drat·ed, ·drat·ing) **2** combine chemically with water **3** cause to absorb water —**hy·dra'tion** n. [Fr, rel. to HYDRO-]

hy·drau·lic /hīdrô'lik/ adj. **1** (of water, oil, etc.) conveyed through pipes or channels **2** (of a mechanism, etc.) operated by moving or compressing liquid in this way —**hy·drau'li·cal·ly** adv. [Gk HYDR(O)- + *aulos* pipe]

hy·drau·lics /hīdrô'liks/ n. pl. (usu. as *sing.*) science of the conveyance of liquids through pipes, etc., esp. as motive power

hydro- *comb. form* **1** having to do with water (*hydroelectric*) **2** combined with hydrogen (*hydrochloric*) [fr. Gk *hydōr* water]

hy·dro·car·bon /hī'drəkär'bən/ n. compound of hydrogen and carbon

hy·dro·chlo·ric ac'id /hī'drəklôr'ik/ n. solution of the colorless gas hydrogen chloride in water

hy·dro·dy·nam·ics /hī'drōdī'nam'iks/ n. pl. (usu. treated as *sing.*) science of forces acting on or exerted by fluids (esp. liquids) —**hy'dro·dy·nam'ic** adj.

hy·dro·e·lec·tric /hī'drō·ilek'trik/ adj. **1** generating electricity by water power **2** (of electricity) so generated —**hy'dro·e·lec·tric'i·ty** /-'tris'ətē/ n.

HYDROFOIL 1

hy·dro·foil /hī'drəfoil'/ n. **1** boat with finlike members on struts for lifting its hull out of the water to increase speed **2** such a device

hy·dro·gen /hī'drəjən/ n. tasteless odorless gas, the lightest element, occurring in water and all organic compounds; *symb.* **H** —**hy·drog·e·nous** /hīdräj'ənəs/ adj. [Fr, rel. to HYDRO- + -GEN]

hy·drog·e·nate /hīdräj'ənāt'/ v. (·nat·ed, ·nat·ing) charge with or cause to combine with hydrogen —**hy'drog·en·a'tion** n.

hy'dro·gen bomb' n. immensely powerful bomb utilizing the explosive fusion of hydrogen nuclei

hy'dro·gen per·ox'ide n. colorless liquid used as an antiseptic and bleach

hy·drol·o·gy /hīdräl′əjē/ n. science of the properties of water, esp. of its movement in relation to land —**hy·drol′o·gist** n.

hy·drol·y·sis /hīdräl′əsis/ n. chemical reaction of a substance with water, usu. resulting in decomposition [Gk HYDRO- + lysis dissolving]

hy·dro·lyze /hī′drəlīz/ v. (**·lyzed, ·lyz·ing**) decompose by hydrolysis

hy·drom·e·ter /hīdräm′ətər/ n. instrument for measuring the density of liquids

hy·dro·pho·bi·a /hī′drəfō′bēə/ n. 1 aversion to water 2 rabies, esp. in humans —**hy′dro·pho′bic** /-bik/ adj.

hy·dro·plane /hī′drəplän′/ n. 1 light fast motorboat that skims over water 2 seaplane —v. (**·planed, ·plan·ing**) 3 (of a tire) lose traction on wet pavement

hy·dro·pon·ics /hī′drəpän′iks/ n. growing plants without soil, in sand, gravel, or liquid, with added nutrients —**hy′dro·pon′ic** adj.; **hy′dro·pon′i·cal·ly** adv. [Gk HYDRO- + ponos labor]

hy·dro·sphere /hī′drəsfēr′/ n. waters of the earth's surface

hy·dro·ther·a·py /hī′drəTHer′əpē/ n. use of water, esp. swimming, in the treatment of arthritis, paralysis, etc.

hy·drous /hī′drəs/ adj. containing water [rel. to HYDRO-]

hy·e·na /hīē′nə/ n. doglike flesh-eating mammal [L fr. Gk]

hy·giene /hī′jēn′/ n. 1 conditions or practices, esp. cleanliness, conducive to maintaining health 2 science of maintaining health —**hy·gi·en·ic** /hījē′nik, ·jen′ik; hī′jē·en′ik/ adj.; **hy′gi·en′i·cal·ly** adv.; **hy·gien·ist** /hījē′nist, -jen′ist/ n. [Gk hygiēs healthy]

hy·grom·e·ter /hīgräm′ətər/ n. instrument for measuring humidity [Gk hygros wet + -METER]

hy·men /hī′mən/ n. membrane at the opening of the vagina [Gk hymēn membrane]

hymn /him/ n. 1 song of esp. Christian praise 2 crusading theme —v. 3 praise or celebrate in hymns [Gk hymnos]

hym·nal /him′nəl/ n. book of hymns

hype /hīp/ Slang. n. 1 extravagant or intensive promotion of a product, etc. —v. (**hyped, hyp·ing**) 2 promote with hype

hy·per /hī′pər/ adj. Colloq. hyperactive; high-strung [abbr. of HYPERACTIVE]

hyper- prefix meaning: 1 over; beyond; above (hypersonic) 2 too (hypersensitive) [Gk hyper over]

hy·per·ac·tive /hī′pərak′tiv/ adj. (of a person) abnormally active

hy·per·bo·la /hīpər′bələ/ n. (pl. **·las** or **·lae** /-lē/) plane curve produced when a cone is cut by a plane that makes a greater angle with the base than the side of the cone —**hy·per·bol·ic** /hī′pərbäl′ik/ adj. [Gk hyperbolē excess, rel. to HYPER- + bolē throw]

hy·per·bo·le /hīpər′bəlē/ n. exaggeration, esp. for effect —**hy·per·bol·ic** /hī′pərbäl′ik/, **hy′per·bol′i·cal** adj.

hy·per·crit·i·cal /hī′pərkrit′ikəl/ adj. excessively critical —**hy′per·crit′i·cal·ly** adv.

hy·per·gly·ce·mi·a /hī′pərglīsē′mēə/ n. excess of glucose in the bloodstream [fr. HYPER- + Gk glykys sweet + haima blood]

hy·per·me′di·a n. MULTIMEDIA

hy·per·sen·si·tive /hī′pərsen′sətiv/ adj. excessively sensitive —**hy′per·sen′si·tiv′i·ty** n.

hy·per·ten·sion /hī′pərten′SHən/ n. abnormally high blood pressure

hy·per·text /hī′pərtekst′/ n. provision of several texts on one computer system, with cross references from one to another

hy·per·ther·mi·a /hī′pərTHər′mēə/ n. abnormally high body temperature [fr. HYPER- + Gk thermē heat]

hy·per·thy·roid·ism /hī′pərTHī′roid′iz′əm/ n. overactivity of the thyroid gland, resulting in an increased rate of metabolism

hy·per·ven·ti·la·tion /hī′pərvent′l-ā′SHən/ n. abnormally rapid breathing —**hy′per·ven′ti·late** /-tlāt/ v. (**·lat·ed, ·lat·ing**)

hy·phen /hī′fən/ n. 1 sign (-) used to join words (e.g., pick-me-up, rock-forming), to indicate the division of a word at the end of a line, or to indicate a missing or implied element (as in man- and womankind) —v. 2 HYPHENATE [Gk hyphen together]

hy·phen·ate /hī′fənāt′/ v. (**·at·ed, ·at·ing**) write or join (a word or words) with a hyphen —**hy′phen·a′tion** n.

hyp·no·sis /hipnō′sis/ n. state like sleep in which the subject acts only on external suggestion [Gk hypnos sleep]

hyp·no·ther·a·py /hip′nōTHer′əpē/ n. treatment of mental disorders by hypnosis

hyp·not·ic /hipnät′ik/ adj. 1 of or producing hypnosis 2 inducing sleep —n. 3 hypnotic drug or influence —**hyp·not′i·cal·ly** adv. [Gk, rel. to HYPNOSIS]

hyp·no·tism /hip′nətiz′əm/ n. the study or practice of hypnosis —**hyp′no·tist** /-tist/ n.

hyp·no·tize /hip′nətīz′/ v. (**·tized, ·tiz·ing**) 1 produce hypnosis in 2 fascinate

hy·po /hī′pō/ n. (pl. **·pos**) Colloq. HYPODERMIC

hypo- prefix 1 under (hypodermic) 2 below normal (hypotension) [Gk hypo under]

hy·po·chon·dri·a /hī′pəkän′drēə/ n. abnormal anxiety about one's health —**hy′po·chon′dri·ac** /-ak/ n.; **hy·po·chon·dri·ach·al** /hī′pōkändrī′əkəl/ adj. [L fr. Gk: abdomen, where melancholy was thought to arise]

hy·poc·ri·sy /hipäk′rəsē/ n. (pl. **·sies**) 1 false claim to virtue; insincerity; pretense 2 instance of this [Gk hypokrisis acting; feigning]

hyp·o·crite /hip′əkrit′/ n. person given to hypocrisy —**hyp′o·crit′i·cal** adj.; **hyp′o·crit′i·cal·ly** adv.

hy·po·der·mic /hī′pədər′mik/ adj. 1 of or penetrating the area beneath the skin —n. 2 hypodermic injection or syringe [fr. HYPO- + Gk derma skin]

hy·po·gly·ce·mi·a /hī′pōglīsē′mēə/ n. abnormally low blood sugar —**hy′po·gly·ce′mic** /-mik/ adj.

hy·po·ten·sion /hī′pōten′SHən/ n. abnormally low blood pressure

hy·pot·e·nuse /hīpät′n-(y)ōōs′, -(y)ōōz′/ n. side opposite the right angle of a right triangle (see illustration at TRIANGLE) [Gk: subtending line]

hy·po·thal·a·mus /hī′pəTHal′əməs/ n. (pl. **·mi** /-mī′/) region of the brain controlling body temperature, thirst, hunger, etc. —**hy′po·tha·lam′ic** /-pōTHələm′ik/ *adj.* [L, rel. to HYPO- + Gk *thalamos* inner room]

hy·po·ther·mi·a /hī′pōTHər′mēə/ *n.* abnormally low body temperature [fr. HYPO- + Gk *thermē* heat]

hy·poth·e·sis /hīpäTH′əsis/ *n.* (*pl.* -ses /-sēz′/) proposition or supposition as the basis for reasoning or investigation —**hy·poth′e·size** /-sīz/ *v.* (-sized, -siz·ing) [Gk: foundation]

hy·po·thet·i·cal /hī′pəTHet′ikəl/ *adj.* 1 of, based on, or serving as a hypothesis 2 supposed —**hy·po·thet′i·cal·ly** *adv.*

hy·po·thy·roid·ism /hī′pōTHī′roid′iz′əm/ *n.* subnormal activity of the thyroid gland —**hy′po·thy′roid** *n. & adj.*

hys·ter·ec·to·my /his′tərek′təmē/ *n.* (*pl.* **-mies**) surgical removal of the womb [Gk *hystera* womb + -ECTOMY]

hys·te·ri·a /hister′ēə, -stēr′-/ *n.* 1 wild uncontrollable emotion 2 *Psychol.* psychoneurotic disorder marked by violent emotional outbreaks, apparent organic dysfunction, etc. [Gk *hystera* womb]

hys·ter·i·cal /hister′ikəl/ *adj.* 1 of or affected with hysteria 2 uncontrollably emotional 3 extremely funny —**hys·ter′i·cal·ly** *adv.*

hys·ter′ics *n.* 1 fit of hysteria 2 overwhelming laughter

Hz *abbr.* hertz

I

i, I /ī/ *n.* (*pl.* **i′s; I′s, Is**) ninth letter of the English alphabet; a vowel

I /ī/ *pron.* (*obj.* **me;** *poss.* **my, mine;** *pl.* **we**) used by a speaker or writer to refer to himself or herself [OE]

i or **i.** *abbr.* 1 incisor 2 interest 3 intransitive 4 island 5 isle(s)

I or **I.** *abbr.* 1 independent 2 interstate 3 island(s) 4 isle(s) 5 *Rom. num.* (usu. I) one

IA, Ia. *abbr.* for Iowa (postal abbr. **IA**)

-ial *suffix* var. of -AL

i·amb /ī·am′/ *n.* metrical foot consisting of one unstressed or short followed by one stressed or long syllable [Gk *iambos*]

i·am·bic /ī·am′bik/ *Pros. adj.* 1 of or using iambs —*n.* 2 (usu. *pl.*) verse in iambs

-ian *suffix* var. of -AN

I·ba·dan /ibäd′n/ *n.* city in SW Nigeria. Pop. 1,295,000

I·ba·gué /ē′bägä′/ *n.* city in Colombia. Pop. 269,500

I·be·ri·an Pen·in·su·la /ībēr′ēən/ *n.* (also called **I·ber′i·a**) peninsula in SW Europe, comprising Spain and Portugal

i·bex /ī′beks/ *n.* (*pl.* **-bex·es**) wild mountain goat with curved ridged horns [L]

ibid. /ib′id/ *abbr.* in the same book or passage, etc. [L *ibidem* in the same place]

-ibility *suffix* forming nouns from, or corresponding to, adjectives in *-ible*

i·bis /ī′bis/ *n.* (*pl.* **-bis·es**) tropical wading bird with a curved bill and long legs [Gk, fr. Egyptian]

-ible *suffix* forming adjectives meaning 'that may or may be' (*forcible; possible*) [L]

-ibly *suffix* forming adverbs corresponding to adjectives in *-ible*

Ibn Sa·ud /ib′ən sä·ōōd′/, **Abdul-Aziz** c. 1880–1953; king of Saudi Arabia (1932–53)

Ib·sen /ib′sən/, **Henrik** 1828–1906; Norwegian dramatist

i·bu·pro·fen /ī′byōōprō′fən/ *n. Pharm.* drug used to reduce pain, inflammation, and fever

-ic *suffix* forming adjectives (*Arabic; classic; public*) and nouns (*epic; mechanic; music*) [L *-icus* or Gk *-ikos*]

-ical *suffix* forming adjectives corresponding to nouns or adjectives ending in *-ic* or *-y* (*classical; historical*)

ICBM *abbr.* intercontinental ballistic missile

ICC *abbr.* 1 Indian Claims Commission 2 International Claims Commission 3 Interstate Commerce Commission

ice /īs/ *n.* 1a frozen water b sheet of this 2 dessert of crushed ice flavored with fruit syrup —*v.* (**iced, ic·ing**) 3 mix with or cool in ice 4 cover (a cake, etc.) with icing 5 **ice over** (or up): a cover or become covered with ice b freeze 6 **on ice:** a performed by skaters b *Colloq.* in waiting or reserve 7 **on thin ice** in a risky situation [OE]

ice′ age′ *n.* glacial period

ice′berg /īs′bərg′/ *n.* 1 large floating mass of ice 2 **the tip of the iceberg** small perceivable part of something very large or complex [Du]

ice′berg let′tuce *n.* type of crisp, round-headed lettuce

ice′box *n.* refrigerator

ice′break′er *n.* 1 ship designed to break through ice 2 joke, incident, etc., that eases social discomfort

ice′ cap′ *n.* permanent covering of ice, esp. in polar regions

ice′ cream′ *n.* sweet, creamy frozen food, usu. flavored

ice′ cube′ *n.* small block of ice for drinks, etc.

ice′ hock′ey *n.* hockey played on ice

Ice·land /īs′lənd/ *n.* republic in the N Atlantic Ocean between Greenland and Scandinavia. Capital: Reykjavik. Pop. 261,000

Ice·land·ic /īslan′dik/ *adj.* 1 of Iceland —*n.* 2 language of Iceland

ice′ milk′ *n.* frozen dessert of flavored milk

ice′ skate′ *n.* 1 boot with a blade beneath, for skating on ice —*v.* (**ice′-skate**) (-skat·ed, -skat·ing) 2 skate on ice —**ice′ skat′er** *n.*

ich·thy·ol·o·gy /ik′THēäl′əjē/ *n.* the study of fishes —**ich′thy·o·log′i·cal** /-əläj′ikəl/ *adj.*; **ich′thy·ol′o·gist** *n.* [Gk *ichthys* fish]

-ician *suffix* forming nouns denoting persons skilled in subjects having nouns usu. ending in *-ic* or *-ics* (*magician; politician*) [Fr *-icien*]

i·ci·cle /ī′sik′əl/ *n.* hanging piece of ice formed from dripping water [fr. ICE + obs. *ickle* icicle]

ic·ing /ĭ′sĭNG/ *n.* **1** sweet coating spread on a cake, etc.; frosting **2** formation of ice on a ship or aircraft **3 icing on the cake** attractive addition or enhancement

i·con /ĭ′kän′/ *n.* **1** representation; image **2** *Comp.* screen symbol for a selectable program or option **3** painting of Christ, etc., esp. in the Eastern Church —**i·con′ic** *adj.* [Gk *eikōn* image]

i·con·o·clast /īkän′əklast′/ *n.* person who attacks cherished beliefs —**i·con′o·clasm′** /-klaz′əm/ *n.*; **i·con′o·clas′tic** *adj.* [Gk, rel. to ICON + *klan* break]

-ics *suffix* (as *sing.* or *pl.*) forming nouns denoting arts, sciences, etc. (*athletics; politics*)

ICU *abbr.* INTENSIVE CARE UNIT

i·cy /ĭ′sē/ *adj.* (**-ci·er, -ci·est**) **1** very cold **2** covered with or full of ice **3** (of a tone or manner) unfriendly; hostile —**i′ci·ly** *adv.*; **i′ci·ness** *n.*

id /ĭd/ *n.* person's inherited unconscious psychological impulses [L: that]

ID *abbr.* **1** identification (*ID card*) **2** postal abbr. for Idaho

i.d. *abbr.* inside diameter

I'd /īd/ *v. contr.* **1** I had **2** I should; I would

Ida. abbr. for Idaho

I·da·ho /ī′də·hō′/ *n.* NW state of the US. Capital: Boise. Pop. 1,006,749. Abbr. ID; Ida. —I′da·ho′an *n.* & *adj.*

-ide *suffix Chem.* forming nouns denoting binary compounds (*sodium chloride; calcium carbide*) [extended fr. OXIDE]

i·de·a /īdē′ə/ *n.* **1** conception or plan formed by mental effort **2** mental impression, conception, or notion **3** intention or purpose **4** archetype or pattern **5** ambition or aspiration **6 have no idea:** **a** not know at all **b** be completely incompetent [Gk: form; kind]

i·de·al /īdē′əl/ *adj.* **1** answering to one's highest conception; perfect **2** existing only in the mind —*n.* **3** perfect model or standard [Fr, rel. to IDEA]

i·de·al·ism *n.* **1** forming or pursuing ideals, esp. unrealistically **2** representation of things in their ideal form —**i·de·al·ist** /-ist/ *n.*; **i·de·al·is′tic** *adj.*; **i·de·al·is′ti·cal·ly** *adv.*

i·de·al·ize /īdē′əlīz/ *v.* (**-ized, -iz·ing**) regard or represent as ideal or perfect —**i·de′al·i·za′tion** *n.*

i·de·al·ly /īdē′əlē/ *adv.* **1** in ideal circumstances **2** according to an ideal

i·dée fixe /ēdā′ fēks′/ *n.* (*pl.* **i·dées fixes**, pronunc. same) dominating idea; obsession [Fr: fixed idea]

i·den·ti·cal /īden′tĭkəl/ *adj.* **1** (of different things) absolutely alike **2** one and the same **3** (of twins) developed from a single ovum —**i·den′ti·cal·ly** *adv.* [L *identicus,* rel. to IDENTITY]

● Usage: See note at SAME.

i·den·ti·fi·ca·tion /īden′təfĭkā′SHən/ *n.* **1** identifying **2** means of identifying

i·den·ti·fy /īden′təfī′/ *v.* (**-fied, -fy·ing**) **1** establish the identity of; recognize **2** select or discover **3** associate inseparably or very closely (with a party, policy, etc.) —**i·den′ti·fi′a·ble** *adj.* [MedL *identificare,* rel. to IDENTITY]

i·den·ti·ty /īden′tətē/ *n.* (*pl.* **-ties**) **1a** condition of being a specified person or thing **b** individuality; personality **2** identification or the result of it (*mistaken identity*) **3** absolute sameness [L *identitas* fr. *idem* same]

id·e·o·gram /id′ēəgram′, ī′dē-/ *n.* (also **id′e·o·graph′** /-graf′/) character symbolizing a thing without indicating the sounds in its name (e.g., a numeral, Chinese characters) —**id′e·o·graph′ic** *adj.*; **id′e·og′ra·phy** /-äg′rəfē/ *n.* [Gk *idea* form + -GRAM]

id·e·o·logue /id′ēəlôg, -läg′/ *n. often Derog.* adherent of an ideology [Fr, rel. to IDEA]

id·e·ol·o·gy /īd′ē-äl′əjē, id′ē-/ *n.* (*pl.* **-gies**) ideas at the basis of an economic, political, or social theory —**i′de·o·log′i·cal** /-əläj′ikəl/ *adj.*; **i′de·o·log′i·cal·ly** *adv.*; **i′de·ol′o·gist** *n.* [IDEA + -LOGY]

ides /īdz/ *n. pl.* day in the ancient Roman month (15th of March, May, July, and October; 13th of other months) [L *idus*]

id·i·o·cy /id′ēəsē/ *n.* (*pl.* **-cies**) foolishness; foolish act

id·i·om /id′ēəm/ *n.* **1** phrase established by usage whose meaning is not literally based on the words used (e.g., *pull one's leg*) **2** form or manner of expression characteristic of a particular language, etc. **3** language of a people or country **4** characteristic mode of expression in art, etc. —**id′i·o·mat′ic** /-mat′ik/ *adj.*; **id′i·o·mat′i·cal·ly** *adv.* [Gk *idios* own]

id·i·o·syn·cra·sy /id′ē-ōsiNG′krəsē/ *n.* (*pl.* **-sies**) attitude, behavior, or opinion peculiar to a person —**id′i·o·syn·crat′ic** /-krat′ik/ *adj.*; **id′i·o·syn·crat′i·cal·ly** *adv.* [Gk *idios* private + *sun* with + *krasis* mixture]

id·i·ot /id′ēət/ *n.* **1** stupid person **2** *Obs.* mentally deficient person incapable of rational conduct —**id·i·ot·ic** /id′ē-ät′ik/ *adj.*; **id·i·ot′i·cal·ly** *adv.* [Gk *idiōtēs* private citizen; ignorant person]

i·dle /īd′l/ *adj.* (**i·dler, i·dlest**) **1** lazy; indolent **2** not in use; not working **3** (of time, etc.) unoccupied **4** purposeless; groundless **5** useless; ineffective —*v.* (**·dled, ·dling**) **6** be idle **7** run (an engine) or (of an engine) be run slowly **8** pass (time, etc.) in idleness —**i′dle·ness, i′dler** *n.*; **i′dly** *adv.* [OE]

i·dol /īd′l/ *n.* **1** image of a deity, etc., as an object of worship **2** object of excessive or supreme adulation [Gk *eidōlon* image; phantom]

i·dol·a·ter /īdäl′ətər/ *n.* **1** worshiper of idols **2** devoted admirer —**i·dol′a·trous** *adj.*; **i·dol′a·try** /-ətrē/ *n.* [rel. to IDOL + Gk *latreia* worship]

i·dol·ize /īd′əlīz′/ *v.* (**·ized, ·iz·ing**) **1** venerate or love excessively **2** make an idol of —**i·dol·i·za′tion** *n.*

IDP *abbr.* **1** integrated data processing **2** International Driving Permit

i·dyll /īd′l/ *n.* **1** short description, esp. in verse, of a peaceful pastoral scene or incident **2** such a peaceful scene, interlude, etc. —**i·dyl′lic** /-dil′ik/ *adj.*; **i·dyl′li·cal·ly** *adv.* [Gk *eidyllion*]

IE *abbr.* **1** Indo-European **2** industrial engineer(ing)

-ie *suffix* see -Y²

i.e. *abbr.* that is to say [L *id est*]

if /if/ *conj.* **1** introducing a conditional clause: **a** on the condition or supposition that; in the event that (*if he comes I will tell him*) **b** (with *past* tense) implying that the condition is not

fulfilled (*if I knew I would say*) 2 even though (*I'll finish it, if it takes me all day*) 3 whenever (*if I am not sure I ask*) 4 whether (*see if you can find it*) 5 expressing a wish, surprise, or request (*if only I had known!*) —*n.* 6 uncertainty (*too many ifs about it*) [OE]

if·fy /if'ē/ *adj.* (**·fi·er, ·fi·est**) *Colloq.* uncertain; dubious

IGLOO

ig·loo /ig'lōō/ *n.* Inuit dome-shaped dwelling, esp. of snow [Esk: house]

Ig·na·tius of Loy·o·la, St. /igna͞'SHəs, loiō'lə/ 1491–1556; Spanish ecclesiastic; founder of Jesuit religious order

ig·ne·ous /ig'nēəs/ *adj.* 1 of fire; fiery 2 (esp. of rocks) volcanic [L *ignis* fire]

ig·nite /ignīt'/ *v.* (**·nit·ed, ·nit·ing**) 1 set fire to 2 catch fire 3 provoke or excite (feelings, etc.) [L *ignitus* fr. *ignire* set on fire]

ig·ni·tion /igniSH'ən/ *n.* 1 mechanism for or action of starting an internal-combustion engine 2 igniting or being ignited

ig·no·ble /ignō'bəl/ *adj.* (**·bler, ·blest**) 1 dishonorable 2 of low birth, position, or reputation —**ig·no'bly** *adv.* [L, rel. to IN⁻¹ + NOBLE]

ig·no·min·i·ous /ig'nəmin'ēəs/ *adj.* shameful; humiliating —**ig'no·min'i·ous·ly** *adv.* [L, rel. to IGNOMINY]

ig·no·mi·ny /ig'nəmin'ē/ *n.* dishonor [L, rel. to IN⁻¹ + *nomen* name]

ig·no·ra·mus /ig'nərā'məs/ *n.* (*pl.* **·mus·es**) ignorant person [L: we do not know]

ig·no·rance /ig'nərəns/ *n.* lack of knowledge —**ig'no·rant** *adj.*; **ig'no·rant·ly** *adv.* [Fr fr. L, rel. to IGNORE]

ig·nore /ignôr'/ *v.* (**·nored, ·nor·ing**) refuse to take notice of; intentionally disregard [L *ignorare* not know]

i·gua·na /igwä'nə/ *n.* tropical American lizard with a dorsal crest [Sp fr. Carib *iwana*]

I·guas·sú Falls /ē'gwäsōō'/ *n.* waterfall 210 ft. high on the Iguassú River on the Argentina-Brazil boundary

Ikh·na·ton /iknä'tən/ see AMENHOTEP, 4

IL postal abbr. for Illinois

il- *prefix* var. of IN⁻¹ or IN⁻² before words beginning with *l*

ilk /ilk/ *n. Colloq.* sort, family, class, etc. [OE]

ill /il/ *adj.* (**worse, worst**) 1 not in good health; unwell 2 unfavorable; bad (*ill fortune*) 3 harmful (*ill effects*) 4 hostile; unkind (*ill feeling*) —*adv.* (**worse, worst**) 5 badly; wrongly 6 scarcely (*can ill afford it*) 7 unfavorably (*spoke ill of them*) —*n.* 8 injury; harm 9 evil 10 ill at ease embarrassed; uneasy [ON]

ill. *abbr.* 1 illustrated 2 illustration 3 illustrator

Ill. abbr. for Illinois

I'll /īl/ *v. contr.* I shall; I will

---

279   **iffy / ILO**

ill-ad·vised /il'advīzd'/ *adj.* foolish; imprudent

ill'-bred' *adj.* badly brought up; rude

il·le·gal /ilē'gəl/ *adj.* 1 not legal 2 criminal —**il'le·gal'i·ty** /-gal'itē/ *n.* (*pl.* **·ties**); **il·le'gal·ly** *adv.*

il·leg·i·ble /ilej'əbəl/ *adj.* not legible —**il·leg'i·bil'i·ty** *n.*; **il·leg'i·bly** *adv.*

il·le·git·i·mate /il'əjit'əmət/ *adj.* 1 born of parents not married to each other 2 unlawful 3 inauthentic —**il'le·git'i·ma·cy** /-məsē/ *n.*; **il'le·git'i·mate·ly** *adv.*

ill-fat·ed /il fāt'əd/ *adj.* destined to or bringing bad fortune

ill'-fa'vored *adj.* unattractive

ill'-got'ten *adj.* gained unlawfully or wickedly

ill' hu'mor *n.* irritability

il·lib·er·al /il(l)ib'ərəl/ *adj.* 1 intolerant; narrow-minded 2 vulgar 3 stingy; mean —**il·lib'er·al'i·ty** /-al'ətē/ *n.*; **il·lib'er·al·ly** *adv.*

il·lic·it /ilis'it/ *adj.* unlawful; forbidden —**il·lic'it·ly** *adv.*; **il·lic'it·ness** *n.*

Il·li·nois /il'ənoi', -noiz'/ *n.* state in the central US. Capital: Springfield. Pop. 11,430,602. Abbr. **IL; Ill.** —**Il'li·nois'an, Il'li·noi'an** /-noi'ən/ *n.* & *adj.*

il·lit·er·ate /ilit'ərət/ *adj.* 1 unable to read 2 uneducated —*n.* 3 illiterate person —**il·lit'er·a·cy** /-əsē/ *n.*; **il·lit'er·ate·ly** *adv.*

ill'-man'nered *adj.* having bad manners; rude

ill·ness /il'nəs/ *n.* 1 disease 2 being ill

il·log·i·cal /iläj'ikəl/ *adj.* devoid of or contrary to logic —**il·log'i·cal·i·ty** /iläj'ikal'ətē/ *n.* (*pl.* **·ties**); **il·log'i·cal·ly** *adv.*

ill-starred /il'stärd'/ *adj.* ill-fated; doomed; unlucky

ill'-tem'pered *adj.* morose; irritable

ill'-timed' *adj.* done or occurring at an inappropriate time

ill'-treat' *v.* treat unkindly; abuse

il·lu·mi·nate /ilōō'mənāt'/ *v.* (**·nat·ed, ·nat·ing**) 1 light up; make bright 2 decorate with lights 3 decorate (a manuscript, etc.) with gold, color, etc. 4 help to explain 5 enlighten spiritually or intellectually —**il·lu'mi·nat'ing** *adj.*; **il·lu'mi·na'tion** *n.* [L *lumen* light]

il·lu·mine /ilōō'min/ *v.* (**·mined, ·min·ing**) 1 light up; make bright 2 enlighten

ill'-use' *v.* (**·used, ·us·ing**) ILL-TREAT

il·lu·sion /ilōō'ZHən/ *n.* 1 false impression or belief 2 state of being deceived by appearances 3 figment of the imagination —**il·lu'sive** /-siv/, **il·lu'so·ry** *adj.* [L *illudere* mock]

il·lu'sion·ist *n.* magician

il·lus·trate /il'əstrāt'/ *v.* (**·trat·ed, ·trat·ing**) 1a provide (a book, etc.) with pictures b elucidate by drawings, pictures, examples, etc. 2 serve as an example of —**il'lus·tra'tor** *n.* [L *lustrare* light up]

il'lus·tra'tion *n.* 1 drawing or picture in a book, magazine, etc. 2 explanatory example 3 illustrating

il·lus·tra·tive /iləs'trətiv/ *adj.* explanatory; exemplary

il·lus·tri·ous /iləs'trēəs/ *adj.* distinguished; renowned [L *illustris*, rel. to ILLUSTRATE]

ill' will' *n.* bad feeling; animosity

ILO *abbr.* International Labor Organization

I'm /īm/ *v. contr.* I am

im- *prefix* var. of IN-[1] or IN-[2] before *b*, *m*, or *p*

im·age /im'ij/ *n.* 1 representation of an object, e.g., a statue 2 reputation or public perception of a person, company, etc. 3 appearance in a mirror, through a lens, etc. 4 mental picture or idea 5 simile or metaphor —*v.* (·aged, ·ag·ing) 6 make an image of; portray 7 reflect; mirror 8 imagine vividly 9 **be the image of** be or look exactly like [L *imago*]

im·age·ry /im'ijrē/ *n.* 1 figurative illustration, esp. in literature 2 images; statuary 3 mental images collectively

i·mag·i·nar·y /imaj'əner'ē/ *adj.* 1 existing only in the imagination 2 *Math.* being the square root of a negative quantity [L, rel. to IMAGE]

● Usage: *Imaginary* means 'make-believe; unreal'; *imaginative* means 'creative; original.' Science fiction, which deals with imaginary people, places, and events, may, in another sense, be imaginative also; ghosts are imaginary (unless you believe them to be real), but are not necessarily imaginative.

i·mag·i·na·tion /imaj'ənā'sHən/ *n.* 1 mental faculty of forming images or concepts of objects or situations not existent or not directly experienced 2 mental creativity or resourcefulness

i·mag·i·na·tive /imaj'ənətiv/ *adj.* having or showing imagination —**i·mag'i·na·tive·ly** *adv.*; **i·mag'i·na·tive·ness** *n.*

● Usage: See note at IMAGINARY.

i·mag·ine /imaj'ən/ *v.* (·ined, ·in·ing) 1a form a mental image or concept of **b** picture to oneself 2 think as probable 3 guess 4 suppose —**i·mag'in·a·ble** *adj.* [L *imaginari*]

i·ma·go /imā'gō/ *n.* (*pl.* ·goes, ·gi·nes /-gənēz'/) adult insect

i·mam /imäm'/ *n.* 1 leader of prayers in a mosque 2 title of various Islamic leaders [Ar]

im·bal·ance /imbal'əns/ *n.* 1 lack of balance 2 disproportion

im·be·cile /im'bəsəl, -sil'/ *n.* stupid person —**im'be·cil'ic** *adj.*; **im'be·cil'i·ty** *n.* (*pl.* ·ties) [Fr fr. L]

im·bed /imbed'/ *v.* var. of EMBED

im·bibe /imbīb'/ *v.* (·bibed, ·bib·ing) 1 drink (esp. alcohol) 2 assimilate (ideas, etc.) [L *bibere* drink]

im·bro·glio /imbrōl'yō/ *n.* (*pl.* ·glios) confused or complicated situation or misunderstanding [It, rel. to IN-[2] + BROIL]

im·bue /imbyōō'/ *v.* (·bued, ·bu·ing) 1 inspire or permeate (with feelings, opinions, or qualities) 2 saturate 3 dye [L *imbuere*]

IMF *abbr.* International Monetary Fund

im·i·tate /im'ətāt'/ *v.* (·tat·ed, ·tat·ing) 1 follow the example of; copy 2 mimic 3 make a copy of 4 be like —**im'i·ta·ble** *adj.*; **im'i·ta'tor** *n.* [L *imitatus* fr. *imitari* copy]

im'i·ta'tion *n.* 1 imitating or being imitated 2 copy 3 counterfeit

im·i·ta·tive /im'ətā'tiv/ *adj.* imitating; following a model or example

im·mac·u·late /imak'yələt/ *adj.* 1 perfectly clean and tidy 2 perfect 3 innocent; faultless —**im·mac'u·late·ly** *adv.*; **im·mac'u·late·ness** *n.* [L, rel. to IN-[1] + *macula* spot]

Im·mac'u·late Con·cep'tion *n. RC Ch.* doc-

trine that the Virgin Mary was without original sin when she was conceived

im·ma·nent /im'ənənt/ *adj.* 1 naturally present; inherent 2 (of God) omnipresent —**im'ma·nence** *n.* [L, rel. to IN-[2] + *manere* remain]

● Usage: See note at EMINENT.

im·ma·te·ri·al /im'ətēr'ēəl/ *adj.* 1 unimportant; irrelevant 2 incorporeal —**im'ma·te·ri·al'i·ty** /-al'ətē/ *n.*

im·ma·ture /im'ət(y)ŏŏr', -əCHŏŏr'/ *adj.* 1 not mature 2 undeveloped, esp. emotionally 3 unripe —**im'ma·ture'ly** *adv.*; **im'ma·tu'ri·ty** *n.*

im·meas·ur·a·ble /imezH'(ə)rəbəl/ *adj.* not measurable; immense —**im·meas'ur·a·bly** *adv.*

im·me·di·ate /imē'dēət/ *adj.* 1 occurring or done at once 2 nearest; next; direct 3 most pressing or urgent (*our immediate concern*) —**im·me'di·a·cy** /-əsē/ *n.*; **im·me'di·ate·ly** *adv.*; **im·me'di·ate·ness** *n.* [L, rel. to IN-[1] + MEDIATE]

im·me·mo·ri·al /im'məmôr'ēəl/ *adj.* beyond memory or record

im·mense /imens'/ *adj.* 1 huge 2 considerable (*immense difference*) —**im·mense'ly** *adv.*; **im·mense'ness, im·men'si·ty** *n.* [L, rel. to IN-[1] + *mensus* fr. *metiri* measure]

im·merse /imərs'/ *v.* (·mersed, ·mers·ing) 1a dip; plunge **b** submerge (a person) 2 absorb or involve deeply (in) —**im·mer·sion** /-zHən/ *n.* [L, rel. to IN-[2] + *mergere* dip]

im·mi·grant /im'əgrənt/ *n.* 1 person who immigrates —*adj.* 2 immigrating 3 of immigrants

im·mi·grate /im'əgrāt'/ *v.* come into a country and settle —**im'mi·gra'tion** *n.* [rel. to IN-[2] + MIGRATE]

● Usage: See note at EMIGRATE.

im·mi·nent /im'ənənt/ *adj.* impending; about to happen —**im'mi·nence** *n.*; **im'mi·nent·ly** *adv.* [L *imminere* be impending]

● Usage: See note at EMINENT.

im·mo·bile /imō'bəl, -bēl', -bīl'/ *adj.* 1 not moving 2 unable to move or be moved —**im'mo·bil'i·ty** /-bil'ətē/ *n.*

im·mo·bi·lize /imō'bəlīz'/ *v.* (·lized, ·liz·ing) 1 make or keep immobile 2 keep (a patient or limb) still for healing purposes —**im·mo'bi·li·za'tion** *n.*

im·mod·er·ate /imäd'ərət/ *adj.* excessive; lacking moderation —**im·mod'er·ate·ly** *adv.*

im·mod·est /imäd'ist/ *adj.* 1 lacking modesty; conceited 2 shameless; indecent —**im·mod'est·ly** *adv.*; **im·mod'es·ty** *n.*

im·mo·late /im'əlāt'/ *v.* (·lat·ed, ·lat·ing) kill or offer as a sacrifice —**im'mo·la'tion** *n.* [L: sprinkle with meal]

im·mor·al /imôr'əl, imär'-/ *adj.* 1 not conforming to accepted morality 2 sexually promiscuous or deviant —**im·mo·ral'i·ty** /im'ôral'ətē/ *n.* (*pl.* ·ties); **im·mor'al·ly** *adv.*

● Usage: *Immoral* means 'lacking moral standards'; *amoral* means 'unrelated to morals.' An *immoral* person commits acts that violate moral principles and standards; but *amoral* describes a person who has no sense or knowledge of right and wrong.

im·mor·tal /imôrt'l/ *adj.* 1a living forever **b** divine 2 lasting 3 famous for all time —*n.* 4a immortal being **b** (*pl.*) gods of antiquity 5 great person remembered long after death

—im·mor·tal·i·ty /im'ôrtal'ətē/ n.; im·mor'tal·ize v. (·ized, ·iz·ing); im·mor'tal·ly adv.

im·mov·a·ble /imoo'vəbəl/ adj. 1 not able to be moved 2 steadfast; unyielding —im·mov'a·bil'i·ty n.; im·mov'a·bly adv.

im·mune /imyoon'/ adj. 1a protected against infection through inoculation, etc. b relating to immunity 2 exempt from [L immunis exempt]

im·mu·ni·ty /imyoo'nətē/ n. (pl. ·ties) 1 ability of an organism to resist infection by means of antibodies and white blood cells 2 freedom; exemption

im·mu·nize /im'yənīz'/ v. (·nized, ·niz·ing) make immune, usu. by inoculation —im'mu·ni·za'tion n.

im·mu·nol·o·gy /im'yənäl'əjē/ n. the study of immunity —im'mu·no·log'i·cal /-näläj'əkəl/ adj.; im'mu·nol'o·gist n.

im·mure /imyoor'/ v. (·mured, ·mur·ing) confine within walls [L murus wall]

im·mu·ta·ble /imyoo'təbəl/ adj. unchangeable —im·mu'ta·bil'i·ty n.; im·mu'ta·bly adv.

imp /imp/ n. 1 mischievous child 2 small devil or sprite [OE: young shoot]

im·pact /im'pakt'/ n. 1 forceful contact; collision 2 strong effect or impression —v. /impakt'/ 3 press or fix firmly 4 (of a tooth) wedge between another tooth and the jaw 5 have an impact on —im·pac'tion /-pak'SHən/ n. [L, rel. to IMPINGE]

im·pair /imper'/ v. damage; weaken —im·pair'ment n. [L in- (intensive) + pejor worse]

im·pa·la /impal'ə, -pä'lə/ n. (pl. same or ·las) small African antelope [Zulu]

im·pale /impāl'/ v. (·paled, ·pal·ing) transfix or pierce with a sharp stake, etc. —im·pale'ment n. [L palus PALE²]

im·pal·pa·ble /impal'pəbəl/ adj. 1 not easily grasped by the mind; intangible 2 imperceptible to the touch —im·pal'pa·bil'i·ty n.; im·pal'pa·bly adv.

IMPALA

im·pan·el /impan'l/ (also empanel) v. (·eled or ·elled, ·el·ing or ·el·ling) Law. officially establish (a jury)

im·part /impärt'/ v. 1 communicate (news, etc.) 2 give a share of (a thing) [L, rel. to PART]

im·par·tial /impär'SHəl/ adj. unprejudiced; fair —im·par'ti·al'i·ty /-pär'SHē-al'ətē/ n.; im·par'tial·ly adv.

im·pass·a·ble /impas'əbəl/ adj. not able to be traversed —im·pass'a·bil'i·ty, im·pass'a·ble·ness n.; im·pass'a·bly adv.

im·passe /im'pas', impas'/ n. deadlock [Fr, rel. to PASS¹]

im·pas·si·ble /impas'əbəl/ adj. incapable of feeling, emotion, or injury —im·pas'si·bil'i·ty n.; im·pas'si·bly adv. [LL impassibilis, rel. to PASSION]

im·pas·sioned /impasH'ənd/ adj. filled with passion; ardent [It impassionato, rel. to PASSION]

im·pas·sive /impas'iv/ adj. incapable of or not showing emotion; serene —im·pas'

sive·ly adv.; im·pas'sive·ness, im·pas·siv'i·ty /-siv'ətē/ n.

im·pas·to /impas'tō, -päs'-/ n. Art. technique of laying on paint thickly [It]

im·pa·tient /impā'SHənt/ adj. 1 lacking or showing a lack of patience or tolerance 2 restlessly eager —im·pa'tience n.; im·pa'tient·ly adv.

im·peach /impēCH'/ v. 1 charge (a public official) with misconduct 2 call in question; disparage —im·peach'a·ble adj.; im·peach'ment n. [Fr empecher fr. L pedica fetter]

im·pec·ca·ble /impek'əbəl/ adj. faultless; exemplary —im·pec'ca·bil'i·ty n.; im·pec'ca·bly adv. [rel. to IN-¹ + L peccare sin]

im·pe·cu·ni·ous /im'pikyoo'nēəs/ adj. having little or no money —im·pe·cu'ni·os'i·ty /-kyoo'nē-äs'ətē/, im'pe·cu'ni·ous·ness n. [rel. to PECUNIARY]

im·ped·ance /impēd'ns/ n. Electr. total effective resistance of a circuit, etc., to an alternating current [fr. IMPEDE]

im·pede /impēd'/ v. (·ped·ed, ·ped·ing) obstruct; hinder [L impedire fr. pes pedis foot]

im·ped·i·ment /imped'əmənt/ n. 1 hindrance; obstruction 2 speech defect [L, rel. to IMPEDE]

im·ped·i·men·ta /imped'əmen'tə/ n. pl. 1 encumbrances 2 baggage, esp. of an army

im·pel /impel'/ v. (·pelled, ·pel·ing) 1 drive; force; urge 2 propel [L pellere drive]

im·pend /impend'/ v. 1 (of a danger, event, etc.) be threatening or imminent 2 hang —im·pend'ing adj. [L pendere hang]

im·pen·e·tra·ble /impen'ətrəbəl/ adj. 1 not able to be penetrated 2 inscrutable 3 inaccessible to ideas, influences, etc. —im·pen'e·tra·bil'i·ty, im·pen'e·tra·ble·ness n.; im'pen'e·tra·bly adv.

im·pen·i·tent /impen'ətənt/ adj. not sorry; unrepentant —im·pen'i·tence n.

im·per·a·tive /imper'ətiv/ adj. 1 urgent; obligatory 2 commanding; peremptory 3 Gram. (of a mood) expressing a command (e.g., come here!) —n. 4 Gram. imperative mood 5 command [L imperare command]

im·per·cep·ti·ble /im'pərsep'təbəl/ adj. 1 not perceptible 2 very slight, gradual, or subtle —im'per·cep'ti·bil'i·ty n.; im'per·cep'ti·bly adv.

im·per·fect /impər'fikt/ adj. 1 faulty; incomplete 2 Gram. (of a tense) denoting action in progress but not completed (e.g., they were singing) —n. 3 imperfect tense —im·per'fect·ly adv.

im·per·fec·tion /im'pərfek'SHən/ n. 1 state of being imperfect 2 fault; blemish

im·pe·ri·al /impēr'ēəl/ adj. 1 of or characteristic of an empire or similar sovereign government 2a of an emperor b authoritative —im·pe'ri·al·ly adv. [L imperium dominion]

im·pe'ri·al gal'lon n. British gallon, equivalent to 1-1/5 US gallons

im·pe·ri·al·ism /impēr'ēəliz'əm/ n. 1 imperial rule or system 2 usu. Derog. policy of dominion over colonies, weaker nations, etc. —im·pe'ri·al·ist /-ist/ n. & adj.; im·pe'ri·al·is'tic adj.

Im·pe'ri·al Val'ley n. valley in the Colorado Desert in S central Calif.

im·per·il /imper'əl/ v. (-iled or -illed, -il·ing or -il·ling) endanger

im·pe·ri·ous /impēr'ēəs/ adj. overbearing; domineering —**im·pe'ri·ous·ly** adv.; **im·pe'ri·ous·ness** n.

im·per·ish·a·ble /imper'ishəbəl/ adj. indestructible

im·per·ma·nent /impər'mənənt/ adj. not permanent —**im·per'ma·nence, im·per'ma·nen·cy** n.

im·per·me·a·ble /impər'mēəbəl/ adj. not allowing fluids to pass through —**im·per'me·a·bil'i·ty** n.

im·per·mis·si·ble /im'pərmis'əbəl/ adj. not allowable

im·per·son·al /impər'sənəl/ adj. 1 objective; impartial 2 cold; unfeeling 3 Gram. a (of a verb) used esp. with it as a subject (it is snowing) b (of a pronoun) INDEFINITE —**im·per'son·al·ly** adv.

im·per·son·ate /impər'sənāt/ v. (-at·ed, ·at·ing) pretend to be (another person) —**im·per'son·a'tion, im·per'son·a'tor** n. [fr. IN-², L persona]

im·per·ti·nent /impərt'n·ənt/ adj. insolent; disrespectful —**im·per'ti·nence** n.; **im·per'ti·nent·ly** adv.

im·per·turb·a·ble /im'pərtər'bəbəl/ adj. not excitable; calm —**im·per·turb'a·bil'i·ty** n.; **im'per·turb'a·bly** adv.

im·per·vi·ous /impər'vēəs/ adj. 1 impenetrable 2 not responsive (to argument, etc.)

im·pe·ti·go /impeti'gō/ n. contagious skin infection forming pustules [L impetere assail]

im·pet·u·ous /impech'ōōəs/ adj. acting or done rashly or suddenly —**im·pet·u·os·i·ty** /-äs'ətē/ n.; **im·pet'u·ous·ly** adv.; **im·pet'u·ous·ness** n. [L, rel. to IMPETUS]

im·pe·tus /im'pətəs/ n. 1 force with which a body moves 2 driving force or impulse [L impetere assail]

im·pi·e·ty /impī'ətē/ n. (pl. ·ties) 1 lack of piety or reverence 2 act of disrespect

im·pinge /impinj'/ v. (·pinged, ·ping·ing) 1 make an impact or effect 2 encroach —**im·pinge'ment** n. [MedL impingere strike against]

im·pi·ous /im'pēəs, impī'əs/ adj. 1 not pious 2 wicked; profane —**im'pi·ous·ly** adv.; **im'pi·ous·ness** n.

imp·ish /im'pish/ adj. of or like an imp; mischievous —**imp'ish·ly** adv.; **imp'ish·ness** n.

im·pla·ca·ble /implak'əbəl/ adj. unable to be appeased —**im·pla'ca·bil'i·ty** n.; **im·plac'a·bly** adv.

im·plant v. /implant'/ 1 insert; fix 2 instill (an idea, etc.) in a person's mind 3 plant 4a insert (tissue, etc.) in a living body b (of a fertilized ovum) become attached to the womb's wall —n. /im'plant/ 5 thing implanted —**im·plan·ta'tion** n. [IM- + PLANT]

im·plau·si·ble /implô'zəbəl/ adj. not plausible —**im·plau'si·bil'i·ty** n.; **im·plau'si·bly** adv.

im·ple·ment n. /im'pləmənt/ 1 tool; instrument; utensil —v. /·ment/ 2 put (a plan, contract, etc.) into effect —**im'ple·men·ta'tion** n. [L implere fill up]

im·pli·cate /im'plikāt/ v. (·cat·ed, ·cat-

ing) show (a person) to be involved (in a crime, etc.) [L implicare interweave]

im·pli·ca·tion n. 1 thing implied 2 act of implicating or implying

im·plic·it /implis'it/ adj. 1 implied though not plainly expressed 2 absolute; unquestioning —**im·plic'it·ly** adv. [L, rel. to IMPLICATE]

im·plode /implōd'/ v. (·plod·ed, ·plod·ing) (cause to) burst inwards —**im·plo'sion** /-plō'zhən/ n. [fr. IN-²; cf. EXPLODE]

im·plore /implôr'/ v. (·plored, ·plor·ing) 1 entreat (a person) 2 beg earnestly for [L implorare entreat]

im·ply /implī'/ v. (·plied, ·ply·ing) 1 suggest indirectly or insinuate 2 signify, esp. as a consequence [L, rel. to IMPLICATE]

• Usage: See note at INFER.

im·po·lite /im'pəlīt'/ adj. not courteous; rude —**im'po·lite'ly** adv.; **im·po·lite'ness** n.

im·pol·i·tic /impäl'ətik/ adj. inexpedient; unwise

im·pon·der·a·ble /impän'dərəbəl/ adj. 1 not able to be estimated —n. 2 imponderable thing —**im·pon'der·a·bil'i·ty** n.; **im·pon'der·a·bly** adv.

im·port v. /impôrt', im'pôrt/ 1 bring in (goods) to a country 2 indicate; signify —n. /im'pôrt/ 3 (esp. pl.) imported article 4 meaning 5 importance —**im·por·ta'tion** /-tä'shən/, **im·port'er** n. [L importare carry in; signify]

im·por·tant /impôrt'nt, -pôr'tənt/ adj. 1 of great effect or consequence; momentous 2 having high rank or authority —**im·por'tance** n.; **im·por'tant·ly** adv.

im·por·tu·nate /impôr'chənət/ adj. making persistent requests —**im·por·tu·ni·ty** /im'pərt(y)ōō'nətē/ n. [L importunus inconvenient]

im·por·tune /im'pərt(y)ōōn'/ v. (·tuned, ·tun·ing) pester with requests

im·pose /impōz'/ v. (·posed, ·pos·ing) 1 lay (a tax, duty, charge, or obligation) on or upon 2 place a burden (on a person) —**im·po·si'tion** /-pəzish'ən/ n. [L imponere place in]

im·pos·ing adj. impressive; formidable, esp. in appearance

im·pos·si·ble /impäs'əbəl/ adj. 1 not possible 2 Colloq. not easy, convenient, or believable 3 Colloq. (esp. of a person) outrageous; intolerable —**im·pos'si·bil'i·ty** n. (pl. ·ties); **im·pos'si·bly** adv.

im·post /im'pōst/ n. tax; duty; tribute [L imponere, impost- impose]

im·pos·tor /impäs'tər/ n. (also **im·pos'ter**) 1 person who pretends to be someone else 2 swindler

im·pos·ture /impäs'chər/ n. fraudulent deception

im·po·tent /im'pətənt/ adj. 1 powerless; ineffective 2 (of a male) unable to achieve an erection or orgasm —**im'po·tence** n.

im·pound /impound'/ v. 1 take legal possession of 2 shut up (animals) in a pound

im·pov·er·ish /impäv'(ə)rish/ v. make poor —**im·pov'er·ish·ment** n. [Fr, ult. fr. L in + pauper poor]

im·prac·ti·ca·ble /imprak'tikəbəl/ adj. not able to be put into practice —**im·prac'ti·ca·bly** adv.

im·prac·ti·cal /imprak'tikəl/ adj. 1 not prac-

283

im·pre·ca·tion /im'prĭkā'shən/ n. *Formal.* oath; curse [L *imprecari* pray to]

im·pre·cise /im'prĭsīs'/ adj. not precise —im'pre·cise'ly adv.; im'pre·cise'ness, im'pre·ci'sion /-siзн'ən/ n.

im·preg·na·ble /impreg'nəbəl/ adj. strong enough to be secure against attack —im·preg·na·bil'i·ty n.; im·preg'na·bly adv. [Fr fr. L *prehendere* lay hold of; gain]

im·preg·nate /impreg'nāt'/ v. (·nat·ed, ·nat·ing) 1 fill or saturate (with) 2 imbue (with feelings, etc.) 3a make (a female) pregnant b fertilize (an ovum) —im'preg·na'tion n. [LL *impraegnare*, fr. L *praegnatis* pregnant]

im·pre·sa·ri·o /im'prĭsä're·ō/ n. (*pl.* -os) organizer of public entertainment, esp. a theatrical, etc., manager [It]

im·press v. /imprĕs'/ 1a affect or influence deeply b affect (a person) favorably (*was most impressed*) 2 emphasize (an idea, etc.) (*impress on you the need to be prompt*) 3a imprint or make (a mark) on b mark (a thing) with a stamp, seal, etc. —n. /im'prĕs'/ 4 mark made by a seal, stamp, etc. 5 characteristic mark or quality —im·press'i·ble adj. [L *impressus* fr. *imprimere* press upon]

im·pres·sion /imprĕsH'ən/ n. 1 effect (esp. on the mind or feelings) 2 vague notion or belief 3 imitation of a person or sound, esp. as entertainment 4 imprint or mark impressed 5 act or instance of impressing

im·pres·sion·a·ble /imprĕsH'ənəbəl/ adj. easily influenced

im·pres·sion·ism /imprĕsH'əniz'əm/ n. style or movement in art, music, etc., that seeks to convey a brief impression or emotion without close, realistic detail —im·pres'sion·ist /-ist/ n.; im·pres'sion·is'tic adj.

im·pres·sive /imprĕs'iv/ adj. arousing respect, approval, or admiration —im·pres'sive·ly adv.; im·pres'sive·ness n.

im·pri·ma·tur /im'prĭmä'tŏŏr'/ n. 1 RC Ch. permission to print (a religious book, etc.) 2 official approval [L: let it be printed]

im·print v. /imprint'/ 1 mark or stamp as by pressing —n. /im'print'/ 2 impression; stamp 3 printer's or publisher's name, etc., printed in a book

im·pris·on /impriz'ən/ v. 1 put in prison 2 confine —im·pris'on·ment n.

im·prob·a·ble /impräb'əbəl/ adj. 1 unlikely 2 difficult to believe —im·prob·a·bil'i·ty n.; im·prob'a·bly adv.

im·promp·tu /imprämp't(y)ŏŏ/ adj. & adv. 1 extemporaneous; unrehearsed —n. (*pl.* ·tus) 2 extemporaneous performance [Fr fr. L *in promptu* in readiness]

im·prop·er /impräp'ər/ adj. 1 unseemly; indecent 2 incorrect —im·prop'er·ly adv.

im·pro·pri·e·ty /im'prəprī'ətē/ n. (*pl.* ·ties) 1 indecency 2 instance of this 3 incorrectness

im·prove /improov'/ v. (·proved, ·prov·ing) 1 make or become better 2 develop, e.g., real estate —im·prov'a·ble adj.; im·prove'ment n. [AngFr *en-* in + *prou* profit]

im·prov·i·dent /impräv'ədənt/ adj. 1 lacking foresight 2 wasteful —im·prov'i·dence n.; im·prov'i·dent·ly adv.

im·pro·vise /im'prəvīz'/ v. (·vised, ·vis·ing) 1 compose or perform (music, verse, etc.) without preparation 2 make or use materials not intended for the purpose —im·prov'i·sa'tion n.; im·prov'i·sa'tion·al adj. [L *improvisus* unforeseen]

im·pru·dent /improod'nt/ adj. unwise; indiscreet —im·pru'dence n.; im·pru'dent·ly adv.

im·pu·dent /im'pyədənt/ adj. impertinent —im'pu·dence n.; im'pu·dent·ly adv. [L in not + *pudere* be ashamed]

im·pugn /impyoon'/ v. challenge as false; call into question —im·pugn'ment n. [L *impugnare* attack]

im·pulse /im'pəls'/ n. 1 sudden urge to act 2 tendency to follow such urges (*man of impulse*) 3 impelling; a push 4 impetus 5 surge in electrical current or flow [L *impulsus*]

im·pul·sion /impəl'shən/ n. 1 impelling 2 mental impulse 3 impetus

im·pul·sive /impəl'siv/ adj. 1 tending to act on impulse 2 done on impulse 3 tending to impel —im·pul'sive·ly adv.; im·pul'sive·ness n.

im·pu·ni·ty /impyoo'nitē/ n. 1 exemption from punishment, bad consequences, etc. 2 **with impunity** without punishment, etc. [L *in* not + *punire* punish]

im·pure /impyoor'/ adj. 1 adulterated 2 dirty 3 unchaste

im·pu·ri·ty /impyoor'itē/ n. (*pl.* ·ties) 1 being impure 2 impure thing or part

im·pute /impyoot'/ v. (·put·ed, ·put·ing) attribute (a fault, etc.) to —im·pu·ta'tion n. [L *imputare* reckon]

in /in, ən, n/ *prep.* 1 expressing inclusion or position within limits of space, time, circumstance, etc. (*in England; in bed; in 1998; in the rain*) 2a within (a certain time) (*finished it in two hours*) b after (a certain time) (*leaving in an hour*) 3 with respect to (*blind in one eye*) 4 as a proportionate part of (*one in three failed*) 5 with the form or arrangement of (*packed in tens; falling in folds*) 6 as a member of (*in the army*) 7 involved with (*is in banking*) 8 as the content of (*there is something in what you say*) 9 within the ability of (*does he have it in him?*) 10 having the condition of; affected by (*in bad health; in danger*) 11 having as a purpose (*in reply to*) 12 by means of or using as material (*drawn in pencil*) 13 using for expression (*written in French*) 14 (of a word) having as a part (*words in un-*) 15 wearing (*dressed in blue*) 16 with the identity of (*found a friend in Mary*) 17 into (with a verb of motion or change: *put it in the box; cut it in two*) —adv. expressing position within limits, or motion to such a position: 18 into a room, house, etc. (*come in*) 19 to or at a place (*she is not in*) 20 so as to be enclosed or included (*locked in; is our story in?*) 21 in or to the inward side (*rub it in*) 22 in fashion or season (*long skirts are in*) 23 (of a season, harvest, order, etc.) having arrived or been received 24 (of the tide) at the highest point (*in is in*) 25 internal; inside 26 fashionable (*the in thing to do*) 27 confined to a small group (*in-joke*) 28 **have it in for** *Colloq.* hold a grudge against 29 **in**

on sharing in; privy to **30 ins and outs** all the details 31 in that because; insofar as 32 in with associated with [OE]

In *symb.* indium

IN postal abbr. for Indiana

in-[1] *prefix* (also **il-, im-, ir-**) added to: **1** adjectives, meaning 'not' (*inedible; insane*) **2** nouns, meaning 'without; lacking' (*inaction*) [L]

in-[2] *prefix* (also **il-, im-, ir-**) in; on; into; toward; within (*induce; influx; insight; intrude*) [fr. IN, or fr. L *in* (prep.)]

in. *abbr.* inch(es)

in ab·sen·tia /in' absen'SH(ē)ə/ *adv.* Latin (in his, her, or their) absence

in·ad·ver·tent /in'ədver'nt/ *adj.* **1** unintentional **2** negligent —**in'ad·ver'tence** *n.*; **in'ad·ver'tent·ly** *adv.*

in·a·lien·a·ble /ināl'yənəbəl/ *adj.* that cannot be transferred or taken away (*inalienable rights*)

in·am·o·ra·to /inam'ərät'ō/ *n.* (*pl.* **-tos;** *fem.* **-ta** /-tə/, *pl.* **-tas**) *Lit.* lover [It]

in·ane /inān'/ *adj.* **1** silly; senseless **2** empty; void —**in·ane'ly** *adv.*; **in·an·i·ty** /inan'ətē/ *n.* (*pl.* **-ties**) [L *inanis*]

in·ar·tic·u·late /in'ärtik'yələt/ *adj.* **1** unable to express oneself clearly **2** (of speech) indistinct **3** mute —**in·ar·tic'u·late·ly** *adv.*

in·as·much as /in'əzməCH' əz'/ *adv.* **1** since; because **2** to the extent that

in·au·gu·ral /inôg'yərəl/ *adj.* **1** of or for an inauguration —*n.* **2** opening speech, lecture, etc.

in·au·gu·rate /inôg'yərāt'/ *v.* (**-rat·ed, -rat·ing**) **1** admit formally to office **2** make a beginning or commence use, esp. formally —**in·au'gu·ra'tion, in·au'gu·ra'tor** *n.* [L *inaugurare* take auguries}

in'·be·tween' *adj. Colloq.* intermediate

in·board /in'bôrd'/ *adv. & adj.* **1** within the sides or toward the center of a ship, aircraft, or vehicle —*n.* **2** boat with a motor mounted in its hull **3** such a motor

in·born /in'bôrn'/ *adj.* existing from birth; natural

in·breed·ing /in'brēd'iNG/ *n.* breeding from closely related animals or persons —**in' breed'** *v.* (**·bred, ·breed·ing**)

Inc. *abbr.* Incorporated

In·ca /iNG'kə/ *n.* member of a people of Peru before the Spanish conquest —**In'can** *adj.* [Quechua: lord]

in·cal·cu·la·ble /inkal'kyələbəl/ *adj.* **1** too many or too great for calculation **2** unpredictable —**in·cal'cu·la·bil'i·ty** *n.*; **in·cal'cu·la·bly** *adv.*

in·can·des·cent /in'kəndes'ənt/ *adj.* **1** glowing with heat **2** shining **3** (of artificial light) produced by a glowing filament, etc. —**in·can·des'cence** *n.* [L *incandescere* glow]

in·can·ta·tion /in'kan'tä'SHən/ *n.* magical spell —**in·can·ta'tion·al** *adj.* [L *incantare* put a spell on]

in·ca·pac·i·tate /in'kəpas'ətāt'/ *v.* (**·ta·ted, ·tat·ing**) make incapable or unfit

in·ca·pac·i·ty /in'kəpas'ətē/ *n.* **1** inability **2** legal disqualification

in·car·cer·ate /inkär'sərāt'/ *v.* (**·at·ed, ·at·ing**) imprison —**in·car'cer·a'tion** *n.* [MedL *in-* in + *carcer* prison]

in·car·nate *adj.* /inkär'nət, -nāt'/ **1** embodied in human form (*the devil incarnate*) —*v.* /inkär'nāt', or kär'nāt'/ (**·nat·ed, ·nat·ing**) **2** embody in flesh **3** put (an idea, etc.) into concrete form **4** be the embodiment of (a quality) [L *in-* in + *carn-* flesh]

in·car·na·tion /in'kärnā'SHən/ *n.* **1** embodiment in (esp. human) flesh **b** (*cap.*) *Christianity.* the embodiment of God in Christ **2** living type (of a quality, etc.)

in·cen·di·ar·y /insen'dēˌer'ē/ *adj.* **1** (of a bomb) designed to cause fires **2** pertaining to arson **3** inflammatory —*n.* (*pl.* **·ies**) **4** firebomb **5** arsonist —**in·cen'di·a·rism** /-ˌriz'əm/ *n.* [L *incendere* set fire to]

in·a·bil'i·ty *n.*
in·ac·ces'si·bil'i·ty *n.*
in·ac·ces'si·ble *adj.*
in·ac'cu·ra·cy *n.*
in·ac'cu·rate *adj.*
in·ac'cu·rate·ly *adv.*
in·ac'tion *n.*
in·ad'e·qua·cy *n.*
in·ad'e·quate *adj.*
in·ad'e·quate·ly *adv.*
in·ad·mis'si·ble *adj.*
in·ad·vis'a·ble *adj.*
in·an'i·mate *adj.*
in·ap'pli·ca·ble *adj.*
in·ap·pre'ci·a·tive *adj.*
in·ap·proach'a·ble *adj.*
in·ap·pro'pri·ate *adj.*
in·ap·pro'pri·ate·ly *adv.*
in·apt' *adj.*
in·ar·gu·a·ble *adj.*
in·ar·tis'tic *adj.*
in·au'di·ble *adj.*
in·au'di·bly *adv.*

in·aus·pi'cious *adj.*
in·ca'pa·ble *adj.*
in·cau'tious *adj.*
in·ci·vil'i·ty *n.*
in·com·bus'ti·ble *adj.*
in·com·men'su·rate *adj.*
in·com·mo'di·ous *adj.*
in·com·mu'ni·ca·ble *adj.*
in·com·pre·hen'si·ble *adj.*
in·con·clu'sive *adj.*
in·con·sist'en·cy *n.*
in·con·sist'ent *adj.*
in·cor·rect' *adj.*
in·cor·rect'ly *adv.*
in·cur'a·ble *adj.*
in·cur'a·bly *adv.*
in·dec'o·rous *adj.*
in·dec'o·rous·ly *adv.*
in·de·fin'a·ble *adj.*
in·de·fin'a·bly *adv.*
in·dis·cern'i·ble *adj.*
in·dis·put'a·ble *adj.*

in·dis·put'a·bly *adv.*
in·dis·tinct' *adj.*
in·dis·tinct'ly *adv.*
in·dis·tin'guish·a·ble *adj.*
in·di·vis'i·bil'i·ty *n.*
in·di·vis'i·ble *adj.*
in·di·vis'i·bly *adv.*
in·ed'i·ble *adj.*
in·ed'u·ca·ble *adj.*
in·ef·fec'tive *adj.*
in·ef·fec'tive·ly *adv.*
in·ef·fi·ca·cy *n.*
in·e·las'tic *adj.*
in·el·i·gi·bil'i·ty *n.*
in·el'i·gi·ble *adj.*
in·eq·ui·ta·ble *adj.*
in·eq·ui·ta·bly *adv.*
in·ex·act' *adj.*
in·ex·cus'a·ble *adj.*
in·ex·cus'a·bly *adv.*
in·ex·pe'di·ence *n.*
in·ex·pe'di·en·cy *n.*
in·ex·pe'di·ent *adj.*
in·ex·pen'sive *adj.*
in·ex·pen'sive·ly *adv.*

in·fer'tile *adj.*
in·fer·til'i·ty *n.*
in·har·mo'ni·ous *adj.*
in·hu·mane' *adj.*
in·ju·di'cious *adj.*
in·ju·di'cious·ly *adv.*
in·op'por·tune' *adj.*
in·op'por·tune'ly *adv.*
in·op·por·tu'ni·ty *n.*
in·sep'a·ra·ble *adj.*
in·sep'a·ra·bly *adv.*
in·sig·nif'i·cance *n.*
in·solv'a·ble *adj.*
in·suf·fi'cient *adj.*
in·suf·fi'cient·ly *adv.*
in·sur·mount'a·ble *adj.*
in·sur·mount'a·bly *adv.*
in·sus·cep'ti·ble *adj.*
in·var·i·a·bil'i·ty *n.*
in·var·i·a·ble *adj. & n.*
in·var·i·a·bly *adv.*

in·cense¹ /ˈinˈsens/ *n.* **1** gum or spice producing a sweet smell when burned **2** smoke or odor from this [ChL *incensum* something kindled, rel. to L *incendere* burn]

in·cense² /inˈsens/ *v.* (**·censed, ·cens·ing**) make angry [L *incensus* set on fire]

in·cen·tive /inˈsentˈiv/ *n.* motive or incitement to effort [L *incentivus* that sets the tune]

in·cep·tion /inˈsepˈSHən/ *n.* beginning [L *inception- fr. incipere* begin]

in·ces·sant /inˈsesˈənt/ *adj.* unceasing; continual; repeated —**in·ces'sant·ly** *adv.* [L *not + cessare* cease]

in·cest /ˈinˈsest/ *n.* sexual intercourse between persons too closely related to marry legally [L *incestus* impure]

in·ces·tu·ous /inˈsesˈCHŌōəs/ *adj.* **1** of or guilty of incest **2** having relationships restricted to a particular group or organization —**in·ces'tu·ous·ly** *adv.*

inch /inCH/ *n.* **1** measure of length equivalent to 1/12 of a foot (2.54 cm) **2** small amount (*not yield an inch*) —*v.* **3** move gradually **4** *every inch* entirely (*every inch a champion*) **5** *within an inch of* almost to the point of [OE fr. L *uncia* twelfth part]

in·cho·ate /inkōˈit/ *adj.* **1** just begun **2** undeveloped [L *inchoare* begin]

In·chon /ˈinˈCHän/ *n.* seaport in South Korea. Pop. 1,818,200

in·ci·dence /ˈinˈsədəns/ *n.* **1** range, extent, or rate of occurrence or influence **2** falling of a line, ray, particles, etc., on a surface [L *incidere* befall]

• **Usage:** *Incidence* and *incidents* sound identical, but *incidence* is more often used in technical contexts, referring to the frequency with which an event takes place: *the incidence of TB increased. Incidents* is simply the plural of *incident*, the event itself: *How many incidents of theft were reported?* The form "*incidences*" should be avoided.

in·ci·dent /ˈinˈsədənt/ *n.* **1** occurrence, esp. a minor one **2** minor conflict or disturbance —*adj.* **3** apt to occur; naturally attaching **4** (of light, etc.) falling on or upon [L *incidere* befall]

in·ci·den·tal /ˈinˈsədentˈl/ *adj.* **1** relatively unimportant; secondary **2** not essential —*n.* **3** (usu. *pl.*) minor details, expenses, etc.

in·ci·den·tal·ly /ˈinˈsədentˈlē/ *adv.* **1** by the way **2** in an incidental way

in·cin·er·ate /insinˈərātˈ/ *v.* (**·at·ed, ·at·ing**) burn to ashes —**in·cin·er·a'tion** *n.* [MedL fr. L *in-* + *ciner-* ashes]

in·cin·er·a·tor /insinˈərātˈər/ *n.* furnace for incineration

in·cip·i·ent /insipˈēənt/ *adj.* in an early stage [L *incipere* begin]

in·cise /insizˈ/ *v.* (**·cised, ·cis·ing**) **1** make a cut in **2** engrave [L *incidere* cut into]

in·ci·sion /insizHˈən/ *n.* **1** cutting, esp. by a surgeon **2** cut made in this way

in·ci·sive /insiˈsiv/ *adj.* **1** sharp **2** clear and effective

in·ci·sor /insiˈzər/ *n.* cutting tooth, esp. at the front of the mouth

in·cite /insitˈ/ *v.* (**·cit·ed, ·cit·ing**) urge or stir up —**in·cite'ment** *n.* [L *incitare* excite]

in·clem·ent /inklemˈənt/ *adj.* (of weather) severe; stormy —**in·clem'en·cy** *n.*

in·cli·na·tion /ˈinˈklināˈSHən/ *n.* **1** disposition; propensity **2** liking; affection **3** slope; slant [L, rel. to INCLINE]

in·cline *v.* /inklinˈ/ (**·clined, ·clin·ing**) **1a** make willing; influence (*inclined to think so*) **b** have a tendency **2a** be disposed (*I incline to your view*) **b** tend **3** (cause to) lean; slope —*n.* /inˈklinˈ/ **4** slope [L *inclinare* bend toward]

in·clined' plane' *n.* sloping plane used, e.g., to reduce work in raising a load

in·clude /inklōōdˈ/ *v.* (**·clud·ed, ·clud·ing**) **1** comprise or contain as a part **2** put in a certain category, etc. —**in·clu'sion** /-klōōˈzHən/ *n.* [L *includere* enclose; shut in]

in·clud'ing *prep.* if we include (*six, including me*)

in·clu·sive /inklōōˈsiv/ *adj.* **1** including all or much (*inclusive terms*) **2** including the limits stated (*pages 7 to 26 inclusive*) **3** (foll. by *of*) including —**in·clu'sive·ly** *adv.*; **in·clu'sive·ness** *n.*

in·cog·ni·to /inˈkägˈnēˈtō, inkägˈnēˈ-/ *adj. & adv.* **1** with name or identity kept secret —*n.* **2** pretended identity [It: unknown]

in·co·her·ent /ˈinˈkōhērˈənt/ *adj.* **1** unintelligible **2** lacking logic or consistency —**in·co·her'ence** *n.*; **in·co·her'ent·ly** *adv.*

in·come /ˈinˈkəm, ˈiNGˈkəm/ *n.* money received from one's work, investments, etc.

in·com·ing /ˈinˈkəmˈiNG/ *adj.* **1** coming in (*incoming telephone calls*) **2** entering; beginning (*incoming students*) **3** succeeding another (*incoming tenant*)

in·com·mu·ni·ca·do /ˈinˈkəmyōōˈnikädˈō/ *adj.* without means of communication [Sp]

in·com·pa·ra·ble /inkämˈp(ə)rəbəl/ *adj.* without an equal —**in·com·pa·ra·bil'i·ty** *n.*; **in·com'pa·ra·bly** *adv.*

in·com·pat·i·ble /ˈinˈkəmpatˈəbəl/ *adj.* **1** not able to live in harmony **2** opposed; discordant —**in·com·pat'i·bil'i·ty** *n.*

in·com·pe·tent /inkämˈpətənt/ *adj.* **1** lacking the necessary skill —*n.* **2** incompetent person —**in·com'pe·tence** *n.*

in·com·plete /ˈinˈkəmplētˈ/ *adj.* **1** lacking something **2** not finished

in·con·ceiv·a·ble /ˈinˈkənsēˈvəbəl/ *adj.* **1** unimaginable **2** *Colloq.* most unlikely —**in·con·ceiv'a·bly** *adv.*

in·con·gru·ous /inˈkäNGˈgrōōəs/ *adj.* **1** out of place; absurd **2** out of keeping —**in·con·gru·i·ty** /ˈinˈkən-grōōˈətē/ *n.* (*pl. ·ties*); **in·con'gru·ous·ly** *adv.*

in·con·se·quen·tial /ˈinˈkänsikwenˈSHəl/ *adj.* of no consequence —**in·con·se·quen'tial·ly** *adv.*

in·con·sid·er·a·ble /ˈinˈkənsidˈ(ə)rəbəl/ *adj.* of small size, value, etc.

in·con·sid·er·ate /ˈinˈkənsidˈ(ə)rət/ *adj.* lacking regard for others; thoughtless —**in·con·sid'er·ate·ly** *adv.*; **in·con·sid'er·ate·ness** *n.*

in·con·sol·a·ble /ˈinˈkənsōˈləbəl/ *adj.* (of a person, grief, etc.) that cannot be comforted —**in·con·sol'a·bly** *adv.*

in·con·spic·u·ous /ˈinˈkənspikˈyōōəs/ *adj.* not easily noticed —**in·con·spic'u·ous·ly** *adv.*; **in·con·spic'u·ous·ness** *n.*

in·con·stant /inkän'stənt/ *adj.* changeable; variable —**in·con'stan·cy** *n.* (*pl.* ·cies)

in·con·test·a·ble /in'kəntes'təbəl/ *adj.* unquestionable —**in'con·test'a·bly** *adv.*

in·con·ti·nent /inkän'tinənt/ *adj.* 1 unable to control the bowels or bladder 2 lacking self-restraint (esp. in sexual matters) —**in·con'ti·nence** *n.*

in·con·tro·vert·i·ble /inkän'trəvərt'əbəl/ *adj.* indisputable; undeniable —**in·con'tro·vert'i·bly** *adv.*

in·con·ven·ience /in'kənvēn'yəns/ *n.* 1 lack of ease or comfort; trouble 2 cause or instance of this —*v.* (·ienced, ·ienc·ing) 3 cause inconvenience to

in'con·ven'ient *adj.* causing trouble, difficulty, or discomfort; awkward —**in'con·ven'ient·ly** *adv.*

in·cor·po·rate *v.* /inkôr'pərāt/ (·rat·ed, ·rat·ing) 1 include as a part or ingredient 2 unite (in one body) 3 form into a legal corporation —*adj.* /inkôr'p(ə)rət/ 4 incorporated —**in·cor'po·ra'tion** *n.* [L *incorporare* embody]

in·cor·po·re·al /in'kôrpôr'ēəl/ *adj.* without physical or material existence

in·cor·ri·gi·ble /inkôr'ijəbəl, -kär'-/ *adj.* (of a person or habit) that cannot be corrected or improved —**in·cor'ri·gi·bil'i·ty** *n.*; **in·cor'ri·gi·bly** *adv.*

in·cor·rupt·i·ble /in'kərəp'təbəl/ *adj.* that cannot be corrupted, esp. morally —**in·cor·rupt'i·bil'i·ty** *n.*; **in·cor·rupt'i·bly** *adv.*

in·crease *v.* /inkrēs', in'krēs/ (·creased, ·creas·ing) 1 make or become greater or more numerous —*n.* /in'krēs, inkrēs'/ 2 growth; enlargement 3 multiplication 4 amount or extent of an increase 5 **on the increase** increasing [L *increscere* grow]

in·creas'ing·ly /inkrē'siNGlē/ *adv.* more and more

in·cred·i·ble /inkred'əbəl/ *adj.* 1 not believable 2 *Colloq.* amazing —**in·cred'i·bly** *adv.*
● Usage: *Incredible* describes actions or things that are unbelievable: *the incredible shrinking man.* It should not be confused with *incredulous,* which describes a person who finds it very difficult to believe something: *She was incredulous when told she had won the lottery.*

in·cred·u·lous /inkrej'ələs, -kred'yələs/ *adj.* unwilling to believe; showing disbelief —**in·cre·du·li·ty** /in'krid(y)oo'lətē/ *n.*; **in·cred'u·lous·ly** *adv.*

in·cre·ment /iNG'krəmənt/ *n.* increase or amount of increase —**in'cre·men'tal** /ment'l/ *adj.* [L *incrementum*]

in·crim·i·nate /inkrim'ənāt/ *v.* (·nat·ed, ·nat·ing) 1 make (a person) appear to be guilty 2 charge with a crime —**in·crim'i·na'tion** *n.*; **in·crim'i·na·to·ry** /-nətôr'ē/ *adj.* [L *incriminare* accuse]

in·crus·ta·tion /in'krəs'tā'sHən/ *n.* 1 encrusting 2 crust or hard coating [L, rel. to CRUST]

in·cu·bate /iNG'kyəbāt/ *v.* (·bat·ed, ·bat·ing) 1 sit on (eggs) or keep warm to cause to hatch 2 cause to develop 3 develop slowly [L *incubare* lie on]

in·cu·ba·tion *n.* 1 incubating 2 period between infection and the appearance of the first symptoms

in·cu·ba·tor *n.* warming apparatus for hatching eggs, protecting premature babies, etc.

in·cu·bus /iNG'kyəbəs/ *n.* (*pl.* ·bus·es or ·bi /-bī/, -bē'/) 1 demon formerly believed to have sexual intercourse with sleeping women 2 nightmare 3 oppressive burden [L *incubare* lie on]

in·cul·cate /inkəl'kāt/ *v.* (·cat·ed, ·cat·ing) urge or impress (a habit or idea) persistently —**in·cul·ca'tion** *n.* [L *inculcare* trample]

in·cum·ben·cy /inkəm'bənsē/ *n.* (*pl.* ·cies) office or tenure of an incumbent

in·cum·bent /inkəm'bənt/ *adj.* 1 resting as a duty (*incumbent on you to do it*) 2 currently holding office (*the incumbent president*) —*n.* 3 holder of an office or post [L *incumbere* lie upon]

in·cu·nab·u·lum /in'kyənab'yələm/ *n.* (*pl.* ·la /-lə/) 1 early printed book from before 1501 2 (*pl.*) early stages of a thing [L *in* in + *cunabula* cradle; origin]

in·cur /inkər'/ *v.* (·curred, ·cur·ring) bring on oneself (danger, blame, loss, etc.) [L *incurrere* run into]

in·cu·ri·ous /inkyoor'ēəs/ *adj.* lacking curiosity

in·cur·sion /inkər'zHən/ *n.* invasion or raid [L, rel. to INCUR]

Ind. *abbr.* for Indiana

in·debt·ed /indet'id/ *adj.* owing gratitude or money —**in·debt'ed·ness** *n.* [OFr *endetté*, rel. to DEBT]

in·de·cent /indē'sənt/ *adj.* 1 offending decency 2 improper (*indecent haste*) —**in·de'cen·cy** *n.* (*pl.* ·cies); **in·de'cent·ly** *adv.*

in·de·ci·pher·a·ble /in'disī'f(ə)rəbəl/ *adj.* that cannot be deciphered

in·de·ci·sion /in'disizH'ən/ *n.* inability to decide; hesitation

in·de·ci·sive /in'disī'siv/ *adj.* 1 (of a person) not decisive; hesitating 2 not conclusive (*an indecisive battle*) —**in·de·ci'sive·ly** *adv.*; **in'de·ci'sive·ness** *n.*

in·deed /indēd'/ *adv.* 1 in truth; really 2 admittedly —*interj.* 3 expressing irony, incredulity, etc.

indef. *abbr.* indefinite

in·de·fat·i·ga·ble /in'difat'igəbəl/ *adj.* unwearying; unremitting —**in'de·fat'i·ga·bly** *adv.*

in·de·fen·si·ble /in'difen'səbəl/ *adj.* that cannot be defended or justified —**in'de·fen'si·bil'i·ty** *n.*; **in'de·fen'si·bly** *adv.*

in·def·i·nite /indef'ənət/ *adj.* 1 vague; undefined 2 unlimited 3 *Gram.* not determining the person, etc., referred to (e.g., *some, someone, anyhow*) —**in·def'i·nite·ly** *adv.*

in·def'i·nite ar'ti·cle *n.* word (as *a* or *an*) preceding a noun and implying 'any of several'

in·del·i·ble /indel'əbəl/ *adj.* that cannot be erased or removed —**in·del'i·bly** *adv.* [L *delebilis* indestructible]

in·del·i·cate /indel'ikət/ *adj.* 1 coarse; unrefined 2 tactless —**in·del'i·ca·cy** /-kəsē/ *n.* (*pl.* ·cies); **in·del'i·cate·ly** *adv.*

in·dem·ni·fy /indem'nəfī'/ *v.* (·fied, ·fy·ing) 1 secure or exempt from harm, a loss, etc. 2 compensate for a loss —in·dem′ni·fi·ca′tion /-fikā′sHən/ n. [L *indemnis* free from loss]

in·dem·ni·ty /indem′nətē/ n. (pl. ·ties) 1 compensation for damage 2 security against loss 3 exemption from penalties

in·dent v. /indent′/ 1 make or impress marks, notches, dents, etc., in 2 start (a line of print or writing) further from the margin than others —n. /indent′, indent′/ 3 indented line 4 indentation [MedL *indentatus* notched, fr. L *dent*- tooth]

in·den·ta·tion /in′den′tā′sHən/ n. 1 indenting or being indented 2 notch 3 spacing in from a margin of text

in·den·tion /inden′sHən/ n. 1 indenting, esp. in printing 2 notch

in·den·ture /inden′sHər/ n. 1 (usu. pl.) sealed agreement or contract —v. (·tured, ·tur·ing) 2 *Hist.* bind by indentures, esp. as a worker [AngFr, rel. to INDENT]

In·de·pend·ence /in′dipen′dəns/ n. city in Mo. Pop. 112,301

In·de·pend′ence Day′ n. (also Fourth′ of Ju·ly′) US national holiday, July 4, commemorating the adoption of the Declaration of Independence in 1776

in·de·pend·ent /in′dipen′dənt/ adj. 1a not subject to authority or control b self-governing 2 not dependent on another person for income, ideas, etc. 3 self-reliant; aloof 4 not affiliated with any political party —n. 5 person who is politically independent —in′de·pend′ent n.; in′de·pend′ent·ly adv.

in-depth /indepTH′, in′depTH′/ adj. thorough

in·de·scrib·a·ble /in′diskrī′bəbəl/ adj. beyond what can be described —in′de·scrib′a·bly adv.

in·de·struc·ti·ble /in′distrək′təbəl/ adj. that cannot be destroyed —in′de·struc′ti·bil′i·ty n.; in′de·struct′i·bly adv.

in·de·ter·min·a·ble /in′ditər′mənəbəl/ adj. that cannot be ascertained or settled —in′de·ter′min·a·bly adv.

in·de·ter·mi·nate /in′ditər′mənət/ adj. 1 not fixed in extent, character, etc. 2 left doubtful; vague —in′de·ter′mi·na·cy n.

in·dex /in′deks/ n. (pl. in·dex·es or in·di·ces) 1 alphabetical list of subjects, etc., with references, as in a book 2 measure of prices or wages compared with a previous month, year, etc. (*retail price index*) 3 pointer; sign; indicator —v. 4 provide with an index 5 enter in an index 6 relate (wages, etc.) to a price index [L]

• Usage: The plural *indexes* is suitable for all senses of *index*; for some technical senses, the plural *indices* is an alternative.

in′dex fin′ger n. forefinger

In·di·a /in′dēə/ n. republic in S Asia on the Indian Ocean and Arabian Sea. Capital: New Delhi. Pop. 889,700,000

In′di·a ink′ n. black liquid ink

In·di·an /in′dēən/ n. 1a native or national of India b person of Indian descent 2 (in full A·mer′i·can In′di·an; also NATIVE AMERICAN) a original inhabitant of America b any of the languages of the American Indians —adj. 3 of India or the subcontinent comprising India, Pakistan, and Bangladesh 4 of the original peoples of America

In·di·an·a /in′dēan′ə/ n. state in the central US. Capital: Indianapolis. Pop. 5,544,159. Abbr. IN; Ind. —In′di·an′an n. & adj.

In·di·an·ap·o·lis /in′dēanap′ələs/ n. capital of Ind., in the central part. Pop. 731,327

In′di·an corn′ n. corn on the cob, esp. with hard kernels of various colors

In′di·an file′ n. SINGLE FILE

In′di·an O′cean n. ocean S of Asia, between Africa and Australia

In′di·an sum′mer n. dry warm weather in late autumn following a frost

in·di·cate /in′dikāt′/ v. (·cat·ed, ·cat·ing) 1 point out; make known 2 show the presence of 3 call for; require (*stronger measures are indicated*) 4 state briefly 5 give as a reading —in′di·ca′tion n. [L *indicare* make known]

in·dic·a·tive /indik′ətiv/ adj. 1 serving as an indication 2 *Gram.* (of a mood) stating a fact —n. 3 *Gram.* indicative mood

in·di·ca·tor /in′dikāt′ər/ n. 1 person or thing that indicates 2 device giving a measurement or showing a condition or status 3 flashing light showing the direction a vehicle is about to turn

in·di·ces /in′dəsēz′/ n. pl. of INDEX

in·dict /indīt′/ v. accuse formally by legal process —in·dict′a·ble adj.; in·dict′ment n. [AngFr fr. L *indicere* proclaim]

in·dif·fer·ent /indif′(ə)rənt/ adj. 1 showing lack of interest 2 neither good nor bad 3 of poor quality or ability —in·dif′fer·ence n.; in′dif′fer·ent·ly adv.

in·dig·e·nous /indij′ənəs/ adj. native or belonging naturally to a place [L *indigen*- native]

in·di·gent /in′dijənt/ adj. needy; poor —in′di·gence n. [L *indigere* need]

in·di·gest·i·ble /in′dijes′təbəl, -dī′-/ adj. difficult or impossible to digest

in·di·ges·tion /in′dijes′cHən, -dī′-/ n. difficulty in digesting food

in·dig·nant /indig′nənt/ adj. feeling or showing indignation —in·dig′nant·ly adv. [L *in*- not + *dignus* worthy]

in·dig·na·tion /in′dignā′sHən/ n. anger at supposed injustice, etc.

in·dig·ni·ty /indig′nətē/ n. (pl. ·ties) humiliating treatment; insult

in·di·go /in′digō′/ n. (pl. ·gos) color between blue and violet in the spectrum [Sp ult. fr. Gk *indikon* Indian dye]

in·di·rect /in′dərekt′, -dī′-/ adj. 1 not straight to the point 2 not straight 3a not directly sought (*indirect result*) b not primary (*indirect cause*) —in·di·rect′ly adv.

in′di·rect ob′ject n. *Gram.* person or thing affected by a verbal action but not primarily acted on (e.g., *him* in *give him the book*)

in·dis·creet /in′diskrēt′/ adj. injudicious; unwary —in′dis·creet′ly adv.

in·dis·cre·tion /in′diskresH′ən/ n. indiscreet conduct or action

in·dis·crim·i·nate /in′diskrim′ənət/ adj. making no distinctions; done or acting at random —in′dis·crim′i·nate·ly adv.

in·dis·pens·a·ble /in′dispen′səbəl/ adj. necessary —in′dis·pens′a·bly adv.

in·dis·posed /in′dispōzd′/ adj. 1 slightly unwell 2 averse; unwilling —in′dis·po·si′tion /-pəzisH′ən/ n.

in·dis·sol·u·ble /in'disäl'yəbəl/ *adj.* that cannot be dissolved; lasting **—in'dis·sol'u·bly** *adv.*

in·dite /indīt'/ *v.* (**·dit·ed, ·dit·ing**) *Formal* or *Joc.* put into words; write [rel. to INDICT]

in·di·um /in'dēəm/ *n.* soft silvery-white metallic element in zinc ores; *symb.* **In** [INDIGO + -*ium*]

in·di·vid·u·al /in'dəvij'(ōō)əl/ *adj.* **1** of, for, or characteristic of a single person, etc. **2a** single (*individual words*) **b** particular; not general **3** having a distinct character **—n. 4** single member of a class **5** single human being [MedL fr. L *individuus* indivisible]

in·di·vid·u·al·ism /in'dəvij'(ōō)əlizəm/ *n.* **1** social theory favoring free action by individuals **2** being independent or different **—in'di·vid'u·al·ist** /-ist/ *n.*; **in'di·vid·u·al·is'tic** *adj.*

in·di·vid·u·al·i·ty /in'dəvij'ōō·al'ətē/ *n.* **1** individual character, esp. when strongly marked **2** separate existence

in·di·vid·u·al·ize /in'dəvij'(ōō)əlīz'/ *v.* (**·ized, ·iz·ing**) **1** give an individual character to **2** note or consider individually

in·di·vid·u·al·ly /in'dəvij'(ōō)əlē'/ *adv.* **1** one by one **2** distinctively

Indo- *comb. form* Indian; Indian and

In·do·chi·na /in'dōCHī'nə/ *n.* peninsula in SE Asia between the S China Sea and the Bay of Bengal, comprising Vietnam, Cambodia, Laos, Thailand, W Malaysia, and Burma

in·doc·tri·nate /indäk'trənāt'/ *v.* (**·nat·ed, ·nat·ing**) teach to accept a particular belief uncritically **—in'doc·tri·na'tion** *n.*

In·do-Eu·ro·pe·an /in'dōyŏŏr'əpē'ən/ *adj.* of the family of languages spoken over most of Europe and Asia as far as N India, or the hypothetical parent language of this family

in·do·lent /in'dələnt/ *adj.* lazy **—in'do·lence** *n.*; **in'do·lent·ly** *adv.* [L *in* not + *dolere* be in pain]

in·dom·i·ta·ble /indäm'itəbəl/ *adj.* **1** unconquerable **2** unyielding **—in·dom'i·ta·bly** *adv.* [L *in* not + *domitus* tamed]

In·do·ne·sia /in'dənē'zhə/ *n.* SE Asian republic of the Malay Archipelago. Capital: Jakarta. Pop. 184,796,000 **—In'do·ne'sian** *n.* & *adj.*

in·door /in'dôr'/ *adj.* of, done, or for use in a building or under cover

in·doors /indôrz'/ *adv.* into or in a building

In·dore /indôr'/ *n.* city in central India. Pop. 1,086,700

in·dorse /indôrs'/ *v.* var. of ENDORSE

in·du·bi·ta·ble /ind(y)ŏŏ'bitəbəl/ *adj.* that cannot be doubted **—in·du'bi·ta·bly** *adv.* [L *in* not + *dubitare* doubt]

in·duce /ind(y)ŏŏs'/ *v.* (**·duced, ·duc·ing**) **1** prevail on; persuade **2** bring about **3** bring on or speed up birth **4** produce (a current) by induction **5** infer; deduce **—in·duc'i·ble** *adj.* [L *inducere* lead in; persuade]

in·duce'ment *n.* incentive; bribe

in·duct /indəkt'/ *v.* **1** install in office **2** enroll in the armed services **—in·duc·tee'** *n.* [rel. to INDUCE]

in·duc·tance /indək'təns/ *n.* property of an electric circuit to produce a magnetic field or induce another current by virtue of a varying current flowing through it

in·duc·tion /indək'sHən/ *n.* **1** act of induct-

ing or inducing **2** act of bringing on (esp. labor) by artificial means **3** inference from particular instances **4** *Electr.* production of an electric or magnetic state by the proximity of another current flow or magnetic field **—in·duc'tive** *adj.*

in·due /ind(y)ŏŏ'/ *v.* var. of ENDUE

in·dulge /indəlj'/ *v.* (**·dulged, ·dulg·ing**) **1** take pleasure in freely **2** gratify the wishes of **3** *Colloq.* take alcoholic liquor [L *indulgere* grant; yield]

in·dul·gence /indəl'jəns/ *n.* **1** indulging or being indulgent **2** thing indulged in **3** privilege granted **4** *RC Ch.* remission of punishment for sin after absolution

in·dul·gent /indəl'jənt/ *adj.* lenient; indulging **—in·dul'gent·ly** *adv.*

In·dus Riv·er /in'dəs/ *n.* river in S Asia flowing 1,900 mi. SW from W Tibet into the Arabian Sea

in·dus·tri·al /indəs'trēəl/ *adj.* **1** pertaining to industry **2** having developed industries **—in·dus'tri·al·ly** *adv.*

in·dus'tri·al arts' *n.* instruction in techniques and skills for using machinery and tools

in·dus·tri·al·ism /indəs'trēəlizəm/ *n.* system in which manufacturing industries are prevalent

in·dus·tri·al·ist *n.* owner or manager in industry

in·dus·tri·al·ize /indəs'trēəlīz'/ *v.* (**·ized, ·iz·ing**) make (a nation, etc.) industrial **—in·dus'tri·al·i·za'tion** *n.*

in·dus'tri·al park' *n.* complex of factories and other businesses, usu. separate from an urban center

in·dus·tri·ous /indəs'trēəs/ *adj.* hard-working **—in·dus'tri·ous·ly** *adv.*

in·dus·try /in'dəstrē/ *n.* (*pl.* **·tries**) **1a** branch of production or manufacture; commercial enterprise **b** these collectively **2** steady effort; diligence [L]

-ine *suffix* **1** forming adjectives, meaning 'belonging to; of the nature of' (*Alpine; asinine*) **2** forming feminine nouns (*heroine*) [L *-inus*]

in·e·bri·ate *v.* /inē'brēāt'/ (**·at·ed, ·at·ing**) **1** make drunk **2** excite **—adj.** /inē'brēət/ **3** drunken **—n.** /inē'brēət/ **4** drunkard **—in·e'bri·a'tion** *n.* [L *inebriare* make drunk]

in·ef·fa·ble /inef'əbəl/ *adj.* **1** too great for description in words **2** that must not be uttered **—in·ef'fa·bil'i·ty** *n.*; **in·ef'fa·bly** *adv.* [L *in* not + *effari* speak out]

in·ef·fec·tu·al /in'ifek'CHŏŏəl/ *adj.* ineffective; feeble **—in'ef·fec'tu·al·ly** *adv.*; **in'ef·fec'tu·al·ness** *n.*

in·ef·fi·cient /in'ifisH'ənt/ *adj.* **1** not efficient or fully capable **2** wasteful **—in'ef·fi'cien·cy** *n.*; **in'ef·fi'cient·ly** *adv.*

in·el·e·gant /inel'igənt/ *adj.* ungraceful; crude **—in·el'e·gance** *n.*; **in·el'e·gant·ly** *adv.*

in·e·luc·ta·ble /in'ilək'təbəl/ *adj.* inescapable; unavoidable [L *in* not + *eluctari* surmount]

in·ept /inept'/ *adj.* **1** unskillful **2** absurd; silly **3** out of place **—in·ep·ti·tude** /inep'tit(y)ŏŏd'/ *n.*; **in·ept'ly** *adv.* [L, rel. to APT]

in·e·qual·i·ty /in'ikwäl'ətē/ *n.* (*pl.* **·ties**) **1** lack of equality **2** unevenness

in·eq·ui·ta·ble /inek'wətəbəl/ *adj.* unfair; unjust

in·ert /inərt'/ *adj.* **1** without inherent power of action or resistance **2** not reacting chemically with other substances **3** sluggish; lifeless [L *iners* lacking skill; rel. to ART]

in·er·tia /inər'SHə/ *n.* **1** *Physics.* property of matter by which it continues in its existing state of rest or motion unless an external force is applied **2** tendency not to move or act —**in·er'tial** *adj.* [L, rel. to INERT]

in·es·cap·a·ble /in'iskā'pəbəl/ *adj.* that cannot be escaped or avoided

in·es·ti·ma·ble /inest'iməbəl/ *adj.* too great, precious, etc., to be estimated —**in·es'ti·ma·bly** *adv.*

in·ev·i·ta·ble /inev'itəbəl/ *adj.* **1** unavoidable **2** *Colloq.* tiresomely familiar —**in·ev'i·ta·bil'i·ty** *n.*; **in·ev'i·ta·bly** *adv.* [L *in* not + *evitare* avoid]

in·ex·haust·i·ble /in'igzô'stəbəl/ *adj.* **1** that cannot be used up **2** untiring

in·ex·o·ra·ble /inek'sərəbəl, -eg'-/ *adj.* relentless; unstoppable —**in·ex'o·ra·bly** *adv.* [L *in* not + *exorare* entreat; appease]

in·ex·pe·ri·ence /in'ikspēr'ēəns/ *n.* lack of experience, knowledge, or skill —**in'ex·pe'ri·enced** *adj.*

in·ex·pert /inek'spərt'/ *adj.* unskillful; lacking expertise

in·ex·pi·a·ble /inek'spēəbəl/ *adj.* that cannot be expiated or appeased

in·ex·pli·ca·ble /in'iksplik'əbəl, inek'splikəbəl/ *adj.* that cannot be explained —**in'ex·pli'ca·bly** *adv.*

in·ex·press·i·ble /in'ikspres'əbəl/ *adj.* that cannot be expressed —**in·ex·press'i·bly** *adv.*

in·ex·tin·guish·a·ble /in'iksting'gwiSHəbəl/ *adj.* that cannot be extinguished or destroyed

in extremis /in' ikstrē'mis, -strā'-/ *adj. Latin.* **1** at the point of death **2** in great difficulties

in·ex·tri·ca·ble /in'ikstrik'əbəl, inek'strikəbəl/ *adj.* **1** inescapable **2** that cannot be separated, loosened, or solved —**in'ex·tri'ca·bly** *adv.*

inf. *abbr.* **1** infantry **2** inferior **3** infinitive

in·fal·li·ble /infal'əbəl/ *adj.* **1** incapable of error **2** sure to succeed —**in·fal'li·bil'i·ty** *n.*; **in·fal'li·bly** *adv.*

in·fa·mous /in'fəməs/ *adj.* notoriously bad —**in'fa·mous·ly** *adv.*

in·fa·my /in'fəmē/ *n.* (*pl.* **-mies**) **1** very bad reputation **2** notorious wickedness **3** infamous act

in·fant /in'fənt/ *n.* **1** child during the earliest period of its life —*adj.* **2** in an early stage of its development —**in'fan·cy** *n.* [L *infans* unable to speak]

in·fan·ti·cide /infant'əsīd'/ *n.* **1** killing of an infant **2** person who kills an infant

in·fan·tile /in'fəntīl'/ *adj.* **1** of or like infants **2** childish; immature

in·fan·tile pa·ral'y·sis *n.* POLIOMYELITIS

in·fan·try /in'fən·trē/ *n.* (*pl.* **-tries**) body of foot-soldiers; foot-soldiers collectively —**in'fan·try·man** /-mən/ *n.* [It *infante* youth; foot-soldier]

in·farct /in'färkt', -färkt'/ *n.* area of dead tissue caused by an inadequate blood supply —**in·farc·tion** /infärk'SHən/ *n.* [L *infarcire, infarct-* stuff]

in·fat·u·ate /infaCH'oo͞-āt'/ *v.* (**-at·ed**, **-at·ing**) inspire with fondness or admiration

—**in·fat'u·at'ed** *adj.*; **in·fat'u·a'tion** *n.* [L, rel. to FATUOUS]

in·fect /infekt'/ *v.* **1** affect or contaminate with a germ, virus, or disease **2** imbue; taint [L *inficere, infect-* taint]

in·fec·tion /infek'SHən/ *n.* **1** infecting or being infected **2** instance of this; disease

in·fec·tious /infek'SHəs/ *adj.* **1** infecting **2** transmissible by infection **3** (of emotions, etc.) quickly affecting others —**in·fec'tious·ly** *adv.*; **in·fec'tious·ness** *n.*

in·fe·lic·i·ty /infəlis'ətē/ *n.* (*pl.* **-ties**) inapt expression, etc. —**in·fe·lic'i·tous** *adj.*

in·fer /infər'/ *v.* (**-ferred**, **-fer·ring**) **1** deduce; conclude **2** *Loosely.* imply —**in·fer'a·ble** *adj.* [L *inferre* bring into]

● Usage: Often used where *imply* is intended, *infer* means to 'draw an understanding or conclusion' from what was said or a particular event: *When I saw him at the airport, I inferred that he was leaving town.* *Imply* means to 'suggest or hint': *When I spoke with him, he implied that he was leaving town.*

in·fer·ence /in'f(ə)rəns/ *n.* **1** act of inferring **2** thing inferred —**in·fer·en'tial** /in'fəren'SHəl/ *adj.*

in·fe·ri·or /infēr'ēər/ *adj.* **1** lower in rank, quality, etc. **2** of poor quality **3** situated below —*n.* **4** person inferior to another —**in·fe·ri·or'i·ty** /-ôr'ətē/ *n.* [L: lower]

in·fer·nal /infərn'l/ *adj.* **1** of hell; hellish **2** *Colloq.* detestable —**in·fer'nal·ly** *adv.* [L *infernus* below]

in·fer·no /infər'nō/ *n.* (*pl.* **-nos**) **1** raging fire **2** hell [It fr. L, rel. to INFERNAL]

in·fest /infest'/ *v.* (esp. of vermin) overrun (a place) —**in·fes·ta'tion** /-tā'SHən/ *n.* [L *infestus* hostile]

in·fi·del /in'fədəl, -del'/ *n.* unbeliever in a particular religion [L *infidelis* faithless]

in·fi·del·i·ty /in'fədel'ətē/ *n.* (*pl.* **-ties**) unfaithfulness, esp. adultery [L, rel. to INFIDEL]

in'field *n. Baseball.* **1** the part of the field near the bases **2** players positioned there

in'fight'ing *n.* **1** conflict between colleagues **2** boxing within arm's length

in·fil·trate /infil'trāt', in'filtrāt'/ *v.* (**-trat·ed**, **-trat·ing**) **1a** enter (a region, group, etc.) gradually and imperceptibly **b** cause to do this **2** permeate by filtration —**in'fil·tra'tion, in'fil·tra'tor** *n.* [fr. IN-², FILTRATE]

in·fi·nite /in'fənət/ *adj.* **1** boundless; endless **2** very great or many —**in'fi·nite·ly** *adv.* [L, rel. to IN-¹, FINITE]

in·fin·i·tes·i·mal /in'fənətes'əməl/ *adj.* infinitely or very small —**in'fin·i·tes'i·mal·ly** *adv.*

in·fin·i·tive /infin'ətiv/ *n. Gram.* verb form without a particular subject, tense, etc. (e.g., *see in* we came to see, let him see)

● Usage: Centuries ago, writers who insisted that English be modeled after Latin created the "rule" that the English infinitive should not be split: *to boldly go* was wrong; one must use *to go boldly*. The Latin infinitive (like that in French, German, and many other languages) is one word, and cannot be split. This arbitrary rule does not apply well in English, and if used strictly can lead to awkward, stilted sentences.

in·fin·i·tude /infin′ət(y)ōōd′/ *n.* INFINITY, 1, 2

in·fin·i·ty /infin′ətē/ *n.* (*pl.* ·ties) 1 being infinite; boundlessness 2 infinite number or extent 3 infinite distance

in·firm /infûrm′/ *adj.* weak; frail

in·fir·ma·ry /infər′mərē/ *n.* (*pl.* ·ries) place that treats injuries and illnesses, as at a school

in·fir·mi·ty /infər′mətē/ *n.* (*pl.* ·ties) physical weakness

in fla·gran·te de·lic·to /in′ fləgrant′ē dəlik′ tō/ *adv. Latin.* in the very act of committing an offense [L: in blazing crime]

in·flame /inflām′/ *v.* (·flamed, ·flam·ing) 1 provoke to strong feeling, esp. anger 2 cause inflammation in; make hot 3 aggravate

in·flam·ma·ble /inflam′əbəl/ *adj.* easily set on fire or excited —**in·flam′ma·bil′i·ty** *n.*
● Usage: Because the prefix *in-* means 'not' in so many words, some people misunderstand *inflammable* to mean 'incombustible, unburnable,' although it means the opposite. To avoid confusion, the *in-* has been dropped in the labeling of combustible products, which are now said to be *flammable.*

in·flam·ma·tion /in′fləmā′SHən/ *n.* 1 inflaming 2 bodily condition with heat, swelling, redness, and usu. pain

in·flam·ma·to·ry /inflam′ətôr′ē/ *adj.* 1 tending to cause anger, etc. 2 of inflammation

in·flat·a·ble /inflāt′əbəl/ *adj.* 1 that can be inflated —*n.* 2 inflatable object

in·flate /inflāt′/ *v.* (·flat·ed, ·flat·ing) 1 distend with air or gas 2 puff up (with pride, etc.) 3a cause inflation of (the currency) b raise (prices) artificially [L *inflare, flat-* blow into]

in·fla′tion *n.* 1 inflating 2 *Econ.* a general increase in prices b increase in the money supply causing this —**in·fla′tion·ar·y** /-ər′ē/ *adj.*

in·flect /inflekt′/ *v.* 1 change the pitch of (the voice) 2a change the form of (a word) to express grammatical relation b undergo such a change [L *inflectere* bend in]

in·flec·tion /inflek′SHən/ *n.* 1 modulation of the voice 2 change in form of a word to indicate person, tense, etc. —**in·flec′tion·al** *adj.* [L, rel. to INFLECT]

in·flex·i·ble /inflek′səbəl/ *adj.* 1 unbendable 2 unyielding —**in·flex′i·bil′i·ty** *n.*; **in·flex′i·bly** *adv.*

in·flict /inflikt′/ *v.* 1 deal (a blow, etc.) 2 impose (suffering, oneself, etc.) on —**in·flic′ tion** /-flik′SHən/, **in·flic′tor** *n.* [L *infligere, -flict-* strike against]

in·flo·res·cence /in′flôres′əns/ *n.* 1a flowerhead of a plant b arrangement of this 2 flowering [L *in* + *florescere* bloom]

in·flu·ence /in′flōō′əns, inflōō′-/ *n.* 1 effect a person or thing has on another 2 moral ascendancy or power 3 thing or person exercising this —*v.* (·enced, ·enc·ing) 4 exert influence on; affect 5 **under the influence** drunk [L *influere* flow into]

in·flu·en·tial /in′flōō·en′SHəl/ *adj.* having great influence —**in′flu·en′tial·ly** *adv.*

in·flu·en·za /in′flōōen′zə/ *n.* virus infection causing fever, aches, and congestion [MedL, rel. to INFLUENCE]

in·flux /in′fləks′/ *n.* flowing in, esp. of people or things [L, rel. to FLUX]

in·fo /in′fō′/ *n. Colloq.* information [abbr.]

in·fo·mer·cial /in′fōmər′SHəl/ *n.* television program promoting a commercial product

in·form /infôrm′/ *v.* 1 tell 2 give incriminating information about a person —**in·for′ mant** /-mənt/, **in·form′er** *n.* [L *informare* fashion; describe]

in·for·mal /infôr′məl/ *adj.* 1 without formality 2 not formal —**in′for·mal′i·ty** /-mal′ətē/ *n.* (*pl.* ·ties); **in·for′mal·ly** *adv.*

in′for·ma′tion *n.* 1 something told; knowledge 2 *Comp.* data stored or generated by a program

in′for·ma′tion su′per·high′way *n.* (also **in′ for·ma′tion high′way**′) nationwide computer network offering information, shopping, and other services

in·for·ma·tive /infôr′mətiv/ *adj.* giving information; instructive

in·formed /infôrmd′/ *adj.* knowledgeable

in·formed′ con·sent′ *n.* agreement by a patient to a medical procedure after being informed of the risks involved

in·fo·tain·ment /in′fōtān′mənt/ *n.* 1 factual information presented in dramatized form on television 2 television program mixing news and entertainment

in·fra /in′frə/ *adv. Latin.* below; further on (in a book, etc.)

infra- *comb. form* below

in·frac·tion /infrak′SHən/ *n.* violation of a law, rule, etc. [L, rel. to INFRINGE]

in·fra dig /in′frə dig′/ beneath one's dignity [L *infra dignitatem*]

in·fra·red /in′frəred′/ *adj.* of or using rays with a wavelength just longer than the red end of the visible spectrum

in·fra·struc·ture /in′frəstrək′CHər/ *n.* basic structural foundations, esp. roads, bridges, sewers, etc.

in·fre·quent /infrē′kwənt/ *adj.* happening rarely —**in·fre′quen·cy** *n.*; **in·fre′quent·ly** *adv.*

in·fringe /infrinj′/ *v.* (·fringed, ·fring·ing) 1 break or violate (a law, another's rights, etc.) 2 encroach; trespass —**in·fringe′ment** *n.* [L *infringere* break]

in·fu·ri·ate /infyŏŏr′ē·āt′/ *v.* make furious; irritate greatly —**in·fu′ri·at·ing** *adj.*; **in·fu′ri· at′ing·ly** *adv.* [MedL, rel. to FURY]

in·fuse /infyŏŏz′/ *v.* (·fused, ·fus·ing) 1 fill (with a quality) 2 steep (tea leaves, etc.) in liquid to extract the content 3 instill; impart —**in·fu′sion** /-ZHən/ *n.* [L *infundere, infus-* pour into]

-ing[1] *suffix* forming nouns from verbs denoting: 1 verbal action or its result (*rendering*) 2 material associated with a process, etc. (*piping; washing*) 3 occupation; event (*banking; wedding*) [OE]

-ing[2] *suffix* 1 forming the present participle of verbs (*asking; fighting*), often as adjectives (*charming; strapping*) 2 forming adjectives from nouns (*hulking*) and verbs (*balding*) [OE]

Inge /inj/, **William** 1913–73; US dramatist

in·ge·nious /injēn′yəs/ *adj.* 1 clever at inventing, organizing, etc. 2 cleverly contrived —**in·ge′nious·ly** *adv.* [L *ingenium* cleverness]

in·gé·nue /an'jənŏŏ′, än′-; aN′ZHƏ-/ *n.* 1 unsophisticated young woman 2 such a role in a play [Fr fr. L *ingenuus* native; natural]

in·ge·nu·i·ty /in'jən(y)ŏŏ′ətē/ *n.* inventiveness; cleverness [rel. to INGENIOUS]

in·gen·u·ous /injen′yŏŏəs/ *adj.* 1 naive 2 frank —**in·gen′u·ous·ly** *adv.* [L *ingenuus* native; natural]

in·gest /injest′/ *v.* take in, as food, knowledge, etc. —**in·ges′tion** /-jes′CHən/ *n.* [L *ingerere, ingest-* pour into]

In·gle·wood /iNG′gəlwŏŏd′/ *n.* city in Calif. Pop. 109,602

in·glo·ri·ous /iNGlôr′ēəs/ *adj.* 1 shameful 2 not famous

in·got /iNG′gət/ *n.* bar of cast metal

in·grained /iNGrānd′/ *adj.* 1 deeply rooted; inveterate 2 deeply embedded

in·gra·ti·ate /iNGrā′sHē·āt′/ *v.* (·at·ed, ·at·ing) bring oneself into favor —**in·gra′ti·at·ing** *adj.*; **in·gra′ti·at′ing·ly** *adv.* [L in *gratiam* into favor]

in·grat·i·tude /iNGrat′ət(y)ŏŏd′/ *n.* lack of due gratitude

in·gre·di·ent /iNGrēd′ēənt/ *n.* component part in a mixture [L *ingredi* enter into]

In·gres /aNgr/, **Jean** 1780–1867; French painter

in·gress /in′gres′/ *n.* act or right of entry [L *ingressus* going into]

in·grow·ing /in′grō′iNG/ *adj.* (esp. of a toenail) growing into the flesh —**in′grown′** *adj.*

in·gui·nal /iNG′gwinəl/ *adj.* of the groin [L *inguen* groin]

in·hab·it /inhab′it/ *v.* dwell in; occupy —**in·hab′it·a·ble** *adj.* [L, rel. to HABIT]

in·hab·i·tant /inhab′ətənt/ *n.* person, etc., who inhabits a place

in·hal·ant /inhā′lənt/ *n.* medicinal substance for inhaling

in·hale /inhāl′/ *v.* (·haled, ·hal·ing) breathe in (air, gas, smoke, etc.) —**in′ha·la′tion** *n.* [L *halare* breathe]

in·hal·er *n.* device for administering an inhalant

in·here /inhēr′/ *v.* (·hered, ·her·ing) be inherent [L *inhaerere* stick]

in·her·ent /inher′ənt, -hir′-/ *adj.* existing in something as an essential or permanent attribute —**in·her′ence** *n.*; **in·her′ent·ly** *adv.*

in·her·it /inher′it/ *v.* 1 receive (property, rank, title, etc.) by legal succession 2 derive from heredity or from a predecessor —**in·her′it·a·ble** *adj.*; **in·her′i·tor** *n.* [LL *inhereditare* make heir]

in·her·i·tance /inher′itəns/ *n.* 1 thing inherited 2 inheriting

in·hib·it /inhib′it/ *v.* hinder; restrain; repress [L *inhibere, inhibit-* hinder]

in·hi·bi·tion /in′(h)əbisH′ən/ *n.* 1 restraint or resistance to a thought, action, etc. 2 inhibiting or being inhibited

in·hos·pi·ta·ble /in′häs′pit′əbəl, inhäs′pitəbəl/ *adj.* not affording shelter, favorable conditions, etc. —**in·hos·pi′ta·bly** *adv.*

in′-house *adj. & adv.* within an institution, company, etc.

in·hu·man /in(h)yŏŏ′mən/ *adj.* brutal; unfeeling; barbarous —**in·hu·man′i·ty** /-man′ ətē/ *n.* (*pl.* ·ties); **in·hu′man·ly** *adv.*

in·im·i·cal /inim′ikəl/ *adj.* 1 hostile 2 harmful —**in·im′i·cal·ly** *adv.* [L *inimicus* enemy]

in·im·i·ta·ble /inim′itəbəl/ *adj.* impossible to imitate —**in·im′i·ta·bly** *adv.*

in·iq·ui·ty /inik′wətē/ *n.* (*pl.* ·ties) 1 wickedness 2 gross injustice —**in·iq′ui·tous** /-wətəs/ *adj.* [L *iniquitas* inequality]

in·i·tial /inisH′əl/ *adj.* 1 of or at the beginning —*n.* 2 initial letter, (esp. *pl.*) those of a person's names —*v.* (·tialed, ·tial·ing) 3 mark or sign with one's initials —**in·i′tial·ly** *adv.* [L *initium* beginning]

in·i·ti·ate *v.* /inisH′ē·āt′/ (·at·ed, ·at·ing) 1 begin; set going 2a admit (a person) into a society, office, etc., esp. with a ritual b instruct (a person) in a subject —*n.* /inisH′(ē)ət/ 3 initiated person —**in·i′ti·a′tion, in·i′ti·a·tor** *n.*; **in·i′ti·a·to·ry** /-ətôr′ē/ *adj.* [L *initium* beginning]

in·i·ti·a·tive /inisH′ətiv/ *n.* 1 ability to initiate things; enterprise (*lacks initiative*) 2 first step 3 legislative proposal introduced by popular petition [rel. to INITIATE]

in·ject /injekt′/ *v.* 1 drive (a solution, medicine, etc.) by or as if by a syringe 2 place (a quality, money, etc.) into something —**in·jec′tion** /-jek′sHən/, **in·jec′tor** *n.* [L *injicere, -ject-* throw in]

in·junc·tion /in′jəNGk′sHən/ *n.* command, esp. a judicial order restraining or compelling some action [L *injungere* join to; inflict]

in·jure /in′jər/ *v.* (·jured, ·jur·ing) 1 harm; damage 2 do wrong to [back formation fr. INJURY]

in·ju·ri·ous /injŏŏr′ēəs/ *adj.* 1 harmful 2 (of language) insulting

in·ju·ry /in′jərē/ *n.* (*pl.* ·ries) 1 harm or damage 2 harmful or wrongful action [L *injuria* injustice]

in·jus·tice /injəs′tis/ *n.* 1 lack of fairness 2 unjust act [Fr fr. L *injustitia*]

ink /iNGk/ *n.* 1 colored fluid or paste used for writing, printing, etc. 2 black liquid ejected by a cuttlefish, etc. —*v.* 3 mark or cover with ink [Gk *enkauston* purple ink]

ink′-jet *adj.* Printing. pertaining to a process in which electrostatically charged droplets of ink are projected onto paper in computer-controlled patterns

ink·ling /iNGk′liNG/ *n.* slight knowledge or suspicion; hint

ink′well *n.* pot or hole for ink

ink′y *adj.* (·i·er, ·i·est) of, as black as, or stained with ink —**ink′i·ness** *n.*

is·land /ī′lənd/ *n.* 1 of or in the interior of a country —*adv.* -land/ 2 in or toward the interior of a country

in·law /in′lô′/ *n.* (often *pl.*) relative by marriage

in·lay *v.* /inlā′, in′lā′/ (·laid, ·lay·ing) 1 embed (a thing in another) so that the surfaces are even 2 decorate (a thing with inlaid work) —*n.* /in′lā′/ 3 inlaid work 4 material inlaid 5 filling shaped to fit a tooth-cavity [fr. IN-², LAY¹]

in·let /in′lət/ *n.* small arm of the sea, a lake, or a river [fr. IN, LET¹]

in lo·co pa·ren·tis /in lō′kō pəren′tis/ *adv.* Latin. (acting) for or instead of a parent

in·mate /in′māt′/ *n.* occupant of a prison, etc. [fr. IN-², MATE¹]

in·me·mo·ri·am /in məmôr′ēəm/ *prep.* in memory of (a dead person) [L]

in·most /in′mōst′/ *adj.* most inward [OE]

inn /in/ *n.* 1 small hotel 2 restaurant or tavern (used in names) [OE]

in·nards /in′ərdz/ *n. pl. Colloq.* entrails [special pronunciation of INWARD]

in·nate /ināt′/ *adj.* inborn; natural —**in′nate′ly** *adv.* [L in in + *nasci* be born]

in·ner /in′ər/ *adj.* 1 inside; interior 2 (of thoughts, feelings, etc.) deeper —**in′ner·most′** *adj.* [OE, comp. of *inne* within]

in′ner cit′y *n.* crowded, often run-down districts in a large city

in′ner tube′ *n.* separate inflatable tube inside a pneumatic tire

in·ning /in′iNG/ *n. Baseball.* 1 turn at bat for a team 2 division of a game in which both teams bat [OE *innung* fr. *innian* go in]

inn′keep′er *n.* person who manages an inn

in·no·cent /in′əsənt/ *adj.* 1 free from moral wrong 2 not guilty (of a crime, etc.) 3 simple; guileless 4 harmless —*n.* 5 innocent person, esp. a young child —**in′no·cence** *n.*; **in′no·cent·ly** *adv.* [L in- not + *nocere* harm]

in·noc·u·ous /inäk′yōōəs/ *adj.* harmless [L *innocuus,* rel. to INNOCENT]

in·no·vate /in′əvāt′/ *v.* (·vat·ed, ·vat·ing) bring in new methods, ideas, etc. —**in′no·va′tion** *n.*; **in′no·va′tive** *adj.*; **in′no·va′tor** *n.* [L *novus* new]

Inns·bruck /inz′brŏŏk/ *n.* city in Austria on the Inn River. Pop. 115,000

in·nu·en·do /in′yōō-en′dō′/ *n.* (*pl.* ·does or ·dos) allusive remark or hint, usu. disparaging [L; hint; literally, by nodding at, fr. in- in + *nuo* nod]

in·nu·mer·a·ble /in(y)ōō′mərəbəl/ *adj.* too many to be counted —**in·nu′mer·a·bly** *adv.*

in·nu·mer·ate /in(y)ōō′mərət/ *adj.* having no knowledge of basic mathematics —**in·nu′mer·a·cy** /-əsē/ *n.*

in·oc·u·late /inäk′yəlāt′/ *v.* (·lat·ed, ·lat·ing) treat with vaccine or serum to provide immunity against a disease —**in·oc′u·la′tion** *n.* [L *inoculare* graft by budding; implant]

in·of·fen·sive /in′əfen′siv/ *adj.* not objectionable; harmless

in·op·er·a·ble /inäp′(ə)rəbəl/ *adj. Surg.* that cannot successfully be operated on

in·op·er·a·tive /inäp′(ə)rətiv/ *adj.* not working or taking effect

in·or·di·nate /inôrd′n-ət/ *adj.* excessive —**in·or′di·nate·ly** *adv.* [L in- not + *ordinatus* orderly]

in·or·gan·ic /in′ôrgan′ik/ *adj. Chem.* (of a compound) not organic, usu. of mineral origin

in′pa′tient *n.* patient who stays in a hospital for treatment

in·put /in′pŏŏt′/ *n.* 1 what is put in or taken in, as power in an electrical circuit or data for a computer 2 contribution of information, etc. —*v.* (·put or ·put·ted, ·put·ting) 3 *Comp.* supply or enter data

in·quest /in′kwest′/ *n. Law.* inquiry by a coroner into the cause of a death [L in- in + *quaesitum* question]

in·qui·e·tude /inkwī′it(y)ōōd′/ *n.* uneasiness [L, rel. to QUIET]

in·quire /inkwīr′/ *v.* (·quired, ·quir·ing) 1

make a formal investigation 2 ask [L *inquirere* seek]

in·qui·ry /inkwīr′ē, in′kwərē/ *n.* (*pl.* ·ries) 1 investigation, esp. an official one 2 question

in·qui·si·tion /in′kwəziSH′ən/ *n.* 1 judicial or official inquiry 2 **(the Inquisition)** *RC Ch. Hist.* tribunal for the violent suppression of heresy, esp. in Spain 3 intensive questioning —**in′qui·si′tion·al** *adj.*; **in·quis′i·tor** *n.* [L, rel. to INQUIRE]

in·quis·i·tive /inkwiz′ətiv/ *adj.* 1 seeking knowledge 2 unduly curious; prying —**in·quis′i·tive·ly** *adv.*; **in·quis′i·tive·ness** *n.*

in re /in rē′, rā′/ *prep. Latin.* in the matter of

INRI *abbr.* Jesus of Nazareth, King of the Jews [L *Iesus Nazarenus Rex Iudaeorum*]

in·road /in′rōd′/ *n.* 1 encroachment 2 hostile attack

INS *abbr.* Immigration and Naturalization Service

in·sane /insān′/ *adj.* 1 mad 2 *Colloq.* extremely foolish —**in·sane′ly** *adv.*; **in·san′i·ty** /-san′ətē/ *n.* (*pl.* ·ties)

in·sa·tia·ble /insā′SHəbəl/ *adj.* 1 unable to be satisfied 2 extremely greedy —**in·sa′tia·bil′i·ty** *n.*; **in·sa′tia·bly** *adv.*

in·scribe /inskrīb′/ *v.* (·scribed, ·scrib·ing) 1 mark or carve (words, etc.) on a surface, page, etc. 2 write an informal dedication to (as in a book, etc.) 3 enter the name of (a person) on a list or in a book [L in- in + *scribere* write]

in·scrip·tion /inskrip′SHən/ *n.* 1 words inscribed 2 inscribing —**in·scrip′tion·al** *adj.* [L, rel. to INSCRIBE]

in·scru·ta·ble /inskrōōt′əbəl/ *adj.* mysterious; impenetrable —**in·scru′ta·bil′i·ty** *n.*; **in·scru′ta·bly** *adv.* [L in- not + *scrutari* search]

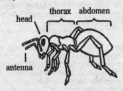

INSECT

in·sect /in′sekt′/ *n.* small invertebrate of a large class, including flies, beetles, bees, etc., with three pairs of thoracic legs and usu. one or two pairs of thoracic wings [L *insecare* cut up; incise]

in·sec·ti·cide /insek′təsīd′/ *n.* substance for killing insects

in·sec·ti·vore /insek′təvôr′/ *n.* animal or plant that feeds on insects —**in′sec·tiv′o·rous** /-tiv′(ə)rəs/ *adj.* [fr. INSECT, L *vorare* devour]

in·se·cure /in′sikyŏŏr′/ *adj.* 1a unsafe b (of a surface, etc.) liable to give way 2 lacking confidence —**in·se·cur′i·ty** *n.* (*pl.* ·ties)

in·sem·i·nate /insem′ənāt′/ *v.* (·nat·ed, ·nat·ing) 1 introduce semen into 2 sow; implant —**in·sem′i·na′tion** *n.* [L, rel. to SEMEN]

in·sen·sate /insen′sāt′, -sit/ *adj.* 1 without

physical sensation 2 without regard 3 stupid [L, rel. to SENSE]

in·sen·si·ble /insen′sibəl/ *adj.* 1 unconscious 2 unaware (*insensible of her needs*) 3 callous 4 too small or gradual to be perceived —**in·sen′si·bil′i·ty** *n.*; **in·sen′si·bly** *adv.*

in·sen·si·tive /insen′sitiv/ *adj.* 1 unfeeling; boorish 2 not sensitive to physical stimuli —**in·sen′si·tive·ly** *adv.*; **in·sen′si·tive·ness**, **in·sen′si·tiv′i·ty** *n.*

in·sen·ti·ent /insen′SHənt/ *adj.* not sentient; inanimate

in·sert *v.* /insərt′/ 1 place or put (a thing) into another —*n.* /in′sərt/ 2 something inserted [L *in-* in + *serere, sert-* join]

in·ser·tion /insər′SHən/ *n.* 1 inserting 2 thing inserted

in·set *n.* /in′set′/ 1 thing inserted 2 small map, etc., within the border of a larger one —*v.* /inset′, in′set′/ (·**set**, ·**set·ting**) 3 put in as an inset 4 decorate with an inset

in·shore /in′SHôr′/ *adv. & adj.* at sea but close to the shore

in·side /insīd′, in′sīd′/ *n.* 1a inner side 2 inner part; interior 3 (usu. *pl.*) *Colloq.* stomach and bowels —*adj.* 3 situated on or in the inside —*adv.* 4 on, in, or to the inside —*prep.* 5 on the inner side of; within 6 in less than (*inside an hour*) 7 **inside out: a** with the inner surface turned outward **b** thoroughly (*knew his subject inside out*)

in·sid·er /insīd′ər, in′sīd′ər/ *n.* 1 person who is within an organization, etc. 2 person privy to a secret

in′sid·er trad′ing *n. Stock Exch.* illegal practice of trading while having access to confidential information

in·sid·i·ous /insid′ēəs/ *adj.* proceeding inconspicuously but harmfully 2 crafty —**in·sid′i·ous·ly** *adv.*; **in·sid′i·ous·ness** *n.* [L *insidiae* ambush]

in·sight /in′sīt′/ *n.* 1 capacity of understanding hidden truths, etc. 2 instance of this

in·sig·ni·a /insig′nēə/ *n.* (*pl.* ·**ni·a** or ·**ni·as**) badge; emblem [L *signum* sign]

● Usage: In Latin, *insignia* is the plural of *insigne.* Staunch traditionalists insist on *insigne* as the singular, but *insignia* and its plural, *insignias*, are accepted as standard.

in·sig·nif·i·cant /in′signif′ikənt/ *adj.* 1 unimportant 2 meaningless

in·sin·cere /in′sinsēr′/ *adj.* not sincere —**in′sin·cere′ly** *adv.*; **in′sin·cer′i·ty** /-ser′ətē/ *n.* (*pl.* ·**ties**)

in·sin·u·ate /insin′yŏo-āt′/ *v.* (·**at·ed**, ·**at·ing**) 1 hint indirectly 2 introduce into favor, etc., deviously or by subtle manipulation —**in·sin′u·a′tion** *n.* [L *insinuare* introduce by windings or turnings, fr. *sinuare* curve]

in·sip·id /insip′id/ *adj.* 1 lacking vigor or character; dull 2 tasteless —**in′si·pid′i·ty** *n.*; **in·sip′id·ly** *adv.* [L *in-* not + *sapor* taste; flavor]

in·sist /insist′/ *v.* 1 maintain or demand assertively 2 state firmly [L *in-* in + *sistere* stand]

in·sis·tent /insis′tənt/ *adj.* 1 insisting 2 forcing itself on the attention —**in·sis′tence** *n.*; **in·sis′tent·ly** *adv.*

in si·tu /in si′t(y)ŏo, sī′tŏo/ *adv. Latin.* in its proper or original place

in·so·bri·e·ty /in′səbrī′ətē/ *n.* intemperance, esp. in drinking

in·so·far /in′səfär′/ *adv.* to such a degree (as)

in·sole /in′sōl′/ *n.* inner sole of a boot or shoe

in·so·lent /in′sələnt/ *adj.* impertinently insulting —**in′so·lence** *n.*; **in′so·lent·ly** *adv.* [L *in-* not + *solere* be accustomed]

in·sol·u·ble /insäl′yəbəl/ *adj.* 1 incapable of being solved 2 incapable of being dissolved —**in·sol′u·bil′i·ty** *n.*; **in·sol′u·bly** *adv.*

in·sol·vent /insäl′vənt/ *adj.* unable to pay one's debts; bankrupt —**in·sol′ven·cy** *n.*

in·som·ni·a /insäm′nēə/ *n.* sleeplessness, esp. habitual [L *in-* not + *somnus* sleep]

in·som·ni·ac /insäm′nē·ak′/ *n.* person suffering from insomnia

in·so·much /in′səməCH′/ *adv.* 1 to such an extent (that) 2 (foll. by *as*) inasmuch

in·sou·ci·ant /insōō′sēənt/ *adj.* carefree; unconcerned —**in·sou′ci·ance** *n.* [Fr *in-* not + *soucier* worry]

insp. *abbr.* 1 inspected 2 inspector

in·spect /inspekt′/ *v.* 1 look closely at 2 examine officially —**in·spec′tion** /-spek′SHən/ *n.* [L *inspicere, inspect-* look into]

in·spec·tor *n.* 1 person who inspects 2 police officer, usu. ranking below superintendent —**in·spec′to·rate** /-tərit/ *n.*

in·spi·ra·tion /in′spərā′SHən/ *n.* 1 creative force or influence stimulating creativity, etc. 2 divine influence, esp. on the writing of Scripture, etc. 3 sudden brilliant idea —**in′spi·ra′tion·al** *adj.*

in·spire /inspīr′/ *v.* (·**spired**, ·**spir·ing**) 1 stimulate to creative activity **2a** animate (a person) with a feeling **b** create (a feeling) in a person 3 prompt; give rise to —**in·spir′ing** *adj.* [L *inspirare* breathe into]

in·spired *adj.* characterized by inspiration

inst. *abbr.* 1 instant; instance 2 institute 3 institution 4 instrument

in·sta·bil·i·ty /in′stəbil′ətē/ *n.* 1 lack of stability 2 unpredictability in behavior, etc.

in·stall /instôl′/ *v.* (·**stalled**, ·**stall·ing**) 1 place (equipment, etc.) in position ready for use 2 place (a person) in an office or rank with ceremony 3 establish in a place —**in′stal·la′tion** /-stələ′SHən/ *n.* [rel. to STALL¹]

in·stall′ment *n.* 1 any of several usu. equal payments 2 any of several parts, as of a broadcast or story [OFr *estaler* fix; place, fr. Gmc *estal* place]

in·stall′ment plan′ *n.* purchase arrangement in which payments are made over a period of time

in·stance /in′stəns/ *n.* 1 example or illustration of 2 particular case (*in this instance*) —*v.* (·**stanced**, ·**stan·cing**) 3 cite as an instance 4 **for instance** as an example [Fr fr. L *instantia* presence]

in·stant /in′stənt/ *adj.* 1 occurring immediately 2 (of food, etc.) processed for quick preparation 3 urgent; pressing —*n.* 4 precise moment 5 short space of time [L *in-* in + *stare* stand]

in·stan·ta·ne·ous /in′stəntā′nēəs/ *adj.* occurring or done in an instant —**in′stan·ta′ne·ous·ly** *adv.*

in·stant·ly /ín'stəntlē/ *adv.* immediately; at once

in'stant re'play *n.* 1 immediate playback of a televised scene, as a sports play 2 *Colloq.* re-enactment of a recent occurrence

in·stead /instéd/ *adv.* 1 as an alternative 2 **instead of** in place of

in·step /ín'step/ *n.* 1 inner arch of the foot between the toes and the ankle 2 part of a shoe, etc., over or under this

in·sti·gate /ín'stigāt/ *v.* (·gat·ed, ·gat·ing) 1 bring about by incitement or persuasion 2 urge on; incite —**in'sti·ga'tion, in'sti·ga'tor** *n.* [L *instigare* stimulate; incite]

in·still or **in·stil** /instíl'/ *v.* (·stilled, ·still·ing) 1 introduce (a feeling, idea, etc.) gradually 2 put (a liquid) into drops —**in'stil·la'tion, in·still'ment** *n.* [L *in-* + *stillare* drop]

in·stinct /ín'stiNGkt'/ *n.* 1 innate pattern of behavior, esp. in animals 2 talent or skill —**in·stinc'tive** *adj.*; **in·stinc'tive·ly** *adv.*; **in·stinc·tu·al** /instíNGk'CHŌōəl/ *adj.* [L *instinguere* incite]

in·sti·tute /ín'stit(y)ōōt'/ *n.* 1 society or organization for the promotion of science, education, etc. 2 educational establishment specializing in technical training —*v.* (·tut·ed, ·tut·ing) 3 establish; found 4 initiate (an inquiry, etc.) [L *in-* + *statuere* erect; found]

in·sti·tu·tion /ín'stit(y)ōō'SHən/ *n.* 1 organization or society founded for a particular purpose 2 established law, practice, or custom 3 *Colloq.* long-established, as in an office or duty 4 instituting or being instituted —**in'sti·tu'tion·al** *adj.*; **in'sti·tu'tion·al·ly** *adv.*

in·sti·tu·tion·al·ize /ín'stit(y)ōō'SHə)nəlīz'/ *v.* (·ized, ·iz·ing) 1 place or keep (a person) in an institution, esp. for treatment 2 make into an institution

in·struct /instrəkt'/ *v.* 1 teach (a person) a subject, etc.; train 2 direct; command [L *instruere, -struct-* build; teach]

in·struc·tion /instrək'SHən/ *n.* 1 (often *pl.*) a order b direction (as to how a thing works, etc.) 2 something taught —**in·struc'tion·al** *adj.*

in·struc·tive /instrək'tiv/ *adj.* tending to instruct; enlightening

in·struc'tor *n.* 1 teacher 2 college teacher below professorial rank

in·stru·ment /ín'strəmənt/ *n.* 1 tool or implement, esp. for delicate or scientific work 2 device for producing musical sounds 3a thing used in performing an action b person made use of 4 gauge, as in an airplane 5 *Law.* formal document [L *instrumentum*, rel. to INSTRUCT]

in·stru·men·tal /ín'strəment'l/ *adj.* 1 serving as an instrument or means 2 *Mus.* performed on instruments

in'stru·men'tal·ist *n.* performer on a musical instrument

in·stru·men·tal·i·ty /ín'strəmen'tal'ətē/ *n.* agency or means

in'stru·men·ta'tion *n.* 1a provision or use of instruments b instruments collectively 2a *Mus.* arrangement for instruments b the particular instruments used in a piece

in·sub·or·di·nate /ín'səbôrd'n·ət/ *adj.* disobedient; rebellious —**in'sub·or'di·na'tion** *n.*

in·sub·stan·tial /ín'səbstan'SHəl/ *adj.* 1 lacking solidity or substance 2 not real

in·suf·fer·a·ble /insəf'(ə)rəbəl/ *adj.* intolerable; unbearable —**in·suf'fer·a·bly** *adv.*

in·su·lar /ín's(y)ələr/ *adj.* 1 of or like an island 2 narrow-minded —**in·su·lar'i·ty** /-lar'ətē/ *n.* [L *insula* island]

in·su·late /ín's(y)əlāt'/ *v.* (·lat·ed, ·lat·ing) 1 prevent the passage of electricity, heat, etc., by use of nonconducting material or design 2 isolate —**in'su·la'tion, in'su·la'tor** *n.* [L *insula* island]

in·su·lin /ín's(y)əlin/ *n.* hormone regulating the amount of glucose in the blood [L *insula* island]

in·sult *v.* /insəlt'/ 1 speak to or treat with scornful abuse 2 offend the self-respect or modesty of —*n.* /ín'səlt'/ 3 insulting remark or action —**in·sult'ing** *adj.*; **in·sult'ing·ly** *adv.* [L *insultare* leap on; assail]

in·su·per·a·ble /insōō'p(ə)rəbəl/ *adj.* impossible to surmount or overcome —**in·su'per·a·bil'i·ty** *n.*; **in·su'per·a·bly** *adv.* [L *in-* not + *superare* overcome]

in·sup·port·a·ble /ín'səpôrt'əbəl/ *adj.* 1 unable to be endured 2 unjustifiable

in·sur·ance /inSHŏŏr'əns/ *n.* 1 insuring 2 (also **in·sur'ance pol'i·cy**) contract that guarantees compensation for theft, damage, etc., for a fee 3 value of such a contract [Fr, rel. to ENSURE]

in·sure /inSHŏŏr'/ *v.* (·sured, ·sur·ing) purchase or issue a contract of insurance [var. of ENSURE]

• **Usage:** *Insure* is the choice for the sense 'protect against loss' (*assure* was also used for this sense formerly). In the sense 'make sure' it is interchanged freely with *ensure*: *My recommendation will ensure* (or *insure*) *you only an interview, not the job.*

in·sured /inSHŏŏrd'/ *n.* person, etc., covered by insurance

in·sur·er /inSHŏŏr'ər/ *n.* person or company selling insurance policies

in·sur·gent /insər'jənt/ *adj.* 1 in active revolt —*n.* 2 rebel —**in·sur'gence** *n.* [L *insurgere, -surrect-* rise to or against]

in·sur·rec·tion /ín'sərek'SHən/ *n.* rebellion —**in·sur·rec'tion·ist** *n.* [L, rel. to INSURGENT]

in·tact /intakt'/ *adj.* 1 undamaged; entire 2 untouched —**in·tact'ness** *n.* [L *in-* not + *tangere, tact-* touch]

in·ta·glio /intal'yō, -täl'-/ *n.* (*pl.* **·glios**) incised or engraved design [It *in* in + *tagliare* cut]

in·take /ín'tāk'/ *n.* 1 action of taking in 2 number or amount taken in or received 3 place where water, fuel, air, etc., is taken in

in·tan·gi·ble /intan'jəbəl/ *adj.* 1 unable to be touched 2 unable to be grasped mentally 3 without quantifiable value —*n.* 4 thing that cannot be precisely assessed or defined —**in·tan'gi·bil'i·ty** *n.*; **in·tan'gi·bly** *adv.* [L *in-* not + *tangere* touch]

in·te·ger /ín'təjər/ *n.* whole number [L: untouched; whole]

in·te·gral /ín'tigrəl, integ'-/ *adj.* 1a of or necessary to a whole b forming a whole c complete 2 of or denoted by an integer —**in'tegral·ly** /ín'teg·/ *adv.* [L, rel. to INTEGER]

in·te·grate /int'igrāt/ v. (·grat·ed, ·grat·ing) 1a combine (parts) into a whole b complete by the addition of parts 2 remove barriers that segregate, esp. by race —**in'te·gra'tion** n.

in'te·grat·ed cir'cuit n. Electronics. board or chip replacing several separate components in a conventional circuit

in·teg·ri·ty /integ'rətē/ n. 1 moral excellence; honesty 2 wholeness; soundness [L, rel. to INTEGER]

in·teg·u·ment /integ'yəmənt/ n. natural outer covering, as a skin, husk, rind, etc. [L in- in + tegere cover]

in·tel·lect /in'təlekt'/ n. 1a faculty of reasoning, knowing, and thinking b understanding 2 clever or knowledgeable person [L, rel. to INTELLIGENT]

in·tel·lec·tu·al /in'təlek'chōōəl/ adj. 1 of or appealing to the intellect 2 possessing a highly developed intellect 3 requiring the intellect —n. 4 person with intellectual interests —**in'tel·lec'tu·al'i·ty** /-al'ətē/ n.; **in'tel·lec'tu·al·ize'** /-īz/ v. (·ized, ·iz·ing); **in'tel·lec'tu·al·ly** adv.

in'tel·lec'tu·al prop'er·ty n. creative work that is protected by copyright, patent, or trademark law

in·tel·li·gence /intel'əjəns/ n. 1a intellect; understanding b quickness of understanding 2a the collecting of information, esp. of military or political value b information so collected c people employed in this

in·tel'li·gence quo'tient n. number denoting the ratio of a person's intelligence to the average; abbr. **IQ**

in·tel·li·gent /intel'əjənt/ adj. 1 having or showing intelligence, esp. of a high level 2 clever —**in·tel'li·gent·ly** adv. [L intelligere understand]

in·tel·li·gent·si·a /intel'əjent'sēə/ n. intellectuals, considered as a class [Russ fr. L intelligentia]

in·tel·li·gi·ble /intel'əjəbəl/ adj. able to be understood —**in·tel'li·gi·bil'i·ty** n.; **in·tel'li·gi·bly** adv.

in·tem·per·ate /intem'p(ə)rət/ adj. 1 immoderate 2 given to excessive drinking of alcohol —**in·tem'per·ance** n.

in·tend /intend'/ v. 1 have as one's purpose 2 design or mean for 3 mean; signify [L intendere stretch toward]

in·tend·ed /intend'id/ adj. 1 done on purpose —n. 2 Colloq. one's fiancé or fiancée

in·tense /intens'/ adj. 1 existing in a high degree; violent; forceful; extreme 2 very emotional —**in·tense'ly** adv.; **in·tense'ness** n. [L intensus stretched]

in·ten·si·fy /inten'səfī'/ v. (·fied, ·fy·ing) make or become intense or more intense —**in·ten'si·fi·ca'tion** /-fikā'shən/ n.

in·ten·si·ty /inten'sətē/ n. 1 intenseness 2 amount of some quality, e.g., force, brightness, etc.

in·ten·sive /inten'siv/ adj. 1 thorough; vigorous; directed to a single point, area, or subject 2 Gram. expressing intensity (really in my feet are really cold) —**in·ten'sive·ly** adv.; **in·ten'sive·ness** n.

in·ten'sive care' u'nit n. section of a hospital providing constant monitoring, etc., of seriously ill patients; abbr. **ICU**

in·tent /intent'/ n. 1 intention; purpose —adj. 2a resolved; determined b attentively occupied 3 (esp. of a look) earnest; eager 4 to (or for) all intents and purposes practically; virtually —**in·tent'ly** adv.; **in·tent'ness** n. [L intentus]

in·ten·tion /inten'shən/ n. 1 thing intended; aim; purpose 2 intending (done without intention)

in·ten'tion·al adj. done on purpose —**in·ten'tion·al·ly** adv.

in·ter /intər'/ v. (·terred, ·ter·ring) bury (a corpse, etc.) [L in in + terra earth]

inter- comb. form 1 between; among (intercontinental) 2 mutually; reciprocally (interbreed) [L inter- between; among]

in·ter·act /int'ərakt'/ v. act on each other —**inter·ac'tion** n.

in·ter·ac·tive /int'ərak'tiv/ adj. 1 reciprocally active 2 (of a computer or other electronic device) allowing a two-way flow of information between it and a user —**in·ter·ac'tive·ly** adv.

in·ter a'li·a /int'ər ā'lēə, äl'ēə/ adv. Latin. among other things

in·ter·breed /int'ərbrēd'/ v. (·bred, ·breed·ing) 1 (cause to) breed with members of a different race or species to produce a hybrid 2 breed within one family, etc.

in·ter·cede /int'ərsēd'/ v. (·ced·ed, ·ced·ing) intervene on behalf of another; plead [L, rel. to CEDE]

in·ter·cept /int'ərsept'/ v. 1 seize, catch, or stop (a person or thing) going from one place to another 2 cut off (light, etc.) —**in'ter·cep'tion** /-sep'shən/ n.; **in'ter·cep'tor** or **in'ter·cep'tor** n. [L intercipere, -cept- fr. capere take]

in·ter·ces·sion /int'ərsesh'ən/ n. interceding —**in'ter·ces'sor** n. [L, rel. to INTERCEDE]

in·ter·change v. /int'ərchānj'/ (·changed, ·chang·ing) 1 (of two people) exchange (things) with each other 2 put each of (two things) in the other's place; alternate —n. /int'ərchānj/ 3 exchange between two people, etc. 4 alternation 5 road junction where traffic streams do not cross —**in·ter·change'a·ble** adj.

in·ter·com /int'ərkäm'/ n. Colloq. 1 system of intercommunication by radio or telephone 2 instrument used in this

in·ter·con·nect /int'ərkənekt'/ v. connect with each other —**in'ter·con·nec'tion** n.

in·ter·con·ti·nen·tal /int'ərkänt'n·ent'l/ adj. connecting or traveling between continents

in·ter·course /int'ərkôrs'/ n. 1 communication or dealings between individuals, nations, etc. 2 SEXUAL INTERCOURSE [L, rel. to COURSE]

in·ter·de·nom·i·na·tion·al /int'ərdinäm'ənā'shənəl/ adj. concerning more than one (religious) denomination

in·ter·de·part·men·tal /int'ərdipärt'ment'l/ adj. concerning more than one department

in·ter·de·pen·dent /int'ərdipen'dənt/ adj. dependent on each other —**in'ter·de·pend'ence** n.

in·ter·dict n. /int'ərdikt'/ 1 authoritative prohibition —v. /int'ərdikt'/ 2 prohibit (an action) 3 forbid the use of 4 restrain (a person) **5** forbid (a thing) to a person —**in′ter·dic′tion** /-dik′sнən/ n.; **in′ter·dic′to·ry** /-tôrē/ adj. [L *interdicere* forbid]

in·ter·dis·ci·plin·ar·y /int′ərdis′əplənər′ē/ adj. of or between more than one branch of learning

in·ter·est /in′trəst, int′ərest′, int′ərəst/ n. **1a** concern; curiosity (*no interest in fishing*) **b** quality exciting curiosity, etc. (*this book lacks interest*) **2** subject, hobby, etc., in which one is concerned **3** advantage or profit (*in my interest to go*) **4** money paid for the use of money lent **5a** thing in which one has a stake or concern (*business interests*) **b** financial stake (in an undertaking, etc.) **c** legal concern, title, or right (in property) **6** party or group with a common interest (*the banking interest*) —v. **7** excite the curiosity or attention of **8** cause (a person) to take a personal interest [L: it matters]

in′ter·est·ing adj. causing curiosity; holding the attention —**in′ter·est·ing·ly** adv.

in·ter·face /int′ərfās′/ n. **1** surface forming a boundary between two regions **2** means or place of interaction between two systems, etc.; interaction **3** *Comp.* apparatus for connecting two pieces of equipment so that they can be operated jointly —v. (**·faced, ·fac·ing**) **4** connect with; interact

in·ter·fere /int′ərfēr′/ v. (**·fered, ·fer·ing**) **1a** (of a person) meddle; obstruct a process, etc. **b** (of a thing) be a hindrance **2** intervene, esp. without invitation or necessity [L *inter-* between + *ferire* strike]

in·ter·fer·ence /int′ərfēr′əns/ n. **1** act of interfering **2** fading or disturbance of received radio signals

in·ter·fer·on /int′ərfēr′än′/ n. any of various proteins inhibiting the development of a virus in a cell, etc.

in·ter·fuse /int′əfyōōz′/ v. (**·fused, ·fus·ing**) **1a** mix (a thing) with; intersperse **b** blend (things) **2** (of two things) blend with each other —**in′ter·fu′sion** /-zнən/ n. [L *interfundere* pour between]

in·ter·im /int′ərim/ n. **1** intervening time —adj. **2** provisional; temporary [L: in the meantime]

in·te·ri·or /intēr′ēər/ adj. **1** inner **2** inland **3** internal; domestic **4** situated further in or within **5** coming from inside —n. **6** interior part; inside **7** domestic affairs of a country [L]

interj. abbr. interjection

in·ter·ject /int′ərjekt′/ v. **1** utter (words) abruptly or parenthetically **2** interrupt [L *interjicere* throw between]

in·ter·jec·tion /int′ərjek′sнən/ n. exclamation, esp. as a part of speech (*ah!; dear me!*) [L]

in·ter·lace /int′ərlās′/ v. (**·laced, ·lac·ing**) bind intricately together; interweave —**in′ter·lace′ment** n.

in·ter·lard /int′ərlärd′/ v. mix (writing or speech) with special elements or features [MFr]

in·ter·leave /int′ərlēv′/ v. (**·leaved, ·leav·ing**) insert white (usu. blank) leaves between the leaves of (a book, etc.)

in·ter·lin·ing /in′tərli′ninG/ n. extra layer of

material between the fabric of (a garment) and its lining

in·ter·lock /int′ərläk′/ v. **1** engage with each other by overlapping **2** lock or clasp within each other

in·ter·loc·u·tor /int′ərläk′yətər/ n. *Formal.* person who takes part in a conversation [L *interloqui* speak between]

in·ter·loc·u·to·ry /int′ərläk′yətôr′ē/ adj. *Formal.* **1** of dialogue **2** *Law.* given provisionally

in·ter·lop·er /int′ərlō′pər/ n. intruder; one who interferes [after *landloper* vagabond, fr. Du *loopen* run]

in·ter·lude /int′ərlōōd/ n. pause between the acts of a play, etc., or something performed during this pause [MedL *inter-* between + *ludus* play]

in·ter·mar·ry /int′ərmar′ē/ v. (**·ried, ·ry·ing**) (of races, castes, families, etc.) become connected by marriage —**in′ter·mar′riage** /-mar′ij/ n.

in·ter·me·di·ar·y /int′ərmēd′ē·er′ē/ n. (pl. **·ies**) **1** intermediate person or thing, esp. a mediator —adj. **2** acting as mediator; intermediate

in·ter·me·di·ate /int′ərmēd′ēət/ adj. **1** coming between two things in time, place, order, character, etc. —n. **2** intermediate thing [L *intermedius*]

in·ter·ment /intər′mənt/ n. burial

● Usage: *Interment,* which means 'burial,' should be distinguished from *internment,* which means 'imprisonment.'

in·ter·mez·zo /int′ərmet′sō/ n. (pl. **·zi** /-sē/) **1** short instrumental movement in a musical work **2** short light dramatic or other performance inserted between the acts of a play [It]

in·ter·mi·na·ble /intər′mənəbəl/ adj. **1** endless **2** tediously long —**in·ter′mi·na·bly** adv.

in·ter·min·gle /int′ərminG′gəl/ v. (**·gled, ·gling**) mix together; mingle

in·ter·mis·sion /int′ərmisн′ən/ n. pause or interval, as between acts of a play [L *intermittere* pause; interrupt]

in·ter·mit·tent /int′ərmit′nt/ adj. occurring at intervals; not continuous —**in·ter·mit′tent·ly** adv. [L *intermittere* pause; interrupt]

in·tern n. /in′tərn/ **1** doctor in training at a hospital **2** apprentice —v. /in′tərn, intərn′/ **3** oblige (a prisoner, alien, etc.) to reside within prescribed limits [Fr, rel. to INTERNAL]

in·ter·nal /intər′nəl/ adj. **1** of or situated in the inside **2** of the inside of the body (*internal injuries*) **3** of a nation's domestic affairs **4** used or applying within an organization **5a** intrinsic to the mind or soul —**in·ter′nal·ly** adv. [L *internus* internal]

in·ter′nal-com·bus′tion en′gine n. engine powered by the explosion of fuel and air in a cylinder

in·ter·nal·ize /intərn′l-īz′/ v. (**·ized, ·iz·ing**) *Psychol.* make (attitudes, behavior, etc.) part of one's nature by learning or unconscious assimilation —**in·ter·nal·i·za′tion** n.

in·ter·na·tion·al /int′ərnasн′(ə)nəl/ adj. **1** existing or carried on between nations **2** agreed on or used by all or many nations —**in′ter·na′tion·al′i·ty** /-al′ətē/ n.; **in·ter·na′tion·al·ly** adv.; **in′ter·na′tion·al·ize** v. (**·ized, ·iz·ing**)

in·ter·na·tion·al·ism /int′ərnasн′(ə)nəliz

…əm/ n. advocacy of a community of interests among nations —in'ter·na'tion·al·ist n.

in·ter·ne·cine /int'ərnēsēn', -nē'sīn/ adj. mutually destructive [L internecinus deadly]

in·tern·ment /intərn'mənt/ n. imprisonment; confinement
● Usage: See note at INTERMENT.

in·ter·per·son·al /int'ərpər'sənəl/ adj. between persons; social (interpersonal skills)

in·ter·plan·e·tar·y /int'ərplan'ətər'ē/ adj. between planets

in·ter·play /int'ərplā/ n. reciprocal action

In·ter·pol /int'ərpäl', -pōl/ n. International Criminal Police Organization [shortening]

in·ter·po·late /intər'pəlāt'/ v. (·lat·ed, ·lat·ing) 1a insert (words) in a book, etc. b make such insertions in (a book, etc.) 2 estimate (values) between known ones in the same range —in·ter·po·la'tion, in·ter'po·la'tor n. [L interpolare refurbish]

in·ter·pose /int'ərpōz'/ v. (·posed, ·pos·ing) 1 insert (a thing) between others 2 say (words) as an interruption; interrupt 3 intervene (between parties) —in'ter·po·si'tion /-zi'sHən/ n. [L interponere set between]

in·ter·pret /intər'prit/ v. 1 explain the meaning of (words, a dream, etc.) 2 make out or bring out the meaning of (creative work) 3 act as an interpreter 4 explain or understand (behavior, etc.) in a specified manner —in·ter'pre·ta'tion /-tā'sHən/ n.; in·ter'pre·ta·tive /-tā'tiv/, in·ter'pre·tive adj. [L interpres, -pret- explainer]

in·ter·pret·er /intər'prətər/ n. person who interprets, esp. one who translates foreign speech orally

in·ter·ra·cial /int'ə(r)rā'sHəl/ adj. between or affecting different races

in·ter·re·late /int'ə(r)rilāt'/ v. (·lat·ed, ·lat·ing) 1 relate (two or more things) to each other 2 (of two or more things) relate to each other —in'ter·re·la'tion, in'ter·re·la'tion·ship' n.

interrog. abbr. interrogative

in·ter·ro·gate /inter'əgāt'/ v. (·gat·ed, ·gat·ing) question (a person), esp. closely or formally —in·ter'ro·ga'tion, in·ter'ro·ga'tor n. [L interrogare question]

in·ter·rog·a·tive /int'əräg'ətiv/ adj. of, like, or used in a question

in·ter·rog·a·to·ry /int'əräg'ətôr'ē/ adj. questioning (interrogatory tone)

in·ter·rupt /int'ərəpt'/ v. 1 break the continuous progress of (an action, speech, person speaking, etc.) 2 break in; interfere —in'ter·rupt'er, in'ter·rup'tion /-rəp'sHən/ n. [L, rel. to RUPTURE]

in·ter·sect /int'ərsekt'/ v. 1 divide (a thing) by crossing it 2 (of lines, roads, etc.) cross each other [L intersecare cut apart]

in·ter·sec·tion /int'ərsek'sHən/ n. 1 intersecting 2 place where two lines, roads, etc., intersect

in·ter·sperse /int'ərspərs'/ v. (·spersed, ·spers·ing) 1 scatter 2 vary (a thing) by scattering other things among it —in·ter·sper'sion /-spər'zHən/ n. [L inter- between + spargere scatter]

in·ter·state /int'ərstāt'/ adj. existing or carried on between states, esp. those of the US

in·ter·stel·lar /int'ərstel'ər/ adj. between stars

in·ter·stice /intər'stis/ n. (pl. ·sti·ces /-stəsēz/) 1 intervening space 2 chink or crevice [L intersistere stand between]

in·ter·sti·tial /int'ərstisH'əl/ adj. of, forming, or occupying interstices —in'ter·sti'tial·ly adv.

in·ter·twine /int'ərtwīn'/ v. (·twined, ·twin·ing) entwine (together)

in·ter·val /int'ərvəl/ n. 1 intervening time or space 2 pause or break, esp. between the parts of a performance 3 difference in pitch between two sounds 4 at intervals here and there; now and then [L intervallum space between ramparts]

in·ter·vene /int'ərvēn'/ v. (·vened, ·ven·ing) 1 occur in time between events 2 interfere; prevent or modify events 3 be situated between things [L intervenire come between]

in·ter·ven·tion /int'ərven'sHən/ n. 1 intervening 2 interference, esp. by a state

in·ter·view /int'ərvyoō'/ n. 1 oral examination of an applicant 2 conversation with a reporter, for a broadcast or publication 3 meeting face to face, esp. for consultation —v. 4 have an interview with —in'ter·view·ee, in'ter·view'er n. [MFr entrevoir glimpse]

in·ter·weave /int'ərwēv'/ v. (·wove or ·wo·ven, ·weav·ing) 1 weave together 2 blend intimately

in·tes·tate /intes'tāt'/ adj. not having made a will before death —in·tes'ta·cy /-təsē/ n. [L in not + testari make a will]

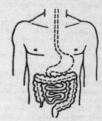

INTESTINE

in·tes·tine /intes'tin/ n. (sing. or pl.) lower part of the alimentary canal —in·tes'ti·nal adj. [L intus within]

in·ti·mate[1] /int'əmət/ adj. 1 closely acquainted; familiar 2 private and personal 3 having sexual relations 4 (of knowledge) detailed; thorough —n. 5 close friend —in'ti·ma·cy n. (pl. ·cies); in'ti·mate·ly adv. [L intimus inmost]

in·ti·mate[2] /int'əmāt'/ v. (·mat·ed, ·mat·ing) 1 state or make known 2 imply; hint —in'ti·ma'tion n. [L intimare announce, rel. to INTIMATE[1]]

in·tim·i·date /intim'ədāt'/ v. (·dat·ed, ·dat·ing) frighten or overawe, esp. to subdue or influence —in·tim'i·da'tion n. [MedL intimidare]

in·to /in'toō/ prep. 1 expressing motion or direction to a point on or within (walked into a tree; ran into the house) 2 expressing direction of attention, etc. (will look into it) 3 expressing a change of state (*turned into a dragon; separated into groups*) **4** after the beginning of (*five minutes into the game*) **5** *Colloq.* interested in [OE, rel. to IN + TO]

in·tol·er·a·ble /intäl'(ə)rəbəl/ *adj.* that cannot be endured —**in·tol'er·a·bly** *adv.*

in·tol·er·ant /intäl'ərənt/ *adj.* not tolerant, esp. of others' beliefs or behavior —**in·tol'er·ance** *n.*

in·to·na·tion /in'tənā'SHən/ *n.* **1** modulation of the voice; accent **2** intoning **3** accuracy of musical pitch [MedL, rel. to INTONE]

in·tone /intōn'/ *v.* (**·toned, ·ton·ing**) **1** recite (prayers, etc.) with prolonged sounds, esp. in a monotone **2** utter with a particular tone [MedL, rel. to IN² + TONE]

in to·to /in tōt'ō/ *adv.* *Latin.* completely

in·tox·i·cant /intäk'sikənt/ *adj.* **1** intoxicating —*n.* **2** intoxicating substance

in·tox·i·cate /intäk'sikāt'/ *v.* (**·cat·ed, ·cat·ing**) **1** make drunk **2** excite or elate beyond self-control —**in·tox'i·ca'tion** *n.* [MedL, rel. to TOXIC]

intr. *abbr.* intransitive

intra- *prefix* on the inside; within [L *intra* inside]

in·trac·ta·ble /intrak'təbəl/ *adj.* hard to control; stubborn —**in·trac'ta·bil'i·ty** *n.*; **in·trac'ta·bly** *adv.*

in·tra·mu·ral /in'trəmyoor'əl/ *adj.* situated or done within an institution, etc. [L *intra*-within + *murus* wall]

in·tra·mus·cu·lar /in'trəməs'kyələr/ *adj.* in or into muscle tissue

in·tran·si·gent /intran'səjənt, -zəjənt/ *adj.* uncompromising; stubborn —**in·tran'si·gence** *n.* [Sp fr L *in* not + *transigere* come to an agreement]

in·tran·si·tive /intran'sətiv/ *adj.* *Gram.* (of a verb) not taking a direct object

in·tra·u·ter·ine /in'trəyoot'ərən, -rīn'/ *adj.* within the womb

in·tra·ve·nous /in'trəvē'nəs/ *adj.* in or into a vein or veins —**in·tra·ve'nous·ly** *adv.*

in·trep·id /intrep'id/ *adj.* fearless; very brave —**in·trep'id·ly** *adv.* [L *in*- not + *trepidus* alarmed]

in·tri·cate /in'trikət/ *adj.* very complicated; perplexingly detailed —**in·tri·ca·cy** /-kəsē/ *n.* (*pl.* **·cies**) **in'tri·cate·ly** *adv.* [L *intricare* entangle]

in·trigue *v.* /intrēg'/ (**·trigued, ·trigu·ing**) **1a** carry on an underhand plot **b** use secret influence **2** arouse the curiosity of —*n.* /in'trēg/ **3** underhand plot or plotting **4** secret arrangement —**in·trigu'ing** *adj.*; **in·trigu'ing·ly** *adv.* [Fr fr. It *intrigare* fr. L *intricare* entangle]

in·trin·sic /intrin'zik, -sik/ *adj.* inherent; essential —**in·trin'si·cal·ly** *adv.* [MedL *intrinsecus* inwardly]

intro- *comb. form* into; within [L]

intro. *abbr.* **1** introduction **2** introductory

in·tro·duce /in'trəd(y)oos'/ *v.* (**·duced, ·duc·ing**) **1** make (a person or oneself) known by name to another, esp. formally **2** announce or present **3** bring (a custom, etc.) into use **4** offer (legislation) for consideration **5** initiate (a person) in a subject **6** insert **7**

bring in; usher in; bring forward —**in'tro·duc'i·ble** *adj.* [L *introducere* lead into]

in·tro·duc·tion /in'trədək'SHən/ *n.* **1** introducing or being introduced **2** formal presentation of one person to another **3** explanatory section at the beginning of a book, etc.

in·tro·duc·to·ry /in'trədək't(ə)rē/ *adj.* serving as an introduction; preliminary

in·tro·spec·tion /in'trəspek'SHən/ *n.* examination of one's own thoughts —**in'tro·spec'tive** /-tiv/ *adj.* [L *introspicere* look within]

in·tro·vert /in'trəvert'/ *n.* **1** person predominantly concerned with his or her own thoughts **2** shy thoughtful person —**in'tro·ver'sion** /-vər'ZHən/ *n.*; **in'tro·vert'ed** *adj.*

in·trude /introod'/ *v.* (**·trud·ed, ·trud·ing**) **1** come uninvited or unwanted **2** force on a person —**in·tru'sion** /-troo'ZHən/ *n.*; **in·tru'sive** /-siv/ *adj.*; **in·tru'sive·ness** *n.* [L *intrudere* thrust in]

in·trud·er /introod'ər/ *n.* person who intrudes, esp. a trespasser

in·trust /intrast'/ *v.* var. of ENTRUST

in·tu·i·tion /in't(y)oo·iSH'ən/ *n.* immediate insight or understanding without conscious reasoning —**in·tu·it** /int(y)oo'it/ *v.*; **in·tu·i'tion·al** *adj.* [L *intueri* look at]

in·tu·i·tive /int(y)oo'ətiv/ *adj.* of, possessing, or perceived by intuition —**in·tu'i·tive·ly** *adv.*; **in·tu'i·tive·ness** *n.* [MedL, rel. to IN-TUITION]

In·u·it /in'(y)oo·it/ *n.* (also **In'nu·it**) (*pl.* same or **·its**) aboriginal peoples of N America; formerly called Eskimos [Esk: people]

in·un·date /in'əndāt', -dat-/ *v.* (**·dat·ed, ·dat·ing**) **1** flood **2** overwhelm —**in'un·da'tion** *n.* [L *inundare* overflow]

in·ure /in(y)oor'/ *v.* (**·ured, ·ur·ing**) accustom (a person) to an esp. unpleasant thing —**in·ure'ment** *n.* [AngFr *in* in + *ure* work, fr. L *opera* work]

in·vade /invād'/ *v.* (**·vad·ed, ·vad·ing**) **1** enter (a country, etc.) with hostility **2** swarm into **3** (of a disease) attack **4** encroach upon —**in·vad'er** *n.* [L *invadere* go into; assault]

in·val·id¹ /in'vəlid/ *n.* **1** person enfeebled or disabled by illness or injury —*adj.* **2** of or for invalids **3** sick; disabled —**in'va·lid'ism** /-izəm/, /-ətē/ *n.* [F fr. L *invalidus* weak]

in·val·id² /inval'id/ *adj.* not valid —**in·val·id·i·ty** /-in'vəlid'ətē/ *n.*

in·val·i·date /inval'ədāt'/ *v.* (**·dat·ed, ·dat·ing**) make (a claim, etc.) invalid —**in·val·i·da'tion** *n.*

in·val·u·a·ble /inval'y(oo)əbəl/ *adj.* above valuation; very valuable —**in·val'u·a·bly** *adv.*

in·va·sion /invā'ZHən/ *n.* invading or being invaded

in·va·sive /invā'siv/ *adj.* **1** tending to spread **2** (of surgery) involving large incisions, etc. **3** tending to encroach

in·vec·tive /invek'tiv/ *n.* strong verbal attack [L, rel. to INVEIGH]

in·veigh /invā'/ *v.* speak or write with strong hostility (against) [L *invehi* assail]

in·vei·gle /invā'gəl/ *v.* (**·gled, ·gling**) entice; persuade by guile —**in·vei'gle·ment** *n.* [AngFr fr. OFr *avogler* blind]

in·vent /invent'/ *v.* **1** create by thought; originate (a method, device, etc.) **2** concoct (a

in·ven·tion /inven′sHən/ *n.* 1 inventing or being invented 2 thing invented 3 fictitious story 4 inventiveness

in·ven·tive /invent′iv/ *adj.* able to invent; imaginative —**in·ven′tive·ly** *adv.*; **in·ven′tive·ness** *n.*

in·ven·to·ry /in′vəntôr′ē/ *n.* (*pl.* **-ries**) 1 complete list of goods, etc. 2 goods listed in this —*v.* (**-ried, -ry·ing**) 3 make an inventory of 4 enter (goods) in an inventory [MedL, rel. to INVENT]

in·verse /invərs′, in′vərs/ *adj.* 1 inverted in position, order, or relation —*n.* 2 inverted state or thing [L *invertere* turn upside down]

in′verse pro·por′tion *n.* (also **in′verse ra′tio**) relation between two quantities such that one increases in proportion as the other decreases

in·ver·sion /invər′zHən, -sHən/ *n.* 1 turning upside down 2 reversal of a normal order, position, or relation

in·vert /invərt′/ *v.* 1 turn upside down 2 reverse the position, order, or relation of [L *invertere* turn inside out]

in·ver·te·brate /invərt′əbrət/ *adj.* 1 (of an animal) not having a backbone —*n.* 2 invertebrate animal

in·vest /invest′/ *v.* 1a apply or use (money), esp. for profit b put money for profit in (stocks, etc.) 2 devote (time, etc.) to an enterprise 3 *Colloq.* buy (something useful) 4a provide or credit (a person, etc., with qualities) (*invested his tone with irony*) b attribute or entrust (qualities or feelings) to (a person, etc.) (*power invested in the doctor*) 5 ceremoniously install in an office —**in·ves′tor** *n.* [L *in-* + *vestis* clothing]

in·ves·ti·gate /inves′tigāt′/ *v.* (**-gat·ed, -gat·ing**) 1 inquire into; examine 2 make a systematic inquiry —**in·ves′ti·ga′tion** *n.*; **in·ves′ti·ga′tive** *adj.*; **in·ves′ti·ga′tor** *n.*; **in·ves′ti·ga·to′ry** /-gətôr′ē/ *adj.* [L *investigare* track]

in·ves·ti·ture /inves′təCHər/ *n.* formal investing of a person with honors or rank [MedL *investire* install]

in·vest′ment *n.* 1 investing 2 money invested 3 property, etc., in which money is invested

in·vet·er·ate /invet′ərət/ *adj.* 1 (of a person) confirmed in a habit, etc. 2 (of a habit, etc.) long-established —**in·vet′er·a·cy** *n.* [L *inveterare* grow old]

in·vid·i·ous /invid′ēəs/ *adj.* likely to cause resentment or anger [L *invidiosus* envious]

in·vig·o·rate /invig′ərāt′/ *v.* (**-rat·ed, -rat·ing**) give vigor or strength to —**in·vig′or·at′ing** *adj.* [rel. to VIGOR]

in·vin·ci·ble /invin′səbəl/ *adj.* unconquerable —**in·vin′ci·bil′i·ty** *n.*; **in·vin′ci·bly** *adv.* [L *in-* not + *vincere* conquer]

in·vi·o·la·ble /invī′ələbəl/ *adj.* not to be violated or dishonored —**in·vi′o·la·bil′i·ty** *n.*; **in·vi′o·la·bly** *adv.*

in·vi·o·late /invī′ələt/ *adj.* 1 not violated 2 safe (from violation or harm) —**in·vi′o·la·cy** *n.*

in·vis·i·ble /inviz′əbəl/ *adj.* not visible to the eye —**in·vis′i·bil′i·ty** *n.*; **in·vis′i·bly** *adv.*

in·vis′i·ble ink′ *n.* ink for writing that is invisible until exposed to heat, vapor, or chemicals

in·vi·ta·tion /invətā′sHən/ *n.* 1 inviting or being invited 2 letter or card, etc., used to invite

in·vite *v.* /invīt′/ (**-vit·ed, -vit·ing**) 1 ask (a person) courteously to come or to do something 2 make a formal courteous request for 3 tend to call forth unintentionally 4 attract —*n.* /in′vīt′/ 5 *Colloq.* invitation [L *invitare*]

in·vit′ing *adj.* 1 attractive 2 tempting —**in·vit′ing·ly** *adv.*

in vi·tro /in vē′trō/ *adv.* taking place in a test-tube or other laboratory environment [L: in glass]

in·vo·ca·tion /invəkā′sHən, -vō-/ *n.* 1 invoking or being invoked, esp. in prayer 2 summoning of a source of inspiration, e.g., the Muses [L *invocatio* calling upon]

in·voice /in′vois/ *n.* 1 bill for usu. itemized goods or services —*v.* (**-voiced, -voic·ing**) 2 send an invoice to 3 put on an invoice [earlier *invoyes* pl. of *invoy*, rel. to ENVOY]

in·voke /invōk′/ *v.* (**-voked, -vok·ing**) 1 call on (a deity, etc.) in prayer or as a witness 2 appeal to (the law, a person's authority, etc.) 3 summon (a spirit) by charms, etc. 4 ask earnestly for (vengeance, etc.) [L *invocare* call]

in·vol·un·tar·y /inväl′ənter′ē/ *adj.* 1 done without exercising the will; unintentional 2 (of a muscle) not under conscious control —**in·vol′un·tar′i·ly** *adv.*; **in·vol′un·tar′i·ness** *n.*

in·vo·lu·tion /invəlōō′sHən/ *n.* 1 an involving 2 intricacy 3 curling inwards

in·volve /invälv′, -vôlv′/ *v.* (**-volved, -volv·ing**) 1 cause (a person or thing) to share the experience or effect (of a situation, activity, etc.) 2 imply; entail; make necessary 3 implicate (a person) in a charge, crime, etc. 4 include or affect —**in·volve′ment** *n.* [L *involvere* roll in, to, or upon]

in·volved′ *adj.* 1 concerned 2 complicated in thought or form 3 amorously involved

in·vul·ner·a·ble /invəl′nərəbəl, -vooln′rəbəl/ *adj.* that cannot be wounded, damaged, or hurt —**in·vul′ner·a·bil′i·ty** *n.*; **in·vul′ner·a·bly** *adv.*

in·ward /in′wərd/ *adj.* 1 directed toward the inside; going in 2 situated within 3 mental; spiritual —*adv.* (also **in′wards**) 4 toward the inside 5 in the mind or soul [OE, rel. to IN + -WARD]

in′ward·ly *adv.* 1 on the inside 2 in the mind or soul 3 not aloud

in′-your-face′ *adj.* aggressively confrontational in manner

I/O *abbr. Comp.* input/output

i·o·dide /ī′ədīd′/ *n.* any compound of iodine with another element or group

i·o·dine /ī′ədīn′/ *n.* 1 chemical element forming a violet vapor when heated 2 solution of this as an antiseptic; *symb.* I [Fr *iode* fr. Gk *iōdēs* violet-like]

i·on /ī′ən, ī′än/ *n.* atom or group of atoms that has lost one or more electrons (CATION) or gained one or more electrons (ANION) [Gk: going]

-ion *suffix* forming nouns denoting: 1 verbal

action (*excision*) 2 instance of this (*a suggestion*) 3 resulting state or product (*vexation; concoction*) [L *-io*]

Io·nes·co /ēənes′kō/, **Eugène** 1912–94; Romanian-born French dramatist

i·on·ic /ī·on′ik/ *adj.* of or using ions —**i·on′i·cal·ly** *adv.*

I·on·ic *adj.* of the order of Greek architecture characterized by a column with scroll-shapes on either side of the capital (see illustration at CAPITAL) [fr. *Ionia* in Gk Asia Minor]

i·on·ize /ī′əniz′/ *v.* (**·ized**, **·iz·ing**) convert or be converted into an ion or ions —**i·on′i·za′tion, i′on·iz′er** *n.*

i·ono·sphere /ī·än′əsfēr′/ *n.* ionized region of the atmosphere above the stratosphere, reflecting radio waves —**i′on·o·spher′ic** /-sfer′ik/ *adj.*

i·o·ta /ī-ōt′ə/ *n.* 1 ninth letter of the Greek alphabet (I, ι) 2 tiny bit; scintilla [Gk]

IOU /ī′ō·yōō′/ *n.* signed document acknowledging a debt [fr. *I owe you*]

I·o·wa /ī′əwə/ *n.* state in the central US. Capital: Des Moines. Pop. 2,776,755. Abbr. IA; Ia. —**I′o·wan** *n.* & *adj.*

I′o·wa Cit′y *n.* city in Iowa. Pop. 59,738

ip·e·cac /ip′ikak′/ *n.* root of a S American shrub, used as an emetic [Port fr. SAmerInd *ipekaaguene*]

I·poh /ē′pō/ *n.* city in Malaysia. Pop. 293,800

ips *abbr.* (also **i.p.s.**) inches per second

ip·so fac·to /ip′sō fak′tō/ *adv. Latin.* by that very fact

Ips·wich /ip′swich/ *n.* city in E England. Pop. 131,100

IQ *abbr.* intelligence quotient

I·qui·tos /ikēt′ōs/, *n.* city in Peru on the Amazon River. Pop. 269,500

ir- *prefix* var. of IN-¹, IN-² before *r*

IRA *abbr.* 1 Individual Retirement Account 2 Irish Republican Army

I·rák·li·on /ēr·ak′lēən/ *n.* (also **Heraklion**) seaport on Crete in Greece. Pop. 117,200

I·ran /iran′, irän′, iran′/ *n.* (formerly called **Persia**) republic in SW Asia on the Persian Gulf and Caspian Sea. Capital: Teheran. Pop. 59,570,000 —**I·ra·ni·an** /irā′nēən/ *n.* & *adj.*

I·raq /irak′, iräk′, īrak′/ *n.* republic in SW Asia. Capital: Baghdad. Pop. 18,828,000 —**I·ra·qi** /irä′kē/ *n.* & *adj.*

i·ras·ci·ble /iras′əbəl/ *adj.* irritable; hot-tempered —**i·ras′ci·bil′i·ty** *n.*; **i·ras′ci·bly** *adv.* [L *irasci* grow angry]

i·rate /īrāt′, ī′rāt′/ *adj.* angry; enraged —**i·rate′ly** *adv.*; **i·rate′ness** *n.* [L *irasci* be angry]

Ir·bid /ēr′bid′/ *n.* city in Jordan. Pop. 314,700

Ir·bil /ir′bil/ *n.* see ERBIL

ire /īr/ *n. Lit.* anger [L *ira*]

Ire·land /īr′lənd/ *n.* 1 island lying W of Great Britain in the N Atlantic Ocean 2 (also called **Eire**) republic including most of the island of Ireland. Capital: Dublin. Pop. 3,519,000. See also NORTHERN IRELAND

ir·i·des·cent /ir′ədes′ənt/ *adj.* showing rainbowlike luminous colors —**ir′i·des′cence** *n.*

i·rid·i·um /irid′ēəm/ *n.* hard white metallic element of the platinum group; *symb.* Ir

i·ris /ī′ris/ *n.* 1 circular colored membrane behind the cornea of the eye, with a circular opening (pupil) in the center 2 plant of a family with sword-shaped leaves and showy flowers [Gk]

I·rish /ī′rish/ *adj.* 1 of Ireland or its people —*n.* 2 Celtic language of Ireland 3 (prec. by *the*; treated as *pl.*) the people of Ireland —**I′rish·man** /-mən/ (*pl.* **·men**; *fem.* **·wom′an**, *pl.* **·wom′en**) *n.*

I′rish cof′fee *n.* coffee with Irish whiskey and sugar, topped with whipped cream

I′rish Sea′ *n.* part of the Atlantic between Ireland and England

irk /ərk/ *v.* irritate; bore; annoy

irk·some /ərk′səm/ *adj.* annoying; tiresome —**irk′some·ly** *adv.*

Ir·kutsk /ērkōōtsk′/ *n.* city in S Russia. Pop. 640,500

i·ron /ī′ərn/ *n.* 1 gray metallic element used for tools and constructions and found in some foods; *symb.* Fe 2 strength or firmness 3 implement with a flat base which is heated to smooth cloth 4 golf club with a metal sloping face 5 (*pl.*) fetters —*adj.* 6 made of iron 7 robust 8 unyielding; merciless —*v.* 9 smooth (cloth, etc.) with an iron 10 iron out remove (difficulties, etc.) [OE]

I′ron Age′ *n.* period when iron replaced bronze in the making of tools and weapons

i·ron·clad /ī′ərnklad′/ *adj.* 1 clad or protected with iron 2 unchangeable 3 unassailable —*n.* 4 *Hist.* warship protected by iron plates

I′ron Cur′tain *n. Hist.* barrier to the passage of people and information from the former Soviet bloc

i·ron·ic /īrän′ik/ *adj.* (also **i·ron′i·cal**) using or displaying irony —**i·ron′i·cal·ly** *adv.*

i·ron·ing /ī′ərning/ *n.* clothes, etc., for ironing or just ironed

i′ron·ing board′ *n.* narrow folding table on which clothes, etc., are ironed

i′ron·stone′ *n.* a hard white pottery

i′ron·ware′ *n.* articles made of iron

i·ro·ny /ī′rənē, ī′ərnē/ *n.* (*pl.* **·nies**) 1 humorous or sarcastic use of language of a different or opposite meaning 2 event or circumstance opposite from what is expected [Gk *eirōneia* pretended ignorance]

Ir·o·quois /ir′əkwoi′, -kwoiz′/ 1 one of an American Indian people in N New York state —*adj.* 2 of the Iroquois —**Ir′o·quois′, Ir′o·quoi′an** *n.* & *n.*

ir·ra·di·ate /ir(r)ād′ē·āt′/ *v.* (**·at·ed**, **·at·ing**) 1 subject to radiation 2 shine upon; light up 3 throw light on —**ir·ra′di·a′tion** *n.* [L *irradiare* shine on, fr. *radius* ray]

ir·ra·tion·al /ir(r)ash′(ə)nəl/ *adj.* 1 illogical; unreasonable 2 not endowed with reason —**ir·ra′tion·al′i·ty** /-al′itē/ *n.*; **ir·ra′tion·al·ly** *adv.*

ir·ra′tion·al num′ber *n. Math.* number that cannot be expressed as a ratio between two integers

ir·rec·on·cil·a·ble /ir(r)ek′ənsīl′əbəl/ *adj.* 1 implacably hostile 2 incompatible —**ir·rec′on·cil′a·bil′i·ty** *n.*; **ir·rec′on·cil′a·bly** *adv.*

ir·re·cov·er·a·ble /ir′ikəv′(ə)rəbəl/ *adj.* not able to be recovered or remedied —**ir′re·cov′er·a·bly** *adv.*

ir·re·deem·a·ble /ir'idē'məbəl/ adj. 1 not able to be redeemed 2 hopeless —ir're·deem'a·bly adv.

ir·re·duc·i·ble /ir'id(y)ōō'səbəl/ adj. not able to be reduced or simplified —ir're·duc'i·bil'i·ty n.; ir·re·duc'i·bly adv.

ir·re·fut·a·ble /iref'yətəbəl, ir'ifyōōt'əbəl/ adj. that cannot be refuted —ir·re'fut·a·bly adv.

ir·re·gard·less /ir'igärd'ləs/ adv. Nonstand. regardless
• Usage: As the -less suffix changes regard to mean 'without regard, disregarding,' the addition of the negative prefix ir- is not only unnecessary but contradictory: avoid using "irregardless."

ir·reg·u·lar /ir(r)eg'yələr/ adj. 1 not regular; unsymmetrical; uneven; varying in form 2 not occurring at regular intervals 3 contrary to a rule, principle, or custom; abnormal 4 (of a verb, noun, etc.) not inflected according to the usual rules 5 disorderly —ir·reg'u·lar'i·ty /-lar'ətē/ n. (pl. -ties); ir·reg'u·lar·ly adv.

ir·rel·e·vant /ir(r)el'əvənt/ adj. not relevant —ir·rel'e·vance, ir·rel'e·van·cy n. (pl. -cies)

ir·re·li·gious /ir'ilij'əs/ adj. lacking or hostile to religion; irreverent

ir·re·me·di·a·ble /ir'imēd'ēəbəl/ adj. that cannot be remedied —ir·re·me'di·a·bly adv.

ir·rep·a·ra·ble /ir(r)ep'(ə)rəbəl/ adj. that cannot be repaired or made good —ir·rep'a·ra·bly adv.

ir·re·place·a·ble /ir'iplā'səbəl/ adj. that cannot be replaced

ir·re·press·i·ble /ir'ipres'əbəl/ adj. that cannot be repressed or restrained —ir·re·press'i·bly adv.

ir·re·proach·a·ble /ir'iprō'CHəbəl/ adj. faultless; blameless —ir·re·proach'a·bly adv.

ir·re·sist·i·ble /ir'izis'təbəl/ adj. too strong, delightful, or convincing to be resisted —ir·re·sist'i·bly adv.

ir·res·o·lute /ir(r)ez'əlōōt/ adj. 1 hesitant 2 lacking in resoluteness —ir·res'o·lute'ly adv.; ir·res'o·lute'ness, ir·res'o·lu'tion n.

ir·re·spec·tive /ir'ispek'tiv/ adj. regardless (of)

ir·re·spon·si·ble /ir'ispän'səbəl/ adj. 1 acting or done without due sense of responsibility 2 not responsible for one's conduct —ir·re·spon'si·bil'i·ty n.; ir're·spon'si·bly adv.

ir·re·triev·a·ble /ir'itrē'vəbəl/ adj. that cannot be retrieved or restored —ir·re·triev'a·bly adv.

ir·rev·er·ent /ir(r)ev'(ə)rənt/ adj. lacking reverence —ir·rev'er·ence n.; ir·rev'er·ent·ly adv.

ir·re·vers·i·ble /ir'ivar'səbəl/ adj. not reversible or alterable —ir're·vers'i·bly adv.

ir·re·vo·ca·ble /ir(r)ev'ikəbəl/ adj. unalterable; gone beyond recall —ir·rev'o·ca·bly adv.

ir·ri·gate /ir'əgāt/ v. (-gat·ed, -gat·ing) 1 supply (land) with water, as by channels, etc. 2 clean (a wound, etc.) with a flow of water, etc. —ir'ri·ga·ble /-gəbəl/ adj.; ir'ri·ga'tion, ir'ri·ga'tor n. [L irrigare water; moisten]

ir·ri·ta·ble /ir'ətəbəl/ adj. 1 easily annoyed 2 Med. very sensitive to contact —ir'ri·ta·bil'i·ty n.; ir'ri·ta·bly adv. [L, rel. to IRRITATE]

ir·ri·tant /ir'ətənt/ adj. 1 causing irritation —n. 2 irritant substance

ir·ri·tate /ir'ətāt'/ v. (-tat·ed, -tat·ing) 1 excite to anger; annoy 2 stimulate discomfort in (a part of the body) —ir'ri·ta'tion n.; ir'ri·ta'tive adj. [L irritare]

ir·rupt /ir(r)əpt'/ v. enter forcibly or violently —ir·rup'tion /-rəp'sHən/ n. [L irrumpere break into]

IRS abbr. Internal Revenue Service

Ir·vine /ər'vIn/ n. city in Calif. Pop. 110,330

Ir·ving /ər'viNG/ n. city in Texas. Pop. 155,037

Ir·ving /ər'viNG/, Washington 1783–1859: US writer

is /iz/ v. 3rd sing. present of BE

is. abbr. island

I·sa·bel·la I /iz'əbel'ə/ 1474–1504; queen of Castile and Aragon; supporter of Christopher Columbus

Is·fa·han /is'fəhän'/ n. (also Es'fahan' or Is'pahan') city in central Iran; former capital of Persia. Pop. 986,800

-ish suffix forming adjectives: 1 from nouns, meaning: a having the qualities of (boyish) b of the nationality of (Danish) 2 from adjectives, meaning: a 'somewhat' (tallish) 3 Colloq. denoting an approximate age or time of day (fortyish; six-thirtyish) [OE]

Ish·er·wood /isH'ərwŏŏd/, Christopher 1904–86; British-born US novelist

Ish·tar /isH'tär/ n. ancient Near Eastern goddess of war and love

i·sin·glass /I'ziNG-glas', I'zən-/ n. 1 gelatin obtained from fish and used in making jellies, glue, etc. 2 mica, usu. in thin sheets [MDu huisenblas sturgeon's bladder]

I·sis /I'sis/ n. Egyptian fertility goddess

isl. abbr. island

Is·lam /isläm', iz-; is'läm', iz'-/ n. 1 the religion of the Muslims, proclaimed by Muhammad 2 the Muslim world —Is·lam'ic /isläm'ik, iz-, -lam'-/ adj. [Ar: submission (to God)]

Is·lam·a·bad /isläm'əbäd'/ n. capital of Pakistan. Pop. 204,400

is·land /I'lənd/ n. 1 land smaller than a continent and surrounded by water 2 detached or isolated thing (of safety) [OE igland; first syllable influenced by ISLE]

is'land·er n. native or inhabitant of an island

isle /Il/ n. island, esp. a small one [Fr ile fr. L insula]

is·let /I'lit/ n. 1 small island 2 Anat. structurally distinct portion of tissue [Fr dim. of ISLE]

ism /iz'əm/ n. any distinctive doctrine or practice [fr. -ISM]

-ism suffix forming nouns, esp. denoting: 1 action or its result (terrorism) 2 system or principle (Conservatism) 3 state or quality (heroism) 4 basis of prejudice or discrimination (racism; sexism) [Gk -ismos]

iso- comb. form equal [Gk isos equal]

i·so·bar /I'sōbär/ n. line on a map connecting places with the same atmospheric pres-

sure —**i·so·bar·ic** /ˈī'səbär'ik, -bar'-/ *adj.* {Gk *isobares* of equal weight}

i·so·late /ˈī'səlāt'/ *v.* (**·lat·ed, ·lat·ing**) 1 place apart or alone 2 separate (a substance) from a mixture —*n.* [It fr. L *insulatus* made into an island]

i·so·la·tion·ism /ˈī'sələ'sHəniz'əm/ *n.* policy of holding aloof from the affairs of other countries or groups —**i·so·la'tion·ist** /-ist/ *n.*

i·so·mer /ˈī'səmər/ *n.* one of two or more compounds with the same molecular formula but a different arrangement of atoms —**i·so·mer'ic** /-mer'ik/ *adj.*; **i·som·er·ism** /ī'säm'əriz'əm/ *n.* [Gk *isomeres* having equal parts]

i·so·met·ric /ˈī'sə'me'trik/ *adj.* 1 of equal measure 2 (of muscle action) developing tension while the muscle is prevented from contracting [Gk *isometria* equality of measure]

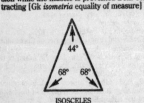

ISOSCELES

i·sos·ce·les /ˈī'säs'əlēz'/ *adj.* (of a triangle) having two sides equal [Gk *isoskeles* with equal legs]

i·so·tope /ˈī'sətōp'/ *n.* one of two or more forms of an element differing from each other in atomic weight —**i·so·top·ic** /ī'sətäp'ik, -tō'pik/ *adj.* [fr. ISO-, Gk *topos* place]

Is·pa·han /is'pəhän'/ *n.* see ISFAHAN

Is·ra·el /iz'rēəl, -rāəl/ *n.* 1 republic in SW Asia on the E coast of the Mediterranean Sea. Capital: Jerusalem. Pop. 5,239,000 (excluding territory occupied after 1967) 2 ancient biblical country of the Hebrews —**Is·rae·li** /izrā'lē/ *n.* & *adj.*

is·sue /isH'ōō/ *n.* 1a outgoing; outflow b exit; outlet 2a act of giving out or circulating stamps, bonds, etc. b quantity of coins, copies of a newspaper, etc., circulated at one time c each of a regular series of a magazine, etc. (*the May issue*) 3 point in question; important subject of debate 4 result; outcome —*v.* (**·sued, ·su·ing**) 5 *Lit.* go or come out 6a publish; put into circulation b supply, esp. officially 7a be derived or result b end; result 8 emerge from a condition 9 at issue under discussion; in dispute 10 take issue disagree or argue [L *exitus* exit]

-ist *suffix* forming personal nouns denoting: 1 adherent of a system, etc., in *-ism* (*Marxist; fatalist*) 2 person pursuing, using, or concerned with something (*balloonist; tobacconist*) 3 person who does something expressed by a verb in *-ize* (*plagiarist*) 4 person who subscribes to a prejudice or practices discrimination (*racist; sexist*) [Gk *-istēs*]

Is·tan·bul /is'tänbōōl'/ *n.* (formerly Constantinople; ancient name Byzantium) port in NW Turkey, on the Bosporus. Pop. 6,620,200

isth·mus /is'məs/ *n.* (*pl.* **·mus·es**) narrow piece of land connecting two larger bodies of land [Gk *isthmos* neck (of land)]

it /it/ *pron.* (*poss.* **its**; *pl.* **they**) 1 thing (or occasionally an animal or child) previously named or in question (*took a stone and threw it*) 2 person in question (*Who is it? It is I*) 3 as the subject of an impersonal verb (*it is raining*) 4 as a substitute for a deferred subject or object (*it is silly to talk like that; I take it that you agree*) 5 as a substitute for a vague object (*brazen it out*) 6 as the antecedent to a relative word or clause (*it was an owl that I heard*) 7 (in children's games) player who must catch others 8 **that's it** *Colloq.* that is: a what is required b the difficulty c the end; enough 9 **with it** *Colloq.* alert; informed [OE]

I·tal·ian /ital'yən/ *n.* 1a native or national of Italy b person of Italian descent 2 language of Italy —*adj.* 3 of Italy, its people, or its language

I·tal·ian·ate /ital'yənāt'/ *adj.* of Italian style or appearance

i·tal·ic /ital'ik/ *adj.* 1 slanting type used esp. for emphasis and in foreign words (*this is italic*) —*n.* 2 letter in italic type 3 this type [L *italicus* fr. Gk *Italikos*, rel. to ITALIAN]

i·tal·i·cize /ital'əsīz'/ *v.* (**·cized, ·ciz·ing**) print in italics

It·a·ly /it'l·ē/ *n.* republic in S Europe on the Mediterranean Sea. Capital: Rome. Pop. 57,158,000

itch /icH/ *n.* 1 irritation in the skin 2 impatient desire —*v.* 3 feel an irritation in the skin 4 feel a desire to do something (*itching to tell you*) [OE]

itch·y *adj.* (**·i·er, ·i·est**) 1 having or causing an itch 2 **have itchy feet**: *Colloq.* a be restless b have a strong urge to travel —**itch'i·ness** *n.*

-ite *suffix* forming nouns meaning 'a person or thing connected with' (*Israelite; Trotskyite; dynamite*) [Gk *-itēs*]

i·tem /ˈīt'əm/ *n.* 1 any of a number of enumerated things 2 bit of news, etc. [L: in like manner]

i·tem·ize /ˈīt'əmīz'/ *v.* (**·ized, ·iz·ing**) state item by item —**i'tem·i·za'tion** *n.*

it·er·ate /it'ərāt'/ *v.* (**·at·ed, ·at·ing**) repeat; state repeatedly —**it'er·a'tion** *n.*; **it·er·a·tive** /it'ərativ/ *adj.* [L *iterare* repeat]

i·tin·er·ant /ītin'ərənt/ *adj.* 1 traveling from place to place —*n.* 2 itinerant person [L *itinerari* journey]

i·tin·er·ar·y /ītin'ərer'ē/ *n.* (*pl.* **·ies**) 1 detailed route 2 record of travel 3 travel plan

-itis *suffix* forming nouns, esp.: 1 names of inflammatory diseases (*appendicitis*) 2 *Colloq.* with ref. to conditions compared to diseases (*electionitis*) [Gk]

its /its/ *poss. pron.* of it; of itself

it's /its/ *v. contr.* 1 it is 2 it has

it·self /itself'/ *pron.* 1 emphat. or refl. form of IT 2 **in itself** viewed in its essential qualities (*not in itself a bad thing*) [OE, rel. to IT + SELF]

-ity *suffix* forming nouns denoting: 1 quality or condition (*purity*) 2 instance of this (*monstrosity*) [L *-itas*]

IUD *abbr.* intrauterine (contraceptive) device

IV *abbr.* **1** intravenous **2** intravenously

I·van IV /ī'vən/ (called **"Ivan the Terrible"**) 1530–84; first czar of Russia (1547–84)

I·va·no·vo /ēvän'əvə/ *n.* city in W Russia. Pop. 482,200

I've /īv/ *v. contr.* I have

-ive *suffix* forming adjectives meaning 'tending to,' and corresponding nouns (*suggestive; corrosive; palliative*) [L *-ivus*]

Ives /īvz/, **Charles** 1874–1954; US composer

i·vo·ry /ī'v(ə)rē/ *n.* (*pl.* **-ries**) **1** hard substance of the tusks of an elephant, etc. **2** creamy-white color of this (usu. *pl.*) *Slang.* a piano key [L *ebur*]

I'vo·ry Coast' *n.* (official name **Côte d'Ivoire**) republic in W Africa on the Atlantic Ocean. Capital: Abidjan. Pop. 12,951,000 —**I·vo·ri·an** /ivôr'ēən/ *n. & adj.*

i'vo·ry tow'er *n.* seclusion or withdrawal from the harsh realities of life

i·vy /ī'vē/ *n.* (*pl.* **-vies**) climbing evergreen shrub with shiny five-angled leaves [OE]

I·wo Ji·ma /ē'wə jē'mə, ē'wō/ *n.* island S of Japan; site of major World War II battle

-ize *suffix* forming verbs, meaning: **1** make or become such (*Americanize; realize*) **2** treat in such a way (*monopolize; pasteurize*) **3a** follow a special practice (*economize*) **b** have a specified feeling (*sympathize*)

I·zhevsk /ē'zнefsk/ *n.* city in Russia. Pop. 646,800

Iz·mir /izmēr'/ *n.* (formerly **Smyrna**) seaport in Turkey. Pop. 1,757,400

Iz·mit /izmit'/ *n.* city in Turkey. Pop. 256,900

J

j, J /jā/ *n.* (*pl.* **j's; J's, Js**) tenth letter of the English alphabet; a consonant

J or J. *abbr.* **1** *Cards.* jack **2** Jewish **3** journal **4** *Physics.* (also **j**) joule(s) **5** judge **6** justice

jab /jab/ *v.* (**jabbed, jab·bing**) **1** poke roughly **b** stab **2** thrust (a thing) hard or abruptly —*n.* **3** abrupt blow, thrust, or stab {var. of *job*: prod}

jab·ber /jab'ər/ *v.* **1** chatter volubly **2** utter (words) in this way —*n.* **3** chatter; gabble [imit.]

ja·bot /zнabō'/ *n.* ornamental frill, etc., on the front of a shirt or blouse [Fr: bird's crop]

jack /jak/ *n.* **1** device for raising heavy objects, esp. vehicles **2** playing card with a picture of a soldier, royal servant, etc. **3** ship's flag, esp. showing nationality **4** device to connect an electrical circuit **5a** pronged metal piece used with a ball in a tossing game **b** (*pl.*) game of jacks **6** (*cap.*) familiar form of *John*, esp. typifying the common man, male animal, etc. —*v.* **7** raise with or as with a jack (in sense 1) **8** *Colloq.* raise (e.g., prices) [familiar form of the name *John*]

jack·al /jak'əl/ *n.* African or Asian wild animal of the dog family [Pers *shaghal*]

jack·ass /jak'as'/ *n.* **1** male donkey **2** stupid person

jack·daw /jak'dô'/ *n.* gray-headed bird of the crow family

jack·et /jak'it/ *n.* **1a** short coat with sleeves **b** protective or supporting garment (*life jacket*) **2** casing or outer covering

Jack' Frost' *n.* frost personified

jack'-in-the-box' *n.* toy figure that springs out of a box

jack'-in-the-pul'pit *n.* N American plant having an upright flower spike and an over-arching hoodlike spathe

jack·knife' *n.* **1** large pocket knife **2** dive in which the body is bent and then straightened —*v.* (**·knifed, ·knif·ing**) **3** double over or bend

jack' of all' trades' *n.* multi-skilled person

jack'-o'-lan'tern *n.* pumpkin lantern

jack'pot' *n.* **1** large prize, esp. accumulated in a game, lottery, etc. **2 hit the jackpot:** *Colloq.* **a** win a large prize **b** have remarkable luck or success

jack'rab'bit *n.* large prairie hare

Jack·son /jak'sən/ *n.* capital of Miss., in the central part. Pop. 196,637

Jack·son /jak'sən/ **1 Andrew** 1767–1845; US general and 7th US president (1828–37) **2 "Stonewall"** (Thomas Jonathan) 1824–63; general of Confederate forces in American Civil War **3 Glenda** 1936– ; English actress and politician **4 Jesse** 1941– ; US politician, civil-rights leader, and clergyman **5 Michael** 1958– ; US pop singer and songwriter

Ja·cob /jā'kəb/ *n.* Hebrew patriarch

Jac·quard /jak'ärd/ *n.* **1** loom controlled by perforated cards, for weaving figured fabrics **2** fabric or article so made [for J. *Jacquard*, French inventor]

Ja·cuz·zi /jəkōō'zē/ *n.* (*pl.* **-zis**) *Tdmk.* bath with massaging underwater jets

jade¹ /jād/ *n.* **1** hard usu. green stone used for ornaments, etc. **2** green color of this [Sp *ijada* fr. L *ilia* flanks (named as a cure for colic)]

jade² *n.* **1** inferior or worn-out horse **2** *Derog.* disreputable woman

jad·ed /jā'did/ *adj.* tired out; surfeited

jag¹ /jag/ *n.* sharp projection of rock, etc.

jag² *n.* *Slang.* **1** drinking bout **2** period of indulgence

jag·ged /jag'id/ *adj.* unevenly cut or torn; deeply indented —**jag'ged·ly** *adv.*; **jag'ged·ness** *n.*

jag·uar /jag'wär'/ *n.* large flesh-eating spotted animal of the cat family [Port fr. Tupi]

jai a·lai /hī' (ə)lī'/ *n.* game similar to handball played with long wicker rackets

jail /jāl/ *n.* **1** place for the detention of prisoners **2** confinement in a jail —*v.* **3** put in jail [OFr *jaiole*, ult. fr. L *cavea* cage]

jail'break' *n.* escape from jail

jail'er *n.* person in charge of a jail

Jai·pur /jī'pŏŏr'/ *n.* city in NW India. Pop. 1,454,700

Ja·kar·ta /jəkärt'ə/ n. capital of Indonesia. Pop. 6,503,400

Ja·la·pa /həläp'ə/ n. capital of the Mexican state of Veracruz. Pop. 111,800

ja·la·pe·ño /ha'lapän'yō, -pēn'-/ n. hot Mexican pepper used in cooking

Ja·lis·co /həlis'kō/ n. SW state of Mexico, on the Pacific Ocean. Capital: Guadalajara. Pop. 5,302,700

ja·lop·y /jəläp'ē/ n. (*pl.* ·ies) *Colloq.* dilapidated old car

jal·ou·sie /jal'əsē/ n. slatted blind or shutter to keep out rain, etc., and control light [Fr fr. It, rel. to JEALOUSY]

jam¹ /jam/ v. (**jammed, jam·ming**) 1a squeeze, cram, or wedge into a space b become wedged 2 cause to become stuck or make stuck and unworkable 3 block (a passage, road, etc.) by crowding, etc. 4 apply (brakes, etc.) forcefully or abruptly 5 make (a radio transmission) unintelligible by interference 6 *Colloq. Mus.* improvise with other musicians —n. 7 squeeze; crush 8 crowded mass (*traffic jam*) 9 *Colloq.* predicament 10 stoppage due to jamming 11 (in full **jam session**) *Colloq. Mus.* improvised playing [imit.]

jam² n. fruit preserve, usu. sweetened [perh. fr. JAM¹]

Ja·mai·ca /jəmā'kə/ n. island republic in the Caribbean Sea, S of Cuba. Capital: Kingston. Pop. 2,445,000

jamb /jam/ n. side post or side face of a doorway, etc. [Fr *jambe* leg, ult. fr. Gk *kampē*]

jam·bo·ree /jam'bərē'/ n. 1 celebration 2 large gathering of Boy Scouts

James /jāmz/ 1 William 1842–1910; US philosopher and psychologist 2 Henry 1843–1916; US-born British novelist and critic 3 Jesse 1847–82; US outlaw

James I 1566–1625; king of England and Ireland (1603–25) —Ja·co·be'an *adj.* & *n.*

James, St. /jāmz/ 1 ("the Less" or "the Just") one of the twelve Apostles; called the brother of Jesus 2 ("the Great") one of the twelve Apostles; brother of St. John the Evangelist

jam'-packed' *adj. Colloq.* full to capacity

Jan. *abbr.* January

Jane Doe /jān dō/ n. fictitious name for a woman whose identity is unknown or concealed

jan·gle /jaNG'gəl/ v. (·gled, ·gling) 1 (cause to) make a (usu. harsh) metallic sound 2 irritate (the nerves, etc.) by discord, etc. —n. 3 harsh metallic sound [Fr fr. MDu *jangelen* haggle; whine]

jan·i·tor /jan'ətər/ n. person who cleans and maintains public areas in a building [L: doorkeeper, fr. *janus* doorway]

Jan·u·ar·y /jan'yōō·er'ē/ n. (*pl.* ·ies) first month of the year in the Gregorian calendar [L *Janus*, god of doors and beginnings]

ja·pan /jəpan'/ n. 1 hard usu. black varnish, orig. from Japan —v. (·panned, ·pan·ning) 2 varnish with japan 3 make black and glossy

Ja·pan /jəpan'/ n. island nation off the E coast of Asia. Capital: Tokyo. Pop. 124,330,000

Ja·pan', Sea' of n. part of the Pacific, between Japan and mainland Asia

Jap·a·nese /jap'ənēz'/ n. (*pl.* same) 1a native or national of Japan b person of Japanese descent 2 language of Japan —*adj.* 3 of Japan, its people, or its language

Jap'a·nese bee'tle n. iridescent green and brown beetle; garden and crop pest

jape /jāp/ n. 1 practical joke —v. (**japed, jap·ing**) 2 play a joke

jar¹ /jär/ n. 1 container, usu. of glass and cylindrical 2 contents of this [MFr fr. Ar *jar·rah*]

jar² v. (**jarred, jar·ring**) 1 (of sound, manner, etc.) sound discordant; grate (on the nerves, etc.) 2a (cause to) strike (esp. part of the body) with vibration or shock (*jarred his neck*) b vibrate with shock, etc. 3 be at variance or in conflict —n. 4 jarring sound or sensation 5 physical shock or jolt [imit.]

jar·di·nière /järd'n·ēr', zhärd'n-(y)er'/ n. 1 ornamental pot or stand for plants 2 dish of mixed vegetables [Fr: gardener]

jar·gon /jär'gən/ n. 1 words or expressions used by a particular group or profession (*medical jargon*) 2 unintelligible language [OFr]

jas·mine /jaz'mən/ n. ornamental shrub with white or yellow flowers [Fr fr. Ar fr. Pers *yasmin*]

jas·per /jas'pər/ n. opaque quartz, usu. red, yellow, or brown [Fr fr. L fr. Gk *iaspis* fr. Sem]

jaun·dice /jôn'dis, jän'-/ n. 1 yellowing of the skin, etc., caused by liver disease, bile disorder, etc. 2 envy —v. (·diced, ·dic·ing) 3 affect (a person) with envy, resentment, etc. [OFr *jaune* yellow]

jaunt /jônt, jänt/ n. 1 short pleasure trip —v. 2 take a jaunt

jaun·ty /jônt'ē, jänt'ē/ adj. (·ti·er, ·ti·est) 1 cheerful and self-confident 2 sprightly —jaunt'i·ly *adv.*; jaunt'i·ness n. [Fr, rel. to GENTLE]

Ja·va /jäv'ə, jav'ə/ n. 1 main island of Indonesia 2 (often j-) a a coffee grown there b *Slang.* any coffee

Jav·a·nese /jav'ənēz', jäv'-/ n. (*pl.* same) 1a native of Java b person of Javanese descent 2 language of Java —*adj.* 3 of Java, its people, or its language [*Java* in Indonesia]

jav·e·lin /jav'ələn/ n. light spear used in competition or, formerly, as a weapon [MFr, prob. fr. Celt]

jaw /jô/ n. 1a upper or lower bony structure in vertebrates, containing the teeth b corresponding parts of certain invertebrates 2 (*pl.*) the mouth with its bones and teeth 3 gripping parts of a tool, etc. —v. 4 *Colloq.* speak, esp. at tedious length [OFr *joue*]

jaw'bone' /jô'bōn'/ n. lower jaw in most mammals

jaw'break'er n. *Colloq.* 1 type of round, very hard candy 2 long or hard word

Jaws' of Life' n. *Tdmk.* emergency apparatus that can cut or pry apart metal, used esp. to free people trapped in vehicles in highway collisions

jay /jā/ n. any of several birds, usu. with vivid plumage [LL *gaius, gaia*, perh. fr. the name *Gaius*; cf. *robin*]

jay'walk' v. cross a road carelessly or dangerously —jay'walk'er n.

jazz /jaz/ n. 1 rhythmic, syncopated music, often improvised, of S US origin 2 *Slang.* pre tentious talk or behavior —*v.* **3** play or dance to jazz **4 jazz up** brighten or enliven

jazz'y *adj.* (**·i·er, ·i·est**) **1** of or like jazz **2** vivid; showy

J.C.D. *abbr. Law.* Doctor of Canon Law [L *Juris Canonici Doctor*]

JCS *abbr.* (also **J.C.S.**) Joint Chiefs of Staff

jct. *abbr.* junction

jeal·ous /jel'əs/ *adj.* **1** resentful of rivalry in love **2** envious (of a person, etc.) **3** fiercely protective (of rights, etc.) **4** of inquiry, supervision, etc.) vigilant —**jeal'ous·ly** *adv.* [ME fr. OF *gelos*, ult. fr. LL *zelus*, rel. to ZEAL]

jeal'ou·sy *n.* (*pl.* **·sies**) **1** jealous state or feeling **2** instance of this [ME fr. OFr, rel. to JEALOUS]

jeans /jēnz/ *n. pl.* casual trousers, esp. denim [earlier *gene fustian*, material from Genoa]

Jeep /jēp/ *n. Tdmk.* sturdy vehicle with four-wheel drive [US Army use, fr. initials of *general purpose*]

jeer /jēr/ *v.* **1** scoff derisively; deride —*n.* **2** taunt —**jeer'ing·ly** *adv.*

Jef·fer·son /jef'ərsən/, **Thomas** 1743–1826; US patriot and politician; 3rd US president (1801–09) —**Jef'fer·so'ni·an** /-sō'nēən/ *adj.*

Jef'fer·son Cit'y *n.* capital of Mo., in the central part. Pop. 35,481

Je·ho·vah /jəhō'və/ *n.* Hebrew name of God in the Old Testament [Heb *yahveh*]

je·june /jijōōn'/ *adj.* **1** intellectually unsatisfying; meager **2** puerile [L *jejunus* empty]

je·ju·num /jijōō'nəm/ *n.* small intestine between the duodenum and ileum [L, rel. to JEJUNE]

jell /jel/ *v. Colloq.* **1a** set, as jelly **b** (of ideas, etc.) take a definite form **2** cohere [back formation fr. JELLY]

jel·ly /jel'ē/ *n.* (*pl.* **·lies**) **1** food preparation set with gelatin, as a jam, condiment, or similar preparation **2** any similar substance —*v.* (**·lied, ·ly·ing**) **1** (cause to) set as or in a jelly; congeal —**jel'ly·like'** *adj.* [ME fr. OFr *gelée* fr. L *gelare* freeze]

jel'ly·fish' /jel'ēfish'/ *n.* (*pl.* same or **·fishes**) **1** marine animal with a jellylike body and stinging tentacles **2** *Slang.* weak or weak-willed person

jel'ly roll' *n.* rolled sponge cake with a jelly filling

Je·na /yā'nə/ *n.* city in Germany. Pop. 102,500

jeop·ar·dize /jep'ərdīz/ *v.* (**·dized, ·diz·ing**) endanger

jeop·ar·dy /jep'ərdē/ *n.* danger, esp. severe [ME fr. OFr *jeu parti* divided play]

jer·e·mi·ad /jer'əmī'ad, -əd/ *n.* doleful complaint or lamentation [rel. to JEREMIAH]

Jer·e·mi·ah /jer'əmī'ə/ *n.* dismal prophet; denouncer of the times [OT prophet]

Je·rez de la Fron·te·ra /hərās' də lä frən'tār'ə/. *n.* city in Spain. Pop. 182,939

jerk¹ /jərk/. *n.* **1** sharp sudden pull, twist, twitch, start, etc. **2** spasmodic muscular twitch **3** *Slang.* fool —*v.* **4** move, pull, thrust, twist, throw, etc., with a jerk [perh. fr. *yerk* pull stitches tight (on shoes)]

jerk² *v.* cure (beef) by cutting it in long slices and drying it in the sun [back formation fr. JERKY²]

jer·kin /jər'kin/ *n.* close-fitting sleeveless jacket, esp. leather

jerk'wa'ter *adj. Colloq.* insignificant; remote

JERKIN

jer'ky¹ *adj.* (**·ki·er, ·ki·est**) **1** moving suddenly or abruptly **2** spasmodic —**jerk'i·ly** *adv.*; **jerk'i·ness** *n.*

jer·ky² *n.* meat, esp. beef, dried by jerking [Sp fr. Quechua *charqui* strips of meat dried in the sun]

Je·rome, **St.** /jərōm'/ c. 342–420; early Christian ecclesiastic and scholar; chief preparer of the Latin Bible (Vulgate)

jer·ry-built /jer'ēbilt'/ *adj.* made of cheap materials

jer·sey /jər'zē/ *n.* (*pl.* **·seys**) **1a** close-fitting, knitted sweater **b** knitted fabric **2** close-fitting, pullover shirt worn by athletes, etc. **3** (*cap.*) breed of light brown dairy cattle [*Jersey* in the Channel Islands, Great Britain]

Jer'sey Cit'y /jər'zē/ *n.* city in N.J. Pop. 228,537

Je·ru·sa·lem /jərōō's(ə)ləm/ *n.* capital of Israel. Pop. 504,100

jest /jest/ *n.* **1** joke; fun **2a** banter **b** object of derision —*v.* **3** joke; jeer **4 in jest** in fun [ME fr. L *gesta* exploits]

jest'er *n.* professional clown at a medieval court, etc.

Jes·u·it /jezH'ōōət, jez'-/ *n.* member of the Society of Jesus, a Roman Catholic order

Je·sus /jē'zəs, -zəz/ (also **Je'sus Christ'** or **Je'sus of Na'zareth**) c. 4 B.C.– c. A.D. 30; source of the Christian religion

jet¹ /jet/ *n.* **1** forceful stream of water, steam, gas, flame, etc., esp. from a small opening **2** spout or nozzle for this purpose **3** jet engine or jet plane —*v.* (**jet·ted, jet·ting**) **4** spurt out in jets **5** *Colloq.* send or travel by jet plane [Fr *jeter* fr. L *jactare* throw]

jet² *n.* **1** hard, black mineral often carved and highly polished **2 jet black** deep glossy black [OFr *jaiet* fr. Gk *Gagai* in Asia Minor]

jet' lag' *n.* exhaustion, etc., felt after a long flight across time zones

jet' pro·pul'sion *n.* propulsion by the backward ejection of a high-speed jet of gas, etc.

jet·sam /jet'səm/ *n.* objects washed ashore, esp. jettisoned from a ship [contr. of JETTISON]

jet' set' *n.* wealthy people who travel widely, esp. for pleasure —**jet'-set'ter** *n.*; **jet'-set'** ting *n. & adj.*

jet·ti·son /jet'isən/ *v.* **1** throw (esp. heavy material) off or out to lighten a ship, etc. **2** abandon; get rid of —*n.* **3** jettisoning [ME fr. OFr *getaison* fr. L, rel. to JET¹]

jet·ty /jet'ē/ *n.* (*pl.* **·ties**) **1** pier or breakwater to protect or defend a harbor, coast, etc. **2** landing pier [OFr *jetee*, rel. to JET¹]

Jew /jōō/ *n.* person of Hebrew descent or whose religion is Judaism [Gk *ioudaios*, ult. fr. Heb]

jew·el /jōō'əl, jōōl/ *n.* **1a** precious stone **b** this used in watchmaking **2** jeweled personal ornament **3** precious person or thing —*v.*

(-eled, -el·ing) 4 adorn or set with jewels [OFr *jouel* fr. L *jocus* joke; trifle]

jew'el box' *n.* plastic case for a compact disk or CD-ROM

jew·el·er *n.* maker of or dealer in jewels or jewelry

jew·el·ry /jōō'əlrē, jōōl'rē/ *n.* rings, necklaces, etc., regarded collectively

● Usage: Avoid the pronunciation "joo-luh-ree," which many regard as unacceptable.

Jew·ish /jōō'ish/ *adj.* 1 of Jews 2 of Judaism —**Jew'ish·ness** *n.*

Jew·ry /jōōr'ē, jōō'rē/ *n.* Jews collectively

jew's harp' *n.* small musical instrument held between the teeth

Jez·e·bel /jez'əbel/ *n.* shameless or immoral woman [for *Jezebel* in the Old Testament]

jg or **J.G.** *abbr.* US Navy. junior grade

jib /jib/ *n.* 1 triangular staysail 2 projecting arm of a crane

jibe¹ /jīb/ *v.* agree; go together; harmonize

● Usage: *Gibe* means 'jeer; deride.' Though pronounced identically to *jibe*, which means 'agree; go together,' the two should not be confused in writing. Neither should be confused with *jive*, a term from jazz, often heard in informal use in place of *jibe*.

jibe² /jīb/ *v.* (also **gybe**) (**jibed, jib·ing**) 1 (of a fore-and-aft sail or boom) swing across the vessel 2 cause (a sail) to do this 3 (of a ship or its crew) cause this to happen [Du]

Jid·da /jid'ə/ *n.* seaport in Saudi Arabia on the Red Sea. Pop. 1,500,000

jif·fy /jif'ē/ *n.* (*pl.* -fies) (also **jiff**) *Colloq.* short time; moment

jig /jig/ *n.* 1 a lively leaping dance b music for this 2 device that holds a piece of work and guides the tools operating on it —*v.* (**jigged, jig·ging**) 3 dance a jig 4 work on or equip with a jig or jigs

jig·ger /jig'ər/ *n.* 1 measure, esp. of liquor, equivalent to 1.5 ounces 2 small glass holding this [rel. to JIG]

jig·gle /jig'əl/ *v.* (-gled, -gling) 1 shake or jerk lightly; fidget —*n.* 2 light shake [fr. JIG]

jig'saw *n.* mechanical saw with a fine blade for cutting on a curve

jig'saw puz'zle *n.* picture cut into irregular interlocking pieces to be reassembled as a pastime

ji·had /jihäd', -had'/ *n.* (also **je·had'**) Muslim holy war [Ar: strife]

Ji·lin /jē'lin'/ *n.* (formerly **Chi'lin**) port in China on the Songhua River. Pop. 1,036,900

jil·lion /jil'yən/ *n. Colloq.* very large indefinite number

jilt /jilt/ *v.* abruptly reject or abandon (esp. a lover)

Jim Crow *n.* segregation of or discrimination against black people [fr. a minstrel song]

jim-dan·dy /jim' dan'dē/ *n.* (*pl.* -dies) *Colloq.* 1 something excellent; a superior example of its kind —*adj.* 2 pleasing; superior

Ji·nan /jē'nän'/ *n.* (formerly **Chi'nan**) city in E China. Pop. 1,480,900

jin·gle /jiNG'gəl/ *n.* 1 ringing or clinking noise 2 short, catchy verse or song in advertising, etc. —*v.* (-gled, -gling) 3 (cause to) make a jingling sound [imit.]

jinn /jin/ *n.* (*pl.* **jinn** or **djinn**) (also **djinn; jin·nee, jin·ni** /jinē'/) *Muslim Myth.* spirit in human or animal form having power over people [Ar *jinni* demon]

Jin·nah /jin'ə/, **Muhammed Ali** 1876–1948; founder and first governor-general of Pakistan (1947–48)

jin·rik·i·sha /jinrik'shò/ (also **jin·rick'sha, jin·rik'sha**) RICKSHAW

jinx /jiNGks/ *n. Colloq.* 1 person or thing that seems to cause bad luck —*v.* 2 subject to bad luck 3 wish bad luck (on) [perh. var. of L *jynx* wryneck (bird used in divination)]

jit·ney /jit'nē/ *n.* passenger bus or van

jit·ter·bug /jit'ərbəg/ *n.* 1 fast popular dance —*v.* (-bugged, -bug·ging) 2 dance the jitterbug

jit·ters /jit'ərz/ *n. Colloq.* extreme nervousness —**jit'ter·y** *adj.*; **jit'ter·i·ness** *n.*

jive /jīv/ *n.* 1 lively jazz music popular esp. in the 1950s 2 *Slang.* foolish or deceptive talk —*v.* 3 play jive 4 *Slang.* deceive

● Usage: See note at JIBE¹.

Joan of Arc, St. /jōn/ c. 1412–31; French national heroine

job /jäb/ *n.* 1 piece of work to be done; task 2 position in, or piece of, paid employment 3 *Slang.* crime, esp. a robbery —*v.* (**jobbed, job·bing**) 4 trade as a jobber 5 subcontract (work) 6 **make a job** (of good job) of do well 7 **on the job** *Colloq.* at work 8 **out of a job** unemployed

job' ac'tion *n.* strike or other protest by employees

job'ber *n.* 1 person who does piecework 2 wholesale merchant

job' lot' *n.* mixed lot bought at auction, etc.

job'-shar'ing *n.* sharing of a full-time job by two or more people —**job'-share'** *n.* & *v.*

jock /jäk/ *n. Slang.* athlete

jock·ey /jäk'ē/ *n.* (*pl.* -eys) 1 rider in horse-races, esp. professional —*v.* (-eyed, -ey·ing) 2 trick; cheat; outwit 3 maneuver for advantage [dim. of Scot *Jock* Jack]

jock·strap /jäk'strap/ *n.* support or protection for the male genitals, worn during exercise [slang *jock* male genitals]

jo·cose /jōkōs', jə-/ *adj.* playful; jocular —**jo·cose'ly** *adv.*; **jo·cos'i·ty** /-käs'ətē/ *n.* (*pl.* -ties) [L *jocus* joke]

joc·u·lar /jäk'yələr/ *adj.* 1 fond of joking 2 humorous —**joc'u·lar'i·ty** /-lar'ətē/ *n.* (*pl.* -ties); **joc'u·lar·ly** *adv.*

jo·cund /jäk'ənd/ *adj. Lit.* merry; cheerful —**jo·cun·di·ty** /jəkən'dətē/ *n.* (*pl.* -ties); **jo'cund·ly** *adv.* [ME fr. L *jucundus* pleasant]

Jodh·pur /jäd'pŏŏr'/ *n.* city in NW India. Pop. 648,600

jodh·purs /jäd'pərz/ *n. pl.* riding breeches that are baggy above the knee [for JODHPUR]

Joe Blow /jō blō/ *n.* fictitious name for an average person

jog /jäg, jôg/ *v.* (**jogged, jog·ging**) 1 run slowly, esp. as exercise 2 push or jerk, esp. unsteadily 3 nudge, esp. to alert 4 stimulate (the memory) —*n.* 5 spell of jogging; slow walk or trot 6 push; jerk; nudge —**jog'ger** *n.*

Jog·ja·kar·ta /jŏg'jəkärt'ə/ *n.* city in Indonesia on Java. Pop. 398,700

Jo·han·nes·burg /jōhan'əsbərg/ *n.* city in South Africa. Pop. 632,400

john /jän/ *n. Slang.* **1** lavatory **2** customer of a prostitute

John /jän/ **("John Lackland")** 1165–1216; king of England (1199–1216); signer of the Magna Carta (1215)

John, St. **("the Evangelist"** or **"the Divine")** one of the twelve Apostles; credited as writer of the fourth Gospel

John' Bull' *n.* England or the typical Englishman (character in an 18th-cent. satire)

John' Doe' *n.* fictitious name for a man whose identity is unknown or concealed

John' Han'cock *n. Colloq.* signature [for JOHN HANCOCK]

johnny-come-lately /jän'ēkəm'lāt'lē/ *n. Colloq.* newcomer; upstart

John Paul II (born **Karol Jozef Wojtyla**) 1920– ; Polish-born pope (1978–)

Johns /jänz/, **Jasper** 1930– ; US artist

John·son /jän'sən/ **1 Samuel** 1709–84; English lexicographer and writer **2 Andrew** 1808–75; 17th US president (1865–69) **3 Lyndon Baines ("L.B.J.")** 1908–73; 36th US president (1963–69)

John the Bap·tist, St. early 1st cent. A.D.; cousin and baptizer of Jesus

joie de vivre /zhwä′ də vēv′(rə)/ *n.* exuberance; high spirits [Fr: joy of living]

join /join/ *v.* **1** put together; fasten; unite (with one or several things or persons) **2** connect (points) by a line, etc. **3** become a member of (a club, organization, etc.) **4a** take one's place with (a person, group, etc.) **b** take part with (others) in an activity, etc. **5** come together; be united —*n.* **6** point, line, or surface at which things are joined **7 join battle** begin fighting **8 join forces** combine efforts **9 join hands** a clasp hands **b** combine in an action, etc. **10 join in** take part in (an activity) **11 join up** a enlist, as for military service **b** unite; connect [L *jungere*]

join·er /join′ər/ *n.* **1** maker of finished woodwork **2** *Colloq.* person who joins an organization or who readily joins societies, etc. —**join'er·y** *n.* (in sense 1)

joint /joint/ *n.* **1** place at which two or more things or parts of a structure are joined; device for joining these **2** point at which two bones fit together **3** cut of meat with the bone **4** *Slang.* restaurant, bar, etc. **5** *Slang.* marijuana cigarette **6** *Geol.* crack in rock —*adj.* **7** held, done by, or belonging to, two or more persons etc. (*joint account*) **8** sharing with another (*joint owner*) —*v.* **9** connect by joint(s) **10** divide at a joint or into joints **11 out of joint: a** (of a bone) dislocated **b** out of order —**joint'ly** *adv.* [ME fr. OFr fr. L, rel. to JOIN]

joist /joist/ *n.* supporting beam in a floor, ceiling, etc. [ME fr. OFr fr. L *jacere* lie]

jo·jo·ba /həhō′bə/ *n.* plant with seeds yielding an oily extract used in cosmetics, etc. [MexSp]

joke /jōk/ *n.* **1** thing said or done to cause laughter; witticism **2** ridiculous person or thing —*v.* (**joked, jok·ing**) **3** make jokes; tease **4 no joke** *Colloq.* serious matter —**jok'ing·ly** *adv.* [L *jocus* jest]

jok'er *n.* **1** person who jokes **2** *Slang.* person **3** extra playing card used in some games

Jo·li·et /jō′lē-et′/ *n.* city in Ill. Pop. 76,836

Jo·li·et /zhōlyā′/, **Louis** 1645–1700; French-Canadian explorer

jol·li·ty /jäl′ətē/ *n.* (*pl.* **-ties**) merrymaking; festivity [ME fr. OFr *joliveté*, rel. to JOLLY]

jol·ly /jäl′ē/ *adj.* (**-li·er, -li·est**) **1** cheerful; merry **2** festive; jovial **3** *Colloq.* pleasant; delightful —*v.* (**-lied, -ly·ing**) **4** *Colloq.* coax or humor (along) in a friendly way **5** josh; kid —**jol′li·ly** *adv.;* **jol′li·ness** *n.* [ME *jolif* gay; pretty: perh. rel. to YULE]

Jol·son /jōl′sən/, **Al** 1886–1950; Russianborn US singer

jolt /jōlt/ *v.* **1** disturb or shake (esp. in a moving vehicle) with a jerk **2** shock; perturb **3** move along jerkily —*n.* **4** jerk **5** surprise; shock —**jolt′y** *adj.* (**-i·er, -i·est**)

Jo·nah /jō′nə/ *n.* person who seems to bring bad luck [for *Jonah* in the Old Testament]

Jones /jōnz/ **1 Inigo** 1573–1652; British architect and stage designer **2 John Paul** (born **John Paul**) 1747–92; Scottish-born US naval hero **3 Daniel** 1881–1967; British linguist and phonetician

jon·quil /jäng′kwəl, jän′-/ *n.* narcissus with small fragrant yellow or white flowers [ult. fr. L *juncus* rush plant]

Jon·son /jän′sən/, **Ben (Benjamin)** 1572–1637; English dramatist and poet

Jor·dan /jôrd′n/ *n.* **1** kingdom in SW Asia, E of Israel. Capital: Amman. Pop. 3,636,000 **2** river in SW Asia flowing S into the Dead Sea —**Jor·da·ni·an** /jôrdā′nēən/ *n. & adj.*

Jo·seph, St. /jō′zəf, -səf/ *n.* husband of the Virgin Mary and foster father of Jesus

Jo·se·phus /jōsē′fəs/, **Flavius** c. 37 – c. 100; Jewish historian and general

josh /jäsh, jōsh/ *Slang. v.* **1** tease; banter **2** indulge in ridicule —*n.* **3** good-natured or teasing joke

jos·tle /jäs′əl/ *v.* (**-tled, -tling**) **1** push against; elbow, esp. roughly or in a crowd **2** struggle roughly —*n.* **3** jostling [fr. JOUST]

jot /jät/ *v.* (**jot·ted, jot·ting**) **1** write briefly or hastily —*n.* **2** very small amount (*not one jot*) [Gk IOTA]

joule /jōōl/ *n.* metric unit of work or energy [for J. *Joule*, English physicist]

jour·nal /jərn′l/ *n.* **1** newspaper or periodical **2** daily record of events; diary **3** book in which transactions are entered **4** part of a shaft or axle that rests on bearings [OFr: daily, fr. L *diurnalis* DIURNAL]

jour·nal·ese /jərn′l-ēz′/ *n.* hackneyed writing characteristic of newspapers

jour·nal·ism *n.* profession of writing for or editing newspapers, etc. —**jour′nal·ist** /-ist/ *n.;* **jour′nal·is′tic** *adj.*

jour·ney /jər′nē/ *n.* (*pl.* **-neys**) **1** act of going from one place to another **2** time taken for this (*a day's journey*) —*v.* **3** make a journey [ME fr. OFr *journee* day; day's work or travel, fr. L *diurnus* daily]

jour·ney·man /jər′nēmən/ *n.* (*pl.* **-men**) **1** qualified mechanic or artisan who works for another **2** reliable but not outstanding worker

joust /joust/ *Hist. n.* **1** combat between two knights on horseback with lances —*v.* **2** engage in a joust —**joust′er** *n.* [OFr *jouste* fr. L *juxta* near]

Jove /jōv/ *n. Rom. Myth.* JUPITER

jo·vi·al /jō′vēəl/ *adj.* merry; convivial —**jo-**

307   **john / jovial**

vi·al·i·ty /jō'vē·al'ətē/ n.; **jo'vi·al·ly** adv. [MedL jovialis, rel. to JOVE, JUPITER]

jowl¹ /joul/ n. 1 jaw or jawbone 2 cheek (cheek by jowl) [OE]

jowl² n. loose skin hanging from the jaw —**jowl'y** adj. [OE]

joy /joi/ n. 1 pleasure; extreme gladness 2 thing causing joy —**joy'ful** adj.; **joy'ful·ly** adv.; **joy'ful·ness** n.; **joy'less, joy'ous** /-əs/ adj.; **joy'ous·ly** adv. [Fr joie fr. L gaudium]

Joyce /jois/, **James** 1882–1941; Irish novelist

joy'ride Colloq. n. 1 ride for pleasure in a car, usu. reckless —v. (**rode, rid·den, rid·ing**) 2 go for a joyride —**joy'rid'er** n.

joy'stick n. 1 Colloq. control column of an aircraft 2 lever controlling movement of an image on a video screen, etc.

JP abbr. Justice of the Peace

Jr. abbr. Junior

Juan Car·los /(h)wän kär'lōs/ n. 1938– ; king of Spain (1975–)

Juan de Fu·ca, Strait of /wän' də f(y)ŌŌ'kə/ n. body of water separating Vancouver Island, Canada, from US

Juá·rez /(h)wär'əs/, **Benito** 1806–72; president of Mexico (1857–72)

ju·bi·lant /jŌŌ'bələnt/ adj. exultant; rejoicing —**ju'bi·lance** n.; **ju'bi·lant·ly** adv.; **ju·bi·la'tion** /-lā'sHən/ n. [L jubilare shout]

ju·bi·lee /jŌŌ'bəlē'/ n. 1 anniversary, esp. the 25th or 50th 2 time of rejoicing [L jubilare shout, ult. fr. Heb yobhel ram's-horn trumpet]

Ju·da·ism /jŌŌ'dāiz'əm, jŌŌ'dē·iz-/ n. religion of the Jews —**Ju·da'ic** /-dā'ik/ adj.

Ju·das /jŌŌ'dəs/ n. traitor [for JUDAS ISCARIOT]

Ju·das see JUDE, ST.

Ju·das Is·car·i·ot /iskar'ēət/ apostle who betrayed Jesus

Ju·das Mac·ca·be·us see MACCABEUS, JUDAS

Jude, St. /jŌŌd/ (also called **Ju'das**; not Iscariot) one of the twelve Apostles

judge /jəj/ n. 1 public official appointed to try legal cases 2 person appointed to decide in a contest, dispute, etc. 3a person who decides a question b person regarded as qualified to decide or pronounce (good judge of art) —v. (**judged, judg·ing**) 4 form an opinion or judgment (about); estimate; appraise 5 act as a judge (of) 6a try (a case) at law b pronounce sentence on 7 conclude; consider [L judicare]

judg·ment /jəj'mənt/ n. (also **judge'ment**) 1 critical faculty; discernment (error of judgment) 2 good sense 3 opinion or estimate (in my judgment) 4 sentence of a court of justice 5 against one's better judgment contrary to what one really feels to be advisable

judg·men·tal /jəjment'əl/ adj. making judgments, esp. critical or subjective ones —**judg'men·tal·ly** adv.

Judg'ment Day' n. Relig. day on which mankind will be judged by God

ju·di·ca·ture /jŌŌd'ikəcHŌŌr/ n. 1 administration of justice 2 jurisdiction 3 judges collectively [MedL, rel. to JUDGE]

ju·di·cial /jŌŌdisH'əl/ adj. 1 of, done by, or proper to a judge or court of law 2 having the function of judgment (judicial assembly) 3 impartial —**ju·di'cial·ly** adv. [L judicium judgment]

● Usage: judicial, like the more formal juridical, means 'relating to judgment and the administration of justice': the judicial system. It should not be confused with judicious, which means 'wise, prudent, reasonable': a judicious choice.

ju·di·ci·ar·y /jŌŌdisH·ē·er'ē, -disH'ərē/ n. (pl. **·ies**) judges of a state collectively

ju·di·cious /jŌŌdisH'əs/ adj. sensible; prudent —**ju·di'cious·ly** adv.

ju·do /jŌŌd'ō/ n. sport derived from jujitsu [Japn: gentle way, fr. Chin]

jug /jəg/ n. 1 vessel for liquids, with a handle and a small opening for pouring 2 Slang. prison

jug·ger·naut /jəg'ərnôt/ n. overwhelming force or object [Hindi fr. Skt Jagannatha lord of the world]

jug·gle /jəg'əl/ v. (**·gled, ·gling**) 1a keep several objects in the air at once by throwing and catching b perform such feats with balls, etc. 2 deal with (several activities) at once 3 misrepresent or rearrange (facts) adroitly —**jug'gler** n. [OFr fr. L jocus jest]

jug·u·lar /jəg'yələr/ adj. 1 of the neck or throat —n. 2 JUGULAR VEIN [L jugulum collarbone; throat]

jug'u·lar vein' n. any of several large veins in the neck carrying blood from the head

juice /jŌŌs/ n. 1 liquid part of plants or fruits 2 fluid from animal tissue 3 Colloq. fuel; electricity 4 Slang. alcoholic drink [OFr fr. L jus]

juice' box' n. container of coated paper for juice, etc., usu. a single serving

juiced /jŌŌst/ adj. intoxicated

juic'er n. device for extracting juice from fruit

juic'y adj. (**·i·er, ·i·est**) 1 full of juice 2 Colloq. interesting, esp. for being improper 3 Colloq. profitable —**juic'i·ly** adv.; **juic'i·ness** n.

ju·jit·su /jŌŌjit'sŌŌ/ n. Japanese system of unarmed combat and physical training [Japn: gentle skill, fr. Chin]

ju·jube /jŌŌ'jŌŌb', jŌŌ'jəbē'/ n. flavored jellylike lozenge [Gk zizuphon]

juke·box /jŌŌk'bäks'/ n. coin-operated music-playing machine [Gullah juke disorderly]

Jul. abbr. July

ju·lep /jŌŌ'ləp/ n. 1 sweet drink, esp. one with alcohol or medicated 2 MINT JULEP [Pers guläb rose-water]

ju·li·enne /jŌŌ'lē·en'/ adj. cut into thin strips as vegetables [Fr, prob. fr. name Julienne]

Jul·ius Cae·sar /jŌŌl'yəs/ CAESAR, GAIUS JULIUS

Jul·lun·dur /jəl'əndər/ n. city in NW India. Pop. 519,500

Ju·ly /jŌŌlī'/ n. (pl. **·lys**) seventh month of the year in the Gregorian calendar [for Julius CAESAR]

jum·ble /jəm'bəl/ v. (**·bled, ·bling**) 1 confuse; mix up; muddle —n. 2 confused state or heap [prob. imit.]

jum·bo /jəm'bō/ n. (pl. **·bos**) Colloq. 1 large animal, person, or thing —adj. 2 very large

jump /jəmp/ v. 1 rise off or leave the ground, a height, etc., by sudden muscular effort in the legs 2 move suddenly or hastily (jumped into the car) 3 jerk; twitch 4a change, esp. suddenly (*prices jumped*) **b** cause to do this **5** change the subject, etc., rapidly **6** go on to (another level, etc.) or skip over suddenly **7** attack (a person) unexpectedly —*n.* **8** act of jumping **9** sudden jerk caused by shock or excitement **10** abrupt rise in amount, value, status, etc. **11** obstacle to be jumped **12a** sudden transition **b** gap in a series, logical sequence, etc. **13 jump at** accept eagerly **14 jump bail** fail to appear for trial having been released on bail **15 jump down a person's throat** *Colloq.* reprimand or contradict a person fiercely **16 jump the gun** *Colloq.* begin prematurely **17 jump on (or all over)** *Colloq.* attack or criticize severely **18 jump out of one's skin** *Colloq.* be extremely startled **19 have (or get) the jump on** have an early start or advantage

jump·er[1] /jəm′pər/ *n.* **1** one-piece, sleeveless dress worn over a blouse **2** loose jacket **3** pinafore dress [prob. *jump* short coat]

jump·er[2] *n.* **1** person or animal that jumps **2** short wire used, esp. temporarily, on an electrical circuit

jump′er ca′bles *n.* paired cable with clamplike connectors for conveying current from one battery to another

jump′-start′ *v.* **1** start (a vehicle) with jumper cables —*n.* **2** act of jump-starting

jump′ suit′ *n.* one-piece garment for the whole body

jump·y *adj.* (**·i·er, ·i·est**) **1** nervous; easily startled **2** making sudden movements —**jump′i·ness** *n.*

Jun. *abbr.* **1** June **2** Junior

jun·co /jəNG′kō/ *n.* small N American finch

junc·tion /jəNG′SHən/ *n.* **1** joint; joining-point **2** place where railroad lines or roads join or cross **3** joining [L *jungere* join]

junc′tion box′ *n.* box containing a junction of electric cables, etc.

junc·ture /jəNGk′CHər/ *n.* **1** critical moment in a series of events **2** joining-point **3** joining

June /jōōn/ *n.* sixth month of the year in the Gregorian calendar [L *Junius*]

Ju·neau /jōō′nō/ *n.* capital of Alaska, in the SE part. Pop. 26,751

Jung /yŏŏNG/, **Carl Gustav** 1875–1961; Swiss psychologist —**Jung′i·an** /–ēən/ *adj.*

Jung·frau /yŏŏNG′frou/ *n.* mountain in the Bernese Alps in S Switzerland; 13,642 ft.

jun·gle /jəNG′gəl/ *n.* **1a** land with dense vegetation, esp. in the tropics **b** an area of this **2** place or mass of bewildering complexity, confusion, or struggle **3 law of the jungle** state of ruthless competition —**jun′gly** *adj.* [Hindi fr. Skt]

jun′gle·gym′ *n.* playground structure with bars, ladders, etc., for children to climb

jun·ior /jōōn′yər/ *adj.* **1** inferior in age, standing, or position **2** the younger (esp. appended to the name of a son with the same name as his father) —*n.* **3** junior person **4** person at the lowest level (in an office, etc.) **5** third-year high school or college student [L: younger]

jun′ior col′lege *n.* institution offering courses equivalent to the first two years of a college education

jun′ior high′ school′ *n.* school usu. for grades 7, 8, and 9

ju·ni·per /jōō′nipər/ *n.* evergreen shrub or

tree with dark-purple berrylike cones [L *juniperus*]

junk[1] /jəNGk/ *n.* **1** discarded articles; rubbish **2** anything regarded as of little value **3** *Slang.* narcotic drug, esp. heroin —*v.* **4** discard as junk

junk[2] *n.* flat-bottomed sailing-vessel in the China seas [Javanese *djong*]

junk′ bond′ *n.* bond bearing high interest but deemed to be a risky investment

jun·ket /jəNG′kit/ *n.* **1** pleasure outing **2** official's tour at public expense **3** sweetened and flavored milk curds [OFr *jonquette* rush basket, fr. L *juncus* rush]

junk′ food′ *n.* snack food with low nutritional value

junk·ie /jəNG′kē/ *n. Slang.* **1** drug addict **2** person who craves a substance such as food, etc. **3** enthusiastic fan, practitioner, follower, etc.

junk′ mail′ *n.* unsolicited advertising matter sent by mail

jun·ta /hōōnt′ə, hənt′ə, jənt′ə/ *n.* (usu. military) clique taking power in a coup d'état [Sp fr. L, rel. to JOIN]

Ju·pi·ter /jōō′pitər/ *n. Rom. Myth.* **1** (also **Jove**) the king of the gods **2** largest planet in the solar system, fifth from the sun

Jur·as·sic /jŏŏras′ik/ *Geol. adj.* **1** of the second period of the Mesozoic era, noted for the presence of dinosaurs —*n.* **2** this era or system [Fr fr. *Jura* Mountains]

ju·rid·i·cal /jŏŏərid′ikəl/ *n.* of the law or judicial proceedings [L *jus, jur-* law + *dicere* say]

ju·ris·dic·tion /jŏŏər′əsdik′SHən/ *n.* **1** legal or other authority **2** extent of this; territory it extends over —**ju′ris·dic′tion·al** *adj.*

ju·ris·pru·dence /jŏŏr′əsprŏŏd′ns/ *n.* science or philosophy of law [L *juris prudentia*]

ju·rist /jŏŏr′ist/ *n.* expert in law

ju·ror /jŏŏr′ər, -ôr′/ *n.* member of a jury

ju·ry /jŏŏr′ē/ *n.* (*pl.* **-ries**) **1** body of people giving a verdict or decision in a court of justice **2** body of people awarding prizes in a competition

ju′ry-rigged′ *adj.* having temporary, improvised rigging or repair

just /jəst/ *adj.* **1** morally right or fair **2** (of treatment, etc.) deserved (*just reward*) **3** well-grounded; justified (*just anger*) **4** right in amount, etc.; proper —*adv.* **5** exactly (*just what I need*) **6** a little time ago; very recently (*has just seen them*) **7** *Colloq.* simply; merely (*just doesn't make sense*) **8** barely; no more than (*just enough*) **9** *Colloq.* positively; indeed (*just splendid*) **10** quite (*not just yet*) **11 just about** *Colloq.* almost exactly; almost completely **12 just in case** as a precaution **13 just the same** nevertheless **14 just so: a** exactly arranged (*everything just so*) **b** exactly as you say —**just′ly** *adv.*; **just′ness** *n.* [L *justus* righteous]

jus·tice /jəs′tis/ *n.* **1** justness; fairness **2** authority exercised in the maintenance of law or right **3** judicial proceedings (*Court of Justice*) **4** magistrate; judge **5 do justice to: a** treat fairly **b** appreciate properly [L *justitia*]

jus′tice of the peace′ *n.* magistrate who tries minor cases, performs marriages, etc.

jus·ti·fy /jəs′tif ī′/ *v.* (**·fied, ·fy·ing**) **1** show the justice or correctness of (a person, act, assertion, etc.) 2 (esp. *passive*) cite or constitute adequate grounds for (conduct, a claim, etc.); vindicate 3 (as **jus'ti-fied** *adj.*) just; right (*justified in assuming*) 4 *Printing.* adjust (a line of type) to give even margins —**jus'ti-fi'a-ble** *adj.*; **jus'ti-fi'a-bly** *adv.*; **jus'ti-fi-ca'tion** /-fikā'sнən/ *n.*; **jus-ti-fi-ca-to-ry** /jəs'tif'ikətòr'ē/ *adj.*

Jus-tin-i-an /jəstin'ēən/ 483–565; Byzantine emperor (527–565) and codifier of Roman law (529)

jut /jət/ *v.* (**jut-ted, jut-ting**) 1 protrude; project —*n.* 2 projection [var. of JET[1]]

jute /jōōt/ *n.* 1 fiber from the bark of an E Indian plant, used esp. for sacking, mats, etc. 2 plant yielding this [Bengali]

Ju-ve-nal /jōō'vən-l/ c. 60 – c. 49 B.C.; Roman satirist

ju-ve-nile /jōō'vənīl', -nəl/ *adj.* 1a youthful b of or for young people 2 immature —*n.* 3 young person 4 actor playing a youthful part [L *juvenilis* youthful]

ju've-nile' de-lin'quen-cy *n.* antisocial or illegal behavior of minors —**ju've-nile de-lin' quent** *n.*

jux-ta-pose /jək'stəpōz'/ *v.* (**-posed, -posing**) 1 place (things) side by side 2 place (a thing) beside another —**jux'ta-po-si'tion** /-zi'sнən/ *n.* [Fr fr. L *juxta* next to + F *poser* put]

JV *abbr.* junior varsity

K

k, K /kā/ *n.* (*pl.* **k's; K's, Ks**) eleventh letter of the English alphabet; a consonant

k or **k.** *abbr.* 1 *Electr.* capacity 2 (also *cap.*) karat 3 kilogram(s) 4 *Chess.* king 5 knight 6 knot 7 kopeck

K or **K** *abbr.* 1 *Physics.* Kelvin 2 kilo- 3 kindergarten 4 *Chess.* king 5 kitchen 6 1000 7 *Comp.* unit of 1,024 (i.e., 2[10]) bytes or bits, or loosely 1,000 8 *Baseball.* strikeout 9 (as **K**) *symb.* potassium

Ka-bul /kä'bool/, käb'əl/ *n.* capital of Afghanistan. Pop. 1,424,400

Kaf-ka /käf'kə/, **Franz** 1883–1924; Czech writer

Ka-go-shi-ma /käg'ōshē'mə, kägō'sнēmə/ *n.* seaport in Japan, on Kyushu. Pop. 536,900

kai-ser /kī'zər/ *n. Hist.* emperor, esp. of Germany, Austria, or the Holy Roman Empire [L CAESAR]

Ka-la-ha-ri /kal'əhär'ē, käl'-/ *n.* desert in SW Africa, mainly in Botswana

Kal-a-ma-zoo /kal'əməzōō'/ *n.* city in Mich. Pop. 80,277

kale /kāl/ *n.* variety of cabbage with wrinkled leaves [ME *col(e)* cabbage]

ka-lei-do-scope /kəlīd'əskōp/ *n.* 1 tube containing mirrors and pieces of colored glass, etc., producing visual patterns when turned or shaken 2 constantly changing pattern, group, etc. —**ka-lei-do-scop'ic** /-skäp'ik/ *adj.* [Gk *kalos* beautiful + *eidos* form + -SCOPE]

Ka-li-nin /kəlē'n(y)in/ *n.* (formerly **Tver**) city in W Russia, on the Volga River. Pop. 455,300

Ka-li-nin-grad /kəlē'n(y)іnGrad'/ *n.* seaport in W Russia. Pop. 408,100

Ka-lu-ga /kəlōō'gə/ *n.* city in W Russia. Pop. 366,300

Kal-yan /kəl'yän'/ *n.* city in W India. Pop. 1,014,100

Kamchatka /kamcнät'kə/ *n.* peninsula in E Russia between the Bering Sea and the Sea of Okhotsk

Ka-me-ha-me-ha I /kəmä'əmä'hä/ c. 1758–1819; king of Hawaii (1810–19)

ka-mi-ka-ze /käm'ikäz'ē/ *n.* (in World War

II) explosive-laden Japanese aircraft flown on a suicide mission to crash on a ship, etc. [Japn: divine wind]

Kam-pa-la /kämpäl'ə/ *n.* capital of Uganda. Pop. 773,500

Kam'pu-che'a /kam'pōōcнē'ə/ *n.* see CAMBODIA

Kan. abbr. for Kansas

Ka-nan-ga /kənäNG'gə/ *n.* city in central Zaire. Pop. 371,900

Kan-din-sky /kandin'skē/, **Wassily** 1866–1944; Russian painter

kan-ga-roo /kaNG'gərōō'/ *n.* (*pl.* **-roos**) Australian marsupial with strong hind legs for jumping [Austral Aborig]

kan'ga-roo court' *n.* tribunal lacking proper authority that renders illegal or mock judgments

Ka-no /kän'ō/ *n.* city in Nigeria. Pop. 699,900

Kan-pur /kän'pōōr'/ *n.* city in India on the Ganges River. Pop. 1,958,300

Kan-sas /kan'zəs/ *n.* state in the central US. Capital: Topeka. Pop. 2,477,574. Abbr. **KS**; **Kan.; Kans.** —**Kan'san** *n.* & *adj.*

Kan'sas Cit'y *n.* 1 city in Mo. Pop. 435,146 2 city in Kan. Pop. 149,767

Kant /känt, kant/, **Immanuel** 1724–1804; German philosopher

Kao-hsiung /gou'sнē-ōōNG'/ *n.* seaport in Taiwan. Pop. 1,386,700

ka-o-lin /kā'əlin/ *n.* fine white clay used esp. for porcelain [Chin *kao-ling* high hill (source of clay)]

ka-pok /kā'päk'/ *n.* fibrous substance from a tropical tree, used for stuffing life preservers, etc. [Malay]

Ka-po'si's sar-co'ma /kəpō'sēz, kap'ə-/ *n. Med.* disease causing cancerous lesions, usu. of the skin [for Hungarian dermatologist M.K. *Kaposi*]

kap-pa /kap'ə/ *n.* tenth letter of the Greek alphabet (K, κ)

ka-put /kəpōōt'/ *adj. Slang.* broken; ruined [Ger]

Ka-ra-chi /kəräcнē'ē/ *n.* seaport in Pakistan. Pop. 5,208,100

Ka·ra·gan·da /kar′əgəndä′/ *n.* city in W Kazakhstan. Pop. 608,600

Ka·raj /kəräj′/ *n.* city in N Iran. Pop. 275,100

kar·a·kul /kar′əkəl/ *n.* (also **car′a·cul**) 1 Asian sheep with curled fleece, dark when young and brown or gray in adults 2 fur of or like this [Russ]

ka·ra·o·ke /kar′ē-ō′kē, kərō′kē/ *n.* entertainment of singing to a recorded musical track, esp. of popular songs [Japn: empty orchestra]

ka·rat /kar′ət/ *n.* unit for measurement of the purity of gold; *abbr.* **K, Kt.**

ka·ra·te /kərät′ē/ *n.* Japanese system of unarmed combat using the hands and feet [Japn: empty hand]

Karl-Marx-Stadt /kärl märks′ SHtät′/ *n.* former name of CHEMNITZ

Karls·ruh·e /kärlz′rōō′ə/ *n.* city in Germany. Pop. 275,100

kar·ma /kär′mə/ *n.* Buddhism. & Hinduism. person's actions in previous lives, believed to determine fate in future existences [Skt: action; fate]

Kath·man·du or **Kat·man·du** /kat′man′dōō′/ *n.* capital of Nepal. Pop. 235,200

Ka·to·wi·ce /kät′əvēt′sə/ *n.* city in S Poland. Pop. 366,500

ka·ty·did /kā′tēdid/ *n.* N American insect related to the grasshopper

Kau·nas /kou′nəs/ *n.* city in Lithuania. Pop. 433,200

Ka·un·da /kä-ōōn′də/, **Kenneth** 1924– ; president of Zambia (1964–91)

Ka·wa·ba·ta /käwəbät′ə, kawäb′ətə/, **Yasunari** 1899–1972; Japanese writer; Nobel prize 1968

Ka·wa·sa·ki /kä′wəsäk′ē/ *n.* seaport in Japan, on Honshu. Pop. 1,187,000

KAYAK

kay·ak /kī′ak′/ *n.* small, enclosed canoe with an opening for the paddler [Esk]

Kay·se·ri /kī′zərē′/ *n.* city in central Turkey. Pop. 421,400

Ka·zakh·stan /kəzäkstän′/ *n.* republic in NW Asia, on the E coast of the Caspian Sea, formerly part of the USSR. Capital: Almaty. Pop. 17,008,000 —**Ka·zakh′** *n.*

Ka·zan /kəzän′(yə)/ *n.* city in Russia. Pop. 1,107,300

Ka·zan /kəzan′/, **Elia** 1909– ; Turkish-born US film and theater director

ka·zoo /kəzōō′/ *n.* toy musical instrument into which the player sings or hums

Keats /kēts/, **John** 1795–1821; English poet

ke·bab /kəbäb′, kā′bäb′/ *n.* chunks of meat, vegetables, etc., cooked on a skewer [Ar fr. Turk *kebap* roast meat]

keel /kēl/ *n.* 1 main lengthwise member of the base of a ship, etc. —*v.* 2 (cause to) fall

---

311   **Karaganda / Kelvin scale**

down or over 3 turn keel upwards 4 **on an even keel** steady; balanced [ON]

keel′haul′ *v.* 1 drag (a person) under the keel of a ship as a punishment 2 scold or rebuke severely

Kee·lung /kē′lōōNG′/ *n.* see CHILUNG

keen¹ /kēn/ *adj.* 1 enthusiastic; eager 2 (foll. by *on*) enthusiastic about; fond of 3 (of the senses) sharp 4 intellectually acute 5 (of a knife, etc.) sharp 6 penetrating; intense; acute —**keen′ly** *adv.*; **keen′ness** *n.* [OE]

keen² *n.* 1 Irish wailing funeral song —*v.* 2 wail mournfully, esp. for the dead [Ir *caoine* fr. *caoinim* wail]

keep /kēp/ *v.* (**kept, keep·ing**) 1 have continuous charge of; retain possession of 2 retain or reserve for (a future time) (*kept it for later*) 3 retain or remain in a specified condition, position, place, etc. (*keep cool; keep out; keep them happy; knives are kept here*) 4 hold back (from) 5 detain (*what kept you?*) 6 observe, honor, or respect (a law, custom, commitment, etc.) (*keep one's word; keep the sabbath*) 7 provide for; look after 8 (foll. by *in*) maintain (a person) with a supply of 9 maintain (a diary, house, accounts, etc.) regularly and in proper order 10 guard or protect (a person or place) 11 preserve (*keep order*) 12 continue; repeat habitually (*keeps telling me*) 13 continue to follow (a way or course) 14 remain fresh; not spoil 15 remain in (one's bed, room, etc.) —*n.* 16 maintenance, food, etc. (*hardly earn your keep*) 17 *Hist.* tower, esp. the central stronghold of a castle 18 **for keeps** *Colloq.* permanently; indefinitely 19 **keep at** (cause to) persist with 20 **keep away** prevent from being near 21 **keep back: a** remain or keep at a distance **b** retard the progress of **c** conceal **d** withhold 22 **keep down: a** hold in subjection **b** prevent from going up **c** not vomit (food eaten) 23 **keep off: a** (cause to) stay away from **b** ward off 24 **keep out: a** remain outside **b** exclude 25 **keep to: a** adhere to **b** confine oneself to 26 **keep to oneself: a** avoid contact with others **b** maintain as secret 27 **keep up: a** maintain (progress, morale, etc.) **b** keep in repair, etc. **c** carry on (a correspondence, etc.) **d** prevent from going to bed **e** (foll. by *with*) not fall behind [OE]

keep′er *n.* 1 person who looks after or is in charge of animals, people, or a thing 2 custodian; guard 3 *Colloq.* thing worth keeping

keep′ing *n.* 1 observance 2 custody; charge 3 **in keeping with** in conformity with

keep′sake′ *n.* souvenir, esp. of a person

keg /keg, kāg/ *n.* small barrel [ON *kaggi*]

Kel·ler /kel′ər/, **Helen** 1880–1968; US writer, social reformer, and academic; blind and deaf from infancy

Kel·logg /kel′ôg′, -äg′/, **W(ill) K(eith)** 1860–1951; US manufacturer of prepared cereals

Kel·ly /kel′ē/ 1 **Emmett** 1898–1979; US circus clown 2 **Grace** 1928–82; US actress; became princess of Monaco

kelp /kelp/ *n.* large, brown seaweed used as a food and mineral source

Kel′vin scale′ /kel′vin/ *n.* scale of temperature with zero at absolute zero [for its developer]

Ke·me·ro·vo /kem'ərəvə, -rō'və/ *n.* city in S Russia. Pop. 520,700

Kem·pis /kem'pəs/, **Thomas à** (born Thomas Hemerken) c. 1379–1471; German monk and writer

ken /ken/ *n.* range of knowledge or sight (*beyond my ken*) [OE: make known, rel. to CAN¹]

Ken·ne·dy /ken'ədē/ 1 John F(itzgerald) ("J.F.K.") 1917–63; 35th US president (1961–63); assassinated 2 Robert F. 1925–68; US politician; assassinated 3 Edward Moore (Ted) 1932– ; US politician

ken·nel /ken'l/ *n.* 1 small shelter for a dog 2 (often *pl.*) breeding or boarding place for dogs —*v.* (·neled or ·nelled, ·nel·ing or ·nel·ling) 3 put into or keep in a kennel [Fr *chenil* fr. L *canis* dog]

Ken·tuck·y /kəntak'ē/ *n.* state in the S central US. Capital: Frankfort. Pop. 3,685,296. Abbr. KY; Ky. —**Ken·tuck'i·an** *n.* & *adj.*

Ken·ya /ken'yə, kē'-/ *n.* republic in E Africa, on the Indian Ocean. Capital: Nairobi. Pop. 26,985,000

Ken·yat·ta /kenyät'ə/, **Jomo** c. 1891–1978; Kenyan prime minister (1963) and president (1964–78)

Ke'ogh plan' /kē'ō/ *n.* pension plan for self-employed people or unincorporated businesses

kep·i /kā'pē, kep'ē/ *n.* (*pl.* **·is**) French military cap with a horizontal peak [Fr fr. SwissGer]

Kep·ler /kep'lər/, **Johannes** 1571–1630; German astronomer

kept /kept/ *v.* past and past part. of KEEP

ker·a·tin /ker'ət·n/ *n.* fibrous protein in hair, feathers, hooves, claws, horns, etc. [Gk *keras, kerat-* horn]

ker·chief /kər'CHif, -CHēf'/ *n.* 1 headscarf; neckerchief 2 handkerchief [ME *courchef* fr. OFr *covrechef*, rel. to COVER, CHIEF]

Ker·man /kərmän'/ *n.* city in Iran. Pop. 257,300

Kern /kərn'/, **Jerome** 1885–1945; US composer and songwriter

ker·nel /kər'nl/ *n.* 1 (usu. soft) center within the hard shell of a nut, fruit stone, seed, etc. 2 whole seed of a cereal 3 essence of anything [OE, rel. to CORN¹]

ker·o·sene /ker'əsēn', ker'əsēn'/ *n.* (also **ker'o·sine**) petroleum distillate used as a solvent, fuel, etc. [Gk *kēros* wax]

Ker·ou·ac /ker'ōō·ak'/, **Jack** 1922–69; US novelist and poet

kes·trel /kes'trəl/ *n.* small hovering falcon

ketch /keCH/ *n.* two-masted sailboat with aftermast set forward of the rudder [ME *cache* CATCH]

ketch·up /keCH'əp, kaCH'əp/ *n.* (also **cat·sup** /kat'səp/) spicy tomato condiment [Malay perh. fr. Chin]

ke·tone /kē'tōn'/ *n.* any of a class of ketone compounds, including acetone [Ger *Keton*, alter. of *Aketon* ACETONE]

ket·tle /ket'l/ *n.* 1 vessel for boiling or cooking 2 a fine (or pretty) kettle of fish an awk-

ward state of affairs [ME fr. ON fr. L *catillus* pot]

ket'tle·drum' *n.* large bowl-shaped drum

KETTLEDRUMS

key¹ /kē/ *n.* (*pl.* **keys**) 1 (usu. metal) instrument for moving the bolt of a lock for locking or unlocking something 2 similar implement for winding a clock, etc. 3 finger-operated button or lever on a typewriter, piano, computer terminal, etc. 4 means of advance, access, etc. (*key to success*) 5 essential element 6a solution or explanation b word or system for solving a cipher or code c explanatory list of symbols used in a map, table, etc. 7 *Mus.* system of notes related to each other and based on a particular note (*key of C major*) —*adj.* 8 essential; important —*v.* (keyed, key·ing) 9 regulate or modify to fit a particular purpose or situation 10 fasten with a pin, wedge, bolt, etc. 11 enter (data) by means of a keyboard 12 align or link (one thing to another) 13 keyed up tense; nervous [OE]

key² *n.* low-lying island or reef, esp. off Florida or in the W Indies [Sp *cayo*]

Key /kē/, **Francis Scott** 1779–1843; US lawyer; composed lyrics to "The Star-Spangled Banner"

key'board' *n.* 1 set of keys on a typewriter, computer, piano, etc. 2 electronic musical instrument with keys arranged as on a piano —*v.* 3 enter (data) by means of a keyboard —**key'board·er** *n.* (in sense 1); **key'board·ist** *n.* (in sense 2)

key'hole' *n.* hole in a door, etc., for a key

Keynes /kānz/, **John Maynard** 1883–1946; English economist

key·note /kē'nōt'/ *n.* 1 (esp. *attrib.*) prevailing tone or idea, esp. in a speech, conference, etc. 2 *Mus.* note on which a key is based

key'pad' *n.* small keyboard, etc., for a calculator, telephone, etc.

key'punch' *n.* 1 device for recording data by means of punched holes or notches on cards or paper tape —*v.* 2 record (data) thus

key'stone' *n.* 1 central principle of a system, policy, etc. 2 central locking stone in an arch

key'stroke' *n.* single depression of a key on a keyboard, esp. as a measure of work

key'word' *n.* 1 key to a code, etc. 2a word of great significance b significant word used in indexing

kg *abbr.* kilogram(s)

Kha·ba·rovsk /kəbär'əfsk/ *n.* port in Russia on the Amur River. Pop. 613,300

kha·ki /kak'ē, käk'ē/ *adj.* 1 dull brownish-yellow —*n.* (*pl.* **·kis**) 2 strong fabric of this color 3 dull brownish-yellow color 4 (usu.

pl.) uniform of this fabric [Urdu fr. Pers: dusty]

khan /kän, kan/ *n.* title of rulers and officials in Central Asia, Afghanistan, etc. **—khan'ate** /-ät/ *n.* [Turk: lord]

Khar·kiv /kär'kif/ *n.* (formerly **Khar'kov**) city in Ukraine. Pop. 1,623,000

Khar·toum /kärtoom'/ *n.* capital of Sudan. Pop. 476,200

Khmer /kmer/ *n. & adj.* (of or relating to) the major ethnic group of Cambodia, or their language

Kho·mei·ni /khōmā'nē, kō-, hō-/, **Ayatollah Ruhollah** c. 1900–89; Islamic religious leader; head of state of Iran (1979–89)

Khru·shchev /krōōshchōf', krōōsh'(ch)ev'/, **Nikita** 1894–1971; Russian political leader; premier of the USSR (1958–64)

Khu·fu /kōō'fōō/ see CHEOPS

Khul·na /kōōl'nə/ *n.* city in Bangladesh. Pop. 545,800

kHz *abbr.* kilohertz

kib·butz /kibōōts', -bōōts'/ *n.* (*pl.* **·but·zim** /-bōōt'sēm', -bōōt'-/) communal settlement in Israel, esp. a collective farm [Heb *qibbus* gathering]

kib·itz /kib'its/ *v.* offer unsolicited advice, esp. to card players **—kib'itz·er** *n.* [Yiddish]

ki·bosh /kī'bäsh/ *n.* Colloq. as in **put the kibosh** on put an end to

kick /kik/ *v.* 1 strike, strike out, or propel forcibly, with the foot or hoof 2 protest at; rebel against 3 *Slang.* give up (a habit) 4 drive (out) 5 *refl.* be annoyed with oneself 6 *Football.* score (a goal) by a kick **—n.** 7 kicking action or blow 8 *Colloq.* a strength or stimulant effect, esp. of alcohol b (often *pl.*) enjoyment (*did it for kicks*) 9 *Colloq.* temporary interest (*on a jogging kick*) 10 recoil of a gun when fired 11 **kick around**: *Colloq.* a drift idly from place to place b be unused or unwanted c treat roughly d discuss unsystematically 12 **kick in** *Slang.* pay in; contribute 13 **kick the bucket** *Slang.* die 14 **kick off**: a *Football.* start or resume a match b *Colloq.* begin 15 remove (shoes, etc.) by kicking

kick'back' *n.* Colloq. 1 recoil 2 (usu. illegal) payment for help or favors, esp. in business

kick'er *n.* 1 person who kicks 2 *Colloq.* surprising turn of events, consequence, or conclusion

kick'·off' *n.* Football. kick that starts play

kick'·stand' *n.* rod for supporting a bicycle or motor cycle when stationary

kick'-start' *v.* start (a motorcycle, etc.) by downward push on a starting pedal **—kick'start·er** *n.*

kid[1] /kid/ *n.* 1 young goat 2 leather from this 3 *Colloq.* child 4 **handle with kid gloves** treat carefully [ON]

 • Usage: The use of *kid* for child is appropriate to informal speech but should be avoided in writing.

kid[2] *v.* (also *refl.*) (**kid·ded, kid·ding**) *Colloq.* 1 deceive; trick; tease (*don't kid yourself; only kidding*) 2 **no kidding** *Slang.* that is the truth

Kidd /kid/, **William** ("Captain Kidd") 1645–1701; Scottish pirate

kid·die /kid'ē/ *n.* (also **kid'dy**) (*pl.* **·dies**) *Colloq.* KID[1], 3

kid·nap /kid'nap'/ *v.* (**·napped** or **·naped**, **·nap·ping** or **·nap·ing**) 1 abduct (a person, etc.), esp. to obtain a ransom 2 steal (a child) **—kid'nap·per** *n.* [fr. KID[1] + *nap* NAB]

kid·ney /kid'nē/ *n.* (*pl.* **·neys**) 1 either of two organs in the abdominal cavity of vertebrates which remove wastes from the blood and excrete urine 2 animal's kidney as food

kid'ney bean' *n.* red-skinned kidney-shaped bean

kiel·ba·sa /ki(l)bä'sä/ *n.* Polish-style smoked sausage [Pol: sausage]

Kier·ke·gaard /kėr'kəgär(d)', -gôr'/, **Søren** 1813–55; Danish philosopher; a founder of existentialism

Ki·ev /kē'ef, -ev/ *n.* capital of Ukraine. Pop. 2,635,000

Ki·ga·li /kigäl'ē/ *n.* capital of Rwanda. Pop. 232,700

Ki·lau·e·a /kil'əwä'ə/ *n.* active volcano on the island of Hawaii

Kil·i·man·ja·ro, Mount /kil'imənjär'ō/ *n.* volcanic peak in N Tanzania; highest in Africa: 19,340 ft.

kill /kil/ *v.* 1 cause death or the death of 2 destroy; remove 3 make ineffectual 4 pass (time, or a specified period) usu. while waiting (*an hour to kill before the interview*) 5 defeat (legislation) 6 *Sports.* a hit (the ball) so that it cannot be returned b stop (the ball) dead **—n.** 7 act of killing 8 animal(s) killed, esp. by a hunter 9 *Milit.* destruction or disablement of an enemy aircraft, etc. 10 **kill two birds with one stone** achieve two aims at once 11 **kill with kindness** spoil with overindulgence [perh. rel. to QUELL]

kill'er *n.* 1 person, animal, or thing that kills 2 *Colloq.* impressive; formidable; excellent thing

kill'er bee' *n.* Apis mellifera adansonii, a very aggressive honeybee orig. from Africa

kill'er in'stinct *n.* 1 innate tendency to kill 2 ruthless streak

kill'er whale' *n.* predatory dolphin with a prominent dorsal fin

kill'ing *n.* 1a causing of death b instance of this 2 *Colloq.* great (esp. financial) success (*make a killing*) **—adj.** *Colloq.* 3 exhausting

kill'joy' *n.* gloomy person, esp. at a party, etc.

kiln /kiln, kil/ *n.* furnace or oven for burning, baking, or drying, esp. bricks, pottery, etc. [OE, fr. L *culina* kitchen]

ki·lo /kē'lō/ *n.* (*pl.* **·los**) kilogram [Fr, abbr.]

kilo· *comb. form* 1,000 (esp. in metric units) [Gk *khilioi*]

kil·o·byte /kil'əbīt', kē'lə-/ *n.* Comp. 1,024 (i.e., 2[10]), or, loosely 1,000 bytes as a measure of memory size, etc.

ki·lo·cy·cle /-sī'kəl/ *n.* former term for KILO-HERTZ

kil·o·gram /-gram'/ *n.* metric unit of mass, approx. 2.205 lb

kil·o·hertz /-hərts'/ *n.* 1,000 hertz; 1,000 cycles per second

kil·o·me·ter /kiläm'ətər, kil'əmēt'ər/ *n.* 1,000 meters (approx. 0.62 miles)

kil·o·ton /kil'ətən, kĕ"lə-/ *n.* unit of explosive power equivalent to 1,000 tons of TNT

kil·o·watt /-wät'/ *n.* 1,000 watts

kil·o·watt'-hour' *n.* electrical power consumption of 1,000 watts for one hour

kilt /kilt/ *n.* pleated knee-length usu. tartan skirt, traditionally worn by Scottish Highland men [Scand]

kil·ter /kil'tər/ *n.* as in **out of kilter** not in working order

Kim Il Sung /kim il sŏoNG/ 1912–94; first premier of North Korea (1948–72); president (1972–94)

ki·mo·no /kimō'nō/ *n.* (*pl.* ·nos) 1 long Japanese robe with a sash 2 similar dressing-gown [Japn *ki* wear + *mono* thing]

kin /kin/ *n.* one's relatives or family [OE]

-kin *suffix* forming diminutive nouns (*catkin; manikin*) [ME fr. MDu]

kind /kīnd/ *n.* 1 race, species, or natural group of animals, plants, etc. (*human kind*) 2 class; type; sort; variety —*adj.* 3 friendly, generous, or benevolent (to) 4 **in kind: a** in the same form; likewise (*was insulted and replied in kind*) **b** (of payment) in goods or labor, not money 5 **kind of** *Colloq.* to some extent (*I kind of expected it*) 6 **of a kind** alike [OE]

KIMONO 1

● Usage: 1. *Kind of* is sometimes used by a speaker to be deliberately vague: *He was kind of worried.* More often, it marks speakers' inability to express themselves clearly: *She is kind of good-looking.* It is used with precision, of course, in *A poodle is a kind of dog.* 2. Difficulty arises in knowing how to handle plurals: with *this* or *that,* it is best to use a singular: *This (or That) kind of dog makes a good pet;* with *these* or *those* switch to the plural: *These (or Those) kinds of dogs make good hunters.* The same recommendations apply to *sort* and *sorts.*

kin·der·gar·ten /kin'dərgärt'n, -gärd'n/ *n.* class or school for children before first grade; *abbr.* K [Ger: children's garden]

kind-heart·ed /kīnd'härt'id/ *adj.* of a kind disposition —**kind'-heart'ed·ly** *adv.*; **kind'-heart'ed·ness** *n.*

kin·dle /kind'l/ *v.* (**·dled, ·dling**) 1 light, catch, or set on fire 2 arouse; inspire 3 become aroused or animated [ON *kynda*]

kin·dling /kin(d)'liNG/ *n.* dry sticks, etc., for lighting fires

kind·ly /kīn'dlē/ *adv.* 1 in a kind manner (*spoke kindly*) 2 please (*kindly go away*) —*adj.* (**·li·er, ·li·est**) 3 kind 4 pleasant —**kind'li·ness** *n.*

kind·ness /kīn(d)'nəs/ *n.* 1 being kind 2 kind act

kin·dred /kindrid/ *adj.* 1 related, allied, or similar —*n.* 2 one's relatives collectively [ME]

ki·ne·mat·ics /kin'əmat'iks/ *n. pl.* (usu. treated as *sing.*) branch of mechanics concerned with the motion of objects without reference to cause —**ki'ne·mat'ic** *adj.* [Gk *kinēma* motion]

ki·net·ic /kənet'ik, kī-/ *adj.* of or due to motion —**ki·net'i·cal·ly** *adv.* [Gk *kinetikos* moving]

ki·net'ic en'er·gy *n.* energy of motion

ki·net·ics /kənet'iks, kī-/ *n. pl.* (usu. treated as *sing.*) branch of mechanics studying forces and motions

kin·folk /kin'fōk'/ *n. Colloq.* kin; relatives

king /kiNG/ *n.* 1 male sovereign, esp. a hereditary ruler 2 preeminent person or thing (*oil king*) 3 (*attrib.*) large (or the largest) kind of plant, animal, etc. (*king penguin*) 4 *Chess.* piece which must be checkmated for a win 5 crowned piece in checkers 6 playing card depicting a king —**king'ly** *adj.*; **king ship** *n.* [OE]

King /kiNG/, **Martin Luther, Jr.** 1929–68; US civil-rights leader; assassinated. Birthday celebrated as a national holiday on third Mon. in Jan.

king·dom /kiNG'dəm/ *n.* 1 territory or state ruled by a king or queen 2 spiritual reign or sphere of God 3 domain; sphere 4 division of the natural world (*plant kingdom*) [OE]

king·fish·er /kiNG'fish'ər/ *n.* small bird with brightly colored plumage that dives for fish, etc.

king'pin' *n.* 1 main, large, or frontmost pin or bolt 2 essential person or thing

king'-size' *adj.* (also **-sized**) very large

Kings·ton /kiNG'stən/ *n.* capital of Jamaica. Pop. 103,800

Kings·ton up·on Hull *n.* HULL

Kings·town /kiNG'toun'/ *n.* capital of St. Vincent and the Grenadines. Pop. 15,700

kink /kiNGk/ *n.* 1a twist or bend in wire, etc. **b** tight wave in hair 2 mental twist or quirk, esp. when perverse —*v.* 3 (cause to) form a kink [LGer or Du]

kink·y *adj.* (**·i·er, ·i·est**) 1 *Colloq.* a sexually perverted or unconventional **b** (of clothing, etc.) bizarre and sexually provocative **c** having kinks —**kink'i·ly** *adv.*; **kink'i·ness** *n.*

kins·folk /kinz'fōk'/ *n. pl.* KINFOLK

Kin·sha·sa /kinSHäs'ə/ *n.* capital of Zaire. Pop. 3,804,000

kin'ship' *n.* 1 blood relationship 2 likeness; sympathy

kins·man /kinz'mən/ *n.* (*pl.* ·men; *fem.* ·wom·an, *pl.* ·wom·en) blood relative

ki·osk /kē'äsk'/ *n.* 1 open-fronted booth selling food, newspapers, tickets, etc. 2 columnar structure on which notices are posted for the public [Turk fr. Pers *kushk* palace]

Kip·ling /kip'liNG/, **(Joseph) Rudyard** 1865–1936; British writer and poet

kip·per /kip'ər/ *n.* 1 fish, esp. a herring, split, salted, dried, and usu. smoked —*v.* 2 cure (a herring, etc.) thus

Ki·ri·ba·ti /kĕrĕbä'tē', kir'ibas/ *n.* republic comprising 33 islands in the mid-Pacific Ocean. Capital: Tarawa. Pop. 74,700

kirk /kərk/ *n. Scot. & No.Engl.* church

Kir·kuk /kərkōōk'/ *n.* city in N Iraq. Pop. 570,000

kirsch /kērSH/ *n.* cherry brandy [Ger: cherry]

Ki·shi·nev /kiSH'inef'/ *n.* (also **Chi'sinau'; Kish'inyov'**) capital of Moldova. Pop. 676,700

kis·met /kiz'met′, -mət/ n. destiny; fate [Turk fr. Ar]

kiss /kis/ v. **1** touch with the lips, esp. as a sign of love, affection, greeting, or reverence **2** lightly touch —n. **3a** touch with the lips **b** light touch **4** cone-shaped candy, usu. chocolate **5 kiss and tell** (of a book, etc.) recounting sexual exploits [OE]

kiss′ing cous′in n. (also **kiss′in′**) **1** relative known well enough to kiss upon greeting **2** something closely related to one or more other things

Kis·sin·ger /kis′ənjər/, **Henry** 1923– ; German-born US statesman

kiss′ of death′ n. **1** apparent sign of good will that actually portends ruin **2** destructive action

kit /kit/ n. **1** articles, equipment, etc., for a specific purpose (*first-aid kit*) **2** box or bag for carrying such things **3** set of parts needed to assemble furniture, a model, etc. **4 (the whole) kit and caboodle** *Colloq.* everything involved; the entire lot [MDu *kitte* jug]

Ki·ta·kyu·shu /kētäk′ē-ōō′sHŌō/ n. seaport in Japan, on Kyushu. Pop. 1,021,800

kit·bag /kit′bag′/ n. bag used by a soldier or traveler

kitch·en /kiCH′ən/ n. place where food is prepared and cooked [L *coquina* fr. *coquere* cook]

Kitch·e·ner /kiCH′(ə)nər/ n. city in SE Ontario, Canada. Pop. 168,300

Kitch·e·ner /kiCH′(ə)nər/, **(Horatio) Herbert (1st Earl Kitchener of Khartoum)** 1850–1916; British soldier and statesman

kitch·en·ette /kiCH′ənet′/ n. small kitchen or cooking area

kitch′en·ware′ n. cooking utensils

kite /kīt/ n. **1** light framework with a thin covering flown on a string in the wind **2** soaring bird of prey [OE]

kith /kiTH/ n. as in **kith and kin** friends and relations [OE *cyth*, orig. 'knowledge,' rel. to CAN¹]

kitsch /kiCH/ n. (often *attrib.*) vulgar, pretentious, or worthless art —**kitsch′y** adj. (·i·er, ·i·est) [Ger *kitschen* throw together]

kit·ten /kit′n/ n. **1** young cat, ferret, etc. **2 have kittens** *Colloq.* be very upset or anxious [AngFr dim. of *chat* CAT]

kit·ten·ish /kit′n-iSH/ adj. playful, lively, or flirtatious

kit·ty¹ /kit′ē/ n. (pl. ·ties) **1** fund of money for communal use **2** pool in some card games

kit·ty² n. (pl. ·ties) playful name for a kitten or cat

kit′ty-cor′ner adj. (also **kit′ty-cor′nered**) CATER-CORNERED

Kit′ty Lit′ter n. *Tdmk.* granular clay used in boxes to absorb pet (esp. cat) waste

Ki·twe /kē′twä′/ n. city in Zambia. Pop. 338,200

ki·wi /kē′wē/ n. (pl. ·wis) **1** flightless long-billed New Zealand bird **2** (*cap.*) *Colloq.* New Zealander [Maori]

ki′wi fruit′ n. green-fleshed fruit with fuzzy skin

Klee /klā/, **Paul** 1879–1940; Swiss painter

Klee·nex /klē′neks/ n. (pl. same or ·nex·es) *Tdmk.* disposable paper handkerchief

klep·to·ma·nia /klep′təmā′nēə/ n. obsessive urge to steal —**klep′to·ma′ni·ac** n. & adj. [Gk *kleptēs* thief + -MANIA]

klutz /klʌts/ n. *Colloq.* clumsy or stupid person [fr. Yiddish *klots* wooden block]

km abbr. kilometer(s)

kmph abbr. kilometers per hour

kmps abbr. kilometers per second

knack /nak/ n. **1** acquired faculty or trick of doing a thing **2** habit (*a knack of offending people*)

knack·wurst /näk′wərst/ n. var. of KNOCK-WURST

knap·sack /nap′sak′/ n. bag of possessions, supplies, etc., carried on the back [LGer *knapp* bite + SACK¹]

knave /nāv/ n. **1** rogue; scoundrel **2** JACK, 2 —**knav′er·y** /-ərē/ n. (pl. ·ies); **knav′ish** adj. [OE *cnafa* orig. boy; servant]

knead /nēd/ v. **1** prepare dough, paste, etc., by pressing, folding, and squeezing **2** massage (muscles, etc.) as if kneading [OE]

knee /nē/ n. **1** joint between the thigh and the lower leg in humans and larger animals **2** part of a garment covering the knee —v. (**kneed, knee·ing**) **3** touch or strike with the knee (*kneed him in the groin*) [OE]

knee′cap′ n. bone in front of the knee joint

knee′-deep′ adj. **1** up to the knees (in) **2** deeply involved (in)

knee′-jerk′ n. **1** reflex kick caused by a blow on the tendon just below the knee **2** predictable; automatic

kneel /nēl/ v. (**knelt** or **kneeled, kneel·ing**) fall or rest on the knees or a knee [OE, rel. to KNEE]

knell /nel/ n. **1** sound of a bell, esp. for a death or funeral **2** announcement, event, etc., regarded as an ill omen —v. **3** ring a knell **4** proclaim by or as by a knell [OE]

knelt /nelt/ v. past and past part. of KNEEL

knew /n(y)ōō/ v. past of KNOW

knick·ers /nik′ərz/ n. pl. loose-fitting breeches gathered at the knee [fr. *Knickerbocker*, pseud. of W. IRVING]

knick-knack /nik′nak′/ n. (also **nick′-nack′**) trinket or small dainty ornament, etc. [fr. KNACK in the obs. sense 'trinket']

knife /nīf/ n. (pl. **knives**) **1** cutting implement, usu. with a sharp-edged blade in a handle **2** cutting blade in a machine —v. (**knifed, knif·ing**) **3** cut or stab with a knife **4 under the knife** *Colloq.* undergoing surgery [OE]

knight /nīt/ n. **1** *Hist.* man, usu. noble, raised to special military rank and pledged to honorable service, as to a monarch **2** man awarded a nonhereditary title (*Sir*) by a sovereign **3** *Chess.* piece usu. shaped like a horse's head —v. **4** confer a knighthood on —**knight′hood** n.; **knight′ly** adj. [OE *cniht* boy; servant]

knight′ er·rant /er′ənt/ n. **1** medieval knight in search of chivalrous adventures **2** chivalrous or quixotic man

knit /nit/ v. (**knit·ted** or **knit, knit·ting**) **1** make (a garment, etc.) by interlocking loops of yarn or thread with special needles **2** momentarily wrinkle (the forehead) or (of the forehead) become momentarily wrinkled **3** make or become close or compact **4** (of a broken bone) become joined; heal —**knit′ter** *n*. [OE]

knit′ting *n*. work being knitted

knives /nīvz/ *n. pl.* of KNIFE

knob /näb/ *n.* rounded lump or protuberance, esp. at the end or on the surface of a thing, as the handle of a door or a control device on an appliance —**knob′by, knob′like** *adj.* [MLGer *knobbe* knot; knob]

knock /näk/ *v.* **1a** strike with an audible sharp blow **b** strike (a door, etc.) to gain admittance **2** make (a hole, etc.) by knocking **3** drive (a thing, person, etc.) by striking (*knocked the ball into the hole*) **4** *Colloq.* criticize **5** (of an engine) make a thumping or rattling noise —*n.* **6** act or sound of knocking **7** knocking sound in an engine **8** knock about (or around): *Colloq.* a strike repeatedly; treat roughly **b** wander aimlessly or adventurously **9** knock back *Slang.* eat or drink, esp. quickly **10** knock down: a strike (esp. a person) to the ground **b** demolish **c** (at an auction) sell (to) a bidder by a knock with a hammer **d** *Colloq.* lower the price of (an article) **11** knock off: a strike off with a blow **b** *Colloq.* finish (work) (*knocked off work early*) **c** *Colloq.* produce (a work of art, etc.) or do (a task) rapidly **d** deduct (a sum) from a price, etc. **e** *Slang.* steal **f** *Slang.* kill **12** knock out: a make unconscious by a blow on the head **b** defeat, esp. in competition **c** *Slang.* astonish **d** (often *refl.*) *Colloq.* exhaust **13** knock together assemble hastily or roughly **14** knock up: a make hastily **b** *Slang.* make pregnant [OE]

knock′er *n.* hinged, esp. metal, instrument on a door for knocking with

knock′ knees′ *n. pl.* abnormal curvature of the legs inward at the knee —**knock′-kneed′** *adj.*

knock′off *n.* unauthorized, usu. cheaper copy, of expensive fashionable clothing, watches, perfume, etc.

knock′out *n.* **1** act of making unconscious by a blow **2** *Boxing.* victory by rendering an opponent unable to continue **3** *Colloq.* outstanding or irresistible person or thing

knock·wurst /näk′wərst/ *n.* (also **knack′wurst**) variety of thick, seasoned sausage [Ger *knackwurst*]

knoll /nōl/ *n.* hillock; mound [OE]

knot /nät′/ *n.* **1a** intertwining or looping and tightening of rope, string, hair, etc., so as to fasten **b** set method of this (*reef knot*) **c** knotted ribbon, etc., as an ornament **d** tangle in hair, knitting, etc. **2** unit of a ship's or aircraft's speed, equivalent to one nautical mile per hour **3** cluster (*knot of journalists*) **4** bond, esp. of marriage **5** hard lump of organic tissue **6a** hard mass in a tree trunk where a branch grows out **b** round cross-grained piece in lumber marking this **7** central point in a problem, etc. —*v.* (**knot·ted, knot·ting**) **8** tie in a knot **9** entangle **10** unite closely **11** tie the knot get married [OE]

knot′hole′ *n.* hole in lumber where a knot has fallen out

knot′ty *adj.* (**·ti·er, ·ti·est**) **1** full of knots **2** puzzling (*knotty problem*)

know /nō/ *v.* (**knew, know·ing, known**) **1a** have in the mind; have learned; be able to recall (*knows a lot about cars*) **b** (also *absol.*) be aware of (a fact) (*know the answer*) **c** have a good command of (*knew German*) **2** be acquainted or friendly with **3a** recognize; identify (*I knew him at once*) **b** be able to distinguish (*know good from bad*) **4** be subject to (*joy knew no bounds*) **5** in the know *Colloq.* knowing inside information **6** know of be aware of; have heard of **7** know what's what have knowledge of the world, life, etc. **8** you never know it is possible —**know′a·ble** *adj.* [OE]

know′how′ *n.* practical knowledge; natural skill

know′ing *adj.* **1** suggesting that one has inside information (*a knowing look*) **2** showing knowledge; shrewd —**know′ing·ly** *adv.*

knowl·edge /näl′ij/ *n.* **1a** awareness or familiarity (of or with a person or thing) **b** person's range of information **2a** understanding of a subject, etc. (*good knowledge of Greek*) **b** sum of what is known (*every branch of knowledge*) **3** to (the best of) one's knowledge as far as one knows

knowl·edge·a·ble /näl′ijəbəl/ *adj.* well-informed; aware —**knowl′edge·a·bly** *adv.*

known /nōn/ *v.* **1** *past. part.* of KNOW —*adj.* **2** familiar **3** acknowledged; proven

Knox /näks/ **1 John** 1505–72; Scottish Protestant religious leader **2 Henry** 1750–1806; first US Secretary of War (1785–94)

Knox·ville /näks′vil′/ *n.* city in Tenn. Pop. 165,121

knuck·le /nək′əl/ *n.* **1** bone at a finger-joint, esp. that connecting the finger to the hand **2** knee- or ankle-joint of an animal, used as food —*v.* (**·led, ·ling**) **3** strike, press, or rub with the knuckles **4** knuckle down apply oneself seriously (to a task, etc.) **5** knuckle under give in; submit [dim. of LGer *Knochen* or Du *knok* bone]

knuck′le·head′ *n.* *Colloq.* stupid or inept person

knurl /nərl/ *n.* **1** small projecting knob, ridge, etc. —*v.* **2** put ridges along an edge, as of a coin [MLGer or MDu]

Knut /knŏōt/ *n.* see CANUTE

KO *abbr.* knockout

ko·a·la /kō·äl′ə/ *n.* small Australian marsupial with thick gray fur [Aborig]

Ko·be /kō′bā′, -bē/ *n.* seaport in Japan, on Honshu. Pop. 1,488,600

Ko·blenz /kō′blents/ *n.* see COBLENZ

Ko′di·ak Is′land /kōd′ē-ak′/ *n.* island off the S coast of Alaska

Kohl /kōl/, **Helmut** 1930– ; German politician; chancellor of the Federal Republic of Germany (1982–90); of unified Germany (1990–)

kohl·ra·bi /kōlräb′ē, -rab′ē/ *n.* (*pl.* **-bies**) cabbage with an edible turniplike stem [Ger, fr. It *cavolrape*]

Köln /koeln/ *n.* see COLOGNE

Kol·we·zi /kōlwä′zē/ *n.* city in Zaire. Pop. 544,500

Kom·so·molsk /käm′səmôlsk′/ *n.* city in Russia on the Amur River. Pop. 318,800

Kon·ya /kŏnyä′/ *n.* city in Turkey. Pop. 513,300

kook /kŏŏk/ *n. Slang.* crazy or eccentric person —**kook′y** *adj.* (·i·er, ·i·est) [prob. fr. CUCKOO]

kook·a·bur·ra /kŏŏk′əbər′ə/ *n.* Australian kingfisher with a strange laughing cry [Aborig.]

ko·pek /kō′pek/ *n.* (also **ko′peck**) Russian coin worth one-hundredth of a ruble [Russ *kopeĭka*]

Ko·ran /kəran′, -rän′, kôr′an′/ *n.* Islamic sacred book [Ar: recitation]

Ko·re·a /kərē′ə/ *n.* peninsula in E Asia on the Sea of Japan and the Yellow Sea. Separated into two countries: **North Korea** (capital: Pyongyang; pop. 22,227,000) and **South Korea** (capital: Seoul; pop. 43,663,000) —**Ko·re′ an** *n. & adj.*

Kos·ci·us·ko /kŏSHCHŎŎSH′kō; käs′ē-əs′kō, käz′-/, **Thaddeus** 1746–1817; Polish-born general in the American Revolutionary army

ko·sher /kō′SHər/ *adj.* 1 *Judaism.* (of food) fulfilling the requirements of dietary law 2 *Colloq.* correct; genuine; legitimate [Heb: proper]

Kos·suth /kō′SHŏŏt, käs′ŏŏTH, käsōŏTH′/, **Lajos** 1802–94; Hungarian statesman and patriot

Ko·tah /kōt′ə/ *n.* city in India on the Chambal River. Pop. 536,400

kow·tow /kou′tou′/ *n.* 1 *Hist.* Chinese custom of kneeling with the forehead touching the ground, esp. in submission —*v.* 2 act obsequiously (to) [Chin: knock the head]

KP *abbr. Milit.* kitchen police (kitchen duties)

k.p.h. *abbr.* kilometers per hour

Kr *symb.* krypton

kraal /kräl/ *n. S. Afr.* 1 village of huts enclosed by a fence 2 enclosure for cattle or sheep [Afrik]

Kra·ka·to·a /krak′ətō′ə/ *n.* (also **Kra′ka·tau**) volcano in Indonesia; noted for 1883 eruption

Kra·ków /kra′kou, krä′kŏŏf/ *n.* see CRACOW

Kras·no·dar /kräs′nədär′/ *n.* city in Russia. Pop. 631,200

Kras·no·yarsk /kräs′nəyärsk′/ *n.* city in central Russia. Pop. 924,400

krem·lin /krem′lən/ *n.* 1a (*cap.*) citadel in Moscow b Russian government housed within it 2 citadel within a Russian town [Russ]

krill /kril/ *n.* tiny planktonic crustaceans [Norw *kril* tiny fish]

Krish·na /kriSH′nə/ *n. Hinduism.* manifestation of Vishnu

Kris Krin·gle /kris′ kriNG′gəl/ (also **Kriss′ Krin′gle**) see SANTA CLAUS

Kroc /kräk/, **Ray A.** 1902–1984; US businessman; developer of McDonald's restaurant chain

kro·na /krō′nə/ *n.* 1 (*pl.* ·nor) chief monetary unit of Sweden 2 (kró·na, *pl.* ·nur) chief monetary unit of Iceland [Sw, Icel: CROWN]

kro·ne /krō′nə/ *n.* (*pl.* ·ner) 1 chief monetary unit of Denmark 2 chief monetary unit of Norway [Dan, Norw: CROWN]

kru·ger·rand /krōō′gərand′, -ränt′/ *n.* S African gold coin

kryp·ton /krip′tän′/ *n.* inert gaseous element used in fluorescent lamps, etc.; *symb.* **Kr** [Gk *kruptŏn* hidden]

KS postal abbr. for Kansas

kt *abbr.* karat

K2 *n.* (also called **God′win Aus′ten**) peak in N Kashmir; second highest in the world: 28,250 ft

Kua·la Lum·pur /kwäl′ə ləmpŏŏr′/ *n.* capital of Malaysia. Pop. 565,300

Ku·blai Khan /kŏŏ′blə kän′, kŏŏ′blī′/ c. 1215–94; Mongol emperor (c. 1260–94); founder of the Chinese Yuan dynasty

Ku·brick /kŏŏ′brik/, **Stanley** 1928– ; US-born film director, producer, and writer

ku·dos /k(y)ŏŏ′däs′, -dōs′/ *n. Colloq.* glory; renown [Gk]
  • Usage: *Kudos* was originally used in English, as in the Greek, as a singular noun meaning 'praise, honor.' However, because of the *-s* ending, *kudos* has come to be widely used as a plural noun meaning 'compliments, accolades,' and the (etymologically incorrect) singular form, *kudo*, also meaning 'praise, honor,' has resulted from back formation.

kud·zu /kəd′zŏŏ/ *n.* fast-growing vine planted to retain soil [Japan]

Kuei·yang /kwäyäNG′/ *n.* see GUIYANG

Kui·by·shev /kwē′bəsHef′/ *n.* port in Russia on the Volga River. Pop. 1,257,300

Ku Klux Klan /k(y)ŏŏ′ kləks′klan′/ *n.* secret white supremacist society of the US; *abbr.* KKK

Ku·ma·mo·to /kŏŏ′məmōt′ō/ *n.* city in Japan, on Kyushu. Pop. 630,900

Ku·ma·si /kŏŏmäs′ē/ *n.* city in Ghana. Pop. 385,200

kum·quat /kəm′kwät′/ *n.* (also **cum′quat**) 1 small orange-like fruit 2 shrub or small tree yielding this [Chin *gamgwat* gold orange]

kung fu /kəNG′fŏŏ′/ *n.* Chinese form of self defense, similar to karate [Chin: skill]

Kung Fu-tzu /kŏŏNG′ fŏŏ′dzə/ see CONFUCIUS

Kun·ming /kŏŏn′miNG′/ *n.* city in S China. Pop. 1,127,400

Kurd /kərd/ *n.* an Islamic people of Iraq, Iran, and Turkey —**Kur′dish** *n. & adj.*

Ku·ro·sa·wa /kŏŏr′əsä′wə/, **Akira** 1910– ; Japanese film director

Kursk /kŏŏrsk/ *n.* city in W Russia. Pop. 433,300

Ku·wait /kəwāt′/ *n.* 1 monarchy in W Asia, on the Persian Gulf. Pop. 1,190,000 2 (also **Ku·wait′ Cit′y**) capital city of the monarchy of Kuwait. Pop. 44,200 —**Ku·wai′ti** /-tē/ *n. & adj.*

kvetch /kveCH/ *v. Slang.* to complain, nag, or whine, esp. continually —**kvetch′er** *n.* [Yiddish *kvetshn* to squeeze or pinch]

kW *abbr.* kilowatt(s)

Kwang·ju /gwäNG′jŏŏ′/ *n.* city in SW South Korea. Pop. 1,144,700

Kwei·yang /kwā′yäNG′/ *n.* see GUIYANG

kWh *abbr.* kilowatt-hour(s)

KY, Ky. abbr. for Kentucky (postal abbr. **KY**)

Kyo·to /kē-ōt′ō/ *n.* city in Japan, on Honshu. Pop. 1,458,600

Kyr·gyz·stan /kir′gistän′, -stan′/ *n.* republic in NW Asia; formerly a part of the USSR. Capital: Bishkek. Pop. 4,533,000

Kyu·shu /kyŏŏ′sHŏŏ/ *n.* island in SW Japan

L

l, L /el/ *n.* (*pl.* **l's; L's, Ls**) twelfth letter of the English alphabet; a consonant

l or **l.** *abbr.* **1** latitude **2** law **3** leaf **4** league **5** left **6** line **7** liter(s) **8** long

L or **L.** *abbr.* **1** *Rom. num.* (usu. **L**) fifty **2** lake **3** Latin **4** long **5** longitude **6** *Theat.* stage left

la /lä/ *n. Mus.* sixth note of a major scale

La *symb.* lanthanum

LA *abbr.* Los Angeles

LA, La. *abbr.* for Louisiana (postal abbr. **LA**)

lab /lab/ *n. Colloq.* laboratory [abbr.]

la·bel /lā'bəl/ *n.* **1** piece of paper, etc., attached to an object to give information about it **2** short classifying phrase applied to a person, etc. —*v.* (**·beled** or **·belled, ·bel·ing** or **bel·ling**) **3** attach a label to **4** classify as [MFr]

la·bi·al /lā'bēəl/ *adj.* **1a** of the lips **b** of, like, or serving as a lip **2** (of a sound) requiring partial or complete closure of the lips —*n.* **3** labial sound (e.g., *p, m, v*) [L *labia* lips]

la·bi·um /lā'bēəm/ *n.* (*pl.* **·bi·a** /-bēə/) each fold of skin of the two pairs enclosing the vulva [L: lip]

la·bor /lā'bər/ *n.* **1** physical or mental work; exertion **2** workers, esp. manual, considered as a political and economic force **3** process of childbirth **4** particular task —*v.* **5** work hard; exert oneself **6a** elaborate needlessly (*don't labor the point*) **b** do with great effort; not spontaneously **7** suffer (*labor under a delusion*) **8** proceed with trouble or difficulty [Fr fr. L *labor* work]

lab·o·ra·to·ry /lab'(ə)rətôr'ē/ *n.* (*pl.* **·ries**) room, building, or establishment for scientific experiments, research, etc. [L, rel. to LABOR]

La'bor Day' *n.* the first Monday in September, celebrated in honor of working people

la'bor·er *n.* person doing unskilled, usu. manual, work for wages

la'bor·in·ten'sive *adj.* requiring many hours of work, esp. relative to capital investment

la·bo·ri·ous /ləbôr'ēəs/ *adj.* **1** needing or performing hard work or toil **2** (esp. of literary style) showing signs of toil —**la·bo'ri·ous·ly** *adv.* [L, rel. to LABOR]

la'bor un'ion *n.* association of workers to protect and advance the working conditions, wages, etc., of its members

Lab'ra·dor re·triev'er /lab'rədôr/ *n.* breed of dog with a black or golden coat, originally bred in Labrador [*Labrador* in Canada]

la·bur·num /ləbər'nəm/ *n.* tree with drooping golden flowers yielding poisonous seeds [L]

lab·y·rinth /lab'ərinTH, -ərənTH/ *n.* **1** complicated network of passages, etc. **2** intricate or tangled arrangement —**lab'y·rin'thine** /-THən, -THīn', -THēn'/ *adj.* [L fr. Gk]

lac /lak/ *n.* resinous substance secreted by a SE Asian insect; used in lacquer, etc. [Hindi fr. Skt]

lace /lās/ *n.* **1** fine open fabric or trimming, made by weaving thread in patterns **2** cord, etc., passed through holes or hooks for fastening shoes, etc. —*v.* (**laced, lac·ing**) **3** fasten or tighten (up) with a lace or laces **4** add alcohol to (a drink) **5** pass (a shoelace, etc.) through [L *laqueus* noose]

lac·er·ate /las'ərāt'/ *v.* (**·at·ed, ·at·ing**) mangle or tear (esp. flesh, etc.) —**lac'er·a'tion** *n.* [L *lacerare* tear up]

lach·ry·mal /lak'rəməl/ *adj.* (also **lac'ri·mal**) of or for tears [L *lacrima* tear]

lach·ry·mose /lak'rəmōs'/ *adj. Formal.* given to weeping; tearful

lack /lak/ *n.* **1** want; deficiency (of) —*v.* **2** be without or deficient in —**lack'ing** *adj.* [MLGer or MDu LACK deficiency]

lack·a·dai·si·cal /lak'ədā'zikəl/ *adj.* unenthusiastic; listless; idle —**lack'a·dai'si·cal·ly** *adv.* [fr. archaic *lackaday*]

lack·ey /lak'ē/ *n.* (*pl.* **·eys**) **1** servile follower; toady **2** footman; manservant [Catalan *alacayo*]

lack·luster /lak'ləs'tər/ *adj.* **1** lacking in vitality, etc. **2** dull

la·con·ic /ləkän'ik/ *adj.* terse; using few words —**la·con'i·cal·ly** *adv.* [Gk *Lakōn* Laconian (Spartan)]

lac·quer /lak'ər/ *n.* **1** varnish made of shellac or a synthetic substance —*v.* **2** coat with lacquer [Fr, ult. fr. Skt, rel. to LAC]

la·crosse /ləkrôs'/ *n.* game played by two teams in which a ball is passed by means of sticks having a netted pocket [CanFr *la* the + *crosse* stick]

lac·tate /lak'tāt'/ *v.* (**·tat·ed, ·tat·ing**) (of mammals) secrete milk [L *lactare* contain milk]

lac·ta'tion *n.* **1** secretion of milk **2** period of secretion [L, rel. to LACTATE]

lac·te·al /lak'tēəl/ *adj.* of milk; milky [L *lacteus,* rel. to LACTATE]

lac·tic /lak'tik/ *adj.* of or from milk [L *lac, lactis* milk]

lac'tic ac'id *n.* acid formed in sour milk and muscle metabolism

lac·tose /lak'tōs'/ *n.* sugar that occurs in milk

la·cu·na /lək(y)ōō'nə/ *n.* (*pl.* **·nae** /-nē, -nī/) **1** gap **2** missing portion, etc., esp. in a text, etc. [L: pit; defect]

lac·y /lā'sē/ *adj.* (**·i·er, ·i·est**) of or resembling lace

lad /lad/ *n.* boy; youth

lad·der /lad'ər/ *n.* **1** set of horizontal bars fixed between two uprights and used for climbing up or down **2** hierarchical structure, esp. as a means of career advancement [OE]

lade /lād/ *v.* (**lad·en, lad·ing**) **1a** load (a ship) **b** ship (goods) **2** (as **lad·en** *adj.*) loaded; burdened [OE]

la·di·da /lä'dēdä'/ *adj. Colloq.* pretentious or snobbish, esp. in manner or speech [imit.]

la'dies' man' *n.* (also **la'dy's man'**) man fond of female company

la·dle /lād'l/ *n.* **1** long-handled spoon or cuplike device used for serving liquids —*v.* (**·dled, ·dling**) **2** transfer (liquid) with a ladle [OE]

La·do·ga, Lake /läd'əgə, lad'-/ *n.* lake in NW Russia, N of St. Petersburg; largest in Europe

la·dy /lā'dē/ *n.* (*pl.* **·dies**) 1 woman regarded as being of superior social status or as having refined manners 2 woman; female (*ask that lady*) 3 *Colloq.* wife; girlfriend 4 (*cap.*) British title for certain women of noble rank [OE]

la'dy·bug' *n.* (also **la'dy·bird'**) small beetle, usu. red with black spots

la'dy·fin'ger *n.* small finger-shaped sponge cake

la'dy-in-wait'ing *n.* lady attending a queen or princess

la'dy·like' *adj.* like or befitting a lady

la'dy·ship' *n.* respectful form of reference or address to a Lady

la'dy's slip'per *n.* plant of the orchid family with a slipper-shaped lip on its flowers

La·fa·yette or La Fa·yette /läf'ē·et', laf'-/, **Marie Joseph (Marquis de)** 1757–1834; French soldier; served in the American Revolutionary army

La·Fol·lette /ləfäl'ət/, **Robert M.** 1855–1925; US politician

La Fon·taine /lä fônten'/, **Jean de** 1621–95; French poet and fabulist

lag /lag/ *v.* (**lagged, lag·ging**) 1 fall behind; not keep pace —*n.* 2 delay

la·ger /läg'ər/ *n.* mild-flavored beer, aged in storage [Ger: store]

lag·gard /lag'ard/ *n.* person who lags behind

lag·ging *n.* material used to insulate a boiler, etc., against loss of heat

la·gniappe /lanyap'/ *n.* 1 something extra given with a purchase 2 gratuity

la·goon /lagōōn'/ *n.* 1 stretch of salt water separated from the sea by a sandbank, reef, etc. 2 shallow pond connected with a larger body of water 3 man-made pool for liquid waste, sewage, etc. [L *lacuna* pool]

La·hore /ləhôr', -hōr'/ *n.* city in Pakistan. Pop. 2,952,700

laid /lād/ *v.* *past* and *past part.* of LAY[1]

laid'-back' *adj.* relaxed; easygoing

laid' up' *adj.* confined to bed or the house

lain /lān/ *v.* *past part.* of LIE[1]

lair /lar', ler/ *n.* 1 wild animal's resting place 2 person's hiding place [OE]

lais·sez-faire /les'ā far', lez'-, -fer'/ *n.* (also **lais·ser-faire**) *French.* policy of noninterference, esp. by a government [Fr: let act]

la·i·ty /lā'ətē/ *n.* lay people, as distinct from the clergy [fr. LAY[2]]

lake /lāk/ *n.* large body of water surrounded by land [L *lacus*]

Lake' Dis'trict *n.* region of lakes in NW England

Lake·wood /lāk'wŏŏd/ *n.* city in Colo. Pop. 126,481

lal·ly·gag /lal'ēgag/ *v.* (also **lol·ly·gag**) (**·gagged, ·gag·ging**) *Colloq.* loaf; waste time

lam /lam/ *n. Slang.* as in **on the lam** in flight, esp. from authorities

la·mé /lämā', lamā'/ *n.* fabric with gold or silver threads interwoven [Fr]

la·ma /läm'ə/ *n.* Tibetan or Mongolian Buddhist monk [Tibetan: superior one]

la·ma·ser·y /läm'əser'ī/ *n.* (*pl.* **·ies**) monastery of lamas [Fr]

La Ma·tan·za /lä mətän'sə/ *n.* suburb of Buenos Aires, Argentina. Pop. 1,121,200

La·maze' meth'od /ləmäz'/ *n. Med.* childbirth technique employing patterned breathing, physical exercises, etc., to avoid the need for anesthetic [for Fr. physician Fernand *Lamaze*]

lamb /lam/ *n.* 1 young sheep 2 its flesh as food 3 mild, gentle, or kind person

lam·ba·da /lambäd'ə/ *n.* fast, erotic Brazilian dance [Port: a beating]

lam·baste /lambāst'/ *v.* (**·bast·ed, ·bast·ing**) (also **lam·bast'** /-bast'/) *Colloq.* 1 thrash; beat 2 scold harshly [fr. E *lam* to beat + *baste* to flog]

lamb·da /lam'də/ *n.* eleventh letter of the Greek alphabet (Λ, λ)

lam·bent /lam'bənt/ *adj.* 1 (of a flame or a light) playing on a surface 2 (of the eyes, sky, wit, etc.) softly or gently bright or radiant —**lam'ben·cy** *n.* [L *lambere* lick]

lame /lām/ *adj.* 1 limping or disabled in the foot or leg 2 (of an excuse, etc.) unconvincing; feeble —*v.* (**lamed, lam·ing**) 3 make lame; disable —**lame'ly** *adv.*; **lame'ness** *n.* [OE]

lame' duck' *n.* person completing a term of office whose successor has been elected or named

la·ment /ləment'/ *n.* 1 passionate expression of grief 2 song, etc., of mourning, etc. —*v.* 3 express or feel grief for or about —**lam'en·ta'tion** /-tā'sнən/ *n.* [L *lamentari* wail]

la·men·ta·ble /lam'əntəbəl, ləment'-/ *adj.* deplorable; regrettable —**la'men·ta·bly** *adv.*

lam·i·na /lam'ənə/ *n.* (*pl.* **·nae** /-nē', -nī'/) thin plate or scale —**lam'i·nar** *adj.* [L]

lam·i·nate *v.* /lam'ənāt'/ (**·nat·ed, ·nat·ing**) 1 cover with a thin layer or protective coating 2 make with successive thin layers —*n.* /lam'ənat, -nāt'/ 3 laminated structure, esp. of layers fixed together —*adj.* /-nət, -nāt'/ 4 in the form of thin plates —**lam'i·na'tion** *n.*

lamp /lamp/ *n.* 1 device for producing a steady light, esp.: **a** an electric bulb, and usu. its holder **b** an oil- or gas-burning light 2 device producing esp. ultraviolet or infrared radiation [Gk *lampas* torch]

lamp'black' *n.* pigment made from soot

lam·poon /lampōōn'/ *n.* 1 satirical attack on a person, etc. —*v.* 2 satirize —**lam·poon'ist** *n.* [Fr *lampon*]

lamp'post' *n.* tall post supporting a street-light

lam·prey /lam'prē/ *n.* (*pl.* **·preys**) eel-like aquatic animal with a sucker mouth [LL *lampreda*]

LAN /lan/ *abbr.* LOCAL AREA NETWORK

lance /lans/ *n.* 1 long spear, esp. one used by a horseman 2 lancet —*v.* (**lanced, lanc·ing**) 3 pierce or cut open with a lance [Fr fr. L]

lanc·er /lan'sər/ *n. Hist.* soldier armed with a lance

lan·cet /lan'sit/ *n.* small, two-edged surgical knife with a sharp point

Lan·chou see LANZHOU

land /land/ *n.* 1 solid part of the earth's surface 2 expanse of country; ground; soil 3 country; nation 4 real estate —*v.* **5a** set or go ashore **b** leave (a ship) and go ashore **c** come to a port **d** arrive at a place or in a position or situation (*land in jail*) **6** bring (an aircraft) to the ground or another surface **7** alight on the ground, etc. **8** bring (a fish) to land **9** (also *refl.*) *Colloq.* bring to, reach, or find oneself in a certain situation or place **10** *Colloq.* win or obtain (a prize, job, etc.) [OE]

land·ed /lan'did/ *adj.* owning land

land'fall *n.* sighting or reaching land, esp. after a sea or air journey

land'fill *n.* **1** waste material, etc., used to landscape or reclaim land **2** place where garbage is buried and the land reclaimed

land' grant' *n.* tract of land given, as by a government, for a university, railroad, etc.

land'ing *n.* **1** platform at the top of or part way up a flight of stairs **2** coming to land **3** place where ships, etc., land

land'ing craft' *n.* craft designed for putting troops and equipment ashore

land'ing gear' *n.* wheels, pontoons, etc., of an aircraft

land·la·dy /lan(d)'lād'ē/ *n.* **1** woman who owns and lets land or premises **2** woman who keeps a public house, boarding-house, etc.

land·locked /land'läkt'/ *adj.* almost or entirely enclosed by land

land·lord /lan(d)'lôrd'/ *n.* **1** man who owns and lets land or premises **2** man who keeps an inn, boarding-house, etc.

land·lub·ber /lan(d)'ləb'ər/ *n.* person unfamiliar with the sea

land·mark /land'märk'/ *n.* **1** conspicuous object in a district, landscape, etc. **2** prominent and critical event, etc.

land' mass' *n.* large area of land

land' mine' *n.* explosive mine laid in or on the ground

land'own'er *n.* owner of (esp. much) land —**land'own'ing** *adj. & n.*

land·scape /lan(d)'skāp'/ *n.* **1** scenery as seen in a broad view **2** picture representing this; this genre of painting —*adj.* **3** *Comp.* viewed or read as from a landscape painting, i.e., printed across a page that is wider in its horizontal dimension —*v.* (·scaped, ·scaping) **4** improve (a piece of land) by changing grading, with plantings, etc. [Du *landschap*]

land·slide /lan(d)'slīd'/ *n.* **1** sliding down of a mass of land from a mountain, cliff, etc. **2** overwhelming victory in an election

lane /lān/ *n.* **1** narrow path or road **2** division of a road for a stream of traffic **3** path regularly followed by a ship, aircraft, etc. [OE]

Lang·land /laNG'lənd/, **William** c. 1330 – c. 1400; English poet

lan·guage /laNG'(g)wij/ *n.* **1** use of words as a method of human communication **2** system of words of a particular community or country, etc. **3a** ability to use language **b** style of expression; use of words, etc. (*poetic language*) **4** system of symbols and rules for writing computer programs **5** any method of communication **6** professional or specialized vocabulary [AngFr *langue* fr. L *lingua* tongue]

lan·guid /laNG'gwid/ *adj.* lacking vigor; idle; inert —**lan'guid·ly** *adv.* [L *languidus* weak; faint]

lan·guish /laNG'gwish/ *v.* **1** lose or lack vitality **2** droop or pine for **3** suffer under (depression, confinement, etc.) [L *languere*]

lan·guor /laNG'(g)ər/ *n.* **1** lack of energy; idleness **2** soft or tender mood or effect —**lan'guor·ous** *adj.*

lank /laNGk/ *adj.* **1** (of hair, grass, etc.) long and limp **2** thin and tall [OE]

lank'y *adj.* (·i·er, ·i·est) very thin and long or tall —**lank'i·ness** *n.*

lan·o·lin /lan'l-in/ *n.* fat from sheep's wool used in cosmetics, etc. [L *lana* wool + *oleum* oil]

Lan·sing /lan'siNG/ *n.* capital of Mich., in the S central part. Pop. 127,321

lan·tern /lant'ərn/ *n.* **1** lamp with a transparent case protecting a flame, etc. **2** raised structure on a dome, room, etc., glazed to admit light [Gk *lamptēr* torch]

lan'tern jaws' *n. pl.* long, thin jaws and chin

lan'tha·nide se'ries /lan'thənīd', -nid/ *n. Chem.* series of rare-earth elements

lan·tha·num /lan'THənəm/ *n.* metallic element, first of the lanthanide series; *symb.* **La** [Gk *lanthanein* escape notice]

lan·yard /lan'yərd/ *n.* **1** cord worn around the neck or the shoulder, to which a knife, etc., may be attached **2** *Naut.* short line for securing, tightening, etc. [OFr *lasniere* + YARD[1]]

Lan·zhou /län'jō'/ *n.* (formerly Lanchou) city in N China. Pop. 1,194,640

Lao /lou/ *n. & adj.* (of or relating to) people of Laos and Thailand, or their language

La·os /lä'ōs/ *n.* country in SE Asia, E of Thailand. Capital: Vientiane. Pop. 4,409,000 —**La·o·tian** /lā-ō'sHən/ *n. & adj.*

Lao-tse /loud'zŏŏ', -zō'/ (also **Lao-tsze, Lao-tsu**) c. 604 – c. 531 B.C.; Chinese philosopher

lap[1] /lap/ *n.* **1** front of the body from the waist to the knees of a sitting person **2** clothing covering this [OE]

lap[2] *n.* **1** one circuit of a racetrack, length of a swimming pool, etc. **2a** amount of overlapping **b** overlapping part —*v.* (lapped, lapping) **3** lead or overtake (a competitor in a race) by one or more laps **4** fold or wrap around; enfold **5** cause to overlap [prob. fr. LAP[1]]

lap[3] *v.* **1a** (esp. of an animal) drink by licking up **b** (foll. by *up*) consume (gossip, praise, etc.) greedily **2** (of waves, etc.) ripple; make a rippling sound against (the shore) —*n.* **3a** act of lapping **b** amount of liquid taken up **4** sound of wavelets [OE]

La Paz /lə päz', päs'/ *n.* **1** administrative capital of Bolivia. Pop. 669,400 **2** capital of the Mexican state of Baja California del Sur. Pop. 161,000

lap' dog' *n.* **1** small pet dog **2** person so treated

la·pel /ləpel'/ *n.* part of either side of a coatfront folded back against itself [fr. LAP[1]]

lap·i·dar·y /lap'əder'ē/ *adj.* **1** concerned with stone or stones —*n.* (*pl.* ·ies) **2** cutter, polisher, or engraver of gems [L *lapidarius* of stone]

lap·is laz·u·li /lap'is laz'(y)əlē, lazH'əlē/ *n.* bright blue semiprecious stone [L *lapis* stone + MedL *lazuli*, ult. fr. Pers *lazhuward* AZURE]

La Pla·ta /lə plät'ə/ *n.* seaport in Argentina. Pop. 542,600

Lapp /lap/ *n.* **1** member of a Mongol people

of N Scandinavia and NW Russia 2 (also **Lap'pish**) their language [Sw]

lap·pet /lap'it/ *n.* small flap or fold of a garment, etc. [fr. LAP¹]

lapse /laps/ *n.* 1 slight error 2 weak decline into an inferior state 3 passage of time —*v.* (**lapsed, laps·ing**) 4 fail to maintain a position or standard 5 fall back into (an inferior or previous state) 6 (of a right or privilege, etc.) become invalid through disuse, failure to renew, etc. [L *lapsus* fr. *labor* slip; fall]

lap'top' *n.* (often *attrib.*) portable microcomputer suitable for use while traveling

lar·board /lär'bərd/ *n.* & *adj. Archaic.* PORT³ [ME *laddeborde*, perh. 'side on which cargo was taken in,' rel. to LADE]

lar·ce·ny /lär'sənē/ *n.* (*pl.* **·nies**) theft of personal property —**lar'ce·nous** /-əs/ *adj.* [AngFr fr. L *latrocinium*]

larch /lärCH/ *n.* 1 deciduous coniferous tree with bright foliage 2 its wood [L *larix, -icis*]

lard /lärd/ *n.* 1 pig fat used in cooking, etc. —*v.* 2 insert strips of fat or bacon in (meat, etc.) before cooking 3 garnish (talk, etc.) with strange terms —**lard'y** *adj.* [Fr fr. L *laridum* bacon fat]

lar·der /lär'dər/ *n.* 1 room or large cupboard for storing food 2 supply of food

La·re·do /lərād'ō/ *n.* city in Texas. Pop. 122,899

large /lärj/ *adj.* 1 of relatively great size or extent 2 of the larger kind 3 comprehensive 4 pursuing an activity on a large scale (*large store*) 5 **at large:** a at liberty b as a body or whole —**large'ness** *n.*; **larg'ish** *adj.* [L *largus* copious]

large·ly /lärj'lē/ *adv.* to a great extent

lar·gess /lärzHes', -jes'/ *n.* (also **lar·gesse'**) money or gifts freely given [L *largus* rich, rel. to LARGE]

lar·go /lär'gō/ *Mus. adv.* & *adj.* 1 in a slow tempo and dignified style —*n.* (*pl.* **·gos**) 2 largo passage or movement [It: broad]

lar·i·at /lar'ēət/ *n.* 1 lasso 2 tethering-rope [Sp *la reata*]

lark¹ /lärk/ *n.* bird with a tuneful song, esp. the skylark [OE]

lark² *n. Colloq.* 1 frolic; amusing incident —*v.* 2 play tricks

lark'spur' *n.* plant with a spur-shaped calyx

La Roche·fou·cauld /lä rōsH'fōōkō'/, François (Duc de) 1613–80; French writer

La·rousse /lärōōs', lə-/, Pierre 1817–75; French lexicographer and encyclopedist

lar·va /lär'və/ *n.* (*pl.* **·vae** /-vē/ or **·vas**) stage of an insect's development between egg and pupa —**lar'val** *adj.* [L: ghost]

lar·yn·gi·tis /lar'injīt'əs/ *n.* inflammation of the larynx

lar·ynx /lar'iNGks/ *n.* (*pl.* **la·ryn·ges** /lərin'jēz / or **·ynx·es**) hollow organ in the throat holding the vocal cords —**la·ryn'geal** /-rin'jēəl/ *adj.* [L fr. Gk]

la·sa·gna /ləzän'yə/ *n.* 1 pasta in wide strips 2 dish made with this and cheese, tomato sauce, etc. [It fr. L fr. Gk *lasana* trivet]

La Salle /lä säl', lə sal'/, René Robert Cavalier (Sieur de) 1643–87; French explorer

las·civ·i·ous /ləsiv'ēəs/ *adj.* 1 lustful 2 inciting to lust —**las·civ'i·ous·ly** *adv.* [L]

Las Cru·ces /läs krōō'səs/ *n.* city in N. Mex. Pop. 62,126

la·ser /lā'zər/ *n.* device that generates an intense beam of light in one direction [light amplification by stimulated emission of radiation]

la'ser disc' *Comp.* disk on which text, music, etc., is stored digitally and retrieved by laser

lash /lasH/ *v.* 1 make a sudden whiplike movement 2 beat with a whip, etc. 3 (of rain, etc.) beat; strike 4 criticize harshly 5 fasten with a cord, etc. —*n.* 6 sharp blow by a whip, etc. 7 eyelash 8 **lash out** speak or hit out angrily

lash'ings *n. pl. Colloq.* a lot of

Las Pal·mas /läs päl'məs/ *n.* seaport of the Canary Islands. Pop. 342,000

lass /las/ *n. Scot.* & *No. Engl.* or *Poet.* girl [prob. ON]

Las·sa fe'ver /las'ə/ *n.* acute febrile viral disease of tropical Africa [*Lassa* in Nigeria]

las·si·tude /las'ət(y)ōōd'/ *n.* 1 languor 2 lack of desire to exert oneself [L *lassus* tired]

las·so /las'ō, lasō̄'/ *n.* (*pl.* **·sos** or **·soes**) 1 rope with a noose at one end, esp. for catching cattle —*v.* (**·soed, ·so·ing**) 2 catch with a lasso [Sp *lazo* fr. L *laqueus* noose]

last¹ /last/ *adj.* 1 after all others; coming at or belonging to the end 2 most recent 3 only remaining 4 (prec. by *the*) least likely 5 lowest in rank (*last place*) 6 final —*adv.* 7 after all others 8 on the most recent occasion 9 lastly —*n.* 10 person or thing that is last 11 end 12 **at (long) last** finally [superl. of LATE]

  ● Usage: When *latest* 'most recent' is meant, many purists think it best to use it in preference to *last* 'final.' Despite the meaning of *last*, people say (and write), *The last time I saw Paris* and *At Peggy's last visit we had a cookout. Latest* should be chosen when it is important to distinguish between 'most recent' and 'final': *On my last day of work, they gave me a gold watch. I saw Jim on my latest visit to the hospital.* See note at FORMER.

last² *v.* 1 remain unexhausted or alive for a time 2 continue for a time [OE]

last³ *n.* model for shaping a shoe [OE]

last'-ditch' *adj.* (of an attempt, etc.) final; desperate

last'ing *adj.* permanent; durable —**last'ing·ly** *adv.*

last'ly *adv.* finally; in the last place

last' name' *n.* family name or surname

last' rites' *n. pl.* rites for a person about to die

last' straw' *n.* (prec. by *the*) slight addition to a burden that makes it unbearable

last' word' *n.* 1 final or definitive statement 2 latest fashion

Las Ve·gas /läs vā'gəs/ *n.* city in Nev. Pop. 258,295

lat. *abbr.* latitude

Lat·a·ki·a /lat'əkē'ə/ *n.* seaport in Syria. Pop. 284,000

latch /lacH/ *n.* 1 fastening for a gate, etc. 2 lock needing a key to be opened from the outside —*v.* 3 fasten with a latch 4 **latch on** or **onto** *Colloq.* attach oneself (to) 5 understand [OE]

late /lāt/ *adj.* (**lat·er** or **lat·ter, lat·est** or **last**) 1 after the due or usual, expected, or proper time 2a far on in a specified period b far on in development 3 no longer alive or functioning 4 recent —*adv.* (**lat·er, lat·est**

or last) **5** after the due or usual time **6** far on in time **7** at or till a late hour —**late′ness** *n.* [OE]

● Usage: See note on **latest** at LAST¹.

late·ly /lāt′lē/ *adv.* recently [OE]

la·tent /lāt′nt/ *adj.* undeveloped; dormant —**la′ten·cy** *n.* [L *latere* be hidden]

lat·er·al /lat′ərəl/ *adj.* of, at, toward, or from the side —**lat′er·al·ly** *adv.* [L *lateris* side]

lat′er·al think′ing *n.* method of solving problems other than by using conventional logic

la·tex /lā′teks/ *n.* milky fluid of esp. the rubber tree [L: liquid]

lath /laTH, laTH/ *n.* (*pl.* **laths** /laTHz, laTHs/) thin flat strip of wood [OE]

lathe /lāTH/ *n.* machine for shaping wood, metal, etc., by rotating it against a cutting tool

lath·er /laTH′ər/ *n.* **1** froth produced by agitating soap and water **2** frothy sweat **3** *Colloq.* agitated state —*v.* **4** form or cover with lather

Lat·in /lat′n/ *n.* **1** language of ancient Rome and its empire **2** person who speaks a language derived from Latin, as Spanish or Italian —*adj.* **3** of or in Latin **4** of the countries or peoples using languages descended from Latin [L *Latium* district near Rome]

Lat′in A·mer′i·ca *n.* the part of the Western Hemisphere S of the US where Spanish, Portuguese, or French is officially spoken —**Lat′in A·mer′i·can** *n. & adj.*

La·ti·no /lətē′nō/ *n.* (*pl.* **-nos**; *fem.* **La·ti·na** /-nä/, *pl.* **-nas**) **1** Latin American person **2** person of Spanish-speaking or Latin American descent

lat·ish /lāt′ish/ *adj. & adv.* fairly late

LINES OF LATITUDE 1a

lat·i·tude /lat′it(y)ōōd′/ *n.* **1a** angular distance on a meridian north or south of the equator **b** (usu. *pl.*) regions or climes **2** tolerated action or opinion —**lat′i·tu′di·nal** /-dinəl/ *adj.* [L *latus* broad]

la·trine /lətrēn′/ *n.* communal toilet, esp. in a military camp [L *latrina*]

lat·ter /lat′ər/ *adj.* **1** second mentioned of two **2** near the end **3** recent —**lat′ter·ly** *adv.* [old comp. of LATE]

● Usage: See note at FORMER.

lat·tice /lat′əs/ *n.* structure of crossed laths with spaces between, used as a screen, fence, etc. —**lat′ticed** *adj.* [Fr *lattis* fr. *latte* LATH]

Lat·vi·a /lat′vēə/ *n.* republic in NW Europe, on the Baltic Sea; formerly part of the USSR. Capital: Riga. Pop. 2,685,000 —**Lat′vi·an** *n. & adj.*

laud /lôd/ *v.* praise or extol [L *laudare*]

laud·a·ble /lôd′əbəl/ *adj.* commendable —**laud′a·bil′i·ty** *n.*; **laud′a·bly** *adv.*

lau·da·num /lôd′n-əm/ *n.* solution prepared from opium

lau·da·to·ry /lôd′ətôr′ē/ *adj.* praising

laugh /laf/ *v.* **1** make the sounds and movements in expressing amusement, scorn, etc. **2** (foll. by *at*) **a** ridicule; make fun of **b** be amused by —*n.* **3** sound, act, or manner of laughing **4** *Colloq.* comical thing **5** **laugh off** get rid of (embarrassment or humiliation) by joking [OE]

laugh·a·ble /laf′əbəl/ *adj.* ludicrous; amusing —**laugh′a·bly** *adv.*

laugh′ing *n.* laughter —**laugh′ing·ly** *adv.*

laugh′ing gas′ *n.* nitrous oxide as an anesthetic

laugh′ing·stock′ *n.* person or thing ridiculed

laugh·ter /laf′tər/ *n.* act or sound of laughing

laugh′ track′ *n.* recorded laughter added to a comedy show

launch¹ /lônch, länch/ *v.* **1** set (a vessel) afloat **2** hurl or send forth (a rocket, etc.) **3** start or set in motion (an enterprise, attack, etc.) **4** formally introduce (a new product) —*n.* **5** act of launching —**launch′er** *n.* [AngFr *lancher*, rel. to LANCE]

launch² *n.* open or partly open motor boat [Sp & Port *lancha*]

launch′ pad′ *n.* (also **launch′ing pad′**) platform with a support for launching rockets

laun·der /lôn′dər, län′-/ *v.* **1** wash and iron (clothes, etc.) **2** *Colloq.* transfer (funds) to conceal their origin [Fr fr. L *lavare* wash]

Laun·dro·mat /lôn′drəmat′/ *n. Tdmk.* self-service laundry with coin-operated equipment

laun·dry /lôn′drē, län′-/ *n.* (*pl.* **-dries**) **1a** place for washing clothes, etc. **b** firm washing clothes, etc., commercially **2** clothes or linen for laundering or newly laundered —**laun′dress**, **laun′dry·man′** /-mən/ (*pl.* **-men**; *fem.* ·**wom′an**, *pl.* ·**wom′en**) *n.*

laun′dry list′ *n. Colloq.* long list of items

lau·re·ate /lôr′ēət, lär′-/ *adj.* wreathed with laurel as a mark of honor —**lau′re·ate·ship′** *n.* [rel. to LAUREL]

lau·rel /lôr′əl, lär′-/ *n.* **1** (*sing.* or *pl.*) wreath of bay leaves as an emblem of victory or poetic merit **2** (usu. *pl.*) honor; glory; fame **3** an evergreen plant with dark-green glossy leaves; bay [L *laurus* bay]

Laur·el /lôr′əl/, **Stan** (born **Arthur Stanley Jefferson**) 1890–1965; English-born US comedian; partner of OLIVER HARDY

Lau·sanne /lōzän′, -zan′/ *n.* city in Switzerland on Lake of Geneva. Pop. 123,200

la·va /läv′ə, lav′ə/ *n.* matter flowing from a volcano and solidifying as it cools [It, perh. fr. L *labi* slide]

La·val /lävál′, ləvál′/ *n.* city in Quebec, Canada. Pop. 314,400

lav·a·to·ry /lav′ətôr′ē/ *n.* (*pl.* **-ries**) room or compartment containing a washbasin and toilet [L *lavare* wash]

lave /lāv/ *v.* **1** (**laved**, **lav·ing**) *Lit.* wash; bathe [L *lavare* wash]

lav·en·der /lav′əndər/ *n.* **1a** evergreen shrub with purple aromatic flowers **b** its flowers and stalks dried and used to scent linen, etc. **2** pale mauve color [L *lavandula*]

lav·ish /lav'ISH/ *adj.* **1** abundant; profuse **2** generous —*v.* **3** (often foll. by *on*) bestow or spend (money, effort, praise, etc.) abundantly —**lav'ish·ly** *adv.*; **lav'ish·ness** *n.* [MFr *lavasse* deluge, fr. L *lavare* wash]

law /lô/ *n.* **1a** rule enacted or customary in a community that commands or forbids certain actions **b** body of such rules **2** respect for laws **3** laws collectively as a social system or subject of study **4** binding force (*her word is law*) **5** (prec. by *the*) **a** the legal profession **b** *Colloq.* the police **6** regularity in natural occurrences (*law of gravity*) [OE, perh. fr. ON: thing laid down]

law'·a·bid'ing *adj.* obedient to the laws

law'break'er *n.* person who breaks the law —**law'break'ing** *n.* & *adj.*

law·ful /lô'fəl/ *adj.* conforming with or recognized by law; not illegal —**law'ful·ly** *adv.*; **law'ful·ness** *n.*

law'giv'er *n.* lawmaker; legislator

law·less *adj.* **1** having no laws or law enforcement **2** disregarding laws; unruly —**law'less·ness** *n.*

law'mak'er *n.* legislator

lawn[1] /lôn, län/ *n.* area of closely mown grass, esp. near a house, in a garden, etc. [MFr *launde* glade fr. Celt]

lawn[2] *n.* fine linen or cotton [prob. fr. *Laon*, France]

lawn' bowl'ing *n.* game played with wooden balls on a smooth, level lawn

lawn'mow'er *n.* machine for cutting lawns

law' of av·er·ag·es *n.* concept that probability will show its effects over time

Law·rence /lôr'əns, lär'-/ *n.* city in Mass. Pop. 70,207

Law·rence /lôr'əns, lär'-/ *n.* **1** D(avid) H(erbert) 1885–1930; English writer **2** T(homas) E(dward) 1888–1935; British soldier and writer; called "Lawrence of Arabia"

law·ren·ci·um /lôren'sēəm/ *n.* transuranic metallic element; *symb.* **Lr** [for E.O. *Lawrence*, U.S. physicist]

law'suit' *n.* bringing of a dispute, claim, etc., before a court of law

law·yer /lô'yər, loi'ər/ *n.* legal practitioner

lax /laks/ *adj.* **1** lacking care or precision **2** not strict —**lax'i·ty** *n.*; **lax'ly** *adv.*; **lax'ness** *n.* [L *laxus* loose]

lax·a·tive /lak'sətiv/ *adj.* **1** easing evacuation of the bowels —*n.* **2** laxative medicine [L, rel. to LAX]

lay[1] /lā/ *v.* (**laid, lay·ing**) **1** place on a surface, esp. horizontally or in the proper or specified place **2** (of a hen bird) produce (an egg) **3** (usu. foll. by *on*) place or attach (blame, etc.) **4** prepare (a plan or trap) **5** prepare (a table) for a meal **6** put down as a wager; stake —*n.* **7** way, position, or direction in which something lies **8 lay aside:** **a** put to one side **b** cease to consider **9 lay at the door of** impute to **10 lay away, by,** *or* **in** store for later use **11 lay bare** expose; reveal **12 lay claim to** claim as one's own **13 lay down:** **a** formulate (a rule) **b** store (wine) for maturing **c** sacrifice (one's life) **14 lay it on thick** (*or* **with a trowel**) *Colloq.* flatter or exaggerate grossly **15 lay off:** **a** discharge (unneeded workers) temporarily **b** *Colloq.* desist **16 lay open:** **a** break the skin of **b** (foll. by *to*) ex-

---

323   **lavish / lead**

pose (to criticism, etc.) **17 lay out:** **a** spread out; expose to view **b** prepare (a corpse) for burial **c** *Colloq.* knock unconscious **d** arrange (grounds, etc.) according to a design **e** spend (money) **18 lay to rest** bury in a grave **19 lay waste** ravage; destroy [OE]

● Usage: The intransitive verb *lie* 'rest in bed' and the transitive verb *lay* 'put (something) down' are usually confused because of their past tenses and past participles. The past of *lie* is *lay: As he lay dying*; its past participle is *lain: He has lain in bed for three days.* The past of *lay* is *laid: I laid the plates on the table*; the past participle is the same: *I have laid table settings for nine.* The lyric "Now I lay me down to sleep" illustrates well that *lay* is the transitive verb. Formal usage calls for *lie low* 'remain concealed'; but *lay low* in that sense has become so common that it is also accepted as standard. (*Lay low* in the slang sense of 'knock out' remains as before.)

lay[2] *adj.* **1a** nonclerical **b** not ordained into the clergy **2a** not professionally qualified **b** of or done by such persons [Gk *laos* people]

lay[3] *n.* **1** short poem meant to be sung **2** song [OFr]

lay[4] *v.* past of LIE[1]

Lay·a·mon /lī'əmən, lä'-/ late 12th cent.; English poet and chronicler

lay·a·way /lā'əwā'/ *n.* purchase by a series of payments in advance of delivery

lay·er /lā'ər/ *n.* **1** thickness of matter, esp. one of several, covering a surface **2** person or thing that lays **3** hen that lays eggs —*v.* **4** arrange in layers

lay·ette /lā·et'/ *n.* set of clothing, etc., for a newborn child [Fr fr. MDu]

lay·man /lā'mən/ *n.* (*pl.* **·men;** *fem.* **·wom'an,** *pl.* **·wom'en**) (*also* **lay'per'son**) **1** person without professional knowledge **2** person not in the clergy

lay'off' *n.* temporary discharge of workers

lay' of the land' *n. Colloq.* LIE OF THE LAND

lay'out' *n.* **1** way in which land, a building, printed matter, etc., is arranged or set out **2** something displayed or laid out **3** *Slang.* plan

Laz·a·rus /laz'(ə)rəs/ *n.* (in the Bible) figure raised from the dead by Jesus

laze /lāz/ *v.* (**lazed, laz·ing**) spend time idly

la·zy /lā'zē/ *adj.* (**·zi·er, ·zi·est**) **1** disinclined to work; doing little work **2** slow; sluggish —**la'zi·ly** *adv.*; **la'zi·ness** *n.* [LGer]

la'zy·bones' *n. Colloq.* lazy person

lb. *abbr.* pound(s) [L *libra*]

LC *abbr.* (*also* **L.C.**) **1** landing craft **2** Library of Congress

l.c. *abbr.* **1** LOC. CIT. **2** lower case

LCD *abbr.* **1** liquid crystal display **2** lowest (or least) common denominator

LCM *abbr.* lowest (or least) common multiple

LDC *abbr.* less developed countries

LDPE *abbr.* low density polyethylene

lea /lē/ *n. Poet.* meadow; field [OE]

leach /lēCH/ *v.* **1** make (a liquid) percolate through some material **2** (foll. by *away, out*) remove (soluble matter) or be removed in this way [prob. OE]

lead[1] /lēd/ *v.* (**led, lead·ing**) **1** cause to go with one, esp. by guiding or going in front **2** direct the actions or opinions of, as by persuasion or example **3** provide access to **4** go through (a life of a specified kind) **5** have first place in **6** be in charge of (*leads a team*) **7** (foll. by *to*) result in **8** come or go first —*n.* **9** guidance given by going in front; example **10a** leading place **b** amount by which a competitor is ahead of the others **11** clue **12** leash **13a** chief part in a play, etc. **b** person playing this **14** *Cards.* **a** act or right of playing first **b** card led **15** lead off begin **16** lead on entice dishonestly **17** lead up to prepare (someone) for something [OE]

lead² /led/ *n.* **1** heavy bluish-gray soft metallic element; *symb.* Pb **2** graphite, esp. a thin length of this in a pencil **3** bullets —*v.* (**lead‧ed, lead‧ing**) **4** cover, weight, or frame with lead —*adj.* **5** made of or with lead [OE]

lead‧en /led'n/ *adj.* **1** of or like lead **2** heavy or slow **3** lead-colored

lead‧er /lēd'ər/ *n.* **1** person or thing that leads **2** person followed by others —**lead'er‧ship'** *n.*

lead‧ing /lēd'iNG/ *adj.* chief; most important

lead'ing ques'tion *n.* question prompting the answer wanted

leaf /lēf/ *n.* . (*pl.* **leaves**) **1** each of several flattened usu. green structures of a plant, growing usu. on the side of a stem **2** single thickness of paper **3** very thin sheet of metal, etc. **4** hinged part, section, or flap of a table, etc. —*v.* **5** put forth leaves **6** (foll. by *through*) turn over the pages of (a book, etc.) —**leaf'age** *n.*; **leaf'y** *adj.* (**·i·er, ·i·est**)

leaf‧let /lē'flit/ *n.* **1** sheet of paper, pamphlet, etc., giving information **2** young leaf

league¹ /lēg/ *n.* **1** people, countries, groups, etc., combining for a purpose **2** group of sports teams that compete for a championship —*v.* (**leagued, leagu‧ing**) **3** (often foll. by *together*) join in a league **4** in league allied; conspiring [L *ligare* bind]

league² *n. Hist.* measure of distance, usu. about three miles [L fr. Celt]

leak /lēk/ *n.* **1a** hole through which matter passes accidentally in or out **b** matter passing through thus **c** act of passing through thus **2** disclosure of secret information —*v.* **3** pass through a leak **4** disclose (secret information) **5** (often foll. by *out*) become known —**leak'y** *adj.* (**·i·er, ·i·est**) [ON]

leak‧age /lē'kij/ *n.* action or result of leaking

lean¹ /lēn/ *v.* (**leaned** or **leant** /lent/, **lean‧ing**) **1** (often foll. by *across, back, over,* etc.) be or place in a sloping position; incline from upright **2** (cause to) rest for support against **3** (foll. by *on, upon*) rely on **4** (foll. by *to, toward*) be partial to **5** lean on *Colloq.* put pressure on (a person) to act in a certain way [OE]

lean² *adj.* **1** thin; containing little fat **2** meager —*n.* **3** lean part of meat —**lean'ness** *n.* [OE]

Lean /lēn/, (**Sir**) **David** 1908–91; English film director

lean'ing *n.* tendency or partiality

lean'-to' *n.* (*pl.* **·tos**) building with its roof leaning against a wall

leap /lēp/ *v.* (**leaped** or **leapt, leap‧ing**) **1** jump or spring forcefully —*n.* **2** forceful jump [OE]

leap'frog' *n.* **1** game in which players vault with parted legs over others bending down —*v.* (**·frogged, ·frog‧ging**) **2** perform such a vault (over) **3** advance by skipping usual steps between

leapt /lept, lēpt/ *v.* *past* and *past. part.* of LEAP

leap' year' *n.* year with 366 days (adding Feb. 29th)

Lear /lēr/, **Edward** 1812–88; English humorist and illustrator

learn /lərn/ *v.* (**learned** /lərnd/ or **learnt** /lərnt/, **learn‧ing**) **1** gain knowledge of or skill in **2** memorize **3** (foll. by *of* or *about*) be told about **4** (foll. by *that, how,* etc.) become aware of —**learn'er** *n.* [OE]

learn‧ed /lər'nid/ *adj.* **1** having much learning **2** showing or requiring learning (*a learned work*)

learn'ing *n.* knowledge acquired by study

learn'ing curve' *n.* **1** graph showing time needed to acquire a new skill, knowledge of a subject, etc. **2** time represented by such a graph

learn'ing dis‧a‧bil'i‧ty condition that prevents learning to read, write, etc. —**learn'ing‧dis‧a'bled** *adj.*

lease /lēs/ *n.* **1** contract by which the owner of property rents it for a specified time, usu. in return for payment —*v.* (**leased, leas‧ing**) **2** grant or take on lease [AngFr *lesser* let, fr. L *laxare* loosen]

lease'hold' *n.* **1** holding of property by lease **2** property held by lease —**lease'hold'er** *n.*

leash /lēsH/ *n.* **1** strap for holding a dog, etc. —*v.* **2** put a leash on **3** restrain [ME fr. OFr *laisse,* rel. to LEASE]

least /lēst/ *adj.* **1** smallest; slightest **2** (of a species, etc.) very small —*n.* **3** the smallest amount —*adv.* **4** in the smallest degree **5 at least: a** at any rate **b** (also **at the least**) not less than **6 not in the least** at all (*not in the least offended*) [OE, superl. of *læssa* LESS]

least' com'mon de‧nom'i‧na'tor *n.* LOWEST COMMON DENOMINATOR

least'wise' *adv.* (also **least'ways'**) *Colloq.* in any case; at least

leath‧er /leTH'ər/ *n.* material made from the skin of an animal by tanning, etc. —**leath'er‧y** *adj.* [OE]

leath'er‧back' *n.* large marine turtle with a leathery shell

leath‧er‧ette /leTH' əret'/ *n.* imitation leather

leath'er‧neck' *n. Slang.* member of the US Marine Corps

leave¹ /lēv/ *v.* (**left, leav‧ing**) **1** go away (from) **2** cause to or let remain **3** abandon **4** have remaining after one's death **5** bequeath **6** allow to remain or cause to be in a specified state (*leave the door open*) **7** leave off discontinue **8** leave out omit; exclude [OE]

● *Usage:* A useful distinction can be made between *leave* and *let. Leave* means 'depart from': *We left together.* The common expression, *Leave me alone,* means 'leave (me), so that I remain by myself.' *Let* means 'allow': *Let me be. Let me alone.* These mean 'don't bother me.'

leave² *n.* **1** permission **2a** (**leave of absence**) permission to be absent from duty **b** period for which this lasts **3 on leave** legitimately

leav·en /lev'ən/ n. (also **leav'en·ing**) 1 substance causing dough to ferment and rise 2 transforming influence or substance —v. 3 raise (dough) with leaven 4 modify with a tempering element [L *levare* lift]

leaves /lēvz/ n. pl. of LEAF

leave'-tak'ing n. act of departing

leav·ings /lē'vĭNGz/ n. pl. things left over

Leb·a·non /leb'ənän', -nən/ n. republic in SW Asia, N of Israel. Capital: Beirut. Pop. 2,803,000 —**Leb·a·nese'** /-nēz/ n. & adj.

lech·er /lecH'ər/ n. one with excessive sexual desire, esp. a man —**lech'er·ous** adj.; **lech'er·ous·ly** adv.; **lech'er·ous·ness, lech'er·y** n. [ME fr. OFr *lechier* lick]

lec·i·thin /les'i·THin/ n. fatty compound found in egg yolk and other living tissue; used as an additive in food and medicine

lec·tern /lek'tərn/ n. stand for holding a book for a lecturer, etc. [MedL *lectrum* fr. L *legere* read]

lec·ture /lek'CHər/ n. 1 talk giving information to students, etc. 2 long reprimand —v. (·tured, ·tur·ing) 3 deliver lecture(s) 4 reprimand —**lec'tur·er, lec'ture·ship** n. [MedL *lectura* reading]

led /led/ v. past and past part. of LEAD[1]

LED abbr. light-emitting diode

ledge /lej/ n. narrow horizontal or shelflike projection

led·ger /lej'ər/ n. main record of the accounts of a business [ME, perh. fr. MDu]

lee /lē/ n. 1 shelter 2 side away from the wind [OE]

Lee /lē/ 1 Henry ("Lighthorse Harry") 1756–1818; officer during the American Revolution 2 Robert E(dward) 1807–70; commander of Confederate forces during the American Civil War

leech /lēcH/ n. 1 bloodsucking worm formerly much used medically 2 person who imposes on others [OE]

Leeds /lēdz/ n. city in N England. Pop. 451,800

leek /lēk/ n. plant of the onion family [OE]

leer /lēr/ v. 1 look slyly, lasciviously, or maliciously —n. 2 leering look [OE, perh. fr. *leer* cheek]

leer'y adj. (·i·er, ·i·est) (foll. by of) wary

lees /lēz/ n. pl. sediment of a liquid, esp. wine; dregs [MFr]

lee·ward /lē'wərd, lōō'ərd/ adj. & adv. 1 on or toward the side sheltered from the wind —n. 2 sheltered region or side

Lee·ward Is'lands /lē'wərd, lōō'ərd/ n. group of Caribbean islands extending from Puerto Rico SE to Martinique

lee·way /lē'wā'/ n. 1 Colloq. allowable scope of action 2 sideways drift off course to leeward

left[1] /left/ adj. 1 on or toward the west side of the human body or of any object when facing north 2 (also cap.) Polit. socialistic —adv. 3 on or to the left side —n. 4 left-hand side, region, or direction 5 (often cap.) group or section favoring socialism; socialists collectively [OE, orig. 'weak; worthless']

left[2] v. past and past part. of LEAVE[1]

left' brain' n. left cerebral hemisphere, esp.

as regards its purported control over mental abilities such as logic, mathematics, and language

left'-hand' adj. 1 on or toward the left side of a person or thing 2 done with the left hand 3 (of a screw) LEFT-HANDED, 3b

left'-hand'ed adj. 1 using the left hand for writing, etc. 2 for use by or done by the left hand 3a turning to the left b (of a screw) turned counterclockwise to tighten 4a (of a compliment) ambiguous b of doubtful sincerity —adv. 5 with the left hand —**left'-hand'ed·ly** adv.; **left'-hand'ed·ness** n.

left'ist n. & adj. socialist —**left'ism** /-iz'əm/ n.

left'most /left'mōst'/ adj. furthest to the left

left'o·ver n. (usu. pl.) surplus items

left' wing' n. & adj. more socialist section of a political party or system —**left'-wing'er** n.

left'y n. (pl. ·ies) Colloq. left-handed person

leg /leg/ n. 1 each of the limbs on which a person or animal walks and stands 2 part of a garment covering a leg 3 support of a chair, table, etc. 4 section of a journey, relay race, competition, etc. 5 **leg it** Colloq. walk or run hard —**legged** /leg'id, legd/ adj. (also in comb.) [ON]

leg·a·cy /leg'əsē/ n. (pl. ·cies) 1 gift left in a will 2 thing handed down by a predecessor [L *legare* bequeath]

le·gal /lē'gəl/ adj. 1 of or based on law 2 appointed or required by law 3 permitted by law —**le'gal·ly** adv. [L *lex, leg-* law]

le'gal age' n. age at which a person assumes adult rights and privileges by law

le'gal aid' n. state assistance for legal advice or action

le·gal·ese /lē'gəlēz/ n. technical language of legal documents

le·gal·is·tic /lē'gəlis'tik/ adj. adhering excessively to a law or formula —**le'gal·ism** /-iz'əm/, **le'gal·ist** n.

le·gal·i·ty /ligal'ətē/ n. (pl. ·ties) 1 lawfulness 2 (pl.) obligations imposed by law

le·gal·ize /lē'gəliz'/ v. (·ized, ·iz·ing) make lawful or legal —**le'gal·i·za'tion** n.

le'gal ten'der n. currency that cannot legally be refused in payment of a debt

le·gate /leg'ət/ n. ambassador [L *legare* depute]

leg·a·tee /leg'ətē'/ n. person who receives a legacy [L *legare* bequeath]

le·ga·tion /ligā'sHən/ n. 1 diplomatic minister and staff 2 official headquarters of this group [L *legatio* embassy]

le·ga·to /ligät'ō/ Mus. adv. & adj. 1 in a smooth flowing manner —n. (pl. ·tos) 2 legato passage 3 legato playing [It fr. L *ligare* bind]

leg·end /lej'ənd/ n. 1a traditional story; myth b these collectively 2 Colloq. famous or remarkable event or person 3 inscription 4 explanation of symbols on a map, etc. [ME fr. L *legere* read]

leg·end·ar·y /lej'əndər'ē/ adj. 1 of, based on, or described in a legend 2 Colloq. remarkable —**leg'end·ar'i·ly** adv.

leg·er·de·main /lej'ərdəmān'/ n. 1 sleight of hand 2 trickery [MFr: light of hand]

leg·ging /leg'iNGn/ *n.* (usu. *pl.*) close-fitting knitted trousers

leg·gy /leg'ē/ *adj.* (**·gi·er**, **·gi·est**) **1** long-legged **2** long-stemmed and weak **—leg'gi·ness** *n.*

Leg·horn /leg'hôrn'/ *n.* (Italian name Livorno) seaport in W Italy. Pop. 171,300

leg·i·ble /leg'əbəl/ *adj.* clear enough to read; readable **—leg·i·bil'i·ty** *n.*; **leg'i·bly** *adv.* [L *legere* read]

le·gion /lē'jən/ *n.* **1** division of 3,000–6,000 men in the ancient Roman army **2** large or organized body **—adj.** **3** great in number **—le'gion·naire'** /-jəner'/ *n.* [L *legio*, *-onis*]

le·gion·naires'' dis·ease' *n.* form of bacterial pneumonia

leg·is·late /lej'əslāt'/ *v.* (**·lat·ed**, **·lat·ing**) make laws **—leg'is·la'tor** *n.* [fr. LEGISLATION]

leg'is·la'tion *n.* **1** law-making **2** laws collectively [L *lex*, *legis* law + *latio* bringing]

leg·is·la·tive /lej'əslāt'iv/ *adj.* **1** of a legislature or legislation **2** of or empowered to make laws

leg·is·la·ture /lej'əslā'CHər/ *n.* legislative body

le·git /ləjit'/ *adj. Colloq.* LEGITIMATE, 2

le·git·i·mate /ləjit'əmət/ *adj.* **1** (of a child) born of parents married to each other **2** lawful; proper; regular **3** logically acceptable **4** of a professional stage play (*legitimate theater*) **—le·git'i·ma·cy** *n.*; **le·git'i·mate·ly** *adv.* [MedL *legitimare* make lawful]

le·git·i·ma·tize /ləjit'əmətīz'/ *v.* (**·tized**, **·tizing**) LEGITIMIZE

le·git·i·mize /lijit'əmīz'/ *v.* (**·mized**, **·miz·ing**) **1** make legitimate **2** serve as a justification for **—le·git'i·mi·za'tion** *n.*

leg'room' *n.* (sufficient) space for the legs of a seated person

leg·ume /leg'(y)ōōm'/ *n.* leguminous plant [F fr. L *legere* gather]

le·gu·mi·nous /ləgyōō'mənəs/ *adj.* of the family of plants with seeds in pods (e.g., peas and beans)

Le Ha·vre /lə häv'(rə)/ *n.* seaport in France. Pop. 197,200

lei /lā'(ē)/ *n.* Polynesian garland of flowers [Haw]

Leib·niz /līp'nits, līb'nəts/, **Gottfried Wilhelm** 1646–1716; German philosopher and mathematician

Leices·ter /les'tər/ *n.* city in central England. Pop. 328,800

Lei·den /līd'n/ *n.* city in the Netherlands. Pop. 111,900

Leip·zig /līp'sig, -sik/ *n.* city in Germany. Pop. 511,100

lei·sure /lē'zHər, lezH'-/ *n.* **1** free time, as for recreation **2 at leisure** not occupied **3 at one's leisure** when one has time [OFr fr. L *licere* be allowed]

lei'sure·ly *adj.* **1** unhurried; relaxed **—adv.** **2** without hurry **—lei'sure·li·ness** *n.*

lei'sure·wear' *n.* informal clothes; sportswear

leit·mo·tif /līt'mōtēf'/ *n.* (also **leit'mo·tiv'**) repeated or main theme [Ger: leading motive]

Le·man, Lake /lē'mən/ *n.* see GENEVA, LAKE

Le Mans /lə män/ *n.* city in France. Pop. 148,500

lem·ming /lem'iNG/ *n.* small Arctic rodent reputed to rush into the sea in such numbers during migration that many drown [Norw]

lem·on /lem'ən/ *n.* **1 a** yellow oval sour citrus fruit **b** tree bearing it **2** pale yellow color **3** *Colloq.* defective thing, esp. a car **—lem'on·y** *adj.* [Pers *līmun*]

lem·on·ade /lem'ənād'/ *n.* drink made from lemon juice

le·mur /lē'mər/ *n.* tree-dwelling primate of Madagascar [L *lemures* ghosts]

lend /lend/ *v.* (**lent**, **lend·ing**) **1** grant the temporary use of (a thing) **2** allow the use of (money) at interest **3** bestow or contribute (*lends a certain charm*) **4 lend an ear** listen **5 lend a hand** help **6 lend itself to** (of a thing) be suitable for **—lend'er** *n.* [OE]
● Usage: See note at LOAN.

L'En·fant /länfän'/, **Pierre Charles** 1754–1825; French-born US engineer; designer of Washington, D.C.

length /leNGTH, lenTH/ *n.* **1** extent from end to end **2** extent in or of time **3** distance a thing extends **4** length of a swimming pool as a measure of distance swum **5 at length: a** in full detail **b** finally [OE]

length·en /leNG'THən, len'-/ *v.* make or become longer

length·wise /leNGTH'wīz', lenTH'-/ *adv. & adj.* (also **length'ways'**) lying or moving parallel to the length

length'y *adj.* (**·i·er**, **·i·est**) of unusual or tedious length **—length'i·ly** *adv.*; **length'i·ness** *n.*

le·ni·ent /lēn'yənt/ *adj.* merciful; not severe **—le'ni·ence**, **le'ni·en·cy** *n.*; **le'ni·ent·ly** *adv.* [L *lenire* alleviate]

Le·nin /len'ən/, **Vladimir** (real surname Ulyanov) 1870–1924; Russian Communist revolutionary and leader; premier of the USSR (1918–24)

Le·nin·grad /len'iNGrad/ *n.* see SAINT PETERSBURG

Len·non /len'ən/, **John** 1940–80; English pop and rock musician and composer

lens /lenz/ *n.* **1** piece of a transparent substance with one or (usu.) both sides curved for concentrating or dispersing light rays, esp. in optical instruments **2** electronic or electromagnetic device for focusing electromagnetic waves **3** transparent substance behind the iris of the eye [L *lens*, *lent-* lentil]

lent /lent/ *v.* past and past part. of LEND

Lent /lent/ *n. Christianity.* period of fasting and penitence preceding Easter **—Lent'en** *adj.* [OE: spring]

len·til /lent'l/ *n.* **1** pealike plant **2** its seed, esp. used as food [L *lens*]

len·to /len'tō/ *adj. & adv. Mus.* slow [It fr. L *lentus*]

Le·o /lē'ō/ *n.* (*pl.* **·os**) **1** constellation and fifth sign of the zodiac (the Lion) **2** person born under this sign [L fr. Gk]

Le·ón /lāōn'/ *n.* **1** city in NW Spain. Pop. 144,100 **2** city in central Mexico. Pop. 593,000

Le·o·nar·do da Vin·ci /lē'ənärd'ō də vin'CHē/ 1452–1519; Italian painter, scientist, and engineer

le·o·nine /lē'ənīn'/ *adj.* like a lion [L, rel. to LEO]

leop·ard /lep′ərd/ *n.* large African or Asian cat with a black-spotted yellowish or all black coat; panther [Gk *leōn* lion + *pardos* panther]

le·o·tard /lē′ətärd/ *n.* close-fitting one-piece garment worn by dancers, etc. [for *Léotard*, a trapeze artist]

lep·er /lep′ər/ *n.* person with leprosy [Gk *lepros* scaly]

lep·re·chaun /lep′rəkòn′,-kän′/ *n.* small mischievous sprite in Irish folklore [OIr *lu* small + *corp* body]

lep·ro·sy /lep′rəsē/ *n.* contagious, deforming disease that damages the skin and nerves —**lep·rous** *adj.* [rel. to LEPER]

Ler·ner /lər′nər/, **Alan Jay** 1918–86 US lyricist and librettist

les·bi·an /lez′bēən/ *n.* 1 homosexual woman —*adj.* 2 of female homosexuality —**les′bi·an·ism′** *n.* [Gk island of *Lesbos*]

lese maj·es·ty /lēz′ maj′es·tÿ/ *n.* 1 treason 2 crime against a sovereign 3 bold conduct [Fr: injured sovereignty]

le·sion /lē′zHən/ *n.* injury to an organ affecting its function [L *laedere, laes-* injure]

Le·so·tho /ləsō′tō-sōō′tōō/ *n.* (formerly **Basutoland**) monarchy in southern Africa. Capital: Maseru. Pop. 1,854,000

less /les/ *adj.* 1 smaller in extent, degree, duration, number, etc. 2 smaller in quantity (*less meat*) 3 *Colloq.* fewer (*less biscuits*) —*adv.* 4 to a smaller extent —*n.* 5 smaller amount —*prep.* 6 minus [OE]

• Usage: See note at FEW.

-less *suffix* forming adjectives and adverbs: 1 from nouns, meaning 'not having; without' (*powerless*) 2 from verbs, meaning 'not accessible to, affected by, or performing the action of the verb' (*fathomless; ceaseless*)

less·ee /lesē′/ *n.* person holding a property by lease [AngFr, rel. to LEASE]

less·en /les′ən/ *v.* make or become less; diminish; reduce

Les·seps /lāseps′, leseps′/, **Ferdinand, Vicomte de** 1805–94; French diplomat and engineer who promoted the Suez Canal

less·er /les′ər/ *adj.* not so great as the other(s) (*lesser evil; lesser mortals*)

Less·er An·til·les *n.* group of smaller islands in the Caribbean Sea comprising the Leeward and Windward islands. See also GREATER ANTILLES

les·son /les′ən/ *n.* 1 time spent teaching 2 systematic instruction 3 thing learned by a pupil 4 experience that serves to warn or encourage 5 passage from the Bible for reading aloud [OFr *leçon* fr. L *legere* read]

les·sor /les′ôr′/ *n.* person who lets a property by lease [AngFr, rel. to LEASE]

lest /lest/ *conj.* in order that not; for fear that (*lest he forget*) [OE, rel. to LESS]

let[1] /let/ *v.* (**let, let·ting**) 1a allow to b cause to 2 rent 3 allow or cause (liquid or air) to escape 4 *aux.* supplying the first and third persons of commands 5 **let alone:** a refrain from bothering b not to mention 6 **let be** not interfere with or do 7 **let down:** a lower b disappoint c lengthen (a garment) 8 **let go: a** release **b** lose hold of 9 **let oneself**

327

go: a act spontaneously **b** neglect one's appearance or habits 10 **let off: a** punish lightly or not at all **b** emit 11 **let on** reveal a secret 12 **let out: a** release **b** reveal (a secret, etc.) **c** enlarge (a garment) 13 **let up:** a ease; relax **b** stop 14 **to let** for rent [OE]

• Usage: See note at LEAVE[1].

let[2] *n.* 1 obstruction of a ball or player in tennis, etc., requiring the ball to be served again 2 **without let or hindrance** unimpeded [OE, rel. to LATE]

-let *suffix* forming nouns, usu. diminutive (*booklet*) or denoting articles of ornament or dress (*anklet*) [MFr]

let′down′ *n.* disappointment

le·thal /lē′THəl/ *adj.* causing death; deadly; fatal —**le′thal·ly** *adv.* [L *letum* death]

leth·ar·gy /leTH′ərjē/ *n.* 1 lack of energy 2 abnormal drowsiness —**le·thar·gic** /ləTHär′jik/ *adj.*; **le·thar′gi·cal·ly** /-jik(ə)lē/ *adv.* [Gk *lēthargikos* forgetful]

let·ter /let′ər/ *n.* 1 alphabetic character 2 written or printed message, usu. sent by mail 3 precise terms of a statement 4 (*pl.*) a literature b learning; erudition —*v.* 5 inscribe letters on [OFr fr. L *littera*]

let′ter-bomb′ *n.* terrorist explosive device in the form of a mailed package

let′ter car·ri·er *n.* person employed to deliver mail

let·tered /let′ərd/ *adj.* well-read or educated

let′ter·head′ *n.* printed heading on stationery

let′ter·ing *n.* act of inscribing letters individually, or such letters

let′ter of cred′it *n.* letter from a bank authorizing the bearer to draw money from another bank

let′ter-per′fect *adj.* exactly right

let′ter·press′ *n.* printing from raised type

let·tuce /let′əs/ *n.* plant with crisp leaves used in salads [prob. OFr fr. L *lactuca*]

let′up′ *n. Colloq.* 1 reduction in intensity 2 relaxation of effort 3 pause

leu·ke·mi·a /lōōkē′mēə/ *n.* malignant disease in which too many leukocytes are produced [Gk *leukos* white + *haima* blood]

leu·ko·cyte /lōō′kəsīt′/ *n.* white blood cell —**leu′ko·cyt′ic** /-sit′ik/ *adj.*

Le·vant, the /ləvant′/ *n. Hist.* the countries bordering the E coast of the Mediterranean Sea, including Syria, Lebanon, and Israel

lev·ee /lev′ē/ *n.* embankment against river floods [Fr *levée* fr. L *levare* raise]

lev·el /lev′əl/ *n.* 1 horizontal line or plane 2 height or value reached (*eye level; sugar level*) 3 social, moral, or intellectual standard 4 instrument giving a horizontal line 5 level surface —*adj.* 6 flat and even 7 horizontal 8 even with something else 9 **on the level** honestly; honest —*v.* (**·eled** or **·elled, ·el·ing** or **·el·ling**) 10 make level 11 raze 12 aim (a missile or gun) 13 direct (an accusation, etc.) 14 **level with** *Slang.* be forthright and honest with —**lev′el·er, lev′el·ler** *n.*

lev′el·head′ed *adj.* mentally well-balanced; sensible —**lev′el·head′ed·ly** *adv.*; **lev′el·head′ed·ness** *n.*

lev·er /lev'ər, lē'vər/ *n.* **1** bar used to pry **2** bar pivoted about a fulcrum (fixed point) acted upon by a force (effort) to move a load **3** handle moved to operate a mechanism —*v.* **4** use a lever **5** lift, move, etc., with a lever [L *levare* raise]

LEVER 1, 2

lev·er·age /lev'(ə)rij/ *n.* **1** action or power of a lever **2** power to accomplish a purpose

le·vi·a·bil·i·ty /lavī'əTHən/ *n.* **1** *Bibl.* sea monster **2** anything large or powerful [LL fr. Heb]

Le·vis /lē'vīz/ *n. pl. Tdmk.* type of (orig. blue) denim jeans reinforced with rivets [for *Levi* Strauss, manufacturer]

lev·i·tate /lev'ətāt'/ *v.* (**·tat·ed, ·tat·ing**) **1** rise and float in the air without visible support **2** cause to do this —**lev·i·ta'tion** *n.* [rel. to LEVITY]

Lev·it·town /lev'it-toun'/ *n.* town in N.Y. Pop. 53,286

lev·i·ty /lev'ətē/ *n.* lack of serious thought; frivolity [L *levitas* lightness]

lev·y /lev'ē/ *v.* (**·ied, ·y·ing**) **1** impose or collect (payment, etc.) **2** enroll (troops, etc.) **3** wage (war) —*n.* (*pl.* **·ies**) **4a** collecting of a tax, etc. **b** contribution, etc., levied **5a** act of enrolling troops **b** (*pl.*) troops enrolled [L *levare* raise]

lewd /lōod/ *adj.* **1** lascivious **2** obscene [OE: lay; vulgar]

Lew·is /lōo'əs/ **1** Meriwether 1774–1809; US explorer (with William Clark) of the American continent (1804–06) **2** (Harry) Sinclair 1885–1951; US novelist **3** C(live) S(taples) 1898–1963; Northern Irish novelist, theologian, and scholar **4** C(ecil) Day 1904–72; English poet and critic

lex·i·cal /lek'sikal/ *adj.* **1** of the words of a language **2** of or as of a lexicon [Gk, rel. to LEXICON]

lex·i·cog·ra·phy /lek'sikäg'rəfē/ *n.* compiling of dictionaries —**lex'i·cog'ra·pher** *n.* [fr. LEXICON + -GRAPHY]

lex·i·con /lek'sikän', -kən/ *n.* **1** dictionary **2** vocabulary of a person, field, etc. [Gk *lexis* word]

Lex·ing·ton /lek'siNGtən/ *n.* **1** city in Ky. Pop. 225,366 **2** Mass. town; site of the opening battle of the American Revolution (1775)

Li *symb.* lithium

li·a·bil·i·ty /lī'əbil'ətē/ *n.* (*pl.* **·ties**) **1** being liable **2** troublesome responsibility; handicap **3** (*pl.*) debts, etc., for which one is liable

li·a·ble /lī'(ə)bəl/ *adj.* **1** legally bound **2** subject to **3** under an obligation **4** apt; likely [AngFr *lier* bind]

li·aise /lē·āz'/ *v.* (**·aised, ·ais·ing**) *Colloq.* act as a link [back formation fr. LIAISON]

li·ai·son /lē'əzän', lē·ā'zän'/ *n.* **1** communication or cooperation **2** illicit sexual relationship [Fr fr. L *ligare* bind]

li·ar /lī'ər/ *n.* person who tells a lie or lies

lib /lib/ *n. Colloq.* (in names of political movements) liberation [abbr.]

Lib. *abbr.* Liberal

li·ba·tion /lībā'SHən/ *n.* **1** pouring out of a drink, esp. wine, as an offering to a god **2** such an offering **3** alcoholic beverage [L *libare* pour]

li·bel /lī'bəl/ *n.* **1** *Law.* a published false statement damaging to a person's reputation **b** act of publishing this —*v.* (**·beled** or **·belled, ·bel·ing** or **·bel·ling**) **2** defame by libelous statements —**li'bel·ous** or **li'bel·lous** *adj.* [L *libellus*, dim. of *liber* book]

lib·er·al /lib'(ə)rəl/ *adj.* **1** abundant; ample **2** generous **3** open-minded **4** not strict or rigorous **5** broadening (*liberal studies*) **6** favoring political and social reform —*n.* **7** person of liberal views —**lib'er·al·ism, lib'er·al'i·ty** /-al'ətē/ *n.*; **lib'er·al·ly** *adv.* [L *liber* free]

liberal arts *n. pl.* literary, artistic, and historical subjects as a course of study

lib·er·al·ize /lib'(ə)rəlīz'/ *v.* (**·ized, ·iz·ing**) make or become liberal —**lib'er·al·i·za'tion** *n.*

lib·er·ate /lib'ərāt'/ *v.* (**·at·ed, ·at·ing**) set free —**lib'er·a'tion, lib'er·a·tor** *n.* [L *liberare, liberat-* free]

Li·be·ri·a /lībēr'ēə/ *n.* republic in W Africa on the Atlantic Ocean, founded in 1822 by freed American slaves. Capital: Monrovia. Pop. 2,780,000 —**Li·be'ri·an** *n. & adj.*

lib·er·tar·i·an /lib'ərtār'ēən/ *n.* **1** person favoring individual freedoms —*adj.* **2** reflecting such views

lib·er·tine /lib'ərtēn'/ *n.* **1** sexually promiscuous person —*adj.* **2** licentious [L: freedman]

lib·er·ty /lib'ərtē/ *n.* (*pl.* **·ties**) **1** freedom from captivity, bondage, etc. **2** freedom to do as one pleases **3** free time from duties for a sailor in the navy **4 at liberty:** **a** free **b** permitted **5 take liberties** behave in an unduly familiar manner [L *liber* free]

li·bid·i·nous /libid'n-əs/ *adj.* lustful [L, rel. to LIBIDO]

li·bi·do /labēd'ō, lib'ədō'/ *n.* (*pl.* **·dos**) psychic drive or energy, esp. that associated with sexual desire —**li·bid·i·nal** /labid'n-əl/ *adj.* [L: lust]

Li·bra /lē'brə/ *n.* **1** constellation and seventh sign of the zodiac (the Scales) **2** person born under this sign [L: pair of scales]

li·brar·i·an /lībrer'ēən/ *n.* person in charge of or assisting in a library —**li·brar'i·an·ship** *n.*

li·brar·y /lī'brer'ē/ *n.* (*pl.* **·ies**) **1a** collection of books **b** place where these are kept **2a** collection of films, records, computer routines, etc. **b** place where these are kept [L *liber* book]

● Usage: Avoid the pronunciation "lie-berry," which many regard as unacceptable.

li·bret·to /labret'ō/ *n.* (*pl.* **·ti** /-tē/ or **·tos**) text of an opera, etc. —**li·bret′tist** *n*. [It: little book]

Li·bre·ville /lĕ′brəvĭl/ *n*. capital of Gabon. Pop. 352,000

Lib·y·a /lĭb′ēə/ *n*. republic in N Africa, W of Egypt. Capital: Tripoli. Pop. 4,447,000 —**Lib′y·an** *n*. & *adj*.

lice /līs/ *n. pl.* of LOUSE

li·cense /lī′səns/ *n*. **1** official permit or permission to own or use something, do something, or carry on a trade **2** liberty of action, esp. when excessive **3** deviation from fact, correct grammar, etc. (*poetic license*) —*v*. (·**censed**, ·**cens·ing**) **4** grant a license to **5** authorize [L *licere* be allowed]

li·cen·see /lī′sənsē′/ *n*. holder of a license

li·cen·ti·ate /līsen′SHēət/ *n*. holder of a professional license [MedL *licentiare* authorize]

li·cen·tious /līsen′SHəs/ *adj*. sexually promiscuous [L *licentiosus* unrestrained]

li·chee /lē′CHē/ *n*. (also **li′chee nut′**) var. of LITCHI

li·chen /lī′kən/ *n*. plant composed of a fungus and an alga, growing on rocks, tree trunks, etc. [Gk *leichēn*]

lic·it /lĭs′ĭt/ *adj*. permitted; lawful —**lic′it·ly** *adv*. [L *licitus*]

lick /lĭk/ *v*. **1** pass the tongue over **2** bring into a specified condition by licking (*licked it clean*) **3** (of a flame, etc.) play lightly over **4** *Colloq*. defeat **5** *Colloq*. thrash —*n*. **6** act of licking with the tongue **7** small amount (*not a lick of work*) **8 lick a person's boots** be servile **9 lick one's lips** (or **chops**) look forward with relish **10 lick and a promise** *Colloq*. hasty performance of a task [OE]

lick′ing *n*. beating

lic·o·rice /lĭk′(ə)rĭSH, -rəs/ *n*. **1** black root extract used in medicine and candy **2** plant yielding this [Gk *glykys* sweet + *rhiza* root]

lid /lĭd/ *n*. **1** hinged or removable cover, esp. for a container **2** EYELID **3 put the lid on** *Colloq*. put a stop to —**lid′ded** *adj*. [OE]

lie¹ /lī/ *v*. (**lay, ly·ing, lain**) **1** be in or assume a horizontal position **2** rest flat on a surface **3** be kept, remain, or be in a specified state or place (*lie hidden; lie to the south*) —*n*. **4** way, direction, or position in which a thing lies; lay [OE]

● Usage: See note at LAY¹.

lie² *n*. **1** intentionally false statement —*v*. (**lied, ly·ing**) **2** tell a lie or lies [OE]

Liech·ten·stein /lĭkH′tənSHtīn′, lĭk′tənstīn′/ *n*. principality in central Europe between Austria and Switzerland. Capital: Vaduz. Pop. 29,600 —**Liech′ten·stein′er** *n*. & *adj*.

lie′ de·tec′tor *n*. instrument that tests for certain physiological changes, used esp. to tell if a person is lying; polygraph

lief /lēf/ *adv*. as in **would** or **had as lief** soon; gladly; willingly [OE *leof* dear]

liege /lēj/ *adj*. **1** entitled to receive or bound to give feudal service or allegiance —*n*. **2** (**liege lord**) feudal superior **3** (usu. *pl.*) vassal; subject [OFr, prob. fr. Gmc]

Liège /lē-ezH′/ *n*. city in Belgium on the Meuse River. Pop. 194,600

lien /lēn, lē′ən/ *n. Law*. right to hold another's property until a debt is paid [L *ligare* bind]

lie′ of the land′ *n*. (also *Colloq*. **lay′ of the land′**) state of affairs

329

lieu /lōō/ *n*. as in **in lieu of** instead; in the place (of) [Fr fr. L *locus* place]

Lieut. *abbr*. Lieutenant

lieu·ten·ant /lōōten′ənt/ *n*. **1** *Milit.* **a** army officer next in rank below captain **b** naval officer next in rank below lieutenant commander **2** deputy —**lieu·ten′an·cy** *n*. (*pl.* ·**cies**) [MFr *lieu* place + *tenant* holding]

lieu·ten′ant colo′nel *n*. military officer ranking next below colonel

lieu·ten′ant gov′er·nor *n*. elected official ranking second to a governor

lieu·ten′ant jun′ior grade′ *n*. rank in the US Navy or Coast Guard above an ensign and below a lieutenant

life /līf/ *n*. (*pl.* **lives**) **1** capacity for growth, functional activity, and continual change until death **2** living things (*insect life*) **3** period of existence or during which life lasts; period from birth to the present or from the present to death **4a** state of existence as a living individual (*sacrificed their lives*) **b** living person (*many lives were lost*) **5a** individual's actions or fortunes; manner of existence (*start a new life*) **b** particular aspect of this (*private life*) **6** business and pleasures of the world (*in Paris you really see life*) **7** energy; liveliness (*full of life*) **8** biography **9** *Colloq*. life sentence of imprisonment [OE]

life′belt′ *n*. buoyant belt for keeping a person afloat

life′blood′ *n*. **1** blood, as being necessary to life **2** vital factor or influence

life′boat′ *n*. ship's small boat for use in emergency

life′bu′oy *n*. buoyant support for keeping a person afloat

life′guard′ *n*. expert swimmer employed to rescue bathers from drowning

life′ in·sur′ance *n*. insurance for a sum paid on the death of the insured

life′ jac′ket *n*. (also **life′ vest′**) buoyant jacket for keeping a person afloat

life′less *adj*. **1** dead **2** unconscious **3** lacking movement or vitality —**life′less·ly** *adv*.; **life′less·ness** *n*.

life′like′ *adj*. closely resembling life or the person or thing represented

life′line′ *n*. **1** rope used for life-saving **2** sole means of communication or transport

life′long′ *adj*. lasting a lifetime

life′ pre·serv′er *n*. any buoyant device, esp. a ring, for keeping a person afloat

lif′er *n. Slang*. person serving a life sentence

life′ sci′enc·es *n. pl.* biology and related subjects

life′-size′ *adj*. (also **-sized′**) of the same size as the person or thing represented

life′style′ *n*. way of life of a person or group

life′time′ *n*. **1** duration of a person's life **2** a long time

lift /lĭft/ *v*. **1** raise or remove to a higher position **2** go up; rise **3** remove (a barrier or restriction) **4** transport (supplies, troops, etc.) by air **5a** *Colloq*. steal **b** plagiarize (a passage of writing, etc.) —*n*. **6** lifting or being lifted **7** ride in another person's vehicle **8** upward pressure that air exerts on an airfoil **9** supporting or elevating influence; feeling of elation **10** *Brit*. elevator [ON, rel. to LOFT]

lift'-off' *n.* vertical take-off of a spacecraft or rocket

lig·a·ment /lig′əmənt/ *n.* band of tough fibrous tissue linking bones [L *ligare* bind]

lig·a·ture /lig′əCHər/ *n.* **1** tie; bandage **2** *Mus.* slur; tie **3** two or more letters joined, e.g., æ, fi **4** bond; thing that unites —*v.* (·tured, ·tur·ing) **5** bind or connect with a ligature [L *ligare* bind]

light¹ /līt/ *n.* **1** the electromagnetic radiation that stimulates sight and makes things visible **2** radiation not visible by the unaided eye (*infrared light; ultraviolet light*) **3** source of light, e.g., the sun, fire, etc. **4** (often *pl.*) traffic-light **5a** flame or spark serving to ignite **b** device producing this **6** aspect in which a thing is regarded (*seen in a new light*) **7** mental or spiritual revelation (*see the light*) **8** public knowledge (*bring to light*) **9** eminent person (*leading light*) **10** window or opening in a wall to let light in —*v.* (**light·ed** or **lit, light·ing**) **11** ignite **12** (often foll. by *up*) provide with light or lighting; make or become prominent by means of light **13** (usu. foll. by *up*) brighten with animation, pleasure, etc. —*adj.* **14** well-provided with light; not dark **15** (of a color) pale (*light blue*) **16** bring (or come) to light reveal (or be revealed) **17** in a good (or bad) light giving a favorable (or unfavorable) impression **18 in (the) light of** taking account of **19 light up** *Colloq.* begin to smoke a cigarette, etc. [OE]

light² *adj.* **1** not heavy **2** relatively low in weight, amount, density, intensity, etc. (*light arms, traffic, metal, rain*) **3** carrying or suitable for small loads (*light truck*) **4** (of food) easy to digest **5** (of entertainment, music, etc.) intended for amusement only; not profound **6** (of sleep or a sleeper) easily disturbed **7** easily borne or done (*light duties*) **8** nimble; quick-moving (*light step*) **9a** unburdened (*light heart*) **b** giddy (*light in the head*) **10** making small products (*light manufacturing*) —*adv.* **11** in a light manner (*sleep light*) **12** with a minimum load (*travel light*) —*v.* (**light·ed** or **lit, light·ing**) **13** (foll. by *on, upon*) come upon by chance **14 make light of** treat as unimportant —**light′ish** *adj.*; **light′ly** *adv.*; **light′ness** *n.* [OE]

light·en¹ /līt′n/ *v.* **1** shed light on **2** make or grow bright

light·en² *v.* **1a** make or become lighter in weight **b** reduce the weight or load of **2** bring relief to (the mind, etc.) **3** reduce (a penalty)

ligh·ter¹ /līt′ər/ *n.* device for lighting a fire, etc.

ligh·ter² *n.* boat for transferring goods from a ship [ME fr. MDu, rel. to LIGHT¹ in the sense 'unload']

light′er-than-air′ *adj.* (of an aircraft) weighing less than the air it displaces

light′-fin′gered *adj.* given to stealing

light′-foot′ed *adj.* nimble

light′-head′ed *adj.* giddy; delirious —**light′-head′ed·ness** *n.*

light′-heart′ed *adj.* **1** cheerful **2** (unduly) casual —**light′-heart′ed·ly** *adv.*

light′ hea′vy·weight *n.* *Sports.* weight class for competitors; in professional boxing, includes fighters usu. up to 175 lbs.

light′house′ *n.* tower containing a beacon light to warn or guide ships at sea at night

light′ing *n.* equipment in a room, street, theater, etc., for producing light

light′ me′ter *n.* instrument for measuring light intensity, esp. for correct photographic exposure

light·ning /līt′ning/ *n.* **1** flash of bright light in the sky produced by discharge of electricity in the atmosphere between clouds and the ground —*adj.* **2** very quick [fr. LIGHTEN¹]

light′ning bug′ *n.* FIREFLY

light′ning-rod′ *n.* metal rod or wire fixed to a building to divert lightning

light′ship′ *n.* moored or anchored ship with a beacon light

light′weight′ *adj.* **1** of below average weight **2** of little importance or influence **3** *Colloq.* of below average intelligence —*n.* **4** *Sports.* weight class for competitors; in professional boxing, includes fighters up to 135 lbs.

light′year′ *n.* distance light travels in one year, nearly 6 trillion miles

lig·nite /lig′nīt′/ *n.* brown coal of woody texture

lik·a·ble /līk′əbəl/ *adj.* (also **like′a·ble**) pleasant; easy to like —**lik′a·bil′i·ty** or **like′a·bil′i·ty, lik′a·ble·ness** or **like′a·ble·ness** *n.*; **lik′a·bly** or **like′a·bly** *adv.*

like¹ /līk/ *adj.* **1** having some or all of the qualities —*prep.* **2** characteristic of (*not like them to be late*) **3** in a suitable state or mood for (*felt like working*) **4** in the manner of; to the same degree as (*act like an idiot*) —*adv.* **5** indicative of **6** *Colloq.* so to speak (*did a quick getaway, like*) **7** *Colloq.* likely; probably (*as like as not*) —*conj. Colloq.* **8** as (*do it like you do*) **9** as if (*ate like they were starving*) —*n.* **10** counterpart; equal **11 and the like** and similar things **12 like anything** *Colloq.* very much; vigorously [ON]

• Usage: In standard English, *like*, which is a preposition, is used before nouns and pronouns: *She sings like a nightingale. A man like him was seen. Their car is like ours.* The terms *as, as if,* and *as though* are adverbs or conjunctions, and introduce clauses that contain a verb: *Do as I say, not as I do. He looks as if he wants to fight.* (*As* is also used in comparisons—*Their house is not as big as mine*—but that usage causes no problems.) The most common difficulty occurs when *like* is used for *as* or *as if*: "Do like I do" and "He looks like he wants to fight" are both colloquial uses that should be avoided in formal contexts.

like² *v.* (**liked, lik·ing**) **1** find agreeable or enjoyable **2a** choose to have; prefer **b** wish for (*would like a nap*) —*n.* (*pl.*) **3** things one prefers [OE]

-like *comb. form* forming adjectives from nouns, meaning 'similar to, characteristic of' (*doglike; shell-like*)

like·li·hood /līk′lēhŏŏd′/ *n.* probability

like·ly /līk′lē/ *adj.* (·li·er, ·li·est) **1** probable **2** reasonably expected (*likely to come*) **3** credible **4** suitable (*a likely spot for a picnic*) —*adv.* **5** probably [ON, rel. to LIKE¹]

like′-mind′ed *adj.* having the same tastes, opinions, etc. —**like′mind′ed·ly** *adv.*; **like′ mind′ed·ness** *n.*

lik·en /līk′ən/ *v.* point out the resemblance of

like·ness /līk'nəs/ *n.* 1 resemblance 2 portrait; representation

like·wise /līk'wīz'/ *adv.* 1 also 2 similarly (*do likewise*)

lik·ing *n.* 1 what one likes; one's taste 2 regard or fondness; taste

li·lac /lī'lək, -lak, -läk'/ *n.* 1 shrub with fragrant pinkish-violet or white blossoms 2 pale pinkish-violet color —*adj.* 3 of this color [Pers]

Lille /lēl/ *n.* city in N France. Pop. 178,300

Lil·li·pu·tian /lil'əpyōō'sнən/ *n.* 1 diminutive person or thing —*adj.* 2 diminutive [*Lilliput* in SWIFT's *Gulliver's Travels*]

Li·long·we /lilong'wä/ *n.* administrative capital of Malawi. Pop. 223,300. See also ZOMBA

lilt /lilt/ *n.* 1 light springing rhythm 2 tune with this —*v.* 3 speak, etc., in a lilting way [ME]

lil·y /lil'ē/ *n.* (*pl. ·ies*) 1 plant with trumpet-shaped flowers on a tall stem 2 similar plant, as water lily 3 fleur-de-lis [L *lilium*]

lil'y-liv'ered *adj.* cowardly

lil'y of the val'ley *n.* plant with white bell-shaped fragrant flowers

Li·ma /lē'mə/ *n.* capital of Peru. Pop. 421,600

li'ma bean' /lī'mə/ *n.* plant with broad, flat, edible seed [LIMA, Peru]

limb¹ /lim/ *n.* 1 arm, leg, or wing 2 large branch of a tree 3 out on a limb precariously isolated [OE]

limb² *n.* edge of the sun, moon, etc. [L *limbus* border]

lim·ber /lim'bər/ *adj.* 1 lithe 2 flexible —*v.* (usu. foll. by *up*) 3 make or become limber

lim·bo¹ /lim'bō/ *n.* (*pl. ·bos*) 1 (sometimes *cap.*) (in some Christian beliefs) abode of the souls of unbaptized infants, and of the just who died before Christ 2 intermediate state or condition [L: border; edge]

lim·bo² *n.* (*pl. ·bos*) W Indian dance in which the dancer bends backwards to pass under a horizontal bar that is progressively lowered [WInd word, perh. rel. to LIMBER]

lime¹ /līm/ *n.* 1 white substance (calcium oxide) obtained by heating limestone; quicklime 2 calcium hydroxide obtained by reacting quicklime with water, used as a fertilizer and in mortar; slaked lime —*v.* (**limed, lim·ing**) 3 treat with lime —**lim'y** *adj.* (**·i·er, ·i·est**) [OE]

lime² *n.* 1a citrus fruit like a lemon but green, rounder, smaller, and more acid b tree which produces this fruit 2 yellowish-green color [Sp fr. Pers *limun*]

lime'light' *n.* 1 intense white light used formerly in theaters 2 glare of publicity

lim·er·ick /lim'ərik/ *n.* humorous five-line verse with a rhyme-scheme *aabba*

lime'stone' *n.* rock composed mainly of calcium carbonate

Lim·ey /lī'mē/ *n.* (*pl. ·eys*) *Slang. Offens.* British person (orig. a sailor) [fr. LIME², for former enforced consumption of lime juice in the Brit. Navy]

lim·it /lim'ət/ *n.* 1 point, line, or level beyond which something does not or may not extend 2 greatest or smallest amount permissible —*v.* 3 set or serve as a limit to —**lim'i·ta'tion** /-tā'sнən/, **lim'it·er** *n.*; **lim'it·less** *adj.* [L *limes, limit-* boundary]

---

likeness / lineal

lim'it·ed *adj.* 1 confined 2 (of a conveyance) making few stops

lim·o /lim'ō/ *n.* (*pl. ·os*) *Colloq.* limousine

Li·moges /lēmōzн'/ *n.* city in France. Pop. 136,400

lim·ou·sine /lim'əzēn', lim'əzēn/ *n.* spacious usu. luxurious car, esp. with a chauffeur [Fr]

limp¹ /limp/ *v.* 1 walk lamely or awkwardly —*n.* 2 lame walk [perh. ME *lympen* or back formation fr. obs. *limphault*]

limp² *adj.* 1 not stiff or firm 2 without energy or will —**limp'ly** *adv.*; **limp'ness** *n.* [prob. rel. to LIMP¹]

lim·pet /lim'pit/ *n.* marine gastropod that sticks tightly to rocks [OE]

lim·pid /lim'pid/ *adj.* clear; transparent —**lim·pid'i·ty** /-pid'itī/ *n.*; **lim'pid·ly** *adv.* [L]

lin·age /lī'nij/ *n.* number of lines in printed or written matter

linch·pin /lincн'pin'/ *n.* pin through the end of an axle to keep a wheel on [OE *lynis* axletree]

Lin·coln /ling'kən/ *n.* capital of Nebr., in the SE part. Pop. 191,972

Lin·coln /ling'kən/, **Abraham** 1809–65; 16th US president (1861–65); assassinated

Lind·bergh /lin(d)'bərg/, **Charles** 1902–74; US aviator

lin·den /lin'dən/ *n.* tree with heart-shaped leaves and fragrant creamy blossom [OE]

Lind·say /lin(d)'zē/, **(Nicholas) Vachel** 1879–1931; US poet

line¹ /līn/ *n.* 1 continuous mark on a surface 2 straight or curved continuous extent of length without breadth; track of a moving point 3 contour or outline 4 limit or boundary 5 row of persons or things, as of printed or written words 6 portion of verse written in one line 7 (*pl.*) words of an actor's part 8 short letter or note 9 cord, rope, etc. 10a wire or cable for a telephone or telegraph b connection by means of this c channel of communication 11 branch or route of a railway system or an entire system under one management 12a regular succession of buses, ships, aircraft, etc., plying between certain places b company conducting this 13 lineage 14 course or manner of procedure, conduct, thought, etc. 15 business or occupation 16 specific design of a product 17 arrangement of soldiers or ships side by side, esp. that closest to the enemy 18 *Football.* players on the line of scrimmage —*v.* (**lined, lin·ing**) 19 mark with lines 20 stand at intervals along (*crowds lined the route*) 21 bring into line make conform 22 draw the line set a limit 23 in line for likely to receive 24 in (or out of) line in (or not in) accordance with 25 line up: a arrange or be arranged in a line or lines b have ready 26 out of line: a not aligned b inappropriate [L *linea* fr. *linum* flax]

line² *v.* (**lined, lin·ing**) cover the inside surface of (a garment, box, etc.) [ME *line* linen, fr. L *linum* flax]

lin·e·age /lin'ē·ij/ *n.* lineal descent; ancestry [OFr fr. VL, rel. to LINE¹]

lin·e·al /lin'ēəl/ *adj.* 1 in the direct line of

descent or ancestry 2 linear —**lin′e·al·ly** adv.

lin·e·a·ment /lin′ēəmənt/ n. (usu. pl.) distinctive characteristic, esp. of the face [L, rel. to LINE[1]]

lin·e·ar /lin′ēər/ adj. 1 of or in lines 2 long and narrow and of uniform breadth —**lin′e·ar′i·ty** /-ar′ətē/ n.; **lin′e·ar·ly** adv.

line·back·er /līn′bak′ər/ n. Football. defensive player positioned behind the line

line′ drive′ n. Baseball. ball struck hard enough to move with a low trajectory

line′ i′tem n. single entry in an accounting ledger, government budget, etc.

line·man /līn′mən/ n. (pl. ·men) 1 person who installs or repairs telephone or power lines 2 Football. player on the line of scrimmage

lin·en /lin′ən/ n. 1 cloth woven from flax 2 (collect.) sheets, shirts, underwear, etc. —adj. 3 made of linen [OE, rel. to L linum flax]

lin′en clos′et n. closet for sheets, towels, table linens, etc.

line′ of scrim′mage n. Football. line along which a play begins

line′ print′er n. machine that prints output from a computer a line at a time

lin·er[1] /līn′ər/ n. ship, aircraft, etc., carrying passengers on a regular line

lin·er[2] n. 1 removable lining 2 EYELINER

lin′er notes′ n. printed information packaged with records, cassette tapes, and compact disks

lines·man /līnz′mən/ n. (pl. ·men) 1 Tennis. official who decides whether a ball has fallen within the playing area or not 2 Football. official who marks yardage gained or lost

line′-up′ n. 1 line of people 2 list of players for a game

-ling suffix denoting a diminutive (duckling), often derogatory (lordling) [OE]

lin·ger /liNG′gər/ v. 1 loiter 2 dally (linger over dinner) 3 continue past its expected end [OE lengan, rel. to LONG[1]]

lin·ge·rie /län′jərā′, län′zHə-, -rē′/ n. women's underwear and nightclothes [MFr linge linen, fr. L lineus flax]

lin·go /liNG′gō/ n. (pl. ·gos or ·goes) Colloq. 1 foreign language 2 vocabulary of a special subject or group [prob. fr. Port lingoa fr. L lingua language]

lin·gua fran·ca /liNG′gwə fraNG′kə/ n. (pl. lin·gua fran·cas) language used in common by speakers with different native languages [It: Frankish tongue]

lin·gual /liNG′gwəl/ adj. 1 of or formed by the tongue 2 of languages —**lin′gual·ly** adv. [L lingua tongue; language]

lin·guist /liNG′gwist/ n. 1 person who speaks several languages 2 linguistics scholar

lin·guis·tic /liNG-gwis′tik/ adj. of language or the study of languages —**lin·guis′ti·cal·ly** adv.

lin·guis′tics n. the study of language and its structure

lin·i·ment /lin′əmənt/ n. medication for rubbing on the skin [L linere smear]

lin·ing /lī′niNG/ n. material for covering an inside surface

link /liNGk/ n. 1 loop or ring of a chain 2a

connecting part; one in a series b state or means of connection 3 cuff link —v. 4 connect or join [ON hlekkr link, or ODan lænka chain]

link·age /liNG′kij/ n. 1 linking or being linked 2 system of links

link′ing verb′ n. verb used between a subject and a predicate, e.g., seem, appear; copula

links /liNGks/ n. pl. golf course [OE: rising ground]

link′up′ n. act or result of linking up

Lin·nae·us /lənē′əs, -nā′-/, **Carolus** 1707–78; Swedish botanist —**Lin·nae′an, Lin·ne′an** /-nē′ən/ adj.

lin·net /lin′it/ n. brown-gray finch [MFr linette fr. L lin flax, because it eats flaxseed]

li·no·le·um /lənō′lēəm/ n. canvas-backed material coated with linseed oil, powdered cork, etc., esp. as a floor covering [L lin flax + oleum oil]

lin·seed /lin′sēd/ n. seed of flax [OE, rel. to LINE[1]]

lin′seed oil′ n. oil extracted from linseed and used in paint and varnish

lint /lint/ n. fluff [perh. fr. MFr linette fr. lin flax]

lin·tel /lint′l/ n. horizontal crosspiece over the top of a door or window [MFr, rel. to LIMIT]

Linz /lins/ n. port in Austria on the Danube River. Pop. 202,900

li·on /lī′ən/ n. 1 (fem. li′on·ess) large tawny flesh-eating wild cat of Africa and S Asia 2 (the Li′on) zodiacal sign or constellation Leo 3 brave or celebrated person [L leo fr. Gk]

li′on·heart′ed n. courageous

li′on·ize′ v. (·ized, ·iz·ing) treat as a celebrity

li′on′s share′ n. largest or best part

lip /lip/ n. 1 either of the two fleshy parts forming the edges of the mouth-opening 2 edge of a vessel, etc. 3 Colloq. impudent talk 4 **lip′ ser′vice** token but insincere support [OE]

lip′ gloss′ n. cosmetic, either clear or lightly tinted, to give shine to lips

lip·id /lip′id/ n. any of a group of fatlike substances, including fatty acids, oils, waxes, and steroids [Gk lipos fat]

li·po·suc·tion /lī′pəsək′sHən, lip′ə-/ n. removal of excess fat from under the skin by suction

lip·o·trop·ic /lip′ətrō′pik, -träp′ik/ adj. having an affinity for lipids, thus preventing fat buildup in the liver

lip·o·tro·pin /lip′ətrō′pin, -träp′in/ n. Physiol. pituitary hormone that stimulates the release of fat from tissue

lip·read /lip′ rēd′/ v. understand (speech) from observing a speaker's lip-movements —**lip′read′er, lip′read′ing** n.

lip′stick′ n. stick of cosmetic for coloring the lips

lip-synch /lip′siNGk′/ v. (also **lip′-sync′**) synchronize lip movements to recorded sound to appear to be singing or talking

liq·ue·fy /lik′wəfī′/ v. (·fied, ·fy·ing) make or become liquid —**liq′ue·fac′tion** /-fak′sHən/ n.

li·queur /likər', -k(y)ŏōr'/ *n.* any of several sweet alcoholic beverages [Fr]

liq·uid /lik'wid/ *adj.* **1** having a consistency like that of water or oil **2** (of sounds) clear and flowing **3** (of assets) easily converted into cash —*n.* **4** liquid substance **5** *Phonet.* sound of *l* or *r* —**li·quid'i·ty** -wid'itē/ *n.* [L *liquere* be liquid]

liq·ui·date /lik'widāt'/ *v.* (·dat·ed, ·dat·ing) **1** close out the affairs of (a business) by paying debts and distributing assets **2** pay (a debt) **3** convert into cash **4** kill —**liq'ui·da'tion, liq'ui·da'tor** *n.* [LL, rel. to LIQUID]

liq·uid·ize /lik'widīz'/ *v.* (·ized, ·iz·ing) reduce to a liquid state —**liq'uid·iz'er** *n.*

liq·uor /lik'ər/ *n.* **1** alcoholic (esp. distilled) drink **2** other liquid, esp. that produced in cooking [L: liquid]

li·ra /lēr'ə/ *n.* (*pl.* **li·re** or **li·ras**) **1** monetary unit of Italy **2** monetary unit of Turkey [L *libra* pound]

Lis·bon /liz'bən/ *n.* capital of Portugal. Pop. 677,800

lisle /līl/ *n.* fine cotton thread for stockings, etc. [*Lisle* (now LILLE), France]

lisp /lisp/ *n.* **1** speech in which *s* is pronounced like *th* in *thick* and *z* is pronounced like *th* in *this* —*v.* **2** speak or utter with a lisp [OE]

lis·some /lis'əm/ *adj.* (also **lis'som**) lithe; agile [ult. fr. LITHE]

list[1] /list/ *n.* **1** number of items, names, etc., written or printed together as a record —*v.* **2** make a list of **3** enter in a list [Fr fr. It fr. Gmc]

list[2] *v.* **1** (of a ship, etc.) lean over to one side —*n.* **2** process or instance of listing

lis·ten /lis'ən/ *v.* **1** make an effort to hear **2** take notice of; heed —**lis'ten·er** *n.* [OE]

Lis·ter /lis'tər/, **Joseph** 1827–1912; English surgeon; developer of antiseptic surgery

list·less /list'ləs/ *adj.* lacking energy or enthusiasm —**list'less·ly** *adv.*; **list'less·ness** *n.* [ME, fr. obs. *list* inclination]

list' price' *n.* price of something as shown in a published list

Liszt /list/, **Franz** 1811–86; Hungarian composer

lit /lit/ *v.* past and past part. of LIGHT[1] and LIGHT[2]

lit·a·ny /lit'n-ē/ *n.* (*pl.* ·nies) **1** series of supplications to God with set responses **2** tedious recital [Gk *litaneia* prayer]

li·tchi /lē'CHē'/ *n.* (also **li'tchi nut; li'chee, ly'chee**) (*pl.* -s) **1** sweet white (or brown when dried) fruit in a brown skin **2** tree bearing this [Chin]

Lit.D. (also **Litt.D.**) *abbr.* Doctor of Letters [L *Litterarum Doctor*]

lite /līt/ *adj.* var. of LIGHT

li·ter /lēt'ər/ *n.* measure of capacity, a metric unit equal to 1.0567 quarts [Fr fr. Gk *litra*]

lit·er·a·cy /lit'ərəsē/ *n.* ability to read and write [L, rel. to LITERATE]

lit·er·al /lit'ərəl/ *adj.* **1** taking words in their basic sense without metaphor or allegory **2** corresponding exactly to the original wording (*literal translation*) **3** prosaic; matter-of-fact **4** so called without exaggeration (*literal bankruptcy*) **5** of a letter of the alphabet —**lit'er·al·ly** *adv.* [L *littera* letter]

● Usage: There is no dispute over the meaning of *literally*: it means 'not figuratively.' Yet,

out of exaggeration, some speakers persist in saying (or writing) things like, *We were literally frying in the 100-degree heat.*

lit·er·ary /lit'ərer'ē/ *adj.* **1** of or concerned with literature **2** (of a word or phrase) formal **3** knowledgeable about literature —**lit'er·ar·i·ness** *n.*

lit·er·ate /lit'ərət/ *adj.* **1** able to read and write; educated —*n.* **2** literate person [L *literatus* learned; scholarly]

li·te·ra·ti /lit'ərä'tē/ *n. pl.* learned people

lit·er·a·ture /lit'ərəCHər/ *n.* **1** written works, esp. those valued for form and style **2** writings of a country or period or on a particular subject **3** *Colloq.* printed matter, leaflets, etc.

lithe /līтН/ *adj.* flexible; supple [OE]

lith·i·um /liтн'ēəm/ *n.* soft silver-white metallic element; *symb.* Li [Gk *lithion* fr. *lithos* stone]

lith·o·graph /liтн'əgraf'/ *n.* **1** lithographic print —*v.* **2** print by lithography —**li·thog'ra·pher** /-тНäg'rəfər/ *n.* [Gk *lithos* stone + -GRAPHY]

li·thog·ra·phy /liтНäg'rəfē/ *n.* process of printing from a plate so treated that ink adheres only to the design to be printed —**lith'o·graph'ic** /-əgraf'ik/ *adj.*; **lith·o·graph'i·cal·ly** *adv.*

Lith·u·a·ni·a /liтн'əwä'nēə/ *n.* republic in E Europe, on the Baltic Sea; formerly part of the USSR. Capital: Vilnius. Pop. 3,801,000

Lith·u·a·ni·an /liтн'(y)ōō-ä'nēən/ *n.* **1** language of Lithuania **2** native or national of Lithuania —*adj.* **3** of Lithuania, its people, or language

lit·i·gant /lit'əgənt/ *n.* party to a lawsuit [L *litigare* go to law]

lit·i·gate /lit'əgāt'/ *v.* (·gat·ed, ·gat·ing) pursue by means of the law —**lit'i·ga'tion, lit'i·ga'tor** *n.* [L *litigare* go to law]

li·ti·gious /litij'əs/ *adj.* **1** fond of litigation **2** quarrelsome [L, rel. to LITIGATE]

lit·mus /lit'məs/ *n.* dye from lichens, turned red by acid and blue by alkali [ON: dye-moss]

lit'mus pa'per *n.* paper stained with litmus, used to test for acids or alkalis

lit'mus test' *n. Colloq.* real or practical test

li·tre /lēt'ər/ *n. Brit.* LITER

lit·ter /lit'ər/ *n.* **1a** refuse, esp. scraps of paper; rubbish **b** odds and ends lying about **2** young animals brought forth at one birth **3** vehicle containing a couch and carried on people's shoulders or by animals **4** stretcher for the sick and wounded **5** straw, etc., as bedding for animals **6** granulated material for a cat's waste —*v.* **7** make (a place) untidy with refuse **8** scatter carelessly [L *lectus* bed]

lit·ter·bug /lit'ərbəg'/ *n. Colloq.* person who drops litter in public places

lit·tle /lit'l/ *adj.* (**lit·tler, lit·tlest;** *less* or *les·ser, least*) **1** small in size, amount, degree, etc. **2a** short in stature **b** of short distance or duration **3** trivial (*every little thing*) **4** petty (*a little mind*) **5** young or younger (*little boy; my little sister*) —*n.* **6** not much; only a small amount (*little does she know*) **7a** a certain but no great amount (*knows a little of everything*) **b** short time or distance (*after a little*) —*adv.* (**less, least**) **8** to a small extent only (*little more than speculation*) **9** not at all; hardly **10** somewhat (*is a little deaf*) **11 little by little** gradually [OE]

Lit'tle Bear' *n.* BEAR[2]

Lit·tle Rock /lit'l räk'/ *n.* capital of Ark., in the central part. Pop. 175,795

lit'tle slam' *n. Bridge.* the taking of twelve of the thirteen tricks available

lit·to·ral /lit'ərəl/ *adj.* **1** of or on the shore —*n.* **2** region lying along a shore [L *litus, litor-* shore]

lit·ur·gy /lit'ərjē/ *n.* (*pl.* **-gies**) prescribed form of public worship —**li·tur'gi·cal** /-tər'jikəl/ *adj.*; **li·tur'gi·cal·ly** *adv.* [Gk *leitourgia* public worship]

liv·a·ble /liv'əbəl/ *adj.* (also **live'a·ble**) **1** *Colloq.* (of a dwelling) fit to live in **2** (of a life) worth living

live[1] /liv/ *v.* (**lived, liv·ing**) **1** have life; be or remain alive **2** have one's home (*lives up the road*) **3** feed or subsist (*lives on fruit; lives on a pension*) **4** conduct oneself in a specified way (*live quietly*) **5** survive; endure **6** enjoy life to the full (*not really living*) **7 live down** cause (guilt, a scandal, etc.) to be forgotten by blameless conduct **8 live for** regard as one's life's purpose (*lives for her music*) **9 live it up** *Colloq.* live gaily and extravagantly **10 live up to** fulfill **11 live with: a** share a home with **b** tolerate [OE]

live[2] /līv/ *adj.* **1** that is alive; living **2** (of a broadcast, performance, etc.) heard, seen, or recorded at the time of its performance **3** of current importance (*a live issue*) **4** glowing (*live coals*) **5** (of a bomb, etc.) not yet exploded **6** (of a wire, etc.) carrying electricity —*adv.* **7** *Sports.* actively in play **8** to make a live broadcast (*we go live now to the White House*) **9** as a live performance, etc. (*show went out live*)

live·a·ble /līv'əbəl/ *adj.* var. of LIVABLE

lived-in /livd'in'/ *adj.* showing signs of habitation

live·li·hood /līv'lēhŏŏd'/ *n.* means of living; job; income [OE]

live·long /liv'lông'/ *adj.* entire (*the livelong day*) [ME *leve longe* fr. obs. *lief*]

live·ly /līv'lē/ *adj.* (**-li·er, -li·est**) **1** full of life; energetic **2** vivid (*lively imagination*) **3** cheerful —**live'li·ness** *n.* [OE]

liv·en /lī'vən/ *v.* (often foll. by *up*) *Colloq.* make or become lively; cheer up

liv·er /liv'ər/ *n.* **1** large glandular organ in the abdomen of vertebrates **2** liver of some animals as food [OE]

Liv·er·pool /liv'ərpool'/ *n.* seaport in England. Pop. 544,900 —**Liv·er·pud·li·an** /liv'ərpəd'lēən/ *n. & adj.*

liv'er spot' *n.* brownish pigmentation on the skin, esp. of older people

liv·er·wurst /liv'ərwərst'/ *n.* sausage of ground liver [Ger *Leberwurst*]

liv·er·y /liv'(ə)rē/ *n.* (*pl.* **-er·ies**) **1** distinctive uniform of a servant **2** maintenance of horses as a business **3** hiring out of horses or vehicles [OFr *livree* fr. L *liberare*, rel. to LIBERATE]

lives /līvz/ *n. pl.* of LIFE

live·stock /līv'stäk'/ *n.* (usu. treated as *pl.*) farm animals kept for use or sale

liv·id /liv'id/ *adj.* **1** of abnormal color (*livid*

with rage) **2** of a bluish leaden color (*livid bruise*) [L]

liv·ing /liv'iNG/ *n.* **1** being alive **2** livelihood **3** enjoyment of life —*adj.* **4** contemporary; now alive **5** (of a likeness) exact; lifelike **6** (of a language) still in use

liv'ing room' *n.* room in a residence for social activity

Liv·ing·stone /liv'iNGstən/, **David** 1813–73; Scottish missionary and explorer

liv'ing wage' *n.* wage on which one can live comfortably

liv'ing will' *n.* document in which a person requests that no extraordinary means, such as life support machines, be used to prolong his or her life

Li·vo·ni·a /livō'nēə/ *n.* city in Mich., near Detroit. Pop. 100,850

Li·vor·no /lēvôr'nō/ *n.* see LEGHORN

Liv·y /liv'ē/ (Latin name **Titus Livius**) 59 B.C.–A.D. 17; Roman historian

liz·ard /liz'ərd/ *n.* slender reptile with usu. a tail, four legs, and a rough or scaly hide [L *lacerta*]

Lju·blja·na /l(y)oo͞'blē-än'ə/ *n.* capital of Slovenia. Pop. 323,300

'll *v. contr.* shall; will (*I'll; that'll*)

LLAMA

lla·ma /läm'ə/ *n.* S American ruminant kept as a beast of burden and for its soft woolly fleece [Sp fr. Quechua]

lla·no /lä'nō/ *n.* grassy plain of the southwestern US and Latin America

Lla·no Es·ta·ca·do /län'ō es'təkäd'ō/ *n.* (also called **Staked' Plain'**) large plateau in W Texas and SE N. Mex.

LL.B. *abbr.* Bachelor of Laws [L *Legum Baccalaureus*]

LL.D. *abbr.* Doctor of Laws [L *Legum Doctor*]

Lloyd George /loid' jôrj'/, **David** 1863–1945; prime minister of Great Britain (1916–22)

Lloyd Web·ber /loid' web'ər/, **(Sir) Andrew** 1948– ; English composer

lo /lō/ *interj. Archaic.* look [OE]

load /lōd/ *n.* **1** what is carried or to be carried at one time **2** burden or commitment of work, responsibility, etc. **3** *Colloq.* **a** (*pl.*) plenty; a lot (*loads of money, people*) **b** a quantity (*a load of nonsense*) **4** amount of power carried by an electric circuit —*v.* **5** charge added to price of shares in a mutual fund for profit and expenses **6** put a load on or aboard **7** (of a vehicle or person) take a load aboard **8** overburden; overwhelm **9a** put ammunition in (a gun), film in (a camera), a cassette in (a tape recorder), a program in (a computer), etc. **b** put (a film, cassette, etc.) into a device —**load'er, load'ing** n. [OE: course; carrying]

load·ed /lōd'id/ *adj.* **1** *Slang.* **a** rich **b** drunk **c** drugged **2** (of dice) weighted **3** (of a question or statement) carrying hidden implication

load·stone /lōd'stōn'/ *n.* var. of LODESTONE

loaf[1] /lōf/ *n.* (*pl.* **loaves**) **1** unit of baked bread **2** other food made in the shape of a loaf and cooked [OE]

loaf[2] *v.* spend time idly [back formation fr. LOAFER]

loaf'er *n.* **1** idle person **2** moccasin-like leather shoe [perh. fr. Ger *Landläufer*]

loam /lōm/ *n.* rich soil of clay, sand, and humus —**loam·y** (·**i·er**, ·**i·est**) *adj.* [OE]

loan /lōn/ *n.* **1** thing lent, esp. money **2** lending or being lent —*v.* **3** lend [OE fr. ON]

● Usage: Traditionally, *loan* was used as a noun and *lend* as a verb: *We went to the bank for a loan. Can you lend me five dollars?* But *loan* has come to be used as a verb, especially but not necessarily when referring to financial matters.

loan' shark' *n. Colloq.* person who lends money at usurious rates of interest

loath /lōTH, lōTH/ *adj.* disinclined; reluctant (*loath to admit it*) [OE]

loathe /lōTH/ *v.* (**loathed, loath·ing**) detest; hate —**loath'ing** *n.* [OE]

loath·some /lōTH'səm, lōTH-/ *adj.* arousing hatred or disgust; repulsive —**loath'some·ness** *n.*

loaves /lōvz/ *n. pl.* of LOAF[1]

lob /läb/ *v.* (**lobbed, lob·bing**) **1** hit or throw (a ball, etc.) slowly or in a high arc —*n.* **2** such a ball [OE: spider, perh. fr. MLGer or MDu]

lob·by /läb'ē/ *n.* (*pl.* **·bies**) **1** entrance hall **2** body of lobbyists —*v.* (**·bied, ·by·ing**) **3** solicit the support of (an influential person) **4** act as a lobbyist [OHGer *lauba* arbor, or perh. LL *lobia* lodge]

lob'by·ist *n.* person who lobbies legislators, esp. professionally

lobe /lōb/ *n.* **1** lower soft pendulous part of the outer ear **2** similar part of other organs, esp. the brain, liver, and lung —**lo·bar** /lō'bär/, **lo·bate** /lō'bāt/, **lobed** *adj.* [Gk *lobos* lobe; pod]

lo·bot·o·my /ləbät'əmē/ *n.* (*pl.* **·mies**) incision into the frontal lobe of the brain, formerly used in some cases of mental disorder [fr. LOBE]

lob·ster /läb'stər/ *n.* edible marine crustacean with two pincerlike claws [OE]

lo·cal /lō'kəl/ *adj.* **1** belonging to, existing in, or peculiar to a particular place (*local history*) **2** of or affecting only a part **3** (of a train, bus, etc.) stopping at all stations on its route —*n.* **4** local train, bus, etc. **5** inhabitant of a particular place —**lo'cal·ly** *adv.* [L *locus* place]

lo'cal ar'e·a net'work *n.* system for linking telecommunications or computer equipment in several offices, a group of buildings, etc.; *abbr.* LAN

lo'cal col'or *n.* characteristics of a place and its inhabitants, esp. as presented in literature, etc.

lo·cale /lōkal'/ *n.* scene or locality of an event or occurrence [Fr]

lo·cal·i·ty /lōkal'ətē/ *n.* (*pl.* **·ties**) **1** district **2** site or scene of a thing

lo·cal·ize /lō'kəlīz'/ *v.* (**·ized, ·iz·ing**) restrict or assign to a particular place —**lo'cal·i·za'tion** *n.*

lo·cate /lō'kāt', lōkāt'/ *v.* (**·cat·ed, ·cat·ing**) **1** discover the place of **2** establish in a place; situate [L *locare* place]

● Usage: *Locate* properly means 'set the position of': *The corral should be located near the pasture.* It is useful to distinguish between *locate* and *find* (*They found the child wandering in the shopping center.*)

lo·ca'tion *n.* **1** place **2** locating **3 on location** *Film.* in a natural, not studio setting

loc. cit. *abbr.* in the place cited [L *loco citato*]

loch /läk, läkн/ *n.* lake or narrow inlet of the sea [ScotGael & OIr]

Loch' Ness' /nes/ *n.* lake in NW Scotland

lo·ci /lō'sī', -kī', -kē/ *pl.* of LOCUS

lock[1] /läk/ *n.* **1** mechanism for fastening a door, box, etc., that requires a key or combination to open it **2** section of a canal or river within gates for raising or lowering the water level **3** mechanism for exploding the charge of a gun —*v.* **4** fasten or shut up with or as with a lock **5** (foll. by *up*) imprison (a person) **6** make or become rigidly fixed **7** (cause to) jam or catch **8** link; interlock —**lock'a·ble** *adj.* [OE]

lock[2] *n.* **1** curl or tress of hair **2** (*pl.*) the hair of the head (*golden locks*) [OE]

Locke /läk/, **John** 1632–1704; English philosopher

lock·er /läk'ər/ *n.* lockable cupboard or compartment, esp. for public use

lock·et /läk'it/ *n.* small ornamental case for a portrait or lock of hair, worn on a chain around the neck [AngFr dim. of *loc* latch, LOCK[1]]

lock'jaw' *n.* form of tetanus in which the jaws become rigidly closed

lock'out' *n.* employer's exclusion of employees until certain terms are agreed to

lock'smith' *n.* maker and mender of locks

lock'up' *n.* jail

lo·co /lō'kō/ *adj. Slang.* crazy [Sp: insane]

lo·co·mo·tion /lō'kəmō'sнən/ *n.* motion or the power of motion from place to place [L LOCUS + MOTION]

lo·co·mo·tive /lō'kəmō'tiv/ *n.* **1** engine for pulling trains —*adj.* **2** of, having, or effecting locomotion

lo·co·weed /lō'kōwēd'/ *n.* plant of the southwestern US and Mexico causing disease in livestock

lo·cus /lō'kəs/ *n.* (*pl.* **lo·ci**) **1** position **2** curve, surface, etc., formed by all points satisfying certain conditions [L: place]

lo·cust /lō'kəst/ *n.* **1** grasshopper migrating in swarms and consuming all vegetation **2** CICADA **3** N American flowering tree yielding durable wood [L *locusta*]

lo·cu·tion /lōkyōō'sнən/ *n.* word, phrase, or idiom [L *loquor, locut-* speak]

lode /lōd/ *n.* vein of metal ore [OE]

lode'star' *n.* star used as a guide, esp. the North Star

lode'stone' *n.* (also **load'stone'**) magnetic oxide of iron

lodge /läj/ *n.* **1** small house used in the sporting seasons (*hunting lodge*) **2** branch or meeting-place of a society such as the Freemasons **3** beaver's or otter's lair —*v.* **(lodged, lodging) 4** reside or live, esp. as a lodger **5** submit (a complaint, etc.) **6** become fixed or caught [OFr *loge* fr. MedL *lobia*]

lodg'er *n.* person paying for accommodation in another's house

lodg'ing *n.* **1** temporary accommodation **2** (*pl.*) room or rooms rented for lodging

Lódz /lŏŏj/ city in central Poland. Pop. 846,500

Loewe /lō/, **Frederick** 1904– ; Austrian-born US composer

loft /lôft/ *n.* **1** attic **2** gallery in a church or hall **3** open area in a warehouse, etc., used as a studio or living space **4** height of a struck or thrown ball —*v.* **5** send (a ball, etc.) high up [OE fr. ON *lopt* air; upper room]

loft'y *adj.* (**·i·er, ·i·est**) **1** (of things) of imposing height **2** haughty; aloof **3** exalted; noble —**loft'i·ly** *adv.*; **loft'i·ness** *n.*

log¹ /lôg, läg/ *n.* **1** unhewn trunk of a felled tree **2** device for gauging a ship's speed **3** record of events, esp. during the voyage of a ship or aircraft; logbook —*v.* **(logged, logging) 4** enter (data) in a log **5** attain (a distance, speed, etc., thus recorded) **6** cut into logs **7 log in** or **on** (or **off**) open (or close) one's online access to a computer system —**log'ger, log'ging** *n.* [ME]

log² *n.* logarithm [abbr.]

lo·gan·ber·ry /lō'gənber'ē/ *n.* (*pl.* **·ries**) dark red fruit, hybrid of a blackberry and a raspberry [*Logan*, name of horticulturalist]

log·a·rithm /lôg'ərĭTH'əm, läg'-/ *n. Math.* exponent showing the power to which a number must be raised to equal a given number —**log a·rith'mic** *adj.*; **log·a·rith'mi·cal·ly** *adv.* [Gk *logos* reckoning + *arithmos* number]

log'book *n.* book containing a log (LOG, 3)

log·ger·head /lôg'ərhed'/ *n.* as in **at loggerheads** disagreeing or disputing [prob. fr. *logger* wooden block]

log·ic /läj'ĭk/ *n.* **1a** science of reasoning **b** particular system or method of reasoning **2** expected procedure or outcome —**lo·gi·cian** /lōjĭSH'ən/ *n.* [Gk *logos* word; reason]

log·i·cal /läj'ĭkəl/ *adj.* **1** of or according to logic **2** consistent —**log'i·cal·i·ty** /-kal'ĭtē/ *n.*; **log'i·cal·ly** *adv.*

lo·gis·tics /lōjĭs'tĭks/ *n. pl.* organization of (orig. military) services and supplies —**lo·gis'tic, lo·gis'ti·cal** *adj.*; **lo·gis'ti·cal·ly** *adv.* [Fr *logistique* fr. *loger* lodge (troops)]

log'jam' *n.* deadlock

lo·go /lō'gō/ *n.* (*pl.* **·gos**) short for LOGOTYPE

lo·go·type /lō'gətīp'/ *n.* emblem or trademark of a company, organization, etc. [Gk *logos* word + TYPE]

log'roll'ing *n.* **1** *Sports.* competition involving two people who stand on a log in water, rotating it to dislodge the opponent **2** exchange of favors, esp. among legislators for political gain

lo·gy /lō'gē/ *adj.* (**·gi·er, ·gi·est**) sluggish; slow

-logy *comb. form* forming nouns denoting: **1** a subject of study (*biology*) **2** speech or discourse or a characteristic of this (*trilogy*; *tautology*) [Gk -*logia* fr. *logos* word]

loin /loin/ *n.* **1** (*pl.*) lower back of the body between the ribs and the hipbones **2** meat from this part of an animal [MFr *loigne* fr. L *lumbus*]

loin'cloth' *n.* cloth worn around the hips

loi·ter /loit'ər/ *v.* **1** stand about idly; linger **2** go slowly with frequent stops —**loi'ter·er** *n.* [perh. MDu]

loll /läl/ *v.* **1** stand or lounge in a lazy attitude **2** hang loosely

lol·li·pop /läl'ēpäp'/ *n.* hard candy on a stick

lol·ly·gag /läl'ēgag'/ *v.* var. of LALLYGAG

Lo·mas de Za·mo·ra /lō'mäs də zəmōr'ə/ *n.* suburb of Buenos Aires, Argentina. Pop. 572,500

Lo·mé *n.* /lōmā'/ capital of Togo. Pop. 366,500

Lon·don /lən'dən/ *n.* **1** capital of England and the United Kingdom, on the River Thames. Pop. 6,677,900 **2** city in SE Ontario, Canada. Pop. 303,200

Lon·don /lən'dən/, **Jack** 1876–1916; US novelist

lone /lōn/ *adj.* **1** solitary; without companions **2** isolated [fr. ALONE]

lone'ly *adj.* (**·li·er, ·li·est**) **1** solitary **2** sad because of this **3** uninhabited —**lone'li·ness** *n.*

lon'er *n.* person or animal that prefers to be alone

lone·some /lōn'səm/ *adj.* **1** lonely **2** uninhabited

long¹ /lôNG/ *adj.* **1** measuring much from end to end in space or time **2** in length or duration (*2 yards long; two months long*) **3** consisting of many items (*a long list*) **4** seemingly more than the stated amount; tedious (*ten long miles*) **5** elongated **6** lasting much time (*long friendship*) **7** far-reaching **8** (of odds or a chance) of low probability **9** (of stocks) bought with the expectation of a rise in price **10** (foll. by *on*) *Colloq.* well supplied with —*n.* **11** long interval or period (*won't be long*) —*adv.* **12** for a long time (*long ago*) **13** throughout a specified time (*all day long*) **14** as (or so) long as provided that **15** before long soon —**long'ish** *adj.* [OE]

long² *v.* have a strong wish or desire [OE]

Long /lôNG/, **Huey** 1893–1935; US politician; assassinated

long. *abbr.* longitude

Long' Beach' *n.* city in Calif., near Los Angeles. Pop. 429,433

long'boat' *n.* sailing ship's largest boat

long'-dis'tance *adj.* **1** traveling or operating between distant places —*adv.* **2** between distant places (*phone long-distance*)

long' di·vi'sion *n.* division of numbers with details of the calculations written down

lon·gev·i·ty /lônjev'ətē, län'-/ *n.* long life [L *longus* long + *aevum* age]

long' face' *n.* dismal expression —**long'-faced'** *adj.*

Long·fel·low /lôNG'fel'ō/, **Henry Wadsworth** 1807–82; US poet

long'hair' *n. Slang.* **1** person with long hair **2** intellectual **3** devotee of classical music

long·hand *n.* ordinary handwriting

long·ing *n.* 1 intense desire —*adj.* 2 having or showing this —**long'ing·ly** *adv.*

Long' Is'land *n.* island off S N.Y. in the Atlantic Ocean that includes sections of New York City

Long' Is'land Sound' *n.* arm of the Atlantic 90 mi. long, separating Long Island, N.Y., from Conn.

MERIDIANS OF LONGITUDE

lon·gi·tude /län'jət(y)ōōd'/ *n.* angular distance east or west of the prime meridian, expressed in degrees or time [L *longitudo* length, fr. *longus* long]

lon·gi·tu·di·nal /län'jət(y)ōōd'n-əl/ *adj.* 1 of or in length 2 running lengthwise 3 of longitude —**lon'gi·tu'di·nal·ly** *adv.*

long' johns' *n. pl.* Colloq. long underwear

long' jump' *n.* athletic contest of jumping as far as possible along the ground in one leap

long-lived /lông'līvd', -livd'/ *adj.* having a long life

long'-play'ing *adj.* (of a phonograph record) playing for about 20–30 minutes on each side

long'-range' *adj.* extending a long distance or time (*long-range forecast*)

long'-run'ning *adj.* continuing for a long time

long·shore·man /lông'shôr'mən/ *n.* (*pl.* ·men) person employed in loading and unloading ships; stevedore

long' shot' *n.* 1 Colloq. wild guess or venture 2 bet at long odds 3 not by a long shot not by any means

long'-stand'ing *adj.* existing for a long time

long'-suf'fer·ing *adj.* enduring pain, trouble, etc., patiently

long'-term' *adj.* of or for a long time (*long-term plans*)

long' ton *n.* Brit. 2240 lbs. avoirdupois

Lon·gueuil /lông-gāl'/ *n.* city in Quebec, Canada. Pop. 129,900

long'-wind'ed *adj.* (of a speech or writing) tediously lengthy

look /lōōk/ *v.* 1a use one's sight; turn one's eyes in some direction b turn one's eyes on; examine (*looked us up and down*) 2 make a search 3 (foll. by *at*) consider; examine (*look at the facts*) 4 have a specified appearance; seem (*look the part; future looks bleak*) 5 (foll. by *into*) investigate —*n.* 6 act of looking; gaze; glance 7a (*sing.* or *pl.*) appearance of a face; expression b appearance of a thing 8 style; fashion —*interj.* 9 (also **look here!**) calling attention, expressing a protest, etc. 10 **look after** take care of 11 **look down on** or **upon** (or **look down one's nose at**) regard with contempt or superiority 12 **look for-**

ward to await with specified feelings 13 **look on** regard; view 14 **look out** be vigilant or prepared 15 **look over** inspect 16 **look up:** a search for (esp. in a book) b Colloq. visit c improve in prospect 17 **look up to** respect or admire [OE]

look'-a·like' *n.* person or thing closely resembling another

look·er *n.* Colloq. attractive woman

look'ing-glass' *n.* mirror

look'out' *n.* 1 watch or looking out 2a observation-post b person stationed to keep watch 3 prospect 4 Colloq. person's own concern

Look·out Moun'tain *n.* ridge in SE Tenn. near Chattanooga; site of Civil War battle

look'-see' *n.* Colloq. quick glance

loom[1] /lōōm/ *n.* apparatus for weaving [OE]

loom[2] *v.* 1 appear dimly, esp. as a threatening shape 2 (of an event) be ominously close

loon /lōōn/ *n.* a kind of diving bird [ON]

loon·y /lōō'nē/ *adj.* (·ni·er, ·ni·est) Slang. crazy —**loo'ni·ness** *n.* [fr. LUNATIC]

loop /lōōp/ *n.* 1 figure produced by a curve, or a doubled thread, etc., that crosses itself 2 anything similarly shaped 3 contraceptive coil 4 endless band of tape or film allowing continuous repetition 5 sequence of computer operations repeated until some condition is satisfied —*v.* 6 form or bend into a loop 7 fasten with a loop or loops 8 form a loop 9 (also **loop the loop**) fly in a circle vertically [ME]

loop'hole' *n.* means of evading a rule, etc., without infringing it

loop'y *adj.* (·i·er, ·i·est) Slang. crazy

loose /lōōs/ *adj.* 1 not tightly held, fixed, etc. 2 free from bonds or restraint 3 not compact or dense 4 inexact 5 morally lax 6 Colloq. relaxed —*v.* (loosed, loos·ing) 7 free; untie 8 discharge (a missile) 9 at loose ends disorganized; uncertain 10 on the loose: a escaped from captivity b enjoying oneself freely —**loose'ly** *adv.*; **loose'ness** *n.* [ON]

• Usage: The adjective *loose* means 'not tight' (*This belt is loose around my waist*) and should not be confused with the verb *loose*, which means 'let go': *They loosed the bloodhounds to track the fugitive.* This verb should also not be confused with the verb *lose*, which means 'be deprived of, fail to keep in one's possession': *They lose money by giving poor service. You will lose your keys if you don't put them in your pocket.*

loose'-leaf' *adj.* (of a notebook, etc.) with pages that can be removed and replaced

loos·en /lōō'sən/ *v.* make or become loose or looser

loot /lōōt/ *n.* 1 spoil; booty 2 Slang. money —*v.* 3 plunder —**loot'er** *n.* [Hindi]

lop /läp/ *v.* (lopped, lop·ping) 1 cut or remove (a part or parts) from a whole, esp. branches from a tree 2 remove (items) as superfluous [ME]

lope /lōp/ *v.* (loped, lop·ing) 1 run with a long bounding stride —*n.* 2 long bounding stride [ON *hlaupa* or MDu *lopen*]

lop·sid·ed /läp'sīd'əd/ *adj.* unevenly balanced —**lop'sid'ed·ly** *adv.*; **lop'sid'ed·ness** *n.* [rel. to LOB]

lo·qua·cious /lōkwā′SHəs/ *adj.* talkative —**lo·quac·i·ty** /lōkwas′ətē/ *n.* [L *loquor* speak]

lord /lôrd/ *n.* **1** master or ruler **2** *Hist.* feudal superior, esp. of a manor **3** (in Great Britain) peer of the realm or person with the title Lord **4** (*cap.*) (often prec. by *the*) God or Christ **5 lord it over** domineer [OE: bread-keeper, rel. to LOAF[1], WARD]

lord′ly *adj.* (**·li·er, ·li·est**) **1** haughty; imperious **2** noble —**lord′li·ness** *n.*

Lord's′ Day′ *n.* Sunday

lord′ship′ *n.* **1** (usu. *cap.*) title used in addressing or referring to a Lord **2** dominion; rule

Lord's′ Prayer *n.* prayer beginning "Our Father" (Matt. 6:9-13; Luke 11:2-4)

lore /lôr/ *n.* traditions and knowledge on a subject [OE]

lor·gnette /lôrnyet′/ *n.* pair of eyeglasses or opera glasses on a long handle [Fr *lorgner* peep; squint]

lo·ris /lô′ris, lôr′is/ *n.* small nocturnal Asiatic lemur with large eyes [Du]

lorn /lôrn/ *adj. Archaic.* desolate; forlorn [OE]

lor·ry /lôr′ē, lär′ē/ *n.* (*pl.* **·ries**) *Brit.* truck

Los An·ge·les /lôs an′jələs, -lēz′/ *n.* city in S Calif. Pop. 3,485,398 —**An·ge·le·no** /an′jəlē′nō/, **Los An·ge·le·no, Los An·ge·le·an** /an′jəlē′ən/ *n.*

lose /lo͞oz/ *v.* (**lost, los·ing**) **1** be deprived of or cease to have, esp. by negligence **2** be deprived of (a person) by death **3** become unable to find, follow, or understand **4** let or have pass from one's control or reach **5** be defeated in (a game, lawsuit, battle, etc.) **6** get rid of **7** be lost (or **lose oneself**) **in** be engrossed in **8 be lost on** be wasted on; not noticed or appreciated by **9 lose face** be deprived of one's dignity —**los′er** *n.* [OE]

● Usage: See note at LOOSE.

loss /lôs/ *n.* **1** losing or being lost **2** thing or amount lost **3** damage or disadvantage resulting from losing **4 at a loss** puzzled; uncertain [OE *los*]

loss-lead·er /lôs′ lēd′ər/ *n.* item sold at a loss to attract customers

lost /lôst/ *v. past* and *past part.* of LOSE

lost′-and-found′ *n.* area for keeping items left by their owners

lot /lät/ *n.* **1** *Colloq.* (often *pl.*) a large number or amount (*a lot of people; lots of milk*) **b** much (*a lot warmer; smiles a lot*) **2a** set of objects from which a chance selection is made **b** share or responsibility resulting from it **3** destiny, fortune, or condition **4** plot; allotment of land **5** article or set of articles for sale at an auction, etc. **6** cast (or draw) lots decide by lots [OE]

lo·tion /lō′SHən/ *n.* medicinal or cosmetic liquid preparation applied externally [L *lavare, lot-* wash]

lot·ter·y /lät′ərē/ *n.* (*pl.* **·ies**) **1** game in which numbered tickets are sold and prizes are won by the holders of numbers drawn at random **2** thing whose success is governed by chance [MDu, rel. to LOT]

lot·to /lät′ō/ *n.* **1** game of chance like bingo **2** LOTTERY, 1 [It fr. Gmc]

lo·tus /lōt′əs/ *n.* **1** legendary plant inducing luxurious languor when eaten **2** a kind of water lily [Gk *lōtos*]

lo·tus po·si′tion *n.* cross-legged position of meditation with the feet resting on the thighs

loud /loud/ *adj.* **1** strongly audible; noisy **2** *Colloq.* (of colors, etc.) gaudy; obtrusive —*adv.* **3** loudly **4 out loud** aloud —**loud′ish** *adj.*; **loud′ly** *adv.*; **loud′ness** *n.* [OE]

loud′speak′er *n.* apparatus that converts electrical signals into sound

Lou′ Gehr′ig's dis·ease′ /lo͞o′ ger′igs/ *n.* AMYOTROPHIC LATERAL SCLEROSIS

Lou·is /lo͞o(ə)wē′, lo͞oē′/ name of 18 kings of France, including: **1 Louis XIV** 1638–1715, reigned 1643–1715; called "the Sun King" **2 Louis XVI** 1754–93, reigned 1774–92 (until French Revolution)

Lou·is /lo͞o′əs/, **Joe** 1914–81; US boxer; called "the Brown Bomber"

Lou·ise, Lake /lo͞o-ēz′, lo͞o-/ *n.* glacial lake in SW Alberta, Canada

Lou·i·si·an·a /lo͞o-ē′zē-an′ə/ *n.* S state of the US. Capital: Baton Rouge. Pop. 4,219,973. Abbr. **LA; La.** —**Lou·i′si·an′an** *n.* & *adj.*; **Lou·i′si·an′i·an** -an′ēən/ *n.* & *adj.*

Louis Phi·lippe /lo͞o(ə)wē′ filēp′, lo͞oē′/ 1773–1850; king of France (1830–48)

Lou·is·ville /lo͞o′ēvil′, -ival/ *n.* city in Ky. Pop. 269,063 —**Lou·is·vill·ian** /lo͞o′ivil′ēən/ *n.*

lounge /lounj/ *v.* (**lounged, loung·ing**) **1** recline comfortably; loll **2** stand or move about idly —*n.* **3** place for lounging **4** sofa **5** waiting room **6** public lavatory

Lourdes /lo͞ord(z)/ *n.* city in SW France; site of a Roman Catholic shrine famous for cures. Pop. 18,100

Lou·ren·ço Mar·ques /ləren′sō märkes′, mär′kəs/ *n.* see MAPUTO

louse /lous/ *n.* **1** (*pl.* **lice**) parasitic insect **2** (*pl.* **lous·es**) *Slang.* contemptible person —*v.* (**loused, lous·ing**) **3 louse up** *Slang.* spoil [OE]

lous·y /lou′zē/ *adj.* (**·i·er, ·i·est**) **1** *Slang.* very bad; disgusting; ill (*feel lousy*) **2** *Colloq.* well supplied; teeming **3** infested with lice —**lous′i·ly** *adv.*; **lous′i·ness** *n.*

lout /lout/ *n.* boorish person —**lout′ish** *adj.*

lou·ver /lo͞o′vər/ *n.* (also **lou·vre**) each of a set of overlapping slats, often adjustable, designed to admit air and light and exclude rain —**lou′vered** or **lou′vred** *adj.* [MFr *lovier* fr. MDu *love* gallery]

love /ləv/ *n.* **1** deep affection or fondness **2** sexual passion **3** sexual relations **4** beloved one; sweetheart **5** *Tennis.* no score; zero —*v.* (**loved, lov·ing**) **6** feel love or a deep fondness for **7** delight in; admire; greatly cherish **8 for love** for pleasure, not profit **9 in love** enamored (of) **10 make love** have sexual intercourse —**lov′a·ble** or **love′a·ble, love′less** *adj.* [OE]

love′-bird′ *n.* kind of small parrot that seems to show great affection for its mate

love′-hate′ re·la′tion·ship *n.* intense relationship involving ambivalent emotions

love′ life′ *n.* one's amorous or sexual relationships

love′lorn′ *adj.* pining from unreciprocated love

love'ly adj. (**·li·er, ·li·est**) 1 beautiful 2 delightful; pleasing —n. (pl. **·lies**) 3 Colloq. pretty woman —**love'li·ness** n.

love'mak'ing n. 1 sexual play, esp. intercourse 2 Archaic. courtship

love'-nest' n. Colloq. secluded place for (esp. illicit) lovers

lov·er /ləv′ər/ n. 1 person in love with another 2 person with whom another is having sexual relations 3 (pl.) unmarried couple in love or having sexual relations 4 person who enjoys a specified thing (music lover)

love'-seat' n. small sofa for two

lov'ing adj. 1 feeling or showing love; affectionate —**lov'ing·ly** adv.

lov'ing cup' n. two-handled drinking cup

low¹ /lō/ adj. 1 not high or tall 2 not elevated 3 of or in humble rank 4 of small or less than normal amount, extent, or intensity 5 dejected; lacking vigor 6 not shrill or loud 7 commonplace; vulgar 8 unfavorable (low opinion) —n. 9 low or the lowest level or number 10 Meteorol. area of low pressure —adv. 11 in or to a low position or state 12 in a low tone or pitch 13 lay low slay or overcome 14 lie low remain hidden —**low'ish** adj.; **low'ness** n. [ON]

low² n. 1 sound made by cattle; moo —v. 2 make this sound [OE]

low'-ball' n. (also **low'ball'**) 1 Cards. type of poker —v. 2 underestimate or underbid a price (usu. for a service) deliberately

low' beam' n. automobile headlight providing short-range illumination

low' blow' n. 1 Boxing. illegal blow below the belt 2 any unfair or unsportsmanlike attack

low'-born' adj. of humble birth

low'brow' adj. 1 not intellectual or cultured —n. 2 lowbrow person

Low' Coun'tries n. low-lying countries along the North Sea: Belgium, the Netherlands, and Luxembourg

low·down adj. /lō′doun′/ 1 mean; dishonorable —n. /lō′doun/ 2 Colloq. (prec. by the) accurate information

Low·ell /lō′əl/ n. city in Mass. Pop. 103,439

Low·ell /lō′əl/ 1 **James Russell** 1819–91; US poet and critic 2 **Amy** 1874–1925; US poet 3 **Robert** 1917–77; US poet

low'-end' adj. Colloq. inexpensive compared to others

low·er¹ /lō′ər/ adj. 1 less high in position or status 2 situated below another part 3a situated on less high land (Lower Egypt) b situated to the south (Lower California) —adv. 4 in or to a lower position, status, etc. —v. 5 let or haul down 6 degrade comp. of **LOW¹** —**low'er·most** adj.

low·er² /lour, lō′ər/ v. 1 frown; look sullen —n. 2 (of the sky) look dark or threatening [ME louren]

low·er·case /lō′ərkās′/ n. 1 small letters —adj. & adv. 2 in lower-case

low'est com'mon de·nom'i·na·tor n. Math. smallest common multiple of the denominators of several fractions

low' fre'quen·cy n. radio frequency between 30 to 300 kilohertz

low' gear' n. gear that has a high ratio of output relative to the power input

low'-grade' adj. of low quality

low'-key' adj. (also **low'-keyed'**) lacking intensity; restrained

low·land /lō′lənd/ n. 1 low-lying country —adj. 2 of or in lowland 3 **the Lowlands** lowland area of S Scotland —**low'land·er** n.

low-lev'el adj. (of a computer language) close in form to machine code

low'ly adj. (**·li·er, ·li·est**) 1 humble; unpretentious —adv. 2 humbly —**low'li·ness** n.

low'-ly'ing adj. near to the ground or sea level

low'-pitch'ed adj. 1 (of a sound) low 2 (of a roof) almost horizontal

low'-pres'sure adj. 1 of low degree of activity or exertion 2 (of atmospheric pressure) below average

low' pro'file n. a modest or retiring state

low' tide' n. (also **low' wa'ter**) time or level of the tide at its ebb

lox¹ /loks/ n. smoked salmon [Yiddish]

lox² n. (also LOX) liquid oxygen [abbr.]

loy·al /loi′əl/ adj. faithful —**loy'al·ly** adv.; **loy'al·ty** n. (pl. **·ties**) [OFr fr. L, rel. to LEGAL]

loy·al·ist n. person who remains loyal to the legitimate sovereign, government, etc. —**loy'al·ism** /-izəm/ n.

loz·enge /läz′ənj, läs′-/ n. 1 small piece of candy or medicinal tablet to be dissolved in the mouth 2 diamond-shaped object [OFr]

LP abbr. long-playing (record)

LPG abbr. liquefied petroleum gas

LPN abbr. (also L.P.N.) licensed practical nurse

LSAT abbr. Law School Admissions Test

LSD abbr. lysergic acid diethylamide, a powerful hallucinogenic drug

Lt. abbr. Lieutenant

Ltd. abbr. Limited

Lu symb. lutetium

Lu·an·da /lōō·än′də/ n. capital of Angola. Pop. 1,544,400

lu·au /lōō′ou′/ n. Hawaiian feast

lub·ber /ləb′ər/ n. clumsy person

Lub·bock /ləb′ək/ n. city in Texas. Pop. 186,206

lube /lōōb/ n. Colloq. 1 lubricant 2 lubrication of parts, esp. of a car

Lü·beck /ly′bek′/ n. seaport in NW Germany. Pop. 214,800

Lu·blin /lōō′blin/ n. city in E Poland. Pop. 352,200

lu·bri·cant /lōō′brikənt/ n. substance used to reduce friction

lu·bri·cate /lōō′brikāt′/ v. (**·cat·ed, ·cat·ing**) 1 apply oil or grease to 2 make slippery —**lu'bri·ca'tion, lu'bri·ca·tor** n. [L lubricare make slippery]

Lu·bum·ba·shi /lōō′bōōmbäsH′ē/ n. city in Zaire. Pop. 739,100

lu·cid /lōō′sid/ adj. 1 expressing or expressed clearly 2 sane —**lu·cid'i·ty** n.; **lu'cid·ly** adv.; **lu'cid·ness** n. [L lucidus, rel. to lux light]

Lu·ci·fer /lōō′səfər/ n. Satan

luck /lək/ n. 1 good or bad fortune 2 circumstances of life (beneficial or not) brought by this 3 good fortune; success owing to chance 4 **luck out** Colloq. be lucky —**luck'less** adj. [LGer or MDu]

Luck·now /lək'nou'/ *n.* city in N India. Pop. 1,592,000

luck'y *adj.* (·i·er, ·i·est) 1 having or resulting from good luck 2 bringing good luck —**luck' i·ly** *adv.*; **luck'i·ness** *n.*

lu·cra·tive /lōō'krətiv/ *adj.* profitable —**lu' cra·tive·ly** *adv.*; **lu'cra·tive·ness** *n.* [L *lucrari* make a profit]

lu·cre /lōō'kər/ *n. Derog.* financial gain [L *lucrum* gain]

Lu·cre·tius /lōōkrē'sHəs/ (**Titus Lucretius Carus**) c. 94 – c. 55 B.C.; Roman poet and philosopher

Lu·dhi·a·na /lōōd'ē-än'ə/ *n.* city in N India. Pop. 1,012,100

lu·di·crous /lōōd'ikrəs/ *adj.* absurd; ridiculous; laughable —**lu'di·crous·ly** *adv.*; **lu'di· crous·ness** *n.* [L *ludere* play]

luff /ləf/ *v.* steer (a sailing vessel) to point into the wind so that its sails flap [ME fr. MDu]

lug /ləg/ *v.* (**lugged, lug·ging**) 1 drag or carry with effort —*n.* 2 projection on an object by which it may be carried, fixed in place, etc. 3 strong nut for fastening a wheel to an axle [prob. Scand]

Lu·gansk /lōōgänsk'/ *n.* (formerly **Vo'ro·shi'lov·grad**) city in Ukraine. Pop. 504,000

lug·gage /ləg'ij/ *n.* suitcases, bags, etc., for a traveler's belongings [fr. LUG]

lug·ger /ləg'ər/ *n.* small sailing vessel with a quadrilateral mainsail [fr. LUGSAIL]

lug·sail /ləg'sāl', -səl/ *n.* quadrilateral sail on a yard [perh. ME *lugge* pole, or fr. LUG]

lu·gu·bri·ous /lōōgōō'brēəs/ *adj.* doleful —**lu·gu'bri·ous·ly** *adv.*; **lu·gu'bri·ous·ness** *n.* [L *lugere* mourn]

Luke, St. /lōōk/ one of the twelve Apostles; credited as writer of the third Gospel

luke·warm /lōōk'wôrm'/ *adj.* 1 moderately warm; tepid 2 unenthusiastic; indifferent [OE]

lull /ləl/ *v.* 1 soothe or send to sleep 2 (usu. foll. by *into*) bring (a person) into a specified frame of mind or feeling 3 (of noise, a storm, etc.) abate or calm down —*n.* 4 calm period [imit.]

lul·la·by /ləl'əbī'/ *n.* (*pl.* ·bies) soothing song to send a child to sleep [rel. to LULL]

lum·ba·go /ləm'bā'gō/ *n.* rheumatic pain in the lower back [L *lumbus* loin]

lum·bar /ləm'bər, -bär'/ *adj.* of the lower back area [L *lumbus* loin]

lum·ber¹ /ləm'bər/ *n.* 1 timber sawn into boards 2 disused and cumbersome articles —*v.* 3 cut and prepare forest timber

lum·ber² *v.* move clumsily [ME]

lum'ber·jack *n.* person who fells and transports lumber

lum'ber·jack'et *n.* thick woolen plaid jacket

lum·ber·man /ləm'bərmən/ *n.* (*pl.* ·men) person dealing in lumber

lu·mi·nar·y /lōō'mənər'ē/ *n.* (*pl.* ·ies) 1 natural light-giving body 2 celebrity [MedL *luminaria* lamp, rel. to L *lumen*]

lu·mi·nes·cence /lōō'mənes'əns/ *n.* emission of light without heat —**lu'mi·nes'cent** *adj.*

lu·mi·nous /lōō'mənəs/ *adj.* 1 shedding light 2 clear 3 phosphorescent; visible in darkness (*luminous paint*) —**lu'mi·nos'i·ty** /-näs'ətē/ *n.*

lum·mox /ləm'əks/ *n. Slang.* lout; clumsy or stupid person

lump¹ /ləmp/ *n.* 1 compact shapeless mass 2 tumor; swelling; bruise 3 heavy, dull, or ungainly person 4 (*pl.*) punishment; bad treatment —*v.* 5 treat as all alike; put together 6 (of sauce, etc.) become lumpy —**lump'i·ly** *adv.*; **lump'i·ness** *n.*; **lump'ish** *adj.*; **lump'y** *adj.* (·i·er, ·i·est) [ME]

lump² *v. Colloq.* put up with ungraciously (*like it or lump it*)

lump' sum' *n.* 1 sum covering a number of items 2 money paid down at one time

lu·na·cy /lōō'nəsē/ *n.* (*pl.* ·cies) 1 insanity 2 great folly [L, rel. to LUNATIC]

lu·nar /lōō'nər/ *adj.* of, like, concerned with, or determined by the moon [L *luna* moon]

lu'nar mod'ule *n.* small craft for traveling between the moon and a spacecraft in orbit around it

lu'nar month' *n.* 1 interval between new moons (about 29-1/2 days) 2 (in general use) four weeks

lu·nate /lōō'nāt'/ *adj.* crescent-shaped

lu·na·tic /lōō'nətik'/ *n.* 1 insane person 2 wildly foolish person —*adj.* 3 insane 4 extremely reckless or foolish [LL *lunaticus* moonstruck; crazy]

lunch / lənCH/ *n.* 1 midday meal —*v.* 2 take lunch [shortening of LUNCHEON]

lun·cheon /lən'CHən/ *n. Formal.* lunch [prob. fr. ME *noneschench* noon drink]

lun·cheon·ette /lən'CHənet'/ *n.* restaurant serving light meals; diner

lun'cheon meat' *n.* ready-to-eat meat in a loaf, sausage, etc.

lung /ləNG/ *n.* either of the pair of respiratory organs in humans and many other vertebrates [OE]

lunge /lənj/ *n.* 1 sudden movement forward 2 the basic attacking move in fencing —*v.* (**lunged, lung·ing**) 3 deliver or make a lunge [Fr *allonger* lengthen fr. LL]

lu·pine /lōō'pīn'/ *adj.* of or like a wolf [L *lupinus* fr. *lupus* wolf]

lu·pus /lōō'pəs/ *n.* autoimmune inflammatory skin disease [L: wolf]

lurch¹ /lərCH/ *n.* 1 stagger; sudden unsteady movement —*v.* 2 stagger

lurch² *n.* as in **leave in the lurch** desert (a person) in difficulties [MFr *lourche* game similar to backgammon]

lure /lŏŏr/ *v.* (**lured, lur·ing**) 1 entice 2 attract —*n.* 3 thing used to entice [OFr, perh. fr. Gmc]

lu·rid /lŏŏr'id/ *adj.* 1 bright and glaring in color 2 sensational; shocking; gruesome 3 ghastly; wan —**lu'rid·ly** *adv.* [L]

lurk /lərk/ *v.* 1 linger furtively 2a lie in ambush b hide, esp. for sinister purposes [perh. fr. LOWER²]

Lu·sa·ka /lōōsäk'ə/ *n.* capital of Zambia. Pop. 982,400

lus·cious /ləsH'əs/ *adj.* 1 richly pleasing in taste or smell 2 voluptuously attractive [prob. rel. to DELICIOUS]

lush[1] /lƏsh/ *adj.* **1** (of vegetation) luxuriant and succulent **2** luxurious

lush[2] *n. Slang.* alcoholic; drunkard

lust /lƏst/ *n.* **1** strong sexual desire **2** passionate desire for —*v.* **3** have a strong desire —**lust′ful** *adj.*; **lust′ful·ly** *adv.*; **lust′ful·ness** *n.* [OE]

lus·ter /lƏs′tƏr/ *n.* (also esp. *Brit.* **lus′tre**) **1** gloss; shining surface **2** brilliance; splendor —**lus′trous** /-trƏs/ *adj.*; **lus′trous·ly** *adv.*; **lus′trous·ness** *n.* [L *lustrare* purify; illuminate]

lust·y /lƏs′tē/ *adj.* (·i·er, ·i·est) **1** healthy **2** vigorous —**lust′i·ly** *adv.*; **lust′i·ness** *n.* [fr. LUST]

LUTE

lute /lōōt/ *n.* guitarlike instrument with a long neck and a pear-shaped body [OFr fr. Ar]

lu·te·ti·um /lōōtē′shƏm/ *n.* silvery metallic element; *symb.* **Lu** [L *Lutetia* Paris]

Lu·ther /lōō′thƏr/, **Martin** 1483–1546; German theologian; principal figure of the German Protestant Reformation

Lu·ther·an /lōō′thƏrƏn/ *n.* **1** follower of Luther **2** member of the Lutheran Church —*adj.* **3** of Luther, or the doctrines associated with him —**Lu′ther·an·ism** *n.* [for MARTIN LUTHER]

Lux·em·bourg /lƏk′sƏmbƏrg/ *n.* **1** country and grand duchy in W Europe. Pop. 387,000 **2** city, capital of Luxembourg. Pop. 75,600 **3** province in SE Belgium —**Lux′em·bourg′er** *n.*; **Lux′em·bourg′i·an** /-bƏrg′ēƏn/ *n.* & *adj.*

lux·u·ri·ant /lƏg′zhŏŏr′ēƏnt/ *adj.* **1** growing profusely **2** florid —**lux·u′ri·ance** *n.*; **lux·u′ri·ant·ly** *adv.* [L, rel. to LUXURY]
● Usage: See note at LUXURIOUS.

lux·u·ri·ate /lƏg′zhŏŏr′ē·āt′/ *v.* (·at·ed, ·at·ing) **1** enjoy as a luxury **2** relax in luxury

lux·u·ri·ous /lƏg′zhŏŏr′ēƏs/ *adj.* **1** supplied with luxuries **2** rich; comfortable —**lux·u′ri·ous·ly** *adv.* [L, rel. to LUXURY]
● Usage: *Luxurious*, which means 'characterized by luxury, lavish,' should be distinguished from *luxuriant*, which is often applied to foliage or hair and means 'flourishing, abundant.' Often, *luxury* is used as an adjective meaning 'luxurious': *a luxury hotel.*

lux·u·ry /lƏk′shƏrē, lƏg′zhƏ-/ *n.* (*pl.* ·ries) **1** choice or costly surroundings, possessions, etc., usu. nonessential—*adj.* **2** comfortable and expensive [L *luxuria*]
● Usage: See note at LUXURIOUS.

Lviv /lƏvēf′/ *n.* city in W Ukraine. Pop. 802,000

Lw *symb.* lawrencium

-ly[1] *suffix* forming adjectives, esp. from nouns, meaning: **1** having the qualities of (*princely*) **2** recurring at intervals of (*daily*) [OE]

-ly[2] *suffix* forming adverbs from adjectives (*boldly*; *happily*) [OE]

Ly·all·pur /lī′Əlpŏŏr′/ *n.* see FAISALABAD

ly·chee /lī′chē, lichē′/ *n.* (also **ly′chee nut′**) var. of LITCHI

Ly·cur·gus /līkƏr′gƏs/ fl. 9th cent. B.C.; Spartan lawgiver

Lyd·i·a /lid′ēƏ/ *n.* ancient kingdom in W Asia Minor —**Lyd′i·an** *n.* & *adj.*

lye /lī/ *n.* alkaline solution as for washing [OE]

ly·ing /lī′ing/ *v. pres. part.* of LIE[1], LIE[2]

Lyl·y /lil′ē/, **John** c. 1554–1606; English writer and dramatist

Lyme′ dis·ease′ /līm/ *n.* disease carried by ticks, characterized by fatigue, joint aches, and general malaise [for *Lyme*, CT, where first described]

lymph /limf/ *n.* colorless fluid from the tissues of the body —**lymph′oid** *adj.* [L *lympha* water]

lym·phat·ic /limfat′ik/ *adj.* **1** of, secreting, or conveying lymph **2** flabby; sluggish

lymph′ gland′ *n.* (also **lymph′ node′**) small mass of tissue in the bodily system that conveys lymph

lym·pho·ma /limfō′mƏ/ *n.* (*pl.* ·mas or ·ma·ta /-mƏtƏ/) tumor of the lymph nodes

lynch /linch/ *v.* (of a mob) put (a person) to death without a legal trial —**lynch′ing** *n.* [prob. fr. *Lynch*, 18th-cent. Va. vigilance committee member]

lynch′ law′ *n.* procedure followed when a person is lynched

Lynn /lin/ *n.* city in Mass. Pop. 81,245

lynx /lingks/ *n.* (*pl.* same or -es) wild cat with a short tail and spotted fur [Gk]

lynx-eyed /lingks′īd′/ *adj.* keen-sighted

Ly·on /lī′Ən/, **Mary** 1797–1849; US educator

Ly·ons /lē-ôN′/ *n.* (also **Ly·on′**) city in E France. Pop. 422,400

lyre /līr/ *n.* ancient U-shaped harplike instrument [Gk *lyra*]

lyre′-bird′ *n.* Australian bird, the male of which has a lyre-shaped tail display

LYRE

lyr·ic /lir′ik/ *adj.* **1** (of poetry) expressing the writer's emotions **2** (of a singing voice) high-pitched and flexible —*n.* **3** lyric poem **4** (*pl.*) words of a song [Gk, rel. to LYRE]

lyr·i·cal /lir′ikƏl/ *adj.* **1** LYRIC **2** highly enthusiastic —**lyr′i·cal·ly** *adv.*

lyr·i·cism /lir′Əsiz′Əm/ *n.* quality of being lyric

lyr·i·cist /lir′Əsist/ *n.* writer of (esp. popular) lyrics

ly·ser·gic ac·id di·eth·yl·am·ide /līsƏr′jik as′id dī′eth′Əlam′īd′/ *n.* LSD

-lysis *comb. form* forming nouns denoting disintegration or decomposition (*electrolysis*) [Gk *lysis* loosening]

-lyte *comb. form* forming nouns denoting substances that can be decomposed (*electrolyte*) [Gk *lytos* soluble]

M

m, M /em/ *n.* (*pl.* **m's; M's, Ms**) thirteenth letter of the English alphabet; a consonant

m or **m.** *abbr.* **1** male **2** married **3** masculine **4** *Physics.* mass **5** meter(s) **6** middle **7** mile **8** million **9** month

M or **M.** *abbr.* **1** Majesty **2** Marquis **3** Master **4** medicine **5** mega- **6** meridian **7** milli- **8** minute(s) **9** Monsieur **10** Monday **11** *Rom. num.* (usu. **M**) one thousand

ma /mä/ *n. Colloq.* mother

MA *abbr.* **1** (also **M.A.**) Master of Arts **2** postal abbr. for Massachusetts

ma'am /mam/ *n.* madam (used in addressing a woman)

Maas·tricht /mäs′triкнt/ *n.* city in the Netherlands, on the Maas River. Pop. 117,400

ma·ca·bre /məkäb′(rə), -käb′ər/ *adj.* grim; gruesome [Fr]

mac·ad·am /məkad′əm/ *n.* broken stone used for roadbuilding —**mac·ad′am·ize′** *v.* (**·ized, ·iz·ing**) [for J.A. *McAdam*, Scottish engineer]

mac·a·da·mia /mak′ədä′mēə/ *n.* edible seed of an Australian tree [for J. *Macadam*, Australian chemist]

mac·a·ro·ni /mak′ərō′nē/ *n.* small pasta tubes [It fr. Gk]

mac·a·roon /mak′ərōōn′/ *n.* small almond cake or biscuit [It, rel. to MACARONI]

Mac·Ar·thur /məkär′тнər/, **Douglas** 1880–1964; US general

Ma·cau·lay /məkô′lē/, **Thomas Babington** 1800–59; English historian, essayist, and philanthropist

ma·caw /məkô′/ *n.* long-tailed brightly colored parrot of Central and S America [Port *macao* fr. Tupi]

Mac·beth /məkbeтн, mak-/ *c.* 1005–57; king of Scotland (1040–57); subject of Shakespearian tragedy

Mac·ca·be·us /mak′əbē′əs/, **Judas** d. 160 B.C.; Jewish patriot and military leader

Mac·Don·ald /məkdän′ld/, **(James) Ramsay** 1866–1937; British prime minister (1924; 1929–35)

mace¹ /mäs/ *n.* **1** staff used as a symbol of office **2** medieval heavy spiked club used as a weapon [OFr, prob. fr. VL]

mace² *n.* dried outer covering of the nutmeg used as a spice [L *maccis*]

Mace /mäs/ *n. Tdmk.* self-defense spray used to temporarily stun an attacker

Mac·e·do·ni·a /mas′ədō′nēə/ *n.* **1** ancient country on the Balkan Peninsula, N of Greece **2** independent state, formerly part of Yugoslavia. Capital: Skopje. Pop. 2,050,000 —**Mac′e·do′ni·an** ·nēən/ *n. & adj.*

mac·er·ate /mas′ərāt′/ *v.* (**·at·ed, ·at·ing**) **1** soften by soaking **2** chew, chop, or tear into bits —**mac′er·a′tion** *n.* [L *macerare*]

Mach /mäk/ *n.* (also **Mach′ num′ber**) ratio of the speed of a body to the speed of sound in the surrounding medium [for ERNST MACH]

Mach /mäk, mäk/, **Ernst** 1836–1916; Austrian physicist

ma·che·te /məsнet′ē/ *n.* large sharp knife for clearing underbrush, cutting sugar cane, etc., in Central and S America [Sp fr. L]

Mach·i·a·vel·li /mak′ēəvel′ē/, **Niccolò di Bernardo** 1469–1527; Italian statesman and political theorist

mach·i·a·vel·li·an /mak′ēəvel′ēən/ *adj.* elaborately cunning; scheming; unscrupulous —**mach′i·a·vel′li·an·ism** /-izəm/ *n.* [fr. MACHIAVELLI]

mach·i·na·tion /mak′ənā′sнən, masн′-/ *n.* (usu. *pl.*) plot; intrigue —**mach·i·nate** /mak′ənāt′/ *v.* (**·nat·ed, ·nat·ing**) [L, rel. to MACHINE]

ma·chine /məsнēn′/ *n.* **1** apparatus for applying mechanical power, having several interrelated parts **2** particular machine, esp. a vehicle or an electrical or electronic apparatus **3** controlling system of an organization **4** VENDING MACHINE —*v.* (**·chined, ·chin·ing**) **5** make, shape, etc., with a machine [L fr. Gk *māchanā*]

ma·chine′ code′ *n.* (also **ma·chine′ lan′ guage**) computer language for a particular computer

ma·chine′ gun′ *n.* **1** automatic gun giving continuous fire —*v.* (**gunned, gun·ning**) **2** shoot with a machine gun

ma·chine′ read·a·ble *adj.* in a form that a computer can process

ma·chin·er·y /məsнē′nərē, -sнēn′rē/ *n.* (*pl.* **·ies**) **1** machines **2** mechanism **3** means devised

ma·chine′ tool′ *n.* mechanically operated tool

ma·chin′ist *n.* person who operates, makes, or maintains machines

ma·chis·mo /məснēz′mō, -cнiz′-, -kiz′-/ *n.* being macho; masculine pride [Sp]

ma·cho /mäcн′ō/ *adj.* aggressively masculine [Sp: male]

Mac·ken·zie /məkenˈzē/ **1 (Sir) Alexander** 1764–1820; Scottish explorer of Canada **2 Alexander** 1822–92; prime minister of Canada (1873–78)

Mac·ken·zie Riv·er /məkenˈzē/ *n.* river in NW Canada, flowing 1,120 mi. NW from Great Slave Lake to the Arctic Ocean

mack·er·el /mak′rəl/ *n.* (*pl.* same or **·els**) marine fish used as food [OFr]

mack·in·tosh /mak′əntäsн/ *n.* (also **mac′ in·tosh′**) waterproof coat or cloak [for C. *Macintosh*, its inventor]

Mac·Leish /məklēsн′/, **Archibald** 1892–1982; US poet and dramatist

Mac·mil·lan /məkmilˈən/, **(Maurice) Harold** 1895–1987; prime minister of Great Britain (1957–63)

Ma·con /māˈkən/ *n.* city in Ga. Pop. 106,612

mac·ra·mé /mak′ramā′/ *n.* **1** art of knotting cord to make decorative articles **2** work so made [Ar *miqrama* coverlet]

macro- *comb. form* **1** long **2** large; large-scale [Gk *makros* long]

mac·ro·bi·ot·ic /mak′rōbī-ät′ik/ *adj.* **1** of a diet intended to prolong life, esp. consisting of natural, organic foods —*n.* **2** (*pl.*; treated as

mac·ro·cosm /mak′rəkäz′əm/ *n.* **1** universe **2** the whole of a complex structure [fr. MACRO- + COSMOS]

ma·cron /mā′krän′, mak′rän′/ *n.* mark (‾) over a long or stressed vowel [Gk *makros* long]

mac·ro·scop·ic /mak′rəskäp′ik/ *adj.* visible to the naked eye

mad /mad/ *adj.* (**mad′der, mad′dest**) **1** insane; frenzied **2** wildly foolish **3** (often foll. by *about*) *Colloq.* wildly excited or infatuated **4** angry **5** (of an animal) rabid **6** like mad *Colloq.* with great energy or enthusiasm —**mad′ly** *adv.*; **mad′ness** *n.* [OE]

Mad·a·gas·car /mad′əgas′kər/ *n.* (formerly **Malagasy Republic**) island country in the Indian Ocean, off the E coast of Africa. Capital: Antananarivo. Pop. 12,803,000 —**Ma′da·gas′can** *n.* & *adj.*

mad·am /mad′əm/ *n.* (*pl.* **mes·dames** /mādäm′, -dam′/) **1** polite or respectful form of address or mode of reference to a woman **2** (*pl.* **-ams**) woman in charge of a brothel [rel. to MADAME]

ma·dame /mad′əm/ *n.* (*pl.* **mes·dames** /mādäm′, -dam′/) **1** Mrs. or madam **2** MADAM, 1 [Fr *ma dame* my lady]

mad′cap′ *adj.* **1** wildly impulsive —*n.* **2** wildly impulsive person

mad·den /mad′n/ *v.* **1** make or become mad **2** irritate —**mad′den·ing** *adj.*; **mad′den·ing·ly** *adv.*

mad·der /mad′ər/ *n.* **1** herbaceous plant with yellowish flowers **2** red dye from its root [OE]

made /mād/ *v.* *past* and *past part.* of MAKE

Ma·dei·ra /mədēr′ə, -der′ə/ *n.* **1** island group off the NW coast of Africa; part of Portugal **2** the major island of this group **3** (often **m-**) a rich wine resembling sherry, originally made there

ma·de·moi·selle /mad′(ə)mwəzel′/ *n.* (*pl.* **mes′de·moi·selles′** /mādm-/) unmarried woman; girl; Miss [Fr *ma* my + *demoiselle* DAMSEL]

made′-to-meas′ure *adj.* made from different fitted parts

made′-to-or′der *adj.* made from yard goods; custom-made

mad′house′ *n.* **1** *Colloq.* scene of confused uproar **2** *Archaic.* mental home or hospital

Mad·i·son /mad′isən/ *n.* capital of Wis., in the S part. Pop. 191,262

Mad·i·son /mad′isən/ *n.*, **James** 1751–1836; 4th US president (1809–17)

Mad′i·son Av′e·nue *n.* **1** street in New York City considered the center of the US advertising industry **2** the advertising industry generally

mad′man′ *n.* (*pl.* **-men′**) man who is mad —**mad′wom′an** *n. fem.* (*pl.* **-wom′en**)

mad′ mon′ey *n. Colloq.* cash kept for unforeseen expenses

Ma·don·na /mədän′ə/ *n.* **1** the Virgin Mary **2** (**m-**) picture or statue of her [It: my lady]

Ma·dras /madras′, -dräs′/ *n.* seaport in SE India on the Bay of Bengal. Pop. 3,795,000

Ma·drid /madrid′/ *n.* capital of Spain. Pop. 2,909,800 —**Mad·ri·le·ni·an** /mad′rilĕ′nēən/ *n.* & *adj.*

mad·ri·gal /mad′rigəl/ *n.* part song, usu. unaccompanied, for several voices [It fr. MedL]

Ma·du·ra /mäj′ərə/ *n.* city in S India. Pop. 951,700

mael·strom /māl′strəm/ *n.* **1** great whirlpool **2** state of confusion [Du]

maes·tro /mī′strō, mäəs′-/ *n.* (*pl.* **-tros** or **-tri** /-trē′/) **1** distinguished musician, esp. a conductor, composer, or teacher **2** great performer in any sphere [It: master]

Mae·ter·linck /māt′ərlinGk′, met′-/, **Count Maurice** 1862–1947; Belgian poet and naturalist

Ma·fi·a /mäf′ēə, maf′-/ *n.* organized body of criminals —**Ma·fi·o·so** *n.* (*pl.* **-o·si** /-sē/) [It, perh. fr. Sicilian]

mag·a·zine /mag′əzēn′/ *n.* **1** periodical containing articles, stories, etc. **2** chamber for cartridges in a firearm **3** similar device in a camera, slide projector, etc. **4** military store for arms, ammunition, etc. [Ar *makhāzin* storehouse]

Mag·de·burg /mag′dəbərg′/ *n.* city in Germany. Pop. 278,800

Ma·gel·lan /məjel′ən/, **Ferdinand** c. 1480–1521; Portuguese navigator

ma·gen·ta /məjent′ə/ *n.* **1** shade of crimson **2** aniline crimson dye —*adj.* **3** of or colored with magenta [*Magenta* in N. Italy]

mag·got /mag′ət/ *n.* larva, esp. of the housefly or bluebottle —**mag′got·y** *adj.* [ME, perh. alter. of *maddock*, fr. ON]

ma·gi /mā′jī′/ *n. pl.* of MAGUS

mag·ic /maj′ik/ *n.* **1** supposed art of influencing or controlling events supernaturally **2** conjuring tricks **3** enchanting quality or phenomenon —*adj.* **4** of magic **5** producing surprising results —**mag′i·cal** *adj.*; **mag′i·cal·ly** *adv.* [Gk *magikos*, rel. to MAGUS]

ma·gi·cian /məjish′ən/ *n.* person skilled in magic

Mag′ic Mark′er *n. Tdmk.* broad felt-tipped pen

mag′ic num′ber *n.* **1** *Physics.* number of neutrons or protons in very stable atomic nuclei **2** *Baseball.* number of combined wins and opponent's losses needed for a team to secure a championship

mag·is·te·ri·al /maj′əstēr′ēəl/ *adj.* **1** imperious **2** of a magistrate —**mag·is·te′ri·al·ly** *adv.* [L *magisterium* mastery]

mag·is·trate /maj′əstrāt′/ *n.* **1** civil officer administering the law **2** lesser official, as a justice of the peace [L, rel. to MASTER]

mag·ma /mag′mə/ *n.* molten rock under the earth's crust, which forms igneous rock [Gk]

Mag·na Car·ta /mag′nə kärt′ə/ *n.* (also **Mag′na Char′ta** /kär′tə/) charter of liberty for English people obtained from King John in 1215 [MedL: great charter]

mag·nan·i·mous /magnan′əməs/ *adj.* nobly generous; not petty in feelings or conduct —**mag·na·nim·i·ty** /mag′nənim′ətē/ *n.*; **mag·nan′i·mous·ly** *adv.* [L *magnus* great + *animus* mind]

mag·nate /mag′nāt′/ *n.* wealthy and influential person, usu. in business [L *magnus* great]

mag·ne·sia /magnē′zhə, -shə/ *n.* magnesium oxide used as an antacid and laxative [*Magnesia* in Asia Minor]

mag·ne·si·um /magnē-zēəm/ *n.* silvery, light-weight metallic element; *symb.* Mg

mag·net /mag'nit/ *n.* piece of iron, alloy, etc., that attracts iron and points approximately north and south when suspended [Gk *mag-nēta*, rel. to MAGNESIA]

mag·net·ic /magnet'ik/ *adj.* **1a** having the properties of a magnet **b** produced or acting by magnetism **2** strongly attractive —**mag·net'i·cal·ly** *adv.*

mag·net'ic field' *n.* area of force around a magnet

mag·net'ic res'o·nance im'ag·ing *n.* see MRI

mag·net'ic tape' *n.* plastic strip coated with magnetic material for recording sound or pictures

mag·ne·tism /mag'nətiz'əm/ *n.* **1a** magnetic phenomena and their science **b** property of producing these **2** attraction; personal charm

mag·ne·tize /mag'nətīz'/ *v.* (**·tized, ·tiz·ing**) **1** give magnetic properties to **2** attract —**mag·ne·tiz'a·ble** *adj.*; **mag·ne·ti·za'tion** *n.*

mag·ne·to /magnet'ō/ *n.* (*pl.* **·tos**) electric generator using permanent magnets

mag·nif·i·cent /magnif'əsənt/ *adj.* **1** splendid; stately **2** *Colloq.* fine; excellent —**mag·nif'i·cence** *n.*; **mag·nif'i·cent·ly** *adv.* [L *magnificus* fr. *magnus* great]

mag·ni·fy /mag'nəfī'/ *v.* (**·fied, ·fy·ing**) **1** make (a thing) appear larger than it is, as with a lens **2** exaggerate **3** intensify —**mag'ni·fi'a·ble** *adj.*; **mag·ni·fi·ca'tion** /·fikā'sHən/, **mag'ni·fi·er** *n.* [L *magnificare* make great]

Mag·ni·to·gorsk /mag'nətōgôrsk'/ *n.* city in Russia on the Ural River. Pop. 444,500

mag·ni·tude /mag'nət(y)ōod/ *n.* **1** largeness **2** size **3** importance **4** degree of brightness of a star [L *magnus* great]

mag·no·lia /magnōl'yə/ *n.* **1** tree with dark-green foliage and waxy flowers **2** creamy-pink color [for P. *Magnol*, French botanist]

mag·num /mag'nəm/ *n.* (*pl.* **·nums**) wine bottle twice the normal size [L fr. *magnus* great]

mag·num o·pus /mag'nəm ō'pəs/ *n. Latin.* great work of art, literature, etc.; masterpiece

mag·pie /mag'pī'/ *n.* **1** a kind of crow with a long tail and black and white plumage **2** chatterer **3** indiscriminate collector [fr. *Mag*, abbr. of *Margaret* + L *pie*]

Ma·gritte /mägrēt'/, **René** 1898–1967; Belgian painter

ma·gus /mā'gəs/ *n.* (*pl.* **ma·gi**) **1** priest of ancient Persia **2** (**the Magi**) the 'wise men' from the East who brought gifts to Jesus (Matt. 2:1–12) [Pers]

Mag·yar /mag'yär', mäg'-/ *n.* **1** member of the chief ethnic group in Hungary **2** their language —*adj.* **3** of this people

Ma·hal·la al-Ku·bra /məhal'ə al kōō'brə/ *n.* city in Egypt. Pop. 358,800

ma·ha·ra·jah /mä'hərä'jə/ *n.* (also **ma'ha·ra'ja**) *Hist.* title of some Indian princes —**ma·ha·ra·ni** /mä'härä'nē/ (or **ma'ha·ra'nee**) *n. fem.* [Hindi: great king]

ma·ha·ri·shi /mä'hərisH'ē/ *n.* (*pl.* **·shis**) great Hindu sage [Skt: great saint]

ma·hat·ma /məhat'mə/ *n.* **1** (in India, etc.) revered person **2** one of a class of persons

supposed by some Buddhists to have special powers [Skt: great soul]

Mah·fouz /mäf'ōoz'/, **Naguib** 1911– ; Egyptian writer; Nobel prize 1988

mah·jongg /mä' zHäNG', jäNG'-; -ONG'/ *n.* (also **-jong**) table game played with pieces called tiles [Chin dial. *ma-tsiang* sparrows]

Mah·ler /mäl'ər/, **Gustav** 1860–1911; Austrian composer and conductor

ma·hog·a·ny /məhäg'ənē/ *n.* (*pl.* **·nies**) **1a** a reddish-brown tropical tree **b** its wood, used for furniture **2** its color

Ma·ho·met /məhäm'it/ see MUHAMMAD

ma·hout /məhout'/ *n.* (in India, etc.) elephant driver [Hindi fr. Skt]

maid /mād/ *n.* **1** female servant **2** *Archaic or Poet.* girl; young woman [abbr. of MAIDEN]

maid·en /mād'n/ *n.* **1a** *Archaic* or *Poet.* young unmarried woman **b** unmarried (**maiden aunt**) **2** first (**maiden voyage**) —**maid'en·hood** *n.*; **maid·en·ly** *adj.* [OE]

maid'en·hair' *n.* delicate fern

maid'en·head' *n.* **1** virginity **2** hymen

maid'en name' *n.* woman's surname before marriage

maid' of hon'or *n.* principal bridesmaid, if unmarried

maid'ser'vant *n.* female servant

mail¹ /māl/ *n.* **1** letters, parcels, etc., carried by the postal service **2** postal system **3** one complete delivery or collection of mail —*v.* **4** send by mail [OFr *malle* wallet, fr. Gmc]

mail² *n.* body armor of metal rings or plates [OFr *maille* fr. L *macula* spot; mesh]

mail'bag' *n.* large sack for carrying mail

mail'box' *n.* box to which mail is delivered or from which it is picked up

mail' car'rier *n.* person who delivers mail

Mail·er /mā'lər/, **Norman** 1923– ; US writer

mail'ing list' *n.* list of people to whom advertising matter, etc., is mailed

mail'man' *n.* (*pl.* **·men'**) male letter carrier

mail' or'der *n.* purchase of goods by mail —**mail'-or·der** *adj.*

mail'wom'an *n.* (*pl.* **·wom'en**) female letter carrier

maim /mām/ *v.* cripple; disable; mutilate [AngFr, rel. to MAYHEM]

Mai·mon·i·des /mīmän'ədēz'/, **Moses** (born **Moses ben Maimon**) 1135–1204; Spanish-born Jewish scholastic philosopher

main /mān/ *adj.* **1** chief; principal **2** exerted to the full —*n.* **3** principal duct, etc., for water, sewage, etc. **4** *Poet.* high seas **5** in the main mostly [OE]

Maine /mān/ *n.* northeasternmost US state. Capital: Augusta. Pop. 1,227,928. Abbr. ME; Me. —**Main'er** *n.*

main'frame' *n.* **1** central processing unit of a large computer **2** large computer

main·land /mān'land', -lənd/ *n.* large continuous extent of land, excluding neighboring islands

main' line' *n.* railway line linking large cities

main'line' *v.* (**·lined, ·lin·ing**) *Slang.* inject (drugs) intravenously —**main'lin'er** *n.*

main'ly *adv.* mostly; chiefly

main·mast /mān'mast', -məst'/ *n.* principal mast of a ship

main·sail /mān'sāl', -səl/ *n.* **1** (in a square-rigged vessel) lowest sail on the mainmast **2**

(in a fore-and-aft rigged vessel) sail set on the after part of the mainmast

main'spring *n.* **1** principal spring of a watch, clock, etc. **2** chief motivating force; incentive

main'stay *n.* **1** chief support **2** stay leading forward from the top of the mainmast

main'stream *n.* prevailing trend in opinion, fashion, etc.

main·tain /māntān'/ *v.* **1** cause to continue; keep up (an activity, etc.) **2** support by work, providing funds, etc. **3** assert as true **4** preserve in good repair **5** provide means for [L *manus* hand + *tenere* hold]

main·te·nance /mān'tənəns/ *n.* **1** maintaining or being maintained **2** provision of the means to support life [MFr, rel. to MAINTAIN]

Mainz /mīnts/ *n.* port in W Germany. Pop. 179,500

ma·iol·i·ca /məyäl'ikə/ *n.* var. of MAJOLICA

maî·tre d'hô·tel /met'r dōtel'/ *n.* (*pl.* **maî' tres d'hô·tel** /met'r/-; also *Colloq.* **maî·tre d'** /mā'tər dē'/) person in charge of service in a restaurant who seats customers

maize /māz/ *n.* **1** *Brit.* CORN¹ **2** yellow [Sp]

Maj. *abbr.* Major

ma·jes·tic /məjes'tik/ *adj.* stately and dignified; imposing —**ma·jes'ti·cal·ly** *adv.*

maj·es·ty /maj'əstē/ *n.* (*pl.* **·ties**) **1** stateliness, dignity, or authority, esp. of bearing, language, etc. **2** (*cap.*) form of address for a sovereign or a sovereign's wife or widow [L *majestas*, rel. to MAJOR]

ma·jol·i·ca /məjäl'ikə/ (also **ma·iol'i·ca**) colorfully decorated earthenware [It, fr. former name of Majorca]

ma·jor /mā'jər/ *adj.* **1** relatively great in size, intensity, or importance **2** (of surgery) serious **3** *Mus.* **a** (of a scale) having intervals of a semitone above its third and seventh notes **b** (of an interval) greater by a semitone than a minor interval (*major third*) **c** (of a key) based on a major scale —*n.* **4** *Milit.* army officer ranking just below lieutenant-colonel **5a** student's main course of study **b** student of this —*v.* **6** (foll. by *in*) specialize in (a subject) [L, comp. of *magnus* great]

Ma·jor /mā'jər/, **John** 1943– ; English politician; prime minister of Great Britain (1990–)

ma·jor·do·mo /mā'jər dō'mō/ *n.* (*pl.* **·mos**) chief steward of a great household [MedL *major* MAJOR + *domus* house]

ma'jor gen·er·al *n.* officer next below a lieutenant general

ma·jor·i·ty /məjôr'ətē, -jär'-/ *n.* (*pl.* **·ties**) **1** greater number or part **2** number of votes or voters amounting to more than half **3** full legal age **4** rank of major [MedL, rel. to MAJOR]
● Usage: *Majority* means more than half: *The majority—51 people out of 100—voted for our candidate. Plurality* describes the largest number among three or more: if Adam received 30 votes, Bob received 34, and Cathy received 36, than the plurality was Cathy's and no candidate won a majority; if Adam got 20 votes, Bob 29, and Cathy 51, then Cathy won both the plurality and the majority.

ma·jor'i·ty lead'er *n.* leader of the party that has the majority of members in a legislative body

ma'jor med'ical (in·sur'ance) *n.* insurance policy covering long-term illnesses, major surgery, etc.

Ma·ju·ro /məjŏŏr'ō/ *n.* capital of the Marshall Islands. Pop. 17,600

Ma·kar·i·os III /məkär'ē·ōs', -kar'-/ 1913–77; Greek Cypriot archbishop and politician; president of Cyprus (1960–77)

make /māk/ *v.* (**made, mak·ing**) **1** construct; create; form from parts or other materials **2** cause or compel **3a** bring about (*made a noise*) **b** cause to become or seem (*made him angry*) **4** compose; prepare; deliver (*make a speech*) **5** constitute; amount to; be reckoned as (*2 and 2 make 4*) **6a** undertake (*made a promise; make an effort*) **b** perform (an action, etc.) (*made a bow*) **7** gain; acquire; procure **8** prepare **9** arrange (a bed) for use **10a** arrive at (a place) or in time for (a train, etc.) **b** manage to attend **c** *Colloq.* achieve a place in (*made the first team*) **11** enact **12** consider to be; estimate as **13** secure the success of (*make my day*) **14** accomplish (a distance, speed, score, etc.) **15** form in the mind (*make a decision*) —*n.* **16** type or brand **17** way a thing is made **18** make away with (or **off**) with steal **19** make believe pretend **20** make do manage with the inadequate means available **21** make for: **a** tend to result in **b** proceed toward **22** make good: **a** repay, repair, or compensate for **b** achieve (a purpose); be successful **23** make it *Colloq.* succeed, esp. in reaching in time **24** make love see LOVE **25** make out: **a** discern or understand **b** assert; pretend **c** *Colloq.* progress; fare *d Slang.* engage in sexual foreplay **e** engage in sexual intercourse **f** write out (a check, etc.) or fill in (a form) **26** make over: **a** transfer the possession of **b** refashion **27** make up: **a** act to overcome (a deficiency) **b** be reconciled **c** concoct **d** apply cosmetics (to) **28** make up one's mind decide **29** make up to curry favor with **30** make water urinate **31** make way: **a** allow room to pass **b** be superseded by **32** make one's way go; prosper **33** on the make *Colloq.* intent on gain [OE]

make'·be·lieve' *n.* **1** pretense —*adj.* **2** pretended

make'shift *adj.* **1** temporary —*n.* **2** temporary substitute or device

make' up' *n.* (also **make'-up'**) **1** cosmetics, as used generally or by actors **2** character, temperament, etc. **3** composition (of a thing)

mal- *comb. form* **1a** bad; badly (*malpractice; maltreat*) **b** faulty (*malfunction*) [OFr *mal* badly, fr. L *male*]

Ma·la·bo /məläb'ō/ *n.* capital of Equatorial Guinea. Pop. 31,600

mal·ad·just·ed /mal'əjəs'tid/ *adj.* unable to adapt to or cope with the demands of a social environment —**mal'ad·just'ment** *n.*

mal·a·droit /mal'ədroit'/ *adj.* clumsy; bungling [Fr]

mal·a·dy /mal'ədē/ *n.* (*pl.* **·dies**) ailment; disease [OFr *malade* sick]

Má·la·ga /mal'əgə/ *n.* seaport in S Spain. Pop. 512,100

Mal·a·gas·y /mal'əgas'ē/ *n.* **1** native or national of Madagascar **2** language of Madagascar

Mal'a·gas'y Re·pub'lic *n.* former name of Madagascar

mal·aise /məlāz', -lez'/ *n.* **1** general bodily discomfort **2** feeling of unease or demoralization [OFr]

Mal·a·mud /mal'əməd/, **Bernard** 1914–86; US writer

mal·a·mute /mal'əmyōōt'/ *n.* hardy breed of dog developed for pulling sleds [fr. *Malimiut*, a people of N Alaska]

Ma·lang /mäläNG'/ *n.* city in Indonesia, on Java. Pop. 511,800

mal·a·prop·ism /mal'əpräpiz'əm/ *n.* comical misuse of a word for one sounding similar, e.g., *alligator* for *allegory* [Mrs. *Malaprop*, character in Sheridan's *The Rivals*]

ma·lar·i·a /məler'ēə/ *n.* recurrent fever caused by a parasite transmitted by a mosquito bite **—ma·lar'i·al** *adj.* [It: bad air]

ma·lar·key /məlär'kē/ *n.* (also **ma·lar'ky**) *Colloq.* nonsense

Ma·la·tya /mäl'ätyä'/ *n.* city in central Turkey. Pop. 281,800

Ma·la·wi /mälä'wē/ *n.* republic on Lake Malawi. Capital: Lilongwe. Pop. 9,484,000

Ma·la'wi, Lake/ *n.* see NYASA, LAKE

Ma·lay /mälā', mā'lā'/ *n.* **1** member of a people in Malaysia and Indonesia **2** their language **—***adj.* **3** of this people or language **—Ma·lay'an** *n.* & *adj.* [Malay *mălāyŭ*]

Ma·lay·a /mälā'ə/ *n.* **1** MALAY PENINSULA **2** former federation of states on the Malay Peninsula; now part of Malaysia

Mal·a·ya·lam /mal'əyä'ləm/ *n.* language of SW India

Ma'lay Ar·chi·pel·a·go *n.* extensive island group between Australia and Asia, including Indonesia and the Philippines

Ma'lay Pen·in·su·la *n.* peninsula of SE Asia; includes parts of Thailand, Burma, and Malaysia

Ma·lay·sia /məlä'zHə/ **1** constitutional monarchy in SE Asia. Capital: Kuala Lumpur. Pop. 18,630,000 **2** see MALAY ARCHIPELAGO **—Ma·lay'sian** *n.* & *adj.*

Mal·colm X /mal'kəm eks'/ (born **Malcolm Little**) 1925–65; US black-rights activist; assassinated

mal·con·tent /mal'kəntent'/ *n.* **1** discontented person **—***adj.* **2** discontented [OFr]

Mal·dives /môl'dēvz, -dīvz/ *n.* republic comprising about 2,000 islands in the Indian Ocean. Capital: Male. Pop. 230,000 **—Mal·div'i·an** /-div'ēən/ *n.* & *adj.*

male /māl/ *adj.* **1** of the sex that can beget offspring by fertilization **2** of men or male animals, plants, etc.; masculine **3** (of plants or flowers) containing stamens but no pistil **4** (of parts of machinery, etc.) designed to enter or fill the corresponding hollow part **—***n.* **5** male person or animal **—male'ness** *n.* [L *masculus* fr. *mas* male]

Ma·le /mäl'ē/ *n.* capital of the Maldives. Pop. 55,100

mal·e·dic·tion /mal'ədik'sHən/ *n.* curse **—mal'e·dic'to·ry** *adj.* [L *maledictio* slander]

mal·e·fac·tor /mal'əfak'tər/ *n.* criminal; evildoer **—mal·e·fac'tion** *n.* [L *male* badly + *facere, fact*- do]

ma·lev·o·lent /məlev'ələnt/ *adj.* wishing evil

to others **—ma·lev'o·lence** *n.*; **ma·lev'o·lent·ly** *adv.* [L *male* badly + *velle, volent*- wish]

mal·fea·sance /malfē'zəns/ *n.* misconduct, esp. in an official capacity [OFr *mal* badly + *faisance* fr. *faire* do]

mal·for·ma·tion /mal'fôrma'sHən/ *n.* faulty formation **—mal·formed'** *adj.*

mal·func·tion /malfəNGk'sHən/ *n.* **1** failure to function normally **—***v.* **2** fail to function normally

Ma·li /mäl'ē/ *n.* republic in W Africa. Capital: Bamako. Pop. 8,464,000 **—Ma'li·an** *n.* & *adj.*

mal·ice /mal'əs/ *n.* **1** desire to harm or cause difficulty to others; ill will **2** *Law*. harmful intent [L *malitia*]

mal'ice a·fore'thought' *n. Law*. intention to commit a crime, esp. murder

ma·li·cious /məlisH'əs/ *adj.* given to or arising from malice **—ma·li'cious·ly** *adv.*; **ma·li'cious·ness** *n.*

ma·lign /məlīn'/ *adj.* **1** (of a thing) injurious **2** (of a disease) malignant **3** malevolent **—***v.* **4** speak ill of; slander **—ma·lig·ni·ty** /məlig'nətē/ *n.* [L *malignus*]

ma·lig·nant /məlig'nənt/ *adj.* **1a** (of a disease) very virulent or infectious **b** (of a tumor) likely to be fatal **2** harmful; feeling or showing intense ill-will **—ma·lig·nan·cy** *n.* (*pl.* ·**cies**); **ma·lig'nant·ly** *adv.* [L *malignare* act maliciously]

ma·lin·ger /məliNG'gər/ *v.* pretend to be ill, esp. to escape work **—ma·lin'ger·er** *n.* [Fr *malingre* sickly]

Ma·li·now·ski /mal'ənôf'skē/, **Bronislaw** 1884–1942; Polish-born anthropologist

mall /môl/ *n.* **1** shopping center, esp. an enclosed one **2** sheltered walk or promenade [*The Mall*, street in London]

mal·lard /mal'ərd/ *n.* common wild duck [OFr]

Mal·lar·mé /mälärmā'/, **Stéphane** 1842–98; French poet

mal·le·a·ble /mal'ēəbəl/ *adj.* **1** (of metal, etc.) that can be shaped by hammering **2** easily influenced; pliable **—mal'le·a·bil'i·ty** *n.*; **mal'le·a·bly** *adv.* [MedL, rel. to MALLET]

mal·let /mal'ət/ *n.* **1** hammer, usu. of wood **2** similar long-handled implement used in croquet, polo, etc. [L *malleus* hammer]

mal·low /mal'ō/ *n.* plant with hairy stems and leaves and pink or purple flowers [L *malva*]

Mal·mö /mäl'mə(r)/ *n.* seaport in S Sweden. Pop. 234,800

mal·nour·ished /malnər'isHt/ *adj.* suffering from malnutrition **—mal·nour'ish·ment** *n.*

mal·nu·tri·tion /mal'n(y)ōōtrisH'ən/ *n.* condition resulting from lack of healthful foods

mal·o·dor·ous /malōd'ərəs/ *adj.* foul-smelling

Mal·o·ry /mal'ərē/, (Sir) **Thomas** d. 1471; English writer

mal·prac·tice /malprak'tis/ *n.* improper, negligent, or criminal professional conduct

Mal·raux /malrō'/, **André** 1901–76; French statesman and writer

malt /môlt/ *n.* **1** barley or other grain steeped, germinated, and dried for brewing beer, ale, etc. **2** *Colloq.* malt whiskey **—***v.* **3** convert (grain) into malt **—malt'y** *adj.* (·**i·er**, ·**i·est**) [OE]

Mal·ta /môl'tə/ *n.* independent island state

in the Mediterranean Sea, S of Sicily. Capital: Valletta. Pop. 360,000

malt′ed milk′ *n.* powder of dried milk and malt added to fresh milk to make a drink

Mal·tese /môltēz′/ *n.* **1** native or language of Malta —*adj.* **2** of Malta

Mal·thus /mal′THəs, môl′-/, **Thomas Robert** 1766–1834; English economist and clergyman

mal·treat /maltrēt′/ *v.* ill-treat —**mal·treat′ment** *n.* [Fr]

malt′ whis′key *n.* whiskey made solely from malted barley

Mal·vi·nas, Is·las /malvē′nəs, ēs′ləs/ *n.* see FALKLAND ISLANDS

ma·ma /mäm′ə/ *n.* (also **mam′ma**) mother [imit.]

mam·ba /mäm′bə/ *n.* venomous African snake [Zulu *imamba*]

mam·bo /mäm′bō, mam′-/ *n.* (*pl.* **·bos**) Latin American dance like the rumba [AmerSp]

mam·mal /mam′əl/ *n.* warm-blooded vertebrate of the class secreting milk to feed its young —**mam·ma·li·an** /məmā′lēən/ *adj.* & *n.* [L *mamma* breast]

mam·ma·ry /mam′ərē/ *adj.* of the breasts

mam·mo·gram /mam′əgram′/ *n.* image obtained by mammography [L *mamma* breast]

mam·mog·ra·phy /mamäg′rəfē/ *n.* x-ray technique for screening the breasts for tumors, etc.

Mam·mon /mam′ən/ *n.* (also **m-**) wealth regarded as an evil influence or a god [Aram *māmōn* riches]

MAMMOTH 1

mam·moth /mam′əTH/ *n.* **1** large extinct elephant with a hairy coat and curved tusks —*adj.* **2** huge [Russ]

man /man/ *n.* (*pl.* **men**) **1** adult human male **2a** human being; person **b** the human race **3a** workman **b** manservant; valet **4** (usu. *pl.*) soldiers, sailors, etc., esp. nonofficers **5** piece in chess, checkers, etc. —*v.* (**manned, man·ning**) **6** supply with a person or people for work or defense **7** work, service, or defend **8 as one man** in unison **9 to a man** without exception —**man′like** *adj.* [OE]

● Usage: The use of *man* generically to mean 'human being' or 'the human race' is considered offensive and sexist by many.

Man, Isle of /man/ *n.* island in the Irish Sea between Britain and Ireland —**Manx** /maNGks/ *n.* & *adj.*

man′ a·bout town′ *n.* fashionable socializer

man·a·cle /man′ikəl/ *n.* **1** (usu. *pl.*) handcuff

2 restraint —*v.* (**·cled, ·cling**) **3** restrain, esp. with manacles [L *manicula* small hand, fr. *manus* hand]

man·age /man′ij/ *v.* (**·aged, ·ag·ing**) **1** organize; regulate; run; operate **2** succeed in achieving; contrive **3** control —**man′age·a·ble** *adj.* [L *manus* hand]

man′age·ment *n.* **1** managing or being managed **2** people engaged in administration of a business, public institution, workforce, etc.

man′ag·er *n.* **1** person who manages **2** person controlling the affairs, training, etc., of a person or team in sports, entertainment, etc. —**man′a·ge′ri·al** /-jēr′ēəl/ *adj.*

Ma·na·gua /mənäg′wə/ *n.* capital of Nicaragua. Pop. 682,100

Ma·na·ma /mənam′ə/ *n.* capital of Bahrain. Pop. 151,500

ma·ña·na /mənyän′ə/ *adv. Spanish.* **1** tomorrow (esp. to indicate procrastination) —*n.* **2** indefinite future

Ma·náos /mänous′/ *n.* (also **Ma·naus′**) port in Brazil. Pop. 613,000

man·a·tee /man′ətē′/ *n.* large aquatic plant-eating mammal [Sp fr. Carib]

Man·ches·ter /man′CHestər, -CHəstər/ *n.* **1** city in N. Hamp. Pop. 99,600 **2** city in NW England. Pop. 448,600 —**Man·cu·ni·an** /mankyōō′nēən/ *n.* & *adj.*

man·da·la /mən′dələ, man′-/ *n.* circular figure as a religious symbol of the universe [Skt: circle]

Man·da·lay /man′dəlā′/ *n.* city on the Irrawaddy River in Burma (Myanmar). Pop. 532,900

man·da·rin /man′dərin/ *n.* **1** (*cap.*) main dialect and official language of China **2** *Hist.* Chinese official **3** powerful person, esp. a top civil servant [Hindi & Skt]

man·date /man′dāt′/ *n.* **1** official command or instruction **2** authority given by electors to a government, trade union, etc. **3** authority to act for another —*v.* (**·dat·ed, ·dat·ing**) **4** instruct (a delegate) how to act or vote [L *mandatum* fr. *mandare* command]

man·da·to·ry /man′dətôr′ē/ *adj.* **1** compulsory **2** of or conveying a command —**man′da·to′ri·ly** *adv.*

Man·de·la /mandel′ə/, **Nelson** 1918– ; South African black-rights activist; president (1994–); Nobel prize 1993

man·di·ble /man′dəbəl/ *n.* **1** jaw, esp. the lower jaw in mammals and fishes **2** either part of a bird's beak, insect's mouth parts, etc. [L *mandere* chew]

man·do·lin /man′dəlin′, man′dəlin/ *n.* a kind of lute with paired metal strings plucked with a plectrum —**man′do·lin′ist** *n.* [It]

man·drake /man′drāk′/ *n.* poisonous narcotic plant with a forked root like human legs [Gk *mandragoras*]

man·drel /man′drəl/ *n.* **1** shaft to which work is fixed on a lathe **2** cylindrical tapered steel for shaping or forging other metal objects

man·drill /man′drəl/ *n.* large W African baboon [prob. fr. MAN + DRILL[4]]

mane /mān/ *n.* long hair on the neck of a horse, lion, etc. [OE]

man-eat·er /man′ ē′tər/ *n.* **1** wild carnivore

that attacks people 2 *Colloq.* aggressive woman who mistreats men

ma·nège /manezH', mə-/ *n.* (also **ma·nege'**) 1 movements of a trained horse 2 horsemanship [Fr fr. It, rel. to MANAGE]

Man·et /mana', mä-/, **Édouard** 1832–83; French painter

ma·neu·ver /mɑnōō'vǝr/ *n.* 1 planned and controlled movement of military personnel, ships, etc. 2 skillful movement; artful plan —*v.* 3 move carefully or skillfully 4 perform or cause to perform maneuvers 5 handle adroitly 6 use artifice —**ma·neu'ver·a·bil'i·ty** *n.;* **ma·neu'ver·a·ble** *adj.* [Fr fr. L *manus* hand + *operare* work]

man' **Fri'day** *n.* male helper [fr. character in novel by DEFOE]

man'ful *adj.* brave; resolute —**man'ful·ly** *adv.*

man·ga·nese /maNG'gǝnēz'/ *n.* gray metallic element; *symb.* **Mn** [It, fr. rel. to MAGNESIA]

mange /mānj/ *n.* skin disease in hairy and woolly animals [Fr *mangeue* itch, fr. L *manducare* chew]

man·ger /mān'jǝr/ *n.* box or trough for feeding horses or cattle [MFr fr. L *manducare* chew]

man·gle¹ /maNG'gǝl/ *n.* machine of two or more cylinders for ironing [Du *mangel* fr. LL]

man·gle² *v.* (·gled, ·gling) 1 hack or mutilate by blows 2 spoil; ruin [AngFr *ma(ha)ngler*, prob. rel. to MAIM]

man·go /maNG'gō/ *n.* (*pl.* ·goes or ·gos) 1 tropical fruit with yellowish flesh 2 tree bearing this [Tamil *mānkāy*]

man·grove /maNG'grōv, man'-/ *n.* tropical tree with many tangled roots above ground

man·gy /mān'jē/ *adj.* (·gi·er, ·gi·est) 1 having mange 2 squalid; shabby; dirty

man'han·dle *v.* (·dled, ·dling) handle roughly

man'hole' *n.* covered opening in a pavement for workmen to gain access to utilities below

man'hood' *n.* 1 state of being a man 2a manliness; courage b a man's sexual potency 3 men of a country, etc.

man'-hour' *n.* work done by one person in one hour

man'hunt' *n.* search for an escaped criminal

ma·ni·a /mā'nēǝ/ *n.* 1 mental illness marked by excitement and violence 2 excessive enthusiasm; obsession [Gk: madness]

-mania *comb. form* 1 denoting a specified type of mental disorder (*megalomania*) 2 denoting enthusiasm or admiration (*Beatlemania*)

ma·ni·ac /mā'nē·ak'/ *n.* person suffering from mania —**ma·ni·a·cal** /mǝnī'ǝkǝl/ *adj.;* **ma·ni'a·cal·ly** *adv.*

ma·nic /man'ik/ *adj.* 1 of or affected by mania 2 *Colloq.* wildly excited; frenzied; excitable —**man'i·cal·ly** *adv.*

man'ic-de·pres'sive *adj.* 1 relating to a mental disorder with alternating periods of elation and depression —*n.* 2 person with such a disorder

man·i·cure /man'ikyōōr'/ *n.* 1 cosmetic treatment of the hands and fingernails —*v.* (·cured, ·cur·ing) 2 give a manicure to (the hands or a person) —**man'i·cur'ist** *n.* [L *manus* hand + *cura* care]

man·i·fest /man'ǝfest'/ *adj.* 1 clear or obvious —*v.* 2 show plainly to the eye or mind —*n.* 3 cargo or passenger list —**man'i·fes·ta'tion** /-tā'sHǝn/ *n.;* **man'i·fest·ly** *adv.* [L *manifestus*]

man'i·fest des'ti·ny *n.* (often *cap.*) 1 *US Hist.* 19th-cent. doctrine that the US ought to expand across N America 2 any such territorial expansion 3 inevitable outcome

man·i·fes·to /man'ǝfes'tō/ *n.* (*pl.* ·tos) declaration of policies, esp. by a political party [It, rel. to MANIFEST]

man·i·fold /man'ǝfōld'/ *adj.* 1 many and various 2 having various forms, parts, applications, etc. —*n.* 3 manifold thing 4 pipe or chamber branching into several openings [OE, rel. to MANY + -FOLD]

man·i·kin /man'ikǝn/ *n.* (also **man·ni·kin**) 1 little man; dwarf 2 MANNEQUIN [Du]

Ma·nil·a¹ /mǝnil'ǝ/ *n.* capital of the Philippines. Pop. 1,587,000

Ma·nil·a² /mǝnil'ǝ/ *n.* 1 (in full **Ma·nil'a hemp'**) strong fiber made from a Philippine plant 2 (also m-) strong brown paper made from this

man' in the street' *n.* ordinary person

ma·nip·u·late /mǝnip'yǝlāt'/ *v.* (·lat·ed, ·lat·ing) 1 handle, esp. with skill 2 manage (a person, situation, etc.) to one's own advantage, esp. unfairly 3 move (part of a patient's body) by hand —**ma·nip'u·la·ble** /-yǝlǝbǝl/ *adj.;* **ma·nip'u·la'tion** *n.;* **ma·nip'u·la'tive** *adj.;* **ma·nip'u·la'tive·ly** *adv.;* **ma·nip'u·la'tor** *n.* [back formation fr. *manipulation*, fr. L *manus* hand]

Man·i·to·ba /man'itō'bǝ/ *n.* province of Canada, in the central part. Capital: Winnipeg. Pop. 1,116,000

Ma·ni·za·les /män'isäl'es/ *n.* city in Colombia. Pop. 275,000

man'kind' *n.* 1 human species 2 /man'kind'/ male people

Man·ley /man'lē/, **Michael Norman** 1923– ; prime minister of Jamaica (1972–80; 1989–)

man·ly /man'lē/ *adj.* (·li·er, ·li·est) 1 having qualities associated with a man (e.g., strength and courage) 2 befitting a man —**man'li·ness** *n.*

man'-made' *adj.* artificial; synthetic

Mann /man/ 1 **Horace** 1796–1859; US educator 2 /män/ **Thomas** 1875–1955; German writer

man·na /man'ǝ/ *n.* 1 substance miraculously supplied as food to the Israelites in the wilderness (Exod. 16) 2 unexpected benefit (esp. *manna from heaven*) [OE, ult. fr. Heb]

manned /mand/ *adj.* (of a spacecraft, etc.) having a human crew

man·ne·quin /man'ikǝn/ *n.* 1 fashion model 2 (also **man'i·kin**) window dummy [Fr: MANIKIN]

man·ner /man'ǝr/ *n.* 1 way a thing is done or happens 2 (*pl.*) a social behavior (*good manners*) b polite behavior (*no manners*) 3 style 4 kind; sort 5 to the manner born naturally at ease in a particular situation, etc. [AngFr fr. L *manus* hand]

man·nered /man'ǝrd/ *adj.* 1 (*in comb.*) having specified manners (*ill-mannered*) 2 artificial

man·ner·ism /man'ǝriz'ǝm/ *n.* 1 habitual gesture or way of speaking, etc. 2a stylistic trick in art, etc. **b** excessive use of these —**man'ner·ist** /-ist/ n. & adj.

man'ner·ly adj. well-mannered; polite

Mann·heim /män'hīm'/ n. city on the Rhine River in Germany. Pop. 310,400

man·ni·kin /man'əkin/ n. var. of MANIKIN

man·nish /man'isн/ adj. **1** (of a woman) masculine in appearance or manner **2** characteristic of a man —**man'nish·ly** adv.; **man' nish·ness** n.

ma·no a ma·no /mä'nō ä mä'nō/ adv. **1** Bullfighting. with two fighters alternating **2** in direct confrontation [Sp: hand to hand]

ma·noeu·vre /mənōō'vər/ n. & v. (·vred, ·vring) var., esp. Brit., of MANEUVER

man' of let'ters n. scholar or writer

man'-of-war' n. (pl. men'-) warship

ma·nom·e·ter /manom'mitər/ n. instrument for measuring fluid pressure (esp. blood pressure) [Gk manós sparse + -METER]

man·or /man'ər/ n. (also **man'or·house'**) large country house with lands —**ma·no·ri·al** /mənôr'ēəl/ adj. [L manere remain]

man'pow'er n. number of people available for work, service, etc.

manqué /mänkā', mäNG-/ adj. (placed after noun) French. that might have been but is not; would-be (an actor manqué)

Man Ray see RAY, Man

MANSARD

man·sard /man'särd, -sərd/ n. roof with four sloping sides, which become steeper halfway down [for N. Mansart, French architect]

manse /mans/ n. ecclesiastical residence [MedL fr. L manere remain; dwell]

man'ser·vant n. (pl. men'ser'vants) male servant

man·sion /man'shən/ n. grand house [L mansio stopping place]

man·slaugh·ter /man'slôt'ər/ n. unintentional but unlawful killing of a human being

man·tel /mant'l/ n. (also **man'tel·piece'**) structure of wood, marble, etc., above and around a fireplace [var. of MANTLE]

man·til·la /man-tē'(y)ə, -til'ə/ n. lace scarf worn, esp. by Spanish women, over the hair and shoulders [Sp, dim. of manta blanket]

man·tis /mant'is/ n. (pl. ·tis·es or ·tes /-tēz/) (in full **pray'ing man'tis**) predatory insect that holds its forelegs like hands folded in prayer [Gk: prophet]

man·tis·sa /man·tis'ə/ n. part of a logarithm after the decimal point [L: makeweight]

man·tle /mant'l/ n. **1** loose sleeveless cloak **2** covering (mantle of snow) **3** lacelike tube fixed around a gas jet to give an incandescent light **4** region between the crust and the core of the earth —v. (·tled, ·tling) **5** clothe; conceal; envelop [L mantellum]

man·tra /man'trə, män'-/ n. **1** Hindu or Buddhist devotional incantation **2** Vedic hymn [Skt: instrument of thought]

man·u·al /man'yōōəl, -yəl/ adj. **1** of or done with the hands **2** worked by hand, not automatically —n. **3** reference book **4** military drill for handling a rifle —**man'u·al·ly** adv. [L manus hand]

man·u·fac·ture /man'yəfak'CHər/ n. **1** making of articles, esp. in a factory —v. (·tured, ·tur·ing) **2** make (articles), esp. on an industrial scale **3** invent or fabricate (evidence, a story, etc.) —**man'u·fac'tur·er** n. [LL manufactum made by hand]

man·u·mit /man'yəmit'/ v. (·mit·ted, ·mit·ting) release from servitude or slavery [L manumittere send away; set free]

ma·nure /mən(y)ŏŏr'/ n. **1** fertilizer, esp. dung —v. (·nured, ·nur·ing) **2** apply manure to (land, etc.) [MFr manouvrer do manual work, rel. to MANEUVER]

man·u·script /man'yəskript'/ n. **1** text written by hand or typed **2** handwritten form —adj. **3** written by hand [MedL manuscriptus written by hand]

Manx /maNGks/ adj. **1** of the Isle of Man —n. **2** former Celtic language of the Isle of Man **3** Manx people [ON]

Manx' cat' n. tailless variety of cat

man·y /men'ē/ adj. (more, most) **1** great in number; numerous —n. **2** many people or things [OE]

man-year /man' yēr'/ n. work done by one person in one year

Mao·ism /mou'iz'əm/ n. Communist doctrines of Mao Zedong —**Mao'ist** /-ist/ n. & adj.

Mao·ri /mou'rē/ n. (pl. same or ·ris) **1** member of the aboriginal people of New Zealand **2** their language —adj. **3** of this people

Mao Ze·dong /mou' dzə'dŏŏNG'/ (also **Mao Tse-tung**) 1893–1976; Chinese Communist revolutionary and leader

map /map/ n. **1** flat representation of the earth's surface, or part of it **2** similar representation of the stars, sky, moon, etc. —v. (mapped, map·ping) **3** represent on a map **4** map out plan in detail [L mappa napkin]

ma·ple /mā'pəl/ n. **1** any of various trees grown for shade, ornament, wood, or sugar **2** its wood [OE]

ma'ple sug'ar n. sugar produced by evaporating the sap of some kinds of maple

ma'ple syr'up n. syrup made by evaporating maple sap or dissolving maple sugar

Ma·pu·to /mäpōōt'ō/ n. (formerly Lourenço Marques /lərēn'sō märkes', mär' kəs/) capital of Mozambique. Pop. 931,600

mar /mär/ v. (marred, mar·ring) spoil; disfigure [OE]

Mar. abbr. March

mar·a·bou /mar'əbŏŏ/ n. **1** large W African stork **2** its down as trimming, etc. [Fr fr. Ar]

ma·ra·ca /mərāk'ə, -rak'ə/ n. dried gourd containing beans or pebbles shaken rhythmically as a musical instrument [Port]

Mar·a·cai·bo /mar'əkī'bō/ n. seaport in NW Venezuela. Pop. 1,207,500

Ma·ra·cay /mär'əkī'/ n. city in NE Venezuela. Pop. 354,400

mar·a·schi·no /mar′əskē′nō, -SHē′-/ *n.* (*pl.* ·nos) sweet liqueur made from black cherries [It]

mar′a·schi′no cher′ry *n.* cherry with maraschino flavor used in cocktails, etc.

Ma·rat /märä′/, **Jean Paul** 1743–93; French revolutionary leader

Ma·ra·thi /mərä′tē/ *n.* language of central and W India

mar·a·thon /mar′əтнän′/ *n.* 1 long-distance running race, usu. of 26 miles, 385 yards (42.195 km) 2 long-lasting or difficult undertaking [*Marathon* in Greece, scene of a decisive battle in 490 B.C.]

ma·raud /mərôd′/ *v.* make a plundering raid (on) **—ma·raud′er** *n.* [Fr *maraud* rogue]

mar·ble /mär′bəl/ *n.* 1 crystalline limestone capable of being polished, used in sculpture and architecture 2a anything of marble b anything like marble in hardness, coldness, etc. 3a small, esp. glass, ball as a toy b (*pl.*) game using these 4 (*pl.*) Slang. one's mental faculties —*v.* (*·bled, ·bling*) 5 stain or color (paper, soap, etc.) to look like marble 6 cause meat to be striped with fat [L *marmor* fr. Gk]

march[1] /märcH/ *v.* 1 (cause to) walk in a military manner with a regular tread (*army marched past; marched him away*) 2a walk purposefully b (of events, etc.) continue unrelentingly (*time marches on*) **—**n. 3a act of marching b uniform military step 4 progress or continuity 5 music to accompany a march **—march′er** *n.* [OFr *marchier*]

march[2] *n. Hist.* (usu. *pl.*) boundary; frontier [OFr *marche* fr. Gmc]

March *n.* third month of the year in the Gregorian calendar [L *Martius* of Mars]

march′ing or′ders *n. pl.* 1 order for troops to mobilize, etc. 2 dismissal

Mar·ci·a·no /mär′sē·an′ō, -SHē-, -än′ō/, **Rocky** 1923–69; US boxer

Mar·co·ni /märkō′nē/, **Guglielmo** 1874–1937; Italian engineer and inventor; pioneer in wireless telegraphy

Mar·co Po·lo see POLO, MARCO

Mar·cos /mär′kōs/, **Ferdinand** 1917–89; Phillipine president (1965–86)

Mar·cus Au·re·li·us /mär′kəs ôrē′lēəs/ 121–180; Stoic philosopher; emperor of Rome (161–180)

Mar·cuse /märkōō′zə/, **Herbert** 1898–1979; German-born US philosopher

Mar·di Gras /märd′ē grä′, ·grô′/ *n.* last day of a pre-Lenten carnival; Shrove Tuesday [Fr: fat Tuesday]

mare[1] /mar, mer/ *n.* female equine animal, esp. a horse [OE]

ma·re[2] /mär′ā/ *n.* (*pl.* ·ri·a /-rēə/ or ·res) large dark flat area on the moon, once thought to be sea [L: sea]

Mare, Walter de la see DE LA MARE, WALTER

mare's′ nest′ /marz, mərz/ *n.* 1 delusion or hoax 2 confused mess

mar·ga·rine /märj′(ə)rin, -ərēn′/ *n.* butter substitute made from vegetable oils or animal fats with milk [Gk *margaron* pearl]

mar·ga·ri·ta /mär′gərē′tə/ *n.* cocktail of tequila, lemon or lime juice, and orange-flavored liqueur

mar·gin /mär′jən/ *n.* 1 edge or border of a surface 2 blank border around print 3 profit 4 amount or interval 5 **on margin** (of stocks) paid for in part by credit **—mar′gin·al** *adj.*; **mar′gin·al·ly** *adv.* [L *margo, margin-* border]

mar·gi·na·lia /mär′jənā′lēə/ *n. pl.* marginal notes

mar·gin·al·ize /mär′jənəlīz′/ *v.* (·ized, ·iz·ing) make or treat as insignificant **—mar′gin·al·i·za′tion** *n.*

mar′gin of er′ror *n.* (also **mar′gin for er′ror**) allowance for miscalculation

Mar·gre·the II /märgret′ə/ 1940– ; queen of Denmark (1972–)

ma·ri·a·chi /mär′ēä′cHē, mar′-/ *n.* 1 Mexican strolling band 2 music played by such a band [MexSp]

Mar′i·an′a Trench′ /mar′ē·an′ə, mer′-/ *n.* Pacific depression SW of the Mariana Islands; greatest known ocean depth: 36,201 ft.

Ma·rie An·toi·nette /mərē′ an′twanet′/ 1755–93; queen of France (1774–92), wife of Louis XVI

Ma·rie de Mé·di·cis /mərē′ də mädēsēs′, med′-/ (Italian name **Maria de′ Medici** /mäd′əcHē/) 1573–1642; queen of France (1610–17)

mar·i·gold /mar′əgōld′, mer′-/ *n.* plant with golden or bright yellow flowers [*Mary* (prob. the Virgin) + *gold*]

mar·i·jua·na /mar′ə(h)wän′ə/ *n.* (also **mar·i·hua′na**) dried leaves, etc., of hemp, smoked as a drug [MexSp]

ma·rim·ba /mərim′bə/ *n.* xylophone with a resonator under each bar [Congo]

ma·ri·na /mərē′nə/ *n.* harbor for pleasure-yachts, etc. [L, rel. to MARINE]

mar·i·nade /mar′ənād′/ *n.* 1 mixture of wine, vinegar, oil, spices, etc., for soaking meat, fish, etc., before cooking 2 meat, fish, etc., so soaked —*v.* (·nad·ed, ·nad·ing) 3 MARINATE [Fr fr. Sp *marinar* pickle in brine]

ma·ri·na·ra /mar′ənar′ə, mä′rinä′rä/ *Cookery.* *n.* 1 meatless tomato sauce **—**adj. 2 served with or in such a sauce

mar·i·nate /mar′ənāt′/ *v.* (·nat·ed, ·nat·ing) soak in a marinade **—mar′i·na′tion** *n.* [It *marinare* pickle]

ma·rine /mərēn′/ *adj.* 1 of, found in, or produced by the sea 2 of shipping or naval matters (*marine insurance*) **—**n. 3 soldier trained to serve on land or sea 4 (often *cap.*) member of the US Marine Corps 5 country's shipping or navy (*merchant marine*) [L *mare* sea]

Ma·rine′ Corps′ *n.* branch of the US armed forces trained for combat on land, on sea, and in the air

mar·i·ner /mar′ənər/ *n.* seaman

mar·i·o·nette /mar′ēənet′/ *n.* puppet worked by strings [Fr, rel. to *Mary*]

mar·i·tal /mar′ət·l/ *adj.* of marriage or marriage relations [L *maritus* husband]

mar·i·time /mar′ətīm′/ *adj.* 1 connected with the sea or seafaring 2 living or found near the sea [L *maritimus*]

Mar′i·time Prov′in·ces *n.* Canadian provinces of Prince Edward Island, New Brunswick, and Nova Scotia

Ma·ri·u·pol /mär′ē·ōō′pōl/ *n.* (formerly Zhda′nov) city on the Sea of Azov in Ukraine. Pop. 522,000

mar·jo·ram /mär′jərəm/ *n.* aromatic herb used in cookery [L fr. Gk *amārakos*]

mark[1] /märk/ *n.* 1 spot, sign, stain, scar, etc., on a surface, etc. 2 (esp. in *comb.*) a written or printed symbol (*question mark*) b number or letter denoting proficiency, conduct, etc. (*black mark; high marks for effort*) 3 sign of quality, character, feeling, etc. 4a target, etc. b line, etc., indicating a position 5 fixed object used as a guide to position 6 (usu. *cap.*) particular design, model, etc., of a car, aircraft, etc. 7 impression; effect 8 starting-point in a race —*v.* 9a make a mark on b mark with initials, name, etc., to identify 10 correct and assess (a student's work, etc.) 11 attach a price to 12 notice or observe 13 characterize (*day was marked by storms*) 14 beside (or off or wide of) the mark: a irrelevant b not accurate 15 make one's mark attain distinction 16 mark down: a reduce the price of (goods, etc.) b make a written note of 17 mark time: a march on the spot without moving forward b wait 18 mark up: a add a profit to the cost of (goods, etc.) b mark or correct (text, etc.) [OE]

mark[2] *n.* DEUTSCHE MARK [Gmc]

Mark, St. /märk/ one of the twelve Apostles; credited as writer of the second Gospel

Mark An·to·ny see ANTONY, MARK

mark′-down′ *n.* reduction in price

marked /märkt/ *adj.* 1 having a visible mark 2 clearly noticeable 3 (of playing-cards) marked on their backs to assist cheating —**mark·ed·ly** /mär′kədlē/ *adv.*

mark·er /mär′kər/ *n.* 1 thing marking a position 2 person or thing that marks 3 *Slang.* I.O.U.

mar·ket /mär′kit/ *n.* 1 gathering of buyers and sellers of provisions, livestock, etc. 2 space for this 3 demand (for a commodity) 4 place or group providing such a demand 5 conditions, etc., for buying or selling; trade 6 STOCK MARKET —*v.* 7 offer for sale —**mar′ket·a·bil′i·ty** *n.*; **mar′ket·a·ble** *adj.*; **mar′ket·er, mar′ket·eer′** /-kitēr′/, **mar′ket·ing** *n.* [L *mercatus* market; trade]

mar′ket-place′ *n.* 1 open space for a market 2 commercial world

mar′ket re·search′ *n.* surveying of consumers' needs and preferences

Mark·ham /mär′kəm/ *n.* city in Ontario, Canada. Pop. 153,800

Mark·ham /mär′kəm/, **(Charles) Edwin** 1852–1940; US poet

mark′ing *n.* (usu. *pl.*) 1 identification mark 2 coloring of an animal's fur, etc.

marks·man /märks′mən/ *n.* (*pl.* ·men) skilled shot, esp. with a pistol or rifle —**marks′man·ship′** *n.*

mark′-up′ *n.* amount added to cost for profit

Marl·bor·ough, 1st Duke of /môl′brə/ see CHURCHILL, JOHN

mar·lin /mär′lən/ *n.* (*pl.* same or ·lins) long-nosed marine gamefish [fr. MARLINSPIKE]

mar′lin·spike′ *n.* pointed metal tool for separating strands of rope for splicing, etc. [*marling* fr. Du *marlen* fr. MDu *marren* bind]

Mar·lowe /mär′lō/, **Christopher** 1564–93; English dramatist and poet

mar·ma·lade /mär′məlād′/ *n.* preserve of citrus fruit, usu. oranges [Port *marmelo* quince fr. L fr. Gk *melimēlon*]

Mar·ma·ra, Sea of /mär′mərə/ *n.* sea in NW Turkey between Mediterranean and Black Sea

mar·mo·set /mär′məset′/ *n.* small monkey with a long bushy tail [OFr]

mar·mot /mär′mət/ *n.* heavyset burrowing rodent with a short bushy tail [OFr]

ma·roon[1] /mərōōn′/ *adj.* & *n.* brownish-crimson [Fr *marron* chestnut]

ma·roon[2] *v.* leave (a person) isolated, esp. on an island [Fr *marron* wild person, fr. Sp *cimarrón*]

Mar·quand /märkwänd′/, **J(ohn) P(hillips)** 1893–1960; US writer

marque /märk/ *n.* make of car, as distinct from a specific model [Fr: MARK[1]]

mar·quee /märkē′/ *n.* projecting roof over an entry [Fr *marquise*]

mar·quess /mär′kwis/ *n.* British nobleman ranking between duke and earl [var. of MARQUIS]

mar·quet·ry /mär′kitrē/ *n.* inlaid work in wood, ivory, etc. [MFr, rel. to MARK[1]]

Mar·quette /märket′/, **Jacques** 1637–75; French Jesuit missionary and explorer in N America

Már·quez, Gabriel García see GARCÍA MÁRQUEZ, GABRIEL

mar·quis /mär′kwis, märkē′/ *n.* foreign nobleman ranking between duke and count [MFr, rel. to MARCH[2]]

mar·quise /märkēz′/ *n.* 1 wife or widow of a marquis 2 woman holding the rank of marquis

Mar·ra·kesh /mar′əkesh′/ *n.* city in Morocco. Pop. 439,700

mar·riage /mar′ij, mer′-/ *n.* 1 legal union of a man and a woman 2 wedding 3 intimate union; combination —**mar′riage·a·bil′i·ty** *n.*; **mar′riage·a·ble** *adj.* [OFr *marier* MARRY]

mar·ried /mar′ēd, mer′-/ *adj.* 1 united in marriage 2 of marriage (*married name; married life*) —*n.* 3 (usu. *pl.*) married person (*young marrieds*)

mar·row /mar′ō/ *n.* soft fatty substance in the cavities of bones [OE]

mar·ry /mar′ē, mer′ē/ *v.* (·ried, ·ry·ing) 1 take, join, or give in marriage 2a unite intimately; combine b pair (socks, etc.) 3 marry off find a spouse for [L *maritus* conjugal; husband]

Mars /märs/ *n.* 1 Roman god of war 2 fourth farthest planet from the sun

Mar·seilles /märsā′/ *n.* seaport in SE France. Pop. 807,700

marsh /märsh/ *n.* low watery land —**marsh′y** *adj.* (·i·er, ·i·est); **marsh′i·ness** *n.* [OE]

mar·shal /mär′shəl/ *n.* 1 high-ranking officer in the armed forces of foreign countries (*Field Marshal*) 2 officer arranging ceremonies, controlling racecourses, crowds, etc. 3 administrative officer of judicial district, similar to a sheriff —*v.* (·shaled or ·shalled, ·shal·ing or ·shal·ling) 4 arrange (one's thoughts, etc.) in order [Fr *mareschal* fr. Gmc]

Mar·shall /mär′shəl/ 1 **John** 1755–1835; US jurist; Chief Justice of the Supreme Court (1801–35) 2 **George C(atlett)** 1880–1959; US general; Secretary of State (1947–49) 3

Thurgood 1908–93; US Supreme Court justice

Mar'shall Is'lands /mär'SHəl/ *n.* Pacific island group and republic, NE of New Guinea. Capital: Majuro. Pop. 50,000

marsh' gas' *n.* methane

marsh·mal·low /märSH'mal'ō, -mel'ō/ *n.* soft white confection made of sugar, gelatin, etc. [fr. *marsh mallow*, a plant]

mar·su·pi·al /märsōō'pēəl/ *n.* 1 mammal giving birth to underdeveloped young subsequently carried in a pouch —*adj.* 2 of or like a marsupial [Gk *marsupion* pouch]

mart /märt/ *n.* market [MDu, rel. to MARKET]

Mar·tel, Charles see CHARLES MARTEL

mar·ten /märt'n/ *n.* weasellike carnivore with dark brown fur [OFr or MLGer]

mar·tial /mär'SHəl/ *adj.* 1 of warfare 2 warlike [L *martialis* of Mars]

Mar·tial /mär'SHəl/ 1st cent. A.D.; Roman writer of epigrams

mar'tial arts' *n. pl.* oriental fighting sports, such as judo and karate

mar'tial law' *n.* military government with ordinary law suspended

Mar·tian /mär'SHən/ *adj.* 1 of the planet Mars —*n.* 2 hypothetical inhabitant of Mars [L]

mar·tin /märt'n/ *n.* a kind of swallow [prob. Scot *Martin*, 4th-cent. bishop]

Mar·tin Lu·ther King's Birth·day see KING, MARTIN LUTHER, JR.

mar·ti·net /märt'n-et'/ *n.* strict disciplinarian [for *Martinet*, a drill-master]

mar·ti·ni /märtē'nē'/ *n.* (*pl.* **·nis**) cocktail of gin and French vermouth [prob. *Martini*, name of a firm selling vermouth]

Mar·ti·nique /märt'n-ēk'/ *n.* resort island in the Caribbean; overseas department of France

mar·tyr /mär'tər/ *n.* 1 person who suffers or is put to death for a cause or belief 2 constant sufferer —*v.* 3 torment or put to death as a martyr —**mar'tyr·dom** *n.* [Gk *martys* witness]

mar·vel /mär'vəl/ *n.* 1 wonderful thing —*v.* (**·veled** or **·velled, ·vel·ing** or **·vel·ling**) 2 (foll. by *at* or *that*) feel or express wonder [L *mirabilia* marvels; wonders]

mar·vel·ous /mär'vələs/ *adj.* (also chiefly *Brit.* **mar·vel·lous**) 1 astonishing 2 excellent —**mar'vel·ous·ly** *adv.* [Fr, rel. to MARVEL]

Marx /märks/ 1 **Karl Heinrich** 1818–83; German political philosopher 2 **"Harpo" (Adolph)** 1888–1964; US comedian; his brother: 3 **"Groucho" (Julius Henry)** 1890–1977; US comedian

Marx·ism /märk'siz'əm/ *n.* anti-capitalist political and economic theories of Karl Marx, advocating communism and socialism —**Marx'ist** /-ist/ *n. & adj.*

Mar·y /mer'ē, mär'ē, mā'rē/ mother of Jesus; also called "(Blessed) Virgin Mary"; "St. Mary"; "Our Lady"

Mar·y I (Mary Tudor) 1516–58; queen of England (1553–58), daughter of Henry VIII; called "Bloody Mary"

Mar·y, Queen of Scots 1542–87; queen of Scotland (1542–67). Also called **Mary Stuart**

Mar·y·land /mer'ələnd/ *n.* E state of the US.

Capital: Annapolis. Pop. 4,781,468. Abbr. **MD; Md.** —**Mar'y·land·er** *n.*

Mar·y Mag·da·lene, St. /mag'dələn, -lēn'/ follower of Jesus

mar·zi·pan /märt'səpan', mär'zə-/ *n.* paste of ground almonds, sugar, etc., used in confectionery [Ger fr. It]

Ma·sa·ryk /mä'särik/, **Tomáš** 1850–1937; first president of Czechoslovakia (1918–35)

mas·car·a /maskar'ə// *n.* cosmetic for darkening the eyelashes [Sp: mask, fr. It *maschera*]

mas·cot /mas'kät'/ *n.* person, animal, or thing supposed to bring luck [Prov *mascoto* charm, fr. *masco* witch]

mas·cu·line /mas'kyələn/ *adj.* 1 of males 2 having manly qualities 3 of or denoting the male gender —*n.* 4 masculine gender or word —**mas·cu·lin'i·ty** /-lin'ətē/ *n.* [L, rel. to MALE]

Mase·field /mās'fēld'/, **John Edward** 1878–1967; English poet and novelist

ma·ser /mā'zər/ *n.* device for amplifying coherent electromagnetic radiation [microwave amplification by stimulated emission of radiation]

Ma·se·ru /maz'ərōō'/ *n.* capital of Lesotho. Pop. 109,400

mash /masH/ *n.* 1 soft or confused mixture 2 mixture of boiled grain, bran, etc., fed to horses, etc. 3 mixture of malt and hot water used in brewing 4 soft pulp —*v.* 5 crush (potatoes, etc.) to a pulp —**mash'er** *n.* [OE]

MASH /masH/ *abbr.* Mobile Army Surgical Hospital

mask /mask/ *n.* 1 covering for all or part of the face as a disguise or for protection (see illustration at SNORKEL) 2 likeness of a person's face, esp. one from a mold —*v.* 3 cover to conceal or protect [It *maschera*, perh. fr. Ar *maskhara* buffoon]

mas·och·ism /mas'əkiz'əm/ *n.* 1 sexual perversion involving one's own pain or humiliation 2 *Colloq.* enjoyment of what appears to be painful —**mas'och·ist** /-ist/ *n.*; **mas·o·chis'tic** *adj.*; **mas·o·chis'ti·cal·ly** *adv.* [for von Sacher-*Masoch*, a novelist]

ma·son /mā'sən/ *n.* 1 person who builds with stone 2 (*cap.*) Freemason [OFr]

Ma·son-Dix'on Line' /dik'sən/ *n.* boundary between Pennsylvania and Maryland, viewed as dividing the North from the South [for *Mason* and *Dixon*, its surveyors]

Ma·son·ic /məsän'ik/ *adj.* of Freemasons

ma·son·ry /mā'sənrē/ *n.* 1a stonework b work of a mason 2 (*cap.*) Freemasonry

masque /mask/ *n.* 1 musical drama with mime, esp. in the 16th and 17th cent. 2 masquerade [var. of MASK]

mas·quer·ade /mas'kərād'/ *n.* 1 false show; pretense 2 masked ball —*v.* (**·ad·ed, ·ad·ing**) 3 appear falsely or in disguise [MFr *mascarade*, rel. to MASK]

mass /mas/ *n.* 1 body of matter indefinite in shape 2 dense collection of objects 3 large number or amount 4 (prec. by *the*) a the majority b (*pl.*) ordinary people 5 *Physics.* quantity of matter a body contains —*adj.* 6 on a large scale (*mass hysteria; mass audience*) —*v.* 7 assemble into a mass [L *massa* fr. Gk]

Mass /mas/ *n.* celebration of the Eucharist,

Mass. *abbr.* Massachusetts

Mas·sa·chu·setts /mas'əCHŌŌ'sits/ *n.* NE state of the US. Capital: Boston. Pop. 6,016,425. Abbr. MA; cf. MASSACHUSE

mas·sa·cre /mas'ikər/ *n.* 1 mass killing —*v.* (**·cred, ·cring**) 2 kill (many people) esp. cruelly or violently [OFr]

mas·sage /məsäzH', -säj'/ *n.* 1 rubbing and kneading of the body to relieve stiffness, cure strains, etc. —*v.* (**·saged, ·sag·ing**) 2 apply massage to [Fr]

mas·seur /məsŏŏr'/ *n.* (*fem.* **mas·seuse** /məsŏŏs'/) person whose work is giving massages [Fr, rel. to MASSAGE]

mas·sive /mas'iv/ *adj.* 1 large and heavy or solid 2 exceptionally large or severe (*massive heart attack*) —**mas'sive·ly** *adv.*; **mas'sive·ness** *n.* [ME, rel. to MASS, 1]

mass'·mar'ket *adj.* pertaining to a product meant to be widely sold

mass' me'di·a *n. pl.* MEDIA, 2

mass' noun' *n. Gram.* noun that is not normally countable and cannot be used with the indefinite article (e.g., *bread*)

mass' pro·duc'tion *n.* mechanical production of large quantities of a standardized article —**mass'-pro·duce'** *v.* (**·duced, ·duc·ing**)

mast[1] /mast/ *n.* 1 long upright post for supporting a ship's sails, etc. 2 post or metal structure for supporting an antenna 3 flagpole —**mast'ed** *adj.* (also in *comb.*); **mas'ter** *n.* (also in *comb.*) [OE]

mast[2] *n.* fruit of the beech, oak, etc., esp. as food for pigs [OE]

mas·tec·to·my /mastek'təmē/ *n.* (*pl.* **·mies**) surgical removal of a breast [Gk *mastos* breast]

mas·ter /mas'tər/ *n.* 1 person having control or ownership (*master of the house; dog obeyed his master*) 2 captain of a merchant ship 3 skilled practitioner (*master carpenter; master of innuendo*) 4 great artist 5 *Chess, etc.* player at international level 6 original of a movie, recording, etc., from which others can be made 7 (*cap.*) title for a boy not old enough to be called *Mr.* —*adj.* 8 main; principal (*master bedroom*) 9 over-all; main (*master plan*) —*v.* 10 overcome; defeat 11 gain full knowledge of or skill in [L *magnus* great]

mas'ter cyl'in·der *n.* hydraulic piston-pump for a vehicle's braking system

mas·ter·ful /mas'tərfəl/ *adj.* 1 imperious; domineering 2 expert —**mas'ter·ful·ly** *adv.*

mas'ter key' *n.* key that opens several different locks

mas'ter·ly *adj.* very skillful

mas'ter·mind' *n.* 1 person with an outstanding intellect 2 person directing a scheme, etc. —*v.* 3 plan and direct (a scheme, etc.)

Mas'ter of Arts' *n.* (also of Sci'ence, etc.) post-graduate college/ or university degree given to a qualified student

Mas'ter of Cer'e·mo·nies *n.* (also **em·cee, MC, M.C.**) person in charge of a ceremonial or social occasion

mas'ter·piece' *n.* 1 outstanding piece of artistry or workmanship 2 person's best work

Mas·ters /mas'tərz/, **Edgar Lee** 1869–1950; US poet

mas'ter ser'geant *Milit.* next to highest ranking noncommissioned officer

mas'ter·stroke' *n.* skillful tactic, etc.

mas'ter·work' *n.* masterpiece

mas'ter·y *n.* 1 control; dominance 2 comprehensive knowledge or skill

mast'head' *n.* 1 top of a ship's mast 2 record of ownership, staff, etc., of a newspaper, magazine, etc.

mas·ti·cate /mas'tikāt'/ *v.* (**·cat·ed, ·cat·ing**) grind or chew with or as with one's teeth —**mas'ti·ca'tion** *n.*; **mas'ti·ca·to'ry** /-kətôr'ē/ *adj.* [L *masticare* chew]

mas·tiff /mas'tif/ *n.* large strong breed of dog [ME, perh. fr. L *mansuetus* tame]

mas·to·don /mas'tədän'/ *n.* large extinct mammal resembling the elephant [Gk *mastos* breast + *odon* tooth]

mas·toid /mas'toid'/ *adj.* 1 shaped like a nipple or breast —*n.* 2 conical prominence on the temporal bone behind the ear [Gk *mastos* breast]

mas·tur·bate /mas'tərbāt'/ *v.* (**·bat·ed, ·bat·ing**) sexually arouse by manual stimulation of the genitals —**mas'tur·ba'tion** *n.*; **mas'tur·ba·to'ry** *adj.* [L]

mat[1] /mat/ *n.* 1 small flat piece of material on a floor 2 piece of cork, rubber, etc., for protecting a surface 3 padded floor covering in gymnastics, wrestling, etc. 4 thickly tangled mass of hair, grass, etc. —*v.* (**mat·ted, mat·ting**) 5 entangle or become entangled in a thick mass [OE]

mat[2] *n.* 1 cardboard border framing a picture 2 MATTE —*v.* (**mat·ted, mat·ting**) 3 frame using a mat

mat[3] *n.* abbr. form of MATRIX

mat·a·dor /mat'ədôr'/ *n.* bullfighter whose task is to kill the bull [Sp fr. *matar* kill]

Mat·a·mo·ros /mat'əmôr'əs/ *n.* port in Mexico on the Rio Grande. Pop. 188,700

match[1] /maCH/ *n.* 1 contest or game 2a equal contender b person or thing exactly like or corresponding to another 3 marriage —*v.* 4 correspond (to); be like or alike; harmonize (with) 5 equal 6 place in conflict or competition with 7 make a match between (things or people) 8 fit together [OE]

match[2] *n.* short thin piece of wood, etc., with a combustible tip [OFr *mesche*]

match'book' *n.* paper folder for holding matches

match'box' *n.* box for matches

match'less *adj.* incomparable

match'mak·er *n.* person who arranges marriages, boxing matches, etc. —**match'mak'ing** *n.*

match' point' *n. Tennis, etc.* 1 situation in which one side needs only one more point to win the match 2 this point

match'stick' *n.* sliver of wood or cardboard, as for a match (MATCH[2])

mate[1] /māt/ *n.* 1 friend; fellow worker 2 partner in marriage 3 (in *comb.*) fellow member or joint occupant of (*roommate*) 4 officer on a merchant ship —*v.* (**mat·ed, mat·ing**) 5 come or bring together for marriage or breeding [MLGer]

mate[2] *n. & v.* (**mat·ed, mat·ing**) *Chess.* CHECKMATE

ma·te·ri·al /mətər'ēəl/ *n.* **1** matter from which a thing is made **2** cloth; fabric **3** (*pl.*) things needed for an activity **4** information, etc., for a book, etc. —*adj.* **5** of matter; physical **6** of bodily comfort, etc. **7** important; relevant [LL *materialis* of MATTER]

ma·te·ri·al·ism /mətər'ēəliz'əm/ *n.* **1** greater interest in material possessions and comfort than in spiritual values **2** *Philos.* theory that nothing exists but matter —**ma·te'ri·al·ist'** *n.*; **ma·te'ri·al·is'tic** *adj.*; **ma·te'ri·al·is'ti·cal·ly** *adv.*

ma·te·ri·al·ize /mətēr'ēəlīz'/ *v.* (·**ized, ·iz·ing**) **1** become actual fact; happen **2** *Colloq.* appear or be present **3** represent in or assume bodily form —**ma·te'ri·al·i·za'tion** *n.*

ma·te'ri·al·ly *adv.* substantially; significantly

ma·te·ri·el /mətēr'ē·el'/ *n.* (also **ma·te'ri·el'**) means, esp. materials and equipment in warfare [Fr]

ma·ter·nal /mətərn'l/ *adj.* **1** of or like a mother; motherly **2** related through the mother —**ma·ter'nal·ism** *n.*; **ma·ter'nal·is'tic** *adj.*; **ma·ter'nal·is'ti·cal·ly**, **ma·ter'nal·ly** *adv.* [L *mater* mother]

ma·ter·ni·ty /mətər'nətē/ *n.* **1** motherhood **2** for women during pregnancy and childbirth (*maternity leave; maternity dress*) [Fr fr. MedL, rel. to MATERNAL]

math /maTH/ *n. Colloq.* mathematics

math·e·mat·i·cal /maTH'(ə)mat'ikəl/ *adj.* **1** of mathematics **2** rigorously precise —**math'e·mat'i·cal·ly** *adv.*

math·e·mat·ics /maTH'(ə)mat'iks/ *n. pl.* **1** (treated as *sing.*) abstract science of number, quantity, and space **2** (*sing.* or *pl.*) use of this in calculation, etc. —**math'e·ma·ti'cian** /-mətiSH'ən/ *n.* [Gk *mathēma* science; learning]

mat·i·nee /mat'n·ā'/ *n.* (also **mat'i·née'**) afternoon performance in the theater, etc. [Fr fr. *matin* morning, rel. to MATINS]

mat'i·nee' i'dol *n.* handsome, popular actor

mat·ins /mat'nz/ *n.* (*sing.* or *pl.*) morning prayer, esp. as a church service [L *matutinus* of the morning]

Ma·tisse /mätēs'/, **Henri** 1869–1954; French painter

ma·tri·arch /mā'trē·ärk'/ *n.* female head of a family or tribe —**ma'tri·ar'chal** *adj.*; **ma'tri·ar'chy** *n.* (*pl.* ·**chies**) [L *mater* mother]

ma·tri·ces /mā'trisēz/ *n. pl.* of MATRIX

mat·ri·cide /ma'trəsīd', mā'-/ *n.* **1** killing of one's mother **2** person who does this [L, rel. to *mater* mother + -CIDE]

ma·tric·u·late /mətrik'yəlāt'/ *v.* (·**lat·ed, ·lat·ing**) enroll at a college or university —**ma·tric'u·la'tion** *n.* [MedL fr. *matricula* list]

mat·ri·mo·ny /ma'trəmō'nē/ *n.* rite or state of marriage —**mat'ri·mo'ni·al** *adj.* [L *matrimonium*, rel. to MOTHER]

ma·trix /mā'triks/ *n.* (*pl.* ·**tri·ces** /-trəsēz/ or ·**trix·es**) mold in which a thing is cast or shaped [L: womb]

ma·tron /mā'trən/ *n.* **1** married or widowed, esp. staid, woman **2** woman supervisor, as in an institution —**ma'tron·ly** *adv.* [L *matrona*]

ma'tron of hon'or *n.* bride's principal attendant, if married

---

matte /mat/ *adj.* **1** not shiny or glossy; dull —*n.* **2** dull flat finish [OFr fr. LL *mattus* soft]

mat·ter /mat'ər/ *n.* **1** physical substance having mass and occupying space that can be detected by the senses **2** specified substance **3** (thing) amiss (*something is the matter with him*) **4** content as distinct from style, form, etc. **5** situation, etc., under consideration or as an occasion (*matter for concern*) **6** pus or a similar substance discharged from the body —*v.* **7** be of importance; have significance **8** **as a matter of fact** in reality; actually **9 no matter:** a regardless of **b** it is of no importance [L *materia* substance]

Mat·ter·horn /mat'ərhôrn'/ *n.* Alpine mountain on the border of Switzerland and Italy: 14,692 ft.

mat'ter-of-fact' *adj.* **1** unimaginative; prosaic **2** unemotional —**mat'ter-of-fact'ly** *adv.*; **mat'ter-of-fact'ness** *n.*

Mat·thew, St. /maTH'yōō/ one of the twelve Apostles; credited as writer of the first Gospel

Mat·thi·as, St. /məthī'əs/ Apostle chosen to replace Judas Iscariot

mat·ting /mat'iNG/ *n.* fabric for mats

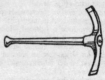

MATTOCK

mat·tock /mat'ək/ *n.* agricultural tool like a pickaxe, with an adze and a chisel edge [OE]

mat·tress /ma'tris/ *n.* cushion stuffed with air or water put on a bed for sleeping [Ar *al-mara* mat; cushion]

ma·ture /mət(y)ŏŏr', -CHŏŏr'/ *adj.* (·**tur·er, ·tur·est**) **1a** fully developed; adult **b** sensible; wise **2** ripe; seasoned **3** (of an insurance policy, etc.) due; payable —*v.* (·**tured, ·tur·ing**) **4** develop fully; ripen **5** (of an insurance policy, etc.) become payable —**ma·ture'ly** *adv.*; **ma·ture'ness, ma·tu'ri·ty** *n.* [L *maturus* timely]

mat·zo /mätsə/ *n.* (also **mat'zoh**) unleavened bread, served esp. at Passover

maud·lin /môd'lən/ *adj.* weakly or tearfully sentimental, esp. from drunkenness [Fr *Madeleine* fr. *Mary Magdalen*, shown in art usu. weeping]

Maugham /môm/, **W(illiam) Somerset** 1874–1965; British writer

Mau·i /mou'ē/ *n.* island of central Hawaii

maul /môl/ *v.* **1** tear the flesh of; claw **2** handle roughly —*n.* **3** heavy hammer [L *malleus* hammer]

Mau·na Lo·a /mou'nə lō'ə/ *n.* volcanic mountain on the island of Hawaii; includes Kilauea volcano

maun·der /môn'dər/ *v.* talk ramblingly

Mau·pas·sant /mōpäsäN'/, **(Henri) Guy de** 1850–93; French writer

Mau·riac /môryäk'/, **François** 1885–1970; French writer

Mau·ri·ta·ni·a /môr'itā'nē·/ *n.* republic in W

Africa, on the Atlantic Ocean. Capital: Nouakchott. Pop. 2,108,000

Mau·ri·tius /mȯrish′əs/ n. island republic in the Indian Ocean, E of Madagascar. Capital: Port Louis. Pop. 1,081,000

mau·so·le·um /mȯ′sōlē′əm, -zə-/ n. magnificent tomb [fr. tomb of *Mausolus*, king of Caria]

mauve /mōv, môv/ adj. 1 pale purple —n. 2 this color —**mauv′ish** adj. [L, rel. to MALLOW]

mav·er·ick /mav′(ə)rik/ n. 1 unorthodox or independent-minded person 2 unbranded calf [for S. *Maverick*, an owner of unbranded cattle]

maw /mȯ/ n. 1 stomach of an animal 2 jaws or throat of a voracious animal [OE]

mawk·ish /mȯ′kish/ adj. feebly sentimental —**mawk′ish·ly** adv.; **mawk′ish·ness** n. [obs. *mawk* MAGGOT, fr. ON]

max. abbr. maximum

max·i /mak′sē/ n. (pl. ·is) Colloq. 1 long skirt 2 garment, as a dress, with a long skirt

maxi- comb. form very large or long [abbr. of MAXIMUM]

max·il·la /maksil′ə/ n. (pl. ·lae /-lē/) jaw or jawbone, esp. (in vertebrates) the upper jaw —**max′il·la′ry** /-er′ē/ adj. [L]

max·im /mak′səm/ n. general truth or rule of conduct briefly expressed [MedL *maxima propositio* axiom]

Max·i·mil·ian /mak′səmil′yən/ 1832–67; emperor of Mexico (1864–67)

max·i·mize /mak′səmīz′/ v. (·mized, ·mizing) make as large or great as possible —**max′i·mi·za′tion** n. [L, rel. to MAXIMUM]

max·i·mum /mak′səməm/ n. (pl. ·mums or ·ma) 1 highest possible amount, size, etc. —adj. 2 greatest in amount, size, etc. [L *maximus* greatest]

may /mā/ v. aux. (past might) expressing: 1 possibility 2 permission 3 a wish 4 uncertainty or irony [OE]

● Usage: Some insist that care should be taken to distinguish between *may* (present tense) and *might* (past tense) in expressing possibility: *We may still go despite the weather. We might have gone, had it not rained.* But in casual use, *may* and *might* are often interchanged: *We might still go. She might have been here.* For *may* vs. *can,* see note at CAN[1].

May n. 1 fifth month of the year in the Gregorian calendar 2 (m-) hawthorn, esp. in blossom [L *Maius* of the goddess Maia]

Ma·ya /mä′yə, mī′ə/ n. 1 (pl. same or ·yas) member of an ancient Indian people of Central America 2 their language —**Ma′yan** adj. & n.

Ma·ya·güez /mī′əgwäs′/ n. seaport in Puerto Rico. Pop. 100,400

may·be /mā′bē/ adv. perhaps [fr. *it may be*]

May′ Day′ n. May 1 as a spring festival or holiday in honor of workers

May·day /mā′dā′/ n. international radio distress signal [approximate pronunc. of Fr *m'aidez* help me]

may′flow′er n. any of various flowers that bloom in May

may′fly′ n. a kind of insect living briefly in spring

may·hem /mā′hem′/ n. destruction; havoc [AngFr *mahaim* fr. Gmc]

may·on·naise /mā′ənāz′, mā′ənāz′/ n. (also Colloq. **may′o**) thick creamy dressing of egg yolks, oil, vinegar, etc. [Fr]

may·or /mā′ər, mer/ n. official head of a city or town —**may′or·al** adj.; **may′or·ess**[1] n. fem. [MedL, rel. to MAJOR]

may·or·al·ty /mā′ərəltē, mer′-/ n. (pl. ·ties) 1 office of mayor 2 period of this

may′pole′ n. decorated pole for dancing around on May Day

Maz·a·rin /măzăran′/, **Jules** 1602–61; Italian-born French cardinal and prime minister (1642–61)

Ma·za·tlán /măz′ətlän′/ seaport in Mexico. Pop. 199,800

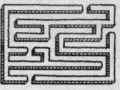

MAZE 1

maze /māz/ n. 1 network of paths designed as a puzzle 2 confused network, mass, etc. [rel. to AMAZE]

ma·zel tov /mä′zəl tôf′/ interj. good luck [Heb]

ma·zur·ka /məzər′kə/ n. 1 lively Polish dance in triple time 2 music for this [Fr or Ger fr. Pol]

MBA abbr. (also **M.B.A.**) Master of Business Administration

Mba·bane /m-bəbän′, em-/ n. capital of Swaziland. Pop. 38,300

Mboy·a /(e)mboi′ə/, **Tom** 1930–69; Kenyan political leader

MC abbr. (also **M.C.**) 1 Master of Ceremonies 2 Member of Congress

Mc·Al·len /məkal′ən/ n. city in Texas. Pop. 84,000

Mc·Car·thy /məkär′THē/ 1 **Joseph R.** 1908–57; US politician 2 **Mary** 1912–89; US novelist and critic

Mc·Cart·ney /məkärt′nē/, **(James) Paul** 1942– ; English pop and rock musician and composer

Mc·Clel·lan /məklel′ən/, **George Brinton** 1826–85; US general and politician

Mc·Cor·mick /məkôr′mik/, **Cyrus Hall** 1809–84; US inventor and manufacturer

Mc·Coy /məkoi′/ n. Colloq. as in the real McCoy the real thing; the genuine article

Mc·Kin·ley /məkin′lē/, **William** 1843–1901; 25th US president (1897–1901); assassinated

Mc·Kin′ley, Mount′ /məkin′lē/ n. mountain in Alaska; highest in N America: 20,320 ft.

Mc·Lu·han /məklōō′ən/, **(Herbert) Marshall** 1911–80; Canadian communications scholar

Md symb. mendelevium

MD abbr. 1 (also **M.D.**) Doctor of Medicine [L *Medicinae Doctor*] 2 postal abbr. for Maryland

Md. abbr. Maryland

me /mē/ pron. objective case of I [OE]

ME, Me. abbr. for Maine (postal abbr. ME)

mead /mēd/ n. alcoholic drink of fermented honey and water [OE]

Mead /mēd/, Margaret 1901–78; US anthropologist

Meade /mēd/, George Gordon 1815–72; general of Union forces in American Civil War

mead·ow /med′ō/ n. area of grassland, esp. one used for hay [OE]

mea·ger /mē′gər/ adj. (also esp. Brit. mea·gre) 1 scant in amount or quality 2 lean; thin [OFr maigre fr. L macer]

meal¹ /mēl/ n. 1 occasion when food is eaten 2 the food eaten at a meal [OE]

meal² n. grain or pulse ground to powder —meal′y adj. (·i·er, ·i·est) [OE]

meal′ tick′et n. Colloq. source of maintenance or income

meal·y-mouthed /mēl′ē mouᵀᴴd′/ adj. afraid to speak plainly

mean¹ /mēn/ v. (meant, mean·ing) 1 have as one's purpose or intention 2 design or destine for a purpose 3 intend to signify or refer to 4 be of specified importance to 5 mean well have good intentions [OE]

mean² adj. 1 stingy; not generous 2 petty; small-minded 3 inferior; poor 4 shabby 5a malicious; ill-tempered b vicious or aggressive 6 Colloq. skillful; formidable —mean′ly adv.; mean′ness n. [OE]

mean³ n. 1a term midway between extremes b quotient of the sum of several quantities and their number; average —adj. 2 (of a quantity) equally far from two extremes 3 calculated as a mean [L medianus MEDIAN]

• Usage: The difference between median and mean is useful: mean, which is synonymous with average, refers to the result obtained by dividing the sum of a set of quantities in the set: The mean or average of 5, 7, 8, and 12 is 32 divided by 4, or 8. The median is the middle number in a sequence or, if their number is even, the average between the two middle numbers: The median of 5, 7, 8, and 12 is 7.5, that is, the mean or the average of 7 and 8.

me·an·der /mē·an′dər/ v. 1 wander at random 2 (of a stream) wind about [Gk Maiandros, a winding river in ancient Phrygia]

mean·ie /mē′nē/ n. (also mean′y) (pl. ·ies) Colloq. cruel or selfish person

mean′ing n. 1 what is meant 2 significance —adj. 3 expressive; meaningful —mean′ing·less adj.; mean′ing·less·ly adv.; mean′ing·less·ness n.; mean′ing·ly adv.

mean·ing·ful /mē′niNGfəl/ adj. 1 full of meaning; significant 2 able to be interpreted —mean′ing·ful·ly adv.; mean′ing·ful·ness n.

mean·ing·less /mē′niNGləs/ adj. having no significance —mean′ing·less·ly adv.; mean′ing·less·ness n.

means /mēnz/ n. pl. 1 (often treated as sing.) action, agent, device, or method producing a result 2a resources b wealth 3 by all means certainly 4 by means of by the agency of 5 by no means certainly not [fr. MEAN³]

meant /ment/ v. past and past part. of MEAN¹

mean·time /mēn′tīm′/ adv. 1 MEANWHILE —n. 2 intervening period

mean·while /mēn′wīl′/ adv. 1 in the intervening period 2 at the same time —n. 3 intervening period

mean′y n. var. of MEANIE

mea·sles /mē′zəlz/ n. pl. (treated as sing.) infectious viral disease marked by a red rash [Ger Masern measles, or perh. fr. MDu masel spot]

mea·sly /mēz′lē/ adj. (·sli·er, ·sli·est) Colloq. meager; contemptible

meas·ure /mezH′ər/ n. 1 size or quantity found by measuring 2 system or unit of measuring 3 instrument for measuring 4 standard used for valuing 5 (usu. pl.) suitable action to achieve some end 6 legislative bill, act, etc. 7 brief passage of poetry or music 8 BAR¹ —v. (·ured, ·ur·ing) 9 ascertain the extent or quantity of (a thing) by comparison with a standard 10 be of a specified size 11 mark (a line, etc., of a given length) 12 (foll. by out) distribute in measured quantities 13 beyond measure excessively 14 for good measure as a finishing touch 15 measure up have the qualifications —meas′ur·a·ble adj.; meas′ur·a·bly adv.; meas′ure·less adj.; meas′ure·less·ly adv.; meas′ure·less·ness n. [L mensura fr. metior measure]

meas′ured adj. rhythmical; regular

meas′ure·ment n. 1 measuring 2 amount measured 3 (pl.) dimensions

meat /mēt/ n. 1 animal flesh as food 2 (often foll. by of) substance; chief part —meat′less adj.; meat′i·ness n.; meat′y adj. (·i·er, ·i·est) [OE]

Mec·ca /mek′ə/ n. city in W Saudi Arabia; Islamic holy site. Pop. 550,000

me·chan·ic /məkan′ik/ n. person skilled in using or repairing machinery [Gk mēchanikos, rel. to MACHINE]

me·chan·i·cal /məkan′ikəl/ adj. 1 of machines or mechanisms 2 working or produced by machinery 3 (of an action, etc.) automatic; repetitive 4 impersonal; unemotional —me·chan′i·cal·ly adv. [L, rel. to MECHANIC]

me·chan·ics /məkan′iks/ n. pl. (treated as sing.) 1 branch of applied mathematics dealing with motion, etc. 2 science of machinery 3 routine technical aspects of a thing

mech·a·nism /mek′əniz′əm/ n. 1 structure or parts of a machine 2 system of parts working together 3 process; method —mech′a·nis′tic /-nis′tik/ adj. [Gk, rel. to MACHINE]

mech·a·nize /mek′əniz′/ v. (·nized, ·niz·ing) 1 introduce machines in (a factory, etc.) 2 make mechanical 3 equip with tanks, armored cars, etc. —mech′a·ni·za′tion n.

med·al /med′l/ n. commemorative metal disk or the like, esp. awarded for military or sporting prowess [it fr. LL medialis middle]

med′al·ist n. winner of a medal

me·dal·lion /mədal′yən/ n. 1 large medal 2 thing so shaped, e.g., a decorative panel, etc. [It, rel. to MEDAL]

Me·dan /mädän′/ n. city in Indonesia, on Sumatra. Pop. 1,379,000

med·dle /med′l/ v. (·dled, ·dling) interfere in another's concerns —med′dler n.; med′dle·some adj. [OFr mesler fr. L miscere mix]

Me·del·lín /med′əyĕn′/ *n.* city in Colombia. Pop. 1,418,600

med·e·vac /med′əvak′, -ēvak′/ *v.* (·vacked, ·vack·ing) **1** transport injured people (as from an accident scene) by medically equipped helicopter or ambulance —*n.* **2** helicopter or ambulance for medical emergencies —*adj.* **3** pertaining to medical personnel involved in such transportation [medical evacuation]

me·di·a /mēd′ēə/ *n. pl.* **1** *pl.* of MEDIUM **2** (usu. prec. by *the*) mass communications (esp. newspapers and broadcasting) collectively
● Usage: See note at MEDIUM.

me·di·al /mēd′ēəl/ *adj.* **1** situated in the middle **2** average —**me′di·al·ly** *adv.* [LL *medialis* middle]

me·di·an /mēd′ēən/ *adj.* **1** situated in the middle —*n.* **2** straight line from any vertex of a triangle to the middle of the opposite side **3** middle value of a series **4** strip separating opposing traffic on a divided highway [L, rel. to MEDIAL]
● Usage: See note at MEAN³.

me·di·ate /mēd′ē-āt′/ *v.* (·at·ed, ·at·ing) **1** intervene to settle a quarrel, etc. **2** act as an intermediary —**me′di·a′tion, me′di·a′tor** *n.* [LL *mediare* be in the middle]

med·ic /med′ik/ *n. Colloq.* **1** medical practitioner **2** medical corpsman [L *medicus* physician]

Med·ic·aid /med′əkād′/ *n.* government-funded program paying medical expenses for those of limited income

med·i·cal /med′ikəl/ *adj.* of medicine —**med′i·cal·ly** *adv.*

med′i·cal ex·am′i·na′tion *n.* examination to determine a person's physical condition

Med·i·care /med′iker′, -kar′/ *n.* government-funded health insurance program for the elderly

med·i·cate /med′ikāt′/ *v.* (·cat·ed, ·cat·ing) **1** treat medically **2** impregnate with medicine —**med′i·ca′tion** *n.*; **med′i·ca′tive** *adj.* [L *medicare, medicat-*]

Me·di·ci /med′ichē, me′dēchē/ **1 Cosimo de′** (called **"the Elder"**) 1389-1464; Florentine banker, art patron, and ruler **2 Lorenzo de′** (called **"the Magnificent"**) 1449-92; ruler of Florence and patron of the arts **3 Catherine de′** see CATHERINE DE MEDICI **4 Cosimo de′** (called **"the Great"**) 1519-74; duke of Florence

me·dic·i·nal /mədis′ənəl/ *adj.* (of a substance) healing —**me·dic′i·nal·ly** *adv.*

med·i·cine /med′əsən/ *n.* **1** art and practice of the diagnosis, treatment, and prevention of disease **2** drug for the treatment or prevention of disease [L *medicina* healing]

med′i·cine man′ *n.* tribal, esp. N American Indian, practitioner of folk remedies, magical cures, etc.

me·di·e·val /med′(ē-)ē′vəl, med′-, mid′-/ *adj.* of the Middle Ages [L *medius* middle + *aevum* age]

me′di·e′val Lat′in *n.* Latin of about A.D. 600–1500

Me·di·na /mədē′nə/ *n.* city in Saudi Arabia. Pop. 290,000

me·di·o·cre /mēd′ē-ō′kər/ *adj.* **1** indifferent in quality **2** second-rate —**me·di·oc·ri·ty** /mē′dēok′ritē/ *n.* [L *mediocris*]

med·i·tate /med′ətāt′/ *v.* (·tat·ed, ·tat·ing) **1** engage in deep thought **2** plan mentally —**med′i·ta′tion** *n.*; **med′i·ta′tive** *adj.*; **med′i·ta·tive·ly** *adv.*; **med′i·ta′tive·ness, med′i·ta′tor** *n.* [L *meditari*]

Med·i·ter·ra·ne·an /med′itərā′nēən/ *adj.* **1** of the sea (**Mediterranean Sea**) bordered by S Europe, SW Asia, and N Africa, or its surrounding region **2** designating the weather, culture, etc., of this region [L *mediterraneus* inland]

me·di·um /mēd′ēəm/ *n.* (*pl.* ·di·a /dēə/ or ·ums) **1** middle quality, degree, etc., between extremes **2** means, esp. of communication **3** substance, e.g., air, through which sense impressions are conveyed **4** material or form used by an artist, composer, etc. **5** (*pl.* ·ums) person claiming to communicate with the dead —*adj.* **6** between two qualities, degrees, sizes, etc. [L *medius* middle]
● Usage: The noun *medium*, borrowed from Latin in the sense of 'means for distributing information, entertainment, etc.,' is singular, with its plural *media: The newspaper is a good advertising medium. We must use all media to reach our customers.* Because it occurs so often in the plural, many speakers use the plural as a singular in the 'information; press' connotation: *The media was invited to a press conference.* (The plural of *medium* in the spiritualist sense is *mediums*.)

med·ley /med′lē/ *n.* **1** varied mixture **2** collection of tunes, etc., played as one piece [AngFr fr. *medler*]

me·dul·la /mədəl′ə/ *n.* (*pl.* ·las or ·lae /-lē/) **1** inner part of certain organs, e.g., the kidney **2** MEDULLA OBLONGATA

me·dul·la ob·lon·ga·ta /′äb′lôNG′gät′ə/ *n.* (also **me·dul·la**) lowest part of the brain, a continuation of the spinal cord

meek /mēk/ *adj.* humble; submissive; gentle —**meek′ly** *adv.*; **meek′ness** *n.* [ON]

meer·schaum /mēr′SHəm, -shôm′/ *n.* **1** soft, white, claylike substance **2** tobacco pipe with bowl made from this [Ger: sea-foam]

Mee·rut /mē′rət/ *n.* city in N India. Pop. 752,100

meet¹ /mēt/ *v.* (**met, meet·ing**) **1** encounter; come together; come face to face (with) **2** be present at the arrival of (a person, train, etc.) **3** come into contact (with); join **4** make the acquaintance of **5a** deal with; answer (*met the proposal with hostility*) **b** satisfy; conform with **6** pay (a bill, etc.) **7** experience; receive (*met their death*) **8** confront in battle, etc. —*n.* **9** assembly (*track meet*) **10** meet the eye be visible or evident **11** meet halfway compromise **12** meet with receive (a reaction) (*met with her approval*) [OE]

meet² *adj. Archaic.* fitting; proper [rel. to METE]

meet′ing *n.* **1** coming together **2** assembly; gathering

mega- *comb. form* (before vowels also **meg-**) **1** large **2** one million (*megabyte*) [Gk *megas* great]

meg·a·buck /meg′əbək′/ *n. Slang.* **1** one million dollars **2** (*pl.*) a very large sum of money

meg·a·byte /meg′əbīt′/ *n. Comp.* 1,048,576 (2^{20}) bytes; loosely 1,000,000 bytes

meg·a·hertz /meg'əhərts'/ *n.* (*pl.* same) one million hertz

meg·a·lith /meg'əlĭth'/ *n.* large stone, esp. a prehistoric monument —**meg'a·lith'ic** *adj.* [Gk *lithos* stone]

meg·a·lo·ma·ni·a /meg'əlōmā'nēə/ *n.* mental disorder marked by delusions of grandeur —**meg·a·lo·ma'ni·ac** *adj.* & *n.* [Gk *megas* great, MANIA]

meg·a·lop·o·lis /meg'əläp'əlis/ *n.* urban area of great extent [Gk: great city]

meg·a·phone /meg'əfōn'/ *n.* funnel-shaped device for sound amplification [Gk *megas* great + *phōnē* sound]

meg·a·ton /meg'ətən'/ *n.* explosive power equal to one million tons of TNT

meg·a·watt /meg'əwät'/ *n.* one million watts

Mei·ji Ten·no /mā'jē ten'nō/ (born **Mutsuhito**) 1852–1912; emperor of Japan (1867–1912)

mei·o·sis /mī-ō'sis/ *n.* (*pl.* **mei·o'ses** /-sēz'/) cell division resulting in gametes with half the normal chromosome number [Gk *meiōn* less]

Me·ir /me-ēr'/, **Golda** 1898–1978; prime minister of Israel (1969–74)

meit·ner·i·um /mītnər'ēəm/ *n.* artificially produced chemical element, atomic number 109; *symb.* **Mt** [for Austrian physicist Lise *Meitner*]

Mek·nès /meknes'/ *n.* city in Morocco. Pop. 319,800

Me'kong Riv'er /mā'kông'/ *n.* river in SE Asia flowing 2,600 mi. from SW China to the South China Sea

mê·lée /mā'lā', mālā'/ *n.* (also **me'lee**) 1 confused fight, skirmish, or scuffle 2 muddle [Fr, rel. to MEDLEY]

mel·a·mine /mel'əmēn'/ *n.* 1 white crystalline compound producing resins 2 (in full **mel'a·mine res'in**) plastic or laminate made from this [fr. arbitrary *melam*, AMINE]

mel·an·cho·li·a /mel'ənkō'lēə/ *n.* depression; anxiety [L, rel. to MELANCHOLY]

mel·an·chol·y /mel'ənkäl'ē/ *n.* 1 pensive sadness; depression —*adj.* 2 sad; depressing; expressing sadness —**mel'an·chol'ic** *adj.* [Gk *melas* black, *kholē* bile]

Mel·a·ne·sia /melənē'zhə, -shə/ *n.* region of Pacific islands NE of Australia

mé·lange /mālänzh'/ *n.* mixture; medley [Fr *mêler* mix]

mel·a·nin /mel'ənin/ *n.* dark pigment in the hair, skin, etc. [Gk *melas* black]

mel·a·no·ma /mel'ənō'mə/ *n.* malignant skin tumor arising in melanin cells

Mel·ba /mel'bə/, (**Dame**) **Nellie** (born **Helen Porter Mitchell**) 1861–1931; Australian operatic soprano

Mel'ba toast' /mel'bə/ *n.* very thin, crisp toast [for N. *Melba*, Australian soprano]

Mel·bourne /mel'bərn, -bôrn'/ *n.* port city in SE Australia. Pop. 3,022,200

meld /meld/ *v.* merge; blend

mel·lif·lu·ous /məlif'lōōəs/ *adj.* (of a voice, etc.) pleasing; musical; flowing —**mel·lif'luous·ly** *adv.*; **mel·lif'lu·ous·ness** *n.* [L *mel* honey + *fluere* flow]

Mel·lon /mel'ən/, **Andrew W.** 1855–1937; US financier, industrialist, and art patron

mel·low /mel'ō/ *adj.* 1 (of sound, light, etc.) soft; rich; free from harshness 2 (of character) gentle 3 mature 4 genial; jovial —*v.* 5 make or become mellow —**mel'low·ly** *adv.*; **mel'low·ness** *n.*

me·lo·di·ous /məlō'dēəs/ *adj.* 1 producing or having melody 2 sweet-sounding —**me·lo'di·ous·ly** *adv.*; **me·lo'di·ous·ness** *n.* [Fr, rel. to MELODY]

mel·o·dra·ma /mel'ədräm'ə, -dram'ə/ *n.* 1 drama appealing blatantly to the emotions 2 theatrical language, behavior, etc. —**mel·o·dra·mat·ic** /mel'ədrəmat'ik/ *adj.*; **mel'o·dra·mat'i·cal·ly** *adv.* [Gk *melos* music, DRAMA]

mel·o·dy /mel'ədē/ *n.* (*pl.* **-dies**) 1 single notes arranged in a distinctive, recognizable pattern; tune 2 principal part in harmonized music —**me·lod·ic** /məläd'ik/ *adj.*; **me·lod'i·cal·ly** *adv.* [Gk *melos* song, rel. to ODE]

mel·on /mel'ən/ *n.* sweet, fleshy fruit of various climbing gourds [Gk *mēlon* apple]

melt /melt/ *v.* 1 change to liquid by the action of heat; dissolve 2 soften, or be softened, by pity, love, etc. 3 merge imperceptibly; change into 4 leave or disappear unobtrusively 5 **melt in one's mouth** be delicious [OE]

melt'down' *n.* 1 melting of the overheated core of a nuclear reactor 2 disastrous event

melt'ing point' *n.* temperature at which a solid becomes liquid

melt'ing pot' *n.* place, country, etc., where various races, theories, etc., are blended

Mel·ville /mel'vil', -vəl/, **Herman** 1819–91; US writer

mem·ber /mem'bər/ *n.* 1 person, etc., belonging to a society, team, group, etc. 2 part of a larger structure 3 part or organ of the body, esp. a limb [L *membrum* limb]

mem'ber·ship' *n.* 1 being a member 2 number or body of members

mem·brane /mem'brān'/ *n.* 1 thin, pliable, sheetlike tissue connecting or lining organs in plants and animals 2 thin, pliable sheet or layer —**mem'bra·nous** /-brənəs/ *adj.* [L *membrana* skin; parchment, rel. to MEMBER]

me·men·to /məmen'tō/ *n.* (*pl.* **-tos** or **-toes**) souvenir; reminder [L, imperative of *memini* remember]

me·men·to mo·ri /məmen'tō môr'ē/ *n.* reminder of death [L: remember you must die]

mem·o /mem'ō/ *n.* (*pl.* **-os**) MEMORANDUM [abbr.]

mem·oir /mem'wä(r)'/ *n.* 1 historical account written from personal knowledge 2 (*pl.*) autobiography [Fr *mémoire*, rel. to MEMORY]

mem·o·ra·bil·i·a /mem'ərəbil'ēə/ *n. pl.* souvenirs of memorable events [L, rel. to MEMORABLE]

mem·o·ra·ble /mem'(ə)rəbəl/ *adj.* 1 worth remembering 2 easily remembered —**mem'o·ra·bil'i·ty** *n.*; **mem'o·ra·bly** *adv.* [L *memor* mindful]

mem·o·ran·dum /mem'əran'dəm/ *n.* (*pl.* **-da** /-də/ or **-dums**) 1 note or record for future use 2 informal written message [L: thing to be remembered]

me·mo·ri·al /məmôr'ēəl/ *n.* 1 object, etc., established in memory of a person or event —*adj.* 2 commemorating (*memorial service*) [L, rel. to MEMORY]

Me·mo′ri·al Day′ *n.* US holiday observed the last Monday in May to honor deceased soldiers of all wars (also called **Decoration Day**)

mem·o·rize /mem′ərīz/ *v.* (**·rized, ·riz·ing**) commit to memory

mem·o·ry /mem′(ə)rē/ *n.* (*pl.* **·ries**) 1 mental faculty by which things are recalled 2 store of things remembered 3 recollection; remembrance 4 storage capacity of a computer, etc. 5 posthumous reputation 6 length of remembered time of a specific person, group, etc. 7 remembering (*deed worthy of memory*) 8 from memory as remembered [L *memoria* fr. *memor* mindful]

Mem·phis /mem′fis/ *n.* city in Tenn. Pop. 610,337

men /men/ *n. pl.* of MAN

men·ace /men′is/ *n.* 1 threat 2 *Joc.* pest; nuisance —*v.* (**·aced, ·ac·ing**) 3 threaten —**men′ac·ing·ly** *adv.* [L *minari* threaten]

mé·nage /mänäZH′/ *n.* (also **me·nage′**) household [L, rel. to MANOR]

me·nag·er·ie /mənaj′(ə)rē/ *n.* 1 small zoo 2 varied collection or group [Fr, rel. to MÉNAGE]

Me·nan·der /mənan′dər/ *c.* 342–292 B.C.; Greek dramatist

men·ar·che /mənär′kē/ *n.* first menstrual period

Men·ci·us /men′CHēəs/ (Latinized name of Meng-tzu or Meng′zi) *c.* 371– *c.* 289 B.C.; Chinese philosopher; developed Confucianism

Menck·en /meNG′kən/, **H(enry) L(ouis)** 1880–1956; US journalist and literary critic

mend /mend/ *v.* 1 restore to good condition; repair 2 regain health 3 improve —*n.* 4 darn or repair 5 **mend one's ways** reform oneself 6 **on the mend** recovering —**mend′er** *n.* [AngFr, rel. to AMEND]

men·da·cious /mendā′SHəs/ *adj.* lying; untruthful —**men·dac′i·ty** /-das′ətē/ *n.* (*pl.* **·ties**) [L *mendax*]

Men·del /men′dəl/, **Gregor Johann** 1822–84; Austrian monk and botanist

men·de·le·vi·um /men′dəlē′vēəm/ *n.* artificial transuranic radioactive metallic element; *symb.* Md [for D.I. *Mendeleev*, a chemist]

Men·de·li·an /mendē′lēən/ *adj.* of Mendel's theory of genetic heredity [for G. MENDEL]

Men·dels·sohn /men′dəlsən/, **Felix** 1809–47; German composer

men·di·cant /men′dikənt/ *adj.* 1 begging —*n.* 2 beggar 3 friar subsisting largely on alms [L *mendicus* beggar]

Me·nes /mē′nēz/ Egyptian pharaoh (reigned *c.* 3100 B.C.)

men′folk′ *n. pl. Colloq.* men

Meng·zi or **Meng·tzu** see MENCIUS

me·ni·al /mē′nēəl/ *adj.* 1 degrading; servile —*n.* 2 domestic servant [AngFr *meinie* retinue]

me·nin·ges /mənin′jēz/ *n. pl.* three membranes enclosing the brain and spinal cord [Gk *mēninx* membrane]

men·in·gi·tis /men′inji′tis/ *n.* infection and inflammation of the meninges

me·nis·cus /mənis′kəs/ *n.* (*pl.* **·ci** /-(k)ī′/) 1 concave or convex surface of liquid in a tube 2 lens convex on one side and concave on the other [Gk *mēniskos* crescent, from *mēnē* moon]

men·o·pause /men′əpôz′/ *n.* permanent

ceasing of menstruation —**men′o·paus′al** *adj.* [Gk *mēn* month, PAUSE]

me·no·rah /mənôr′ə/ *n.* seven- or nine-branched Judaic candelabrum [Heb: candlestick]

Me·not·ti /mənôt′ē/, **Gian Carlo** 1911– ; Italian-born US composer

men·ses /men′sēz/ *n. pl.* flow of blood in menstruation [L, pl. of *mensis* month]

men′stru·al cy′cle /men′strōōəl/ *n.* process of ovulation and menstruation

men·stru·a·tion /men′strōō-ā′SHən/ *n.* process of discharging blood, etc., from the uterus, usu. at monthly intervals —**men·stru·al** /men′strōō-əl/ *adj.*; **men′stru·ate** (**·at·ed, ·at·ing**) *v.* [L *menstruus* monthly]

men·su·ra·tion /men′sərā′SHən/ *n.* measuring [L, rel. to MEASURE]

mens′wear′ *n.* clothes for men

-ment *suffix* 1 forming nouns expressing means or result (*abridgment; embankment*) 2 forming nouns from adjectives (*merriment; oddment*) [L *-mentum*]

men·tal /ment′l/ *adj.* 1 of, in, or done by the mind 2 *Colloq.* mentally ill —**men′tal·ly** *adv.* [L *mens ment-* mind]

men′tal age′ *n.* degree of mental development compared to chronological age

men·tal·i·ty /mental′ətē/ *n.* (*pl.* **·ties**) 1 character or disposition 2 mental capacity

men·thol /men′THôl/ *n.* organic alcohol found in oil of peppermint, etc., used as a flavoring and to relieve local pain —**men·tho·lat·ed** /men′THəlāt′id/ *adj.* [L, rel. to MINT[1]]

men·tion /men′SHən/ *v.* 1 refer to briefly 2 reveal or disclose —*n.* 3 reference 4 **not to mention** and also [L *mentio*]

men·tor /men′tôr′/ *n.* 1 experienced and trusted adviser or teacher —*v.* 2 act as a mentor [*Mentor* in Homer's *Odyssey*]

men·u /men′yōō/ *n.* 1 list of dishes available in a restaurant, etc., or to be served at a meal 2 *Comp.* list of program options displayed on a computer screen [L, rel. to MINUTE[2]]

me·ow /mē·ou′, myou/ *n.* 1 characteristic cry of a cat —*v.* 2 make this cry [imit.]

mer·can·tile /mər′kantīl′/ *adj.* 1 of trade or trading 2 commercial [L, rel. to MERCHANT]

Mer·ca·tor /mərkāt′ər/, **Gerardus** 1512–94; Flemish geographer; invented system of map projection

mer·ce·nar·y /mər′səner′ē/ *adj.* 1 primarily concerned with money; working only for payment —*n.* (*pl.* **·ies**) 2 hired soldier in foreign service —**mer′ce·nar′i·ness** *n.* [L fr. *merces* reward]

mer·cer·ize /mər′sərīz′/ *v.* (**·ized, ·iz·ing**) treat (cotton) with caustic alkali to strengthen and make lustrous [for J. *Mercer*, its supposed inventor]

mer·chan·dise *n.* /mər′CHəndīz′, -dīs′/ 1 goods for sale —*v.* /-dīz/ (**·dised, ·dis·ing**) 2 trade; traffic (in) 3 advertise; promote [Fr, rel. to MERCHANT]

mer·chant /mər′CHənt/ *n.* 1 one who buys and sells goods 2 retailer; storekeeper [L *mercari* trade]

mer·chant·man /mər′CHəntmən/ *n.* (*pl.* **·men**) merchant ship

mer'chant ma·rine' *n.* **1** commercial shipping fleet of a nation **2** personnel of this fleet

mer'chant ship' *n.* ship carrying merchandise

mer·ci·ful /mər'sifəl/ *adj.* showing mercy —**mer'ci·ful·ly** *adv.*; **mer'ci·ful·ness** *n.*

mer·ci·less /mər'siləs/ *adj.* showing no mercy —**mer'ci·less·ly** *adv.*; **mer'ci·less·ness** *n.*

mer·cu·ri·al /mərkyŏŏr'ēəl/ *adj.* **1** volatile; fickle **2** of or containing mercury [L, rel. to MERCURY]

mer·cu·ry /mər'kyərē/ *n.* **1** silvery, heavy, liquid metallic element used in barometers, thermometers, etc.; *symb.* Hg **2** (*cap.*) planet nearest to the sun **3** HERMES —**mer·cu'ric** /-kyŏŏ'rik/, **mer·cu'rous** *adj.* [L *Mercurius*, Roman messenger-god]

mer·cy /mər'sē/ *n.* (*pl.* ·**cies**) **1** compassion or forbearance, esp. toward enemies, etc. **2** act of forgiveness, clemency, etc. **3** thing to be thankful for **4** at the mercy of in the power of [L *merces* reward; pity]

mere /mēr/ *adj.* solely or only what is specified —**mere'ly** *adv.* [L *merus* unmixed]

Mer·e·dith /mer'ədɪTH/, George 1828–1909; English novelist and poet

mer·e·tri·cious /merˈə'trɪSH'əs/ *adj.* showily but artificially attractive [L *meretrix* prostitute]

mer·gan·ser /mərgan'sər/ *n.* (*pl.* same or ·**sers**) a diving duck [L *mergus* diver, *anser* goose]

merge /mərj/ *v.* (**merged**, **merg·ing**) **1a** combine **b** join or blend gradually **2** (cause to) lose character and identity [L *mergere* dip]

merg'er *n.* combining, esp. of two businesses, etc., into one

Mé·ri·da /mer'idə/ *n.* capital of the Mexican state of Yucatán. Pop. 595,100

me·rid·i·an /mərid'ēən/ *n.* **1a** circle of constant longitude, passing through a given place and the terrestrial poles **b** corresponding line on a map **2** point of greatest power, achievement, etc. [L *meridies* midday]

me·ringue /mərɑNG'/ *n.* baked mixture of whipped egg whites and sugar [Fr]

me·ri·no /mərē'nō/ *n.* (*pl.* ·**nos**) **1** (in full **me·ri'no sheep'**) variety of sheep with long, fine wool **2** wool of this sheep, or cloth made from this [Sp]

mer·it /mer'it/ *n.* **1** excellence; worth **2** (*usu. pl.*) thing deserving reward or gratitude **3** intrinsic rights and wrongs —*v.* **4** deserve [L *meritum* value]

mer·i·toc·ra·cy /mer'itäk'rəsē/ *n.* (*pl.* ·**cies**) **1** government by those selected for merit **2** those so selected **3** society governed thus

mer·i·to·ri·ous /mer'itôr'ēəs/ *adj.* praiseworthy —**mer'i·to'ri·ous·ly** *adv.*; **mer'i·to'ri·ous·ness** *n.*

mer·maid /mər'mād'/ *n.* legendary sea creature with a woman's head and trunk and a fish's tail [ME *mere* sea + MAID]

mer·ry /mer'ē/ *adj.* (·**ri·er**, ·**ri·est**) **1a** joyous **b** full of laughter or fun **2** make merry be festive —**mer'ri·ly** *adv.*; **mer'ri·ment**, **mer'ri·ness** *n.* [OE]

mer'ry-go-round' *n.* **1** carnival ride with revolving model horses or cars as seats **2** cycle of high activity

mer'ry·mak'ing *n.* festivity; fun —**mer'ry·mak'er** *n.*

Mer·sin /mersēn'/ *n.* seaport in Turkey. Pop. 422,400

Me·sa /mā'sə/ *n.* city in Ariz. Pop. 288,091

mes·cal /meskal'/ *n.* peyote cactus [Sp fr. Nahuatl]

mes·ca·line /mes'kəlin/ *n.* hallucinogenic drug present in mescal

mes·dames /mādäm', -dam'/ *n. pl.* of MADAME

mes·de·moi·selles /mā'dəm(w)əzel'/ *n. pl.* of MADEMOISELLE

mesh /meSH/ *n.* **1** network fabric or structure **2** the open spaces in a net, sieve, etc. **3** (*pl.*) snare —*v.* **4** be engaged (as the teeth of a wheel) or entangled **5** be harmonious [Du]

Me·shed /məsHed'/ *n.* city in Iran. Pop. 1,463,500

mes·mer·ize /mez'mərīz'/ *v.* (·**ized**, ·**iz·ing**) **1** hypnotize **2** fascinate; spellbind —**mes'mer·ism** /-izəm/ *n.*; **mes'mer·iz'ing·ly** *adv.* [for F.A. *Mesmer*, Austrian physician]

meso- *comb. form* middle; intermediate [Gk *mesos* middle]

me·so·morph /mez'əmôrf'/ *n.* person with a compact muscular body [Gk *mesos* middle + *morphē* form]

me·son /mes'än', mez'än'/ *n.* elementary particle with a mass between that of an electron and a proton [fr. MESO-]

Mes·o·po·ta·mia /mes'əpətä'mēə/ *n.* ancient region between the Tigris and Euphrates rivers (part of present-day Iraq)

me·so·sphere /mez'əsfēr'/ *n.* region of the atmosphere extending in altitude from 20 to 50 miles

Me·so·zo·ic /mes'əzō'ik/ *adj.* **1** of the geological era marked by the development of dinosaurs, the first mammals, birds, and flowering plants —*n.* **2** this era [Gk *zōion* animal]

mes·quite or **mes·quit** /meskēt'/ *n.* thorny shrub or tree of SW North America [fr. AmerInd *mizquitl*]

Mes·quite /məskēt'/ *n.* city in Texas. Pop. 101,484

mess /mes/ *n.* **1a** dirty or untidy state **b** spill **2** state of confusion, embarrassment, or trouble **3** disagreeable concoction **4a** soldiers, etc., dining together **b** MESS HALL **c** meal taken there **5** portion of food —*v.* **6** make a mess of; dirty; muddle **7** (foll. by *with*) interfere **8** mess about (or around) putter; fiddle —**mess'i·ly** *adv.*; **mess'i·ness** *n.*; **mess'y** *adj.* (·**i·er**, **i·est**) [L *missus* course of a meal, rel. to MESSAGE]

mes·sage /mes'ij/ *n.* **1** communication sent by one person to another **2** main theme or idea of an artist's, writer's, or performer's work **3** get the message *Colloq.* understand (a hint, etc.) [L *mittere miss-* send]

mes·sen·ger /mes'ənjər/ *n.* person who carries a message

mess' hall' *n.* army dining hall

Mes·si·ah /məsī'ə/ *n.* **1a** promised deliverer of the Jews **b** *Christianity*. Jesus **2** liberator of an oppressed people —**Mes·si·an·ic** /mes'ēan'ik/ *adj.* [Heb: anointed] mes·sieurs /māsyərz′/ *n. pl.* of MONSIEUR

Mes·si·na /məsē′nə/ *n.* seaport of Sicily. Pop. 274,800

mess′ kit′ *n.* cooking and eating utensils for a soldier, hiker, camper, etc.

Mes·srs. /mes′ərz/ *n. pl.* of MR. [abbr. of MESSIEURS]

met /met/ *v.* past and *past part.* of MEET¹

met. *abbr.* 1 meteorological 2 metropolitan

meta- *comb. form* 1 denoting change of position or condition (*metabolism*) 2 behind, after, higher, or beyond (*metaphysics; metalanguage*) [Gk *meta* with; after]

me·tab·o·lism /mətab′əliz′əm/ *n.* chemical processes in a living organism producing energy and growth —met·a·bol·ic /met′əbäl′ik/ *adj.*; me·tab·o·lize /metab′əliz′/ *v.* (·lized, ·liz·ing) [Gk *metabol* change, rel. to META-, Gk *ballein* throw]

met·a·car·pus /met′əkär′pəs/ *n.* (*pl.* ·car·pi /-pī′, -pē/) 1 part of the hand between the wrist and the fingers 2 set of five bones in this —met′a·car′pal *adj.* [rel. to META- + CARPUS]

Met·air·ie /met′ərē/ *n.* suburb of New Orleans, La. Pop. 149,428

met·al /met′l/ *n.* 1a any of a class of elements such as gold, silver, iron, or tin, usu. good conductors of heat and electricity and exhibiting luster b alloy of any of these —*adj.* 2 made of metal [Gk *metallon* mine]

met·a·lan·guage /met′əlaNG′(g)wij/ *n.* language or system used to discuss or analyze another language or system

me·tal·lic /mətal′ik/ *adj.* 1 of or like metal or metals 2 sounding like struck metal 3 lustrous —me·tal′li·cal·ly *adv.*

met·al·lur·gy /met′l-ər′jē/ *n.* science of metals and their application, extraction, and purification —met′al·lur′gic, met′al·lur′gi·cal *adj.*; met′al·lur′gist *n.* [Gk *metallon* METAL, *-ourgia* working]

met·a·mor·phic /met′əmôr′fik/ *adj.* 1 of metamorphosis 2 (of rock) transformed, usu. by heat or pressure —met′a·mor′phism *n.* [fr. META-, Gk *morphē* form]

met·a·mor·phose /met′əmôr′fōz′/ *v.* (·phosed, ·phos·ing) change in form or nature

met·a·mor·pho·sis /met′əmôr′fəsis, -môrfō′sis/ *n.* (*pl.* ·pho·ses /-sēz′/) 1 change of form in an animal, esp. from a pupa to an insect, etc. 2 change of character, conditions, etc. [Gk *morphē* form]

met·a·phor /met′əfôr′/ *n.* application of a name or description to something to which it is not literally applicable (*a glaring error*) —met′a·phor′ic, met′a·phor′i·cal *adj.*; met′a·phor′i·cal·ly *adv.* [L fr. Gk]

met·a·phys·i·cal /met′əfiz′ikəl/ *adj.* 1 of metaphysics 2 excessively abstract or theoretical

met·a·phys·ics /met′əfiz′iks/ *n. pl.* (usu. treated as *sing.*) 1a branch of philosophy dealing with the nature of existence, truth, and knowledge b any branch of abstract philosophy 2 *Colloq.* abstract talk; mere theory [Gk, for its following *Physics* in Aristotle's works]

me·tas·ta·sis /metas′təsis/ *n.* (*pl.* ·ta·ses /-sēz′/) transference of disease from one part or organ to another, esp. the spread of can-

cerous cells —me·tas′ta·size′ *v.* (·sized, ·siz·ing) [Gk: removal]

met·a·tar·sus /met′ətär′səs/ *n.* (*pl.* ·si /-sī′, -sē/) 1 part of the foot between the ankle and the toes 2 set of five bones in this —met′a·tar′sal *adj.* [rel. to META-, TARSUS]

mete /mēt/ *v.* (met·ed, met·ing) apportion or allot [OE]

me·te·or /mēt′ēər/ *n.* 1 small, solid body of natural rock or metal from outer space that becomes incandescent when entering the earth's atmosphere 2 visible streak of light from a meteor [Gk *meteōros* lofty]

me·te·or·ic /mēt′ē-ôr′ik, -är′-/ *adj.* 1 rapid; dazzling 2 of meteors —me·te·or′i·cal·ly *adv.*

me·te·or·ite /mēt′ēərīt′/ *n.* fallen meteor found on the earth's surface

me·te·or·oid /mēt′ēəroid′/ *n.* METEOR

me·te·or·ol·o·gy /mēt′ēərāl′əjē/ *n.* the study of atmospheric phenomena, esp. for forecasting the weather —me′te·o·ro·log′i·cal *adj.*; me′te·o·rol′o·gist *n.* [Gk *meteōrologia*, rel. to METEOR]

me·ter¹ /mē′tər/ *n.* 1 instrument that measures or records, esp. quantity or distance —*v.* 2 measure or record by meter [fr. METE]

me·ter² *n.* 1 poetic rhythm, esp. as determined by number and stress of syllables 2 basic rhythm of music [Gk *metron* measure]

me·ter³ *n.* basic metric measure of length, equal to 39.37 inches —me′ter·age /-ij/ *n.* [Gk *metron* measure]

-meter *comb. form* 1 forming nouns denoting measuring instruments (*barometer*) 2 forming nouns denoting lines of poetry with a specified number of measures (*pentameter*) [Gk *metron* measure]

me′ter maid′ *n.* woman officer who issues tickets for parking meter violations

meth·a·done /meTH′ədōn′/ *n.* narcotic analgesic drug used esp. as a substitute for morphine or heroin [abbr. fr. 6-dimethylamino-4, 4-diphenyl-3-heptanone]

meth·ane /meTH′ān′/ *n.* colorless, odorless, flammable gas, the main constituent of natural gas [fr. METHYL]

meth·a·nol /meTH′ənôl′/ *n.* (also meth′yl al′co·hol) colorless, volatile, flammable, poisonous liquid, used as a solvent [fr. METHANE, ALCOHOL]

me·thinks /mēTHiNGks′/ *v.* (me·thought /mēTHôt′/) *Archaic.* it seems to me [OE, rel. to ME, THINK]

meth·od /meTH′əd/ *n.* 1 way of doing something; systematic procedure 2 orderliness; regular habits [Gk, rel. to META-, *hodos* way]

me·thod·i·cal /məTHäd′ikəl/ *adj.* (also me·thod′ic) characterized by method or order —me·thod′i·cal·ly *adv.*

Meth·od·ist /meTH′ədist/ *n.* 1 member of a Protestant denomination originating in the teachings of John Wesley —*adj.* 2 of Methodists or Methodism —Meth′od·ism′ /-iz′əm/ *n.*

meth·od·ol·o·gy /meTH′ədäl′əjē/ *n.* (*pl.* ·gies) system or science of methods —meth′od·o·log′i·cal /-dəläj′ikəl/ *adj.*; meth′od·o·log′i·cal·ly *adv.*

meth·yl /meTH'əl/ *n.* hydrocarbon radical found in many organic compounds [Gk *methu* wine, *hulē* wood]

meth'yl al'co·hol *n.* METHANOL

me·tic·u·lous /mətik'yələs/ *adj.* giving great attention to detail; scrupulous; precise —**me·tic'u·lous·ly** *adv.*; **me·tic'u·lous·ness** *n.* [L *metus* fear]

mé·tier /me'tyā'/ *n.* one's trade, profession, or field of activity [Fr]

me·ton·y·my /mitän'əmē/ *n.* substitution of the name of an attribute or adjunct for that of the thing meant (*Crown* for *king*) [Gk, rel. to META-, *onuma* name]

me·tre /mē'tər/ *n. Brit.* var. of METER

met·ric /me'trik/ *adj.* 1 of or based on the meter 2 of the metric system [Fr, rel. to ME-TER[1]]

-metric *comb. form* (also **-metrical**) forming adjectives corresponding to nouns in *-meter* and *-metry* (*geometric*)

met·ri·cal /me'trikəl/ *adj.* 1 of or composed in meter (*metrical psalms*) 2 of or involving measurement (*metrical geometry*) —**met'ri·cal·ly** *adv.* [Gk, rel. to METER[2]]

met'ric sys'tem *n.* decimal measuring system with the meter, liter, and gram (or kilogram) as basic units

met'ric ton' *n.* (also **tonne** /tən/) 1,000 kilograms (2,205 lb.)

met·ro /me'trō/ *n.* (*pl.* **·ros**) subway system, as in Paris, etc. [fr. metropolitan]

met·ro·nome /me'trənōm'/ *n.* device ticking at a set rate to mark time [Gk *metron* measure + *nomos* law]

me·trop·o·lis /məträp'əlis/ *n.* chief city; capital —**met·ro·pol·i·tan** /me'trōpäl'itən/ *adj.* [Gk *mētēr* mother, *polis* city]

-metry *comb. form* forming nouns denoting procedures and systems involving measurement (*geometry*)

Met·ter·nich /met'ərnik, -niKH/, **(Prince) Klemens** 1773–1859; Austrian statesman and diplomat

met·tle /met'l/ *n.* 1 strength of character; spirit; courage 2 **on one's mettle** ready to do one's best —**met'tle·some** /-səm/ *adj.* [fr. METAL *n.*]

Metz /mets/ *n.* city in NE France. Pop. 123,900

mew /myōō/ *n.* 1 characteristic cry of a cat, gull, etc. —*v.* 2 utter this sound [imit.]

mewl /myōōl/ *v.* 1 whimper 2 mew like a cat [imit.]

mews /myōōz/ *n. pl.* (treated as *sing.*) *Brit.* stables or carriage houses, esp. in an alley; often converted to housing [orig. sing. *mew* 'cage for hawks': Fr fr. L *mutare* change]

Mex·i·cal·i /mek'sikal'ē/ *n.* capital of the Mexican state of Baja California Norte. Pop. 602,300

Mex·i·co /mek'sikō/ *n.* country of N America, S of the US. Capital: Mexico City. Pop. 84,439,000 —**Mex'i·can** *n.* & *adj.*

Mex'i·co', Gulf' of *n.* arm of the Atlantic Ocean E of Mexico and S of US

Mex'i·co' Cit'y *n.* capital of Mexico. Pop. 8,235,700

mez·za·nine /mez'ənēn'/ *n.* story between two others (usu. between the first and second floors) [It, rel. to MEDIAN]

mez·zo /met'sō/ *Mus. adv.* 1 half; moderately —*n.* 2 (in full **mez'zo·so·pran'o**) (*pl.* **·nos**) female voice or singer between soprano and contralto [L *medius* middle]

M.F.A. *abbr.* Master of Fine Arts

mfg. *abbr.* manufacturing

m.f.n. *abbr.* most favored nation

mfr. *abbr.* manufacturer; manufactured

mg or **mg.** *abbr.* milligram(s)

Mg *symb.* magnesium

Mgr. *abbr.* 1 Manager 2 Monseigneur 3 Monsignor

MHz *abbr.* megahertz

mi /mē/ *n. Mus.* third note of a major scale

MI postal abbr. for Michigan

mi. *abbr.* mile(s)

MIA *abbr.* missing in action

Mi·am·i /mī-am'ē/ *n.* city in Fla. Pop. 358,548

Mi·am'i Beach' *n.* city and resort in Fla. Pop. 92,639

mi·as·ma /mē·az'mə/ *n.* (*pl.* **·ma·ta** /-mətə/ or **·mas**) infectious or noxious vapor [Gk: defilement]

mi·ca /mī'kə/ *n.* silicate mineral found as glittering scales in granite, etc., or in crystals, separable into thin, transparent layers [L: crumb]

mice /mīs/ *n. pl.* of MOUSE

Mich. abbr. for Michigan

Mi·chel·an·ge·lo /mī'kəlan'jəlō', mik'əl-/ (surname **Buonarroti**) 1475–1564; Italian sculptor, painter, and architect

Mich·i·gan /misH'igən/ *n.* peninsular state in the central US. Capital: Lansing. Pop. 9,295,297. Abbr. **MI**; **Mich.** —**Mich·i·gan·der** /misH'igan'dər/, **Mich'i·gan·ite'** /-gənit'/ *n.*

Mich'i·gan, Lake' *n.* one of the Great Lakes, W of the lower peninsula of Mich.

Mi·cho·a·cán /mē'CHō-äkän'/ *n.* SW state of Mexico. Capital: Morelia. Pop. 3,548,200

Mick·ey Finn /mik'ē fin'/ *n.* (also **Mick'ey** or **mick'ey**) *Slang.* drugged drink intended to make an unsuspecting victim unconscious

Mick·ey Mouse /mik'ē mous'/ *adj.* smalltime or inadequate; insignificant [fr. the DISNEY cartoon character]

micro- *comb. form* 1 small (*microchip*) 2 one millionth (10^{-6}) (*microgram*) [Gk *mikros* small]

mi·crobe /mī'krōb'/ *n.* microorganism, esp. one causing disease —**mi·cro'bi·al** /-bēal/, **mi·cro'bic** *adj.* [Gk *mikros* small + *bios* life]

mi·cro·bi·ol·o·gy /mī'krōbī·äl'əjē/ *n.* the study of microorganisms —**mi·cro·bi·ol·o·gist** *n.*

mi·cro·brew·er·y /mī'krōbrōō'ərē/ *n.* limited-production brewery, usu. selling only locally

mi·cro·chip /mī'krōCHip'/ *n.* INTEGRATED CIRCUIT

mi·cro·com·put·er /mī'krōkəmpyōōt'ər/ *n.* compact or portable computer using a microprocessor

mi·cro·cosm /mī'krəkäz'əm/ *n.* miniature representation, e.g., a community seen as a small-scale model of the universe —**mi'cro·cos'mic** *adj.* [fr. MICRO- + COSMOS]

mi·cro·dot /mī'krōdät'/ *n.* photograph of a document, etc., reduced to the size of a dot

mi·cro·ec·o·nom·ics /mī'krōek'ənäm'iks/ *n.* branch of economics concerned with individual factors within a closed system

mi·cro·e·lec·tron·ics /mī'krō-ilekträn'iks/ *n.* design, manufacture, and use of miniaturized electronic components

mi·cro·fiche /mī'krōfēsh/ *n.* (*pl.* same or ·**fich'es**) small, flat piece of film bearing miniaturized photographs of documents, etc. [fr. MICRO- + Fr *fiche* slip of paper]

mi·cro·film /mī'krəfilm'/ *n.* 1 length of film bearing miniaturized photographs of documents, etc. —*v.* 2 photograph on microfilm

mi·cro·light /mī'krəlīt'/ *n.* a kind of motorized hang glider

MICROMETER

mi·crom·e·ter /mīkräm'ətər/ *n.* instrument for accurate small-scale measurement

mi·cron /mī'krän'/ *n.* one millionth of a meter [Gk *mikros* small]

Mi·cro·ne·sia /mī'krənē'zhə, -shə/ *n.* 1 region of Pacific island groups N of the Equator and E of the Philippines 2 (**Federated States of**) federation of islands in the S Pacific Ocean. Capital: Palikir. Pop. 114,000

mi·cro·or·gan·ism /mī'krōôr'gənizəm'/ *n.* microscopic organism, e.g., bacteria, protozoa, and viruses

mi·cro·phone /mī'krəfōn'/ *n.* instrument for converting sound waves into electrical energy [fr. MICRO- + Gk *phōnē* sound]

mi·cro·pro·ces·sor /mī'krōpräs'esər/ *n. Comp.* integrated circuit that functions as a central processing unit

mi·cro·scope /mī'krəskōp'/ *n.* instrument with lenses for magnifying objects or details —**mi·cros·co·py** /mīkräs'kəpē/ *n.* [fr. MICRO- + -SCOPE]

mi·cro·scop·ic /mī'krəskäp'ik/ *adj.* 1 visible only with a microscope; extremely small 2 of or by means of a microscope —**mi'cro·scop'i·cal·ly** *adv.*

mi·cro·sur·ger·y /mī'krōsər'jərē/ *n.* intricate surgery using microscopes

mi·cro·wave /mī'krəwāv'/ *n.* 1 electromagnetic wave with a wavelength in the range 300,000 to 300 megahertz 2 (in full **mi·cro·wave' ov'en**) oven using microwaves to cook or heat food quickly —*v.* (·**waved, ·wav·ing**) 3 cook in a microwave oven —**mi'cro·wave'a·ble** *adj.*

mid /mid/ *adj.* middle [OE]

Mi·das /mī'dəs/ *n. Gk. Myth.* legendary king whose touch turned everything into gold 2 **Midas touch** knack for moneymaking

mid·day /mid'dā'/ *n.* noon

mid·dle /mid'l/ *attrib. adj.* 1 at an equal distance, time, or number from extremities; central 2 intermediate; average —*n.* 3 central or halfway point, position, or part 4 waist [OE]

mid'dle age' *n.* period between youth and old age —**mid'dle-aged'** *adj.*

Mid·dle Ag'es *n.* period of European history

363   **microeconomics / mien**

between ancient times and the Renaissance, from c. 476 to 1453

Mid'dle A·mer'i·ca *n.* 1 middle-class Americans considered as a group 2 central US states

mid'dle-brow' *adj. Colloq.* having or appealing to nonintellectual or conventional tastes

mid'dle class' *n.* social class between the upper and the lower socially, economically, etc. —**mid'dle-class'** *adj.*

mid'dle ear' *n.* cavity behind the eardrum

Mid'dle East' *n.* (also **Near' East'**) region of N Africa and SW Asia, roughly from Libya to Afghanistan

Mid'dle Eng'lish *n.* the English language in use from c. A.D. 1150 to 1500

mid'dle·man' *n.* (*pl.* ·**men**) 1 trader who handles a commodity between producer and consumer 2 intermediary

mid'dle-of-the-road' *adj.* moderate; avoiding extremes

mid'dle school' *n.* school for children in grades 5 to 8

mid'dle·weight' *n. Sports.* weight class for competitors; in professional boxing, includes fighters up to 160 lbs.

mid·dling /mid'liNG/ *adj.* 1 moderately good; medium —*adv.* 2 fairly; moderately

midge /mij/ *n.* gnatlike insect [OE]

midg·et /mij'it/ *n.* extremely small person or thing

mid·land /mid'lənd/ *n.* 1 middle part of a country —*adj.* 2 of or in the midland; inland

Mid·land /mid'lənd/ *n.* city in Texas. Pop. 89,443

mid'night' *n.* 12 o'clock at night [OE]

mid·riff /mid'rif'/ *n.* front of the body just above the waist [OE: mid-belly]

mid·ship·man /mid'ship'mən/ *n.* (*pl.* ·**men**) student at the US Naval Academy

mid'ships' *adv.* AMIDSHIPS

midst /midst, mitst/ *prep.* 1 *Poet.* amidst —*n.* 2 **middle 3 in the midst of:** a among b during 4 **in our** (or **your** or **their**) **midst** among us (or you or them) [rel. to MID]

mid'stream' *n.* 1 middle of a stream, etc. —*adv.* 2 (also **in midstream**) in the middle of an action, etc.

mid'sum'mer *n.* 1 period of or near the summer solstice, about June 21 2 middle of summer [OE]

mid'term' *adj.* 1 in the middle of a term or semester —*n.* 2 *Colloq.* exam during or esp. in the middle of a term

mid'way' *adv.* 1 in or toward the middle of the distance between two points; halfway —*n.* 2 part of a fair or carnival containing sideshows, games of chance, etc.

Mid·west /midwest'/ *n.* (also called **Mid'dle West'**) region of the N central US from the Allegheny Mountains W into the Great Plains

mid'wife' *n.* (*pl.* ·**wives** /-wīvz/) person trained to assist at childbirth —**mid·wife·ry** /midwif'ərē/ *n.* [orig. with-woman]

mid'win'ter *n.* 1 period of or near the winter solstice, about Dec 22 2 middle of winter [OE]

mien /mēn/ *n.* person's look or bearing [prob. obs. *demean*]

Mies van der Rohe /mēs′ vän′ də rō′ə/, Ludwig 1886–1969; German-born US architect and designer

miff /mif/ v. Colloq. (usu. as **miffed** /mift/ adj.) offend

might[1] /mīt/ v. past of MAY, used esp. in 1 reported speech, expressing possibility or permission (cf. MAY, 1, 2) 2 expressing a possibility based on a condition not fulfilled (if you'd looked you might have found it) 3 expressing complaint that an obligation or expectation is not or has not been fulfilled (they might have asked) 4 expressing a request (5 Colloq. instead of may (it might be so; might I be told why?)
● Usage: See note at MAY.

might[2] n. 1 strength; power 2 **with might and main** with all one's power [OE, rel. to MAY]

might·y /mī′tē/ adj. (·i·er, ·i·est) 1 powerful; strong 2 massive; bulky 3 Colloq. great; considerable —adv. 4 Colloq. very (mighty difficult) —**might′i·ly** adv.; **might′i·ness** n. [OE, rel. to MIGHT[2]]

mi·graine /mī′grān/ n. intense headache often affecting vision [Gk hēmikrania, rel. to HEMI-, CRANIUM]

mi·grant /mī′grənt/ adj. 1 migrating —n. 2 migrant person or animal, esp. a bird

mi·grate /mī′grāt/ v. (·grat·ed, ·grat·ing) 1 move from one place and settle in another, esp. abroad 2 (of a bird or fish) change its habitation seasonally —**mi·gra′tion**, **mi′grator** n.; **mi′gra·to·ry** /-tôr′ē/ adj. [L migrare]

mi·ka·do /mikä′dō/ n. (pl. ·dos) Hist. emperor of Japan [Japn: exalted (palace) door]

mike /mīk/ n. Colloq. 1 microphone —v. 2 record or amplify by microphone [abbr.]

mil /mil/ n. one thousandth of an inch [L mille thousand]

mi·la·dy /milā′dē/ n. (pl. ·dies) 1 noblewoman 2 woman of fashion [Fr fr. my lady]

Mi·lan /milan′, -län′/ n. city in N Italy. Pop. 1,432,200 —**Mil·an·ese** /mil′ənēz′/ n. & adj.

milch /milch, milcH/ adj. giving milk [OE, rel. to MILK]

mild /mīld/ adj. 1 gentle; conciliatory 2 not severe or harsh; moderate 3 (of flavor) not sharp or strong 4 tame; feeble; lacking vivacity —**mild′ish** adj.; **mild′ly** adv.; **mild′ness** n. [OE]

mil·dew /mil′d(y)ōō′/ n. 1 destructive growth of minute fungi on plants, damp paper, leather, etc. —v. 2 taint or be tainted with mildew —**mil′dew·y** adj. (·i·er, ·i·est) [OE]

mile /mīl/ n. (also **sta′tute mile′**) measure of distance, equal to 1,760 yards (approx. 1.6 kilometers) [L mille thousand]

mile·age /mī′lij/ n. 1 number of miles traveled, esp. by a vehicle, per unit of fuel 2 an allowance per mile for cost of travel 3 Colloq. use; advantage

mile′ post′ n. sign or marker showing distance to or from a place, esp. in miles

mil·er /mī′lər/ n. person or horse specializing in races of one mile

mile·stone /mīl′stōn′/ n. 1 stone marking a distance in miles 2 significant event or point in a life, history, project, etc.

mi·lieu /milyōō′, -yōō′/ n. (pl. **mi·lieux** or **·lieus** /-yōōz′, -yōōz′/) environment or social surroundings [Fr]

mil·i·tant /mil′ətənt/ adj. 1 combative; aggressive 2 engaged in warfare —n. 3 militant person —**mil′i·tan·cy** n.; **mil′i·tant·ly** adv. [L, rel. to MILITATE]

mil·i·ta·rism /mil′ətəriz′əm/ n. 1 aggressive military policy, etc. 2 military spirit —**mil′ita·rist** /-ist/ n.; **mil′i·ta·ris′tic** adj.

mil·i·ta·rize /mil′ətərīz′/ v. (·rized, ·riz·ing) 1 equip with military resources 2 make military or warlike —**mil′i·ta·ri·za′tion** n.

mil·i·tar·y /mil′əter′ē/ adj. 1 of or characteristic of soldiers or armed forces —n. 2 (with the) the armed forces, collectively —**mil′itar′i·ly** adv. [L miles milit- soldier]

mil′i·tar·y po·lice′ n. (as pl.) soldiers who act as police in the army

mil·i·tate /mil′ətāt′/ v. (·tat·ed, ·tat·ing) have force or effect (against) [L, rel. to MILITARY]
● Usage: Militate, usually followed by against, means 'have a profound effect': His poor marks militated against his entering college. It should be kept distinct from mitigate, which means 'make less intense or severe': With a plea of self-defense, her lawyer tried to mitigate the charge from murder to manslaughter.

mi·li·tia /məlish′ə/ n. citizen army, esp. serving in an emergency —**mi·li′tia·man** /-mən/ n. (pl. ·men) [L: military service]

milk /milk/ n. 1 white fluid secreted by female mammals for the nourishment of their young 2 milk of cows, etc., as food 3 milklike juice of the coconut, etc. —v. 4 draw milk from (a cow, etc.) 5 exploit (a person or situation) [OE]

milk′maid′ n. girl or woman who milks cows or works in a dairy

milk′man n. (pl. ·men) man who sells or delivers milk

milk′ run′ n. routine expedition, etc.

milk′ shake′ n. shaken or blended drink of milk, flavoring, and ice cream

milk′sop′ /milk′säp′/ n. weak or timid person

milk′ tooth′ n. temporary tooth in young mammals

milk·y adj. (·i·er, ·i·est) 1 of, like, or mixed with milk 2 (of a gem or liquid) cloudy; not clear —**milk′i·ness** n.

Milk′y Way′ n. luminous band of stars; the Galaxy containing earth's solar system

mill[1] /mil/ n. 1a building fitted with a mechanical device for grinding grain b such a device 2 device for grinding, crushing, or cutting solid material 3 factory —v. 4 grind or crush in a mill 5 produce a ribbed edge on (a coin) 6 cut or shape (metal) with a rotating tool 7 move aimlessly (around) 8 **go** (or **put**) **through the mill** undergo (or cause to undergo) intensive work, pain, training, etc. [L mola]

mill[2] n. one tenth of a cent [L mille thousand]

Mill /mil/, **J(ohn) S(tuart)** 1806–73; English philosopher and economist

mill·age /mil′ij/ n. taxation rate; mills per dollar valuation

Mil·lay /məlā′/, **Edna St. Vincent** 1892–1950; US poet

mil·len·ni·um /məlen′ēəm/ n. (pl. ·ums or ·ni·a) 1 period of 1,000 years 2 1,000-year period prophesied for Christ to reign on earth **3** (esp. future) period of happiness and prosperity —**mil·len′ni·al** *adj.* [L *mille* thousand + *annus* year]

● Usage: The words *millennium, millennia,* etc., come from *milli-* 'thousand' and *-ennium* 'year' (as in *biennial*), the same root that appears in *annual*. It is spelled as shown, with a double *n*.

mill′er /mil′ər/ *n.* owner or operator of a mill, esp. a flour mill [rel. to MILL]

Mil·ler /mil′ər/ **1 (Alton) Glenn** 1904–44; US jazz trombonist and band-leader **2 Arthur** 1915– ; US dramatist

mil·let /mil′it/ *n.* **1** cereal plant bearing small, nutritious seeds **2** seed of this [L *milium*]

Mil·let /mē·ye′, -le′/, **Jean François** 1814–75; French painter

milli- *comb. form* one thousandth [L *mille* thousand]

mil·li·gram /mil′igram′/ *n.* one thousandth of a gram

mil·li·li·ter /mil′ilē′tər/ *n.* one thousandth of a liter

mil·li·me·ter /mil′imē′tər/ *n.* one thousandth of a meter

mil·li·ner /mil′inər/ *n.* person who makes or sells women's hats —**mil′li·ner′y** /-er′ē/ *n.* [*Milan* in Italy]

mil·lion /mil′yən/ *n.* one thousand thousand —**mil′lionth** *adj. & n.* [Fr, prob. fr. It *mille* thousand]

mil·lion·aire /mil′yəner′/ *n.* person who has over a million dollars, pounds, etc. [Fr *millionnaire,* rel. to MILLION]

mil·li·pede /mil′ipēd′/ *n.* small crawling invertebrate with many legs [L *mille* thousand + *pes ped-* foot]

mil·li·sec·ond /mil′isek′ənd/ *n.* one thousandth of a second

mill′race′ *n.* current of water that drives a mill wheel

mill′stone′ *n.* **1** each of two circular stones for grinding grain **2** heavy burden or responsibility

mill′wheel′ *n.* water-driven wheel that powers mill machinery

mill′wright′ *n.* person who designs, builds, or repairs mills or mill machinery

Milne /mil(n)/, **A(lan) A(lexander)** 1882–1956; English writer

mi·lord /milôrd′/ *n.* English nobleman [Fr fr. *my lord*]

milt /milt/ *n.* reproductive gland or sperm of a male fish [OE]

Mil·ton /milt′n/, **John** 1608–74; English poet

Mil·wau·kee /milwô′kē/ *n.* city in Wis. Pop. 628,088

mime /mīm/ *n.* **1** acting using only gestures **2** mime performer —*v.* (**mimed, mim·ing**) **3** convey by mime [Gk *mimos*]

mim·e·o·graph /mim′ēəgraf′/ *n.* **1** machine that makes copies from a stencil **2** copy so produced —*v.* **3** reproduce by this process [Gk *mimeisthai* imitate]

mi·met·ic /məmet′ik, mī-/ *adj.* of or practicing imitation or mimicry [Gk *mimētikos* imitative]

mim·ic /mim′ik/ *v.* (**-icked, -ick·ing**) **1** imitate (a person, gesture, etc.), esp. to entertain or ridicule **2** copy or resemble closely —*n.*

365 **miller / mineralogy**

3 person skilled in imitation —**mim′ic·ry** *n.* [Gk *mimikos,* rel. to MIME]

mi·mo·sa /məmō′sə/ *n.* **1** shrub with globular usu. yellow flowers **2** acacia plant with showy yellow flowers **3** cocktail of champagne and orange juice [L, rel. to MIME]

min. *abbr.* **1** minute(s) **2** minimum

min·a·ret /min′əret′/ *n.* slender turret attached to a mosque [Fr or Sp fr. Turk fr. Ar]

mi·na·to·ry /min′ətôr′ē/ *adj.* threatening; menacing [L *minari* threaten]

MINARET

mince /min(t)s/ *v.* (**minced, minc·ing**) **1** cut up or grind in small bits **2** speak or walk effeminately or affectedly **3** mince matters (or one's words) (usu. with *neg.*) speak evasively or candidly mildly —**minc′er** *n.* [L *minutia* something small]

mince′meat′ *n.* **1** mixture of raisins, apples, sugar, spices, suet, etc., used as pie filling **2 make mincemeat of** utterly defeat

mind /mīnd/ *n.* **1a** seat of consciousness, thought, volition, and feeling **b** attention; concentration **2** intellect **3** memory **4** opinion **5** way of thinking or feeling **6** sanity —*v.* **7** object; be upset (*do you mind if I smoke?*) **8** heed; take care (to) **9** look after (*mind the house*) **10** apply oneself to; concern oneself with **11** bear (or keep) in mind remember **12** have (it) in mind intend **13** make up one's mind decide **14** never mind let or leave alone; not to mention **15** on one's mind in one's thoughts, concerns, etc. **16** out of one's mind insane [OE]

mind′-bog′gling *adj. Colloq.* unbelievable; startling

mind′ed *adj.* **1** having a specified kind of mind or interest **2** disposed; inclined

mind′ful /mīnd′fəl/ *adj.* taking heed or care; giving thought (to) —**mind′ful·ly** *adv.*

mind′less *adj.* **1** lacking intelligence; brutish **2** not requiring thought or skill **3** heedless (of advice, etc.) —**mind′less·ly** *adv.*; **mind′less·ness** *n.*

mind-read /mīnd′rēd′/ *v.* discern the thoughts of (another person) —**mind′ read′er** *n.*

mine¹ /mīn/ *poss. pron.* the one(s) of or belonging to me (*it is mine*) [OE]

mine² *n.* **1** excavation to extract ore, coal, salt, etc. **2** abundant source (of information, etc.) **3** military explosive device placed in the ground or in the water —*v.* (**mined, min·ing**) **4** dig for or obtain (ore, coal, etc.) from a mine **5** tunnel **6** lay explosive mines under or in —**min′ing** *n.* [Fr]

mine′field′ *n.* **1** area planted with explosive mines **2** *Colloq.* hazardous subject or situation

min′er *n.* person who works in a mine

min·er·al /min′(ə)rəl/ *n.* **1** inorganic substance **2** substance obtained by mining [Fr or MedL, rel. to MINE²]

min·er·al·o·gy /min′ərāl′əjē, -ral′-/ *n.* the study of minerals —**min′er·al·og′i·cal** /-əläj′ikəl/ *adj.*; **min′er·al′o·gist** *n.*

min·er·al oil′ *n.* colorless oil obtained from petroleum, used as a laxative, lubricant, etc.

min·er·al wa′ter *n.* natural or artificial water containing dissolved salts or minerals

Mi·ner·va /minər′və/ *n.* see ATHENA

min·e·stro·ne /min′əstrō′nē/ *n.* thick vegetable soup [It]

mine′sweep′er *n.* ship for clearing explosive mines from the sea

min·gle /miNG′gəl/ *v.* (**·gled, ·gling**) 1 mix; blend 2 mix socially [OE]

mini- *comb. form* miniature

min·i·a·ture /min′(ē)əCHər/ *adj.* 1 much smaller than normal 2 represented on a small scale —*n.* 3 any miniature object 4 detailed small-scale portrait —**min′i·a·tur′ist** *n.* [L *miniare* paint red]

min·i·a·tur·ize /min′(ē)əCHərīz′/ *v.* (**·ized, ·iz·ing**) produce in a smaller version; make small —**min′i·a·tur′i·za′tion** *n.*

min·i·cam /min′ēkam′/ *n.* portable TV or video camera

min·i·com·put·er /min′ēkəmpyōō′tər/ *n.* computer of medium power

min·i·ma /min′əmə/ *n. pl.* of MINIMUM

min·i·mal /min′əməl/ *adj.* very minute; smallest; least —**min′i·mal·ly** *adv.*

min·i·mal·ism /min′əmlizəm/ *n. Art & Mus.* movement using simple or primary forms, designs, or phrases —**min′i·mal·ist** /-ist/ *n. & adj.*

min·i·mize /min′əmīz′/ *v.* (**·mized, ·miz·ing**) reduce to, or estimate at, a minimal degree, value, or importance —**min′i·mi·za′tion** *n.*

min·i·mum /min′əməm/ *n.* (*pl.* **·mums** or **·ma** /-mə/) 1 least possible or attainable amount —*adj.* 2 least; smallest possible [L *minimus* smallest]

min′i·mum-se·cu′ri·ty *adj.* designating a prison where inmates are permitted some liberties

min·ion /min′yən/ *n.* servile subordinate [MFr *mignon*]

min·i·ser·ies /min′ēsēr′ēz/ *n.* (*pl.* same) short series of related television programs

min·i·skirt /min′ēskərt/ *n.* very short skirt

min·is·ter /min′istər/ *n.* 1 (in some countries) head of a government department 2 clergyman, esp. in Protestant churches 3 diplomat, usu. ranking below an ambassador —*v.* 4 give help or aid (to) 5 serve as a minister —**min·is·te·ri·al** /min′əstēr′ēəl/ *adj.* [L: servant]

min·is·tra·tion /min′istrā′sHən/ *n.* 1 help; service 2 supplying of help, justice, etc. —**min·is·trant** /min′əstrənt/ *adj. & n.* [L, rel. to MINISTER]

min·is·try /min′istrē/ *n.* (*pl.* **·tries**) 1 (in some countries) government department headed by a minister 2 (prec. by *the*) vocation, office, profession, or tenure of a religious minister 3 body of ministers of a government or religion 4 ministering; ministration [L, rel. to MINISTER]

min·i·van /min′ēvan′/ *n.* vehicle, smaller than a full-sized van, for passengers, cargo, etc.

mink /miNGk/ *n.* (*pl.* same or **-s**) 1 semiaquatic weasellike animal bred for its thick

brown fur 2 this fur or garment, etc., made from it [Sw]

Minn. *abbr.* Minnesota

Min·ne·ap·o·lis /min′ē·ap′ələs/ *n.* city in Minn. Pop. 368,383

Min·ne·so·ta /min′əsō′tə/ *n.* state in the central US. Capital: St. Paul. Pop. 4,375,099. Abbr. **MN; Minn.** —**Min′ne·so′tan** *n. & adj.*

min·now /min′ō/ *n.* small freshwater fish [OE]

Mi·no·an /minō′ən/ *adj.* 1 of the Bronze Age civilization centered on Crete c. 3000–1100 B.C.) —*n.* 2 person of this civilization [*Minos*, legendary king of Crete]

mi·nor /mī′nər/ *adj.* 1 lesser or comparatively small in size, importance, etc. 2 *Mus.* a halftone lower than the corresponding major —*n.* 3 person under full legal age 4 student's subsidiary course of study —*v.* 5 (foll. by *in*) study (a subject) as a subsidiary [L: less]

mi·nor·i·ty /mīnôr′ətē, -när′-/ *n.* (*pl.* **·ties**) 1 smaller number or part; less than half 2 small group of people differing from others in race, religion, language, etc. 3 being under full legal age [Fr or MedL, rel. to MINOR]

mi·nor′i·ty lead′er *n.* legislative leader whose party is not in the majority

mi′nor scale′ *n. Mus.* diatonic scale having a half step between the second and third tones

min·ox·i·dil /minak′sidil′/ *n.* drug used to treat hypertension or baldness

Minsk /minsk/ *n.* capital of Belarus. Pop. 1,633,600

min·strel /min′strəl/ *n.* 1 medieval singer or musician 2 performer in a former variety show involving comedy sketches and songs performed with blackened faces [rel. to MINISTER]

mint¹ /mint/ *n.* 1 aromatic herb used in cooking 2 mint-flavored candy —**mint′y** *adj.* (**·i·er, ·i·est**) [L *menta* fr. Gk]

mint² *n.* 1 establishment where money is coined 2 *Colloq.* vast sum —*v.* 3 make (a coin) by stamping metal 4 invent; coin (a word, phrase, etc.) 5 **in mint condition** as new [L *moneta*]

mint′ ju′lep /jōō′lip/ *n.* drink of bourbon, mint, and sugar syrup, served on ice

min·u·et /min′yōō·et′/ *n.* 1 slow, stately dance for two in triple time 2 music for this [Fr dim.]

Min·u·it /min′yōōit/, Peter 1580–1638; Dutch colonial administrator in America

mi·nus /mī′nəs/ *prep.* 1 with the subtraction of (*7 minus 4 equals 3*) 2 below zero 3 *Colloq.* lacking (*returned minus their dog*) —*adj.* 4 negative —*n.* 5 MINUS SIGN 6 *Math.* negative quantity 7 *Colloq.* disadvantage [L, neut. of MINOR]

mi·nus·cule /min′əskyōōl′, minəs′-/ *adj. Colloq.* extremely small or unimportant [L dim., rel. to MINUS]

● Usage: Avoid misspelling this as "miniscule."

mi′nus sign′ *n.* the symbol (−) indicating subtraction or a negative value

min·ute¹ /min′it/ *n.* 1a sixtieth part of an hour b sixtieth part of a degree of an arc 2 distance covered in one minute 3 moment 4 (*pl.*) official memorandum or summary of a meeting, etc. 5 **up to the minute** completely up to date [L *minuere* lessen]

mi·nute² /mīn(y)ōōt'/ *adj.* (·nut·er, ·nut·est) 1 very small 2 accurate; detailed —**mi·nute'ly** *adv.* [L *minutus*, rel. to MINUTE¹]

min·ute·man /min'itman'/ *n.* (*pl.* -men) member of the American militia in the Revolutionary War

mi·nu·ti·ae /mən(y)ōō'SHē-ē', -SHē-ī'/ *n. pl.* very small, precise, or minor details [L, rel. to MINUTE¹]

minx /miNGks/ *n.* pert, sly, or playful girl

mir·a·cle /mir'ikəl/ *n.* 1 extraordinary or remarkable occurrence or development, esp. one apparently supernatural 2 remarkable specimen (*a miracle of ingenuity*) [L *mirus* wonderful]

mi·rac·u·lous /mərak'yələs/ *adj.* 1 being or having the character of a miracle 2 able to perform miracles —**mi·rac'u·lous·ly** *adv.* [Fr or MedL, rel. to MIRACLE]

mi·rage /məräzH'/ *n.* 1 optical illusion caused by atmospheric conditions 2 illusory thing [L *mirare* look at]

mire /mīr/ *n.* 1 area of swampy ground 2 mud; dirt —*v.* (mired, mir·ing) 3 plunge or sink in a mire 4 involve in difficulties 5 bespatter; besmirch —**mir'y** *adj.* [ON]

Mi·ró /mē-rō'/, **Joan** 1893–1983; Spanish painter

mir·ror /mir'ər/ *n.* 1 polished surface, usu. of coated glass, reflecting an image 2 anything reflecting truly or accurately —*v.* 3 reflect in or as in a mirror [L *mirare* look at]

mirth /mərTH/ *n.* merriment; laughter —**mirth'ful** *adj.*; **mirth'ful·ly** *adv.*; **mirth'ful·ness** *n.*; **mirth'less** *adj.*; **mirth'less·ly** *adv.*; **mirth'less·ness** *n.* [OE, rel. to MERRY]

mis- *prefix* occurring in some verbs, nouns, and adjectives meaning 'improperly,' 'badly,' 'wrongly,' 'amiss,' 'ill,' or having a negative force (*mislead; misadventure; mistrust*) [OE or L *minus*]

mis·ad·ven·ture /mis'ədven'CHər/ *n.* bad luck; misfortune

mis·an·thrope /mis'ənTHrōp'/ *n.* (also **mis·an·thro·pist** /misan'THrəpist/) person who hates or avoids human society —**mis·an·throp'ic** /-THrāp'ik/ *adj.*; **mis·an·throp'i·cal·ly** *adv.*; **mis·an·thro·py** /misan'THrəpē/ *n.* [Gk *misos* hatred + *anthrōpos* man]

mis·ap·ply /mis'əplī'/ *v.* (·plied, ·ply·ing) apply (esp. funds) improperly —**mis·ap·pli·ca'tion** /-plikā'SHən/ *n.*

mis·ap·pre·hend /mis'ap'rihend'/ *v.* misunderstand —**mis·ap·pre·hen'sion** /-SHən/ *n.*

mis·ap·pro·pri·ate /mis'əprō'prē-āt'/ *v.* (·at·ed, ·at·ing) take for one's own use; embezzle —**mis·ap·pro'pri·a'tion** *n.*

mis·be·got·ten /mis'bēgät'n/ *adj.* 1 illegitimate 2 contemptible; disreputable

mis·be·have /mis'bihāv'/ *v.* (·haved, ·having) behave improperly —**mis·be·ha'vior** *n.*

misc. *abbr.* miscellaneous

mis·car·riage /mis'kar'ij/ *n.* 1 spontaneous premature expulsion of a fetus 2 failure of a system, plan, etc.

mis·car·ry /miskar'ē/ *v.* (·ried, ·ry·ing) 1 have a miscarriage 2 (of a plan, etc.) fail

mis·cast /miskast'/ *v.* (·cast, ·cast·ing) cast an actor or play badly or unsuitably

mis·ce·ge·na·tion /misej'ənā'SHən, mis'əjə-/ *n.* interbreeding of races [rel. to MIX, GENUS]

mis·cel·la·ne·ous /mis'ələ'nēəs/ *adj.* of

mixed composition, character, or kinds —**mis·cel·la·ne·ous·ly** *adv.* [L *miscere* mix]

mis·cel·la·ny /mis'ələnē/ *n.* (*pl.* -nies) mixture; medley, esp. a varied literary collection [L, rel. to MISCELLANEOUS]

mis·chance /misCHans/ *n.* bad luck [Fr, rel. to MIS-]

mis·chief /mis'CHif/ *n.* 1 pranks or tricks 2 playfulness; malice (*eyes full of mischief*) 3a harm; injury b a cause of this [OFr, rel. to MIS-, *chever* happen]

mis·chie·vous /mis'CHivəs/ *adj.* 1 (of a person) inclined to mischief 2 (of conduct) playful; malicious 3 harmful —**mis'chie·vous·ly** *adv.*; **mis'chie·vous·ness** *n.*
● Usage: Do not pronounce with an extra syllable, as "mis-chee-vee-uhs."

mis·ci·ble /mis'əbəl/ *adj.* capable of being mixed —**mis·ci·bil'i·ty** *n.* [MedL, rel. to MIX]

mis·con·ceive /mis'kənsēv'/ *v.* (·ceived, ·ceiv·ing) 1 have a wrong idea or conception 2 plan or organize badly —**mis·con·cep'tion** /-sep'SHən/ *n.* [fr. MIS-, CONCEIVE]

mis·con·duct /mis'kän'dəkt/ *n.* improper or unprofessional behavior

mis·con·strue /mis'kənstrōō'/ *v.* (·strued, ·stru·ing) interpret wrongly —**mis·con·struc'tion** /-strək'SHən/ *n.*

mis·count *v.* /miskount'/ 1 count inaccurately —*n.* /mis'kount'/ 2 inaccurate count

mis·cre·ant /mis'krēənt/ *n.* villain [Fr, rel. to MIS-, *creant* believer]

mis'deal' *Cards. v.* (·dealt, ·deal·ing) 1 deal improperly —*n.* 2 an improper deal

mis·deed /misdēd'/ *n.* evil deed; wrongdoing [OE]

mis·de·mean·or /mis'dimē'nər/ *n. Law.* offense less serious than a felony [fr. MIS-, DEMEANOR]

mis·di·rect /mis'dərekt'/ *v.* direct improperly —**mis·di·rec'tion** *n.*

mis·do·ing /misdōō'iNG/ *n.* misdeed

mi·ser /mī'zər/ *n.* person who hoards wealth greedily —**mi'ser·li·ness** *n.*; **mi·ser·ly** *adj.* [L: wretched]

mis·er·a·ble /miz'(ə)rəbəl/ *adj.* 1 unhappy or uncomfortable 2 contemptible; mean 3 causing wretchedness or discomfort 4 inadequate —**mis'er·a·ble·ness** *n.*; **mis'er·a·bly** *adv.* [L, rel. to MISER]

mis·er·y /miz'ərē/ *n.* (*pl.* -ies) 1 condition or feeling of discontent; distress 2 cause of this [L, rel. to MISER]

mis·fire /misfīr'/ *v.* (·fired, ·fir·ing) 1 (of a gun, engine, etc.) fail to go off or function smoothly 2 (of a plan, etc.) fail to have the intended effect —*n.* 3 such failure

mis·fit /mis'fit'/ *n.* 1 person unsuited to an environment, occupation, etc. 2 clothing, etc., that does not fit

mis·for·tune /misfôr'CHən/ *n.* bad luck

mis·giv·ing /misgiv'iNG/ *n.* (often *pl.*) feeling of mistrust or apprehension

mis·gov·ern /misgəv'ərn/ *v.* govern badly —**mis'gov'ern·ment** *n.*

mis·guid·ed /misgī'did/ *adj.* mistaken in thought or action —**mis'guid·ed·ly** *adv.*; **mis'guid·ed·ness** *n.*

mis·han·dle /mis-han'dəl/ *v.* (·dled, ·dling)

1 deal with improperly **2** handle roughly or rudely

mis·hap /mis′hap′/ *n.* unlucky accident

mis·hear /mis·hēr′/ *v.* (·**heard**, ·**hear·ing**) hear incorrectly or imperfectly

mish-mash /miSH′maSH′/ *n.* confused mixture [reduplication of MASH]

mis·in·form /mis′infôrm′/ *v.* give wrong information to; mislead —**mis′in·for·ma′tion** *n.*

mis·in·ter·pret /mis′intər′prit/ *v.* **1** interpret wrongly **2** draw a wrong inference from —**mis′in·ter′pre·ta′tion** /-pritā′SHən/ *n.*

mis·judge /misjəj′/ *v.* (·**judged**, ·**judg·ing**) **1** judge wrongly **2** have a wrong opinion of —**mis′judg′ment** *n.*

mis·lay /mislā′/ *v.* (·**laid**, ·**lay·ing**) inadvertently put (a thing) where it cannot readily be found

mis·lead /mislēd′/ *v.* (·**led** /-led/, ·**lead·ing**) cause to infer what is not true; deceive —**mis·lead′ing** *adj.* [OE]

mis·man·age /misman′ij/ *v.* (·**aged**, ·**aging**) manage improperly —**mis′man′age·ment** *n.*

mis·match *v.* /mismaCH′/ **1** match unsuitably or incorrectly —*n.* /mis′maCH′/ **2** bad match

mis·no·mer /misnō′mər/ *n.* wrong or inappropriate name or term [AngFr, rel. to MIS-, *nommer* to name]

mi·sog·y·ny /misäj′ənē/ *n.* hatred of women —**mi·sog′y·nist** *n.*; **mi·sog′y·nis′tic** *adj.* [Gk *misos* hatred, *gynē* woman]

mis·place /misplās′/ *v.* (·**placed**, ·**plac·ing**) **1** put in the wrong place **2** bestow (affections, confidence, etc.) on an inappropriate object —**mis′place′ment** *n.*

mis·print *n.* /mis′print′/ **1** printing error —*v.* /misprint′/ **2** print wrongly

mis·pri·sion /mispriZH′ən/ *n.* misuse of office by a public official [AngFr, rel. to MIS-, *prendre* take]

mis·pro·nounce /mis′prənouns′/ *v.* (·**nounced**, ·**nounc·ing**) pronounce (a word, etc.) wrongly —**mis′pro·nun′ci·a′tion** /-nən′sēā′SHən/ *n.*

mis·quote /miskwōt′/ *v.* (·**quot·ed**, ·**quot·ing**) quote inaccurately —**mis′quo·ta′tion** *n.*

mis·read /misrēd′/ *v.* (·**read** /-red/, ·**read·ing**) read or interpret wrongly

mis·rep·re·sent /mis′rep′rizent′/ *v.* give a false account or idea of —**mis′rep·re·sen·ta′tion** /-tā′SHən/ *n.*

mis·rule /misrōōl′/ *n.* **1** bad government; disorder —*v.* (·**ruled**, ·**rul·ing**) **2** govern badly

miss[1] /mis/ *v.* **1** fail to hit, reach, find, catch, see, hear, meet, etc. **2** fail to seize (an opportunity, etc.) **3** notice or regret the loss or absence of **4** avoid **5** (of an engine, etc.) fail; misfire —*n.* **6** failure to hit, reach, attain, connect, etc. [OE]

miss[2] *n.* **1** (*cap.*) **a** title of an unmarried woman or girl **b** title of a beauty queen (*Miss World*) **2** girl or unmarried woman [fr. MISTRESS]

Miss. abbr. for Mississippi

mis·sal /mis′əl/ *n.* RC Ch. book containing

texts for the Mass and prayers [L *missa* MASS]

mis·shap·en /mis-SHā′pən/ *adj.* deformed; distorted [fr. MIS-, *shapen* (archaic) shaped]

mis·sile /mis′əl/ *n.* object or weapon designed to be thrown or propelled, esp. one directed by remote control or automatically [L *mittere miss-* send]

miss·ing /mis′iNG/ *adj.* lost; absent

mis·sion /miSH′ən/ *n.* **1** task or goal assigned to or assumed by a person or group **2** military or scientific operation or expedition **3** persons sent to conduct negotiations or propagate a religious faith **4** missionary or diplomatic post [L, rel. to MISSILE]

mis·sion·ar·y /miSH′əner′ē/ *adj.* **1** of or concerned with religious missions —*n.* (*pl.* ·**ies**) **2** person doing missionary work [L, rel. to MISSION]

mis·sis /mis′iz, -is/ *n.* (also **mis·sus** /mis′əz, -əs/) *Colloq.* or *Joc.* **1** form of address to a woman **2** wife; fema′e head of a household [fr. pronunc. of MRS.]

Mis·sis·sau·ga /mis′isô′gə/ *n.* city in Ontario, Canada. Pop. 463,400

Mis·sis·sip·pi /mis′isip′ē/ *n.* S state of the US. Capital: Jackson. Pop. 2,573,216. Abbr. **Miss.; MS**

Mis·sis·sip·pi·an /mis′əsip′ēən/ *adj.* **1** of or pertaining to the Mississippi River or the state of Mississippi **2** *Geol.* of or pertaining to a Paleozoic Era period from about 345 million to 310 million years ago, an age of amphibians and coal-forming —*n.* **3** native or inhabitant of the state of Mississippi

Mis′sis·sip′pi Riv′er *n.* chief river of the US, flows 2,470 mi. from Minn. to the Gulf of Mexico

mis·sive /mis′iv/ *n.* letter; message [L, rel. to MISSILE]

Mis·sour·i /mizōōr′ē, -ə/ *n.* state in the central US. Capital: Jefferson City. Pop. 5,117,073. Abbr. **MO; Mo.** —**Mis·sour′i·an** *n.* & *adj.*

Mis·sour′i Riv′er *n.* river in central US, flows 2,700 mi. from SW Mont. into the Mississippi near St. Louis, Mo.

mis·spell /misspel′/ *v.* (·**spelled** or ·**spelt**, ·**spell·ing**) spell wrongly

mis·spend /misspend′/ *v.* (·**spent**, ·**spend·ing**) spend wrongly or wastefully

mis·state /misstāt′/ *v.* (·**stat·ed**, ·**stat·ing**) state improperly —**mis′state′ment** *n.*

mist /mist/ *n.* **1a** water vapor cloud or mass limiting visibility, usu. less dense than fog **b** condensed vapor obscuring glass, etc. **2** anything resembling or obscuring like mist —*v.* **3** cover or become covered with mist or as with mist [OE]

mis·take /mistāk′/ *n.* **1** incorrect idea, judgment, or opinion; thing incorrectly done or thought —*v.* (·**took** /-tŏŏk′/, ·**tak·en**, ·**tak·ing**) **2** misunderstand **3** perceive, identify, or choose wrongly [ON, rel. to MIS-, TAKE]

mis·tak·en /mistā′kən/ *adj.* wrong; misunderstood; incorrect —**mis·tak′en·ly** *adv.*

mis·ter /mis′tər/ *n.* form of address to a man [fr. MASTER; cf. MR.]

mis·time /mistīm′/ *v.* (·**timed**, ·**tim·ing**) say or do at the wrong time

mis·tle·toe /mis′əltō′/ *n.* parasitic evergreen plant with white berries [OE]

mis·took /mistŏŏk′/ *v.* past of MISTAKE

mis·treat /mistrēt'/ v. treat improperly —**mis'treat'ment** n.

mis·tress /mis'tris/ n. 1 female head of a household 2 woman in authority 3 Brit. female teacher 4 woman having an illicit (usu. extramarital) sexual relationship with a man [Fr maistre MASTER + -ESS]

mis·tri·al /mis'trī'əl/ n. trial rendered invalid by error

mis·trust /mistrəst'/ v. be suspicious of 2 doubt —n. 3 suspicion 4 lack of confidence —**mis·trust'ful** adj.; **mis·trust'ful·ly** adv.

mist·y /mis'tē/ adj. (·i·er, ·i·est) 1 of or covered with mist 2 obscure; vague; dim —**mist'i·ly** adv.; **mist'i·ness** n. [OE, rel. to MIST]

mis·un·der·stand /mis'ən'dərstand'/ v. (·stood /stŏŏd'/, ·stand·ing) 1 understand incorrectly 2 misinterpret

mis'un·der·stand'ing n. 1 failure to understand correctly 2 slight disagreement or quarrel

mis·use v. /misyōōz'/ (·used, ·us·ing) 1 use wrongly; apply to the wrong purpose 2 ill-treat —n. /misyōōs'/ 3 wrong or improper use or application

Mitch·ell /miCH'əl/, Margaret 1900–49; US writer

mite /mīt/ n. 1 small, often parasitic arachnid 2 small sum of money 3 small object or person [OE]

mi·ter /mī'tər/ n. 1 tall, deeply-cleft headdress worn by bishops and abbots 2 (also **mi'ter joint'**) beveled joint of two pieces of wood, etc., at an angle of 90° —v. 3 join with a miter joint [Gk mitra turban]

Mit·ford /mit'fərd/ English novelists and social commentators: 1 Nancy 1904–73 2 Jessica 1917–

Mith·ri·da·tes VI /miTH'rədāt'ēz/ ("the Great") c. 132–63 B.C.; MITER 2 king of Pontus (120–63)

mit·i·gate /mit'igāt'/ v. (·gat·ed, ·gat·ing) make less intense or severe —**mit'i·ga'tion** n. [L mitis mild]

● Usage: See note at MILITATE.

mi·to·sis /mītō'sis/ n. Biol. type of cell division that results in two nuclei each having the full number of chromosomes —**mi·tot'ic** /-tät'ik/ adj. [Gk mitos thread]

mitt /mit/ n. 1 glove leaving the fingers and thumb tip exposed 2 Slang. hand or fist 3 padded baseball glove 4 see MITTEN [L, rel. to MOIETY]

mit·ten /mit'n/ n. glove with two compartments, one for the thumb and the other for all four fingers

Mit·ter·rand /mēterän'/, François 1916– ; French politician; president (1981–)

mix /miks/ v. 1 combine; blend; put together 2 prepare by combining ingredients 3 join, be mixed, or combine, esp. readily 4a be compatible b be sociable (must learn to mix) c participate 5 combine (sound signals, etc.) electronically —n. 6a mixing; mixture b proportion of materials in a mixture 7 ingredients prepared commercially for making a cake, concrete, etc. 8 audio recording produced by combining several separately recorded tracks 9 be mixed up in (or with) be involved in or

with 10 mix up: a mix thoroughly b confuse [back formation fr. MIXED]

mixed /mikst/ adj. 1 of diverse qualities or elements 2 containing persons from various backgrounds, both genders, etc. [L miscere mix]

mixed'-up' adj. Colloq. mentally or emotionally confused; socially ill-adjusted

mix·er /mik'sər/ n. 1 machine for mixing foods, etc. 2 drink to be mixed with another 3 device that combines two or more separate audio signals 4 informal social gathering, as a dance

mix·ture /miks'CHər/ n. 1 process or result of mixing 2 combination of ingredients, qualities, characteristics, etc. [L, rel. to MIXED]

mix'-up n. confusion; misunderstanding

miz·zen·mast /miz'ənmast'/ n. mast next aft of the mainmast of a ship [It, rel. to MEZZANINE]

ml or **ml.** abbr. milliliter(s)

Mlle. abbr. (pl. -s) Mademoiselle

mm abbr. millimeter(s)

MM abbr. Messieurs

Mme. abbr. (pl. -s) Madame

Mn symb. manganese

MN postal abbr. for Minnesota

mne·mon·ic /nimän'ik/ adj. 1 of or designed to aid the memory —n. 2 word, verse, etc., that aids memory —**mne'mon'i·cal·ly** adv. [Gk mnēmōn mindful]

Mo symb. molybdenum

MO, Mo. abbr. for Missouri (postal abbr. MO)

moan /mōn/ n. 1 long, low, plaintive sound 2 Colloq. complaint; grievance —v. 3 make a moan or moans 4 Colloq. complain; grumble —**moan'er** n. [OE]

moat /mōt/ n. defensive ditch around a castle, etc., usu. filled with water [Fr mote mound]

mob /mäb/ n. 1a disorderly crowd; rabble b any crowd 2 (prec. by the) usu. Derog. the people; the masses 3 (cap.) the US Mafia —v. (mobbed, mob·bing) 4 crowd around in order to attack or admire [L mobile vulgus excitable crowd]

mo·bile /mō'bəl, -bil/ adj. 1 movable; able to move easily 2 expressive; changeable 3 transportable in a motor vehicle 4 easily able to change social status —n. (also /-bēl, -bil/) 5 decoration that may be hung so as to turn freely —**mo·bil'i·ty** /-bil'ətē/ n. [L movere move]

Mo·bile /mōbēl', mō'bēl'/ n. city in Ala. Pop. 196,278

Mo'bile Bay' /mōbēl'/ n. inlet of the Gulf of Mexico on the SW coast of Ala.

mo'bile home' /mō'bəl/ n. residential trailer usu. permanently parked

mo·bi·lize /mō'bəlīz'/ v. (·lized, ·liz·ing) make or become ready for service or action —**mo'bi·li·za'tion** n.

mob·ster /mäb'stər/ n. Slang. gangster

Mo·bu·tu Se·se Se·ko /məbōō'tōō ses'ā sek'ō/ 1930– ; president of Zaire (1965–)

moc·ca·sin /mäk'əsin/ n. soft, flat-soled, usu. leather shoe [AmerInd]

mo·cha /mō'kə/ n. 1 coffee of fine quality —adj. 2 flavored with coffee or with coffee and chocolate [Mocha, port on the Red Sea]

mock /mäk/ *v.* **1** ridicule; scoff (at) **2** mimic contemptuously **3** defy or delude contemptuously —*adj* **4** sham; imitation **5** trial —**mock′er** *n.*; **mock′ing·ly** *adv.* [Fr *moquer*]

mock·er·y /mäk′(ə)rē/ *n.* (*pl.* **-ies**) **1** derision; ridicule **2** absurdly inadequate or futile action, etc.

mock′ing·bird′ *n.* bird that mimics the calls of other birds

mock′-up′ *n.* experimental model or replica

mod /mäd/ *adj. Colloq.* modern; stylish [abbr.]

mod·al /mōd′l/ *adj.* **1** of mode or form **2** *Gram.* **a** of the mood of a verb **b** (of an auxiliary verb, e.g., *would*) used to express the mood of another verb **3** *Mus.* denoting a style of music using a particular mode [L, rel. to MODE]

mode /mōd/ *n.* **1** way in which a thing is done **2** prevailing fashion or custom **3** *Mus.* any of several types of scale **4** *Gram.* mood [L *modus* measure]

mod·el /mäd′l/ *n.* **1** small-scale representation in three dimensions of an existing or proposed structure, etc. **2** simplified description of a system, etc., to assist calculations and predictions **3** particular design or style, esp. of a car **4** exemplary person or thing **5** person employed to pose for an artist or photographer or to wear clothes, etc., for display —*v.* (**·eled** or **·elled, ·el·ing** or **·el·ling**) **6** fashion, shape, or form a model **7a** act or pose as a model **b** display (a garment) [L, rel. to MODE]

mo·dem /mō′dəm/ *n.* device for transmitting data between computers, esp. over a telephone line [fr. *modulation* and *demodulation*]

Mo·de·na /mōd′n-ə/ *n.* city in N Italy. Pop. 177,500

mod·er·ate *adj.* /mäd′ərət/ **1** avoiding extremes; temperate; reasonable **2** fairly large or good **3** calm —*n.* /-rət/ **4** person who holds moderate views —*v.* /-rāt/ (**·at·ed, ·at·ing**) **5** make or become moderate **6** act as moderator of or to —**mod′er·ate·ly** *adv.*; **mod′er·ate·ness** *n.* [L]

mod·er·a·tion /mäd′ərā′SHən/ *n.* **1** avoidance of extremes **2** moderating

mod·er·a·tor /mäd′ərā′tər/ *n.* **1** arbitrator; mediator **2** presiding officer

mod·ern /mäd′ərn/ *adj.* **1** of present or recent times **2** in current fashion —*n.* **3** person living in modern times —**mo·der·ni·ty** /mädər′nitē/ *n.* [L *modo* just now]

Mod′ern Eng′lish *n.* the English language in use from about 1500 onward

mod·ern·ism /mäd′ərniz′əm/ *n.* modern ideas, methods, or practices —**mod′ern·ist** /-ist/ *n. adj.*; **mod′ern·is′tic** *adj.*

mod·ern·ize /mäd′ərnīz′/ *v.* (**·ized, ·iz·ing**) make or become modern; adapt to modern needs or habits —**mod′ern·i·za′tion** *n.*

mod·est /mäd′ist/ *adj.* **1** humble; not vain **2** diffident; bashful **3** decorous **4** unpretentious; not extravagant; restrained —**mod′est·ly** *adv.*; **mod′es·ty** *n.* [Fr fr. L]

Mo·des·to /mədes′tō/ *n.* city in Calif. Pop. 164,730

mod·i·cum /mäd′ikəm/ *n.* small quantity [L, rel. to MODE]

mod·i·fy /mäd′ifī′/ *v.* (**·fied, ·fy·ing**) **1**

make less severe or extreme **2** make partial changes in **3** *Gram.* qualify or expand the sense of (a word, etc.) —**mod′i·fi·ca′tion** /-fikā′SHən/ *n.* [L, rel. to MODE]

Mo·di·glia·ni /mō′dēlyän′ē/, **Amedeo** 1884–1920; Italian painter and sculptor

mod·ish /mō′diSH/ *adj.* fashionable —**mod′ish·ly** *adv.*; **mod′ish·ness** *n.*

mod·u·late /mäj′ələt′/ *v.* (**·lat·ed, ·lat·ing**) **1a** regulate or adjust **b** moderate **2** adjust or vary the tone, pitch, or key of **3** alter the amplitude or frequency of (a wave) —**mod′u·la′tion, mod′u·la′tor** *n.* [L, rel. to MODULE]

mod·ule /mäj′ōōl/ *n.* **1** standardized part or independent unit designed to fit in a system or structure **2** independent self-contained unit of a spacecraft **3** unit or period of training or education —**mod′u·lar** /-ələr/ *adj.* [L *modulus* measure]

mo·dus o·per·an·di /mō′dəs äp′əran′dē/ *n.* (*pl.* **mo·di o·per·an·di** /mō′dē/) method of working [L]

mo·dus vi·ven·di /mō′dəs viven′dē/ *n.* (*pl.* **mo·di vi·ven·di** /mō′dē/) **1** way of living **2** arrangement between people who agree to differ [L: way of living]

Mo·ga·di·shu /mō′gədiSH′ōō, -dē′SHōō/ *n.* capital of Somalia. Pop. 700,000

Mo·gi·lyov /mō′gilyôf′/ *n.* city in E Belarus. Pop. 363,000

mo·gul /mō′gəl/ *n. Colloq.* important or influential person [Pers, rel. to *Mongol*]

mo·hair /mō′her′/ *n.* **1** hair of the angora goat **2** yarn or fabric from this [ult. fr. Ar: choice]

Mo·ham·med /mōhäm′id/ *see* MUHAMMAD

moi·e·ty /moi′ətē/ *n.* (*pl.* **·ties**) **1** half **2** each of two parts **3** indefinite part or portion [L *medietas* fr. *medius* middle]

moire /moir, mwär/ *n.* (also **moi·re** /mwärā′/) watered fabric, usu. silk, with wavy pattern [Fr, rel. to MOHAIR]

moist /moist/ *adj.* slightly wet; damp —**moist′ly** *adv.*; **moist′ness** *n.* [Fr]

moist·en /moi′sən/ *v.* make or become moist

mois·ture /mois′CHər/ *n.* water or other liquid causing slight dampness

mois·tur·ize /mois′CHərīz′/ *v.* (**·ized, ·iz·ing**) make less dry —**mois′tur·iz′er** *n.*

Mo·ja·ve Des·ert /məhä′vē, mō–/ *n.* desert in SE Calif.; site of Death Valley

mol·ar /mō′lər/ *adj.* **1** (of a tooth) serving to grind —*n.* **2** molar tooth [L *mola* millstone]

mo·las·ses /məlas′iz/ *n.* thick, blackish syrup extracted from raw sugar [Port fr. L *mel* honey]

mold¹ /mōld/ *n.* **1** hollow container into which a substance is poured or pressed to harden into the shape of the container **2** form; shape **3** frame; template **4** character; type **5** something formed or shaped in or on a mold —*v.* **6** make (an object) in a required shape or from certain ingredients **7** shape; form **8** influence [OFr *modle* fr. L *modulus*]

mold² *n.* **1** furry growth of fungi occurring esp. in moist, warm conditions —*v.* **2** become moldy

mold³ *n.* loose earth, esp. when rich in organic matter

mold·er /mōl′dər/ *v.* decay to dust; deteriorate [fr. MOLD³]

mold·ing *n.* ornamentally shaped plaster or woodwork as an architectural feature

Mol·do·va /môldō'və/ *n.* (formerly **Molda'via**) republic in NE Europe; formerly part of the USSR. Capital: Kishinev. Pop. 4,394,000

moldy *adj.* (**·i·er, ·i·est**) 1 covered with mold 2 stale; out of date —**mold'i·ness** *n.*

mole[1] /môl/ *n.* 1 small, burrowing mammal with dark, velvety fur 2 spy established in a position of trust in an organization [LGer or Du]

mole[2] *n.* small, permanent dark spot on the skin [OE]

mole[3] *n.* pier, breakwater, or causeway [L *moles* mass]

mol·e·cule /mäl'ikyōōl'/ *n.* 1 *Chem.* smallest fundamental unit of an element or compound 2 small particle —**mo·lec·u·lar** /məlek'yələr/ *adj.*; **mo·lec·u·lar·i·ty** /məlek'yələr'itē/ *n.* [L dim., rel. to MOLE[3]]

mole'hill' *n.* small mound thrown up by a mole in burrowing

mole'skin' *n.* 1 fur of the mole 2 heavy cotton fabric with napped finish

mo·lest /məlest'/ *v.* 1 annoy or pester 2 attack or make advances to, esp. sexually —**mol·les·ta'tion** /-tā'sHən/, **mo·lest'er** *n.* [L *molestus* troublesome]

Mo·lière /môlyer'/ (pseudonym of Jean-Baptiste Poquelin) 1622–73; French dramatist

mol·li·fy /mäl'əfī'/ *v.* (**·fied, ·fy·ing**) appease —**mol'li·fi·ca'tion** /-fikā'sHən/ *n.* [L *mollis* soft]

mol·lusk /mä'ləsk/ *n.* invertebrate with a soft body and usu. a hard shell, e.g., a snail or oyster [L *molluscus* soft]

mol·ly·cod·dle /mäl'ēkädl'/ *v.* (**·dled, ·dling**) 1 coddle; pamper —*n.* 2 one who is used to being coddled [fr. name *Molly* + CODDLE]

Mol·nár /môlnär'/, **Ferenc** 1878–1952; Hungarian writer

Mo·lo·kai /mäl'əkī', mō'-/ *n.* island in central Hawaii

molt /môlt/ *v.* shed (feathers, hair, a shell, etc.) in the process of renewing plumage, a coat, etc. [L *mutare* change]

mol·ten /môlt'n/ *adj.* melted, esp. made liquid by heat [fr. MELT]

Mo·luc·cas /məlәk'əz/ *n.* (also called **Spice Islands**) S Pacific islands in the Malay Archipelago, between Sulawesi and New Guinea

mo·lyb·de·num /məlib'dənəm/ *n.* silver-white metallic element used in alloys of steel; *symb.* **Mo** [Gk *molubdos* lead]

mom /mäm/ *n. Colloq.* mother [abbr. of *momma*]

mom'-and-pop' *adj.* designating a business, esp. a retail store, etc., in which the owners are the principal workers

Mom·ba·sa /mämbäs'ə/ *n.* seaport in Kenya. Pop. 425,600

mo·ment /mō'mənt/ *n.* 1 very brief portion of time 2 an exact point of time 3 importance 4 product of a force and the distance from its line of action to a point [L, rel. to MOMENTUM]

mo·men·tar·y /mō'məntər'ē/ *adj.* lasting only a moment —**mo'men·tar'i·ly** *adv.* [L, rel. to MOMENT]

mo·men·tous /mōmen'təs/ *adj.* very impor-

---

371   **molding / monger**

---

tant —**mo·men'tous·ly** *adv.*; **mo·men'tous·ness** *n.*

mo·men·tum /mōment'əm/ *n.* (*pl.* **·tums** or **·ta** /-tə/) 1 quantity of motion of a moving body, the product of its mass and velocity 2 strength, impetus, or continuity derived from an initial effort [L *movere* move]

mom·ma /mäm'ə/ *n. Colloq.* mother [var. of MAMA]

Momm·sen /môm'sən/, **Theodor** 1817–1903; German historian

mom·my /mäm'ē/ *n.* (*pl.* **·mies**) *Colloq.* mother

Mon. *abbr.* Monday

Mon·a·co /män'ikō/ *n.* principality on the Mediterranean Sea. Capital: Monaco. Pop. 30,300

mon·arch /män'ərk, -ärk'/ *n.* 1 ruler of a country, esp. hereditary, as a king, queen, etc. 2 large N American butterfly with orange and black wings —**mo·nar'chic** /-när'kik/, **mo·nar'chi·cal** *adj.* [Gk, rel. to MONO-, *archein* rule]

mon·ar·chism /män'ərkizəm/ *n.* advocacy of monarchy —**mon'ar·chist** /-kist/ *n.* [Fr, rel. to MONARCH]

mon·ar·chy /män'ərkē/ *n.* (*pl.* **·chies**) state or form of government with a monarch at the head —**mo·nar'chi·al** /-när'kēəl/ *adj.* [Gk, rel. to MONARCH]

mon·as·ter·y /män'əster'ē/ *n.* (*pl.* **·ies**) residence of a community of monks [L *monasterium* fr. Gk *monazein* be alone]

mo·nas·tic /mənas'tik/ *adj.* of or like monasteries or monks, nuns, etc. —**mo·nas'ti·cal·ly** *adv.*; **mo·nas'ti·cism** *n.* [Gk, rel. to MONASTERY]

Mön·chen·glad·bach /mOEN'KHən-glät'bäKH/ *n.* city in W Germany. Pop. 259,400

Mon·day /mən'dā', -dē/ *n.* day of the week following Sunday; *abbr.* **M, Mon.** [OE]

Mon·dri·an /môn'drēän/, **Piet** 1872–1944; Dutch painter

Mo·net /mōnā'/, **Claude** 1840–1926; French painter

mon·e·tar·y /män'iter'ē/ *adj.* 1 of the currency in use 2 of or consisting of money —**mon'e·tar'i·ly** *adv.* [L, rel. to MONEY]

mon·ey /mən'ē/ *n.* 1 coins and paper notes as a medium of exchange 2 (*pl.* **·eys** or **·ies**) sums of money 3 wealth 4 **for my money** in my opinion; for my preference 5 **in the money:** *Colloq.* **a** as one of the top finishers in a race, etc. **b** wealthy [L *moneta*]

mon'ey·bags' *n. Colloq.* usu. *Derog.* wealthy person

mon·eyed /mən'ēd/ *adj.* wealthy

mon'ey·grub·ber /-grəb'ər/ *n. Colloq.* person greedily intent on amassing money —**mon'ey·grub'bing** *n.* & *adj.*

mon'ey·mak·er *n.* person, thing, idea, etc., that produces or earns much money —**mon'ey·mak'ing** *n.* & *adj.*

mon'ey mar'ket *n.* short-term trade in money, esp. by governments, etc.

mon'ey or'der *n.* order for payment of a specified sum, issued by a bank, post office, etc.

mon·ger /məNG'gər, mäNG'-/ *n.* (usu. in *comb.*) dealer; trader; promoter [L *mango* dealer]

Mon·go·li·a /mänˈgōˈlēə, mäNG-/ *n.* republic in E central Asia bordered by China and Russia. Capital: Ulan Bator. Pop. 2,182,000 —**Mon·goˈli·an** *n.*

mon·gol·ism /mäNGˈgəlizˈəm/ *n.* former name for DOWN SYNDROME

Mon·gol·oid /mäNGˈgəloid/ *adj.* 1 characteristic of the Mongolians, esp. in having a broad, flat, yellowish face 2 (m-) *Offens.* (no longer in technical use) having the characteristic symptoms of Down syndrome

mon·goose /mänˈgōos/ *n.* (*pl.* ·goos'es) small, flesh-eating, civetlike mammal [Marathi]

mon·grel /məNGˈgrəl, mäNGˈ-/ *n.* 1 dog or other animal or plant of mixed breed 2 of mixed origin, nature, or character [rel. to MINGLE]

mon·i·ker /mänˈikər/ *n.* (also **mon'ick·er**) name or nickname

mon·i·tor /mänˈitər/ *n.* 1 person or device for checking or warning 2 student with disciplinary or other special duties 3a television receiver used to select or verify the picture being broadcast b *Comp.* visual display device —*v.* 4 act as a monitor 5 watch over; check on [L *monere* warn]

monk /məNGk/ *n.* member of a religious community of men living under vows —**monk'ish** *adj.* [Gk *monakhos* fr. *monos* alone]

mon·key /məNGˈkē/ *n.* 1 any of various primates, including marmosets, baboons, etc. 2 mischievous person, esp. a child —*v.* 3 tamper; play around

mon'key busꞌi·ness *n. Colloq.* mischief

mon'key·shines' *n. pl. Colloq.* mischief

mon'key wrench' *n.* 1 wrench with an adjustable jaw 2 thing that interferes

mon·o /mänˈō/ *adj.* 1 monophonic —*n.* 2 mononucleosis [abbr.]

mono- *comb. form* one; alone; single [Gk *monos* alone]

mon·o·chro·mat·ic /mänˈəkrōmatˈik/ *adj.* 1 of a single color or wavelength 2 containing only one color —**mon'o·chro·matꞌi·cal·ly** *adv.*

mon·o·chrome /mänˈəkrōm/ *n.* 1 photograph or picture done in one color or different tones of this, or in black, white, and gray only —*adj.* 2 having or using only one color or in black, white, and gray only [fr. MONO-, Gk *khrōma* color]

mon·o·cle /mänˈikəl/ *n.* single eyeglass —**mon'o·cled** /-kəld/ *adj.* [L, rel. to MONO-, *oculus* eye]

mon·o·clon·al /mänˈəklōˈnəl/ *adj.* cloned from one cell

mon·o·cot·y·le·don /mänˈəkätˈlˈēdˈn/ *n.* flowering plant with one cotyledon —**mon'o·cot'y·le·don·ous** *adj.*

mon·oc·u·lar /mänäkˈyələr/ *adj.* with or for one eye [rel. to MONOCLE]

mo·nog·a·my /mənägˈəmē/ *n.* practice or state of being married to or sexually involved with one person at a time —**mo·nog'a·mous** *adj.* [Gk *gamos* marriage]

mon·o·gram /mänˈəgram/ *n.* a person's initials interwoven as a device

mon·o·graph /mänˈəgraf/ *n.* treatise on a single subject

mon·o·lin·gual /mänˈəliNGˈgwəl/ *adj.* speaking or using only one language

mon·o·lith /mänˈlˈiTH/ *n.* 1 single block of stone, esp. shaped into a pillar, etc. 2 massive, immovable, or solidly uniform person or thing —**mon'o·lith'ic** *adj.* [Gk *lithos* stone]

mon·o·logue /mänˈlˈôg, -äg/ *n.* 1a soliloquy b play or skit for one performer 2 long speech as part of a conversation, etc. [Fr fr. Gk *monologos* speaking alone]

mon·o·ma·ni·a /mänˈəmāˈnēə/ *n.* obsession over a single idea or interest —**mon'o·maꞌni·ac** /-nēak/ *n.* & *adj.*; **mon'o·ma·niꞌac·al** /-nīˈəkəl/ *adj.*

mon·o·nu·cle·o·sis /mänˈōn(y)ōōklēōˈsis/ *n.* (fully **in·fecꞌtious mon'o·nu·cle·oꞌsis**) viral disease characterized by fever, lethargy, and swollen lymph nodes

mon·o·phon·ic /mänˈəfänˈik/ *adj.* (of sound-reproduction) using only one channel of transmission [Gk *phōnē* sound]

mo·nop·o·list /mənäpˈəlist/ *n.* person who has or advocates a monopoly —**mo·nop'o·lisꞌtic** *adj.*

mo·nop·o·lize /mənäpˈəlīzˈ/ *v.* (·lized, ·liz·ing) 1 obtain a monopoly 2 dominate or prevent others from sharing in —**mo·nop'o·li·zaꞌtion, mo·nop'o·liz·er** *n.*

mo·nop·o·ly /mənäpˈəlē/ *n.* (*pl.* ·lies) 1a exclusive possession or control of a commodity or service b this conferred as a privilege by the government 2 a commodity or service held as a monopoly [Gk *monos* single, *pōlein* sell]

mon·o·rail /mänˈərāl/ *n.* railway with a single track

mon·o·so·di·um glu·ta·mate /mänˈəsōˈdēəm glōōˈtəmāt/ *n.* sodium salt of glutamic acid used to enhance the flavor of food; *abbr.* MSG

mon·o·syl·la·ble /mänˈasilˈəbəl/ *n.* word of one syllable —**mon'o·syl·lab'ic** /-labˈik/ *adj.*

mon·o·the·ism /mänˈəTHēˈizˈəm/ *n.* doctrine that there is only one god —**mon'o·the'ist** /-ist/ *n.*; **mon'o·the·isꞌtic** *adj.*

mon·o·tone /mänˈətōn/ *n.* 1 sound or utterance continuing or repeated without change of pitch 2 sameness of color, style, etc. —*adj.* 3 without change of pitch

mo·not·o·nous /mənätˈənəs/ *adj.* lacking in variety; tedious through sameness —**mo·not'o·nous·ly** *adv.*; **mo·not'o·ny** *n.*

Mon·roe /mənrōˈ/ 1 **James** 1758–1831; 5th US president (1817–25) 2 **Marilyn** 1926–62; US actress

Mon·ro·vi·a /mənrōˈvēə/ *n.* capital of Liberia. Pop. 421,100

mon·sieur /məsyōˈ(r)/ *n.* (*pl.* **mes·sieurs** /mesyərˈ(z)/) French title corresponding to *Mr.* or *sir* [Fr *mon* my, *sieur* lord]

mon·si·gnor /mänsēnˈyər/ *n.* (*pl.* **·gno·ri** /-sēnˈyôrˈē/) title of various Roman Catholic priests and officials [It: my lord]

mon·soon /mänsōōnˈ/ *n.* 1 seasonal wind in S Asia, esp. in the Indian Ocean 2 rainy season accompanying the summer monsoon [Ar *mawsim*]

mon·ster /mänˈstər/ *n.* 1 frightening imaginary creature 2 cruel or wicked person 3 large, usu. ugly or misshapen, animal or thing —*adj.* 4 huge [L *monstrum* fr. *monere* warn]

mon·strance /'män'strəns/ *n.* RC Ch. vessel in which the consecrated Host is exposed for veneration [L *monstrare* show]

mon·strous /'män'strəs/ *adj.* 1 like a monster; abnormally formed 2 huge 3a outrageously wrong or absurd b atrocious —**mon·stros·i·ty** /mänsträs'itē/ *n.*; **mon'strous·ly** *adv.*; **mon'strous·ness** *n.* [L, rel. to MONSTER]

Mont. abbr. for Montana

mon·tage /mäntäzн', mōn-/ *n.* composite visual image or scene made from juxtaposed photographs, film sequences, etc. [Fr, rel. to MOUNT[1]]

Mon·taigne /mônten'(yə)/, **Michel de** 1533–92; French essayist

Mon·tan·a /mäntan'ə/ *n.* NW state of the US. Capital: Helena. Pop. 799,065. Abbr. **Mont.**; **MT** —**Mon·tan'an** *n.* & *adj.*

Mont·calm /mônkälm'/, **Louis Joseph** 1712–59; French general

Mon·te·ne·gro /mäntə'nē'grō/ *n.* republic in SE Europe, on the Balkan Peninsula. Capital: Podgorica. Pop. 550,000 —**Mon'te·ne'gran** *n.* & *adj.*

Mon·ter·rey /mänt'ərā'/ *n.* capital of the Mexican state of Nuevo León. Pop. 2,549,400

Mon·tes·quieu /mänt'əskyōō'/ 1689–1755; French political philosopher

Mon·tes·so·ri /mänt'əsôr'ē/, **Maria** 1870–1952; Italian educator

Mon·te·ver·di /mänt'əverd'ē/, **Claudio** 1567–1643; Italian composer

Mon·te·vi·de·o /mänt'əvidā'ō/ *n.* capital of Uruguay. Pop. 1,251,600

Mon·te·zu·ma II /mänt'əzōō'mə/ 1466–1520; Aztec emperor (1502–20)

Mont·gom·er·y /mantgom'(ə)rē, mänt-/ capital of Ala., in the E central part. Pop. 187,106

month /mənтн/ *n.* 1a each of twelve periods into which a year is divided b period of time between the same dates in successive calendar months 2 period of 30 days or 4 weeks [OE]

month'ly *adj.* 1 done, produced, or occurring once every month —*adv.* 2 every month —*n.* (*pl.* **·lies**) 3 monthly periodical

Mont·pel·ier /mäntpēl'yər/ *n.* capital of Vt., in the central part. Pop. 8,247

Mont·pel·lier /môn'pelyā'/ *n.* city in S France. Pop. 210,900

Mont·re·al /män'trē-ôl'/ *n.* city in Quebec, Canada, on St. Lawrence River. Pop. 1,017,700

mon·u·ment /män'yəmənt/ *n.* 1 anything enduring that serves to commemorate or celebrate, esp. a structure, gravestone, etc. 2 model or example of enduring significance 3 ancient building or site [L *monere* remind]

mon·u·men·tal /män'yəment'l/ *adj.* 1a extremely great; stupendous b massive and permanent 2 of or serving as a monument —**mon'u·men'tal·ly** *adv.*

moo /mōō/ *n.* (*pl.* **·s**) 1 cry of a cow —*v.* (**mooed**, **moo·ing**) 2 make this sound [imit.]

mooch /mōōCH/ *v. Colloq.* beg; impose upon [prob. fr. Fr *muchier* skulk]

mood[1] /mōōd/ *n.* 1 state of mind or feeling 2 fit of bad temper or depression [OE]

373   **monstrance / mop**

mood[2] *n. Gram.* form or set of forms of a verb indicating whether it expresses a fact, command, wish, etc. [alter. of MODE]

mood' swing *n.* marked change in temperament, as from euphoria to depression

mood·y /mōō'dē/ *adj.* (**·i·er**, **·i·est**) given to changes of mood; gloomy; sullen —**mood'i·ly** /-əlē/ *adv.*; **mood'i·ness** *n.* [rel. to MOOD[1]]

| full | waxing, crescent | waning, gibbous |

MOON 1a

moon /mōōn/ *n.* 1a the primary natural satellite of the earth, orbiting it monthly b anything resembling the moon, as an orb or crescent 2 natural satellite of any planet —*v.* 3 behave dreamily or listlessly —**moon'less** *adj.* [OE]

Moon /mōōn/, **Sun Myung** 1920– ; Korean religious leader

moon'beam *n.* ray of moonlight

moon'light *n.* 1 light of the moon —*v.* (**·light·ed**, **·light·ing**) 2 *Colloq.* have two paying jobs, esp. one by day and one by night —**moon'light·er** *n.*; **moon'lit** *adj.*

moon'scape *n.* 1 surface or landscape of the moon 2 area resembling this; wasteland

moon'shine *n.* 1 foolish talk or ideas 2 *Slang.* illicitly distilled or smuggled alcohol 3 moonlight

moon'shot *n.* launching of a spacecraft to the moon

moon'stone *n.* feldspar of pearly appearance

moon'struck *adj.* slightly mad

moor[1] /mōōr/ *n. Brit.* open uncultivated land, esp. when covered with heather [OE]

moor[2] *v.* attach (a boat, etc.) to a fixed object —**moor'age** /-ij/ *n.* [prob. LGer]

Moor /mōōr/ *n.* member of a Muslim people of NW Africa —**Moor'ish** *adj.* [Gk *Mauros*]

Moore /môr, mōr, mōōr/ 1 G(eorge) E(dward) 1873–1958; English philosopher 2 **Marianne** 1887–1972; US poet 3 **Henry** 1898–1986; English sculptor

moor'ing *n.* 1 (often *pl.*) place where a boat, etc., is moored 2 (*pl.*) set of permanent anchors and chains

m.o. or **M.O.** *abbr.* 1 MODUS OPERANDI 2 MONEY ORDER

moose /mōōs/ *n.* (*pl.* same) large deer of northern N America, having broad, flattened antlers in the male [Narragansett]

moot /mōōt/ *adj.* debatable; undecided [OE]

moot' court' *n.* enactment of law court procedure, as for student training

mop /mäp/ *n.* 1a bundle of yarn or cloth or a sponge on the end of a stick, for cleaning floors, etc. b similarly shaped implement for various purposes 2 thick mass of hair —*v.* (**mopped**, **mop·ping**) 3 wipe or clean with or as with a mop 4 **mop up:** *Colloq.* a dispatch; make an end of b complete the occupation of (a district, etc.) by capturing or killing enemy troops left there

mope /mōp/ v. (**moped, mop·ing**) be depressed or listless —**mop′y** adj. (·**i·er**, ·**i·est**)

mo·ped /mō′ped/ n. two-wheeled, low-powered motor vehicle with pedals [Sw, rel. to MO-TOR, PEDAL]

mo·raine /mərān′/ n. area of debris carried down and deposited by a glacier [Fr]

mor·al /môr′əl, mär′-/ adj. **1a** concerned with the distinction between right and wrong **b** concerned with accepted rules and standards of human behavior **2** virtuous; capable of moral action **3** founded on moral not actual law **4** psychological rather than physical (*moral support*) —n. **5** moral lesson of a fable, story, event, etc. **6** (*pl.*) moral behavior or standards —**mor′al·ly** adv. [L *mos mor-custom*]

mo·rale /məral′/ n. confidence, determination, etc., of a person or group [Fr *moral*, rel. to MORAL]

mor·al·ist /môr′əlist, mär′-/ n. person who practices, teaches, or imposes morality —**mor′al·is′tic** adj.

mo·ral·i·ty /məral′ətē/ n. (*pl.* ·**ties**) **1** degree of conformity to moral principles **2** right moral conduct **3** particular system of morals

mor·al·ize /môr′əlīz′, mär′-/ v. (·**ized**, ·**iz·ing**) indulge in moral reflection or talk —**mor′al·i·za′tion** n.

mo·rass /məras′/ n. **1** entanglement; confusion **2** bog; swamp [Fr *marais*, rel. to MARSH]

mor·a·to·ri·um /môr′ətôr′ēəm/ n. (*pl.* ·**ums** or ·**ri·a** /-ə/) **1** temporary prohibition or suspension (of an activity) **2a** legal authorization to postpone payment **b** period of this postponement [L *morari* delay]

mor·bid /môr′bid/ adj. **1** unwholesome; gruesome **2** *Med.* of the nature of or indicative of disease —**mor·bid′i·ty** n.; **mor′bid·ly** adv. [L *morbus* disease]

mor·dant /môrd′nt/ adj. **1** caustic; biting; sarcastic **2** serving to fix dye —n. **3** mordant substance [L *mordere* bite]

more /môr/ adj. **1** greater in quantity or degree; additional —n. **2** greater quantity, number, or amount —adv. **3** to a greater degree or extent **4** forming the comparative of some adjectives and adverbs (*more easily*) **5** more or less approximately; effectively; nearly [OE]

More /môr/, (Sir) **Thomas** 1478–1535; English scholar and statesman

Mo·re·lia /mərēl′yə/ n. capital of the Mexican state of Michoacán. Pop. 489,700

Mo·re·los /mərä′ləs/ n. state in S central Mexico. Capital: Cuernavaca. Pop. 1,195,100

Mo·re·no Val·ley /mərē′nō/ n. city in Calif. Pop. 118,779

more·o·ver /môrō′vər/ adv. besides; in addition

mo·res /môr′āz/ n. pl. customs or conventions of a community [L, pl. of *mos* custom]

Mor·gan /môr′gən/, **J(ohn) P(ierpont)** 1837–1913; US financier and philanthropist

morgue /môrg/ n. **1** temporary mortuary for victims of violence or accidents **2** (in a newspaper office) room or file of unused material, back issues, etc. [Fr, orig. the name of a Paris mortuary]

mor·i·bund /môr′ibənd/ adj. dying [L *mor ibundus*]

Mor·i·son /môr′əsən/, **Samuel Eliot** 1887–1976; US historian

Mo·ri·sot /môr′isō′/, **Berthe** 1841–95; French painter

Mor·mon /môr′mən/ n. member of the Church of Jesus Christ of Latter-Day Saints —**Mor′mon·ism** /-izəm/ n. [name of the man believed to be the author of their sacred book]

morn /môrn/ n. *Poet.* morning [OE]

morn·ing /môr′niNG/ n. early part of the day, ending at noon or lunchtime [fr. MORN]

morn′ing glo′ry n. twining plant with trumpet-shaped flowers

morn′ing sick′ness n. nausea felt esp. in the morning in early pregnancy

mo·roc·co /mərak′ō/ n. (*pl.* ·**cos**) fine flexible goatskin leather [for MOROCCO, where orig. made]

Mo·roc·co /mərak′ō/ n. kingdom in NW Africa. Capital: Rabat. Pop. 26,239,000 —**Mo·roc′can** /-kən/ n. & adj.

mo·ron /môr′än/ n. *Colloq.* very stupid person —**mo·ron′ic** /-än′ik/ adj. [Gk *mōros* foolish]

Mo·rón /môrōn′/ n. suburb of Buenos Aires, Argentina. Pop. 641,500

Mo·ro·ni /môrō′nē/ n. capital of Comoros. Pop. 22,000

mo·rose /mərōs′/ adj. sullen; gloomy —**mo·rose′ly** adv.; **mo·rose′ness** n. [L *mos mor-manner*]

morph /môrf/ v. (in movies, videos, etc.) change form or appearance, as from person to animal, by computer-controlled special effects

mor·pheme /môr′fēm′/ n. *Ling.* smallest meaningful unit of a language [Gk *morphē* form]

mor·phine /môr′fēn/ n. narcotic drug from opium, used to relieve pain [L *Morpheus* god of sleep]

mor·phol·o·gy /môrfäl′əjē/ n. the study of the forms or structures of things —**mor′pho·log′i·cal** /-fəläj′ikəl/ adj. [Gk *morphē* form]

Mor·ris /môr′əs, mär′-/ **1 Robert** 1734–1806; English-born statesman and financier of the American Revolution **2 Gouverneur** 1752–1816; US statesman

Mor·ri·son /môr′əsən, mär′-/, **Toni** 1931–; US novelist; Nobel prize 1993

mor·row /mär′ō, môr′ō/ n. *Old-fash.* the following day [rel. to MORN]

Morse /môrs/ n. (in full **Morse′ code′**) telegraphic code in which letters are represented by combinations of long and short light or sound signals [for MORSE]

Morse /môrs/, **Samuel F(inley) B(reese)** 1791–1872; US inventor and painter; developed Morse code

mor·sel /môr′səl/ n. mouthful; small piece [L *morsus* bite]

mor·tal /môrt′l/ adj. **1** subject to death **2** causing death; fatal **3** associated with death **4** intense; very serious; implacable —n. **5** human being —**mor′tal·ly** adv. [L *mors mort-death*]

mor·tal·i·ty /môrtal′itē/ n. (*pl.* ·**ties**) **1** being subject to death **2** loss of life on a large scale **3** death rate

mor·tar /môrt′ər/ *n.* 1 mixture of lime or cement, sand, and water, for bonding bricks or stones 2 short large-bore cannon for firing shells at high angles 3 bowl in which ingredients are pounded with a pestle [L *mortarium*]

MORTAR 3 and PESTLE

mor′tar·board′ *n.* 1 academic cap with a stiff, flat, square top 2 flat board for holding mortar

mort·gage /môr′gij/ *n.* 1a conveyance of property to a creditor as security for a debt b deed effecting this 2 sum of money lent by this —*v.* (-gaged, -gag·ing) 3 convey (a property) by mortgage 4 promise in advance; pledge —**mort′gage·a·ble** *adj.* [Fr: dead pledge, rel. to GAGE¹]

mort·gag·ee /môr′gijē′/ *n.* creditor in a mortgage

mort·gag·or /môr′gijər/ *n.* (also **mort′gag·er**) debtor in a mortgage

mor·ti·cian /môrtish′ən/ *n.* UNDERTAKER [L *mors mort-* death]

mor·ti·fy /môr′tifī′/ *v.* (-fied, -fy·ing) 1 shame; humiliate 2 bring (bodily desires, etc.) into subjection by self-denial or discipline 3 (of flesh) be affected by gangrene or necrosis —**mor′ti·fi·ca′tion** /-fikā′shən/ *n.*; **mor′ti·fy′ing** *adj.* [L, rel. to MORTICIAN]

mor·tise /môr′tis/ *n.* 1 hole in a framework designed to receive the end of another part, esp. a tenon —*v.* (-tised, -tis·ing) 2 join securely, esp. by mortise and tenon 3 cut a mortise in [Fr fr. Ar]

mor·tu·ar·y /môr′cho͞o-er′ē/ *n.* (*pl.* -ies) room or building in which dead bodies are kept until burial or cremation [MedL *mortuus* dead]

mo·sa·ic /mōzā′ik/ *n.* 1 picture or pattern produced by arranging small, colored pieces of glass or stone, etc. 2 of or like a mosaic [Gk: ult. rel. to MUSE]

Mo·sa·ic /mōzā′ik/ *adj.* of Moses or the laws attributed to him

Mos·cow /mäs′kou′, -kō′/ *n.* capital of Russia and former capital of the USSR. Pop. 8,801,500

Mo·ses /mō′ziz/ *n.* c. 14th–13th cent. B.C.; Hebrew prophet and lawgiver

Mo·ses /mō′ziz/, **Anna Mary** (called "Grandma Moses") 1860–1961; US painter

Mo·ses ben Mai·mon see MAIMONIDES

mo·sey /mō′zē/ *v. Slang.* move along in a leisurely manner

Mos·lem /mäz′ləm/ *n. & adj.* var. of MUSLIM

mosque /mäsk/ *n.* Muslim place of worship [Ar *masgid*]

mos·qui·to /məskē′tō/ *n.* (*pl.* -toes) flying insect, of which the female sucks the blood of animals and humans [Sp and Port, dim. of *mosca* fly]

moss /môs/ *n.* small, flowerless plant growing in dense clusters on the ground, trees, stones, etc. —**moss′y** *adj.* (-i·er, -i·est) [OE]

most /mōst/ *adj.* 1 greatest in quantity or degree 2 the majority of —*n.* 3 greatest quantity or number 4 the majority —*adv.* 5 in the highest degree 6 forming the superlative of some adjectives and adverbs (*most absurd; most easily*) 7 *Colloq.* almost 8 at most no more or better than (*this is at most a compromise*) 9 make the most of employ to the best advantage [OE]

-most *suffix* forming superlative adjectives and adverbs from prepositions and other words indicating relative position (*foremost; uttermost*) [OE]

most′-fa′vored na′tion *adj.* US-government designation for countries granted favorable trade benefits

most′ly *adv.* 1 mainly 2 usually

Mo·sul /mōso͞ol′/ *n.* city in Iraq on the Tigris River. Pop. 570,900

mote /mōt/ *n.* speck of dust [OE]

mo·tel /mōtel′/ *n.* roadside hotel for motorists [fr. *motor hotel*]

moth /môth/ *n.* 1 nocturnal insect similar to a butterfly 2 insect of this type, the larva of which feeds on wool, etc. [OE]

moth′ball′ *n.* ball of naphthalene placed in stored clothes to deter moths

moth′-eat′en *adj.* 1 damaged by moths 2 time-worn

moth·er /məth′ər/ *n.* 1 female parent 2 that which gives rise to something else 3 (in full **moth′er su·pe′ri·or**) head of a female religious community —*v.* 4 treat as a mother does 5 give birth to; be the mother or origin of —**moth′er·hood** *n.*; **moth′er·less** *adj.* [OE]

Moth′er Goose′ *n.* fictitious author of a collection of nursery rhymes

moth′er-in-law′ *n.* (*pl.* **moth′ers-in-law′**) husband's or wife's mother

moth′er·land′ *n.* native country

moth′er·ly *adj.* kind or tender like a mother —**moth′er·li·ness** *n.*

moth′er-of-pearl′ *n.* iridescent inner layer of the shell of oysters, etc.

Moth′er Te·re′sa see TERESA, MOTHER

moth′er tongue′ *n.* native language

mo·tif /mōtēf′/ *n.* 1 theme that is repeated and developed in an artistic work 2 decorative design or pattern [Fr, rel. to MOTIVE]

mo·tile /mō′til/ *adj.* capable of moving spontaneously —**mo·til′i·ty** *n.*

mo·tion /mō′shən/ *n.* 1 moving; changing position 2 gesture 3 formal proposal put to a committee, legislature, court, etc. —*v.* 4 direct (a person) by a gesture 5 make a gesture directing 6 go through the motions do something perfunctorily or superficially 7 in motion moving; not at rest —**mo′tion** *adj.* [L, rel. to MOVE]

mo′tion pic′ture *n.* MOVIE

mo·ti·vate /mō′təvāt′/ *v.* (-vat·ed, -vat·ing) 1 supply a motive to; be the motive of 2 stimulate the interest of —**mo′ti·va′tion** *n.*; **mo′ti·va′tion·al** *adj.*

mo·tive /mō′tiv/ *n.* 1 thing that induces a person to act in a particular way; incentive 2 MOTIF —*adj.* 3 causing or concerned with movement [L *motivus*, rel. to MOVE]

mot·ley /mät′lē/ *adj.* (·li·er, ·li·est) diversified in color, character, or makeup

mo·to·cross /mō′tōkrôs/ *n.* cross-country racing on motorcycles

mo·tor /mō′tər/ *n.* 1 thing that imparts motion 2 engine, esp. one powered by electricity or internal combustion —*adj.* 3 giving, imparting, or producing motion 4 driven by a motor 5 of or for motor vehicles 6 *Anat.* relating to muscular movement or the nerves activating it —*v.* 7 go or convey in a motor vehicle [L, rel. to MOVE]
● Usage: See note at ENGINE.

mo′tor bike′ *n.* motorized bicycle or lightweight motorcycle

mo·tor·cade /mō′tərkād/ *n.* procession of motor vehicles [blend of MOTOR, CAVALCADE]

mo′tor·cy·cle *n.* two-wheeled motor vehicle without pedal propulsion —**mo′tor·cy′clist** *n.*

mo′tor home′ *n.* van or trucklike vehicle outfitted as a residence

mo·tor·ist /mō′tərist/ *n.* driver of a car

mo·tor·ize /mō′tərīz/ *v.* (·ized, ·iz·ing) provide with a motor or motor transport

mo′tor pool′ *n.* vehicles kept ready for assignment as needed, as for a military unit

mo′tor ve′hi·cle *n.* powered road vehicle, as a car, truck, etc.

Mott /mät/, **Lucretia Coffin** 1793–1880; US social reformer

mot·tle /mät′l/ *v.* (·tled, ·tling) mark with spots or smears of color —**mot′tled** *adj.* [back formation fr. MOTLEY]

mot·to /mät′ō/ *n.* (*pl.* ·toes or ·tos) maxim adopted as a rule of conduct, ideal, etc. [It: word]

mound /mound/ *n.* heap or pile of earth, stones, etc.

mount[1] /mount/ *v.* 1 ascend; climb on to 2a set on horseback b serving on horseback (*mounted police*) 3 accumulate; increase 4 set (an object) on a support or in a backing, frame, etc. 5 organize; arrange; set in motion —*n.* 6 backing or support on which something is set for display 7 horse for riding [L, rel. to MOUNT[2]]

mount[2] *n.* mountain [L *mons mont-*]

moun·tain /mount′n/ *n.* 1 large, natural elevation of the ground 2 large heap or pile; huge quantity [L, rel. to MOUNT[2]]

moun′tain bike′ *n.* sturdy bicycle suitable for rough terrain

moun′tain dew′ *n. Colloq.* home-distilled (illegal) whiskey

moun·tain·eer /mount′n-ēr/ *n.* person who climbs mountains for sport —**moun′tain·eer′ing** *n.*

moun′tain goat′ *n.* goatlike animal of the Rocky Mountains

moun′tain li′on *n.* COUGAR

moun′tain·ous *adj.* 1 having many mountains 2 huge

moun′tain range′ *n.* continuous line of mountains

moun′tain sick′ness *n.* sickness caused by thin air at great heights

Moun′tain State′ *n.* any US state containing part of the Rocky Mountain range: Ariz., Colo., Idaho, Mont., Nev., N. Mex., Utah, Wyo.

Mount·bat·ten /mountbat′n/, **Louis (1st Earl Mountbatten of Burma)** 1900–79; British naval officer and statesman

moun·te·bank /moun′tibaNGk/ *n.* swindler; charlatan [It: mount on bench]

Moun·tie /moun′tē/ *n. Colloq.* member of the Royal Canadian Mounted Police [abbr.]

mount′ing *n.* MOUNT[1], 6

mourn /môrn/ *v.* feel or show deep sorrow or regret for (a dead person, a lost thing, etc.) —**mourn′er** *n.* [OE]

mourn′ful /môrn′fəl/ *adj.* doleful; sad; expressing mourning —**mourn′ful·ly** *adv.*; **mourn′ful·ness** *n.*

mourn′ing *n.* 1 expression of sorrow for a dead person 2 black clothes worn to express such sorrow

mouse *n.* /mous/ (*pl.* mice) 1 common small rodent 2 timid or feeble person 3 (*pl.* mice or mous′es) *Comp.* small hand-held device controlling the cursor on a monitor —*v.* /mous, mouz/ (moused, mous·ing) 4 hunt mice —**mous′er** *n.* [OE]

mousse /mōōs/ *n.* 1a flavored, whipped dessert of cream, eggs, etc. b meat or fish purée made with whipped cream, etc. 2 foamy substance applied to the hair to enable styling [Fr: froth]

Mous·sorg·sky /mōōsôrg′skē/ (also **Mus·sorgsky**), **Modest** 1839–81; Russian composer

mous·tache /mus′tasH, məstasH′/ *n.* var. of MUSTACHE

mous·y /mou′sē/ *adj.* (·i·er, ·i·est) 1 of or like a mouse 2 timid; feeble 3 nondescript light brown —**mous′i·ness** *n.*

mouth *n.* /mouTH/ (*pl.* mouths /mouTHz/) 1 opening in the head through which most animals take in food and emit communicative sounds 2 opening of a container, cave, trumpet, etc. 3 place where a river enters the sea —*v.* /mouTH/ 4 say or speak by moving the lips but with no sound 5 utter or speak insincerely 6 down at (or in) the mouth *Colloq.* sad; depressed [OE]

mouth·ful /mouTH′fəl/ *n.* (*pl.* ·fuls) 1 quantity of food, etc., that fills the mouth 2 small quantity 3 *Colloq.* long or complicated word or phrase

mouth′ or′gan *n.* HARMONICA

mouth′piece′ *n.* 1 part of a musical instrument, telephone, etc., placed next to or near the mouth 2 *Slang* lawyer

mouth′wash′ *n.* liquid antiseptic, etc., for rinsing the mouth or gargling

mouth′-wa′ter·ing *adj.* having a delicious smell or appearance

mov′a·ble /mōōv′əb′l/ *adj.* (also **move′a·ble**) 1 that can be moved 2 variable in date from year to year —**mov′a·bil′i·ty** *n.*; **mov′a·bly** *adv.* [rel. to MOVE]

move /mōōv/ *v.* (moved, mov·ing) 1 change or cause to change position, posture, or place 2 put or keep in motion; rouse; stir 3 take a turn in a board game 4 go; proceed; make progress 5 take action, esp. promptly 6 be socially active in 7 affect with emotion 8 prompt; incline; provoke 9 (cause to) change one's attitude 10a cause (the bowels) to be evacuated b (of the bowels) be evacuated 11 make a formal request or proposal, as in a meeting **12** sell; be sold —*n.* **13** act or process of moving **14** change of house, premises, etc. **15** step taken to secure an object, goal, etc. **16** player's turn in a board game **17** get a move on *Colloq.* hurry up **18** on the move moving —**mov'er** *n.* [L *movere*]

move'a·ble *adj.* var. of MOVABLE

move'ment *n.* **1** moving or being moved **2** moving parts of a mechanism (esp. a clock or watch) **3a** body of persons with a common object **b** campaign undertaken by them **4** (*pl.*) activities and whereabouts of a person or group **5** *Mus.* principal division of a longer musical work **6** bowel evacuation **7** progress

mov·ie /moo͞'ve̅/ *n.* **1** sequence of photographs or images shown in rapid succession to create an illusion of movement **2** story, event, etc., so depicted **3** the movies: **a** the movie industry **b** the showing of a movie

mov·ie·dom /moo͞'ve̅dəm/ *n.* the film industry and associated businesses, people, etc.

mow[1] /mo͞/ *v.* (**mowed** or **mown** /mo͞n/, **mow·ing**) **1** cut (grass, hay, etc.) with a scythe or machine **2** mow down kill or destroy randomly or in great numbers —**mow'er** *n.* [OE *mawan*]

mow[2] /mou/ *n.* **1** storage place for grain, hay, etc., in a barn **2** pile of hay, grain, etc. [OE *muga*]

Mo·zam·bique /mo̅'zambe̅k'/ *n.* republic in SE Africa, W of Madagascar. Capital: Maputo. Pop. 14,842,000 —**Mo'zam·bi'can** *n.* & *adj.*

Mo·zart /mo̅t'särt'/, **Wolfgang Amadeus** 1756–91; Austrian composer

MP *abbr.* **1** Military Police **2** *Brit.* Member of Parliament

mpg *abbr.* miles per gallon

mph *abbr.* miles per hour

Mr. /mis'tər/ *n.* (*pl.* **Messrs.**) **1** title for a man **2** title prefixed to a designation of office, etc. (*Mr. President*) [abbr. of MISTER]

MRI *abbr. Med.* diagnostic technique producing an image of the structure of a solid (esp. body tissue) using computer technology and radio waves [magnetic resonance imaging]

Mrs. /mis'iz/ *n.* (*pl.* same) title for a married woman [abbr. of MISTRESS]

MS *abbr.* **1** postal abbr. for Mississippi **2** multiple sclerosis **3** (*pl.* **MSS**) manuscript

Ms. /miz/ *n.* title for a married or unmarried woman [combination of MRS., MISS[2]]

M.S. or **M.Sc.** *abbr.* Master of Science

MS-DOS /em'es'däs', -dôs'/ *abbr. Tdmk. Comp.* Microsoft disk operating system

MSG *abbr.* MONOSODIUM GLUTAMATE

Msgr. *abbr.* MONSIGNOR

MST *abbr.* mountain standard time

MSW *abbr.* Master of Social Work

Mt *symb.* meitnerium

MT postal abbr. for Montana

Mt. *abbr.* Mount

mu /m(y)o͞o/ *n.* twelfth Greek letter (M, μ) [Gk]

much /məCH/ *adj.* (**more, most**) **1** existing or occurring in a great quantity —*n.* **2** a great quantity **3** noteworthy or outstanding example (*not much to look at*) —*adv.* **4** in a great degree **5** often **6** nearly [ME fr. OE *micel* great]

mu·ci·lage /myo͞o'silij/ *n.* **1** viscous sub-

stance obtained from plants **2** adhesive gum; glue [L, rel. to MUCUS]

muck /mək/ *n.* **1** *Colloq.* dirt or filth; anything disgusting **2** manure —*v.* **3** muck up: *Colloq.* **a** bungle (a job) **b** make dirty or untidy —**muck'y** *adj.* (**·i·er, ·i·est**) [Scand]

muck'rake' *v.* (**·raked, ·rak·ing**) search out and reveal scandal —**muck'rak·er, muck' rak'ing** *n.*

mu·cous /myo͞o'kəs/ *adj.* of or covered with mucus —**mu·cos·i·ty** /myo͞okäs'ətē/ *n.* [L *mucosus*, rel. to MUCUS]

mu'cous mem'brane *n.* mucus-secreting tissue lining body cavities, etc.

mu·cus /myo͞o'kəs/ *n.* slimy substance that moistens and protects internal tissues, organs, etc. [L]

mud /məd/ *n.* **1** soft wet earth **2** disparaging or slanderous remarks [Ger]

mud·dle /məd'l/ *v.* (**·dled, ·dling**) **1** bring into disorder **2** bewilder; confuse —*n.* **3** disorder **4** confusion [perh. Du, rel. to MUD]

mud'dle·head'ed *adj.* mentally confused

mud·dy /məd'ē/ *adj.* (**·di·er, ·di·est**) **1** like or covered with mud **2** not clear; impure **3** vague; confused —*v.* (**·died, ·dy·ing**) **4** make muddy —**mud'di·ness** *n.*

mud'flat' *n.* stretch of muddy land uncovered at low tide

mud'sling'er *n. Colloq.* person given to making abusive or disparaging remarks —**mud' sling'ing** *n.*

mu·ez·zin /mo͞o·ez'in/ *n.* Muslim crier who proclaims the hours of prayer [Ar]

muff /məf/ *n.* **1** covering, esp. of fur, for keeping the hands or ears warm —*v.* *Colloq.* **2** bungle **3** miss (a catch, ball, etc.) [Du *mof*]

muf·fin /məf'in/ *n.* small, round, quick bread, fried or baked

muf·fle /məf'əl/ *v.* (**·fled, ·fling**) **1** wrap or cover for warmth, or to deaden sound **2** stifle or deaden (a sound) [perh. Fr *moufle* thick glove, MUFF]

muf·fler /məf'lər/ *n.* **1** scarf worn for warmth **2** thing used to deaden sound, esp. the exhaust noise of a motor vehicle

muf·ti /məf'tē/ *n.* civilian clothes [Ar]

mug /məg/ *n.* **1a** drinking vessel, usu. cylindrical with a handle **b** its contents **2** *Slang.* face **3** *Slang.* criminal —*v.* (**mugged, mugging**) **4** make a face, as for a photograph **5** attack and rob, esp. in public —**mug'ger** *n.*; **mug'ful** *n.* (*pl.* **·fuls**); **mug'ging** *n.* [Scand]

Mu·ga·be /mo͞ogäb'ē/, **Robert** 1924– ; Zimbabwean politician; prime minister (1980–87); president (1987–)

mug·gy /məg'ē/ *adj.* (**·gi·er, ·gi·est**) oppressively humid —**mug'gi·ness** *n.* [ON]

mug'shot' *n. Slang.* photograph of a face, esp. for police records

Mu·ham·mad /mo͞ohäm'əd, mō-/ (also **Mo·ham'med; Ma·hom'et**) c. 570–632; Arab prophet and founder of Islam

Mu·ham·mad A·li see ALI, MUHAMMAD

Muir /myo͞or/, **John** 1838–1914; Scottish-born US naturalist, explorer, and conservationist

mu·ja·hi·din /mo͞o'jəhədēn'/ *n. pl.* (also **mu·ja'he·din', ·deen'**) guerrilla fighters in Islamic countries [Pers and Ar, rel. to JIHAD]

muk·luk /mӘk'lӘk/ *n.* **1** fur-lined boot worn by the Inuits **2** any similar soft-soled boot

mu·lat·to /m(y)ŏŏlat'ō,-lät'ō/ *n.* (*pl.* ·tos or ·toes) person of mixed white and black parentage [Sp *mulato* young mule]

mul·ber·ry /mӘl'ber'ē/ *n.* (*pl.* ·ries) **1** tree bearing edible purple or white berries **2** its fruit **3** dark-red or purple [L *morum* mulberry, BERRY]

mulch /mӘlCH/ *n.* **1** layer of straw, leaves, plastic, etc., spread around plantings to insulate, retain moisture, etc. —*v.* **2** treat with mulch [OE: soft]

mule¹ /myŏŏl/ *n.* **1** offspring of a male donkey and a female horse **2** *Colloq.* stupid or obstinate person —**mul'ish** *adj.*; **mul'ish·ly** *adv.*; **mul'ish·ness** *n.* [L *mulus*]

mule² *n.* backless slipper [Fr]

mu·le·teer /myŏŏ'lӘtēr'/ *n.* mule driver [Fr *muletier*, rel. to MULE¹]

mull¹ /mӘl'/ *v.* ponder; consider [prob. Du]

mull² *v.* warm (wine or beer) with added sugar, spices, etc.

mul·lah /mŏŏl'Ә/ *n.* Muslim learned in theology and sacred law [ult. Ar *mawlā*]

mul·let /mӘl'it/ *n.* (*pl.* same) any of several kinds of marine fish valued for food [Gk *mullos*]

mul·li·gan /mӘl'igӘn/ *n. Golf.* second attempt allowed after a poor shot

mul·li·ga·taw·ny /mӘl'igatô'nē/ *n.* highly seasoned soup orig. from India [Tamil: pepper-water]

mul·lion /mӘl'yӘn/ *n.* vertical bar dividing the panes or sections of a window —**mul'lioned** *adj.* [prob. Fr *moinel* middle, rel. to MEAN³]

Mul·tan /mŏŏltän'/ *n.* city in Pakistan. Pop. 730,100

multi- *comb. form* many [L *multus* much; many]

mul·ti·cul·tur·al /mӘl'tēkӘl'CH(Ә)rӘl/ *adj.* of or including several cultural groups —**mul'ti·cul'tur·al·ism** *n.*

mul·ti·far·i·ous /mӘl'tifar'ēӘs/ *adj.* **1** many and various **2** diverse —**mul'ti·far'i·ous·ly** *adv.*; **mul'ti·far'i·ous·ness** *n.* [L *multifarius*]

mul·ti·lat·er·al /mӘl'tēlat'ӘrӘl/ *adj.* **1** (of an agreement, etc.) in which three or more parties participate **2** having many sides —**mul'ti·lat'er·al·ly** *adv.*

mul·ti·lin·gual /mӘl'tēlinG'gwӘl/ *adj.* in, speaking, or using several languages

mul·ti·me·di·a /mӘl'tēmē'dēӘ/ *adj.* **1** using more than one medium of communication **2** having several media, as a computer system incorporating audio, text, and graphics

mul·ti·na·tion·al /mӘl'tēnash'(Ә)nӘl/ *adj.* **1** operating in several countries **2** of several nationalities —*n.* **3** multinational company

mul·ti·ple /mӘl'tӘpӘl/ *adj.* **1** having several parts, elements, or components **2** many and various —*n.* **3** number that contains another without a remainder (*56 is a multiple of 7*) [L *multiplus*, rel. to MULTIPLEX]

mul'ti·ple-choice' *adj.* accompanied by several possible answers from which the correct one is to be chosen

mul·ti·ple scle·ro'sis *n.* progressive disease

of the nervous system marked by loss of muscle control

mul·ti·plex /mӘl'tipleks/ *adj.* **1** manifold; of many elements **2** *Electronics.* of a circuit, etc., allowing transmission of more than one signal simultaneously —*n.* **3** cluster of movie theaters, usu. partitioned sections of one structure —**mul'ti·plex'er, mul'ti·plex'or** *n.* [L, rel. to MULTI-, *-plex*]

mul·ti·pli·cand /mӘl'tiplikand'/ *n.* quantity to be multiplied by another

mul·ti·pli·ca·tion /mӘl'tiplikā'sHӘn/ *n.* multiplying

mul'ti·pli·ca'tion sign' *n.* sign (× or ·) to indicate that one quantity is to be multiplied by another

mul·ti·plic·i·ty /mӘl'tiplis'itē/ *n.* (*pl.* ·ties) **1** manifold variety **2** great number

mul·ti·pli·er /mӘl'tiplī'Әr/ *n.* quantity by which a given number is multiplied

mul·ti·ply /mӘl'tiplī'/ *v.* (·plied, ·ply·ing) **1** increase a number by a specified number of times (*multiply 6 by 4*) **2** increase in number [L *multiplicare*]

mul·ti·proc·es·sor /mӘl'tēprä'ses'Әr/ *n. Comp.* system utilizing two or more processing units

mul·ti·ra·cial /mӘl'tērā'sHӘl/ *adj.* of, concerning, or including several races

mul·ti·tude /mӘl'tit(y)ŏŏd'/ *n.* great number; crowd [Fr fr. L]

mul·ti·tu·di·nous /mӘl'tit(y)ŏŏd'n-Әs/ *adj.* **1** very numerous **2** many [L, rel. to MULTITUDE]

mum¹ /mӘm/ *n. Colloq.* CHRYSANTHEMUM [abbr.]

mum² *adj. Colloq.* **1** silent **2** mum's the word say nothing [imit.]

mum·ble /mӘm'bӘl/ *v.* (·bled, ·bling) **1** speak or utter indistinctly —*n.* **2** indistinct utterance or sound [rel. to MUM²]

mum·ble·ty·peg /mӘm'bӘltēpeg'/ *n.* children's game involving skillful tricks with a penknife

mum·bo-jum·bo /mӘm'bō jӘm'bō/ *n.* (*pl.* ·bos) meaningless or ignorant ritual [name of a supposed African idol]

mum·mer /mӘm'Әr/ *n.* actor in a traditional mime [fr. MUM²]

mum·mer·y /mӘm'Әrē/ *n.* (*pl.* ·ies) **1** ridiculous or flamboyant ceremonial **2** performance by mummers [Fr *momerie*, rel. to MUMMER]

mum·mi·fy /mӘm'Әfī'/ *v.* (·fied, ·fy·ing) preserve (a body) as a mummy —**mum'mi·fi·ca'tion** /-fikā'sHӘn/ *n.*

mum·my /mӘm'ē/ *n.* (*pl.* ·mies) body embalmed for burial, esp. in ancient Egypt [Pers *mūm* wax]

mumps /mӘmps/ *n. pl.* (treated as *sing.*) infectious disease with swelling of the neck and face [obs. *mump* grimace]

munch /mӘnCH/ *v.* eat steadily with a marked action of the jaws [imit.]

munch·ies /mӘn'CHēz/ *n. pl. Colloq.* **1** snack foods **2** urge to snack

mun·dane /mӘn'dān'/ *adj.* **1** dull; routine **2** of this world —**mun·dane'ly** *adv.* [L *mundus* world]

Mu·nich /myŏŏ'nik, -nikH/ *n.* city in SW Germany. Pop. 1,229,000

mu·nic·i·pal /myŏŏnis'ӘpӘl/ *adj.* of a munic-

mu·nic'i·pal bond' *n.* interest-bearing instrument offered by a local government to finance public projects

mu·nic·i·pal·i·ty /myŏŏnis'ipal'ətē/ *n.* (*pl.* ·ties) town or district having local government

mu·nif·i·cent /myŏŏnif'əsənt/ *adj.* splendidly generous, esp. in giving —**mu·nif'i·cence** *n.* [L *munus* gift, *facere fic-* make]

mu·ni·tions /myŏŏnish'ənz/ *n. pl.* military weapons, ammunition, etc. [L *munire* fortify]

Mun·ro /mənrō'/, **H**(ector) **H**(ugh) ("**Saki**") 1870–1916; British writer

Mün·ster /myn'stər, mən'-/ *n.* city in NW Germany. Pop. 259,400

muon /myŏŏ'än/ *n.* Physics. unstable elementary particle with a greater mass than an electron [fr. use of Greek MU as its symbol]

mu·ral /myŏŏr'əl/ *n.* 1 painting executed directly on a wall —*adj.* 2 of, on, or like a wall [L *murus* wall]

Mu·rat /myŏŏrä'/, **Joachim** c. 1767–1815; French general and king of Naples (1808–15)

Mur·cia /mər'SH(ē)ə/ *n.* city in SE Spain. Pop. 318,800

mur·der /mər'dər/ *n.* 1 intentional unlawful killing of a human being by another 2 Colloq. unpleasant, troublesome, or dangerous state of affairs —*v.* 3 kill (a human being) intentionally and unlawfully 4 Colloq. a utterly defeat b spoil by a bad performance, mispronunciation, etc. —**mur'der·er, mur'der·ess** *n.* [OE]

mur·der·ous /mər'dərəs/ *adj.* 1 capable of, intending, or involving murder or great harm 2 Colloq. extremely arduous or unpleasant

Mur·doch /mər'däk/, **Rupert** 1931– ; Australian publisher and communications magnate

mu'ri·at'ic ac'id /myŏŏr'ēat'ik/ *n.* HYDROCHLORIC ACID

murk /mərk/ *n.* darkness; poor visibility [prob. Scand]

murk·y /mər'kē/ *adj.* (·i·er, ·i·est) 1 dark; gloomy; obscure 2 thick; dirty —**murk'i·ly** /-əlē/ *adv.*; **murk'i·ness** *n.*

Mur·mansk /mŏŏrmansk'/ *n.* seaport in NW Russia. Pop. 472,900

mur·mur /mər'mər/ *n.* 1 subdued continuous sound, as made by waves, a brook, etc. 2 softly spoken or nearly inarticulate utterance —*v.* 3 make a murmur 4 utter (words) in a low voice, esp. as a complaint [L]

Mur·ray /mər'ē/, (**Sir**) **James Augustus Henry** 1837–1915; Scottish philologist and lexicographer

mus·cat /məs'kat', -kət/ *n.* 1 (also **mus'ca·tel'**) sweet, usu. fortified white wine made from musk-flavored grapes 2 this grape [Prov, rel. to MUSK]

Mus·cat /məs'kät', -kət/ *n.* capital of Oman. Pop. 85,000

mus·cle /məs'əl/ *n.* 1 fibrous tissue that can contract to produce movement in or maintain the position of an animal body 2 bodily part composed of muscles 3 strength; power —*v.* (·cled, ·cling) Colloq. 4 force through 5 muscle in (or in on) force oneself on others; intrude [L dim. of *mus* mouse]

379   municipal bond / Mussolini

mus·cle-bound' *adj.* lacking agility through excessive muscularity

mus·cu·lar /məs'kyələr/ *adj.* 1 of or affecting the muscles 2 having well-developed muscles —**mus'cu·lar'i·ty** *n.*

mus'cu·lar dys'tro·phy /dis'trəfē/ *n.* hereditary disease marked by progressive wasting of the muscles

mus·cu·la·ture /məs'kyələCHər/ *n.* muscular system of a body or organ

muse /myŏŏz/ *v.* (mused, mus·ing) 1 ponder; reflect 2 say meditatively [Fr]

Muse /myŏŏz/ *n. Gk. & Rom. Myth.* one of nine sister goddesses thought to inspire creative effort

mu·se·um /myŏŏzē'əm/ *n.* building used for storing and exhibiting objects of historical, scientific, or cultural interest [Gk, rel. to MUSE]

mush[1] /məsh/ *n.* 1 soft pulp 2 feeble sentimentality 3 porridge —**mush'y** *adj.* (·i·er, ·i·est); **mush'i·ness** *n.* [appar. var. of MASH]

mush[2] *interj.* 1 cry to encourage sled dogs —*v.* 2 travel with a dogsled across snow or ice

mush'room' *n.* 1 edible fungus with a stem and domed cap —*v.* 2 appear or develop rapidly —*adj.* 3 of or similar to a mushroom [Fr *mousseron* fr. L]

mu·sic /myŏŏ'zik/ *n.* 1 art of combining vocal or instrumental sounds in a harmonious or expressive way 2 composition or performance of this 3 pleasant natural sound [Gk, rel. to MUSE]

mu·si·cal /myŏŏ'zikəl/ *adj.* 1 of music 2 melodious; harmonious 3 fond of, sensitive to, or skilled in music 4 set to or accompanied by music —*n.* 5 movie or play featuring songs, dance, etc. —**mu'si·cal'i·ty** /-kal'itē/ *n.*; **mu'si·cal·ly** *adv.*

mu·si·cian /myŏŏzish'ən/ *n.* person who performs or studies music, esp. professionally —**mu·si'cian·ly** *adj.*; **mu·si'cian·ship'** *n.* [Fr, rel. to MUSIC]

mu·si·col·o·gy /myŏŏ'zikäl'əjē/ *n.* the academic study of music —**mu'si·col'o·gist** *n.*; **mu'si·co·log'i·cal** /-kəläj'ikəl/ *adj.*

musk /məsk/ *n.* substance secreted by the male musk deer, used in perfumes —**musk'y** *adj.* (·i·er, ·i·est); **musk'i·ness** *n.* [L *muscus* fr. Pers]

musk' deer' *n.* small, hornless Asian deer

mus·kel·lunge /məs'kələnj'/ *n.* (also **mus·kie** /məs'kē/) large, edible N American pike

mus·ket /məs'kit/ *n. Hist.* smooth-bored light gun [It *moschetto* crossbow bolt]

mus·ke·teer /məs'kətēr'/ *n. Hist.* soldier armed with a musket

musk'ox' *n.* shaggy N American arctic ox

musk'rat' *n.* 1 large N American aquatic rodent with a musky smell 2 its fur

Mus·lim /mŏŏz'ləm, maz'-, mŏŏs'-/ (also **Mos'lem**) *n.* 1 follower of Islam —*adj.* 2 of Islam or its believers [Ar, rel. to ISLAM]

mus·lin /məz'lin/ *n.* strong, woven cotton fabric [It *Mussolo* Mosul in Iraq]

muss /məs/ *n. Colloq.* 1 mess —*v.* 2 make messy —**muss'y** *adj.* (·i·er, ·i·est)

mus·sel /məs'əl/ *n.* bivalve mollusk, esp. an edible kind [OE, rel. to MUSCLE]

Mus·so·li·ni /mŏŏ'səlē'nē, mŏŏs'ə-/, **Benito**

(called **"Il Duce"**) 1883–1945; Italian Fascist
leader; dictator of Italy (1922–43)

Mus·sorg·sky see MOUSSORGSKY

must /məst/ *v. aux.* (*past* must) 1 be
obliged to 2 be certainly 3 ought to —*n.* 4
Colloq. thing that should not be missed [OE]

mus·tache /məs´tasн´, məstasн´/ *n.* (also
mous´tache) hair left to grow on a man's upper lip [Gk *mustax*]

mus·tang /məs´taNG´/ *n.* small, wild horse of
W North America [Sp]

mus·tard /məs´tərd/ *n.* 1a plant with slender
pods and yellow flowers b seeds of this
ground and used as a spicy condiment 2
brownish-yellow [ME fr. OFr for relish made
with *must* 'grape juice']

mus´tard gas´ *n.* colorless oily liquid whose
vapor is a powerful irritant

mus·ter /məs´tər/ *v.* 1 collect; gather together 2 summon —*n.* 3 assembly of persons for inspection 4 **pass muster** be accepted as adequate [L *monstrare* show]

must·y /məs´tē/ *adj.* (·i·er, ·i·est) 1 moldy;
stale 2 dull; antiquated —**must´i·ly** *adv.*;
must´i·ness *n.* [perh. rel. to MOIST]

mu·ta·ble /myōō´təbəl/ *adj.* liable to change;
easily changed —**mu´ta·bil´i·ty** *n.* [L *mutare*
change]

mu·ta·gen /myōō´təjən/ *n.* agent promoting
genetic mutation —**mu´ta·gen´ic** /-jenik/
adj.; **mu´ta·gen´e·sis** /-əsis/ *n.* [fr. MUTA-
TION, -GEN]

mu·tant /myōōt´nt/ *adj.* 1 resulting from mutation —*n.* 2 mutant organism or gene

mu·ta·tion /myōōtā´sнən/ *n.* 1 change; alteration 2 genetic, heritable change 3 mutant
—**mu´tate** *v.* (·tat·ed, ·tat·ing) [L *mutare*
change]

mute /myōōt/ *adj.* 1 silent; refraining from
speech 2 incapable of speech 3 (also
muted) subdued —*n.* 4 person incapable of
speech 5 device for damping the sound of a
musical instrument —*v.* (mut·ed, mut·ing)
6 deaden or soften the sound, color, etc., of
—**mute´ly** *adv.*; **mute´ness** *n.* [L *mutus*]

mu·ti·late /myōōt´l-āt´/ *v.* (·lat·ed, ·lat·ing)
1 cut off; disfigure or destroy, esp. by cutting
2 damage part of (a limb, organ, book, etc.)
—**mu´ti·la´tion** *n.* [L *mutilus* maimed]

mu·ti·ny /myōōt´n-ē/ *n.* (*pl.* ·nies) 1 open
revolt, esp. by soldiers or sailors against their
officers —*v.* (·nied, ·ny·ing) 2 revolt
—**mu´ti·neer´** /-ēr/ *n.*; **mu´ti·nous** /-tinəs/
adj.; **mu´ti·nous·ly** *adv.*

mutt /mət/ *n.* Slang. dog, esp. a mongrel
[abbr. of *mutton-head*]

mut·ter /mət´ər/ *v.* 1 utter (words) in a
barely audible manner 2 murmur; grumble
—*n.* 3 muttered words or sounds 4 mutter-
ing [rel. to MUTE]

mut·ton /mət´n/ *n.* flesh of sheep as food
[MedL *multo* sheep]

mu·tu·al /myōō´cнōōəl/ *adj.* 1 experienced
or done by each of two or more parties to or
towards the other(s) 2 *Colloq.* common to two
or more persons —**mu´tu·al´i·ty** /-al´itē/ *n.*;
mu´tu·al·ly *adv.* [L *mutuus* borrowed]

mu´tu·al fund´ *n.* Finance. investment fund
in which shares are sold and capital is invested
in several companies, etc.

muu-muu /mōō´mōō´/ *n.* loose, traditionally
Hawaiian dress

Mu·zak /myōō´zak´/ *n.* 1 *Tdmk.* system of
piped music used in public places 2 (m-) recorded background music, esp. if bland or artless [fanciful var. of MUSIC]

muz·zle /məz´əl/ *n.* 1 projecting part of an
animal's face, including the nose and mouth 2
guard put over an animal's nose and mouth to
stop it biting or feeding 3 open end of a firearm —*v.* (·zled, ·zling) 4 put a muzzle on
5 impose silence on [MedL *musum*]

MVP *abbr.* Sports. most valuable player

Mwan·za /mwän´zə/ *n.* city in Tanzania on
Lake Victoria. Pop. 252,100

my /mī/ *pron.* of, or belonging to me [fr.
MINE¹]

my·al·gia /mī-al´jə/ *n.* muscular pain —**my-
al´gic** *adj.* [Gk *mus* muscle]

My·an·mar /myän´mär´/ *n.* see BURMA

My·ce·nae·an /mīsə´nē´ən/ *adj.* 1 of the late
Bronze Age civilization in Greece (c. 1500–
1100 B.C.), depicted in the Homeric poems
—*n.* 2 person of this civilization [L *Mycenae*,
ancient Greek city]

my·col·o·gy /mīkäl´əjē/ *n.* 1 the study of
fungi 2 fungi of a particular region —**my·col´
o·gist** *n.* [Gk *mukēs* mushroom]

My·lar /mī´lär/ *n. Tdmk.* a durable, lightweight polyester film

my·na /mī´nə/ *n.* (also **my´nah**) talking bird
of the starling family [Hindi]

my·o·pi·a /mī-ō´pēə/ *n.* 1 near-sightedness
2 lack of imagination or insight —**my·op´ic**
/-äp´ik/ *adj.*; **my·op´i·cal·ly** *adv.* [Gk *muein*
shut, *ōps* eye]

myr·i·ad /mēr´ēəd/ *n.* 1 an indefinitely great
number —*adj.* 2 innumerable [Gk: 10,000]

My·ron /mī´rən/ fl. c. 480–440 B.C.; Greek
sculptor

myrrh /mər/ *n.* aromatic gum resin used in
perfume, incense, etc. [L *myrrha* fr. Gk]

myr·tle /mərt´l/ *n.* evergreen shrub with
shiny leaves and white scented flowers [Gk
murtos]

my·self /mīself´/ *pron.* 1 *emphat.* form of I
or ME (*I saw it myself*) 2 *refl.* form of ME (*I
was angry with myself*)

My·sore /mīsôr´/ *n.* city in S India. Pop.
480,000

mys·te·ri·ous /mistēr´ēəs/ *adj.* full of or
wrapped in mystery —**mys·te´ri·ous·ly** *adv.*;
mys·te´ri·ous·ness *n.* [Fr, rel. to MYSTERY]

mys·ter·y /mis´t(ə)rē/ *n.* (*pl.* ·ies) 1 secret,
hidden, or inexplicable matter 2 secrecy; obscurity 3 fictional work dealing with a puzzling event, esp. a crime [Gk *mustērion*, rel. to
MYSTIC]

mys·tic /mis´tik/ *n.* 1 person who seeks spiritual truths or experiences —*adj.* 2 MYSTICAL
—**mys´ti·cism´** /-təsizəm/ *n.* [Gk *mustēs* initiated person]

mys·ti·cal /mis´tikəl/ *adj.* 1 of mystics or
mysticism 2 mysterious; occult 3 spiritually
allegorical or symbolic —**mys´ti·cal·ly** *adv.*

mys·ti·fy /mis´təfī´/ *v.* (·fied, ·fy·ing) 1 bewilder; confuse 2 wrap in mystery —**mys´ti-
fi·ca´tion** /-fikā´sнən/ *n.* [Fr, rel. to MYSTIC/
MYSTERY]

mys·tique /mistēk´/ *n.* atmosphere of mystery and usu. admiration attending some activity, person, profession, etc. [Fr, rel. to MYSTIC]

myth /mɪth/ *n.* **1a** traditional story embodying popular ideas on natural or supernatural and social phenomena, etc. **b** such narratives collectively **2** widely held but false notion **3** fictitious person, thing, or idea —**myth'i·cal** *adj.*; **myth'i·cal·ly** *adv.* [Gk *muthos*]

my·thol·o·gy /mɪˈthäl'əjē/ *n.* (*pl.* -**gies**) **1**

body of myths **2** the study of myths —**myth'o·log'i·cal** /-ˈläj'ikəl/ *adj.*; **my·thol'o·gize'** /-jīz/ *v.* (-**gized**, -**giz·ing**) [Gk: MYTH, -LOGY]

Myu·ko·la·yiv /myōō'kəli'if/ *n.* (formerly Nikolayev) city in Ukraine. Pop. 512,000

N

n, N /en/ *n.* (*pl.* **n's**; **N's, Ns**) fourteenth letter of the English alphabet; a consonant

N *symb.* nitrogen

n or **n.** *abbr.* **1** name **2** born [L *natus, nata*] **3** neuter **4** new **5** nominative **6** noon **7** noun **8** number

N or **N.** *abbr.* **1** navy **2** north; northern **3** noon **4** November

Na *symb.* sodium

N.A. *abbr.* **1** North America **2** (also **NA; N/A**) not applicable

NAACP *abbr.* National Association for the Advancement of Colored People

nab /nab/ *v.* (**nabbed, nab·bing**) *Slang.* **1** arrest; catch **2** grab

Na·be·re·zhny·e Chel·ny /nä'bərizH'nēə cHēl'nē/ *n.* city in E Russia. Pop. 513,100

na·bob /nā'bäb/ *n.* important, wealthy person

Na·bo·kov /nəbô'kəf, nab'əkôf'/, **Vladimir** 1899–1977; Russian-born US novelist

na·cho /näcH'ō/ *n.* (*pl.* -**chos**) tortilla chips topped with melted cheese, peppers, etc.

na·cre /nā'kər/ *n.* mother-of-pearl —**na'cre·ous** /-krēəs/ *adj.* [Fr]

Na·der /nād'ər/, **Ralph** 1934– ; US consumer advocate

na·dir /nā'dēr', -dər/ *n.* **1** part of the celestial sphere directly below an observer **2** lowest point [Ar: opposite]

NAFTA /naf'tə/ *abbr.* North American Free Trade Agreement

nag[1] /nag/ *v.* (**nagged, nag·ging**) **1** persistently criticize, urge, scold, etc. **2** be persistent, as a pain, trouble, etc. —*n.* **3** person who nags [orig. a dial. word]

nag[2] *n. Colloq.* horse, esp. an old or worthless one

Na·ga·sa·ki /nä'gəsäk'ē/ *n.* seaport in Japan, on Kyushu; target of second atomic bomb, 1945. Pop. 443,800

Na·go·ya /nəgoi'ə, nä'gəyä'/ *n.* city in Japan, on Honshu. Pop. 2,158,800

Nag·pur /näg'pōōr'/ *n.* city in central India. Pop. 1,622,200

Na·hua·ti /nä'wätl/ *n.* language used mainly by Indians of Central America

nai·ad /nī'ad'/ *n.* water nymph [L fr. Gk]

nail /nāl/ *n.* **1** small, metal spike hammered in to join things together or as a peg or decoration **2** horny growth at the tip of a finger or toe —*v.* **3** fasten or secure with or as if with nails **4** keep (attention, etc.) fixed **5** expose or discover [OE]

Nai·ro·bi /nīrō'bē/ *n.* capital of Kenya. Pop. 1,504,900

na·ïve /nī-ēv'/ *adj.* (also **na·ive**) innocent; unaffected; credulous —**na·ïve'ly** *adv.*; **na·**

ïve·ty /nī-ē'vətē/, **na·ïve·té** /nä'ēvtä'/ *n.* [L *nativus* NATIVE]

na·ked /nā'kid/ *adj.* **1** without clothes; nude **2** without its usual covering or protection **3** undisguised —**na'ked·ly** *adv.*; **na'ked·ness** *n.* [OE]

nam·by-pam·by /nam'bē pam'bē/ *adj.* **1** insipid; weak —*n.* (*pl.* -**bies**) **2** timid or weak person [sarcastic play on the name of writer *Ambrose* Philips]

name /nām/ *n.* **1** word or phrase by which an individual person, family, animal, place, thing, or class of things is spoken of, etc. **2** abusive term used of a person, group, etc. **3** famous person **4** reputation —*v.* (**named, nam·ing**) **5** give a name to **6** state the name of **7** mention; specify; cite **8** nominate **9** *in the name of* as representing; by virtue of **10** *in name only* not in reality —**name'a·ble** *adj.* [OE]

name'less *adj.* **1** having or showing no name **2** unnamed **3** too horrific to be named

name'ly *adv.* that is to say; in other words

name'sake' *n.* person or thing having the same name as another [prob. fr. *for the name's sake*]

Na·mib·i·a /nəmib'ēə/ *n.* republic in SW Africa on the Atlantic Ocean. Capital: Windhoek. Pop. 1,431,000 —**Na·mib'i·an** *n.* & *adj.*

Nam·p'o /nam'pō/ *n.* city in North Korea. Pop. 370,000

Nam·pu·la /nampōō'lə/ *n.* city in Mozambique. Pop. 250,500

Nan·chang /nän'cHäng'/ *n.* city in SE China. Pop. 1,086,100

Nan·cy /nänsē', nan'sē/ *n.* city in NE France. Pop. 102,400

Nan·jing /nän'jiNG'/ *n.* (formerly **Nan'king**) port in E China. Pop. 2,090,200

nan·ny /nan'ē/ *n.* (*pl.* -**nies**) **1** child's nurse **2** (in full **nan'ny goat'**) female goat [fr. proper name *Nanny*]

nano- *comb. form* denoting a factor of 10^{-9}; one billionth (*nanosecond*) [Gk *nanos* dwarf]

Nantes /nänt/ *n.* seaport in W France. Pop. 251,100

nap[1] /nap/ *v.* (**napped, nap·ping**) **1** sleep lightly or briefly —*n.* **2** short sleep or doze, esp. by day [OE]

nap[2] *n.* raised pile on textiles [LGer or Du]

na·palm /nā'pä(l)m'/ *n.* **1** jellied incendiary mixture used in bombs —*v.* **2** attack with napalm bombs [fr. NAPHTHALENE, PALMATE]

nape /nāp/ *n.* back of the neck

naph·tha /naf'THə, nap'-/ *n.* flammable hydrocarbon distilled from coal, etc. [L fr. Gk]

naph·tha·lene /naf'THəlēn', nap'-/ *n.* crystalline distillate of coal tar used in moth repellent, etc.

nap·kin /nap'kin/ *n.* small cloth or paper for wiping the lips, fingers, etc., at meals [Fr *nappe* fr. L *mappa*]

Na·ples /nā'pəlz/ *n.* (Italian name **Napoli**) seaport in SW Italy. Pop. 1,206,000

Na·po·le·on I /nəpō'lēən/ (surname **Bonaparte**) 1769–1821; Corsican-born French general and politician; emperor of France (1804–15) —**Na·po'le·on'ic** /-lēä'nək/ *adj.*

Na·po·le·on III (**Louis Napoleon Bonaparte**) 1808–73; president of France (1848–52); emperor of France (1852–70)

narc /närk/ *n.* (also **nark**) *Slang.* undercover police officer charged with enforcing narcotics laws [fr. NARCOTIC]

nar·cis·sism /när'səsiz'əm/ *n.* excessive interest in oneself —**nar'cis·sist** /-sist/ *n.* & *adj.*; **nar'cis·sis'tic** *adj.* [*Narkissos*, youth in Gk myth who fell in love with his reflection]

nar·cis·sus /närsis'əs/ *n.* (*pl.* **-cis·si** /-sī'/) any of several flowering bulbs, including the daffodil [L fr. Gk]

nar·co·sis /närkō'sis/ *n.* state of insensibility [Gk *narkē* numbness]

nar·cot·ic /närkät'ik/ *adj.* 1 inducing drowsiness, etc. 2 (of a drug) affecting the mind —*n.* 3 narcotic substance, drug, or influence [Gk *narkōtikos*]

nar·co·tize /när'kətīz'/ *v.* (**·tized, ·tiz·ing**) treat with or subject to a narcotic —**nar'co·ti·za'tion** *n.*

Nar·ra·gan·sett /nar'əgan'sit/ *n.* Algonquian language used by the Narragansett people of NE North America

nar·rate /nar'āt, narāt'/ *v.* (**·rat·ed, ·rat·ing**) 1 tell 2 provide a spoken accompaniment for —**nar·ra'tion, nar'ra·tor** *n.* [L *narrare*]

nar·ra·tive /nar'ətiv/ *n.* 1 ordered account of connected events —*adj.* 2 of or by narration

nar·row /nar'ō/ *adj.* (**·row·er, ·row·est**) 1a of small width b confined; confining 2 of limited scope 3 with little margin (*narrow escape*) —*n.* 4 (usu. *pl.*) narrow part of a strait, river, pass, street, etc. —*v.* 5 become or make narrow; contract; lessen —**nar'row·ly** *adv.*; **nar'row·ness** *n.* [OE]

nar'row-mind'ed *adj.* rigid or restricted in one's views; intolerant —**nar'row-mind'ed·ness** *n.*

nar·whal /när'wäl', -wəl/ *n.* Arctic white whale, the male of which has a long tusk [Du fr. Dan]

nar·y /ner'ē/ *adj. Dial.* or *Joc.* none; not any

NASA /nas'ə/ *abbr.* National Aeronautics and Space Administration

na·sal /nā'zəl/ *adj.* 1 of the nose 2 pronounced or spoken with the breath passing through the nose —*n.* 3 nasal letter or sound —**na'sal·i·za'tion** /-izā'sHən/ *n.*; **na'sal·ize** *v.* (**·ized, ·iz·ing**); **na'sal·ly** *adv.* [L *nasus* nose]

nas·cent /nas'ənt, nā'sənt/ *adj.* 1 in the act of being born 2 just beginning to be —**nas'cen·cy** *n.* [L, rel. to NATAL]

NASDAQ /naz'dak/ *abbr.* National Association of Securities Dealers Automated Quotations

Nash /nasH/, **Ogden** 1902–71; US writer of humorous poetry

Nash·u·a /nasH'ōōə/ *n.* city in N. Hamp. Pop. 79,662

Nash·ville /nasH'vil', -vəl/ *n.* capital of Tenn., in the N central part. Pop. 487,969

Na·sik /näs'ik/ *n.* (also **Nashik**) city in W central India. Pop. 646,900

Nas·sau /nas'ô/ *n.* capital of the Bahamas. Pop. 172,200

Nas·ser /nas'ər/, **Gamal Abdel** 1918–70; Egyptian leader; president (1956–58)

nas·tur·tium /nəstər'sHəm/ *n.* trailing plant with edible leaves and bright orange, yellow, or red flowers [L]

nas·ty /nas'tē/ *adj.* (**·ti·er, ·ti·est**) 1 highly unpleasant; ill-natured 2 difficult to negotiate 3 obscene; offensive —**nas'ti·ly** *adv.*; **nas'ti·ness** *n.*

na·tal /nā'tl/ *adj.* of or from one's birth [L *natalis* fr. *nasci nat-* be born]

na·tion /nā'sHən/ *n.* 1 usu. self-governing community of people with a common history, language, etc., inhabiting a territory 2 country [L, rel. to NATAL]

Na·tion /nā'sHən/, **Carry** 1846–1911; US temperance advocate

na·tion·al /nasH'(ə)nəl/ *adj.* 1 of or characteristic of a nation —*n.* 2 citizen of a specified country —**na'tion·al·ly** *adv.*

Na'tion·al Guard' *n.* federally subsidized state militia, called into service in cases of emergency

na·tion·al·ism /nasH'(ə)nəliz'əm/ *n.* 1 patriotic feeling, principles, etc. 2 policy of national independence —**na'tion·al·ist** /-ist/ *n.* & *adj.*; **na'tion·al·is'tic** *adj.*

na·tion·al·i·ty /nasH'ənal'ətē/ *n.* (*pl.* **·ties**) 1 status of belonging to a particular nation 2 ethnic group forming a part of one or more political nations

na·tion·al·ize /nasH'(ə)nəlīz'/ *v.* (**·ized, ·iz·ing**) 1 take (industry, land, etc.) into government control or ownership 2 make national —**na'tion·al·i·za'tion** *n.*

Na'tion·al Road' *n.* (also called **National Old Trail Road; Cumberland Road**) first federal road in the US, extending from Cumberland, Md. to St. Louis, Mo.

na·tion·wide /nā'sHənwīd'/ *adj.* & *adv.* extending over the whole nation

na·tive /nā'tiv/ *n.* 1a person born in a specified place b local inhabitant 2 indigenous animal or plant —*adj.* 3 inherent; innate 4 of one's birth 5 belonging to a specified place 6 indigenous 7 found in a pure or uncombined state [L, rel. to NATAL]

Na'tive A·mer'i·can *n.* 1 term (sometimes preferred) for AMERICAN INDIAN —*adj.* (**Na'tive-A·mer'i·can**) 2 pertaining to the cultures or languages of these people

na·tiv·i·ty /nətiv'ətē/ *n.* (*pl.* **·ties**) 1 (*cap.*) Christ's birth 2 birth [L, rel. to NATIVE]

natl. *abbr.* national

NATO /nā'tō/ *abbr.* North Atlantic Treaty Organization

nat·ty /nat'ē/ *adj.* (**·ti·er, ·ti·est**) *Colloq.* trim; stylish; neat —**nat'ti·ly** *adv.* [cf. NEAT]

nat·u·ral /nacH'(ə)rəl/ *adj.* 1a existing in or caused by nature b uncultivated c not artificial in content or preparation 2 in the course of nature 3 not surprising; to be expected 4 unaffected; spontaneous 5 innate 6 not disguised or altered 7 likely or suited by its or their nature to be such (*natural enemies*) 8 *Mus.* (of a note) not sharpened or flatted —*n.* 9 *Colloq.* person or thing naturally suitable, adept, etc. 10 *Mus.* a sign (♮) denoting a return to natural pitch b natural note —nat′u·ral·ness *n.* [L, rel. to NATURE]

nat′u·ral gas′ *n.* gas extracted from the earth, used as fuel

nat′u·ral his′to·ry *n.* the study of earth history, animals, and plants

nat·u·ral·ism /nacH′(ə)rəliz′əm/ *n.* 1 realistic representation in art, literature, etc. 2a theory of the world that excludes the supernatural or spiritual b moral or religious system based on this —nat′u·ral·is′tic /-is′tik/ *adj.*

nat′u·ral·ist *n.* 1 person who studies natural history 2 adherent of naturalism

nat·u·ral·ize /nacH′(ə)rəliz/ *v.* (-ized, -iz-ing) 1 admit (an alien) to citizenship 2 successfully introduce (an animal, plant, etc.) into another region —nat′u·ral·i·za′tion *n.*

nat′u·ral law′ *n.* moral principles, etc., thought to be common to all human beings

nat′u·ral·ly *adv.* 1 in a natural manner 2 as might be expected; of course

nat′u·ral num′ber *n.* whole number greater than zero

nat′u·ral re·sourc·es *n. pl.* materials or conditions occurring in nature and capable of economic exploitation

nat′u·ral sci′ence *n.* the study of the natural or physical world

nat′u·ral se·lec′tion *n.* Darwinian theory of the survival of the most adaptable organisms

nature /nā′CHər/ *n.* 1 innate or essential qualities or character 2 (often *cap.*) a physical power causing all material phenomena b these phenomena 3 kind or class 4 inherent impulses 5 the natural world 6 by nature innately [L *natura*, rel. to NATAL]

-na·tured *comb. form* having a specified disposition (*good-natured*)

Naug·a·hyde /nô′gəhīd′/ *n. Tdmk.* an imitation leather material [fr. *Nauga*tuck, CT, where developed + var. of *hide*]

naught /nôt/ *n.* 1 nothing 2 the digit zero —*adj.* 3 worthless; useless [OE, rel. to NO², WIGHT]

naugh·ty /nô′tē/ *adj.* (-ti·er, -ti·est) 1 disobedient; badly behaved 2 *Colloq.* indecent; slightly obscene —naugh′ti·ly *adv.*; naugh′ti·ness *n.* [fr. NAUGHT]

Na·u·ru /nä·ōō′rōō/ *n.* Pacific island republic W of Kiribati. Pop. 9,600

nau·se·a /nô′zēə, -zhə/ *n.* 1 inclination to vomit 2 revulsion [Gk *naus* ship]

nau·se·ate /nô′zē·āt′/ *v.* (-at·ed, -at·ing) affect with nausea —nau′se·at′ing *adj.*; nau′se·at′ing·ly *adv.*

● Usage: *Nauseated* originally meant 'affected with nausea,' while *nauseous* meant 'causing nausea.' Purists insist that the difference should be maintained. But so many people use *nauseous* to mean 'affected with nausea' that it is considered standard by many commentators.

nau·seous /nô′sHəs, -zēəs/ *adj.* 1 causing nausea 2 inclined to vomit

nau·ti·cal /nô′tikəl/ *adj.* of sailors, navigation, or vessels —naut′i·cal·ly *adv.* [Gk *nautēs* sailor]

nau′ti·cal mile′ *n.* unit of distance equal to approx. 2,025 yards (1,852 meters)

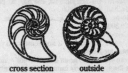

cross section   outside

NAUTILUS

nau·ti·lus /nôt′l-əs/ *n.* (*pl.* -lus·es or -li /-lī/) cephalopod mollusk with a spiral shell, esp. one having a chambered shell [Gk *nautilos*, rel. to NAUTICAL]

Nav·a·jo /nav′əhō/ *n.* (*pl.* -jo or -jos) (also Nav′a·ho; *pl.* -ho or -hos) SW US American Indian people

na·val /nā′vəl/ *adj.* of a navy or ships [L *navis* ship]

nave /nāv/ *n.* central part of a church, usu. from the main entrance to the chancel [L *navis* ship]

na·vel /nā′vəl/ *n.* depression or scar in the center of the abdomen at the site of attachment of the umbilical cord [OE]

na′vel or′ange *n.* orange with a navellike formation opposite the stem

nav·i·ga·ble /nav′igəbəl/ *adj.* 1 (of a river, etc.) suitable for ships to pass through 2 steerable —nav′i·ga·bil′i·ty /-bil′itē/ *n.* [L, rel. to NAVIGATE]

nav·i·gate /nav′igāt′/ *v.* (-gat·ed, -gat·ing) 1 manage or direct the course of (a ship or aircraft) 2a sail on b fly through 3 assist a driver or pilot by map-reading, etc. —nav′i·ga′tor *n.* [L *navigare* fr. *navis*]

nav·i·ga·tion /nav′igā′sHən/ *n.* 1 act or process of navigating 2 art or science of navigating —nav′i·ga′tion·al *adj.*

na·vy /nā′vē/ *n.* (*pl.* -vies) 1 (often *cap.*) a nation's ships of war, including crews, maintenance systems, etc. b officers and enlisted personnel of a navy 2 (in full na′vy blue′) dark blue [Rom *navia* ship, rel. to NAVAL]

nay /nā/ *adv.* 1 or rather; and even; and more than that 2 'no,' esp. as a vote —*n.* 3 utterance of 'nay'; 'no' vote [ON: not ever]

Na·ya·rit /nī′ərēt′/ *n.* central W state of Mexico, on the Pacific Ocean. Capital: Tepic. Pop. 824,600

nay·say·er /nā′sā′ər/ *n.* person who consistently or habitually opposes or expresses negative views

Na·zi /nät′sē, nat′-/ *n.* (*pl.* -zis) 1 *Hist.* member of the German National Socialist party 2 adherent of this party's tenets —*adj.* 3 of the Nazis or Nazism —Na′zism /-sizəm/ *n.* [fr. pronunc. of *Nati-* in Ger *Nationalsozialist*]

Nb *symb.* niobium

NB *abbr.* note well [L *nota bene*]

NC, N.C., N. Car. *abbr.* North Carolina (postal abbr. NC)

NCO *abbr.* noncommissioned officer

Nd *symb.* neodymium

ND, N.D., N. Dak. *abbr.* North Dakota (postal abbr. ND)

n.d. *abbr.* no date

N'Dja·me·na /en'jəmä′nə, -mē′nə/ *n.* capital of Chad. Pop. 687,800

Ndo·la /(e)n-dō′lə/ *n.* city in Zambia. Pop. 376,300

Ne *symb.* neon

NE *abbr.* 1 northeast 2 northeastern 3 postal abbr. for Nebraska

Ne·an·der·thal /nē-an′dərThôl′, -tôl′/ *adj.* 1 of the type of early human widely distributed in paleolithic Europe 2 regressive; unenlightened; primitive —*n.* 3 Neanderthal person [for a valley in Germany]

neap /nēp/ *n.* (in full **neap tide**) tide at the times of the month when high tides are lowest [OE]

Ne·a·pol·i·tan /nē′əpäl′ət-n/ *n.* 1 native or citizen of Naples —*adj.* 2 of Naples [Gk *Neapolis* Naples]

Ne·a·pol·i·tan ice′ cream′ *n.* ice cream made in layers, each of a different flavor and color

near /nēr/ *adv.* 1 at a short distance in space or time 2 closely —*prep.* 3 to or at a short distance from 4 (in *comb.*) almost —*adj.* 5 close (to); not far (in place or time) 6a closely related b intimate 7 close; narrow (*near escape*) 8 similar (to) —*v.* 9 approach; draw close to —**near′ish** *adj.*; **near′ness** *n.* [orig. fr. a comp. of NIGH]

near′by′ *adj.* 1 near in position —*adv.* 2 close; not far away

Near′ East′ *n.* see MIDDLE EAST

near′ly *adv.* 1 almost 2 closely

near′ miss′ *n.* 1 narrowly avoided collision 2 not quite successful attempt

near′sight′ed *adj.* unable to see distant objects clearly; myopic —**near′sight′ed·ness** *n.*

neat /nēt/ *adj.* 1 tidy and methodical 2 elegantly simple 3 brief, clear, and pointed 4a cleverly executed b dexterous 5 undiluted 6 *Slang.* great; nice —**neat′ly** *adv.*; **neat′ness** *n.* [Fr *net* fr. L *nitidus* shining]

neat·en /nēt′n/ *v.* make neat

Nebr. abbr. for Nebraska

Ne·bras·ka /nəbras′kə/ *n.* state in the central US. Capital: Lincoln. Pop. 1,578,385. Abbr. NE; Nebr. —**Ne·bras′kan** *n. & adj.*

Neb·u·chad·nez·zar /neb′(y)əkadnez′ər/ *n.* king of Babylon (605-562 B.C.)

neb·u·la /neb′yələ/ *n.* (*pl.* **·lae** /-lē/) interstellar cloud of gas and dust —**neb′u·lar** *adj.* [L: mist]

neb·u·lous /neb′yələs/ *adj.* 1 cloudlike 2 indistinct; vague [L, rel. to NEBULA]

nec·es·sar·y /nes′əser′ē/ *adj.* 1 requisite; essential 2 inevitable —*n.* (*pl.* **·ies**) 3 (usu. *pl.*) basic requirements —**nec′es·sar′i·ly** *adv.* [L *necesse* needful]

ne·ces·si·tate /nəses′ətāt′/ *v.* (·**tat·ed**, ·**tat·ing**) make necessary or unavoidable

ne·ces·si·ty /nəses′ətē/ *n.* (*pl.* **·ties**) 1 indispensable thing 2 imperative need 3 want; poverty 4 of **necessity** unavoidably

neck /nek/ *n.* 1a part of the body connecting the head to the shoulders b part of a garment around the neck 2 something resembling a neck; narrow part of a cavity, vessel, or other object —*v.* 3 *Colloq.* kiss and caress amorously 4 **neck and neck** even in a race, etc. 5 **up to one's neck** *Colloq.* very deeply involved [OE]

neck·er·chief /nek′ərchif, -chēf′/ *n.* square of cloth worn around the neck [fr. KERCHIEF]

neck·lace /nek′ləs/ *n.* chain or string of beads, precious stones, or metal, etc., worn around the neck

neck′line′ *n.* edge or shape of a garment opening at the neck

neck′tie′ *n.* TIE, 6

necro- *comb. form* corpse [Gk *nekros* corpse]

nec·ro·man·cy /nek′rəman′sē/ *n.* 1 divination by supposed communication with the dead 2 magic —**nec′ro·man′cer** *n.* [fr. NECRO-, *mantis* seer]

ne·cro·sis /nəkrō′sis/ *n.* death of tissue —**ne·crot′ic** /-krät′ik/ *adj.*

nec·tar /nek′tər/ *n.* 1 sugary substance produced by plants and made into honey by bees 2 *Gk. & Rom. Myth.* the drink of the gods 3 any delicious drink —**nec′tar·ous** *adj.* [L fr. Gk]

nec·tar·ine /nek′tərēn′/ *n.* smooth-skinned variety of peach [fr. NECTAR]

née /nā/ *adj.* (also **nee**) born (*Mrs. Ann Hall, née Brown*) [Fr, fem. past part. of *naître* to be born]

need /nēd/ *v.* 1 stand in want of; require 2 be under the obligation (*needs to be done well*) —*n.* 3 requirement 4 circumstances requiring action (*friend in need*) 5 poverty 6 crisis; emergency 7 if need be if required [OE]

need·ful /nēd′fəl/ *adj.* requisite —**need′ful·ly** *adv.*

nee·dle /nēd′l/ *n.* 1a very thin pointed rod of smooth steel, etc., with a slit ('eye') for thread at the blunt end, used in sewing b larger plastic, wooden, etc., slender rod without an eye, used in knitting, etc. 2 pointer on a dial 3a the pointed end of a hypodermic syringe b STYLUS, 1 4 pointed rock, peak, or structure 5 leaf of a fir or pine tree —*v.* (·**dled**, ·**dling**) 6 *Colloq.* irritate; provoke [OE]

nee′dle·point′ *n.* 1 lace made with needles 2 embroidery on canvas

need′less *adj.* 1 unnecessary 2 uncalled for —**need′less·ly** *adv.*; **need′less·ness** *n.*

nee′dle·work′ *n.* sewing or embroidery

needs /nēdz/ *adv. Archaic.* of necessity (*he needs must go*)

need·y *adj.* (·**i·er**, ·**i·est**) poor; destitute —**need′i·ness** *n.*

ne′er /ner/ *adv. Poet.* NEVER [contr.]

ne′er′-do-well′ *n.* 1 good-for-nothing person —*adj.* 2 good for nothing

ne·far·i·ous /nəfar′ēəs, -fer′-/ *adj.* wicked —**ne·far′i·ous·ly** *adv.*; **ne·far′i·ous·ness** *n.* [L *nefas* wrong]

Nef·er·ti·ti /nef′ərtē′tē/ *n.* fl. 14th cent. B.C.; Egyptian queen; wife of Amenhotep IV

ne·gate /nigāt′/ *v.* (·**gat·ed**, ·**gat·ing**) 1 nullify 2 deny [L *negare* deny]

ne·ga·tion /nigā′SHən/ *n.* 1 absence or opposite of something actual or positive 2 act of denying

neg·a·tive /neg′ətiv/ *adj.* 1 expressing or implying denial, prohibition, or refusal 2 lacking positive attributes 3 marked by the absence of qualities 4 opposite to a thing regarded as positive **5** of a quantity less than zero; to be subtracted from others or from zero **6** *Electr.* **a** of the kind of charge carried by electrons **b** containing or producing such a charge —*n.* **7** negative statement, word, viewpoint, etc. **8** *Photog.* **a** image with light and dark areas reversed or colors replaced by their complements **b** developed film or plate bearing such an image **9 in the negative** in refusal or denial —**neg′a·tive·ly** *adv.*; **-ty** *n.*

neg·a·tiv·ism /ˈnegˈətivizˈəm/ *n.* pessimistic attitude; extreme skepticism

Neg′ev Des′ert /negˈev/ *n.* desert in S Israel, along the Sinai Peninsula

ne·glect /niglekt′/ *v.* **1** fail to care for or to do; be remiss about **2** not pay attention to; disregard —*n.* **3** negligence **4** neglecting or being neglected —**ne·glect′ful** *adj.*; **ne·glect′ful·ly** *adv.* [L *neglegere* neglect-]

neg·li·gée /negˈlizHāˊ/ *n.* (also neg·li·gee′) woman's sheer or revealing dressing gown [Fr, past part. of *négliger* NEGLECT]

neg·li·gence /negˈlijəns/ *n.* **1** lack of proper care and attention **2** culpable carelessness —**neg′li·gent** *adj.*; **neg′li·gent·ly** *adv.* [L, rel. to NEGLECT]

neg·li·gi·ble /negˈlijəbəl/ *adj.* not worth considering; insignificant —**neg′li·gi·bly** *adv.* [Fr, rel. to NEGLECT]

ne·go·ti·ate /nigōˈsHē-āt′/ *v.* (·at·ed, ·at·ing) **1** discuss in order to reach an agreement **2** arrange or bring about by negotiating **3** find a way over, through, etc. **4** convert (a check, etc.) into money —**ne·go′tia·ble** /-sHēəbəl, -sHəbəl/ *adj.*; **ne·go′ti·a′tion**, **ne·go′ti·a′tor** *n.* [L *negotium* business]

Ne·gro /nēˈgrō/ *n.* (*pl.* **·groes**) **1** (sometimes considered *Offens.*) member of a dark-skinned race orig. native to Africa; black person —*adj.* **2** of black people —**Ne·groid** /nēˈgroid/ *adj.* [L *niger nigri* black]

Neh·ru /nerˈōō, nāˈrōō/, **Jawaharlal** 1889–1964; prime minister of India (1947–64)

neigh /nā/ *n.* **1** cry of a horse —*v.* **2** make a neigh [OE]

neigh·bor /nāˈbər/ *n.* **1** person or thing near or living near or next to another **2** fellow human being —*v.* **3** border on; adjoin [OE form of NIGH + (*ge*)*bur* farmer]

neigh′bor·hood′ *n.* **1** district; vicinity **2** people of a district **3 in the neighborhood of** roughly; about

neigh·bor·ly /nāˈbərlē/ *adj.* like a good neighbor; friendly; kind —**neigh′bor·li·ness** *n.*

nei·ther /nēˈтнər, nīˈ-/ *adj. & pron.* **1** not the one nor the other (of two); not either (*neither of the accusations is true*) —*adv.* **2** not either; not on the one hand (*neither the teachers nor the parents*) **3** also not —*conj.* **4** *Archaic.* nor yet; nor (*I know not, neither can I guess*) [OE, rel. to NO², WHETHER]

Nel·son /nelˈsən/, **Horatio** 1758–1805; British admiral

nem·a·tode /nemˈətōd′/ *n.* worm with a slender unsegmented cylindrical shape [Gk *nēma* thread]

nem·e·sis /nemˈəsis/ *n.* (*pl.* **·ses** /-sēz′/) **1** retributive justice **2** downfall caused by this **3** something that one cannot conquer, achieve, etc. [Gk: retribution]

---

neo- *comb. form* **1** new; modern **2** new form of [Gk *neos* new]

ne·o·clas·si·cism /nēˈōklasˈəsizˈəm/ *n.* revival of classical style in the arts, etc. —**ne′o·clas′sic** /-ik/, **ne′o·clas′si·cal** *adj.*

ne·o·dym·i·um /nēˈōdimˈēəm/ *n.* metallic element; *symb.* **Nd** [fr. NEO-, Gk *didumos* twin]

ne·o·lith·ic /nēˈəlĩтнˈik/ *adj.* of the later part of the Stone Age [Gk *lithos* stone]

ne·ol·o·gism /nē-älˈəjizˈəm/ *n.* **1** new word or meaning **2** coining of new words [Gk *logos* word]

ne·on /nēˈän′/ *n.* inert gaseous element giving an orange glow when electricity is passed through it; *symb.* **Ne** [Gk: new]

ne·o·phyte /nēˈəfĩt′/ *n.* **1** new convert **2** beginner; novice [Gk *phuton* plant]

ne·o·prene /nēˈəprēn′/ *n.* oil- and heat-resistant synthetic rubber

Ne·pal /nipôl′, -pal′/ *n.* constitutional monarchy in S Asia, between Tibet and N India. Capital: Kathmandu. Pop. 19,795,000 —**Ne·pa·lese** /nepˈəlēzˈ, -lēsˈ/ *n. & adj.*

Ne·pal·i /nəpôˈlē, -pä′-/ *n.* language of Nepal

neph·ew /nefˈyōō/ *n.* son of one's brother or sister or of one's spouse's brother or sister [L *nepos*]

ne·phrit·ic /nəfritˈik/ *adj.* **1** of or in the kidneys **2** of nephritis [Gk *nephros* kidney]

ne·phri·tis /nəfrīˈtis/ *n.* inflammation of the kidneys

ne plus ul·tra /nēˈ pləs′ əlˈtrə, nä′-/ *n.* furthest attainable point; acme [L: not further beyond]

nep·o·tism /nepˈətizˈəm/ *n.* favoritism to relatives in employment, etc. [It *nepote* nephew]

Nep·tune /nepˈt(y)ōōn/ *n.* **1** eighth planet from the sun **2** POSEIDON

nep·tu·ni·um /nept(y)ōōˈnēəm/ *n.* transuranic metallic element; *symb.* **Np** [NEPTUNE, planet]

nerd /nərd/ *n. Slang.* **1** person lacking in social skills, esp. one more interested in intellectual pursuits **2** foolish, feeble, or uninteresting person

Ne·ro /nērˈō/ 37–68; Roman emperor (54–68)

nerve /nərv/ *n.* **1** fiber or bundle of fibers that transmits impulses between the brain or spinal cord and other parts of the body **2a** coolness in danger; bravery **b** *Colloq.* impudence **3** (*pl.*) nervousness; mental or physical stress —*v.* (**nerved, nerv·ing**) **4** give strength, vigor, or courage to **5 get on a person's nerves** irritate a person [L *nervus* sinew; bowstring]

nerve′ cell′ *n.* cell transmitting impulses in nerve tissue

nerve′ cen′ter *n.* center of control

nerve′ gas′ *n.* poisonous gas affecting the nervous system

nerve′less *adj.* **1** lacking vigor **2** cool under pressure —**nerve′less·ly** *adv.*; **nerve′less·ness** *n.*

nerve′rack′ing *adj.* (also **nerve′wrack′ing**) causing mental strain

ner·vous /nərˈvəs/ *adj.* **1** easily upset; timid **2** made up of or affecting the nerves **3** anxious; afraid —**ner′vous·ly** *adv.*; **ner′vous·ness** *n.*

ner'vous break'down *n. Informal.* period of mental illness

ner'vous sys'tem *n.* network of nerve tissue in an organism, including, in vertebrates, the brain and spinal cord

nerv'y *adj.* (**·i·er, ·i·est**) *Colloq.* brash; courageous

-ness *suffix* forming nouns from adjectives, expressing state or condition, or an instance of this (*happiness*) [OE]

nest /nest/ *n.* **1** structure or place where a bird lays eggs and shelters its young **2** any creature's breeding place or lair **3** snug retreat or shelter **4** group or set of similar objects, often graduated in size and fitting together (*nest of tables*) —*v.* **5** use or build a nest **6** fit objects together or one inside another [OE]

nest' egg' *n.* sum of money saved for the future

nes·tle /nes'əl/ *v.* (**·tled, ·tling**) **1** settle oneself comfortably **2** press oneself against another in affection, etc. **3** lie half hidden or embedded [OE]

nest·ling /nes(t)'liNG/ *n.* bird too young to leave its nest

net¹ /net/ *n.* **1** open-meshed fabric of cord, rope, etc. **2** piece of this, used esp. to restrain, contain, catch fish, etc. —*v.* (**net·ted, net·ting**) **3** cover, confine, or catch with a net [OE]

net² *adj.* **1** remaining after all necessary deductions **2** ultimate; actual —*n.* **3** profit, weight, etc., after deductions —*v.* (**net·ted, net·ting**) **4** gain or yield as net profit, weight, etc. [Fr, rel. to NEAT]

neth·er /neTH'ər/ *adj.* LOWER¹ [OE]

Neth·er·lands, the /neTH'ərləndz/ *n.* (also called **Hol'land**) kingdom in W Europe, on the North Sea. Capital: Amsterdam; seat of government: The Hague. Pop. 15,163,000 —**Neth'er·land·er** *n.*

Neth·er·lands An·til'les *n.* Caribbean islands off the coast of Venezuela; territory of the Netherlands

neth·er re'gions *n. pl.* (also **neth'er world'**) hell; the underworld

net'ting *n.* **1** fabric of net **2** piece of this

net·tle /net'l/ *n.* **1** plant with jagged leaves covered with stinging hairs —*v.* (**·tled, ·tling**) **2** irritate; provoke [OE]

net·tle·some /net'lsəm/ *adj.* irritating

net'work *n.* **1** arrangement of intersecting horizontal and vertical lines **2** complex system of railways, roads, people, computers, etc., that interconnect or communicate **3** group of broadcasting stations connected for the simultaneous broadcast of programs —*v.* **4** broadcast on a network —**net'work·ing** *n.*

Ne·tza·hual·có·yotl /netsä'wälkô'yôt'l/ *n.* suburb of Mexico City, Mexico. Pop. 1,341,200

neu·ral /n(y)ŏŏr'əl/ *adj.* of a nerve or the central nervous system [Gk *neuron* nerve]

neu·ral·gia /n(y)ŏŏral'jə/ *n.* intense pain along a nerve —**neu·ral'gic** /-jik/ *adj.*

neu·ri·tis /n(y)ŏŏrī'tis/ *n.* inflammation of a nerve or nerves —**neu·rit'ic** /-rit'ik/ *adj.*

neuro- *comb. form* nerve or nerves [Gk *neuron* nerve]

neu·rol·o·gy /n(y)ŏŏräl'əjē/ *n.* the study of nerve systems —**neu'ro·log'i·cal** /-läj'ikal/ *adj.;* **neu·rol'o·gist** *n.*

neu·ron /n(y)ŏŏr'än/ *n.* nerve cell —**neu·ron'ic** *adj.*

neu·ro·sis /n(y)ŏŏrō'sis/ *n. Psychiat.* (*pl.* **·ses** /-sēz/) behavioral disorder marked by anxiety, obsessions, compulsive acts, etc.

neu·ro·sur·ger·y /n(y)ŏŏr'ōsər'jərē/ *n.* surgery on the brain or spinal cord —**neu'ro·sur'geon** /-jən/ *n.;* **neu'ro·sur'gi·cal** *adj.*

neu·rot·ic /n(y)ŏŏrät'ik/ *adj.* **1** caused by, relating to, or suffering from neurosis **2** *Colloq.* abnormally sensitive or obsessive —*n.* **3** neurotic person —**neu·rot'i·cal·ly** *adv.*

neut. *abbr.* neuter

neu·ter /n(y)ŏŏ'tər/ *adj.* **1** neither masculine nor feminine **2** *Biol. & Bot.* lacking or having undeveloped sexual organs in an adult —*n.* **3** neuter gender or word **4a** nonfertile insect **b** castrated animal —*v.* **5** castrate or spay [L *ne* not + *uter* either]

neu·tral /n(y)ŏŏ'trəl/ *adj.* **1** not supporting either of two opposing sides; impartial **2** indistinct; vague; indeterminate **3** (of a gear) in which the engine is disconnected from the driven parts **4** not strongly colored; gray or beige **5** *Chem.* neither acid nor alkaline **6** *Electr.* neither positive nor negative —*n.* **7** neutral government or person **8** neutral gear —**neu·tral'i·ty** /-tral'itē/ *n.;* **neu'tral·ly** *adv.* [L *neutralis* of neut. gender]

neu·tral·ize /n(y)ŏŏ'trəlīz/ *v.* (**·ized, ·iz·ing**) **1** make or declare to be neutral **2** make ineffective by an opposite force or effect —**neu'tral·i·za'tion, neu'tral·iz'er** *n.*

neu·tri·no /n(y)ŏŏtrē'nō/ *n.* (*pl.* **·nos**) elementary particle with no electric charge and probably without mass [It, dim. of *neutro* neutral]

neu·tron /n(y)ŏŏ'trän/ *n.* uncharged elementary particle of about the same mass as a proton [fr. NEUTRAL]

neu'tron bomb' *n.* thermonuclear bomb producing neutrons and limited blast, destroying life but not property

Nev. *abbr.* for Nevada

Ne·va·da /nəvad'ə, -väd'ə/ *n.* W state of the US. Capital: Carson City. Pop. 1,201,833. Abbr. **Nev.; NV** —**Ne·vad'an, Ne·vad'i·an** /-dēən/ *n. & adj.*

nev·er /nev'ər/ *adv.* **1** at no time; on no occasion; not ever **2** not at all [OE: not ever]

nev'er·more' *adv.* at no future time

nev'er·nev'er land *n.* unrealistic or imaginary place

nev'er·the·less' *adv.* in spite of that; notwithstanding

ne·vus /nē'vəs/ *n.* (*pl.* **·vi** /-vī'/) **1** raised red birthmark **2** MOLE² [L]

new /n(y)ŏŏ/ *adj.* **1** arrived, made, discovered, acquired, experienced recently or now for the first time **2** in original condition; not worn or used **3a** renewed; reformed **b** reinvigorated **4** different from a recent previous one **5** unfamiliar; strange (*all new to me*) **6** modern; newfangled; advanced —*adv.* **7** newly; recently —**new'ish** *adj.;* **new'ness** *n.* [OE]

New' Age' *n.* set of beliefs and practices combining alternative approaches to religion, medicine, the environment, etc., with traditional Western culture

New·ark /n(y)ŏŏ′ərk/ *n.* city in N.J. Pop. 275,221

New′ Bed′ford /bed′fərd/ *n.* city in Mass. Pop. 99,922

new′blood′ *n.* new members of a group, etc., as a source of ideas, vitality, etc.

new′born *adj.* & *n.* (*pl.* same or ·**borns**) 1 recently born 2 reborn

New′ Bruns′wick /brənz′wik/ *n.* province of Canada on the Gulf of St. Lawrence. Capital: Fredericton. Pop. 751,000

New·cas·tle /n(y)ŏŏ′kas′əl, n(y)ŏŏkas′-/ *n.* seaport in SE Australia. Pop. 427,700

New′cas′tle up·on′ Tyne′ *n.* seaport on the Tyne River in England. Pop. 203,600

new′com′er *n.* 1 person who has recently arrived 2 beginner in some activity

New Del·hi /del′ē/ *n.* capital of India. Pop. 294,100

new·el /n(y)ŏŏ′əl/ *n.* 1 supporting central post of winding stairs 2 (also **new′el post′**) top or bottom supporting post of a stair rail [L *nodus* knot]

New′ Eng′land /ĭNG′(g)lənd/ *n.* region of thè NE US; includes Conn., Maine, Mass., N. Hamp., R.I., and Vt.

new·fan·gled /n(y)ŏŏ′faNG′gəld/ *adj.* new or novel, esp. in an objectionable way [ME *newefangel* fond of what is new]

New·found·land /n(y)ŏŏ′fən(d)lənd, n(y)ŏŏ′fən(d)lənd/ *n.* 1 island off the E Atlantic coast of Canada 2 province of Canada, including the island of Newfoundland and Labrador (mainland). Capital: St. John's. Pop. 581,000 **—New′found·land·er** *n.*

New′ Guin′ea /gin′ē/ *n.* large island in the East Indies, N of Australia

New′ Hamp′shire /hamp′SHər/ *n.* NE state of the US. Capital: Concord. Pop. 1,109,252. Abbr. NH; N.H.; N. Hamp. **—New′ Hamp′shir·ite, New′ Hamp′shire·man** /-mən/ *n.*

New′ Ha′ven /hā′vən/ *n.* city in Conn. Pop. 130,474

New′ Jer′sey /jər′zē/ *n.* NE state of the US. Capital: Trenton. Pop. 7,730,188. Abbr. NJ; N.J. **—New′ Jer′sey·ite, New′ Jer′sey·an** *n.*

new′ly *adv.* 1 recently 2 afresh; anew

New·man /n(y)ŏŏ′mən/ 1 John Henry 1801–91; English theologian 2 Paul 1925– ; US actor, director, and producer

New′ Mex′i·co /mek′sikō′/ *n.* SW state of the US. Capital: Santa Fe. Pop. 1,515,069. Abbr. NM; N. Mex. **—New′ Mex′i·can** *n.* & *adj.*

new′ moon′ *n.* moon in its dark phase and immediately after, when seen as a thin crescent

New′ Or′le·ans /ôr′lēənz, ôr′lənz, ôrlēnz′/ *n.* city in La. Pop. 496,938 **—New′ Or·lea′ni·an** /ôrli′nēən/ *n.*

New·port News /n(y)ŏŏ′pôrt n(y)ŏŏz, -pərt/ *n.* city in Va. Pop. 170,045

news /n(y)ŏŏz/ *n. pl.* (usu. treated as *sing.*) 1 information about important or interesting recent events 2 broadcast report of news 3 newly received or noteworthy information [fr. NEW]

news′cast′ *n.* radio or television broadcast of news reports **—news′cast′er** *n.*

news′deal′er *n.* person selling newspapers, periodicals, etc.

news′ flash′ *n.* brief news report of a recent, usu. important, event

news′let′ter *n.* concise periodical of news, events, etc., of special interest

news′pa′per *n.* 1 printed publication containing news, advertisements, correspondence, etc., usu. published daily or weekly 2 NEWSPRINT, 1

news′print′ *n.* 1 low-quality paper on which newspapers are printed 2 ink on the fingers from handling a newspaper

news′reel′ *n.* short movie of recent events

news′stand′ *n.* stand or booth for the sale of newspapers and other periodicals

news·week·ly /n(y)ŏŏz′wēk′lē/ *n.* periodical covering current events, issued weekly

news′wor′thy *adj.* noteworthy as news

news′y *adj.* (·**i·er**, ·**i·est**) *Colloq.* full of news

newt /n(y)ŏŏt/ *n.* small amphibian with a well-developed tail [fr. ME *(a)n + ewt*]

New′ Tes′ta·ment *n.* part of the Bible concerned with the life and teachings of Christ and his earliest followers

new·ton /nyŏŏt′n/ *n.* unit of force used in physics [for Isaac NEWTON]

New·ton /n(y)ŏŏt′n/, (**Sir**) **Isaac** 1642–1727; English mathematician, scientist, and philosopher

New′ World′ *n.* North and South America

New′ Year′s′ Day′ *n.* January 1

New′ Year′s′ Eve′ *n.* December 31

New′ York′ /yôrk/ *n.* 1 NE state of the US. Capital: Albany. Pop. 17,990,455. Abbr. NY; N.Y. 2 (also **New York City**) city in N.Y.; US financial and commercial center. Pop. 7,322,564. Abbr. NYC **—New′ York′er** *n.*

New′ Zea′land /zē′lənd/ *n.* Pacific island country SE of Australia. Capital: Wellington. Pop. 3,434,900 **—New′ Zea′land·er** *n.*

next /nekst/ *adj.* 1 being, positioned, or living nearest in space or time **—***adv.* 2 in the nearest place, degree, or time **—***n.* 3 next person or thing 4 next to almost (*next to nothing left*) [OE, superl. of NIGH]

next′door′ *adv.* in the next house or room **—next′-door′** *adj.*

nex·us /nek′səs/ *n.* (*pl.* same) connected group or series [L]

Ngo Dinh Di·em /nō′ din′ dē-em′/ 1901–63; president of South Vietnam (1956–63)

NH, N.H., N. Hamp. *abbr.* New Hampshire (postal abbr. **NH**)

Ni *symb.* nickel

ni·a·cin /nī′əsin/ *n.* NICOTINIC ACID [shortening]

Ni·ag′a·ra Falls′ /nī-ag′(ə)rə/ *n.* scenic falls of the Niagara River, along the US-Canada border

Nia·mey /nē-äm′ā/ *n.* capital of Niger. Pop. 398,300

nib /nib/ *n.* pen point [LGer or Du]

nib·ble /nib′əl/ *v.* (·**bled**, ·**bling**) 1a take small bites (at) b take cautious interest in 2 eat in small amounts 3 bite at gently, cautiously, or playfully **—***n.* 4 very small amount [LGer or Du]

nibs /nibz/ *n.* as in **his** (or **her**) **nibs** *Joc.* & *Colloq.* mock title used for a self-important person

Nic·a·ra·gua /nik′ərag′wə/ *n.* republic in

Central America. Capital: Managua. Pop. 4,131,000 —**Nic·a·ra'guan** *n.* & *adj.*

nice /nīs/ *adj.* 1 pleasant; satisfactory 2 kind; good-natured 3 fine; subtle (*nice distinction*) 4 fastidious; delicately sensitive —**nice'ly** *adv.*; **nice'ness** *n.* [orig. ME: foolish, fr. L *nescius* ignorant]

• Usage: *Nice* is an effective adjective when used to mean 'precise, discriminating, subtle': *He had developed a nice sense of what to say when his friend was upset.* However, colloquial overuse of *nice* to mean 'pleasant, agreeable, attractive' has rendered the word trite in these contexts: *What a nice child! That is a nice car.*

Nice /nēs/ *n.* port in SE France. Pop. 345,600

ni·ce·ty /nī'sitē/ *n.* (*pl.* **·ties**) 1 subtle distinction or detail 2 precision 3 refined or dainty thing

niche /niCH/ *n.* 1 shallow recess, esp. in a wall 2 comfortable or apt position [L *nidus* nest]

Nich·o·las II /nik'(ə)ləs/ 1868–1918; last Russian czar (1894–1917); assassinated

Nich·o·las, St. fl. 4th cent.; bishop in Asia Minor; prototype of Santa Claus

nick /nik/ *n.* 1 small cut or notch —*v.* 2 make a nick or nicks in 3 cut or wound slightly 4 in the nick of time only just in time

nick·el /nik'əl/ *n.* 1 silver-white metallic element, used esp. in magnetic alloys; *symb.* **Ni** 2 US or Canadian five-cent coin [Ger]

nick·el-and-dime' *Colloq. adj.* 1 pertaining to trivial amounts of money 2 cheap or unimportant —*v.* (**·dimed, ·dim·ing**) 3 niggle in commercial transactions

nick·el·o·de·on /nik'əlō'dēən/ *n.* type of early jukebox

Nick·laus /nik'ləs/, **Jack William** 1940– ; US golfer

nick'name' *n.* 1 familiar or humorous name given to a person or thing instead of or as well as the real name —*v.* (**·named, ·nam·ing**) 2 give a nickname to [earlier *eke-name*, with *n* fr. *an*: OE *eke* addition]

Nic·o·si·a /nik'əsē'ə/ *n.* capital of Cyprus. Pop. 168,800

nic·o·tine /nik'ətēn/ *n.* poisonous alkaloid present in tobacco [for J. *Nicot*, introducer of tobacco into France]

nic'o·tin'ic ac'id *n.* (also **ni·a·cin**) vitamin of the B complex

nic'ti·tat'ing mem'brane /nik'titāt'iNG/ *n.* transparent third eyelid in amphibians, birds, etc.

Nie·buhr /nē'bŏŏr/, **Reinhold** 1892–1971; US theologian

niece /nēs/ *n.* daughter of one's brother or sister or of one's spouse's brother or sister [L *neptis* granddaughter]

niels·bohr·i·um /nēls'bôr'ēəm/ *n.* artificially produced radioactive element; atomic number 107; *symb.* **Ns** [for Danish physicist *Niels Bohr*]

Nie·tzsche /nē'CHə, -CHē/, **Friedrich Wilhelm** 1844–1900; German philosopher

nif·ty /nif'tē/ *adj.* (**·ti·er, ·ti·est**) *Colloq.* 1 clever; adroit 2 stylish

Ni·ger /nī'jər, nēzнer'/ *n.* republic in NW Africa, north of Nigeria. Capital: Niamey. Pop. 8,281,000 —**Ni·ge·ri·en** /nījēr'ēən/ *n.* & *adj.*

Ni·ge·ri·a /nījēr'ēə/ *n.* republic in W Africa on the Gulf of Guinea. Capital: Abuja. Pop. 89,666,000 —**Ni·ge'ri·an** *n.* & *adj.*

Ni·ger Riv·er /nī'jər/ *n.* river in W Africa flowing SW 2,600 mi. to the Gulf of Guinea

nig·gard /nig'ərd/ *n.* stingy person —**nig'gard·ly** *adj.*; **nig'gard·li·ness** *n.* [prob. Scand]

nig·gle /nig'əl/ *v.* (**·gled, ·gling**) 1 be overattentive to details 2 find fault in a petty way —**nig'gling** *adj.*

nigh /nī/ *adv.*, *prep.* & *adj. Archaic.* or *Dial.* near [OE]

night /nīt/ *n.* 1 period of darkness between one day and the next; time from sunset to sunrise 2 darkness of or similar to night [OE]

night'cap' *n.* 1 *Hist.* cap worn to bed 2 *Colloq.* alcoholic drink taken at bedtime

night'club' *n.* club providing entertainment, refreshment, etc., late at night

night' crawl'er *n.* earthworm, esp. one used as bait

night'fall' *n.* end of daylight

night'gown' *n.* loose dress worn to bed by girls or women

night' hawk *n.* nocturnal bird related to the whippoorwill

night·in·gale /nīt'n-gāl'/ *n.* reddish-brown bird, noted for the males' melodious songs at night [OE: night-singer]

Night·in·gale /nīt'n-gāl'/, **Florence** 1820–1910; English nurse and medical reformer

night' life' *n.* entertainment available at night in a city, etc.

night'ly *adj.* 1 happening, done, or existing in the night 2 recurring every night —*adv.* 3 every night

night·mare /nīt'mer'/ *n.* 1 frightening dream 2 frightening experience or situation —**night'mar'ish** *adj.* [NIGHT + OE *mare* demon]

night' owl' *n.* person active or more active at night

night·shade /nīt'sнād'/ *n.* any of various plants with poisonous berries [OE]

night'shirt' *n.* long shirt worn to bed

night'spot' *n.* nightclub

night'stick' *n.* police officer's club

night'time' *n.* time of darkness

NIH *abbr.* National Institutes of Health

ni·hil·ism /nī'əliz'əm, nē'-/ *n.* rejection of all religious and moral principles —**ni'hil·ist** /-ist/ *n.*; **ni'hil·is'tic** *adj.* [L *nihil* nothing]

Ni·jin·sky /nəzнin'skē, -jin'-/, **Vaslav** 1890–1950; Russian ballet dancer and choreographer

-nik *suffix* forming nouns denoting a person associated with a specified thing or quality (*beatnik*) [Russ (as SPUTNIK) and Yiddish]

Ni·ko·la·yev /nik'əlä'yəf/ *n.* see MYUKOLAYIV

nil /nil/ *n.* nothing; no number or amount [fr. L *nihil* nothing]

Nile /nīl/ *n.* river in E Africa, flowing 3,470 mi. N from Lake Victoria to the Mediterranean; longest river in the world

nim·ble /nim'bəl/ *adj.* (**·bler, ·blest**) quick and light in movement or function; agile —**nim'bly** *adv.* [OE: quick to seize]

nim·bus /nim'bəs/ *n.* (*pl.* **nim·bi** /-bī', -bē/) or **·bus·es**) 1 halo 2 rain cloud [L: cloud]

NIMBY /nim'bē/ *abbr.* not in my back yard (in reference to unwanted industrial sites, etc.)

Nîmes /nēm/ *n.* city in S France. Pop. 133,600

Nim·itz /nim'its/, **Chester William** 1885–1966; US admiral

nin·com·poop /niNG'kəmpōōp'/ *n.* foolish person

nine /nīn/ *adj. & n.* **1** one more than eight **2** symbol for this (9, ix, IX) —**ninth** /nīnTH/ *adj. & n.* [OE]

nine'fold *adj. & adv.* nine times as much or as many

nine'pins *n. pl.* (usu. treated as *sing.*) bowling game using nine pins

nine·teen /nīn'tēn'/ *adj. & n.* **1** one more than eighteen **2** symbol for this (19, xix, XIX) —**nine'teenth** *adj. & n.* [OE]

nine·ty /nīn'tē/ *adj. & n.* (*pl.* **·ties**) **1** nine times ten **2** symbol for this (90, xc, XC) **3** (*pl.*) numbers fr. 90 to 99, esp. as years —**nine'ti·eth** /-əTH/ *adj. & n.* [OE]

nin·ja /nin'jə/ *n.* person trained in a style of Japanese martial arts emphasizing stealth

nin·ny /nin'ē/ *n.* (*pl.* **·nies**) foolish person

ni·o·bi·um /nī-ō'bēəm/ *n.* rare metallic element; *symb.* Nb [*Niobe* in Gk legend]

nip[1] /nip/ *v.* (**nipped, nip·ping**) **1** pinch, squeeze, or bite sharply **2** remove by pinching, etc. **3** (of the cold, etc.) cause pain or harm to —*n.* **4a** pinch; sharp squeeze **b** bite **5** biting cold **6 nip and tuck** very close, as in a contest **7 nip in the bud** suppress or destroy (esp. an idea) at an early stage [LGer or Du]

nip[2] *n.* small quantity of alcohol [fr. *nipperkin* small measure]

nip·per /nip'ər/ *n.* **1** person or thing that nips **2** claw of a crab, etc. **3** (*pl.*) any tool for gripping or cutting **4** *Colloq.* young child

nip·ple /nip'əl/ *n.* **1** small projection on the breast or udder of mammals from which, in females, milk is secreted for the young **2** teat of a baby bottle **3** device like a nipple in shape or function [perh. fr. *neb* tip]

nip·py /nip'ē/ *adj.* (**·pi·er, ·pi·est**) *Colloq.* chilly; biting [fr. NIP[1]]

nir·va·na /nərvä'nə, nər-/ *n.* (in Buddhism) perfect bliss attained by the extinction of individuality [Skt: extinction]

ni·sei /nē'sā/ *n.* (*pl.* same or **·seis**) (also *cap.*) child born in the US to immigrant Japanese parents

nit /nit/ *n.* egg or young form of a louse or other parasitic insect [OE]

ni·ter /nī'tər/ *n.* saltpeter [Gk *nitron*]

nit'pick'ing *n. & adj. Colloq.* fault-finding in a petty manner —**nit'pick'er** *n.*

ni·trate /nī'trāt'/ *n.* **1** any salt or ester of nitric acid **2** potassium or sodium nitrate as a fertilizer —*v.* (**·trat·ed, ·trat·ing**) **3** treat, combine, or impregnate with nitric acid —**ni·tra'tion** *n.* [Fr, rel. to NITER]

ni'tric ac'id /nī'trik/ *n.* a colorless, corrosive, poisonous acid of nitrogen

nitro- *comb. form* of or containing nitric acid, niter, or nitrogen [Gk, rel. to NITER]

ni·tro·gen /nī'trəjən/ *n.* gaseous element that forms four fifths of the atmosphere; *symb.* N —**ni·trog·e·nous** /nīträj'ənəs/ *adj.* [Fr]

ni·tro·glyc·er·in /nī'trōglis'ərin/ *n.* (also **ni'**

tro·glyc'er·ine; *Colloq.* **ni'tro**) explosive yellow liquid made by reacting glycerin with sulfuric and nitric acids

ni'trous ox'ide /nī'trəs/ *n.* colorless gas used as an anesthetic [L, rel. to NITER]

nit·ty-grit·ty /nit'ē grit'ē/ *n. Slang.* realities or practical details of a matter

nit'wit' *n. Colloq.* stupid person [perh. fr. NIT, WIT]

nix /niks/ *adv.* **1** no —*v.* **2** veto

Nix·on /nik'sən/, **Richard Milhous** 1913–94; 37th US president (1969–74)

Nizh·ni Ta·gil /nizH'nē təgil'/ *n.* city in Russia. Pop. 439,200

NJ, N.J. abbr. for New Jersey (postal abbr. NJ)

Nkru·mah /enkrōō'mə/, **Kwame** 1909–72; prime minister of Ghana (1957–60); president (1960–66)

NLRB *abbr.* National Labor Relations Board

NM, N. Mex. *abbr.* New Mexico (postal abbr. NM)

no[1] /nō/ *adj.* **1** not any (*no reason for it*) **2** not a; quite other than (*he's no fool*) **3** hardly any (*did it in no time*) [rel. to NONE]

no[2] *adv.* **1** indicating a negative, refusal, or denial **2** by no amount; not at all (*no better than before*) —*n.* (*pl.* **noes**) **3** denial; refusal **4** 'no' vote [OE]

No *symb.* nobelium

no. or **No.** *abbr.* number [L *numero,* abl. of *numerus* number]

NOAA /nō'ə/ *abbr.* National Oceanic and Atmospheric Administration

No·ah /nō'ə/ Hebrew patriarch; builder of Ark in Biblical flood story

No·bel /nōbel'/, **Alfred Bernhard** 1833–96; Swedish chemist; inventor of dynamite; endowed Nobel Prizes

No·bel·ist /nōbel'ist/ (also **No'bel lau're·ate** /lôr'ēət/) *n.* person who has been awarded a Nobel prize

no·bel·i·um /nōbē'lēəm/ *n.* artificially produced radioactive transuranic metallic element; *symb.* No [for A. NOBEL]

No'bel prize' *n.* any of six prizes awarded annually for physics, chemistry, physiology or medicine, literature, economics, and the promotion of peace [for A. NOBEL]

no·bil·i·ty /nōbil'itē/ *n.* (*pl.* **·ties**) **1** nobleness of character, mind, birth, or rank **2** highest social class

no·ble /nō'bəl/ *adj.* (**·bler, ·blest**) **1** of the social class with inherited rank; aristocratic **2** of excellent character; magnanimous **3** distinguished —*n.* **4** nobleman; noblewoman —**no'ble·ness** *n.*; **no'bly** *adv.* [L (*g*)*nobilis*]

no·ble·man /nō'bəlmən/ *n.* (*pl.* **·men**) man of noble rank

no·blesse o·blige /nōbles' oblēzH'/ *n.* responsibility of the privileged to behave nobly toward the less privileged [Fr: nobility obliges]

no'ble·wom'an *n.* (*pl.* **·wom'en**) woman of noble rank

no·bod·y /nō'bädē, -bəd'ē, -bäd'ē/ *pron.* **1** no person —*n.* (*pl.* **·ies**) **2** person of no importance

no'brain'er *n. Slang.* decision, etc., requiring little mental effort

noc·tur·nal /näktərn'l/ adj. of or in the night; done or active by night [L nox noct- night]

noc·turne /näk'tərn/ n. Mus. short romantic composition, usu. for piano [Fr]

nod /näd/ v. (**nod·ded, nod·ding**) 1 incline one's head slightly and briefly in assent, greeting, or command 2 let one's head fall forward in drowsiness 3 signify (assent, etc.) by a nod 4 bend forward —n. 5 nodding of the head 6 **nod off** Colloq. fall asleep

node /nōd/ n. 1a part of a plant stem from which leaves emerge b knob on a root or branch 2 natural swelling 3 point of minimum disturbance in a standing wave system 4 component in a computer network —**nod'al** adj. [L nodus knot]

nod·ule /näj'ōōl'/ n. small, rounded lump, tumor, node, or swelling —**nod'u·lar** adj. [L dim., rel. to NODE]

No·el /nō·el'/ n. Christmas [L, rel. to NATAL]

no'-fault' adj. without assigned liability or blame (no-fault insurance; no-fault divorce)

nog·gin /näg'in/ n. 1 small mug b Slang. head

no'-go' adj. Colloq. 1 canceled 2 not functional 3 impossible

noise /noiz/ n. 1 sound, esp. loud or unpleasant 2 interference in electronically transmitted information —v. (**noised, nois·ing**) 3 (of a rumor, fact, etc.) make public; spread abroad 4 **make noises** speak vaguely or insincerely [L NAUSEA]

noise'less adj. making little or no noise —**noise'less·ly** adv.

noi·some /noi'səm/ adj. 1 harmful; noxious 2 evil-smelling [fr. ANNOY]
● Usage: Noisome means 'foul-smelling' and has nothing to do with the word noise.

nois·y /noi'zē/ adj. (**·i·er, ·i·est**) 1 making much noise 2 full of noise —**nois'i·ly** adv.; **nois'i·ness** n.

no'·load' adj. Finance. designating investment purchases for which no sales commission is charged

no·mad /nō'mad'/ n. 1 member of a tribe roaming from place to place for pasture 2 wanderer —**no·mad'ic** adj. [Gk nomas nomad- fr. nemein to pasture]

no' man's' land' n. 1 space between two opposing armies 2 unclaimed tract of land 3 area of uncertainty

nom de plume /näm' də ploom'/ n. (pl. **noms de plume**, pronunc. same) pen name [quasi-Fr]

Nome /nōm/ n. city in Alaska. Pop. 3,500

no·men·cla·ture /nō'mənklā'CHər/ n. system of names; set of terminology [L nomen name, calare call]

nom·i·nal /näm'ən·l/ adj. 1 existing in name only; not real or actual 2 very small, as a fee 3 of or in names 4 of, as, or like a noun —**nom'i·nal·ly** adv. [L nomen name]

nom·i·nate /näm'ənāt'/ v. (**·nat·ed, ·nat·ing**) 1 propose (a candidate) for election 2 name or appoint —**nom'i·na'tion, nom'i·na'tor** n. [L, rel. to NOMINAL]

nom·i·na·tive /näm'ənətiv/ n. Gram. case expressing the subject of a verb; subjective

nom·i·nee /näm'ənē'/ n. person who is nominated

non- prefix giving the negative sense of words with which it is combined [L non not]

no·na·ge·nar·i·an /nō'nəjəner'ēən/ n. person from 90 to 99 years old [L nonageni ninety each]

no·na·gon /nō'nəgän'/ n. plane figure with nine sides and angles [L nonus ninth, after HEXAGON]

non'a·bra'sive adj.
non'ab·sor'bent adj.
non'a·bu'sive adj.
non'ac·a·dem'ic adj.
non'ac·cept'ance n.
non'ac'tive adj. & n.
non'ad·dic'tive adj.
non'ad·he'sive adj.
non'ad·ja'cent adj.
non'ad·just'a·ble adj.
non'ad·min'is·tra'tive adj.
non'al·co·hol'ic adj.
non'al·ler'gic adj.
non'al·lied' adj.
non·ap'pli·ca·ble adj.
non'ap·proved' adj.
non'ar·riv'al n.
non'as·sign'a·ble adj.
non'ath·let'ic adj.
non'at·tend'ance n.
non'au·to·mo'tive adj.
non'a·vail·a·bil'i·ty n.
non·ba'sic adj.
non·be·liev'er n.
non·break'a·ble adj.
non·burn'a·ble adj.
non·cak'ing adj.

non'ca·lor'ic adj.
non·can'cer·ous adj.
non-Cath'o·lic adj. & n.
non·charge'a·ble adj.
non-Chris'tian adj. & n.
non·cler'i·cal adj. & n.
non·clin'i·cal adj.
non·clot'ting adj.
non'co·her'ent adj.
non'col·lect'a·ble adj.
non'com·bus'ti·ble adj.
non'com·mer'cial adj.
non'com·mu'ni·ca·ble adj.
non-Com'mu·nist adj. & n.
non'com·pet'ing adj.
non'com·pet'i·tive adj.
non'com·pet'i·tive·ly adv.
non'com·pli'ance n.
non'com·ply'ing adj.
non'com·pre·hend'ing adj.

non'com·pre·hen'sion n.
non'com·pre·hen'sive adj.
non'con·duct'ing adj.
non'con·form'ing adj.
non'-Con·gres'sion·al adj.
non'con·sec'u·tive adj.
non'con·struc'tive adj.
non'con·ta'gious adj.
non'con·tig'u·ous adj.
non'con·trib'ut·ing adj.
non'con·trib'u·to'ry adj.
non'con·tro·ver'sial adj.
non'con·ven'tion·al adj.
non'con·vert'i·ble adj.
non'co·op'er·a'tion n.
non'cor·rod'ing adj.
non'cor·ro'sive adj.
non·crim'i·nal adj. & n.

non·crit'i·cal adj.
non·crys'tal·line adj.
non·cum'u·la·tive adj.
non·cus·to'di·al adj.
non·dead'ly adj.
non'de·duct'i·ble adj.
non'de·liv'er·y n.
non'de·part·men'tal adj.
non'de·pre'ci·at'ing adj.
non'de·struc'tive adj.
non'de·tach'a·ble adj.
non'dip·lo·mat'ic adj.
non'dis·ci·pli·nar'y adj.
non'dis·crim·i·na'tion n.
non'di·vis'i·ble adj.
non'dog·mat'ic adj.
non'do·mes'tic adj. & n.
non·dom'i·nant adj.
non'dra·mat'ic adj.
non·driv'er n.
non·drug' adj.
non·dry'ing adj.

non·a·ligned /nän'əlīnd'/ *adj.* not aligned with a major power —**non·a·lign'ment** *n.*

non·bel·lig·er·ent /nän'bəlij'ərənt/ *adj.* not engaged in hostilities

nonce /näns/ *n.* as in **for the nonce** for the time being; for the present occasion [ME *for then anes* for the one]

nonce' word' *n.* word coined for one occasion

non·cha·lant /nän'shəlänt'/ *adj.* calm and casual —**non'cha·lance'** *n.*; **non'cha·lant'ly** *adv.* [Fr *chaloir* be concerned]

non·com /nän'käm'/ *n. Colloq.* noncommissioned officer [abbr.]

non·com·ba·tant /nän'kəmbat'nt, -käm'bətänt/ *n.* person not fighting in a war, esp. a civilian, army chaplain, etc.

non·com·mis·sioned /nän'kəmish'ənd/ *adj.* not holding an officer's commission

non·com·mit·tal /nän'kəmit'l/ *adj.* avoiding commitment to a definite opinion or course of action

non com·pos men·tis /nän' käm'pəs men'tis/ *adj. Latin.* not in one's right mind

non·con·duc·tor /nän'kəndək'tər/ *n.* substance that does not conduct heat or electricity

non·con·form·ist /nän'kənfôr'mist/ *n.* person who does not conform to a prevailing principle —**non'con·form'i·ty** *n.*

non·de·script /nän'diskript'/ *adj.* lacking distinctive characteristics; not easily classified [rel. to DESCRIBE]

non·drink'er *n.* person who does not drink alcoholic liquor

none /nən/ *pron.* **1a** not any (of); no part

---

non'ed·u·ca'tion·al *adj.*
non'ef·fec'tive *adj.*
non·e·lec'tric *adj.*
non·el'i·gi·ble *adj.*
non'e·mer'gen·cy *adj. & n.* (*pl.* ·cies)
non'en·force'a·ble *adj.*
non-Eng'lish *adj. & n.*
non'e·quiv'a·lent *adj. & n.*
non·es·sen'tial *adj.*
non·ex·change'a·ble *adj.*
non·ex·clu'sive *adj.*
non'ex·empt' *adj. & n.*
non'ex·ist'ence *n.*
non'ex·ist'ent *adj.*
non'ex·plo'sive *adj. & n.*
non·fac'tu·al *adj.*
non·fad'ing *adj.*
non'fat' *adj.*
non·fa'tal *adj.*
non·flam'ma·ble *adj.*
non·flow'er·ing *adj.*
non·fluc'tu·at'ing *adj.*
non·fly'ing *adj.*
non·food' *n. & adj.*
non·freez'ing *adj.*
non·func'tion·al *adj.*
non·func'tion·ing *adj.*
non·gas'e·ous *adj.*
non'gov·ern·men'tal *adj.*
non·gran'u·lar *adj.*
non·greas'y *adj.*
non·haz'ard·ous *adj.*
non'he·red'i·tar·y *adj.*
non'hi·er·ar'chi·cal *adj.*
non'his·tor'i·cal *adj.*
non·hu'man *adj.*
non'i·den'ti·cal *adj.*
non'in·clu'sive *adj.*
non'in·de·pend'ent *adj.*
non'in·dus'tri·al *adj.*

non'in·flect'ed *adj.*
non'in·flam'ma·to'ry *adj.*
non'in·fla'tion·ar·y *adj.*
non'in·tel·lec'tu·al *adj. & n.*
non·in'te·grat'ed *adj.*
non'in·ter·change'a·ble *adj.*
non'in·ter·fer'ence *n.*
non'in·ter·sect'ing *adj.*
non'in·tox'i·cat'ing *adj.*
non·ir'ri·tat'ing *adj.*
non·is'sue *n.*
non·join'er *n.*
non·ju·di'cial *adj.*
non·le'gal *adj.*
non·le'thal *adj.*
non·lin'e·ar *adj.*
non·lit'er·ar·y *adj.*
non·liv'ing *adj. & n.*
non'mag·net'ic *adj.*
non·ma·lig'nant *adj.*
non·mem'ber *n.*
non·mi'gra·to'ry *adj.*
non·mil'i·tant *adj.*
non·mil'i·tar·y *adj.*
non'nar·cot'ic *adj. & n.*
non'ne·go'ti·a·ble *adj.*
non'nu·mer'i·cal *adj.*
non'ob·jec'tive *adj.*
non'ob·lig'a·to'ry *adj.*
non'ob·serv'ant *adj.*
non'oc·cu·pa'tion·al *adj.*
non'oc·cur'rence *n.*
non·of·fi'cial *adj.*
non'op·er·a'tion·al *adj.*
non·op'er·a·tive *adj.*
non·or·gan'ic *adj.*
non'par·al·lel' *adj. & n.*
non'par·tic'i·pant *n.*
non'par·tic'i·pat'ing *adj.*
non'par·tic'i·pa'tion *n.*

non·par'ti·san *adj.*
non·pay'ing *adj.*
non·pay'ment *n.*
non·per'ish·a·ble *adj.*
non·phys'i·cal *adj.*
non·poi'son·ous *adj.*
non'po·lit'i·cal *adj.*
non·pol·lut'ing *adj.*
non·po'rous *adj.*
non·prac'tic·ing *adj.*
non'prej·u·di'cial *adj.*
non'pro·duc'tive *adj.*
non'pro·fes'sion·al *adj. & n.*
non·prof'it·a·ble *adj.*
non·pub'lic *adj.*
non·pun'ish·a·ble *adj.*
non·ra'cial *adj.*
non·re·ac'tive *adj.*
non're·cip'ro·cal *adj. & n.*
non're·ceipt' *n.*
non're·cip'ro·cat'ing *adj.*
non'rec·og·ni'tion *n.*
non're·cov'er·a·ble *adj.*
non're·cur'ring *adj.*
non're·deem'a·ble *adj.*
non're·fill'a·ble *adj.*
non're·li'gious *adj.*
non're·new'a·ble *adj.*
non'rep·re·sen·ta'tion·al *adj.*
non're·sid'u·al *adj. & n.*
non're·sist'ant *adj.*
non're·spon'sive *adj.*
non're·turn'a·ble *adj.*
non·rhyth'mic *adj.*
non·rig'id *adj.*
non·sal'a·ried *adj.*
non'sci·en·tif'ic *adj.*
non·scor'ing *adj.*
non·sea'son·al *adj.*
non'sec·tar'i·an *adj.*
non·sec'u·lar *adj.*
non·sen'si·tive *adj.*
non·sex'ist *adj.*

non·sex'u·al *adj.*
non'skid' *adj.*
non·slip' *adj.*
non·smok'er *n.*
non·smok'ing *adj.*
non·so'cial *adj.*
non·speak'ing *adj.*
non·spe'cial·ist *n. & adj.*
non·spe'cial·iz'ing *adj.*
non·spe·cif'ic *adj.*
non·spir'it·u·al *adj. & n.*
non·stain'ing *adj.*
non'stan'dard *adj.*
non'stick' *adj.*
non'stra·te'gic *adj.*
non·strik'ing *adj.*
non'suc·ces'sive *adj.*
non'sup·port'ing *adj.*
non·sur'gi·cal *adj.*
non'sus·tain'ing *adj.*
non·swim'mer *n.*
non·sym'pa·thiz'er *n.*
non·tar'nish·a·ble *adj.*
non·tax'a·ble *adj.*
non·tech'ni·cal *adj.*
non'the·at'ri·cal *adj.*
non·think'ing *adj.*
non·threat'en·ing *adj.*
non·tox'ic *adj.*
non'trans·fer'a·ble *adj.*
non'trans·par'ent *adj.*
non·trop'i·cal *adj.*
non·u'ni·form *adj.*
non·us'er *n.*
non·ven'om·ous *adj.*
non·ver'bal *adj.*
non·vir'u·lent *adj.*
non·vo'cal *adj.*
non'vo·ca'tion·al *adj.*
non'vol·can'ic *adj.*
non·vot'er *n.*
non·vot'ing *adj.*
non·white' *n. & adj.*
non·work'ing *adj.*
non·yield'ing *adj.*

(*none of this is true*) **b** not any one; no one (*none left alive*) **2** no person(s) (*none but fools believe it*) **3** not any (*you have money and I have none*) *—adv.* **4** by no amount; not at all (*am none the wiser*) [OE: not one]

non·en·ti·ty /nänen'tətē/ *n.* (*pl.* **·ties**) person or thing of no importance [MedL]

none·the·less /nun'THəles/ *adv.* (also **none' the less'**) nevertheless

non·e·vent /näněvent'/ *n.* insignificant event, esp. contrary to hopes or expectations

non·fer·rous /nänfer'əs/ *adj.* not containing iron

non·fic'tion *n.* literary work other than fiction

non'in·ter·ven'tion *n.* (esp. political) principle or practice of not becoming involved in others' affairs

non·nu'cle·ar *adj.* **1** not involving nuclei or nuclear energy **2** not having nuclear weapons

no'-no' *n.* (*pl.* **-noes**) *Colloq.* something disallowed or forbidden

non·pa·reil /nän'pərel'/ *adj.* unrivalled or unique [Fr *pareil*]

non·plus /nän'plus'/ *v.* (·plussed, ·plus·sing) completely perplex [L *non plus* not more]

non·prof'it *adj.* not conducted primarily to make a profit

non·pro·lif·er·a·tion /nän'prəlif'ərā'SHən/ *n.* prevention of an increase in something, esp. possession of nuclear weapons

non·res'i·dent *adj.* **1** not residing in the place where one works, seeks office, etc. *—n.* **2** nonresident person **—non·res'i·den'tial** /-denSHəl/ *adj.*

non·re·sis'tance *n.* practice or principle of not resisting authority

non're·stric'tive *adj. Gram.* (of a clause, etc.) not essential to the sense

non·sense /nän'sens, -səns/ *n.* absurd or meaningless words, ideas, or actions **—non·sen'si·cal** *adj.*; **non·sen'si·cal·ly** *adv.*

non se·qui·tur /nän sek'wətər/ *n.* **1** conclusion that does not logically follow from the premises **2** statement or remark that does not follow from the previous conversation [L: it does not follow]

non·start'er *n.* **1** *Colloq.* person or scheme that is unlikely to succeed **2** worthless notion

non·stop' *adj.* **1** not stopping at intermediate places **2** done without a stop or intermission *—adv.* **3** without stopping

non·sup·port' *n.* failure to pay legally obligated support

non·u'nion *adj.* **1** not belonging to a trade union **2** not done or made by trade union members

non·vi'o·lence *n.* avoidance of violence, esp. as a principle **—non·vi'o·lent** *adj.*

noo·dle[1] /nood'l/ *n.* strip or ring of pasta [Ger]

noo·dle[2] *n. Slang.* head [orig. unknown]

nook /nook/ *n.* corner or recess; secluded place

noon /noon/ *n.* twelve o'clock in the day; midday [L *nona* (*hora*) ninth (hour)]

no' one' *n.* no person; nobody

noose /noos/ *n.* **1** loop of rope with a slipknot, tightening when pulled **2** snare; bond [Fr fr. L *nodus* NODE]

nor /nôr/ *conj.* and not; and not either (*neither one thing nor the other*) [ME *nother* not other]

Nor·dic /nôr'dik/ *adj.* of the tall, blond Germanic people of Scandinavia [Fr *nord* north]

nor'east·er /nôrē'stər/ *n.* **1** northeasterly wind **2** storm from the northeast

Nor·folk /nôr'fək, -fôk'/ *n.* city in Va. Pop. 261,229

norm /nôrm/ *n.* **1** standard; pattern; type **2** customary behavior, etc. [L *norma* carpenter's square]

nor·mal /nôr'məl/ *adj.* **1** conforming to a standard; regular; usual; typical; average **2** free from mental or emotional disorder *—n.* **3** usual state, level, value, etc. **—nor'mal·cy, nor'mal'i·ty** /-mal'itē/ *n.*; **nor'mal·ize'** *v.* (·ized, ·iz·ing); **nor'mal·i·za'tion** *n.* [L *normalis,* rel. to NORM]

● Usage: *Normalcy* is criticized as an alternative of *normality,* but actually appears quite frequently in American usage and can be taken as standard.

nor'mal·ly *adv.* **1** in a normal manner **2** usually

Nor·man /nôr'mən/ *n.* **1** native or inhabitant of medieval or modern Normandy **2** the people of medieval Normandy who conquered England in 1066 *—adj.* **3** of the Normans, their architecture, etc. [ON: *Northman*]

Nor·man /nôr'mən/ *n.* city in Okla. Pop. 80,071

Nor'man Con'quest *n.* conquest of England by William of Normandy in 1066

nor·ma·tive /nôr'mətiv/ *adj.* of or establishing a norm [L, rel. to NORM]

Norse /nôrs/ *n.* **1** Norwegian language **2** Scandinavian language group *—adj.* **3** of ancient Scandinavia, esp. Norway **—Norse'man** /-mən/ *n.* (*pl.* **-men**) [Du *noor(d)sch* northern]

north /nôrTH/ *n.* **1a** point of the horizon 90° counterclockwise from east **b** compass point or direction corresponding to this **2** (usu. **the North**) part of a country or town lying to the north *—adj.* **3** toward, at, near, or facing the north **4** from the north (*north wind*) *—adv.* **5** toward, at, or near the north [OE]

North /nôrTH/, **Frederick ("Lord North")** 1732–92; prime minister of Great Britain (1770–82) during American Revolution

North' Af'ri·ca *n.* the part of Africa N of the Sahara Desert

North' A·mer'i·ca *n.* continent of the Western Hemisphere; includes Canada, the United States, Mexico, and Central America **—North' A·mer'i·can** *n.* & *adj.*

North·amp·ton /nôrTH(h)amp'tən/ *n.* city in central England. Pop. 155,700

North Car·o·li·na /kar'əlī'nə/ *n.* SE state of the US. Capital: Raleigh. Pop. 6,628,637. Abbr. NC; N.C.; N. Car. **—North Car·o·lin'i·an** /-lin'ēən/ *n.*

North Da·ko·ta /dəkōt'ə/ *n.* N central state of the US. Capital: Bismarck. Pop. 638,800. Abbr. ND; N.D.; N. Dak. **—North Da·ko'tan** /-kōt'n/ *n.*

north·east' *n.* **1** point of the horizon midway between north and east **2** direction in which this lies *—adj.* **3** of, toward, or coming from the northeast *—adv.* **4** toward, at, or near the northeast **—north'east'er·ly** *adj., adv.* & *n.*;

north·east·ern *adj.*; **north·east·ward** *adj.* & *adv.*

north·er·ly /nôr'THə(r)lē/ *adj.* & *adv.* 1 in a northern position or direction 2 from the north

north·ern /nôr'THərn/ *adj.* of, in, or toward the north —**north'ern·most** *adj.* [OE]

north·ern·er *n.* native or inhabitant of the north

North'ern Hem'i·sphere *n.* the half of the earth north of the equator

North'ern Ire'land *n.* part of the United Kingdom, in the NE of the island of Ireland. Capital: Belfast. Pop. 1,583,000

● Usage: See note at GREAT BRITAIN.

north'ern lights' *n. pl.* aurora borealis

North'ern Mar'i·an·a Is'lands /mar'ē-an'ə, mer'-/ *n.* group of Pacific islands N of Guam; US possession. Pop. 43,300

North Ko·re·a *n.* see KOREA

North' Pole' *n.* northernmost point of the earth's axis of rotation

North' Sea' *n.* arm of the Atlantic between N Europe and Britain

North' Star' *n.* pole star

north·ward /nôrTH'wərd/ *adj.* & *adv.* (also **north'wards**) toward the north

north·west' *n.* 1 point of the horizon midway between north and west 2 direction in which this lies —*adj.* 3 of, toward, or coming from the northwest —*adv.* 4 toward, at, or near the northwest —**north'west'er·ly** *adj., adv.* & *n.*; **north'west'ern** *adj.*; **north'west'ward** *adj.* & *adv.*

North'west Ter'ri·to·ries *n.* territory of Canada, in the NW part. Capital: Yellowknife. Pop. 63,000

Nor·way /nôr'wā/ *n.* kingdom of N Europe, on the W part of the Scandinavian peninsula. Capital: Oslo. Pop. 4,283,000

Nor·we·gian /nôrwē'jən/ *n.* 1a native or national of Norway b person of Norwegian descent 2 language of Norway —*adj.* 3 of or relating to Norway [MedL *Norvegia* fr. ON: northway]

Nor·we'gian Sea' *n.* part of the Arctic Ocean between Norway and Greenland

nor'west·er /nôr'wes'tər/ *n.* northwesterly wind

Nor·wich /nôr'ij, -iCH/ *n.* city in E England. Pop. 173,300

nose /nōz/ *n.* 1 organ above the mouth of a human or animal, used for smelling and breathing 2a sense of smell b ability to detect a particular thing (*a nose for scandal*) 3 front end or projecting part of a thing —*v.* (**nosed, nos·ing**) 4 pry; search 5 perceive the smell of; discover or detect by smell 6 make one's way cautiously forward 7 **by a nose** by a very narrow margin 8 **keep one's nose clean** *Slang.* stay out of trouble 9 **on the nose** exactly 10 **put a person's nose out of joint** *Colloq.* annoy; make envious 11 **turn up one's nose** *Colloq.* show disdain 12 **under a person's nose** right before a person 13 **with one's nose in the air** haughtily [OE]

nose'bleed' *n.* bleeding from the nose

nose'cone' *n.* projecting front cone of an aircraft or spacecraft

nose'dive' *n.* 1 steep downward plunge by an airplane 2 sudden plunge or drop —*v.* (**·dived, ·div·ing**) 3 make a nosedive

nose·gay /nōz'gā'/ *n.* small bunch of flowers

nose' guard' *n.* (also **nose' tack'le**) *Football.* defensive lineman playing opposite the center

nose' job' *n. Colloq.* plastic surgery to reshape the nose

nosh /näSH/ *Slang. v.* 1 eat —*n.* 2 snack [Yiddish]

nos·tal·gia /nästal'jə, nə-/ *n.* 1 yearning for a past period 2 severe homesickness —**nos·tal'gic** /-jik/ *adj.*; **nos·tal'gi·cal·ly** *adv.* [Gk *nostos* return home]

Nos·tra·da·mus /näs'trədä'məs, nôs'-, -däm'əs/ 1503–66; French astrologer

nos·tril /näs'trəl/ *n.* either of the two openings in the nose [OE: nose-hole]

nos·trum /näs'trəm/ *n.* 1 quack remedy 2 pet scheme, esp. for political or social reform [L: our, ours]

nos·y or **nos·ey** /nō'zē/ *adj.* (**·i·er, ·i·est**) *Colloq.* inquisitive; prying —**nos'i·ly** *adv.*; **nos'i·ness** *n.*

not /nät/ *adv.* expressing negation or denial [contr. of NAUGHT]

no·ta·ble /nō'təbəl/ *adj.* 1 worthy of note; remarkable; eminent —*n.* 2 eminent person —**no'ta·bil'i·ty** *n.*; **no'ta·bly** *adv.* [L *notare* NOTE]

no·ta·ry /nō'tərē/ *n.* (*pl.* **·ries**) (in full **no'ta·ry pub'lic**) person authorized to certify signatures, deeds, etc. —**no·tar'i·al** /nōter'ēəl/ *adj.* [L *notarius* secretary]

no·ta·tion /nōtā'sHən/ *n.* 1 representation of numbers, quantities, musical notes, etc., by symbols 2 any set of such symbols [L, rel. to NOTE]

notch /näCH/ *n.* 1 V-shaped indentation on an edge or surface 2 narrow mountain pass —*v.* 3 make notches in 4 record or score with or as with notches [AngFr]

note /nōt/ *n.* 1 brief written record as an aid to memory 2 observation, written or unwritten, of experiences, etc. 3 short or informal letter 4 short annotation or additional explanation in a book, etc. 5 written promise of payment 6a notice; attention (*worthy of note*) b eminence (*person of note*) 7a single musical tone of definite pitch b written sign representing its pitch and duration 8 quality or tone of speaking, expressing mood or attitude, etc. (*note of optimism*) —*v.* (**not·ed, not·ing**) 9 observe; notice; give attention to 10 record as a thing to be remembered or observed 11 be well known [L *nota* mark]

note'book' *n.* small book for making notes in

note'book com·put'er *n.* light-weight, portable computer that closes to notebook size

note'pa'per *n.* paper for writing letters

note'wor'thy *adj.* worthy of attention; remarkable

noth·ing /nəTH'iNG/ *n.* 1 not anything; no thing 2 person or thing of no importance 3 nonexistence; what does not exist 4 no amount —*adv.* 5 not at all; in no way 6 **for nothing:** a at no cost b to no purpose 7 **nothing doing:** *Colloq.* a no prospect of success or agreement b I refuse [OE, rel. to NO[1], THING]

noth'ing·ness *n.* 1 nonexistence 2 worthlessness; triviality

no·tice /nō'tis/ *n.* 1 attention; observation 2

displayed sign bearing an announcement **3** intimation or warning, esp. a formal declaration of intention to end an agreement, leave employment, etc. **4** short published review of a new play, book, etc. —*v.* (**·ticed, ·tic·ing**) **5** perceive; observe **6** take notice of; observe; act upon [L *notus* known]

no'tice·a·ble *adj.* perceptible; noteworthy —**no'tice·a·bly** *adv.*

no·ti·fy /nō'təfī'/ *v.* (**·fied, ·fy·ing**) **1** inform or give formal notice to **2** make known —**no' ti·fi·ca'tion** /·fikā'sHən/ *n.* [L *notus* known]

no·tion /nō'sHən/ *n.* **1a** concept or idea **b** opinion **c** general or imprecise idea **2** inclination or intention **3** (*pl.*) buttons, thread, and other small articles displayed for sale [L *notio*, rel. to NOTIFY]

no'tion·al *adj.* hypothetical; imaginary —**no' tion·al·ly** *adv.*

no·to·ri·ous /nōtôr'ēəs/ *adj.* well known, esp. unfavorably —**no·to·ri·e·ty** /nō'tərī'itē/ *n.*; **no·to'ri·ous·ly** *adv.* [L *notus* known]

Not·ting·ham /nät'iNGəm/ *n.* city in central England. Pop. 277,200

not·with·stand·ing /nät'wiTHstan'diNG/ *prep.* **1** in spite of —*adv.* **2** nevertheless [fr. NOT, WITHSTAND]

Nouak·chott /nōō·äk'sHät'/ *n.* capital of Mauritania. Pop. 393,300

nou·gat /nōō'gət/ *n.* candy made from sugar or honey, nuts, and egg white [Fr fr. Prov]

nought /nôt/ *n.* NAUGHT

noun /noun/ *n.* Gram. word used to name a person, place, thing, or concept [L *nomen* name]

nour·ish /nər'isH/ *v.* **1** sustain with food **2** foster or cherish —**nour'ish·ing** *adj.* [L *nu·trire* to feed]

nour'ish·ment *n.* sustenance; food

nou·veau riche /nōō'vō' rēsH'/ *n.* (*pl.* **nou' veaux riches'**, pronunc. same) person who has recently acquired (usu. ostentatious) wealth [Fr: new rich]

Nov. *abbr.* November

no·va /nō'və/ *n.* (*pl.* **no·vae** /·vē/ or **·vas**) star showing a sudden burst of brightness and then subsiding [L: new]

No·va Sco·tia /nō'və skō'sHə/ *n.* Atlantic province of Canada. Capital: Halifax. Pop. 923,000 —**No'va Sco'tian** *n. & adj.*

nov·el /näv'əl/ *adj.* **1** of a new kind or nature —*n.* **2** fictitious prose story of book length [L *novus* new]

nov·el·ette /näv'əlet'/ *n.* short novel

nov'el·ist *n.* writer of novels

nov·el·ize *v.* (**·ized, ·iz·ing**) make a movie, play, etc., into a novel

no·vel·la /nəvel'ə/ *n.* (*pl.* **·las**) short novel or narrative story [It, rel. to NOVEL]

nov·el·ty /näv'əltē/ *n.* (*pl.* **·ties**) **1** newness **2** new or unusual thing or occurrence **3** small toy or trinket [rel. to NOVEL]

No·vem·ber /nōvem'bər/ *n.* eleventh month of the year in the Gregorian calendar [L *novem* nine; 9th month of the Roman year]

no·ve·na /nōvē'nə/ *n.* RC Ch. devotion consisting of special prayers or services on nine successive days [L *novem* nine]

Nov·go·rod /näv'gəräd'/ *n.* city in W Russia. Pop. 233,800

nov·ice /näv'is/ *n.* **1a** probationary member of a religious order **b** new convert **2** beginner [L *novicius*, fr. *novus* new]

no·vi·ti·ate /nəvisH'(ē)ət/ *n.* **1** period of being a novice **2** residence for religious novices [MedL, rel. to NOVICE]

No·vo·caine /nō'vəkān'/ *n. Tdmk.* a local anesthetic

No·vo·kuz·netsk /nō'vōkŏŏznetsk'/ *n.* city in S Russia. Pop. 601,900

No·vo·si·birsk /nō'vō'sibērsk'/ *n.* city in SW Russia. Pop. 1,446,300

now /nou/ *adv.* **1a** at the present or mentioned time **b** immediately **2** nowadays **3** under the present circumstances **4** on this further occasion (*what do you want now?*) **5** (esp. in a narrative) then; next —*conj.* **6** as a consequence —*n.* **7** this time; the present **8** just now in the immediate past **9** now and again (or then) from time to time; intermittently [OE]

NOW' ac·count' *n.* checking account that pays interest on unused balance [Negotiable Order of Withdrawal]

now·a·days /nou'ədāz'/ *adv.* at the present time or age; in these times

no·where /nō'wer'/ *adv.* **1** in or to no place —*pron.* **2** no place **3** nowhere near not nearly [OE]

no'-win' *adj.* of or designating a situation in which success is impossible

no·wise /nō'wīz'/ *adv.* in no way

nox·ious /näk'sHəs/ *adj.* harmful; unwholesome [L *noxius*]

Noyes /noiz/, **Alfred** 1880–1958; English poet and critic

noz·zle /näz'əl/ *n.* spout on a hose, etc., from which a jet issues [dim. of NOSE]

Np *symb.* neptunium

NRC *abbr.* Nuclear Regulatory Commission

ns or **nsec** *abbr.* nanosecond

Ns *abbr.* nielsbohrium

NSF *abbr.* National Science Foundation

n.s.f. or **N.S.F.** *abbr.* not sufficient funds

NT *abbr.* New Testament

n't *comb. form* not (*aren't; wouldn't*)

nth /enTH/ *adj.* of or designating a quantity represented by n, esp. an indefinite large quantity

nt. wt. *abbr.* net weight

nu /n(y)ōō/ *n.* thirteenth letter of the Greek alphabet (N, ν) [Gk]

nu·ance /n(y)ōō'äns'/ *n.* subtle shade of meaning, feeling, color, etc. [Fr: shade]

nub /nəb/ *n.* **1** point or gist **2** small lump or piece —**nub'bly** *adj.* [rel. to KNOB]

Nu'bi·an Des'ert /n(y)ōō'bēən/ *n.* arid region in NE Sudan

nu·bile /n(y)ōō'bīl'/ *adj.* (of a woman) marriageable or sexually attractive —**nu·bil'i·ty** /·bil'itē/ *n.* [L *nubere* become the wife of]

nu·cle·ar /n(y)ōō'klēər/ *adj.* **1** of, relating to, or constituting a nucleus **2** using nuclear energy

• Usage: Avoid the pronunciation "noo·kyoo·luhr," which many regard as unacceptable.

nu'cle·ar en'er·gy *n.* energy obtained by nuclear fission or fusion

nu'cle·ar fam'i·ly *n.* a couple and their child or children

nu'cle·ar fis'sion *n.* nuclear reaction in which

a heavy nucleus splits, accompanied by the release of energy

nu'cle·ar fu'sion *n.* nuclear reaction in which atomic nuclei of low atomic number fuse to form a heavier nucleus, accompanied by the release of energy

nu'cle·ar med'i·cine *n. Med.* specialty utilizing electromagnetic radiation for diagnosis and treatment

nu'cle·ar phys'ics *n. pl.* (treated as *sing.*) physics of atomic nuclei

nu'cle·ar pow'er *n.* **1** power generated by a nuclear reactor **2** country that has nuclear weapons

nu'cle·ar re·ac'tor *n.* device in which a nuclear fission chain reaction is used to produce energy

nu'cle·ar weap'on *n.* weapon using the release of energy by nuclear fission or fusion or both

nu·cle·ate *adj.* /n(y)ōō'klē·it'/ **1** having a nucleus —*v.* /-āt'/ (**·at·ed, ·at·ing**) **2** form or form into a nucleus [L, rel. to NUCLEUS]

nu·cle'ic ac'id /n(y)ōōklē'ik, -klā'-/ *n.* either of two complex organic molecules (DNA and RNA) present in all living cells

nu·cle·o·lus /nōōklē'ələs/ *n.* (*pl.* **-li** /-lī/) *Biol.* rounded body within the nucleus of most cells

nu·cle·on /n(y)ōō'klēän/ *n.* proton or neutron, esp. as part of a nucleus

nu·cle·us /n(y)ōō'klēəs/ *n.* (*pl.* **-cle·i** /-klē·ī'/) **1a** central part or thing around which others are collected **b** kernel of an aggregate or mass **2** initial part meant to receive additions **3** central core of an atom **4** *Biol.* specialized, often central part of a cell, containing the genetic material —**nu·cle·ic** /nōōklē'ik, -klā'-/ *adj.* [L: kernel]

nude /n(y)ōōd/ *adj.* **1** naked; bare; unclothed —*n.* **2** nude human figure or a representation of such **3** state of being naked —**nu'di·ty** *n.* [L *nudus*]

nudge /nəj/ *v.* (**nudged, nudg·ing**) **1** prod gently with the elbow to attract attention **2** push gradually —*n.* **3** prod; gentle push

nud·ist /nyōō'dist/ *n.* person who advocates or practices going nude —**nud'ism** /-iz'əm/ *n.*

Nue·vo La·re·do /nōō·ā'vō lərād'ō/ *n.* city on the Rio Grande in Mexico. Pop. 201,700

Nue·vo Le·ón /nōō·ā'vō lā·ōn'/ *n.* state in NE Mexico. Capital: Monterrey. Pop. 3,098,700

nu·ga·to·ry /n(y)ōō'gətôr'ē/ *adj.* **1** worthless **2** inoperative; not valid [L *nugae* jests]

nug·get /nag'it/ *n.* lump of gold, etc., esp. as found in the earth [appar. fr. dial. *nug* lump]

nui·sance /n(y)ōō'səns/ *n.* person, thing, or circumstance causing trouble or annoyance [Fr, ult. fr. L *nocere* to hurt]

nuke /n(y)ōōk/ *Colloq. n.* **1** nuclear weapon **2** nuclear-powered electricity-generating plant —*v.* (**nuked, nuk·ing**) **3** attack or destroy with nuclear weapons **4** cook in a microwave oven [abbr.]

Nu·ku·a·lo·fa /nōō'kōōälō'fə, -lō'fə/ *n.* capital of Tonga. Pop. 21,400

null /nəl/ *adj.* **1** (esp. **null and void**) invalid **2** nonexistent **3** without value, content, or significance —**nul'li·ty** *n.* [L *nullus* none]

nul·li·fy /nəl'əfī'/ *v.* (**·fied, ·fy·ing**) neutral-

ize; invalidate —**nul'li·fi·ca'tion** /-fikā'sHən/ *n.*

num. *abbr.* number; numerical

numb /nəm/ *adj.* **1** deprived of feeling; paralyzed —*v.* **2** make numb —**numb'ness** *n.* [obs. *nome* past part. of *niman* take]

num·ber /nəm'bər/ *n.* **1a** arithmetical word or symbol representing a particular quantity **b** arithmetical value showing position in a series **2** total count or aggregate; total amount **3** (*pl.*) numerical preponderance (*force of numbers*) **4** person or thing having a place in a series, esp. a single issue of a magazine, an item in a program, etc. **5** company; collection; group (*among our number*) **6** *Gram.* classification of words by their singular or plural forms —*v.* **7** include **8** assign a number or numbers to **9** amount to (a specified number) **10** count **11** do a number on thwart; defeat **12** a number of several (of) **13** have a person's number *Colloq.* understand a person's real motives, character, etc. [L *numerus*]

num'ber·less *adj.* innumerable

num'ber one' *n.* **1** *Colloq.* oneself —*adj.* **2** most important

nu·mer·a·ble /n(y)ōō'm(ə)rəbəl/ *adj.* countable [L, rel. to NUMBER]

nu·mer·al /n(y)ōō'm(ə)rəl/ *n.* **1** symbol or group of symbols denoting a number —*adj.* **2** of or denoting a number [L, rel. to NUMBER]

nu·mer·ate[1] /n(y)ōō'mərət/ *adj.* acquainted with the basic principles of mathematics —**nu·mer·a·cy** /n(y)ōō'mərəsē'/ *n.* [L *numerus* number, after *literate*]

nu·mer·ate[2] /n(y)ōō'mərāt'/ *v.* (**·at·ed, ·at·ing**) count out; enumerate

nu·mer·a·tor /n(y)ōō'mərā'tər/ *n.* number above or to the left of the line in a common fraction [L, rel. to NUMBER]

nu·mer·i·cal /n(y)ōōmer'ikəl/ *adj.* of or relating to a number or numbers —**nu·mer'i·cal·ly** *adv.* [MedL, rel. to NUMBER]

nu·mer·ol·o·gy /n(y)ōō'mərôl'əjē/ *n.* the study of the occult significance of numbers

nu·me·ro u·no /nōō'mərō ōō'nō/ *n.* **1** *Colloq.* head, chief, or most important of a kind **2** *Joc.* oneself [It: number one]

nu·mer·ous /n(y)ōō'mərəs/ *adj.* **1** many **2** consisting of many [L, rel. to NUMBER]

nu·mi·nous /n(y)ōō'mənəs/ *adj.* **1** indicating the presence of a divinity **2** spiritual; awe-inspiring [L *numen* deity]

nu·mis·mat·ics /n(y)ōō'mizmat'iks/ *n. pl.* (usu. treated as *sing.*) the study of coins or medals —**nu·mis·mat'ic** *adj.*; **nu·mis'ma·tist'** /-mətist/ *n.* [Gk *nomisma* coin]

num·skull /nəm'skəl/ *n.* stupid person [fr. NUMB]

nun /nən/ *n.* member of a religious community of women living under certain vows [LL *nonna*]

nun·ci·o /nən'sē·ō', nōōn'-/ *n.* (*pl.* **·os**) papal ambassador [L *nuntius* messenger]

nun·ner·y /nən'ərē/ *n.* (*pl.* **·ies**) religious house of nuns

nup·tial /nəp'sHəl/ *adj.* **1** of marriage or weddings —*n.* **2** (*pl.*) wedding [L *nubere nupt-* wed]

Nu·rem·berg /nōōr'əmbərg'/ *n.* (German

name **Nürnberg**) city in Germany. Pop. 493,700

Nu·re·yev /nŏŏrā′əf, nŏŏr′ē-ef′/, **Rudolf** 1939–93; Russian ballet dancer

nurse /nərs/ *n.* **1** person trained to care for the sick or infirm and assist doctors or dentists **2** NURSEMAID —*v.* (**nursed, nurs·ing**) **3a** work as a nurse **b** attend to (a sick person) **4** feed or be fed at the breast **5** hold or treat carefully **6** foster; encourage [L, rel. to NOURISH]

nurse′maid′ *n.* woman in charge of a child or children

nurse′ prac·ti′tion·er *n.* nurse with advanced training to provide medical care, give physical exams, and diagnose and treat minor illnesses

nurs·er·y /nərs′(ə)rē/ *n.* (*pl.* **·ies**) **1a** a room or place equipped for young children **b** day-care facility for children **2** place where plants are raised for sale [prob. AngFr, rel. to NURSE]

nurs·er·y·man /nər′s(ə)rēmən/ *n.* (*pl.* **·men**) owner of or worker in a plant nursery

nur′ser·y rhyme′ *n.* simple traditional song or rhyme for children

nur′ser·y school′ *n.* school for children between the ages of three and five

nurs′ing home′ *n.* residential institution providing care for invalids, old people, etc.

nur·ture /nər′CHər/ *n.* **1** bringing up; training **2** nourishment —*v.* (**·tured, ·tur·ing**) **3** bring up; rear [Fr, rel. to NOURISH]

NUTS 3

nut /nət/ *n.* **1a** fruit consisting of a hard or tough shell around an edible kernel **b** this kernel **2** pod containing hard seeds **3** small, usu. hexagonal, piece of metal, etc., with a threaded hole through it for securing a bolt **4**

Slang. **a** a crazy or eccentric person **b** fanatic; devotee [OE]

nut′case′ *n. Slang.* crazy person

nut′crack′er *n.* device for cracking nutshells

nut·hatch /nət′hacH/ *n.* small bird that climbs trees, feeding on small nuts

nut′meat′ *n.* edible kernel of a nut

nut·meg /nət′meg/ *n.* hard aromatic seed used as a spice and in medicine [ME *note-mugge*, fr. OFr: NUT + MUSK]

nu·tri·a /n(y)ŏŏ′trēə/ *n.* **1** large S American rodent **2** its fur [Sp: otter]

nu·tri·ent /n(y)ŏŏ′trēənt/ *n.* **1** substance that provides essential nourishment —*adj.* **2** nutritious [L *nutrire* nourish]

nu·tri·ment /n(y)ŏŏ′trəmənt/ *n.* anything nourishing; food

nu·tri·tion /n(y)ŏŏtrish′ən/ *n.* **1** food; nourishment **2** study of diet and its relation to health —**nu·tri′tion·al,** nu′tri·tive /-trətiv/ *adj.*; **nu·tri′tion·ist** *n.*

nu·tri·tious /n(y)ŏŏtrish′əs/ *adj.* nourishing as food

nuts /nəts/ *adj.* **1** *Slang.* crazy; mad **2** **be nuts about** *Colloq.* be very fond of

nuts′ and bolts′ *n. pl. Colloq.* practical details

nut′shell′ *n.* **1** hard exterior covering of a nut **2 in a nutshell** in a few words

nut·ty /nət′ē/ *adj.* (**·ti·er, ·ti·est**) **1a** full of nuts **b** tasting like nuts **2** *Slang.* crazy —**nut′ti·ness** *n.*

nuz·zle /nəz′əl/ *v.* (**·zled, ·zling**) **1** prod or rub gently with the nose **2** nestle [fr. NOSE]

NV postal abbr. for Nevada

NW *abbr.* **1** northwest **2** northwestern

NWT *abbr.* Northwest Territories

NY, N.Y. *abbr.* New York (postal abbr. **NY**)

Nya·sa, Lake /nī-as′ə/ *n.* (also called **Lake Malawi**) freshwater lake in E Africa

NYC *abbr.* New York City

ny·lon /nī′län/ *n.* **1** tough, light, elastic, synthetic fiber or fabric made of this **2** (*pl.*) stockings of nylon [invented word]

nymph /nimf/ *n.* **1** mythological female spirit associated with aspects of nature, esp. rivers and woods **2** beautiful young woman **3** immature form of some insects [Gk *nymphē* nymph; bride]

NYSE *abbr.* New York Stock Exchange

NZ *abbr.* New Zealand

O

o, O /ō/ *n.* (*pl.* **o's**; **O's, Os**) fifteenth letter of the English alphabet; a vowel

O *interj.* **1** var. of OH **2** prefixed to a name in the vocative (*O God*) [natural exclamation]

o or **o.** *abbr.* **1** octavo **2** off **3** old **4** only **5** order **6** *Baseball.* out(s)

O or **O.** *abbr.* **1** Ocean **2** October **3** Ohio **4** Old **5** Ontario **6** Oregon **7** (as O) *symb.* oxygen **8** a blood type

o′ *prep.* of; on (*o'clock; will-o'-the-wisp*) [abbr.]

-o *suffix* forming slang variants or derivatives (*cheapo; wino*) [perh. fr. OH]

oaf /ōf/ *n.* (*pl.* **-s**) awkward or stupid person

—**oaf′ish** *adj.*; **oaf′ish·ly** *adv.*; **oaf′ish·ness** *n.* [ON, rel. to ELF]

O·a·hu /ō-ä′hŏŏ/ *n.* Hawaiian island, location of Honolulu

oak /ōk/ *n.* **1** acorn-bearing tree with lobed leaves **2** its durable wood —**oak′en** *adj.* [OE]

Oak·land /ō′klənd/ *n.* city in Calif. Pop. 372,242

Oak·ley /ō′klē/, **Annie** (full name **Phoebe Anne Oakley Mozee**) 1860–1926; US sharpshooter

oa·kum /ō′kəm/ *n.* loose fiber obtained by picking apart old rope and used esp. in caulking [OE: off-comb]

oar /ôr/ *n.* pole with a blade used to propel a boat [OE]

oar'lock *n.* device for holding an oar in position while rowing

oars·man /ôrz'mən/ *n.* (*pl.* ·men; *fem.* ·wom·an, *pl.* ·wom'en) rower —**oars'man·ship'** *n.*

OAS *abbr.* Organization of American States

o·a·sis /ō·ā'sis/ *n.* (*pl.* ·ses /-sēz/) 1 fertile place in a desert 2 area or period of calm in the midst of turbulence [L fr. Gk]

oat /ōt/ *n.* **1a** hardy cereal plant grown as food **b** (*pl.*) grain yielded by this —**oat'en** *adj.* [OE]

oat'cake' *n.* thin oatmeal cake

oath /ōTH/ *n.* (*pl.* oaths /ōTHz/) 1 solemn declaration naming God as witness 2 profanity; curse [OE]

oat'meal' *n.* 1 meal ground from oats 2 porridge made with this

Oa·xa·ca /wähäk'ə/ *n.* state in S Mexico, on the Pacific Ocean. Capital: Oaxaca. Pop. 3,019,600

ob- *prefix* used to mean: 1 meeting or facing 2 resistance; concealment 3 finality; completeness [L *ob* toward; against; in the way of]

ob. *abbr.* he or she died [L *obiit*]

ob·bli·ga·to /äb'ligät'ō/ *n.* (*pl.* ·tos) *Mus.* complicated accompaniment forming an integral part of a composition [It: obligatory]

ob·du·rate /äb'd(y)ərət/ *adj.* 1 stubborn 2 hardened —**ob'du·ra·cy** /-sē/ *n.* [L *ob-* (intens.) + *durus* hard]

o·be·di·ent /ōbē'dēənt/ *adj.* obeying or ready to obey; submissive —**o·be'di·ence** *n.*; **o·be'di·ent·ly** *adv.* [L, rel. to OBEY]

o·bei·sance /ōbē'səns, ōbā'-/ *n.* 1 bow, curtsy, or other respectful gesture 2 homage —**o·bei'sant** *adj.* [Fr, rel. to OBEY]

ob·e·lisk /äb'əlisk/ *n.* tapering, usu. four-sided stone pillar [Gk *obelus* pointed pillar]

o·bese /ōbēs'/ *adj.* very fat —**o·be'si·ty** *n.* [L *edere* eat]

o·bey /ōbā'/ *v.* **1a** carry out the command or request of **b** carry out (a command or request) 2 be actuated or guided by [L *obedire* fr. *audire* hear]

ob·fus·cate /äb'fəskāt'/ *v.* (·cat·ed, ·cat·ing) 1 obscure or confuse 2 stupefy; bewilder —**ob'fus·ca'tion** *n.* [L *fuscus* dark]

ob·gyn *abbr.* (also **OB-GYN**) 1 obstetrician-gynecologist 2 obstetrics and gynecology

o·bit·u·ary /ōbiCH'ōō·er'ē/ *n.* (*pl.* ·ies) (also *Colloq.* **o'bit**) 1 notice of a death or deaths 2 account of the life of a deceased person [L *obitus* death]

obj. *abbr.* objective

ob·ject *n.* /äb'jikt, -jekt/ 1 material thing that can be seen or touched 2 person or thing to which action or feeling is directed 3 goal 4 *Gram.* noun or its equivalent governed by an active transitive verb or by a preposition —*v.* /əbjekt'/ 5 express opposition, disapproval, or reluctance 6 protest —**ob·jec'tor** *n.* [L *jacere ject-* throw]

ob·jec·ti·fy /əbjek'təfī'/ *v.* (·fied, ·fy·ing) present as an object

ob·jec·tion /əbjek'shən/ *n.* 1 expression or feeling of opposition or disapproval 2 adverse reason or statement [L, rel. to OBJECT]

ob·jec'tion·a·ble *adj.* 1 offensive 2 open to objection —**ob·jec'tion·a·bly** *adv.*

ob·jec·tive /əbjek'tiv/ *adj.* 1 external to the mind; actually existing 2 dealing with outward things or exhibiting unbiased facts 3 *Gram.* (of a case or word) in the form appropriate to an object of a verb or preposition —*n.* 4 goal —**ob·jec'tive·ly** *adv.*; **ob·jec'tive·ness, ob'jec·tiv'i·ty** *n.* [MedL, rel. to OBJECT]

ob'ject les'son *n.* striking practical example of some principle

ob·jet d'art /ōb'zHä där'/ *n.* (*pl.* **ob·jets d'art,** pronunc. same) small object of artistic worth [Fr: object of art]

ob·late /äblāt'/ *adj.* *Geom.* flattened at the poles [NeoL *oblatus* lengthened]

ob·la·tion /əblā'shən/ *n.* offering to a divine being [L *oblatio,* fr. *offerre* offer]

ob·li·gate /äb'ligāt'/ *v.* (·gat·ed, ·gat·ing) bind legally or morally [L, rel. to OBLIGE]

ob'li·ga'tion *n.* 1 constraining power of a law, duty, contract, etc. 2 duty; task 3 binding agreement 4 indebtedness for a service or benefit [L, rel. to OBLIGE]

ob·lig·a·to·ry /əblig'ətôr'ē/ *adj.* 1 binding 2 compulsory —**ob·lig·a·to'ri·ly** *adv.* [L, rel. to OBLIGE]

o·blige /əblīj'/ *v.* (·bliged, ·blig·ing) 1 constrain; compel 2 do a small favor; help [L *obligare* bind]

o·blig'ing *adj.* accommodating; helpful —**o·blig'ing·ly** *adv.*

ob·lique /əblēk', əblīk', ō-/ *adj.* 1 slanting; at an angle 2 indirect —**ob·lique'ly** *adv.*; **oblique'ness, ob·liq·ui·ty** /əblik'witē/ *n.* [Fr fr. L]

ob·lit·er·ate /əblit'ərāt'/ *v.* (·at·ed, ·at·ing) blot out; destroy; leave no clear traces of —**ob·lit'er·a'tion** *n.* [L *obliterare* erase, fr. *litera* letter]

ob·liv·i·on /əbliv'ēən/ *n.* state of having or being forgotten [L *oblivisci* forget]

ob·liv·i·ous /əbliv'ēəs/ *adj.* unaware or unmindful —**ob·liv'i·ous·ly** *adv.*; **ob·liv'i·ous·ness** *n.*

ob·long /äb'lôNG/ *adj.* 1 rectangular with adjacent sides unequal —*n.* 2 oblong figure or object [L *oblongus* longish]

ob·lo·quy /äb'ləkwē/ *n.* 1 ill spoken of 2 abuse; censure [L *obloqui* speak against]

ob·nox·ious /əbnäk'shəs/ *adj.* offensive; objectionable —**ob·nox'ious·ly** *adv.*; **ob·nox'ious·ness** *n.* [L *noxa* injury]

OBOE

o·boe /ō'bō/ *n.* woodwind double-reed instrument with a piercing, plaintive tone —**o'bo·ist** *n.* [Fr *hautbois* fr. *haut* high, *bois* wood]

obs. *abbr.* obsolete

ob·scene /əbsēn′/ *adj.* **1** offensively indecent **2** *Colloq.* highly offensive —**ob·scene′ly** *adv.*; ob·scen′i·ty /-sen′itē/ *n.* (*pl.* ·ties) [L *obsc(a)enus* abominable]

ob·scu·ran·tism /äbskyŏŏr′əntiz′əm/ *n.* opposition to knowledge and enlightenment —**ob·scu′ran·tist** /-tist/ *n.* & *adj.* [L *Obscurus* dark]

ob·scure /əbskyŏŏr′/ *adj.* **1** not clearly expressed, explained, or easily understood **2** dark **3** indistinct **4** hidden; unnoticed **5** undistinguished; hardly known —*v.* (·scured, ·scur·ing) **6** make obscure —**ob·scure′ly** *adv.*; ob·scu′ri·ty *n.* [Fr fr. L]

ob·se·quies /äb′sikwēz′/ *n. pl.* funeral rites [L *obsequiae*]

ob·se·qui·ous /əbsē′kwēəs/ *adj.* servile; fawning —**ob·se′qui·ous·ly** *adv.*; ob·se′qui·ous·ness *n.* [L *obsequi* comply with]

ob·serv·ance /əbzʉr′vəns/ *n.* **1** keeping or performing of a law, duty, etc. **2** rite; ceremony

ob·serv′ant *adj.* **1** acute in taking notice **2** attentive in observance —**ob·serv′ant·ly** *adv.*

ob·ser·va·tion /äb′zərvā′shən/ *n.* **1** observing or being observed **2** power of perception **3** remark; comment **4** thing observed, esp. by scientific study —**ob·ser·va′tion·al** *adj.*

ob·ser·va·to·ry /əbzər′vətôr′ē/ *n.* (*pl.* ·ries) building for astronomical or other observation

ob·serve /əbzʉrv′/ *v.* (·served, ·serv·ing) **1** perceive; become aware of **2** watch carefully **3a** follow or keep **b** celebrate or perform **4** remark **5** take note of scientifically —**ob·serv′a·ble** *adj.*; ob·serv′er *n.* [L *servare* watch; keep]

ob·sess /əbses′/ *v.* **1** fill the mind continually; preoccupy **2** be unduly preoccupied —**ob·ses′sive** *adj.* & *n.*; ob·ses′sive·ly *adv.*; ob·ses′sive·ness *n.* [L *obsidere obsess-* besiege]

ob·ses·sion /əbsesh′ən/ *n.* **1** obsessing or being obsessed **2** persistent idea dominating a person's mind —**ob·ses′sion·al** *adj.*; ob·ses′sion·al·ly *adv.*

ob·ses′sive·com·pul′sive *adj.* marked by neurotic behavior that includes repetitive actions and irresistible urges

ob·sid·i·an /əbsid′ēən/ *n.* dark, glassy rock formed from lava [L fr. *Obsius*, discoverer of a similar stone]

ob·so·les·cent /äb′səles′ənt/ *adj.* becoming obsolete —**ob′so·les′ce** *v.* (·lesced, ·lesc·ing); ob′so·les′cence n. [L *obsolescere* go out of use]

ob·so·lete /äb′səlēt′/ *adj.* no longer used; antiquated

ob·sta·cle /äb′stikəl/ *n.* thing that obstructs progress [L *obstare* stand in the way]

ob·stet·rics /əbste′triks/ *n. pl.* (treated as *sing.*) branch of medicine dealing with pregnancy and childbirth —**ob·stet′ric** *adj.*; ob·ste·tri·cian /äb′stətrish′ən/ *n.* [L *obstetrix* midwife]

ob·sti·nate /äb′stənət/ *adj.* stubborn; intractable —**ob′sti·na·cy** *n.*; ob′sti·nate·ly *adv.* [L *obstinare* persist]

ob·strep·er·ous /əbstrep′ərəs/ *adj.* **1** turbulent; unruly **2** noisy —**ob·strep′er·ous·ly**

adv.; ob·strep′er·ous·ness *n.* [L *obstrepere* shout at]

ob·struct /əbstrəkt′/ *v.* **1** block up; clog **2** prevent or retard the progress of —**ob·struc′tive** *adj.*; ob·struc′tive·ly *adv.*; ob·struc′tive·ness *n.* [L *obstruere obstruct-*]

ob·struc·tion /əbstrək′shən/ *n.* **1** obstructing or being obstructed **2** thing that obstructs; blockage —**ob·struc′tion·ist** *n.*

ob·tain /əbtān′/ *v.* **1** acquire; secure **2** prevail —**ob·tain′a·ble** *adj.*; ob·tain′ment *n.* [L *tenere* hold]

ob·trude /əbtrōōd′/ *v.* (·trud·ed, ·trud·ing) **1** stick out; push forward **2** thrust importunately forward —**ob·tru′sion** /-trōō′zhən/, ob·tru′sive·ness /-sivnes/ *n.*; ob·tru′sive *adj.*; ob·tru′sive·ly *adv.* [L *obtrudere* thrust against]

ob·tuse /əbt(y)ōōs′/ *adj.* **1** dull-witted **2** (of an angle) between 90° and 180° **3** blunt; not sharp —**ob·tuse′ly** *adv.*; ob·tuse′ness *n.* [L *obtundere obtus-* beat against; blunt]

ob·verse /äb′vərs/ *n.* **1** counterpart; opposite **2** side of a coin, medal, etc., bearing the head or principal design **3** front or top side of a thing [L *obvertere obvers-* turn toward]

ob·vi·ate /äb′vēāt′/ *v.* (·at·ed, ·at·ing) prevent; do away with [L *obviare* prevent]

ob·vi·ous /äb′vēəs/ *adj.* easily seen, recognized, or understood —**ob′vi·ous·ly** *adv.*; ob′vi·ous·ness *n.* [L *ob viam* in the way]

oc·a·ri·na /äk′ərē′nə/ *n.* small wind instrument [It *oca* goose, after its shape]

O′Ca·sey /ōkā′sē/, Sean 1880–1964; Irish dramatist

oc·ca·sion /əkā′zhən/ *n.* **1a** special event or happening **b** time of this **2** reason; need **3** suitable juncture; opportunity **4** subordinate cause —*v.* **5** cause **6** on occasion now and then [L *occidere occas-* go down]

oc·ca·sion·al /əkā′zh(ə)nəl/ *adj.* **1** happening irregularly or infrequently **2** for or of a special occasion —**oc·ca′sion·al·ly** *adv.*

Oc·ci·dent /äk′sədənt/ *n. Poet.* or *Rhet.* **1** West **2** Europe and N and S America —**Oc′ci·den′tal** or oc′ci·den′tal *adj.* & *n.* [L *occidens -entis* setting; sunset; west]

oc·ci·put /äk′səpət/ *n.* back of the head —**oc·cip·i·tal** /äksip′ət·l/ *adj.* [L *caput* head]

oc·clude /əklōōd′/ *v.* (·clud·ed, ·clud·ing) **1** stop up or close **2** shut in or shut out —**oc·clu′sion** /-klōō′zhən/ *n.*; oc·clu′sive /-siv/ *adj.* [L *occludere occlus-* close up]

oc·cult /əkəlt′, ä-/ *adj.* **1** supernatural; mystical **2** esoteric [L *occultus* hidden]

oc·cu·pant /äk′yəpənt/ *n.* person who occupies —**oc′cu·pan·cy** *n.* (*pl.* ·cies) [L, rel. to OCCUPY]

oc·cu·pa·tion /äk′yəpā′shən/ *n.* **1** person's employment, profession, pastime, etc. **2** occupying or being occupied **3** holding of a country, etc., by force —**oc′cu·pa′tion·al** *adj.*

oc·cu·py /äk′yəpī′/ *v.* (·pied, ·py·ing) **1** live in **2** take up or fill (space, time, or a place) **3** hold (a position or office) **4** take possession of forcibly or without authority **5** keep busy or engaged [L *occupare* seize]

oc·cur /əkʉr′/ *v.* (·curred, ·cur·ring) **1** come into being **2** exist or be encountered **3** come into the mind of [L *occurrere* befall]

oc·cur·rence *n.* **1** occurring **2** incident or event

o·cean /ō′shən/ *n.* **1** large expanse of sea, esp. the Atlantic, Pacific, Indian, and Arctic Oceans **2** (often *pl.*) *Colloq.* very large expanse or quantity —**o·ce·an·ic** /ō′shē·an′ik/ *adj.* [Gk *ōkeanos*]

o′cean-front′ *adj.* at the seashore

o′cean-go′ing *adj.* able to cross or travel on oceans

O·ce·an·i·a /ō′shē·an′ē·ə/ *n.* collective term for the Pacific islands and Australia

o·ce·a·nog·ra·phy /ō′shən·ag′rəfē/ *n.* the study of the oceans —**o′cea·nog′ra·pher** *n.*; **o′cea·no·graph′ic** /·nōgraf′ik/, **o′cea·no·graph′i·cal** *adj.*

O·cean·side /ō′shənsīd′/ *n.* city in Calif. Pop. 128,398

o·ce·lot /äs′əlät′/ *n.* leopardlike cat of S and Central America [Fr fr. Nahuatl]

o·cher /ō′kər/ *n.* (also o′chre) **1** a clay used as yellow, brown, or red pigment **2** pale brownish-yellow —**o·chre·ous** /ō′krēəs/ *adj.* [Gk *ōkhra*]

o′clock /əkläk′, ō-/ *adv.* of the clock (*six o′clock*)

O′Con·nell /ōkän′l/, **Daniel** 1775–1847; Irish nationalist leader

OCR *abbr.* optical character recognition; optical character reader

Oct. *abbr.* October

octa- *comb. form* (oct- before a vowel) eight [Gk *oktō* eight]

oc·ta·gon /äk′təgän/ *n.* plane figure with eight sides and angles —**oc·tag·o·nal** /äktag′ənl/ *adj.* [OCTA-, Gk *gōnos* -angled]

oc·ta·he·dron /äk′təhē′drən/ *n.* (*pl.* -drons) solid figure contained by eight plane faces —**oc′ta·he′dral** *adj.* [Gk]

oc·tane /äk′tān/ *n.* flammable hydrocarbon present in gasoline [fr. OCTA-]

oc·tave /äk′tiv/ *n.* **1** *Mus.* **a** interval between (and including) two notes, one having twice or half the frequency of vibration of the other **b** eight notes occupying this interval **c** each of the two notes at the extremes of this interval **2** group of eight [L *octavus* eighth]

OCTAHEDRON

Oc·ta·vi·an /äktā′vēən/ *see* AUGUSTUS

oc·ta·vo /äktä′vō, -tä′vō/ *n.* (*pl.* -vos) **1** standard book size, approx. 6 by 9 ins., orig. from a sheet folded to form eight leaves **2** book or sheet of this size [L, rel. to OCTAVE]

oc·tet /äktet′/ *n.* (also oc·tette′) **1a** musical composition for eight performers **b** the performers **2** group of eight [It or Ger, rel. to OCTA-]

octo- *comb. form* (oct- before a vowel) eight [see OCTA-]

Oc·to·ber /äktō′bər/ *n.* tenth month of the year in the Gregorian calendar [L *octo* eight; the 8th month of the Roman year]

oc·to·ge·nar·i·an /äk′təjəner′ēən/ *n.* person from 80 to 89 years old [L *octogeni* 80 each]

oc·to·pus /äk′təpəs/ *n.* (*pl.* ·pus·es or ·pi /-pī′/) sea mollusk with eight tentacles [Gk, rel. to OCTO-, *pous* foot]

oc·u·lar /äk′yələr/ *adj.* of, for, or by the eyes; visual [L *oculus* eye]

oc·u·list /äk′yəlist/ *n.* **1** *Old-fash.* ophthalmologist **2** optometrist

OD /ōdē′/ *Slang. n.* **1** drug overdose —*v.* **2** (OD′s, OD′d, OD′ing) take an overdose [abbr.]

o.d. *abbr.* outside diameter

O.D. *abbr.* **1** Doctor of Optometry **2** overdraft

odd /äd/ *adj.* **1** strange; remarkable; eccentric **2** casual; occasional **3** not normally considered; unconnected; disconnected **4a** (of numbers) not integrally divisible by two, e.g., 1, 3, 5 **b** bearing such a number **5** one item of a pair (*odd sock*) **6** (usu. in comb.) somewhat more than (*forty-odd people*) **7** remaining after taking a set sum or round number —**odd′ly** *adv.*; **odd′ness** *n.* [ON *oddi* angle; point; third or odd number]

odd′ball′ *n. Colloq.* eccentric person

odd′i·ty *n.* (*pl.* ·ties) **1** strange person, thing, trait, or occurrence **2** strangeness

odds /ädz/ *n. pl.* **1** ratio between the amounts staked by the parties to a bet, based on the expected probability either way **2** balance of probability or advantage **3** at odds in conflict; at variance [appar. fr. ODD]

odds′ and ends′ *n. pl.* miscellaneous articles or remnants

odds′-on′ *adj.* (of a chance) better than even; likely

ode /ōd/ *n.* lyric poem of exalted style and tone [Gk *ōidē* song]

O·den·se /ōd′n·sə/ *n.* seaport in S Denmark. Pop. 139,000

O·der Riv·er /ōd′ər/ *n.* river in central Europe flowing 560 mi. from Czech Republic to the Baltic Sea

O·des·sa /ōdes′ə/ *n.* seaport in S Ukraine on the Black Sea. Pop. 1,101,000.

O·dets /ōdets′/, **Clifford** 1906–63; US dramatist

O·din /ō′din/ *n. Norse Myth.* supreme deity

o·di·ous /ō′dēəs/ *adj.* hateful; repulsive —**o′di·ous·ly** *adv.*; **o′di·ous·ness** *n.* [rel. to ODIUM]

o·di·um /ō′dēəm/ *n.* widespread dislike or disapproval [L: hatred]

o·dom·e·ter /ōdäm′ətər/ *n.* instrument for measuring distance traveled [Gk *hodos* way]

o·dor /ō′dər/ *n.* **1** smell; fragrance **2** quality; trace **3** regard; repute —**o′dor·less, o′dor·ous** *adj.* [L]

o·dor·if·er·ous /ō′dərif′ərəs/ *adj.* emitting a strong odor [L, rel. to ODOR]

od·ys·sey /äd′əsē/ *n.* (*pl.* ·seys) long adventurous journey [title of the Homeric epic poem on the adventures of Odysseus]

OE *abbr.* Old English

OED *abbr.* Oxford English Dictionary

Oed·i·pus com′plex /ed′əpəs, ē′də-/ *n. Psychol.* child's subconscious sexual desire for the parent of the opposite sex —**Oed′i·pal** /-pəl/ *adj.* [for the legendary Greek king who unknowingly married his mother]

OEM *abbr.* original equipment manufacturer

oe·no·phile /ē′nəfīl/ *n.* wine connoisseur [Gk *oinos* wine]

o′er /ōr, ôr/ *adv. & prep. Poet.* OVER [contr.]

o′er·ween′ing *adj.* arrogant; presumptuous

œu·vre /OEvr, œrv(r)/ *n.* works of a creative artist regarded collectively [Fr: work]

of /əv, äv/ *prep.* expressing: **1** origin or cause **2** material or substance **3** belonging or connection **4** identity or relation **5** removal or separation **6** reference or direction (*beware of the dog; short of money*) **7** partition; classification; inclusion (*part of the story; this sort of book*) **8** description; quality; condition (*person of tact; girl of ten*) **9** time in relation to the following hour (*quarter of three*) [OE]

off /ôf/ *adv.* **1** away; at or to a distance (*three miles off*) **2** out of position; not on, touching, or attached (*a part fell off*) **3** so as to be rid of (*sleep it off*) **4** so as to be discontinued or stopped (*turn off the radio*) **5** (of food, etc.) beginning to decay **6** less; discounted by (*ten cents off*) —*prep.* **7a** from; away, down, or up from **b** not on (*off campus*) **8** temporarily relieved of or abstaining from (*off duty*) **9** using as a source or means of support (*live of the land*) **10** leading from (*off Main Street*) —*adj.* **11** far; further **12** *Colloq.* somewhat unwell (*feeling a bit off*) —*v.* **13** *Slang.* kill; murder **14 off and on** intermittently; now and then [var. of OF]

-off *comb. form* contest or tie-breaker (*playoff; bake-off*)

of·fal /ôʹfəl/ *n.* **1** innards of a carcass **2** refuse; scraps [Du *afval*, rel. to OFF, FALL]

off′beat′ *adj.* **1** not coinciding with the beat **2** eccentric; unconventional —*n.* **3** *Mus.* any of the unaccented beats in a bar

off′ chance′ *n.* remote possibility

off′-col′or *adj.* somewhat indecent

Of·fen·bach /ôʹfənbäkh, -bäk/, **Jacques** 1819–80; German-born French composer

of·fend /əfendʹ/ *v.* **1** cause offense to; upset **2** displease; anger **3** do wrong; transgress —**of·fendʹer** *n.*; **of·fendʹing** *adj.* [L *offendere offens-* strike against, displease]

of·fense /əfensʹ, ôfʹens/ *n.* **1** illegal act **2** upsetting of feelings; insult **3** aggressive action **4** *Sports.* squad or players seeking to score points [rel. to OFFEND]

of·fen·sive *adj.* **1** causing offense; insulting **2** disgusting **3a** aggressive; attacking **b** for attacking —*n.* **4** aggressive action, attitude, or campaign —**of·fenʹsive·ly** *adv.*; **of·fenʹsive·ness** *n.*

of·fer /ôʹfər/ *v.* **1** present for acceptance, refusal, or consideration **2** express readiness or show intention **3** provide; give an opportunity for **4** present itself; occur (*as opportunity offers*) **5** attempt (violence, resistance, etc.) —*n.* **6** expression of readiness to do or give if desired, or to buy or sell **7** amount offered **8** proposal **9** bid [L *offerre*]

of·fer·ing *n.* **1** contribution or gift, esp. of money **2** thing offered as a sacrifice, etc.

of·fer·to·ry /ôʹfə(r)tôr′ē/ *n.* (*pl.* **-ries**) *Christianity.* **1** offering of the bread and wine at the Eucharist **2** collection of money at a religious service [ChL, rel. to OFFER]

off′hand′ *adj.* **1** curt or casual in manner —*adv.* **2** without preparation or thought —**off′handʹed** *adj.*; **off′handʹed·ly** *adv.*; **off′handʹed·ness** *n.*

of·fice /ôʹfis/ *n.* **1** room or building used as a place of business, for clerical work, etc. **2** room or area for a particular business (*ticket office*) **3** position with duties attached to it **4** duty; task; function **5** (usu. *pl.*) kindness; service **6** form of worship; ceremony [L *officium* fr. *opus* work, *facere fic-* do]

off′fice-holdʹer *n.* person who holds an official position

of·fi·cer /ôʹfisər/ *n.* **1a** person holding a position of authority or trust **b** such a person with a commission in the armed forces **2** policeman; policewoman

of′ficer of the day′ *n. Milit.* officer in charge of security, etc., at a base for the day

of·fi·cial /əfiSHʹəl/ *adj.* **1** of an office or its tenure **2** characteristic of officials and bureaucracy **3** properly authorized —*n.* **4** person holding office —**of·fiʹcial·dom** /-dəm/ *n.*; **of·fiʹcial·ly** *adv.*

of·fi·ci·ate /əfiSHʹē-āt/ *v.* (**·at·ed, ·at·ing**) **1** act in an official capacity **2** conduct a religious service —**of·fiʹci·ant** /-fiSHʹənt, -ēənt/, **of·fiʹci·aʹtion, of·fiʹci·aʹtor** *n.*

of·fi·cious /əfiSHʹəs/ *adj.* **1** domineering **2** intrusive; meddlesome —**of·fiʹcious·ly** *adv.*; **of·fiʹcious·ness** *n.*

off′ing *n.* **1** distant part of the sea in view **2 in the offing** likely to appear or happen soon [prob. fr. OFF]

off′-key′ *adj.* & *adv.* **1** out of tune **2** not quite fitting

off′-limʹits *adj.* prohibited; not allowed, esp. to a certain group

off′line′ *adj. Comp.* **1** not operational; operating independently —*adv.* **2** not under direct computer control

off′load′ *v.* **1** get rid of (esp. something unpleasant) by passing it to someone else **2** (also **off′-load′**) remove cargo

off′-peak′ *adj.* used for or for use at times other than those of greatest demand

off′-put′ting *adj.* causing annoyance, uneasiness, etc.

off′-road′ *adj.* made for or done on unpaved ground, such as trails, beaches, etc.

off′screen′ *adj.* & *adv.* **1** beyond the range of a camera, etc. **2** not being filmed

off′-sea′son *n.* time of the year when business, etc., is slack

off′set′ *n.* **1** compensation; consideration or amount balancing the effect of a contrary one **2** (also **off′set print′ing**) process in which the inked impression is transferred to a rubber roller and from there to paper, etc. —*v.* (**·set, ·set·ting**) **3** counterbalance; compensate **4** print by the offset process

off′shoot′ *n.* **1** side shoot or branch **2** derivative

off′shore′ *adj.* **1** at sea some distance from the shore **2** (of the wind) blowing seaward **3** done in a foreign country (*offshore banking*)

off′side′ *adj.* (also **off′sides′**) *Sports.* in an illegal position to play

off′spring′ *n.* (*pl.* same) children; descendants [OE: see OFF, SPRING]

off′stage′ *adj.* & *adv.* not on the stage; not visible to the audience

off′-the-wall′ /ôfʹ THə wôlʹ/ *adj. Slang.* crazy; absurd; outlandish

off′-white′ *adj.* & *n.* white with a gray or yellowish tinge

off′ year′ *n.* **1** year in which a specified event

oft /ôft/ *adv. Lit.* or *Joc.* often [OE]

of·ten /ô′fən, ôf′tən/ *adv.* (**of·ten·er, of·ten·est**) **1** frequently; many times **2** at short intervals

● Usage: Some speakers sound the *-t-*, pronouncing the word "off-ten"; for others, it is silent, as in *soften*. Both pronunciations are acceptable.

Og·bo·mo·sho /äg′bəmō′shō/ *n.* city in SW Nigeria. Pop. 660,600

o·gle /ō′gəl/ *v.* (**o·gled, o·gling**) **1** look amorously or lecherously (at) —*n.* **2** amorous or lecherous look —**o′gler** *n.* [prob. LGer or Du]

O·gle·thorpe /ō′gəlthôrp′/, **James Edward** 1696–1785; English philanthropist and founder of Georgia colony

o·gre /ō′gər/ *n.* (*fem.* **o·gress** /ō′gris/) **1** man-eating giant in folklore **2** hideous person —**o′gre·ish** *adj.* [Fr]

oh /ō/ *interj.* (also *cap.* or O) expression of surprise, pain, entreaty, etc.

OH postal abbr. for Ohio

O. Hen·ry /ō hen′rē/ (pseudonym of William Sydney Porter) 1862–1910; US writer

O'Hig·gins /ōhig′inz/, **Bernardo** c. 1778–1842; Chilean revolutionary leader and head of state (1817–23)

O·hi·o /ōhī′ō/ *n.* state in the E central US. Capital: Columbus. Pop. 10,847,115. Abbr. O.; OH —**O·hi′o·an** *n. & adj.*

O·hi′o Riv′er *n.* river flowing 980 mi. from W Penn., joining the Mississippi at Cairo, Ill.

ohm /ōm/ *n.* unit of electrical resistance [for G. *Ohm*, Ger physicist]

o·ho /ōhō′/ *interj.* expression of surprise or exultation

-oid *suffix* forming adjectives and nouns denoting form or resemblance (*humanoid*) [Gk *eidos* form]

oil /oil/ *n.* **1** any of various viscous, usu. flammable liquids insoluble in water **2** petroleum **3a** (usu. *pl.*) OIL PAINT **b** picture painted in oil paints —*v.* **4** apply oil to; lubricate [L *oleum* olive oil]

oil′cloth′ *n.* fabric, esp. canvas, waterproofed with oil or another substance

oil′ paint′ *n.* paint made by mixing powdered pigment in (esp. linseed) oil —**oil′ paint′ing** *n.*

oil′skin′ *n.* **1** cloth waterproofed with oil **2** (often *pl.*) garment or suit of this

oil′ slick′ *n.* patch of oil, esp. on the sea

oil′stone′ *n.* fine-grained flat stone used with oil for sharpening knives and tools

oil′y *adj.* (**-i·er, -i·est**) **1** of or like oil **2** covered or soaked with oil **3** fawning; unctuous; ingratiating —**oil′i·ness** *n.*

oint·ment /oint′mənt/ *n.* greasy healing or cosmetic preparation for the skin [L *unguentum*]

OK¹ /ōkā′/ (also **O.K.; okay**) *Colloq. adj.* **1** (often as *interj.*) all right; satisfactory —*adv.* **2** well; satisfactorily —*n.* **3** approval; sanction —*v.* (**OK'd, OK′ing**) **4** approve; sanction [prob. abbr. of *ori* (or *oll*) *korrect*, jocular form of 'all correct']

OK² postal abbr. for Oklahoma

O·ka·ya·ma /ō′kəyä′mə/ *n.* city in Japan, on Honshu. Pop. 597,200

O·kee·cho·bee, Lake /ō′kəchō′bē/ *n.* lake in N part of the Everglades, in S Fla.

O'Keeffe /ōkēf′/, **Georgia** 1887–1986; US painter

O·ke·fe·no·kee Swamp /ō′kēfənō′kē/ *n.* extensive wooded swamp in SW Ga.

o·key-doke /ō′kē dōk′/ (also **o·key-do·key** /-dō′kē/) *adj. & interj. Slang.* OK

O·khotsk, Sea′ of /əkhôtsk′, ōkätsk′/ *n.* arm of the N Pacific enclosed by the Kamchatka Peninsula

O·ki·na·wa /ōkinä′wə/ *n.* largest of the Ryukyu Islands SW of Japan

Okla. abbr. for Oklahoma

O·kla·ho·ma /ō′kləhō′mə/ *n.* S state of the US. Capital: Oklahoma City. Pop. 3,145,585. Abbr. OK; Okla. —**O′kla·ho′man** *n. & adj.*

O′kla·ho′ma Cit′y *n.* capital of Okla., in the central part. Pop. 444,719

ok·ra /ō′krə/ *n.* tall plant with long ridged seed pods used for food [WAfr native name]

old /ōld/ *adj.* (**old·er, old·est** or **eld·er, eld·est**) **1a** advanced in age **b** not young or new **2** made long ago **3** long in use **4** worn, dilapidated, or shabby from age or use **5** having the characteristics of age **6** practiced; inveterate **7** belonging to the past; former; dating from long ago; ancient; primeval **8** of a certain age (*four years old*) —*n.* **9** time gone by (*knights of old*) —**old′ish** *adj.*; **old′ness** *n.*

old′ age′ *n.* later part of normal life

old′ boy′ net′work *n. Colloq.* preferment in employment, esp. for members of the same college, social class, etc.

old′ coun′try *n.* native country of immigrants, etc.

old′en *adj. Archaic.* old; of old

Old′ Eng′lish *n.* Germanic language spoken in Anglo-Saxon England from the 5th to the 12th cent.

old′-fash′ioned *adj.* showing or favoring the tastes of former times

Old′ Glo′ry *n.* nickname for the US national flag

old′ guard′ *n.* long-standing or conservative members of a group

old′ hat′ *adj. Colloq.* hackneyed

old·ie /ōl′dē/ *n. Colloq.* old person or thing

old′ la′dy *n. Slang.* one's mother or wife

old′-line′ *adj.* traditional or conservative

old′ maid′ *n.* **1** elderly unmarried woman **2** *Colloq.* prim and fussy person

old′ man′ *n. Slang.* one's husband or father

old′ mas′ter *n.* **1** great European artist, esp. of the 13th–17th cent. **2** painting by such a painter

Old′ Norse′ *n.* Germanic language from which the Scandinavian languages were derived

old′ school′ *n.* traditional attitudes or people having them

Old′ Tes′ta·ment *n.* part of the Bible containing the Judaic scriptures

old′-time′ *adj.* belonging to former times

old′ tim′er *n.* **1** experienced person **2** an elderly person

old′ wives′′ tale′ *n.* unscientific belief

Old′ World′ *n.* Europe, Asia, and Africa

o·lé /ōlā′/ *interj. & n. Span.* shout of approval, joy, etc.

o·le·ag·i·nous /ō′lē-aj′ənəs/ *adj.* like or producing oil [L, rel. to OIL]

o·le·an·der /ō′lē-an′dər/ *n.* evergreen flowering shrub [L]

o·le·o·mar·ga·rine /ō′lēōmär′jərin/ *n.* MARGARINE

ol·fac·to·ry /olfak′tərē, äl-/ *adj.* of the sense of smell [L *olere* smell, *facere* make]

ol·i·garch /äl′igärk, ōl′i-/ *n.* member of an oligarchy [Gk *oligoi* few, *archos* ruler]

ol·i·gar·chy /äl′igär′kē, ō′li-/ *n.* (*pl.* -chies) 1 government or nation governed by a small group of people 2 members of such a government —ol′i·gar′chic /-kik/ *adj.*; ol′i·gar′chi·cal *adj.*

ol·ive /äl′iv/ *n.* 1 small, oval, hard-stoned, edible fruit 2a tree bearing this b its wood 3 dull yellowish green color —*adj.* 4 olive-colored [L *oliva* fr. Gk]

ol′ive branch′ *n.* branch of the olive tree, symbol of reconciliation or peace

ol′ive oil′ *n.* oil extracted from olives

O·liv·i·er /əliv′ē-ā′, ō-/, (Sir) Laurence 1907–89; English actor and director

Olm·sted /ōm′stid/, Frederick L. 1822–1903; US landscape architect

OLIVE BRANCH

O·lym·pi·a /ōlim′pēə/ *n.* capital of Wash., in the W part. Pop. 33,840

O·lym·pi·ad /əlim′pē-ad′, ō-/ *n.* 1 period of four years between Olympic games, used by the ancient Greeks in dating events 2 celebration of the modern or ancient Olympic Games [Gk, rel. to OLYMPIC]

O·lym·pi·an /əlim′pēən, ō-/ *adj.* 1 of Mount Olympus 2 superior; aloof 3 OLYMPIC —*n.* 4 any of the Greek gods said to dwell on Olympus 5 competitor in the Olympic games [fr. Mt. OLYMPUS]

O·lym·pic /əlim′pik, ō-/ *adj.* 1 of the Olympic games —*n.* 2 (*pl.*) Olympic games [fr. *Olympia* in S Greece]

O·lym′pic games′ *n. pl.* 1 ancient Greek athletic festival held at Olympia every four years 2 modern international athletic festival

O·lym·pus /ōlim′pəs/ *n.* mountain in N Greece; in Greek mythology, the home of the gods

O·ma·ha /ō′məhä′, -hô′/ *n.* city in Nebr. Pop. 335,795

O·man /ōmän′, ōman′/ *n.* independent sultanate on the Gulf of Oman. Capital: Muscat. Pop. 1,640,000

O·man′, Gulf′ of *n.* inlet of the Arabian Sea at the entrance to the Persian Gulf

O·mar Khay·yám /ōmär′ kī-äm′, kī-am′/ d. 1123; Persian poet, mathematician, and astronomer

OMB *abbr.* Office of Management and Budget

om·buds·man /äm′bŏŏdz′mən, -bədz-/ *n.* (*pl.* ·men) official appointed to investigate complaints against public authorities [Sw: legal representative]

Om·dur·man /äm′dərmän′/ *n.* city in Sudan. Pop. 526,300

o·me·ga /ōmē′gə, -mā′-, omeg′ə/ *n.* 1 last

(24th) letter of the Greek alphabet (Ω, ω) 2 last of a series; final development

om·e·let or **om·e·lette** /äm′lət/ *n.* beaten eggs cooked and often folded around a filling [Fr]

o·men /ō′mən/ *n. Latin.* event or object portending good or evil

om·i·cron /äm′ikrän′, ō′mi-/ *n.* fifteenth letter of the Greek alphabet (O, o)

om·i·nous /äm′ənəs/ *adj.* 1 threatening 2 of evil omen —om′i·nous·ly *adv.* [L, rel. to OMEN]

o·mis·sion /ōmisH′ən/ *n.* 1 omitting or being omitted 2 thing omitted

o·mit /ōmit′/ *v.* (·mit·ted, ·mit·ting) 1 leave out; not insert or include 2 leave undone; fail; neglect [L *omittere*]

omni- *comb. form* all [L *omnis* all]

om·ni·bus /äm′nibəs, -bəs′/ *n.* 1 bus —*adj.* 2 serving several purposes; comprising several items [L: for all]

om·nip·o·tent /ämnip′ətənt/ *adj.* having great or absolute power —om·nip′o·tence *n.* [L, rel. to POTENT]

om·ni·pres·ent /äm′niprez′ənt/ *adj.* present everywhere —om′ni·pres′ence *n.*

om·ni·scient /ämnisH′ənt/ *adj.* knowing everything —om·ni′science *n.* [L *scire* know]

om·niv·o·rous /ämniv′ərəs/ *adj.* 1 feeding on both plants and animals 2 reading, observing, etc., everything that comes one's way —om·ni·vore /äm′nivôr′/ *n.*; om·niv′o·rous·ly *adv.*; om·niv′o·rous·ness *n.* [L *vorare* devour]

Omsk /ômsk, ämsk/ *n.* city in W Russia. Pop. 1,166,800

on /ôn, än/ *prep.* 1 supported by; attached to; in contact with; covering (*sat on a stool; hung on the wall*) 2 in the direction of; near to (*on your left*) 3 exactly at the time of (*on the hour*) 4 as a result of (*lost on a bet*) 5 having as a situation or location (*on the school board; on the next street*) 6 through the use of (*runs on diesel*) 7 in the direction of; against 8 having as a basis (*on good authority; did it on purpose*) 9 concerning (*essay on politics*) 10 using or engaged with (*on a diet; here on business*) 11 at the expense of (*drinks are on me*) 12 added to (*disaster on disaster*) 13 in a specified manner or state (*on the run*) —*adv.* 14 (so as to be) wearing 15 in the appropriate direction; toward (*look on*) 16 further forward (*move on*) 17 with continued action or operation (*sing on; light is on*) 18 set to take place, happen, function, etc. (*party is on; a good show on*) 19 be on to *Colloq.* realize the significance or intentions of 20 on and off intermittently 21 on and on continually; at tedious length 22 on time punctual; punctually [OE]

once /wəns/ *adv.* 1 on one occasion only 2 at some time in the past 3 ever or at all —*conj.* 4 as soon as —*n.* 5 one time or occasion 6 at once: a immediately b simultaneously 7 for once on only one occasion 8 once and for all conclusively; in conclusion 9 once (or every once) in a while occasionally 10 once upon a time at some unspecified time in the past [orig. gen. of ONE]

once′-o′ver *n. Colloq.* rapid inspection

on·co·gene /äNG′kəjēn′/ *n.* gene that can

transform a cell into a cancer cell [Gk *onkos* mass]

on·col·o·gy /ăngkăl'əjē/ *n.* the study or treatment of tumors [Gk *onkos* mass]

on'com'ing *adj.* approaching from the front

one /wən/ *adj.* **1** single and integral in number **2** being a singular member of a group, class, etc. (*one type of boat*) **3** particular but undefined (*one night last week*) **4** only (*the one man who can do it*) **5** united (*speaking with one voice*) **6** identical; the same —*n.* **7a** lowest cardinal number **b** symbol for this (1, i, I) **8** unity; a unit **9** single thing, person, or example —*pron.* **10** person of a specified kind **11** any person (*one never knows*) **12** *l*; me **13** **at one** in agreement **14 one and all** everyone **15 one by one** singly; successively [OE]

one'-horse' *adj.* **1** using a single horse **2** *Colloq.* small; poorly equipped

O'Neill /ōnēl'/, **Eugene Gladstone** 1888–1953; US dramatist

one·ness /wən'nis/ *n.* **1** singleness **2** uniqueness **3** agreement **4** sameness

one'-on-one' *adj. & adv.* of or in direct person-to-person conflict

on·er·ous /ō'nərəs, än'ər-/ *adj.* burdensome —**on'er·ous·ness** *n.* [L, rel. to ONUS]

one·self' /wən'self'/ *pron.* **1** reflexive and emphatic form of ONE **2** be oneself act in one's normal manner

one'-shot' *adj. Colloq.* subject to happening just once

one'-sid'ed *adj.* unfair; partial —**one'-sid'ed·ly** *adv.*; **one'-sid'ed·ness** *n.*

one'time' *adj.* former

one'-to-one' *adj. & adv.* **1** involving or between only two people **2** with correspondence of one individual to another

one'-track' mind' *n.* mind preoccupied with one subject

one'-up' *adj. Colloq.* having a particular advantage —**one'-up'man·ship** /-mənSHip/ *n.*

one'-way' *adj.* allowing movement, travel, etc., in one direction only

on'go'ing *adj.* **1** continuing **2** in progress

on·ion /ən'yən/ *n.* vegetable with an edible bulb of a pungent smell and flavor —**on'ion·y** *adj.* [L *unio -onis*]

on'line' *Comp. adj.* **1** directly connected to a computer; under direct computer control —*adv.* **2** while connected to a computer

on'look'er *n.* spectator —**on'look'ing** *adj.*

on·ly /ōn'lē/ *adv.* **1** solely; merely; exclusively; **2** as soon or as recently as **3** with no better result than —*adj.* **4** existing alone of its or their kind **5** best or alone worth considering —*conj.* **6** *Colloq.* except that; but **7 only too** extremely [OE, rel. to ONE]

on·o·mat·o·poe·ia /än'əmat'əpē'ə, -mät'-/ *n.* formation of a word by an imitation of sound (e.g., *buzz, cuckoo*) —**on'o·mat'o·poe'ic, on'-o·mat'o·po·et'ic** /-pōe'tik/ *adj.* [Gk *onoma* name, *poiein* make]

on'rush' *n.* onward rush

on'screen' *adj. & adv.* within the range of a camera, etc., when being filmed

on'set' *n.* **1** attack **2** impetuous beginning

on'shore' *adj.* **1** on the shore **2** (of the wind) blowing landwards from the sea

on'side kick' *n. Football.* short kickoff in which the kicking team attempts recovery of the ball

on·slaught /ŏn'slôt', än'-/ *n.* fierce attack [Du, rel. to ON, *slag* blow]

On·tar·i·o /änter'ēŏ, -tar'-/ *n.* most populous province of Canada, N of the Great Lakes. Capital: Toronto. Pop. 10,746,000

On·tar'i·o, Lake' *n.* easternmost of the Great Lakes, between N.Y. and Ontario, Canada

on·to /ŏn'tŏŏ, än'-/ *prep.* **1** to a place or position on **2** *Colloq.* aware of

on·tog·e·ny /äntäj'ənē/ *n.* life cycle or development of a single organism

o·nus /ō'nəs/ *n.* (*pl.* **·nus·es**) *Latin.* burden; duty

on·ward /ŏn'wərd, än'-/ *adj. & adv.* (also **on'wards**) forward; advancing

on·yx /än'iks/ *n.* semiprecious variety of agate with colored layers [Gk *onyx* fingernail]

oo·dles /ŏŏd'lz/ *n. pl. Colloq.* great many; large amount

oops /ŏŏps, ŏŏps/ *interj. Colloq.* exclamation on making an obvious mistake

ooze[1] /ŏŏz/ *v.* (**oozed, ooz·ing**) **1** trickle or leak slowly out **2** exude —*n.* **3** sluggish flow —**ooz'y** *adj.* (**·i·er, ·i·est**) [OE]

ooze[2] *n.* wet mud; slime —**ooz'y** *adj.* [OE]

o·pal /ō'pəl/ *n.* iridescent mineral used as a gem —**o'pal·es'cent** /-es'ənt/ *adj.*; **o'pal·es'cence** *n.* [L]

o·paque /ōpāk'/ *adj.* (**·paqu·er, ·paqu·est**) **1** not transmitting light **2** impenetrable to sight **3** unintelligible; obscure **4** unintelligent; stupid —**o·pac'i·ty** /ōpas'ĭtē/, **o·paque'ly** *adv.*; **opaque'ness** *n.* [L *opacus* shaded]

op' art' /äp/ *n. Colloq.* art using contrasting colors, patterns, etc., to create optical illusions [abbr. for optical art]

op. cit. *abbr.* in the work already cited [L *opere citato*]

OPEC /ō'pek'/ *abbr.* Organization of Petroleum Exporting Countries

Op-Ed /äp'ed'/ *adj.* denoting a newspaper page that features commentary and opinion, etc. [Opposite the Editorial page]

o·pen /ō'pən/ *adj.* **1** not closed, locked, or blocked up; allowing access **2** unenclosed; unconfined (*the open road*) **3** uncovered; exposed (*open wound*) **4** undisguised; public (*open hostilities*) **5** unfolded; spread out (*the book was open*) **6** (of a fabric) with gaps **7** frank and communicative **8** accessible; ready **9a** willing to receive (*open to offers*) **b** available **c** vulnerable —*v.* **10** make or become open or more open **11** give access **12** start; begin; establish; set going —*n.* **13a** open space, country, or air **b** public notice; general attention —**o'pen·er, o'pen·ness** *n.*; **o'pen·ly** *adv.* [OE]

o'pen air' *n.* outdoors —**o'pen-air'** *adj.*

o'pen-and-shut' *adj.* straightforward

o'pen-end'ed *adj.* having no predetermined limit

o'pen-faced' *adj.* designating a sandwich with no covering slice of bread

o'pen-hand'ed *adj.* generous

o'pen-heart'ed *adj.* frank and kindly

o'pen-heart' sur'gery *n.* surgery with the heart exposed and the blood made to bypass it

o'pen house' *n.* reception welcoming visitors

o·pen·ing *n.* 1 gap 2 opportunity 3 beginning; initial part 4 job vacancy —*adj.* 5 initial; first

o·pen-mind'ed *adj.* accessible to new ideas

o'pen ques'tion *n.* undecided matter

o·pen·work *n.* surface or design with intervening spaces

op·er·a[1] /ˈäp(ə)rə/ *n.* drama set to music for singers and usu. orchestra —**op'er·at'ic** /-ratˈik/ *adj.*; **op'er·at'i·cal·ly** *adv.* [It fr. L: work]

o·pe·ra[2] /ˈōˈpärə, äpˈ-/ *n. pl.* of OPUS

op·er·a·ble /ˈäp(ə)rəbəl/ *adj.* 1 workable 2 treatable by surgery [L, rel. to OPERATE]

op'er·a glass'es *n. pl.* small binoculars for use at the theater, etc.

op·er·ate /ˈäpˈərät/ *v.* (·at·ed, ·at·ing) 1 work; control 2 be in action; function 3 perform a surgical or military operation 4 bring about [L *operari* work, rel. to OPUS]

op'er·at·ing sys'tem *n. Comp.* basic software that enables the running of a computer

op'er·a'tion *n.* 1 act, action, scope, or method of operating 2 active process 3 piece of work, esp. one in a series 4 act of surgery on a patient 5 military maneuver [L, rel. to OPERATE]

op'er·a'tion·al *adj.* 1 of or engaged in or used for operations 2 able or ready to function —**op'er·a'tion·al·ly** *adv.*

op·er·a·tive /ˈäˈp(ə)rətiv/ *adj.* 1 in operation; having effect 2 having the main relevance 3 of or by surgery —*n.* 4 detective; spy [L, rel. to OPERATE]

op'er·a'tor *n.* 1 person controlling a machine, etc. 2 person engaging in business *n. Colloq.* person skilled in a specified way (*smooth operator*)

op·er·et·ta /ˈäpˈəretˈə/ *n.* 1 light or humorous opera 2 one-act or short opera [It, dim. of OPERA[1]]

oph·thal·mic /ˈäfTHalˈmik/ *adj.* of or relating to the eye and its diseases [Gk *ophthalmos* eye]

oph·thal·mol·o·gy /ˈäfˈTHə(l)mälˈəjē, äpˈ-/ *n.* the study of the eye —**oph'thal·mol'o·gist** *n.*

o·pi·ate /ˈōˈpēət/ *adj.* 1 containing opium 2 narcotic; soporific —*n.* 3 drug containing opium 4 soothing influence [L, rel. to OPIUM]

o·pine /ōpīnˈ/ *v.* (·pined, ·pin·ing) hold or express as an opinion [L *opinari* believe]

o·pin·ion /əpinˈyən/ *n.* 1 unproven but probable belief 2 what one thinks about something 3 piece of professional advice [L, rel. to OPINE]

o·pin·ion·at·ed /əpinˈyənātˈəd/ *adj.* stubborn in one's opinions

o·pi·um /ˈōˈpēəm/ *n.* narcotic drug made from the juice of a certain poppy [L fr. Gk *opion*]

O·por·to /ōpôrtˈō/ *n.* (also **Pôr'to**) port in NW Portugal. Pop. 350,000

o·pos·sum /əpäsˈəm/ *n.* tree-dwelling American marsupial [Algonquian]

opp. *abbr.* opposite

Op·pen·heim·er /ˈäpˈənhīˈmər/, **J(ulius) Robert** 1904–67; US physicist

op·po·nent /əpōˈnənt/ *n.* person who opposes [L *opponere opposit-* set against]

op·por·tune /ˈäpˈərt(y)ōōnˈ/ *adj.* 1 well-chosen or especially favorable 2 well-timed [L *opportunus* (of the wind) towards the PORT[1]]

op·por·tu·nism /ˈäpˈərt(y)ōōˈnizˈəm/ *n.* adaptation to circumstances or opportunity, esp regardless of principle —**op'por·tun'ist** /-ist/ *n.*; **op'por·tu·nis'tic** *adj.*; **op'por·tu·nis'ti·cal·ly** *adv.*

op·por·tu·ni·ty /ˈäpˈərt(y)ōōˈnətē/ *n.* (*pl.* ·ties) favorable chance or opening offered by circumstances

op·pos·a·ble /əpōzˈəbəl/ *adj. Zool.* (of the thumb) capable of touching the other digits on the same hand

op·pose /əpōzˈ/ *v.* (·posed, ·pos·ing) 1 resist; argue or compete against 2 place in opposition or contrast —**op·pos'er** *n.* [L, rel. to OPPONENT]

op·po·site /ˈäpˈəzit/ *adj.* 1 facing; on the other side 2 contrary; diametrically different —*n.* 3 anything opposite —*adv.* 4 facing; on the other side —*prep.* 5 facing 6 in a complementary role to (another actor, etc.)

op'po·site num'ber *n.* person holding an equivalent position in another group, etc.

op'po·site sex' *n.* either sex in relation to the other

op·po·si·tion /ˈäpˈəziˈsHən/ *n.* 1 resistance; antagonism; hostility 2 contrast; antithesis 3a group or party of opponents or competitors b (*cap.*) political party opposed to that in office [L, rel. to POSITION]

op·press /əpresˈ/ *v.* 1 keep in subservience; govern; treat cruelly 2 weigh on the mind or spirit —**op·pres'sion** /-presHˈən/, **op·pres'sor** *n.* [L, rel. to PRESS[1]]

op·pres·sive /əpresˈiv/ *adj.* 1 harsh; tyrannical 2 uncomfortable —**op·pres'sive·ly** *adv.*; **op·pres'sive·ness** *n.*

op·pro·bri·ous /əprōˈbrēəs/ *adj.* very scornful; abusive

op·pro·bri·um /əprōˈbrēəm/ *n. Latin.* 1 disgrace 2 cause of this

opt /äpt/ *v.* 1 make a choice; decide 2 **opt out** (of) choose not to participate (in) [L *optare* choose]

op·tic /ˈäpˈtik/ *adj.* of the eye or sight [Gk *optikos* seen]

op'ti·cal *adj.* 1 of sight; visual 2 of or according to optics 3 aiding sight —**op'ti·cal·ly** *adv.*

op'ti·cal char'ac·ter rec·og·ni'tion *n. Comp.* scanning of written characters, esp. in printed text, for conversion to a digital file; *abbr.* OCR

op'ti·cal disk' *n. Comp.* data-storage disk read and recorded by laser

op'ti·cal fi'ber *n.* thin glass fiber that conducts light to carry signals

op'ti·cal il·lu'sion *n.* image that deceives the eye

op·ti·cian /äptisHˈən/ *n.* maker, seller, or prescriber of eyeglasses, contact lenses, etc.

op'tics *n. pl.* (treated as *sing.*) science of light and vision

op·ti·mal /ˈäpˈtəməl/ *adj.* best or most favorable [L *optimus* best]

op·ti·mism /ˈäpˈtəmizˈəm/ *n.* 1 inclination to hopefulness and confidence 2 *Philos.* belief that good must ultimately prevail over evil —**op'ti·mist** /-ist/ *n.*; **op'ti·mis'tic** *adj.*; **op'ti·mis'ti·cal·ly** /-tiklē/ *adv.* [L *optimus* best]

op·ti·mize /ˈäpˈtəmīz/ *v.* (·mized, ·miz·ing)

make the best or most effective use of —**op′ti·mi·za′tion** n.

op·ti·mum /äp′təməm/ n. (pl. **·mums** or **·ma** /-mə/) **1** most favorable conditions, solution, etc. —adj. **2** OPTIMAL [L, neut. of *optimus* best]

op·tion /äp′sHən/ n. **1a** choosing; choice **b** thing chosen **2** liberty to choose **3** right to buy or sell at a specified price within a set time [L, rel. to OPT]

op′tion·al adj. not obligatory —**op′tion·al·ly** adv.

op·tom·e·try /äptäm′ətrē/ n. science of detecting and correcting defects of vision —**op′tom′e·trist′** /-trist/ n.

op·u·lent /äp′yələnt/ adj. **1** wealthy **2** luxurious **3** abundant —**op′u·lence** n. [L *opes* wealth]

o·pus /ō′pəs/ n. (pl. **·pus·es** or **o·pe·ra**) composition or other artistic work, esp. one numbered as part of a composer's works [L: work]

or /ôr, ər/ conj. **1** introducing an alternative **2** introducing an alternative word or name **3** **or else: a** otherwise **b** Colloq. expressing a warning or threat (be good or else) [OE]

OR postal abbr. for Oregon

O.R. abbr. operating room

-or suffix forming nouns denoting esp. an agent (*actor; escalator*) or condition (*error; horror*) [L]

or·a·cle /ôr′ikəl, är′-/ n. **1a** place at which divine advice or prophecy was sought in classical antiquity **b** response given **c** prophet or prophetess at an oracle **2** source of wisdom, etc. —**or·ac·u·lar** /ôrak′yələr/ adj. [L *oraculum* fr. *orare* speak]

o·ral /ôr′əl, är′-/ adj. **1** by word of mouth; spoken, not written **2** done or taken by the mouth —**o′ral·ly** adv. [L *os oris* mouth]

O·ran /ôrän′/ n. seaport in NW Algeria. Pop. 628,600

or·ange /ôr′inj, är′inj/ n. **1a** round, reddishyellow, juicy citrus fruit **b** tree bearing this **2** its color —adj. **3** orange-colored [Ar *nāranj*]

Or·ange n. city in Calif. Pop. 110,658

o·rang·u·tan /əraNG′ətan′/ n. large, reddishhaired, long-armed, anthropoid ape of the E Indies [Malay: wild man]

O·ran·je·stad /ôrän′yəstäd′, -jəstäd′/ n. capital of Aruba. Pop. 19,800

o·rate /ôrāt′, ō-/ v. (**·rat·ed, ·rat·ing**) deliver an oration; speak pompously

o·ra′tion /ôrä′sHən/ n. formal or ceremonial speech [L *oratio* discourse, fr. *orare* speak; pray]

or·a·tor /ôr′ətər, är′-/ n. **1** person making a formal speech **2** eloquent public speaker [L, rel. to ORATION]

or·a·to·ri·o /ôr′ətôr′ē-ō′, är′-/ n. (pl. **·os**) semidramatic work for orchestra and voices, esp. on a sacred theme [It: small chapel]

or·a·to·ry /ôr′ətôr′ē/ n. (pl. **·ries**) art of or skill in public speaking —**or′a·tor′i·cal** adj. [Fr and L *oratorium* place of prayer]

orb /ôrb/ n. sphere; globe [L *orbis* ring]

or·bit /ôr′bit/ n. **1a** course of a planet, satellite, etc., around another body **b** one complete passage around a body **2** range or sphere of action —v. **3** move in orbit around **4** put into orbit —**or′bit·al** adj.; **or′bit·er** n. [L *orbitus* circular]

or·ca /ôr′kə/ n. any of various cetaceans, esp. the killer whale [L]

or·chard /ôr′CHərd/ n. piece of land with fruit trees [L *hortus* garden]

or·ches·tra /ôr′kəstrə, -kes′-/ n. **1** group of instrumentalists performing as a unit, typically combining strings, woodwinds, brass, and percussion **2** (in full **or′ches′tra pit′**) part (usu. in front of the stage) of a theater, etc., where the orchestra plays **3** main floor of seats in a theater, etc. —**or·ches′tral** adj. [Gk: area for the chorus in drama]

or·ches·trate /ôr′kəstrāt′/ v. (**·trat·ed, ·trat·ing**) **1** arrange or compose for an orchestra **2** arrange (elements) to achieve a desired result —**or′ches·tra′tion** n.

or·chid /ôr′kid/ n. any of various plants with brilliant flowers [Gk *orkhis* testicle, for shape of its roots]

or·dain /ôrdān′/ v. **1** confer priestly status on **2** decree; order [L *ordinare*, rel. to ORDER]

or·deal /ôrdēl′/ n. painful or horrific experience; severe trial [OE]

or·der /ôr′dər/ n. **1a** condition in which every part, unit, etc., is in its right place; tidiness **b** specified sequence, succession, etc. **2** authoritative command, direction, etc. **3** state of obedience to law, authority, etc. **4a** direction to supply or pay something **b** goods, etc., to be supplied **5** social class **6** kind; sort **7** constitution or nature of the world, society, etc. (*the order of things*) **8** taxonomic rank below a class and above a family **9** religious, social, or military fraternity or company **10** rank of the ordained Christian ministry **11** any of the classical styles of architecture **12** system of rules or procedure —v. **13** command; bid; prescribe **14** put in order; regulate **15 in order: a** in the correct sequence or position **b** fit for use **c** according to the rules of a meeting, etc. **16 in order that** so that **17 in order to** with the purpose of **18 on the order of** approximately **19 on order** ordered but not yet received **20 to order** as specified by the customer **21 out of order: a** not functioning **b** out of proper sequence or position **c** not according to the rules of a meeting, etc. [L *ordo ordin-* row, command, etc.]

or·der·ly /ôr′dərlē/ adj. **1** methodically arranged; tidy **2** well-behaved —n. (pl. **·lies**) **3** male attendant in a hospital **4** soldier who carries orders for an officer, etc. —**or′der·li·ness** n.

or·di·nal /ôrd′n-əl/ n. (in full **or′di·nal num′ber**) number defining position in a series, e.g., first, second, third, etc. [L, rel. to ORDER]

or·di·nance /ôrd′n-əns/ n. **1** decree **2** statute, esp. municipal [L, rel. to ORDAIN]

or·di·nar·y /ôrd′n-er′ē/ adj. **1** normal; usual **2** commonplace; unexceptional **3 out of the ordinary** unusual —**or′di·nar′i·ly** adv.; **or′di·nar′i·ness** n. [L, rel. to ORDER]

or·di·nate /ôrd′n-ət/ n. Math. coordinate measured usu. along the vertical or y-axis (see illustration at ABSCISSA) [L, rel. to ORDAIN]

or·di·na·tion /ôrd′n-ā′sHən/ n. conferring of priestly status

ord·nance /ôrd′n-əns/ n. artillery; military supplies [contr. of ORDINANCE]

or·dure /ôr′jər/ *n.* dung [L *horridus*, rel. to HORRID]

Or·dzho·ni·ki·dze /ôr′jän′ikid′zə/ *n.* (also **Vla′dikav′kaz**) city in Russia. Pop. 306,000

ore /ôr/ *n.* rock or mineral from which metal or other valuable minerals may be extracted [OE]

Ore. abbr. for Oregon

o·reg·a·no /əreg′ənō′/ *n.* dried wild marjoram as seasoning [Sp]

Or·e·gon /ôr′igən, är′-, -gän′/ *n.* NW state of the US. Capital: Salem. Pop. 2,842,321. Abbr. **OR; Ore.** —**Or·e·go·ni·an** /ôr′igō′nēən,är′-/ *n. & adj.*

Or′e·gon Trail′ *n.* 19th-century pioneers' route extending W 2,000 mi. from Independence, Mo., to Oregon

O·ren·burg /ôr′ənbərg, ōr′-/ *n.* city in W Russia. Pop. 556,500

-orexia *comb. form* desire; appetite [Gk]

or·gan /ôr′gən/ *n.* **1a** keyboard instrument producing sound by compressed air directed through tuned pipes or reeds **b** instrument producing similar sounds electronically **2** part of an animal or plant body serving a particular function **3** periodical publication, esp. of a group, party, etc. [Gk *organon* tool]

or·gan·dy or **or·gan·die** /ôr′gəndē/ *n.* (*pl.* **·dies**) fine translucent muslin, usu. stiffened [Fr]

or·gan·elle /ôr′gənel′/ *n. Biol.* specialized cell structure having a specific function

or·gan·ic /ôrgan′ik/ *adj.* **1** of or affecting a bodily organ or organs **2** relating to or derived from living organisms **3** produced without the use of artificial fertilizers, pesticides, etc. **4** (of a chemical compound) containing carbon **5** structural; inherent **6** organized; systematic —**or·gan′i·cal·ly** *adv.* [Gk, rel. to ORGAN]

or·gan·ism /ôr′gəniz′əm/ *n.* **1** individual plant or animal **2** any living being or system with interdependent parts [Fr, rel. to ORGANIZE]

or·gan·ist /ôr′gənist/ *n.* organ player

or·ga·ni·za·tion /ôr′gənizā′SHən/ *n.* **1** organizing or being organized **2** organized body, system, or society —**or′ga·ni·za′tion·al** *adj.*

or·gan·ize /ôr′gəniz′/ *v.* (**·ized, ·iz·ing**) **1** give an orderly structure to; systematize **2** initiate; arrange for **3a** enlist (a person or group) in a trade union, political party, etc. **b** form (a trade union, etc.) —**or′gan·iz′er** *n.* [L, rel. to ORGAN]

or′gan·ized crime′ *n.* established criminal hierarchy

or·gan·za /ôrgan′zə/ *n.* thin, stiff, transparent silk or synthetic fabric

or·gasm /ôr′gaz′əm/ *n.* climax of sexual excitement —**or·gas′mic** *adj.* [Gk: excitement]

or·gy /ôr′jē/ *n.* (*pl.* **-gies**) **1** wild party with open sexual activity **2** excessive indulgence in an activity —**or′gi·as′tic** /-as′tik/ *adj.* [Gk *orgia* secret rites]

o·ri·el /ôr′ēəl/ *n.* projecting window of an upper story [Fr]

o·ri·ent /ôr′ēənt, -ē-ent′/ *n.* **1** (*cap.*) Asia, esp. E Asia —*v.* (also **o·ri·en·tate** /ôr′ē-entāt′/) (**·tat·ed, ·tat·ing**) **2a** find the bearings of **b** direct **3** turn or place eastward or in a specified direction [L *oriens -entis* rising; sunrise; east]

o·ri·en·tal /ôr′ē-ent′l/ *adj.* **1** of the Orient —*n.* **2** *Derog.* person or people from the Orient

o·ri·en·ta·tion /ôr′ēəntā′SHən/ *n.* **1** orienting or being oriented **2a** relative position **b** person's attitude or adjustment **3** introduction; briefing —**o′ri·en·ta′tion·al** *adj.*

or·i·fice /ôr′əfis, är′-/ *n.* opening, esp. the mouth of a cavity [L *os or-* mouth, *facere* make]

orig. abbr. original; originally

o·ri·ga·mi /ôr′igäm′ē/ *n.* art of folding paper into decorative shapes [Japn]

or·i·gin /ôr′əjin, är′-/ *n.* **1** starting point; source **2** ancestry; parentage [L *origo orig-* fr. *oriri* rise]

o·rig·i·nal /ərij′ən-l/ *adj.* **1** existing from the beginning; earliest; innate **2** inventive; creative **3** not copied or translated —*n.* **4** original model, pattern, picture, etc., from which another is copied or translated —**o·rig′i·nal′i·ty** *n.*; **o·rig′i·nal·ly** *adv.*

o·rig·i·nate /ərij′ənāt′/ *v.* (**·nat·ed, ·nat·ing**) **1** cause to begin; initiate **2** have as an origin; begin —**o·rig′i·na′tion, o·rig′i·na′tor** *n.*

o·ri·ole /ôr′ē-ōl, -əl/ *n.* American bird with black and orange plumage in the male [L *aurum* gold]

Ork′ney Is′lands /ôrk′nē/ *n.* group of islands off the NE tip of Scotland

Or·lan·do /ôrlan′dō/ *n.* city in Fla., tourist center. Pop. 164,693

Or·lé·ans /ôrlā-än′/ *n.* city in central France. Pop. 108,000

Or·lon /ôr′län/ *n. Tdmk.* synthetic acrylic fiber

or·mo·lu /ôr′məlōō′/ *n.* **1** gilded bronze; gold-colored alloy **2** articles made of or decorated with ormolu [Fr *or moulu* powdered gold]

or·na·ment *n.* /ôr′nəmənt/ **1** thing used to adorn or decorate; decoration **2** quality or person bringing honor, distinction, credit, etc. —*v.* /-ment, -mənt/ **3** adorn; beautify —**or′na·men′tal** /-men′təl/ *adj.*; **or′na·men·ta′tion** /-məntā′SHən/ *n.* [L *ornare* adorn; equip]

or·nate /ôrnāt′/ *adj.* elaborately adorned; showy —**or·nate′ly** *adv.*; **or·nate′ness** *n.* [L, rel. to ORNAMENT]

or·ner·y /ôr′nərē/ *adj.* **1** unpleasant; nasty **2** stubborn —**or′ner·i·ness** *n.*

or·ni·thol·o·gy /ôr′nəTHäl′əjē/ *n.* the study of birds —**or′ni·tho·log′i·cal** /-äläj′ikəl/ *adj.*; **or′ni·thol′o·gist** *n.* [Gk *ornis ornith-* bird]

o·ro·tund /ôr′ətənd, är′-, -tənd/ *adj.* **1** (of the voice) round; imposing **2** pompous; pretentious [L *ore rotundo* with rounded mouth]

or·phan /ôr′fən/ *n.* **1** child whose parents are dead —*v.* **2** deprive of parents [Gk *orphanos*]

or·phan·age /ôr′fənij/ *n.* home for orphans

or·rer·y /ôr′ərē/ *n.* (*pl.* **·ies**) clockwork model of the solar system [for the Earl of *Orrery,* for whom first made]

ortho- *comb. form* **1** straight **2** right; correct [Gk *orthos* straight]

or·tho·don·tics /ôr′THədän′tiks/ *n. pl.*

(treated as *sing.*) correction of irregularities in the teeth and jaws —**or'tho·don'tic** *adj.*; **or'tho·don'tist** *n.* [Gk *odous odont-* tooth]

or·tho·dox /ôr'THədäks'/ *adj.* holding usual or established beliefs, esp. on religion, morals, etc.; conventional —**or'tho·dox'y** *n.* [L *doxa* opinion]

Or'tho·dox Church' *n.* Eastern Christian Church, including the national churches of Greece, Russia, etc.

or·thog·ra·phy /ôrTHäg'rəfē/ *n.* (*pl.* **·phies**) spelling, esp. as to correctness —**or'tho·graph'ic** /-THōgraf'ik/ *adj.* [Gk *orthographia*]

or·tho·pe·dics /ôr'THəpē'diks/ *n. pl.* (treated as *sing.*) (also **or·tho·pae'dics**) branch of medicine dealing with the correction of diseased, deformed, or injured bones or muscles —**or'tho·pe'dic** or **or'tho·pae'dic** *adj.*; **or'tho·pe'dist** or **or'tho·pae'dist** *n.* [ORTHO- + Gk *pais paid-* child]

or·thot·ics /ôrTHät'iks/ *n.* 1 *Med.* specialty that treats joint or muscle disorders using mechanical support, braces, etc. 2 devices, as inserts for athletic shoes, that provide such support

Or·well /ôr'wel', -wəl/, **George** (pseudonym of Eric Arthur Blair) 1903–50; British novelist and essayist

-ory *suffix* 1 forming nouns denoting a place (*dormitory*) 2 forming adjectives and nouns relating to or involving a verbal action (*accessory; compulsory*) [L *-orius, -orium*]

Os *symb.* osmium

OS *abbr.* 1 old style 2 Old Saxon

O·sa·ka /ōsäk'ə/ *n.* city in Japan, on Honshu. Pop. 2,613,200

os·cil·late /äs'əlāt'/ *v.* (**·lat·ed**, **·lat·ing**) 1 (cause to) swing to and fro 2 vacillate 3 *Sci.* undergo alternations between (extreme) values —**os'cil·la'tion, os'cil·la'tor** *n.* [L *oscillare* swing]

os·cil·lo·scope /əsil'əskōp'/ *n.* device for displaying oscillation in electrical current, etc.

os·cu·late /äs'kyəlāt'/ *v.* (**·lat·ed**, **·lat·ing**) kiss [L *osculum*]

-ose *suffix* denoting possession of a quality (*verbose*) [L *-osus*]

OSHA /ō'sHə/ *abbr.* Occupational Safety and Health Administration

Osh·a·wa /äsH'əwə, -wä', -wô'/ *n.* city in Ontario, Canada. Pop. 129,300

Osh·kosh /äsH'käsH/ *n.* city in Wis. Pop. 55,006

o·sier /ō'zHər/ *n.* willow used in basketwork [Fr]

O·si·ris /ōsī'ris/ *n. Egypt. Myth.* god associated with death, nature, and renewal

-osis *suffix* denoting a process or condition (*metamorphosis*), often a pathological state (*neurosis*) [L or Gk]

Os·lo /äz'lō, äs'-/ *n.* capital of Norway. Pop. 467,100

Os·man I /äz'mən, äs'-/ (also **Oth'man**) 1259–1326; Turkish conqueror, founder of the Ottoman dynasty and empire

os·mi·um /äz'mēəm/ *n.* heavy, hard, bluish-white metallic element; *symb.* **Os** [Gk *osmē* smell]

os·mo·sis /äzmō'sis, äs-/ *n.* 1 passage of a solvent through a semipermeable partition into another solution 2 absorption of influ-

ence, ideas, etc. —**os·mot'ic** /-mät'ik/ *adj.* [Gk *ōsmos* push]

os·prey /äs'prē, -prā'/ *n.* (*pl.* **·preys**) large bird of prey feeding on fish [L *ossifraga* fr. *os* bone, *frangere* break]

os·si·fy /äs'əfī'/ *v.* (**·fied**, **·fy·ing**) 1 turn into bone 2 make or become rigid; harden —**os'si·fi·ca'tion** /-fikā'sHən/ *n.* [L *os oss-* bone]

os·ten·si·ble /ästen'səbəl/ *adj.* apparent; professed —**os·ten'si·bly** *adv.* [L *ostendere ostens-* show]

os·ten·sive /ästen'siv/ *adj.* directly showing

os·ten·ta·tion /äs'tentāsHən/ *n.* pretentious display of wealth, etc. —**os'ten·ta'tious** *adj.*; **os'ten·ta'tious·ly** *adv.*

osteo- *comb. form* bone [Gk *osteon*]

os·te·o·ar·thri·tis /äs'tē·ō'ärTHrī'tis/ *n.* disease marked by degeneration of joint cartilage —**os'te·o·ar·thrit'ic** /-THrit'ik/ *adj.*

os·te·op·a·thy /äs'tē·äp'əTHē/ *n.* medical specialty providing treatment and therapy through manipulation of bones, muscles, etc. —**os'te·o·path** /äs'tēəpaTH'/ *n.*

os·te·o·po·ro·sis /äs'tē·ō'pərō'sis/ *n.* condition of brittle bones

os·tra·cize /äs'trəsīz'/ *v.* (**·cized**, **·ciz·ing**) banish; refuse to associate with —**os'tra·cism'** /-cizəm/ *n.* [Gk *ostrakon* potsherd, used in ancient Athens to record votes of banishment]

O·stra·va /ō'strəvə/ *n.* city in E Czech Republic. Pop. 327,600

os·trich /äs'triCH/ *n.* 1 large, swift-running, flightless bird of Africa and SW Asia 2 person who ignores an awkward truth [L *avis* bird, *struthio* (fr. Gk) ostrich]

Os·wald /äz'wôld', -wäld/, **Lee Harvey** 1939–63; accused assassin of US president John F. Kennedy

OT *abbr.* Old Testament

o.t. *abbr.* 1 occupational therapist; occupational therapy 2 overtime

OTB *abbr.* off-track betting

oth·er /əTH'ər/ *adj.* 1 not the same as one or some already mentioned or implied 2a further; additional; remaining (*see other side*) 2b second of two (*the other shoe*) —*adv.* 3 otherwise —*n.* or *pron.* 4 other person or thing 5 **other than** except; apart from [OE]

oth'er day' *n.* (also **oth'er night'**) (prec. by *the*) a few days (or nights) ago

oth·er·wise /əTH'ərwīz'/ *adv.* 1 or else; in different circumstances 2 in other respects 3 in a different way —*adj.* 4 different [OE, rel. to WISE²]

oth'er·world'ly *adj.* 1 of another world 2 dreamily distracted from mundane life

Oth·man /äTH'mən/ *see* OSMAN

o·ti·ose /ō'tēōs'/ *adj.* useless; futile [L *otium* leisure]

O·tis /ōt'əs/, **James** 1725–83; American Revolutionary War patriot

Ot·ta·wa /ät'əwə, -wä', -wô'/ *n.* capital city of Canada, in province of Ontario. Pop. 314,000

ot·ter /ät'ər/ *n.* 1 aquatic fish-eating mammal with webbed feet and thick brown fur 2 its fur [OE]

ot·to·man /ät'əmən/ *n.* (*pl.* **·mans**) upholstered seat without back or arms; footstool [Fr fr. Ar]

Oua·ga·dou·gou /wä′gədōō′gōō′/ *n.* capital of Burkina Faso. Pop. 441,500

ouch /ouCH/ *interj.* expression of sharp or sudden pain

ought /ôt/ *v. aux.* expressing duty; rightness; advisability; probability (*ought to do it; ought to see a dentist; it ought to rain soon*) [OE, past of OWE]

Oui·ja /wē′jə, -jē/ *n. Tdmk.* board game purporting to give advice, etc. [Fr *oui* yes, Ger *ja* yes]

Ouj·da /ōōzhdä′/ *n.* city in NE Morocco. Pop. 260,100

ounce /ouns/ *n.* 1 unit of weight, equal to 1/16 lb. (avoirdupois) or 1/12 lb. (troy) 2 fluid ounce, equal to 1/16 pint 3 very small quantity [L *uncia* twelfth part of a pound or a foot]

our /our, är/ *poss. pron.* of or belonging to us or society [OE]

ours /ourz, ärz/ *poss. pron.* the one or ones belonging to or associated with us

our·selves /our′selvz′, är-/ *pron.* 1a *emphat. form* of US (*we ourselves did it*) b *refl. form* of US (*we are pleased with ourselves*) 2 in our normal state of body or mind (*not quite ourselves today*)

-ous *suffix* forming adjectives meaning abounding in, characterized by, of the nature of (*envious; poisonous*) [AngFr *-ous*, fr. L *asus*]

oust /oust/ *v.* drive out or expel; dispossess [L *obstare* oppose]

oust′er *n.* expulsion

out /out/ *adv.* 1 away from or not in or at a place, etc. 2 indicating: a dispersal from a center, etc. b coming or bringing into the open (*bring out the best*) 3 not in one's house, office, etc. 4 to or at an end; completely (*tired out*) 5 (of a fire, candle, etc.) not burning 6 *Colloq.* unconscious 7 not in office, on the job, etc. 8 (of a product, etc.) available; on sale 9 no longer in fashion 10 *Baseball.* (of a batter or baserunner) having failed to reach base or advance home 11 not worth considering (*that idea is out*) 12 (of a mark, etc.) removed (*washed the stain out*) —*prep.* 13 out of (*looked out the window*) —*n.* 14 way of escape 15 *Baseball.* failure to reach or advance base —*v.* 16 come or go out; emerge 17 *Colloq.* reveal (a person) as a homosexual 18 **out for** intent on; determined to get 19 **out of:** a from within; from among b not within c beyond the range of (*out of reach*) d so as to be without; lacking (*out of luck*) e from (*get money out of him*) f because of (*asked out of curiosity*) 20 **out to** determined to [OE]

out- *prefix* 1 so as to surpass or exceed (*outdo*) 2 external; separate (*outline*) 3 out of; away from; outward (*outgrowth*)

out·age /out′ij/ *n.* period during which a power supply, etc., is not operating

out′-and-out′ *adj.* (also out′ and out′) 1 thorough; complete —*adv.* 2 thoroughly

out′back′ *n.* remote inland areas, esp. those of Australia

out′bal′ance *v.* (·anced, ·anc·ing) outweigh

out′bid′ *v.* (·bid, ·bid·ding) bid higher than

out′board′ mo′tor *n.* engine with propeller attached to the outside of a boat

out′break′ *n.* sudden eruption of anger, war, disease, fire, etc.

out′build′ing *n.* shed, barn, etc., detached from a main building

out′burst′ *n.* 1 verbal explosion of anger, etc. 2 bursting out

out′cast′ *n.* 1 person rejected by family or society —*adj.* 2 rejected

out′class′ *v.* surpass in quality

out′come′ *n.* result

out′crop′ *n.* (also **out′crop′ping**) 1a emergence of a stratum, etc., at a surface b stratum, etc., emerging 2 noticeable manifestation

out′cry′ *n.* (*pl.* ·cries) strong public protest

out′dat′ed *adj.* no longer fresh, current, etc.

out′dis′tance *v.* (·tanced, ·tanc·ing) leave (a competitor) behind completely

out′do′ *v.* (·did, ·done, ·do·ing) exceed; surpass

out′door′ *adj.* 1 done, existing, or used out of doors 2 fond of the open air (*an outdoor type*)

out′doors′ *adv.* 1 in or into the open air —*n.* 2 area outside of a building, esp. a natural area

out′er *adj.* 1 outside; external 2 farther from the center or the inside —**out′er·most** *adj.*

out′er space′ *n.* universe beyond the earth's atmosphere

out′field′ *n.* outer part of a baseball field —**out′field′er** *n.*

out′fit′ *n.* 1 set of clothes or equipment 2 *Colloq.* group of people regarded as an organization —*v.* (·fit·ted, ·fit·ting) 3 supply or furnish with an outfit —**out′fit′ter** *n.*

out′flank′ *v.* 1 extend beyond the flank of (an enemy) 2 outmaneuver; outwit

out′fox′ *v.* outwit

out′go′ing *adj.* 1 friendly 2 retiring from office 3 going out

out′grow′ *v.* (·grew, ·grow, ·grow·ing) 1 grow too big for 2 leave behind (a childish habit, etc.) 3 grow faster or taller than

out′growth′ *n.* 1 offshoot 2 natural product or development

out′house′ *n.* small building apart from a house used as a toilet

out′ing *n.* pleasure trip; excursion

out′land′ish *adj.* bizarre; strange —**out′land·ish·ly** *adv.*; **out′land′ish·ness** *n.* [OE, fr. *outland* foreign country]

out′last′ *v.* last longer than

out′law′ *n.* 1 fugitive from the law 2 *Hist.* person denied protection of the law —*v.* 3 declare or make illegal

out′lay′ *n.* expenditure

out′let *n.* 1 means of exit or escape 2 means of expressing feelings 3a market for goods b retail store 4 *Electr.* socket from which current may be taken to power appliances, etc.

out′line′ *n.* 1 rough draft 2 summary of main features 3 sketch consisting of only contour lines 4 (*sing.* or *pl.*) lines enclosing or indicating an object —*v.* (·lined, ·lin·ing) 5 draw or describe in outline 6 mark the outline of

out·live /out′liv′/ *v.* (·lived, ·liv·ing) 1 live longer than (a person) 2 live beyond (a period or date)

out·look *n.* 1 prospect; view 2 mental attitude

out·ly·ing *adj.* far from a center; remote

out·ma·neu·ver *v.* secure an advantage over by skillful maneuvering

out·match *v.* be superior to

out·mod·ed *adj.* outdated; out of fashion

out'-of-doors' *adj. & adv.* in or into the open air

out·pa·tient *n.* nonresident hospital patient

out·place·ment *n.* assistance in finding a new job after a layoff

out·post *n.* 1 detachment posted at a distance from an army 2 distant branch or settlement

out·put *n.* 1 amount produced (by a machine, worker, etc.) 2 power, etc., delivered by an apparatus 3 *Comp.* printout, results, etc. —*v.* (·put *or* ·put·ted, ·put·ting) 4 *Comp.* supply (results, etc.)

out·rage *n.* 1 extreme violation of others' rights, sentiments, etc. 2 gross offense or indignity 3 fierce resentment —*v.* (·raged, ·rag·ing) 4 subject to outrage 5 commit an outrage against [Fr *outrer* exceed, fr. L *ultra* beyond]

out·ra·geous / out'rā'jəs/ *adj.* 1 exceedingly shocking or offensive 2 grossly injurious —**out·ra·geous·ly** *adv.*

out·rank *v.* be superior in rank to

ou·tré /ōōtrā'/ *adj.* eccentric; unconventional [Fr, past part. of *outrer:* see OUTRAGE]

out·rid·er *n.* mounted rider ahead of or alongside a procession, etc.

OUTRIGGER 1

out·rig·ger /out'rig'ər/ *n.* 1 spar or framework with an attached float, projecting from the side of a boat or canoe to give stability 2 boat fitted with this

out·right' *adv.* 1 altogether; entirely 2 without reservation; openly —*adj.* 3 downright; complete 4 undisputed

out·run' *v.* (·ran, ·run, ·run·ning) 1 run faster or farther than 2 go beyond

out·sell' *v.* (·sold, ·sel·ling) 1 sell more than 2 be sold in greater quantities than

out·set' *n.* beginning

out·shine' *v.* (·shone, ·shin·ing) 1 shine brighter than 2 surpass

out·side' *n.* 1 external side or surface; outer parts 2 external appearance; outward aspect —*adj.* 3 of, on, or nearer the outside; outer 4 not belonging; not part of 5 remote; very unlikely (*outside chance*) 6 extreme (*outside price*) —*adv.* 7 on or to the outside 8 in or to the open air 9 not within, enclosed, or included —*prep.* 10 not in; to or at the exterior of 11 external to; not included in; beyond the limits of

out·sid·er *n.* nonmember of some group, or ganization, profession, etc.

out·size' *adj.* unusually large

out·skirts' *n. pl.* outer area of a town, etc.

out·smart' *v.* outwit; be cleverer than

out·source' *v.* (·sourced, ·sourc·ing) acquire from vendors or foreign sources —**out'sourc'ing** *n.*

out·spo·ken *adj.* saying openly what one thinks; frank —**out·spo·ken·ly** *adv.*; **out·spo·ken·ness** *n.*

out·spread' *adj.* spread out; expanded

out·stand·ing *adj.* 1 conspicuous because of excellence 2 not yet settled or dealt with —**out·stand·ing·ly** *adv.*

out·sta·tion *n.* remote branch or outpost

out·strip' *v.* (·stripped, ·strip·ping) 1 go faster than 2 surpass, esp. competitively

out·take' *n.* film or tape sequence rejected in editing

out·vote' *v.* (·vot·ed, ·vot·ing) defeat by a majority of votes

out·ward /out'wərd/ *adj.* 1 situated on or directed toward the outside 2 going out 3 bodily; external; apparent —*adv.* (also **out'wards**) 4 in an outward direction —**out'ward·ly** *adv.* [OE, rel. to OUT-, -WARD]

out·weigh' *v.* exceed in weight, value, importance, or influence

out·wit' *v.* (·wit·ted, ·wit·ting) overcome by greater cleverness

o·va /ō'və/ *n. pl.* of OVUM

o·val /ō'vəl/ *adj.* 1 egg-shaped; ellipsoidal; elliptical —*n.* 2 egg-shaped or elliptical closed curve [L, rel. to OVUM]

o·va·ry /ō'vərē/ *n.* (*pl.* ·ries) 1 each of the female reproductive organs in which ova are produced 2 hollow base of the carpel of a flower —**o·var·i·an** /-var'ē·ən/ *adj.*

o·va·tion /ōvā'SHən/ *n.* enthusiastic reception, esp. applause [L *ovare* exult]

ov·en /əv'ən/ *n.* enclosed compartment for heating or cooking food, etc. [OE]

o·ver /ō'vər/ *adv.* expressing movement, position, or state above or beyond something stated or implied: 1 outward and downward from an edge or an erect position (*knocked me over*) 2 so as to cover or touch a whole surface (*paint over*) 3 so as to produce a fold or reverse position (*fold over*) 4a across a street or other space **b** for a visit, etc. (*invited them over*) 5 with change from one hand, part, etc., to another (*went over to the enemy*) 6 with motion above something; so as to pass across something (*climb over; fly over*) 7a from beginning to end (*think it over*) **b** again (*do it over*) 8 in excess; in addition (*left over*) 9 for or until a later time (*hold it over*) 10 at an end; settled; (*game is all over*) —*prep.* 11 above, in, or to a position higher than 12 out and down from; down from the edge of (*over the cliff*) 13 so as to cover 14 above and across (*flew right over us*) 15 concerning (*laughed over it*) 16a superior to; in charge of **b** in preference to 17 so as to deal with completely (*went over the plans*) 18 during (*over the years*) 19 beyond; more than (*over the limit*) —*adj.* 20 upper; outer 21 superior 22 extra 23 over **against** in contrast with 24 over and over repeatedly [OE]

over- *prefix* **1** excessively (*overuse*) **2** above; upper; outer (*overhead*) **3** across; beyond (*overdo*)

o'ver·a·chieve' *v.* (·**chieved**, ·**chiev·ing**) **1** perform beyond expectations **2** push oneself to unreasonable expectations —**o'ver·a·chieve'ment**, **o'ver·a·chiev'er** *n.*

o'ver·act' *v.* act in an exaggerated manner

o·ver·all *adj.* /ō'vərôl/ **1** total; inclusive of all (*overall cost*) **2** taking everything into account; general —*adv.* /ō'vərôl'/ **3** including everything **4** on the whole; generally —*n.* /ō'vərôl'/ **5** (*pl.*) protective loose trousers having a bib and shoulder straps

o'ver·arm' *adj.* done or made with the arm above the shoulder

o'ver·awe' *v.* (·**awed**, ·**aw·ing**) overcome with awe

o'ver·bal'ance *v.* (·**anced**, ·**anc·ing**) **1** lose balance and fall **2** cause to do this

o'ver·bear'ing *adj.* **1** domineering; bullying **2** overpowering

o'ver·bite' *n.* condition in which teeth of the upper jaw project forward over the lower ones

o·ver·blown /ō'vərblōn'/ *adj.* inflated or pretentious

o'ver·board' *adv.* **1** from a ship into the water (*fall overboard*) **2** behave immoderately **3 go overboard** *Colloq.* be highly enthusiastic

o'ver·book' *v.* make too many bookings for (an aircraft, hotel, etc.)

o'ver·came' *v.* *past* of **OVERCOME**

o'ver·cast' *adj.* covered with cloud

o·ver·charge *v.* /ō'vərCHärj'/ (·**charged**, ·**charg·ing**) **1** charge or load excessively —*n.* /ō'vərCHärj'/ **2** excessive charge or load

o'ver·coat' *n.* warm outdoor coat

o'ver·come' *v.* (·**came**, ·**come**, ·**com·ing**) **1** prevail over; master **2** make faint, weak, or helpless

o'ver·de·vel'op *v.* **1** develop too much **2** *Photog.* treat with developer for longer than normal

o'ver·do' *v.* (·**did**, ·**done**, ·**do·ing**) **1** carry to excess; go too far **2** overcook **3** *Colloq.* exhaust oneself

o·ver·dose *n.* /ō'vərdōs'/ **1** excessive dose of a drug, etc. —*v.* /ō'vərdōs'/ (·**dosed**, ·**dos·ing**) **2** suffer an overdose

o'ver·draft' *n.* **1** overdrawing of a bank account **2** amount by which an account is overdrawn

o'ver·draw' *v.* (·**drew**, ·**drawn**, ·**draw·ing**) draw more from (a bank account) than the amount credited

o'ver·drive' *n.* **1** gear above top gear for economy at high speeds **2** state of high activity

o'ver·dub' *v.* (·**dubbed**, ·**dub·bing**) **1** superimpose one recording over another —*n.* **2** recording so made

o'ver·due' *adj.* past the due time for payment, arrival, return, etc.

o·ver·es'ti·mate *v.* /ō'vəres'təmāt'/ (·**mat·ed**, ·**mat·ing**) **1** form too high an estimate of —*n.* /·mit/ **2** too high an estimate —**o'ver·es'ti·ma'tion** *n.*

o'ver·ex·pose' *v.* (·**posed**, ·**pos·ing**) **1** expose too much to the public **2** expose (film) too long —**o'ver·ex·po'sure** /·pōZHər/ *n.*

o·ver·flow *v.* /ō'vərflō'/ **1** flow over (the brim, etc.) **2** be filled beyond capacity **3** flood; flow out **4** be very abundant —*n.* /ō'vərflō'/ **5** what overflows or is superfluous **6** outlet for excess water, etc.

o'ver·grown' *adj.* **1** grown too big **2** wild; covered with weeds, etc. —**o'ver·grow'** *v.* (·**grew**, ·**grown**, ·**grow·ing**); **o'ver·growth'** *n.*

o'ver·hand' *adj.* with the arm moving above the shoulder (*throw overhand*)

o·ver·hang *v.* /ō'vərhaNG'/ (·**hung**, ·**hang·ing**) **1** project or hang over —*n.* /ō'vərhaNG'/ **2** projection over **3** projecting part

o·ver·haul *v.* /ō'vərhôl'/ **1** thoroughly examine and repair as necessary **2** overtake —*n.* /ō'vərhôl'/ **3** thorough examination and repair

o·ver·head /ō'vərhed'/ *adv.* **1** above head height **2** in the sky —*adj.* **3** placed overhead —*n.* /ō'vərhed'/ **4** routine, continuing expenses of a business

o'ver·hear' *v.* (·**heard**, ·**hear·ing**) hear unintentionally or as an eavesdropper

o·ver·joyed /ō'vərjoid'/ *adj.* filled with great joy

o'ver·kill' *n.* **1** excess of capacity to kill or destroy **2** excess

o·ver·land /ō'vərland', ·lənd/ *adj. & adv.* by land

O·ver·land Park /ō'vərland' pärk', ·lənd/ *n.* city in Kan. Pop. 111,790

o'ver·a·bun'dance *n.*	**o'ver·en·thu'si·asm** *n.*
o'ver·a·bun'dant *adj.*	**o'ver·en·thu'si·as'tic** *adj.*
o'ver·ac'tive *adj.*	**o'ver·en·thu'si·as'ti·cal·ly** *adv.*
o'ver·am·bi'tious *adj.*	**o'ver·ex·cite'** *v.*
o'ver·anx'ious *adj.*	**o'ver·ex·cite'ment** *n.*
o'ver·bur'den *v.*	**o'ver·ex'er·cise'** *v.*
o'ver·cau'tious *adj.*	**o'ver·ex·ert'** *v.*
o'ver·con'fi·dent *adj.*	**o'ver·ex·er'tion** *n.*
o'ver·cook' *v.*	**o'ver·ex·tend'** *v.*
o'ver·crit'i·cal *adj.*	**o'ver·feed'** *v.*
o'ver·crowd' *v.*	**o'ver·fond'** *adj.*
o'ver·crowd'ed *adj.*	**o'ver·full'** *adj.*
o'ver·crowd'ing *n.*	**o'ver·gen'er·ous** *adj.*
o'ver·ea'ger *adj.*	**o'ver·heat'** *v.*
o'ver·eat' *v.*	**o'ver·in·dulge'** *v.*
o'ver·em'pha·size' *v.*	

o'ver·in·dul'gence *n.*	**o'ver·sen'si·tive** *adj.*
o'ver·in·dul'gent *adj.*	**o'ver·sen'si·tive·ness** *n.*
o'ver·large' *adj.*	**o'ver·sen'si·tiv'i·ty** *n.*
o'ver·load' *v.*	**o'ver·size'** *adj.*
o'ver·long' *adj. & adv.*	**o'ver·spe'cial·i·za'tion** *n.*
o'ver·par·tic'u·lar *adj.*	**o'ver·spe'cial·ize** *v.*
o'ver·pay' *v.*	**o'ver·spend'** *v.*
o'ver·pop'u·late' *v.*	**o'ver·spill'** *n. & v.*
o'ver·pop'u·lat'ed *adj.*	**o'ver·spread'** *v.*
o'ver·pop'u·la'tion *n.*	**o'ver·stim'u·late'** *v.*
o'ver·pro·tec'tive *adj.*	**o'ver·stock'** *v.*
o'ver·re·fined' *adj.*	**o'ver·strain'** *v.*
o'ver·ripe' *adj.*	**o'ver·strict'** *adj.*
o'ver·sell' *v.*	**o'ver·sup·ply'** *n.*
	o'ver·tire' *v.*
	o'ver·wind' *v.*

o·ver·lap v. /ō'vərlap'/ (-lapped, ·lap·ping) 1 (cause to) partly cover and extend beyond 2 partly coincide —n. /ō'vərlap'/ 3 extension over 4 extending part or amount

o·ver·lay v. /ō'vərlā'/ (-laid, ·lay·ing) 1 lay over 2 cover, as with a coating, etc. —n. /ō'vərlā/ 3 thing put over another

o·ver·leaf' adv. on the other side of the leaf of a book

o·ver·look' v. 1 fail to notice; tolerate 2 have a view of from above 3 supervise

o·ver·lord' n. supreme lord

o·ver·ly adv. excessively; too

o·ver·mas'ter v. overcome

o·ver·much' adj. 1 to too great an extent —adj. 2 excessive

o·ver·night' adv. /ō'vərnīt'/ 1 for or during the night 2 instantly; suddenly —adj. /ō'vərnīt'/ 3 done or for use overnight 4 instant

o·ver·pass' n. road or railway line that passes over another by means of a bridge

o·ver·play v. 1 give undue importance to; overemphasize 2 **overplay one's hand** act on an unduly optimistic estimation of one's chances

o·ver·pop·u·lat'ed adj. having too large a population —o'ver·pop·u·la'tion n.

o·ver·pow'er v. 1 subdue; conquer; overwhelm —o'ver·pow'er·ing adj.; o'ver·pow'er·ing·ly adv.

o·ver·price' v. (-priced, ·pric·ing) price too highly

o·ver·print v. /ō'vərprint'/ 1 print over (a surface already printed) —n. /ō'vərprint'/ 2 words, etc., overprinted

o·ver·pro·duce' v. (-duced, ·duc·ing) 1 produce more of (a commodity) than is wanted 2 produce (a play, recording, etc.) to an excessive degree —o'ver·pro·duc'tion /-dək'-SHən/ n.

o·ver·qual'i·fied adj. too highly qualified for a particular job, etc.

o·ver·rate' v. (-rat·ed, ·rat·ing) assess or value too highly

o·ver·reach' v. 1 reach past or beyond 2 **overreach oneself** fail by attempting too much —o'ver·reach'ing adj.

o·ver·re·act' v. respond more forcibly or emotionally than is justified —o'ver·re·ac'tion /-ak'SHən/ n.

o·ver·ride v. /ō'vərīd'/ (-rode, ·rid·den, ·rid·ing) 1a intervene and make ineffective b interrupt the action of, esp. to take manual control of an automatic device —n. /ō'vərīd'/ 2 suspension of an automatic function 3 device for this

o·ver·rule' v. (-ruled, ·rul·ing) set aside (a decision, etc.) made by a lesser authority

o·ver·run' v. (-ran, -run, ·run·ning) 1 swarm or spread over 2 conquer by force 3 exceed stated limits —n. /ō'vərən/ 4 excess of produced items

o·ver·seas' adv. 1 across the sea; abroad —adj. 2 of places across the sea; foreign

o·ver·see' v. (-saw, -seen, ·see·ing) officially supervise; superintend —o'ver·se'er /-sē'ər, -sēr/ n.

o·ver·shad·ow v. 1 appear much more prominent or important than 2 cast into the shade

o·ver·shoe' n. outer protective shoe worn over an ordinary one

o·ver·shoot' v. (-shot, ·shoot·ing) pass, send, or extend beyond

o·ver·sight' n. 1 failure to do or notice something 2 inadvertent mistake 3 supervision

o·ver·sim'pli·fy v. (-fied, ·fy·ing) distort (a problem, etc.) by stating it in too simple terms —o'ver·sim'pli·fi·ca'tion /-fikā'SHən/ n.

o·ver·size' adj. (also ·sized') of greater than the usual size

o·ver·sleep' v. (-slept, ·sleep·ing) sleep beyond the intended time of waking

o·ver·spe'cial·ize v. (-ized, ·iz·ing) concentrate too much on one aspect or area —o'ver·spe'cial·i·za'tion n.

o·ver·state' v. (-stat·ed, ·stat·ing) 1 assert too strongly 2 exaggerate —o'ver·state'ment n.

o·ver·stay' v. stay longer than wanted

o·ver·steer n. /ō'vərster'/ 1 tendency of a vehicle to turn more sharply than was intended —v. /ō'vərstēr'/ 2 (of a vehicle) exhibit oversteer

o·ver·step' v. (-stepped, ·step·ping) pass beyond (a permitted or acceptable limit)

o·ver·strung' adj. too tense or highly strung

o·ver·stuffed' adj. 1 (of furniture) made soft and comfortable by thick upholstery 2 stuffed too full

o·vert /ōvərt'/ adj. done openly; unconcealed —o·vert'ly adv. [Fr, past part. of ouvrir open]

o·ver·take' v. (-took, ·tak·en, ·tak·ing) 1 catch up with and pass 2 come suddenly upon

o·ver·tax' v. 1 make excessive demands on 2 tax too heavily

o·ver-the-count'er adj. 1 available for purchase without a prescription 2 designating stocks, etc., that may be sold directly to buyers

o·ver-the-top' adj. Colloq. excessive

o·ver·throw v. /ō'vərTHrō'/ (-threw, ·thrown, ·throw·ing) 1 remove forcibly from power 2 conquer; overcome —n. /ō'vərTHrō'/ 3 defeat; downfall

o·ver·time n. 1 time worked in addition to regular hours 2 payment for this —adv. 3 in addition to regular hours

o·ver·tone' n. 1 Mus. any of the tones above the lowest in a harmonic series 2 subtle extra quality or implication

o·ver·ture /ō'və(r)CHOŏr'/ n. 1 orchestral piece opening an opera, etc. 2 (usu. pl.) a opening of negotiations b formal proposal or offer [Fr, rel. to OVERT]

o·ver·turn' v. 1 (cause to) fall down or over 2 reverse; overthrow

o·ver·use v. /ō'vər-yōōz'/ (-used, ·us·ing) 1 use too much —n. /ō'vər-yōōs'/ 2 excessive use

o·ver·view' n. general survey

o·ver·weight' adj. above an allowed or suitable weight

o·ver·whelm' v. 1 overpower with emotion, burden, force, etc. 2 bury or drown beneath a huge mass —o'ver·whelm'ing adj.; o'ver·whelm'ing·ly adv.

o·ver·work v. /ō'vərwərk'/ 1 (cause to) work too hard 2 weary or exhaust with too much work —n. /ō'vərwərk'/ 3 excessive work

o·ver·wrought adj. /ō'vər-rôt'/ adj. 1 overexcited; nervous; distraught 2 too elaborate

ovi- *comb. form* egg; ovum [fr. OVUM]

Ov·id /äv'id/ (**Pub'lius Ovid'ius Na'so**) 43 B.C. – c. A.D. 17; Roman poet

o·vi·duct /ō'vidəkt'/ *n.* tube through which an ovum passes from the ovary

O·vi·e·do /ō'vēä'dō/ *n.* city in NW Spain. Pop. 194,900

o·vine /ō'vīn/ *adj.* of or like sheep [L *ovis* sheep]

o·vip·a·rous /ōvip'ərəs/ *adj.* producing young from eggs hatching after leaving the body [fr. OVUM, L *-parus* bearing]

o·void /ō'void/ *adj.* egg-shaped [rel. to OVUM]

ov·u·late /äv'yəlāt/ *v.* (**·lat·ed, ·lat·ing**) produce ova or ovules, or discharge them from the ovary —**ov'u·la'tion** *n.* [rel. to OVUM]

ov·ule /äv'yōōl'/ *n.* structure that contains the germ cell in a female plant —**ov'u·lar** *adj.* [rel. to OVUM]

o·vum /ō'vəm/ *n.* (*pl.* **o·va**) female egg cell [L: egg]

ow /ou/ *interj.* expression of sudden pain

owe /ō/ *v.* (**owed, ow·ing**) **1** be under obligation; be in debt **2** have a duty to render **3** be indebted (to a person or thing) for [OE]

Ow·en /ō'ən/ **1 Wilfred** 1893–1918; English poet **2 David** 1938– ; British politician

Ow·ens /ō'ənz/, **Jesse** (born **James Cleveland Owens**) 1913–80; US Olympic athlete

ow·ing /ō'iNG/ *adj.* **1** owed; yet to be paid **2** (foll. by *to*) a caused by b because of

owl /oul/ *n.* **1** nocturnal bird of prey with large eyes and a hooked beak **2** solemn or wise-looking person —**owl'ish** *adj.* [OE]

owl'et *n.* small or young owl

own /ōn/ *adj.* **1** belonging to oneself or itself **2** individual; peculiar; particular —*v.* **3** have as property; possess **4** admit as valid, true, etc. **5** acknowledge **6** confess **7** hold one's own maintain one's position **8** on one's own alone; independently **9** own up confess frankly —**owned** *adj.*; **own'er, own'er·ship'** *n.* [OE]

ox /äks/ *n.* (*pl.* **ox·en** /äk'sin/) **1** large, usu. horned, ruminant used esp. as a draft animal **2** castrated male of a domesticated species of cattle [OE]

ox·bow /äks'bō'/ *n.* **1** loop formed by a horseshoe bend in a river **2** lower, looped part of an ox yoke

ox·ford /äks'fərd/ *n.* **1** (in full **ox'ford cloth'**) cotton fabric used for shirts, etc. **2** (in full **ox'ford shoe'**) low shoe laced at the instep

Ox·ford /äks'fərd/ *n.* city in S England; site of Oxford University. Pop. 119,900

ox·i·da·tion /äk'sədā'sHən/ *n.* process of oxidizing [Fr, rel. to OXIDE]

ox·ide /äk'sīd'/ *n.* binary compound of oxygen [Fr, rel. to OXYGEN]

ox·i·dize /äk'sədīz/ *v.* (**·dized, ·diz·ing**) combine with oxygen, as in burning or rusting —**ox'i·di·za'tion, ox'i·diz'er** *n.*

Ox·nard /äks'närd/ *n.* city in Calif. Pop. 142,216

ox·y·a·cet·y·lene /äk'sēəset'l-ēn'/ *adj.* of or using a mixture of oxygen and acetylene, esp. in a torch for cutting or welding metals

ox·y·gen /äk'sijən/ *n.* tasteless, odorless, gaseous element essential to plant and animal life; *symb.* O [Fr fr. Gk *oxys* sharp (because it was thought to occur in all acids) + -GEN]

ox·y·gen·ate *v.* (**·at·ed, ·at·ing**) supply, treat, or mix with oxygen; oxidize —**ox'y·gen·a'tion** *n.*

ox'y·gen tent' *n.* tentlike enclosure supplying a patient with air rich in oxygen

ox·y·mo·ron /äk'səmôr'än'/ *n.* (*pl.* **·mo·ra** /-môr'ə/ or **·rons**) figure of speech in which apparently contradictory terms appear in conjunction (*make haste slowly*) [Gk: pointedly foolish, fr. *oxys* sharp, *mōros* dull]

oys·ter /oi'stər/ *n.* bivalve mollusk, esp. an edible kind, sometimes producing a pearl [Gk *ostreon*]

oz. *abbr.* ounce(s) [It *onza* ounce]

O·zarks, the /ō'zärks'/ *n.* range of low peaks in S central US

o·zone /ō'zōn'/ *n.* **1** *Chem.* unstable form of oxygen with three atoms in a molecule, having a pungent odor **2** *Colloq.* a invigorating air b exhilarating influence [Gk *ozein* smell (v.)]

o'zone-friend'ly *adj.* not containing chemicals destructive to the ozone layer

o'zone lay'er *n.* layer of ozone concentration in the stratosphere that absorbs most of the sun's ultraviolet radiation

---

P

---

p, P /pē/ *n.* (*pl.* **p's; P's, Ps**) sixteenth letter of the English alphabet; a consonant

p or **p.** *abbr.* **1** after [L *post*] **2** father [L *pater*] **3** page **4** part **5** participal **6** past **7** pastor **8** *Chess.* pawn **9** penny **10** per **11** *Mus.* softly [It *piano*] **12** pint **13** pipe **14** *Baseball.* pitcher **15** poor **16** post **17** president **18** pressure **19** progressive

P or **P.** *abbr.* **1** Protestant **2** pass; passing grade **3** (as P) *symb.* phosphorus

pa /pä/ *n. Colloq.* father [abbr. of PAPA]

Pa *symb.* protactinium

PA *abbr.* public address (system)

PA, Pa. *abbr.* Pennsylvania (postal abbr. PA)

p.a. *abbr.* per annum

PAC /pak/ *abbr.* political action committee

pace /pās/ *n.* **1a** single step in walking or running b distance covered in this **2** speed in walking or running **3** rate of movement or progression **4** gait —*v.* (**paced, pac·ing**) **5a** walk slowly and evenly b (of a horse) amble **6** traverse or measure by pacing **7** set the pace for **8** keep pace advance at an equal rate (to) **9** put (one) through (one's) paces test qualities, skills, etc. [Fr *pas* fr. L *passus*]

pace'mak'er *n.* **1** competitor who sets the

pace in a race 2 surgically implanted electronic mechanism that regulates heartbeat

pace′set′ter n. 1 leader 2 PACEMAKER, 1

Pa·chu·ca /pəchōō′ka/ n. capital of the Mexican state of Hidalgo. Pop. 179,400

pach·y·derm /pak′idərm′/ n. thick-skinned mammal, esp. an elephant or rhinoceros —**pach′y·der′ma·tous** /-mətəs/ adj. [Gk pakhys thick, derma skin]

pa·cif·ic /pəsif′ik/ adj. peaceful; tranquil

Pa·cif′ic O′cean n. ocean separating Americas from Asia and Australia; area approx. 70,000,000 sq. mi.

Pa·cif′ic Rim′ n. the Pacific coastal regions of N and S America, Asia, and Australia

pac·i·fi·er /pas′əfi′ər/ n. 1 person or thing that pacifies 2 nipple-shaped device for soothing a baby

pac·i·fism /pas′əfiz′əm/ n. belief that war and violence are morally unjustifiable —**pac′i·fist** /-fist/ n. & adj.

pac·i·fy /pas′əfi′/ v. (·fied, ·fy·ing) 1 appease 2 bring (a country, etc.) to a state of peace —**pac′i·fi·ca′tion** /-fika″shən/ n. [L pax pacis peace + -FY]

pack[1] /pak/ n. 1a collection of things wrapped up or tied together for carrying b BACKPACK 2 set of packaged items, as playing cards, cigarettes, etc. 3 group or collection, esp. a group of wild animals —v. 4a fill (a suitcase, bag, etc.) with clothes, etc. b put (things) in a bag or suitcase 5 crowd or cram; fill tightly (room was packed; crowds packed the streets) 6 cover (a thing) with packaging 7 be capable of delivering with force 8 form a pack —adj. 9 used to carry packs (pack mule) 10 **pack in** Colloq. stop; give up 11 **send packing** Colloq. dismiss summarily —**pack′er** n. [LGer or Du]

pack[2] v. select (a jury, etc.) or fill (a meeting) so as to secure a decision in one's favor [prob. fr. PACT]

pack·age /pak′ij/ n. 1a bundle of things packed b parcel, box, etc., in which things are packed 2 (in full **pack′age deal′**) set of proposals or items offered or agreed to as a whole —v. (·aged, ·ag·ing) 3 make up into or enclose in a package —**pack′ag·er, pack′ag·ing** n.

pack′age store′ n. retail store selling alcoholic beverages in sealed containers

pack′ag·ing n. 1 wrapping or container for goods 2 process of packing goods

pack·et /pak′it/ n. 1 small package 2 (in full **pack′et-boat′**) Hist. mail boat or passenger ship

pack′ ice′ n. crowded, floating ice in the sea

pack′ing n. material used to pack esp. fragile articles

pack′ing house′ n. factory where meat is processed or packed for sale

pact /pakt/ n. agreement; treaty [L pactum]

pad[1] /pad/ n. 1 thick piece of soft material used to protect, fill out hollows, hold or absorb liquid, etc. 2 sheets of writing paper fastened together at one edge 3 fleshy underpart of an animal's foot or of a human finger 4 flat surface for helicopter or rocket takeoff or launching 5 Slang. lodgings, apartment, etc. 6 floating leaf of a water lily —v. (pad·ded, pad·ding) 7 provide with a pad or padding; stuff

8 lengthen or fill out with unnecessary or extraneous material [prob. LGer or Du]

pad[2] v. (pad·ded, pad·ding) 1 walk with a soft, dull, steady step —n. 2 sound of soft, steady steps [LGer pad PATH]

Pa·dang /päd′äNG′/ n. seaport in Indonesia, on Sumatra. Pop. 480,900

pad′ding n. soft material used to pad or stuff

pad·dle /pad′l/ n. 1 short, broad-bladed oar 2 any paddle-shaped instrument or implement —v. (·dled, ·dling) 3 move on water or propel a boat by paddles 4 beat or spank with or as with a paddle

PADDLE WHEEL

pad′dle wheel′ n. wheel with radiating paddles around it for propelling a ship

pad·dock /pad′ək/ n. 1 small field, esp. for keeping horses in 2 turf enclosure at a racetrack [OE pearroc enclosure]

pad·dy /pad′ē/ n. (pl. ·dies) field where rice is grown [Malay]

pad′dy wag′on n. Colloq. police van for transporting those under arrest [fr. patrol wagon]

Pa·de·rew·ski /pad′əref′skē, -rev′-/, Ignace 1860–1941; Polish pianist and statesman

pad′lock′ n. 1 detachable lock hanging by a pivoted hook on the object fastened —v. 2 secure with a padlock

pa·dre /pä′drā/ n. 1 priest in Spain, Italy, etc. 2 chaplain [It, Sp, and Port: father; priest]

Pad·u·a /paj′əwə/ n. city in NE Italy. Pop. 218,200

pae·an /pē′ən/ n. song of praise or triumph [L fr. Gk]

pa·el·la /pī-el′ə, pä-ā′(y)ə/ n. Spanish dish of rice, saffron, chicken, seafood, etc. [Sp fr. Catalan: pan]

pa·gan /pā′gən/ n. 1 nonreligious person, pantheist, or heathen —adj. 2a of pagans b irreligious 3 pantheistic —**pa′gan·ism** n. [L paganus fr. pagus country district]

Pa·ga·ni·ni /pag′ənē′nē/, Nicolò 1782–1840; Italian violinist and composer

page[1] /pāj/ n. 1a leaf of a book, periodical, etc. b each side of this 2 episode; memorable event —v. (paged, pag·ing) 3 PAGINATE [L pagina]

page[2] n. 1 person employed to run errands, attend to a door, etc. —v. (paged, pag·ing) 2 summon, esp. by making an announcement 3 summon by pager [Fr]

pag·eant /paj′ənt/ n. 1 brilliant spectacle, esp. an elaborate parade 2 spectacular procession or play illustrating historical events

pag·eant·ry /paj′əntrē/ n. spectacular show; pomp

pag·er /pāj′ər/ *n.* beeping radio device, signaling its wearer to the telephone, etc.

pag·i·nate /paj′ənāt′/ *v.* (-nat·ed, -nat·ing) assign numbers to the pages of (a book, etc.) —**pag′i·na′tion** *n.* [L, rel. to PAGE¹]

pa·go·da /pəgō′də/ *n.* Hindu or Buddhist temple, esp. a many-tiered tower, in India, China, etc. [Port]

Pa·go Pa·go /päNG′gō päNG′gō/ *n.* capital of American Samoa. Pop. 3,500

Pah·la·vi /päl′əvē/, **Mohammed Riza** (also **Pah′levi**) 1919–79; shah of Iran (1941–78)

paid /pād/ *v.* past and past part. of PAY

pail /pāl/ *n.* 1 bucket 2 amount contained in this —**pail′ful** *n.* (*pl.* -fuls) [OE]

pain /pān/ *n.* 1 any unpleasant bodily sensation produced by illness, accident, etc. 2 mental suffering 3 (also **pain in the neck**) *Colloq.* troublesome person or thing; nuisance —*v.* 4 cause pain to 5 **take pains** take great care 6 **on** (or **under**) **pain of** with (death, etc.) as the penalty —**pain′ful** *adj.*; **pain′ful·ly** *adv.*; **pain′less** *adj.*; **pain′less·ly** *adv.*; **pain′less·ness** *n.* [L *poena* penalty]

Paine /pān/, **Thomas** 1737–1809; English-born US writer and patriot

pain′kill′er *n.* drug for alleviating pain —**pain′kill′ing** *adj.*

pains·tak·ing /pānz′tāk′iNG/ *adj.* using or requiring great care —**pains′tak′ing·ly** *adv.*

paint /pānt/ *n.* 1 pigment, esp. in liquid form, for coloring a surface 2 this as a dried coating —*v.* 3a cover with paint **b** apply paint of a specified color to 4 depict (an object, scene, etc.) in paint; produce (a picture) thus 5 describe vividly [L *pingere* *pict-*]

Paint′ed Des′ert *n.* region of multicolored rock surfaces in N central Ariz.

paint′er¹ *n.* person who paints; artist or decorator

paint·er² *n.* rope attached to the bow of a boat for mooring

paint′ing *n.* 1 process or art of using paint 2 painted picture

pair /per/ *n.* 1 set of two people or things used together or regarded as a unit 2 article (e.g., scissors) consisting of two joined or corresponding parts 3 mated couple of people or animals 4 two playing cards of the same denomination —*v.* 5 arrange or be arranged in couples 6 mate [L *paria*, rel. to PAR]

PAISLEY

pais·ley /pāz′lē/ *n.* (*pl.* -leys) ornate pattern of colorful swirls [*Paisley* in Scotland]

pa·ja·mas /pəjäm′əz, -jam′-/ *n. pl.* 1 loose suit, usu. of shirt and pants, worn for sleeping 2 loose trousers worn by both sexes in some Asian countries [Urdu: leg-clothing]

Pa·ki·stan /pak′istan′, päk′istän′/ *n.* republic in central Asia. Capital: Islamabad. Pop. 130,129,000 —**Pa′ki·stan′i** *n.* & *adj.*

pal /pal/ *n. Colloq.* friend; comrade [Romany]

pal·ace /pal′is/ *n.* 1 official residence of a sovereign, etc. 2 splendid or spacious building [L *Palatium* site of the emperor's palace]

palaeo- *comb. form* PALEO-

pal·at·a·ble /pal′ətəbəl/ *adj.* 1 pleasant to taste 2 acceptable; satisfactory

pal·a·tal /pal′ət-l/ *adj.* 1 of the palate 2 (of a sound) made by placing the tongue against the hard palate (e.g., y in *yes*) —*n.* 3 palatal sound

pal·ate /pal′ət/ *n.* 1 structure closing the upper part of the mouth cavity in vertebrates 2 taste; liking [L *palatum*]

pa·la·tial /pəlā′sнəl/ *adj.* like a palace; spacious and splendid —**pa·la′tial·ly** *adv.* [L, rel. to PALACE]

Pa·lat·i·nate /pəlat′n-āt′/ *n.* district in SW Germany W of the Rhine

pal·a·tine /pal′ətīn′/ *adj. Hist.* having or subject to sovereign authority [L, rel. to PALACE]

pa·la·ver /pəlav′ər, -läv′-/ *n. Colloq.* tedious fuss and bother [LL, rel. to PARABLE]

pale¹ /pāl/ *adj.* 1 light or faint; whitish; ashen 2 of faint luster; dim —*v.* (**paled, pal·ing**) 3 grow or make pale 4 seem feeble —**pale′ly** *adv.*; **pale′ness** *n.*; **pal′ish** *adj.* [L *pallidus*]

pale² /pāl/ *n.* 1 pointed piece of wood for fencing, etc.; stake 2 boundary 3 **beyond the pale** outside the bounds of acceptable behavior [L *palus*]

pale′face′ *n.* person of the white race (name supposedly used by N American Indians)

Pa·lem·bang /päl′əmbäNG′/ *n.* city in Indonesia, on Sumatra. Pop. 787,200

paleo- *comb. form* ancient; prehistoric [Gk *palaios*]

pa·le·og·ra·phy /pā′lē·äg′rəfē/ *n.* the study of ancient writing and documents —**pa′le·og′ra·pher** *n.* [Fr, rel. to PALEO-]

pa·le·o·lith·ic /pā′lē·əli′тнik/ *adj.* of the early part of the Stone Age [Gk *lithos* stone]

pa·le·on·tol·o·gy /pā′lē·äntäl′əjē/ *n.* the study of life in the geological past —**pa′le·on·tol′o·gist** *n.* [Gk *ōn* *ont-* being]

Pa·le·o·zo·ic /pā′lē·əzō′ik/ *adj.* 1 of an era of geological time marked by the appearance of plants and animals, esp. invertebrates —*n.* 2 this era [Gk *zōion* animal]

Pa·ler·mo /pəler′mō/ *n.* seaport in Sicily. Pop. 734,200

ᴾal·es·tine /pal′əstīn′, -stēn′/ *n.* 1 ancient country in SW Asia on the E coast of the Mediterranean Sea 2 British-controlled region (1923–48); divided between Israel, Jordan, and Egypt —**Pal′es·tin′i·an** /-stin′ēən/ *n.* & *adj.*

pal·ette /pal′it/ *n.* 1 artist's board or slab for arranging and mixing colors on 2 range of colors used by an artist, video display, etc. [Fr fr. L *pala* spade]

pal·i·mo·ny /pal′əmō′nē/ *n. Colloq.* allowance paid to a former partner after separation of an unmarried couple [fr. PAL, ALIMONY]

pa·limp·sest /pal′impsest′/ *n.* writing material or manuscript on which the original writing has been erased for reuse [Gk *palin* again, *psēstos* rubbed]

pal·in·drome /pal′indrōm′/ *n.* word or

phrase reading the same backward as forward (e.g., *nurses run*) —**pal'in·drom'ic** /-dräm'ik/ *adj.* [Gk *palindromos* running backward]

pal·ing /pāl'iNG/ *n.* fence of pales

pal·i·sade /pal'əsād'/ *n.* 1 fence of pales or iron railings 2 (*pl.*) line of cliffs [Fr, rel. to PALE[2]]

pall[1] /pôl/ *n.* 1 cloth spread over a coffin, etc. 2 dark covering [L *pallium* cloak]

pall[2] /pôl/ *v.* 1 become uninteresting or distasteful (to) 2 become satiated (with) [fr. APPALL]

Pal·la·dio /pəläd'ē·ō'/, **Andrea** 1508–80; Italian architect

pal·la·di·um /pəläd'ēəm/ *n.* rare, white metallic element used as a catalyst and in jewelry; *symb.* Pd [*Pallas*, name of an asteroid]

pall·bear·er /pôl'ber'ər/ *n.* person helping to carry or escort a coffin at a funeral

pal·let[1] /pal'it/ *n.* 1 straw mattress 2 makeshift bed [L *palea* straw]

pal·let[2] /pal'it/ *n.* portable platform on which crates, boxes, etc., are stored and shipped [Fr, rel. to PALETTE]

pal·li·ate /pal'ē·āt'/ *v.* (·at·ed, ·at·ing) 1 alleviate (disease) without curing it 2 excuse; extenuate —**pal'li·a·tive** /-ətiv/ *n. & adj.* [L, rel. to PALL[1]]

pal·lid /pal'id/ *adj.* pale, esp. from illness [L, rel. to PALE[1]]

pal·lor /pal'ər/ *n.* paleness [L *pallere* be pale]

palm[1] /pä(l)m/ *n.* 1 (also **palm' tree'**) usu. tropical treelike plant with no branches and a mass of large leaves at the top 2 leaf of this as a symbol of victory [L *palma*]

palm[2] *n.* 1 inner surface of the hand between the wrist and fingers —*v.* 2 conceal in the hand 3 **palm off** impose on or dispose of fraudulently [L *palma*]

Pal·ma /päl'mə/ *n.* (also **Pal'ma de Ma·llor'ca** /dä mä(l)yôr'kə/) seaport on Majorca, Spain. Pop. 296,754

pal·mate /pal'māt'/ *adj.* shaped like an open hand [L *palmatus*, rel. to PALM[2]]

Pal·mer /pä(l)mər/, **Arnold** 1929– ; US golfer

pal·met·to /palmet'ō/ *n.* (*pl.* ·tos) small palm tree [Sp *palmito* dim. of *palma* PALM[1]]

palm·ist·ry /pä(l)m'istrē/ *n.* fortunetelling from lines, etc., on the palm of the hand —**palm'ist** *n.*

Palm' Sun'day *n.* Sunday before Easter, celebrating Christ's entry into Jerusalem

palm·y /päm'ē/ *adj.* (·i·er, ·i·est) 1 of, like, or abounding in palms 2 triumphant; flourishing

Pal·o Al·to /pal'ō al'tō/ *n.* city in Calif. Pop. 55,900

pal·o·mi·no /pal'əmē'nō/ *n.* (*pl.* ·nos) golden or cream-colored horse with light-colored mane and tail [L *palumba* dove]

pal·pa·ble /pal'pəbəl/ *adj.* 1 able to be touched or felt 2 readily perceived —**pal'pa·bly** *adv.* [L *palpare* caress]

pal·pate /pal'pāt'/ *v.* (·pat·ed, ·pat·ing) examine (esp. medically) by touch —**pal·pa'tion** *n.*

pal·pi·tate /pal'pətāt'/ *v.* (·tat·ed, ·tat·ing) pulsate; throb; tremble —**pal·pi·ta'tion** *n.* [L *palpitare* freq. of *palpare* touch gently]

pal·sy /pôl'zē/ *n.* (*pl.* ·sies) 1 paralysis, esp. with involuntary tremors —*v.* (·sied, ·sy·ing) 2 affect with palsy [Fr, rel. to PARALYSIS]

pal·try /pôl'trē/ *adj.* (·tri·er, ·tri·est) worthless; contemptible —**pal'tri·ness** *n.* [LGer *paltrig* ragged]

pam·pas /pam'pəs, päm'-/ *n. pl.* treeless plains of S America [Sp fr. Quechua]

pam·per /pam'pər/ *v.* overindulge; spoil [obs. *pamp* cram]

pam·phlet /pam'flit/ *n.* 1 small, usu. unbound booklet or leaflet —*v.* 2 distribute pamphlets to —**pam'phlet·eer** /-tēr/ *n.* [*Pamphilus*, name of medieval poem]

Pam·plo·na /pamplō'nə/ *n.* city in N Spain. Pop. 179,300

pan[1] /pan/ *n.* 1 broad, usu. metal vessel used for cooking, heating, etc. 2 any similar shallow container —*v.* (**panned, pan·ning**) 3 *Colloq.* criticize severely 4 wash (gold-bearing gravel) in a pan 5 **pan out** turn up; work out —**pan'ful** *n.* (*pl.* ·fuls); **pan'like** *adj.* [OE]

pan[2] *v.* (**panned, pan·ning**) 1 swing (a camera) horizontally to give a panoramic effect or to follow a moving object —*n.* 2 panning movement [fr. PANORAMA]

Pan /pan/ *n. Gk. Myth.* horned, goat-legged god of field and forest

pan- *comb. form* 1 all; the whole of 2 relating to or comprising the whole (*pan-American*) [Gk *pan*, neut. of *pas pantos* all]

pan·a·ce·a /pan'əsē'ə/ *n.* universal remedy [Gk, rel. to PAN-, *akos* remedy]

pa·nache /pənaSH', -näSH'/ *n.* assertive flamboyance; confidence of style or manner [Fr: plume]

Pan·a·ma (**hat'**) /pan'əmä', -mô'/ *n.* straw hat with a brim and indented crown [for PANAMA]

Pan·a·ma /pan'əmä', -mô'/ *n.* 1 republic in Central America. Pop. 2,515,000 2 (**Pan'a·ma' Cit'y**) capital of Panama. Pop. 411,500 —**Pan·a·ma·ni·an** /pan'əmä'nēən/ *n. & adj.*

Pan'a·ma' Ca·nal' *n.* canal extending through the Isthmus of Panama, connecting the Atlantic and Pacific oceans

Pan'-A·mer'i·can *adj.* including N, S, and Central America

pan'cake' *n.* 1 thin, flat cake of fried batter 2 flat cake of make-up, etc.

Pan·chi·ao /pän'CHē·ou'/ *n.* suburb of Taipei, Taiwan. Pop. 539,000

pan·chro·mat·ic /pan'krōmat'ik/ *adj.* sensitive to all colors of the spectrum, as film

pan·cre·as /paNG'krēəs/ *n.* gland near the stomach supplying digestive fluid and secreting insulin —**pan·cre·at·ic** /paNG'krē·at'ik/ *adj.* [Gk *kreas* flesh]

pan·da /pan'də/ *n.* 1 (also **gi'ant pan'da**) bearlike black-and-white mammal native to China and Tibet 2 (also **red' pan'da**) reddish-brown racoonlike Himalayan mammal [Nepali]

pan·dem·ic /pandem'ik/ *adj.* widespread; universal [Gk *dēmos* people]

pan·de·mo·ni·um /pan'dəmō'nēəm/ *n.* uproar; utter confusion [place in hell in Milton's *Paradise Lost*, rel. to PAN-, DEMON]

pan·der /pan'dər/ *v.* 1 gratify or indulge —*n.* (also **pan'der·er**) 2 procurer; pimp 3 person who encourages vice, etc. [*Pandare*, name of a character in the story of Troilus and Cressida]

Pan·do·ra's box' /pandôr'əz/ *n.* process that will generate many unmanageable problems once begun [in Gk myth. a box from which many ills were released on humankind]

pane /pān/ *n.* single sheet of glass in a window or door [L *pannus* a cloth]

pan·e·gyr·ic /pan'əjir'ik, -jī'rik/ *n.* eulogy; speech or essay of praise [Gk *panēgyrikos* solemn assembly]

pan·el /pan'l/ *n.* 1 distinct, usu. rectangular, flat section of a surface (e.g., of a wall, door, etc.) 2 surface for instruments and controls 3 strip of material in a garment 4 group of people discussing, judging, etc., as a team 5a list of available jurors b jury —*v.* (·eled or ·elled, ·el·ing or ·el·ling) 6 fit, cover, or decorate with panels [L dim. of *pannus*, rel. to PANE]

pan'el·ing or **pan'el·ling** *n.* 1 paneled work 2 sheets of wood, plastic, etc., used as panels

pan'el·ist *n.* member of a panel

pan'el truck' *n.* small truck with enclosed rear storage area

pang /paNG/ *n.* (often *pl.*) sudden sharp pain or painful emotion [obs. *pronge*]

pan·han·dle¹ *n.* narrow strip of land whose shape resembles the handle of a pan

pan·han·dle² *v.* (·dled, ·dling) beg on the streets for change —**pan'han'dler** *n.*

pan·ic /pan'ik/ *n.* 1 sudden, uncontrollable fear 2 infectious fright —*v.* (·icked, ·icking) 3 affect or be affected with panic —**pan'icky** *adj.* [fcn PAN]

pan'ic-strick'en *adj.* (also **pan'ic-struck'**) affected with panic

Pank·hurst /paNGk'hərst/, **Emmeline Goulden** 1858–1928; English suffragist

pan·nier /pan'yər/ *n.* basket, bag, or box, esp. one of a pair for transporting loads [L *panis* bread]

pan·o·ply /pan'əplē/ *n.* (*pl.* ·plies) 1 complete or splendid array 2 complete suit of armor [Gk *hopla* arms]

pan·o·ra·ma /pan'əram'ə/ *n.* 1 unbroken view of a surrounding region 2 complete survey of a subject, series of events, etc. 3 continuous passing scene —**pan'o·ram'ic** *adj.* [Gk *horama* view]

pan·sy /pan'zē/ *n.* (*pl.* ·sies) cultivated plant with flowers of various rich colors [Fr *pensée* thought; pansy]

pant /pant/ *v.* 1 breathe with short quick breaths 2 utter breathlessly 3 yearn; crave —*n.* 4 panting breath [Gk, rel. to FANTASY]

pan·ta·loons /pant'l-ōōnz'/ *n. pl.* baggy trousers gathered at the ankles [Fr fr. It]

pan·the·ism /pan'THē-iz'əm/ *n.* 1 belief that God is in all nature 2 worship that admits or tolerates all gods —**pan'the·ist'**/-ist/ *n.*; **pan'the·is'tic** *adj.* [Gk *theos* god]

pan·the·on /pan'THē-än'/ *n.* 1 building in which illustrious dead are buried or have memorials 2 the deities or heroes of a people, group, etc., collectively 3 temple dedicated to all the gods [Gk *theion* divine]

pan·ther /pan'THər/ *n.* 1 leopard, esp. with black fur 2 cougar [Gk *panthēr*]

pant·ies /pan'tēz/ *n. pl. Colloq.* underpants worn by women and girls [dim. of PANTS]

pan·to·mime /pan'təmīm'/ *n.* 1 gestures and facial expression conveying meaning without words, esp. in drama and dance —*v.* (·mimed, ·mim·ing) 2 act or express in pantomime —**pan'to·mim'ic** /-mim'ik/ *adj.*; **pan'to·mim'ist** /-mīm'ist/ *n.* [Gk, rel. to PAN-, MIME]

pan·try /pan'trē/ *n.* (*pl.* ·tries) small room or cupboard for storage of packaged food, kitchen supplies, etc. [L *panis* bread]

pants /pants/ *n. pl.* 1 trousers 2 underpants [abbr. of PANTALOONS]

pant'suit' *n.* women's garment of matching jacket and pants

pan·ty·hose /pan'tēhōz'/ *n.* women's stockings, usu. of nylon, extending to the waist

pap /pap/ *n.* 1 soft or semiliquid food for infants or invalids 2 light or trivial reading matter [LGer or Du]

pa·pa /päp'ə, pəpä'/ *n.* father (esp. as a child's word) [Gk *papas*]

pa·pa·cy /pā'pəsē/ *n.* (*pl.* ·cies) 1 pope's office or tenure 2 papal system [MedL *papatia*, rel. to POPE]

pa·pal /pā'pəl/ *adj.* of a pope or the papacy [MedL, rel. to POPE]

Pa·pan·dre·ou /päp'ändrā'ōō/, **George** 1888–1968; Greek politician

pa·paw /pô'pô'/ 1 central and southern N American tree with an edible, yellowish fruit 2 PAPAYA

pa·pa·ya /pəpī'ə/ *n.* tropical American tree with an edible, yellow fruit

pa·per /pā'pər/ *n.* 1 flexible material made in thin sheets from wood pulp, rags, etc., used for writing, printing on, as wrapping material, etc. 2 NEWSPAPER 3a printed document b (*pl.*) identification or other legal documents 4 WALLPAPER 5 report, essay, or dissertation 6 piece of paper —*adj.* 7 made of or similar to paper —*v.* 8 decorate with wallpaper 9a cover with paper b (foll. by *over*) disguise or try to hide —**pa'per·y** *adj.* [L PAPYRUS]

pa'per·back' *n.* book bound in paper or cardboard covers

pa'per·boy' *n.* (also **pa'per·girl'**) youth who delivers or sells newspapers

pa'per clip' *n.* clip of bent wire or plastic for fastening papers together

pa'per ti'ger *n.* apparently threatening but ineffectual person or thing

pa'per trail' *n. Colloq.* documentary record, as of activities, transactions, etc.

pa'per·weight' *n.* small heavy object for keeping loose papers in place

pa'per·work' *n.* routine clerical or administrative work

pa·pier mâ·ché /pā'pər məsHā', pap'yā'/ *n.* paper pulp molded into boxes, trays, etc. [Fr: chewed paper]

pa·pil·la /pəpil'ə/ *n.* (*pl.* ·pil·lae /-pil'ē/) small, nipplelike protuberance in or on the body —**pap·il·lar·y** /pap'əler'ē/ *adj.* [L]

pa·poose /papōōs'/ *n.* N American Indian young child [Algonquian]

pa·pri·ka /paprē'kə/ *n.* powdered spice ground from a type of red pepper [Magyar]

Pap' test' *n.* test for cervical or vaginal cancer [for US cytologist, G. Papanicolaou, who developed its method]

Pap·u·a New Guin·ea /păp′ōōə n(y)ōō
gin′ē/ *n.* republic in the W Pacific consisting
of E New Guinea and nearby islands. Capital:
Port Moresby. Pop. 3,834,000

pa·py·rus /pəpī′rəs/ *n.* (*pl.* **-ri** /-rē, -rī′/) 1
aquatic plant of N Africa 2 writing material
made in ancient Egypt from the pithy stem of
this [L fr. Gk]

par /pär/ *n.* 1 average or normal amount, degree, condition, etc. 2 equality; equal footing
3 *Golf.* number of strokes a skilled player
should normally require for a hole or course
4 face value of stocks and shares, etc. 5 recognized value of one country's currency in
terms of another's —*adj.* 6 average; at par 7
par for the course *Colloq.* what is normal or
to be expected [L: equal]

para- *prefix* (also **par-**) 1 beside; beyond
(*paranormal*) 2 ancillary (*paralegal*) [Gk]

par·a·ble /par′əbəl/ *n.* 1 story used to illustrate a moral or spiritual lesson 2 allegory
[Gk *parabolē* comparison]

PARABOLA

pa·rab·o·la /pərab′ələ/ *n.* open plane curve
formed by the intersection of a cone with a
plane parallel to its side —**par·a·bol·ic** /par′-
əbäl′ik/ *adj.* [Gk *parabolē* placing side by
side, rel. to PARABLE]

par·a·chute /par′əshōōt/ *n.* 1 rectangular
or umbrella-shaped apparatus allowing a slow
and safe descent, esp. from an aircraft —*v.*
(·**chut·ed**, ·**chut·ing**) 2 descend by parachute —**par·a·chut·ist** *n.* [fr. It *parare* ward
off + CHUTE¹]

pa·rade /pərād′/ *n.* 1 public procession 2
ceremonial muster of troops for inspection 3
ostentatious display —*v.* (·**rad·ed**, ·**rad·ing**)
4 march ceremonially 5 display ostentatiously [L *parare* prepare]

par·a·digm /par′ədīm/ *n.* example or pattern, esp. a set of noun or verb inflections
—**par·a·dig·mat·ic** /par′ədigmat′ik/ *adj.* [L
fr. Gk]

par·a·dise /par′ədīs/ *n.* 1 heaven 2 place
or state of complete happiness 3 abode of
Adam and Eve; garden of Eden —**par·a·di-
sa·ic** /-dəsā′ik/, **par·a·di·sa·ical** /-dəsā′-
ikəl/ *adj.* [Gk *paradeisos*]

Par·a·dise /par′ədīs/ *n.* suburb of Sacramento, Calif. Pop. 124,682

par·a·dox /par′ədäks′/ *n.* 1a seemingly contradictory though often true statement b self-
contradictory statement 2 person or thing
having contradictory qualities, etc. —**par′a·
dox′i·cal** *adj.*; **par′a·dox′i·cal·ly** *adv.* [Gk,
rel. to PARA-, *doxa* opinion]

par·af·fin /par′əfin/ *n.* waxy substance used
to seal jars, etc., and in candle-making [L
parum barely, *affinis* connected, for its inert-
ness]

par·a·gon /par′əgän′/ *n.* model of excellence
[Gk *parakonē*]

par·a·graph /par′əgraf′/ *n.* 1 distinct section
of a piece of writing, beginning on a new, often
indented, line 2 symbol (usu. ¶ or §) used to
mark a new paragraph 3 short item in a newspaper —*v.* 4 arrange in paragraphs [Gk, rel.
to PARA-¹, -GRAPH]

Par·a·guay /par′əgwī′, -gwā′/ *n.* republic in
central S America. Capital: Asunción. Pop.
4,519,000 —**Par·a·guay′an** *n.* & *adj.*

par·a·keet /par′əkēt′/ *n.* small, usu. long-
tailed parrot [Fr, rel. to PARROT]

par·a·le·gal /par′əlē′gəl/ *n.* 1 person trained
to assist lawyers —*adj.* 2 pertaining to training or work in legal research, etc., to assist a
lawyer

par·al·lax /par′əlaks/ *n.* apparent difference
in the position or direction of an object caused
when the observer's position is changed [Gk:
change]

par·al·lel /par′əlel′/ *adj.* 1 continuously side
by side and equidistant 2 precisely similar;
analogous or corresponding; simultaneous
—*n.* 3 person or thing precisely analogous to
another 4 comparison 5a each of the imaginary parallel circles of constant latitude on the
earth's surface b corresponding line on a map
—*v.* (·**leled** or ·**lelled**, ·**lel·ing** or ·**lel·ling**)
6 be parallel, or correspond, to 7 represent
as similar; compare —**par′al·lel′ism** *n.* [Gk:
alongside one another]

par·al·lel·o·gram /par′əlel′əgram′/ *n.* four-
sided plane rectilinear figure with opposite
sides parallel

pa·ral·y·sis /pəral′əsis/ *n.* 1 impairment or
loss of the motor or sensory function of the
nerves; immobility 2 powerlessness —**par·a·
lyt·ic** /par′əlit′ik/ *n.* & *adj.* [Gk *paralyein*
loosen on one side]

par·a·lyze /par′əlīz′/ *v.* (·**lyzed**, ·**lyz·ing**) 1
affect with paralysis 2 render powerless; cripple [back formation fr. PARALYSIS]

Par·a·mar·i·bo /par′əmar′ibō′/ *n.* capital of
Suriname. Pop. 77,600

par·a·me·ci·um /par′əmē′sē·əm/ *n.* ciliated,
freshwater protozoan

par·a·med·ic /par′əmed′ik/ *n.* paramedical
worker, as in an ambulance

par·a·med·i·cal /par′əmed′ikəl/ *adj.* supplementing and assisting medical work

pa·ram·e·ter /pəram′ətər/ *n.* 1 *Math.* quantity constant in the case considered but varying in different cases 2a characteristic or feature b (usu. *pl.*) limit or boundary [Gk PARA-,
-METER]

par·a·mil·i·tar·y /par′əmil′əter′ē/ *adj.* organized on military lines or assisting a military
organization

par·a·mount /par′əmount′/ *adj.* supreme;
most important [AngFr *paramont* above]

par·a·mour /par′əmŏŏr′/ *n.* illicit lover of a
married person [Fr *par amour* by love]

par·a·noi·a /par′ənoi′ə/ *n.* 1 mental disorder
with delusions of persecution and self-impor-
tance 2 abnormal suspicion and mistrust
—**par′a·noi′ac** *adj.* & *n.*; **par·a·noi′a·cal·ly**
adv.; **par·a·no′ic** /-nō′ik, -noi′ik/ *adj.*; **par·a·
no′i·cal·ly** *adv.*; **par·a·noid′** /-noid/ *adj.* & *n.*
[Gk]

par·a·nor·mal /par′ənôr′məl/ *adj.* beyond

the scope of normal scientific investigation or explanation

par·a·pet /par'əpit/ *n.* 1 low wall at the edge of a roof, balcony, bridge, etc. 2 defense of earth or stone [It *parare* guard, *petto* breast]

par·a·pher·na·li·a /par'əfə(r)nāl'yə/ *n. pl.* (also treated as *sing.*) miscellaneous belongings, equipment, etc. [Gk, rel. to PARA-, *phernē* dower]

par·a·phrase /par'əfrāz/ *n.* 1 expression of a passage in other words —*v.* (·phrased, ·phras·ing) 2 express the meaning of (a passage) thus [Gk PARA-, *phrazein* say]

par·a·ple·gi·a /par'əplē'jə/ *n.* paralysis of both legs —**par·a·ple'gic** *adj.* & *n.* [Gk, rel. to PARA-, *plēgē* blow; stroke]

par·a·pro·fes'sion·al *n.* person trained to assist a professional, e.g., a doctor

par·a·psy·chol·o·gy /par'əsīkäl'əjē/ *n.* the study of mental phenomena outside the sphere of ordinary psychology

par·a·quat /par'əkwät/ *n.* a quick-acting, highly toxic herbicide [fr. PARA-, QUATERNARY]

par·a·site /par'əsīt/ *n.* 1 organism living in or on another and feeding on it 2 person exploiting another or others —**par·a·sit'ic** /-sit'ik/ *adj.*; **par·a·sit'i·cal·ly** *adv.*; **par·a·sit·ism'** /-iz'əm/ *n.* [Gk, rel. to PARA-, *sitos* food]

par·a·sol /par'əsôl', -säl'/ *n.* light umbrella giving shade from the sun [It *parare* ward off, *sole* sun]

par·a·sym'pa·thet'ic *adj.* designating that part of the autonomic nervous system controlling the slowing of the heartbeat, constriction of the pupils, etc.

par·a·thy·roid /par'əTHĪ'roid/ *adj.* situated near the thyroid, esp. ref. to several small glands there

par·a·troops /par'ətrōōps/ *n. pl.* troops deployed to parachute into a combat area —**par'a·troop'er** *n.* [blend of *parachute* + *troops*]

par·boil /pär'boil'/ *v.* boil until partly cooked [L *par-* PER-, confused with PART]

par·cel /pär'səl/ *n.* 1 goods, etc., wrapped in a package 2 piece of land —*v.* (·celed or ·celled, ·cel·ing or ·cel·ling) 3 (foll. by *out*) divide into portions [L, rel. to PARTICLE]

parch /pärCH/ *v.* make or become hot and dry

parch·ment /pärCH'mənt/ *n.* 1 a skin, esp. of sheep or goat, prepared for writing b manuscript written on this 2 high-grade paper resembling parchment [fr. L *Pergamum*, city in Asia Minor where made]

par·don /pärd'n/ *n.* 1 forgiveness for an offense, error, etc. 2 remission of the legal consequences of a crime or conviction —*v.* 3 forgive; excuse 4 grant a legal pardon to —**par'don·a·ble** *adj.*; **par'don·a·bly** *adv.* [L, rel. to PER-, *donare* give]

pare /per/ *v.* (**pared, par·ing**) 1 trim or shave the surface of 2 diminish little by little [L *parare* prepare]

par·ent /par'ənt, per'-/ *n.* 1 person who has or adopts a child; father or mother 2 animal or plant from which others are derived 3 source, origin, etc. —*v.* 4 be the parent of or act as parent to —*adj.* 5 describing a corporation in relation to its subsidiaries —**par·en-**

tal /pərent'l/ *adj.*; **par'ent·hood** *n.* [L *parere* bring forth]

par·ent·age /par'əntij, per'-/ *n.* lineage; descent from or through parents

pa·ren·the·sis /pəren'THəsis/ *n.* (*pl.* ·ses /-sēz/) 1 explanatory or qualifying word, clause, or sentence 2 (*pl.*) curved brackets ( ) used for this in writing or printing —**par·en·thet·ic** /par'ənTHet'ik/, **par'en·thet'i·cal** *adj.*; **par'en·thet'i·cal·ly** *adv.* [Gk, rel. to PARA-, EN-, THESIS]

par'ent·ing *n.* skill of bringing up children

pa·reve /pär'əvə, pärˈvə/ *adj.* made without milk or meat, thus suitable for kosher use

par ex·cel·lence /pär ek'sələns/ *adv.* being the supreme example of its kind (*the short story par excellence*) [Fr]

par·fait /pärfā'/ *n.* 1 dish of ice cream, syrup, fruit, etc., in alternating layers, served in a tall glass 2 rich frozen dessert of whipped cream, eggs, etc. [Fr *parfait* PERFECT]

pa·ri·ah /pərī'ə/ *n.* 1 social outcast 2 member of a low caste or of no caste in S India [Tamil]

pa·ri·etal /pərī'ət-l/ *adj.* 1 of the wall of the body or any of its cavities 2 of the area at the side and top of the skull [L *paries* wall]

pari·mu·tu·el /par'imyōō'CHōōəl/ *n.* system of horse-race betting in which winners gain a share of the total amount bet

par·ing /per'iNG/ *n.* strip or piece cut off

Par·is /par'is, pärē'/ *n.* capital of France. Pop. 2,175,100 —**Pa·ri·sian** /pərē'zHən/ *n.* & *adj.*

par·ish /par'iSH/ *n.* 1 area having its own church and clergyman 2 county-equivalent district in Louisiana, etc. 3 inhabitants or members of a parish [L *parochia* fr. Gk *oikos* dwelling]

pa·rish·ion·er /pəriSH'ənər/ *n.* inhabitant or member of a parish

par·i·ty /par'ətē/ *n.* 1 equality; equal status or pay 2 equivalence of one currency with another; being at par [L *paritas*, rel. to PAR]

park /pärk/ *n.* 1 public land set aside for recreation or as a preserve 2 area for a specified purpose (*business park*) 3 setting in an automatic transmission that immobilizes the drive wheels —*v.* 4 leave (a vehicle) temporarily 5 maneuver or drive into a parking space [Fr fr. Gmc]

par·ka /pär'kə/ *n.* hooded winter jacket [Esk]

Par·ker /pär'kər/, **Dorothy** 1893–1967; US writer

park'ing me'ter *n.* coin-operated meter to charge for and limit the use of a parking space

Par·kin·son's dis·ease' /pär'kinsənz/ *n.* (also Par'kin·son·ism') progressive disease of the nervous system marked by tremors, muscle rigidity, etc. [for Brit. physician who described it]

Par'kin·son's law' *n.* notion that work expands to fill the time available for it [for Brit. author who conceived it]

Park·man /pärk'mən/, **Francis** 1823–93; US historian

park'way' *n.* wide, landscaped highway

par·lance /pär'ləns/ *n.* vocabulary or idiom [Fr fr. *parler* speak]

par·lay /pär'lā, -lē/ *v.* 1 gamble (a bet and

winnings) on a subsequent contest or race
—n. 2 parlayed bet

par·ley /pär'lē/ n. (pl. ·leys) 1 conference,
esp. to discuss peace terms, etc. —v. (·leyed,
·ley·ing) 2 hold a parley [Fr parler, rel. to
PARLANCE]

Par·lia·ment /pär'ləmənt/ n. legislature of
various countries, as the United Kingdom [Fr,
rel. to PARLANCE]

par·lia·men·tar·i·an /pär'ləmen'ter'ēən/ n.
1 person skilled in parliamentary procedures
2 member of a parliament

par·lia·men·ta·ry /pär'ləmen't(ə)rē/ adj. 1
of a parliament or other legislative body 2 enacted or established by a parliament

par·lor /pär'lər/ n. 1 Old-fash. living room in
a private house 2 shop providing specified
goods or services (beauty parlor) [AngFr, rel.
to PARLEY]

Par·ma /pär'mə/ n. city in N Italy. Pop.
174,000

Par·men·i·des /pärmen'ədēz'/ early 5th
cent. B.C.; Greek philosopher

Par·me·san /pär'mizän',-zhän'/ n. hard, dry
cheese usu. grated [It parmegiano of PARMA]

Par·nell /pärnel', pärn'l/, Charles Stewart
1846–91; Irish nationalist leader

pa·ro·chi·al /pərō'kēəl/ adj. 1 of a parish 2
local; narrow; provincial —pa·ro'chi·al·ism'
/-iz'əm/ n.; pa·ro'chi·al·ly adv. [L, rel. to
PARISH]

pa·ro'chi·al school' n. school run or supported by a church

par·o·dy /par'ədē/ n. (pl. ·dies) 1 humorous exaggerated imitation of an author, literary work, style, etc. —v. (·died, ·dy·ing) 2
compose a parody of —par'o·dist /-dist/ n.
[L or Gk, rel. to PARA-, ODE]

pa·role /pərōl'/ n. 1 provisional release of a
prisoner before a sentence is fully served, on
the promise of good behavior —v. (·roled,
·rol·ing) 2 put (a prisoner) on parole [Fr:
word, rel. to PARLANCE]

par·ox·ysm /par'əksiz'əm/ n. sudden attack
or outburst —par'ox·ys'mal adj. [Gk oxus
sharp]

par·quet /pärkā'/ n. 1 flooring of parquetry
2 main floor area of a theater —v. (·queted
/-kād'/, ·quet·ing /-kā'iNG/) 3 floor with
parquetry [Fr, dim. of parc PARK]

par·quet·ry /pär'kətrē/ n. use of wooden
blocks arranged in a pattern to make floors or
inlay for furniture

par·ri·cide /par'əsīd'/ n. 1 murder of a near
relative, esp. of a parent 2 person who commits parricide —par'ri·ci'dal adj. [L: see
PARENT, -CIDE]

par·rot /par'ət/ n. 1 mainly tropical bird with
a short, hooked bill, often vivid plumage, and
the ability to mimic speech 2 person who mechanically repeats another's words or actions
—v. (·rot·ed, ·rot·ing) 3 repeat mechanically [Fr, dim. of Pierre Peter]

par·ry /par'ē/ v. (·ried, ·ry·ing) 1 avert or
ward off 2 deal skillfully with (an awkward
question, etc.) —n. (pl. ·ries) 3 act of par-
rying [It parare ward off]

parse /pärs, pärz/ v. (parsed, pars·ing) describe the function and forms (of a sentence
or a word in context) grammatically [perh. fr.
Fr pars parts, rel. to PART]

par·sec /pär'sek/ n. unit of stellar distance,

equal to about 3.25 light-years [fr. PARALLAX,
SECOND²]

par·si·mo·ny /pär'səmō'nē/ n. stinginess
—par'si·mo'ni·ous adj. [L parcere spare]

pars·ley /pär'slē/ n. herb with aromatic
leaves, used to season and garnish food [Gk
petra rock, selinon parsley]

pars·nip /pär'snip/ n. 1 plant with a pale-yellow tapering root 2 this root eaten as a vegetable [L pastinaca]

par·son /pär'sən/ n. minister; clergyman [L,
rel. to PERSON]

par·son·age /pär'sənij/ n. house provided
for a minister by the church

part /pärt/ n. 1 some but not all of a thing or
group of things 2 essential member, constituent, or component 3 division of a book,
broadcast series, etc. 4 each of several equal
portions of a whole (3 parts sugar to 2 parts
flour) 5a allotted share b person's share in
an action, etc. 6a role of an actor on stage b
melody, etc., assigned to a particular voice or
instrument c printed or written copy of an actor's or musician's part 7 side in an agreement
or dispute 8 (pl.) region or district (not from
these parts) 9 dividing line combed into the
hair —v. 10 divide or separate into parts 11
leave; say goodbye to 12 (foll. by with) give
up; hand over 13 comb hair to form a part
—adv. 14 in part; partly 15 for one's part
as far as one is concerned 16 in part partly
17 part and parcel (of) an essential part 18
take part assist; have a share (in) [L pars
part-]

par·take /pärtāk'/ v. (·took, ·tak·en, ·tak·
ing) 1 take a share or part 2 eat or drink
something [part + taker]

par·terre /pärter'/ n. 1 level space in a formal garden occupied by flower beds 2 rear
seating area of a theater [Fr: on the ground]

par·the·no·gen·e·sis /pär'THənōjen'əsis/ n.
reproduction without fertilization [Gk par-
thenos virgin]

par·tial /pär'SHəl/ adj. 1 not complete; forming only part 2 biased; having a liking for —n.
3 denture replacing one or several teeth
—par·ti·al·i·ty /pär'SHē·al'ətē/ n.; par'tial·
ly adv.; par'tial·ness n. [L, rel. to PART]

● Usage: In the sense of 'in part, to some extent,' traditionalists prefer partly: His testimony was partly true. The job was partly completed. The form partial, however, has been
adopted in many phrases as the adjective form
for part (partial blindness, partial denture,
partial derivative, partial fraction, partial vacuum, etc.); hence partially is in wide use with
the same sense as partly: He is partially blind.

par·tic·i·pate /pärtis'əpāt'/ v. (·pat·ed, ·pat·
ing) take part or a share (in) —par·tic'i·
pant /-pənt/, par·tic'i·pa'tion, par·tic'i·pa'
tor n.; par·tic'i·pa·to'ry /-pətōr'ē/ adj. [L
participere -cip- take part]

par·ti·ci·ple /pärt'əsip'əl/ n. Gram. word
formed from a verb and used in compound
verb forms or as an adjective —par'ti·cip'i·
al /-sip'ēəl/ adj. [L, rel. to PARTICIPATE]

par·ti·cle /pär'tikəl/ n. 1 minute portion of
matter 2 smallest possible amount 3 minor
part of speech, esp. a short, undeclinable one
[L particula dim. of pars PART]

par·ti·cle board' *n.* building material made in flat sheets from scrap wood bonded with adhesive

par·ti·col·ored /pär'tēkal'ard/ *adj.* of more than one color [rel. to PART, COLOR]

par·tic·u·lar /pə(r)tik'yələr/ *adj.* 1 relating to or considered as a distinct thing or person; individual 2 more than is usual; special 3 scrupulously exact; fastidious —*n.* 4 detail; item 5 (*pl.*) information; detailed account 6 **in particular** especially; specifically —**par·tic'u·lar'i·ty** /-lar'ətē/ *n.* (*pl.* ·**ties**) [L, rel. to PARTICLE]

par·tic·u·lar·ize /pə(r)tik'yələrīz'/ *v.* (·**ized**, ·**iz·ing**) 1 name specially or one by one; specify 2 give details (of) —**par·tic·u·lar·i·za'tion** *n.*

par·tic·u·lar·ly *adv.* 1 especially; very 2 specifically

part'ing *n.* 1 leave-taking or departure 2 division; separating

par·ti·san /pär'tizən/ (also **par'ti·zan**) *n.* 1 strong, esp. unreasoning, supporter of a party, cause, etc. 2 guerrilla —*adj.* 3 of or like partisans —**par'ti·san·ship** [It, rel. to PART]

par·ti·tion /pärtisH'ən/ *n.* 1 structure dividing a space, esp. a light interior wall 2 division into parts —*v.* 3 divide into parts 4 separate with a partition —**par·ti'tioned** *adj.* [L *partiri* divide]

part'ly *adv.* to some extent; not entirely
● Usage: See note at PARTIAL

part·ner /pärt'nər/ *n.* 1 person who shares or takes part with another or others 2 companion in dancing 3 player on the same side in a game 4 either member of a married or unmarried couple —*v.* 5 be the partner of —**part'ner·ship'** *n.* [ME, alter. of *parcener* joint heir]

part' of speech' *n.* one of eight classes of words based on function, meaning, etc.

par·took /pärtŏŏk'/ *v. past of* PARTAKE

par·tridge /pär'trij/ *n.* (*pl.* same or ·**tridg·es**) any of various species of game bird [Gk *perdix*]

part' song' *n.* song with three or more voice-parts, often unaccompanied

part'-time' *adj.* 1 (of a job, study schedule, etc.) occupying less than the usual or full time —*adv.* 2 (also **part' time'**) as a part-time activity —**part'-tim'er** *n.*

par·tu·ri·tion /pär'tyŏŏrisH'ən/ *n.* giving birth [L *parere part*- bring forth]

part'way' *adv.* not entirely or completely

par·ty /pär'tē/ *n.* (*pl.* ·**ties**) 1 social gathering 2 people working or traveling together 3 organized political group putting forward candidates in elections 4 each side in an agreement or dispute 5 *Law.* accessory (to an action) 6 *Colloq.* person —*v.* (·**tied,** ·**ty·ing**) 7 attend a party; celebrate [Rom, rel. to PART]

par'ty line' *n.* 1 policy adopted by a political party 2 shared telephone line

par·ve·nu /pär'vən(y)ŏŏ'/ *n.* (*pl.* ·**nus**; *fem.* **par've·nue',** *pl.* ·**nues**) newly rich social climber; upstart [L, rel. to PER-, *venire* come]

Pas·a·de·na /pas'ədēnə/ *n.* city in Calif. Pop. 131,591

Pas·cal /paskal'/, **Blaise** 1623–62; French philosopher

pas·chal /pas'kəl/ *adj.* 1 of Passover 2 of Easter [Heb *pesach*]

pa·sha /pä'sHə/ *n.* historical Turkish title (placed after the name) [Turk]

pass¹ /pas/ *v.* 1a move onward, past, etc. b overtake, esp. in a vehicle 2 (cause to) be transferred from one person or place to another 3 surpass; exceed 4 get through 5a go unremarked or uncensured b be accepted or known (as) 6 move; cause to go 7a be successful or adequate, esp. in an examination, course, etc. b judge (a candidate) to be satisfactory 8a (of a bill) be approved by a legislature b cause or allow (a bill) to proceed c be approved 9 occur; elapse; happen 10 (cause to) circulate; be current 11 spend (time or a period) 12 *Sports.* throw; send (a ball, etc.) 13 forgo one's turn or chance 14 come to an end 15 discharge from the body 16 utter (legal sentence, criticism) upon; adjudicate —*n.* 17 act of passing 18 success in an examination, course, etc. 19 ticket or permit giving free entry, access, leave, travel, etc. 20 *Sports.* transference of the ball to a teammate 21 desperate position 22 **in passing** in the course of conversation, etc. 23 **make a pass at** *Colloq.* make sexual advances to 24 **pass away** *Euphem.* die 25 **pass off:** a misrepresent; disguise b evade or falsely dismiss (an awkward remark, etc.) 26 **pass out:** a become unconscious b distribute 27 **pass over** omit; ignore; disregard 28 **pass up** *Colloq.* refuse or neglect (an opportunity, etc.) —**pass'er** *n.* [L *passus* PACE]

pass² *n.* narrow way through mountains [var. of PACE]

pass'a·ble *adj.* 1 barely satisfactory; adequate 2 (of a road, etc.) that can be traversed —**pass'a·bly** *adv.*

pas·sage /pas'ij/ *n.* 1 process or means of passing; transit 2 PASSAGEWAY 3 liberty or right to pass through 4 journey by sea or air 5 transition 6 short extract from a book, piece of music, etc. [Fr, rel. to PASS¹]

pas'sage·way' *n.* narrow path or way; corridor

pass'book' *n.* booklet for recording bank deposits and withdrawals

pas·sé /pasā'/ *adj.* 1 old-fashioned 2 past its prime [Fr]

pas·sel /pas'əl/ *n. Colloq.* bunch; quite a few [dial. *parcel*]

pas·sen·ger /pas'injər/ *n.* traveler in or on a vehicle (other than the driver, pilot, crew, etc.) [Fr *passager,* rel. to PASSAGE]

pass'er·by' *n.* (*pl.* **pass'ers·by'**) person who goes past, esp. by chance

pass'-fail' *adj. & n.* (pertaining to) an academic grading system with only two grades, one yielding credit, the other not

pas·sim /pas'im/ *adv.* throughout; at several points in a book, article, etc. [L]

pass'ing *adj.* 1 moving past, by, etc. 2 cursory; brief; casual 3 having achieved satisfactory results (*passing grade*) —*n.* 4 death

pas·sion /pasH'ən/ *n.* 1 strong emotion or enthusiasm 2 emotional outburst 3 object arousing passion 4 (*cap.*) suffering of Christ during his last days —**pas'sion·less** *adj.;* **pas'sion·less·ly** *adv.;* **pas'sion·less·ness** *n.* [L *pati* pass- suffer]

pas·sion·ate /pasH'ənət/ *adj.* dominated, displaying, or caused by strong emotion —**pas′-sion·ate·ly** *adv.*

pas·sive /pas′iv/ *adj.* **1** acted upon, though not acting **2** showing no interest or initiative; submissive **3** *Chem.* not active; inert **4** *Gram.* indicating that the subject undergoes the action of the verb —**pas′sive·ly** *adv.*; **pas·siv′i·ty** *n.* [L, rel. to PASSION]

pas·sive re·sis′tance *n.* nonviolent refusal to cooperate

pas′sive smok′ing *n.* involuntary inhalation of others′ cigarette smoke

pass′key′ *n.* **1** private key to a gate, etc. **2** master key

Pass·o·ver /pas′ō′vər/ *n.* Jewish spring festival commemorating the Exodus from Egypt [fr. PASS¹, OVER]

pass′port′ *n.* **1** official document certifying the holder′s identity and citizenship and authorizing travel abroad **2** thing that ensures admission or attainment [Fr *passeport*, rel. to PASS¹, PORT¹]

pass′word′ *n.* prearranged word or phrase securing recognition, admission, etc.

past /past/ *adj.* **1** gone by in time **2** recently gone by **3** of a former time **4** *Gram.* expressing a past action or state —*n.* **5a** past time **b** past events **6** person′s past life, esp. if discreditable **7** past tense or form —*prep.* **8** beyond in time or place **9** beyond the range, duration, or compass of —*adv.* **10** so as to pass by [fr. old form of *passed*, past tense of PASS¹]

pas·ta /pä′stə/ *n.* flour paste made in various shapes (e.g., spaghetti) [It, rel. to PASTE]

paste /pāst/ *n.* **1** any moist, fairly stiff mixture **2** dough of flour with shortening, water, etc. **3** liquid adhesive used for sticking paper, etc. **4** hard, glasslike composition used for imitation gems —*v.* (**past·ed, past·ing**) **5** fasten or coat with paste **6** *Slang.* beat or thrash [LL *pasta* dough, fr. Gk]

paste′board′ *n.* stiff material made by pasting together sheets of paper

pas·tel /pastel′/ *n.* **1** less intense shade of a color **2** crayon of powdered pigments **3** drawing in pastel [Fr *pastel*, or It *pastello* dim. of PASTA]

pas·tern /pas′tərn/ *n.* part of a horse′s foot between fetlock and hoof [fr. Fr, rel. to L]

Pas·ter·nak /pas′tərnak′/, **Boris** 1890–1960; Russian poet and novelist

Pas·teur /pastōr′/, **Louis** 1822–95; French chemist and bacteriologist

pas·teur·ize /pas′CHəriz′/ *v.* (**·ized, ·iz·ing**) sterilize (milk, etc.) by heating —**pas′teur·i·za′tion** *n.* [for L. PASTEUR]

pas·tiche /pastēSH′/ *n.* literary or artistic work from or imitating various sources [LL *pasta*]

pas·time /pas′tīm′/ *n.* recreation; hobby [fr. PASS¹, TIME]

past′ mas′ter *n.* expert

pas·tor /pas′tər/ *n.* minister or priest leading a congregation —**pas′tor·ate** /-it/ *n.* [L: shepherd]

pas·tor·al /pas′tərəl/ *adj.* **1** of shepherds, flocks, or herds **2** of or portraying (esp. romanticized) country life **3** of a pastor —*n.* **4** pastoral poem, play, picture, etc. [L *pastoralis*, rel. to PASTOR]

past′ par·ti·ci·ple *n. Gram.* participle used to

421

passive / path

express completed action, form the passive voice, or as an adjective

pas·tra·mi /pəsträ′mē/ *n.* seasoned smoked beef [Yiddish]

pas·try /pā′strē/ *n.* (*pl.* **·tries**) **1** flaky dough of flour, shortening, and water used as a base and covering for pies, etc. **2** any fancy baked item [fr. PASTE]

pas·tur·age /pas′CHərij/ *n.* land for pasture

pas·ture /pas′CHər/ *n.* **1** grassland suitable for grazing **2** herbage for animals —*v.* (**·tured, ·tur·ing**) **3** put (animals) to pasture [L, rel. to PASTOR]

past·y /pā′stē/ *adj.* (**·i·er, ·i·est**) unhealthily pale —**past′i·ness** *n.*

pat¹ /pat/ *v.* (**pat·ted, pat·ting**) **1** strike or tap gently with a flat palm **2** flatten or mold by patting —*n.* **3** light stroke or tap, esp. with the hand **4** sound made by this **5** small mass (esp. of butter) **6** pat on the back congratulatory gesture [prob. imit.]

pat² *adj.* **1** prepared or known thoroughly **2** so glib as to seem contrived —*adv.* **3** in a pat manner **4** stand pat stand one′s ground; stand by one′s opinion [rel. to PAT¹]

patch /paCH/ *n.* **1** material used to mend a hole or as reinforcement **2** protective shield or bandage, esp. over an eye **3** large or irregular distinguishable area **4** piece of ground **5** scrap; remnant —*v.* **6** repair with a patch or patches **7** (of material) serve as a patch to **8** put together, esp. hastily **9** (usu. foll. by *up*) settle (a quarrel, etc.) [perh. Fr, var. of PIECE]

patch′ test′ *n.* test for allergy by applying patches of allergenic substances to the skin

patch′work′ *n.* **1** stitching together of small pieces of various cloths to form a pattern **2** thing composed of fragments, etc.

patch·y *adj.* (**·i·er, ·i·est**) **1** uneven in quality **2** having or existing in patches —**patch′i·ly** *adv.*; **patch′i·ness** *n.*

pate /pāt/ *n. Colloq.* or *Joc.* head

pâ·té /pätā′, pa-/ *n.* paste of ground and spiced meat or fish [Fr]

pa·tel·la /pətel′ə/ *n.* (*pl.* **·lae** /-ē/) kneecap —**pa·tel′lar** *adj.* [L: pan]

pat·ent *n.* /pat′nt/ **1** official document conferring the sole right to make, use, or sell a specified invention **2** invention or process so protected —*adj.* /pat′nt, pāt′-/ **3** obvious; plain **4** conferred or protected by patent —*v.* /pat′nt/ **5** obtain a patent for —**pat′ent·a·bil′i·ty** *n.*; **pat′ent·a·ble** *adj.*; **pat′ent·ly** *adv.* (in sense 3) [L *patere* lie open]

pat′ent leath′er *n.* glossy leather

pat′ent med′i·cine *n.* trademarked medicine, esp. nonprescription

pa·ter·nal /pətərn′l/ *adj.* **1** fatherly **2** related through the father **3** (of a government, etc.) limiting freedom and responsibility by well-meaning regulations —**pa·ter′nal·ly** *adv.* [L *pater* father]

pa·ter′nal·ism′ *n.* policy of governing or behaving in a paternal way —**pa·ter′nal·is′tic** /-is′tik/ *adj.*

pa·ter·ni·ty /pətər′nitē/ *n.* **1** fatherhood **2** one′s paternal origin

Pat·er·son /pat′ərsən/ *n.* city in N.J. Pop. 140,891

path /paTH/ *n.* (*pl.* **paths** /paTHz/) **1** way

or track made for or by walking 2 line along which a person or thing moves 3 course of action [OE]

pa·thet·ic /pəTHet'ik/ adj. 1 arousing pity, sadness, or contempt 2 Colloq. miserably or pitifully inadequate —**pa·thet'i·cal·ly** adv. [Gk pathos fr. paschein suffer]

path·o·gen /paTH'əjən/ n. agent causing disease —**path'o·gen'ic** /-jen'ik/ adj. [Gk pathos suffering, -GEN]

path·o·log·i·cal /paTH'əläj'ikəl/ adj. 1 of pathology 2 of or caused by physical or mental disorder —**path'o·log'i·cal·ly** adv.

pa·thol·o·gy /pəTHäl'əjē/ n. the study or symptoms of disease —**pa·thol'o·gist** n. [Gk pathos, rel. to PATHETIC]

pa·thos /pā'THäs', -THōs'/ n. evocation of pity or sadness in speech, writing, etc. [Gk, rel. to PATHETIC]

path·way /paTH'wā'/ n. path or its course

-pathy comb. form 1 feeling 2 suffering; disease

pa·tience /pā'SHəns/ n. ability to endure; perseverance; forbearance [L, rel. to PASSION]

pa·tient /pā'SHənt/ adj. 1 having or showing patience —n. 2 person receiving medical treatment —**pa'tient·ly** adv.

pa·ti·na /pətē'nə, pat'n-ə/ n. (pl. **-nas**) 1 oxidized film, usu. green, formed on old bronze 2 similar film or gloss on other surfaces [It: coating, fr. L]

pa·ti·o /pat'ē-ō'/ n. (pl. **-os**) 1 paved, usu. roofless area adjoining a house 2 roofless courtyard [Sp]

Pat·na /pat'nə/ n. city in NE India on the Ganges River. Pop. 917,000

pa·tois /pat'wä'/ n. (pl. same /-twäz'/) regional dialect [Fr]

pat. pend. abbr. patent pending

pa·tri·arch /pā'trē-ärk'/ n. 1 male head of a family or tribe 2 Eccles. a chief bishop in the Orthodox Church b RC Ch. bishop ranking immediately below the pope 3 venerable old man —**pa'tri·ar'chal** adj. [Gk patria family, arkhēs ruler]

pa·tri·arch·ate /pā'trē-är'kət/ n. office, rank, see, or residence of a patriarch

pa·tri·ar·chy /pā'trēär'kē/ n. (pl. **-chies**) male-dominated social system, with descent through the male line

pa·tri·cian /pətriSH'ən/ n. 1a Hist. member of the nobility in ancient Rome b aristocrat —adj. 2 aristocratic [L patricius, rel. to pater father]

Pat·rick, St. /pa'trik/ 5th cent.; patron saint of Ireland

pat·ri·mo·ny /pa'trəmō'nē/ n. (pl. **-nies**) property inherited from one's father or ancestor —**pat'ri·mo'ni·al** adj. [L, rel. to pater father]

pa·tri·ot /pā'trēət, pa'-/ n. person devoted to and supportive of his or her country —**pa'tri·ot'ic** /-āt'ik/ adj.; **pa'tri·ot'i·cal·ly** adv.; **pa'tri·o·tism** /-ətiz'əm/ n. [Gk patris fatherland]

pa·trol /pətrōl'/ n. 1 act of walking or traveling regularly around an area for security or supervision 2 guards, police, troops, etc., sent out to watch or protect —v. (**-trolled, -trol-**

ling) 3 carry out a patrol of 4 act as a patrol [Fr]

pa·trol' car' n. police car used for patrols

pa·tron /pā'trən/ n. (fem. **pat'ron·ess**) 1 person financially supporting a person, cause, etc.; benefactor 2 habitual customer [L patronus, rel. to pater father]

pa·tron·age /pa'trənij, pā'-/ n. 1 patron's or customer's support 2 right or control of political favors 3 patrons as a group; clientele

pa·tron·ize /pa'trəniz', pā'-/ v. (**-ized, -iz-ing**) 1 treat condescendingly 2 be a patron or customer of —**pa'tron·iz'ing** adj.; **pa'tron·iz'ing·ly** adv.

pa'tron saint' n. saint regarded as protecting a person, place, activity, etc.

pat·ro·nym·ic /pa'trənim'ik/ n. name derived from the name of a father or ancestor (e.g., Johnson) [Gk patēr father, onoma name]

pat·ter¹ /pat'ər/ n. 1 sound of quick, light steps or taps —v. 2 make this sound [fr. PAT¹]

pat·ter² n. 1 rapid, glib speech used by a comedian or salesperson —v. 2 talk or say glibly [orig. pater fr. L Pater Noster the Our Father]

pat·tern /pat'ərn/ n. 1 decorative design 2 regular or logical form, order, etc. 3 model, design, or instructions for making something 4 excellent example; model —v. 5 model (a thing) on a design, etc. 6 decorate with a pattern [fr. PATRON]

Pat·ton /pat'n/, **George Smith** 1885–1945; US general

pat·ty /pat'ē/ n. (pl. **-ties**) 1 little pie 2 disk-shaped cake of food [Fr PÂTÉ]

pau·ci·ty /pô'sətē/ n. smallness of number or quantity [L paucus few]

Paul, St. /pôl/ died c. A.D. 67; early Christian missionary; writer of several Epistles

Paul Bun·yan /bən'yən/ hero in American folklore, a giant lumberjack

Paul·ing /pô'liNG/, **Linus Carl** 1901–94; US chemist; Nobel prize 1954, 1962

paunch /pônCH, pänCH/ n. belly, stomach, esp. when protruding —**paunch'y** adj. (**-i·er, -i·est**) [AngFr pa(u)nche fr. L pantices bowels]

pau·per /pô'pər/ n. poor person —**pau'per·ism** /-izəm/ n.; **pau'per·ize** v. (**-ized, -iz-ing**) [L: poor]

pause /pôz/ n. 1 temporary stop or silence —v. (**paused, paus·ing**) 2 make a pause; wait [Gk pauein stop]

Pa·va·rot·ti /päv'ərät'ē, päv'-/, **Luciano** 1935– ; Italian operatic tenor

pave /pāv/ v. (**paved, pav·ing**) 1 cover (a street, etc.) with a durable surface 2 pave the way make preparations —**pav'ing** n. [L pavire ram (v.)]

pave'ment n. paved path, roadway, etc. [L pavimentum, rel. to PAVE]

pa·vil·ion /pəvil'yən/ n. 1 large tent at a show, fair, etc. 2 building or stand for entertainments, exhibits, etc. 3 any group of attached or related buildings [L papilio butterfly]

Pav·lov /päv'lôf', pav'-, -lôv'/, **Ivan** 1849–1936; Russian physiologist

Pav·lo·va /pav'ləvə, pavlō'və/, **Anna** 1881–1931; Russian prima ballerina

Pav·lo·vi·an /pavlō'vēən, -lō'-/ adj. 1 reacting

paw /pô/ *n.* **1** foot of an animal having claws or nails **2** *Colloq.* person's hand —*v.* **3** strike, scrape, etc., with a paw or foot **4** *Colloq.* fondle awkwardly or indecently [Fr *poue* fr. Gmc]

pawl /pôl/ *n.* lever with a catch for the teeth of a gear, wheel, or bar [LGer or Du]

pawn[1] /pôn/ *n.* **1** *Chess.* piece of the smallest size and value **2** person used by others for their own purposes [Fr *poun* fr. L *pedo -onis* foot-soldier]

pawn[2] *v.* **1** deposit (a thing) as security for money lent **2** pledge as wager —*n.* **3** object left in pawn **4 in pawn** held as security [Fr *pan* fr. Gmc]

pawn'bro'ker *n.* person who lends money at interest on the security of personal property

pawn'shop' *n.* pawnbroker's shop

paw·paw /pô'pô/ *n.* var. of PAPAW

pay /pā/ *v.* (**paid, pay·ing**) **1** give (a person) what is due for services done, goods received, debts incurred, etc. **2** give (a sum) for work done, a debt, etc. **3a** give; bestow; express **b** make (a visit) **4** be profitable or advantageous **5** reward or punish **6** let out (a rope) by slackening it —*n.* **7** wages —*adj.* **8** operating only on payment of coins, a set fee, etc. **9 in the pay of** employed by **10 pay back: a** repay **b** punish or have revenge on **11 pay off: a** *Colloq.* yield good results; succeed **b** pay (a debt) in full **c** bribe —**pay·ee** /pā-ē'/, **pay'er** *n.* [L *pacare* appease, rel. to PEACE]

pay'a·ble *adj.* that must or may be paid; due

pay'check' *n.* check in payment of wages

pay' day' *n.* day on which wages are paid

pay' dirt' *n.* **1** mineral-rich ore, soil, etc. **2** *Colloq.* source of wealth or success

pay'load' *n.* **1** *Aeron.* cargo, passengers, etc. **2** explosive warhead carried by a rocket, etc.

pay'mas'ter *n.* official who pays troops, employees, etc.

pay'ment *n.* **1** paying **2** amount paid **3** reward; recompense

pay'off' *n. Slang.* **1** payment **2** climax **3** final reckoning **4** bribe

pay·o·la /pā-ō'lə/ *n. Slang.* bribe offered for unofficial promotion of a product, etc., in the media

pay' phone' *n.* coin-operated telephone

pay'roll' *n.* **1** list of employees receiving regular pay **2** total sum required to pay these

Pb *symb.* lead [L *plumbum*]

PBS *abbr.* Public Broadcasting Service

PC *abbr.* **1** personal computer **2** politically correct

PCB *abbr.* polychlorinated biphenyl, any of several toxic aromatic compounds formed as waste in industrial processes

pct. *abbr.* percent; percentage

Pd *symb.* palladium

pd. *abbr.* paid

P.D. *abbr.* **1** (also **p.d.**) per diem **2** police department **3** public defender

PDT *abbr.* Pacific daylight time

PE *abbr.* physical education

pea /pē/ *n.* **1** climbing plant with edible seeds growing in pods **2** its seed [formerly *pease* mistaken as a pl.]

peace /pēs/ *n.* **1a** quiet; tranquillity **b** mental calm; serenity **2** freedom from or the cessa-

tion of war **3** freedom from civil disorder **4 hold one's peace** keep silent [L *pax pac-*]

peace'a·ble *adj.* **1** disposed to peace **2** peaceful; tranquil —**peace'a·bly** *adv.* [L *placibilis* pleasing, rel. to PLEASE]

peace·ful /pēs'fəl/ *adj.* **1** characterized by peace; tranquil **2** not infringing peace —**peace'ful·ly** *adv.*; **peace'ful·ness** *n.*

peace'mak'er *n.* person who brings about peace —**peace'mak'ing** *n. & adj.*

peace' pipe' *n.* tobacco pipe smoked as a token of peace among N American Indians

peace'time' *n.* **1** period when a country is not at war —*adj.* **2** of such a time

peach /pēch/ *n.* **1a** round, juicy fruit with downy yellow or reddish skin **b** tree bearing this **2** yellowish-pink color **3** *Colloq.* person or thing of superlative quality, attractiveness, etc. —**peach'y** *adj.* (**·i·er, ·i·est**) [L *persica Pers* (apple)]

pea·cock /pē'käk/ *n.* (*pl.* same or **·cocks**) male peafowl, with brilliant plumage and erectile fanlike tail feathers with eyelike markings [fr. L *pavo* peacock, COCK]

pea'fowl' *n.* peacock or peahen

pea'hen' *n.* female peafowl

pea'jack'et (also **pea' coat'**) *n.* heavy wool coat, as worn by seamen

peak /pēk/ *n.* **1** projecting, usu. pointed part, esp.: **a** the pointed top of a mountain **b** a mountain with a peak **c** a stiff brim at the front of a cap **2a** highest point **b** time of greatest success, fitness, etc. —*adj.* **3** maximum; busiest —*v.* **4** reach its highest value, quality, etc. —**peaked** /pēkt/ *adj.* [rel. to PICK]

peak·ed /pē'kid/ *adj.* sharp-featured; pinched or drawn, esp. from illness

peal /pēl/ *n.* **1a** loud ringing of a bell or bells **b** tuned set of bells **2** loud, repeated sound, esp. of thunder, laughter, etc. —*v.* **3** (cause to) sound in a peal [fr. APPEAL]

Peale /pēl/ **1 Charles Willson** 1741–1827; US painter **2 Norman Vincent** 1898–1994; US clergyman and writer

pea·nut /pē'nət'/ *n.* **1** plant of the pea family bearing pods underground that contain seeds used for food and oil **2** seed of this **3** (*pl.*) *Colloq.* paltry thing or amount, esp. of money

pea'nut but'ter *n.* paste of ground, roasted peanuts

pear /per/ *n.* **1** fleshy fruit, tapering toward the stalk **2** tree bearing this [L *pirum*]

pearl /pərl/ *n.* **1a** rounded, usu. white or bluish-gray, lustrous solid formed within the shell of certain oysters, highly prized as a gem **b** imitation of this **2** precious thing; finest example **3** thing like a pearl, e.g., a dewdrop or tear —*v.* **4** fish for pearl oysters —**pearl'y** *adj.* [It *perla*, fr. L *perna* sea mussel]

Pearl' Har'bor *n.* inlet on the S coast of Oahu, Hawaii; site of US naval base

Pea·ry /per'ē/, **Robert Edwin** 1856–1920; US arctic explorer

peas·ant /pez'ənt/ *n.* **1** small farmer; agricultural worker **2** *Derog.* lout; boor —**peas'ant·ry** *n.* (*pl.* **·ries**) [AngFr *paisant* fr. *païs* country]

peat /pēt/ *n.* partly carbonized vegetable matter obtained from marshland, used for fuel, in horticulture, etc. —**peat′y** *adj.* [perh. Celt, rel. to PIECE]

peat′bog *n.* bog composed of peat

peat′moss′ *n.* dried peat from mosses

peb·ble /pebˈəl/ *n.* small stone worn smooth, esp. by the action of water —**peb′bly** *adj.* [OE]

pe·can /pikänˈ, -kanˈ; pēˈkanˈ/ *n.* **1** pinkish-brown, smooth nut with an edible kernel **2** type of hickory producing this [Algonquian]

pec·ca·dil·lo /pekˈədilˈō/ *n.* (*pl.* ·**loes** or ·**los**) trifling offense; venial sin [Sp *pecadillo*, fr. L *peccare* to sin]

peck[1] /pek/ *v.* **1** strike or bite with a beak **2** kiss hastily or perfunctorily **3** make, remove, or pluck by pecking **4** *Colloq.* eat listlessly; nibble at —*n.* **5** stroke, mark, or bite made by a beak **6** hasty or perfunctory kiss [prob. LGer]

peck[2] *n.* dry measure equal to 8 quarts [AngFr]

peck′ing or′der *n.* social hierarchy

pec·tin /pekˈtin/ *n.* soluble gelatinous carbohydrate found in ripe fruits, etc., and used as a setting agent in jams and jellies —**pec′tic** *adj.* [Gk *pectos* congealed]

pec·to·ral /pekˈtərəl/ *adj.* **1** of or worn on the breast or chest —*n.* **2** pectoral muscle or fin [L *pectus -tor-* chest]

pec·u·late /pekˈyəlāt/ *v.* (·**lat·ed**, ·**lat·ing**) embezzle —**pec·u·la′tion, pec′u·la′tor** *n.* [L, rel. to PECULIAR]

pe·cu·liar /pikyōōlˈyər/ *adj.* **1** strange; odd; unusual **2a** belonging exclusively to; belonging to the individual **3** particular; special —**pe·cu′liar·ly** *adv.* [L *peculium* private property, fr. *pecu* cattle]

pe·cu·li·ar·i·ty /pikyōōˈlē·ar′ətē/ *n.* (*pl.* ·**ties**) **1** oddity; idiosyncrasy **2** characteristic [pe·cu·liar]

pe·cu·ni·ar·y /pikyōōˈnē·er′ē/ *adj.* of or concerning money [L *pecunia* money, fr. *pecu* cattle]

ped·a·gogue /pedˈəgäg′/ *n.* schoolmaster; pedantic teacher —**ped·a·gog·ic** /pedˈəgō′jik/, **ped′a·gog′i·cal** *adj.* [Gk *pais paid-* child, *agein* lead]

ped·a·go·gy /pedˈəgäj′ē, -gō′jē/ *n.* science of teaching

ped·al *n.* /pedˈl/ **1** lever or control operated by foot, esp. in a vehicle, on a bicycle, etc. —*v.* /pedˈl/ (·**aled** or ·**alled**, ·**al·ing** or ·**al·ling**) **2** operate the pedals of **3** propel (a bicycle, etc.) with the pedals —*adj.* /pēdˈl/ **4** of the foot or feet [L *pes ped-* foot]

ped·ant /pedˈnt/ *n.* person, esp. a teacher, who insists on adherence to formal rules or literal meaning —**pe·dan·tic** /pədant′ik/, *adj.*; **pe·dan′ti·cal·ly** *adv.*; **ped′ant·ry** *n.* [Fr fr. It]

ped·dle /pedˈl/ *v.* (·**dled**, ·**dling**) **1a** sell (goods) while traveling **b** advocate or promote **2** sell (drugs) illegally —**ped′dler** *n.*

ped·er·as·ty /pedˈərasˈtē/ *n.* anal intercourse between a man and a boy —**ped′er·ast** *n.* [Gk *pais paid-* boy, *erastēs* lover]

ped·es·tal /pedˈəstal/ *n.* base supporting a column, pillar, statue, etc. [It *piedestallo* foot of stall]

pe·des·tri·an /pədesˈtrēən/ *n.* **1** person who is walking —*adj.* **2** prosaic; dull; uninspired

3 of or for pedestrians —**pe·des′tri·an·ize** *v.* (·**ized**, ·**iz·ing**) [L, rel. to PEDAL]

pe·di·at·rics /pēˈdē·a′triks/ *n. pl.* (treated as *sing.*) branch of medicine dealing with children and their diseases —**pe′di·at′ric** *adj.*; **pe′di·a·tri′cian** /-ətrish′ən/ *n.* [Gk *pais, paid-* child, *iatros* physician]

ped·i·cure /pedˈikyōōr′/ *n.* care or treatment of the feet, esp. the toenails [L *pes ped-* foot, *cura* care]

ped·i·gree /pedˈigrē′/ *n.* **1** recorded line of descent **2** genealogical table —**ped′i·greed** *adj.* [fr. MFr *pie de grue* crane's foot, thought to resemble lines in a family tree]

PEDIMENT

ped·i·ment /pedˈəmənt/ *n.* triangular part crowning the front of a building, esp. over a doorway, etc. [fr. *periment*, perh. a corruption of PYRAMID]

ped·lar /pedˈlər/ *n.* a former spelling of PEDDLER

pe·dom·e·ter /pidämˈətər/ *n.* instrument for measuring distance walked [L *pes ped-* foot, rel. to -METER]

pe·dun·cle /pēˈdəNGˈkəl, pidəNGˈ/ *n.* stalk of a flower, fruit, or cluster —**pe·dun′cu·lar** /-kyələr/ *adj.* [L *pedunculus*, dim. of *pes, ped-* foot]

peek /pēk/ *v.* **1** look slyly; glance —*n.* **2** quick or sly look

peel /pēl/ *v.* **1a** strip the skin, rind, wrapping, etc., from **b** strip (skin, peel, etc.) **2a** become bare of skin, paint, etc. **b** flake off —*n.* **3** rind of a fruit, vegetable, etc. —**peel′er** *n.* [OE fr. L *pilo* strip of hair]

Peel /pēl/, (**Sir**) **Robert** 1788–1850; British prime minister (1834–35; 1841–46)

peel′ing *n.* (usu. *pl.*) stripped-off piece of peel

peen /pēn/ *n.* ball- or wedge-shaped end of a hammerhead [prob. Scan]

peep[1] /pēp/ *v.* **1** look through a narrow opening; look furtively **2** come slowly into view; emerge —*n.* **3** furtive or peering glance

peep[2] *v.* **1** make a shrill feeble sound as of young birds, mice, etc. —*n.* **2** such a sound **3** slight sound, utterance, or complaint [imit.]

peep′hole′ *n.* small hole for peeping through

peep′ing Tom′ *n.* furtive voyeur

peer[1] /pēr/ *v.* look closely or with difficulty

peer[2] *n.* **1a** (*fem.* **peer′ess**) member of the British nobility **b** noble of any country **2** person who is equal in ability, standing, rank, or value —**peer′age** /-ij/ *n.* [L *par* equal]

peer′less *adj.* unequalled; superb

peeve /pēv/ *Colloq. v.* (**peeved, peev·ing**) **1** irritate; annoy —*n.* **2** cause or state of irritation [back formation fr. PEEVISH]

pee·vish *adj.* irritable —**pee′vish·ly** *adv.*

pee·wee /pēˈwē/ *n.* any thing or person that is unusually small

peg /peg/ *n.* **1** pin or bolt of wood, metal, etc., for holding, hanging, or supporting things **2** pin for marking position, e.g., on a map, cribbage board, etc. **3** degree or notch **4** *Slang.*

fast, accurate throw —*v.* (**pegged, peg·ging**) **5** fix, stabilize, secure, etc., with or as if with pegs **6** throw accurately **7 peg away (at)** work consistently [prob. LGer or Du]

Peg·a·sus /pĕg′əsəs/ *Gk. Myth.* legendary winged horse

peg′board′ *n.* board with small holes for pegs or other fittings, used for displays, storage, etc.

Pei /pā/, **I(eoh) M(ing)** 1917– ; Chinese-born US architect

pe·jo·ra·tive /pijôr′ətiv, -jär′-/ *adj.* **1** derogatory —*n.* **2** derogatory word —**pe′jo·ra′tion** /-rā′sHən/ *n.;* **pe·jor·a·tive·ly** *adv.* [L *pejor* worse]

Pe·king /pākiNG′, pē′-/ *n.* see BEIJING

Pe·king·ese /pē′kinēz′, -ēs′/ *n.* (also **Pe′kin·ese′**) (*pl.* same) short-legged lap dog with long hair and a snub nose [fr. *Peking* (Beijing) in China]

pe·koe /pē′kō/ *n.* black tea grown in Sri Lanka and India

pe·lag·ic /pəlaj′ik/ *adj.* of the open ocean

pelf /pelf/ *n. Derog.* or *Joc.* money; wealth [Fr, rel. to PILFER]

pel·i·can /pel′ikən/ *n.* water bird with a large bill and a pouch in its throat for carrying fish [Gk *pelekan*]

pel·la·gra /pəlag′rə, -lā′grə/ *n.* disease caused by niacin deficiency, marked by cracking of the skin and mental disorders [It fr. L *pellis* skin, Gk *agra* seizure]

pel·let /pel′it/ *n.* **1** small compressed ball of paper, medicine, etc. **2** piece of small shot [Fr *pelote* fr. L *pila* ball]

pell-mell /pel′mel′/ *adv.* **1** headlong; recklessly **2** in disorder or confusion [Fr *pêle-mêle*]

pel·lu·cid /pilōō′sid/ *adj.* **1** transparent **2** clear; easily understood [L, rel. to PER-]

pelt[1] /pelt/ *v.* **1** strike repeatedly with thrown objects **2** fall quickly and torrentially

pelt[2] *n.* undressed skin, usu. of a fur-bearing mammal [Fr, ult. fr. L *pellis* skin]

pel·vis /pel′vis/ *n.* basin-shaped cavity in most vertebrates, formed from the hip bones, sacrum, and other vertebrae —**pel′vic** *adj.* [L: basin]

pen[1] /pen/ *n.* **1** instrument for writing, etc., with ink —*v.* (**penned, pen·ning**) **2** write [L *penna* feather]

pen[2] *n.* **1** small enclosure for cows, sheep, poultry, etc. —*v.* (**penned, pen·ning**) **2** enclose or shut up, esp. in a pen [OE]

pen[3] *n. Slang.* penitentiary

pe·nal /pēn′l/ *adj.* of or concerning punishment or its infliction —**pe′nal·ly** *adv.* [L *poena* PAIN]

pe·nal·ize /pēn′l-īz′/ *v.* (**·ized, ·iz·ing**) subject (a person) to a penalty or disadvantage

pen·al·ty /pen′l-tē/ *n.* (*pl.* **·ties**) **1** punishment **2** disadvantage, loss, etc., esp. as a result of one's own actions **3** *Sports.* disadvantage imposed for a breach of the rules, etc. [MedL, rel. to PENAL]

pen·ance /pen′əns/ *n.* act of self-punishment as reparation for guilt, sins, etc. [rel. to PENITENT]

pen·chant /pen′CHənt/ *n.* inclination or liking [Fr]

pen·cil /pen′səl/ *n.* **1** instrument for writing or drawing, usu. a thin rod of graphite, etc.,

enclosed in a wooden cylinder or metal case —*v.* (**·ciled** or **·cilled, ·cil·ing** or **·cil·ling**) **2** write, draw, or mark with a pencil **3** write, note, or arrange provisionally [L *penicillum* paintbrush]

pend /pend/ *v.* await decision or settlement

pen·dant /pen′dənt/ *n.* hanging jewel, etc., esp. one attached to a necklace, bracelet, etc. [Fr *pendre* hang]

pen·dent /pen′dənt/ *adj.* **1a** hanging **b** overhanging **2** undecided; pending —**pen′den·cy** *n.*

pend′ing *adj.* **1** awaiting decision or settlement; undecided —*prep.* **2** during **3** until [after Fr: see PENDANT]

pen·du·lous /pen′jələs/ *adj.* hanging down; drooping and swinging [L *pendulus* fr. *pendere* hang]

pen·du·lum /pen′jələm/ *n.* (*pl.* **·lums**) weight suspended so as to swing freely, esp. one regulating a clock [L neut. adj., rel. to PENDULOUS]

pen·e·trate /pen′ətrāt′/ *v.* (**·trat·ed, ·trat·ing**) **1a** find access into or through **b** pierce **c** permeate **2** see into or through; find out; discern **3** be absorbed by the mind —**pen′e·tra·ble** /-trəbəl/ *adj.;* **pen′e·tra·bil′i·ty, pen′e·tra′tion** *n.;* **pen′e·tra·tive** *adj.* [L]

PENDULUM

pen′e·trat′ing *adj.* **1** insightful; sensitive **2** easily heard; piercing

pen·guin /peNG′gwin, pen′-/ *n.* flightless black and white sea bird of the southern hemisphere with flipperlike wings used in swimming

pen·i·cil·lin /pen′əsil′ən/ *n.* antibiotic produced naturally from mold or synthetically [L *penicillum,* rel. to PENCIL]

pen·in·su·la /pənin′s(y)ələ/ *n.* piece of land almost surrounded by water —**pen·in′su·lar** *adj.* [L *paene* almost, *insula* island]

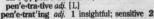

PENGUIN

pe·nis /pē′nis/ *n.* male organ of copulation and (in mammals) urination —**pe·nile** /pē′nīl/ *adj.* [L]

pen·i·tent /pen′ətənt/ *adj.* **1** repentant —*n.* **2** repentant person —**pen′i·tence** *n.;* **pen′i·ten′tial** /-ten′sHəl/ *adj.;* **pen′i·tent·ly** *adv.* [L *paenitere* repent]

pen·i·ten·tia·ry /pen′əten′sHərē/ *n.* (*pl.* **·ries**) **1** federal or state prison —*adj.* **2** of penance **3** of reformatory treatment [L, rel. to PENITENT]

pen′knife′ *n.* (*pl.* **knives** /-nīvz′/) pocket-knife

pen·light /pen′līt′/ *n.* small flashlight

pen′man·ship′ *n.* art of fine handwriting

Penn /pen/, **William** 1644–1718; English founder of Pennsylvania (1682)

Penn., Penna. abbr. for Pennsylvania

pen′ name′ *n.* literary pseudonym

pen·nant /pen′ənt/ *n.* **1** long, tapering flag **2**

sports championship or a flag representing this [blend of PENDANT and PENNON]

pen·ni·less /pen'ēlis, pen'i-/ adj. having no money; destitute

pen·non /pen'ən/ n. pennant; flag [L penna feather]

Penn·syl·va·nia /pen'səlvā'nyə/ n. NE state of the US. Capital: Harrisburg. Pop. 11,881,643. Abbr. PA; Pa.; Penn.; Penna.

Penn·syl·va·nian /pen'səlvān'yən, -vā'nēən/ adj. 1 of or pertaining to the state of Pennsylvania 2 Geol. of or pertaining to a Paleozoic Era period from about 310 to 280 million years ago, an age of insect and reptile development —n. 3 native or inhabitant of Pennsylvania

pen·ny /pen'ē/ n. (pl. ·nies) 1 US or Canadian cent 2a coin in the UK equal to one hundredth of a pound b Hist. coin in the UK equal to 1/240 of a pound [OE]

pen'ny an'te /an'tē/ n. 1 poker game with small stakes —adj. 2 Colloq. small-time; small-scale

pen'ny ar·cade' n. amusement center containing coin-operated games, etc.

pen'ny-pinch'ing n. 1 frugality —adj. 2 frugal —pen'ny-pinch'er n.

pen'ny-weight' n. unit of troy weight, 1/20 of an ounce or 24 grains

pe·nol·o·gy /pēnäl'əjē/ n. the study of the punishment of crime and prison management —pe·nol'o·gist n. [L poena penalty]

pen' pal' n. Colloq. friend, esp. one from abroad, communicated with by letter

Pen·sa·co·la /pen'səkō'lə/ n. city in Fla. Pop. 58,165

pen·sion /pen'SHən/ n. 1 regular payment made to the disabled, retirees, etc. —v. 2 grant a pension to —pen'sion·a·ble adj.; pen'sion·er n. [L pensio paying]

pen·sive /pen'siv/ adj. deep in thought —pen'sive·ly adv.; pen'sive·ness n. [Fr penser think]

pent /pent/ adj. closely confined; shut in (fr. PEN²]

penta- comb. form five [Gk pente five]

pen·ta·cle /pen'tikəl/ n. figure used as a symbol, esp. in magic, e.g., a pentagram [MedL pentaculum, rel. to PENTA-]

pen·ta·gon /pen'təgän/ n. 1 plane figure with five sides and angles 2 (cap.) pentagonal building in Washington, DC, headquarters of the US Defense Department —pen·tag·o·nal /pentag'ənl/ adj. [PENTA-, Gk gonia angle]

pen·ta·gram /pen'təgram/ n. five-pointed star [Gk PENTA-, -GRAM]

pen·tam·e·ter /pentam'ətər/ n. line of verse with five metrical feet [Gk PENTA-, -METER]

Pen·ta·teuch /pent'ət(y)ook'/ n. first five books of the Old Testament [Gk PENTA-, teukhos book]

pen·tath·lon /pentaTH'län/ n. athletic event comprising five different events for each competitor —pen·tath'lete' /-təTH'lēt'/ n. [Gk PENTA-, athlon contest]

Pen·te·cost /pen'tikôst', -käst'/ n. 1 Christian festival held on the seventh Sunday after Easter; Whitsunday 2 Jewish harvest festival, on the fiftieth day after the second day of Passover [Gk pentēkostē fiftieth (day)]

pen·te·cos'tal adj. of or describing esp. fun-

damentalist Christian groups that emphasize the activity of the Holy Spirit, as healing power, speaking in tongues, etc.

pent·house /pent'hous'/ n. apartment on the roof or top floor of a tall building [L, rel. to APPEND]

pe·nu·che /pənoo'CHē/ n. type of brown-sugar fudge

pen·ul·ti·mate /pinəl'təmət/ adj. & n. last but one [L paene almost, ultimus last]
 • Usage: Avoid using penultimate to mean 'ultimate.'

pen·um·bra /pinəm'brə/ n. (pl. ·bras or ·brae /-brē/) 1 partly shaded region around the shadow of an opaque body, esp. that around the shadow of the moon or earth in an eclipse 2 partial shadow —pen·um'bral adj. [L paene almost, UMBRA]

pe·nu·ri·ous /pin(y)oor'ēəs/ adj. 1 poor 2 stingy; grudging [MedL, rel. to PENURY]

pen·u·ry /pen'yərē/ n. (pl. ·ries) 1 destitution; poverty 2 lack; scarcity [L]

Pen·za /pen'zä/ n. city in W Russia. Pop. 551,500

pe·on /pē'än, -ən/ n. 1 in Latin America, a day-laborer 2 person held in servitude to work off a debt [Port and Sp, rel. to PAWN¹]

pe·o·ny /pē'ənē/ n. (pl. ·nies) plant with globular red, pink, or white flowers [Gk paiōnia]

peo·ple /pē'pəl/ n. (pl. except sense 1) 1 persons composing a community, tribe, race, nation, etc. 2 persons in general or of a specified kind 3 the mass of people in a country, etc. 4 family 5 subjects, followers, congregation, etc. 6 humans generally —v. (·pled, ·pling) 7 populate; inhabit [L populus]
 • Usage: See note at PERSON.

Pe·o·ri·a /pē·ôr'ēə, -ōr'-/ n. city in Ill. Pop. 113,504

pep /pep/ Colloq. n. 1 vigor; spirit —v. (pepped, pep·ping) 2 (foll. by up) fill with vigor —pep'py adj. (·pi·er, ·pi·est) [abbr. of PEPPER]

Pep·in /pep'in/ (called "the Short") c. 714-768; king of the Franks (751-768); father of Charlemagne

pep·per /pep'ər/ n. 1 hot, aromatic condiment from the dried berries of certain plants 2 plant with a red, green, or yellow many-seeded fruit, grown as a vegetable —v. 3 sprinkle or treat with or as if with pepper 4 pelt with missiles [Gk peperi]

pep'per·corn' n. dried pepper berry

pep'per mill' n. device for grinding peppercorns

pep'per·mint' n. 1a mint plant grown for its strong-flavored oil b this oil 2 candy flavored with peppermint

pep·per·o·ni /pep'ərō'nē/ n. beef and pork sausage seasoned with pepper [It peperone chili]

pep'per shak'er n. small container with a perforated lid for sprinkling ground pepper

pep'per·y adj. 1 of, like, or containing pepper 2 hot-tempered 3 pungent

pep·sin /pep'sin/ n. enzyme contained in the gastric juice [Gk pepsis digestion]

pep' talk' n. talk intended to create enthusiasm, etc.

pep·tic /pep'tik/ adj. 1 concerning or promoting digestion **2** of or caused by pepsin [Gk *peptikos* able to digest]

Pepys /pēps/, **Samuel** 1633–1703; English diarist

per /pər/ *prep.* **1** for each **2** by means of; by; through **3** (in full **as per**) in accordance with [L]

per- *prefix* **1** through; all over **2** completely; very [L *per*, rel. to PER]

per·ad·ven·ture /pər'adven'CHər/ *adv. Archaic.* or *joc.* perhaps [Fr, rel. to PER, ADVENTURE]

per·am·bu·late /pəram'byəlāt'/ *v.* (**·lat·ed, ·lat·ing**) walk through, over, or about —**per·am'bu·la'tion** *n.* [L *perambulare*, rel. to AMBLE]

per an'num /an'əm/ *adv.* for each year [L]

per·cale /pərkāl'/ *n.* closely woven cotton fabric [Fr]

per cap·i·ta /kap'itə/ *adv. & adj.* for each person [L: by heads]

per·ceive /pərsēv'/ *v.* (**·ceived, ·ceiv·ing**) **1** observe; take notice of **2** understand; see or regard —**per·ceiv'a·ble** *adj.* [L *percipere -cept-* seize; understand]

per·cent /pərsent'/ (also **per' cent'**) *adv.* **1** in every hundred —*n.* **2** percentage [L *per centum* per hundred]

● Usage: Some still insist on the spelling as two words, *per cent*, rather than as one word, *percent*. Both are acceptable, but one should be consistent.

per·cent'age /-ij/ *n.* **1** rate or proportion; per-cent **2** proportion

per·cen·tile /pərsen'tīl'/ *n. Stat.* each of 100 groups of equal size into which a range of data is divided, or the points dividing each group

per·cep·ti·ble /pəsep'təbəl/ *adj.* capable of being perceived —**per·cep'ti·bil'i·ty** *n.*; **per·cep'ti·bly** *adv.* [L, rel. to PERCEIVE]

per·cep·tion /pərsep'SHən/ *n.* **1** act or faculty of perceiving **2** intuitive recognition; way of seeing or understanding —**per·cep'tion·al, per·cep'tu·al** /-CHŌōəl/ *adj.*; **per·cep'tu·al·ly** *adv.*

per·cep·tive /pərsep'tiv/ *adj.* **1** sensitive; discerning **2** capable of perceiving —**per·cep'tive·ly** *adv.* —**per·cep'tive·ness, per·cep·tiv'i·ty** *n.*

perch¹ /pərCH/ *n.* **1** bar, branch, etc., used by a bird to rest on **2** high place for a person or thing to rest on —*v.* **3** settle or rest on or as on a perch, etc. [L *pertica* pole]

perch² *n.* (*pl.* same or **-es**) edible spiny-finned, freshwater fish [L *perca* fr. Gk]

per·chance /pərCHans'/ *adv. Archaic.* or *Poet.* **1** by chance **2** maybe [AngFr *par by*]

per·co·late /pər'kəlāt'/ *v.* (**·lat·ed, ·lat·ing**) **1a** (of liquid, etc.) filter or ooze gradually **b** (of an idea, etc.) permeate gradually **2** strain (a liquid, powder, etc.) through a fine mesh, etc. —**per'co·la'tion** *n.* [L *colum* strainer]

per·co·la·tor *n.* device for making coffee by circulating boiling water through ground beans

per·cus·sion /pərkəSH'ən/ *n.* **1a** playing of music by striking instruments with sticks, etc. **b** such instruments collectively **2** gentle or forcible striking of one solid body against another —**per·cus'sion·ist** *n.*; **per·cus'sive** /-kəs'iv/ *adj.* [L *percutere -cuss-* strike]

per·cus'sion cap' *n.* small amount of explo-

sive powder contained in metal or paper and exploded by striking

per di·em /pər dē'əm/ *adv.* **1** daily —*n.* **2** daily allowance for expenses

per·di·tion /pərdiSH'ən/ *n.* damnation [L *perdere -dit-* destroy]

per·e·gri·nate /per'əgrināt'/ *v.* (**·nat·ed, ·nat·ing**) travel across, through, etc.

per·e·grine /per'əgrin, -grēn'/ *n.* (in full **per'e·grine fal'con**) very fast-flying falcon used in hawking [L *peregrinus* foreign]

pe·remp·to·ry /pəremp't(ə)rē/ *adj.* **1** admitting no denial or refusal **2** imperious; dictatorial —**pe·remp'to·ri·ly** *adv.*; **pe·remp'to·ri·ness** *n.* [L *peremptorius* deadly; decisive]

pe·ren·ni·al /pəren'ēəl/ *adj.* **1** lasting through a year or several years **2** (of a plant) lasting several years **3** lasting a long time or forever —*n.* **4** perennial plant —**pe·ren'ni·al·ly** *adv.* [L *perennis* fr. *annus* year]

pe·re·stroi·ka /per'əstroi'kə/ *n.* (in the former USSR) reform of the economic and political system [Russ: restructuring]

Pé·rez de Cué·llar /per'ez de kwā'yär/, **Javier** 1920– ; Peruvian diplomat; Secretary-General of the United Nations (1982–92)

per·fect *adj.* /pər'fikt/ **1** complete; not deficient; faultless **2** very enjoyable; excellent **3** exact; precise **4** entire; unqualified **5** *Gram.* (of a tense) denoting a completed action or event (e.g., *he has gone*) —*v.* /pərfekt'/ **6** make perfect **7** complete —*n.* /pər'fikt/ **8** *Gram.* the perfect tense —**per·fect'i·ble** *adj.*; **per·fect'i·bil'i·ty** *n.*; **per'fect·ly** *adv.*; **per'fect·ness** *n.* [L *perficere -fect-* complete (v.)]

● Usage: Purists maintain that *perfect, unique*, etc., are absolute words and should not be modified in such phrases as "more perfect, more unique," etc.

per·fec·ta /pərfek'tə/ *n.* bet won by picking the first and second finishers in a race

per·fec·tion /pərfek'SHən/ *n.* **1** making, becoming, or being perfect **2** faultlessness **3** perfect person, thing, or example **4** to **perfection** exactly; completely [L, rel. to PERFECT]

per·fec'tion·ism' *n.* uncompromising pursuit of excellence —**per·fec'tion·ist** *n. & adj.*

per'fect pitch' *n.* ability to identify or sound any given pitch

per·fi·dy /pər'fidē/ *n.* breach of faith; treachery —**per·fid'i·ous** /-fid'ēəs/ *adj.* [L *perfidia* fr. *fides* faith]

per·fo·rate /pər'fərāt'/ *v.* (**·rat·ed, ·rat·ing**) **1** make a hole or holes through; pierce **2** make a row of small holes in (paper, etc.) so that a part may be torn off easily —**per'fo·ra'tion** *n.* [L *perforare* pierce through]

per·force /pərfôrs'/ *adv. Archaic.* unavoidably; necessarily [Fr *par force* by FORCE]

per·form /pə(r)fôrm'/ *v.* **1** do; execute **2** act in a play; play music, sing, etc.; execute tricks **3** function —**per·form'er** *n.* [AngFr, rel. to PER-, FURNISH]

per·for·mance /pə(r)fôr'məns/ *n.* **1a** act, process, or manner of performing or functioning **b** execution (of a duty, etc.) **2a** performing of a play, music, etc. **b** instance of this

per·form'ing arts' *n. pl.* drama, music, dance, etc.

per·fume *n.* /pər'fyōōm/ **1** sweet smell **2** fluid containing the essence of flowers, etc.; scent —*v.* /pər'fyōōm', pərfyōōm'/ (·**fumed**, ·**fum·ing**) **3** scent with perfume [It *parfumare* smoke through]

per·fum'er *n.* maker or seller of perfumes —**per·fum'er·y** *n.* (*pl.* ·**ies**)

per·func·to·ry /pərfəNGK't(ə)rē/ *adj.* done merely out of duty; superficial; careless —**per·func'to·ri·ly** *adv.*; **per·func'to·ri·ness** *n.* [L, rel. to FUNCTION]

per·go·la /pər'gələ/ *n.* arbor or covered walk formed of growing plants trained over a trellis [It]

per·haps /pərhaps'/ *adv.* it may be; possibly

peri- *prefix* around; about [Gk]

per·i·car·di·um /per'əkär'dēəm/ *n.* (*pl.* ·**di·a** /-dēə/) membranous sac enclosing the heart [Gk *kardia* heart]

Per·i·cles /per'əklēz/ *c.* 495–429 B.C.; Athenian statesman and general

per·i·gee /per'əjē'/ *n.* point in the orbit of a planet, satellite, etc., where it is nearest the earth [Gk *perigeion*]

per·i·he·li·on /per'əhē'lēən/ *n.* (*pl.* ·**li·a** /-lēə/) point in the orbit of a planet or comet where it is nearest the sun [rel. to PERI-, Gk *hēlios* sun]

per·il /per'əl/ *n.* serious and immediate danger —**per'il·ous** *adj.*; **per'il·ous·ly** *adv.* [L *peric(u)lum*]

pe·rim·e·ter /pərim'ətər/ *n.* **1** circumference or outline of a closed figure or enclosed area **2** length of this [Gk, rel. to -METER]

per·i·ne·um /per'ənē'əm/ *n.* (*pl.* ·**ne·a** /-nē'ə/) region between the anus and the genitals —**per·i'ne·al** *adj.* [L fr. Gk]

pe·ri·od /pēr'ēəd/ *n.* **1** length or portion of time **2** distinct portion of history, a person's life, a geological era, etc. **3** interval between recurrences of an event **4** portion of time allowed for a lesson, section of a game, etc. **5** occurrence of menstruation **6a** punctuation mark (.) used at the end of a sentence or abbreviation **b** *Colloq.* used at the end of a statement to indicate finality —*adj.* **7** characteristic of some past period [Gk *periodos* cycle]

pe·ri·od·ic /pēr'ē·äd'ik/ *adj.* appearing or occurring at intervals —**pe'ri·od·ic'i·ty** /-ədis'itē/ *n.*

pe'ri·od'i·cal *n.* **1** newspaper, magazine, etc., issued at regular intervals —*adj.* **2** periodic —**pe'ri·od'i·cal·ly** *adv.*

pe'ri·od·ic ta'ble *n.* arrangement of chemical elements in order of increasing atomic number

per·i·o·don·tics /per'ēədän'tiks/ *n. pl.* (treated as *sing.*) branch of dentistry concerned with the structures surrounding and supporting the teeth —**per'i·o·don'tal** *adj.*; **per'i·o·don'tist** *n.* [Gk *odous* tooth]

per·i·pa·tet·ic /per'əpətet'ik/ *adj.* going from place to place; itinerant [Gk *patein* walk]

pe·riph·er·al /pərif'(ə)rəl/ *adj.* **1** of minor importance; marginal **2** of the periphery —*n.* **3** any input, output, or storage device that can be connected to and used with a computer, e.g., a modem or printer

pe·riph·er·y /pərif'(ə)rē/ *n.* (*pl.* ·**ies**) **1** boundary of an area or surface **2** outer or surrounding region [Gk *pherein* bear]

pe·riph·ra·sis /pərif'rəsis/ *n.* (*pl.* ·**ses** /-sēz'/) roundabout way of speaking; circumlocution —**per·i·phras·tic** /per'əfras'tik/ *adj.* [Gk, rel. to PHRASE]

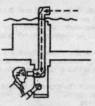

PERISCOPE

per·i·scope /per'əskōp/ *n.* apparatus with a tube and mirrors or prisms by which an observer can see around or over an obstacle, etc. —**per'i·scop'ic** /-skäp'ik/ *adj.*

per·ish /per'isH/ *v.* be destroyed; suffer death or ruin [L *perire*]

per·ish·a·ble /per'isHəbəl/ *adj.* **1** liable to perish; subject to decay —*n.* **2** thing, esp. food, subject to rapid decay

per·i·stal·sis /per'əstal'sis, -stôl'-/ *n.* involuntary muscular wavelike movement by which the contents of the digestive tract are propelled along it [Gk *peristellein* wrap around]

per·i·to·ne·um /per'ət·n-ē'əm/ *n.* (*pl.* ·**ums** or ·**ne·a** /-n·ē'ə/) membrane lining the cavity of the abdomen —**per'i·to·ne'al** *adj.* [Gk *peritonos* stretched around]

per·i·to·ni·tis /per'ət·n-īt'is/ *n.* inflammatory disease of the peritoneum

per·i·wig /per'iwig/ *n. esp. Hist.* wig [alter. of PERUKE]

per·i·win·kle¹ /per'iwiNG'kəl/ *n.* evergreen trailing plant with blue, purple, or white flowers [L *pervinca*]

per·i·win·kle² *n.* small, intertidal, saltwater snail

per·jure /pər'jər/ *v.* (·**jured**, ·**jur·ing**) *Law.* willfully tell a lie when under oath —**per'jur·er** *n.* [Fr fr. L *jurare* swear]

per·ju·ry /pər'j(ə)rē/ *n.* (*pl.* ·**ries**) *Law.* act of willfully telling a lie when under oath

perk¹ /pərk/ *v.* (foll. by *up*) **1** recover or restore confidence, courage, life, or zest **2** smarten up **3** raise (one's head, etc.) briskly —**perk'i·ly** *adv.*; **perk'i·ness** *n.*; **perk'y** *adj.* (·**i·er**, ·**i·est**)

perk² *n. Colloq.* perquisite

perk³ *Colloq. v.* **1** percolate —*n. & adj.* **2** percolation

Per·kins /pər'kinz/, **Frances** 1882–1965; US sociologist; first woman cabinet member

perm /pərm/ *n.* **1** PERMANENT, 2 —*v.* **2** give a permanent to [abbr.]

Perm /perm/ *n.* city on the Kama River in Russia. Pop. 1,100,400

per·ma·frost /pər'məfrôst'/ *n.* subsoil that remains frozen all year [fr. PERMANENT, FROST]

per·ma·nent /pər'mənənt/ *adj.* **1** lasting, or intended to last or function, indefinitely —*n.* **2** (in full **per'ma·nent wave'**) long-lasting artificial wave in the hair —per'ma·nence, per'ma·nen·cy n.; per'ma·nent·ly adv. [L *permanere* remain to the end]

per'ma·nent press' n. process keeping clothing nearly wrinkle-free

per·me·a·ble /pər'mēəbəl/ adj. capable of being permeated —per'me·a·bil'i·ty n. [rel. to PERMEATE]

per·me·ate /pər'mē·āt/ v. (·at·ed, ·at·ing) 1 penetrate throughout; pervade; saturate 2 diffuse —per'me·a'tion n. [L *permeare* pass through]

per·mis·si·ble /pərmis'əbəl/ adj. allowable —per·mis'si·bil'i·ty n. [Fr or MedL, rel. to PERMIT]

per·mis·sion /pərmisн'ən/ n. consent; authorization [L *permissio*, rel. to PERMIT]

per·mis·sive /pərmis'iv/ adj. 1 tolerant; lenient 2 giving permission —per·mis'sive·ly adv.; per·mis'sive·ness n. [Fr or MedL, rel. to PERMIT]

per·mit v. /pərmit'/ (·mit·ted, ·mit·ting) 1 give permission or consent to; authorize; allow 2 give an opportunity (to) —n. /pər'mit/ 3 document giving permission, allowing entry, etc. [L *permittere* ·miss· allow]

per·mu·ta·tion /pər'myōōtā'sнən/ n. 1 one of the possible ordered arrangements or groupings of a set of things 2 transformation; alteration [L *permutare* change thoroughly]

per·ni·cious /pərnisн'əs/ adj. very harmful or destructive; deadly —per·ni'cious·ly adv. [L *pernicies* ruin]

Pe·rón /pərōn', pā-/ 1 Juan Domingo 1895–1974; Argentine political leader; president (1946–55; 1973–74); his wife: 2 Evita (Eva) 1919–52; Argentine political figure

per·o·ra·tion /per'ərā'sнən/ n. concluding part of a speech [L *orare* speak]

per·ox·ide /pərak'sīd'/ n. 1a HYDROGEN PEROXIDE b solution of hydrogen peroxide used esp. to bleach the hair 2 compound of oxygen containing the greatest possible proportion of oxygen —v. (·id·ed, ·id·ing) 3 bleach (the hair) with peroxide [fr. PER-, OXIDE]

per·pen·dic·u·lar /pər'pandik'yələr/ adj. 1 at right angles to a given line, plane, or surface 2 upright; vertical —n. 3 perpendicular line, plane, or direction —per'pen·dic'u·lar'i·ty /-lar'itē/ n. [L *perpendiculum* plumb line]

per·pe·trate /pər'pətrāt'/ v. (·trat·ed, ·trat·ing) commit (a crime, blunder, etc.) —per'pe·tra'tion, per'pe·tra'tor n. [L *perpetrare* perform]

per·pet·u·al /pərpecн'ōōəl/ adj. 1 lasting for ever or indefinitely 2 continuous; uninterrupted —per·pet'u·al·ly adv. [L *perpetuus* continuous]

per·pet·u·ate /pərpecн'ōō·āt'/ v. (·at·ed, ·at·ing) 1 make perpetual 2 preserve from oblivion —per·pet'u·a'tion, per·pet'u·a'tor n. [L *perpetuare*]

per·pe·tu·i·ty /pər'pət(y)ōō'ətē/ n. (pl. ·ties) 1 state or quality of being perpetual 2 in perpetuity for ever [L, rel. to PERPETUAL]

per·plex /pərpleks'/ v. puzzle; bewilder; disconcert —per·plex'ed·ly /-plek'sadlē/ adv.; per·plex'ing adj.; per·plex'i·ty n. (pl. ·ties) [L *perplexus* involved]

per·qui·site /pər'kwazit/ n. customary extra right or privilege in addition to one's main in-

come, etc. [L *perquirere* ·quisit· search diligently for]

Per·ry /per'ē/ 1 Oliver Hazard 1785–1819; US naval officer; his brother: 2 Matthew Calbraith 1794–1858; US commodore

per se /pər' sā'/ adv. by or in itself; intrinsically [L]

per·se·cute /pər'sikyōōt'/ v. (·cut·ed, ·cut·ing) subject to hostility or ill-treatment, esp. on grounds of political or religious belief —per'se·cu'tion, per'se·cu'tor n. [L *persequi* ·secut· pursue]

per·se·vere /pər'səvēr'/ v. (·vered, ·ver·ing) continue steadfastly or determinedly; persist —per'se·ver'ance n. [L, rel. to SEVERE]

Per·shing /pər'sнiNG, -zнiNG/, John Joseph (called "Black Jack") 1860–1948; US general, commander of American forces in Europe during World War I

Per·sia /pûr'zнa/ n. 1 official name (until 1935) of Iran 2 ancient empire in W Asia

Per·sian /pər'zнən, -sнən/ n. 1 native or inhabitant of Persia (now Iran); person of Persian descent 2 language of ancient Persia or modern Iran 3 (in full Per'sian cat') cat of a breed with long silky hair —adj. 4 of or relating to Persia or its people or language

Per'sian Gulf' n. arm of the Arabian Sea between Iran and the Arabian Peninsula

Per'sian lamb' n. fur of a young karakul, used in clothing

per·si·flage /pər'sifläzн'/ n. light raillery; banter [Fr]

per·sim·mon /pərsim'ən/ n. 1 tree bearing an edible plumlike fruit 2 its fruit [Algonquian]

per·sist /pərsist'/ v. 1 continue firmly or obstinately 2 continue in existence; survive —per·sist'ence n.; per·sist'ent adj.; per·sist'ent·ly adv. [L *sistere* stand]

per·snick·e·ty /pərsnik'ətē/ adj. Colloq. overly particular; fussy [Scot]

per·son /pər'sən/ n. 1 individual human being 2 living human body (*found on my person*) 3 Gram. any of three classes of personal pronoun and verb forms: first person, second person, third person 4 (in comb.) used to replace *-man* in positions open to either sex (*salesperson*) 5 in person physically present [L, rel. to PERSONA]

● Usage: Some prefer the plural *persons* to *people*. The former is often considered more formal and more specific, while *people* is considered more general and indefinite; that distinction is not supported by their use. In some contexts, *persons* has pompous overtones, while *people* is friendlier.

per·so·na /pərsō'na/ n. (pl. ·nae /-nē/) aspect of the personality as shown to or perceived by others [L: actor's mask]

per·son·a·ble /pər's(ə)nabəl/ adj. pleasing in appearance and behavior

per·son·age /pər'sənij/ n. person, esp. of rank or importance

per·son·al /pər's(ə)nəl/ adj. 1 one's own; individual; private 2 done or made in person (*my personal attention*) 3 directed to or concerning an individual (*personal letter*) 4 referring to an individual's private life (*no need to be personal*) **5** of the body (*personal hygiene*)

per'son·al com·put'er *n.* computer designed for use by a single individual; *abbr.* PC

per·son·al·i·ty /pər'sənal'itē/ *n.* (*pl.* **-ties**) **1a** person's distinctive character or qualities **b** socially attractive qualities **2** famous person

per·son·al·ize /pər'sənalīz'/ *v.* (**-ized, -iz·ing**) make personal, esp. by marking with one's name, etc.

per'son·al·ly *adv.* **1** in person **2** for one's own part (*personally speaking*) **3** in a personal manner

per'son·al pro'noun *n.* pronoun replacing a noun referring to a person, e.g., *I, we, you, them, us*

per'son·al prop'er·ty *n. Law.* all one's property except land and interests in land

per·so·na non gra·ta /pərsō'nə nän grät'ə/ *n.* (*pl.* **per·so·nae non gra·tae** /-nē, -ē/) unwelcome person [L]

per·son·i·fy /pərsän'əfī'/ *v.* (**-fied, -fy·ing**) **1** represent (an abstraction or thing) as human **2** be a typical example of; embody **—per·son'i·fi·ca'tion** /-fikā'SHən/ *n.*

per·son·nel /pər'sənel'/ *n.* workers or staff of an organization [Fr: personal]

per·spec·tive /pərspek'tiv/ *n.* **1a** art of drawing solid objects on a two-dimensional surface to suggest third dimension **b** picture so drawn **2** apparent relation between visible objects as to position, distance, etc. **3** mental view of or ability to discern the relative importance of things **4** view, esp. stretching into the distance [L *perspicere* -spect- look at]

per·spi·ca·cious /pər'spikā'SHəs/ *adj.* having mental discernment **—per'spi·cac'i·ty** /-kas'itē/ *n.* [L *perspicax*, rel. to PERSPECTIVE]

per·spic·u·ous /pərspik'yōōəs/ *adj.* **1** easily understood; clear **2** expressing things clearly **—per'spi·cu'i·ty** /-itē/ *n.* [L, rel. to PERSPECTIVE]

per·spi·ra·tion /pər'spərā'SHən/ *n.* **1** sweat **2** sweating [Fr, rel. to PERSPIRE]

per·spire /pərspīr'/ *v.* (**-spired, -spir·ing**) sweat [L *spirare* breathe]

per·suade /pərswād'/ *v.* (**-suad·ed, -suad·ing**) **1** cause to believe; convince **2** induce **—per·suad'a·ble** or **per·sua'si·ble** *adj.* [L *persuadere* induce]

per·sua·sion /pərswā'ZHən/ *n.* **1** persuading **2** persuasiveness **3** belief or conviction, or the group holding it [L, rel. to PERSUADE]

per·sua·sive /pərswā'siv, -ziv/ *adj.* good at or successful in persuading **—per·sua'sive·ly** *adv.*; **per·sua'sive·ness** *n.* [Fr or MedL, rel. to PERSUADE]

pert /pərt/ *adj.* saucy; impudent **—pert'ly** *adv.*; **pert'ness** *n.* [L *apertus* open]

pert. *abbr.* pertaining

per·tain /pərtān'/ *v.* **1a** relate or have reference (to) **b** belong to as a part, appendage, or accessory **2** be appropriate [L *pertinere* belong to]

Perth /pərTH/ *n.* city in SW Australia. Pop. 1,143,300

per·ti·na·cious /pərt'n·ā'SHəs/ *adj.* stubborn; persistent **—per'ti·nac'i·ty** /-as'itē/ *n.* [L *pertinax*, rel. to PERTAIN]

per·ti·nent /pərt'n-ənt/ *adj.* relevant **—per'ti·nence** *n.* [L, rel. to PERTAIN]

per·turb /pərtərb'/ *v.* disturb mentally; throw into confusion **—per'tur·ba'tion** *n.* /-bāSHən/ [Fr fr. L]

per·tus·sis /pərtus'is/ *n.* WHOOPING COUGH

Pe·ru /pərōō'/ *n.* republic in western S America on the Pacific Ocean. Capital: Lima. Pop. 22,454,000 **—Pe·ru'vi·an** /-vēən/ *n. & adj.*

pe·ruke /pərōōk'/ *n. Hist.* wig [Fr fr. It]

pe·ruse /pərōōz'/ *v.* (**-rused, -rus·ing**) read or study carefully **—pe·rus'al** *n.* [PER + USE]

per·vade /pərvād'/ *v.* (**-vad·ed, -vad·ing**) spread throughout; permeate **—per·va'sion** /-vāZHən/ *n.*; **per·va'sive** /-siv/ *adj.* [L *pervadere* penetrate]

per·verse /pərvərs'/ *adj.* **1** deliberately or stubbornly departing from what is reasonable or required **2** wicked; deviant **—per·verse'ly** *adv.*; **per·ver'si·ty** *n.* (*pl.* **-ties**) [L, rel. to PERVERT]

per·ver·sion /pərvər'ZHən/ *n.* **1** perverting or being perverted **2** preference for abnormal sexual activity [L, rel. to PERVERT]

per·vert /v. pərvərt'/ **1** turn (a person or thing) aside from its proper use or nature **2** misapply (words, etc.) **3** lead astray from right conduct; corrupt **—***n.* /pər'vərt'/ **4** perverted person, esp. sexually [L *vertere* vers- turn]

pe·se·ta /pəsā'tə/ *n.* chief monetary unit of Spain [Sp]

Pe·sha·war /pəshā'wər/ *n.* city in N Pakistan. Pop. 566,300

pes·ky /pes'kē/ *adj.* (**-ki·er, -ki·est**) *Colloq.* troublesome; annoying

pe·so /pā'sō/ *n.* (*pl.* **-sos**) chief monetary unit of Mexico and other Latin American countries and of the Philippines [Sp]

pes·si·mism /pes'əmiz'əm/ *n.* **1** tendency to be gloomy or expect the worst **2** *Philos.* belief that all things tend to evil **—pes'si·mist** /-mist/ *n.*; **pes·si·mis'tic** *adj.*; **pes·si·mis'ti·cal·ly** *adv.* [L *pessimus* worst]

pest /pest/ *n.* troublesome or harmful person, animal, or thing [L *pestis* plague]

pes·ter /pes'tər/ *v.* trouble or annoy, esp. with frequent or persistent requests [prob. Fr *empestrer* encumber, influenced by PEST]

pes·ti·cide /pes'təsīd'/ *n.* substance for destroying pests, esp. insects

pes·ti·lence /pes'tələns/ *n.* fatal epidemic disease; plague [L *pestis* plague]

pes·ti·lent /pes'tələnt/ *adj.* **1** deadly **2** harmful or morally destructive **3** troublesome; annoying **—pes'ti·len'tial** /-len'SHəl/ *adj.*

pes·tle /pes'(t)əl/ *n.* club-shaped instrument for pounding substances in a mortar (see illustration at MORTAR) [L *pistillum* fr. *pinsere* pound]

pes·to /pes'tō/ *n.* pasta sauce of olive oil, basil, garlic, pine nuts, and cheese

pet¹ /pet/ *n.* **1** domestic or tamed animal kept for pleasure or companionship **2** darling; favorite **—***adj.* **3** kept as a pet **4** of or for pet animals **5** favorite or particular (*pet peeve*) **6** expressing fondness or familiarity (*pet name*) **—***v.* (**-ted, -ting**) **7** treat as a pet; stroke; pat **8** fondle, kiss, etc., esp. mutually

pet² *n.* fit of ill-humor

PET (**scan**) *abbr.* POSITRON EMISSION TOMOG-
RAPHY

Pé·tain /pätaN'/, Henri Philippe 1856–1951;
French politician; premier of Vichy France
(1940–44)

pet·al /pet'l/ *n.* leaflike part of a flower
—**pet'aled** *adj.* [Gk *petalon* leaf]

pe·tard /potärd'/ *n. Hist.* small bomb used to
blast down a door, etc. [Fr]

PETE *abbr.* polyethylene terephthalate

pe·ter /pē'tər/ *v.* as in **peter out** diminish;
come to an end

Pe·ter I /pē'tər/ (called "the Great") 1672–
1725; emperor of Russia (1682–1725)

Pe·ter, St. (also **Si'mon Pe'ter**) died c. A.D.
67; one of the twelve Apostles

pet·i·ole /pet'ē-ōl'/ *n.* slender stalk joining a
leaf to a stem [Fr fr. L]

petite /potēt'/ *adj.* (of a woman) small and
trim [Fr: little]

pe·tit four /pet'ē fôr'/ *n.* (*pl.* **pet'its fours'**
/pet'ē fôrz'/) very small fancy cake [Fr:
small oven]

pe·ti·tion /pətish'ən/ *n.* 1 appeal; request 2
formal written appeal, esp. one signed by
many people 3 *Law.* application to a court for
a writ, etc. —*v.* 4 make or address a petition
to 5 appeal earnestly or humbly [L *petere pe-
tit-* ask]

pet'peeve' *n. Colloq.* something especially annoying to an individual

Pe·trarch /pē'trärk, pe'-/ 1304–74; Italian
poet

pet·rel /pe'trəl/ *n.* sea bird, usu. flying far
from land

pe'tri dish' /pē'trē/ *n.* shallow covered dish
used for the culture of bacteria, etc. [for J.R.
Petri, German bacteriologist]

pet·ri·fy /pe'trəfī'/ *v.* (**-fied, -fy·ing**) 1 paralyze with fear, astonishment, etc. 2 change
(organic matter) into a stony substance 3 become like stone —**pet'ri·fac'tion** /-fak'SHən/
n. [L *petra* rock, fr. Gk]

pet·ro·chem·i·cal /pe'trōkem'ikəl/ *n.* product made from petroleum or natural gas

pet·ro·dol·lar /pe'trōdäl'ər/ *n.* dollar's worth
of earnings realized by a petroleum-exporting
country

pet·rol /pe'trəl/ *n. Brit.* gasoline [fr. PETRO-
LEUM]

pe·tro·le·um /pətrō'lēəm/ *n.* hydrocarbon
oil found in the upper strata of the earth, refined for use as fuel, etc. [L *petra* rock, *oleum*
oil]

pe·tro·le·um jel'ly *n.* (also **pet·ro·la·tum**
/pe'trəlā'təm/) translucent, greasy, jellylike
substance used as a lubricant, ointment, etc.

pet' shop' *n.* store selling animals to be kept
as pets

pet·ti·coat /pet'ēkōt'/ *n.* woman's or girl's
underskirt or slip, often full, trimmed with
lace, etc. [*petty* + *coat*]

pet·ti·fog /pet'ēfôg', -fäg'/ *v.* (**-fogged, -fog-
ging**) 1 practice legal trickery 2 quibble or
wrangle about trivial points —**pet'ti·fog'ger,
pet'ti·fog'ger·y** *n.*

pet·tish /pet'isH/ *adj.* peevish; petulant [fr.
PET²]

pet·ty /pet'ē/ *adj.* (**-ti·er, -ti·est**) 1 unimportant; minor; trivial 2 small-minded —**pet'
ti·ly** *adv.*; **pet'ti·ness** *n.* [Fr *petit* small]

pet'ty cash' *n.* cash kept, as at an office, etc.,
for small expenses

pet'ty of'fi·cer *n. US Navy.* noncommissioned
officer

pet·u·lant /pecH'ələnt/ *adj.* peevishly impatient or irritable —**pet'u·lance** *n.*; **pet'u·
lant·ly** *adv.* [L *petere* seek]

pe·tu·nia /pət(y)ōōn'yə/ *n.* cultivated plant
with white, purple, red, etc., funnel-shaped
flowers [ult. fr. AmerInd]

pew /pyōō/ *n.* (in a church) long bench with
a back [L PODIUM]

pew·ter /pyōō'tər/ *n.* 1 any of various gray
alloys, e.g., of tin, antimony, and copper 2
utensils made of this [Fr *peutre*]

pey·o·te /pā·ō'tē/ *n.* 1 type of Mexican cactus; mescal 2 hallucinogenic drug prepared
from this [AmerSp fr. Nahuatl]

Pfc. *abbr.* private first class

PG *abbr.* (of a movie) classified as suitable for
all ages subject to parental guidance

PG-13 *abbr.* (of a movie) classified as containing material unsuitable for children under 13
years old unless under parental guidance

pg. *abbr.* page

pH *n.* numerical scale measuring the relative
acidity or alkalinity of a solution [Ger *Potenz*
power, *H* (for hydrogen)]

phag·o·cyte /fag'əsīt'/ *n.* leukocyte that destroys foreign matter in blood, etc. [Gk *phag-
ein* eat, *kutos* cell]

pha·lanx /fā'laNGks'/ *n.* (*pl.* **-lanx·es** or
-lan·ges /-lan'jēz'/) 1 *Gk. Antiq.* line of infantry drawn up in close order 2 any mass or
united band of people [L fr. Gk]

phal·lus /fal'əs/ *n.* (*pl.* **-li** /-lī/ or **-lus·es**)
1 penis 2 image of this as a symbol of natural
generative power —**phal'lic** *adj.* [L fr. Gk]

phan·tasm /fan'taz'əm/ *n.* illusion; phantom
—**phan·tas'mal** /-məl/ *adj.* [L fr. Gk *phantasma*]

phan·tas·ma·go·ri·a /fantaz'məgôr'ēə/ *n.*
series of images, as in a dream —**phan·tas'
ma·go'ric** /-rik/ *adj.* [Fr *fantasmagorie,* rel. to
PHANTASM]

phan·tom /fan'təm/ *n.* 1 ghost; apparition;
specter 2 mental illusion —*adj.* 3 illusory
[Gk *phantasma*]

phar. or **Phar.** *abbr.* (also **pharm.** or
Pharm.) 1 pharmaceutical 2 pharmacist 3
pharmacy

Pha·raoh /fer'ō, far'ō, fā'rō/ *n.* title of a ruler
of ancient Egypt [OE, ult. fr. Egyptian]

Phar·i·see /far'əsē'/ *n.* 1 member of an ancient Jewish sect that strictly observed both
traditional and written law 2 self-righteous
person; hypocrite —**Phar'i·sa'ic** /-sā'ik/
adj. [Heb *pārūs*]

phar·ma·ceu·ti·cal /fär'məsōō'tikəl/ *adj.* 1
of the use or sale of medicinal drugs —*n.* 2
(also **phar'ma·ceu'tic**) medicinal drug [L fr.
Gk *pharmakon* drug]

phar·ma·ceu·tics /fär'məsōō'tiks/ *n. pl.*
(usu. treated as *sing.*) PHARMACY, 1

phar·ma·cist /fär'məsist/ *n.* person licensed
to prepare and dispense drugs

phar·ma·col·o·gy /fär'məkäl'əjē/ *n.* the
study of the action of drugs on the body
—**phar'ma·co·log'i·cal** /-kəläj'ikəl/ *adj.*;
phar'ma·col'o·gist *n.*

phar·ma·co·poe·ia /fär'məkəpē'ə/ *n.* official directory of medicinal drugs with directions for use [Gk *pharmakopoios* drugmaker]

phar·ma·cy /fär'məsē/ *n.* (*pl.* ·cies) 1 preparation and (esp. medicinal) dispensing of drugs 2 drugstore

phar·ynx /far'iNGks/ *n.* (*pl.* **pha·ryn·ges** /fəriɴ'jēz/ or ·ynx·es) cavity behind the nose and mouth —**pha·ryn'ge·al** /-rin'jēəl/ *adj.* [L fr. Gk]

phase /fāz/ *n.* 1 stage in a process of change or development 2 each of the aspects of the moon or a planet, according to its illumination —*v.* (**phased, phas·ing**) 3 carry out (a program, etc.) in phases or stages 4 **phase in** (or **out**) bring gradually into (or out of) use [Gk *phasis* appearance]

Ph.D. *abbr.* Doctor of Philosophy [L *philosophiae doctor*]

pheas·ant /fez'ənt/ *n.* long-tailed game bird [Gk *Phasianos* of Phasis, a river associated with the bird]

phe·no·bar·bi·tal /fē'nōbär'bitôl/ *n.* narcotic and sedative drug, used esp. to treat epilepsy [fr. PHENOL, BARBITURATE]

phe·nol /fē'nôl/ *n.* hydroxyl derivative of benzene, used in synthetic resins and, in solution, as an antiseptic [Fr]

phe·nom·e·nal /finäm'ənəl/ *adj.* 1 extraordinary; remarkable 2 of the nature of a phenomenon —**phe·nom'e·nal·ly** *adv.*

phe·nom·e·non /finäm'ənən, -nän'/ *n.* (*pl.* ·na /-nə/) 1 fact or occurrence that appears or is perceived; object of consciousness or the senses 2 remarkable person or thing [Gk *phainesthai* show]

● Usage: The singular is *phenomenon*, the plural *phenomena*, reflecting the word's Greek origin.

pher·o·mone /fer'əmōn'/ *n.* substance secreted by an animal for detection and response by another, usu. of the same species [Gk *pherein* convey, HORMONE]

phi /fī/ *n.* twenty-first letter of the Greek alphabet (Φ, φ) [Gk]

phi·al /fī'əl/ *n.* small glass bottle [Gk *phialē*]

Phid·i·as /fid'ēəs/ fl. 5th cent. B.C.; Athenian sculptor

phil- *prefix* var. of PHILO-

-phil *suffix* var. of -PHILE

Phil·a·del·phi·a /fil'ədel'fēə/ *n.* city in Penn. Pop. 1,585,577

Phil·a·del·phi·a law·yer *n.* lawyer shrewd in exploiting legal subtleties and technicalities

phi·lan·der /fəlan'dər/ *v.* flirt or have casual affairs with women —**phi·lan'der·er** *n.* [Gk *philandros* one who loves]

phi·lan·thro·py /fəlan'THrəpē/ *n.* concern for fellow humans, esp. through gifts promoting social welfare —**phil'an·throp'ic** /-THräp'ik/ *adj.*; **phi·lan'thro·pist** *n.* [Gk PHIL- + *anthrōpos* human being]

phi·lat·e·ly /fəlat'l-ē/ *n.* the study and collecting of postage stamps —**phi·lat'e·list** *n.* [Gk PHIL- + *atelēs* not taxed further (i.e., postpaid)]

-phile *comb. form* (also **-phil**) forming nouns and adjectives denoting fondness for what is specified (*bibliophile*) [Gk *philos* loving]

phil·har·mon·ic /fil'(h)ärmän'ik/ *adj.* 1 fond of music (usu. in the names of orchestras, etc.) —*n.* 2 orchestra or musical society [PHIL- + HARMONIC]

Phil·ip II /fil'əp/ c. 382–336 B.C.; king of Macedonia (359–336); father of Alexander the Great

Phil'ip, St. one of the twelve Apostles

phi·lip·pic /fəlip'ik/ *n.* bitter verbal attack [for Demosthenes' speeches denouncing PHILIP II]

Phil·ip·pines /fil'ipēnz', fil'ipēnz'/ *n.* republic comprising several large islands and many smaller ones in the Pacific Ocean, SE of China. Capital: Manila. Pop. 63,609,000

Phi·lis·tine /fil'əstēn, -stīn'/ *n.* 1 member of a people of ancient Palestine 2 (usu. p-) person hostile or indifferent to culture —*adj.* 3 (usu. p-) hostile or indifferent to culture —**phil'is·tin·ism'** *n.*

Phil·lips /fil'əps/ *n.* denoting a screw with a cross-shaped slot, or a corresponding screwdriver [name of its US designer]

philo- *comb. form* (also **phil-** before a vowel or *h*) denoting a liking for what is specified [Gk *philos* loving]

phil·o·den·dron /fil'əden'drən/ *n.* (*pl.* ·drons or ·dra /-drə/) ornamental climbing plant [Gk PHILO- + *dendron* tree]

phi·lol·o·gy /fəläl'əjē/ *n.* the study of language, esp. in its historical and comparative aspects; linguistics —**phil'o·log'i·cal** /-əläj'ikəl/ *adj.*; **phi·lol'o·gist** *n.* [PHILO-, -LOGY]

phi·los·o·pher /fəläs'əfər/ *n.* 1 expert in or student of philosophy 2 person who lives by a philosophy

phil·o·soph·i·cal /fil'əsäf'ikəl/ *adj.* (also **phil'o·soph'ic**) 1 of or according to philosophy 2 skilled in or devoted to philosophy 3 calm in adversity —**phil'o·soph'i·cal·ly** *adv.*

phi·los·o·phize /fəläs'əfīz'/ *v.* (·**phized,** ·**phiz·ing**) 1 reason like a philosopher 2 speculate; theorize —**phi·los'o·phiz'er** *n.*

phi·los·o·phy /fəläs'əfē/ *n.* (*pl.* ·**phies**) 1 use of reason and argument to seek knowledge of the causes and nature of things and of the principles governing existence 2a particular system or set of beliefs reached by this b personal rule of life [Gk, rel. to PHILO-, *sophia* wisdom]

phil·ter /fil'tər/ *n.* (also esp. *Brit.* **philtre**) love potion [Gk *philein* to love]

phle·bi·tis /fləbī'tis/ *n.* inflammation of a vein —**phle·bit'ic** /-bit'ik/ *adj.* [Gk *phleps phleb-* vein]

phlegm /flem/ *n.* 1 viscous substance secreted by the mucous membranes of the respiratory passages, discharged by coughing 2a calmness b sluggishness [Gk *phlegma*]

phleg·mat·ic /flegmat'ik/ *adj.* unexcitable; sluggish —**phleg·mat'i·cal·ly** *adv.*

phlo·em /flō'em/ *n.* tissue conducting sap in plants [Gk *phloos* bark]

phlox /fläks/ *n.* (*pl.* same or -es) plant with scented clusters of esp. white, blue, or red flowers [Gk for the plant (literally, 'flame')]

Phnom Penh /pənäm' pen'/ *n.* capital of Cambodia. Pop. 800,000

-phobe *comb. form* forming nouns denoting a person with a specified fear or aversion (*xenophobe*) [Gk *phobos* fear]

pho·bi·a /fō'bēə/ *n.* abnormal or morbid fear

or aversion —pho′bic /-bik/ adj. & n. [fr. -PHOBIA]

-phobia comb. form forming nouns denoting a specified fear or aversion (agoraphobia) [Gk phobos fear]

phoe·nix /fē′niks/ n. mythical bird that burns itself on a pyre, then rises from the ashes to live again [Gk phoinix]

Phoe·nix /fē′niks/ n. capital of Ariz., in the central part. Pop. 983,403

phone /fōn/ n. & v. (phoned, phon·ing) TELEPHONE

pho·neme /fō′nēm′/ n. unit of sound perceived as distinctive in a specified language despite slight variations (as p in English pun and spun) —pho·ne′mic adj.; pho·ne′mi·cal·ly adv. [Gk phōnēma sound]

pho·net·ic /fənet′ik/ adj. 1 representing vocal sounds 2 (of spelling, etc.) corresponding to pronunciation —pho·net′i·cal·ly adv. [Gk phōnē voice]

pho·net·ics /fənet′iks/ n. pl. (usu. treated as sing.) 1 vocal sounds 2 the study of these —pho·ne·ti·cian /fō′nətiSH′ən/ n.

phon·ics /fän′iks/ n. pl. (treated as sing.) method of teaching reading by sound-letter identification [Gk phōnē voice]

phono- comb. form sound [Gk phōnē voice; sound]

pho·no·graph /fō′nəgraf′/ n. RECORD PLAYER

pho·nol·o·gy /fənäl′əjē/ n. the study of sounds in language or a particular language —pho′no·log′i·cal /-nōläj′ikəl/ adj.; pho′no·log′i·cal·ly adv.

pho·ny /fō′nē/ adj. (also pho′ney) adj. (·ni·er, ·ni·est) 1 sham; counterfeit 2 not genuine or sincere; false; dishonest —n. (pl. ·nies) 3 phony person or thing —pho′ni·ness n.

phos·phate /fäs′fāt′/ n. salt or ester of phosphoric acid, esp. used as a fertilizer [Fr, rel. to PHOSPHORUS]

phos·phor /fäs′fər/ n. synthetic fluorescent or phosphorescent substance [L PHOSPHORUS]

phos·pho·res·cence /fäs′fəres′əns/ n. 1 luminous radiation that continues after the source stimulating it is removed 2 emission of light without combustion or perceptible heat —phos′pho·resce′ v. (·resced, ·resc·ing); phos′pho·res′cent adj.

phos·pho·rus /fäs′f(ə)rəs/ n. Chem. nonmetallic element existing esp. as a whitish waxy substance that burns slowly at ordinary temperatures and is luminous in the dark; symb. P —phos·pho′ric /-fôr′ik/ adj. [Gk phōs light, phoros bringing]

pho·to /fō′tō/ n. PHOTOGRAPH, 1

photo- comb. form denoting: 1 light 2 photography [Gk phōs phōt- light]

pho·to·cop·y /fō′täkäp′ē/ n. (pl. ·ies) 1 photographic or xerographic copy of printed or written material —v. (·ied, ·y·ing) 2 make a photocopy of —pho′to·cop′i·er n.

pho·to·e·lec·tric /fō′tō-ēlek′trik/ adj. marked by or using emissions of electrons from substances exposed to light —pho′to·e·lec·tric′i·ty /-ris′itē/ n.

pho′to·e·lec′tric cell′ n. device using the effect of light to generate current

pho′to·fin′ish n. finish of a race so close that the winner can be identified only on a photograph

pho·to·gen·ic /fō′təjen′ik/ adj. 1 looking attractive in photographs 2 Biol. producing or emitting light

pho·to·graph /fō′təgraf′/ n. 1 picture formed by means of the chemical action of light or other radiation on sensitive film —v. 2 take a photograph of (a person, etc.) —pho·tog′ra·pher /-tägrəfər/ n.; pho′to·graph′ic adj.; pho′to·graph′i·cal·ly adv.

pho·tog·ra·phy /fətäg′rəfē/ n. the art and technique of taking and processing photographs

pho·to·jour·nal·ism /fō′tōjərn′l-iz′əm/ n. the relating of news by photographs, esp. in magazines, etc. —pho′to·jour′nal·ist /-ist/ n.

pho·ton /fō′tän′/ n. quantum of electromagnetic radiation energy [Gk photos light, after ELECTRON]

pho′to op′ n. PHOTO OPPORTUNITY [abbr.]

pho′to op·por·tu′ni·ty n. (also pho′to op′) opportunity for the press to photograph a celebrity, etc., arranged for publicity

pho·to·sen·si·tive /fō′tōsen′sətiv/ adj. reacting to light

Pho·to·stat /fō′təstat′/ n. Tdmk. (also p-) 1 type of photocopier 2 copy made by it —v. (·stat·ted, ·stat·ting) 3 make a Photostat of

pho·to·syn·the·sis /fō′tōsin′THəsis/ n. process in which the energy of sunlight is used by organisms, esp. green plants, to synthesize carbohydrates from carbon dioxide and water —pho′to·syn′the·size′ /-sīz/ v. (·sized, ·siz·ing); pho′to·syn·thet′ic adj.

phrase /frāz/ n. 1 group of words forming a conceptual unit but not a clause or sentence 2 common or current expression 3 Mus. group of notes forming a distinct unit within a melody —v. (phrased, phras·ing) 4 express in words —phras′al adj. [Gk phrasis fr. phrazein tell]

phra·se·ol·o·gy /frā′zē-äl′əjē/ n. (pl. ·gies) 1 choice or arrangement of words 2 mode of expression —phra′se·o·log′i·cal /-əläj′ikəl/ adj.

phre·nol·o·gy /frinäl′əjē/ n. Hist. the study of the shape and size of the skull as a supposed indication of character and mental faculties —phre·nol′o·gist n. [Gk phrēn mind]

phy·lac·ter·y /fəlak′tərē/ n. (pl. ·ies) small leather box containing Hebrew texts, worn by Jewish men at prayer [Gk phylaktērion amulet]

phy·lum /fī′ləm/ n. (pl. ·la /-lə/) Biol. taxonomic rank below a kingdom, comprising a class or classes and subordinate taxa [Gk phulon race]

phys. ed. /fiz′ ed′/ abbr. PHYSICAL EDUCATION

phys·i·cal /fiz′ikəl/ adj. 1 of the body 2 of matter; material 3a of, or according to, the laws of nature b of physics and its laws —n. 4 medical examination —phys′i·cal·ly adv.

phys′i·cal ed·u·ca′tion n. instruction on exercise, sports, etc.; abbr. PE, Phys. Ed.

phys′i·cal sci′ence n. science(s) used in the study of inanimate natural objects

phy·si·cian /fiziSH′ən/ n. medical doctor; M.D.

phys·ics /fiz′iks/ n. pl. (treated as sing.) science dealing with the properties and interactions of matter and energy —**phys'i·cist** /-əsist/ *n.* [L *physica* (pl.) fr. Gk *physis* nature]

phys·i·og·no·my /fiz'ē-ä(g)'nəmē/ *n.* (*pl.* **·mies**) cast or form of a person's features, expression, etc. [ult. fr. Gk *physiognomon*]

phy·si·og·ra·phy /fizēäg'rəfē/ *n.* study of the earth's surface, oceans, etc.

phys·i·ol·o·gy /fiz'ē-äl'əjē/ *n.* 1 science of the functions of living organisms and their parts 2 these functions in a particular organism —**phys'i·o·log'i·cal** /-əläj'ikəl/ *adj.*; **phys'i·o·log'i·cal·ly** *adv.*; **phys·i·ol'o·gist** *n.* [Gk *physis* nature, -LOGY]

phys·i·o·ther·a·py /fiz'ē-ōtʜer'əpē/ *n.* treatment of disease, injury, etc., by massage, heat treatment, and remedial exercise —**phys'i·o·ther'a·pist** *n.* [Gk *physis* nature, THERAPY]

phy·sique /fizēk'/ *n.* bodily structure; build [Fr fr. Gk *physis* nature]

pi /pī/ *n.* 1 sixteenth letter of the Greek alphabet (Π, π) 2 (as π) the symbol of the ratio of the circumference of a circle to its diameter (approx. 3.14) [Gk]

Pi·af /pēäf'/, **Edith** (born **Edith Giovanna Gassion**) 1915–63; French singer

Pia·get /pyäzhā'/, **Jean** 1897–1980; Swiss psychologist

pia ma·ter /pī'ə mā'tər/ *n.* delicate innermost membrane enveloping the brain and spinal cord [L: tender mother]

pi·a·nis·si·mo /pē'anis'imō'/ *Mus. adj.* 1 very soft —*adv.* 2 very softly —*n.* (*pl.* **·mos** or **·mi** /-mē/) 3 very soft playing or passage [It, superl. of PIANO²]

pi·an·o¹ /pē·an'ō, pyan'ō/ *n.* (*pl.* **·os**) keyboard instrument with metal strings struck by hammers, or producing sound electronically —**pi·a·nist** /pē'ənist, pyan'ist/ *n.* [It, abbr. of PIANOFORTE]

pi·a·no² /pyä'nō/ *adj. & adv. Mus.* softly [L *planus* flat, (of sound) soft]

pi·an·o·forte /pē·an'əfôrt'(ē)/ *n.* PIANO¹ [It *piano e forte* soft and loud]

pi·az·za /pē·at'sə, -ät'sə/ *n.* 1 public square or marketplace 2 large porch [It, rel. to PLACE]

pi·broch /pē'bräk', -brôkʜ/ *n.* martial or funerary bagpipe music [Gaelic]

pi·ca /pī'kə/ *n.* unit of type size, 12 point or 10 characters per inch

pic·a·dor /pik'ədôr'/ *n.* man on a horse with a lance in a bullfight [Sp]

pic·a·resque /pik'əresk'/ *adj.* (of a style of fiction) dealing with the episodic adventures of rogues, etc. [Sp *pícaro* rogue]

Pi·cas·so /pikäs'ō, -kas'-/, **Pablo** 1881–1973; Spanish painter

pic·a·yune /pik'ē(y)ōōn'/ *adj. Colloq.* trifling; paltry; petty [Fr *picaillon*]

pic·ca·lil·li /pik'əlil'ē/ *n.* pickle of chopped vegetables, mustard, and hot spices

pic·co·lo /pik'əlō'/ *n.* (*pl.* **·los**) small flute sounding an octave higher than the standard one [It: small]

pick¹ /pik/ *v.* 1 choose 2 detach or pluck (a flower, fruit, etc.) 3a probe with the fingernail, an instrument, etc., to remove unwanted matter b clear (a bone, carcass, etc.) of scraps of meat, etc. 4 open (unlock) with a wire, etc., not a key 5 steal, as from a person's pocket

6 eat (food, a meal, etc.) in small bits —*n.* 7 act of picking 8a selection; choice b right to select (*had first pick*) 9 best (*pick of the bunch*) 10 pick and choose select fastidiously 11 pick at: a eat (food) without interest b find fault with 12 pick off: a pluck (leaves, etc.) off b shoot (people, etc.) one by one 13 pick on abuse; annoy 14 pick up: a grasp and raise b learn or master without effort or unmethodically c stop for and take along with one d acquire e become acquainted with (a person) casually, esp. for sexual purposes f recover, improve, etc. g arrest h resume —**pick'er** *n.* [fr. PIKE]

pick² *n.* 1 any of various pointed devices or tools for picking, as used for breaking up hard ground, ice, etc. 2 plectrum [fr. PIKE]

pick·ax /pik'aks'/ *n.* (also **pick'axe'**) PICK², 1 [Fr, rel. to PIKE]

pick·et /pik'it/ *n.* 1 demonstration, esp. outside a business, to persuade others not to enter during a strike, etc. 2 pointed stake driven into the ground or used with others to form a fence 3 small body of troops on watch for the enemy —*v.* 4a act as a picket b beset or guard with a picket or pickets 5 secure (a place) with stakes [Fr *piquer* prick]

pick'et line' *n.* line of workers on strike

Pick·ett /pik'ət/, **George Edward** 1825–75; Confederate general in American Civil War

pick'ings *n. pl.* 1 profits or gains acquired easily or dishonestly 2 leftovers

pick·le /pik'əl/ *n.* 1a cucumber or other vegetable preserved in liquid, esp. brine or vinegar b the liquid used for this —*v.* (**·led, ·ling**) 3 preserve in or treat, esp. with brine solution 4 in a pickle in a difficult situation [LGer or Du *pekel*]

pick'pock'et *n.* person who steals from people's pockets

pick'up' *n.* 1 *Colloq.* person met casually, esp. for sexual purposes 2 small open truck 3 part of a record player carrying the stylus 4 device on an electric guitar, etc., that converts string vibrations into electrical signals 5 act of picking up

pick·y /pik'ē/ *adj.* (**·i·er, ·i·est**) excessively fastidious

pic·nic /pik'nik/ *n.* 1 outing including an outdoor meal 2 *Colloq.* something agreeable or easily accomplished —*v.* (**·nicked, ·nicking**) 3 take part in a picnic —**pic'nick·er** *n.* [Fr]

pico- *comb. form* denoting a factor of 10^{-12}; one trillionth (*picosecond*) [Sp *pico* beak; little bit]

pic·to·graph /pik'təgraf'/ *n.* (also **pic'to·gram'** /-gram'/) 1 pictorial symbol for a word or phrase 2 pictorial representation of statistics, etc. —**pic'to·graph'ic** *adj.* [L *pingere pict-* paint]

pic·to·ri·al /piktôr'ēəl/ *adj.* 1 of or expressed in a picture or pictures 2 illustrated —**pic·to'ri·al·ly** *adv.* [L *pictor* painter]

pic·ture /pik'ʜʜər/ *n.* 1 painting, drawing, photograph, etc. 2 scene imagined or observed 3 movie 4 perfect image or likeness —*v.* (**·tured, ·tur·ing**) 5 imagine (*pictured it to herself*) 6 represent in a picture 7 describe graphically 8 get the picture comprehend the situation [L *pingere pict-* paint]

pic·tur·esque /pĭk'CHəresk'/ *adj.* 1 charmingly beautiful or scenic 2 (of language, etc.) strikingly graphic [It *pittoresco,* assimilated to PICTURE]

pic'ture tube' *n.* cathode-ray tube of a television set

PICTURE WINDOW

pic'ture win'dow *n.* large window with a view

pid·dle /pĭd'l/ *v.* (**·dled, ·dling**) *Colloq.* 1 urinate 2 dawdle

pid'dling /pĭd'lĭNG/ *adj.* *Colloq.* trivial; trifling

pid·gin /pĭj'ən/ *n.* simplified language used between people not having a common language [perh. fr. Chin pronunc. of *business*]

pie /pī/ *n.* 1 baked dish of fruit, etc., with a pastry crust 2 thing resembling a pie (*mud pie*) 3 easy as pie very easy

pie·bald /pī'bôld'/ *adj.* 1 (esp. of a horse) having irregular patches of two colors, esp. black and white —*n.* 2 piebald animal [fr. *pie* (obs.) magpie + BALD]

piece /pēs/ *n.* 1a distinct portion forming part of or broken off from a larger object b each of the parts of something (*five-piece band*) 2 coin 3 (usu. short) literary or musical composition; picture; play 4 item 5 object moved in a board game 6 definite quantity in which a thing is sold —*v.* (**pieced, piec·ing**) 7 (foll. by *together*) form into a whole; join 8 go to pieces collapse 9 piece of cake very easy thing (to do) 10 piece of one's mind sharp rebuke or lecture [AngFr, prob. fr. Celt]

pièce de ré·sis·tance /pyes' də räzēstäns'/ *n.* most important or remarkable item, esp. a dish at a meal [Fr]

piece'meal' *adv.* 1 piece by piece; gradually —*adj.* 2 gradual; unsystematic [fr. PIECE, MEAL']

piece'work' *n.* work paid for at a rate per piece produced

pie' chart' *n.* graph using a circle divided into sectors to represent relative quantities

pied /pīd/ *adj.* having patches of two or more colors [fr. *pie* magpie]

pied-à-terre /pyä'dáter'/ *n.* (*pl.* **pieds-à-terre,** pronunc. same) (usu. small) residence for occasional use [Fr, literally 'foot to earth']

pie' in the sky' *n.* (used without an article) unrealistic prospect of future happiness

pier /pēr/ *n.* 1 structure built out into water as a landing-place, promenade, etc. 2a support of an arch or of the span of a bridge; pillar b solid masonry between windows, etc. [L *pera*]

pierce /pērs/ *v.* (**pierced, pierc·ing**) 1 make a hole in or through as with a sharp-pointed instrument 2 pass into or through;

penetrate [Fr *percer* fr. L *pertundere* bore through]

Pierce /pērs/, **Franklin** 1804–69; 14th US president (1853–57)

Pierre /pēr/ *n.* capital of S. Dak., in the central part. Pop. 12,906

pi·e·ty /pī'ətē/ *n.* (*pl.* **·ties**) 1 quality of being pious 2 pious act [L, rel. to PIOUS]

pig /pĭg/ *n.* 1 omnivorous hoofed bristly broad-snouted mammal, esp. a domesticated kind 2 its flesh as food 3 greedy, dirty, gross, or unpleasant person 4 oblong mass of metal (esp. iron or lead) from a smelting furnace 5 buy a pig in a poke acquire something without previous sight or knowledge of it 6 pig out *Slang.* eat gluttonously [OE]

pi·geon /pĭj'ən/ *n.* bird of the dove family [L *pipio -onis*]

pi'geon·hole' *n.* 1 each of a set of compartments on a wall, etc., for papers, letters, etc. —*v.* (**·holed, ·hol·ing**) 2 assign to a category 3 deposit in a pigeonhole 4 put aside for future consideration

pi'geon-toed' *adj.* having the toes turned inward

pig'gish /pĭg'ĭsH/ *adj.* greedy; dirty —**pig'gish·ly** *adv.*; **pig'gish·ness** *n.*

pig·gy /pĭg'ē/ *n.* (*pl.* **·gies**) 1 *Colloq.* little pig —*adj.* (**·gi·er, ·gi·est**) 2 like a pig

pig'gy·back' *adj. & adv.* 1 on the back and shoulders of another person 2 (of freight) on a flatbed

pig'gy bank' 1 pig-shaped portable bank, esp. for coins 2 any such small bank

pig'head'ed *adj.* obstinate —**pig'head'ed·ness** *n.*

pig' i'ron *n.* crude iron from a smelting furnace

pig'let *n.* young pig

pig·ment /pĭg'mənt/ *n.* 1 coloring matter used in paint or dye 2 natural coloring matter of animal or plant tissue [L *pingere* paint]

pig·men·ta·tion /pĭg'məntā'sHən/ *n.* natural coloring of plants, animals, etc.

Pig·my /pĭg'mē/ *n.* var. of PYGMY

pig'pen' *n.* 1 enclosure for pigs 2 filthy or messy place

pig'skin' *n.* 1 hide of a pig 2 leather made from this 3 *Colloq.* a football

pig·sty /pĭg'stī'/ *n.* (*pl.* **·sties**) PIGPEN

pig'tail' *n.* plait of hair hanging from the back of the head

pike /pīk/ *n.* (*pl.* same or **-s**) 1 large voracious freshwater fish with a long narrow snout 2 *Hist.* weapon with a pointed metal head on a long wooden shaft [OE]

Pikes Peak /pīks/ *n.* peak in Colo., in the Front Range of the Rocky Mountains

pi·laf /pĭ·läf', -lôf/ *n.* (also **pi·laff'**) dish of seasoned rice, usu. boiled with meat, vegetables, etc. [Turk]

pi·las·ter /pĭ'las'tər/ *n.* rectangular column projecting slightly from a wall [L *pīla* pillar]

Pi·late /pī'lət/, **Pontius** 1st cent. A.D.; Roman governor of Judea (26–36); presided at the trial of Jesus

pil·chard /pĭl'CHərd/ *n.* small marine fish of the herring family

pile[1] /pīl/ *n.* 1 heap of gathered or clustered

things 2 large imposing building 3 *Colloq.* a large quantity b large amount of money —*v.* (**piled, pil·ing**) 4 heap up 5 crowd hurriedly or tightly 6 **pile it on** *Colloq.* exaggerate [L *pila*]

pile² *n.* (also **pil'ing**) heavy support beam driven vertically into the ground [L *pilum* javelin]

pile³ *n.* soft, raised surface on a carpet, velvet, etc. [L *pilus* hair]

pile' driv'er *n.* machine for driving piles into the ground

piles /pīlz/ *n. pl. Colloq.* hemorrhoids [L *pila* ball]

pile'up' *n. Colloq.* multiple crash of road vehicles

pil·fer /pil'fər/ *v.* steal (objects), esp. in small quantities [Fr *pelfre*]

pil·grim /pil'grəm/ *n.* 1 person who journeys to a sacred place 2 traveler 3 (also **Pil'grim Fa'thers**) English Puritans who founded the colony of Plymouth, Mass., in 1620 [L, rel. to PEREGRINE]

pil·grim·age /pil'grəmij/ *n.* 1 pilgrim's journey 2 any journey taken earnestly

pill /pil/ *n.* 1a ball or flat disk of solid medicine for swallowing whole b (usu. prec. by *the*) contraceptive pill 2 *Slang.* tiresome or irritating person [L *pila* ball]

pil·lage /pil'ij/ *v.* (**·laged, ·lag·ing**) 1 plunder; sack —*n.* 2 pillaging, esp. in war [Fr *piller* plunder]

pil·lar /pil'ər/ *n.* 1 vertical structure of stone, etc., used as a support or for ornament 2 person regarded as a mainstay (*pillar of the faith*) 3 upright mass of air, water, rock, etc. 4 **from pillar to post** (rushing, etc.) aimlessly or helplessly from one place to another [L *pila* pillar]

pill'box' *n.* 1 small box for carrying pills in the pocket, etc. 2 shallow, cylindrical hat 3 *Milit.* concrete fort or gun emplacement

pil·lion /pil'yən/ *n.* extra seat for a passenger behind a motorcyclist or rider on a saddled horse [Gaelic *pillean* small cushion]

pil·lo·ry /pil'ərē/ *n.* (*pl.* **·ries**) 1 *Hist.* wooden framework with holes for the head and hands, securing a person for public ridicule —*v.* (**·ried, ·ry·ing**) 2 expose to ridicule 3 *Hist.* put in the pillory [Fr]

pil·low /pil'ō/ *n.* 1 soft support or cushion, as under the head in sleeping —*v.* 2 absorb pressure or shock 3 rest on or as if on a pillow [L *pulvinus* cushion]

pil'low·case' *n.* washable cover for a pillow

pi·lot /pī'lət/ *n.* 1 person who operates the controls of an aircraft 2 person qualified to take charge of a ship entering or leaving harbor 3 guide —*v.* 4 act as a pilot of 5 conduct or initiate as a pilot —*adj.* 6 done as a trial; experimental [Gk *pēdon*]

pi'lot·house' *n.* enclosed structure on a ship's deck for the helmsman

pi'lot light' *n.* small gas flame kept burning to light a main burner

pi·men·to /pəmen'tō/ (or **pi·mien·to** /pəmyen'tō/) *n.* (*pl.* **·tos**) red, ripe bell pepper [Sp fr. L *pigmentum* pigment]

pimp /pimp/ *n.* 1 man who lives off the earn-

ings of a prostitute or a brothel —*v.* 2 act as a pimp

pim·ple /pim'pəl/ *n.* 1 small raised spot on the skin 2 anything resembling a pimple —**pim'ply** *adj.* [OE]

pin /pin/ *n.* 1 thin pointed piece of metal used (as in sewing) for holding things in place, attaching one thing to another, etc. 2 peg of wood or metal for various purposes 3 badge or ornament worn on the clothing 4 *Bowling.* club at which the ball is rolled —*v.* (**pinned, pin·ning**) 5a fasten with a pin or pins b transfix with a pin, lance, etc. 6 seize and hold fast 7 **pin down:** a bind (a person, etc.) to a promise, arrangement, etc. b force (a person) to declare his or her intentions c restrict the actions of (an enemy, etc.) d specify (a thing) precisely 8 **pin on** put (blame, responsibility, etc.) on (a person, etc.) [OE *pinn* peg, perh. rel. to L *pinna* quill]

PIN /pin/ *abbr.* personal identification number

pi·na co·la·da /pēnə kōlä'də/ (also **pi·ña** /pē'nyə/) *n.* cocktail of pineapple juice, rum, and cream of coconut [Sp]

pin·a·fore /pin'əfôr'/ *n.* apron or similar sleeveless garment worn over a dress [fr. PIN, -AFORE]

pin'ball ma·chine' *n.* usu. coin-operated game in which a metal ball is directed at various targets on a slanted board, with electrical scoring as targets are touched

pince-nez /pansnā'/ *n.* (*pl.* same) pair of eyeglasses with a nose clip [Fr: pinch-nose]

PINCERS 1, 2

pin·cers /pin'sərz/ *n. pl.* 1 gripping tool resembling pliers 2 front claws of lobsters and some other crustaceans [rel. to PINCH]

pinch /pinCH/ *v.* 1a squeeze tightly, esp. between finger and thumb b (of a shoe, etc.) constrict painfully 2 (of cold, hunger, etc.) affect painfully 3 *Slang.* a steal b arrest —*n.* 4 act of pinching 5 small amount (*pinch of salt*) 6 the stress caused by poverty, etc. 7 **in a pinch** in an emergency [Fr *pincer*]

pinch'·hit' *v.* (**·hit, ·hit·ting**) 1 *Baseball.* to go to bat in place of another 2 *Colloq.* to substitute (for another) in an emergency

pin'cush'ion *n.* small pad for holding pins

Pin·dar /pin'dər, -där'/ 518–438 B.C.; Greek lyric poet

pine¹ /pīn/ *n.* 1 evergreen coniferous tree with needle-shaped leaves 2 its wood [L *pinus*]

pine² *v.* (**pined, pin·ing**) 1 decline or waste (away) from grief, etc. 2 long eagerly [OE]

pin·e·al bod'y /pin'ēəl/ n. (also **pin'e·al gland'**) conical gland in the brain, secreting a hormonelike substance

pine·ap·ple /pīn'ap'əl/ n. 1 juicy tropical fruit with yellow flesh and tough segmented skin 2 plant bearing this [fr. PINE[1], APPLE]

pine' cone' n. fruit of the pine

ping /pinG/ n. 1 short high ringing sound —v. 2 (cause to) make a ping [imit.]

Ping-Pong /pinG'pònG'/ n. Tdmk. TABLE TENNIS

pin'head' n. 1 head of a pin 2 very small thing or spot 3 Slang. stupid person

pin'hole' n. hole made by or for a pin

pin·ion[1] /pin'yən/ n. 1 outer part of a bird's wing —v. 2 cut off the pinion of (a wing or bird) to prevent flight 3 bind the arms of (a person) [L pinna]

pin·ion[2] n. toothed gear engaging with a larger one or a toothed rod (rack), etc. [L pinea pine-cone, rel. to PINE[1]]

pink[1] /pinGk/ n. 1 pale red color 2 cultivated plant with fragrant flowers 3 best condition (in the pink) —adj. 4 of a pale red color 5 tending to socialism —**pink'ish** adj.; **pink'ness** n.

pink[2] v. 1 cut a scalloped or zigzag edge on 2 pierce [perh. fr. LGer or Du]

Pink·er·ton /pinGk'kərtən/, **Allan** 1819–84; Scottish-born US detective

pink'ing shears' n. pl. dressmaker's serrated shears for cutting a zigzag edge

pink' slip' n. notice of dismissal or layoff given to an employee

pin' mon'ey n. small sum of money for minor expenses

pin·na·cle /pin'əkəl/ n. 1 culmination or climax 2 natural peak 3 small ornamental turret crowning a buttress, roof, etc. [L pinna]

pin·nate /pin'āt'/ adj. (of a compound leaf) having leaflets on either side of the leaf stalk [L pinnatus feathered, rel. to PINNACLE]

Pi·no·chet U·gar·te /pē'nōCHet' ōōgär'tā/, **Augusto** 1915– ; Chilean leader; president (1973–89)

pin'point' n. 1 point of a pin 2 something very small or sharp —v. 3 locate with precision

pin'prick' n. 1 tiny puncture 2 trifling irritation

pins' and nee'dles n. pl. 1 tingling sensation in a limb recovering from numbness 2 **on pins and needles** nervous; apprehensive

pin'stripe' n. 1 narrow stripe in cloth 2 (pl.) pinstripe suit, uniform, etc. —**pin'striped'** adj.

pint /pīnt/ n. 1 liquid measure equal to 1/2 of a quart or 1/8 of a gallon (.47 l.) 2 dry measure equal to 1/2 quart [Fr]

Pin·ter /pint'ər/, **Harold** 1930– ; English dramatist

pint'-sized' adj. (also **pint'-size'**) Colloq. very small

pin-up /pin'əp'/ n. 1 photograph of a popular or attractive person, hung on the wall 2 person in such a photograph

pin'wheel' n. 1 small wheel of paper, plastic, etc., made to spin in a breeze 2 spinning firework

Pin·yin /pin'yin'/ n. system of romanized spelling for transliterating Chinese [Chin]

pi·o·neer /pī'ənēr'/ n. 1 initiator of an enterprise; pathfinder in a subject, etc. 2 explorer or settler; colonist —v. 3 initiate (an enterprise, etc.) for others to follow 4 be a pioneer [Fr pionnier, rel. to PAWN[1]]

pi·ous /pī'əs/ adj. 1 devout; religious 2 sanctimonious —**pi'ous·ly** adv.; **pi'ous·ness** n. [L]

pip[1] /pip/ n. seed of an apple, pear, orange, grape, etc. [abbr. of PIPPIN]

pip[2] n. any of the spots on a playing card, domino, or dice

pipe /pīp/ n. 1 tube used to convey water, gas, etc. 2a narrow tube with a bowl at one end containing tobacco for smoking b quantity of tobacco held by this 3a musical wind instrument of a single straight tube b any of the tubes by which sound is produced in an organ c (pl.) BAGPIPE 4 tubular organ, vessel, etc. —v. (piped, pip·ing) 5 convey (oil, water, gas, etc.) by pipes 6 play (a tune, etc.) on a pipe or pipes 7 transmit (recorded music, etc.) by wire or cable 8 **pipe down** Slang. make less noise —**pipe'ful** n. [L pipare chirp]

pipe' clean'er n. piece of flexible tufted wire for cleaning a tobacco pipe

pipe' dream' n. unattainable or fanciful hope or scheme

pipe'line' n. 1 long, usu. underground, pipe for oil, etc. 2 channel supplying goods, information, etc. 3 **in the pipeline** being prepared; on the way

pipe' or'gan n. organ, as in a church, with sound emanating from tuned pipes

pip'er n. person who plays a pipe, esp. the bagpipes

pi·pette /pīpet'/ n. slender tube for transferring or measuring small quantities of liquids [Fr dim., rel. to PIPE]

pip'ing n. 1 pipelike fold or cord for decorative edging 2 segments of or a network of pipes 3 **piping hot** (of food, water, etc.) very hot

pip·it /pip'it/ n. small bird resembling a lark [imit.]

pip·pin /pip'in/ n. a type of apple [Fr]

pip·squeak /pip'skwēk'/ n. Colloq. insignificant or contemptible person or thing [imit.]

pi·quant /pē'kənt, -känt/ adj. 1 agreeably pungent, sharp, or appetizing 2 pleasantly stimulating to the mind —**pi'quan·cy** /-känsē/ n. [Fr piquer prick]

pique /pēk/ v. (piqued, piqu·ing) 1 wound the pride of; irritate 2 arouse (curiosity, interest, etc.) —n. 3 resentment; hurt pride [Fr, rel. to PIQUANT]

pi·ra·cy /pī'rəsē/ n. (pl. ·cies) 1 robbery of ships at sea 2 similar illegal or unauthorized practice, as infringement of copyright, etc. [rel. to PIRATE]

Pi·rae·us /pīrē'əs, pirä'-/ n. seaport in Greece. Pop. 169,600

Pi·ran·del·lo /pir'əndel'ō/, **Luigi** 1867–1936; Italian writer

pi·ra·nha /pərä'nə/ n. voracious S American freshwater fish [Port]

pi·rate /pī'rət/ n. 1 seafaring robber attacking ships 2 infringer of copyright, business rights, etc. —v. (·rat·ed, ·rat·ing) 3 reproduce (a book, etc.) or market (goods) without permission —pi·rat'i·cal /·rat'ikəl/ adj. [L *pirata* fr. Gk]

pir·ou·ette /pir'ŏŏ·et'/ n. 1 dancer's spin on one foot or the point of the toe —v. (·et·ted, ·et·ting) 2 perform a pirouette [Fr: spinning-top]

Pi·sa /pē'zə/ n. city in Italy, on the Arno River. Pop. 101,500

pis·ca·to·ri·al /pis'kətôr'ē·əl/ adj. of fishermen or fishing —pis'ca·to'ri·al·ly adv. [L *piscator* angler, fr. *piscis* fish]

Pi·sces /pī'sēz/ n. (pl. same) 1 constellation and twelfth sign of the zodiac (the Fish or Fishes) 2 person born under this sign [L, pl. of *piscis* fish]

Pi·sis·tra·tus /pisis'trətəs/ fl. 6th cent. B.C.; ruler of Athens

Pis·sar·ro /pisär'ō/, Camille 1830–1903; French painter

pis·tach·i·o /pəstasH'(ē)ō/ n. (pl. ·os) 1 edible pale-green nut 2 tree yielding this [Pers *pistah*]

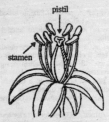

PISTIL and STAMEN

pis·til /pis'təl/ n. female organs of a flower, comprising the stigma, style, and ovary —pis'til·late /·lit, ·lāt/ adj. [L, rel. to PESTLE]

pis·tol /pis'təl/ n. small handgun [Czech *pišt'al*]

pis'tol-whip' v. (-whipped, -whip·ping) beat with a pistol

pis·ton /pis'tən/ n. 1 cylindrical part that slides up and down within a cylindrical sleeve, as in an internal-combustion engine, pump, etc. 2 sliding valve in a trumpet, etc. [It, rel. to PESTLE]

pis'ton ring' n. sealing ring on a piston

pis'ton rod' n. rod attached to a piston to impart motion

pit[1] /pit/ n. 1 usu. large hole in the ground 2 hollow or indentation on a surface 3 enclosed area for an orchestra in front of a stage 4 (the pits) *Slang.* worst imaginable place, situation, etc. 5 service area at the side of an auto racetrack —v. (pit·ted, pit·ting) 6 set (one's wits, strength, etc.) in competition (against) 7 make pits, scars, craters, etc., in [OE fr. L *puteus* well]

pit[2] n. 1 stone of a fruit —v. (pit·ted, pit·ting) 2 remove stones from (fruit)

pi·ta /pē'tə/ n. flat, hollow, unleavened bread that can be split and filled [ModGk: a kind of cake]

pit·a·pat /pit'əpat', pit'ē-/ (also pit'ter-pat'ter) adv. 1 with a sound like quick light steps 2 falteringly (*heart went pitapat*) —n. 3 such a sound [imit.]

pit' bull' ter'ri·er n. compactly built breed of dog noted for ferocity

pitch[1] /picH/ v. 1 erect and fix (a tent, camp, etc.) 2a throw b *Baseball.* act as the pitcher 3 express in a particular style or at a particular level 4 fall heavily, esp. headlong 5 (of a ship, etc.) plunge backward and forward in a lengthwise direction —n. 6 height, degree, intensity, etc. 7 degree of slope, esp. of a roof 8 *Mus.* highness or lowness of a sound governed by rate of vibrations 9a act of throwing b *Baseball.* pitcher's delivery of the ball to the batter 10 pitching motion of a ship, etc. 11 *Colloq.* persuasive sales talk 12 pitch in *Colloq.* set to work vigorously

pitch[2] n. 1 dark resinous substance from the distillation of tar or turpentine, used for caulking and paving —v. 2 coat with pitch [L *pix pic-*]

pitch'-black' adj. (also pitch'-dark') very or completely dark

pitch·blende /picH'blend'/ n. uranium ore occurring in pitchlike masses, also yielding radium [Ger, rel. to PITCH[2]]

pitched' bat'tle /picHt/ n. 1 battle between sides in prepared positions 2 concerted dispute, argument, etc.

pitched' roof' n. sloping roof

pitch·er[1] /picH'ər/ n. container for liquid with a lip and a handle [rel. to BEAKER]

pitch·er[2] n. *Baseball.* player who delivers the ball to the batter

pitch'fork' n. long-handled fork for pitching hay, etc.

pitch·man /picH'mən/ n. (pl. ·men) 1 booth attendant at a carnival 2 salesman

pit·e·ous /pit'ē·əs/ adj. deserving or arousing pity; wretched —pit'e·ous·ly adv.; pit'e·ous·ness n. [Rom, rel. to PITY]

pit·fall /pit'fôl'/ n. 1 unsuspected danger or drawback 2 covered pit for trapping animals

pith /pitH/ n. 1 spongy white tissue lining the rind of an orange, etc. 2 essential part 3 spongy tissue in the stems and branches of plants 4 strength; vigor; energy [OE]

pith·y /pitH'ē/ adj. (·i·er, ·i·est) 1 (of style, speech, etc.) terse and cogent 2 of or like pith —pith'i·ly adv.; pith'i·ness n.

pit·i·a·ble /pit'ēəbəl/ adj. deserving or arousing pity or contempt —pit'i·a·bly adv. [Fr, rel. to PITY]

pit·i·ful /pit'ifəl/ adj. 1 causing pity 2 contemptible —pit'i·ful·ly adv.

pit·i·less /pit'ilis/ adj. showing no pity —pit'i·less·ly adv.; pit'i·less·ness n.

pi·ton /pē'tän/ n. metal peg driven into rock or a crack to support a climber or rope [Fr]

Pitt /pit/ 1 William ("the Elder"), Earl of Chatham (called "the Great Commoner") 1708–78; British statesman; his son: 2 William ("the Younger") 1759–1806; British statesman; prime minister (1783–1801; 1804–06)

pit·tance /pit'ns/ n. very small allowance or payment [Rom, rel. to PITY]

pit'ter-pat'ter n. var. of PITAPAT

Pitts·burgh /pits'bərg/ *n.* city in Penn. Pop. 369,879

439

Pittsburgh / plane

pi·tu·i·tar·y /pit'yŏŏ'ətər'ē/ *n.* (*pl.* ·ies) (also pi·tu'i·tar·y gland') small ductless gland at the base of the brain [L *pituita* phlegm]

pit·y /pit'ē/ *n.* 1 sorrow and compassion for another's suffering 2 cause for regret (*what a pity!*) —*v.* (·ied, ·y·ing) 3 feel pity for —pit'y·ing *adj.*; pit'y·ing·ly *adv.* [L, rel. to PIETY]

Piu·ra /pyŏŏ'rä/ *n.* city in N Peru. Pop. 315,800

piv·ot /piv'ət/ *n.* 1 shaft or pin on which something turns or oscillates 2 crucial or essential person, point, etc. —*v.* 3 turn on or as on a pivot 4 provide with a pivot —piv'ot·al *adj.* [Fr]

pix·el /pik'səl/ *n.* any of the minute dots, etc., that comprise an image on a display screen [fr. *picture element*]

pix·ie /pik'sē/ *n.* (also pix'y) (*pl.* ·ies) fairy-like being

Pi·zar·ro /pizär'ō/, Francisco c. 1478–1541; Spanish conquistador

piz·za /pēt'sä/ *n.* Italian-style dish of a layer of dough baked with various toppings [It: pie]

piz·ze·ri·a /pēt'sərē'ə/ *n.* pizza restaurant

piz·zi·ca·to /pit'sikä'tō/ *adv.* & *adj.* *Mus.* (played) by plucking [It]

pkg. *abbr.* package

pl. *abbr.* 1 plural 2 (also *cap.*) place

plac·ard /plak'ərd, -ärd/ *n.* 1 large notice for public display —*v.* 2 set up placards on (a wall, etc.) [Fr fr. Du *placken* glue (v.)]

pla·cate /plā'kāt', plak'āt'/ *v.* (·cat·ed, ·cat·ing) pacify; conciliate —pla'ca·to'ry /-kətôr'ē/ *adj.* [L *placare* appease]

place /plās/ *n.* 1a particular space b space occupied by a person or thing c proper or natural position 2 city, town, village, etc.; locale 3 residence; home 4 rank; status 5 space, esp. a seat, for a person 6 building or area for a specific purpose (*place of work*) 7 point reached in a book, etc. (*lost my place*) 8 particular spot or position on a surface 9 employment or office 10 position; rank; prerogative 11 second position in finishing a race 12 position of a digit in a series indicated in decimal or similar notation —*v.* (placed, plac·ing) 13 put in a particular or proper place, state, or order; arrange 14 assign to a particular place, class, or rank 15 identify, classify, or remember correctly 16 find employment for 17 make or state (an order, bet, etc.) 18 finish among the first three in a race 19 go places *Colloq.* be successful 20 in place of in exchange for; instead of 21 put a person in his (or her) place humble a person 22 take place occur 23 take the place of be substituted for —place'ment *n.* [L *platea* broad way]

pla·ce·bo /pləsē'bō/ *n.* (*pl.* ·bos) preparation administered like medicine but having no physiological effect, prescribed for psychological reasons or in a test [L: I shall placate]

place' mat' *n.* mat for a place at a dining table

place'name' *n.* name of a town, natural feature, etc.

pla·cen·ta /pləsen'tə/ *n.* (*pl.* ·tae /-tē/ or ·tas) organ in the uterus of pregnant mammals that nourishes the fetus —pla·cen'tal *adj.* [Gk: flat cake]

plac·er /plas'ər/ *n.* deposit of sand, gravel, etc., containing valuable minerals in particles [AmerSp]

place' set'ting /plās'/ *n.* set of plate(s), flatware, etc., for one person at a table

plac·id /plas'id/ *adj.* 1 calm; not easily excited or irritated 2 tranquil; serene —pla·cid'i·ty *n.*; plac'id·ly *adv.*; plac'id·ness *n.* [L *placere* please]

plack·et /plak'it/ *n.* opening or slit in a garment [var. of PLACARD]

pla·gia·rize /plā'jarīz'/ *v.* (·rized, ·riz·ing) 1 take and pass off (another's thoughts, writings, etc.) as one's own 2 pass off the thoughts, etc., of (another person) as one's own —pla'gia·rism', pla'gia·rist /-rist/, pla' gia·riz'er *n.* [L *plagiarius* kidnapper]

plague /plāg/ *n.* 1a deadly contagious disease b (the plague) BUBONIC PLAGUE 2 infestation of a pest, etc. 3 great trouble or affliction —*v.* (plagued, plagu·ing) 4 pester; annoy 5 afflict; hinder (*plagued by back pain*) [L *plaga* infection]

plaid /plad/ *n.* 1 cloth with crossbarred or tartan pattern, esp. wool 2 any tartanlike pattern [Gaelic]

plain /plān/ *adj.* 1 clear; evident 2 readily understood; simple 3 unadorned 4 not beautiful or luxurious; homely 5 straightforward —*adv.* 6 clearly 7 simply —*n.* 8 level tract of country —plain'ly *adv.*; plain'ness *n.* [L *planus*]

plain'clothes' *adj.* designating a police officer, esp. a detective, who wears ordinary clothing on duty —plain'clothes'man /-mən/ *n.*

plain'song' *n.* unaccompanied church music chanted in unison

plain'-spo'ken *adj.* frank

plaint /plānt/ *n.* 1 *Law.* accusation 2 *Lit.* complaint [Fr *plainte* fr. L *plangere* lament]

plain·tiff /plān'tif/ *n.* person who brings a case against another into court [Fr *plaintif*, rel. to PLAINTIVE]

plain·tive /plān'tiv/ *adj.* expressing sorrow; mournful —plain'tive·ly *adv.* [Fr, rel. to PLAINT]

plain'va·nil'la *adj.* ordinary; undistinguished

plait /plāt, plat/ *n.* 1 braid of hair, straw, etc. 2 pleat —*v.* 3 weave (hair, etc.) into a plait 4 make by interlacing strands [Fr *pleit* fr. L *plicare* fold]

plan /plan/ *n.* 1 method or procedure for doing something; design, scheme, or intention 2 drawing or diagram of a structure 3 map of a town or district —*v.* (planned, plan·ning) 4 arrange beforehand; intend 5 develop a procedure or design for —plan'ner, plan'ning *n.* [Fr]

Planck /plängk, plaNGk/, Max 1858–1947; German physicist; originated quantum theory

plane[1] /plān/ *n.* 1a flat, level surface b *Geom.* surface such that any two points on it may be connected by a straight line 2 AIRPLANE 3 level, as of attainment, knowledge, etc. —*adj.* 4 (of a surface, etc.) perfectly level 5 (of an angle, figure, etc.) lying in a plane [L *planus* PLAIN]

plane² *n.* 1 tool for smoothing a usu. wooden surface by paring shavings from it —*v.* (**planed, plan·ing**) 2 smooth with a plane [L, rel. to PLANE¹]

PLANE² 1

plan·et /plan'it/ *n.* celestial body orbiting around a star —**plan'e·tar'y** /-iter'ē/ *adj.* [Gk: wanderer]

plan·e·tar·i·um /plan'ater'ēəm/ *n.* (*pl.* **·ums** or **·i·a** /-ēə/) 1 domed area on which images of stars, planets, constellations, etc., are projected 2 device for such projection

plane' tree' *n.* type of tree with maplelike leaves and bark that peels in uneven patches [Gk *platanos*]

plan·gent /plan'jənt/ *adj.* 1 loud and reverberating 2 plaintive [L, rel. to PLAINT]

plank /plaNGk/ *n.* 1 long, flat piece of timber 2 item in a political or other program —*v.* 3 provide or cover with planks 4 *Colloq.* put (down) or deposit with force [L *planca*]

plank'ing *n.* planks as flooring, etc.

plank·ton /plaNGk'tən/ *n.* chiefly microscopic organisms drifting in the sea or fresh water [Gk: wandering]

Pla·no /plā'nō/ *n.* city in Texas. Pop. 128,713

plant /plant/ *n.* 1a organism usu. containing chlorophyll to synthesize food and lacking the power of voluntary movement b organism of this kind smaller than a shrub or tree 2a machinery, fixtures, etc., used in industry b factory —*v.* 3 place (seeds, plants, etc.) in soil for growing 4 put or fix in position 5 instill; implant 6 place (something incriminating) for later discovery —**plant'like'** *adj.* [L *planta*]

plan·tain /plant'n/ *n.* 1 a kind of banana plant, grown for its fruit 2 bananalike fruit of this [Sp]

plan·ta·tion /plantā'sHən/ *n.* 1 estate on which cotton, tobacco, etc., is cultivated 2 area planted with trees, etc. [L, rel. to PLANT]

plant'er /plant'ər/ *n.* 1 manager or owner of a plantation 2 container for houseplants

plaque /plak/ *n.* 1 commemorative tablet, esp. fixed to a building 2 deposit on teeth where bacteria proliferate [Du *plak* tablet, rel. to PLACARD]

plas·ma /plaz'mə/ *n.* 1a fluid part of blood, lymph, or milk b this taken from blood for transfusions 2 PROTOPLASM 3 gas of positive ions and free electrons in about equal numbers —**plas'mic** *adj.* [Gk: molded thing]

plas·ter /plas'tər/ *n.* 1 mixture, usu. of lime, sand, and water, applied wet to walls, ceilings, etc., to dry into a smooth hard surface 2 pasty material spread on a cloth and applied to the body as a healing treatment 3 PLASTER OF PARIS —*v.* 4 cover (a wall, etc.) with plaster 5 daub or cover thickly 6 stick or apply (a thing) 7 smooth (esp. hair) with water, etc. —**plas'ter·er** *n.* [Gk *emplastron* salve]

plas'ter·board' *n.* construction board of paper-covered plaster for partitions, walls, etc.

plas'ter of Par'is *n.* fine white gypsum powder, mixed with water to mold casts, etc.

plas·tic /plas'tik/ *n.* 1 resin-based, esp. synthetic, substance that can be molded into any shape, used in manufacturing, etc. 2 credit card(s) —*adj.* 3 made of plastic 4 capable of being molded; pliant —**plas·tic'i·ty** /-tis'itē/ *n.*; **plas'ti·cize** /-sīz'/ *v.* (**·cized, ·ciz·ing**); **plas'ti·ciz'er** *n.* [Gk *plassein* mold]

plas'tic sur'ger·y *n.* reconstruction or repair of damaged or unsightly skin, muscle, etc., esp. by the transfer of tissue —**plas'tic sur'geon** *n.*

plate /plāt/ *n.* 1a shallow dish from which food is eaten or served b contents of this 2 similar vessel used for a collection in church, etc. 3 (*collect.*) utensils or objects coated with silver, gold, etc. 4 piece of metal with a name or inscription for affixing to a door, etc. 5 illustration on special paper in a book 6 *Photog.* thin sheet of metal, glass, etc., coated with a light-sensitive film 7 flat, thin, usu. rigid sheet of metal, etc., often part of a mechanism 8a smooth piece of metal, glass, etc., for engraving b impression from this 9a plastic dental device to hold artificial teeth b *Colloq.* denture 10 *Baseball.* HOME PLATE —*v.* (**plat·ed, plat·ing**) 11 apply a thin coat, esp. of silver, gold, or tin, to 12 cover with plates of metal, for protection —**plate'ful** *n.* [L *plata* fr. *plattus* flat]

pla·teau /platō'/ *n.* (*pl.* **·teaus**) 1 area of fairly level high ground 2 phase of little change, progress, etc. [Fr, rel. to PLATE]

plate' glass' *n.* clear, flat glass for windows, etc.

plate'let *n.* disk of protoplasm found in blood and involved in clotting

plat·en /plat'n/ *n.* 1 plate in a printing press that presses the paper against the type 2 cylindrical roller in a typewriter [Fr *platine*, rel. to PLATE]

plate' tec·ton'ics *n. pl.* (usu. treated as *sing.*) theory that the earth's surface is composed of moving 'plates' that cause continental drift, etc.

plat·form /plat'fôrm/ *n.* 1 raised level surface, as for a speaker, for freight loading, etc. 2 declared policy of a political party [Fr, rel. to PLATE, FORM]

Plath /plaTH/, **Sylvia** 1932–63; US poet and novelist

plat·i·num /plat'n-əm/ *n.* *Chem.* white, heavy, precious metallic element that does not tarnish; *symb.* Pt [earlier *platina* fr. Sp, dim. fr. *plata* silver]

plat·i·tude /plat'ət(y)ōōd'/ *n.* commonplace remark, esp. one solemnly delivered —**plat'i·tu'di·nous** /-dənəs/ *adj.* [Fr, rel. to PLATE]

Pla·to /plāt'ō/ 429–347 B.C.; Greek philosopher; disciple of Socrates

Pla·ton·ic /plətän'ik/ *adj.* 1 of Plato or his ideas 2 (usu. p-) (of love or friendship) not sexual [for PLATO]

Pla·to·nism /plāt'n·iz'əm/ *n.* philosophy of Plato or his followers —**Pla'to·nist** /-nist/ *n.*

pla·toon /plətōōn'/ *n.* 1 subdivision of a military company 2 *Sports.* specialized squad

—v. (·tooned, ·toon·ing) 3 *Sports.* alternate (players) at a position [Fr *peloton* dim. of *pelote* PELLET]

plat·ter /plat'ər/ *n.* large flat dish or plate [AngFr *plater*, rel. to PLATE]

plat·y·pus /plat'əpəs, -pŏŏs/ *n.* (*pl.* ·puses) Australian aquatic egg-laying mammal with a ducklike bill and flat tail [Gk: flat foot]

plau·dit /plô'dit/ *n.* (usu. *pl.*) tribute; applause [L *plaudite*, imper. of *plaudere* clap]

plau·si·ble /plô'zəbəl/ *adj.* 1 reasonable; probable 2 (of a person) persuasive but possibly deceptive —**plau'si·bil'i·ty** *n.*; **plau'si·bly** *adv.* [L, rel. to PLAUDIT]

Plau·tus /plôt'əs/, **Titus Maccius** c. 250–184 B.C.; Roman comic dramatist

play /plā/ *v.* 1 occupy or amuse oneself pleasantly or idly 2 trifle (with a person's feelings, etc.) 3a perform on or be able to perform on (a musical instrument) b perform (a piece of music) c cause (a recording, radio, etc.) to produce sounds 4 *Theat.* perform (a role, in a theater, etc.) 5 behave or act as (*play the fool*) 6 perform (a trick or joke) on (a person) 7a *Sports & Games.* take part in b compete with (another player or team) c occupy a specified position on a team d assign (a player) to a position —*n.* 8 recreation or amusement, esp. as the spontaneous activity of children 9a playing of a game b action or manner of this 10 dramatic piece for the stage, etc. 11 activity or operation (*the play of fancy*) 12a freedom of movement b space or scope for this 13 **play along** cooperate or feign cooperation 14 **play down** minimize the importance of 15 **play for time** seek to gain time by delaying 16 **play it cool** *Colloq.* be relaxed or apparently indifferent 17 **play up to** flatter, esp. to win favor 18 **play with fire** take foolish risks [OE]

play·act' *v.* pretend; behave insincerely —**play'act'ing** *n.*

play'back' *n.* reproduction of recorded sound, images, etc.

play'bill' *n.* program for or notice of a play

play'boy' *n.* pleasure-seeking man

play-by-play *adj.* 1 pertaining to a description, esp. of a sports event, with continuous commentary —*n.* 2 such a description

play·er /plā'ər/ *n.* 1 participant in a game 2 person playing a musical instrument 3 actor

play·ful /plā'fəl/ *adj.* 1 fond of or inclined to play 2 done in fun —**play'ful·ly** *adv.*; **play'ful·ness** *n.*

play'go'er *n.* person who goes often to the theater

play'ground' *n.* outdoor area for children to play in, esp. one with swings, climbing equipment, etc.

play'house' *n.* 1 theater 2 small structure for children's play

play'ing card' *n.* one of a set of usu. 52 oblong cards, divided into four suits and used in games

play'mate' *n.* child's companion in play

play·off /plā'ôf'/ *n.* game(s) played to determine a champion or resolve a tie

play' on words' *n.* pun

play'pen' *n.* portable enclosure for a young child to play in

play'thing *n.* toy

play·wright /plā'rīt/ *n.* person who writes plays

pla·za /plä'zə/ *n.* 1 city square or open area 2 shopping center 3 service and rest area on a turnpike, etc.

plea /plē/ *n.* 1 appeal; entreaty 2 *Law.* formal statement by or on behalf of a defendant 3 excuse [L *placitum* decree, rel. to PLEASE]

plea' bar'gain *Law. n.* 1 agreement in a criminal case in which the prosecution accepts a defendant's plea of guilty to a lesser charge in exchange for information, etc. —*v.* 2 negotiate such an agreement —**plea' bar'gain·ing** *n.*

plead /plēd/ *v.* (**plead·ed** or **pled**, **plead·ing**) 1 make an earnest appeal 2 (of an attorney) address a court 3 argue (a case) in a court 4 answer (guilty or not guilty) to a charge 5 allege as an excuse (*plead insanity*) —**plead'er**, **plead'ing** *n.* [AngFr *pleder*, rel. to PLEA]

pleas·ant /plez'ənt/ *adj.* pleasing to the mind, feelings, or senses —**pleas'ant·ly** *adv.*; **pleas'ant·ness** *n.* [Fr, rel. to PLEASE]

pleas·ant·ry /plez'əntrē/ *n.* (*pl.* ·ries) amusing or polite remark

please /plēz/ *v.* (**pleased**, **pleas·ing**) 1 be agreeable to; give pleasure 2a be glad or willing to b derive pleasure or satisfaction (from) 3 desire or think fit (*take as many as you please*) 4 expression in polite requests (*come in, please*) —**pleas'ing** *adj.* [Fr *plaisir* fr. L *placere*]

pleas·ur·a·ble /plezH'(ə)rəbəl/ *adj.* causing pleasure —**pleas'ur·a·bly** *adv.*

pleas·ure /plezH'ər/ *n.* 1 feeling of satisfaction or joy; enjoyment 2 source of pleasure or gratification 3 one's will or desire (*what is your pleasure?*) 4 sensual gratification [Fr, rel. to PLEASE]

pleat /plēt/ *n.* 1 fold or crease, esp. a flattened fold of cloth —*v.* 2 make a pleat or pleats in [fr. PLAIT]

plebe /plēb/ *n.* first-year cadet, esp. at a US military academy

ple·be·ian /pləbē'ən/ *n.* 1 commoner, esp. in ancient Rome 2 working-class person, esp. an uncultured one —*adj.* 3 uncultured; coarse [L *plebs* common people]

pleb·i·scite /pleb'əsit/ *n.* direct, popular vote on an issue [L *plebiscitum*, rel. to PLEBE·IAN]

plec·trum /plek'trəm/ *n.* (*pl.* ·trums or ·tra /-trə/) thin flat piece of plastic, etc., for plucking the strings of a guitar, etc. [L fr. Gk *plēssein* strike]

pled /pled/ *past* of PLEAD

pledge /plej/ *n.* 1 solemn promise 2 security against a debt, etc. 3 thing given as a token —*v.* (**pledged**, **pledg·ing**) 4 deposit as security 5 promise solemnly by the pledge of (one's honor, word, etc.) 6 bind by a solemn promise [Fr *plege*]

ple·na·ry /plē'nərē, plen'ə-/ *adj.* 1 (of an assembly) to be attended by all members 2 entire; unqualified [L *plenus* full]

plen·i·po·ten·ti·ar·y /plenəpəten'sHərē, -sHēer'ē/ *n.* (*pl.* ·ies) 1 person (esp. a diplomat) invested with full authority to act —*adj.* 2

having such authority [L, rel. to PLENARY, PO-TENT]

plen·i·tude /plen'ət(y)ōōd'/ *n.* **1** fullness; completeness **2** abundance [L, rel. to PLE-NARY]

plen·te·ous /plent'ēəs/ *adj.* plentiful [Fr *plentivous*, rel. to PLENTY]

plen·ti·ful /plen'tifəl/ *adj.* abundant; copious —**plen'ti·ful·ly** *adv.*

plen·ty /plen'tē/ *n.* **1** abundant or sufficient quantity or number —*adv.* **2** *Colloq.* fully; quite [L *plenitas*, rel. to PLENARY]

ple·o·nasm /plē'ōnaz'əm/ *n.* use of redundant words (e.g., *true facts*) —**ple'o·nas'tic** /-nas'tik/ *adj.* [Gk *pleon* more]

pleth·o·ra /pleTH'ərə/ *n.* overabundance [Gk: fullness]

pleu·ra /plŏŏr'ə/ *n.* (*pl.* **-rae** /-ē/) membrane enveloping the lungs —**pleu'ral** *adj.* [Gk: rib]

pleu·ri·sy /plŏŏr'əsē/ *n.* inflammation of the pleura —**pleu·rit'ic** /-rit'ik/ *adj.* [Gk, rel. to PLEURA]

Plex·i·glas /plek'sēglas'/ *n. Tdmk.* durable transparent plastic used for windows, furniture, etc.

plex·us /plek'səs/ *n.* (*pl.* same or **-us·es** *Anat.* network of nerves or vessels (*solar plexus*) [L *plectere*]

pli·a·ble /plī'əbəl/ *adj.* **1** bending easily; supple **2** yielding; compliant —**pli'a·bil'i·ty** *n.* [Fr, rel. to PLY¹]

pli·ant /plī'ənt/ *adj.* PLIABLE —**pli'an·cy** *n.*

PLIERS

pli·ers /plī'ərz/ *n. pl.* tool with parallel flat surfaces for holding small objects, bending wire, etc. [fr. dial. *ply* bend, rel. to PLIABLE]

plight¹ /plīt/ *n.* unfortunate condition or state [AngFr *plit* PLAIT]

plight² *v. Archaic.* pledge [OE]

plinth /plinTH/ *n.* lower square slab at the base of a column, vase, statue, etc. [Gk: tile]

Plin·y /plin'ē/ **1** ("the Elder") c. 23–79; Roman statesman and scholar; his nephew: **2** ("the Younger") c. 61 – c. 112; Roman senator and writer

PLO *abbr.* Palestine Liberation Organization

plod /pläd/ *v.* (**plod·ded, plod·ding**) **1** walk doggedly or laboriously; trudge **2** work slowly and steadily —**plod'der** *n.* [prob. imit.]

Plo·ies·ti /plō·yeSHt'(ē)/ *n.* (also Ploiesti) city in S Romania. Pop. 252,000

plop /pläp/ *n.* **1** sound as of an object dropping into water —*v.* (**plopped, plop·ping**) **2** fall or drop with a plop [imit.]

plot /plät/ *n.* **1** defined and usu. small piece of land **2** sequence or progress of events in a play, novel, film, etc. **3** conspiracy or secret plan —*v.* (**plot·ted, plot·ting**) **4** make a plan or map of **5** plan or contrive secretly (a crime, etc.) **6** mark on a chart or diagram —**plot'ter** *n.* [OE]

Plov·div /plôf'dif/ *n.* city in Bulgaria, on the Maritsa River. Pop. 379,100

plo·ver /plav'ər, plō'var/ *n.* plump-breasted wading bird, e.g., the lapwing [L *pluvia* rain]

pkow /plou/ (also, esp. *Brit.* **plough** /plou/) *n.* **1** implement for cutting furrows in the soil and turning it up **2** implement resembling this (*snowplow*) —*v.* **3** turn up, furrow, or move with a plow **4** produce (a furrow or line) thus **5** advance laboriously, esp. through work, a book, etc. **6** move violently like a plow [OE]

plow'share' *n.* cutting blade of a plow

ploy /ploi/ *n.* cunning maneuver to gain advantage

pluck /pluk/ *v.* **1** pick or pull out or away **2** strip (a bird) of feathers **3** tug or snatch (at) **4** sound (the string of a musical instrument) with a finger or plectrum —*n.* **5** courage: spirit **6** plucking [OE]

pluck·y /pluk'ē/ *adj.* (**-i·er, -i·est**) brave; spirited —**pluck'i·ly** *adv.*; **pluck'i·ness** *n.*

plug /plag/ *n.* **1** piece of solid material fitting tightly into a hole **2** device fitting into holes in a socket for making an electrical connection **3** *Colloq.* piece of free publicity for an idea, product, etc. **4** cake of tobacco for chewing —*v.* (**plugged, plug·ging**) **5** stop (up) with a plug **6** *Slang.* shoot or hit (a person, etc.) **7** *Colloq.* promote (an idea, product, etc.) **8** *Colloq.* work steadily (at) [LGer or Du]

plum /pləm/ *n.* **1a** sweet, oval, fleshy fruit with a flattish stone **b** tree bearing this **2** reddish-purple color **3** *Colloq.* something prized [L, rel. to PRUNE¹]

plum·age /plŏŏ'mij/ *n.* bird's feathers [Fr, rel. to PLUME]

plumb /pləm/ *n.* **1** lead weight at the end of a line for finding depth of water or testing for vertical —*adv.* **2** exactly (*plumb in the center*) **3** vertically **4** *Colloq.* totally (*plumb crazy*) —*adj.* **5** vertical —*v.* **6** sound or test with a plumb **7** learn, reach, or experience [L *plumbum* lead]

plumb·er /pləm'ər/ *n.* person who fits and repairs water pipes, fixtures, etc.

plumb·ing /pləm'iNG/ *n.* **1** system or apparatus of water supply, etc. **2** work of a plumber

plume /plŏŏm/ *n.* **1** feather, esp. a large one used for ornament **2** ornament of feathers, etc., worn on a helmet or hat or in the hair **3** something resembling this (*plume of smoke*) —*v.* (**plumed, plum·ing**) **3** decorate or provide with a plume or plumes **5** (of a bird) preen (itself or its feathers) —**plum'y** *adj.* (**-i·er, -i·est**) [L *pluma*]

PLUMB 1

plum·met /pləm'it/ *n.* **1** PLUMB, 1 —*v.* **2** fall or plunge rapidly [Fr, rel. to PLUMB]

plump¹ /pləmp/ *adj.* **1** full or rounded in shape; fleshy —*v.* **2** make or become plump (*plumped up the cushion*) —**plump'ness** *n.* [LGer or Du *plomp* blunt]

plump² *v.* **1** drop or fall abruptly —*n.* **2** abrupt or heavy fall —*adv.* **3** directly; unmistakably [LGer or Du *plompen*, imit.]

plun·der /plən'dər/ *v.* **1** rob or steal; loot **2**

exploit (another's property) for profit —*n.* 3 activity of plundering 4 property so acquired [Ger *plündern*]

plunge /plənj/ *v.* (**plunged, plung·ing**) **1a** thrust forcefully or abruptly **b** dive **c** (cause to) enter or embark impetuously **2** immerse completely **3** fall suddenly or dramatically —*n.* 4 plunging action or movement; dive **5 take the plunge:** *Colloq.* **a** take a decisive step **b** place a large, risky bet [Rom, rel. to PLUMB]

plung·er /plən'jər/ *n.* **1** mechanism with a plunging or thrusting movement **2** rubber suction cup on a handle for clearing blocked pipes

plu·ral /ploor'əl/ *adj.* **1** more than one in number **2** *Gram.* (of a word or form) denoting more than one —*n.* 3 *Gram.* plural word or form [L, rel. to PLUS]

plu·ral·ism /ploor'əliz'əm/ *n.* social theory or form that embraces diverse cultures, races, etc. —**plu'ral·ist** /-ist/ *n.*; **plu·ral·is'tic** *adj.*

plu·ral·i·ty /plooral'ətē/ *n.* (*pl.* **-ties**) **1** state of being plural **2a** leading total of votes, etc., as in an election involving three or more candidates **b** excess of votes of a leading candidate over the second finisher

• **Usage:** See note at MAJORITY.

plus /pləs/ *prep.* **1** with the addition of **2** along with —*adj.* 3 (after a number) at least (*fifteen plus*) **4** (after a grade, etc.) somewhat better than **5** *Math.* positive **6** *Electr.* having a positive charge **7** additional; extra —*n.* 8 the symbol (+) **9** additional or positive quantity **10** advantage —*conj.* 11 *Colloq.* also; and furthermore [L: more]

plush /pləsh/ *n.* **1** cloth of silk, cotton, etc., with a long soft nap —*adj.* **2** made of plush **3** *Colloq.* luxurious —**plush'ly** *adv.*; **plush' ness** *n.* [L, rel. to PILE²]

Plu·tarch /ploo'tärk/ *c.* 46–*c.* 120; Greek philosopher and biographer

Plu·to /ploo'tō/ *n.* **1** *Gk. & Rom. Myth.* god of the underworld; Hades **2** outermost known planet of the solar system

plu·toc·ra·cy /plootäk'rəsē/ *n.* (*pl.* **-cies**) **1** government by the wealthy **2** wealthy elite —**plu·to·crat** /ploo'təkrat/ *n.*; **plu'to·crat' ic** *adj.* [Gk *ploutos* wealth]

plu·to·ni·um /plootō'nēəm/ *n.* radioactive metallic element; *symb.* **Pu** [fr. PLUTO]

plu·vi·al /ploo'vēəl/ *adj.* **1** of rain; rainy **2** *Geol.* caused by rain [L *pluvia* rain]

ply¹ /plī/ *n.* (*pl.* **plies**) **1** thickness or layer of cloth, wood, etc. **2** strand of yarn, rope, etc. [Fr *pli*, rel. to PLAIT]

ply² *v.* (**plied, ply·ing**) **1** use or wield (a tool, weapon, etc.) **2** work steadily at (*ply one's trade*) **3** supply continuously (with food, drink, etc.) **4** (of a vehicle, etc.) travel regularly to and fro [fr. APPLY]

Plym·outh /plim'əTH/ *n.* seaport in SW England. Pop. 242,600

ply'wood *n.* strong board made by gluing together thin sheets of wood

Pm *symb.* promethium

p.m. *abbr.* after noon [L *post meridiem*]

PMS *abbr.* premenstrual syndrome

pneu·mat·ic /n(y)oomat'ik/ *adj.* **1** filled with air or wind **2** operated by compressed air [Gk *pneuma* wind]

pneu·mo·nia /n(y)oomōn'yə/ *n.* inflammation of one or both lungs [Gk *pneumōn* lung]

Po *symb.* polonium

PO *abbr.* **1** post office **2** purchase order

poach¹ /pōCH/ *v.* cook (an egg without its shell, fish, etc.) in or over boiling water [Fr *pochier*, rel. to POKE²]

poach² *v.* **1** catch (game or fish) illegally **2** trespass or encroach (on another's property, territory, etc.) —**poach'er** *n.* [earlier *poche*, rel. to POACH¹]

Po·ca·hon·tas /pō'kəhänt'əs/ (English name Rebecca Rolfe) d. 1616; American Indian woman in early colonial Virginia

pock /päk/ *n.* (also **pock'mark**) small pus-filled spot on the skin, esp. caused by chickenpox or smallpox —**pock'-marked'** *adj.* [OE]

pock·et /päk'it/ *n.* **1** small pouch sewn into or on clothing, for carrying small articles **2** pouchlike compartment or holder **3** isolated group or area (*pockets of resistance*) —*adj.* 4 small enough to fit a pocket **5** small —*v.* 6 put into one's pocket **7** appropriate, esp. dishonestly [AngFr dim., rel. to POKE²]

pock'et·book *n.* **1** woman's purse **2** folding case for papers or money carried in a pocket

pock'et·knife *n.* knife with one or several blades that fold into the handle

pock'et ve'to *n.* indirect veto by a president who fails to sign a bill presented by Congress within ten days of its adjournment

pod /päd/ *n.* long seed vessel, esp. of a pea or bean

Pod·go·ri·ca /pôd'gôrē'tsä/ *n.* capital of Montenegro. Pop. 54,500

po·di·a·try /pōdī'ətrē/ *n.* care of the human foot —**po·di'a·trist** *n.*

po·di·um /pō'dēəm/ *n.* (*pl.* **-ums** or **-di·a** /-dēə/) **1** platform, as for an orchestra conductor **2** lectern [Gk *podion* dim. of *pous* podfoot]

Poe /pō/, Edgar Allan 1809–49; US short-story writer and poet

po·em /pō'əm, pōm/ *n.* metrical composition, usu. concerned with feeling or imaginative description [Gk *poiein* make]

po·e·sy /pō'əsē/ *n. Archaic.* poetry [Fr, ult. fr. Gk *poiēsis*]

po·et /pō'ət/ *n.* (*fem.* **po'et·ess**) **1** writer of poems **2** highly imaginative or expressive person [Gk *poiētēs*, rel. to POEM]

po·et·ic /pōet'ik/ *adj.* (also **po·et'i·cal**) of or like poetry or poets —**po·et'i·cal·ly** *adv.*

po·et'ic jus'tice *n.* appropriate punishment or reward, esp. not administered by law

po·et'ic li'cense *n.* writer's or artist's disregard of conventions or rules for effect

po'et lau're·ate *n.* (*pl.* **po'ets lau'reate**) nation's preeminent or official poet

po·et·ry /pō'ətrē/ *n.* **1** art or work of a poet **2** poems collectively **3** poetic or tenderly pleasing quality [MedL, rel. to POET]

po·grom /pō'grəm, pəgräm'/ *n.* organized massacre (orig. of Jews in Russia) [Russ]

poign·ant /poin'yənt/ *adj.* **1** painfully sharp to the emotions or senses; deeply moving **2** arousing sympathy —**poign'ance, poign'an·cy** *n.*; **poign'ant·ly** *adv.* [L, rel. to POINT]

poin·set·ti·a /poinset'ēə, -set'ə/ *n.* plant with

large, usu. scarlet, bracts surrounding small yellow flowers [for J.R. Poinsett, US diplomat]

point /point/ *n.* 1 sharp or tapered end of a tool, weapon, pencil, etc. 2 tip or extreme end 3 *Geom.* that which has position but not magnitude 4 particular place or position 5 precise or critical moment 6 very small mark; dot 7 DECIMAL POINT 8 stage or degree in progress or increase 9 temperature at which a change of state occurs (*freezing point*) 10 single item or particular 11 unit of scoring in games or of measuring value, etc. 12 significant or essential thing; sense 13 purpose; benefit (*no point in staying*) 14 characteristic (*strong point*) 15a each of 32 directions marked at equal distances around a compass b corresponding direction toward the horizon 16 (usu. *pl.*) electrical contact in the distributor of an engine 17 promontory —*v.* 18a direct or aim (a finger, weapon, etc.) b direct attention 19 aim; be directed to 20 indicate; be evidence of (*it all points to murder*) 21 at (or on) **the point of** on the verge of 22 **beside the point** irrelevant 23 **point out** indicate; draw attention to 24 **point up** emphasize 25 **to the point** relevant; relevantly 26 **up to a point** to some extent but not completely [L *pungere punct-* prick]

Point′ Bar′row /bar′ō/ *n.* northernmost point of the US, at the N tip of Alaska

point′-blank′ *adj.* 1 (of a shot) aimed or fired at very close range 2 blunt; direct —*adv.* 3 at very close range 4 directly; bluntly

point′ed *adj.* 1 sharpened or tapering to a point 2 (of a remark, etc.) cutting 3 emphasized —**point′ed·ly** *adv.*

Pointe-Noire /pwänt′n(ə)wär′/ *n.* seaport in the Congo. Pop. 576,200

point·er /point′ər/ *n.* 1 thing that points or indicates 2 rod for pointing to features on a chart, etc. 3 bit of helpful advice; tip 4 dog of a breed that on scenting game stands rigid looking toward it

poin·til·lism /pwan′til·iz′əm/ *n.* technique of impressionist painting using tiny dots of pure color (that become blended in the viewer's eye) —**poin′til·list** /-list/ *n.* & *adj.* [Fr *pointiller* mark with dots]

point′less *adj.* lacking purpose or meaning; ineffective; fruitless —**point′less·ly** *adv.*; **point′less·ness** *n.*

point′ man′ *n.* soldier, player, etc., positioned at the front

point′ of or′der *n.* parliamentary query as to correct procedure

point′ of view′ *n.* 1 position from which a thing is viewed 2 way of considering a matter

poise /poiz/ *n.* 1 composure 2 equilibrium 3 carriage (of the head, etc.) —*v.* (**poised, pois·ing**) 4 balance; hold suspended or supported 5 be balanced or suspended [L *pendere pens-* weigh]

poised /poizd/ *adj.* 1a composed; self-assured b carrying oneself gracefully or with dignity 2 ready for action

poi·son /poi′zən/ *n.* 1 substance causing an organism death or injury, esp. in a small quantity 2 harmful influence —*v.* 3 administer poison to 4 kill, injure, or infect with poison

5 treat (something) with poison 6 corrupt; pervert; spoil —**poi′son·er** *n.*; **poi′son·ous** *adj.* [L, rel. to POTION]

poi′son i′vy *n.* climbing plant secreting an irritant oil from its leaves

poke¹ /pōk/ *v.* (**poked, pok·ing**) 1a thrust or push with the hand, a stick, etc. b be thrust forward; protrude 2 thrust the end of a finger, etc., against 3 produce (a hole, etc., in) by poking 4 move (along) slowly 5 pry or search (into) —*n.* 6 thrust; jab 7 **poke fun at** ridicule [Ger or Du]

poke² *n. Dial.* bag; sack [Fr dial.]

pok·er¹ /pōk′ər/ *n.* metal rod for stirring a fire

pok·er² *n.* card game in which bluff is used as players bet on the value of their hands

pok′er face′ *n.* impassive or expressionless look, as on a poker player —**pok′er-faced′** *adj.*

pok·y /pōk′ē/ *adj.* (**·i·er, ·i·est**) 1 slow or dull 3 (of a room, etc.) small and cramped —**pok′i·ness** *n.* [fr. POKE¹]

Po·land /pō′lənd/ *n.* republic in central Europe. Capital: Warsaw. Pop. 38,429,000

po·lar /pō′lər/ *n.* 1 *adj.* of or near a pole of the earth 2 having magnetic or electric polarity 3 directly opposite in character [L, rel. to POLE²]

po′lar bear′ *n.* large white bear of Arctic regions

po·lar·i·ty /pōlar′ətē/ *n.* (*pl.* ·ties) 1 tendency of a magnet to point to the magnetic poles of the earth or of a body's axis to lie in a particular direction 2 state of having two poles with contrary qualities 3 state of two opposing tendencies, opinions, etc. 4 *Electr.* positive or negative condition

po·lar·ize /pō′lərīz′/ *v.* (**·ized, ·iz·ing**) 1 restrict the vibrations of (light waves, etc.) to one direction 2 give magnetic or electric polarity to 3 divide into two opposing groups —**po′lar·i·za′tion** *n.*

Po·la·roid /pō′ləroid′/ *n. Tdmk.* 1 transparent material polarizing light passing through it 2 camera with film that produces a print rapidly after each exposure

pole¹ /pōl/ *n.* 1 long slender rounded piece of wood, metal, etc. —*v.* (**poled, pol·ing**) 2 propel with thrusts of a pole [L *palus* stake]

pole² *n.* 1a each of the two points in the celestial sphere about which the stars appear to revolve b each of the ends of the axis of rotation of the earth 2 each of the two opposite points on a magnet at which magnetic forces are strongest 3 each of two terminals (positive and negative) of an electric cell or battery 4 be **poles apart**; differ greatly [Gk: axis]

Pole /pōl/ *n.* 1 native or national of Poland 2 person of Polish descent [Ger fr. Pol]

pole·cat /pōl′kat′/ *n.* 1 small brownish-black mammal of the weasel family 2 skunk

po·lem·ic /pəlem′ik/ *n.* 1 forceful verbal or written controversy or argument 2 (*pl.*) art or practice of disputation —*adj.* (also **po·lem′i·cal**) 3 involving dispute; controversial —**po·lem′i·cist** /-sist/ *n.* [Gk *polemos* war]

pole′star′ *n.* 1 star near the North Pole in the sky 2 thing serving as a guide

pole′ vault′ *n.* 1 vault, or sport of vaulting,

over a high bar with the aid of a pole —*v.* 2 perform this —**pole′ vault′er** *n.*

po·lice /pəlēs′/ *n.* 1 (usu. prec. by *the*) civil force responsible for maintaining public order 2 its members 3 force with similar functions (*military police*) —*v.* (·**liced**, ·**lic·ing**) 4 keep (a place or people) in order by means of police, etc. 5 provide with police 6 make or keep neat or orderly [L, rel. to POLICY[1]]

po·lice·man /pəlēs′mən/ *n.* (*pl.* ·**men;** *fem.* ·**wom′an,** *pl.* ·**wom′en**) member of a police force

po·lice′ of′fi·cer *n.* member of a police force

po·lice′ state′ *n.* totalitarian state controlled by political police

pol·i·cy[1] /päl′əsē/ *n.* (*pl.* ·**cies**) 1 plan or course of action adopted by a government, business, individual, etc. 2 prudent conduct; sagacity [L *politia* POLITY]

pol·i·cy[2] *n.* (*pl.* ·**cies**) insurance contract [Fr *police*, ult. fr. Gk *apodeixis* proof]

pol′i·cy·hold′er *n.* person or body holding an insurance policy

po·li·o·my·e·li·tis /pō′lē·ō·mī′əlī′tis/ *n.* (also **po·li·o** /pō′lēō/) infectious viral disease of the gray matter of the central nervous system with temporary or permanent paralysis [Gk *polios* gray, *myelos* marrow]

pol·ish /päl′ish/ *v.* 1 make or become smooth or glossy by rubbing 2 refine or improve; add the finishing touches to —*n.* 3 substance used for polishing 4 smoothness or glossiness produced by rubbing 5 refinement; elegance 6 **polish off** finish (esp. food) quickly [L *polire*]

Po·lish /pō′lish/ *adj.* 1 of Poland 2 of the Poles or their language —*n.* 3 language of Poland

po·lite /pəlīt′/ *adj.* 1 having good manners; courteous 2 cultivated; refined —**po·lite′ly** *adv.*; **po·lite′ness** *n.* [L *politus*, rel. to POLISH]

pol·i·tesse /päl′ites′/ *n.* formal courtesy

pol·i·tic /päl′ətik/ *adj.* 1 (of an action) judicious; expedient 2 (of a person) prudent; sagacious —*v.* (·**ticked,** ·**tick·ing**) 3 engage in politics [Gk, rel. to POLITY]

po·lit·i·cal /pəlit′ikəl/ *adj.* 1 of or concerning government or public affairs 2 taking or belonging to a side in politics 3 concerned with seeking power, status, etc. (*political decision*) —**po·lit′i·cal·ly** *adv.* [L, rel. to POLITIC]

po·lit′i·cal ac′tion com·mit′tee *n.* permanent organization that collects and distributes funds for political purposes; *abbr.* **PAC**

po·lit′i·cal cor·rect′ness *n.* preoccupation with eliminating language or behavior that might offend a group; *abbr.* **PC**

po·lit′i·cal·ly cor·rect′ *adj.* in conformance with POLITICAL CORRECTNESS; *abbr.* **PC**

po·lit′i·cal sci′ence *n.* the study of politics and systems of government

pol·i·ti·cian /päl′ətish′ən/ *n.* 1 person engaged in politics, esp. an elected official 2 opportunistic or manipulative person; smooth schemer

po·lit·i·cize /pəlit′əsīz′/ *v.* (·**cized,** ·**ciz·ing**) 1a give a political character to b make politically aware 2 engage in or talk politics —**po·lit′i·ci·za′tion** *n.*

po·lit·i·co /pəlit′ikō′/ *n.* (*pl.* ·**cos**) politician [Sp]

pol·i·tics /päl′ətiks′/ *n. pl.* 1 (treated as *sing.* or *pl.*) a art and science of government b public life and affairs 2 (usu. treated as *pl.*) political principles or practice (*what are his politics?*) 3 activities concerned with seeking power, status, etc.

pol·i·ty /päl′ətē/ *n.* (*pl.* ·**ties**) 1 form or process of civil government 2 organized society; state [Gk *politēs* citizen, fr. *polis* city]

Polk /pōk/, **James Knox** 1795–1849; 11th US president (1845–49)

pol·ka /pōl′kə, pō′kə/ *n.* 1 lively dance of Bohemian origin 2 music for this —*v.* (·**kaed,** ·**ka·ing**) 3 dance the polka [Czech *půlka*]

pol′ka dot′ *n.* round dot as one of many forming a regular pattern on a textile fabric, etc.

poll /pōl/ *n.* 1a (often *pl.*) voting b result of voting or number of votes recorded 2 survey of opinion —*v.* 3a take the vote or votes of b receive (so many votes) 4 survey (a person or group) for opinion [perh. fr. LGer or Du]

pol·len /päl′ən/ *n.* fine dustlike grains discharged from the male part of a flower, each containing the fertilizing element [L]

pol′len count′ *n.* index of the amount of pollen in the air

pol·li·nate /päl′ənāt′/ *v.* (·**nat·ed,** ·**nat·ing**) convey pollen to or sprinkle (a pistil) with pollen —**pol′li·na′tion, pol′li·na′tor** *n.*

Pol·lock /päl′ək/, **Jackson** 1912–56; US painter

poll′ster /pōl′stər/ *n.* person who conducts an opinion poll

pol·lute /pəlōōt′/ *v.* (·**lut·ed,** ·**lut·ing**) 1 contaminate (the environment) 2 make foul or impure —**pol·lu′tant** *adj. & n.*; **pol·lut′er, pol·lu′tion** *n.* [L *polluere* -*lut*-]

Pol·lux /päl′əks/ *n.* see CASTOR

po·lo /pō′lō/ *n.* game played on horseback with a long-handled mallet and wooden ball [Tibetan: ball]

Po·lo /pō′lō/, **Marco** 1254–1324; Venetian traveler in E Asia

po·lo·naise /päl′ənāz′/ *n.* 1 slow dance of Polish origin 2 music for this [Fr, rel. to POLE]

po·lo·ni·um /pəlō′nēəm/ *n.* radioactive metallic element; *symb.* **Po** [MedL *Polonia* Poland]

Pol Pot /päl′ pät′, pōl′/ c. 1925– ; Cambodian political leader; prime minister (1976–79)

pol·ter·geist /pōl′tərgīst′/ *n.* noisy mischievous ghost, esp. one causing physical damage [Ger]

pol·troon /pältrōōn′/ *n.* utter coward —**pol·troon′er·y** *n.* [It *poltro* sluggard]

poly- *comb. form* 1 many (*polygamy*) 2 polymerized (*polyunsaturated; polyester*) [Gk: many]

pol·y·an·dry /päl′ē·an′drē/ *n.* polygamy in which a woman has more than one husband —**pol′y·an′drous** *adj.* [Gk *anēr andr-* male]

pol·y·chro·mat·ic /päl′ēkrōmat′ik/ *adj.* 1 many-colored 2 (of radiation) containing more than one wavelength

pol·y·chrome /päl′ēkrōm′/ *adj.* 1 in many colors —*n.* 2 polychrome work of art [Gk, rel. to POLY-, CHROME]

pol·y·es·ter /päl′ĕs′tər/ *n.* synthetic fiber or resin

pol·y·eth·yl·ene /päl′ĕ-ĕTH′əlēn′/ *n.* Chem. plastic polymer of ethylene used for containers, packaging, etc.

po·lyg·a·my /pəlig′əmē/ *n.* practice of having more than one spouse at a time —**po·lyg′a·mist** /-mist/ *n.*; **po·lyg′a·mous** *adj.* [Gk *gamos* marriage]

pol·y·glot /päl′ēglät′/ *adj.* 1 knowing, using, or written in several languages —*n.* 2 polyglot person [Gk *glötta* tongue]

pol·y·gon /päl′igän′/ *n.* plane figure with usu. five or more sides and angles —**po·lyg·o·nal** /pəlig′ən-l/ *adj.* [Gk *gönos* angled]

pol·y·graph /päl′igraf′/ *n.* machine recording variations in pulse, etc., esp. to detect lying

pol·y·he·dron /päl′ēhē′drən/ *n.* (*pl.* **-dra** /-drə/ or **-drons**) solid figure with many (usu. more than six) faces —**pol′y·he′dral** /-drəl/ *adj.* [Gk *hedra* base]

pol·y·math /päl′imaTH′/ *n.* person of great or varied learning [Gk *manthanein math-* learn]

pol·y·mer /päl′imər/ *n.* compound of large molecules formed from repeated units of smaller molecules —**pol′y·mer′ic** /-mer′ik/ *adj.*; **pol′y·mer·ize′** /-īz/ *v.* (**·ized, ·iz·ing**); **po·lym′er·i·za′tion** *n.* [Gk *polymeros* having many parts]

Pol·y·ne·sia /päl′ənē′zhə, -shə/ *n.* central Pacific islands from the Hawaiian Islands S to New Zealand —**Pol′y·ne′sian** *n.* & *adj.*

pol·y·no·mi·al /päl′inō′mēəl/ *n.* 1 expression of more than two algebraic terms —*adj.* 2 of or being a polynomial [fr. POLY-, BINOMIAL]

pol·yp /päl′əp/ *n.* 1 simple organism with a tube-shaped body 2 small usu. benign growth on a mucous membrane [Gk *poly* many, *pous* foot]

po·lyph·o·ny /pəlif′ənē/ *n.* (*pl.* **·nies**) Mus. contrapuntal music —**pol′y·phon′ic** /päl′əfän′ik/ *adj.* [Gk *phōnē* sound]

pol·y·pro·pyl·ene /päl′ēprō′pəlēn′/ *n.* Chem. plastic polymer of propylene, used for packaging, molded parts, etc.

pol·y·sac·cha·ride /päl′isak′ərīd′/ *n.* any of a group of complex carbohydrates, e.g., starch [rel. to SACCHARIN]

pol·y·sty·rene /päl′esti′rēn/ *n.* Chem. plastic polymer of styrene, used for packaging, insulation, etc. [*styrene* fr. Gk *sturax* a resin]

pol·y·syl·lab·ic /päl′ēsəlab′ik/ *adj.* 1 having many syllables 2 using words of many syllables —**pol′y·syl′la·ble** /-labəl/ *n.* [MedL fr. Gk]

pol·y·tech·nic /päl′ĕtek′nik/ *n.* 1 school of-fering courses in many (esp. vocational) subjects —*adj.* 2 giving instruction in various vocational or technical subjects [Gk *tekhnē* art]

pol·y·the·ism /päl′ēTHē′iz′əm/ *n.* belief in or worship of more than one god —**pol′y·the·ist** /-ist/ *n.*; **pol′y·the·is′tic** *adj.* [Gk *theos* god]

pol·y·un·sat·u·rat·ed /päl′ē-ən′sacH′ərā′tid/ *adj.* (of a fat or oil) having a chemical structure capable of further reaction and not con-tributing to the accumulation of cholesterol in the blood

pol·y·u·re·thane /päl′ĕyŏŏr′əTHān′/ *n.* synthetic resin or plastic used in coatings, foam, etc. [rel. to UREA, ETHANE]

pol′y·vi·nyl chlo′ride /päl′ēvīn′əl/ *n.* a vinyl plastic used in piping, insulation, etc.; *abbr.* PVC

po·made /pämäd′, -mäd′/ *n.* scented oint-ment for the hair and head [It]

po·man·der /pō′man′dər/ *n.* 1 ball of mixed aromatic substances 2 container for this [AngFr fr. MedL]

pome·gran·ate /päm′əgran′it/ *n.* 1 tropical fruit with a tough rind, reddish pulp, and many seeds 2 tree bearing this [Fr *pome grenate* fr. Rom: many-seeded apple]

pom·mel /pəm′əl, päm′-/ *n.* 1 knob, esp. at the end of a sword hilt 2 upward projecting front of a saddle —*v.* (**·meled** or **·melled, ·mel·ing** or **mel·ling**) 3 PUMMEL [L *pomum* apple]

Po·mo·na /pəmō′nə/ *n.* city in Calif. Pop. 131,723

pomp /pämp/ *n.* 1 splendid display; splendor 2 vainglory [L fr. Gk *pompe*]

Pom′pa·no′ Beach′ /päm′pənō/ *n.* city in Fla. Pop. 72,411

Pom·pey /päm′pē/ ("the Great") 106–48 B.C.; Roman general and politician

Pom·pi·dou /pōN′pēdōō′/, Georges 1911–74; French politician; president (1969–74)

pom·pom /päm′päm′/ *n.* (also **pom′pon′** /-pän′/) ornamental tuft or bobble on a hat, shoes, etc. [Fr]

pomp·ous /päm′pəs/ *n.* affectedly grand or solemn; self-important —**pom·pos′i·ty** /-päs′ətē/ *n.* (*pl.* **·ties**); **pomp′ous·ly** *adv.*; **pomp′ous·ness** *n.* [L, rel. to POMP]

Ponce /pôn′sā/ *n.* seaport in Puerto Rico. Pop. 187,700

Ponce de Le·ón /pän(t)s′ də lē′ən, pōn(t)′sə dā lē·ōn′/, Juan c. 1460–1521; Spanish explorer; discovered Florida

pon·cho /pän′CHō/ *n.* (*pl.* **·chos**) blanket-like cloak with a slit for the head [SAmerSp]

pond /pänd/ *n.* body of water smaller than a lake [var. of POUND³]

pon·der /pän′dər/ *v.* think over; consider [L *ponderare* weigh]

pon·der·ous /pän′dərəs/ *adj.* 1 slow and awkward, esp. because of great weight 2 (of style, etc.) laborious; dull —**pon′der·ous·ly** *adv.*; **pon′der·ous·ness** *n.* [L *pondus -der-* weight]

Pon·di·cher·ry /pän′dicHer′ē, -sHer′-/ *n.* seaport in India. Pop. 202,600

pon·iard /pän′yərd/ *n.* dagger [Fr *poignard* fr. L *pugnus* fist]

Pont·char·train, Lake /pän′CHərtrān, pän′-CHərträn′/ *n.* shallow extension of the Gulf of Mexico N of New Orleans, La.

Pon·ti·ac /pänt′ē-ak′/ *n.* d. 1769; Ottawa Indian chief

Pon·ti·a·nak /pän′tē·ä′näk/ *n.* seaport in Indonesia. Pop. 304,800

pon·tiff /pän′tif/ *n.* pope [L *pontifex* priest]

pon·tif′i·cal *adj.* 1 papal 2 pompously dog-matic —**pon·tif′i·cal·ly** *adv.*

pon·tif·i·cate /päntif′ikät′/ *v.* (**·cat·ed, ·cat·ing**) 1 be pompously dogmatic 2 act as the pontiff

pon·toon /päntoon'/ *n.* **1** flat-bottomed boat **2** each of several boats or floats used to support a temporary bridge **3** float on a seaplane [L *pons* bridge]

PONTOON 3

po·ny /po'nē/ *n.* (*pl.* ·**nies**) **1** horse of any small breed **2** small liqueur glass **3** small bottle of liquor, wine, etc. [perh. fr. Fr *poulenet* foal]

po'ny·tail' *n.* hair drawn back, tied, and hanging down behind the head

poo·dle /pood'l/ *n.* dog of a breed with a curly coat usu. distinctively trimmed [Ger *Pudel*]

pooh-pooh /poo'poo'/ *v.* express contempt for; ridicule

pool[1] /pool/ *n.* **1** small body of still water **2** small shallow body of any liquid **3** swimming pool [OE]

pool[2] /pool/ *n.* **1a** common supply of persons, vehicles, commodities, etc., for sharing by a group **b** group sharing duties, etc. **2** common fund, e.g., of profits or of players' stakes in gambling **3** game on a billiard table with usu. 16 balls —*v.* **4** put into a common fund **5** share in common [Fr *poule*]

Poo·na /poo'nə/ *n.* city in W India. Pop. 1,559,600

poop /poop/ *n.* stern of a ship; deck farthest aft and highest [L *puppis*]

poor /poor/ *adj.* **1** without enough money to live comfortably **2** deficient (in a possession or quality) **3a** scanty; inadequate **b** less good than is usual or expected (*poor visibility*) **4** unfortunate [L *pauper*]

poor'house' *n.* *Hist.* public institution for paupers

poor'ly *adv.* **1** in a poor manner; badly —*adj.* **2** unwell

poor'-mouth' *v.* *Colloq.* use poverty as an excuse or complain about it

pop[1] /päp/ *n.* **1** sudden sharp explosive sound, as of a cork when drawn **2** *Colloq.* effervescent soft drink —*v.* (**popped, popping**) **3** (cause to) make a pop **4** *Baseball.* hit the ball high but not far **5** put or move (in) quickly or suddenly **6** pop the question *Colloq.* propose marriage [imit.]

pop[2] /päp/ *n.* **1** (in full **pop music**) commercially promoted contemporary music, esp. of a style popular since the 1950s —*adj.* **2** of or relating to popular music, culture, etc. [fr. POPULAR]

pop[3] *n.* *Colloq.* father [fr. PAPA]

pop. *abbr.* population

pop'art' *n.* art based on modern popular culture and the mass media

pop'corn' *n.* corn that bursts open when heated, esp. eaten as a snack

pop'cul'ture *n.* commercial culture based on popular taste

pope /pop/ *n.* (also *cap.*) head of the Roman Catholic Church [Gk *papas* patriarch]

Pope /pop/, **Alexander** 1688–1744; English poet

pop·in·jay /päpinjā'/ *n.* fop; conceited person [Ar *babagha* parrot]

pop·lar /päp'lər/ *n.* **1** fast-growing tree with a straight trunk **2** wood of this tree [L *populus*]

pop·lin /päp'lən/ *n.* fabric, usu. of cotton, with a finely corded surface [Fr *papeline*]

Po·po·cat·e·petl /po'pōkat'əpet'l/ *n.* volcano in SW Mexico: 17,887 ft.

pop·py /päp'ē/ *n.* (*pl.* ·**pies**) plant with showy esp. scarlet flowers and a milky sap [L *papaver*]

pop·py·cock /päp'ēkäk'/ *n.* *Slang.* nonsense [Du *pappekak*]

Pop·si·cle /päp'sikəl/ *n.* *Tdmk.* flavored ice confection on a stick

pop·u·lace /päp'yələs/ *n.* the common people [It, rel. to POPULAR]

pop·u·lar /päp'yələr/ *adj.* **1** liked by many people **2** of, for, or common among the general public **3** adapted to the understanding, taste, or means of the general public (*popular science*) —pop'u·lar'i·ty /-lar'ətē/ *n.*; pop' u·lar·ly *adv.* [AngL *populus* PEOPLE]

pop·u·lar·ize /päp'yələriz'/ *v.* (·**ized, ·izing**) **1** make popular **2** present (a difficult subject) in a readily understandable form —pop'u·lar·i·za'tion *n.*

pop·u·late /päp'yəlāt'/ *v.* (·**lat·ed, ·lat·ing**) **1** inhabit; form the population of **2** supply with inhabitants [MedL, rel. to PEOPLE]

pop·u·la·tion /päp'yəlā'sHən/ *n.* **1** inhabitants **2** total number of these or any group of living things

pop·u·list /päp'yəlist/ *n.* **1** politician claiming to represent the ordinary people —*adj.* **2** of a populist —pop'u·lism' /-liz'əm/ *n.* [L *populus* people]

pop·u·lous /päp'yələs/ *adj.* thickly inhabited

pop'-up' *adj.* having parts that spring or extend up automatically (*pop-up book*)

por·ce·lain /pôr'sələn/ *n.* **1** hard translucent ceramic with a transparent glaze **2** objects made of this [It dim. of *porca* sow]

por·ce·lain e·nam'el *n.* durable enamel finish fused to a surface by heat

porch /pôrcH/ *n.* covered entrance to a building [L *porticus*]

por·cine /pôr'sin'/ *adj.* of or like pigs [L, rel. to PORK]

por·cu·pine /pôr'kyəpin'/ *n.* rodent with a body and tail covered with erectile spines [Prov, rel. to PORK, SPINE]

pore[1] /pôr/ *n.* minute opening in a surface through which fluids, etc., may pass [Gk *poros*]

pore[2] *v.* (**pored, por·ing**) (foll. by *over*) **1** be absorbed in studying (a book, etc.) **2** meditate on

pork /pôrk/ *n.* **1** flesh of a pig, used as food **2** *Slang.* legislated benefits added to a bill for political advantage [L *porcus* pig]

por·ky /pôr'kē/ *adj.* (·**ki·er, ·ki·est**) **1** *Colloq.* fat **2** of or like pork

porn /pôrn/ *n.* (also *por'no*) **1** *Colloq.* pornography —*adj.* **2** pornographic [abbr.]

por·nog·ra·phy /pôrnäg'rəfē/ *n.* **1** explicit, prurient representation of sexual activity in literature, movies, etc. **2** literature, etc., containing this —**por'no·graph'ic** /-nəgra′fik/ *adj.* [Gk *pornē* prostitute]

po·rous /pôr′əs/ *adj.* **1** full of pores **2** letting through air, water, etc. —**po·ros·i·ty** /pôräs′itē/ *n.* [L, rel. to PORE¹]

por·phy·ry /pôr′fərē/ *n.* (*pl.* **·ries**) hard rock composed of crystals of white or red feldspar in a red matrix —**por'phy·rit'ic** /-rit′ik/ *adj.* [Gk, rel. to PURPLE]

por·poise /pôr′pəs/ *n.* **1** sea mammal of the whale family with a blunt snout **2** dolphin [L *porcus* pig, *piscis* fish]

por·ridge /pôr′ij, pär′-/ *n.* dish of oatmeal or cereal boiled in water or milk [alter. of POTTAGE]

por·rin·ger /pôr′injər, pär′-/ *n.* small bowl, often with a handle, for soup, etc. [Fr *potager*, rel. to POTTAGE]

Porsche /pôr′shə/, **Ferdinand** 1875–1952; Austrian car designer

port¹ /pôrt/ *n.* **1** harbor **2** town with a harbor [L *portus*]

port² *n.* a kind of sweet fortified wine [*Oporto* in Portugal]

port³ *n.* **1** left-hand side of a ship or aircraft as one looks forward —*v.* **2** turn (the helm) to port [prob. orig. the side turned to PORT¹]

port⁴ *n.* **1** opening in the side of a ship for entrance, loading, etc. **2** porthole [L *porta* gate]

por·ta·ble /pôrt′əbəl/ *adj.* **1** easily movable, convenient for carrying —*n.* **2** portable version of an item, e.g., a television set —**por'ta·bil'i·ty** *n.* [L *portare* carry]

por·tage /pôr′tij/ *n.* **1** carrying of boats or goods overland between navigable waters **2** place where this is necessary —*v.* (**·taged, ·tag·ing**) **3** convey (a boat or goods) over a portage [L *portare* carry]

por·tal /pôrt′l/ *n.* doorway or gate, esp. an elaborate one [L, rel. to PORT⁴]

Port-au-Prince /pôrt′ōprins′, -praNs′/ *n.* capital of Haiti. Pop. 752,600

port·cul·lis /pôrtkəl′əs/ *n.* heavy grating lowered to block a gateway in a castle, etc. [Fr: sliding door]

Port' E·liz'a·beth *n.* seaport in South Africa. Pop. 272,800

por·tend /pôrtend′/ *v.* **1** foreshadow as an omen **2** give warning of [L *portendere* stretch forth]

por·tent /pôr′tent′/ *n.* significant sign of something to come; omen [L *portentum*, rel. to PORTEND]

por·ten·tous /pôrtent′əs/ *adj.* **1** like or being a portent **2** pompously solemn

por·ter¹ /pôrt′ər/ *n.* **1** person employed to carry luggage, etc. **2** type of dark beer [L *portare* carry]

por·ter² *n.* gatekeeper or doorman [L, rel. to PORT⁴]

Por·ter /pôrt′ər, pôrt′ər/ **1 Katherine Anne** 1890–1980; US writer **2 Cole** 1891–1964; US composer and lyricist **3 William Sydney** see O. HENRY

por'ter·house steak' *n.* cut of beef between the tenderloin and sirloin

port·fo·li·o /pôrtfō′lē-ō′/ *n.* (*pl.* **·os**) **1a** folder or case for loose sheets of paper, draw-

ings, etc. **b** samples of an artist's work **2** investments held by a person, company, etc. **3** office of a minister of state [It *portafogli* sheet-carrier]

port'hole' *n.* aperture in a ship's side for letting in light

PORTICO

por·ti·co /pôr′tikō/ *n.* (*pl.* **·coes** or **·cos**) roof supported by columns, usu. attached as a porch to a building [L *porticus* porch]

por·tion /pôr′shən/ *n.* **1** part or share **2** amount of food allotted to one person **3** one's destiny or lot —*v.* **4** divide (a thing) into portions **5** (foll. by *out*) distribute [L *portio*]

Port·land /pôrt′lənd/ *n.* **1** city in Ore. Pop. 437,319 **2** city in Maine. Pop. 64,358

Port'land ce·ment' (also **p-**) *n.* cement manufactured from limestone and clay [for its resemblance to stone from the Isle of *Portland* in England]

Port' Lou'is /lōō′is, lōō-ē′/ *n.* capital of Mauritius. Pop. 141,900

port·ly /pôrt′lē/ *adj.* (**·li·er, ·li·est**) corpulent; stout [L *portare* carry]

port·man·teau /pôrt′man′tō/ *n.* (*pl.* **·teaus** or **·teaux** /-tōz′/) trunk for clothes, etc., opening into two equal parts [Fr *porter* carry, *manteau* cloak]

port·man'teau word' *n.* word combining two others (e.g., *motel* from *motor hotel*)

Port' Mores'by /môrz′bē/ *n.* capital of Papua New Guinea. Pop. 152,100

Pôr·to *n.* see OPORTO

Pôr·to A·le·gre /pôr′tōō əleg′rə/ *n.* seaport in S Brazil. Pop. 1,108,900

port' of call' *n.* place where a ship or a person stops on a journey

Port'-of-Spain' *n.* capital of Trinidad and Tobago. Pop. 50,900

Por·to No·vo /pôr′tō nō′vō/ *n.* de facto capital of Benin. Pop. 208,300. See also COTONOU

por·trait /pôr′trət/ *n.* **1** drawing, painting, photograph, etc., of a person, esp. of the face **2** description in words —*adj.* **3** *Comp.* (of a printing format) with printed lines parallel to the shorter dimension —**por'trait·ist** *n.* [Fr, rel. to PORTRAY]

por·trai·ture /pôr′trəchər/ *n.* the making of portraits

por·tray /pôrtrā′/ *v.* **1** make a likeness of **2** describe in words —**por·tray'al, por·tray'er** *n.* [Fr *portraire* -*trait* depict]

Port' Sa·id' /sä-ēd′/ *n.* seaport in Egypt. Pop. 461,000

Ports·mouth /pôrt′sməTH/ *n.* **1** seaport in S England. Pop. 177,900 **2** city in Va. Pop. 103,907

Por·tu·gal /pôr′CHəgəl/ *n.* republic in SW Europe on the Iberian Peninsula with Spain. Capital: Lisbon. Pop. 10,429,000

Por·tu·guese /pôr′CHəgēz′, -gēs′/ *n.* (*pl.* same) **1a** native or national of Portugal **b** person of Portuguese descent 2 language of Portugal and Brazil —*adj.* 3 of Portugal, its people, or language [MedL]

pose /pōz/ *v.* (**posed, pos·ing**) 1 assume a certain attitude of the body, esp. when being photographed or painted 2 (foll. by *as*) pretend to be (another person, etc.) 3 behave affectedly to impress others 4 put forward or present (a question, etc.) —*n.* 5 attitude of body or mind 6 affectation; pretense [L *pausare* stop]

Po·sei·don /pōsīd′n, pə-/ *n.* Gk. Myth. god of the sea, identified with Roman Neptune

po·seur /pōzər′/ *n.* person who behaves affectedly [Fr *poser* POSE]

posh /päSH/ *adj.* luxurious —**posh′ly** *adv.;* **posh′ness** *n.* [perh. fr. slang *posh* a dandy]

pos·it /päz′it/ *v.* assume as a fact; postulate [L, rel. to POSITION]

po·si·tion /pəzisH′ən/ *n.* 1 place occupied by a person or thing 2 placement or arrangement 3 proper place (*in position*) 4 advantage (*jockey for position*) 5 situation; circumstance 7 rank; status 8 paid employment —*v.* 9 place in a certain way 10 **in a position to** able to —**po·si′tion·al** *adj.* [L *ponere* posit- place]

pos·i·tive /päz′ətiv/ *adj.* 1 explicit; definite (*positive proof*) 2 (of a person) convinced, confident, or overconfident in an opinion 3 in agreement; affirmative 4 optimistic 5 constructive (*positive thinking*) 6 (of medical tests, etc.) confirming as present; indicative of (a condition) 7 esp. Philos. dealing only with matters of fact; practical 8 tending toward increase or progress 9 Math. greater than zero 10 Electr. of, containing, or producing the kind of electrical charge produced by rubbing glass with silk; lacking electrons 11 (of a photographic image) showing light and dark areas and shades or colors naturally —*n.* 12 something favorable or encouraging 13 positive photograph, quantity, etc. —**pos′i·tive·ly** *adv.;* **pos′i·tive·ness** *n.* [L, rel. to POSITION]

pos·i·tron /päz′iträn/ *n.* Physics. elementary particle with the same mass as but opposite (positive) charge to an electron [*positive electron*]

pos′i·tron e·mis′sion to·mog′ra·phy *n.* Med. (abbr. **PET**) diagnostic technique utilizing a computer-generated scanning (**PET scan**) of positrons emitted by radioactive isotopes administered to a patient

poss. *abbr.* possible

pos·se /päs′ē/ *n.* 1 force or company having a common purpose 2 summoned body of law enforcers [L: be able]

pos·sess /pəzes′/ *v.* 1 hold as property; own 2 have (a faculty, quality, etc.) 3 occupy or dominate the mind of (*possessed by the devil; possessed by fear*) —**pos·ses′sor** *n.* [L *possidere* possess-]

pos·ses·sion /pəzesH′ən/ *n.* 1 possessing or being possessed 2 thing possessed 3 holding or occupancy 4 (*pl.*) property, assets, subject territory, etc.

pos·ses·sive /pəzes′iv/ *adj.* 1 wanting to retain what one has; reluctant to share 2 jealous and domineering 3 Gram. indicating possession —*n.* 4 (in full **pos·ses′sive case'**)

449   **pose / postmodern**

Gram. case of nouns and pronouns expressing possession —**pos·ses′sive·ness** *n.*

pos·si·bil·i·ty /päs′əbil′ətē/ *n.* (*pl.* **·ties**) 1 state or fact of being possible 2 thing that may exist or happen 3 (usu. *pl.*) potential (*have possibilities*) [L *posse* be able]

pos·si·ble /päs′əbəl/ *adj.* 1 capable of existing, happening, being done, etc. 2 potential (*a possible solution*)

pos·si·bly /päs′əblē/ *adv.* 1 perhaps 2 by any means; conceivably (*cannot possibly go*)

pos·sum /päs′əm/ *n.* Colloq. 1 OPOSSUM, 1 2 **play possum:** a pretend to be dead, asleep, etc. b feign ignorance

post[1] /pōst/ *n.* 1 upright piece of wood or metal used as a support, marker, etc. 2 pole, etc., marking the start or finish of a race —*v.* 3 attach (a notice, etc.) in a prominent place 4 announce or advertise by poster or list [L *postis*]

post[2] *n.* 1 chiefly Brit. (the) mail —*v.* 2 chiefly Brit. put (a letter, etc.) in the mail 3 supply with information (*keep me posted*) [L, rel. to POSITION]

post[3] *n.* 1 station; place of duty 2 troop installation, base, etc. 3 job —*v.* 4 place (soldiers, an employee, etc.) [Fr, rel. to POST[2]]

post- *prefix* after; behind [L *post* (adv. and prep.)]

post·age /pōst′ij/ *n.* charge for sending an item of mail

post′age stamp′ *n.* official stamp affixed to a letter, etc., showing the amount of postage paid

post·al /pōs′tal/ *adj.* of or by mail [Fr, rel. to POST[2]]

post′card′ *n.* card for sending by mail

post′date′ *v.* (**·dat·ed, ·dat·ing**) 1 give a date later than the actual one to (a document, etc.) 2 follow in time

post·er /pōs′tər/ *n.* 1 placard in a public place 2 large printed picture

pos·te·ri·or /pōstēr′ēər, päs-/ *adj.* 1 later; coming after 2 at the back —*n.* 3 buttocks [L, comp. of *posterus*, rel. to POST-]

pos·ter·i·ty /päster′ətē/ *n.* 1 succeeding generations 2 person's descendants [L, rel. to POSTERIOR]

post′ ex·change′ *n.* general store on a military installation; *abbr.* **PX**

post′grad′u·ate *adj.* 1 engaged in a course of study after taking a first degree 2 of or concerning postgraduates

post′haste′ *adv.* with great speed

post·hu·mous /päs′CHəməs/ *adj.* 1 occurring after death 2 (of a book, etc.) published after the author's death 3 (of a child) born after the death of its father —**post′hu·mous·ly** *adv.* [L *postumus* last]

post·man /pōst′mən/ *n.* (*pl.* **·men**) mailman

post′mark′ *n.* 1 official dated postage cancellation mark on a piece of mail —*v.* 2 mark (an envelope, etc.) with this

post′mas′ter *n.* (*fem.* **post′mis′tress** /-mis′trəs/) official in charge of a post office

post′mod′ern *adj.* (in the arts, etc.) of the movement reacting against modernism, esp. by drawing attention to former conventions

—post′mod′ern·ism′ *n.*; post′mod′ern·ist *n.* & *adj.*

post-mor′tem *n.* 1 examination made after death, esp. to determine its cause 2 discussion and analysis of a game, election, etc. —*adv.* & *adj.* 3 after death [L]

post′na′tal *adj.* of the period after childbirth

post′of′fice *n.* 1 department officially responsible for postal services 2 room or building where postal business is carried on

post′paid′ *adj.* & *adv.* with postage already paid

post·pone /pōs(t)pōn′/ *v.* (·poned, ·pon·ing) cause or arrange to take place at a later time —**post·pone′ment** *n.* [L *ponere* put; place]

post′script /pōs(t)′skript′/ *n.* additional paragraph or remark at the end of a letter, etc., introduced by "P.S."

pos·tu·late *v.* /päs′CHəlīt, -lāt′/ (·lat·ed, ·lat·ing) 1 assume as a necessary condition, esp. as a basis for reasoning; take for granted 2 claim —*n.* /-lit, -lāt′/ 3 thing postulated 4 prerequisite or condition —**pos′tu·la′tion** *n.* [L *postulare* demand]

pos·ture /päs′CHər/ *n.* 1 bodily carriage; bearing 2 mental attitude 3 condition or state (of affairs, etc.) —*v.* (·tured, ·tur·ing) 4 assume a mental or physical attitude, esp. for effect —**pos′tur·al** *adj.* [L, rel. to POSIT]

po·sy /pō′zē/ *n.* (*pl.* ·sies) small bunch of flowers [alter. of POESY]

pot[1] /pät/ *n.* 1 round vessel for holding liquids, food to be cooked, etc. 2 contents of a pot 3 total amount bet in a game, etc. 4 (usu. *pl.*) *Slang:* large sum (*pots of money*) —*v.* (pot·ted, pot·ting) 5 place in a pot 6 go to pot deteriorate; be ruined —**pot′ful** *n.* (*pl.* ·fuls) [OE fr. L]

pot[2] *n. Slang:* marijuana [MexSp *potiguaya*]

po·ta·ble /pō′təbəl/ *adj.* drinkable [L *potare* drink]

pot·ash /pät′asH′/ *n.* an alkaline potassium compound [Du, rel. to POT[1], ASH[1]]

po·tas·si·um /pətas′ēəm/ *n.* soft silver-white metallic element; *symb.* K [fr. POTASH]

po·ta·to /pōtā′tō/ *n.* (*pl.* ·toes) 1 starchy plant tuber used for food 2 plant bearing this [Sp *patata* fr. Taino *batata*]

pot′bel′ly *n.* protruding stomach —**pot′bel′lied** *adj.*

pot′boil′er *n.* piece of writing, art, etc., done merely to earn money

po·tent /pōt′nt/ *adj.* 1 powerful; strong 2 (of a reason) cogent; forceful 3 (of a male) capable of sexual erection or orgasm —**po′ten·cy** *n.* [L *potens* -*ent*- fr. *posse* be able]

po·ten·tate /pōt′n-tāt′/ *n.* monarch or ruler [L, rel. to POTENT]

po·ten·tial /pəten′sHəl/ *adj.* 1 capable of coming into being or action; latent —*n.* 2 capacity for use or development 3 usable resources 4 *Physics.* quantity determining the energy of mass in a gravitational field or of charge in an electric field —**po·ten′ti·al′i·ty** /-sHē·al′itē/ *n.*; **po·ten′tial·ly** *adv.* [L, rel. to POTENT]

poth·er /päTH′ər/ *n.* commotion; fuss

pot′herb *n.* herb cooked in a pot as food or added for flavoring

pot′hole′ *n.* 1 deep hole, as in rock 2 hole in a road surface

pot′hook′ *n.* 1 hook over a fire for hanging or lifting a pot 2 curved stroke in handwriting

po·tion /pō′sHən/ *n.* dose of a liquid drug, magical substance, poison, etc. [L *potare* drink]

pot′ luck′ *n.* 1 whatever is available —*adj.* 2 designating a dinner to which each person brings a prepared dish to share

Po·to·mac Riv′er /pətō′mik/ *n.* river flowing SE 290 mi. from W. Va. to Chesapeake Bay; flows between Md. and Va. and past Washington, D.C.

pot·pour·ri /pō′pŏŏrē′/ *n.* (*pl.* ·ris) 1 fragrant mixture of dried petals and spices 2 musical or literary medley 3 mixture; miscellany [Fr: rotten pot]

pot′ roast′ *n.* cut of beef cooked slowly in a covered dish —**pot′-roast′** *v.*

Pots·dam /päts′dam′/ *n.* city in Germany. Pop. 139,800

pot′sherd /pät′sHərd/ *n.* esp. *Archaeol.* broken piece of pottery

pot′shot′ *n.* 1 random shot 2 incidental attack or criticism 3 casual attempt

pot·tage /pät′ij/ *n.* thick soup [Fr, rel. to POT[1]]

pot′ter /pät′ər/ *n.* maker of ceramic vessels [OE, rel. to POT[1]]

Pot·ter /pät′ər/ *n.*, (**Helen**) **Beatrix** 1866–1943; English writer of children's books

pot′ter's field′ *n.* burial ground for the poor and the unmourned

pot′ter's wheel′ *n.* revolving horizontal disk to carry clay during molding

pot′ter·y *n.* (*pl.* ·ies) 1 vessels, etc., made of fired clay 2 potter's work 3 potter's workshop [Fr, rel. to POTTER]

pot·ty /pät′ē/ *n.* (*pl.* ·ties) child's small toilet chair or pot

pouch /pouCH/ *n.* 1 small bag or outside pocket 2 pocketlike receptacle of kangaroos, etc. —*v.* 3 put or make into a pouch [Fr, rel. to POKE[2]]

poul·tice /pōl′tis/ *n.* 1 soft medicated usu. heated mass applied to the body to relieve soreness and inflammation —*v.* (·ticed, ·tic·ing) 2 apply a poultice to [L *puls* pottage]

poul·try /pōl′trē/ *n.* domestic fowl (turkeys, chickens, etc.), esp. as a source of food [Fr, rel. to PULLET]

pounce /pouns/ *v.* (pounced, pounc·ing) 1 spring or swoop, esp. as in capturing prey 2 make a sudden attack (on, upon) —*n.* 3 act of pouncing

pound[1] /pound/ *n.* 1 measure of weight equal to 16 oz. avoirdupois or 12 oz. troy 2 (in full **pound sterling**) chief monetary unit of the UK, etc. —**pound′age** /-ij/ *n.* [L *pondo*]

pound[2] *v.* 1 crush or beat with blows 2 deliver heavy blows or gunfire 3 (of the heart) beat heavily [OE]

pound[3] *n.* enclosure for stray animals [OE]

Pound /pound/, **Ezra** 1885–1972; US-born poet and critic

pound′ sign′ *n.* 1a the symbol, used to denote weight in pounds b the symbol, used to denote a numerical value 2 the symbol (£), denoting pounds sterling (Brit. currency)

pour /pôr/ *v.* 1 flow or cause to flow, esp.

downward 2 dispense (a drink) by pouring **3** rain heavily **4** come or go in profusion or rapidly

pout /pout/ v. **1** push the lips forward, as in displeasure or sulking —n. **2** this action —**pout′er** n.

pov·er·ty /păv′ərtē/ n. **1** being poor; need **2** scarcity or deficiency [L *pauper*]

pov·er·ty-strick′en adj. very poor

POW abbr. prisoner of war

pow·der /pou′dər/ n. **1** mass of fine dustlike particles **2** medicine or cosmetic in this form **3** GUNPOWDER —v. **4** apply powder to **5** reduce to a fine powder —**pow′der·y** adj. [L *pulvis -ver-* dust]

pow′der puff′ n. soft pad for applying cosmetic powder

pow′der room′ n. Euphem. women's toilet

Pow·ell /pou′l/, Colin 1937– ; US general

pow·er /pou′ər/ n. **1** ability to do or act **2** particular faculty of body or mind **3** influence; authority; control (*the party in power*) **4** authorization; delegated authority **5** influential person, body, government, etc. **6** vigor; energy **7** active property or function (*heating power*) **8** mechanical or electrical energy as distinct from manual labor **9a** electricity supply **b** source or form of energy (*hydroelectric power*) **10** Physics. rate of energy output **11** Math. product obtained when a number is multiplied by itself a certain number of times (*2 to the power of 3 = 8*) **12** magnifying capacity of a lens —v. **13** supply with mechanical or electrical energy **14** the powers that be those in authority [L *posse* be able]

pow·er·boat′ n. motorboat

pow·er·ful /pou′ərfəl/ adj. having much power or influence —**pow′er·ful·ly** adv.; **pow′er·ful·ness** n.

pow·er·house′ n. **1** POWER STATION **2** person or thing of great energy

pow·er·less adj. **1** without power **2** wholly unable —**pow′er·less·ly** adv.; **pow′er·less·ness** n.

pow′er of at·tor′ney n. authority to act for another person in legal and financial matters

pow′er sta′tion n. building where electrical power is generated

Pow·ha·tan /pou′ətan′, pouhat′n/ c. 1550–1618; American Indian chief in early colonial Virginia

pow·wow /pou′wou′/ n. **1** meeting for discussion (orig. among N American Indians) —v. **2** hold a powwow [Algonquian]

pox /päks/ n. **1** virus disease leaving pockmarks **2** SYPHILIS [alter. of *pocks* pl. of POCK]

Poz·nan /pōz′nan′(yə)/ n. city in Poland on the Warta River. Pop. 590,100

pp abbr. pianissimo

PP abbr. polypropylene

pp. abbr. pages

ppd. abbr. **1** postpaid **2** prepaid

ppm abbr. parts per million

P.P.S. abbr. additional postscript [fr. *post-postscript*]

Pr symb. praseodymium

PR or **P.R.** abbr. **1** public relations **2** Puerto Rico

pr. abbr. pair

prac·ti·ca·ble /prak′tikəbəl/ adj. **1** that can be done or used **2** feasible —**prac′ti·ca·bil′i·ty** n. [Fr, rel. to PRACTICAL]

prac·ti·cal /prak′tikəl/ adj. **1** of or concerned with practice rather than theory **2** useful; functional **3** (of a person) good at organizing, mending, etc. **4** sensible; realistic **5** so in practice or effect —**prac′ti·cal′i·ty** /-kal′itē/ n. (pl. **-ties**) [Gk *praktikos* fr. *prassein* do]

● Usage: *Practical* and *practicable*, sometimes confused, can be kept apart if one notes that *practical* is the adjective form for *practice* (*practice + -al*), meaning 'concerning practice,' in other words, 'useful; for actual use,' and that *practicable* comes from *practice + -able*, meaning 'able to be practiced,' in other words, 'able to be done.' Some things—especially ideas—can be both: Plans for landing on Mars by 2010 may be both practical (that is, there is something to be gained) and practicable (that is, present technology makes it possible).

prac′ti·cal joke′ n. humorous trick played on a person

prac′ti·cal·ly adv. **1** virtually; almost **2** in a practical way

prac′ti·cal nurse′ n. Med. nurse who has less training than a registered nurse, often one licensed by the state for specific duties (*licensed practical nurse*)

prac·tice /prak′tis/ n. **1** habitual action or performance **2a** repeated activity to improve a skill **b** session of this **3** action as opposed to theory **4** the work or place of business of a doctor, lawyer, etc. —v. (**-ticed, -tic·ing**) **5** perform habitually; carry out in action **6** do repeatedly as an exercise to improve a skill; exercise oneself in (an activity requiring skill) **7** be engaged in (a profession, religion, etc.) [L, rel. to PRACTICAL]

prac′ticed adj. experienced; skilled

prac·ti·tion·er /praktish′ənər/ n. person practicing a profession, esp. medicine

Prae·to′ri·an Guard′ /prētôr′ēən/ n. Hist. bodyguard of the ancient Roman emperor

prag·mat·ic /pragmat′ik/ adj. dealing with matters from a practical point of view —**prag·mat′i·cal·ly** adv.; **prag′ma·tism′** /-mətiz′əm/, **prag′ma·tist** /-tist/ n. [Gk *pragma -mat-* deed]

Prague /präg/ n. capital of the Czech Republic. Pop. 1,212,000

Prai·a /prī′ə/ n. capital of Cape Verde. Pop. 61,800

prai·rie /prar′ē, prer′ē/ n. large area of treeless grassland, esp. in N America [L *pratum* meadow]

prai′rie dog′ n. N American burrowing rodent that makes a barking sound

Prai′rie Prov′in·ces n. the Canadian provinces of Alberta, Saskatchewan, and Manitoba

praise /prāz/ v. (**praised, prais·ing**) **1** express warm approval or admiration of **2** glorify (God) in words —n. **3** praising; commendation [Fr *preisier* fr. L *pretium* price]

praise′wor′thy adj. worthy of praise

pra·line /prä′lēn, prā′-/ n. candy made by browning nuts in boiling sugar [Fr]

prance /prans/ v. (**pranced, pranc·ing**) **1** (of a horse) raise the forelegs and spring from the hind legs **2** walk or behave in an elated or arrogant manner —n. **3** prancing

prank /praNGk/ n. practical joke; caper

prank'ster *n.* practical joker

pra·se·o·dym·i·um /prā'zē-ōdim'ēəm/ *n.* soft silvery metallic element having green salts; *symb.* Pr [Gk *prasios* green]

prate /prāt/ *v.* (**prat·ed, prat·ing**) 1 chatter; talk too much 2 talk foolishly or irrelevantly —*n.* 3 prating; idle talk [LGer or Du]

prat·tle /prat'l/ *v.* (**·tled, ·tling**) 1 chatter in a childish or foolish way —*n.* 2 childish or inconsequential chatter [LGer *pratelen*, rel. to PRATE]

prawn /prôn/ *n.* edible shrimplike shellfish

Prax·it·e·les /praksit'l-ēz/ mid-4th cent. B.C.; Athenian sculptor

pray /prā/ *v.* 1 say prayers; make devout supplication 2 ask earnestly; implore 3 hope earnestly 4 (*as imper.*) *Archaic.* please (*pray tell me*) —**pray·er** /prā'ər/ *n.* [L *precari*]

prayer /prer/ *n.* 1a request, praise, or thanksgiving to God b formula used in praying (*the Lord's Prayer*) c act of praying 2 entreaty to a person

prayer' book *n.* book of set prayers

pray'ing man'tis *n.* MANTIS

pre- *prefix* before (in time, place, order, degree, or importance) [L *prae*]

preach /prēch/ *v.* 1 deliver (a sermon); proclaim or expound (the gospel, etc.) 2 give moral advice in an obtrusive way; proselytize 3 advocate or inculcate (a quality or practice, etc.) —**preach'er** *n.* [L *praedicare* proclaim]

pre·am·ble /prē'am'bəl/ *n.* 1 preliminary statement 2 introductory part of a statute or deed, etc. [L, rel. to AMBLE]

pre·ar·range /prē'ərānj'/ *v.* (**·ranged, ·ranging**) arrange beforehand —**pre'ar·range'ment** *n.*

Pre·cam·bri·an /prēkam'brēən, -kām'-/ *Geol. adj.* 1 of the earliest geological era —*n.* 2 this era

pre·car·i·ous /prikar'ēəs, -ker'-/ *adj.* 1 uncertain; dependent on chance 2 insecure; perilous —**pre·car'i·ous·ly** *adv.*; **pre·car'i·ous·ness** *n.* [L *precarius* reliant on entreaty]

pre·cau·tion /prikô'shən/ *n.* care taken beforehand to avoid risk or ensure a good result —**pre·cau'tion·ar·y** /-erē/ *adj.* [L, rel. to CAUTION]

pre·cede /prisēd'/ *v.* (**·ced·ed, ·ced·ing**) come or go before in time, order, importance, etc. [L, rel. to CEDE]

prec·e·dence /pres'əd·ns/ *n.* priority in time, order, importance, etc.

prec·e·dent *n.* /pres'əd·nt/ 1 previous case, instance, etc., taken as a guide or justification —*adj.* /prisē'dənt, pre'sədənt/ 2 preceding in time, order, importance, etc. [Fr, rel. to PRECEDE]

pre·cept /prē'sept'/ *n.* rule or guide, esp. for conduct [L *praeceptum* maxim; order]

pre·cep·tor /prisep'tər/ *n.* teacher; instructor —**pre·cep·to·ri·al** /prē'septôr'ēəl/ *adj.* [L, rel. to PRECEPT]

pre·ces·sion of the e'qui·noxes /prēsesh'ən/ *n.* earlier occurrence of equinoxes in each successive sidereal year, from the slow retrograde motion of equinoctial points along the ecliptic

pre·cinct /prē'singkt'/ *n.* 1 official district, esp. for voting or police authority 2 space or place of defined boundaries 3 (*pl.*) environs [L *praecingere* -*cinct*- encircle]

pre·ci·os·i·ty /presh'ē-äs'ətē, pres'-/ *n.* affected refinement in art, etc., esp. in the choice of words [rel. to PRECIOUS]

pre·cious /presh'əs/ *adj.* 1 of great value or worth 2 beloved; treasured 3 affectedly refined —**pre'cious·ness** *n.* [L *pretium* price]

pre'cious met'als *n. pl.* gold, silver, and platinum

prec·i·pice /pres'əpis/ *n.* 1 vertical or steep face of a rock, cliff, mountain, etc. 2 dangerous situation [L *praeceps* -*cipit*- headlong]

pre·cip·i·tate *v.* /prisip'ətāt'/ (**·tat·ed, ·tat·ing**) 1 hasten the occurrence of; cause to occur prematurely 2 throw down headlong 3 *Chem.* cause (a substance) to be deposited in solid form from a solution 4a *Physics.* condense (vapor) into drops and so deposit it b *Meteorol.* (of clouds, etc.) condense into rain, snow, etc. —*adj.* /-tət/ 5 headlong; violently hurried (*precipitate departure*) 6 (of a person or act) hasty; rash —*n.* /-tət/ 7 *Chem.* substance precipitated from a solution

● Usage: *Precipitate*, the adjective, means 'sudden, hasty': *a precipitate decision. Precipitous*, also an adjective, means 'steep': *a precipitous incline.*

pre·cip·i·ta·tion /prisip'ətā'shən/ *n.* 1 precipitating or being precipitated 2 rash haste 3 rain, snow, etc., falling to the ground

pre·cip·i·tous /prisip'ətəs/ *adj.* 1a of or like a precipice b dangerously steep 2 PRECIPITATE

pré·cis /prāsē', prā'sē/ *n.* (*pl.* same, /-sēz'/) summary; abstract [Fr]

pre·cise /prisīs'/ *adj.* 1a accurately expressed b definite; exact 2 scrupulous in being exact —**pre·cise'ly** *adv.* [L *praecidere* -*cis*- cut short]

pre·ci·sion /prisizh'ən/ *n.* 1 accuracy 2 marked by or adapted for precision (*precision instruments*)

pre·clude /priklood'/ *v.* (**·clud·ed, ·clud·ing**) prevent; make impossible [L *praecludere*, rel. to CLOSE¹]

pre·co·cious /prikō'shəs/ *adj.* 1 (of esp. a child) prematurely developed in some respect 2 (of an action, etc.) indicating such development —**pre·co'cious·ly** *adv.*; **pre·co'cious·ness, pre·coc'i·ty** /-käs'ətē/ *n.* [L *praecox* -*cocis* premature]

pre·cog·ni·tion /prē'kägnish'ən/ *n.* supposed foreknowledge, esp. of a supernatural kind

pre·con·ceive /prē'kənsēv'/ *v.* (**·ceived, ·ceiv·ing**) form (an idea or opinion) beforehand

pre·con·cep·tion /prē'kənsep'shən/ *n.* preconceived idea; prejudice

pre·con·di·tion /prē'kəndish'ən/ *n.* condition that must be fulfilled in advance

pre·cur·sor /prikur'sər/ *n.* 1 forerunner 2 predecessor [L *praecurrere* -*curs*- run before]

pred. *abbr.* predicate

pre·date /prēdāt'/ *v.* (**·dat·ed, ·dat·ing**) precede in time

pred·a·tor /pred'ətər/ *n.* predatory animal [L]

pred·a·to·ry /pred'ətôr'ē/ *adj.* 1 (of an animal) preying naturally upon others 2 victimizing or exploiting others

pre·de·cease /prē'disēs'/ v. (**·ceased**, **·ceas·ing**) die earlier than (another person)

pre·de·ces·sor /pred'əses'ər, prē'-/ n. person or thing coming before, as a former holder of an office or position [L prae before + decedere depart]

pre·des·tine /prēdes'tin/ v. (**·tined**, **·tin·ing**) 1 determine beforehand 2 ordain in advance by divine will or as if by fate —**pre·des'ti·na'tion** /-nā'SHən/ n. [Fr or ChL]

pre·de·ter·mine /prē'ditər'mən/ v. (**·mined**, **·min·ing**) 1 decree beforehand 2 predestine

pre·dic·a·ment /pridik'məm/ n. difficult or unpleasant situation [L, rel. to PREDICATE]

pred·i·cate v. /pred'ikāt'/ 1 assert (something) about the subject of a proposition 2 found or base (a statement, etc., on) —n. /-ikət/ 3 Gram. & Logic. what is said about the subject of a sentence or proposition, etc. (e.g., went home in John went home) —**pred'i·ca·ble** /-ikəbəl/ adj.; **pred'i·ca'tion** n. [L praedicare-dicat- declare]

pred·i·ca·tive /pred'ikətiv/ adj. (of an adjective or noun) forming or contained in the predicate, as old in the dog is old 2 that predicates [L, rel. to PREDICATE]

pre·dict /prēdikt'/ v. foretell; prophesy —**pre·dic'tor** n. [L praedicare-dict- foretell]

pre·dict'a·ble adj. that can be predicted or is to be expected —**pre·dict'a·bil'i·ty** n.; **pre·dict'a·bly** adv.

pre·dic·tion /prēdik'SHən/ n. 1 predicting or being predicted 2 thing predicted

pred·i·lec·tion /pred'l·ek'SHən, prēd'-/ n. preference or special liking [L praediligere prefer]

pre·dis·pose /prē'dispōz'/ v. (**·posed**, **·pos·ing**) 1 influence favorably in advance 2 render liable or inclined beforehand —**pre'dis·po·si'tion** /-pəzi'SHən/ n.

pre·dom·i·nant /pridäm'ənənt/ adj. 1 superior 2 being the strongest or main element —**pre·dom'i·nance** n.; **pre·dom'i·nant·ly** adv.

pre·dom·i·nate /pridäm'ənāt'/ v. (**·nat·ed**, **·nat·ing**) 1 have control (over) 2 be superior 3 be the strongest or main element

pre·em·i·nent /prēem'ənənt/ adj. 1 excelling others 2 outstanding —**pre·em'i·nence** n.; **pre·em'i·nent·ly** adv.

pre·empt /prēempt'/ v. 1a forestall b appropriate in advance 2 obtain by preemption 3 TV & Radio. replace (another program) [back formation fr. PREEMPTION]

pre·emp·tion /prēemp'SHən/ n. acquisition by one party before the opportunity is offered to others [MedL emere empt- buy]

pre·emp·tive /prēemp'tiv/ adj. 1 preempting 2 (of military action) intended to prevent attack by disabling the enemy

preen /prēn/ v. 1 (of a bird) groom (the feathers or itself) with its beak 2 (of a person) smarten or admire (oneself, one's hair, clothes, etc.)

pre·fab /prē'fab'/ n. prefabricated building [abbr.]

pre·fab·ri·cate /prēfab'rikāt'/ v. (**·cat·ed**, **·cat·ing**) manufacture sections of (a building, etc.) prior to their assembly for use

pref·ace /pref'əs/ n. 1 introduction to a book —v. (**·aced**, **·ac·ing**) 2 (foll. by with) introduce or begin (a speech or event) 3 provide (a book, etc.) with a preface —**pref'a·to·ry** /-tôr'ē/ adj. [L praefatio]

pre·fect /prē'fekt'/ n. administrator; overseer [L praeficere-fect- set in authority over]

pre·fec·ture /prē'fek'CHər/ n. administrative district [L, rel. to PREFECT]

pre·fer /prifər'/ v. (**·ferred**, **·fer·ring**) 1 like better 2 submit (information, an accusation, etc.) for consideration 3 promote or advance (a person) [L praeferre -lat-]

pref·er·a·ble /pref'(ə)rəbəl/ adj. to be preferred; more desirable —**pref'er·a·bly** adv.

pref·er·ence /pref'(ə)rəns/ n. 1 preferring or being preferred 2 thing preferred 3 favoring of one person, etc., before others —**pref'er·en'tial** /-en'SHəl/ adj.; **pref'er·en'tial·ly** adv.

pre·fer·ment /prifər'mənt/ n. promotion to a higher office

pre·fig·ure /prēfig'yər/ v. (**·ured**, **·ur·ing**) represent or imagine beforehand

pre·fix /prē'fiks'/ n. 1 element at the beginning of a word that modifies its meaning (e.g., ex-, non-) —v. 2 add as an introduction 3 join (a word or element) as a prefix

preg·nant /preg'nənt/ adj. 1 having a child or young developing in the uterus 2 full of meaning; significant; suggestive (a pregnant pause) —**preg'nan·cy** n. (pl. **·cies**) [L praegnans]

pre·hen·sile /prēhen'səl, -sīl'/ adj. Zool. (of a tail or limb) capable of or aiding in grasping [L prehendere -hens- grasp]

pre·his·tor·ic /prē'(h)istôr'ik, -stär'ik/ adj. 1 of the period before written records 2 Slang. utterly out of date —**pre·his'to·ry** n.

pre·judge /prējəj'/ v. (**·judged**, **·judg·ing**) form a premature judgment on (a person, issue, etc.) —**pre·judg'ment** n.

prej·u·dice /prej'ədəs/ n. 1a preconceived opinion b bias; partiality 2 detriment (to the prejudice of) —v. (**·diced**, **·dic·ing**) 3 impair the validity or force of (a right, claim, statement, etc.) 4 cause (a person) to have a prejudice [L, rel. to JUDGE]

prej·u·di·cial /prej'ədiSHəl/ adj. causing prejudice; detrimental

prel·ate /prel'ət/ n. high ecclesiastical dignitary, e.g., a bishop —**prel'a·cy** n. [L, rel. to PREFER]

pre·lim·i·nar·y /prilim'əner'ē/ adj. 1 introductory; preparatory —n. (pl. **·ies**) (usu. pl.) 2 preliminary matter, step, etc. (dispense with the preliminaries) 3 preliminary trial or contest [L limen threshold]

prel·ude /prel'yōōd, prā'l(y)ōōd/ n. 1 action, event, or situation serving as an introduction 2 introductory part of a poem, etc. 3 Mus. a introductory piece to a fugue, suite, etc. b short piece of a similar type [L ludere lus- play]

pre·mar·i·tal /prēmar'it·l/ adj. existing or (esp. of sexual relations) occurring before marriage

pre·ma·ture /prēmət(ə)ŏor', -CHŏor'/ adj. 1 occurring or done before the usual or proper time (a premature decision) 2 (of a baby) born (esp. three or more weeks) before the end of full gestation —**pre'ma·ture'ly** adv. [L, rel. to PRE-, MATURE]

pre·med·i·tate /prēmed'ətāt'/ v. (·tat·ed, ·tat·ing) think out or plan beforehand (*premeditated murder*) —**pre'med·i·ta'tion** n. [L, rel. to MEDITATE]

pre·men·stru·al /prēmen'strōōəl/ adj. of the time preceding each menstruation

pre·men'stru·al syn'drome n. physical and psychological symptoms experienced by some women prior to menstruation; *abbr.* **PMS**

pre·mier /primēr', -myēr'/ n. 1 prime minister or other head of government —adj. 2 first in importance, order, or time —**pre·mier'ship** n. [Fr: first]

pre·miere or **pre·mière** /primēr', -myēr'/ n. 1 first performance or showing —v. (·miered, ·mier·ing) 2 have an initial performance or showing [Fr fem., rel. to PREMIER]

prem·ise /prem'is/ n. 1 *Logic.* previous statement from which another is inferred 2 (*pl.*) house or other building with its grounds, outbuildings, etc. [L *praemissa* set in front]

pre·mi·um /prē'mēəm/ n. 1 amount to be paid for a contract of insurance 2 sum added to interest, wages, price, etc. 3 reward or prize —adj. 4 of the best quality and therefore more expensive 5 at a premium: a highly valued b scarce and in demand [L *praemium* reward]

prem·o·ni·tion /prem'ənisH'ən/ n. forewarning; presentiment —**pre·mon·i·to·ry** /primän'itôr'ē/ adj. [L *monere* warn]

pre·na·tal /prēnāt'l/ adj. of the period before childbirth

pre·oc·cu·py /prēäk'yəpī'/ v. (·pied, ·py·ing) 1 (of a thought, etc.) dominate the mind of (a person) 2 distract mentally —**pre·oc'cu·pa'tion** /-pā'sHən/ n. [L *praeoccupare* seize beforehand]

pre·or·dain /prē'ôrdān'/ v. ordain or determine beforehand

prep /prep/ adj. 1 short for *preparatory*, esp. in *prep school* —v. (**prepped, prep·ping**) 2 prepare, as for surgery

prep. *abbr.* 1 preparation 2 preparatory 3 preposition

pre·paid /prē'pād'/ v. past and past part. of PREPAY

prep·a·ra·tion /prep'ərā'sHən/ n. 1 preparing or being prepared 2 (often *pl.*) something done to make ready 3 prepared substance

pre·par·a·to·ry /pripar'ətôr'ē/ adj. 1 serving to prepare; introductory —adv. 2 in a preparatory manner

pre·par'a·to·ry school n. private secondary school that prepares students for college

pre·pare /priper'/ v. (·pared, ·par·ing) 1 make or get ready for use, consideration, etc. 2 assemble (a meal, etc.) 3a make (a person or oneself) ready or disposed in some way b get ready [L *parare* make ready]

pre·par·ed·ness /pripar'ədnəs, -per'-/ n. readiness, esp. for war

pre·pay /prēpā'/ v. (·paid, ·pay·ing) pay (a charge) in advance —**pre·pay'ment** n.

pre·pon·der·ate /pripän'dərāt'/ v. (·at·ed, ·at·ing) be greater in influence, quantity, or number; predominate (over) —**pre·pon'der·ance** /-əns/ n.; **pre·pon'der·ant** adj. [L *pondus·der·* weight]

prep·o·si·tion /prep'əzisH'ən/ n. *Gram.* word with (usu. preceding) a noun or pronoun that expresses a relation to another word, as in: "the man *on* the platform," "came *after* dinner," "went *by* train" —**prep'o·si'tion·al** adj. [L *praeponere -posit-* place before]

• Usage: It is a natural feature of the English language that many sentences and clauses end with a preposition, and has been since the earliest times. The "rule" that forbids the placing of a preposition at the end of a clause or sentence should be disregarded.

pre·pos·sess /prē'pəzes'/ v. 1 (usu. prepossessed) (of an idea, feeling, etc.) take possession of (a person) 2 (usu. prepossessing) a prejudice (usu. favorably) b impress favorably —**pre'pos·ses'sion** /-zesH'ən/ n.

pre·pos·ter·ous /pripäs't(ə)rəs/ adj. utterly absurd; outrageous —**pre·pos'ter·ous·ly** adv. [L: before (and) behind]

prep·py /prep'ē/ (also **prep·pie**) n. (*pl.* ·pies) 1 student of an expensive preparatory school —adj. 2 of a manner of thought, dress, etc., regarded as typical of such students

prep' school n. PREPARATORY SCHOOL [abbr.]

pre·puce /prē'pyōōs/ n. 1 FORESKIN 2 fold of skin surrounding the clitoris [L *praeputium*]

pre·quel /prē'kwəl/ n. story with the same characters, etc., of a previous story, but set in an earlier time

pre·re·cord /prē'rikôrd'/ v. record (esp. material for broadcasting) in advance

pre·req·ui·site /prērek'wəzit/ adj. 1 required as a precondition —n. 2 prerequisite thing

pre·rog·a·tive /priräg'ətiv/ n. right or privilege exclusive to an individual or class [L *praerogare* ask first]

Pres. *abbr.* President

pres·age n. /pres'ij/ 1 omen; portent 2 presentiment; foreboding —v. /prēsāj', pri-/ (·aged, ·ag·ing) 3 portend; foreshadow [L *praesagium*]

Pres·by·te·ri·an /prez'bətēr'ēən/ adj. 1 of a church governed by elders (**pres'by·ters**) all of equal rank —n. 2 member of a Presbyterian Church —**Pres'by·te'ri·an·ism'** n.

pre'school' adj. 1 of the time before a child is old enough to go to school —n. 2 NURSERY SCHOOL

pre·scient /presH'(ē)ənt/ adj. having foreknowledge or foresight —**pre'science** n. [L *praescire* know before]

pre·scribe /priskrīb'/ v. (·scribed, ·scrib·ing) 1a advise the use of (a medicine, etc.) b recommend 2 lay down or impose authoritatively [L *praescribere*]

• Usage: *Prescribe* means 'set forth rules to be followed' or 'specify medication, treatment': *We abide by the prescribed regulations. The doctor prescribed an antihistamine.* The common noun for what is prescribed is *prescription*. *Proscribe* means 'forbid; outlaw': *The doctor proscribed eating red meat.* The noun for the act of proscribing is *proscription*.

pre·scrip·tion /priskrip'sHən/ n. 1 act of prescribing **2a** a doctor's (usu. written) instruction for a patient's medicine **b** medicine prescribed

pre·scrip·tive /priskrip'tiv/ *adj.* prescribing; laying down rules

pres·ence /prez'əns/ *n.* **1** being present **2** place where a person is **3** person's appearance or bearing, esp. when imposing **4** person or spirit that is present (*aware of a presence in the room*) [L, rel. to PRESENT[1]]

pres·ence of mind' *n.* calmness and quickwittedness in difficulty, etc.

pres·ent[1] /prez'ənt/ *adj.* **1** being in the place in question **2a** now existing or occurring **b** now being considered, etc. (*in the present case*) **3** *Gram.* expressing an action, etc., now going on or habitually performed —*n.* **4** (prec. by *the*) the time now passing (*no time like the present*) **5** *Gram.* present tense **6 at present** now [L *praesens* -*ent*- being before]

pre·sent[2] /prizent'/ *v.* **1** introduce, offer, deliver, or exhibit **2a** offer or give as a gift **b** make available to; cause to have (*that presents us with a problem*) **3a** put (a piece of entertainment) before the public **b** introduce (*may I present my fiancé?*) **4** (of an idea, etc.) offer or suggest itself **5 present arms** hold a rifle vertically in front of the body as a salute —**pre·sent'er** *n.* [rel. to PRESENT[1]]

pres·ent[3] /prez'ənt/ *n.* thing given; gift [Fr, rel. to PRESENT[1]]

pre·sent·a·ble /prizent'əbəl/ *adj.* of good appearance; fit to be presented —**pre·sent'a·bil'i·ty** *n.*; **pre·sent'a·bly** *adv.*

pre·sen·ta·tion /prez'əntā'sHən, prē'zən-/ *n.* **1a** presenting or being presented **b** thing presented **2** manner or quality of presenting **3** demonstration, display, or lecture

pres·ent-day' /prez'ənt/ *adj.* of this time; modern

pre·sen·ti·ment /prizent'əmənt/ *n.* vague expectation; foreboding (esp. of misfortune)

pres·ent·ly /prez'əntlē/ *adv.* **1** soon; after a short time **2** currently

● Usage: In *He will be here presently*, the meaning is 'soon'; in *She is presently in New York*, the meaning is clearly 'at this moment.' Both senses are in wide use.

pre·ser·va·tive /prizur'vətiv/ *n.* **1** substance for preserving perishable foodstuffs, wood, etc. —*adj.* **2** tending to preserve

pre·serve /prizurv'/ *v.* (**·served, ·serv·ing**) **1** keep safe or intact **2** maintain or retain **3** treat (food) to prevent decomposition or fermentation —*n.* **4** (*sing.* or *pl.*) preserved fruit; jam **5** place where wildlife, game, etc., is preserved **6** sphere of activity regarded as a person's own —**pres·er·va·tion** /prez'ərvā'sHən/ *n.* [L *servare* keep]

pre·set /prēset'/ *v.* (**·set, ·set·ting**) set or fix (a device) in advance of its operation

pre·shrunk /prē'sHrəNGk'/ *adj.* (of fabric) treated to shrink in manufacture and not later

pre·side /prizīd'/ *v.* (**·sid·ed, ·sid·ing**) **1** be chairperson or president of a meeting, etc. **2** exercise control or authority [L *praesidere* sit before]

pres·i·den·cy /prez'ədənsē/ *n.* (*pl.* **·cies**) **1** office of president **2** period of this

pres·i·dent /prez'ədənt/ *n.* **1** head of a republican government, as executive or formal leader **2** head of a society, council, university,

company, etc. —**pres'i·den'tial** /-den'sHəl/ *adj.*

Pres'i·den'tial Range' *n.* range of peaks in the White Mountains, in northern N. Hamp., most named for US presidents

Pres·ley /prez'lē, pres'-/, Elvis 1935–77; US pop singer

press[1] /pres/ *v.* **1** apply steady force to (a thing in contact) **2a** compress or squeeze a thing to flatten, shape, or smooth it **b** squeeze (as for juice) **3** be urgent; demand immediate action **4** crowd **5** hasten (on) insistently **6** (often *passive*) (of an enemy, etc.) bear heavily on **7** urge or entreat **8** insist on (*did not press the point*) **9** manufacture by pressure shaping a sheet of material —*n.* **10** act of pressing **11** device for compressing, flattening, shaping, extracting juice, etc. **12a** PRINTING PRESS **b** publishing firm **13** (prec. by *the*) journalism, generally or collectively **14** publicity **15** crowding **16** the pressure of affairs **17 be pressed for** have barely enough (time, etc.) [L *premere* press-]

press[2] *v.* **1** *Hist.* force to serve in the army or navy **2** bring into use as a makeshift (*was pressed into service*) [obs. *prest* fr. Fr: loan]

press' a'gent *n.* person employed to obtain publicity

press' con'fer·ence *n.* interview given to a number of journalists

press'ing *adj.* urgent —**press'ing·ly** *adv.*

press' re·lease' *n.* statement issued to news media

pres·sure /presH'ər/ *n.* **1a** exertion of continuous force on or against a body by another **b** amount of this **2** urgency (*work under pressure*) **3** stress or difficulty (*under financial pressure*) **4** constraining influence (*put pressure on us*) —*v.* (**·sured, ·sur·ing**) **5** prevail upon; coerce [L, rel. to PRESS[1]]

pres'sure cook'er *n.* **1** airtight pot for cooking quickly under steam pressure **2** stressful situation

pres'sure group' *n.* group formed to influence public policy

pres·sur·ize /presH'ərīz'/ *v.* (**·ized, ·iz·ing**) maintain normal atmospheric pressure in (an aircraft cabin, etc.) at a high altitude —**pres'sur·i·za'tion** *n.*

pres·ti·dig·i·ta·tor /pres'tədij'ətā'tər/ *n.* magician or sleight-of-hand artist —**pres'ti·dig'i·ta'tion** /-itā'sHən/ *n.* [Fr, rel. to PRESTO, DIGIT]

pres·tige /prestēzH'/ *n.* **1** acquired or earned respect or reputation —*adj.* **2** having or conferring prestige —**pres·ti'gious** /-stij'əs/ *adj.* [L *praestigiae* juggler's tricks]

pres·to /pres'tō/ *adv. & adj.* **1** *Mus.* in quick tempo —*interj.* **2** word used by magicians, etc., meaning 'lo!,' 'look!,' etc. [L *praestus* quick]

pre·sum·a·bly /prizōō'məblē/ *adv.* as may reasonably be presumed

pre·sume /prizōōm'/ *v.* (**·sumed, ·sum·ing**) **1** suppose to be true; take for granted **2a** dare (to) **b** venture (*may I presume to ask?*) **3** be presumptuous [L *praesumere*]

pre·sump·tion /prizəm(p)'sHən/ *n.* **1** arrogant behavior **2a** presuming a thing to be true-

b thing presumed to be true [L, rel. to PRE-SUME]

pre·sump·tive /prizəm(p)'tiv/ *adj.* giving grounds for presumption

pre·sump·tu·ous /prizəm(p)'CHŏŏəs/ *adj.* unduly or overbearingly forward or confident —**pre·sump'tu·ous·ly** *adv.*; **pre·sump'tu·ous·ness** *n.*

pre·sup·pose /prē'səpōz'/ *v.* (·posed, ·posing) **1** assume beforehand **2** imply —**pre'sup·po·si'tion** /-səp'əzisн'ən/ *n.*

pre-tax /prē'taks'/ *adj.* (of income, etc.) before deduction of taxes

pre·tend /pritend'/ *v.* **1** claim or assert falsely so as to deceive **2** imagine to oneself in play (*pretended it was night*) **3** (foll. by *to*) **a** lay claim to (a right or title, etc.) **b** profess to have (a quality, etc.) [L *praetendere* stretch forth]

pre·tend'er *n.* person who claims a throne, title, etc.

pretense /prē'tens, pritens'/ *n.* **1** pretending; make-believe **2** false show of feelings, sincerity, etc. **3** (foll. by *to*) claim, esp. a false one **4** display; ostentation [AngL, rel. to PRETEND]

pre·ten·sion /pritensн'ən/ *n.* **1a** assertion of a claim **b** justifiable claim **2** pretentiousness [MedL, rel. to PRETEND]

pre·ten·tious /pritensн'əs/ *adj.* **1** making an excessive claim to merit or importance **2** ostentatious —**pre·ten'tious·ly** *adv.*; **pre·ten'tious·ness** *n.*

pret·er·it or **pret·er·ite** /pret'ərit/ *Gram. adj.* **1** expressing a past action or state —*n.* **2** preterit tense or form [L *praeteritum* past]

pre·ter·nat·u·ral /prēt'ərnacн'(ə)rəl/ *adj.* **1** beyond what is natural; abnormal **2** supernatural [L *praeter* beyond]

pre·text /prē'tekst'/ *n.* ostensible reason; excuse offered [L *praetextus*, rel. to TEXT]

Pre·to·ri·a /pritôr'ēə/ *n.* executive capital of South Africa. Pop. 443,100

pret·ti·fy /prit'əfī'/ *v.* (·fied, ·fy·ing) make pretty, esp. in an affected way

pret·ty /prit'ē/ *adj.* (·ti·er, ·ti·est) **1** attractive in a fine or charming way **2** fine or good of its kind —*adv.* **3** *Colloq.* rather; fairly; moderately —*v.* (·tied, ·ty·ing) **4** (often foll. by *up*) make pretty —**pret'ti·ly** *adv.*; **pret'ti·ness** *n.* [OE]

pret·zel /pret'səl/ *n.* baked snack made from a biscuit dough, usu. salted and shaped in a knot or stick [Ger]

pre·vail /privāl'/ *v.* **1** be victorious or gain mastery **2** be the more usual or predominant **3** exist or occur in general use or experience **4** (foll. by *on, upon*) persuade [L *praevalere*, rel. to AVAIL]

PRETZEL

prev·a·lent /prev'ələnt/ *adj.* **1** generally existing or occurring **2** predominant —**prev'a·lence** *n.* [rel. to PREVAIL]

pre·var·i·cate /privar'ikāt'/ *v.* (·cat·ed, ·cating) **1** speak or act evasively or misleadingly **2** lie —**pre·var'i·ca'tion**, **pre·var'i·ca'tor** *n.* [L: walk crookedly]

pre·vent /privent'/ *v.* stop from happening or

doing something; make impossible —**pre·vent'a·ble** *adj.* (also **pre·vent'i·ble**); **pre·ven'tion** /-ven'sнən/ *n.* [L *praevenire -vent-* hinder]

pre·ven·tive /priven'tiv/ (also **pre·ven·ta·tive** /priven'tətiv/) *adj.* **1** serving to prevent, esp. disease —*n.* **2** preventive agent, measure, drug, etc.

● Usage: Avoid using "preventative," a less accepted variant of *preventive*, as in *preventive medicine, preventive measures, preventive care.*

pre·view /prē'vyōō'/ *n.* **1** showing of a film, exhibition, etc., before it is open to the general public —*v.* **2** see or show in advance

Pre·vin /prev'ən/, **André** (born **Andreas Priwin**) 1929– ; German-born US pianist, conductor, and composer

pre·vi·ous /prē'vēəs/ *adj.* **1** coming before in time or order **2** *previous to* before —**pre'vi·ous·ly** *adv.* [L *praevius* fr. *via* way]

prey /prā/ *n.* **1** animal hunted or killed by another for food **2** person or thing influenced by or vulnerable to (something undesirable) (*prey to morbid fears*) —*v.* (foll. by *on, upon*) **3** seek or take as prey **4** (of a disease, emotion, etc.) torment (*it preyed on his mind*) [L *praeda*]

price /prīs/ *n.* **1** amount of money for which a thing is bought or sold **2** what is or must be given, done, sacrificed, etc., to obtain or achieve something —*v.* (priced, pric·ing) **3** fix or find the price or value of (a thing for sale) **4 at a price** at a high cost [L *pretium*]

Price /prīs/, **(Mary) Leontyne** 1927– ; US operatic soprano

price'less *adj.* **1** invaluable **2** wonderfully amusing or absurd —**price'less·ness** *n.*

pric·ey /prī'sē/ *adj.* (·i·er, ·i·est) expensive

prick /prik/ *v.* **1** pierce slightly; make a small hole in **2** pain; trouble —*n.* **3** act of pricking **4** small hole or mark made by pricking **5** pain **6 prick up one's ears: a** (of a dog, etc.) make the ears erect when alert **b** (of a person) become suddenly attentive [OE]

prick·le /prik'əl/ *n.* **1** (also **prick'er**) small thorn **2** hard-pointed spine of a hedgehog, etc. **3** prickling sensation —*v.* (·led, ·ling) **4** affect or be affected with a sensation of multiple pricking [OE]

prick'ly *adj.* (·li·er, ·li·est) **1** having prickles **2** tingling **3** (of a person) ready to take offense —**prick'li·ness** *n.*

prick'ly heat' *n.* itchy inflammation of the skin

prick'ly pear' *n.* **1** cactus with pear-shaped prickly fruit **2** its fruit

pride /prīd/ *n.* **1a** elation or satisfaction at one's achievements, qualities, possessions, etc. **b** object of this feeling **2** high or overbearing opinion of one's worth or importance **3** self-respect **4** group (of certain animals, esp. lions) —*v.* (prid·ed, prid·ing) **5** (foll. by *on, upon*) be proud of **6 take pride in: a** be proud of **b** maintain in good condition or appearance [OE, rel. to PROUD]

priest /prēst/ *n.* **1** ordained minister of the Roman Catholic, Orthodox, or Anglican Church **2** (*fem.* **priest'ess**) official minister of a religion, esp. non-Christian —**priest'hood** *n.*; **priest'ly** *adj.* [ult. fr. Gk *presbys* old]

Priest·ley /prēst'lē/, **Joseph** 1733–1804; English chemist and theologian

prig /prig/ n. self-righteous or moralistic person —**prig'gish** adj.; **prig'gish·ness** n.

prim /prim/ adj. (**prim·mer, prim·mest**) stiffly formal and precise; prudish —**prim'ly** adv.; **prim'ness** n. [Fr., rel. to PRIME[1]]

pri·ma bal·le·ri·na /prē'mə bal'ərē'nə/ n. chief female dancer in a ballet [It]

pri·ma·cy /prī'məsē/ n. (pl. **·cies**) 1 preeminence 2 office of a primate [L, rel. to PRIMATE]

pri·ma don·na /prē'mə dän'ə/ n. (pl. **pri·ma don·nas**) 1 chief female singer in an opera 2 temperamentally self-important person [It]

pri·ma fa·cie /prī'mə fā'SHə, -SHē(ē')/ adj. (of evidence) based on the first impression [L]

pri·mal /prī'məl/ adj. 1 primitive; primeval 2 chief; fundamental [L, rel. to PRIME[1]]

pri·mar·y /prī'mer'ē/ adj. 1a of the first importance; chief b fundamental; basic 2 earliest; original 3 designating the colors red, green, and blue, or (for pigments) red, blue, and yellow —n. (pl. **·ies**) 4 thing that is primary 5 (in full **pri'mar·y e·lec'tion**) preliminary election to appoint delegates or select candidates —**pri·mar·i·ly** /prīmer'əlē/ adv. [L, rel. to PRIME[1]]

pri'mar·y school' n. a school including the first three or four grades, and sometimes kindergarten

pri·mate /prī'māt/ n. 1 member of the highest order of mammals, including apes, monkeys, and humans 2 -mit/ archbishop [L primas -at-chief]

prime[1] /prīm/ adj. 1 chief; most important 2 first-rate; excellent 3 primary; fundamental 4 Math. (of a number, etc.) divisible only by itself and 1 (e.g., 2, 3, 5, 7, 11) —n. 5 state of the highest perfection (prime of life) 6 the best part [L primus first]

prime[2] v. (**primed, prim·ing**) 1 prepare (a thing) for use or action 2 prepare for firing or detonation 3 pour (liquid) into a pump to start it 4 prepare (wood, etc.) for painting by applying a substance that prevents paint from being absorbed 5 equip (a person) with information, etc.

prime' min·is·ter n. (in some countries) chief executive of the government

prim·er[1] /prīm'ər/ n. substance used to prime wood, etc.

prim·er[2] /prim'ər/ n. 1 elementary textbook for teaching children to read 2 introductory book [L, rel. to PRIME[1]]

prime' time' /prīm/ n. (in broadcasting) time when audiences are largest

pri·me·val /prīmē'vəl/ adj. 1 of the first age of the world 2 ancient; primitive —**pri·me'val·ly** adv. [L, rel. to PRIME[1], aevum age]

prim·i·tive /prim'ətiv/ adj. 1 at an early stage of civilization 2 undeveloped; crude; simple (primitive methods) —n. 3 primitive person or thing —**prim'i·tive·ly** adv.; **prim'i·tive·ness** n. [L, rel. to PRIME[1]]

pri·mo·gen·i·ture /prī'mōjen'əCHər/ n. 1 state of being the firstborn child 2 right of inheritance of the firstborn [MedL, rel. to PRIME[1], L genitura birth]

pri·mor·di·al /prīmôr'dēəl/ adj. existing at or from the beginning; primeval —**pri·mor'di·al·ly** adv. [L, rel. to PRIME[1], ordiri begin]

primp /primp/ v. 1 make (the hair, clothes,

etc.) neat 2 refl. groom (oneself) [var. of PRIM]

prim·rose /prim'rōz'/ n. 1a wild plant bearing pale yellow spring flowers b its flower 2 pale yellow color [Fr and MedL: first rose]

prim'rose path' n. way or behavior that is easy but ultimately destructive

prince /prins/ n. 1 male member of a royal family other than the reigning king 2 ruler of a small state 3 noble man in some countries 4 chief or greatest male exemplar (the prince of novelists) [L princeps -cip-]

Prince' Ed'ward Is'land n. island province of Canada, in the Gulf of St. Lawrence. Capital: Charlottetown. Pop. 132,000

prince'ly adj. (**·li·er, ·li·est**) 1 of or worthy of a prince 2 splendid; generous

Prince' of Wales' n. (title conferred on) the eldest son and heir apparent of the British monarch

prin·cess /prin'sis, -ses'/ n. 1 wife of a prince 2 female member of a royal family other than a queen [Fr, rel. to PRINCE]

Prince' Wil'liam Sound' n. inlet of the Gulf of Alaska

prin·ci·pal /prin'səpəl/ adj. 1 first in rank or importance; chief 2 main; leading —n. 3 chief person 4 head of a school 5 leading performer 6 capital sum as distinct from interest or income —**prin'ci·pal·ly** adv. [L, rel. to PRINCE]

• Usage: Always carefully distinguish in writing between principal 'important; person in charge' (as at a school) and principle 'rule.'

prin·ci·pal·i·ty /prin'səpal'ətē/ n. (pl. **·ties**) state ruled by or government of a prince

prin'ci·pal parts' n. pl. Gram. forms of a verb from which all other forms can be deduced

prin·ci·ple /prin'səpəl/ n. 1 fundamental truth or law as the basis of reasoning or action 2a personal code of conduct b (pl.) personal rules of conduct 3 general law in physics, etc. 4 law of nature or science 5 in principle in theory 6 on principle on the basis of a moral attitude [L principium source]

• Usage: See note at PRINCIPAL.

prin·ci·pled /prin'səpəld/ adj. based on or having (esp. praiseworthy) principles of behavior

print /print/ v. 1 produce or cause (a book, picture, etc.) to be produced by applying inked types, blocks, or plates to paper, etc. 2 express or publish in print 3 impress or stamp 4 write (letters) without connecting them 5 produce (a photograph) from a negative 6 Comp. (usu. foll. by out) display (data, a file, etc.) in printed form —n. 7 indentation or residual mark 8 FINGERPRINT 9a printed lettering or writing b words in printed form 10 picture or design printed from a block or plate 11 photograph 12 fabric, garment, etc., with a printed design 13 in print (of a book, etc.) available from the publisher 14 out of print no longer available from the publisher [L premere press]

print·er /print'ər/ n. 1 person who prints books, etc. 2 owner of a printing business 3 device that prints, esp. from a computer

print·ing *n.* **1** production of printed books, etc. **2** copies of a book printed at one time **3** block letters, etc., each written separately

print'ing press *n.* machine for printing from inked types, plates, etc.

print'out *n.* computer output in printed form

pri·or /prī'ər/ *adj.* **1** earlier **2** coming before in time, order, or importance —*adv.* **3** (foll. by *to*) before —*n.* (*fem.* **pri'or·ess**) **4** superior of a religious house or order [L: earlier]

pri·or·i·ty /prī-ôr'ətē, -är'-/ *n.* (*pl.* ·ties) **1** thing regarded as more important than others **2** right to be first; precedence —**pri·or'i·tize'** /-tīz/ *v.* (·tized, ·tiz·ing) [MedL, rel. to PRIOR]

pri·o·ry /prī'ərē/ *n.* (*pl.* ·ries) monastery governed by a prior or nunnery governed by a prioress [AngFr and MedL, rel. to PRIOR]

prise /prīz/ *v.* var. of PRIZE²

PRISM 1

prism /priz'əm/ *n.* **1** solid figure whose two ends are equal parallel rectilinear figures and whose sides are parallelograms **2** transparent body in this form, usu. triangular, that separates white light into a spectrum of colors —**pris·mat'ic** /-mat'ik/ *adj.* [Gk *prisma -mat-* thing sawn]

pris·on /priz'ən/ *n.* **1** place of confinement for convicted criminals or persons awaiting trial **2** custody; confinement [L *prehendere* seize]

pris'on camp' *n.* **1** camp for prisoners of war **2** camplike prison, with minimum security and restriction

pris'on·er *n.* **1** person kept in prison **2** person or thing confined by illness, another's domination, etc. [AngFr, rel. to PRISON]

pris·sy /pris'ē/ *adj.* (·si·er, ·si·est) prim; prudish —**pris'si·ly** *adv.*; **pris'si·ness** *n.* [perh. fr. PRIM, SISSY]

pris·tine /pristēn'/ *adj.* **1** in its original condition; unspoiled **2** spotless; fresh as if new [L *pristinus* former]

pri·va·cy /prī'vəsē/ *n.* **1a** being private and undisturbed **b** right to this **2** freedom from intrusion or public attention

pri·vate /prī'vət/ *adj.* **1** belonging to an individual; one's own; personal **2** confidential (*private talks*) **3** kept or removed from public knowledge or observation **4** not open to the public **5** secluded **6** (of a person) not holding public office or an official position —*n.* **7** *Milit.* lowest-ranking enlisted soldier **8** (*pl.*) genitals **9** in private privately —**pri'vate·ly** *adv.* [L *privare* deprive]

pri'vate de·tec'tive *n.* professional detective for hire by private individuals

pri'vate en'ter·prise *n.* businesses not under state control

pri'vate eye' *n.* *Slang.* PRIVATE DETECTIVE

pri'vate parts' *n. pl. Euphem.* genitals

pri'vate sec'tor *n.* the part of the economy free of direct governmental control

pri·va·tion /prīvā'shən/ *n.* lack of the comforts or necessities of life [L, rel. to PRIVATE]

pri·vat·ize /prī'vətīz'/ *v.* (·ized, ·iz·ing) transfer (a business, etc.) from governmental to private ownership —**pri·va·ti·za'tion** *n.*

priv·et /priv'it/ *n.* bushy evergreen shrub used for hedges

priv·i·lege /priv'(ə)lij/ *n.* **1** right, advantage, or immunity **2** special benefit or honor (*a privilege to meet you*) —*v.* (·leged, ·leg·ing) **3** invest with a privilege —**priv'i·leged** *adj.* [L, rel. to PRIVY, *lex leg-* law]

priv·y /priv'ē/ *adj.* **1** (foll. by *to*) sharing in the secret of (a person's plans, etc.) **2** *Archaic.* hidden; secret —*n.* (*pl.* ·ies) **3** outhouse [Fr *privé* private place]

prize¹ /prīz/ *n.* **1** something won in a competition, lottery, etc. **2** reward given as a symbol of victory or superiority **3** something worth striving for —*adj.* **4** excellent of its kind —*v.* (prized, priz·ing) **5** value highly [Fr, rel. to PRAISE]

prize² *v.* (also **prise**) (prized, priz·ing) force open or out by leverage [Fr fr. L *prehendere* seize]

prize'fight' *n.* boxing match fought for a prize of money —**prize'fight'er** *n.*

prize'win'ner *n.* winner of a prize —**prize'win'ning** *adj.*

pro¹ /prō/ *n.* (*pl.* pros) professional [abbr.]

pro² *adj.* **1** for; in favor —*n.* (*pl.* pros) **2** reason in favor —*prep.* **3** in favor of [L: for; on behalf of]

pro-¹ *prefix* **1** favoring or supporting (*pro-government*) **2** acting as a substitute or deputy for (*pronoun*) **3** forward (*produce*) **4** forward and downward (*prostrate*) **5** onward (*progress*) **6** in front of (*protect*) [L *pro* in front (of)]

pro-² *prefix* before in time, place, order, etc. [Gk *pro* before]

pro·ac·tive /prōak'tiv/ *adj.* (of a person, policy, etc.) taking the initiative [fr. PRO-², after REACTIVE]

prob. *abbr.* **1** probable; probably **2** problem

prob·a·bil·i·ty /präb'əbil'ətē/ *n.* (*pl.* ·ties) **1** being probable **2** likelihood of something happening **3** probable or most probable event **4** *Stat.* extent to which an event is likely to occur, expressed as the ratio of the actual cases to the total number of possible cases **5** **in all probability** most probably

prob·a·ble /präb'əbəl/ *adj.* **1** expected to happen or prove true; likely —*n.* **2** probable candidate, member of a team, etc. —**prob'a·bly** *adv.* [L, rel. to PROVE]

pro·bate /prō'bāt/ *adj.* designating a judge, court, etc., authorized to establish the legal validity of documents, as wills [L *probare* PROVE]

pro·ba·tion /prōbā'shən/ *n.* **1** *Law.* system of supervising the behavior in society of criminal offenders **2** period of testing, as for a new employee, etc. —**pro·ba'tion·ar·y** /-erē/ *adj.* [L, rel. to PROVE]

pro·ba·tion·er /prōbā'shənər/ *n.* person on probation

pro·ba'tion of'fi·cer *n.* official supervising offenders on probation

probe /prōb/ *n.* **1** penetrating investigation **2** small device for measuring, testing, etc. **3** surgical exploratory instrument **4** (in full **space' probe'**) unmanned exploratory spacecraft —v. (probed, prob·ing) 5 examine or inquire into closely 6 explore with a probe [L *proba*, rel. to PROVE]

pro·bi·ty /prō′bĭtē/ n. uprightness; honesty [L *probus* good]

prob·lem /prăb′ləm/ n. 1 doubtful or difficult matter requiring a solution 2 something hard to understand or accomplish [Gk *problēma -mat-*]

prob·lem·at·ic /prăb′ləmăt′ik/ adj. (also prob′lem·at′i·cal) attended by difficulty; doubtful or questionable —prob′lem·at′i·cal·ly adv. [Gk, rel. to PROBLEM]

pro bo·no /prō′ bō′nō/ adj. pertaining to service, esp. legal work, for which no fee is charged [L *pro bono publico* for the public good]

pro·bos·cis /prəbăs′is, -kis/ n. (pl. ·cis·es) 1 long flexible trunk or snout of some mammals, e.g., an elephant or tapir 2 elongated mouth parts of some insects [Gk *boskein* feed]

pro·ce·dure /prəsē′jər/ n. 1 way of acting, advancing, performing, etc.; method 2 series of actions conducted in a certain order or manner —pro·ce′dur·al adj. [Fr, rel. to PROCEED]

pro·ceed /prəsēd′/ v. 1 go forward or on further; make one's way 2 continue on with (something) 3 (of an action) be carried on or continued 4 take action 5 go on to say [L *cedere cess-* go]

pro·ceed·ing n. 1 action or piece of conduct 2 (pl.) (in full le′gal pro·ceed′ings) lawsuit 3 (pl.) published report of discussions or a conference

pro·ceeds /prō′sēdz/ n. pl. profits [pl. of obs. *proceed* (n.) fr. PROCEED]

pro·cess[1] /prăs′es, prō′ses/ n. 1 course of action or proceeding, esp. as a series of stages 2 progress or course (in the process of construction) 3 natural evolution or change (process of growing old) 4 Law. summons or writ 5 natural projection of a bone, stem, etc. —v. 6 deal with by a particular process 7 treat (food, esp. to prevent decay) (processed cheese) [L, rel. to PROCEED]

pro·cess[2] /prəses′/ v. walk in procession [back formation fr. PROCESSION]

pro·ces·sion /prəsesH′ən/ n. 1 people, vehicles, etc., advancing in orderly or ceremonial succession 2 movement of such a group [L, rel. to PROCEED]

pro·ces·sion·al adj. 1 of processions 2 used, carried, or sung in processions

pro·ces·sor /prăs′es·ər, prō′ses′-/ n. machine that processes things, e.g., a food processor

pro-choice /prō′CHOIS′/ adj. in favor of the right to legal abortion

pro·claim /prōklām′/ v. 1 announce or declare publicly or officially 2 declare to be (king, a traitor, etc.) —proc·la·ma·tion /prŏk′ləmā′sHən/ n. [L, rel. to CLAIM]

pro·cliv·i·ty /prōkliv′ətē/ n. (pl. ·ties) tendency; inclination [L *clivus* slope]

pro·cras·ti·nate /prōkrăs′tənāt/ v. (·nat·ed, ·nat·ing) defer action —pro·cras′ti·na′tion, pro·cras′ti·na′tor n. [L *cras* tomorrow]

pro·cre·ate /prō′krē·āt′/ v. (·at·ed, ·at·ing) produce (offspring) naturally —pro′cre·a′tion n.; pro′cre·a′tive adj. [L, rel. to CREATE]

Pro·crus·te·an bed /prōkrəs′tē·ən/ adj. situation that enforces ruthless or violent conformity [for *Prokroustēs*, robber in Gk myth

459   **probity / professed**

who fitted his victims to a bed by stretching or cutting off parts of their bodies]

proc·tor /prăk′tər/ n. disciplinary supervisor or monitor [L *procurator* agent]

pro·cure /prəkyōōr′/ v. (·cured, ·cur·ing) 1 obtain, esp. by care or effort; acquire 2 bring about 3 obtain (women) for prostitution —pro·cure′ment n. [L *curare* look after]

pro·cur·er /prəkyōor′ər/ n. (fem. pro·cur′ess) pimp [L *procurator* agent]

prod /prăd/ v. (prod·ded, prod·ding) 1 poke with a finger, stick, etc. 2 stimulate to action —n. 3 poke; thrust 4 stimulus to action

prod·i·gal /prăd′igəl/ adj. 1 recklessly wasteful 2 lavish —n. 3 person who has exhausted resources wastefully —prod′i·gal′i·ty /-gal′itē/ n. [L *prodigus* lavish]

pro·di·gious /prədij′əs/ adj. 1 marvelous or amazing 2 enormous [L, rel. to PRODIGY]

prod·i·gy /prăd′əjē/ n. (pl. ·gies) 1 exceptionally gifted or able person, esp. a precocious child 2 marvelous, esp. extraordinary, thing [L *prodigium* portent]

pro·duce v. /prəd(y)ōōs′/ (·duced, ·duc·ing) 1 manufacture or prepare (goods, etc.) 2 bring forward for consideration, inspection, or use 3 bear, yield, or bring into existence 4 cause or bring about 5 supervise the production of (a play, film, broadcast, etc.) —n. /prä′dōos, prō′-/ 6 what is produced 7 agricultural products, esp. fresh fruits and vegetables —pro·duc′i·ble adj. [L *ducere duct-* lead]

pro·duc·er n. 1 person who produces goods, etc. 2 person who supervises the production of a play, film, broadcast, etc.

prod·uct /prăd′əkt/ n. 1 thing produced, esp. by manufacture 2 result 3 quantity obtained by multiplication [L, rel. to PRODUCE]

pro·duc·tion /prədək′sHən/ n. 1 producing or being produced, esp. in large quantities (go into production) 2 total yield 3 thing produced, esp. a film, play, book, etc. [L, rel. to PRODUCE]

pro·duc·tive /prədək′tiv/ adj. 1 of or engaged in the production of goods 2 producing much 3 (foll. by of) causing or yielding —pro·duc′tive·ly adv.; pro·duc′tive·ness n. [L, rel. to PRODUCE]

pro·duc·tiv·i·ty /prăd′əktiv′ətē, prō′dək-/ n. 1 capacity to produce 2 amount produced or rate of production efficiency in an industry, work force, etc.

Prof. abbr. Professor

pro·fane /prəfān′/ adj. 1a irreverent; blasphemous b (of language) obscene 2 not sacred; secular —v. (·faned, ·fan·ing) 3 treat (esp. a sacred thing) irreverently; disregard 4 violate; defile —pro·fa·na·tion /prăf′ənā′ sHən/ n. [L *fanum* temple]

pro·fan·i·ty /prəfăn′ətē/ n. (pl. ·ties) 1 profane act or language; blasphemy 2 swear word

pro·fess /prəfes′/ v. 1 claim openly to have (a quality or feeling) 2 declare, esp. as an excuse (profess ignorance) 3 affirm one's faith in or allegiance to [L *profiteri -fess-* declare]

pro·fessed /prəfest′/ adj. 1 self-acknowledged 2 alleged; ostensible —**pro·fess'ed·ly** /-fes'edlē/ adv.

pro·fes·sion /prəfesʜ'ən/ n. 1 work requiring specialized, advanced training, as law, medicine, etc. 2 people in a profession 3 declaration or avowal

pro·fes'sion·al adj. 1 of, belonging to, or connected with a profession 2a skillful b worthy of a professional (*professional conduct*) 3 engaged in a specified activity as one's main paid occupation —n. 4 professional person —**pro·fes'sion·al·ism** n.; **pro·fes'sion·al·ly** adv.

pro·fes·sor /prəfes'ər/ n. 1a (often as a title) highest college or university teaching rank b person who holds this rank c (loosely) any college or university teacher 2 person who professes a religion, etc. —**pro·fes·so·ri·al** /prāf'əsōr'ēəl/ adj.; **pro·fes'sor·ship** n.

prof·fer /prāf'ər/ v. offer [Fr, rel. to PRO-¹, OFFER]

pro·fi·cient /prəfisʜ'ənt/ adj. adept; expert —**pro·fi'cien·cy** n.; **pro·fi'cient·ly** adv. [L *proficere -fect-* advance]

pro·file /prō'fīl'/ n. 1a outline, esp. of a human face, as seen from one side b representation of this 2 short biographical or character sketch —v. (filed, fil·ing) 3 represent or describe by a profile 4 keep a low profile remain inconspicuous [It *profilare* draw in outline]

prof·it /prāf'it/ n. 1 advantage or benefit 2 financial return after deducting costs —v. 3 be beneficial to 4 obtain advantage or benefit 5 at a profit with financial gain —**prof'it·a·ble** adj.; **prof'it·a·bil'i·ty** n.; **prof'it·a·bly** adv. [L *profectus*, rel. to PROFICIENT]

prof·i·teer /prāf'itēr'/ v. 1 make or seek excessive profits, esp. illegally —n. 2 person who profiteers

prof·li·gate /prāf'ligət/ adj. 1 recklessly extravagant 2 licentious; dissolute —n. 3 profligate person —**prof'li·ga·cy** n.; **prof'li·gate·ly** adv. [L *profligare* ruin]

pro for·ma /prō fôr'mə/ adv. & adj. as or being a matter of form [L]

pro·found /prəfound'/ adj. (·er, ·est) 1 having or demanding great knowledge, study, or insight; substantial 2 deep; intense; thorough (a *profound sleep; profound indifference*) 3 deeply felt —**pro·found'ly** adv.; **pro·found'ness** n.; **pro·fun·di·ty** /prəfən'dətē/ n. (pl. ·ties) [L *profundus*]

pro·fuse /prəfyōōs'/ adj. 1 lavish; extravagant 2 exuberantly plentiful; copious (*profuse variety*) —**pro·fuse'ly** adv.; **pro·fu'sion** /-fyōō'zʜən/ n. [L *fundere fus-* pour]

pro·gen·i·tor /prōjen'ətər/ n. 1 ancestor 2 predecessor [L *progignere* beget]

prog·e·ny /prāj'ənē/ n. 1 offspring; descendant(s) [L, rel. to PROGENITOR]

pro·ges·ter·one /prōjes'tərōn/ n. a steroid hormone that stimulates preparation of the uterus for pregnancy and maintains it during pregnancy [Ger, rel. to PRO-¹, GESTATION]

prog·no·sis /prāgnō'sis/ n. (pl. ·ses /-sēz/) forecast, esp. of the course of a disease [Gk *gignōskein* know]

prog·nos·tic /prāgnäs'tik/ n. 1 advance indication, esp. of the course of a disease 2 predicting; forecast —adj. 3 foretelling; predictive [L, rel. to PROGNOSIS]

prog·nos·ti·cate /prāgnäs'tikāt'/ v. (·cat·ed, ·cat·ing) foretell; prophesy —**prog·nos'ti·ca'tion, prog·nos'ti·ca'tor** n. [MedL, rel. to PROGNOSTIC]

pro·gram /prō'gram', -grəm/ n. 1 list of events, performers, etc., at a public function, etc. 2 radio or television broadcast 3 plan of events 4 course or series of studies, lectures, etc. 5 *Comp.* series of coded instructions, etc. —v. (·grammed or ·gramed, ·gram·ming or ·gram·ing) 6 make a program of 7 express (a problem) or instruct (a computer) by means of a program —**pro·gram'ma·ble** /-gram'əbəl/, **pro·gram·mat·ic** /prō'grəmat'ik/ adj.; **pro·gram·mer** n. (sense 7) [Gk *graphein* write]

prog·ress —n. /prāg'rəs/ 1 forward or onward movement toward a destination 2 advance; improvement —v. /prəgres'/ 3 move or be moved forward or onward; continue 4 advance, develop, or improve (*science progresses*) 5 in progress developing; going on [L *progrediri -gress-* go forward]

pro·gres·sion /prəgresʜ'ən/ n. 1 progressing 2 succession; series [L, rel. to PROGRESS]

pro·gres·sive /prəgres'iv/ adj. 1 moving forward 2 proceeding step by step; cumulative 3a favoring rapid political or social reform b modern 4 (of disease, violence, etc.) increasing in severity or extent 5 *Gram.* (of a tense) expressing action in progress, e.g., *am writing, was writing* —n. 6 advocate of progressive political policies —**pro·gres'sive·ly** adv. [Fr or MedL, rel. to PROGRESS]

pro·hib·it /prōhib'it/ v. 1 forbid 2 prevent —**pro·hib'i·tor** n.; **pro·hib'i·to'ry** /-itô'rē/ adj. [L *prohibere -hibit-*]

pro·hi·bi·tion /prō'(h)əbisʜ'ən/ n. 1 forbidding or being forbidden 2 order that forbids 3 (cap.) legal ban on the manufacture or sale of alcohol, esp. in the US (1920–33) —**pro'hi·bi'tion·ist** n. (sense 3)

pro·hib·i·tive /prōhib'ətiv/ adj. 1 prohibiting 2 (of prices, taxes, etc.) extremely high —**pro·hib'i·tive·ly** adv.

proj·ect —n. /prāj'ekt/ 1 plan; scheme 2 extensive undertaking, academic assignment, etc. —v. /prəjekt'/ 3 protrude; jut out 4 throw 5 extrapolate (results, etc.); forecast 6 cause (light, shadow, images, etc.) to fall on a surface 7 cause (a sound, esp. the voice) to be heard at a distance 8 express or promote forcefully or effectively 9a attribute (an emotion, etc.) to an external object or person, esp. unconsciously b imagine (oneself) having another's feelings, being in the future, etc. [L *projicere -ject-* throw forth]

pro·jec·tile /prəjek'təl/ n. 1 missile, esp. fired by a rocket 2 bullet, shell, etc.

pro·jec·tion /prəjek'sʜən/ n. 1 projecting or being projected 2 thing that projects or obtrudes 3 presentation of an image, etc., on a surface 4 forecast 5a mental image viewed as an objective reality b unconscious transfer of feelings, etc., to external objects or persons 6 representation on a plane surface of any part of the surface of the earth —**pro·jec'tion·ist** n. (sense 3)

pro·jec·tor /prəjek'tər/ n. apparatus for projecting slides or film onto a screen

Pro·ko·fiev /prəkôf'yev', -yef', -yəf/, **Sergei** 1891–1953; Russian composer

pro·lapse /prōlaps'/ n. (also **pro·lap'sus** /-lap'səs/) 1 forward or downward displacement of a part or organ —v. (·lapsed, ·laps·ing) 2 undergo prolapse [L, rel. to LAPSE]

pro·le·tar·i·at /prō'liter'ēət/ n. 1 the working class 2 esp. Derog. lowest, esp. uneducated, class —**pro'le·tar'i·an** adj. [L proletarius citizen of the lowest class]

pro'-life' adj. opposed to the right to legal abortion

pro·lif·er·ate /prəlif'ərāt'/ v. (·at·ed, ·at·ing) 1 reproduce; produce (cells, etc.) rapidly 2 increase rapidly in numbers —**pro·lif'er·a'tion** n. [L proles offspring]

pro·lif·ic /prəlif'ik/ adj. 1 producing many offspring or much output 2 abundantly productive —**pro·lif'i·cal·ly** adv. [MedL, rel. to PROLIFERATE]

pro·lix /prōliks', prō'liks/ adj. (of speech, writing, etc.) lengthy; tedious —**pro·lix'i·ty** /-lik'sitē/ n. [L]

pro·logue /prō'lôg', -läg'/ n. 1 preliminary speech, poem, etc., esp. of a play 2 introductory event [Gk logos word]

pro·long /prəlông'/ v. extend in time or space —**pro'lon·ga'tion** /-gā'sHən/ n. [L longus long]

prom /präm/ n. formal school or college dance [fr. PROMENADE]

prom·e·nade /präm'ənād', -näd'/ n. 1 paved public walk, esp. with a scenic view 2 outing for display or pleasure —v. (·nad·ed, ·nad·ing) 3 make a promenade (through) [Fr]

Pro·me·the·an /prəmē'THēən/ adj. daring or inventive [Prometheus, mortal in Gk myth who stole fire from the gods]

pro·me·thi·um /prəmē'THēəm/ n. radioactive metallic element of the lanthanide series; symb. Pm [Prometheus: see PROMETHEAN]

prom·i·nent /präm'ənənt/ adj. 1 jutting out; projecting 2 conspicuous 3 distinguished; important —**prom'i·nence** n.; **prom'i·nent·ly** adv. [L prominere project]

pro·mis·cu·ous /prəmis'kyōōəs/ adj. 1 having frequent, esp. casual, sexual relationships 2 random or indiscriminate —**prom·is·cu·i·ty** /präm'əskyōō'ətē/ n.; **pro·mis'cu·ous·ly** adv. [L miscere mix]

prom·ise /präm'is/ n. 1 assurance that one will or will not undertake a certain action, etc. 2 potential for achievement —v. (·ised, ·is·ing) 3 make a promise 4 seem likely (to) (promises to be a good book) 5 assure [L promissum fr. mittere miss- send]

Prom'ised Land' n. 1 Bibl. Canaan, land promised by God to Abraham and his people 2 fervent goal

prom'is·ing adj. likely to turn out well; hopeful —**prom'is·ing·ly** adv.

prom·is·so·ry /präm'əsôr'ē/ adj. conveying a promise [MedL, rel. to PROMISE]

prom'is·so'ry note' n. signed document containing a promise to pay a stated sum

pro·mo /prō'mō/ n. (pl. ·mos) Colloq. 1 promotional video, demonstration, etc. —v. (·moed, ·mo·ing) 2 promote; publicize [abbr.]

prom·on·to·ry /präm'əntôr'ē/ n. (pl. ·ries) point of high coastal land; headland [L]

pro·mote /prəmōt'/ v. (·mot·ed, ·mot·ing) 1 raise (a person) to a higher office, rank, etc. 2 encourage (a cause, process, etc.) 3 publicize and sell —**pro·mo'tion** n.; **pro·mo'tion·al** adj. [L promovere -mot-]

pro·mot·er n. 1 person who promotes 2 person who arranges for and publicizes a sports event, show, etc. [MedL, rel. to PROMOTE]

prompt /prämpt/ adj. 1 acting, made, or done without delay —adv. 2 punctually —v. 3 incite; urge (prompted them to action) 4 assist (an actor or hesitating speaker) with a cue or suggestion 5 give rise to; inspire —n. 6 something that prompts 7 Comp. symbol on a monitor showing that the system is waiting for input —**promp'ti·tude** n.; **prompt'ly** adv.; **prompt'ness** n. [L]

prompt'er n. person or thing that prompts actors, etc.

pro·mul·gate /präm'əlgāt'/ v. (·gat·ed, ·gat·ing) 1 make known; disseminate; promote 2 proclaim (a decree, news, etc.) —**pro·mul'ga'tion, prom'ul·ga'tor** n. [L]

prone /prōn/ adj. 1a lying face downward b lying flat; prostrate 2 disposed; liable (to) —**prone'ness** n. [L]

prong /prông/ n. each of two or more projections at the end of a fork, etc.

pro·noun /prō'noun/ n. Gram. word used instead of and to indicate a noun already mentioned or known, esp. to avoid repetition (e.g., we, their, this, ourselves) [fr. PRO-¹, NOUN]

pro·nounce /prənouns'/ v. (·nounced, ·nounc·ing) 1 utter or speak (words, sounds, etc.) in a certain or prescribed way 2 utter or proclaim (a judgment, sentence, etc.) 3 officially or formally state as one's opinion —**pro·nounce'a·ble** adj.; **pro·nounce'ment** n. [L nuntiare announce]

pro·nounced' adj. strongly marked; noticeable (pronounced limp)

pron·to /prän'tō/ adv. Colloq. promptly; quickly [L, rel. to PROMPT]

pro·nun·ci·a·tion /prənun'sē·ā'sHən/ n. 1 pronouncing of a word, esp. with reference to a standard 2 act of pronouncing 3 way of pronouncing words, etc. [L, rel. to PRONOUNCE]

proof /prōōf/ n. 1 facts, evidence, etc., establishing or helping to establish a truth 2 demonstration; proving 3 test; trial (put them to the proof) 4 standard of strength of distilled alcohol 5 trial impression before final printing 6 step by step resolution of a mathematical or philosophical problem 7 photographic print made for selection, etc. —adj. 8 impervious to penetration, ill effects, etc. (proof against corruption) [L proba, rel. to PROVE]

proof·read /prōōf'rēd'/ v. (·read, ·read·ing) read and correct (typed or printed words) —**proof'read'er** n.

prop¹ /präp/ n. 1 rigid, esp. separate, support 2 person or thing that supports, comforts, etc. —v. (propped, prop·ping) 3 (often foll. by up) support with or as if by a prop 4 lean (up) against a wall, etc. [LGer or Du]

prop² n. PROPERTY, 3 [abbr.]

prop³ n. PROPELLER [abbr.]

pro·pa·gan·da /präp'əgan'də/ n. 1 organized propagation of a doctrine by use of publicity, exaggeration, etc. 2 usu. Derog. ideas, etc., so propagated —**prop'a·gan'dist** n. & adj.; **pro'**

pa·gan·dize /-dīz/ v. (**·dized, ·diz·ing**) [L, rel. to PROPAGATE]

prop·a·gate /präpəgāt'/ v. (**·gat·ed, ·gat·ing**) **1a** breed (a plant, animal, etc.) from the parent stock **b** (of a plant, animal, etc.) reproduce itself **2** disseminate (a belief, theory, etc.) —**prop'a·ga'tion, prop'a·ga'tor** n. [L *propagare*]

pro·pane /prō'pān'/ n. gaseous hydrocarbon used as bottled fuel [*propionic acid*, rel. to PRO-², Gk *pīōn* fat]

pro·pel /prəpel'/ v. (**·pelled, ·pel·ling**) drive or push forward; urge on —**pro·pel'·lant** n. & adj. [L *pellere puls*- drive]

pro·pel'ler n. revolving shaft with blades, esp. for propelling a ship or aircraft

pro·pen·si·ty /prəpen'sitē/ n. (pl. ·ties) inclination; tendency [L *propensus* inclined]

prop·er /präp'ər/ adj. **1a** accurate; correct **b** fit; suitable; right (at the proper time) **2** decent; respectable, esp. excessively so **3** belonging or relating (respect proper to them) **4** (usu. placed after the noun) strictly so called; per se (this is the crypt, not the cathedral proper) [L *proprius* one's own]

prop·er·ly adv. **1** fittingly; suitably **2** correctly; precisely (properly speaking) **3** rightly **4** with decency; respectably (behave properly)

prop·er noun n. (also **prop'er name'**) noun that specifies a particular person, place, animal, country, etc., e.g., 'Jane,' 'Everest'

prop·er·tied /präp'ərtēd/ adj. having property, esp. land

prop·er·ty /präp'ərtē/ n. (pl. ·ties) **1** thing(s) owned; possession(s), esp. a house, land, etc. **2** attribute, quality, or characteristic **3** movable object used in a play, movie, etc. [L *proprietas*, rel. to PROPER]

proph·e·cy /präf'əsē/ n. (pl. ·cies) **1a** prophetic utterance, esp. biblical **b** prediction of future events **2** faculty, practice, etc., of prophesying (gift of prophecy) [Gk, rel. to PROPHET]

• Usage: Be careful to note that *prophesy* is the verb, *prophecy* the noun.

proph·e·sy /präf'əsī'/ v. (**·sied, ·sy·ing**) **1** foretell (an event, etc.) **2** speak as a prophet; foretell the future [Fr *profecier*, rel. to PROPH-ECY]

proph·et /präf'it/ n. (fem. **proph'et·ess**) **1** religious seer or interpreter **2a** person who foretells events **b** spokesman; advocate (prophet of the new order) [Gk *prophētēs* spokesman]

pro·phet·ic /prəfet'ik/ adj. **1** containing a prediction; predicting **2** of a prophet —**pro·phet'i·cal·ly** adv. [L, rel. to PROPHET]

pro·phy·lac·tic /prō'filak'tik/ adj. **1** tending to prevent disease, etc. —n. **2** preventive medicine or action **3** condom [Gk: keeping guard before]

pro·phy·lax·is /prō'filak'sis/ n. preventive treatment against disease [fr. PRO-², Gk *phulaxis* guarding]

pro·pin·qui·ty /prəpiNG'kwətē/ n. nearness in space; proximity [L *prope* near]

pro·pi·ti·ate /prəpish'ē·āt'/ v. (**·at·ed, ·at·ing**) appease (an offended person, etc.) —**pro·pi'ti·a'tion, pro·pi'ti·a·tor·n.; pro·pi'ti·a·to·ry** /-ətō'rē/ adj. [L, rel. to PROPITIOUS]

pro·pi·tious /prəpish'əs/ adj. **1** favorable; auspicious **2** advantageous [L *propitius*]

pro·po·nent /prəpō'nənt/ n. advocate of a cause, proposal, etc. [L, rel. to PROPOSE]

pro·por·tion /prəpôr'sHən/ n. **1a** comparative part or share **b** comparative ratio (proportion of births to deaths) **2** correct or pleasing relation of things or parts of a thing **3** (pl.) dimensions; size (man of huge proportions) **4** Math. equality of ratios between two pairs of quantities, e.g., 3:5 and 9:15 —v. **5** make proportionate —**pro·por'tion·al** adj.; **pro·por'tion·al·ly** adv.; **pro·por'tion·ate** /-nit/ adj.; **pro·por'tion·ate·ly** adv. [L, rel. to PORTION]

• Usage: Except in fixed phrases like *proportional representation*, *proportional* and *proportionate* may be treated as variants.

pro·pos·al /prəpō'zəl/ n. **1a** act of proposing something **b** course of action, etc., proposed **c** something proposed, e.g., an outline for a book, etc.; prospectus **2** offer of marriage

pro·pose /prəpōz'/ v. (**·posed, ·pos·ing**) **1** put forward for consideration or as a plan; suggest **2** intend; purpose **3** offer oneself in marriage **4** nominate —**pro·pos'er** n. [L *ponere posit*- place]

prop·o·si·tion /präp'əzisH'ən/ n. **1** statement; assertion **2** scheme proposed; proposal **3** Logic. statement subject to proof or disproof **4** problem (difficult proposition) **5** Math. formal statement of a theorem or problem **6** sexual advance —v. **7** make a sexual advance to [L, rel. to PROPOSE]

pro·pound /prəpound'/ v. offer for consideration; propose [*propo(u)ne* fr. L, rel. to PRO-POSE]

pro·pri·e·tar·y /prəprī'əter'ē/ adj. **1a** of or holding property (proprietary classes) **b** of a proprietor (proprietary rights) **2** held in private ownership [L *proprietarius*, rel. to PROP-ERTY]

pro·pri·e·tor /prəprī'ətər/ n. (fem. **pro'pri'e·tress** /-tris/) owner —**pro·pri·e·to'ri·al** /-tō'rial/ adj. [rel. to PROPRIETARY]

pro·pri·e·ty /prəprī'ətē/ n. (pl. ·ties) **1** fitness; rightness **2** correctness of behavior or morals **3** (pl.) details or rules of correct conduct [Fr, rel. to PROPERTY]

pro·pul·sion /prəpəl'sHən/ n. **1** driving or pushing forward **2** impelling influence —**pro·pul'sive** /-siv/ adj. [L, rel. to PROPEL]

pro ra·ta /prō rä'tə, -rä'-/ adj. **1** proportional —adv. **2** proportionally [L]

pro·rate /prō'rāt'/ v. (**·rat·ed, ·rat·ing**) divide or dispense proportionately

pro·sa·ic /prōzā'ik/ adj. **1** like prose; lacking poetic beauty **2** unromantic; dull; commonplace —**pro·sa'i·cal·ly** adv. [L, rel. to PROSE]

pros' and cons' n. pl. points for and against a proposition, etc.

pro·sce·ni·um /prōsē'nēəm/ n. (pl. ·ums or ·a /-ə/) Theatr. vertical arched opening to the stage [Gk, rel. to SCENE]

pro·scribe /prōskrīb'/ v. (**·scribed, ·scrib·ing**) **1** forbid, esp. by law **2** reject or denounce **3** outlaw (a person) —**pro·scrip'·tion** /-skrip'sHən/ n.; **pro·scrip'tive** /-tiv/ adj. [L: publish in writing]

• Usage: See note at PRESCRIBE.

prose /prōz/ *n.* ordinary written or spoken language not in verse [L *prosa* fr. *prorsus* straightforward]

pros·e·cute /präs′ikyŌōt′/ *v.* (·cuted, ·cuting) 1 institute legal proceedings against (a person), or with reference to (a claim, crime, etc.) 2 carry on (a trade, pursuit, etc.) —**pros′e·cu′tion, pros′e·cu′tor** *n.* [L *prose-qui -secut-* pursue]

pros·e·lyte /präs′əlīt′/ *n.* person converted from one opinion, creed, party, etc., to another —**pros′e·ly·tism′** /-lətiz′əm/, *n.* [L *proselytus* fr. Gk]

pros·e·lyt·ize /präs′ələtīz′/ *v.* (·ized, ·izing) convert or seek to convert from one belief, etc., to another

pros·o·dy /präs′ədē/ *n.* versification; study of meter, rhyme, etc. [Gk *pros* to, rel. to ODE]

pros·pect /präs′pekt′/ *n.* 1a (often *pl.*) expectation, esp. of success in a career, etc. b something anticipated 2 extensive view of landscape, etc. 3 possible or probable customer, subscriber, etc. —*v.* 4 search (esp. a region) for gold, etc. —**pros′pec′tor** *n.* [L, rel. to PROSPECTUS]

pro·spec·tive /prəspek′tiv/ *adj.* expected; future [L, rel. to PROSPECTUS]

pro·spec·tus /prəspek′təs/ *n.* (*pl.* ·tus·es) promotional or descriptive document or brochure [L]

pros·per /präs′pər/ *v.* be successful; thrive [L *prosperus* prosperous]

pros·per·i·ty /präsper′ətē/ *n.* prosperous state; wealth; success

pros·per·ous /präs′p(ə)rəs/ *adj.* successful; rich; thriving —**pros′per·ous·ly** *adv.* [Fr fr. L]

pros·tate /präs′tāt′/ *n.* gland near the bladder in male mammals, releasing part of the semen —**pros·tat′ic** /-tat′ik/ *adj.* [Gk *prostatēs* one who stands before]

pros·the·sis /präsтнē′sis/ *n.* (*pl.* ·ses /-sēz/) 1 artificial replacement for a body part amputated, etc. 2 branch of surgery dealing with prostheses —**pros·thet′ic** /-тнet′ik/ *adj.* [Gk: placing in addition]

pros·ti·tute /präs′tit(y)ŌŌt′/ *n.* 1 person who engages in sexual activity for payment —*v.* (·tut·ed, ·tut·ing) 2 make a prostitute of (esp. oneself) 3 misuse (one's talents, skills, name, etc.) for money, etc. —**pros′ti·tu′tion** *n.* [L *prostituere -tut-* offer for sale]

pros·trate /präs′trāt′/ *adj.* 1a lying face downward, esp. in submission b lying horizontally 2 overcome, esp. by grief, exhaustion, etc. —*v.* (·trat·ed, ·trat·ing) 3 lay or throw (esp. a person) flat 4 throw (oneself) down in submission, etc. 5 overcome; make weak —**pros·tra′tion** *n.* [L *prosternere -strat-* throw in front]

pros·y /prō′zē/ *adj.* (·i·er, ·i·est) commonplace; dull

Prot. *abbr.* Protestant

prot·ac·tin·i·um /prō′taktin′ēəm/ *n.* radioactive metallic element; *symb.* Pa [Ger, rel. to ACTINIUM]

pro·tag·o·nist /prōtag′ənist/ *n.* leading character in a drama, story, etc. [Gk, rel. to PROTO-, *agōnistēs* actor]

pro·te·an /prō′tēən/ *adj.* taking many forms; versatile; variable [*Proteus*, Gk sea-god who could assume various shapes]

pro·tect /prətekt′/ *v.* keep (a person, thing, etc.) safe; defend; guard —**pro·tec′tor** *n.* [L *tegere tect-* cover]

pro·tec·tion /prətek′sнən/ *n.* 1a protecting or being protected; defense b thing, person, or animal that protects 2 *Colloq.* immunity from violence, etc., obtained by payment (protection money) to gangsters, etc. —**pro·tec′tion·ist** *n. & adj.*

pro·tec·tive /prətek′tiv/ *adj.* protecting —**pro·tec′tive·ly** *adv.*; **pro·tec′tive·ness** *n.*

pro·tec·tor·ate /prətek′tərət/ *n.* 1 state controlled and protected by another 2 this relation

pro·té·gé /prō′təzнā′/ *n.* (*fem.* **pro·té·gée**, *pronunc.* same) person under the protection, patronage, tutelage, etc., of another [Fr, rel. to PROTECT]

pro·tein /prō′tēn, prō′tēən/ *n.* one of numerous organic compounds composed of amino acids, essential to all living organisms [Gk *prōtos* first]

pro tempore /prō tem′pərē/ *adj. & adv.* (also, *abbr.* **pro tem** /prō′tem′/) for the time being [L]

Prot·er·o·zo·ic /prō′tərəzō′ik/ *Geol. adj.* 1 of the later part of the Precambrian era —*n.* 2 this time [Gk *proteros* former, *zōē* life]

pro·test /prō′test′/ *n.* 1 statement or act of dissent or disapproval —*v.* /prōtest′, prə-/ 2 make a protest 3 affirm (one's innocence, etc.) solemnly 4 object to (a decision, etc.) 5 under protest unwillingly —**pro·test′er** or **pro·tes′tor** *n.* [L *protestari* declare formally]

Prot·es·tant /prät′əstənt/ *n.* 1 member or follower of a church separated from the Roman Catholic Church after the Reformation —*adj.* 2 of the Protestant Churches or their members, etc. —**Prot′es·tant·ism′** /-iz′əm/ *n.* [rel. to PROTEST]

prot·es·ta·tion /prät′əstā′sнən/ *n.* 1 strong affirmation 2 protest [L, rel. to PROTEST]

proto- *comb. form* first (*prototype*) [Gk *prōtos*]

pro·to·col /prō′təkôl′/ *n.* 1 official formality and etiquette 2 original draft, esp. terms of a treaty 3 formal statement of a transaction [Gk *kolla* glue]

pro·ton /prō′tän′/ *n.* elementary particle with a positive electric charge, occurring in all atomic nuclei [Gk *prōtos* first]

pro·to·plasm /prō′təplazəm/ *n.* complex substance comprising the living part of a cell —**pro′to·plas′mic** /-plaz′mik/ *adj.* [Gk, rel. to PROTO-, PLASMA]

pro·to·type /prō′tətīp′/ *n.* 1 original as a pattern for imitations, improved forms, etc. 2 trial model or preliminary version —**pro′to·typ′ic** /-tip′ik/, **pro′to·typ′i·cal** *adj.* [Gk, rel. to PROTO-]

pro·to·zo·an /prō′təzō′ən/ *n.* (also **pro′to·zo′on** /-zō′än′/) (*pl.* ·zo·a /-ə/ or ·ans) 1 unicellular microscopic organism —*adj.* 2 (also **pro′to·zo′ic** /-zō′ik/) of this group [fr. PROTO-, Gk *zōion* animal]

pro·tract /prōtrakt′/ *v.* prolong or lengthen —**pro·trac′tion** /-trak′sнən/ *n.* [L *trahere tract-* draw]

pro·trac·tor *n.* instrument for measuring angles, usu. in the form of a graduated semicircle

PROTRACTOR

pro·trude /prōtrōōd′/ *v.* (**·trud·ed, ·trud·ing**) thrust forward; stick out; project —**pro·tru′sion** /-trōō′zHən/ *n.*; **pro·tru′sive** /-siv/ *adj.* [L *trudere trus-* thrust]

pro·tu·ber·ant /prōt(y)ōō′bərənt/ *adj.* bulging out; prominent —**pro·tu′ber·ance** *n.* [L, rel. to TUBER]

proud /proud/ *adj.* 1 feeling greatly honored or pleased 2a haughty; arrogant b having a proper pride; satisfied (*proud of a job well done*) 3 (of an occasion, action, etc.) worthy of pride (*proud day*) 4 imposing; splendid —**proud′ly** *adv.* [Fr *prud* valiant]

Prou·dhon /prōōdôN′/, **Pierre Joseph** 1809–65; French writer

Proust /prōōst/, **Marcel** 1871–1922; French writer and critic

prove /prōōv/ *v.* (**proved, proved** *or* **prov·en, prov·ing**) 1 demonstrate the truth of by evidence or argument 2a be found (*it proved to be untrue*) b emerge as (*will prove the winner*) 3 test the accuracy of (a calculation) 4 prove oneself show one's abilities, courage, etc. —**prov′a·ble** *adj.* [L *probare* test; approve]

prov·e·nance /präv′ənəns/ *n.* origin or place of origin [Fr *provenir* fr. L]

Pro·ven·çal /prō′vänsäl′, präv′ən-/ *adj.* 1 of Provence, region in SE France —*n.* 2 native or language of Provence 3 medieval language and literature of Provence [Fr, rel. to PROVINCE]

prov·en·der /präv′əndər/ *n.* animal fodder [L *praebere* give]

prov·erb /präv′ərb/ *n.* short pithy saying in popular use, held to embody a general truth [L *proverbium* fr. *verbum* word]

pro·ver·bi·al /prəvər′bēəl/ *adj.* 1 well known; notorious (*his proverbial honesty*) 2 of or referred to in a proverb (*proverbial ill wind*) —**pro·ver′bi·al·ly** *adv.* [L, rel. to PROVERB]

pro·vide /prəvīd′/ *v.* (**·vid·ed, ·vid·ing**) 1 supply; furnish 2a make due preparation b take care of a person, etc., with money, food, etc. (*provides for a large family*) 3 stipulate in a will, statute, etc. —**pro·vid′er** *n.* [L *providere vis-* foresee]

pro·vid·ed *conj.* (also **pro·vid′ing**) on the condition or understanding (that)

prov·i·dence /präv′ədəns/ *n.* 1 protective care of God or nature 2 (*cap.*) God in this aspect 3 foresight; thrift [L, rel. to PROVIDE]

Prov·i·dence /präv′ədəns/ *n.* capital of R.I., in the NE part. Pop. 160,728

prov·i·dent *adj.* having or showing foresight;

thrifty —**prov′i·dent·ly** *adv.* [L, rel. to PROVIDE]

prov·i·den·tial /präv′əden′CHəl/ *adj.* 1 of or by divine foresight or interposition 2 opportune; lucky —**prov′i·den′tial·ly** *adv.*

prov·ince /präv′ins/ *n.* 1 principal administrative division of a country, etc. 2 (*pl.*) country outside a capital city, esp. regarded as uncultured or unsophisticated 3 field, area, or sphere of action [L *provincia*]

pro·vin·cial /prəvin′SHəl/ *adj.* 1 of a province or provinces 2 unsophisticated or uncultured —*n.* 3 inhabitant of a province or the provinces 4 unsophisticated or uncultured person —**pro·vin′cial·ism′** /-iz′əm/ *n.*

pro·vi·sion /prəvizH′ən/ *n.* 1a act of providing b preparation, esp. for the future 2 (*pl.*) food, drink, etc., esp. for an expedition 3 legal or formal stipulation or proviso —*v.* 4 supply with provisions [L, rel. to PROVIDE]

pro·vi·sion·al *adj.* providing for immediate needs only; temporary —**pro·vi′sion·al·ly** *adv.*

pro·vi·so /prəvī′zō/ *n.* (*pl.* **·sos** *or* **·soes**) 1 stipulation 2 clause containing this —**pro·vi′so·ry** *adj.* [L: it being provided]

Pro·vo /prō′vō/ *n.* city in Utah. Pop. 86,835

prov·o·ca·tion /präv′əkā′sHən/ *n.* 1 provoking or being provoked 2 cause of annoyance

pro·voc·a·tive /prəväk′ətiv/ *adj.* 1 tending to provoke, as anger or sexual desire 2 intentionally annoying or controversial —**pro·voc′a·tive·ly** *adv.*; **pro·voc′a·tive·ness** *n.*

pro·voke /prəvōk′/ *v.* (**·voked, ·vok·ing**) 1 rouse or incite 2 call forth; instigate; cause 3 irritate or anger [L *provocare* call forth]

pro·vo·lo·ne /prō′vəlō′nē, -lōn′/ *n.* an Italian-style medium hard cheese

pro·vost /prō′vōst′/ *n.* high official of a church or college [L *propositus* fr. *ponere* place]

pro′vost mar′shal /prō′vō/ *n.* head of military police force or detail

prow /prou/ *n.* forepart or bow of a ship [Fr *proue* fr. Gk *prōira*]

prow·ess /prou′is/ *n.* 1 skill; expertise 2 valor; gallantry [Fr, rel. to PROUD]

prowl /proul/ *v.* 1 roam (a place), esp. stealthily or restlessly or in search of prey, loot, etc. —*n.* 2 act of prowling —**prowl′er** *n.*

prox·i·mate /präk′səmət/ *adj.* 1 nearest or next before or after 2 approximate [L *proximus* nearest]

prox·im·i·ty /präksim′ətē/ *n.* nearness in space, time, etc. [L, rel. to PROXIMATE]

prox·y /präk′sē/ *n.* (*pl.* **·ies**) 1 authorization given to a substitute or deputy (*proxy vote; married by proxy*) 2 person authorized to act thus [obs. *procuracy* procuration]

prude /prōōd/ *n.* excessively (often affectedly) proper or sexually modest person —**prud′er·y** *n.*; **prud′ish** *adj.*; **prud′ish·ly** *adv.*; **prud′ish·ness** *n.* [Fr, rel. to PROUD]

pru·dent /prōōd′nt/ *adj.* 1 sound in judgment 2 careful; cautious —**pru′dence** *n.*; **pru′dent·ly** *adv.* [L *prudens -ent-*, rel. to PROVIDENT]

pru·den·tial /prōōden′SHəl/ *adj.* of or showing prudence —**pru·den′tial·ly** *adv.*

prune¹ /prōōn/ *n.* dried plum [L *prunum* fr. Gk]

prune² v. (**pruned, prun·ing**) **1** trim (a bush, etc.) by cutting away dead or unwanted branches, etc. **2a** clear or remove superfluities from **b** remove (superfluities) [Fr *prooignier* fr. Rom, rel. to ROUND]

pru·ri·ent /prŏŏr′ēənt/ adj. having or encouraging unhealthy sexual curiosity —**pru′ri·ence** n. [L *prurire* itch]

Prus·sian /prəsh′ən/ adj. **1** of Prussia (former state of N Europe) or esp. its rigidly militaristic tradition —n. **2** native of Prussia

prus′sic ac′id /prə′sik/ n. hydrocyanic acid [Fr]

pry¹ /prī/ n. **1** tool, as a crowbar or lever —v. (**pried, pry·ing**) **2** raise, move, or open with such a tool **3** obtain with difficulty

pry² v. (**pried, pry·ing**) inquire impertinently

PS or **P.S.** abbr. **1** postscript **2** polystyrene

psalm /sä(l)m/ n. (also cap.) sacred song, esp. from the Book of Psalms (Old Testament) —**psalm′ist** n. [L *psalmus* fr. Gk]

Psal·ter /sôl′tər/ n. **1** the Book of Psalms **2** (**p-**) version of this for use in religious services [OE and Fr fr. Gk *psalterion* stringed instrument]

p's and q's n. as in mind one's p's and q's: **1** attend to one's own conduct and manners **2** attend to one's own accuracy in work

PSAT abbr. Preliminary Scholastic Assessment Test

pseud. abbr. pseudonym

pseudo- comb. form (also **pseud-** before some vowels) **1** false; not genuine (*pseudo-intellectual*) **2** resembling or imitating [Gk *pseudes* false]

pseu·do·nym /sŏŏd′n-im′/ n. fictitious name, esp. of an author [Gk, rel. to PSEUDO-, *onoma* name]

psf. or **p.s.f.** abbr. pounds per square foot

psi /(p)sī/ n. twenty-third letter of the Greek alphabet (Ψ, ψ) [Gk]

psi or **p.s.i.** abbr. pounds per square inch

psit·ta·co·sis /sit′əkō′sis/ n. contagious viral disease, esp. of parrots, transmissible to human beings [Gk *psittakos* parrot]

pso·ri·a·sis /sərī′əsis/ n. skin disease marked by red scaly patches [Gk *psōra* itch]

psst /pst/ interj. whispered sound to attract a person's attention [imit.]

PST abbr. Pacific standard time

psych /sīk/ v. Colloq. **1** prepare (oneself or another) mentally for an ordeal, etc. **2** (usu. foll. by *out*) intimidate or confuse (a person), esp. for one's own advantage [abbr.]

psych. /sīk/ abbr. (also **psychol.**) psychological; psychology

psy·che /sī′kē/ n. the soul, spirit, or mind [L fr. Gk]

psy·che·del·ic /sī′kədel′ik/ adj. **1a** expanding the mind's awareness, etc., esp. with hallucinogenic drugs **b** (of a drug) producing hallucinations **2** hallucinatory in effect, color, design, etc. **3** of or associated with hallucinogenic drugs [Gk *psukhē* mind, *dēlos* clear]

psy·chi·a·try /səkī′ətrē, sī-/ n. the study and medical treatment of mental disorders —**psy·chi·at·ric** /sī′kē-a′trik/ adj.; **psy·chi′a·trist** /-trist/ n. [fr. PSYCHO-, Gk *iatros* physician]

psy·chic /sī′kik/ adj. **1** (of a person) considered to have occult powers such as telepathy, clairvoyance, etc. **2** of the soul or mind —n.

465

3 person considered to have psychic powers; medium —**psy′chi·cal** adj.; **psy′chi·cal·ly** adv. [Gk *psukhē* soul, mind]

psy·cho /sī′kō/ Slang. n. (pl. **-chos**) **1** psychopath —adj. **2** psychopathic [abbr.]

psycho- comb. form of the mind or psychology (*psychoanalysis*) [Gk, rel. to PSYCHIC]

psy·cho·a·nal·y·sis /sī′kōənal′əsis/ n. treatment of mental disorders by discussion and analysis of repressed fears and conflicts —**psy′cho·an′a·lyst** /-an′əlist/ n.; **psy·cho·an′a·lyt′ic** /-an′əlit′ik/, **psy·cho·an·a·lyt′i·cal** adj.; **psy′cho·an′a·lyze** /-an′əlīz/ v. (**-lyzed, -lyz·ing**)

psy·cho·bab·ble /sī′kōbab′l/ n. language marked by popularized psychological jargon

psy·cho·gen·ic /sī′kəjen′ik/ adj. Psychol. originating in the mind or in a mental or emotional condition

psy·cho·log·i·cal /sī′kəläj′ikəl/ adj. **1** of or arising in the mind **2** of psychology **3** (of an ailment, etc.) imaginary —**psy′cho·log′i·cal·ly** adv.

psy′cho·log′i·cal war′fare n. campaign directed at reducing an opponent's morale

psy·chol·o·gy /sīkäl′əjē/ n. (pl. **-gies**) **1** the study of the human mind **2** treatise on or theory of this **3** mental characteristics, etc., of a person, group, situation, etc. —**psy·chol′o·gist** /-jist/ n.

psy·cho·path /sī′kəpaтн/ n. **1** mentally deranged person, esp. showing abnormal or violent social behavior **2** mentally or emotionally unstable person —**psy·cho·path′ic** adj.; **psy·cho·pa·thy** /-käp′əтнē/ n.

psy·cho·pa·thol·o·gy /sī′kōpəтнäl′əjē/ n. **1** the study of mental disorders **2** mentally or behaviorally disordered state

psy·cho·sis /sīkō′sis/ n. (pl. **-ses** /-sēz′/) severe mental disorder with loss of contact with reality [Gk, rel. to PSYCHE]

psy·cho·so·mat·ic /sī′kōsōmat′ik/ adj. (of a bodily disorder) mental, not physical, in origin

psy·cho·ther·a·py /sī′kōтнer′əpē/ n. professional treatment of mental disorder by psychoanalysis, counseling, etc. —**psy′cho·ther′a·peu′tic** /-тнer′əpyŏŏt′ik/ adj.; **psy·cho·ther′a·pist** /-pist/ n.

psy·chot·ic /sīkät′ik/ adj. **1** of or suffering from a psychosis —n. **2** psychotic person

Pt symb. platinum

PT abbr. **1** physical therapy **2** part-time

pt. abbr. **1** part **2** pint **3** point **4** Naut. port

PTA abbr. Parent-Teacher Association

ptar·mi·gan /tär′migən/ n. game bird with a grouselike appearance [Gaelic]

pter·o·dac·tyl /ter′ədak′təl/ n. extinct flying reptile [Gk *pteron* wing, DACTYL]

Ptol·e·my /täl′əmē/ fl. 127–151; ancient astronomer and geographer in Alexandria

pto·maine /tō′mān′/ n. any of various esp. toxic amine compounds in putrefying matter [Gk *ptōma* corpse]

Pu symb. plutonium

pub /pəb/ n. tavern; bar [abbr. of *public house*]

pub. or **publ.** abbr. **1** public **2** publication **3** published; publisher; publishing

pu·ber·ty /pyŏŏ′bərtē/ n. period of sexual maturation —**pu′ber·tal** adj. [L *puber* adult]

pu·bes /pyōō′bēz/ *n.* (*pl.* same) 1 lower part of the abdomen at the front of the pelvis 2 /pyōō̄z/ *Colloq.* pubic hair [L]

pu·bes·cence /pyōōbes′əns/ *n.* 1 beginning of puberty 2 soft down on plants or on animals, esp. insects —**pu·bes′cent** *adj.* [L, rel. to PUBES]

pu·bic /pyōō′bik/ *adj.* of the genital area

pu·bis /pyōō′bis/ *n.* (*pl.* **·bes** /-bēz/) either of a pair of bones forming the two sides of the pelvis [L *os pubis* bone of the PUBES]

pub·lic /pəb′lik/ *adj.* 1 of the people as a whole 2 open to or shared by all 3 done or existing openly (*public apology*) 4 provided by, concerning, or serving government (*public records*) —*n.* 5 community, or members of it, in general 6 specified section of the community (*reading public*) 7 **go public: a** sell stock in a company on a public market **b** reveal one's plans, etc. 8 **in public** openly; publicly —**pub′lic·ly** *adv.* [L]

pub′lic-ad·dress′ sys′tem *n.* loudspeakers, microphones, amplifiers, etc., for addressing large audiences

pub·li·can /pəb′likən/ *n.* 1 *Rom. Hist.* tax collector 2 *Brit.* keeper of a pub [L, rel. to PUB-LIC]

pub·li·ca·tion /pəb′likā′shən/ *n.* 1a preparation and issuing of a book, newspaper, etc. **b** book, etc., so issued 2 making something publicly known [L, rel. to PUBLIC]

pub′lic do·main′ *n.* 1 literary work, etc., without copyright, or an invention, process, etc., without a patent 2 land owned by the government

pub′lic health′ *n.* provision of adequate community sanitation, immunization, etc., as by government

pub·li·cist /pəb′ləsist/ *n.* publicity or public relations agent

pub·lic·i·ty /pəblis′ətē/ *n.* 1 public exposure 2a advertising **b** material used for this [Fr, rel. to PUBLIC]

pub·li·cize /pəb′ləsīz′/ *v.* (·**cized**, ·**ciz·ing**) advertise; make publicly known

pub′lic re·la′tions *n. pl.* professional promotion of a favorable public image, esp. for a company, famous person, etc.

pub′lic school′ *n.* 1 *US.* elementary or secondary school supported primarily by taxes 2 *Brit.* private boarding school

pub′lic sec′tor *n.* government-controlled part of an economy, industry, etc.

pub′lic u·til′i·ty *n.* organization supplying water, gas, etc., to the community

pub·lish /pəb′lish/ *v.* 1 prepare and issue (a book, newspaper, etc.) for public sale 2 make generally known [L, rel. to PUBLIC]

pub′lish·er *n.* person or (esp.) company that publishes books, etc., for sale

Puc·ci·ni /pōōchē′nē/, **Giacomo** 1858–1924; Italian operatic composer

puce /pyōōs/ *adj. & n.* dark red or purple-brown [L *pulex* flea]

puck¹ /pək/ *n.* hard rubber disk used in ice hockey

puck² *n.* mischievous or evil sprite —**puck′ish** *adj.*; **puck′ish·ly** *adv.*; **puck′ish·ness** *n.* [OE]

puck·er /pək′ər/ *v.* 1 gather into wrinkles,

folds, or bulges —*n.* 2 such a wrinkle, fold, etc.

pud·ding /pōōd′ing/ *n.* any of various flavored desserts with a consistency of thickened cream [ME *poding* sausage]

pud·dle /pəd′l/ *n.* small pool, esp. of rain-water [OE]

pu·den·dum /pyōōden′dəm/ *n.* (*pl.* **·da** /-də/) (usu. *pl.*) genitals, esp. of a woman [L *pudere* be ashamed]

pudg·y /pəj′ē/ *adj.* (·**i·er**, ·**i·est**) (esp. of a person) short and fat —**pudg′i·ness** *n.*

Pue·bla /pweb′lä/ *n.* state in E central Mexico. Capital: Puebla. Pop. 4,126,100

pueb·lo /pweb′lō/ *n.* communal dwelling, often terraced, multi-storied, and of adobe, built by American Indians of the southwestern U.S. [Sp fr. L *populus* people]

Pueb·lo /p(y)ōō-eb′lō, pweb′lō/ *n.* city in Colo. Pop. 98,640

pu·er·ile /pyōō′ərəl, -rīl′/ *adj.* childish; immature —**pu′er·il′i·ty** /-il′itē/ *n.* (*pl.* **·ties**) [L *puer* boy]

Puer·to Ri·co /pôrt′ə rē′kō, pwer′tō/ *n.* self-governing island commonwealth of the US in the Caribbean Sea. Capital: San Juan. Pop. 3,522,037. Abbr. **PR**, **P.R.** —**Puer′to Ri′can** /-kan/ *n. & adj.*

Puer′to Ri′co Trench′ *n.* ocean depression N of Puerto Rico; deepest part of the Atlantic: 28,374 ft.

puff /pəf/ *n.* 1a short quick blast of breath, wind, vapor, etc. **b** sound of or like this 2 light pastry cake containing jam, cream, etc. 3 draw of smoke from a cigarette, etc. 4 extravagantly enthusiastic review, advertisement, etc. 5 POWDER PUFF —*v.* 6 emit a puff of air or breath; blow with short blasts 7 draw in and exhale (cigarette smoke, etc.) 8 breathe hard; pant 9 inflate; swell (*his eye was puffed up*) 10 (foll. by *up*) elate; make proud or boastful 11 promote in an exaggerated way [imit.]

puff′ball′ *n.* ball-shaped fungus emitting clouds of spores

puf·fin /pəf′in/ *n.* northern sea bird with a short neck and brightly colored triangular bill

puff′ pas′try *n.* multilayered pastry dough that puffs when baked

puff′y *adj.* (·**i·er**, ·**i·est**) swollen; puffed out —**puff′i·ness** *n.*

pug /pəg/ *n.* dog of a dwarf breed with a broad flat nose and wrinkled face

Pu·get Sound /pyōō′jit/ *n.* inlet of the Pacific Ocean in NW Wash.

pu·gil·ist /pyōō′jəlist/ *n.* boxer —**pu′gi·lism′** /-iz′əm/ *n.*; **pu·gil·is′tic** *adj.* [L *pugil* boxer]

pug·na·cious /pəgnā′shəs/ *adj.* quarrelsome; eager to fight —**pug·na′cious·ly** *adv.*; **pug·nac′i·ty** /-nas′ətē/ *n.* [L *pugnax -acis* fr. *pugnare* fight]

pug′ nose′ *n.* short squat or snub nose —**pug′ nosed′** *adj.*

puke /pyōōk/ *v. & n.* (**puked, puk·ing**) *Slang.* vomit [imit.]

Pu·las·ki /pəlas′kē, pyōō-/, (**Count**) **Casimir** c. 1748–79; Polish general in the American Revolutionary army

pul·chri·tude /pəl′krit(y)ōōd′/ *n.* beauty —**pul′chri·tu′di·nous** /-dənəs/ *adj.* [L *pulcher* beautiful]

pule /pyo͞ol/ v. (**puled, pul·ing**) cry whiningly or weakly; whimper [imit.]

Pu·litz·er /po͞ol'ətsər, pyo͞o'lət-/, Joseph 1847–1911; Hungarian-born US newspaper publisher; established Pulitzer Prizes

pull /po͞ol/ v. **1** exert force upon (a thing, person, etc.) to move it to oneself or the origin of the force **2** exert force to draw or attract **3** extract; pluck out **4** damage (a muscle, etc.) by abnormal strain **5** bring out (a weapon) **6** tear or pluck (at) **7** inhale or drink deeply; draw or suck (on a pipe, etc.) **8** remove (a plant) by the root —n. **9** act of pulling **10** force exerted by this **11** influence; advantage **12** attraction or attention-getter **13** suck at a cigarette, etc. **14** **pull back** retreat **15** **pull in: a** (of a bus, train, etc.) arrive to take passengers **b** (of a vehicle) arrive or come to a halt **c** Colloq. earn or acquire **d** Colloq. arrest **16** **pull a person's leg** deceive playfully **17** **pull off: a** remove by pulling **b** succeed in achieving or winning **18** **pull out: a** take out by pulling **b** depart **c** withdraw from an undertaking **d** (of a bus, train, etc.) leave a station, stop, etc. **e** (of a vehicle) move into the road and accelerate **19** **pull over** (of a vehicle) drive off or direct to drive off the road and stop **20** **pull one's punches** avoid using one's full force **21** **pull the plug on** put an end to (by withdrawing resources, etc.) **22** **pull strings** exert (esp. clandestine) influence **23** **pull together: a** work in harmony **b** assemble; make **24** **pull up** (cause to) stop moving **25** **pull one's weight** do one's fair share of work [OE]

pul·let /po͞ol'it/ n. young hen, esp. one less than one year old [L pullus]

pul·ley /po͞ol'ē/ n. grooved wheel or wheels for a cord, etc., to pass over and used for changing the direction of or transmitting force [Fr polie, rel. to POLE²]

Pull·man /po͞ol'mən/ n. (pl. **-mans**) railroad sleeping car [for its designer]

pull·o·ver n. garment put on over the head and covering the top half of the body

pul·mo·nar·y /po͞ol'məner'ē/ adj. pertaining to the lungs [L pulmo -onis lung]

pulp /pəlp/ n. **1** soft fleshy part of fruit, etc. **2** soft thick wet material from wood, rags, etc., used in paper making —v. **3** reduce to or become pulp —**pulp'y** adj.; **pulp'i·ness** n. [L]

pul·pit /po͞ol'pit, pəl-/ n. **1** platform at the front of a church for preaching, etc. **2** (prec. by the) preachers collectively; preaching [L pulpitum platform]

pul·sar /pəl'sär'/ n. cosmic source of regular rapid pulses of radiation, e.g., a rotating neutron star [fr. pulsating star, after quasar]

pul·sate /pəl'sāt'/ v. (**·sat·ed, ·sat·ing**) **1** expand and contract rhythmically; throb **2** vibrate; quiver —**pul·sa'tion** n. [L, rel. to PULSE]

pulse /pəls/ n. **1a** rhythmical arterial throbbing, esp. in the wrists, temples, etc. **b** each beat of the arteries or heart **2** throb or thrill of life or emotion **3** general feeling or opinion **4** single burst of sound, light, etc. **5** rhythmical beat, esp. of music —v. (**pulsed, puls·ing**) **6** pulsate [L pellere puls-; beat, beat]

pul·ver·ize /pəl'vəriz'/ v. (**·ized, ·iz·ing**) **1** reduce or crumble to fine particles or dust **2**

Colloq. demolish; defeat utterly —**pul'ver·i·za'tion** n. [L pulvis -ver- dust]

pu·ma /p(y)o͞o'mə, po͞o-/ n. COUGAR

pum·ice /pəm'is/ n. (also **pum'ice stone**) **1** light porous volcanic rock used in cleaning or polishing **2** piece of this used for removing hard skin, etc. [L pumex pumic-]

pum·mel /pəm'əl/ v. (**·meled** or **·melled**, **·mel·ing** or **·mel·ling**) strike repeatedly, esp. with the fists [fr. POMMEL]

pump¹ /pəmp/ n. **1** machine or device for raising or moving liquids, compressing gases, inflating tires, etc. —v. **2** raise or remove (liquid, gas, etc.) with a pump **3** (often foll. by up) fill (a tire, etc.) with air **4** work a pump **5** persistently question (a person) to obtain information **6** move vigorously up and down **7** **pump iron** exercise with weights

pump² n. low-cut shoe without ties, straps, etc.

pum·per·nick·el /pəm'pərnik'əl/ n. type of dark rye bread [Ger]

pump·kin /pəmp'kin/ n. rounded yellow or orange gourdlike fruit [Gk pepōn melon]

pun /pən/ n. **1** humorous use of a word or words with two or more meanings; play on words —v. (**punned, pun·ning**) **2** make a pun or puns —**pun'ster** /-stər/ n.

punch¹ /pənCH/ v. **1** strike, esp. with a closed fist **2a** pierce a hole in (metal, paper, etc.) as or with a punch **b** pierce (a hole) thus —n. **3** blow with a fist **4** vigor; momentum **5** tool or machine for punching holes or impressing a design in leather, metal, etc. [var. of pounce emboss]

punch² n. drink of mixed juices, spices, etc., often with wine or liquor added

punch-drunk adj. stupefied from or as if from punches to the head

punch line n. words giving the point of a joke or story

punch·y adj. (**·i·er, ·i·est**) **1** vigorous; forceful **2** PUNCH-DRUNK

punc·til·i·o /pəngk'til'ē·ō'/ n. (pl. **-os**) delicate point of ceremony or etiquette [It and Sp, rel. to POINT]

punc·til·i·ous /pəngk'til'ēəs/ adj. **1** attentive to formality or etiquette **2** precise in behavior —**punc·til'i·ous·ly** adv.; **punc·til'i·ous·ness** n. [It, rel. to PUNCTILIO]

punc·tu·al /pəngk'CHo͞oəl/ adj. keeping to the appointed time; prompt —**punc·tu·al'i·ty** /-al'itē/ n.; **punc·tu·al·ly** adv. [MedL, rel. to POINT]

punc·tu·ate /pəngk'CHo͞o·āt'/ v. (**·at·ed, ·at·ing**) **1** insert punctuation marks in **2** interrupt at intervals (as with applause) **3** pause, gesture, etc., for emphasis [MedL, rel. to PUNCTUAL]

punc·tu·a'tion n. **1** system of marks used to punctuate a written passage **2** use of, or skill in using, these

punc·tu·a'tion mark n. any of the marks (e.g., period and comma) used in writing to separate sentences, etc., and clarify meaning

punc·ture /pəngk'CHər/ n. **1** piercing, as of a tire **2** hole made in this way —v. (**·tured, ·tur·ing**) **3** make or undergo a puncture (in) **4** prick, pierce, or deflate (pomposity, etc.) [L punctura, rel. to POINT]

pun·dit /ˈpən'dit/ n. expert authority or commentator —**pun'dit·ry** n. [Hindustani fr. Skt]

pun·gent /ˈpən'jənt/ adj. 1 sharp or strong in taste or smell 2 (of remarks) biting; caustic —**pun'gen·cy** n. [L, rel. to POINT]

pun·ish /ˈpən'ish/ v. 1 inflict retribution on (an offender) or for (an offense) 2 hurt, abuse, or treat severely or improperly —**pun'ish·a·ble, pun'ish·ing** adj. [L punīre]

pun'ish·ment n. 1 punishing or being punished 2 loss or suffering inflicted in this 3 severe treatment or suffering

pu·ni·tive /ˈpyoo'nitiv/ adj. inflicting or intended to inflict punishment [Fr or MedL, rel. to PUNISH]

punk /pəNGk/ n. 1 Derog. Slang. inferior or insignificant person 2 Slang. young person, esp. one regarded as malicious 3a (in full **punk' rock'**) anti-establishment and deliberately outrageous style of rock music b (in full **punk' rock'er**) devotee of this

punt[1] /pənt/ v. 1 kick (a football) after it has dropped from the hands and before it reaches the ground —n. 2 such a kick

punt[2] n. 1 square-ended flat-bottomed pleasure boat propelled by a long pole —v. 2 propel (a punt) with a pole 3 go or carry in a punt [LGer or Du]

pu·ny /ˈpyoo'nē/ adj. (·ni·er, ·ni·est) 1 undersized 2 weak; feeble [Fr puisné born afterwards]

pup /pəp/ n. young dog, wolf, rat, seal, etc. [fr. PUPPY]

pu·pa /ˈpyoo'pə/ n. (pl. ·pae /-pē/) insect in the stage between larva and adult forms —**pu'pal** adj. [L: doll]

pu·pil[1] /ˈpyoo'pəl/ n. person taught by another [L dim. pupillus, ·illa fr. pupus boy, pupa girl]

pu·pil[2] n. dark opening in the center of the iris of the eye [rel. to PUPIL[1]]

pup·pet /ˈpəp'it/ n. 1 small figure controlled by hands or by strings as entertainment 2 person controlled by another —**pup'pet·ry** n. [ult. fr. L pupa doll]

pup·py /ˈpəp'ē/ n. (pl. ·pies) 1 young dog 2 conceited or arrogant young man [Fr, rel. to PUPPET]

pup'py love' n. infatuation, esp. among adolescents

pup' tent' n. small tent for one or two persons, as for camping

pur·blind /ˈpər'blīnd'/ adj. 1 partly blind; dim-sighted 2 obtuse; dimwitted —**pur'blind'ness** n. [fr. pur(e) ('utterly') blind]

pur·chase /ˈpər'CHəs/ v. (·chased, ·chas·ing) 1 buy 2 obtain or achieve at some cost —n. 3 buying 4 thing bought 5 firm hold to prevent slipping; leverage —**pur'chas·er** n. [AngFr, rel. to PRO-[1], CHASE, 1]

pure /pyoor/ adj. 1 unmixed; unadulterated 2 chaste 3 not morally corrupt 4 guiltless 5 (of a subject of study) abstract, not applied —**pure'ness** n. [L pūrus]

pu·rée /ˈpyoorā', -rē/ (also **pu·ree**) n. 1 smooth pulp of vegetables, fruit, etc. —v. 2 make a purée of [Fr]

pure'ly adv. 1 in a pure manner 2 merely; solely; exclusively

pur·ga·tive /ˈpər'gətiv/ adj. 1 serving to purify 2 strongly laxative —n. 3 purgative thing 4 laxative [L, rel. to PURGE]

pur·ga·to·ry /ˈpər'gətôr'ē/ n. (pl. ·ries) 1 RC Ch. supposed place or state of expiation of sins after death and before entering heaven 2 place or state of temporary suffering or expiation —adj. 3 purifying —**pur'ga·to'ri·al** adj. [MedL, rel. to PURGE]

purge /pərj/ v. (purged, purg·ing) 1 make physically or spiritually clean 2 remove by cleansing 3 rid (an organization, party, etc.) of unacceptable members 4 empty (the bowels) —n. 5 act of purging 6 purgative [L purgāre purify]

pu·ri·fy /ˈpyoor'əfī'/ v. (·fied, ·fy·ing) 1 clear of extraneous elements; make pure 2 make ceremonially pure or clean —**pu'ri·fi·ca'tion** /-fikā'SHən/ n.

pu·rist /ˈpyoor'ist/ n. advocate of scrupulous purity, esp. in language or art —**pur'ism** /-izəm/ n.; **pu·ris'tic** adj.

pu·ri·tan /ˈpyoor'ət-n/ n. 1 (cap.) Hist. member of a group of English Protestants who sought to simplify and regulate forms of worship 2 strict observer of religion or morals —adj. 3 (cap.) Hist. of the Puritans 4 scrupulous and austere in religion or morals —**pu'ri·tan·ism'** n. [L, rel. to PURE]

pu·ri·tan·i·cal /ˌpyoo'ri'tan'ikəl/ adj. strictly religious or moral in behavior —**pu·ri·tan'i·cal·ly** adv.

pu·ri·ty /ˈpyoor'itē/ n. pureness; cleanness

purl[1] /pərl/ n. 1 type of inverted knitting stitch 2 chain of minute loops decorating the edges of lace, etc. —v. 3 knit with a purl stitch

purl[2] v. (of a brook, etc.) flow with a babbling sound

pur·loin /pərˈloin'/ v. steal; pilfer [AngFr purloigner fr. loign far]

pur·ple /ˈpər'pəl/ n. 1 color combining red and blue 2 purple robe, esp. as a mark of royalty 3 (prec. by the) position of rank, authority, or privilege —adj. 4 of a purple color [Gk porphura, a shellfish yielding dye]

pur'ple pas'sage' n. (also **Brit. pur'ple patch'**) ornate or elaborate literary passage

pur·port v. /pərˈpôrt'/ 1 profess; claim (purports to be an officer) 2 (of a document or speech) have as its meaning; state —n. /ˈpər'pôrt'/ 3 ostensible intent or meaning —**pur·port'ed·ly** adv. [L, rel. to PRO-[1], portare carry]

pur·pose /ˈpər'pəs/ n. 1 object to be attained; thing intended 2 intention to act 3 resolution; determination —v. (·posed, ·pos·ing) 4 intend; plan 5 on purpose intentionally 6 to no purpose with no result or effect [L proponere PROPOSE]

pur·pose·ful /ˈpər'pəsfəl/ adj. 1 having or indicating purpose 2 intentional 3 resolute —**pur'pose·ful·ly** adv.; **pur'pose·ful·ness** n.

pur'pose·less adj. having no aim or plan

pur'pose·ly adv. on purpose

pur·pos·ive /ˈpər'pəsiv/ adj. 1 having, serving, or done with a purpose 2 purposeful; resolute

purr /pər/ v. 1 (as of a cat) make a low vibratory sound expressing contentment 2 (of machinery, etc.) run smoothly and quietly —n. 3 purring sound [imit.]

purse /pərs/ n. 1 small pouch for carrying

money on the person **2** handbag **3** money; funds **4** sum as a present or prize in a contest —*v.* (**pursed, purs·ing**) **5** pucker or contract (the lips, etc.) **6 hold the purse strings** have control of expenditure [Gk *bursa* hide]

purs·er /pərs´əs/ *n.* ship's officer who keeps accounts, secures valuables, etc.

pur·su·ance /pərsōō´əns/ *n.* carrying out or observance (of a plan, idea, etc.)

pur·su·ant /pərsōō´ənt/ *adv.* (foll. by *to*) esp. *Law.* in accordance with [Fr, rel. to PURSUE]

pur·sue /pərsōō´/ *v.* (**·sued, ·su·ing**) **1** follow with intent to overtake, capture, or do harm to **2** continue or proceed by (a route, plan, or course of action) **3** follow or engage in (study or other activity) **4** seek after; aim at **5** continue to investigate or discuss (a topic) **6** importune (a person) persistently —**pur·su´er** *n.* [L *sequi* follow]

pur·suit /pərsōōt´/ *n.* **1** act of pursuing **2** occupation or activity pursued **3 in pursuit** of pursuing [Fr, rel. to SUIT]

pu·ru·lent /pyŏŏr´(y)ələnt/ *adj.* of, containing, or discharging pus —**pu´ru·lence** *n.* [L, rel. to PUS]

pur·vey /pərvā´/ *v.* provide or supply (food, etc.) —**pur·vey´ance, pur·vey´or** *n.* [L, rel. to PROVIDE]

pur·view /pər´vyōō/ *n.* **1** scope or range of a document, scheme, etc. **2** range of physical or mental vision [AngFr past part., rel. to PURVEY]

pus /pəs/ *n.* thick yellowish liquid produced by infected tissue [L *pus puris*]

Pu·san /pōō´sän´/ *n.* seaport in South Korea. Pop. 3,797,600

push /pŏŏSH/ *v.* **1** exert a force on (a thing) to move it or cause it to move away **2** exert such a force (*do not push*) **3a** thrust forward or upward **b** (cause to) project (*pushes out new roots*) **4** move forward or make (one's way) by force or persistence **5** exert oneself, esp. to surpass others **6** urge, impel, or press (a person) hard **7** pursue or demand persistently (*pushed for change*) **8** promote **9** *Slang.* sell (a drug) illegally —*n.* **10** act of pushing; shove; thrust **11** force exerted in this **12** vigorous effort **13** enterprise; ambition **14 push around** bully **15 push one's luck: a** take undue risks **b** act presumptuously [L, rel. to PULSATE]

push´ but´ton *n.* button to be pushed, esp. to operate an electrical device

push´er *n.* **1** person or thing that pushes or for pushing **2** *Slang.* seller of illegal drugs

push´ing *adj.* **1** pushy **2** *Colloq.* having nearly reached (a specified age)

Push·kin /pŏŏSH´kin/, **Alexander** 1799–1837; Russian writer; first national poet of Russia

push´o´ver *n. Colloq.* **1** something easily done **2** person easily persuaded, defeated, etc.

push-up /pŏŏSH´əp´/ *n.* exercise of raising one's body, in prone position, by straightening the arms, with palms and knees or toes on the ground

push´y *adj.* (**·i·er, ·i·est**) *Colloq.* excessively persistent —**push´i·ly** *adv.*; **push´i·ness** *n.*

pu·sil·lan·i·mous /pyōō´sələn´iməs/ *adj.* cowardly; timid —**pu·sil·la·nim´i·ty** /-lənim´ ətē/ *n.* [L *pusillus* very small, *animus* mind]

puss /pŏŏs/ *n. Slang.* **1** face **2** mouth [LGer or Du]

puss·y /pŏŏs´ē/ *n.* (*pl.* **·ies**) (also **puss, puss´y·cat´**) cat

puss´y·foot´ *v. Colloq.* **1** move stealthily **2** equivocate; stall

puss´y wil´low *n.* willow with furry catkins

pus·tule /pəs´CHŌŏl´/ *n.* pimple or blister containing pus —**pus´tu·lar** /-CHələr/ *adj.*; **pus´tu·late** /-CHələt/ *v.* (**·lat·ed, ·lat·ing**) [L *pustula*]

put /pŏŏt/ *v.* (**put, put·ting**) **1** move to or cause to be in a specified place or position **2** bring into a specified condition or state **3** impose, enforce, assign, or apply (*put a tax on beer; put it to good use*) **4** place (a person) or imagine (oneself) in a specified position (*put them at their ease*) **5** express in a specified way **6** (foll. by *at*) state (an amount, etc.) **7** (foll. by *in, into*) express or translate (words, or another language) **8** invest **9** (foll. by *on*) wager **10** submit for attention (*put it to a vote*) **11** throw (esp. a shot or weight) as a sport **12** (of a ship, etc.) proceed in a specified direction —*n.* **13** throw of the shot **14** option to sell stock at a fixed price **15 put across** communicate (an idea, etc.) effectively **16 put away: a** (also put by) store; save **b** consume (food and drink), esp. in large quantities **17 put down: a** suppress by force **b** snub; humiliate **c** record or enter in writing **d** enter the name of (a person) on a list **e** (foll. by *to*) attribute (*put it down to bad planning*) **f** put (an old or sick animal) to death **g** pay as a deposit **18 put off: a** postpone **b** evade (a person) **c** hinder; dissuade **d** offend; disconcert **19 put on: a** clothe oneself with **b** stage (a play, show, etc.) **c** pretend to (an emotion) **d** attempt to trick **e** increase one's weight by (a specified amount) **f** make (one) aware of (*put us on to their new accountant*) **20 put out: a** disconcert or annoy **b** inconvenience (*don't put yourself out*) **c** extinguish (a fire or light) **21 put up: a** build; erect **b** provide with accommodation (*put me up for the night*) **c** engage in (a defensive fight, struggle, etc.) **d** offer **e** provide (money) as a backer **f** display (a notice) **22 put upon** take advantage of (a person) unfairly or excessively **23 put up with** endure; tolerate [OE]

pu·ta·tive /pyōō´tətiv/ *adj.* reputed; supposed [L *putare* think]

put´-down´ *n. Colloq.* belittling remark or act

put´-on´ *n. Colloq.* deception or hoax

pu·tre·fy /pyōō´trəfī´/ *v.* (**·fied, ·fy·ing**) become or make putrid or rotten —**pu´tre·fac´tion** /-fak´SHən/ *n.*; **pu´tre·fac´tive** /-tiv/ *adj.* [L *puter putris* rotten]

pu·tres·cent /pyōō´tres´ənt/ *adj.* rotting —**pu·tres´cence** *n.* [L, rel. to PUTRID]

pu·trid /pyōō´trid/ *adj.* **1** decomposed; rotten **2** foul; noxious [L *putrere* rot (v.)]

putsch /pŏŏCH/ *n.* sudden revolution; violent uprising [Swiss Ger]

putt /pət/ *v.* **1** strike (a golf ball) gently on a putting green. —*n.* **2** putting stroke —**putt´ er** *n.* [fr. PUT]

put·tee /pə´tē´/ *n. Hist.* strip of cloth wound around the leg from ankle to knee, worn esp. by soldiers [Hindi]

put·ter /pət'ər/ v. 1 work or occupy oneself in an aimless manner 2 go slowly; dawdle [dial. *pote* push]

put·ty /pət'ē/ n. soft, pliable mixture used for fixing panes of glass, filling holes, etc. —v. (·ties, ·tied) 2 cover, fix, join, or fill with putty [Fr *potée*, rel. to POT]

puz·zle /pəz'əl/ n. 1 difficult or confusing problem 2 problem or toy designed to test knowledge or ingenuity —v. (·zled, ·zling) 3 confound or disconcert mentally 4 be perplexed (over) 5 require much mental effort —puz'zle·ment, puz'zler n.

pvt. or **Pvt.** abbr. private

PX abbr. post exchange

pyg·my /pig'mē/ n. (also **pig'my**) (pl. ·mies) 1 (cap.) member of a dwarf people of esp. equatorial Africa 2 very small person, animal, or thing [L fr. Gk]

py·lon /pī'län/ n. tall towerlike structure for supporting electric power cables, etc. [Gk *pulē* gate]

Pyong·yang /pyôNG'yäNG'/ n. capital of N Korea. Pop. 2,355,000

py·or·rhe·a /pī'ərē'ə/ n. gum disease causing loosening of the teeth and discharge of pus [Gk *puon* pus, *rheein* flow]

PYRAMID 1

pyr·a·mid /pir'əmid/ n. 1 monumental, esp. stone, structure with a square base and slop-ing triangular sides meeting at an apex, esp. an ancient Egyptian royal tomb 2 Geom. solid with a square or triangular base and triangular sides that have a common vertex —py·ram·i·dal /piram'id'l/ adj. [Gk *puramis* ·mid-]

pyre /pīr/ n. heap of combustible material, esp. for burning a corpse [Gk, rel. to PYRO-]

Pyr·e·nees /pěr'ənēz'/ n. mountain range between Spain and France

Py·rex /pī'reks/ n. Tdmk. hard heat-resistant glass, used esp. for ovenware [invented word]

py·rite /pī'rīt/ (also **py·rites**) n. lustrous yellow mineral that is a sulphide of iron [Gk, rel. to PYRE]

pyro- comb. form 1 denoting fire 2 denoting a mineral, etc., altered by heat or fiery in color [Gk *pur* fire]

py·ro·ma·ni·a /pī'rōmā'nēə/ n. obsessive desire to start fires —py'ro·ma'ni·ac /·nēak/ n. & adj.

py·ro·tech·nics /pī'rōtek'niks/ n. pl. 1 art of making fireworks 2 display of fireworks 3 any brilliant display —py'ro·tech'nic adj.

pyr·rhic /pir'ik/ adj. (of a victory) won at too great a cost [for *Pyrrhus* of Epirus, who defeated the Romans in 279 B.C., but suffered heavy losses]

Py·thag·o·ras /pəTHag'(ə)rəs, pī-/ fl. late 6th cent. B.C.; Greek philosopher

Py·thag·o·re·an the·o·rem /pǐTHag'ərē'ən/ n. theorem that the square of the hypotenuse of a right-angled triangle is equal to the sum of the squares of the other two sides [for PYTHAGORAS]

py·thon /pī'THän', -THən/ n. large tropical constricting snake [Gk *Puthōn*, name of a monster]

pyx /piks/ n. vessel for the consecrated bread of the Eucharist [Gk *puxis* BOX[1]]

Q

q, Q /kyōō/ n. (pl. q's; Q's, Qs) seventeenth letter of the English alphabet; a consonant

q or **q.** abbr. 1 Brit. Hist. farthing [L *quadrans*] 2 quarterly 3 quart(s) 4 query 5 question 6 quire

Q or **Q.** abbr. 1 Quebec 2 Queen

Qa·dha·fi /kədäf'ē, -daf'-/ (also **Gaddafi**), **Muammar (Muhammad)** al- 1942– ; Libyan chief of state (1969–)

Qa·tar /kät'ər, gət'ər/ n. emirate on the Persian Gulf. Capital: Doha. Pop. 520,000 —**Qa·tar'i** n. & adj.

qb abbr. quarterback

QED abbr. which was to be proved [L *quod erat demonstrandum*]

Qing·dao /CHiNG'dou'/ n. (also **Tsingtao**) seaport in E China. Pop. 1,459,200

Qom /kōm/ n. city in NW Iran on the Qom River; Islamic holy site. Pop. 543,100

qt. abbr. quart(s)

Q'-tip' n. Tdmk. double-ended cotton swab on a thin stick

qty. abbr. quantity

qua /kwä, kwä/ conj. in the function of; as [L]

quack[1] /kwak/ n. 1 harsh sound made by ducks —v. 2 utter this sound [imit.]

quack[2] n. unqualified practitioner, esp. of medicine —**quack'er·y** n. [abbr. of *quacksalver* fr. Du, prob. rel. to QUACK[1], SALVE, 1]

quad /kwäd/ n. 1 quadrangle 2 quadrant [abbr.]

quad·ran·gle /kwäd'raNG'gəl/ n. 1 four-sided plane figure, esp. a square or rectangle 2 four-sided courtyard —**quad·ran'gu·lar** /-gyələr/ adj. [L, rel. to QUADRI-, ANGLE[1]]

quad·rant /kwäd'rənt/ n. 1 quarter of a circle's circumference 2 quarter of a circle enclosed by two radii at right angles 3 Naut. instrument for measuring angular elevation [L *quadrans* ·ant-]

qua·drat·ic /kwädrat'ik/ adj. Math. involving the square (and no higher power) of an unknown quantity or variable (*quadratic equation*)

quadri- comb. form four [fr. L *quattuor* four]

quad·ri·ceps /kwäd'rəseps/ n. four-headed

muscle, as at the front of the thigh [QUADRI-, (BI)CEPS]

quad·ri·lat·er·al /kwäd′rəlat′ərəl/ *adj.* 1 having four sides —*n.* 2 four-sided figure

QUADRILATERALS 2

qua·drille /kwädril′/ *n.* 1 a kind of square dance 2 music for this [Fr]

quad·ri·ple·gia /kwäd′riplē′jə/ *n.* paralysis of all four limbs —**quad′ri·ple′gic** /-jik/ *adj.* & *n.* [QUADRI-, Gk *plēgē* a blow]

quad·ru·ped /kwäd′rəped/ *n.* four-footed animal, esp. a mammal [L, rel. to QUADRI-, *pes ped*-foot]

qua·dru·ple /kwädrōō′pəl, -drəp′əl/ *adj.* 1 fourfold; having four parts —*n.* 2 fourfold number or amount —*v.* (**·pled, ·pling**) 3 multiply by four [L, rel. to QUADRI-]

qua·dru·plet /kwädrōō′plit, -drəp′lit/ *n.* each of four children born at one birth

qua·dru·pli·cate —*adj.* /kwädrōō′plikət/ 1 fourfold 2 of which four copies are made —*v.* /-pləkāt/ (**·cat·ed, ·cat·ing**) 3 multiply by four

quag·mire /kwag′mīr, kwäg′-/ *n.* 1 muddy or boggy area 2 hazardous situation [fr. *quag* bog + MIRE]

quail[1] /kwāl/ *n.* (*pl.* same or **·s**) small game bird related to the partridge [Fr *quaille*]

quail[2] *v.* flinch; show fear

quaint /kwänt/ *adj.* attractively odd or old-fashioned —**quaint′ly** *adv.*; **quaint′ness** *n.* [Fr *cointe* fr. L *cognoscere* ascertain]

quake /kwāk/ *v.* (**quaked, quak·ing**) 1 shake; tremble —*n.* 2 earthquake [OE]

Quak·er /kwāk′ər/ *n.* member of the Society of Friends —**Quak′er·ism** /-iz′em/ *n.*

qual·i·fi·ca·tion /kwäl′ifikā′SHən/ *n.* 1 skill or accomplishment fitting a person for a position or purpose 2 thing that modifies or limits 3 qualifying or being qualified [Fr or MedL, rel. to QUALIFY]

qual·i·fy /kwäl′əfī′/ *v.* (**·fied, ·fy·ing**) 1 make competent or fit for a position or purpose 2 make legally entitled 3 satisfy conditions or requirements 4 modify or limit (a statement, etc.) (*qualified approval*) —**qual′i·fi′er** *n.* [L *qualis* of what kind, -FY]

qual·i·ta·tive /kwäl′ətā′tiv/ *adj.* of quality or qualities —**qual′i·ta′tive·ly** *adv.* [L, rel. to QUALITY]

qual·i·ty /kwäl′ətē/ *n.* (*pl.* **·ties**) 1 degree of excellence 2 general excellence 3 attribute; faculty 4 nature or characteristic [L *qualis* of what kind]

qual′i·ty con·trol′ *n.* methodology for maintaining standards in products or services

qual′i·ty time′ *n.* periods of usu. limited duration devoted to close interaction, as with one's family

qualm /kwä(l)m/ *n.* 1 misgiving 2 scruple of conscience 3 momentary faint or sick feeling

471 **quadrilateral / quarterly**

quan·da·ry /kwän′d(ə)rē/ *n.* (*pl.* **·ries**) 1 perplexed state 2 practical dilemma

quan·ta /kwän′tə/ *n. pl.* of QUANTUM

quan·ti·fy /kwänt′əfī′/ *v.* (**·fied, ·fy·ing**) 1 determine the quantity of 2 express as a quantity —**quan′ti·fi′a·ble** *adj.*; **quan′ti·fi·ca′tion** /-fikā′SHən/ *n.* [MedL, rel. to QUANTITY]

quan·ti·ta·tive /kwän′tətā′tiv/ *adj.* pertaining to quantity

quan·ti·ty /kwän′tətē/ *n.* (*pl.* **·ties**) 1 property of things that is measurable 2 amount; number 3 specified portion, number, or amount 4 (*pl.*) large amounts or numbers 5 *Math.* value, component, etc., that may be expressed in numbers [L *quantus* how much]

quan·tum /kwän′təm/ *n.* (*pl.* **·ta** /-tə/) 1 *Physics.* discrete amount of radiant energy 2 a required or allowed amount [L *quantus* how much]

quan′tum jump′ *n.* (also **quan′tum leap′**) 1 sudden large increase or advance 2 *Physics.* abrupt transition in an atom or molecule from one quantum state to another

quan′tum me·chan′ics *n. pl.* (also **quan′tum the′o·ry**) *Physics.* theory of molecular and atomic motion and energy

quar·an·tine /kwôr′əntēn, kwär′-/ *n.* 1 isolation imposed on persons or animals to prevent infection or contagion 2 period of this —*v.* (**·tined, ·tin·ing**) 3 put in quarantine [It *quaranta* forty]

quark /kwôrk, kwärk/ *n. Physics.* hypothetical subatomic particle [fr. word in J. Joyce's *Finnegans Wake*]

quar·rel /kwôr′əl, kwär′-/ *n.* 1 severe or angry dispute 2 cause of complaint or dispute —*v.* (**·reled** or **·relled, ·rel·ing** or **·rel·ling**) 3 find fault 4 dispute; break off friendly relations [L *querela* fr. *queri* complain]

quar·rel·some /kwôr′əlsəm, kwär′-/ *adj.* given to quarreling

quar·ry[1] /kwôr′ē, kwär′ē/ *n.* (*pl.* **·ries**) 1 place from which stone, etc., may be extracted —*v.* (**·ried, ·ry·ing**) 2 extract (stone) from a quarry [L *quadrum* square]

quar·ry[2] *n.* (*pl.* **·ries**) 1 intended victim or prey 2 object of pursuit [L *cor* heart]

quart /kwôrt/ *n.* 1 liquid measure equal to 1/4 of a gallon 2 dry measure equal to 1/8 of a peck [L *quartus* fourth]

quar·ter /kwôr′tər/ *n.* 1 each of four equal parts into which a thing is divided 2 period of three months 3a 25 US or Canadian cents b coin for this 4 district or section 5 source of supply (*help from any quarter*) 6 (*pl.*) a lodgings b accommodations for troops, etc. 7 mercy toward an enemy, etc., on condition of surrender —*v.* 8 divide into quarters 9 provide with lodgings [L *quartarius*, rel. to QUART]

quar′ter·back′ *n.* player in football who directs offensive play

quar′ter·deck′ *n.* part of a ship's upper deck near the stern

quar′ter·fi′nal *n. Sports.* match or round preceding the semifinal

quar′ter horse′ *n.* muscular horse notable for its swiftness in quarter-mile races

quar′ter·ly *adj.* 1 produced or occurring once

every quarter of a year —*adv.* 2 once every quarter of a year —*n.* (*pl.* ·lies) 3 quarterly journal

quar′ter·mas′ter *n.* 1 military officer in charge of quartering, rations, etc. 2 naval petty officer in charge of steering, signals, etc.

quar·tet /kwôrtet′/ *n.* 1 *Mus.* a composition for four performers **b** the performers 2 any group of four [L *quartus*]

quar·to /kwô′rtō/ *n.* (*pl.* ·tos) 1 size of a book or page (approx. 9 by 12 in.) made from a printed sheet folded twice to form four leaves 2 book of this size [L, rel. to QUART]

quartz /kwôrts/ *n.* silica in various crystalline forms [Ger fr. Slavonic]

qua·sar /kwā′zär′/ *n. Astron.* remote starlike object that emits radio waves and light [fr. quasi-stellar]

quash /kwäSH, kwôSH/ *v.* 1 reject as invalid, esp. by a legal procedure 2 suppress; crush [Fr *quasser* fr. L]

quasi- *comb. form* 1 seemingly; not really 2 almost [L *quasi* as if]

qua·ter·na·ry /kwät′ərner′ē, kwətər′nərē/ *adj.* 1 having four parts 2 (*cap.*) *Geol.* of the most recent period in the Cenozoic era —*n.* 3 (*cap.*) *Geol.* this period [L *quaterni* four each]

quat·rain /kwä′trān′/ *n.* four-line stanza [Fr *quatre* four]

qua·ver /kwā′vər/ *v.* 1 (esp. of a voice or sound) vibrate; shake; tremble 2 sing or say with a quavering voice —*n.* 3 trembling quality in speech, singing, etc. —**qua′ver·y** *adj.* [prob. imit.]

quay /kē, kā/ *n.* artificial landing place for loading and unloading ships [Fr]

quea·sy /kwē′zē/ *adj.* (·si·er, ·si·est) 1a (of a person) affected by nausea **b** (of the stomach) easily upset 2 (of the conscience, etc.) overscrupulous —**quea′si·ly** *adv.*; **quea′si·ness** *n.*

Que·bec /k(w)ibek′/ *n.* 1 largely French-speaking province of Canada, in the SE part. Pop. 7,209,000 2 (also **Quebec′ Cit′y**) capital of Quebec province. Pop. 645,600 —**Que·beck′er, Que·bec·ois** /kā′bekwä′/ —*n.*

Quech·ua /keCH′wä, -wə/ *n.* 1 native peoples of South America who were dominant in the former Inca empire 2 family of languages spoken esp. by native peoples of central South America

queen /kwēn/ *n.* 1 female sovereign 2 king's wife 3 woman, country, or thing pre-eminent of its kind 4 fertile female among ants, bees, etc. 5 *Chess.* most powerful piece 6 playing card depicting a queen —**queen′ly** *adj.* (·li·er, ·li·est); **queen′li·ness** *n.* [OE]

queen′ bee′ *n.* 1 fertile female bee 2 self-important woman

Queens /kwēnz/ *n.* one of the five boroughs of New York City. Pop. 1,925,100

queer /kwēr/ *adj.* 1 strange; odd; eccentric 2 *Offens. Slang.* homosexual —*n.* 3 *Offens. Slang.* homosexual —*v.* 4 spoil; put out of order

quell /kwel/ *v.* 1 crush or put down (a rebellion, etc.) 2 suppress (fear, etc.) [OE]

quench /kwenCH/ *v.* 1 satisfy (thirst) by

drinking 2 extinguish (a fire or light) 3 cool, esp. with water [OE]

Que·ré·ta·ro /kərät′ərō′/ *n.* state in central Mexico. Capital: Querétaro. Pop 1,051,200

quer·u·lous /kwer′(y)ələs/ *adj.* complaining; peevish —**quer′u·lous·ly** *adj.* [L *queri* complain]

que·ry /kwēr′ē/ *n.* (*pl.* ·ries) 1 question 2 question mark —*v.* (·ried, ·ry·ing) 3 ask or inquire 4 call in question [L *quaerere* inquire]

quest /kwest/ *n.* 1 search or seeking 2 journey in search of something [L *quaerere quae-sit-* seek]

ques·tion /kwes′CHən/ *n.* 1 sentence worded or expressed so as to seek information or an answer 2 doubt or dispute about a matter 3 matter to be discussed or decided 4 problem requiring a solution —*v.* 5 ask questions of; interrogate 6 throw doubt upon; raise objections to 7 **be a question of** be at issue; be a problem 8 **call in (or into) question** express doubts about 9 **in question** that is being discussed or referred to 10 **out of the question** not worth discussing; impossible —**ques′tion·er** *n.*; **ques′tion·ing** *adj.* & *n.*; **ques′tion·ing·ly** *adv.* [L, rel. to QUEST]

ques′tion·a·ble *adj.* doubtful as regards truth, quality, honesty, wisdom, etc.

ques′tion mark′ *n.* punctuation mark (?) indicating a question

ques·tion·naire /kwes′CHəner′/ *n.* written series of questions [Fr, rel. to QUESTION]

queue /kyōō/ *n.* esp. *Brit.* 1 line or sequence of persons, vehicles, etc., waiting their turn —*v.* (**queued, queu·ing**) 2 line (up) [L *cauda* tail]

Que′zon Cit′y /kāsōn′/ *n.* city on Luzon in the Philippines. Pop. 1,632,000

quib·ble /kwib′əl/ *n.* 1 petty objection; trivial point of criticism 2 evasion; argument relying on ambiguity —*v.* (·bled, ·bling) 3 use quibbles —**quib′bling** *adj.*

quiche /kēsH/ *n.* custard dish in a pastry shell, usu. with cheese and other ingredients [Fr]

quick /kwik/ *adj.* 1 taking only a short time 2 arriving or occurring after a short time; prompt 3 with only a short interval (*in quick succession*) 4 lively; intelligent; alert 5 (of a temper) easily roused 6 *Archaic.* alive (*the quick and the dead*) —*adv.* 7 quickly —*n.* 8 soft sensitive flesh, esp. below the nails 9 seat of emotion (*cut to the quick*) —**quick′ly** *adv.* [OE]

quick·en /kwik′ən/ *v.* 1 make or become quicker; accelerate 2 give life or vigor to; rouse

quick′ie *n.* thing done or made quickly

quick′lime′ *n.* LIME[1]

quick′sand′ *n.* 1 area of loose wet sand that sucks anything placed on it 2 treacherous situation, etc.

quick′sil′ver *n.* mercury

quick′-tem′pered *adj.* easily angered

quick′-wit′ted *adj.* quick to grasp a situation, make repartee, etc. —**quick′-wit′ted·ly** *adv.*; **quick′-wit′ted·ness** *n.*

quid /kwid/ *n.* lump of tobacco for chewing [var. of CUD]

quid pro quo /kwid′ prō kwō′/ *n.* (*pl.* **quid**

pro quos /-kwōz'/) return made (for a gift, favor, etc.) [L: something for something]

qui·es·cent /kwī-es'ənt, kwē-/ *adj.* inert; dormant —**qui·es'cence** *n.* [rel. to QUIET]

qui·et /kwī'ət/ *adj.* 1 with little or no sound or motion 2 of gentle or peaceful disposition 3 unobtrusive; not overt 4 undisturbed or uninterrupted 5 calm; peaceful 6 not busy (*it is very quiet at work*) —*n.* 7 silence; stillness 8 undisturbed state; tranquillity —*v.* 9 make or become quiet or calm —**qui'et·ly** *adv.*; **qui'et·ness** *n.* [L *quiescere* become quiet]

qui·e·tude /kwī'ət(y)ōōd'/ *n.* state of quiet

qui·e·tus /kwī-ē'təs/ *n.* 1 release; discharge 2 death [MedL, rel. to QUIET]

quill /kwil/ *n.* 1 large feather in a wing or tail 2 hollow stem of this 3 (in full **quill'-pen'**) pen made of a quill 4 spine on a porcupine, etc. [prob. LGer *quiele*]

Quil·mes /kēl'mäs/ *n.* city in E Argentina. Pop. 509,400

quilt /kwilt/ *n.* 1 bed cover filled with stuffing material and often stitched in a colorful pattern —*v.* 2 make quilts —**quilt'er, quilt'ing** *n.* [L *culcita* cushion]

quince /kwins/ *n.* 1 acid pear-shaped fruit used in jams, etc. 2 tree bearing this [orig. a pl., fr. Fr *cooin*, fr. *Cydonia* in Crete]

qui·nine /kwī'nīn'/ *n.* bitter extract of cinchona bark, used as a tonic and to reduce fever [Sp *quina* cinchona bark, fr. Quechua *kina* bark]

Quin·ta·na Ro·o /kēntän'ə rō'(ō)/ *n.* NE state of Mexico, on the Gulf of Mexico. Capital: Chetumal. Pop. 493,300

quin·tes·sence /kwintes'əns/ *n.* purest and most perfect form, manifestation, type, or embodiment (of a quality, etc.) —**quin'tes·sen'tial** /-təsen'sHəl/ *adj.*; **quin·tes·sen'tial·ly** *adv.* [L *quinta essentia* fifth substance (underlying the four ancient elements)]

quin·tet /kwintet'/ *n.* 1 *Mus.* a composition for five performers **b** the performers 2 any group of five [L *quintus* fifth]

quin·tu·ple /kwint(y)ōō'pəl, -təp'əl/ *adj.* 1 fivefold; having five parts —*n.* 2 fivefold number or amount —*v.* (·pled, ·pling) 3 multiply by five [L *quintus* fifth]

quin·tu·plet /kwint(y)ōō'plət, -təp'lət/ *n.* each of five children born at one birth

quip /kwip/ *n.* 1 clever saying; epigram —*v.* (quipped, quip·ping) 2 make quips [perh. fr. L *quippe* forsooth]

quire /kwīr/ *n.* 25 (formerly 24) sheets of paper [L, rel. to QUATERNARY]

quirk /kwərk/ *n.* 1 peculiar feature 2 trick of fate —**quirk'y** *adj.* (·i·er, ·i·est)

quis·ling /kwiz'liNG/ *n.* traitorous collaborator [for V. *Quisling,* Norwegian collaborator with the Nazis]

quit /kwit/ *v.* (quit or quit·ted, quit·ting) 1 give up; let go; abandon (a task, etc.) 2 cease; stop 3 leave or depart from [L, rel. to QUIET]

quite /kwīt/ *adv.* 1 completely; entirely; wholly 2 to some extent; rather 3 **quite a few** a fairly large number of [var. of QUIT]

Qui·to /kēt'ō/ *n.* capital of Ecuador. Pop. 1,100,800

quits /kwits/ *adj.* 1 on even terms by retaliation or repayment 2 **call it quits: a** cease activity; stop working **b** give up [prob. rel. to QUIT]

quit'ter *n.* person who gives up easily

quiv·er¹ /kwiv'ər/ *v.* 1 tremble or vibrate with a slight rapid motion —*n.* 2 quivering motion or sound [obs. *quiver* nimble]

quiv·er² *n.* case for arrows [AngFr fr. Gmc]

quix·ot·ic /kwiksät'ik/ *adj.* foolishly idealistic; romantically unrealistic —**quix·ot'i·cal·ly** *adv.* [Don *Quixote,* in Cervantes' romance]

quiz /kwiz/ *n.* (*pl.* quiz'zes) 1 test of knowledge, esp. as entertainment 2 brief school examination —*v.* (quizzed, quiz·zing) 3 examine by questioning

quiz·zi·cal /kwiz'ikəl/ *adj.* expressing or done with mild or amused perplexity —**quiz'zi·cal·ly** *adv.*

quoin /k(w)oin/ *n.* 1 external angle of a building 2 cornerstone 3 wedge [var. of COIN]

quoit /k(w)oit/ *n.* 1 ring thrown to encircle an iron peg 2 (*pl.*) game using these

quon·dam /kwän'dəm/ *adj.* that once was; sometime; former [L]

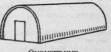

QUONSET HUT

Quon'set hut' /kwän'sit/ *n. Tdmk.* semicylindrical metal building used for storage, barracks, etc., esp. by US military [for Quonset Naval Base, R.I., where first made]

quo·rum /kwôr'əm/ *n.* minimum number of members that must be present to constitute a valid meeting [L: of whom]

quo·ta /kwō'tə/ *n.* 1 share to be contributed to, or received from, a total 2 number of goods, people, etc., stipulated or permitted [L *quota (pars)* how great a part]

quo·ta·tion /kwōtā'sHən/ *n.* 1 passage or remark quoted 2 quoting or being quoted 3 cost estimate [MedL, rel. to QUOTE]

quota'tion marks' *n. pl.* raised marks (' ' or " ") used to mark quoted speech, for emphasis, etc.

quote /kwōt/ *v.* (quot·ed, quot·ing) 1 cite or appeal to (an author, book, etc.) in confirmation of some view 2 repeat or copy out a passage from 3 state the price of —*interj.* 4 word spoken to note that quoted speech follows —*n.* 5 passage quoted 6 price quoted 7 (*pl.*) quotation marks —**quot'a·ble** *adj.* [L *quotus* of what number]

quoth /kwōTH/ *v. Archaic.* said [OE]

quo·tid·i·an /kwōtid'ēən/ *adj.* 1 daily 2 commonplace; trivial [L *cotidie* daily]

quo·tient /kwō'sHənt/ *n. Math.* result of a division [L *quoties -ent-* how many times]

q.v. *abbr.* which see (in references) [L *quod vide*]

qwerty /kwər'tē/ *attrib. adj.* denoting the standard English-language keyboard [for the first letter keys in the top row]

R

r, R /är/ *n.* (*pl.* **r's**; **R's, Rs**) eighteenth letter of the English alphabet; a consonant

r or **r.** *abbr.* 1 rabbi 2 radius 3 railroad 4 recipe 5 replacing 6 residence 7 right 8 river 9 road 10 royal 11 *Baseball.* run(s)

R or **R.** *abbr.* 1 Radical 2 Regina (queen) 3 (also ®) registered as a trademark 4 Republican 5 *Chess.* rook 6 *Theat.* stage right 7 (of a movie) classified as restricted; children under 17 years old must be accompanied by an adult

Ra *symb.* radium

Ra·bat /rəbät'/ *n.* capital of Morocco. Pop. 518,600

rab·bet /rab'it/ *n.* 1 step-shaped channel cut into wood, etc., usu. to receive the edge or tongue of another piece —*v.* 2 join or fix with a rabbet 3 make a rabbet in [Fr *rab*(*b*)*at*, rel. to REBATE]

rab·bi /rab'ī'/ *n.* (*pl.* **·bis**) 1 Jewish scholar or teacher, esp. of the law 2 Jewish religious leader —**rab·bin·i·cal** /rəbin'ikəl/ *adj.* {Heb: my master]

rab·bit /rab'it/ *n.* 1 large-eared burrowing plant-eating mammal related to the hare 2 its fur

rab'bit ears' *n.* TV antenna consisting of two rods, usu. on top of the set

rab'bit punch' *n.* short chop to the nape of the neck

rab·ble /rab'əl/ *n.* 1 disorderly crowd; mob 2 contemptible or inferior set of people

rab'ble-rous'er *n.* person who stirs up the rabble or a crowd

Rab·e·lais /rab'əlā'/, François c. 1494–1553; French humanist and satirist

Rab·e·lai·si·an /rab'əlā'zēən, -ᴢHən/ *adj.* of or like Rabelais or his writings, esp. as being marked by satire and coarse humor

ra·bid /rab'id/ *adj.* 1 affected with rabies; mad 2 violent; fanatical —**ra·bid·i·ty** /rəbid'itē/ *n.* [L *rabidus*]

ra·bies /rā'bēz/ *n.* acute, contagious viral disease transmissible to humans by the bite, saliva, etc., of an infected animal [L, rel. to RABID]

rac·coon /rakōon'/ *n.* (*pl.* same or **·coons**) 1 N American mammal with a bushy tail and sharp snout 2 its fur [Algonquian]

race¹ /rās/ *n.* 1 competition of speed between runners, horses, vehicles, etc. 2 contest between persons to be first to achieve something 3a strong sea or river current **b** channel with swift current —*v.* (**raced, rac·ing**) 4 take part in a race 5 have a race with 6 cause to race 7a go at full or excessive speed **b** cause to do this [ON]

race² *n.* 1 any of the major divisions of humankind having distinct physical characteristics 2 fact or concept of division into races 3 category, genus, species, breed, or variety of animals or plants [It *razza*]

race'horse' *n.* horse bred or kept for racing

ra·ceme /rāsēm'/ *n.* flower cluster with separate flowers attached by short stalks at equal

distances along the stem [L *racemus* grapebunch]

race'track' *n.* track for horse or motor racing

Rach·ma·ni·noff /räkmän'ənôf'/, **Sergei** 1873–1943; Russian composer

ra·cial /rā'SHəl/ *adj.* 1 of or concerning race 2 on the grounds of or connected with difference in race —**ra'cial·ly** *adv.*

Ra·cine /rəsēn', rä-/ *n.* city in Wis. Pop. 84,298

Ra·cine /rasēn'/, **Jean** 1639–99; French dramatist

rac·ism /rā'sizəm/ *n.* 1 belief in the superiority of a particular race; prejudice based on this 2 antagonism toward other races —**rac'ist** /-ist/ *n.* & *adj.*

rack¹ /rak/ *n.* 1 framework, usu. with rails, bars, etc., for holding things 2 cogged or toothed bar or rail engaging with a wheel or pinion, etc. 3 *Hist.* instrument of torture used to stretch the victim's limbs —*v.* 4 (of disease or pain) inflict suffering on 5 place in or on a rack 6 **rack one's brains** make a great mental effort [LGer or Du]

rack² *n.* destruction (esp. *rack and ruin*) [fr. WRACK]

rack·et¹ /rak'it/ *n.* (also **rac'quet**) bat with a round or oval frame strung with catgut, nylon, etc., used in tennis, squash, etc. [Fr *raquette* fr. Ar *rahat* palm of the hand]

rack·et² *n.* 1 uproar; din 2 scheme for obtaining money, etc., by dishonest means, extortion, etc. 3 *Slang.* line of business [perh. imit.]

rack·e·teer /rak'ətēr'/ *n.* person who operates an illegal business —**rack'e·teer'ing** *n.*

ra·con·teur /rak'əntər'/ *n.* teller of anecdotes [Fr, rel. to RECOUNT]

rac·quet /rak'it/ *n.* var. of RACKET¹

rac'quet·ball' *n.* racket game played on a four-walled court

rac·y /rā'sē/ *adj.* (**·i·er, ·i·est**) 1 lively and vigorous in style 2 risqué 3 of distinctive quality (*a racy wine*) —**rac'i·ly** *adv.*; **rac'i·ness** *n.* [fr. RACE²]

rad /rad/ *n.* unit of absorbed dose of ionizing radiation [fr. radiation absorbed dose]

ra·dar /rā'där'/ *n.* system for detecting the direction, range, or presence of objects by reflection of transmitted radio waves [fr. *radio detection and ranging*]

ra·di·al /rā'dēəl/ *adj.* 1 of or in rays 2 arranged like rays or radii; radiating in lines from the center 3 (of a tire) having fabric layers laid radially, i.e., at right angles to the center of the tread —*n.* 4 radial tire —**ra'di·al·ly** *adv.* [MedL, rel. to RADIUS]

ra·di·ant /rā'dēənt/ *adj.* 1 emitting rays of light or energy 2 (of eyes or looks) beaming with joy, hope, or love 3 (of beauty) splendid or dazzling —**ra'di·ance** *n.*; **ra'di·ant·ly** *adv.*

ra·di·ate /rā'dēāt/ *v.* (**·at·ed, ·at·ing**) 1a emit rays of light, heat, etc. **b** (of light or heat) emit or be emitted in rays 2 transmit or demonstrate (joy, etc.) 3 diverge or spread from a center

ra·di·a·tion /rā'dēā'sнən/ *n.* **1** radiating or being radiated **2** *Physics.* energy or its emission as electromagnetic waves or as moving particles **3** (in full **ra'di·a'tion ther'a·py**) RADIOTHERAPY

ra·di·a·tor /rā'dēā'tər/ *n.* **1** device through which hot water or steam circulates to heat a room, etc. **2** heat-dissipating device in a motor vehicle, etc.

rad·i·cal /rad'ikəl/ *adj.* **1** fundamental; primary **2** far-reaching; thorough **3** representing or holding extreme political views; revolutionary **4** of the root of a number or quantity —*n.* **5** person holding radical views or belonging to a radical party **6** *Chem.* a atom(s) with one or more unpaired electrons b atom(s) normally forming part of a compound and remaining unaltered during ordinary chemical changes **7** *Math.* quantity forming or expressed as the root of another —**rad'i·cal·ism'** *n.*; **rad'i·cal·ly** *adv.* [L *radix* root]

ra·dic·chio /rədē'kē·ō/ *n.* (*pl.* **·os**) chicory with reddish-purple leaves [It: chicory]

ra·di·i /rā'dēī/ *n. pl.* of RADIUS

ra·di·o /rā'dē·ō'/ *n.* (*pl.* **·os**) **1** a transmission and reception of sound messages, etc., in the form of beamed electromagnetic waves b apparatus for this **2** sound broadcasting (*prefers the radio*) —*v.* (**·oed, ·o·ing**) **3** a send a (message) by radio b send a message to (a person) by radio [short for *radio-telegraphy*]

radio- *comb. form* **1** denoting radio or broadcasting **2** connected with radioactivity **3** connected with rays or radiation [fr. L *radius* ray]

ra'di·o·ac'tive *adj.* of or exhibiting radioactivity

ra'di·o·ac·tiv'i·ty *n.* spontaneous disintegration of atomic nuclei, with emission of radiation or particles

ra'di·o·i'so·tope *n.* radioactive isotope

ra·di·ol·o·gy /rā'dē·äl'əjē/ *n.* the study of x-rays and other high-energy radiation, esp. as used in medicine —**ra'di·ol'o·gist** /-jist/ *n.*

ra·di·om·e·ter /rā'dēäm'itər/ *n.* measuring instrument containing vanes that rotate when exposed to radiant energy [RADIO- + METER]

ra·di·os·co·py /rā'dē·äs'kəpē/ *n.* examination by x-rays, etc., of objects opaque to light

ra'di·o tel'e·scope *n.* directional aerial system for collecting and analyzing radiation in the radio frequency range from stars, etc.

ra'di·o·ther'a·py (also **ra'di·a'tion ther'a·py**) *n.* treatment of disease by x-rays and other forms of radiation

rad·ish /rad'ish/ *n.* **1** plant with a fleshy pungent root **2** this root, eaten, esp. raw [L *radix* root]

ra·di·um /rā'dēəm/ *n.* radioactive metallic element orig. obtained from pitchblende, etc.; *symb.* **Ra**

ra·di·us /rā'dēəs/ *n.* (*pl.* **·di·i** /-dē·ī'/ or **·us·es**) **1** a straight line from the center to the circumference of a circle or sphere b length of this **2** distance from a center (*in a radius*

of 20 miles) **3** thicker and shorter of the two bones in the human forearm [L]

ra·don /rā'dän/ *n.* gaseous radioactive element arising from the disintegration of radium; *symb.* **Rn**

RAF *abbr.* Royal Air Force

raf·fi·a /raf'ēə/ *n.* **1** palm tree native to Madagascar **2** fiber from its leaves, used for weaving, tying plants, etc. [Malagasy]

raff·ish /raf'ish/ *adj.* **1** disreputable; rakish **2** vulgar; tawdry [*raff* rubbish]

raf·fle /raf'əl/ *n.* **1** fund-raising lottery with prizes —*v.* (**·fled, ·fling**) **2** sell (off) by means of a raffle [Fr *raf(f)le*, a dice game]

raft /raft/ *n.* floating flat structure of logs or other buoyant material for conveying persons or things [ON]

raf·ter /raf'tər/ *n.* each of the sloping beams forming the framework of a roof [OE]

rag[1] /rag/ *n.* **1** torn, frayed, or worn piece of woven material **2** (*pl.*) old or worn clothes **3** *Derog.* newspaper **4** **in rags** much torn **5** **rags to riches** poverty to affluence [prob. a back formation fr. RAGGED]

rag[2] *v.* (**ragged, rag·ging**) tease; play rough jokes on

rag[3] *n.* ragtime composition [abbr.]

rag·a·muf·fin /rag'əmuf'in/ *n.* child in ragged, dirty clothes [prob. fr. RAG[1]]

rag'bag' *n.* **1** bag for scraps of fabric, etc. **2** miscellaneous collection

rage /rāj/ *n.* **1** fierce or violent anger **2** fit of this **3** violent action of a natural force —*v.* (**raged, rag·ing**) **4** be full of anger **5** speak furiously or madly **6** (of wind, battle, etc.) be violent; have force **7** **all the rage** very popular; fashionable [L RABIES]

rag·ged /rag'id/ *adj.* **1** torn; frayed **2** in ragged clothes **3** with a broken or jagged outline or surface **4** lacking finish, smoothness, or uniformity [ON]

rag·lan /rag'lən/ *adj.* **1** (of a sleeve) set into the neck of a garment —*n.* **2** overcoat with such sleeves [for Brit. general Lord *Raglan*]

ra·gout /ragōō'/ *n.* meat stewed with vegetables and highly seasoned [Fr]

rag'tag' *adj.* **1** disheveled; shabby **2** very diverse or mixed [fr. RAG[1]]

rag'time' *n.* form of highly syncopated early jazz, esp. for the piano

rag' trade' *n.* *Slang.* the clothing business

RAGLAN 1

rag'weed' *n.* any of various plants whose pollen is highly allergenic

raid /rād/ *n.* **1** rapid surprise attack, esp.: a in warfare **2** to commit a crime, steal, or do harm c by police, etc., to arrest suspects or seize illicit goods —*v.* **2** make a raid on —**raid'er** *n.* [Scots form of ROAD]

rail[1] /rāl/ *n.* **1** level or sloping bar or series of bars: a used to hang things on b as the top of a banister c forming part of a fence or barrier **2** steel bar or continuous line of bars laid on the ground, usu. as a railroad **3** RAILROAD,

RADIOMETER

1, 2 —*v.* 4 furnish with a rail or rails 5 enclose with rails [Fr *reille* fr. L *regula* RULE]

rail² *v.* complain or protest strongly; rant [Fr *railler*]

rail³ *n.* wading bird often inhabiting marshes [Fr]

rail'ing *n.* fence or barrier made of rails

rail·ler·y /rā'lərē/ *n.* good-humored ridicule [Fr *raillerie*, rel. to RAIL²]

rail'road' *n.* 1 track or set of parallel tracks of steel rails upon which trains run 2 system providing such transportation —*v.* 3 coerce; rush (*railroaded through Congress*)

rail'way' *n.* 1 RAILROAD, 1, 2 2 path laid with railroad tracks

rai·ment /rā'mənt/ *n. Archaic.* clothing [*arrayment*, rel. to ARRAY]

rain /rān/ *n.* 1a condensed atmospheric moisture falling in drops b fall of such drops 2 (*pl.*) a (prec. by *the*) rainy season b rainfalls 3 rainlike falling of liquid, particles, objects, etc. —*v.* 4 (prec. by *it* as subject) rain falls 5a rain fall like rain b (prec. by *it* as subject) send in large quantities 6 repeatedly bestow, inflict, etc. (*rained blows upon him*) 7 rain out cause (an event, etc.) to be canceled because of rain —rain'y *adj.* (·i·er, ·i·est) [OE]

rain'bow' *n.* 1 arch of spectral colors formed by reflection, refraction, and dispersion of the sun's rays in rain or mist —*adj.* 2 many-colored [OE, rel. to RAIN, BOW¹]

rain' check' *n.* 1 ticket given for later use when an outdoor event is canceled by rain 2 **take a rain check (on)** reserve the right to accept (an offer) when more convenient

rain'coat' *n.* waterproof or water-resistant coat

rain'drop' *n.* single drop of rain

rain'fall' *n.* 1 fall of rain 2 quantity of rain falling within a given area in a given time

rain' for'est *n.* luxuriant tropical forest with heavy rainfall

Rai·nier, Mt. /rənēr', rā-/ *n.* dormant volcanic peak in W central Wash.

rain'proof' *adj.* impervious to rain

rain'storm' *n.* storm with heavy rain

rain'wa'ter *n.* water collected from fallen rain

raise /rāz/ *v.* (**raised, rais·ing**) 1 put or take into a higher position 2 cause to rise, stand, or be vertical 3 increase the amount, value, or strength of 4 construct or build 5 levy, collect, or bring together (*raise money*) 6 cause to be heard or considered (*raise an objection*) 7 engender or encourage; inspire (*raise hopes*) 8 bring up (children) 9 breed; grow 10 (foll. by *to*) multiply a quantity to a power 11 *Cards.* bet more than (another player) 12 remove (a barrier, etc.) —*n.* 13 *Cards.* increase in a stake or bid 14 increase in salary 15 **raise Cain:** *Slang.* a become angry b be disruptive [ON]

rai·sin /rā'zən/ *n.* dried grape [L, rel. to RACEME]

rai·son d'ê·tre /rā'zōn de't(rə)/ *n.* (*pl.* **rai' sons d'ê'tre,** pronunc. same) purpose or reason for a thing's existence [Fr]

raj /räj/ *n.* (*cap.,* prec. by *the*) *Hist.* British sovereignty in India [Hindi]

ra·ja /rä'jə/ *n.* (also *ra'jah*) *Hist.* 1 Indian king or prince 2 petty dignitary or noble in India [Hindi fr. Skt]

Raj·kot /räj'kōt'/ *n.* city in W India. Pop. 556,100

Raj·sha·hi /räjshä'hē/ *n.* city on Ganges River in Bangladesh. Pop. 299,700

rake¹ /rāk/ *n.* 1 gathering or soil-smoothing implement consisting of a pole with a toothed crossbar at the end —*v.* (**raked, rak·ing**) 2 collect (leaves, etc.) or smooth (soil, etc.) with or as with a rake 3 direct gunfire along (a line) from end to end 4 scratch or scrape 5 **rake in** amass (profits, etc.) 6 **rake up** revive the (unwelcome) memory of [OE]

rake² *n.* dissolute or licentious man [*rakehell*, rel. to RAKE¹, HELL]

rake³ *v.* (**raked, rak·ing**) 1 set or be set at a sloping angle; slant —*n.* 2 slanting position

rak'ish *adj.* 1 dashing; jaunty 2 dissolute —rak'ish·ly *adv.* [fr. RAKE²]

Ra·leigh /rô'lē, rä'lē/ *n.* capital of N. Car., in the central part. Pop. 207,951

Ra·leigh /rô'lē, rä'lē/, (Sir) **Walter** c. 1552–1618; English navigator, colonizer, and historian

ral·ly /ra'lē/ *v.* (·**lied,** ·**ly·ing**) 1 bring or come together as support for or action 2 recover after illness, etc.; revive 3 revive (courage, etc.) 4 (of stock prices, etc.) increase after a fall —*n.* (*pl.* ·**lies**) 5 rallying or being rallied 6 mass meeting for a cause 7 (also **ral'lye**) competition for motor vehicles, mainly over public roads 8 (in tennis, etc.) extended exchange of strokes [Fr *rallier*, rel. to RE-, ALLY]

ram /ram/ *n.* 1 male sheep 2 (**the Ram**) zodiacal sign or constellation Aries 3 *Hist.* BATTERING RAM —*v.* (**rammed, ram·ming**) 4 force or squeeze into place by pressure 5 beat or drive by heavy blows 6 (of a ship, vehicle, etc.) strike violently; crash against [OE]

RAM *n. abbr.* random access memory

Ram·a·dan /räm'ədän'/ *n. Islam.* ninth month of the Muslim year, with strict fasting from sunrise to sunset [Ar]

ram·ble /ram'bəl/ *v.* (·**bled,** ·**bling**) 1 walk for pleasure 2 talk or write incoherently 3 wander; travel irregularly —*n.* 4 walk taken for pleasure [Du *rammelen*]

ram'bler *n.* 1 person who rambles 2 straggling or spreading rose

ram·i·fi·ca·tion /ram'əfikā'sHən/ *n.* (usu. *pl.*) 1 consequence 2 subdivision of a complex structure or process [Fr, rel. to RAMIFY]

ram·i·fy /ram'əf ī'/ *v.* (·**fied,** ·**fy·ing**) (cause to) form branches, subdivisions, or offshoots; branch out [L *ramus* branch]

ramp /ramp/ *n.* 1 slope, esp. joining two levels of ground, floor, etc. 2 movable staircase for entering or leaving an aircraft [Fr *ramper* crawl]

ram·page *v.* /rampāj', ram'pāj/ (·**paged,** ·**pag·ing**) 1 rush wildly or violently about 2 rage; storm —*n.* /ram'pāj/ 3 wild or violent behavior 4 **on the rampage** rampaging

ram·pant /ram'pənt/ *adj.* 1 flourishing excessively or unchecked 2 fanatical or violent [Fr, rel. to RAMP]

ram·part /ram'pärt/ *n.* 1 defensive wall with a broad top and usu. a stone parapet 2 walkway on top of this [Fr *remparer* fortify]

ram'rod' *n.* 1 rod for ramming down the charge of a muzzle-loading firearm 2 thing that is very straight or rigid

Ram·ses /ram'sēz'/ name of several pharaohs of ancient Egypt

ram·shack·le /ram'sHakəl/ adj. tumbledown; rickety [rel. to RANSACK]

ran /ran/ v. past of RUN

ranch /ranCH/ n. **1** farm where animals are bred, such as cattle, sheep, etc. —v. **2** farm on a ranch —**ranch'er** n. [Sp rancho group of persons eating together]

ranch' house' n. house with all rooms on ground level

Ran·chi /rän'CHē/ n. city in E India. Pop. 598,500

Ran·cho Cu·ca·mon·ga /ran'CHō kōō'kəmäNG'gə/ n. city in Calif. Pop. 101,409

ran·cid /ran'sid/ adj. smelling or tasting like rank, stale fat —**ran·cid'i·ty** n. [L rancidus stinking]

ran·cor /raNG'kər/ n. inveterate bitterness; malignant hate —**ran'cor·ous** adj. [L rancor, rel. to RANCID]

R & B abbr. rhythm and blues

R & D abbr. research and development

ran·dom /ran'dəm/ adj. made, done, etc., without method or conscious choice —**ran'dom·ly** adv.; **ran'dom·ness** n. [Fr randon fr. randir gallop]

ran'dom-ac'cess adj. Comp. (of a memory or file) having all data immediately accessible, not needing to be read sequentially

R and R abbr. rest and recreation (or relaxation)

ran·dy /ran'dē/ adj. (·di·er, ·di·est) lustful —**ran'di·ness** n. [perh. rel. to RANT]

ra·nee /rä'nē/ n. (also **ra'ni**, pronunc. same) Hist. raja's wife or widow [Hindi]

rang /raNG/ v. past of RING[2]

range /rānj/ n. **1a** region between limits of occurrence, dispersal, variation, etc.; extent; scope **b** such limits **2** distance attainable by a gun or projectile **3** row, series, etc., esp. of mountains **4** area with targets for shooting **5** cooking stove **6** maximal travel distance for a vehicle, rocket, etc. **7** distance between a camera and the object to be photographed **8** large area of open land for grazing or hunting —v. (**ranged, rang·ing**) **9** reach; lie spread out; extend **10** rove; wander [Fr, rel. to RANK[1]]

rang·er /rān'jər/ n. **1** government employee who cares for public forests **2** member of an armed law-enforcement patrol **3** soldier highly trained in hand-to-hand combat, raiding tactics, etc. **4** one who ranges

Ran·goon /raNG-gōōn'/ n. (also **Yangon**) capital of Burma (Myanmar). Pop. 2,513,000

rang·y /rān'jē/ adj. (·i·er, ·i·est) tall and slim

ra·ni /rä'nē/ n. var. of RANEE

rank[1] /raNGk/ n. **1a** position or grade in a hierarchy **b** high social position **c** place in a scale **2** row or line **3** row of soldiers drawn up abreast **4** place where taxis await customers **5** order; array —v. **6** have a rank or place **7** classify or grade **8 close ranks** maintain solidarity [Fr ranc]

rank[2] adj. **1** luxuriant and coarse; choked with or apt to produce weeds or excessive foliage **2a** foul-smelling **b** loathsome; corrupt **3** complete; utter (rank outsider) [OE]

rank' and file' n. ordinary members of an organization

Ran·kin /raNG'kin/, **Jeannette** 1880–1973; US politician; first woman elected to US Congress (1917–19; 1941–43)

ran·kle /raNG'kəl/ v. (·kled, ·kling) (of envy, disappointment, etc., or their cause) cause persistent annoyance or resentment [Fr (d)rancler fester, fr. MedL dra(cu)nculus little serpent]

ran·sack /ran'sak'/ v. **1** pillage or plunder (a house, country, etc.) **2** thoroughly search [ON rannsaka fr. rann house, -saka seek]

ran·som /ran'səm/ n. **1** money demanded or paid for the release of a captive **2** liberation of a captive in return for this —v. **3** buy the freedom or restoration of; redeem [L, rel. to REDEMPTION]

rant /rant/ v. **1** speak loudly, bombastically, violently, or theatrically —n. **2** piece of ranting **3** rant and rave express anger noisily and forcefully [Du]

rap[1] /rap/ n. **1** smart slight blow **2** sharp tapping sound **3** Slang. blame; punishment **4a** rhythmic monologue recited to music **b** (in full **rap music**) style of popular music with words recited rhythmically —v. (**rapped, rap·ping**) **5** strike smartly **6** knock; make a sharp tapping sound **7** criticize adversely **8** perform a rap **9 take the rap** Slang. suffer the consequences —**rap'per** n. [prob. imit.]

ra·pa·cious /rəpā'SHəs/ adj. grasping; extortionate; predatory —**ra·pac·i·ty** /rəpas'ətē/ n. [L rapax, rel. to RAPE[1]]

rape[1] /rāp/ n. **1** act of forcing a person to have sexual intercourse against his or her will **2** violent assault or plunder (of a city, etc.) —v. (**raped, rap·ing**) **3** commit rape on —**rap'ist** n. [L rapire seize]

rape[2] n. plant grown as fodder, and for its seed (**rape'seed'**) from which oil is extracted [L rapum, rapa turnip]

Raph·a·el /raf'ēəl, rä'fē-, räf'ē-/ 1483–1520; Italian painter

rap·id /rap'id/ adj. **1** quick; swift; brief **2** (of a slope) descending steeply —n. **3** (usu. pl.) steep descent in a riverbed, with swift currents —**ra·pid·i·ty** /rəpid'ətē/ n.; **rap'id·ly** adv.; **rap'id·ness** n. [L, rel. to RAPE[1]]

rap'id eye' move'ment n. (also **REM**) type of jerky movement of the eyes during dreaming

ra·pi·er /rā'pēər/ n. **1** light slender sword for thrusting —adj. **2** sharp (rapier wit) [Fr rapière]

rap·ine /ra'pīn/ n. plundering [L, rel. to RAPE[1]]

rap·port /rapôr'/ n. relationship or communication, esp. when useful and harmonious [L portare carry]

rap·proche·ment /ra'prōSHmän/ n. resumption of harmonious relations, esp. between governments [Fr, rel. to APPROACH]

rap·scal·lion /rapskal'yən/ n. rascal [perh. fr. RASCAL]

rapt /rapt/ adj. **1** fully absorbed or intent **2** carried away with feeling or lofty thought [L raptus, rel. to RAPE[1]]

rap·ture /rap'CHər/ n. **1** ecstatic delight (pl.) great pleasure or enthusiasm or the expression of this —**rap·tur·ous** adj. [Fr MedL, rel. to RAPE[1]]

ra·ra a·vis /rer′ə ā′vis/ *n.* being or thing that is rare [L: rare bird]

rare[1] /rer/ *adj.* (**rar′er, rar′est**) **1** seldom done, found, or occurring; uncommon; unusual **2** exceptionally good **3** of less than the usual density (*rare gases*) —**rare′ness** *n.* [L *rarus*]

rare[2] *adj.* (**rar′er, rar′est**) (of meat) cooked so that the inside is still red and juicy [OE]

rare′ earth[1] *n.* lanthanide element

rar·e·fy /rer′əfī′/ *v.* (**·fied, ·fy·ing**) make or become less dense or solid —**rar′e·fac′tion** /-fak′shən/ *n.* [For or MedL, rel. to RARE[1]]

rare·ly /rer′lē/ *adv.* **1** seldom; not often **2** exceptionally

rar′ing *adj. Colloq.* enthusiastic; eager (*raring to go*) [participle of *rare,* dial. var. of ROAR or REAR[2]]

rar·i·ty /rer′ətē/ *n.* (*pl.* **·ties**) **1** rareness **2** uncommon thing [L, rel. to RARE[1]]

ras·cal /ras′kəl/ *n.* dishonest or mischievous person —**ras′cal·ly** *adj.* [Fr *rascaille* rabble]

rash[1] /rash/ *adj.* reckless; impetuous; hasty —**rash′ly** *adv.;* **rash′ness** *n.* [prob. OE]

rash[2] *n.* **1** eruption of the skin in spots or patches **2** sudden widespread appearance (of)

rash′er *n.* slice or serving of (esp.) bacon

Rasht /räsht/ *n.* city in NW Iran. Pop. 290,900

rasp /rasp/ *n.* **1** coarse kind of file **2** grating noise or utterance —*v.* **3** scrape with a rasp **4a** make a grating sound **b** say gratingly —**rasp′i·ness** *n.;* **rasp′y** *adj.* (**·i·er, ·i·est**) [Fr *raspe(r)*]

rasp·ber·ry /raz′ber′ē/ *n.* (*pl.* **·ries**) **1a** red blackberrylike fruit **b** plant bearing this **2** *Colloq.* sound made by blowing through the lips, expressing derision or disapproval

Ra·spu·tin /rasp(y)ōōt′n/, **Grigori** 1871–1916; Russian monk; influential at court of Czar Nicholas II

rat /rat/ *n.* **1a** rodent like a large mouse **b** similar rodent (*water rat*) **2** *Slang.* turncoat; betrayer; informer; deserter **3** *Slang.* unpleasant or treacherous person **4** (*pl.*) *Slang.* exclamation of annoyance, etc. —*v.* (**rat·ted, rat·ting**) **5** inform (on); betray [OE]

ra·ta·tou·ille /rat′ətōō′ē, -twē′/ *n.* dish of stewed onions, zucchini, tomatoes, eggplant, and peppers [Fr dial.]

ratch·et /rach′it/ *n.* **1** set of teeth on the edge of a bar or wheel with a catch permitting motion in one direction only **2** (in full **ratch′et wheel′**) wheel with a rim so toothed [Fr *rochet* lance-head]

rate[1] /rāt/ *n.* **1** numerical proportion or amount expressed in units (*a rate of 50 m.p.h.*) or as a basis of calculating (*rate of interest*) **2** fixed or appropriate charge, cost, or value (*postal rates*) **3** pace of movement or change **4** (in *comb.*) class or rank (*first-rate*) —*v.* (**rat·ed, rat·ing**) **5a** estimate the worth or value of **b** assign a value to **6** consider; regard as **7** rank or be considered (as) **8** be worthy of; deserve **9** *Slang.* at any rate in any case; whatever happens **10** at this rate if this example is typical [L *rata,* rel. to RATIO]

rate[2] *v.* (**rat·ed, rat·ing**) scold angrily

rath·er /rath′ər/ *adv.* **1** by preference (*would rather not go*) **2** more truly; as a more

likely alternative (*stupid rather than dishonest*) **3** more precisely (*a book or, rather, a pamphlet*) **4** slightly; to some extent (*rather drunk*) [OE comp. of *rathe* early]

rat·i·fy /rat′əfī′/ *v.* (**·fied, ·fy·ing**) confirm or accept by formal consent, signature, etc. —**rat′i·fi·ca′tion** /-fikā′shən/ *n.* [MedL, rel. to RATE[1]]

rat·ing /rāt′ing/ *n.* **1** placing in a rank or class **2** estimated standing of a person as regards credit, etc. **3** rank on a ship or in the military **4** relative popularity of a broadcast program as determined by the estimated size of the audience

ra·ti·o /rā′shē·ō′/ *n.* (*pl.* **·os**) quantitative relation between two comparable magnitudes (*in the ratio of three to two*) [L: reckoning]

ra·ti·oc·i·nate /rash′ē·äs′ənāt′/ *v.* (**·nat·ed, ·nat·ing**) reason —**ra′ti·oc·i·na′tion** *n.* [L, rel. to RATIO]

ra·tion /rash′ən, rā′shən/ *n.* **1** official allowance of food, clothing, etc., in a time of shortage **2** (usu. *pl.*) fixed daily allowance of food, esp. in the armed forces —*v.* **3** limit (persons or provisions) to a fixed ration **4** share out (food, etc.) in fixed quantities [L, rel. to RATIO]

ra·tion·al /rash′ənəl/ *adj.* **1** of or based on reason **2** sensible or sane **3** endowed with reason **4** (of a quantity or ratio) expressible as a ratio of whole numbers —**ra′tion·al′i·ty** /-al′itē/ *n.;* **ra′tion·al·ly** *adv.* [L, rel. to RATION]

ra·tion·ale /rash′ənal′/ *n.* fundamental reason; logical basis [neut. of L *rationalis,* rel. to RATIONAL]

ra′tion·al·ism′ *n.* practice of treating reason as the basis of belief and knowledge —**ra′tion·al·ist** /-ist/ *n.* & *adj.;* **ra′tion·al·is′tic** *adj.*

ra·tion·al·ize /rash′ənəlīz′/ *v.* (**·ized, ·iz·ing**) offer a rational but specious explanation of (one's behavior or attitude) —**ra′tion·al·i·za′tion** *n.*

rat·line /rat′lin/ *n.* (also **rat′lin,** pronunc. same) (usu. *pl.*) any of the lines fastened across a sailing-ship's shrouds, serving as ladder rungs

rat′ race′ *n. Colloq.* hectic working routine; struggle to get ahead

rat·tan /ratan′/ *n.* climbing palm with long thin jointed pliable stems, used for furniture, etc. [Malay]

rat·tle /rat′l/ *v.* (**·tled, ·tling**) **1a** give out a rapid succession of short sharp hard sounds **b** cause such sounds by shaking something **2** move (along) with a rattling noise **3** disconcert; alarm —*n.* **4** rattling sound **5** device or plaything made to rattle **6 rattle off** say rapidly —**rat′tly** *adj.* [prob. LGer or Du]

rat′tle·snake′ *n.* poisonous American snake with rattling horny rings at the end of its tail

rat′tling *adj.* **1** that rattles **2** brisk; vigorous (*rattling pace*) —*adv.* **3** remarkably (*rattling good story*)

rat·ty /rat′ē/ *adj.* (**·ti·er, ·ti·est**) shabby —**rat′ti·ness** *n.*

rau·cous /rô′kəs/ *adj.* **1** harsh-sounding **2** loud —**rau′cous·ly** *adv.;* **rau′cous·ness** *n.* [L]

raun·chy /rôn′chē/ *adj.* (**·chi·er, ·chi·est**)

rav·age /rav'ij/ *v.* (·**aged, ·ag·ing**) **1** devastate; plunder —*n.* **2** (usu. *pl.*) destructive effect [Fr alter. fr. *ravine* rush of water]

rave /rāv/ *v.* (**raved, rav·ing**) **1** talk wildly or furiously in or as in delirium **2** speak with rapturous admiration (about) —*n.* **3** highly enthusiastic review [prob. Fr dial. *raver*]

rav·el /rav'əl/ *v.* (·**eled** or ·**elled,** ·**el·ing** or ·**el·ling**) disentangle; separate into threads [prob. Du *ravelen*]

Ra·vel /rəvel'/, **Maurice** 1875–1937; French composer

ra·ven /rā'vən/ *n.* glossy blue-black crow with a hoarse cry [OE]

rav·en·ing /rav'əniNG/ *adj.* hungrily seeking prey; voracious [Fr *raviner* fr. L, rel. to RAPINE]

Ra·ven·na /rəven'ə/ *n.* city in NE Italy. Pop. 136,700

rav·en·ous /rav'ənəs/ *adj.* **1** very hungry **2** voracious **3** rapacious —**rav'en·ous·ly** *adv.* [obs. *raven* plunder, fr. Fr *raviner* ravage]

ra·vine /rəvēn'/ *n.* deep narrow gorge [L, rel. to RAPINE]

rav'ing *n.* **1** (usu. *pl.*) wild or delirious talk —*adj.* & *adv.* **2** exceeding(ly) (*a raving beauty; raving mad*)

rav·i·o·li /rav'ē-ō'lē/ *n.* small pasta casings filled with cheese, meat, etc. [It]

rav·ish /rav'isH/ *v.* **1** seize and carry away **2** *Archaic.* rape (a woman) **3** enrapture —**rav'ish·ment** *n.* [L, rel. to RAPE¹]

rav'ish·ing *adj.* lovely; beautiful —**rav'ish·ing·ly** *adv.*

raw /rô/ *adj.* **1** uncooked **2** in the natural state; not processed or manufactured **3** inexperienced; untrained **4** (of a wound, etc.) a stripped of skin b sensitive to the touch from being exposed **5** (of the atmosphere, day, etc.) cold and damp **6** crude; coarse **7 in the raw: a** in its natural state **b** naked [OE]

Ra·wal·pin·di /rä'wəlpin'dē/ *n.* city in N Pakistan. Pop. 794,800

raw-boned /rô' bônd'/ *adj.* gaunt

raw'hide' *n.* **1** untanned hide **2** rope or whip of this

raw' ma·te'ri·al *n.* material from which manufactured goods are made

ray¹ /rā/ *n.* **1** narrow beam of light from a small or distant source **2** straight line in which radiation travels to a given point **3** (*pl.*) radiation of a specified type (*x-rays*) **4** promising trace (*ray of hope*) **5** any of a set of radiating lines, parts, or things [L RADIUS]

ray² *n.* marine fish with a broad, flat body and a long slender tail [L *raia*]

Ray /rā/, **Man** 1890–1976; US painter and photographer

ray·on /rā'än/ *n.* textile fiber or fabric made from cellulose [fr. RAY¹]

raze /rāz/ *v.* (**razed, raz·ing**) completely destroy; tear down [L *radere ras-* scrape]

ra·zor /rā'zər/ *n.* instrument with a sharp blade used in cutting hair, esp. in shaving [Fr *rāsor*, rel. to RAZE]

ra'zor wire' *n.* wire with sharpened projections, often coiled atop walls for security

raz·zle-daz·zle /raz'əl daz'əl/ *n. Colloq.* **1** excitement; bustle **2** extravagant publicity [reduplication of DAZZLE]

razz·ma·tazz /raz'mətaz'/ *n. Colloq.* glamorous excitement; bustle [prob. an alter. of RAZZLE-DAZZLE]

Rb *symb.* rubidium

R.C. *abbr.* Roman Catholic

RD *abbr.* **1** registered dietician **2** rural delivery

rd. *abbr.* road

RDA *abbr.* recommended daily (or dietary) allowance

re¹ /rē, rā/ *n. Mus.* second note of a major scale [L *resonare*, word arbitrarily taken]

re² *prep.* in the matter of; regarding; as to [L, abl. of *res* thing]

Re *symb.* rhenium

re- *prefix* **1** attachable to almost any verb or its derivative, meaning: **a** once more; afresh; anew **b** back; with return to a previous state **2** (also **red-** before a vowel, as in *redolent*) in verbs and verbal derivatives denoting: **a** in return; mutually (*react*) **b** opposition (*resist*) **c** behind or after (*relic*) **d** retirement or secrecy (*recluse*) **e** off; away; down (*recede; recline; repress*) **f** frequentative or intensive force (*redouble; resplendent*) **g** negative force (*recant; reveal*) [L]

re'ac·quire' *v.*	re'as·sess'ment *n.*	re·con·nect' *v.*	re·draft' *v.*
re'ad·mis'sion *n.*	re'as·sign' *v.*	re·con·nec'tion *n.*	re·draw' *v.*
re'ad·mit' *v.*	re'as·sign'ment *n.*	re·con'quer *v.*	re·ed'it *v.*
re'a·dopt' *v.*	re'a·wa'ken *v.*	re·con'quest *n.*	re·e·lect' *v.*
re'a·dop'tion *n.*	re·bid' *v.*	re·con·sign' *v.*	re'e·lec'tion *n.*
re'af·firm' *v.*	re·bind' *v.*	re·con·vene' *v.*	re·em·bark' *v.*
re'af·fir·ma'tion *n.*	re·boot' *v.*	re·con·ver'sion *n.*	re·em·bod'y *v.*
re·al'lo·cate *v.*	re·broad'cast' *v.*	re·con'vert' *v.*	re·e·merge' *v.*
re·al'lo·ca'tion *n.*	re·build' *v.*	re·co'py *v.*	re·em'pha·size' *v.*
re'ap·pear' *v.*	re·charge' *v.* & *n.*	re·cov'er *v.*	re·em·ploy' *v.*
re'ap·pear'ance *n.*	re·charge'a·ble *adj.*	re·cross' *v.*	re·em·ploy'ment *n.*
re'ap·pli·ca'tion *n.*	re·check' *v.* & *n.*	re·ded'i·cate' *v.*	re·en·gage' *v.*
re'ap·ply' *v.*	re·chris'ten *v.*	re·de·fine' *v.*	re·en'ter *v.*
re'ap·point' *v.*	re·clas'si·fi·ca'tion *n.*	re·def·i·ni'tion *n.*	re·e·quip' *v.*
re'ap·point'ment *n.*	re·clas'si·fy *v.*	re·de·sign' *v.*	re'es·tab'lish *v.*
re'ap·prais'al *n.*	re·clothe' *v.*	re·di'al *v.*	re'es·tab'lish·ment *n.*
re'ap·praise' *v.*	re·co'lor *v.*	re'dis·cov'er *v.*	
re'ar·rest' *v.* & *n.*	re·com·bine' *v.*	re'dis·cov'er·y *n.*	re·e·val'u·ate' *v.*
re'as·sem'ble *v.*	re·com·mence' *v.*	re'dis·trib'ute *v.*	re'ex·am'i·na'tion *n.*
re'as·sem'bly *n.*	re·com·mence'ment *n.*	re'dis·tri·bu'tion *n.*	re'ex·am'ine *v.*
re'as·sess' *v.*		re'di·vide' *v.*	re'ex·plain' *v.*

reach /rēCH/ v. **1** stretch out; extend **2** stretch out the hand, etc., (for); make a stretch or effort (for) **3** get as far as **4** get to or attain **5** make contact with the hand, etc., or by telephone, etc. **6** hand; pass (*reach me that book*) —n. **7** extent to which a hand, etc., can be reached out, influence exerted, motion carried out, etc. **8** act of reaching out **9** continuous extent, esp. of a river —**reach′a·ble** *adj.* [OE]

re·ac·quaint /rē′əkwānt′/ v. make acquainted again —**re′ac·quaint′ance** n.

re·act /rē·akt′/ v. **1** respond (to a stimulus, etc.) **2** respond in a reverse or contrary way (against) **3** (of a substance or particle) be the cause of chemical activity or interaction (with)

re·ac·tion /rēak′SHən/ n. **1** reacting; response **2** bad physical response to a drug, etc. **3** response in a reverse or contrary way **4** interaction of substances undergoing chemical change

re·ac·tion·ar·y /rēak′SHəner′ē/ adj. **1** tending to oppose (esp. political) change or reform —n. (pl. ·ar·ies) **2** reactionary person

re·ac·ti·vate /rē·ak′tivāt′/ v. (·vat·ed, ·vat·ing) restore to a state of activity —**re·ac′ti·va′tion** n.

re·ac·tive /rēak′tiv/ adj. **1** showing reaction **2** reacting rather than taking the initiative **3** susceptible to chemical reaction

re·ac′tor n. **1** person or thing that reacts **2** NUCLEAR REACTOR

read /rēd/ v. (**read** /red/, **read·ing**) **1** reproduce mentally or vocally written or printed words **2** convert or be able to convert (characters, symbols, etc.) into the intended words or meaning (*can′t read music*) **3** understand by observing; interpret **4** find (a thing) stated in print, etc. **5** assume as intended or deducible (*read too much into it*) **6a** (of a registering instrument) show (a specified figure, etc.) **b** interpret (a registering instrument) **7** convey meaning or an effect (*it reads persuasively; reads from left to right*) **8** Comp. access (data), as to copy or display **9** hear and understand (over a radio) (*Are you reading me?*) —n. **10** spell of reading **11** Colloq. book, etc., as regards readability (*a good read*) **12** read between the lines look for or find nonexplicit meaning **13** read up (on) make a special study of (a subject) [OE]

read′a·ble adj. **1** able to be read **2** interesting to read —**read′a·bil′i·ty** n.

read′er n. **1** person who reads **2** book intended to give reading practice, esp. in a foreign language **3** person appointed to read aloud, esp. in church

read′er·ship′ n. readers of a newspaper, etc.

read·i·ly /red′l-ē/ adv. **1** without reluctance; willingly **2** without difficulty

read·ing /rēd′iNG/ n. **1a** act of reading **b** matter to be read **2** literary knowledge **3** entertainment at which a play, poems, etc., are read **4** figure, etc., shown by a recording instrument **5** interpretation [OE, rel. to READ]

Read·ing /red′iNG/ n. **1** city in S England. Pop. 198,300 **2** city in Penn. Pop. 78,380

re·ad·just /rē′əjəst′/ v. adjust again or to a former state —**re·ad·just′ment** n.

read·y /red′ē/ adj. (·i·er, ·i·est) **1** with preparations complete **2** in a fit or usable state **3** willing, inclined, or resolved (*He is always ready to complain*) **4** within reach; easily secured (*ready source of income*) **5** immediate; unqualified (*found ready acceptance*) **6** prepared (*ready to burst*) —adv. **7** (usu. in comb.) beforehand; immediately usable (*ready-to-wear*) —v. (·ied, ·y·ing) **8** make ready; prepare **9** make ready prepare [OE]

Rea·gan /rā′gən/, **Ronald Wilson** 1911– ; 40th US president (1981–89)

re·a·gent /rē·ā′jənt/ n. Chem. substance used to cause a reaction, esp. to detect another substance

re·al /rē′əl, rēl/ adj. **1** actually existing or occurring **2** genuine; rightly so called; not artificial **3** Law. consisting of immovable property such as land or houses (*real estate*) **4** appraised by purchasing power (*real value*) —adv. **5** Colloq. really; very **6** for real Colloq. seriously; in earnest **7** the real thing (of an object or emotion) genuine; not inferior [AngFr and L *realis* fr. *res* thing]

re·face′ v.	re′in·spect′ v.	re·or′ga·nize′ v.	re·shape′ v.
re·fa′shion v.	re′in·ter′pret v.	re·pack′age v.	re·spray′ v. & n.
re·fas′ten v.	re′in·ter′pre·ta′tion	re·paint′ v.	re·start′ v.
re′fi·nance′ v.	n.	re·pave′ v.	re·state′ v.
re·fo′cus v.	re′in·vest′ v.	re·pop′u·late′ v.	re·stock′ v.
re·for′mat v.	re′in·vest′ment v.	re·price′ v.	re·string′ v.
re·for·mu·la′tion	re·is′sue v. & n.	re·pro′cess v.	re·stud′y v.
n.	re·kin′dle v.	re·pro′gram v.	re·style′ v.
re·freeze′ v.	re·la′bel v.	re′pro·gram′ma·ble	re′sub·scribe′ v.
re·fur′nish v.	re·learn′ v.	adj.	re·sup·ply′ v.
re·grade′ v.	re·light′ v.	re′pub·li·ca′tion n.	re·tell′ v.
re·grow′ v.	re·load′ v.	re·pub′lish v.	re·test′ v.
re·growth′ n.	re·match′ v.	re·pur′chase v. &	re·tie′ v.
re·hang′ v.	re·name′ v.	n.	re·tri′al n.
re·hear′ v.	re′ne·go′ti·ate′ v.	re·read′ v.	re·tune′ v.
re·heat′ v.	re′ne·go′ti·a′tion	re′re·cord′ v.	re·type′ v.
re·hire′ v.	n.	re′re·lease′ v.	re′up·hol′ster v.
re′im·pose′ v.	re·nom′i·nate′ v.	re·route′ v.	re·use′ v. & n.
re·house′ v.	re′oc·cu·pa′tion n.	re·sched′ule v.	re·vis′it v.
re·in·fect′ v.	re·oc′cu·py v.	re·seal′ v.	re·vi′tal·ize′ v.
re′in·oc′u·late′ v.	re·oc·cur′ v.	re·seal′a·ble adj.	re·weigh′ v.
re′in·sert′ v.	re·o′pen v.	re·sell′ v.	re·work′ v.
		re·set′tle v.	re·zone′ v.

ings and improvements

re·al·ism' *n.* 1 practice of regarding things in their true nature and dealing with them as they are 2 fidelity to appearance in represen- tation —**re'al·ist** /-ist/ *n.*

re·al·is'tic *adj.* 1 regarding things as they are 2 based on facts rather than ideals —**re·al·is' ti·cal·ly** *adv.*

re·al·i·ty /rē·al'ətē/ *n.* (*pl.* ·ties) 1 what is real or existent or underlies appearances 2 the real nature (of) 3 real existence; state of being real 4 **in reality** in fact [MedL or Fr, rel. to REAL]

re·al·ize /rē'əlīz'/ *v.* (·ized, ·iz·ing) 1 be fully aware of; conceive as real 2 understand clearly 3 present as real 4 convert into actu- ality 5 obtain, as profit —**re'al·iz·a·ble** *adj.*; **re'al·i·za'tion** *n.*

re·al-life' *adj.* actual, not fictional (*her real-life husband*)

re·al·ly *adv.* 1 in reality 2 very; genuinely (*re- ally useful*) 3 indeed; truly —*interj.* 4 ex- pression of mild protest or surprise

realm /relm/ *n.* 1 kingdom 2 domain (*realm of myth*) [L REGIMEN]

re·al time' *n.* 1 actual time during which a process occurs —*adj.* 2 (**real-time**) *Comp.* (of a system) in which the processing or re- sponse is ongoing and occurs during the ac- tual time of an event

re·al·ty /rē'əltē/ *n.* REAL ESTATE

ream /rēm/ *n.* 1 quantity of paper, usu. 500 sheets 2 (*pl.*) large quantity [Ar: bundle]

re·an'i·mate' *v.* (·mat·ed, ·mat·ing) 1 re- store to life 2 restore to activity or liveliness —**re·an'i·ma'tion** *n.*

reap /rēp/ *v.* 1 cut or gather (esp. grain) as a harvest 2 harvest the crop of (a field, etc.) 3 receive as a result of one's own or others' actions [OE]

reap'er *n.* 1 person who reaps 2 reaping ma- chine 3 (**the Reaper** or **Grim Reaper**) death personified

re·ap·por·tion /rē'əpôr'sHən/ *v.* apportion again or differently (esp. legislative districts)

rear[1] /rēr/ *n.* 1 back part of anything 2 space behind or position at the back of anything 3 buttocks —*adj.* 4 at the back 5 **bring up the rear** come last [prob. fr. ARREARS]

rear[2] *v.* 1a bring up and educate (children) b breed and care for (animals) c cultivate (crops) 2 (of a horse, etc.) raise itself on its hind legs 3 set upright; build [OE]

rear' ad'mi·ral *n.* naval officer ranking above captain

rear'guard' *n.* body of troops detached to pro- tect the rear, esp. in retreats [Fr *rereguarde*]

rear'guard' ac'tion *n.* 1 engagement under- taken by a rearguard 2 defensive stand or struggle, esp. when losing

re·arm' *v.* arm again, esp. with improved weapons —**re·ar'ma·ment** *n.*

rear'most' *adj.* furthest back

re·ar·range' /rē'ərānj'/ *v.* (·ranged, ·rang- ing) arrange again in a different way —**re'ar· range'ment** *n.*

rear'ward /rēr'wərd/ *adj.* 1 to the rear —*adv.* (also **rearwards**) 2 toward the rear [AngFr *rerewarde* REARGUARD]

rea·son /rē'zən/ *n.* 1 motive, cause, or justi- fication 2 fact adduced or serving as this 3

intellectual faculty by which conclusions are drawn from premises 4 sanity (*lost his reason*) 5 sense; moderation —*v.* 6 form or try to reach conclusions by connected thought 7 use argument (with) by way of persuasion 8 conclude or assert in argument 9 **stand to reason** be logical [L *ratio*]

• Usage: Since *reason* means 'cause or basis,' it is poor style to use *the reason is because*; the preferred usage is *the reason is that: The rea- son Max can't come is that* (not *because*) *his leg is broken.*

rea'son·a·ble *adj.* 1 having sound judgment 2 wise 3a not excessive or expensive b tolerable; fair —**rea'son·a·ble·ness** *n.*; **rea' son·a·bly** *adv.*

re·as·sert' /rē'əsert'/ *v.* assert again, esp. with renewed emphasis —**re·as·ser'tion** *n.*

re·as·sure /rē'əsHŏŏr'/ *v.* (·sured, ·sur- ing) 1 restore confidence to; dispel the ap- prehensions of 2 confirm in an opinion or im- pression —**re·as·sur'ance** *n.*; **re·as·sur'ing** *adj.*

re·bate *n.* /rē'bāt/ 1 partial refund —*v.* /rē' bāt, ribāt'/ (·bat·ed, ·bat·ing) 2 pay back, as a refund [Fr *rabattre*, rel. to RE-, ABATE]

reb·el *n.* /reb'əl/ 1 person who fights against or resists established authority —*adj.* /reb' əl/ 2 rebellious 3 of rebels 4 in rebellion —*v.* /ribel'/ (·belled, ·bel·ling) 5 act as a rebel; revolt 6 feel or display repugnance [L, rel. to RE-, *bellum* war]

re·bel·lion /ribel'yən/ *n.* open resistance to authority, esp. organized armed resistance to an established government [L, rel. to REBEL]

re·bel·lious /ribel'yəs/ *adj.* 1 tending to rebel 2 in rebellion 3 (of a thing) unmana- geable —**re·bel'lious·ly** *adv.*; **re·bel'lious· ness** *n.*

re·birth /rēberTH'/ *n.* 1 new incarnation 2 spiritual enlightenment 3 revival —**re·born'** *adj.*

re·bound /ribound', rē'bound/ *v.* 1 spring back after impact —*n.* /rē'bound, ribound'/ 2 act of rebounding; recoil; reaction 3 **on the rebound** while still recovering from an emo- tional shock, esp. after the end of a romantic relationship [Fr *rebonder*, rel. to BOUND[3]]

re·buff' /ribəf'/ *n.* 1 rejection of another's overtures, request, offer, etc. 2 snub —*v.* 3 give a rebuff to [Fr fr. It]

re·buke /ribyŏŏk'/ *v.* (·buked, ·buk·ing) 1 express sharp disapproval to (a person) for a fault; censure —*n.* 2 rebuking or being re- buked [AngFr]

re·bus /rē'bəs/ *n.* (*pl.* ·bus·es) represen- tation of a word or phrase by pictures, etc., suggesting its parts [L *rebus*, abl. pl. of *res* thing]

re·but /ribət'/ *v.* (·but·ted, ·but·ting) 1 re- fute or disprove (evidence or a charge) 2 force or turn back; check —**re·but'tal** *n.* [AngFr *rebuter*, rel. to BUTT[1]]

rec. *abbr.* 1 receipt 2 record 3 recreation

re·cal·ci·trant /rikal'sitrənt/ *adj.* 1 obsti- nately disobedient 2 objecting to restraint —**re·cal'ci·trance** *n.* [L *recalcitrare* kick out, fr. *calx* heel]

re·call *v.* /rikôl'/ 1a summon to return b (of a product) request return to fix a defect 2 recollect; remember **3** bring back to memory; serve as a reminder of **4** revoke or annul (an action or decision) **5** take back (a gift) —*n.* (also /rē'kôl'/) **6a** summons to come back **b** request to return a product to fix a defect **7** act of remembering **8** ability to remember

re·cant /rikant'/ *v.* withdraw and renounce (a former belief or statement) as erroneous or heretical —**re'can·ta'tion** /-kantä'sHən/ *n.* [L, rel. to CHANT]

re·cap *v.* /rē'kap', rēkap'/ (**·capped, ·cap·ping**) **1** recapitulate —*n.* /rē'kap'/ **2** recapitulation [abbr.]

re·ca·pit·u·late /rē'kəpicH'əlāt'/ *v.* (**·lat·ed, ·lat·ing**) go briefly through again; summarize [L, rel. to CAPITAL]

re'ca·pit'u·la'tion *n.* **1** act of recapitulating **2** *Mus.* section in which themes are restated [L, rel. to RECAPITULATE]

re·cap'ture *v.* (**·tured, ·tur·ing**) **1** capture again; recover by capture **2** reexperience (a past emotion, etc.) —*n.* **3** act of recapturing

re·cast' *v.* (**·cast, ·cast·ing**) **1** cast again (a play, net, votes, etc.) **2** put into a new form —*n.* **3** recasting **4** recast form

re·cede /risēd'/ *v.* (**·ced·ed, ·ced·ing**) **1** go or shrink back or further off **2** diminish; fade **3** slope backward (*a receding chin*) [L *recedere -cess-*, rel. to CEDE]

re·ceipt /risēt'/ *n.* **1** receiving or being received **2** written acknowledgment of payment received **3** (usu. *pl.*) amount of money, etc., received —*v.* **4** write a receipt for (a bill) [AngFr *receite*, rel. to RECEIVE]

re·ceive /risēv'/ *v.* (**·ceived, ·ceiv·ing**) **1** take or accept **2** acquire; be provided with **3** have conferred or inflicted on one **4** react to (news, a play, etc.) in a particular way **5** admit; provide accommodation for **6** (of a receptacle) be able to hold **7** greet or welcome, esp. in a specified manner **8** (of electronic equipment) convert (broadcast signals) into sound or pictures [L *recipere -cept-* get back again]

re·ceiv'er *n.* **1** person or thing that receives **2** telephone earpiece **3** (in full *offi'cial re·ceiv'er*) *Law.* person appointed by a court to administer the property of a bankrupt or insane person, or property under litigation **4** radio or television receiving apparatus

re·ceiv'er·ship' *n.* *Law.* state of being dealt with by a receiver (sense 3)

re·cent /rē'sənt/ *adj.* **1** not long past; of late **2** not long established; lately begun; modern **3** (*cap.*) *Geol.* of the most recent epoch of the Quaternary period, including modern humans —*n.* **4** (*cap.*) *Geol.* this epoch —**re'cent·ly** *adv.* [L *recens -ent-*]

re·cep·ta·cle /risep'tikal/ *n.* containing vessel, place, or space [L, rel. to RECEIVE]

re·cep·tion /risep'SHən/ *n.* **1** receiving or being received **2** way in which a person or thing is met or welcomed (*cool reception*) **3** social occasion for greeting guests **4** arrival area at a hotel, office, etc. **5a** receiving of broadcast signals **b** quality of this [L, rel. to RECEIVE]

re·cep'tion·ist *n.* person employed to receive guests, answer the telephone, etc.

re·cep·tive /risep'tiv/ *adj.* able or quick to receive impressions or ideas —**re·cep'tive·ly** *adv.*; **re·cep'tive·ness, re'cep·tiv'i·ty** *n.* [Fr or MedL, rel. to RECEIVE]

re·cess /rises', rē'ses'/ *n.* **1** space set back in a wall **2** (often *pl.*) remote or secret place **3** temporary cessation from school, proceedings, etc. —*v.* **4** make a recess in **5** place in a recess **6** take a recess; adjourn [L *recessus*, rel. to RECEDE]

re·ces·sion /risesH'ən/ *n.* **1** temporary decline in economic activity or prosperity **2** receding or withdrawal from a place or point [L, rel. to RECESS]

re·ces'sion·al *n.* hymn sung while the clergy and choir withdraw after a service

re·ces·sive /rises'iv/ *adj.* **1** tending to recede **2** *Genetics.* appearing in offspring only when not masked by an inherited dominant characteristic

re·cher·ché /rəsHer'sHā'/ *adj.* carefully sought out; rare; exotic [Fr]

re·cid·i·vist /risid'əvist/ *n.* person who relapses into crime, etc. —**re·cid'i·vism'** /-viz'əm/ *n.* [L *recidivus* falling back, rel. to RE-CEDE]

Re·ci·fe /rəsē'fə/ *n.* (formerly Per'nam·bu'co) seaport in NE Brazil. Pop. 1,184,200

rec·i·pe /res'əpē/ *n.* **1** statement of ingredients and procedure required for preparing a cooked dish **2** certain means to (an outcome) (*recipe for disaster*) [2nd sing. imper. of L *recipere* RECEIVE]

re·cip·i·ent /risip'ēənt/ *n.* person who receives something [It or L, rel. to RECEIVE]

re·cip·ro·cal /risip'rəkəl/ *adj.* **1** in return (*a reciprocal greeting*) **2** mutual **3** *Math.* expression or function so related to another that their product is one (*1/2 is the reciprocal of 2*) —**re·cip'ro·cal·ly** *adv.* [L *reciprocus* moving to and fro]

re·cip·ro·cate /risip'rəkāt/ *v.* (**·cat·ed, ·cat·ing**) **1** do, feel, give, etc. in return **2** interchange **3** (of a part of a machine) move backwards and forwards —**re·cip'ro·ca'tion** *n.*

rec·i·proc·i·ty /res'iprās'ətē/ *n.* **1** condition of being reciprocal **2** mutual action **3** give and take, esp. the interchange of privileges

re·cit·al /risīt'l/ *n.* **1** reciting **2** concert of classical music given by a soloist or small group **3** detailed account; narrative

rec·i·ta·tion /res'ətā'sHən/ *n.* **1** reciting **2** thing recited

rec·i·ta·tive /res'ətətēv'/ *n.* musical declamation in the narrative and dialogue parts of opera and oratorio [It *recitativo*, rel. to RECITE]

re·cite /risīt'/ *v.* (**·cit·ed, ·cit·ing**) **1** repeat aloud or declaim (a poem or passage) from memory **2** give a recitation **3** enumerate [L *recitare* read out]

reck·less /rek'ləs/ *adj.* heedless; rash —**reck'less·ly** *adv.*; **reck'less·ness** *n.* [OE *reck* concern oneself]

reck·on /rek'ən/ *v.* **1** be of the considered opinion; think **2** consider or regard **3** count; compute **4** estimate **5** **reckon with** take into account [OE]

reck'on·ing *n.* **1** counting or calculating **2** consideration **3** settlement of an account

re·claim /riklām'/ *v.* **1** seek or recover (one's property, rights, etc.) **2** make (land) useful, esp. after being under water **3** win back —**re-**

claim·a·ble *adj.*; **rec'la·ma'tion** /-kləmā′-sHən/ *n.* [L *reclamare* cry out against]

re·cline /riklīn′/ *v.* (**·clined, ·clin·ing**) assume or be in a horizontal or relaxed leaning position [L *reclinare*]

rec·luse /rek′lōōs, riklōōs′/ *n.* person given to or living in seclusion or isolation; hermit —**re·clu'sive** *adj.* [L *recludere* -*clus*- shut away]

rec·og·ni·tion /rek′əgnisH′ən/ *n.* recognizing or being recognized [L, rel. to RECOGNIZE]

re·cog·ni·zance /rikäg′nizəns/ *n.* *Law.* charge to observe some condition, as to appear when summoned [OFr, rel. to RECOGNIZE]

rec·og·nize /rek′əgnīz′/ *v.* (**·nized, ·niz·ing**) 1 identify as already known 2 realize or discover the nature of 3 realize or admit 4 acknowledge or countenance 5 show appreciation of; reward —**rec'og·niz·a·ble** *adj.* [L *recognoscere*]

re·coil *v.* /rikoil′/ 1 suddenly move or spring back in fear, horror, or disgust 2 shrink mentally in this way 3 (of a gun) be driven backward by its discharge —*n.* /rē′koil, rikoil′/ 4 act or sensation of recoiling [Fr *reculer* fr. L *culus* buttocks]

rec·ol·lect /rek′əlekt′/ *v.* remember —**rec'ol·lec'tion** /-lek′sHən/ *n.* [L *recolligere*, rel. to COLLECT¹]

rec·om·mend /rek′əmend′/ *v.* 1 suggest as fit for some purpose or use 2 advise as a course of action, etc. 3 make acceptable or desirable 4 commend or entrust (to a person or a person's care) —**rec'om·men·da'tion** *n.* [MedL, rel. to RE- + L *commendare*]

rec·om·pense /rek′əmpens/ *v.* (**·pensed, ·pens·ing**) 1 make amends to (a person) or for (a loss, etc.) 2 reward or punish (a person or action) —*n.* 3 reward; requital 4 retribution [L, rel. to COMPENSATE]

rec·on·cile /rek′ənsīl′/ *v.* (**·ciled, ·cil·ing**) 1 make or become friendly again after an estrangement 2 make acquiescent or contentedly submissive (to something disagreeable) 3 settle (a quarrel, etc.) 4 make or show to be compatible —**rec'on·cil'a·ble** *adj.*; **rec'on·cil'i·a'tion** /-sil′ēā′sHən/ *n.* [L, rel. to CONCILIATE]

re·con·dite /rek′əndīt′/ *adj.* 1 (of a subject or knowledge) abstruse; little known 2 (of an author or style) obscure [L *recondere* -*dit*- put away]

re'con·di'tion *v.* overhaul; make usable again

re·con·nais·sance /rikän′əsəns/ *n.* survey of a region, esp. to locate an enemy or ascertain strategic features [Fr, rel. to RECOGNIZE]

re·con·noi·ter /rē′kənoi′tər/ *v.* make a reconnaissance (of) [Fr, rel. to RECOGNIZE]

re'con·sid'er /rē′kənsid′ər/ *v.* consider again or anew, esp. with a view to change —**re'con·sid'er·a'tion** *n.*

re'con·sti·tute' *v.* (**·tut·ed, ·tut·ing**) 1 reconstruct; reorganize 2 restore (dried food, etc.) to liquid form —**re'con·sti·tu'tion** *n.*

re·con·struct /rēkənstrəkt′/ *v.* 1 build again 2 recall (past events or their order) by assembling the evidence for them —**re'con·struc'tion** /-strək′sHən/ *n.*

re·cord *n.* /rek′ərd/ 1a evidence or information constituting a (esp. official) account of something that has occurred, been said, etc.; b document, etc., preserving this 2 state of being set down or preserved in writing, etc. 3 disk carrying recorded sound in grooves on each surface, for reproduction by a record player 4 official report of legal proceedings 5a facts known about a person's past b list of a person's previous criminal convictions 6 best performance or most remarkable event of its kind —*v.* /rikôrd′/ 7 set down in writing, etc., for later reference 8 convert (sound, a broadcast, etc.) into permanent form for later reproduction 9 off the record unofficially; confidentially [L *cor cordis* heart]

re·cord'er *n.* 1 apparatus for recording, esp. a video or tape recorder 2 wooden or plastic wind instrument with holes covered by the fingers 3 keeper of records

re·cord'ing *n.* 1 process by which audio or video signals are recorded for later reproduction 2 material or a program recorded 3 recorded tape, disk, etc.

rec'ord play'er *n.* apparatus for reproducing sound from phonograph records

re·count *v.* /rikount′/ 1 count again —*n.* /rē′kount/ 2 re-counting, esp. of votes in an election

re·count /rikount′/ *v.* 1 narrate 2 tell in detail [AngFr *reconter*, rel. to RE-, COUNT¹]

re·coup /rikōōp′/ *v.* recover or regain (a loss) —**re·coup'a·ble** *adj.*; **re·coup'ment** *n.* [Fr *recouper* cut back]

re·course /rē′kôrs, -rē′/ *n.* 1 resort to a possible source of help 2 person or thing resorted to 3 have recourse to turn to (a person or thing) for help [L, rel. to COURSE]

re·cov·er *v.* 1 regain possession, use, or control of 2 return to health, consciousness, or to a normal state or position 3 obtain or secure by legal process 4 retrieve or make up for (a loss, setback, etc.) 5 retrieve; salvage —**re·cov'er·a·ble** *adj.* [L, rel. to RECUPERATE]

re·cov·er·y *n.* (*pl.* **·ies**) recovering or being recovered [AngFr *recoverie*, rel. to RECOVER]

rec·re·ant /rek′rēənt/ *Lit. adj.* 1 craven; cowardly —*n.* 2 coward [MedL, rel. to CREED]

re·cre·ate /rē′krēāt′/ *v.* (**·at·ed, ·at·ing**) create over again; reproduce —**re'cre·a'tion** /-ā′sHən/ *n.*

rec·re·a·tion /rek′rēā′sHən/ *n.* 1 process or means of refreshing or entertaining oneself 2 pleasurable activity —**rec're·a'tion·al** *adj.* [L, rel. to CREATE]

re·crim·i·nate /rikrim′ənāt′/ *v.* (**·nat·ed, ·nat·ing**) make mutual or counter accusations —**re·crim'i·na'tion** *n.*; **re·crim'i·na·to'ry** /-nətôr′ē/ *adj.* [MedL, rel. to CRIME]

re·cru·desce /rē′krōōdes′/ *v.* (**·desced, ·desc·ing**) (of a disease, problem, etc.) break out again —**re'cru·des'cence** *n.*; **re'cru·des' cent** *adj.* [L, rel. to CRUDE]

re·cruit /rikrōōt′/ *n.* 1 newly enlisted serviceman or servicewoman 2 new member or beginner —*v.* 3 enlist (a person) as a recruit 4 form (an army, etc.) by enlisting recruits 5 get or seek recruits —**re·cruit'ment** *n.* [Fr dial. *recrute*, rel. to CREW]

rec·tal /rek′təl/ *adj.* of or by means of the rectum

rec·tan·gle /rek′taNG′gəl/ *n.* plane figure

with four straight sides and four right angles, esp. other than a square —**rec·tan·gu·lar** /rektaNG'gyələr/ *adj.* [Fr or MedL]

rec·ti·fy /rek'təfī'/ *v.* (**·fied, ·fy·ing**) 1 adjust; make right 2 convert (alternating current) to direct current —**rec'ti·fi'a·ble** *adj.*; **rec'ti·fi·ca'tion** /-fikā'sHən/, **rec'ti·fi'er** *n.* [L *rectus* straight; right]

rec·ti·lin·ear /rek'təlin'ēər/ *adj.* 1 bounded or characterized by straight lines 2 in or forming a straight line [L, rel. to RECTIFY]

rec·ti·tude /rek'tit(y)ōōd'/ *n.* 1 moral uprightness 2 correctness [L *rectus* right]

rec·to /rek'tō/ *n.* (*pl.* **·tos**) 1 right-hand page of an open book 2 front of a printed leaf [L: on the right]

rec·tor /rek'tər/ *n.* 1 clergy member in charge of a parish or religious institution 2 head of some universities and colleges —**rec' tor·ship** *n.* [L *regere rect-* rule]

rec·to·ry /rek'tərē/ *n.* (*pl.* **·ries**) rector's house [Fr or MedL, rel. to RECTOR]

rec·tum /rek'təm/ *n.* (*pl.* **·tums**) final section of the large intestine, terminating at the anus [L: straight]

re·cum·bent /rikəm'bənt/ *adj.* lying down; reclining [L *cumbere* lie]

re·cu·per·ate /rikōō'pərāt'/ *v.* (**·at·ed, ·at·ing**) 1 recover from illness, exhaustion, loss, etc. 2 regain (health, a loss, etc.) —**re·cu' per·a'tion** *n.*; **re·cu'per·a·tive** /-ətiv/ *adj.* [L *recuperare*]

re·cur /rikər'/ *v.* (**·curred, ·cur·ring**) 1 occur again; be repeated 2 return to the mind [L *currere* run]

● Usage: *Recur* and *recurrence* are generally preferred to *reoccur* and *reoccurrence*.

re·cur·rent /rikər'ənt, -kə'rənt/ *adj.* recurring; happening repeatedly —**re·cur'rence** *n.*

re·cy·cle /rēsī'kəl/ *v.* (**·cled, ·cling**) 1 convert (waste) to reusable material 2 return (empty cans, etc.) for reuse —**re·cy'cla·ble** *adj.*

red /red/ *adj.* (**red'der, red'dest**) 1 of a color like blood 2 flushed in the face with shame, anger, etc. 3 (of the eyes) bloodshot or red-rimmed 4 (of the hair) reddish-brown; tawny 5 communist; socialist —*n.* 6 red color or pigment 7 communist or socialist 8 **in the red** in debt or deficit —**red'dish** *adj.*; **red'ness** *n.* [OE]

red' blood' cell' *n.* ERYTHROCYTE

red'-blood'ed *adj.* vigorous; robust

red'cap' *n.* railroad baggage porter

red' car'pet *n.* grand welcome to or treatment of a visitor

red' cell' *n.* (also **red' cor'pus·cle**) ERYTHROCYTE

red'coat' *n. Hist.* British soldier

Red' Cross' *n.* international organization bringing relief to victims of war or disaster

red'den *v.* 1 make or become red 2 blush

re·dec·o·rate' *v.* (**·rat·ed, ·rat·ing**) decorate (a room, etc.) again or differently —**re·dec'o· ra'tion** *n.*

re·deem /ridēm'/ *v.* 1 recover by a stipulated payment 2 make a single payment to cancel (a regular charge or obligation) 3 convert (tokens, bonds, etc.) into goods or cash 4 deliver

from sin and damnation 5 make up or compensate for (*has one redeeming feature*) 6 save (oneself) from blame —**re·deem'a·ble** *adj.* [L *emere* buy]

re·deem'er *n.* 1 person who redeems 2 (*cap.*) Christ

re·demp·tion /ridemp'sHən/ *n.* 1 redeeming or being redeemed 2 thing that redeems [L, rel. to REDEEM]

re·de·ploy /rē'deploi'/ *v.* send (troops, workers, etc.) to a new place or task —**re·de·ploy' ment** *n.*

re·de·vel'op *v.* replan or rebuild (esp. an urban area) —**re·de·vel'op·ment** *n.*

Red·grave /red'grāv'/ family of English actors, including: 1 (Sir) **Michael** 1908–85 2 **Vanessa** 1937–

red'-hand'ed *adv.* in the act of committing a crime, doing wrong, etc.

red'head' *n.* person with red hair

red' her'ring *n.* misleading clue; diversion

red'-hot' *adj.* 1 heated until red 2 highly exciting 3 completely new or fresh 4 intensely excited, angry, etc.

red' lead' /led'/ *n.* red form of lead oxide used as a pigment

red'-let'ter day' *n.* day that is pleasantly noteworthy or memorable

red' light' *n.* 1 signal to stop on a road, railroad, etc. 2 warning

red'-light' dis'trict *n.* district where many prostitutes work

red'neck' *n. Derog.* 1 politically conservative working-class white 2 ignorant bigot

re·do /rēdōō'/ *v.* (**·did, ·done, ·do·ing**) 1 do again 2 redecorate

red·o·lent /red'l-ənt/ *adj.* 1 strongly suggestive or smelling (of) 2 fragrant —**red'o·lence** *n.* [L *olere* smell]

re·dou·ble /rēdəb'əl/ *v.* (**·bled, ·bling**) make or grow greater or more intense or numerous

re·doubt /ridout'/ *n. Milit.* outwork or fieldwork without flanking defenses [Fr *redoute*, rel. to REDUCE]

re·doubt·a·ble /ridou'təbəl/ *adj.* formidable

re·dound /ridound'/ *v.* 1 make a great contribution (as to one's credit, advantage, etc.) 2 come back or recoil (up)on) [L *unda* wave]

red'-pen'cil *v.* (**·ciled** or **·cilled, ·cil·ing** or **·cil·ling**) revise, correct, or censor, usu. text

red' pep'per *n.* 1 cayenne pepper 2 ripe red fruit of the capsicum plant

re·dress *v.* /ridres'/ 1 remedy or rectify (a wrong, grievance, etc.) —*n.* /rē'dres, ridres'/ 2 reparation for a wrong 3 (foll. by *of*) redressing (a grievance, etc.) [Fr, rel. to DRESS]

Red' Riv'er *n.* 1 river flowing 1,300 mi. E from NW Texas into the Mississippi River in La. 2 **Red River of the North** river flowing 530 mi. N along the Minn.-N. Dak. border into Lake Winnipeg in S Canada

Red' Sea' *n.* arm of the Indian Ocean between Africa and the Arabian Peninsula

red' tape' *n.* excessive bureaucracy or formality, esp. in governmental administration

re·duce /rid(y)ōōs'/ *v.* (**·duced, ·duc·ing**) 1 make or become smaller or less 2 bring by force or necessity (to some undesirable state or action) (*reduced them to tears; reduced to begging*) 3 convert to another (esp. simpler) form (*reduced it to a powder*) **4** convert (a fraction) to the form with the lowest terms **5** simplify **6** make lower in status, price, etc. **7** lessen one's weight or size —**re·duc′i·ble** *adj.* [L *ducere* bring]

re·duc·ti·o ad ab·sur·dum /ridəc′tēō′ ad′ absər′dəm, -zər-, -SHēō′/ *n.* proof of the falsity of a premise by showing that its logical consequence is absurd [L: reduction to the absurd]

re·duc·tion /ridək′SHən/ *n.* **1** reducing or being reduced **2** amount by which prices, etc., are reduced —**re·duc′tive** /-tiv/ *adj.*

re·dun·dant /ridən′dənt/ *adj.* **1** superfluous **2** that can be omitted without any loss of significance —**re·dun·dan·cy** *n.* (*pl.* ·**cies**); **re·dun′dant·ly** *adv.* [L, rel. to REDOUND]

re·du′pli·cate′ *v.* (·**cat·ed**, ·**cat·ing**) **1** make double **2** repeat —**re·du′pli·ca′tion** *n.*

red′wood′ *n.* very large California conifer yielding red wood

re·ech′o *v.* (·**oed**, ·**o·ing**) echo repeatedly; resound

reed /rēd/ *n.* **1a** water or marsh plant with a firm stem **b** tall straight stalk of this **2** *Mus.* a strip of cane, etc., vibrating to produce the sound in some wind instruments **b** (esp. *pl.*) such an instrument [OE]

Reed /rēd/, **Walter C.** 1851–1902; US army physician

reed′y *adj.* (·**i·er**, ·**i·est**) **1** full of reeds **2** like a reed **3** (of a voice) like a reed instrument in tone —**reed′i·ness** *n.*

reef¹ /rēf/ *n.* ridge of rock, coral, etc., at or near the surface of the sea [ON *rif*]

reef² *n.* **1** part of a sail, folded and tied to reduce its surface area in a high wind —*v.* **2** take in a reef or reefs of (a sail) [Du fr. ON]

reef′er¹ *n. Slang.* marijuana cigarette [fr. REEF²]

reef·er² *n. Slang.* refrigerator car, truck, etc. [abbr.]

reek /rēk/ *v.* **1** smell strongly and unpleasantly **2** have unpleasant or suspicious associations (*reeks of corruption*) —*n.* **3** foul or stale smell [OE]

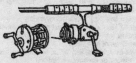

REELS 1, 3

reel /rēl/ *n.* **1** cylindrical device on which film, fishing line, etc., is wound **2** quantity wound on a reel **3** device for winding and unwinding a line as required, esp. in fishing **4** revolving part in various machines **5a** lively folk dance **b** music for this —*v.* **6** wind (fishing line, etc.) on a reel **7** (foll. by *in*) draw (fish, etc.) with a reel **8** stand or move unsteadily **9** be shaken mentally or physically **10** reel off say or recite very rapidly and without apparent effort [OE]

re·en·act′ /rē′enakt′/ *v.* act out (a past event) —**re′·en·act′ment** *n.*

re′·en·list′ *v.* enlist again, esp. in the armed services

re·en′try *n.* (*pl.* ·**tries**) act of entering again,

---

esp. (of a spacecraft, missile, etc.) into the earth's atmosphere

ref /ref/ *n.* referee in sports [abbr.]

re·fec·to·ry /rifek′tərē/ *n.* (*pl.* ·**ries**) dining room, esp. in a monastery or college [L *reficiere* renew]

re·fer /rifər′/ *v.* (·**ferred**, ·**fer·ring**) **1** appeal or have recourse (to some authority or source of information) (*referred to his notes*) **2** send on or direct (a person, or a question for decision) **3** make an allusion or direct attention (*did not refer to our problems*) **4** pertain **5** send (a person) to a medical specialist, etc. —**ref·er′a·ble** *adj.*; **re·fer′ral** *n.* [L *referre relat*- carry back]

ref·er·ee /ref′ərē′/ *n.* **1** umpire, esp. in football or boxing **2** person turned to in a dispute, etc. —*v.* (·**eed**, ·**ee·ing**) **3** act as referee (for)

ref·er·ence /ref′(ə)rəns/ *n.* **1** referring of a matter to some authority **2a** direction to a book, passage, etc. **b** book or passage so cited **3a** written testimonial supporting an applicant for employment, etc. **b** person giving this **4** with (or in) reference to regarding; as regards; about —**ref·er·en′tial** /ref′ərenˈSHəl/ *adj.*

ref′er·ence book′ *n.* book containing information organized for ready access, as a dictionary, atlas, etc.

ref·er·en·dum /ref′ərenˈdəm/ *n.* (*pl.* ·**dums** or ·**da** /-də/) direct popular vote on a political question [L, rel. to REFER]

re·fill *v.* /rēfil′/ **1** fill again —*n.* /rē′fil/ **2** thing that refills, esp. another container **3** act of refilling —**re·fill′a·ble** *adj.*

re·fine /rifīn′/ *v.* (·**fined**, ·**fin·ing**) **1** free from impurities or defects **2** make or become more polished, elegant, or cultured —**re·fined′** *adj.*; **re·fin′er** *n.*

re·fine′ment *n.* **1** refining or being refined **2** fineness of feeling or taste **3** polish or elegance in behavior **4** added improvement (*car with several refinements*)

re·fin·er·y /rifīn′(ə)rē/ *n.* (*pl.* ·**ies**) plant where oil, sugar, etc., is refined

re·fit *v.* /rēfit′/ (·**fit·ted**, ·**fit·ting**) **1** make or become serviceable again by repairs, renewals, etc. —*n.* /rē′fit/ **2** refitting

refl. *abbr.* reflex; reflexive

re·flect /riflekt′/ *v.* **1** (of a surface or body) throw back (heat, light, sound, etc.) **2** (of a mirror) show (back) an image of **3** manifest or testify to (*their behavior reflects their upbringing*) **4** (of an action, result, etc.) show or bring (credit, discredit, etc.) **5** meditate; consider [L *flectere flex*- bend]

re·flec·tion /riflekˈSHən/ *n.* **1** reflecting or being reflected **2a** reflected light, heat, or color **b** reflected image **3** reconsideration (*on reflection*) **4** discredit or thing bringing discredit (on) **5** idea arising in the mind; comment

re·flec·tive /riflekˈtiv/ *adj.* **1** reflecting **2** (of mental faculties) concerned in reflection or thought **3** pensive; given to meditation —**re·flec′tive·ly** *adv.*; **re·flec′tive·ness** *n.*

re·flec′tor *n.* **1** piece of glass, metal, etc., for reflecting light in a required direction **2a** tel-

escope, etc., using a mirror to produce images
b the mirror itself

re·flex /rē'fleks'/ *adj.* 1 (of an action) independent of will or as an automatic response to the stimulation of a nerve 2 (of an angle) exceeding 180° —*n.* 3 reflex action [L, rel. to REFLECT]

re·flex'ive *Gram. adj.* 1 (of a word or form, esp. of a pronoun) referring back to the subject of a sentence (e.g., *myself*) 2 (of a verb) having a reflexive pronoun as its object (as in *to wash oneself*) —*n.* 3 reflexive word or form, esp. a pronoun (e.g., *myself*)

re·form /rifôrm'/ *v.* 1 make or become better by the removal of faults and errors 2 abolish or cure (an abuse or malpractice) —*n.* 3 removal of faults or abuses, esp. moral, political, or social 4 improvement —**re·for'ma·tive** *adj.*

re·-form /rēfôrm'/ *v.* form again

ref·or·ma·tion /ref'ərmā'SHən/ *n.* 1 reforming or being reformed, esp. concerted change for the better in political, religious, or social affairs 2 (*cap.*) *Hist.* 16th-cent. movement for the reform of abuses in the Roman Catholic Church

re·for·ma·to·ry /rifôr'mətôr'ē/ *n.* (*pl.* -ries) 1 institution for the reform of young offenders —*adj.* 2 producing reform

re·form·er /rifôrm'ər/ *n.* person who advocates or brings about (esp. political or social) reform

re·fract /rifrakt'/ *v.* (of water, air, glass, etc.) deflect (a ray of light, etc.) at a certain angle when it enters from another medium —**re·frac'tion** /-frak'SHən/ *n.*; **re·frac'tive** *adj.* [L *refringere -fract-* break open]

re·frac·tor *n.* 1 refracting medium or lens 2 telescope using a lens to produce an image

re·frac·to·ry /rifrak'tərē/ *adj.* stubborn; unmanageable; rebellious [L, rel. to REFRACT]

re·frain¹ /rifrān'/ *v.* (foll. by *from*) avoid doing (an action) [L *frenum* bridle]

re·frain² *n.* 1 recurring phrase or lines, esp. at the ends of stanzas 2 music accompanying this [L, rel. to REFRACT]

re·fresh *v.* 1 give new spirit or vigor to 2 revive (the memory) —**re·fresh'ing** *adj.*; **re·fresh'ing·ly** *adv.* [Fr, rel. to FRESH]

re·fresh'ment *n.* 1 refreshing or being refreshed 2 (usu. *pl.*) food or drink

re·'fried beans' /rē'frīd/ *n. Cookery.* Mexican-style cooked beans, seasoned and partially mashed, then fried

re·frig·er·ant /rifrij'ərənt/ *n.* 1 substance used for refrigeration —*adj.* 2 cooling [L, rel. to REFRIGERATE]

re·frig·er·ate /rifrij'ərāt'/ *v.* (-at·ed, -at·ing) 1 make or become cool or cold 2 subject (food, etc.) to cold in order to freeze or preserve it —**re·frig·er·a'tion** *n.* [L *refrigerare* fr. *frigus* cold]

re·frig'er·a'tor *n.* electric appliance, etc., in which food, etc., is kept cold

re·fu·el /rēfyōō'əl/ *v.* (-eled, -el·ing) 1 replenish a fuel supply 2 supply with more fuel

ref·uge /ref'yōōj/ *n.* 1 shelter from pursuit, danger, or trouble 2 person or place offering this [L *refugium* fr. *fugire* flee]

ref·u·gee /ref'yōōjē'/ *n.* person taking ref-

uge, esp. in a foreign country, from war, persecution, or natural disaster [Fr *réfugié*, rel. to REFUGE]

re·ful·gent /rifəl'jənt/ *adj.* shining; gloriously bright —**re·ful'gence** *n.* [L *refulgere* shine brightly]

re·fund *v.* /rifənd'/ 1 pay back (money or expenses) —*n.* /rē'fənd'/ 2 act of refunding 3 sum refunded —**re·fund'a·ble** *adj.* [L *fundere* pour]

re·fur·bish /rēfər'biSH/ *v.* 1 brighten up 2 restore and redecorate —**re·fur'bish·ment** *n.*

re·fuse¹ /rifyōōz'/ *v.* (-fused, -fus·ing) 1 withhold acceptance of or consent to 2 indicate unwillingness or inability 3 (often with double object) not grant (a request) made by (a person) —**re·fus'al** *n.* [Fr *refuser*]

re·fuse² /ref'yōōs/ *n.* waste material [Fr, rel. to REFUSE¹]

re·fute /rifyōōt'/ *v.* (-fut·ed, -fut·ing) 1 prove the falsity or error of (a statement, opponent's reasoning, etc.) 2 rebut by argument —**ref·u·ta·tion** /ref'yōōtā'SHən/ *n.* [L *refutare*]

re·gain' *v.* obtain possession or use of after loss (*regain consciousness*)

re·gal /rē'gəl/ *adj.* 1 of or by a monarch or monarchs 2 fit for a monarch; magnificent —**re·gal'i·ty** /-gal'itē/ *n.*; **re·gal·ly** *adv.* [L *rex reg-* king]

re·gale /rigāl'/ *v.* (-galed, -gal·ing) 1 entertain lavishly with feasting 2 entertain (with talk, etc.) [Fr *régaler*, rel. to GALLANT]

re·ga·li·a /rigāl'yə/ *n. pl.* 1 insignia of royalty 2 decorations, finery, etc. [MedL, rel. to REGAL]

re·gard /rigärd'/ *v.* 1 gaze on steadily (usu. in a specified way) (*regarded them suspiciously*) 2 heed; take into account 3 think of in a specified way (*regard it as an insult*) —*n.* 4 gaze; steady or significant look 5 attention or care 6 esteem; kindly feeling 7 matter; respect (*in this regard*) 8 (*pl.*) expression of friendliness in a letter, etc. 9 **as regards** about; concerning; in respect of 10 in (or with) **regard to** in respect of [Fr *regard(er)*, rel. to GUARD]

re·gard'ing *prep.* about; concerning

re·gard'less *adj.* 1 without regard or consideration for —*adv.* 2 no matter what 3 **regardless of** in spite of

re·gat·ta /rigä'tə, -gat'ə/ *n.* event consisting of rowing or yacht races [It]

re·gen·er·ate *v.* /rijen'ərāt'/ (-at·ed, -at·ing) 1 generate again 2 improve the moral condition of 3 impart new, more vigorous, or spiritually higher life or nature to 4 *Biol.* regrow or cause (new tissue) to regrow —*adj.* /rijen'ərit/ 5 spiritually born again; reformed —**re·gen'er·a'tion** *n.*; **re·gen'er·a'tive** *adj.* [L *regere* rule]

re·gent /rē'jənt/ *n.* 1 person appointed to rule when a monarch is a minor or is absent or incapacitated 2 member of a governing board, as of a university [L *regere* rule]

reg·gae /reg'ā/ *n.* W Indian style of music with a strongly accented subsidiary beat

reg·i·cide /rej'əsīd'/ *n.* 1 person who kills or helps to kill a king 2 killing of a king [L *rex reg-* king, -CIDE]

re·gime /rāzHēm'/ *n.* (also **ré·gime'**, pronunc. same) 1 system of government 2 particular government or administration **3** *regimen* [Fr. rel. to REGIMEN]

reg·i·men /rej'əmən/ *n.* prescribed course of exercise, way of life, and diet [L *regere* rule]

reg·i·ment *n.* /rej'əmənt/ **1** military unit below division level **2** large or formidable array or number —*v.* /rej'əment'/ **3** organize (esp. oppressively) in groups or according to a system —**reg·i·men'tal** /-men'təl/ *adj.*; **reg·i·men·ta'tion** /-mentə'sHən/ *n.* [L, rel. to REGIMEN]

Re·gi·na /riji'nə/ *n.* capital of the Canadian province of Saskatchewan. Pop. 191,700

re·gion /rē'jən/ *n.* **1** geographical area or division (*fertile region*) **2** part of the body **3** sphere or realm (*region of metaphysics*) **4** in the region of approximately —**re'gion·al** *adj.*; **re'gion·al·ly** *adv.* [L *regere* rule]

reg·is·ter /rej'istər/ *n.* **1** official list, e.g., of births, marriages, property transactions, merchant ships, etc. **2** book in which items are recorded for reference **3a** compass of a voice or instrument **b** part of this compass (*lower register*) **4** CASH REGISTER **5** *Ling.* level or variety of a language (colloquial, literary, etc.) used in particular circumstances —*v.* **6** set down formally; record in writing **7** enter or cause to be entered in a particular register **8a** express (an emotion) facially or by gesture (*registered surprise*) **b** (of an emotion) show in a person's face or gestures [L *regerere -gest-* transcribe; record]

reg·is·tered nurse' *n.* state-certified, trained nurse

reg·is·trar /rej'isträr'/ *n.* **1** official responsible for keeping a register **2** enrollment administrator in a university, college, etc. [MedL, rel. to REGISTER]

reg·is·tra·tion /rejistrā'sHən/ *n.* registering or being registered [Fr or MedL, rel. to REGISTER]

reg'is·try *n.* (*pl.* -tries) place where registers or records are kept [MedL, rel. to REGISTER]

re·gress *v.* /rigres'/ **1** move backwards; return to a former, esp. worse, state **2** *Psychol.* (cause to) return mentally to a former phase of life —*n.* /rē'gres/ **3** act of regressing —**re·gres'sion** /-sHən/ *n.*; **re·gres'sive** *adj.* [L *regrediri -gress-* go back]

re·gret /rigret'/ *v.* (·gret·ted, ·gret·ting) **1** feel or express sorrow, repentance, or distress over (an action, loss, etc.) —*n.* **2** feeling of sorrow, repentance, etc., over an action or loss, etc. **3** give (or send) one's **regrets** politely decline an invitation —**re·gret'ful** *adj.*; **re·gret'ful·ly** *adv.*; **re·gret'ta·ble** *adj.*; **re·gret'ta·bly** *adv.* [Fr *regretter*]

re·group' *v.* **1** group or arrange again or differently **2** *Milit.* prepare for a fresh attack

reg·u·lar /reg'yələr/ *adj.* **1** acting, done, or recurring uniformly or calculably in time or manner; habitual; constant **2** conforming to a rule, standard, or principle; systematic **3** harmonious; symmetrical **4** proper or full-time (*regular soldier*) **5** *Gram.* (of a noun, verb, etc.) following the normal type of inflection **6** *Colloq.* genuine; absolute (*a regular hero*) **7** (of a person) defecating or menstruating at predictable times —*n.* **8** regular soldier **9** *Colloq.* regular customer, visitor, etc. —**reg·u·lar'i·ty** /-lar'itē/ *n.*; **reg'u·lar·ize** *v.* (·ized, ·iz·ing); **reg'u·lar·ly** *adv.* [L *regula* rule]

reg·u·late /reg'yəlāt'/ *v.* (·lat·ed, ·lat·ing) **1** control by rule **2** subject to restrictions **3** adapt to requirements **4** alter the speed of (a machine or clock) so that it works accurately —**reg·u·la'tor** *n.*; **reg·u·la·to·ry** /-lətôr'ē/ *adj.* [L, rel. to REGULAR]

reg·u·la'tion *n.* **1** regulating or being regulated **2** prescribed rule **3** in accordance with regulations; of the correct type, etc.

re·gur·gi·tate /rēgər'jətāt'/ *v.* (·tat·ed, ·tat·ing) **1** bring (swallowed food) up again to the mouth **2** reproduce; rehash (information, etc.) —**re·gur'gi·ta'tion** *n.* [L *gurges -git-* whirlpool]

re·ha·bil·i·tate /rē'həbil'ətāt/ *v.* (·tat·ed, ·tat·ing) **1** restore to effectiveness or normal life by training, etc., esp. after imprisonment or illness **2** restore to former privileges or reputation **3** restore to proper condition —**re'ha·bil'i·ta'tion** *n.* [MedL, rel. to RE-, ABILITY]

re·hash *v.* /rēhasH'/ **1** present or use (old material) again, esp. without freshness —*n.* /rē'hasH/ **2** material rehashed **3** rehashing

re·hears·al /rihər'səl/ *n.* **1** trial performance or practice of a play, music, etc. **2** process of rehearsing

re·hearse /rihərs'/ *v.* (·hearsed, ·hears·ing) **1** practice (a play, music, etc.) for later public performance **2** hold a rehearsal **3** train (a person) by rehearsal **4** recite or say over [AngFr, rel. to HEARSE]

Reich /rīk, rīKH/ *n.* the former German state, esp. the Third Reich (1933–45) [Ger: empire]

reign /rān/ *v.* **1** be king or queen **2** prevail (*confusion reigns*) —*n.* **3** sovereignty; rule **4** period of power, dominance, etc. [L *regnum*]

re·im·burse' *v.* (·bursed, ·burs·ing) **1** repay (a person who has spent money) **2** repay (expenses) —**re·im·burse'ment** *n.*

Reims /reNs, rēmz/ *n.* city in NE France. Pop. 185,200

rein /rān/ *n.* (usu. *pl.*) **1** long narrow strap with each end attached to the bit, used to guide or check a horse, etc. **2** means of control —*v.* **3** check or manage with reins **4** hold (in) as with reins **5** govern; restrain; control **6** give free rein to allow freedom of action or expression **7** keep a tight rein on allow little freedom to [Fr *rene* fr. L *retinēre* RETAIN]

re·in·car·na·tion /rē'inkär'nā'sHən/ *n.* rebirth of a soul in a new body —**re'in·car'nate** /-nāt'/ *v.* (·nat·ed, ·nat·ing); **re'in·car'nate** /-nət/ *adj.*

rein'deer' *n.* (*pl.* same or -s) subarctic deer with large antlers [ON]

re·in·force /rēinfôrs'/ *v.* (·forced, ·forc·ing) strengthen or support, esp. with additional personnel, material, etc. [Fr *renforcer*]

re'in·forced con'crete *n.* concrete with metal bars or wire embedded to increase its strength

re'in·force'ment *n.* **1** reinforcing or being reinforced **2** thing that reinforces **3** (*pl.*) reinforcing personnel, equipment, etc.

re·in·state' *v.* (·stat·ed, ·stat·ing) **1** replace in a former position **2** restore (a person, etc.) to former privileges —**re·in·state'ment** *n.*

REIT *abbr.* real estate investment trust

re·it·er·ate /rēīt′ərāt′/ v. (·at·ed, ·at·ing) say or do again or repeatedly —**re·it′er·a′tion** n.; **re·it′er·a·tive** /-ətiv/ adj.

re·ject v. /rijekt′/ 1 put aside, send back, or turn down 2 refuse to accept or believe in 3 rebuff or withhold affection from (a person) 4 show an immune response to (a transplant) so that it fails —n. /rē′jekt′/ 5 thing or person rejected as unfit or below standard —**re·jec′tion** /-jek′sнən/ n. [L rejicere -ject- throw back]

re·joice /rijois′/ v. (·joiced, ·joic·ing) feel great joy; be glad [Fr réjoir, rel. to JOY]

re·join[1] v. 1 join together again; reunite 2 join (a companion, etc.) again

re·join[2] v. 1 say in answer; retort 2 reply to a charge or pleading in a lawsuit —**re·join′der** n. [Fr rejoindre, rel. to JOIN]

re·ju·ve·nate /rijoo′vənāt′/ v. (·nat·ed, ·nat·ing) make (as if) young again —**re·ju′ve·na′tion** n. [L juvenis young]

rel. abbr. 1 relating; relative 2 religion; religious

re·lapse v. /rilaps′/ (·lapsed, ·laps·ing) 1 fall back or sink again (into a worse state after improvement) —n. /rilaps′, rē′laps/ 2 relapsing, esp. a deterioration in a patient's condition after partial recovery [L labi laps- slip]

re·late /rilāt′/ v. (·lat·ed, ·lat·ing) 1 narrate or recount 2 connect (two things) in thought or meaning; associate 3 have reference (to) 4 feel connected or sympathetic (to) [L, rel. to REFER]

re·lat′ed adj. connected

re·la′tion n. 1 the way in which one person or thing is related or connected to another 2 relative 3 (pl.) a dealings (with others) b sexual intercourse 4 RELATIONSHIP 5 in relation to as regards [L, rel. to REFER]

re·la′tion·ship′ n. 1 state or instance of being related 2a particular association (good working relationship) b emotional (esp. sexual) association between two people

rel·a·tive /rel′ətiv/ adj. 1 considered in relation to something else (relative velocity) 2 implying comparison or contextual relation ("heat" is a relative word) 3 comparative (their relative merits) 4 having mutual relations; corresponding in some way; related to each other 5 (foll. by to) having reference or relating to (the facts relative to the issue) 6 Gram. referring to an expressed or implied antecedent —n. 7 person connected by blood or marriage 8 species related to another by common origin 9 Gram. relative word, esp. a pronoun —**rel′a·tive·ly** adv. [L, rel. to REFER]

rel′a·tiv′i·ty n. 1 being relative 2 Physics. a (special theory of relativity) theory based on the principle that all motion is relative and that light has a constant velocity b (general theory of relativity) theory extending this to gravitation and accelerated motion

re·lax /rilaks′/ v. 1 make or become less stiff, rigid, tense, or formal 2 cease work or effort [L relaxare, rel. to LAX]

re·lax′ant n. 1 causing relaxation, esp. of the muscles —n. 2 substance (a drug, etc.) causing relaxation

re·lax·a·tion /ri′laksā′sнən/ n. 1 relaxing or being relaxed 2 recreation

re·lay n. /rē′lā′/ 1 fresh set or supply of people, materials, etc. 2 RELAY RACE 3 device activating an electric circuit, etc., in response to changes affecting itself 4 device to receive, reinforce, and transmit a message, broadcast, etc. —v. /rilā′, rē′lā′/ 5 receive (a message, broadcast, etc.) and transmit it to others [Fr relai fr. L laxare, rel. to LAX]

re′lay race′ n. team race in which each member in turn covers part of the distance

re·lease /rilēs′/ v. (·leased, ·leas·ing) 1 set free; liberate 2 allow to move from a fixed position; open, unfasten, etc. 3 make (information, a film, etc.) publicly available —n. 4 liberation from restriction, duty, pain, etc. 5 handle or catch that frees a mechanism 6 news item, etc., made available for publication (press release) 7a film, record, etc., that has been released b releasing or being released in this way [Fr relesser fr. L relaxare RELAX]

rel·e·gate /rel′igāt′/ v. (·gat·ed, ·gat·ing) 1 consign or dismiss to an inferior position 2 banish —**rel′e·ga′tion** n. [L relegere send away]

re·lent /rilent′/ v. relax severity; abandon a harsh intention; yield to compassion, etc. [MedL lentus flexible]

re·lent′less adj. unrelenting; oppressively constant —**re·lent′less·ly** adv.

rel·e·vant /rel′əvənt/ adj. bearing on or having reference to the matter in hand —**rel′e·vance** or **rel′e·van·cy** n. [L relevare, rel. to RELIEVE]

re·li·a·ble /rilī′əbəl/ adj. of consistently good character or quality; dependable —**re·li′a·bil′i·ty** n.; **re·li′a·bly** adv.

re·li·ance /rilī′əns/ n. trust; confidence —**re·li′ant** adj.

rel·ic /rel′ik/ n. 1 object valued because of its age or association 2 part of a dead holy person's remains, etc., kept out of reverence 3 surviving custom or belief, etc., from a past age 4 memento or souvenir 5 (pl.) fragments, ruins, etc. [L reliquiae remains, rel. to RELINQUISH]

re·lief /rilēf′/ n. 1a alleviation of or deliverance from pain, distress, anxiety, etc. b lightened feeling accompanying such deliverance 2 assistance (esp. financial) given to those in need 3a replacing of a person or persons on duty b person or persons replacing others in this way 4a method of molding, carving, or stamping in which the design is raised from the surface b piece of sculpture, etc., in relief 5 vivid contrast (in sharp relief) 6 reinforcement or rescue [Fr and It, rel. to RELIEVE]

re·lief′ map′ n. map indicating hills and valleys by shading, contour lines, etc.

re·lieve /rilēv′/ v. (·lieved, ·liev·ing) 1 bring or give relief to 2 mitigate the tedium or monotony of 3 release (a person) from a duty by acting as or providing a substitute 4 take (esp. a burden or duty) away from (a person) 5 relieve oneself urinate or defecate —**re·lieved′** adj. [L relevare raise again; alleviate]

re·li·gion /rilij′ən/ n. 1 belief in a personal God or gods entitled to obedience and worship 2 expression of this in worship 3 particular system of faith and worship 4 thing that one is devoted to [L *religio* bond]

re·lig·i·os·i·ty /rilij'ē·äs'ətē/ *n.* state of being religious or too religious [L, rel. to RELIGIOUS]

re·li·gious /rilij'əs/ *adj.* 1 devoted to religion; pious; devout 2 of or concerned with religion 3 of or belonging to a monastic order 4 scrupulous; conscientious —**re·li'gious·ly** *adv.* [L *religiosus*, rel. to RELIGION]

re·lin·quish /riling'kwish/ *v.* 1 surrender or resign (a right or possession) 2 give up or cease from (a habit, plan, belief, etc.) 3 relax hold of; let go —**re·lin'quish·ment** *n.* [L *relinquere* -*lict*- leave behind]

rel·ish /rel'ish/ *n.* 1 great liking or enjoyment 2 appetizing flavor 3 condiment eaten with plainer food to add flavor —*v.* 4 get pleasure out of; enjoy greatly 5 anticipate with pleasure [Fr *reles* remainder, rel. to RELEASE]

re·live /rēliv'/ *v.* (**·lived, ·liv·ing**) live (an experience, etc.) over again, esp. in the imagination

re·lo·cate *v.* (**·cat·ed, ·cat·ing**) 1 locate in a new place 2 move to a new place —**re'lo·ca'tion** *n.*

re·luc·tant /rilək'tənt/ *adj.* unwilling or disinclined —**re·luc'tance** *n.*; **re·luc'tant·ly** *adv.* [L *luctari* struggle]

re·ly /rilī'/ *v.* (**·lied, ·ly·ing**) (foll. by *on, upon*) depend on with confidence or assurance [L *religare* bind closely]

REM *abbr.* rapid eye movement

re·main /rimān'/ *v.* 1 be left over after others or other parts have been removed, used, etc. 2 stay (*remained at home*) 3 continue to be [L *remanere*]

re·main'der *n.* 1 residue 2 remaining persons or things 3 number left after division or subtraction 4 copy of a book left unsold —*v.* 5 dispose of (a remainder of books) at a reduced price [AngFr, rel. to REMAIN]

re·mains' *n. pl.* 1 what remains after other parts have been removed or used, etc. 2 relics of antiquity, esp. of buildings 3 dead body

re·make *v.* /rēmāk'/ (**·made, ·mak·ing**) make again or differently —*n.* /rē'māk'/ 2 thing that has been remade, esp. a movie

re·mand /rimand'/ *v.* return (a prisoner) to custody [L *remandare*]

re·mark /rimärk'/ *v.* 1 say by way of comment; note; observe 2 make a comment (on or upon) —*n.* 3 written or spoken comment; anything said 4 noting or noticing (*worthy of remark*) [Fr *remarquer*, rel. to MARK¹]

re·mark'a·ble *adj.* worth notice; exceptional; striking —**re·mark'a·bly** *adv.* [Fr *remarquable*, rel. to REMARK]

Re·marque /rəmärk'/, **Erich Maria** 1898–1970; German-born US writer

Rem·brandt /rem'brant'/ 1606–69; Dutch painter

re·me·di·al /rimē'dēəl/ *adj.* 1 affording or intended as a remedy 2 (of teaching, etc.) for slow or disadvantaged pupils [L, rel. to REMEDY]

rem·e·dy /rem'ədē/ *n.* (*pl.* **·dies**) 1 medicine or treatment 2 means of counteracting or removing a wrong —*v.* (**·died, ·dy·ing**) 3 rectify; make good —**re·me·di·a·ble** /rimē'dēəbəl/ *adj.* [L *remedium* fr. *mederi* heal]

re·mem·ber /rimem'bər/ *v.* 1 keep in the

memory; not forget 2 bring back into one's thoughts 3 convey greetings from (one person) to (another) (*remember me to John*) [L, rel. to MEMORY]

re·mem·brance /rimem'brəns/ *n.* 1 remembering or being remembered 2 a memory or recollection 3 keepsake; souvenir 4 (*pl.*) greetings conveyed through a third person [Fr, rel. to REMEMBER]

re·mind /rimīnd'/ *v.* cause (a person) to remember or think of (someone or something)

re·mind'er *n.* 1 thing that reminds, esp. a memo or note 2 memento

rem·i·nisce /rem'ənis'/ *v.* (**·nisced, ·nisc·ing**) indulge in reminiscence

rem·i·nis·cence /rem'ənis'əns/ *n.* 1 remembering things past 2 (*pl.*) collection in literary form of incidents and experiences remembered [L *rememini* remember]

rem·i·nis·cent /rem'ənis'ənt/ *adj.* 1 reminding or suggestive (of) 2 concerned with reminiscence

re·miss /rimis'/ *adj.* careless of duty; lax; negligent [L, rel. to REMIT]

re·mis·sion /rimish'ən/ *n.* 1 reduction of a prison sentence on account of good behavior 2 remitting of a debt or penalty, etc. 3 diminution of or period of relief from (esp. disease or pain) 4 forgiveness (of sins, etc.) [L, rel. to REMIT]

re·mit /rimit'/ *v.* (**·mit·ted, ·mit·ting**) 1 cancel or refrain from exacting or inflicting (a debt, punishment, etc.) 2 abate or slacken; cease partly or entirely 3 send (money, etc.) in payment 4 refer (a matter for decision, etc.) to some authority 5 pardon (sins, etc.) [L *remittere* -*miss*-]

re·mit·tance /rimit'ns/ *n.* 1 payment sent, esp. by mail 2 sending of money

rem·nant /rem'nənt/ *n.* 1 small remaining quantity 2 piece of leftover cloth, etc. [Fr, rel. to REMAIN]

re·mod·el *v.* (**·eled or ·elled, ·el·ing or ·el·ling**) 1 model again or differently 2 reconstruct

re·mon·strate /rimän'strāt'/ *v.* (**·strat·ed, ·strat·ing**) make a protest; argue forcibly —**re·mon'strance** /-strəns/ *n.* [MedL *monstrare* show]

re·morse /rimôrs'/ *n.* 1 deep regret for a wrong committed 2 compassion —**re·morse'ful** *adj.*; **re·morse'ful·ly** *adv.*; **re·morse'less** *adj.*; **re·morse'less·ly** *adv.* [MedL *mordere mors*- bite]

re·mote /rimōt'/ *adj.* (**·mot·er, ·mot·est**) 1 far away; far apart; distant 2 isolated; secluded 3 distantly related (*remote ancestor*) 4 slight; faint (*not the remotest chance*) 5 aloof; not friendly —**re·mote'ly** *adv.*; **re·mote'ness** *n.* [L *remotus*, rel. to REMOVE]

re·mote' con·trol' *n.* 1 control of an apparatus from a distance by means of signals transmitted from a radio or electronic device 2 such a device

re·move /rimōōv'/ *v.* (**·moved, ·mov·ing**) 1 take off or away from the place occupied 2 get rid of; dismiss 3 take away 4 move away; be distant or remote —*adj.* 5 (as removed) (esp. of cousins) separated by a specified number of steps of descent (*a first cousin twice* *removed* refers to a grandchild of a first cousin) —*n.* **6** degree of remoteness; distance **7** stage in a gradation; degree (*several removes from what I expected*) —re·mov'a·ble *adj.*; re·mov'al *n.* [L *removere -mot-*]

re·mu·ner·ate /rimyo͞o′nərāt/ *v.* (·ated, ·ating) serve as or provide recompense for (work, etc.) or to (a person) —re·mu'ner·a′tion *n.*; re·mu'ner·a·tive /-rətiv/ *adj.* [L *munus -ner-* gift]

Ren·ais·sance /ren′əsäns/ *n.* **1** revival of European art and literature in the 14th–16th cent. **2** period of this **3** style of art, architecture, etc., developed at this time **4** (r-) any similar revival [Fr *naissance* birth]

Ren·ais·sance man' *n.* person with many talents or pursuits, esp. in the humanities

re·nal /rēn′l/ *adj.* of the kidneys [L *renes* kidneys]

re·nas·cent /rinas′ənt, -nā′sənt/ *adj.* springing up anew; being reborn —re·nas'cence *n.*

Re·nault /rēnō′/, **Mary** (pseudonym of **Mary Challans**) 1905–83; British novelist

rend /rend/ *v.* (**rent, rend·ing**) tear or wrench forcibly [OE]

rend·er /ren′dər/ *v.* **1** cause to be or become (*rendered us helpless*) **2** give or pay (money, service, etc.), esp. in return or as a thing due **3a** give (assistance) **b** show (obedience, etc.) **c** do (a service, etc.) **4a** represent or portray **b** perform; execute **5** translate **6** melt (fat, etc.) —ren'der·ing *n.* (esp. in senses 4 and 5) [L *reddere* give back]

ren·dez·vous /rän′divo͞o/, -dā-/ *n.* (*pl.* same /-vo͞oz/) **1** agreed or regular meeting place **2** meeting by arrangement —*v.* (·voused /-vo͞od′/, ·vous·ing /-vo͞oiNG/) **3** meet at a rendezvous [Fr: betake yourselves]

ren·di·tion /rendisH′ən/ *n.* interpretation or rendering, esp. artistic [Fr, rel. to RENDER]

ren·e·gade /ren′igād′/ *n.* person who deserts a party or principles [MedL, rel. to RENEGE]

re·nege /rinig′, -neg′/ *v.* (·neged, ·neg·ing) go back (on one's word, etc.) [L *negare* deny]

re·new /rino͞o′/ *v.* **1** revive; refresh; restore **2** reinforce; resupply; replace **3** resume or reestablish (*renewed our acquaintance*) **4** grant or be granted continuation of (a license, lease, etc.) —re·new'a·ble *adj.*; re·new'al *n.*

Rennes /ren/ *n.* city in NW France. Pop. 203,500

ren·net /ren′it/ *n.* preparation made from the stomach membrane of a calf or from certain fungi, used in making cheese [prob. OE, rel. to RUN]

Re·no /rē′nō/ *n.* city in Nev. Pop. 133,850

Re·noir /rənwär′/, **Pierre Auguste** 1841–1919; French painter

re·nounce /rinouns′/ *v.* (·nounced, ·nounc·ing) **1** formally abandon (a claim, right, etc.) **2** repudiate; reject [L *nuntiare* announce]

ren·o·vate /ren′əvāt′/ *v.* (·vat·ed, ·vat·ing) restore to good condition; repair —ren'o·va′tion, ren'o·va'tor *n.* [L *novus* new]

re·nown /rinoun′/ *n.* fame; high distinction [Fr *renomer* make famous]

re·nowned' *adj.* famous; celebrated

rent[1] /rent/ *n.* **1** tenant's periodical payment to an owner for use of land, etc. **2** payment for the use of equipment, etc. —*v.* **3** take, occupy, or use for a fee to the owner **4** hire (a thing) for rent [Fr *rente*, rel. to RENDER]

rent[2] *n.* large tear in a garment, etc. [fr. REND]

rent[3] *v.* *past* and *past part.* of REND

rent'al *n.* **1** amount paid or received as rent **2** act of renting [AngFr or AngL, rel. to RENT[1]]

re·nun·ci·a·tion /rinən′sē·ā′sHən/ *n.* **1** renouncing or giving up **2** self-denial

re·or·der *v.* **1** order again **2** put into a new order —*n.* **3** renewed or repeated order for goods

re·o·ri·ent /rēôr′ēənt/ *v.* **1** give a new direction or outlook to (ideas, a person, etc.) **2** help (a person) find his or her bearings again **3** adjust oneself (to)

re·o′ri·en·tate′ *v.* (·tat·ed, ·tat·ing) see RE-ORIENT —re·o'ri·en·ta′tion *n.*

Rep. *abbr.* **1** Representative **2** Republican

re·pair[1] /riper′/ *v.* **1** restore to good condition after damage or wear **2** set right or make amends (a loss, wrong, etc.) —*n.* **3** restoring to sound condition (*in need of repair*) **4** relative condition or suitability (*in bad repair*) —re·pair'a·ble *adj.*; re·pair'er *n.* [L *parare* make ready]

re·pair[2] *v.* (foll. by *to*) resort; have recourse; go [L, rel. to REPATRIATE]

rep·a·ra·ble /rep′(ə)rəbəl/ *adj.* (of a loss, etc.) that can be made good [L, rel. to RE-PAIR[1]]

rep·a·ra·tion /rep′ərā′sHən/ *n.* **1** making amends **2** (esp. *pl.*) compensation for war damages

rep·ar·tee /rep′ärtē′/ *n.* **1** practice or skill of making witty retorts **2** witty banter [Fr *repartie* fr. *repartir* reply promptly, rel. to PART]

re·past /ripast′, rē′past′/ *n.* **1** meal **2** food and drink for this [L *repascere -past-* feed]

re·pa·tri·ate /rē′pā′trē·āt′/ *v.* (·at·ed, ·at·ing) **1** return (a person) to his or her native land —*n.* /-trēat/ **2** repatriated person —re·pa'tri·a′tion *n.* [L *repatriare* go back home, fr. *patria* native land]

re·pay /rēpā′/ *v.* (**paid, ·pay·ing**) **1** pay back (money) **2** make repayment to (a person) **3** requite; reward (a service, action, etc.) (*repaid their kindness*) —re·pay'a·ble *adj.*; re·pay'ment *n.*

re·peal /ripēl′/ *v.* **1** revoke or annul (a law, etc.) —*n.* **2** repealing [Fr, rel. to APPEAL]

re·peat /ripēt′/ *v.* **1** say or do over again **2** recite, rehearse, or report (something learned or heard) **3** recur; appear again —*n.* **4a** repeating **b** thing repeated **5** repeated broadcast —re·peat'a·ble *adj.*; re·peat'ed·ly *adv.* [L *petere* seek]

re·pel /ripel′/ *v.* (**·pelled, ·pel·ling**) **1** drive back; ward off **2** refuse to accept **3** be repulsive or distasteful to **4** resist mixing with or admitting (*surface repels moisture*) —re·pel'lent *adj.* & *n.* [L *repellere -puls-*]

● Usage: *Repellent* and *repulsive* are very close in meaning, but the latter is felt to be stronger. When used as a noun to mean a 'substance for repelling insects,' *repellent* is sometimes spelled *repellant*.

re·pent /ripent′/ *v.* **1** feel deep sorrow about one's actions, etc. **2** wish one had not done; resolve not to continue (a wrongdoing, etc.) —re·pen′tance *n.*; re·pen′tant *adj.* [L *paenitere*]

re·per·cus·sion /rē′pərkəsH′ən/ *n.* **1** indirect effect or reaction **2** recoil after impact **3** echo [L, rel. to RE-]

rep·er·toire /rep'ərtwär'/ *n.* stock of works that a performer, etc., is prepared to perform [L, rel. to REPERTORY]

rep·er·to·ry /rep'ə(r)tôr'ē/ *n.* (*pl.* ·ries) **1** performance of various plays for short periods by one company **2** repertory theaters collectively **3** store or collection, esp. of information, instances, etc. **4** REPERTOIRE [L *reperire* find]

rep·e·ti·tion /rep'ətish'ən/ *n.* **1** repeating or being repeated **2** thing repeated —**rep'e·ti'tious** /-SHəs/ *adj.*; **rep'e·ti'tious·ly** *adv.*; **re·pet·i·tive** /ripet'ətiv/ *adj.*; **re·pet'i·tive·ly** *adv.*

re·place' *v.* (·placed, ·plac·ing) **1** put back in place **2** take the place of; succeed; be substituted for **3** find or provide a substitute for —**re·place'ment** *n.*

re·plen·ish /riplen'ish/ *v.* **1** fill up again **2** renew (a supply, etc.) —**re·plen'ish·ment** *n.* [Fr *plenir* fr. *plein* full]

re·plete /riplēt'/ *adj.* **1** well-fed; gorged **2** filled or well-supplied —**re·ple'tion** *n.* [L *plere* fill]

rep·li·ca /rep'likə/ *n.* **1** exact copy, esp. of an art work **2** copy or model, esp. on a smaller scale [It *replicare* REPLY]

re·ply /riplī'/ *v.* (·plied, ·ply·ing) **1** make an answer; respond in word or action **2** say in answer —*n.* (*pl.* ·plies) **3** replying (*What did they say in reply?*) **4** what is replied; response [L *replicare* fold back]

re·port /ripôrt'/ *v.* **1a** give an account of; relate the facts of **b** state as fact or news **c** relate as spoken by another **2** make an official or formal statement about **3** bring (an offender or offense) to the attention of authorities, etc. **4** present oneself to a person as having returned or arrived **5** cover events as a journalist **6** make or send in a report **7** be responsible (to a superior, etc.) —*n.* **8** account given or opinion formally expressed after investigation, research, etc. **9** account of an event, esp. for publication or broadcast **10** common talk; rumor **11** way a person or thing is spoken of **12** periodic statement on academic performance, work, conduct, etc. **13** sound of a gunshot, etc. —**re·port'ed·ly** *adv.* [L *portare* bring]

re·port·age /rep'ärtäzн'/ *n.* **1** art or practice of news reporting **2** factual journalistic material in a book, etc. [fr. REPORT, after Fr]

re·port' card' *n.* evaluation of a student, usu. with number or letter grades and comments

re·port'er *n.* person employed to report news, etc., for the media

re·pose[1] /ripōz'/ *n.* **1** calmness or rest; peace; quietude **2** sleep —*v.* (·posed, ·pos·ing) **3** lie down in rest **4** lie, esp. in death [L, rel. to PAUSE]

re·pose[2] *v.* (·posed, ·pos·ing) place (trust, etc.) in [fr. RE-, POSE]

re·pos·i·to·ry /ripäz'ətôr'ē/ *n.* (*pl.* ·ries) **1** place where things are stored, esp. a warehouse or museum **2** receptacle **3** book, person, etc., regarded as a store of information, etc. [L, rel. to REPOSE[2]]

re·pos·sess /rē'pəzes'/ *v.* regain possession of (esp. goods on which payment is owed) —**re'pos·ses'sion** /-ze'sHən/ *n.*

re·pre·hend /rep'rihend'/ *v.* rebuke; find fault with [L *prehendere* seize]

rep·re·hen·si·ble /rep'rihen'səbəl/ *adj.* blameworthy

rep·re·sent /rep'rizent'/ *v.* **1** stand for or correspond to **2** be a specimen or example of **3** embody; symbolize **4** depict **5** describe; delineate **6** be a substitute, deputy, or agent for; be entitled to act or speak for **7** be elected as a member of a legislature, etc., by [L, rel. to PRESENT]

rep·re·sen·ta·tion /rep'rizentā'sHən/ *n.* **1** representing or being represented **2** thing that represents another **3** (esp. *pl.*) allegation or opinion —**rep're·sen·ta'tion·al** *adj.*

rep·re·sen·ta·tive /rep'rizen'tətiv/ *adj.* **1** typical of a class or as a specimen; exemplary (*representative sample*) **2** *Polit.* a consisting of elected deputies, etc. **b** based on representation by these (*representative government*) **3** serving as a portrayal or symbol (of) —*n.* **4** sample, specimen, or typical embodiment **5** agent, spokesperson, etc. **6** legislative delegate, deputy, etc. [Fr or MedL, rel. to REPRESENT[1]]

re·press /ripres'/ *v.* **1** keep under or down **2a** hold in subjection **b** put down; quell **3** *Psychol.* actively exclude (a painful thought or memory) from conscious awareness —**re·pres'sion** /-sHən/ *n.*; **re·pres'sive** *adj.* [L, rel. to PRESS[1]]

re·prieve /riprēv'/ *v.* (·prieved, ·priev·ing) **1** remit or postpone the execution of (a condemned person) **2** give respite to —*n.* **3** reprieving or being reprieved **4** respite [*repry* fr. Fr *reprendre* ·*pris* take back]

rep·ri·mand /rep'rimand'/ *n.* **1** (esp. official) rebuke —*v.* **2** administer this to [L, rel. to REPRESS]

re·print /rēprint'/ **1** print again —*n.* /rē'print'/ **2** reprinting of a book, etc. **3** book, etc., reprinted

re·pri·sal /riprī'zəl/ *n.* act of retaliation [MedL, rel. to REPREHEND]

re·prise /riprēz'/ *n.* **1** repeated passage in music **2** repeated item in a musical program [Fr, rel. to REPRIEVE]

re·proach /riprōcH'/ *v.* **1** express disapproval to (a person or oneself) for a fault —*n.* **2** rebuke or censure **3** thing that brings disgrace or discredit **4** state of disgrace or discredit **5** above (or beyond) reproach perfect; blameless —**re·proach'ful** *adj.*; **re·proach'ful·ly** *adv.* [Fr *reprochier*]

rep·ro·bate /rep'rōbāt'/ *n.* unprincipled or immoral person [L, rel. to PROVE]

re·pro·duce /rēprədōōs'/ *v.* (·duced, ·duc·ing) **1** produce a copy or representation of **2** cause to be seen or heard, etc., again (*reproduce the sound exactly*) **3** produce further members of the same species by natural means **4** produce offspring —**re'pro·duc'i·ble** *adj.*

re·pro·duc·tion /rēprədək'sHən/ *n.* **1** reproducing or being reproduced, esp. offspring **2** copy; imitation **3** quality of reproduced sound —**re'pro·duc'tive** /-tiv/ *adj.*

re·proof /riprōōf'/ *n.* **1** blame **2** rebuke [Fr *reprove*, rel. to REPROVE]

re·prove /riprōōv'/ *v.* (·proved, ·prov·ing)

rebuke (a person, conduct, etc.) [L, rel. to REPROBATE]

rep·tile /rep'tīl'/ *n.* cold-blooded scaly animal of a class including snakes, lizards, crocodiles, turtles, and tortoises —**rep·til·i·an** /reptil'ēən/ *adj.* & *n.* [L *repere rept-* creep]

re·pub·lic /ripəb'lik/ *n.* government in which power is exercised by elected representatives of the people [L *res* concern, rel. to PUBLIC]

re·pub·li·can /ripəb'likən/ *adj.* 1 of or constituted as a republic 2 characteristic of a republic 3 advocating or supporting republican government —*n.* 4 person advocating or supporting republican government 5 (*cap.*) supporter of the Republican Party —**re·pub'li·can·ism'** /-iz'əm/ *n.*

re·pu·di·ate /ripyōōd'ē-āt'/ *v.* (·at·ed, ·at·ing) 1a disown; disavow; reject b refuse dealings with c deny 2 refuse to recognize or obey (authority or a treaty) 3 refuse to discharge (an obligation or debt) —**re·pu'di·a'tion** *n.* [L *repudium* divorce]

re·pug·nance /ripəg'nəns/ *n.* 1 antipathy; aversion 2 inconsistency or incompatibility of ideas, etc. —**re·pug'nant** *adj.* [L *pugnare* fight]

re·pulse /ripəls'/ *v.* (·pulsed, ·puls·ing) 1 drive back by force of arms 2a rebuff b refuse —*n.* 3 repulsing; being repulsed [L, rel. to REPEL]

re·pul·sion /ripəl'SHən/ *n.* 1 aversion; disgust 2 *Physics.* tendency of bodies to repel each other

re·pul·sive /ripəl'siv/ *adj.* causing aversion or loathing; disgusting —**re·pul'sive·ly** *adv.* [Fr *répulsif* or REPULSE]

rep·u·ta·ble /rep'yətəbəl/ *adj.* of good repute; respectable [Fr or MedL, rel. to REPUTE]

rep·u·ta·tion /rep'yotā'SHən/ *n.* 1 what is generally said or believed about a person's or thing's character 2 good repute; respectability (*lost its reputation*) [L, rel. to REPUTE]

re·pute /ripyōōt'/ *n.* 1 reputation —*v.* 2 be generally considered; be said to be —**re·put'ed·ly** /-pyōō'tidlē/ *adv.* [L *putare* think]

re·quest /rikwest'/ *n.* 1 act of asking for something 2 thing asked for —*v.* 3 ask to be given, allowed, or favored with 4 ask (a person) to do something 5 ask (that) 6 by (or on) request in response to an expressed wish [L, rel. to REQUIRE]

re·qui·em /rek'wēəm/ *n.* 1 (*cap.*) *chiefly RC Ch.* Mass for the repose of the souls of the dead 2 music for this [L: rest]

re·quire /rikwīr'/ *v.* (·quired, ·quir·ing) 1 need; call for; depend on 2 ordain or prescribe (*required by law*) 3 command; insist on —**re·quire'ment** *n.* [L *requirere -quisit-* seek]

req·ui·site /rek'wozit/ *adj.* 1 required by circumstances; necessary —*n.* 2 thing needed (for some purpose) [L, rel. to REQUIRE]

req·ui·si·tion /rek'wəzi'SHən/ *n.* 1 formal demand or official request 2 written order for supplies 3 being called or put into service —*v.* 4 demand the use or supply of, esp. by requisition order [L, rel. to REQUIRE]

re·quite /rikwīt'/ *v.* (·quit·ed, ·quit·ing) 1 make return for (a service) 2 reward (a favor)

or avenge (an injury) 3 repay (a person) —**re·quit'al** *n.* [fr. RE-, *quite* QUIT]

re·ran /rēran'/ *v.* *past of* RERUN

re·run *v.* /rēran'/ (·ran, ·run, ·run·ning) 1 run (a race, tape, etc.) again —*n.* /rē'ran'/ 2 act of rerunning 3 TV program, etc., shown again 4 repetition (of events)

Res. *abbr.* Reservation

re'sale *n.* sale of a thing previously bought

re·scind /risind'/ *v.* abrogate; revoke; cancel —**re·scis'sion** /-siZH'ən/ *n.* [L *rescindere -sciss-* cut off]

res·cue /res'kyōō/ *v.* (·cued, ·cu·ing) 1 save or set free from danger, harm, etc. —*n.* 2 rescuing or being rescued —**res'cu·er** *n.* [ult. fr. L *quatere* shake]

re·search /risərCH', rē'sərCH'/ *n.* 1 systematic investigation and study of materials, sources, etc., in order to establish facts or advance knowledge —*v.* 2 do research into or for —**re·search'er** *n.* [Fr, rel. to SEARCH]

re·search' and de·vel'op·ment *n.* work directed toward the innovation, introduction, and improvement of products and processes

re·sem·blance /rizem'bləns/ *n.* likeness; similarity [AngFr, rel. to RESEMBLE]

re·sem·ble /rizem'bəl/ *v.* (·bled, ·bling) be like; have a similarity to [Fr *sembler* seem]

re·sent /rizent'/ *v.* feel indignation at; be aggrieved by —**re·sent'ful** *adj.*; **re·sent'ful·ly** *adv.* [L *sentire* feel]

re·sent'ment *n.* indignant or bitter feelings [It or Fr, rel. to RESENT]

res·er·va·tion /rez'ərvā'SHən/ *n.* 1 reserving or being reserved 2 thing booked, e.g., a hotel room 3 spoken or unspoken limiting consideration; qualification; misgiving 4 area of land reserved for occupation by American Indians [L, rel. to RESERVE]

re·serve /rizərv'/ *v.* (·served, ·serv·ing) 1 put aside or keep back for a later occasion or special use 2 order to be specially retained or allocated for a particular person or at a particular time 3 retain or secure (*reserve the right to*) —*n.* 4 thing reserved for future use; extra amount 5 self-restraint; reticence; lack of cordiality 6 (*sing.* or *pl.*) assets kept readily available 7 (*sing.* or *pl.*) standby or supplemental troops 8 RESERVIST 9 substitute player on a team 10 land reserved for special use, esp. as a habitat (*nature reserve*) 11 **in reserve** unused and available if required 12 **reserve judgment** postpone giving one's opinion [L *servare* keep]

re·served' *adj.* 1 not forthcoming; uncommunicative 2 set apart or aside; destined for a particular use

re·serv'ist *n.* member of the military reserve

res·er·voir /rez'ə(r)vwär', -vôr'/ *n.* 1 large lake as a source of water supply 2 receptacle for fluid 3 supply of information, etc. [Fr, rel. to RESERVOIR]

re·set' *v.* (·set, ·set·ting) set (a bone, gems, a clock, etc.) again or differently

re·shuf'fle *v.* (·fled, ·fling) 1 shuffle (cards) again 2 change the positions of (government officials, etc.) —*n.* 3 act of reshuffling

re·side /rizīd'/ *v.* (·sided, ·sid·ing) 1 have one's home; dwell permanently 2 (of power, a right, etc.) be vested in 3 (of a quality) be present or inherent in [L *sedere* sit]

res·i·dence /rez'ədəns/ *n.* 1 process of residing or being resident **2** place where a person resides **3 in residence** living or working at a specified place, esp. for the performance of duties (artist in residence)

res·i·den·cy /rez′ədənsē/ n. (pl. ·cies) **1** RESIDENCE, 1, 2 **2** period of hospital staff training for a physician

res·i·dent /rez′ədənt/ n. **1** permanent inhabitant **2** physician with duties on a hospital staff during a training period —adj. **3** residing; in residence **4** having quarters at one's workplace, etc. (resident housekeeper) **5** existing; immanent **6** (of birds, etc.) nonmigratory

res·i·den·tial /rez′əden′CHəl/ adj. **1** pertaining to or used as a residence (residential hotel) **2** (of a district) having houses or apartments; not commercial

re·sid·u·al /rizij′ōōəl/ adj. **1** left as a residue —n. **2** residual quantity **3** (pl.) pay to actors for reruns of dramas, commercials, etc.

res·i·due /rez′əd(y)ōō′/ n. what is left over or remains; remainder [L residuum remaining]

re·sign /rizīn′/ v. **1** give up office, one's employment, etc. **2** relinquish (a right, task, etc.) **3** reconcile (oneself) to the inevitable [L signare sign]

res·ig·na·tion /rez′ignā′SHən/ n. **1** resigning, esp. from one's job or office **2** letter, etc., conveying this **3** reluctant acceptance of the inevitable [MedL, rel. to RESIGN]

re·signed /rēzīnd′/ adj. **1** having resigned oneself; resolved to endure **2** indicative of this —re·sign′ed·ly /-zi′nidlē/ adv.

re·sil·ient /rizil′yənt/ adj. **1** resuming its original shape after compression, etc. **2** readily recovering from a setback —re·sil′ience n. [L salire jump]

res·in /rez′ən/ n. **1** adhesive substance secreted by some plants and trees **2** (in full **synthetic resin**) (also **ros·in**) organic compound made by polymerization, etc., and used in plastics —res′in·ous adj. [L]

re·sist /rizist′/ v. **1** withstand the action or effect of **2** abstain from (pleasure, temptation, etc.) **3** strive or struggle against; refuse to comply with (resist arrest) —n. **4** protective coating of a resistant substance —re·sis′tant, re·sist′i·ble adj. [L sistere stop]

re·sis′tance /rizis′təns/ n. **1** resisting; refusal to comply **2** power of resisting **3** ability to withstand disease **4** impeding or stopping effect exerted by one thing on another **5** Physics. property of hindering the conduction of electricity, heat, etc. **6** secret organization resisting a regime, esp. in an occupied country [L, rel. to RESIST]

re·sis′tor n. device having resistance to the passage of an electric current

res·o·lute /rez′əlōōt′/ adj. firm of purpose; determined —res′o·lute′ly adv. [L, rel. to RESOLVE]

res′o·lu′tion n. **1** resolute temper or character **2** thing resolved on; intention **3** formal expression of opinion or intention by a legislative body, public meeting, etc. **4** solving of a doubt, problem, or question **5a** separation into components **b** optical or visual clarity or sharpness

re·solve /rizôlv′, -zälv′/ v. (·solved, ·solv·ing) **1** make up one's mind; decide firmly **2** solve, explain, or settle (a doubt, argument,

etc.) **3** (of an assembly or meeting) pass a resolution by vote **4** (cause to) separate into constituent parts —n. **5** firm mental decision or intention; determination [L, rel. to SOLVE]

re·solved′ adj. resolute; determined

res·o·nant /rez′ənənt/ adj. **1** (of sound) echoing; resounding **2** (of a body, room, place, etc.) tending to reinforce or prolong sounds **3** richly abundant or intensely present —res′o·nance n. [L, rel. to RESOUND]

res·o·nate /rez′ənāt′/ v. (·nat·ed, ·nat·ing) produce or show resonance; resound —res′o·na′tor n. [L, rel. to RESONANT]

re·sort /rizôrt′/ n. **1** place frequented for recreation, vacation, health, etc. **2a** thing to which one has recourse; expedient; measure **b** access or turning (to) (without resort to violence) —v. **3** turn (to) as an expedient **4** as **a last resort** when all else has failed [Fr sortir go out]

re·sound /rizound′/ v. **1** (of a place) ring or echo **2** produce echoes; go on sounding [L, rel. to SOUND¹]

re·sound′ing adj. **1** ringing; echoing **2** notable; emphatic (a resounding success)

re·source /rē′sôrs, -zôrs/ n. **1** expedient or device **2** (often pl.) means or material available; asset **3** (pl.) country's collective wealth **4** skill in devising expedients (person of great resource) **5** (pl.) one's inner strength, ingenuity, etc. —re·source′ful adj. (in sense 4); re·source′ful·ly adv.; re·source′ful·ness n. [Fr, rel. to SOURCE]

re·spect /rispekt′/ n. **1** deference felt or shown toward a person or quality **2** heed or regard **3** aspect, detail, etc. (correct in all respects) **4** reference or relation (with respect to) **5** (pl.) greetings or best wishes (give her my respects) —v. **6** regard with deference or esteem **7a** avoid interfering with or harming **b** treat with consideration or discretion —re·spect′er n. [L respicere -spect- look back at]

re·spect′a·ble adj. **1** decent and proper in appearance or behavior **2** fairly competent (a respectable try) **3** reasonably good in condition, appearance, number, size, etc. —re·spect·a·bil′i·ty n.; re·spect′a·bly adv.

re·spect·ful /rispekt′fəl/ adj. showing deference —re·spect′ful·ly adv.

re·spect′ing prep. with regard to; concerning

re·spec′tive adj. of or relating to each of several individually (go to your respective seats) —re·spec′tive·ly adv. [Fr or MedL, rel. to RESPECT]

res·pi·ra·tion /res′pərā′SHən/ n. **1a** breathing **b** single breath in or out **2** Biol. (in organisms) absorption of oxygen and the release of energy and carbon dioxide [L spirare breathe]

res·pi·ra·tor /res′pərā′tər/ n. **1** apparatus worn over the face to warm, filter, or purify inhaled air **2** apparatus for maintaining artificial respiration

re·spire /rispīr′/ v. (·spired, ·spir·ing) **1** breathe (air, etc.); inhale and exhale **2** (of a plant) carry out respiration —res·pi·ra·to·ry /res′p(ə)rətôr′ē, rispīr′-/ adj.

res·pite /res′pət, rispīt′/ n. **1** interval of rest or relief **2** delay permitted before the discharge of an obligation or the suffering of a penalty [L, rel. to RESPECT]

re·splen·dent /risplen'dənt/ *adj.* dazzlingly or gloriously bright; brilliant —**re·splen'dence** *n.* [L *resplendere* shine]

re·spond /rispänd'/ *v.* 1 answer; reply 2 react 3 show sensitiveness (to) by behavior or change (*does not respond to kindness*) [L *respondere* *-spons-*]

re·spon'dent *n. Law.* defendant, esp. in an appeal or divorce case

re·sponse /rispäns'/ *n.* 1 answer given in a word or act; reply 2 feeling, movement, or change caused by a stimulus or influence 3 *Eccles.* (often *pl.*) any part of the liturgy said or sung in answer to the priest [L, rel. to RE-SPOND]

re·spon·si·bil·i·ty /rispän'səbil'ətē/ *n.* (*pl.* ·ties) 1a being responsible b authority and obligation (*job with more responsibility*) 2 person or thing for which one is responsible; duty; commitment

re·spon·si·ble /rispän'səbəl/ *adj.* 1 liable to be called to account (to a person or for a thing) 2 morally accountable for one's actions; capable of rational conduct 3 of good credit, position, or repute; respectable 4 being the primary cause 5 involving responsibility —**re·spon'si·bly** *adv.*

re·spon·sive /rispän'siv/ *adj.* 1 responding readily (to some influence) 2 sympathetic 3 answering —**re·spon'sive·ness** *n.*

rest[1] /rest/ *v.* 1 cease from exertion, action, etc.; pause 2 be still or asleep, esp. to refresh oneself or recover strength 3 give relief or repose to; allow to rest 4 lie (on); be supported (by) 5 depend or be based (on) 6 (of a look) alight or be steadily directed (on) 7 place for support (on) 8 be left without further investigation or discussion 9a lie in death b lie buried (in a churchyard, etc.) 10 refresh by resting —*n.* 11 cessation of exertion, activity, etc. 12 repose or sleep 13 period of resting 14 support for holding or steadying something 15 *Mus.* a interval of silence b sign denoting this 16 **at rest:** a motionless b dead 17 **rest one's case** conclude one's argument, etc. 18 **rest on one's laurels** not seek further success [OE]

rest[2] *n.* 1 (prec. by *the*) the remaining part or parts; the others; the remainder —*v.* 2 remain in a specified state (*rest assured*) 3 be left in the hands or charge of (*decision rests with you*) [Fr *rester* remain]

res·tau·rant /res't(ə)ränt, -ränt'/ *n.* public premises where meals can be bought and eaten [Fr fr. *restaurer* RESTORE]

res·tau·ra·teur /res'tərətər'/ *n.* owner or operator of a restaurant

• Usage: There is no *n* in this word. None should be used in either its spelling or its pronunciation.

rest·ful /rest'fəl/ *adj.* giving rest or a feeling of rest; quiet; undisturbed —**rest'ful·ly** *adv.*; **rest'ful·ness** *n.*

rest' home' *n.* place where old or convalescent people are cared for

res·ti·tu·tion /res'tit(y)ōō'shən/ *n.* 1 restoring of a thing to its proper owner 2 reparation [L]

res·tive /res'tiv/ *adj.* 1 resisting control; unruly 2 restless —**res'tive·ly** *adv.*; **res'tive·ness** *n.* [Fr, rel. to REST[2]]

rest·less *adj.* 1 without rest or sleep 2 uneasy; agitated 3 constantly in motion; fidgety —**rest'less·ly** *adv.*; **rest'less·ness** *n.* [OE, rel. to REST[1]]

res·to·ra·tion /res'tərā'shən/ *n.* 1 restoring or being restored 2 model or representation of the supposed original form of a thing 3 (*cap.*) *Hist.* a (prec. by *the*) reestablishment of the British monarchy in 1660 b literary period following this (*Restoration comedy*)

re·stor·a·tive /ristôr'ətiv/ *adj.* 1 tending to restore health or strength —*n.* 2 restorative medicine, food, etc.

re·store /ristôr'/ *v.* (·**stored**, ·**stor·ing**) 1 bring back to the original state by rebuilding, repairing, etc. 2 bring back to health, etc. 3 give back to the original owner 4 reinstate 5 replace; put or bring back —**re·stor'er** *n.* [L *restaurare*]

re·strain /ristrān'/ *v.* 1 check or hold in; keep under control or within bounds 2 repress; keep down 3 deprive of liberty; incarcerate [L *restringere* *-strict-*]

re·straint /ristrānt'/ *n.* 1 restraining or being restrained 2 restraining agency or influence 3 moderation; self-control 4 reserve of manner 5 confinement, esp. because of insanity

re·strict /ristrikt'/ *v.* 1 confine; limit 2 withhold from general circulation or disclosure —**re·strict'ed** *adj.*; **re·stric'tion** *n.* [L, rel. to RESTRAIN]

re·stric'tive *adj.* 1 restricting 2 *Gram.* denoting a modifier that uniquely identifies a preceding noun and has no punctuation —**re·stric'tive·ly** *adv.* [Fr or MedL, rel. to RE-STRICT]

rest' room' *n.* public toilet

re·struc·ture /rēstrak'chər/ *v.* (·**tured, ·tur·ing**) give a new structure or form to; rebuild; rearrange

re·sult /rizolt'/ *n.* 1 consequence, issue, or outcome of something 2 (*pl.*) satisfactory outcome (*gets results*) 3 end product of calculation 4 (*pl.*) list of scores, winners, etc., in examinations or sporting events —*v.* 5 arise as the actual or follow as a logical consequence 6 have a specified end or outcome (*resulted in a large profit*) —**re·sul'tant** *adj.* & *n.* [L *resultare* spring back]

re·sume /rizōōm'/ *v.* (·**sumed, ·sum·ing**) 1 begin again or continue after an interruption 2 begin to speak, work, or use again; recommence 3 get back; take back (*resume one's seat*) [L *sumere sumpt-* take]

ré·su·mé /rez'əmā'/ *n.* (also **re'su·me', re'su·me'**) summary, esp. of professional or work experience [Fr, rel. to RESUME]

re·sump·tion /rizamp'shən/ *n.* resuming —**re·sump'tive** *-tiv/ adj.* [L, rel. to RESUME]

re·sur·face *v.* (·**faced, ·fac·ing**) 1 lay a new surface on (a road, etc.) 2 return to the surface 3 turn up again

re·sur·gent /risər'jənt/ *adj.* rising or arising again —**re·sur'gence** *n.* [L *resurgere -surrect-* rise again]

res·ur·rect /rez'ərekt'/ *v.* 1 revive the practice, use, or memory of 2 raise or rise from the dead [back formation fr. RESURRECTION]

res·ur·rec·tion /rez'ərek'shən/ *n.* 1 rising

from the dead **2** (*cap.*) Christ's rising from the dead **2** revival after disuse, inactivity, or decay [L, rel. to RESURGENT]

re·sus·ci·tate /risǝs′ǝtāt′/ *v.* (·tat·ed, ·tat·ing) **1** revive from unconsciousness or apparent death **2** revive; restore —**re·sus·ci·ta′tion** *n.* [L *suscitare* raise]

re·tail /rē′tāl′/ *n.* **1** sale of goods in small quantities to the public —*adj. & adv.* **2** by retail; at a retail price —*v.* **3** sell (goods) by retail **4** (of goods) be sold in this way (esp. for a specified price) —**re′tail·er** *n.* [Fr *tailier* cut, rel. to TALLY]

re·tain /ritān′/ *v.* **1a** keep possession of; not lose **b** not abolish, discard, or alter **2** keep in one's memory **3** keep in place; hold fixed **4** secure the services of (a person, esp. a lawyer) with a preliminary payment [L *retinere* -*tent*-]

re·tain′er *n.* **1** fee or initial fee for securing a person's services **2** faithful servant (esp. *old retainer*) **3** person or thing that retains

re·take *v.* /rētāk′/ (·took, ·tak·en, ·tak·ing) **1** take (a photograph, exam, etc.) again **2** recapture —*n.* /rē′tāk′/ **3** act of filming a scene or recording music, etc., again **4** film or recording obtained in this way

re·tal·i·ate /rital′ē·āt′/ *v.* (·at·ed, ·at·ing) repay an injury, insult, etc., in kind; attack in return —**re·tal′i·a′tion** *n.*; **re·tal′i·a·to′ry** /-tal′yǝtȯr′ē/ *adj.* [L *talis* such]

re·tard /ritärd′/ *v.* **1** make slow or late **2** delay the progress or accomplishment of —**re·tar′dant** *adj. & n.*; **re′tar·da′tion** *n.* [L *tardus* slow]

re·tard′ed *adj.* limited in mental or physical development

retch /recH/ *v.* make a motion of vomiting, esp. involuntarily and without effect [OE]

re·ten·tion /riten′sHǝn/ *n.* **1** retaining or being retained **2** condition of retaining bodily fluid (esp. urine) normally evacuated [L, rel. to RETAIN]

re·ten·tive /riten′tiv/ *adj.* **1** tending to retain **2** (of memory, etc.) not forgetful [Fr or MedL, rel. to RETAIN]

re·think /rēTHiNGk′/ *v.* (·thought, ·think·ing) **1** consider again, esp. with a view to making changes —*n.* /rē′THiNGk′/ **2** reassessment; rethinking

ret·i·cence /ret′ǝsǝns/ *n.* **1** personal hesitancy or avoidance; reluctance **2** disposition to silence —**ret′i·cent** *adj.* [L *reticere* keep silent]

re·tic·u·late *v.* /ritik′yǝlāt′/ (·lat·ed, ·lat·ing) **1** divide or be divided in fact or appearance into a network —*adj.* /ritik′yǝlǝt/ **2** reticulated —**re·tic′u·la′tion** *n.* [L *reticulum* dim. of *rete* net]

ret·i·na /ret′n·ǝ/ *n.* (*pl.* ·nas or ·nae /-ē/) layer at the back of the eyeball sensitive to light —**ret′i·nal** *adj.* [L *rete* net]

ret·i·nue /ret′n·(y)ōō′/ *n.* body of attendants accompanying an important person [Fr, rel. to RETAIN]

re·tire /ritīr′/ *v.* (·tired, ·tir·ing) **1a** leave office or employment, esp. because of age **b** cause (a person) to do this **2** withdraw; go away; retreat **3** seek seclusion or shelter **4** go to bed —**re·tir′ee′**, **re·tire′ment** *n.* [Fr *tirer* draw]

re·tir′ing *adj.* shy; fond of seclusion

re·took /rētŏŏk′/ *v.* past of RETAKE

re·tort[1] /ritȯrt′/ *n.* **1** incisive, witty, or angry reply —*v.* **2a** say by way of a retort **b** make a retort [L *retorquere* -*tort*- twist]

RETORT[2]

re·tort[2] *n.* vessel with a long neck turned downward, used in distilling liquids [MedL, rel. to RETORT[1]]

re′touch′ *v.* improve (a picture, photograph, etc.) by minor alterations

re·trace *v.* (·traced, ·trac·ing) **1** go back over (one's steps, etc.) **2** trace back to a source or beginning

re·tract /ritrakt′/ *v.* **1** withdraw (a statement or undertaking) **2** draw or be drawn back or in —**re·tract′a·ble** *adj.*; **re·trac′tion** /-trak′sHǝn/ *n.* [L *retrahere* -*tract*- draw back]

re·trac·tile /ritrak′tǝl, -tīl′/ *adj.* capable of being retracted

re·tread *v.* /rētred′/ **1** (·trod, ·trod·den or trod, ·tread·ing) tread (a path, etc.) again **2** (·tread·ed) put a fresh tread on (a tire) —*n.* /rē′tred/ **3** retreaded tire

re·treat /ritrēt′/ *v.* **1** (esp. of military forces) go back; retire **2** recede —*n.* **3a** act of retreating **b** *Milit.* signal for this **4** withdrawal into privacy or security **5** place of shelter, seclusion, or religious contemplation **6** *Milit.* bugle call at sunset [L, rel. to RETRACT]

re·trench *v.* cut down expenses; economize —**re·trench′ment** *n.* [Fr, rel. to TRENCH]

ret·ri·bu·tion /re′trǝbyōō′sHǝn/ *n.* requital, usu. for evil done; vengeance —**re·trib′u·tive** /ritrib′yǝtiv/ *adj.* [L, rel. to TRIBUTE]

re·trieve /ritrēv′/ *v.* (·trieved, ·triev·ing) **1a** regain possession of **b** recover by investigation or effort of memory **2** obtain (information stored in a computer, etc.) **3** (of a dog) find and bring in (killed or wounded game, etc.) **4** rescue (esp. from a bad state) —**re·triev′a·ble** *adj.*; **re·triev′al** *n.* [Fr *trouver* find]

re·triev′er *n.* breed of dog used for retrieving game

ret·ro /re′trō/ *adj. Colloq.* (of a style, design, etc.) reviving or harking back to the past

retro- *comb. form* **1** denoting action back or in return **2** *Anat. & Med.* denoting location behind [L]

re·tro·ac·tive /re′trō·ak′tiv/ *adj.* effective from a past date

re·trod /rēträd′/ *v.* past of RETREAD

re·trod·den /rēträd′ǝn/ *v.* past part. of RETREAD

ret·ro·fit /re′trōfit′/ *v.* (·fit·ted, ·fit·ting) install after manufacture, as a replacement part

ret·ro·grade /re′trōgrād′/ *adj.* **1** directed backward **2** reverting, esp. to an inferior state; declining **3** reversed (*retrograde order*) —*v.*

4 move backward; recede 5 decline; revert [L *retrogradi -gress-* move backward]

ret·ro·gress /re'tragres'/ *v.* 1 move backward 2 deteriorate —**ret'ro·gres'sion** /-gre'SHən/ *n.*; **ret'ro·gres'sive** /-siv/ *adj.*

ret'ro·rock'et *n.* auxiliary rocket for slowing down a spacecraft, etc.

ret·ro·spect /re'trəspekt'/ *n.* as in **in retrospect** when looking back [fr. RETRO-, PROSPECT]

ret·ro·spec·tion /retrəspek'SHən/ *n.* looking back into the past

ret·ro·spec·tive /re'trəspek'tiv/ *adj.* 1 looking back on or dealing with the past 2 (of a statute, etc.) applying to the past as well as the future —*n.* 3 exhibition, recital, etc., showing an artist's lifetime development —**ret'ro·spec'tive·ly** *adv.*

ret·rous·sé /rətrŏŏ'sā'/ *adj.* (of the nose) turned up at the tip [Fr]

ret·ro·vi·rus /re'trəvī'rəs/ *n.* any of a group of RNA viruses that form DNA during the replication of their RNA, and so transfer genetic material into the DNA of host cells

re·try /re'trī'/ *v.* (·tried, ·try·ing) try (a defendant or lawsuit) a second or further time

ret·si·na /retsē'nə/ *n.* Greek white wine flavored with resin [ModGk]

re·turn /ritərn'/ *v.* 1 come or go back 2 bring, put, or send back 3 pay back or reciprocate; give in response 4 yield (a profit) 5 say in reply; retort 6 (in tennis, etc.) hit or send (the ball) back 7 restore or reelect (a politician, etc.) —*n.* 8 coming or going back 9a giving, sending, putting, or paying back b thing given or sent back 10 (*sing.* or *pl.*) proceeds or profit of an undertaking 11 formal statement compiled or submitted by order (*tax return*) 12 **in return** as an exchange or reciprocal action 13 **many happy returns (of the day)** greeting on a birthday —**re·turn'a·ble** *adj.* [Rom, rel. to TURN]

re·turn'ee' *n.* person who returns home from abroad, esp. after war service

re·u·ni·fy /rēyŏŏ'nəfī'/ *v.* (·fied, ·fy·ing) restore (esp. separated territories) to a political unity —**re·u'ni·fi·ca'tion** /-fikā'SHən/ *n.*

re·un·ion /rēyŏŏn'yən/ *n.* 1 reuniting or being reunited 2 social gathering of people formerly associated

re·u·nite /rē'yŏŏnīt'/ *v.* (·nit·ed, ·nit·ing) (cause to) come together again

rev *Colloq.* /rev/ *n.* 1 (*pl.*) number of revolutions of an engine per minute —*v.* (**revved, rev·ving**) 2 (of an engine) revolve; turn over 3 cause (an engine) to run quickly [abbr.]

Rev. *abbr.* Reverend

re·vamp /rēvamp'/ *v.* renovate; revise; improve

re·veal /rivēl'/ *v.* 1 display or show; allow to appear 2 disclose; divulge; betray 3 come to sight or knowledge [L *velum* veil]

rev·eil·le /rev'əlē/ *n.* military waking signal [Fr *réveillez* wake up]

rev·el /rev'əl/ *v.* (·eled or ·elled, ·el·ing or ·el·ling) 1 have a good time; be extravagantly festive 2 take keen delight (in) —*n.* 3 (*sing.* or *pl.*) reveling —**rev'el·er** or **rev'el·ler** *n.*; **rev'el·ry** *n.* (*pl.* ·ries) [L, rel. to REBEL]

rev·e·la·tion /rev'əlā'SHən/ *n.* 1a revealing,

esp. by a divine or supernatural agency b knowledge disclosed in this way 2 striking disclosure 3 (*cap.*) last book of the New Testament

re·venge /rivenj'/ *n.* 1 retaliation for an offense or injury 2 desire for this; vindictive feeling 3 (in games) win after an earlier defeat —*v.* (**·venged, ·veng·ing**) 4 inflict retaliation for (an offense) —**re·venge'ful** *adj.*; **re·venge'ful·ly** *adv.* [L, rel. to VINDICATE]

rev·e·nue /rev'ən(y)ŏŏ'/ *n.* 1a income, esp. when substantial b (*pl.*) items constituting this 2 governmental income from which public expenses are met [Fr *revenu* fr. L *revenire* return]

re·ver·ber·ate /rivər'bərāt'/ *v.* (·at·ed, ·at·ing) 1 (of sound, light, or heat) be returned, echoed, or reflected repeatedly 2 return (a sound, etc.) in this way 3 (of an event, etc.) produce a continuing effect, shock, etc. —**re·ver'ber·ant** *adj.*; **re·ver'ber·a'tion** *n.*; **re·ver'ber·a·tive** /-ətiv/ *adj.* [L *verberare* beat]

re·vere /rivēr'/ *v.* (**·vered, ·ver·ing**) hold in deep or religious respect [L *vereri* fear]

Re·vere /rəvēr'/, **Paul** 1735–1818; American patriot and silversmith

rev·er·ence /rev'(ə)rəns/ *n.* 1 revering or being revered 2 capacity for revering —*v.* (**·enced, ·enc·ing**) 3 regard or treat with reverence [L, rel. to REVERE]

rev·er·end /rev'(ə)rənd/ *adj.* (esp. as the title of a clergyman) deserving reverence [L *reverendus*, rel. to REVERE]

rev·er·ent /rev'(ə)rənt/ *adj.* feeling or showing reverence —**rev'er·ent·ly** *adv.* [L, rel. to REVERE]

rev·er·en·tial /rev'ərən'SHəl/ *n.* of the nature of, due to, or characterized by reverence —**rev'er·en'tial·ly** *adv.* [MedL, rel. to REVERENCE]

rev·er·ie /rev'ərē/ *n.* spell of abstracted musing; daydreaming [Fr]

re·vers /rivēr', -ver'/ *n.* (*pl.* same /-vērz', -verz'/) 1 turned-back edge of a garment revealing the undersurface 2 material on this surface [Fr, rel. to REVERSE]

re·verse /rivərs'/ *v.* (**·versed, ·vers·ing**) 1 turn the other way around or up or inside out 2 change to the opposite character or effect 3 (cause to) travel backward; back up 4 revoke or annul (a decree, act, etc.) —*adj.* 5 backward or upside-down 6 opposite or contrary in character or order; inverted —*n.* 7 opposite or contrary (*the reverse is the case*) 8 piece of misfortune; defeat 9a reverse gear or motion b gear used to make a vehicle go backward 10 reverse side 11 **reverse the charges** have the recipient of a telephone call pay for it —**re·ver'sal** *n.*; **re·vers'i·ble** *adj.* [L *vertere vers- turn*]

re·vert /rivərt'/ *v.* 1 (foll. by *to*) return to a former state, practice, opinion, etc. 2 (of property, an office, etc.) return to a former owner —**re·ver'sion** /-vər'ZHən/ *n.*; **re·vert'i·ble** *adj.*

re·view /rivyŏŏ'/ *n.* 1 general survey or assessment of a subject or thing 2 survey of the past 3 revision or reconsideration 4 display and formal inspection of troops, etc. 5 criticism of a book, play, etc. 6 periodical with critical articles on current events, the arts, etc. —*v.* 7 survey or look back on 8 reconsider or revise 9 hold a review of (troops, etc.) 10 write a review of (a book, play, etc.) —re·view'er n. [rel. to VIEW]

re·vile /rivīl'/ v. (·viled, ·vil·ing) abuse verbally —re·vile'ment, re·vil'er n. [Fr, rel. to VILE]

re·vise /rivīz'/ v. (·vised, ·vis·ing) 1 examine and improve or correct (esp. written or printed matter) 2 change (an opinion, etc.) —re·vi·sion /rivizH'ən/ n.; re·vi'so·ry adj. [L revisere fr. videre vis- see]

Re·vised' Stan'dard Ver'sion n. revision (1946-57) of the Bible

Re·vised' Ver'sion n. revision (1881-95) of the Bible

re·vi·sion·ism /riviZH'əniz'əm/ n. revision or modification of conventional views or an established system of thought —re·vi'sion·ist n. & adj.

re·viv·al /rivī'vəl/ n. 1 reviving or being revived 2 new production of an old play, etc. 3 reawakening of religious fervor —re·viv'al·ism n.; re·viv'al·ist n. & adj.

re·vive /rivīv'/ v. (·vived, ·viv·ing) 1 come or bring back to consciousness, life, or strength 2 come or bring back to existence or to use or notice, etc. [L vivere live]

re·viv·i·fy /rivīv'əfī'/ v. (·fied, ·fy·ing) restore to animation, vigor, or life —re·viv'i·fi·ca'tion n. [L, rel. to VIVIFY]

re·voke /rivōk'/ v. (·voked, ·vok·ing) withdraw; cancel —re·vo·ca·ble /rev'əkəbəl/ adj.; rev·o·ca·tion /rev'əkā'SHən/ n. [L vocare call]

re·volt /rivōlt'/ v. 1 rise in rebellion 2 affect with strong disgust 3 feel strong disgust —n. 4 act of rebelling —re·volt'ing adj.; re·volt'ing·ly adv. [It, rel. to REVOLVE]

rev·o·lu·tion /rev'əlōō'SHən/ n. 1 forcible overthrow of a government or social order 2 any fundamental change or reversal of conditions 3 revolving 4 completion of an orbit or rotation 5 periodic recurrence —rev'o·lu'tion·ar'y adj. & n. (pl. ·ar·ies) [L, rel. to REVOLVE]

Rev'o·lu'tion·ar'y War' see AMERICAN REVOLUTION

rev'o·lu'tion·ize' v. (·ized, ·iz·ing) cause to change fundamentally

re·volve /rivälv'/ v. (·volved, ·volv·ing) 1 (cause to) turn around, esp. on an axis; rotate 2 move in a circular orbit 3 ponder (a problem, etc.) 4 (foll. by around) be centered upon [L revolvere -volut-]

re·volv'er n. pistol with revolving chambers holding several cartridges

re·vue /rivyōō'/ n. entertainment of short usu. satirical sketches and songs [Fr, rel. to REVIEW]

re·vul·sion /rivəl'SHən/ n. abhorrence; disgust [L vellere vuls- pull]

re·ward /riwôrd'/ n. 1 return or recompense for service or merit 2 money offered for the detection of a criminal, restoration of lost property, etc. —v. 3 give a reward to (a person) or for (a service, etc.) [AngFr reward(er) REGARD]

re·ward'ing adj. (of an activity, etc.) worthwhile; satisfying

re·wind /rēwīnd'/ v. (·wound, ·wind·ing) wind (a film, tape, etc.) back on its spool or reel

---

497   revile / rhinitis

---

re·wire /rēwīr'/ v. (·wired, ·wir·ing) provide with new electrical wiring

re·word /rēwərd'/ v. express in different words

re·write v. /rērīt'/ (·wrote, ·writ·ten, ·writ·ing) 1 write again, esp. differently —n. /rē'rīt'/ 2 rewriting 3 thing rewritten

Reye's' syn'drome /rīz, rāz/ n. Med. acute, often fatal brain disease of children, associated with use of aspirin [for Australian pediatrician Ralph D.K. Reye]

Rey·kja·vik /rā'kyəvik'/ n. capital of Iceland. Pop. 99,600

Reyn·olds /ren'ldz/, (Sir) Joshua 1723-92; English painter

Rf symb. rutherfordium

RF abbr. radio frequency

RFD abbr. rural free delivery

Rh symb. rhodium

r.h. abbr. right hand

Rhae·to-Ro·man·ic /rē'tō rōman'ik/ n. various Romance languages of Alpine Switzerland and Italy

rhap·so·dize /rap'sədīz'/ v. (·dized, ·diz·ing) express oneself enthusiastically (about)

rhap·so·dy /rap'sədē/ n. (pl. ·dies) 1 enthusiastic or extravagant speech or composition 2 instrumental music of irregular form that suggests improvisation —rhap·sod·ic /rapsäd'ik/ adj. [Gk rhaptein stitch, rel. to ODE]

rhe·a /rē'ə/ n. S American flightless ostrich-like bird [Gk Rhea mother of Zeus]

Rhee /rē/, Syngman 1875-1965; first president of the Republic of Korea (1948-60)

rhe·ni·um /rē'nēəm/ n. rare metallic element; symb. Re [L Rhenus Rhine]

rhe·o·stat /rē'əstat'/ n. device for controlling an electric current by varying the resistance [Gk rheos stream]

rhe·sus /rē'səs/ n. small N Indian monkey [Rhesus, mythical king of Thrace]

rhe'sus fac'tor n. (also Rh fac'tor) antigen occurring in the red blood cells of most humans; those who have it are Rh positive; those who do not are Rh negative

rhet·o·ric /ret'ərik/ n. 1 art of effective or persuasive speaking or writing 2 overblown or meaningless language designed to persuade or impress —rhe·tor'i·cal /-tôr'ikəl/ adj.; rhe·tor'i·cal·ly adv. [Gk rhētōr orator]

rhe·tor'i·cal ques'tion n. question used for effect but not seeking an answer

rheu·ma·tism /rōō'mətiz'əm/ n. disease marked by inflammation and pain in the joints, muscles, or fibrous tissue; arthritis —rheu·mat'ic /-mat'ik/ adj.; rheu·mat'i·cal·ly adv.; rheu'ma·toid /-mətoid/ adj.

rheu'ma·toid ar·thri'tis n. chronic progressive disease causing inflammation and stiffening of the joints

Rh fac'tor n. RHESUS FACTOR

Rhine Riv·er /rīn/ n. river in W Europe flowing 820 mi. from Switzerland to the North Sea

rhine'stone' n. glass cut as imitation diamond [river Rhine in Germany]

rhi·ni·tis /rīnī'tis/ n. inflammation of the mucous membranes of the nose [Gk rhinnose, -ITIS]

rhi·no /rī′nō/ *n.* (*pl.* same or **·nos**) *Colloq.* rhinoceros [abbr.]

rhi·noc·er·os /rīnäs′(ə)rəs/ *n.* (*pl.* same or **·os·es**) large thick-skinned mammal with one or two horns on its nose [Gk *rhis rhin-* nose, *keras* horn]

rhi·zome /rī′zōm/ *n.* underground rootlike stem bearing both roots and shoots [Gk *rhizoma*]

rho /rō/ *n.* seventeenth letter of the Greek alphabet (P, ρ) [Gk]

Rhode′ Is′land /rōd/ *n.* NE state of the US. Capital: Providence. Pop. 1,003,464. Abbr. **RI; R.I. —Rhode′ Is′land·er** *n.*

Rhodes /rōdz/ Greek island in the Aegean Sea off the coast of Turkey

Rhodes /rōdz/, **Cecil John** 1853–1902 British colonial administrator in South Africa

Rho·de·sia /rōdē′zнə, -sнə/ *n.* former region of S Africa under British control; became independent as countries of Zimbabwe (Southern Rhodesia) and Zambia (Northern Rhodesia)

rho·di·um /rō′dēəm/ *n.* hard, white metallic element; *symb.* **Rh** [Gk *rhodon* rose]

rho·do·den·dron /rō′dəden′drən/ *n.* evergreen shrub with large clusters of bell-shaped flowers [Gk *rhodon* rose, *dendron* tree]

RHOMBOID 2

rhom·boid /räm′boid/ *adj.* (also **rhom·boi′ dal**) 1 like a rhombus —*n.* 2 quadrilateral of which only the opposite sides and angles are equal [Gk, rel. to RHOMBUS]

rhom·bus /räm′bəs/ *n.* (*pl.* **·bus·es** or **·bi** /-bī/) *Geom.* parallelogram with oblique angles and equal sides [Gk *rhombos*]

Rhone Riv·er /rōn/ *n.* river in W Europe flowing 500 mi. from Switzerland to the Mediterranean Sea

RHOMBUS

rhu·barb /rōō′bärb/ *n.* 1 plant with long, fleshy, dark-red stalks used to make pies, etc. 2 *Slang.* noisy argument [Gk *rha* rhubarb, *barbaros* foreign]

rhyme /rīm/ *n.* (also **rime**) 1 identity of sound between words or their endings, esp. in verse 2 verse or a poem having rhymes 3 word providing a rhyme —*v.* (**rhymed, rhym·ing**) 4a (of words or lines) produce a rhyme b act as or treat (a word) as a rhyme (with another) 5 make or write rhymes 6 **rhyme or reason** sense; logic [L, rel. to RHYTHM]

rhyme·ster /rīm′stər/ *n.* writer of mediocre verse

rhythm /riTH′əm/ *n.* 1 pattern of accent and duration of notes in music 2 measured regular flow of verse or prose determined by the length of syllables and stress —**rhyth′mic, rhyth′mi·cal** *adj.*; **rhyth′mi·cal·ly** *adv.* [Gk *rhuthmos*]

rhythm′ and blues′ *n.* popular music with blues themes and a strong rhythm

rhythm′ meth′od *n.* abstention from sexual intercourse near the time of ovulation, as a method of birth control

RI, R.I. abbr. for Rhode Island (postal abbr. RI)

rib /rib/ *n.* 1 each of the curved bones joined to the spine in pairs and protecting the chest 2 supporting ridge, timber, rod, etc. —*v.* (**ribbed, rib·bing**) 3 provide with ribs 4 *Colloq.* make fun of; tease [OE]

rib·ald /rib′əld/ *adj.* coarsely or disrespectfully humorous; obscene —**rib′ald·ry** *n.* [Fr *riber* be licentious]

rib·bon /rib′ən/ *n.* 1 narrow strip or band of fabric, used esp. for trimming or decoration 2 long, narrow strip of anything (*typewriter ribbon*) 3 (*pl.*) ragged strips [fr. Fr *riban*]

ri·bo·fla·vin /rī′bəflā′vin/ *n.* vitamin of the B complex, found in liver, milk, eggs, etc. [*ribose* sugar, L *flavus* yellow]

ri′bo·nu·cle′ic ac′id /rī′bōnōōklē′ik, -klā-/ *n.* nucleic acid in living cells, involved in protein synthesis; *abbr.* RNA [*ribose* sugar]

rice /rīs/ *n.* 1 cereal grass cultivated esp. in Asian marshes 2 grains of this, used as food —*v.* (**riced, ric·ing**) 3 crush food in a kitchen device that forces it through holes as in a sieve [Fr *ris* ult. fr. Gk *oruza*]

rich /rich/ *adj.* 1 having much money or many possessions 2 splendid; costly; elaborate 3 copious; abundant; fertile 4 (of food or diet) containing much fat, sugar, etc. 5 (of the fuel mixture in an engine) containing a high proportion of fuel 6 (of color, sound, or smell) mellow and deep; strong and full 7 highly amusing —**rich′ly** *adv.*; **rich′ness** *n.* [OE and Fr]

Ri·chard /rich′ərd/ name of three kings of England: 1 **Richard I** ("Lionheart") 1157–99; reigned 1189–99 2 **Richard II** 1367–1400; reigned 1377–99 3 **Richard III** 1452–85; reigned 1483–85

Rich·ard·son /rich′ərdsən/, **Samuel** 1689–1761; English writer

Rich·e·lieu /rish′əl(y)ōō′, **Armand Jean du Plessis (Duc de)** 1585–1642; French cardinal and statesman

rich′es *n. pl.* wealth [Fr *richesse*, rel. to RICH]

Rich·mond /rich′mənd/ *n.* capital of Va., in the E part. Pop. 203,056

Rich′ter scale′ /rik′tər/ *n.* logarithmic scale of 0–10 for representing the strength of an earthquake [for C. *Richter*, US seismologist]

rick /rik/ *n.* stack of hay, etc. [OE]

rick·ets /rik′its/ *n.* deficiency disease, chiefly of children, with softening of the bones

rick·et·y /rik′ətē/ *adj.* 1 insecure; shaky 2 suffering from rickets —**rick′et·i·ness** *n.*

Rick·o·ver /rik′ō′vər/, **Hyman** 1900–86; US naval officer

rick′rack′ *n.* ribbon of zigzag braiding used for trimming [fr. RACK[1]]

rick·shaw /rik′shô/ *n.* (also **rick′sha, jin· rik′i·sha, jin·rick′sha, jin·rik′sha**) light, two-wheeled hooded vehicle drawn by one or more persons [abbr. of *jinricksha* fr. Japn]

ric·o·chet /rik′əshā′ *n.* 1 rebounding, esp. of a shell or bullet off a surface —*v.* (**·cheted** /-shād′/, **·chet·ing** /-shā′iNG/) 2 (of a projectile) make a ricochet [Fr]

ri·cot·ta /rikät′ə/ *n.* soft Italian cheese simi-

ric·rac /rik'rak'/ *n.* var. of RICKRACK

rid /rid/ *v.* (**rid** or **rid·ded, rid·ding**) 1 free (a person or place) of something unwanted 2 **get rid of** dispose of [ON]

rid·dance /rid'ns/ *n.* 1 getting rid of something 2 **good riddance** expression of relief at getting rid of something

rid·den /rid'n/ *adj.* dominated; overwhelmed [past part. of RIDE]

rid·dle¹ /rid'l/ *n.* 1 verbal puzzle or test, often with a trick answer 2 puzzling fact, thing, or person —*v.* (**·dled, ·dling**) 3 speak in riddles [OE, rel. to READ]

rid·dle² *v.* (**·dled, ·dling**) 1 make many holes in; perforate —*n.* 2 coarse sieve [OE]

rid'dled *adj.* filled; permeated

ride /rīd/ *v.* (**rode, rid·den, rid·ing**) 1 travel or be carried on any means of transportation 2 be seated on and direct the movement of a horse or other animal 3 traverse 4 lie at anchor; float buoyantly 5 give a ride to —*n.* 6 journey or spell of riding 7 amusement for riding on at a carnival, amusement park, etc. 8 **let ride** leave undisturbed 9 **ride out** come safely through (a storm, danger, etc.) 10 **ride up** (of a garment) work upward out of place 11 **take for a ride: a** *Slang.* kidnap and murder **b** *Colloq.* hoax; deceive [OE]

rid'er *n.* 1 person who rides (esp. a horse) 2 addition to a document —**rid'er·less** *adj.*

ridge /rij/ *n.* 1 line of the junction of two surfaces sloping upward toward each other 2 long, narrow hilltop, mountain range, or watershed 3 any narrow elevation —*v.* (**ridged, ridg·ing**) 4 mark with ridges —**ridg'y** *adj.* [OE]

ridge'pole' *n.* horizontal roof pole

rid·i·cule /rid'ikyōōl'/ *n.* 1 derision; mockery —*v.* (**·culed, ·cul·ing**) 2 mock [L *ridere* laugh]

ri·dic·u·lous /rədik'yələs/ *adj.* deserving of or inviting ridicule —**ri·dic'u·lous·ly** *adv.*; **ri·dic'u·lous·ness** *n.*

Ries·ling /rēz'liNG/ *n.* 1 a kind of grape 2 white wine made from this [Ger]

rife /rīf/ *adj.* 1 widespread 2 abounding in [OE, prob. fr. ON]

riff /rif/ *n.* short, repeated phrase in jazz, etc. [abbr. of RIFFLE]

rif·fle /rif'əl/ *v.* (**·fled, ·fling**) 1 leaf quickly through (pages) 2 shuffle (playing cards), esp. by flexing and combining the two halves of a pack —*n.* 3 act of riffling 4 patch of waves or ripples [perh. var. of RUFFLE]

riff-raff /rif'raf'/ *n.* rabble; disreputable people [Fr *rif et raf*]

ri·fle¹ /rī'fəl/ *n.* 1 gun with a long, rifled barrel, esp. one fired from the shoulder —*v.* (**·fled, ·fling**) 2 make spiral grooves in (a gun barrel) to make a projectile spin [Fr]

ri·fle² *v.* (**·fled, ·fling**) search and rob [Fr]

ri·fle·man /rī'fəlmən/ *n.* (*pl.* **·men**) soldier armed with a rifle

ri'fle range' *n.* place for rifle practice

ri'fling *n.* grooves in a gun barrel

rift /rift/ *n.* 1 crack; split; opening 2 disagreement; breach —*v.* 3 tear or burst apart [Scand, rel. to *riven*]

rig /rig/ *v.* (**rigged, rig·ging**) 1 provide (a vessel) with sails, rigging, etc. 2 assemble 3 fit out; equip 4 establish or change fraudulently —*n.* 5 arrangement of a vessel's masts, sails, etc. 6 special equipment 7 oil-drilling equipment 8 *Colloq.* tractor-trailer [perh. fr. Scand]

Ri·ga /rē'gə/ *n.* capital of Latvia. Pop. 910,200

rig·ger /rig'ər/ *n.* 1 worker on an oil rig 2 person who rigs or who arranges rigging

rig·ging /rig'iNG/ *n.* vessel's spars, ropes, etc.

right /rīt/ *adj.* 1 just; morally or socially correct 2 correct; proper 3 suitable; preferable 4 sound or normal; healthy; satisfactory 5 on or toward the east side of the human body or of anything when facing north 6 (of a side of fabric, etc.) meant for display or use 7 (also *cap.*) of the political Right —*n.* 8 that which is correct or just 9 justification or fair claim 10 legal or moral authority to act 11 right-hand part, region, or direction 12 (often *cap.*) conservative political group —*v.* 13 restore to a proper, straight, or vertical position 14 correct or avenge (mistakes, wrongs, etc.) —*adv.* 15 straight; directly 16 *Colloq.* immediately 17a (foll. by *to, through,* etc.) all the way (*right to the bottom*) b completely (*came right off its hinges*) 18 exactly 19 properly; correctly; satisfactorily 20 on or to the right side —*interj.* 21 expressing agreement or assent 22 **right away** immediately —**right'ly** *adv.*; **right'ness** *n.* [OE]

right' an'gle *n.* angle of 90°

right' brain' *n.* the half of the cerebral cortex that controls the left side of the body, associated with perception of music, visual patterns, emotions, etc.

right·eous /rī'CHəs/ *adj.* morally right; virtuous; law-abiding —**right'eous·ly** *adv.*; **right'eous·ness** *n.* [OE]

right·ful /rīt'fəl/ *adj.* 1 legitimate 2 equitable; fair —**right'ful·ly** *adv.* [OE]

right'-hand' *adj.* 1 on or toward the right side of a person or thing 2 done with the right hand 3 indispensable

right'-hand'ed *adj.* 1 naturally using the right hand for writing, etc. 2 (of a tool, etc.) for use by the right hand —*adv.* 3 with or toward the right hand —**right'-hand'ed·ly** *adv.*; **right'-hand'ed·ness** *n.*

right·ism /rīt'izəm/ *n.* political conservatism —**right'ist** *n.* & *adj.*

right'-mind'ed *adj.* (also **right'-think'ing**) having sound views and principles

right'most' *adj.* furthest to the right

right' of way' *n.* 1 right established by usage to pass over another's land 2 path subject to such a right 3 right of a vehicle to precedence

right'-size' *v. Business.* reduce staff according to real needs

right'-to-die' *adj.* pertaining to the avoidance of artificial life support in case of severe illness or injury

right'-to-life' *adj.* pertaining to the social movement opposing abortion

right'-to-work' *adj.* pertaining to (legislation) outlawing obligatory union membership

right' tri'an·gle *n.* triangle with a 90° angle (see illustration at TRIANGLE)

right' wing' *n.* 1 more conservative section of a political party or system —*adj.* (**right'-**

wing') 2 conservative; reactionary —**right'-wing·er** *n.*

rig·id /rij'id/ *adj.* 1 not flexible; unbendable 2 inflexible; harsh —**ri·gid·i·ty** /rəjid'ətē/ *n.*; **rig'id·ly** *adv.*; **rig'id·ness** *n.* [L *rigidus* fr. *rigere* be stiff]

rig·ma·role /rig'mərōl/ *n.* 1 lengthy, complicated procedure 2 rambling or meaningless talk [orig. *ragman roll* catalogue]

rig·or /rig'ər/ *n.* strictness; severity —**rig'or·ous** *adj.*; **rig'or·ous·ly** *adv.*; **rig'or·ous·ness** *n.* [L *rigere* be stiff]

rig·or mor·tis /rig'ər môr'tis/ *n.* stiffening of the body after death

rile /rīl/ *v.* (**riled, ril·ing**) *Colloq.* anger; irritate [Fr fr. L]

rill /ril/ *n.* small stream [prob. LGer or Du]

rim /rim/ *n.* 1 edge or border 2 outer edge of a wheel, holding the tire 3 part of frames around the lenses of eyeglasses —**rim'less, rimmed** *adj.* [OE]

rime¹ /rīm/ *n.* light covering of frost [OE]

rime² *n. & v.* (**rimed, rim·ing**) var. of RHYME

Rim·i·ni /rim'inē/ *n.* seaport in NE Italy. Pop. 130,900

Rim·sky-Kor·sa·kov /rim'skē kôr'səkôf'/, **Nikolai** 1844–1908; Russian composer

rind /rīnd/ *n.* tough outer skin of fruit, vegetables, cheese, etc. [OE]

ring¹ /riNG/ *n.* 1 circular band, usu. of metal, worn on a finger 2 circular band of any material 3 circular line or band around an object 4 enclosure for a circus performance, boxing, etc. 5 people or things in a circle 6 group of people combined illicitly for profit, etc. —*v.* 7 make or draw a circle around 8 **run rings around** *Colloq.* outclass or outwit (another person) [OE]

ring² *v.* (**rang, rung, ring·ing**) 1 give a clear resonant or vibrating sound of or as of a bell 2 make to sound like a bell 3 call by telephone 4 (of a place) resound with a sound (*theater rang with applause*) 5 (of the ears) experience a ringing sensation 6 convey a specified impression; seem (*rang true*) —*n.* 7 ringing sound or tone 8 act or sound of ringing a bell 9 telephone call 10 impression conveyed by words, etc. (*a melancholy ring*) 11 **ring a bell** *Colloq.* begin to revive a memory 12 **ring down (or up) the curtain** cause a theater curtain to be lowered or raised [OE]

ring·er¹ *n.* thrown horseshoe, etc., that encircles the peg

ring·er² *n.* 1 bell-ringer 2 person who closely resembles another 3 substitute in a contest who outclasses the competition

ring' fin'ger *n.* third finger of the hand

ring'lead·er *n.* leading instigator of a crime, mischief, etc.

ring'let /riNG'lit/ *n.* curly lock of hair

ring'mas'ter *n.* person directing a circus performance

ring'side' *n.* area alongside a boxing, wrestling, etc., ring

ring'worm' *n.* fungal skin infection causing circular inflamed patches, esp. on the scalp

rink /riNGk/ *n.* 1 area of ice for skating 2 enclosed area for roller-skating [appar. fr. Fr *renc* RANK¹]

rinse /rins/ *v.* (**rinsed, rins·ing**) 1 wash lightly with clean water 2 remove detergent, etc., from with clean water —*n.* 3 rinsing 4 temporary hair tint [Fr *rincer*]

Ri·o de Ja·nei·ro /rē'ō dā zHaner'ō/ *n.* city and seaport in SE Brazil. Pop. 5,090,700

Ri·o Gran·de /rē'ō grand'(ē)/ *n.* major river in N America, flowing 1800 mi., forming the border of Texas with Mexico

riot /rī'ət/ *n.* 1 violent disturbance by a crowd of people 2 lavish display or sensation 3 *Colloq.* very amusing thing or person —*v.* 4 engage in a riot 5 **read the riot act** to act firmly to suppress insubordination 6 **run riot** throw off all restraint —**ri'ot·er** *n.*; **ri'ot·ous** *adj.* [Fr]

rip /rip/ *v.* (**ripped, rip·ping**) 1 tear or cut (a thing) quickly or forcibly away or apart 2 make a tear in 3 come violently apart; split 4 *Colloq.* rush along —*n.* 5 long tear 6 act of ripping 7 **rip into** *Colloq.* attack (a person) verbally 8 **rip off:** *Slang.* a swindle b steal —**rip'per** *n.*

RIP *abbr.* may he, she, or they rest in peace [L *requiesca(n)t in pace*]

ri·par·i·an /rīper'ēən, ri-/ *adj.* of or on a river-bank [L *ripa* bank]

rip' cord' *n.* cord for releasing a parachute from its pack

ripe /rīp/ *adj.* 1 (of grain, fruit, cheese, etc.) ready to be reaped, picked, or eaten 2 mature; fully developed 3 (of a person's age) advanced 4 fit or ready —**ripe'ly** *adv.*; **ripe'ness** *n.* [OE]

rip'en *v.* make or become ripe

rip'-off' *n. Slang.* swindle; theft

ri·poste /ripōst'/ *n.* quick retort [It, rel. to RESPOND]

rip·ple /rip'əl/ *n.* 1 ruffling of the water's surface 2 gentle, lively sound, e.g., of laughter or applause —*v.* (**·pled, ·pling**) 3 (cause to) form or flow in ripples 4 show or sound like ripples —**rip'ply** *adj.*

rip'-roar'ing *adj. Colloq.* wildly noisy or boisterous

rip'saw' *n.* coarse-toothed saw for cutting wood along the grain

rip'tide' *n.* disturbance in the sea where opposing tidal currents meet

rise /rīz/ *v.* (**rose, ris·en** /riz'ən/, **ris·ing**) 1 come or go up 2 grow, project, expand, or incline upward; become higher 3 appear above the horizon 4 get up from lying, sitting, kneeling, or from bed 5 come to life again 6 (of dough) swell by the action of yeast, etc. 7 rebel 8 originate; start up —*n.* 9 rising 10 hill; elevation 11 increase 12 increase in status or power 13 origin 14 **get a rise out of** *Colloq.* provoke a reaction from (a person) 15 **give rise to** cause 16 **rise above** be superior to [OE]

ris'er *n.* 1 person who rises from bed 2 vertical section between the treads of a staircase

ris·i·ble /riz'əbəl/ *adj.* laughable; ludicrous [L *ridere ris-* laugh]

ris·ing /rīz'iNG/ *adj.* 1 advancing to maturity or high standing —*n.* 2 uprising

risk /risk/ *n.* 1 chance or possibility of danger, loss, injury, etc. 2 person or thing regarded in relation to risk (*a poor risk*) —*v.* 3 expose to risk 4 accept the chance of —**risk'**

i·ly *adv.*; **risk′i·ness** *n.*; **risk′y** *adj.* (**·i·er**, **·i·est**) [Fr *risque*(r) fr. It]

risqué /riskā′/ *adj.* slightly indecent [Fr, rel. to RISK]

rite /rīt/ *n.* religious or solemn observance, act, or procedure [L *ritus*]

rite′ of pas′sage *n.* event marking a change or stage in life, e.g., marriage

rit·u·al /riCH′ōōəl/ *n.* 1 prescribed order of a ceremony, etc. 2 habitual procedure —*adj.* 3 of or done as a ritual or rite —**rit′u·al·ism′** /-iz′əm/ *n.*; **rit′u·al·is′tic** *adj.*; **rit′u·al·is′ti·cal·ly**, **rit′u·al·ly** *adv.* [L, rel. to RITE]

ritz·y /rit′sē/ *adj.* (**·i·er**, **·i·est**) *Colloq.* high-class; luxurious; showily smart [for C. *Ritz*, Swiss hotel founder]

riv. *abbr.* river

ri·val /rī′vəl/ *n.* 1 person competing with another —*v.* (**·valed** or **·valled**, **·val·ing** or **·val·ling**) 2 be, seem, or claim to be the rival of or comparable to —**ri′val·ry** *n.* (*pl.* **·ries**) [L *rivus* stream]

rive /rīv/ *v.* (**rived**, **rived** or **riv·en** /riv′ən/, **riv·ing**) split; tear apart [ON]

riv·er /riv′ər/ *n.* copious natural stream of water flowing to a larger body of water [L *ripa* bank]

Ri·ve·ra /river′ə/, **Diego** 1886–1957; Mexican painter

riv′er·side′ *n.* bank of a river

Riv·er·side /riv′ərsīd′/ *n.* city in Calif. Pop. 226,505

RIVET 1

riv·et /riv′it/ *n.* 1 bolt for joining parts with the headless end widened by beating to secure it in place —*v.* 2 join or fasten with rivets 3 fix immovably [Fr *river* fasten]

Riv·i·er·a /riv′ē·er′ə/ *n.* Mediterranean coast of SE France and NW Italy; resort area [It: seashore]

riv·u·let /riv′yəlit/ *n.* small stream [L *rivus* stream]

Ri·yadh /rē(y)äd′/ *n.* capital of Saudi Arabia. Pop. 1,308,000

rm. *abbr.* 1 ream 2 room

Rn *symb.* radon

RN or **R.N.** *abbr.* registered nurse

RNA *abbr.* ribonucleic acid

roach /rōCH/ *n.* shortened form of COCK-ROACH

road /rōd/ *n.* 1 narrow path with a prepared surface, for vehicles, pedestrians, etc. 2 one's way or route 3 (often *pl.*) anchorage near the shore 4 hit the road *Slang.* start going away 5 on the road traveling, esp. as a sales representative [OE, rel. to RIDE]

road′bed′ *n.* foundation of a railroad, road, etc.

road′block′ *n.* barrier set up on a road to stop and inspect vehicles

road′hog′ *n. Colloq.* driver who prevents other cars from passing

road′run′ner *n.* kind of fast-running cuckoo of SW US

road′show′ *n.* theatrical performance by a touring company of performers

road′side′ *n.* strip of land alongside a road

road·ster /rōd′stər/ *n.* open car without rear seats

road′way *n.* road, esp. the part for vehicles

road′work′ *n.* distance running as an exercise, esp. for boxers

roam /rōm/ *v.* ramble; wander —**roam′er** *n.*

roan /rōn/ *adj.* 1 (of esp. a horse) having a coat thickly interspersed with another color —*n.* 2 roan animal [Fr]

Ro·a·noke /rō′ənōk′/ *n.* city in Va. Pop. 96,397

roar /rôr/ *n.* 1 loud, deep, hoarse sound —*v.* 2 utter loudly or make a roar, roaring laugh, etc. [OE]

roar′ing for′ties *n. pl.* stormy, windy ocean areas between latitude 40° and 50° S

roast /rōst/ *v.* 1 cook (food, esp. meat) or (of food) be cooked in an oven or by open heat 2 expose to heat 3a criticize severely b honor at a roast (sense 8) —*adj.* 4 roasted —*n.* 5 roast meat 6 piece of meat for roasting 7 picnic with roasted or grilled food 8 banquet for a celebrity, etc., with guest speakers offering light-hearted mockery of the guest of honor —**roast′er** *n.* [Fr *rost*(ir) fr. Gmc]

rob /räb/ *v.* (**robbed**, **rob·bing**) 1 take unlawfully from, esp. by force or threat 2 deprive of what is due or normal —**rob′ber**, **rob′ber·y** *n.* (*pl.* **·ies**) [Fr *rob*(b)*er* fr. Gmc]

Rob·bins /räb′inz/, **Jerome** 1918– ; US choreographer and director

robe /rōb/ *n.* 1a long, loose outer garment b (often *pl.*) this worn as an indication of rank, office, profession, etc. 2 dressing gown —*v.* (**robed**, **rob·ing**) 3 clothe in a robe; dress [Fr]

Robert I /räb′ərt/ (called "**Robert the Bruce**") 1274–1329; king of Scotland (1306–29)

Robe·son /rōb′sən/, **Paul** 1898–1976; US actor and singer

Robes·pierre /rōbz′pēr′, -pyer′/, **Maximilien** 1758–94; French revolutionary leader

rob·in /räb′in/ *n.* (**also rob′in red′breast′**) red-breasted thrush [pet form of *Robert*]

Rob′in Hood′ *n.* legendary English outlaw who stole from the rich to give to the poor

Rob·in·son /räb′insən/ 1 **Edwin Arlington** 1869–1935; US poet 2 **Jackie (John)** 1919–72; US baseball player

ro·bot /rō′bät′, -bət/ *n.* 1 machine resembling or functioning like a human to perform a mechanical task 2 person who acts mechanically —**ro·bot′ic** *adj.*; **ro′bot·ize′** /-bətīz′/ *v.* (**·ized**, **·iz·ing**) [Czech]

ro·bot′ics *n. pl.* (usu. treated as *sing.*) science. technology, or study of robot design and operation

ro·bust /rōbəst′, rō′bəst′/ *adj.* strong and sturdy, esp. in physique or construction —**ro·bust′ly** *adv.*; **ro·bust′ness** *n.* [L *robur* strength]

Roch·es·ter /räCH′es′tər, -əstər/ *n.* city in N.Y. Pop. 231,636

rock¹ /räk/ *n.* 1 hard material of the earth's crust; stone 2 *Geol.* any natural material, hard or soft (e.g., clay), consisting of one or more minerals 3 stone of any size 4 firm and dependable support or protection 5 **on the**

rocks: *Colloq.* **a** (of a marriage, etc.) broken down **b** (of a drink) served with ice cubes [Fr *roque*, *roche*]

rock² *v.* **1** move gently to and fro; set, maintain, or be in such motion **2** (cause to) sway; shake; reel —*n.* **3** rocking movement **4** ROCK-AND-ROLL [OE]

rock·a·bil·ly /ˈräkˌbiləˈē/ *n.* rock-and-roll with elements of hillbilly music

rock'-and-roll' *n.* (also **rock 'n' roll**) popular music, originating in the 1950s, with a heavy beat and often a blues element

rock' bot'tom *adj.* **1** (of prices, etc.) the very lowest —*n.* **2** very lowest level

rock' can'dy *n.* sugar in large, hard crystals

Rock·e·fel·ler /ˈräkˌefelˈər/ US family prominent in industry, politics, and philanthropy, including: **1** John D(avison) 1839–1937; US oil magnate; his son: **2** John D(avison), Jr. 1874–1960; oil magnate; his son: **3** Nelson 1908–79; US politician

rock'er *n.* **1** curved bar on which a chair, cradle, etc., can rock **2** rocking chair **3** devotee of rock music **4** off one's rocker *Slang.* crazy

rock·et /ˈräkˈit/ *n.* **1** cylindrical firework, signal, etc., propelled by thrust against burnt fuel, independent of air intake **2** engine operating on the same principle **3** rocket-propelled device, vehicle, etc. —*v.* **4** move rapidly upward **5** increase rapidly [Fr *roquette* fr. It]

rock·et·ry /ˈräkˈitrē/ *n.* science or practice of rocket propulsion, designing and building rockets, etc.

Rock·ford /ˈräkˈfərd/ *n.* city in Ill. Pop. 173,645

rock' gar'den *n.* arrangement of rocks and soil for planting flowers, etc.

rock'ing horse' *n.* toy horse on rockers or springs for a child to ride

rock' salt' *n.* common salt in large crystals

rock·y¹ *adj.* (**·i·er**, **·i·est**) of, like, or full of rock or rocks —**rock'i·ness** *n.*

rock·y² *adj.* (**·i·er**, **·i·est**) *Colloq.* unsteady; tottering; unstable —**rock'i·ness** *n.*

Rock'y Moun'tains *n.* (also **the Rockies**) major mountain range in W N America, running SW to NE more than 3,000 mi.

ro·co·co /rəkōˈkō/ *adj.* **1** of a late baroque style of 18th-cent. decoration **2** (of literature, music, architecture, etc.) highly ornate —*n.* **3** this style [Fr]

rod /räd/ *n.* **1** slender, straight, cylindrical bar or stick **2** cane for flogging **3** (also **fish'ing rod'**) pole with line and reel used for fishing **4** measure of length equivalent to 5-1/2 yards [OE]

rode¹ /rōd/ *v.* past of RIDE

rode² *n. Naut.* vessel's anchor rope or chain [fr. RODE¹]

ro·dent /ˈrōdˈnt/ *n.* mammal with strong incisors, e.g., the rat, mouse, porcupine, etc. [L *rodere* gnaw]

ro·de·o /ˈrōˈdēˈō, rədāˈō/ *n.* (*pl.* **·os**) exhibition of cowboys' skills in handling animals [Sp]

Rodg·ers /ˈräjˈərz/, **Richard** 1902–79; US composer

Ro·din /rōdanˈ/, (**François**) **Auguste** 1840–1917; French sculptor

roe¹ /rō/ *n.* fish eggs [LGer or·Du]

roe² *n.* (*pl.* same or **·s**) (also **roe' deer'**) small deer of Europe and Asia [OE]

roe'buck' *n.* male roe deer

roent·gen /ˈrəntˈgən, -jənˈ/ *n.* unit of radiation produced by x-rays, etc. [for W.C. RÖNTGEN German physicist]

Roentgen see RÖNTGEN, WILHELM CONRAD

Rog·er /ˈräjˈər/, *interj.* (also **r-**) (used in radio communication) your message has been received and understood [the name used as code for *R*]

Rog·ers /ˈräjˈərz/, **Will** 1879–1935; US humorist

rogue /rōg/ *n.* **1** dishonest or unprincipled person **2** mischievous person **3** fierce, wild animal driven away or living apart from others **4** (often *attrib.*) inexplicable result or phenomenon —**ro'guer·y** *n.*; **ro'guish** *adj.*; **ro'guish·ly** *adv.*; **ro'guish-ness** *n.*

roil /roil/ *v.* **1** disturb sediment in a liquid and make it cloudy **2** rile

rois·ter /roisˈtər/ *v.* act uproariously —**rois'ter·er** *n.* [L, rel. to RUSTIC]

role /rōl/ *n.* (also **rôle**) **1** actor's part in a play, film, etc. **2** function [Fr, rel. to ROLL]

role' mod'el *n.* person on whom others model themselves

role'-play'ing *n.* acting of characters or situations as an aid in psychotherapy, language teaching, etc.

roll /rōl/ *v.* **1** (cause to) move or go in some direction by turning on an axis **2** (also **roll' up'**) make cylindrical or spherical by revolving between two surfaces or over on itself **3** (cause to) move, advance, or be conveyed on wheels, etc. **4** (of a time period) pass **5** rotate **6a** (of a moving vehicle) sway to and fro sideways **b** walk unsteadily **7** give the appearance of hills, waves, etc. **8** sound or utter with vibrations or a trill (*thunder rolled; rolls his rs*) —*n.* **9** rolling motion or gait **10** rolling **11** rhythmic rumbling sound of thunder, etc. **12** complete revolution of something around its longitudinal axis **13** anything formed into a cylinder by being turned over on itself **14** individual portion of bread baked separately **15** official list or register **16 on a roll:** *Slang.* **a** winning at gambling **b** continually successful [L *rota* wheel]

roll' call' *n.* calling out of a list of names to establish who is present

rolled' gold' *n.* thin coating of gold applied to a base metal by rolling

roll'er *n.* **1** revolving cylinder for smoothing, spreading, crushing, stamping, hanging a towel on, etc., used alone or in a machine **2** small cylinder on which hair is rolled for setting **3** long, swelling wave

roll'er bear'ing *n.* bearing using cylinders to reduce friction

Roll'er·blade /ˈrōˈlərblādˈ/ *n.* **1** *Tdmk.* (usu. *pl.*) roller skates with wheels in a straight line, used like ice skates; in-line skates —*v.* **2** use Rollerblades

roll'er coast'er *n.* amusement ride consisting of cars on a track that twists and dips sharply

roll'er skate' *n.* **1** metal frame with small wheels, fitted to shoes for riding on a hard surface —*v.* (**roller-skate**; **-skat·ed**, **-skat·ing**) **2** move on roller skates —**roll'er skat'er** *n.*

rol·lick·ing /räl′ikiNG/ *adj.* jovial; exuberant

roll′ing pin′ *n.* cylinder for rolling out dough

roll′-top′ *n.* flexible cover sliding in curved grooves

Röl·vaag /rôl′väg/, **Ole Edvart** 1876–1931; Norwegian-born US writer

roly-poly /rō′lē pō′lē/ *adj.* 1 plump —*n.* (*pl.* **-lies**) 2 such a person or thing [prob. ROLL]

ROM *abbr. Comp.* read-only memory

Rom. *abbr.* 1 Roman 2 Romance 3 Romania; Romanian; Romanic

Ro·man /rō′mən/ *adj.* 1 of ancient or modern Rome, its territory, people, etc. 2 ROMAN CATHOLIC 3 (r-) (of type) plain and upright, used in ordinary print 4 based on the ancient Roman alphabet —*n.* 5 native or inhabitant of Rome 6 (r-) roman type [L]

Ro′man can′dle *n.* firework discharging colored balls of fire

Ro′man Cath·o·lic *adj.* (also **Ro′man**) 1 of the part of the Christian Church acknowledging the Pope as its head —*n.* 2 member of this Church —**Ro′man Ca·thol′i·cism′** /-isiz′əm/

ro·mance /rōmans′, rō′mans/ *n.* 1 idealized, poetic, or unworldly atmosphere or tendency 2a love affair b sentimental or idealized love 3 literary works concerning romantic love, adventurous action, etc. —*adj.* 4 denoting languages descended from Latin, e.g., French, Spanish, Italian, etc. —*v.* (**-manced, -manc·ing**) 5 court; woo [ult. fr. L *Romanicus* Roman]

Ro′man Em′pire *n.* empire established by Augustus in 27 B.C., including much of Europe, N Africa, and SW Asia

Ro·ma·ni·a /rōmā′nēə, rōō-/ *n.* (also **Ru·ma′ni·a** /rōō-/) republic in SE Europe. Capital: Bucharest. Pop. 23,332,000

Ro·ma·ni·an /rōmā′nēən/ (also **Ru·ma′ni·an** /rōō-/) *n.* 1a native or national of Romania b person of Romanian descent 2 language of Romania —*adj.* 3 of Romania, its people, or language

Ro′man nu′mer·al *n.* any of the Roman letters representing numbers: I=1, V=5, X=10, L=50, C=100, D=500, M=1000

Ro·mansh /rōmänsH′, -mänsH′/ *n.* dialect of the Rhaeto-Romanic, an official language of Switzerland

ro·man·tic /rōman′tik/ *adj.* 1 of, characterized by, or suggestive of romance 2 inclined toward or suggestive of love 3 (of a person) imaginative, visionary, idealistic 4a (of style in art, music, etc.) concerned more with feeling and emotion than with form and esthetic qualities b (also *cap.*) of the 18th–19th-cent. movement or style in the European arts 5 unpractical; fantastic —*n.* 6 romantic person 7 romanticist —**ro·man′ti·cal·ly** *adv.* [Fr, rel. to ROMANCE]

ro·man·ti·cism /rōman′tēsiz′əm/ *n.* adherence to a romantic style in art, music, etc. —**ro·man′ti·cist** /-cist/ *n.*

ro·man·ti·cize /rōman′təsīz/ *v.* (**·cized, ·ciz·ing**) 1 embellish; exaggerate 2 indulge in romantic thoughts, etc.

Rom·a·ny /räm′ənē/ *n.* language of the Gypsies

Rom·berg /räm′bərg/, **Sigmund** 1887–1951; Hungarian-born US composer

Rome /rōm/ *n.* city, capital of Italy, and center of the ancient Roman Empire. Pop. 2,791,400

Ro·me·o /rō′mē·ō′/ *n.* (*pl.* **-os**) passionate male lover or seducer [character in Shakespeare's *Romeo and Juliet*]

Rom·mel /räm′əl/, **Erwin** 1891–1944; German general

romp /rämp/ *v.* 1 play energetically, in a lively manner, etc. —*n.* 2 spell of romping 3 *Colloq.* easy win [perh. fr. RAMP]

romp′ers *n. pl.* young child's one-piece garment covering the body, arms, and legs

Rönt·gen /rent′gən, ren′CHən/ (also **Roent′gen**), **Wilhelm Conrad** 1845–1923; German physicist who discovered x-rays

rood /rōōd/ *n.* crucifix [OE]

roof /rōōf, rŏŏf/ *n.* (*pl.* **-s**) 1 upper covering of a building 2 top of any enclosed space —*v.* 3 cover with or as with a roof 4 **go through the roof** *Colloq.* (of prices, etc.) rise dramatically —**roof′er** *n.* [OE]

roof′ing *n.* material for a roof

roof′top′ *n.* top of a house

rook¹ /rŏŏk/ *n.* 1 black bird of the crow family —*v.* 2 *Colloq.* charge (a customer) extortionately [OE]

rook² *n. Chess.* piece with a battlement-shaped top [Fr fr. Ar]

rook·er·y *n.* (*pl.* **-ies**) colony of rooks, penguins, or seals

rook·ie /rŏŏk′ē/ *n. Slang.* 1 new recruit 2 *Sports.* first-year player [corruption of *recruit*]

room /rōōm, rŏŏm/ *n.* 1 space for or occupied by something; capacity 2 part of a building enclosed by walls, floor, and ceiling —*v.* 3 have lodging; lodge —**room′er** *n.* [OE]

room′ and board′ *n.* lodging and meals

room·ette /rōōmet′/ *n.* cabinlike accommodation on a train

room′ing house′ *n.* house providing room and board

room′mate′ *n.* person sharing living accommodations

room·y /rōō′mē, rŏŏm′ē/ *adj.* (**·i·er, ·i·est**) having much room; spacious —**room′i·ness** *n.*

Roo·se·velt /rō′zəvəlt, -velt′, rōō′-/ 1 **Teddy** (**Theodore**) 1858–1919; US soldier and politician; 26th US president (1901–08) 2 **Franklin Delano** 1882–1945; US politician; 32nd US president (1933–45); his wife: 3 (**Anna**) **Eleanor** 1884–1962; US diplomat and writer

roost /rōōst/ *n.* 1 branch or perch for a bird, esp. to sleep —*v.* 2 settle for rest or sleep 3 **come home to roost** (of a plan, etc.) boomerang [OE *hrōst*]

roost′er /rōō′stər/ *n.* male domestic chicken

root¹ /rōōt, rŏŏt/ *n.* 1 part of a plant normally below the ground, conveying nourishment from the soil 2 (*pl.*) attachment, esp. to one's place of origin 3 embedded part of a hair, tooth, nail, etc. 4 basic cause, source, nature, or origin 5 number that when multiplied by itself a specified number of times gives a specified number or quantity (*cube root of eight is two*) 6 core of a word, without prefixes, suffixes, etc. —*v.* 7 (cause to) grow roots 8 fix firmly; establish 9 **root out** find and get rid of **10 take root** begin to grow and draw nourishment from the soil; become established —**root′less** *adj.* [OE]

root[2] *v.* **1** turn up (the ground) with the snout, etc., in search of food **2** rummage; find or extract by rummaging **3** (foll. by *for*) *Colloq.* encourage by applause or support [OE and ON]

root′ beer′ *n.* carbonated soft drink flavored with various roots, etc.

root′ ca·nal′ *n. Dentistry.* **1** channel in a tooth for the nerve **2** *Colloq.* treatment involving removal of a tooth's nerve, filling of the channel, etc.

rope /rōp/ *n.* **1** strong cord made by twisting together strands of hemp, wire, etc. **2** onions, pearls, etc., strung together —*v.* (**roped, rop·ing**) **3** fasten, secure, or catch with rope **4** (usu. foll. by *off, in*) enclose with rope **5 the ropes** knowledge of how to do a thing properly **6 rope in** *Slang.* persuade to take part [OE]

Roque·fort /rōk′fərt/ *n. Tdmk.* blue-veined cheese made from ewes' milk [for town in France where made]

Ror′schach test′ /rôr′SHäk′/ *n.* personality test based on the subject's interpretation of a standard set of inkblots [for H. Rorschach, its Swiss developer]

Ro·sa·ri·o /rōsär′ē-ō′, -zär′-/ *n.* port on the Paraná River in Argentina. Pop. 875,700

ro·sa·ry /rō′zərē/ *n.* (*pl.* **-ries**) *RC Ch.* repeated sequence of prayers, usu. said with a string of beads for keeping count of them [L *rosarium* rose-garden]

rose[1] /rōz/ *n.* **1** thorny bush or shrub bearing usu. fragrant red, pink, yellow, or white flowers **2** this flower **3** pinkish-red color —*adj.* **4** rose-colored [L *rosa*]

rose[2] *v. past of* RISE

ro·sé /rōzā′/ *n.* light pink wine [Fr]

Ro·seau /rōzō′/ *n.* capital of Dominica. Pop. 20,800

rose′bud′ *n.* bud of a rose

rose′bush′ *n.* rose plant

rose′mar′y *n.* fragrant evergreen shrub used as an herb [*rosmarine* fr. L *ros* dew, rel. to MARINE]

ro·sette /rōzet′/ *n.* rose-shaped ornament of ribbon [Fr dim., rel. to ROSE[1]]

rose′wa′ter *n.* perfume made from roses

rose′win′dow *n.* circular window with rose-like tracery

rose′wood′ *n.* any of several fragrant close-grained woods used in making furniture

Rosh Ha·sha·nah /rōsH′ həsHä′nə, -sHô′nə/ *n.* the Jewish New Year

ros·in /räz′in/ *n.* resin, esp. in solid form [alter. of RESIN]

Ross /rôs/, **Betsy** 1752–1836; maker of the first US flag

Ros·set·ti /rōzet′ē, -set′-/ English poets: **1** Dante Gabriel 1828–82; his sister: **2** Christina Georgina 1830–94

Ros·si·ni /rəsē′nē, rô-/, **Gioachino** 1792–1868; Italian composer

Ross Sea /rôs, räs/ *n.* arm of the Antarctic Ocean S of the Ross Shelf

Ros·tand /rôstän′, rästand′/, **Edmond** 1868–1918; French dramatist

ros·ter /räs′tər/ *n.* list or plan of turns of duty, etc. [Du *rooster*, literally 'gridiron']

Ros·tock /räs′täk′, -tôk′/ *n.* seaport in Germany on the Baltic Sea. Pop. 248,100

Ro·stov /rəstôf′/ *n.* seaport in Russia on the Don River. Pop. 1,027,600

ros·trum /räs′trəm/ *n.* (*pl.* **-tra** or **-trums**) platform for public speaking, an orchestral conductor, etc. [L]

ros·y /rō′zē/ *adj.* (**-i·er, -i·est**) **1** pink; red **2** optimistic; hopeful —**ros′i·ly** *adv.*; **ros′i·ness** *n.*

rot /rät/ *v.* (**rot·ted, rot·ting**) **1** decompose; decay **2** gradually perish or waste away —*n.* **3** rotting; decay **4** *Slang.* nonsense **5** disease marked by evil-smelling decay [OE]

ro·ta·ry /rō′tərē/ *adj.* **1** acting by rotation —*n.* (*pl.* **-ries**) **2** rotary machine **3** TRAFFIC CIRCLE [L *rota* wheel]

ro·tate /rō′tāt′/ *v.* (**-tat·ed, -tat·ing**) **1** revolve around an axis or center **2** act, arrange, or take place in rotation —**ro′tat·a·ble** *adj.*; **ro·ta′tion** *n.*; **ro′ta·to·ry** /rō′tətôr′ē/ *adj.* [L *rota* wheel]

ROTC /rät′sē/ *abbr.* Reserve Officers Training Corps

rote /rōt/ *n.* **1** mechanical method of doing something **2 by rote** by memorization alone, without attention to meaning

rot′·gut′ *n. Slang.* cheap, low-grade whiskey

Roth /rôTH/, **Philip** 1933– ; US novelist

Roth·schild /rô(TH)s′CHīld′, rôTH′-/ **1** Mayer Amschel (Meyer Anselm) 1743–1812; German banker; established Rothschild international banking firm **2** Lionel Nathan (Baron de) 1809–79; English banker; first Jewish member of British Parliament

ro·tis·ser·ie /rōtis′ərē/ *n.* rotating spit for roasting or barbecuing meat [Fr, rel. to ROAST]

ro·tor /rō′tər/ *n.* **1** rotary part of a machine **2** rotary airfoil on a helicopter [rel. to ROTATE]

rot·ten /rät′n/ *adj.* **1** decomposed; rotting or rotted **2** morally or politically corrupt **3** *Slang.* **a** disagreeable; unpleasant **b** worthless **c** sick —**rot′ten·ness** *n.* [ON, rel. to ROT]

Rot·ter·dam /rät′ərdam′/ *n.* seaport in the Netherlands. Pop. 582,300

ro·tund /rōtänd′/ *adj.* plump; round —**ro·tun′di·ty, ro·tund′ness** *n.* [L *rotundus*]

ro·tun·da /rōtän′də/ *n.* circular building, hall, or room, esp. domed [It *rotonda*, rel. to ROTUND]

rou·é /rōō-ā′/ *n.* rake; debauchee [Fr]

Rou·en /rōō-än′/ *n.* city in France on the Seine River. Pop. 105,500

rouge /rōōzH/ *n.* **1** red cosmetic for coloring the cheeks **2** reddish metal polish —*v.* (**rouged, roug·ing**) **3** color with or apply rouge [L *rubeus* red]

rough /rəf/ *adj.* **1** uneven; bumpy; not smooth, level, or polished **2** shaggy; coarse-haired **3** boisterous; coarse; violent; not mild, quiet, or gentle **4** harsh; insensitive **5** unpleasant; severe; demanding **6** hard; unfair (toward) **7** incomplete; rudimentary; approximate —*adv.* **8** in a rough manner —*n.* **9** rough ground, esp. on a golf course **10** unfinished or natural state —*v.* **11** (foll. by *out, in*) shape, plan, or sketch roughly **12 rough it** *Colloq.* do without basic comforts **13 rough**

up Slang. attack violently **—rough'ly** adj.; **rough'ness** n. [OE]

rough·age /rəf'ij/ n. coarse, fibrous material in food

rough'en v. make or become rough

rough'-hewn' adj. **1** cut to shape coarsely **2** uncouth; unrefined

rough'house' n. Slang. **1** disturbance or row; boisterous play **—v.** (**·housed, ·hous·ing**) **2** engage in boisterous play

rough'neck' n. Colloq. **1** worker on an oil rig **2** rough or rowdy person

rough'shod' adj. **1** (of a horse) having shoes with nailheads projecting to prevent slipping **2 ride roughshod over** treat harshly

rou·lette /rōōlet'/ n. gambling game in which a ball is dropped on to a revolving numbered wheel [Fr: little wheel]

round /round/ adj. **1** shaped like a circle, sphere, or cylinder; convex; circular; curved **2** entire; complete (round dozen) **3** candid; outspoken **4** (of a number) expressed for brevity as a whole number **—n. 5** round object or form **6** recurring series of activities, meetings, etc.; fixed route for deliveries **7** drink for each member of a group **8** bullet or shell **9** set, series, or sequence of actions in turn, esp.: **a** one spell of play in a game, etc. **b** one stage in a competition **10** song overlapping at intervals **—adv. 11** with circular motion **12** around **—prep. 13** around **—v. 14** give or take a round shape **15** pass around (a corner, etc.) **16** express (a number) approximately, for brevity **17 round up** collect or bring together **—round'ish** adj.; **round'ness** n. [L, rel. to ROTUND]

round'a·bout' adj. indirect

roun·de·lay /round'älā'/ n. short, simple song with a refrain [alter. of Fr rondelet]

round'ly adv. **1** energetically **2** fully; completely

round'-shoul'dered adj. having shoulders bent forward and a rounded upper back

Round' Ta'ble n. **1** circular table around which King Arthur and his knights sat **2** (round table) assembly for discussion, esp. at a conference

round'-the-clock' adj. & adv. continuously throughout the day and night

round' trip' n. trip to one or more places and back again

round'-up' n. **1** driving together of cattle, etc., for branding, shipping to market, etc. **2** summary or résumé

round'worm' n. worm with a cylindrical body; nematode

rouse /rouz/ v. (**roused, rous·ing**) **1** (cause to) wake **2** stir up; make or become active or excited

Rous·seau /rōōsō'/, **Jean-Jacques** 1712–78; Swiss-born French philosopher and writer

roust·a·bout /roust'əbout'/ n. **1** laborer on an oil rig **2** unskilled or casual laborer, as in a circus [roust rout out, rouse]

rout[1] /rout/ n. **1** disorderly retreat **2** overthrow; defeat **—v. 3** put to flight; defeat [Fr, rel. to ROUTE]

rout[2] v. (also **rout out**) **1** get rid of; drive out **2** hollow out **—rout'er** n. [var. of ROOT[2]]

route /rōōt, rout/ n. **1** way or course taken,

esp. routinely **—v.** (**rout·ed, rout·ing**) **2** send, forward, or direct by a particular route [Fr route road, fr. L rupta (via)]

● Usage: The pronunciation that rhymes this word with out is standard, but the pronunciation that rhymes it with root is heard among older and more conservative speakers.

rou·tine /rōōtēn'/ n. **1** regular course or procedure **2** set sequence in a dance or act **—adj. 3** performed as part of a routine **—rou·tine'ly** adv. [Fr, rel. to ROUTE]

rove /rōv/ v. (**roved, rov·ing**) wander without settling; roam **—rov'er** n. [prob. Scand]

row[1] /rō/ n. **1** line of persons or things **2** line of seats across a theater, etc. **3 in a row: a** in succession **b** in a line [OE]

row[2] v. **1** propel (a boat) by means of oars **2** convey (a passenger) thus. **—n. 3** trip in a rowboat **—row'er** n. [OE]

row[3] /rou/ n. **1** commotion; quarrel **—v. 2** engage in a row

row'boat' n. small boat propelled by oars

row·dy /rou'dē/ adj. (**·di·er, ·di·est**) **1** noisy and disorderly **—n.** (pl. **·dies**) **2** rowdy person **—row'di·ly** adv.; **row'di·ness, row'dy·ism'** n.

row·el /rou'əl, roul/ n. spiked revolving disk at the end of a spur [L rota wheel]

roy·al /roi'əl/ adj. **1** of, suited to, or worthy of a king or queen; majestic **2** in the service or under the patronage of a king or queen **—n. 3** Colloq. member of the royal family **—roy'al·ly** adv. [L, rel. to REGAL]

Roy'al Ca·na'di·an Mount'ed Po·lice' n. Canadian national police force

roy'al·ist n. supporter of monarchy

roy'al·ty n. (pl. **·ties**) **1** royal office, dignity, or power; being royal **2** royal persons **3** percentage of profit from a book, song, patent, etc., paid to the author [Fr, rel. to ROYAL]

rpm abbr. revolutions per minute

rps or **r.p.s.** abbr. revolutions per second

RR or **R.R.** abbr. **1** railroad **2** rural route

RSV abbr. Revised Standard Version (of the Bible)

RSVP abbr. (in an invitation, etc.) please answer [Fr répondez s'il vous plaît]

rt. abbr. right

rte. abbr. route

Ru symb. ruthenium

rub /rəb/ v. (**rubbed, rub·bing**) **1** move (one's hand, a rag, etc.) with firm pressure over the surface of **2** apply (one's hand, etc.) in this way **3** clean, polish, chafe, or make dry, sore, or bare by rubbing **4** apply (polish, etc.) by rubbing **5** move with contact or friction (objects) against each other **6** (foll. by out, off) remove; erase **—n. 7** act or spell of rubbing **8 rub down** massage **9 rub it in** remind a person of a fault or failing **10 rub shoulders with** associate with **11 rub the wrong way** irritate [LGer]

ru·ba·to /rōōbä'tō/ n. Mus. (pl. **·tos** or **·ti** /-tē/) temporary disregard of strict tempo [It: robbed]

rub·ber[1] /rəb'ər/ n. **1** tough, elastic substance made from the latex of plants or synthetically **2** eraser **3** Colloq. condom **4** rub-

ber overshoes —*adj.* **5** made of rubber
—**rub′ber·y** *adj.*; **rub′ber·i·ness** *n.* [fr. RUB]

rub·ber² *adj.* designating the deciding game
or match in a series

rub′ber band′ *n.* loop of rubber for holding
papers, etc., together

rub′ber check′ *n.* check drawn against insufficient funds

rub·ber·ize /rəb′ərīz′/ *v.* (**-ized**, **-iz·ing**)
treat or coat with rubber

rub′ber·neck′ *Colloq. n.* **1** tourist or sightseer
—*v.* **2** behave like a rubberneck

rub′ber plant′ *n.* **1** evergreen tropical plant
often cultivated as a house plant **2** (also **rub′
ber tree′**) tropical tree yielding latex

rub′ber stamp′ *n.* **1** device for inking and im-
printing on a surface —*v.* **2** approve automatically

rub·bish /rəb′ISH/ *n.* **1** waste material; refuse; litter **2** nonsense —**rub′bish·y** *adj.*
[AngFr *rubbous*]

rub·ble /rəb′əl/ *n.* rough fragments of stone,
brick, etc., esp. from a demolished building
[Fr *robe* spoils]

rub′-down′ *n.* massage

ru·bel·la /r $ō$ōbel′ə/ *n.* German measles [L
rubellus reddish]

Ru·bens /r $ō$ō′bənz/, (Sir) **Peter Paul** 1577–
1640; Flemish painter

Ru·bi·con /r $ō$ō′bikän′/ *n.* point of no return
[*Rubicon*, ancient river frontier of Italy]

ru·bi·cund /r $ō$ō′bikənd/ *adj.* ruddy; reddish
[L *ruber* red]

ru·bid·i·um /r $ō$ōbid′ēəm/ *n.* silvery metallic
element; *symb.* **Rb** [L *rubidus* red]

Ru·bin·stein /r $ō$ō′bənstīn′/, **Artur** 1886–
1982; Polish-born US concert pianist

ru·ble /r $ō$ō′bəl/ *n.* monetary unit of Russia
and other former states of the USSR

ru·bric /r $ō$ō′brik/ *n.* **1** heading in red or special lettering **2** explanatory words; direction
[L *ruber* red]

ru·by /r $ō$ō′bē/ *n.* (*pl.* **-bies**) **1** precious
stone red in color **2** deep red —*adj.* **3** of this
color [L *rubeus* red]

ruck·sack /rək′sak′, r $ō$ōk′-/ *n.* bag carried on
the back, esp. by hikers [Ger]

ruck·us /rək′əs/ *n. Colloq.* row; commotion
[perh. fr. *ruction* uproar + RUMPUS]

rud·der /rəd′ər/ *n.* flat piece for steering,
hinged vertically to the stern of a vessel or on
the stabilizer of an aircraft —**rud′der·less**
adj. [OE]

rud·dy /rəd′ē/ *adj.* (**-di·er**, **-di·est**) freshly
or healthily red —**rud′di·ly** *adv.*; **rud′di·
ness** *n.* [OE]

rude /r $ō$ōd/ *adj.* **1** impolite; offensive **2**
roughly made or done; crude **3** primitive **4**
indecent; lewd —**rude′ly** *adv.*; **rude′ness** *n.*
[L *rudis*]

ru·di·ment /r $ō$ō′dəmənt/ *n.* **1** (*pl.*) elements
or first principles of a subject **2** (*pl.*) imperfect or undeveloped beginning of something
—**ru′di·men′ta·ry** /-men′terē/ *adj.* [L, rel. to
RUDE]

rue¹ /r $ō$ō/ *v.* (**rued**, **ru·ing**) **1** repent of **2**
regret —**rue′ful** *adj.*; **rue′ful·ly** *adv.*; **rue′
ful·ness** *n.* [OE]

rue² *n.* evergreen shrub with bitter strong-
scented leaves [Gk *rhutē*]

ruff¹ /rəf/ *n.* **1** projecting, starched, frilly collar of the 16th cent. **2** projecting or colored
ring of feathers or hair around a bird's or animal's neck [perh. ROUGH]

RUFF¹ 1

ruff² *v.* **1** trump at cards —*n.* **2** trumping [Fr
ro(u)ffle]

ruf·fi·an /rəf′ēən/ *n.* violent, lawless person
[It *ruffiano*]

ruf·fle /rəf′əl/ *v.* (**-fled**, **-fling**) **1a** disturb
the smoothness or tranquility of **b** undergo
this **2** gather into a ruffle **3** anger; disturb or
become disturbed —*n.* **4** frill of fabric, lace,
etc.

rug /rəg/ *n.* floor covering, usu. smaller than
a carpet [prob. Scand]

rug·by /rəg′bē/ *n.* team game played with an
oval ball that may be kicked or carried [for
English school where first played]

rug·ged /rəg′id/ *adj.* **1** rough; uneven; wrinkled **2** unpolished; lacking refinement **3**
harsh **4** robust; hardy —**rug′ged·ly** *adv.*;
rug′ged·ness *n.* [prob. Scand]

ru·in /r $ō$ō′in/ *n.* **1** destroyed, wrecked, or
spoiled state **2** utter destruction **3** destroyed
building, etc. **4** cause of ruin —*v.* **5** bring to
ruin **6** spoil; damage —**ru′in·a′tion** *n.*; **ru′
in·ous** *adj.*; **ru′in·ous·ly** *adv.* [L *ruere* fall]

rule /r $ō$ōl/ *n.* **1** compulsory principle governing action **2** custom; standard **3** government;
dominion **4** ruler —*v.* (**ruled**, **rul·ing**) **5**
dominate; keep under control **6** control **7**
pronounce authoritatively **8** make parallel
lines across (paper) **9** as a rule usually **10**
rule out exclude [L *regula*]

rule′ of thumb′ *n.* rule based on experience
or practice rather than theory

rul′er *n.* **1** person exercising government or
dominion **2** straight, usu. graduated, rigid
strip of wood, metal, or plastic used to draw
or measure

rul′ing *n.* authoritative pronouncement, as of
a court

rum /rəm/ *n.* spirit distilled from sugar cane
or molasses

Ru·ma·ni·a /r $ō$ōmā′nēə/ *n.* var. of ROMANIA

Ru·ma·ni·an /r $ō$ōmā′nēən/ *n. & adj.* var. of
ROMANIAN

rum·ba /rəm′bə/ *n.* **1** dance orig. from Cuba
2 music for this —*v.* **3** dance the rumba
[AmerSp]

rum·ble /rəm′bəl/ *v.* (**-bled**, **-bling**) **1** make
a continuous, deep, resonant, thunderlike
sound **2** move with a rumbling noise —*n.* **3**
rumbling sound [prob. Du *rommelen*]

ru·mi·nant /r $ō$ō′mənənt/ *n.* **1** cud-chewing
animal —*adj.* **2** of ruminants **3** meditative
[rel. to RUMINATE]

ru·mi·nate /r $ō$ō′mənāt′/ *v.* (**-nat·ed**, **-nat·
ing**) **1** meditate; ponder **2** chew the cud

—ru·mi·na'tion n.; ru'mi·na'tive /-tiv/ adj. [L rumen throat]

rum·mage /rəm'ij/ v. (·maged, ·mag·ing) 1 search, esp. unsystematically —n. 2 rummaging [Fr arrumage fr. arrumer stow cargo]

rum'mage sale' n. informal sale of miscellaneous, usu. donated, articles, esp. for charity

rum·my /rəm'ē/ n. card game, the object of which is to make matched sets and sequences

ru·mor /rōō'mər/ n. 1 unconfirmed information passed about orally —v. 2 (usu. in passive) report by way of rumor [L rumor noise]

rump /rəmp/ n. hind part of a mammal or bird, esp. the buttocks [prob. Scand]

rum·ple /rəm'pəl/ v. (·pled, ·pling) crease; ruffle [Du rompelen]

rum·pus /rəm'pəs/ n. Colloq. disturbance; brawl; uproar

run /rən/ v. (ran, run, run·ning) 1 go with quick steps, without having both feet on the ground at once 2 flee 3 go briefly 4a advance by or as by rolling or on wheels, or smoothly or easily b (cause to) be in action or operation or go in a specified way 5 be current or in effect 6 (of a play, etc.) be staged or presented 7 extend 8 have a course, order, or tendency 9a compete in (a race, election, etc.) b finish a race in a specified position 10 cause (water, etc.) to flow 11 spread or flow rapidly 12 traverse (a route, race, or distance) 13 perform (an errand) 14 publish in a periodical 15 direct or manage (a business, etc.) 16 own and use (a vehicle) regularly 17 transport in a private vehicle 18 smuggle 19 (of a dyed color) spread 20a (of a thought, the eye, the memory, etc.) pass quickly b pass (one's eye) quickly 21 (of stockings, etc.) unravel 22 exude liquid —n. 23 running 24 short excursion 25 distance traveled 26 general tendency 27 regular route 28 spell 29 high general demand 30 quantity produced at one time 31 average type or class 32 point scored in baseball 33 (foll. by of) free use of or access to 34 ladderlike unraveling in knitwear, esp. stockings, etc. 35 in the long run eventually 36 on the run fleeing 37 run across (or into) happen to meet or find 38 run down: a knock down b (of a mechanism, etc.) stop c discover after a search d Colloq. disparage 39 run in Colloq. arrest 40 run into: a collide with b encounter 41 run off: a flee b produce (copies, etc.) on a machine 42 run out: a come to an end b (foll. by of) exhaust one's stock of c (foll. by on) Colloq. desert (a person) 43 run over: a (of a vehicle, etc.) knock down or crush b overflow c study or repeat quickly 44 run through: a spend (money) rapidly or recklessly b pierce with a sword, etc. 45 run up accumulate (a debt, etc.) 46 run up against meet with (a difficulty, etc.) [OE]

run'a·bout' n. small, light car, boat, etc.

run'a·round' n. as in give a person the runaround Colloq. evasive treatment

run'a·way' n. 1 fugitive —adj. 2 escaping 3 out of control

run'-down' adj. 1 stopped by loss of power 2 weakened or in poor health 3 fallen into disrepair

run'down' n. detailed analysis

rune /rōōn/ n. 1 letter of the earliest Germanic alphabet 2 mark of mysterious or magic significance —ru'nic adj. [OE]

rung[1] /rəNG/ n. 1 step of a ladder 2 strengthening crosspiece in a chair, etc. [OE]

rung[2] v. past part. of RING[2]

run'-in' n. Colloq. quarrel

run·nel /rən'l/ n. brook [OE]

run'ner n. 1 one that runs in a race, as a messenger, etc. 2 creeping, rooting plant stem 3 rod, groove, roller, or blade on which a sled, etc., slides 4 long, narrow rug

run'ner-up' n. (pl. run'ners-up') competitor or team taking second place

run'ning n. 1 action of runners in a race, etc. —adj. 2 continuous 3 consecutive 4 in (or out of) the running (of a competitor) with a good (or poor) chance of success

run'ning light' n. one of several night lights on a vessel or aircraft

run'ning mate' n. candidate for a secondary office in relation to an associate running for a primary office

run'ny adj. (·ni·er, ·ni·est) 1 tending to run or flow 2 excessively fluid

run'-off' n. 1 additional election, race, etc., after a tie 2 surface water not absorbed by the ground

run'-of-the-mill' adj. ordinary; undistinguished

runt /rənt/ n. 1 smallest animal in a litter 2 Colloq. Derog. undersized person

run'-through' n. rehearsal

run'way' n. 1 surface for aircraft taking off and landing 2 walkway as a stage extension, as for models to display clothing, etc.

ru·pee /rōō'pē, rōōpē'/ n. chief monetary unit of India, Pakistan, etc. [Hindustani]

rup·ture /rəp'CHər/ n. 1 breaking; breach; disagreement 2 abdominal hernia —v. (·tured, ·tur·ing) 3 cause or undergo a rupture [L rumpere rupt- break]

ru·ral /rōōr'əl/ adj. in, of, or suggesting the country [L rus rur- country]

ru'ral de·liv'er·y serv'ice n. (formerly ru'ral free' de·liv'er·y) postal delivery to mailboxes in rural areas

ruse /rōōz/ n. stratagem; trick [Fr]

rush[1] /rəsh/ v. 1 move, flow, or act precipitately or with great speed 2 move or transport with great haste 3a move suddenly toward b begin or attack impetuously 4 force or induce (a person) to act hastily —n. 5 rushing 6 great activity 7 great haste or speed 8 sudden movement of large numbers [Fr ruser, rel. to RUSE]

rush[2] n. marsh plant with slender stems, used for making chair seats, baskets, etc. —rush'y adj. Colloq.

Rush·die /rōōsh'dē, rəsh'-/, (Ahmed) Salman 1947– ; Indian-born British novelist

rush' hour' n. time each day when traffic is heaviest

Rush'more, Mt. /rəsh'môr', -môr'/ n. peak in Black Hills of S. Dak. with monumental carving of the faces of US presidents Washington, Jefferson, T. Roosevelt, and Lincoln

rusk /rəsk/ n. slice of bread rebaked as a light biscuit [Sp or Port rosca twist]

Rus·kin /rəs'kin/, **John** 1819–1900; English art and social critic

Rus·sell /rəs'əl/, **Bertrand** 1873–1970; British philosopher, mathematician, and reformer

rus·set /rəs'it/ *adj.* 1 reddish-brown —*n.* 2 russet color 3 russet-colored fruit or vegetable [L *russus*]

Rus·sia /rəSH'ə/ *n.* republic in E Europe and Asia. Capital: Moscow. Pop. 149,469,000. Formerly chief republic of the USSR

Rus·sian /rəSH'ən/ *n.* 1 native or national of Russia or (loosely) the former Soviet Union 2 Slavic language of Russia —*adj.* 3 of Russia, (loosely) the former Soviet Union, its people, or their language

Rus'sian rou·lette' *n.* pulling the trigger of a revolver, with one chamber loaded, at one's head after spinning the chamber

rust /rəst/ *n.* 1 reddish corrosive coating formed on iron, steel, etc., by oxidation, esp. when wet 2 fungal plant disease with rust-colored spots 3 impaired state due to disuse or inactivity 4 reddish-brown —*v.* 5 affect or be affected with rust 6 become impaired through disuse [OE]

rust' belt' *n.* region of the east central US, once dependent on steel-making and heavy industry

rus·tic /rəs'tik/ *adj.* 1 of or like country people or country life 2 unsophisticated 3 rude; rough —*n.* 4 country person —**rus'ti·cal·ly** *adv.*; **rus·tic'i·ty** /-tis'itē/ *n.* [L *rus* the country]

rus·ti·cate /rəs'tikāt'/ *v.* (·cat·ed, ·cat·ing) 1 retire to or live in the country 2 make rustic —**rus'ti·ca'tion** *n.*

rus·tle /rəs'əl/ *v.* (·tled, ·tling) 1 (cause to) make a gentle sound as of dry, blown leaves 2 steal (cattle or horses) —*n.* 3 rustling sound 4 **rustle up** *Colloq.* produce on short notice —**rus'tler** *n.* [imit.]

rust'proof' *adj.* 1 not susceptible to corrosion by rust —*v.* 2 make rustproof

rust·y /rəs'tē/ *adj.* (·ti·er, ·ti·est) 1 rusted or affected by rust 2 impaired by neglect —**rust'i·ness** *n.*

rut[1] /rət/ *n.* 1 deep track made by the passage of wheels 2 established (esp. tedious) routine —*v.* (**rut·ted, rut·ting**) 3 mark with ruts [prob. Fr. rel. to ROUTE]

rut[2] *n.* 1 periodic sexual excitement of certain male animals —*v.* (**rut·ted, rut·ting**) 2 be affected with rut [L *rugire* roar]

ru·ta·ba·ga /rōō'təbā'gə/ *n.* root vegetable [Sw dial. *rotabagge*]

Ruth /rōōTH/, **"Babe"** (George Herman) 1895–1948; US baseball player

ru·the·ni·um /rōōTH'nē'əm/ *n.* rare metallic element; *symb.* **Ru** [MedL *Ruthenia* Russia]

Ruth·er·ford /rəTH'ə(r)fərd/, **(Sir) Ernest** 1871–1937; New Zealand-born British nuclear physicist

ruth·er·for·di·um /rəTH'ərfôr'dēəm/ *n.* artificial metallic element; *symb.* **Rf** [for E. RUTHERFORD]

ruth·less /rōōTH'ləs/ *adj.* having no pity or compassion —**ruth'less·ly** *adv.*; **ruth'less·ness** *n.* [*ruth* pity, fr. RUE[1]]

RV *abbr.* 1 recreational vehicle; camper, trailer, etc. 2 Revised Version (of the Bible)

Rwan·da /rōō·än'də/ *n.* republic in central Africa. Capital: Kigali. Pop. 7,347,000 —**Rwan'dan** *n. & adj.*

Rwy. *abbr.* railway

Rya·zan /rē'əzän'/ *n.* city in W Russia. Pop. 527,200

Ry·binsk /rib'insk'/ *n.* city in W Russia on the Volga River. Pop. 252,600

rye /rī/ *n.* 1a cereal plant b grain of this used for bread and fodder 2 (**rye' whis'key**) whiskey distilled from fermented rye [OE]

Ryle /rīl/, **Gilbert** 1900–76; English philosopher

S

s, S /es/ *n.* (*pl.* **s's**; **S's, Ss**) nineteenth letter of the English alphabet; a consonant

S *symb.* sulfur

s or **s.** *abbr.* 1 satisfactory 2 second 3 signature 4 signed 5 small 6 soft 7 son 8 *Mus.* soprano

S or **S.** *abbr.* 1 Sabbath 2 Saint 3 Saturday 4 Saxon 5 Senate 6 September 7 Signor 8 Socialist 9 Society 10 south; southern 11 Sunday

's *abbr.* 1 is (*he's*) 2 has (*she's got it*) 3 us (*let's*)

-'s *suffix* denoting the possessive case of singular nouns and of plural nouns not ending in -s (*John's book; book's cover; children's shoes*)

-s' *suffix* denoting the possessive case of plural nouns and sometimes of singular nouns ending in s (*the boys' shoes; Charles' book*) [OE inflection]

S.A. *abbr.* 1 South Africa 2 South America 3 South Australia

sab·bath /sab'əTH/ *n.* religious day of rest kept by Christians on Sunday and Jews on Saturday [Heb: rest]

sab·bat·i·cal /səbat'ikəl/ *adj.* 1 (of leave) granted at intervals from one's usual work, as to a teacher for study or travel 2 (*cap.*) of the Sabbath —*n.* 3 period of sabbatical leave [Gk, rel. to SABBATH]

sa·ber /sā'bər/ *n.* (also **sa'bre**) 1 curved cavalry sword 2 tapered fencing sword [Fr fr. Ger *Sabel*]

sa'ber-rat'tling *n.* display or threat of military force

sa'ber saw' *n.* portable electric jigsaw

Sa·bin /sā'bin/, **Albert Bruce** 1906–93; Russian-born US microbiologist; developed oral polio vaccine

Sa'bin vac'cine *n.* oral vaccine immunizing against poliomyelitis [for A.B. SABIN]

sa·ble /sā'bəl/ *n.* (*pl.* same or **·bles**) 1 small, brown-furred mammal of N Europe and N Asia 2 its skin or fur [Slavonic]

sa·bot /sabō´/ *n.* shoe carved from a block of wood [Fr]

sab·o·tage /sab´ətäzH´/ *n.* 1 deliberate damage to productive capacity, esp. by enemy agents, as a political act, etc. —*v.* (·taged, ·tag·ing) 2 commit sabotage on —**sa·bo·teur** /sab´ətur´/ *n.* [Fr, rel. to SABOT]

sac /sak/ *n.* membranous bag in an animal or plant [L, rel. to SACK¹]

SAC /sak/ *abbr.* Strategic Air Command

Sac·a·ja·we·a /sak´əjəwē´ə, -wä´ə/ ("Bird Woman") *c.* 1788–1812; Shoshone Indian guide and interpreter for the Lewis and Clark expedition

sac·cha·rin /sak´(ə)rən/ *n.* a sugar substitute [MedL *saccharum* sugar]

sac·cha·rine /sak´(ə)rən/ *adj.* excessively sentimental or sweet

sac·er·do·tal /sas´ərdōt´l, sak´-/ *adj.* of priests or priestly office [L *sacerdos -dot- priest*]

sa·chem /sā´cHəm/ *n.* (in some American Indian tribes) chief [AmerInd]

sa·chet /saSHā´/ *n.* small bag or packet containing fragrance, etc. [Fr dim., rel. to SAC]

sack¹ /sak/ *n.* 1a large, strong bag for storage or conveyance **b** quantity contained in a sack 2 (prec. by *the*) *Slang.* dismissal from employment 3 (prec. by *the*) *Slang.* bed —*v.* 4 put into a sack or sacks 5 *Slang.* dismiss from employment [L *saccus*]

sack² /sak/ *v.* 1 plunder and destroy (a captured town, etc.) —*n.* 2 such sacking [Fr *mettre à sac* put in a sack]

sack³ *n. Hist.* white wine from Spain and the Canaries [Fr *vin sec* dry wine]

sack´cloth´ *n.* (also **sack´ing**) 1 coarse fabric used for sacks **b** clothing for mourning (esp. **sackcloth and ashes**)

sac·ra·ment /sak´rəmənt/ *n.* symbolic Christian ceremony, e.g., baptism and Eucharist —**sac´ra·men´tal** /-men´təl/ *adj.* [L, rel. to SACRED]

Sac·ra·men·to /sak´rəmen´tō/ *n.* capital of Calif., in the N central part. Pop. 369,365

sa·cred /sā´krid/ *adj.* 1a dedicated to a god **b** connected with religion 2 safeguarded or required, esp. by tradition —**sa´cred·ly** *adv.*; **sa´cred·ness** *n.* [L *sacer* holy]

sa´cred cow´ *n. Colloq.* hallowed idea or institution

sac·ri·fice /sak´rəfīs´/ *n.* 1a voluntary giving up of something valued **b** thing given up **c** the loss involved 2a slaughter of an animal or person or surrender of a possession, as an offering to a deity **b** animal, person, or thing offered —*v.* (·ficed, ·fic·ing) 3 give up (a thing) as a sacrifice —**sac´ri·fi´cial** /-fiSH´əl/ *adj.* [L, rel. to SACRED]

sac·ri·lege /sak´rəlij´/ *n.* violation of what is regarded as sacred —**sac´ri·le´gious** /-lij´əs/ *adj.* [L, rel. to SACRED, *legere* take]

sac·ris·tan /sak´ristən/ *n.* person in charge of a sacristy

sac·ris·ty /sak´ristē/ *n.* (*pl.* **·ties**) room in a church for vestments, sacred vessels, etc. [MedL, rel. to SACRED]

sac·ro·il·i·ac /sak´rōil´ēak, sā´krō-/ *n.* joint in the back between the pelvis and the fused bottom vertebra

sac·ro·sanct /sak´rōsaNGkt´/ *adj.* most sacred; inviolable —**sac´ro·sanc´ti·ty, sac´ro·sanct´ness** *n.* [L, rel. to SACRED, SAINT]

sad /sad/ *adj.* (**sad·der, sad·dest**) 1 unhappy 2 causing sorrow 3 regrettable 4 shameful; deplorable —**sad´den** *v.*; **sad´ly** *adv.*; **sad´ness** *n.* [OE]

Sa·dat /sədät´, -dat´/, **Anwar el-** 1918–81; president of Egypt (1970–81); assassinated

sad·dle /sad´l/ *n.* 1 seat usu. of leather strapped on a horse, etc., for riding 2 seat on a bicycle, etc. 3 cut of meat consisting of the two loins —*v.* (·dled, ·dling) 4 put a saddle on (a horse, etc.) 5 burden (a person) 6 **in the saddle** at work; in control [OE]

sad´dle·bag´ *n.* 1 each of a pair of bags laid across the back of a horse, etc. 2 bag attached to a bicycle saddle, etc.

sad´dle shoes´ *n.* laced shoes with yokes that contrast in color with the rest of the upper

Sad·du·cee /saj´əsē´/ *n.* member of an ancient fundamentalist Jewish sect [Heb]

Sade /säd/, **Donatien (Comte de)** (called "**Marquis de Sade**") 1740–1814; French novelist and pornographer

sa·dism /sad´iz´əm, sā´diz/- *n.* pleasure derived from inflicting cruelty on others —**sad´ist** *n.*; **sa·dis´tic** /-dis´tik/ *adj.*; **sa·dis´ti·cal·ly** *adv.* [for Marquis de SADE]

sa·do·mas·och·ism /sad´ōmas´əkizm, sā´dō-/ *n.* sexual pleasure from sadism or masochism or both —**sa´do·mas´o·chist** *n.*; **sa´do·mas´o·chis´tic** *adj.*

sa·fa·ri /səfär´ē/ *n.* expedition, esp. in Africa, to observe or hunt animals [Swahili fr. Ar *safara* to travel]

safe /sāf/ *adj.* 1 free of danger or injury 2 secure; not risky 3 reliable; certain 4 uninjured —*n.* 5 strong, lockable cabinet, etc., for valuables —**safe´ly** *adv.*; **safe´ness** *n.* [Fr *sauf* fr. L *salvus*]

safe´-con´duct *n.* 1 immunity given from arrest or harm 2 document securing this

safe´-de·pos´it *adj.* offering vaults and safes for hire

safe´guard´ *n.* 1 something ensuring security or safety —*v.* 2 guard; protect

safe´ house´ *n.* place of refuge, etc., for spies, terrorists, etc.

safe´keep´ing *n.* preservation in a safe place

safe´ sex´ *n.* sexual activity in which precautions are taken against sexually transmitted diseases

safe·ty /sāf´tē/ *n.* 1 being safe 2 *Football.* defensive position farthest from the line of scrimmage

safe´ty match´ *n.* match igniting only on a specially prepared surface

safe´ty pin´ *n.* doubled pin with a guarded point

safe´ty ra´zor *n.* razor with a guard to prevent cutting the skin

safe´ty valve´ *n.* automatic valve relieving excess pressure

saf·flow·er /saf´flou´ər/ *n.* thistlelike herb yielding reddish dye and edible oil [Du *saf- floer*]

saf·fron /saf´rən/ *n.* 1 stigmas of a variety of crocus yielding flavoring and yellowish-or-ange coloring 2 color of this —*adj.* 3 deep yellowish orange [Fr fr. Ar]

sag /sag/ v. (**sagged, sag·ging**) **1** sink or subside, esp. unevenly **2** bulge or curve downward in the middle **3** fall in price —n. **4** state or extent of sagging [LGer or Du]

sa·ga /säʹgə/ n. **1** long, heroic story, esp. medieval Icelandic or Norwegian **2** any long, involved story [ON, rel. to SAW³]

sa·ga·cious /səgāʹshəs/ adj. showing insight or good judgment —**sa·gac′i·ty** /-gasʹitē/ n. [L sagax -acis]

Sa·ga·mi·ha·ra /sägäʹmēhär′ə/ n. city in Japan, on Honshu. Pop. 542,000

sage¹ /sāj/ n. **1** herb with dull grayish-green leaves **2** SAGEBRUSH [Fr fr. L salvus safe, for its reputed healing power]

sage² n. **1** wise man —adj. (**sag·er, sag·est**) **2** wise; judicious —**sage′ly** adv. [Fr fr. L sapere be wise]

sage′brush′ n. shrubby aromatic plant in semi-arid regions of western US

Sag·it·tar·i·us /saj′əter′ēəs/ n. **1** constellation and ninth sign of the zodiac (**the Archer**) **2** person born under this sign —**Sag′it·tar′i·an** adj. & n. [L: archer]

sa·gua·ro /səgwäʹrō/ n. (pl. **-ros**) tall cactus of the SW US [MexSp]

Sa·har′a Des′ert /səharʹə, -härʹə/ n. vast arid region extending across N Africa

Sa·hel /səhälʹ, -hēlʹ/ n. arid region S of the Sahara from Senegal to Chad

sa·hib /säʹ(h)ib/ n. (in colonial India) form of address to European man [Ar: lord]

said /sed/ v. **1** past and past part. of SAY —adj. **2** referred to earlier **3** reputed

Sai·gon /sīgänʹ, sīʹgänʹ/ n. former name of HO CHI MINH CITY

sail /sāl/ n. **1** piece of fabric extended on rigging to catch the wind and propel a vessel **2** vessel's sails collectively **3** voyage in a vessel, esp. a sailing vessel **4** wind-catching apparatus of a windmill —v. **5** travel on water (or a body of water) by the use of sails or engine-power **6** begin a voyage **7** navigate (a vessel) **8** glide or move smoothly **9 sail into** Colloq. attack physically or verbally **10 under sail** with sails set [OE]

sail′board′ n. board with a mast and sail, used in windsurfing —**sail′board′er, sail′board′ing** n.

sail′boat′ n. boat driven by a sail or sails

sail′cloth′ n. **1** fabric used for sails **2** canvaslike material for awnings, tents, etc.

sail′fish′ n. (pl. **-fish** or **-fish·es**) large marine fish having a large saillike dorsal fin

sail′or n. **1** member of a vessel's crew, esp. one below the rank of officer **2** person whose hobby is sailing or boating [orig. sailer]

sail′plane′ n. light, one-person glider

saint /sānt/ n. **1** holy or (in some Churches) formally canonized person regarded as worthy of special veneration **2** very virtuous person —**saint′ed** adj.; **saint′hood** n.; **saint′like** adj.; **saint′li·ness** n.; **saint′ly** adj. (**·li·er, ·li·est**) [L sanctus holy]

Saint′ Ber·nard′ /bärnärdʹ/ n. large dog of a breed orig. kept in the Alps for rescue

Saint′ Cath′a·rines /kaTHʹ(ə)rinz/ n. city in Ontario, Canada. Pop. 129,300

St. Chris·to·pher & Ne·vis /sänt krisʹtəfər, nēʹvis, səntʹ/ n. see ST. KITTS AND NEVIS

Saint-Gau·dens /sänt gōdʹnz/, **Augustus** 1848–1907; Irish-born US sculptor

Saint′ George′s /jorʹjəz/ n. capital of Grenada. Pop. 4,400

St. Hel′ens, Mt. /helʹənz/ n. active volcano in the Cascade Mountains of Wash.

St. John′s /sänt jänz′, sənt′/ n. **1** capital of Antigua and Barbuda. Pop 36,000 **2** capital of the Canadian province of Newfoundland. Pop. 171,900

Saint′ John′s′ bread′ n. see CAROB

St. Jo·seph /jōʹsəf, -zəf/ n. city in Mo. Pop. 71,852

St. Kitts and Ne·vis /kits, nēʹvis/ n. (formerly **St. Christopher & Nevis**) two-island state in the West Indies. Capital: Basseterre. Pop. 43,100

St. Law′rence Riv′er /lorʹəns, lär′-/ n. river flowing 760 mi. from Lake Ontario into the Atlantic on the US-Canada border

St. Law′rence Sea′way n. international waterway for oceangoing ships connecting the Atlantic Ocean and the Great Lakes

St. Lou·is /lōōʹis/ n. city in Mo. Pop. 396,685

St. Lu·cia /lōōʹshə/ n. island country in the West Indies. Capital: Castries. Pop. 135,000

Saint′ Pat′rick′s Day′ /patʹriks/ n. March 17, observed esp. by the Irish to honor the patron saint of Ireland

St. Paul /pôlʹ/ n. capital of Minn., across the Mississippi River from Minneapolis. Pop. 272,235

Saint Pe·ters·burg /pētʹərzbərg/ n. (called **Leningrad** fr. 1924–91) city and port in NW Russia. Pop. 4,466,800

St. Pe·ters·burg /pētʹərzbərg/ n. city in Fla. Pop. 238,629

Saint-Saëns /saN sänsʹ/, **Charles Camille** 1835–1921; French composer

Saint′ Val′en·tine′s Day′ /valʹəntīnz/ n. February 14, observed by exchange of notes and tokens of affection

Saint′ Vi′tus's dance′ /vīʹtəsiz/ n. disease producing involuntary convulsive movements

Sa·kai /säʹkīʹ/ n. seaport in Japan, on Honshu. Pop. 808,100

sake¹ /sāk/ n. **1** benefit; advantage **2** cause; purpose [OE]

sa·ke² /säkʹē/ n. Japanese rice wine [Japn]

Sa·kha·lin Is·land /sakʹəlēn′/ n. island off the SE coast of Russia, N of Japan

Sa·kha·rov /säKHʹərôf, sakʹ-/, **Andrei** 1921–89; Russian nuclear physicist

Saki /säkʹē/ pseudonym of MUNRO, H(ECTOR) H(UGH)

sa·laam /səlämʹ/ n. Muslim greeting, often with a low bow and the right palm on the forehead [Ar: peace]

sal·a·ble or **sale·a·ble** /sāʹləbəl/ adj. suitable to be sold; subject to sale —**sa′la·bil′i·ty** n.

sa·la·cious /səlāʹshəs/ adj. **1** indecent **2** lecherous —**sa·la′cious·ly** adv.; **sa·la′cious·ness** n. [L salax -acis, rel. to SALIENT]

sal·ad /salʹəd/ n. mixture of usu. cold vegetables, meats, eggs, etc., often with a dressing [Fr salade fr. L sal salt]

sal′ad bar′ n. restaurant buffet offering diners ingredients for salad making

sal′ad days′ n. period of youthful inexperience

sal′ad dress′ing n. mixture of oil, vinegar, spices, etc., used to flavor salad

Sal·a·din /sal'əd-n, -ədin'/ 1137–93; sultan of Egypt and Syria (1175–93)

Sal·a·man·ca /săl'əmăNG'kə/ n. city in W Spain. Pop. 162,500

sal·a·man·der /sal'əman'dər/ n. 1 tailed newtlike amphibian once thought able to endure fire 2 similar mythical creature [Gk *salamandra*]

sa·la·mi /sələ'mē/ n. type of highly seasoned sausage [It]

sal·a·ry /sal'(ə)rē/ n. (pl. **·ries**) fixed regular wages —**sal'a·ried** adj. [L *salarium* money for buying salt]

Sa·la·zar /săl'əzär'/, António de Oliveira 1899–1970; Portuguese politician; premier (1932–68)

sale /sāl/ n. 1 exchange of a commodity for money, etc.; act or instance of selling 2 amount sold 3 event at which goods are sold, esp. at a reduced price 4 **for sale** offered for purchase 5 **on sale** offered for purchase, esp. at a reduced price [OE]

Sa·lem /sā'ləm/ n. capital of Ore., in the NW part. Pop. 107,786

Sa·ler·no /sələr'nō/ n. seaport in SW Italy. Pop. 151,300

sales·clerk /sālz'klərk'/ n. person employed to sell goods in a store

sales'girl' n. girl or woman employed to sell goods in a store

sales'la·dy n. woman employed to sell goods in a store

sales·man /sālz'mən/ n. (pl. **·men**) man employed to sell goods

sales'man·ship' n. skill in selling

sales'per'son n. salesman or saleswoman —**sales'peo'ple** n. pl.

sales' rep·re·sen'ta·tive n. (also *Colloq.* **sales' rep'**) person who sells for a manufacturer, etc., esp. one who travels

sales' slip' n. receipt

sales' talk' n. persuasive talk promoting goods, an idea, etc.

sales'wom'an n. (pl. **·wom'en**) woman employed to sell goods

sal·i·cyl'ic ac'id /sal'əsil'ik/ n. chemical used as a preservative and in aspirin and dyes [L *salix* willow]

sa·lient /sā'lēənt/ adj. 1 prominent; conspicuous 2 (of a fortification) pointing outward —n. 3 salient angle or part of a fortification [L *salire* leap]

Sa·li·nas /sālē'nəs/ n. city in Calif. Pop. 108,777

sa·line /sā'lēn', -līn'/ adj. 1 containing or like salt —n. 2 saline solution —**sa·lin·i·ty** /səlin'ətē/, **sal·in·i·za·tion** /sal'inizā'sHən/ n. [L *sal* salt]

Sal·in·ger /sal'injər/, J(erome) D(avid) 1919– ; US novelist and short-story writer

sa·li·va /səlī'və/ n. watery liquid secreted into the mouth by glands —**sal'i·var·y** /sal'əver'ē/ adj. [L]

sal·i·vate /sal'əvāt'/ v. (**·vat·ed, ·vat·ing**) secrete saliva —**sal'i·va'tion** n. [L *salivare*, rel. to SALIVA]

Salk /sô(l)k/, Jonas 1914– ; US physician and bacteriologist; developed polio vaccine

sal·low /sal'ō/ adj. (esp. of the skin) yellowish; sickly [OE]

Sal·lust /sal'əst/ (Gaius Sallustius Cris-

pus) 86–34 B.C.; Roman historian and politician

sal·ly /sal'ē/ n. (pl. **·lies**) 1 sudden charge; sortie 2 excursion 3 witticism —v. (**·lied, ·ly·ing**) 4 make a sally [Fr *saillie* fr. L *salire* leap]

salm·on /sam'ən/ n. (pl. same or **·ons**) 1 large edible fish with orange-pink flesh —adj. 2 salmon-pink [L *salmo*]

sal·mo·nel·la /sal'mənel'ə/ n. (pl. **·lae** /-lē/) bacterium causing food poisoning [for D. *Salmon*, US pathologist]

sa·lon /səlän', sal'än'/ n. 1 room or establishment of a hairdresser, beautician, etc. 2 meeting of eminent people in the home of a lady of fashion 3 reception room [Fr, rel. to SALOON]

Sa·lon·i·ka /sələn'ikə/ n. see THESSALONIKE

sa·loon /səlōōn'/ n. 1 public barroom 2 large room or hall [Fr *salon*]

sal·sa /säl'sə/ n. 1 a kind of dance music of Cuban origin, with jazz and rock elements 2 spicy sauce, usu. containing tomatoes, onions, chilies, etc. [Sp, rel. to SAUCE]

salt /sôlt/ n. 1 (also **com'mon salt', ta'ble salt'**) sodium chloride, esp. mined or evaporated from sea water, and used for seasoning, preserving food, etc. 2 chemical compound formed from the reaction of an acid with a base 3 piquancy; wit 4 (sing. or pl.) a substance resembling salt in taste, form, etc. (**bath salts**) b (pl.) substance used as a laxative 5 (also **old' salt'**) experienced sailor —adj. 6 containing, tasting of, or preserved with salt —v. 7 cure, preserve, sprinkle, or season with salt 8 **salt away** *Colloq.* put (money, etc.) aside; save 9 **salt of the earth** best person or people (Matt. 5:13) 10 **with a grain of salt** regard skeptically 11 **worth one's salt** efficient; capable [OE]

SALT /sôlt/ abbr. Strategic Arms Limitation Talks (or Treaty)

salt·cel·lar /sôlt'sel'ər/ n. container for salt at table [earlier *salt saler* fr. Fr *salier* salt-box]

Sal·ti·llo /sältē'(y)ō/ n. capital of the Mexican state of Coahuila. Pop. 440,800

sal·tine /sôltēn'/ n. slightly salted, square, flat cracker

Salt' Lake' Cit'y n. capital of Utah, in the N part. Pop. 159,936

salt' lick' n. place where animals lick salt

Sal·ton Sea /sôlt'n/ n. shallow, saline lake in S Calif. NE of San Diego, 240 ft. below sea level

salt·pe·ter /sôlt'pē'tər/ n. potassium nitrate, used in gunpowder, etc. [L *sal petrae* salt of rock]

salt' pork' n. pork preserved in salt

salt' shak'er n. dispenser for salt, with a perforated top

salt'·wa'ter adj. of or living in the sea

salt'y adj. (**·i·er, ·i·est**) 1 tasting of or containing salt 2 (of wit, etc.) piquant 3 risqué —**salt'i·ness** n.

sa·lu·bri·ous /səlōō'brēəs/ adj. health-giving; healthy —**sa·lu'bri·ous·ly** adv.; **sa·lu' bri·ous·ness, sa·lu'bri·ty** /-brītē/ n. [L *salus* health]

sal·u·tar·y /sal'yəter'ē/ adj. 1 having a good effect 2 healthful [L, rel. to SALUTE]

sal·u·ta·tion /sal'yōōtā'sHən/ *n.* expression of greeting, vocal or in a letter, etc.

sa·lute /səlōōt'/ *n.* 1 gesture of respect, homage, greeting, etc. 2 *Milit. & Naval.* prescribed gesture or use of weapons or flags as a sign of respect, etc. 3 ceremonial discharge of a gun or guns —*v.* (·lut·ed, ·lut·ing) 4a make a salute to b perform a salute 5 greet 6 commend [L *salus -ut-* health]

Sal·va·dor /sal'vədôr, sal'vədôr'/ *n.* seaport in E Brazil. Pop. 1,506,600

sal·vage /sal'vij/ *n.* 1 rescue of property from the sea, a fire, etc. 2 property so saved 3a saving and use of waste materials b materials salvaged —*v.* (·vaged, ·vag·ing) 4 save from a wreck, disaster, etc. —**sal'vage·a·ble** *adj.* [L, rel. to SAVE¹]

sal·va·tion /salvā'sHən/ *n.* 1 saving or being saved 2 deliverance from sin and damnation 3 person or thing that saves [L, rel. to SAVE¹]

salve /sav/ *n.* 1 healing ointment 2 thing that soothes or consoles —*v.* (salved, salv·ing) 3 soothe [OE]

sal·ver /sal'vər/ *n.* small tray, esp. of silver [Sp *salva* food-tasting]

sal·vo /sal'vō/ *n.* (*pl.* ·vos or ·voes) simultaneous discharge of guns [It *salva*]

Salz·burg /sôlz'bərg, sälz'-, zälts'-/ *n.* city in W Austria. Pop. 144,000

SAM /sam/ *abbr.* surface-to-air missile

Sa·ma·ra /səmär'ə/ *n.* see KUIBYSHEV

Sam·a·rin·da /sam'ərin'də/ *n.* city in Indonesia, on Borneo. Pop. 264,700

Sa·mar·i·tan /səmar'ət·n/ *n.* as in **good Samaritan** charitable or helpful person (Luke 10:33)

sa·mar·i·um /səmar'ēəm/ *n.* metallic element of the lanthanide series; *symb.* **Sm** [ult. fr. V.E. *Samarski*, Russian mining engineer]

Sam·ar·kand /sam'ərkand'/ *n.* city in E Uzbekistan. Pop. 370,500

sam·ba /sam'bə, säm'-/ *n.* 1 ballroom dance of Brazilian origin 2 music for this —*v.* (·baed, ·ba·ing) 3 dance the samba [Port]

same /sām/ *adj.* 1 identical; not different or another 2 unvarying 3 just mentioned —*pron.* 4 the same person or thing —*adv.* 5 (usu. prec. by *the*) similarly; in the same way —**same'ness** *n.* [ON]

● Usage: Care should be taken not to use *same* of objects, in place of 'identical': To say that Tom and Jan bought the same car describes an unlikely situation: they might have bought identical cars, but to say they bought the same car would literally mean they each paid for one car.

sa·miz·dat /säm'ēzdät'/ *n.* clandestine publication of banned literature [Russ]

Sa·mo·a /səmō'ə/ *n.* see AMERICAN SAMOA; WESTERN SAMOA

sam·o·var /sam'əvär'/ *n.* Russian urn for making tea [Russ]

sam·pan /sam'pan'/ *n.* small boat used in the Far East [Chin]

sam·ple /sam'pəl/ *n.* 1 small representative part or quantity 2 illustrative or typical example —*v.* (·pled, ·pling) 3 take or try samples of [AngFr, rel. to EXAMPLE]

sam·pler /sam'plər/ *n.* 1 one who samples 2 piece of embroidery using various stitches as a specimen of proficiency 3 collection of samples —**sam'pling** *n.* [Fr, rel. to EXEMPLAR]

Sam·son /sam'sən/ *n.* person of great strength [*Samson* in the Old Testament]

Sam·sun /sämsōōn'/ *n.* city in N Turkey. Pop. 304,000

sam·u·rai /sam'ərī'/ *n.* (*pl.* same) member of a former Japanese military caste [Japn]

Sa·naa /sanä'/ *n.* political capital of Yemen. Pop. 427,200

San' An·dre'as Fault' /san' andrā'əs/ *n.* extensive earthquake zone extending N to S along the N Calif. coast

San An·to·ni·o /san' antō'nēō, əntō'-/ *n.* city in Texas. Pop. 935,933

san·a·to·ri·um /san'ətôr'ēəm/ *n.* (*pl.* ·ums or ·ri·a /-ə/) (esp. *Brit.*) sanitarium

San Ber·nar·di·no /san' bər'nə(r)dē'nō/ *n.* city in Calif. Pop. 164,164

San Bue·na·ven·tu·ra /san' bwen' əvent(y)ōōr'ə/ *n.* (also Ven·tu'ra) city in Calif. Pop. 92,575

San·chung /san'CHəNG'/ *n.* suburb of Taipei, Taiwan. Pop. 376,000

sanc·ti·fy /saNGK'təfī'/ *v.* (·fied, ·fy·ing) 1 treat as holy 2 free from sin —**sanc'ti·fi·ca'tion** /-fikā'sHən/ *n.* [L *sanctus* holy]

sanc·ti·mo·ni·ous /saNGK'təmō'nēəs/ *adj.* ostentatiously pious or righteous —**sanc'ti·mo'ni·ous·ly** *adv.;* **sanc'ti·mo'ni·ous·ness**, **sanc'ti·mo·ny** *n.* [L *sanctimonia* sanctity]

sanc·tion /saNGK'sHən/ *n.* 1 approval; express permission 2 support; confirmation of a law, etc. 3 penalty for disobeying a law or rule, esp. economic action by a state against another —*v.* 4 authorize or agree to (an action, etc.) 5 ratify; make (a law, etc.) binding [L *sancire sanct-* make sacred]

● Usage: Interestingly, *sanction* has meanings that are almost opposite, depending on whether domestic or foreign relations are under discussion. In the first case, *sanction* means 'approval; permission': *Her father gave the groom his official sanction.* In the second, it means 'penalty; deterrent': *The sanctions against the republic have been canceled.*

sanc·ti·ty /saNGK'tətē/ *n.* holiness; sacredness; inviolability [L *sanctus* holy]

sanc·tu·ar·y /saNGK'CHōō·er'ē/ *n.* (*pl.* ·ies) 1 holy place, esp. in a temple, etc. 2 place of refuge, esp. where wildlife is protected

sanc·tum /saNGK'təm/ *n.* (*pl.* ·tums) 1 holy place 2 *Colloq.* study; den

Sand /sän(d), sand/, **George** (pseudonym of Amandine-Aurore Dupin) 1804–76; French novelist

sand /sand/ *n.* 1 loose grains resulting from the erosion of rocks and forming the seashore, deserts, etc. 2 (*pl.*) a grains of sand b expanse of sand —*v.* 3 smooth with sandpaper —**sand'er** *n.* [OE]

san·dal /san'dəl/ *n.* shoe with an openwork upper or no upper, usu. fastened by straps [L fr. Gk]

san'dal·wood' *n.* sweet-scented wood of an Asian tree

sand'bag' *n.* 1 bag filled with sand, used for fortifications, retaining walls, etc. —*v.* (·bagged, ·bag·ging) 2 defend or hit with sandbag(s) 3 *Colloq.* make a person do something 4 *Colloq.* withhold full effort

sand'blast' *v.* 1 roughen, treat, or clean with a jet of sand driven by compressed air or steam —*n.* 2 this jet —**sand'blast'er** *n.*

sand'box' *n.* large open box containing sand for children to play in

Sand·burg /san(d)'bərg/, **Carl** 1878–1967; US poet and biographer

sand'hog' *n.* worker esp. in underwater construction

San Di·e·go /san' dē·ā'gō/ *n.* city in Calif. Pop. 1,110,549

sand'man' *n.* imaginary person said to put sand in children's eyes to make them sleepy

sand'pa'per *n.* 1 paper with an abrasive coating for smoothing or polishing —*v.* 2 rub with this

SANDPIPER

sand·pip·er /sand'pī'pər/ *n.* shore bird with a piping call

sand'stone' *n.* sedimentary rock of compressed sand

sand'storm' *n.* storm with clouds of sand raised by the wind

sand·wich /san(d)'wich/ *n.* 1 two or more slices of bread with a filling —*v.* 2 put between two other things [for the Earl of *Sandwich*]

sand'y *adj.* (·i·er, ·i·est) 1 having much sand 2 sandlike in color, texture, n. 3 reddish-yellow —**sand'i·ness** *n.*

sane /sān/ *adj.* 1 of sound mind; rational 2 moderate; sensible [L *sanus* healthy]

San Fran·cis·co /san' frənsis'kō, fran-/ *n.* city in Calif. Pop. 723,959 —**San' Fran·cis' can** *n.*

San' Fran·cis'co Bay' *n.* inlet of the Pacific Ocean on W central coast of Calif.

sang /saNG/ *v. past* of SING

Sang·er /saNG'ər/, **Margaret** 1883–1966; US nurse; proponent of birth control

sang·froid /sän'frwä'/ *n.* calmness in danger or difficulty [Fr: cold blood]

san·gri·a /saNG·grē'ə, san-grē'ə/ *n.* drink of red wine with lemonade, fruit, etc. [Sp: bleeding]

san·gui·nar·y /saNG'gwəner'ē/ *adj.* 1 bloody 2 bloodthirsty [L *sanguis·guin·* blood]

san·guine /saNG'gwin/ *adj.* 1 optimistic; confident 2 (of the complexion) florid; ruddy

san·i·tar·i·um /san'əter'ēəm/ *n.* (*pl.* ·ums or ·i·a /-ə/) resort or medical facility for restoration of health [rel. to SANITARY]

san·i·tar·y /san'əter'ē/ *adj.* 1 (of conditions, etc.) affecting health 2 hygienic [L *sanitas*, rel. to SANE]

san'i·tar·y nap'kin *n.* absorbent pad used during menstruation

san·i·ta·tion /san'ətā'sHən/ *n.* 1 study, design, and maintenance of sanitary conditions 2 disposal of sewage, refuse, etc.

san·i·tize /san'ətīz/ *v.* (·ized, ·iz·ing) 1 make sanitary; disinfect 2 *Colloq.* censor (information, etc.) to make it acceptable

san·i·ty /san'ətē/ *n.* 1 state of being sane 2 soundness of judgment [L *sanitas*, rel. to SANE]

San Joa·quin Val·ley /san' wäkēn'/ *n.* rich agricultural area in the S portion of the Central Valley of Calif.

San' Jo·se' /hōzā', əzā'/ *n.* 1 (usu. **San José**) capital of Costa Rica. Pop. 299,500 2 city in Calif. Pop. 782,248

San Juan' /(h)wän'/ *n.* capital of Puerto Rico. Pop. 437,700

San Jus'to /hōō'stō/ *n.* suburb of Buenos Aires, Argentina. Pop. 946,700

sank /saNGk/ *v. past* of SINK

San Lu·is Po·to·si /sän' lōō·ēs' pōt'əsē'/ *n.* state in central Mexico. Capital: San Luis Potosí. Pop. 2,003,200

San Ma·ri·no /san' mərē'nō/ *n.* small republic in E Italy; oldest independent country in Europe. Pop. 23,600 —**San' Mar'i·nese'** /mar'ənēz', -nēs'/ *n. & adj.*

San Ni·co·lás' de los Gar'zas /nē'kōläs' de lōs gär'säs/ *n.* city in Mexico. Pop. 280,700

San Pe'dro Su'la /pā'drō sōō'lä/ *n.* city in NW Honduras. Pop. 300,400

sans /sanz/ *prep.* without [Fr]

San Sal·va·dor /san sal'vədôr/ *n.* capital of El Salvador. Pop. 481,400

San·skrit /san'skrit/ *n.* 1 ancient and sacred language of the Hindus in India —*adj.* 2 of or in this language

sans ser·if /sanz' ser'if/ *n.* typeface without serifs

San·ta An·a /sant'ə an'ə/ *n.* city in Calif. Pop. 293,742

San'ta An'na /an'ə/, **Antonio López de** (also **Santa Ana**) c. 1795–1876; Mexican military and political leader

San'ta Bar'ba·ra /bär'b(ə)rə/ *n.* city in Calif. Pop. 85,571

San'ta Cat·a·li'na Is'land /kat'l-ē'nə/ *n.* (also **Cat·a·li'na Is·land**) resort island in the Pacific Ocean near Long Beach, Calif.

San'ta Cla'ra /klar'ə, kler'ə/ *n.* city in Calif. Pop. 93,613

San'ta Cla·ri'ta /klərēt'ə/ *n.* city in Calif. Pop. 110,642

San'ta Claus /sant'ə klôz'/ *n.* legendary fat, jolly old man who brings children presents at Christmas [Du: St. Nicholas]

San'ta Cruz /sän'tä krōōz'/ *n.* city in central Bolivia. Pop. 529,200

San'ta Cruz' de Te·ne·rife' /dä ten'ərēf', -rif', -rē'fä/ *n.* seaport on Tenerife Island, Spain. Pop. 189,300

San'ta Fe /sant'ə fā'/ *n.* capital of N. Mex., in the N central part. Pop. 55,859

San'ta Mon'i·ca /män'ikə/ *n.* city in Calif. Pop. 86,905

San'ta Ro'sa /rō'zə/ *n.* city in Calif. Pop. 113,313

San·ta·ya·na /sant'əyän'ə/, **George** 1863–1952; Spanish-born US philosopher and poet

San·ti·a·go /sänt'ē·ä'gō, sant'-/ *n.* administrative capital of Chile. Pop. 5,342,900

San·ti·a·go de Cu·ba /säntyäg′ō dä k(y)ōō′bä/ *n.* seaport in Cuba. Pop. 397,000

San·to Do·min·go /sant′ə dəmiNG′gō/ *n.* capital of Dominican Republic. Pop. 1,600,000

San·to To·mé de Gua·ya·na /sän′tō tōmä′ dä gī′ən′ä/ *n.* (also **Ciu·dad′ Gua·ya·na** /see(y)ōōdäd/) city in Venezuela on the Orinoco River. Pop. 536,500

São Pau·lo /sou′ pou′lō/ *n.* city in Brazil. Pop. 7,033,600

São To·mé and Prin·ci·pe /sou′ təmä′, prin′səpə/ *n.* republic in W Africa, on the Gulf of Guinea. Capital: São Tomé (pop. 35,000). Pop. 126,000

sap¹ /sap/ *n.* **1** vital juice circulating in plants **2** vigor, vitality **3** *Slang.* foolish person —*v.* (**sapped, sap·ping**) **4** drain of sap [OE]

sap² *v.* (**sapped, sap·ping**) **1** undermine **2** weaken [Fr *sappe* or It *zappa* spade]

sa·pi·ent /sā′pēənt/ *adj.* wise —**sa′pi·ence** *n.* [L *sapire* be wise]

sap·ling /sap′liNG/ *n.* young tree [fr. SAP¹]

sap·phire /saf′īr′/ *n.* **1** transparent, deep-blue precious stone **2** its color —*adj.* **3** deep blue [Gk *sappheiros* lapis lazuli]

Sap·pho /saf′ō/ *b.* 7th cent. B.C.; Greek lyric poet

Sap·po·ro /säpōr′ō, -pôr′ō/ *n.* city in Japan, on Hokkaido. Pop. 1,696,100

sap′py *adj.* (**·pi·er, ·pi·est**) **1** full of sap **2** *Slang.* silly; foolish

sap·ro·phyte /sap′rəfīt′/ *n.* plant or microorganism living on dead or decayed organic matter [Gk *sapros* rotten, *phyton* plant]

sap′suck′er *n.* American woodpecker that makes holes in trees to eat the sap and insects

Sar·a·cen /sar′əsən/ *n. Hist.* Arab or Muslim at the time of the Crusades [Gk *sarakēnos*]

Sar·a·gos·sa /sar′əgōs′ə/ *n.* (also **Zar′a·go′za**) city on the Ebro River in NE Spain. Pop. 586,200

Sa·ra·je·vo /sar′əyä′vō, sär′-/ *n.* capital of Bosnia and Hercegovina. Pop. 526,000

sa·ran /səran′/ *n.* thermoplastic used in making pipes, thin film for packaging, etc. [former Tdmk.]

Sar·a·so·ta /sar′əsōt′ə/ *n.* city in Fla. Pop. 50,961

Sa·ra·tov /sərät′əf/ *n.* city in SW Russia on the Volga River. Pop. 911,100

sar·casm /sär′kaz′əm/ *n.* ironically scornful language —**sar·cas′tic** /-kas′tik/ *adj.*; **sar·cas′ti·cal·ly** *adv.* [Gk *sarkazein* speak bitterly]

sar·co·ma /särkō′mə/ *n.* (*pl.* **·mas** or **·ma·ta** /-mətə/) malignant tumor of connective tissue [Gk *sarx* sark- flesh]

sar·coph·a·gus /särkäf′əgəs/ *n.* (*pl.* **·a·gi** /-gī′, -jī′/ or **·gus·es**) stone coffin [Gk: flesh-consumer]

sar·dine /särdēn′/ *n.* small, edible fish in tightly packed tins [Fr fr. L]

Sar·din·i·a /särdin′ēə/ *n.* large Mediterranean island W of Italy

sar·don·ic /särdän′ik/ *adj.* bitterly mocking or cynical —**sar·don′i·cal·ly** *adv.* [Gk *sardonios* Sardinian]

sarge /särj/ *n. Slang.* sergeant

Sar·gent /sär′jənt/, **John Singer** 1856–1925; US portrait painter

sa·ri /sär′ē/ *n.* length of cloth draped around the body, traditionally worn by Hindu women [Hindi]

sa·rong /sərôNG′/ *n.* Malay and Javanese garment of a long strip of cloth tucked around the waist or under the armpits [Malay]

sar·sa·pa·ril·la /sas′(ə)pəril′ə, särs′-/ *n.* preparation of the dried roots of various plants, used esp. to flavor a carbonated drink [Sp]

SARI

sar·to·ri·al /särtôr′ēəl/ *adj.* of men's clothes or tailoring —**sar·to′ri·al·ly** *adv.* [L *sartor* tailor]

Sar·tre /särt(rə)/, **Jean-Paul** 1905–80; French philosopher, writer, and critic

SASE *abbr.* (also **S.A.S.E., s.a.s.e.**) self-addressed stamped envelope

sash¹ /sasH/ *n.* strip or loop of cloth, etc., worn over one shoulder or around the waist [Ar: muslin]

sash² *n.* frame holding the glass in a fixed or sliding window [fr. CHASSIS]

sa·shay /sasHā′/ *v. Colloq.* walk or move ostentatiously or casually [Fr *chassé*]

Sas·katch·e·wan /səskaCH′əwən, sas-, -wän′/ *n.* province of Canada, in the central part. Capital: Regina. Pop. 1,003,000

Sas·ka·toon /sas′kətōōn′/ *n.* city in Saskatchewan, Canada. Pop. 186,100

sass /sas/ *Colloq. n.* **1** impudence —*v.* **2** be impudent to —**sass′y** *adj.* (**·i·er, ·i·est**) [var. of SAUCE]

sas·sa·fras /sas′əfras/ *n.* **1** small N American tree **2** medicinal preparation from its leaves or bark [Sp or Port]

sat /sat/ *v.* past and past part. of SIT

SAT *abbr.* Scholastic Assessment (formerly Aptitude) Test

Sat. *abbr.* Saturday

Sa·tan /sāt′n/ *n.* the Devil; Lucifer [Heb: enemy]

sa·tan·ic /sətan′ik/ *adj.* of or like Satan; hellish; evil —**sa·tan′i·cal·ly** *adv.*

Sa′tan·ism′ *n.* **1** worship of Satan **2** pursuit of evil —**Sa′tan·ist** *n.* & *adj.*

satch·el /saCH′əl/ *n.* small bag for carrying schoolbooks, etc. [L, rel. to SACK¹]

sate /sāt/ *v.* (**sat·ed, sat·ing**) gratify fully; satiate [prob. dial. *sade* satisfy]

sa·teen /saten′/ *n.* glossy, satinlike, cotton fabric [*satin* after *velveteen*]

sat·el·lite /sat′l-īt′/ *n.* **1** natural or artificial body orbiting the earth or another planet **2** small country controlled by another [L *satelles -lit-* attendant]

sat′el·lite dish′ *n.* dish-shaped antenna for receiving transmitted signals from a satellite

sa·ti·ate /sā′sHē-āt′/ *v.* (**·at·ed, ·at·ing**) SATE —**sa·tia·ble** /sā′sHəbəl/ *adj.*; **sa′ti·a′tion** *n.* [L *satis* enough]

sa·ti·e·ty /sətī′ətē/ *n.* being sated [L, rel. to SATIATE]

sat·in /sat′n/ *n.* **1** fabric, glossy on one side —*adj.* **2** smooth as satin —**sat′in·y** *adj.* [L *zaitūnī*]

sat'in·wood *n.* a kind of yellow glossy timber

sat·ire /sa'tīr'/ *n.* 1 ridicule, irony, etc., used to expose folly, evil, etc. 2 work using this —**sa·tir·i·cal** /sətir'ikəl/ *adj.*; **sa·tir'i·cal·ly** *adv.*; **sat'i·rist** *n.* [L *satira* medley]

sat·i·rize /sat'ərīz'/ *v.* (·**rized**, ·**riz·ing**) attack or describe with satire

sat·is·fac·tion /sat'isfak'sHən/ *n.* 1 satisfying or being satisfied 2 thing that satisfies 3 atonement; compensation

sat·is·fac·to·ry /sat'isfak't(ə)rē/ *adj.* adequate; giving satisfaction —**sat'is·fac'to·ri·ly** *adv.*

sat·is·fy /sat'isfī'/ *v.* (·**fied**, ·**fy·ing**) 1a meet the requirements, expectations, or desires of **b** be adequate 2 meet (an appetite or want) 3 pay (a debt or creditor) 4 convince, esp. with proof, etc. [L *satisfacere*]

sa·trap /sā'trap', sa'-/ *n.* subordinate, often despotic ruler [Pers: protector of the land]

sat·u·rate /sacH'ərāt'/ *v.* (·**rat·ed**, ·**rat·ing**) 1 fill with moisture 2 cause (a substance, etc.) to absorb, hold, etc., as much as possible of another substance, etc. —**sat'u·ra'tion** *n.* [L *satur* full]

Sat·ur·day /sat'ərdā', -dē/ *n.* day of the week following Friday [L *Saturni dies* Saturn's day]

Sat'ur·day night' spe'cial *n. Slang.* inexpensive handgun

Sat·urn /sat'ərn/ *n.* 1 *Rom. Myth.* god of agriculture 2 second largest planet in the solar system, and sixth from the sun; surrounded by a series of rings of particles

sat·ur·nine /sat'ərnīn'/ *adj.* of gloomy temperament or appearance [under influence of planet SATURN]

sa·tyr /sat'ər, sā'-/ *n.* 1 *Gk. & Rom. Myth.* woodland god with some manlike and goatlike features 2 lecherous man [Gk *saturos*]

sauce /sôs/ *n.* 1 liquid or viscous accompaniment to a dish 2 something adding piquancy or excitement 3 *Colloq.* impudence; impertinence [L *salsus* salted]

sauce'pan' *n.* cooking pan, usu. with a lid and a projecting handle

sau·cer /sô'sər/ *n.* shallow circular dish for a cup [Fr *saussier*]

sau·cy *adj.* (·**ci·er**, ·**ci·est**) impudent —**sau'ci·ly** *adv.*; **sau'ci·ness** *n.*

Sau·di A·ra·bi·a /soud'ē ərā'bēə, sôd'ē/ *n.* kingdom on the Arabian Peninsula. Capital: Riyadh. Pop. 15,267,000 —**Sau'di, Sau'di A·ra'bi·an** *n. & adj.*

sau·er·kraut /sou'ərkrout'/ *n.* pickled cabbage [Ger]

Saul /sôl/ 11th cent. B.C.; first king of Israel

sau·na /sô'nə, sou'nə/ *n.* special dry, hot room in which one sits to cleanse the skin [Finn]

saun·ter /sôn'tər/ *v.* 1 walk slowly; stroll —*n.* 2 leisurely walk

sau·ri·an /sôr'ēən/ *adj.* of or like a lizard [Gk *saura* lizard]

sau·sage /sô'sij/ *n.* seasoned ground meat, etc., stuffed into a tubeshaped edible casing [Fr *saussiche*]

Saus·sure /sōsŏŏr'/, **Ferdinand de** 1857–1913; Swiss linguist

sau·té /sôtā', sô-/ *v.* (·**téed**, ·**té·ing**) brown or fry in a pan with a little oil or fat [Fr *sauter* jump]

Sau·ternes /sōtərn'/ *n.* (also **sau·terne'**) sweet white wine from the Bordeaux region [town in France]

sav·age /sav'ij/ *adj.* 1 fierce; cruel 2 wild; primitive —*n.* 3 *Derog.* member of a primitive tribe 4 cruel or barbarous person —*v.* (·**aged**, ·**ag·ing**) 5 attack —**sav'age·ly** *adv.*; **sav'age·ry** *n.* [Fr fr. L *silva* wood]

sa·van·na /səvan'ə/ *n.* (also **sa·van'nah**) grassy plain with few trees [Sp]

Sa·van·nah /səvan'ə/ *n.* city in Ga. Pop. 137,560

Sa·van'nah Riv'er *n.* river of S US, flowing 300 mi to the Atlantic Ocean N of Savannah, Ga.

sa·vant /savänt', -vän'/ *n.* learned person [Fr]

save¹ /sāv/ *v.* (**saved**, **sav·ing**) 1 rescue or keep from danger, harm, etc. 2 keep for future use 3 eliminate the need for 4 preserve from damnation 5 avoid wasting —*n.* 6 prevention of an opponent's goal —**sav'er** *n.* [L *salvare* fr. *salvus* safe]

save² *prep. & conj.* except; but [L *salvare, salvus* safe]

sav·ing *adj.* 1 (often in *comb.*) making economical use of (*labor-saving*) —*n.* 2 anything saved; an economy 3 (*pl.*) money saved 4 act of rescuing

● Usage: *Savings* is necessary in modifying position: *savings bank, savings bond.* It is used as a plural when referring to money saved in a bank: *Your savings are safe at our bank.* When used in the sense of an 'act of saving,' as in the realization of a discount on a purchase, the preferred form is *saving: Present this coupon for a saving* (not *savings*) *of $5.*

sav'ings and loan' *as·so·ci·a'tion* *n.* banking institution making loans from funds deposited by customers as savings

sav·ior or **sav·iour** /sāv'yər/ *n.* 1 person who saves from danger, etc. 2 (*cap.*) (prec. by *the, our*) Christ [L, rel. to SAVE¹]

sa·voir-faire /sav'wär(r) fer'/ *n.* knowledge of how to behave properly; tact [Fr]

Sav·o·na·ro·la /sav'ənərō'lə/, **Girolamo** 1452–98; Italian religious reformer

sa·vor /sā'vər/ *n.* 1 characteristic flavor or quality —*v.* 2 appreciate; enjoy 3 have a characteristic flavor, etc. [L *sapor*]

sa'vor·y¹ *adj.* 1 having an appetizing taste or smell 2 acceptable; pleasant

sa'vor·y² *n.* aromatic herb [L *satureia*]

sav·vy /sav'ē/ *Slang. n.* 1 knowingness; understanding —*adj.* (·**vi·er**, ·**vi·est**) 2 shrewd; wise [Pidgin alter. of Sp *sabe* you know]

saw¹ /sô/ *n.* 1 toothed metal blade or disk used to cut firm or hard materials —*v.* (**sawn** or **sawed, saw·ing**) 2 use a saw 3 move with a sawing motion 4 **saw wood** *Colloq.* snore [OE]

saw² *v.* *past of* SEE¹

saw³ *n.* proverb; maxim [OE, rel. to SAY]

saw'dust' *n.* powdery wood particles produced in sawing

sawed'-off' *adj.* (also **sawn'-off'**) (of a shotgun) with part of the barrel cut off

saw'horse' *n.* rack or holder for sawing wood

saw′mill′ *n.* factory for sawing planks from logs

sawn /sôn/ *v. past part.* of SAW[1]

saw′-toothed′ *adj.* notched, like the cutting edge of a saw

saw·yer /sô′yər, soi′ər/ *n.* person whose work is sawing timber

sax /saks/ *n. Colloq.* SAXOPHONE

Sax·on /sak′sən/ *n.* 1 *Hist.* a member of the Germanic people that conquered parts of England in the 5th–6th cent. b (usu. Old Saxon) language of the Saxons 2 ANGLO-SAXON —*adj.* 3 *Hist.* of the Saxons 4 Anglo-Saxon [L *Saxo -onis*]

SAXOPHONE

sax·o·phone /sak′səfōn/ *n.* metal-bodied single reed instrument —**sax′o·phon′ist** *n.* [for A. *Sax*, Belgian inventor]

say /sā/ *v.* (**said, say·ing**) 1a utter (specified words); remark b express 2a state; promise; prophesy b have specified wording; indicate 3 judge; estimate 4 recite or repeat (prayers, lessons, etc.) 5 mean —*n.* 6 opportunity to speak 7 influence 8 **that is to say** in other words [OE]

say′ing *n.* 1 maxim, proverb, etc. 2 **go without saying** be too obvious to need mention

say′-so′ *n. Colloq.* 1 authority 2 mere assertion

Sb *symb.* antimony [L *stibium*]

SBA *abbr.* Small Business Administration

Sc *symb.* scandium

SC postal abbr. for South Carolina

s.c. *abbr.* small capitals

scab /skab/ *n.* 1 crust over a healing cut, sore, etc. 2 worker who replaces a striking union member —*v.* (**scabbed, scab·bing**) 3 *Colloq.* act as a scab 4 form a scab; heal over —**scab′by** *adj.* (**·bi·er, ·bi·est**) [ON: cf. SHABBY]

scab·bard /skab′ərd/ *n.* sheath of a sword, etc. [AngFr]

sca·bies /skā′bēz/ *n.* contagious skin disease causing itching [L]

sca·brous /skab′rəs/ *adj.* 1 rough; scaly 2 indecent; salacious [L]

scaf·fold /skaf′əld, -ōld/ *n.* 1 platform for the execution of criminals, esp. by hanging 2 (also **scaf′fold·ing**) strong framework for workers, materials, etc., during erection, repair, etc., of a building, etc. [Rom, rel. to EX-[1], CATAFALQUE]

scal·a·wag /skal′əwag/ *n.* scamp; rascal

scald /skôld/ *v.* 1 burn (the skin, etc.) with hot liquid or steam 2 heat (esp. milk) to near

boiling point 3 clean with boiling water —*n.* 4 burn caused by scalding [L *excaldare* fr. *calidus* hot]

scale[1] /skāl/ *n.* 1 each of the thin, horny plates protecting the skin of fish and reptiles 2 deposit formed in a kettle, on teeth, etc. —*v.* (**scaled, scal·ing**) 3 remove scale(s) from 4 form or come off in scales —**scal′y** *adj.* (**·i·er, ·i·est**) [Fr *escale*]

scale[2] *n.* 1a (often *pl.*) weighing device b either of the dishes on a simple balance 2 (**the Scales**) zodiacal sign or constellation Libra 3 weigh 4 **tip the scales** be the decisive factor [ON *skál* bowl]

scale[3] *n.* 1 graded classification system (*high on the social scale*) 2 ratio that the size of a map, model, etc., bears to what it represents (*scale of 1/8 in. to the foot*) 3 *Mus.* set of notes at fixed intervals, arranged in order of pitch 4a set of regular marked intervals on a line used in measuring b device on which these are marked —*v.* (**scaled, scal·ing**) 5 climb (a wall, height, etc.) 6 **scale up** (or **down**) represent proportionally; reduce to a common scale [L *scala* ladder]

sca·lene /skā′lēn′/ *adj.* (esp. of a triangle) having unequal sides [Gk *skalēnos* unequal]

scal·lion /skal′yən/ *n.* variety of onion with long, green stalk and a small bulb [L fr. *Ascalon* in ancient Palestine]

SCALLOP 2

scal·lop /skal′əp, skäl′-/ *n.* 1 edible mollusk with two fan-shaped ridged shells 2 single shell of a scallop, used in cooking, etc. 3 (also **scal′lop·ing**) ornamental edging of semicircular curves —*v.* 4 ornament with scallops [OFr *escalope*]

scalp /skalp/ *n.* 1 skin on the head, usu. with the hair —*v.* 2 cut or tear off the scalp of (an enemy) 3 *Colloq.* resell tickets for sports events, etc., at a high profit [prob. Scand]

scal·pel /skal′pəl/ *n.* surgeon's small razor-sharp knife [L *scalpere* scratch]

scam /skam/ *n. Slang.* swindle; con game

scamp /skamp/ *n.* rascal; rogue [prob. Du]

scam·per /skam′pər/ *v.* 1 run quickly —*n.* 2 act of scampering [perh. fr. SCAMP]

scam·pi /skam′pē/ *n. pl.* large, edible prawns, esp. served with garlic sauce [It]

scan /skan/ *v.* (**scanned, scan·ning**) 1 examine analytically 2 look at superficially or quickly 3a analyze the metrical structure of (verse) b (of verse) be metrically consistent 4 obtain an image of using a scanner —*n.* 5 scanning 6 image obtained by scanning [L *scandere* climb; scan]

scan·dal /skan′dəl/ *n.* 1 disgraceful behavior, esp. by a public figure 2 public outrage so caused 3 malicious gossip —**scan′dal·ous** *adj.*; **scan′dal·ous·ly** *adv.* [Gk *skandalon* snare]

scan·dal·ize′ *v.* (**·ized, ·iz·ing**) offend morally; shock

scan·dal·mon'ger *n.* person who habitually spreads scandal or gossip

Scan·di·na·vi·a /skan'dinā'vēə/ *n.* 1 region of N Europe; includes Norway, Sweden, Denmark, and sometimes Finland, Iceland, and the Faeroe Islands 2 (**Scan'di·na'vi·an Pen·in'su·la**) peninsula including Norway and Sweden

Scan·di·na·vi·an /skan'dənā'vēən/ *n.* 1a native or inhabitant of Scandinavia b person of Scandinavian descent 2 family of languages of Scandinavia —*adj.* 3 of Scandinavia [L]

scan·di·um /skan'dēəm/ *n.* natural metallic element; *symb.* Sc [L *Scandia* Scandinavia]

scan·ner /skan'ər/ *n.* 1 device for obtaining an electronic image of something 2 *Comp.* such a device that uses software to convert an image into digital data for processing by computer

scan·sion /skan'sHən/ *n.* metrical scanning of verse [L, rel. to SCAN]

scant /skant/ *adj.* 1 barely sufficient 2 deficient [ON]

scant'y *adj.* (·i·er, ·i·est) 1 of small extent or amount 2 barely sufficient —**scant'i·ly** *adv.*; **scant'i·ness** *n.*

scape·goat /skāp'gōt/ *n.* person blamed for others' shortcomings (with ref. to Lev. 16) [obs. *scape* escape]

scap·u·la /skap'yələ/ *n.* (*pl.* ·**lae** /-lē/ or ·**las**) shoulder blade —**scap'u·lar** *adj.* [L]

scar /skär/ *n.* 1 usu. permanent mark on the skin from a wound, etc., after healing —*v.* (**scarred, scar·ring**) 2 mark with a scar 3 form a scar [Fr *eschar(r)e*]

S. Car. *abbr.* South Carolina

scar·ab /skar'əb/ *n.* 1 sacred beetle of ancient Egypt 2 ancient Egyptian gem cut in the form of a beetle [L *scarabaeus* fr. Gk]

Scar·bor·ough /skär'b(ə)rə/ *n.* city in Ontario, Canada, near Toronto. Pop. 524,600

scarce /skers/ *adj.* 1 in short supply 2 rare —*adv.* 3 **make oneself scarce** *Colloq.* keep out of the way [Fr *scars* L *excerptere* picked out]

scarce'ly *adv.* 1 hardly; only just 2 surely not

scar·ci·ty /sker'sətē/ *n.* (*pl.* ·**ties**) lack or shortage

scare /sker/ *v.* (**scared, scar·ing**) 1 frighten, esp. suddenly 2 become scared or intimidated —*n.* 3 sudden attack of fright 4 alarm 5 **scare away** or **off** chase away or off by frightening 6 **scare up** *Colloq.* find with effort [ON]

scare'crow *n.* human figure dressed in old clothes and set up in a field to scare birds away

scarf¹ /skärf/ *n.* (*pl.* **scarves** /skärvz/ or **scarfs**) piece of fabric worn esp. around the neck or over the head for warmth or ornament [Fr *escarpe*]

scarf² *v.* 1 join overlapping, beveled ends of (timber, etc.) by bolting, gluing, etc. —*n.* (*pl.* ·**s**) 2 (also **scarf' joint**) joint made by scarfing [prob. Fr *escarf*]

scar·i·fy /skar'əfī'/ *v.* (·**fied, ·fy·ing**) make slight incisions in —**scar'i·fi·ca'tion** /-fikā'shən/ *n.* [Gk *skariphos* stylus]

Scar·lat·ti /skärlät'ē/ Italian composers: 1 **Alessandro** 1659–1725; his son: 2 (**Giuseppe**) **Domenico** 1683–1757

scar·let /skär'lət/ *adj.* 1 of brilliant red

tinged with orange —*n.* 2 scarlet color [Fr *escarlate*]

scar'let fe'ver *n.* infectious bacterial fever with a scarlet rash

scarp /skärp/ *n.* steep slope [It *scarpa*]

scar·y /sker'ē/ *adj.* (·i·er, ·i·est) *Colloq.* frightening

scat¹ /skat/ *v.* (**scat·ted, scat·ting**) (usu. in *imper.*) *Colloq.* depart quickly [perh. abbr. of SCATTER]

scat² *Mus. n.* 1 vocalization using meaningless syllables, as in a song —*v.* (**scat·ted, scat·ting**) 2 sing scat [prob. imit.]

scath·ing /skā'THiNG/ *adj.* bitterly scornful —**scath'ing·ly** *adv.* [ON]

sca·tol·o·gy /skətäl'əjē/ *n.* excessive interest in excrement or obscenity —**scat'o·log'i·cal** /-əläj'ikəl/ *adj.* [Gk *skōr skat-* dung]

scat·ter /skat'ər/ *v.* 1 throw about; strew 2 disperse or cause (hopes, clouds, animals, etc.) to disperse [prob. var. of SHATTER]

scat'ter·brain' *n.* person lacking concentration —**scat'ter·brained'** *adj.*

scav·enge /skav'inj/ *v.* (·**enged, ·eng·ing**) search for and collect (discarded items) [back formation fr. SCAVENGER]

scav·en·ger /skav'injər/ *n.* 1 person who collects usable items from waste or cast-offs 2 animal that feeds on carrion, refuse, etc. [AngFr *scawager*, rel. to SHOW]

sce·nar·i·o /sənar'ē·ō', -ner'-, -när'-/ *n.* (*pl.* ·**os**) 1 outline of the plot of a play, film, etc. 2 supposed sequence of future events [It]

scene /sēn/ *n.* 1 place where events occur 2 public display of emotion, temper, etc. 3 portion of a play, film, etc., in a fixed setting 4 piece of scenery in a play 5 landscape; view 6 *Colloq.* area of interest, activity, etc.; milieu 7 **behind the scenes** offstage; in the background; secretly [Gk *skēnē* tent, stage]

scen·er·y /sēn'ərē/ *n.* 1 natural features of a landscape 2 painted backdrops, properties, etc., used in a play, etc. [It, rel. to SCENARIO]

sce·nic /sēn'ik/ *adj.* 1a picturesque b of natural scenery 2 of stage scenery —**sce'ni·cal·ly** *adv.*

scent /sent/ *n.* 1 distinctive, esp. pleasant, smell 2 perfume 3 perceptible smell left by an animal 4 sense of smell —*v.* 5a discern by scent 5 sense (*scented danger*) 6 make fragrant [Fr *sentir* perceive]

scep·ter /sep'tər/ *n.* (also esp. *Brit.* **scep·tre**) staff or rod as a symbol of sovereignty [Gk *skēptron* staff]

sch. *abbr.* school

sched·ule /skej'ōōl/ *n.* 1a list of intended or regular events, times, etc.; timetable b plan of work 2 list of rates, details, prices, etc. —*v.* (·**uled, ·ul·ing**) 3 include in a schedule [L *schedula* slip of paper]

sche·mat·ic /skimat'ik/ *adj.* 1 of or as a scheme or diagram —*n.* 2 diagram, esp. of an electronic circuit —**sche·mat'i·cal·ly** *adv.*

scheme /skēm/ *n.* 1 systematic plan or arrangement 2 cunning plot —*v.* (**schemed, schem·ing**) 3 plan, esp. secretly or deceitfully —**schem'er** *n.* [Gk *schema* a form]

Sche·nec·ta·dy /skənek'tadē/ *n.* city in N.Y. Pop. 65,566

scher·zo /skert'sō/ *n.* (*pl.* ·**zos** or ·**zi** /-tsē/)

Mus. vigorous, often playful piece, esp. as part of a larger work [It: jest]

Schil·ler /sHil'ər/, **Johann Christoph Friedrich von** 1759–1805; German dramatist and poet

schism /siz'əm, skiz'-/ *n.* division of a group (esp. religious) into sects, etc., usu. over doctrine —**schis·mat'ic** /-mat'ik/ *adj. & n.* [Gk *skhizein* to split]

schist /sHist/ *n.* layered crystalline rock [Gk *skhizein* to split]

schiz·o /skit'sō/ *Slang. adj.* 1 schizophrenic —*n.* (*pl.* ·os) 2 schizophrenic person

schiz·o·phre·ni·a /skit'səfrē'nēə/ *n.* mental disease marked by a breakdown in the relation between thoughts, feelings, and actions, and often with delusions and retreat from society —**schiz·oid** /skit'zoid/ *adj. & n.;* **schizo'phren'ic** /-fren'ik/ *adj. & n.* [Gk *skhizein* split, *phrēn* mind]

schle·miel /sHləmēl'/ *n. Slang.* unlucky, awkward person [Yiddish]

schlep /sHlep/ (also **shlepp**) *Colloq. v.* (**schlepped, schlep·ping**) 1 to drag or carry around with difficulty —*v.* 2 long haul 3 person regarded as a clumsy or ineffectual bungler [Yiddish *shlepn* to drag]

Schlie·mann /sHlē'män'/, **Heinrich** 1822–90; German archaeologist

schlock /sHläk/ *n. Slang.* trash [Yiddish *shlak* a blow]

schmaltz /sHmälts, sHmôlts/ *n.* (also **shmaltz**) *Slang.* sentimentality, esp. in music, drama, etc. —**schmaltz'y** *adj.* [Yiddish]

schmo /sHmō/ *n. Slang.* fool [shortening of SCHMUCK]

schmuck /sHmək/ *n. Slang.* foolish or contemptible person [Yiddish]

schnapps /sHnäps/ *n.* any of various alcoholic drinks, often flavored [Ger]

schnau·zer /sHnou'zər/ *n.* wire-haired dog of German breed [Ger]

schnit·zel /sHnit'səl/ *n.* veal cutlet [Ger]

schol·ar /skäl'ər/ *n.* 1 learned person; academic 2 pupil —**schol'ar·ly** *adj.* [L, rel. to SCHOOL¹]

schol'ar·ship' *n.* 1a academic achievement, esp. of a high level b standards of a good scholar 2 financial award for a student

scho·las·tic /skəlas'tik/ *adj.* of schools, education, etc.; academic [Gk, rel. to SCHOOL¹]

Schön·berg /sHœ(r)n'bärg'/, **Arnold** 1874–1951; Austrian composer

school¹ /skŏŏl/ *n.* 1 educational institution 2 school buildings, pupils, staff, etc. 3 time of teaching; the teaching itself (*no school today*) 4 university department 5 group of similar artists, like-minded people, etc. —*v.* 6 educate 7 discipline; train; control [Gk *skholē*]

school² *n.* shoal of fish, etc. [LGer or Du]

school'book' *n.* textbook

school'boy' *n.* boy attending school

school'child' *n.* (*pl.* ·chil'dren) child attending school

school'girl' *n.* girl attending school

school'house' *n.* school building, esp. a small one

school'ing *n.* education, esp. at school

school·marm /skŏŏl'märm/ *n.* 1 *Old-fash.*

---

woman schoolteacher 2 *Colloq.* pedant —**school'marm'ish** *adj.*

school'mas'ter *n.* male head of a school; principal

school'mis'tress *n.* female head of a school; principal

school'room' *n.* room used for lessons

school'teach'er *n.* teacher in a school

school'work' *n.* studying, assignments, etc., done as part of one's schooling

school'yard' *n.* (esp. in urban schools) area near school for sports, recreation, etc.

schoo·ner /skŏŏ'nər/ *n.* 1 fore-and-aft rigged vessel with two or more masts, the foremast of which is shorter than the other(s) 2 tall beer glass

Scho·pen·hau·er /sHō'pənhou'ər/, **Arthur** 1788–1860; German philosopher

schrod /skräd/ *n.* var. of SCROD

Schrö·ding·er /sHräd'iNGər, sHrôd'-/, **Erwin** 1887–1961; German theoretical physicist

Schu·bert /sHŏŏ'bərt/, **Franz** 1797–1828; Austrian composer

Schulz /sHŏŏlts/, **Charles** 1922– ; US cartoonist

Schu·mann /sHŏŏ'män', -mən/, **Robert** 1810–56; German composer

schuss /sHŏŏs, sHŏŏs/ *Skiing. n.* 1 straight downhill run —*v.* 2 make such a run [Ger: shot]

Schuyl·kill Riv·er /skŏŏl'kil', skŏŏ(l)'kəl/ *n.* river rising in central Penn., flowing 130 mi. SE into the Delaware River at Philadelphia

schwa /sHwä/ *n.* 1 imprecise vowel sound of *a* in *above, e* in *baker, i* in *easily, o* in *major, u* in *circus* 2 symbol for schwa (ə) [Ger fr. Heb *shewa*]

Schweit·zer /sHwīt'sər/, **Albert** 1875–1965; Alsatian theologian and medical missionary in Africa

sci·at·ic /sī·at'ik/ *adj.* of the hip or its nerves [Gk *iskhion* hip]

sci·at·i·ca /sī·at'ikə/ *n.* neuralgia of the hip and leg [L, rel. to SCIATIC]

sci·at'ic nerve' *n.* nerve running from pelvis to thigh

sci·ence /sī'əns/ *n.* 1 branch of knowledge involving systematic observation and experiment 2a knowledge so gained, or on a specific subject b pursuit or principles of this 3 skillful technique [L *scire* know]

sci'ence fic'tion *n.* fiction with a scientific theme, esp. concerned with the future, space, other worlds, etc.

sci·en·tif·ic /sī'əntif'ik/ *adj.* 1a following the systematic methods of science b systematic; accurate 2 of, used in, or engaged in science —**sci'en·tif'i·cal·ly** *adv.*

sci·en·tist /sī'əntist/ *n.* expert in a science

sci-fi /sī'fī'/ *n. Colloq.* science fiction [abbr.]

Scil·ly Is·lands /sil'ē/ *n.* group of islands in the Atlantic off the SW tip of England

scim·i·tar /sim'ətər/ *n.* curved oriental sword [Fr and It]

scin·til·la /sintil'ə/ *n.* trace [L: spark]

scin·til·late /sint'lāt'/ *v.* (·lat·ed, ·lat·ing) 1 talk cleverly; be brilliant 2 sparkle; twinkle —**scin'til·la'tion** *n.* [L, rel. to SCINTILLA]

sci·on /sī'ən/ *n.* 1 shoot of a plant, etc., esp. for grafting or planting 2 descendant [Fr]

Scip·i·o /sip'ēō'/ name of two Roman generals: 1 **Publius Cornelius Scipio Africanus**

Major 236–184/3 B.C.; defeated Hannibal; his adopted grandson: **2 Publius Cornelius Scipio Aemilianus Africanus** 185–129 B.C.; destroyed Carthage

scis·sors /siz'ərz/ *n. pl.* manual cutting instrument with two pivoted blades [LL *cisorium* cutting tool]

scle·ro·sis /sklərō'sis/ *n.* **1** abnormal hardening of body tissue **2** MULTIPLE SCLEROSIS —**scle·rot'ic** /-rät'ik/ *adj.* [Gk *sklēros* hard]

scoff /skäf, skôf/ *v.* **1** speak scornfully; mock —*n.* **2** mocking words; taunt [perh. fr. Scand]

scold /skōld/ *v.* **1** rebuke **2** find fault angrily —*n.* **3** *Archaic.* nagging woman —**scold'ing** *n.* [prob. ON]

sconce /skäns/ *n.* wall bracket for candles or electric lights [L (*ab*)*sconsa* covered (light)]

scone /skōn, skän/ *n.* small, biscuitlike cake

scoop /skōop/ *n.* **1** shovel-shaped object, esp.: **a** spoonlike dispenser for ice cream, etc. **b** the excavating part of a digging-machine, etc. **2** quantity taken up by a scoop **3** scooping movement **4** exclusive news item —*v.* **5** hollow out with or as if with a scoop **6** lift with or as if with a scoop **7** precede (a rival newspaper, etc.) with news [LGer or Du]

scoot /skōot/ *v. Colloq.* depart quickly; flee

scoot·er /skōot'ər/ *n.* **1** child's toy consisting of a footboard on two wheels and a long steering-handle **2** (**motor scooter**) similar low-powered motor vehicle with a seat

scope /skōp/ *n.* **1** range; opportunity **2** extent of mental ability, outlook, etc. [Gk *target*]

-scope *comb. form* forming nouns denoting an instrument for observing or showing (*oscilloscope*) —**·scopic** *comb. form* forming adjectives relating to viewing (*telescopic*); **-scopy** *comb. form* forming nouns indicating observation (*microscopy*) [Gk *skopein* look at]

scor·bu·tic /skôrbyōō'tik/ *adj.* of, like, or affected with scurvy [L *scorbutus* scurvy]

scorch /skôrCH/ *v.* **1** burn or discolor the surface of with dry heat **2** become so discolored, etc. —*n.* **3** mark made by scorching —**scorch'er** *n.*; **scorch'ing** *adj.*

scorched' earth' pol·i·cy *n.* policy of destroying anything that might be of use to an invading enemy

score /skôr/ *n.* **1** number of points made by a player or side in some games **2** (*pl.* same or **-s**) twenty or a set of twenty **3** (*pl.*) a great many **4** reason; motive **5** *Mus.* a copy of a composition showing all the vocal and instrumental parts arranged one below the other **b** music for a film or play **6** notch, line, etc., cut or scratched into a surface **7** *Colloq.* facts —*v.* (**scored, scor·ing**) **8a** win or gain (a goal, points, success, etc.) **b** make (a score) in a test, game, etc. **9** mark with notches, etc. **10** *Mus.* orchestrate or arrange (music) —**score'less** *adj.*; **scor'er** *n.* [ON, rel. to SHEAR]

score'board' *n.* large board for displaying the score in a game

scorn /skôrn/ *n.* **1** disdain; contemptuous derision —*v.* **2** hold in contempt **3** reject or refuse to do as unworthy —**scorn'ful** *adj.*; **scorn'ful·ly** *adv.* [Fr *escarnir*]

Scor·pi·o /skôr'pē·ō'/ *n.* (*pl.* **-os**) **1** constellation and eighth sign of the zodiac (the Scorpion) **2** person born under this sign [Gk *skorpios* scorpion]

scor·pi·on /skôr'pēən/ *n.* **1** arachnid with pincers and a jointed, stinging tail **2** (**the Scorpion**) zodiacal sign or constellation Scorpio

SCORPION

Scot /skät/ *n.* **1** native of Scotland **2** person of Scottish descent [L *Scottus*]

scotch /skäcH/ *v.* **1** put an end to; frustrate **2** *Archaic.* wound without killing

Scotch /skäcH/ *adj. & n.* **1** var. of SCOTTISH or SCOTS —*n.* **2** SCOTCH WHISKEY [fr. Scot]
● Usage: *Scots* or *Scottish* is generally preferred to *Scotch* except in certain fixed expressions, e.g., *Scotch whisky*.

Scotch' tape' *n. Tdmk.* an adhesive tape for paper, etc., usu. clear when applied

Scotch' ter'ri·er *n.* (also **Scot'tish ter'ri·er**) small wire-haired terrier

Scotch' whis'key *n.* (also **Scotch' whis'ky**) whiskey distilled in Scotland

scot'-free' *adv.* unharmed; unpunished [obs. *scot* tax]

Scot·land /skät'lənd/ *n.* division of the United Kingdom, N of England. Capital: Edinburgh. Pop. 4,770,600
● Usage: See note at GREAT BRITAIN.

Scots /skäts/ *adj.* **1** SCOTTISH **2** in the dialect, accent, etc., of (esp. Lowlands) Scotland —*n.* **3** SCOTTISH **4** Scots English [var. of SCOT]

Scots' Gael'ic *n.* Gaelic of the Hebrides, Scottish Highlands, and Nova Scotia

Scots'man /skäts'mən/ *n.* (*pl.* **·men**; *fem.* **·wom·an**, *pl.* **·wom'en**) SCOT

Scott /skät/ *n.* **1** (Sir) **Walter** 1771–1832; Scottish novelist and poet **2 Winfield** 1786–1866; US general **3 Dred** c. 1795–1858; US slave; subject of a US Supreme Court proslavery decision (1857)

Scot'tie *n.* SCOTCH TERRIER

Scot·tish /skät'isH/ *adj.* (also **Scotch**) **1** of Scotland or its inhabitants —*n.* **2** (prec. by *the*; treated as *pl.*) people of Scotland

Scotts·dale /skäts'dāl'/ *n.* city in Ariz. Pop. 130,069

scoun·drel /skoun'drəl/ *n.* unscrupulous villain; rogue

scour¹ /skour/ *v.* **1** cleanse by rubbing **2** clear out (a pipe, channel, etc.) by flushing —**scour'er** *n.* [Fr *escurer*]

scour² *v.* search thoroughly, esp. by scanning (*scoured the newspaper*)

scourge /skərj/ *n.* **1** anything regarded as a cause of suffering **2** whip —*v.* (**scourged, scourg·ing**) **3** whip **4** punish; oppress [L *corrigia* whip]

scout /skout/ *n.* **1** soldier, vessel, etc., sent ahead, esp. to get military intelligence **2** (*cap.*) Boy Scout or Girl Scout —*v.* **3** go about searching for information, etc. 4 act as a scout [Fr *escoute(r)* fr. L *auscultare* listen]

scout′ing *n.* 1 action of a scout 2 (often *cap.*) activities of Boy Scouts or Girl Scouts

scout′mas′ter *n.* person in charge of a group of Boy Scouts

scow /skou/ *n.* flat-bottomed boat for freight; barge [Du]

scowl /skoul/ *n.* 1 frowning or sullen expression —*v.* 2 make a scowl [Scand]

scrab·ble /skrab′əl/ *v.* (·bled, ·bling) scratch or grope about, esp. in search of something [Du]

scrag·gly /skrag′lē/ *adj.* (·gli·er, ·gli·est) jagged; rough; uneven

scram /skram/ *v.* (**scrammed, scram·ming**) (esp. in *imper.*) *Slang.* go away [perh. fr. SCRAMBLE]

scram·ble /skram′bəl/ *v.* (·bled, ·bling) 1 clamber, crawl, climb, etc., esp. hurriedly or anxiously 2 struggle with competitors (for a thing or share) 3 mix together indiscriminately 4 cook (beaten eggs) 5 make, esp. an electronically transmitted message, unintelligible 6 (of fighter aircraft or pilots) take off quickly for action —*n.* 7 act of scrambling 8 difficult climb or walk 9 eager struggle or competition 10 emergency takeoff by fighter aircraft

scram·bler /skram′blər/ *n.* device for scrambling transmitted messages

Scran·ton /skran′tn/ *n.* city in Penn. Pop. 81,805

scrap¹ /skrap/ *n.* 1 small, detached piece; fragment 2 rubbish or waste material 3 (*pl.*) uneaten food —*v.* (**scrapped, scrap·ping**) 4 discard as useless [ON, rel. to SCRAPE]

scrap² *Colloq. n.* 1 fight or rough quarrel —*v.* (**scrapped, scrap·ping**) 2 have a scrap [perh. fr. SCRAPE]

scrap′book′ *n.* blank book for clippings, memorabilia, etc.

scrape /skrāp/ *v.* (**scraped, scrap·ing**) 1 move a hard or sharp edge across (a surface), esp. to make smooth. 2 remove by scraping 3 scratch or damage by scraping 4 move with a scraping sound 5 narrowly achieve (a living, passing examination, etc.) 6 barely manage 7 bring together with difficulty —*n.* 8 act or sound of scraping 9 abrasion 10 predicament —**scrap′er** *n.* [ON]

scrap′heap′ *n.* 1 pile of scrap 2 state of being discarded as useless

scrap′py *adj.* (·pi·er, ·pi·est) argumentative; aggressive

scrap′yard′ *n.* place where scrap is collected for reuse

scratch /skrach/ *v.* 1 score, mark, or wound superficially, esp. with a sharp object 2 scrape, esp. with the nails to relieve itching 3 strike (out) (writing, etc.) 4 withdraw (a competitor) —*n.* 5 mark or wound made by scratching 6 sound of scratching —*adj.* 7 (of paper, a pad, etc.) for scribbling, hasty notes, etc. 8 **from scratch** from the beginning 9 **up to scratch** up to the required standard —**scratch′y** *adj.* (·i·er, ·i·est); **scratch′i·ly** *adv.*; **scratch′i·ness** *n.*

scrawl /skrôl/ *v.* 1 write or make (marks) in

a hurried, untidy way —*n.* 2 hurried, untidy manner of writing —**scrawl′y** *adj.*

scraw·ny /skrô′nē/ *adj.* (·ni·er, ·ni·est) lean; skinny [dial.]

scream /skrēm/ *n.* 1 loud high-pitched cry of fear, pain, etc. 2 similar sound or cry 3 *Colloq.* hilarious occurrence or person —*v.* 4 emit a scream 5 laugh uncontrollably [OE]

screech /skrēch/ *n.* 1 harsh, piercing scream —*v.* 2 utter with or make a screech —**screech′y** *adj.* (·i·er, ·i·est) [OE (imit.)]

screed /skrēd/ *n.* long usu. boring speech or piece of writing [prob. fr. SHRED]

screen /skrēn/ *n.* 1 fixed or movable partition for separating, concealing, or protecting 2 thing used to conceal or shelter 3 blank surface on which a photographic image is projected, a television image is formed, etc. 4 sieve or riddle —*v.* 5 shelter or hide, as behind a screen 6 show (a film, television program, etc.) 7 sift or check by or as if passing through a screen [Fr]

screen′play′ *n.* movie script

screen′ test′ *n.* audition for a part in a movie

screen′writ′er *n.* person who writes screenplays

screw /skrōō/ *n.* 1 thin, metal cylinder or cone with a ridge or thread spiraling along its length 2 (in full **screw′ pro·pel′ler**) propeller with pitched blades that act like a screw on the water or air —*v.* 3 fasten or tighten with or as with a screw 4 twist or turn around like a screw 5 *Slang.* swindle 6 **have a screw loose** *Colloq.* be slightly crazy 7 **put the screws on** *Colloq.* pressure; intimidate 8 **screw up: a** contract or contort **b** summon up (one's courage, etc.) **c** *Slang.* bungle **d** *Slang.* ruin [Fr *escroue*]

screw′ball′ *n. Slang.* crazy or eccentric person

screw′driv′er *n.* tool with a tip that fits into the head of a screw to turn it

screw′y *adj.* (·i·er, ·i·est) *Slang.* 1 crazy; eccentric 2 absurd —**screw′i·ness** *n.*

scrib·ble /skrib′əl/ *v.* (·bled, ·bling) 1 write or draw carelessly or hurriedly —*n.* 2 scrawl [MedL *scribillare* dim. of *scribere* write]

scribe /skrīb/ *n.* 1 ancient or medieval copyist of manuscripts 2 writer —**scrib′al** *adj.* [L *scriba* fr. *scribere* write]

scrim /skrim/ *n.* 1 open-weave cotton or linen fabric for lining, etc. 2 scenic or semitransparent backdrop

scrim·mage /skrim′ij/ *Football. n.* 1 action from the moment the ball is in play till it is dead 2 practice game —*v.* (·maged, ·mag·ing) 3 engage in this [fr. SKIRMISH]

scrimp /skrimp/ *v.* skimp

scrip /skrip/ *n.* certificate entitling the holder to receive later payment in currency, goods, etc. [fr. *subscription receipt*]

script /skript/ *n.* 1 text of a play, movie, or broadcast 2 handwriting; written characters —*v.* 3 *Colloq.* write a script for (a movie, etc.) [L *scriptum* fr. *scribere* write]

scrip·ture /skrip′chər/ *n.* 1 sacred writings 2 (**Scripture** or **the Scriptures**) the Bible —**scrip′tur·al** *adj.* [L, rel. to SCRIPT]

script′writ′er *n.* person who writes scripts for movies, TV, etc. —**script′writ′ing** *n.*

scrod /skräd/ *n.* (*pl.* same) (also **schrod**) young cod or haddock, esp. a filet for cooking [MDu *schrode*]

scrof·u·la /skräf'yələ/ *n.* disease with glandular swellings, a form of tuberculosis —**scrof'u·lous** *adj.* [L *scrofa* a sow]

SCROLL 1

scroll /skrōl/ *n.* 1 roll of parchment or paper, esp. written on 2 ornamental design imitating a roll of parchment —*v.* 3 move (a display on a computer screen) vertically [orig. (*sc*)*rowle* ROLL]

scro·tum /skrō'təm/ *n.* (*pl.* **·ta** /-tə/ or **·tums**) pouch of skin containing the testicles —**scro'tal** *adj.* [L]

scrounge /skrounj/ *Colloq. v.* (**scrounged, scroung·ing**) 1 obtain by begging or borrowing without returning —*n.* 2 person who does this habitually; scrounger [dial. *scrunge* steal]

scrub[1] /skrəb/ *v.* (**scrubbed, scrub·bing**) 1 clean by rubbing vigorously 2 *Colloq.* scrap or cancel 3 remove impurities from (gases, smoke, etc.) —*n.* 4 scrubbing or being scrubbed —**scrub'ber** *n.* [LGer or Du]

scrub[2] *n.* 1 brushwood or stunted forest growth 2 *Sports.* person who plays as a substitute —**scrub'by** *adj.* [fr. SHRUB]

scruff /skrəf/ *n.* back of the neck [perh. fr. ON *skoft* hair]

scruff'y *adj.* (**·i·er, ·i·est**) shabby; slovenly; untidy —**scruff'i·ly** *adv.*; **scruff'i·ness** *n.* [*scruff* SCURF]

scrump·tious /skrəmp'SHəs/ *adj. Colloq.* 1 delicious 2 delightful

scrunch /skrənCH/ *v.* 1 crumple 2 crunch —*n.* 3 crunching sound [var. of CRUNCH]

scru·ple /skrōō'pəl/ *n.* 1 moral concern 2 doubt caused by this —*v.* (**·pled, ·pling**) 3 hesitate because of scruples [L]

scru·pu·lous /skrōō'pyələs/ *adj.* 1 conscientious; thorough 2 careful to avoid doing wrong —**scru'pu·los'i·ty** /-läs'i·tē/, **scru'pu·lous·ness** *n.*; **scru'pu·lous·ly** *adv.* [L, rel. to SCRUPLE]

scru·ti·nize /skrōōt'n·īz/ *v.* (**·nized, ·niz·ing**) subject to scrutiny

scru·ti·ny /skrōōt'n·ē/ *n.* (*pl.* **·nies**) 1 critical examination 2 close investigation [L *scrutinium* fr. *scrutari* examine]

scu·ba /skōō'bə/ *n.* (*pl.* **·bas**) compressed-air tanks and apparatus for underwater diving [*self*-*c*ontained *u*nderwater *b*reathing *a*pparatus]

scud /skəd/ *v.* (**scud·ded, scud·ding**) 1 move straight and fast; skim along —*n.* 2 scudding [perh. fr. ON]

scuff /skəf/ *v.* 1 abrade or mark by brushing against something 2 shuffle or drag the feet —*n.* 3 mark of scuffing 4 backless slipper; mule

scuf·fle /skəf'əl/ *n.* 1 confused struggle or

fight at close quarters —*v.* (**·fled, ·fling**) 2 engage in a scuffle [prob. Scand, rel. to SHOVE]

scull /skəl/ *n.* 1 oar over the stern of a boat to propel it, usu. by a twisting motion 2 light racing rowboat —*v.* 3 propel (a boat) with sculls

scul·ler·y /skəl'(ə)rē/ *n.* (*pl.* **·ies**) kitchen room for washing pots, dishes, etc. [AngFr *squillerie*]

scul·lion /skəl'yən/ *n. Archaic.* cook's young assistant

sculpt /skəlpt/ *v.* sculpture [fr. SCULPTURE]

sculp·tor /skəlp'tər/ *n.* (*fem.* **sculp·tress** /skəlp'trəs/) artist who sculptures [L, rel. to SCULPTURE]

sculp·ture /skəlp'CHər/ *n.* 1 art of making three-dimensional or relief forms 2 work of sculpture —*v.* (**·tured, ·tur·ing**) 3 represent in sculpture 4 practice sculpture —**sculp'tur·al** *adj.* [L *sculpere* sculpt·carve]

scum /skəm/ *n.* 1 layer of dirt, froth, etc., at the top of liquid 2 *Derog.* worst part, person, or group (*scum of the earth*) —*v.* (**scummed, scum·ming**) 3 remove scum from 4 form a scum (on) —**scum'my** *adj.* (**·mi·er, ·mi·est**) [LGer or Du]

scum'bag' *n.* contemptible person

scup·per /skəp'ər/ *n.* hole in a vessel's side to drain water from the deck [Fr *escopir* to spit]

scurf /skərf/ *n.* dandruff —**scurf'y** *adj.* [OE]

scur·ri·lous /skər'ələs/ *adj.* grossly or indecently abusive —**scur·ril'i·ty** /skəril'ətē/ *n.* (*pl.* **·ties**); **scur'ri·lous·ly** *adv.*; **scur'ri·lous·ness** *n.* [L *scurra* buffoon]

scur·ry /skər'ē/ *v.* (**·ried, ·ry·ing**) 1 run or move hurriedly; scamper —*n.* (*pl.* **·ries**) 2 scurrying [fr. *hurry-scurry* reduplication of HURRY]

scur·vy /skər'vē/ *n.* 1 disease caused by a deficiency of vitamin C —*adj.* (**·vi·er, ·vi·est**) 2 paltry; contemptible —**scur·vi·ly** /skər'vəlē/ *adv.*; **scur'vi·ness** *n.* [fr. SCURF]

scut·tle[1] /skət'l/ *n.* metal bucket for carrying or storing coal [ON fr. L *scutella* dish]

scut·tle[2] *v.* (**·tled, ·tling**) 1 scurry —*n.* 2 scurry [perh. rel. to dial. *scuddle* freq. of SCUD]

scut·tle[3] *n.* 1 hole with a lid in a vessel's deck or side —*v.* 2 sink (a vessel) by letting in water [Sp *escotilla* hatchway]

scut·tle·butt /skət'əlbət'/ *n.* 1 *Naval.* drinking fountain 2 *Colloq.* rumor [SCUTTLE[1] + BUTT[4]]

scuz·zy /skəz'ē/ *adj.* (**·zi·er, ·zi·est**) *Slang.* scruffy; grimy; repulsive

SCYTHE

scythe /sīTH/ *n.* farming implement with a long handle and curved blade swung over the ground for mowing, etc. [OE]

SD, S. Dak. *abbr.* South Dakota (postal abbr. SD)

SDI *abbr.* Strategic Defense Initiative

Se *symb.* selenium

SE *abbr.* 1 southeast 2 southeastern

sea /sē/ *n.* 1 expanse of salt water that covers

most of the earth's surface **2** any part of this **3** large inland lake (*Caspian Sea*) **4** waves of the sea; their motion or state (*choppy seas*) **5** vast quantity or expanse **6 at sea: a** in a vessel on the sea **b** perplexed; confused [OE]

sea′ an′chor *n.* open canvas bag to retard the drifting of a vessel

sea′ a·nem′o·ne *n.* marine animal with tube-shaped body and petal-like tentacles

sea′bed′ *n.* ocean floor

sea′board′ *n.* **1** seashore or coastline **2** coastal region

sea·borg·i·um /sēbôrg′ēəm/ *n.* artificially produced chemical element, atomic number 106; *symb.* **Sg** [for US chemist Glenn T. *Seaborg*]

sea′ cow′ *n.* plant-eating marine mammal, esp. the manatee

sea′ ea′gle *n.* large fish-eating eagle; erne

sea·far·er /sē′fer′ər/ *n.* **1** sailor **2** traveler by sea —**sea′far′ing** *adj. & n.*

sea′food′ *n.* edible sea fish or shellfish

sea′go′ing *adj.* (of vessels) fit for crossing the open sea

sea′ green′ *adj. & n.* bluish-green

sea′ gull′ *n.* GULL[1]

sea′ horse′ *n.* small, upright fish with a head like that of a horse

seal[1] /sēl/ *n.* **1** piece of stamped wax, lead, paper, etc., attached to a document, envelope, etc., to guarantee authenticity or security **2** engraved die for stamping a design on a seal **3** substance or device for closing a gap **4** anything regarded as a guarantee **5** decorative adhesive stamp —*v.* **6** close; secure **7** stamp, fasten, or fix with a seal **8** certify as correct with a seal or stamp **9** confine securely —**seal′a·ble** *adj.* [L *sigillum*]

seal[2] *n.* **1** fish-eating amphibious marine mammal with flippers **2** fur of certain seals —*v.* **3** hunt for seals —**seal′er** *n.* [OE]

seal·ant /sē′lənt/ *n.* material for sealing

sea′ legs′ *n. pl.* ability to keep one's footing and avoid seasickness at sea

sea′ lev′el *n.* mean level of the sea's surface, used in reckoning land elevations and as a barometric standard

sea′ li′on *n.* large, eared seal

seal′skin′ *n.* **1** skin or prepared fur of a seal **2** garment made from this

seam /sēm/ *n.* **1** line where two edges join, esp. of cloth or boards **2** line between parallel edges **3** wrinkle **4** stratum of coal, etc. —*v.* **5** join with or as with a seam —**seam′less** *adj.* [OE]

sea·man /sē′mən/ *n.* (*pl.* ·men) **1** sailor **2** US Navy. enlisted rank below petty officer

sea′man·ship′ *n.* skill in managing a vessel

seam·stress /sēm′stris/ *n.* woman who sews, esp. for a living [OE, rel. to SEAM]

seam′y *adj.* (·i·er, ·i·est) disreputable; sordid (*seamy side*) —**seam′i·ness** *n.*

se·ance /sā′äns/ *n.* meeting at which a spiritualist attempts to make contact with the dead [Fr]

sea′plane′ *n.* aircraft designed to take off from and land on water

sea′port′ *n.* harbor for ocean-going vessels

sear /sēr/ *v.* **1** scorch; cauterize **2** parch **3** brown (meat) quickly at a high temperature [OE]

search /sərcH/ *v.* **1** go over thoroughly to find something **2** examine or feel over (a person) to find anything concealed **3** probe **4** (foll. by *for*) look thoroughly in order to find —*n.* **5** searching; investigation **6 in search of** trying to find —**search′er** *n.* [AngFr *cerchier*]

search′ing *adj.* **1** penetrating **2** probing —**search′ing·ly** *adv.*

search′light′ *n.* **1** outdoor electric light with a powerful directional beam **2** beam from this

search′ war′rant *n.* legal authorization to enter and search premises

sea′scape′ *n.* picture or view of the sea

sea′shell′ *n.* shell of a saltwater mollusk

sea′shore′ *n.* land next to the sea

sea′sick′ *adj.* nauseated from the motion of the sea —**sea′sick′ness** *n.*

sea′side′ *n.* seashore

sea·son /sē′zən/ *n.* **1** each of the climatic divisions of the year (spring, summer, fall, winter) **2** proper or suitable time **3** time when something is plentiful, active, etc. —*v.* **4** flavor (food) with salt, herbs, etc. **5** enhance, harden, mature, or condition by aging or exposure to the weather or experience **6 in season** at the proper time [L *satio* sowing, fr. *serere* sow]

sea′son·a·ble *adj.* **1** suitable or usual to the season **2** opportune **3** apt

sea′son·al *adj.* of, depending on, or varying with the season [L *season*] —**sea′son·al·ly** *adv.*

sea′son·ing *n.* salt, herbs, etc., added to food to enhance its flavor

sea′son tick′et *n.* ticket for specified series of events, unlimited access, etc., in a given period

seat /sēt/ *n.* **1** thing made or used for sitting on **2a** buttocks **b** part of a garment covering them **3** part of a chair, etc., on which the buttocks rest **4** place for one person to sit **5** position as a committee member, etc., or the right to occupy it **6** center or main site (*seat of learning*) —*v.* **7** cause to sit **8** provide seating for **9** put or fit in position **10 be seated** or **take a seat** sit down [ON, rel. to SIT]

seat′ belt′ *n.* belt for securing a motor vehicle or aircraft passenger

seat′ing *n.* **1** seats collectively **2** sitting accommodation

Se·at·tle /sē·at′l/ *n.* port city in Wash. Pop. 516,259

sea′ ur′chin *n.* small marine animal with a shell radiating needle-sharp spines

sea·ward /sē′wərd/ *adv.* (also **sea′wards**) **1** toward the sea —*adj.* **2** going or facing toward the sea

sea′way′ *n.* inland waterway open to seagoing ships

sea′weed′ *n.* plant growing in the sea

sea′wor′thy *adj.* fit to put to sea —**sea′wor′thi·ness** *n.*

se·ba·ceous /sibā′sHəs/ *adj.* fatty; secreting oily matter [L *sebum* tallow]

seb·or·rhe·a or **seb·or·rhoe·a** /seb′ərē′ə/ *n.* excessive discharge from the sebaceous glands [L *sebum* tallow, Gk *-rrhein* run]

sec[1] *abbr.* secant

sec² /sek/ *n. Colloq.* (in phrases) second; moment (*wait a sec*) [abbr.]

sec³ *adj.* (of wine) dry [Fr]

SEC *abbr.* Securities and Exchange Commission

sec. *abbr.* second(s)

Sec. *abbr.* (also **sec.**) secretary

se·cant /sē'kant'/ *n. Math.* **1** (in a right triangle) ratio of the hypotenuse to the side adjacent to an acute angle **2** line cutting a curve at one or more points [Fr]

se·cede /sisēd'/ *v.* (**·ced·ed, ·ced·ing**) withdraw formally from an organization [L *secedere* *-cess-*]

se·ces·sion /sisesH'ən/ *n.* **1** act of seceding **2** (*cap.*) *US Hist.* the secession of 11 southern states from the Union in 1860–61, bringing on the Civil War **—se·ces'sion·ist'** *n. & adj.* [L, rel. to SECEDE]

se·clude /siklōōd'/ *v.* (**·clud·ed, ·clud·ing**) keep (a person or place) apart from others [L *secludere* *-clus-*]

se·clu·sion /siklōō'zhən/ *n.* secluded state or place **—se·clu'sive** /-siv/ *adj.;* **se·clu'sive·ness** *n.*

sec·ond¹ /sek'ənd/ *adj.* **1** next after first **2** additional **3** subordinate; inferior **—***n.* **4** runner-up **5** person or thing besides the first or previously mentioned one **6** second gear **7** (*pl.*) inferior goods **8** (*pl.*) second helping **9** assistant to a boxer, etc. **—***v.* **10** support; back up **—***adv.* **11** in the second place, group, etc. [L *secundus* fr. *sequi* follow]

● Usage: See notes at FIRST and FORMER.

sec·ond² *n.* **1** sixtieth of a minute of time or of an angle **2** *Colloq.* moment; instant [MedL *secunda* (*minuta*) secondary (minute)]

sec·ond·ar·y /sek'ənder'ē/ *adj.* **1** coming second **2** derived from or supplementing what is primary **3** (of education, a school, etc.) following primary, esp. from the 7th grade **—***n.* (*pl.* **·ies**) **4** secondary thing **5** *Football.* defensive backfield **—sec'ond·ar'i·ly** *adv.* [L, rel. to SECOND¹]

sec'ond·ary col'or *n.* result of mixing two primary colors

sec'ond class' *n.* **1** group, category, postal service, accommodation, etc., coming after and inferior to the first **—***adj. & adv.* **2** (**sec'ond-class'**) of or by the second class

sec'ond cous'in *n.* son or daughter of one's parent's cousin

sec'ond-guess' *v. Colloq.* criticize with hindsight

sec'ond-hand' *adj.* **1** having had a previous owner; not new **2** (of information, etc.) indirectly acquired **—***adv.* **3** on a second-hand basis **4** indirectly

sec'ond lieu·ten'ant *n. US Milit.* officer of the lowest commissioned rank

sec'ond·ly *adv.* **1** furthermore **2** as a second item

sec'ond na'ture *n.* acquired tendency that has become instinctive

sec'ond per'son see PERSON, 3

sec'ond-rate' *adj.* mediocre; inferior

sec'ond string' *n.* alternative, secondary team

sec'ond thoughts' *n. pl.* revised opinion or resolution

sec'ond wind' *n.* **1** recovery of normal breathing during exercise after initial breathlessness **2** renewed energy to continue

se·cre·cy /sē'krəsē/ *n.* state of being secret; habit or faculty of keeping secrets

se·cret /sē'krit/ *adj.* **1** kept or meant to be kept private, unknown, or hidden **2** acting or operating secretly **—***n.* **3** thing to be kept secret **—se'cret·ly** *adv.* [L *secernere secret-* separate]

se'cret a'gent *n.* spy

sec·re·tar·i·at /sek'rəter'ēət/ *n.* administrative department [MedL, rel. to SECRETARY]

sec·re·tar·y /sek'rəter'ē/ *n.* (*pl.* **·ies**) **1** employee who assists with correspondence, records, making appointments, etc. **2** official of a society or company who writes letters, organizes business, etc. **3** principal of a governmental department **4** writing desk **—sec're·tar'i·al** *adj.;* **se·cre'tar·y·ship'** *n.* [L *secretarius,* rel. to SECRET]

se·crete /sikrēt'/ *v.* (**·cret·ed, ·cret·ing**) **1** (of a cell, organ, etc.) produce and discharge (a substance) **2** conceal **—se·cre'to·ry** /sikrēt'ərē/ *adj.* [fr. SECRET]

se·cre·tion /sikrē'shən/ *n.* **1a** process of secreting **b** secreted substance **2** act of concealing [L, rel. to SECRET]

se·cre·tive /sē'kritiv/ *adj.* inclined to make or keep secrets; uncommunicative **—se'cre·tive·ly** *adv.;* **se'cre·tive·ness** *n.*

Se'cret Serv'ice *n.* US government agency, a branch of the US Treasury Department, that provides protection for the US president and other officials, and enforces laws against counterfeiting

sect /sekt/ *n.* **1** group sharing (sometimes unorthodox) religious, political, or philosophical doctrines **2** religious denomination [L *sequi* follow]

sec·tar·i·an /sekter'ēən/ *adj.* **1** of a sect **2** devoted, esp. narrow-mindedly, to one's sect **—***n.* **3** member of a sect **—sec·tar'i·an·ism'** *n.* [MedL *sectarius* adherent]

sec·tion /sek'shən/ *n.* **1** each of the parts of a thing or out of which a thing can be fitted together **2** part cut off **3a** cutting of a solid by a plane **b** resulting figure **4** surgical cutting **—***v.* **5** arrange in or divide into sections [L *secare sect-* cut]

sec·tion·al *adj.* **1** made in sections **2** local rather than general **—sec'tion·al·ly** *adv.*

sec·tor /sek'tər/ *n.* **1** distinct military subdivision of an area **2** plane figure enclosed by two radii of a circle, ellipse, etc., and the arc between them [L, rel. to SECTION]

sec·u·lar /sek'yələr/ *adj.* not concerned with religion; worldly **—sec'u·lar·ism'** *n.;* **sec'u·lar·ize'** *v.* (**·ized, ·iz·ing**) **sec'u·lar·i·za'tion** *n.* [L *saeculum* an age]

se·cure /sikyŏŏr'/ *adj.* **1** untroubled by danger or fear **2** safe **3** reliable; stable; fixed **—***v.* (**·cured, ·cur·ing**) **4** make secure or safe **5** fasten or close securely **6** succeed in obtaining **—se·cure'ly** *adv.* [L *se* without, *cura* care]

se·cu·ri·ty /sikyŏŏr'ətē/ *n.* (*pl.* **·ties**) **1** secure condition or feeling **2** thing that guards or guarantees **3** deposit given as a guarantee of a loan, etc. **4** (often *pl.*) stocks, bonds, etc.

secy. *abbr.* secretary

se·dan /sidan'/ *n.* enclosed car with seats for four or more people se·date /sidāt'/ adj. 1 tranquil and dignified; serious —v. (·dat·ed, ·dat·ing) 2 put under sedation —se·date'ly adv.; se·date'ness n. [L sedare settle; calm]

se·da·tion /sidā'shən/ n. state of calm induced esp. by a sedative [L, rel. to SEDATE]

sed·a·tive /sed'ətiv/ n. 1 calming drug or influence —adj. 2 calming; soothing [MedL, rel. to SEDATE]

sed·en·tar·y /sed'n·terē/ adj. 1 sitting 2 (of work, etc.) done while sitting [L sedere sit]

sedge /sej/ n. waterside or marsh plant resembling coarse grass —sedg'y adj. [OE]

sed·i·ment /sed'əmənt/ n. 1 grounds; dregs 2 matter deposited by water or wind —sed·i·men'ta·ry /-men'terē/ adj.; sed·i·men·ta'tion /-mentā'shən/ n. [L sedere sit]

se·di·tion /sidish'ən/ n. conduct or speech inciting to rebellion —se·di·tious /-dish'əs/ adj. [L seditio]

se·duce /sid(y)ōōs/ v. (·duced, ·duc·ing) entice into sexual activity or wrongdoing —se·duc'er, se·duc'tion /-dək'shən/ n.; se·duc'tive adj.; se·duc'tive·ly adv.; se·duc'tive·ness n.; se·duc'tress /-tris/ n. fem. [L se away, ducere duct- lead]

sed·u·lous /sej'ələs/ adj. persevering; diligent; painstaking —se·du·li·ty /sid(y)ōō'lətē/ n.; sed'u·lous·ly adv. [L sedulous zealous]

se·dum /sē'dəm/ n. fleshy-leaved plant with yellow, pink, or white flowers [L: houseleek]

see[1] /sē/ v. (saw, seen, see·ing) 1 perceive with the eyes 2 understand 3 learn; find out 4 meet and recognize 5 visit or be visited by 6 meet regularly as a boyfriend or girlfriend 7 wait for clarification 8 experience 9 ensure 10 think 11a (in poker, etc.) equal (a bet) b equal the bet of (a player) 12 see through: a detect the true nature of b complete c support in difficulty 13 see to or about attend to [OE]

see[2] n. office or jurisdiction of a bishop or archbishop [L sedes seat]

seed /sēd/ n. 1a part of a plant capable of developing into another such plant b seeds collectively 2 semen 3 prime cause 4 descendants —v. 5 place seeds in 6 produce seed 7 go (or run) to seed: a cease flowering as seed develops b become degenerate, unkempt, etc. —seed'less adj.; seed'less·ness n. [OE]

seed'ling n. plant raised from seed

seed' mon·ey n. money for starting a new enterprise

seed·y adj. (·i·er, ·i·est) 1 shabby; unkempt 2 full of or going to seed —seed'i·ness n.

see'ing conj. considering (that); inasmuch as; because

seek /sēk/ v. (sought, seek·ing) 1 search; inquire 2 try to find or get or reach 3 endeavor —seek'er n. [OE]

seem /sēm/ v. 1 appear to be, feel, etc. 2 appear to be likely 3 give the appearance; pretend to be [ON]

seem'ing adj. apparent but perhaps doubtful —seem'ing·ly adv.

seem'ly adj. (·li·er, ·li·est) in good taste; proper —seem'li·ness n. [ON, rel. to SEEM]

seen /sēn/ v. past part. of SEE[1]

seep /sēp/ v. ooze; percolate —seep'age /-ij/ n. [OE]

seer /sēr/ n. (also fem. seer'ess) prophet; visionary

seer·suck·er /sēr'sək(ə)r/ n. linen, cotton, etc., fabric with a puckered surface [Pers]

see'-saw n. 1 long plank balanced on a central support, for children to sit on at each end and move up and down alternately 2 up-and-down or back-and-forth motion —v. 3 move up and down or back and forth [reduplication of SAW[1]]

seethe /sēTH/ v. (seethed, seeth·ing) 1 boil; bubble over 2 be very angry, resentful, etc. [OE]

seg·ment n. /seg'mənt/ 1 each part into which a thing is or can be divided —v. /-ment'/ 2 divide into segments —seg·men'tal /-men'təl/ adj.; seg·men·ta'tion n. [L secare cut]

Se·go·vi·a /səgō'vēə/, Andrés 1893–1987; Spanish classical guitarist

seg·re·gate /seg'rigāt/ v. (·gat·ed, ·gat·ing) isolate; separate (esp. an ethnic group) from the rest of the community [L grex greg- flock]

seg·re·ga·tion /seg'rigā'shən/ n. enforced separation of ethnic groups in a community, etc. —seg·re·ga'tion·ist n. & adj.

se·gue /seg'wā, sā'gwā/ v. (·gued, ·gue·ing) 1 continue without stopping (into the next section) —n. 2 such a transition [It fr. seguire follow]

sei·gneur /sānyər', sēn-/ n. (also sei·gnior /sān'yər, sānyôr', sēn-/) feudal lord —sei·gneur'i·al or sei·gnio'ri·al /-rēəl/ adj. [Fr fr. L senior SENIOR]

seine /sān/ n. 1 fishing-net with floats at the top and weights at the bottom —v. (seined, sein·ing) 2 fish or catch with a seine [OE segne]

Seine riv·er /sān, sen/ n. river in N France flowing 480 mi. NW through Paris to the English Channel

seis·mic /sīz'mik/ adj. of earthquakes —seis'mi·cal·ly adv. [Gk seismos earthquake]

seis·mo·graph /sīz'məgraf'/ n. instrument that records the force, direction, etc., of earthquakes —seis·mo·graph'ic adj.

seis·mol·o·gy /sīzmäl'əjē/ n. the study of earthquakes —seis·mo·log'i·cal /-məläj'ikəl/ adj.; seis·mol'o·gist n.

seize /sēz/ v. (seized, seiz·ing) 1 take hold or possession of forcibly or suddenly or by legal power 2 affect suddenly 3 take advantage of (an opportunity, etc.) 4 (of a mechanism) become jammed —sei·zure /sē'zhər/ n. [Fr saisir]

sel·dom /sel'dəm/ adv. rarely; not often [OE]

se·lect /silekt'/ v. 1 choose, esp. with care —adj. 2 chosen for excellence or suitability —se·lec'tive /-tiv/ adj.; se·lec'tive·ly adv.; se·lec'tive·ness, se·lec·tiv'i·ty, se·lect'ness, se·lec'tor n. [L seligere -lect-]

se·lec·tion /silek'shən/ n. 1 selecting or being selected 2 selected person or thing

se·le·ni·um /silē'nēəm/ n. nonmetallic element; symb. Se [Gk selēnē moon]

Se·leu·cus I /səlōō'kəs/ c. 358–280 B.C.; Macedonian general; founder of the Seleucid dynasty

self /self/ *n.* (*pl.* **selves**) 1 individuality; personality; essence 2 one's own interests or pleasure [OE]

self- *comb. form* expressing reflexive action: 1 of or by oneself or itself (*self-locking*) 2 on, in, for, or of oneself or itself (*self-absorbed*)

self'-a·base'ment *n.* self-humiliation; cringing

self'-a·buse' *n.* masturbation

self'-ad·dressed' *adj.* (of an envelope) bearing one's own address for a reply

self'-ag·gran'dize·ment *n.* process of enriching oneself or making oneself powerful —**self'-ag·gran'diz·ing** *adj.*

self'-ap·point'ed *adj.* designated so by oneself, not by others

self'-as·sured' *n.* self-confident —**self'-as·sur'ance** *n.*

self'-a·ware' *adj.* conscious of one's character, feelings, motives, etc. —**self'-a·ware'ness** *n.*

self'-cen'tered *adj.* preoccupied with oneself; selfish

self'-clean'ing *adj.* (esp. of an oven) cleaning itself when heated

self'-con·fessed' *adj.* openly admitting oneself to be

self'-con'fi·dent *adj.* having confidence in oneself —**self'-con'fi·dence** *n.*; **self'-con'fi·dent·ly** *adv.*

self'-con'scious *adj.* nervous; shy; embarrassed —**self'-con'scious·ly** *adv.*; **self'-con'scious·ness** *n.*

self'-con·tained' *adj.* 1 (of a person) uncommunicative; independent 2 complete in itself

self'-con·trol' *n.* power to control one's behavior, emotions, etc. —**self'-con·trolled'** *adj.*

self'-de·cep'tion *n.* deceiving of oneself, esp. about one's motives or feelings —**self'-de·ceit'** *n.*

self'-de·feat'ing *adj.* (of an action, etc.) doomed to failure because of internal inconsistencies

self'-de·fense' *n.* physical or verbal defense of one's body, property, rights, reputation, etc.

self'-de·ni'al *n.* asceticism, esp. to discipline oneself

self'-dep're·ca'tion *n.* belittling of oneself —**self'-dep're·cat'ing** *adj.*

self'-de·struct' *v.* (of a spacecraft, bomb, etc.) preset to disintegrate automatically —**self'-de·struc'tion** *n.*; **self'-de·struc'tive** *adj.*; **self'-de·struc'tive·ly** *adv.*

self'-de·ter'mi·na'tion *n.* 1 nation's right to determine its own government, etc. 2 ability to act with free will

self'-dis'ci·pline *n.* 1 ability to apply oneself 2 self-control —**self'-dis'ci·plined** *adj.*

self'-doubt' *n.* lack of confidence in oneself

self'-ed'u·cat'ed *adj.* educated by one's own reading, etc., without formal instruction

self'-ef·fac'ing *adj.* retiring; modest —**self'-ef·face'ment** *n.*

self'-em·ployed' *adj.* working freelance or for one's own business, etc. —**self'-em·ploy'ment** *n.*

self'-es·teem' *n.* good opinion of oneself

self'-ev'i·dent *adj.* obvious; without the need of further explanation —**self'-ev'i·dent·ly** *adv.*

self'-ex·am'i·na'tion *n.* 1 examining of one's own conduct, etc. 2 examining of one's own body for signs of illness

self'-ex·plan'a·to'ry *adj.* not needing explanation

self'-ex·pres'sion *n.* artistic or free expression

self'-ful·fill'ing *adj.* (of a prophecy, etc.) bound to come true as a result of its being made —**self'-ful·fill'ment** *n.*

self'-gov'ern·ing *adj.* governing itself or oneself —**self'-gov'ern·ment** *n.*

self'-help' *adj.* designating a method of using one's own resources, etc., to solve one's problems

self'-im'age *n.* one's conception of oneself

self'-im·port'ant *adj.* conceited; pompous —**self'-im·port'ance** *n.*

self'-in·dul'gent *adj.* indulging in one's own pleasure, feelings, etc. —**self'-in·dul'gence** *n.*

self'-in'ter·est *n.* one's personal advantage

self'ish *adj.* concerned chiefly with one's own interests or pleasure —**self'ish·ly** *adv.*; **self'ish·ness** *n.*

self'-know'ledge *n.* understanding of oneself

self'less *adj.* unselfish —**self'less·ly** *adv.*; **self'less·ness** *n.*

self'-made' *adj.* successful or rich by one's own effort

self'-pit'y *n.* feeling sorry for oneself —**self'-pit'y·ing** *adj.*

self'-por'trait *n.* portrait or description of oneself by oneself

self'-pos·sessed' *adj.* calm and composed —**self'-pos·ses'sion** *n.*

self'-pres·er·va'tion *n.* preservation of oneself from harm or destruction

self'-pro·pelled' *adj.* (of a vehicle, etc.) propelled by its own power —**self'-pro·pel'ling** *adj.*

self'-reg'u·lat'ing *adj.* regulating oneself or itself without intervention —**self'-reg·u·la'tion** *n.*; **self'-reg·u·la·to'ry** *adj.*

self'-re·li'ance *n.* reliance on one's own resources, etc.; independence —**self'-re·li'ant** *adj.*

self'-re·spect' *n.* respect for oneself —**self'-re·spect'ing** *adj.*

self'-re·straint' *n.* self-control

self'-right'eous *adj.* smugly sure of one's rightness —**self'-right'eous·ly** *adv.*; **self'-right'eous·ness** *n.*

---

self'-ab·sorp'tion *n.*	**self'-crit'i·cism** *n.*
self'-ab·sorbed' *adj.*	**self'-de·lu'sion** *n.*
self'-ad·vance'ment *n.*	**self'-fer·til·i·za'tion** *n.*
self'-com·mand' *n.*	**self'-im·posed'** *adj.*
self'-com·pla'cent *adj.*	**self'-im·prove'ment** *n.*
self'-crit'i·cal *adj.*	**self'-in·crim'i·na'tion** *n.*

self'-in·duced' *adj.*	**self'-pol'li·nat'ing** *adj.*
self'-in·flict'ed *adj.*	**self'-pro·claimed'** *adj.*
self'-jus'ti·fi·ca'tion *n.*	**self'-pro·tec'tion** *n.*
self'-love' *n.*	**self'-re·proach'** *n.*
self'-per·pet'u·at'ing *adj.*	**self'-sus·tain'ing** *adj.*
self'-pol'li·na'tion *n.*	

self-rule' *n.* self-government

self'-sac'ri·fice' *n.* selflessness; self-denial **—self'-sac'ri·fic'ing** *adj.*

self'same' *adj.* very same; identical

self'-sat'is·fied' *adj.* smug; self-righteous **—self'-sat'is·fac'tion** *n.*

self'-seek'ing *adj. & n.* selfish

self'-ser'vice *adj.* 1 (of a store, restaurant, etc.) with customers serving themselves **—n.** 2 such a system

self'-start'er *n.* 1 electrical appliance for starting an engine 2 ambitious person with initiative

self'-styled' *adj.* called so by oneself

self'-suf·fi'cient *adj.* able to supply one's own needs; independent **—self'-suf·fi'cien·cy** *n.*

self'-sup·port'ing *adj.* financially self-sufficient

self'-taught' *adj.* self-educated

self'-willed' *adj.* obstinately pursuing one's own wishes

self'-worth' *n.* SELF-ESTEEM

sell /sel/ *v.* (**sold, sell·ing**) 1 exchange or be exchanged for money 2 offer for sale 3 have a specified price 4 cause to be accepted or purchased **—n.** 5 *Colloq.* manner of selling (*soft sell*) 6 **sell off** get rid of, esp. by selling at reduced prices 7 **sell out: a** sell (all of one's wares, shares, etc.) **b** betray **—sell'er** *n.* [OE]

sell'-by' date' *n.* latest recommended date for sale, esp. of a perishable item

sell'-out' *n.* 1 commercial success, esp. the selling of all tickets for a show 2 betrayal

selt·zer /selt'sər/ *n.* untreated carbonated water [fr. *Selters* German spring]

sel·vage /sel'vij/ *n.* (also **sel'vedge**) fabric edging woven to prevent cloth from fraying [fr. SELF, EDGE]

selves /selvz/ *n. & adj. pl.* of SELF

se·man·tic /siman'tik/ *adj.* of meaning in language **—se·man'ti·cal·ly** *adv.* [Gk *sēmainein* to mean]

se·man·tics /siman'tiks/ *n. pl.* branch of linguistics concerned with meaning

sem·a·phore /sem'əfôr'/ *n.* 1 system of signaling with the arms or two flags 2 railway signaling apparatus consisting of a post with a movable arm or arms, etc. [Gk *sēma* sign, *pherein* bear]

Se·ma·rang /səmär'äNG/ *n.* seaport in Indonesia, on Java. Pop. 1,026,700

sem·blance /sem'bləns/ *n.* appearance; show [Fr *sembler* resemble]

se·men /sē'mən/ *n.* reproductive fluid of males [L *semen semin-* seed]

se·mes·ter /simes'tər/ *n.* half an academic year [L *semestris* fr. *sex* six, *mensis* month]

sem·i /sem'ē, -ī'/ *n.* (*pl.* **-is**) shortening of SEMITRAILER

semi- *prefix* 1 half 2 partly [L]

sem·i·cir·cle /sem'isər'kəl/ *n.* half of a circle or of its circumference **—sem'i·cir'cu·lar** *adj.*

sem'i·co'lon *n.* punctuation mark (;) of intermediate value between a comma and a period

sem'i·con·duc'tor *n.* substance that has conductivity intermediate between insulators and metals

sem'i·con'scious *adj.* partly or imperfectly conscious

sem'i·fi'nal *n.* match or round preceding the final **—sem'i·fi'nal·ist** *n.*

sem·i·nal /sem'ən-l/ *adj.* 1 of seed, semen, or reproduction 2 (of ideas, etc.) original and fruitful [L, rel. to SEMEN]

sem·i·nar /sem'ənär'/ *n.* 1 advanced class with limited attendance 2 conference of specialists [Ger, rel. to SEMINARY]

sem·i·nar·y /sem'əner'ē/ *n.* (*pl.* **·ies**) 1 training college for priests, rabbis, etc. 2 school, esp. for young women **—sem'i·nar'i·an** *n.* [L, rel. to SEMEN]

se·mi·ot·ics /sē'mē-ät'iks/ *n.* the study of signs and symbols and their use, esp. in language **—se'mi·ot'ic** *adj.* [Gk *sēmeiōtikos* of signs]

sem·i·per·me·a·ble /sem'ipər'mēəbəl/ *adj.* (of a membrane, etc.) allowing certain substances to pass through

sem'i·pre'cious *adj.* (of a gem) less valuable than a precious stone

sem'i·pro·fes'sion·al *adj.* 1 (of a footballer, musician, etc.) paid for an activity but not relying on it for a living 2 of semiprofessionals **—n.** 3 semiprofessional person

sem'i·skilled' *adj.* (of work or a worker) needing or having some training

Sem·ite /sem'īt'/ *n.* member of the peoples said to be descended from Shem (Gen. 10), including esp. the Jews and Arabs [Gk *Sēm* Shem]

Se·mit·ic /simit'ik/ *adj.* 1 of the Semites, esp. the Jews 2 of languages of the family including Hebrew and Arabic **—n.** 3 the subfamily of such languages

sem'i·tone' *n.* half a tone in the musical scale

sem'i·trail'er *n.* detachable freight trailer hauled by a truck tractor

sem'i·trop'i·cal *adj.* (of climate) nearly tropical

Sem·tex /sem'teks'/ *n.* malleable, odorless plastic explosive [fr. *Semtín* in the Czech republic, where orig. made]

Sen. *abbr.* 1 Senator 2 Senior

sen·ate /sen'it/ *n.* 1 legislative body 2 (*cap.*) upper and smaller assembly in the US Congress [L *senatus* fr. *senex* old man]

sen·a·tor /sen'ətər/ *n.* member of a senate **—sen'a·to'ri·al** /-tôr'ēəl/ *adj.* [L, rel. to SENATE]

send /send/ *v.* (**sent, send·ing**) 1 order or cause to go or be conveyed 2 drive 3 *Slang.* put into ecstasy 4 **send for: a** (also **send away for**) order (goods) by post **b** summon **—send'er** *n.* [OE]

Sen·dai /sen'dī'/ *n.* city in Japan, on Honshu. Pop. 930,500

send'-off' *n.* party, etc., at the departure of a person, start of a project, etc.

Sen·e·ca /sen'ikə/, **Lucius Annaeus** c. 4 B.C.–A.D. 65; Roman philosopher and writer

Sen·e·gal /sen'əgôl'/ *n.* republic in W Africa on the Atlantic Ocean. Capital: Dakar. Pop. 7,691,000 **—Sen·e·gal·ese'** /-ēz/ *n. & adj.*

se·nile /sē'nīl'/ *adj.* 1 of old age 2 mentally or physically infirm because of old age **—se·nil·i·ty** /sinil'ətē/ *n.* [ult. fr. L *senex* old]

se·nior /sēn'yər/ *adj.* 1 more or most advanced in age, standing, or position 2 (placed after a person's name) senior to a relative of

the same name **3** of or for senior citizens —*n.*
4 senior person **5** one's elder or superior **6** student in his last year of high school or college —**se·nior'i·ty** /sēnyôr'itē, -yär'-/ *n.* [L comp. of *senex* old]

se'nior cit'i·zen *n.* retired or elderly person

sen·na /sen'ə/ *n.* **1** cassia **2** laxative from the dried pod of this [Ar]

Sen·nach·er·ib /sənak'ərib/ d. 681 B.C.; king of Assyria (704–681 B.C.)

se·ñor /sānyôr'/ *n.* (*pl.* **·ñor·es** /-nyôr'ās/) title used of or to a Spanish man [Sp fr. L *senior* SENIOR]

se·ño·ra /sānyôr'ə/ *n.* title used of or to a Spanish woman, esp. one who is married

se·ño·ri·ta /sān'yərēt'ə/ *n.* title used of or to a young Spanish woman, esp. one who is unmarried

sen·sa·tion /sensā'sнən/ *n.* **1** feeling in one's body detected by the senses **2** awareness; impression **3a** intense interest, excitement, etc., felt by a large group **b** person, event, etc., causing this [MedL, rel. to SENSE]

sen·sa'tion·al *adj.* **1** causing excitement, etc. **2** dazzling; wonderful —**sen·sa'tion·al·ism'** /-iz'əm/, **sen·sa'tion·al·ist** /-ist/ *n.*; **sen·sa'tion·al·ize'** *v.* (·ized, ·iz·ing); **sen·sa'tion·al·ly** *adv.*

sense /sens/ *n.* **1** any of the five bodily faculties transmitting sensation **2** ability to perceive or feel **3** consciousness; awareness **4** quick or accurate appreciation, understanding, or instinct **5** common sense **6a** meaning of a word, etc. **b** intelligibility; coherence —*v.* (sensed, sens·ing) **7** perceive by a sense or senses **8** be vaguely aware of **9** in a (or one) sense in a way; to some degree **10** make sense be intelligible or practicable [L *sensus* fr. *sentire sens-* feel]

sense'less *adj.* **1** pointless; foolish **2** unconscious **3** meaningless —**sense'less·ly** *adv.*; **sense'less·ness** *n.*

sen·si·bil·i·ty /sen'səbil'ətē/ *n.* (*pl.* **·ties**) **1** capacity to feel **2** sensitiveness

sen·si·ble /sen'səbəl/ *adj.* **1** having or showing wisdom or common sense **2a** perceptible by the senses **b** great enough to be perceived **3** aware —**sen'si·bly** *adv.*

sen·si·tive /sen'sətiv/ *adj.* **1** acutely susceptible to external stimuli or impressions; having sensibility **2** (of an instrument, film, etc.) responsive to or recording slight changes **3** (of a topic, etc.) requiring tactful treatment or secrecy —**sen'si·tive·ly** *adv.*; **sen'si·tive·ness, sen'si·tiv'i·ty** *n.*

sen·si·tize /sen'sətīz'/ *v.* (·tized, ·tiz·ing) make sensitive —**sen'si·ti·za'tion** *n.*

sen·sor /sen'sər, -sôr'/ *n.* device for detecting or measuring a physical property [fr. SENSORY]

sen'so·ry *adj.* of sensation or the senses [L *sentire sens-* feel]

sen·su·al /sen'sнoōəl/ *adj.* **1** of or giving physical, esp. sexual, pleasure **2** showing sensuality —**sen'su·al·ism, sen'su·al'i·ty** /-al'itē/ *n.*; **sen'su·al·ly** *adv.* [L, rel. to SENSE]

sen·su·ous /sen'sнoōəs/ *adj.* of or affecting the senses, esp. aesthetically —**sen'su·ous·ly** *adv.*; **sen'su·ous·ness** *n.* [L, rel. to SENSE]

sent /sent/ *v.* past and past part. of SEND

sen·tence /sent'ns/ *n.* **1** statement, question,

exclamation, or command containing or implying a subject and predicate **2** decision of a court, esp. the punishment set for a convicted criminal —*v.* (·tenced, ·tenc·ing) **3** declare the sentence of (a convicted criminal) [L *sententia* fr. *sentire* consider]

sen·ten·tious /senten'sнəs/ *adj.* **1** pompously moralizing **2** aphoristic; using maxims —**sen·ten'tious·ly** *adv.*; **sen·ten'tious·ness** *n.* [L, rel. to SENTENCE]

sen·tient /sen'sнənt/ *adj.* capable of perception and feeling —**sen'tience, sen'tien·cy** *n.*; **sen'tient·ly** *adv.* [L *sentire* feel]

sen·ti·ment /sent'əmənt/ *n.* **1** mental feeling **2** what one feels; opinion **3** exaggerated emotion

sen·ti·men·tal /sent'əmen'tl/ *adj.* **1** of or showing sentiment **2** showing or affected by emotion rather than reason —**sen'ti·men'tal·ism', sen'ti·men'tal·ist, sen'ti·men·tal'i·ty** /-tal'itē/ *n.*; **sen'ti·men·tal·ize'** *v.* (·ized, ·iz·ing); **sen'ti·men'tal·ly** *adv.*

sen·ti·nel /sent'n·əl/ *n.* sentry; guard [Fr fr. It]

sen·try /sen'trē/ *n.* (*pl.* **·tries**) soldier standing guard [perh. fr. obs. *centrinel*, var. of SENTINEL]

Seoul /sōl/ *n.* capital of South Korea. Pop. 10,627,800

Sep. *abbr.* September

se·pal /sē'pəl/ *n.* division or leaf of a calyx [perh. fr. SEPARATE, PETAL]

sep·a·ra·ble /sep'(ə)rəbəl/ *adj.* able to be separated —**sep'a·ra·bil'i·ty** *n.*; **sep'a·ra·bly** *adv.* [L, rel. to SEPARATE]

sep·a·rate *adj.* /sep'(ə)rət/ **1** forming a unit by itself; existing apart; disconnected; distinct; individual —*n.* /-rət/ **2** (*pl.*) trousers, skirts, etc., that are not parts of suits —*v.* /sep'(ə)rāt'/ (·rat·ed, ·rat·ing) **3** make separate; sever **4** prevent union or contact of **5** go different ways **6** divide or sort into parts or sizes —**sep'a·rate·ly** *adv.*; **sep'a·rate·ness** *n.* [L *separare*]

sep·a·ra·tion /sep'ərā'sнən/ *n.* **1** separating or being separated **2** legal arrangement by which a couple remain married but live apart [L, rel. to SEPARATE]

sep·a·rat·ist /sep'(ə)rətist/ *n.* person who favors separation, esp. political independence —**sep'a·rat·ism'** /-tiz'əm/ *n.*

sep·a·ra·tor /sep'ərā'tər/ *n.* machine for separating, e.g., cream from milk

Se·phar·di /sifär'dē/ *n.* (*pl.* **·dim** /-dim/) Jew of Spanish or Portuguese descent —**Se·phar'dic** *adj.* [Heb: Spaniard]

se·pi·a /sē'pēə/ *n.* **1** dark reddish-brown color or paint **2** brown tint used in photography [Gk: cuttlefish]

sep·sis /sep'sis/ *n.* septic condition [Gk, rel. to SEPTIC]

Sept. *abbr.* September

Sep·tem·ber /septem'bər/ *n.* ninth month of the year in the Gregorian calendar [L *septem* seven, orig. the 7th month of the Roman year]

sep·ten·ni·al /septen'ēəl/ *adj.* **1** lasting for seven years **2** recurring every seven years —**sep·ten'ni·al·ly** *adv.*

sep·tet /septet'/ *n.* **1** *Mus.* a composition for

seven performers **b** the performers **2** any group of seven [L *septem* seven]

sep·tic /sep′tik/ *adj.* contaminated with bacteria; putrefying [Gk *sēpein* rot]

sep·ti·ce·mi·a /sep′təsē′mēə/ *n.* blood poisoning —**sep′ti·ce′mic** *adj.* [fr. SEPTIC, Gk *haima* blood]

sep′tic tank′ *n.* tank in which sewage decomposes through bacterial activity

sep·tu·a·ge·nar·i·an /sep′t(y)ōōəjəner′ēən/ *n.* person from 70 to 79 years old [L -*arius* fr. *septuaginta* seventy]

Sep·tu·a·gint /sep′t(y)ōōəjint′/ *n.* Greek version of the Old Testament [L *septuaginta* seventy, said to have been translated by 70 scholars]

sep·tum /sep′təm/ *n.* (*pl.* -ta /-tə/) partition, esp. that between the nostrils [L *s(a)eptum* fr. *saepire* enclose]

sep·ul·cher /sep′əlkər/ *n.* tomb or burial place [L *sepelire* bury]

se·pul·chral /sipəl′krəl/ *adj.* 1 of a tomb or interment 2 funereal; gloomy

seq. *abbr.* 1 sequel 2 the following (thing) 3 (as *seqq.*) the following ones [L *sequens,* pl. *sequentia*]

se·quel /sē′kwəl/ *n.* 1 what follows (esp. as a result) 2 novel, film, etc., that continues the story of an earlier one [L *sequi* follow]

se·quence /sē′kwəns/ *n.* 1 succession 2 order of succession 3 series of things belonging next to one another 4 part of a film dealing with one scene or topic; episode —**se·quen′tial** /-kwen′SHəl/ *adj.;* **se·quen′tial·ly** *adv.* [L, rel. to SEQUEL]

se·ques·ter /sikwes′tər/ *v.* seclude; isolate —**se′ques·tra′tion** /-trā′SHən/ *n.* [L *sequester* trustee]

se·quin /sē′kwin/ *n.* circular spangle, esp. sewn on to clothing —**se′quined** or **se′quinned** *adj.* [It *zecchino* a gold coin]

se·quoi·a /sikwoi′ə/ *n.* extremely tall Californian evergreen conifer [for SEQUOYA]

Se·quoy·a /sikwoi′ə/ c. 1770–1843; Cherokee Indian leader and scholar

se·ra /sir′ə/ *n. pl.* of SERUM

se·ragl·io /sərâl′yō/ *n.* (*pl.* -ios) harem [It *serraglio* fr. Turk]

se·ra·pe /sərä′pē/ *n.* shawl or blanket worn in Latin America [MexSp]

ser·aph /ser′əf/ *n.* (*pl.* -aphs or -a·phim /-əfim′/) angelic being of the highest order of the celestial hierarchy —**se·raph·ic** /səraf′ik/ *adj.* [Heb]

Ser·bi·a /sər′bēə/ *n.* republic in SE Europe on the Balkan Peninsula. Capital: Belgrade. Pop. 9,800,000 —**Serb** *n.* & *adj.*

Ser·bi·an /sər′bēən/ *n.* 1 dialect of the Serbs 2 Serb; native or inhabitant of Serbia —*adj.* 3 of Serbia

Ser·bo-Cro·a·tian /sər′bō krōā′SHən/ (also **Ser′bo-Cro′at** /-krō′at/) *n.* 1 language of Serbians and Croatians —*adj.* 2 of this language

ser·e·nade /ser′ənād′/ *n.* 1 romantic music performed at night, esp. by a man beneath his beloved's window —*v.* (**·nad·ed, ·nad·ing**) 2 perform a serenade [It, rel. to SERENE]

ser·en·dip·i·ty /ser′əndip′ətē/ *n.* faculty of making happy discoveries by accident —**ser′-**

en·dip′i·tous *adj.* [coined by Horace Walpole]

se·rene /sərēn′/ *adj.* 1 clear and calm 2 tranquil; unperturbed —**se·rene′ly** *adv.;* **se·rene′ness,** se·ren′i·ty /-ren′ətē/ *n.* [L]

serf /sərf/ *n.* laborer who was not allowed to leave the land on which he worked —**serf′dom** *n.* [L *servus* slave]

serge /sərj/ *n.* durable, twilled fabric [Fr *sarge, serge*]

ser·geant /sär′jənt/ *n.* 1 *Milit.* noncommissioned officer ranking just above a corporal 2 police officer ranking just below a lieutenant or captain [Fr *sergent* fr. L *serviens* -*ent*- servant]

ser′geant ma′jor *n.* (*pl.* ser′geants ma′jor) *US Milit.* highest-ranking noncommissioned officer

se·ri·al /sēr′ēəl/ *n.* 1 story, etc., published, broadcast, or shown in installments —*adj.* 2 of, in, or forming a series —**se′ri·al·ly** *adv.* [fr. SERIES]

se·ri·al·ize /sēr′ēəlīz′/ *v.* (**·ized, ·iz·ing**) publish or produce in installments —**se′ri·al·i·za′tion** *n.*

se′ri·al num′ber *n.* number identifying one of a series of items, people, etc.

se·ries /sēr′ēz/ *n.* (*pl.* same) 1 number of similar or related things, events, etc.; succession; row; set 2 set of related but individual programs [L *serere* join]

ser·if /ser′if/ *n.* slight projection at the extremities of a printed letter (as in T contrasted with T)

se·ri·ous /sēr′ēəs/ *adj.* 1 thoughtful; sober; earnest 2 important; demanding consideration 3 not trivial; dangerous 4 not joking or funny; sincere —**se′ri·ous·ly** *adv.;* **se′ri·ous·ness** *n.* [L *seriosus*]

ser·mon /sər′mən/ *n.* 1 discourse on religion or morals, etc., esp. delivered in church 2 serious warning; lecture —**ser′mon·ize** *v.* (**·ized, ·iz·ing**) [L *sermo -onis* speech]

se·rous /sēr′əs/ *adj.* 1 of or like serum; watery 2 (of a gland or membrane) having a serous secretion [rel. to SERUM]

ser·pent /sər′pənt/ *n.* snake, esp. large [L *serpere* creep]

ser·pen·tine /sər′pəntīn′/ *adj.* 1 of or like a serpent 2 coiling; meandering 3 cunning; treacherous

ser·rat·ed /serāt′id, ser′āt′id/ *adj.* (also **ser′rate**) with a sawlike edge —**ser·ra′tion** *n.* [L *serra* saw]

ser·ried /ser′ēd/ *adj.* (of ranks of soldiers, etc.) close together [Fr *serrer* to close]

se·rum /sēr′əm/ *n.* (*pl.* **·rums** or **·ra** /-rə/) 1 liquid that separates from a clot when blood coagulates, esp. used for inoculation 2 watery fluid in animal bodies [L: whey]

ser·vant /sər′vənt/ *n.* 1 person employed to do domestic duties 2 devoted follower or helper [Fr, rel. to SERVE]

serve /sərv/ *v.* (**served, serv·ing**) 1 do a service for (a person, community, etc.) 2 be a servant to 3 carry out duties 4 spend a period (e.g., in the navy, in prison) 5 meet a purpose; perform a function 6 act as a waiter 7 attend to (a customer, etc.) 8 deliver (a subpoena, etc.) to (someone) 9 (in tennis, etc.) deliver (a ball, etc.) to begin or resume play —*n.* 10 delivery of a ball, etc., as in tennis

11 serve a person right be a person's deserved punishment, etc. [L *servire*]

serv'er *n.* 1 person who serves 2 utensil or plate for serving

serv·ice /sɜr'vis/ *n.* 1 work or the doing of work for another, for a community, etc. 2 assistance or benefit given 3 supplying of a public need, e.g., of water, gas, etc. 4 employment as a servant 5 state or period of employment 6 public department or organization (*civil service*) 7 the armed forces 8 ceremony of worship 9 maintenance of a machine, etc. 10 serving of food, drinks, etc. 11 set of dishes, etc., for serving meals 12 act of serving in tennis, etc. —*v.* (·viced, ·vic·ing) 13 maintain or repair (a machine, etc.) 14 supply with a service 15 at a person's service ready to serve a person 16 in service: a employed as a servant b functioning 17 of service to 18 out of service not working [L *servitium* fr. *servus* slave]

serv·ice·a·ble /sɜr'visəbəl/ *adj.* 1 useful or usable 2 durable but plain —**serv'ice·a·bil'i·ty** /-bil'itē/ *n.*

serv'ice a'rea *n.* area beside a major road providing fuel, refreshments, toilets, etc.

serv'ice in'dus·try *n.* business that provides services, not goods

serv·ice·man /sɜr'vismən/ *n.* (*pl.* ·men') 1 man in the armed forces 2 man providing maintenance, etc.

serv'ice sta'tion *n.* place for servicing cars, selling fuel, etc.

serv'ice·wom'an *n.* (*pl.* ·wom'en) woman in the armed forces

ser·vile /sɜr'vil'/ *adj.* 1 of or like a slave 2 fawning; subservient —**ser·vil·i·ty** /sərvil'itē/ *n.* [L *servus* slave]

ser·vi·tor /sɜr'vitər/ *n.* servant; attendant [L, rel. to SERVE]

ser·vi·tude /sɜr'vit(y)ōōd'/ *n.* slavery [L *servus* slave]

ser·vo /sɜr'vō/ *n.* (*pl.* ·vos) shortening of SERVOMECHANISM or SERVOMOTOR

ser'vo·mech'an·ism *n.* system for automatic control of electrical, hydraulic, etc., devices

ser'vo·mo'tor *n.* electric motor used in a servomechanism

ses·a·me /ses'əmē/ *n.* 1 E Indian plant with edible oil-yielding seeds 2 its seeds [Gk]

ses·qui·cen·ten·ni·al /ses'kwisenten'ēəl/ *n.* 1 period of 150 years 2 150th anniversary —*adj.* 3 relating to 150 years or a 150th anniversary

ses·sion /sesH'ən/ *n.* 1 period devoted to an activity 2 assembly of a parliament, court, etc. 3 academic year [L *sedere sess-* sit]

set¹ /set/ *v.* (**set**, **set·ting**) 1 put, lay, or stand in a certain position, place, etc. 2 make ready; fix in position; arrange suitably for use, action, or display 3 adjust (a clock, mechanical device, etc.) 4 insert (a jewel) in a ring, etc. 5 lay (a table) for a meal 6 style (the hair) 7 (of jelly, cement, etc.) harden; solidify 8 (of the sun, moon, etc.) move below the horizon 9 establish (a story, etc.) as happening in a certain time or place 10 give as a matter to be dealt with 11 exhibit as a model, etc. 12 initiate; lead 13 establish (a record, etc.) 14a put parts of (a broken or dislocated bone, limb, etc.) together for healing b deal with (a fracture, etc.) in this way 15 (in full **set to** music) provide (words, etc.) with music for singing 16a compose (type, etc.) b compose the type for (a book, etc.) 17 (of a hen) to sit on eggs 18 set about begin 19 set down: a record in writing b alight 20 set forth: a begin a journey b describe 21 set off: a begin a journey b detonate (a bomb, etc.) c initiate d enhance 22 set on (or upon) attack violently 23 set out: a begin a journey b intend 24 set up: a place in position or view b establish [OE]

● Usage: *Set* means either 'to place or put,' or, in a limited sense, 'to decline or wane': *I set the book on the table; The sun sets in the evening.* *Sit* means 'to be seated': *The child sits quietly in her chair.*

set² *n.* 1 group of linked, related, or similar things or persons 2 radio or television receiver 3 (in tennis, etc.) group of games counting as a unit toward winning a match 4 stage furniture, etc., for a play, film, etc. [senses 1–3 fr. *sette*; sense 4 fr. SET¹]

set³ *adj.* 1 determined; fixed 2 prepared for action 3 rigid; firm 4 stubborn [past part. of SET¹]

Set /set/ *n. Egypt. Myth.* god of evil, opponent of Osiris

set'back' *n.* reversal or arrest of progress

Se·ton /sēt'n/, **St. Elizabeth Ann (Bayley)** (called "Mother Seton") 1774–1821; US nun and educator; first American-born saint (1975)

set' screw' *n.* screw for tightening a fixed to a movable part

set·tee /setē'/ *n.* benchlike seat, usu. with a back, often upholstered

set'ter *n.* dog of a long-haired breed trained to stand rigid when scenting game

set'ting *n.* 1 position or manner in which a thing is set 2 immediate surroundings 3 period, place, etc., of a story, etc. 4 mounting for a jewel 5 cutlery, dishes, etc., for one person at a table

set·tle /set'l/ *v.* (·tled, ·tling) 1 establish or become established in an abode or lifestyle 2a regain calm after disturbance b apply oneself 3 (cause to) sit, alight, or come down to stay for some time 4 determine, decide, or agree upon 5 agree to terminate (a lawsuit) 6 pay (a debt, account, etc.) 7 colonize 8 subside; fall to the bottom or on to a surface —**set'tler** *n.* [OE, rel. to SIT]

set'tle·ment *n.* 1 settling or being settled 2 place occupied by settlers 3 agreement

set'-to' *n.* (*pl.* ·tos) *Colloq.* fight; argument

set'-up' *n.* 1 arrangement; organization 2 manner, structure, or position of this 3 fraudulent scheme or trick

Seu·rat /sərä'/, **Georges** 1859–91; French painter

Se·vas·to·pol /səvas'təpōl', -pōl'/ *n.* seaport in S Ukraine. Pop. 366,000

sev·en /sev'ən/ *adj. & n.* 1 one more than six 2 symbol for this (7, vii, VII) —**sev'enth** *adj. & n.* [OE]

sev·en·teen /sev'əntēn'/ *adj. & n.* 1 one more than sixteen 2 symbol for this (17, xvii, XVII) —**sev'en·teenth'** *adj. & n.* [OE]

sev'enth heav'en *n.* state of rapture

sev·en·ty /sev'əntē/ *adj. & n.* (*pl.* ·ties) 1 seven times ten 2 symbol for this (70, lxx,

LXX) **3** (*pl.*) numbers from 70 to 79, esp. the years of a century or of a person's life —**sev'en·ti·eth** /-tēəTH/ *adj. & n.* [OE]

sev·er /sev'ər/ *v.* divide, break, or make separate, esp. by cutting [AngFr *severer* fr. L *parare*]

sev·er·al /sev'(ə)rəl/ *adj. & pron.* **1** more than two but not many; a few —*adj.* **2** separate or respective —**sev'er·al·ly** *adv.* [L *separ* distinct]

sev·er·ance /sev'(ə)rəns/ *n.* **1** act of severing **2** noting payment to an employee upon dismissal

se·vere /sivēr'/ *adj.* **1** rigorous and harsh **2** serious **3** forceful; intense **4** plain —**se·vere'ly** *adv.*; **se·ver·i·ty** /siver'ətē/ *n.* [L *severus*]

Se·ville /səvil'/ *n.* port in SW Spain. Pop. 659,100

sew /sō/ *v.* (**sewed, sewn** or **sewed, sew·ing**) **1** fasten, join, etc., with a needle and thread **2 sew up:** **a** join or enclose by sewing **b** *Colloq.* conclude satisfactorily —**sew'er** *n.* [OE]

sew·age /sōō'ij/ *n.* waste matter conveyed in sewers [fr. SEWER]

Sew·ard /sōō'ərd/, **William** 1801–72; US politician; urged US purchase of Alaska

sew·er /sōō'ər/ *n.* conduit, usu. underground, for draining water and sewage [AngFr *sever(e)*, rel. to EX-[1], *aqua* water]

sew·er·age /sōō'ərij/ *n.* system of or drainage by sewers

sew·ing /sō'iNG/ *n.* material or work to be sewn

sew'ing ma·chine' *n.* machine for sewing or stitching

sex /seks/ *n.* **1** each of the main groups (male and female) into which living things are categorized on the basis of their reproductive functions **2** sexual instincts, desires, etc., or their manifestation **3** SEXUAL INTERCOURSE [L *sexus*]

sex·a·ge·nar·i·an /sek'səjəner'ēən/ *n.* person from 60 to 69 years old [L *-arius* fr. *sexaginta* sixty]

sex' ap·peal' *n.* sexual attractiveness

sex' chro'mo·some *n.* chromosome determining the sex of an organism

sex·ism *n.* prejudice or discrimination, esp. against women, on the grounds of sex —**sex'ist** /-ist/ *adj. & n.*

sex·ol·o·gy /seksäl'əjē/ *n.* the study of sexual relationships or practices —**sex·ol'o·gist** *n.*

sex' sym'bol *n.* person noted for sex appeal

SEXTANT

sex·tant /seks'tənt/ *n.* instrument for measuring the angular distance of objects [L *sextans -ntis* sixth part]

sex·tet /sekstet'/ *n.* (also **sex·tette**) **1** *Mus.* a composition for six performers **b** the performers **2** any group of six [L *sex* six]

sex·ton /seks'tən/ *n.* person who looks after a church and churchyard [AngFr *segerstaine* fr. L *sacristanus*]

sex·tu·plet /sekstəp'lit/ *n.* each of six children born at one birth

sex·u·al /sek'sнōōəl/ *adj.* of sex, the sexes, or relations between them —**sex·u·al·i·ty** /-al'itē/ *n.*; **sex·u·al·ly** *adv.*

sex·u·al in·ter·course *n.* act involving insertion of the penis into the vagina, usu. followed by ejaculation

sex·y *adj.* (**·i·er, ·i·est**) sexually attractive or stimulating —**sex'i·ly** *adv.*; **sex'i·ness** *n.*

Sey·chelles /sāshel(z)'/ *n.* island republic in the Indian Ocean, NE of Madagascar. Capital: Victoria. Pop. 71,000

sf or **SF** *abbr.* science fiction

Sg *symb.* seaborgium

Sgt. *abbr.* Sergeant

sh /sн/ *interj.* hush! quiet!

shab·by /sнab'ē/ *adj.* (**·bi·er, ·bi·est**) **1** faded and worn; neglected **2** contemptible —**shab'bi·ly** *adv.*; **shab'bi·ness** *n.* [rel. to SCAB]

shack /sнak/ *n.* roughly built hut or cabin [perh. fr. MexSp *jacal* wooden hut]

shack·le /sнak'əl/ *n.* **1** metal loop or link, closed by a bolt, used to connect chains, etc. **2** fetter for the ankle or wrist **3** (usu. *pl.*) restraint; impediment —*v.* (**·led, ·ling**) **4** impede; restrain [OE]

shad /sнad/ *n.* (*pl.* same or **-s**) coastal and river edible fish [OE]

shade /sнād/ *n.* **1** comparative darkness given by shelter from direct light **2** area so sheltered **3** color, esp. as darker or lighter than one of similar hue **4** slight amount **5** screen to block or diffuse light **6** (*pl.*) *Colloq.* sunglasses **7** *Lit.* ghost —*v.* (**shad·ed, shad·ing**) **8** screen from light **9** moderate or exclude the light of **10** darken (area of a drawing, etc.) [OE]

shad'ing *n.* light and shade shown on a map or drawing by hatching, etc.

shad·ow /sнad'ō/ *n.* **1** shade; patch of shade projected by a body intercepting light **2** slightest trace; weak or insubstantial remnant **3** shaded part of a picture **4** gloom; sadness —*v.* **5** cast a shadow over **6** secretly follow and watch —**shad'ow·y** *adj.* [OE, rel. to SHADE]

shad'ow·box' *v.* box with an imaginary opponent as training —**shad'ow·box'ing** *n.*

shad·y /sнā'dē/ *adj.* (**·i·er, ·i·est**) **1** giving shade **2** situated in shade **3** *Colloq.* disreputable; of doubtful honesty —**shad'i·ly** *adv.*; **shad'i·ness** *n.*

shaft /sнaft/ *n.* **1** narrow usu. vertical space, as access to a mine, for an elevator, vent, etc. **2** long shape as an arrow, spear, handle of a tool, bolt of lightning, etc. **3** long narrow part transmitting motion between other parts **4** hurtful or provocative remark (*shafts of wit*) **5** stem of a feather —*v.* **6** *Slang.* cheat; bilk [OE]

shag[1] /sнag/ *n.* rough mass of hair, nap of a carpet, etc. [OE]

shag[2] *v.* (**shagged, shag·ging**) *Baseball & Golf.* retrieve balls hit in practice

shag·gy *adj.* (·gi·er, ·gi·est) **1** hairy; rough-haired **2** unkempt —**shag′gi·ness** *n.*

shah /SHä/ *n.* former monarch of Iran [Pers]

shake /SHāk/ *v.* (**shook, shak·en, shak·ing**) **1** move forcefully or quickly up and down or to and fro **2** (cause to) tremble or vibrate **3** upset the composure of **4** *Colloq.* shake hands —*n.* **5** shaking or being shaken **6** (*pl.*; prec. by *the*) *Colloq.* fit of trembling **7** short for MILK SHAKE **8 no great shakes** *Colloq.* mediocre; disappointing **9 shake down:** a settle or cause to fall by shaking b *Slang.* extort money from **10 shake hands** clasp another's hand as a greeting, farewell, etc. **11 shake off** get rid of **12 shake up:** a mix by shaking b make uncomfortable c rouse from apathy [OE]

shake′down′ *n.* **1** extortion **2** thorough search —*adj.* **3** test done (of a new vessel, airplane, etc.) for operation, function, etc.

shak′er *n.* **1** person or thing that shakes **2** container or dispenser for shaking together ingredients, salt, etc. **3** (*cap.*) religious sect that advocates a simple manner of community living

Shake·speare /SHāK′spēr′/, **William** 1564–1616; English poet and dramatist —**Shake·spear′i·an** or **Shake·spear′e·an** *adj.*

shake′-up′ *n.* upheaval or drastic reorganization

shak′y *adj.* (·i·er, ·i·est) **1** unsteady; trembling **2** unsound; infirm **3** unreliable —**shak′i·ly** *adv.*; **shak′i·ness** *n.*

shale /SHāl/ *n.* soft rock of hardened mud or clay that splits easily [Ger, rel. to SCALE²]

shall /SHal/ *v. aux.* (*past* **should**) **1** (in the 1st person) expressing the future tense or (with *shall* stressed) emphatic intention (*I shall return*) **2** (in the 2nd and 3rd persons) expressing strong determination [OE]

● Usage: Formerly *shall* and *should* were used after *I* or *we*, and *will* and *would* after other pronouns to express the ordinary future. *Shall* was sometimes used after *you, he, she, it,* and *they* to indicate an order: *You shall behave or be punished. Should* is still heard, especially in British English, in first-person conditional sentences: *I should like to have an opportunity.* But these distinctions are all but lost today except among the most formal users of the language.

shal·lot /SHAl′ət, SHälät′/ *n.* onionlike plant with a cluster of small bulbs, used in cookery [Fr, rel. to SCALLION]

shal·low /SHAl′ō/ *adj.* **1** not deep **2** superficial; trivial —*n.* **3** (*pl.*) shallow place —**shal′low·ly** *adv.*; **shal′low·ness** *n.* [OE]

shalt /SHAlt/ *v. Archaic.* 2nd person sing. of SHALL

sham /SHAm/ *v.* (**shammed, sham·ming**) **1** feign; pretend —*n.* **2** fraud —*adj.* **3** counterfeit

sham·ble /SHAm′bəl/ *v.* (·bled, ·bling) **1** walk or run awkwardly, dragging the feet —*n.* **2** shambling gait [perh. rel. to SHAMBLES]

sham·bles *n. pl.* (usu. treated as *sing.*) **1** slaughterhouse **2** scene of carnage [pl. of *shamble* butcher's table]

shame /SHām/ *n.* **1** distress or humiliation caused by awareness of one's guilt, dishonor, or folly **2** state of disgrace or discredit **3** person or thing that brings disgrace —*v.* (**shamed, sham·ing**) **4** bring shame on; make ashamed **5** force by shame **6** put to shame humiliate by causing to feel shame or by being greatly superior —**shame′ful** *adj.*; **shame′ful·ly** *adv.*; **shame′ful·ness** *n.* [OE]

shame′faced′ *adj.* **1** showing shame **2** bashful —**shame′fac′ed·ly** /-făs′edlē/ *adv.*

shame′less *adj.* **1** having or showing no shame **2** impudent —**shame′less·ly** *adv.*; **shame′less·ness** *n.*

sham·poo /SHAmpo͞o′/ *n.* **1** substance for washing the hair, a carpet, upholstery, etc. —*v.* (·pooed, ·poo·ing) **2** wash with shampoo [Hindi]

sham·rock /SHAm′räk/ *n.* three-leaved plant; emblem of Ireland [Ir]

shang·hai /SHANGhī′/ *v.* (·haied, ·hai·ing) trick or force (a person) into serving as a sailor [for SHANGHAI]

Shang·hai /SHANGhī′, SHANG′hī′/ *n.* seaport in E China. Pop. 7,496,500

shank /SHANGk/ *n.* **1** lower part of the leg **2** leg **3** shaft or stem, esp. the part of a tool joining the handle to the working end [OE]

Shan·kar /SHäNG′kär/, **Ravi** 1920– ; Indian sitar player

shan't /SHant/ *v. contr.* shall not

shan·tung /SHantəNG′/ *n.* soft undressed Chinese silk [*Shantung*, Chinese province]

shan·ty /SHan′tē/ *n.* (*pl.* ·ties) hut

shape /SHāp/ *n.* **1** effect produced by the outline of something or somebody **2** external form or appearance **3** good or specified condition **4** vague or indistinct outline —*v.* (**shaped, shap·ing**) **5** give a certain form to; fashion **6** adapt or make conform **7** shape up *Colloq.* conform **8 take shape** take on a definite form —**shape′less** *adj.*; **shape′less·ly** *adv.*; **shape′less·ness** *n.* [OE]

shape′ly *adj.* (·li·er, ·li·est) pleasing in form; well-proportioned —**shape′li·ness** *n.*

shard /SHärd/ *n.* broken piece of pottery, etc. [OE]

share¹ /SHer/ *n.* **1** portion of a whole allotted to or taken from a person **2** each of the equal parts of a company's capital —*v.* (**shared, shar·ing**) **3** have or use with another or others **4** participate [OE, rel. to SHEAR]

share² *n.* short for PLOWSHARE

share′crop′ *v.* (·cropped, ·crop·ping) farm (land) in return for a share of the crop —**share′crop′per** *n.*

share′hold′er *n.* owner of shares in a company

share·ware /SHer′wer′/ *n. Comp.* software distributed free or sold at nominal cost

shark¹ /SHärk/ *n.* large, voracious marine fish

shark² *n. Colloq.* swindler; profiteer

shark′skin′ *n.* **1** skin of a shark **2** smooth, slightly shiny fabric

sharp /SHärp/ *adj.* **1** having an edge or point able to cut or pierce **2** tapering to a point or edge **3** abrupt; steep **4** well-defined; clean-cut **5a** severe; intense **b** (of a taste) pungent **6** (of a voice, etc.) shrill **7** acute; quick to understand **8** artful; unscrupulous **9** brisk **10** *Mus.* a semitone higher than a specified pitch (*C sharp*) **11** *Slang.* stylish —*n.* **12** *Mus.* a note a semitone above natural pitch **b** sign (♯) indicating this **13** *Colloq.* expert (*card* *sharp*) —*adv.* 14 punctually 15 suddenly 16 *Mus.* above true pitch —**sharp′ly** *adv.*; **sharp′ness** *n.* [OE]

sharp′en *v.* make or become sharp —**sharp′en·er** *n.*

sharp′er *n.* swindler, esp. at cards

sharp′shoot′er *n.* skilled marksman

sharp′-wit′ted *adj.* keenly perceptive or intelligent

shat·ter /SHat′ər/ *v.* 1 break suddenly into pieces 2 damage severely; destroy 3 greatly upset

shave /SHāv/ *v.* (**shaved, shaved** or **shav·en, shav·ing**) 1 remove (bristles or hair) with a razor (from) 2 reduce by a small amount 3 miss or pass narrowly —*n.* 4 shaving or being shaved 5 narrow miss or escape [OE]

shav′er *n.* 1 thing that shaves 2 *Colloq.* young lad

shav′ing *n.* thin strip cut off wood, etc.

Shaw /SHô/, **George Bernard** 1856–1950; Irish dramatist

shawl /SHôl/ *n.* usu. rectangular piece of fabric worn over the shoulders or head [Urdu fr. Pers *shāl*]

she /SHē/ *pron.* 1 the woman, girl, female animal, ship, country, etc., previously named or in question —*n.* 2 female; woman [OE]
● Usage: See note at EVERYBODY.

sheaf /SHēf/ *n.* (*pl.* **sheaves** /SHēvz/) bundle of things laid and tied lengthwise together, esp. stalks of wheat, etc. [OE]

shear /SHēr/ *v.* (**sheared, sheared** or **shorn, shear·ing**) 1 clip the wool off (a sheep, etc.) 2 remove by cutting 3 cut with scissors, shears, etc. —*n.* 4 (*pl.*) (also **pair of shears** *sing.*) large scissor-shaped cutting instrument —**shear′er** *n.* [OE]

sheath /SHēth/ *n.* (*pl.* **sheaths** /SHēThz, SHēThs/) 1 close-fitting cover for the blade of a knife or sword 2 enclosing case, covering, or tissue 3 woman's close-fitting dress [OE]

sheathe /SHēTH/ *v.* (**sheathed, sheath·ing**) 1 put into a sheath 2 encase; protect with a sheath

she·bang /SHibaNG′/ *n.* *Colloq.* as in **the whole shebang** everything

shed[1] /SHed/ *n.* structure for storage, shelter, etc., or as a workshop, esp. having a roof with a single slope (**shed′roof**) [fr. SHADE]

shed[2] *v.* (**shed, shed·ding**) 1 let or cause to fall off 2 take off (clothes) 3 cause to fall or flow 4 disperse; diffuse; radiate 5 get rid of [OE]

she'd /SHēd/ *v. contr.* 1 she had 2 she would

sheen /SHēn/ *n.* 1 gloss; luster 2 brightness —**sheen′y** *adj.* (**·i·er, ·i·est**) [OE: beautiful]

sheep /SHēp/ *n.* (*pl.* same) 1 domesticated mammal with a thick woolly coat 2 timid, silly, or easily led person [OE]

sheep′dog′ *n.* dog trained to guard and herd sheep

sheep′fold′ *n.* pen for sheep

sheep′ish *adj.* embarrassed or shy; ashamed —**sheep′ish·ly** *adv.*; **sheep′ish·ness** *n.*

sheep′skin′ *n.* 1 sheep's skin with the wool on 2 leather from sheep's skin; parchment 3 *Colloq.* diploma

sheer[1] /SHēr/ *adj.* 1 complete 2 perpendic-

ular 3 (of a textile) almost transparent —*adv.* 4 completely 5 perpendicularly [OE]

sheer[2] *v.* swerve or change course

sheet[1] /SHēt/ *n.* 1 rectangle of cotton, linen, etc., used for bedclothes 2 flat piece of paper, metal, etc. 3 wide expanse of water, ice, flame, falling rain, etc. [OE]

sheet[2] *n.* rope attached to the lower corner of a sail to control it [OE, rel. to SHEET[1]]

sheet′ing *n.* material for making bed sheets

sheet′ met′al *n.* metal in thin sheets

sheet′ mu′sic *n.* music published on unbound pages

Shef·field /SHef′ēld/ *n.* city in N England. Pop. 477,300

sheik or **sheikh** /SHēk, SHāk/ *n.* chief or head of an Arab tribe, family, or village —**sheik(h)′dom** *n.* [Ar]

shek·el /SHek′əl/ *n.* 1 chief monetary unit of modern Israel 2 coin and unit of weight in ancient Israel, etc. 3 (*pl.*) *Colloq.* money; riches [Heb]

shelf /SHelf/ *n.* (*pl.* **shelves**) 1 flat board projecting from a wall, or as part of a unit, for holding books, dishes, etc. 2 **on the shelf** put aside as no longer useful [LGer]

shelf′ life′ *n.* period during which a stored item remains usable

shell /SHel/ *n.* 1 outer case of mollusks, tortoises, eggs, nuts, etc. 2 explosive projectile for use in a gun 3 light racing boat 4 the walls of an unfinished or gutted building, ship, etc. —*v.* 5 remove the shell or pod from 6 bombard with shells 7 **shell out** *Colloq.* pay out (money) —**shell′-like′** *adj.* [OE]

she'll /SHēl/ *v. contr.* she will; she shall

shel·lac or **shel·lack** /SHəlak′/ *n.* 1 resin used for making varnish —*v.* (**·lacked, ·lack·ing**) 2 cover with shellac 3 *Colloq.* defeat utterly [fr. SHELL, LAC]

Shel·ley /SHel′ē/ 1 **Percy Bysshe** 1792–1822; English poet; his wife: 2 **Mary Wollstonecraft** 1797–1851; English novelist

SHELLFISH

shell′fish′ *n.* (*pl.* same) edible aquatic animal having a shell, as a mollusk, lobster, crab, etc.

shell′ shock′ *n.* mental breakdown caused by warfare —**shell′shocked′** *adj.*

shel·ter /SHel′tər/ *n.* 1 protection from danger, bad weather, etc. 2 place giving refuge —*v.* 3 serve as a shelter to; protect 4 find refuge

shelve /SHelv/ *v.* (**shelved, shelv·ing**) 1 put aside, esp. temporarily 2 put on a shelf 3 fit with shelves —**shelv′ing** *n.*

shelves /SHelvz/ *n. pl.* of SHELF

she·nan·i·gan /SHinan′igən/ *n.* (esp. *pl.*) *Colloq.* mischievous or dubious behavior

Shen·yang /SHən′yäNG′/ *n.* city in NE China. Pop. 3,603,700

shep·herd /SHɛp'ərd/ n. 1 (fem. **shep'herd·ess**) person employed to tend sheep 2 member of the clergy in charge of a congregation —v. 3 guide 4 herd (a crowd, etc.) [OE, rel. to SHEEP, HERD]

sher·bet /SHər'bət/ n. frozen fruit-flavored dessert [Turk and Pers fr. Ar]
• Usage: Avoid the pronunciation "sher-bert," which many regard as unacceptable. The word has only one r, in the first syllable.

Sher·i·dan /SHɛr'əd·n/ 1 **Richard Brinsley** 1751–1816; Irish dramatist 2 **Phillip Henry** 1831–88; general of Union forces in American Civil War

sher·iff /SHɛr'əf/ n. civil law-enforcement official [ult. fr. OE for 'shire official']

Sher·man /SHär'mən/ 1 **Roger** 1721–93; American statesman and patriot 2 **William Tecumseh** 1820–91; general of Union forces in American Civil War

Sher·pa /SHɛr'pə/ n. (pl. same or **·pas**) member of a people living on the Nepal-Tibet borders

sher·ry /SHɛr'ē/ n. (pl. **·ries**) fortified wine orig. from S Spain [Xeres in Andalusia]

she's /SHēz/ v. contr. 1 she is 2 she has

Shet'land Is'lands /SHɛt'lənd/ n. group of islands off the NE coast of Scotland

Shev·ard·na·dze /SHɛv'ərdnäd'zə/, **Eduard** 1928– ; former Soviet foreign minister; president of Georgia (1992–)

shib·bo·leth /SHĭb'ələTH/ n. 1 long-standing doctrine, phrase, etc., held to be true by a party or sect 2 password [Heb (Judg. 12:6)]

shied /SHīd/ v. past and past part. of SHY[1], SHY[2]

shield /SHēld/ n. 1a piece of armor held in front of the body for protection when fighting b person or thing giving protection 2 shield-shaped trophy, protective screen on a machine, etc. —v. 3 protect; screen [OE]

shi·er /SHī'ər/ adj. compar. of SHY[1]

shi·est /SHī'əst/ adj. superl. of SHY[1]

shift /SHĭft/ v. 1 (cause to) change or move from one position to another 2 change (gear) in a vehicle 3 get along; survive —n. 4 act of shifting 5a relay of workers b time for which they work 6 woman's straight un-waisted dress or petticoat 7 typewriter key for switching between capital and small letters, etc. 8 gear lever in a vehicle [OE]

shift'less adj. lacking resourcefulness; lazy

shift'y adj. Colloq. (**·i·er**, **·i·est**) evasive; deceitful —**shift'i·ly** adv.; **shift'i·ness** n.

Shi·jia·zhuang /SHē'jē·ä'zHᴕ·äNG'/ n. (formerly **Shih'chia'chuang**) city in NE China. Pop. 1,068,400

Shi·ko·ku /SHĭkō'kōō/ n. island in SW Japan, S of Honshu

shill /SHĭl/ Slang. n. 1 person pretending to be a customer to attract others, as at an auction, gambling casino, etc. —v. 2 act as a shill

shil·le·lagh /SHĭlā'lē/ n. cudgel [for village in Ireland]

shil·ling /SHĭl'ĭNG/ n. former British coin and monetary unit worth one-twentieth of a pound [OE]

shil·ly-shal·ly /SHĭl'ēSHAl'ē/ v. (**·lied**, **·ly·ing**) be undecided; vacillate [fr. shall I?]

shim /SHĭm/ n. 1 thin wedge for filling space to make parts fit properly —v. (**shimmed**, **shim·ming**) 2 fit or fill up with a shim

shim·mer /SHĭm'ər/ v. 1 shine faintly —n. 2 faint light [OE]

shin /SHĭn/ n. 1 front of the leg below the knee —v. (**shinned**, **shin·ning**) 2 climb by clinging with the arms and legs [OE]

shin'·bone n. TIBIA

shin'dig n. Colloq. lively, noisy party [prob. fr. shindy brawl]

shine /SHīn/ v. (**shone** or **shined**, **shin·ing**) 1 emit or reflect light; be bright; glow 2 (of the sun, a star, etc.) be visible 3 focus the light of (a lamp, etc.) 4 (**shined**, **shin·ing**) polish 5 be brilliant; excel —n. 6 light; brightness 7 polish [OE]

shin'er n. Colloq. black eye

shin·gle[1] /SHĭNG'gəl/ n. 1 thin, rectangular tile used on roofs, etc., in overlapping rows 2 shingled haircut —v. (**·gled**, **·gling**) 3 roof with shingles 4 cut (hair) short [L scindula]

shin·gle[2] n. small, smooth pebbles, esp. on the seashore —**shin'gly** adj.

shin'gles n. pl. (treated as pl. or sing.) HERPES ZOSTER [L cingulum girdle]

Shin·to /SHĭn'tō/ n. Japanese religion based on the worship of ancestors —**Shin'to·ism** /-izəm/, **Shin'to·ist** /-ist/ n. [Chin: way of the gods]

shin'y adj. (**·i·er**, **·i·est**) 1 having a shine 2 (of clothing) with the nap worn off —**shin'i·ness** n.

ship /SHĭp/ n. 1 large seagoing vessel 2 aircraft 3 crew of a vessel —v. (**shipped**, **ship·ping**) 4 put, take, or send, as in a ship, etc. 5a take in (water) over a vessel's side, etc. b remove (oars) from rowlocks 6 embark —**ship'per** n. [OE]

-ship suffix forming nouns denoting: 1 quality or condition (hardship) 2 status, office, etc. (authorship) 3 tenure (chairmanship) 4 skill (workmanship) 5 members of a group (readership) [OE]

ship'board' adj. used or occurring on board a ship

ship'build'er n. person, company, etc., that constructs ships —**ship'build'ing** n.

ship'mate' n. fellow member of a crew

ship'ment n. 1 amount of goods shipped 2 act of shipping goods, etc.

ship'ping n. 1 transport of goods, etc. 2 ships, as a navy, transports collectively, etc.

ship'shape' adv. & adj. trim; neat

ship'wreck' n. 1a destruction of a ship by a storm, foundering, etc. b ship so destroyed 2 ruin; destruction —v. 3 inflict shipwreck on 4 suffer shipwreck

ship'wright' n. 1 shipbuilder 2 ship's carpenter

ship'yard' n. place where ships are built

Shi·raz /SHĭräz'/ n. city in SW Iran. Pop. 848,300

shire /SHīr/ n. county in Great Britain [OE]

shirk /SHərk/ v. avoid (duty, work, etc.) —**shirk'er** n. [Ger Schurke scoundrel]

shirr /SHər/ n. 1 gathered threads in a fabric to form smocking —v. 2 gather (fabric) with parallel threads 3 bake eggs —**shirr'ing** n.

shirt /SHərt/ n. 1 loose-fitting tailored upper-body garment 2 keep one's shirt on Colloq. keep one's temper —**shirt'less** adj. [OE]

shirt'-tail' n. tails of a shirt below the waist

shirt'waist' *n.* **1** woman's tailored blouse styled like a shirt **2** (usu. **shirt'waist' dress'**) dress styled like a long shirt

shish ke-bab /SHISH′ kəbäb′/ *n.* pieces of meat and vegetables grilled on skewers [Turk. rel. to KEBAB]

shiv /SHIV/ *n.* *Slang.* knife, esp. as a weapon [prob. fr. Rom *chiv* blade]

Shi-va /SHĒ′və/ *n.* Hindu god of destruction and regeneration

shiv-er[1] /SHIV′ər/ *v.* **1** tremble with cold, fear, etc. —*n.* **2** sudden trembling movement —**shiv′er·y** *adj.*

shiv-er[2] *n.* **1** small fragment or splinter —*v.* **2** break into shivers [rel. to dial. *shive* slice]

shlep /SHlep/ *v.* (**shlepped, shlep·ping**) var. sp. of SCHLEP

shmaltz /SHmälts/ *n.* var. sp. of SCHMALTZ

shoal[1] /SHŌl/ *n.* **1** multitude, esp. of fish swimming together —*v.* **2** (of fish) form shoals [Du: cf. SCHOOL[2]]

shoal[2] *n.* **1a** area of shallow water **b** submerged sandbar exposed at low water —*v.* **2** (of water) get shallower [OE]

shock[1] /SHäk/ *n.* **1** violent collision, impact, tremor, etc. **2** sudden and disturbing effect on the emotions, etc. **3** acute prostration following a wound, pain, etc. **4** discharge of electricity through a person **5** short for SHOCK ABSORBER —*v.* **6** horrify; outrage **7** affect with an electric or pathological shock [Fr *choc, choquer*]

shock[2] *n.* **1** sheaves of grain bundled together —*v.* **2** arrange (grain stalks) in shocks

shock[3] *n.* unkempt or shaggy mass of hair

shock′ ab·sorb′er *n.* pistonlike device for absorbing vibrations, etc.

shock′ cord′ *n.* elastic cord or rope for binding loose things together, tautening loose rigging, etc.; bungee cord

shock′er *n.* *Colloq.* **1** shocking person or thing **2** sensational novel, etc.

shock′ing *adj.* **1** causing shock; scandalous **2** *Colloq.* very bad —**shock′ing·ly** *adv.*

shock′ing pink′ *adj. & n.* vibrant shade of pink

shock′proof′ *adj.* resistant to the effects of shock

shock′ ther′a·py *n.* (also **shock′ treat′ment**) treatment of mental patients by electric shock, etc.

shock′ troops′ *n. pl.* troops specially trained for assault

shock′ wave′ *n.* moving volume of high air pressure caused by an explosion, etc.

shod /SHäd/ *v.* *past* and *past part.* of SHOE

shod′dy *adj.* (**·di·er, ·di·est**) **1** of inferior material or workmanship **2** counterfeit —*n.* (*pl.* **·dies**) **3** low-grade fabric made from rags —**shod′di·ly** *adv.*; **shod′di·ness** *n.*

shoe /SHōō/ *n.* **1** outer foot-covering, esp. one not reaching above the ankle **2** protective metal rim for a horse's hoof **3** (also **brake′ shoe′**) part of a brake that presses against a wheel or drum —*v.* (**shod** or **shoed, shoe·ing**) **4** fit with shoes [OE]

shoe′horn′ *n.* spoonlike implement for easing the heel into a shoe —*v.* **2** fit forcibly, as into a small space

shoe′lace′ *n.* cord for lacing up a shoe

shoe′mak′er *n.* maker or repairer of shoes —**shoe′mak′ing** *n.*

shoe′string′ *n.* **1** shoelace **2** *Colloq.* small, esp. inadequate amount of money

shoe′ tree′ *n.* shaped device for keeping an empty shoe in shape

sho-far /SHŌ′fär′/ *n.* *Judaism.* ram's horn used as a ceremonial wind instrument [Heb *shōphār*]

sho-gun /SHŌ′gən/ *n.* any of the former Japanese military leaders, hereditary absolute rulers till 1868 [Japn fr. Chin *chiang chun* army leader]

shone /SHōn/ *v.* *past* and *past part.* of SHINE

shoo /SHōō/ *interj.* **1** exclamation used to frighten away animals, etc. —*v.* (**shooed, shoo·ing**) **2** utter the word "shoo!" to drive away

shook /SHŏŏk/ *v.* *past* of SHAKE

shoot /SHōōt/ *v.* (**shot, shoot·ing**) **1** cause (a weapon) to discharge its missile **2** kill or wound with a bullet, arrow, etc. **3** send out, discharge, etc., esp. swiftly **4** come or go swiftly or vigorously **5** film or photograph **6a** score (a goal) **b** take aim at (the goal) **7** (of a pain) seem to stab **8** *Slang.* inject (a drug) —*n.* **9** young branch or new growth of a plant **10** hunting expedition, etc. —**shoot′er** *n.* [OE]

shoot′ing star′ *n.* meteor

shoot′out′ *n.* gunfight

shop /SHäp/ *n.* **1** place for the retail sale of goods or services; small store **2** place for manufacture or repair (*body shop*) **3** one's work or workplace —*v.* (**shopped, shop·ping**) **4** go to buy goods, etc. **5 shop around** search out a bargain **6 talk shop** discuss one's work —**shop′per** *n.* [Fr *eschoppe*]

shop′keep′er *n.* owner or manager of a shop

shop′lift′ *v.* steal goods while appearing to shop —**shop′lift′er** *n.*

shop′ping cen′ter *n.* (also **shop′ping mall′**) area or complex of stores

shop′talk′ *n.* **1** discussion about one's work **2** language specialized to describe a trade or profession

shop′worn′ *adj.* worn from handling, display, etc., in a shop

shore[1] /SHôr/ *n.* land adjoining the sea, a lake, etc. [LGer or Du]

shore[2] *v.* (**shored, shor·ing**) (often foll. by *up*) prop (up); support —**shor′ing** *n.* [LGer or Du]

shore′line′ *n.* line where shore and water meet

shore′ pa·trol′ *n.* *Milit.* US Navy, etc., police who serve ashore

shorn /SHôrn/ *v.* *past part.* of SHEAR

short /SHôrt/ *adj.* **1a** measuring little from head to foot, top to bottom, or end to end; not long or tall **b** not long in duration **2** deficient **3** not far-reaching **4a** concise; brief **b** curt; uncivil **5** (of the memory) unable to remember distant events **6** (of pastry) easily crumbled; flaky **7** (of stocks, etc.) sold or selling when not in hand, hoping to profit from a lower price at delivery —*adv.* **8** abruptly **9** so as not to reach a destination **10** without possessing stocks one has sold **11** rudely —*n.* **12** short circuit **13** short film —*v.* **14** short-circuit **15 be caught** (or **taken**) **short**

be put at a disadvantage **16 be short for** be an abbreviation for **17 for short** as a short name **18 in short** briefly —**short′ish** *adj.*; **short′ness** *n.* [OE]

short′age *n.* deficiency; lack

short′bread *n.* rich cake or cookie of butter, flour, and sugar

short′cake *n.* dessert of pastry, sponge cake, or biscuit topped with fruit and whipped cream

short′-change *v.* (**-changed, -chang·ing**) *Colloq.* cheat, esp. by giving insufficient change

short′ cir′cuit *n.* **1** electric circuit through small resistance, esp. instead of the resistance of a normal circuit —*v.* (**short′-cir′cuit**) **2** cause a short circuit (in) **3** shorten or avoid by taking a more direct route, etc.

short′com′ing *n.* deficiency; defect

short′cut′ *n.* route or method shorter than the usual one

short·en *v.* become or make shorter or short

short′en·ing *n.* fat for pastry, frying, etc.

short′fall′ *n.* deficit

short′hand′ *n.* system of rapid writing using special symbols

short′-hand′ed *adj.* understaffed·

short′horn′ *n.* animal of a breed of cattle with short horns

short′ie *n.* var. of SHORTY

short′ list′ *n.* **1** list of selected candidates from which a final choice is made —*v.* (**short′-list′**) **2** put on a short list

short′-lived′ /-livd′, -livd′/ *adj.* ephemeral

short′ly *adv.* **1** soon **2** curtly [OE]

short′ or′der *n.* order for food that can be served quickly

short′-range′ *adj.* of limited extent in space or time

short′ ribs′ *n.* ends of beef ribs cut from the forequarter and usu. boiled or stewed

shorts /shôrtz/ *n. pl.* **1** trousers reaching to the knees or higher **2** underpants

short′ shrift′ *n.* curt or dismissive treatment [OE *shrift* confession, rel. to SHRIVE]

short′-sight′ed *adj.* **1** NEAR-SIGHTED **2** lacking imagination or foresight —**short′-sight′ed·ly** *adv.*; **short′-sight′ed·ness** *n.*

short′stop′ *n.* Baseball. fielder's position between second and third bases

short′ sto′ry *n.* piece of prose fiction, shorter than a novella

short′ sub′ject *n.* short, usu. nonfiction, motion picture

short′-tem′pered *adj.* irritable; testy

short′-term′ *adj.* of or for a short period of time

short′ ton′ *n.* unit of weight equal to 2000 pounds

short′ wave′ *n.* radio wave of 120 meters or less, or frequency greater than 2.3 MHz

short′-wind′ed *adj.* easily becoming breathless

short′y *n.* (also **short′ie**) (*pl.* **-ies**) *Colloq.* person or garment shorter than average

Sho·sta·ko·vich /shäs′təkō′vich/, **Dmitri** 1906–75; Russian composer

shot[1] /shät/ *n.* **1** firing of a gun, cannon, etc. **2** attempt at hitting by shooting or throwing, etc. **3a** single nonexplosive missile for a gun, etc. **b** (*pl.*) these collectively **4a** photograph **b** continuous film sequence of same scene **5** *Colloq.* person of specified shooting skill **6**

ball thrown by a shot-putter **7** *Colloq.* **a** drink of liquor **b** hypodermic injection [OE]

shot[2] *v.* **1** *past* and *past part.* of SHOOT —*adj.* **2** (of colored fabric) woven so as to show different colors at different angles **3** *Colloq.* in ruined condition; inoperable

shot′gun′ *n.* gun for firing small shot

shot′put′ *n.* athletic contest in which a heavy metal ball is thrown for distance —**shot′-put′ter, shot′-put′ting** *n.*

should /shŏŏd/ *v. aux.* *past* of SHALL, used esp.: **1** to express obligation or likelihood (*you should have read it; they should have arrived by now*) **2** to express a tentative suggestion (*I should like to add*) **3** expressing a condition (*I should have been killed if I had gone; if you should see him*)

● Usage: See note at SHALL.

shoul·der /shōl′dər/ *n.* **1** part of the body at which the arm, foreleg, or wing is attached **2** either of the two sideways projections at the base of the neck **3** strip of land next to a road —*v.* **4** shove, esp. roughly, with the shoulder **5** take on (a burden, etc.) **6 from the shoulder** directly; frankly [OE]

shoul′der blade *n.* either of the large flat bones of the upper back; scapula

shouldn′t /shood′nt/ *v. contr.* should not

shout /shout/ *v.* **1** speak or cry loudly **2** say or express loudly —*n.* **3** loud cry [perh. rel. to SHOOT]

shove /shəv/ *v.* (**shoved, shov·ing**) **1** push vigorously **2** *Colloq.* put casually —*n.* **3** act of shoving **4 shove off** start off in a boat [OE]

shov·el /shəv′əl/ *n.* **1** spadelike tool with raised sides, for shifting coal, snow, etc. —*v.* (**-eled** or **-elled, -el·ing** or **-el·ling**) **2** move (as if) with a shovel **3** *Colloq.* move in large quantities or roughly —**shov′el·ful** *n.* (*pl.* **·fuls**) [OE]

show /shō/ *v.* (**showed, shown** or **showed, show·ing**) **1** be, allow, or cause to be, visible **2** offer for scrutiny **3** indicate or reveal (one's feelings) **4** grant (favor, mercy, etc.) **5** be or make manifest **6** demonstrate **7** conduct or lead **8** finish third in a horse race —*n.* **9** showing **10** spectacle, display, exhibition, etc. **11** outward appearance or display **12 show off: a** display to advantage **b** act pretentiously **13 show up: a** make or be conspicuous or clearly visible **b** *Colloq.* appear; arrive [OE]

Showa /shō′wə/ see HIROHITO

show′case′ *n.* **1** glass case for exhibiting goods, etc. **2** event, etc., designed to exhibit someone or something to advantage —*v.* (**·cased, ·cas·ing**) **3** display in or as if in a showcase

show′down′ *n.* final test or confrontation; climax

show·er /shou′ər/ *n.* **1** brief fall of rain, snow, etc. **2** brisk flurry of bullets, dust, etc. **3** sudden copious arrival of gifts, honors, etc. **4a** spray of water for bathing **b** apparatus used for this **5** party for giving presents to a prospective bride, etc. —*v.* **6** discharge (water, missiles, etc.) in a shower **7** bathe in a shower **8** lavishly bestow (gifts, etc.) **9** descend in a shower —**show′er·y** *adj.* [OE]

show·girl /shō′gərl′/ *n.* female performer in musicals, variety shows, etc.

show′ing *n.* **1** display; performance **2** performance judged for its quality

show·man /shō′mən/ *n.* (*pl.* ·men) **1** proprietor or manager of a show **2** person skilled at theatrical presentation —**show′man·ship** *n.*

shown /shōn/ *v. past part.* of SHOW

show′-off′ *n. Colloq.* person who shows off

show′ of hands′ *n.* raised hands indicating a vote

show′-piece′ *n.* **1** item presented for display **2** outstanding specimen

show′-place′ *n.* **1** stately home, estate, etc., open to the public **2** place known for its beauty, tasteful elegance, etc.

show′room′ *n.* room used for displaying goods for sale

show′-stop′per *n. Colloq.* action that interrupts a theatrical performance by its enthusiastic reception

show′y *adj.* (·i·er, ·i·est) **1** brilliant; gaudy **2** striking —**show′i·ly** *adv.*; **show′i·ness** *n.*

shrank /shraNGk/ *v.* (also **shrunk**) *past* of SHRINK

shrap·nel /shrap′nəl/ *n.* **1** fragments of an exploded shell, etc. **2** shell containing pieces of metal, etc. [for H. *Shrapnel*, English inventor]

shred /shred/ *n.* **1** scrap; bit; fragment —*v.* (**shred·ded, shred·ding**) **2** tear or cut into shreds —**shred′der** *n.* [OE]

Shreve·port /shrēv′pôrt′, -pōrt′/ *n.* city in La. Pop. 198,525

shrew /shrōō/ *n.* **1** mouselike long-nosed mammal **2** bad-tempered or scolding woman —**shrew′ish** *adj.* [OE]

shrewd /shrōōd/ *adj.* astute; clever and judicious —**shrewd′ly** *adv.*; **shrewd′ness** *n.* [perh. fr. obs. *shrew* to curse]

shriek /shrēk/ *n.* **1** shrill scream or sound —*v.* **2** make or utter a shriek [ON]

shrift /shrift/ *n.* SHORT SHRIFT

shrike /shrīk/ *n.* bird of prey with a strong hooked and toothed bill [OE]

shrill /shril/ *adj.* **1** piercing and high-pitched in sound —*v.* **2** utter with or make a shrill sound —**shrill′ness** *n.*; **shril′ly** *adv.*

shrimp /shrimp/ *n.* **1** (*pl.* same or -s) small edible crustacean **2** *Colloq.* very small person

shrine /shrīn/ *n.* **1** place for worship or devotion **2** tomb; receptacle, esp. for the remains of a saint **3** hallowed place [L *scrinium* bookcase]

shrink /shriNGk/ *v.* (**shrank** or **shrunk, shrunk** or **shrunk·en, shrink·ing**) **1** make or become smaller, esp. from moisture, heat, or cold **2** recoil; flinch —*n.* **3** *Slang.* psychiatrist [OE]

shrink·age /shriNGk′ij/ *n.* **1** process or degree of shrinking **2** allowance made for loss by wastage, theft, etc.

shrink′-wrap′ *v.* (-wrapped, -wrap·ping) enclose (an article) in plastic film that shrinks tightly to it

shrive /shrīv/ *v.* (**shrived** or **shrove, shriv·en** or **shrived, shriv·ing**) *Archaic* hear the confession of and absolve (a penitent) [OE *scrīfan* impose as penance]

shriv·el /shriv′əl/ *v.* (·eled or ·elled, ·el·ing or ·el·ling) contract into a wrinkled or dried-up state [perh. fr. ON]

shroud /shroud/ *n.* **1** wrapping for a corpse **2** thing that conceals **3** rope or cable supporting a mast —*v.* **4** clothe (a body) for burial **5** cover or conceal [OE: garment]

shrove /shrōv/ *v. past* of SHRIVE

Shrove′ Tues′day *n.* day before Ash Wednesday; Mardi Gras

shrub /shrəb/ *n.* any woody plant smaller than a tree; bush —**shrub′by** *adj.* [OE]

shrub·ber·y /shrəb′ərē/ *n.* shrubs collectively

shrug /shrəg/ *v.* (**shrugged, shrug·ging**) **1** slightly and momentarily raise (the shoulders) to express indifference, doubt, ignorance, etc. —*n.* **2** act of shrugging **3** shrug off dismiss as unimportant

shrunk /shrəNGk/ *v.* **1** (also **shrank**) *past* of SHRINK **2** (also **shrunk·en**) *past part.* of SHRINK

shrunk·en *adj.* **1** shriveled up —*v.* (also **shrunk**) **2** *past* of SHRINK

shtick /shtik/ *n. Slang. Colloq.* **1** show-business routine, esp. comic **2** something that concerns or engages someone [Yiddish fr. Ger *Stück* piece; act]

Shub·ra al-Khay·mah /shōōbrä′ al′kīmä(KH)′/ *n.* suburb of Cairo, Egypt. Pop. 811,000

shuck /shək/ *v.* **1** remove the outer covering from (corn, peas, etc.) —*n.* **2** outer covering

shucks /shəks/ *interj. Slang.* used as an expression of disappointment or disgust

shud·der /shəd′ər/ *v.* **1** shiver, esp. convulsively, from fear, cold, horror, repugnance, etc. —*n.* **2** act of shuddering [LGer or Du]

shuf·fle /shəf′əl/ *v.* (·fled, ·fling) **1** drag (the feet) in walking **2** rearrange or intermingle (cards or papers) —*n.* **3** act of shuffling **4** shuffling dance [LGer]

shuf′fle·board′ *n.* game in which disks are pushed with sticks along a diagram on a floor to reach scoring sections

shun /shən/ *v.* (**shunned, shun·ning**) avoid; keep clear of [OE]

shunt /shənt/ *v.* **1** move (a train) between sidings, etc.; (of a train) be shunted **2** move or put aside; redirect —*n.* **3** shunting **4** *Electr.* bypass for diverting current **5** *Surg.* bypass for the circulation of the blood [ME *schunten* shy (of a horse); akin to SHUN]

shush /shŏŏsh, shəsh/ *interj.* **1** hush! —*v.* **2** order or request (a person or people) to be quiet by saying "shush" [imit.]

shut /shət/ *v.* (**shut, shut·ting**) **1a** move (a door, window, lid, etc.) to block an opening **b** close (a room, box, eye, etc.); block by moving a door, etc. **2** become or be capable of being closed **3** fold or contract (a book, telescope, etc.) **4** keep in or out of a place, etc. **5** **shut down: a** stop (a business, etc.) from operating **b** (of a business, etc.) stop operating **6** **shut off** stop the flow of (water, gas, money, etc.) **7** **shut out: a** exclude **b** prevent from scoring **8** **shut up: a** imprison **b** *Colloq.* stop talking [OE]

shut′-down′ *n.* closure of a factory, etc.

shut′-eye′ *n. Colloq.* sleep

shut′-in′ *n.* invalid confined indoors

shut·ter /shət′ər/ *n.* **1** movable often louvered cover for a window **2** device that exposes the film in a camera —*v.* **3** provide or close with shutters

shut·tle /SHət'l/ *n.* **1** (in a loom) spool-like instrument for threading the weft into the warp **2** train, bus, etc., used regularly for traveling back and forth over a short route —*v.* (**·tled, ·tling**) **3** (cause to) move to and fro like a shuttle [OE, rel. to SHOOT]

shut'tle·cock' *n.* cork with a ring of feathers, or a similar plastic device, struck in badminton

shy[1] /SHĪ/ *adj.* (**shy·er** or **shi·er, shy·est** or **shi·est**) **1** timid and nervous in company **2** (in *comb.*) disliking or fearing (*gun-shy*) **3** *Colloq.* lacking —*v.* (**shied, shy·ing**) **4** turn suddenly aside in fright **5** avoid —**shy'ly** *adv.*; **shy'ness** *n.* [OE]

shy[2] *v.* (**shied, shy·ing**) fling; throw

shy·ster /SHĪ'stər/ *n. Colloq.* dishonest or unscrupulous lawyer

Si *symb.* silicon

Si·am /sī-am'/ *n.* see THAILAND

Si·a·mese /sī'əmēz', -mēs'/ *n.* (*pl.* same) **1** native or language of Thailand **2** (**Si'a·mese cat'**) cat of a cream-colored, short-haired breed with dark markings and blue eyes —*adj.* **3** of Siam, its people, or language

Si'a·mese twins' *n. pl.* twins born joined at some part of the body

Si·an *n.* see XIAN

Si·be·li·us /sibā'lēəs/, **Jean** 1865–1957; Finnish composer

sib·i·lant /sib'ələnt/ *adj.* **1** sounded with a hiss **2** hissing —*n.* **3** sibilant letter or sound —**sib'i·lance, sib'i·lan·cy** *n.*; **sib'i·late** /-lāt/ *v.* (**·lat·ed, ·lat·ing**) [L]

sib·ling /sib'liNG/ *n.* brother or sister [OE]

sib·yl /sib'əl/ *n.* pagan prophetess —**sib'yl·line'** /-līn, -lēn/ *adj.* [Gk *sibulla*]

sic /sik/ *adv.* used, spelled, etc., as written [L: so]

sic or **sick** /sik/ *v.* (**sicced** or **sicked, sic·cing** or **sick·ing**) urge (a dog) to attack [fr. SEEK]

Sic·i·ly /sis'əlē/ *n.* island in the Mediterranean Sea S of mainland Italy. Capital: Palermo

sick /sik/ *adj.* **1** unwell; ill **2** nauseated **3** disgusted by having had enough **4** *Colloq.* (of a joke, etc.) cruel; morbid [OE]

sick' bay' *n.* infirmary for those who are sick, esp. aboard ship

sick'bed' *n.* invalid's bed

sick·en /sik'ən/ *v.* disgust —**sick'en·ing** *adj.*; **sick'en·ing·ly** *adv.*

sick·le /sik'əl/ *n.* short-handled tool with a semicircular blade, used for reaping, etc. [OE]

sick' leave' *n.* leave granted because of illness

sick'le cell' *n.*-shaped or abnormal **·e·mi·a** *n.* form of anemia marked by misshapen red blood cells, pain, and ulcers, chiefly afflicting black people

sick'ly *adj.* (**·li·er, ·li·est**) **1** weak; apt to be ill **2** faint; pale **3** causing ill health **4** sentimental or mawkish [rel. to SICK]

sick'ness *n.* **1** being ill **2** disease **3** nausea

sick' pay' *n.* pay given during sick leave

Sid·dhar·tha /sidär'tə, -THə/ see BUDDHA

side /sīd/ *n.* **1a** each of the surfaces bounding an object **b** inner or outer surface **c** such a surface as distinct from the top or bottom, front or back **2a** right or left part of a person or animal, esp. of the torso **b** left or right half or a specified part of a thing **3** direction **4**

either surface of a thing having two surfaces **5** aspect of an issue, etc. **6** each of two competing groups in war, politics, games, etc. **7** one of two or more lines of a plane figure **8** line of descent through one parent —*v.* (**sid·ed, sid·ing**) **9** associate (oneself) with a faction **10 on the side: a** as a sideline **b** illicitly **c** as a side dish **11 side by side** standing together; facing in the same direction **12 take sides** support a faction, cause, etc. [OE]

side' arm' *n.* **1** weapon, as a pistol, dagger, etc., worn at the belt —*adj. & adv.* (**side' arm'**) **2** done or made with the arm below shoulder height

side'board' *n.* cupboard for dishes, table linen, etc.

side'burns' *n. pl.* man's facial hair in front of the ears [earlier *burnsides*, after US Gen. A.E. BURNSIDE]

side'car' *n.* pod for a passenger attached to the side of a motorcycle

side' dish' *n.* vegetable or other food served with a main course

side'kick' *n. Colloq.* **1** friend **2** henchman

side'light' *n.* item of incidental information

side'line *n.* **1** work done in addition to one's main activity **2** auxiliary line of merchandise **3** line bounding the side of a playing field —*v.* (**·lined, ·lin·ing**) **4** put on the sidelines **5 on the sidelines** not directly concerned

side'long *adj.* **1** oblique —*adv.* **2** obliquely

side'man' *n.* (*pl.* **·men'**) musician in a band

si·de·re·al /sīdir'ēəl/ *adj.* of the stars [L *sidus sider-* star]

side'sad'dle *n.* **1** saddle for riding with both legs on the same side —*adv.* **2** riding in this position

side'show' *n.* small show or stall at a circus, fair, etc.

side'split'ting *adj.* causing hearty laughter

side'step' *n.* **1** step to the side —*v.* (**·stepped, ·step·ping**) **2** avoid by stepping sideways **3** evade

side'swipe' *n.* **1** glancing blow on or from the side —*v.* (**·swiped, ·swip·ing**) **2** hit with a sideswipe

side'track' *v.* divert or diverge from the main course or issue

side'walk' *n.* paved track for pedestrians

side'wall' *n.* side casing of a tire, between the rim and the tread

side·ways /sīd'wāz/ (also **side'wise'** /-wīz'/) *adv.* **1** to or from a side **2** with the front facing toward the side —*adj.* **3** to or from a side

sid'ing *n.* **1** short track at the side of a railway line, used for loading, etc. **2** exterior covering for the sides of a frame building

si·dle /sī'd'l/ *v.* (**·dled, ·dling**) walk sideways, esp. timidly or furtively [shortening of SIDELONG]

Si·don /sī'd'n/ *n.* seaport in Lebanon Pop. 100,000

SIDS /sidz/ *abbr.* sudden infant death syndrome; crib death

siege /sēj, sēZH/ *n.* **1** surrounding and blockading of a town, building, etc. **2 lay siege to** conduct the siege of [ME & OFr *sege* seat]

Sie·mens /sē'mənz, zē'-/, (**Ernst**) **Werner**

von 1816–92; German electrical engineer and inventor

si·er·ra /sē·er'ə/ n. long, jagged mountain chain [Sp fr. L *serra* saw]

Si·er·ra Le·one /sē·er'ə lē·ōn'/ n. republic in W Africa on the Atlantic Ocean. Capital: Freetown. Pop. 4,373,000 —**Si·er·ra Le·o'ne·an** /·nēon/ n. & adj.

si·es·ta /sē·es'tə/ n. afternoon sleep or rest, esp. in hot countries [Sp fr. L *sexta (hora)* sixth hour]

sieve /siv/ n. 1 perforated or meshed utensil for separating solids or coarse material from liquids or fine particles —v. (**sieved, sieving**) 2 sift [OE]

sift /sift/ v. 1 put through a sieve 2 separate (finer or coarser parts) from material 3 examine (evidence, facts, etc.) [OE]

sigh /sī/ v. 1 emit an audible breath in sadness, weariness, relief, etc. 2 (foll. by *for*) yearn for —n. 3 act or sound of sighing [OE]

sight /sīt/ n. 1 faculty of seeing; eyesight 2 act of seeing or being seen 3 thing seen 4 range of vision 5 noteworthy feature of a place 6a device on a gun, telescope, etc., for assisting aim or observation b aim or observation so gained 7 *Colloq.* unsightly person or thing —v. 8 see 9 aim (a gun, etc.) 10 at (or on) **sight** as soon as seen 11 **in sight** visible 12 **out of sight: a** beyond one's view b *Slang.* marvelous; excellent [OE, rel. to SEE[1]]

sight'ed adj. 1 not blind 2 (in comb.) having specified kind of vision (*long-sighted*)

sight'less adj. blind

sight'ly adj. attractive to look at

sight'-read /·rēd'/ v. read (music) at sight

sight'seer /sīt'sē'ər/ n. person visiting the sights of a place —**sight'see'ing** n.

sig·ma /sig'mə/ n. eighteenth letter of the Greek alphabet (Σ, σ, or, when final, ς) [L fr. Gk]

sign /sīn/ n. 1 thing indicating a quality, state, future event, etc. 2 mark, symbol, etc. 3 gesture or action conveying an order, etc. 4 signboard; signpost 5 each of the twelve divisions of the zodiac —v. 6a write (one's name) b sign (a document) 7 communicate by gesture 8 engage or be engaged by signing a contract, etc. 9 **sign away** relinquish (property, etc.) by signing 10 **sign in** sign or cause to sign a register 11 **sign off** end broadcasting 12 **sign on** or **up** sign or cause to sign a contract; enlist [L *signum*]

sig·nal /sig'nəl/ n. 1 conventional sign conveying information 2 direct cause of action, etc. 3 electrical impulse or impulses or radio waves transmitted as a signal —v. (**·naled** or **·nalled, ·nal·ing** or **·nal·ling**) 4 make signals 5 transmit or express by signal; announce —**sig'nal·er** or **sig'nal·ler** n. [L: *signum* sign]

sig'nal·ize' v. (**·ized, ·iz·ing**) 1 make noteworthy or remarkable 2 indicate

sig·nal·man /sig'nəlman/ n. (pl. **·men**) operator of signals, as in the army or on a railroad

sig·na·to·ry /sig'nətôr'ē/ n. (pl. **·ries**) 1 party that has signed an agreement —adj. 2 having signed an agreement [L, rel. to SIGN]

sig·na·ture /sig'nəCHər/ n. 1 person's name,

initials, etc., used in signing 2 *Mus.* a group of sharps or flats indicating the key b notation showing the tempo of a piece. 3 *Printing.* section of a book made from one folded sheet [MedL, rel. to SIGNATORY]

sign'board' n. board displaying a name, poster, advertisement, etc.

sig·net /sig'nit/ n. small seal [Fr or MedL, rel. to SIGN]

sig·nif·i·cance /signif'ikəns/ n. 1 importance 2 meaning 3 being significant [L, rel. to SIGNIFY]

sig·nif·i·cant /signif'ikənt/ adj. 1 having a meaning; indicative 2 noteworthy; important —**sig·nif'i·cant·ly** adv. [L, rel. to SIGNIFY]

sig·ni·fy /sig'nifī'/ v. (**·fied, ·fy·ing**) 1 be a sign or indication of; mean 2 make known 3 be of importance; matter —**sig'ni·fi·ca'tion** /·fikā'sнən/ n. [L, rel. to SIGN]

sign' lan'guage n. system of communication by gestures, used esp. by the deaf

sign' of the cross' n. sign made by tracing a cross with the hand

si·gnor /sēnyôr'/ n. (pl. **·gno·ri** /·nyôr'ē/) title used of or to an Italian man [L *senior* SENIOR]

si·gno·ra /sēnyôr'ə/ n. (pl. **·re** /·re/) title used of or to an Italian woman, esp. one who is married

si·gno·ri·na /sēn'yərē'nə/ n. (pl. **·ne** /·ne/) title used of or to an Italian woman, esp. one who is unmarried

sign'post' n. 1 post with a sign indicating direction, etc. 2 indication; guide

Si·kor·sky /sikôr'skē/, Igor 1889–1972; Russian-born US aircraft designer

si·lage /sī'lij/ n. green fodder stored in a silo [fr. SILO]

si·lence /sī'ləns/ n. 1 absence of sound 2 abstinence from speech or noise 3 avoidance of mentioning —v. (**·lenced, ·lenc·ing**) 4 make silent 5 suppress [L, rel. to SILENT]

si'lenc·er n. device for reducing the noise of a gun

si·lent /sī'lənt/ adj. 1 not speaking; not making or accompanied by any sound 2 (of a partner) inactive —**si'lent·ly** adv. [L *sileo* be silent]

si'lent ma·jor'i·ty n. the mass of citizens whose opinions are not publicly expressed, usu. considered politically moderate

SILHOUETTE 1

sil·hou·ette /sil'ŏŏ·et'/ n. 1 picture showing the outline only, usu. in black on white 2 dark shadow or outline against a lighter background —v. (**·et·ted, ·et·ting**) 3 show in silhouette [for E. de *Silhouette*, French politician]

sil·i·ca /sil'ikə/ n. silicon dioxide, occurring

as quartz, etc. —**si·li·ceous** /səlɪsн'əs/ *adj.* [L *silex* -*lic*- flint]

sil'i·ca gel' *n.* hydrated silica in a granular form used as a drying agent

sil·i·cate /sɪl'ɪkāt/ *n.* compound of a metal with silicon and oxygen

sil·i·con /sɪl'ɪkən, -kän/ *n. Chem.* nonmetallic element occurring widely in silica and silicates; *symb.* Si

sil'i·con chip' *n.* microchip made of silicon

sil·i·cone /sɪl'ɪkōn/ *n.* any organic compound of silicon

Sil'i·con Val'ley *n.* area south of San Francisco with concentration of computer firms

sil·i·co·sis /sɪl'ɪkō'sɪs/ *n.* lung fibrosis caused by inhaling dust containing silica

silk /sɪlk/ *n.* 1 fine, soft, lustrous fiber produced by silkworms 2 thread or cloth from this —**silk'en** *adj.* [OE *sioloc*]

silk' screen' *n.* (also **silk-screen**) printing process in which ink is pressed through a silk stencil bearing a design to the surface below

silk'worm' *n.* caterpillar that spins a cocoon of silk

silk'y *adj.* (·i·er, ·i·est) 1 soft and smooth; like silk 2 suave —**silk'i·ly** *adv.*; **silk'i·ness** *n.*

sill /sɪl/ *n.* slab of stone, wood, or metal at the foot of a window or doorway [OE]

sil·ly /sɪl'ē/ *adj.* (·li·er, ·li·est) 1 foolish; imprudent 2 weak-minded —**sil'li·ness** *n.* [OE: happy]

SILO 1

si·lo /sɪ'lō/ *n.* (*pl.* ·los) 1 pit or airtight structure in which green crops are kept for fodder 2 underground storage chamber for a guided missile [Sp fr. L]

silt /sɪlt/ *n.* 1 sediment at the bottom of a body of water —*v.* 2 choke or be choked with silt [perh. Scand]

sil·ver /sɪl'vər/ *n.* 1 grayish-white lustrous precious metallic element; *symb.* Ag 2 color of this 3 silver coins 4 household cutlery —*adj.* 5 of or colored like silver 6 noting a 25th anniversary —*v.* 7 coat or plate with silver or a similar substance —**sil'ver·y** *adj.* [OE]

sil'ver·fish' *n.* (*pl.* same) silvery, wingless insect

sil'ver lin'ing *n.* consolation or hope in misfortune

sil'ver plate' *n.* vessels, cutlery, etc., plated with silver —**sil'ver·plat'ed** *adj.*

sil'ver screen' *n.* movies collectively

sil'ver·smith' *n.* worker in silver

sil'ver·tongued' /-təNGd/ *adj.* eloquent

sil'ver·ware' *n.* articles of or plated with silver

sim·i·an /sɪm'ēən/ *adj.* 1 of the anthropoid apes 2 like an ape or monkey —*n.* 3 ape or monkey [L *simia* ape]

539

silica gel / Sinclair

sim·i·lar /sɪm'ələr/ *adj.* 1 like; alike 2 having a resemblance —**sim·i·lar·i·ty** /sɪm'əlar'ətē/ *n.* (*pl.* ·ties); **sim'i·lar·ly** *adv.* [L *similis* like]

sim·i·le /sɪm'əlē/ *n.* comparison of one thing with another using the words *like* or *as* (e.g., *as brave as a lion*) [L, neut. of *similis* like]

si·mil·i·tude /simɪl'ət(y)ŏŏd/ *n.* likeness; resemblance [L, rel. to SIMILE]

Si·mi Val'ley /sɪmē', sē'mē/ *n.* city in Calif. Pop. 100,217

sim·mer /sɪm'ər/ *v.* 1 bubble or boil gently 2 be in a state of suppressed anger or excitement —*n.* 3 simmering condition 4 **simmer down** become less agitated

Si·mon /sɪ'mən/, (**Marvin**) **Neil** 1927– ; US dramatist

Si'mon Pe'ter see PETER, ST.

si·mo·ny /sɪ'mənē/ *n.* buying or selling of ecclesiastical privileges [fr. *Simon* Magus (Acts 8:18)]

sim·per /sɪm'pər/ *v.* 1 smile in a silly or affected way —*n.* 2 such a smile

sim·ple /sɪm'pəl/ *adj.* (·pler, ·plest) 1 understood or done easily 2 plain 3 not compound or complex 4 unqualified; straightforward 5 foolish; feeble-minded —**sim'ple·ness** *n.* [L *simplus*]

sim'ple in'ter·est *n.* interest payable on a capital sum only

sim'ple-mind'ed *adj.* foolish; feeble-minded —**sim'ple-mind'ed·ness** *n.*

sim·ple·ton /sɪm'pəltən/ *n.* fool

sim·plic·i·ty /simplɪs'ətē/ *n.* fact or condition of being simple

sim·pli·fy /sɪm'pləfī'/ *v.* (·fied, ·fy·ing) make simple or simpler —**sim'pli·fi·ca'tion** /-fɪkā'sнən/ *n.*

sim·plis·tic /simplɪs'tɪk/ *adj.* excessively or affectedly simple —**sim·plis'ti·cal·ly** *adv.*

sim'ply *adv.* 1 in a simple manner 2 absolutely 3 merely

sim·u·late /sɪm'yəlāt'/ *v.* (·lat·ed, ·lat·ing) 1 pretend 2 imitate; counterfeit —**sim'u·la'tion**, **sim'u·la'tor** *n.* [L, rel. to SIMILAR]

si·mul·ta·ne·ous /sɪ'məltə'nēəs/ *adj.* happening, functioning, etc., at the same time —**si'mul·ta·ne'i·ty** /-tənā'ətē/ *n.*; **si'mul·ta'ne·ous·ly** *adv.* [L *simul* at the same time]

sin[1] /sɪn/ *n.* 1a breaking of divine or moral law, esp. deliberately b such an act 2 offense against good taste or propriety, etc. —*v.* (**sinned, sin·ning**) 3 commit a sin —**sin'ful** *adj.*; **sin'ful·ly** *adv.*; **sin'ful·ness** *n.* [OE]

sin[2] *abbr.* sine

Si·na·lo·a /sē'nəlō'ə/ *n.* state of NW Mexico, on the Gulf of California. Capital: Culiacán. Pop. 2,204,100

Si·na·tra /sənä'trə/, **Frank (Francis Albert)** 1915– ; US singer and film actor

since /sɪns/ *prep.* 1 throughout or during the period after —*conj.* 2 during the time after 3 because —*adv.* 4 from that time or event until now 5 ago [OE: after that]

sin·cere /sinsɛr'/ *adj.* (·cer·er, ·cer·est) 1 free from pretense 2 genuine; honest; frank —**sin·cere'ly** *adv.*; **sin·cer'i·ty** /-ser'ətē/ *n.* [L]

Sin·clair /sɪn'klâr/, sɪNG', -klər/, **Upton** 1878–1968; US novelist

sine /sīn/ *n.* ratio of the side opposite a given angle (in a right-angled triangle) to the hypotenuse [L SINUS]

si·ne·cure /sī'nəkyŏŏr', sin'ə-/ *n.* profitable or prestigious position requiring little or no work [L *sine cura* without care]

si·ne qua non /sin'ā kwä' nōn', nän'/ *n.* indispensable condition or qualification [L: without which not]

sin·ew /sin'yōō/ *n.* 1 tough, fibrous tissue uniting muscle to bone; a tendon 2 muscles; bodily strength —**sin'ew·y** *adj.* [OE]

sing /siNG/ *v.* (**sang, sung, sing·ing**) 1 utter musical sounds, esp. words with a set tune 2 utter or produce by singing 3 (of the wind, a kettle, etc.) hum, buzz, or whistle 4 *Slang.* turn informer —*n.* 5 act or spell of singing —**sing'er** *n.* [OE]

sing. *abbr.* singular

Sin·ga·pore /siNG'(g)əpôr'/ *n.* republic at the S tip of the Malay Peninsula. Capital: Singapore. Pop. 2,792,000 —**Sin'ga·po're·an** /-rēən/ *n.*

singe /sinj/ *v.* (**singed, singe·ing**) 1 burn superficially; scorch —*n.* 2 superficial burn [OE]

Sing·er /siNG'ər/ 1 Isaac Merrit 1811–75; US inventor 2 Isaac Bashevis 1904–91; Polish-born US writer

sin·gle /siNG'gəl/ *adj.* 1 one only 2 united; undivided 3 for or done by one person, etc. 4 separate 5 not married —*n.* 6 single thing, as accommodation for one 7 pop record with one item on each side 8 *Baseball.* hit enabling the batter to reach first base 9 racquet game with one player on each side 10 (*pl.*) unmarried people —*v.* (**·gled, ·gling**) 11 (foll. by *out*) choose for special attention, treatment, etc. 12 *Baseball.* hit a single —**sin'gle·ness** *n.*; **sin'gly** *adv.* [L *singulus*]

sin·gle-breast·ed *adj.* (of a coat, etc.) overlapping little down the front

sin'gle file' *n.* 1 line of people one behind another —*adv.* 2 one behind the other

sin'gle-hand'ed *adv.* without help —**sin'gle-hand'ed·ly** *adv.*

sin'gle-mind'ed *adj.* having or intent on only one aim —**sin'gle-mind'ed·ly** *adv.*; **sin'gle-mind'ed·ness** *n.*

sin'gle par'ent *n.* person bringing up a child or children alone

sin·gle·ton /siNG'gəltən/ *n.* one card only of a suit in a player's hand

sing'song *n.* monotonously rising and falling

sin·gu·lar /siNG'gyələr/ *adj.* 1 unique; outstanding; extraordinary; strange 2 *Gram.* (of a word or form) denoting a single person or thing —*n.* 3 *Gram.* singular word or form —**sin'gu·lar'i·ty** /-lar'ətē/ *n.*; **sin'gu·lar·ly** *adv.* [L, rel. to SINGLE]

Sin·ha·lese /sin'(h)əlēz', -lēs'/ *n.* (*pl.* same) 1 member of a people forming most of the population of Sri Lanka 2 their language —*adj.* 3 of this people or language

sin·is·ter /sin'istər/ *adj.* 1 evil or villainous in appearance or manner 2 ominous [L: left]

sink /siNGk/ *v.* (**sank** or **sunk, sunk, sink·ing**) 1 fall or come slowly downward 2 disappear below the horizon 3 go below the surface of a liquid, esp. the sea 4 decline in

strength, etc. —*n.* 5 basin 6 place where foul liquid collects 7 place of vice 8 **sink in:** a penetrate; permeate b become understood —**sink'a·ble** *adj.* [OE]

sink'er *n.* weight used to sink a fishing line

sink'ing fund' *n.* money set aside bit by bit for the eventual repayment of a debt

Sino- *comb. form* Chinese; Chinese and (*Sino-American*) [Gk *Sinai*]

si·nu·ous /sin'yōōəs/ *adj.* having many curves; winding —**sin'u·os'i·ty** /-äs'ətē/ *n.* [L, rel. to SINUS]

si·nus /sī'nəs/ *n.* cavity in bone, esp. in the skull connecting with the nostrils [L: bosom; recess]

si·nus·i·tis /sī'nəsī'tis/ *n.* inflammation of a sinus

Sioux Cit'y /sōō/ *n.* city in Iowa. Pop. 80,505

Sioux Falls' *n.* city in S. Dak. Pop. 100,814

sip /sip/ *v.* (**sipped, sip·ping**) 1 drink in small mouthfuls —*n.* 2 small mouthful of liquid [perh. var. of SUP¹]

si·phon /sī'fən/ *n.* 1 tube for conveying liquid from a container to a lower level by atmospheric pressure 2 bottle from which aerated water is forced by the pressure of gas —*v.* 3 (cause to) flow through a siphon 4 divert or set aside (funds, etc.) [Gk: pipe]

sip'per *n.* 1 one who sips 2 drinking straw

sir /sər/ *n.* 1 polite form of address or reference to a man 2 (*cap.*) title prefixed to the forename of a knight, etc. [fr. SIRE]

sire /sīr/ *n.* 1 male parent of an animal, esp. a stallion 2 *Archaic.* form of address to a king 3 *Archaic.* father or male ancestor —*v.* (**sired, sir·ing**) 4 (esp. of an animal) beget [Fr fr. L *senior* SENIOR]

si·ren /sī'rən/ *n.* 1 device for making a loud wailing or warning sound 2 *Gk. Myth.* woman or winged creature whose singing lured unwary sailors on to rocks 3 temptress; seductress [Gk *seirēn*]

sir·loin /sər'loin'/ *n.* choicer part of a loin of beef [Fr, rel. to SUR-¹, LOIN]

si·roc·co /səräk'ō/ *n.* (*pl.* **·cos**) hot Saharan wind that blows over S Europe [Ar *sharūk*]

sir·up /sir'əp/ *n.* var. of SYRUP

sis /sis/ *n.* *Colloq.* sister

si·sal /sī'səl/ *n.* 1 fiber made from a Mexican agave 2 this plant [*Sisal*, the port of Yucatan]

sis·sy /sis'ē/ *n.* (*pl.* **·sies**) *Colloq.* effeminate or cowardly man or boy [fr. SIS]

sis·ter /sis'tər/ *n.* 1 woman or girl in relation to her siblings 2 female fellow member of a trade union, feminist group, etc. 3 nun 4 thing of the same type, design, or origin, etc. (*sister ship*) —**sis'ter·hood** *n.*; **sis'ter·ly** *adj.* [OE]

sis'ter-in-law' *n.* (*pl.* **sis'ters-in-law'**) 1 sister of one's spouse 2 wife of one's brother

Sis·y·phe·an /sis'əfē'ən/ *adj.* (of toil) endless and fruitless like that of the mythical Sisyphus (who endlessly pushed a stone uphill in Hades)

sit /sit/ *v.* (**sat, sit·ting**) 1 rest the buttocks on the ground or a seat while keeping the torso upright 2a (of a bird) perch or warm the eggs in its nest b (of an animal) rest with the forelegs straight and the buttocks on the ground 3 (of a committee, etc.) be in session 4 pose (for a portrait) 5 babysit 6 **sit down** sit after standing 7 **sit in:** a occupy a place

as a protest **b** (foll. by *for*) take the place of **c** (foll. by *on*) be present as a guest or observer at (a meeting, etc.) **8 sit out:** a take no part in (a dance, etc.) **b** wait till the end of **9 sit tight** *Colloq.* remain firmly in place **10 sit up: a** rise from lying to sitting **b** sit firmly upright **—sit′ter** *n.* [OE]
● Usage: See note at SET.

si·tar /sitär′/ *n.* long-necked Indian lute [Hindi]

sit·com /sit′käm/ *n. Colloq.* situation comedy

sit′-down′ *adj.* **1** (of a meal) eaten sitting at a table **2** (of a protest, etc.) with demonstrators refusing to leave a place **—n. 3** spell of sitting **4** sit-down protest, etc.

site /sīt/ *n.* **1** place; location **—v.** (sit·ed, sit·ing) **2** locate; place [L *situs*]

sit′-in *n.* protest in which a group of people occupy a usu. public place and refuse to leave

sit′ting *n.* **1** continuous period spent engaged in an activity **2** session

Sit·ting Bull /sit′iNG bŏŏl′/ c. 1831–90; Sioux Indian leader; defeated Gen. Custer's forces

sit′ting duck′ *n. Colloq.* easy target

sit′ting room′ *n.* living room; parlor

sit·u·ate /siCH′ŏŏ·āt′/ *v.* (·at·ed, ·at·ing) put in a certain position or circumstances; locate [LL *situare situat-*, rel. to SITE]
● Usage: See note at LOCATE.

sit′u·a′tion *n.* **1** place and its surroundings **2** circumstances; position; state of affairs **3** *Formal.* paid job **—sit′u·a′tion·al** *adj.*

sit′u·a′tion com′e·dy *n.* serialized television comedy in which the same characters are placed in ludicrous situations

sit′-up′ *n.* physical exercise of sitting up from a supine position without using the arms or hands

six /siks/ *adj. & n.* **1** one more than five **2** symbol for this (6, vi, VI) **3 at sixes and sevens** in confusion or disagreement **—sixth** /siksTH/ *adj. & n.* [OE]

six′-pack′ *n.* package of six bottles or cans of beer, a soft drink, etc.

six′-shoot′er *n.* (also **six′-gun′**) revolver with six chambers

six·teen /sikstēn′/ *adj. & n.* **1** one more than fifteen **2** symbol for this (16, xvi, XVI) **—six·teenth** *adj. & n.* [OE]

sixth′ sense′ *n.* supposed intuitive or extrasensory faculty

six·ty /siks′tē/ *adj. & n.* (*pl.* ·ties) **1** six times ten **2** symbol for this (60, lx, LX) **3** (*pl.*) numbers from 60 to 69, esp. the years of a century or of a person's life **—six′ti·eth** /-tēiTH/ *adj. & n.* [OE]

siz′a·ble /sīz′əbəl/ *adj.* (also **size′a·ble**) large or fairly large

size¹ /sīz/ *n.* **1** relative dimensions; magnitude **2** each of the classes into which similar things are divided according to dimensions **—v.** (sized, siz·ing) **3** sort in sizes or according to size **4 size up** *Colloq.* form a judgment of [Fr *sise*]

size² *n.* (also **siz′ing**) **1** sticky solution used in glazing paper, stiffening textiles, etc. **—v.** (sized, siz·ing) **2** treat with size [perh. SIZE¹]

-sized *comb. form* (also *Colloq.* **-size**) of a specified size (*economy-sized*)

siz·zle /siz′əl/ *v.* (·zled, ·zling) **1** sputter or hiss, esp. in frying **2** *Colloq.* be very hot or

excited, etc. **—n. 3** sizzling sound **—siz′zling** *adj. & adv.* [imit.]

S.J. *abbr.* Society of Jesus (Jesuit)

skate¹ /skāt/ *n.* **1** ICE SKATE **2** ROLLER SKATE **—v.** (skat·ed, skat·ing) **3** move on skates **—skat′er** *n.* [Du *schaats* fr. Fr]

skate² *n.* (*pl.* same or ·s) flat, raylike marine fish [ON]

skate′board′ *n.* **1** short narrow board on two pairs of wheels for riding on while standing **—v. 2** ride on a skateboard **—skate′board′er** *n.*

ske·dad·dle /skidad′l/ *v.* (·dled, ·dling) *Colloq.* depart quickly; flee

skeet /skēt/ *n.* (also **skeet′ shoot′ing**) sport of shooting at targets released into the air

skein /skān/ *n.* **1** loosely coiled bundle of yarn or thread **2** flock of wild geese, etc., in flight [Fr *escaigne*]

skel·e·ton /skel′ət·n/ *n.* **1** hard framework of bones of an animal **2** supporting framework or structure of a thing **—skel′e·tal** *adj.* [Gk *skeletos* dried up]

skel′e·ton key′ *n.* key designed to fit many locks

skep·tic /skep′tik/ *n.* **1** person inclined to doubt accepted opinions, ideas, etc. **2** philosopher who questions the possibility of knowledge **—skep′ti·cal** *adj.*; **skep′ti·cal·ly** *adv.*; **skep′ti·cism** /-tisiz′əm/ *n.* [Gk *skeptikos* inquiring]

sketch /skeCH/ *n.* **1** rough or unfinished drawing or painting **2** rough draft or general outline **3** short usu. humorous play or story **—v. 4** make or give a sketch of **5** draw sketches [Gk *skhēdios* extempore]

sketch′y *adj.* (·i·er, ·i·est) imprecise; rough; vague **—sketch′i·ly** *adv.*; **sketch′i·ness** *n.*

skew /skyŏŏ/ *n.* **1** slant **—v. 2** distort **3** move obliquely [Fr, rel. to ESCHEW]

skew·er /skyŏŏ′ər/ *n.* **1** wooden or metal pin for holding meat together while cooking **—v. 2** fasten together or pierce (as) with a skewer

ski /skē/ *n.* (*pl.* ·s) **1** each of a pair of long narrow strips of wood, etc., for gliding over snow **—v.** (skied, ski·ing) **2** travel on skis **—ski′er** *n.* [Norw fr. ON]

skid /skid/ *v.* (skid·ded, skid·ding) **1** slide on slippery ground, esp. sideways or obliquely **—n. 2** act of skidding **3** strong base for supporting heavy objects during moving **4** runner beneath an aircraft for use when landing **5 on the skids** *Colloq.* on the way out; failing **6 put the skids under** *Colloq.* hasten the downfall of

skid′ row′ /rō′/ *n.* part of a town frequented by vagrants, etc.

skiff /skif/ *n.* light boat for rowing, sailing, etc. [Fr *esquif*, rel. to SHIP]

ski′ jump′ *n.* steep slope leveling off sharply to allow a skier to leap through the air **—ski′ jump′er, ski′ jump′ing** *n.*

ski′ lift′ *n.* device for carrying skiers up a slope, usu. a cable with hanging seats

skill /skil/ *n.* ability to do something well; technique **—skilled** *adj.* [ON: difference]

skil·let /skil′it/ *n.* frying pan [Fr]

skill·ful /skil′fəl/ *adj.* having or showing skill **—skill′ful·ly** *adv.*; **skill′ful·ness** *n.*

skim /skim/ v. (**skimmed, skim·ming**) 1 take a floating layer from the surface of (a liquid) 2 barely touch (a surface) in passing over 3 deal with or treat, read or look over superficially 4 go or glide lightly —**skim′mer** n. [Fr, rel. to SCUM]

skim′ milk′ n. (also **skimmed′ milk′**) milk from which the cream has been removed

skimp /skimp/ v. (also **scrimp**) be stingy [cf. SCRIMP]

skimp′y adj. (**·i·er, ·i·est**) meager; insufficient —**skimp′i·ness** n.

skin /skin/ n. 1 flexible covering of the body of a living being 2 hide 3 outer layer or covering, esp. of a fruit, sausage, etc. —v. (**skinned, skin·ning**) 4 remove the skin from 5 graze (part of the body) 6 Slang. swindle —**skin′less** adj. [ON]

skin′ deep′ adj. superficial

skin′-div′er n. underwater swimmer without a diving-suit, usu. with scuba and flippers —**skin′-div′ing** n.

skin′flint′ n. miser

skin′head′ n. youth with a shaven head, esp. one of a gang

Skin·ner /skin′ər/, **B(urrhus) F(rederic)** 1904–90; US psychologist

skin′ny adj. (**·ni·er, ·ni·est**) thin; emaciated —**skin′ni·ness** n.

skin′-tight′ adj. (of a garment) very close-fitting

skip /skip/ v. (**skipped, skip·ping**) 1 move along lightly, esp. with alternate hops 2 move quickly from one point, subject, etc., to another 3 omit parts of (a text, subject, etc.) 4 Colloq. avoid 5 Colloq. leave hurriedly —n. 6 skipping movement or action [prob. Scand]

skip′per n. 1 captain of a ship or aircraft —v. 2 be captain of [LGer or Du schipper]

skir·mish /skər′mish/ n. 1 minor battle —v. 2 engage in a skirmish [Fr fr. Gmc]

skirt /skərt/ n. 1 woman's garment hanging from the waist 2 the part of a coat, etc., hanging below the waist —v. 3 go or lie along or around the edge of 4 avoid [ON, rel. to SHIRT]

ski′ run′ n. slope prepared for skiing

skit /skit/ n. light, usu. short, piece of satire or burlesque [perh. fr. ON, rel. to SHOOT]

ski′ tow′ n. apparatus for towing skiers up a slope on their skis

skit·tish /skit′ish/ adj. 1 lively; playful 2 (of a horse, etc.) nervous [perh. rel. to SKIT]

skiv·vy /skiv′ē/ n. (pl. **-vies**) 1 T-shirt 2 (pl.) men's underwear

Skop·je /skòp′ye, -yä/ n. capital of Macedonia. Pop. 563,300

skul·dug·ger·y /skəl′dəg′(ə)rē/ n. trickery; unscrupulous behavior

skulk /skəlk/ v. move stealthily; lurk; hide [Scand]

skull /skəl/ n. 1 bony case of the brain of a vertebrate 2 head as the seat of intelligence

skull′cap′ n. brimless cap covering the crown

skunk /skəngk/ n. 1 (pl. same or -s) 1 black mammal with white stripes on the back that emits a powerful stench when attacked 2 Colloq. contemptible person [AmerInd]

sky /skī/ n. (pl. **skies**) atmosphere and outer space as seen from the earth [ON: cloud]

sky′cap′ n. airport porter

sky′ div′ing n. sport of performing acrobatic maneuvers under free fall from an airplane before opening a parachute —**sky′ div′er** n.

Skye /skī/ n. island in the Hebrides, off W Scotland

sky′-high′ adv. & adj. very high

sky′jack′ v. Colloq. hijack (an aircraft)

sky′lark′ n. 1 lark that sings while soaring —v. 2 play tricks; frolic

sky′light′ n. window in a roof

sky′line′ n. outline of buildings, etc., against the sky

sky′-rock′et n. 1 firework rocket —v. 2 (esp. of prices) rise very rapidly

sky′scrap′er n. very tall building

sky·ward /skī′wərd/ adj. & adv. (also **sky′wards**) (moving) toward the sky

sky′-writ′ing n. writing in airplane smoke-trails —**sky′writ′er** n.

slab /slab/ n. flat, thick piece of solid material

slack[1] /slak/ adj. 1 (of rope, etc.) loosely hanging; not taut 2 inactive; sluggish 3 negligent; remiss 4 (of tide, etc.) neither ebbing nor flowing —n. 5 slack part of a rope 6 slack period 7 (pl.) informal trousers —v. 8 loosen (rope, etc.) —**slack′ness** n. [OE]

slack[2] n. coal dust or fragments of coal [prob. LGer or Du]

slack·en /slak′ən/ v. make or become slack

slack′er n. shirker

slag /slag/ n. refuse left after smelting [LGer]

slain /slān/ v. past part. of SLAY

slake /slāk/ v. (**slaked, slak·ing**) 1 satisfy (thirst, a desire, etc.) 2 temper (quicklime) by combination with water [OE, rel. to SLACK[1]]

sla·lom /slä′ləm/ n. ski race down a zigzag obstacle course [Norw]

slam[1] /slam/ v. (**slammed, slam·ming**) 1 shut forcefully and loudly 2 Slang. criticize severely —n. 3 sound or action of slamming [prob. Scand]

slam[2] n. Bridge. winning of 12 (**lit′tle slam′**) or 13 (**grand′ slam′**) tricks

slan·der /slan′dər/ n. 1 false and damaging utterance about a person 2 uttering of this —v. 3 utter slander about —**slan′der·ous** adj. [Fr esclandre, rel. to SCANDAL]

slang /slang/ n. words, phrases, or meanings, regarded as very informal or taboo, or as used by a specific profession, group, etc. —**slang′y** adj. (**·i·er, ·i·est**)

slant /slant/ v. 1 slope; lie or (cause to) go at an angle 2 present (information) in a biased or particular way —n. 3 slope; oblique position 4 point of view, esp. a biased one —adj. 5 sloping [Scand]

slap /slap/ v. (**slapped, slap·ping**) 1 strike with the palm or a flat object, or so as to make a similar noise 2 lay (down) forcefully 3 put hastily or carelessly —n. 4 blow with the palm or a flat object 5 rebuke; insult [LGer, imit.]

slap′dash′ adj. 1 hasty and careless —adv. 2 in this manner

slap′-hap′py adj. Colloq. 1 befuddled 2 silly

slap′stick′ n. boisterous comedy

slash /slash/ v. 1 cut or gash with a knife, etc. 2 deliver or aim cutting blows 3 reduce (prices, etc.) drastically —n. 4 slashing cut or stroke 5 slanting mark

slat /slat/ *n.* thin, narrow piece of wood, etc. [Fr *esclat* splinter]

slate /slāt/ *n.* 1 (esp. bluish-gray) rock easily split into flat smooth plates 2 piece of this as a tile or for writing on 3 bluish gray 4 list of nominees for office, etc. —*v.* (slat·ed, slat·ing) 5 roof with slates 6 nominate for office, etc. —*adj.* 7 of slate or the color of slate [Fr *esclate*, fem. of *esclat*, rel. to SLAT]

slath·er /slaTH′ər/ *v.* lavish on thickly

slat·tern /slat′ərn/ *n.* slovenly woman —slat′tern·ly *adj.*

slaugh·ter /slôt′ər/ *v.* 1 kill (animals) 2 kill (people) ruthlessly or on a great scale —*n.* 3 act of slaughtering —slaugh′ter·er *n.* [ON, rel. to SLAY]

slaugh′ter·house *n.* place for the butchering of animals for food

Slav /släv/ *n.* 1 member of a group of peoples in central and eastern Europe speaking Slavonic languages —*adj.* 2 of the Slavs [L *Sclavus*, ethnic name]

slave /slāv/ *n.* 1 person who is owned by and has to serve another 2 drudge; hard worker 3 obsessive devotee —*v.* (slaved, slav·ing) 4 work very hard [Fr *esclave* fr. L *Sclavus* SLAV (captive)]

slave′driv·er *n.* 1 overseer of slaves 2 *Colloq.* demanding boss

sla·ver¹ /slā′vər/ *n.* ship or person engaged in the slave trade

sla·ver² /slav′ər/ *v.* dribble; drool [LGer or Du]

slav·er·y /slā′v(ə)rē/ *n.* 1 condition of a slave 2 drudgery 3 practice of having slaves

slave′trade′ *n.* dealing in slaves

Slav·ic /släv′ik/ *adj.* 1 of the group of languages including Russian, Polish, and Czech 2 of the Slavs —*n.* 3 Slavic language-group [rel. to SLAV]

slav·ish /slā′vish/ *adj.* 1 like slaves 2 without originality —slav′ish·ly *adv.*

slay /slā/ *v.* (slew, slain, slay·ing) 1 kill 2 *Slang.* overwhelm, esp. with humor —slay′er *n.* [OE]

sleaze /slēz/ *n. Colloq.* sleaziness [back formation fr. SLEAZY]

slea·zy *adj.* (·zi·er, ·zi·est) 1 vulgar; tawdry 2 (of fabric) flimsy; of poor texture —slea′zi·ly *adv.*; slea′zi·ness *n.*

sled /sled/ *n.* 1 vehicle on runners for use on snow —*v.* (sled·ded, sled·ding) 2 ride on a sled [LGer]

sledge /slej/ *n.* sled, esp. a large, heavy one [Du *sleedse*]

sledge′ham·mer *n.* long-handled hammer with a heavy steel head for breaking stone, etc. [OE *slecg*, rel. to SLAY]

sleek /slēk/ *adj.* 1 (of hair, skin, etc.) smooth and glossy 2 looking well-fed and comfortable —*v.* 3 make sleek —sleek′ly *adv.*; sleek′ness *n.* [var. of SLICK]

sleep /slēp/ *n.* 1 natural recurring condition of suspended consciousness, with the eyes closed and the muscles relaxed 2 state like sleep —*v.* (slept, sleep·ing) 3 be in a state of sleep 4 accommodate for sleeping 5 have sexual intercourse (with) 6 put to sleep: a anesthetize b *Euphem.* kill mercifully (an animal) —sleep′less *adj.*; sleep′less·ness *n.*; sleep′less·ly *adv.*; sleep′er *n.* [OE]

sleep′er *n.* 1 person or animal that sleeps 2

horizontal beam supporting a railway track 3 sleeping car

sleep′ing bag′ *n.* padded bag to sleep in when camping, etc.

sleep′ing car′ *n.* railroad car with sleeping berths

sleep′ing sick′ness *n.* tropical disease causing extreme lethargy

sleep′walk′ *v.* walk about while asleep —sleep′walk′er, sleep′walk′ing *n.*

sleep·y *adj.* (·i·er, ·i·est) 1 drowsy 2 quiet; inactive —sleep′i·ly *adv.*; sleep′i·ness *n.*

sleet /slēt/ *n.* 1 snow and rain falling together —*v.* 2 fall as sleet —sleet′y *adj.* [OE]

sleeve /slēv/ *n.* 1 part of a garment that encloses an arm 2 cover of a phonograph record 3 tube enclosing a rod, etc. 4 up one's sleeve concealed and in reserve —sleeved, sleeve′less *adj.* [OE]

sleigh /slā/ *n.* sled [Du *slee*, rel. to SLEDGE]

sleight′ of hand′ /slīt/ *n.* dexterity, esp. in conjuring [ON, rel. to SLY]

slen·der /slen′dər/ *adj.* 1a of small girth or breadth b gracefully thin 2 relatively small; scanty; inadequate

slept /slept/ *v. past* and *past part.* of SLEEP

sleuth /slōōth/ *n. Colloq.* detective [ON]

slew¹ /slōō/ *n. Colloq.* large amount [Ir *sluagh* army]

slew² *v.* SLUE

slew³ *v. past* of SLAY

slice /slīs/ *n.* 1 thin, flat piece or wedge cut off or out 2 share; part —*v.* (sliced, slic·ing) 3 cut into slices 4 cut off as a slice 5 cut (as) with a knife 6 strike (a ball) so it curves right or left [Fr *esclice* fr. Gmc]

slick /slik/ *adj.* 1 *Colloq.* a skillful; efficient b superficially or pretentiously smooth and dexterous; glib 2 sleek; smooth —*n.* 3 patch of oil, etc., esp. on the sea —*v.* 4 *Colloq.* smooth down (the hair) as with oil 5 (usu. foll. by *up*) make sleek or smart —slick′ly *adv.*; slick′ness *n.* [OE]

slick′er *n.* oilskin

slide /slīd/ *v.* (slid, slid·ing) 1 move easily along a smooth surface with continuous contact 2 move quietly or smoothly —*n.* 3 act of sliding 4 decline 5 incline down which children, goods, etc., slide 6a mounted transparency viewed with a projector b piece of glass holding an object for a microscope 7 avalanche; landslide 8 let slide be negligent —slid′er *n.* [OE]

slide′fas′ten·er *n.* ZIPPER

slide′rule′ *n.* frame with a sliding central strip for making rapid calculations

slid′ing scale′ *n.* scale of fees, taxes, wages, etc., that varies according to some factor

slight /slīt/ *adj.* 1 small; insignificant 2 inadequate 3 slender; frail-looking —*v.* 4 treat disrespectfully; ignore —*n.* 5 act of slighting —slight′ly *adv.*; slight′ness *n.* [ON]

slim /slim/ *adj.* (slim·mer, slim·mest) 1 slender 2 slight; insufficient —*v.* (slimmed, slim·ming) 3 become slimmer by dieting, exercise, etc. 4 make smaller —slim′mish *adj.*; slim′ness *n.* [LGer or Du]

slime /slīm/ *n.* thick slippery or sticky substance —slim′y *adj.* (·i·er, ·i·est); slim′i·ness *n.* [OE]

sling /sliNG/ *n.* **1** strap, etc., for supporting or raising a thing **2** straplike device for flinging a stone or other missile —*v.* (**slung**, **sling·ing**) **3** throw **4** suspend with a sling [ON or LGer or Du]

sling'shot' *n.* frame shaped like a Y with an elastic band across the arms, for shooting stones, etc.

slink /sliNGk/ *v.* (**slunk**, **slink·ing**) move in a stealthy or guilty manner [OE]

slink'y *adj.* (**·i·er**, **·i·est**) **1** stealthy or sneaky in movement **2** (of a woman's garment) close-fitting and sinuous

slip[1] /slip/ *v.* (**slipped**, **slip·ping**) **1** slide unintentionally or momentarily; lose one's footing or balance **2** go or move with a sliding or stealthy motion **3** escape or fall from being slippery or not being held properly **4** go unobserved or quietly **5** make a careless or slight error **6** fall below standard **7** (foll. by *on*, *off*) don or doff (a garment) easily or hastily **8** escape from; evade —*n.* **9** act of slipping **10** careless or slight error **11** petticoat **12** bay in a dock for mooring a vessel **13** let slip utter unintentionally **14** slip up *Colloq.* make a mistake [prob. fr. LGer *slippen*]

slip[2] *n.* **1** small piece of paper **2** piece cut from a plant for grafting or planting **3** slip of a small and slim (*slip of a girl*) [LGer or Du]

slip[3] *n.* clay and water mixture for decorating earthenware [OE: *slime*]

slip'cov'er *n.* fitted fabric covering for a chair, sofa, etc.

slip'knot' *n.* knot undone by a pull

slip'-on' *adj.* easily slipped on and off

slip·page /slip'ij/ *n.* act, instance, or amount of slipping

slipped' disk' *n.* displaced disk between vertebrae

slip'per *n.* light, loose, soft, indoor shoe

slip'per·y *adj.* **1** causing sliding or slipping; slick **2** difficult to hold **3** unreliable; unscrupulous —**slip'per·i·ness** *n.* [OE]

slip'shod' *adj.* careless; slovenly

slip'-up' *n.* *Colloq.* mistake

slit /slit/ *n.* **1** straight, narrow incision or opening —*v.* (**slit**, **slit·ting**) **2** make a slit in **3** cut into strips [OE]

slith·er /sliTH'ər/ *v.* **1** slide unsteadily —*n.* **2** act of slithering —**slith'er·y** *adj.* [var. of *slidder*, rel. to SLIDE]

sliv·er /sliv'ər/ *n.* **1** thin piece cut or split off —*v.* **2** break off as a sliver **3** break or form into slivers [OE]

slob /släb/ *n.* *Colloq.* lazy, untidy person [Ir *slab* mud]

slob·ber /släb'ər/ *v.* **1** drool **2** behave in a foolishly sentimental way [Du]

sloe /slō/ *n.* **1** BLACKTHORN **2** its small, sour bluish-black fruit [OE]

slog /släg/ *v.* (**slogged**, **slog·ging**) **1** work or walk doggedly —*n.* **2** hard, steady work or walk

slo·gan /slō'gən/ *n.* **1** catchy phrase used in advertising, etc. **2** party cry; watchword [Gaelic: war cry]

sloop /slōop/ *n.* one-masted fore-and-aft rigged vessel [Du *sloep*]

slop /släp/ *v.* (**slopped**, **slop·ping**) **1** spill over the edge of a container —*n.* **2** liquid spilled or splashed **3** dirty waste water **4** unappetizing, weak, liquid food [OE]

slope /slōp/ *n.* **1** inclined position, direction, or state **2** piece of rising or falling ground **3** difference in level between the two ends or sides of a thing —*v.* (**sloped**, **slop·ing**) **4** have or take a slope; slant **5** cause to slope [*aslope* crosswise]

slop·py /släp'ē/ *adj.* (**·pi·er**, **·pi·est**) **1** watery; slushy; too liquid **2** careless; untidy **3** foolishly sentimental —**slop'pi·ly** *adv.*; **slop'pi·ness** *n.*

slosh /släsh/ *v.* **1** walk through mud, water, etc. **2** splash about, as liquid in a partly empty container **3** *Colloq.* pour (liquid) untidily [var. of SLUSH]

sloshed /shläsht/ *adj.* *Slang.* drunk

slot /slät/ *n.* **1** slit, esp. in a machine, for a coin **2** allotted place in a schedule —*v.* (**slot·ted**, **slot·ting**) **3** place or be placed (as if) into a slot **4** provide with slots [Fr *esclot* hollow of breast]

sloth /slôTH, slōTH/ *n.* **1** laziness; indolence **2** slow-moving S American mammal that hangs upside down in trees —**sloth'ful** *adj.*; **sloth'ful·ly** *adv.*; **sloth'ful·ness** *n.* [fr. SLOW]

slot' ma·chine' *n.* machine, esp. a gambling device, worked by the insertion of a coin

slouch /slouCH/ *v.* **1** stand, move, or sit in a drooping fashion —*n.* **2** slouching posture or movement **3** *Slang.* incompetent or slovenly worker —**slouch'y** *adj.* (**·i·er**, **·i·est**)

slough[1] /slō, slou/ *n.* **1** swamp; miry place **2** state of helpless depression [OE]

slough[2] /sləf/ *n.* **1** part that an animal molts, esp. a snake's cast skin —*v.* **2** cast or drop off as a slough [ME *slughe* skin]

Slo·vak /slō'väk'/ *n.* **1** native of Slovakia **2** language of Slovakia —*adj.* **3** of the Slovaks or their language

Slo·va·ki·a /slavāk'ēa, slō-/ *n.* (also called **Slovak Republic**) republic in central Europe, the E part of the former Czechoslovakia. Capital: Bratislava. Pop. 5,300,000

slov·en /sləv'ən/ *n.* untidy or careless person —**slov'en·li·ness** *n.*; **slov'en·ly** *adj.* (**·li·er**, **·li·est**)

Slo·ve·ni·a /slōvē'nēa, slō-/ *n.* republic on the Balkan Peninsula, formerly part of Yugoslavia. Capital: Ljubljana. Pop. 1,985,000 —**Slo·ve'ni·an** *n.* & *adj.*

slow /slō/ *adj.* **1a** taking a relatively long time to do a thing **b** acting, moving, or done without speed; not quick **2** not conducive to speed **3** (of a clock, etc.) showing a time earlier than is correct **4** (of a person) not understanding or learning readily **5** slack; sluggish **6** *Photog.* (of a film) needing long exposure —*adv.* **7** slowly —*v.* **8** (usu. foll. by *down* or *up*) **a** reduce one's speed or the speed of (a vehicle, etc.) **b** reduce one's pace of life —**slow'ish** *adj.*; **slow'ly** *adv.*; **slow'ness** *n.* [OE]

slow'down' *n.* deliberate slowing of work pace and productivity

slow' mo'tion *n.* speed of a motion-picture film, etc., in which actions appear slower than normal

SLR *abbr.* single lens reflex (camera)

sludge /sləj/ *n.* **1** thick, greasy mud or sediment **2** sewage —**sludg'y** *adj.* [cf. SLUSH]

slue /slōō/ *v.* (also **slew**) turn or swing forcibly to a new position

slug[1] /sləg/ *n.* 1 small, snaillike mollusk without a shell, a common garden pest 2 bullet; missile for an airgun 3 counterfeit coin 4 *Slang.* drink of liquor [Scand]

slug[2] *v.* (**slugged, slug·ging**) 1 hit hard —*n.* 2 hard blow —**slug'ger** *n.*

slug·gard /sləg'ərd/ *n.* lazy person [rel. to SLUG[1]]

slug'gish *adj.* slothful; slow-moving —**slug'gish·ly** *adv.*; **slug·gish·ness** *n.*

sluice /sloōs/ *n.* 1 (also **sluice' gate', sluice' valve'**) sliding gate, etc., for regulating the flow of water 2 water so regulated 3 (**sluice' way'**) artificial water-channel, esp. for washing ore —*v.* (**sluiced, sluic·ing**) 4 provide or wash with a sluice or sluices [Fr *escluse*]

slum /sləm/ *n.* 1 overcrowded and squalid district in a city —*v.* (**slummed, slum·ming**) 2 visit slums, esp. out of curiosity —**slum'my** *adj.* (**·mi·er, ·mi·est**)

slum·ber /sləm'bər/ *v. & n.* sleep [OE]

slump /sləmp/ *n.* 1 sudden fall in prices and trade —*v.* 2 undergo a slump 3 adopt a limp, drooping stance or sitting position [imit.]

slung /sləNG/ *v. past* and *past part.* of SLING

slunk /sləNGk/ *v. past* and *past part.* of SLINK

slur /slər/ *v.* (**slurred, slur·ring**) 1 pronounce indistinctly with sounds running into one another 2 *Mus.* perform (notes) legato 3 put a slur on (a person or a person's character) 4 pass over (a fact, fault, etc.) lightly —*n.* 5 accusation of wrongdoing 6 act of slurring 7 *Mus.* curved line joining notes to be slurred

slurp /slərp/ *Slang. v.* 1 eat or esp. drink noisily —*n.* 2 sound of this [Du]

slur·ry /slər'ē/ *n.* (*pl.* **·ries**) thin, semi-liquid cement, mud, etc. [rel. to dial. *slur* thin mud]

slush /sləSH/ *n.* 1 thawing, muddy snow 2 silly sentimentality —**slush'y** *adj.* (**·i·er, ·i·est**)

slush' fund' *n.* reserve fund, esp. for political bribery

slut /slət/ *n.* 1 slovenly woman 2 promiscuous woman —**slut'tish** *adj.*

sly /slī/ *adj.* (**sli·er** or **sly·er, sli·est** or **sly·est**) 1 cunning; crafty; wily 2 knowing; insinuating 3 **on the sly** secretly —**sly'ly** *adv.*; **sly'ness** *n.* [ON, rel. to SLAY]

Sm *symb.* samarium

smack[1] /smak/ *n.* 1 sharp slap or blow 2 loud kiss 3 loud, sharp sound —*v.* 4 slap 5 part (one's lips) noisily in anticipation of food 6 move, hit, etc., with a smack —*adv.* 7 *Colloq.* with a smack 8 suddenly; directly; violently 9 exactly [imit.]

smack[2] *v.* (foll. by *of*) 1 have a flavor of; suggest —*n.* (foll. by *of*) 2 flavor 3 barely discernible quality [OE]

smack[3] *n.* single-masted sailboat [LGer or Du]

smack[4] *n. Slang.* heroin [prob. alter. of Yiddish *schmeck* sniff]

smack'er *n. Slang.* dollar bill

small /smôl/ *adj.* 1 less in dimension compared with others of the same class 2 of lesser importance, amount, number, power, etc. 3 mean; miserly 4 young —*n.* 5 slenderest part of a thing, esp. of the back —*adv.* 6 into small pieces 7 feel (or **look**) **small** be humiliated or ashamed —**small'ish** *adj.*; **small' ness** *n.* [OE]

small' arms' *n. pl.* portable firearms

small' fry' *n.* 1 children 2 unimportant people

small'-mind'ed *adj.* petty; narrow in outlook

small'pox' *n.* acute contagious disease with fever and pustules

small' print' *n.* unfavorable conditions in a contract, usu. printed in small type

small' talk' *n.* light social conversation

small'-time' *adj. Colloq.* unimportant; petty

smart /smärt/ *adj.* 1 clever; ingenious; quick-witted 2 quick; brisk 3 painfully severe 4 well-groomed; neat 5 stylish; fashionable —*v.* 6 feel or give pain 7 suffer the consequences (of) —*n.* 8 sharp pain 9 (*pl.*) *Slang.* wisdom —**smart'ly** *adv.*; **smart'ness** *n.* [OE]

smart' al'eck /al'ek/ *n.* (also **smart' al'ec**) *Colloq.* conceited know-it-all —**smart'-al'eck·y** *adj.*

smart'en *v.* make or become smart

smash /smaSH/ *v.* 1 break into pieces; shatter 2 bring or come to sudden destruction, defeat, or disaster 3 (foll. by *into, through*) strike with great force —*n.* 4 act of smashing; collision 5 sound of this 6 (in full **smash hit**) very successful play, song, performer, etc. —*adv.* 7 with a smash [imit.]

smash'ing *adj. Colloq.* excellent; wonderful

smash'-up *n.* violent collision

smat·ter·ing /smat'əriNG/ *n.* slight, superficial knowledge

smear /smēr/ *v.* 1 daub or mark with a sticky or greasy substance 2 smudge 3 defame —*n.* 4 act of smearing 5 *Med.* material smeared on a microscopic slide, etc., for examination —**smear'y** *adj.* (**·i·er, ·i·est**) [OE]

smell /smel/ *n.* 1 faculty of perceiving odors 2 quality that is perceived by this 3 act of sniffing to ascertain smell —*v.* (**smelled** or **smelt, smell·ing**) 4 perceive or examine by smell 5 emit an odor 6 perceive; detect 7 have or use a sense of smell 8 **smell a rat** suspect trickery, etc. [OE]

smell'ing salts' *n. pl.* sharp-smelling ammonia compound smelled for relieving faintness, etc.

smell'y *adj.* (**·i·er, ·i·est**) having a strong or unpleasant smell —**smell'i·ness** *n.*

smelt[1] /smelt/ *v.* 1 extract metal from (ore) by melting 2 refine (metal) in this way —**smelt'er** *n.* [LGer or Du *smelten*]

smelt[2] *v. past* and *past part.* of SMELL

smelt[3] *n.* (*pl.* same or *-s*) small, edible green and silver fish [OE]

Sme·ta·na /smet'n-ə, sme'tänä/, **Bedřich** 1824–84; Czech composer

smid·gen /smij'ən/ *n.* (also **smid'gin, smid'geon**) *Colloq.* small bit [perh. fr. *smitch*]

smile /smīl/ *v.* (**smiled, smil·ing**) 1 have or assume a happy, kind, or amused expression, with the corners of the mouth turned up 2 (foll. by *on, upon*) favor —*n.* 3 act of smiling 4 smiling expression [perh. fr. Scand]

smirch /smərCH/ *v.* 1 soil; discredit —*n.* 2 spot; stain

smirk /smərk/ *n.* 1 conceited or silly smile —*v.* 2 make a smirk [OE]

smite /smīt/ *v.* (**smote, smit·ten, smit·ing**) 1 *Archaic.* or *Lit.* hit 2 affect strongly [OE]

smith /smiTH/ n. 1 blacksmith 2 worker in metal [OE]

Smith /smiTH/ 1 **John** 1580–1631; English colonist in Virginia 2 **Adam** 1723–90; Scottish philosopher and economist 3 **Joseph** 1805–44; founder of the Mormon Church

smith·er·eens /smiTH'ǝrēnz/ n. pl. small fragments [dial. smithers]

smith·y /smiTH'ē/ n. (pl. ·ies) blacksmith's workshop; forge [rel. to SMITH]

smit·ten /smit'n/ v. past part. of SMITE

smock /smäk/ n. loose, shirtlike garment for protecting the clothing [OE]

smock'ing n. ornamental effect on cloth made by gathering it tightly with stitches

smog /smäg, smôg/ n. smoke-laden fog —**smog'gy** adj. (·gi·er, ·gi·est) [blend of smoke and fog]

smoke /smōk/ n. 1 visible vapor from a burning substance 2 act of smoking tobacco 3 Colloq. cigarette or cigar —v. (smoked, smok·ing) 4a inhale and exhale the smoke of (a cigarette, etc.) b do this habitually 6 emit smoke or visible vapor 6 preserve with smoke 7 smoke out drive out by or as by means of smoke —smoke'less adj.; smok'er, smok'i·ness n.; smok'y adj. (·i·er, ·i·est) [OE]

smoke' and mir'rors n. deception or false appearance; sleight of hand

smoke'screen' n. 1 cloud of smoke concealing (esp. military) operations 2 ruse for disguising one's activities

smoke'stack' n. chimney

smol·der /smōl'dǝr/ v. 1 burn slowly without flame 2 (of emotions) be fierce but suppressed 3 (of a person) show suppressed emotion —n. 4 smoldering

Smo·lensk /smǝlensk'/ n. city in W Russia. Pop. 349,800

Smol·lett /smäl'it/, **Tobias George** 1721–71; English novelist

smooch /smōōCH/ Colloq. n. 1 kiss —v. 2 kiss —smooch'y adj.

smooth /smōōTH/ adj. 1 having an even, slick surface 2 uninterrupted 3 pleasant sound or taste; not harsh 4 suave; slick 5 even in motion; not jerky —v. 6 make or become smooth 7 reduce or get rid of (differences, faults, difficulties, etc.) —adv. 8 smoothly —smooth'ly adv.; smooth'ness n. [OE]

smooth'ie n. Colloq. suave, often slick person

smooth'-spo'ken adj. speaking in a gentle, polished manner

smooth'-tongued' adj. insincerely flattering

smor·gas·bord /smôr'gǝsbôrd/ n. various hot and cold dishes as hors d'oeuvres or a buffet meal [Sw]

smote /smōt/ v. past of SMITE

smoth·er /smǝTH'ǝr/ v. 1 suffocate; stifle 2 (foll. by in, with) overwhelm or cover with 3 extinguish (a fire) by covering it [OE]

smudge /smǝj/ n. 1 blurred or smeared line, mark, blot, etc. —v. (smudged, smudg·ing) 2 make a smudge on or of 3 become smeared or blurred —smudg'y adj. (·i·er, ·i·est)

smug /smǝg/ adj. (smug'ger, smug'gest)

self-satisfied —smug'ly adv.; smug'ness n. [LGer smuk pretty]

smug·gle /smǝg'ǝl/ v. (·gled, ·gling) 1 import or export illegally, esp. without paying duties 2 (foll. by in, out) convey secretly —smug'gler, smug'gling n. [LGer]

smut /smǝt/ n. 1 small flake of soot, etc. 2 spot or smudge made by this 3 obscene talk, pictures, or stories 4 fungous disease, esp. of cereals —smut'ty adj. (·ti·er, ·ti·est)

Smuts /smɪts, smæts/, **Jan** 1870–1950; South African leader; prime minister (1919–24; 1939–48)

Smyr·na /smǝr'nǝ/ n. see IZMIR

Sn symb. tin [L stannun]

snack /snak/ n. 1 small amount of food, esp. eaten between meals —v. 2 eat snacks, esp. habitually [Du]

snack' bar' n. place where snacks are sold

snaf·fle /snaf'ǝl/ n. bridle-bit without a curb [LGer or Du perh. fr. snavel beak]

snag /snag/ n. 1 unexpected obstacle or drawback 2 jagged projection 3 tear in fabric —v. (snagged, snag·ging) 4 catch or tear on a snag [prob. Scand]

snail /snāl/ n. slow-moving mollusk with a spiral shell [OE]

snail' mail' n. Colloq. standard mail service, esp. in contrast to electronic mail

snake /snāk/ n. 1 long, limbless reptile 2 (also snake' in the grass') traitor; secret enemy —v. (snaked, snak·ing) 3 move or twist like a snake [OE]

snake' charm'er n. person appearing to make poisonous snakes move by music, etc.

Snake' Riv'er n. river rising in Yellowstone National Park, Wyo., flowing 1,040 mi. SW and NW into the Columbia River in Wash.

snak'y adj. (·i·er, ·i·est) 1 of or like a snake 2 winding; sinuous 3 cunning; treacherous

snap /snap/ v. (snapped, snap·ping) 1 break suddenly or with a cracking sound 2 (cause to) emit a sudden sharp crack 3 speak or say irritably 4 make a sudden, audible bite 5 move quickly 6 take a snapshot (of) 7 act or sound of snapping 8 crisp cookie 9 snapshot 10 (in full cold snap) sudden, brief spell of cold weather 11 Colloq. vigor; liveliness 12 (also snap' fas'ten·er) two-piece device consisting of a knob and a receptacle for it, used to fasten clothing, etc. 13 Colloq. easy job —adv. 14 with a snap —adj. 15 done without forethought 16 closing with a snap fastener 17 snap out of Slang. get rid of (a mood, lethargy, etc.) by a sudden effort 18 snap up accept (an offer, etc.) quickly or eagerly —snap'per n.; snap'pish adj. [LGer or Du snappen seize]

snap'drag·on n. plant with a two-lipped flower

snap'py adj. (·pi·er, ·pi·est) Colloq. 1 brisk; lively 2 neat and elegant 3 irritable; impatient 4 make it snappy be quick —snap'pi·ly adv.

snap'shot' n. casual or informal photograph

snare /snar/ n. 1 trap for birds or small animals 2 trap, trick, or temptation 3 twisted strings of gut, hide, or wire stretched across the lower head of a drum —v. (snared, snar·ing) 4 catch in a snare; trap [ON]

snarl¹ /snärl/ v. 1 growl with bared teeth 2 speak, say, or express angrily —n. 3 act or sound of snarling [snar fr. LGer]

snarl² v. entangle or become entangled or

congested —**snarl'y** *adj.* (·i·er, ·i·est) [fr. SNARE]

snatch /snaCH/ *v.* 1 seize or remove quickly, eagerly, or unexpectedly 2 steal (a handbag, etc.) by grabbing 3 *Slang.* kidnap 4 (foll. by *at*) try to seize —*n.* 5 act of snatching 6 fragment 7 *Slang.* kidnapping 8 short spell of activity, etc. [rel. to SNACK]

snaz·zy /snaz'ē/ *adj.* (·zi·er, ·zi·est) *Slang.* smart; stylish; showy —**snaz·zi·ly** /snaz'əlē/ *adv.*; **snaz'zi·ness** *n.*

sneak /snēk/ *v.* (sneaked or snuck, sneak·ing) 1 go or convey furtively —*n.* 2 mean-spirited, underhand person —*adj.* 3 acting or done without warning; secret —**sneak'y** *adj.* (·i·er, ·i·est)

sneak'er *n.* rubber-soled shoe for sports or casual wear

sneer /snēr/ *n.* 1 contemptuous smile or remark —*v.* 2 smile or speak derisively 3 say with a sneer —**sneer'ing** *adj.*; **sneer'ing·ly** *adv.*

sneeze /snēz/ *v.* 1 sudden, loud, involuntary expulsion of air from the nose and mouth —*v.* (sneezed, sneez·ing) 2 make a sneeze [OE]

snick·er /snik'ər/ *n.* 1 half-suppressed laugh —*v.* 2 laugh in this way [imit.]

snide /snīd/ *adj.* sneering; slyly derogatory

sniff /snif/ *v.* 1 inhale air suddenly through the nose 2 draw in through the nose 3 smell the scent of by sniffing —*n.* 4 act or sound of sniffing 5 amount sniffed 6 **sniff at** show contempt for 7 **sniff out** detect —**snif'fer** *n.* [imit.]

snif·fle /snif'əl/ *v.* (·fled, ·fling) 1 sniff slightly or repeatedly —*n.* 2 act of sniffling 3 (often *pl.*) cold in the head causing sniffling [imit.; cf. SNIVEL]

snif·ter /snif'tər/ *n.* globular brandy glass with a narrow opening

snig·ger /snig'ər/ *n. & v.* SNICKER

snip /snip/ *v.* (snipped, snip·ping) 1 cut with scissors, etc., esp. in small quick strokes —*n.* 2 act of snipping 3 piece snipped off 4 small cut [LGer or Du *snippen*]

snipe /snīp/ *n.* (*pl.* same or -s) 1 wading bird with a long straight bill —*v.* (sniped, snip·ing) 2 fire a rifle from hiding, usu. at long range 3 make a sly critical attack —**snip'er** *n.* [prob. Scand]

snip·pet /snip'it/ *n.* 1 small piece cut off 2 scrap, esp. of information

snit /snit/ *n.* brief fit of agitation [dial.]

snitch /sniCH/ *v.* 1 steal 2 inform on a person —*n.* 3 informer

sniv·el /sniv'əl/ *v.* (·eled or ·elled, ·el·ing or ·el·ling) 1 weep with sniffling 2 run at the nose 3 whine 4 show weak or tearful sentiment [OE]

snob /snäb/ *n.* person who despises those considered inferior in social position, wealth, intellect, taste, etc. —**snob'bery** *n.*; **snob'bish**, **snob'by** *adj.* (·i·er, ·i·est)

snood /snōōd/ *n.* woman's ornamental hairnet, worn usu. at the back of the head [OE]

snoop /snōōp/ *Colloq. v.* 1 pry —*n.* 2 person who snoops —**snoop'er** *n.*; **snoop'y** *adj.* (·i·er, ·i·est) [Du]

snoot /snōōt/ *n. Slang.* nose [fr. SNOUT]

snoot·ful /snōōt'fəl/ *n. Slang.* as in **have a snootful** drunk

snoot·y /snōō'tē/ *adj.* (·i·er, ·i·est) *Colloq.*

supercilious; conceited; snobbish —**snoot'i·ly** *adv.*; **snoot'i·ness** *n.* [fr. SNOOT]

snooze /snōōz/ *Colloq. n.* 1 short sleep; nap —*v.* (snoozed, snooz·ing) 2 take a snooze

snore /snôr/ *n.* 1 snorting or grunting sound of breathing during sleep —*v.* (snored, snor·ing) 2 make this sound —**snor'er** *n.* [imit.]

snor·kel /snôr'kəl/ *n.* 1 breathing tube for an underwater swimmer 2 device for supplying air to a submerged submarine —*v.* (·keled or ·kelled, ·kel·ing or ·kel·ling) 3 use a snorkel —**snor'kel·er** *n.* [Ger *Schnorchel*]

snort /snôrt/ *n.* 1 explosive sound made by the sudden forcing of breath through the nose 2 *Colloq.* small drink of liquor 3 *Slang.* inhaled dose of powdered cocaine, etc. —*v.* 4 make a snort 5 *Slang.* inhale (esp. cocaine) 6 utter with a snort —**snort'er** *n.*

SNORKEL 1 and MASK 1

snot /snät/ *n. Slang.* nasal mucus [prob. LGer or Du, rel. to SNOUT]

snot'ty *adj.* (·ti·er, ·ti·est) *Slang.* 1 running or covered with nasal mucus 2 snooty 3 mean; contemptible —**snot'ti·ly** *adv.*; **snot'ti·ness** *n.*

snout /snout/ *n.* projecting nose and mouth of an animal [LGer or Du]

snow /snō/ *n.* 1 frozen atmospheric vapor falling to earth in light white flakes 2 fall or layer of this 3 *Slang.* cocaine —*v.* 4 fall as snow 5 *Slang.* deliberately overwhelm so as to deceive 6 **snowed under** overwhelmed, esp. with work —**snow'y** *adj.* (·i·er, ·i·est) [OE]

snow'ball' *n.* 1 ball of compressed snow for throwing —*v.* 2 increase in size, momentum, etc., steadily and rapidly

snow'bound' *adj.* prevented by snow from going out or traveling

snow'drift' *n.* bank of snow heaped up by the wind

snow'drop' *n.* early spring plant with white drooping flowers

snow'fall' *n.* 1 fall of snow 2 amount of this

snow'flake' *n.* each of the flakes in which snow falls

snow'man' *n.* (*pl.* ·men) figure resembling a human, made of packed snow

snow·mo·bile /snō'mōbēl'/ *n.* motor vehicle for travel over snow equipped with runners and driven by continuous tractor tread

snow'plow' *n.* bladelike device on a vehicle, train, etc., for clearing snow

snow'shoe' *n.* racket-shaped attachment to a boot for walking on snow without sinking in

snow'storm' *n.* heavy fall of snow, esp. with a high wind

snow'suit' *n.* child's overall-style insulated garment

snow'tire' *n.* vehicle tire with deep treads for traction in snow

snub /snəb/ *v.* (snubbed, snub·bing) 1 rebuff or humiliate **—n.** 2 act of snubbing **—adj.** 3 short and blunt in shape [ON: chide]

snuck /snək/ **v.** past and past part. of SNEAK
● Usage: Although in formal writing the form *sneaked* is usually preferred, *snuck* has become an accepted variant in colloquial use.

snuff[1] /snəf/ **v.** 1 trim the wick of (a candle) 2 (usu. foll. by *out*) extinguish (a candle flame) **—snuff'er** n.

snuff[2] **n.** 1 powdered tobacco taken by sniffing 2 sniff **—v.** 3 sniff **4 up to snuff** *Colloq.* meeting a satisfactory standard [Du]

snuff'box' **n.** small box for holding snuff

snuf·fle /snəf'əl/ **v.** (·fled, ·fling) 1 sniff; sniffle **—n.** 2 sniffle **—snuf'fly** adj. [LGer or Du *snuffelen*]

snug /snəg/ **adj.** (·ger, ·gest) 1 cozy; comfortable 2 close-fitting **—snug'ly** adv.; **snug'ness** n. [prob. LGer or Du]

snug·gle /snəg'əl/ **v.** (·gled, ·gling) settle into a warm comfortable position; cuddle

so[1] /sō/ **adv.** 1 to such an extent (*stop complaining so*) 2 in this or that way; in a specified manner, position, or state (*place your feet so*) 3 also (*he went and so did I*) 4 indeed; actually (*you said it was good, and so it is*) 5 very (*I am so glad*) 6 (with verbs of saying or thinking, etc.) thus; this; that (*I think so; he said*) **—conj.** 7 consequently (*I was ill, so couldn't come*) 8 in order to or that (*I came early so that I could see you*) 9 and then; as the next step (*so then I gave up*) **10 and so on** (or **forth**): a and others of the same kind b and in other similar ways **11 so as to** in order to **12 so long!** *Colloq.* goodbye **13 so so** SO-SO **14 so what?** *Colloq.* what is significant about that? [OE]

so[2] **n.** *Mus.* SOL

soak /sōk/ **v.** 1 make or become thoroughly wet through saturation 2 (foll. by *in*, *up*) absorb (liquid, knowledge, etc.) 3 (of liquid) go or penetrate by saturation 4 *Slang.* overcharge **—n.** 5 soaking [OE]

so'-and-so' **n.** (*pl.* -sos) 1 particular but unspecified person or thing 2 *Colloq.* objectionable person

soap /sōp/ **n.** 1 cleansing agent yielding lather when rubbed in water 2 *Colloq.* SOAP OPERA **—v.** 3 apply soap to **—soap'y** adj. (·i·er, ·i·est) [OE]

soap'box' **n.** makeshift stand for a speaker in the street, etc.

soap' op·er·a **n.** *Colloq.* (also **soap**) broadcast melodramatic serial

soap'stone' **n.** talc in the form of stone

soap'suds' **n.** pl. SUDS

soar /sôr/ **v.** 1 fly or rise high 2 reach a high level 3 fly without using power [Fr *essorer*]

sob /säb/ **v.** (**sobbed, sob·bing**) 1 weep convulsively, usu. with gasping 2 utter with sobs **—n.** 3 act or sound of sobbing

so·ber /sō'bər/ **adj.** 1 not drunk 2 abstaining from alcoholic drinks 3 moderate; tranquil; sedate; serious 4 (of a color, etc.) quiet; dull **—v.** 5 (often foll. by *down*, *up*) make or become sober **—so'ber·ly** adv.; **so'ber·ness** n. [Fr fr. L]

so·bri·e·ty /səbrī'ətē/ **n.** being sober

so·bri·quet /sō'brikā', -ket'/ **n.** (also **sou'bri·quet'**) nickname [Fr]

---

sob' sis'ter **n.** *Colloq.* usu. female journalist who writes sentimental human-interest stories

Soc. *abbr.* 1 Socialist 2 Society

so'-called' **adj.** commonly called, often incorrectly

soc·cer /säk'ər/ **n.** form of football in which a spherical ball is kicked to score goals [fr. Association football, -ER[1]]

so·ci·a·ble /sō'shəbəl/ **adj.** liking company; gregarious; friendly **—so'cia·bil'i·ty** n.; **so'cia·bly** adv. [L *socius* companion]

so·cial /sō'shəl/ **adj.** 1 of society or its organization, esp. of the relations between people or classes of people 2 living in organized communities 3 needing companionship; gregarious **—n.** 4 social gathering, esp. of a club **—so'cial·ly** adv. [L *socialis*]

so'cial climb'er **n.** person anxious to gain a higher social status **—so'cial climb'ing** n. & adj.

so'cial dis·ease' **n.** venereal disease

so·cial·ism /sō'shəliz'əm/ **n.** 1 political and economic theory advocating state ownership and control of the means of production, distribution, and exchange 2 social system based on this **—so'cial·ist** /-ist/ **n. & adj.; so'cial·is'tic** adj. [Fr, rel. to SOCIAL]

so·cial·ite /sō'shəlīt'/ **n.** person moving in fashionable society

so·cial·ize /sō'shəlīz/ **v.** (·ized, ·iz·ing) 1 mix socially 2 make social 3 organize on socialistic principles **—so'cial·i·za'tion** n.

so'cial sci'ence **n.** study of society and social relationships **—so'cial sci'en·tist** n.

so'cial se·cu'ri·ty **n.** (often *caps.*) federal system providing payments to the elderly, disabled, etc.

so'cial ser'vic·es **n.** pl. welfare services provided by the government, esp. education, health, and housing

so'cial work' **n.** professional or voluntary welfare work **—so'cial work'er** n.

so·ci·e·ty /səsī'ətē/ **n.** (*pl.* -ties) 1 organized and interdependent community 2 system and organization of this 3 aristocratic or wealthy part of this; its members 4 companionship; company 5 club; association **—so·ci'e·tal** /-təl/ adj. [L *societas*]

So·ci'e·ty Is'lands **n.** Pacific island group, part of French Polynesia; includes Tahiti

So·ci'e·ty of Friends' **n.** pacifist Christian sect with no written creed or ordained ministers; Quakers

So·ci'e·ty of Je'sus **n.** JESUIT

so·ci·ol·o·gy /sō'sē-äl'əjē, sō'shē-/ **n.** the study of society and social problems **—so'ci·o·log'i·cal** /-läj'ikəl/ adj.; **so'ci·o·log'i·cal·ly** adv.; **so'ci·ol'o·gist** n. [Fr, rel. to SOCIAL]

so·ci·o·path /sō'sēəpaTH', -shē-/ **n.** person who is an antisocial psychopath

sock[1] /säk/ **n.** stocking for the foot and lower leg [OE *socc* fr. Gk *sukkhos* slipper]

sock[2] *Colloq.* **v.** 1 hit hard **—n.** 2 hard blow

sock·et /säk'it/ **n.** hollow for something to fit into [AngFr]

Soc·ra·tes /säk'rətēz'/ 469–399 B.C.; Athenian philosopher; teacher of Plato **—So·crat'ic** /səkra'tik/ adj.

So·crat'ic meth'od **n.** procedure of teaching by question and answer

sod /säd/ **n.** 1 turf; piece of turf 2 surface of the ground [LGer or Du]

so·da /sṓdə/ *n.* **1** sodium bicarbonate **2** (also **so'da pop'**) effervescent water, esp. flavored [perh. fr. L *sodanum* fr. Ar]

so'da foun'tain *n.* counter for making and serving sodas, ice cream, etc.

so'da wa'ter *n.* seltzer; club soda

sod·den /sädʹn/ *adj.* saturated; soaked through; soggy [archaic past part. of SEETHE]

so·di·um /sṓdēəm/ *n.* soft silver-white metallic element; *symb.* Na [fr. SODA]

so'di·um bi·car'bon·ate *n.* white crystalline compound used in baking powder, as an antacid, etc.

so'di·um chlo'ride *n.* common salt

so'di·um hy·drox'ide *n.* (also **caus'tic so'da**) strongly alkaline compound used in making soap, etc.

sod·om·y /sädʹəmē/ *n.* any form of sexual intercourse considered abnormal —**sod'om·ize**/ /-mīz/ *v.* (·ized, ·iz·ing); **sod'om·ite'** /-īt/ *n.* [L fr. *Sodom*: Gen. 18,19]

so·ev·er /sṓevʹər/ *adv. Lit.* of any kind; to any extent

so·fa /sṓfə/ *n.* long, upholstered seat with a back and arms [Ar *shuffa*]

so'fa bed' *n.* sofa convertible into a bed

sof·fit /säfʹit/ *n.* undersurface of an arch, etc. [Fr *soffite*, It *soffitta*]

So·fi·a /sōfēʹə, sō-/ *n.* capital of Bulgaria. Pop. 1,141,100

soft /sôft/ *adj.* **1** yielding; easily cut or dented; malleable **2** (of cloth, etc.) smooth; fine; not rough **3** (of water) low in mineral salts **4** (of sound) low; not loud **5** not harsh; gentle; mild **6** (of an outline, etc.) vague; blurred **7** easy-going; conciliatory; compassionate; sympathetic **8** *Colloq.* (of a job, etc.) easy **9** (of drugs) not highly addictive **10** not garish; soothing (*soft colors*) **11** (of currency) likely to fall in value —*adv.* **12** quietly; softly —**soft'ly** *adv.*; **soft'ness** *n.* [OE]

soft'ball' *n.* form of baseball using a larger ball

soft'-boiled' *adj.* (of an egg) boiled leaving the yolk soft

soft' drink' *n.* nonalcoholic drink

soft·en /sôfʹən/ *v.* make or become soft or softer —**soft'en·er** *n.*

soft'-heart'ed *adj.* tender; compassionate —**soft'-heart'ed·ly** *adv.*; **soft'-heart'ed·ness** *n.*

soft' pal'ate *n.* rear part of the palate; velum

soft' ped'al *n.* **1** piano pedal that softens the tone —*v.* (**soft'-ped'al**; ·aled or ·alled, ·al·ing or ·al·ling) **2** refrain from emphasizing; be restrained

soft' sell' *n.* subtle, low-pressure selling

soft' soap' *Colloq. n.* **1** persuasive flattery —*v.* **2** (**soft'-soap'**) persuade with flattery

soft'-spo'ken *adj.* having a gentle voice

soft' touch' *n. Colloq.* person easily imposed upon

soft'ware' *n.* programs for a computer

soft'wood' *n.* easily sawn wood

soft'y *n.* weak or soft-hearted person

sog·gy /sägʹē/ *adj.* (·gi·er, ·gi·est) sodden; saturated; too moist —**sog'gi·ly** *adv.*; **sog'gi·ness** *n.* [dial. *sog* marsh]

soil¹ /soil/ *n.* **1** upper layer of earth in which plants grow **2** territory belonging to a nation [L *solium* seat, *solum* ground]

soil² *v.* **1** make dirty; smear; stain **2** defile;

---

discredit —*n.* **3** dirty mark **4** filth; refuse [Fr *soill(i)er*]

soi·rée /swärāʹ/ *n.* evening party [Fr]

so·journ /sṓjərn, sōjörnʹ/ *n.* **1** temporary stay —*v.* **2** stay temporarily [Fr *sojorner*]

sol /sôl/ *n.* (also so) *Mus.* fifth note of a major scale [L *solve*, word arbitrarily taken]

sol·ace /sälʹəs/ *n.* **1** comfort —*v.* (·aced, ·ac·ing) **2** give solace to [L *solatium*]

so·lar /sṓlər/ *adj.* of, coming from, or reckoned by the sun [L *sol* sun]

so'lar bat'ter·y *n.* (also **so'lar cell'**) device converting solar radiation into electricity

so·lar·i·um /sōlerʹēəm/ *n.* (*pl.* ·i·a /-ēə/) room with sun lamps or a glass roof, etc., for sunbathing [L, rel. to SOLAR]

so'lar plex'us *n.* complex of nerves at the pit of the stomach

so'lar sys'tem *n.* the sun and the celestial bodies whose motion it governs

sold /sōld/ *v.* past and past part. of SELL

sol·der /sädʹər/ *n.* **1** fusible alloy used to join metals or wires, etc. —*v.* **2** join with solder [L, rel. to SOLID]

sol·dier /sōlʹjər/ *n.* **1** member of an army **2** enlisted person in an army **3** serve as a soldier —**sol'dier·ly** *adj.* [Fr *soulde*, orig. soldier's pay]

sol'dier of for'tune *n.* mercenary; adventurer

sole¹ /sōl/ *n.* **1** undersurface of the foot **2** part of a shoe, sock, etc., under the foot, esp. excluding the heel —*v.* (soled, sol·ing) **3** provide (a shoe, etc.) with a sole [L *solea* sandal]

sole² *n.* (*pl.* same or ·s) flatfish used as food [L *solea* sandal, which the fish resembles]

sole³ *adj.* one and only; single; exclusive [Fr fr. L *solus*]

sol·e·cism /sälʹəsizʹəm/ *n.* mistake of grammar or idiom —**so'le·cis'tic** /-sisʹtik/ *adj.* [Gk *soloikos* speaking incorrectly]

sole'ly *adv.* **1** alone; exclusively **2** only; merely

sol·emn /sälʹəm/ *adj.* **1** serious and dignified **2** formal **3** awe-inspiring **4** serious or cheerless in manner; grave; sober —**sol'emn·ly** *adv.*; **sol'emn·ness** *n.* [L *solemnis*]

so·lem·ni·ty /səlemʹnətē/ *n.* (*pl.* ·ties) **1** being solemn **2** rite; ceremony

sol·em·nize /sälʹəmnīz/ *v.* (·nized, ·niz·ing) **1** duly perform (esp. a marriage ceremony) **2** formalize —**sol'em·ni·za'tion** *n.*

so·le·noid /sṓlənoid, sälʹə-/ *n.* cylindrical coil of electrical wire acting as a magnet when charged [Fr fr. Gk *sōlēn* tube]

so·lic·it /səlisʹit/ *v.* **1** seek (esp. business) repeatedly or earnestly **2** accost as a prostitute —**so·lic'i·ta'tion** /-itāʹsнən/ *n.* [L *sollicitus* anxious]

so·lic'i·tor *n.* **1** person who solicits business **2** *Brit.* lawyer qualified to advise clients and instruct barristers **3** legal official (*solicitor general*)

so·lic·i·tous /səlisʹətəs/ *adj.* **1** showing interest or concern **2** eager; anxious —**so·lic'i·tous·ly** *adv.* [L, rel. to SOLICIT]

so·lic·i·tude /səlisʹət(y)ōōd/ *n.* being solicitous

sol·id /sälʹid/ *adj.* **1** firm and stable in shape; not liquid or fluid **2** of such material throughout; not hollow **3** of the same substance, color, etc., throughout **4** sturdily built; not flimsy or slender **5** three-dimensional **6** sound; reliable **7** unbroken; undivided **8** unanimous —*n.* **9** solid substance or body **10** (*pl.*) solid food —*adv.* **11** solidly —**sol'id·ly** *adv.*; **sol'id·ness** *n.* [L *solidus*]

sol·i·dar·i·ty /säl'ədar'ətē/ *n.* unity, esp. political or in an industrial dispute [Fr, rel. to SOLID]

so·lid·i·fy /səlid'əfī'/ *v.* (·fied, ·fy·ing) make or become solid —**so·lid'i·fi·ca'tion** /-fikā'sHən/ *n.*

so·lid·i·ty /solid'ətē/ *n.* being solid; firmness

sol'id-state' *adj.* using semiconductors instead of tubes

sol·i·dus /säl'idəs/ *n.* (*pl.* /-dī'/) virgule (/) [L, rel. to SOLID]

so·lil·o·quy /səlil'əkwē/ *n.* (*pl.* ·quies) **1** talking without or regardless of hearers, esp. in a play **2** this part of a play —**so·lil'o·quist'** /-kwist'/ *n.*; **so·lil'o·quize'** /-kwīz'/ *v.* (·quized, ·quiz·ing) [L *solus* alone, *loqui* speak]

sol·i·taire /säl'ater'/ *n.* **1** jewel set by itself **2** card game for one player [Fr: see SOLITARY]

sol·i·tar·y /säl'ater'ē/ *adj.* **1** living or being alone; not gregarious **2** secluded **3** single; sole [L *solitarius* fr. *solus* alone]

sol·i·tude /säl'ət(y)ōōd'/ *n.* **1** being solitary **2** lonely place [L *solitudo*, rel. to SOLITARY]

so·lo /sō'lō/ *n.* (*pl.* ·los or ·li /-lē/) **1** musical piece or passage, dance, etc., performed by one person **2** thing done by one person, esp. an unaccompanied flight —*v.* (·loed, ·lo·ing) **3** perform a solo —*adv.* **4** unaccompanied; alone —**so'lo·ist** *n.* [It fr. L, rel. to SOLE³]

Sol·o·mon /säl'əmən/ 10th cent. B.C.; king of Israel; son of David

Sol'o·mon Is'lands *n.* Pacific island group and country, E of New Guinea. Capital: Honiara. Pop. 339,000

So·lon /sō'lən/ c. 638–559 B.C.; Athenian statesman and poet

sol·stice /säl'stis/ *n.* either of the times of the year when the sun is farthest from the equator [L *solstitium* 'the sun standing still']

sol·u·ble /säl'yəbəl/ *adj.* **1** that can be dissolved, esp. in water **2** solvable —**sol'u·bil'i·ty** /-bil'itē/ *n.* [L *solvere solut-* release]

so·lute /säl'yōōt'/ *n.* dissolved substance

so·lu·tion /səlōō'sHən/ *n.* **1** solving or means of solving a problem **2a** conversion of a solid or gas into a liquid by mixture with a liquid **b** mixture resulting from this

solve /sälv/ *v.* (solved, solv·ing) answer or effectively deal with (a problem) —**solv'a·ble** *adj.*; **solv'er** *n.*

sol·vent /säl'vənt/ *adj.* **1** able to pay one's debts; not in debt **2** able to dissolve or form a solution with something —*n.* **3** solvent liquid, etc. —**sol'ven·cy** *n.*

Sol·zhe·ni·tsyn /sōl'zHəniʹt'sin, sōl'-/, Alexander 1918– ; Russian novelist

So·ma·li·a /səmäl'yə, -ēə/ *n.* republic on the E coast of Africa. Capital: Mogadishu. Pop. 7,872,000 —**So·ma'li** *n.*; **So·ma'li·an** *adj.*

so·mat·ic /sōmat'ik/ *adj.* of the body, not of the mind —**so·mat'i·cal·ly** *adv.* [Gk *sōma -mat-* body]

som·ber /säm'bər/ *adj.* dark; gloomy; dismal —**som'ber·ly** *adv.*; **som'ber·ness** *n.* [L *sub ombra* under shade]

SOMBRERO

som·bre·ro /səmbrer'ō/ *n.* (*pl.* ·ros) broad-brimmed hat worn esp. in Latin America [Sp *sombra* shade, rel. to SOMBER]

some /səm/ *adj.* **1** unspecified amount or number of (*some water; some apples*) **2** unknown or unspecified (*some day*) **3** approximately (*some ten days*) **4** considerable (*went to some trouble*) **5** at least a modicum of (*have some consideration*) —*pron.* **6** some number or amount (*some remained*) —*adv.* **7** Colloq. to some extent (*do it some more*) [OE]

-some¹ *suffix* forming adjectives meaning: **1** producing (*fearsome*) **2** characterized by being (*meddlesome*) [OE]

-some² *suffix* forming nouns from numerals, meaning 'a group of' (*foursome*) [OE]

-some³ *suffix* forming technical words, meaning 'body' (*chromosome*)

some·bod·y /səm'bəd'ē, -bäd'ē/ *pron.* **1** some or any person —*n.* (*pl.* ·ies) **2** important person

some'day' *adv.* at some time in the future

some'how' *adv.* for some unstated reason or way

some'one' *n. & pron.* SOMEBODY

some'place' *adv.* SOMEWHERE

som·er·sault /səm'ərsôlt'/ *n.* **1** leap or roll forward or backward so that the body turns in a circle —*v.* **2** perform this [Fr *sobre* above, *saut* jump]

some'thing *n. & pron.* **1** unspecified or unknown event (*something happened*) **2** unexpressed or intangible quantity, quality, or extent (*something strange*) **3** Colloq. notable person or thing —*adv.* **4** approximately (*something like*) **something else** Colloq. something exceptional [OE, rel. to SOME, THING]

some'time' *adv.* **1** at some time **2** formerly —*adj.* **3** former

some'times' *adv.* occasionally

some'what' *adv.* to some extent

some'where' *adv.* **1** in or to some place **2** approximately —*pron.* **3** some unspecified place

som·nam·bu·lism /sämnam'byəliz'əm/ *n.* sleepwalking —**som·nam'bu·lant** /-lənt/ *adj.*; **som·nam'bu·list** /-list/ *n.* [L *somnus* sleep, *ambulare* walk]

som·no·lent /säm'nələnt/ *adj.* **1** sleepy; drowsy **2** inducing drowsiness —**som'no·lence** *n.* [L, rel. to SOMNAMBULISM]

son /sən/ *n.* **1** boy or man in relation to his parent(s) **2** male descendant [OE]

so·nar /sō'när'/ *n.* **1** system for the underwater detection of objects by reflected sound 2 apparatus for this [sound navigation and ranging]

so·na·ta /sənät′ə/ *n.* *Mus.* composition for one or two instruments, usu. in three or four movements [It: sounded]

Sond·heim /sänd′hīm′/, **Stephen** 1930– ; US songwriter and lyricist

song /sông/ *n.* 1 words set to music or meant to be sung 2 vocal music 3 cry of some birds 4 for a song *Colloq.* very cheaply [OE, rel. to SING]

song′ and dance *n.* *Colloq.* fuss; commotion

song′bird *n.* bird with a musical call

son·ic /sän′ik/ *adj.* of or using sound or sound waves [L *sonus* sound]

son′ic bar′ri·er *n.* SOUND BARRIER

son′ic boom *n.* noise made when an aircraft passes the speed of sound

son′-in-law *n.* (*pl.* **sons′-in-law**) daughter's husband

son·net /sän′it/ *n.* poem of 14 lines with any of several rhyme patterns and usu. ten syllables per line [Fr *sonnet* or It *sonetto*]

son·ny /sən′ē/ *n.* *Colloq.* familiar form of address to a young boy

son·o·gram /sän′əgram′, sō′nə-/ *n.* *Med.* image produced by ultrasound waves, used for diagnostic purposes

So·no·ra /sənôr′ə/ *n.* state of NW Mexico, bordering Ariz. and the Gulf of California. Capital: Hermosillo. Pop. 1,823,600

So·no′ran Des′ert /sənôr′ən/ *n.* arid region in SW Ariz. and SE Calif., extending into Mexico

so·no·rous /sənôr′əs, sän′ərəs/ *adj.* 1 having a loud, full, or deep sound; resonant 2 (of language, style, etc.) imposing —**so·nor′i·ty** /-nôr′ətē/ *n.* [L *sonor* sound]

soon /sōōn/ *adv.* 1 in a short time 2 readily; willingly (*would as soon stay*) 3 quickly; before long (*as soon as possible*) 4 **sooner or later** at some future time; eventually [OE]

soot /sōōt/ *n.* black, powdery deposit from smoke [OE]

sooth /sōōth/ *n.* *Archaic.* truth [OE]

soothe /sōōth/ *v.* (**soothed, sooth·ing**) 1 calm (a person, feelings, etc.) 2 soften or alleviate (pain, etc.) [OE]

sooth·say·er /sōōth′sā′ər/ *n.* seer; prophet

soot′y *adj.* (**·i·er, ·i·est**) 1 covered with soot 2 like soot; black

sop /säp/ *n.* 1 thing given or done to pacify or bribe 2 piece of bread, etc., dipped in gravy, milk, etc. *—v.* (**sopped, sop·ping**) 3 drench 4 (foll. by *up*) soak or mop up [OE]

SOP or **S.O.P.** *abbr.* standard operating procedure

soph /säf/ *abbr.* sophomore

soph·ism /säf′iz′əm/ *n.* false argument, esp. one intended to deceive [Gk *sophos* wise]

soph·ist /säf′ist/ *n.* captious or clever but fallacious reasoner —**so·phis′tic** or **so·phis′ti·cal** *adj.* [Gk, rel. to SOPHISM]

so·phis·ti·cate /səfis′tikat/ 1 sophisticated person *—v.* /-kāt′/ (**·cat·ed, ·cat·ing**) 2 make worldly wise 3 complicate [MedL, rel. to SOPHISM]

so·phis·ti·cat·ed /səfis′tikä′tid/ *adj.* 1 (of a person) worldly wise; cultured; elegant 2 (of a thing, idea, etc.) highly developed and complex —**so·phis′ti·ca′tion** *n.*

soph·ist·ry /säf′istrē/ *n.* (*pl.* **·ries**) 1 use of sophism 2 a sophism

Soph·o·cles /säf′əklēz′/ c. 496–406 B.C.; Greek tragedian

soph·o·more /säf′(ə)môr′/ *n.* second-year university or high-school student [earlier *sophumer*, rel. to SOPHISM]

so·po·rif·ic /säp′ərif′ik/ *adj.* 1 inducing sleep *—n.* 2 soporific drug or influence —**sop′o·rif′i·cal·ly** *adv.* [L *sopor* sleep]

sop·py /säp′ē/ *adj.* (**·pi·er, ·pi·est**) 1 *Colloq.* overly sentimental 2 drenched —**sop·pi·ly** /säp′əlē/ *adv.*; **sop′pi·ness** *n.* [fr. SOP]

so·pran·o /səpran′ō/ *n.* (*pl.* **·os**) 1a highest singing voice b singer with this voice 2 instrument of a high or the highest pitch in its family *—adj.* 3 of a soprano 4 in the range of a soprano [It *sopra* above]

sor·bet /sôrbā′, sôr′bit/ *n.* sherbet [Ar *sharba* to drink]

Sorb·i·an /sôr′bēən/ *n. & adj.* (pertaining to) a west Slavic people or their language (also called **Lusatian** or **Wendish**)

sor·cer·er /sôr′sərər/ *n.* (*fem.* **sor′cer·ess**) magician; wizard —**sor′cer·y** *n.* (*pl.* **·ies**) [Fr *sourcier*, rel. to SORT]

sor·did /sôr′did/ *adj.* 1 dirty; squalid 2 ignoble; mercenary —**sor′did·ly** *adv.*; **sor′did·ness** *n.* [L *sordidus*]

sore /sôr/ *adj.* 1 (of a part of the body) painful 2 suffering pain 3 *Colloq.* aggrieved; vexed 4 grievous; severe *—n.* 5 inflamed place on the skin or flesh *—adv.* 6 *Archaic.* grievously; severely —**sore′ness** *n.* [OE]

sore′ly *adv.* extremely

sore′ point′ *n.* subject to which a person is particularly sensitive

sor·ghum /sôr′gəm/ *n.* tropical cereal grass [It *sorgo*]

sor·rel¹ /sôr′əl, sär′-/ *n.* sour-leaved herb [Gmc, rel. to SOUR]

sor·rel² *adj.* 1 of a light reddish-brown color *—n.* 2 this color 3 sorrel animal, esp. a horse [Fr]

sor·row /sär′ō, sôr′ō/ *n.* 1 mental distress caused by loss or disappointment, etc.; sadness 2 cause of sorrow *—v.* 3 feel sorrow; mourn —**sor′row·ful** *adj.*; **sor′row·ful·ly** *adv.* [OE]

sor·ry /sär′ē, sôr′ē/ *adj.* (**·ri·er, ·ri·est**) 1 regretful; penitent 2 (foll. by *for*) feeling pity or sympathy for 3 wretched; miserable [OE, rel. to SORE]

sort /sôrt/ *n.* 1 group of similar things, people, etc.; class; kind 2 undistinguished, quasi type (*sort of artist*) *—v.* 3 arrange systematically; put in order 4 **of a sort** or **of sorts** *Colloq.* mediocre; inferior 5 **out of sorts** *Colloq.* slightly unwell 6 **sort of** *Colloq.* more or less; to some extent [L *sors sort-* lot]
    ● Usage: See note at KIND.

sor·tie /sôr′tē/ *n.* 1 sally, esp. from a besieged garrison 2 operational military flight [Fr]

SOS /es′ō·es′/ *n.* international signal of extreme distress

so'-so' *adj.* (also **so' so'**) **1** mediocre; passable —*adv.* **2** indifferently

sot /sät/ *n.* drunkard —**sot'tish** *adj.* [OE]

sot·to vo·ce /sät'ō vō'CHē/ *adv.* in an undertone [It]

sou·bri·quet /sōō'brəkā'/ *n.* var. of SOBRIQUET

soufflé /sōōflā'/ *n.* light, spongy, baked dish made with stiffly beaten egg whites [Fr: blown]

sough /sou, səf/ *v.* **1** moan or whisper like the wind in trees, etc. —*n.* **2** this sound [OE]

sought /sôt/ *v.* past and past part. of SEEK

soul /sōl/ *n.* **1** spiritual part of a person, often regarded as immortal **2** moral, emotional, or intellectual nature of a person **3** personification; pattern **4** an individual **5** animating or essential part **6** of, pertaining to, or deriving from American black culture (*soul music; soul food*) [OE]

soul·ful /sōl'fəl/ *adj.* having, expressing, or evoking deep feeling —**soul'ful·ly** *adv.*; **soul'ful·ness** *n.*

soul'less *adj.* lacking sensitivity or noble qualities

soul' mate' *n.* person ideally suited to another

soul' mu'sic *n.* music with rhythm and blues, gospel, and rock elements

sound[1] /sound/ *n.* **1** sensation caused in the ear by the vibration of air or other medium **2** vibrations causing this sensation **3** what is or may be heard **4** idea or impression conveyed by words —*v.* **5** (cause to) emit sound **6** seem; appear —**sound'less** *adj.* [L *sonus*]

sound[2] *adj.* **1** healthy; not diseased, injured, or rotten **2** (of an opinion, policy, etc.) correct; well-founded **3** undisturbed **4** thorough —*adv.* **5** soundly (*sound asleep*) —**sound'ly** *adv.*; **sound'ness** *n.* [OE]

sound[3] *v.* **1** test the depth or quality of the bottom of (a body of water) **2** (often foll. by *out*) inquire (esp. indirectly) into the opinions or feelings of (a person) [Fr *sonder* fr. L *sub unda* under the wave]

sound[4] *n.* **1** body of water between an island and the mainland **2** strait [OE: swimming]

sound' bar·ri·er *n.* hypothetical limit once thought to prevent speeds beyond the speed of sound

sound' bite' *n.* short pithy recorded extract from an interview, speech, etc.

sound' ef·fect' *n.* sound other than speech or music made artificially for a film, etc.

sound'ing *n.* **1** measurement of the depth of water **2** (*pl.*) waters close to shore

sound'ing board' *n.* **1** person used to test opinion **2** device for directing sound

sound'proof' *adj.* **1** impervious to sound —*v.* **2** make soundproof

sound'track' *n.* the sound element of a film or videotape

soup /sōōp/ *n.* **1** liquid food made by boiling meat, fish, or vegetables —*v.* **2 soup up:** *Colloq.* **a** increase the power of (an engine) **b** enliven **3 in the soup** *Colloq.* in trouble [Fr]

soup·çon /sōōpsōn'/ *n.* small quantity; trace [Fr, rel. to SUSPICION]

soup'y *adj.* (**-i·er, -i·est**) **1** like soup **2** sentimental **3** foggy

sour /sour/ *adj.* **1** acid in taste or smell **2** (of milk, etc.) fermented **3** morose; bitter **4** unpleasant; distasteful —*v.* **5** make or become sour —**sour'ly** *adv.*; **sour'ness** *n.* [OE]

source /sôrs/ *n.* **1** place from which a thing issues or originates **2** person, document, etc., providing information [Fr, rel. to SURGE]

sour' grapes' *n. pl.* seeming disdain for something unattainable

sour'puss' *n. Colloq.* sour-tempered, cranky person; grouch

Sou·sa /sōō'zə/, **John Philip** 1854–1932; US composer of march music

souse /sous/ *v.* (**soused, sous·ing**) **1** immerse in pickling or other liquid **2** soak (a thing) in liquid; drench —*n.* **3** pickled food **4** pickling liquid **5** plunge or drench in water [Fr *sous*]

south /souTH/ *n.* **1** point of the horizon 90° clockwise from east **2** compass point corresponding to this **3** direction in which this lies **4a** (usu. **the South**) part of the world, a country, or a town to the south **b** southern US states, esp. those of the Confederacy —*adj.* **5** toward, at, near, or facing the south **6** from the south —*adv.* **7** toward, at, or near the south **8** (foll. by *of*) further south than [OE]

South' Af'ri·ca *n.* republic at the S tip of Africa. Capitals: Cape Town; Pretoria; Bloemfontein. Pop. 41,688,400 —**South' Af'ri·can** *n. & adj.*

South' A·mer'i·ca *n.* continent of the Western Hemisphere extending S from the Isthmus of Panama —**South' A·mer'i·can** *n. & adj.*

South·amp'ton /souTH(h)am(p)'tən/ *n.* seaport in S England. Pop. 214,800

South' Bend' *n.* city in Ind. Pop. 105,511

South' Car·o·li'na /kar'əlī'nə/ *n.* S state of the US. Capital: Columbia. Pop. 3,486,703. Abbr. SC; S.C.; S. Car. —**South Car·o·lin·i·an** /-lin'ēən/ *n. & adj.*

South' Chi'na Sea' *n.* part of the W Pacific enclosed by the Philippines and Borneo

South' Da·ko'ta /dəkōt'ə/ *n.* state in the central US. Capital: Pierre. Pop. 696,004. Abbr. SD; S.D.; S. Dak. —**South' Da·ko'tan** *n. & adj.*

south·east' *n.* **1** point midway between south and east **2** direction in which this lies —*adj.* **3** of, toward, or coming from the southeast —*adv.* **4** toward, at, or near the southeast —**south·east'er** *n.*; **south'east'ern** *adj.*; **south'east'er·ly** *adv. & adj.*; **south'east'ward** *adv., adj. & n.*; **south'east'wards** *adv.*

south·er·ly /səTH'ərlē/ *adj. & adv.* **1** in a southern position or direction **2** (of a wind) from the south —*n.* (*pl.* **-lies**) **3** such a wind

south·ern /səTH'ərn/ *adj.* **1** of, toward, or in the south —**south'ern·er** *n.*; **south'ern·most'** *adj.*

South'ern Hem'i·sphere' *n.* the half of the earth south of the equator

south'ern lights' *n. pl.* AURORA

Sou·they /səTH'ē, souTH'ē/, **Robert** 1774–1843; English poet and writer

South' Ko·re'a *n.* see KOREA

south'paw' *n. Colloq.* left-handed person, esp. a baseball pitcher

South' Pole' *n.* S end of the earth's axis of rotation, on Antarctica

South' Seas' *n.* southern Pacific Ocean

south·ward /soUTH′wərd/ *adj. & adv.* (also **south′wards**) toward the south

south·west′ *n.* **1** point of the horizon midway between south and west **2** direction in which this lies —*adj.* **3** of, toward, or coming from the southwest —*adv.* **4** toward, at, or near the southwest —**south′west′er** *n.*; **south′west′ern** *adj.*; **south′west′er·ly** *adv. & adj.*; **south′west′ward** *adv., adj. & n.*; **south′west′wards** *adv.*

sou·ve·nir /sŌo′vənēr′/ *n.* memento of an occasion, place, etc. [Fr]

sou′west·er /sou′wes′tər/ *n.* **1** waterproof hat with a broad flap covering the neck **2** southwest wind

sov·er·eign /säv′(ə)rin/ *n.* **1** supreme ruler, esp. a monarch **2** former British gold coin nominally worth £1 —*adj.* **3** supreme **4** self-governing [Fr *so(u)verain*, -*g*- by association with *reign*]

sov′er·eign·ty *n.* (*pl.* -**ties**) **1** supremacy **2a** self-government **b** self-governing state

So·vi·et /sŌ′vē·et′/ *adj.* **1** of the former USSR or its people —*n.* **2** (**s-**) elected council in the USSR **3** (**s-**) revolutionary council of workers, peasants, etc. [Russ]

sow¹ /sō/ *v.* (**sowed**, **sown** /sōn/ or **sowed**, **sow·ing**) **1a** scatter (seed) on or in the earth **b** plant with seed **2** engender [OE]

sow² /sou/ *n.* adult female pig [OE]

So·we·to /səwet′ō, -wāt′ō/ *n.* group of townships in South Africa. Pop. 864,000

sox /säks/ *n.* var. pl. of SOCKS

soy /soi/ *n.* (also **soy·a** /soi′ə/) **1a** leguminous plant yielding edible oil and flour and used to replace animal protein **b** (in full **soy′** or **soy′a bean′**) seed of this **2** (in full **soy′ sauce′**) sauce from fermented soy beans [Japn]

So·yin·ka /SHŌ·yiNG′kə/, **Wole** 1934– ; Nigerian dramatist and novelist; Nobel prize 1986

spa /spä/ *n.* **1** resort with curative mineral spring **2** facility offering use of exercise equipment, steam baths, etc. [*Spa* in Belgium]

space /spās/ *n.* **1a** continuous expanse in which things exist and move **b** amount of this taken by a thing or available **2** interval between points or objects **3** empty area **4** OUTER SPACE **5** interval of time **6** freedom to think, be oneself, etc. —*v.* (**spaced, spac·ing**) **7** set or arrange at intervals —**spac′er** *n.* [L *spatium*]

space′ age′ *n.* **1** era of space travel —*adj.* **2** (**space′-age′**) very modern

space′craft′ *n.* (*pl.* -**craft**) vehicle for traveling in outer space

space′man′ *n.* (*pl.* -**men′**; *fem.* -**wom·an**, *pl.* -**wom′en**) astronaut

space′ship′ *n.* spacecraft

space′ shut′tle *n.* spacecraft for repeated use

space′ sta′tion *n.* artificial satellite as a base for operations in outer space

space′suit′ *n.* sealed pressurized suit for an astronaut in outer space

space′-time′ *n.* fusion of the concepts of space and time as a four-dimensional continuum

spac·y *adj.* (also **spac′y**) (**-i·er, -i·est**) *Slang.* flighty; eccentric

spa·cious /spä′SHəs/ *adj.* having ample

space; roomy —**spa′cious·ly** *adv.*; **spa′cious·ness** *n.* [L, rel. to SPACE]

spade¹ /spād/ *n.* **1** long-handled digging tool with a broad metal blade often squared off at the end **2** call a spade a spade speak bluntly —*v.* (**spad·ed, spad·ing**) **3** dig using a spade —**spade′ful** *n.* (*pl.* -**fuls**) [OE]

spade² *n.* **1a** playing card of a suit denoted by black inverted heart-shaped figures with short stalks **b** (*pl.*) this suit **2** in spades: *Slang.* **a** definitely; absolutely **b** to extreme [It *spada* sword, rel. to SPADE¹]

spade′work′ *n.* hard, preparatory work

spa·ghet·ti /spəget′ē/ *n.* pasta in long thin strands [It]

Spain /spān/ *n.* monarchy in SW Europe on the Iberian Peninsula. Capital: Madrid. Pop. 39,085,000

span /span/ *n.* **1** full extent from end to end or side to side **2** each part of a bridge between supports **3** maximum distance between the tips of the thumb and little finger (approx. 9 in.) —*v.* (**spanned, span·ning**) **4** stretch from side to side of; extend across **5** bridge (a river, etc.) [OE]

Span. *abbr.* **1** Spaniard **2** Spanish

span·dex /span′deks/ *n.* synthetic elastic fiber used in swimwear, etc.

SPANDREL

span·drel /span′drəl/ *n. Archit.* space between an arch and a cornice or exterior wall [prob. AngFr]

span·gle /spaNG′gəl/ *n.* **1** sequin —*v.* (-**gled, -gling**) **2** cover with or as with spangles [obs. *spang* fr. Du]

Span·iard /span′yərd/ *n.* **1** native or inhabitant of Spain **2** person of Spanish descent [Fr *Espaigne* Spain]

span·iel /span′yəl/ *n.* dog of a breed with a long silky coat and drooping ears [Fr *espaignneul* Spanish (dog)]

Span·ish /span′iSH/ *adj.* **1** of Spain, its people, or language —*n.* **2** the Romance language of Spain and Spanish America **3** (**the Spanish**) (*pl.*) the people of Spain

Span·ish A·mer′i·ca *n.* parts of N and S America where Spanish is the main language —**Span′ish-A·mer′i·can** *n. & adj.*

Span′ish Main′ *n. Hist.* NE coast of S America and adjoining parts of the Caribbean Sea

spank /spaNGk/ *v.* **1** slap, esp. on the buttocks as punishment —*n.* **2** slap, esp. on the buttocks [imit.]

spank′er *n. Naut.* fore-and-aft sail set aft of the mizzenmast

spank′ing *adj.* **1** brisk **2** *Colloq.* striking; excellent —*adv.* **3** *Colloq.* very —*n.* **4** slapping on the buttocks

spar¹ /spär/ *n.* stout pole, esp. as a ship's mast, etc. [ON *sperra* or Fr *esparre*]

spar[2] *v.* (sparred, spar·ring) 1 make the motions of boxing without heavy blows 2 argue [OE]

spare /sper/ *adj.* 1 extra 2 lean; thin 3 frugal —*n.* 4 spare part —*v.* (spared, spar·ing) 5 afford to give 6 refrain from killing, hurting, etc. 7 be frugal or grudging of 8 *Bowling.* knocking down of all pins with two rolls —spare′ly *adv.*; spare′ness *n.* [OE]

spare′ribs′ *n. pl.* closely trimmed ribs of pork

spar′ing *adj.* frugal; economical —spar′ing·ly *adv.*

spark /spärk/ *n.* 1 fiery particle from a fire 2 tiny amount 3 flash of light between electric conductors, etc. 4 flash of wit, etc. —*v.* 5 emit a spark or sparks 6 stir into activity; set off; ignite —spark′y *adj.* [OE]

spar·kle /spär′kəl/ *v.* (·kled, ·kling) 1 emit or seem to emit sparks; glitter; scintillate 2 (of beverages) effervesce —*n.* 3 glitter; effervescence; scintillation 4 lively quality

spar′kler *n.* 1 hand-held sparkling firework 2 *Colloq.* diamond

spark′ plug′ *n.* fuel-igniting device in an internal-combustion engine

spar·row /spar′ō/ *n.* small, brownish-gray bird [OE]

sparse /spärs/ *adj.* thinly dispersed or scattered —sparse′ly *adv.*; sparse′ness, spar′si·ty *n.* [L *spargere spars-* scatter]

Spar·ta·cus /spärt′ikəs/ 1st cent. B.C.; Thracian gladiator; led a slave revolt against Rome

Spar·tan /spärt′n/ *adj.* 1 of Sparta in ancient Greece 2 austere; rigorous; frugal —*n.* 3 citizen of Sparta [L]

spasm /spaz′əm/ *n.* 1 sudden, involuntary, convulsive muscular contraction 2 *Colloq.* brief spell [Gk *spasmos*]

spas·mod·ic /spazmäd′ik/ *adj.* of or in spasms; intermittent —spas·mod′i·cal·ly *adv.* [Gk, rel. to SPASM]

spas·tic /spas′tik/ *adj.* 1 of or afflicted with spasms —*n.* 2 spastic person [Gk, rel. to SPASM]

spat[1] /spat/ *v.* esp. *Brit. & Archaic.* past and past part. of SPIT[1]

spat[2] *n.* (usu. *pl.*) short gaiter covering a shoe [abbr. of *spatterdash*, rel. to SPATTER]

spat[3] *Colloq. n.* 1 petty or brief quarrel —*v.* (spat·ted, spat·ting) 2 quarrel [prob. imit.]

spat[4] *n.* spawn of shellfish, esp. the oyster

spate /spāt/ *n.* unexpectedly frequent occurrence of similar events

spathe /spāTH/ *n.* large bract(s) enveloping a flower cluster [Gk *spathē* broad blade]

spa·tial /spā′shəl/ *adj.* of space —spa′tial·ly *adv.* [L, rel. to SPACE]

spat·ter /spat′ər/ *v.* 1 splash or scatter in drops —*n.* 2 splash 3 spattering [imit.]

spat·u·la /spaCH′ələ/ *n.* broad-bladed flexible implement used for spreading, stirring, etc. [L dim., rel. to SPATHE]

spawn /spôn/ *v.* 1a (of a fish, frog, etc.) produce (eggs) b be produced as eggs or young 2 produce or generate in large numbers —*n.* 3 eggs of fish, frogs, etc. [AngFr *espaundre*, rel. to EXPAND]

spay /spā/ *v.* sterilize (a female animal) by removing the ovaries [AngFr, rel. to ÉPÉE]

speak /spēk/ *v.* (spoke, spok·en, speak·ing) 1 utter words 2 utter (words, the truth, etc.) 3a (foll. by *to* or *with*) converse; talk b (foll. by *of*, *about*) mention c (foll. by *for*) support 4 make a speech 5 use or be able to use (a specified language) 6 so to speak that is to say 7 speak up: a make oneself heard b (foll. by *for*) defend 8 speak volumes be significant [OE]

speak′eas′y *n.* (*pl.* ·ies) *Slang.* place where alcoholic liquor is sold illicitly

speak′er *n.* 1 person who speaks, esp. in public 2 person who speaks a specified language (esp. in *comb.: French-speaker*) 3 (*cap.*) presiding officer in a legislative assembly, esp. the House of Representatives 4 short for LOUDSPEAKER

spear /spēr/ *n.* 1 weapon with a long shaft and a pointed usu. metal tip 2 tip and stem of asparagus, broccoli, grass, etc. —*v.* 3 pierce or strike (as) with a spear [OE]

spear′fish′ *n.* (*pl.* same or -es) 1 any marine fish having a long, pointed bill —*v.* 2 fish with a spear, esp. under water

spear′head′ *n.* 1 point of a spear 2 person or group leading an attack, etc. —*v.* 3 act as the spearhead of (an attack, etc.)

spear′mint′ *n.* common garden mint, used in flavoring

spec[1] /spek/ *n. Colloq.* 1 speculation 2 on spec as a gamble

spec[2] *n. Colloq.* short for SPECIFICATION, 2

spe·cial /spesh′əl/ *adj.* 1a exceptional b peculiar; specific 2 for a particular purpose 3 (of education, etc.) for children, etc., with disabilities —*n.* 4 special edition of a newspaper, dish on a menu, etc. —spe′cial·ly *adv.* [L, rel. to SPECIES]

spe′cial de·liv′er·y *n.* delivery of mail outside the normal delivery schedule

spe′cial ef·fects′ *n. pl.* illusions created by props, studio techniques, etc.

spe′cial·ist *n.* person trained in a particular branch of a profession

spe′cial·ize *v.* (·ized, ·iz·ing) 1 be or become a specialist 2 devote oneself to a single interest, skill, etc. 3 adapt for a particular purpose —spe′cial·i·za′tion *n.* [Fr, rel. to SPECIAL]

spe·cial·ty /spe′SHəltē/ *n.* (*pl.* ·ties) 1 special subject, product, activity, etc. 2 special feature or skill

spe·cie /spē′SHē/ *n.* coin as contrasted with paper money [rel. to SPECIES]

spe·cies /spē′SHēz/ *n.* (*pl.* same) 1 class of things having certain common characteristics 2 group of animals or plants within a genus 3 kind; sort [L: appearance, rel. to *specere* look]

spe·cif·ic /spəsif′ik/ *adj.* 1 clearly defined 2 particular 3 exact; precise; giving full details 4 (of a medication) having a distinct effect in curing a certain disease —*n.* 5 specific medication 6 particular aspect or factor —spe·cif′ic·al·ly *adv.*; spec·i·fic′i·ty /spes′əfis′ətē/ *n.* [L, rel. to SPECIES]

spec·i·fi·ca·tion /spes′ifikā′SHən/ *n.* 1 act of specifying 2 detail of the design and materials, etc., of work done or to be done [MedL, rel. to SPECIFY]

spe·cif′ic grav′i·ty *n.* the ratio between the mass of a substance and that of the same volume of a substance used as a standard (usu. water or air)

spec·i·fy /ˈspesˈəfī/ v. (**-fied, ·fy·ing**) 1 name or mention expressly or as a condition 2 include in a specification [L, rel. to SPECIFIC]

spec·i·men /ˈspesˈəmin/ n. 1 individual or sample taken as an example of a class or whole 2 sample of urine for testing [L specere look]

spe·cious /ˈspēSHəs/ adj. plausible but wrong —**spe'cious·ly** adv.; **spe'cious·ness** n. [L, rel. to SPECIES]

speck /spek/ n. 1 small spot or stain 2 particle —v. 3 mark with specks [OE]

speck·le /ˈspekˈəl/ n. 1 speck, esp. one of many —v. (**·led, ·ling**) 2 mark with speckles [Du spekkel]

specs /speks/ n. pl. Colloq. 1 specifications 2 spectacles

spec·ta·cle /ˈspektikəl/ n. 1 striking, impressive, or ridiculous sight 2 public show 3 (pl.) Old-fash. eyeglasses [L specere spect- look]

spec·tac·u·lar /spekˈtakˈyələr/ adj. 1 striking; impressive; lavish —n. 2 spectacular show —**spec·tac'u·lar·ly** adv.

spec·ta·tor /ˈspekˈtātˈər/ n. person who watches a show, game, etc. [L, rel. to SPECTACLE]

spec·ter /ˈspekˈtər/ n. (also **spec'tre**) 1 ghost 2 haunting presentiment [L spectrum fr. specere look]

spec·tral /ˈspekˈtrəl/ adj. 1 of or like a specter 2 of a spectrum —**spec'tral·ly** adv.

spec·trom·e·ter /spekˈträmˈətər/ n. instrument for measuring observed spectra

spec·tro·scope /ˈspekˈtrəskōp/ n. instrument for recording spectra for examination —**spec'tro·scop'ic** /-skäpˈik/ adj.; **spec·tros·co·py** /spekˈträsˈkəpē/ n.

spec·trum /ˈspekˈtrəm/ n. (pl. **·tra** /-trə/) 1 band of colors as seen in a rainbow, etc. 2 entire or wide range of a subject, emotion, etc. 3 distribution of visible electromagnetic radiation arranged by wavelength [L specere look]

spec·u·late /ˈspekˈyəlāt/ v. (**·lat·ed, ·lat·ing**) 1 theorize; conjecture 2 deal in a commodity or asset in the hope of profiting from fluctuating prices —**spec·u·la'tion** n.; **spec'u·la·tive** /-lətiv/ adj.; **spec'u·la·tor** n. [L specula watchtower, fr. specere]

spec·u·lum /ˈspekˈyələm/ n. (pl. **·la** /-lə/) 1 instrument for dilating orifices of the body 2 mirror of polished metal in a telescope [L: mirror]

sped /sped/ v. past and past part. of SPEED

speech /spēCH/ n. 1 faculty, act, or manner of speaking 2 formal public address 3 language of a nation, group, etc. —**speech'less** adj.; **speech'less·ly** adv.; **speech'less·ness** n. [OE, rel. to SPEAK]

speed /spēd/ n. 1 rapidity of movement 2 rate of progress or motion 3 gear appropriate to a range of speeds, esp. of a bicycle 4 Photog. a sensitivity of film to light b light-gathering power of a lens c duration of an exposure 5 Slang. amphetamine drug —v. (**sped** or **speed·ed, speed·ing**) 6 go or send quickly 7 (past and past part. **speed·ed**) travel at an illegal or dangerous speed 8 **speed up** move or work faster —**speed'er, speed'ster** n. [OE]

speed'boat' n. high-speed motor boat

speed·om·e·ter /spiˈdämˈətər/ n. instrument on a vehicle indicating its speed

speed'way' n. race track for cars, motorcycles, etc.

speed'y adj. (**·i·er, ·i·est**) 1 rapid 2 done without delay; prompt —**speed'i·ly** adv.; **speed'i·ness** n.

spe·le·ol·o·gy /ˌspēˈlēˈälˈəjē/ n. study of caves —**spe'le·ol'o·gist** n. [Gk spēlaion cave]

spell¹ /spel/ v. (**spelled** or **spelt, spell·ing**) 1 write or name correctly the letters of (a word, etc.) 2 (of letters) form (a word, etc.) 3 result in 4 **spell out: a** make out (words, etc.) letter by letter **b** explain in detail [Fr espeller, rel. to SPELL²]

spell² n. 1 words used as a charm or incantation, etc. 2 effect of these 3 fascination exercised by a person, activity, etc. [OE]

spell³ n. 1 fairly short period 2 period of some activity or work —v. (**spelled, spell·ing**) 3 relieve (a person) at work by temporary substitution [OE: substitute]

spell·bind /ˈspelˈbīnd/ v. (**·bound, ·bind·ing**) hold the attention as if with a spell; entrance —**spell'bind'er** n.; **spell'bind'ing** adj.

spell' check'er (also **spell'ing check'er**) n. Comp. software that checks text for spelling errors —**spell'·check'** v.

spell'er n. 1 book listing words to show their spelling 2 person who spells words, esp. with reference to skill (good or bad speller)

spell'ing bee' n. contest in which competitors are eliminated for misspelling a word

spe·lunk·er /spəˈləNGˈkər/ n. explorer of caves [Gk spēlynx cave]

spend /spend/ v. (**spent** /spent/, **spend·ing**) 1 pay out (money) 2 use or consume (time, energy, etc.) —**spend'a·ble** adj.; **spend'er** n. [L, rel. to EXPEND]

spend'thrift' n. 1 extravagant person —adj. 2 extravagant

Spen·ser /ˈspenˈsər/, **Edmund** c. 1552–99; English poet

sperm /spərm/ n. (pl. same or **-s**) 1 SPERMATOZOON 2 semen [Gk sperma -mat-]

sper·ma·to·zo·on /ˌspərmatˈəˈzōˈən, spərˈmətə-/ n. (pl. **·zo·a** /-zōˈə/) mature sex cell in semen [fr. SPERM, Gk zōion animal]

sper·mi·cide /ˈspərˈməsīd/ n. substance for killing spermatozoa —**sper'mi·cid'al** adj.

sperm' whale' n. large whale yielding valuable oil

spew /spyoō/ v. 1 vomit 2 (cause to) gush [OE]

SPF abbr. sun protection factor

sp. gr. abbr. specific gravity

sphere /sfēr/ n. 1 solid figure with every point on its surface equidistant from its center 2 ball; globe 3 field of action, influence, etc. —**spher·i·cal** /ˈsferˈəkəl/ adj.; **spher'i·cal·ly** adv. [Gk sphaira ball]

spher·oid /ˈsferˈoid, sfer'-/ n. 1 spherelike but not perfectly spherical body —adj. 2 spherelike —**sphe·roi'dal** adj.

sphinc·ter /ˈsfiNGˈktər/ n. ring of muscle surrounding and closing an opening in the body [Gk sphingein bind tight]

sphinx /sfiNGks/ *n.* 1 *Gk. Myth.* winged monster with a woman's head and a lion's body 2 ancient Egyptian stone figure with a lion's body and a human or animal head 3 (*cap.*) statue of a huge sphinx at Giza, Egypt 4 inscrutable person [Gk]

SPHINX 2

sphyg·mo·ma·no·me·ter /sfig'mōmənom' itər/ *n.* instrument for measuring blood pressure [Gk *sphygmós* pulse, *manós* sparse, -METER]

spice /spīs/ *n.* 1 aromatic or pungent vegetable substance used to flavor food 2 piquant quality —*v.* (**spiced, spic·ing**) 3 flavor with spice —**spic'y** *adj.* (**·i·er, ·i·est**); **spic'i·ness** *n.* [Fr *espice*]

Spice Is'lands *n.* see MOLUCCAS

spick' and span' /spik/ *adj.* 1 neat and clean 2 fresh and new [earlier *spick and span new* 'brand new']

spi·der /spī'dər/ *n.* 1 arachnid, of which many species spin webs, esp. to capture insects as food 2 cast-iron frying pan [OE, rel. to SPIN]

spi'der·y *adj.* elongated and thin

spiel /spēl, shpēl/ *n. Slang.* glib speech or story; sales pitch [Ger: game]

spiff·y /spif'ē/ *adj.* (**·i·er, ·i·est**) *Slang.* smartly dressed

spig·ot /spig'ət/ *n.* 1 small peg, esp. in a cask 2 faucet [rel. to SPIKE²]

spike¹ /spīk/ *n.* 1 pointed piece of metal, as at the top of an iron railing 2a metal point in the sole of a shoe to prevent slipping b (*pl.*) spiked shoes 3 large nail —*v.* (**spiked, spik·ing**) 4 fit with spikes 5 fix on a spike 6 *Colloq.* lace (a drink) with alcohol, etc. 7 *Colloq.* thwart; frustrate 8 invalidate; reject —**spik'y** *adj.* (**·i·er, ·i·est**) [LGer or Du, rel. to SPOKE¹]

spike² *n.* 1 cluster of flower-heads on a long stem 2 ear of grain [L *spica*]

spill /spil/ *v.* (**spilled** or **spilt** /spilt/, **spill·ing**) 1 fall or run or cause (liquid, powder, etc.) to fall or run out of a container, esp. accidentally 2 throw from a vehicle, saddle, etc. 3 (foll. by *into, out,* etc.) (esp. of a crowd) leave a place 4 *Slang.* disclose (information, etc.) 5 shed (blood) —*n.* 6 spilling or being spilled 7 tumble, esp. from a horse, bicycle, etc. 8 **spill the beans** *Colloq.* divulge secret information, etc. —**spill'age** *n.* [OE]

spill'way' *n.* sluice for surplus water from a dam

spin /spin/ *v.* (**spun, spin·ning**) 1 (cause to) turn or whirl around quickly 2a draw out and twist (wool, cotton, etc.) into threads b make (yarn) in this way 3 (of a spider, silkworm, etc.) make (a web, cocoon, etc.) by extruding a fine thread 4 (esp. of the head) be dizzy through excitement, etc. 5 tell or write (a story, etc.) —*n.* 6 spinning motion; whirl 7 rotating dive of an aircraft 8 twisting motion, e.g., of a ball in flight 9 *Colloq.* brief drive, esp. in a car 10 **spin off** create something new from an existing entity, e.g., a separate company from a parent —**spin'ner** *n.* [OE]

spi·na bi·fi·da /spī'nə bif'ədə/ *n.* congenital spinal defect [L: cleft spine]

spin·ach /spin'ich/ *n.* green vegetable with edible leaves [Fr *espinache*]

spi·nal /spīn'l/ *adj.* of the spine [L, rel. to SPINE]

spi'nal col'umn *n.* spine

spi'nal cord' *n.* cylindrical nervous structure within the spine

spin·dle /spin'dəl/ *n.* 1 slender rod or bar, often tapered, for twisting and winding thread 2 pin or axis that revolves or on which something revolves 3 turned piece of wood used as a banister, chair leg, etc. [OE, rel. to SPIN]

spin·dly /spin(d)'lē/ *adj.* (**·dli·er, ·dli·est**) long or tall and thin; thin and weak

spine /spīn/ *n.* 1 vertebrae extending from the skull to the coccyx; backbone 2 needle-like outgrowth of an animal or plant 3 back part of a book where the pages are fastened 4 sharp ridge or projection —**spin'y** *adj.* (**·i·er, ·i·est**) [L *spina*]

spine'-chill'ing *adj.* frightening; horrifying

spine'less *adj.* 1 having no spine; invertebrate 2 lacking resolve; feeble

spin·et /spin'ət/ *n.* upright piano with short strings [It *spinetta*]

spin·ner·et /spin'əret'/ *n.* spinning organ in a spider, etc.

spin'ning jen'ny *n.* machine for spinning fibers with more than one spindle at a time

spin'ning wheel' *n.* household device for spinning yarn or thread, having a spindle driven by a wheel spun usu. by a treadle

spin'-off' *n.* 1 new entity created from one already in existence 2 ancillary benefit; bonus

Spi·no·za /spinō'zə/, **Baruch (Benedict de)** 1632–77; Dutch philosopher

spin·ster /spin'stər/ *n.* 1 unmarried woman 2 esp. elderly woman thought unlikely to marry —**spin'ster·ish** *adj.* [orig. woman who spins]

spi·ral /spī'rəl/ *adj.* 1 coiled in a plane or as if around a cylinder or cone —*n.* 2 spiral curve or thing 3 progressive rise or fall —*v.* (**·raled** or **·ralled, ·ral·ing** or **·ral·ling**) 4 move in a spiral course 5 (of prices, wages, etc.) rise or fall continuously —**spi'ral·ly** *adv.* [Gk *speira* coil]

spire /spīr/ *n.* tapering structure, esp. on a church tower [OE]

spi·re·a /spīrē'ə/ *n.* (also **spi·rae'a**) shrub with white or pink flowers [Gk, rel. to SPIRAL]

spir·it /spir'it/ *n.* 1 person's essence or intelligence; soul 2 ghost 3a person's character b attitude; essential characteristic 4 type of person 5 (usu. *pl.*) distilled liquor 6 courage; vivacity 7 (*pl.*) state of mind; mood —*v.* 8 essential meaning 9 (usu. foll. by *away, off,* etc.) convey rapidly or mysteriously —**spir'it·less** *adj.* [L *spiritus* breathing]

spir·it·ed *adj.* lively; courageous —**spir·it·ed·ly** *adv.*

spir·it lev·el *n.* device with a glass tube nearly filled with alcohol, used to test horizontality

spir·i·tu·al /spir'iCHŌŌəl/ *adj.* 1 of the spirit or soul as contrasted with bodily or worldly 2 religious; divine; inspired —*n.* 3 religious song orig. of American blacks —**spir'i·tu·al'i·ty** /-al'itē/ *n.*; **spir'i·tu·al·ly** *adv.*

spir·i·tu·al·ism *n.* belief in communication with the dead, esp. through mediums —**spir'it·u·al·ist** /-ist/ *n.*; **spir'i·tu·al·is'tic** *adj.*

spir·i·tu·ous /spir'iCHŌŌəs/ *adj.* alcoholic

spi·ro·chete /spi'rōkēt'/ *n.* any of various flexible spiral-shaped bacteria [L fr. Gk *speira* coil, *khaitē* long hair]

spit¹ /spit/ *v.* (**spit** or **spat**, **spit·ting**) **1a** eject (esp. saliva) from the mouth in contempt or anger; sputter; splutter **2** (of a fire, gun, etc.) throw out with an explosion —*n.* 3 saliva **4** act of spitting [OE]

spit² *n.* 1 rod for skewering meat for roasting on a fire, etc. 2 point of land projecting into the sea —*v.* (**spit·ted**, **spit·ting**) 3 pierce (as) with a spit [OE]

spit' and pol'ish *n.* *Colloq.* esp. military cleaning and polishing

spit'ball' *n.* 1 wad of chewed paper used as a missile 2 *Baseball.* pitched ball smeared with spit, etc., to make it curve

spite /spīt/ *n.* 1 ill will; malice —*v.* (**spit·ed**, **spit·ing**) 2 hurt, harm, or frustrate (a person) through spite **3 in spite of** notwithstanding; despite —**spite'ful** *adj.*; **spite'ful·ly** *adv.*; **spite'ful·ness** *n.* [Fr, rel. to DESPITE]

spit'fire' *n.* woman of fiery temper

spit'ting dis'tance *n.* *Colloq.* short distance

spit'ting im'age *n.* *Colloq.* double (of a person)

spit·tle /spit'l/ *n.* saliva [rel. to SPIT¹]

spit·toon /spitōōn'/ *n.* vessel to spit into

splash /splash/ *v.* 1 scatter or cause (liquid) to scatter in drops 2 wet with spattered liquid, etc. 3 move while spattering liquid, etc. 4 display prominently —*n.* 5 splashing 6 quantity splashed 7 mark made by splashing 8 **make a splash** attract attention —**splash'y** *adj.* (·i·er, ·i·est) [imit.]

splash'down' *n.* landing of a spacecraft on the sea —**splash' down** *v.*

splat¹ /splat/ *Colloq.* *n.* 1 sharp splattering sound —*adv.* 2 with a splat —*v.* (**splat·ted**, **splat·ting**) 3 fall or hit with a splat [abbr. of SPLATTER]

splat² *n.* wide, flat, wooden piece forming the center upright of a chair back [rel. to SPLIT]

splat'ter *v.* splash, esp. with a continuous noisy action; spatter [imit.]

splay /splā/ *v.* 1 spread apart —*adj.* 2 splayed [fr. DISPLAY]

spleen /splēn/ *n.* 1 abdominal organ regulating blood quality 2 moroseness [Gk *splēn*]

splen·did /splen'did/ *adj.* 1 magnificent; sumptuous 2 impressive; glorious 3 excellent; fine —**splen'did·ly** *adv.* [L, rel. to SPLENDOR]

splen·dor /splen'dər/ *n.* dazzling brightness; magnificence [L *splendere* shine]

sple·net·ic /splinet'ik/ *adj.* bad-tempered; peevish —**sple·net'i·cal·ly** *adv.* [L, rel. to SPLEEN]

splice /splīs/ *v.* (**spliced**, **splic·ing**) 1 join (ends of ropes) by interweaving strands 2 join (ends of pieces of wood, tape, etc.) by overlapping 3 *Colloq.* join in marriage —*n.* 4 join made by splicing [prob. Du *splissen*]

splint /splint/ *n.* 1 strip of wood, etc., bound to a broken limb to keep it rigid 2 thin wooden strip used in basket weaving —*v.* 3 secure with a splint [LGer or Du]

splin·ter /splin'tər/ *n.* 1 small, sharp fragment of wood, stone, glass, etc. —*v.* 2 break into splinters; shatter —**splint'er·y** *adj.* [Du, rel. to SPLINT]

split /split/ *v.* (**split**, **split·ting**) 1 break, esp. with the grain or into halves 2 divide into parts, esp. equal shares 3 remove or be removed by breaking or dividing **4a** divide into factions **b** quarrel or cease association 5 *Slang.* leave, esp. suddenly —*n.* 6 act or result of splitting 7 disagreement; schism 8 feat of sinking to the floor with the legs at right angles to the body in front and behind or on either side [Du]

split' in·fin'i·tive *n.* infinitive with a word between *to* and the verb (*to boldly go*)

  ● Usage: See note at INFINITIVE.

split'-lev'el *adj.* (of a house) with more than one level

split' pea' *n.* pea dried and split in half for cooking

split' per·son·al'i·ty *n.* psychological condition in which a person seems to have two or more alternating personalities

split'ting *adj.* excruciatingly painful

splotch /spläch/ *Colloq.* *n.* 1 daub; blot; smear —*v.* 2 make a splotch on —**splotch'y** *adj.* (·i·er, ·i·est)

splurge /splərj/ *Colloq.* *n.* 1 sudden extravagance 2 ostentatious display or effort —*v.* (**splurged**, **splurg·ing**) 3 spend large sums of money [prob. imit.]

splut·ter /splət'ər/ *v.* **1a** speak, say, or express in a choking manner **b** emit spitting sounds 2 speak rapidly or incoherently —*n.* 3 spluttering speech or sound [fr. SPUTTER]

Spock /späk/, **Benjamin** 1903– ; US pediatrician and writer

spoil /spoil/ *v.* (**spoiled** or **spoilt**, **spoil·ing**) 1 make or become useless, unsatisfactory, rotten, inedible, etc. 2 overindulge (esp. a child) 3 despoil —*n.* 4 (usu. *pl.*) plunder 5 profit or advantage from success or position 6 **be spoiling for** aggressively seek (a fight, trouble, etc.) —**spoil'age** /-ij/, **spoil'er** *n.* [L *spoliare*]

spoil'sport' *n.* person who spoils others' enjoyment

Spo·kane /spōkan'/ *n.* city in Wash. Pop. 177,196

spoke¹ /spōk/ *n.* each of the rods running from the hub to the rim of a wheel [OE]

spoke² *v.* *past* of SPEAK

spo·ken /spō'kən/ *v.* 1 *past part.* of SPEAK —*adj.* 2 (in *comb.*) speaking in a specified way (*well-spoken*) 3 oral 4 **spoken for** claimed

spokes·man /spōks'mən/ *n.* (*pl.* **·men**; *fem.* **·wom'an**, *pl.* **·wom'en**) person speaking for a group, etc. [fr. SPOKE²]

spokes′per′son *n.* (*pl.* **·sons** or **spokes′peo′ ple**) spokesman or spokeswoman

spo·li·a·tion /spō′lē-ā′sʜən/ *n.* plundering; pillage [L, rel. to SPOIL]

spon·dee /spän′dē′/ *n.* metrical foot consisting of two long syllables —**spon·da·ic** /-dā′ ik/ *adj.* [Gk *spondē* libation, with which songs in this meter were associated]

sponge /spənj/ *n.* 1 sea animal with a porous skeleton 2 this skeleton or a synthetic imitation of it 3 thing like a sponge in absorbent quality, consistency, etc. —*v.* (**sponged, spong·ing**) 4 wipe, cleanse, or absorb (as) with a sponge 5 live as a parasite —**spong′er** *n.*; **spon′gi·form** /-jifôrm′/ *adj.*; **spong′i·ness** *n.*; **spong′y** *adj.* (**·i·er, ·i·est**) [L *spongia*]

sponge′ cake′ *n.* light, spongy cake

spon·sor /spän′sər/ *n.* 1 person who supports an activity; backer 2 company paying for advertising time on radio or television 3 godparent —*v.* 4 be a sponsor for —**spon′ sor·ship′** *n.* [L *spondere spons-* pledge]

spon·ta·ne·ous /späntā′nēəs/ *adj.* 1 acting, done, or occurring without external cause 2 instinctive; automatic; natural —**spon·ta·ne· i·ty** /spän′tänä′ətē, -nē′-/ *n.*; **spon·ta′ne·ous· ly** *adv.* [L *sponte* of one's own accord]

spon·ta′ne·ous com·bus′tion *n.* ignition of a substance from internal heat

spoof /spo͞of/ *n. & v.* 1 parody 2 hoax [invented word]

spook /spo͞ok/ *Colloq. n.* 1 ghost —*v.* 2 frighten; unnerve; cause to shy —**spook′i·ly** *adv.*; **spook′i·ness** *n.*; **spook′y** *adj.* (**·i·er, ·i· est**) [LGer or Du]

spool /spo͞ol/ *n.* 1 reel for winding magnetic tape, yarn, etc. 2 revolving cylinder of an angler's reel —*v.* 3 wind on a spool [Fr *espole* or Gmc *spole*]

spoon /spo͞on/ *n.* 1a utensil with a bowl and a handle for lifting food to the mouth, stirring, etc. b spoonful —*v.* 2 take (liquid, etc.) with a spoon 3 *Colloq.* kiss and cuddle —**spoon′ ful** *n.* (*pl.* **·fuls**) [OE]

spoon′bill′ *n.* wading bird with a broad flat-tipped bill

spoo·ner·ism /spo͞o′nəriz′əm/ *n.* transposition of the initial sounds, etc., of two or more words, as *roaring pain* for *pouring rain* [for the Rev. W.A. *Spooner*, noted for this]

spoon′feed′ *v.* (**·fed, ·feed·ing**) 1 feed with a spoon 2 give so much help to (a person) that no further effort need be made

spoor /spo͞or/ *n.* animal's track or scent [Du]

spo·rad·ic /spərad′ik/ *adj.* occasional —**spo·rad′i·cal·ly** *adv.* [Gk *sporas -ad-* scattered]

spore /spôr/ *n.* 1 reproductive cell of many plants and microorganisms —*v.* (**spored, spor·ing**) 2 produce spores [Gk *spora* seed]

sport /spôrt/ *n.* 1 game or competitive activity, usu. played outdoors and involving physical skill, training, etc., e.g., football, running 2 amusement; fun 3 *Colloq.* fair or generous person 4 object of fun or derision —*v.* 5 amuse oneself; play about 6 wear or exhibit, esp. ostentatiously —*adj.* 7 informal (*sport jacket*) 8 **in sport** jestingly 9 **make sport of** ridicule [fr. DISPORT]

sport′ing *adj.* 1 interested or concerned in sport 2 generous; fair 3 involving sport or gaming 4 **sporting chance** some possibility of success —**sport′ing·ly** *adv.*

sport′ive *adj.* playful

sports′ car′ *n.* low-built fast car

sports·man /spôrts′mən/ *n.* (*pl.* **·men;** *fem.* **·wom·an,** *pl.* **·wom′en**) 1 person who takes part in sports 2 fair and generous person —**sports′man·like** *adj.*; **sports′man·ship′** *n.*

sports′wear′ *n.* clothes for sports or informal wear

sport′y *adj.* (**·i·er, ·i·est**) *Colloq.* 1 fond of sport 2 rakish; showy —**sport′i·ly** *adv.*; **sport′i·ness** *n.*

spot /spät/ *n.* 1 small, roundish area or mark differing in color, texture, etc., from the surface it is on 2 blemish; defect 3 particular place; locality 4 small amount 5 SPOTLIGHT —*v.* (**spot·ted, spot·ting**) 6 mark with spots 7 identify; recognize; catch sight of 8 watch for and take note of (trains, talent, etc.) —*adj.* 9 random (*spot check*) 10 immediately available 11 **hit the spot:** a fulfill ideally b satisfy a need 12 **in a** (**tight**) **spot** in a precarious situation 13 **on the spot:** a at the scene of an event b *Colloq.* in a position demanding response or action —**spot′less** *adj.*; **spot′ less·ly** *adv.*; **spot′less·ness,** **spot′ter** *n.*; **spot′ti·ly** *adv.*; **spot′ti·ness** *n.*; **spot′ty** *adj.* (**·ti·er, ·ti·est**) [perh. fr. LGer or Du]

spot′light′ *n.* 1a (also **spot**) beam of light directed on a small area b lamp projecting this 2 full publicity —*v.* (**·lighted** or **·lit, light· ing**) 3 direct a spotlight on 4 draw attention to

spouse /spous/ *n.* husband or wife [L *sponsus* betrothed]

spout /spout/ *n.* 1 projecting tube or lip used for pouring from a teapot, kettle, jug, etc., or on a fountain, roof-gutter, etc. 2 jet or column of liquid, etc. —*v.* 3 discharge or issue forcibly in a jet 4 utter or speak at length or pompously [Du]

sprain /sprān/ *v.* 1 wrench (an ankle, wrist, etc.), causing pain or swelling —*n.* 2 such a wrench

sprang /spraNG/ *v. past* of SPRING

sprat /sprat/ *n.* small, edible marine fish [OE]

sprawl /sprôl/ *v.* 1a sit, lie, or fall with limbs flung out untidily b spread (one's limbs) thus 2 (of writing, a plant, a town, etc.) be irregular or straggling —*n.* 3 sprawling movement, position, or mass [OE]

spray¹ /sprā/ *n.* 1 liquid flying in small drops 2 device for creating this —*v.* 3 throw (liquid) as spray 4 sprinkle (an object) thus —**spray′er** *n.*

spray² *n.* sprig of flowers or leaves [OE]

spray′ can′ *n.* can containing an aerosol

spray′ gun′ *n.* device for spraying paint, etc.

spread /spred/ *v.* (**spread, spread·ing**) 1a open; extend; unfold b cause to cover a surface or larger area 2 have a wide, increasing extent 3 become or make widely known, felt, etc. 4 set (a table) 5 extend sideways —*n.* 6 act of spreading 7 extent of spreading 8 diffusion 9 increased girth 10 difference between two rates, prices, etc. 11 *Colloq.* elaborate meal 12 food for spreading on bread, etc. 13 bedspread 14 matter printed across more than one column 15 property; acreage [OE]

spread′ ea′gle *adj.* 1 in the shape of an eagle with legs and wings extended —*v.* (**-gled, -gling**) 2 place (a person) in this position

spread′sheet′ *n. Comp.* program for the manipulation of tabulated figures

spree /sprē/ *n. Colloq.* 1 extravagant outing 2 bout of fun or drinking, etc.

sprig /sprig/ *n.* small branch or shoot [LGer *sprick*]

spright·ly /sprīt′lē/ *adj.* (**-li·er, -li·est**) vivacious; lively; brisk —**spright′li·ness** *n.* [fr. *spright*, var. of SPRITE]

spring /spriNG/ *v.* (**sprang** or **sprung, spring·ing**) 1 rise rapidly or suddenly; leap; jump 2 move rapidly by or as by the action of a spring 3 originate (from ancestors, a source, etc.) 4 act or appear suddenly or unexpectedly 5 present (a thing, circumstance, etc.) suddenly or unexpectedly 6 *Slang.* contrive the release of (a person from prison, etc.) —*n.* 7 jump; leap 8 recoil 9 elasticity 10 elastic device, usu. of coiled metal, used to drive clockwork, for cushioning in furniture or vehicles, etc. 11 season of the year in which new vegetation begins to appear 12 earliest stage 13 place where water, oil, etc., wells up from the earth 14 spring a leak develop a leak —**spring′like′** *adj.* [OE]

SPRING 10

spring′board′ *n.* 1 flexible board for leaping or diving from 2 point of departure

spring′ fe′ver *n.* restlessness or lethargy associated with spring

Spring·field /spriNG′fēld′/ *n.* 1 capital of Ill., in the central part. Pop. 105,227 2 city in Mass. Pop. 156,983 3 city in Mo. Pop. 140,494

spring′on′ion *n.* young onion; scallion

spring′time′ *n.* season of spring

spring′y *adj.* (**-i·er, -i·est**) resilient; elastic —**spring′i·ness** *n.*

sprin·kle /spriNG′kəl/ *v.* (**-kled, -kling**) 1 scatter in small drops or particles 2 subject to sprinkling with liquid, etc. 3 distribute in small amounts —*n.* 4 light shower 5 SPRINKLING —**sprin′kler** *n.*

sprin′kling *n.* sparse number or amount

sprint /sprint/ *v.* 1 run a short distance at full speed —*n.* 2 such a run 3 short burst in cycling, swimming, etc. —**sprint′er** *n.* [ON]

sprite /sprīt/ *n.* elf; fairy [*sprit*, contr. of SPIRIT]

spritz·er /sprit′sər/ *n.* drink of wine with soda water [Ger: a splash]

sprock·et /spräk′it/ *n.* each of several teeth on a wheel engaging with links of a chain

sprout /sprout/ *v.* 1 put forth (shoots, hair, etc.) 2 begin to grow —*n.* 3 shoot of a plant [OE]

spruce¹ /sprōōs/ *adj.* 1 neatly dressed, etc.; smart —*v.* (**spruced, spruc·ing**) 2 (usu. foll. by *up*) make or become neat or dapper —**spruce′ly** *adv.*; **spruce′ness** *n.* [perh. fr. SPRUCE²]

spruce² *n.* 1 conifer with dense foliage 2 its wood [*Spruce* Prussia]

sprung /spruNG/ *v. past* and *past. part.* of SPRING

spry /sprī/ *adj.* (**spri·er** or **spry·er, spri·est** or **spry·est**) lively; nimble —**spry′ly** *adv.*; **spry′ness** *n.*

spud /spud/ *n. Colloq.* potato

spume /spyōōm/ *n. & v.* (**spumed, spum·ing**) froth; foam —**spum′y** *adj.* (**-i·er, -i·est**) [L *spuma*]

spun /spun/ *v. past* and *past part.* of SPIN

spunk /spuNGk/ *n. Colloq.* courage; mettle; spirit —**spunk′y** *adj.* (**-i·er, -i·est**)

spur /spər/ *n.* 1 small spike or spiked wheel worn on a rider's heel for urging on a horse 2 stimulus; incentive 3 projection from a mountain 4 branch railroad track —*v.* (**spurred, spur·ring**) 5 urge (a horse) onward with spurs 6 incite or stimulate 7 **on the spur of the moment** on impulse [OE]

spurge /spərj/ *n.* plant with an acrid, milky juice [L *expurgare* to clean out]

spu·ri·ous /spyŏŏr′ēəs/ *adj.* not genuine; fake [L]

spurn /spərn/ *v.* reject with disdain or contempt [OE]

spurt /spərt/ *v.* 1 (cause to) gush out in a jet or stream 2 make a sudden effort —*n.* 3 sudden gushing out; jet 4 short burst of speed, growth, etc.

sput·nik /spŏŏt′nik, spət′-/ *n.* Russian artificial earth-orbiting satellite [Russ]

sput·ter /spət′ər/ *v.* 1 make a series of quick explosive sounds 2 splutter —*n.* 3 sputtering [Du (imit.)]

spu·tum /spyōō′təm/ *n.* (*pl.* **spu·ta** /-tə/) 1 saliva 2 expectorated matter, used esp. in diagnosis [L]

spy /spī/ *n.* (*pl.* **spies**) 1 person who collects and reports secret information for a government, company, etc. 2 person watching others secretly —*v.* (**spied, spy·ing**) 3 discern; see 4 act as a spy [Fr *espie, espier*]

spy′glass′ *n.* small hand-held telescope

sq. *abbr.* square

squab /skwäb/ *n.* young pigeon or other bird [perh. fr. Scand]

squab·ble /skwäb′əl/ *n.* 1 petty or noisy quarrel —*v.* (**-bled, -bling**) 2 engage in this [prob. imit.]

squad /skwäd/ *n.* 1 small group sharing a task, etc., esp. of soldiers or policemen 2 *Sport.* team [Fr *escouade*]

squad′ car′ *n.* police car

squad·ron /skwäd′rən/ *n.* unit of aircraft, warships, etc. [It *squadrone*, rel. to SQUAD]

squal·id /skwäl′id/ *adj.* 1 filthy 2 mean or poor [L]

squall /skwôl/ *n.* 1 sudden or violent wind, esp. with rain, snow, or sleet 2 discordant cry; scream (esp. of a baby) —*v.* 3 utter a squall; scream —**squall′y** *adj.* (**-i·er, -i·est**) [prob. alter. of SQUEAL after BAWL]

squa·lor /skwäl′ər/ *n.* filthy or squalid state [L]

squan·der /skwän′dər/ *v.* spend wastefully

Squan·to /skwän′tō/ *d.* 1622; Indian who befriended Pilgrims at Plymouth Colony

square /skwer/ *n.* 1 rectangle with four equal sides 2 open (usu. four-sided) area surrounded by buildings 3 product of a number multiplied by itself (*16 is the square of 4*) **4** L- or T-shaped instrument for obtaining or testing right angles **5** *Slang.* conventional or old-fashioned person —*adj.* **6** square-shaped **7** having or in the form of a right angle **8** angular; not round **9** designating the area of a square whose side is one of the unit specified (*square mile*) **10** level; parallel **11** at right angles **12** equal; settled **13** fair and honest **14** *Slang.* conventional; old-fashioned —*adv.* **15** squarely —*v.* (**squared, squar·ing**) **16** make square **17** multiply (a number) by itself **18** reconcile **19** settle or pay (a debt, etc.) **20** place (one's shoulders, etc.) squarely forwards **21** square one *Colloq.* starting-point **22** square off make ready to hit someone —**square′ly** *adv.*; **square′ness** *n.*; **squar′ish** *adj.* [Fr *esquare*, ult. fr. L *quadrare*]

square′ dance′ *n.* dance with usu. four couples facing inwards from four sides —**square′-dance′** *v.* (**-danced, -danc·ing**)

square′ meal′ *n.* substantial meal

square′-rigged′ *adj.* with the principal sails at right angles to the length of the ship

square′ root′ *n.* number that multiplied by itself gives a specified number

squash[1] /skwäsh, skwôsh/ *v.* **1** crush or squeeze, esp. flat or into pulp **2** suppress (a proposal, allegation, etc.) —*n.* **3** game played with rackets and a small ball in a closed court —**squash′y** *adj.* (**·i·er, ·i·est**) [Fr *esquasser*, rel. to EX-[1], QUASH]

squash[2] *n.* (*pl.* same or **-es**) plant that yields an edible gourd [Narragansett]

squat /skwät/ *v.* (**squat·ted, squat·ting**) **1** sit on one's heels or on the ground with the knees drawn up **2** occupy a building as a squatter —*adj.* (**squat·ter, squat·test**) **3** short and thick; dumpy —*n.* **4** squatting posture [Fr *esquatir* flatten]

squat′ter *n.* person who inhabits unoccupied premises without permission

squaw /skwô/ *n.* *Offens.* N American Indian woman or wife [Narragansett]

squawk /skwôk/ *n.* **1** loud, harsh cry, esp. of a bird **2** complaint —*v.* **3** utter a squawk [imit.]

squeak /skwēk/ *n.* **1** short, high-pitched cry or sound **2** (also **close** or **narrow squeak**) narrow escape —*v.* **3** make a squeak **4** utter (words) shrilly **5** (foll. by *by, through*) *Colloq.* barely pass —**squeak′er** *n.*; **squeak′i·ly** *adv.*; **squeak′i·ness** *n.*; **squeak′y** *adj.* (**·i·er, ·i·est**) [imit., rel. to SQUEAL, SHRIEK]

squeal /skwēl/ *n.* **1** prolonged shrill sound or cry —*v.* **2** make or utter with a squeal **3** *Slang.* turn informer [imit.]

squeam·ish /skwē′mish/ *adj.* **1** easily nauseated or disgusted **2** fastidious —**squeam′ish·ly** *adv.*; **squeam′ish·ness** *n.* [AngFr *escoymos*]

squee·gee /skwē′jē/ *n.* rubber-edged implement on a handle, for wiping water from a window, etc. [squeege, alter. of SQUEEZE]

squeeze /skwēz/ *v.* (**squeezed, squeezing**) **1** exert pressure on **2** reduce in size or alter in shape by squeezing **3** make smaller in order to force or push into or through a small or narrow space **4** harass or pressure (a person) **5** obtain by extortion, entreaty, etc.

---

6 hug tightly —*n.* **7** squeezing or being squeezed **8** close embrace **9** crowded state **10** small quantity produced by squeezing **11** restriction in a financial crisis **12** *Slang.* lover **13** **put the squeeze on** *Colloq.* coerce or pressure

squeeze′ box′ *n.* *Colloq.* accordion; concertina

squelch /skwelch/ *v.* **1a** make a sucking sound as of treading in thick mud **b** move with a squelching sound **2** suppress; silence —*n.* **3** crushing rebuke —**squelch′y** *adj.* (**·i·er, ·i·est**) [imit.]

squib /skwib/ *n.* **1** small, hissing firework that finally explodes **2** witty saying or essay [perh. imit.]

squid /skwid/ *n.* (*pl.* same or **-s**) ten-armed marine cephalopod

squig·gle /skwig′əl/ *n.* **1** short, curly line, esp. in handwriting —*v.* (**·gled, ·gling**) **2** make such lines —**squig′gly** *adj.* [imit.]

squint /skwint/ *v.* **1** have eyes that do not move together but look in different directions; be cross-eyed **2** look obliquely or with half-closed eyes —*n.* **3** condition causing cross-eye **4** stealthy or sidelong glance [obs. *asquint*, perh. fr. Du *schuinte* slant]

squire /skwīr/ *n.* **1** (esp. *Brit.*) country gentleman or landowner **2** *Hist.* knight's attendant —*v.* (**squired, squir·ing**) **3** (of a man) attend or escort (a woman) [rel. to ESQUIRE]

squirm /skwərm/ *v.* **1** wriggle; writhe **2** show or feel embarrassment —*n.* **3** squirming movement —**squirm′y** *adj.* (**·i·er, ·i·est**)

squir·rel /skwər′əl, skwə′rəl/ *n.* **1** bushy-tailed usu. tree-dwelling rodent **2** its fur —*v.* (**·reled** or **·relled, ·rel·ing** or **·rel·ling**) **3** hoard [Gk *skia* shadow, *oura* tail]

squirt /skwərt/ *v.* **1** eject (liquid, etc.) in a jet **2** be ejected in this way **3** splash with a squirted substance —*n.* **4a** jet of water, etc. **b** small quantity squirted **5** *Colloq.* insignificant but self-assertive person [imit.]

squish /skwish/ *n.* **1** slight squelching sound —*v.* **2** move with a squishing sound —**squish′y** *adj.* (**·i·er, ·i·est**) [imit.]

Sr *symb.* strontium

Sr. *abbr.* **1** Senior **2** Señor **3** Sister

Sri Lan·ka /srē läng′kə, shrē/ *n.* (formerly Ceylon) island republic in the Indian Ocean, SE of India. Capital: Colombo. Pop. 17,464,000 —**Sri Lank′an** *n.* & *adj.*

SRO *abbr.* standing room only

SS *abbr.* **1** steamship **2** *Hist.* Nazi special police force [Ger *Schutz-Staffel*] **3** Saints

SSA *abbr.* Social Security Administration

SSS *abbr.* Selective Service System

SST *abbr.* supersonic transport

St. *abbr.* **1** Saint **2** Street

stab /stab/ *v.* (**stabbed, stab·bing**) **1** pierce or wound with a knife, etc. **2** thrust, plunge, jab, etc., with or as if with such a weapon —*n.* **3** stabbing thrust **4** wound from this **5** sharp pain **6** attempt

sta·bil·i·ty /stəbil′ətē/ *n.* being stable [L, rel. to STABLE]

sta·bi·lize /stā′bəlīz′/ *v.* (**·lized, ·liz·ing**) make or become stable —**sta′bi·li·za′tion** *n.*

sta′bi·liz′er *n.* **1** device used to keep stable a ship, aircraft, etc. **2** food additive for preserving texture

sta·ble /stā′bəl/ *adj.* **1** firmly fixed or established **2** (of a person) not easily upset or disturbed —*n.* **3** building for keeping horses **4** establishment for training racehorses **5** group of persons, products, etc., having a common origin or affiliation —*v.* (·**bled,** ·**bling**) **6** put or keep in a stable —**sta′bly** *adv.* [L *stabilis* fr. *stare* to stand]

stac·ca·to /stəkä′tō/ *adv. & adj. Mus.* with each sound or note sharply distinct [It]

stack /stak/ *n.* **1** (esp. orderly) pile or heap **2** HAYSTACK **3** large quantity (*a stack of work; stacks of money*) **4** SMOKESTACK **5** (usu. *pl.*) part of a library where books are stored —*v.* **6** pile in a stack or stacks **7a** arrange (cards) secretly for cheating **b** manipulate (circumstances, etc.) to suit one [ON]

sta·di·um /stā′dēəm/ *n.* (*pl.* ·**ums** or ·**di·a** /dēə/) sports field with tiered seats for spectators [Gk *stadion*]

staff /staf/ *n.* **1a** stick or pole for use in walking or as a weapon **b** stick or rod as a sign of office, etc. **2a** people employed in a business, etc. **b** employees with specific duties **c** body of military officers (*general staff*) **3** (*pl.* **staffs** or **staves**) *Mus.* set of usu. five parallel lines on or between which notes are indicated —*v.* **4** provide (an institution, etc.) with staff [OE]

stag /stag/ *n.* **1** adult male deer —*adj.* **2** of a party, etc.) for men only [OE]

stage /stāj/ *n.* **1** point or period in a process or development **2a** raised platform, esp. for performances **b** (prec. by *the*) theatrical profession **c** scene of action **3a** regular stopping place on a route **b** distance between two of these **4** *Astronaut.* section of a rocket with a separate engine —*v.* (**staged, stag·ing**) **5** present (a play, etc.) on stage **6** organize; create (*staged a demonstration*) [Fr *estage,* ult. fr. L *stare* stand]

stage′coach′ *n. Hist.* closed horse-drawn coach running on a regular route by stages

stage′craft′ *n.* theatrical skill or experience

stage′fright′ *n.* fear of a live audience

stage′hand′ *n.* worker who moves stage scenery, etc.

stag·fla·tion /stagflā′shən/ *n. Econ.* inflation without a corresponding increase of demand and employment [blend of *stagnation, inflation*]

stag·ger /stag′ər/ *v.* **1** (cause to) walk unsteadily **2** shock; confuse **3** arrange (events, etc.) so that they do not coincide **4** arrange (objects) so that they are not in line —*n.* **5** tottering movement **6** (*pl.*) disease, esp. of horses and cattle, causing staggering [ON]

stag′ger·ing *adj.* astonishing; bewildering —**stag′ger·ing·ly** *adv.*

stag·nant /stag′nənt/ *adj.* **1** (of liquid) motionless; having no current **2** dull; lifeless —**stag′nan·cy** *n.* [L *stagnum* pool]

stag·nate /stag·nāt′/ *v.* (·**nat·ed,** ·**nat·ing**) be or become stagnant —**stag·na′tion** *n.*

staid /stād/ *adj.* of quiet and steady character; sedate [*stayed,* past part. of STAY[1]]

stain /stān/ *v.* **1** discolor or be discolored by the action of liquid, etc. **2** damage (a reputation, character, etc.) **3** color (wood, glass, etc.) with a penetrating substance **4** impregnate (a specimen) with a coloring agent for microscopic examination —*n.* **5** discoloration; spot; mark **6** moral or character blemish; damage to a reputation, etc. **7** substance

used in staining [earlier *distain* fr. Fr *desteindre*]

stained′ glass′ *n.* pieces of colored glass assembled to form a design, as in a leaded window, etc.

stain′less steel′ *n.* steel alloyed with chromium, etc., resisting rust or tarnish

stair /ster/ *n.* **1** each of a set of fixed indoor steps **2** (usu. *pl.*) set of these [OE]

stair′case′ *n.* flight(s) of stairs and the supporting structure

stair′way′ *n.* STAIRCASE

stair′well′ *n.* shaft for a staircase

stake[1] /stāk/ *n.* **1** stout, sharpened stick driven into the ground as a support, boundary mark, etc. **2** *Hist.* post to which a condemned person was tied to be burned alive —*v.* (**staked, stak·ing**) **3** secure or support with a stake or stakes **4** (foll. by *off, out*) mark off (an area) with stakes **5** establish (a claim) **6** stake out *Colloq.* place under surveillance [OE]

stake[2] *n.* **1** sum of money wagered **2** interest or concern, esp. financial **3** (*pl.*) prize money, esp. in a horse race **4** wager **5** support, esp. financially **6 at stake** risked; to be won or lost [OE]

Staked′ Plain′ /stākt/ *n.* see LLANO ESTACADO

stake′out′ *n.* period of surveillance

sta·lac·tite /stəlak′tīt′/ *n.* iciclelike deposit of calcium carbonate hanging from the roof of a cave, etc. [Gk *stalaktos* dripping]

sta·lag·mite /stəlag′mīt′/ *n.* cone-shaped deposit of calcium carbonate rising from the floor of a cave, etc. [Gk *stalagma* a drop]

stale /stāl/ *adj.* **1** not fresh; flat; musty **2** trite; worn; unoriginal —*v.* (**staled, stal·ing**) **3** make or become stale —**stale′ness** *n.* [AngFr *estaler* halt]

stale′mate′ *n.* **1** *Chess.* position counting as a draw, in which a player cannot move except into check **2** deadlock —*v.* (·**mat·ed,** ·**mat·ing**) **3** *Chess.* bring (a player) to a stalemate **4** bring to a deadlock [obs. *stale,* rel. to STALE, MATE[2]]

Sta·lin /stäl′ən, stal′-/, Josef (born Joseph Dzhugashvili) 1879–1953; Soviet political leader; premier (1941–53)

Sta·lin·grad /stä′lingrad′/ *n.* see VOLGOGRAD

stalk[1] /stôk/ *n.* main stem of a plant, leaf, flower, fruit, etc. [dim. of (now dial.) *stale* rung]

stalk[2] *v.* **1** pursue (game or an enemy) stealthily **2** stride boldly **3** move threateningly through (a place); haunt (*fear stalked the land*) —*n.* **4** stalking of game **5** haughty gait [OE, rel. to STEAL]

stall[1] /stôl/ *n.* **1** booth or table at a market, exhibition, etc. **2** compartment for one animal in a stable, etc. **3** fixed, usu. partly enclosed, seat in a church **4** compartment for one person in a lavatory, bathhouse, etc. **5** loss of engine power —*v.* **6** (of a vehicle or its engine) stop or lose power because of an overload on the engine or inadequate fuel **7** cause to stall [OE]

stall[2] *v.* **1** play for time when being questioned, etc. **2** delay; obstruct [*stall* 'decoy,' prob. rel. to STALL[1]]

stal·lion /stal'yən/ *n.* uncastrated adult male horse [Fr *estalon*]

stal·wart /stôl'wərt/ *adj.* **1** strong; sturdy **2** courageous; resolute; reliable —*n.* **3** stalwart person, esp. a loyal comrade [OE: place, WORTH]

sta·men /stā'mən/ *n.* organ producing pollen in a flower (see illustration at PISTIL) [L: warp, thread]

Stam·ford /stam'fərd/ *n.* city in Conn. Pop. 108,056

stam·i·na /stam'ənə/ *n.* physical or mental endurance [L, pl. of STAMEN]

stam·mer /stam'ər/ *v.* **1** speak haltingly, esp. with pauses or rapid repetitions of the same syllable **2** utter (words) in this way —*n.* **3** tendency to stammer **4** instance of stammering [OE]

stamp /stamp/ *v.* **1a** bring down (one's foot) heavily **b** crush or flatten in this way **c** walk heavily **2a** impress (a design, mark, etc.) on a surface **b** impress (a surface) with a pattern, etc. **3** affix a postage or other stamp to **4** assign a specific character to; mark out —*n.* **5** instrument for stamping **6** mark or design made by this, esp. as an official authorization or certification **7** small adhesive piece of paper indicating that payment has been made, esp. a postage stamp **8** act or sound of stamping the foot **9** characteristic mark or quality **10** stamp out: **a** produce by cutting out with a die, etc. **b** put an end to; destroy; suppress [OE]

stam·pede /stampēd'/ *n.* **1** sudden flight or hurried movement of animals or people **2** immediate or impulsive response by many —*v.* (·ped·ed, ·ped·ing) **3** (cause to) take part in a stampede [Sp *estampida* crash, uproar]

stamp'ing ground' *n. Colloq.* favorite haunt

stance /stans/ *n.* **1** standpoint; attitude **2** attitude or position of the body, esp. when hitting a ball, etc. [It *stanza* standing]

stanch /stänCH, stänCH, stônCH/ *v.* (also **staunch**) **1** restrain the flow of (esp. blood) **2** restrain the flow from (a wound) [Fr *estanchier*]

stan·chion /stan'CHən/ *n.* **1** upright post or support **2** upright bar or frame for confining cattle in a stall [AngFr]

stand /stand/ *v.* (**stood**, **stand·ing**) **1** have, take, or maintain an upright position, esp. on the feet or a base **2** be situated (*here once stood a village*) **3** be of a specified height **4** be in a specified state (*stands accused*) **5** set in an upright or specified position (*stood it against the wall*) **6a** move to and remain in a specified position (*stand aside*) **b** take a specified attitude (*stand aloof*) **7** remain valid or unaltered **8** endure; tolerate **9** provide at one's own expense (*stood him a drink*) —*n.* **10** cessation from progress; halting **11** *Milit.* resistance to attack or compulsion (esp. *make a stand*) **12** rack, set of shelves, etc., for storage **13** open-fronted stall for a vendor, exhibitor, etc. **14** standing place for vehicles **15a** raised structure to sit or stand on **b** *Law.* witness-box **16** group of growing plants (*stand of trees*) **17 as it stands: a** in its present condition **b** in the present circumstances **18 stand by: a** stand nearby **b** uphold; support

(a person) **c** adhere to (a promise, etc.) **d** be ready for action **19 stand corrected** accept correction **20 stand for: a** represent; signify; imply **b** endure; tolerate **21 stand out** be prominent or outstanding **22 stand to reason** be obvious or outstanding **23 stand up: a** rise to one's feet **b** (of an argument, etc.) be valid **c** *Slang.* fail to keep an appointment with **24 stand up to: a** face (an opponent) courageously **b** be resistant to (wear, use, etc.) [OE]

stan·dard /stan'dərd/ *n.* **1** object, quality, or measure serving as a basis, example, or principle by which others are judged **2** level of excellence required or specified (*not up to standard*) **3** distinctive flag **4** upright support **5** tune or song of established popularity —*adj.* **6** serving or used as a standard **7** of a normal or prescribed quality, type, or size **8** of recognized and permanent value; authoritative (*standard book on jazz*) **9** (of language) conforming to established educated usage [OFr]

stan·dard-bear'er *n.* **1** soldier who carries a standard **2** prominent leader in a cause

stand·ard·ize /stan'dərdīz'/ *v.* (·ized, ·iz·ing) cause to conform to a standard —**stand'ard·i·za'tion** *n.*

stan·dard of liv'ing *n.* level of material comfort of a person or group

stan·dard time' *n.* uniform time for places in any of the 24 worldwide zones based generally on longitude and established by law or custom

stand·by *n.* (*pl.* ·bys) **1** person or thing ready if needed in an emergency or as a substitute **2** readiness for duty (*on standby*)

stand·in *n.* deputy or substitute

stand·ing *n.* **1** esteem or repute; status **2** duration (*of long standing*) —*adj.* **3** upright **4** established; permanent (*standing rule*) **5** (of a jump, start, etc.) performed in place **6** (of water) stagnant

Stan·dish /stan'diSH/, **Myles** c. 1584–1656; English colonial settler in America

stand·off' *n.* tie, as in a contest

stand·off'ish *adj.* cold or distant in manner

stand·pipe' *n.* **1** water fixture, as on the side of a building, to supply fire hoses **2** vertical pipe extending from a water supply

stand·point' *n.* point of view

stand·still' *n.* stoppage; inability to proceed

stand·up' *adj.* (of a comedian) telling jokes to an audience

Stan·i·slav·sky /stan'əsläv'skē/, **Konstantin** 1863–1938; Russian acting teacher and director

stank /staNGk/ *v. past of* STINK

Stan·ley /stan'lē/, **(Sir) Henry Morton** (born **John Rowlands**) 1841–1904; Welsh-born explorer and writer

Stan·ton /stant'n/, **Elizabeth Cady** 1815–1902; US social reformer

stan·za /stan'zə/ *n.* basic unit of a poem, etc., typically of four or more lines [It]

staph·y·lo·coc·cus /staf'ələkäk'əs/ *n.* (*pl.* ·coc·ci /-käk'(s)ī', -käk'(s)ē/) (also *Colloq.* **staph**) bacterium sometimes forming pus —**staph'y·lo·coc'cal** /-kəl/ *adj.* [Gk *staphulē* bunch of grapes, *kokkos* berry]

sta·ple[1] /stā'pəl/ *n.* **1** U-shaped metal bar or piece of wire with often bendable pointed ends, for driving into and holding papers together, etc. —v. (·pled, ·pling) 2 fasten or provide with a staple —sta′pler n. [OE]

sta·ple² n. 1 principal or important article of commerce 2 chief element or main component 3 fiber of cotton, wool, etc., with regard to its quality (*cotton of fine staple*) —adj. 4 main or principal (*staple diet*) 5 important as a product or export [Fr *estaple* market]

star /stär/ n. 1 celestial body appearing as a luminous point in the night sky 2 large, naturally luminous, gaseous body such as the sun 3 celestial body regarded as influencing fortunes, etc. 4a conventional closed figure with five or more points b asterisk 5 decoration or mark of rank or excellence, usu. with radiating points 6a famous or brilliant person; principal performer (*star of the show*) b outstanding (*star pupil*) —v. (starred, star·ring) 7 appear or present as principal performer(s) —star′dom n. [OE]

star′board /stär′bärd/ n. 1 right-hand side of a ship or aircraft as one faces forward —adj. & adv. 2 of, at, to, or on this side [OE: *steer board*]

starch /stärCH/ n. 1 polysaccharide obtained chiefly from cereals and potatoes 2 preparation of this for stiffening fabric 3 stiffness of manner; formality 4 Colloq. bold vigor; energy —v. 5 stiffen (clothing) with starch [OE, rel. to STARK]

starch′y adj. (·i·er, ·i·est) of, like, or containing starch —starch′i·ly adv.; starch′i·ness n.

stare /ster/ v. (stared, star·ing) 1 look fixedly, as in curiosity, surprise, horror, etc. —n. 2 staring gaze [OE]

star′fish′ n. (pl. same or -es) echinoderm with five or more radiating arms

star′gaz′er n. astronomer; astrologer

stark /stärk/ adj. 1 sharply evident (*in stark contrast*) 2 desolate; bare 3 absolute (*stark madness*) —adv. 4 completely; wholly (*stark naked*) —stark′ly adv.; stark′ness n. [OE]

star′let n. promising young performer, esp. a film actress

star′light′ n. light of the stars

star′ling n. gregarious bird with blackish speckled lustrous plumage [OE]

star′lit adj. 1 lit by stars 2 with stars visible

Star′ of Da′vid n. two interlaced equilateral triangles used as a Jewish and Israeli symbol

Starr /stär/, Ringo 1940– ; British rock musician

starred /stärd/ adj. mark, set, or adorn with a star or stars

star′ry adj. (·ri·er, ·ri·est) 1 full of stars 2 like a star

star′ry-eyed′ adj. enthusiastic but impractical; unrealistically romantic

Stars′ and Stripes′ n. pl. national flag of the US

Star′-Span·gled Ban′ner n. US national anthem

start /stärt/ v. 1 begin 2 set in motion or action (*started a fire*) 3 set oneself in motion or action 4 begin a journey, etc. 5 (cause to) begin operating 6a cause or enable (a person) to make a beginning (*started me in business*) b cause (a person) to begin (*started me coughing*) 7 jump in surprise, pain, etc. 8 spring out, up, etc. —n. 9 beginning 10

563

staple / stationary

place from which a race, etc., begins 11 sudden movement of surprise, pain, etc. [OE]

start′er n. 1 device for starting a vehicle engine, etc., automatically 2 first course of a meal 3 person giving the signal for the start of a race

start′ing block′ n. block for the feet used at the start of a race

star·tle /stärt′l/ v. (·tled, ·tling) shock; surprise [OE]

starve /stärv/ v. (starved, starv·ing) 1 (cause to) die of hunger or suffer from malnourishment 2 Colloq. feel very hungry (*I'm starving*) 3 feel a strong need or craving (for) 4 deprive (of) 5 compel by starving (*starved into surrender*) —star·va·tion /stärvä′sHən/ n. [OE: die]

stash /stasH/ Colloq. v. 1 conceal; put in a safe place 2 hoard —n. 3 hiding place 4 thing hidden

stat. abbr. 1 at once [L *statim*] 2 statistics 3 statute

state /stät/ n. 1 existing condition or position of a person or thing 2 Colloq. a excited or agitated mental condition b untidy condition 3a political community under one government b this as part of a federal republic 4 civil government 5 (the States) US —v. (stat·ed, stat·ing) 6 express in speech or writing 7 specify 8 Mus. introduce (a theme, etc.) 9 lie in state be laid in a public place of honor before burial [partly fr. ESTATE, partly fr. L STATUS]

state′less adj. having no nationality or citizenship —state′less·ness n.

state′ly adj. (·li·er, ·li·est) dignified; imposing —state′li·ness n.

state′ment n. 1 stating or being stated; expression in words 2 thing stated 3 formal account of facts 4 record of transactions in a bank account, etc. 5 periodic summary of unpaid bills

Stat′en Is′land /stat′n/ n. island in N.Y. Bay; one of the five boroughs of New York City. Pop. 380,000

state′ of the art′ n. 1 current stage of esp. technological development —adj. 2 (usu. state-of-the-art) absolutely up-to-date

state′room′ n. large private cabin in a passenger ship

states·man /stäts′mən/ n. (pl. ·men; fem. ·wom·an, pl. ·wom·en) distinguished and capable politician or diplomat —states′man·like′ adj.; states′man·ship′ n.

stat·ic /stat′ik/ adj. 1 stationary; not acting or changing 2 Physics. concerned with bodies at rest or forces in equilibrium —n. 3 interference in receiving a broadcast signal —stat′i·cal·ly adv. [Gk *statikos* fr. *sta-* stand]

stat′ic e·lec·tric′i·ty n. electricity produced by a difference in potential within an object

sta·tion /stä′sHən/ n. 1a regular stopping-place on a railroad, bus, route, etc. b building at this 2 allotted place or post for a person or thing 3 establishment involved in broadcasting 4 military or naval base 5 position in life; rank; status —v. 6 assign a station to 7 put in position [L *statio* fr. *stare stat-* stand]

sta·tion·ar·y /stä′sHəner′ē/ adj. 1 not moving 2 not meant to be moved 3 unchanging [L, rel. to STATION]

• Usage: Writers should take care to distinguish *stationary* 'fixed' from *stationery* 'writing paper and other supplies.'

sta'tion·er *n.* dealer in stationery

sta'tion·er'y /stä'sʜəner'ē/ *n.* writing materials, office supplies, etc.

sta'tion wag'on *n.* car with additional rear seating, enclosed storage space, and a rear door

sta·tis'tic /stətis'tik/ *n.* statistical fact or item [Ger, rel. to STATE]

sta·tis'tics *n. pl.* 1 (usu. treated as *sing.*) science of collecting and analyzing numerical data 2 such analyzed data —**sta·tis'ti·cal** *adj.*; **sta·tis'ti·cal·ly** *adv.*; **stat·is·ti·cian** /stat'istish'ən/ *n.*

stat·u·ar·y /stacʜ'ōo·er'ē/ *adj.* 1 of or for statues (*statuary art*) —*n.* (*pl.* ·**ies**) 2 statues collectively [L, rel. to STATUE]

stat·ue /stacʜ'ōo/ *n.* sculptured figure of a person or animal, esp. life-size or larger [L *statua*]

stat·u·esque /stacʜ'ōo·esk'/ *adj.* 1 like or having the dignity or beauty of a statue 2 (of a person) tall

stat·u·ette /stacʜ'ōo·et'/ *n.* small statue

stat·ure /stacʜ'ər/ *n.* 1 height of a (esp. human) body 2 caliber, esp. moral; eminence [L *statura*]

sta·tus /stä'təs, stat'əs/ *n.* 1 condition or state of affairs 2 rank, social position, or relative importance 3 prestige [L, rel. to STATURE]

sta'tus quo' *n.* existing state of affairs [L]

sta'tus sym'bol *n.* possession, object, etc., considered prestigious

stat·ute /stacʜ'ōot/ *n.* 1 written law passed by a legislative body 2 rule of a corporation, founder, etc., intended to be permanent [L *statutum* fr. *statuere* set up]

stat·u·to·ry /stacʜ'ətôr'ē/ *adj.* required or enacted by statute —**stat'u·to·ri·ly** *adv.*

staunch /stôncʜ, stäncʜ/ *adj.* 1 loyal 2 (of a ship, joint, etc.) strong, watertight, airtight, etc. —**staunch'ly** *adv.* [Fr *estanche*]

staunch² *v.* var. of STANCH

stave /stäv/ *n.* 1 each of the curved slats forming the sides of a cask, pail, etc. 2 stick; staff 3 stanza; verse —*v.* **staved** or **stove, stav·ing**) 4 break a hole (line crush by) forcing inwards 5 **stave off** avert or defer (danger, etc.) [fr. STAFF]

Stav·ro·pol /stävrō'pəl, -rō'-/ *n.* city in Russia. Pop. 328,500

stay¹ /stä/ *v.* 1 continue in the same place or condition; not depart or change 2 reside temporarily 3 *Archaic.* or *Lit.* **a** stop or check **b** (esp. in *imper.*) pause 4 postpone (judgment, etc.) —*n.* 5 act or period of staying 6 suspension or postponement of a sentence, judgment, etc. 7 prop; support 8 **stay put** *Colloq.* remain where it is placed or where one is 9 **stay up** not go to bed (until late) [AngFr fr. L *stare* stand]

stay² *n.* 1 *Naut.* guy supporting a mast, flagstaff, etc. 2 supporting cable on an aircraft, etc. [OE fr. Gmc]

stay'ing pow'er *n.* endurance

STD *abbr.* sexually transmitted disease

STD *abbr.* sexually transmitted disease

std. *abbr.* standard

stead /sted/ *n.* as in 1 **in a person's** (or **thing's) stead** as a substitute; in a person's or thing's place 2 **stand (someone) in good stead** be advantageous or useful to [OE: place]

stead'fast' *adj.* constant; firm; unwavering —**stead'fast'ly** *adv.*; **stead'fast'ness** *n.* [OE, rel. to STEAD]

stead·y /sted'ē/ *adj.* (·**i·er**, ·**i·est**) 1 firmly fixed or supported; unwavering 2 uniform and regular 3 constant; persistent 4 (of a person) serious and dependable 5 established (*steady girlfriend*) —*v.* (·**ied**, ·**y·ing**) 6 make or become steady —*adv.* 7 steadily —*n.* (*pl.* ·**ies**) 8 *Colloq.* regular boyfriend or girlfriend 9 **go steady** *Colloq.* be or have as a regular boyfriend or girlfriend —**stead'i·ly** *adv.*; **stead'i·ness** *n.* [fr. STEAD]

stead'y state' *n.* unvarying condition, esp. in a physical process

steak /stāk/ *n.* thick slice of meat (esp. beef) or fish, usu. grilled or fried [ON]

steal /stēl/ *v.* (**stole, sto·len, steal·ing**) 1 take (another's property) illegally or without right or permission, esp. in secret 2 obtain surreptitiously, insidiously, or artfully (*stole a kiss*) 3 move, esp. silently or stealthily 4 *Baseball.* (of a baserunner) advance to the next base without a hit, walk, etc. —*n.* 5 *Colloq.* good bargain 6 *Baseball.* extra base gained by stealing 7 **steal a march on** get an advantage over by surreptitious means 8 **steal the show** outshine other performers, esp. unexpectedly 9 **steal a person's thunder** take away the attention due someone else [OE]

stealth /stelʜ/ *n.* 1 furtive or secret behavior —*adj. Milit.* 2 designed to foil detection by radar, etc. [OE, rel. to STEAL]

stealth'y *adj.* (·**i·er**, ·**i·est**) done or moving with stealth; furtive —**stealth'i·ly** *adv.*; **stealth'i·ness** *n.*

steam /stēm/ *n.* 1 vapor from heated water 2**a** power obtained from steam **b** *Colloq.* power or energy —*v.* 3**a** cook (food) in steam **b** treat with steam 4 give off steam 5**a** move under steam power **b** (foll. by *ahead*, *away*, etc.) proceed or travel fast or with vigor 6 cover or become covered with condensed steam 7 *Colloq.* angry [OE]

steam'boat' *n.* steam-driven boat

steam' en'gine *n.* 1 engine that uses steam to generate power 2 locomotive powered by this

steam'er *n.* 1 steamship 2 vessel for steaming food in

steam' i'ron *n.* electric iron that emits steam

steam'roll'er *n.* 1 heavy, slow-moving vehicle with a roller, used to flatten newly laid roads 2 a crushing power or force —*v.* 3 crush or move forcibly or indiscriminately; force

steam'ship' *n.* steam-driven ship

steam'y *adj.* (·**i·er**, ·**i·est**) 1 like or full of steam 2 *Colloq.* erotic —**steam'i·ly** *adv.*; **steam'i·ness** *n.*

steed /stēd/ *n. Archaic.* or *Poet.* horse [OE]

steel /stēl/ *n.* 1 strong alloy of iron and carbon, used esp. for making tools, weapons, etc. 2 strength; firmness (*nerves of steel*) —*adj.* 3 of or like steel —*v.* 4 harden; make resolute

—**steel′y** *adj.* (·i·er, ·i·est); **steel′i·ness** *n.* [OE]

steel′ wool′ *n.* abrasive substance consisting of woven, fine, wirelike steel shavings

steel′works′ *n. pl.* (usu. treated as *sing.*) factory producing steel —**steel′work′er** *n.*

steel′yard′ *n.* balance with a graduated arm along which a weight is moved

steep¹ /stēp/ *adj.* 1 sloping sharply 2 (of a rise or fall) rapid 3 exorbitant; unreasonable —**steep′en** *v.*; **steep′ly** *adv.*; **steep′ness** *n.* [OE]

steep² *v.* 1 soak or bathe in liquid 2 make deeply acquainted with (a subject, etc.) 3 **steep in** pervade; imbue with [OE]

stee·ple /stē′pal/ *n.* 1 tall tower, esp. with a spire, above the roof of a church 2 spire [OE, rel. to STEEP¹]

stee′ple·chase′ *n.* race with ditches, fences, etc., to jump —**stee′ple·chas′ing** *n.*

stee′ple·jack′ *n.* repairer of tall chimneys, steeples, etc.

steer¹ /stēr/ *v.* 1 guide (a vehicle, ship, etc.) with a wheel, rudder, etc. 2 direct or guide (one's course, other people, a conversation, etc.) in a specified direction 3 **steer clear of** avoid —**steer′ing** *n.* [OE]

steer² *n.* castrated male of cattle raised for beef [OE]

steer·age /stēr′ij/ *n.* 1 act of steering 2 *Hist.* cheapest part of a ship's accommodation

steer′ing wheel′ *n.* wheel by which a vehicle is steered

steg·o·sau·rus /steg′əsôr′əs/ *n.* (*pl.* ·rus·es) plant-eating dinosaur with a double row of bony plates along the spine [Gk *stegē* covering, *sauros* lizard]

Stein /stīn/, **Gertrude** 1874–1946; US writer

Stein·beck /stīn′bek′/, **John** 1902–68; US writer

ste·la /stē′lə/ *n.* (*pl.* **ste·lae** /-lē/) (also **ste·le** /stēl, stē′lē/) *Archaeol.* upright slab or pillar, usu. inscribed and sculpted, esp. as a gravestone [L and Gk]

stel·lar /stel′ər/ *adj.* of a star or stars [L *stella* star]

stem¹ /stem/ *n.* 1 main body or stalk of a plant, fruit, flower, leaf, etc. 2 stem-shaped part, as: **a** the slender part of a wineglass **b** the tube of a tobacco pipe **c** a vertical stroke in a letter or musical note 3 *Gram.* root or main part of a noun, verb, etc., to which inflections are added 4 main upright timber at the bow of a ship (*from stem to stern*) —*v.* (**stemmed, stem·ming**) 5 spring or originate (from) [OE]

stem² *v.* (**stemmed, stem·ming**) check; stop [ON]

stench /stench/ *n.* foul smell [OE, rel. to STINK]

sten·cil /sten′səl/ *n.* 1 thin sheet into which a pattern, letters, etc., are cut, placed on a surface, and printed or inked over to reproduce the pattern 2 pattern so produced —*v.* (·ciled or ·cilled, ·cil·ing or ·cil·ling) 3 produce (a pattern) with a stencil 4 mark (a surface) in this way [Fr *estanceler* sparkle, fr. L *scintilla* spark]

Sten·dhal /stendäl′, ständäl′/ (pseudonym of **Henri Beyle**) 1783–1842; French novelist

ste·nog·ra·pher /stənäg′rəfər/ *n.* typist, secretary, etc., using shorthand —**ste·nog′ra·phy** *n.* [Gk *stenos* narrow]

sten·to·ri·an /stentôr′ēən/ *adj.* loud and powerful [for *Stentor*, a herald in Homer's *Iliad*]

step /step/ *n.* 1a complete movement of one leg in walking or running **b** distance so covered 2 foot movement in dancing 3 action taken, esp. one of several 4 surface of a stair, stepladder, etc.; tread 5 short distance 6 footfall 7 manner of walking, etc. 8 degree in the scale of promotion or precedence, etc. 9 stepping in unison or to music (esp. *in* or *out of step*) —*v.* (**stepped, step·ping**) 10 lift and set down one's foot or alternate feet in walking 11 come or go in a specified direction by stepping 12 make progress in a specified way (*stepped into a new job*) 13 **step by step** gradually; cautiously 14 **step down** resign 15 **step in:** **a** enter **b** intervene 16 **step on it** *Colloq.* accelerate; hurry up 17 **step out:** **a** be active socially **b** cease participation 18 **step out of line** behave inappropriately or disobediently 19 **step up: a** increase; intensify **b** move forward [OE]

step- *comb. form* denoting a relationship resulting from a parent's later marriage [OE: orphaned]

step′ aer·o′bics *n.* exercise regimen using a step-climbing motion

step′broth′er *n.* son of one's step-parent by a previous partner

step′child′ *n.* one's husband's or wife's child by a previous partner

step′daugh′ter *n.* female stepchild

step′fa′ther *n.* male step-parent

step′lad′der *n.* short, folding ladder with flat steps

step′moth′er *n.* female step-parent

step′par′ent *n.* mother's or father's spouse who is not one's own parent

steppe /step/ *n.* level, grassy, unforested plain [Russ]

step′ping·stone′ *n.* 1 large stone in a stream, etc., helping one to cross 2 means of progress

step′sis′ter *n.* daughter of one's step-parent by a previous partner

step′son′ *n.* male stepchild

-ster *suffix* denoting a person engaged in or associated with a particular activity or quality (*gangster; youngster*) [OE]

ste·re·o /ster′ē-ō′, stēr′-/ *n.* (*pl.* ·os) 1a stereophonic sound system **b** stereophonic sound reproduction (see STEREOPHONIC) 2 STEREOSCOPE —*adj.* 3 STEREOPHONIC 4 stereoscopic (see STEREOSCOPE) [abbr.]

stereo- *comb. form* solid; having three dimensions [Gk *stereos* solid]

ster·e·o·phon·ic /ster′ēəfän′ik/ *adj.* using two or more channels, giving the effect of naturally distributed sound

ster′e·o·scope′ *n.* device for producing a three-dimensional effect by viewing two slightly different photographs of the same scene together —**ster′e·o·scop′ic** /-skäp′ik/ *adj.*

ster′e·o·type′ *n.* 1a person or thing seeming to conform to a widely accepted type **b** such a type, idea, or attitude 2 printing plate cast from a mold of composed type —*v.* (·typed,

·typ·ing] 3 cause to conform to a type; standardize 4a print from a stereotype b make a stereotype of [Fr, rel. to STEREO-]

ster·ile /ster′əl/ adj. 1 unable to produce a crop, fruit, or young; barren 2 unproductive (sterile discussion) 3 free from living microorganisms, etc. —ste·ril′i·ty n. [L]

ster·il·ize /ster′əlīz′/ v. (·ized, ·iz·ing) 1 make sterile 2 deprive of reproductive powers —ster′il·i·za′tion n.

ster·ling /stər′liNG/ adj. 1 of or made of sterling silver 2 of or in British money (pound sterling) 3 (of a person, etc.) genuine; reliable —n. 4 British money 5 sterling silver [OE: penny]

ster′ling sil′ver n. silver that is at least 92.5% pure

stern[1] /stərn/ adj. severe; grim; authoritarian —stern′ly adv.; stern′ness n. [OE]

stern[2] n. rear part, esp. of a vessel [ON, rel. to STEER[1]]

Sterne /stərn/, Laurence 1713–68; British novelist

ster·num /stər′nəm/ n. (pl. ·na /-nə/ or ·nums) breastbone [Gk sternon chest]

ste·roid /stēr′oid′, ster′-/ n. any of a group of organic compounds including many hormones, alkaloids, and vitamins [fr. STEROL]

ste·rol /stēr′ôl′, ster′-/ n. naturally occurring steroid alcohol [fr. CHOLESTEROL, etc.]

ster·to·rous /stər′tərəs/ adj. (of breathing) labored and noisy [L stertere snore]

stet /stet/ v. (stet·ted, stet·ting) ignore or cancel (an alteration to printed text); let the original stand [L: let it stand]

steth·o·scope /steTH′əskōp′/ n. instrument used in listening to the heart, lungs, etc. [Gk stēthos breast]

stet·son /stet′sən/ n. style of hat with a very wide brim and high crown [for its maker]

Steu·ben /st(y)ŌŌ′bən, SHtoi′-/, Friedrich von 1730–94; Prussian military leader; trained American Revolutionary army

ste·ve·dore /stē′vədôr′/ n. person employed in loading and unloading ships [Sp estivador]

Ste·vens /stē′vənz/, Wallace 1878–1955; US poet

Ste·ven·son /stē′vənsən/ 1 Robert Louis Balfour 1850–94; British novelist 2 Adlai E. 1900–65; US statesman and politician

stew /st(y)ŌŌ/ v. 1 cook by long simmering 2 fret; be anxious —n. 3 dish of stewed meat, etc. 4 agitated or angry state 5 stew in one's own juice suffer the consequences of one's actions [Fr estuver]

stew·ard /st(y)ŌŌərd/ n. 1 passengers' attendant on a ship, aircraft, or train 2 person responsible for supplies of food and drink 3 property manager —v. 4 act as a steward (of) —stew′ard·ship n. [OE: house-warden]

stew·ard·ess /st(y)ŌŌərdis/ n. female steward, esp. on a ship or aircraft

stick[1] /stik/ n. 1a short, slender length of wood b this as a support or weapon 2 implement used to propel the ball in hockey, polo, etc. 3 gear lever 4 sticklike piece of celery, dynamite, etc. [OE]

stick[2] v. (stuck, stick·ing) 1 (foll. by in, into, through) insert or thrust (a thing or its point) 2 stab 3 (foll. by in, into, on, etc.) fix or be

fixed on a pointed end or thing 4 fix or be fixed (as) by adhesive, etc. 5 remain (in the mind) 6 not open, release, etc.; jam 7 Colloq. a put in a specified position or place b remain in a place 8 be stuck on Colloq. be infatuated with 9 be stuck with Colloq. be unable to get rid of 10 stick around Colloq. linger; remain 11 stick by (or with) stay loyal or close to 12 stick it out Colloq. endure something resignedly 13 stick one's neck out be rashly bold 14 stick out (cause to) protrude 15 stick to: a remain fixed on or to b keep to (a subject, etc.) 16 stick up: a be or make erect or protruding upwards b fasten to an upright surface c Colloq. rob or threaten with a gun 17 stick up for support or defend [OE]

stick′er n. adhesive label

stick′er shock′ n. Colloq. surprise at a higher than expected retail price

stick′-in-the-mud′ n. Colloq. unenterprising or old-fashioned person

stick·le·back /stik′əlbak′/ n. small spinybacked fish [OE: thorn-back]

stick·ler /stik′lər/ n. person who insists on something (stickler for accuracy) [obs. stickle be umpire]

stick′up′ n. Colloq. robbery using a gun

stick·y /stik′ē/ adj. (·i·er, ·i·est) 1 tending or intended to stick or adhere; glutinous; viscous 2 humid 3 difficult; awkward; unpleasant —stick′i·ly adv.; stick′i·ness n.

stiff /stif/ adj. 1 rigid; inflexible 2 hard to bend, move, or turn 3 requiring strength or effort (stiff climb) 4 severe (stiff penalty) 5 formal; constrained 6 (of a muscle, person, etc.) aching owing to exertion, injury, etc. 7 (of a wind, alcoholic drink, motive, etc.) strong; powerful —adv. 8 Colloq. to the extreme (bored stiff) —n. 9a Slang. corpse b foolish or useless person —stiff′ish adj.; stiff′ly adv.; stiff′ness n. [OE]

stiff′en v. make or become stiff —stiff′en·ing n.

stiff′-necked′ adj. obstinate; haughty

stiff′ up′per lip′ n. appearance of being calm in adversity

sti·fle /sti′fəl/ v. (·fled, ·fling) 1 suppress 2 feel or make unable to breathe easily; suffocate 3 kill by suffocating —sti′fling adj.

stig·ma /stig′mə/ n. (pl. ·mas or, esp. in sense 3, ·ma·ta /-mät′ə/) 1 burden of shame or disgrace; blot; curse 2 part of the pistil that receives the pollen in pollination 3 (pl.) Christianity. marks like those of the crucified Christ appearing on the bodies of certain saints, etc. [Gk stigma -mat- brand, dot]

stig·ma·tize /stig′mətīz′/ v. (·tized, ·tiz·ing) brand as unworthy or disgraceful [Gk stigmatizein, rel. to STIGMA]

stile /stīl/ n. steps allowing people but not animals to climb over or pass through a barrier [OE]

sti·let·to /stəlet′ō/ n. (pl. ·tos) 1 short dagger 2 (in full sti·let′to heel′) a long tapering heel of a shoe b shoe with such a heel [It dim., rel. to STYLE]

still[1] /stil/ adj. 1 not or hardly moving 2 with little or no sound; calm and tranquil —n. 3 deep silence (still of the night) 4 static photograph or single frame from a movie film —adv. 5 without moving (sit still) 6 now or at a particular time (is he still here?) 7

nevertheless **8** (with *compar.*) even, yet, increasingly (*still greater efforts*) —*v.* **9** make or become still —**still'ness** *n.* [OE]

still[2] *n.* apparatus for distilling alcoholic liquor [obs. *still* (v.) DISTIL]

still'birth' *n.* birth of a dead child

still'born' *adj.* **1** born dead **2** abortive

still' life' *n.* (*pl.* **still lifes**) painting or drawing of inanimate objects, as fruit or flowers

stilt /stilt/ *n.* **1** either of a pair of poles with foot supports for walking with the body elevated **2** each of a set of piles or posts supporting a building, etc. [LGer or Du]

stilt'ed *adj.* (of literary style, etc.) stiff and unnatural; bombastic

stim·u·lant /stim'yələnt/ *n.* stimulating substance or influence [L, rel. to STIMULATE]

stim·u·late /stim'yəlāt'/ *v.* (·lat·ed, ·lat·ing) **1** act as a stimulus to **2** animate; excite; arouse —**stim·u·la'tion** *n.*; **stim·u·la'tive** /-tiv/ *adj.*; **stim·u·la'tor** *n.* [L, rel. to STIMULUS]

stim·u·lus /stim'yələs/ *n.* (*pl.* **·li** /-lī', -lē'/) thing that rouses to activity [L: goad]

sting /stiNG/ *n.* **1** sharp, wounding organ of an insect, snake, nettle, etc. **2a** infliction of such a wound **b** the wound itself or the pain caused by it **3** painful quality or effect **4** pungency; vigor **5** *Slang.* swindle —*v.* (**stung, sting·ing**) **6a** wound or pierce with a sting **b** be able to sting **7** feel or give a tingling physical or sharp mental pain **8** (foll. by *into*) incite, esp. painfully (*stung into replying*) **9a** *Slang.* swindle **b** law-enforcement operation in which officers pose as law-breakers to catch suspects in the act of a crime —**sting'er** *n.* [OE]

sting'ray' *n.* broad flatfish with a poisonous spine at the base of its tail

stin·gy /stin'jē/ *adj.* (·gi·er, ·gi·est) miserly —**stin'gi·ly** *adv.*; **stin'gi·ness** *n.* [perh. fr. STING]

stink /stiNGk/ *v.* (**stank** or **stunk, stunk, stink·ing**) **1** emit a strong, offensive smell **2** (foll. by *up*) fill (a place) with a stink —*n.* **3** strong or offensive smell **4** *Colloq.* fuss —**stink'ing** *adj.* & *adv.* [OE]

stink'er *n. Colloq.* troublesome, mean, or difficult person or thing

stint /stint/ *v.* **1** supply (food, aid, etc.) meanly or grudgingly —*n.* **2** limitation of supply or effort (*without stint*) **3** allotted amount of work (*do one's stint*) [OE]

sti·pend /stī'pend'/ *n.* **1** salary **2** periodic allowance, esp. to a student or scholar [L *stipendium*]

stip·ple /stip'əl/ *v.* (·**pled, ·pling**) **1** draw, paint, engrave, etc., with dots instead of lines —*n.* **2** stippling **3** effect of stippling [Du]

stip·u·late /stip'yəlāt'/ *v.* (·**lat·ed, ·lat·ing**) demand or specify as part of an agreement —**stip'u·la'tion** *n.* [L *stipulari*]

stir[1] /stər/ *v.* (**stirred, stir·ring**) **1** move a utensil circularly in (a liquid, etc.), esp. to mix ingredients **2** move, esp. slightly **3** rise from sleep **4** arouse, inspire, or excite (the emotions, a person, etc.) —*n.* **5** act of stirring **6** commotion; excitement **7** stir up stimulate; excite; provoke —**stir'rer** *n.* [OE]

stir[2] *n. Slang.* prison

stir'-fry' *v.* (·**fried, ·fry·ing**) **1** fry rapidly while stirring —*n.* **2** stir-fried dish

stir·rup /stər'əp/ *n.* metal loop at the side of a saddle to hold a rider's foot [OE: climbing-rope]

stitch /stich/ *n.* **1** (in sewing, knitting, or crocheting) single pass of a needle, or the resulting thread, loop, etc. **2** least bit of clothing (*not a stitch on*) **3** sharp pain in the side —*v.* **4** sew; make stitches (in) **5** in stitches laughing uncontrollably [OE, rel. to STICK[2]]

stoat /stōt/ *n.* mammal of the weasel family with brown fur turning mainly white in the winter

stock /stäk/ *n.* **1** store of goods ready for sale or distribution **2** supply; quantity **3** equipment or raw material for manufacture or trade, etc. **4** farm animals or equipment **5** ownership of capital in a business, esp. as shares **6** reputation or popularity (*his stock is rising*) **7** line of ancestry **8** liquid base for soup, etc., made by stewing bones, vegetables, etc. **9** plant into which a graft is inserted **10** (*pl.*) *Hist.* timber frame with holes for the limbs in which offenders were locked as a public punishment **11** base, support, or handle on an implement or machine **12** shoulder rest of a rifle —*adj.* **13** kept in stock and so regularly available **14** hackneyed; conventional —*v.* **15** have (goods) in stock **16** supply **17** stock up provide with or get stocks or supplies (of) **18** take stock: **a** make an inventory of one's stock **b** review and assess (a situation, etc.) [OE]

stock·ade /stäkād'/ *n.* **1** line or enclosure of upright stakes **2** military prison [Sp *estacada*]

stock'brok'er *n.* dealer in stocks, bonds, etc. —**stock'brok·ing** *n.*

stock' car' *n.* production-model car for use in racing

stock' ex·change' *n.* **1** place for dealing in shares of stock **2** dealers working there

stock'hold'er *n.* owner of shares of stock

Stock·holm /stäk'hō(l)m'/ *n.* capital of Sweden. Pop. 679,400

stock'ing *n.* long, knitted fabric covering for the leg and foot [fr. STOCK]

stock' in trade' *n.* **1** requisite(s) of a trade or profession **2** characteristic or essential ability

stock' mar'ket *n.* STOCK EXCHANGE

stock'pile' *n.* **1** accumulated stock of goods, etc., held in reserve —*v.* (·**piled, ·pil·ing**) **2** accumulate a stockpile of

stock'room' *n.* room for storing goods

stock'-still' *adj.* motionless

stock'tak'ing *n.* **1** making an inventory of stock **2** review and appraisal of one's position, actions, etc.

Stock·ton /stäk'tən/ *n.* city in Calif. Pop. 210,943

stock'y *adj.* (·i·er, ·i·est) short and sturdy —**stock'i·ly** *adv.*; **stock'i·ness** *n.*

stock'yard' *n.* enclosure for livestock coming to market

stodg·y /stäj'ē/ *adj.* (·i·er, ·i·est) ponderously dull, stale, or uninteresting —**stodg'i·ly** *adv.*; **stodg'i·ness** *n.*

Sto·ic /stō'ik/ *n.* **1** member of the ancient Greek school of philosophy that taught control of one's feelings and passions **2** (s-) stoical person —*adj.* 3 of or like the Stoics 4 (s-) STOICAL [Gk *stoa* portico]

sto·i·cal /stō′ikal/ *adj.* having or showing great self-control in adversity —**sto′i·cal·ly** *adv.*

Sto·i·cism /stō′isiz′əm/ *n.* 1 philosophy of the Stoics 2 (s-) stoical attitude

stoke /stōk/ *v.* (**stoked, stok·ing**) feed and tend (a fire or furnace) [Du *stoken*]

Stoke-on-Trent /stō′ än trent′/ *n.* city on the Trent River in England. Pop. 275,200

STOL /stōl/ *abbr.* short take-off and landing

stole¹ /stōl/ *n.* 1 woman's garment like a long, wide scarf, worn over the shoulders 2 strip of silk, etc., worn similarly by a priest [Gk *stolē* equipment, clothing]

stole² *v.* past of STEAL

sto·ken /stō′lən/ *v.* past part. of STEAL

stol·id /stäl′id/ *adj.* not easily excited or moved; impassive; unemotional —**sto·lid′i·ty** *n.*; **stol′id·ly** *adv.* [L]

stom·ach /stam′ik/ *n.* 1a internal organ in which food is digested b any of several such organs in animals 2 lower front of the body 3 appetite or inclination (for) —*v.* 4 find palatable 5 endure (usu. *neg.*: *cannot stomach it*) [Gk *stoma* mouth]

stom′ach·ache′ *n.* pain in the belly or bowels

stomp /stämp, stômp/ *v.* 1 tread or stamp heavily —*n.* 2 lively jazz dance with heavy stamping [var. of STAMP]

stone /stōn/ *n.* 1a solid nonmetallic mineral matter; rock b small piece of this 2a thing resembling stone, e.g., the hard case of the kernel in some fruits b (often *pl.*) hard mass forming in certain body organs 3 *Brit.* (*pl.* same) unit of weight equal to 14 lb. —*adj.* 4 gem, esp. as used in jewelry —*v.* (**stoned, ston·ing**) 5 pelt with stones 6 leave no stone unturned try all possible means 7 a stone's throw a short distance [OE]

Stone /stōn/, Lucy 1818–93; US suffragist

Stone′ Age′ *n.* prehistoric period when weapons and tools were made of stone

stoned *adj.* *Slang.* under the influence of drugs or alcohol

stone′ma′son *n.* person who cuts, prepares, and builds with stone

stone′wall′ *v.* obstruct (a discussion or investigation) with evasive answers, etc.

stone·ware /stōn′wer′/ *n.* ceramic ware that is partly vitrified

stone′washed′ *adj.* (esp. of denim) washed with abrasives to give a worn or faded look

stone′work′ *n.* masonry

ston′y *adj.* (**-i·er, -i·est**) 1 full of stones 2a (of eyes, looks, etc.) cold; hard b unfeeling; uncompromising —**ston′i·ly** *adv.*; **ston′i·ness** *n.*

stood /stŏod/ *v.* past and past part. of STAND

stooge /stŏoj/ *n.* 1 butt or foil, esp. for a comedian 2 subordinate or hireling, esp. for routine or unpleasant work

stool /stŏol/ *n.* 1 single seat without a back or arms 2 FOOTSTOOL 3 (usu. *pl.*) FECES [OE]

stool′ pi′geon *n.* *Slang.* police informer or decoy

stoop¹ /stŏop/ *v.* 1 lower the body, sometimes bending the knee; bend down 2 stand or walk with the shoulders habitually bent forward 3 condescend 4 degrade by descent (to) —*n.* 5 stooping posture [OE]

stoop² *n.* porch, small veranda, or steps in front of a house [Du *stoep*]

stop /stäp/ *v.* (**stopped, stop·ping**) 1a put an end to the continuation, progress, motion, or operation of b effectively hinder or prevent 2 come to an end 3 cease from motion, speaking, action, etc. 4 defeat 5 stay for a short time 6 block or close (a hole, leak, etc.) —*n.* 7 stopping or being stopped 8 designated stopping place for a bus, train, etc. 9 plug or other device for stopping motion 10a (in an organ) row of pipes of one character b knob. etc., operating these 11 pull out all the stops make extreme effort 12 stop at nothing be ruthless [OE]

stop′cock′ *n.* externally operated valve regulating flow through a pipe, etc.

stop′gap′ *n.* temporary substitute

stop′o′ver *n.* break in a journey, esp. overnight

stop·page /stäp′ij/ *n.* 1 stopping or being stopped; cessation 2 blockage; obstruction

Stop·pard /stäp′ärd′, -ərd/, Tom 1937– ; Czech-born English dramatist

stop′per *n.* 1 plug for closing a bottle, etc. —*v.* 2 close with this

stop′watch′ *n.* watch that records elapsed time, used for races, etc.

stor·age /stôr′ij/ *n.* 1a storing of goods, etc. b space for storing 2 cost of storing 3 storing of data in a computer

stor′age bat′tery *n.* rechargeable unit for storing electricity

store /stôr/ *n.* 1 quantity of something kept available for use 2 (*pl.*) a articles gathered for a particular purpose b supply of or capacity for keeping these 3 retail shop or outlet 4 warehouse —*v.* (**stored, stor·ing**) 5 accumulate for future use 6 put (furniture, etc.) in storage 7 stock or provide with something useful 8 keep (data) for retrieval 9 in store: a kept in readiness b coming in the future c (foll. by *for*) awaiting 10 set store by consider important [Fr *estore(r)* fr. L *instaurare* renew]

store′house′ *n.* storage place

store′keep′er *n.* person with a shop or outlet for retail selling

store′room′ *n.* storage room

sto·rey /stôr′ē/ *n.* STOREY²

sto·ried /stôr′ēd/ *adj.* celebrated in or associated with stories or legends

stork /stôrk/ *n.* long-legged usu. white wading bird [OE]

storm /stôrm/ *n.* 1 violent atmospheric disturbance with strong winds and usu. thunder, rain, or snow 2 violent political, etc., disturbance 3 (foll. by *of*) outbreak of applause, hisses, etc. 4 direct assault by troops on a fortified place —*v.* 5 attack or capture by storm 6 move violently or angrily (*stormed out*) 7 take by storm: a capture by direct assault b rapidly captivate [OE]

storm′ troop′er *n.* member of the storm troops

storm′ troops′ *n. pl.* 1 SHOCK TROOPS 2 *Hist.* Nazi political militia

storm′y *adj.* (**-i·er, -i·est**) 1 of or affected by storms 2 full of angry feeling or outbursts; tempestuous (*stormy meeting*) —**storm′i·ly** *adv.*; **storm′i·ness** *n.*

storm'y pet'rel *n.* 1 small black and white N Atlantic petrel 2 person causing unrest

sto·ry[1] /stôr′ē/ *n.* (*pl.* **·ries**) 1 account of imaginary or past events; tale; anecdote 2 history of a person, institution, etc. 3 (in full **sto'ry line'**) narrative or plot of a novel, play, etc. 4 facts or experiences worthy of narration 5 fib [AngFr *estorie* fr. L, rel. to HISTORY]

sto·ry[2] *n.* (*pl.* **·ries**) (also **sto'rey**) horizontal division of a building, from floor to ceiling in each —**sto'ried** *adj.* [AngL, rel. to HISTORY, perh. orig. meaning a tier of painted windows]

sto'ry·board' *n.* Film. one of a series of sketches used for designing scenes in a movie, etc.

sto'ry·tell'er *n.* person who tells stories —**sto'ry·tell'ing** *n.* & *adj.*

stoup /stoop/ *n.* 1 basin for holy water 2 *Archaic.* flagon; beaker [ON]

stout /stout/ *adj.* 1 rather fat; corpulent; bulky 2 thick; strong 3 brave; resolute —*n.* 4 strong, dark beer —**stout'ly** *adv.*; **stout'ness** *n.* [AngFr fr. Gmc]

stout'-heart'ed *adj.* courageous —**stout'heart'ed·ly** *adv.*; **stout'heart'ed·ness** *n.*

stove[1] /stōv/ *n.* closed apparatus burning fuel or using electricity for heating or cooking [LGer or MDu]

stove[2] *v.* *past* and *past part.* of STAVE

stove'pipe' *n.* 1 pipe carrying smoke and gases from a stove to a chimney 2 (also **stove' pipe' hat'**) tall, black top hat

stow /stō/ *v.* 1 pack (goods, cargo, etc.) compactly 2 **stow away: a** place (a thing) out of the way **b** be a stowaway on a ship, etc. [OE: a place]

stow'a·way' *n.* person who hides on a ship, aircraft, etc., to travel free, escape, etc.

Stowe /stō/, **Harriet Beecher** 1811–96; US novelist

stra·bis·mus /strəbiz′məs/ *n.* *Med.* squint; crossed eyes [Gk *strabos* squinting]

strad·dle /strad′l/ *v.* (**·dled, ·dling**) 1 sit or stand over with the legs spread 2 be situated on both sides of [fr. STRIDE]

Stra·di·va·ri /strad′əvär′ē, -var′-/, **Antonio** c. 1644–1737; Italian violin-maker

strafe /strāf/ *v.* (**strafed, straf·ing**) attack from an airplane with gunfire [Ger: punish]

strag·gle /strag′əl/ *v.* (**·gled, ·gling**) 1 lack compactness or tidiness 2 be dispersed or sporadic 3 trail behind or wander from a group —**strag'gler** *n.*; **strag'gly** *adj.* (**·gli·er, ·gli·est**)

straight /strāt/ *adj.* 1 extending uniformly in the same direction; not bent or curved 2 successive, uninterrupted (*three straight wins*) 3 ordered; tidy (*put things straight*) 4 *Colloq.* honest; candid 5a unmodified b (of a drink) undiluted 6 *Colloq.* **a** (of a person) conventional; respectable **b** heterosexual 7 direct; undeviating —*n.* 8 straight condition 9 *Cards.* sequence of five cards in poker 10 *Colloq.* conventional person; heterosexual —*adv.* 11 in a straight line; direct; upright 12 correctly 13 **go straight** (of a criminal) become honest 14 **straight off** *Colloq.* without hesitation —**straight'ness** *n.* [orig. a past part. of STRETCH]

straight'a·way' *n.* 1 straight road, course, track, etc. —*adv.* 2 without delay; at once

straight·en /strāt′n/ *v.* 1 make or become

straight in position, form, conduct, etc. 2 (foll. by *up*) stand erect after bending

straight' face' *n.* intentionally expressionless face —**straight'-faced'** *adj.*

straight' flush' *n.* Cards. flush in numerical sequence

straight'for'ward *adj.* 1 honest or frank 2 (of a task, etc.) simple

straight' man' *n.* comedian's foil

strain[1] /strān/ *v.* 1 stretch tightly; make or become taut or tense 2 injure by overuse or excessive demands 3 exercise (oneself, one's senses, a thing, etc.) intensely; press to extremes 4 strive intensively 5 (foll. by *at*) tug; pull 6 distort from the true intention or meaning 7 clear (a liquid) of solid matter by passing it through a sieve, etc.; filter —*n.* 8a act of straining b force exerted in this 9 injury caused by straining a muscle, etc. 10 severe mental or physical demand or exertion 11 short segment of music or poetry 12 tone or tendency in speech or writing (*more in the same strain*) [Fr estrei(g)n- fr. L *stringere*]

strain[2] *n.* 1 breed or stock of animals, plants, etc. 2 tendency; characteristic [OE: beget-ting]

strained /strānd/ *adj.* 1 constrained; artificial 2 (of a relationship) mutually distrustful or tense

strain'er *n.* sieve for straining liquids, etc.

strait /strāt/ *n.* 1 (*sing.* or *pl.*) narrow channel connecting two large bodies of water 2 (usu. *pl.*) difficulty; distress [Fr *estreit* fr. L *strictus* narrow]

strait·ened /strāt′nd/ *adj.* of or marked by poverty

strait'jack'et *n.* 1 strong garment with long sleeves for confining a violent person 2 restrictive measures

strait'-laced' *adj.* puritanical

strand[1] /strand/ *v.* 1 run aground 2 leave in difficulties, esp. without money or transport —*n.* 3 beach [OE]

strand[2] *n.* 1 each of the twisted threads or wires making a rope, cable, etc. 2 single thread or strip of fiber 3 lock of hair 4 element; component

strange /strānj/ *adj.* (**strang·er, strang·est**) 1 unusual; peculiar; surprising; eccentric 2 unfamiliar; foreign 3 not at ease —**strange'ly** *adv.*; **strange'ness** *n.* [Fr *estrange* fr. L *extraneus*]

strang'er *n.* 1 person new to a particular place or company 2 person one does not know 3 person unacquainted with or unaccustomed to something (*no stranger to controversy*)

stran·gle /strang′gəl/ *v.* (**·gled, ·gling**) 1 squeeze the windpipe or neck of, esp. so as to kill 2 hamper; suppress —**stran'gler** *n.* [Gk *strangos* twisted]

stran'gle·hold' *n.* 1 throttling hold in wrestling 2 deadly grip 3 force or action that restricts freedom

stran·gu·late /strang′gyəlāt′/ *v.* (**·lat·ed, ·lat·ing**) compress (a vein, intestine, etc.), preventing circulation [L, rel. to STRANGLE]

stran·gu·la'tion *n.* 1 strangling or being strangled 2 strangulating

strap /strap/ *n.* 1 strip of leather, etc., often with a buckle, for securing or holding things together 2 narrow strip of fabric worn over the shoulders as part of a garment —v. (**strapped, strap·ping**) 3 secure or bind with a strap —**strap'less** adj. [dial.: STROP]

strap'ping adj. large and sturdy

Stras·bourg /sträsbŏŏrg′, sträs′bärg′/ n. city in NE France. Pop. 255,900

stra·ta /strä′ta, strā′-/ n. pl. of STRATUM
• Usage: The standard singular is *stratum*; its plural, *strata*.

strat·a·gem /strat′əjəm, -jem′/ n. 1 cunning plan or scheme 2 trickery [Gk *stratēgos* a general]

stra·te·gic /strətē′jik/ adj. 1 of or promoting strategy; purposive and long-term 2 (of materials) essential in war 3 (of bombing or weapons) done or for use as a longer-term military objective —**stra·te'gi·cal·ly** adv.

strat·e·gy /strat′əjē/ n. (pl. **-gies**) 1 longterm plan, policy, or management (*economic strategy*) 2 art of war or military deployment —**strat'e·gist** /-jist/ n.

strat·i·fy /strat′əfī′/ v. (**-fied, -fy·ing**) arrange in strata, grades, etc. —**strat'i·fi·ca'tion** /-fikā′SHən/ n. [Fr. rel. to STRATUM]

strat·o·sphere /strat′əsfēr′/ n. layer of atmosphere above the troposphere, extending to about 30 miles (50 km) from the earth's surface —**strat'o·spher'ic** /-sfer′ik/ adj. [fr. STRATUM]

stra·tum /strat′əm, strā′təm/ n. (pl. **-ta** /-ə/) 1 layer or set of layers of any deposited substance, esp. of rock 2 atmospheric layer 3 social class [L *sternere* strew]

Strauss /strous, SHrous/ 1 **Johann II** (called "**the Waltz King**") 1825–99; Austrian composer 2 **Richard** 1864–1949; German composer

Stra·vin·sky /strəvin′skē/, **Igor** 1882–1971; Russian-born US composer

straw /strô/ n. 1 dry cut stalks of grain as fodder, packing, etc. 2 single stalk of straw 3 thin tube for sucking drink through 4 pale yellow color 5 **clutch at straws** try any remedy in desperation [OE]

straw·ber·ry /strô′ber′ē, -b(ə)rē/ n. (pl. **-ries**) 1 pulpy, red fruit with a seed-studded surface 2 plant with white flowers bearing this [OE, rel. to STRAW, perh. for the fruit's appearance]

straw' vote' n. (also **straw' poll'**) unofficial ballot as a test of opinion

stray /strā/ v. 1 wander from the right place or from one's companions; go astray 2 deviate morally or mentally —n. 3 strayed person, animal, or thing —adj. 4 strayed; lost 5 isolated; occasional [AngFr *strey*, perh. rel. to L *strata* street]

streak /strēk/ n. 1 long, thin, usu. irregular line or band, esp. of color 2 strain or tendency in a person's character 3 consecutive run; spell; series (*winning streak*) —v. 4 mark with streaks 5 move very rapidly 6 run naked in public —**streak'er** n. [OE: pen-stroke]

streak'y adj. (**-i·er, -i·est**) 1 full of streaks 2 irregular or unpredictable; erratic

stream /strēm/ n. 1 flowing body of water, esp. a small river 2 flow of a fluid or of a mass of people 3 current; direction (*against the stream*) —v. 4 move as a stream 5 course; flow [OE]

stream'er n. 1 long, narrow strip of ribbon or paper 2 long, narrow flag

stream'line' v. (**-lined, -lin·ing**) 1 give (a vehicle, etc.) the form that presents the least resistance to motion 2 make simple, trim, or more efficient

street /strēt/ n. 1a public road in a city, town, or village b this with the houses, etc., on each side, or as a local community 2 **on the streets: a** homeless **b** without a job **c** out of prison [OE]

street'car' n. electrically powered passenger road vehicle running on rails

street'walk·er n. prostitute seeking customers in the street

street'wise' n. (also **street'-smart**) experienced and shrewd regarding life in a harsh urban or ghetto environment

strength /streNGTH, strenTH/ n. 1 being strong; degree or manner of this 2a person or thing giving strength b positive attribute 3 number of people present or available; full number 4 **in strength** in large numbers 5 **on the strength of** on the basis of [OE, rel. to STRONG]

strength·en /streNG′THən, stren′-/ v. make or become stronger

stren·u·ous /stren′yŏŏəs/ adj. 1 requiring or using great effort 2 energetic —**stren'u·ous·ly** adv.; **stren'u·ous·ness** n. [L]

strep·to·coc·cus /strep′təkäk′əs/ n. (pl. **-coc·ci** /-käk′(s)ī, -(s)ē/) bacterium of a type often causing infectious diseases —**strep'to·coc'cal** /-kəl/ adj. [Gk *streptos* twisted, *kokkos* berry]

strep·to·my·cin /strep′təmī′sin/ n. antibiotic effective against many disease-producing bacteria [Gk *streptos* twisted, *mukēs* fungus]

stress /stres/ n. 1 pressure; tension 2 physical or mental strain or distress 3a emphasis b pronunciation emphasis on a syllable or word —v. 4 emphasize 5 subject to stress [shortening of DISTRESS]

stress'ful adj. causing stress

stretch /streCH/ v. 1 draw, be drawn, or be able to be drawn out in length or size 2 make or become taut 3 place or lie at full length or spread out 4a extend (a limb, etc.) b thrust out a limb and tighten one's muscles, as in exercising 5 have a specified length or extension; extend 6 strain; exaggerate (*stretch the truth*) —n. 7 continuous extent, expanse, or period 8 stretching or being stretched 9 elastic (*stretch fabric*) 10 *Colloq.* period of imprisonment, etc. 11 straight side of a racetrack 12 **at a stretch** in one period 13 **stretch a point** agree to something not normally allowed —**stretch'y** adj. (**-i·er, -i·est**) [OE]

stretch'er n. two poles with canvas, etc., between, for carrying a person in a lying position

strew /strŏŏ/ v. (**strewed, strewn** or **strewed, strew·ing**) 1 scatter or spread about over a surface 2 spread (a surface) with scattered things [OE, rel. to STRAW]

stri·ate adj. /strī′it, -āt′/ (also **stri'at·ed** /-ā′ tid/) 1 marked with parallel lines, ridges, etc. —v. /strī′āt′/ (**-at·ed, -at·ing**) 2 mark with parallel lines, ridges, etc. —**stri·a'tion** n.

strick·en /strik′ən/ adj. overcome with illness, misfortune, etc. [past part. of STRIKE]

strict /strikt/ *adj.* **1** precisely limited or defined; undeviating **2** requiring complete obedience or exact performance **3** strictly speaking applying words or rules in their strict sense —**strict′ly** *adv.*; **strict′ness** *n.* [L *stringere* strict- draw tight]

stric·ture /strik′CHər/ *n.* (usu. *pl.*) critical or censorious remark [L, rel. to STRICT]

stride /strīd/ *v.* (**strode, strid·den** /strid′ən/, **strid·ing**) **1** walk with long, firm steps **2** cross with one step **3** bestride —*n.* **4a** single, long step **b** length of this **5** gait as determined by the length of stride **6** (usu. *pl.*) progress (*great strides*) **7** hit one's stride achieve a level or state of successful functioning or productivity **8** take in stride manage or adapt to easily [OE]

stri·dent /strīd′nt/ *adj.* loud and harsh —**stri′den·cy** *n.*; **stri′dent·ly** *adv.* [L *stridere* creak]

strife /strīf/ *n.* conflict; struggle [Fr *estrif*, rel. to STRIVE]

strike /strīk/ *v.* (**struck, struck** or **strick·en, strik·ing**) **1** deliver (a blow) or inflict a blow on; hit **2** come or bring sharply into contact with (*ship struck a rock*) **3** propel with a blow **4** induce (*struck terror into him*) **5** ignite (a match) or produce (sparks, etc.) by friction **6** make (a coin) by stamping **7** produce (a musical note) by striking **8** (of a clock) indicate (the time) with a chime, etc. **9a** attack suddenly **b** (of a disease) afflict **10** cause to become suddenly (*struck dumb*) **11** reach or achieve (*strike a balance*) **12** agree on (a bargain) **13** assume (a pose, etc.) **14** discover or find (oil, etc.) **15** occur to or appear to (*strikes me as silly*) **16** (of employees) engage in a strike **17** lower or take down (a flag, tent, stage set, etc.) —*n.* **18** act of striking **19** organized refusal to work until a grievance is remedied **20** sudden find or success **21** attack, esp. from the air **22** *Baseball.* pitch called good by the umpire or swung at and not successfully hit **23 on strike** taking part in an industrial, etc., strike **24 strike home:** a deal an effective blow **b** have the intended effect **25 strike out:** a act vigorously **b** delete **c** set off (*struck out eastward*) **d** *Baseball.* to retire or be retired on three pitches ruled strikes **e** to fail **26 strike up:** a start (an acquaintance, conversation, etc.), esp. casually **b** begin playing (a tune, etc.) —**strik′er** *n.* [OE: go, stroke]

strike′break·er *n.* person working or employed in place of strikers

strik′ing *adj.* impressive; attracting attention —**strik′ing·ly** *adv.*

Strind·berg /strin(d)′bərg/, (Johan) August 1849–1912; Swedish writer

string /strinG/ *n.* **1** twine or narrow cord **2** piece of this **3** length of catgut, wire, etc., on a musical instrument, producing a note by vibration **4a** (*pl.*) stringed instruments in an orchestra **b** stringed instruments (*string quartet*) **5** (*pl.*) condition; complication (*no strings attached*) **6** set of things strung together; series; line —*v.* (**strung, strung, string·ing**) **7** fit (a racket, violin, violin's or archer's bow, etc.) with a string or strings or the like **8** thread on a string **9** arrange in or as a string **10 string along: a** deceive **b** keep company (with) **11 string out** extend; prolong **12**

string up: a hang up on strings, etc. **b** kill by hanging [OE]

stringed /strinGd/ *adj.* (of musical instruments) having strings

strin·gent /strin′jənt/ *adj.* (of rules, etc.) strict; precise —**strin′gen·cy** *n.*; **strin′gent·ly** *adv.* [L, rel. to STRICT]

string·er /strinG′ər/ *n.* **1** longitudinal structural member in a framework, esp. of a ship or aircraft **2** freelance newspaper correspondent

string·y /strinG′ē/ *adj.* (**·i·er, ·i·est**) like string; fibrous —**string′i·ness** *n.*

strip[1] /strip/ *v.* (**stripped, strip·ping**) **1** undress; remove the covering from **2** deprive (a person) of property or titles **3** leave bare **4** remove the accessory fittings of or take apart (a machine, etc.) **5** damage the thread of (a screw) or the teeth of (a gearwheel) —*n.* **6** act of stripping, esp. in striptease [OE]

strip[2] *n.* long, narrow piece [LGer *strippe* strap]

stripe /strīp/ *n.* **1** long narrow band or strip differing in color or texture from the surface on either side of it **2** *Milit.* chevron, etc., denoting military rank **3** (of a person) type or makeup —*v.* (**striped, strip·ing**) **4** make with a stripe or stripes [perh. fr. LGer or Du]

strip·ling /strip′linG/ *n.* youth not yet fully grown [fr. STRIP[2]]

strip′ min′ing *n.* mining of a mineral deposit near the surface by excavation —**strip′-mine′** *v.* (**·mined, -min·ing**) & *n.*

strip′per *n.* **1** person or thing that strips something **2** striptease performer

strip′-search′ *n.* **1** thorough body search requiring removal of all clothing —*v.* **2** search in this way

strip′tease′ *n.* entertainment in which the performer slowly and erotically undresses, usu. to music

strive /strīv/ *v.* (**strove** or **strived, striv·en** /striv′ən/ or **strived, striv·ing**) **1** try hard **2** struggle [Fr *estriver*]

strobe /strōb/ *n.* stroboscope [abbr.]

stro·bo·scope /strō′bəskōp/ *n.* **1** *Physics.* instrument for determining speeds of rotation, etc., by shining a bright light at intervals so that a rotating object appears stationary **2** lamp made to flash intermittently —**stro′bo·scop′ic** /-skäp′ik/ *adj.* [Gk *strobos* whirling]

strode /strōd/ *v. past of* STRIDE

stroke /strōk/ *n.* **1** act of striking; blow; hit **2** sudden disabling attack caused esp. by thrombosis **3a** action or movement, esp. as one of a series **b** slightest action (*stroke of work*) **4** single complete motion of a wing, oar, piston, etc. **5** specified mode of swimming **6** specially successful or skillful effort (*a stroke of diplomacy*) **7** mark made by a single movement of a pen, paintbrush, etc. **8** sound of a striking clock **9** (in full **stroke′ oar′**) oar or oarsman nearest the stern, setting the time of the stroke **10** act or spell of stroking —*v.* (**stroked, strok·ing**) **11** caress with the hand **12** encourage; praise **13** act as the stroke of (a boat or crew) **14 at a stroke** by a single action **15 on the stroke (of)** punctually (at) [OE, rel. to STRIKE]

stroll /strōl/ *v.* **1** walk in a leisurely way —*n.*

2 short, leisurely walk [prob. fr. Ger *Strolch* vagabond]

strong /strȯNG/ *adj.* (**strong·er** /strȯNG′gər/, **strong·est** /strȯNG′gist/) 1 able to resist; not easily damaged, overcome, or disturbed 2 healthy 3 physically robust; muscular; powerful 4 forceful (*strong wind*) 5 firmly held (*strong suspicion*) 6 (of an argument, etc.) convincing 7 intense; concentrated 8 formidable (*strong candidate*) 9 of a specified number (*200 strong*) 10 *Gram.* (of a verb) forming inflections by a change of vowel within the stem (e.g., *swim, swam*) —*adv.* 11 strongly 12 come on strong behave aggressively 13 going strong *Colloq.* continuing vigorously; in good health, etc. —**strong′ish** *adj.*; **strong′ly** *adv.* [OE]

strong′-arm′ *adj.* using force (*strong-arm tactics*)

strong′box′ *n.* small, strongly made chest for valuables

strong′hold′ *n.* 1 fortified place 2 secure refuge

strong′room′ *n.* room, esp. in a bank, for keeping valuables safe from fire or theft

stron·ti·um /strän′tēəm/ *n.* soft silver-white metallic element; *symb.* Sr [*Strontian* in Scotland]

stron′ti·um-90 *n.* radioactive isotope of strontium

strop /sträp/ *n.* 1 device, esp. a strip of leather, for sharpening razors —*v.* (**stropped, strop·ping**) 2 sharpen on a strop [LGer or Du]

strove /strōv/ *v. past* of STRIVE

struck /strək/ *v. past* and *past part.* of STRIKE

struc·tur·al /strək′CHərəl/ *adj.* 1 of a structure 2 of order, sequence, or arrangement; organizational —**struc′tur·al·ly** *adv.*

struc·ture /strək′CHər/ *n.* 1a a constructed unit, esp. a building b way in which a building, etc., is constructed 2 framework —*v.* (**-tured, -tur·ing**) 3 give structure to; organize [L *struere struct-* build]

stru·del /strōōd′l/ *n.* thin-leaved pastry rolled around a filling and baked [Ger]

strug·gle /strəg′əl/ *v.* (**-gled, -gling**) 1 energetically try to get free of restraint 2 try hard under difficulties 3 (foll. by *with, against*) contend; fight 4 progress with difficulty 5 have difficulty in gaining recognition or a living —*n.* 6 act or spell of struggling 7 hard or troublesome contest 8 ordeal; hardship

strum /strəm/ *v.* (**strummed, strum·ming**) 1 play on (a guitar, etc.), with light rolls of the fingers, esp. casually 2 play (a tune, etc.) in this way —*n.* 3 sound or spell of strumming [imit.: cf. THRUM]

strum·pet /strəm′pit/ *n. Archaic* or *Rhet.* prostitute

strung /strəNG/ *v. past* and *past part.* of STRING

strut /strət/ *n.* 1 bar in a framework, designed to resist compression 2 strutting gait —*v.* (**strut·ted, strut·ting**) 3 walk stiffly and pompously [OE]

strych·nine /strik′nēn′, -nīn′/ *n.* highly poisonous alkaloid used in small doses as a stimulant [Gk *strukhnos* nightshade]

Sts. *abbr.* 1 Saints 2 Streets

Stu·art /stōō′ərt/ 1 **Gilbert Charles** 1755-1828; US painter 2 "**Jeb**" **J**(ames) **E**(well) **B**(rown) 1833-64; Confederate general during the American Civil War

stub /stəb/ *n.* 1 remnant of a pencil, cigarette, etc. 2 retained part of a check, receipt, etc. 3 stump —*v.* (**stubbed, stub·bing**) 4 strike (one's toe) against something 5 extinguish (a cigarette) by pressure [OE]

stub·ble /stəb′əl/ *n.* 1 stalks of corn, etc., left in the ground after the harvest 2 short, stiff hair or bristles —**stub′bly** *adj.* [L *stupula*]

stub·born /stəb′ərn/ *adj.* obstinate; inflexible —**stub′born·ly** *adj.*; **stub′born·ness** *n.*

stub′by *adj.* (**·bi·er, ·bi·est**) short and thick

stuc·co /stək′ō/ *n.* (*pl.* **·coes**) 1 plaster or cement for coating walls —*v.* (**·coed, ·co·ing**) 2 coat with stucco [It]

stuck /stək/ *v. past* and *past part.* of STICK²

stuck′-up′ *adj. Colloq.* conceited; snobbish [STICK²]

stud¹ /stəd/ *n.* 1 large-headed projecting nail, boss, or knob, esp. for ornament 2 double button for a collar, shirt-front, etc. —*v.* (**stud·ded, stud·ding**) 3 set with or as with studs 4 thickly set or strew (with) [OE]

stud² *n.* 1 stallion 2 *Colloq.* young man, esp. one noted for sexual prowess 3 (in full **stud′po′ker**) form of poker in which some cards are dealt face up 4 **at stud** (of a male animal) hired out for breeding [OE]

stu·dent /st(y)ōōd′nt/ *n.* person who is studying, esp. one enrolled at a school, college, etc. —**stu′dent·ship** *n.* [L, rel. to STUDY]

stud·ied /stəd′ēd/ *adj.* deliberate; affected

stu·di·o /st(y)ōō′dē·ō′/ *n.* (*pl.* **-os**) 1 workroom of a painter, photographer, etc. 2 place for making films, recordings, or broadcast programs [It]

stu′di·o couch′ *n.* couch convertible into a bed

stu·di·ous /st(y)ōō′dēəs/ *adj.* 1 assiduous in study 2 painstaking —**stu′di·ous·ly** *adv.* [L, rel. to STUDY]

study /stəd′ē/ *n.* (*pl.* **·ies**) 1 acquisition of knowledge, esp. from books 2 (*pl.*) pursuit of academic knowledge 3 private room used for reading, writing, etc. 4 piece of work, esp. a drawing, done for practice or as an experiment or preliminary treatment 5 thing worth observing (*his face was a study*) 6 investigation; analysis; treatment —*v.* (**·ied, ·y·ing**) 7 make a study of; investigate (a subject) 8 apply oneself to study 9 scrutinize closely (a visible object) 10 learn (one's role, etc.) [L *studium*]

stuff /stəf/ *n.* 1 material; fabric 2 unspecified content, things, etc. 3 one's particular knowledge or activity (*know one's stuff*) —*v.* 4 pack (a receptacle) tightly 5 (foll. by *in, into*) force, push, or cram (a thing) 6 fill (an animal skin, etc.) with material to restore the original shape 7 fill (food, esp. poultry) with a mixture, esp. before cooking 8 fill with food; eat greedily 9 block (the nose, etc.) [Fr *estoffe*]

stuffed′ shirt′ *n.* pompous person

stuff′ing *n.* 1 padding for cushions, etc. 2 mixture used to stuff food, esp. before cooking

stuff′y *adj.* (**·i·er, ·i·est**) 1 (of a room, etc.) lacking fresh air 2 (of the nose, etc.) stuffed up 3 dull and conventional —**stuff′i·ly** adv.; **stuff′i·ness** n.

stul·ti·fy /stəl′təfī′/ v. (**·fied, ·fy·ing**) make ineffective or useless, esp. by routine —**stul′ti·fi·ca′tion** /·fikā′SHən/ n. [L *stultus* foolish]

stum·ble /stəm′bəl/ v. (**·bled, ·bling**) 1 involuntarily lurch forward or almost fall 2 walk with repeated stumbles 3 speak haltingly 4 (foll. by *on, upon, across*) find by chance —n. 5 act of stumbling [rel. to STAMMER]

stum′bling block n. obstacle

stump /stəmp/ n. 1 part of a cut or fallen tree still in the ground 2 similar part cut off or worn down —v. 3 (of a question, etc.) be too hard for; baffle 4 traverse (a district) making political speeches [LGer or Du]

stun /stən/ v. (**stunned, stun·ning**) 1 knock senseless; stupefy 2 bewilder; shock [Fr, rel. to ASTONISH]

stung /stəNG/ v. *past* and *past part.* of STING

stunk /stəNGk/ v. *past* and *past part.* of STINK

stun′ning adj. extremely attractive or impressive —**stun′ning·ly** adv.

stunt[1] /stənt/ v. retard the growth or development of [obs. *stunt* foolish; short]

stunt[2] n. 1 something unusual done for publicity 2 trick or daring feat

stunt′ man′ n. (pl. **·men**) man employed to perform dangerous stunts in place of an actor

stu·pe·fy /st(y)ŏŏ′pəfī′/ v. (**·fied, ·fy·ing**) 1 make stupid or insensible 2 astonish; amaze —**stu′pe·fac′tion** /·fak′SHən/ n. [Fr fr. L *stupere* be amazed]

stu·pen·dous /st(y)ŏŏpen′dəs/ adj. amazing or prodigious, esp. in magnitude —**stu·pen′dous·ly** adv. [L, rel. to STUPEFY]

stu·pid /st(y)ŏŏ′pid/ adj. (**·pid·er, ·pid·est**) 1 unintelligent; foolish 2 typical of stupid persons 3 uninteresting; boring —**stu·pid′i·ty** n. (pl. **·ties**); **stu′pid·ly** adv. [L, rel. to STUPENDOUS]

stu·por /st(y)ŏŏ′pər/ n. dazed, torpid, or helplessly amazed state [L, rel. to STUPEFY]

stur·dy /stər′dē/ adj. (**·di·er, ·di·est**) 1 robust; strongly built 2 vigorous (*sturdy resistance*) —**stur′di·ly** adv.; **stur′di·ness** n. [Fr *esturdi*]

stur·geon /stər′jən/ n. (pl. *same* or **·geons**) large, edible, sharklike fish yielding caviar [AngFr fr. Gmc]

stut·ter /stət′ər/ v. 1 stammer, esp. by involuntary repetition of initial consonants of words —n. 2 act or habit of stuttering [dial. *stut*]

Stutt·gart /SHtŏŏt′gärt′/ n. city in S Germany. Pop. 570,700

Stuy·ve·sant /stī′vəsənt/, **Peter** 1592–1672; Dutch colonial administrator in America

sty[1] /stī/ n. (pl. **sties**) PIGSTY [OE]

sty[2] n. (also **stye**) (pl. **sties** or **styes**) inflamed swelling on the edge of an eyelid [OE]

Styg·i·an /stij′ēən/ adj. Lit. dark; gloomy [literally 'of the *Styx,*' river around Hades in Gk myth]

style /stīl/ n. 1 evident kind or sort, esp. in regard to appearance and form (*elegant style of house*) 2 manner of writing, speaking, or performing 3 distinctive manner of a person, artistic school, or period 4 superior quality or manner (*do it in style*) 5 fashion in dress, etc. —v. (**styled, styl·ing**) 6 design or make, etc., in a particular (esp. fashionable) style 7 designate in a specified way [L *stilus*]

styl′ish adj. fashionable; elegant —**styl′ish·ly** adv.; **styl′ish·ness** n.

styl′ist n. 1a designer of fashionable styles, etc. b hairdresser 2 stylish writer or performer

sty·lis′tic adj. of esp. literary style —**sty·lis′ti·cal·ly** adv.

styl·ized /stī′līzd/ adj. painted, drawn, etc., in a conventional nonrealistic style

sty·lus /stī′ləs/ n. (pl. **·lus·es** or **·li** /·lī/) 1 needle that follows each groove in a phonograph record and transmits the recorded sound for reproduction 2 pointed writing tool [L, rel. to STYLE]

sty·mie /stī′mē/ (also **stimy**) n. (pl. **·mies**) 1 *Golf.* situation where an opponent's ball lies between one's ball and the hole —v. (**·mied, ·my·ing** or **·mie·ing**) 2 obstruct; thwart

styp·tic /stip′tik/ adj. 1 checking bleeding —n. 2 styptic substance [Gk *stuphein* contract]

sty·rene /stī′rēn, stēr′ēn/ n. *Chem.* colorless liquid, not soluble in water, that is used to make synthetic rubbers

Sty·ro·foam /stī′rəfōm′/ n. *Tdmk.* lightweight plastic foam from polystyrene used for cups, insulation, packing material, etc.

Su abbr. Sunday

sua·sion /swā′ZHən/ n. persuasion (*moral suasion*) [L *suadere suas-* urge]

suave /swäv/ adj. smooth; polite; sophisticated —**suave′ly** adv.; **suav′i·ty** n. [L *suavis*]

sub /səb/ *Colloq.* n. 1a submarine b submarine sandwich 2 substitute —v. (**subbed, sub·bing**) 3 act as a substitute (for) [abbr.]

sub- prefix 1 at, to, or from a lower position (*subordinate; submerge; subtract*) 2 secondary or inferior position (*subclass; subtotal*) 3 nearly; more or less (*subarctic*) [L]

sub·a·tom·ic /səb′ətäm′ik/ adj. occurring in or smaller than an atom

sub′com·mit′tee n. committee formed from a main committee for a special purpose

sub·com′pact n. & adj. car model smaller than a compact

sub·con′scious adj. 1 of the part of the mind which is not fully conscious but influences actions, etc. —n. 2 this part of the mind —**sub·con′scious·ly** adv.

sub·con′ti·nent n. large land mass, smaller than a continent

sub·con·tract /səbkän′trakt/ n. 1 secondary contract —v. 2 employ another contractor to do (work) as part of a larger project —**sub′con′trac·tor** n.

sub′cul′ture n. distinct cultural group or movement within a larger culture

sub·cu·ta·ne·ous /səb′kyŏŏtā′nēəs/ adj. under the skin

sub′di·vide′ v. (**·vid·ed, ·vid·ing**) divide again after a first division —**sub′di·vi′sion** n.

sub·due /səbd(y)ŏŏ′/ v. (**·dued, ·du·ing**) 1 conquer; subjugate; tame 2 make less intense; tone down [L *subducere*]

sub′head′ing n. subordinate heading or title

sub·hu′man adj. (of behavior, intelligence, etc.) less than human

subj. abbr. 1 subject; subjective 2 subjunctive

sub·ject *n.* /'səb'jikt/ 1 matter, theme, etc., to be discussed, described, represented, etc. 2 field of study 3 *Gram.* noun or its equivalent that performs the action of the verb or about which the verb makes a statement 4 person living under a government 5 person scientifically observed, studied, etc. —*adj.* /'səb'jikt/ 6 (foll. by *to*) conditional 7 (foll. by *to*) liable or exposed (*subject to infection*) 8 under the power or jurisdiction of —*adv.* /'səb'jikt/ 9 (foll. by *to*) conditionally (*subject to your consent, I shall go*) —*v.* /'səbjekt'/ 10 impose on or expose (to) —**sub·jec'tion** /-jek'SHən/ *n.* [L *subjectus* placed under]

sub·jec·tive /'səbjek'tiv/ *adj.* 1 (of art, written history, an opinion, etc.) not impartial or literal; personal 2 esp. *Philos.* of the individual consciousness or perception; imaginary, partial, or distorted —**sub·jec'tive·ly** *adv.*; **sub'jec·tiv'i·ty** *n.* [L, rel. to SUBJECT]

sub·join /'səbjoin'/ *v.* add (an illustration, anecdote, etc.) at the end [L *subjungere* -*junct*-]

sub·ju·gate /'səb'jəgāt'/ *v.* (·gat·ed, ·gat·ing) bring into subjection; vanquish —**sub'ju·ga'tion, sub'ju·ga'tor** *n.* [L *jugum* yoke]

sub·junc·tive /'səbjəNGk'tiv/ *Gram. adj.* 1 (of a mood) expressing what is imagined, wished, or possible (e.g., *if I were you; be that as it may*) —*n.* 2 this mood or form [L, rel. to SUBJOIN]

sub·lease *n.* /'səb'lēs'/ 1 lease granted by a tenant to a subtenant —*v.* /'səb'lēs'/ (·leased, ·leas·ing) 2 lease to a subtenant

sub·let *n.* /'səb'let'/ 1 SUBLEASE, 1 —*v.* /'səb'let'/ (·let, ·let·ting) 2 SUBLEASE, 2

sub·li·mate /'səb'ləmāt'/ *v.* (·mat·ed, ·mat·ing) 1 divert (esp. sexual energy) into socially more acceptable activity 2 convert (a substance) from the solid state directly to vapor by heat, and usu. allow it to solidify again 3 refine; purify; idealize —**sub'li·ma'tion** *n.* [L, rel. to SUBLIME]

sub·lime /'səblīm'/ *adj.* (·lim·er, ·lim·est) 1 of the most exalted or noble kind; awe-inspiring 2 to a heedless degree; utter (*sublime indifference*) —*v.* 3 SUBLIMATE, 2 —**sub·lime'ly** *adv.*; **sub·lim'i·ty** /-lim'ətē/ *n.* [L *sublimis*]

sub·lim·i·nal /'səblim'ən-l/ *adj. Psychol.* (of a stimulus, etc.) below the threshold of sensation or consciousness —**sub·lim'i·nal·ly** *adv.* [L *limen* -*min*- threshold]

sub·ma·chine' gun' *n.* hand-held, lightweight machine gun

sub·ma·rine /'səb'mərēn', səb'mərēn'/ *n.* 1 vessel, esp. an armed warship, capable of operating under water —*adj.* 2 existing, occurring, done, or used under the sea —**sub·mar·i·ner** /'səb'mərē'nər, -mar'ənər/ *n.*

sub·ma·rine' sand'wich *n.* sandwich made with a tubelike bread roll

sub·merge /'səbmərj'/ *v.* (·merged, ·merg·ing) place, go, or dive under water —**sub·mer'gence** *n.* [L *mergere mers*- dip]

sub·merse /'səbmərs'/ *v.* (·mersed, ·mers·ing) submerge —**sub·mer'sion** /-mər'ZHən, -SHən/ *n.*

sub·mers·i·ble /'səbmər'səbəl/ *n.* 1 submarine operating under water for short periods —*adj.* 2 capable of submerging

sub·mis·sion /'səbmisH'ən/ *n.* 1a submitting

or being submitted **b** thing submitted 2 submissiveness [L *submissio*, rel. to SUBMIT]

sub·mis·sive /'səbmis'iv/ *adj.* humble; obedient —**sub·mis'sive·ly** *adv.*; **sub·mis'sive·ness** *n.*

sub·mit /'səbmit'/ *v.* (·mit·ted, ·mit·ting) 1 (usu. foll. by *to*) cease resistance; yield 2 present for consideration 3 subject (a person or thing) to a process, treatment, etc. [L *mittere miss*- send]

sub·nor'mal *adj.* below or less than normal, esp. in intelligence

sub·or'der *n.* taxonomic category between an order and a family

sub·or·di·nate *adj.* /'səbôrd'n-ət/ 1 of inferior importance or rank; secondary; subservient —*n.* /'səbôrd'n-ət/ 2 person working under another —*v.* /-āt'/ (·nat·ed, ·nat·ing) 3 make or treat as subordinate —**sub·or'di·na'tion** *n.* [L, rel. to ORDAIN]

sub·or'di·nate clause' *n.* clause modifying or dependent on a main sentence

sub·orn /'səbôrn'/ *v.* induce by bribery, etc., to commit perjury, etc. [L *ornare* equip]

sub'plot' *n.* secondary plot in a play, etc.

sub·poe·na /'səpē'nə/ *n.* 1 writ ordering a person to appear or submit evidence in court —*v.* (·naed, ·na·ing) 2 serve a subpoena on [L: under penalty]

sub ro·sa /'səb rō'zə/ *adj. & adv.* in secrecy or confidence [L: under the rose]

sub·scribe /'səbskrīb'/ *v.* (·scribed, ·scrib·ing) 1a pay, esp. regularly, for membership in an organization, receipt of a publication, etc. **b** contribute money to a fund, cause, etc. 2 agree with and support an opinion, etc. —**sub·scrib'er** *n.* [L *scribere script*- write]

sub·script /'səb'skript'/ *adj.* 1 written or printed below the line —*n.* 2 subscript number, etc.

sub·scrip·tion /'səbskrip'SHən/ *n.* 1 subscribing 2 membership fee, esp. paid regularly —*adj.* 3 paid for mainly by advance sales of tickets (*subscription concert*)

sub·se·quent /'səb'sikwənt/ *adj.*, following, esp. as a consequence —**sub'se·quent·ly** *adv.* [L *sequor* follow]

sub·ser·vi·ent /'səbsər'vēənt/ *adj.* 1 servile 2 subordinate —**sub·ser'vi·ence** *n.*; **sub·ser'vi·ent·ly** *adv.* [L *subservire*]

sub'set' *n.* set of which all the elements are contained in another set

sub·side /'səbsīd'/ *v.* (·sid·ed, ·sid·ing) 1 become tranquil; abate (*excitement subsided*) 2 (of water, etc.) sink —**sub·sid·ence** /'səbsīd'ns, səb'sədəns/ *n.* [L *subsidere*]

sub·sid·i·ar·y /'səbsid'ē-er'ē/ *adj.* 1 supplementary; auxiliary 2 (of a company) controlled by another —*n.* (*pl.* ·ies) 3 subsidiary thing, person, or company [L, rel. to SUBSIDY]

sub·si·dize /'səb'sədīz'/ *v.* (·dized, ·diz·ing) 1 pay a subsidy to 2 partially pay for by subsidy

sub·si·dy /'səb'sədē/ *n.* (*pl.* ·dies) money granted esp. by the government [L *subsidium* help]

sub·sist /'səbsist'/ *v.* 1 keep oneself alive; be kept alive 2 continue to be; exist [L *subsistere*]

sub·sis·tence /'səbsis'təns/ *n.* 1 state or instance of subsisting 2a means of support;

livelihood **b** minimal level of existence or income

sub'soil' *n.* soil immediately under the surface
soil

sub·son·ic /səb'sän'ik/ *adj.* of speeds less
than that of sound

subst. *abbr.* **1** substantive **2** substitute

sub·stance /səb'stəns/ *n.* **1** particular kind
of material having uniform properties **2** reality; solidity **3** content or essence as opposed
to form, etc. **4** wealth and possessions
(*woman of substance*) [L *substantia*]

sub·stand·ard *adj.* of less than the required
or normal quality or state

sub·stan·tial /səb'stan'SHəl/ *adj.* **1a** of real
importance or value **b** large **2** solid; sturdy **3**
commercially successful; wealthy **4** essential; largely true **5** real; existing —**sub·stan'**
tial·ly *adv.* [L, rel. to SUBSTANCE]

sub·stan·ti·ate /səb'stan'SHē-āt'/ *v.* (**·at·ed,**
·at·ing) prove the truth of (a charge, claim,
etc.) —**sub·stan'ti·a'tion** *n.*

sub·stan·tive /səb'stəntiv/ *adj.* (also
/səbstan'tiv/) **1** genuine; actual; real **2** not
slight; substantial —*n.* **3** *Gram.* word or
words used as a noun —**sub'stan·tive·ly** *adv.*

sub·sti·tute /səb'stit(y)ōōt'/ *n.* **1** person or
thing acting or used in place of another —*v.*
(**·tut·ed, ·tut·ing**) **2** (cause to) act as a substitute —**sub'sti·tu'tion** *n.* [L *substituere*
-tut-]

sub·stra·tum /səb'strā'təm, -strat'əm/ *n.*
(*pl.* **·ta** /-tə/) underlying layer or substance

sub'struc'ture *n.* underlying or supporting
structure

sub·sume /səbsōōm'/ *v.* (**·sumed, ·sum-**
ing) include (an instance, idea, category,
etc.) in a rule, class, etc. [L *sumere* take]

sub·ter·fuge /səb'tərfyōōj'/ *n.* **1** evasive or
conspiratorial lying or deceit **2** statement, action, etc., used for such a purpose [L]

sub·ter·ra·ne·an /səb'tərā'nēən/ *adj.* underground [L *terra* land]

sub'text' *n.* underlying theme

sub'ti'tle *n.* **1** secondary or additional title of
a book, etc. **2** caption in a film, etc., esp. trans-
lating dialogue —*v.* (**·tled, ·tling**) **3** provide
with a subtitle or subtitles

sub·tle /sət'l/ *adj.* (**·tler, ·tlest**) **1** elusive;
mysterious; not obvious **2** (of scent, color,
etc.) faint; delicate **3a** perceptive (*subtle in-*
tellect) **b** ingenious (*subtle device*) —**sub'tle·**
ty *n.* (*pl.* **·ties**); **sub'tly** *adv.* [L *subtilis*]

sub'to'tal *n.* **1** total of one part of a group of
figures to be added —*v.* (**·taled** or **·talled,**
·tal·ing or **·tal·ling**) **2** calculate a subtotal

sub·tract /səbtrakt'/ *v.* deduct (a number,
etc.) from another —**sub·trac'tion** /-trak'
SHən/ *n.* [L *subtrahere* draw away]

sub·trop·ics /səb'trä'piks/ *n. pl.* regions adjacent to the tropics —**sub·trop'i·cal** *adj.*

sub·urb /səb'ərb/ *n.* outlying district of a city
[L *urbs* city]

sub·ur·ban /səbər'bən/ *adj.* of or characteristic of suburbs —**sub·ur'ban·ite'** *n.*

sub·ur·bi·a /səbər'bēə/ *n.* suburbs, their inhabitants, their way of life

sub·ver·sive /səbvər'siv/ *adj.* **1** seeking to
subvert (esp. a government) —*n.* **2** subversive person —**sub·ver'sion** /-ZHən/ *n.*;
sub·ver'sive·ly *adv.*; **sub·ver'sive·ness** *n.*
[MedL *subversivus*, rel. to SUBVERT]

sub·vert /səbvərt'/ *v.* overthrow or weaken
(a government, etc.) [L *vertere vers-* turn]

sub'way' *n.* underground usu. urban electric
railroad

suc- *prefix* var. of SUB- before *c*

suc·ceed /səksēd'/ *v.* **1** have success; be successful **2** follow; come next after **3** come into
an inheritance, office, title, or property (*suc-*
ceeded to the throne) [L *succedere -cess-* come
after]

suc·cess /səkses'/ *n.* **1** accomplishment of
an aim; favorable outcome **2** attainment of
wealth, fame, or position **3** successful thing
or person —**suc·cess'ful** *adj.*; **suc·cess'ful·**
ly *adv.* [L, rel. to SUCCEED]

suc·ces·sion /səkseSH'ən/ *n.* **1a** process of
following in order; succeeding **b** series or sequence **2a** succeeding to the throne, an office, inheritance, etc. **b** those having such a
right **3 in succession** one after another

suc·ces·sive *adj.* following one after another;
consecutive —**suc·ces'sive·ly** *adv.*

suc·ces·sor *n.* person or thing that succeeds
another

suc·cinct /səksiNGkt'/ *adj.* brief; concise
—**suc·cinct'ly** *adv.*; **suc·cinct'ness** *n.* [L
cingere cinct- gird]

suc·cor /sək'ər/ *n.* **1** aid, esp. in time of need
—*v.* **2** give succor to [L *succurrere* run to
help]

suc·cu·lent /sək'yələnt/ *adj.* **1** juicy; palatable **2** *Bot.* (of a plant, its leaves, or stems)
thick and fleshy —*n.* **3** *Bot.* succulent plant
—**suc'cu·lence** *n.* [L *succus* juice]

suc·cumb /səkəm'/ *v.* **1** surrender **2** die
(*succumbed to his injuries*) [L *cumbere* lie]

such /səCH/ *adj.* **1** of the kind or degree indicated (*such people; people such as these*) **2** so
great or extreme (*not such a fool as that*) **3** of
a more than normal kind or degree (*such awful*
food) —*pron.* **4** such a person; such a thing
5 as such as being what has been indicated
or named; in itself (*there is no theater as such*)
6 such as for example [OE: so like]

such'like' *adj.* **1** of such a kind —*pron.* **2**
things, people, etc., of such a kind

suck /sək/ *v.* **1** draw (a fluid) into the mouth
by suction **2** draw fluid from (a thing) in this
way **3** roll the tongue around (a sweet, etc.)
4 engulf or drown in a sucking movement **5**
Slang. be of very poor quality —*n.* **6** act or
period of sucking **7 suck dry** exhaust the
contents of by sucking **8 suck in:** **a** absorb
b lure (a person) into involvement **9 suck up:**
a *Slang.* behave obsequiously **b** absorb [OE]

suck'er *n.* **1a** gullible person **b** (foll. by *for*)
person susceptible to **2a** rubber cup, etc., adhering by suction **b** similar organ of an organism **3** shoot springing from a root or stem
below ground

suck·le /sək'əl/ *v.* (**·led, ·ling**) **1** feed
(young) from the breast or udder **2** rear;
bring up **3** suck at the breast, etc.

suck'ling *n.* unweaned child or animal

Su·cre /sōō'krä/ *n.* judicial capital of Bolivia.
Pop. 105,800. See also LA PAZ

su·crose /sōō'krōs'/ *n.* sugar from sugar
cane, sugar beet, etc. [Fr *sucre* SUGAR]

suc·tion /sək'SHən/ *n.* **1** act of sucking **2a**
production of a partial vacuum by removal of

air, etc., so that liquid, etc., is forced in or adhesion effected **b** force so produced [L *sugere* *suct-* suck]

Su·dan /soōdan', -dän'/ *n.* republic in Africa, S of Egypt. Capital: Khartoum. Pop. 29,971,000

sud·den /sad'n/ *adj.* **1** done or occurring unexpectedly or abruptly **2 all of a sudden** suddenly —**sud'den·ly** *adv.*; **sud'den·ness** *n.* [L *subitaneus*]

sudden death *n. Sports.* situation or period after a tie in regulation time when the first score wins

sudden in'fant death' syn'drome *n.* condition in which an infant dies while asleep without symptoms of illness; *abbr.* SIDS

suds /sadz/ *n. pl.* froth of soap and water —**sud'sy** *adj.* [LGer *sudde* or Du *sudse* marsh; bog]

sue /soō/ *v.* (**sued, su·ing**) **1** begin a law suit against **2** make application to a court for redress **3** make entreaty to a person for a favor [AngFr *suer* fr. L *sequi* follow]

suede /swād/ *n.* **1** leather with the flesh side rubbed to a nap **2** cloth imitating it [Fr: Sweden]

su·et /soō'it/ *n.* hard white fat on the kidneys or loins of oxen, sheep, etc. —**su'et·y** *adj.* [AngFr *seu*, fr. L *sebum*]

Sue·to·ni·us /swētō'nēas/ 75–150; Roman historian

Su·ez /soō·ez', soō'ez/ *n.* seaport in Egypt on the Suez Canal. Pop. 392,000

Su·ez' Ca·nal' *n.* canal in NE Egypt connecting the Red and Mediterranean seas

suf- *prefix* var. of SUB- before *f*

suf·fer /saf'ar/ *v.* **1** undergo pain, grief, damage, etc. **2** undergo, experience, or be subjected to pain, loss, grief, defeat, change, etc. **3** tolerate (*does not suffer fools gladly*) **4** *Archaic.* allow —**suf'fer·er** *n.* [L *sufferre*]

suf'fer·ance *n.* **1** tacit consent **2** capacity to endure pain, suffering, etc. [L, rel. to SUFFER]

suf·fice /saf īs'/ *v.* (**·ficed, ·fic·ing**) be adequate; satisfy [L *sufficere*]

suf·fi·cien·cy /safisH'ansē/ *n.* (*pl.* **·cies**) adequate amount

suf·fi·cient /safisH'ant/ *adj.* adequate; enough —**suf·fi'cient·ly** *adv.*

suf·fix /saf'iks/ *n.* letter(s) added at the end of a word to form a derivative [L *figere fix-* fasten]

suf·fo·cate /saf'əkāt'/ *v.* (**·cat·ed, ·cat·ing**) **1** choke or kill by stopping breathing, esp. by pressure, fumes, etc. **2** produce a choking or breathlessness in **3** be or feel suffocated —**suf'fo·cat'ing** *adj.*; **suf'fo·ca'tion** *n.* [L *suffocare* fr. *fauces* throat]

suf·fra·gan /saf'ragan, -jən/ *n.* bishop assisting a diocesan bishop [MedL *suffraganeus*]

suf·frage /saf'rij/ *n.* right of voting in political elections —**suf'fra·gist** *n.* [L *suffragium*]

suf·fra·gette /saf'rəjet'/ *n. Hist.* woman advocating female suffrage

suf·fuse /səfyoōz'/ *v.* (**·fused, ·fus·ing**) (of color, moisture, etc.) overspread throughout —**suf·fu'sion** /-fyoō'zHən/ *n.* [L *suffundere* pour over]

Su·fi /soō'fē/ *n.* (*pl.* **·fis**) Muslim mystic —**Su'fic** *adj.*; **Su'fism** *n.* [Ar]

sug- *prefix* assim. form of SUB- before *g*

sug·ar /sHoog'ar/ *n.* **1** sweet crystalline substance, esp. from sugar cane and sugar beet, used in cooking, etc.; sucrose **2** *Chem.* soluble usu. sweet crystalline carbohydrate, e.g., glucose —*v.* **3** sweeten or coat with sugar [Fr *sukere*, fr. Ar *sukkar*]

sug'ar beet' *n.* beet yielding sugar

sug'ar cane' *n.* tropical grass yielding sugar

sug'ar-coat' *v.* **1** coat with sugar **2** make something unpleasant seem more acceptable

sug'ar-dad'dy *n.* (*pl.* **·dies**) *Colloq.* wealthy older man who spends lavishly on a young woman

sug'ar·y *adj.* **1** containing or like sugar **2** excessively sweet or sentimental —**sug'ar·i·ness** *n.*

sug·gest /sə(g)jest'/ *v.* **1** propose (a theory, plan, etc.) **2a** evoke (an idea, etc.) **b** hint at [L *suggerere -gest-*]

sug·gest·i·ble /sə(g)jes'təbəl/ *adj.* easily influenced —**sug·gest'i·bil'i·ty** /-bil'itē/ *n.*

sug·ges·tion /sə(g)jes'CHən/ *n.* **1** suggesting or being suggested **2** theory, plan, etc. suggested **3** slight trace, hint [L, rel. to SUGGEST]

sug·ges·tive /sə(g)jes'tiv/ *adj.* **1** hinting (at) **2** (of a remark, joke, etc.) indecent —**sug·ges'tive·ly** *adv.*

su·i·cid·al /soō'əsīd'l/ *adj.* **1** inclined to commit suicide **2** of suicide **3** self-destructive; rash —**su'i·cid'al·ly** *adv.*

su·i·cide /soō'əsīd'/ *n.* **1a** intentional killing of oneself **b** person who commits suicide **2** self-destructive action or course (*political suicide*) [L *sui* of oneself, *-CIDE*]

su·i ge·ne·ris /soō'ī' jen'əris, soō'ē', gen'-/ *adj.* of its own kind; unique [L]

suit /soōt/ *n.* **1** set of matching clothes, usu. a jacket and trousers or skirt **2** (esp. in *comb.*) clothes for a special purpose (*swimsuit*) **3** any of the four sets (spades, hearts, diamonds, clubs) in a pack of cards **4** lawsuit **5** *Archaic.* courting a woman (*paid suit to her*) —*v.* **6** go well with (a person's appearance, etc.) **7** meet the demands or requirements of; satisfy **8** make fitting; accommodate **9 suit oneself** do as one chooses [AngFr *siute*]

suit'a·ble *adj.* appropriate —**suit'a·bil'i·ty** *n.*; **suit'a·bly** *adv.*

suit'case' *n.* case for carrying clothes while traveling

suite /swēt/ *n.* **1** set, esp. of rooms in a hotel **2** *Mus.* set of instrumental pieces performed as a unit **3** group of attendants; retinue **4** set of furniture, usu. for one room [Fr, rel. to SUIT]

suit·or /soōt'ər/ *n.* **1** man wooing a woman **2** plaintiff or petitioner in a lawsuit [AngFr fr. L]

Su·kar·no /soōkär'nō/, **Achmed** 1901–70; Indonesian political leader; president (1945–67)

Su·la·we·si /soō' läwä'sē/ *n.* (formerly Celebes) island in Malay Archipelago in central Indonesia

Su·lei·man I /soō'lämän', -li-/ ("the Magnificent") c. 1495–1566; sultan of Turkey (1520–66)

sul·fa (drug) /səl'fə/ *n.* any of various sulfonamides [abbr.]

sul·fate /səl'fāt'/ *n.* salt or ester of sulfuric acid [L SULFUR]

sul·fide /səl'fīd'/ *n.* binary compound of sulfur

sul·fite /səl'fīt'/ *n.* salt or ester of sulfurous acid [Fr, rel. to SULFATE]

sul·fon·a·mide /səlfän'əmīd'/ *n.* any of a class of antibiotic drugs containing sulfur [Ger *Sulfon* (rel. to SULFUR), *amide* a deriv. of AMMONIA]

sul·fur /səl'fər/ *n.* pale-yellow nonmetallic element burning with a blue flame and a suffocating smell; *symb.* S —**sul·fur'ic**, **sul'fur·ous** *adj.* [AngFr fr. L]

sul'fur di·ox'ide *n.* colorless pungent gas formed by burning sulfur in air and dissolving it in water

sul·fu·ric ac·id /səlfyŏŏ'rik/ *n.* dense, oily, highly corrosive acid

sulk /sŏlk/ *v.* 1 be sulky —*n.* 2 period of sullen silence [perh. a back formation fr. SULKY]

sulk'y *adj.* (·i·er, ·i·est) sullen or silent, esp. from resentment —**sulk'i·ly** *adv.*; **sulk'i·ness** *n.* [perh. fr. obs. *sulke* sluggish, ult. prob. fr. OE]

Sul·la /sŏŏl'ə, sŏŏl'ə/, **Lucius Cornelius** c. 138–78 B.C.; Roman general and dictator

sul·len /səl'ən/ *adj.* 1 passively resentful; sulky; morose 2 gloomy; dismal —**sul'len·ly** *adv.*; **sul'len·ness** *n.* [prob. fr. L *solus* alone]

sul·ly /səl'ē/ *v.* (·lied, ·ly·ing) disgrace; tarnish [Fr *souiller*, rel. to SOIL²]

sul·tan /səlt'n/ *n.* Muslim sovereign —**sul'tan·ate** /·it, ·āt/ *n.* [Ar]

sul·ta·na /səl'tan'ə/ *n.* sultan's mother, wife, concubine, or daughter [It]

sul·try /səl'trē/ *adj.* (·tri·er, ·tri·est) 1 (of weather, etc.) hot and close 2 (of a person, etc.) passionate; sensual —**sul'tri·ly** *adv.*; **sul'tri·ness** *n.* [obs. *sulter* (v.), rel. to SWELTER]

sum /səm/ *n.* 1 total resulting from addition 2 amount of money 3 arithmetical problem —*v.* (**summed, sum·ming**) 4 find the sum of 5 **sum up:** a (esp. of a judge) give a summary b summarize [L *summa*]

su·mac /sŏŏ'mak, SHŎŏ-/ *n.* (also **su'mach**) 1 shrub, usu. with reddish conical fruits; some species having poisonous foliage 2 dried and ground leaves of this used in tanning and dyeing [Fr fr. Ar]

Su·ma·tra /sŏŏmä'trə/ *n.* large island in the W part of Indonesia

Sum·ga·it /sŏŏm'gä·ēt'/ *n.* city in Azerbaijan on the Caspian Sea. Pop. 236,200

sum·ma·rize /səm'ərīz'/ *v.* (·rized, ·riz·ing) make or be a summary of

sum·ma·ry /səm'ərē/ *n.* (*pl.* ·ries) 1 brief account —*adj.* 2 without details or formalities; brief —**sum·mar'i·ly** /·mer'ilē/ *adv.* [L, rel. to SUM]

sum·ma·tion /səmā'SHən/ *n.* 1 finding of a total 2 summary, as of final arguments at a trial

sum·mer /səm'ər/ *n.* 1 warmest season of the year —*v.* 2 spend the summer —**sum'mer·y** *adj.* [OE]

sum'mer·house' *n.* airy building in a garden, etc., for use in warm weather

sum'mer sol'stice *n.* solstice about June 21

sum'mer·time' *n.* season or period of summer

sum·mit /səm'it/ *n.* 1 highest point; top 2 highest degree 3 (in full **sum'mit meet'ing, talks,** etc.) conference of heads of government [L *summus* highest]

sum·mon /səm'ən/ *v.* 1 order to come or appear, esp. at a court 2 call upon 3 call together 4 gather (courage, spirits, resources, etc.) [L *summonere*]

sum'mons *n.* (*pl.* ·mons·es) authoritative call to attend or do something, esp. to appear in court

sumo /sŏŏ'mō/ *n.* Japanese form of wrestling practiced by very heavy competitors [Japn]

sump /səmp/ *n.* pit, well, hole, etc., to collect liquid [LGer or Du]

sump·tu·ous /səmp'CHŏŏəs/ *adj.* rich; lavish; costly —**sump'tu·ous·ly** *adv.*; **sump'tu·ous·ness** *n.* [L *sumptus* expense]

sun /sən/ *n.* 1 star around which the earth orbits and from which it receives light and warmth 2 any star —*v.* (**sunned, sun·ning**) 3 *refl.* bask in the sun —**sun'less** *adj.* [OE]

Sun. *abbr.* Sunday

sun'bathe' *v.* (·bathed, ·bath·ing) bask in the sun, esp. to tan the body —**sun'bath'er** *n.*

sun'beam' *n.* ray of sunlight

sun'burn' *n.* inflammation and reddening of the skin from exposure to the sun —**sun'burnt'** *adj.* (also **sun'burned'**)

Sun·chon /sŏŏn'CHŎn'/ *n.* city in North Korea. Pop. 356,000

sun·dae /sən'dā, ·dē/ *n.* ice cream with fruit, nuts, syrup, etc. [perh. fr. SUNDAY]

Sun·da Is'lands /sən'də, sŏŏn'dä/ *n.* islands of the Malay Archipelago, including Borneo, Sumatra, Java, and smaller islands

Sun·day /sən'dā, ·dē/ *n.* first day of the week, a Christian day of worship; *abbr.* **Sun., Su** [OE]

sun·der /sən'dər/ *v. Archaic* or *Lit.* separate; break apart [OE: cf. ASUNDER]

SUNDIAL

sun'di·al *n.* instrument showing the time by the shadow of a pointer in sunlight

sun'down' *n.* sunset

sun·dry /sən'drē/ *adj.* 1 various; several —*n.* (*pl.* ·dries) 2 miscellaneous items [OE, rel. to SUNDER]

sun'fish' *n.* (*pl.* same or ·es) freshwater fish with lustrous scales and a broad, flat body

sun'flow'er *n.* plant with large, golden-rayed flowers

sung /səNG/ *v. past part.* of SING

sun'glass'es *n. pl.* eyeglasses tinted as protection against sunlight or glare

sunk /səNGk/ *v. past* and *past part.* of SINK

sunk'en *adj.* **1** at a lower level; submerged **2** (of the cheeks) hollow; depressed [past part. of SINK]

sun'lamp' *n.* lamp giving ultraviolet rays for therapy, tanning, etc.

sun'light' *n.* light from the sun

sun'lit' *adj.* illuminated by sunlight

Sun·ni /soon'ē/ *n.* (*pl.* same or **-nis**) one of the two main branches of Islam (cf. **Shiite**) **2** adherent of this branch **—Sun'nite** /-īt/ *adj.* [Ar *Sunna* way, rule]

sun·ny /sən'ē/ *adj.* (**-ni·er, -ni·est**) **1** bright with or warmed by sunlight **2** cheery; bright **—sun'ni·ly** *adv.;* **sun'ni·ness** *n.*

Sun·ny·vale /sən'ēvāl'/ *n.* city in Calif. Pop. 117,229

sun'rise' *n.* **1** sun's rising **2** time of this

sun'roof' *n.* panel in a car's roof that opens

sun'screen' *n.* (also **sun'block'**) lotion, etc., to protect the skin against ultraviolet rays and sunburn

sun'set' *n.* **1** sun's setting **2** time of this **—***adj.* **3** of or designating a law that requires termination of its provisions, programs, etc., after a specified period of time, unless specifically renewed by legislation

sun'shine' *n.* **1a** light of the sun **b** area lit by the sun **2** fine weather **3** cheerfulness

sun'spot' *n.* any of the dark patches cyclically appearing on the sun's surface

sun'stroke' *n.* acute prostration from excessive exposure to the sun

sun'tan' *n.* brownish skin color caused by exposure to the sun **—sun'tanned'** *adj.*

sun'up' *n.* sunrise

Sun Yat-sen /soon' yät'sen'/ (also **Sun Yixian**) 1866–1925; Chinese revolutionary leader

sup /səp/ *v.* (**supped, sup·ping**) *Archaic.* eat supper [Fr]

sup- *prefix* var. of SUB- before *p*

su·per /soo'pər/ *Colloq. adj.* **1** (also as *interj.*) excellent; splendid **—***n.* **2** superintendent [L: above]

super- *comb. form* forming nouns, adjectives, and verbs, meaning: **1** above, beyond, or over (*superstructure; supernatural*) **2** to an extreme degree (*superabundant*) **3** extra good or large of its kind (*supertanker*) **4** of a higher kind (*superintendent*) [L]

su·per·a·bun'dant *adj.* abounding beyond what is normal **—su'per·a·bun'dance** *n.* [L, rel. to SUPER-, ABOUND]

su·per·an·nu·ate /soo'pərən yoo-āt'/ *v.* (**-at·ed, -at·ing**) **1** pension (a person) off **2** dismiss or discard as too old **3** deem too old for work or use **—su'per·an'nu·a'tion** *n.* [L *annus* year]

su·perb' /soopərb'/ *adj.* **1** excellent **2** magnificent **—su·perb'ly** *adv.* [L: proud]

su'per·charge' *v.* (**-charged, -charg·ing**) **1** charge (the atmosphere, etc.) with energy, emotion, etc. **2** increase the power of an engine by using a supercharger

su'per·charg·er *n.* device supplying compressed air to an internal-combustion engine for added power

su·per·cil·ious /soo'pərsil'ēəs/ *adj.* contemptuous; haughty **—su'per·cil'ious·ly**
adv.; **su'per·cil'ious·ness** *n.* [L *supercilium* eyebrow]

su·per·con·duc·tiv·i·ty /soo'pərkən'dəktiv'itē/ *n. Physics.* lowered electrical resistance in some substances, esp. at very low temperatures **—su'per·con·duct'ing** *adj.;* **su'per·con·duc'tor** *n.*

su·per·e'go *n.* (*pl.* **-gos**) *Psychol.* part of the mind that acts as a conscience

su·per·er·o·ga·tion /soo'pərer'əgā'shən/ *n.* doing more than duty requires [L *supererogare* pay in addition]

su·per·fi·cial /soo'pərfish'əl/ *adj.* **1** of or on the surface; lacking depth **2** swift; cursory **3** apparent but not real (*superficial resemblance*) **4** (esp. of a person) shallow **—su'per·fi'ci·al'i·ty** /-al'itē/ *n.* (*pl.* **-ties**); **su'per·fi'cial·ly** *adv.* [L, rel. to FACE]

su·per·flu·i·ty /soo'pərfloo'itē/ *n.* (*pl.* **-ties**) **1** state of being superfluous **2** superfluous amount or thing [L *fluere* to flow]

su·per·flu·ous /soopər'flooəs/ *adj.* more than is required; unnecessary [L *fluere* to flow]

su·per·hu'man *adj.* **1** above what is human; supernatural; divine **2** exceeding normal human capability

su·per·im·pose' *v.* (**-posed, -pos·ing**) lay (a thing) on something else **—su'per·im·po·si'tion** *n.*

su·per·in·tend' /soo'pərintend'/ *v.* supervise; direct **—su'per·in·ten'dence** *n.*

su·per·in·tend'ent *n.* **1** person who superintends; director **2** maintenance custodian of a building

su·pe·ri·or /soopēr'ēər/ *adj.* **1** in a higher position; of higher rank **2a** of high quality **b** supercilious; haughty **3** better or greater in some respect **4** written or printed above the line **—***n.* **5** person superior to another, esp. in rank **6** head of a monastery, etc. (*mother superior*) **—su·pe'ri·or'i·ty** /-ôr'itē/ *n.* [L comp. of *superus* above]

Su·pe·ri·or, Lake /soopēr'ēər/ *n.* largest and northernmost of the Great Lakes

su·per·la·tive /soopər'lətiv/ *adj.* **1** of the highest quality or degree; excellent **2** *Gram.* (of an adjective or adverb) expressing the highest degree of a quality (*e.g.,* *bravest, most fiercely*) **—***n.* **3** *Gram.* superlative form of an adjective or adverb **4** (*pl.*) high praise; exaggerated language [Fr fr. L]

su·per·man' *n.* (*pl.* **-men**) man of exceptional strength or ability

su·per·mar'ket *n.* large self-service store selling food, housewares, etc.

su·per·nat'u·ral *adj.* **1** not attributable to or explicable by the laws of nature **—***n.* **2** (prec. by *the*) supernatural realm, forces, etc. **—su'per·nat'u·ral·ly** *adv.*

su·per·no·va /soo'pərnō'və/ *n.* (*pl.* **-vae** /-vē/ or **-vas**) exploding star that increases suddenly in brightness

su·per·nu·mer·ar·y /soo'pərn(y)oo'mərer'ē/ *adj.* **1** in excess of the normal number; extra **—***n.* (*pl.* **-ies**) **2** supernumerary person or thing **3** actor without a speaking part; extra [L, rel. to NUMBER]

su'per·pow'er *n.* extremely powerful nation

su'per·script' *adj.* **1** written or printed above **—***n.* **2** superscript number or symbol [L *scribere* write]

su·per·sede /soo͞'pərsēd'/ v. (·sed·ed, ·sed·ing) take the place of; succeed or supplant; make obsolete —**su'per·ses'sion** /-seSH'ən/ n. [L *supersedere*]

su'per·son'ic adj. of or having a speed greater than that of sound —**su·per·son'i·cal·ly** adv.

su'per·star' n. extremely famous actor, musician.

su·per·sti·tion /soo͞'pərstiSH'ən/ n. 1 belief in the supernatural; irrational fear of the unknown 2 practice or belief based on this —**su'per·sti'tious** adj.; **su'per·sti'tious·ly** adv. [L]

su'per·struc'ture n. 1 structure built on top of another 2 part of a building above the foundation

su'per·tank'er n. very large tanker ship

su·per·vene /soo͞'pərvēn'/ v. (·vened, ·ven·ing) Formal. occur as something unexpected or additional —**su·per·ven'tion** /-ven'SHən/ n. [L *supervenire*]

su·per·vise /soo͞'pərvīz'/ v. (·vised, ·vis·ing) superintend; oversee —**su'per·vi'sion** /-vizH'ən/, **su'per·vi'sor** n.; **su'per·vi'so·ry** adj. [L *supervidere* vis-]

su·pine /soo͞pīn', soo͞'pīn'/ adj. 1 lying face upwards 2 inert; indolent [L]

supp. or **suppl.** abbr. 1 supplement 2 supplementary

sup·per /səp'ər/ n. evening meal [Fr *souper*]

sup·plant /səplant'/ v. take the place of, esp. by underhand means [L *supplantare* trip up]

sup·ple /səp'əl/ adj. (·pler, ·plest) 1 flexible; pliant 2 limber 3 adaptable, esp. mentally —**sup'ple·ness** n. [L *supplex*]

sup·ple·ment n. /səp'ləmənt/ 1 thing or part added to improve or provide further information 2 separate section of a newspaper, etc. —v. /səp'ləment'/ 3 provide a supplement for —**sup'ple·men'tal, sup'ple·men'ta·ry** adj.; **sup'ple·men·ta'tion** n. /-mentā'SHən/ n. [L *supplementum*]

sup·pli·ant /səp'lēənt/ adj. 1 supplicating —n. 2 supplicating person [L, rel. to SUPPLICATE]

sup·pli·cate /səp'likāt'/ v. (·cat·ed, ·cat·ing) petition humbly; entreat —**sup'pli·cant** adj. & n.; **sup'pli·ca'tion** n.; **sup'pli·ca·to·ry** /-kətô'rē/ adj. [L *supplicare*]

sup·ply /səplī'/ v. (·plied, ·ply·ing) 1 provide (a thing needed) 2 provide (a person, etc., with a thing) 3 meet or make up for (a deficiency or need) —n. (pl. ·plies) 4 providing of what is needed 5 stock, store, amount, etc. 6 (pl.) provisions; equipment —**sup·pli'er** n. [L *supplere* fill up]

sup·ply'-side' adj. Econ. denoting a policy of low taxation, etc., to encourage production and investment

sup·port /səpôrt'/ v. 1 carry all or part of the weight of; keep from falling, sinking, or failing 2 provide for (a family, etc.) 3 strengthen; encourage 4 bear out; substantiate 5 give help or approval to; further 6 speak in favor of —n. 7 supporting or being supported 8 thing or person that supports —**sup·port'er** n. [L *portare* carry]

sup·port'ive adj. providing (esp. emotional) support or encouragement —**sup·por'tive·ly** adv.; **sup·por'tive·ness** n.

sup·pose /səpōz'/ v. (·posed, ·pos·ing) 1 assume; be inclined to think 2 take as a pos-

sibility or hypothesis 3 require as a condition (*that supposes we're on time*) 4a be expected or required (*was supposed to write to you*) b (with neg.) ought not; not be allowed to [Fr, rel. to POSE]

sup·pos·ed·ly /səpō'zədlē/ adv. allegedly

sup·po·si·tion /səp'əziSH'ən/ n. 1 thing supposed 2 act of supposing

sup·pos·i·to·ry /səpäz'ətôr'ē/ n. (pl. ·ries) medical preparation melting in the rectum or vagina [L *suppositorius* placed underneath]

sup·press /səpres'/ v. 1 put an end to, esp. forcibly 2 prevent from being done, seen, heard, or known —**sup·press'i·ble** adj.; **sup·pres'sion** /-SHən/, **sup·pres'sor** n. [L, rel. to PRESS¹]

sup·pu·rate /səp'yərāt'/ v. (·rat·ed, ·rat·ing) 1 form pus 2 fester —**sup'pu·ra'tion** n. [L, rel. to PUS]

supra- prefix above

su·pra·na·tion·al /soo͞'prənaSH'(ə)nəl/ adj. transcending national limits

su·prem·a·cy /soo͞prem'əsē/ n. (pl. ·cies) being supreme

su·preme /soo͞prēm'/ adj. 1 highest in authority or rank 2 greatest; most important 3 (of a penalty or sacrifice) involving death —**su·preme'ly** adv. [L]

Su·preme' Court' n. 1 highest court of the US 2 highest court in a state

suprv. abbr. supervisor

supt. abbr. superintendent

sur-¹ prefix SUPER- (*surcharge; surrealism*) [Fr]

sur-² prefix var. of SUB- before r

Su·ra·ba·ya /soor'əbī'ə/ n. seaport in Indonesia, on Java. Pop. 2,027,900

Su·rat /soor'ət, soorät'/ n. seaport in W India. Pop. 1,496,900

sur·charge n. /sər'CHärj'/ 1 additional charge or payment —v. /sər'CHärj', sər'CHärj'/ (·charged, ·charg·ing) 2 exact a surcharge from [Fr, rel. to SUR-¹]

surd /sərd/ Math. adj. 1 (of a number) irrational —n. 2 surd number, esp. the root of an integer [L: deaf]

sure /SHoor, SHər/ adj. 1 convinced 2 having adequate reason for a belief or assertion 3 confident 4 reliable; unfailing 5 certain; positive 6 undoubtedly true or truthful —adv. 7 Colloq. certainly 8 **make sure** make certain; ensure 9 **to be sure** admittedly; indeed —**sure'ness** n. [Fr fr. L *securus*]

● Usage: In formal contexts use the adverb *surely*, not *sure*: *He surely was silly to run away.*

sure'fire' adj. certain to succeed

sure'foot'ed adj. never stumbling or making a mistake

sure'ly adv. 1 with certainty or safety 2 certainly; to be sure

● Usage: See note at SURE.

sure·ty /SHoor'ətē, SHər'-/ n. (pl. ·ties) 1 certainty 2 money given as a pledge, guarantee, etc. 3 person who takes responsibility for another's debt, obligation, etc. [Fr fr. L]

surf /sərf/ n. 1 foam of the sea breaking on the shore or reefs —v. 2 practice surfing —**surf'er** n.

sur·face /sər'fis/ n. 1 outside of a thing 2 any of the limits of a solid 3 top of a liquid, the ground, etc. 4 outward or superficial aspect **5** *Geom.* set of points with length and breadth but no thickness —*v.* (**·faced, ·fac·ing**) **6** give the required surface to (a road, paper, etc.) **7** rise or bring to the surface **8** become visible or known [Fr, rel. to SUR-¹]

surf′board′ *n.* long, narrow board used in surfing

sur·feit /sər′fit/ *n.* **1** an excess, esp. in eating or drinking; overindulgence **2** resulting fullness —*v.* **3** overfeed **4** (cause to) be wearied through excess [Fr, rel. to SUR-¹, FEAT]

surf′ing *n.* sport of riding the surf on a board

surg. *abbr.* surgeon; surgery; surgical

surge /sərj/ *n.* **1** sudden rush **2** heavy forward or upward motion **3** sudden increase in price, activity, etc. **4** sudden increase in voltage —*v.* (**surged, surg·ing**) **5** move suddenly and powerfully forward **6** increase suddenly **7** (of the sea, etc.) swell [L *surgere* rise]

sur·geon /sər′jən/ *n.* medical practitioner qualified in surgery

sur·ger·y /sər′jərē/ *n.* (*pl.* **·ies**) **1** medical treatment by incision or manipulation as opposed to drugs **2** operating room [L *chirurgia,* fr. Gk *kheir* hand, *ergon* work]

sur·gi·cal /sər′jikəl/ *adj.* **1** of or used by surgeons or in surgery **2** (esp. of military action) swift and precise —**sur′gi·cal·ly** *adv.*

Su·ri·na·me /sŏŏr′inäm′, -nam′/ *n.* republic on the NE coast of S America. Capital: Paramaribo. Pop. 404,000 —**Su·ri·na·mese** /sŏŏr′ənəmēz′, -mēs′/ *n.* & *adj.*

sur·ly /sər′lē/ *adj.* (**·li·er, ·li·est**) bad-tempered; rude —**sur′li·ness** *n.* [obs. *sirly* haughty, rel. to SIR]

sur·mise /sərmīz′/ *n.* **1** conjecture —*v.* (**·mised, ·mis·ing**) **2** guess; suppose [L *supermittere ·miss·* accuse]

sur·mount /sərmount′/ *v.* **1** overcome; prevail over **2** be on top of **3** get over or across —**sur·mount′a·ble** *adj.* [Fr, rel. to SUR-¹]

sur·name /sər′nām′/ *n.* family or last name [obs. *surnoun* fr. AngFr, rel. to SUR-¹]

sur·pass /sərpas′/ *v.* **1** be greater or better than; outdo **2** be preeminent [Fr, rel. to SUR-¹]

sur·plice /sər′plis/ *n.* loose, white vestment worn by clergy and choristers [AngFr *surplis*]

sur·plus /sər′pləs/ *n.* **1** amount left over **2** excess of revenue over expenditure —*adj.* **3** exceeding what is needed or used [AngFr]

sur·prise /sə(r)prīz′/ *n.* **1** unexpected or astonishing thing **2** emotion caused by this **3** catching or being caught unawares —*v.* (**·prised, ·pris·ing**) **4** turn out contrary to the expectations of **5** astonish **6** capture or attack by surprise **7** come upon (a person) unawares —**sur·pris′ing** *adj.;* **sur·pris′ing·ly** *adv.* [OFr]

SURPLICE

sur·re·al /sərē′əl, -rēl′/ *adj.* unreal; dreamlike; bizarre [back formation fr. SURREALISM]

sur·re·al·ism /sərē′əlizəm/ *n.* 20th-cent. movement in art and literature attempting to express the subconscious mind by dream im-

agery, bizarre juxtapositions, etc. —**sur′re′al·ist** /-ist/ *n.* [adj.]; **sur·re′al·is′tic** *adj.;* **sur·re′al·is′ti·cal·ly** *adv.* [Fr, rel. to REAL]

sur·ren·der /sər5en′dər/ *v.* **1** hand over; relinquish **2** submit, esp. to an enemy **3** *refl.* (foll. by *to*) yield to a habit, emotion, influence, etc. **4** abandon (hope, etc.) —*n.* **5** act of surrendering [AngFr, rel. to SUR-¹]

sur·rep·ti·tious /sər′əptish′əs/ *adj.* done by stealth; clandestine —**sur′rep·ti′tious·ly** *adv.* [L *surripere* seize secretly]

sur·ro·gate /sər′əgət, -gāt′/ *n.* **1** substitute **2** deputy, esp. a judicial or ecclesiastical one —**sur′ro·ga·cy** /-gəsē/ *n.* [L *rogare* ask]

sur′ro·gate moth′er *n.* woman who bears a child on behalf of another woman, usu. by artificial insemination of her own egg by the other woman's partner

sur·round /səround′/ *v.* come or be all around; encircle; enclose [L, rel. to SUR-¹, *unda* wave]

sur·round′ings *n. pl.* objects or conditions around or affecting a person or thing; environment

sur·tax /sər′taks/ *n.* additional tax [Fr, rel. to SUR-¹]

sur·veil·lance /sərvā′ləns/ *n.* close observation by the police, etc. [Fr, rel. to SUR-¹, *veiller* watch]

sur·vey *v.* /sərvā′/ **1** view or consider as a whole **2** examine the condition of (a building, etc.) **3** determine the boundaries, extent, ownership, etc., of (a tract of land) —*n.* /sər′vā′/ **4** general view or consideration **5** act of surveying property **6** investigation of public opinion, etc. **7** map or plan made by surveying [L, rel. to SUPER-, *videre* see]

sur·vey′or *n.* person who surveys land and buildings, esp. as a profession

sur·viv·al /sərvī′vəl/ *n.* **1** surviving **2** relic

sur·vive /sərvīv′/ *v.* (**·vived, ·viv·ing**) **1** continue to live or exist **2** live or exist longer than **3** remain alive despite (a danger, accident, etc.) —**sur·vi′vor** *n.* [AngFr *survivre* fr. L *supervivere*]

sus- *prefix* var. of SUB- before *c, p, t*

sus·cep·ti·bil·i·ty /səsep′təbil′ətē/ *n.* (*pl.* **·ties**) **1** being susceptible **2** (*pl.*) person's feelings

sus·cep·ti·ble /səsep′təbəl/ *adj.* **1** impressionable; sensitive **2a** liable or vulnerable to **b** allowing; admitting of (proof, etc.) —**sus·cep′ti·bly** *adv.* [L *suscipere ·cept·* take up]

su·shi /sŏŏ′shē/ *n.* Japanese dish of rolls of cold rice with raw fish, etc. [Japn]

sus·pect *v.* /səspekt′/ **1** be inclined to think **2** have an impression or sense of **3** mentally accuse **4** doubt the genuineness or truth of —*n.* /səs′pekt′/ **5** suspected person —*adj.* /səs′pekt′/ **6** subject to or deserving suspicion [L *suspicere ·spect·*]

sus·pend /səspend′/ *v.* **1** hang up **2** keep inoperative or undecided for a time **3** debar temporarily from a function, office, etc.

sus·pend′ed *adj.* (of particles or a body in a fluid) remaining between the top and bottom [L *suspendere ·pens·*]

sus·pend′ed an·i·ma′tion *n.* temporary deathlike condition

sus·pend′ers *n. pl.* straps over the shoulders for holding up trousers

sus·pense /səspens'/ *n.* state of anxious uncertainty or expectation —**sus·pense'ful** *adj.* [L *suspendere* suspend]

sus·pen·sion /səspen'SHən/ *n.* 1 suspending or being suspended 2 springs, etc., supporting a vehicle on its axles 3 substance consisting of particles suspended in a medium

sus·pen·sion bridge' *n.* bridge suspended from cables supported by towers

sus·pi·cion /səspish'ən/ *n.* 1 unconfirmed belief; distrust 2 suspecting or being suspected 3 slight trace of [L, rel. to SUSPECT]

sus·pi·cious /səspish'əs/ *adj.* 1 prone to or feeling suspicion 2 prompting suspicion —**sus·pi'cious·ly** *adv.*

sus·tain /səstān'/ *v.* 1 support or bear the weight of, esp. for a long period 2 encourage; support 3 (of food) nourish 4 endure; stand 5 suffer (defeat, injury, etc.) 6 (of a court) uphold or decide in favor of (an objection, etc.) 7 corroborate 8 maintain —**sus·tain'a·ble** *adj.* [L *sustinere* keep up]

sus·te·nance /səs'tənəns/ *n.* 1 nourishment; food 2 means of support [AngFr, rel. to SUSTAIN]

Suth·er·land /səTH'ərlənd/, **Joan** 1926– ; Australian operatic soprano

su·ture /sōō'CHər/ *n.* 1 stitching together of the edges of a wound or incision 2 thread or wire used for this [L *suere* sut- sew]

Su·va /sōō'və/ *n.* capital of Fiji. Pop. 69,700

Su·won /sōō'wən/ *n.* city in South Korea. Pop. 645,000

svelte /svelt/ *adj.* slender; lissome; graceful [Fr fr. It]

Sverd·lovsk /sferdlôfsk'/ *n.* (also **Yeka'terinburg'**) city in W Russia. Pop. 1,375,400

SW *abbr.* 1 southwest 2 southwestern

swab /swäb/ *n.* 1a absorbent pad used in surgery b specimen of a secretion taken for examination 2 mop —*v.* (**swabbed, swabbing**) 3 clean with a swab 4 mop clean (a ship's deck) [Du]

swad·dle /swäd'l/ *v.* (**-dled, -dling**) wrap (esp. a baby) tightly [fr. SWATHE]

swag /swag/ *n.* flowers, foliage, drapery, etc., hanging decoratively in a curve —**swagged** *adj.* [prob. Scand]

swag·ger /swag'ər/ *v.* 1 walk or behave arrogantly —*n.* 2 swaggering gait or manner [fr. SWAG]

swag'ger stick' *n.* baton carried by a military officer

Swa·hi·li /swähē'lē/ *n.* (*pl.* same) 1 member of a Bantu people of Zanzibar and adjacent coasts 2 their language [Ar]

swain /swān/ *n.* 1 *Archaic.* country youth 2 *Poet.* young lover or suitor [ON: lad]

swal·low[1] /swäl'ō/ *v.* 1 cause or allow (food, etc.) to pass down the throat 2 perform the muscular movement required to do this 3 accept meekly or credulously 4 repress (*swallow one's pride*) 5 engulf; absorb —*n.* 6 act of swallowing 7 amount swallowed at one time [OE]

swal·low[2] *n.* migratory swift-flying bird with a forked tail [OE]

swam /swam/ *v. past of* SWIM

swa·mi /swä'mē/ *n.* (*pl.* **-mis**) Hindu male religious teacher [Hindi *svami*]

swamp /swämp, swômp/ *n.* 1 (area of) waterlogged ground —*v.* 2 overwhelm, flood, or sink (as a boat) with water 3 overwhelm with a large amount of something —**swamp'y** *adj.* (**·i·er, ·i·est**)

swan /swän/ *n.* large, usu. white, water bird with a long, flexible neck [OE]

swank /swangk/ *n.* ostentation; swagger —**swank'y** *adj* (**·i·er, ·i·est**)

Swan·sea /swän'zē/ *n.* seaport in Wales, United Kingdom. Pop. 175,200

swan' song' *n.* person's last work or act before death, retirement, etc.

swap /swäp/ (also **swop**) *v.* (**swapped, swap·ping**) —*n.* 1 exchange or barter 2 act of swapping 3 thing swapped [orig. 'hit,' imit.]

sward /swôrd/ *n.* expanse of turf [OE: skin]

swarm /swôrm/ *n.* 1 cluster of bees leaving the hive with the queen to establish a new colony 2 large cluster of insects, birds, or people 3 great numbers —*v.* 4 move in or form a swarm 5 (of a place) be overrun, crowded, or infested with [OE]

swarth·y /swôr'THē, -THē/ *adj.* (**·i·er, ·i·est**) dark; dark-complexioned [obs. *swarty* fr. *swart* black, fr. OE]

swash /swäsh, swôsh/ *v.* 1 splash 2 dash

swash'buck'ler /-buk'lər/ *n.* swaggering adventurer —**swash'buck'ling** *adj. & n.* [*swash* swagger, BUCKLER]

swat /swät/ *v.* (**swat·ted, swat·ting**) 1 crush (a fly, etc.) with a sharp blow 2 hit hard and abruptly —*n.* 3 swatting blow [dial. var. of SQUAT]

SWAT *n.* (also **SWAT team**) heavily armed police unit trained for assault, etc. [Special Weapons and Tactics]

swatch /swäch/ *n.* sample, esp. of cloth

swath /swäTH, swôTH/ *n.* 1 ridge of cut grass or corn, etc. 2 space left clear by a mower, etc. 3 broad strip [OE]

swathe /swäTH, swôTH, swāTH/ *v.* (**swathed, swath·ing**) bind or wrap in bandages, garments, etc. [OE]

sway /swā/ *v.* 1 (cause to) lean or move unsteadily from side to side; waver 2a control the motion or direction of b influence —*n.* 3 rule, influence, or government (*hold sway*) 4 swaying motion

Swa·zi·land /swäz'ēland/ *n.* kingdom in SE Africa. Capital: Mbabane. Pop. 826,000

swear /swer/ *v.* (**swore, sworn, swear·ing**) 1a state or promise solemnly or on oath b (cause to) take (an oath) 2 insist (*swore he was fit*) 3 use profane or obscene language 4a appeal to as a witness in taking an oath (*swear by Almighty God*) b *Colloq.* have great confidence in (*swears by yoga*) 5 say certainly (*could not swear to it*) 6 swear off promise to abstain from (drink, etc.) [OE]

swear'word' *n.* profane or indecent word

sweat /swet/ *n.* 1 moisture exuded through the pores, from heat, nervousness, illness, etc.

2 state or period of sweating 3 drudgery; effort —v. (**sweat** or **sweat·ed, sweat·ing**) 4 exude sweat 5 be terrified or suffer 6 (of a wall, etc.) exhibit surface moisture 7 (cause to) drudge or toil 8 emit like sweat 9 **in a sweat** very worried; in a state of dread 10 **no sweat** *Colloq.* no bother; no trouble 11 **sweat blood:** *Colloq.* a work strenuously **b** be very anxious 12 **sweat it out** *Colloq.* endure a difficult experience to the end —**sweat′y** *adj.* (·**i·er,** ·**i·est**) [OE]

sweat′band′ *n.* band fitted inside a hat or worn around a wrist, etc., to absorb sweat

sweat′er *n.* knitted garment for the upper body, usu. worn over a shirt, etc.

sweat′shirt′ *n.* heavy, absorbent pullover jersey

Swe·den /swēd′n/ *n.* kingdom in N Europe, on the Scandinavian Peninsula. Capital: Stockholm. Pop. 8,673,000 —**Swede** /swēd/ *n.*

Swed·ish /swē′dish/ *adj.* 1 of Sweden, its people, or language —*n.* 2 language of Sweden

sweep /swēp/ *v.* (**swept, sweep·ing**) 1 clean or clear (as) with a broom 2 clean a room, etc., in this way 3 collect or remove (dirt, etc.) by sweeping 4a push (as) with a broom **b** dismiss abruptly 5 carry or drive along with force 6 remove or clear forcefully 7 traverse swiftly or lightly 8a glide swiftly; speed along **b** go majestically 9 win all the prizes, etc., in (a competition, etc.) —*n.* 10 act or motion of sweeping 11 range; scope 12 **make a clean sweep of** completely abolish or expel —**sweep′er** *n.* [OE]

sweep′ing *adj.* 1 wide in range or effect 2 generalized; too comprehensive (*sweeping statement*) —*n.* 3 (*pl.*) dirt, etc., collected by sweeping

sweep′stakes′ *n.* (*pl.* same) 1 form of gambling in which all stakes are pooled and paid to the winners 2 race with betting of this kind 3 prize(s) won in a sweepstakes

sweet /swēt/ *adj.* 1 tasting of sugar 2 fragrant 3 melodious; harmonious 4 gratifying; attractive 5 charming; amiable; pleasant 6 (foll. by *on*) *Colloq.* fond of; in love with —*n.* 7 (*pl.*) confections; candy —**sweet′ish** *adj.*; **sweet′ly** *adv.* [OE]

sweet′bread′ *n.* pancreas or thymus of an animal, esp. as food

sweet′bri′er *n.* (also **eg′lantine′**) wild rose with small fragrant leaves

sweet′en *v.* 1 make or become sweet or sweeter 2 make agreeable or less painful 3 *Colloq.* increase the value of (an offer, etc.) —**sweet′en·ing** *n.*

sweet′en·er *n.* 1 substance used to sweeten food or drink 2 bribe or inducement

sweet′heart′ *n.* 1 lover or darling 2 term of endearment

sweet′meat′ *n.* candy

sweet′ness *n.* 1 being sweet 2 fragrance

sweet′ pea′ *n.* climbing plant with fragrant flowers

sweet′ pep′per *n.* mild pepper

sweet′ po·ta′to *n.* 1 tropical trailing plant with sweet tuberous roots used for food 2 root of this

sweet′ talk′ *Colloq.* *n.* 1 flattery; blandishment —*v.* 2 (**sweet′-talk′**) flatter in order to persuade

sweet′ tooth′ *n.* liking for sweet-tasting things

swell /swel/ *v.* (**swelled, swol·len** or **swelled, swell·ing**) 1 (cause to) grow bigger, louder, or more intense 2 rise or raise up 3 bulge 4 (of the heart, etc.) feel full of joy, pride, relief, etc. 5 (foll. by *with*) be hardly able to restrain (pride, etc.) —*n.* 6 act or state of swelling 7 heaving of the sea with unbreaking waves 8 crescendo 9 *Slang.* stylish person —*adj.* 10 *Colloq.* fine; excellent [OE]

swell′ing *n.* abnormal protuberance

swel·ter /swel′tər/ *v.* 1 be uncomfortably hot —*n.* 2 sweltering condition [OE]

swept /swept/ *v.* *past* and *past part.* of SWEEP

swerve /swərv/ *v.* (**swerved, swerv·ing**) 1 (cause to) change direction, esp. abruptly —*n.* 2 swerving movement [OE: scour]

swift /swift/ *adj.* 1 quick; rapid 2 prompt —*n.* 3 swift-flying migratory bird with long wings —**swift′ly** *adv.*; **swift′ness** *n.* [OE]

Swift /swift/, **Jonathan** 1667–1745; Anglo-Irish poet and satirist

swig /swig/ *v.* (**swigged, swig·ging**) *Colloq.* 1 drink in large gulps —*n.* 2 swallow of drink, esp. a long one

swill /swil/ *v.* 1 drink greedily —*n.* 2 mainly liquid refuse as pig food [OE]

swim /swim/ *v.* (**swam, swum, swim·ming**) 1 propel the body through water with limbs, fins, or tail 2 traverse (a stretch of water or distance) by swimming 3 perform (a swimming stroke) 4 feel dizzy (*my head swam*) 5 (foll. by *in, with*) be flooded —*n.* 6 period or act of swimming —**swim′mer** *n.* [OE]

swim′suit′ *n.* garment worn for swimming

Swin·burne /swin′bərn/, **Algernon Charles** 1837–1909; English poet and critic

swin·dle /swin′dəl/ *v.* (·**dled,** ·**dling**) 1 cheat (a person, etc.) of money, etc. —*n.* 2 act of swindling —**swin′dler** *n.* [back formation fr. *swindler* fr. Ger]

Swin·don /swin′dən/ *n.* city in S England. Pop. 128,500

swine /swīn/ *n.* (*pl.* same) 1 pig; hog 2 (*pl.* same or -s) contemptible person —**swin′ish** *adj.* [OE]

swing /swing/ *v.* (**swung, swing·ing**) 1a (cause to) move with a to-and-fro or curving motion; sway **b** hang so as to be free to swing 2 oscillate; revolve 3 move by gripping and leaping 4 walk easily or airily 5 (foll. by *around*) move to face the opposite direction 6 change one's opinion or mood 7 (foll. by *at*) attempt to hit 8 play (music) with compelling or jazzy rhythm 9 *Colloq.* (of a party, etc.) be lively, etc. 10 have a decisive influence on (voting, etc.) 11 *Colloq.* achieve; manage —*n.* 12 act, motion, or extent of swinging 13 swinging or smooth gait, rhythm, or action 14 seat slung by ropes, etc., for swinging on or in 15a rhythmic jazz or dance music **b** rhythmic feeling of this —**swing′er** *n.* [OE]

swipe /swīp/ *Colloq.* *v.* (**swiped, swip·ing**) 1 make a swinging or sweeping grab or blow

2 steal —*n.* **3** swinging or sweeping grab or blow [perh. var. of SWEEP]

swirl /swərl/ *v.* **1** move, flow, or carry along with a whirling motion —*n.* **2** swirling motion **3** twist; curl —**swirl′y** *adj.* [perh. fr. LGer or Du]

swish /swiSH/ *v.* **1** swing (a thing) audibly through the air, grass, etc. **2** move with or make a swishing sound —*n.* **3** swishing action or sound [imit.]

Swiss /swis/ *adj.* **1** of Switzerland, its people, or its culture —*n.* **2** native or inhabitant of Switzerland

Swiss′ cheese′ *n.* firm, pale yellow cheese with large holes

switch /swiCH/ *n.* **1** device for opening, closing, or diverting an electric current or circuit **2a** transfer; change-over; deviation **b** exchange **3** flexible shoot cut from a tree **4** light, tapering rod **5** railroad track-changing device with movable rails —*v.* **6** turn (an electrical device) on or off **7** change or transfer **8** exchange **9** whip or flick with a switch [LGer]

switch′back′ *n.* steep road or route with zigzags or sharp curves

switch′board′ *n.* apparatus for making connections between electric circuits, esp. in telephony

switch′ hit′ter *n. Baseball.* player able to bat left-handed or right-handed

Switz·er·land /swit′sərlənd/ *n.* mountainous, landlocked republic in central Europe. Capital: Bern. Pop. 6,911,000

swiv·el /swiv′əl/ *n.* **1** coupling between two parts enabling one to revolve without turning the other —*v.* (**·eled** or **·elled, ·el·ing** or **·el·ling**) **2** turn on or as on a swivel [OE]

swiz′zle stick′ /swiz′l/ *n.* small rod for stirring drinks

swol·len /swō′lən/ *v. past part.* of SWELL

swoon /swo͞on/ *v. & n.* faint [OE]

swoop /swo͞op/ *v.* **1** descend rapidly like a bird of prey **2** make a sudden attack —*n.* **3** swooping movement or action [OE]

swop /swäp/ *v.* (**swopped, swop·ping**) var. of SWAP

sword /sôrd/ *n.* weapon with a long blade and hilt with a hand guard [OE]

sword′fish′ *n.* (*pl.* same or **·fish′es**) large marine fish with swordlike upper jaw

sword′ of Dam′o·cles /dam′əklēz′/ *n.* an impending peril [fr. Gk. legend of *Damocles*, who had a sword suspended by a hair over him]

swords·man /sôrdz′mən/ *n.* (*pl.* **·men**) person of (usu. specified) skill with a sword —**swords′man·ship′** *n.*

swore /swôr/ *v. past* of SWEAR

sworn /swôrn/ *v.* **1** *past part.* of SWEAR —*adj.* **2** bound (as) by an oath

swum /swəm/ *v. past part.* of SWIM

swung /swəNG/ *v. past* and *past part.* of SWING

syb·a·rite /sib′ərīt′/ *n.* self-indulgent or voluptuous person —**syb′a·rit′ic** /-rit′ik/ *adj.* [*Sybaris*, ancient city in S. Italy]

syc·a·more /sik′əmôr′/ *n.* **1** N American plane tree or its wood **2** large Eurasian maple or its wood [Gk *sukomoros*]

syc·o·phant /sik′əfənt, -fant′, sī′kə-/ *n.* flat-

terer; toady —**syc′o·phan′cy** *n.*; **syc′o·phan′tic** *adj.* [Gk *sukophantēs*]

Syd·ney /sid′nē/ *n.* seaport in SE Australia. Pop. 3,539,000

syl- *prefix* assim. form of SYN- before *l*

syl·lab·ic /səlab′ik/ *adj.* of or in syllables —**syl·lab′i·cal·ly** *adv.*

syl·lab·i·fy /səlab′əfī′/ *v.* (**·fied, ·fy·ing**) (also **syl·lab′i·cate** /-kāt/, **·cat·ed, ·cat·ing**) divide into syllables —**syl·lab′i·ca′tion, syl·lab′i·fi·ca′tion** /-fikā′SHən/ *n.*

syl·la·ble /sil′əbəl/ *n.* **1** unit of pronunciation forming the whole or part of a word and usu. having one vowel sound **2** character(s) representing a syllable [Gk *sullabē*]

syl·la·bus /sil′əbəs/ *n.* (*pl.* **·bus·es** or **·bi** /-bī′/) outline of a course of study, teaching, etc. [misreading of Gk *sittuba* label]

syl·lo·gism /sil′əjiz′əm/ *n.* reasoning in which a conclusion is drawn from two propositions —**syl′lo·gis′tic** /-jis′tik/ *adj.* [Gk *logos* reason]

sylph /silf/ *n.* **1** elemental spirit of the air **2** slender, graceful woman or girl —**sylph′like′** *adj.* [L]

syl·van /sil′vən/ *adj.* (also **sil′van**) **1** of the woods **2** wooded; rural [L *silva* a wood]

sym- *prefix* assim. form of SYN- before *b, m, p*

sym. *abbr.* **1** symbol **2** symphony

sym·bi·o·sis /sim′bē·ō′sis, -bī-/ *n.* (*pl.* **·o·ses** /-sēz′/) **1** close coexistence and interaction of two different organisms usu. to the advantage of both **2** any mutually advantageous association —**sym′bi·ot′ic** /-ät′ik/ *adj.* [Gk: living together]

sym·bol /sim′bəl/ *n.* **1** thing regarded as typifying or representing something **2** representative mark, sign, logo, etc. —**sym·bol′ic** /-bäl′ik/ *adj.*; **sym·bol′i·cal·ly** *adv.* [Gk *sumbolon*]

sym·bol·ism /sim′bəlizəm/ *n.* **1a** use of symbols **b** symbols collectively **2** artistic and poetic movement or style using symbols to express ideas, emotions, etc. —**sym′bol·ist** /-ist/ *n.*

sym·bol·ize /sim′bəlīz′/ *v.* (**·ized, ·iz·ing**) **1** be a symbol of **2** represent by symbols [Fr, rel. to SYMBOL]

sym·me·try /sim′ətrē/ *n.* (*pl.* **·tries**) **1** correct or beautiful proportion of parts; aesthetic evenness or balance **2** counterbalance of exactly similar parts facing each other or a center —**sym·met′ri·cal** /-me′trikəl/ *adj.*; **sym·met′ri·cal·ly** *adv.* [Gk *summetria*]

sym·pa·thet·ic /sim′pəTHet′ik/ *adj.* **1** of or expressing sympathy **2** pleasant; likable **3** favoring —**sym′pa·thet′i·cal·ly** *adv.*

sym·pa·thize /sim′pəTHīz/ *v.* (**·thized, ·thiz·ing**) **1** feel or express sympathy **2** agree —**sym′pa·thiz′er** *n.*

sym·pa·thy /sim′pəTHē/ *n.* (*pl.* **·thies**) **1a** sharing of another's feelings **b** capacity for this **2** (*sing.* or *pl.*) compassion; commiseration; condolences **3** (*sing.* or *pl.*) agreement in opinion or desire [Gk: fellow-feeling]

sym·pho·ny /sim(p)′fənē/ *n.* (*pl.* **·nies**) **1** large-scale composition in several movements for full orchestra **2** instrumental interlude in a large-scale vocal work **3** SYMPHONY ORCHESTRA **4** harmony of sounds, colors, etc. —**sym-**

phon·ic /simfǎn'ik/ *adj.*; **sym·phon'i·cal·ly** *adv.* [fr. SYN-, Gk *phōnē* sound]

sym'pho·ny or'ches·tra *n.* large orchestra suitable for playing symphonies.

sym·po·si·um /simpō'zēəm/ *n.* (*pl.* **·si·ums** or **·si·a**) 1 conference on a particular subject 2 collected articles or essays on a particular subject [Gk *sumposion* drinking party]

symp·tom /sim(p)'təm/ *n.* 1 physical or mental sign of disease 2 telltale sign —**symp'tom·at'ic** /-təmat'ik/ *adj.* [Gk *piptein* fall]

syn- *prefix* with together, alike [Gk: with]

syn. *abbr.* synonym; synonymous; synonymy

syn·a·gogue /sin'əgäg/ *n.* 1 building for Jewish religious observance and instruction 2 Jewish congregation [Gk: assembly]

syn·apse /sin'aps', sənaps'/ *n. Anat.* junction of two nerve cells [Gk *haptein* join]

sync /siNGk/ (also **synch,** pronunc. same) *Colloq. n.* 1 synchronization —*v.* 2 synchronize 3 **in** (or **out of**) **sync** according or agreeing well (or badly) with [abbr.]

syn·chron·ic /siNGkrän'ik/ *adj.* concerned with a subject as it exists at a given time —**syn·chron'i·cal·ly** *adv.* [fr. SYN-, Gk *khronos* time]

syn·chro·nize /siNG'krəniz/ *v.* (**·nized, ·niz·ing**) 1 make or be synchronous (with) 2 make the sound and picture of (a film, etc.) coincide 3 cause (clocks, etc.) to show the same time —**syn'chro·ni·za'tion** *n.*

syn·chro·nous /siNG'krənəs/ *adj.* existing or occurring at the same time

syn·co·pate /siNG'kəpät/ *v.* (**·pat·ed, ·pat·ing**) 1 displace the beats or accents in (music), esp. by stress of the weak beat 2 shorten (a word) by dropping interior letters —**syn'co·pa'tion** *n.* [ult. fr. Gk *synkopē* cutting short]

synd. *abbr.* syndicate; syndicated

syn·di·cate *n.* /sin'dikət/ 1 combination of individuals or businesses to promote a common interest 2 agency that supplies newspapers with features, columns, etc. 3 criminal enterprise —*v.* /sin'dikāt/ (**·cat·ed, ·cat·ing**) 4 form into a syndicate 5 publish or sell (material) through a syndicate —**syn'di·ca'tion** *n.* [Gk SYN-, *dikē* justice]

syn·drome /sin'drōm/ *n.* 1 group of characteristic symptoms of a disease 2 characteristic combination of opinions, emotions, behavior, etc. [Gk: running together]

syn·ec·do·che /sənek'dəkē/ *n.* figure of speech in which a part is made to represent the whole or vice versa (e.g., *new faces at the club; Boston lost to Detroit*) [Gk: taking together]

syn·er·gism /sin'ərjizəm/ *n.* combined interaction of elements, factors, etc., that is greater than the sum of their effects individually [Gk SYN-, *ergon* work]

Synge /siNG/, **(Edmund) John Millington** 1871–1909; Irish dramatist

syn·od /sin'əd/ *n.* 1 church council of delegated clergy and sometimes laity 2 governing body in certain Christian churches [Gk: meeting]

syn·o·nym /sin'ənim/ *n.* word or phrase that means the same as another (e.g., *shut* and *close*) [Gk *onoma* name]

syn·on·y·mous /sənän'əməs/ *adj.* 1 having the same meaning 2 suggestive of; tantamount to (*his name is synonymous with terror*)

syn·op·sis /sənäp'sis/ *n.* (*pl.* **·ses** /-sēz/) summary or outline —**syn·op'tic** *adj.* [Gk *opsis* view]

syn·o·vi·a /sənō'vēə, sī-/ *n. Physiol.* viscous fluid lubricating joints, etc. —**sy·no'vi·al** *adj.* [MedL]

syn·tax /sin'taks/ *n.* 1 grammatical arrangement of words 2 rules or analysis of this —**syn·tac'tic** /-tak'tik/ *adj.*; **syn·tac'ti·cal·ly** *adv.* [Gk arrangement]

syn·the·sis /sin'THəsis/ *n.* (*pl.* **·ses** /-sēz/) 1 combining of elements into a whole 2 *Chem.* artificial production of compounds from their constituents [Gk: placing together]

syn·the·size /sin'THəsiz/ *v.* (**·sized, ·siz·ing**) make a synthesis of

syn'the·siz'er *n.* electronic console or keyboard reproducing varied instrumental sounds

syn·thet·ic /sinTHet'ik/ *adj.* 1 made by chemical synthesis, esp. to imitate a natural product 2 affected; insincere —*n.* 3 synthetic substance —**syn·thet'i·cal·ly** *adv.*

syph·i·lis /sif'əlis/ *n.* contagious venereal disease —**syph'i·lit'ic** *adj.* [*Syphilus,* name of a character in a poem of 1530]

Syr·a·cuse /ser'əkyoōs, ser'-, -kyoōz'/ *n.* city in N.Y. Pop. 163,860

Syr·i·a /ser'ēə/ *n.* republic in SW Asia on the E coast of the Mediterranean Sea. Capital: Damascus. Pop. 12,958,000 —**Syr'i·an** *n.* & *adj.*

SYRINGE 1

sy·ringe /sərinj'/ *n.* 1 device for drawing in and ejecting liquid in a fine stream —*v.* (**·ringed, ·ring·ing**) 2 sluice or inject with a syringe [Gk *syrinx* pipe]

syr·up /sir'əp, sər'-/ *n.* 1 sweet sauce of sugar dissolved in boiling water 2 any thick and esp. sweet liquid —**syr'up·y** *adj.* [Ar *sharab*]

sys·tem /sis'təm/ *n.* 1 interrelated or complex whole; organized arrangement or network 2a set of organs in the body with a common structure or function b human or animal body as a whole 3 scheme of action, procedure, or classification; method 4 orderliness 5 (prec. by *the*) prevailing political or social order [Gk *systēma -mat-*]

sys·tem·at·ic /sis'təmat'ik/ *adj.* 1 methodical; according to a system 2 regular; deliberate —**sys'tem·at'i·cal·ly** *adv.*

sys·tem·a·tize /sis'təmətiz/ *v.* (**·tized, ·tiz·ing**) make systematic —**sys'tem·a·ti·za'tion** *n.*

sys·tem·ic /sistem'ik/ *adj. Physiol.* of the whole body —**sys·tem'i·cal·ly** *adv.*

sys·to·le /sis'təlē/ *n.* normal rhythmic contraction of the heart —**sys·tol'ic** /-täl'ik/ *adj.* [Gk SYN-, *stellein* set up]

Szcze·cin /SHCHet'sēn/ *n.* seaport in NW Poland. Pop. 413,600

T

t, T /tē/ *n.* (*pl.* **t's; T's, Ts**) 1 twentieth letter of the English alphabet; a consonant 2 **to a T** exactly; to a nicety

T *symb.* tritium

t or **t.** *abbr.* 1 *Football.* tackle 2 tare 3 teaspoon; teaspoonful 4 temperature 5 in the time of 6 *Mus.* tenor 7 time 8 ton 9 town 10 troy

T or **T.** *abbr.* 1 tablespoon; tablespoonful 2 Territory 3 Township 4 Tuesday

Ta *symb.* tantalum

tab /tab/ *n.* 1 small flap or strip attached for grasping, fastening, or hanging up, or for identification 2 *Colloq.* check; bill (*picked up the tab*) 3 keep tabs (or a tab) on *Colloq.* have under observation or in check [prob. dial.]

Ta·bas·co /təbas′kō/ *n.* 1 *Tdmk.* pungent hot pepper sauce 2 state of SE Mexico, on the Gulf of Mexico. Capital: Villahermosa. Pop. 1,501,700

tab·by /tab′ē/ *n.* (*pl.* **·bies**) 1 gray or brownish cat with dark stripes 2 domestic and esp. female cat [Fr fr. Ar]

tab·er·na·cle /tab′ərnak′əl/ *n.* 1 *Hist.* tent used as a sanctuary by the Israelites during the Exodus 2 large place of worship 3 niche or receptacle, esp. for the consecrated Eucharistic elements [L, rel. to TAVERN]

ta·bla /täb′lə/ *n.* pair of small drums played with the hands, esp. in Indian music [Ar: drum]

ta·ble /tā′bəl/ *n.* 1 flat surface usu. on a leg or legs, used for eating, working at, etc. 2a food set out for eating b group seated for dinner, etc. 3 set of facts or figures in columns, etc. (*table of contents; multiplication table*) —*v.* (**·bled, ·bling**) 4 postpone discussion of (a topic, legislation, etc.) at a meeting 5 **turn the tables** reverse circumstances to one's advantage [L *tabula* board]

tab·leau /tablō′/ *n.* (*pl.* **·leaux** or **·leaus** /-lōz′/) 1 picturesque presentation 2 group of silent, motionless people portraying a scene [Fr: picture, dim. of TABLE]

ta′ble·cloth′ *n.* cloth spread over a table, esp. for meals

ta·ble d'hôte /täbəl dōt′/ *n.* meal from a set menu at a fixed price [Fr: host's table]

ta′ble·land′ *n.* plateau

ta′ble·spoon′ *n.* 1 large spoon for serving food 2 volume measure, 1/2 fluid ounce or 3 teaspoons —**ta′ble·spoon′ful** *n.* (*pl.* **·fuls**)

tab·let /tab′lit/ *n.* 1 solid dose of a medicine, etc., for swallowing or chewing 2 flat slab of esp. stone, usu. inscribed 3 writing pad [L dim., rel. to TABLE]

ta′ble ten′nis *n.* ball game played with small paddles on a table divided by a net; Ping Pong

tab·loid /tab′loid′/ *n.* small-sized, usu. sensationalized, illustrated newspaper [fr. TABLET]

ta·boo /təbōō′, ta-/ (also **ta·bu′**) *n.* (*pl.* **·boos** or **·bus**) 1 ritual isolation of a person or thing as sacred or accursed 2 prohibition imposed by social custom —*adj.* 3 avoided or prohibited, esp. by social custom (*taboo words*) —*v.* (**·booed** or **·bued, ·boo·ing** or

·bu·ing) 4 put under taboo 5 exclude or prohibit, esp. socially [Tongan]

Ta·briz /təbrēz′/ *n.* city in NW Iran. Pop. 971,500

tab·u·lar /tab′yələr/ *adj.* of or arranged in tables or lists [L, rel. to TABLE]

tab·u·late /tab′yəlāt′/ *v.* (**·lat·ed, ·lat·ing**) arrange (figures or facts) in tabular form —**tab′u·la′tion, tab′u·la′tor** *n.*

ta·chom·e·ter /təkäm′ətər/ *n.* instrument measuring velocity or rate of rotation of a shaft (esp. in a vehicle)

tac·it /tas′it/ *adj.* understood or implied without being stated —**tac′it·ly** *adv.* [L *tacere* be silent]

tac·i·turn /tas′itərn/ *adj.* saying little; uncommunicative —**tac′i·turn′i·ty** *n.* [L, rel. to TACIT]

Tac·i·tus /tas′ətəs/, **Cornelius** c. 55 – c. 120; Roman historian

tack /tak/ *n.* 1 small, sharp, broad-headed nail 2 THUMBTACK 3 long stitch for joining fabrics lightly or temporarily together 4 (in sailing) direction, or temporary change of direction, esp. taking advantage of a wind 5 course of action or policy —*v.* 6 fasten with tacks 7 stitch lightly together 8 add or append 9a change a ship's course to take advantage of a wind b make a series of such changes [prob. rel. to Fr *tache* clasp, nail]

tack·le /tak′əl/ *n.* 1 equipment for a task or sport 2 mechanism, esp. of ropes, pulleys, etc., for lifting weights, etc. 3 act of tackling in football, etc. 4 *Football.* either of two linemen —*v.* (**·led, ·ling**) 5 try to deal with (a problem or difficulty) 6 grapple with (an opponent) 7 confront (a person) in discussion or argument 8 *Football.* stop (a player with the ball) usu. by throwing him to the ground —**tack′ler** *n.* [LGer]

tack·y¹ *adj.* (**·i·er, ·i·est**) slightly sticky —**tack′i·ness** *n.* [fr. TACK]

tack·y² *adj.* (**·i·er, ·i·est**) 1 in poor taste; cheap 2 shabby —**tack′i·ness** *n.*

ta·co /tä′kō/ *n.* (*pl.* **·cos**) tortilla filled with chopped meat, beans, lettuce, etc. [MexSp]

Ta·co·ma /təkō′mə/ *n.* city in Wash. Pop. 176,664

tact /takt/ *n.* skill in dealing with others, esp. in delicate situations; intuitive social grace —**tact′ful** *adj.*; **tact′ful·ly** *adv.* [L *tangere* *tact-* touch]

tac·tic /tak′tik/ *n.* tactical maneuver —**tac′ti·cal** *adj.*; **tac′ti·cal·ly** *adv.* [Gk fr. *tassein* arrange]

tac′tics *n. pl.* 1 (also treated as *sing.*) disposition of armed forces, esp. in warfare 2 procedure to achieve an end; purposive method —**tac·ti′cian** /-tish′ən/ *n.*

tac·tile /tak′təl, -tīl′/ *adj.* 1 of the sense of touch 2 perceived by touch; tangible —**tac·til′i·ty** /-til′itē/ *n.* [L, rel. to TACT]

tact′less *adj.* having or showing no tact —**tact′less·ly** *adv.*; **tact′less·ness** *n.*

tad·pole /tad′pōl′/ *n.* larva, esp. of a frog or toad [rel. to TOAD, POLL]

Ta·dzhik·i·stan /täje′kistan′, -stän′/ *n.* republic in central Asia, NE of Afghanistan; formerly part of the USSR. Capital: Dushanbe. Pop. 5,568,000 **—Ta·dzhik'** *n.*

Tae·gu /tag'ōō'/ *n.* city in South Korea. Pop. 2,228,800

Tae·jon /taj'ŏn'/ *n.* city in South Korea. Pop. 1,062,100

taf·fe·ta /taf'itə/ *n.* fine, lustrous silk or silk-like fabric [Pers *tāftah*]

taff'rail /-rāl'/ *n.* rail around a ship's stern [Du *taffereel* panel]

Taft /taft/ **1 William Howard** 1857–1930; 27th US president (1909–13) and Supreme Court justice; father of: **2 Robert A(lphonse)** 1889–1953; US politician

tag[1] /tag/ *n.* **1** label, esp. attached to an object **2** metal, etc., point on a shoelace, cord, etc. **3** loop or flap for handling or hanging a thing **4** loose or ragged end **5** epithet; nickname **—v.** (**tagged, tag·ging**) **6** provide with a tag or tags **7** join; attach **8** tag along follow; accompany passively

tag[2] *n.* **1** children's chasing game **—v.** (**tagged, tag·ging**) **2** touch in a game of tag

Ta·ga·log /təgä'lŏg/ *n.* **1** member of ethnic group native to Manila and environs **2** Austronesian language, the national language of the Philippines

Ta·gore /təgôr', -gōr'/, **(Sir) Rabindranath** 1861–1941; Indian poet

Ta·gus Riv·er /tā'gəs/ *n.* river in SW Europe, flowing W 570 mi. through Spain and Portugal to the Atlantic

Ta·hi·ti /təhēt'ē/ *n.* S Pacific island; one of the Society Islands. Capital: Papeete **—Ta·hi'tian** /-SHən/ *n. & adj.*

Ta·hoe, Lake /tä'hō'/ *n.* glacial lake in the Sierra Nevadas on Calif.-Nev. border, 6,228 ft. above sea level

t'ai chi /tī' CHē'/ *n.* (in full **t'ai' chi' ch'uan'** /CHwän/) Chinese martial art and system of calisthenics with slow, controlled movements [Chin: great ultimate boxing]

Tai·chung /tī'CHəNG'/ *n.* city in Taiwan. Pop. 761,800

Ta·if /tä'if/ *n.* city in Saudi Arabia. Pop. 300,000

tail /tāl/ *n.* **1** hindmost part of an animal, esp. extending beyond the body **2a** thing like a tail, esp. a rear extension **b** rear of a procession, etc. **3** rear part of an airplane, vehicle, or rocket **4** luminous trail following a comet **5** part of a shirt or coat below the waist at the back **6** (*pl.*) *Colloq.* **a** TAILCOAT **b** man's evening dress including this **7** (*pl.*) reverse of a coin **8** *Colloq.* person following another **9** *Slang.* human posterior **—v.** **10** *Colloq.* follow closely **11 with one's tail between one's legs** rebuffed; humiliated **—tail'less** *adj.* [OE]

tail'back' *n. Football.* offensive back farthest from the line of scrimmage

tail'coat' *n.* man's formal coat with a long divided flap at the back

tail'gate' *n.* **1** hinged or removable gate or door at the back of a truck, wagon, etc. **—v.** (**-gat·ed, -gat·ing**) **2** follow (another vehicle) too closely **3** have a picnic on or from a car's tailgate, as while parked for a sports event

tail'light' *n.* rear light on a vehicle

tai·lor /tā'lər/ *n.* **1** maker or fitter of clothes **—v.** **2** make (clothes) as a tailor **3** make or adapt for a special purpose **—tai'lored** *adj.* [AngFr *taillour*, fr. LL *taliare* cut]

tai'lor-made' *adj.* **1** made to order by a tailor **2** made or suited for a particular purpose

tail'pipe' *n.* rear exhaust pipe

tail'spin' *n.* **1** spin by an aircraft with the tail spiraling **2** rapid decline or collapse

tail'wind' *n.* wind blowing in the direction of travel

Tai·nan /tī'nän'/ *n.* city in Taiwan. Pop. 683,300

Tai·no /tī'nō/ *n.* language of the extinct Taino Indians of the West Indies

taint /tānt/ *n.* **1** spot or trace of decay, infection, corruption, etc. **—v.** **2** affect with a taint **3** (foll. by *with*) affect slightly [L, rel. to TINGE]

Tai·pei /tī'pā', -bā'/ *n.* capital of Taiwan. Pop. 2,719,700

Tai·wan /tīwän'/ *n.* island nation off the SE coast of China. Capital: Taipei. Pop. 20,727,000 **—Tai·wan·ese** /tī'wənēz'/ *n. & adj.*

Tai·yuan /tī'yŏŏ·än'/ *n.* city in N China. Pop. 1,533,900

take /tāk/ *v.* (**took, tak·en, tak·ing**) **1** lay hold of; get into one's hands **2** acquire; capture; earn; win **3** get by purchase, hire, or formal agreement (*took a taxi*) **4** (in a recipe) use **5** occupy (*take a chair*) **6** make use of (*take the next left; take the bus*) **7** consume (food or medicine) **8** be effective (*inoculation did not take*) **9** require or use up (*will only take a minute*) **10** carry; convey (*bus will take you*) **11** remove; steal **12a** experience (*take pleasure*) **b** exert (*take no notice*) **13** find out and note (*took his address; took her temperature*) **14** understand (*I took you to mean yes*) **15** treat, deal with, or regard in a specified way (*took it badly*) **16** (foll. by *for*) regard as being (*do you take me for an idiot?*) **17a** accept; receive **b** hold (*takes 3 pints*) **18** wear (*takes size 10*) **19** choose; assume (*took the initiative*) **20** get; derive **21** subtract (*take 3 from 9*) **22** perform; produce; undertake (*take notes; take an oath*) **23** be taught or examined in (a subject) **24** make (a photograph) **25** use as an example (*take Napoleon*) **26** *Gram.* have or require as part of a construction (*this verb takes an object*) **27** have sexual intercourse with (a woman) **28** (in *passive*) be attracted or charmed (by) **29** *Colloq.* deceive; swindle **—n.** **30** amount taken or caught at a time, etc. **31** film sequence photographed continuously at one time **32 have what it takes** have the necessary qualities, etc., for success **33 take after** resemble (a parent, etc.) **34 take away** subtract **35 take back:** **a** retract (a statement) **b** carry in thought to a past time **c** return (goods) to a store **d** (of a store) accept such goods **e** accept or welcome (a person) back **36 take down:** **a** write down (spoken words) **b** remove; dismantle **37 take heart** be encouraged **38 take in:** **a** receive as a guest, etc. **b** make (a garment, etc.) smaller **c** include **d** deceive **39 take it:** **a** assume **b** endure in a specified way (*took it badly*) **40 take it or leave it** accept it or not **41 take it out on** relieve one's frustration by treating (another) aggressively **42 take off:**

a deduct **b** *Colloq.* depart, esp. hastily **c** become airborne **d** (of a scheme, enterprise, etc.) become successful **e** have (a period) away from work **43 take on: a** undertake (work, etc.) **b** be willing or ready to meet (an opponent, etc.) **c** acquire (new meaning, etc.) **44 take out: a** remove; extract; borrow **b** escort socially; date **c** purchase (prepared food) for consumption elsewhere **d** *Slang.* murder; destroy **45 take over** take control **46 take to: a** begin or fall into the habit of (*took to smoking*) **b** form a liking for **47 take up: a** become interested or engaged in (a pursuit) **b** occupy (time or space) **c** begin (residence, etc.) **d** shorten (a garment) **e** pursue (a matter, etc.) further **48 take (a person) up on** accept (a person's offer, etc.) —**tak′er** *n.* [OE fr. ON]

take′off′ *n.* **1** act of becoming airborne **2** act of mimicking

take′out′ *adj.* **1** (of food) bought cooked for eating elsewhere —*n.* **2** this food

take′o′ver *n.* **1** assumption of control (esp. of a business)

tak′ing *adj.* **1** engaging; attractive **2** (*pl.*) receipts; earnings

talc /talk/ *n.* **1** magnesium silicate used as a lubricant **2** TALCUM POWDER [Ar fr. Pers *talk*]

tal′cum pow′der /tal′kəm/ *n.* (also **tal′cum**) powdered talc for the body, usu. scented [MedL: see TALC]

tale / tāl/ *n.* **1** (usu. fictitious) narrative or story **2** gossip **3** false story; lie [OE]

tal·ent /tal′ənt/ *n.* **1** special aptitude or faculty **2** natural ability or competency valued for success **3** person or persons of talent **4** ancient esp. Greek weight and unit of currency —**tal′ent·ed** *adj.* [Gk *talanton*]

tal·is·man /tal′əsmən, -əz-/ *n.* (*pl.* **·mans**) ring, stone, etc., thought to have magic powers, esp. to bring good luck —**tal′is·man′ic** /-man′ik/ *adj.* [Fr and Sp fr. MGk]

talk / tôk/ *v.* **1** converse or communicate by speech **2** have the power of speech **3a** discuss; express; utter (*talking nonsense*) **b** (in *imper.*) as an emphatic statement (*talk about expense!*) **4** use (a language) in speech (*talking Spanish*) **5** divulge secrets **6** gossip (*people will talk*) **7** have influence (*money talks*) —*n.* **8** conversation; talking **9** particular mode of speech (*baby talk*) **10** address or lecture **11a** rumor or gossip (*talk of a merger*) **b** its theme (*the talk was of mergers*) **12** empty promises; boasting **13** (often *pl.*) discussions; negotiations **14 talk back** reply defiantly **15 talk down** to speak condescendingly to **16 talk of: a** discuss; mention **b** express some intention of (*talked of moving*) **17 talk** over discuss at length **18 talk shop** talk about one's occupation, etc. **19 talk to: a** speak privately with **b** rebuke; scold —**talk′er** *n.* [fr. TALE or TELL]

talk′a·tive *adj.* fond of or given to talking

talk′ie *n.* (esp. early) movie with a soundtrack

talk′ing book′ *n.* recorded reading of a book, esp. for the blind

talk′ show′ *n.* television or radio program featuring interviews of guests and often questions from callers in the broadcast audience

tall / tôl/ *adj.* **1** of more than average height **2** of a specified height (*about six feet tall*) —

adv. **3** as if tall; proudly (*sit tall*) —**tall′ish** *adj.*; **tall′ness** *n.* [OE: swift]

Tal·la·has·see /tal′əhas′ē/ *n.* capital of Fla., in the NW part. Pop. 124,773

tall′boy′ *n.* tall chest of drawers

Tal·ley·rand-Pé·ri·gord /tal′ērand per′əgôr′/, **Charles Maurice de** 1754–1838; French statesman

Tal·linn / tä′l(y)in, tal′in/ *n.* capital of Estonia. Pop. 481,500

tal·low /tal′ō/ *n.* hard (esp. animal) fat melted down to make candles, soap, etc. —**tal′low·y** *adj.* [LGer]

tal·ly / tal′ē/ *n.* (*pl.* **·lies**) **1** reckoning of a debt or score **2** total amount or score **3** mark registering the number of objects delivered or received **4** identification ticket or label —*v.* (**·lied**, **·ly·ing**) **5** agree; correspond [L *talea* rod]

tal·ly·ho /tal′ēhō′/ *interj.* **1** huntsman's cry on sighting a fox —*n.* (*pl.* **·hos**) **2** cry of this —*v.* (**·hoed**, **·ho·ing**) **3** utter a cry of 'tally-ho' **4** indicate (a fox) or urge (hounds) with this cry [cf. Fr *taïaut*]

Tal·mud / täl′mŏŏd, -məd/ *n.* body of Jewish civil and ceremonial law and tradition —**Tal·mu′dic** /-m(y)ŏŏ′dik, -mŏŏd′ik/ *adj.*; **Tal′mu·dist** *n.* [Heb: instruction]

tal·on /tal′ən/ *n.* claw, esp. of a bird of prey [L *talus* ankle]

ta·lus / tā′ləs/ *n.* (*pl.* **·li** /-lī′/) anklebone supporting the tibia [L: ankle]

ta·ma·le /təmä′lā/ *n.* Mexican dish of chopped meat, etc., wrapped in cornmeal dough and steamed in corn husks [MexSp]

tam·a·rind /tam′ərind/ *n.* **1** tropical evergreen tree **2** its fruit [Ar: Indian date]

Ta·mau·li·pas /täm′oulā′päs/ *n.* state of NE Mexico, bordering Texas and the Gulf of Mexico. Capital: Ciudad Victoria. Pop. 2,249,600

tam·bou·rine /tam′bərēn′/ *n.* small, shallow, hand drum with jingling disks in its rim, shaken or banged as an accompaniment [prob. fr. Ar *tanbur* lute]

tame / tām/ *adj.* **1** (of an animal) domesticated; not wild or shy **2** insipid; dull **3** (of a person) docile —*v.* (**tamed**, **tam·ing**) **4** make tame; domesticate **5** subdue; curb —**tam′a·ble** *adj.*; **tame′ly** *adv.*; **tame′ness**, **tam′er** *n.* [OE]

TAMBOURINE

Tam·er·lane /tam′ərlān/ *c.* 1336–1405; Tartar conqueror; ruler of Samarkand (1369–1405)

Tam·il /täm′əl, tam′-/ *n.* **1** member of a people of South India and Sri Lanka **2** language of this people —*adj.* **3** of this people or language [native name]

tam-o′-shanter /tam′əsHan′tər/ *n.* floppy, round, esp. woolen beret, of Scottish origin [hero of a poem by Burns]

tamp /tamp/ *v.* ram down hard or tightly by a series of taps [*tampion* stopper for gun muzzle, fr. Fr *tampon*]

Tam·pa /tam′pə/ *n.* city in Fla. Pop. 280,015

tam·per /tam′pər/ *v.* (foll. by *with*) **1** meddle with or change illicitly **2** exert a secret or corrupt influence upon; bribe [var. of TEMPER]

Tam·pi·co /tampē´kō/ *n.* seaport in E Mexico. Pop. 268,000

tam·pon /tam´pän´/ *n.* plug of soft material used esp. to absorb blood [Fr, rel. to TAMP]

tan¹ /tan/ *n.* **1** SUNTAN **2** yellowish-brown color —*adj.* **3** yellowish-brown —*v.* (**tanned, tan·ning**) **4** make or become brown by exposure to sunlight **5** convert (raw hide) into leather **6** *Colloq.* beat; thrash [MedL *tannum* oak bark]

tan² *abbr.* tangent

tan·dem /tan´dəm/ *n.* **1** set of two, with one following the other **2** in tandem: **a** one behind another **b** in association [L: at length]

tan·door·i /tändŏŏr´ē/ *n.* Indian food spiced and cooked over charcoal in a clay oven [Hindustani]

tang /taNG/ *n.* **1** strong taste or smell **2** characteristic quality **3** projection on a blade fitting into a handle [ON *tange* point]

Tan·gan·yi·ka, Lake /tan´ganyē´kə, taNG´-/ *n.* freshwater lake in central Africa between Zaire and Tanzania

tan·gent /tan´jənt/ *n.* **1** straight line, curve, or surface that meets a curve but does not intersect it **2** ratio of two sides (other than the hypotenuse) opposite and adjacent to an acute angle in a right-angled triangle **3** at (or on) a tangent diverging from a previous course or from what is relevant or central (*go off at a tangent*) [L *tangere* tact- touch]

tan·gen·tial /tanjen´SHəl/ *adj.* **1** of or along a tangent **2** divergent **3** peripheral —**tan·gen´ tial·ly** *adv.*

tan·ger·ine /tan´jərēn, tan´jərēn´/ *n.* **1** small, sweet, thin-skinned citrus fruit like an orange **2** deep orange-yellow color [TANGIER]

tan·gi·ble /tan´jəbəl/ *adj.* **1** perceptible by touch **2** definite; clearly intelligible; not elusive (*tangible proof*) —**tan´gi·bil´i·ty, tan´gi· ble·ness** *n.*; **tan´gi·bly** *adv.* [L, rel. to TANGENT]

Tan·gier /tanjēr´/ *n.* (also **Tangiers**) seaport in Morocco. Pop. 266,300

tan·gle /taNG´gəl/ *v.* (**-gled, -gling**) **1** intertwine (threads, hairs, etc.) or become entwined in a confused mass; entangle **2** *Colloq.* become involved (esp. in conflict) with (*don't tangle with me*) —*n.* **3** confused, intertwined mass **4** confused state

tan·go /taNG´gō/ *n.* (*pl.* **-gos**) **1** slow S American ballroom dance **2** music for this —*v.* (**-goed, -go·ing**) **3** dance the tango [AmerSp]

Tang·shan /täNG´SHän´/ *n.* city in NE China. Pop. 1,044,200

tang·y /taNG´ē/ *adj.* (**-i·er, -i·est**) having a strong usu. acid tang

tank /taNGk/ *n.* **1** large container, usu. for liquid or gas **2** heavy, armored fighting vehicle moving on continuous tracks —**tank´ful** *n.* (*pl.* **-fuls**) [perh. Gujarati: reservoir]

tan·kard /taNG´kärd/ *n.* tall beer mug with a handle [prob. MDu *tankaert*]

tank´er *n.* ship, aircraft, or truck for carrying liquids, esp. oil, in bulk

tan·ner /tan´ər/ *n.* person who tans hides

tan´ner·y *n.* (*pl.* **-ies**) place where hides are tanned

tan·nic ac´id /tan´ik/ *n.* (also **tan·nin** /tan´ in/) natural, yellowish organic compound used in tanning and dyeing

tan·sy /tan´zē/ *n.* (*pl.* **-sies**) plant with yellow flowers and aromatic leaves [Gk *athanasia* immortality]

tan·ta·lize /tant´l-īz´/ *v.* (**-lized, -liz·ing**) torment or tease by the sight or promise of the unobtainable —**tan´tal·i·za´tion** *n.* [*Tantalus*, mythical king punished in Hades with sight of water and fruit that drew back whenever he tried to reach them]

tan·ta·lum /tant´l-əm/ *n.* rare, hard, white metallic element; *symb.* Ta [rel. to TANTALIZE]

tan·ta·mount /tan´təmount´/ *adj.* equivalent (to) [It *tanto montare* amount to so much]

tan·tra /tən´trə, tän´-/ *n.* any of a class of Hindu or Buddhist mystical or magical writings [Skt: doctrine]

tan·trum /tan´trəm/ *n.* (esp. child's) outburst of bad temper or petulance

Tan·za·ni·a /tan´zanē´ə/ *n.* republic in E Africa, the merger of Tanganyika and Zanzibar. Capital: Dar es Salaam. Pop. 25,809,000 —**Tan·za·ni´an** *n.* & *adj.*

Tao·ism /dou´iz´əm, tou´-/ *n.* Chinese philosophy and religion advocating humility and piety —**Tao´ist** /-ist/ *n.* [Chin *dao* right way]

tap¹ /tap/ *n.* **1** device controlling a flow of liquid or gas from a pipe or vessel **2** wiretapping —*v.* (**tapped, tap·ping**) **3** provide (a cask) or let out (liquid) with a tap **4** draw sap from (a tree) by cutting into it **5** obtain information or supplies from **6** extract or obtain; discover and exploit **7** install a secret listening device [OE]

tap² *v.* (**tapped, tap·ping**) **1** strike a gentle but audible blow on **2** make by a tap or taps (*tapped out the rhythm*) **3** tap-dance —*n.* **4a** light blow; rap **b** sound of this **5a** tap-dancing **b** metal attachment on a tap-dancer's shoe [imit.]

tap´-dance´ *n.* **1** rhythmic dance performed with shoes with metal taps —*v.* **2** perform a tap dance —**tap´-danc´er, tap´-danc´ing** *n.*

tape /tāp/ *n.* **1** narrow strip of woven material for tying up, fastening, etc. **2** this across the finishing line for a race **3** (in full **ad·he´sive tape´**) strip of adhesive plastic, etc., for fastening, masking, etc. **4a** MAGNETIC TAPE **b** tape recording **5** TAPE MEASURE —*v.* (**taped, tap·ing**) **6** cover, seal, mark off, fasten, join, etc., with tape **7** record on magnetic tape [OE]

tape´ deck´ *n.* machine for playing and recording audiotape

tape´ meas´ure *n.* strip of marked tape or flexible metal for measuring

ta·per /tā´pər/ *n.* **1** wick coated with wax, etc., for conveying a flame **2** slender candle —*v.* **3** diminish or reduce in thickness toward one end **4** make or become gradually less [OE]

tape´ re·cord´er *n.* apparatus for recording and replaying sounds on magnetic tape —**tape´-re·cord´** *v.*; **tape´ re·cord´ing** *n.*

tap·es·try /tap´əstrē/ *n.* (*pl.* **-tries**) thick fabric in which colored weft threads are woven to form pictures or designs [*tapissery* fr. Fr *tapis* carpet]

tape'worm' *n.* parasitic intestinal flatworm with a segmented body

tap·i·o·ca /tap'ē·ō'kə/ *n.* starchy substance in hard white grains, obtained from cassava and used for puddings, etc. [Tupi-Guarani]

ta·pir /tā'pər, -pēr'/ *n.* nocturnal Central and S American or Malaysian hoofed mammal with a short, flexible snout [Tupi]

tap·pet /tap'it/ *n.* lever or projecting part in machinery giving intermittent motion [fr. TAP²]

tap' root' *n.* tapering main root growing vertically downwards

tar¹ /tär/ *n.* 1 dark, thick liquid distilled from wood, coal, etc., used as a preservative of wood and iron, in making roads, etc. 2 similar substance formed in the combustion of tobacco —*v.* (tarred, tar·ring) 3 cover with tar 4 tar and feather smear with tar and then cover with feathers as a punishment —**tar'ry** *adj.* [OE]

tar² *n. Colloq.* sailor [fr. TARPAULIN]

tar·an·tel·la /tar'əntel'ə/ *n.* 1 whirling S Italian dance 2 music for this [It fr. *Taranto* in Italy]

ta·ran·tu·la /təran'CHələ/ *n.* 1 large, hairy tropical spider 2 large, black S European spider [MedL, rel. to TARANTELLA]

tar·dy /tär'dē/ *adj.* (·di·er, ·di·est) 1 slow to act, come, or happen 2 delaying; delayed; late —**tar'di·ly** *adv.*; **tar'di·ness** *n.* [L *tardus* slow]

tare¹ /ter/ *n.* 1 vetch, esp. as a cornfield weed or fodder 2 (*pl.*) *Bibl.* an injurious cornfield weed (Matt. 13:24-30)

tare² *n.* 1 allowance made for the weight of packing or wrapping around goods 2 weight of a vehicle without fuel or load [Ar *tarha*]

tar·get /tär'git/ *n.* 1 mark fired or aimed at, esp. a circular object marked with concentric circles 2 person or thing aimed or fired at 3 objective 4 butt for criticism, abuse, etc. —*v.* 5 identify or single out as a target 6 aim or direct (*missiles targeted on major cities*) [MFr *targe* shield]

tar·iff /tar'əf/ *n.* 1 table of fixed charges (*hotel tariff*) 2 duty on a particular class of goods [Ar: notification]

Tar·king·ton /tär'kiNGtən/, **(Newton)** Booth 1869–1946; US writer

tarn /tärn/ *n.* small mountain lake [ON]

tar·nish /tär'niSH/ *v.* 1 (cause to) lose luster 2 sully —*n.* 1 loss of luster, esp. as a film on a metal's surface 2 blemish; stain [Fr *ternir* fr. *terne* dark]

ta·ro /tar'ō, tär'ō/ *n.* (*pl.* -ros) tropical plant with tuberous roots used as food [Polynesian]

ta·rot /tar'ō, tərō'/ *n.* 1 (*sing.* or *pl.*) pack of mainly picture cards used in fortunetelling 2 any card from a tarot pack [Fr]

tar·pau·lin /tärpô'lən, tär'pələn/ *n.* 1 heavy-duty, waterproofed canvas or other material 2 sheet or covering of this [fr. TAR¹, PALL¹]

tar·pon /tär'pən/ *n.* large, silvery game fish of the Atlantic coastal waters

tar·ra·gon /tar'əgən/ *n.* bushy herb used in salads, stuffings, vinegar, etc. [MedL fr. Gk]

tar·ry /tar'ē/ *v.* (·ried, ·ry·ing) linger; stay; wait

tar·sus /tär'səs/ *n.* (*pl.* -si /-sī'/) bones of the ankle and upper foot [Gk]

tart¹ /tärt/ *n.* small pastry containing jam, etc. —**tart'let** *n.* [Fr *tarte*]

tart² *n. Colloq.* prostitute; promiscuous woman [prob. abbr. of SWEETHEART]

tart³ *adj.* 1 sharp or acid in taste 2 (of a remark, etc.) cutting; bitter —**tart'ly** *adv.*; **tart'ness** *n.* [OE]

TARTAN 2

tar·tan /tärt'n/ *n.* 1 plaid pattern, esp. denoting a Scottish Highland clan 2 woolen cloth woven in this pattern

tar·tar /tär'tər/ *n.* 1 hard deposit that forms on the teeth 2 deposit that forms a hard crust in wine [MedL fr. Gk]

Tar·tar /tär'tər/ *n.* 1 (also **Ta'tar**) a member of a group of Central Asian peoples including Mongols and Turks b Turkic language of these peoples 2 (t-) harsh or formidable person —*adj.* 3 of Tartars or of Central Asia east of the Caspian Sea [Fr or MedL]

tar'tar sauce' *n.* sauce of mayonnaise and chopped pickles, etc. [fr. TARTAR]

Tash·kent /tasHkent'/ *n.* capital of Uzbekistan. Pop. 2,113,300

task /task/ *n.* 1 piece of work to be done —*v.* 2 make great demands on (a person's powers, etc.) 3 take to task rebuke; scold [MedL *tasca*, prob. fr. L *taxare* reckon]

task' force' *n.* armed force or other group organized for a specific operation or task

task'mas'ter *n.* (*fem.* **task'mis'tress**) person who makes others work hard

Tas·ma·ni·a /tazmā'nē·ə/ *n.* island and state of Australia; S of Australia

tas·sel /tas'əl/ *n.* 1 decorative tuft of loosely hanging threads or cords 2 tassellike flowerhead of some plants, esp. corn —**tas'seled** *adj.* [Fr *tas(s)el* clasp]

taste /tāst/ *n.* 1a sensation caused in the mouth by contact with the taste buds with a substance b faculty of perceiving this 2 small sample of food or drink 3 slight experience (*taste of success*) 4 liking or predilection (*expensive tastes*) 5 aesthetic discernment in art, clothes, conduct, etc. (*in poor taste*) —*v.* (tast·ed, tast·ing) 6 sample the flavor of (food) 7 perceive the flavor of (*cannot taste with a cold*) 8 eat or drink a small portion of (*had not tasted food for days*) 9 experience (*never tasted failure*) 10 have a specified flavor (*tastes of onions*) —**tast'er** *n.* [Fr fr. Rom]

taste' bud' *n.* cell or nerve ending on the surface of the tongue by which things are tasted

taste'ful *adj.* having or done in good taste —**taste'ful·ly** *adv.*; **taste'ful·ness** *n.*

taste'less *adj.* 1 lacking flavor 2 having or done in bad taste —**taste'less·ly** *adv.*; **taste'less·ness** *n.*

tast·y /tās'tē/ *adj.* (·i·er, ·i·est) pleasing in

flavor; appetizing —tast′i·ly adv.; tast′i·ness n.

tat¹ /tat/ v. (tat·ted, tat·ting) do or make by tatting

tat² n. TIT²

Ta·tar /tä′tər/ var. of TARTAR

tat·ter /tat′ər/ n. (usu. pl.) 1 rag; irregularly torn cloth or paper 2 in tatters: a torn in many places b destroyed; ruined —tat′tered adj. [ON]

tat′ting n. 1 a kind of handmade, knotted lace for trimming, etc. 2 process of making this

tat·tle /tat′l/ v. (·tled, ·tling) 1 chatter; gossip 2 divulge personal secrets —tat′tler n. [Du tatelen, imit.]

tat·too¹ /tatōō′/ n. 1 evening drum or bugle signal recalling soldiers to quarters 2 rhythmic tapping or drumming [earlier tap-too fr. Du taptoe, literally 'close the tap' (of the cask)]

tat·too² v. (·tooed, ·too·ing) 1 mark (skin) indelibly by puncturing it and inserting pigment 2 make (a design) in this way —n. 3 such a design —tat·too′er, tat·too′ist n. [Polynesian]

tau /tou, tô/ n. nineteenth letter of the Greek alphabet (T, τ) [Gk]

taught /tôt/ v. past and past part. of TEACH

taunt /tônt/ n. 1 insult; provocation —v. 2 insult; provoke contemptuously [Fr tant pour tant tit for tat, smart rejoinder]

taupe /tōp/ adj. & n. dark, brownish gray [Fr: MOLE¹]

Tau·rus /tôr′əs/ n. (pl. ·rus·es) 1 constellation and second sign of the zodiac (the Bull) 2 person born under this sign —Tau′re·an /·rēən/ adj. & n. [L: bull]

taut /tôt/ adj. 1 (of a rope, etc.) tight; not slack 2 (of nerves, etc.) tense 3 (of a ship, etc.) in good condition —taut′en v.; taut′ly adv.; taut′ness n. [ME toght tight]

tau·tol·o·gy /tôtäl′əjē/ n. (pl. ·gies) needless repetition using different words, esp. as a fault of style —tau·to·log·i·cal /tôt′l·äj′ikəl/, tau·tol·o·gous /tôtäl′əgəs/ adj. [Gk tauto the same]

tav·ern /tav′ərn/ n. saloon [L taberna]

tav·er·na /täver′nə/ n. Greek restaurant [ModGk, rel. to TAVERN]

taw·dry /tô′drē/ adj. (·dri·er, ·dri·est) showy but worthless; gaudy —taw′dri·ly adv.; taw′dri·ness n. [tawdry lace fr. St Audrey's lace]

taw·ny /tô′nē/ adj. (·ni·er, ·ni·est) orange-brown or yellow-brown [AngFr tauné, rel. to TAN¹]

tax /taks/ n. 1 money compulsorily levied by government authority on individuals, property, businesses, etc. 2 strain; heavy demand or burden —v. 3 impose a tax on 4 deduct tax from (income, etc.) 5 make heavy demands on —tax′a·ble adj. [L taxare censure; compute]

tax·a·tion /taksā′SHən/ n. imposition or payment of tax [L, rel. to TAX]

tax·i /tak′sē/ n. (pl. ·is or ·ies) 1 (in full tax′i·cab′ /·cab′/) car licensed for hire and usu. fitted with a meter —v. (·ied, ·i·ing or ·y·ing) 2 (of an aircraft or pilot) drive on the ground before takeoff or after landing 3 go or convey in a taxi [abbr. of taximeter cab]

tax·i·der·my /tak′sədər″mē/ n. art of preparing, stuffing, and mounting the skins of animals —tax′i·der′mist /·mist/ n. [Gk taxis arrangement, derma skin]

tax·i·me·ter /tak′sēmē″tər/ n. device that registers the fare in a taxi [rel. to TAX + ·METER]

tax·on /tak′sän/ n. (pl. tax·a /tak′sə/) a taxonomic category, as a family, genus, species, etc. [Gk tassein arrange]

tax·on·o·my /taksän′əmē/ n. (pl. ·mies) classification of living and extinct organisms —tax·o·nom·ic /tak′sənäm″ik/, tax·o·nom′i·cal adj.; tax·o·nom′i·cal·ly adv.; tax·on′o·mist n. [Gk taxis arrangement, ·nomia distribution]

tax′pay′er n. person who pays taxes

Tay·lor /tā′lər/ Zachary 1784–1850; 12th US president (1849–50)

Tb symb. terbium

TB abbr. 1 tubercle bacillus 2 tuberculosis

Tbi·li·si /təbälē′sē/ n. capital of the E European republic of Georgia. Pop. 1,279,000

T-bone /tē′bōn′/ n. T-shaped bone, esp. in steak from the thin end of a loin

tbsp. abbr. 1 tablespoon(s) 2 tablespoonful(s)

Tc symb. technetium

T cell n. white blood cell developed in the thymus that regulates the immune system

Tchai·kov·sky /CHīkôf′skē, ·kôv′·/, Peter 1840–93; Russian composer

TD abbr. 1 (also td) touchdown 2 Treasury Department

tdmk. abbr. trademark

Te symb. tellurium

tea /tē/ n. 1a (in full tea plant) Asian evergreen shrub or small tree b its dried leaves 2 drink made by infusing tea leaves in boiling water 3 infusion of herbal or other leaves (chamomile tea) 4 (chiefly Brit.) light afternoon meal of tea, bread, cakes, etc. [prob. Du tee fr. Chin]

tea′ bag′ n. small, porous bag of tea for infusion

teach /tēCH/ v. (taught, teach·ing) 1a give systematic information, instruction, or training to (a person) or about (a subject or skill) b practice this professionally c cause to learn by experience (taught forgiveness) 2 impress upon by example or punishment (that will teach you not to disobey) —teach′a·ble adj. [OE]

teach′er n. person who teaches, esp. in a school

teach′ing n. 1 profession of a teacher 2 (often pl.) what is taught; doctrine

tea′ co′zy n. cover to keep a teapot warm

ten′cup′ n. 1 cup from which tea is drunk 2 amount held by this —tea′cup·ful′ n. (pl. ·fuls)

teak /tēk/ n. 1 a hard, durable timber 2 large Indian or SE Asian deciduous tree yielding this [Port fr. Malayalam]

teal /tēl/ n. (pl. same) 1 small freshwater duck 2 dark, greenish blue color

team /tēm/ n. 1 set of players forming one side in a game 2 two or more people working together 3 set of draft animals —v. 4 join in a team or in common action [OE]

team′mate′ n. fellow member of a team

team'ster *n.* driver of a truck or a team of animals

team'work' *n.* combined action; cooperation

tea'pot' *n.* pot with a handle, spout, and lid, for brewing and pouring tea

tear[1] /ter/ *v.* (**tore, torn, tear·ing**) 1 pull apart or to pieces with some force 2 make a hole or rent in this way; undergo this (*have torn my coat; curtain tore*) 3 pull violently (*tore down the notice*) 4 emotionally torment, confuse, etc. (*torn by guilt*) 5 go hurriedly —*n.* 6 hole or split caused by tearing 7 torn part of cloth, etc. 8 **be torn between** have difficulty in choosing between 9 **tear apart:** a search (a place) exhaustively b criticize forcefully c distress greatly 10 **tear one's hair** out behave with extreme desperation 11 **tear into:** *Colloq.* a severely attack or reprimand b start (an activity) vigorously 12 **tear oneself away** leave reluctantly [OE]

tear[2] /tēr/ *n.* 1 drop of clear, salty liquid secreted by glands from the eye 2 tearlike thing; drop 3 **in tears** crying; weeping [OE]

tear-drop /tēr'dräp'/ *n.* single tear

tear·ful /tēr'fəl/ *adj.* 1 crying or inclined to cry 2 sad (*tearful event*) —**tear'ful·ly** *adv.*

tear gas /tēr' gas'/ *n.* gas irritating the eyes, used by police, etc., to disable

tear·jerk·er /tēr'jər'kər/ *n.* *Colloq.* sentimental story, film, etc.

tea'room' *n.* small restaurant serving tea, coffee, etc.

tease /tēz/ *v.* (**teased, teas·ing**) 1a make fun of playfully, unkindly, or annoyingly b tempt or tantalize, esp. sexually c coax 2 pick (wool, etc.) into separate fibers 3 dress (cloth) esp. with teasels 4 comb or brush hair toward the scalp to make it appear fuller —*n.* 5 person fond of teasing 6 act of teasing (*only a tease*) —**teas'er** *n.* [OE]

tea·sel /tē'zəl/ *n.* 1 plant with large, prickly heads that are dried and used to raise the nap on woven cloth 2 other device used for this purpose —**tea'sel·er** *n.* [OE, rel. to TEASE]

tea'spoon' *n.* 1 spoon for stirring tea, etc. 2 amount held by this, 1/6 fluid ounce —**tea'spoon·ful'** *n.* (*pl.* **·fuls**)

teat /tēt, tit/ *n.* mammary nipple, esp. of an animal [Fr fr. Gmc]

tech. *abbr.* technical; technician; technology

tech·ne·tium /teknē'SH(ē)əm/ *n.* artificially produced radioactive metallic element; *symb.* Tc [Gk *tekhnētos* artificial]

tech·ni·cal /tek'nikəl/ *adj.* 1 of the mechanical arts and applied sciences (*technical college*) 2 (of a book, discourse, etc.) using scientific or specialized language 3 due to mechanical failure (*technical problem*) 4 strictly or legally interpreted (*technical point*) —**tech'ni·cal·ly** *adv.* [Gk *tekhnē* art]

tech·ni·cal·i·ty /tek'nikal'ətē/ *n.* (*pl.* **·ties**) 1 being technical 2 technical expression 3 minor or specialized point or detail

tech'ni·cal knock'out *n.* ruling by the referee that a boxer has lost because he is not fit to continue; *abbr.* TKO

tech·ni·cian /teknisH'ən/ *n.* person skilled in scientific, mechanical, artistic, etc., technique

Tech·ni·col·or /tek'nikal'ər/ *n.* *Tdmk.* process of color cinematography

tech·nique /teknēk'/ *n.* 1 manual or mechanical skill; applicable method 2 manner of artistic execution in music, painting, etc. [Fr]

tech·noc·ra·cy /teknäk'rəsē/ *n.* (*pl.* **·cies**) rule or control by technical experts —**tech·no·crat** /tek'nəkrat'/ *n.*; **tech'no·crat'ic** *adj.* [Gk *tekhnē* art]

tech·nol·o·gy /teknäl'əjē/ *n.* (*pl.* **·gies**) 1 knowledge or use of the mechanical arts and applied sciences 2 these subjects collectively —**tech'no·log'i·cal** /-nəläj'ikəl/ *adj.*; **tech'no·log'i·cal·ly** *adv.*; **tech·nol'o·gist** *n.* [Gk *tekhnologia* systematic treatment, fr. *tekhnē* art]

tec·ton·ic /tektän'ik/ *adj.* 1 of building or construction 2 of the deformation and subsequent structural changes of the earth's crust [Gk *tektōn* craftsman]

tec·ton'ics *n. pl.* (usu. treated as *sing.*) study of the earth's large-scale structural features

Te·cum·seh /tikəm'sə/ *c.* 1768–1813; Shawnee Indian leader

ted'dy bear' /ted'ē/ *n.* soft toy bear [for *Teddy* (Theodore) Roosevelt]

te·di·ous /tē'dēəs/ *adj.* tiresomely long; wearisome —**te'di·ous·ly** *adv.*; **te'di·ous·ness** *n.* [L, rel. to TEDIUM]

te·di·um /tē'dēəm/ *n.* tediousness [L *taedium* fr. *taedet* it bores]

tee /tē/ *Golf. n.* 1 cleared space from which the golf ball is struck at the start of play for each hole 2 small wooden or plastic support for a golf ball —*v.* (**teed, tee·ing**) 3 (often foll. by *up*) place (a ball) on a golf tee

tee-hee /tē'hē'/ *interj.* 1 expression of esp. derisive amusement —*n.* 2 titter; giggle —*v.* (**·heed, ·hee·ing**) 3 titter; giggle [imit.]

teem /tēm/ *v.* 1 be abundant 2 be full of or swarming (*teeming with ideas*) [OE: give birth to]

-teen *suffix* forming numerals from 13 to 19 [OE]

teen'age' *adj.* of or characteristic of teenagers —**teen'aged'** *adj.*

teen'ag'er *n.* person from 13 to 19 years of age

teens /tēnz/ *n. pl.* years of age from 13 to 19

tee·ny /tē'nē/ *adj.* (**·i·er, ·i·est**) (also **teen·sy** /tēnz'ē/) (**·si·er, ·si·est**) tiny [var. of TINY]

tee·ny-wee·ny /tē'nē wē'nē/ *adj.* (also **teen·sy-ween·sy** /tēn'zē wēn'zē, -sē/) very tiny

tee·pee /tē'pē/ *n.* var. of TEPEE

tee·ter /tē'tər/ *v.* totter; move unsteadily [dial. *titter*]

teeth /tēTH/ *n. pl.* of TOOTH

teethe /tēTH/ *v.* (**teethed, teeth·ing**) grow or cut teeth

tee·to·tal /tē'tōt'l/ *adj.* of or advocating total abstinence from alcohol —**tee·to'tal·ism'**, **tee·to'tal·er** or **tee·to'tal·ler** *n.* [reduplication of TOTAL]

Tef·lon /tef'län/ *n. Tdmk.* nonstick coating used on kitchen utensils, etc. [fr. tetra-, fluor-, -on]

Te·gu·ci·gal·pa /təgōō'sigal'pə, -gäl'-/ *n.* capital of Honduras. Pop. 608,100

Teh·ran /tā'(ə)ran', -rän'/ *n.* (also **Teheran,** pronunc. same) capital of Iran. Pop. 6,042,600

Teil·hard de Char·din /tā·yär' də SHärdän'/, **Pierre** 1881–1955; French Jesuit philosopher

Te Ka·na·wa /tā kä′nəwə/, **Kiri** 1944– ; New Zealand operatic soprano

tel. *abbr.* telephone

Tel A·viv-Jaf·fa /tel′ əvēv′ jäf′ə/ *n.* (also **Tel Aviv** or **Tel Aviv-Yafo**) city in Israel. Pop. 321,700

tele- *comb. form* 1 at or to a distance (*telekinesis, telescope*) 2 television (*telecast*) 3 by telephone (*telemarketing*) [Gk *tēle* far off]

tel·e·cast /tel′əkast′/ *n.* 1 television broadcast —*v.* 2 transmit by television —**tel′e·cast′er** *n.*

tel·e·com·mu·ni·ca·tion /tel′əkəmyōō′nikā′ SHən/ *n.* 1 communication over a distance by circuits using cable, fiber optics, satellites, radio, etc. 2 (usu. *pl.*) technology of this

tel·e·com·mute /tel′ikəmyōōt′/ *v.* (**·mut·ed, ·mut·ing**) work, esp. at home, communicating with one's employer, etc., electronically by computer, fax, telephone, etc.

tel·e·con′fer·ence *n.* conference with participants linked by telephone, etc. —**tel′e·con′fer·enc·ing** *n.*

tel·e·gram /tel′əgram/ *n.* message sent by telegraph and delivered in printed form

tel·e·graph *n.* 1 device or system for transmitting messages or signals to a distance, esp. by making and breaking an electrical connection —*v.* 2 send a message by telegraph to 3 send or communicate by telegraph 4 give advance indication of (*telegraphed his punch*) —**tel′e·graph′ic** *adj.* 1 of or by telegraphs or telegrams 2 economically worded —**tel′e·graph′i·cal·ly** *adv.*

te·leg·ra·phy /təleg′rəfē/ *n.* communication by telegraph —**te·leg′ra·phist** /-fist/ *n.*

tel·e·ki·ne·sis /tel′əkinē′səs/ *n.* supposed paranormal force moving objects at a distance —**tel′e·ki·net′ic** /-net′ik/ *adj.* [Gk *kinein* move]

tel·e·mar·ket·ing *n.* marketing by unsolicited telephone calls

te·lem·e·try /təlem′ətrē/ *n.* process of recording the readings of an instrument and transmitting them by radio —**te·lem′e·ter** *n.*

tel·e·pa·thy /təlep′əTHē/ *n.* supposed paranormal communication of thoughts —**tel·e·path′ic** /-paTH′ik/ *adj.*; **tel·e·path′i·cal·ly** *adv.*

tel·e·phone /tel′əfōn/ *n.* 1 apparatus for transmitting and receiving sound (esp. speech) over a distance, esp. by using optical or electrical signals 2 handset, etc., used in this 3 system of communication using a network of telephones —*v.* (**·phoned, ·phon·ing**) 4 speak to or send a (message) by telephone 5 make a telephone call —**tel′e·phon′ic** /-fän′ik/ *adj.*; **tel′e·phon′i·cal·ly** *adv.*

tel′e·phone booth′ *n.* booth, etc., with a telephone for public use

te·leph·o·ny /təlef′ənē/ *n.* transmission of sound by telephone

tel·e·pho·to /tel′əfō′tō/ *n.* (*pl.* **·tos**) (in full **tel′e·pho′to lens′**) lens used in telephotography

tel·e·pho·tog′ra·phy *n.* photographing of distant objects with a system of lenses to magnify the image —**tel′e·pho′to·graph′ic** *adj.*

Tel·e·Promp·Ter /tel′əpräm(p)′tər/ *n.* *Tdmk.* device used for television scripts, speeches, etc., that continuously displays the text to be read by the speaker

tel·e·scope /tel′əskōp/ *n.* 1 optical instrument using lenses or mirrors to magnify distant objects 2 RADIO TELESCOPE —*v.* (**·scoped, ·scop·ing**) 3 press or drive (sections of a tube, etc.) together so that one slides into another 4 be capable of closing in this way 5 compress in space or time —**tel·e·scop·ic** /tel′əskäp′ik/ *adj.*; **tel′e·scop′i·cal·ly** *adv.*

tel·e·thon /tel′əTHän′/ *n.* long television program, esp. to raise money for charity [fr. TELE-, MARATHON]

Tel·e·type /tel′ətīp/ *n.* *Tdmk.* telegraphic apparatus for direct exchange of printed messages

tel·e·vise /tel′əvīz′/ *v.* (**·vised, ·vis·ing**) broadcast on television

tel·e·vi·sion /tel′əviZHən/ *n.* 1 system for reproducing on a screen visual images transmitted (usu. with sound) by broadcast or cable 2 (in full **tel′e·vi·sion set′**) device with a screen for receiving these signals 3 television broadcasting

tel·ex /tel′eks/ *n.* 1 system of telegraphy for printed messages using a public telecommunications network —*v.* 2 communicate by telex [fr. *teletypewriter* + EXCHANGE]

tell /tel/ *v.* (**told, tell·ing**) 1 relate in speech or writing 2 make known; express in words (*tell me your name*) 3 reveal or signify to (a person) (*your face tells me everything*) 4a divulge information, etc.; reveal a secret, the truth, etc. b (foll. by *on*) *Colloq.* inform against 5 instruct; order (*tell them to wait*) 6 assure (*it's true, I tell you*) 7 decide; distinguish (*tell one from the other*) 8 produce a noticeable effect or influence (*strain told on me*) 9 tell apart distinguish between 10 tell off upbraid; scold 11 tell tales make known another person's faults, etc. [OE, rel. to TALE]

tell·er /tel′ər/ *n.* 1 person working at the counter of a bank, etc. 2 person who tells esp. stories (*teller of tales*)

Tel·ler /tel′ər/, **Edward** 1908– ; Hungarian-born US nuclear physicist

tell′ing *adj.* having a marked effect; striking; impressive —**tell′ing·ly** *adv.*

tell′tale′ *n.* 1 person who reveals secrets about another 2 that reveals or betrays (*telltale smile*) 3 automatic monitoring or registering device

tel·lu·ri·um /telōōr′ēəm/ *n.* rare, lustrous, silver-white element used in semiconductors; *symb.* Te —**tel·lu′ric** *adj.* [L *tellus -ur-* earth]

te·mer·i·ty /təmer′ətē/ *n.* rashness; audacity [L *temere* rashly]

temp /temp/ *Colloq.* *n.* 1 temporary employee, esp. a secretary —*v.* 2 work as a temp [abbr.]

temp. *abbr.* 1 temperature 2 temporary

Tem·pe /tem′pē/ *n.* city in Ariz. Pop. 141,865

tem·per /tem′pər/ *n.* 1 mental disposition; mood 2 irritation; anger (*fit of temper*) 3 tendency to lose one's temper (*have a temper*) 4 composure; calmness (*lose one's temper*) 5 hardness or elasticity of metal —*v.* 6 bring (metal or clay) to a proper hardness or consistency 7 moderate (*temper justice with mercy*) [L *temperare* mingle]

tem·per·a /tem′p(ə)rə/ *n.* 1 method of painting using an emulsion, e.g., of pigment with egg yolk and water, esp. on canvas 2 this emulsion [It]

tem·per·a·ment /tem′prəmənt, -pər-/ *n.* person's or animal's nature and character [L, rel. to TEMPER]

tem·per·a·men·tal /tem′prəmen′təl, -pər-/ *adj.* 1 of temperament 2 (of a person) unreliable; moody —**tem′per·a·men′tal·ly** *adv.*

tem·per·ance /tem′p(ə)rəns/ *n.* 1 moderation, esp. in eating and drinking 2 abstinence, esp. total, from alcohol [L, rel. to TEMPER]

tem·per·ate /tem′p(ə)rət/ *adj.* 1 avoiding excess 2 moderate 3 (of a region or climate) mild [L, rel. to TEMPER]

tem·per·a·ture /tem′prəCHər/ *n.* 1 measured or perceived degree of heat or cold of a thing, region, etc. 2 body temperature above normal (*have a temperature*) [L, rel. to TEMPER]

tem·pest /tem′pist/ *n.* violent storm —**tem·pes·tu·ous** /tempes′CHŌŌəs/; **tem·pes′tu·ous·ly** *adv.* [L *tempus* time]

tem·plate /tem′plit, -plāt′/ *n.* piece of thin board or metal plate used as a pattern in cutting, drilling, etc. [orig. *templet*, dim. of *temple*, device in a loom to keep the cloth stretched]

tem·ple¹ /tem′pəl/ *n.* building for the worship of a god or gods [L *templum*]

tem·ple² *n.* flat part of either side of the head between the forehead and the ear [Fr fr. L]

tem·po /tem′pō/ *n.* (*pl.* ·**pos** *or* ·**pi** /-pē/) 1 speed at which music is or should be played 2 rate or pace of activity, movement, etc. [L *tempus por-* time]

tem·po·ral /tem′p(ə)rəl/ *adj.* 1 worldly as opposed to spiritual; secular 2 of time [L *tempus -por-* time]

tem·po·rar·y /tem′pərer′ē/ *adj.* 1 lasting or meant to last only for a limited time —*n.* (*pl.* ·**ies**) 2 person employed temporarily —**tem′po·rar′i·ly** *adv.*; **tem′po·rar′i·ness** *n.*

tem·po·rize /tem′pərīz′/ *v.* (·**rized**, ·**riz·ing**) 1 avoid committing oneself so as to gain time; procrastinate 2 comply temporarily; adopt a timeserving policy

tempt /tem(p)t/ *v.* 1 entice or incite (a person) to do what is wrong or forbidden 2 allure; attract 3 risk provoking (fate, etc.) —**tempt′er**, **tempt′ress** *n.* [L *temptare* try; test]

temp·ta·tion /tem(p)tā′SHən/ *n.* 1 tempting or being tempted; incitement, esp. to wrongdoing 2 alluring thing or course of action

tempt′ing *adj.* attractive; inviting —**tempt′ing·ly** *adv.*

tem·pu·ra /tem′pərə, tempŏŏr′ə/ *n.* Japanese dish of fish, shellfish, etc., fried in batter [Japan]

ten /ten/ *adj. & n.* 1 one more than nine 2 symbol for this (10, x, X) 3 **ten to one** very probably [OE]

ten·a·ble /ten′əbəl/ *adj.* maintainable or defensible against attack or objection —**ten′a·bil′i·ty** /-bil′itē/ *n.* [Fr *tenir* hold]

te·na·cious /tənā′SHəs/ *adj.* 1 keeping a firm hold 2 persistent; resolute 3 (of memory) retentive —**te·na′cious·ly** *adv.*; **te·nac′i·ty** /nas′ətē/ *n.* [L *tenax -acis* fr. *tenere* hold]

ten·an·cy /ten′ənsē/ *n.* (*pl.* ·**cies**) 1 status of or possession as a tenant 2 duration of this

ten·ant /ten′ənt/ *n.* 1 person who rents land

or property from a landlord 2 occupant of a place [Fr, rel. to TENABLE]

Ten′ Com·mand′ments *n. pl.* (prec. by *the*) rules of conduct given by God to Moses (Exod. 20:1–17)

tend¹ /tend/ *v.* 1 be apt or incline (to) 2 be moving; hold a course (*tends in our direction*) [L *tendere* tens- or tent- stretch]

tend² *v.* take care of; look after [fr. ATTEND]

ten·den·cy /ten′dənsē/ *n.* (*pl.* ·**cies**) leaning; inclination [MedL, rel. to TEND¹]

ten·den·tious /tenden′SHəs/ *adj.* calculated to promote a particular cause or viewpoint; biased —**ten·den′tious·ly** *adv.*; **ten·den′tious·ness** *n.*

ten·der¹ /ten′dər/ *adj.* 1 easily cut or chewed; not tough 2 susceptible to pain or grief; compassionate 3 sensitive; fragile; delicate 4 loving; affectionate 5 (of age) immature (*of tender years*) —**ten′der·ly** *adv.*; **ten′der·ness** *n.* [L *tener*]

tend·er² *v.* 1 offer; present (one's services, resignation, payment, etc.) —*n.* 2 offer, esp. in writing, to execute work or supply goods at a stated price [Fr, rel. to TEND¹]

tend·er³ *n.* 1 person who looks after people or things 2 supply ship attending a larger one, etc. 3 railroad car coupled to a steam locomotive to carry fuel and water [fr. TEND²]

ten′der-heart′ed *adj.* easily moved; compassionate —**ten′der-heart′ed·ly** *adv.*; **ten′der-heart′ed·ness** *n.*

ten′der·ize *v.* (·**ized**, ·**iz·ing**) make (esp. meat) tender by beating, hanging, marinating, etc. —**ten′der·iz′er** *n.*

ten′der·loin *n.* tender cut of beef or pork loin

ten·don /ten′dən/ *n.* cord of strong connective tissue attaching a muscle to a bone, etc. [L *tendere* stretch]

ten·dril /ten′drəl/ *n.* slender, leafless shoot by which some climbing plants cling [prob. fr. Fr *tendrillon*]

ten·e·ment /ten′əmənt/ *n.* (also **ten′e·ment house′**) overcrowded or run-down apartment house [L *tenere* hold]

ten·et /ten′it/ *n.* doctrine; principle [L: he holds]

ten′fold′ *adj. & adv.* 1 ten times as much or as many 2 consisting of ten parts

Tenn. abbr. for Tennessee

Ten·nes·see /ten′əsē′/ *n.* state in the S central US. Capital: Nashville. Pop. 4,877,185. Abbr. **Tenn.**; **TN** —**Ten′nes·se′an** *n. & adj.*

Ten′nes·see′ Riv′er *n.* river rising in Tenn., flowing 650 mi. SW to the Ohio River

ten·nis /ten′is/ *n.* game in which two or four players strike a ball with rackets over a net stretched across a court [prob. Fr *tenez* take! (as a server's call)]

ten′nis el′bow *n.* elbow strain and inflammation caused by overuse

Ten·ny·son /ten′əsən/, **Alfred, Lord** 1809–92; English poet

ten·on /ten′ən/ *n.* wooden projection made for insertion into a cavity, esp. a mortise, in another piece [L, rel. to TENOR]

ten·or /ten′ər/ *n.* 1 **a** male singing voice between baritone and alto or countertenor **b** singer with this voice 2 drift or general meaning; purport 3 prevailing course, esp. of a person's life or habits [L *tenere* hold]

tense[1] /tens/ *adj.* 1 stretched tight; strained 2 causing tenseness (*tense moment*) —*v.* (**tensed, tens·ing**) 3 make or become tense —**tense′ly** *adv.*; **tense′ness** *n.* [L *tensus*, rel. to TEND[1]]

tense[2] *n.* form of a verb indicating the time (also the continuance or completeness) of the action, etc. [L *tempus* time]

ten·sile /ten′sɪl/ *adj.* 1 of tension 2 capable of being stretched —**ten·sil′i·ty** /-sil′ətē/ *n.* [MedL, rel. to TENSE[1]]

ten·sion /ten′shən/ *n.* 1 stretching or being stretched; tenseness 2 mental strain or emotional suspense; edginess 3 strained (political, social, etc.) state or relationship 4 stress produced by forces pulling apart 5 voltage (*high tension; low tension*) [L, rel. to TEND[1]]

tent /tent/ *n.* 1 portable canvas, etc., shelter or dwelling supported by poles and ground pegs 2 tentlike enclosure [L, rel. to TEND[1]]

ten·ta·cle /ten′tikal/ *n.* long, slender, flexible appendage of an (esp. invertebrate) animal, used for feeling, grasping, or moving —**ten′ta·cled** *adj.* [L, rel. to TEMPT]

ten·ta·tive /ten′tətiv/ *adj.* 1 experimental 2 hesitant or provisional (*tentative suggestion*) —**ten′ta·tive·ly** *adv.*; **ten′ta·tive·ness** *n.* [MedL, rel. to TEMPT]

ten·ter·hook /ten′tərhŏŏk/ *n.* 1 hook to which cloth is fastened for stretching 2 **on tenterhooks** in a state of anxiety or uncertainty

tenth /tentH/ *adj. & n.* 1 next after ninth 2 any of ten equal parts of a thing —**tenth′ly** *adv.*

ten·u·ous /ten′yŏŏəs/ *adj.* 1 slight; insubstantial; oversubtle 2 thin; slender; small 3 rarefied —**te·nu·i·ty** /ten(y)ŏŏ′ətē/ *n.*; **ten′u·ous·ly** *adv.* [L *tenuis*]

ten·ure /ten′yər/ *n.* 1 right or title under which (esp. real) property is held 2 period of this 3 guaranteed permanent employment, esp. as a professor or teacher —**ten′ured** *adj.* [L *tenere*]

te·pee /tē′pē/ *n.* (also **tee′pee**) N American Indian's conical tent [Dakota]

Te·pic /tāpēk′/ *n.* capital of the Mexican state of Nayarit. Pop. 238,100

tep·id /tep′id/ *adj.* 1 lukewarm 2 unenthusiastic —**te·pid′i·ty** /-ətē/ *n.*; **tep′id·ly** *adv.* [L]

te·qui·la /təkē′lə/ *n.* Mexican liquor made from an agave [for a town in Mexico]

tera- *comb. form* denoting a factor of 10^{12} (*terabyte*) [Gk *teras* monster]

ter·a·byte /ter′əbīt/ *n. Comp.* one trillion bytes

ter·bi·um /tər′bēəm/ *n.* silvery metallic element of the lanthanide series; *symb.* **Tb** [*Ytterby* in Sweden]

ter·cen·te·nar·y /tər′senten′ərē/ *n.* (*pl.* **-ies**) 1 three-hundredth anniversary 2 celebration of this [L *ter*: three times]

ter·eph·thal·ate /ter′efthal′āt, -it, tərəf′thəlāt′/ *n. Chem.* salt or ester of terephthalic acid

ter′eph·thal′ic ac′id /ter′efthal′ik, tər′-/ *n.*

Chem. white crystalline solid, not soluble in water, used to make resins and fibers

Te·re·sa, Moth·er /tərē′sə, -rā′zə/ (born **Ag·nes Gonxha Bojaxhiu**) 1910– ; Albanian-born Roman Catholic nun and missionary; Nobel prize 1979

term /tərm/ *n.* 1 word for a definite concept, esp. specialized 2 (*pl.*) language used; mode of expression (*in no uncertain terms*) 3 (*pl.*) relationship (*on good terms*) 4 (*pl.*) a stipulations (*accepts your terms*) b charge; price (*reasonable terms*) 5 limited, usu. specified, period (*term of five years; in the short term*) 6 *Math.* each of the quantities in a ratio, series, or expression 7 completion of a normal length of pregnancy —*v.* 8 call; name (*was termed a bigot*) 9 **come to terms with** reconcile oneself to (a difficulty, etc.) 10 **in terms of** in the language peculiar to; referring to —**term′ly** *adj. & adv.* [L TERMINUS]

ter·ma·gant /tər′məgənt/ *n.* overbearing woman; virago [Fr *Tervagan* fr. It]

ter·mi·na·ble /tər′mənəbəl/ *adj.* able to be terminated

ter·mi·nal /tər′mənəl/ *adj.* 1a (of a condition or disease) fatal b dying 2 of or forming a limit or end point —*n.* 3 terminating thing; extremity 4 terminus for planes, trains, or long-distance buses 5 point of connection for closing an electric circuit 6 apparatus for the transmission of messages to and from a computer, communications system, etc. —**ter′mi·nal·ly** *adv.* [L, rel. to TERMINUS]

ter·mi·nate /tər′mənāt′/ *v.* (**·nat·ed, ·nat·ing**) 1 bring or come to an end 2 (foll. by *in*) (of a word) end in (a specified letter, etc.) —**ter′mi·na′tion** *n.*

ter·mi·nol·o·gy /tər′mənäl′əjē/ *n.* (*pl.* **-gies**) 1 system of specialized terms 2 science of the use of terms —**ter′mi·no·log′i·cal** /-nəläj′ikəl/ *adj.* [Ger, rel. to TERMINUS]

ter·mi·nus /tər′mənəs/ *n.* (*pl.* **·ni** /-nī/ or **·nus·es**) end of a bus route, pipeline, etc. [L: end]

ter·mite /tər′mīt′/ *n.* antlike social insect destructive to timber [L *termes -mitis*]

tern /tərn/ *n.* marine gull-like bird with a long, forked tail [Scand]

terr. *abbr.* 1 terrace 2 territory

ter·race /ter′əs/ *n.* 1 flat area made on a slope for cultivation 2 patio 3 flat roof of a building projection used as a patio, etc., for an apartment —*v.* (**·raced, ·rac·ing**) 4 form into or provide with a terrace or terraces [L *terra* earth]

ter·ra cot·ta /ter′ə kät′ə/ *n.* unglazed usu. brownish-red earthenware [It: baked earth]

ter·ra fir·ma /ter′ə fər′mə/ *n.* dry land; firm ground [L]

ter·rain /tərān′/ *n.* tract of land, esp. in geographical or military contexts [L, rel. to *terra* land]

ter·ra·pin /ter′əpin/ *n.* N American edible freshwater turtle [Algonquian]

ter·rar·i·um /tərer′ēəm/ *n.* (*pl.* **·ums** or **·ri·a** /-rēə/) usu. glass enclosure for plants or small land animals [L *terra* earth, after *aquarium*]

ter·raz·zo /tərät′sō, -raz′ō/ *n.* smooth flooring material of stone chips set in concrete [It: terrace]

ter·res·tri·al /təres´trēəl/ *adj.* **1** of or on the earth; earthly **2** of or on dry land [L, rel. to *terra* land]

ter·ri·ble /ter´əbəl/ *adj.* **1** very great or bad (*terrible bore*) **2** very incompetent (*terrible at math*) **3** causing or likely to cause terror; dreadful [L *terrere* frighten]

ter·ri·bly *adv.* **1** very; extremely **2** in a terrible manner

ter·ri·er /ter´ēər/ *n.* small dog of various breeds originally used to ferret out game [Fr *chien terrier* dog that chases to earth]

ter·rif·ic /tərif´ik/ *adj.* **1** huge; intense (*terrific noise*) **2** excellent (*did a terrific job*) **3** causing terror —**ter·rif´i·cal·ly** *adv.* [L, rel. to TERRIBLE]

ter·ri·fy /ter´əfī/ *v.* (**·fied, ·fy·ing**) fill with terror —**ter´ri·fy·ing** *adj.*; **ter´ri·fy·ing·ly** *adv.*

ter·ri·to·ri·al /ter´ətôr´ēəl/ *adj.* **1** of territory or a district **2** tending to defend one's territory —**ter´ri·to´ri·al·ly** *adv.* [fr. TERRITORY]

ter·ri·to·ry /ter´ətôr´ē/ *n.* (**·ries**) **1** extent of land under a ruler or government **2** (*cap.*) division of a country, esp. one not yet having full rights **3** sphere of action or interest; province **4** designated business or sales area **5** animal's or human's defended space or area [L *terra* land]

ter·ror /ter´ər/ *n.* **1** extreme fear **2a** terrifying person, thing, or force **b** formidable or troublesome person or thing, esp. a child [L *terrere* frighten]

ter´ror·ist *n.* person using esp. organized violence against a government, etc. —**ter´ror·ism´** /-iz´əm/ *n.* [Fr, rel. to TERROR]

ter·ror·ize /ter´ərīz/ *v.* (**·ized, ·iz·ing**) **1** fill with terror **2** use terrorism against —**ter´ror·i·za´tion** *n.*

ter·ry /ter´ē/ *n.* looped pile fabric used esp. for towels

terse /tərs/ *adj.* (**ters·er, ters·est**) **1** brief; concise **2** curt; abrupt —**terse´ly** *adv.*; **terse´ness** *n.* [L *tergere ters-* wipe]

ter·ti·ar·y /tər´shēer´ē, -shərē/ *adj.* **1** third in order or rank, etc. **2** (*cap.*) of the first period in the Cenozoic era —*n.* **3** (*cap.*) Tertiary period [L *tertius* third]

tes·la /tes´lə/ *n.* unit of magnetic induction [for N. TESLA]

Tes·la /tes´lə/, **Nikola** 1856–1943; US physicist and inventor

tes·sel·lat·ed /tes´əlā´tid/ *adj.* **1** of or resembling a mosaic **2** regularly checkered —**tes´sel·la´tion** /-SHən/ *n.* [L *tessellatus* mosaic]

test /test/ *n.* **1** critical examination or trial of a person's or thing's qualities **2** means, procedure, or standard for so appraising **3** oral or written examination —*v.* **4** cause to undergo a test **5** try or burden severely **6** *Chem.* examine by means of a reagent —**test´a·ble** *adj.* [OFr fr. L *testu(m)* earthenware pot (for its later use in assaying gold)]

Test. *abbr.* Testament

tes·ta·ment /tes´təmənt/ *n.* **1** will (esp. last will and testament) **2** evidence; proof **3** *Bibl.* a covenant; dispensation **b** (*cap.*) division of the Bible (see OLD TESTAMENT, NEW TESTAMENT) —**tes´ta·men´ta·ry** /-men´terē/ *adj.* [L *testamentum* will, rel. to TESTATE]

tes·tate /tes´tāt/ *adj.* having left a valid will at death [L *testari* testify, fr. *testis* witness]

tes·ta·tor /tes´tā´tər/ *n.* (*fem.* **tes·ta·trix** /testā´triks/) (esp. deceased) person who has made a will [L, rel. to TESTATE]

test´ case´ *n.* case setting a precedent for other similar cases

tes·tes /tes´tēz/ *n. pl.* of TESTIS

tes·ti·cle /tes´tikəl/ *n.* male organ that produces spermatozoa, etc., esp. one of a pair in the scrotum in man and most mammals [L, dim. of *testis* witness]

tes·ti·fy /tes´tifī´/ *v.* (**·fied, ·fy·ing**) **1** (of a person or thing) bear witness; be evidence of **2** give evidence **3** affirm; declare [L *testificari* fr. *testis* witness]

tes·ti·mo·ni·al /tes´təmō´nēəl/ *n.* **1** statement attesting to the virtues or qualifications of a person or thing; recommendation; endorsement **2** gift presented to a person (esp. in public) as a token of esteem or gratitude [Fr, rel. to TESTIMONY]

tes·ti·mo·ny /tes´təmō´nē/ *n.* (*pl.* **·nies**) **1** witness's statement under oath, etc. **2** declaration or statement of fact **3** evidence; demonstration [L *testimonium* fr. *testis* witness]

tes·tis /tes´tis/ *n.* (*pl.* **·tes**) *Anat. & Zool.* testicle [L: witness (cf. TESTICLE)]

tes·tos·ter·one /testäs´tərōn´/ *n.* male sex hormone formed in the testicles [fr. TESTIS, STEROL]

test´ tube´ *n.* thin glass tube closed at one end, used for chemical tests, etc.

test´-tube ba´by *n.* baby conceived by *in vitro* fertilization

tes·ty *adj.* (**·ti·er, ·ti·est**) irritable; touchy —**tes´ti·ly** *adv.*; **tes´ti·ness** *n.* [MFr *testu* headstrong]

tet·a·nus /tet´nəs, tet´n-əs/ *n.* bacterial disease causing painful spasm of the voluntary muscles [Gk *tetanos* spasm]

tête-à-tête /tāt´ ə tāt´/ *n.* **1** private conversation between two persons —*adv.* **2** privately without a third person [Fr, literally 'head-to-head']

teth·er /teTH´ər/ *n.* **1** rope, etc., confining a grazing animal —*v.* **2** tie with a tether **3** **at the end of one's tether** at the limit of one's patience, resources, etc. [ON]

tetra- *comb. form* four [Gk *tettares* four]

tet·ra·he·dron /te´trahē´drən/ *n.* (*pl.* **·drons** or **·dra** /-drə/) four-sided solid; triangular pyramid —**tet´ra·he´dral** *adj.* [Gk *hedra* base]

TETRAHEDRON

te·tral·o·gy /teträl´əjē, -tral´-/ *n.* (*pl.* **·gies**) group of four related novels, plays, operas, etc.

te·tram·e·ter /tetram´itər/ *n. Pros.* verse of four measures

Teu·ton /t(y)ōōt´n/ *n.* member of a Teutonic nation, esp. a German [L *Teutones*, ancient tribe of N Europe]

Teu·ton·ic /t(y)ōōtän´ik/ *adj.* **1** of the Germanic peoples or languages **2** German [L, rel. to TEUTON]

Tex. abbr. for Texas

Tex·as /tek´səs/ *n.* state in the S US on

the Mexican border. Capital: Austin. Pop. 16,986,510. Abbr. **Tex.; TX** —**Tex′an** *n.* & *adj.*

Tex-Mex /teks′ meks′/ *adj.* combining cultural elements from Texas and Mexico, as in cooking, music, etc.

text /tekst/ *n.* 1 main body of a book as distinct from notes, etc. 2 original or primary version of a book or document 3 passage from Scripture, esp. as the subject of a sermon 4 subject; theme 5 TEXTBOOK 6 written or printed matter [L *texere text-* weave]

text′book′ *n.* 1 instructional book, esp. a standard introduction to a school subject —*adj.* 2 instructively typical or exemplary

tex-tile /teks′tīl′, -tal/ *n.* 1 (often *pl.*) fabric, cloth, or fibrous material, esp. woven 2 fiber; yarn —*adj.* 3 of weaving or cloth (*textile industry*) 4 woven (*textile fabrics*) [L, rel. to TEXT]

tex-tu-al /teks′CHŌŏəl/ *adj.* of, in, or concerning a text —**tex′tu-al-ly** *adv.*

tex-ture /teks′CHər/ *n.* 1 feel or appearance of a surface or substance 2 arrangement of threads, etc., in textile fabric —**tex′tur-al** *adj.* [L, rel. to TEXT]

Th *symb.* thorium

-th *suffix* (also -eth) forming ordinal and fractional numbers from *four* onward [OE]

Thack-er-ay /THak′ərā′/, **William Makepeace** 1811–63; English novelist

Thai /tī/ *n.* (*pl.* same or -s) 1a native or national of Thailand b person of Thai descent 2 language of Thailand —*adj.* 3 of Thailand [Thai: free]

Thai-land /tī′land, -lənd/ *n.* (formerly **Siam**) kingdom in SE Asia on the Gulf of Thailand. Capital: Bangkok. Pop. 56,801,000

Tha-les /THā′lēz/ fl. early 6th cent. B.C.; Greek philosopher

tha-lid-o-mide /THəlid′əmīd′/ *n.* sedative drug found to cause fetal malformation when taken early in pregnancy

thal-li-um /THal′ēəm/ *n.* rare, soft, white metallic element; *symb.* **Tl** [Gk *thallos* green shoot]

Thames /temz/ *n.* river in S England flowing 210 mi. E, past London to the North Sea

than /THan, THən/ *conj.* introducing a comparison (*plays better than he did before; cost more than $100; you are older than he*) [OE, orig. THEN]

Thana /tän′ə/ *n.* suburb of Bombay, India. Pop. 796,600

thane /THān/ *n. Hist.* former English or Scottish noble rank [OE]

thank /THaNGk/ *v.* 1 express gratitude to 2 hold responsible (*you can thank yourself for that*) —*n.* 3 (*pl.*) a gratitude b expression of gratitude 4 (*pl.*) thank you (*thanks for your help*) 5 **thanks to** as the result of (*thanks to my foresight*) 6 **thank you** polite formula expressing gratitude [OE]

thank′ful *adj.* 1 grateful; pleased 2 expressive of thanks

thank′ful-ly *adv.* 1 in a thankful manner 2 fortunately

thank′less *adj.* 1 not expressing or feeling gratitude 2 (of a task, etc.) giving no pleasure

or profit; unappreciated —**thank′less-ly** *adv.*; **thank′less-ness** *n.*

thanks′giv′ing *n.* 1 expression of gratitude, esp. to God 2 (*cap.*, often with **Day**) fourth Thursday in November (a national holiday)

that /THat/ *demons. pron.* (*pl.* **those** /THōz/) 1 person or thing indicated, named, or understood (*I heard that; who is that in the garden?*) 2 contrasted with **this** (*this is much better than that*) 3 (esp. in relative constructions) the one, the person, etc. (*a table like that described above*) 4 (*pl.* **that**) used instead of **which** or **whom** to introduce a defining clause (*the books that you sent me; there is nothing here that matters*) —*demons. adj.* (*pl.* **those** /THōz/) 5 designating the person or thing indicated, named, understood, etc. (cf. sense 1 of *pron.*) —*adv.* 6 to such a degree; so (*have done that much*) 7 very (*not that good*) —*conj.* 8 introducing a subordinate clause indicating: **a** statement or hypothesis (*they say that he is better*) **b** purpose (*we eat that we may live*) **c** result (*am so sleepy that I cannot work*) 9 **all that** very (*not all that good*) 10 **that is** (or **that is to say**) formula introducing or following an explanation of a preceding word or words [OE]

● Usage: See note at WHICH.

thatch /THaCH/ *n.* 1 roof covering of straw, reeds, etc. —*v.* 2 cover with thatch —**thatch′er, thatch′ing** *n.* [OE]

Thatch-er /THaCH′ər/, **(Lady) Margaret** 1925– ; British politician; prime minister (1979–90)

thaw /THô/ *v.* 1 pass from a frozen into a liquid or unfrozen state 2 become warm enough to melt ice, etc. 3 become or make genial 4 cause to thaw —*n.* 5 thawing 6 warmth of weather that thaws [OE]

the /THə, THē/ *adj.* (called the definite article) 1 denoting person(s) or thing(s) already mentioned, under discussion, implied, or familiar (*gave the man a wave*) 2 describing as unique (*the Mississippi*) 3a (foll. by defining adj.) which is, who are, etc. (*Edward the Seventh*) **b** (foll. by adj. used *absol.*) denoting a class described (*from the sublime to the ridiculous*) 4 commonly known (with the stressed: *do you mean the Kipling?*) 5 indicating a following defining clause or phrase (*the book that you borrowed*) 6 speaking generically (*the cat is a mammal*) —*adv.* 7 (preceding comparatives in expressions of proportional variation) in or by that (or such a) degree (*the more the merrier*) [OE]

theat. *abbr.* theater; theatrical

the-a-ter /THē′ətər/ *n.* (also **the′a-tre**) 1 building or outdoor area for dramatic performances 2 writing and production of plays 3 event, phenomenon, etc., that is engagingly dramatic 4 room or hall for lectures, etc., with seats in tiers 5 scene or field of action (*the theater of war*) [Gk *theatron*]

the-at-ri-cal /THē:a′trikəl/ *adj.* 1 of or for the theater or acting 2 calculated for effect; showy —*n.* 3 (*pl.*) dramatic performances (*amateur theatricals*) —**the-at′ri-cal′i-ty** /-kal′itē/ *n.*; **the-at′ri-cal-ly** *adv.*

thee /THē/ *pron.* objective case of THOU[1]

theft /THeft/ *n.* act of stealing [OE, rel. to THIEF]

their /THer/ *poss. pron.* of or belonging to them [ON]

• Usage: *Their* is a possessive pronoun; *there* is an adverb meaning 'at that place'; and *they're* is a contraction of 'they are': *They're planning to leave their house in an hour and will meet us there.*

theirs /THerz/ *poss. pron.* 1 the one or ones of or belonging to them (*it is theirs; theirs are over here*) 2 of theirs of or belonging to them (*a friend of theirs*)

the·ism /THēˈizˌəm/ *n.* belief in gods or a god —**the·ist** *n.*; **the·is·tic** *adj.* [Gk *theos* god]

them /THem/ *pron.* 1 *objective case* of THEY 2 *Colloq.* they (*it's them again*) [ON]

theme /THēm/ *n.* 1 subject, topic, or recurrent focus 2 *Mus.* prominent melody in a composition 3 school exercise on a given subject —**the·mat·ic** /THēˈmatˈik/ *adj.*; **the·mat´i·cal·ly** *adv.* [Gk *thema -mat-*]

theme´ park´ *n.* amusement park organized around a unifying idea, historical period, etc.

them·selves /THəmselvz´, THem-/ *pron.* 1 *emphat. form* of THEY or THEM 2 *refl. form* of THEM 3 be themselves act in their normal, unconstrained manner 4 by themselves see *by oneself*

then /THen/ *adv.* 1 at that time 2a next; after that b and also 3a in that case (*then you should have said so*) b implying grudging or impatient concession (*all right then, if you must*) c used parenthetically to resume a narrative, etc. (*the policeman, then, knocked on the door*) —*adj.* 4 such at the time in question (*the then king*) —*n.* 5 that time (*until then*) 6 then and there immediately and on the spot [OE]

thence /THens/ *adv.* 1 from that place 2 for that reason [OE]

thence´forth´ *adv.* (also **thence´for´ward**) from that time onward

theo- *comb. form* God or god(s) [Gk *theos* god]

the·oc·ra·cy /THēˈäkˈrəsē/ *n.* (*pl.* **·cies**) form of government founding its authority on God or through a priestly order, etc. —**the·o·crat´ic** /-əkrat´ik/ *adj.*

theol. *abbr.* theological; theology

the·o·lo·gian /THēˈəlōˈjən/ *n.* expert in theology [Fr, rel. to THEOLOGY]

the·ol·o·gy /THēˈälˈəjē/ *n.* (*pl.* **·gies**) the study or a system of doctrines on divinity and religion —**the·o·log´i·cal** /-əläj´ikəl/ *adj.*; **the·o·log´i·cal·ly** *adv.* [Gk, rel. to THEO-]

the·o·rem /THēˈərəm, THēr´əm/ *n. esp. Math.* 1 general proposition that is not self-evident but is proved by reasoning 2 rule in algebra, etc., esp. one expressed by symbols or formulas [Gk *theōrein* look at]

the·o·ret·i·cal /THēˈəret´ikəl/ *adj.* 1 concerned with knowledge but not with its practical application 2 based on theory rather than experience —**the´o·ret´i·cal·ly** *adv.*

the·o·rist /THē´ərist/ *n.* holder or inventor of a theory

the·o·rize /THē´ərīz´/ *v.* (**·rized**, **·riz·ing**) evolve or indulge in theories

the·o·ry /THē´ərē, THēr´ē/ *n.* (*pl.* **·ries**) 1 supposition or system of ideas explaining something, esp. one based on general principles; abstract knowledge; speculation 2 speculative (esp. fanciful) view (*one of my pet theories*) 3 exposition of the principles of a science, etc. (*the theory of music*) 4 collection of mathematical propositions [Gk, rel. to THEOREM]

the·os·o·phy /THēˈäsˈəfē/ *n.* (*pl.* **·phies**) any of various philosophies professing to achieve knowledge of God by spiritual ecstasy, direct intuition, or special individual relations, esp. a modern movement following Hindu and Buddhist teachings and seeking universal brotherhood —**the·o·soph´i·cal** /THēˈəsäf´ikəl/ *adj.*; **the·os´o·phist** *n.* [Gk *theosophos* wise concerning God]

ther·a·peu·tic /THerˈəpyōō´tik/ *adj.* 1 of, for, or contributing to the cure of disease 2 healing; soothing —**ther´a·peu´ti·cal·ly** *adv.* [Gk *therapeuō* wait on, cure]

ther´a·peu´tics *n. pl.* (usu. treated as *sing.*) branch of medicine concerned with cures and remedies

ther·a·py /THer´əpē/ *n.* (*pl.* **·pies**) nonsurgical treatment of disease or disability —**ther´a·pist** /-pist/ *n.* [Gk *therapeia* healing]

there /THer/ *adv.* 1 in, at, or to that place or position (*lived there for a year; goes there daily*) 2 at that point (in speech, performance, writing, etc.) 3 in that respect (*I agree with you there*) 4 used for emphasis in calling attention (*you there!*) 5 used to indicate the fact or existence of something (*there is a house on the corner*) —*n.* 6 that place (*lives near there*) —*interj.* 7 expressing confirmation, triumph, etc. (*there! what did I tell you?*) 8 used to soothe a child, etc. (*there, there, never mind*) [OE]

• Usage: See note at THEIR.

there´about´ *adv.* (also **there´abouts´**) 1 near that place 2 near that number, quantity, etc.

there´af´ter *adv.* after that

there´by´ *adv.* by that means; as a result of that

there´fore´ *adv.* for that reason; accordingly; consequently

there´in´ *adv.* 1 in that place, etc. 2 in that respect

there´of´ *adv.* of that or it

there´to´ *adv.* 1 to that or it 2 in addition

there´up·on´ *adv.* 1 in consequence of that 2 immediately after that

ther·mal /THər´məl/ *adj.* 1 of, for, or producing heat 2 promoting the retention of heat —*n.* 3 rising current of warm air —**ther´mal·ly** *adv.* [Fr, rel. to THERMO-]

thermo- *comb. form* heat [Gk *thermē* heat]

ther·mo·dy·nam·ics /THərˈmōdīnam´iks/ *n. pl.* (usu. treated as *sing.*) science of the relations between heat and other forms of energy —**ther´mo·dy·nam´ic** *adj.*

ther·mom·e·ter /THə(r)mäm´ətər/ *n.* instrument for measuring temperature, as a graduated glass tube containing mercury or alcohol [Fr, rel. to THERMO-, -METER]

ther·mo·nu·cle·ar /THərˈmōn(y)ōō´klēər/ *adj.* 1 relating to the fusion of atomic nuclei at very high temperatures 2 (of weapons) using thermonuclear reactions

ther·mo·plas·tic /THərˈmōˈplas´tik/ *adj.* 1 that becomes plastic on heating and hardens on cooling —*n.* 2 thermoplastic substance

ther·mos /THər´məs/ *n.* bottle or jug with a

double wall enclosing a vacuum, used to keep liquids hot or cold [fr. Gk. rel. to THERMO- (orig. a trademark)]

ther·mo·stat /ˈTHərˈməstat/ n. device that automatically regulates or responds to temperature —**ther'mo·stat'ic** adj.; **ther·mo·stat'i·cal·ly** adv. [fr. THERMO-, Gk statos standing]

the·sau·rus /THisôrˈəs/ n. (pl. ·rus·es or ·ri /-ī′, -ē′/) book that categorizes or lists synonyms and related concepts [fr. L to THEASURE]

these /THēz/ pron. & adj. pl. of THIS

the·sis /THēˈsis/ n. (pl. ·ses /-sēz′/) 1 proposition to be maintained or proved 2 dissertation, esp. by a candidate for a higher degree [Gk: putting]

thes·pi·an /THesˈpēən/ (often cap.) adj. 1 of drama —n. 2 actor or actress [for Thespis, a Greek tragedian]

Thes·sa·lo·ni·ke /THesˈəlônēˈkē/ n. (also **Sa·lon'ika**) seaport in Greece. Pop. 378,000

the·ta /THāˈtə/ n. eighth letter of the Greek alphabet (Θ, θ) [Gk]

they /THā/ pron. (obj. **them**; poss. **their**, **theirs**) 1 pl. of HE, SHE, IT 2 people in general (so they say) 3 those in authority (they have raised taxes) [ON]

• Usage: See notes at EVERYBODY; THEIR.

they'd /THād/ v. contr. 1 they had 2 they would

they'll /THāl/ v. contr. 1 they will 2 they shall

they're /THer/ v. contr. they are

they've /THāv/ v. contr. they have

thi·a·mine /THīˈəmin, -mēn′/ n. (also **thi'a·min**) B vitamin found in unrefined cereals, beans, and liver [Gk theion sulfur, amin fr. VITAMIN]

thick /THik/ adj. 1 of great or specified extent between opposite surfaces 2 (of a line, etc.) broad; not fine 3 arranged closely; crowded together; dense 4 densely permeated (air thick with smoke) 5a firm in consistency; containing much solid matter b made of thick material (a thick coat) 6 muddy; cloudy; impenetrable by sight 7 stupid 8a (of a voice) indistinct b (of an accent) very marked —n. 9 thick part of anything —adv. 10 thickly 11 **in the thick of** at the busiest part of 12 **lay it on thick** praise extravagantly; flatter 13 **through thick and thin** under all conditions; in spite of all difficulties —**thick'ish** adj.; **thick'ly** adv. [OE]

thick·en v. 1 make or become thick or thicker 2 become more complicated (plot thickens) —**thick'en·er** n.

thick·et /THikˈit/ n. tangle of shrubs or trees [OE, rel. to THICK]

thick·ness n. 1 being thick 2 extent of this 3 layer of material

thick'set' adj. 1 heavily or solidly built 2 set or growing close together

thick'-skinned' adj. 1 having a thick skin or rind 2 not sensitive to criticism

thief /THēf/ n. (pl. **thieves** /THēvz/) person who steals, esp. secretly [OE]

thieve /THēv/ v. (**thieved, thiev·ing**) 1 be a thief 2 steal (a thing) —**thiev'ish** adj. [OE, rel. to THIEF]

thiev·er·y /THēvˈərē/ n. stealing

thigh /THī/ n. part of the leg between the hip and the knee [OE]

thigh'bone' n. FEMUR

thim·ble /THimˈbəl/ n. metal or plastic cap worn to protect the finger and push the needle in sewing —**thim'ble·ful** n. (pl. ·fuls) [OE, rel. to THUMB]

Thim·phu /THimpōō′/ n. official capital of Bhutan. Pop. 15,000. See also PARO

thin /THin/ adj. (**thin·ner, thin·nest**) 1 having opposite surfaces close together; of small thickness 2 (of a line) narrow or fine 3 made of thin material (thin dress) 4 lean; not plump 5 not dense or copious (thin hair) 6 of slight consistency 7 weak; lacking an important ingredient (thin blood; a thin voice) 8 (of an excuse, etc.) flimsy or transparent —adv. 9 so as to be thin (cut the bread very thin) —v. (**thinned, thin·ning**) 10 make or become thin or thinner 11 make or become less dense, crowded, or numerous 12 **thin on top** balding —**thin'ly** adv.; **thin'ness** n.; **thin'nish** adj. [OE]

thine /THīn/ poss. pron. 1 of or belonging to thee 2 (before a vowel) THY [OE]

thing /THiNG/ n. 1 entity, idea, action, etc., that exists or may be thought about or perceived 2 inanimate material object 3 unspecified item (a few things to buy) 4 act, idea, or utterance (silly thing to do) 5 event (unfortunate thing to happen) 6 fashion (latest thing in hats) 7 Colloq. one's main interest or specialty (not my thing) 8 (pl.) personal belongings or clothing (where are my things?) 9 (pl.) affairs in general (not in the nature of things) 10 (pl.) circumstances; prospects (things look good) 11 **have a thing about** Colloq. be obsessed or prejudiced about [OE]

think /THiNGk/ v. (**thought, think·ing**) 1 be of the opinion 2 judge or consider (is thought to be a fraud) 3 exercise the mind 4 (foll. by of or about) consider; imagine 5 have a half-formed intention (I think I'll stay) 6 **think again** revise one's plans or opinions 7 **think aloud** utter one's thoughts as they occur 8 **think better of** change one's mind about (an intention) after reconsideration 9 **think little (or nothing) of** consider to be insignificant 10 **think much (or a lot or highly) of** have a high opinion of 11 **think out** consider carefully 12 **think over** reflect upon in order to reach a decision 13 **think through** reflect fully upon (a problem, etc.) 14 **think twice** use careful consideration, avoid hasty action, etc. 15 **think up** devise —**think'er** n. [OE]

think'ing adj. 1 intelligent; rational —n. 2 opinion or judgment

think' tank' n. body or institute of experts fostering problem-solving advice and progressive ideas

thin·ner /THinˈər/ n. solvent for diluting paint, etc.

thin'-skinned' adj. 1 having a thin skin or rind 2 sensitive to criticism

third /THərd/ adj. & n. 1 next after second 2 each of three equal parts of a thing —**third'ly** adv. [OE, rel. to THREE]

• Usage: See note at FIRST.

third' de·gree' n. severe or harsh treatment in questioning to obtain information or a confession

third' per'son n. Gram. see PERSON

third´-rate´ *adj.* inferior; very poor

Third´ Reich´ /rīk/ *n.* Nazi regime, 1933–45

Third´ World´ *n.* developing countries of Asia, Africa, and Latin America

thirst /THərst/ *n.* 1 need to drink; discomfort caused by this 2 desire; craving —*v.* 3 feel thirst 4 have a strong desire —**thirst´y** *adj.*; **thirst´i·ly** *adv.*; **thirst´i·ness** *n.* [OE]

thir·teen /THər´tēn´/ *adj. & n.* 1 one more than twelve 2 symbol for this (13, xiii, XIII) —**thir·teenth´** *adj. & n.* [OE, rel. to THREE]

thir·ty /THər´tē/ *adj. & n.* (*pl.* **·ties**) 1 three times ten 2 symbol for this (30, xxx, XXX) 3 (*pl.*) numbers from 30 to 39, esp. in years —**thir´ti·eth** /-əTH/ *adj. & n.* [OE, rel. to THREE]

this /THis/ *demons. pron.* (*pl.* these /THēz/) 1 person or thing close at hand or indicated or already named or understood (*can you see this?; this is my cousin*) 2 (contrasted with *that*) the person or thing nearer to hand or more immediately in mind —*demons. adj.* (*pl.* these /THēz/) 3 designating the person or thing close at hand, etc. (cf. senses 1, 2 of *pron.*) 4 (of time) the present or current (*am busy all this week*) 5 *Colloq.* (in narrative) designating a person or thing previously unmentioned (*then up came this policeman*) —*adv.* 6 to the degree or extent indicated (*knew him when he was this high*) 7 **this and that** various unspecified things [OE]

THISTLE

this·tle /THis´əl/ *n.* prickly plant, usu. with globular heads of purple flowers [OE]

thith·er /THĬTH´ər, THĬTH´ər/ *adv.* to or toward that place [OE]

tho´ /THō/ *conj.* (also tho) var. of THOUGH

Thom·as /täm´əs/, Dylan 1914–53; Welshborn poet

Thom·as à Kem·pis see KEMPIS, THOMAS À

thong /THÔNG, THĔNG/ *n.* narrow strip of hide or leather [OE]

Thor /THôr/ *n. Myth.* Norse god of thunder and war

tho·rax /THôr´aks´/ *n.* (*pl.* **·rax·es** or **ra·ces** /-rəsēz´/) *Anat. & Zool.* part of the trunk between the neck and the abdomen —**tho·rac´ic** /-ras´ik/ *adj.* [L fr. Gk]

Tho·reau /THərō´, THôr´ō/, Henry David 1817–62; US writer

tho·ri·um /THôr´ēəm/ *n. Chem.* radioactive metallic element; *symb.* Th [THOR]

thorn /THôrn/ *n.* 1 sharp-pointed projection on a plant 2 thorn-bearing shrub or tree [OE]

thorn´y *adj.* (**·i·er**, **·i·est**) 1 having many thorns 2 problematic; causing disagreement ╌**thorn´i·ly** *adv.*; **thorn´i·ness** *n.* [OE, rel. to THORN]

thor·ough /THər´ō, THə´rō/ *adj.* 1 complete and unqualified; not superficial 2 acting or done with great care and completeness 3 absolute (*thorough nuisance*) —**thor´ough·ly** *adv.*; **thor´ough·ness** *n.* [rel. to THROUGH]

thor´ough·bred´ *adj.* 1 of pure breed —*n.* 2 thoroughbred animal, esp. (*cap.*) a horse

thor´ough·fare´ *n.* road or path open at both ends, esp. a highway

thor´ough·go´ing *adj.* thorough; complete

those /THōz/ *pron. & adj. pl.* of THAT

thou¹ /THOU/ *pron.* (*obj.* thee /THē/; *poss.* thy or thine; *pl.* ye or you) *Archaic.* second person singular pronoun [OE]

thou² *n.* (*pl.* same or **-s**) *Colloq.* thousand [abbr.]

though /THō/ (also tho´ or tho) *conj.* 1 despite the fact that; in spite of being 2 (introducing a possibility) even if (*ask him, though he may refuse*) 3 and yet; nevertheless —*adv.* 4 however; all the same [ON]

thought¹ /THôt/ *n.* 1 process or power of thinking; faculty of reason 2 way of thinking associated with a particular time, group, etc. 3 attention, reflection, or consideration 4 idea, conception, or piece of reasoning 5 (usu. *pl.*) what one is thinking; one's opinion [OE, rel. to THINK]

thought² *v. past and past part.* of THINK

thought´ful *adj.* 1 engaged in or given to rumination or meditation 2 having reflective or intellectual substance 3 considerate —**thought´ful·ly** *adv.*; **thought´ful·ness** *n.*

thought´less *adj.* 1 careless of consequences or of others' feelings 2 due to lack of thought —**thought´less·ly** *adv.*; **thought´less·ness** *n.*

thou·sand /THOU´zənd/ *adj. & n.* (*pl.* **thousands** or, in sense 1, **thousand**) (in *sing.* prec. by *a* or *one*) 1 ten hundred 2 symbol for this (1,000; m, M; k, K) 3 (in *sing.* or *pl.*) *Colloq.* large number —**thou´sand·fold´** *adj. & adv.*; **thou´sandth** /-zən(d)TH/ *adj. & n.* [OE]

Thou´sand Is´lands *n.* group of 1,700 islands in the St. Lawrence River between N.Y. and Ontario, Canada

Thou´sand Oaks´ *n.* city in Calif. Pop. 104,352

thrall /THrôl/ *n.* 1 slave 2 slavery (*in thrall*) —**thrall´dom** *n.* [OE fr. ON]

thrash /THrash/ *v.* 1 beat or whip severely 2 defeat thoroughly 3 move or fling (esp. the limbs) about violently 4 THRESH —*n.* 5 act of thrashing 6 **thrash out** discuss to a conclusion [OE]

thread /THred/ *n.* 1a spun cotton, silk, glass, etc.; yarn b length of this 2 thin cord of twisted yarns used esp. in sewing and weaving 3 continuous aspect of a thing (*the thread of life; thread of his argument*) 4 spiral ridge of a screw —*v.* 5 pass a thread through (a needle) 6 insert (a strip of film, tape, etc.) into equipment 7 make (one's way) carefully through a crowded place, etc. [OE, rel. to THROW]

thread´bare´ *adj.* 1 (of cloth) with the nap worn away and the thread visible 2 (of a person) wearing such clothes 3 hackneyed

threat /THret/ *n.* 1 declaration of an intention to punish or hurt if an order, etc., is not obeyed

2 imminence of something undesirable (*threat of war*) 3 person or thing as a likely cause of harm, etc. [OE]

threat′en *v.* 1 make a threat or threats against 2 be a sign of (something undesirable) 3 (also *absol.*) presents imminent danger 4 endanger (a species, etc.) —**threat′en·ing** *adj.*; **threat′en·ing·ly** *adv.* [OE]

three /THrē/ *adj. & n.* 1 one more than two 2 symbol for this (3, iii, III) [OE]

three′-deck′er *n.* thing with three levels or divisions

three′-di·men′sion·al *adj.* having or appearing to have length, breadth, and depth

three′fold *adj. & adv.* 1 three times as much or as many 2 consisting of three parts

three R′s *n. pl.* (prec. by *the*) reading, writing, and arithmetic

three′score *n. & adj. Archaic.* sixty

three·some /THrē′səm/ *n.* group of three persons

thren·o·dy /THren′ədē/ *n.* (*pl.* ·**dies**) song of lamentation or mourning [Gk]

thresh /THresh/ *v.* beat out or separate grain from (corn, etc.) —**thresh′er** *n.* [OE]

thresh·old /THresh′(h)ōld/ *n.* 1 strip of wood or stone forming the bottom of a doorway 2 point of entry or beginning; crucial demarcation 3 limit [OE, rel. to THRASH in the sense 'tread']

threw /THrōō/ *v. past of* THROW

thrice /THrīs/ *adv. Archaic.* or *Lit.* 1 three times 2 (esp. in *comb.*) highly (*thrice-blessed*) [rel. to THREE]

thrift /THrift/ *n.* frugality [ON, rel. to THRIVE]

thrift′y *adj.* (·**i·er**, ·**i·est**) economical —**thrift′i·ly** *adv.*; **thrift′i·ness** *n.*

thrill /THril/ *n.* 1 wave or nervous tremor of emotion or sensation (*a thrill of joy*) 2 throb; pulsation —*v.* 3 (cause to) feel a thrill 4 quiver or throb with or as with emotion —**thrill′ing** *adj.*; **thrill′ing·ly** *adv.* [OE: pierce, rel. to THROUGH]

thrill′er *n.* exciting or sensational story, film, etc., esp. about crime or espionage

thrive /THrīv/ *v.* (**thrived** or **throve**, **thrived** or **thriv·en** /THriv′ən/, **thriv·ing**) 1 prosper; flourish 2 grow rich 3 grow vigorously [ON]

throat /THrōt/ *n.* 1a windpipe or gullet b front part of the neck 2 narrow passage, entrance, or exit 3 cut one's own throat harm oneself or one's interests [OE]

throat′y *adj.* (·**i·er**, ·**i·est**) (of a voice) hoarsely resonant —**throat′i·ly** *adv.*; **throat′i·ness** *n.*

throb /THräb/ *v.* (**throbbed, throb·bing**) 1 pulsate, esp. with more than the usual force or rapidity 2 vibrate with a persistent rhythm or with emotion —*n.* 3 throbbing 4 (esp. violent) pulsation [imit.]

throe /THrō/ *n.* (usu. *pl.*) 1 violent pangs, esp. of childbirth or death 2 **in the throes of** struggling with the experience of [OE, alter. of orig. *throwe*, perh. by association with *woe*]

throm·bo·sis /THrämbō′sis/ *n.* (*pl.* ·**ses** /-sēz/) coagulation of the blood in a blood vessel or organ [Gk: curdling]

throne /THrōn/ *n.* 1 official chair for a sovereign, bishop, etc. 2 sovereign power (*came to the throne*) [Gk *thronos*]

throng /THrông, THräng/ *n.* 1 crowd, esp. of people —*v.* 2 come in great numbers 3 flock into or crowd around; fill with or as with a crowd [OE]

throt·tle /THrät′l/ *n.* 1a valve controlling flow of fuel, steam, etc., in an engine b lever or pedal operating this valve —*v.* (·**tled**, ·**tling**) 3 choke; strangle 4 prevent the utterance, etc., of 5 control (an engine or steam, etc.) with a throttle [perh. fr. THROAT]

through /THrōō/ (also **thru**) *prep.* 1a from end to end or side to side of b going in one side or end and out the other of 2 between or among 3 from beginning to end of (*read through the letter; went through many difficulties*) 4 because of (*lost it through carelessness*) 5 up to and including (*Monday through Friday*) —*adv.* 6 through a thing; from side to side, end to end, or beginning to end —*adj.* 7 (of traffic) going through a place to its destination 8 (of a road) open at both ends 9 finished 10 have no further prospects; defeated; doomed 11 **through and through** thoroughly; completely [OE]

through′out′ *prep.* 1 right through; from end to end of —*adv.* 2 in every part or respect

through′put′ *n.* amount of material, data, etc., put through a process

throve /THrōv/ *v. past of* THRIVE

throw /THrō/ *v.* (**threw, thrown** /THrōn/, **throw·ing**) 1 propel with force through the air 2 force or relegate violently (*thrown on the rocks; threw themselves down*) 3 turn or move (part of the body) quickly or suddenly (*threw an arm out*) 4 project or cast (light, a shadow, etc.) 5a bring to the ground in wrestling b (of a horse) unseat (its rider) 6 *Colloq.* disconcert (*the question threw me*) 7 (foll. by *on, off*) put (clothes, etc.) hastily on or off 8a cast (dice) b obtain (a specified number) by throwing dice 9 extend or provide (*threw a bridge across the river*) 10 operate (a switch or lever) 11 have (a fit or tantrum) —*n.* 12 act of throwing or being thrown 13 distance a thing is or may be thrown 14 (prec. by *a*) *Slang.* each; per item 15 **throw away:** a discard as useless or unwanted b waste or fail to make use of (an opportunity, etc.) 16 **throw in the towel** (or **sponge**) admit defeat 17 **throw off:** a discard; get rid of b write or utter in an offhand manner c emit 18 **throw out:** a put out forcibly or suddenly b discard 19 **throw together:** a assemble hastily b bring into casual contact 20 **throw up:** a vomit b erect hastily [OE: twist]

throw′-a·way′ *adj.* 1 meant to be thrown away after (one) use 2 spoken in a deliberately casual way

throw′back′ *n.* 1 reversion to former or earlier time, type, etc. 2 instance of this

thru /THrōō/ *prep. & adv.* var. of THROUGH

thrum /THrəm/ *v.* (**thrummed, thrumming**) 1 play (a stringed instrument) monotonously or unskillfully 2 drum idly —*n.* 3 such playing 4 resulting sound [imit.]

thrush /THrəsh/ *n.* any of various songbirds [OE]

thrust /THrəst/ *v.* (**thrust, thrust·ing**) 1 push with a sudden impulse or with force 2 (foll. by *on*) impose (a thing) forcibly 3 stab; lunge suddenly —*n.* 4 sudden or forcible push or lunge 5 propulsive force produced by a jet or rocket engine **6** military offensive **7** stress between the parts of an arch, etc. **8** chief theme or gist of remarks, etc. [ON]

Thu·cyd·i·des /ᴛ H(y)ōōsid′∂dēz′/ c. 455 – c. 400 B.C.; Greek historian

thud /ᴛ H∂d/ n. **1** low, dull sound as of a blow on a nonresonant surface —v. (**thud·ded, thud·ding**) **2** make or fall with a thud [prob. OE]

thug /ᴛ H∂g/ n. violent brute; hoodlum —**thug′ger·y** n.; **thug′gish** adj. [Hindi]

thu·li·um /ᴛ H(y)ōō′lēəm/ n. metallic element of the lanthanide series; symb. **Tm** [L *Thule* region in the remote north]

thumb /ᴛ H∂m/ n. **1** short, thick finger on the human hand, set apart from the other four **2** part of a glove, etc., for a thumb —v. **3** turn over pages with or as with a thumb **4** request or get (a lift) by signaling with a raised thumb **5 thumb one's nose** make a contemptuous gesture with the thumb to the nose and the fingers spread and wiggling **6 thumbs down** indication of rejection **7 thumbs up** indication of satisfaction or approval **8 under a person's thumb** completely dominated by a person [OE]

thumb′nail′ n. **1** nail of a thumb —adj. **2** concise (*thumbnail sketch*)

thumb′tack′ n. wide-headed tack to be pushed with the thumb

thump /ᴛ H∂mp/ v. **1** beat or strike heavily, esp. with the fist **2** throb strongly **3** knock loudly —n. **4** heavy blow **5** dull sound of this [imit.]

thun·der /ᴛ H∂n′dər/ n. **1** loud noise caused by lightning and due to the expansion of rapidly heated air **2** resounding, loud, deep noise —v. **3** produce sounds of thunder **4** make a noise like thunder **5** utter (threats, etc.) loudly **6** (foll. by *against*, etc.) make violent threats, etc., against [OE]

thun′der·bolt′ n. **1** flash of lightning with a simultaneous crash of thunder **2** unexpected occurrence or announcement

thun′der·clap′ n. crash of thunder

thun′der·cloud′ n. cumulus cloud charged with electricity and producing thunder and lightning

thun′der·ous adj. **1** like thunder **2** very loud

thun′der·storm′ n. storm with thunder and lightning and usu. heavy rain

thun′der·struck′ adj. amazed

Thur. abbr. (also **Thurs.**) Thursday

Thur·ber /ᴛ Hər′bər/, **James** 1894–1961; US humorist, writer, and cartoonist

Thurs·day /ᴛ Hərz′dā, -dē/ n. day of the week following Wednesday; abbr. **Th., Thur.,** or **Thurs.** [OE]

thus /ᴛ H∂s/ adv. **1a** in this way **b** as indicated **2a** accordingly **b** as a result or inference **3** to this extent; so (*thus far*) [OE]

• Usage: The adverb *thus* does not need to be expanded to "thusly" in any context.

thwart /ᴛ Hwôrt/ v. **1** frustrate or foil (a person, plan, etc.) —n. **2** rower's seat [ON: across]

thy /ᴛ Hī/ poss. pron. (also **thine** /ᴛ Hīn/ predic. or before a vowel) Archaic. of or belonging to thee [fr. THINE]

thyme /tīm/ n. any of several herbs with aromatic leaves [Gk *thymon*]

thy·mus /ᴛ Hī′məs/ n. (pl. **·mus·es** or **·mi**

/-mī′/) lymphoid organ situated in the neck of vertebrates [Gk]

thy·roid /ᴛ Hī′roid′/ n. (in full **thy′roid gland′**) **1** large, ductless gland in the neck of vertebrates, secreting a hormone that regulates growth and development **2** extract prepared from the thyroid gland of animals and used in treating goiter, etc. [Gk *thyreos* oblong shield]

thy·self /ᴛ Hīself′/ pron. Archaic. emphatic & refl. form of THOU[1], THEE

ti / tē/ n. Mus. seventh note of a major scale [earlier *si*: fr. fr. It]

Ti symb. titanium

Tian·jin / tē-än′jin′, tē-en′-/ n. (formerly **Tientsin**) port in NE China. Pop. 4,574,700

ti·ar·a / tē-ar′ə, -är′ə/ n. **1** jeweled ornamental band worn at the front of a woman's hair **2** three-crowned diadem worn by a pope [L fr. Gk]

Ti·be·ri·us / tībēr′ēəs/ 42 B.C.–A.D. 37; Roman emperor (A.D. 14–37)

Ti·bet / tibet′/ n. autonomous region of SW China. Capital: Lhasa

Ti·bet·an / tibet′n/ n. **1** people and language of Tibet —adj. **2** of or pertaining to the people or language of Tibet

tib·i·a / tib′ēə/ n. (pl. **·i·ae** /-ē-ē′/) Anat. inner of two bones extending from the knee to the ankle —**tib′i·al** adj. [L]

tic / tik/ n. occasional involuntary contraction of the muscles, esp. of the face [Fr fr. It]

tick[1] / tik/ n. **1** slight recurring click, esp. that of a watch or clock **2** mark (/) to denote correctness, check items in a list, etc. —v. **3** (of a clock, etc.) make ticks **4a** mark with a tick **b** mark (an item) with a tick in checking **5 what makes a person tick** person's motivation [prob. imit.]

tick[2] n. parasitic arachnid on the skin of warm-blooded vertebrates [OE]

tick[3] n. **1** cover of a mattress or pillow **2** TICKING [Gk *thēkē* case]

tick′er n. Colloq. **1** heart **2** device displaying stock prices, etc., as a continuous moving strip

tick′er-tape′ n. **1** paper strip from a ticker machine **2** this material thrown from windows, etc., to greet a celebrity

tick·et / tik′it/ n. **1** written or printed piece of paper or card entitling the holder to admittance, travel by public transport, etc. **2** notification of a traffic violation, etc. **3** certificate or license **4** price, etc., label **5** list of a political party's candidates —v. **6** attach or give a ticket to [obs. Fr *étiquet*]

tick′ing n. strong usu. striped material used to cover mattresses, etc. [fr. TICK[3]]

tick·le / tik′əl/ v. (**·led, ·ling**) **1** touch or stroke (a person, etc.) playfully or lightly so as to produce laughter and spasmodic movement **2** excite agreeably; amuse —n. **3** act of tickling **4** tickling sensation **5 tickled pink (or to death)** Colloq. extremely amused or pleased —**tick′ly** adj. [prob. freq. of TICK[1]]

tick·lish / tik′(ə)lis H/ adj. **1** sensitive to tickling **2** (of a matter or person) difficult to handle

tick-tack-toe or **tic-tac-toe** / tik′tak-tō′/ n. game of marking "Xs" and "Os" in a grid

tick·tock /ˈtikˌtäk/ *n.* ticking of a large clock, etc.

tid·al /ˈtīdʼl/ *adj.* relating to, like, or affected by tides **—tidʼal·ly** *adv.*

tidal wave *n.* **1** exceptionally large ocean wave, esp. one caused by an underwater earthquake **2** widespread manifestation of feeling, etc.

tid·bit /ˈtidˈbitʼ/ *n.* **1** dainty morsel **2** curious item of news, etc. [perh. from dial. *tid* tender]

tid·dly·winks /ˈtidˈlēwiNGks/ *n. pl.* game in which a counter is flicked with another into a cup

tide /tīd/ *n.* **1a** periodic rise and fall of the sea due to the attraction of the moon and sun **b** water as affected by this **2** time or season (usu. in *comb.*: *Eastertide*) **3** marked trend of opinion, fortune, or events **—v.** **(tid·ed, tid·ing) 4 tide over** provide (a person) with what is needed during a difficult period [OE: TIME]

tideʼway *n.* tidal part of a river

ti·dings /ˈtīdiNGz/ *n.* (as *sing.* or *pl.*) news [OE, prob. fr. ON]

ti·dy /ˈtīdē/ *adj.* (·di·er, ·di·est) **1** neat; orderly **2** considerable (*a tidy sum*) **—v.** (·died, ·dy·ing) **3** put in good order; make tidy **—tiʼdi·ly** *adv.*; **tiʼdi·ness** *n.* [orig. timely, etc., fr. TIDE]

tie /tī/ *v.* (tied, ty·ing) **1** attach or fasten with string, cord, etc. **2a** form (a string, ribbon, etc.) into a knot or bow **b** form (a knot or bow) in this way **3** restrict (a person) in some way **4** achieve the same score or place as another competitor **—n.** **5** cord, wire, etc., used for fastening **6** strip of material worn around the collar and tied in a knot at the front **7** bond (*family ties*) **8** draw, dead heat, or equality of score among competitors **9 tie up: a** bind securely with cord, etc. **b** invest or reserve (capital, etc.) so that it is not immediately available for use **c** (usu. in *passive*) fully occupy (a person) **d** bring to a satisfactory conclusion [OE]

tieʼbreakʼer *n.* means of deciding a winner when a contest ends in a tie

tieʼ-dyeʼ *n.* method of producing irregular dyed patterns by tying string, etc., to expose the dye to only parts of the fabric

tieʼ-inʼ *n.* **1** connection or association **2** joint promotion of related commodities (e.g., a book and a movie)

Tien·tsin /tinˈtsin/ *n.* see TIANJIN

tieʼpinʼ *n.* ornamental pin for holding a tie in place

tier /tēr/ *n.* vertical or sloped row, rank, or unit of a structure (*tiers of seats*) **—tiered** *adj.* [Fr *tire* fr. *tirer* draw, elongate]

Ti·er·ra del Fue·go /tēˈerʼə del fwāˈgō/ *n.* group of islands at the S tip of S America

tiff /tif/ *n.* slight or petty quarrel

ti·ger /ˈtīgər/ *n.* **1** large Asian animal of the cat family, with a yellow-brown coat with black stripes **2** fierce, energetic, or formidable person [Gk *tigris*]

tiʼger liʼly *n.* tall garden lily with dark-spotted orange flowers

tight /tīt/ *adj.* **1** closely held, exerted, drawn, fastened, fitting, etc. **2** too closely fitting **3**

impermeable or impervious, esp. (in *comb.*) to a specified thing (*watertight*) **4** tense; stretched **5** *Slang.* drunk **6** stingy **7** (of money or materials) not easily obtainable **8a** (of precautions, etc.) stringent **b** presenting difficulties (*tight situation*) **—adv.** **9** tightly (*hold tight!*) **—tightʼly** *adv.*; **tightʼness** *n.* [ON]

tightʼen *v.* make or become tighter

tightʼfistʼed *adj.* stingy

tightʼ-lippedʼ *adj.* determinedly taciturn; secretive

tightʼropeʼ *n.* rope stretched tightly high above the ground, on which acrobats perform

tights /tīts/ *n. pl.* thin close-fitting wool garment covering the lower body

tightʼwadʼ *n.* miserly person

ti·gress /ˈtīgris/ *n.* female tiger

Ti·gris Riv·er /ˈtīgris/ *n.* river in SW Asia flowing 1,150 mi. from SE Turkey to the Euphrates River

Ti·jua·na /tihwänʼə, tēˈəwänʼə/ *n.* city in NW Mexico. Pop. 429,500

tike /tīk/ *n.* var. of TYKE

Til·burg /ˈtilˈbärg/ *n.* city in the Netherlands. Pop. 158,800

til·de /ˈtilˈdə/ *n.* mark (˜) put over a letter, e.g., over a Spanish *n* when pronounced *ny* (as in *señor*) [L, rel. to TITLE]

tile /tīl/ *n.* **1** thin slab of concrete, baked clay, etc., used for roofing or paving, etc. **2** similar slab of glazed pottery, cork, linoleum, etc., for covering a wall, floor, etc. **3** thin, flat piece used in a game (esp. in mah-jongg) **—v.** **(tiled, til·ing) 4** cover with tiles **—tilʼer** *n.* [L *tegula*]

tilʼing *n.* **1** process of fixing tiles **2** aggregate or area of tiles

till [1] /til/ *prep.* **1** up to or as late as (*wait till six o'clock*) **2** up to the time of (*faithful till death*) **—conj.** **3** up to the time when (*wait till I return*) **4** so long that (*laughed till I cried*) [ON, rel. to TILL [2]]
● **Usage:** See note at UNTIL.

till [2] *n.* drawer for money in a shop, bank, etc.

till [3] *v.* cultivate (land) **—tillʼer** *n.* [OE: strive for]

till·age /ˈtilʼij/ *n.* **1** preparation of land for growing crops **2** tilled land

tillʼer *n.* bar fitted to a boat's rudder to turn it in steering [AngFr *telier* weaver's beam]

Til·lich /ˈtilˈik/, **Paul Johannes** 1886–1965; German-born US Protestant theologian

tilt /tilt/ *v.* **1** (cause to) assume a sloping position; heel over **2** (foll. by *at*) strike, thrust, or run at with a weapon **3** (foll. by *with*) engage in a contest **—n.** **4** tilting **5** sloping position **6** (of medieval knights, etc.) charging with a lance against an opponent or at a mark **7 full (or at full) tilt: a** at full speed **b** with full force [OE: unsteady]

tim·ber /ˈtimˈbər/ *n.* **1** wood suitable for building, carpentry, etc. **2** piece of wood or beam, esp. as the rib of a vessel **3** large standing trees **4** quality or qualification (*presidential timber*) [OE: building]

timʼber·lineʼ *n.* line or level above which no trees grow

tim·bre /ˈtamˈbər, timʼ-/ *n.* distinctive character of a musical sound or voice apart from its pitch and volume [Gk, rel. to TYMPANUM]

time /tīm/ *n.* **1** indefinite continuing progress of existence, events, etc., in the past, present, and future, regarded as a whole **2** progress of this as affecting persons or things **3** portion of time; period **4** allotted or available portion of time (*no time to eat*) **5** point of time, esp. in hours and minutes (*the time is 7:30*) **6** (prec. by *a*) indefinite period **7** particular reckoning of time (*eight o'clock New York time*) **8** occasion (*last time*) **9** opportune occasion or moment (*the time to act*) **10** (*pl.*) expressing multiplication (*five times six is thirty*) **11** (*sing.* or *pl.*) conditions of life or of a period (*hard times*) **12** *Slang.* prison sentence (*did time*) **13** date or expected date of childbirth or death **14** any of several rhythmic patterns of music —*v.* (**timed, tim·ing**) **15** choose the time for **16** do at a chosen or correct time **17** arrange the time of arrival of **18** ascertain the time taken by **19** ahead of time earlier than expected **20** all the time: a throughout **b** constantly **21** at one time: **a** in a known but unspecified past period **b** simultaneously **22** at the same time: **a** simultaneously **b** nevertheless **23** at times intermittently **24** for the time being until some other arrangement is made **25** half the time as often as not **26** in no time: **a** very soon **b** very quickly **27** in time: **a** eventually **b** in accordance with a given rhythm **28** on time punctual **29** time and (or time and time) again on many occasions **30** the time of one's life period of exceptional enjoyment [OE]

time' and a half' *n.* one and a half times the normal rate of payment

time' bomb' *n.* bomb designed to explode at a preset time

time' clock' *n.* clock with a device for recording employees' hours of work

time' ex·po'sure *n.* exposure of photographic film for longer than the slowest normal shutter setting

time'-hon'ored *adj.* esteemed by tradition or through custom

time'keep'er *n.* **1** person who records time, esp. of workers or in a game **2** watch or clock as regards accuracy —**time'keep'ing** *n.*

time'less *adj.* **1** everlasting **2** not affected by the passage of time —**time'less·ly** *adv.*; **time'less·ness** *n.*

time'ly *adj.* (**·li·er, ·li·est**) opportune —**time'li·ness** *n.*

time'-out' *n.* **1** pause or break in activity **2** *Sports.* brief suspension of play

time'piece' *n.* clock or watch

tim·er /tīm'ər/ *n.* person or device that measures or records time taken

time'serv'er *n.* person who changes his or her view to suit prevailing circumstances, fashion, etc. —**time'serv'ing** *adj.*

time'-share' *n.* share in a property under a time-sharing contract

time'-shar'ing *n.* use of a vacation home at contractually agreed different times by several joint owners

time' sheet' *n.* sheet of paper for recording hours of work, etc.

time'ta'ble *n.* **1** list of times of trains on a schedule, esp. arrivals and departures of public trans-

portation **2** any anticipated sequence or schedule

time' zone' *n.* range of longitudes where a common standard time is used

tim·id /tim'id/ *adj.* easily frightened; apprehensive —**ti·mid'i·ty** *n.*; **tim'id·ly** *adv.* [L *timere* fear]

tim'ing *n.* **1** way an action or process is timed **2** opportuneness of an occurrence

Ti·mi·soa·ra /tē'mĭshwär'ə/ *n.* city in W Romania. Pop. 334,300

tim·o·rous /tim'ərəs/ *adj.* timid; fearful —**tim'o·rous·ly** *adv.* [MedL, rel. to TIMID]

Tim·o·thy, St. /tim'əTHē/ 1st cent. A.D.; colleague of St. Paul

tim·pa·ni /tim'pənē/ *n. pl.* (also **tym'pa·ni**) kettledrums —**tim'pa·nist** /-nist/ *n.* [It, pl. of *timpano* TYMPANUM]

tin /tin/ *n.* **1** silvery-white metallic element, used esp. in alloys and in making tin plate; *symb.* **Sn 2** esp. *Brit.* can, esp. of tin-plated steel, for food storage, etc. **3** TIN PLATE —*v.* (**tinned, tin·ning**) **4** cover or coat with tin [OE]

tin' can' *n.* tin-plated container, esp. an empty one

tinc·ture /tiNGK'CHər/ *n.* **1** slight flavor or trace **2** tinge (of a color) **3** medicinal solution (of a drug) in alcohol (*tincture of quinine*) —*v.* (**·tured, ·tur·ing**) **4** color slightly; tinge; flavor **5** (often foll. by *with*) affect slightly (with a quality) [L, rel. to TINGE]

tin·der /tin'dər/ *n.* dry substance that readily catches fire from a spark [OE]

tin'der·box' *n.* **1** *Hist.* box containing tinder, flint, and steel, for kindling fires **2** volatile or potentially explosive place, situation, etc.

tine /tīn/ *n.* prong, tooth, or point of a fork, comb, antler, etc. [OE]

tin' foil' *n.* foil made of tin, aluminum, or tin alloy, used for wrapping food

tinge /tinj/ *v.* (**tinged, tinge·ing** or **ting·ing**) **1** color slightly **2** affect slightly —*n.* **3** tendency toward or trace of some color **4** slight admixture of a feeling or quality [L *tingere tinct-* dye]

tin·gle /tiNG'gəl/ *v.* (**·gled, ·gling**) **1** feel a slight prickling, stinging, or throbbing sensation —*n.* **2** tingling sensation —**tin'gly** *adj.* [prob. fr. TINKLE]

tin·ker /tiNG'kər/ *n.* **1** itinerant mender of kettles, pans, etc. —*v.* **2** (foll. by *at, with*) work or repair in an amateurish or desultory way

tin·kle /tiNG'kəl/ *v.* (**·kled, ·kling**) **1** (cause to) make a succession of short, light, ringing sounds —*n.* **2** tinkling sound —**tin'kly** *adj.* [imit.]

tin·ni·tus /tinī'təs, tin'i-/ *n. Med.* condition with ringing in the ears [L *tinnire tinnit-* ring; tinkle]

tin·ny /tin'ē/ *adj.* (**·ni·er, ·ni·est**) **1** of or like tin **2** flimsy; insubstantial **3** (of sound) thin and metallic

Tin' Pan' Al'ley *n.* composers and publishers of popular music, collectively

tin' plate' *n.* sheet iron or sheet steel coated with tin

tin·sel /tin'səl/ *n.* **1** glittering metallic strips, threads, etc., used as decoration 2 superficial brilliance or splendor —**tin′seled** or **tin′selled** *adj.* [L *scintilla* spark]

tint /tint/ *n.* 1 light or delicate variety of a color 2 tendency toward or admixture of a different color (*red with a blue tint*) 3 hair dye —*v.* 4 apply a tint to; color [*tinct*, rel. to TINGE]

tin·tin·nab·u·la·tion /tin′tənab′yələ′sHən/ *n.* ringing or tinkling of bells [L *tintinnabulum* bell]

Tin·to·ret·to /tin′təret′ō/ 1518–94; Venetian painter

ti·ny /tī′nē/ *adj.* (**·ni·er, ·ni·est**) very small or slight —**ti′ni·ness** *n.*

-tion *suffix* see -ION

tip¹ /tip/ *n.* 1 extremity or end, esp. of a small or tapering thing 2 small piece or part attached to the end of a thing —*v.* (**tipped, tip·ping**) 3 provide with a tip 4 **tip of the iceberg** small visible part of something much larger [ON]

tip² *v.* (**tipped, tip·ping**) 1a lean or slant b cause to do this —*n.* 2 slight push or tilt

tip³ *v.* (**tipped, tip·ping**) 1 make a small present of money to, esp. for a service given 2 strike or touch lightly —*n.* 3 small money present, esp. for a service given 4 piece of private or special information, esp. regarding betting or investment 5 small or casual piece of advice 6 **tip off** give (a person) helpful information or a warning —**tip′per, tip′ster** *n.*

tip′-off′ *n.* tip, hint, or warning

tip·ple /tip′əl/ *v.* (**·pled, ·pling**) drink intoxicating liquor habitually —**tip′pler** /-lər/ *n.*

tip·sy /tip′sē/ *adj.* (**·si·er, ·si·est**) slightly drunk —**tip′si·ly** *adv.*; **tip′si·ness** *n.* [fr. TIP²]

tip′toe′ *n.* 1 the tips of the toes —*v.* (**·toed, ·toe·ing**) 2 walk on tiptoe or very stealthily —*adv.* (also **on tiptoe**) 3 with the heels of the ground

tip′top′ *Colloq. adj.* 1 highest in excellence —*n.* 2 highest point of excellence —*adv.* 3 most excellently

ti·rade /tī′rād′/ *n.* long, vehement denunciation or declamation [Fr fr. It]

Ti·ra·në /tirän′ə/ *n.* capital of Albania. Pop 239,400

tire¹ /tīr/ *v.* (**tired, tir·ing**) 1 make or grow weary 2 bore [OE]

tire² *n.* rubber covering, usu. inflated, placed around a wheel to form a soft contact with the road

tired /tīrd/ *adj.* 1 weary; ready for sleep 2 hackneyed —**tired′ly** *adv.*; **tired′ness** *n.*

tire′less *adj.* not tiring easily; energetic —**tire′less·ly** *adv.*; **tire′less·ness** *n.*

tire·some /tīr′səm/ *adj.* wearisome; tedious; boring —**tire′some·ly** *adv.*; **tire′some·ness** *n.*

′tis /tiz/ *v. Poet.* it is

tis·sue /tisH′ōō/ *n.* 1 any coherent mass of specialized cells of which animals or plants are made (*muscular tissue*) 2 TISSUE PAPER 3 disposable piece of thin, soft, absorbent paper for wiping, drying, etc. 4 fine, gauzy fabric [Fr *tissu* woven cloth]

tis′sue pa′per *n.* thin, soft paper for wrapping, etc.

tit¹ /tit/ *n.* any of various small birds [prob. fr. Scand]

tit² *n.* as in **tit for tat** blow for blow; retaliation [earlier *tip* in *tip for tap*: see TIP²]

ti·tan /tīt′n/ *n.* person of very great strength, intellect, or importance [Gk Myth.: member of a race of giants]

ti·tan·ic /tītan′ik/ *adj.* gigantic; colossal —**ti·tan′i·cal·ly** *adv.* [Gk, rel. to TITAN]

ti·ta·ni·um /tītā′nēəm/ *n.* gray metallic element; *symb.* Ti [Gk, rel. to TITAN]

tithe /tīTH/ *n.* 1 one-tenth of the annual produce of land or labor, formerly taken as a tax for the church —*v.* (**tithed, tith·ing**) 2 pay tithes [OE: tenth]

ti·tian /tisH′ən/ *adj.* (of hair) bright auburn [for TITIAN]

Ti·tian /tisH′ən/ c. 1488–1576; Italian painter

Ti·ti·ca·ca, Lake /tit′ēkäk′ə/ *n.* lake on Peru-Bolivia border; 12,508 ft. above sea level

tit·il·late /tit′l-āt′/ *v.* (**·lat·ed, ·lat·ing**) excite, esp. sexually —**tit′il·la′tion** *n.* [L]

ti·tle /tīt′l/ *n.* 1 name of a book, work of art, etc. 2 heading of a chapter, document, etc. 3 book, magazine, etc., in terms of its title (*brought out two new titles*) 4 (usu. *pl.*) caption or credit in a film, etc. 5 name indicating a person's status (e.g., *queen, professor*) or used as a form of address (e.g., *Your Honor*) 6 championship 7 *Law.* a right to ownership of property with or without possession b just or recognized claim —*v.* (**·tled, ·tling**) 8 give a title to; entitle [L *titulus*]

ti′tled *adj.* having a title of nobility or rank

tit·mouse /tit′mous/ *n.* (*pl.* **tit′mice**) small, active tit [OE *tit* little, *māse* titmouse, assimilated to MOUSE]

Ti·to /tē′tō/ (born **Josip Broz**) 1892–1980; Yugoslavian Communist leader; president (1953–80)

tit·ter /tit′ər/ *v.* 1 laugh covertly; giggle —*n.* 2 covert laugh [imit.]

tit·tle /tit′l/ *n.* 1 small stroke or dot 2 particle (*not one jot or tittle*) [L, rel. to TITLE]

tit·u·lar /tiCH′ələr/ *adj.* 1 of or relating to a title 2 in name or title only (*titular ruler*) [Fr, rel. to TITLE]

tiz·zy /tiz′ē/ *n.* (*pl.* **·zies**) *Slang.* state of agitation (*in a tizzy*)

TKO *abbr. Boxing.* technical knockout

Tl *symb.* thallium

Tlax·ca·la /tläskäl′ə, tələ-/ *n.* state of E central Mexico. Capital: Tlaxcala. Pop. 761,300

TLC *abbr.* tender loving care

Tm *symb.* thulium

TM *abbr.* 1 trademark 2 transcendental meditation

TN postal *abbr.* for Tennessee

tnpk. *abbr.* turnpike

TNT *abbr.* trinitrotoluene, a high explosive

to /tōō, tōō/ *prep.* 1 introducing a noun expressing: a what is reached, approached, or touched (*fell to the ground; went to Paris; five minutes to six*) b what is aimed at (*throw it to me*) c as far as (*went on to the end*) d what is followed (*made to order*) e what is considered or affected (*used to that; that is nothing to me*) f what is caused or produced (*turn to stone*) g what is compared (*nothing to what it once was; equal to the occasion*) h what is increased (*add*

it to mine) i what is involved or composed as specified (*there is nothing to it*) **2** introducing the infinitive: **a** as a verbal noun (*to get there*) **b** expressing purpose, consequence, or cause (*we eat to live; left him to starve; I'm sorry to hear that*) **c** as a substitute for *to* + infinitive (*wanted to come but was unable to*) —*adv.* **3** in the normal or required position or condition (*come to; heave to*) **4** (of a door) in a nearly closed position **5 to and fro** backward and forward repeatedly between the same points [OE]

toad /tōd/ *n.* **1** froglike amphibian breeding in water but living chiefly on land **2** repulsive person [OE]

toad'stool *n.* poisonous mushroom

toad'y *n.* (*pl.* **·ies**) **1** sycophant —*v.* (**·ied, ·y·ing**) **2** behave servilely (to) —**toad'y·ism** *n.* [contr. of *toad-eater*]

toast /tōst/ *n.* **1** sliced bread browned on both sides by radiant heat **2a** person or thing in whose honor a company is requested to drink **b** call to such a drink or an instance of it —*v.* **3** brown or warm by radiant heat **4** drink to the health or in honor of (a person or thing) [Fr *toster* roast]

toast'er *n.* electrical device for making toast

toast'mas'ter *n.* (*fem.* **toast'mis'tress**) person presiding at a banquet

to·bac·co /təbak'ō/ *n.* (*pl.* **·cos**) **1** plant with narcotic leaves used for smoking, chewing, or snuff **2** its leaves, esp. as prepared for smoking [Sp *tabaco*, ult. Amer. Indian origin]

to·bog·gan /təbäg'ən/ *n.* **1** narrow, runnerless sled, curled upward in front, for use on snow —*v.* **2** ride on a toboggan [CanFr fr. Algonquian]

Tocque·ville /tōk'vil/, **Alexis de** 1805–59; French statesman and historian

toc·sin /täk'sən/ *n.* alarm bell or signal [Prov *tocasenh*]

to·day /tədā'/ *adv.* **1** on this present day **2** nowadays —*n.* **3** this present day **4** modern times [OE]

tod·dle /täd'l/ *v.* (**·dled, ·dling**) **1** walk with short, unsteady steps like a small child —*n.* **2** act of toddling

tod·dler /täd'lər/ *n.* child who is just learning to walk

tod·dy /täd'ē/ *n.* (*pl.* **·dies**) drink of whiskey with hot water, sugar, etc. [Hindustani *tār* palm]

to-do /tədōō'/ *n.* (*pl.* **-dos**) *Colloq.* commotion or fuss

toe /tō/ *n.* **1** any of the five digits of a foot **2** part of a shoe, etc., that covers the toes —*v.* (**toed, toe·ing**) **3** touch (a starting line, etc.) with the toes **4 on one's toes** alert **5 toe the line** conform, esp. under pressure [OE]

toe'hold' *n.* **1** small foothold **2** small beginning or advantage

toe'nail' *n.* nail of each toe

tof·fee /tô'fē, täf'ē/ *n.* firm or hard candy made by boiling sugar, butter, etc.

to·fu /tō'fōō'/ *n.* curd made from mashed soybeans [Japn]

tog /täg, tôg/ *n.* (usu. *pl.*) item of clothing [appar. orig. cant: ult. rel. to L TOGA]

to·ga /tō'gə/ *n.* ancient Roman citizen's loose, flowing outer garment [L]

TOGA

to·geth·er /təgeTH'ər/ *adv.* **1** in company or conjunction (*walking together; at school together*) **2** simultaneously (*both shouted together*) **3** one with another (*talking together*) **4** so as to unite (*tied them together; put two and two together*) **5** into company or companionship —*adj.* **6** *Slang.* well-organized; self-assured; emotionally stable **7 together with** as well as [OE, rel. to TO, GATHER]

to·geth'er·ness *n.* **1** being together **2** feeling of comfort from this

tog'gle switch' /täg'əl/ *n.* **1** electric switch with a lever to be moved usu. up and down **2** *Comp.* (as **toggle**) switching action or option to select opposite settings —*v.* (**·gled, ·gling**) **3** *Comp.* choose by toggle

To·go /tō'gō/ *n.* country in W Africa on the Gulf of Guinea. Capital: Lomé. Pop. 3,701,000

toil /toil/ *v.* **1** work laboriously or incessantly **2** make slow, painful progress —*n.* **3** intensive labor; drudgery [AngFr *toil(er)* dispute]

toi·let /toi'lit/ *n.* **1a** bowllike receptacle for urine and feces, usu. with disposal by flushing **b** room containing this **2** process of washing oneself, dressing, etc. (*at one's toilet*) [Fr *toilette* dim. of *toile* cloth]

toi'let pa'per *n.* paper for cleaning oneself after excreting

toi·let·ry /toi'litrē/ *n.* (*pl.* **·ries**) (usu. *pl.*) article or cosmetic used in washing, dressing, etc.

toi·lette /twälet'/ *n.* TOILET, 2 [Fr]

toi'let wa'ter *n.* diluted perfume

toil'some *adj.* involving toil

To·jo /tō'jō/, **Hideki** 1885–1948; Japanese general and prime minister (1941–44)

to·ken /tō'kən/ *n.* **1** thing serving as a symbol, reminder, or mark (*as a token of affection*) **2** metal disk used as a special currency **3a** perfunctory; pro forma (*token effort*) **b** chosen by tokenism to represent a group (*token woman*) [OE]

to·ken·ism /tō'kəniz'əm/ *n.* **1** granting of minimum or only visible concessions, esp. to minority groups **2** making of only a token effort

To·ky·o /tō'kē·ō/ *n.* capital of Japan. Pop. 8,154,400

told /tōld/ *v.* past and past part. of TELL

To·le·do /təlēd'ō/ *n.* city in Ohio. Pop. 332,943

tol·er·a·ble /täl'(ə)rəbəl/ *adj.* **1** endurable **2** fairly good —**tol'er·a·bly** *adv.* [L, rel. to TOLERATE]

tol·er·ance /täl'ərəns/ *n.* **1** willingness or ability to tolerate; forbearance **2** capacity to withstand or resist **3** allowable variation or range

tol·er·ant /täl'ərənt/ *adj.* disposed to tolerate; forbearing; patient

tol·er·ate /tāl′ərāt′/ v. (-at·ed, -at·ing) 1 allow the existence or occurrence of without interference 2 endure (suffering, etc.) 3 be able to take or undergo (drugs, treatment, etc.) without adverse effects —**tol′er·a′tion** n. [L tolero]

Tol·kien /tāl′kēn, tōl′-/, J(ohn) R(onald) R(euel) 1892–1973; English writer and scholar

toll[1] /tōl/ n. 1 charge to use a bridge, road, etc. 2a cost or damage caused by a disaster, etc. b number of fatalities from this

toll[2] v. 1a (of a bell) sound with slow, uniform strokes b ring (a bell) in this way 2 strike (the hour) —n. 3 tolling 4 stroke of a bell [ME tollen pull]

toll′gate′ n. gate preventing passage until a toll is paid

toll′ road′ n. road maintained by the tolls collected on it

Tol·stoy /tōl′stoi′, tōl′-, tȧl′-/, (Count) Leo or Lev Nikolaevich 1828–1910; Russian writer

To·lu·ca /təlōō′kə/ n. capital of the Mexican state of Mexico. Pop. 827,300

tol·u·ene /tȧl′yōō-ēn′/ n. colorless aromatic liquid, derivative of benzene, used in the manufacture of explosives, etc. [orig. distilled fr. resin of the tolu tree]

Tom′, **Dick**′, **and Har′ry** n. (usu. prec. by any or every) person taken at random

tom·a·hawk /tȧm′əhȯk′/ n. N American Indian war axe [Algonquian]

to·ma·to /təmā′tō, -mä′tō/ n. (pl. -toes) 1 glossy red or yellow, pulpy, edible fruit 2 plant bearing this [ult. fr. Mexican tomatl]

tomb /tōōm/ n. 1 burial vault 2 grave [Gk tumbos]

tom·boy /tȧm′boi/ n. girl who enjoys sports, etc., traditionally associated with boys —**tom′boy′ish** adj. [fr. TOM]

tomb′stone′ n. memorial stone over a grave, usu. with an epitaph

tom·cat /tȧm′kat′/ n. male cat [abbr. of the name Thomas]

tome /tōm/ n. heavy book or volume [Gk temnō cut]

tom·fool·er·y /tȧmfōōl′ərē/ n. foolish behavior

tom′my gun′ /tȧm′ē/ n. submachine-gun [for J. Thompson, its coinventor]

to·mog·ra·phy /təmȧg′rəfē/ n. method of radiography displaying details in a selected plane within the body [Gk tomē a cutting]

to·mor·row /təmȧr′ō, -mȯr′ō/ adv. 1 on the day after today 2 at some future time —n. 3 the day after today 4 the near future [fr. TO, MORROW]

Tomsk /tȯmsk, tämsk/ n. city in central Russia. Pop. 506,600

tom-tom /tȧm′ tȧm′/ n. 1 primitive drum beaten with the hands 2 tall drum used in jazz bands, etc. [Hindi tamtam, imit.]

ton /tən/ n. 1 (in full short′ ton′) unit of weight equal to 2,000 lb 2 (in full long′ ton′) unit of weight equal to 2,240 lb 3 METRIC TON 4 (in full dis′place′ment ton′) unit of measurement of a ship's weight or volume 5 (usu. pl.) Colloq. large number or amount (tons of people) 6 weigh a ton Colloq. be very heavy [orig. the same word as TUN]

ton·al /tōn′l/ adj. of or relating to tone or tonality —**ton′al·ly** adv. [MedL, rel. to TONE]

to·nal·i·ty /tōnal′ətē/ n. (pl. -ties) 1 Mus. a relationship between the tones of a musical scale b observance of a single tonic key as the basis of a composition 2 color scheme of a picture

tone /tōn/ n. 1 musical or vocal sound, esp. with reference to its pitch, quality, and strength 2 (often pl.) expressive vocal manner or quality (a cheerful tone) 3 manner of expression in writing or speaking 4 Mus. a musical sound, esp. of a definite pitch and character b interval of a major second, e.g., C–D 5a general coloration or contrast in a picture b tint or shade of a color 6 proper firmness of the body, a muscle, etc. —v. (toned, ton·ing) 7 give the desired tone to 8 modify the tone of 9 tone down make or become milder or softer in tone —**tone′less** adj.; **tone′less·ly** adv. [Gk tonos fr. teinein stretch]

tone′-deaf′ adj. unable to perceive differences in musical pitch accurately

to·ner /tōn′ər/ n. powdered ink as used in photocopying, etc.

Ton·ga /tȧng′ga, tȯng′-/ n. island kingdom in the S Pacific, NE of New Zealand. Capital: Nukualofa. Pop. 97,300 —**Ton′gan** n. & adj.

tongs /tȯngz, tängz/ n. pl. implement with two arms for grasping ice, sugar cubes, etc. [OE]

tongue /təng/ n. 1 fleshy, muscular organ in the mouth used in tasting, licking, and swallowing and (in humans) for speech 2 tongue of an ox, etc., as food 3 faculty of or tendency in speech (a sharp tongue) 4 particular language (the German tongue) 5 thing like a tongue in shape or position, esp.: a a long, low promontory b a strip of leather, etc., under the laces in a shoe c a projecting strip on a board, etc., fitting into the groove of another —v. (tongued, tongu·ing) 6 use the tongue in playing a wind instrument 7 hold one's tongue see HOLD[1] 8 on the tip of the (or one's) tongue: a about to be said b just eluding recall [OE]

tongue′-and-groove′ adj. designating planking, etc., with a projecting strip down one side and a groove down the other, allowing pieces to fit securely together

tongue′-in-cheek′ adj. 1 ironic; facetious —adv. 2 insincerely; teasingly

tongue′-tied′ adj. too shy or embarrassed to speak

tongue′ twist′er n. sequence of words difficult to pronounce quickly and correctly

ton·ic /tȧn′ik/ n. 1 invigorating medicine 2 anything serving to invigorate 3 TONIC WATER 4 Mus. keynote —adj. 5 invigorating [Gk, rel. to TONE]

ton′ic wa′ter n. carbonated water flavored with quinine

to·night /tənīt′/ adv. 1 on the present or approaching evening or night —n. 2 the evening or night of the present day [OE]

ton·nage /tən′ij/ n. 1 ship's internal cubic capacity or freight-carrying capacity 2 charge per ton on freight or cargo [rel. to TON]

tonne /tən/ n. METRIC TON [Fr, rel. to TON]

ton·sil /tän′səl/ n. either of two small organs, one on each side of the root of the tongue [L

ton·sil·lec·to·my /tän′sǝlek′tǝmē/ *n.* (*pl.* ·**mies**) surgical removal of the tonsils

ton·sil·li·tis /tän′sǝlī′tis/ *n.* inflammation of the tonsils

ton·so·ri·al /tänsôr′ēǝl/ *adj.* usu. *Joc.* of a barber or haircutting [L *tondere* tons- shave]

ton·sure /tän′sHǝr/ *n.* 1 shaving of the crown of the head or the entire head, esp. of a person entering a monastic order 2 bare patch made in this way —*v.* (·**sured**, ·**sur·ing**) 3 give a tonsure to [L, rel. to TONSORIAL]

too /too͞/ *adv.* 1 to a greater extent than is desirable or permissible (*too large*) 2 very (*not too sure*) 3 in addition (*I'm coming, too*) 4 moreover (*food was bad, and expensive, too*) 5 none too not at all (*feeling none too good*) 6 too much for: a more than a match for b beyond what is endurable by [stressed form of TO]

took /took/ *v.* past of TAKE

tool /too͞l/ *n.* 1 implement used to carry out mechanical functions by hand or by machine 2 thing used in an occupation or pursuit (*tools of one's trade*) 3 person merely used by another —*v.* 4 impress a design on (leather) 5 (foll. by *along, around*, etc.) drive or ride, esp. in a casual or leisurely manner [OE]

tool′mak′er *n.* person who makes precision tools —**tool′mak′ing** *n.*

toot /too͞t/ *n.* 1 short, sharp sound as made by a horn —*v.* 1 sound (a horn, etc.) with a short, sharp sound 3 give out such a sound [prob. imit.]

tooth /too͞TH/ *n.* (*pl.* **teeth**) 1 each of a set of hard, bony enamel-coated structures in the jaws of most vertebrates, used for biting and chewing 2 toothlike part or projection, e.g., the cog of a gearwheel, point of a saw or comb, etc. 3 (*pl.*) force; effectiveness 4 armed to the teeth completely and elaborately armed 5 fight tooth and nail fight very fiercely 6 get one's teeth into devote oneself seriously to 7 in the teeth of: a in spite of (opposition, difficulty, etc.) b contrary to (instructions, etc.) c directly against (the wind, etc.) —**toothed** *adj.*; **tooth′less** *adj.* [OE]

tooth′ache′ *n.* pain in a tooth or teeth

tooth′brush′ *n.* brush for cleaning the teeth

tooth′paste′ *n.* paste for cleaning the teeth

tooth′pick′ *n.* small, sharp stick for removing food lodged between the teeth

tooth′ pow′der *n.* powder for cleaning the teeth

tooth·some /too͞TH′sǝm/ *adj.* delicious

tooth′y *adj.* (·**i·er**, ·**i·est**) having large, numerous, or prominent teeth

too·tle /too͞t′l/ *v.* (·**tled**, ·**tling**) 1 toot gently or repeatedly 2 move casually

top[1] /täp/ *n.* 1 highest point or part 2 highest rank or place 3 upper surface or part 4 stopper; cap; lid 5 garment for the upper part of the body 6 utmost degree; height (*at the top of his voice*) 7 (*pl.*) *Colloq.* person or thing of the best quality —*adj.* 8 highest in position 9 highest in degree or importance —*v.* (**topped, top·ping**) 10 provide with a top, cap, etc. 11 be higher or better than; surpass; be at the top of; head (*topped the list*) 12 on top in a superior position; above; successful 13 on top of: a fully in command of b in close proximity to c in addition to 14 on top

of the world elated; exuberant —**top′most′** *adj.* [OE]

top[2] *n.* twirling toy that spins on a point [OE]

to·paz /tō′paz′/ *n.* transparent mineral, usu. yellow, used as a gem [Gk *topazos*]

top′ brass′ *n. Colloq.* highest-ranking officers or officials

top′coat′ *n.* 1 overcoat 2 last coat of paint, etc.

top′ draw·er′ *n.* high social position or origin

To·pe·ka /tǝpē′kǝ/ *n.* capital of Kan., in the NE part. Pop. 119,883

top·gal·lant /täpgal′ǝnt, tǝgal′-/ *n. Naut.* mast, sail, yard, or rigging immediately above the topmast and topsail

top′ hat′ *n.* tall, silk hat

top′-heav′y *adj.* disproportionately heavy at the top

to·pi·ar·y /tō′pē·er′ē/ *adj.* 1 of or formed by clipping shrubs, trees, etc., into ornamental shapes —*n.* 2 topiary art [Gk *topos* place]

top·ic /täp′ik/ *n.* subject of a discourse, conversation, argument, etc. [Gk *topos* place; commonplace]

top′i·cal *adj.* dealing with the news, current affairs, etc. —**top′i·cal′i·ty** /-kal′ǝtē/ *n.*; **top′i·cal·ly** *adv.*

top′knot′ *n.* 1 tuft, crest, or knot of hair or feathers worn or growing on top of the head 2 knot or bow of ribbon worn on top of the head

top′less *adj.* 1 without a top 2a (of clothes) having no upper part b (of esp. a woman) bare-breasted c (of a place) where women go topless; employing bare-breasted women

top′-lev′el *adj.* of the highest level of importance, prestige, etc.

top·mast /täp′mast′, -mǝst/ *n. Naut.* mast next above the lower mast

top′notch′ *adj.* first-rate

to·pog·ra·phy /tǝpäg′rǝfē/ *n.* 1 detailed description, mapping, etc., of the features of a region, town, etc. 2 such features —**to·pog′ra·pher** *n.*; **top′o·graph′i·cal** /-ǝgraf′ikǝl/ *adj.* [Gk *topos* place, -GRAPHY]

top′ping *n.* thing that tops another thing, as on ice cream, pizza, etc.

top·ple /täp′ǝl/ *v.* (·**pled**, ·**pling**) 1 (cause to) fall as if top-heavy 2 overthrow [fr. TOP[1]]

top′ quark′ *n. Physics.* hypothetical subatomic particle of great mass (also called **truth quark**)

top·sail /täp′sāl′, -sǝl/ *n. Naut.* square sail next above the lowest; fore-and-aft sail on a gaff

top′-se′cret *adj.* of the highest secrecy

top′side′ *n.* 1 side of a ship above the waterline —*adv.* 2 on or to an upper or main deck of a ship

top′soil′ *n.* top layer of soil

top′spin′ *n.* spinning motion imparted to a ball in tennis, etc., by hitting it forward and upward

top·sy-tur·vy /täp′sē·tur′vē/ *adv.* & *adj.* 1 upside down; reversed 2 in utter confusion [fr. TOP[1], obs. *terve* overturn]

toque /tōk/ *n.* woman's small, brimless hat [Fr]

tor /tôr/ *n.* hill or rocky peak [OE]

torch /tôrCH/ *n.* 1 thing lit for illumination 2 source of heat, illumination, or enlightenment

3 carry a torch for suffer from unrequited love for [L, rel. to TORT]

torch′ song *n.* popular song of unrequited love

tore /tôr/ *v.* past of TEAR[1]

TORII

to·ri·i /tōr′ē-ē/ *n. pl.* decorative gateway at the entrance to some Shinto temples

To·ri·no /tōrē′nō/ *n.* see TURIN

tor·ment *n.* /tôr′ment′/ 1 severe physical or mental suffering 2 cause of this —*v.* /tôrment′/ 3 subject to torment 4 tease or worry excessively —**tor·men′tor** *n.* [L *tormentum*]

torn /tôrn/ *v.* past part. of TEAR[1]

tor·na·do /tôrnā′dō/ *n.* (*pl.* **-does**) violent storm with whirling winds in a funnel-shaped cloud, usu. destructive along a narrow path [Sp *tronada* thunderstorm]

To·ron·to /təränt′ō/ *n.* capital of the Canadian province of Ontario. Pop. 3,893,000

tor·pe·do /tôrpē′dō/ *n.* (*pl.* **-does**) 1 cigar-shaped, self-propelled, underwater explosive missile —*v.* (**·doed, ·do·ing**) 2 destroy or attack with a torpedo 3 destroy or damage (a policy, institution, plan, etc.) [L: electric ray]

tor·pid /tôr′pid/ *adj.* 1 sluggish; inactive; apathetic 2 (of a hibernating animal) dormant —**tor·pid′i·ty** *n.* [L, rel. to TORPOR]

tor·por /tôr′pər/ *n.* torpid condition [L *torpere* be numb]

torque /tôrk/ *n. Mech.* twisting or rotating force, esp. in a machine [L *torquere* twist]

Tor·que·ma·da /tôr′kəmäd′ə/, **Tomás de** c. 1420–98; Spanish monk; prominent in Spanish Inquisition

Tor·rance /tôr′əns, tär′-/ *n.* city in Calif. Pop. 133,107

tor·rent /tôr′ənt, tär′-/ *n.* 1 rushing stream of liquid 2 (*pl.*) great downpour of rain 3 violent or copious flow (*torrent of abuse*) —**tor·ren·tial** /təren′SHəl/ *adj.* [L *torrens* rushing]

Tor·re·ón /tôr′ā-ōn′/ *n.* city in N Mexico. Pop. 328,100

tor·rid /tôr′id, tär′-/ *adj.* 1a (of the weather) very hot and dry **b** (of land, etc.) parched by such weather 2 passionate; intense [L *torrere tost-* parch]

tor′rid zone′ *n.* the part of the earth between the Tropics of Cancer and Capricorn

tor·sion /tôr′SHən/ *n.* twisting, esp. of one end of a body while the other is held fixed —**tor′sion·al** *adj.* [L, rel. to TORQUE]

tor·so /tôr′sō/ *n.* (*pl.* **-sos**) 1 trunk of the human body 2 statue of this [Gk *thyrsos* stem]

tort /tôrt/ *n. Law.* breach of duty (other than under contract) leading to liability for damages [L *torquere tort-* twist]

torte /tôrt/ *n.* type of rich dessert cake [Ger fr. It *torta* twisted (bread)]

tor·ti·lla /tôrtē′(y)ə/ *n.* thin, flat, unleavened cornmeal or flour cake [Sp dim. of *torta* cake]

tor·toise /tôr′təs/ *n.* turtle, esp. a land turtle [Gk *tartaroúcha* evil demon]

tor′toise·shell′ *n.* 1 yellowish-brown, mottled or clouded outer shell of some turtles —*adj.* 2 having the coloring or appearance of tortoiseshell

tor·tu·ous /tôr′CHŌŌəs/ *adj.* 1 full of twists and turns 2 devious; circuitous —**tor′tu·ous·ly** *adv.* [L, rel. to TORT]

tor·ture /tôr′CHər/ *n.* 1 infliction of severe bodily pain, esp. as a punishment or means of persuasion 2 severe physical or mental suffering —*v.* (**·tured, ·tur·ing**) 3 subject to torture —**tor′tur·er** *n.*; **tor′tur·ous** *adj.* [L *tortura* twisting, rel. to TORT]

● Usage: Note the difference between *torturous*, which has to do with torture, and *tortuous*, which means 'winding, twisting.'

To·ry /tôr′ē/ *n.* (*pl.* **·ries**) 1 member of the Conservative Party in Great Britain or Canada 2 *Hist.* member of the British party that gave rise to the Conservative Party (opp. WHIG) 3 one loyal to Great Britain during the American Revolution —**To′ry·ism′** *n.* [Ir: outlaw]

Tos·ca·ni·ni /täs′kənē′nē/, **Arturo** 1867–1975; Italian conductor

toss /tôs, täs/ *v.* 1 throw up (a ball, etc.) 2 roll about, throw, or be thrown, restlessly or from side to side 3 throw (a thing) lightly or carelessly 4a throw (a coin) into the air to decide a choice, etc., by the side on which it lands **b** settle a question or dispute with (a person) in this way 5 mix (salad ingredients, etc.) by moving or shaking them —*n.* 6 act of tossing (a coin, the head, etc.)

toss′up′ *n.* 1 an even chance 2 tossing of a coin

tot[1] /tät/ *n.* small child [perh. fr. *totterer*]

tot[2] *v.* (**tot·ted, tot·ting**) 1 add (figures, etc.) 2 (foll. by *up*) (of items) mount up [abbr. of TOTAL or of L *totum* the whole]

to·tal /tōt′l/ *adj.* 1 complete or comprising the whole 2 absolute (*in total ignorance*) —*n.* 3 total number or amount —*v.* (**·taled** or **·tal·led, ·tal·ing** or **·tal·ling**) 4 amount in number to 5 amount to [MedL *totus* entire]

to·tal·i·tar·i·an /tōtal′əter′ēən/ *adj.* of a one-party form of government requiring complete subservience; dictatorial —**to·tal′i·tar′i·an·ism′** *n.*

to·tal′i·ty *n.* (*pl.* **·ties**) entirety; complete amount

to·tal·i·za·tor /tōt′l·əzā′tər/ *n.* device showing the number and amount of bets staked, as for horse races

to′tal·ly *adv.* completely

tote /tōt/ *v.* (**tot·ed, tot·ing**) *Colloq.* carry; convey; transport [orig. US, prob. of dial. orig.]

tote′ bag′ *n.* carrying bag for shopping, etc.

to·tem /tō′təm/ *n.* 1 natural object or animal, adopted esp. by N American Indians as an emblem of a clan or individual 2 image of this —**to·tem′ic** /-tem′ik/ *adj.* [Algonquian]

tot·ter /tät′ər/ *v.* **1** stand or walk unsteadily or feebly **2a** shake as if about to collapse **b** (of a system of government, etc.) be about to fall —**tot′ter·er** *n.*; **tot′ter·y** *adj.* [Du]

tou·can /tōō′kan/ *n.* tropical American fruit-eating bird with an elongated beak [Tupi]

touch /təCH/ *v.* **1** come into or be in physical contact (a thing, each other, etc.) **2** bring the hand, etc., into contact with **3** bring (two things) into contact **4** rouse tender or painful feelings in **5** strike lightly **6** (usu. with *neg.*) a disturb, harm, or affect **b** have any dealings with **c** consume; use (*I don't touch alcohol*) **7** concern **8** (usu. with *neg.*) approach in excellence, etc. (*can't touch him for style*) **9** (as touched) slightly mad —*n.* **10** act of touching **11** faculty of perception through physical contact, esp. with the fingers **12a** small amount; slight trace **b** slightly **13a** manner of playing keys or strings **b** response of the keys or strings **c** distinguishing style of workmanship, writing, etc. **14** special talent or skill **15** *Slang.* act of getting money from a person by asking **16 in touch: a** in communication **b** aware **17 lose touch: a** cease to be informed **b** cease to be in contact **18 out of touch: a** not in correspondence **b** not up to date **c** lacking in awareness **19 touch down** (of an aircraft) make contact with the ground in landing **20 touch off: a** explode by touching with a match, etc. **b** initiate (a process) suddenly **21 touch on** (or **upon**) refer to or mention briefly or casually **22 touch up: a** give finishing touches to **b** retouch [OFr *tochier*]

touch′-and-go′ *adj.* critical; risky

touch′down′ *n.* **1** act of landing by an aircraft **2** *Football.* six-point score made by crossing the goal line with the ball **3** *Colloq.* a success

tou·ché /tōōSHā′/ *interj.* **1** acknowledgment of a justified accusation or retort **2** acknowledgment of a hit by a fencing opponent [Fr: *touched*]

touch′ing *adj.* moving; pathetic —**touch′ing·ly** *adv.*

touch′stone′ *n.* **1** dark schist or jasper used for testing alloys by marking it with them **2** criterion

touch′-type′ *v.* type without looking at the keys —**touch′-typ′ist** *n.*

touch′y *adj.* (·i·er, ·i·est) apt to take offense; oversensitive —**touch′i·ly** *adv.*; **touch′i·ness** *n.*

touch′y-feel′y /-fē′lē/ *adj. Colloq.* **1** readily demonstrative or emotional **2** characterized by emphasis on intuition rather than rationality

tough /təf/ *adj.* **1** hard to break, cut, tear, or chew **2** able to endure hardship; hardy **3** demanding; difficult **4** unpleasant **5a** severe; stringent (*get tough with*) **b** (of circumstances, luck, etc.) severe; hard **6** mean; incorrigible —*n.* **7** tough person, esp. a hoodlum —**tough′en** *v.*; **tough′ness** *n.* [OE]

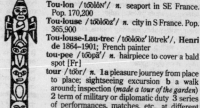

TOTEM
POLE

Tou·lon /tōōlôN′/ *n.* seaport in SE France. Pop. 170,200

Tou·louse /tōōlōōz′/ *n.* city in S France. Pop. 365,900

Tou·louse-Lau·trec /tōōlōōz′lōtrek′/, **Henri de** 1864–1901; French painter

tou·pee /tōōpā′/ *n.* hairpiece to cover a bald spot [Fr]

tour /tōōr/ *n.* **1a** pleasure journey from place to place; sightseeing excursion **b** a walk around; inspection (*made a tour of the garden*) **2** term of military or diplomatic duty **3** series of performances, matches, etc., at different places —*v.* **4** make a tour **5** make a tour of (a country, etc.) [OFr *tourner* turn]

tour de force /tōōr′ də fôrs′/ *n.* (*pl.* **tours de force**, pronunc. same) exceptional or virtuoso feat or performance [Fr]

tour′ism′ *n.* tourist booking and travel

tour′ist *n.* **1** person traveling for pleasure, esp. abroad —*adj.* **2** for tourists

tour·ma·line /tōōr′malēn/ *n.* mineral of various colors used as a gemstone [Fr fr. Sinhalese]

tour·na·ment /tōōr′nəmənt, tər′-/ *n.* **1** large contest of many rounds **2** *Hist.* pageant with jousting [Fr, rel. to TOURNEY]

tour·ney /tōōr′nē, tər′-/ *n.* (*pl.* **-neys**) tournament [Fr *tourner* turn]

tour·ni·quet /tōōr′nikit, tər′-/ *n.* device for constricting heavy, arterial blood flow [Fr]

Tours /tōōr/ *n.* city in W France. Pop. 133,400

tou·sle /tou′zəl, -səl/ *v.* (·sled, ·sling) make (esp. the hair) untidy; muss up [dial. *touse*]

tout /tout/ *v.* **1** promote or advertise; praise highly **2** spy out the movements and condition of racehorses in training —*n.* **3** person who touts [OE: peep]

tow /tō/ *v.* **1** pull along by a rope, etc. —*n.* **2** towing or being towed **3 have in tow: a** be towing **b** be accompanied by and often in charge of (a person) [OE]

toward /tôrd, təwôrd/ *prep.* (also **towards** /-z/) **1** in the direction of (*set out toward town*) **2** as regards; in relation to (*attitude toward death*) **3** as a contribution to; for (*put it toward her vacation*) **4** near (*toward the end of our journey*) [OE: future, rel. to TO, -WARD]

tow·el /tou′əl, toul/ *n.* absorbent cloth or paper used for drying after washing [Fr *toail(l)e* fr. Gmc]

tow′el·ing *n.* (also **tow′el·ling**) thick, soft, absorbent cloth, used esp. for towels

tow·er /tou′ər/ *n.* **1** tall structure, often part of a church, castle, etc. **2** fortress, etc., with a tower **3** tall structure housing machinery, etc. (*cooling tower; control tower*) —*v.* **4** reach or be high or above; be superior [Gk *turris*]

tow′er·ing *adj.* **1** high; lofty (*towering intellect*) **2** extreme (*towering rage*)

tow·head·ed /tou′hed′id/ *adj.* having very light hair —**tow′head′** *n.*

town /toun/ *n.* **1a** densely populated defined area, between a city and a village in size **b** densely populated area, esp. as contrasted with the country **2** central business area in a city **3 go to town** *Colloq.* do something with great energy or enthusiasm [OE]

town' cri'er *n. Hist.* person who made public announcements by loud calls

town' hall' *n.* headquarters of local government, with public meeting rooms, etc.

town' house' *n.* **1** town residence, esp. of a person with a house in the country **2** living unit of two or more stories, as one of a complex of similar units

town·ie /toun'ē/ *n.* (also **town'ee**) town inhabitant, esp. a nonstudent in a college town

towns·folk /tounz'fōk'/ *n. pl.* (also **towns' peo'ple**) inhabitants of a town

towns·man /tounz'mən/ *n.* (*pl.* **-men;** *fem.* **·wom'an,** *pl.* **·wom'en**) inhabitant of a town

tow·path /tō'paTH'/ *n.* path by a river or canal, orig. used for a horse towing a boat

tox·e·mia /täksē'mēə/ *n.* blood poisoning [rel. to TOXIC, Gk *haima* blood]

tox·ic /täk'sik/ *adj.* **1** poisonous **2** of poison —**tox·ic'i·ty** /-sis'itē/ *n.* [Gk *toxikon* poison for arrows]

tox·i·col·o·gy /täk'sikäl'əjē/ *n.* the study of poisons —**tox'i·co·log'i·cal** /-kəläj'ikəl/ *adj.*; **tox'i·col'o·gist** *n.*

tox·in /täk'sin/ *n.* poison produced by a living organism

toy /toi/ *n.* **1** plaything **2** thing regarded as providing amusement **3** diminutive breed of dog, etc. —*v.* (usu. foll. by *with*) **4** trifle; amuse oneself; flirt **5** move a thing idly

Toyn·bee /toin'bē/, **Arnold Joseph** 1889–1975; English historian

tp. *abbr.* **1** (also **t.p.**) title page **2** township **3** troop

tpk. *abbr.* turnpike

trace¹ /trās/ *v.* (**traced, trac·ing**) **1a** observe or find vestiges or signs of by investigation **b** track down or find (a person or thing missing) **c** follow or mark the track or position of **d** follow to its origins **2** copy (a drawing, etc.) by drawing over its lines on superimposed translucent paper **3** mark out, esp. laboriously **4** make one's way along (a path, etc.) —*n.* **5a** indication of something having existed; vestige **b** very small quantity **6** track; footprint —**trace'a·ble** *adj.* [L *trahere* draw]

trace² *n.* **1** each of the two straps, chains, or ropes by which a horse draws a vehicle **2** kick over the traces become insubordinate or reckless [Fr *trais*, pl. of TRAIT]

trace' el'e·ment *n.* chemical element required only in minute amounts by organisms for normal growth

trac'er *n.* **1** person or thing that traces **2** bullet, etc., that is visible in flight because of flames, etc., emitted **3** radioactive isotope that can be followed through the body by the radiation it produces **4** inquiry sent after a missing package, shipment, etc.

trac·er·y /trā'sarē/ *n.* (*pl.* **-ies**) **1** ornamental stone openwork, esp. in the upper part of a Gothic window **2** fine decorative pattern

tra·che·a /trā'kēə/ *n.* (*pl.* **·ae** /-ē', -ī'/ or **·as**) windpipe [L fr. Gk]

tra·che·ot·o·my /trā'kē·ät'əmē/ *n.* (*pl.* **·mies**) incision of the trachea to relieve an obstruction

trac'ing *n.* **1** traced copy of a drawing, etc. **2** act of tracing

track /trak/ *n.* **1** mark(s) left by a person, animal, vehicle, etc. **2** rough path, esp. one beaten by use **3** pair of parallel rails for a railroad **4a** race course; circuit **b** prepared course for runners, etc. **5** section of a record, CD, or magnetic tape containing one song, etc. **6** line of travel (*track of the comet*) **7** line of thought or action —*v.* **8** follow the track of **9** trace (a course, development, etc.) **10** in one's tracks *Colloq.* where one stands; instantly (*stopped him in his tracks*) **11** keep (or lose) track of follow (or fail to follow) the course of **12** make tracks *Colloq.* depart **13** track down reach or capture by tracking —**track'er** *n.* [Fr *trac*]

track·ball /trak'bôl'/ *n. Comp.* input device utilizing a ball that is manipulated to control a cursor on a monitor

track' re'cord *n.* person's past performance

tract¹ /trakt/ *n.* **1** stretch or extent of territory, esp. large **2** bodily organ or system (*digestive tract*) [L *trahere tract-* pull]

tract² *n.* pamphlet, esp. religious or political [appar. LL *tractatus* treatise]

trac·ta·ble /trak'təbəl/ *adj.* easily handled; manageable —**trac'ta·bil'i·ty** /-bil'ətē/ *n.* [L *tractare* handle]

trac·tion /trak'SHən/ *n.* **1** act of hauling or pulling a thing over a surface **2** adhering power on a surface **3** therapeutic pulling on a limb, etc. [Fr or MedL, rel. to TRACT¹]

trac·tor /trak'tər/ *n.* **1** vehicle used for pulling farm machinery, etc. **2** driver's cab for a trailer, etc. [rel. to TRACTION]

trac'tor-trail'er *n.* combination of a tractor and a trailer or semitrailer, used to transport goods

Tra·cy /trā'sē/, **Spencer** 1900–67; US actor

trade /trād/ *n.* **1a** buying and selling **b** this between nations, etc. **c** business conducted for profit (esp. as distinct from a profession) **d** business of a specified nature or time (*Christmas trade; tourist trade*) **2** skilled craft practiced professionally **3** exchanging; swap **4** (*pl.*) TRADE WIND —*v.* (**trad·ed, trad·ing**) **5** engage in trade; buy and sell **6a** exchange in commerce **b** exchange (insults, blows, etc.) **c** swap **7** have a transaction (with a person for a thing) **8** trade in exchange (esp. a used car) in part payment for another **9** trade off exchange, esp. as a compromise **10** trade on take advantage of —**trad'a·ble** or **trade' a·ble** *adj.* [LGer: track, rel. to TREAD]

trade'-in' *n.* thing given in part exchange for another

trade'mark' *n.* **1** device or name secured by law or custom as representing a company, product, etc. **2** distinctive characteristic, etc.

trade' name' *n.* **1** name by which a thing is called in a trade **2** name given to a product **3** name under which a business trades

trade'-off' *n.* balance; compromise

trad'er *n.* person, ship, etc., engaged in trade

trades·man /trādz'mən/ *n.* (*pl.* **·men;** *fem.* **·wom'an,** *pl.* **·wom'en**) person engaged in trade

trade' wind' *n.* (also **trades**) wind blowing continually toward the equator and deflected westward

trad'ing *n.* **1** act of engaging in trade —*adj.* **2** engaged in trade (*trading partner*)

trad'ing post' *n.* store in a remote or unsettled region

tra·di·tion /trədɪsн'ən/ *n.* **1a** custom, opinion, or belief handed down to posterity **b** this process of handing down **2** artistic, literary, etc., principles based on experience and practice **3** valued convention or observance —**tra·di'tion·al** *adj.;* **tra·di'tion·al·ly** *adv.* [L *tradere -dit-* hand on; betray]

tra·di'tion·al·ism *n.* respect or support for tradition —**tra·di'tion·al·ist** /-ist/ *n. & adj.*

tra·duce /trəd(y)ōōs'/ *v.* (**·duced, ·duc·ing**) speak ill of; slander —**tra·duce'ment, tra·duc'er** *n.* [L *trans-* across, *ducere* lead]

traf·fic /traf'ik/ *n.* **1** vehicles moving on a public highway, in the air, or at sea **2** trade, esp. illegal **3** comings and goings **4** dealings between people, etc. (*had no traffic with them*) **5a** transmitted messages **b** volume of these —*v.* (**·ficked, ·fick·ing**) **6** (usu. foll. by *in*) deal in something, esp. illegally **7** deal in; barter —**traf'fick·er** *n.* [Fr fr. It]

traf'fic cir'cle *n.* circular area at the junction of usu. three or more roads to allow the passage of vehicles from one road to another

traf'fic jam' *n.* traffic congestion

traf'fic light' *n.* signal controlling road traffic by colored lights

trag·e·dy /traj'ədē/ *n.* (*pl.* **·dies**) **1** serious accident, disaster, etc.; great misfortune **2a** play dealing with tragic events and ending unhappily, esp. with the downfall of the protagonist **b** such plays as a genre —**tra·ge·di·an** /trəjē'dēən/ *n.* [Gk *tragōidia* goat song]

trag·ic /traj'ik/ *adj.* **1** disastrous; greatly distressing; very sad **2** of tragedy —**trag'i·cal·ly** *adv.*

trag·i·com·e·dy /traj'ikäm'ədē/ *n.* (*pl.* **·dies**) play or situation with a mixture of comedy and tragedy —**trag'i·com'ic** *adj.*

trail /trāl/ *n.* **1** track or scent left by a moving thing, person, etc. **2** beaten path, esp. through a wild region **3** line of people or things following behind something —*v.* **1** draw or be drawn along behind, esp. on the ground **2** walk wearily (behind) **3** follow the trail of; pursue **4** be losing in a contest **5** (usu. foll. by *off*) grow dimmer or weaker **6** (of a plant, etc.) grow or hang over a wall, along the ground, etc. [Fr or LGer]

trail·blaz·er /trāl'blā'zər/ *n.* **1** person who marks a new track through wild country **2** pioneer —**trail'blaz'ing** *n.*

trail'er *n.* **1** scenes from a film used to advertise it in advance **2** vehicle towed by another **3** such a vehicle equipped with living accommodations

train /trān/ *v.* **1a** teach (a person, animal, oneself, etc.) a specified skill, esp. by practice **b** undergo this process (*trained as a teacher*) **2** guide toward or achieve physical fitness by exercise, diet, etc. **3** make (the mind, eye, etc.) discerning through practice, etc. **4** point or aim (a gun, camera, etc.) —*n.* **5** series of railroad cars drawn by an engine **6** thing dragged along behind or forming the back part of a dress, robe, etc. **7** succession or series of people, things, events, etc. **8** train of thought sequence or direction in one's thinking process —**train·ee'**, **train'ing** *n.* [L *trahere* draw]

train'er *n.* **1** person who prepares horses, athletes, etc., for competition **2** aircraft or simulator used to train pilots

traipse /trāps/ *v.* (**traipsed, traips·ing**) *Colloq.* tramp or trudge wearily

trait /trāt/ *n.* characteristic [L *tractus*, rel. to TRACT¹]

trai·tor /trā'tər/ *n.* person who is treacherous or disloyal, esp. to his or her country —**trai'tor·ous** *adj.;* **trait'or·ous·ly** *adv.;* **trait'or·ous·ness** *n.* [L *tradere* betray]

tra·jec·to·ry /trəjek'tərē/ *n.* (*pl.* **·ries**) path of an object moving under given forces [L *trans-* across, *jacere* throw]

tram·mel /tram'əl/ *n.* **1** (usu. *pl.*) impediment; hindrance **2** triple dragnet for fishing —*v.* (**·meled** or **·melled, ·mel·ing** or **·mel·ling**) **3** hamper [MedL *tremaculum*]

tramp /tramp/ *v.* **1a** walk heavily and firmly **b** go on foot, esp. a distance **2** tread on; trample; stamp on —*n.* **3** itinerant vagrant or beggar **4** sound of a person, or esp. people, walking, marching, etc. **5** long walk **6** *Slang. Derog.* promiscuous woman [ME *trampen*]

tram·ple /tram'pəl/ *v.* (**·pled, ·pling**) tread under foot or crush in this way [fr. TRAMP]

tram·po·line /tram'pəlēn/ *n.* **1** strong fabric sheet connected by springs to a horizontal frame, used for gymnastic jumping —*v.* (**·lined, ·lin·ing**) **2** use a trampoline [It *trampolino*]

trance /trans/ *n.* **1** sleeplike state without response to stimuli; hypnotic or cataleptic state **2** abstracted or stuporous state [L *transire* pass over]

tran·quil /traNG'kwil/ *adj.* (**·quil·er** or **·quil·ler, ·quil·est** or **·quil·lest**) calm; serene; undisturbed —**tran·quil'i·ty** or **tran·quil'li·ty** *n.;* **tran'quil·ly** *adv.* [L]

tran·quil·ize /traNG'kwəlīz'/ *v.* (also **tran'quil·lize'**) (**·quil·ized** or **·quil·lized, ·quil·iz·ing** or **·quil·liz·ing**) make tranquil, esp. by a drug, etc.

tran'quil·iz·er *n.* (also **tran'quil·liz'er**) drug used to diminish anxiety

trans- *prefix* **1** across; beyond **2** on or to the other side of **3** through [L]

trans. *abbr.* **1** transaction **2** transfer **3** transitive **4** (also **transl.**) translated; translation; translator **5** transmission **6** transportation **7** transpose; transposition **8** transverse

trans·act /tranzakt'/ *v.* perform or carry out (business) [L, rel. to ACT]

trans·ac'tion *n.* **1a** business agreement or deal **b** transacting of business, etc. **2** (*pl.*) published reports of the proceedings of a learned society

trans·at·lan·tic /tranzətlan'tik/ *adj.* **1** on the other side of the Atlantic Ocean **2** crossing the Atlantic

trans·ceiv·er /transē'vər/ *n.* combined radio transmitter and receiver

tran·scend /transend'/ *v.* **1** be beyond the range or grasp of (human experience, reason, belief, etc.) **2** excel; surpass [L *scandere* climb]

tran·scen'dent *adj.* **1** excelling; surpassing **2** transcending human experience —**tran·scen'dence, tran·scen·den·cy** *n.*

tran·scen·den·tal /tran'səndent'l/ *adj.* **1** *Philos.* a priori; not based on experience; intuitively accepted; innate in the mind **2** visionary; abstract —**tran'scen·den'tal·ly** adv.

tran·scen·den·tal·ism / n. transcendental philosophy —**tran'scen·den'tal·ist** /-ist/ n.

trans·con·ti·nen·tal adj. crossing or extending across a continent

tran·scribe / transkrīb'/ v. (·**scribed**, ·**scrib·ing**) **1** copy out **2** write out (shorthand, notes, etc.) in full **3** arrange (music) for a different instrument, etc. —**tran·scrib'er, tran·scrip'tion** /-skrip'SHən/ n. [L transcribere -script-]

tran·script / tran'skript/ n. written copy

trans·duc·er / tranzd(y)ōō'sər/ n. device for converting energy into another form, as (in a microphone) acoustical pressure into electrical impulses [L, rel. to DUCT]

tran·sept / tran'sept/ n. **1** the part of a cross-shaped church at right angles to the nave **2** either arm of this [L, rel. to SEPTUM]

trans·fer v. /transfər', trans'fər/ (·**ferred**, ·**fer·ring**) **1** (often foll. by to) **a** convey, remove, or hand over **b** make over the possession of (property, rights, etc.) to a person **2** change or move to another group, club, department, etc. **3** change from one public vehicle, route, etc., to another on a journey **4** convey (a design) from one surface to another —n. / trans'fər/ **5** transferring or being transferred **6** design, etc., conveyed or to be conveyed from one surface to another **7** document effecting conveyance of property, a right, etc. **8** ticket for transferring during travel —**trans·fer'a·ble** adj. [L ferre bear]

trans·fer·ence / transfər'əns, trans'fərəns/ n. **1** transferring or being transferred **2** Psychol. redirection of childhood emotions to a new object, esp. to a psychoanalyst

trans·fig·ure v. (·**ured**, ·**ur·ing**) change in form or appearance, esp. so as to elevate or idealize —**trans'fig·u·ra'tion** n. [L]

trans·fix v. **1** paralyze with horror or astonishment **2** pierce with a sharp implement or weapon [L, rel. to FIX]

trans·form v. make a thorough or dramatic change in the form, appearance, character, etc., of —**trans'for·ma'tion** n. [L]

trans·form·er n. apparatus for reducing or increasing the voltage of an alternating current or reducing that of a direct current

trans·fuse / transfyōōz'/ v. (·**fused**, ·**fus·ing**) **1a** transfer (blood) from one person or animal to another **b** inject (liquid) into a blood vessel to replace lost fluid **2** permeate —**trans·fu'sion** /-ZHən/ n. [L, rel. to FOUND³]

trans·gress / tranzgres'/ v. go beyond the bounds or limits set by (a commandment, law, etc.); sin —**trans·gres'sion** /-SHən/, **trans·gres'sor** n. [L transgredi -gress-]

tran·sient / tran'SH(ē)ənt, -zēənt/ adj. **1** of short duration; passing —n. **2** temporary dweller, worker, etc. —**tran'sience** n. [L, rel. to TRANCE]

tran·sis·tor / tranzis'tər/ n. **1** semiconductor device with three connections, capable of amplification in addition to rectification **2** (in full **tran·sis'tor ra'di·o**) portable radio with tran-

sistors —**tran·sis'tor·ize'** v. (·**ized**, ·**iz·ing**) [fr. TRAN(SFER), (RE)SISTOR]

transit / tran'zit/ n. **1** going, conveying, or being conveyed, esp. over a distance **2** passage; route **3** apparent passage of a celestial body across the meridian of a place or across the sun or a planet [L trans over, ire go]

tran·si·tion / tranzish'ən/ n. passing or change from one place, state, condition, style, etc., to another —**tran·si'tion·al** adj.; **tran·si'tion·al·ly** adv. [L, rel. to TRANSIT]

tran·si·tive / tran'sətiv/ adj. Gram. (of a verb) taking a direct object (whether expressed or implied), e.g., saw in saw the donkey; saw that she was ill [L, rel. to TRANSIT]

tran·si·to·ry / tran'sitôr'ē/ adj. not permanent; brief; transient —**tran'si·to'ri·ly** adv.; **tran'si·to'ri·ness** n. [L, rel. to TRANSIT]

trans·late / translāt', tranz-, trans'lāt, tranz'-/ v. (·**lat·ed**, ·**lat·ing**) **1** express the sense of (a word, text, etc.) in another language or in another form **2** be translatable (does not translate well) **3** interpret (translated his silence as dissent) —**trans·lat'a·ble** adj.; **trans·la'tion, trans'la·tor** n. [L, rel. to TRANSFER]

trans·lit·er·ate / tranzlit'ərāt'/ v. (·**ated**, ·**at·ing**) represent (a word, etc.) in the closest corresponding letters of a different script —**trans·lit'er·a'tion** n. [L litera letter]

trans·lu·cent / translōō'sənt, tranz-/ adj. allowing light to pass through; semitransparent —**trans·lu'cence, trans·lu'cen·cy** n. [L lucere shine]

trans·mi·grate v. (·**grat·ed**, ·**grat·ing**) **1** (of the soul) pass into a different body at death **2** migrate —**trans'mi·gra'tion** n. [L]

trans·mis·sion / tranzmisH'ən/ n. **1** transmitting or being transmitted **2** broadcast program **3** mechanism transmitting power from the engine to the axle in a vehicle

trans·mit / tranzmit'/ v. (·**mit·ted**, ·**mit·ting**) **1a** pass or hand on; transfer **b** communicate **2** allow to pass through; conduct **3** broadcast (a radio or television program) —**trans·mis'si·ble** or **trans·mit'ta·ble** adj. [L mittere miss- send]

trans·mit·ter n. **1** person or thing that transmits **2** equipment used to transmit radio or other electronic signals

trans·mog·ri·fy / tranzmäg'rəfī/ v. (·**fied**, ·**fy·ing**) transform, esp. in a magical or surprising manner —**trans·mog'ri·fi·ca'tion** /-fikā'sHən/ n.

trans·mute / tranzmyōōt'/ v. (·**mut·ed**, ·**mut·ing**) **1** change the form, nature, or substance of **2** Hist. (supposedly) change (base metals) into gold —**trans'mu·ta'tion** n. [L mutare change]

trans·oce·an·ic / tranz'ō'SHē·an'ik/ adj. **1** beyond the ocean **2** crossing the ocean

tran·som / tran'səm/ n. **1** horizontal bar of wood or stone across a window or the top of a door **2** window above a door [Fr traversin, rel. to TRAVERSE]

trans·par·en·cy / transpar'ənsē/ n. (pl. ·**cies**) **1** being transparent **2** picture, esp. a photograph, to be viewed by light passing through it [MedL, rel. to TRANSPARENT]

trans·par·ent / transpar'ənt/ adj. **1** allowing light to pass through; perfectly clear and (usu.) colorless **2a** (of a disguise, pretext, etc.) easily seen through **b** (of a quality, etc.)

evident; obvious **3** easily understood; frank —**trans·par'ent·ly** *adv.* [L *parere* appear]

tran·spire /transpī'ər/ *v.* (·**spired, ·spir·ing**) **1** (usu. prec. by *it* as subject) come to be known; turn out (*it transpired he knew nothing about it*) **2** emit (vapor or moisture) or be emitted through the skin, lungs, or leaves; perspire **3** occur; happen —**tran'spi·ra'tion** /-porə'SHən/ *n.* (in sense 2) [L *spirare* breathe]

trans·plant *v.* /transplant'/ **1** plant in another place **2** *Surg.* transfer (living tissue or an organ) to another part of the body or to another body —*n.* /trans'plant'/ **3a** transplanting of an organ or tissue **b** such an organ, etc. **4** thing, esp. a plant, transplanted **5** person who has relocated —**trans'plan·ta'tion** /-tā'SHən/ *n.* [L]

tran·spon·der /transpän'dər/ *n.* device for receiving a radio signal and automatically transmitting a different signal [fr. TRANS(MIT), (RE)SPOND]

trans·port *v.* /transpôrt'/ **1** take or carry to another place **2** affected with strong emotion —*n.* /trans'pôrt/ **3** system or vehicle for conveyance **4** ship, aircraft, etc., used to carry soldiers, stores, etc. **5** (esp. *pl.*) rapture (*transports of joy*) —**trans·port'a·ble** *adj.* [L *portare* carry]

trans·por·ta·tion /trans'pərtā'SHən/ *n.* **1** conveying; being conveyed **2a** system of conveying **b** means of this

trans·pose /transpōz'/ *v.* (·**posed, ·pos·ing**) **1** cause (two or more things) to change places **2** change the order or position of (words or a word) in a sentence **3** put (music) into a different key —**trans'po·si'tion** /-pəzi'SHən/ *n.* [Fr, rel. to POSE]

trans·sex·u·al *adj.* **1** having the physical characteristics of one sex but psychological identification with the other —*n.* **2** transsexual person **3** person who has had a sex change

trans·ship' *v.* (·**shipped, ·ship·ping**) transfer from one ship or form of transport to another —**trans·ship'ment** *n.*

tran·sub·stan·ti·a·tion /tran'səbstan'SHē·ā'SHən/ *n.* *RC Ch.* doctrine that the Eucharistic elements are wholly converted into the body and blood of Christ [MedL, rel. to TRANS-, SUBSTANCE]

Trans·vaal /tranzväl'/ *n.* province in the NE of the Republic of South Africa

trans·verse *adj.* /tranzvərs', tranz'vərs'/ crosswise —*n.* /tranz'vərs/ **2** something that traverses, as a road —**trans·verse'ly** *adv.* [L *transvertere* -*vers*- turn across]

trans·ves·tite /tranzves'tīt/ *n.* person (usu. a man) deriving esp. sexual pleasure from dressing in clothes of the opposite sex —**trans·ves'tism** /-tizəm/ *n.* [L *vestire* clothe]

Tran·syl·va·ni·a /tran'silvā'nēə/ *n.* a region and former province in central Romania

trap /trap/ *n.* **1** device, often baited, for catching animals **2** trick betraying a person into speech or an act **3** arrangement to catch an unsuspecting person **4** device for hurling a clay target into the air to be shot at **5** sealing curve or vertical S-curve in a drainpipe **6** (*pl.*) percussion instruments, as in a band **7** two-wheeled carriage (*pony and trap*) **8** TRAPDOOR **9** *Slang.* mouth —*v.* (**trapped, trap·ping**) **10** catch (an animal) in a trap **11** catch or catch out (a person) by means of a trick, etc. **12** stop and retain in or as in a trap [OE]

trap'door' *n.* hinged door in a horizontal surface

tra·peze /trapēz', trap-/ *n.* crossbar suspended by ropes as a swing for acrobatics, etc. [L, rel. to TRAPEZIUM]

tra·pe·zi·um /trapē'zēəm/ *n.* (*pl.* ·**ums** or ·**zi·a** /-ə/) quadrilateral plane figure with no two sides parallel [Gk *trapeza* table]

trap·e·zoid /trap'əzoid'/ *n.* quadrilateral with one pair of sides parallel [Gk, rel. to TRAPEZIUM]

trap'per *n.* person who traps wild animals, esp. for their fur

trap'pings *n. pl.* **1** ornamental accessories **2** harness of a horse, esp. when ornamental [OFr *drap* cloth]

TRAPEZOID

Trap'pist *n.* monk of an order vowed to silence [*La Trappe* in Normandy]

trash /trasH/ *n.* **1** worthless material or waste; rubbish **2** worthless person or persons —*v.* **3** *Slang.* wreck; vandalize —**trash'y** *adj.* (·**i·er, ·i·est**)

trau·ma /trô'mə, trou'mə/ *n.* (*pl.* ·**mas** or ·**ma·ta** /-mətə/) **1** profound emotional shock **2** physical injury **3** physical shock syndrome following this —**trau'ma·tize** *v.* (·**tized, ·tiz·ing**) [Gk: wound]

trau·mat·ic /trəmat'ik, trô-, trou-/ *adj.* **1** of or causing trauma **2** distressing (*traumatic experience*) —**trau·mat'i·cal·ly** *adv.* [Gk, rel. to TRAUMA]

trav. *abbr.* travel; traveler

tra·vail /travāl', trav'āl'/ *n. Lit.* **1** burdensome effort; toil **2** anguishing hardship **3** pangs of childbirth [Fr *travaillier* torment]

trav·el /trav'əl/ *v.* (·**eled** or ·**elled, ·el·ing** or **el·ling**) **1** go from one place to another; make a journey, esp. a long one or abroad **2a** journey along or through (a country) **b** cover (a distance) in traveling **3** move or proceed as specified (*light travels faster than sound*) **4** (of a machine or part) move or operate in a specified way —*n.* **5a** traveling, esp. in foreign countries **b** (often *pl.*) wanderings or journeys over time **6** range, rate, or mode of motion of a part in machinery —**trav'el·er** or **trav'el·ler** *n.* [orig. TRAVAIL]

trav'el·er's check' *n.* (also **trav'el·ler's check'**) check, issued by a bank, etc., purchased for a fixed amount, to be cashed on signature

trav·e·logue /trav'əlôg', -läg'/ *n.* (also **trav·e·log**) film or illustrated lecture about travel [fr. TRAVEL, after *monologue*]

tra·verse *v.* /travərs', tra-/ (·**versed, ·vers·ing**) **1** travel or lie across (*traversed the country*) —*n.* /trav'ərs/ **2** traversing **3** thing that crosses another —**tra·vers'al** *n.* [Fr, rel. to TRANSVERSE]

trav·es·ty /trav'əstē/ *n.* (*pl.* ·**ties**) **1** grotesque; burlesque —*v.* (·**tied, ·ty·ing**) **2** make or be a travesty of [ult. fr. L *trans* over, *vestire* dress]

trawl /trôl/ *v.* **1** fish with a trawl or seine **2**

catch by trawling —n. 3 act of trawling 4 (in full **trawl′net′**) large, widemouthed fishing net dragged by a boat along the sea bottom [prob. Du *traghel* dragnet]

trawl·er n. boat used for trawling

tray /trā/ n. 1 flat board, usu. with a raised rim, for carrying dishes, etc. 2 shallow lidless box for papers or small articles [OE]

treach·er·ous /treCH′ərəs/ adj. 1 guilty of or involving treachery 2 (of the weather, ice, the memory, etc.) hazardous; unreliable —**treach′er·ous·ly** adv.

treach·er·y /treCH′ərē/ n. (pl. ·ies) violation of faith or trust; betrayal; treason [OFr fr. *trichier* cheat]

trea·cle /trē′kəl/ n. 1 (esp. *Brit.*) molasses 2 cloying sweetness or sentiment —**trea·cly** /trē′klē/ adj. [Fr fr. L *theriaca* antidote against a snakebite]

tread /tred/ v. (**trod**, **trod·den** or **trod**, **tread·ing**) 1 set down one's foot; walk; step 2 walk upon 3 perform (steps, etc.) by walking —n. 4 manner or sound of walking 5 top surface of a step or stair 6 surface pattern on a tire 7 shoe part that rests on the ground 8 **tread water** maintain an upright position in water by moving the feet and hands [OE]

trea·dle /tred′l/ n. lever worked by the foot and imparting motion to a machine [OE, rel. to TREAD]

tread′mill′ n. 1 device for producing motion by the weight of persons or animals stepping on steps attached to a revolving upright wheel 2 similar device used for exercise 3 monotonous routine work

trea·son /trē′zən/ n. betrayal of one's country —**trea′son·a·ble** adj. [L, rel. to TRADITION]

treas·ure /trezH′ər/ n. 1 a precious metals or gems b hoard of these c wealth; valuables 2 thing valued for its rarity, workmanship, associations, etc. (art treasures) 3 much loved or highly valued person —v. (·**ured**, ·**ur·ing**) 4 value highly [Gk *thēsauros*]

treas′ur·er n. person in charge of the funds of an organization, etc.

treas′ure-trove′ n. discovered treasure of unknown ownership

treas′ur·y n. (pl. ·ies) 1 place or building where treasure is stored 2 funds or revenue of a government, institution, or society 3 (*cap*) a department managing the public revenue of a country b offices and officers of this

treat /trēt/ v. 1 act or behave toward or deal with in a certain way 2 apply a process to (treat it with acid) 3 apply medical care or attention to 4 address or present (a subject) in literature or art 5 pay for food, drink, entertainment, etc. 6 negotiate terms (with a person) 7 discuss —n. 8 delightful event or circumstance 9 meal, entertainment, etc., paid for by another —**treat′a·ble** adj. [L *trahere* draw]

trea·tise /trē′tis/ n. a written work dealing formally and systematically with a subject [AngFr, rel. to TREAT]

treat′ment n. 1 process or manner of behaving toward or dealing with a person or thing 2 medical care or attention 3 manner of treating a subject in literature or art

trea·ty /trē′tē/ n. (pl. ·ties) formal agreement between nations or governments [L, rel. to TREAT]

tre·ble /treb′əl/ adj. 1 threefold; triple 2 SOPRANO —n. 3 *Mus.* SOPRANO —v. (·**bled**, ·**bling**) 4 make or become three times as much or many; increase threefold —**tre′bly** adv. [L, rel. to TRIPLE]

tre′ble clef′ n. *Mus.* clef placing the G above middle C on the second lowest line of the staff

tree /trē/ n. 1 branched perennial plant with a woody, self-supporting main stem or trunk 2 piece or frame of wood, etc., for various purposes (shoetree) 3 FAMILY TREE —v. (**treed**, **tree·ing**) 4 force to take refuge in a tree —**tree′less** adj. [OE]

tree′ line′ n. TIMBERLINE

tre·foil /trē′foil, tref′oil/ n. 1 leguminous plant with leaves of three leaflets, esp. clover 2 three-lobed ornamentation in architecture, etc. [ult. fr. L *tri-* three, *folium* leaf]

trek /trek/ v. (**trekked**, **trek·king**) 1 travel or make one's way arduously —n. 2 long or arduous journey or walk 3 organized migration of a body of people —**trek′ker** n. [Du: draw]

trel·lis /trel′is/ n. lattice of light wooden or metal laths, esp. as a support for climbing plants [Fr *trelis*]

trem·a·tode /trem′ətōd/ n. a kind of parasitic flatworm [Gk *trēmatōdēs* perforated]

trem·ble /trem′bəl/ v. (·**bled**, ·**bling**) 1 shake involuntarily from emotion, weakness, etc. 2 be in a state of extreme apprehension 3 quiver —n. 4 trembling; quiver (tremble in his voice) [MedL, rel. to TREMULOUS]

tre·men·dous /trimen′dəs/ adj. 1 huge; enormous 2 remarkable; considerable; excellent 3 awe-inspiring; overpowering 4 dreadful; frightening —**tre·men′dous·ly** adv. [L *tremendus* to be trembled at, rel. to TREMOR]

trem·o·lo /trem′əlō/ n. (pl. ·los) tremulous effect in music [It, rel. to TREMULOUS]

trem·or /trem′ər/ n. 1 shaking; quivering 2 thrill 3 (in full **earth′ trem′or**) slight earthquake [L *tremere* tremble]

trem·u·lous /trem′yələs/ adj. trembling —**trem′u·lous·ly** adv.; **trem′u·lous·ness** n. [L *tremulus*, rel. to TREMOR]

trench /trenCH/ n. 1 long, narrow, usu. deep ditch 2 *Milit.* this dug by troops as a shelter from enemy fire [OFr *trenche*, *-ier* cut]

tren·chant /tren′CHant/ adj. (of style or language, etc.) incisive; terse; vigorous —**tren′chan·cy** n.; **tren′chant·ly** adv. [Fr, rel. to TRENCH]

trench′ coat′ n. military-style belted raincoat

tren·cher·man /tren′CHərmən/ n. (pl. ·men) person who eats well or in a specified manner

trench′ foot′ n. foot disorder from exposure to cold and wet

trench′ mouth′ n. infectious disease affecting mucous membranes of the mouth and throat

trend /trend/ n. general direction and tendency (esp. of events, fashion, or opinion) [OE]

trend·y adj. (·i·er, ·i·est) fashionable —**trend′i·ly** adv.; **trend′i·ness** n.

Tren·ton /trent′n/ n. capital of N.J., in the W central part. Pop. 88,675

trep·i·da·tion /trep′ədā′SHən/ *n.* fear; anxiety [L *trepidus* flurried]

tres·pass /tres′pəs/ *v.* **1** make an unlawful or unauthorized intrusion (esp. on land or property) **2** encroach; transgress (*trespass on your hospitality*) —*n.* **3** *Law.* act of trespassing **4** *Archaic.* sin; offense —**tres′pass·er** *n.* [MedL, rel. to TRANS-, PASS¹]

tress /tres/ *n.* **1** long lock of human hair **2** (*pl.*) woman's or girl's hair [Fr]

tres·tle /tres′əl/ *n.* **1** supporting structure for a table, etc., usu. consisting of a bar with two divergent pairs of legs **2** open braced framework to support a bridge, etc. [L *transtrum* crossbeam]

Trev·i·thick /trev′əTHik′/, **Richard** 1771–1833; English engineer

tri- *comb. form* three or three times [L and Gk]

tri·ad /trī′ad′/ *n.* **1** group of three (esp. notes in a chord) **2** the number three —**tri·ad′ic** *adj.* [L fr. Gk]

tri·age /trēäZH′/ *n. Med.* establishing of priorities for treatment of individual cases, as in emergencies

trial /trī′əl, trīl/ *n.* **1** judicial examination and determination of issues between parties by a judge with or without a jury **2** test; tryout **3** affliction (*trials of old age*) **4 on trial: a** being tried in a court of law **b** to be proved or tested [AngFr, rel. to TRY]

tri′al and er′ror *n.* repeated (usu. unsystematic) attempts continued until successful

tri′al run′ *n.* preliminary operational test

isosceles

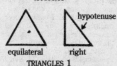
equilateral   right
hypotenuse

TRIANGLES 1

tri·an·gle /trī′aNG′gəl/ *n.* **1** plane figure with three sides and angles **2** any three points not in a straight line but considered relationally **3** implement of this shape **4** steel musical percussion instrument of this shape, struck with a small steel rod **5** situation, esp. an emotional relationship, involving three people —**tri·an′gu·lar** /-gyələr/ *adj.* [L, rel. to TRI-, ANGLE]

tri·an·gu·late /trī-aNG′gyəlāt′/ *v.* (**-lat·ed, -lat·ing**) measure and map out (an area) by dividing it into triangles —**tri·an′gu·la′tion** *n.*

Tri·as·sic /trī-as′ik/ *Geol. adj.* **1** of the earliest period of the Mesozoic era —*n.* **2** this period [rel. to TRIAD]

triathlon /trī-aTH′lən, -län′/ *n.* three-event competition, usu. comprising swimming, bicycling, and running [fr. TRI-, after DECATHLON]

trib. *abbr.* **1** tribunal; tribune **2** tributary

tribe /trīb/ *n.* **1** group of (often primitive) families or communities usu. having a common culture and a recognized leader **2** any

---

615   **trepidation / trident**

similar natural or political division —**trib′al** *adj.*; **trib′al·ism′** *n.* [L *tribus*]

tribes·man /trībz′mən/ *n.* (*pl.* **·men;** *fem.* **·wom′an,** *pl.* **·wom′en**) member of a tribe

trib·u·la·tion /trib′yəlā′SHən/ *n.* great affliction [L *tribulare* press]

tri·bu·nal /trībyōōn′l/ *n.* **1** board appointed to adjudicate in some matter **2** court of justice **3** seat or bench for a judge or judges [L, rel. to TRIBUNE]

trib·une /trib′yōōn′/ *n.* **1** popular leader **2** official in ancient Rome chosen by the people to protect their interests [L *tribunus*, rel. to TRIBE]

trib·u·tar·y /trib′yəter′ē/ *n.* (*pl.* **·ies**) **1** river or stream flowing into a larger river or lake **2** *Hist.* person or government paying or subject to tribute —*adj.* **3** (of a river, etc.) that is a tributary **4** *Hist.* a paying tribute **b** serving as tribute [L, rel. to TRIBUTE]

trib·ute /trib′yōōt′/ *n.* **1** thing said, done, or given as a mark of respect or affection **2** indication of; recompense for (*their success is a tribute to their perseverance*) **3** *Hist.* periodic payment by one government or ruler to another [L *tributum* neut. past part. of *tribuere -ut-* assign; (orig.) divide between tribes]

trice /trīs/ *n.* as in **in a trice** in an instant [MDu *trisen* haul up]

tri·ceps /trī′seps′/ *n.* muscle (esp. in the upper arm) with three points of attachment at one end [TRI- + L *ceps* fr. *caput* head]

tri·cer·a·tops /trīser′ətäps′/ *n.* dinosaur with three sharp horns on the forehead and a wavy neck crest [Gk *keras* horn, *ōps* eye]

trich·i·no·sis /trik′ənō′sis/ *n.* disease caused by hairlike worms usu. ingested in infected, undercooked pork [Gk *trichinos* hairy]

trick /trik/ *n.* **1** action or scheme to deceive or outwit **2** illusion (*trick of the light*) **3** special technique; knack **4** feat of skill or dexterity **5** practical joke **6a** cards played in one round of a card game **b** point gained in this **7** done to deceive or mystify (*trick photography; trick question*) —*v.* **8** deceive by a trick; outwit **9** swindle (*tricked out of his savings*) **10** cause to do something by trickery (*tricked me into agreeing*) **11 do the trick** achieve the required result [Fr]

trick·er·y /trik′ərē/ *n.* (*pl.* **·ies**) deception; use of tricks

trick·le /trik′əl/ *v.* (**·led, ·ling**) **1** (cause to) flow in drops or a small stream **2** come or go slowly or gradually (*information trickles out*) —*n.* **3** small, slow flow [prob. imit.]

trick′le-down′ *adj. Econ.* designating a theory that private business expansion will benefit lower-income groups

trick′ster *n.* deceiver; rogue

trick·y /trik′ē/ *adj.* (**·i·er, ·i·est**) **1** requiring care and adroitness **2** crafty; deceitful —**trick′i·ly** *adv.*; **trick′i·ness** *n.*

tri·col·or /trī′kəl′ər/ *n.* flag with three broad bands of different colors, esp. the French or Irish national flags

tri·cot /trē′kō/ *n.* knitted fabric [Fr]

tri·cy·cle /trī′sikəl/ *n.* three-wheeled pedal-driven vehicle

tri·dent /trīd′nt/ *n.* three-pronged spear [L *dens dent-* tooth]

tried /trīd/ *v.* *past and past part.* of TRY

tri·en·ni·al /trī·en′ēəl/ *adj.* lasting or recurring every three years —**tri·en′ni·al·ly** *adv.* [L *annus* year]

Tri·este /trē·est′/ *n.* seaport in NE Italy. Pop. 231,100

tri·fle /trī′fəl/ *n.* **1** thing of slight value or importance **2a** small amount, esp. of money **b** (prec. by *a*) somewhat (*a trifle annoyed*) —*v.* (**·fled, ·fling**) **3** talk or act frivolously **4** (foll. by *with*) treat or deal with frivolously; flirt heartlessly with [orig. *trufle* fr. *truf(f)e* deceit]

tri′fling *adj.* **1** unimportant; petty **2** frivolous

tri·fo·ri·um /trīfôr′ēəm/ *n.* (*pl.* **·ri·a** /-a/) upper gallery or arcade in a church [AngL]

trig /trig/ *n.* TRIGONOMETRY

trig·ger /trig′ər/ *n.* **1** movable device for releasing a spring or catch and so setting off a mechanism (esp. that of a gun) **2** event, occurrence, etc., that sets off a reaction or series of reactions —*v.* **3** set (an action or process) in motion; precipitate [fr. Du *trekken* pull]

trig′ger-hap·py *adj.* apt to shoot on the slightest provocation

trig·o·nom·e·try /trig′ənäm′ətrē/ *n.* branch of mathematics dealing with the relations of the sides and angles of triangles and with the relevant functions of angles —**trig′o·no·met′ric** /-nəmet′rik/, **trig′o·no·met′ri·cal** *adj.* [Gk *trigōnon* triangle, *metria* measurement]

tri·lat·er·al /trīlat′ərəl/ *adj.* **1** of, on, or with three sides **2** involving three parties [L, rel. to TRI- + LATERAL]

tril·by /tril′bē/ *n.* (*pl.* **·bies**) soft felt hat with a narrow brim and indented crown [fr. *Trilby,* a novel by G. du Maurier]

trill /tril/ *n.* **1** quavering sound, esp. a rapid alternation of sung or played tones **2** bird's warbling **3** pronunciation of *r* with vibration of the tongue —*v.* **4** produce a trill **5** warble (a song) or pronounce (*r,* etc.) with a trill [It]

tril·lion /tril′yən/ *n.* (*pl.* **·lions** or same) a million million (10¹²) —**tril′lionth** *adj. & n.* [Fr or T, rel. to TRI-, MILLION, after *billion*]

tri·lo·bite /trī′ləbīt′/ *n.* a kind of fossil marine arthropod [Gk TRI-, LOBE]

tril·o·gy /tril′əjē/ *n.* (*pl.* **·gies**) group of three related novels, plays, operas, etc.

trim /trim/ *v.* (**trimmed, trim·ming**) **1** make neat or of the required size, fit, or form, esp. by cutting **2** cut off (unwanted parts) **3** ornament; decorate **4** adjust the balance of (a ship) by arranging its cargo, etc. **5** arrange (sails) to suit the wind **6** balance; level off (a plane) —*n.* **7** state of readiness or fitness (*in perfect trim*) **8** ornament; decorative material **9** cutting of a person's hair —*adj.* (**trim·mer, trim·mest**) **10** neat; spruce **11** in good order; well arranged or equipped [OE: make firm]

tri·ma·ran /trī′məran′/ *n.* vessel like a catamaran, with three parallel hulls [fr. CATAMARAN]

trim·e·ter /trim′itər/ *n.* Pros. line of verse of three measures [Gk: see TRI-, -METER]

trim′ming *n.* **1** ornamentation or decoration, esp. for clothing **2** (*pl.*) usual accompaniments, esp. of the main course of a meal

Trin·i·dad and To·ba·go /trin′idad′; təbā′gō/

n. two-island republic in the West Indies. Capital: Port-of-Spain. Pop. 1,261,000

tri·ni·tro·tol·u·ene /trī′nī′trōtäl′yōō-ēn′/ *n.* (also **tri·ni′tro·tol′u·ol** /-täl′yōō-ôl′/) TNT

trin·i·ty /trin′ətē/ *n.* (*pl.* **·ties**) **1** state of being three **2** group of three **3** (*cap.* or Holy Trinity) *Christianity.* the three persons of the Christian Godhead (Father, Son, and Holy Spirit) [L *trinitas* fr. *trinus* threefold]

trin·ket /triNG′kit/ *n.* trifling ornament, esp. a piece of jewelry —**trin′ket·ry** *n.*

tri·o /trē′ō/ *n.* (*pl.* **·os**) **1** group of three **2** *Mus.* a composition for three performers **b** the performers [Fr and It fr. L]

trip /trip/ *v.* (**tripped, trip·ping**) **1a** (cause to) stumble, esp. by catching the feet **b** (cause to) make a slip or blunder **2a** move with quick, light steps **b** (of a rhythm, etc.) run lightly **3** operate (a mechanism) suddenly by knocking aside a catch, etc. **4** *Slang.* have a hallucinatory experience caused by a drug —*n.* **5** journey or excursion, esp. for pleasure **6a** stumble; misstep **b** tripping or being tripped up **7** nimble step **8** *Slang.* drug-induced hallucinatory experience [Du *trippen* skip; hop]

tri·par·tite /trīpär′tīt′/ *adj.* **1** consisting of three parts **2** shared by or involving three parties [L *partire* divide]

tripe /trīp/ *n.* **1** first or second stomach of a ruminant, esp. an ox, as food **2** *Slang.* nonsense; rubbish [Fr]

tri·ple /trip′əl/ *adj.* **1** consisting of three usu. equal parts or things; threefold **2** involving three parties **3** three times as much or many —*n.* **4** threefold number or amount **5** set of three **6** *Baseball.* hit on which the batter reaches third base —*v.* (**·pled, ·pling**) **7** multiply by three —**tri·ply** /-plē/ *adv.* [L *triplus*]

tri′ple jump′ *n.* athletic contest for distance, comprising a hop, step, and jump

trip·let /trip′lit/ *n.* **1** each of three children or animals born at one birth **2** set of three things, esp. three equal musical notes played in the time of two of the same value

trip·li·cate /trip′ləkət/ *adj.* **1** existing in three examples or copies **2** having three corresponding parts **3** tripled —*n.* **4** each of a set of three copies or corresponding parts —**trip·li·ca·tion** /trip′likā′sHən/ *n.* [TRI-, L *plicare* fold]

tri·pod /trī′päd′/ *n.* three-legged stand for a camera, etc. [Gk: three-footed]

Trip·o·li /trip′əlē/ *n.* **1** capital of Libya. Pop. 591,100 **2** seaport in Lebanon. Pop. 500,000

trip·tych /trip′tik/ *n.* picture or relief carving on three usu. hinged panels [Gk]

tri·sect /trīsekt′, trī′sekt′/ *v.* divide into three (usu. equal) parts —**tri·sec′tion** /-sek′sHən/, **tri·sec′tor** *n.* [L *secare sect-* cut]

trite /trīt/ *adj.* hackneyed —**trite′ly** *adv.*; **trite′ness** *n.* [L *terere trit-* wear out]

tri·ti·um /trit′ēəm, trisH′-/ *n.* radioactive isotope of hydrogen with a mass about three times that of ordinary hydrogen [Gk *tritos* third]

tri·umph /trī′əmf/ *n.* **1a** state of victory or success **b** a great success or achievement **2** supreme example (*a triumph of engineering*) —*v.* **3** gain a victory; be successful **4** (often foll. by *over*) exult [Fr fr. L]

tri·um'phal *adj.* of or used in celebrating a triumph (*triumphal arch*)

• Usage: Monuments and parades are *triumphal*, 'commemorating a triumph'; people are *triumphant* when they are 'celebrating a triumph.'

tri·um'phant *adj.* 1 victorious; successful 2 exultant —**tri·um'phant·ly** *adv.*

tri·um·vi·rate /trī-əm'vərət/ *n.* ruling group of three persons [L *trium virum* of three men]

tri·va·lent /trīvā'lənt/ *adj. Chem.* having a valency of three —**tri·va'len·cy** *n.*

triv·et /triv'it/ *n.* iron tripod or bracket for a pot or kettle to stand on [appar. fr. L *tripes* three-footed]

triv·i·a /triv'ēə/ *n. pl.* trifles or trivialities

triv·i·al /triv'ēəl/ *adj.* of small value or importance; trifling —**triv·i·al·i·ty** /triv'ēal'ətē/ *n.* (*pl.* **·ties**); **triv'i·al·ly** *adv.* [L *trivialis* commonplace, fr. *trivium* three-way street corner]

triv'i·al·ize' *v.* (**·ized**, **·iz·ing**) make or treat as trivial; minimize —**triv'i·al·i·za'tion** *n.*

tro·chee /trō'kē/ *n. Pros.* metrical foot consisting of one long followed by one short syllable (‾ ˘) —**tro·cha·ic** /trōkā'ik/ *adj.* [Gk: running]

trod /träd/ *v. past* and *past part.* of TREAD

trod·den /träd'n/ *v. past part.* of TREAD

trog·lo·dyte /träg'lədīt'/ *n.* cave dweller —**trog'lo·dyt'ic** /-dit'ik/ *adj.* [Gk *trōglē* hole]

troi·ka /troi'kə/ *n.* 1a Russian vehicle with a team of three horses abreast b this team 2 group of three people, esp. as an administrative council [Russ]

Tro·jan horse /trō'jən/ *n.* 1 (in Gk. legend) hollow wooden horse used by the Greeks to enter Troy 2 person or device inserted or planted to bring about downfall or disaster

troll¹ /trōl/ *n.* (in Scand. folklore) fabulous being, esp. a giant or dwarf dwelling in a cave [ON]

troll² *v.* fish by drawing bait along in the water [ME *trollen* to roll]

trol·ley /träl'ē/ *n.* (*pl.* **·leys**) 1 table, stand, or basket on wheels for serving food, transporting luggage, etc. 2 TROLLEY CAR 3 wheel attached to a pole, etc., used for collecting current from an overhead electric wire to drive a vehicle [dial., perh. fr. TROLL²]

trol'ley bus' *n.* electric bus powered by a trolley (sense 3)

trol'ley car' *n.* electric rail vehicle powered by a trolley (sense 3)

trol·lop /träl'əp/ *n.* loose woman; prostitute [perh. rel. to archaic *trull* prostitute]

Trol·lope /träl'əp/, **Anthony** 1815–82; English writer

TROMBONE

trom·bone /trämbōn'/ *n.* brass wind instrument usu. with a sliding tube —**trom·bon'ist** *n.* [Fr or It *tromba* TRUMPET]

trompe-l'œil /trômp' lä', loi'/ *n.* painting, etc., designed to give an illusion of reality [Fr: deceives the eye]

-tron *suffix* forming nouns denoting: 1 elementary particle (*positron*) 2 particle accelerator [fr. ELECTRON]

Trond·heim /trän'hām'/ *n.* seaport in central Norway. Pop. 139,700

troop /trōōp/ *n.* 1 assembled company; assemblage of people or animals 2 (*pl.*) soldiers; armed forces 3 cavalry unit under a captain —*v.* 4 come together or move in large numbers [Fr *troupe*]

troop'er *n.* 1 soldier in a cavalry or armored unit 2 mounted or state police officer

troop'ship' *n.* ship used for transporting troops

trop. *abbr.* tropic; tropical

trope /trōp/ *n.* figurative use of a word [Gk *tropos* fr. *trépein* turn]

tro·phy /trō'fē/ *n.* (*pl.* **·phies**) 1 cup, statuette, etc., as a prize in a contest 2 memento or souvenir of success in hunting, war, etc. [Gk *tropaion*]

trop·ic /träpik/ *n.* 1 parallel of latitude approx. 23°27' north (**tropic of Cancer**) or south (**tropic of Capricorn**) of the equator 2 (**the Tropics**) warm-weather region between the tropics of Cancer and Capricorn —**trop'i·cal** *adj.* [Gk *tropikos* turn]

tro·po·sphere /träp'əsfēr', trō'pə-/ *n.* lowest layer of atmosphere, extending 6–12 mi. upward from the earth's surface [Gk *tropos* turn, SPHERE]

trot /trät/ *v.* (**trot·ted**, **trot·ting**) 1 run at a moderate pace 2 (of a horse) proceed at a steady pace faster than a walk, lifting each diagonal pair of legs alternately —*n.* 3 action or exercise of trotting 4 (**the trots**) *Slang.* diarrhea 5 **trot out** *Colloq.* introduce (an opinion, etc.) tediously or repeatedly —**trot'ter** *n.* [Fr]

troth /trôth, trōth/ *n.* 1 faith; loyalty 2 truth 3 **pledge** (or **plight**) **one's troth** pledge one's word, esp. in marriage or betrothal [OE, rel. to TRUTH]

Trot·sky /trät'skē/, **Leon** (born Lev Bronstein) 1879–1940; Russian revolutionary and writer

trou·ba·dour /trōō'bədôr'/ *n.* 1 singer or poet 2 French medieval lyric poet singing of courtly love [Prov *trobar* find; compose]

trou·ble /trəb'əl/ *n.* 1 difficulty or distress; vexation; affliction 2a inconvenience; unpleasant exertion; bother b cause of this 3 perceived failing 4 dysfunction (*kidney trouble*) 5 disturbance —*v.* (**·bled**, **·bling**) 6 cause distress or anxiety to; disturb 7 afflict; cause pain, etc., to 8 subject to inconvenience or unpleasant exertion [L, rel. to TURBID]

trou'ble·mak'er *n.* person habitually causing trouble —**trou'ble·mak'ing** *n.*

trou'ble·shoot'er *n.* 1 mediator in a dispute 2 person who corrects faults in machinery or in an organization, etc. —**trou'ble·shoot'ing** *n.*

trou'ble·some *adj.* causing trouble; nettlesome

trough /trôf, träf/ *n.* 1 long, narrow, open receptacle for water, animal feed, etc. 2 channel or hollow like this **3** elongated region of low barometric pressure [OE]

trounce /trouns/ v. (**trounced, trounc·ing**) **1** defeat heavily **2** beat; thrash

troupe /trōop/ n. company or band, esp. of actors, singers, etc. [Fr: troop]

troup·er n. **1** member of a theatrical troupe **2** staunch colleague

trou·sers /trou'zərz/ n. pl. **1** two-legged outer garment reaching from the waist usu. to the ankles —adj. **2** (trouser) designating part of this (trouser leg) [Gaelic triubhas trews]

trous·seau /trōo'sō', trōosō'/ n. (pl. ·seaux /-sōz/ or seaus) bride's collection of clothes, household linens, etc. [OFr trousse bundle]

trout /trout/ n. (pl. same or -s) food fish related to the salmon [L tructa]

trove /trōv/ n. TREASURE TROVE [AngFr trové fr. trouver find]

trow·el /trou'əl, troul/ n. **1** small, flat-bladed tool for spreading mortar, etc. **2** scoop for lifting small plants or earth [L trulla]

troy /troi/ n. system of weights used for precious metals and gems [prob. Troyes in France]

Troy /troi/ n. **1** ancient city in NW Asia Minor **2** city in N.Y. Pop. 72,884 —**Tro·jan** /trō'jan/ adj.

tru·ant /trōo'ənt/ n. **1** student who stays away from school **2** person who avoids work, etc. —adj. **3** shirking; idle; wandering —**tru'an·cy** n. (pl. ·cies) [Fr, prob. fr. Celt]

truce /trōos/ n. temporary agreement to cease hostilities [ME trewes fr. OE treow covenant]

truck[1] /trək/ n. **1** self-propelled vehicle for carrying loads **2** wheeled cart to aid in moving loads —**truck'er** n. [perh. fr. TRUCKLE]

truck[2] n. **1** dealings **2** have no truck with avoid dealing with [Fr troquer exchange; barter]

truck·le /trək'əl/ n. **1** (in full truck'le bed') TRUNDLE BED —v. (·led, ·ling) **2** submit obsequiously [L trochlea pulley]

tru·cu·lent /trək'yələnt/ adj. **1** cruel; savage **2** aggressively defiant —**tru'cu·lence** n.; **tru'cu·lent·ly** adv. [L trux truc- fierce]

Tru·deau /trōodō'/, Pierre Elliott 1919– ; Canadian politician; prime minister (1968–79; 1980–84)

trudge /trəj/ v. (**trudged, trudg·ing**) **1** go on foot, esp. laboriously —n. **2** trudging walk

true /trōo/ adj. (tru·er, tru·est) **1** in accordance with fact or reality **2** genuine; authentic **3** loyal; faithful **4** accurately conforming to (a type or standard) (true to form) **5** correctly positioned or balanced; upright; level **6** exact; accurate (a true copy) —adv. **7** accurately (aim true) **8** come true actually happen [OE]

true'-blue' adj. extremely loyal or orthodox

truf·fle /traf'əl/ n. **1** edible, rich-flavored underground fungus **2** candy made of a chocolate mixture covered with cocoa [ult. fr. L tuber knob]

tru·ism /trōo'iz'əm/ n. statement too obvious or hackneyed to be worth making

Tru·ji·llo /trōohē'yō/ n. seaport in NW Peru. Pop. 532,000

tru·ly /trōo'lē/ adv. **1** sincerely **2** really; indeed **3** loyally & accurately [OE, rel. to TRUE]

Tru·man /trōo'mən/, Harry S 1884–1972; 33rd US president (1945–53)

trump /trəmp/ n. **1a** playing card of a suit ranking above the others in a hand **b** this suit —v. **2** defeat (a card or its player) with a trump **3** outdo **4** trump up fabricate or invent (an accusation, etc.) [corruption of TRIUMPH in the same (now obs.) sense]

trum·per·y /trəm'parē/ n. (pl. ·ies) **1** worthless finery **2** worthless thing; rubbish [Fr tromperie deceit]

trum·pet /trəm'pit/ n. **1** brass instrument with a flared bell and bright penetrating tone **2** trumpet-shaped thing (ear trumpet) **3** sound of or like a trumpet —v. **4a** blow a trumpet **b** (of an enraged elephant, etc.) make a trumpetlike cry **5** proclaim loudly —**trum'pet·er** n. [Fr trompe]

trun·cate /trəNG'kāt/ v. (·cat·ed, ·cat·ing) cut the top or the end from; shorten —**trun·ca'tion** n. [L, rel. to TRUNK]

trun·cheon /trən'CHən/ n. short club carried by a police officer [Fr tronchon stump; rel. to TRUNK]

trun·dle /trən'dl/ v. (·dled, ·dling) roll or move, esp. heavily or noisily [OE trendan roll, rel. to TREND]

trun'dle bed' n. low, wheeled bed stored under a larger bed

trunk /trəNGk/ n. **1** main stem of a tree **2** body excluding the limbs and head **3** large box with a hinged lid for luggage, storage, etc. **4** usu. rear storage compartment of a car **5** elephant's elongated prehensile nose **6** (pl.) men's shorts worn for swimming, etc. [L truncus cut short]

trunk' line' n. main line of a railroad, etc.

truss /trəs/ n. **1** framework supporting a roof, bridge, etc. **2** surgical appliance worn to support a hernia —v. **3** tie up (a fowl) for cooking **4** tie (a person) up with the arms to the sides **5** support (a roof, bridge, etc.) with a truss or trusses [Fr]

trust /trəst/ n. **1** firm belief in the reliability, truth, or strength of a person or thing **2** confident expectation **3** responsibility (position of trust) **4** commercial credit **5** Law. **a** arrangement whereby a person or group manages property on another's behalf **b** property so held **c** body of trustees **6** association of companies for reducing competition, etc. —v. **7** place trust in; believe in **8** allow to have or use (a thing); entrust (trusted her with my car) **9** have faith, confidence, or hope that a thing will take place (I trust you will come) **10** place reliance in (we trust in you) **11** place (esp. undue) reliance on (trust to luck) **12** in trust (of property) managed by one or more persons on behalf of another [ON]

trus·tee /trəs'tē'/ n. **1** person managing property in trust **2** member of an administrative board **3** TRUSTY, **2** —**trus·tee'ship** n.

trust'ful adj. full of trust or confidence —**trust'ful·ly** adv.; **trust'ful·ness** n.

trust'ing adj. having trust; trustful —**trust'ing·ly** adv.

trust'wor'thy adj. deserving of trust; reliable —**trust'wor'thi·ness** n.

trust'y adj. (·i·er, ·i·est) **1** trustworthy; reliable —n. (pl. -ies) 2 prisoner given special privileges for good behavior

truth /tro͞oTH/ n. (pl. **truths** /tro͞oTHz, tro͞oTHs/) 1 quality or state of being true 2 what is true [OE, rel. to TRUE]

truth'ful adj. 1 speaking the truth 2 (of a story, etc.) true —**truth'ful·ly** adv.; **truth'ful·ness** n.

try /trī/ v. (**tried, try·ing**) 1 make an effort with a view to success 2 make an effort to achieve (*tried my best*) 3 test by use or experiment 4 tax (*tries my patience*) 5 ascertain the state of fastening of (a door, window, etc.) 6a investigate and decide (a case or issue) judicially b subject (a person) to trial (*tried for murder*) 7 aim; strive (*try for a gold medal*) —n. (pl. **tries**) 8 effort to accomplish something 9 **try one's hand** test how skillful one is 10 **try on** put on (clothes, etc.) to see if they fit, etc. 11 **try out** put to the test [orig. separate; distinguish, fr. Fr *trier* sift]

try'ing adj. annoying; vexing

try'out' n. experimental test

TRY SQUARE

try' square' n. carpenter's tool consisting of two straight-edges fixed at right angles, used to test squareness

tryst /trist/ n. meeting, esp. a secret one of lovers [OFr *triste* hunting station]

tsar /tsär, zär/ n. var. of CZAR

tset·se /(t)set'sē, (t)sēt'-/ n. African fly feeding on blood and transmitting esp. sleeping sickness [Tswana: fly]

TSH abbr. thyroid-stimulating hormone

T'-shirt' n. short-sleeved casual top having the form of a T when spread out

Tshom·be /CHôm'bā/, **Moïse Kapenda** 1919–69; African political leader; prime minister of the Republic of the Congo (1964–65)

Tsing·tao /tsĭng'tou'/ n. see QINGDAO

Tsit·si·har /tsē'tsē'här/ n. see QIQIHAR

tsp. abbr. (pl. **tsps.**) teaspoonful

T'-square' n. T-shaped instrument for drawing right angles, parallel lines, etc.

tsu·na·mi /(t)so͞onä'mē/ n. (pl. -**mis**) long, high, sea wave caused by underwater earthquake, etc. [Japn]

Tswa·na /tswä'nē, swä'-/ n. Bantu language used in Botswana and nearby parts of S Africa

tub /təb/ n. 1 open, flat-bottomed, usu. round container of wood or metal 2 tub-shaped carton 3 container for bathing 4 clumsy, slow boat [MDu *tubbe*]

tu·ba /t(y)o͞o'bə/ n. (pl. -**bas**) low-pitched, brass wind instrument [L: trumpet]

tub·by /təb'ē/ adj. (-**bi·er, ·bi·est**) short and fat —**tub'bi·ness** n.

tube /t(y)o͞ob/ n. 1 long, hollow cylinder 2 pliable cylinder sealed at one end and holding a semi-liquid substance (*tube of toothpaste*) 3

hollow, cylindrical organ in the body 4 Brit. subway 5 (prec. by *the*) Colloq. television 6 INNER TUBE [L]

tu·ber /t(y)o͞o'bər/ n. thick, rounded part of a stem or rhizome, usu. found underground, e.g., a potato —**tu'ber·ous** adj. [L: hump; swelling]

tu·ber·cle /t(y)o͞o'bərkəl/ n. small, rounded swelling on the body or in an organ, esp. as characteristic of tuberculosis —**tu·ber·cu·lar** /t(y)o͞obər'kyələr/, **tu·ber'cu·lous** /-ləs/ adj. [L *tuberculum*, dim. of TUBER]

tu·ber·cu·lo·sis /t(y)o͞obər'kyəlō'sis/ n. infectious bacterial disease marked by tubercles, esp. in the lungs

tub'ing n. 1 length of tube 2 quantity of tubes

Tub·man /təb'mən/, **Harriet** 1820–1913; US abolitionist

tu·bu·lar /t(y)o͞o'b(y)ələr/ adj. 1 tube-shaped 2 having or consisting of tubes

tu·bule /t(y)o͞o'byo͞ol'/ n. small tube in a plant or animal body [L *tubulus*, dim., rel. to TUBE]

tuck /tək/ v. 1 draw, fold, or turn the outer or end parts of (cloth or clothes) close together so as to be held; push in the edge of (a thing) 2 draw together into a small space (*tucked its head under its wing*) 3 stow; stash 4 make a stitched fold in (cloth, etc.) —n. 5 flattened, usu. stitched fold in cloth, etc. [MDu *tucken*]

tuck'er v. Colloq. tire; weary

Tuc·son /to͞o'sän/ n. city in Ariz. Pop. 405,390

-tude suffix forming abstract nouns (*altitude; solitude*) [L -*tudo*]

Tu·dor /t(y)o͞o'dər/ adj. 1 of the royal family of England 1485–1603 or this period 2 of the architectural style of this period [for Owen *Tudor*, grandfather of Henry VII]

Tues·day /t(y)o͞oz'dā, -dē/ n. day of the week following Monday; abbr. **Tues., Tue.** [OE]

tuft /təft/ n. bunch or collection of threads, grass, feathers, hair, etc., held or growing together at the base —**tuft'ed, tuft'y** adj. [prob. OFr *tofe*]

tug /təg/ v. (**tugged, tug·ging**) 1 pull hard or violently; jerk 2 tow (a ship, etc.) with a tugboat —n. 3 hard, violent, or jerky pull 4 sudden, strong emotion 5 TUGBOAT [rel. to TOW]

tug'boat' n. sturdy, powerful boat for towing or pushing ships, barges, etc.

tug' of war' n. 1 contest of strength between two sides pulling opposite ways on a rope 2 struggle between two sides or factions

tu·i·tion /t(y)o͞o-ish'ən/ n. 1 fee for instruction, as at a college 2 teaching [L *tueri tuit-* look after]

tu·lip /t(y)o͞o'ləp/ n. 1 bulbous, spring-flowering plant with showy, cup-shaped flowers 2 its flower [Turk *tul(i)band* TURBAN (fr. its shape), fr. Pers]

tulle /t(y)o͞ol/ n. soft, fine silk, etc., net for veils and dresses [for *Tulle*, France]

Tul·sa /təl'sə/ n. city in Okla. Pop. 367,302

tum·ble /təm'bəl/ v. (-**bled, ·bling**) 1 (cause to) fall suddenly, clumsily, or headlong 2 fall rapidly in value, etc. 3 roll or toss to and fro 4 move or rush in a headlong or blunder-

ing manner **5** perform acrobatic feats, esp.
somersaults —*n.* **6** sudden or headlong fall
7 somersault or other acrobatic feat [LGer
tummeln]

tum'ble-down' *adj.* falling or fallen into ruin;
dilapidated

tum'bler *n.* **1** drinking glass **2** acrobat **3** part
of a lock that holds the bolt until lifted by a
key or combination

tum-brel /təm'brəl/ *n.* (also **tum'bril**) *Hist.*
open cart into which condemned persons were
taken to the guillotine in the French Revolution [Fr *tomber* fall]

tu-mes-cent /t(y)ōōmes'ənt/ *adj.* swelling
—**tu-mes'cence** *n.* [L, rel. to TUMOR]

tu-mid /t(y)ōō'mid/ *adj.* **1** swollen; inflated
2 (of style, etc.) inflated; bombastic —**tu-
mid'i-ty** *n.* [L *tumere* swell]

tum-my /təm'ē/ *n.* (*pl.* **-mies**) *Colloq.* stomach

tu-mor /t(y)ōō'mər/ *n.* a swelling, esp. from
an abnormal growth of tissue —**tu'mor-ous**
adj. [L: swelling]

tu-mult /t(y)ōō'məlt/ *n.* **1** uproar or din,
esp. of a disorderly crowd **2** uprising; riot **3**
emotional agitation or stress [L, rel. to TU-
MOR]

tu-mul-tu-ous /t(y)ōōməl'CHōōəs/ *adj.*
noisy; turbulent; violent

tun /tən/ *n.* large beer or wine cask [OE]

tu-na /t(y)ōō'nə/ *n.* (*pl.* same or **-nas**) **1**
large, edible marine fish **2** (in full **tu'na fish'**)
its flesh as food [AmerSp]

tun-dra /tən'drə/ *n.* vast, level, treeless Arctic region with underlying permafrost [Russ
fr. Lappish]

tune /t(y)ōōn/ *n.* **1** melody —*v.* (**tuned,
tun-ing**) **2** put (a musical instrument) in tune
3 adjust (a radio, etc.) to the frequency of a
signal **4** adjust (an engine, etc.) to run efficiently [var. of TONE]

tune'ful *adj.* melodious; musical —**tune'fully** *adv.*

tune'less *adj.* unmelodious; unmusical
—**tune'less-ly** *adv.*

tun'er *n.* **1** person who tunes musical instruments, esp. pianos **2a** part of a radio or television receiver for tuning **b** radio receiver as
a separate unit in a high-fidelity system

tung-sten /təNG'stən/ *n.* (also **wolf'ram**)
dense metallic element with a very high melting point; *symb.* W [Sw: heavy stone]

tu-nic /t(y)ōō'nik/ *n.* **1** blouselike garment
extending to the hips, sometimes belted **2**
loose often sleeveless garment, esp. as worn
in ancient Greece and Rome [L]

TUNING FORK

tun'ing fork' *n.* two-pronged steel fork giving
a particular note when struck

Tu-nis /t(y)ōō'nis/ *n.* capital of Tunisia. Pop.
620,100

Tu-ni-sia /t(y)ōōnē'ZHə, -niZH'ə/ *n.* republic

in N Africa on the Mediterranean Sea. Capital:
Tunis. Pop. 8,413,000 —**Tu-ni'sian** *n.* & *adj.*

tun-nel /tən'l/ *n.* **1** underground passage
dug through a hill or under a road, river, etc.,
esp. for a railway or road **2** underground passage dug by an animal —*v.* (**-neled** or **-nel-
led, -nel-ing** or **-nel-ling**) **3** make a tunnel
through **4** make (one's way) by tunneling [Fr
tonnelle vault]

tun'nel vi'sion *n.* **1** vision that is normal only
in a small central area **2** *Colloq.* inability to
grasp a situation's wider implications

tun-ny /tən'ē/ *n.* (*pl.* same or **-nies**)
TUNA, 1

Tu-pi /tōō'pē, tōōpē'/ *n.* (*pl.* same or **-pis**)
1 member of an American Indian people of the
Amazon valley **2** their language —*adj.* **3** of
this people or language

tur-ban /tər'bən/ *n.* **1** man's headdress of
fabric wound around a cap or the head, worn
esp. by Muslims and Sikhs **2** woman's hat resembling this —**tur'baned** *adj.* [Pers *dul-
band*]

tur-bid /tər'bid/ *adj.* **1** muddy; thick; not
clear **2** (of style, etc.) confused; disordered
—**tur-bid'i-ty** *n.* [L *turba* crowd]

tur-bine /tər'bən, -bīn/ *n.* rotary motor
driven by a flow of water, steam, gas, wind,
etc. [L *turbo* -*in*- thing that spins; whirl]

tur-bo- *comb. form* turbine

tur-bo-charg-er /tər'bōCHär'jər/ *n.* (also
tur'bo; *pl.* **-bos**) supercharger driven by a
turbine powered by the engine's exhaust
gases

tur'bo-jet' *n.* **1** jet engine in which the jet also
operates a turbine-driven air compressor **2**
aircraft powered by this

tur'bo-prop' *n.* **1** jet engine in which a turbine
is used as in a turbojet and also to drive a propeller **2** aircraft powered by this [fr. PROP³]

tur-bot /tər'bət/ *n.* (*pl.* same or **-bots**) any
of several types of flatfish prized as food [Fr
Sw]

tur-bu-lent /tər'byələnt/ *adj.* **1** disturbed; in
commotion **2** (of a flow of air, etc.) varying
irregularly **3** restless; riotous —**tur'bu-
lence** *n.;* **tur'bu-lent-ly** *adv.* [L *turba* crowd]

tu-reen /tərēn', tōōr-/ *n.* deep covered dish
for soup [Fr *terrine* earthenware dish]

turf /tərf/ *n.* **1a** layer of grass, etc., with earth
and its roots; sod **b** piece of this **2** slab of peat
3 (prec. by *the*) a horse racing generally **b**
general term for race tracks —*v.* **4** cover
(ground) with turf —**turf'y** *adj.* [OE]

Tur-ge-nev /tōōrgän'yəf, -gen'-/, **Ivan** 1818–
83; Russian novelist

tur-gid /tər'jid/ *adj.* **1** swollen; inflated **2** (of
language) pompous; bombastic —**tur-gid'i-
ty** *n.* [L *turgere* swell]

Tu-rin /t(y)ōōr'in, t(y)ōōrin'/ *n.* (Italian
name **Torino**) city in NW Italy. Pop. 991,900

Turk /tərk/ *n.* **1a** native or national of Turkey
b person of Turkish descent **2** member of a
Central Asian people from whom the Otto-
mans derived

tur-key /tər'kē/ *n.* **1** large, orig. N American
bird, wild or bred for food **2** its flesh as food
3 *Slang.* theatrical failure; flop **4 talk turkey**
Colloq. talk frankly; get down to business
[orig. of the guinea fowl, imported fr. *Turkey*]

Tur-key /tər'kē/ *n.* republic in W Asia, with

a small part in SE Europe. Capital: Ankara. Pop. 58,584,000

621

Turkish / turret

Tur·kish /ˈtərˈkiSH/ *adj.* **1** of Turkey, the Turks, or their language —*n.* **2** this language

Tur'kish bath' *n.* hot-air or steam bath followed by washing, massage, etc.

Tur'kish tow'el *n.* thick, absorbent towel made of cotton terry

Turk·me·ni·stan /ˌtərkmenˈistän/ *n.* republic in S Asia on the E coast of the Caspian Sea; formerly part of the USSR. Capital: Ashgabat. Pop. 3,859,000 —**Turk·men** *n.*

tur·mer·ic /ˈtərˈmərik/ *n.* **1** E Indian plant of the ginger family **2** its powdered rhizome used as a spice in curry, etc., or for yellow dye [MedL *terra merita*]

tur·moil /ˈtərˈmoil/ *n.* **1** violent confusion; agitation **2** din and bustle

turn /tərn/ *v.* **1** move around a point or axis; give or receive rotary motion **2** change in position; invert; reverse **3a** give a new direction to **b** take a new direction **4** aim in a certain way **5** change in nature, form, or condition (*turned into a frog*) **6** (foll. by *to*) **a** set about (*turned to doing the ironing*) **b** have recourse to (*turned to me for help*) **c** go on to consider next **7** become (*turned nasty*) **8a** (foll. by *against*) make or become hostile to (*has turned her against us*) **b** become hostile to; attack (*suddenly turned on them*) **9** change color **10** (of a dairy product) sour or become sour **11** (of the stomach) nauseate or be nauseated **12** move to the other side of; go around (*turned the corner*) **13** pass the age (*he has turned 40*) **14** perform (a somersault, etc.) **15** make (a profit) **16** give an (esp. elegant) form to (*turn a compliment*) **17** (of the tide) change or cause to change direction —*n.* **18** turning; rotary motion **19** change of direction or tendency (*a sudden turn to the left*) **20** point at which a turning or change occurs **21** change of direction of the tide **22** tendency or disposition; facility of forming (*a mechanical turn of mind*) **23** opportunity or obligation that comes successively (*my turn to pay*) **24** short walk or ride (*took a turn in the park*) **25** short performance; variety act **26** service of a specified kind (*did me a good turn*) **27** momentary nervous shock (*gave me a turn*) **28** by turns in rotation; alternately **29** in turn in succession **30** out of turn: **a** when it is not one's turn **b** inappropriately (*did I speak out of turn?*) **31** take (it in) turns act alternately **32** to a turn (esp. cooked) perfectly **33** turn down: **a** reject (a proposal, etc.) **b** reduce the volume or strength of (sound, heat, etc.) by turning a knob, etc. **34** turn in: **a** hand in; return **b** achieve or register (a performance, score, etc.) **c** go to bed for the night **d** incline inward **e** hand over **35** turn loose release **36** turn off: **a** stop the flow or operation of (water, electricity, etc.) by a tap, switch, etc. **b** operate (a tap, switch, etc.) to achieve this **c** enter a side road **d** *Colloq.* cause to lose interest **37** turn on: **a** start the flow or operation of (water, electricity, etc.) by means of a tap, switch, etc. **b** operate (a tap, switch, etc.) to achieve this **c** *Colloq.* excite; stimulate, esp. sexually **38** turn out: **a** expel **b** extinguish (an electric light, etc.) **c** produce (goods, etc.) **d** prove to be the case;

result (*turned out to be true; see how things turn out*) **39** turn over: **a** reverse the position of (*turn over the page*) **b** cause (an engine) to run **c** (of an engine) start running **d** (foll. by *to*) transfer or delegate **e** hand over **f** earn as gross income **40** turn over a new leaf reform one's conduct **41** turn tail turn one's back; run away **42** turn up: **a** increase the volume or strength of by turning a knob, etc. **b** discover; reveal **c** be found, esp. by chance; appear **d** arrive (*people turned up late*) [Gk *tornos* lathe]

turn'a·bout' *n.* **1** turning in a different direction **2** abrupt change of policy, etc.

turn'a·round' *n.* **1** TURNABOUT **2** complete, often abrupt reversal of policy, attitude, etc. **3** area, as in a driveway, that allows a vehicle to turn around

TURNBUCKLE

turn'buck'le *n.* threaded device for tightly connecting parts of a metal rod or wire

turn'coat' *n.* person who changes sides

Tur·ner /ˈtərnər/, **Joseph Mallord William** 1775–1851; English landscape painter

turn'ing point' *n.* point at which a decisive change occurs

tur·nip /ˈtərˈnip/ *n.* **1** plant with a globular root **2** its root as a vegetable —**tur'nip·y** *adj.* [*turn* (ref. to roundness), ME *nepe* fr. L *napas*]

turn'key' *n.* **1** jailer —*adj.* **2** (of a process, etc.) fully ready to function when started

turn'off' *n.* **1** turning off a main road **2** *Slang.* something that repels or causes a loss of interest

turn'on' *n. Slang.* person or thing that causes (esp. sexual) excitement

turn'out' *n.* **1** number of people attending a meeting, voting at an election, etc. **2** set or display of equipment, clothes, etc.

turn'o·ver *n.* **1** act of turning over **2** gross amount of money taken in a business **3** rate at which goods are sold and replaced **4** rate at which people enter and leave employment, etc. **5** small pie made by folding pastry over a filling

turn·pike /ˈtərnˈpīk/ *n.* highway on which a toll is usu. charged

turn'stile' *n.* gate with revolving arms allowing people through singly

turn'ta'ble *n.* circular revolving disk on which records are played

tur·pen·tine /ˈtərˈpəntīn/ *n.* resin from any of various trees [Gk *terebinthos*]

tur·pi·tude /ˈtərˈpit(y)o͞od/ *n.* depravity; wickedness [L *turpis* vile]

tur·quoise /ˈtərˈk(w)oiz/ *n.* **1** semiprecious stone, usu. opaque and greenish- or sky-blue **2** greenish-blue color —*adj.* **3** of this color [OFr: Turkish (stone)]

tur·ret /ˈtərˈit, ˈtärˈit/ *n.* **1** small tower, esp. decorating a building **2** low, flat, usu. revolving armored tower for a gun and gunners in a ship, aircraft, fort, or tank **3** rotating holder for tools in a lathe, etc. —**tur'ret·ed** *adj.* [Fr dim., rel. to TOWER]

tur·tle /ˈtərt'l/ *n.* **1** aquatic reptile with flippers and a horny shell **2** its flesh, used for soup **3 turn turtle** capsize [Fr *tortue* TORTOISE]

tur·tle·dove *n.* wild dove noted for its soft cooing and affection for its mate [ME, equiv. to TURTLE + DOVE]

tur·tle·neck *n.* **1** high, close-fitting, turned-down collar on a knitted garment **2** such a garment

Tus·ca·loo·sa /ˌtəsˈkəloōˈsə/ *n.* city in Ala. Pop. 77,759

tusk /təsk/ *n.* long, pointed tooth, esp. protruding from a closed mouth, as in the elephant, walrus, etc. —**tusked** *adj.* [OE]

tus·sle /ˈtəsˈəl/ *n.* **1** struggle; scuffle —*v.* (**·sled, ·sling**) **2** engage in a tussle [rel. to TOUSLE]

tus·sock /ˈtəsˈək/ *n.* clump of grass, etc. —**tus·sock·y** *adj.* [perh. fr. dial. *tusk* tuft]

Tut·ankh·a·men /toōˈtängˈkämˈən, -tängˈ-/ *n.* 14th cent. B.C.; Egyptian pharaoh

tu·te·lage /ˈt(y)oōt'l-ij/ *n.* **1** guardianship **2** being under this **3** instruction [L *tutela* protection]

tu·te·lar·y /ˈt(y)oōt'l-erˈē/ *adj.* **1** of or serving as a guardian **2** giving protection [L, rel. to TUTELAGE]

tu·tor /ˈt(y)oōˈtər/ *n.* **1** private teacher —*v.* **2** act as tutor to **3** work as a tutor —**tu'tor·ship'** *n.* [L *tueri tut-* guard]

tu·to·ri·al /ˈt(y)oōtôrˈēəl/ *adj.* **1** of a tutor or tuition —*n.* **2** intensive class for one or a few students [L *tutorius,* rel. to TUTOR]

tut·ti /ˈtoōˈtē/ *Mus. adj. & adv.* **1** with all voices or instruments together —*n.* (*pl.* **·tis**) **2** such a passage [It, pl. of *tutto* all]

tut·ti-frut·ti /ˈtoōˈtē froōˈtē/ *n.* (*pl.* **·tis**) ice cream containing small bits of candied fruit [It: all fruits]

tu·tu /ˈtoōˈtoō/ *n.* ballet dancer's short skirt of stiffened frills [Fr]

Tu·tu /ˈtoōˈtoō/ *n.,* **Desmond** (born **Mpilo**) 1931– ; South African clergyman and civil-rights leader; Nobel prize 1984

Tu·va·lu /ˈt(y)oōvälˈoō, -värˈ-/ *n.* island nation in the S Pacific Ocean. Capital: Funafuti. Pop. 9,500

tux /təks/ *n.* (*pl.* **-es**) TUXEDO [abbr.]

tux·e·do /təksˈēˈdō/ *n.* (*pl.* **-dos**) **1** dressy dinner jacket with silk-faced lapels **2** suit of semiformal clothes including this [*Tuxedo Park,* NY]

Tux·tla (**Gu·tiér·rez**) /ˈtoōstˈlä (goōtyerˈās) /n.* capital of the Mexican state of Chiapas. Pop. 295,600

TV *abbr.* television

TVA *abbr.* Tennessee Valley Authority

Tver /tvər/ *n.* see KALININ

twad·dle /ˈtwädˈl/ *n.* silly writing or talk; nonsense [earlier *twattle,* alter. of TATTLE]

twain /twān/ *adj. & n.* two [OE *twegen* TWO]

Twain /twān/, **Mark** (pseudonym of **Samuel Langhorne Clemens**) 1835–1910; US writer

twang /twang/ *n.* **1** sound made by a plucked string or released bowstring **2** nasal quality of a voice —*v.* **3** (cause to) emit this sound —**twang·y** *adj.* [imit.]

'twas /twəz/ *v. contr.* it was

tweak /twēk/ *v.* **1** pinch and twist sharply —*n.* **2** act of tweaking [OE *twiccan* TWITCH]

tweed /twēd/ *n.* **1** rough-surfaced woolen cloth, usu. of mixed flecked colors **2** (*pl.*) clothes made of tweed —**tweed'y** *adj.* [alter. of *tweel* (Scots var. of TWILL)]

Tweed /twēd/, **"Boss"** (**William Marcy**) 1823–78; US politician

'tween /twēn/ *prep.* BETWEEN

tweet /twēt/ *n.* **1** chirp of a small bird —*v.* **2** make this noise [imit.]

tweet'er *n.* loudspeaker for high frequencies

tweez·ers /ˈtwēˈzərz/ *n. pl.* small pair of pincers for taking up small objects, plucking out hairs, etc. [fr. obs. *tweeze* case for small instruments]

twelfth /twelfTH/ *adj. & n.* **1** next after eleventh **2** each of twelve equal parts of a thing [OE, rel. to TWELVE]

Twelfth' Day' *n.* EPIPHANY

Twelfth' Night' *n.* Jan. 5, eve of Epiphany

twelve /twelv/ *adj. & n.* **1** one more than eleven **2** symbol for this (12, xii, XII) **3** (**the Twelve**) *Christianity.* the apostles [OE]

twelve'fold' *adj. & adv.* **1** twelve times as much or as many **2** consisting of twelve parts

twen·ty /ˈtwenˈtē/ *adj. & n.* (*pl.* **·ties**) **1** product of two and ten **2** symbol for this (20, xx, XX) **3** (*pl.*) numbers from 20 to 29, esp. as years —**twen'ti·eth** /-ith/ *adj. & n.* [OE]

twen·ty-twen·ty vi'sion *n.* (also **20-20 vi'sion**) **1** vision of normal acuity **2** good eyesight

'twere /twər/ *v. contr. Archaic.* it were

twerp /twərp/ *n. Slang.* stupid, insignificant, or objectionable person

twice /twīs/ *adv.* **1** two times; on two occasions **2** in double degree or quantity [OE, rel. to TWO]

twid·dle /ˈtwidˈl/ *v.* (**·dled, ·dling**) **1** twirl, adjust, or play randomly or idly —*n.* **2** act of twiddling **3 twiddle one's thumbs: a** idly make one's thumbs revolve around each other **b** have nothing to do —**twid'dly** *adj.* [prob. imit.]

twig /twig/ *n.* very small, thin branch of a tree or shrub —**twig'gy** *adj.* [OE]

twi·light /ˈtwīˈlīt/ *n.* **1** light from the sky when the sun is below the horizon, esp. in the evening; dusk **2** period of this **3** faint light **4** period of decline or destruction [fr. TWO, LIGHT[1]]

twi·lit /ˈtwīˈlit/ *adj.* dimly illuminated by twilight

twill /twil/ *n.* fabric so woven as to have a surface of diagonal parallel ridges —**twilled** *adj.* [OE: two-thread]

'twill /twil/ *v. contr.* it will

twin /twin/ *n.* **1** each of a closely related or associated pair, esp. of children or animals born at a single birth **2** exact counterpart of a person or thing **3** (**the Twins**) zodiacal sign or constellation Gemini —*adj.* **4** forming or being one of such a pair (**twin brothers**) —*v.* (**twinned, twin·ning**) **5a** join intimately together **b** (foll. by *with*) pair **6** bear twins —**twin'ning** *n.* [OE, rel. to TWO]

twin' bed' *n.* each of a pair of single beds

twine /twīn/ *n.* **1** strong, coarse string of twisted strands of fiber **2** coil; twist —*v.*

(twined, twin·ing) 3 coil; wind 4 (of a plant) grow in this way [OE]

twinge /twinj/ *n.* sharp, momentary local pain or pang [OE]

twin·kle /twiNG′kəl/ *v.* (**·kled, ·kling**) 1 (of a star, light, etc.) shine with rapidly intermittent gleams 2 (of the eyes) sparkle 3 (of the feet) move lightly and rapidly —*n.* 4 sparkle or gleam of the eyes 5 twinkling light 6 light, rapid movement —**twink′ly** *adj.* [OE]

twin′kling *n.* 1 wink of an eye 2 time it takes for a wink; an instant

twirl /twərl/ *v.* 1 spin, swing, or twist quickly and lightly around —*n.* 2 twirling motion 3 flourish made with a pen

twist /twist/ *v.* 1a change the form of by rotating one end and not the other or the two ends in opposite directions b undergo such a change c wrench or pull out of shape with a twisting action (*twisted my ankle*) 2 wind (strands, etc.) about each other 3 produce or take a spiral form 4 (foll. by *off*) break off by twisting 5 misrepresent the meaning of (words) 6 take a winding course —*n.* 7 act of twisting 8 twisted state 9 thing formed by twisting 10 point at which a thing twists or bends 11 unexpected turn in a story, etc. 12 popular 1960s dance, with a twisting movement of the hips 13 **twist a person's arm** coerce, esp. by argument 14 **twist around one's (little) finger** easily persuade or control (a person) —**twist′y** *adj.* (**·i·er, ·i·est**) [rel. to TWIN, TWINE]

twist′ed *adj.* (of a person or mind) neurotic or perverted

twit¹ /twit/ *n. Colloq.* foolish person [orig. dial., perh. fr. TWIT²]

twit² *v.* (**twit·ted, twit·ting**) reproach or taunt, usu. good-humoredly [OE]

twitch /twiCH/ *v.* 1 (of features, muscles, etc.) move or contract spasmodically 2 pull sharply at —*n.* 3 sudden involuntary contraction or movement 4 sudden pull or jerk —**twitch′y** *adj.* (**·i·er, ·i·est**) (in sense 3) [prob. OE]

twit·ter /twit′ər/ *v.* 1 (esp. of a bird) emit a succession of light, tremulous sounds 2 utter or express in this way —*n.* 3 act of twittering 4 tremulously excited state —**twit′ter·y** *adj.* [imit.]

'twixt /twikst/ *prep. contr.* BETWIXT

two /tŌŌ/ *adj. & n.* 1 one more than one 2 symbol for this (2, ii, II) 3 in two in or into two pieces 4 **put two and two together** infer from known facts [OE]

two′-bit′ *adj. Slang.* cheap; petty

two′-di·men·sion·al *adj.* 1 having or appearing to have length and breadth but no depth 2 lacking substance; superficial

two′-faced′ *adj.* insincere; deceitful

two′fold′ *adj. & adv.* 1 twice as much or as many 2 consisting of two parts

two′hand′ed *adj.* 1 having, using, or requiring the use of two hands 2 (of a card game) for two players

two′-ply′ *adj.* having two strands or layers

two·some /tŌŌ′səm/ *n.* two persons together

two′-step′ *n.* dance in march or polka time

two′-time′ *v. Colloq.* 1 be unfaithful to (a lover) 2 swindle —**two′-tim′er** *n.*

two′-tone′ *adj.* having two colors or sounds

'twould /twŎŎd/ *v. contr.* it would

two′-way′ *adj.* 1 involving two directions or participants 2 (of a radio) capable of transmitting and receiving signals

twp. *abbr.* township

TX postal abbr. for Texas

-ty¹ *suffix* forming nouns denoting quality or condition (*cruelty; plenty*) [Fr fr. L *-tas -tatis*]

-ty² *suffix* denoting tens (*ninety*) [OE *-tig*]

ty·coon /tīkŌŌn′/ *n.* business magnate [Japn: great lord]

ty·ing /tī′iNG/ *v. pres. part.* of TIE

tyke /tīk/ *n.* (also **tike**) small child [ON]

Ty·ler /tī′lər/, **John** 1790–1862; 10th US president (1841–45)

tym·pa·ni /tim′pənē/ *n.* var. of TIMPANI

tym·pa·num /tim′pənəm/ *n.* (*pl.* **·nums** or **·na/-nə/**) 1 middle ear 2 eardrum [L fr. Gk *tympanon* drum]

Tyn·dale /tin′dəl, -dāl′/, **William** c. 1494–1536; English translator of the Bible

a a *a*

roman   bold   italic

TYPE 6

type /tīp/ *n.* 1 sort; class; kind 2 person, thing, or event exemplifying a class or group 3 (in *comb.*) made of, resembling, or functioning as (*ceramic-type material*) 4 *Colloq.* person, esp. of a specified character (*a quiet type; not my type*) 5 object, conception, or work serving as a model for subsequent artists 6 *Printing.* a piece of metal, etc., with a raised letter or character on its upper surface for printing b kind or size of such pieces (*printed in large type*) —*v.* (**typed, typ·ing**) 7 write with a typewriter 8 typecast 9 esp. *Biol. & Med.* assign to a type; classify [Gk *typos* mark]

type′cast′ *v.* (**·cast, ·cast·ing**) assign (an actor or actress) repeatedly to the same type of role

type′face′ *n. Printing.* 1 set of characters in one design 2 inked surface of type

type′script′ *n.* typewritten document

type′set′ter *n. Printing.* 1 person who composes type 2 composing machine —**type′ set′ting** *n.*

type′writ′er *n.* machine with keys for producing printlike characters one at a time on paper inserted around a roller

type′writ′ten *adj.* produced on a typewriter

ty·phoid /tī′foid/ *n.* (in full **ty′phoid fe′ver**) infectious bacterial fever attacking the intestines

ty·phoon /tīfŌŌn′/ *n.* tropical hurricane in E Asian seas [Chin: great wind]

ty·phus /tī′fəs/ *n.* infectious fever with a purple rash, headaches, and usu. delirium [Gk: fever]

typ·i·cal /tip′ikəl/ *adj.* 1 serving as a characteristic example; representative 2 characteristic; to be expected (*typical of him to refuse*) —**typ′i·cal′i·ty** /-kal′ətē/ *n.*; **typ′i·cal·ly** *adv.* [MedL, rel. to TYPE]

typ·i·fy /tip′əfī′/ *v.* (**·fied, ·fy·ing**) 1 be typical of 2 represent by or as a type or symbol —**typ′i·fi·ca′tion** /-fikā′sнən/ n. [L, rel. to TYPE]

typ·ist /tī′pist/ n. person who types, esp. for a living

ty·po /tī′pō/ n. (pl. **-pos**) Colloq. typographical error

typo. or **typog.** abbr. typographer; typographical; typography

ty·pog·ra·phy /tīpäg′rəfē, tə-/ n. 1 printing as an art 2 style and appearance of printed matter —**ty·pog′ra·pher** n.; **ty′po·graph′i·cal** /-pōgraf′ikəl/ adj.; **ty′po·graph′i·cal·ly** adv. [TYPE, -GRAPHY]

ty·ran·ni·cal /təran′ikəl, tī-/ adj. despotic; unjustly severe —**ty·ran′ni·cal·ly** adv. [Gk, rel. to TYRANT]

tyr·an·nize /tēr′ənīz′/ v. (**-nized, ·niz·ing**) treat despotically or cruelly [Fr, rel. to TYRANT]

ty·ran·no·sau·rus /təran′əsôr′əs/ n. (pl. **·rus·es**) (also **ty·ran′no·saur**) carnivorous dinosaur with short front legs and a long, well-developed tail [Gk tyrannos tyrant, sauros lizard]

tyr·an·ny /tēr′ənē/ n. (pl. **·nies**) 1 cruel and arbitrary use of authority 2 rule by a tyrant —**tyr′an·nous** adj. [Gk, rel. to TYRANT]

ty·rant /tī′rənt/ n. 1 oppressive or cruel ruler 2 person exercising power arbitrarily or cruelly [Gk tyrannos]

Tyr·i·an pur·ple /tēr′ēən/ n. crimson or purple dye much prized in the ancient world, orig. obtained from certain mollusks and now made synthetically [for Tyre in Phoenicia]

ty·ro /tī′rō/ n. (pl. **·ros**) beginner; novice [L: recruit]

Tzu·po /dzə′bō′/ n. see ZIBO

U

u, U /yōō/ n. (pl. **u's; U's, Us**) twenty-first letter of the English alphabet; a vowel

U symb. uranium

u or **u.** abbr. 1 uniform 2 unit 3 unsatisfactory 4 upper

U or **U.** abbr. 1 Uncle 2 Union 3 United 4 University

UAW abbr. United Auto Workers

u·biq·ui·tous /yōōbik′witəs/ adj. (seemingly) present everywhere simultaneously —**u·biq′ui·tous·ly** adv.; **u·biq′ui·ty** n. [L ubique everywhere]

U-boat /yōō′bōt′/ n. Hist. German submarine [Ger Untersee undersea]

ud·der /ud′ər/ n. baglike mammary organ of cattle, etc., with several teats [OE]

U·fa /ōōfä′/ n. city in W Russia. Pop. 1,097,000

UFO n. (pl. **-s**) unidentified flying object

u·fol·o·gy /yōōfäl′əgē/ n. study of UFOs —**u·fol′o·gist** n.

U·gan·da /(y)ōōgan′də/ n. country in E Africa at the N end of Lake Victoria. Capital: Kampala. Pop. 17,194,000 —**U·gan′dan** n. & adj.

ugh /əg/ interj. expression of disgust, etc. [imit.]

ug·ly /əg′lē/ adj. (**·li·er, ·li·est**) 1 unpleasant to the eye, ear, mind, etc. 2 unpleasantly suggestive; discreditable (ugly rumors) 3 threatening; dangerous 4 morally repulsive —**ug′li·ness** n. [ON]

UHF abbr. ultrahigh frequency

U·jung Pan·dang /ōō′jŏŏNG pändäNG′/ n. seaport on Celebes (Sulawesi) in Indonesia. Pop. 709,000

UK abbr. United Kingdom

u·kase /yōō′kās′, yōōkäz′/ n. authoritative decree

U·kraine /yōōkrān′/ n. republic in E Europe on the N coast of the Black Sea; formerly part of the USSR. Capital: Kiev. Pop. 52,135,000

Ukrai·ni·an /yōōkrā′nēən/ n. 1 native or language of Ukraine 2 person of Ukrainian descent —adj. 3 of Ukraine, its people, or language

u·ku·le·le /yōō′kələ′lē/ n. small, four-stringed Hawaiian guitar [Haw]

U·lan Ba·tor /ōō′län bä′tôr′/ n. (also U′laan·baa′tar′) capital of Mongolia. Pop. 548,400

U·lan-U·de /ōō′län ōōdä′/ n. city in SE Russia. Pop. 362,400

ul·cer /əl′sər/ n. 1 open sore on or in the body, often forming pus 2 corrupting influence, etc. —**ul′cer·ous** adj. [L ulcus -cer-]

ul·cer·ate /əl′sərāt′/ v. (**·at·ed, ·at·ing**) form into or affect with an ulcer —**ul′cer·a′tion** n.

Ulm /ŏŏlm/ n. city on the Danube River in Germany. Pop. 108,900

ul·na /əl′nə/ n. (pl. **·nae** /-nē/ or **·nas**) thinner and longer bone of the two in the forearm —**ul′nar** /-nər/ adj. [L]

Ul·san /ōōl′sän′/ n. city in South Korea. Pop. 683,000

ul·ster /əl′stər/ n. long, loose overcoat of rough cloth [Ulster in Ireland]

ult. abbr. ultimately

ul·te·ri·or /əl′tērēər/ adj. not evident or admitted; hidden; secret (ulterior motive) [L: further]

ul·ti·mate /əl′təmət/ adj. 1 last or last possible; final 2 fundamental; primary; basic —n. 3 best achievable or imaginable 4 final or fundamental fact or principle —**ul′ti·mate·ly** adv. [L ultimus last]

ul·ti·ma·tum /əl′təmā′təm/ n. (pl. **·tums** or **·ta** /-tə/) final statement of terms or a demand in negotiations [L, rel. to ULTIMATE]

ul·tra /əl′trə/ adj. extreme; beyond usual limits

ultra- comb. form 1 extreme(ly); excessive(ly) (ultramodern) 2 beyond [L ultra beyond]

ul′tra·high′ adj. (of a frequency) in the range 300 to 3000 megahertz

ul′tra·ma·rine′ n. 1 brilliant blue pigment or color —adj. 2 of this color [It and MedL: beyond the sea]

ul′tra·son′ic adj. of or using sound waves

pitched above the range of human hearing —**ul′tra·son′i·cal·ly** adv.

ul′tra·sound′ n. ultrasonic waves, esp. as used in medicine

ul′tra·vi′o·let adj. of or using radiation with a frequency just beyond that of the violet end of the visible spectrum

ul·u·late /əl′yəlāt′/ v. (·lat·ed, ·lat·ing) howl; wail —**ul′u·la′tion** n. [L]

Ul·ya·novsk /ŏŏlyän′əfsk/ n. city in W Russia. Pop. 667,300

um /əm/ interj. expression of hesitation or a pause in speech [imit.]

um·bel /əm′bəl/ n. cluster of flower stalks springing from a common center and forming a flat or curved surface —**um′bel·late, um′bel·lif′er·ous** /-if′ərəs/ adj. [L umbella sunshade]

um·ber /əm′bər/ n. 1 natural pigment or color darker brown than ochre —adj. 2 of this color [L umbra shadow]

um·bil·i·cal /əm′bil′ikəl/ adj. of the navel [fr. UMBILICUS]

um·bil′i·cal cord′ n. cordlike structure attaching a fetus to the placenta

um·bi·li·cus /əm′bil′ikəs, -m·/ n. (pl. ·li·ci /-kī′, -sī′/) navel [L]

um·bra /əm′brə/ n. (pl. ·bras or ·brae /-brē/) total shadow, esp. that cast by a planet or satellite [L: shadow]

um·brage /əm′brij/ n. offense taken [L, rel. to UMBRA]

um·brel·la /əm′brel′ə/ n. 1 device held over the head to keep off rain, sun, etc., usu. cloth on a collapsible frame with a stick by which to hold it 2 protection; patronage [It dim., rel. to UMBRA]

u·mi·ak /ŏŏ′mēak′/ n. open, wood-framed, skin boat used by the Inuit [Esk]

um·laut /ŏŏm′lout′, ŏŏm′-/ n. 1 mark (¨) used over a vowel, esp. in Germanic languages, to indicate an altered vowel sound 2 such a vowel change [Ger]

ump /əmp/ n. umpire

um·pire /əm′pīr′/ n. 1 person enforcing rules and settling disputes, esp. an official in certain sports —v. (·pired, ·pir·ing) 2 act as umpire [Fr nonper not equal, rel. to PEER²]

ump·teen /əmp′tēn′, əmp′tēn′/ Colloq. adj. indefinitely many; a lot of —**ump′teenth** adj. [jocular formation on -TEEN]

UN abbr. UNITED NATIONS

un- prefix 1 added to adjectives and participles and their derivative nouns and adverbs, meaning: **a** not (unusable) **b** reverse of (unsociable) 2 added to nouns, meaning lack or reverse of (unrest, untruth) 3 added to verbs and nouns forming verbs denoting: **a** reversal (undress) **b** deprivation (unmask) **c** release from (unburden) **d** causing to be no longer (unman) [OE]

---

un′a·bashed′ adj.
un·ab′le adj.
un′ac·cept′a·ble adj.
un′ac·cept′a·bly adv.
un′ac·knowl′edged adj.
un′ac·quaint′ed adj.
un′af·fil′i·at·ed adj.
un′a·fraid′ adj.
un·aid′ed adj.
un·al′ter·a·ble adj.
un·al′tered adj.
un·am·big′u·ous adj.
un·am·bi′tious adj.
un′an·nounced′ adj.
un·an′swered adj.
un·an·tic′i·pat′ed adj.
un′ap·peal′ing adj.
un′ap·peal′ing·ly adv.
un′ap·pe·tiz′ing adj.
un′ap·pre′ci·at·ed adj.
un′ap·pre′cia·tive adj.
un·asked′ adj.
un′as·sail′a·ble adj.
un′as·sist′ed adj.
un′at·tain′a·ble adj.
un′at·trac′tive adj.
un′at·trac′tive·ly adv.
un·au′thor·ized adj.
un′a·vail′a·bil′i·ty n.
un′a·vail′a·ble adj.
un′a·void′a·ble adj.
un′a·void′a·bly adv.
un·bear′a·ble adj.
un·bear′a·bly adv.
un·beat′a·ble adj.
un·bi′ased adj.

un·bleached′ adj.
un·blem′ished adj.
un′bound′ adj.
un·break′a·ble adj.
un·buck′le v.
un·but′ton v.
un·ceas′ing adj.
un·ceas′ing·ly adv.
un·cen′sored adj.
un·chal′lenged adj.
un·change′a·ble adj.
un·changed′ adj.
un·chang′ing adj.
un·chap′er·oned′ adj.
un′char·ac·ter·is′tic adj.
un′char·ac·ter·is′ti·cal·ly adv.
un·claimed′ adj.
un·clean′ adj.
un·clear′ adj.
un·cloud′ed adj.
un·clut′tered adj.
un·col′ored adj.
un·combed′ adj.
un′com·plain′ing adj.
un′com·plain′ing·ly adv.
un′com·plet′ed adj.
un′com·pli·cat·ed adj.
un′com·pli·men′ta·ry adj.
un′com·pre·hend′ing adj.
un′con·cealed′ adj.
un′con·fined′ adj.
un′con·firmed′ adj.

un′con·quer·a·ble adj.
un′con·strained′ adj.
un′con·tam′i·nat·ed adj.
un′con·test′ed adj.
un′con·trol′la·ble adj.
un′con·trol′la·bly adv.
un′con·trolled′ adj.
un′con·vinced′ adj.
un′con·vin′cing adj.
un′con·vin′cing·ly adv.
un·cooked′ adj.
un′co·op′er·a·tive adj.
un′cor·rob′o·rat′ed adj.
un·crit′i·cal adj.
un·cross′ v.
un·cul′ti·vat′ed adj.
un·cured′ adj.
un·dam′aged adj.
un·dat′ed adj.
un·de·clared′ adj.
un·de·feat′ed adj.
un·de·fend′ed adj.
un·de·fined′ adj.
un·de·mand′ing adj.
un′de·mo·cra′tic adj.
un′de·pend′a·ble adj.
un·de·served′ adj.
un′de·serv′ed·ly adv.
un′de·serv′ing adj.
un′de·tect′a·ble adj.
un′de·tect′ed adj.
un′de·ter′mined adj.

un′de·terred′ adj.
un′de·vel′oped adj.
un′di·gest′ed adj.
un·dig′ni·fied′ adj.
un′di·lut′ed adj.
un′di·min′ished adj.
un′dip·lo·mat′ic adj.
un·dis′ci·plined adj.
un′dis·closed′ adj.
un′dis·co′vered adj.
un′dis·guised′ adj.
un′dis·mayed′ adj.
un′dis·put′ed adj.
un′dis·tin′guished adj.
un′di·sturbed′ adj.
un·di·vid′ed adj.
un·dressed′ adj.
un·drink′a·ble adj.
un·earned′ adj.
un·eat′en adj.
un′e·co·nom′ic adj.
un′e·co·nom′i·cal adj.
un′e·co·nom′i·cal·ly adv.
un·ed′it·ed adj.
un·ed′u·cat·ed adj.
un′em·phat′ic adj.
un′en·cum′bered adj.
un·end′ing adj.
un′en·dur′a·ble adj.
un′en·dur′a·bly adv.
un′en·light′ened adj.
un′en·thu′si·as′tic adj.
un′en·thu′si·as′ti·cal·ly adv.

un·a·bat'ed /-bātəd/ adj. not abated; undiminished

un·ac·com'pa·nied adj. 1 not accompanied 2 Mus. without accompaniment

un·ac·com'plished adj. 1 uncompleted 2 lacking accomplishments

un·ac·count'a·ble adj. 1 without explanation; strange 2 not answerable for one's actions —un·ac·count'a·bly adv.

un·ac·count'ed adj. unexplained; excluded

un·ac·cus'tomed adj. 1 not accustomed 2 unusual (*unaccustomed silence*)

un·a·dorned' adj. plain

un·a·dul'ter·at·ed adj. 1 pure 2 complete; utter

un·ad·vised' adj. 1 indiscreet; rash 2 without advice —un·ad·vis'ed·ly /-vīz'ədlē/ adv.

un·af·fect'ed adj. 1 not affected 2 free from affectation —un·af·fect'ed·ly adv.

un·al·loyed' adj. 1 complete; utter 2 unmixed; pure

un'-A·mer'i·can adj. 1 uncharacteristic of Americans 2 unpatriotic; considered contrary to US interests

u·nan·i·mous /yōōnan'əməs/ adj. (of an opinion, vote, etc.) by all without exception or dissent —u'nan·im'i·ty n.; u·nan'i·mous·ly adv. [L *unus* one, *animus* mind]

un'an·swer·a·ble adj. 1 irrefutable 2 having no known answer

un·ap·proach'a·ble adj. 1 inaccessible 2 unfriendly; aloof

un·armed' adj. not armed; without weapons

un·a·shamed' adj. 1 feeling no guilt 2 blatant; bold —un·a·sham'ed·ly /-shām'ədlē/ adv.

un·as·sum'ing adj. not pretentious; modest —un·as·sum'ing·ly adv.

un·at·tached' adj. 1 not engaged, married, etc. 2 not attached, esp. to a particular organization, etc.

un·at·tend'ed adj. 1 not attended 2 (of a person, vehicle, etc.) alone

un·at·trib'ut·a·ble adj. not able to be attributed to a source, etc.

un·a·vail'ing adj. achieving nothing; futile —un·a·vail'ing·ly adv.

un·a·ware' adj. 1 not aware 2 unperceptive —adv. 3 UNAWARES —un·a·ware'ness n.

un·a·wares' adv. 1 unexpectedly 2 inadvertently

un·bal'anced adj. 1 emotionally unstable 2 biased 3 out of balance

un·bar' v. (·barred, ·bar·ring) unlock; open

un·be·com'ing adj. 1 unflattering 2 not fitting; indecorous —un·be·com'ing·ly adv.

un·be·known' adj. (also un'be·knownst' /-nōnst'/) unknown

un·be·lief' n. lack of esp. religious belief —un·be·liev'er n.; un·be·liev'ing adj.

un·be·liev'a·ble adj. not believable; incredible —un·be·liev'a·bly adv.

---

un·en'vi·a·ble *adj.*	un'gram·mat'i·cal *adj.*	un·in'sured' *adj.*	un·mu'si·cal *adj.*
un·e'vent'ful *adj.*		un·in·tel'li·gi·ble *adj.*	un·mu'si·cal·ly *adv.*
un·e'vent'ful·ly *adv.*	un'gram·mat'i·cal·ly *adv.*	un·in·tend'ed *adj.*	un·named' *adj.*
un·ex·cit'ing *adj.*	un·grate'ful *adj.*	un·in·ten'tion·al *adj.*	un·nat'u·ral·ized' *adj.*
un'ex·pired' *adj.*	un·grate'ful·ly *adv.*	un·in·ten'tion·al·ly *adv.*	un·need'ed *adj.*
un'ex·plained' *adj.*	un·grudg'ing *adj.*		un·no'tice·a·ble *adj.*
un·ex·plored' *adj.*	un·ham'pered *adj.*	un·in'ter·est·ing *adj.*	un·no'tice·a·bly *adv.*
un'ex·posed' *adj.*	un·harmed' *adj.*	un·in'ter·rupt'ed *adj.*	un·no'ticed *adj.*
un'ex·pressed' *adj.*	un·har'ness *v.*	un·in·vit'ed *adj.*	un'ob·jec'tion·a·ble *adj.*
un·fad'ing *adj.*	un·health'ful *adj.*	un·just' *adj.*	
un·fa·mil'iar *adj.*	un·heed'ed *adj.*	un·jus·ti·fi'a·ble *adj.*	un'ob·ser'vant *adj.*
un·fa·mil·iar'i·ty *n.*	un·help'ful *adj.*	un·jus·ti·fi'a·bly *adv.*	un'ob·served' *adj.*
un·fash'ion·a·ble *adj.*	un·help'ful·ly *adv.*	un·jus'ti·fied' *adj.*	un'ob·struct'ed *adj.*
un·fash'ion·a·bly *adv.*	un·hes'i·tat·ing *adj.*	un·just'ly *adv.*	un'ob·tain'a·ble *adj.*
un·fath'o·ma·ble *adj.*	un·hes'i·tat·ing·ly *adv.*	un·la'beled *adj.*	un·oc'cu·pied' *adj.*
un·fa'vor·a·ble *adj.*		un·lace' *v.*	un'of·fi'cial *adj.*
un·fa'vor·a·bly *adv.*	un·hin'dered *adj.*	un·la'den *adj.*	un'of·fi'cial·ly *adv.*
un·fer'ti·lized' *adj.*	un·his·to'ri·cal *adj.*	un·la'dy·like *adj.*	un·o'pened *adj.*
un·filled' *adj.*	un·hook' *v.*	un·latch' *v.*	un·op'posed' *adj.*
un·fit' *adj.*	un·hoped'-for' *adj.*	un·li'censed *adj.*	un·or'tho·dox' *adj.*
un·flag'ging *adj.*	un·hur'ried *adj.*	un·lined' *adj.*	un·paid' *adj.*
un·flag'ging·ly *adv.*	un·hurt' *adj.*	un·list'ed *adj.*	un·paint'ed *adj.*
un·flat'ter·ing *adj.*	un·i·den'ti·fied' *adj.*	un·lit' *adj.*	un·par'don·a·ble *adj.*
un·flat'ter·ing·ly *adv.*	un·i·mag'i·na·ble *adj.*	un·lov'a·ble *adj.*	un·par'don·a·bly *adv.*
un·flinch'ing *adj.*	un·im·paired' *adj.*	un·loved' *adj.*	
un·flinch'ing·ly *adv.*	un·im·ped'ed *adj.*	un·made' *adj.*	un'pat·ri·o'tic *adj.*
un'fore·see'a·ble *adj.*	un·im·por'tant *adj.*	un·man'age·a·ble *adj.*	un·paved' *adj.*
un'fore·seen' *adj.*	un·im·pressed' *adj.*	un·man'age·a·bly *adv.*	un'per·turbed' *adj.*
un·for·giv'a·ble *adj.*	un·im·pres'sive *adj.*	un·man'ly *adj.*	un·planned' *adj.*
un·for·giv'ing *adj.*	un·im·proved' *adj.*	un·marked' *adj.*	un·pleas'ing *adj.*
un·for·got'ten *adj.*	un·in·cor'po·rat·ed *adj.*	un·mar'ried *adj.*	un·pol'ished *adj.*
un·fre'quent·ed *adj.*	un·in·formed' *adj.*	un·matched' *adj.*	un·pol·lut'ed *adj.*
un·ful·filled' *adj.*	un·in·hab'it·a·ble *adj.*	un·mer'it·ed *adj.*	un·prac'ti·cal *adj.*
un·fur'nished *adj.*	un·in·hab'it·ed *adj.*	un'me·thod'i·cal *adj.*	un'pre·dict·a·bil'i·ty *n.*
un·gen'tle·man·ly *adj.*	un·in·hib'it·ed *adj.*	un·mind'ful *adj.*	un'pre·dict'a·ble *adj.*
un·grace'ful *adj.*	un·in'jured *adj.*	un·mixed' *adj.*	un'pre·dict'a·bly *adv.*
un·grace'ful·ly *adv.*	un·in·spir'ing *adj.*	un·mo'di·fied' *adj.*	un·prej'u·diced *adj.*

un·bend' v. (·bent, ·bend·ing) 1 straighten 2 relax; become affable

un'bend'ing adj. 1 inflexible 2 firm; austere

un·bid'den /-bid'n/ adj. not commanded or invited

un'blink'ing adj. 1 not blinking 2 steadfast; stolid

un·blush'ing adj. 1 shameless 2 frank

un·bolt' v. release the bolt of (a door, etc.)

un·born' adj. not yet, or never to be, born

un·bos'om v. disclose (thoughts, etc.); unburden oneself

un·bound'ed adj. 1 infinite 2 unrestrained

un·bri'dle v. (·dled, ·dling) remove a bridle, constraints, etc., from (a horse, one's tongue, etc.)

un·bro'ken adj. 1 not broken 2 untamed (*unbroken horse*) 3 uninterrupted 4 unsurpassed

un·bur'den v. relieve (oneself, one's conscience, etc.) by confession, etc.

un·called'-for' adj. 1 (of a remark, action, etc.) unnecessary 2 improper

un·can'ny adj. (·ni·er, ·ni·est) seemingly supernatural; mysterious —**un·can'ni·ly** adv.; **un·can'ni·ness** n.

un·cared'-for' adj. disregarded; neglected

un·car'ing adj. neglectful; lacking compassion

un'cer·e·mo'ni·ous adj. 1 abrupt; discourteous 2 informal —**un'cer·e·mo'ni·ous·ly** adv.

un·cer'tain adj. 1 not certainly knowing or known 2 unreliable 3 changeable; erratic 4 in no uncertain terms clearly and forcefully —**un·cer'tain·ly** adv.; **un·cer'tain·ty** n. (pl. ·ties)

un·char'i·ta·ble adj. censorious; severe in judgment —**un·char'i·ta·bly** adv.

un·chart'ed adj. 1 not mapped or surveyed 2 unexplored; unknown

un·chris'tian adj. 1 not in keeping with Christian principles 2 uncaring; selfish

un·ci·al /ən'sHəl, -sēəl/ adj. 1 of or written in rounded, unjoined letters similar to capitals, found in manuscripts of the 4th–8th cent. —n. 2 uncial letter, style, or manuscript [L *uncia* inch]

un·civ'il adj. ill-mannered; impolite —**un·civ'il·ly** adv.

un·clasp' v. 1 loosen the clasp(s) of 2 release the grip of (a hand, etc.)

un·cle /əNG'kəl/ n. 1 brother of one's father or mother 2 aunt's husband [L *avunculus*]

un·clean' adj. 1 not clean 2 religiously impure; forbidden

Un'cle Sam' n. US government personified

Un'cle Tom' n. Colloq. disparaging term for a black person considered servile toward whites

un·coil' v. unwind

un·com'fort·a·ble adj. 1 not comfortable 2 uneasy; disquieting —**un·com'fort·a·bly** adv.

un·com·mit'ted adj. 1 not committed 2 not politically attached

un'pre·med'i·tat·ed adj.	**un're·pre·sent'ed** adj.	**un'signed'** adj.	**un'sym·met'ri·cal** adj.
un'pre·pared' adj.	**un're·spon'sive** adj.	**un·sink'a·ble** adj.	**un'sym·pa·thet'ic** adj.
un'pro·duc'tive adj.	**un're·strained'** adj.	**un·skill'ful** adj.	**un'sym·pa·thet'i·cal·ly** adv.
un·prof'it·a·ble adj.	**un're·strict'ed** adj.	**un·sliced'** adj.	
un·prom'is·ing adj.	**un're·ward'ed** adj.	**un·smil'ing** adj.	**un'sys·te·mat'ic** adj.
un'pro·nounce'a·ble adj.	**un·ripe'** adj.	**un·so'cia·ble** adj.	**un'sys·te·mat'i·cal·ly** adv.
un'pro·pi'tious adj.	**un·safe'** adj.	**un·soiled'** adj.	
un·prov'a·ble adj.	**un·said'** adj.	**un·sold'** adj.	**un·taint'ed** adj.
un·proved' adj.	**un·sal'a·ble** adj.	**un·solved'** adj.	**un·tamed'** adj.
un'pro·voked' adj.	**un·salt'ed** adj.	**un·sort'ed** adj.	**un·tar'nished** adj.
un·pub'lished adj.	**un·san'i·tar'y** adj.	**un'spe·cif'ic** adj.	**un·tast'ed** adj.
un·pun'ished adj.	**un'sat·is·fac'to·ri·ly** adv.	**un'spe·ci'fied** adj.	**un·taught'** adj.
un·quench'a·ble adj.		**un'spec·tac'u·lar** adj.	**un·teach'a·ble** adj.
un·read'y adj.	**un'sat·is·fac'to·ry** adj.		**un·ten'a·ble** adj.
un're·a·lis'tic adj.	**un·sat'is·fied** adj.	**un'spec·tac'u·lar·ly** adv.	**un·test'ed** adj.
un're·a·list'i·cal·ly adv.	**un·sat'is·fy'ing** adj.	**un·spoiled'** adj.	**un·tir'ing** adj.
	un·scarred' adj.	**un·sports'man·like'** adj.	**un·tir'ing·ly** adv.
un're·a·liz'a·ble adj.	**un·sche'duled** adj.		**un·trace'a·ble** adj.
un're'a·lized' adj.	**un·sea'soned** adj.	**un·stat'ed** adj.	**un·trained'** adj.
un·rea'son·ing adj.	**un·see'ing** adj.	**un·stop'pa·ble** adj.	**un·tram'melled** adj.
un'rec·og·niz'a·ble adj.	**un·see'ing·ly** adv.	**un'sub·stan'ti·at'ed** adj.	**un·treat'ed** adj.
	un·seg'ment·ed adj.		**un·trou'bled** adj.
un're·cord'ed adj.	**un'self·con'scious** adj.	**un'suc·cess'ful** adj.	**un·trust'wor'thi·ness** n.
un're·deemed' adj.	**un'self·con'scious·ly** adv.	**un'suc·cess'ful·ly** adv.	
un're·fined' adj.		**un'suit·a·bil'i·ty** n	**un·trust'wor'thy** adj.
un're·formed' adj.	**un'self·con'scious·ness** n.	**un·suit'a·ble** adj.	**un·us'a·ble** adj.
un·reg'is·tered adj.		**un·suit'a·bly** adv.	**un·var'y·ing** adj.
un·reg'u·lated adj.	**un·self'ish** adj.	**un·sul'lied** adj.	**un·ver'i·fied'** adj.
un're·hearsed' adj.	**un·self'ish·ly** adv.	**un'su·per·vised'** adj.	**un·want'ed** adj.
un're·lated' adj.	**un·self'ish·ness** n.	**un'sup·port'ed** adj.	**un·washed'** adj.
un're·mark'a·ble adj.	**un·sen'ti·men'tal** adj.	**un·sure'** adj.	**un·wa'ver·ing** adj.
un're·mark'a·bly adv.	**un·shak'en** adj.	**un'sur·passed'** adj.	**un·wa'ver·ing·ly** adv.
	un·shav'en adj.	**un'sus·pect'ed** adj.	**un·wel'come** adj.
un're·pent'ant adj.	**un·shock'a·ble** adj.	**un'sus·pect'ing** adj.	**un·work'a·ble** adj.
un're·pent'ant·ly adv.	**un·sight'ed** adj.	**un'sus·tain'a·ble** adj.	**un·work'a·bly** adv.
		un·sweet'ened adj.	**un·zip'** v.

un·com'mon adj. 1 unusual 2 remarkably great, etc. —**un·com'mon·ly** adv.; **un·com' mon·ness** n.

un'com·mu'ni·ca'tive adj. taciturn

un'com·pro·mis'ing adj. stubborn; unyielding; absolute —**un'com'pro·mis'ing·ly** adv.

un'con·cern' n. 1 calmness 2 indifference; apathy —**un'con·cerned'** adj.; **un'con·cern' ed·ly** /-sərn'əd lē/ adv.

un'con·di'tion·al adj. not subject to conditions; complete —**un'con·di'tion·al·ly** adv.

un'con·di'tioned re'flex n. instinctive response to a stimulus

un'con·nec'ted adj. 1 not physically joined 2 not connected or associated 3 disconnected

un·con·scion·a·ble /ən'kän'SH(ə)nəbəl/ adj. 1 without or contrary to conscience 2 excessive —**un·con'scion·a·bly** adv. [fr. UN-, CONSCIENCE]

un·con'scious adj. 1 not conscious or aware —n. 2 normally inaccessible part of the mind affecting the emotions, etc. —**un·con' scious·ly** adv.; **un·con'scious·ness** n.

un'con·sti·tu'tion·al adj. in breach of a political constitution —**un'con·sti·tu'tion·al·ly** adv.

un'con·ven'tion·al adj. unusual; unorthodox —**un'con·ven·tion·al'i·ty** n.; **un'con·ven' tion·al·ly** adv.

un'co·or'di·nat'ed adj. 1 not coordinated 2 clumsy

un·cork' v. 1 draw the cork from (a bottle) 2 vent (feelings, etc.)

un·count'ed adj. inestimable; immense

un·cou'ple v. (·pled, ·pling) release from couplings; unfasten

un·couth /ən'kōōTH/ adj. uncultured; crude [OE: unknown]

un·cov'er v. 1 remove a cover or covering from 2 disclose 3 remove one's hat, etc., from one's head

unc·tion /əNGK'SHən/ n. 1a anointing with oil, etc., as a religious rite or medical treatment b oil, ointment, etc., so used 2a soothing words or thought b excessive or insincere flattery [L ungere unct- anoint]

unc·tu·ous /əNGK'CHŌŌəs/ adj. 1 unpleasantly flattering; oily 2 greasy or soapy —**unc' tu·ous·ly** adv. [MedL, rel. to UNCTION]

un·cut' adj. 1 not cut 2 (of a book, film, etc.) complete; uncensored 3 (of a gem) not shaped

un·de·ceive' v. (·ceived, ·ceiv·ing) free (a person) from a misconception, deception, or error

un·de·cid'ed adj. 1 not settled 2 irresolute

un'de·mon'stra·tive adj. not emotionally expressive; reserved

un·de·ni'a·ble adj. indisputable; certain —**un·de·ni'a·bly** adv.

un·der /ən'dər/ prep. 1a in or to a position lower than; below; beneath (under the table) b on the inside of (vest under his jacket) 2 inferior to; less than (is under 18) 3a subject to; controlled by (under constraint) b undergoing (is under repair) c classified or subsumed in (under two headings) 4 at the foot of or sheltered by (under the cliff) 5 powered by (sail, steam, etc.) 6 during the reign or rule of —adv. 7 in or to a lower position or con-

dition 8 Colloq. in or into unconsciousness —adj. 9 lower 10 under the sun anywhere in the world 11 under way in motion; in progress —**un'der·most'** adj. [OE]

under- prefix in senses of UNDER: 1 below; beneath 2 lower; subordinate 3 insufficiently; incompletely

un'der·a·chieve' v. (·chieved, ·chiev·ing) do less well than might be expected (esp. academically) —**un'der·a·chiev'er** n.

un'der·act' v. 1 act with insufficient force 2 Theat. act with restraint or without energy

un'der·age' adj. (also **un'der age'**) not old enough, esp. not of legal age

un'der·arm' adj. 1 UNDERHAND, 2 2 under the arm 3 in the armpit —adv. 4 UNDERHAND, 2

un'der·bel'ly n. (pl. ·lies) undersurface of an animal, vehicle, etc., esp. as vulnerable to attack

un'der·bid' v. (·bid, ·bid·ding) 1 make a lower bid than 2 Cards. bid less on (one's hand) than warranted —**un'der·bid'der** n.

un'der·brush' n. dense, low shrubs, etc., as in a forest

un'der·car'riage n. 1 wheeled, retractable structure beneath an aircraft, used for landing, etc. 2 supporting frame of a vehicle

un'der·charge' v. (·charged, ·charg·ing) 1 charge too little to (a person) 2 give too little charge to (a gun, battery, etc.)

un'der·class' n. poor or underprivileged social class

un'der·class'man /-klas'mən/ n. (pl. ·men) first- or second-year student at a high school or college

un'der·clothes' n. pl. (also **un'der·cloth'ing**) UNDERWEAR

un'der·coat' n. 1 layer of paint under a topcoat 2 sealant used to retard rust on the underside of a car 3 animal's under layer of hair, etc. —v. 4 seal with an undercoat

un'der·cov'er adj. 1 surreptitious 2 spying incognito, esp. by infiltration

un'der·cur'rent n. 1 current below the surface 2 underlying often contrary feeling, influence, etc.

un'der·cut' v. (·cut, ·cut·ting) 1 sell or work at a lower price than 2 cut away the part below 3 undermine

un'der·de·vel'oped adj. 1 not fully developed; immature 2 (of a country, etc.) with unexploited potential —**un'der·de·vel'op· ment** n.

un'der·dog' n. 1 oppressed person 2 one expected to be the loser in a contest

un'der·done' adj. not sufficiently cooked

un'der·em·ployed' adj. working below one's potential, training, etc. —**un'der·em·ploy' ment** n.

un·der·es·ti·mate v. /ən'dəres'təmāt'/ (·mat·ed, ·mat·ing) 1 form too low an estimate of —n. /·mit, ·māt'/ 2 estimate that is too low —**un'der·es'ti·ma'tion** n.

un'der·ex·pose' v. (·posed, ·pos·ing) expose (film) for too short a time, etc. —**un' der·ex·po'sure** n.

un'der·foot' adv. (also **un'der foot'**) 1 under one's feet 2 in the way

un'der·gar'ment n. piece of underwear

un'der·go' v. (·went, ·gone, ·go·ing) be subjected to; suffer; endure

un'der·grad'u·ate n. college student who has

not yet received a degree, esp. a bachelor's degree

un·der·ground adv. /ən'dərground'/ 1 beneath the ground 2 in or into secrecy or hiding —adj. /ən'dərground'/ 3 situated underground 4 secret; subversive 5 unconventional; radical —n. /ən'dərground'/ 6 Brit. subway 7 secret subversive group or activity

un'der·growth' n. UNDERBRUSH

un'der·hand' adj. & adv. 1 deceitful; crafty; secret 2 Sports. done or performed with the arm below shoulder level —**un'der·hand'ed·ly** /-ədlē/ adv.

un·der·lie' v. (·lay, ·lain, ·ly·ing) 1 lie under (a stratum, etc.) 2 be the basis of 3 exist beneath the superficial aspect of

un·der·line' v. (·lined, ·lin·ing) 1 draw a line under 2 emphasize; stress

un·der·ling /ən'dərlING/ n. usu. Derog. subordinate

un·der·ly'ing v. 1 pres. part. of UNDERLIE —adj. 2 basic

un·der·mine v. /ən'dərmīn'/ (·mined, ·min·ing) 1 injure secretly or insidiously 2 wear away the base of 3 /ən'dərmīn'/ make an excavation under

un'der·neath' /-nēTH'/ prep. 1 beneath; below —adv. 2 at or to a lower place —n. 3 lower surface or part —adj. 4 lower [OE, rel. to NETHER]

un'der·pants' n. pl. UNDERSHORTS

un'der·pass' n. road, etc., passing under a railroad, another road, etc.

un'der·pay' v. (·paid, ·pay·ing) pay too little to (a person) or for (a thing) —**un'der·pay'ment** n.

un·der·pin' v. (·pinned, ·pin·ning) 1 support from below with masonry, etc. 2 support; strengthen

un'der·play' v. 1 make little of 2 Theat. UNDERACT

un·der·pop'u·lat'ed adj. having an insufficient or very small population

un·der·priv'i·leged adj. less privileged than others; having below average income, rights, etc.

un·der·rate' v. (·rat·ed, ·rat·ing) have too low an opinion of

un'der·score' v. (·scored, ·scor·ing) UNDERLINE

un'der·sea' adj. below the sea or its surface

un'der·sec're·tar'y n. (pl. ·ies) government official subordinate to a secretary

un'der·sell' v. (·sold, ·sell·ing) sell at a lower price than (another seller)

un'der·shirt' n. collarless shirt worn under other clothing

un'der·shorts' n. pl. shorts worn as underwear

un'der·shot' adj. 1 (of a water-wheel) turned by water flowing under it 2 (of a lower jaw) projecting beyond the upper jaw

un'der·side' n. lower or under side or surface

un'der·signed' adj. whose signature is appended (we, the undersigned)

un'der·skirt' n. petticoat or skirt worn beneath another

un'der·staffed' /-staft'/ adj. having too few staff

un'der·stand' v. (·stood, ·stand·ing) 1 perceive the meaning, significance, or cause of 2 sympathize with; know how to deal with 3 infer; take as implied 4 supply (an implied missing word) mentally —**un'der·stand'a·ble** adj.; **un'der·stand'a·bly** adv. [OE, rel. to STAND]

un'der·stand'ing n. 1 ability to understand or think; intelligence 2 individual's perception of a situation, etc. 3 agreement, esp. informal (had an understanding) 4 sympathy; tolerance —adj. 5 having understanding or insight 6 sympathetic —**un'der·stand'ing·ly** adv.

un'der·state' v. (·stat·ed, ·stat·ing) 1 express mildly or in a restrained way 2 represent as less than it actually is —**un'der·state'ment** n.

un'der·stood' v. 1 past and past part. of UNDERSTAND —adj. 2 agreed upon (it was understood that he would wait for us) 3 implied but not stated

un'der·stud'y n. (pl. ·ies) 1 actor ready to take on another's role when required —v. (·ied, ·y·ing) 2 study (a role, etc.) in order to act as understudy 3 act as an understudy to

un'der·take' v. (·took, ·tak·en, ·tak·ing) 1 agree to perform or be responsible for; engage in; enter upon 2 promise; guarantee

un'der·tak'er n. professional funeral organizer

un'der·tak'ing n. 1 work, etc., undertaken; enterprise 2 promise

un'der·the·count'er adj. (also **un'der·the·ta'ble**) Colloq. done secretively, esp. because illegal

un'der·things' n. pl. underwear, esp. a woman's or girl's

un'der·tone' n. 1 subdued tone or color 2 underlying quality or feeling

un'der·tow' n. current below the surface of the sea moving contrary to the surface current

un'der·val'ue v. (·ued, ·u·ing) 1 value insufficiently 2 underestimate —**un'der·val'u·a'tion** n.

un'der·wa'ter adj. situated or done underwater

un'der·wear' n. clothes worn under others, esp. next to the skin

un'der·weight' adj. below normal or desirable weight

un·der·whelm /ən'dər(h)welm'/ v. Joc. fail to impress [alter. of OVERWHELM]

un'der·world' n. 1 those who live by organized crime and vice 2 mythical abode of the dead under the earth

un'der·write' v. (·wrote, ·writ·ten, ·writ·ing) 1a sign and accept liability under b accept (liability) in this way 2 undertake to finance or support 3 agree to buy all the unsold stock in (a company, etc.) —**un'der·writ'er** n.

un'de·signed' adj. unintentional

un'de·sir'a·ble adj. 1 objectionable; unpleasant —n. 2 undesirable person —**un'de·sir'a·bil'i·ty** n.

un·dies /ən'dēz/ n. pl. Colloq. (esp. women's) underwear [abbr.]

un'dif·fer·en'ti·at·ed adj. not differentiated; amorphous

un·do′ v. (·did, ·done, ·do·ing) 1 unfasten; open 2 annul; cancel 3 ruin the prospects, reputation, or morals of

un·doc′u·ment′ed adj. 1 not supported by written evidence 2 not having legal immigration papers

un·do′ing n. 1 ruin or cause of ruin 2 reversing of an action, etc. 3 opening or unfastening

un·done′ adj. 1 not done 2 not fastened 3 ruined

un·doubt′ed adj. certain; not questioned —un·doubt′ed·ly adv.

un·dreamed /ən′drēmd′/ adj. (also un′dreamt′ /-dremt′/) not dreamed, thought, or imagined

un·dress′ v. 1 take off one's clothes 2 take the clothes off (a person) —n. 3a state of dress inappropriate for the public b nakedness

un·due′ adj. excessive; disproportionate —un·du′ly adv.

un·du·late /ən′jəlāt′, ən′dyə-/ v. (·lat·ed, ·lat·ing) (cause to) have a wavy motion or look —un′du·la′tion n. [L *unda* wave]

un·dy′ing adj. immortal; never-ending

un·earned′ in′come /-in′kum/ n. income from investments, etc., not from wages

un·earth′ v. discover by searching, digging, or rummaging

un·earth′ly adj. 1 supernatural; mysterious 2 *Colloq.* absurdly early or inconvenient (*unearthly hour*) —un·earth′li·ness n.

un·ease′ n. nervousness; anxiety

un·eas′y adj. (·i·er, ·i·est) 1 nervous; anxious 2 disturbing —un·eas′i·ly adv.; un·eas′i·ness n.

un·ed′i·fy′ing adj. distasteful; degrading

un′e·mo′tion·al adj. not emotional; lacking emotion

un′em·ploy′a·ble adj. unfit for paid employment —un′em·ploy′a·bil′i·ty n.

un′em·ployed′ adj. 1 out of work 2 not in use —un′em·ploy′ment n.

un·e′qual adj. 1 not equal 2 of varying quality 3 unfair (*unequal contest*) —un·e′qual·ly adv.

un·e′qualed adj. (also un·e′qualled) superior to all others

un′e·quiv′o·cal adj. not ambiguous; plain; unmistakable —un′e·quiv′o·cal·ly adv.

un·err′ing adj. not erring; true; certain —un·err′ing·ly adv.

UNESCO /yo͞ones′kō/ abbr. United Nations Educational, Scientific, and Cultural Organization

un·eth′i·cal adj. not ethical, esp. unscrupulous or unprofessional —un·eth′i·cal·ly adv.

un·e′ven adj. 1 not level or smooth 2 of variable quality, etc. 3 unequal —un·e′ven·ly adv.; un·e′ven·ness n.

un′ex·am′pled adj. without precedent

un′ex·cep′tion·a·ble adj. entirely satisfactory —un′ex·cep′tion·a·bly adv.

un′ex·cep′tion·al adj. usual; ordinary —un′ex·cep′tion·al·ly adv.

un′ex·pect′ed adj. not expected; surprising —un′ex·pect′ed·ly adv.; un′ex·pect′ed·ness n.

un′ex·pur′gat·ed adj. (esp. of a text) complete

un·fail′ing adj. not failing or dwindling; reliable —un·fail′ing·ly adv.

un·fair′ adj. not fair, just, or impartial —un·fair′ly adv.; un·fair′ness n.

un·faith′ful adj. 1 not faithful, esp. adulterous 2 treacherous; disloyal —un·faith′ful·ly adv.; un·faith′ful·ness n.

un·fas′ten v. 1 make or become loose 2 open the fastening(s) of 3 detach

un·feel′ing adj. unsympathetic; harsh

un·feigned′ adj. genuine; sincere

un·fin′ished adj. 1 not finished; incomplete 2 not painted or varnished, esp. of furniture

un·fit′ting adj. not suitable; unbecoming

un·fix′ v. release; loosen; detach

un·flag′ging adj. tireless; persistent

un·flap′pa·ble adj. *Colloq.* imperturbable; calm —un·flap′pa·bil′i·ty n.

un·fold′ v. 1 open the fold or folds of; spread out 2 reveal (thoughts, etc.) 3 become opened out 4 develop

un·forced′ adj. 1 easy; natural 2 not compelled or constrained

un′for·get′ta·ble adj. that cannot be forgotten; memorable; wonderful —un′for·get′ta·bly adv.

un·formed′ adj. 1 not formed; undeveloped 2 shapeless

un·for′tu·nate adj. 1 unlucky or bringing bad luck 2 unhappy 3 regrettable —n. 4 unfortunate person —un·for′tu·nate·ly adv.

un·found′ed adj. without basis (*unfounded rumor*)

un·friend′ly adj. (·li·er, ·li·est) not friendly; hostile

un·fun′ny adj. (·ni·er, ·ni·est) failing to amuse

un·furl′ v. 1 unroll; spread out 2 become unrolled

un·gain′ly adj. awkward; clumsy —un·gain′li·ness n. [obs. *gain* straight, fr. ON]

un·god′ly adj. 1 impious; wicked 2 *Colloq.* outrageous (*ungodly hour*)

un·gov′ern·a·ble adj. 1 that cannot be governed 2 uncontrollable; violent

un·gra′cious adj. discourteous; grudging —un·gra′cious·ly adv.

un·guard′ed adj. 1 incautious; thoughtless 2 not guarded

un·guent /əNG′gwənt/ n. soft ointment or lubricant [L *unguere* anoint]

un·gu·late /əNG′gyo͞olət, -lāt′/ adj. 1 hoofed —n. 2 hoofed mammal [L *ungula* hoof; claw]

un·hal′lowed adj. 1 not consecrated 2 not sacred; wicked

un·hand′ v. take one's hands off (a person); release

un·hap′py adj. (·pi·er, ·pi·est) 1 miserable 2 unfortunate 3 disastrous —un·hap′pi·ly adv.; un·hap′pi·ness n.

un·health′y adj. (·i·er, ·i·est) 1 in poor health 2a harmful to health b unwholesome c *Slang.* dangerous —un·health′i·ly adv.; un·health′i·ness n.

un·heard′ adj. 1 not heard 2 (usu. un·heard′-of′) unprecedented

un·hinge′ v. (·hinged, ·hing·ing) 1 take (a door, etc.) off its hinges 2 make crazy; derange —un·hinged′ adj.

un·hitch′ v. 1 release from a hitched state 2 unhook; unfasten

un·ho'ly *adj.* (**·li·er**, **·li·est**) **1** impious; wicked **2** *Colloq.* dreadful; outrageous

un·horse' *v.* (**·horsed**, **·hors·ing**) throw (a rider) from a horse

uni- *comb. form* one; having or consisting of one (*unicycle*) [L *unus* one]

u·ni·cam·er·al /yo͞o'nikam'(ə)rəl/ *adj.* having a single legislative chamber [L *camera* chamber]

UNICEF /yo͞o'nəsef'/ *abbr.* United Nations Children's (orig., International Children's Emergency) Fund

u·ni·cel·lu·lar /yo͞o'nisel'yələr/ *adj.* (of an organism, etc.) consisting of a single cell

u·ni·corn /yo͞o'nikôrn'/ *n.* mythical horse with a single straight horn in the center of its forehead [L *cornu* horn]

u·ni·cy·cle /yo͞o'nəsī'kəl/ *n.* single-wheeled cycle —**u'ni·cy'clist** /-klist/ *n.*

u·ni·form /yo͞o'nəfôrm'/ *adj.* **1** unvarying **2** conforming to the same standard, rules, etc. —*n.* **3** distinctive clothing worn by soldiers, police, etc. —**u'ni·formed'** *adj.*; **u'ni·for'mi·ty** *n.*; **u'ni·form'ly** *adv.* [L, rel. to FORM]

u·ni·fy /yo͞o'nəfī'/ *v.* (**·fied**, **·fy·ing**) make or become united or uniform —**u'ni·fi·ca'tion** /-fikā'sHən/ *n.* [L, rel. to UNI-]

u·ni·lat·er·al /yo͞o'nilat'ərəl/ *adj.* done by or affecting only one person or party —**u'ni·lat'er·al·ly** *adv.*

un'i·mag'i·na·tive *adj.* lacking imagination; stolid; dull —**un'i·mag'i·na·tive·ly** *adv.*

un'im·peach'a·ble *adj.* beyond reproach or question

un'i·ni'ti·at·ed *adj.* not initiated, admitted, or instructed

un'in·spired' *adj.* not inspired; commonplace; pedestrian

un·in'ter·est·ed *adj.* not interested; indifferent

● Usage: See note at DISINTERESTED.

un'in·vit'ing *adj.* unattractive; repellent

un·ion /yo͞on'yan/ *n.* **1** uniting or being united **2a** whole formed from parts or members **b** political unit so formed **3** LABOR UNION **4** marriage **5** concord **6** *Math.* totality of the members of two or more sets **7** (*cap.*) United States, esp. considered as a nation during the Civil War [L *unus* one]

un'ion·ize' *v.* (**·ized**, **·iz·ing**) organize in or into a labor union —**un'ion·i·za'tion** *n.*

U'nion Jack' *n.* the British flag

Un'ion of So'vi·et So'cial·ist Re·pub'lics *n.* former union of 15 constituent republics under Soviet control, in E Europe and N Asia; dissolved in 1991. Abbr. USSR —**So'vi·et'** *n.* & *adj.*

u·nique /yo͞onēk'/ *adj.* **1** being the only one of its kind; having no like, equal, or parallel **2** remarkable —**u·nique'ly** *adv.* [L *unicus* fr. *unus* one]

● Usage: See note at PERFECT.

u·ni·sex /yo͞o'niseks'/ *adj.* designed or suitable for both sexes

u·ni·son /yo͞o'nəsən, -zən/ *n.* **1** concord **2** coincidence in pitch of sounds or notes [L *sonus* SOUND¹]

u·nit /yo͞o'nit/ *n.* **1a** individual thing, person, or group **b** smallest component of a complex whole **2** quantity as a standard of measurement **3** part of a mechanism with a specified function **4** group of buildings, wards, etc.,

---

631   **unholy / unknowable**

as in a hospital **5a** single-digit number **b** the number "one" [L *unus* one]

U·ni·tar·i·an /yo͞o'nəter'ēən/ *n.* member of a religious body believing that God is one, not a Trinity —**U'ni·tar'i·an·ism'** *n.* [L *unitas* UNITY]

u·ni·tar·y /yo͞o'nəter'ē/ *adj.* **1** of a unit or units **2** marked by unity or uniformity [fr. UNIT or UNITY]

u'nit cost' *n.* cost of producing one item

u·nite /yo͞onīt'/ *v.* (**·nit·ed**, **·nit·ing**) **1** join together; combine **2** join in marriage **3** (cause to) form a physical or chemical whole [L *unire* -*it*- fr. *unus* one]

U·nit'ed Ar'ab E'mir·ates /em'ərəts, -rāts'/ *n.* federation of seven emirates on the Persian Gulf. Capital: Abu Dhabi. Pop. 1,989,000

U·nit'ed King'dom *n.* monarchy in NW Europe comprising England, Scotland, Wales, and Northern Ireland. Capital: London. Pop. 57,730,000. Abbr. **UK, U.K.**

U·nit'ed Na'tions *n. pl.* (as *sing.* or *pl.*) international peace-seeking organization; *abbr.* UN

U·nit'ed States of A·mer'i·ca *n.* federal republic of 50 states in N America and the island state of Hawaii. Capital: Washington, D.C. Pop. 255,414,000. Abbr. **US; U.S.; U.S.A.**

u'nit price' *n.* price charged for each unit of goods supplied

u·ni·ty /yo͞o'nətē/ *n.* (*pl.* **·ties**) **1a** oneness; being one; interconnected parts constituting a whole **b** such a complex whole **2a** being united; solidarity **b** harmony **3** the number "one" [L *unus* one]

univ. *abbr.* **1** universal; universe **2** university

u·ni·va·lent /yo͞o'nivā'lənt/ *adj.* having a valence of one [fr. UNI-, VALENCE]

u·ni·valve /yo͞o'nivalv'/ *Zool. adj.* **1** having one valve —*n.* **2** univalve mollusk

u·ni·ver·sal /yo͞o'nəvər'səl/ *adj.* **1** of, belonging to, or done etc., by all; applicable to all cases —*n.* **2** term, characteristic, or concept of general application —**u'ni·ver·sal'i·ty** /-sal'itē/ *n.*; **u'ni·ver'sal·ly** *adv.* [L, rel. to UNIVERSE]

u'ni·ver'sal joint' *n.* (also **u'ni·ver'sal cou'pling**) joint or coupling that can transmit rotary power by a shaft at any angle

U·ni·ver'sal Prod'uct Code' *n.* coded series of black lines printed on consumer products to be read electronically for price, inventory control, etc.; *abbr.* UPC

u·ni·verse /yo͞o'nəvərs'/ *n.* **1** all existing things; the Cosmos **2** *Stat. & Logic.* all the objects under consideration [L *universus* combined into one]

u·ni·ver·si·ty /yo͞o'nəvər'sitē/ *n.* (*pl.* **·ties**) educational institution conferring degrees in a range of academic disciplines, including bachelor's and usu. advanced degrees [L, rel. to UNIVERSE]

un·kempt /ən'kempt'/ *adj.* untidy; disheveled [UN- + OE *kemben* comb]

un·kind' *adj.* not kind; harsh; cruel —**un·kind'ly** *adv.*; **un·kind'ness** *n.*

un·know'a·ble *adj.* **1** that cannot be known —*n.* **2** unknowable thing **3** (**the Unknowable**) the postulated absolute or ultimate reality

un·know'ing *adj.* not knowing; ignorant; unconscious —**un·know'ing·ly** *adv.*

un·known' *adj.* 1 not known; unfamiliar; unidentified —*n.* 2 unknown thing, person, or quantity

Un'known Sol'dier *n.* unidentified soldier killed in battle, honored as a symbol of a nation's war dead

un·law'ful *adj.* 1 illegal; not permissible 2 immoral; illegitimate —**un·law'ful·ly** *adv.*

un·lead·ed /ənled'əd/ *adj.* (of gasoline, etc.) without added lead

un·learn' *v.* forget, esp. deliberately

un·learn·ed *adj.* 1 /ən'lər'nid/ not well educated; ignorant 2 /ən'lərnd'/ not learned

un·leash' *v.* release from or as if from a leash or restraint

un·leav·ened /ənlev'ənd/ *adj.* not leavened; made without yeast, etc.

un·less /ənles'/ *conj.* if not; except when [ON, LESS]

un·let'tered *adj.* illiterate; not well educated

un·like' *adj.* 1 not like; different from 2 uncharacteristic of 3 dissimilar; different —*prep.* 4 differently from

un·like'ly *adj.* (·li·er, ·li·est) 1 improbable 2 not expected 3 unpromising —**un·like'li·hood', un·like'li·ness** *n.*

un·lim'it·ed *adj.* unrestricted; enormous

un·load' *v.* 1 remove (a load) from 2 remove the ammunition from (a gun, etc.) 3 *Colloq.* get rid of

un·lock' *v.* 1a release the lock of b release or disclose by unlocking 2 release thoughts, feelings, etc., from

un·looked'-for' *adj.* unexpected

un·loose' *v.* (·loosed, ·loos·ing) (also un·loos'en) unfasten; loose; set free

un·luck'y *adj.* (·i·er, ·i·est) 1 not fortunate or successful 2 wretched 3 bringing bad luck 4 ill-judged —**un·luck'i·ly** *adv.*; **un·luck'i·ness** *n.*

un·make' *v.* (·made, ·mak·ing) 1 undo 2 destroy; depose

un·man' *v.* (·manned, ·man·ning) make weak, cowardly, etc.

un·mask' *v.* 1a remove the mask from b expose the true character of 2 remove one's mask

un·men'tion·a·ble *adj.* 1 unsuitable for polite conversation —*n.* 2 (*pl.*) UNDERWEAR

un·mer'ci·ful *adj.* merciless; cruel —**un·mer'ci·ful·ly** *adv.*

un'mis·tak·a·ble *adj.* clear; obvious —**un'mis·tak·a·bly** *adv.*

un·mit'i·gat'ed *adj.* 1 less severe 2 absolute

un·mor'al *adj.* not concerned with morality (cf. IMMORAL) —**un'mo·ral'i·ty** *n.*

un·moved' *adj.* 1 not moved 2 unemotional

un·nat'u·ral *adj.* 1 contrary to nature; not normal 2 cruel or wicked 3 not genuine 4 affected —**un·nat'u·ral·ly** *adv.*

un·nec'es·sar'y *adj.* 1 not necessary 2 superfluous —**un·nec'es·sar'i·ly** *adv.*

un·nerve' *v.* (·nerved, ·nerv·ing) deprive of confidence, etc.

un·num'bered *adj.* 1 without a number 2 not counted 3 countless

un·ob·tru'sive *adj.* not making oneself or itself noticed —**un'ob·tru'sive·ly** *adv.*

un·or'gan·ized' *adj.* 1 not organized 2 not part of or represented by a labor union

un·pack' *v.* 1 open and empty (a package, luggage, etc.) 2 take (a thing) from a package, etc.

un·pal'at·a·ble *adj.* 1 not pleasant to the taste 2 disagreeable; unpleasant

un·par'al·leled' *adj.* unequaled

un·pleas'ant *adj.* not pleasant; disagreeable —**un·pleas'ant·ly** *adv.*; **un·pleas'ant·ness** *n.*

un·plug' *v.* (·plugged, ·plug·ging) 1 remove the plug of (an electrical device) from the socket 2 remove (an obstruction)

un·plumbed' *adj.* 1 not plumbed 2 not fully explored or understood

un·pop'u·lar *adj.* not popular; disliked —**un'pop·u·lar'i·ty** *n.*

un·prac'ticed *adj.* 1 not experienced or skilled 2 not put into practice

un·prec'e·dent'ed *adj.* having no precedent; unparalleled —**un·prec'e·dent'ed·ly** *adv.*

un'pre·pos·sess'ing *adj.* unattractive

un'pre·ten'tious *adj.* modest; unassuming

un·prin'ci·pled *adj.* lacking or not based on moral principles

un·print'a·ble *adj.* too offensive or indecent to be printed

un'pro·fes'sion·al *adj.* 1 contrary to professional standards 2 unskilled; amateurish —**un'pro·fes'sion·al·ly** *adv.*

un·prompt'ed *adj.* spontaneous

un·qual'i·fied' *adj.* 1 not legally or officially qualified 2 complete (*unqualified success*) 3 not competent

un·ques'tion·a·ble *adj.* that cannot be disputed or doubted —**un·ques'tion·a·bly** *adv.*

un·ques'tioned *adj.* not disputed or doubted; definite

un·ques'tion·ing *adj.* 1 asking no questions 2 (of obedience, etc.) absolute —**un·ques'tion·ing·ly** *adv.*

un·qui'et *adj.* 1 restless; agitated 2 anxious

un'quote' *v.* (as *interj.*) verbal formula indicating closing quotation marks

un·rav'el *v.* (·eled or ·elled, ·el·ing or ·el·ling) 1 make or become disentangled, unknotted, unwoven, etc. 2 probe and solve (a mystery, etc.)

un·read' /ən'red'/ *adj.* 1 (of a book, etc.) not read 2 (of a person) not well-read

un·read·a·ble /ənrē'dəbəl/ *adj.* too dull, bad, or difficult to read

un·re'al *adj.* 1 not real 2 imaginary 3 *Slang.* incredible —**un're·al'i·ty** *n.* (*pl.* ·ties)

un·rea'son *n.* madness; chaos

un·rea'son·a·ble *adj.* 1 excessive 2 not heeding reason —**un·rea'son·a·bly** *adv.*

un·rec'og·nized' *adj.* not acknowledged

un're·gen'er·ate /rē'jen'ərət/ *adj.* obstinately wrong or bad

un·re·lent'ing *adj.* 1 not abating or relaxing 2 unmerciful —**un're·lent'ing·ly** *adv.*

un're·li·a·ble *adj.* not reliable; erratic —**un're·li·a·bil'i·ty** *n.*

un·re·lieved' *adj.* not relieved; monotonously uniform

un're·mit'ting *adj.* incessant —**un're·mit'ting·ly** *adv.*

un·re·quit'ed *adj.* (of love, etc.) not returned

un·re·served' *adj.* 1 not reserved 2 total;

without reservation   **—un·re·serv'ed·ly**
/-zər'vidlē/ *adv.*

un're·solved' *adj.* **1** irresolute; undecided **2** undetermined

un·rest' *n.* disturbed or dissatisfied state

un·right'eous *adj.* wicked

un·ri'valled *adj.* (also **un·ri'valled**) having no equal

un·roll' *v.* **1** open out from a rolled-up state **2** display or be displayed like this

un·ruf'fled *adj.* calm

un·ru·ly /ən'rōo'lē/ *adj.* (·i·er, ·i·est) undisciplined; disorderly **—un·rul'i·ness** *n.* [rel. to RULE]

un·sad'dle *v.* (·dled, ·dling) remove the saddle from

un·sat'u·rat'ed *adj.* **1** not saturated **2** *Chem.* (of esp. a fat or oil) having double or triple bonds in its molecule and therefore capable of further reaction

un·sa'vor·y *adj.* **1** disgusting; unpleasant **2** morally offensive

un·scathed /ən'skāTHd'/ *adj.* without injury

un·schooled *adj.* uneducated; untrained

un'sci·en·tif'ic *adj.* not scientific in method, etc. **—un'sci·en·tif'i·cal·ly** *adv.*

un·scram'ble *v.* (·bled, ·bling) decode a scrambled transmission, etc.)

un·screw' *v.* **1** unfasten by removing a screw or screws **2** loosen (a screw, lid, etc.)

un·script'ed *adj.* spoken impromptu

un·scru'pu·lous *adj.* having no scruples; unprincipled **—un·scru'pu·lous·ly** *adv.;* **un·scru'pu·lous·ness** *n.*

un·seal' *v.* break the seal of; open

un·sea'son·a·ble *adj.* **1** not seasonable or appropriate to the season **2** untimely; inopportune **—un·sea'son·a·bly** *adv.*

un·seat' *v.* **1** remove from office **2** dislodge from a seat

un·seem'ly *adj.* (·li·er, ·li·est) **1** indecent **2** unbecoming **—un·seem'li·ness** *n.*

un·set'tle *v.* (·tled, ·tling) **1** disturb; discompose **2** derange

un·set'tled *adj.* **1** restless; disturbed; unpredictable **2** not populated **3** unpaid

un·shak'a·ble *adj.* firm; obstinate **—un·shak'a·bly** *adv.*

un·shrink'ing *adj.* unhesitating; fearless

un·sight'ly *adj.* ugly **—un·sight'li·ness** *n.*

un·skilled *adj.* lacking or not needing special skill or training

un'so·lic'it·ed *adj.* not asked for; voluntary

un'so·phis'ti·cat'ed *adj.* **1** ingenuous; artless **2** not intricate or complex; simple

un·sought' *adj.* **1** not sought for **2** without being requested

un·sound' *adj.* **1** not healthy, sane, etc. **2** rotten; weak; unreliable **3** ill-founded **—un·sound'ness** *n.*

un·spar'ing *adj.* **1** lavish **2** merciless

un·speak'a·ble *adj.* **1** that cannot be expressed in words **2** indescribably bad **—un·speak'a·bly** *adv.*

un·sta'ble *adj.* (·bler, ·blest) **1** not stable; likely to fall **2** not stable emotionally **3** changeable **4** *Chem.* tending toward decomposition **—un·sta'bly** *adv.*

un·stead'y *adj.* (·i·er, ·i·est) **1** not steady or firm **2** changeable; erratic **3** not uniform or regular **—un·stead'i·ly** *adv.;* **un·stead'i·ness** *n.*

un·stint'ing *adj.* lavish; limitless **—un·stint'ing·ly** *adv.*

un·stop' *v.* (·stopped, ·stop·ping) **1** remove an obstruction from **2** remove the stopper from

un·stressed' *adj.* not pronounced with stress

un·string' *v.* (·strung, ·string·ing) **1** remove or relax the string(s) of (a bow, harp, etc.) **2** remove (beads, etc.) from a string **3** unnerve

un·struc'tured *adj.* **1** not structured **2** informal

un·stuck' *adj.* out of control; undone (esp. as in **come unstuck**)

un·stud'ied *adj.* easy; natural; spontaneous

un'sub·stan'tial *adj.* **1** INSUBSTANTIAL **2** lacking substance, solidity, firmness, etc.

un·suit'ed *adj.* **1** not fit (for) **2** not well adapted

un·sung' *adj.* not celebrated; unrecognized

un·swerv'ing *adj.* steady; constant **—un·swerv'ing·ly** *adv.*

un·tamed' *adj.* **1** not tamed **2** unsettled; wild

un·tan'gle *v.* (·gled, ·gling) disentangle

un·tapped' *adj.* not (yet) tapped or used

un·taught' *adj.* **1** (of a person) not taught **2** natural; intuitive

un·ten'a·ble *adj.* (of a theory, etc.) not logically defensible

un·think'a·ble *adj.* **1** unimaginable; inconceivable **2** *Colloq.* highly unlikely or undesirable **—un·think'a·bly** *adv.*

un·think'ing *adj.* **1** thoughtless **2** inadvertent **—un·think'ing·ly** *adv.*

un·ti'dy *adj.* (·di·er, ·di·est) not neat or orderly **—un·ti'di·ly** *adv.;* **un·ti'di·ness** *n.*

un·tie' *v.* (·tied, ·ty·ing) **1** undo (a knot, package, etc.) **2** release from bonds or attachment

un·til /ən'til'/ *prep. & conj.* till; before; up to the time that [ME]

● Usage: Both *till* and *until* are correct, and both have been in the language for a millennium; *till* is not a short form of *until*. The form '*til* is sometimes seen as a contraction for *until*, but should be avoided. The forms "'till" and "untill" are errors.

un·time'ly *adj.* **1** inopportune **2** premature **—un·time'li·ness** *n.*

un·to /ən'tōo/ *prep. Archaic.* TO [ME]

un·told' *adj.* **1** not told or revealed **2** immeasurable

un·touch'a·ble *adj.* **1** that may not be touched **—n.** **2** formerly, member of the lowest Hindu caste **—un'touch·a·bil'i·ty** *n.*

un·touched' *adj.* **1** not touched or touched on **2** not affected physically, emotionally, etc.

un·to·ward /ən'tôrd', -təwôrd'/ *adj.* **1** inconvenient; unlucky **2** awkward **3** unseemly

un·tram'meled *adj.* (also **un·tram'elled**) unhampered

un·tried' *adj.* **1** not tried or tested **2** inexperienced

un·trou'bled *adj.* **1** not troubled **2** calm; tranquil

un·true' *adj.* **1** not true **2** not faithful or loyal **3** deviating from an accepted standard

un·truth' *n.* **1** being untrue **2** lie **—un·truth'ful** *adj.;* **un·truth'ful·ly** *adv.;* **un·truth'ful·ness** *n.*

un·tu'tored *adj.* uneducated; untaught

un·twist' v. open from a twisted or spiraled state

un·used adj. 1 /unyŏŏzd' / a not in use b never having been used 2 /unyŏŏst'/ not accustomed (to)

un·u'su·al adj. 1 not usual 2 remarkable —**un·u'su·al·ly** adv.

un·ut'ter·a·ble adj. inexpressible; beyond description —**un·ut'ter·a·bly** adv.

un·var'nished adj. 1 not varnished 2 plain and straightforward

un·veil' v. 1 uncover ceremonially 2 reveal 3a remove a veil from b remove one's veil

un·voiced' adj. 1 not spoken 2 not sounded with the vocal cords

un·war'rant·ed adj. 1 unauthorized 2 unjustified

un·war'y adj. not cautious —**un·war'i·ly** adv.; **un·war'i·ness** n.

un·washed' adj. 1 not washed or clean 2 the great unwashed Derog. the rabble

un·wea'ry·ing adj. persistent

un·well' adj. ill

un·whole'some adj. 1 detrimental to physical or moral health 2 unhealthy-looking

un·wield'y adj. cumbersome or hard to manage, owing to size, shape, etc. —**un·wield'i·ly** adv.; **un·wield'i·ness** n.

un·will'ing adj. not willing or inclined; reluctant —**un·will'ing·ly** adv.; **un·will'ing·ness** n.

un·wind' /ən'wīnd'/ v. (·wound, ·wind·ing) 1 draw out or become drawn out after having been wound 2 Colloq. relax

un·wise' adj. foolish; imprudent —**un·wise'ly** adv.

un·wit'ting /ənwit'ING/ adj. 1 not knowing or aware 2 unintentional —**un·wit'ting·ly** adv. [OE, rel. to WIT²]

un·wont'ed adj. not customary or usual

un·work'a·ble adj. not workable; impracticable

un·world'ly adj. 1 spiritual 2 naïve —**un·world'li·ness** n.

un·wor'thy adj. (·thi·er, ·thi·est) 1 not worthy of or befitting a person, etc. 2 discreditable; unseemly —**un·wor'thi·ly** adv.; **un·wor'thi·ness** n.

un·wrap' v. (·wrapped, ·wrap·ping) 1 remove the wrapping from 2 open; unfold

un·writ'ten adj. 1 not written 2 based on custom or judicial decision

un·yield'ing adj. 1 not yielding 2 firm; obstinate

up¹ /əp/ adv. 1 at, in, or toward a higher place or a place regarded as higher 2a to or in an erect or required position or condition (stood it up) b in or into an active condition (stirred up trouble; wound up the watch) 3 in a stronger or leading position 4 to a specified place, person, or time 5 higher in price or value 6 completely 7 more loudly or clearly 8 completed; past (time is up) 9 into a compact, accumulated, or secure state 10 awake; having risen 11 happening, esp. unusually (something is up) 12 Baseball. at one's turn at bat —prep. 13 upward and along; through; into 14 from the bottom to the top of 15 toward the source of (a river) —adj. 16 directed upward 17 Comp. functioning nor-

mally —n. 18 spell of good fortune 19 upward slope —v. (upped, up·ping) 20 Colloq. start, esp. abruptly, to speak or act (up and hit him) 21 raise (upped their prices) 22 on the up and up: Colloq. a legitimate b steadily improving 23 up against: a close to b Colloq. confronted with 24 up and about having risen from bed; active 25 up and down: Colloq. in a varying health or spirits b variable in activity, profit, etc. 26 up for available for or standing for (office, etc.) 27 up on informed about 28 up to: a until b below or equal to c incumbent on (it is up to you to say) d capable of or occupied or busy with 29 up with power to [OE]

up² adv. Sports. apiece; each

up- prefix in senses of UP, added: 1 as an adverb to verbs and verbal derivations, meaning 'upward' (update) 2 as a preposition to nouns forming adverbs and adjectives (uphill) 3 as an adjective to nouns (up-stroke)

up'-and-com'ing adj. showing promise; progressing

up'beat' n. 1 unaccented beat in music —adj. 2 Colloq. optimistic; cheerful

up·braid' v. chide; reproach [OE, rel. to BRAID brandish]

up'bring·ing n. care and education, etc., of a child

UPC abbr. UNIVERSAL PRODUCT CODE

up'chuck' v. & n. Slang. vomit

up'com'ing adj. about to happen

up·date' v. /əp'dāt'/ (·dat·ed, ·dat·ing) 1 bring up to date —n. /əp'dāt'/ 2 updating 3 updated information, etc.

Up·dike /əp'dīk'/, John Hoyer 1932– ; US novelist

up·end' v. set or rise up on end

up'front' Colloq. adv. 1 at the front; in front 2 in advance —adj. 3 honest; frank 4 made in advance

up·grade v. /əpgrād', əp'grād'/ (·grad·ed, ·grad·ing) 1 raise in rank, etc. 2 improve (equipment, etc.) —n. /əp'grād/ 3 upward grade or slope 4 improvement

up·heav·al /əphē'vəl/ n. violent or sudden change or disruption [fr. upheave heave or lift up]

up·hill' /əp'hil'/ adv. 1 up a slope —adj. 2 sloping up; ascending 3 arduous

up·hold' v. (·held, ·hold·ing) 1 confirm 2 support; maintain —**up·hold'er** n.

up·hol·ster /əp(h)ōl'stər/ v. provide (furniture) with upholstery —**up·hol'ster·er** n. [ult. fr. ME upholder tradesman]

up·hol'ster·y n. 1 covering, padding, springs, etc., for furniture 2 upholsterer's work

up'keep' n. 1 maintenance in good condition 2 cost or means of this

up·land /əp'lənd, ·land/ n. 1 (usu. pl.) higher or inland parts of a country —adj. 2 of these parts

up·lift v. /əp'lift'/ 1 raise 2 elevate morally or emotionally; inspire —n. /əp'lift'/ 3 Colloq. elevating influence —**up·lift'ing** adj.

up'mar'ket adj. & adv. of or directed at high-income consumers; expensive

up·on /əpän', əpôn'/ prep. ON

up·per¹ /əp'ər/ adj. 1 higher in place; situated above 2 higher in rank, etc. —n. 3 part of a boot or shoe above the sole 4 on one's uppers Colloq. very short of money

up·per² *n. Slang.* amphetamine or other stimulant

up'per case' *n.* capital letters

up'per class' *n.* highest socioeconomic class

up'per·class'man /-klas'mən/ *n.* (*pl.* **-men**) a third- or fourth-year student at a high school or college

up'per crust' *n. Colloq.* UPPER CLASS

up'per·cut' *n.* **1** upward blow delivered with the arm bent —*v.* **2** hit upward with the arm bent

up'per hand' *n.* dominance; control

up'per·most' *adj.* **1** highest **2** predominant —*adv.* **3** at or to the uppermost position

up·pi·ty /əp'ətē/ *adj. Colloq.* haughty; arrogant

Upp·sa·la /əp'sələ', -säl'ə/ *n.* city in SE Sweden. Pop. 170,700

up·rear' *v.* **1** lift; raise (up) **2** bring up; rear

up·right /əp'rīt'/ *adj.* **1** erect; vertical **2** (of a piano) with vertical strings **3** honorable or honest —*n.* **4** upright post or rod, esp. as a structural support **5** upright piano —*adv.* **6** vertically

up'ris'ing *n.* insurrection

up'roar' *n.* tumult; violent disturbance [Du: commotion]

up·roar·i·ous /əp'rôr'ēəs/ *adj.* **1** very noisy **2** boisterous; very funny —**up·roar'i·ous·ly** *adv.*

up·root' *v.* **1** pull up from the ground **2** displace **3** eradicate

ups' and downs' *n. pl.* mixed fortune

up'scale' *adj.* upmarket; expensive

up·set *v.* /əpset'/ (**·set, ·set·ting**) **1** overturn **2** disturb the composure or digestion of **3** disrupt **4** win unexpectedly —*n.* /əp'set'/ **5** emotional or physical disturbance **6** surprising defeat —*adj.* /əp'set', əp,set'/ **7** disturbed **8** overturned

up'shot' *n.* outcome; conclusion

up'side down' *adv. & adj.* **1** with the upper and lower parts reversed; inverted **2** in or into total disorder

up·si·lon /yŏŏp'səlän', əp'-/ *n.* twentieth letter of the Greek alphabet (Υ, υ) [Gk: short U, fr. *psilos* slender, with ref. to its later similarity in sound to Greek *oi*]

up·stage *adj. & adv.* /əp'stāj'/ **1** nearer the back of a stage —*v.* /əpstāj'/ (**·staged, ·stag·ing**) **2** divert attention from (esp. another actor) to oneself

up'stairs' *adv.* **1** to or on an upper floor —*adj.* **2** situated upstairs —*n.* **3** upper floor **4** *Colloq.* mind; intelligence

up·stand'ing *adj.* **1** standing up **2** honest

up'start' *n.* **1** newly successful, esp. arrogant, person —*adj.* **2** of or being an upstart

up'state' *n.* **1** part of a state farther north or farther from the main city —*adv. & adj.* **2** in, to, or of this part

up'stream' *adv. & adj.* in the direction contrary to the flow of a stream, etc.

up'surge' *n.* upward surge

up'swing' *n.* upward movement or trend

up'take' *n.* **1** taking up **2 quick (or slow) on the uptake** *Colloq.* quick or slow to understand

up'thrust' *n.* **1** upward thrust **2** upward displacement of part of the earth's crust

up'tight' *adj. Colloq.* **1** nervously tense or angry **2** rigidly conventional

up'town' *adv. & adj.* **1** of, in, or to the residential part of a town or city —*n.* **2** this part

up·turn *n.* /əp'tərn/ **1** upward trend; improvement —*v.* /əptərn'/ **2** turn up or upside down

up·ward /əp'wərd/ *adv.* (also **up'wards**) **1** toward what is higher, more important, etc. —*adj.* **2** moving or extending upward **3 upward of** more than (*upward of forty*) —**up'ward·ly** *adv.*

up'ward·ly mo'bile /mō'bəl/ *adj.* aspiring to advance socially or professionally

up·wind /əp'wind'/ *adj. & adv.* in the direction from which the wind is blowing

Ü·rüm·qi /ōōrōōm'CHē/ *n.* city in W China. Pop. 1,046,900

U·ral Moun·tains /yŏŏr'əl/ *n.* mountain range in W Russia; considered part of the boundary between Europe and Asia

u·ra·ni·um /yərā'nēəm/ *n.* radioactive, gray, dense, metallic element, capable of nuclear fission and used as a source of nuclear energy; *symb.* U [URANUS]

U·ra·nus /yŏŏrā'nəs, yŏŏr'ənəs/ *n.* **1** seventh planet from the sun **2** *Class. Myth.* sky god, son and consort of Gaea (Earth)

ur·ban /ər'bən/ *adj.* of, living in, or situated in a town or city [L *urbs* city]

ur·bane /ərbān'/ *adj.* suave; elegant —**ur·ban'i·ty** /-ban'ətē/ *n.* [L, rel. to URBAN]

ur·ban·ize /ər'bənīz'/ *v.* (**·ized, ·iz·ing**) make urban, esp. by destroying the rural quality of —**ur'ban·i·za'tion** *n.*

ur·chin /ər'CHin/ *n.* **1** mischievous, esp. ragged, child **2** SEA URCHIN [L *ericius* hedgehog]

Ur·du /ŏŏr'dōō, ər'-/ *n.* language related to Hindi but with many Persian words, used esp. in Pakistan [Hindustani]

-ure *suffix* forming: **1** nouns of action (*seizure*) **2** nouns of result (*creature*) **3** collective nouns (*nature*) [L *-ura*]

u·re·a /yŏŏrē'ə/ *n.* soluble, nitrogenous compound contained esp. in urine [Fr *urée* fr. Gk *ouron* urine]

u·re·ter /yŏŏr'ətər/ *n.* duct conveying urine from a kidney to the bladder [Gk *ourein* urinate]

u·re·thane /yŏŏr'əТНān'/ *n.* water-soluble crystalline compound used as a solvent, etc.

u·re·thra /yŏŏrē'ТНrə/ *n.* (*pl.* **·thrae** /-ТНrē/ or **·thras**) duct conveying urine from the bladder [Gk, rel. to URETER]

Ur·fa /ŏŏrfä'/ *n.* city in SE Turkey. Pop. 276,500

urge /ərj/ *v.* (**urged, urg·ing**) **1** drive energetically; hasten **2** encourage or entreat earnestly or persistently **3** advocate emphatically —*n.* **4** urging impulse or tendency **5** strong desire [L *urgere* press hard]

ur·gent /ər'jənt/ *adj.* **1** requiring immediate action or attention **2** persistent; insistent —**ur'gen·cy** *n.*; **ur'gent·ly** *adv.* [rel. to URGE]

u·ric /yŏŏr'ik/ *adj.* of urine [rel. to URINE]

u·ri·nal /yŏŏr'ən-l/ *n.* place or receptacle for urination by men [L, rel. to URINE]

u·ri·nal·y·sis /yŏŏr'ənal'isis/ *n.* chemical analysis of urine

u·ri·nate /yŏŏr'ənāt'/ *v.* (**·nat·ed, ·nat·ing**) discharge urine —**u'ri·na'tion** *n.*

u·rine /yŏŏr'in/ *n.* waste fluid secreted by

the kidneys and discharged from the bladder —u'ri·nar·y /-er'ē/ adj. [L urina]

urn /ərn/ n. 1 vase with a foot and usu. a rounded body, used esp. for the ashes of the dead 2 large vessel with a faucet in which tea or coffee, etc., is made or kept hot [L urna]

u·ro·gen·i·tal /yŏŏrō'ōjen'ət-l/ adj. of the urinary and reproductive systems [Gk ouron urine + GENITAL]

u·rol·o·gy /yŏŏräl'əjē/ n. the study of the urinary system —u'ro·log'i·cal adj.; u·rol'o·gist n.

URN 1

ur·sine /ər'sīn/ adj. of or like a bear [L ursus bear]

U·ru·guay /(y)ŏŏr'əgwī', -gwä'/ n. republic in SE South America. Capital: Montevideo. Pop. 3,130,000 —U·ru·guay'an n. & adj.

us /əs/ pron. 1 objective case of WE 2 Colloq. ME [OE]

US or U.S. abbr. United States

us·a·ble /yŏŏ'zəbəl/ adj. (also use'a·ble) that can be used —us'a·bil'i·ty or use'a·bil'i·ty n.

USAF abbr. United States Air Force

us·age /yŏŏ'sij/ n. 1 use; treatment 2 customary practice, esp. in the use of a language or as creating a precedent in law
• Usage: Usage means 'manner of use; practice,' while use means the 'act of employing.' In discussions of grammar and style, usage is the term referring to normal practice: Standard usage calls for a plural. However, in describing particular situations, use is preferred: Their use of the plural here is correct.

USA or U.S.A. abbr. 1 United States of America 2 United States Army

U.S.C. abbr. Law. United States Code

USDA or U.S.D.A. abbr. United States Department of Agriculture

use v. /yŏŏz/ (used, us·ing) 1 cause to act or serve for a purpose; bring into service 2 treat in a specified manner 3 exploit for one's own ends 4 did or had habitually —n. /yŏŏs/ 5 using or being used 6 right or power of using 7 benefit; advantage 8 custom; usage 9 purpose; function 10 have no use for: a not need b dislike; be contemptuous of 11 used to familiar by habit; accustomed 12 use up consume completely —us'er n. [Fr us, user, ult. fr. L uti, usus]
• Usage: See note at USAGE.

used /yŏŏzd/ v. 1 past and past part. of USE —adj. 2 previously owned; not new

use·ful /yŏŏs'fəl/ adj. that can be used to advantage; helpful; beneficial —use'ful·ly adv.; use'ful·ness n.

use·less /yŏŏs'ləs/ adj. 1 serving no purpose; unavailing 2 Colloq. feeble; ineffectual —use'less·ly adv.; use'less·ness n.

us'er-friend'ly /yŏŏz'ər-/ adj. easy to use or understand

ush·er /əsh'ər/ n. 1 person who shows people to their seats in a theater, church, etc. 2 attendant to a bridegroom —v. 3 act as usher to 4 announce; herald; show in [L ostium door]

USIA or U.S.I.A. abbr. United States Information Agency

USMC or U.S.M.C. abbr. United States Marine Corps

USN or U.S.N. abbr. United States Navy

USO or U.S.O. abbr. United Service Organizations

USPS or U.S.P.S. abbr. United States Postal Service

USS or U.S.S. abbr. 1 United States Senate 2 United States Ship

USSR abbr. see UNION OF SOVIET SOCIALIST REPUBLICS

Us·ti·nov /(y)ŏŏ'stənôf', -nôv'/, (Sir) Peter 1921– ; British actor, director, and writer

usu. abbr. usual; usually

u·su·al /yŏŏ'ZHŏŏəl/ adj. 1 customary; habitual —n. 2 Colloq. person's usual drink, etc. —u'su·al·ly adv. [L, rel. to USE]

u·surp /yŏŏsərp', -zərp'/ v. seize (power, etc.) wrongfully —u'sur·pa'tion /-pā'SHən/, u·surp'er n. [Fr fr. L]

u·su·ry /yŏŏ'ZHərē/ n. 1 lending of money at an exorbitant or illegal rate of interest 2 exorbitant interest —u'su·rer n.; u·su'ri·ous /-ZHŏŏr'ēəs/ adj. [AngFr or MedL, rel. to USE]

UT, Ut. abbr. for Utah (postal abbr. UT)

U·tah /yŏŏ'tä', -tô'/ n. mountainous W state of the US. Capital: Salt Lake City. Pop. 1,722,850. Abbr. UT; Ut. —U·tah·an /yŏŏtä'ən, -tô'ən; yŏŏ'tän', -tôn'/ n. & adj.

u·ten·sil /yŏŏten'səl/ n. implement or vessel, esp. for kitchen use [MedL, rel. to USE]

u·ter·us /yŏŏ'tərəs/ n. (pl. -ter·i /-ī'/) womb —u'ter·ine /-in, -īn'/ adj. [L]

U Thant /(y)ŏŏ THänt', THänt'/ 1909–74; Burmese diplomat; Secretary-General of the United Nations (1962–71)

u·til·i·tar·i·an /yŏŏtil'əter'ēən/ adj. 1 designed to be useful rather than attractive; severely practical 2 of utilitarianism

u·til'i·tar'i·an·ism' n. doctrine that actions are right if they are useful or benefit a majority

u·til·i·ty /yŏŏtil'ətē/ n. (pl. -ties) 1 usefulness 2 useful thing 3 public water, gas, electric, etc., service; public utility [L utilis useful, rel. to USE]

u·til'i·ty room' n. room for domestic appliances, e.g., a washing machine, furnace, etc.

u·ti·lize /yŏŏt'l-īz'/ v. (-lized, -liz·ing) use; make profitable use of —u'ti·li·za'tion n. [It, rel. to UTILITY]

ut·most /ət'mōst'/ adj. 1 furthest; extreme; greatest —n. 2 utmost point or degree, etc. [OE]

U·to·pi·a /yŏŏtō'pēə/ n. imagined perfect place or state of things —U·to'pi·an (also u-) adj. [title of a book by Thomas More, fr. Gk ou not, topos place]

U·trecht /(y)ŏŏ'trekt'/ n. city in the Netherlands. Pop. 231,200

ut·ter[1] /ət'ər/ adj. complete; absolute —ut'ter·ly adv. [OE]

ut·ter[2] v. 1 emit audibly 2 express in words [ME: outward]

ut'ter·ance n. 1 act of uttering 2 thing spoken 3 power or manner of speaking

ut'ter·most' adj. UTMOST

U-turn /yŏŏ'tərn/ n. 1 turn by a vehicle so

uv or **UV** *abbr.* ultraviolet

u·vu·la /yōō'vyələ/ *n.* (*pl.* **-lae** /-lē', -lī'/) fleshy part of the soft palate hanging above the throat —**u'vu·lar** *adj.* [L dim. of *uva* grape]

ux·o·ri·al /ək'sôr'ēəl/ *adj.* of a wife [L *uxor* wife]

ux·o·ri·ous /ək'sôr'ēəs/ *adj.* greatly or excessively fond of one's wife

Uz·bek·i·stan /ōōzbek'istän', -stan'/ *n.* republic in S central Asia on the S coast of the Aral Sea; formerly part of the USSR. Capital: Tashkent. Pop. 21,363,000 —**Uz'bek** *n.*

V

v, V /vē/ *n.* (*pl.* **v's; V's, Vs**) twenty-second letter of the English alphabet; a consonant

V *symb.* vanadium

v or **v.** *abbr.* **1** valve **2** variable **3** vector **4** vein **5** verb **6** verse **7** version **8** versus **9** very **10** *vide* **11** village **12** violin **13** voice **14** volt; voltage **15** volume

V or **V.** *abbr.* **1** *Rom. num.* (usu. **v**) five **2** Venerable **3** Vicar **4** Victory **5** Vinyl **6** Virgin **7** Viscount

VA, Va. abbr. for Virginia (postal abbr. **VA**)

VA or **V.A.** *abbr.* Veterans Administration

va·can·cy /vā'kənsē/ *n.* (*pl.* **-cies**) **1** being vacant **2** available job, room, office, etc.

va'cant *adj.* **1** not filled or occupied; empty **2** not mentally active; showing no interest —**va' cant·ly** *adv.* [L, rel. to VACATE]

va·cate /vā'kāt', vākāt'/ *v.* (**·cat·ed, ·cat· ing**) leave vacant; cease to occupy (a house, position, etc.) [L *vacare* be empty]

va·ca'tion *n.* **1** extended period of recreation, esp. one spent away from home —*v.* **2** take a vacation —**va·ca'tion·er** *n.* [L, rel. to VACATE]

vac·ci·nate /vak'sənāt'/ *v.* (**·nat·ed, ·nat· ing**) inoculate with a vaccine to immunize against a disease —**vac'ci·na'tion, vac'ci·na' tor** *n.*

vac·cine /vaksēn', vak'sēn'/ *n.* preparation used in vaccination [L *vacca* cow]

vac·il·late /vas'əlāt'/ *v.* (**·lat·ed, ·lat·ing**) be irresolute; fluctuate —**vac'il·la'tion, vac'il· la'tor** *n.* [L]

vac·u·ole /vak'yōō-ōl'/ *n.* tiny space in an organ or cell, containing air, fluid, etc. [L *vacuus* empty]

vac·u·ous /vak'yōōəs/ *adj.* **1** expressionless **2** showing absence of thought or intelligence **3** empty —**vac·u'i·ty** /-kyōō'ətē/ *n.;* **vac'u· ous·ly** *adv.* [L *vacuus* empty]

vac·u·um /vak'yōōəm', -yōōm', -yəm/ *n.* (*pl.* **·ums** or **·u·a** /-yōōə/) **1** space entirely devoid of matter **2** space from which all or most of the air has been pumped out **3** absence of the normal or previous content, activities, etc. —*adj.* **4** working by means of a vacuum —*v.* **5** clean with a vacuum cleaner [L *vacuus* empty]

vac'u·um clean'er *n.* machine for removing dust, etc., by suction

vac'u·um-packed' *adj.* sealed after partial removal of air

vac'u·um tube' *n.* tube with a near-vacuum for modifying electric current

Va·duz /fädōōts'/ *n.* capital of Liechtenstein. Pop. 4,900

vag·a·bond /vag'əbänd'/ *n.* **1** wanderer, esp.

a tramp or beggar —*adj.* **2** wandering; roving —**vag'a·bond·age** /-dij/ *n.* [L *vagari* wander]

va·ga·ry /vā'gərē/ *n.* (*pl.* **·ries**) caprice; whim [L *vagari* wander]

va·gi·na /vəjī'nə/ *n.* (*pl.* **·nas** or **·nae** /-nē/) canal from the uterus to the vulva in female mammals —**vag'i·nal** *adj.* [L: sheath]

va·grant /vā'grənt/ *n.* **1** unemployed itinerant —*adj.* **2** wandering; roving —**va'gran·cy** *n.* [AngFr]

vague /vāg/ *adj.* **1** uncertain; ill-defined **2** imprecise; inexact in thought, expression, or understanding —**vague'ly** *adv.;* **vague'ness** *n.* [L *vagus* wandering]

vain /vān/ *adj.* **1** having too high an opinion of one's looks, abilities, etc. **2** empty; trivial **3** useless; futile **4 in vain: a** without success **b** lightly; profanely —**vain'ly** *adv.* [L *vanus* empty]

vain'glo'ry *n.* boastfulness; extreme vanity —**vain'glo'ri·ous** *adj.* [Fr *vaine gloire*]

val·ance /val'əns, vā'ləns/ *n.* short curtain framing the canopy of a bedstead or above a window, etc. [AngFr *valer* descend]

vale /vāl/ *n.* (*Archaic.* except in place names) valley [L *vallis*]

val·e·dic·tion /val'ədik'sнən/ *n.* **1** bidding farewell **2** words used in this [L *vale* farewell]

val·e·dic·to·ri·an /val'ədiktôr'ēən/ *n.* **1** top student in a graduating class **2** student delivering a valedictory

val·e·dic·to·ry /val'ədik'tərē/ *n.* speech bidding farewell, esp. at a graduation

va·lence /vā'ləns/ *n.* (also **va'len·cy** /-sē/, *pl.* **·cies**) combining power of an atom measured by the number of hydrogen atoms it can displace or combine with [L *valentia* power]

Va·len·ci·a /välen'sēə, -тнуä/ *n.* **1** seaport in E Spain. Pop. 752,900 **2** city in N Venezuela. Pop. 903,100

val·en·tine /val'əntīn/ *n.* **1** card or gift sent as a mark of love on St. Valentine's Day (Feb. 14) **2** sweetheart chosen on this day [for *Valentine*, name of two saints]

Val·en·ti·no /val'əntē'nō/, **Rudolph** 1895–1926; Italian-born US actor

Va·lé·ry /väl'ärē'/, **Paul Ambroise** 1871–1945; French poet and critic

va·let /valā', val'it/ *n.* **1** gentleman's personal servant **2** hotel, etc., employee who cares for patrons' clothing, cars, etc. —*v.* **3** work as a valet (for) [Fr *va(s)let,* rel. to VARLET, VASSAL]

val·e·tu·di·nar·i·an /val'ət(y)ōōd'n·er'ēən/ *n.* **1** person of poor health or who is unduly anxious about health —*adj.* **2** in poor health or anxious about one's health —**val'e·tu'di· nar'i·an·ism'** *n.* [L *valetudo* health]

Val·hal·la /valhal′ə, välhä′lə/ n. Norse Myth. hall where the souls of slain heroes are received

val·iant /val′yənt/ adj. brave —**val′iance** n.; **val′iant·ly** adv. [L valere be strong]

val·id /val′id/ adj. 1 (of a reason, objection, etc.) sound; defensible 2a legally acceptable b not yet expired —**va·lid′i·ty** n.; **val′id·ly** adv.; **val′id·ness** n. [L validus strong, rel. to VALIANT]

val·i·date /val′ədāt′/ v. (·dat·ed, ·dat·ing) make or prove valid; ratify —**val′i·da′tion** n.

va·lise /vəlēs′/ n. Old-fash. suitcase [Fr fr. It]

Val·i·um /val′ēəm/ n. Tdmk. drug (diazepam) used as a tranquilizer

Val·kyr·ie /valkir′ē, val′kirē/ n. Norse Myth. maidens who escort the souls of slain heroes to Valhalla

Va·lla·do·lid /val′ədəlid′, -lēd′/ n. city in N Spain. Pop. 328,400

Val·le·jo /vəlā′ō/ n. city in Calif. Pop. 109,199

Val·let·ta /vəlet′ə/ n. capital of Malta. Pop. 9,200

val·ley /val′ē/ n. low area between hills, usu. with a stream or river flowing through it [L vallis]

val·or /val′ər/ n. courage, esp. in battle —**val′or·ous** adj. [L valere be strong]

Val·pa·rai·so /val′pərī′zō/ n. legislative capital of Chile. Pop. 296,000

val·u·a·ble /val′y(ōō)əbəl/ adj. 1 of great value, price, or worth —n. 2 (usu. pl.) valuable thing —**val′u·a·bly** adv.

val·u·a′tion n. 1 estimation (esp. professional) of a thing's worth 2 worth so estimated

val·ue /val′yōō/ n. 1 worth; desirability; utility 2 worth as estimated 3 amount for which a thing can be exchanged in the open market 4 effectiveness (news value) 5 (pl.) one's principles, priorities, or standards 6 Mus. duration of a note 7 Math. amount denoted by an algebraic term —v. (·ued, ·u·ing) 8 estimate the value of, esp. professionally 9 have a high or specified opinion of —**val′ue·less** adj.; **val′u·er** n. [ult. fr. Fr valoir be worth, fr. L valere]

val′ue-add′ed tax′ n. tax levied on the rise in value of services and goods at each stage of production; abbr. VAT

val′ue judg′ment n. subjective estimate of worth, etc.

valve /valv/ n. 1 device controlling flow through a pipe, etc. 2 structure in an organ, etc., allowing a flow of blood, etc., in one direction only 3 device to vary the effective length of the tube in a trumpet, etc. 4 half-shell of an oyster, mussel, etc. —**val·vu·lar** /val′vyələr/ adj. [L valva leaf of a folding door]

va·moose /vəmōōs′, va-/ v. (·moosed, ·moos·ing) Slang. depart quickly [Sp vamos let us go]

vamp¹ /vamp/ n. 1 upper front part of a boot or shoe —v. 2 improvise a musical accompaniment [Fr avantpié front of the foot]

vamp² Colloq. n. 1 woman who uses sexual attraction to exploit men —v. 2 act as a vamp [abbr. of VAMPIRE]

vam·pire /vam′pīr′/ n. 1 fictitious reani-

mated corpse that sucks the blood of sleeping persons 2 person who preys ruthlessly on others 3 (in full vam′pire bat′) tropical (esp. S American) bloodsucking bat [Fr or Ger fr. Magyar]

van¹ /van/ n. 1 small, enclosed delivery truck, multi-passenger vehicle, etc. 2 large, enclosed truck, used for moving, etc. [abbr. of CARAVAN]

van² n. vanguard; forefront [abbr.]

va·na·di·um /vənā′dēəm/ n. hard, gray, metallic element used to strengthen steel; symb. V [ON Vanadis epithet of the goddess Freyja]

Van Bu·ren /van byŏōr′ən/, **Martin** 1782–1862; 8th US president (1837–41)

Van·cou·ver /vankōō′vər/ n. 1 large island in SW Canada, off the coast of British Columbia 2 seaport in British Columbia. Pop. 471,800

van·dal /van′dəl/ n. person who willfully or maliciously damages property —**van′dal·ism′** n.; **van′dal·ize′** v. (·ized, ·iz·ing) [Vandals, name of a Germanic people who sacked Rome and destroyed works of art in the 5th cent.; L fr. Gmc]

Van·der·bilt /van′dərbilt′/, **Cornelius** 1794–1877; US financier

Van Dyck /van dīk′/, **(Sir) Anthony** 1599–1641; Flemish painter

Van·dyke′ beard′ /vandīk′/ n. short, pointed beard

vane /vān/ n. 1 weather vane 2 blade of a propeller, windmill, etc. [OE fana flag]

Van Eyck /van īk′/, **Jan** d. 1441; Flemish painter

Van Gogh /van gō′, gäкн′/, **Vincent** 1853–90; Dutch painter

van·guard /van′gärd′/ n. 1 foremost part of an advancing army, etc. 2 leaders of a movement, etc. [Fr avan(t)garde fr. avant before, rel. to GUARD]

va·nil·la /vənil′ə/ n. 1a tropical, fragrant, climbing orchid b (in full va·nil′la bean′) fruit of this 2 extract from the vanilla bean, or a synthetic equivalent, used as flavoring [Sp dim. of vaina pod]

van·ish /van′isн/ v. 1 disappear 2 cease to exist [L, rel. to VAIN]

van·i·ty /van′itē/ n. (pl. ·ties) 1 conceit about one's appearance or attainments 2 futility; unsubstantiality 3 ostentatious display 4 table, usu. with a mirror, at which one sits or stands while applying makeup, dressing, etc. [L, rel. to VAIN]

van′i·ty case′ n. woman's small traveling case for make-up, etc.

van·quish /vaNG′kwisн/ v. conquer; overcome [L vincere]

van·tage /van′tij/ n. 1 (also van′tage point′) place giving a good view 2 advantageous position [Fr, rel. to ADVANTAGE]

Va·nu·a·tu /vän′(y)əwä′tōō/ n. island republic in the S Pacific, NE of Australia. Capital: Port-Vila. Pop. 154,000

vap·id /vap′id, vā′pid/ adj. insipid; dull; flat —**va·pid′i·ty** n.; **vap′id·ly** adv.; **vap′id·ness** n. [L vapidus]

va·por /vā′pər/ n. 1 moisture or other substance diffused or suspended in air, e.g., mist, smoke 2 gaseous form of a substance —**va′por·ous**, **va′por·y** adj. [L]

va′por·ize′ v. (·ized, ·iz·ing) change into vapor —**va′por·i·za′tion**, **va′por·iz′er** n.

va·por trail' n. white trail of condensed water from an aircraft, etc.

va·que·ro /väker'ō/ n. SW US. cowboy [Sp *vac(a)* cow + *-ero*]

Va·ra·na·si /vərän'əsē/ n. (formerly **Benares**) city in NE India on the Ganges River. Pop. 926,000

va·ri·a·ble /ver'ēəbəl/ adj. 1 changeable; adaptable 2 apt to vary; not constant 3 *Math.* (of a quantity) indeterminate; able to assume different numerical values —n. 4 variable thing or quantity —**var'i·a·bil'i·ty** n.; **var'i·a·bly** adv.

var·i·ance /ver'ēəns/ n. 1 difference of opinion; dispute 2 discrepancy 3 officially allowed exception to regulations, zoning laws, etc.

var·i·ant /ver'ēənt/ adj. 1 differing in form or details from a standard (*variant spelling*) 2 having different forms —n. 3 variant form, spelling, type, etc.

var·i·a·tion /ver'ēā'sHən/ n. 1 varying; departure from the normal kind, amount, a standard, etc. 2 extent of this 3 variant thing 4 *Mus.* theme in a changed or elaborated form

var·i·col·ored /ver'ēkəl'ərd/ adj. variegated in color 2 of various colors [L *varius* various]

var·i·cose /var'ikōs'/ adj. permanently and abnormally dilated (*varicose veins*) [L *varix* enlarged vein]

var·ied /ver'ēd/ adj. showing variety

var·i·e·gat·ed /ver'ēgā'tid, ver'ē·ə-/ adj. 1 with irregular patches of different colors 2 having leaves of two or more colors —**var'i·e·ga'tion** n. [L, rel. to VARIOUS]

va·ri·e·tal /vəri'ətəl/ n. 1 wine made chiefly from one type of grape —adj. 2 of or designating such a wine 3 of or having variety

va·ri·e·ty /vəri'ətē/ n. (pl. **·ties**) 1 diversity; absence of uniformity 2 quantity or collection of different things 3 different form of a thing, quality, etc. 4 *Biol.* subdivision of a species [L, rel. to VARIOUS]

var·i·ous /ver'ēəs/ adj. 1 different; diverse 2 several —**var'i·ous·ly** adv. [L *varius*]

var·let /vär'lit/ n. *Archaic.* 1 scoundrel 2 menial [OFr var. of *vaslet* VALET]

var·mint /vär'mint/ n. *Colloq.* objectionable or annoying person or animal

Var·na /vär'nə/ n. seaport in Bulgaria on the Black Sea. Pop. 314,900

var·nish /vär'nish/ n. 1 resinous solution used to give a hard, shiny, transparent coating 2 deceptive outward appearance or show —v. 3 apply varnish to 4 give a deceptively attractive appearance to [Fr *vernis*]

var·si·ty /vär'sitē/ n. (pl. **·ties**) *Colloq.* top sports team representing a school, etc. [fr. UNIVERSITY]

var·y /ver'ē, var'ē/ v. (**·ied, ·y·ing**) 1 be or become different; be of different kinds; change 2 make different; modify [L *varius*]

vas·cu·lar /vas'kyələr/ adj. of or containing vessels for conveying blood, sap, etc. [L *vasculum* dim. of *vas* vessel]

vas def·er·ens /vas def'ərenz'/ n. (pl. **va·sa def·er·en·ti·a** /vā'zə def'əren'sH(ē)ə/) sperm duct of the testicle

vase /vās, vāz, väz/ n. vessel used as an ornament or container for flowers [L *vas* vessel]

va·sec·to·my /vəsek'təmē/ n. (pl. **·mies**)

---

removal of part of each vas deferens for sterilization

Vas·e·line /vas'əlēn', vas'əlēn'/ n. *Tdmk.* type of petroleum jelly used as an ointment, etc. [Ger *Wasser* water, Gk *elaion* oil]

vas·o·mo·tor /vas'ōmō'tər/ adj. regulating the change in diameter of blood vessels, e.g., a nerve, drug, etc.

vas·sal /vas'əl/ n. 1 *Hist.* feudal land tenant 2 humble dependent —**vas'sal·age** /-ij/ n. [MedL *vassallus* retainer]

vast /vast/ adj. immense; huge —**vast'ly** adv.; **vast'ness** n. [L]

vat /vat/ n. large tank for holding liquids [OE *fæt*]

VAT abbr. VALUE-ADDED TAX

Vat·i·can Cit'y /vat'ikən/ n. seat of the Roman Catholic Church within the city of Rome, Italy

vaude·ville /vôd'(ə)vil', -vəl/ n. stage show of dances, songs, comedy acts, etc. —**vaude·vil'li·an** /-vil'ēən/ adj. & n. [Fr]

Vaughan /vôn/, **Sarah** 1924–90; US jazz singer

Vaughan Wil·liams /vôn wil'yəmz/, **Ralph** 1872–1958; English composer

vault /vôlt/ n. 1 arched roof 2 vaultlike covering 3 underground storage chamber or place of interment 4 secure storage place for valuables, etc. 5 act of vaulting —v. 6 leap, esp. using the hands or a pole 7 spring over in this way 8 make in the form of a vault [L *volvere* roll]

vault'ing n. 1 arched work in a vaulted roof or ceiling —adj. 2 over-reaching; overly confident

vault'ing horse' n. *Sports.* padded rectangular or cylindrical apparatus used in gymnastics for pushing off in vaulting

vaunt /vônt/ v. & n. boast —**vaunt'ed** adj. [L, rel. to VAIN]

VCR abbr. VIDEOCASSETTE RECORDER

VD abbr. venereal disease

VDT abbr. video display terminal

've v. contr. have (*I've*)

veal /vēl/ n. calf's flesh as food [Fr fr. L *vitulus* calf]

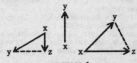

VECTORS 1

vec·tor /vek'tər/ n. 1 *Math. & Physics.* quantity having direction as well as magnitude 2 carrier of disease [L *vehere vect-* convey]

Ve·da /vā'də/ n. (sing. or pl.) oldest Hindu scriptures —**Ve'dic** adj. [Skt: knowledge]

vee·jay /vē'jā'/ n. VIDEO JOCKEY

veep or **Veep** /vēp/ n. vice president

veer /vēr/ v. 1 change direction 2 change in course or opinion, etc. —n. 3 change of direction [Fr *virer* turn]

veg·an /vej'ən, vē'gən/ n. 1 person who does not eat animals or animal products —adj. 2 using or containing no animal products [shortening of VEGETARIAN]

veg·e·ta·ble /vej´(ə)təbəl/ *n.* **1** plant, esp. a herbaceous one used for food **2** *Colloq. Derog.* **a** *Offens.* mentally incapacitated person **b** dull or inactive person —*adj.* **3** of, derived from, or relating to plant life or vegetables as food [L, rel. to VEGETATE]

veg·e·tar·i·an /vej´ətẽr´ēən/ *n.* **1** person who does not eat meat or fish —*adj.* **2** excluding animal food, esp. meat —**veg´e·tar´i·an·ism´** *n.* [fr. VEGETABLE]

veg·e·tate /vej´ətāt´/ *v.* (·**tat·ed, ·tat·ing**) **1** live an uneventful or monotonous life **2** grow as plants do —**veg´e·ta´tive** /-tiv/ *adj.* [L *vegere* animate]

veg·e·ta´tion *n.* plants collectively; plant life [MedL, rel. to VEGETATE]

veg·gie /vej´ē/ *n. Colloq.* **1** vegetarian **2** vegetable

ve·he·ment /vē´əmənt/ *adj.* showing or caused by strong feeling; ardent —**ve´he·mence** *n.*; **ve´he·ment·ly** *adv.* [L *vehemens, -ment-* fr. *vehere* carry]

ve·hi·cle /vē´(h)ikəl/ *n.* **1** means of or device for conveyance **2** medium for expression or action **3** liquid, etc., as a medium for suspending pigments, drugs, etc. —**ve·hic·u·lar** /vēhik´yələr/ *adj.* [L *vehere* carry]

veil /vāl/ *n.* **1** piece of usu. transparent net attached to a woman's hat, headpiece, etc. **2** part of a nun's headdress **3** thing that hides or disguises —*v.* **4** cover with a veil **5 take the veil** become a nun [L *velum*]

veiled /vāld/ *adj.* **1** having a veil **2** partly concealed or hidden; disguised

vein /vān/ *n.* **1a** any of the tubes conveying blood to the heart **b** (in general use) any blood vessel **2** rib of an insect's wing or leaf **3** streak of a different color in wood, marble, cheese, etc. **4** fissure in rock filled with ore **5** specified character or tendency; mood —**veined** *adj.*; **vein´y** *adj.* (·**i·er, ·i·est**) [L *vena*]

Ve·láz·quez /vəläs´kəs, -k(w)ez´/, **Diego** 1599–1660; Spanish painter

Vel·cro /vel´krō´/ *n. Tdmk.* fastener consisting of two strips of fabric that cling when pressed together [blend fr. Fr *velours croché* hooked velvet]

veld /velt/ *n.* (also **veldt** /velt/) *S. Afr.* open country [Afrik, rel. to FIELD]

vel·lum /vel´əm/ *n.* **1a** fine parchment, orig. calfskin **b** manuscript on this **2** smooth writing paper imitating vellum [Fr *vélin*, rel. to VEAL]

ve·loc·i·ty /vəläs´ətē/ *n.* (*pl.* ·**ties**) speed, esp. of inanimate things [L *velox* swift]

ve·lour /vəloor´/ *n.* (also **ve·lours´**, pronunc. same) plushlike fabric [Fr]

ve·lum /vē´ləm/ *n.* (*pl.* ·**la** /-lə/) SOFT PALATE

vel·vet /vel´vit/ *n.* **1** soft fabric with a thick, short pile **2** furry skin on a growing antler —*adj.* **3** of, like, or soft as velvet —**vel´vet·y** *adj.* [L *villus* tuft; down]

vel·ve·teen /vel´vətēn´/ *n.* cotton fabric with a pile like velvet

ve·nal /vēn´l/ *adj.* corrupt; able to be bribed; involving bribery —**ve·nal·i·ty** /-nal´itē/ *n.*; **ve´nal·ly** *adv.* [L *venalis* for sale]

vend /vend/ *v.* offer (small wares) for sale

—**vend´i·ble** *adj.*; **ven´dor** or **vend´er** *n.* [L *vendere* sell]

ven·det·ta /vendet´ə/ *n.* prolonged bitter quarrel or blood feud [It fr. L, rel. to VINDICTIVE]

vend´ing ma·chine´ *n.* coin-operated machine selling small items

ve·neer /vənēr´/ *n.* **1** thin covering of fine wood, etc. **2** deceptively pleasing appearance —*v.* **3** apply a veneer to [Ger *furnieren* to furnish]

ven·er·a·ble /ven´(ə)rəbəl/ *adj.* entitled to respect on account of character, age, etc. —**ven´er·a·bil´i·ty** /-bil´itē/ *n.* [L, rel. to VENERATE]

ven·er·ate /ven´ərāt´/ *v.* (·**at·ed, ·at·ing**) respect deeply —**ven´er·a´tion, ven´er·a´tor** *n.* [L *venerari* worship]

ve·ne·re·al /vənēr´ēəl/ *adj.* **1** of sexual desire or intercourse **2** transmitted through sexual intercourse (*venereal disease*) [L *venus veneris* sexual love]

ve·ne´tian blind´ /vənē´sHən/ *n.* window blind of adjustable horizontal slats

Ve·ne·zia /vənet´sēə/ *n.* see VENICE

Ven·e·zue·la /ven´əz(ə)wā´lə/ *n.* republic in N South America on the Caribbean Sea. Capital: Caracas. Pop. 20,184,000 —**Ven·e·zue´lan** *n.* & *adj.*

ven·geance /ven´jəns/ *n.* **1** punishment inflicted for wrong to oneself or one's cause; revenge **2 with a vengeance** to a high or excessive degree [Fr *venger* fr. L *vindicare* avenge]

venge´ful *adj.* vindictive; seeking vengeance —**venge´ful·ly** *adv.* [obs. *venge* avenge, rel. to VENGEANCE]

ve·ni·al /vē´nēəl/ *adj.* pardonable; not mortal (*venial sin*) —**ve·ni·al´i·ty** /-al´itē/ *n.*; **ve´ni·al·ly** *adv.* [L *venia* grace]

Ven·ice /ven´is/ *n.* (Italian name **Venezia**) seaport in NE Italy. Pop. 317,800 —**Ve·ne·tian** *n.* & *adj.*

ven·i·son /ven´isən/ *n.* deer's flesh as food [L *venatio* hunting]

Venn´ di´a·gram /ven/ *n.* diagram using overlapping and intersecting circles to show the relationships between mathematical sets [for J. *Venn*, English logician]

ven·om /ven´əm/ *n.* **1** poisonous fluid of snakes, spiders, etc. **2** malignity —**ven´om·ous** *adj.*; **ven´om·ous·ly** *adv.* [L *venenum*]

ve·nous /vē´nəs/ *adj.* of, full of, or contained in veins [L, rel. to VEIN]

vent¹ /vent/ *n.* **1** opening allowing the passage of air, etc. **2** outlet; free expression —*v.* **3** make a vent in **4** give free expression to **5** vent one's spleen scold or express displeasure, esp. without cause [L *ventus* wind]

vent² *n.* slit in a garment [Fr *fente* fr. L *findere* split]

ven·ti·late /vent´l-āt´/ *v.* (·**lat·ed, ·lat·ing**) **1** cause air to circulate freely in (a room, etc.) **2** air (a question, grievance, etc.) **3a** *Med.* oxygenate (the blood) **b** admit or force air into (the lungs) —**ven´ti·la´tion** *n.* [L *ventilare* blow, winnow, rel. to VENT¹]

ven´ti·la´tor *n.* appliance or aperture for ventilating a room, etc.

ven·tral /ven´trəl/ *adj.* of or on the abdomen [L *venter* belly]

ven·tri·cle /ven´trikəl/ *n.* hollow part of an organ, esp. the lower chambers of the heart

—ven·tric·u·lar /-yələr/ adj. [L ventriculus dim. of venter belly]

ven·tril·o·quism /ventril'əkwiz'əm/ n. (also ven·tril'o·quy /-kwē/) skill of speaking without moving the lips, esp. as entertainment —ven·tril'o·quist /-kwist/ n. [L venter belly, loqui speak]

Ventura /ventyŏŏr'ə, -CHŏŏr'-/ n. see SAN BUENAVENTURA

ven·ture /ven'CHər/ n. 1 risky undertaking 2 commercial speculation —v. (·tured, ·tur·ing) 3 dare; not be afraid 4 dare to go, make, or put forward 5a expose to risk; stake b take risks [fr. ADVENTURE]

ven·ture·some /ven'CHərsəm/ adj. (also ven'tur·ous) 1 disposed to take risks 2 risky

ven·ue /ven'yōō/ n. 1 place for a match, meeting, concert, etc. 2 Law. place where a crime or trial occurs [Fr fr. venir come]

Ve·nus /vē'nəs/ n. 1 second planet from the sun 2 Rom. Myth. APHRODITE

Ve'nus's fly'·trap' n. insectivorous plant [L Venus goddess of love]

ve·ra·cious /vərā'SHəs/ adj. 1 truthful by nature 2 true —ve·rac'i·ty /-ras'ətē/ n. [L verax fr. verus true]

Ve·ra·cruz /ver'əkrōōs', -krōōz'/ n. 1 state in E central Mexico, on the Gulf of Mexico. Capital: Jalapa. Pop. 6,228,200 2 seaport in this state, on the Gulf of Mexico. Pop. 284,800

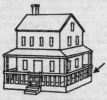

VERANDA

ve·ran·da or ve·ran·dah /vəran'də/ n. (usu. covered) platform along the side of a house [Hindi fr. Port varanda]

verb /vərb/ n. Gram. word used to indicate action, a state, or an occurrence [L verbum word]

ver·bal /vər'bəl/ adj. 1 of words 2 oral; not written 3 of or derived from a verb 4 talkative —n. Gram. 5 word derived from a verb; an infinitive, participle, or gerund —ver'bal·ly adv. [L, rel. to VERB]

ver'bal·ize' v. (·ized, ·iz·ing) put into words

ver'bal noun' n. Gram. noun derived from a verb; gerund (e.g., smoking in smoking is forbidden)

ver·ba·tim /vərbā'təm/ adv. & adj. in exactly the same words [MedL, rel. to VERB]

ver·be·na /vərbē'nə/ n. (pl. same) usu. annual or biennial plant with clusters of fragrant flowers [L]

ver·bi·age /vər'b(ē)ij/ n. too many words or unnecessarily difficult words [Fr, rel. to VERB]

ver·bose /vərbōs'/ adj. using more words than are needed —ver·bos'i·ty /-bäs'ətē/ n. [L verbosus fr. verbum word]

ver·dant /vərd'nt/ adj. 1 green; lush 2 (of a

person) unsophisticated —ver'dan·cy n. [perh. fr. Fr verdeant fr. viridis green]

Ver·di /verd'ē/, Giuseppe 1813–1901; Italian composer

ver·dict /vər'dikt/ n. 1 decision of a judge or jury 2 decision; judgment [AngFr verdit fr. L vere truly + dictum thing said]

ver·di·gris /vər'digrēs, -gris, -grē/ n. greenish-blue substance that forms on copper and its alloys [OFr: green of Greece]

ver·dure /vər'jər/ n. green vegetation or its color [OFr verd green]

verge¹ /vərj/ n. 1 edge; border 2 brink —v. (verged, verg·ing) 3 border on [L virga rod]

verge² v. (verged, verg·ing) 1 incline downward or in a specified direction 2 change gradually [L vergere bend]

verg·er /vər'jər/ n. 1 church caretaker 2 officer with a staff preceding a bishop, etc., in a procession [AngFr, rel. to VERGE¹]

Ver·gil /vər'jəl/ see VIRGIL

ver·i·fy /ver'əfī'/ v. (·fied, ·fy·ing) establish the truth, correctness, accuracy, or validity of by examination, etc. —ver'i·fi'a·ble adj.; ver'i·fi·ca'tion /-fikā'SHən/ n. [MedL, rel. to VERY]

ver·i·ly /ver'əlē/ adv. Archaic. truly [fr. VERY]

ver·i·si·mil·i·tude /ver'əsəmil'ət(y)ōōd'/ n. appearance of being true or real [L verus true, similis like]

ver·i·ta·ble /ver'ətəbəl/ adj. real; rightly so called —ver'i·ta·bly adv. [Fr, rel. to VERITY]

ver·i·ty /ver'ətē/ n. (pl. ·ties) 1 fundamental truth or principle 2 truth [L veritas truth]

Ver·meer /vərmer', vermār'/, Jan 1632–75; Dutch painter

ver·mi·cel·li /vər'məCHel'ē/ n. pasta in long, slender threads [L vermis worm]

ver·mi·cide /vər'məsīd'/ n. drug that kills intestinal worms [L vermis worm]

ver·mic·u·lite /vərmik'yəlīt'/ n. a hydrous silicate mineral used esp. as a medium for plant growth and in insulation [L vermiculatus worm-eaten, fr. vermis worm]

ver·mi·form /vər'miförm'/ adj. worm-shaped [MedL, rel. to VERMICIDE]

ver'mi·form ap·pen'dix n. small, blind tube extending from the cecum in humans and some other mammals

ver·mil·ion /vərmil'yən/ n. 1a brilliant red pigment b color of this —adj. 2 of this color [L vermiculus dim. of vermis worm]

ver·min /vər'min/ n. (usu. treated as pl.) 1 mammals, birds, and insects harmful to game, crops, etc. 2 vile people —ver'min·ous adj. [L vermis worm]

Ver·mont /vərmänt'/ n. NE state of the US. Capital: Montpelier. Pop. 562,758. Abbr. VT; Vt. —Ver·mont'er n.

ver·mouth /vərmōōTH'/ n. wine flavored with aromatic herbs [Ger, rel. to WORMWOOD]

ver·nac·u·lar /vərnak'yələr/ n. 1 language or dialect of a particular country 2 language of a particular class or group 3 common speech —adj. 4 (of language) native; not foreign or formal [L vernaculus native]

ver·nal /vər'nl/ adj. 1 of or in spring 2 young; youthful [L ver spring]

Verne /vərn/, Jules 1828–1905; French novelist

ver·ni·er /vər′nēər/ *n.* small, movable, graduated scale for obtaining fractional parts on a fixed scale [for P. *Vernier*, French mathematician]

Ve·ro·na /vərō′nə/ *n.* city on the Adige River in N Italy. Pop. 258,900

ver·sa·tile /vər′sət·l/ *adj.* **1** adapting easily to or skilled in different subjects or occupations **2** having many uses —**ver′sa·til′i·ty** /-til′ ətē/ *n.* [L *vertere* vers- turn]

verse /vərs/ *n.* **1** poetry **2** stanza of a poem or song **3** each of the short, numbered divisions of the Bible **4** poem [L *versus*, rel. to VERSATILE]

versed /vərst/ *adj.* experienced or skilled in [L *versari* be engaged in]

ver·si·fy /vər′sifī′/ *v.* (**-fied, -fy·ing**) **1** turn into or express in verse **2** compose verses —**ver′si·fi·ca′tion** /-fikā′SHən/, **ver′si·fi′er** *n.*

ver·sion /vər′ZHən, -SHən/ *n.* **1** account of a matter from a particular point of view **2** book, etc., in a particular edition or translation **3** form; variant [L, rel. to VERSE]

ver·so /vər′sō/ *n.* (*pl.* **-sos**) **1** left-hand page of an open book **2** back of a printed leaf [L *verso* (*folio*) on the turned (leaf)]

ver·sus /vər′səs/ *prep.* against; *abbr.* **vs.** [ME fr. L: toward]

ver·te·bra /vər′tibrə/ *n.* (*pl.* **-brae** /-brā′, -brē/) each segment of a backbone —**ver′te·bral** *adj.* [L *vertere* turn]

ver·te·brate /vər′tibrət/ *adj.* **1** having a backbone **2** vertebrate animal [L *vertebratus* jointed, rel. to VERTEBRA]

ver·tex /vər′teks/ *n.* (*pl.* **-tex·es** or **-ti·ces** /-tisēz′/) **1** highest point; top **2a** each angular point of a polygon **b** meeting point of lines that form an angle [L: whirl, crown of a head, fr. *vertere* turn]

ver·ti·cal /vər′tikəl/ *adj.* **1** at right angles to a horizontal plane **2** in a direction from top to bottom **3** of or at the vertex —*n.* **4** vertical line or plane —**ver′ti·cal·ly** *adv.* [L, rel. to VERTEX]

ver·tig·i·nous /vərtij′inəs/ *adj.* of or causing vertigo [L, rel. to VERTIGO]

ver·ti·go /vər′tigō′/ *n.* dizziness, esp. as caused by heights [L: whirling, fr. *vertere* turn]

verve /vərv/ *n.* enthusiasm; vigor [Fr]

ver·y /ver′ē/ *adv.* **1** in a high degree **2** truly; utterly —*adj.* **3** actual; truly such **4** complete; utter **5** not very in a low degree; far from being [L *verus* true]

ves·i·cle /ves′ikəl/ *n.* small bladder, bubble, or blister —**ve·sic′u·lar** /-yələr/, **ve·sic′u·late** /-lit/ *adj.* [L]

ves·pers /ves′pərz/ *n. pl.* an evening prayer service [L: evening]

Ves·puc·ci /vespŏŏ′CHē/, **Amerigo** 1451–1512; Florentine explorer

ves·sel /ves′əl/ *n.* **1** hollow receptacle, esp. for liquid **2** ship or boat, esp. a large one **3** duct or canal, etc., holding or conveying blood or sap, etc. [L *vas*]

vest /vest/ *n.* **1** sleeveless, jacketlike garment, usu. worn by men with a suit **2** bestow (powers, authority, etc.) on **3** clothe (oneself), esp. in vestments [L *vestis* garment]

ves·tal /ves′tl/ *adj.* pure

ves·tal vir·gin *n. Rom. Antiq.* virgin consecrated to Vesta and vowed to chastity [*Vesta*, Roman goddess of the hearth and home]

vest·ed in·ter·est *n.* **1** personal interest in a state of affairs **2** interest or right recognized as belonging to a person

ves·ti·bule /ves′tibyŏŏl′/ *n.* hall or lobby, as of a building [L]

ves·tige /ves′tij/ *n.* **1** trace; sign **2** slight amount; particle **3** atrophied part or organ of an animal or plant —**ves·tig′i·al** /-tij′ēəl, -tij′ əl/ *adj.* [L *vestigium* footprint]

vest′ment *n.* ceremonial garment, esp. one worn by a priest or minister [L, rel. to VEST]

vest′-pock′et *adj.* small enough to fit into a pocket

ves·try /ves′trē/ *n.* (*pl.* **-tries**) **1** church room or building for holding meetings or keeping vestments, etc., in **2** lay committee managing the secular affairs of a church

Ve·su·vi·us /vəsŏŏ′vēəs/ *n.* active volcano near Naples, Italy

vet /vet/ *n.* **1** *Colloq.* veterinarian **2** veteran —*v.* (**vet·ted, vet·ting**) **3** make a careful and critical examination of [abbr.]

vetch /vecH/ *n.* plant of the pea family used chiefly for fodder [L *vicia*]

vet·er·an /vet′ərən, ve′trən/ *n.* **1** old soldier or long-serving member of any group **2** former member of the armed forces —*adj.* **3** of long standing; experienced [L *vetus -er-* old]

Vet′er·ans Day′ *n.* (formerly **Ar′mi·stice Day′**) US holiday on Nov. 11 commemorating the end of WWI and WWII and honoring veterans of the armed services

vet·er·i·nar·i·an /vet′ərəner′ēən, ve′trə-/ *n.* person trained in veterinary medicine

vet·er·i·nar·y /vet′ərəner′ē, ve′trə-/ *adj.* **1** of or for the diseases and injuries of animals —*n.* (*pl.* **-ies**) **2** VETERINARIAN [L *veterinae* beasts of burden]

ve·to /vē′tō/ *n.* (*pl.* **-toes**) **1** right to reject a bill, resolution, etc. **2** rejection; prohibition —*v.* (**-toed, -to·ing**) **3** use one's right of veto **4** forbid; prohibit [L: I forbid]

vex /veks/ *v.* **1** anger; irritate **2** *Archaic.* afflict [L *vexare* annoy]

vex·a′tion *n.* **1** vexing or being vexed **2** annoying or distressing thing —**vex·a′tious** *adj.*

VF or **V.F.** *abbr.* **1** video frequency **2** visual field

VFR *abbr.* visual flight rules

vhf or **VHF** *abbr.* very high frequency

VHS *Tdmk.* videocassette recording system [fr. video home service]

VI or **V.I.** *abbr.* Virgin Islands (postal abbr. VI)

vi·a /vī′ə, vē′ə/ *prep.* through; by means or way of [L: way]

vi·a·ble /vī′əbəl/ *adj.* **1** feasible **2** capable of developing and surviving outside the womb —**vi′a·bil′i·ty** *n.* [Fr *vie* life]

vi·a·duct /vī′ədəkt′/ *n.* long bridge, esp. a series of connected spans, as over a valley, etc. [L *via* way, after AQUEDUCT]

vi·al /vī′əl/ *n.* small bottle or container, esp. for medicines [rel. to PHIAL]

vi·and /vī′ənd/ *n. Formal.* (usu. *pl.*) article of food [L *vivere* live]

vibes /vībz/ *n. pl. Slang.* **1** vibrations, esp.

feelings communicated without speech, etc. 2
VIBRAPHONE

vi·brant /vī′brənt/ *adj.* 1 vibrating 2 thrill-
ing; lively; striking 3 (of sound) resonant
—**vi′bran·cy** *n.*; **vi′brant·ly** *adv.* [L, rel. to
VIBRATE]

vi·bra·phone /vī′brəfōn′/ *n.* instrument like
a xylophone but with electrical resonators [fr.
VIBRATO]

vi·brate /vī′brāt′/ *v.* (**·brat·ed, ·brat·ing**) 1
move rapidly to and fro 2 (of a sound) throb;
resonate 3 quiver; thrill 4 swing to and
fro; oscillate —**vi′bra·tor** *n.*; **vi′bra·to·ry**
/·brətôr′ē/ *adj.* [L *vibrare* shake]

vi·bra′tion *n.* 1 vibrating 2 (*pl.*) VIBES, 1

vi·bra·to /vibrät′ō, vī-/ *n.* rapid slight variation in musical pitch producing a tremulous
effect [It, rel. to VIBRATE]

vi·bur·num /vībər′nəm/ *n.* a shrub, usu.
with white flowers [L: wayfaring-tree]

vic·ar /vik′ər/ *n.* 1 priest of a Church of England parish receiving a stipend rather than
tithes 2 *RC Ch.* bishop's deputy [L *vicarius*
substitute, rel. to VICE²]

vic·ar·age /vik′ərij/ *n.* vicar's house

vi·car·i·ous /vīker′ēəs/ *adj.* 1 experienced
indirectly or second-hand 2 acting or done for
another 3 deputed; delegated —**vi·car′i·
ous·ly** *adv.* [L, rel. to VICAR]

vice¹ /vīs/ *n.* 1 immoral conduct 2 form of
this, esp. prostitution 3 weakness; indulgence
[L *vitium*]

vi·ce² /vī′sə/ *prep.* in the place of [L *vicis*
change]

vice- *comb. form* substitute; deputy; next in
rank (*vice-chairman*) [rel. to VICE²]

vice′ pres′i·dent *n.* (also **vice′-pres′i·dent**)
official ranking below and deputizing for a
president (for US usu. *caps.*) —**vice′ pres′i·
den·cy** *n.* (*pl.* **·cies**); **vice′-pres·i·den′tial**
adj.

vice·roy /vīs′roi′/ *n.* sovereign's deputy ruler
in a colony, province, etc. [Fr, rel. to VICE-, *roy*
king]

vice′ squad′ *n.* police department concerned
with prostitution, etc.

vi·ce ver·sa /vī′sə vər′sə, vīs, vī′sē/ *adj.*
Latin. with the order of the terms changed;
the other way around

vi·chys·soise /vīsH′ēswäz′/ *n.* (usu. chilled)
creamy soup of leeks and potatoes [Fr: of Vi-
chy]

vi·cin·i·ty /vəsin′ətē/ *n.* (*pl.* **·ties**) 1 surrounding district 2 nearness [L *vicinus* near]

vi·cious /visH′əs/ *adj.* 1 bad-tempered; spiteful 2 violent 3 corrupt; depraved 4 faulty;
unsound —**vi′cious·ly** *adv.*; **vi′cious·ness** *n.*
[L, rel. to VICE¹]

vi′cious cir′cle *n.* (also **vi′cious cy′cle**) self-
perpetuating, harmful sequence of cause and
effect

vi·cis·si·tude /vəsis′ət(y)ōōd′/ *n.* change,
esp. of fortune [L, rel. to VICE²]

vic·tim /vik′təm/ *n.* 1 person or thing injured, sacrificed, destroyed, etc. 2 prey; dupe
[L]

vic′tim·ize *v.* (**·ized, ·iz·ing**) make (a person, etc.) a victim —**vic′tim·i·za′tion** *n.*

vic·tor /vik′tər/ *n.* winner in a battle or contest [L *vincere vict-* conquer]

Vic·to·ri·a /viktôr′ēə/ 1819–1901; queen of
Great Britain (1837–1901)

Vic·to·ri·a /viktôr′ēə/ *n.* 1 capital of the Canadian province of British Columbia. Pop.
71,200 2 capital of Seychelles. Pop. 24,300

Vic·to′ri·a Falls′ *n.* waterfalls of the Zambezi
River in S Africa; 420 ft. high

Vic·to′ri·a, Lake′ *n.* freshwater lake in E central Africa; principal source of the Nile River

Vic·to·ri·an /viktôr′ēən/ *adj.* 1 of the time of
Queen Victoria 2 prudish; strict —*n.* 3 person of this time —**Vic·to′ri·an·ism′** *n.*

vic·to·ri·ous /viktôr′ēəs/ *adj.* 1 conquering;
triumphant 2 marked by victory —**vic·to′ri·
ous·ly** *adv.* [L, rel. to VICTOR]

vic·to·ry /vik′t(ə)rē/ *n.* (*pl.* **·ries**) defeat of
an enemy or opponent

vict·ual /vit′l/ *n. Colloq.* (usu. *pl.*) food; provisions [L *victus* food]

vi·cu·ña /vik(y)ōō′nə, -kōōn′yə/ *n.* 1 S American mammal like a llama, with fine silky wool
2 its wool or an imitation [Sp fr. Quechua]

Vi·dal /vidäl′, -dôl′/, **Gore** (born **Eugene Luther Vidal**) 1925– ; US writer

vi·de /vī′dē, vē′dā′/ *v. Latin.* see; consult (a
passage in a book, etc.)

vid·e·o /vid′ē·ō′/ *adj.* 1 of the recording (or
reproduction) of moving pictures on magnetic
tape 2 of television or television broadcasting
3 of a computer terminal display —*n.* (*pl.*
·os) 4 such recording or broadcasting 5 *Colloq.* movie on videotape —*v.* (**·oed, ·o·ing**)
6 record on videotape [L: I see]

vid′e·o·cas·sette *n.* cassette of videotape

vid′e·o·cas·sette re·cord′er *n.* (also **vid′e·o
re·cord′er**) machine for recording and playing back videocassettes; *abbr.* VCR

vid′e·o dis·play′ ter′mi·nal *n. Comp.* monitor

vid′e·o game′ *n.* electronic game played on a
television screen or computer monitor

vid′e·o jock′ey *n.* introducer of music videos,
as on television; *abbr.* veejay, VJ

vid′e·o·tape′ *n.* 1 magnetic tape for recording
moving pictures and sound —*v.* (**·taped,
·tap·ing**) 2 record on this

vid′e·o·tape re·cord′er *n.* VIDEOCASSETTE RE-
CORDER

vie /vī/ *v.* (**vied, vy·ing**) compete; contend
for superiority [prob. Fr, rel. to ENVY]

Vi·en·na /vē·en′ə/ *n.* capital of Austria. Pop.
1,533,200 —**Vi·en·nese** /vē′ənēz′/ *n.* & *adj.*

Vien·tiane /vyentyän′/ *n.* capital of Laos.
Pop. 178,200

Vi·et·cong /vē·et′kONG′/ *n.* Communist-led
forces in South Vietnam that fought for North
Vietnam during the Vietnam War

Vi·et·nam /vē·et′näm′, vē′ət-, -nam′/ *n.* country in SE Asia on the S China Sea. Capital:
Hanoi. Pop. 69,052,000

Vi·et·nam·ese /vē·et′nəmēz′, -mēs′/ *adj.* 1 of
Vietnam —*n.* (*pl.* same) 2 native or language of Vietnam

Vi·et·nam War′ *n.* conflict (1954–75) between
South Vietnam (aided by the US, South Korea,
Australia, etc.) and North Vietnam and the Vi-
etcong

view /vyōō/ *n.* 1 range of vision 2 what is
seen; prospect; scene, etc. 3a opinion b manner of considering a thing (*a long-term view*)
4 inspection by the eye or mind —*v.* 5 look
at; inspect; survey visually or mentally 6 consider 7 see; watch 8 **have in view: a** have

as one's object **b** bear in mind **9 in view of** considering **10 with a view to** with the hope or intention of [L *videre* see]

view·er *n.* **1** person who views **2** device for looking at slides, etc.

view′find′er *n.* device on a camera showing the borders of the proposed photograph

view′point′ *n.* point of view

vig·il /vij′əl/ *n.* **1** keeping awake during the night, etc., esp. to keep watch or pray **2** eve of a festival or holy day [L *vigilia*]

vig·i·lance /vij′ələns/ *n.* watchfulness; caution —**vig′i·lant** *adj.* [L, rel. to VIGIL]

vig·i·lan·te /vij′əlan′tē/ *n.* member of a self-appointed group maintaining order —**vig′i·lan′tism, vig′i·lan′tist** *n.* [Sp: vigilant]

vi·gnette /vinyet′, vēn-/ *n.* **1** short description; character sketch **2** illustration, photograph, etc., without a definite border —**vi·gnet′tist** *n.* [Fr, dim., rel. to VINE]

Vi·go /vē′gō/ *n.* seaport in NW Spain. Pop. 274,600

vig·or /vig′ər/ *n.* **1** physical or mental strength or energy **2** healthy growth **3** forcefulness —**vig′or·ous** *adj.*; **vig′or·ous·ly** *adv.* [Fr fr. L *vigere* thrive]

Vi·ja·ya·wa·da /vij′əyəwäd′ə/ *n.* city in SE India. Pop. 701,400

Vi·king /vī′kiNG/ *n.* Scandinavian pirate and raider of the 8th–11th cent. [ON]

Vi·la /vē′lə/ *n.* capital of Vanuatu. Pop. 19,300

vile /vīl/ *adj.* **1** disgusting **2** depraved **3** *Colloq.* abominable; very bad or unpleasant —**vile′ly** *adv.*; **vile′ness** *n.* [L *vilis* cheap; base]

vil·i·fy /vil′əfī′/ *v.* (·**fied**, ·**fy·ing**) defame; malign —**vil′i·fi·ca′tion** /-fikā′SHən/ *n.* [L, rel. to VILE]

vil·la /vil′ə/ *n.* country house, esp. a luxurious one [It fr. L farm]

Vil·la /vē′(y)ə/, **Pancho (Francisco)** 1877–1923; Mexican revolutionary

vil·lage /vil′ij/ *n.* **1** settlement, usu. smaller than a town **2** self-contained urban community —**vil′lag·er** *n.* [L, rel. to VILLA]

Vi·lla·her·mo·sa /vē(l)yə·ermō′sə/ *n.* capital of the Mexican state of Tabasco. Pop. 390,100

vil·lain /vil′ən/ *n.* **1** wicked person **2** chief evil character in a play, story, etc. —**vil′lain·ous** *adj.*; **vil′lain·y** *n.* (*pl.* ·**ies**) [L, rel. to VILLA]

vil·lein /vil′ən, -ān′/ *n. Hist.* feudal tenant entirely subject to a lord or attached to a manor —**vil′lein·age** /-ij/ *n.* [var. of VILLAIN]

Vil·lon /vē·yōN′/, **François** 1431 – c. 1463; French poet

Vil·ni·us /vil′nēəs/ *n.* capital of Lithuania. Pop. 597,700

vim /vim/ *n.* vigor [L, acc. of *vis* energy]

Vi·ña del Mar /vēn′yə del mär′/ *n.* city in central Chile. Pop. 312,300

vin·ai·grette /vin′əgret′/ *n.* salad dressing of oil, vinegar, and seasoning [Fr, dim., rel. to VINEGAR]

vin·di·cate /vin′dikāt′/ *v.* (·**cat·ed**, ·**cat·ing**) **1** clear of blame or suspicion **2** establish the existence, merits, or justice of **3** justify —**vin′di·ca′tion, vin′di·ca′tor** *n.*; **vin′di·ca·to′ry** /-katō′rē/ *adj.* [L *vindicare* claim]

vin·dic·tive /vindik′tiv/ *adj.* vengeful —**vin·**

dic′tive·ly *adv.*; **vin·dic′tive·ness** *n.* [L *vindicta* vengeance, rel. to VINDICATE]

vine /vīn/ *n.* **1** climbing or trailing plant with a woody stem **2** stem of this **3** grape plant [L *vinea* vineyard]

vin·e·gar /vin′igər/ *n.* sour liquid from fermented wine, cider, etc., used as a condiment or for pickling —**vin′e·gar·y** *adj.* [MFr fr. OFr *vin* wine, *aigre* sour]

vine·yard /vin′yard/ *n.* plantation of grapevines, esp. for wine making

vi·no /vē′nō/ *n. Slang.* wine [It and Sp]

vin·tage /vin′tij/ *n.* **1a** season's produce of grapes **b** wine from this **2** wine of high quality from a particular year and district **3a** period when a thing was made **b** thing made in a particular period —*adj.* **4** of high or peak quality **5** of a past season [L *vinum* wine]

vint·ner /vint′nər/ *n.* wine seller [ME, ult. fr. L *vinetum* vineyard]

vi·nyl /vīn′l/ *n.* plastic made by polymerization [L *vinum* wine]

vi·ol /vī′əl/ *n.* medieval stringed instrument of various sizes [Fr fr. Prov]

vi·o·la /vē·ō′lə/ *n.* instrument larger than the violin and of lower pitch —**vi·ol′ist** *n.* [It & Sp, rel. to VIOL]

vi·o·late /vī′əlāt′/ *v.* (·**lat·ed**, ·**lat·ing**) **1** disregard; break (an oath, treaty, etc.) **2** treat profanely; desecrate **3** disturb **4** rape —**vi′o·la·ble** /-ləbəl/ *adj.*; **vi′o·la′tion, vi′o·la′tor** *n.* [L *violare*]

vi·o·lence /vī′ələns/ *n.* **1** being violent **2** violent conduct or treatment **3** unlawful use of force [L, rel. to VIOLENT]

vi·o·lent /vī′ələnt/ *adj.* **1** involving or using great physical force **2a** intense; vehement **b** lurid (*violent colors*) **3** resulting from or caused by violence —**vi′o·lent·ly** *adv.* [L]

vi·o·let /vī′əlet/ *n.* **1** plant with usu. purple, blue, or white flowers **2** bluish-purple color —*adj.* **3** of this color [L dim. of VIOLA]

VIOLIN

vi·o·lin /vī′əlin′/ *n.* high-pitched stringed instrument played with a bow —**vi′o·lin′ist** *n.* [It dim. of VIOLA]

vi·o·lon·cel·lo /vī′ələnCHel′ō/ *n.* (*pl.* ·**los**) CELLO [It, dim. of *violone* bass viol]

VIP *abbr.* very important person

vi·per /vī′pər/ *n.* **1** small venomous snake **2** treacherous person —**vi′per·ous** *adj.* [L]

vi·ra·go /virä′gō/ *n.* (*pl.* ·**goes**) fierce or abusive woman [L: female warrior]

vi·ral /vī′rəl/ *adj.* of or caused by a virus

vir·e·o /vir′ēō/ *n.* N American songbird

Vir·gil or **Vergil** /vər′jəl/ 70–19 B.C.; Roman poet

vir·gin /vər′jin/ *n.* **1** person who has never had sexual intercourse **2** (**the Virgin**)

Christ's mother, Mary **3** **(the Virgin)** zodiacal sign or constellation Virgo —*adj.* **4** not yet used, explored, etc. **5** chaste; pure —**vir'gin·al** *adj.*; **vir·gin'i·ty** *n.* [L *virgo -gin-*]

Vir·gin·ia /vərjin`yə/ *n.* S state of the US. Capital: Richmond. Pop. 6,187,358. Abbr. **VA**; **Va.** —**Vir·gin'ian** *n.* & *adj.*

Vir·gin'ia Beach' *n.* city in Va. Pop. 393,069

Vir·gin'ia creep'er *n.* ornamental vine [*Virginia* in US]

Vir·gin'ia reel' *n.* American dance done by partners in two facing rows

Vir'gin Is'lands of the U·nit'ed States' *n.* island group in the Caribbean Sea, SE of Puerto Rico; U.S. possession. Pop. 101,800

Vir'gin Mar'y see MARY

Vir·go /vər`gō/ *n.* (*pl.* **-gos**) **1** constellation and sixth sign of the zodiac (the Virgin) **2** person born under this sign [L, rel. to VIRGIN]

vir·gule /vər`gyōōl/ *n.* slash mark (/) used in fractions and dates or as meaning "per" or "or" [L *virgula* small rod]

vir·ile /vir'əl, -il/ *adj.* **1** (of a man) vigorous or strong **2** sexually potent **3** of a man as distinct from a woman or child —**vi·ril'i·ty** *n.* [L *vir* man]

vi·rol·o·gy /vīrāl`əjē/ *n.* study of viruses —**vi·rol'o·gist** *n.*

vir·tu·al /vər`CHŌŌəl/ *adj.* being so in practice or effect, though not in fact or name [MedL, rel. to VIRTUE]

vir'tu·al·ly *adv.* in effect; almost

vir'tu·al re·al'i·ty *n.* computer-generated artificial world in which a person can participate

vir·tue /vər`CHŌŌ/ *n.* **1** moral excellence; goodness **2** particular form of this **3** chastity **4** good quality **5** efficacy, esp. medical **6** by (or in) **virtue** of on account of; because of [L, rel. to VIRILE]

vir·tu·o·so /vər`CHŌŌ-ō´sō, -zō/ *n.* (*pl.* **-sos** or **-si** /-sē, -zē/) highly skilled artist, esp. a musician —**vir·tu·os'i·ty** /-äs'itē/ *n.* [It: skilled]

vir·tu·ous /vər`CHŌŌəs/ *adj.* **1** morally good **2** *Archaic* chaste —**vir'tu·ous·ly** *adv.*; **vir'tu·ous·ness** *n.* [L, rel. to VIRTUE]

vir·u·lent /ver`(y)ələnt/ *adj.* **1** strongly poisonous **2** (of a disease) violent; very infectious **3** bitterly hostile —**vir'u·lence** *n.*; **vir'u·lent·ly** *adv.* [L, rel. to VIRUS]

vi·rus /vī`rəs/ *n.* **1** microscopic organism of ten causing diseases **2** COMPUTER VIRUS [L: poison]

vi·sa /vē`zə/ *n.* (also **vi·sé**) endorsement on a passport, etc., esp. allowing entrance to or exit from a country [L: seen]

vis·age /viz'ij/ *n.* face [L *visus* sight]

Vi·sa·kha·pat·nam /visäk`əpət´nəm/ *n.* seaport in E India, on the Bay of Bengal. Pop. 750,000

vis à vis /vē`zə vē´/ *prep.* **1** in relation to **2** in comparison with —*adv.* **3** opposite [Fr: face to face, rel. to VISAGE]

● **Usage:** The expression literally means 'face to face'; Avoid using it to mean 'about, concerning': *I was sitting vis-à-vis the painting* is a typical usage. "She wanted to talk to me vis-à-vis the problem" is widely considered unacceptable. However, in the sense of 'in contrast, comparison or relation to,' it has gained currency: *One must consider inflation vis-à-vis interest rates.*

vis·cer·a /vis'ərə/ *n. pl.* internal organs of the body [L]

vis·cer·al *adj.* **1** of the viscera **2** of feelings rather than reason

vis·cid /vis'id/ *adj.* glutinous; sticky [L, rel. to VISCOUS]

vis·cose /vis'kōs, -kōz´/ *n.* cellulose in a highly viscous state, used for making rayon, etc. [L, rel. to VISCOUS]

vis·count /vī`kount/ *n.* British nobleman ranking between an earl and a baron —**vis'count·cy** *n.* (*pl.* **-cies**); **vis'count·ess** *n. fem.* [AngFr, rel. to VICE-, COUNT²]

vis·cous /vis'kəs/ *adj.* **1** glutinous; sticky **2** semifluid **3** not flowing freely —**vis·cos'i·ty** /-käs´ətē/ *n.* (*pl.* **-ties**) [L *viscum* birdlime]

VISE

vise /vīs/ *n.* clamp with two jaws holding an object so as to allow work with both hands [L *vitis* vine]

vi·sé /vē`zā/ *n. Old-fash.* VISA

Vish·nu /vish`nōō/ *n.* Hindu god regarded as the preserver, member of the sacred triad with Brahma and Shiva

vis·i·bil·i·ty /viz`əbil´ətē/ *n.* **1** being visible **2** range or possibility of vision as determined by the light and weather

vis·i·ble /viz'ibəl/ *adj.* able to be seen, perceived, or ascertained —**vis'i·bly** *adv.* [L, rel. to VISION]

vi·sion /vizH`ən/ *n.* **1** act or faculty of seeing **2** thing or person seen in a dream or trance **3** mental picture **4** imaginative insight; foresight **5** beautiful person, etc. [L *videre vis-* see]

vi·sion·ar·y /vizH`əner´ē/ *adj.* **1** given to seeing visions or to fanciful theories **2** having vision or foresight **3** impractical —*n.* (*pl.* **-ies**) **4** visionary person

vis·it /viz'it/ *v.* **1** go or come to see or inspect **2** stay temporarily with (a person) or at (a place) **3** (of a disease, calamity, etc.) attack; inflict —*n.* **4a** act of visiting **b** temporary stay, esp. as a guest **5** occasion of going to a doctor, etc. **6** formal or official call —**vis'i·tor** *n.* [L, rel. to VISION]

vis·i·tant /viz'itənt/ *n.* visitor

vis·i·ta·tion /viz`itā´sHən/ *n.* **1** official visit of inspection **2** divine punishment **3** legally permitted visits, as to one's children after a divorce

vi·sor /vī`zər/ *n.* **1** movable part of a helmet covering the face **2** shield for the eyes, esp. the brim of a cap [OFr, rel. to VISAGE]

vis·ta /vis`tə/ *n.* **1** long, narrow view as between rows of trees **2** mental view of a series of events [It]

vis·u·al /vizH`ōōəl, vizH`(w)əl/ *adj.* **1** of or

used in seeing 2 visible —**vis′u·al·ly** adv. [L visus sight]

vis·u·al·ize /vizH′ōōəlīz′, vizH′(w)ə-/ v. (·ized, ·iz·ing) imagine visually —**vi′su·al·i·za′tion** n.

vi·ta /vēt′ə, vī′tə/ n. person's educational and career history; résumé [L: life]

vi·tal /vīt′l/ adj. 1 of or essential to organic life 2 essential; indispensable 3 full of life or activity 4 fatal —n. 5 (pl.) the body's vital organs, e.g., the heart and brain —**vi′tal·ly** adv. [L vita life]

vi·tal·i·ty /vītal′itē/ n. 1 liveliness; animation 2 ability to survive or endure [L, rel. to VITAL]

vi·tal·ize /vīt′l-īz′/ v. (·ized, ·iz·ing) 1 endow with life 2 make lively or vigorous —**vi′tal·i·za′tion** n.

vi′tal signs′ n. pl. signs of life, e.g., pulse, respiration rate, etc.

vi′tal sta·tis′tics n. pl. data on number of births, marriages, deaths, etc.

vi·ta·min /vī′təmin/ n. any of various organic substances essential to health and growth, present in many foods or sometimes produced in the body [L vita life, AMINE]

vi·ti·ate /vish′ē-āt′/ v. (·at·ed, ·at·ing) 1 impair; debase 2 make invalid or ineffectual —**vi′ti·a′tion** /-ā′shən/ n. [L, rel. to VICE[1]]

vit·i·cul·ture /vit′ikəl′chər/ n. cultivation of grapes [L vitis vine]

vit·re·ous /vi′trēəs/ adj. of or like glass [L vitrum glass]

vit′re·ous hu′mor (or **bod′y**) n. clear fluid in the eye between the lens and the retina

vit·ri·fy /vi′trifī′/ v. (·fied, ·fy·ing) change into glass or a glasslike substance, esp. by heat —**vit′ri·fac′tion** /-faksHən/, **vit′ri·fi·ca′tion** /-fikā′shən/ n. [Fr or MedL, rel. to VITREOUS]

vit·ri·ol /vi′trēōl, -əl/ n. 1 sulfuric acid or a sulfate 2 caustic or hostile speech or criticism —**vit′ri·ol′ic** /-äl′ik/ adj. [L vitrum]

vi·tu·per·ate /vīt(y)ōō′pərāt′/ v. (·at·ed, ·at·ing) criticize abusively —**vi·tu′per·a′tion** n.; **vi·tu′per·a·tive** /-ətiv/ adj. [L]

vi·va /vē′və/ interj. long live [It & Sp]

vi·va·ce /vivächˈē, -ā/ adv. Mus. in a lively manner [L, rel. to VIVACIOUS]

vi·va·cious /vivā′shəs, vī-/ adj. lively; animated —**vi·va′cious·ly** adv.; **vi·va′cious·ness, vi·vac′i·ty** /-vas′itē/ n. [L vivax long lived]

Vi·val·di /vivōl′dē, -väl′-/, Antonio 1678–1741; Italian composer and violinist

vive /vēv/ interj. long live [Fr.]

viv·id /viv′id/ adj. 1 of (color) strong; intense 2 clear; lively; graphic —**viv′id·ly** adv.; **viv′id·ness** n. [L]

viv·i·fy /viv′əfī′/ v. (·fied, ·fy·ing) animate; give life to [Fr fr. L]

vi·vip·a·rous /vīvip′ərəs/ adj. Zool. bringing forth live young [L vivus alive, parere produce]

viv·i·sec·tion /viv′əsek′shən/ n. surgery on living animals for scientific research —**viv′i·sect′** v.; **viv′i·sec′tion·al** adj.; **viv′i·sec′tion·ist** n. & adj.; **viv′i·sec′tor** n. [L vivus living, SECTION]

vix·en /vik′sən/ n. 1 female fox 2 spiteful

woman —**vix′en·ish** adj.; **vix′en·ish·ly** adv. [OE fyxe female fox]

viz. /viz/ adv. namely; that is to say [abbr. of videlicet]

vi·zier /vizēr′/ n. Hist. high official in the Ottoman Empire [ult. fr. Ar]

vi·zor /vī′zôr/ n. var. of VISOR

VJ abbr. VIDEO JOCKEY

Vla·di·kav·kaz /vläd′əkäf′käz/ n. see ORDZHONIKIDZE

Vla·di·vos·tok /vlad′iväs′täk′, -vəstäk′/ n. seaport in SE Russia on the Sea of Japan. Pop. 648,000

vlf or **VLF** abbr. very low frequency

V.M.D. abbr. doctor of veterinary medicine [L Veterinariae Medicinae Doctor]

voc. abbr. vocational; vocative

vocab. abbr. vocabulary

vo·cab·u·lar·y /vōkab′yəler′ē/ n. (pl. ·ies) 1 words used by a particular language, book, group, individual, etc. 2 list of these, esp. in alphabetical order with definitions or translations [MedL vocabularium]

vo·cal /vō′kəl/ adj. 1 of or uttered by the voice 2 outspoken 3 sung —**vo′cal·ly** adv. [L, rel. to VOICE]

vo′cal cords′ (or **folds′**) n. voice-producing folds in the larynx

vo·cal·ic /vōkal′ik/ adj. of or like a vowel or vowels

vo′cal·ist n. singer

vo·cal·ize /vō′kəlīz′/ v. (·ized, ·iz·ing) 1 form (a sound), utter (a word), or sing 2 articulate; express —**vo′cal·i·za′tion** n.

vo·ca·tion /vōkā′shən/ n. 1 strong feeling of suitability for a particular career 2 trade; profession —**vo·ca′tion·al** adj. [L vocare call]

voc·a·tive /väk′ətiv/ n. Gram. case of a noun used in addressing a person or thing

vo·cif·er·ate /vōsif′ərāt′/ v. (·at·ed, ·at·ing) shout; bawl —**vo·cif′er·a′tion, vo·cif′er·a′tor** n. [L, rel. to VOICE, ferre to bear]

vo·cif·er·ous /vōsif′ərəs/ adj. 1 noisy; clamorous 2 insistent —**vo·cif′er·ous·ly** adv.

vod·ka /väd′kə/ n. colorless alcoholic spirit distilled from grain, etc. [Russ "little" water]

vogue /vōg/ n. 1 prevailing fashion 2 popularity 3 **in vogue** in fashion —**vogu′ish** adj. [Fr]

voice /vois/ n. 1a sound formed in the larynx and uttered by the mouth, esp. by a person b power of this 2a spoken or written expression b opinion so expressed c right to express an opinion d medium for expression 3 Gram. set of verbal forms showing whether a verb is active or passive 4 Mus. a vocal part in a composition b vocal ability, esp. in singing —v. (**voiced, voic·ing**) 5 express 6 utter with vibration of the vocal cords 7 with one voice unanimously —**voice′less** adj.; **voice′less·ly** adv.; **voice′less·ness** n. [L vox voc-]

voice′ box′ n. larynx

voice′ mail′ n. automatic telephone answering system that records messages for several individuals

voice·o·ver n. commentary in a movie, etc., by an unseen narrator

void /void/ adj. 1 empty; vacant 2 invalid; not legally binding 3 ineffective —n. 4 empty space; vacuum —v. 5 render void 6 excrete; empty [Fr]

voi·la /vwälä'/ *interj.* expression of success [Fr behold]

voile /voil/ *n.* fine, semi-transparent fabric [Fr: VEIL]

vol. *abbr.* volume

vol·a·tile /väl'ət-l/ *adj.* 1 changeable; fickle 2 unstable; likely to erupt in violence 3 *Chem.* evaporating rapidly —**vol'a·til'i·ty, vol'a·til·i·za'tion** *n.*; **vol'a·til·ize'** *v.* (·ized, ·iz·ing) [L *volare* fly]

vol·can·ic /välkan'ik/ *adj.* of, like, or from a volcano —**vol·can'i·cal·ly** *adv.*

vol·ca·no /välkā'nō, vōl-/ *n.* (*pl.* ·noes) mountain from which lava, steam, etc., escape through openings in the earth's crust [L *Volcanus* Vulcan, Roman god of fire]

vole /vōl/ *n.* small, plant-eating rodent [orig. *vole-mouse* fr. Norw *voll* field]

Vol·ga Riv·er /väl'gə, vōl'-, vōl'-/ *n.* river in W Russia flowing 2,320 mi. to the Caspian Sea; longest river in Europe

Vol·go·grad /väl'gəgrad', vōl'-/ *n.* (formerly **Sta'lingrad'**) city on the Volga River in SW Russia. Pop. 1,007,300

vo·li·tion /vōlish'ən/ *n.* act or power of willing —**vo·li'tion·al** *adj.* [L *volo* I wish]

vol·ley /väl'ē/ *n.* (*pl.* ·leys) 1a simultaneous firing of a number of weapons b bullets, etc., so fired 2 torrent (of abuse, words, etc.) 3 playing of a ball in tennis, etc., before it touches the ground —*v.* 4 return or send by or in a volley [MFr *volee* fr. L *volare* fly]

vol'ley·ball' *n.* 1 game for two teams of six hitting a large ball by hand over a high net 2 ball used in this game

volt /vōlt/ *n.* unit of electromotive force [for A. VOLTA]

Vol·ta /vōl'tä/, **(Count) Alessandro** 1745–1827; Italian physicist

volt·age /vōlt'ij/ *n.* electromotive force expressed in volts

vol·ta·ic /vältā'ik/ *adj.* of or using electricity produced by chemical action

Vol·taire /vōltar', vōl-, -ter'/ (pseudonym of **François-Marie Arouet**) 1694–1778; French writer

volt'me'ter *n.* instrument measuring electric potential in volts

vol·u·ble /väl'yəbəl/ *adj.* speaking or spoken at length —**vol'u·bil'i·ty** *n.*; **vol'u·bly** *adv.* [L *volvere* roll]

vol·ume /väl'yōōm', -yəm/ *n.* 1 single book forming part or all of a work 2a space occupied by a gas, solid, or liquid b amount; quantity 3 strength of sound; loudness [L *volumen* scroll, rel. to VOLUBLE]

vo·lu·mi·nous /vəlōō'minəs/ *adj.* 1a loose and ample b bulky 2 written or writing at great length —**vo·lu'min·ous·ly** *adv.* [L, rel. to VOLUME]

vol·un·ta·rism /väl'əntəriz'əm/ *n.* policy or system based on voluntary action

vol·un·tar·y /väl'ənter'ē/ *adj.* 1 acting, done, or given willingly; not compulsory; 2 unpaid 3 brought about by voluntary action 4 controlled by the will —*n.* (*pl.* ·ies) 5 organ solo played before or after a church service —**vol'un·tar'i·ly** *adv.*; **vol'un·tar'i·ness** *n.* [L *voluntas* free will]

vol·un·teer /väl'əntēr'/ *n.* 1 person who vol-

untarily undertakes a task or enters military service —*v.* 2 undertake or offer voluntarily 3 be a volunteer —*adj.* 4 of or being a volunteer [Fr, rel. to VOLUNTARY]

vo·lup·tu·ar·y /vəlⴷp'chⴷⴷ-er'ē/ *n.* (*pl.* ·ies) person who seeks sensual pleasure [L, rel. to VOLUPTUOUS]

vo·lup·tu·ous /vəlⴷp'chⴷⴷəs/ *adj.* of, tending to, occupied with, or derived from sensuous or sensual pleasure —**vo·lup'tu·ous·ly** *adv.*; **vo·lup'tu·ous·ness** *n.* [L *voluptas* pleasure]

VOLUTES

vo·lute /vəlōōt'/ *n.* spiral, esp. a spiral ornament [L *volut-* rolled]

vom·it /väm'it/ *v.* 1 eject (contents of the stomach) through the mouth 2 eject violently —*n.* 3 matter vomited from the stomach [L]

von Braun /vän broun', fôn/, **Wernher** 1912–77; German-born US rocket scientist

Von·ne·gut /vän'igət/, **Kurt** 1922– ; US writer

von Neu·mann /vän n(y)ōō'mən, fôn, noi'män'/, **John** 1903–57; Hungarian-born US mathematician

voo·doo /vōō'dōō/ *n.* 1 religious witchcraft as practiced esp. in the W Indies 2 fetish used in voodoo —*v.* (·dooed, ·doo·ing) 3 affect by voodoo; bewitch —**voo'doo·ism'** *n.* [WAfr]

vo·ra·cious /vərā'shəs/ *adj.* 1 gluttonous; ravenous 2 very eager —**vo·ra'cious·ly** *adv.*; **vo·rac'i·ty** /-ras'itē/ *n.* [L *vorax* fr. *vorare* devour]

Vo·ro·nezh /vərō'nish/ *n.* city in SW Russia. Pop. 900,000

Voroshilovgrad /vər'ōshē'ləfgräd/ *n.* see LUGANSK

vor·tex /vôr'teks/ *n.* (*pl.* ·tex·es or ·ti·ces /-təsēz'/) 1 whirlpool 2 any whirling motion or mass 3 thing viewed as destructive or devouring —**vor'ti·cal** *adj.* [L, rel. to VERTEX]

vo·ta·ry /vō'tərē/ *n.* (*pl.* ·ries) 1 person bound by a vow to religious service 2 devotee of a person, cause, occupation, etc. [L, rel. to VOTE]

vote /vōt/ *n.* 1 formal expression of choice or opinion by a ballot, show of hands, etc. 2 right to vote 3 opinion expressed by a vote 4 votes given by or for a particular group —*v.* (vot·ed, vot·ing) 5 give a vote 6 enact or resolve by vote 7 suggest; urge 8 vote with one's feet *Colloq.* indicate an opinion by one's presence or absence —**vot'er** *n.* [L *votum* vow]

vo·tive /vō'tiv/ *adj.* offered or consecrated in fulfillment of a vow [L, rel. to VOTE]

vouch /vouCH/ v. answer for; be surety for [MFr vo(u)cher summon; invoke]

vouch·er n. 1 document exchangeable for goods or services 2 receipt [fr. AngFr, or fr. VOUCH]

vouch·safe v. (·safed, ·saf·ing) Formal. condescend to grant

vow /vou/ n. 1 solemn, esp. religious, promise —v. 2 promise or declare solemnly [Fr vou(er), rel. to VOTE]

vow·el /vou'əl, voul/ n. 1 speech sound made with vibration of the vocal cords but without audible friction 2 letter representing this, as a, e, i, o, u [L, rel. to VOCAL]

vox po·pu·li /väks' päp'yəlī/ n. public opinion [L: the people's voice]

voy·age /voi'ij/ n. 1 journey, esp. a long one by sea or in space —v. (·aged, ·ag·ing) 2 make a voyage —voy'ag·er n. [L viaticum travel money]

vo·ya·geur /vwäyäzHər'/ n. Hist. French explorer in pre-Revolutionary N America, esp. in Canada

voy·eur /vwäyər', voi·ər'/ n. person who derives sexual pleasure from secretly observing others' sexual activity or organs —voy'eur·ism' /-iz'əm/ n.; voy·eur·is'tic /-yəris'tik/ adj. [Fr voir see]

VP or **V.P.** abbr. VICE PRESIDENT

vs. abbr. versus

V.S. abbr. veterinary surgeon

VT, Vt. abbr. for Vermont (postal abbr. **VT**)

VTOL /vē'tâl', -tôl'/ abbr. vertical take off and landing

Vul·can /vəl'kən/ n. Rom. Myth. HEPHAESTUS

vul·can·ize /vəl'kənīz'/ v. (·ized, ·iz·ing) treat (rubber, etc.) with sulfur at a high temperature to strengthen it —vul'can·i·za'tion n. [for Vulcan, rel. to VOLCANO]

vul·can·ol·o·gy /vəl'kanäl'əjē/ n. the study of volcanoes —vul·can·o·log'i·cal /-əläj'ikəl/ adj.; vul·can·ol'o·gist /-jist/ n.

Vulg. abbr. Vulgate

vul·gar /vəl'gər/ adj. 1 indecent; tasteless 2 of or characteristic of the common people 3 common; prevalent —vul'gar·ly adv. [L vulgus common people]

vul·gar·i·an /vəl'ger'ēən/ n. vulgar (esp. rich) person

vul'gar·ism' n. vulgar word, expression, action, or habit

vul·gar·i·ty /vəl'ger'itē/ n. (pl. ·ties) vulgar act, expression, or state

vul·gar·ize v. (·ized, ·iz·ing) 1 make vulgar 2 popularize —vul'gar·i·za'tion, vul'gar·iz'er n.

vul'gar tongue' n. vernacular language

Vul·gate /vəl'gāt'/ n. 4th-cent. Latin version of the Bible

vul·ner·a·ble /vəl'nərəbəl/ adj. 1 easily wounded or harmed 2 exposed to damage, temptation, etc. —vul'ner·a·bil'i·ty /-əbil'itē/ n.; vul'ner·a·bly adv. [L vulnus -eris wound]

vul·pine /vəl'pīn/ adj. 1 of or like a fox 2 crafty; cunning [L vulpes fox]

vul·ture /vəl'CHər/ n. 1 large, carrion-eating bird of prey 2 rapacious person —vul'tur·ous adj. [ME fr. L]

vul·va /vəl'və/ n. (pl. ·vae /-vē/ or ·vas) external female genitals [L]

vy·ing /vī'iNG/ v. pres. part. of VIE

W

w, W /dub'əl yōō'/ n. (pl. w's; W's, Ws) twenty-third letter of the English alphabet; a semivowel

W symb. tungsten [wolframium, Latinized name]

w or **w.** abbr. 1 warden 2 warehouse 3 water 4 week(s) 5 weight 6 wide; width 7 widowed 8 wife 9 with 10 won

W or **W.** abbr. 1 Wales 2 Washington 3 watt(s) 4 Wednesday 5 west; western 6 Welsh 7 win

WA postal abbr. for Washington

Wa'bash' Riv'er /wô'basH/ n. river flowing 475 mi. SW across Ind. to the Ohio River

WAC /wak/ abbr. 1 Women's Army Corps —n. 2 member of the WAC

wack·o /wak'ō/ Colloq. adj. 1 wacky —n. (pl. ·os) 2 person who is crazy

wack'y adj. (·i·er, ·i·est) Slang. crazy [orig. dial.: left-handed]

Wa·co /wā'kō/ n. city in Texas. Pop. 103,590

wad /wäd/ n. 1 lump of soft material 2 bundle of paper money —v. (wad·ded, wad·ding) 3 stop up or keep in place with a wad 4 compress or crumple into a wad

wad'ding n. soft, fibrous material used for stuffing, etc., or to pack fragile articles

wad·dle /wäd'l/ v. (·dled, ·dling) 1 walk with short steps and a swaying motion —n. 2 waddling gait [fr. WADE]

wade /wād/ v. (wad·ed, wad·ing) 1 walk through water, mud, etc., esp. with difficulty 2 push or go through with difficulty 3 Colloq. attack vigorously [OE]

wad·er n. 1 long-legged, wading water bird 2 (pl.) high, waterproof boots

wa·di /wä'dē/ n. (pl. ·dis) rocky watercourse in N Africa, etc., dry except in the rainy season [Ar]

wa·fer /wā'fər/ n. 1 very thin, light, crisp cookie or cracker 2 Christianity. disk of unleavened bread used in the Eucharist 3 any similar, very thin disk [ME wafre fr. Gmc]

wa'fer-thin' adj. very thin

waf·fle¹ /wäf'əl/ v. (·fled, ·fling) speak or write verbosely or indecisively [dial. Eng. 'wave']

waf·fle² n. flat, crisp batter cake baked on a waffle iron [Du]

waf'fle i'ron n. utensil, usu. of two shallow metal pans with prominent studs and hinged together, for baking waffles

waft /wäft, waft/ v. 1 convey or travel easily and smoothly, as through air or over water —n. 2 whiff; scent 3 light wind gust [orig.

ME *waughter* armed escort vessel fr. Du or LGer *wachter* watchman]

wag[1] /wag/ *v.* (**wagged, wag·ging**) **1** shake or wave to and fro —*n.* **2** wagging motion [OE]

wag[2] *n.* facetious or comic person [OE]

wage /wāj/ *n.* **1** (*sing.* or *pl.*) fixed regular payment to an employee **2** return; recompense —*v.* (**waged, wag·ing**) **3** carry on (a war, etc.) [AngFr fr. Gmc]

wa·ger /wā′jər/ *n.* & *v.* BET [AngFr, rel. to WAGE]

wag·gish /wag′isH/ *adj.* playful; facetious —**wag′gish·ly** *adv.*; **wag′gish·ness** *n.*

wag·gle /wag′əl/ *v.* (**-gled, -gling**) *Colloq.* wag —**wag′gly** *adj.*

Wag·ner /väg′nər/, **Richard** 1813–83; German composer and conductor

wag·on /wag′ən/ *n.* **1** four-wheeled vehicle for heavy loads **2** *Colloq.* STATION WAGON **3 on** (or **off**) **the wagon** *Slang.* abstaining (or no longer abstaining) from alcohol [Du]

waif /wāf/ *n.* **1** homeless or helpless person, esp. a child **2** ownerless object or animal [AngFr, prob. fr. Scand]

wail /wāl/ *n.* **1** prolonged, plaintive cry of pain, grief, etc. —*v.* **2** utter a wail **3** lament or complain persistently or bitterly [ON]

wain /wān/ *n. Archaic.* wagon [OE]

wain·scot /wān′skət, -skät′/ *n.* **1** wooden paneling on the lower part of a wall —*v.* (**·scot·ed** or **·scot·ted, ·scot·ing** or **·scot·ting**) **2** panel with wainscot [LGer *wagenschot* fr. *wagen* WAGON]

wain·scot·ing /wān′skätiNG/ *n.* **1** wainscot **2** material for this

wain·wright /wān′rīt′/ *n.* person who makes or repairs wagons

waist /wāst/ *n.* **1a** part of the human body below the ribs and above the hips **b** circumference of this **2** narrow middle of a violin, wasp, etc. **3a** part of a garment encircling the waist **b** *Old-fash.* blouse —**waist′ed** *adj.* [OE, rel. to WAX[2]]

waist′band′ *n.* strip of cloth forming the waist of a garment

waist′coat′ *n. Brit.* VEST

waist′line′ *n.* outline or size of a person's body at the waist

wait /wāt/ *v.* **1a** defer action or departure for a specified time or until some event occurs **b** be expectant; ready **2** await **3** defer (a meal, etc.) **4a** serve food, drinks, etc. **b** serve as an attendant to —*n.* **5** period of waiting **6 wait and see** await the progress of events **7 wait table(s)** act as a waiter, esp. in a restaurant **8 wait up** not go to bed until a person arrives or an event happens —**wait′ing** *adj.* & *n.* [Gmc, rel. to WAKE[1]]

wait′er *n.* person who serves at table in a hotel, restaurant, etc.

wait′ing game′ *n.* delaying of action in order to have a greater effect later

wait′ing list′ *n.* list of people, esp. applicants for a position, place, etc.

wait′ing room′ *n.* room for people to wait in, esp. to see a doctor, etc., or at a station

wait′per′son *n.* waiter or waitress

wait′ress *n.* woman who serves at table in a hotel, restaurant, etc.

wait′staff′ *n.* restaurant workers who wait tables

waive /wāv/ *v.* (**waived, waiv·ing**) refrain from insisting on or using (a right, claim, opportunity, etc.) [AngFr *weyver*, rel. to WAIF]

● Usage: *Waive* 'surrender' and its noun, *waiver*, should be kept separate from *wave* 'back-and-forth or up-and-down motion' and *waver* 'go back and forth, vacillate': *He waived all rights to the inheritance by signing the waiver. The flag waved in the breeze. She wavered between saying Yes and No to his proposal.*

waiv′er *n. Law.* **1** waiving of a legal right, etc. **2** document recording this

wake[1] /wāk/ *v.* (**waked** or **woke, waked** or **wok·en, wak·ing**) **1** (cause to) cease to sleep **2** (cause to) become alert or attentive **3** *Archaic.* be awake **4** evoke; arouse —*n.* **5** watch beside a corpse before burial [OE]

wake[2] *n.* **1** wave pattern left on the water's surface by a moving ship **2** turbulent air left behind a moving aircraft, etc. **3 in the wake of** following; as a result of [LGer fr. ON]

wake′ful *adj.* **1** unable to sleep **2** sleepless **3** vigilant —**wake′ful·ly** *adv.*; **wake′ful·ness** *n.*

wak·en /wā′kən/ *v.* make or become awake [OE, rel. to WAKE[1]]

Wald·heim /vōld′hīm′/, **Kurt** 1918– ; Austrian politician and diplomat; president (1986–92); Secretary-General of the United Nations (1972–82)

wale /wāl/ *n.* **1** WEAL[1] **2** ridge on corduroy, etc. —*v.* (**waled, wal·ing**) **3** mark with wales [OE]

Wales /wālz/ *n.* division of the United Kingdom, W of England. Chief city: Cardiff. Pop. 2,719,200

● Usage: See note at GREAT BRITAIN.

Wa·łe·sa /vəlen′sə, -wen′-/, **Lech** 1943– ; Polish activist and politician; president (1990–)

walk /wôk/ *v.* **1** travel or go on foot, esp. at a moderate pace **b** go with the slowest gait, as a horse or dog **2** tread the floor or surface of **3** cause to walk with one (*walk the dog*) **4** *Baseball.* advance a batter or as a batter to first base after four balls are pitched —*n.* **5a** act of walking; the ordinary human gait **b** slowest gait of an animal **c** person's manner of walking **6a** distance walked **b** excursion on foot **7** place or track intended or suitable for walking **8** way of life or occupation **9** *Baseball.* four pitched balls advancing a batter to first base **10 walk all over:** *Colloq.* **a** defeat easily **b** take advantage of **11 walk away** (or **off**) **with:** *Colloq.* **a** steal **b** take or win easily **12 walk on air** feel elated **13 walk out: a** depart suddenly or angrily **b** stop work in protest **14 walk out on** desert; abandon —**walk′a·ble** *adj.*

walk′er *n.* **1** one who walks **2a** framework in which a baby can walk unaided **b** tubular metal frame to help the disabled or elderly to walk

walk·ie-talk·ie /wô′kē tô′kē/ *n.* two-way radio carried on the person

walk′ing stick′ *n.* stick carried for support when walking

Walk·man /wôk′mən, -man′/ *n.* (*pl.* **-mans**) *Tdmk.* type of portable stereo with headphones

walk′ of life′ *n.* occupation; profession

walk·'on' *n.* nonspeaking dramatic role

walk·'out' *n.* work stoppage or strike

walk·'up' *n.* apartment in a building with no elevator

walk·'way' *n.* passage or path (esp. raised) for walking

wall /wôl/ *n.* 1 vertical structure of usu. brick or stone, esp. enclosing or dividing a space or supporting a roof —*v.* 2 surround, block off, or enclose with a wall 3 go to the wall forced into a final stand 4 off the wall *Slang.* unorthodox 5 up the wall *Colloq.* crazy; furious —**walled, wall·'less** *adj.* [L *vallum* rampart]

wal·la·by /wäl'əbē/ *n.* (*pl.* ·bies) small kangaroo [Aborig]

Wal·lace /wäl'əs/, **Alfred Russell** 1823–1913; British naturalist

wall·'board' *n.* rigid composite or fibrous material made in panels, used for walls and ceilings

wal·let /wäl'it/ *n.* small, flat case for holding money, identification, etc. [AngFr]

wall·eye /wôl'ī'/ *n.* 1 eye with a streaked or opaque white iris 2 eye squinting outward 3 N American pike —**wall·'eyed'** /-īd/ *adj.* [ON]

wall·'flow'er *n. Colloq.* person sitting out a dance for lack of partners

Wal·loon /wälōōn'/ *n.* 1 member of a French-speaking people inhabiting S and E Belgium 2 French dialect spoken by this people [OHGer *wahl* foreigner]

wal·lop /wäl'əp/ *Colloq. v.* 1 thrash; beat —*n.* 2 heavy blow [Fr *waloper* fr. Gmc, rel. to GALLOP]

wal·low /wäl'ō/ *v.* 1 roll about in mud, etc. 2 indulge in unrestrained pleasure, misery, etc. —*n.* 3 act of wallowing 4 place used for wallowing [OE]

wall·'pa'per *n.* 1 decorative paper for pasting on to interior walls 2 trivial background noise, music, etc. —*v.* 3 decorate with wallpaper

Wall' Street' *n.* financial markets of the US considered as a group [fr. their center on and near *Wall St.*, New York City]

wall·'-to-wall' *adj.* 1 covering a whole room, etc. 2 *Colloq.* ubiquitous

wal·nut /wôl'nət'/ *n.* 1 tree with aromatic leaves and drooping catkins 2 edible nut of this tree 3 its timber [OE: foreign nut]

Wal·pole /wôl'pōl'/, **Horace (4th Earl of Orford)** 1717–97; English writer

wal·rus /wôl'rəs/ *n.* (*pl.* same or ·**rus·es**) large, amphibious, long-tusked, arctic mammal [Du: whale horse]

Wal·ton /wôlt'n/, **Izaak** 1593–1683; English writer

waltz /wôl(t)s/ *n.* 1 ballroom dance in 3/4 time performed by couples 2 music for this —*v.* 3 dance a waltz 4 *Colloq.* move easily, casually, etc. [Ger *Walzer* fr. *walzen* roll; dance]

wam·pum /wäm'pəm/ *n. Hist.* beads made from shells and strung together for use as money, decoration, etc., by N American Indians [Algonquian]

wan /wän/ *adj.* (**wan·ner, wan·nest**) pale; exhausted-looking —**wan'ly** *adv.*; **wan'ness** *n.* [OE: dark]

wand /wänd/ *n.* 1 rod used by a magician, etc. 2 staff as a symbol of office [ON]

wan·der /wän'dər/ *v.* 1 go aimlessly from place to place 2a wind about; meander b stray from a path, etc. 3 talk or think incoherently —**wan'der·er** *n.* [OE, rel. to WEND]

wan'der·lust' *n.* urge for traveling or wandering; restlessness [Ger]

wane /wän/ *v.* (**waned, wan·ing**) 1 (of the moon) decrease in apparent size 2 decrease in power, vigor, etc. —*n.* 3 process of waning 4 on the wane diminishing; declining [OE]

wan·gle /waNG'gəl/ *v.* (·**gled, ·gling**) *Colloq.* contrive to obtain

Wan·kel /väNG'kəl/, **Felix** 1902–88; German engineer

wan·na·be /wän'əbē', wôn'-/ *n. Slang.* anybody who would like to be someone or something else, esp. a fan emulating an admired person [corruption of *want to be*]

want /wônt, wänt/ *v.* 1a desire; wish for; need b require to be attended to 2 lack 3 be without or fall short of 4 seek for, as by the police —*n.* 5 lack; deficiency 6 poverty; need 7 craving [ON]

want'ad' *n. Colloq.* newspaper, etc., advertisement for a job opening

want'ing *adj.* 1 lacking; not equal to requirements 2 absent; not supplied

wan·ton /wônt'n, wänt'n/ *adj.* 1 licentious 2 capricious; arbitrary 3 luxuriant; unrestrained —*n.* 4 licentious person —**wan'ton·ly** *adv.*; **wan'ton·ness** *n.* [OE *wan* not, *teon* disciplined]

wa·pi·ti /wäp'ətē/ *n.* (*pl.* ·**tis**) N American deer; elk [Cree Indian]

war /wôr/ *n.* 1a armed hostilities esp. between nations; conflict b specific instance or period of this 2 hostility or contention between people, groups, etc. 3 sustained campaign against crime, poverty, etc. —*v.* (**warred, war·ring**) 4 rival; fight 5 make war 6 at war engaged in a war 7 go to war declare or begin a war [AngFr fr. Gmc]

war·ble /wôr'bəl/ *v.* (·**bled, ·bling**) 1 sing or speak in a gentle, trilling manner —*n.* 2 warbled song or utterance [ME *werble*]

war·bler /wôr'blər/ *n.* bird that warbles

ward /wôrd/ *n.* 1 section of a hospital, jail, etc. 2 administrative division of a city or town, esp. an electoral district 3 person under the care of a guardian or court 4 (*pl.*) corresponding notches and projections in a key and a lock 5 *Archaic.* guardian's control 6 ward off parry; avert; fend off [OE]

-ward *suffix* (also **-wards**) added to nouns of place or destination and to adverbs of direction, specifying direction in which action occurs or to which action tends [OE]

war·den /wôrd'n/ *n.* supervising official, esp. of a prison [AngFr and Fr, rel. to GUARDIAN]

ward·er /wôr'dər/ *n.* watchman; caretaker [ME]

ward'heel'er *n.* minor worker for a politician or political machine

ward·robe /wôrd'rōb'/ *n.* 1 large cupboard for storing clothes 2 stock of clothes, esp. of an individual or a theater company [ME]

ward'room' *n.* mess in a warship for commissioned officers

ware /wer/ *n.* 1 things of a specified kind,

usu. made for sale (*chinaware; hardware*) **2** (usu. *pl.*) articles for sale **3** ceramics, etc., of a specified kind [OE]

ware'house' *n.* **1** building in which goods are stored —*v.* (·**housed**, ·**hous·ing**) **2** (also /-houz'/) store, esp. temporarily, in a warehouse

war'fare' *n.* waging war; campaigning

war'head' *n.* explosive head of a missile

War·hol /wôr'hôl', -hōl'/, **Andy** 1930–87; US painter and graphic artist

war'horse' *n. Colloq.* veteran soldier, politician, etc.

war·i·ly /wer'əlē/ *adv.* with caution

war'like' *adj.* **1** hostile **2** soldierly

war'lock' *n.* sorcerer [OE: oathbreaker]

war'lord' *n.* military commander, esp. in a warlike nation

warm /wôrm/ *adj.* **1** of or at a fairly high temperature **2** giving or retaining warmth **3a** sympathetic; friendly **b** enthusiastic **4** *Colloq.* **a** close to an object sought **b** near to guessing **5** (of a scent) fresh and strong —*v.* **6** make warm **7** warm oneself **8** become animated or sympathetic **9** **warm up: a** become or become warm **b** prepare for a performance, etc. **c** reach a temperature for efficient working **d** reheat (food) —**warm'er** *n.*; **warm'ish** *adj.*; **warm'ly** *adv.*; **warmth** *n.* [OE]

warm'-blood'ed *adj.* having blood temperature well above that of the environment

warmed'o'ver /wôrmd'/ *adj.* reheated, or as if reheated (as ideas, etc.)

warm'front' *n. Meteorol.* advancing edge of a mass of warm air

warm'heart'ed *adj.* kind; friendly —**warm'heart'ed·ness** *n.*

war·mon·ger /wôr'mäNG'gər, -məNG'gər/ *n.* person who promotes war —**war'mon'ger·ing** *n.* & *adj.*

warm'up' *n.* period of preparatory exercise

warn /wôrn/ *v.* **1a** inform of danger, etc. **b** advise or inform **2** admonish [OE]

warn'ing *n.* **1** act of one who warns **2** thing that warns [OE]

warp /wôrp/ *v.* **1a** make or become distorted **b** make or become perverted or strange —*n.* **2a** warped state, esp. of timber **b** mental distortion or idiosyncrasy **3** lengthwise threads in a loom [OE]

war'path' *n.* as in **on the warpath: 1** going to war **2** *Colloq.* seeking a confrontation **3** *Colloq.* furious

war·rant /wôr'ənt, wär'-/ *n.* **1** authorization; justification **2** written authorization allowing police to search premises, arrest a suspect, etc. —*v.* **3** justify **4** guarantee; attest to [Fr *warant*, fr. Gmc]

war'rant'of'fi·cer *n. Milit.* officer ranking below commissioned officers and above NCOs

war·ran·ty /wôr'əntē, wär'-/ *n.* (*pl.* ·**ties**) guarantee of the ownership or quality of a thing sold, etc., often accepting responsibility for defects or repairs over a specified period [AngFr *warantie*, rel. to WARRANT]

● Usage: *Guarantee* and *guaranty* are interchangeable for both **noun** and **verb**. Many manufacturers **use** *warranty* in their place. *Warrantee* means the 'person to whom a warranty is made'; it is not a spelling variant of *warranty*.

war·ren /wôr'ən, wär'-/ *n.* **1** network of rabbit burrows **2** densely populated or labyrinthine building or district [AngFr *warenne* fr. Gmc]

War·ren /wôr'ən, wär'-/ *n.* city in Mich. Pop. 144,864

War·ren /wôr'ən, wär'-/, **Earl** 1891–1974; US politician; Chief Justice of Supreme Court (1953–69)

war·ri·or /wôr'ēər, wär'-/ *n.* person experienced or distinguished in fighting; soldier [ME *werreior*, rel. to WAR]

War·saw /wôr'sô'/ *n.* capital of Poland. Pop. 1,654,500

war'ship' *n.* ship used in war

wart /wôrt/ *n.* **1** small, hard, round growth on the skin **2** protuberance on the surface of a plant, etc. —**wart'y** *adj.* (·**i·er**, ·**i·est**) [OE]

wart'hog' *n.* African wild pig

war·y /wer'ē/ *adj.* (·**i·er**, ·**i·est**) **1** on one's guard; circumspect **2** cautious —**war'i·ness** *n.* [*ware* look out for; avoid]

was /wəz, wäs/ *v.* *1st* and *3rd sing.* *past* of BE

wash /wäSH, wôSH/ *v.* **1** cleanse with liquid, esp. water **2a** remove (a stain) in this way **b** (of a stain, etc.) be removed by washing **3** wash oneself **4** wash clothes, dishes, etc. **5** (of an argument, etc.) stand scrutiny; be believed or acceptable **6** (of a river, etc.) touch **7** carry along or away (*was washed overboard*) **8** sweep; move; splash **9** sift (ore) by the action of water **10** brush watery paint or ink over **11** moisten; water —*n.* **12** washing **13** clothes, etc., to be or just washed **14** motion of agitated water or air, esp. from the passage of a ship or aircraft **15** surge of water **16** liquid to spread over a surface to cleanse, heal, or color **17** thin coating of watercolor **18** **come out in the wash** *Colloq.* be resolved in the course of time **19** **wash down: a** wash completely **b** accompany or follow (food) with a drink **20** **wash one's hands of** renounce responsibility for —**wash'a·ble** *adj.* [OE]

Wash. abbr. for Washington

wash'-and-wear' *adj.* describing clothing that does not require ironing

wash'board' *n.* ribbed board on which clothes are scrubbed

wash'cloth' *n.* small square of toweling used to wash

washed'out' /wäSHt, wôSHt/ *adj.* (also **washed'-out'**) **1** faded; pale **2** *Colloq.* pale; exhausted **3** *Colloq.* rained out

washed'up' *adj.* (also **washed'-up'**) *Slang.* defeated; having failed

wash'er *n.* **1** person or machine that washes **2** flat ring inserted at a joint to tighten and prevent leakage, or under the head of a screw, etc., to disperse its pressure

wash'er·wom'an *n.* (*pl.* ·**wom'en**) woman who launders clothing, esp. as a business

wash'ing *n.* clothes, etc., to be or just washed

wash'ing ma·chine' *n.* machine for washing clothes

Wash·ing·ton /wäSH'iNGtən, wôSH'-/ *n.* NW state of the US. Capital: Olympia. Pop. 4,866,692. Abbr. **WA**; **Wash.** —**Wash'ing·ton'i·an** /-tō'nēən/ *n.* & *adj.*

Wash·ing·ton /wǒsHˈiNGtən, wôsHˈ-/ 1
George 1732–99; American patriot, general,
and 1st US president (1789–97) 2 Booker T.
1856–1915; US reformer, educator, and writer

Wash·ing·ton, D.C. *n.* capital of the United
States of America, coextensive with the District of Columbia, between Md. and Va. Pop.
606,900

Wash·ing·ton, Mt. *n.* peak in the White
Mountains of N. Hamp.; highest in northeastern US: 6,288 ft.

wash′out′ *n.* 1 *Colloq.* complete failure 2 area
where soil, a bridge, etc., has been washed
away

wash′room′ *n.* bathroom

wash′stand′ *n.* piece of furniture to hold a basin, jug, soap, etc.

wash′y *adj.* (·i·er, ·i·est) WISHY-WASHY
—**wash′i·ly** *adv.*; **wash′i·ness** *n.*

was·n′t /wǒzˈənt, wäzˈ-/ *v. contr.* was not

WASP

wasp /wäsp, wôsp/ *n.* stinging insect with a
narrow waist [OE]

Wasp or **WASP** *n.* White Anglo-Saxon Protestant [abbr.]

wasp′ish *adj.* irritable; snappish

was·sail /wäsˈəl, wäsˈāl/ *n.* 1 festive occasion
2 spiced ale or cider with which toasts, etc.,
were formerly drunk —*v.* 3 make merry;
toast [ON *ves heill* be in health, rel. to WHOLE]

wast·age /wāˈstij/ *n.* 1 amount wasted 2 loss
by use, wear, or leakage

waste /wāst/ *v.* (**wast·ed, wast·ing**) 1 use
to no purpose or extravagantly 2 fail to use 3
(often *passive*) fail to be appreciated or used
properly 4 wear gradually away; make or become weak 5 devastate 6 *Slang.* kill —*adj.*
7 superfluous 8 not inhabited or cultivated
—*n.* 9 act of wasting 10 waste material 11
waste region 12 bodily excretions 13 go to
waste be wasted 14 lay waste (to) destroy;
devastate [L, rel. to VAST]

waste′bas′ket *n.* (also **waste′pa′per bas′
ket**) receptacle for wastepaper

wast′ed *adj. Slang.* under the influence of
drugs or alcohol

waste·ful /wāstˈfəl/ *adj.* 1 extravagant 2
causing or showing waste —**waste′ful·ly**
adv.; **waste′ful·ness** *n.*

waste′land′ *n.* unproductive or useless area of
land, period of time, etc.

waste′pa′per *n.* used or valueless paper

wast·rel /wāˈstrəl/ *n.* good-for-nothing person

watch /wǒCH, wôCH/ *v.* 1 keep the eyes fixed
on 2 keep under observation 3 be in an alert
state; be vigilant 4 look after; take care of
—*n.* 5 small, portable timepiece for the wrist

or pocket 6 state of alert or constant observation or attention 7 *Naut.* a usu. four-hour
spell of duty b ship's crew on watch 8 guard;
security officer 9 watch it (or oneself) *Colloq.* be careful 10 watch out be on one's
guard —**watch′er** *n.* [OE, rel. to WAKE¹]

watch′band′ *n.* band for holding a watch on
the wrist

watch′dog′ *n.* 1 dog guarding property, etc. 2
person or organization monitoring others'
rights, etc.

watch·ful /wǒCHˈfəl, wôCHˈ-/ *adj.* alert; on
the watch —**watch′ful·ly** *adv.*; **watch′ful·
ness** *n.*

watch·man /wǒCHˈmən/ *n.* (*pl.* ·men) man
employed to look after a building, etc., esp. at
night

watch′tow′er *n.* tower for keeping watch, esp.
for fires

watch′word′ *n.* phrase summarizing a guiding
principle

wa·ter /wôˈtər, wätˈər/ *n.* 1 colorless, transparent, liquid compound of oxygen and hydrogen 2 liquid consisting chiefly of this found in
seas, rivers, and rain 3 expanse of water 4
(*pl.*) part of a sea or river 5 (often *pl.*) mineral
water at a spa, etc. 6 state of a tide 7a amniotic fluid, released during labor b other
bodily secretions, esp. urine —*v.* 8 sprinkle
or soak with water 9 supply (a plant or animal) with water 10 secrete water 11 (of silk,
etc.) finish with wavy, glossy markings 12
take on a supply of water 13 drink 14 hold
water be supportable, as a theory, etc. 15
make one's mouth water cause salivation or
anticipation [OE]

wa′ter bed′ or **wa′ter·bed′** *n.* mattress filled
with water

wa′ter buf′fa·lo *n.* common domestic S Asian
buffalo

Wa·ter·bur·y /wôtˈərber′ē, wätˈ-/ *n.* city in
Conn. Pop. 108,961

wa′ter chest′nut *n.* nutlike tuber from a
sedge, used esp. in Chinese cooking

wa′ter clos′et *n.* TOILET, 1a

wa′ter·col′or *n.* 1 pigment diluted with water
2 picture painted with this —**wa′ter·col′or·
ist** *n.*

wa′ter-cooled′ *adj.* cooled by the circulation
of water

wa′ter·course′ *n.* 1 brook or stream 2 bed or
channel of this

wa′ter·craft′ *n.* (*pl.* same) any water vehicle

wa′ter·cress′ *n.* pungent edible plant growing
in running water

wa′ter·fall′ *n.* water flowing over a precipice
or down a steep hillside

wa′ter·fowl′ *n.* (usu. as *pl.*) swimming birds

wa′ter·front′ *n.* part of a town along a harbor,
river, etc.

wa′ter glass′ *n.* 1 solution of sodium or potassium silicate 2 glass for drinking water

wa′ter hole′ *n.* small pond, as for swimming
or fishing

wa′ter·ing hole′ *n. Slang.* bar

wa′ter lil′y *n.* (*pl.* ·ies) aquatic plant with
floating leaves and flowers

wa′ter·line′ *n.* line along which the surface of
water touches a ship's side

wa′ter·logged′ *adj.* saturated or filled with water

Wa·ter·loo /wôˈtərlōō, wätˈ-/ *n.* decisive defeat or contest [*Waterloo*, Belgium, where Napoleon was defeated]

wa'ter main' *n.* main pipe in a water-supply system

wa·ter·man /wô'tərmən, wät'-/ *n.* (*pl.* ·men) man who earns his living on the water, esp. a fisherman, etc.

wa'ter·mark' *n.* 1 faint, identifying design in some paper —*v.* 2 mark with this

wa'ter·mel'on *n.* large, dark green melon with sweet, juicy red pulp

wa'ter moc'ca·sin *n.* poisonous water snake of the SE US

wa'ter pipe' *n.* 1 pipe that carries water 2 hookah

wa'ter po'lo *n.* ball game played by swimmers

wa'ter pow'er *n.* mechanical force derived from the weight or motion of water

wa'ter·proof' *adj.* 1 impervious to water —*v.* 2 make waterproof

wa'ter rat' *n.* aquatic rodent

wa'ter·re·pel'lent *adj.* partially waterproof

wa'ter·shed' *n.* 1 line of separation between waters flowing to different rivers, etc. 2 turning point in affairs [fr. *shed* ridge]

wa'ter ski' *n.* 1 ski, often of a pair, for skimming the surface of the water when towed by a motor boat —*v.* 2 (**wa'ter·ski'**, **-skied**, **-ski·ing**) travel on water skis —**wa'ter·ski'er** *n.*

wa'ter·spout' *n.* whirling column of water and spray between sea and cloud

wa'ter ta'ble *n.* highest level of saturation of ground water

wa'ter·tight' *adj.* 1 closely fastened or fitted so as to prevent the passage of water 2 (of an argument, etc.) unassailable

wa'ter tow'er *n.* tower with an elevated tank to store and distribute water

wa'ter·way' *n.* navigable channel

wa'ter wheel' *n.* wheel driven by the weight or motion of water

wa'ter wings' *n. pl.* inflated floats for a person learning to swim

wa'ter·works' *n.* water-supply system for a city, district, etc.

wa'ter·y *adj.* 1 containing too much water; overly dilute 2 of or consisting of water 3 vapid; uninteresting 4 moist; tearful —**wa'ter·i·ness** *n.*

WATS *abbr.* Wide-Area Telecommunications Service

Wat·son /wät'sən/, **James Dewey** 1928– ; US biologist; Nobel prize 1962

watt /wät/ *n.* unit of electrical power, equivalent to one joule per second [for J. WATT]

Watt /wät/, **James** 1736–1819; Scottish engineer and inventor

watt·age /wät'ij/ *n.* amount of electrical power expressed in watts

Wat·teau /wätō'/, **Jean Antoine** 1684–1721; French painter

wat·tle¹ /wät'l/ *n.* 1 structure of interlaced rods and sticks used for fences, etc. —*v.* (·tled, ·tling) 2 interlace or build with wattle [OE]

wat·tle² *n.* fleshy appendage on the head or throat of a turkey or other birds

Waugh /wô/, **Evelyn** 1903–66; English novelist

wave /wāv/ *v.* (**waved, wav·ing**) 1a move a

---

hand to and fro in greeting or as a signal b move (a hand, etc.) in this way 2 move in a to and fro, sinuous, or sweeping manner 3 direct (a person) by waving 4 express (a greeting, etc.) by waving 5 give an undulating form to (hair, etc.) —*n.* 6 ridge of water between two depressions 7 such a ridge curling into an arch and breaking on the shore 8 fluctuating motion, etc. 9 gesture of waving 10 undulating form, as in the hair 11a *Physics.* disturbance of the particles of a medium for the propagation or direction of motion, heat, light, sound, etc. b single curve in this motion 12 **make waves** *Colloq.* cause trouble [OE]

Wave /wāv/ *n.* member of the WAVES

wave'·form' *n.* curve showing the shape of a wave at a given time

wave'length' *n.* 1 distance between successive crests of a wave 2 *Colloq.* particular mode or range of thought

wave'let *n.* small wave

wa·ver /wā'vər/ *v.* 1 be or become unsteady 2 be irresolute 3 flicker; falter [ON, rel. to WAVE]

WAVES /wāvz/ *abbr.* Women Appointed for Voluntary Emergency Service, former women's branch of the US Navy

wav'y *adj.* (·i·er, ·i·est) having waves or alternate contrary curves —**wav'i·ness** *n.*

wax¹ /waks/ *n.* 1 sticky, plastic, yellowish substance secreted by bees 2 this used for candles, modeling, etc. 3 any similar substance, e.g., the yellow substance secreted by the ear —*v.* 4 cover or treat with wax 5 remove unwanted hair from (legs, etc.) using wax —**wax'y** *adj.* (·i·er, ·i·est) [OE]

wax² *v.* 1 (of the moon) increase in apparent size 2 become larger or stronger 3 pass into a specified state or mood 4 **wax and wane** undergo alternate increases and decreases [OE]

wax' bean' *n.* variety of string bean with waxy, pale yellow pods

wax·en /wak'sən/ *adj.* of, consisting of, or like wax

wax' mu·se'um *n.* exhibit of life-sized wax figures of historical persons, celebrities, etc.

wax' pa'per *n.* (also **waxed' pa'per**) coated paper for kitchen use

wax'wing' *n.* any of various birds with tips like red sealing wax on some wing-feathers

wax'work' *n.* 1 object, esp. a lifelike dummy, modeled in wax 2 (*pl.*) exhibition of wax dummies

way /wā/ *n.* 1 road, track, path, etc. 2 course or route for reaching a place 3 method or plan for attaining an object 4 style; manner 5 person's chosen or habitual course of action 6 normal course of events 7 traveling distance 8 unimpeded opportunity or space to advance (**make way**) 9 impetus; progress 10 specified direction 11 *Colloq.* scope; range 12 specified condition 13 respect (*useful in some ways*) 14 (*pl.*) part into which a thing is divided (*split it three ways*) 15 (*pl.*) structure of timber down which a ship is launched —*adv.* 16 *Colloq.* far 17 **by the way** incidentally 18 **by way of: a** by means of **b** as a form of **c** passing through 19 **give way** yield

20 go out of one's way make a special effort **21** lead the way act as guide or leader **22** under way in progress; advancing [OE]

way'far·er *n.* traveler, esp. on foot —**way'far'ing** *n. & adj.*

way'lay' *v.* (·laid, ·lay·ing) **1** lie in wait for **2** stop to talk to or rob

Wayne /wān/ **1 Anthony** (called **"Mad Anthony"**) 1745–96; US general during the American Revolution **2 John** (born **Marion Michael Morrison**) 1907–79; US actor

way'-out' *adj.* unusual; eccentric

-ways *suffix* forming adjectives and adverbs of direction or manner (*sideways*)

ways' and means' *n. pl.* methods of achieving something, esp. of raising government funds

way'side' *n.* side of a road

way'ward /wā'wərd/ *adj.* self-willed; capricious —**way'ward·ness** *n.* [fr. AWAY, -WARD]

we /wē/ *pron.* (*obj.* **us**; *poss.* **our, ours**) **1** *pl.* of first-person pronoun **2** used for or by a royal person, an editor, etc., when speaking formally or for a group [OE]

weak /wēk/ *adj.* **1** deficient in strength, power, vigor, resolution, or number **2** unconvincing **3** *Gram.* (of a verb) forming inflections by the addition of a suffix to the stem —**weak'ish** *adj.* [ON]

weak'en *v.* make or become weak or weaker

weak'-kneed' *adj.* lacking resolution

weak'ling *n.* feeble person or animal

weak'ly *adv.* **1** in a weak manner —*adj.* (·li·er, ·li·est) **2** sickly; not robust

weak'-mind'ed *adj.* **1** mentally deficient **2** lacking in resolution —**weak'-mind'ed·ly** *adv.*; **weak'-mind'ed·ness** *n.*

weak' mo'ment *n.* time when one is unusually compliant or susceptible

weak'ness *n.* **1** being weak **2** weak point **3** self-indulgent liking (*weakness for chocolate*)

weal[1] /wēl/ *n.* **1** ridge raised on the flesh by a stroke of a rod or whip —*v.* **2** mark with a weal [var. of WALE]

weal[2] *n.* *Lit.* or *Archaic.* welfare [OE]

wealth /welTH/ *n.* **1** riches **2** being rich **3** abundance [OE]

wealth'y *adj.* (·i·er, ·i·est) having an abundance, esp. of money

wean /wēn/ *v.* **1** accustom (an infant or other young mammal) to food other than (esp. its mother's) milk **2** disengage (from a habit, etc.) [OE: accustom]

weap·on /wep'ən/ *n.* **1** thing designed, used, or usable for inflicting bodily harm **2** means for gaining the advantage in a conflict —**weap'on·less** *adj.*

weap·on·ry /wep'ənrē/ *n.* weapons collectively

wear /wer/ *v.* (**wore, worn, wear·ing**) **1** have on one's person as clothing or an ornament, etc. **2** exhibit or present (a facial expression, etc.) **3a** injure the surface of, or partly obliterate or alter, by rubbing, stress, or use **b** undergo such injury or change **4** rub or be rubbed off **5** (often foll. by *out* or *down*) exhaust; overcome by persistence **6** (foll. by *well*, etc.) endure continued use or life —*n.* **7** wearing or being worn **8** things worn; clothing (*sportswear*) **9** damage from continuous use, etc. **10** wear off lose effectiveness or intensity —**wear'a·ble** *adj.*; **wear'er** *n.* [OE]

wear' and tear' *n.* WEAR, 9

wea·ri·some /wē'rēsəm/ *adj.* tedious; tiring by monotony or length —**wea'ri·some·ly** *adv.*

wea·ry /wēr'ē/ *adj.* (·ri·er, ·ri·est) **1** very tired **2** no longer interested in **3** tiring; tedious —*v.* (·ried, ·ry·ing) **4** make or grow weary —**wea'ri·ly** *adv.*; **wea'ri·ness** *n.* [OE]

wea·sel /wē'zəl/ *n.* **1** small, flesh-eating mammal related to the stoat and ferret —*v.* **2** avoid, esp. a decision or commitment —**wea'sel·ly** *adj.* [OE]

weath·er /weTH'ər/ *n.* **1** state of the atmosphere at a place and time as regards heat, cloudiness, wind, rain, etc. —*adj.* **2** designating the windward side —*v.* **3** expose to or affect by atmospheric changes **4** be discolored or worn in this way **5** come safely through (a storm, difficult period, etc.) **6** under the weather *Colloq.* indisposed; ill [OE]

weath'er-beat'en *adj.* affected by exposure to the weather

weath'er·cock' *n.* weather vane in the form of a rooster

weath'er·ize' *v.* (·ized, ·iz·ing) insulate or otherwise protect (esp. a building) from the weather

weath'er·man' *n.* meteorologist, esp. one who broadcasts a weather forecast

weath'er·proof' *adj.* resistant to the effects of bad weather, esp. rain or snow

weath'er·strip' *n.* **1** (also **weath'er·strip'ping**) thin sealing material placed at the edges of doors, windows, etc., to protect from drafts, etc. —*v.* (·stripped, ·strip·ping) **2** install weather strips

weath'er·vane' *n.* **1** revolving pointer on a church spire, etc., to show the direction of the wind **2** inconstant person

WEAVE[1] 1a

weave[1] /wēv/ *v.* (**wove, wo·ven** or **wove, weav·ing**) **1a** form (fabric) by interlacing long threads in two directions **b** interlace straw, etc., in this way **2** spin (as a spider or insect does) **3** make (facts, etc.) into a story or connected whole —*n.* **4** style of weaving —**weav'er** *n.* [OE]

weave[2] *v.* (**weaved, weav·ing**) move repeatedly from side to side [OE]

web /web/ *n.* **1** woven fabric **2** complex series (*web of lies*) **3** cobweb, gossamer, or a similar product of a spider, etc. **4** membrane between the toes of a swimming animal or bird **5** large roll of paper used in printing —**webbed** *adj.* [OE]

web'bing *n.* strong, narrow, closely woven fabric used for belts, etc.

we·ber /web'ər, vā'bər/ *n.* unit of magnetic flux [for W.E. *Weber*, German physicist]

We·ber /vā'bər/, **Max** 1864–1920; German economist

web-foot·ed /web'fŏŏt'əd/ *adj.* having the toes connected by webs

Web·ster /web'stər/ **1** Noah 1758–1843; US lexicographer **2** Daniel 1782–1852; US politician, orator, and lawyer

wed /wed/ *v.* (**wed·ded** or **wed, wed·ding**) **1** marry **2** unite [OE: pledge]

Wed. *abbr.* Wednesday

we'd /wēd/ *v. contr.* **1** we had **2** we should; we would

wed·ded /wed'əd/ *adj.* **1** married **2** obstinately attached (to)

Wed·dell' Sea' /wədel', wed'l/ *n.* arm of the Atlantic E of the Antarctic Peninsula

wed·ding *n.* marriage ceremony [OE, rel. to WED]

WEDGE 1

wedge /wej/ *n.* **1** piece of tapering wood or metal, etc., driven between two objects or parts to secure or separate them **2** anything resembling a wedge —*v.* (**wedged, wedging**) **3** secure or fasten with a wedge **4** force open or apart with a wedge **5** pack or thrust (a thing or oneself) tightly in or into [OE]

Wedg·wood /wej'wŏŏd/, **Josiah** 1730–95; English potter

wed'lock *n.* the married state [OE, rel. to WED]

Wednes·day /wenz'dā, -dē/ *n.* day of the week following Tuesday; *abbr.* **Wed., W** [OE]

wee /wē/ *adj.* (**we·er** /wē'ər/, **we·est** /wē'ist/) **1** little; tiny **2** of very early morning (*wee hours*) [OE]

weed /wēd/ *n.* **1** wild plant growing where it is not wanted **2** *Slang.* **a** marijuana **b** cigarette —*v.* **3** clear (an area) of weeds **4a** sort out and remove (inferior or unwanted parts, etc.) **b** rid of inferior parts, unwanted members, etc. —**weed'er** *n.*; **weed'less** *adj.* [OE]

weeds /wēdz/ *n. pl.* deep mourning clothes [OE: garment]

weed'y *adj.* (**·i·er, ·i·est**) **1** of or like a weed **2** having many weeds

week /wēk/ *n.* **1** period of seven days, esp. one reckoned from midnight on Saturday **2a** the five days Monday to Friday **b** time spent working in this period [OE]

week'day' *n.* day other than Sunday and usu. Saturday

week'end' *n.* **1** Saturday and Sunday **2** this period extended slightly, esp. for a holiday, etc. —*v.* **3** spend the weekend

week'ly *adj.* **1** done, produced, or occurring once a week —*adv.* **2** once a week —*n.* (*pl.* **·lies**) **3** weekly newspaper or periodical

week'night' *n.* night of a weekday

weep /wēp/ *v.* (**wept, weep·ing**) **1** shed tears **2** bewail; lament over **3** exude liquid **4** (of a tree) have drooping branches —**weep'**

er *n.*; **weep'ing, weep'y** *adj.* (**·i·er, ·i·est**) [OE]

wee·vil /wē'vəl/ *n.* destructive beetle feeding on grain, cotton, etc. [LGer]

weft /weft/ *n.* (also **woof**) threads woven across a warp to make fabric [OE, rel. to WEAVE[1]]

weigh /wā/ *v.* **1** find the weight of **2** measure out (a specified weight) **3** compare **4** be equal to (a specified weight) **5** consider carefully **6** exert an influence **7** be heavy or burdensome (to) **8 weigh anchor** *Naut.* raise anchor **9 weigh down** bring down; be oppressive to [OE: carry]

weight /wāt/ *n.* **1** force experienced by a body as a result of the earth's gravitation **2** heaviness of a body **3** quantitative expression of weight **4** body of a known weight for use in weighing or weightlifting **5** heavy body, esp. as used in a mechanism, etc. **6** load; burden **7** influence; importance —*v.* **8a** attach a weight to **b** hold down with a weight **9** impede; burden [OE]

weight'less *adj.* not apparently acted on by gravity —**weight'less·ness** *n.*

weight'lift'ing *n.* sport or exercise of lifting heavy weights —**weight'lift'er** *n.*

weight'y *adj.* (**·i·er, ·i·est**) **1** heavy **2** momentous **3** burdening **4** influential; authoritative —**weight'i·ly** *adv.*; **weight'i·ness** *n.*

Weill /wīl, vīl/, **Kurt** 1900–50; German composer

weir /wēr/ *n.* **1** dam across a river to raise the level of water or regulate its flow **2** fish trap, esp. one like a fence [OE]

weird /wērd/ *adj.* **1** uncanny; supernatural **2** *Colloq.* incomprehensible; strange —**weird'ly** *adv.*; **weird'ness** *n.* [OE *wyrd* destiny]

weird·o /wēr'dō/ *n.* (*pl.* **·os**) *Slang.* odd or eccentric person

Weiz·mann /wīts'mən, vīts'-/, **Chaim** 1874–1952; first president of Israel (1949–52)

wel·come /wel'kəm/ *n.* **1** act of greeting or receiving gladly; kind or glad reception —*interj.* **2** expressing such a greeting —*v.* (**·comed, ·com·ing**) **3** receive with a welcome —*adj.* **4** received with pleasure **5** allowed; invited [OE]

weld /weld/ *v.* **1a** hammer or press (heated pieces of metal) into one piece **b** join by fusion with an electric arc, etc. **c** form by welding into some article **2** unite; join —*n.* **3** welded joint —**weld'a·ble** *adj.*; **weld'er** *n.* [var. of WEAL[2], fr. obs. sense 'boil']

wel·fare /wel'fer'/ *n.* **1** well-being; happiness; health and prosperity **2** financial support given by a government to the unemployed, disadvantaged, etc. **3 on welfare** receiving government support [fr. WELL[1], FARE]

wel·kin /wel'kin/ *n. Poet.* sky [OE: cloud]

we'll /wēl/ *v. contr.* we shall; we will

well[1] /wel/ *adv.* (**bet·ter, best**) **1** in a satisfactory way **2** with some distinction **3** in a kind way **4** thoroughly; carefully **5** with approval (*speak well of*) **6** probably; reasonably **7** to a considerable extent —*adj.* (**bet·ter, best**) **8** in good health **9** satisfactory; advisable —*interj.* **10** expressing surprise, resignation, etc. **11 as well (as)** in addition; along with **12 leave well enough alone** avoid needless change or disturbance [OE]

● Usage: See note at GOOD.

well² n. 1 shaft sunk into the ground to obtain water, oil, etc. **2** enclosed space like a well shaft **3** source **4** small bottle, esp. an inkwell **5** spring or upwelling —v. **6** spring as from a fountain [OE]

well'·ad·vised' adj. prudent

well'·ap·point'ed adj. having all the necessary equipment

well'·bal'anced adj. sane; sensible

well'·be'ing n. state of being contented, healthy, etc.

well'·born' adj. of a good or esteemed family

well'·bred' adj. having or showing good breeding or manners; courteous

well'·dis·posed' adj. friendly; sympathetic

well'·done' adj. cooked completely or thoroughly

well'·fixed' adj. prosperous; wealthy

well'·found'ed adj. based on good evidence

well'·groomed' adj. with carefully tended hair, clothes, etc.

well'·ground'ed adj. knowledgeable about the basics of a subject

well'head' n. source

well'·heeled' adj. Colloq. wealthy

well'·in·formed' adj. having much knowledge or information about a subject

Wel·ling·ton /wel'iNGtən/ n. capital of New Zealand. Pop. 149,600

Wel·ling·ton /wel'iNGtən/, **1st Duke of** 1769–1852; British soldier and statesman

well'·in·ten'tioned adj. having or showing good intentions

well'·known' adj. known to many

well'·mean'ing adj. (also **well'·meant'**) well-intentioned

well'·nigh' adv. almost

well'·off' adj. **1** wealthy **2** in a fortunate situation

well'·pre·served' adj. **1** in good condition **2** showing little sign of age

well'·read' /-red'/ adj. knowledgeable through much reading

well'·round'ed adj. **1** complete and symmetrical **2** having varied talents or abilities

Wells /welz/, **H(erbert) G(eorge)** 1866–1946; English novelist

well'·spo'ken adj. articulate or refined in speech

well'spring n. WELLHEAD

well'·tak'en adj. logical; cogent

well'·to·do' adj. prosperous

well'·worn' adj. **1** much worn by use **2** trite

welsh /welsh/ v. evade an obligation, debt, promise, etc. —**welsh'er** n.

Welsh /welsh/ adj. **1** of or relating to Wales or its people or language —n. **2** the Celtic language of Wales **3** (prec. by *the*; treated as *pl.*) the people of Wales [OE, ult. fr. L *Volcae*, name of a Celtic people]

Welsh' rab'bit n. (also **Welsh' rare'bit**) dish of melted cheese, etc., on toast

welt /welt/ n. **1** leather rim sewn around the edge of a shoe upper attached to the sole **2** WEAL¹

wel·ter /wel'tər/ v. **1** roll; wallow —n. **2** general confusion [LGer or Du]

wel'ter·weight' n. Sports. weight class for competitors; in professional boxing, includes fighters up to 147 lbs.

wen /wen/ n. benign tumor on the skin, esp. on the scalp [OE]

wench /wench/ n. Joc. or Derog. girl or young woman [abbr. of ME *wenchel*, fr. OE *wencel* child]

wend /wend/ v. as in **wend one's way** make one's way [OE: turn]

went /went/ v. past of GO

wept /wept/ v. past of WEEP

we're /wēr/ v. contr. we are

were /wər/ v. 2nd sing. past, pl. past, and past subjunctive of BE

weren't /wər'ənt/ contr. were not

were·wolf /wer'wŏŏlf, wēr'-, wər'-/ n. (pl. ·wolves) mythical being who at times changes from a person to a wolf [OE *wer* man, *wulf* wolf]

Wes·ley /wes'lē, wez'-/, **John** 1703–91; English religious leader; founder of Methodism

west /west/ n. **1a** point of the horizon where the sun sets at the equinoxes **b** compass point corresponding to this **c** direction in which this lies **2** (usu. *cap.*) a European civilization **b** western US and Canada —adj. **3** toward, at, near, or facing the west **4** from the west (*west wind*) —adv. **5** toward, at, or near the west **6** farther west than [OE]

West /west/ **1** Benjamin 1738–1820; US painter **2** Mae 1892–1980; US actress **3** Rebecca (pseudonym of **Cicily Isabel Fairfield**) 1892–1983; English writer

west·er·ly /wes'tərlē/ adj. & adv. **1** in a western position or direction **2** (of a wind) from the west —n. (pl. ·lies) **3** such a wind

west·ern /wes'tərn/ adj. **1** of or in the west —n. **2** movie or novel about cowboys in western N America —**west'ern·most** adj.

west'ern·er n. native or inhabitant of the west

West'ern Hem'i·sphere n. the half of the earth to the west of 0° longitude

west·ern·ize /wes'tərnīz'/ v. (·ized, ·iz·ing) influence with, or convert to, the ideas and customs of the West

West'ern Sa·mo'a n. country in the S Pacific comprising the W Samoan islands. Capital: Apia. Pop. 160,000. See also AMERICAN SAMOA —Sa·mo'an n. & adj.

West' Ger'man·y n. German state created in 1949, under parliamentary government; unified with East Germany in 1990

West' In'dies /in'dēz/ n. numerous islands off the E coast of N and S America, between the Atlantic Ocean and Caribbean Sea

West' Palm' Beach' n. city in Fla. Pop. 67,643

West' Point' n. US Military Academy, in NY state

West' Vir·gin'ia /vərjin'yə/ n. state in the E central US. Capital: Charleston. Pop. 1,793,477. Abbr. WV; W. Va. —**West' Vir·gin'ian** n. & adj.

west·ward /west'wərd/ adj. & adv. (also **westwards**) toward the west

wet /wet/ adj. (**wet·ter, wet·test**) **1** soaked or covered with water or other liquid **2** rainy **3** not yet dried **4** allowing sales of alcohol **5** Colloq. feeble; inept —v. (**wet or wet·ted,**

wet·ting 6 make or become wet —*n.* 7 liquid that wets something 8 rainy weather 9 **wet behind the ears** *Colloq.* immature; inexperienced —**wet'ly** *adv.*; **wet'ness, wet'ter** *n.* [OE]

wet'back' *n. Derog. & Offens.* illegal Mexican alien working in the US

wet' blan'ket *n.* gloomy person hindering others' enjoyment

wet'land' *n.* (often *pl.*) swampland and other damp land areas

wet' nurse' *n.* 1 woman employed to suckle another's child —*v.* (**wet-nurse, -nursed, -nurs·ing**) 2 act as a wet nurse to

wet' suit' *n.* rubber garment worn by skin divers, etc., to keep warm

whack /(h)wak/ *Colloq. v.* 1 strike or beat forcefully —*n.* 2 sharp or resounding blow 3 **have (or take) a whack at** *Slang.* attempt 4 **out of whack:** a not properly balanced b not working —**whack'er** *n.* [imit.]

whale¹ /(h)wāl/ *n.* 1 very large marine mammal with a streamlined body and horizontal tail —*v.* (**whaled, whal·ing**) 2 hunt whales 3 **a whale of a** *Colloq.* an exceedingly large, fine, etc. [OE]

whale² *v.* (**whaled, whal·ing**) beat soundly

whale'bone' *n.* elastic, horny substance in the upper jaw of some whales

whale' oil' *n.* oil from the blubber of whales

whal'er *n.* 1 whaling ship 2 sailor on a whaling ship

wham /(h)wam/ *interj.* 1 *Colloq.* expressing forcible impact —*v.* (**whammed, wham·ming**) 2 strike forcefully, loudly, etc. [imit.]

wham'my *n.* (*pl.* **-mies**) 1 curse 2 blow

wharf /(h)wôrf/ *n.* (*pl.* **wharves** /(h)wôrvz/ or **wharfs**) pier or other structure at which a ship may be moored to load and unload [OE]

Whar·ton /(h)wôrt'n/, **Edith** 1862–1937; US novelist

what /(h)wät, (h)wət/ *adj.* 1 asking for a choice from an indefinite number or for a statement of amount, number, or kind (*what books have you read?*) 2 *Colloq.* WHICH (*what book have you chosen?*) 3 how great or remarkable (*what luck!*) 4 whatever (*will give you what help I can*) —*pron.* 5 what thing or things? (*what is your name?; I don't know what you mean*) 6 how much (*what you must have suffered!*) 7 that or those which (*what followed was worse; tell me what you think*) —*adv.* 8 to what extent (*what does it matter?*) 9 **what about** what is the news or your opinion of 10 **what for:** *Colloq.* a why? b severe reprimand (*give a person what for*) [OE]

what·ev'er *adj. & pron.* 1 WHAT (in relative uses), with the emphasis on indefiniteness (*lend me whatever you can*) 2 though anything (*we are safe whatever happens*) 3 at all; of any kind

what'not' *n. Colloq.* 1 indefinite or trivial thing 2 shelf or shelves for memorabilia, trinkets, etc.

what'so·ev'er *adj. & pron.* WHATEVER

wheal /hwēl/ *n.* small, itchy swelling on the skin, as from an insect bite [OE]

wheat /(h)wēt/ *n.* 1 cereal plant bearing dense, four-sided seed spikes 2 its grain, used in making flour, etc. —**wheat'en** *adj.* [OE]

wheat' germ' *n.* embryo of the wheat grain, extracted as a source of vitamins

Wheat·stone /(h)wēt'stōn/, **(Sir) Charles** 1802–75; English physicist and inventor

whee·dle /(h)wēd'l/ *v.* (**·dled, ·dling**) coax, influence, or get by flattery or endearments

wheel /(h)wēl/ *n.* 1 circular frame or disk that revolves on an axle 2 wheellike thing 3 motion as of a wheel 4 (*pl.*) *Slang.* car 5 STEERING WHEEL 6 (esp. **big wheel**) *Slang.* powerful or important person 7 (*pl.*) progressive force (*wheels of industry*) —*v.* 8 turn on or as on an axis or pivot 9 change direction; face another way 10 push or pull (a wheeled thing) 11 **at the wheel** driving or directing a vehicle, ship, etc. —**wheeled** *adj.* [OE]

WHEELBARROW

wheel'bar'row *n.* small handcart with one wheel and two handles

wheel'base' *n.* distance between the axles of a vehicle

wheel'chair' *n.* chair on wheels for a person unable to walk

wheel'er-deal'er *n.* person who engages in political or commercial scheming

wheel'house' *n.* shelter covering the pilot or helm of a ship

wheel·ie /(h)wē'lē/ *n. Slang.* stunt of riding a bicycle or motorcycle with the front wheel off the ground

Whee·ling /(h)wēl'iNG/ *n.* city in W. Va. Pop. 148,641

wheel'wright' *n.* person who makes or repairs wheels

wheeze /(h)wēz/ *v.* (**wheezed, wheez·ing**) 1 breathe with an audible whistling sound —*n.* 2 sound of wheezing —**wheez'i·ly** *adv.*; **wheez'i·ness** *n.*; **wheez'y** *adj.* (**·i·er, ·i·est**) [fr. ON: hiss]

WHELK

whelk /(h)welk/ *n.* edible marine mollusk with a spiral shell [OE]

whelm /(h)welm/ *v.* 1 engulf 2 crush with weight [OE]

whelp /(h)welp/ *n.* 1 young dog; puppy 2 ill-mannered child or youth —*v.* 3 give birth to (a whelp or whelps) [OE]

when /(h)wen, (h)wən/ *adv.* 1 at what time? 2 on what occasion? 3 (time) at or on which —*conj.* 4 at the or any time that; as soon as (*come when you like*) 5 although 6 after which; and then; but just then (*was nearly* *asleep when the bell rang* —*pron.* **7** what time; which time? (*till when can you stay?*) —*n.* **8** time; occasion (*tell me where and when*) **9** (say) when (tell me) at what point to stop pouring, etc. [OE]

whence /(h)wens/ *adv.* **1** from what place? —*conj.* **2** (to) the place from which **3** and thence [OE, rel. to WHEN]

when·ev'er *conj.* & *adv.* **1** at whatever time; on whatever occasion **2** every time that

when'so·ev'er *conj.* & *adv.* WHENEVER

where /(h)wer, (h)war/ *adv.* **1** in or to what place or position? **2** in what respect? (*where does it concern us?*) **3** in or to which (*places where they meet*) —*conj.* **4** wherever (*go where you like*) —*pron.* **5** what place? (*where do you come from?*) —*n.* **6** place; scene of something [OE]

where'a·bouts' *adv.* **1** approximately where? —*n.* **2** (*sing.* or *pl.*) person's or thing's location

where·as' *conj.* **1** in contrast or comparison with the fact that **2** taking into consideration the fact that

where·at' *conj. Archaic.* at which

where·by' *conj.* by what or which means

where'fore' *Archaic. adv.* **1** for what reason? **2** for which reason —*n.* **3** reason

where·in' *conj.* in what or which place or respect

where·of' *conj.* of what or which

where·up·on' *conj.* immediately after which

wher·ev'er *adv.* **1** in or to whatever place —*conj.* **2** in every place that

where·with·al /(h)wer'wiTHôl', -wiTH/ *n.* money, etc., needed for a purpose

wher·ry /(h)wer'ē/ *n.* (*pl.* ·ries) light rowboat usu. for carrying passengers

whet /(h)wet/ *v.* (**whet·ted, whet·ting**) **1** sharpen (a tool) **2** stimulate (the appetite, a desire, etc.) [OE]

wheth·er /(h)weTH'ar/ *conj.* introducing the first or both of alternative possibilities (*I do not know whether they have arrived or not*) [OE]

whet'stone' *n.* abrasive stone used to sharpen tools

whew /hwyōō, hyōō, fyōō/ *interj.* expression of surprise, consternation, or relief [imit.]

whey /(h)wā/ *n.* watery liquid left when milk forms curds [OE]

which /(h)wiCH/ *adj.* **1** asking for choice from a definite set of alternatives (*which John do you mean?*) **2** being the one just referred to —*pron.* **3** which thing or person? (*which of you is responsible?*) **4** which thing or things (*the house, which is empty, has been damaged*) **5** used in place of *that* after *in* or *that* (*the house in which I was born*) [OE]

● Usage: Careful users should distinguish between *which* and *that*. *Which* should be reserved for nonrestrictive (or nonessential) clauses: *The ring, which was found under the sofa, is mine.* (The *which*-clause merely relates a nonessential fact noted in passing.) But in the following, the *that*-clause is restrictive (or essential), as it indicates a certain ring is being identified as mine: *The ring that was found under the sofa is mine.*

which·ev'er *adj.* & *pron.* any which

whiff /(h)wif/ *n.* **1** puff or breath of air, smoke, etc. **2** odor [imit.]

Whig /(h)wig/ *n. Hist.* **1** member of a British reformist party before the 19th cent. **2** member of a former US political party **3** American colonist supporting the American Revolution —**Whig'ger·y** *n.*; **Whig'gish** *adj.*; **Whig'gism** *n.* [*whiggamer, -more,* nickname of 17th-cent. Scots rebels]

while /(h)wīl/ *n.* **1** period of time (*a long while ago*) —*conj.* **2** during the time that (*while I was away, the house was robbed*) **3** whereas (*while I want to believe it, I cannot*) —*v.* (**whiled, whil·ing**) **4** pass (time, etc.) in a leisurely or interesting way **5** worth (one's) while worth the time or effort [OE]

whim /(h)wim/ *n.* sudden fancy; caprice

whim·per /(h)wim'par/ *v.* **1** make feeble, querulous, or frightened sounds —*n.* **2** such a sound

whim·si·cal /(h)wim'zikal/ *adj.* capricious —**whim'si·cal·i·ty** /-kal'itē/ *n.*; **whim'si·cal·ly** *adv.*

whim·sy /(h)wim'zē/ *n.* (*pl.* ·sies) WHIM

whine /(h)wīn/ *n.* **1** complaining, nasal wail, as of a dog **2** similar shrill, prolonged sound **3** querulous tone or complaint —*v.* (**whined, whin·ing**) **6** emit or utter a whine; complain —**whin'y** *adj.* (·i·er, ·i·est) [OE]

whin·ny /(h)win'ē/ *n.* (*pl.* ·nies) **1** gentle or joyful neigh —*v.* (·nied, ·ny·ing) **2** give a whinny [imit.]

whip /(h)wip/ *n.* **1** lash attached to a stick for urging on animals or punishing, etc. **2** legislative member of a political party appointed to control discipline, tactics, etc. —*v.* (**whipped, whip·ping**) **3** beat or urge on with a whip **4** beat into a froth **5** take or move suddenly, unexpectedly, or rapidly **6** *Slang.* defeat **7** bind with spirally wound twine **8** sew with overcast stitches **9** move rapidly back and forth; flap **10 whip up: a** excite; stir up **b** *Colloq.* prepare rapidly, as a meal —**whip'per, whip'ping** *n.* [LGer or Du]

whip'cord' *n.* tightly twisted cord

whip' hand' *n.* advantage or control in a situation

whip'lash' *n.* **1** flexible end of a whip **2** injury to the neck caused by a jerk of the head, esp. as in an automobile accident

whip'per·snap'per /(h)wip'arsnap'ar/ *n.* unimportant but presumptuous person

whip·pet /(h)wip'it/ *n.* breed of racing dog like a greyhound [prob. fr. obs. *whippet* move briskly, fr. *whip it*]

whip'ping boy' *n.* scapegoat

whip·poor·will /(h)wip'arwil'/ *n.* nocturnal N American bird [imit. of its call]

whir /(h)war/ *n.* (also **whirr**) **1** rapid buzz or soft clicking sound —*v.* (**whirred, whir·ring**) **2** make this sound [Scand]

whirl /(h)warl/ *v.* **1** swing around and around; revolve rapidly **2** send or travel swiftly in an orbit or a curve **3** seem to spin around —*n.* **4** whirling movement **5** state of intense activity **6** state of confusion **7** give it a whirl *Colloq.* attempt it [ON]

whirl·i·gig /(h)war'lēgig/ *n.* spinning or whirling toy

whirl'pool' *n.* powerful circular eddy of water

whirl'wind' *n.* **1** rapidly whirling mass or column of air —*adj.* **2** very rapid

whisk /(h)wisk/ *v.* **1a** brush with a sweeping movement **b** take suddenly **2** convey or go lightly or quickly —*n.* **3** whisking action or motion **4** utensil for whipping cream, etc. **5** small broom [Scand]

whisk·er /(h)wisk'ər/ *n.* **1** (usu. *pl.*) hair growing on a man's face, esp. on the cheeks **2** each of the bristles on the face of a cat, etc. **3** *Colloq.* small distance —**whisk'ered** /-ərd/, **whisk'er·y** *adj.* [fr. WHISK]

whis·key /(h)wis'kē/ *n.* (Brit. & Canad. **whis'ky**) (*pl.* **·keys** or **·kies**) spirit distilled esp. from malted grain, esp. barley or rye [shortening of *usquebaugh* fr. Gaelic: water of life]

whis·per /(h)wis'pər/ *v.* **1a** speak very softly without vibration of the vocal cords **b** talk or say in a barely audible tone **2** rustle; murmur —*n.* **3** whispering speech or sound **4** thing whispered —**whis'pered** /-pərd/ *adj.*; **whis'per·er** *n.*; **whis'per·ing** *adj.* [OE]

whist /(h)wist/ *n.* card game usu. for two pairs of players [earlier *whisk*, perh. fr. WHIST]

whis·tle /(h)wis'əl/ *n.* **1** clear, shrill sound made by forcing breath through a hole between nearly closed lips, etc. **2** similar sound made by a bird, the wind, a missile, etc. **3** instrument used to produce such a sound —*v.* (**·tled**, **·tling**) **4** emit a whistle **5** give a signal or express surprise or derision by whistling **6** produce (a tune) by whistling —**whis'tler** *n.* [OE]

whis·tle-blow·er *n.* person who publicizes fraud, corruption, etc., from within an organization

Whis·tler /(h)wis'lər/, **James Abbott Mc-Neill** 1834–1903; US painter

whis·tle-stop *n.* **1** small, unimportant town **2** politician's brief pause for a speech on tour

whit /(h)wit/ *n.* particle; least possible amount [OE WIGHT]

white /(h)wīt/ *adj.* **1** resembling a surface reflecting sunlight without absorbing any of the visible rays; of the color of milk or snow **2** nearly this color; pale, esp. in the face **3** having light-colored skin **4** lacking or having lost color —*n.* **5** innocent **6** white color or pigment **7** EGG WHITE **8** whitish part of the eyeball around the iris **9** member of a light-skinned race —**white'ness** *n.*; **whit'ish** *adj.* [OE]

white' blood' cell' *n.* LEUKOCYTE

white'cap' *n.* foamy top of a cresting wave

white'-col·lar *adj.* (of a worker or work) clerical; professional

white' el'e·phant *n.* useless possession

white' feath'er *n.* symbol of cowardice

white' flag' *n.* symbol of surrender

white' gold' *n.* platinum-colored alloy of gold

white' goods' *n. pl.* **1** household appliances, as refrigerators, etc. **2** linens, sheets, towels, etc.

white'head' *n. Colloq.* white or white-topped pimple

White·head /(h)wīt'hed/, **Alfred North** 1861–1947; English philosopher and mathematician

white' heat' *n.* **1** temperature at which metal emits white light **2** state of intense passion or activity —**white'-hot'** *adj.*

659

White·horse /(h)wīt'hôrs'/ *n.* capital of the Yukon Territory of Canada. Pop. 17,900

White' House' *n.* **1** US presidential residence in Washington, D.C. **2** executive branch of the US government

white-knuck·le /hwit'nək'əl/ *adj.* causing or showing tense fear

white' lead' /led/ *n.* mixture of lead carbonate and hydrated lead oxide used as pigment

white' lie' *n.* harmless or trivial untruth

white' light' *n.* apparently colorless light, e.g., ordinary daylight

white' mag'ic *n.* magic used for beneficent purposes

white' meat' *n.* lighter-colored meat of chicken, turkey, etc.

whit·en *v.* make or become white —**whit'en·er, whit'en·ing** *n.*

white' noise' *n.* (also **white' sound'**) noise containing many frequencies with equal intensities

white'out' *n.* dense blizzard allowing no visibility

white' pa'per *n.* official government report

white' sale' *n.* sale of sheets, towels, and other household linens

white' tie' *n.* man's white bow tie as part of full evening dress

white'wall' *n.* **1** tire having a white band on the sidewall —*adj.* **2** of or describing such a tire

white'wash' *n.* **1** solution of lime or whiting for whitening walls, etc. **2** means employed to conceal mistakes or faults —*v.* **3** cover with whitewash **4** attempt to conceal facts

white' wa'ter *n.* rapids; foaming water

whith·er /(h)wiTH'ər/ *Archaic.* *adv.* **1** to what place or state? —*conj.* **2** to which place; to whatever place [OE]

whit·ing[1] /(h)wī'tiNG/ *n.* (*pl.* same) small white-fleshed fish used as food [Du, rel. to WHITE]

whit·ing[2] *n.* ground chalk used in whitewash, etc.

Whit·man /(h)wit'mən/, **Walt** 1819–92; US poet

Whit·ney /(h)wit'nē/, **Eli** 1765–1825; US manufacturer and inventor

Whit·ney, Mt. /(h)wit'nē/ *n.* peak in Sierra Nevada in central Calif., tallest in conterminous US: 14,495 ft.

Whit'sun·day' *n.* seventh Sunday after Easter, commemorating Pentecost

Whit·ti·er /(h)wit'ēər/ *n.* city in Calif. Pop. 77,671

Whit·ti·er /(h)wit'ēər/, **John Greenleaf** 1807–92; US poet

whit·tle /(h)wit'l/ *v.* (**·tled**, **·tling**) **1** carve or pare (wood, etc.) with a knife **2** reduce, esp. gradually [OE]

whiz /(h)wiz/ (also **whizz**) *n.* **1** sound made by an object moving through the air at great speed **2** *Slang.* genius; expert —*v.* (**whizzed**, **whiz·zing**) **3** move with or make a whiz [imit.]

whiz' kid' *n.* brilliant or highly successful young person

who /hōō/ *pron.* (*obj.* **whom** or *Colloq.* **who**; *poss.* **whose**) **1a** what or which person or persons? (*who called?; you know who it was*) **b** what sort of person or persons? (*who am I to object?*) **2** (a or the person) that (*anyone who wishes can come; the woman whom you met*) [OE]

● **Usage:** The form *whom*, the objective case of *who*, is properly used where the word functions as an object: *He is the one whom you mean. To whom should I give it?* Usage is variable in informal settings, where *who* often serves as the universal form, but in formal writing it is best to maintain the distinction.

WHO *abbr.* World Health Organization

whoa /(h)wō/ *interj.* used to stop or slow a horse, etc. [var. of *ho*]

who·dun·it /hōōdən′it/ *n. Colloq.* detective story, play, or movie [*who done* (joc. for *did*) *it?*]

who·ev·er *pron.* (*obj.* **who·ev·er** or **whom·ev′er**; *poss.* **whos·ev′er**) **1** the or any person or persons who **2** though anyone **3** emphatic for WHO

whole /hōl/ *adj.* **1** uninjured; unbroken; intact; undiminished **2** not less than; all there is of **3** with no part removed —*n.* **4** thing complete in itself **5** all there is of a thing **6** all members, etc., of **7** **as a whole** as a unity; not as separate parts **8** **on the whole** taking everything relevant into account —**whole′ ness** *n.* [OE]

whole′heart′ed /-härt′əd/ *adj.* **1** completely devoted **2** done with all possible effort or sincerity —**whole′heart′ed·ly** *adv.*

whole′-hog′ *adj. & adv. Slang.* completely

whole′ milk′ *n.* milk containing all of its butterfat, etc.

whole′ num′ber *n.* number without fractions; integer

whole·sale′ *n.* **1** selling of goods in large quantities to be retailed by others —*adj. & adv.* **2** by wholesale **3** on a large scale —*v.* (·saled, ·sal·ing) **4** sell wholesale —**whole′ -sal·er** *n.*

whole·some /hōl′səm/ *adj.* **1** promoting physical, mental, or moral health **2** prudent —**whole′some·ness** *n.* [OE, rel. to WHOLE]

whole′ wheat′ *n.* wheat with none of the bran or germ removed —**whole′-wheat′** *adj.*

whol·ly /hōl′(l)ē/ *adv.* entirely; without limitation; purely

whom /hōōm/ *pron. objective case of* WHO

whom·ev′er *pron. objective case of* WHOEVER

whom′so·ev′er *pron. objective case of* WHOSO-EVER

whoop /hōōp, hŏŏp, wōōp, wŏŏp/ *n.* **1** loud cry of or as of excitement, etc. **2** long, rasping intake of breath in whooping cough —*v.* **3** utter a whoop [imit.]

whoop′ing cough′ *n.* infectious bacterial disease, esp. of children, with a series of short, violent coughs followed by a whoop

whop·per /(h)wäp′ər/ *n. Slang.* **1** something big of its kind **2** great lie

whop′ping *adj. Colloq.* (esp. as an intensifier) huge

whore /hôr/ *n.* prostitute —**whor′ish** *adj.* [OE]

whorl /(h)wôrl, (h)wərl/ *n.* **1** ring of leaves, etc., around a stem **2** one turn of a spiral **3**

spiral pattern of a fingerprint —**whorled** *adj.* [appar. var. of WHIRL]

whose /hōōz/ *pron.* **1** of or belonging to which person (*whose is this book?*) **2** of whom; of which —*adj.* **3** of whom or which (*whose book is this?*)

● **Usage:** Some people mistakenly avoid using *whose* in referring to things, restricting it to people alone. But there is nothing wrong with *I saw many trees whose leaves had turned red*; the alternative, *I saw many trees, the leaves of which had turned red*, is awkward at best.

who′so·ev′er *pron.* **whom′so·ev′er**; *poss.* **whose′so·ev′er** *Archaic.* WHOEVER

why /(h)wī/ *adv.* **1** for what reason or purpose (*why did you do it?*) **2** for which (*the reasons why I did it*) —*interj.* **3** expressing: **a** surprised discovery or recognition (*why, it's you!*) **b** impatience (*why, of course I do!*) **c** reflection (*why, yes, I think so*) **d** objection (*why, what is wrong with it?*) [OE, rel. to WHAT]

WI postal abbr. for Wisconsin

Wich·i·ta /wiCH′ətô′, -tä′/ *n.* city in Kan. Pop. 304,011

wick /wik/ *n.* tape or cord feeding a flame with fuel [OE]

wick·ed /wik′id/ *adj.* **1** sinful; immoral **2** spiteful **3** playfully malicious **4** *Colloq.* very bad **5** *Slang.* excellent —**wick′ed·ly** *adv.*; **wick′ed·ness** *n.*

wick·er /wik′ər/ *n.* braided twigs as material for baskets, furniture, etc. [Scand]

wick′er·work′ *n.* **1** wicker **2** things made of wicker

wick·et /wik′it/ *n.* **1** small door or gate, esp. beside or in a larger one **2** small window or opening **3** wire hoops through which balls must pass in croquet [AngFr *wiket* fr. Fr *guichet*]

wide /wīd/ *adj.* (wid·er, wid·est) **1** having sides far apart; broad, not narrow **2** in width (*a foot wide*) **3a** extending far **b** considerable; not restricted **4** open to the full extent **5** not within a reasonable distance of; far from **6** (in comb.) extending over the whole of (*nation-wide*) —*adv.* **7** widely **8** to the full extent **9** far from the target, etc. —**wide′ness** *n.* [OE]

wide′ a·wake′ *adj.* **1** fully awake **2** *Colloq.* wary; knowing

wide′-eyed′ *adj.* surprised; naive

wide′ly *adv.* **1** to a wide extent; far apart **2** extensively **3** by many people **4** considerably; to a large degree

wid′en *v.* make or become wider

wide′spread′ *adj.* widely distributed

wid·geon /wij′ən/ *n.* (also **wi′geon**, pronunc. same) a kind of wild duck

wid·ow /wid′ō/ *n.* **1** woman who has lost her husband by death and not married again —*v.* **2** make into a widow or widower —**wid′ow·hood** *n.* [OE]

wid′ow·er *n.* man who has lost his wife by death and not married again

width /widTH/ *n.* **1** measurement from side to side **2** large extent **3** strip of material of full width —**width′wise′** or **width′ways′** *adv.* [fr. WIDE]

wield /wēld/ *v.* **1** hold and use **2** command; exert [OE]

wie·ner /wē′nər/ *n.* HOT DOG [Ger *Vienna* fr. Vienna sausage]

Wies·ba·den /vēs'bäd'n/ *n.* city in W Germany. Pop. 256,900

wife /wīf/ *n.* (*pl.* **wives**) married woman, esp. in relation to her husband **—wife'less**, **wife'ly** *adj.* [OE: woman]

wig /wig/ *n.* artificial head of hair [abbr. of PERIWIG]

wig·eon /wij'ən/ *n.* var. of WIDGEON

wig·gle /wig'əl/ *Colloq. v.* (·gled, ·gling) 1 move from side to side, etc. **—n.** 2 act of wiggling **—wig'gler** *n.*; **wig'gly** *adj.* (·gli·er, ·gli·est) [LGer or Du *wiggelen*]

wight /wīt/ *n. Archaic.* person [OE: thing; creature]

Wight, Isle of /wīt/ *n.* island off the S coast of England

wig·wag /wig'wag'/ *v.* (·wagged, ·wag·ging) 1 wag 2 signal by wagging or waving

wig·wam /wig'wäm'/ *n.* N American Indian hut or tent [Algonquian]

wild /wīld/ *adj.* 1 in its original natural state; not domesticated, cultivated, or civilized 2 unrestrained; disorderly 3 tempestuous 4 intensely eager 5 *Colloq.* enthusiastically devoted to 6 haphazard; ill-aimed **—adv. 7a** in a wild manner **b** out of control **—n.** 8 (usu. *pl.*) wild tract of land **—wild'ly** *adv.*; **wild'ness** *n.* [OE]

wild' card' *n.* 1 card having any rank chosen by the player holding it 2 *Comp.* character that will match any character or combination of characters

wild'cat' *n.* 1 any small or medium-sized undomesticated cat, as the lynx, bobcat, etc. 2 hot-tempered or violent person 3 exploratory oil well **—adj.** 4 (of a strike) sudden and unofficial 5 reckless; financially unsound

Wilde /wīld/, **Oscar** 1854–1900; Irish-born dramatist and poet

wil·de·beest /wil'dəbēst'/ *n.* (*pl.* same or ·beests) see GNU [Afrik, rel. to WILD, BEAST]

Wil·der /wīl'dər/, **Thornton** 1897–1975; US writer

wil·der·ness /wil'dərnəs/ *n.* uncultivated or uninhabited region [OE, rel. to WILD, DEER]

wild-eyed' /wīld' īd'/ *adj.* 1 staring in a wild, angry, or insane manner 2 impractical; foolish; extreme

wild'fire' *n.* rapidly spreading fire

wild'fowl' *n.* (*pl.* same) game bird

wild'-goose' chase' *n.* foolish or hopeless quest

wild'life' *n.* wild animals collectively

wild' oat' *n.* 1 western US wild grain 2 sow (one's) wild oats commit youthful follies; be promiscuous

wild' rice' *n.* N American aquatic grass with an edible grain

Wild' West' *n.* western US before the establishment of law and order

wile /wīl/ *n.* 1 (usu. *pl.*) stratagem; trick **—v.** (wiled, wil·ing) 2 lure

wil·ful /wil'fəl/ *adj.* var. of WILLFUL

will¹ /wil/ *v. aux.* (**will**, **would**) 1 expressing a future statement, command, etc. (*you will regret this*) 2 expressing intention (*I will return soon*) 3 wish or desire (*come when you will*) 4 be able to (*it will hold a large amount*) 5 have a habit or tendency to (*accidents will happen*) [OE]

● Usage: See note at SHALL.

will² *n.* 1 faculty by which a person decides what to do 2 strong desire or intention 3 determination; willpower 4 legal written directions for the disposal of one's property after death 5 disposition toward others **—v.** 6 try to cause by willpower 7 intend; desire 8 bequeath by a will 9 **at will** whenever one wishes [OE]

Wil·lard /wil'ərd/, **Emma Hart** 1787–1870; US pioneer of women's education

will·ful /wil'fəl/ *adj.* 1 intentional; deliberate 2 obstinate **—will'ful·ly** *adv.*; **will'ful·ness** *n.* [fr. WILL²]

Wil·liam /wil'yəm/ name of three kings of England, including: 1 **William I** (**"the Conqueror"**) c. 1027–87; reigned 1066–87 2 **William III** 1650–1702; reigned 1689–1702 jointly with his wife, **Mary II**

Wil·liams /wil'yəmz/ 1 **Roger** c. 1603–83; English clergyman; founder of Rhode Island colony 2 **William Carlos** 1883–1963; US poet 3 **Tennessee** (born **Thomas Lanier Williams**) 1911–83; US dramatist

wil·lies /wil'ēz/ *n. pl. Colloq.* nervous discomfort

will'ing *adj.* 1 ready to consent or undertake 2 given or done, etc., by a willing person **—will'ing·ly** *adv.*; **will'ing·ness** *n.*

will-o'-the-wisp /wil'ə ᴛʜə wisp'/ *n.* 1 phosphorescent light seen on marshy ground 2 elusive person or goal [orig. *Will(iam) of the wisp* (torch)]

wil·low /wil'ō/ *n.* tree with pliant branches and narrow leaves, usu. growing near water **—wil'low·y** *adj.* [OE]

will'pow'er *n.* control by deliberate purpose over impulse; self-control

wil·ly-nil·ly /wil'ē nil'ē/ *adv.* whether one likes it or not [later spelling of *will I, nill I* I am willing, I am unwilling]

Wil·ming·ton /wil'miNGtən/ *n.* city in Del. Pop. 71,529

Wil·son /wil'sən/ 1 (**Thomas**) **Woodrow** 1856–1924; 28th US president (1913–21) 2 **Edmund** 1895–1972; US writer and critic 3 (**Lord**) (**James**) **Harold** 1916– ; prime minister of Great Britain (1964–70; 1974–76)

wilt /wilt/ *v.* 1 wither; droop 2 lose energy [orig. dial.]

wil·y /wī'lē/ *adj.* (·i·er, ·i·est) crafty; cunning **—wil'i·ness** *n.*

wimp /wimp/ *n. Colloq.* feeble or ineffectual person **—wimp'ish, wimp'y** *adj.*

wim·ple /wim'pəl/ *n.* headdress also covering the neck and the sides of the face, worn by some nuns [OE]

win /win/ *v.* (**won, win·ning**) 1 secure as a result of a fight, contest, bet, effort, etc. 2 be the victor; be victorious in **—n.** 3 victory in a game, etc. **—win'na·ble** *adj.* [OE: toil]

wince /win(t)s/ *n.* 1 start or involuntary shrinking movement, showing pain or distress **—v.** (**winced, winc·ing**) 2 give a wince [Gmc]

winch /winCH/ *n.* 1 crank of a wheel or axle 2 windlass **—v.** 3 lift with a winch [OE]

wind¹ /wind/ *n.* 1 current of air in natural motion 2a breath b power of breathing 3 empty talk 4 gas generated in the bowels 5 (*pl.*) wind instruments of an orchestra **6** scent or other information carried by the wind; rumor; hint —*v.* **7** cause to be out of breath **8** detect the presence of by a scent **9** get **wind of** suspect the existence of **10 in the wind** about to happen —**wind′less** *adj.* [OE]

wind² /wīnd/ *v.* (**wound, wind·ing**) **1** go in a spiral, curved, or crooked course **2** make (one's way) thus **3** wrap closely; coil **4** surround with or as with a coil **5** tighten the coiled spring of (a clock, etc.) —*n.* **6** bend; turn; twist **7 wind up: a** coil the whole of **b** *Colloq.* excite; provoke **c** bring to a conclusion; end **d** *Baseball.* swing the arm preparatory to pitching [OE]

wind′·bag′ /wind′bag/ *n. Colloq.* person who talks a lot but says little of any value

wind′break′ *n.* thing serving to break the force of the wind —**wind′break′er** *n.*

wind′burn′ *n.* inflammation of the skin caused by exposure to the wind

wind·ed /win′dəd/ *adj.* out of breath

wind′fall′ *n.* **1** fruit blown to the ground by the wind **2** unexpected good fortune

Wind·hoek /vint′hŏŏk′/ *n.* capital of Namibia. Pop. 114,500

wind′ing sheet′ /wīn′diNG/ *n.* sheet in which a corpse is wrapped for burial

wind′ in′stru·ment /wind′/ *n.* musical instrument sounded by an air current, as a flute, clarinet, etc.

wind′jam′mer *n.* merchant sailing ship

WINDLASS

wind·lass /win(d)′ləs/ *n.* machine with a horizontal axle for hauling or hoisting [ON: winding-pole]

wind′mill′ *n.* mill worked by the wind acting on its sails or vanes

WINDMILL

win·dow /win′dō/ *n.* **1a** opening in a wall, etc., usu. with glass to admit light, etc. **b** the

glass itself **2** windowlike opening **3** gap **4** *Comp.* rectangular display area showing a particular application, set of data, etc. —**win′dow·less** *adj.* [ON: wind-eye]

win′dow·box′ *n.* box placed outside a window for growing flowers, etc.

win′dow dress′ing *n.* **1** display in a store window, etc. **2** adroit presentation of facts to give a deceptively favorable impression —**win′dow-dress′** *v.*; **win′dow dress′er** *n.*

win′dow·pane′ *n.* pane of glass in a window

win′dow-shop′ *v.* (**-shopped, -shop·ping**) look at goods displayed in store windows without buying anything

win′dow sill′ *n.* sill below a window

wind′pipe′ /wind′-/ *n.* air passage from the throat to the lungs

wind′ shear′ *n.* sudden updraft or downdraft, esp. affecting an airplane in flight

wind′shield′ *n.* screen of glass at the front of a car

wind′shield wip′er *n.* blade moving in an arc to keep a windshield clear of rain, etc.

wind′sock′ *n.* canvas cylinder or cone on a pole showing the direction of the wind

Wind·sor /win′zər/ *n.* city in Ontario, Canada. Pop. 191,400

wind′surf′ing /wind′-/ *n.* sport of riding on water on a sailboard —**wind′surf** *v.*; **wind′surf·er** *n.*

wind′ tun′nel *n.* tunnellike device producing an airstream flowing past models of aircraft, etc., for aerodynamic study

wind·up /wīnd′əp/ *n.* **1** conclusion; finish **2** *Baseball.* pitcher's arm motion preparatory to pitching

wind·ward /wind′wərd/ *adj. & adv.* **1** on the side from which the wind is blowing —*n.* **2** windward direction

wind′y *adj.* (**·i·er, ·i·est**) **1** stormy; exposed to wind **2** *Colloq.* wordy —**wind′i·ness** *n.* [OE, rel. to WIND¹]

wine /wīn/ *n.* **1** fermented grape juice as an alcoholic drink **2** fermented drink resembling this made from other fruits, etc. **3** dark red color of red wine —*v.* (**wined, win·ing**) (esp. in the phrase **wine and dine**) **4** drink wine **5** entertain, esp. lavishly, with wine [OE]

win·er·y /wīn′ərē/ *n.* (*pl.* **·ies**) place where wine is made

wing /wiNG/ *n.* **1** each of the limbs or organs by which a bird, insect, etc., is able to fly **2** winglike structure supporting an aircraft **3** part of a building, stage, etc., extended in a certain direction **4** polarized section of a political party in terms of its views **5** flank of a battle array **6** air force unit of several squadrons or groups —*v.* **7** travel or traverse on wings **8** wound in a wing or an arm **9** equip with wings **10** enable to fly; send in flight **11 on the wing** flying; in flight **12 take under one's wing** treat as a protégé **13 take wing** fly away **14 wing it** improvise —**winged, wing′less, wing′like** *adj.* [ON]

wing′ nut′ *n.* nut with winglike projections for the fingers

wing′span′ *n.* (also **wing′spread′**) measurement across the wings from tip to tip

wink /wiNGK/ *v.* **1** close and open one eye quickly, esp. as a signal **2** close and open (one or both eyes) quickly **3** twinkle; flash on and off **—n. 4** act of winking **5** *Colloq.* short sleep **6 wink at** purposely avoid noticing **—wink′er** *n.* [OE]

win·ner /win′ər/ *n.* person, etc., that wins

win′ning *adj.* **1** having or bringing victory **2** attractive **—n. 3** (*pl.*) money won **—win′ning·ly** *adv.*

Win·ni·peg /win′ipeg/ *n.* capital of the Canadian province of Manitoba. Pop. 652,400

win·now /win′ō/ *v.* **1** blow (grain) free of chaff, etc. **2** blow (chaff, etc.) from grain **3** sift; examine [OE, rel. to WIND¹]

wi·no /wī′nō/ *n.* (*pl.* **-nos**) *Slang.* alcoholic

win·some /win′səm/ *adj.* attractive; engaging **—win′some·ly** *adv.*; **win′some·ness** *n.* [OE: joyous]

Win·ston-Sa·lem /win′stən sā′ləm/ *n.* city in N. Car. Pop. 143,485

win·ter /win′tər/ *n.* **1** coldest season of the year, between autumn and spring **2** any period of decline or adversity **—adj. 3** characteristic of or fit for winter **—v. 4** pass the winter [OE]

win′ter·green′ *n.* evergreen plant having red berries, source of an aromatic oil used for flavoring

win′ter·ize′ *v.* (**·ized, ·iz·ing**) make ready for winter

win′ter sol′stice *n.* shortest day of the year, about Dec. 22 in the Northern Hemisphere

win′ter·time′ *n.* season or period of winter

win·try /win′trē/ *adj.* (**·tri·er, ·tri·est**) **1** characteristic of winter **2** lacking warmth; unfriendly **—win′tri·ness** *n.*

win·y /wīn′ē/ *adj.* (**·i·er, ·i·est**) wine-flavored

wipe /wīp/ *v.* (**wiped, wip·ing**) **1** clean or dry by rubbing **2** rub (a cloth, etc.) over a surface **3** spread or remove by rubbing **4** erase or eliminate completely **—n. 5** act of wiping **6** piece of material for wiping **7 wipe out** destroy; annihilate **—wip′er** *n.* [OE]

wire /wīr/ *n.* **1a** metal drawn out into a thread or thin, flexible rod **b** piece or length of this **2** *Colloq.* telegram or telegraph **—adj. 3** made of wire **—v.** (**wired, wir·ing**) **4** provide, fasten, strengthen, etc., with wire **5** install electrical circuits in **6** *Colloq.* telegraph [OE]

wired /wīrd/ *adj. Slang.* **1** very excited, active, anxious, etc. **2** equipped with surreptitious microphones for listening or recording **3** well-connected, as to influential people

wire′-haired′ *adj.* (esp. of a dog) with stiff or wiry hair

wire′less′ *adj.* **1** operating without wires, esp. by electromagnetic waves **—n. 2** wireless telegraph or other communication medium

wire′ serv′ice *n.* service supplying news to clients by telegraphy or electronic means

wire′tap′ping *n.* tapping of telephone lines to eavesdrop **—wire′tap′** *v.* (**·tapped, ·tap·ping**)

wir′ing *n.* system or installation of wires providing circuits for electricity, telephones, etc.

wir′y *adj.* (**·i·er, ·i·est**) **1** sinewy **2** of or like wire; tough; coarse **—wir′i·ness** *n.*

Wis. abbr. for Wisconsin

Wis·con·sin /wiskän′sən/ *n.* state in the N

central US. Capital: Madison. Pop. 4,891,769. Abbr. **WI**; **Wis.** **—Wis·con·sin·ite′** *n.*

wis·dom /wiz′dəm/ *n.* **1** experience and knowledge together with the power of applying them **2** prudence; common sense **3** wise sayings [OE, rel. to WISE¹]

wis′dom tooth′ *n.* hindmost molar in a human

wise¹ /wīz/ *adj.* (**wis·er, wis·est**) **1** having, showing, or dictated by wisdom **2** prudent; sensible **3** having knowledge **4** suggestive of wisdom **5** *Colloq.* crafty **6** *Colloq.* impertinent **7** *Colloq.* put or get wise **—wise′ly** *adv.* [OE]

wise² *n. Archaic.* way, manner, or degree [OE]

-wise *suffix* forming adjectives and adverbs of manner (*clockwise; lengthwise*) or respect (*moneywise*)

wise′a′cre *n.* person who affects a wise manner [Du *wijssegger* soothsayer]

wise′crack′ *Colloq. n.* **1** smart, pithy, or flip remark **—v. 2** make a wisecrack

wise′ guy′ *n.* know-it-all

wish /wiSH/ *v.* **1** have or express a desire or aspiration for **2** have as a desire or aspiration **3** want or demand **4** express one's hopes for **—n. 5a** desire; request **b** expression of this **6** thing desired **7** hope felt or expressed for another **—wish′er** *n.* [OE]

wish′bone′ *n.* forked bone between the neck and breast of a fowl

wish·ful /wiSH′fəl/ *adj.* desiring **—wish′ful·ly** *adv.*

wish·y-wash·y /wiSH′ē wäSH′ē/ *adj. Colloq.* **1** feeble in quality or character **2** weak; watery [fr. WASH]

wisp /wisp/ *n.* **1** small bundle or twist of straw, etc. **2** small, separate quantity of smoke, hair, etc. **3** small, delicate person or thing **—wisp′y** *adj.* (**·i·er, ·i·est**)

wis·te·ri·a /wistēr′ēə/ *n.* climbing plant with blue, purple, or white hanging flowers [for C. *Wistar,* US anatomist]

wist·ful /wist′fəl/ *adj.* yearning; mournfully expectant **—wist′ful·ly** *adv.*; **wist′ful·ness** *n.* [appar. an assimilation of obs. *wistly* 'intently' to *wishful*]

wit¹ /wit/ *n.* **1** (*sing.* or *pl.*) intelligence; quick understanding **2a** unexpected or humorous combining or contrasting of ideas or expressions **b** power of giving pleasure by this **3** person possessing such power **4 at one's wit's** (or **wits'**) **end** utterly at a loss [OE]

wit² *v.* (**wist, wit·ting**) **1** know; learn **2 to wit** namely

witch /wiCH/ *n.* **1** woman supposed to have magical powers or dealings with evil spirits **2** *Derog.* old hag **3** fascinating girl or woman [OE]

witch′craft′ *n.* use or power of magic

witch′ doc′tor *n.* tribal magician of primitive cultures

witch′er·y *n.* **1** WITCHCRAFT **2** bewitching charm

witch′ ha′zel *n.* **1** shrub with bark yielding an astringent lotion **2** this lotion

witch′ hunt′ *n.* campaign against persons suspected of unpopular or unorthodox views, usu. with little actual evidence

with /wiTH, wiTH/ *prep.* expressing: **1** instrument or means used (*cut with a knife*) **2a** association or company (*lives with his mother*) **b** parting of company (*dispense with*) **3** cause (*shiver with fear*) **4** possession (*man with dark hair*) **5** circumstances (*sleep with the window open*) **6** manner **7** understanding (*are you with me?*) **8** reference or regard (*how are things with you?*) **9** **with it** *Colloq.* up to date **10** **with that** thereupon [OE]

with·al /wiTHôl′, wiTH-/ *adv.* despite

with·draw /wiTH′drô′/ *v.* (**·drew**, **·drawn**, **·draw·ing**) **1** pull or take aside or back **2** discontinue; cancel; retract **3** remove; take away **4** retire; move apart; remove oneself [fr. WITH away]

with·draw·al /wiTHdrô′əl/ *n.* **1** withdrawing or being withdrawn **2** process of ceasing to take an addictive drug, etc.

with·drawn′ /-/ *v.* **1** *past part.* of WITHDRAW —*adj.* **2** abnormally shy and unsociable

withe /wiTH, wiTH, wiTH/ *n.* tough, flexible shoot, esp. of willow, used for binding, basketwork, etc. [OE]

with·er /wiTH′ər/ *v.* **1** make or become dry and shriveled **2** deprive of or lose vigor or freshness **3** blight with scorn, etc. —**with′er·ing** *adj.;* **with′er·ing·ly** *adv.* [appar. var. of WEATHER]

with·ers *n. pl.* ridge between a horse's shoulder blades [obs. *wither* against (the collar)]

with·hold /wiTHhōld′, wiTH-/ *v.* (**·held**, **·hold·ing**) **1** hold back; restrain **2** refuse to give, grant, or allow **3** deduct, esp. from a paycheck [fr. WITH away]

with·in /wiTHin′/ *adv.* **1** inside **2** indoors **3** in spirit —*prep.* **4** inside **5** not beyond or exceeding **6** not further off than —*n.* **7** inside [OE, rel. to WITH, IN]

with·out′ *prep.* **1** not having **2** with freedom from **3** in the absence of **4** with neglect or avoidance of **5** *Archaic* outside —*adv.* **6** outside **7** out of doors [OE, rel. to WITH, OUT]

with·stand′ *v.* (**·stood**, **·stand·ing**) oppose; hold out against [OE, rel. to WITH, STAND]

wit′less *adj.* foolish; crazy —**wit′less·ly** *adv.;* **wit′less·ness** *n.* [OE, rel. to WIT]

wit·ness /wit′nəs/ *n.* **1** EYEWITNESS **2a** person giving sworn testimony **b** person attesting another's signature on a document **3** testimony; evidence; confirmation —*v.* **4** be an eyewitness to **5** be witness to the authenticity of **6** give or serve as evidence **7** bear witness attest the truth of [OE, rel. to WIT]

Witt·gen·stein /vit′gənSHtīn′, -stīn′/, **Ludwig** 1889–1951; Austrian philosopher

wit·ti·cism /wit′əsiz′əm/ *n.* witty remark [fr. WITTY]

wit·ting·ly /wit′iNGlē/ *adv.* aware of what one is doing; intentionally [fr. WIT]

wit′ty *adj.* (**·ti·er**, **·ti·est**) showing wit —**wit′ti·ly** *adv.;* **wit′ti·ness** *n.* [OE, rel. to WIT]

wives /wīvz/ *n. pl.* of WIFE

wiz·ard /wiz′ərd/ *n.* **1** sorcerer; magician **2** talented person; genius —**wiz′ard·ry** *n.* [fr. WISE¹]

wiz·ened /wiz′ənd/ *adj.* shriveled; withered [OE]

w/o *abbr.* without

wob·ble /wäb′əl/ *v.* (**·bled**, **·bling**) **1** sway from side to side **2** stand or go unsteadily; stagger **3** waver; vacillate —*n.* **4** state or instance of wobbling —**wob′bly** *adj.* (**·bli·er**, **·bli·est**); **wob′bli·ness** *n.* [prob. fr. LGer *wabbeln*]

Wode·house /wŏŏd′hous′/, (**Sir**) **P(elham) G(renville)** 1881–1975; English writer

woe /wō/ *n.* **1** affliction; bitter grief **2** (*pl.*) calamities [OE]

woe′be·gone′ *adj.* dismal-looking; pathetic [fr. WOE + *begone* surrounded]

woe·ful /wō′fəl/ *adj.* **1** sorrowful **2** causing or feeling affliction **3** wretched —**woe′ful·ly** *adv.*

WOK

wok /wäk/ *n.* bowl-shaped pan used esp. in Chinese cookery [Chin]

woke /wōk/ *v. past of* WAKE¹

wok·en /wō′kən/ *v. past part.* of WAKE¹

wolf /wŏŏlf/ *n.* (*pl.* **wolves** /wŏŏlvz/) **1** wild animal related to the dog, usu. hunting in packs **2** *Slang.* man who seduces or flirts with women —*v.* **3** devour greedily **4** **cry wolf** raise a false alarm —**wolf′ish** *adj.* [OE]

Wolfe /wŏŏlf/, **Thomas** 1900–38; US writer

wolf′hound′ *n.* dog of a kind used orig. to hunt wolves

wolf·ram /wŏŏl′frəm/ *n.* see TUNGSTEN [Ger]

Wol·las·ton /wŏŏl′əstən/, **William Hyde** 1766–1828; English chemist and physicist

Wol·sey /wŏŏl′zē/, **Thomas** c. 1474–1530; English cardinal and statesman

Wol·ver·hamp·ton /wŏŏl′vər(h)am(p)′tən/ *n.* city in W England. Pop. 265,600

wol·ver·ine /wŏŏl′vərēn′/ *n.* N American animal of the weasel family [rel. to WOLF]

wom·an /wŏŏm′ən/ *n.* (*pl.* **wom′en**) **1** adult human female **2** females as a group **3** feminine characteristics **4** (*comb. form*) woman of a specified nationality, skill, etc. —*adj.* **5** female [OE]

wom′an·hood′ *n.* **1** female maturity **2** womanly instinct **3** womankind

wom′an·ish *adj. Derog.* effeminate; unmanly

wom′an·ize *v.* (**·ized**, **·iz·ing**) **1** chase after women; philander **2** make womanish —**wom′an·iz′er** *n.*

wom′an·kind *n.* (also **wom′en·kind**′) women in general

wom′an·ly *adj.* having or showing qualities associated with women —**wom′an·li·ness** *n.*

womb /wŏŏm/ *n.* organ of conception and gestation in female mammals [OE]

wom·bat /wäm′bat/ *n.* burrowing, plant-eating Australian marsupial [Aborig.]

wom·en /wim′in/ *n. pl.* of WOMAN

wom′en·folk′ *n. Colloq.* **1** women in general **2** the women in a family

wom′en·kind′ *n.* var. of WOMANKIND

wom′en's lib·er·a′tion *n.* (also **wom′en's lib′**) movement to free women from domestic duties and subservient status

won /wən/ *v.* past and past part. of WIN

won·der /wən'dər/ *n.* 1 emotion excited by what is unexpected, unfamiliar, or inexplicable 2 strange or remarkable thing, specimen, event, etc. —*v.* 3 be filled with wonder 4 be surprised to find 5 desire or be curious to know [OE]

Won·der /wən'dər/, **Stevie** (born **Stephen Judkins**) 1950– ; US pop singer and songwriter

won·der·ful *adj.* very remarkable or admirable —**won'der·ful·ly** *adv.* [OE]

won·der·land *n.* 1 fairyland 2 land of surprises or marvels

won'der·ment *n.* surprise; awe

won·drous /wən'drəs/ *Poet. adj.* 1 wonderful —*adv.* 2 *Archaic* wonderfully

wonk /wäNGk/ *n. Slang.* student, etc., who studies a great deal

wont /wônt, wōnt/ *adj.* 1 accustomed —*n.* 2 what is customary; habit [OE]

won't /wōnt/ *v. contr.* will not

wont·ed /wôn'tid, wōn'-/ *adj.* habitual; usual

won ton /wän' tän'/ *n.* filled Chinese dumpling or noodle, usu. fried or boiled

woo /wō/ *v.* (**wooed, woo·ing**) 1 court; seek the love of 2 try to win 3 coax; importune —**woo'er** *n.* [OE]

wood /wŏŏd/ *n.* 1a hard, fibrous substance of the trunk or branches of a tree or shrub b this for lumber, fuel, etc. 2 (*sing.* or *pl.*) growing trees densely occupying a tract of land 3 wooden-headed golf club —*adj.* 4 made of wood 5 living or growing in a wood 6 **out of the woods** out of danger or difficulty —**wood'ed** *adj.* [OE]

Wood /wŏŏd/, **Grant** 1892–1942; US painter

wood' al'co·hol *n.* METHANOL

wood'bine /-bīn/ *n.* honeysuckle

wood' carv'ing *n.* 1 art object carved from wood 2 art of creating such objects —**wood' carv'er** *n.*

wood'chuck' *n.* N American marmot [AmerInd name]

wood'cock' *n.* game bird related to the snipe

wood'craft' *n.* 1 knowledge of woodland, esp. in camping, etc. 2 skill in woodwork

wood'cut' *n.* 1 relief cut on wood 2 print made from this

wood'cut'ter *n.* person who cuts timber —**wood' cut'ting** *n.*

wood·en /wŏŏd'n/ *adj.* 1 made of or like wood 2a stiff; clumsy b expressionless —**wood'en·ly** *adv.*; **wood'en·ness** *n.*

wood·land /wŏŏd'lənd, -land/ *n.* wooded country; woods

wood'peck'er *n.* bird that taps tree trunks with its beak in search of insects

wood'pile' *n.* pile of wood, esp. for fuel

wood' pulp' *n.* wood fiber prepared for papermaking

wood'shed' *n.* shed where wood for fuel is stored

woods·man or **wood·man** /wŏŏdz'mən, wŏŏd'-/ *n.* (*pl.* **·men**) person who lives or works in the woods

WOODCHUCK

wood'sy *adj.* (**·si·er, ·si·est**) of or like a wood or woods —**wood'si·ness** *n.*

wood'wind' /-wind'/ *n.* 1 wind instruments that were orig. made mostly of wood, e.g., the flute, clarinet, oboe, and saxophone 2 any such instrument —*adj.* 3 composed for woodwinds

wood'work' *n.* 1 making of things in wood 2 things made of wood, esp. paneling, moldings, etc. —**wood'work'er, wood'work'ing** *n.*

wood'y *adj.* (**·i·er, ·i·est**) 1 wooded 2 like or of wood —**wood'i·ness** *n.*

woof¹ /wŏŏf/ *n.* 1 gruff bark of a dog —*v.* 2 give a woof [imit.]

woof² /wŏŏf, wōŏf/ *n.* WEFT [OE, rel. to WEB]

woof·er /wŏŏf'ər/ *n.* loudspeaker for low frequencies [fr. WOOF¹]

wool /wŏŏl/ *n.* 1 fine, soft, wavy hair from the fleece of sheep, etc. 2 woolen yarn, cloth, or clothing 3 woollike substance [OE]

wool'en *adj.* 1 made of wool —*n.* 2 (*pl.*) woolen fabric or clothing [OE]

Woolf /wŏŏlf/, (**Adeline**) **Virginia** 1882–1941; English novelist

wool'-gath'er·ing *n.* absent-mindedness

wool'ly *adj.* (**·li·er, ·li·est**) 1 bearing wool 2 like or made of wool 3 vague or confused 4 **wild and woolly** uncivilized —**wool'li·ness** *n.*

woo·zy /wŏŏ'zē/ *adj.* (**·zi·er, ·zi·est**) *Colloq.* 1 dizzy or unsteady 2 slightly drunk —**woo' zi·ly** *adv.*; **woo'zi·ness** *n.*

Worces·ter /wŏŏs'tər/ *n.* city in Mass. Pop. 169,759

word /wərd/ *n.* 1 meaningful element or unit of speech, writing, or printing 2 speech, esp. as distinct from action 3 one's promise or assurance 4 (*sing.* or *pl.*) remark; conversation 5 (*pl.*) text of a song 6 (*pl.*) angry talk 7 news; message; signal 8 command —*v.* 9 put into words; select words to express 10 **in a word** briefly 11 **in other words** expressing the same thing differently 12 **in so many words** explicitly 13 **the Word** (or **Word of God**) the Gospel or Bible 14 **word for word** in exactly the same or (of translation) corresponding words —**word'less** *adj.*; **word' less·ly** *adv.* [OE]

-word *comb. form Colloq.* used in phrases referring (often jocularly or euphemistically) to a familiar term (e.g., the F-*word*)

word·age /wərd'ij/ *n.* choice or quantity of words

word'ing *n.* form or choice of words used

word' of hon'or *n.* promise or assurance

word' of mouth' *n.* speech (only)

word'play' *n.* witty use of words, esp. punning

word' pro'ces·sor *n. Comp.* program or device to store text entered from a keyboard, make corrections, and provide a printout —**word'·pro'cess** *v.*; **word' pro'cess·ing** *n.*

Words·worth /wərdz'wərTH'/, **William** 1770–1850; English poet

word'y *adj.* (**·i·er, ·i·est**) using or expressed in too many words —**word'i·ly** *adv.*; **word'i·ness** *n.*

wore /wôr/ *v.* past of WEAR

work /wərk/ *n.* 1 application of mental or physical effort to a purpose; use of energy 2 task to be undertaken **3** thing done or made by work; result of an action **4** employment or occupation **5** literary or musical composition **6** (*pl.*) operative part of a clock or machine **7 the works:** *Colloq.* **a** all that is available or needed **b** full treatment **8** (*pl.*) operations of building or repair **9** (*pl.*, often treated as *sing.*) factory **10** (usu. *pl.*) meritorious act —*adj.* **11** of or used for work —*v.* **12** do work; be engaged in bodily or mental activity **13** be employed **14** craft (a material, etc.) **15** operate or function, esp. effectively **16** operate; manage; control **17a** cause to toil **b** manipulate **c** cultivate (land) **18a** bring about; produce as a result **b** *Colloq.* arrange (matters) **19** solve **20** bring to a desired shape or consistency **21** do or make by needlework, etc. **22** make (one's way) gradually or with difficulty **23** gradually become (loose, etc.) by constant movement **24** artificially excite **25a** purchase with one's labor instead of money **b** obtain by labor the money for **26** have influence **27** ferment **28 at work** in action **29 work off** get rid of by work or activity **30 work out: a** solve or calculate **b** solve; understand **c** have a result **d** provide for the details of **e** engage in physical exercise or training **31 work over: a** examine thoroughly **b** *Slang.* beat up **32 work up: a** develop or advance gradually **b** elaborate or excite by degrees **c** develop; devise [OE]

work′a·ble *adj.* that can be worked, will work, or is worth working —**work′a·bil′i·ty** /-bil′ itē/ *n.*

work·a·day′ *adj.* ordinary; everyday

work·a·hol·ic /wərk′əhô′lik, -häl′ik/ *n. Colloq.* person addicted to working

work′bench′ *n.* sturdy table for manual work, esp. carpentry

work′book′ *n.* student's book with exercises

work′day′ *n.* **1** day on which work is usually done **2** part of the day devoted to work

work′er *n.* **1** person who works, esp. for an employer **2** neuter bee or ant **3** person who works hard

work′fare′ *n.* government assistance program with required employment

work′force′ *n.* **1** workers engaged or available **2** number of these

work′horse′ *n.* **1** horse used for work **2** steady or hard worker

work′ing *adj.* **1** engaged in work **2** functioning or able to function —*n.* **3** activity of work

work′ing class′ *n.* social and economic class employed esp. in manual or industrial work —**work′ing-class′** *adj.*

work′load′ *n.* amount of work to be done

work·man /wərk′mən/ *n.* (*pl.* -**men**) man employed to do manual labor

work′man·like′ *adj.* competent; showing practiced skill

work′man·ship′ *n.* degree of skill in doing a task or of finish in the product made

work′out′ *n.* session of physical exercise or training

work′place′ *n.* place at which a person works

work′sheet′ *n.* **1** paper for recording work done or in progress **2** paper listing problems or activities for students, etc., to work through

work′shop′ *n.* **1** room or building in which goods are manufactured **2** place or meeting for concerted discussion or activity

work′sta′tion *n.* **1** specific area where a person works **2** computer terminal or work area where this is located

work′-up′ *n.* complete or thorough study, esp. a medical diagnostic examination

work′week′ *n.* part of the week devoted to work

world /wərld/ *n.* **1a** the earth, or a planetary body like it **b** its countries and people **2** the universe; all that exists **3** secular or individual interests and affairs **4** human affairs; active life **5** a specified class or sphere of activity **6** vast amount **7 for all the world** precisely [OE]

world′-class′ *adj.* of a quality or standard regarded as high throughout the world

world′ly *adj.* (-**li·er**, -**li·est**) **1** temporal; earthly **2** experienced in life; sophisticated —**world′li·ness** *n.*

world′ly-wise′ *adj.* prudent or shrewd in one's dealings with the world

World′ Se′ries *n. Baseball.* US professional championship, determined in a series of games

world′-shak′ing *adj.* momentous

World War I *n.* war (1914–18) between the Central Powers (Germany, Austria-Hungary, etc.) and the Allies (the US, Great Britain, France, Russia, etc.)

World War II *n.* war (1939–45) between the Axis (Germany, Italy, Japan, etc.) and the Allies (the US, Great Britain, France, Soviet Union, etc.)

world′-wea′ry *adj.* bored with human affairs —**world′-wea′ri·ness** *n.*

world′wide′ *adj.* **1** occurring in or known in all parts of the world —*adv.* **2** throughout the world

worm /wərm/ *n.* **1** any of various types of creeping invertebrate animals or insect larvae with long, slender bodies and no limbs **2** (*pl.*) intestinal parasites **3** insignificant or contemptible person **4** spiral part of a screw —*v.* **5** move with a crawling motion **6** insinuate oneself into favor, etc. **7** obtain by cunning means or persistence **8** rid of intestinal worms —**worm′i·ness** *n.*; **worm′y** *adj.* (-**i·er**, -**i·est**) [OE]

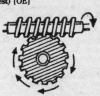

WORM GEAR

worm′ gear′ *n.* gear consisting of a rotating shaft with a screwlike thread that meshes with a toothed wheel

worm′wood′ *n.* **1** plant with a bitter aromatic taste **2** bitter mortification; source of this [OE]

worn /wôrn/ *v.* **1** *past part.* of WEAR —*adj.* **2**

damaged by use or wear **3** looking tired and exhausted

worn'-out' *adj.* **1** no longer usable, working, etc., through wear **2** exhausted

wor·ri·some /wɜr'ēsəm, wə'rē-/ *adj.* causing worry

wor·ry /wɜr'ē, wə'rē/ *v.* (·ried, ·ry·ing) **1** give way to anxiety **2** harass; be a trouble or anxiety to **3** (of a dog, etc.) shake or pull about with the teeth **4** make uneasy —*n.* (*pl.* ·ries) **5** thing that causes anxiety **6** disturbed state of mind; anxiety —**wor'ri·er** *n.* [OE: strangle]

wor'ry·wart' *n. Colloq.* person who worries excessively

worse /wɜrs/ *adj.* (comparative of BAD; ILL) **1** more bad **2** in or into worse health or a worse condition —*adv.* **3** more badly; more ill —*n.* **4** worse thing or things **5** worse condition **6 none the worse (for)** not adversely affected (by) **7 worse off** in a worse position [OE]

wors·en /wɜr'sən/ *v.* make or become worse

wor·ship /wɜr' SHip/ *n.* **1a** homage or service to a deity **b** acts, rites, or ceremonies of this **2** adoration; devotion **3** *Brit.* (*cap.*) form of address for certain magistrates, etc. —*v.* (·shiped or ·shipped, ·ship·ing or ·ship·ping) **4** honor with religious rites or adoration **5** idolize **6** attend or engage in worship —**wor'ship·er** or **wor'ship·per** *n.* [OE, rel. to WORTH, -SHIP]

wor·ship·ful /wɜr'SHipfəl/ *adj.* **1** *Brit.* honorable; distinguished **2** worshiping

worst /wɜrst/ *adj.* (superlative of BAD; ILL) **1** most bad —*adv.* **2** most badly —*n.* **3** worst part or possibility —*v.* **4** get the better of; defeat **5 at (the) worst** in the worst possible case **6 if worst comes to worst** if the worst happens **7 in the worst way** very much [OE, rel. to WORSE]

wors·ted /wŏŏs'tid, wɜr'stid/ *n.* **1** fine woolen yarn **2** fabric made from this [*Worste(a)d* in Norfolk, England]

wort /wɜrt, wôrt/ *n.* infusion of malt before it is fermented into beer [OE]

worth /wɜrTH/ *adj.* **1** of a value equivalent to **2** such as to justify or repay **3** possessing or having wealth amounting to —*n.* **4** what a person or thing is worth; the (usu. high) merit of **5** equivalent of money in a commodity (*ten dollars worth of gas*) **6 for what it is (or it's) worth** without a guarantee of its truth or value [OE]

worth'less *adj.* without value or merit —**worth'less·ness** *n.*

worth'while' *adj.* worth the time, effort, or money spent

wor·thy /wɜr'THē/ *adj.* (·thi·er, ·thi·est) **1** deserving respect; estimable **2** deserving; entitled to —*n.* (*pl.* ·thies) **3** worthy person —**wor'thi·ly** *adv.*; **wor'thi·ness** *n.*

-worthy *comb. form* forming adjectives meaning: **1** deserving of **2** suitable for

would /wŏŏd/ *v. aux. past* of WILL[1], used esp.: **1** in reported speech (*he said he would be home by evening*) **2** to express a condition or probability (*they would have been killed if they had gone*) **3** to express habitual action (*would wait every evening*) **4** to express a question or polite request (*would you come in, please?*) **5** to express consent (*they would not help*) **6 would that** *Archaic.* to express a wish
● Usage: See note at SHALL.

would'·be' *adj.* desiring or aspiring to be

would·n't /wŏŏd'nt/ *v. contr.* would not

wound[1] /wŏŏnd/ *n.* **1** injury done to living tissue by a deep cut, heavy blow, etc. **2** pain or injury inflicted on one's feelings, reputation, etc. —*v.* **3** inflict a wound on [OE]

wound[2] /wound/ *v. past* and *past part.* of WIND[2]

wound up /wound' əp'/ *adj.* excited; tense; angry

wove /wōv/ *v. past* of WEAVE[1]

wo·ven /wō'vən/ *v. past part.* of WEAVE[1]

wow /wou/ *interj.* **1** expression of astonishment or admiration —*v.* **2** *Slang.* impress greatly [imit.]

w.p.m. *abbr.* words per minute

wrack /rak/ *n.* destruction [LGer or Du *wrak*]

wraith /rāTH/ *n.* ghost [Scot]

wran·gle /raNG'gəl/ *n.* **1** noisy argument or dispute —*v.* (·gled, ·gling) **2** engage in a wrangle —**wran'gler** *n.* [LGer or Du]

wran'gler *n.* cowboy —**wran'gle** *v.* (·gled, ·gling) [perh. fr. MexSp *caballerango* stable boy]

wrap /rap/ *v.* (wrapped, wrap·ping) **1** envelop in folded or soft encircling material **2** coil; twist around —*n.* **3** shawl, scarf, etc. **4** wrapping material **5 under wraps** in secrecy **6 wrapped up** in engrossed or absorbed in **7 wrap up** *Colloq.* finish (a matter, etc.)

wrap'a·round' *adj.* **1** designed to wrap around **2** curving or extending around at the edges

wrap'per *n.* **1** that which wraps; cover **2** loose, enveloping robe or gown

wrap'ping *n.* (esp. *pl.*) material used to wrap

wrap'ping pa'per *n.* strong or decorative paper for wrapping parcels

wrap'-up' *n.* conclusion; summary

wrasse /ras/ *n.* any of various usu. bright-colored marine fish [Cornish *wrach*]

wrath /raTH/ *n.* extreme anger —**wrath'ful** *adj.*; **wrath'ful·ly** *adv.* [OE, rel. to WROTH]

wreak /rēk, rek/ *v.* **1** express (vengeance, anger, etc.) **2** cause (damage, etc.) [OE: avenge]

wreath /rēTH/ *n.* (*pl.* **wreaths** /rēTHz/) **1** flowers or leaves fastened in a ring **2** curl or ring of smoke, cloud, etc. [OE, rel. to WRITHE]

wreathe /rēTH/ *v.* (wreathed, wreath·ing) **1** encircle or cover as, with, or like a wreath **2** (of smoke, etc.) move in wreaths **3** make into a wreath

wreck /rek/ *n.* **1** the sinking or running aground of a ship **2** ship that has suffered a wreck **3** greatly damaged thing —*v.* **4** seriously damage; ruin **5** cause the wreck of [perh. fr. AngFr *wrec* fr. Gmc]

wreck·age /rek'ij/ *n.* **1** wrecked material **2** remnants of a wreck **3** act of wrecking

wreck'er *n.* **1** person or thing that wrecks or destroys **2** person who or machine that removes wrecks **3** *Hist.* person who tries to cause shipwrecks for plunder or profit

wren /ren/ n. small, usu. brown songbird with an erect tail [OE]

Wren /ren/, (**Sir**) **Christopher** 1632–1723; English architect

WRENCHES 2

wrench /rench/ n. 1 violent twist or oblique pull or tearing off 2 tool for gripping and turning nuts, etc. 3 painful uprooting or parting —v. 4 twist or pull violently, esp. sideways 5 pull off with a wrench 6 twist the meaning of [OE]

wrest /rest/ v. 1 wrench away from a person's grasp 2 obtain by effort or with difficulty [OE]

wres·tle /res′əl/ n. 1 contest or athletic sport in which two opponents grapple and try to throw each other to the ground 2 hard struggle —v. (**·tled, ·tling**) 3 take part in a wrestle 4 struggle against; deal with —**wres′tler, wres′tling** n. [OE]

wretch /rech/ n. 1 unfortunate or pitiable person 2 reprehensible person [OE: outcast]

wretch·ed /rech′id/ adj. 1 unhappy; miserable; unwell 2 of bad quality; contemptible 3 displeasing; hateful —**wretch′ed·ly** adv.; **wretch′ed·ness** n.

wrig·gle /rig′əl/ v. (**·gled, ·gling**) 1 twist or turn with short, writhing movements 2 make wriggling motions 3 go or travel thus 4 be evasive —n. 5 act of wriggling —**wrig′gler** n.; **wrig′gly** adj. (**·gli·er, ·gli·est**) [LGer wriggelen]

wright /rīt/ n. maker or builder [OE, rel. to WORK]

Wright /rīt/ 1 **Wilbur** 1867–1912; US aeronautical inventor, with his brother, Orville 2 **Frank Lloyd** 1869–1959; US architect 3 **Orville** 1871–1948

wring /ring/ v. (**wrung, wring·ing**) 1a squeeze tightly b squeeze and twist, esp. to remove liquid 2 distress; torture 3 extract by squeezing 4 obtain by pressure or importunity; extort 5 clasp (hands) in a gesture of distress —n. 6 act of wringing [OE]

wring·er n. device for wringing water from washed clothes, etc.

wrin·kle¹ /ring′kəl/ n. 1 crease in the skin 2 similar mark in another flexible surface —v. (**·kled, ·kling**) 3 make wrinkles in 4 form wrinkles —**wrin′kly** adj. (**·kli·er, ·kli·est**) [prob. rel. to OE gewrinclod sinuous]

wrin·kle² n. Colloq. useful tip or clever expedient [OE wrenc a trick]

wrist /rist/ n. 1 joint connecting the hand with the arm 2 part of a garment covering this [OE]

wrist′-watch′ n. small watch worn on a strap, etc., around the wrist

writ /rit/ n. legal document commanding or forbidding action [OE, rel. to WRITE]

write /rīt/ v. (**wrote, writ·ten, writ·ing**) 1 mark symbols, letters, or words onto paper or some other surface 2 compose 3 fill out or complete (a check, etc.) 4 transfer or record (data) in a computer 5 write and send a letter to (a person) 6 **write off: a** cancel the record of; acknowledge the loss of **b** dismiss as insignificant 7 **write out** write in full or in finished form 8 **write up** write a full account of [OE]

write′-in′ n. candidate whose name is written on a ballot by the voter

write′-off′ n. thing written off

writ′er n. person who writes, esp. as a profession; author

write′-up′ n. written or published account; review

writhe /rīth/ v. (**writhed, writh·ing**) 1 twist or roll about 2 suffer mental torture or embarrassment [OE]

writ′ing n. 1 written words, etc. 2 handwriting 3 (usu. pl.) author's works

writ·ten /rit′n/ v. past part. of WRITE

Wroc·ław /vrōt′släf′/ n. city in SW Poland. Pop. 643,100

wrong /rông/ adj. 1 mistaken; not true; in error 2 unsuitable; less or least desirable 3 contrary to law or morality 4 amiss; out of order —adv. 5 in a wrong manner or direction; with an incorrect result —n. 6 what is morally wrong 7 unjust action —v. 8 treat unjustly 9 **in the wrong** on the wrong side; mistaken 10 **wrong side out** inside out —**wrong′ly** adv.; **wrong′ness** n. [OE]

wrong-do·er /rông′dōō′ər/ n. person who behaves immorally or illegally —**wrong′do′ing** n.

wrong·ful /rông′fəl/ adj. unwarranted; unjustified —**wrong′ful·ly** adv.; **wrong′ful·ness** n.

wrong′-head′ed adj. perverse; obstinate

wrote /rōt/ v. past of WRITE

wroth /rôth/ adj. Archaic. angry [OE]

wrought /rôt/ v. 1 Archaic. past and past part. of WORK —adj. 2 (of metals) beaten out or shaped by hammering 3 formed; made

wrought′ i′ron n. tough, malleable form of iron —**wrought′-i′ron** adj.

wrung /rəng/ v. past and past part. of WRING

wry /rī/ adj. (**wry·er, wry·est** or **wri·er, wri·est**) 1 distorted 2 contorted in disgust, disappointment, or mockery 3 (of humor) dry and mocking —**wry′ly** adv.; **wry′ness** n. [OE]

wt. abbr. weight

Wu·han /wōō′hän′/ n. city in E China. Pop. 3,284,200

Wup·per·tal /vōōp′ərtäl′/ n. city in W Germany. Pop. 378,300

wuss /wōōs/ n. Colloq. person seen as a coward or weakling —**wuss′y** adj.

WV postal abbr. for West Virginia

W. Va. abbr. for West Virginia

WWI or **W.W.I** abbr. World War I

WY postal abbr. for Wyoming

Wy·eth /ˈwī′əTH/ family of US painters, including: 1 N(ewell) C(onvers) 1882–1945 2 **Andrew Newell** 1917– 3 **James Browning** 1946–

Wyo. abbr. for Wyoming

Wy·o·ming /wī-ō′miNG/ *n.* W state of the US.

Capital: Cheyenne. Pop. 453,588. Abbr. **WY;** **Wyo.** —**Wy·o′ming·ite′** *n.*

WYSIWYG /ˈwiz′ēwig/ *adj.* (also **wysiwyg**) *Comp.* denoting software that displays text in the same format on screen as it does in printout [acronym of *what you see is what you get*]

X

---

x, X /eks/ *n.* (*pl.* **x's; X's, Xs**) twenty-fourth letter of the English alphabet; a consonant

X *abbr.* 1 *Rom. num.* ten 2 experimental 3 extra 4 extraordinary 5 cross-shaped symbol used esp. to indicate position (*X marks the spot*) or incorrectness, to symbolize a kiss or a vote, or as the signature of a person who cannot write 6 (of a movie) classified as suitable for adults only

x or **x.** *abbr.* 1 excess 2 *Math.* unknown quantity or variable 3 *Math.* horizontal coordinate (see illustration at ABSCISSA)

Xa·vi·er /zā′vēər, igzā′-/, **St. Francis** 1506–52; Spanish Jesuit missionary of Far East

X chro·mo·some /eks′ krō′məsōm′/ *n.* (in humans and some other mammals) sex chromosome of which the number in female cells is twice that in male cells [*X* as an arbitrary label]

Xe *symb.* xenon

xe·non /zē′nän′, zen′än′/ *n.* heavy, inert gaseous element; *symb.* **Xe** [Gk, neut. of *xenos* strange]

xe·no·pho·bi·a /zen′əfō′bēə, zē′nə-/ *n.* hatred or fear of foreigners —**xe′no·phobe′** *n.*; **xe′no·pho′bic** *adj.* [Gk *xenos* strange; *stranger*]

Xen·o·phon /zen′əfən, -fän′/ *c.* 428–*c.* 354 B.C.; Greek writer

xe·rog·ra·phy /zēräg′rəfē/ *n.* dry copying process utilizing powder that adheres to electrically charged areas of a surface [Gk *xēros* dry]

Xe·rox /zēr′äks′/ *n.* 1 *Tdmk.* machine for copying by xerography 2 (x-) copy thus made —*v.* 3 (x-) reproduce by this process

Xerx·es I /zərk′sēz′/ *c.* 519–465 B.C.; king of Persia (486–465 B.C.); son of Darius I; father of Artaxerxes I

xi /zī, sī, ksē/ *n.* fourteenth letter of the Greek alphabet (Ξ, ξ) [Gk]

Xi·an /sHē′än′/ *n.* (also **Si′an**) city in central China. Pop. 1,959,000

XL *abbr.* 1 extra large 2 extra long

X·mas /kris′məs, eks′məs/ *n. Colloq.* CHRISTMAS [abbr., with X for the initial chi of Gk *Khristos* Christ]

x′ ray′ or **x′-ray′** *n.* (also *cap.* X) 1 electromagnetic radiation of short wavelength, able to pass through opaque bodies 2 photograph made by x rays —*v.* 3 photograph, examine, or treat with x rays —*adj.* (x-ray) 4 by, like, or of x rays [X, orig. with ref. to the unknown nature of the rays]

XS *abbr.* extra small

XXL *abbr.* 1 extra extra large 2 extra extra long

xy·lem /zī′ləm/ *n. Bot.* woody tissue [Gk]

xy·lo·phone /zī′ləfōn′/ *n.* musical instrument of graduated wooden or metal bars struck with small, wooden hammers —**xy′lo·phon′ist** *n.* [Gk *xulon* wood]

Y

---

y, Y /wī/ *n.* (*pl.* **y's; Y's, Ys**) twenty-fifth letter of the English alphabet; a semivowel

Y¹ *abbr.* yen; *symb.* ¥

Y² *symb.* yttrium

y or **y.** *abbr.* 1 *Math.* vertical coordinate (see illustration at ABSCISSA) 2 *Math.* second unknown quantity 3 yard(s) 4 year(s)

-y¹ *suffix* forming adjectives: 1 from nouns and adjectives, meaning full of; having the quality of 2 from verbs, meaning inclined to, apt to [OE]

-y² *suffix* (also **-ey, -ie**) forming diminutives [orig. Scot]

-y³ *suffix* forming nouns denoting state, condition, or quality [L *-ia*, Gk *-eia*]

yacht /yät/ *n.* 1 boat for racing, cruising, etc., esp. for pleasure —*v.* 2 race or cruise in a yacht —**yacht′ing** *n.* [Du *jaghtschip* pursuit-ship]

yachts·man /yäts′mən/ *n.* (*pl.* **-men;** *fem.*

-wom′an, *pl.* **-wom′en**) person who sails yachts

ya·hoo /yä′hōō′/ *n.* boorish, crass person [name of a race of brutes in *Gulliver's Travels*]

Yah·weh /yä′wä, -vä/ *n.* (also **Yah·veh** /-vä/) JEHOVAH

yak¹ /yak/ *n.* long-haired Tibetan ox [Tibetan]

yak² *Slang. v.* (**yakked, yak·king**) 1 chat idly or trivially —*n.* 2 such a chat

yam /yam/ *n.* 1a tropical or subtropical climbing plant b edible, starchy tuber of this 2 sweet potato [Port or Sp fr. W Afr]

yam·mer /yam′ər/ *Colloq.* or *Dial. n.* 1 lament; grumble 2 voluble talk —*v.* 3 utter a yammer [OE]

Ya·mous·sou·kro /yäm′ōōsōō′krō/ *n.* capital of Ivory Coast (Côte d'Ivoire). Pop. 120,000

yang /yaNG/ *n.* (in Chinese philosophy) the

active male principle of the universe (see illustration at YIN)

Yan·gon /yän'gōōn/ *n.* see RANGOON

Yang·tze River /yaNG'tsě', -sě/ *n.* see CHANG

yank /yaNGk/ *v. & n. Colloq.* pull with a jerk

Yank /yaNGk/ *n. Colloq.* American [abbr. of YANKEE]

Yan·kee /yaNG'kē/ *Colloq. n.* **1** citizen of the US **2** inhabitant of New England or of the northern states —*adj.* **3** characteristic of Yankees [perh. fr. Du *Janke*, dim. of *Jan* John, as a nickname]

Ya·oun·dé /youndā'/ *n.* capital of Cameroon. Pop. 649,000

yap /yap/ *v.* (**yapped, yap·ping**) **1** bark shrilly **2** *Colloq.* talk noisily, foolishly, or complainingly —*n.* **3** sound of yapping —**yap'py** *adj.* (**·pi·er, ·pi·est**) [imit.]

yard[1] /yärd/ *n.* **1** measure of length (3 ft.; 36 in.) **2** this length of material, etc. **3** spar slung across a mast for a sail to hang from [OE: stick]

yard[2] *n.* piece of enclosed ground, esp. attached to a house or building, or used for a particular purpose [OE: enclosure]

yard·age /yär'dij/ *n.* number of yards of material, etc.

yard'arm' *n. Naut.* either end of a ship's yard

yard'stick' *n.* **1** standard of comparison **2** measuring rod a yard long

Ya·ren /yär'ən/ *n.* capital of Nauru. Pop. 600

yar·mul·ke /yäm'əlkə, yär'malkə/ *n.* skullcap worn by Jewish men [Yiddish]

yarn /yärn/ *n.* **1** spun thread, esp. for knitting, weaving, etc. **2** *Colloq.* story; anecdote [OE]

Ya·ro·slavl /yär'əslävʹəl/ *n.* city in W Russia on the Volga River. Pop. 638,100

yaw /yô/ *v.* **1** (of a ship, aircraft, etc.) fail to hold a straight course; go unsteadily **2** turn or rotate about a vertical axis —*n.* **3** yawing of a ship, etc., from its course

yawl /yôl/ *n.* two-masted sailboat with aftermast set astern of the rudder [LGer *jolle* or Du *jol*]

yawn /yôn/ *v.* **1** open the mouth wide and inhale, esp. involuntarily **2** gape; be wide open —*n.* **3** act of yawning [OE]

yaws /yôz/ *n. pl.* (usu. treated as *sing.*) contagious tropical skin disease

Yb *symb.* ytterbium

Y chro·mo·some /wī' krō'məsōm'/ *n.* (in humans and some other mammals) sex chromosome occurring only in male cells [*Y* as an arbitrary label]

yd. *abbr.* (*pl.* **yds.**) yard (measure)

ye[1] /yē/ *pron. Archaic. pl.* of THOU[1]

ye[2] /yē, THē, THə/ *adj. Pseudo-archaic.* THE [fr. the obs. *y*-shaped letter for *th*]

yea /yā/ *Archaic. adv.* **1** yes **2** indeed —*n.* **3** 'yes' vote or voter [OE]

yeah /ye'ə, ya/ *adv. Colloq.* yes [casual pronunc. of YES]

year /yēr/ *n.* **1** unit of time, one revolution of the earth around the sun, 365–366 days **2** (also **cal'en·dar year'**) this amount of time, reckoned from Jan. 1 to Dec. 31 **3** period of twelve months, starting at any point **4** (also **school' year'**) part of the year when school is in session, usu. from Sept. to June **5** (*pl.*)

age; time of life **6** (usu. *pl.*) *Colloq.* very long time [OE]

year'book' *n.* annual publication dealing with events or aspects of the preceding year

year·ling /yēr'liNG/ *n.* animal between one and two years old

year'ly *adj.* **1** done, produced, or occurring once a year **2** of or lasting a year —*adv.* **3** once a year

yearn /yärn/ *v.* be filled with longing, compassion, or tenderness —**yearn'ing** *n. & adj.* [OE]

yeast /yēst/ *n.* grayish-yellow fungus used as a fermenting agent, to raise bread, etc. [OE]

yeast'y *adj.* (**·i·er, ·i·est**) **1** of, like, containing, or tasting of yeast; frothy **2** in a ferment **3** light and superficial

Yeats /yāts/, **William Butler** 1865–1939; Irish poet and dramatist

Ye·ka·te·rin·burg /yikät'ərinbōōrg'/ *n.* see SVERDLOVSK

yell /yel/ *n.* **1** loud, sharp cry; shout —*v.* **2** cry; shout [OE]

yel·low /yel'ō/ *adj.* **1** of the color of ripe lemons, egg yolks, etc. **2** having a yellowish skin or complexion **3** *Colloq.* cowardly **4** sensationalist —*n.* **5** yellow color or pigment —*v.* **6** turn yellow —**yel'low·ish** *adj.*; **yel'low·ness** *n.*; **yel'low·y** *adj.* [OE]

yel'low fe'ver *n.* tropical virus disease with fever and jaundice

yel'low jack'et *n.* yellow wasp or hornet

Yel·low·knife /yel'ōnīf'/ *n.* capital of the Northwest Territories of Canada. Pop. 15,200

Yel'low Pag'es *n. pl.* telephone directory on yellow paper, listing businesses, etc., by category

Yel'low Riv'er *n.* see HUANG RIVER

Yel'low Sea' *n.* arm of the N Pacific between China and Korea

Yel'low·stone Falls' /yel'əstōn/ *n.* waterfalls of the Yellowstone River in NW Wyo.

yelp /yelp/ *n.* **1** sharp, shrill cry, as of a dog in pain or excitement —*v.* **2** utter a yelp [OE]

Yelt·sin /yelt'sən/, **Boris** 1931– ; Russian politician; president (1990–)

Yem·en /yem'ən, yā'mən/ *n.* Arab republic on the SW Arabian Peninsula. Capitals: Aden; Sanaa. Pop. 12,147,000 —**Yem'en·ite, Yem'en·i** *n. & adj.*

yen[1] /yen/ *n.* (*pl.* same) chief monetary unit of Japan [Japn fr. Chin]

yen[2] *n. Colloq.* longing; yearning [Chin]

yeo·man /yō'mən/ *n.* (*pl.* **·men**) **1** *Hist.* man holding and cultivating a small landed estate **2** *US Navy.* clerical petty officer —**yeo'man·ly** *adj.* [fr. earlier *yoman*, *yeman*, etc., prob. fr. *yongman*, *yengman* young man]

yeo·man·ry /yō'mənrē/ *n.* (*pl.* **·ries**) body or class of yeomen

yep /yəp, yep/ *adv. & n.* (also **yup**) *Colloq.* YES

Ye·re·van /yer'əvän'/ *n.* capital of Armenia. Pop. 1,283,000

yes /yes/ *adv.* **1** indicating affirmation, consent, assent, etc. **2** (*interrog.*) **a** indeed? **b** what do you want? —*n.* **3** affirmation or assent **4** "yes" vote —*v.* (**yessed, yes·sing**) **5** answer affirmatively [OE: *yea let it be*]

ye·shi·va /yəsHē'və/ *n.* (*pl.* **·vas** or **·voth** /·vōt/) **1** Jewish school combining secular and religious education 2 Jewish rabbinical seminary [Heb: a sitting]

yes' man' *n.* (*pl.* **·men**) *Slang.* weakly acquiescent person

yes·ter·day /yes'tərdā,-dē/ *adv.* 1 on the day before today 2 in the recent past —*n.* 3 the day before today 4 the recent past [OE]

yes·ter·year /yes'təryēr'/ *n. Archaic.* or *Rhet.* 1 last year 2 the recent past [OE]

yet /yet/ *adv.* 1 as late as; until; now or then 2 (with *neg.* or *interrog.*) so soon as; by; now or then 3 again; in addition 4 still 5 even 6 nevertheless —*conj.* 7 but nevertheless 8 as yet until now [OE]

yew /yōō/ *n.* 1 evergreen tree bearing berry-like cones 2 its wood [OE]

Ye·zo /yĕ'zō/ *n.* see HOKKAIDO

Yid·dish /yid'ish/ *n.* 1 language used by Jews in or from Europe, orig. a German dialect —*adj.* 2 of or in this language [Ger *jüdisch* Jewish]

yield /yēld/ *v.* 1 produce or return as a fruit, profit, or result 2 give up; surrender 3 submit; defer to 4 give right of way to —*n.* 5 amount yielded or produced [OE: pay]

yield'ing *adj.* compliant; submissive; pliable

YIN and YANG

yin /yin/ *n.* (in Chinese philosophy) the passive female principle of the universe (cf. YANG)

yip /yip/ *n.* & *v.* (**yipped, yip·ping**) YELP

yip·pee /yip'ē/ *interj.* expression of delight or excitement

YMCA *abbr.* Young Men's Christian Association

YMHA *abbr.* Young Men's Hebrew Association

yo·del /yōd'l/ *v.* (**·deled** or **·delled, ·del·ing** or **·del·ling**) 1 sing with melodious sounds and frequent changes between falsetto and normal voice —*n.* 2 yodeling cry —**yo'del·er** or **yo'del·ler** *n.* [Ger]

yo·ga /yō'gə/ *n.* 1 Hindu system of meditation and asceticism designed to effect reunion with the universal spirit 2 system of physical exercises and breathing control used in yoga [Skt: union]

yo·gi /yō'gē/ *n.* (*pl.* **·gis**) devotee or teacher of yoga [Hindustani, rel. to YOGA]

yo·gurt /yō'gərt/ *n.* (also **yo'ghurt**) semi-solid food made from fermented milk [Turk]

YOKE 1

yoke /yōk/ *n.* 1 wooden crosspiece fastened over the necks of two oxen, etc. 2 (*pl.* same

or -s) pair (of harnessed oxen, etc.) 3 object like a yoke in form or function 4 dominion; servitude 5 bond of union, esp. of marriage —*v.* (**yoked, yok·ing**) 6 put a yoke on 7 couple or unite (a pair) 8 harness [OE]

yo·kel /yō'kəl/ *n.* country bumpkin [perh. dial.]

Yo·ko·ha·ma /yō'kəhäm'ə/ *n.* seaport in Japan, on Honshu. Pop. 3,250,900

Yo·ko·su·ka /yō'kəsōō'kə/ *n.* seaport in Japan, on Honshu. Pop. 435,000

yolk /yōk/ *n.* yellow, inner part of an egg [OE, rel. to YELLOW]

Yom Kip·pur /yōm' kipōōr', kip'ər/ *n.* most solemn holy day of the Jewish year, observed by fasting and prayer; Day of Atonement [Heb]

yon /yän/ *adj.* & *adv. Lit.* or *Dial.* yonder [OE]

yon·der /yän'dər/ *adj.* & *adv.* over there; at some distance in that direction

Yon·kers /yäng'kərz/ *n.* city in N.Y., near New York City. Pop. 188,082

yoo-hoo /yōō'hōō'/ *interj.* used to attract a person's attention

yore /yôr/ *n.* 1 long ago 2 of yore a long time ago [OE: long ago]

York /yôrk/ *n.* 1 city in NE England. Pop. 126,400 2 city in Ontario, Canada. Pop. 140,500

York·town /yôrk'toun/ *n.* village in Va.; site of British surrender to Washington (1781)

you /yōō/ *pron.* (*obj.* **you**; *poss.* **your, yours**) 1 the person or persons addressed 2 one; a person; people [OE, orig. objective case of YE[1]]

young /yəng/ *adj.* (**young·er** /yəng'gər/, **young·est** /yəng'gist/) 1 not far advanced in life, development, or existence; not yet old 2 immature; inexperienced 3 of or characteristic of youth —*n.* 4 offspring 5 YOUTH, 4 —**young'ish** *adj.* [OE]

Young /yəng/, **Brigham** 1801–77; US Mormon leader

young' blood' *n.* vigor, enthusiasm, esp. as brought by the young

young·ster /yəng'stər/ *n.* child; young person

Youngs·town /yəng'stoun/ *n.* city in Ohio. Pop. 95,732

your /yôr, yər/ *poss. pron.* of or belonging to you [OE]

you're /yōōr, yôr, yər/ *v. contr.* you are

yours /yōōrz, yôrz/ *pron.* 1 the one or ones belonging to you 2 introducing a formula ending a letter (*yours truly*)

your·self /yərself'/ *pron.* (*pl.* **·selves**) 1a *emphat. form* of YOU b *refl. form* of YOU 2 in your normal state of body or mind (*you'll feel like yourself soon*)

youth /yōōth/ *n.* (*pl.* **youths** /yōōthz/) 1 being young; period between childhood and adulthood 2 vigor, enthusiasm, inexperience, or other characteristic of this period 3 young person 4 (as *pl.*) young people collectively [OE, rel. to YOUNG]

youth'ful *adj.* young or having the characteristics of youth —**youth'ful·ly** *adv.*; **youth'ful·ness** *n.*

you've /yōōv/ *v. contr.* you have

yowl /youl/ *n.* **1** loud, wailing cry —*v.* **2** utter a yowl

yo-yo /yōʹyōʹ/ *n.* (*pl.* **yo-yos**) **1** toy consisting of an attached pair of disks that can be made to fall and rise on a string **2** thing that repeatedly falls and rises **3** *Slang.* inept person —*v.* (**-yoed, -yo-ing**) **4** fall and rise; fluctuate

yr(s). *abbr.* **1** year(s) **2** your(s)

YT *abbr.* Yukon Territory

yt-ter-bi-um /itɑrʹbēəm/ *n.* metallic element of the lanthanide series; *symb.* **Yb** [*Ytterby* in Sweden]

yt-tri-um /iʹtrēəm/ *n.* metallic element resembling the lanthanides; *symb.* **Y** [rel. to YTTERBIUM]

yu-an /yōō-änʹ, yōōʹən/ *n.* (*pl.* same) chief monetary unit of China [Chin]

Yu-ca-tán /yōōkɑtanʹ, -tänʹ/ *n.* state of SE Mexico on the Gulf of Mexico. Capital: Mérida. Pop. 1,362,900

yuc-ca /yakʹə/ *n.* subtropical plant with swordlike leaves, often grown as an ornamental [Carib]

yuck /yak/ *interj. Slang.* expression of strong distaste [imit.]

yuck'y *adj.* (**·i·er, ·i·est**) *Slang.* **1** messy; disgusting **2** sickly; sentimental

Yu-go-sla-vi-a /yōōʹgōslävʹēə/ *n.* former federation (1918–92) in SE Europe that included Serbia, Croatia, Bosnia and Hercegovina, Montenegro, Macedonia, and Slovenia

yuk /yək/ *v.* (**yukked, yuk·king**) **1** laugh —*n.* **2** something humorous

Yu'kon' Riv'er /yōōʹkän/ *n.* river flowing 2,000 mi. from SW Yukon Territory, Canada into the Bering Sea

Yu'kon' Ter'ri·to'ry *n.* territory of Canada, in the NW part, bordering Alaska on the W. Capital: Whitehorse. Pop. 32,000. Abbr. **YT**

yule /yōōl/ (also **yule'tide'**) *n.* the Christmas festival [OE]

yum·my /yamʹē/ *adj.* (**·mi·er, ·mi·est**) *Colloq.* tasty; delicious

yup /yəp/ *adv.* var. of YEP

yup·pie /yapʹē/ *n.* (also **yup'py**) (*pl.* **·pies**) *Colloq.* young, ambitious, usu. affluent professional person [fr. *y*oung *u*rban *p*rofessional]

YWCA *abbr.* Young Women's Christian Association

YWHA *abbr.* Young Women's Hebrew Association

Z

z, Z /zē/ *n.* (*pl.* **z's; Z's, Zs**) **1** twenty-sixth letter of the English alphabet; a consonant **2** *Math.* third unknown quantity

z or **z.** *abbr.* zero

Z or **Z.** *abbr.* zone

Za·ca·te·cas /zäkʹətäʹkəs/ *n.* state of N central Mexico. Capital: Zacatecas. Pop. 1,276,300

Za·greb /zäʹgreb/ *n.* capital of Croatia. Pop. 930,800

Za·ire /zä-ērʹ/ *n.* republic in S central Africa. Capital: Kinshasa. Pop. 41,151,000 —**Za·ir'i·an** *n. & adj.*

Zam·be·zi /zambēʹzē/ *n.* river in southern Africa flowing 1,650 mi. from Zambia to the Indian Ocean

Zam·bi·a /zamʹbēə/ *n.* republic in S central Africa. Capital: Lusaka. Pop. 8,303,000 —**Zam'bi·an** *n. & adj.*

za·ny /zäʹnē/ *adj.* (**·ni·er, ·ni·est**) **1** comically idiotic; crazily ridiculous —*n.* **2** clown —**zan'i·ness** *n.* [It]

Zan·zi·bar /zanʹzibär/ *n.* island off the E coast of Tanzania.

zap /zap/ *Slang. v.* (**zapped, zap·ping**) **1a** kill; destroy; attack **b** hit hard **2** move quickly **3** cook or heat in a microwave oven **4** change a television channel with a remote control —*interj.* **5** expressing the sound or impact of a bullet, ray gun, etc., or any sudden event [imit.]

Za·pa·ta /zəpätʹə/, **Emiliano** c. 1877–1919; Mexican revolutionary

Za·po·pan /säʹpōpänʹ/ *n.* city in W central Mexico. Pop. 345,400

zap·per /zapʹər/ *n. Colloq.* hand-held remote-control device for changing television channels, etc.

Za·ra·go·za /säʹrägōʹsä/ *n.* see SARAGOSSA

Zar·a·thus·tra /zärʹəthōōʹstrə/ *n.* see ZOROASTER

Zar·qa /zärkäʹ/ *n.* (also **al-Zarqa**) city in Jordan. Pop. 515,000

zeal /zēl/ *n.* earnestness or fervor [Gk *zēlos*]

zeal·ot /zelʹət/ *n.* extreme partisan; fanatic —**zeal'ot·ry** *n.*

zeal·ous /zelʹəs/ *adj.* full of zeal; enthusiastic —**zeal'ous·ly** *adv.*

ze·bra /zēʹbrə/ *n.* (*pl.* same or **·bras**) black-and-white striped African animal of the horse family [It or Port]

ze·bu /zēʹb(y)ōō/ *n.* (*pl.* same or **·bus**) humped ox of Asia and Africa [Fr]

zed /zed/ *n. Brit.* letter Z [Gk ZETA]

Zeit·geist /tsītʹgīstʹ, zītʹ-/ *n.* the spirit of the times [Ger]

Zen /zen/ *n.* form of Buddhism emphasizing meditation and intuition [Japn fr. Skt: thinking]

ze·nith /zēʹniTH/ *n.* **1** point in the sky directly above an observer **2** any peak or highest point [L fr. Ar]

zeph·yr /zefʹər/ *n.* mild gentle breeze [Gk: west wind]

Zep·pe·lin /zepʹəlin/ *n.* large German dirigible of the early 20th cent. [for COUNT F. VON ZEPPELIN]

Zep·pe·lin /zepʹəlin/, (**Count**) **Ferdinand von** 1838–1917; German airship pioneer

ze·ro /zērʹō, zērʹō/ *n.* (*pl.* **·ros**) **1** figure 0; naught; cipher **2** point on a scale from which a positive or negative quantity is reckoned **3** not any; nothing **4** lowest or earliest point **5** **zero in on** take aim at; focus attention on **6**

ze′ro-sum′ *adj.* of a system in which gains and losses are equal

zest /zest/ *n.* 1 piquancy; stimulating flavor or quality 2 keen enjoyment or interest; relish 3 scraping of orange or lemon peel as flavoring —**zest′ful** *adj.*; **zest′ful·ly** *adv.*; **zest′ful·ness** *n.* [Fr]

ze·ta /zā′tə, zē′tə/ *n.* sixth letter of the Greek alphabet (Z, ζ) [Gk]

Zeus /zōōs/ *n.* Gk. Myth. chief deity and father of the gods, associated with the Roman Jupiter

Zhdan·ov /ᴢʜdän′əf/ *n.* see MARIUPOL

Zheng·zhou /jəNG′jō′/ *n.* (formerly **Cheng′chou′**) city in E China. Pop. 1,159,700

Zhou En·lai /jō′ enlī′/ see CHOU EN-LAI

Zhu·kov /ᴢʜōō′kôf′, -kôv/, **Georgi ("Marshal")** 1896–1974; Soviet military leader during World War II

Zi·bo /jī′bōō′/ *n.* (formerly **Tzu′po**) city in NE China. Pop. 1,138,100

Zieg·feld /zig′feld′, zēg′-/, **Florenz** 1867–1932; US theatrical producer

zig·gu·rat /zig′ərat′/ *n.* rectangular, stepped pyramidal tower in ancient Mesopotamia, surmounted by a temple [Assyrian]

zig·zag /zig′zag′/ *adj.* 1 with abrupt, alternate right and left turns —*n.* 2 zigzag line; thing having the form of a zigzag —*adv.* 3 with a zigzag course —*v.* (·**zagged**, ·**zag·ging**) 4 move in a zigzag course [Fr fr. Ger]

zilch /zilcʜ/ *n.* Slang. nothing

zil·lion /zil′yən/ *n.* Colloq. indefinite large number [prob. after *million*]

Zim·bab·we /zimbäb′wā/ *n.* republic in S central Africa. Capital: Harare. Pop. 9,871,000

zinc /ziNGk/ *n.* grayish-white metallic element used as a component of brass and in galvanizing; symb. Zn [Ger *Zink*]

zin·fan·del /zin′fəndel′/ *n.* dry or semi-dry wine made esp. in California

zing /ziNG/ Colloq. *n.* 1 vigor; energy —*v.* 2 move swiftly, esp. with a high-pitched ringing sound —**zing′er** *n.* [imit.]

zin·ni·a /zin′ēə/ *n.* garden plant with showy flowers [*Zinn*, name of a physician and botanist]

Zi·on /zī′ən/ *n.* 1 ancient Jerusalem; its holy hill 2 the Jewish people or religion 3 the Kingdom of Heaven [Heb *ṣiyōn*]

Zi′on·ism′ *n.* movement for the reestablishment and development of a Jewish nation in what is now Israel —**Zi′on·ist** /-ist/ *n.* & *adj.*

zip /zip/ *n.* 1 light, fast sound 2 energy; vigor —*v.* (**zipped, zip·ping**) 3 fasten with a zipper 4 move with zip or at high speed [imit.]

ZIP′ code′ *n.* numeric postal code assigned to speed sorting and delivering mail [zone improvement plan]

zip·per /zip′ər/ *n.* fastening device of two flexible strips with interlocking projections, closed or opened by sliding a clip along them

zip′py *adj.* (·**pi·er**, ·**pi·est**) Colloq. lively; speedy

zir·con /zur′kän′/ *n.* zirconium silicate, used as a gemstone [Ger *Zirkon*]

zir·co·ni·um /zərkō′nēəm/ *n.* gray metallic element; symb. Zr

zit /zit/ *n.* Slang. pimple

zith·er /ziᴛʜ′ər, ziᴛʜ′ər/ *n.* stringed instru-

ment with a flat soundbox, placed horizontally and played with the fingers and a plectrum [L fr. Gk]

Zn symb. zinc

zo·di·ac /zō′dē-ak′/ *n.* 1 imaginary belt of the heavens including all apparent positions of the sun, moon, and planets, divided into twelve equal parts named for constellations 2 diagram of these signs —**zo·di′a·cal** /-dī′əkəl/ *adj.* [Gk *zōion* animal]

Zo·la /zō′lə, zōlä′/, **Émile** 1840–1902; French writer

Zom·ba /zäm′bə/ *n.* legislative capital of Malawi. Pop. 43,300. See also LILONGWE

zom·bie /zäm′bē/ *n.* 1 corpse said to have been revived by witchcraft 2 Colloq. person who acts mechanically or lifelessly [WAfr]

zone /zōn/ *n.* 1 area having particular features, properties, purpose, or use 2 well-defined region, belt, or band 3 latitudinal division of the Earth (**temperate zone**) —*v.* (**zoned, zon·ing**) 4 encircle as or with a zone 5 assign as or to a particular area —**zon′al**, **zoned** *adj.* [Gk *zōnē* girdle]

zonked /zäNGkt, zôNGkt/ *adj.* Slang. 1 exhausted 2 intoxicated [*zonk* hit]

zoo /zōō/ *n.* 1 park with a collection of animals for exhibition or study 2 Slang. disorderly or confused place [fr. *zoological garden*]

zool. *abbr.* zoological; zoology

zo·ol·o·gy /zō-äl′əjē, zōō-/ *n.* study of animals —**zo′o·log′i·cal** /-älij′ikəl/ *adj.*; **zo·ol′o·gist** *n.* [Gk *zōion* animal]

zoom /zōōm/ *v.* 1 move quickly, esp. with a buzzing sound 2 cause an airplane to climb at high speed and a steep angle 3 (of a camera) change rapidly from a long shot to a close-up 4 rise sharply —*n.* 5 airplane's steep climb 6 zooming camera shot [imit.]

zoom′ lens′ *n.* lens allowing a camera to zoom by varying the focal length

zo·o·phyte /zō′əfīt′/ *n.* plantlike animal, esp. a coral, sea anemone, or sponge —**zo′o·phyt′ic** /-fit′ik/ *adj.* [Gk *zōion* animal, *phuton* plant]

Zo·ro·as·ter /zôr′ō-as′tər, zōr′-/ (Persian name **Zarathustra**) c. 628–551 B.C. Persian prophet; founder of Zoroastrianism

Zo·ro·as·tri·an /zôr′ō-as′trēən/ *adj.* 1 of Zoroaster or the dualistic religious system taught by him —*n.* 2 follower of Zoroaster —**Zo′ro·as′tri·an·ism′** *n.* [*Zoroaster*, Pers founder of the religion]

Zr symb. zirconium

zuc·chi·ni /zōōkē′nē/ *n.* (*pl.* same or ·**nis**) green summer squash [It, pl. of *zucchino*, dim. of *zucca* gourd]

Zu·lu /zōō′lōō/ *n.* (*pl.* ·**lus**) 1 member of a S African Bantu people 2 their language —*adj.* 3 of this people or language [native name]

Zü·rich /zōōr′ik, tsy′riкʜ/ *n.* city in N Switzerland. Pop. 341,300

zy·de·co /zī′dəkō/ *n.* syncopated Cajun style of music, orig. from Louisiana and incorporating jazz, blues, and other elements

zy·gote /zī′gōt′/ *n. Biol.* cell formed by the union of two gametes [Gk *zugōtos* yoked]

zy·mur·gy /zī′mərjē/ *n.* chemical science of fermentation, esp. in brewing, etc. [Gk]

Standard Weights and Measures
with Metric Equivalents

Linear Measure

1 inch	= 25.4 millimeters exactly
1 foot = 12 inches	= 0.3048 meter exactly
1 yard = 3 feet	= 0.9144 meter exactly
= 36 inches	
1 (statute) mile = 1,760 yards	= 1.609 kilometers
= 5,280 feet	

Square Measure

1 sq. inch	= 6.45 sq. centimeters
1 sq. foot = 144 sq. inches	= 9.29 sq. decimeters
1 sq. yard = 9 sq. feet	= 0.836 sq. meter
1 acre = 4,840 sq. yards	= 0.405 hectare
1 sq. mile = 640 acres	= 259 hectares

Cubic Measure

1 cu. inch	= 16.4 cu. centimeters
1 cu. foot = 1.728 cu. inches	= 0.0283 cu. meter
1 cu. yard = 27 cu. feet	= 0.765 cu. meter

Capacity Measure

DRY MEASURE

1 pint = 33.60 cu. inches	= 0.550 liter
1 quart = 2 pints	= 1.101 liters
1 peck = 8 quarts	= 8.81 liters
1 bushel = 4 pecks	= 35.3 liters

LIQUID MEASURE

1 fluid ounce	= 29.573 milliliters
1 gill = 4 fluid ounces	= 118.294 milliliters
1 pint = 16 fluid ounces	= 0.473 liter
	= 28.88 cu. inches
1 quart = 2 pints	= 0.946 liter
1 gallon = 4 quarts	= 3.785 liters

Avoirdupois Weight

1 grain	= 0.065 gram
1 dram	= 1.772 grams
1 ounce = 16 drams	= 28.35 grams
1 pound = 16 ounces	= 0.4536 kilograms
= 7,000 grains	(0.45359237 exactly)
1 stone (Brit.) = 14 pounds	= 6.35 kilograms
1 ton	= 2,000 pounds
1 hundred weight (US)	= 100 pounds
20 hundred weight (US)	= 2000 pounds

Metric Weights and Measures
with Standard Equivalents

Linear Measure

1 millimeter (mm)	= 0.039 inch
1 centimeter (cm) = 10 millimeters	= 0.394 inch
1 decimeter (dm) = 10 centimeters	= 3.94 inches
1 meter (m) = 10 decimeters	= 1.094 yards
1 decameter = 10 meters	= 10.94 yards
1 hectometer = 100 meters	= 109.4 yards
1 kilometer (km) = 1,000 meters	= 0.6214 mile

Square Measure

1 sq. centimeter	= 0.155 sq. inch
1 sq. meter	= 10,000 sq. centimeters
	= 1.196 sq. yards
1 are = 100 sq. meters	= 119.6 sq. yards
1 hectare = 100 ares	= 2.471 acres
1 sq. kilometer	= 0.386 sq. mile
	= 100 hectares

Cubic Measure

1 cu. centimeter	= 0.061 cu. inch
1 cu. meter = 1,000,000 cu. centimeters	= 1.308 cu. yards

Capacity Measure

1 milliliter (ml)	= 0.034 fluid ounces
1 centiliter (cl) = 10 milliliters	= 0.34 fluid ounces
1 deciliter (dl) = 10 centiliter	= 3.38 fluid ounces
1 liter (l) = 10 deciliters	= 1.06 quarts
1 decaliter = 10 liters	= 2.20 gallons
1 hectoliter = 100 liters	= 2.75 bushels

Weight

1 milligram (mg)	= 0.015 grain
1 centigram = 10 milligrams	= 0.154 grain
1 decigram (dg) = 10 centigrams	= 1.543 grains
1 gram (g) = 10 decigrams	= 15.43 grains
1 decagram = 10 grams	= 5.64 drams
1 hectogram = 100 grams	= 3.527 ounces
1 kilogram (kg) = 1,000 grams	= 2.205 pounds
1 ton (metric ton) = 1,000 kilograms	= 0.984 (long) ton

Metric Prefixes

	Abbr. or Symbol	Factor		Abbr. or Symbol	Factor
deca-	da	10	deci-	d	10^{-1}
hecto-	h	10^2	centi-	c	10^{-2}
kilo-	k	10^3	milli-	m	10^{-3}
mega-	M	10^6	micro-	μ	10^{-6}
giga-	G	10^9	nano-	n	10^{-9}
tera-	T	10^{12}	pico-	p	10^{-12}
peta-	P	10^{15}	femto-	f	10^{-15}
exa-	E	10^{18}	atto-	a	10^{-18}

Temperature

Fahrenheit: Water boils (under standard conditions) at 212° and freezes at 32°.

Celsius or Centigrade: Water boils at 100° and freezes at 0°.

Kelvin: Water boils at 373.15 K and freezes at 273.15 K.

Celsius	Fahren-heit	Fahren-heit	Celsius
−17.8°	0°	0°	−17.8°
−10°	14°	10°	−12.2°
0°	32°	20°	−6.6°
10°	50°	32°	0.0°
20°	68°	40°	3.5°
30°	86°	50°	10.0°
40°	104°	60°	15.5°
50°	122°	70°	21.1°
60°	140°	80°	26.6°
70°	158°	90°	32.2°
80°	176°	98.6°	37.0°
90°	194°	100°	37.6°
100°	212°	212°	100.0°

To convert Celsius into Fahrenheit: multiply by 9, divide by 5, and add 32.

To convert Fahrenheit into Celsius: subtract 32, multiply by 5, and divide by 9.

The Greek Alphabet

α	A	alpha	ι	I	iota	ρ	P	rho
β	B	beta	κ	K	kappa	σ	Σ	sigma
γ	Γ	gamma	λ	Λ	lambda	τ	T	tau
δ	Δ	delta	μ	M	mu	υ	Y	upsilon
ϵ	E	epsilon	ν	N	nu	ϕ	Φ	phi
ζ	Z	zeta	ξ	Ξ	xi	χ	X	chi
η	H	eta	o	O	omicron	ψ	Ψ	psi
θ	Θ	theta	π	Π	pi	ω	Ω	omega

Scientific Units

Physical Quantity	Name	Abbr. or Symbol
Base Units		
length	meter	m
mass	kilogram	kg
time	second	s
electric current	ampere	A
temperature	kelvin	K
amount of substance	mole	mol
luminous intensity	candela	cd
Supplementary Units		
plane angle	radian	rad
solid angle	steradian	sr
Derived Units with Special Names		
frequency	hertz	Hz
energy	joule	J
force	newton	N
power	watt	W
pressure	pascal	Pa
electric charge	coulomb	C
electromotive force	volt	V
electric resistance	ohm	Ω
electric conductance	siemens	S
electric capacitance	farad	F
magnetic flux	weber	Wb
inductance	henry	H
magnetic flux density	tesla	T
luminous	lumen	lm
flux illumination	lux	lx

Formulas from Geometry

The following symbols are used for the measure:
r: radius; h: altitude; b: base; a: base; C: circumference; A: area; S: surface area; B: area of base; V: volume

Circle: $A = \pi r^2$; $C = 2\pi r$
Triangle: $A = \frac{1}{2}bh$
Rectangle and parallelogram: $A = bh$
Trapezoid: $A = \frac{1}{2}(a + b)h$
Right circular cylinder: $V = \pi r^2 h$; $S = 2\pi rh$
Right circular cone: $V = \frac{1}{3}\pi r^2 h$; $S = \pi r\sqrt{r^2 + h^2}$
Sphere: $V = \frac{4}{3}\pi r^3$; $S = 4\pi r^2$
Prism (with parallel bases): $V = Bh$
Pyramid: $V = \frac{1}{3}Bh$

Chemical Elements

Element	Symbol	Atomic Number	Element	Symbol	Atomic Number
actinium	Ac	89	neptunium	Np	93
aluminum	Al	13	nickel	Ni	28
americium	Am	95	nielsbohrium*	Ns	107
antimony	Sb	51	niobium	Nb	41
argon	Ar	18	nitrogen	N	7
arsenic	As	33	nobelium	No	102
astatine	At	85	osmium	Os	76
barium	Ba	56	oxygen	O	8
berkelium	Bk	97	palladium	Pd	46
beryllium	Be	4	phosphorus	P	15
bismuth	Bi	83	platinum	Pt	78
boron	B	5	plutonium	Pu	94
bromine	Br	35	polonium	Po	84
cadmium	Cd	48	potassium	K	19
calcium	Ca	20	praseodymium	Pr	59
californium	Cf	98	promethium	Pm	61
carbon	C	6	protactinium	Pa	91
cesium	Cs	55	radium	Ra	88
cerium	Ce	58	radon	Rn	86
chlorine	Cl	17	rhenium	Re	75
chromium	Cr	24	rhodium	Rh	45
cobalt	Co	27	rubidium	Rb	37
copper	Cu	29	ruthenium	Ru	44
curium	Cm	96	rutherfordium*	Rf	104
dysprosium	Dy	66	samarium	Sm	62
einsteinium	Es	99	scandium	Sc	21
erbium	Er	68	seaborgium*	Sg	106
europium	Eu	63	selenium	Se	34
fermium	Fm	100	silicon	Si	14
fluorine	F	9	silver	Ag	47
francium	Fr	87	sodium	Na	11
gadolinium	Gd	64	strontium	Sr	38
gallium	Ga	31	sulfur	S	16
germanium	Ge	32	tantalum	Ta	73
gold	Au	79	technetium	Tc	43
hafnium	Hf	72	tellurium	Te	52
hahnium*	Ha	105	terbium	Tb	65
hassium*	Hs	108	thallium	Tl	81
helium	He	2	thorium	Th	90
holmium	Ho	67	thulium	Tm	69
hydrogen	H	1	tin	Sn	50
indium	In	49	titanium	Ti	22
iodine	I	53	tungsten	W	74
iridium	Ir	77	(wolfram)		
iron	Fe	26	uranium	U	92
krypton	Kr	36	vanadium	V	23
lanthanum	La	57	xenon	Xe	54
lawrencium	Lr	103	ytterbium	Yb	70
lead	Pb	82	yttrium	Y	39
lithium	Li	3	zinc	Zn	30
lutetium	Lu	71	zirconium	Zr	40
magnesium	Mg	12			
manganese	Mn	25			
meitnerium	Mt	109			
mendelevium	Md	101			
mercury	Hg	80			
molybdenum	Mo	42			
neodymium	Nd	60			
neon	Ne	10			

*There is some dispute about the names for elements 104 through 108; they are also called:

104	Dubnium	Db
105	Joliotium	Jl
106	Rutherfordium	Rf
107	Bohrium	Bh
108	Hahnium	Hn

Signs and Symbols

General

&	and	x	by, as in *an 8′ × 12′ room*
&c.	et cetera (and so forth)	w/	with
©	copyright(ed)	w/o	without
®	registered; of a trademark or service mark	§	section (of a text)
†	death; died	″	ditto marks; repeat the word or sign located in the line above
℞	take (Latin *recipe*); used on prescriptions	☠	poison
#	1. number (before a figure) 2. pound(s) (after a figure) 3. space (in printing)	☢	radioactive; radiation

Suits of Playing Cards

♠	spade	♦	diamond
♥	heart	♣	club

Arabic and Roman Numerals

Arabic	Roman	Arabic	Roman
0		17	XVII
1	I	18	XVIII
2	II	19	XIX
3	III	20	XX
4	IV or IIII	30	XXX
5	V	40	XL
6	VI	50	L
7	VII	60	LX
8	VIII	70	LXX
9	IX or VIIII	80	LXXX
10	X	90	XC
11	XI	100	C
12	XII	400	CD
13	XIII	500	D
14	XIV	900	CM
15	XV	1,000	M
16	XVI	2,000	MM

Science and Mathematics

♂ □	male	=	equal to
♀ ○	female	≠	not equal to
+	1. plus 2. positive (number or charge)	>	greater than
		<	less than
−	1. minus 2. negative (number or charge)	≧	greater than or equal to
		≦	less than or equal to
		≡	identical with
±	plus or minus	≈	approximately equal to
× or · or ∗	multiplied by	≅	congruent to (in geometry)
÷	divided by	:	is to; the ratio of
		!	factorial of

679

Signs and Symbols

Science and Mathematics

Σ	sum		⊥	perpendicular to
π	pi; the ratio of the circumference of a circle to its diameter (3.14159265+)		√	radical sign; root
			°	degree
∞	infinity		′	1. minute(s) of arc
∴	therefore			2. foot, feet
∵	since		″	1. second(s) of arc
∥	parallel to			2. inch(es)
			∅	empty set

Commerce and Finance

$	dollar(s)		@	at the rate of
¢	cent(s)		%	percent
£	pound(s) sterling (UK)		DM	Deutsche mark (Germany)
p	(new) pence (UK)		F	franc (France)
¥	yen (Japan)			

Proofreading Marks

¶	new paragraph		⑨	delete and close up
∧	insert here (caret mark)		#	leave space
℈	delete		=	insert hyphen
‿	close up space		tr	transpose

Signs of the Zodiac

Spring

♈	Aries the Ram
♉	Taurus, the Bull
♊ or ♊	Gemini, the Twins

Summer

♋ or ♋	Cancer, the Crab
♌	Leo, the Lion
♍	Virgo, the Virgin

Autumn

♎	Libra, the Balance
♏	Scorpio, the Scorpion
♐ or ♐	Sagittarius, the Archer

Winter

♑ or ♑	Capricorn, the Goat
♒	Aquarius, the Water Bearer
♓ or ♓	Pisces, the Fishes

Diacritical Marks
(to distinguish sounds or values of letters)

´	acute (as in the French word *née*)
`	grave (as in the French word *père*)
~	tilde (as in the Spanish word *piñata*)
^	circumflex (as in the word *rôle*)
¯	macron (as used in pronunciation: *āge, īce, ūse*)
˘	breve (as used in pronunciation: *tăp, rĭp, fŏb*)
¨	dieresis (as in the word *Noël*)
¸	cedilla (as in the word *façade*)

States of the United States of America

State (with traditional and postal abbreviations)	Capital	ZIP Codes (first 3 digits)	Area Codes
Alabama (Ala., AL)	Montgomery	350–369	205, 334
Alaska (AK)	Juneau	995–999	907
Arizona (Ariz., AZ)	Phoenix	850–865	520, 602
Arkansas (Ark., AR)	Little Rock	716–729	501
California (Calif., CA)	Sacramento	900–966	209, 213, 310, 408, 415, 510, 562, 619, 707, 714, 805, 818, 909, 916
Colorado (Colo., CO)	Denver	800–816	303, 719, 970
Connecticut (Conn., CT)	Hartford	060–069	203, 860
Delaware (Del., DE)	Dover	197–199	302
Florida (Fla., FL)	Tallahassee	320–349	305, 407, 813, 904, 941, 954
Georgia (Ga., GA)	Atlanta	300–319	404, 706, 912
Hawaii (HI)	Honolulu	967–968	808
Idaho (Ida., ID)	Boise	832–838	208
Illinois (Ill., IL)	Springfield	600–629	217, 309, 312, 618, 630, 708, 815
Indiana (Ind., IN)	Indianapolis	460–479	219, 317, 812
Iowa (Ia., IA)	Des Moines	500–528	319, 515, 712
Kansas (Kans., KS)	Topeka	660–679	316, 913
Kentucky (Ky., KY)	Frankfort	400–427	502, 606
Louisiana (La., LA)	Baton Rouge	700–714	318, 504
Maine (Me., ME)	Augusta	039–049	207
Maryland (Md., MD)	Annapolis	206–219	301, 410
Massachusetts (Mass., MA)	Boston	010–027	413, 508, 617
Michigan (Mich., MI)	Lansing	480–499	313, 517, 616, 810, 906
Minnesota (Minn., MN)	St. Paul	550–567	218, 507, 612
Mississippi (Miss., MS)	Jackson	386–397	601
Missouri (Mo., MO)	Jefferson City	630–658	314, 417, 816

States of the United States of America

State (with traditional and postal abbreviations)	Capital	ZIP Codes (first 3 digits)	Area Codes
Montana (Mont., MT)	Helena	590–599	406
Nebraska (Nebr., NE)	Lincoln	680–693	308, 402
Nevada (Nev., NV)	Carson City	889–898	702
New Hampshire (N.H., NH)	Concord	030–038	603
New Jersey (N.J., NJ)	Trenton	070–089	201, 609, 908
New Mexico (N. Mex., NM)	Santa Fe	870–884	505
New York (N.Y., NY)	Albany	004; 090–149	212, 315, 516, 518, 607, 716, 718, 914, 917
North Carolina (N.C., NC)	Raleigh	270–289	704, 910, 919
North Dakota (N. Dak., ND)	Bismarck	580–588	701
Ohio (OH)	Columbus	430–458	216, 419, 513, 614
Oklahoma (Okla., OK)	Oklahoma City	730–749	405, 918
Oregon (Ore., OR)	Salem	970–979	503
Pennsylvania (Pa., PA)	Harrisburg	150–196	215, 412, 610, 717, 814
Rhode Island (R.I., RI)	Providence	028–029	401
South Carolina (S.C., SC)	Columbia	290–299	803
South Dakota (S. Dak., SD)	Pierre	570–577	605
Tennessee (Tenn., TN)	Nashville	370–385	423, 615, 901
Texas (Tex., TX)	Austin	750–799	210, 214, 281, 409, 512, 713, 806, 817, 903, 915
Utah (Ut., UT)	Salt Lake City	840–847	801
Vermont (Vt., VT)	Montpelier	050–059	802
Virginia (Va., VA)	Richmond	220–246	540, 703, 804
Washington (Wash., WA)	Olympia	980–994	206, 360, 509
West Virginia (W. Va., WV)	Charleston	247–268	304
Wisconsin (Wis., WI)	Madison	530–549	414, 608, 715
Wyoming (Wyo., WY)	Cheyenne	820–831	307

Area Codes

Code	State or Province
201	New Jersey
202	District of Columbia
203	Connecticut
204	Manitoba
205	Alabama
206	Washington
207	Maine
208	Idaho
209	California
210	Texas
212	New York
213	California
214	Texas
215	Pennsylvania
216	Ohio
217	Illinois
218	Minnesota
219	Indiana
281	Texas
301	Maryland
302	Delaware
303	Colorado
304	West Virginia
305	Florida
306	Saskatchewan
307	Wyoming
308	Nebraska
309	Illinois
310	California
312	Illinois
313	Michigan
314	Missouri
315	New York
316	Kansas
317	Indiana
318	Louisiana
319	Iowa
334	Alabama
360	Washington
401	Rhode Island
402	Nebraska
403	Alberta
404	Georgia
405	Oklahoma
406	Montana

Code	State or Province
407	Florida
408	California
409	Texas
410	Maryland
412	Pennsylvania
413	Massachusetts
414	Wisconsin
415	California
416	Ontario
417	Missouri
418	Quebec
419	Ohio
423	Tennessee
441	Bermuda
501	Arkansas
502	Kentucky
503	Oregon
504	Louisiana
505	New Mexico
506	New Brunswick
507	Minnesota
508	Massachusetts
509	Washington
510	California
512	Texas
513	Ohio
514	Quebec
515	Iowa
516	New York
517	Michigan
518	New York
519	Ontario
520	Arizona
540	Virginia
562	California
601	Mississippi
602	Arizona
603	New Hampshire
604	British Columbia
605	South Dakota
606	Kentucky
607	New York
608	Wisconsin
609	New Jersey
610	Pennsylvania

Area Codes

Code	State or Province
612	Minnesota
613	Ontario
614	Ohio
615	Tennessee
616	Michigan
617	Massachusetts
618	Illinois
619	California
630	Illinois
701	North Dakota
702	Nevada
703	Virginia
704	North Carolina
705	Ontario
706	Georgia
707	California
708	Illinois
709	Newfoundland
710	US Government
712	Iowa
713	Texas
714	California
715	Wisconsin
716	New York
717	Pennsylvania
718	New York
719	Colorado
801	Utah
802	Vermont
803	South Carolina
804	Virginia
805	California
806	Texas
807	Ontario

Code	State or Province
808	Hawaii
809	The Caribbean Islands
810	Michigan
812	Indiana
813	Florida
814	Pennsylvania
815	Illinois
816	Missouri
817	Texas
818	California
819	Quebec
860	Connecticut
901	Tennessee
902	Nova Scotia
903	Texas
904	Florida
905	Ontario
906	Michigan
907	Alaska
908	New Jersey
909	California
910	North Carolina
911	Universal Emergency
912	Georgia
913	Kansas
914	New York
915	Texas
916	California
917	New York
918	Oklahoma
919	North Carolina
941	Florida
954	Florida
970	Colorado

Presidents of the United States of America

1.	George Washington 1732–99	Federalist 1789–97
2.	John Adams 1735–1826	Federalist 1797–1801
3.	Thomas Jefferson 1743–1826	Democratic-Republican 1801–09
4.	James Madison 1751–1836	Democratic-Republican 1809–17
5.	James Monroe 1758–1831	Democratic-Republican 1817–25
6.	John Quincy Adams 1767–1848	Independent 1825–29
7.	Andrew Jackson 1767–1845	Democrat 1829–37
8.	Martin Van Buren 1782–1862	Democrat 1837–41
9.	William H. Harrison 1773–1841	Whig 1841
10.	John Tyler 1790–1862	Whig, then Democrat 1841–45
11.	James K. Polk 1795–1849	Democrat 1845–49
12.	Zachary Taylor 1784–1850	Whig 1849–50
13.	Millard Fillmore 1800–74	Whig 1850–53
14.	Franklin Pierce 1804–69	Democrat 1853–57
15.	James Buchanan 1791–1868	Democrat 1857–61
16.	Abraham Lincoln 1809–65	Republican 1861–65
17.	Andrew Johnson 1808–75	Democrat 1865–69
18.	Ulysses S. Grant 1822–85	Republican 1869–77
19.	Rutherford B. Hayes 1822–93	Republican 1877–81
20.	James A. Garfield 1831–81	Republican 1881
21.	Chester A. Arthur 1830–86	Republican 1881–85
22.	Grover Cleveland 1837–1908	Democrat 1885–89
23.	Benjamin Harrison 1833–1901	Republican 1889–93
24.	Grover Cleveland (see above)	Democrat 1893–97
25.	William McKinley 1843–1901	Republican 1897–1901
26.	Theodore Roosevelt 1858–1919	Republican 1901–09
27.	William H. Taft 1857–1930	Republican 1909–13
28.	Woodrow Wilson 1856–1924	Democrat 1913–21
29.	Warren G. Harding 1865–1923	Republican 1921–23
30.	Calvin Coolidge 1872–1933	Republican 1923–29
31.	Herbert Hoover 1874–1964	Republican 1929–33
32.	Franklin D. Roosevelt 1882–1945	Democrat 1933–45
33.	Harry S Truman 1884–1972	Democrat 1945–53
34.	Dwight D. Eisenhower 1890–1969	Republican 1953–61
35.	John F. Kennedy 1917–63	Democrat 1961–63
36.	Lyndon B. Johnson 1908–73	Democrat 1963–69
37.	Richard M. Nixon 1913–94	Republican 1969–74
38.	Gerald R. Ford 1913–	Republican 1974–77
39.	James Earl Carter 1924–	Democrat 1977–81
40.	Ronald W. Reagan 1911–	Republican 1981–89
41.	George H. W. Bush 1924–	Republican 1989–93
42.	William J. Clinton 1946–	Democrat 1993–

Countries of the World

Country	Capital	Continent/Area	Nationality
Afghanistan	Kabul	Asia	Afghan
Albania	Tirane	Europe	Albanian
Algeria	Algiers	Africa	Algerian
Andorra	Andorra la Vella	Europe	Andorran
Angola	Luanda	Africa	Angolan
Antigua and Barbuda	Saint John's	North America	Antiguan, Barbudan
Argentina	Buenos Aires	South America	Argentine, *n.*; Argentinian, *adj.*
Armenia	Yerevan	Asia	Armenian
Australia	Canberra	Australia	Australian
Austria	Vienna	Europe	Austrian
Azerbaijan	Baku	Asia	Azerbaijani
Bahamas, The	Nassau	North America	Bahamian
Bahrain	Manama	Asia	Bahraini
Bangladesh	Dhaka	Asia	Bangaldeshi
Barbados	Bridgetown	North America	Barbadian
Belarus	Minsk	Europe	Belarusian
Belgium	Brussels	Europe	Belgian
Belize	Belmopan	North America	Belizean
Benin	Porto-Novo	Africa	Beninese
Bhutan	Thimphu	Asia	Bhutanese
Bolivia	La Paz; Sucre	South America	Bolivian
Bosnia and Herzegovina	Sarajevo	Europe	Bosnian
Botswana	Gaborone	Africa	Batswana, *pl.*; Motswana, *sing.*
Brazil	Brasilia	South America	Brazilian
Brunei	Bandar Seri Begawan	Asia	Bruneian
Bulgaria	Sofia	Europe	Bulgarian
Burkina Faso	Ouagadougou	Africa	Burkinabe
Burma	Rangoon	Asia	Burmese
Burundi	Bujumbura	Africa	Burundian, *n.*; Burundi, *adj.*
Cambodia	Phnom Penh	Asia	Cambodian
Cameroon	Yaoundé	Africa	Cameroonian
Canada	Ottawa	North America	Canadian
Cape Verde	Praia	Africa	Cape Verdean
Central African Republic	Bangui	Africa	Central African
Chad	N'Djamena	Africa	Chadian
Chile	Santiago	South America	Chilean

Countries of the World

Country	Capital	Continent/Area	Nationality
China	Beijing	Asia	Chinese
Colombia	Bogotá	South America	Colombian
Comoros	Moroni	Africa	Comoran
Congo	Brazzaville	Africa	Congolese, *n.*; Congolese *or* Congo, *adj.*
Costa Rica	San José	North America	Costa Rican
Côte d'Ivoire (Ivory Coast)	Yamoussoukro	Africa	Ivorian
Croatia	Zagreb	Europe	Croat, *n.*; Croatian, *adj.*
Cuba	Havana	North America	Cuban
Cyprus	Nicosia	Europe	Cypriot
Czech Republic	Prague	Europe	Czech
Denmark	Copenhagen	Europe	Dane, *n.*; Danish, *adj.*
Djibouti	Djibouti	Africa	Djiboutian
Dominica	Roseau	North America	Dominican
Dominican Republic	Santo Domingo	North America	Dominican
Ecuador	Quito	South America	Ecuadorian
Egypt	Cairo	Africa	Egyptian
El Salvador	San Salvador	North America	Salvadoran
Equatorial Guinea	Malabo	Africa	Equatorial Guinean *or* Equatoguinean
Eritrea	Asmara	Africa	Eritrean
Estonia	Tallinn	Europe	Estonian
Ethiopia	Addis Ababa	Africa	Ethiopian
Fiji	Suva	Oceania	Fijian
Finland	Helsinki	Europe	Finn, *n.*; Finnish, *adj.*
France	Paris	Europe	French
Gabon	Libreville	Africa	Gabonese
Gambia, The	Banjul	Africa	Gambian
Georgia	T'bilisi	Europe	Georgian
Germany	Berlin	Europe	German
Ghana	Accra	Africa	Ghanaian
Greece	Athens	Europe	Greek
Grenada	Saint George's	North America	Grenadian
Guatemala	Guatemala	North America	Guatemalan
Guinea	Conakry	Africa	Guinean
Guinea-Bissau	Bissau	Africa	Guinea-Bissauan
Guyana	Georgetown	South America	Guyanese

Countries of the World

Country	Capital	Continent/Area	Nationality
Haiti	Port-au-Prince	North America	Haitian
Holy See	Vatican City	Europe	
Honduras	Tegucigalpa	North America	Honduran
Hungary	Budapest	Europe	Hungarian
Iceland	Reykjavik	Europe	Icelander, *n.*; Icelandic, *adj.*
India	New Delhi	Asia	Indian
Indonesia	Jakartà	Asia	Indonesian
Iran	Tehran	Asia	Iranian
Iraq	Baghdad	Asia	Iraqi
Ireland	Dublin	Europe	Irish
Israel	Jerusalem	Asia	Israeli
Italy	Rome	Europe	Italian
Jamaica	Kingston	North America	Jamaican
Japan	Tokyo	Asia	Japanese
Jordan	Amman	Asia	Jordanian
Kazakhstan	Almaty	Asia	Kazakhstani
Kenya	Nairobi	Africa	Kenyan
Kiribati	Tarawa	Oceania	I-Kiribati
Korea, North	P'yongyang	Asia	North Korean
Korea, South	Seoul	Asia	South Korean
Kuwait	Kuwait	Asia	Kuwaiti
Kyrgyzstan	Bishkek	Asia	Kyrgyz
Laos	Vientiane	Asia	Lao or Laotian
Latvia	Riga	Europe	Latvian
Lebanon	Beirut	Asia	Lebanese
Lesotho	Maseru	Africa	Mosotho, *sing. n.*; Basotho, *pl. n. & adj.*
Liberia	Monrovia	Africa	Liberian
Libya	Tripoli	Africa	Libyan
Liechtenstein	Vaduz	Europe	Liechtensteiner, *n.*; Liechtenstein, *adj.*
Lithuania	Vilnius	Europe	Lithuanian
Luxembourg	Luxembourg	Europe	Luxembourger, *n.*; Luxembourg, *adj.*
Macedonia, The Former Yugoslav Republic of	Skopje	Europe	Macedonian
Madagascar	Antananarivo	Africa	Malagasy
Malawi	Lilongwe	Africa	Malawian

Countries of the World

Country	Capital	Continent/Area	Nationality
Malaysia	Kuala Lumpur	Asia	Malaysian
Maldives	Male	Asia	Maldivian
Mali	Bamako	Africa	Malian
Malta	Valletta	Europe	Maltese
Marshall Islands	Majuro	Oceania	Marshallese
Mauritania	Nouakchott	Africa	Mauritanian
Mauritius	Port Louis	Africa	Mauritian
Mexico	Mexico	North America	Mexican
Micronesia, Federated States of	Kolonia	Oceania	Micronesian
Moldova	Chisinau	Europe	Moldovan
Monaco	Monaco	Europe	Monegasque
Mongolia	Ulaanbaatar	Asia	Mongolian
Morocco	Rabat	Africa	Moroccan
Mozambique	Maputo	Africa	Mozambican
Namibia	Windhoek	Africa	Namibian
Nauru	Yaren District	Oceania	Nauruan
Nepal	Kathmandu	Asia	Nepalese
Netherlands	Amsterdam; The Hague	Europe	Dutchman or Dutchwoman, n.; Dutch, adj.
New Zealand	Wellington	Oceania	New Zealander, n.; New Zealand, adj.
Nicaragua	Managua	North America	Nicaraguan
Niger	Niamey	Africa	Nigerien
Nigeria	Abuja	Africa	Nigerian
Norway	Oslo	Europe	Norwegian
Oman	Muscat	Asia	Omani
Pakistan	Islamabad	Asia	Pakistani
Palau	Koror	Oceania	Palauan
Panama	Panama	North America	Panamanian
Papua New Guinea	Port Moresby	Oceania	Papua New Guinean
Paraguay	Asunción	South America	Paraguayan
Peru	Lima	South America	Peruvian
Philippines	Manila	Asia	Filipino, n.; Philippine, adj.
Poland	Warsaw	Europe	Polish
Portugal	Lisbon	Europe	Portuguese
Qatar	Doha	Asia	Quatari
Romania	Bucharest	Europe	Romanian

Countries of the World

Country	Capital	Continent/Area	Nationality
Russia	Moscow	Europe & Asia	Russian
Rwanda	Kigali	Africa	Rwandan
Saint Kitts and Nevis	Basseterre	North America	Kittsian; Nevisian
Saint Lucia	Castries	North America	St. Lucian
Saint Vincent and the Grenadines	Kingstown	North America	Vincentian *or* St. Vincentian
San Marino	San Marino	Europe	Sanmarinese
Sao Tome and Principe	Sao Tome	Africa	Sao Tomean
Saudi Arabia	Riyadh	Asia	Saudi *or* Saudi Arabian
Senegal	Dakar	Africa	Senegalese
Seychelles	Victoria	Indian Ocean	Seychellois, *n.*; Seychelles, *adj.*
Sierra Leone	Freetown	Africa	Sierra Leonean
Singapore	Singapore	Asia	Singaporean, *n.*; Singapore, *adj.*
Slovakia	Bratislava	Europe	Slovak
Slovenia	Ljubljana	Europe	Slovene, *n.*; Slovenian, *adj.*
Solomon Islands	Honiara	Oceania	Solomon Islander
Somalia	Mogadishu	Africa	Somali
South Africa	Pretoria; Cape Town; Bloemfontein	Africa	South African
Spain	Madrid	Europe	Spanish
Sri Lanka	Colombo	Asia	Sri Lankan
Sudan	Khartoum	Africa	Sudanese
Suriname	Paramaribo	South America	Surinamer, *n.*; Surinamese, *adj.*
Swaziland	Mbabane	Africa	Swazi
Sweden	Stockholm	Europe	Swede, *n.*; Swedish, *adj.*
Switzerland	Bern	Europe	Swiss
Syria	Damascus	Asia	Syrian
Tajikistan	Dushanbe	Asia	Tajik
Tanzania	Dar es Salaam	Africa	Tanzanian
Thailand	Bangkok	Asia	Thai
Togo	Lome	Africa	Togolese
Tonga	Nuku'alofa	Oceania	Tongan
Trinidad and Tobago	Port-of-Spain	South America	Trinidadian; Tobagonian